YOUTH BIBLE

TODAY'S NEW INTERNATIONAL VERSION

The Holy Bible, Today's New International Version
Copyright © 2004 by Biblica
Full Bible first published in Great Britain 2005

The Book: TNIV Youth Bible first published in Great Britain 2005
Notes and supplementary material copyright© 2005
Hodder & Stoughton

The TNIV text may be quoted for non-commercial use in any form (written, visual, electronic or audio), up to and inclusive of five hundred (500) verses without express written permission of the publisher, providing the verses quoted do not amount to a complete book of the Bible nor do the verses quoted account for 25 per cent or more of the total text of the work in which they are quoted.

The appropriate notice of copyright must appear on the title or copyright page of the work as follows:

Scripture quotations taken from The Holy Bible,
Today's New International Version
Copyright © 2004 by Biblica.
Used by permission of Hodder & Stoughton Publishers,
an Hachette UK company
All rights reserved.
'TNIV' is a registered trademark of Biblica.

When quotations from the TNIV text are used in non-saleable media, such as church bulletins, orders of service, posters, transparencies or similar media, a complete copyright notice is not required, but the initials (TNIV) must appear at the end of each quotation.

Any commentary or other biblical reference work produced for commercial sale that uses the Today's New International Version must obtain written permission for use of the TNIV text.

Permission requests for commercial use within the UK, EEC, and EFTA countries that exceed the above guidelines must be directed to, and approved in writing, by Hodder & Stoughton Publishers, 338 Euston Road, London NW1 3BH, England.

Permission requests for commercial use within the US and Canada that exceed the above guidelines must be directed to, and approved in writing, by Zondervan Publishing House.

Permission requests for non-commercial use that exceed the above guidelines must be directed to, and approved in writing, by Biblica, 1820 Jet Stream Drive, Colorado Springs, CO 80921-3696, USA.

Bible Notes written by Jenny Baker.

*This publication is not included under licenses issued by the Copyright Licensing Agency.
Printed in Italy by Lego SPA.*

INTRODUCING...

... the most important book in the world. The Bible will not only take you through the whole history of the universe from beginning to end, it can also speak clearly to you about your life: Why are you here? How should you live? What does the Bible have to say about your deepest problems and desires? Although the Bible was written by many different authors, Christians believe that each author wrote under the ultimate control of the Holy Spirit, meaning they were divinely inspired - the Bible is God's Word communicated to us through human means.

This particular edition of the Bible has been designed to allow you, its reader, to discover and interpret God's Word for yourself, and at your own pace. Scattered throughout the pages of this Bible you'll find notes that will help you to make sense of what you're reading. They come in five different 'flavours':

Introduction
Starting each book with the basic facts you need about it - who wrote it, when, where and why.

In Other Words
Shedding some light on unfamiliar words or ideas.

People and places
Giving you some background information about key people and places in the Bible.

Sign of the times
Explaining why people acted like they did by exploring what life was like when the Bible was written.

Making connections
Helping you get the big picture by pointing out interesting facts or how different parts of the Bible are linked to each other.

The notes are designed to enable you to get more out of reading the Bible. If a note mentions another passage, why not look that up too? It could give you another perspective on the issue.

We have also included some suggestions on how to find your way around the Bible, and a reading plan to help you structure your study according to what works best for you. It is important to remember that there is no one ideal order in which to read the books of the Bible. Much depends on you - what your particular needs or interests are at any one time. If you are unsure, it might be worth reading through the **What is the Bible?** pages that follow the Contents page, as these will give you a little more background about the various parts that make up the whole of the Bible

Everybody needs help so don't worry if you find parts of the Bible difficult to understand. You are following in the footsteps of millions! All the extra material in this edition is intended to provide a good starting point in getting to grips with the Bible, but be ready to ask someone who might know more.

The Bible was written for you. This is your book. Read it prayerfully and at your own pace. And prepare to be surprised at what you find within.

CONTENTS

What's in the Bible? vi
How to Read the Bible 1325
One-Year Bible Reading Plan 1326

THE OLD TESTAMENT	1	THE NEW TESTAMENT	1005
Genesis	3	Matthew	1007
Exodus	61	Mark	1046
Leviticus	106	Luke	1071
Numbers	139	John	1111
Deuteronomy	187	Acts	1143
Joshua	226	Romans	1181
Judges	254	1 Corinthians	1198
Ruth	281	2 Corinthians	1214
1 Samuel	286	Galatians	1225
2 Samuel	322	Ephesians	1231
1 Kings	353	Philippians	1237
2 Kings	388	Colossians	1242
1 Chronicles	422	1 Thessalonians	1246
2 Chronicles	460	2 Thessalonians	1250
Ezra	499	1 Timothy	1253
Nehemiah	512	2 Timothy	1258
Esther	530	Titus	1262
Job	540	Philemon	1265
Psalms	574	Hebrews	1267
Proverbs	663	James	1280
Ecclesiastes	696	1 Peter	1285
Song of Songs	707	2 Peter	1290
Isaiah	714	1 John	1294
Jeremiah	784	2 John	1299
Lamentations	852	3 John	1301
Ezekiel	860	Jude	1303
Daniel	916	Revelation	1305
Hosea	934		
Joel	945		
Amos	950		
Obadiah	960		
Jonah	962		
Micah	965		
Nahum	973		
Habakkuk	977		
Zephaniah	981		
Haggai	986		
Zechariah	989		
Malachi	1000		

WHAT'S IN THE BIBLE?

One of the most amazing things about the Bible is the huge variety of material in it. If you're reading through the Bible and wondering exactly what it is you've got, this section should help explain.

The Bible consists of two main parts: the Old Testament and the New Testament. 'Testament' means 'agreement' or 'covenant' and so the two parts describe the main covenants that God made with his people. These include the giving of the Law to Moses and the Israelites (Exodus 20 and Deuteronomy 5) and, of supreme importance for Christians, the life, death and resurrection of Jesus, which led to a completely new understanding of how people could relate to God (John 1:17). But that's just for starters... Within these testaments are individual books, sixty-six in all. These books were written at different times in different styles which are generally recognised as being: law, history, wisdom, prophecy, Gospels, letters, apocalyptic literature.

Within the formal categories, you can make your own personal classifications (if it's helpful). For example, you could classify Song of Songs under 'passion'; Jeremiah under 'prophetic anger' and Kings under 'thriller'. Try it once you're familiar with some of the Bible text.

The Old Testament

Law: The five books of the Law given to Israel through Moses (often called the Pentateuch, 'The Five Scrolls' or the Torah): Genesis, Exodus, Leviticus, Numbers, Deuteronomy

These first five books deal with the creation of the world, the calling of Israel as a people, and its early history, including the exodus from Egypt. The story they tell features names such as Noah, Joseph, Moses and ends with the people of Israel about to cross over the Jordan and enter the promised land. One of the most important themes of these books is the giving of the Law to Moses, and its implications for the life of Israel (Leviticus in particular is concerned with the regulation of the life of Israel). Although these books appear at the start of the Bible, unless you are a very able reader or have a very straightforward and easy-read Bible translation, don't start here! Wait until you have read one or more of the Gospels.

History: Joshua, Judges, Ruth, 1 and 2 Samuel, 1 and 2 Kings, 1 and 2 Chronicles, Ezra, Nehemiah, Esther

These books reveal God's activity throughout the history of the people of Israel, his chosen people, from their entry into the promised land of Canaan to the return of the people of Jerusalem from exile in the city of Babylon. These are histories with a special perspective; right from the moment Joshua leads the Israelites into Canaan at the start of the book that bears his name, we are being shown God at work. Be warned: there is much blood and sex in this part of the Bible. The Bible doesn't hide bloody reality from us, neither does it pretend that the great heroes of the faith were perfect. Yet these are the stories of Israel, of how God took a bunch of ex-slaves and turned them into a special nation. Try reading from the start of 1 Samuel to the end of 2 Kings like you would a novel.

Wisdom: Job, Psalms, Proverbs, Ecclesiastes, Song of Songs, Lamentations

These are also earthy books full of realism and passion (the common factor rather than any one literary style). Some of these books have a raw edge about them. If you have never read the Psalms before, you will quickly see why their mixture of pain, anger, joy and praise makes them so popular with Christians. Each of these books stands on its own, although Job, Proverbs, Ecclesiastes and Lamentations are all musings on life, love and death, while Psalms and Song of Songs are written as poetry.

Prophets: Major prophets are Isaiah, Jeremiah, Ezekiel, Daniel; Minor prophets: Hosea, Joel, Amos, Obadiah, Jonah, Micah, Nahum, Habakkuk, Zephaniah, Haggai, Zechariah, Malachi

This section of the Old Testament views part of the story of God's people from within through the eyes of individuals - prophets. Instead of the wide political scope of Chronicles, we get very personal revelations to individuals who have been chosen by God, about what God really feels as a result of his people's constant round of disobedience-obedience-disobedience. Try reading one of the 'minor' (shorter) prophets like Amos before tackling the likes of Jeremiah. Daniel isn't really a major prophet (the other three in that category are much longer than all the other prophets), but he's a bit of an anomaly, containing part story, and part 'apocalyptic' material (apocalypse being a vision of the end of the world).

The New Testament

Gospels: Matthew, Mark, Luke, John

The New Testament starts with four slightly different accounts of the life, death and resurrection of Jesus. Sometimes people think one Gospel would be better than four and start worrying about why they are different. A good response would be that it's a bit like reporting on a football match. In football, you have one referee and two assistants: while the referee is watching the ball, the assistants are looking out for offsides and fouls and what they each remember from a match will be slightly different from the other's memory. So it is with the Gospels, each story has a different twist: Matthew's is filled with practical teaching, Mark's is action-packed, Luke's is intelligent, John's is deep, very deep. But all these different writers highlight one thing: Jesus is the most important person ever to have lived, because he was ... well, why don't you read about it!

Acts

Acts is part two of the Gospel of Luke, and starts off where Luke ends. It provides amazing glimpses into the early church, recording how the good news about Jesus spread from Palestine through Lebanon, Turkey and Greece and on to Italy.

Letters: Romans, 1 and 2 Corinthians, Galatians, Ephesians, Philippians, Colossians, 1 and 2 Thessalonians, 1 and 2 Timothy, Titus, Philemon, Hebrews, James, 1 and 2 Peter, 1, 2 and 3 John, Jude

The New Testament was formed much more quickly than the Old Testament because the length of time it spans is so much shorter. There is a much stronger feel of the here and now about it. That's mainly because of all these special letters written to the new churches by really special people such as Paul.

Apocalypse: Revelation

These two long words actually mean the same thing: a vision especially of the end of the world. Don't worry if you find this book difficult to fathom! It's not all double Dutch. It's written in a highly symbolic way that its readers would have understood. If you want to really get into this book, using a commentary would definitely be a good idea.

The Old Testament

Genesis

INTRODUCTION

GENESIS

Author: Moses

When: Genesis tells the story of the first couple of thousand years of human history.

Did you know? Genesis is the first of the five books of Moses, known as the Pentateuch.

Main theme: The word 'Genesis' means 'the origin, source or creation of something', so it's a good name for a book that's all about beginnings. Genesis tells the story of the creation of the world, how everything went wrong when people disobeyed God, and the start of God's plan to put things right. Genesis also contains the origins of the Israelites, God's chosen people, whose father was Abraham.

The beginning

1 In the beginning God created the heavens and the earth. 2Now the earth was formless and empty, darkness was over the surface of the deep, and the Spirit of God was hovering over the waters.

3And God said, 'Let there be light,' and there was light. 4God saw that the light was good, and he separated the light from the darkness. 5God called the light 'day', and the darkness he called 'night'. And there was evening, and there was morning—the first day.

6And God said, 'Let there be a vault between the waters to separate water from water.' 7So God made the vault and separated the water under the vault from the water above it. And it was so. 8God called the vault 'sky'. And there was evening, and there was morning—the second day.

9And God said, 'Let the water under the sky be gathered to one place, and let dry ground appear.' And it was so. 10God called the dry ground 'land', and the gathered waters he called 'seas'. And God saw that it was good.

> **IN OTHER WORDS**
>
> **Image**
> Genesis 1:26
> The Bible uses the word 'image' to mean a close likeness of something. We are made in the image of God, an image which was damaged in the fall, but can be restored through Jesus.

¹¹Then God said, 'Let the land produce vegetation: seed-bearing plants and trees on the land that bear fruit with seed in it, according to their various kinds.' And it was so. ¹²The land produced vegetation: plants bearing seed according to their kinds and trees bearing fruit with seed in it according to their kinds. And God saw that it was good. ¹³And there was evening, and there was morning—the third day.

¹⁴And God said, 'Let there be lights in the vault of the sky to separate the day from the night, and let them serve as signs to mark seasons and days and years, ¹⁵and let them be lights in the vault of the sky to give light on the earth.' And it was so. ¹⁶God made two great lights—the greater light to govern the day and the lesser light to govern the night. He also made the stars. ¹⁷God set them in the vault of the sky to give light on the earth, ¹⁸to govern the day and the night, and to separate light from darkness. And God saw that it was good. ¹⁹And there was evening, and there was morning—the fourth day.

²⁰And God said, 'Let the water teem with living creatures, and let birds fly above the earth across the vault of the sky.' ²¹So God created the great creatures of the sea and every living and moving thing with which the water teems, according to their kinds, and every winged bird according to its kind. And God saw that it was good. ²²God blessed them and said, 'Be fruitful and increase in number and fill the water in the seas, and let the birds increase on the earth.' ²³And there was evening, and there was morning—the fifth day.

²⁴And God said, 'Let the land produce living creatures according to their kinds: livestock, creatures that move along the ground, and wild animals, each according to its kind.' And it was so. ²⁵God made the wild animals according to their kinds, the livestock according to their kinds, and all the creatures that move along the ground according to their kinds. And God saw that it was good.

²⁶Then God said, 'Let us make human beings in our image, in our likeness, so that they may rule over the fish in the sea and the birds in the sky, over the livestock and all the wild animals,[a] and over all the creatures that move along the ground.'

²⁷So God created human beings
in his own image,
in the image of God he created them;
male and female
he created them.

²⁸God blessed them and said to them, 'Be fruitful and increase in number; fill the earth and subdue it. Rule over the fish in the sea and the birds in the sky and over every living creature that moves on the ground.'

²⁹Then God said, 'I give you every seed-bearing plant on the face of the whole earth and every tree that has fruit with seed in it. They will be yours for food. ³⁰And to all the beasts of the earth and all the birds in the sky and all the creatures that move on the ground—everything that has the breath of life in it—I give every green plant for food.' And it was so.

³¹God saw all that he had made, and it was very good. And there was evening, and there was morning—the sixth day.

---

[a] 26 Probable reading of the original Hebrew text (see Syriac); Masoretic Text *the earth*

2 Thus the heavens and the earth were completed in all their vast array.

²By the seventh day God had finished the work he had been doing; so on the seventh day he rested from all his work. ³Then God blessed the seventh day and made it holy, because on it he rested from all the work of creating that he had done.

Adam and Eve

⁴This is the account of the heavens and the earth when they were created, when the LORD God made the earth and the heavens.

⁵Now no shrub had yet appeared on the earth[a] and no plant had yet sprung up, for the LORD God had not sent rain on the earth and there was no-one to work the ground, ⁶but streams[b] came up from the earth and watered the whole surface of the ground. ⁷Then the LORD God formed a man[c] from the dust of the ground and breathed into his nostrils the breath of life, and the man became a living being.

⁸Now the LORD God had planted a garden in the east, in Eden; and there he put the man he had formed. ⁹The LORD God made all kinds of trees grow out of the ground—trees that were pleasing to the eye and good for food. In the middle of the garden were the tree of life and the tree of the knowledge of good and evil.

¹⁰A river watering the garden flowed from Eden; from there it was separated into four headwaters. ¹¹The name of the first is the Pishon; it winds through the entire land of Havilah, where there is gold. ¹²(The gold of that land is good; aromatic resin[d] and onyx are also there.) ¹³The name of the second river is the Gihon; it winds through the entire land of Cush.[e] ¹⁴The name of the third river is the Tigris; it runs along the east side of Ashur. And the fourth river is the Euphrates.

¹⁵The LORD God took the man and put him in the Garden of Eden to work it and take care of it. ¹⁶And the LORD God commanded the man, 'You are free to eat from any tree in the garden; ¹⁷but you must not eat from the tree of the knowledge of good and evil, for when you eat of it you will certainly die.'

¹⁸The LORD God said, 'It is not good for the man to be alone. I will make a helper suitable for him.'

¹⁹Now the LORD God had formed out of the ground all the wild animals and all the birds in the sky. He brought them to the man to see what he would name them; and whatever the man called each living creature, that was its name. ²⁰So the man gave names to all the livestock, the birds in the sky and all the wild animals.

But for Adam[f] no suitable helper was found. ²¹So the LORD God caused the man to fall into a deep sleep; and while he was sleeping, he took one of the man's ribs[g] and then closed up the place with flesh. ²²Then the LORD God made a woman from the rib[h] he had taken out of the man, and he brought her to the man.

²³The man said,

'This is now bone of my bones
 and flesh of my flesh;
she shall be called "woman",
 for she was taken out of man.'

²⁴For this reason a man will leave his father and mother and be united to his wife, and they will become one flesh.

People and Places

Adam and Eve
Genesis 2:7
The first two people in the history of the world. God formed Adam from dust and gave him his name, which means 'man' or 'humanity'. God then formed Eve from one of Adam's ribs; her name means 'living'.

---

a 5 Or *land*; also in verse 6 *b* 6 Or *mist* *c* 7 The Hebrew for *man* (*adam*) sounds like and may be related to the Hebrew for *ground* (*adamah*); it is also the name *Adam* (see Gen. 2:20). *d* 12 Or *good; pearls* *e* 13 Possibly south-east Mesopotamia *f* 20 Or *the man* *g* 21 Or *took part of the man's side* *h* 22 Or *part*

> **IN OTHER WORDS**
>
> **Fall**
> **Genesis 3:1**
> Genesis 3 describes the fall of the human race, when God's perfect creation was spoilt by the disobedience of Adam and Eve. Every good thing that God had made was damaged in the fall, but one day God will restore it all. Read Colossians 1:15–20 to find out how.

25 The man and his wife were both naked, and they felt no shame.

The fall

3 Now the snake was more crafty than any of the wild animals the LORD God had made. He said to the woman, 'Did God really say, "You must not eat from any tree in the garden"?'

2 The woman said to the snake, 'We may eat fruit from the trees in the garden, 3 but God did say, "You must not eat fruit from the tree that is in the middle of the garden, and you must not touch it, or you will die."'

4 'You will not certainly die,' the snake said to the woman. 5 'For God knows that when you eat of it your eyes will be opened, and you will be like God, knowing good and evil.'

6 When the woman saw that the fruit of the tree was good for food and pleasing to the eye, and also desirable for gaining wisdom, she took some and ate it. She also gave some to her husband, who was with her, and he ate it. 7 Then the eyes of both of them were opened, and they realised that they were naked; so they sewed fig leaves together and made coverings for themselves.

8 Then the man and his wife heard the sound of the LORD God as he was walking in the garden in the cool of the day, and they hid from the LORD God among the trees of the garden. 9 But the LORD God called to the man, 'Where are you?'

10 He answered, 'I heard you in the garden, and I was afraid because I was naked; so I hid.'

11 And he said, 'Who told you that you were naked? Have you eaten from the tree from which I commanded you not to eat?'

12 The man said, 'The woman you put here with me—she gave me some fruit from the tree, and I ate it.'

13 Then the LORD God said to the woman, 'What is this you have done?'

The woman said, 'The snake deceived me, and I ate.'

14 So the LORD God said to the snake, 'Because you have done this,

'Cursed are you above all livestock
    and all wild animals!
You will crawl on your belly
    and you will eat dust
    all the days of your life.
15 And I will put enmity
    between you and the woman,
    and between your offspring[a] and hers;
he will crush[b] your head,
    and you will strike his heel.'

16 To the woman he said,

'I will make your pains in childbearing
    very severe;
with pain you will give birth to
    children.
Your desire will be for your husband,
    and he will rule over you.'

17 To Adam he said, 'Because you listened to your wife and ate from the tree about which I commanded you, "You must not eat of it,"

'Cursed is the ground because of you;
    through painful toil you will eat of it
    all the days of your life.
18 It will produce thorns and thistles for you,
    and you will eat the plants of the field.
19 By the sweat of your brow
    you will eat your food
until you return to the ground,
    since from it you were taken;
for dust you are
    and to dust you will return.'

---

[a] 15 Or *seed*   [b] 15 Or *strike*

20Adam[a] named his wife Eve,[b] because she would become the mother of all the living.
21The LORD God made garments of skin for Adam and his wife and clothed them. 22And the LORD God said, 'The man has now become like one of us, knowing good and evil. He must not be allowed to reach out his hand and take also from the tree of life and eat, and live for ever.' 23So the LORD God banished him from the Garden of Eden to work the ground from which he had been taken. 24After he drove them out, he placed on the east side[c] of the Garden of Eden cherubim and a flaming sword flashing back and forth to guard the way to the tree of life.

Cain and Abel

4 Adam[d] made love to his wife Eve, and she became pregnant and gave birth to Cain.[e] She said, 'With the help of the LORD I have brought forth[f] a man.' 2Later she gave birth to his brother Abel.

Now Abel kept flocks, and Cain worked the soil. 3In the course of time Cain brought some of the fruits of the soil as an offering to the LORD. 4But Abel also brought an offering—fat portions from some of the firstborn of his flock. The LORD looked with favour on Abel and his offering, 5but on Cain and his offering he did not look with favour. So Cain was very angry, and his face was downcast.

6Then the LORD said to Cain, 'Why are you angry? Why is your face downcast? 7If you do what is right, will you not be accepted? But if you do not do what is right, sin is crouching at your door; it desires to have you, but you must rule over it.'

8Now Cain said to his brother Abel, 'Let's go out to the field.'[g] While they were in the field, Cain attacked his brother Abel and killed him.

9Then the LORD said to Cain, 'Where is your brother Abel?'

'I don't know,' he replied. 'Am I my brother's keeper?'

10The LORD said, 'What have you done? Listen! Your brother's blood cries out to me from the ground. 11Now you are under a curse and driven from the ground, which opened its mouth to receive your brother's blood from your hand. 12When you work the ground, it will no longer yield its crops for you. You will be a restless wanderer on the earth.'

13Cain said to the LORD, 'My punishment is more than I can bear. 14Today you are driving me from the land, and I will be hidden from your presence; I will be a restless wanderer on the earth, and whoever finds me will kill me.'

15But the LORD said to him, 'Not so;[h] anyone who kills Cain will suffer vengeance seven times over.' Then the LORD put a mark on Cain so that no-one who found him would kill him. 16So Cain went out from the LORD's presence and lived in the land of Nod,[i] east of Eden.

17Cain made love to his wife, and she became pregnant and gave birth to Enoch. Cain was then building a city, and he named it after his son Enoch. 18To Enoch was born Irad, and Irad was the father of Mehujael, and Mehujael was the father of Methushael, and Methushael was the father of Lamech.

19Lamech married two women, one named Adah and the other Zillah. 20Adah gave birth to Jabal; he was the father of those who live in tents and raise livestock. 21His brother's name was Jubal; he was the father of all who play stringed instruments and pipes. 22Zillah also had a son, Tubal-Cain, who forged all kinds of tools out of[j] bronze and iron. Tubal-Cain's sister was Naamah.

23Lamech said to his wives,

'Adah and Zillah, listen to me;
   wives of Lamech, hear my words.
I have killed a man for wounding me,
   a young man for injuring me.
24If Cain is avenged seven times,
   then Lamech seventy-seven times.'

25Adam made love to his wife again, and she gave birth to a son and named him Seth,[k]

---

[a]20 Or *The man*   [b]20 *Eve* probably means *living*.   [c]24 Or *placed in front*   [d]1 Or *The man*   [e]1 *Cain* sounds like the Hebrew for *brought forth* or *acquired*.   [f]1 Or *have acquired*   [g]8 Samaritan Pentateuch, Septuagint, Vulgate and Syriac; Masoretic Text does not have *'Let's go out to the field.'*   [h]15 Septuagint, Vulgate and Syriac; Hebrew *Very well*   [i]16 *Nod* means *wandering* (see verses 12 and 14).   [j]22 Or *who instructed all who work in*   [k]25 *Seth* probably means *granted*.

saying, 'God has granted me another child in place of Abel, since Cain killed him.' 26Seth also had a son, and he named him Enosh.

At that time people began to call on[a] the name of the LORD.

From Adam to Noah

5 This is the written account of Adam's family line.

When God created human beings, he made them in the likeness of God. 2He created them male and female and blessed them. And when they were created, he called them 'human beings'.

3When Adam had lived 130 years, he had a son in his own likeness, in his own image; and he named him Seth. 4After Seth was born, Adam lived 800 years and had other sons and daughters. 5Altogether, Adam lived a total of 930 years, and then he died.

6When Seth had lived 105 years, he became the father[b] of Enosh. 7After he became the father of Enosh, Seth lived 807 years and had other sons and daughters. 8Altogether, Seth lived a total of 912 years, and then he died.

9When Enosh had lived 90 years, he became the father of Kenan. 10After he became the father of Kenan, Enosh lived 815 years and had other sons and daughters. 11Altogether, Enosh lived a total of 905 years, and then he died.

12When Kenan had lived 70 years, he became the father of Mahalalel. 13After he became the father of Mahalalel, Kenan lived 840 years and had other sons and daughters. 14Altogether, Kenan lived a total of 910 years, and then he died.

15When Mahalalel had lived 65 years, he became the father of Jared. 16After he became the father of Jared, Mahalalel lived 830 years and had other sons and daughters. 17Altogether, Mahalalel lived a total of 895 years, and then he died.

18When Jared had lived 162 years, he became the father of Enoch. 19After he became the father of Enoch, Jared lived 800 years and had other sons and daughters. 20Altogether, Jared lived a total of 962 years, and then he died.

21When Enoch had lived 65 years, he became the father of Methuselah. 22After he became the father of Methuselah, Enoch walked faithfully with God 300 years and had other sons and daughters. 23Altogether, Enoch lived a total of 365 years. 24Enoch walked faithfully with God; then he was no more, because God took him away.

25When Methuselah had lived 187 years, he became the father of Lamech. 26After he became the father of Lamech, Methuselah lived 782 years and had other sons and daughters. 27Altogether, Methuselah lived a total of 969 years, and then he died.

28When Lamech had lived 182 years, he had a son. 29He named him Noah[c] and said, 'He will comfort us in the labour and painful toil of our hands caused by the ground the LORD has cursed.' 30After Noah was born, Lamech lived 595 years and had other sons and daughters. 31Altogether, Lamech lived a total of 777 years, and then he died.

32After Noah was 500 years old, he became the father of Shem, Ham and Japheth.

Wickedness in the world

6 When human beings began to increase in number on the earth and daughters were born to them, 2the sons of God saw that these daughters were beautiful, and they married any of them they chose. 3Then the LORD said, 'My Spirit will not contend with[d] human beings for ever, for they are mortal;[e] their days will be a hundred and twenty years.'

4The Nephilim were on the earth in those days—and also afterwards—when the sons of God went to the daughters of the human beings and had children by them. They were the heroes of old, men of renown.

5The LORD saw how great the wickedness of the human race had become on the earth, and that every inclination of the thoughts of the human heart was only evil all the time. 6The LORD regretted that he had

---

[a] 26 Or to proclaim [b] 6 Father may mean ancestor; also in verses 7-26. [c] 29 Noah sounds like the Hebrew for comfort. [d] 3 Or My spirit will not remain in [e] 3 Or corrupt

Making Connections

Nephilim
Genesis 6:4

These mysterious Nephilim are only mentioned twice in the Bible. Some people think they were the result of fallen angels marrying women on earth and having children. They were certainly people of great size and strength who were seen as heroes of the past.

made human beings on the earth, and his heart was deeply troubled. 7So the LORD said, 'I will wipe from the face of the earth the human race I have created—and with them the animals, the birds and the creatures that move along the ground—for I regret that I have made them.' 8But Noah found favour in the eyes of the LORD.

Noah and the flood

9This is the account of Noah and his family.

Noah was a righteous man, blameless among the people of his time, and he walked faithfully with God. 10Noah had three sons: Shem, Ham and Japheth.

11Now the earth was corrupt in God's sight and was full of violence. 12God saw how corrupt the earth had become, for all the people on earth had corrupted their ways. 13So God said to Noah, 'I am going to put an end to all people, for the earth is filled with violence because of them. I am surely going to destroy both them and the earth. 14So make yourself an ark of cypress[a] wood; make rooms in it and coat it with pitch inside and out. 15This is how you are to build it: the ark is to be three hundred cubits long, fifty cubits wide and thirty cubits high.[b] 16Make a roof for it, leaving below the roof an opening one cubit[c] high all around.[d] Put a door in the side of the ark and make lower, middle and upper decks. 17I am going to bring floodwaters on the earth to destroy all life under the heavens, every creature that has the breath of life in it. Everything on earth will perish. 18But I will establish my covenant with you, and you will enter the ark—you and your sons and your wife and your sons' wives with you. 19You are to bring into the ark two of all living creatures, male and female, to keep them alive with you. 20Two of every kind of bird, of every kind of animal and of every kind of creature that moves along the ground will come to you to be kept alive. 21You are to take every kind of food that is to be eaten and store it away as food for you and for them.'

22Noah did everything just as God commanded him.

7 The LORD then said to Noah, 'Go into the ark, you and your whole family, because I have found you righteous in this generation. 2Take with you seven pairs of every kind of clean animal, a male and its mate, and one pair of every kind of unclean animal, a male and its mate, 3and also seven pairs of every kind of bird, male and female, to keep their various kinds alive throughout the earth. 4Seven days from now I will send rain on the earth for forty days and forty nights, and I will wipe from the face of the earth every living creature I have made.'

5And Noah did all that the LORD commanded him.

6Noah was six hundred years old when the floodwaters came on the earth. 7And Noah and his sons and his wife and his sons' wives entered the ark to escape the waters of the flood. 8Pairs of clean and unclean animals, of birds and of all creatures that move along the ground, 9male and female, came to Noah and entered the ark, as God had commanded Noah. 10And after the seven days the floodwaters came on the earth.

---

[a] 14 The meaning of the Hebrew for this word is uncertain. [b] 15 That is, about 135 metres long, 22.5 metres wide and 13.5 metres high [c] 16 That is, about 45 centimetres [d] 16 The meaning of the Hebrew for this clause is uncertain.

Genesis 7:11

¹¹In the six hundredth year of Noah's life, on the seventeenth day of the second month—on that day all the springs of the great deep burst forth, and the floodgates of the heavens were opened. ¹²And rain fell on the earth for forty days and forty nights.

¹³On that very day Noah and his sons, Shem, Ham and Japheth, together with his wife and the wives of his three sons, entered the ark. ¹⁴They had with them every wild animal according to its kind, all livestock according to their kinds, every creature that moves along the ground according to its kind and every bird according to its kind, everything with wings. ¹⁵Pairs of all creatures that have the breath of life in them came to Noah and entered the ark. ¹⁶The animals going in were male and female of every living thing, as God had commanded Noah. Then the LORD shut him in.

¹⁷For forty days the flood kept coming on the earth, and as the waters increased they lifted the ark high above the earth. ¹⁸The waters rose and increased greatly on the earth, and the ark floated on the surface of the water. ¹⁹They rose greatly on the earth, and all the high mountains under the entire heavens were covered. ²⁰The waters rose and covered the mountains to a depth of more than fifteen cubits.[a,b] ²¹Every living thing that moved on the earth perished—birds, livestock, wild animals, all the creatures that swarm over the earth, and the entire human race. ²²Everything on dry land that had the breath of life in its nostrils died. ²³Every living thing on the face of the earth was wiped out; human beings and animals and the creatures that move along the ground and the birds were wiped from the earth. Only Noah was left, and those with him in the ark.

²⁴The waters flooded the earth for a hundred and fifty days.

8 But God remembered Noah and all the wild animals and the livestock that were with him in the ark, and he sent a wind over the earth, and the waters receded. ²Now the springs of the deep and the floodgates of the heavens had been closed, and the rain had stopped falling from the sky. ³The water receded steadily from the earth. At the end of the hundred and fifty days the water had gone down, ⁴and on the seventeenth day of the seventh month the ark came to rest on the mountains of Ararat. ⁵The waters continued to recede until the tenth month, and on the first day of the tenth month the tops of the mountains became visible.

⁶After forty days Noah opened a window he had made in the ark ⁷and sent out a raven, and it kept flying back and forth until the water had dried up from the earth. ⁸Then he sent out a dove to see if the water had receded from the surface of the ground. ⁹But the dove could find nowhere to perch because there was water over all the surface of the earth; so it returned to Noah in the ark. He reached out his hand and took the dove and brought it back to himself in the ark. ¹⁰He waited seven more days and again sent out the dove from the ark. ¹¹When the dove returned to him in the evening, there in its beak was a freshly plucked olive leaf! Then Noah knew that the water had receded from the earth. ¹²He waited seven more days and sent the dove out again, but this time it did not return to him.

People and Places

Noah
Genesis 8:1

Noah stood out as the only person on the whole earth who walked with God. God was hurt that everyone else was so wicked and he decided to wipe out mankind in a flood. He told Noah to build an ark to save his family and all the animals. Noah trusted God and spent many years building the ark on dry land; imagine the jokes that must have been made about him! But Noah did the right thing, and back on dry land again he built an altar and worshipped God.

---

[a] 20 That is, about 6.8 metres [b] 20 Or *rose more than fifteen cubits, and the mountains were covered*

¹³By the first day of the first month of Noah's six hundred and first year, the water had dried up from the earth. Noah then removed the covering from the ark and saw that the surface of the ground was dry. ¹⁴By the twenty-seventh day of the second month the earth was completely dry.

¹⁵Then God said to Noah, ¹⁶'Come out of the ark, you and your wife and your sons and their wives. ¹⁷Bring out every kind of living creature that is with you—the birds, the animals, and all the creatures that move along the ground—so they can multiply on the earth and be fruitful and increase in number on it.'

¹⁸So Noah came out, together with his sons and his wife and his sons' wives. ¹⁹All the animals and all the creatures that move along the ground and all the birds—everything that moves on the earth—came out of the ark, one kind after another.

²⁰Then Noah built an altar to the LORD and, taking some of all the clean animals and clean birds, he sacrificed burnt offerings on it. ²¹The LORD smelled the pleasing aroma and said in his heart: 'Never again will I curse the ground because of human beings, even though*a* every inclination of the human heart is evil from childhood. And never again will I destroy all living creatures, as I have done.

²²'As long as the earth endures,
  seedtime and harvest,
  cold and heat,
  summer and winter,
  day and night
  will never cease.'

God's covenant with Noah

9 Then God blessed Noah and his sons, saying to them, 'Be fruitful and increase in number and fill the earth. ²The fear and dread of you will fall on all the beasts of the earth and all the birds in the sky, on every creature that moves along the ground, and on all the fish in the sea; they are given into your hands. ³Everything that lives and moves will be food for you. Just as I gave you the green plants, I now give you everything.

⁴'But you must not eat meat that has its lifeblood still in it. ⁵And for your lifeblood I will surely demand an accounting. I will demand an accounting from every animal. And from each human being, too, I will demand an accounting for the life of another human being.

⁶'Whoever sheds human blood,
  by human beings shall their blood be shed;
 for in the image of God
  has God made humanity.

⁷As for you, be fruitful and increase in number; multiply on the earth and increase upon it.'

⁸Then God said to Noah and to his sons with him: ⁹'I now establish my covenant with you and with your descendants after you ¹⁰and with every living creature that was with you—the birds, the livestock and all the wild animals, all those that came out of the ark with you—every living creature on earth. ¹¹I establish my covenant with you: never again will all life be destroyed by the waters of a flood; never again will there be a flood to destroy the earth.'

¹²And God said, 'This is the sign of the covenant I am making between me and you and every living creature with you, a covenant for all generations to come: ¹³I have set my rainbow in the clouds, and it will be the sign of the covenant between me and the earth. ¹⁴Whenever I bring clouds over the earth and the rainbow appears in the clouds, ¹⁵I will remember my covenant between me and you and all living creatures of every kind. Never again will the waters become a flood to destroy all life. ¹⁶Whenever the rainbow appears in the clouds, I will see it and remember the everlasting covenant between God and all living creatures of every kind on the earth.'

¹⁷So God said to Noah, 'This is the sign of the covenant I have established between me and all life on the earth.'

The sons of Noah

¹⁸The sons of Noah who came out of the ark were Shem, Ham and Japheth. (Ham was the father of Canaan.) ¹⁹These were the

---

a 21 Or *human beings, for*

three sons of Noah, and from them came the people who were scattered over the whole earth.

20 Noah, a man of the soil, proceeded[a] to plant a vineyard. 21 When he drank some of its wine, he became drunk and lay uncovered inside his tent. 22 Ham, the father of Canaan, saw his father's nakedness and told his two brothers outside. 23 But Shem and Japheth took a garment and laid it across their shoulders; then they walked in backwards and covered their father's nakedness. Their faces were turned the other way so that they would not see their father's nakedness.

24 When Noah awoke from his wine and found out what his youngest son had done to him, 25 he said,

'Cursed be Canaan!
  The lowest of slaves
  will he be to his brothers.'

26 He also said,

'Praise be to the LORD, the God of Shem!
  May Canaan be the slave of Shem.
27 May God extend Japheth's[b] territory;
  may Japheth live in the tents of
    Shem,
  and may Canaan be the slave of
    Japheth.'

28 After the flood Noah lived 350 years. 29 Noah lived a total of 950 years, and then he died.

The table of nations

10 This is the account of Shem, Ham and Japheth, Noah's sons, who themselves had sons after the flood.

The Japhethites

2 The sons[c] of Japheth:
  Gomer, Magog, Madai, Javan, Tubal, Meshek and Tiras.
3 The sons of Gomer:
  Ashkenaz, Riphath and Togarmah.

4 The sons of Javan:
  Elishah, Tarshish, the Kittites and the Rodanites.[d] 5 (From these the maritime peoples spread out into their territories by their clans within their nations, each with its own language.)

The Hamites

6 The sons of Ham:
  Cush, Egypt, Put and Canaan.
7 The sons of Cush:
  Seba, Havilah, Sabtah, Raamah and Sabteka.
The sons of Raamah:
  Sheba and Dedan.

8 Cush was the father[e] of Nimrod, who became a mighty warrior on the earth. 9 He was a mighty hunter before the LORD; that is why it is said, 'Like Nimrod, a mighty hunter before the LORD.' 10 The first centres of his kingdom were Babylon, Uruk, Akkad and Kalneh, in[f] Shinar.[g] 11 From that land he went to Assyria, where he built Nineveh, Rehoboth Ir,[h] Calah 12 and Resen, which is between Nineveh and Calah—which is the great city.

13 Egypt was the father of
  the Ludites, Anamites, Lehabites, Naphtuhites, 14 Pathrusites, Kasluhites (from whom the Philistines came) and Caphtorites.

15 Canaan was the father of
  Sidon his firstborn,[i] and of the Hittites, 16 Jebusites, Amorites, Girgashites, 17 Hivites, Arkites, Sinites, 18 Arvadites, Zemarites and Hamathites.

Later the Canaanite clans scattered 19 and the borders of Canaan reached from Sidon towards Gerar as far as Gaza, and then towards Sodom, Gomorrah, Admah and Zeboyim, as far as Lasha.

20 These are the sons of Ham by their clans and languages, in their territories and nations.

---

[a] 20 Or *soil, was the first*   [b] 27 *Japheth* sounds like the Hebrew for *extend*.   [c] 2 *Sons* may mean *descendants or successors* or *nations*; also in verses 3, 4, 6, 7, 20-23, 29 and 31.   [d] 4 Some manuscripts of the Masoretic Text and Samaritan Pentateuch (see also Septuagint and 1 Chron. 1:7); most manuscripts of the Masoretic Text *Dodanites*   [e] 8 *Father* may mean *ancestor* or *predecessor* or *founder*; also in verses 13, 15, 24 and 26.   [f] 10 Or *Uruk and Akkad—all of them in*   [g] 10 That is, Babylonia   [h] 11 Or *Nineveh with its city squares*   [i] 15 Or *of the Sidonians, the foremost*

The Semites

21 Sons were also born to Shem, whose elder brother was[a] Japheth; Shem was the ancestor of all the sons of Eber.

22 The sons of Shem:
Elam, Ashur, Arphaxad, Lud and Aram.
23 The sons of Aram:
Uz, Hul, Gether and Meshek.[b]
24 Arphaxad was the father of[c] Shelah, and Shelah the father of Eber.
25 Two sons were born to Eber:
One was named Peleg,[d] because in his time the earth was divided; his brother was named Joktan.
26 Joktan was the father of
Almodad, Sheleph, Hazarmaveth, Jerah, 27 Hadoram, Uzal, Diklah, 28 Obal, Abimael, Sheba, 29 Ophir, Havilah and Jobab. All these were sons of Joktan.

30 The region where they lived stretched from Mesha towards Sephar, in the eastern hill country.

31 These are the sons of Shem by their clans and languages, in their territories and nations.

32 These are the clans of Noah's sons, according to their lines of descent, within their nations. From these the nations spread out over the earth after the flood.

The tower of Babel

11 Now the whole world had one language and a common speech. 2 As people moved eastward,[e] they found a plain in Shinar[f] and settled there.

3 They said to each other, 'Come, let's make bricks and bake them thoroughly.' They used brick instead of stone, and bitumen for mortar. 4 Then they said, 'Come, let us build ourselves a city, with a tower that reaches to the heavens, so that we may make a name for ourselves and not be scattered over the face of the whole earth.'

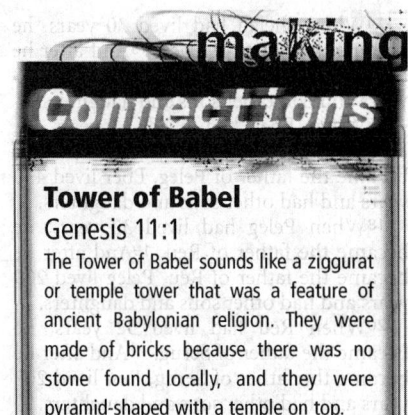

making Connections

Tower of Babel
Genesis 11:1
The Tower of Babel sounds like a ziggurat or temple tower that was a feature of ancient Babylonian religion. They were made of bricks because there was no stone found locally, and they were pyramid-shaped with a temple on top.

5 But the LORD came down to see the city and the tower that they were building. 6 The LORD said, 'If as one people speaking the same language they have begun to do this, then nothing they plan to do will be impossible for them. 7 Come, let us go down and confuse their language so they will not understand each other.'

8 So the LORD scattered them from there over all the earth, and they stopped building the city. 9 That is why it was called Babel[g]—because there the LORD confused the language of the whole world. From there the LORD scattered them over the face of the whole earth.

From Shem to Abram

10 This is the account of Shem's family line.

Two years after the flood, when Shem was 100 years old, he became the father[h] of Arphaxad. 11 And after he became the father of Arphaxad, Shem lived 500 years and had other sons and daughters.

12 When Arphaxad had lived 35 years, he became the father of Shelah. 13 And after he became the father of Shelah, Arphaxad lived 403 years and had other sons and daughters.[i]

---

[a] 21 Or *Shem, the elder brother of* [b] 23 See Septuagint and 1 Chron. 1:17; Hebrew *Mash*. [c] 24 Hebrew; Septuagint *father of Cainan, and Cainan was the father of* [d] 25 *Peleg* means *division*. [e] 2 Or *from the east; or in the east* [f] 2 That is, Babylonia [g] 9 That is, Babylon; *Babel* sounds like the Hebrew for *confused*. [h] 10 *Father* may mean *ancestor*; also in verses 11–25. [i] 12,13 Hebrew; Septuagint (see also Luke 3:35, 36 and note at Gen. 10:24) *35 years, he became the father of Cainan.* 13 *And after he became the father of Cainan, Arphaxad lived 430 years and had other sons and daughters, and then he died. When Cainan had lived 130 years, he became the father of Shelah. And after he became the father of Shelah, Cainan lived 330 years and had other sons and daughters*

14When Shelah had lived 30 years, he became the father of Eber. 15And after he became the father of Eber, Shelah lived 403 years and had other sons and daughters.

16When Eber had lived 34 years, he became the father of Peleg. 17And after he became the father of Peleg, Eber lived 430 years and had other sons and daughters.

18When Peleg had lived 30 years, he became the father of Reu. 19And after he became the father of Reu, Peleg lived 209 years and had other sons and daughters.

20When Reu had lived 32 years, he became the father of Serug. 21And after he became the father of Serug, Reu lived 207 years and had other sons and daughters.

22When Serug had lived 30 years, he became the father of Nahor. 23And after he became the father of Nahor, Serug lived 200 years and had other sons and daughters.

24When Nahor had lived 29 years, he became the father of Terah. 25And after he became the father of Terah, Nahor lived 119 years and had other sons and daughters.

26After Terah had lived 70 years, he became the father of Abram, Nahor and Haran.

Abram's family

27This is the account of Terah's family line.

Terah became the father of Abram, Nahor and Haran. And Haran became the father of Lot. 28While his father Terah was still alive, Haran died in Ur of the Chaldeans, in the land of his birth. 29Abram and Nahor both married. The name of Abram's wife was Sarai, and the name of Nahor's wife was Milkah; she was the daughter of Haran, the father of both Milkah and Iskah. 30Now Sarai was childless because she was not able to conceive.

31Terah took his son Abram, his grandson Lot son of Haran, and his daughter-in-law Sarai, the wife of his son Abram, and together they set out from Ur of the Chaldeans to go to Canaan. But when they came to Harran, they settled there.

32Terah lived 205 years, and he died in Harran.

People and Places

Abraham
Genesis 12:1

Who would you choose to be the founder of a mighty nation of chosen people? God chose Abram, an old man who was unable to have children. But once God had called him into a covenant relationship, anything was possible. God changed his name to 'Abraham' and miraculously gave him a son, Isaac. Abraham became the father of the nation of Israel, one of the great patriarchs and a great example of someone who had faith.

The call of Abram

12 The LORD had said to Abram, 'Go from your country, your people and your father's household to the land I will show you.

2'I will make you into a great nation,
 and I will bless you;
I will make your name great,
 and you will be a blessing.[a]
3I will bless those who bless you,
 and whoever curses you I will curse;
and all peoples on earth
 will be blessed through you.'[b]

4So Abram went, as the LORD had told him; and Lot went with him. Abram was seventy-five years old when he set out from Harran. 5He took his wife Sarai, his nephew Lot, all the possessions they had accumulated and the people they had acquired in Harran, and they set out for the land of Canaan, and they arrived there.

6Abram travelled through the land as far as the site of the great tree of Moreh at Shechem. At that time the Canaanites were in the land. 7The LORD appeared to Abram and said, 'To your offspring[c] I will give this

---

[a] 2 Or great, / and you will be seen as blessed [b] 3 Or earth / I will use your name in blessings (see Gen. 48:20) [c] 7 Or seed

land.' So he built an altar there to the LORD, who had appeared to him.

8From there he went on towards the hills east of Bethel and pitched his tent, with Bethel on the west and Ai on the east. There he built an altar to the LORD and called on the name of the LORD.

9Then Abram set out and continued towards the Negev.

Abram in Egypt

10Now there was a famine in the land, and Abram went down to Egypt to live there for a while because the famine was severe. 11As he was about to enter Egypt, he said to his wife Sarai, 'I know what a beautiful woman you are. 12When the Egyptians see you, they will say, "This is his wife." Then they will kill me but will let you live. 13Say you are my sister, so that I will be treated well for your sake and my life will be spared because of you.'

14When Abram came to Egypt, the Egyptians saw that Sarai was a very beautiful woman. 15And when Pharaoh's officials saw her, they praised her to Pharaoh, and she was taken into his palace. 16He treated Abram well for her sake, and Abram acquired sheep and cattle, male and female donkeys, male and female servants, and camels.

17But the LORD inflicted serious diseases on Pharaoh and his household because of Abram's wife Sarai. 18So Pharaoh summoned Abram. 'What have you done to me?' he said. 'Why didn't you tell me she was your wife? 19Why did you say, "She is my sister," so that I took her to be my wife? Now then, here is your wife. Take her and go!' 20Then Pharaoh gave orders about Abram to his men, and they sent him on his way, with his wife and everything he had.

Abram and Lot separate

13 So Abram went up from Egypt to the Negev, with his wife and everything he had, and Lot went with him. 2Abram had become very wealthy in livestock and in silver and gold.

3From the Negev he went from place to place until he came to Bethel, to the place between Bethel and Ai where his tent had been earlier 4and where he had first built an altar. There Abram called on the name of the LORD.

5Now Lot, who was moving about with Abram, also had flocks and herds and tents. 6But the land could not support them while they stayed together, for their possessions were so great that they were not able to stay together. 7And quarrelling arose between Abram's herders and the herders of Lot. The Canaanites and Perizzites were also living in the land at that time.

8So Abram said to Lot, 'Let's not have any quarrelling between you and me, or between your herders and mine, for we are close relatives. 9Is not the whole land before you? Let's part company. If you go to the left, I'll go to the right; if you go to the right, I'll go to the left.'

10Lot looked around and saw that the whole plain of the Jordan was well watered, like the garden of the LORD, like the land of Egypt, towards Zoar. (This was before the LORD destroyed Sodom and Gomorrah.) 11So Lot chose for himself the whole plain of the Jordan and set out towards the east. The two men parted company: 12Abram lived in the land of Canaan, while Lot lived among the cities of the plain and pitched his tents near Sodom. 13Now the people of Sodom were wicked and were sinning greatly against the LORD.

14The LORD said to Abram after Lot had parted from him, 'Look around from where you are, to the north and south, to the east and west. 15All the land that you see I will give to you and your offspring[a] for ever. 16I will make your offspring like the dust of the earth, so that if anyone could count the dust, then your offspring could be counted. 17Go, walk through the length and breadth of the land, for I am giving it to you.'

18So Abram went to live near the great trees of Mamre at Hebron, where he pitched his tents. There he built an altar to the LORD.

Abram rescues Lot

14 At the time when Amraphel was king of Shinar,[b] Arioch king of Ellasar, Kedorlaomer king of Elam and

---

[a] 15 Or *seed*; also in verse 16   [b] 1 That is, Babylonia; also in verse 9

Tidal king of Goyim, ²these kings went to war against Bera king of Sodom, Birsha king of Gomorrah, Shinab king of Admah, Shemeber king of Zeboyim, and the king of Bela (that is, Zoar). ³All these latter kings joined forces in the Valley of Siddim (that is, the Dead Sea Valley). ⁴For twelve years they had been subject to Kedorlaomer, but in the thirteenth year they rebelled.

⁵In the fourteenth year, Kedorlaomer and the kings allied with him went out and defeated the Rephaites in Ashteroth Karnaim, the Zuzites in Ham, the Emites in Shaveh Kiriathaim ⁶and the Horites in the hill country of Seir, as far as El Paran near the desert. ⁷Then they turned back and went to En Mishpat (that is, Kadesh), and they conquered the whole territory of the Amalekites, as well as the Amorites who were living in Hazezon Tamar.

⁸Then the king of Sodom, the king of Gomorrah, the king of Admah, the king of Zeboyim and the king of Bela (that is, Zoar) marched out and drew up their battle lines in the Valley of Siddim ⁹against Kedorlaomer king of Elam, Tidal king of Goyim, Amraphel king of Shinar and Arioch king of Ellasar—four kings against five. ¹⁰Now the Valley of Siddim was full of tar pits, and when the kings of Sodom and Gomorrah fled, some of the men fell into them and the rest fled to the hills. ¹¹The four kings seized all the goods of Sodom and Gomorrah and all their food; then they went away. ¹²They also carried off Abram's nephew Lot and his possessions, since he was living in Sodom.

¹³A man who had escaped came and reported this to Abram the Hebrew. Now Abram was living near the great trees of Mamre the Amorite, a brother*ᵃ* of Eshkol and Aner, all of whom were allied with Abram. ¹⁴When Abram heard that his relative had been taken captive, he called out the 318 trained men born in his household and went in pursuit as far as Dan. ¹⁵During the night Abram divided his men to attack them and he routed them, pursuing them as far as Hobah, north of Damascus. ¹⁶He recovered all the goods and brought back his relative Lot and his possessions, together with the women and the other people.

¹⁷After Abram returned from defeating Kedorlaomer and the kings allied with him, the king of Sodom came out to meet him in the Valley of Shaveh (that is, the King's Valley).

¹⁸Then Melchizedek king of Salem brought out bread and wine. He was priest of God Most High, ¹⁹and he blessed Abram, saying,

'Blessed be Abram by God Most High,
  Creator of heaven and earth.
²⁰And praise be to God Most High,
  who delivered your enemies into your hand.'

Then Abram gave him a tenth of everything. ²¹The king of Sodom said to Abram, 'Give me the people and keep the goods for yourself.'

²²But Abram said to the king of Sodom, 'With raised hand I have sworn an oath to the LORD, God Most High, Creator of heaven and earth, ²³that I will accept nothing belonging to you, not even a thread or the thong of a sandal, so that you will never be able to say, "I made Abram rich." ²⁴I will accept nothing but what my men have eaten and the share that belongs to the men who went with me—to Aner, Eshkol and Mamre. Let them have their share.'

God's covenant with Abram

15 After this, the word of the LORD came to Abram in a vision:

'Do not be afraid, Abram.
  I am your shield,*ᵇ*
  your very great reward.'*ᶜ*

²But Abram said, 'Sovereign LORD, what can you give me since I remain childless and the one who will inherit*ᵈ* my estate is Eliezer of Damascus?' ³And Abram said, 'You have given me no children; so a servant in my household will be my heir.'

⁴Then the word of the LORD came to him: 'This man will not be your heir, but a son coming from your own body will be your heir.' ⁵He took him outside and said,

---

ᵃ 13 Or *a relative*; or *an ally*   *ᵇ* 1 Or *sovereign*   *ᶜ* 1 Or *shield; I your reward will be very great*   *ᵈ* 2 The meaning of the Hebrew for this phrase is uncertain.

'Look up at the heavens and count the stars—if indeed you can count them.' Then he said to him, 'So shall your offspring^a be.'

6Abram believed the LORD, and he credited it to him as righteousness.

7He also said to him, 'I am the LORD, who brought you out of Ur of the Chaldeans to give you this land to take possession of it.'

8But Abram said, 'Sovereign LORD, how can I know that I shall gain possession of it?'

9So the LORD said to him, 'Bring me a heifer, a goat and a ram, each three years old, along with a dove and a young pigeon.'

10Abram brought all these to him, cut them in two and arranged the halves opposite each other; the birds, however, he did not cut in half. 11Then birds of prey came down on the carcasses, but Abram drove them away.

12As the sun was setting, Abram fell into a deep sleep, and a thick and dreadful darkness came over him. 13Then the LORD said to him, 'Know for certain that for four hundred years your descendants will be strangers in a country not their own and that they will be enslaved and ill-treated there. 14But I will punish the nation they serve as slaves, and afterwards they will come out with great possessions. 15You, however, will go to your ancestors in peace and be buried at a good old age. 16In the fourth generation your descendants will come back here, for the sin of the Amorites has not yet reached its full measure.'

17When the sun had set and darkness had fallen, a smoking brazier with a blazing torch appeared and passed between the pieces. 18On that day the LORD made a covenant with Abram and said, 'To your descendants I give this land, from the Wadi^b of Egypt to the great river, the Euphrates— 19the land of the Kenites, Kenizzites, Kadmonites, 20Hittites, Perizzites, Rephaites, 21Amorites, Canaanites, Girgashites and Jebusites.'

Hagar and Ishmael

16 Now Sarai, Abram's wife, had borne him no children. But she had an Egyptian servant named Hagar; 2so she said to Abram, 'The LORD has kept me from having children. Go, sleep with my servant; perhaps I can build a family through her.'

Abram agreed to what Sarai said. 3So after Abram had been living in Canaan ten years, Sarai his wife took her Egyptian servant Hagar and gave her to her husband to be his wife. 4He slept with Hagar, and she conceived.

When she knew she was pregnant, she began to despise her mistress. 5Then Sarai said to Abram, 'You are responsible for the wrong I am suffering. I put my servant in your arms, and now that she knows she is pregnant, she despises me. May the LORD judge between you and me.'

6'Your servant is in your hands,' Abram said. 'Do with her whatever you think best.' Then Sarai ill-treated Hagar; so she fled from her.

7The angel of the LORD found Hagar near a spring in the desert; it was the spring that is beside the road to Shur. 8And he said, 'Hagar, servant of Sarai, where have you come from, and where are you going?'

'I'm running away from my mistress Sarai,' she answered.

9Then the angel of the LORD told her, 'Go back to your mistress and submit to her.' 10The angel added, 'I will increase your

---

IN OTHER WORDS

Covenant
Genesis 15:18

A special agreement, a contract, showing a close relationship between two parties. This covenant between God and Abraham and the covenant between God and Israel (Genesis 35:9–12) are important examples early in the Bible. When Jesus shared the Last Supper with the disciples he said that he had put in place a new covenant (Matthew 26:28).

---

^{a}5 Or *seed* ^{b}18 Or *river*

descendants so much that they will be too numerous to count.'

11 The angel of the LORD also said to her:

'You are now pregnant
 and you will give birth to a son.
You shall name him Ishmael,[a]
 for the LORD has heard of your misery.
12 He will be a wild donkey of a man;
 his hand will be against everyone
 and everyone's hand against him,
and he will live in hostility
 towards[b] all his brothers.'

13 She gave this name to the LORD who spoke to her: 'You are the God who sees me,' for she said, 'I have now seen[c] the One who sees me.' 14 That is why the well was called Beer Lahai Roi;[d] it is still there, between Kadesh and Bered.

15 So Hagar bore Abram a son, and Abram gave the name Ishmael to the son she had borne. 16 Abram was eighty-six years old when Hagar bore him Ishmael.

The covenant of circumcision

17 When Abram was ninety-nine years old, the LORD appeared to him and said, 'I am God Almighty;[e] walk before me faithfully and be blameless. 2 Then I will make my covenant between me and you and will greatly increase your numbers.'

3 Abram fell face down, and God said to him, 4 'As for me, this is my covenant with you: you will be the father of many nations. 5 No longer will you be called Abram;[f] your name will be Abraham,[g] for I have made you a father of many nations. 6 I will make you very fruitful; I will make nations of you, and kings will come from you. 7 I will establish my covenant as an everlasting covenant between me and you and your descendants after you for the generations to come, to be your God and the God of your descendants after you. 8 The whole land of Canaan, where you now reside as a foreigner, I will give as an everlasting possession to you and your descendants after you; and I will be their God.'

> **IN OTHER WORDS**
>
> **Circumcision**
> **Genesis 17:10**
> This was a special ritual given by God to set the Jews apart from other peoples in Palestine. Every male child was to have his foreskin removed.

9 Then God said to Abraham, 'As for you, you must keep my covenant, you and your descendants after you for the generations to come. 10 This is my covenant with you and your descendants after you, the covenant you are to keep: every male among you shall be circumcised. 11 You are to undergo circumcision, and it will be the sign of the covenant between me and you. 12 For the generations to come every male among you who is eight days old must be circumcised, including those born in your household or bought with money from a foreigner—those who are not your offspring. 13 Whether born in your household or bought with your money, they must be circumcised. My covenant in your flesh is to be an everlasting covenant. 14 Any uncircumcised male, who has not been circumcised in the flesh, will be cut off from his people; he has broken my covenant.'

15 God also said to Abraham, 'As for Sarai your wife, you are no longer to call her Sarai; her name will be Sarah. 16 I will bless her and will surely give you a son by her. I will bless her so that she will be the mother of nations; kings of peoples will come from her.'

17 Abraham fell face down; he laughed and said to himself, 'Will a son be born to a man a hundred years old? Will Sarah bear a child at the age of ninety?' 18 And Abraham said to God, 'If only Ishmael might live under your blessing!'

19 Then God said, 'Yes, but your wife Sarah will bear you a son, and you will call him Isaac.[h] I will establish my covenant with

---

[a] 11 *Ishmael* means *God hears.*   [b] 12 Or *live to the east / of*   [c] 13 Or *seen the back of*   [d] 14 *Beer Lahai Roi* means *well of the Living One who sees me.*   [e] 1 Hebrew *El-Shaddai*   [f] 5 *Abram* means *exalted father.*   [g] 5 *Abraham* probably means *father of many.*   [h] 19 *Isaac* means *he laughs.*

him as an everlasting covenant for his descendants after him. ²⁰And as for Ishmael, I have heard you: I will surely bless him; I will make him fruitful and will greatly increase his numbers. He will be the father of twelve rulers, and I will make him into a great nation. ²¹But my covenant I will establish with Isaac, whom Sarah will bear to you by this time next year.' ²²When he had finished speaking with Abraham, God went up from him.

²³On that very day Abraham took his son Ishmael and all those born in his household or bought with his money, every male in his household, and circumcised them, as God told him. ²⁴Abraham was ninety-nine years old when he was circumcised, ²⁵and his son Ishmael was thirteen; ²⁶Abraham and his son Ishmael were both circumcised on that same day. ²⁷And every male in Abraham's household, including those born in his household or bought from a foreigner, was circumcised with him.

The three visitors

18 The LORD appeared to Abraham near the great trees of Mamre while he was sitting at the entrance to his tent in the heat of the day. ²Abraham looked up and saw three men standing nearby. When he saw them, he hurried from the entrance of his tent to meet them and bowed low to the ground.

³He said, 'If I have found favour in your eyes, my lord,[a] do not pass your servant by. ⁴Let a little water be brought, and then you may all wash your feet and rest under this tree. ⁵Let me get you something to eat, so you can be refreshed and then go on your way—now that you have come to your servant.'

'Very well,' they answered, 'do as you say.'

⁶So Abraham hurried into the tent to Sarah. 'Quick,' he said, 'get three seahs[b] of the finest flour and knead it and bake some bread.'

⁷Then he ran to the herd and selected a choice, tender calf and gave it to a servant, who hurried to prepare it. ⁸He then brought some curds and milk and the calf that had been prepared, and set these before them. While they ate, he stood near them under a tree.

⁹'Where is your wife Sarah?' they asked him.

'There, in the tent,' he said.

¹⁰Then the LORD[c] said, 'I will surely return to you about this time next year, and Sarah your wife will have a son.'

Now Sarah was listening at the entrance to the tent, which was behind him. ¹¹Abraham and Sarah were already very old, and Sarah was past the age of childbearing. ¹²So Sarah laughed to herself as she thought, 'After I am worn out and my lord is old, will I now have this pleasure?'

¹³Then the LORD said to Abraham, 'Why did Sarah laugh and say, "Will I really have a child, now that I am old?" ¹⁴Is anything too hard for the LORD? I will return to you at the appointed time next year and Sarah will have a son.'

¹⁵Sarah was afraid, so she lied and said, 'I did not laugh.'

But he said, 'Yes, you did laugh.'

Abraham pleads for Sodom

¹⁶When the men got up to leave, they looked down towards Sodom, and Abraham walked along with them to see them on their way. ¹⁷Then the LORD said, 'Shall I hide from Abraham what I am about to do? ¹⁸Abraham will surely become a great and powerful nation, and all nations on earth will be blessed through him.[d] ¹⁹For I have chosen him, so that he will direct his children and his household after him to keep the way of the LORD by doing what is right and just, so that the LORD will bring about for Abraham what he has promised him.'

²⁰Then the LORD said, 'The outcry against Sodom and Gomorrah is so great and their sin so grievous ²¹that I will go down and see if what they have done is as bad as the outcry that has reached me. If not, I will know.'

²²The men turned away and went towards Sodom, but Abraham remained standing before the LORD.[e] ²³Then Abraham approached him and said: 'Will

---

[a] 3 Or *eyes, Lord* [b] 6 That is, probably about 16 kilograms [c] 10 Hebrew *Then he* [d] 18 Or *will use his name in blessings* (see Gen. 48:20) [e] 22 Masoretic Text; an ancient Hebrew scribal tradition *but the LORD remained standing before Abraham*

you sweep away the righteous with the wicked? 24What if there are fifty righteous people in the city? Will you really sweep it away and not spare*a* the place for the sake of the fifty righteous people in it? 25Far be it from you to do such a thing—to kill the righteous with the wicked, treating the righteous and the wicked alike. Far be it from you! Will not the Judge of all the earth do right?'

26The LORD said, 'If I find fifty righteous people in the city of Sodom, I will spare the whole place for their sake.'

27Then Abraham spoke up again: 'Now that I have been so bold as to speak to the Lord, though I am nothing but dust and ashes, 28what if the number of the righteous is five less than fifty? Will you destroy the whole city for lack of five people?'

'If I find forty-five there,' he said, 'I will not destroy it.'

29Once again he spoke to him, 'What if only forty are found there?'

He said, 'For the sake of forty, I will not do it.'

30Then he said, 'May the Lord not be angry, but let me speak. What if only thirty can be found there?'

He answered, 'I will not do it if I find thirty there.'

31Abraham said, 'Now that I have been so bold as to speak to the Lord, what if only twenty can be found there?'

He said, 'For the sake of twenty, I will not destroy it.'

32Then he said, 'May the Lord not be angry, but let me speak just once more. What if only ten can be found there?'

He answered, 'For the sake of ten, I will not destroy it.'

33When the LORD had finished speaking with Abraham, he left, and Abraham returned home.

Sodom and Gomorrah destroyed

19 The two angels arrived at Sodom in the evening, and Lot was sitting in the gateway of the city. When he saw them, he got up to meet them and bowed down with his face to the ground. 2'My lords,' he said, 'please turn aside to your servant's house. You can wash your feet and spend the night and then go on your way early in the morning.'

'No,' they answered, 'we will spend the night in the square.'

3But he insisted so strongly that they did go with him and entered his house. He prepared a meal for them, baking bread without yeast, and they ate. 4Before they had gone to bed, all the men from every part of the city of Sodom—both young and old—surrounded the house. 5They called to Lot, 'Where are the men who came to you tonight? Bring them out to us so that we can have sex with them.'

6Lot went outside to meet them and shut the door behind him 7and said, 'No, my friends. Don't do this wicked thing. 8Look, I have two daughters who have never slept with a man. Let me bring them out to you, and you can do what you like with them. But don't do anything to these men, for they have come under the protection of my roof.'

9'Get out of our way,' they replied. 'This fellow came here as a foreigner, and now he wants to play the judge! We'll treat you worse than them.' They kept bringing pressure on Lot and moved forward to break down the door.

10But the men inside reached out and pulled Lot back into the house and shut the door. 11Then they struck the men who were at the door of the house, young and old, with blindness so that they could not find the door.

12The two men said to Lot, 'Do you have anyone else here—sons-in-law, sons or daughters, or anyone else in the city who belongs to you? Get them out of here, 13because we are going to destroy this place. The outcry to the LORD against its people is so great that he has sent us to destroy it.'

14So Lot went out and spoke to his sons-in-law, who were pledged to marry*b* his daughters. He said, 'Hurry and get out of this place, because the LORD is about to destroy the city!' But his sons-in-law thought he was joking.

15With the coming of dawn, the angels urged Lot, saying, 'Hurry! Take your wife and your two daughters who are here, or

---

a 24 Or *forgive*; also in verse 26   *b* 14 Or *were married to* you will be swept away when the city is punished.'

16When he hesitated, the men grasped his hand and the hands of his wife and of his two daughters and led them safely out of the city, for the LORD was merciful to them. 17As soon as they had brought them out, one of them said, 'Flee for your lives! Don't look back, and don't stop anywhere in the plain! Flee to the mountains or you will be swept away!'

18But Lot said to them, 'No, my lords,[a] please! 19Your[b] servant has found favour in your[c] eyes, and you[d] have shown great kindness to me in sparing my life. But I can't flee to the mountains; this disaster will overtake me, and I'll die. 20Look, here is a town near enough to run to, and it is small. Let me flee to it—it is very small, isn't it? Then my life will be spared.'

21He said to him, 'Very well, I will grant this request too; I will not overthrow the town you speak of. 22But flee there quickly, because I cannot do anything until you reach it.' (That is why the town was called Zoar.[e])

23By the time Lot reached Zoar, the sun had risen over the land. 24Then the LORD rained down burning sulphur on Sodom and Gomorrah—from the LORD out of the heavens. 25Thus he overthrew those cities and the entire plain, destroying all those living in the cities—and also the vegetation in the land. 26But Lot's wife looked back, and she became a pillar of salt.

27Early the next morning Abraham got up and returned to the place where he had stood before the LORD. 28He looked down towards Sodom and Gomorrah, towards all the land of the plain, and he saw dense smoke rising from the land, like smoke from a furnace.

29So when God destroyed the cities of the plain, he remembered Abraham, and he brought Lot out of the catastrophe that overthrew the cities where Lot had lived.

Lot and his daughters

30Lot and his two daughters left Zoar and settled in the mountains, for he was afraid to stay in Zoar. He and his two daughters lived in a cave. 31One day the elder daughter said to the younger, 'Our father is old, and there is no man round here to give us children—as is the custom all over the earth. 32Let's get our father to drink wine and then sleep with him and preserve our family line through our father.'

33That night they got their father to drink wine, and the elder daughter went in and slept with him. He was not aware of it when she lay down or when she got up.

34The next day the elder daughter said to the younger, 'Last night I slept with my father. Let's get him to drink wine again tonight, and you go in and sleep with him so we can preserve our family line through our father.' 35So they got their father to drink wine that night also, and the younger daughter went in and slept with him. Again he was not aware of it when she lay down or when she got up.

36So both of Lot's daughters became pregnant by their father. 37The elder daughter had a son, and she named him Moab;[f] he is the father of the Moabites of today. 38The younger daughter also had a son, and she named him Ben-Ammi;[g] he is the father of the Ammonites[h] of today.

Pillar of salt
Genesis 19:26
What a horrible way to go! Sodom and Gomorrah were in the Jordan valley near the south end of the Dead Sea, the lowest point on earth. Oddly-shaped rock-salt formations are found naturally in this area; that's what Lot's wife was turned into when she ignored the angels and looked back at the cities.

---

[a] 18 Or *No, Lord*; or *No, my lord*   [b] 19 The Hebrew is singular.   [c] 19 The Hebrew is singular.   [d] 19 The Hebrew is singular.   [e] 22 *Zoar* means *small*.   [f] 37 *Moab* sounds like the Hebrew for *from father*.   [g] 38 *Ben-Ammi* means *son of my father's people*.   [h] 38 Hebrew *Bene-Ammon*

Abraham and Abimelek

20 Now Abraham moved on from there into the region of the Negev and lived between Kadesh and Shur. For a while he stayed in Gerar, 2and there Abraham said of his wife Sarah, 'She is my sister.' Then Abimelek king of Gerar sent for Sarah and took her.

3But God came to Abimelek in a dream one night and said to him, 'You are as good as dead because of the woman you have taken; she is a married woman.'

4Now Abimelek had not gone near her, so he said, 'Lord, will you destroy an innocent nation? 5Did he not say to me, "She is my sister," and didn't she also say, "He is my brother"? I have done this with a clear conscience and clean hands.'

6Then God said to him in the dream, 'Yes, I know you did this with a clear conscience, and so I have kept you from sinning against me. That is why I did not let you touch her. 7Now return the man's wife, for he is a prophet, and he will pray for you and you will live. But if you do not return her, you may be sure that you and all who belong to you will die.'

8Early the next morning Abimelek summoned all his officials, and when he told them all that had happened, they were very much afraid. 9Then Abimelek called Abraham in and said, 'What have you done to us? How have I wronged you that you have brought such great guilt upon me and my kingdom? You have done things to me that should never be done.' 10And Abimelek asked Abraham, 'What was your reason for doing this?'

11Abraham replied, 'I said to myself, "There is surely no fear of God in this place, and they will kill me because of my wife." 12Besides, she really is my sister, the daughter of my father though not of my mother; and she became my wife. 13And when God caused me to wander from my father's household, I said to her, "This is how you can show your love to me: everywhere we go, say of me, 'He is my brother.'"'

14Then Abimelek brought sheep and cattle and male and female slaves and gave them to Abraham, and he returned Sarah his wife to him. 15And Abimelek said, 'My land is before you; live wherever you like.'

16To Sarah he said, 'I am giving your brother a thousand shekels[a] of silver. This is to cover the offence against you before all who are with you; you are completely vindicated.'

17Then Abraham prayed to God, and God healed Abimelek, his wife and his female slaves so they could have children again, 18for the LORD had kept all the women in Abimelek's household from conceiving because of Abraham's wife Sarah.

The birth of Isaac

21 Now the LORD was gracious to Sarah as he had said, and the LORD did for Sarah what he had promised. 2Sarah became pregnant and bore a son to Abraham in his old age, at the very time God had promised him. 3Abraham gave the name Isaac[b] to the son Sarah bore him. 4When his son Isaac was eight days old, Abraham circumcised him, as God commanded him. 5Abraham was a hundred years old when his son Isaac was born to him.

People and Places

Isaac
Genesis 21:3

Both Abraham and Sarah laughed when they were told they were going to have a son in their old age, and so that's what they called their baby when he finally arrived; Isaac means 'laughter'. God tested Abraham's faith by asking him to sacrifice his precious son Isaac, and then provided a ram at the last minute instead. Isaac married Rebekah and had two sons, Jacob and Esau.

---

[a] 16 That is, about 11.5 kilograms   [b] 3 *Isaac* means *he laughs*.

6Sarah said, 'God has brought me laughter, and everyone who hears about this will laugh with me.' 7And she added, 'Who would have said to Abraham that Sarah would nurse children? Yet I have borne him a son in his old age.'

Hagar and Ishmael sent away

8The child grew and was weaned, and on the day Isaac was weaned Abraham held a great feast. 9But Sarah saw that the son whom Hagar the Egyptian had borne to Abraham was mocking, 10and she said to Abraham, 'Get rid of that slave woman and her son, for that slave woman's son will never share in the inheritance with my son Isaac.'

11The matter distressed Abraham greatly because it concerned his son. 12But God said to him, 'Do not be so distressed about the boy and your servant. Listen to whatever Sarah tells you, because it is through Isaac that your offspring[a] will be reckoned. 13I will make the son of the servant into a nation also, because he is your offspring.'

14Early the next morning Abraham took some food and a skin of water and gave them to Hagar. He set them on her shoulders and then sent her off with the boy. She went on her way and wandered in the Desert of Beersheba.

15When the water in the skin was gone, she put the boy under one of the bushes. 16Then she went off and sat down about a bow-shot away, for she thought, 'I cannot watch the boy die.' And as she sat there, she[b] began to sob.

17God heard the boy crying, and the angel of God called to Hagar from heaven and said to her, 'What is the matter, Hagar? Do not be afraid; God has heard the boy crying as he lies there. 18Lift the boy up and take him by the hand, for I will make him into a great nation.'

19Then God opened her eyes and she saw a well of water. So she went and filled the skin with water and gave the boy a drink.

20God was with the boy as he grew up. He lived in the desert and became an archer. 21While he was living in the Desert of Paran, his mother got a wife for him from Egypt.

The treaty at Beersheba

22At that time Abimelek and Phicol the commander of his forces said to Abraham, 'God is with you in everything you do. 23Now swear to me here before God that you will not deal falsely with me or my children or my descendants. Show to me and the country where you now reside as a foreigner the same kindness that I have shown to you.'

24Abraham said, 'I swear it.'

25Then Abraham complained to Abimelek about a well of water that Abimelek's servants had seized. 26But Abimelek said, 'I don't know who has done this. You did not tell me, and I heard about it only today.'

27So Abraham brought sheep and cattle and gave them to Abimelek, and the two men made a treaty. 28Abraham set apart seven ewe lambs from the flock, 29and Abimelek asked Abraham, 'What is the meaning of these seven ewe lambs you have set apart by themselves?'

30He replied, 'Accept these seven lambs from my hand as a witness that I dug this well.'

31So that place was called Beersheba,[c] because the two men swore an oath there.

32After the treaty had been made at Beersheba, Abimelek and Phicol the commander of his forces returned to the land of the Philistines. 33Abraham planted a tamarisk tree in Beersheba, and there he called on the name of the LORD, the Eternal God. 34And Abraham stayed in the land of the Philistines for a long time.

Abraham tested

22 Some time later God tested Abraham. He said to him, 'Abraham!'

'Here I am,' he replied.

2Then God said, 'Take your son, your only son, whom you love—Isaac—and go to the region of Moriah. Sacrifice him there as a burnt offering on a mountain that I will show you.'

3Early the next morning Abraham got up and loaded his donkey. He took with him two of his servants and his son Isaac. When he had cut enough wood for the burnt offering, he set out for the place God had

---

[a] 12 Or *seed* [b] 16 Hebrew; Septuagint *the child* [c] 31 *Beersheba* can mean *well of seven* or *well of the oath*.

told him about. ⁴On the third day Abraham looked up and saw the place in the distance. ⁵He said to his servants, 'Stay here with the donkey while I and the boy go over there. We will worship and then we will come back to you.'

⁶Abraham took the wood for the burnt offering and placed it on his son Isaac, and he himself carried the fire and the knife. As the two of them went on together, ⁷Isaac spoke up and said to his father Abraham, 'Father?'

'Yes, my son?' Abraham replied.

'The fire and wood are here,' Isaac said, 'but where is the lamb for the burnt offering?'

⁸Abraham answered, 'God himself will provide the lamb for the burnt offering, my son.' And the two of them went on together.

⁹When they reached the place God had told him about, Abraham built an altar there and arranged the wood on it. He bound his son Isaac and laid him on the altar, on top of the wood. ¹⁰Then he reached out his hand and took the knife to slay his son. ¹¹But the angel of the LORD called out to him from heaven, 'Abraham! Abraham!'

'Here I am,' he replied.

¹²'Do not lay a hand on the boy,' he said. 'Do not do anything to him. Now I know that you fear God, because you have not withheld from me your son, your only son.'

¹³Abraham looked up and there in a thicket he saw a ram[a] caught by its horns. He went over and took the ram and sacrificed it as a burnt offering instead of his son. ¹⁴So Abraham called that place The LORD Will Provide. And to this day it is said, 'On the mountain of the LORD it will be provided.'

¹⁵The angel of the LORD called to Abraham from heaven a second time ¹⁶and said, 'I swear by myself, declares the LORD, that because you have done this and have not withheld your son, your only son, ¹⁷I will surely bless you and make your descendants as numerous as the stars in the sky and as the sand on the seashore. Your descendants will take possession of the cities of their enemies, ¹⁸and through your offspring[b] all nations on earth will be blessed,[c] because you have obeyed me.'

¹⁹Then Abraham returned to his servants, and they set off together for Beersheba. And Abraham stayed in Beersheba.

Nahor's sons

²⁰Some time later Abraham was told, 'Milkah is also a mother; she has borne sons to your brother Nahor: ²¹Uz the firstborn, Buz his brother, Kemuel (the father of Aram), ²²Kesed, Hazo, Pildash, Jidlaph and Bethuel.' ²³Bethuel became the father of Rebekah. Milkah bore these eight sons to Abraham's brother Nahor. ²⁴His concubine, whose name was Reumah, also had sons: Tebah, Gaham, Tahash and Maakah.

The death of Sarah

23 Sarah lived to be a hundred and twenty-seven years old. ²She died at Kiriath Arba (that is, Hebron) in the land of Canaan, and Abraham went to mourn for Sarah and to weep over her.

³Then Abraham rose from beside his dead wife and spoke to the Hittites.[d] He said, ⁴'I am a foreigner and stranger among you. Sell me some property for a burial site here so that I can bury my dead.'

⁵The Hittites replied to Abraham, ⁶'Sir, listen to us. You are a mighty prince among us. Bury your dead in the choicest of our tombs. None of us will refuse you his tomb for burying your dead.'

⁷Then Abraham rose and bowed down before the people of the land, the Hittites. ⁸He said to them, 'If you are willing to let me bury my dead, then listen to me and intercede with Ephron son of Zohar on my behalf ⁹so that he will sell me the cave of Machpelah, which belongs to him and is at the end of his field. Ask him to sell it to me for the full price as a burial site among you.'

¹⁰Ephron the Hittite was sitting among his people and he replied to Abraham in the hearing of all the Hittites who had come to the gate of his city. ¹¹'No, my lord,' he said. 'Listen to me; I give[e] you the field, and I give[f]

---

[a] 13 Many manuscripts of the Masoretic Text, Samaritan Pentateuch, Septuagint and Syriac; most manuscripts of the Masoretic Text *a ram behind | him |*   [b] 18 Or *seed*   [c] 18 Or *and all nations on earth will use the name of your offspring in blessings* (see Gen. 48:20)   [d] 3 Or *the descendants of Heth;* also in verses 5, 7, 10, 16, 18 and 20   [e] 11 Or *sell*   [f] 11 Or *sell*

you the cave that is in it. I give^a it to you in the presence of my people. Bury your dead.'

¹²Again Abraham bowed down before the people of the land ¹³and he said to Ephron in their hearing, 'Listen to me, if you will. I will pay the price of the field. Accept it from me so that I can bury my dead there.'

¹⁴Ephron answered Abraham, ¹⁵'Listen to me, my lord; the land is worth four hundred shekels^b of silver, but what is that between me and you? Bury your dead.'

¹⁶Abraham agreed to Ephron's terms and weighed out for him the price he had named in the hearing of the Hittites: four hundred shekels of silver, according to the weight current among the merchants.

¹⁷So Ephron's field in Machpelah near Mamre—both the field and the cave in it, and all the trees within the borders of the field—was legally made over ¹⁸to Abraham as his property in the presence of all the Hittites who had come to the gate of the city. ¹⁹Afterwards Abraham buried his wife Sarah in the cave in the field of Machpelah near Mamre (which is at Hebron) in the land of Canaan. ²⁰So the field and the cave in it were legally made over to Abraham by the Hittites as a burial site.

Isaac and Rebekah

24 Abraham was now very old, and the LORD had blessed him in every way. ²He said to the senior servant in his household, the one in charge of all that he had, 'Put your hand under my thigh. ³I want you to swear by the LORD, the God of heaven and the God of earth, that you will not get a wife for my son from the daughters of the Canaanites, among whom I am living, ⁴but will go to my country and my own relatives and get a wife for my son Isaac.'

⁵The servant asked him, 'What if the woman is unwilling to come back with me to this land? Shall I then take your son back to the country you came from?'

⁶'Make sure that you do not take my son back there,' Abraham said.

⁷'The LORD, the God of heaven, who brought me out of my father's household and my native land and who spoke to me and promised me on oath, saying, "To your offspring^c I will give this land"—he will send his angel before you so that you can get a wife for my son from there. ⁸If the woman is unwilling to come back with you, then you will be released from this oath of mine. Only do not take my son back there.' ⁹So the servant put his hand under the thigh of his master Abraham and swore an oath to him concerning this matter.

¹⁰Then the servant left, taking with him ten of his master's camels loaded with all kinds of good things from his master. He set out for Aram Naharaim^d and made his way to the town of Nahor. ¹¹He made the camels kneel down near the well outside the town; it was towards evening, the time the women go out to draw water.

¹²Then he prayed, 'LORD, God of my master Abraham, make me successful today, and show kindness to my master Abraham. ¹³See, I am standing beside this spring, and the daughters of the townspeople are coming out to draw water. ¹⁴May it be that when I say to a girl, "Please let down your jar that I may have a drink," and

Finding a bride
Genesis 24:3

Forget hanging out at discos or advertising in personal columns, this is how to find a partner Old Testament style! Abraham is determined that his son should marry a woman from his home country and so he sends his servant back to find someone. The servant prays for success, and look what happens: the first woman he sees is Rebekah, Abraham's grand-niece, and she offers him water for his camels just as he prayed. What's more, she's happy to go back with him to marry Isaac. Job done!

---

^a 11 Or *sell*   ^b 15 That is, about 4.6 kilograms   ^c 7 Or *seed*   ^d 10 That is, North-west Mesopotamia

she says, "Drink, and I'll water your camels too"—let her be the one you have chosen for your servant Isaac. By this I will know that you have shown kindness to my master.'

15Before he had finished praying, Rebekah came out with her jar on her shoulder. She was the daughter of Bethuel son of Milkah, who was the wife of Abraham's brother Nahor. 16The girl was very beautiful, a virgin; no man had ever slept with her. She went down to the spring, filled her jar and came up again.

17The servant hurried to meet her and said, 'Please give me a little water from your jar.'

18'Drink, my lord,' she said, and quickly lowered the jar to her hands and gave him a drink.

19After she had given him a drink, she said, 'I'll draw water for your camels too, until they have had enough to drink.' 20So she quickly emptied her jar into the trough, ran back to the well to draw more water, and drew enough for all his camels. 21Without saying a word, the man watched her closely to learn whether or not the LORD had made his journey successful.

22When the camels had finished drinking, the man took out a gold nose ring weighing a beka[a] and two gold bracelets weighing ten shekels.[b] 23Then he asked, 'Whose daughter are you? Please tell me, is there room in your father's house for us to spend the night?'

24She answered him, 'I am the daughter of Bethuel, the son that Milkah bore to Nahor.' 25And she added, 'We have plenty of straw and fodder, as well as room for you to spend the night.'

26Then the man bowed down and worshipped the LORD, 27saying, 'Praise be to the LORD, the God of my master Abraham, who has not abandoned his kindness and faithfulness to my master. As for me, the LORD has led me on the journey to the house of my master's relatives.'

28The girl ran and told her mother's household about these things. 29Now Rebekah had a brother named Laban, and he hurried out to the man at the spring. 30As soon as he had seen the nose ring, and the bracelets on his sister's arms, and had heard Rebekah tell what the man said to her, he went out to the man and found him standing by the camels near the spring. 31'Come, you who are blessed by the LORD,' he said. 'Why are you standing out here? I have prepared the house and a place for the camels.'

32So the man went to the house, and the camels were unloaded. Straw and fodder were brought for the camels, and water for him and his men to wash their feet. 33Then food was set before him, but he said, 'I will not eat until I have told you what I have to say.'

'Then tell us,' Laban said.

34So he said, 'I am Abraham's servant. 35The LORD has blessed my master abundantly, and he has become wealthy. He has given him sheep and cattle, silver and gold, male and female servants, and camels and donkeys. 36My master's wife Sarah has borne him a son in her old age, and he has given him everything he owns. 37And my master made me swear an oath, and said, "You must not get a wife for my son from the daughters of the Canaanites, in whose land I live, 38but go to my father's family and to my own clan, and get a wife for my son."

39'Then I asked my master, "What if the woman will not come back with me?"

40'He replied, "The LORD, before whom I have walked faithfully, will send his angel with you and make your journey a success, so that you can get a wife for my son from my own clan and from my father's family. 41Then, when you go to my clan, you will be released from my oath even if they refuse to give her to you—you will be released from my oath."

42'When I came to the spring today, I said, "O LORD, God of my master Abraham, if you will, please grant success to the journey on which I have come. 43See, I am standing beside this spring. If a young woman comes out to draw water and I say to her, 'Please let me drink a little water from your jar,' 44and if she says to me, 'Drink, and I'll draw water for your camels too,' let her

---

[a] 22 That is, about 5.7 grams   [b] 22 That is, about 115 grams

be the one the LORD has chosen for my master's son."

45'Before I finished praying in my heart, Rebekah came out, with her jar on her shoulder. She went down to the spring and drew water, and I said to her, "Please give me a drink."

46'She quickly lowered her jar from her shoulder and said, "Drink, and I'll water your camels too." So I drank, and she watered the camels also.

47'I asked her, "Whose daughter are you?"

'She said, "The daughter of Bethuel son of Nahor, whom Milkah bore to him."

'Then I put the ring in her nose and the bracelets on her arms, 48and I bowed down and worshipped the LORD. I praised the LORD, the God of my master Abraham, who had led me on the right road to get the granddaughter of my master's brother for his son. 49Now if you will show kindness and faithfulness to my master, tell me; and if not, tell me, so I may know which way to turn.'

50Laban and Bethuel answered, 'This is from the LORD; we can say nothing to you one way or the other. 51Here is Rebekah; take her and go, and let her become the wife of your master's son, as the LORD has directed.'

52When Abraham's servant heard what they said, he bowed down to the ground before the LORD. 53Then the servant brought out gold and silver jewellery and articles of clothing and gave them to Rebekah; he also gave costly gifts to her brother and to her mother. 54Then he and the men who were with him ate and drank and spent the night there.

When they got up the next morning, he said, 'Send me on my way to my master.'

55But her brother and her mother replied, 'Let the girl remain with us ten days or so; then you*a* may go.'

56But he said to them, 'Do not detain me, now that the LORD has granted success to my journey. Send me on my way so I may go to my master.'

57Then they said, 'Let's call the girl and ask her about it.' 58So they called Rebekah and asked her, 'Will you go with this man?'

'I will go,' she said.

59So they sent their sister Rebekah on her way, along with her nurse and Abraham's servant and his men. 60And they blessed Rebekah and said to her,

'Our sister, may you increase
  to thousands upon thousands;
may your offspring possess
  the cities of their enemies.'

61Then Rebekah and her attendants got ready and mounted their camels and went back with the man. So the servant took Rebekah and left.

62Now Isaac had come from Beer Lahai Roi, for he was living in the Negev. 63He went out to the field one evening to meditate,*b* and as he looked up, he saw camels approaching. 64Rebekah also looked up and saw Isaac. She got down from her camel 65and asked the servant, 'Who is that man in the field coming to meet us?'

'He is my master,' the servant answered. So she took her veil and covered herself.

66Then the servant told Isaac all he had done. 67Isaac brought her into the tent of his mother Sarah, and he married Rebekah. So she became his wife, and he loved her; and Isaac was comforted after his mother's death.

The death of Abraham

25 Abraham had taken another wife, whose name was Keturah. 2She bore him Zimran, Jokshan, Medan, Midian, Ishbak and Shuah. 3Jokshan was the father of Sheba and Dedan; the descendants of Dedan were the Ashurites, the Letushites and the Leummites. 4The sons of Midian were Ephah, Epher, Hanok, Abida and Eldaah. All these were descendants of Keturah.

5Abraham left everything he owned to Isaac. 6But while he was still living, he gave gifts to the sons of his concubines and sent them away from his son Isaac to the land of the east.

---

a 55 Or *she* *b* 63 The meaning of the Hebrew for this word is uncertain.

People and Places

Ishmael
Genesis 25:12

Ishmael was Isaac's older half-brother; his father was Abraham and his mother was Hagar, Sarah's servant girl. Once Isaac was born, Ishmael fell out of favour and was banished to the wilderness where he grew up and became an archer. God promised to bless Ishmael and make him a great nation too. Muslims claim Ishmael as their ancestor.

[7] Abraham lived a hundred and seventy-five years. [8] Then Abraham breathed his last and died at a good old age, an old man and full of years; and he was gathered to his people. [9] His sons Isaac and Ishmael buried him in the cave of Machpelah near Mamre, in the field of Ephron son of Zohar the Hittite, [10] the field Abraham had bought from the Hittites.[a] There Abraham was buried with his wife Sarah. [11] After Abraham's death, God blessed his son Isaac, who then lived near Beer Lahai Roi.

Ishmael's sons

[12] This is the account of the family line of Abraham's son Ishmael, whom Sarah's servant, Hagar the Egyptian, bore to Abraham.

[13] These are the names of the sons of Ishmael, listed in the order of their birth: Nebaioth the firstborn of Ishmael, Kedar, Adbeel, Mibsam, [14] Mishma, Dumah, Massa, [15] Hadad, Tema, Jetur, Naphish and Kedemah. [16] These were the sons of Ishmael, and these are the names of the twelve tribal rulers according to their settlements and camps. [17] Ishmael lived a hundred and thirty-seven years. He breathed his last and died, and he was gathered to his people. [18] His descendants settled in the area from Havilah to Shur, near the eastern border of Egypt, as you go towards Ashur. And they lived in hostility towards[b] all the tribes related to them.

Jacob and Esau

[19] This is the account of the family line of Abraham's son Isaac.

Abraham became the father of Isaac, [20] and Isaac was forty years old when he married Rebekah daughter of Bethuel the Aramean from Paddan Aram[c] and sister of Laban the Aramean.

[21] Isaac prayed to the LORD on behalf of his wife, because she was childless. The LORD answered his prayer, and his wife Rebekah became pregnant. [22] The babies jostled each other within her, and she said, 'Why is this happening to me?' So she went to enquire of the LORD.

[23] The LORD said to her,

'Two nations are in your womb,
 and two peoples from within you will
  be separated;
one people will be stronger than the
  other,
 and the elder will serve the younger.'

[24] When the time came for her to give birth, there were twin boys in her womb. [25] The first to come out was red, and his whole body was like a hairy garment; so they named him Esau.[d] [26] After this, his brother came out, with his hand grasping Esau's heel; so he was named Jacob.[e] Isaac was sixty years old when Rebekah gave birth to them.

[27] The boys grew up, and Esau became a skilful hunter, a man of the open country, while Jacob was content to stay at home among the tents. [28] Isaac, who had a taste for wild game, loved Esau, but Rebekah loved Jacob.

[29] Once when Jacob was cooking some stew, Esau came in from the open country, famished. [30] He said to Jacob, 'Quick, let me have some of that red stew! I'm famished!' (That is why he was also called Edom.[f])

[31] Jacob replied, 'First sell me your birthright.'

---

[a] 10 Or *the descendants of Heth*   [b] 18 Or *lived to the east of*   [c] 20 That is, North-west Mesopotamia   [d] 25 *Esau* may mean *hairy*.   [e] 26 *Jacob* means *he grasps the heel*, a Hebrew idiom for *he deceives*.   [f] 30 *Edom* means *red*.

³²'Look, I am about to die,' Esau said. 'What good is the birthright to me?'

³³But Jacob said, 'Swear to me first.' So he swore an oath to him, selling his birthright to Jacob.

³⁴Then Jacob gave Esau some bread and some lentil stew. He ate and drank, and then got up and left.

So Esau despised his birthright.

Isaac and Abimelek

26 Now there was a famine in the land—besides the previous famine in Abraham's time—and Isaac went to Abimelek king of the Philistines in Gerar. ²The LORD appeared to Isaac and said, 'Do not go down to Egypt; live in the land where I tell you to live. ³Stay in this land for a while, and I will be with you and will bless you. For to you and your descendants I will give all these lands and will confirm the oath I swore to your father Abraham. ⁴I will make your descendants as numerous as the stars in the sky and will give them all these lands, and through your offspring^a all nations on earth will be blessed,^{b} ⁵because Abraham obeyed me and did everything I required of him, keeping my commands, my decrees and my instructions.' ⁶So Isaac stayed in Gerar.

⁷When the men of that place asked him about his wife, he said, 'She is my sister,' because he was afraid to say, 'She is my wife.' He thought, 'The men of this place might kill me on account of Rebekah, because she is beautiful.'

⁸When Isaac had been there a long time, Abimelek king of the Philistines looked down from a window and saw Isaac caressing his wife Rebekah. ⁹So Abimelek summoned Isaac and said, 'She is really your wife! Why did you say, "She is my sister"?'

Isaac answered him, 'Because I thought I might lose my life on account of her.'

¹⁰Then Abimelek said, 'What is this you have done to us? One of the men might well have slept with your wife, and you would have brought guilt upon us.'

¹¹So Abimelek gave orders to all the people: 'Anyone who harms this man or his wife shall surely be put to death.'

¹²Isaac planted crops in that land and the same year reaped a hundredfold, because the LORD blessed him. ¹³The man became rich, and his wealth continued to grow until he became very wealthy. ¹⁴He had so many flocks and herds and servants that the Philistines envied him. ¹⁵So all the wells that his father's servants had dug in the time of his father Abraham, the Philistines stopped up, filling them with earth.

¹⁶Then Abimelek said to Isaac, 'Move away from us; you have become too powerful for us.'

¹⁷So Isaac moved away from there and camped in the Valley of Gerar, where he settled. ¹⁸Isaac reopened the wells that had been dug in the time of his father Abraham, which the Philistines had stopped up after Abraham died, and he gave them the same names his father had given them.

¹⁹Isaac's servants dug in the valley and discovered a well of fresh water there. ²⁰But the herders of Gerar quarrelled with those of Isaac and said, 'The water is ours!' So he named the well Esek,^{c} because they disputed with him. ²¹Then they dug another well, but they quarrelled over that one also; so he named it Sitnah.^{d} ²²He moved on from there and dug another well, and no-one quarrelled over it. He named it Rehoboth,^{e} saying, 'Now the LORD has given us room and we will flourish in the land.'

²³From there he went up to Beersheba. ²⁴That night the LORD appeared to him and said, 'I am the God of your father Abraham. Do not be afraid, for I am with you; I will bless you and will increase the number of your descendants for the sake of my servant Abraham.'

²⁵Isaac built an altar there and called on the name of the LORD. There he pitched his tent, and there his servants dug a well.

²⁶Meanwhile, Abimelek had come to him from Gerar, with Ahuzzath his personal advisor and Phicol the commander of his forces. ²⁷Isaac asked them, 'Why have you

---

^{a} 4 Or *seed* ^{b} 4 Or *and all nations on earth will use the name of your offspring in blessings* (see Gen. 48:20) ^{c} 20 *Esek* means *dispute*. ^{d} 21 *Sitnah* means *opposition*. ^{e} 22 *Rehoboth* means *room*.

come to me, since you were hostile to me and sent me away?'

28 They answered, 'We saw clearly that the LORD was with you; so we said, "There ought to be a sworn agreement between us"—between us and you. Let us make a treaty with you 29 that you will do us no harm, just as we did not harm you but always treated you well and sent you away peacefully. And now you are blessed by the LORD.'

30 Isaac then made a feast for them, and they ate and drank. 31 Early the next morning the men swore an oath to each other. Then Isaac sent them on their way, and they went away peacefully.

32 That day Isaac's servants came and told him about the well they had dug. They said, 'We've found water!' 33 He called it Shibah,[a] and to this day the name of the town has been Beersheba.[b]

Jacob takes Esau's blessing

34 When Esau was forty years old, he married Judith daughter of Beeri the Hittite, and also Basemath daughter of Elon the Hittite. 35 They were a source of grief to Isaac and Rebekah.

27 When Isaac was old and his eyes were so weak that he could no longer see, he called for his elder son Esau and said to him, 'My son.'

'Here I am,' he answered.

2 Isaac said, 'I am now an old man and don't know the day of my death. 3 Now then, get your equipment—your quiver and bow—and go out to the open country to hunt some wild game for me. 4 Prepare me the kind of tasty food I like and bring it to me to eat, so that I may give you my blessing before I die.'

5 Now Rebekah was listening as Isaac spoke to his son Esau. When Esau left for the open country to hunt game and bring it back, 6 Rebekah said to her son Jacob, 'Look, I overheard your father say to your brother Esau, 7 "Bring me some game and prepare me some tasty food to eat, so that I may give you my blessing in the presence of the LORD before I die." 8 Now, my son, listen carefully and do what I tell you: 9 go out to the flock and bring me two choice young goats, so that I can prepare some tasty food for your father, just the way he likes it. 10 Then take it to your father to eat, so that he may give you his blessing before he dies.'

11 Jacob said to Rebekah his mother, 'But my brother Esau is a hairy man while I have smooth skin. 12 What if my father touches me? I would appear to be tricking him and would bring down a curse on myself rather than a blessing.'

13 His mother said to him, 'My son, let the curse fall on me. Just do what I say; go and get them for me.'

14 So he went and got them and brought them to his mother, and she prepared some tasty food, just the way his father liked it. 15 Then Rebekah took the best clothes of her elder son Esau, which she had in the house, and put them on her younger son Jacob. 16 She also covered his hands and the smooth part of his neck with the goatskins. 17 Then she handed to her son Jacob the tasty food and the bread she had made.

People and Places

Jacob and Esau
Genesis 27:1

How would you like to be remembered for being hairy? Well, that was Esau's claim to fame! Esau and Jacob were twin brothers who just didn't get on with each other. Jacob was the younger twin by a few minutes, but he was determined not to let that stand in his way. He stole the special blessing that their dad Isaac should have given to Esau, his older son. Jacob did more than his fair share to turn Abraham's ancestors into a great nation. Abraham had one son, Isaac had two, and Jacob had twelve sons who became the twelve tribes of Israel.

---

[a] 33 *Shibah* can mean *oath* or *seven*.   [b] 33 *Beersheba* can mean *well of the oath* or *well of seven*.

¹⁸He went to his father and said, 'My father.'

'Yes, my son,' he answered. 'Who is it?'

¹⁹Jacob said to his father, 'I am Esau your firstborn. I have done as you told me. Please sit up and eat some of my game, so that you may give me your blessing.'

²⁰Isaac asked his son, 'How did you find it so quickly, my son?'

'The LORD your God gave me success,' he replied.

²¹Then Isaac said to Jacob, 'Come near so I can touch you, my son, to know whether you really are my son Esau or not.'

²²Jacob went close to his father Isaac, who touched him and said, 'The voice is the voice of Jacob, but the hands are the hands of Esau.' ²³He did not recognise him, for his hands were hairy like those of his brother Esau; so he proceeded to bless him. ²⁴'Are you really my son Esau?' he asked.

'I am,' he replied.

²⁵Then he said, 'My son, bring me some of your game to eat, so that I may give you my blessing.'

Jacob brought it to him and he ate; and he brought some wine and he drank. ²⁶Then his father Isaac said to him, 'Come here, my son, and kiss me.'

²⁷So he went to him and kissed him. When Isaac caught the smell of his clothes, he blessed him and said,

'Ah, the smell of my son
  is like the smell of a field
  that the LORD has blessed.
²⁸May God give you of heaven's dew
  and of earth's richness—
  an abundance of grain and new wine.
²⁹May nations serve you
  and peoples bow down to you.
Be lord over your brothers,
  and may the sons of your mother bow down to you.
May those who curse you be cursed
  and those who bless you be blessed.'

³⁰After Isaac finished blessing him and Jacob had scarcely left his father's presence, his brother Esau came in from hunting. ³¹He too prepared some tasty food and brought it to his father. Then he said to him, 'My father, please sit up and eat some of my game, so that you may give me your blessing.'

³²His father Isaac asked him, 'Who are you?'

'I am your son,' he answered, 'your firstborn, Esau.'

³³Isaac trembled violently and said, 'Who was it, then, that hunted game and brought it to me? I ate it just before you came and I blessed him—and indeed he will be blessed!'

³⁴When Esau heard his father's words, he burst out with a loud and bitter cry and said to his father, 'Bless me—me too, my father!'

³⁵But he said, 'Your brother came deceitfully and took your blessing.'

³⁶Esau said, 'Isn't he rightly named Jacob?ᵃ This is the second time he has taken advantage of me: he took my birthright, and now he's taken my blessing!' Then he asked, 'Haven't you reserved any blessing for me?'

³⁷Isaac answered Esau, 'I have made him lord over you and have made all his relatives his servants, and I have sustained him with grain and new wine. So what can I possibly do for you, my son?'

³⁸Esau said to his father, 'Do you have only one blessing, my father? Bless me too, my father!' Then Esau wept aloud.

³⁹His father Isaac answered him,

'Your dwelling will be
  away from the earth's richness,
  away from the dew of heaven above.
⁴⁰You will live by the sword
  and you will serve your brother.
But when you grow restless,
  you will throw his yoke
  from off your neck.'

⁴¹Esau held a grudge against Jacob because of the blessing his father had given him. He said to himself, 'The days of mourning for my father are near; then I will kill my brother Jacob.'

⁴²When Rebekah was told what her elder son Esau had said, she sent for her younger son Jacob and said to him, 'Your brother Esau is planning to avenge himself by killing

---

ᵃ 36 *Jacob* means *he grasps the heel,* a Hebrew idiom for *he takes advantage of* or *he deceives.*

you. ⁴³Now then, my son, do what I say: flee at once to my brother Laban in Harran. ⁴⁴Stay with him for a while until your brother's fury subsides. ⁴⁵When your brother is no longer angry with you and forgets what you did to him, I'll send word for you to come back from there. Why should I lose both of you in one day?'

⁴⁶Then Rebekah said to Isaac, 'I'm disgusted with living because of these Hittite women. If Jacob takes a wife from among the women of this land, from Hittite women like these, my life will not be worth living.'

28 So Isaac called for Jacob and blessed him. Then he commanded him: 'Do not marry a Canaanite woman. ²Go at once to Paddan Aram,ᵃ to the house of your mother's father Bethuel. Take a wife for yourself there, from among the daughters of Laban, your mother's brother. ³May God Almightyᵇ bless you and make you fruitful and increase your numbers until you become a community of peoples. ⁴May he give you and your descendants the blessing given to Abraham, so that you may take possession of the land where you now reside as a foreigner, the land God gave to Abraham.' ⁵Then Isaac sent Jacob on his way, and he went to Paddan Aram, to Laban son of Bethuel the Aramean, the brother of Rebekah, who was the mother of Jacob and Esau.

⁶Now Esau learned that Isaac had blessed Jacob and had sent him to Paddan Aram to take a wife from there, and that when he blessed him he commanded him, 'Do not marry a Canaanite woman,' ⁷and that Jacob had obeyed his father and mother and had gone to Paddan Aram. ⁸Esau then realised how displeasing the Canaanite women were to his father Isaac; ⁹so he went to Ishmael and married Mahalath, the sister of Nebaioth and daughter of Ishmael son of Abraham, in addition to the wives he already had.

Jacob's dream at Bethel

¹⁰Jacob left Beersheba and set out for Harran. ¹¹When he reached a certain place, he stopped for the night because the sun had set. Taking one of the stones there, he put it under his head and lay down to sleep. ¹²He had a dream in which he saw a stairwayᶜ resting on the earth, with its top reaching to heaven, and the angels of God were ascending and descending on it. ¹³There above itᵈ stood the LORD, and he said: 'I am the LORD, the God of your father Abraham and the God of Isaac. I will give you and your descendants the land on which you are lying. ¹⁴Your descendants will be like the dust of the earth, and you will spread out to the west and to the east, to the north and to the south. All peoples on earth will be blessed through you and your offspring.ᵉ ¹⁵I am with you and will watch over you wherever you go, and I will bring you back to this land. I will not leave you until I have done what I have promised you.'

¹⁶When Jacob awoke from his sleep, he thought, 'Surely the LORD is in this place, and I was not aware of it.' ¹⁷He was afraid and said, 'How awesome is this place! This is none other than the house of God; this is the gate of heaven.'

¹⁸Early the next morning Jacob took the stone he had placed under his head and set it up as a pillar and poured oil on top of it. ¹⁹He called that place Bethel,ᶠ though the city used to be called Luz.

²⁰Then Jacob made a vow, saying, 'If God will be with me and will watch over me on this journey I am taking and will give me food to eat and clothes to wear ²¹so that I return safely to my father's household, then the LORDᵍ will be my God ²²andʰ this stone that I have set up as a pillar will be God's house, and of all that you give me I will give you a tenth.'

Jacob arrives in Paddan Aram

29 Then Jacob continued on his journey and came to the land of the eastern peoples. ²There he saw a well in the open country, with three flocks of sheep

---

ᵃ 2 That is, North-west Mesopotamia; also in verses 5, 6 and 7   ᵇ 3 Hebrew *El-Shaddai*   ᶜ 12 Or *ladder*   ᵈ 13 Or *There beside him*   ᵉ 14 Or *will use your name and the name of your offspring in blessings* (see Gen. 48:20)   ᶠ 19 *Bethel* means *house of God*.   ᵍ 20,21 Or *Since God... father's household, the LORD*   ʰ 21,22 Or *household, and the LORD will be my God,* ²²*then* lying near it because the flocks were watered from that well. The stone over the mouth of the well was large. ³When all the flocks were gathered there, the shepherds would roll the stone away from the well's mouth and water the sheep. Then they would return the stone to its place over the mouth of the well.

⁴Jacob asked the shepherds, 'My brothers, where are you from?'

'We're from Harran,' they replied.

⁵He said to them, 'Do you know Laban, Nahor's grandson?'

'Yes, we know him,' they answered.

⁶Then Jacob asked them, 'Is he well?'

'Yes, he is,' they said, 'and here comes his daughter Rachel with the sheep.'

⁷'Look,' he said, 'the sun is still high; it is not time for the flocks to be gathered. Water the sheep and take them back to pasture.'

⁸'We can't,' they replied, 'until all the flocks are gathered and the stone has been rolled away from the mouth of the well. Then we will water the sheep.'

⁹While he was still talking with them, Rachel came with her father's sheep, for she was their shepherd. ¹⁰When Jacob saw Rachel daughter of Laban, his mother's brother, and Laban's sheep, he went over and rolled the stone away from the mouth of the well and watered his uncle's sheep. ¹¹Then Jacob kissed Rachel and began to weep aloud. ¹²He had told Rachel that he was a relative of her father and a son of Rebekah. So she ran and told her father.

¹³As soon as Laban heard the news about Jacob, his sister's son, he hurried to meet him. He embraced him and kissed him and brought him to his home, and there Jacob told him all these things. ¹⁴Then Laban said to him, 'You are my own flesh and blood.'

Jacob marries Leah and Rachel

After Jacob had stayed with him for a whole month, ¹⁵Laban said to him, 'Just because you are a relative of mine, should you work for me for nothing? Tell me what your wages should be.'

¹⁶Now Laban had two daughters; the name of the elder one was Leah, and the name of the younger was Rachel. ¹⁷Leah had weak*ᵃ* eyes, but Rachel had a lovely figure and was beautiful. ¹⁸Jacob was in love with Rachel and said, 'I'll work for you seven years in return for your younger daughter Rachel.'

¹⁹Laban said, 'It's better that I give her to you than to some other man. Stay here with me.' ²⁰So Jacob served seven years to get Rachel, but they seemed like only a few days to him because of his love for her.

²¹Then Jacob said to Laban, 'Give me my wife. My time is completed, and I want to make love to her.'

²²So Laban brought together all the people of the place and gave a feast. ²³But when evening came, he took his daughter Leah and brought her to Jacob, and Jacob made love to her. ²⁴And Laban gave his servant Zilpah to his daughter as her attendant.

²⁵When morning came, there was Leah! So Jacob said to Laban, 'What is this you have done to me? I served you for Rachel, didn't I? Why have you deceived me?'

²⁶Laban replied, 'It is not our custom here to give the younger daughter in marriage before the elder one. ²⁷Finish

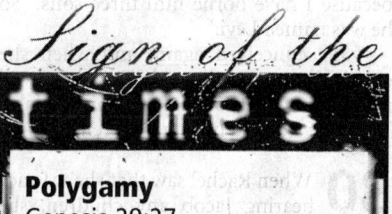

Sign of the times

Polygamy
Genesis 29:27
Having more than one wife at a time was common throughout the ancient world and is known as 'polygamy'. The Bible says that monogamy is God's ideal – that's one man and one woman married to each other for life – but sometimes habits from local cultures crept in among God's people. The most famous polygamist in the Bible was King Solomon who had seven hundred wives and three hundred concubines (1 Kings 11:3).

ᵃ 17 Or *delicate*

this daughter's bridal week; then we will give you the younger one also, in return for another seven years of work.'

28And Jacob did so. He finished the week with Leah, and then Laban gave him his daughter Rachel to be his wife. 29Laban gave his servant Bilhah to his daughter Rachel as her attendant. 30Jacob made love to Rachel also, and his love for Rachel was greater than his love for Leah. And he worked for Laban another seven years.

Jacob's children

31When the LORD saw that Leah was not loved, he enabled her to conceive, but Rachel remained childless. 32Leah became pregnant and gave birth to a son. She named him Reuben,[a] for she said, 'It is because the LORD has seen my misery. Surely my husband will love me now.'

33She conceived again, and when she gave birth to a son she said, 'Because the LORD heard that I am not loved, he gave me this one too.' So she named him Simeon.[b]

34Again she conceived, and when she gave birth to a son she said, 'Now at last my husband will become attached to me, because I have borne him three sons.' So he was named Levi.[c]

35She conceived again, and when she gave birth to a son she said, 'This time I will praise the LORD.' So she named him Judah.[d] Then she stopped having children.

30 When Rachel saw that she was not bearing Jacob any children, she became jealous of her sister. So she said to Jacob, 'Give me children, or I'll die!'

2Jacob became angry with her and said, 'Am I in the place of God, who has kept you from having children?'

3Then she said, 'Here is Bilhah, my servant. Sleep with her so that she can bear children for me and I too can build a family through her.'

4So she gave him her servant Bilhah as a wife. Jacob slept with her, 5and she became pregnant and bore him a son. 6Then Rachel said, 'God has vindicated me; he has listened to my plea and given me a son.' Because of this she named him Dan.[e]

7Rachel's servant Bilhah conceived again and bore Jacob a second son. 8Then Rachel said, 'I have had a great struggle with my sister, and I have won.' So she named him Naphtali.[f]

9When Leah saw that she had stopped having children, she took her servant Zilpah and gave her to Jacob as a wife. 10Leah's servant Zilpah bore Jacob a son. 11Then Leah said, 'What good fortune!'[g] So she named him Gad.[h]

12Leah's servant Zilpah bore Jacob a second son. 13Then Leah said, 'How happy I am! The women will call me happy.' So she named him Asher.[i]

14During the wheat harvest, Reuben went out into the fields and found some mandrake plants, which he brought to his mother Leah. Rachel said to Leah, 'Please give me some of your son's mandrakes.'

15But she said to her, 'Wasn't it enough that you took away my husband? Will you take my son's mandrakes too?'

'Very well,' Rachel said, 'he can sleep with you tonight in return for your son's mandrakes.'

16So when Jacob came in from the fields that evening, Leah went out to meet him. 'You must sleep with me,' she said. 'I have hired you with my son's mandrakes.' So he slept with her that night.

17God listened to Leah, and she became pregnant and bore Jacob a fifth son. 18Then Leah said, 'God has rewarded me for giving my servant to my husband.' So she named him Issachar.[j]

19Leah conceived again and bore Jacob a sixth son. 20Then Leah said, 'God has presented me with a precious gift. This time my husband will treat me with honour, because I have borne him six sons.' So she named him Zebulun.[k]

21Some time later she gave birth to a daughter and named her Dinah.

---

[a]32 *Reuben* sounds like the Hebrew for *he has seen my misery*; the name means *see, a son*. [b]33 *Simeon* probably means *one who hears*. [c]34 *Levi* sounds like and may be derived from the Hebrew for *attached*. [d]35 *Judah* sounds like and may be derived from the Hebrew for *praise*. [e]6 *Dan* here means *he has vindicated*. [f]8 *Naphtali* means *my struggle*. [g]11 Or *'A troop is coming!'* [h]11 *Gad* can mean *good fortune* or *a troop*. [i]13 *Asher* means *happy*. [j]18 *Issachar* sounds like the Hebrew for *reward*. [k]20 *Zebulun* probably means *honour*.

22Then God remembered Rachel; he listened to her and enabled her to conceive. 23She became pregnant and gave birth to a son and said, 'God has taken away my disgrace.' 24She named him Joseph,*a* and said, 'May the LORD add to me another son.'

Jacob's flocks increase

25After Rachel gave birth to Joseph, Jacob said to Laban, 'Send me on my way so that I can go back to my own homeland. 26Give me my wives and children, for whom I have served you, and I will be on my way. You know how much work I've done for you.'

27But Laban said to him, 'If I have found favour in your eyes, please stay. I have learned by divination that the LORD has blessed me because of you.' 28He added, 'Name your wages, and I will pay them.'

29Jacob said to him, 'You know how I have worked for you and how your livestock has fared under my care. 30The little you had before I came has increased greatly, and the LORD has blessed you wherever I have been. But now, when may I do something for my own household?'

31'What shall I give you?' he asked.

'Don't give me anything,' Jacob replied. 'But if you will do this one thing for me, I will go on tending your flocks and watching over them: 32let me go through all your flocks today and remove from them every speckled or spotted sheep, every dark-coloured lamb and every spotted or speckled goat. They will be my wages. 33And my honesty will testify for me in the future, whenever you check on the wages you have paid me. Any goat in my possession that is not speckled or spotted, or any lamb that is not dark-coloured, will be considered stolen.'

34'Agreed,' said Laban. 'Let it be as you have said.' 35That same day he removed all the male goats that were streaked or spotted, and all the speckled or spotted female goats (all that had white on them) and all the dark-coloured lambs, and he placed them in the care of his sons. 36Then he put a three-day journey between himself and Jacob, while Jacob continued to tend the rest of Laban's flocks.

37Jacob, however, took fresh-cut branches from poplar, almond and plane trees and made white stripes on them by peeling the bark and exposing the white inner wood of the branches. 38Then he placed the peeled branches in all the watering troughs, so that they would be directly in front of the flocks when they came to drink. When the flocks were in heat and came to drink, 39they mated in front of the branches. And they bore young that were streaked or speckled or spotted. 40Jacob set apart the young of the flock by themselves, but made the rest face the streaked and dark-coloured animals that belonged to Laban. Thus he made separate flocks for himself and did not put them with Laban's animals. 41Whenever the stronger females were in heat, Jacob would place the branches in the troughs in front of the animals so that they would mate near the branches, 42but if the animals were weak, he would not place them there. So the weak animals went to Laban and the strong ones to Jacob. 43In this way the man grew exceedingly prosperous and came to own large flocks, and female and male servants, and camels and donkeys.

Jacob flees from Laban

31 Jacob heard that Laban's sons were saying, 'Jacob has taken everything our father owned and has gained all this wealth from what belonged to our father.' 2And Jacob noticed that Laban's attitude towards him was not what it had been.

3Then the LORD said to Jacob, 'Go back to the land of your fathers and to your relatives, and I will be with you.'

4So Jacob sent word to Rachel and Leah to come out to the fields where his flocks were. 5He said to them, 'I see that your father's attitude towards me is not what it was before, but the God of my father has been with me. 6You know that I've worked for your father with all my strength, 7yet your father has cheated me by changing my wages ten times. However, God has not allowed him to harm me. 8If he said, "The speckled ones will be your wages," then all the flocks gave birth to speckled young; and

---

a 24 *Joseph means may he add.*

if he said, "The streaked ones will be your wages," then all the flocks bore streaked young. 9So God has taken away your father's livestock and has given them to me. 10'In the breeding season I once had a dream in which I looked up and saw that the male goats mating with the flock were streaked, speckled or spotted. 11The angel of God said to me in the dream, "Jacob." I answered, "Here I am." 12And he said, "Look up and see that all the male goats mating with the flock are streaked, speckled or spotted, for I have seen all that Laban has been doing to you. 13I am the God of Bethel, where you anointed a pillar and where you made a vow to me. Now leave this land at once and go back to your native land."'

14Then Rachel and Leah replied, 'Do we still have any share in the inheritance of our father's estate? 15Does he not regard us as foreigners? Not only has he sold us, but he has used up what was paid for us. 16Surely all the wealth that God took away from our father belongs to us and our children. So do whatever God has told you.'

17Then Jacob put his children and his wives on camels, 18and he drove all his livestock ahead of him, along with all the goods he had accumulated in Paddan Aram,*a* to go to his father Isaac in the land of Canaan.

19When Laban had gone to shear his sheep, Rachel stole her father's household gods. 20Moreover, Jacob deceived Laban the Aramean by not telling him he was running away. 21So he fled with all he had, crossed the River Euphrates, and headed for the hill country of Gilead.

Laban pursues Jacob

22On the third day Laban was told that Jacob had fled. 23Taking his relatives with him, he pursued Jacob for seven days and caught up with him in the hill country of Gilead. 24Then God came to Laban the Aramean in a dream at night and said to him, 'Be careful not to say anything to Jacob, either good or bad.'

25Jacob had pitched his tent in the hill country of Gilead when Laban overtook him, and Laban and his relatives camped there too. 26Then Laban said to Jacob, 'What have you done? You've deceived me, and you've carried off my daughters like captives in war. 27Why did you run off secretly and deceive me? Why didn't you tell me, so that I could send you away with joy and singing to the music of tambourines and harps? 28You didn't even let me kiss my grandchildren and my daughters good-bye. You have done a foolish thing. 29I have the power to harm you; but last night the God of your father said to me, "Be careful not to say anything to Jacob, either good or bad." 30Now you have gone off because you longed to return to your father's household. But why did you steal my gods?'

31Jacob answered Laban, 'I was afraid, because I thought you would take your daughters away from me by force. 32But if you find anyone who has your gods, that person shall not live. In the presence of our relatives, see for yourself whether there is anything of yours here with me; and if so, take it.' Now Jacob did not know that Rachel had stolen the gods.

33So Laban went into Jacob's tent and into Leah's tent and into the tent of the two female servants, but he found nothing. After he came out of Leah's tent, he entered Rachel's tent. 34Now Rachel had taken the household gods and put them inside her camel's saddle and was sitting on them. Laban searched through everything in the tent but found nothing.

35Rachel said to her father, 'Don't be angry, my lord, that I cannot stand up in your presence; I'm having my period.' So he searched but could not find the household gods.

36Jacob was angry and took Laban to task. 'What is my crime?' he asked Laban. 'How have I wronged you that you hunt me down? 37Now that you have searched through all my goods, what have you found that belongs to your household? Put it here in front of your relatives and mine, and let them judge between the two of us.

38'I have been with you for twenty years now. Your sheep and goats have not miscarried, nor have I eaten rams from your flocks. 39I did not bring you animals torn by

---

a 18 That is, North-west Mesopotamia

Genesis 32:6

wild beasts; I bore the loss myself. And you demanded payment from me for whatever was stolen by day or night. 40This was my situation: the heat consumed me in the daytime and the cold at night, and sleep fled from my eyes. 41It was like this for the twenty years I was in your household. I worked for you fourteen years for your two daughters and six years for your flocks, and you changed my wages ten times. 42If the God of my father, the God of Abraham and the Fear of Isaac, had not been with me, you would surely have sent me away empty-handed. But God has seen my hardship and the toil of my hands, and last night he rebuked you.'

43Laban answered Jacob, 'The women are my daughters, the children are my children, and the flocks are my flocks. All you see is mine. Yet what can I do today about these daughters of mine, or about the children they have borne? 44Come now, let's make a covenant, you and I, and let it serve as a witness between us.'

45So Jacob took a stone and set it up as a pillar. 46He said to his relatives, 'Gather some stones.' So they took stones and piled them in a heap, and they ate there by the heap. 47Laban called it Jegar Sahadutha, and Jacob called it Galeed.[a]

48Laban said, 'This heap is a witness between you and me today.' That is why it was called Galeed. 49It was also called Mizpah,[b] because he said, 'May the LORD keep watch between you and me when we are away from each other. 50If you ill-treat my daughters or if you take any wives besides my daughters, even though no-one is with us, remember that God is a witness between you and me.'

51Laban also said to Jacob, 'Here is this heap, and here is this pillar I have set up between you and me. 52This heap is a witness, and this pillar is a witness, that I will not go past this heap to your side to harm you and that you will not go past this heap and pillar to my side to harm me. 53May the God of Abraham and the God of Nahor, the God of their father, judge between us.' So Jacob took an oath in the name of the Fear of his father Isaac. 54He offered a sacrifice there in the hill country and invited his relatives to a meal. After they had eaten, they spent the night there. *55Early the next morning Laban kissed his grandchildren and his daughters and blessed them. Then he left and returned home.

Jacob prepares to meet Esau

32 *Jacob also went on his way, and the angels of God met him. 2When Jacob saw them, he said, 'This is the camp of God!' So he named that place Mahanaim.'

3Jacob sent messengers ahead of him to his brother Esau in the land of Seir, the country of Edom. 4He instructed them: 'This is what you are to say to my lord Esau: "Your servant Jacob says, I have been staying with Laban and have remained there till now. 5I have cattle and donkeys, sheep and goats, male and female servants. Now I am sending this message to my lord, that I may find favour in your eyes."'

6When the messengers returned to Jacob, they said, 'We went to your brother Esau, and now he is coming to meet you, and four hundred men are with him.'

Stone memorials
Genesis 31:45

Leaving behind this pile of rocks was a visual and permanent reminder of the agreement between Jacob and Laban. They both gave it names meaning 'a pile of rocks to remind us'!

---

sign of the times

---

*a 47 The Aramaic Jegar Sahadutha and the Hebrew Galeed both mean witness heap.   b 49 Mizpah means watchtower.   c 2 Mahanaim means two camps.   * 31:55 is numbered 32:1 in Hebrew texts.   * 32:1-32 is numbered 32:2-33 in Hebrew texts.*

Genesis 32:7

7In great fear and distress Jacob divided the people who were with him into two groups,[a] and the flocks and herds and camels as well. 8He thought, 'If Esau comes and attacks one group,[b] the group[c] that is left may escape.'

9Then Jacob prayed, 'O God of my father Abraham, God of my father Isaac, LORD, you who said to me, "Go back to your country and your relatives, and I will make you prosper," 10I am unworthy of all the kindness and faithfulness you have shown your servant. I had only my staff when I crossed this Jordan, but now I have become two camps. 11Save me, I pray, from the hand of my brother Esau, for I am afraid he will come and attack me, and also the mothers with their children. 12But you have said, "I will surely make you prosper and will make your descendants like the sand of the sea, which cannot be counted."'

13He spent the night there, and from what he had with him he selected a gift for his brother Esau: 14two hundred female goats and twenty male goats, two hundred ewes and twenty rams, 15thirty female camels with their young, forty cows and ten bulls, and twenty female donkeys and ten male donkeys. 16He put them in the care of his servants, each herd by itself, and said to his servants, 'Go ahead of me, and keep some space between the herds.'

17He instructed the one in the lead: 'When my brother Esau meets you and asks, "Who do you belong to, and where are you going, and who owns all these animals in front of you?" 18then you are to say, "They belong to your servant Jacob. They are a gift sent to my lord Esau, and he is coming behind us."'

19He also instructed the second, the third and all the others who followed the herds: 'You are to say the same thing to Esau when you meet him. 20And be sure to say, "Your servant Jacob is coming behind us."' For he thought, 'I will pacify him with these gifts I am sending on ahead; later, when I see him, perhaps he will receive me.' 21So Jacob's gifts went on ahead of him, but he himself spent the night in the camp.

---

a 7 Or camps   b 8 Or camp   c 8 Or camp   d 28 Israel probably means he struggles with God.   e 30 Peniel means face of God.

Jacob wrestles with God

22That night Jacob got up and took his two wives, his two female servants and his eleven sons and crossed the ford of the Jabbok. 23After he had sent them across the stream, he sent over all his possessions. 24So Jacob was left alone, and a man wrestled with him till daybreak. 25When the man saw that he could not overpower him, he touched the socket of Jacob's hip so that his hip was wrenched as he wrestled with the man. 26Then the man said, 'Let me go, for it is daybreak.'

But Jacob replied, 'I will not let you go unless you bless me.'

27The man asked him, 'What is your name?'

'Jacob,' he answered.

28Then the man said, 'Your name will no longer be Jacob, but Israel,[d] because you have struggled with God and with human beings and have overcome.'

29Jacob said, 'Please tell me your name.'

But he replied, 'Why do you ask my name?' Then he blessed him there.

30So Jacob called the place Peniel,[e] saying, 'It is because I saw God face to face, and yet my life was spared.'

People and Places

Israelites

Genesis 32:28

God changed Jacob's name to 'Israel' after he struggled with God, and Israel also became the name of the nation of God's chosen people. Its most famous kings were Saul, David and Solomon. At one time, the people of Israel were split into two nations; Israel was the name of the northern kingdom and Judah the southern kingdom. Today Israel is the name of the whole Jewish nation.

³¹The sun rose above him as he passed Peniel,ᵃ and he was limping because of his hip. ³²Therefore to this day the Israelites do not eat the tendon attached to the socket of the hip, because the socket of Jacob's hip was touched near the tendon.

Jacob meets Esau

33 Jacob looked up and there was Esau, coming with his four hundred men; so he divided the children among Leah, Rachel and the two female servants. ²He put the female servants and their children in front, Leah and her children next, and Rachel and Joseph in the rear. ³He himself went on ahead and bowed down to the ground seven times as he approached his brother.

⁴But Esau ran to meet Jacob and embraced him; he threw his arms around his neck and kissed him. And they wept. ⁵Then Esau looked up and saw the women and children. 'Who are these with you?' he asked.

Jacob answered, 'They are the children God has graciously given your servant.'

⁶Then the female servants and their children approached and bowed down. ⁷Next, Leah and her children came and bowed down. Last of all came Joseph and Rachel, and they too bowed down.

⁸Esau asked, 'What do you mean by all these flocks and herds I met?'

'To find favour in your eyes, my lord,' he said.

⁹But Esau said, 'I already have plenty, my brother. Keep what you have for yourself.'

¹⁰'No, please!' said Jacob. 'If I have found favour in your eyes, accept this gift from me. For to see your face is like seeing the face of God, now that you have received me favourably. ¹¹Please accept the present that was brought to you, for God has been gracious to me and I have all I need.' And because Jacob insisted, Esau accepted it.

¹²Then Esau said, 'Let us be on our way; I'll accompany you.'

¹³But Jacob said to him, 'My lord knows that the children are tender and that I must care for the ewes and cows that are nursing their young. If they are driven hard just one day, all the animals will die. ¹⁴So let my lord go on ahead of his servant, while I move along slowly at the pace of the flocks and herds before me and the pace of the children, until I come to my lord in Seir.'

¹⁵Esau said, 'Then let me leave some of my men with you.'

'But why do that?' Jacob asked. 'Just let me find favour in the eyes of my lord.'

¹⁶So that day Esau started on his way back to Seir. ¹⁷Jacob, however, went to Sukkoth, where he built a place for himself and made shelters for his livestock. That is why the place is called Sukkoth.ᵇ

¹⁸After Jacob came from Paddan Aram,ᶜ he arrived safely at theᵈ city of Shechem in Canaan and camped within sight of the city. ¹⁹For a hundred pieces of silver,ᵉ he bought from the sons of Hamor, the father of Shechem, the plot of ground where he pitched his tent. ²⁰There he set up an altar and called it El Elohe Israel.ᶠ

Dinah and the Shechemites

34 Now Dinah, the daughter Leah had borne to Jacob, went out to visit the women of the land. ²When Shechem son of Hamor the Hivite, the ruler of that area, saw her, he took her and raped her. ³His heart was drawn to Dinah daughter of Jacob; he loved the young woman and spoke tenderly to her. ⁴And Shechem said to his father Hamor, 'Get me this young woman as my wife.'

⁵When Jacob heard that his daughter Dinah had been defiled, his sons were in the fields with his livestock; so he did nothing about it until they came home.

⁶Then Shechem's father Hamor went out to talk with Jacob. ⁷Meanwhile, Jacob's sons had come in from the fields as soon as they heard what had happened. They were shocked and furious, because Shechem had done an outrageous thing inᵍ Israel by sleeping with Jacob's daughter—a thing that should not be done.

⁸But Hamor said to them, 'My son Shechem has his heart set on your daughter.

ᵃ 31 Hebrew *Penuel*, a variant of *Peniel*   ᵇ 17 *Sukkoth* means *shelters*.   ᶜ 18 That is, North-west Mesopotamia
ᵈ 18 Or *arrived at Shalem, a*   ᵉ 19 Hebrew *hundred kesitahs*; a kesitah was a unit of money of unknown weight and value.   ᶠ 20 *El Elohe Israel* can mean *El is the God of Israel* or *mighty is the God of Israel*.   ᵍ 7 Or *against*

Please give her to him as his wife. ⁹Intermarry with us; give us your daughters and take our daughters for yourselves. ¹⁰You can settle among us; the land is open to you. Live in it, trade*ᵃ* in it, and acquire property in it.'

¹¹Then Shechem said to Dinah's father and brothers, 'Let me find favour in your eyes, and I will give you whatever you ask. ¹²Make the price for the bride and the gift I am to bring as great as you like, and I'll pay whatever you ask me. Only give me the young woman as my wife.'

¹³Because their sister Dinah had been defiled, Jacob's sons replied deceitfully as they spoke to Shechem and his father Hamor. ¹⁴They said to them, 'We can't do such a thing; we can't give our sister to a man who is not circumcised. That would be a disgrace to us. ¹⁵We will enter into an agreement with you on one condition only: that you become like us by circumcising all your males. ¹⁶Then we will give you our daughters and take your daughters for ourselves. We'll settle among you and become one people with you. ¹⁷But if you will not agree to be circumcised, we'll take our sister and go.'

¹⁸Their proposal seemed good to Hamor and his son Shechem. ¹⁹The young man, who was the most honoured of all his father's family, lost no time in doing what they said, because he was delighted with Jacob's daughter. ²⁰So Hamor and his son Shechem went to the gate of their city to speak to the men of their city. ²¹'These men are friendly towards us,' they said. 'Let them live in our land and trade in it; the land has plenty of room for them. We can marry their daughters and they can marry ours. ²²But the men will agree to live with us as one people only on the condition that our males be circumcised, as they themselves are. ²³Won't their livestock, their property and all their other animals become ours? So let us agree to their terms, and they will settle among us.'

²⁴All the men who went out of the city gate agreed with Hamor and his son Shechem, and every male in the city was circumcised.

²⁵Three days later, while all of them were still in pain, two of Jacob's sons, Simeon and Levi, Dinah's brothers, took their swords and attacked the unsuspecting city, killing every male. ²⁶They put Hamor and his son Shechem to the sword and took Dinah from Shechem's house and left. ²⁷The sons of Jacob came upon the dead bodies and looted the city where*ᵇ* their sister had been defiled. ²⁸They seized their flocks and herds and donkeys and everything else of theirs in the city and out in the fields. ²⁹They carried off all their wealth and all their women and children, taking as plunder everything in the houses.

³⁰Then Jacob said to Simeon and Levi, 'You have brought trouble on me by making me obnoxious to the Canaanites and Perizzites, the people living in this land. We are few in number, and if they join forces against me and attack me, I and my household will be destroyed.'

³¹But they replied, 'Should he have treated our sister like a prostitute?'

Jacob returns to Bethel

35 Then God said to Jacob, 'Go up to Bethel and settle there, and build an altar there to God, who appeared to you when you were fleeing from your brother Esau.'

²So Jacob said to his household and to all who were with him, 'Get rid of the foreign gods you have with you, and purify yourselves and change your clothes. ³Then come, let us go up to Bethel, where I will build an altar to God, who answered me in the day of my distress and who has been with me wherever I have gone.' ⁴So they gave Jacob all the foreign gods they had and the rings in their ears, and Jacob buried them under the oak at Shechem. ⁵Then they set out, and the terror of God fell on the towns all around them so that no-one pursued them.

⁶Jacob and all the people with him came to Luz (that is, Bethel) in the land of Canaan. ⁷There he built an altar, and he called the place El Bethel,*ᶜ* because it was there that God revealed himself to him when he was fleeing from his brother.

---

*ᵃ*10 Or *move about freely*; also in verse 21   *ᵇ*27 Or *because*   *ᶜ*7 *El Bethel* means *God of Bethel*.

Genesis 36:2

El
Genesis 35:1

In the ancient world, knowing someone's name was a special privilege that let you in on who they really were. God showed his love for his people by telling them several of his names, each of which revealed something about his character. One of the oldest names for God is El, which can be found at the beginning or end of names like Israel and Elizabeth. The name El Shaddai means 'God Almighty', and shows that God is a source of power and blessing.

⁸Now Deborah, Rebekah's nurse, died and was buried under the oak below Bethel. So it was named Allon Bakuth.[a]

⁹After Jacob returned from Paddan Aram,[b] God appeared to him again and blessed him. ¹⁰God said to him, 'Your name is Jacob,[c] but you will no longer be called Jacob; your name will be Israel.'[d] So he named him Israel.

¹¹And God said to him, 'I am God Almighty;[e] be fruitful and increase in number. A nation and a community of nations will come from you, and kings will come from your body. ¹²The land I gave to Abraham and Isaac I also give to you, and I will give this land to your descendants after you.' ¹³Then God went up from him at the place where he had talked with him.

¹⁴Jacob set up a stone pillar at the place where God had talked with him, and he poured out a drink offering on it; he also poured oil on it. ¹⁵Jacob called the place where God had talked with him Bethel.[f]

The deaths of Rachel and Isaac

¹⁶Then they moved on from Bethel. While they were still some distance from Ephrath, Rachel began to give birth and had great difficulty. ¹⁷And as she was having great difficulty in childbirth, the midwife said to her, 'Don't despair, for you have another son.' ¹⁸As she breathed her last—for she was dying—she named her son Ben-Oni.[g] But his father named him Benjamin.[h]

¹⁹So Rachel died and was buried on the way to Ephrath (that is, Bethlehem). ²⁰Over her tomb Jacob set up a pillar, and to this day that pillar marks Rachel's tomb.

²¹Israel moved on again and pitched his tent beyond Migdal Eder. ²²While Israel was living in that region, Reuben went in and slept with his father's concubine Bilhah, and Israel heard of it.

Jacob had twelve sons:

²³The sons of Leah:

Reuben the firstborn of Jacob, Simeon, Levi, Judah, Issachar and Zebulun.

²⁴The sons of Rachel:

Joseph and Benjamin.

²⁵The sons of Rachel's servant Bilhah:

Dan and Naphtali.

²⁶The sons of Leah's servant Zilpah:

Gad and Asher.

These were the sons of Jacob, who were born to him in Paddan Aram.

²⁷Jacob came home to his father Isaac in Mamre, near Kiriath Arba (that is, Hebron), where Abraham and Isaac had stayed. ²⁸Isaac lived a hundred and eighty years. ²⁹Then he breathed his last and died and was gathered to his people, old and full of years. And his sons Esau and Jacob buried him.

Esau's descendants

36 This is the account of the family line of Esau (that is, Edom).

²Esau took his wives from the women of Canaan: Adah daughter of Elon the Hittite, and Oholibamah daughter of Anah and

---

[a] 8 *Allon Bakuth* means *oak of weeping*. [b] 9 That is, North-west Mesopotamia; also in verse 26 [c] 10 *Jacob* means *he grasps the heel*, a Hebrew idiom for *he deceives*. [d] 10 *Israel* probably means *he struggles with God*. [e] 11 Hebrew *El-Shaddai* [f] 15 *Bethel* means *house of God*. [g] 18 *Ben-Oni* means *son of my trouble*. [h] 18 *Benjamin* means *son of my right hand*.

granddaughter of Zibeon the Hivite— ³also Basemath daughter of Ishmael and sister of Nebaioth.

⁴Adah bore Eliphaz to Esau, Basemath bore Reuel, ⁵and Oholibamah bore Jeush, Jalam and Korah. These were the sons of Esau, who were born to him in Canaan.

⁶Esau took his wives and sons and daughters and all the members of his household, as well as his livestock and all his other animals and all the goods he had acquired in Canaan, and moved to a land some distance from his brother Jacob. ⁷Their possessions were too great for them to remain together; the land where they were staying could not support them both because of their livestock. ⁸So Esau (that is, Edom) settled in the hill country of Seir.

⁹This is the account of the family line of Esau the father of the Edomites in the hill country of Seir.

¹⁰These are the names of Esau's sons:
Eliphaz, the son of Esau's wife Adah, and Reuel, the son of Esau's wife Basemath.

¹¹The sons of Eliphaz:
Teman, Omar, Zepho, Gatam and Kenaz.

¹²Esau's son Eliphaz also had a concubine named Timna, who bore him Amalek. These were grandsons of Esau's wife Adah.

¹³The sons of Reuel:
Nahath, Zerah, Shammah and Mizzah. These were grandsons of Esau's wife Basemath.

¹⁴The sons of Esau's wife Oholibamah daughter of Anah and granddaughter of Zibeon, whom she bore to Esau:
Jeush, Jalam and Korah.

¹⁵These were the chiefs among Esau's descendants:

The sons of Eliphaz the firstborn of Esau:
Chiefs Teman, Omar, Zepho, Kenaz, ¹⁶Korah,[a] Gatam and Amalek. These were the chiefs descended from Eliphaz in Edom; they were grandsons of Adah.

¹⁷The sons of Esau's son Reuel:
Chiefs Nahath, Zerah, Shammah and Mizzah. These were the chiefs descended from Reuel in Edom; they were grandsons of Esau's wife Basemath.

¹⁸The sons of Esau's wife Oholibamah:
Chiefs Jeush, Jalam and Korah. These were the chiefs descended from Esau's wife Oholibamah daughter of Anah.

¹⁹These were the sons of Esau (that is, Edom), and these were their chiefs.

²⁰These were the sons of Seir the Horite, who were living in the region:
Lotan, Shobal, Zibeon, Anah, ²¹Dishon, Ezer and Dishan. These sons of Seir in Edom were Horite chiefs.

²²The sons of Lotan:
Hori and Homam.[b] Timna was Lotan's sister.

²³The sons of Shobal:
Alvan, Manahath, Ebal, Shepho and Onam.

²⁴The sons of Zibeon:
Aiah and Anah. This is the Anah who discovered the hot springs[c] in the desert while he was grazing the donkeys of his father Zibeon.

²⁵The children of Anah:
Dishon and Oholibamah daughter of Anah.

²⁶The sons of Dishon:[d]
Hemdan, Eshban, Ithran and Keran.

²⁷The sons of Ezer:
Bilhan, Zaavan and Akan.

²⁸The sons of Dishan:
Uz and Aran.

---

[a] 16 Masoretic Text; Samaritan Pentateuch (see also Gen. 36:11 and 1 Chron. 1:36) does not have *Korah*.   [b] 22 Hebrew *Hemam*, a variant of *Homam* (see 1 Chron. 1:39)   [c] 24 Vulgate; Syriac *discovered water*; the meaning of the Hebrew for this word is uncertain.   [d] 26 Hebrew *Dishan*, a variant of *Dishon*

29These were the Horite chiefs:
Lotan, Shobal, Zibeon, Anah, 30Dishon, Ezer and Dishan. These were the Horite chiefs, according to their divisions, in the land of Seir.

The rulers of Edom

31These were the kings who reigned in Edom before any Israelite king reigned:
32Bela son of Beor became king of Edom. His city was named Dinhabah.
33When Bela died, Jobab son of Zerah from Bozrah succeeded him as king.
34When Jobab died, Husham from the land of the Temanites succeeded him as king.
35When Husham died, Hadad son of Bedad, who defeated Midian in the country of Moab, succeeded him as king. His city was named Avith.
36When Hadad died, Samlah from Masrekah succeeded him as king.
37When Samlah died, Shaul from Rehoboth on the river succeeded him as king.
38When Shaul died, Baal-Hanan son of Akbor succeeded him as king.
39When Baal-Hanan son of Akbor died, Hadad*a* succeeded him as king. His city was named Pau, and his wife's name was Mehetabel daughter of Matred, the daughter of Me-Zahab.

40These were the chiefs descended from Esau, by name, according to their clans and regions:
Timna, Alvah, Jetheth, 41Oholibamah, Elah, Pinon, 42Kenaz, Teman, Mibzar, 43Magdiel and Iram. These were the chiefs of Edom, according to their settlements in the land they occupied.

This was Esau the father of the Edomites.

Sign of the times

Joseph's robe
Genesis 37:3
Joseph's robe didn't just make him look good, it meant something too. It probably had long sleeves like the robes of wealthy men, which showed that Joseph wasn't expected to do manual labour. It definitely showed that Joseph was his dad's favourite. No wonder his brothers were jealous!

Joseph's dreams

37 Jacob lived in the land where his father had stayed, the land of Canaan.

2This is the account of Jacob's family line.

Joseph, a young man of seventeen, was tending the flocks with his brothers, the sons of Bilhah and the sons of Zilpah, his father's wives, and he brought their father a bad report about them.

3Now Israel loved Joseph more than any of his other sons, because he had been born to him in his old age; and he made a richly ornamented*b* robe for him. 4When his brothers saw that their father loved him more than any of them, they hated him and could not speak a kind word to him.

5Joseph had a dream, and when he told it to his brothers, they hated him all the more. 6He said to them, 'Listen to this dream I had: 7we were binding sheaves of corn out in the field when suddenly my sheaf rose and stood upright, while your sheaves gathered round mine and bowed down to it.'

8His brothers said to him, 'Do you intend to reign over us? Will you actually

---

a 39 Many manuscripts of the Masoretic Text, Samaritan Pentateuch and Syriac (see also 1 Chron. 1:50); most manuscripts of the Masoretic Text *Hadar*   *b* 3 The meaning of the Hebrew for *richly ornamented* is uncertain; also in verses 23 and 32.

rule us?' And they hated him all the more because of his dream and what he had said.

9Then he had another dream, and he told it to his brothers. 'Listen,' he said, 'I had another dream, and this time the sun and moon and eleven stars were bowing down to me.'

10When he told his father as well as his brothers, his father rebuked him and said, 'What is this dream you had? Will your mother and I and your brothers actually come and bow down to the ground before you?' 11His brothers were jealous of him, but his father kept the matter in mind.

Joseph sold by his brothers

12Now his brothers had gone to graze their father's flocks near Shechem, 13and Israel said to Joseph, 'As you know, your brothers are grazing the flocks near Shechem. Come, I am going to send you to them.'

'Very well,' he replied.

14So he said to him, 'Go and see if all is well with your brothers and with the flocks, and bring word back to me.' Then he sent him off from the Valley of Hebron.

When Joseph arrived at Shechem, 15a man found him wandering around in the fields and asked him, 'What are you looking for?'

16He replied, 'I'm looking for my brothers. Can you tell me where they are grazing their flocks?'

17'They have moved on from here,' the man answered. 'I heard them say, "Let's go to Dothan."'

So Joseph went after his brothers and found them near Dothan. 18But they saw him in the distance, and before he reached them, they plotted to kill him.

19'Here comes that dreamer!' they said to each other. 20'Come now, let's kill him and throw him into one of these cisterns and say that a ferocious animal devoured him. Then we'll see what comes of his dreams.'

21When Reuben heard this, he tried to rescue him from their hands. 'Let's not take his life,' he said. 22'Don't shed any blood. Throw him into this cistern here in the wilderness, but don't lay a hand on him.' Reuben said this to rescue him from them and take him back to his father.

23So when Joseph came to his brothers, they stripped him of his robe—the richly ornamented robe he was wearing— 24and they took him and threw him into the cistern. The cistern was empty; there was no water in it.

25As they sat down to eat their meal, they looked up and saw a caravan of Ishmaelites coming from Gilead. Their camels were loaded with spices, balm and myrrh, and they were on their way to take them down to Egypt.

26Judah said to his brothers, 'What will we gain if we kill our brother and cover up his blood? 27Come, let's sell him to the Ishmaelites and not lay our hands on him; after all, he is our brother, our own flesh and blood.' His brothers agreed.

28So when the Midianite merchants came by, his brothers pulled Joseph up out of the cistern and sold him for twenty shekels*a* of silver to the Ishmaelites, who took him to Egypt.

29When Reuben returned to the cistern and saw that Joseph was not there, he tore his clothes. 30He went back to his brothers and said, 'The boy isn't there! Where can I turn now?'

31Then they got Joseph's robe, slaughtered a goat and dipped the robe in the blood. 32They took the ornamented robe back to their father and said, 'We found this. Examine it to see whether it is your son's robe.'

33He recognised it and said, 'It is my son's robe! Some ferocious animal has devoured him. Joseph has surely been torn to pieces.'

34Then Jacob tore his clothes, put on sackcloth and mourned for his son many days. 35All his sons and daughters came to comfort him, but he refused to be comforted. 'No,' he said, 'in mourning will I go down to the grave to my son.' So his father wept for him.

36Meanwhile, the Midianites*b* sold Joseph in Egypt to Potiphar, one of Pharaoh's officials, the captain of the guard.

---

a 28 That is, about 230 grams *b* 36 Samaritan Pentateuch, Septuagint, Vulgate and Syriac (see also verse 28); Masoretic Text *Medanites*

People and Places

Joseph
Genesis 37:36

Perhaps best known for the special coat his father gave him, Joseph was Jacob's eleventh son. His brothers got so fed up with him that they sold him into slavery in Egypt where he led a bit of a roller-coaster life. He went from being a slave to running Potiphar's household; from being in prison to being in charge of the whole of Egypt. Throughout it all, he kept trusting God. Eventually he was reunited with his family and they all moved to join him in Egypt.

Judah and Tamar

38 At that time, Judah left his brothers and went down to stay with a man of Adullam named Hirah. ²There Judah met the daughter of a Canaanite man named Shua. He married her and made love to her; ³she became pregnant and gave birth to a son, who was named Er. ⁴She conceived again and gave birth to a son and named him Onan. ⁵She gave birth to still another son and named him Shelah. It was at Kezib that she gave birth to him.

⁶Judah got a wife for Er, his firstborn, and her name was Tamar. ⁷But Er, Judah's firstborn, was wicked in the LORD's sight; so the LORD put him to death.

⁸Then Judah said to Onan, 'Sleep with your brother's wife and fulfil your duty to her as a brother-in-law to raise up offspring for your brother.' ⁹But Onan knew that the child would not be his; so whenever he slept with his brother's wife, he spilled his semen on the ground to avoid providing offspring for his brother. ¹⁰What he did was wicked in the LORD's sight; so he put him to death also.

¹¹Judah then said to his daughter-in-law Tamar, 'Live as a widow in your father's household until my son Shelah grows up.' For he thought, 'He may die too, just like his brothers.' So Tamar went to live in her father's household.

¹²After a long time Judah's wife, the daughter of Shua, died. When Judah had recovered from his grief, he went up to Timnah, to the men who were shearing his sheep, and his friend Hirah the Adullamite went with him.

¹³When Tamar was told, 'Your father-in-law is on his way to Timnah to shear his sheep,' ¹⁴she took off her widow's clothes, covered herself with a veil to disguise herself, and then sat down at the entrance to Enaim, which is on the road to Timnah. For she saw that, though Shelah had now grown up, she had not been given to him as his wife.

¹⁵When Judah saw her, he thought she was a prostitute, for she had covered her face. ¹⁶Not realising that she was his daughter-in-law, he went over to her by the roadside and said, 'Come now, let me sleep with you.'

'And what will you give me to sleep with you?' she asked.

¹⁷'I'll send you a young goat from my flock,' he said.

'Will you give me something as a pledge until you send it?' she asked.

¹⁸He said, 'What pledge should I give you?'

'Your seal and its cord, and the staff in your hand,' she answered. So he gave them to her and slept with her, and she became pregnant by him. ¹⁹After she left, she took off her veil and put on her widow's clothes again.

²⁰Meanwhile Judah sent the young goat by his friend the Adullamite in order to get his pledge back from the woman, but he did not find her. ²¹He asked the men who lived there, 'Where is the shrine-prostitute who was beside the road at Enaim?'

'There hasn't been any shrine-prostitute here,' they said.

²²So he went back to Judah and said, 'I didn't find her. Besides, the men who lived there said, "There hasn't been any shrine-prostitute here."'

²³Then Judah said, 'Let her keep what she has, or we will become a laughing-stock.

After all, I did send her this young goat, but you didn't find her.'

24About three months later Judah was told, 'Your daughter-in-law Tamar is guilty of prostitution, and as a result she is now pregnant.'

Judah said, 'Bring her out and let her be burned to death!'

25As she was being brought out, she sent a message to her father-in-law. 'I am pregnant by the man who owns these,' she said. And she added, 'See if you recognise whose seal and cord and staff these are.'

26Judah recognised them and said, 'She is more righteous than I, since I wouldn't give her to my son Shelah.' And he did not sleep with her again.

27When the time came for her to give birth, there were twin boys in her womb. 28As she was giving birth, one of them put out his hand; so the midwife took a scarlet thread and tied it on his wrist and said, 'This one came out first.' 29But when he drew back his hand, his brother came out, and she said, 'So this is how you have broken out!' And he was named Perez.[a] 30Then his brother, who had the scarlet thread on his wrist, came out and he was given the name Zerah.[b]

Joseph and Potiphar's wife

39 Now Joseph had been taken down to Egypt. Potiphar, an Egyptian who was one of Pharaoh's officials, the captain of the guard, bought him from the Ishmaelites who had taken him there.

2The LORD was with Joseph so that he prospered, and he lived in the house of his Egyptian master. 3When his master saw that the LORD was with him and that the LORD gave him success in everything he did, 4Joseph found favour in his eyes and became his attendant. Potiphar put him in charge of his household, and he entrusted to his care everything he owned. 5From the time he put him in charge of his household and of all that he owned, the LORD blessed the household of the Egyptian because of Joseph. The blessing of the LORD was on everything Potiphar had, both in the house and in the field. 6So Potiphar left everything he had in Joseph's care; with Joseph in charge, he did not concern himself with anything except the food he ate.

Now Joseph was well-built and handsome, 7and after a while his master's wife took notice of Joseph and said, 'Come to bed with me!'

8But he refused. 'With me in charge,' he told her, 'my master does not concern himself with anything in the house; everything he owns he has entrusted to my care. 9No-one is greater in this house than I am. My master has withheld nothing from me except you, because you are his wife. How then could I do such a wicked thing and sin against God?' 10And though she spoke to Joseph day after day, he refused to go to bed with her or even to be with her.

11One day he went into the house to attend to his duties, and none of the household servants was inside. 12She caught him by his cloak and said, 'Come to bed with me!' But he left his cloak in her hand and ran out of the house.

13When she saw that he had left his cloak in her hand and had run out of the house, 14she called her household servants. 'Look,' she said to them, 'this Hebrew has been brought to us to make sport of us! He came in here to sleep with me, but I screamed. 15When he heard me scream for help, he left his cloak beside me and ran out of the house.'

16She kept his cloak beside her until his master came home. 17Then she told him this story: 'That Hebrew slave you brought us came to me to make sport of me. 18But as soon as I screamed for help, he left his cloak beside me and ran out of the house.'

19When his master heard the story his wife told him, saying, 'This is how your slave treated me,' he burned with anger. 20Joseph's master took him and put him in prison, the place where the king's prisoners were confined.

But while Joseph was there in the prison, 21the LORD was with him; he showed him kindness and granted him favour in the eyes of the prison warder. 22So the warder put Joseph in charge of all those held in the prison, and he was made responsible for all

---

[a] 29 Perez means breaking out. [b] 30 Zerah can mean scarlet or brightness.

that was done there. ²³The warder paid no attention to anything under Joseph's care, because the LORD was with Joseph and gave him success in whatever he did.

The cupbearer and the baker

40 Some time later, the cupbearer and the baker of the king of Egypt offended their master, the king of Egypt. ²Pharaoh was angry with his two officials, the chief cupbearer and the chief baker, ³and put them in custody in the house of the captain of the guard, in the same prison where Joseph was confined. ⁴The captain of the guard assigned them to Joseph, and he attended them.

After they had been in custody for some time, ⁵each of the two men—the cupbearer and the baker of the king of Egypt, who were being held in prison—had a dream the same night, and each dream had a meaning of its own.

⁶When Joseph came to them the next morning, he saw that they were dejected. ⁷So he asked Pharaoh's officials who were in custody with him in his master's house, 'Why do you look so sad today?'

⁸'We both had dreams,' they answered, 'but there is no-one to interpret them.'

Then Joseph said to them, 'Do not interpretations belong to God? Tell me your dreams.'

⁹So the chief cupbearer told Joseph his dream. He said to him, 'In my dream I saw a vine in front of me, ¹⁰and on the vine were three branches. As soon as it budded, it blossomed, and its clusters ripened into grapes. ¹¹Pharaoh's cup was in my hand, and I took the grapes, squeezed them into Pharaoh's cup and put the cup in his hand.'

¹²'This is what it means,' Joseph said to him. 'The three branches are three days. ¹³Within three days Pharaoh will lift up your head and restore you to your position, and you will put Pharaoh's cup in his hand, just as you used to do when you were his cupbearer. ¹⁴But when all goes well with you, remember me and show me kindness; mention me to Pharaoh and get me out of this prison. ¹⁵I was forcibly carried off from the land of the Hebrews, and even here I

Interpreting dreams
Genesis 40:8

Dreams often seem to be a weird jumble of images, people and words that are a strange variation of real life, but in the Bible God spoke through dreams at significant times. God gives Joseph the ability to understand the prophetic dreams of the cupbearer and baker, and he tells them what's going to happen. Later, he interprets Pharaoh's dreams and gets to run the country as a result! But he's always quick to point out that the interpretation comes from God, not him.

have done nothing to deserve being put in a dungeon.'

¹⁶When the chief baker saw that Joseph had given a favourable interpretation, he said to Joseph, 'I too had a dream: on my head were three baskets of bread.ᵃ ¹⁷In the top basket were all kinds of baked goods for Pharaoh, but the birds were eating them out of the basket on my head.'

¹⁸'This is what it means,' Joseph said. 'The three baskets are three days. ¹⁹Within three days Pharaoh will lift off your head and impale your body on a pole. And the birds will eat away your flesh.'

²⁰Now the third day was Pharaoh's birthday, and he gave a feast for all his officials. He lifted up the heads of the chief cupbearer and the chief baker in the presence of his officials: ²¹he restored the chief cupbearer to his position, so that he once again put the cup into Pharaoh's hand— ²²but he impaled the chief baker, just as Joseph had said to them in his interpretation.

²³The chief cupbearer, however, did not remember Joseph; he forgot him.

ᵃ 16 Or *three wicker baskets*

Pharaoh's dreams

41 When two full years had passed, Pharaoh had a dream: he was standing by the Nile, 2when out of the river there came up seven cows, sleek and fat, and they grazed among the reeds. 3After them, seven other cows, ugly and gaunt, came up out of the Nile and stood beside those on the river-bank. 4And the cows that were ugly and gaunt ate up the seven sleek, fat cows. Then Pharaoh woke up.

5He fell asleep again and had a second dream: seven ears of corn, healthy and good, were growing on a single stalk. 6After them, seven other ears of corn sprouted—thin and scorched by the east wind. 7The thin ears of corn swallowed up the seven healthy, full ears. Then Pharaoh woke up; it had been a dream.

8In the morning his mind was troubled, so he sent for all the magicians and wise men of Egypt. Pharaoh told them his dreams, but no-one could interpret them for him.

9Then the chief cupbearer said to Pharaoh, 'Today I am reminded of my shortcomings. 10Pharaoh was once angry with his servants, and he imprisoned me and the chief baker in the house of the captain of the guard. 11Each of us had a dream the same night, and each dream had a meaning of its own. 12Now a young Hebrew was there with us, a servant of the captain of the guard. We told him our dreams, and he interpreted them for us, giving each man the interpretation of his dream. 13And things turned out exactly as he interpreted them to us: I was restored to my position, and the other man was impaled.'

14So Pharaoh sent for Joseph, and he was quickly brought from the dungeon. When he had shaved and changed his clothes, he came before Pharaoh.

15Pharaoh said to Joseph, 'I had a dream, and no-one can interpret it. But I have heard it said of you that when you hear a dream you can interpret it.'

16'I cannot do it,' Joseph replied to Pharaoh, 'but God will give Pharaoh the answer he desires.'

17Then Pharaoh said to Joseph, 'In my dream I was standing on the bank of the Nile, 18when out of the river there came up seven cows, fat and sleek, and they grazed among the reeds. 19After them, seven other cows came up—scrawny and very ugly and lean. I had never seen such ugly cows in all the land of Egypt. 20The lean, ugly cows ate up the seven fat cows that came up first. 21But even after they ate them, no-one could tell that they had done so; they looked just as ugly as before. Then I woke up.

22'In my dream I saw seven ears of corn, full and good, growing on a single stalk. 23After them, seven other ears sprouted—withered and thin and scorched by the east wind. 24The thin ears of corn swallowed up the seven good ears. I told this to the magicians, but none of them could explain it to me.'

25Then Joseph said to Pharaoh, 'The dreams of Pharaoh are one and the same. God has revealed to Pharaoh what he is about to do. 26The seven good cows are seven years, and the seven good ears of corn are seven years; it is one and the same dream. 27The seven lean, ugly cows that came up afterwards are seven years, and so are the seven worthless ears of corn scorched by the east wind: they are seven years of famine.

28'It is just as I said to Pharaoh: God has shown Pharaoh what he is about to do. 29Seven years of great abundance are coming throughout the land of Egypt, 30but seven years of famine will follow them. Then all the abundance in Egypt will be forgotten, and the famine will ravage the land. 31The abundance in the land will not be remembered, because the famine that follows it will be so severe. 32The reason the dream was given to Pharaoh in two forms is that the matter has been firmly decided by God, and God will do it soon.

33'And now let Pharaoh look for a discerning and wise man and put him in charge of the land of Egypt. 34Let Pharaoh appoint commissioners over the land to take a fifth of the harvest of Egypt during the seven years of abundance. 35They should collect all the food of these good years that are coming and store up the grain under the authority of Pharaoh, to be kept in the cities for food. 36This food should be held in reserve for the country, to be used during the seven years of famine that will come upon Egypt, so that the country may not be ruined by the famine.'

37The plan seemed good to Pharaoh and to all his officials. 38So Pharaoh asked them, 'Can we find anyone like this man, one in whom is the spirit of God?'[a]

39Then Pharaoh said to Joseph, 'Since God has made all this known to you, there is no-one so discerning and wise as you. 40You shall be in charge of my palace, and all my people are to submit to your orders. Only with respect to the throne will I be greater than you.'

Joseph in charge of Egypt

41So Pharaoh said to Joseph, 'I hereby put you in charge of the whole land of Egypt.' 42Then Pharaoh took his signet ring from his finger and put it on Joseph's finger. He dressed him in robes of fine linen and put a gold chain round his neck. 43He made him ride in a chariot as his second-in-command,[b] and people shouted before him, 'Make way!'[c] Thus he put him in charge of the whole land of Egypt.

44Then Pharaoh said to Joseph, 'I am Pharaoh, but without your word no-one will lift hand or foot in all Egypt.' 45Pharaoh gave Joseph the name Zaphenath-Paneah and gave him Asenath daughter of Potiphera, priest of On,[d] to be his wife. And Joseph went throughout the land of Egypt.

46Joseph was thirty years old when he entered the service of Pharaoh king of Egypt. And Joseph went out from Pharaoh's presence and travelled throughout Egypt. 47During the seven years of abundance the land produced plentifully. 48Joseph collected all the food produced in those seven years of abundance in Egypt and stored it in the cities. In each city he put the food grown in the fields surrounding it. 49Joseph stored up huge quantities of grain, like the sand of the sea; it was so much that he stopped keeping records because it was beyond measure.

50Before the years of famine came, two sons were born to Joseph by Asenath daughter of Potiphera, priest of On. 51Joseph named his firstborn Manasseh[e] and said, 'It is because God has made me forget all my trouble and all my father's household.' 52The second son he named Ephraim[f] and said, 'It is because God has made me fruitful in the land of my suffering.'

53The seven years of abundance in Egypt came to an end, 54and the seven years of famine began, just as Joseph had said. There was famine in all the other lands, but in the whole land of Egypt there was food. 55When all Egypt began to feel the famine, the people cried to Pharaoh for food. Then Pharaoh told all the Egyptians, 'Go to Joseph and do what he tells you.'

56When the famine had spread over the whole country, Joseph opened all the storehouses and sold grain to the Egyptians, for the famine was severe throughout Egypt. 57And all the world came to Egypt to buy grain from Joseph, because the famine was severe everywhere.

Joseph's brothers go to Egypt

42 When Jacob learned that there was grain in Egypt, he said to his sons, 'Why do you just keep looking at each other?' 2He continued, 'I have heard that there is grain in Egypt. Go down there and buy some for us, so that we may live and not die.'

Sign of the times

Famine in Egypt
Genesis 41:41

There's lots of archaeological evidence of famines in Egypt, and Joseph's story in Genesis has plenty of details that tie in with Egyptian records of the time. Pharaoh made Joseph vizier of Egypt, second in power to himself and rather like a prime minister.

---

[a] 38 Or *of the gods* [b] 43 Or *in the chariot of his second-in-command*; or *in his second chariot* [c] 43 Or *Bow down*
[d] 45 That is, Heliopolis; also in verse 50 [e] 51 *Manasseh* sounds like and may be derived from the Hebrew for *forget*.
[f] 52 *Ephraim* sounds like the Hebrew for *twice fruitful*.

³Then ten of Joseph's brothers went down to buy grain from Egypt. ⁴But Jacob did not send Benjamin, Joseph's brother, with the others, because he was afraid that harm might come to him. ⁵So Israel's sons were among those who went to buy grain, for the famine was in the land of Canaan also.

⁶Now Joseph was the governor of the land, the person who sold grain to all its people. So when Joseph's brothers arrived, they bowed down to him with their faces to the ground. ⁷As soon as Joseph saw his brothers, he recognised them, but he pretended to be a stranger and spoke harshly to them. 'Where do you come from?' he asked.

'From the land of Canaan,' they replied, 'to buy food.'

⁸Although Joseph recognised his brothers, they did not recognise him. ⁹Then he remembered his dreams about them and said to them, 'You are spies! You have come to see where our land is unprotected.'

¹⁰'No, my lord,' they answered. 'Your servants have come to buy food. ¹¹We are all the sons of one man. Your servants are honest men, not spies.'

¹²'No!' he said to them. 'You have come to see where our land is unprotected.'

¹³But they replied, 'Your servants were twelve brothers, the sons of one man, who lives in the land of Canaan. The youngest is now with our father, and one is no more.'

¹⁴Joseph said to them, 'It is just as I told you: you are spies! ¹⁵And this is how you will be tested: as surely as Pharaoh lives, you will not leave this place unless your youngest brother comes here. ¹⁶Send one of your number to get your brother; the rest of you will be kept in prison, so that your words may be tested to see if you are telling the truth. If you are not, then as surely as Pharaoh lives, you are spies!' ¹⁷And he put them all in custody for three days.

¹⁸On the third day, Joseph said to them, 'Do this and you will live, for I fear God: ¹⁹if you are honest men, let one of your brothers stay here in prison, while the rest of you go and take grain back for your starving households. ²⁰But you must bring your youngest brother to me, so that your words may be verified and that you may not die.' This they proceeded to do.

²¹They said to one another, 'Surely we are being punished because of our brother. We saw how distressed he was when he pleaded with us for his life, but we would not listen; that's why this distress has come on us.'

²²Reuben replied, 'Didn't I tell you not to sin against the boy? But you wouldn't listen! Now we must give an accounting for his blood.' ²³They did not realise that Joseph could understand them, since he was using an interpreter.

²⁴He turned away from them and began to weep, but then came back and spoke to them again. He had Simeon taken from them and bound before their eyes.

²⁵Joseph gave orders to fill their bags with grain, to put each man's silver back in his sack, and to give them provisions for their journey. After this was done for them, ²⁶they loaded their grain on their donkeys and left.

²⁷At the place where they stopped for the night one of them opened his sack to get feed for his donkey, and he saw his silver in the mouth of his sack. ²⁸'My silver has been returned,' he said to his brothers. 'Here it is in my sack.'

Their hearts sank and they turned to each other trembling and said, 'What is this that God has done to us?'

²⁹When they came to their father Jacob in the land of Canaan, they told him all that had happened to them. They said, ³⁰'The man who is lord over the land spoke harshly to us and treated us as though we were spying on the land. ³¹But we said to him, "We are honest men; we are not spies. ³²We were twelve brothers, sons of one father. One is no more, and the youngest is now with our father in Canaan."

³³'Then the man who is lord over the land said to us, "This is how I will know whether you are honest men: leave one of your brothers here with me, and take food for your starving households and go. ³⁴But bring your youngest brother to me so I will know that you are not spies but honest men. Then I will give your brother back to you, and you can trade*a* in the land."'

---

a 34 Or *move about* freely

35As they were emptying their sacks, there in each man's sack was his pouch of silver! When they and their father saw the money pouches, they were frightened. 36Their father Jacob said to them, 'You have deprived me of my children. Joseph is no more and Simeon is no more, and now you want to take Benjamin. Everything is against me!'

37Then Reuben said to his father, 'You may put both of my sons to death if I do not bring him back to you. Entrust him to my care, and I will bring him back.'

38But Jacob said, 'My son will not go down there with you; his brother is dead and he is the only one left. If harm comes to him on the journey you are taking, you will bring my grey head down to the grave in sorrow.'

The second journey to Egypt

43 Now the famine was still severe in the land. 2So when they had eaten all the grain they had brought from Egypt, their father said to them, 'Go back and buy us a little more food.'

3But Judah said to him, 'The man warned us solemnly, "You will not see my face again unless your brother is with you." 4If you will send our brother along with us, we will go down and buy food for you. 5But if you will not send him, we will not go down, because the man said to us, "You will not see my face again unless your brother is with you."'

6Israel asked, 'Why did you bring this trouble on me by telling the man you had another brother?'

7They replied, 'The man questioned us closely about ourselves and our family. "Is your father still living?" he asked us. "Do you have another brother?" We simply answered his questions. How were we to know he would say, "Bring your brother down here"?'

8Then Judah said to Israel his father, 'Send the boy along with me and we will go at once, so that we and you and our children may live and not die. 9I myself will guarantee his safety; you can hold me personally responsible for him. If I do not bring him back to you and set him here before you, I will bear the blame before you all my life. 10As it is, if we had not delayed, we could have gone and returned twice.'

11Then their father Israel said to them, 'If it must be, then do this: put some of the best products of the land in your bags and take them down to the man as a gift—a little balm and a little honey, some spices and myrrh, some pistachio nuts and almonds. 12Take double the amount of silver with you, for you must return the silver that was put back into the mouths of your sacks. Perhaps it was a mistake. 13Take your brother also and go back to the man at once. 14And may God Almighty^a grant you mercy before the man so that he will let your other brother and Benjamin come back with you. As for me, if I am bereaved, I am bereaved.'

15So the men took the gifts and double the amount of silver, and Benjamin also. They hurried down to Egypt and presented themselves to Joseph. 16When Joseph saw Benjamin with them, he said to the steward of his house, 'Take these men to my house, slaughter an animal and prepare a meal; they are to eat with me at noon.'

17The man did as Joseph told him and took the men to Joseph's house. 18Now the men were frightened when they were taken to his house. They thought, 'We were brought here because of the silver that was put back into our sacks the first time. He wants to attack us and overpower us and seize us as slaves and take our donkeys.'

19So they went up to Joseph's steward and spoke to him at the entrance to the house. 20'We beg your pardon, our lord,' they said, 'we came down here the first time to buy food. 21But at the place where we stopped for the night we opened our sacks and each of us found his silver—the exact weight—in the mouth of his sack. So we have brought it back with us. 22We have also brought additional silver with us to buy food. We don't know who put our silver in our sacks.'

23'It's all right,' he said. 'Don't be afraid. Your God, the God of your father, has given you treasure in your sacks; I received your

---
^{a} 14 Hebrew *El-Shaddai*

silver.' Then he brought Simeon out to them.

24 The steward took the men into Joseph's house, gave them water to wash their feet and provided fodder for their donkeys. 25 They prepared their gifts for Joseph's arrival at noon, because they had heard that they were to eat there.

26 When Joseph came home, they presented to him the gifts they had brought into the house, and they bowed down before him to the ground. 27 He asked them how they were, and then he said, 'How is your aged father you told me about? Is he still living?' 28 They replied, 'Your servant our father is still alive and well.' And they bowed down, prostrating themselves before him.

29 As he looked about and saw his brother Benjamin, his own mother's son, he asked, 'Is this your youngest brother, the one you told me about?' And he said, 'God be gracious to you, my son.' 30 Deeply moved at the sight of his brother, Joseph hurried out and looked for a place to weep. He went into his private room and wept there.

31 After he had washed his face, he came out and, controlling himself, said, 'Serve the food.'

32 They served him by himself, the brothers by themselves, and the Egyptians who ate with him by themselves, because Egyptians could not eat with Hebrews, for that is detestable to Egyptians. 33 The men had been seated before him in the order of their ages, from the firstborn to the youngest; and they looked at each other in astonishment. 34 When portions were served to them from Joseph's table, Benjamin's portion was five times as much as anyone else's. So they feasted and drank freely with him.

A silver cup in a sack

44 Now Joseph gave these instructions to the steward of his house: 'Fill the men's sacks with as much food as they can carry, and put each man's silver in the mouth of his sack. 2 Then put my cup, the silver one, in the mouth of the youngest one's sack, along with the silver for his grain.' And he did as Joseph said.

3 As morning dawned, the men were sent on their way with their donkeys. 4 They had

Sign of the times

Cup divination
Genesis 44:5
Rather like reading tea-leaves, cup divination was the practice of looking for signs in drops of oil poured into a cup of water. The Bible forbids this kind of divination (Leviticus 19:26), and it must have been a practice that Joseph picked up in Egypt.

not gone far from the city when Joseph said to his steward, 'Go after those men at once, and when you catch up with them, say to them, "Why have you repaid good with evil? 5 Isn't this the cup my master drinks from and also uses for divination? This is a wicked thing you have done."'

6 When he caught up with them, he repeated these words to them. 7 But they said to him, 'Why does my lord say such things? Far be it from your servants to do anything like that! 8 We even brought back to you from the land of Canaan the silver we found inside the mouths of our sacks. So why would we steal silver or gold from your master's house? 9 If any of your servants is found to have it, he will die; and the rest of us will become my lord's slaves.'

10 'Very well, then,' he said, 'let it be as you say. Whoever is found to have it will become my slave; the rest of you will be free from blame.'

11 Each of them quickly lowered his sack to the ground and opened it. 12 Then the steward proceeded to search, beginning with the eldest and ending with the youngest. And the cup was found in Benjamin's sack. 13 At this, they tore their clothes. Then they all loaded their donkeys and returned to the city.

14 Joseph was still in the house when Judah and his brothers came in, and they threw themselves to the ground before him.

¹⁵Joseph said to them, 'What is this you have done? Don't you know that a man like me can find things out by divination?'

¹⁶'What can we say to my lord?' Judah replied. 'What can we say? How can we prove our innocence? God has uncovered your servants' guilt. We are now my lord's slaves—we ourselves and the one who was found to have the cup.'

¹⁷But Joseph said, 'Far be it from me to do such a thing! Only the man who was found to have the cup will become my slave. The rest of you, go back to your father in peace.'

¹⁸Then Judah went up to him and said: 'Pardon your servant, my lord, let me speak a word to my lord. Do not be angry with your servant, though you are equal to Pharaoh himself. ¹⁹My lord asked his servants, "Do you have a father or a brother?" ²⁰And we answered, "We have an aged father, and there is a young son born to him in his old age. His brother is dead, and he is the only one of his mother's sons left, and his father loves him."

²¹'Then you said to your servants, "Bring him down to me so I can see him for myself." ²²And we said to my lord, "The boy cannot leave his father; if he leaves him, his father will die." ²³But you told your servants, "Unless your youngest brother comes down with you, you will not see my face again." ²⁴When we went back to your servant my father, we told him what my lord had said.

²⁵'Then our father said, "Go back and buy a little more food." ²⁶But we said, "We cannot go down. Only if our youngest brother is with us will we go. We cannot see the man's face unless our youngest brother is with us."

²⁷'Your servant my father said to us, "You know that my wife bore me two sons. ²⁸One of them went away from me, and I said, 'He has surely been torn to pieces.' And I have not seen him since. ²⁹If you take this one from me too and harm comes to him, you will bring my grey head down to the grave in misery."

³⁰'So now, if the boy is not with us when I go back to your servant my father, and if my father, whose life is closely bound up with the boy's life, ³¹sees that the boy isn't there, he will die. Your servants will bring the grey head of our father down to the grave in sorrow. ³²Your servant guaranteed the boy's safety to my father. I said, "If I do not bring him back to you, I will bear the blame before you, my father, all my life!"

³³'Now then, please let your servant remain here as my lord's slave in place of the boy, and let the boy return with his brothers. ³⁴How can I go back to my father if the boy is not with me? No! Do not let me see the misery that would come on my father.'

Joseph makes himself known

45 Then Joseph could no longer control himself before all his attendants, and he cried out, 'Make everyone leave my presence!' So there was no-one with Joseph when he made himself known to his brothers. ²And he wept so loudly that the Egyptians heard him, and Pharaoh's household heard about it.

³Joseph said to his brothers, 'I am Joseph! Is my father still living?' But his brothers were not able to answer him, because they were terrified at his presence.

⁴Then Joseph said to his brothers, 'Come close to me.' When they had done so, he said, 'I am your brother Joseph, the one you sold into Egypt! ⁵And now, do not be distressed and do not be angry with yourselves for selling me here, because it was to save lives that God sent me ahead of you. ⁶For two years now there has been famine in the land, and for the next five years there will be no ploughing and reaping. ⁷But God sent me ahead of you to preserve for you a remnant on earth and to save your lives by a great deliverance.ᵃ

⁸'So then, it was not you who sent me here, but God. He made me father to Pharaoh, lord of his entire household and ruler of all Egypt. ⁹Now hurry back to my father and say to him, "This is what your son Joseph says: God has made me lord of all Egypt. Come down to me; don't delay. ¹⁰You shall live in the region of Goshen and be near me—you, your children and grandchildren, your flocks and herds, and all you

---

ᵃ 7 Or *save you as a great band of survivors*

have. ¹¹I will provide for you there, because five years of famine are still to come. Otherwise you and your household and all who belong to you will become destitute."

¹²'You can see for yourselves, and so can my brother Benjamin, that it is really I who am speaking to you. ¹³Tell my father about all the honour accorded me in Egypt and about everything you have seen. And bring my father down here quickly.'

¹⁴Then he threw his arms around his brother Benjamin and wept, and Benjamin embraced him, weeping. ¹⁵And he kissed all his brothers and wept over them. Afterwards his brothers talked with him.

¹⁶When the news reached Pharaoh's palace that Joseph's brothers had come, Pharaoh and all his officials were pleased. ¹⁷Pharaoh said to Joseph, 'Tell your brothers, "Do this: load your animals and return to the land of Canaan, ¹⁸and bring your father and your families back to me. I will give you the best of the land of Egypt and you can enjoy the fat of the land."

¹⁹'You are also instructed to tell them, "Do this: take some carts from Egypt for your children and your wives, and get your father and come. ²⁰Never mind about your belongings, because the best of all Egypt will be yours."'

²¹So the sons of Israel did this. Joseph gave them carts, as Pharaoh had commanded, and he also gave them provisions for their journey. ²²To each of them he gave new clothing, but to Benjamin he gave three hundred shekels*a* of silver and five sets of clothes. ²³And this is what he sent to his father: ten donkeys loaded with the best things of Egypt, and ten female donkeys loaded with grain and bread and other provisions for his journey. ²⁴Then he sent his brothers away, and as they were leaving he said to them, 'Don't quarrel on the way!'

²⁵So they went up out of Egypt and came to their father Jacob in the land of Canaan. ²⁶They told him, 'Joseph is still alive! In fact, he is ruler of all Egypt.' Jacob was stunned; he did not believe them. ²⁷But when they told him everything Joseph had said to them, and when he saw the carts Joseph had sent to carry him back, the spirit of their father Jacob revived. ²⁸And Israel said, 'I'm convinced! My son Joseph is still alive. I will go and see him before I die.'

Jacob goes to Egypt

46 So Israel set out with all that was his, and when he reached Beersheba, he offered sacrifices to the God of his father Isaac.

²And God spoke to Israel in a vision at night and said, 'Jacob! Jacob!'

'Here I am,' he replied.

³'I am God, the God of your father,' he said. 'Do not be afraid to go down to Egypt, for I will make you into a great nation there. ⁴I will go down to Egypt with you, and I will surely bring you back again. And Joseph's own hand will close your eyes.'

⁵Then Jacob left Beersheba, and Israel's sons took their father Jacob and their children and their wives in the carts that Pharaoh had sent to transport him. ⁶So Jacob and all his offspring went to Egypt, taking with them their livestock and the possessions they had acquired in Canaan. ⁷Jacob brought with him to Egypt his sons and grandsons and his daughters and granddaughters—all his offspring.

⁸These are the names of the sons of Israel (Jacob and his descendants) who went to Egypt:

People and Places

Egypt
Genesis 46:3

Egypt is a country in the north-east of Africa, known for the River Nile and its impressive pyramids. Joseph was brought here as a slave and rose to be in charge of the whole country because God was with him. His descendants spent 430 years here, the last of them in horrific slavery, before Moses led them out of captivity.

---

a 22 That is, about 3.5 kilograms

Reuben the firstborn of Jacob. ⁹The sons of Reuben:

Hanok, Pallu, Hezron and Karmi.

¹⁰The sons of Simeon:

Jemuel, Jamin, Ohad, Jakin, Zohar and Shaul the son of a Canaanite woman.

¹¹The sons of Levi:

Gershon, Kohath and Merari.

¹²The sons of Judah:

Er, Onan, Shelah, Perez and Zerah (but Er and Onan had died in the land of Canaan).

The sons of Perez:

Hezron and Hamul.

¹³The sons of Issachar:

Tola, Puah,^{a} Jashub^b and Shimron.

¹⁴The sons of Zebulun:

Sered, Elon and Jahleel.

¹⁵These were the sons Leah bore to Jacob in Paddan Aram,^{c} besides his daughter Dinah. These sons and daughters of his were thirty-three in all.

¹⁶The sons of Gad:

Zephon,^{d} Haggi, Shuni, Ezbon, Eri, Arodi and Areli.

¹⁷The sons of Asher:

Imnah, Ishvah, Ishvi and Beriah. Their sister was Serah.

The sons of Beriah:

Heber and Malkiel.

¹⁸These were the children born to Jacob by Zilpah, whom Laban had given to his daughter Leah—sixteen in all.

¹⁹The sons of Jacob's wife Rachel:

Joseph and Benjamin. ²⁰In Egypt, Manasseh and Ephraim were born to Joseph by Asenath daughter of Potiphera, priest of On.^{e}

²¹The sons of Benjamin:

Bela, Beker, Ashbel, Gera, Naaman, Ehi, Rosh, Muppim, Huppim and Ard.

²²These were the sons of Rachel who were born to Jacob—fourteen in all.

²³The son of Dan:

Hushim.

²⁴The sons of Naphtali:

Jahziel, Guni, Jezer and Shillem.

²⁵These were the sons born to Jacob by Bilhah, whom Laban had given to his daughter Rachel—seven in all.

²⁶All those who went to Egypt with Jacob—those who were his direct descendants, not counting his sons' wives—numbered sixty-six persons. ²⁷With the two sons^f who had been born to Joseph in Egypt, the members of Jacob's family, which went to Egypt, were seventy^g in all.

²⁸Now Jacob sent Judah ahead of him to Joseph to get directions to Goshen. When they arrived in the region of Goshen, ²⁹Joseph had his chariot made ready and went to Goshen to meet his father Israel. As soon as Joseph appeared before him, he threw his arms around his father^h and wept for a long time.

³⁰Israel said to Joseph, 'Now I am ready to die, since I have seen for myself that you are still alive.'

³¹Then Joseph said to his brothers and to his father's household, 'I will go up and speak to Pharaoh and will say to him, "My brothers and my father's household, who were living in the land of Canaan, have come to me. ³²The men are shepherds; they tend livestock, and they have brought along their flocks and herds and everything they own." ³³When Pharaoh calls you in and asks, "What is your occupation?" ³⁴you should answer, "Your servants have tended livestock from our boyhood on, just as our fathers did." Then you will be allowed to settle in the region of Goshen, for all shepherds are detestable to the Egyptians.'

47

Joseph went and told Pharaoh, 'My father and brothers, with their flocks and herds and everything they own, have come from the land of Canaan and are now in Goshen.' ²He chose five of his

---

^{a} 13 Samaritan Pentateuch and Syriac (see also 1 Chron. 7:1); Masoretic Text *Puvah* ^{b} 13 Samaritan Pentateuch and some Septuagint manuscripts (see also Num. 26:24 and 1 Chron. 7:1); Masoretic Text *Iob* ^{c} 15 That is, North-west Mesopotamia ^{d} 16 Samaritan Pentateuch and Septuagint (see also Num. 26:15); Masoretic Text *Ziphion* ^{e} 20 That is, Heliopolis ^{f} 27 Hebrew; Septuagint *the nine children* ^{g} 27 Hebrew (see also Exodus 1:5 and footnote); Septuagint (see also Acts 7:14) *seventy-five* ^{h} 29 Hebrew *around him* brothers and presented them before Pharaoh.

3 Pharaoh asked the brothers, 'What is your occupation?'

'Your servants are shepherds,' they replied to Pharaoh, 'just as our fathers were.' 4 They also said to him, 'We have come to live here for a while, because the famine is severe in Canaan and your servants' flocks have no pasture. So now, please let your servants settle in Goshen.'

5 Pharaoh said to Joseph, 'Your father and your brothers have come to you, 6 and the land of Egypt is before you; settle your father and your brothers in the best part of the land. Let them live in Goshen. And if you know of any among them with special ability, put them in charge of my own livestock.'

7 Then Joseph brought his father Jacob in and presented him before Pharaoh. After Jacob blessed[a] Pharaoh, 8 Pharaoh asked him, 'How old are you?'

9 And Jacob said to Pharaoh, 'The years of my pilgrimage are a hundred and thirty. My years have been few and difficult, and they do not equal the years of the pilgrimage of my fathers.' 10 Then Jacob blessed[b] Pharaoh and went out from his presence.

11 So Joseph settled his father and his brothers in Egypt and gave them property in the best part of the land, the district of Rameses, as Pharaoh directed. 12 Joseph also provided his father and his brothers and all his father's household with food, according to the number of their children.

Joseph and the famine

13 There was no food, however, in the whole region because the famine was severe; both Egypt and Canaan wasted away because of the famine. 14 Joseph collected all the money that was to be found in Egypt and Canaan in payment for the grain they were buying, and he brought it to Pharaoh's palace. 15 When the money of the people of Egypt and Canaan was gone, all Egypt came to Joseph and said, 'Give us food. Why should we die before your eyes? Our money is all gone.'

16 'Then bring your livestock,' said Joseph. 'I will sell you food in exchange for your livestock, since your money is gone.' 17 So they brought their livestock to Joseph, and he gave them food in exchange for their horses, their sheep and goats, their cattle and donkeys. And he brought them through that year with food in exchange for all their livestock.

18 When that year was over, they came to him the following year and said, 'We cannot hide from our lord the fact that since our money is gone and our livestock belongs to you, there is nothing left for our lord except our bodies and our land. 19 Why should we perish before your eyes—we and our land as well? Buy us and our land in exchange for food, and we with our land will be in bondage to Pharaoh. Give us seed so that we may live and not die, and that the land may not become desolate.'

20 So Joseph bought all the land in Egypt for Pharaoh. The Egyptians, one and all, sold their fields, because the famine was too severe for them. The land became Pharaoh's, 21 and Joseph reduced the people to servitude,[c] from one end of Egypt to the other. 22 However, he did not buy the land of the priests, because they received a fixed allowance from Pharaoh and had food enough from the allowance Pharaoh gave them. That is why they did not sell their land.

23 Joseph said to the people, 'Now that I have bought you and your land today for Pharaoh, here is seed for you so you can plant the ground. 24 But when the crop comes in, give a fifth of it to Pharaoh. The other four-fifths you may keep as seed for the fields and as food for yourselves and your households and your children.'

25 'You have saved our lives,' they said. 'May we find favour in the eyes of our lord; we will be in bondage to Pharaoh.'

26 So Joseph established it as a law concerning land in Egypt—still in force today—that a fifth of the produce belongs to Pharaoh. It was only the land of the priests that did not become Pharaoh's.

---

[a] 7 Or greeted [b] 10 Or said farewell to [c] 21 Samaritan Pentateuch and Septuagint (see also Vulgate); Masoretic Text and he moved the people into the cities

²⁷Now the Israelites settled in Egypt in the region of Goshen. They acquired property there and were fruitful and increased greatly in number.

²⁸Jacob lived in Egypt seventeen years, and the years of his life were a hundred and forty-seven. ²⁹When the time drew near for Israel to die, he called for his son Joseph and said to him, 'If I have found favour in your eyes, put your hand under my thigh and promise that you will show me kindness and faithfulness. Do not bury me in Egypt, ³⁰but when I rest with my fathers, carry me out of Egypt and bury me where they are buried.'

'I will do as you say,' he said.

³¹'Swear to me,' he said. Then Joseph swore to him, and Israel worshipped as he leaned on the top of his staff.[a]

Manasseh and Ephraim

48 Some time later Joseph was told, 'Your father is ill.' So he took his two sons Manasseh and Ephraim along with him. ²When Jacob was told, 'Your son Joseph has come to you,' Israel rallied his strength and sat up on the bed.

³Jacob said to Joseph, 'God Almighty[b] appeared to me at Luz in the land of Canaan, and there he blessed me ⁴and said to me, "I am going to make you fruitful and increase your numbers. I will make you a community of peoples, and I will give this land as an everlasting possession to your descendants after you."

⁵'Now then, your two sons born to you in Egypt before I came to you here will be reckoned as mine; Ephraim and Manasseh will be mine, just as Reuben and Simeon are mine. ⁶Any children born to you after them will be yours; in the territory they inherit they will be reckoned under the names of their brothers. ⁷As I was returning from Paddan,[c] to my sorrow Rachel died in the land of Canaan while we were still on the way, a little distance from Ephrath. So I buried her there beside the road to Ephrath' (that is, Bethlehem).

⁸When Israel saw the sons of Joseph, he asked, 'Who are these?'

⁹'They are the sons God has given me here,' Joseph said to his father.

Then Israel said, 'Bring them to me so that I may bless them.'

¹⁰Now Israel's eyes were failing because of old age, and he could hardly see. So Joseph brought his sons close to him, and his father kissed them and embraced them.

¹¹Israel said to Joseph, 'I never expected to see your face again, and now God has allowed me to see your children too.'

¹²Then Joseph removed them from Israel's knees and bowed down with his face to the ground. ¹³And Joseph took both of them, Ephraim on his right towards Israel's left hand and Manasseh on his left towards Israel's right hand, and brought them close to him. ¹⁴But Israel reached out his right hand and put it on Ephraim's head, though he was the younger, and crossing his arms, he put his left hand on Manasseh's head, even though Manasseh was the firstborn.

¹⁵Then he blessed Joseph and said,

'May the God before whom my fathers
 Abraham and Isaac walked faithfully,
 the God who has been my shepherd

making Connections

Ephraim and Manasseh
Genesis 48:18

In ancient Israel, firstborn sons were given special privileges and responsibilities. Manasseh was the eldest of Joseph's sons and should have got a special blessing, but Jacob gave the blessing to Ephraim, the younger son. What was he up to? Well, years ago, Jacob tricked his dad into giving him the blessing of the firstborn son instead of his older brother Esau (Genesis 27:1–39). And now he's choosing the same for his own grandsons.

---

[a] 31 Or *Israel bowed down at the head of his bed* [b] 3 Hebrew *El-Shaddai* [c] 7 That is, North-west Mesopotamia

all my life to this day,
¹⁶the Angel who has delivered me from all harm
—may he bless these boys.
May they be called by my name
and the names of my fathers Abraham and Isaac,
and may they increase greatly
on the earth.'

¹⁷When Joseph saw his father placing his right hand on Ephraim's head he was displeased; so he took hold of his father's hand to move it from Ephraim's head to Manasseh's head. ¹⁸Joseph said to him, 'No, my father, this one is the firstborn; put your right hand on his head.'

¹⁹But his father refused and said, 'I know, my son, I know. He too will become a people, and he too will become great. Nevertheless, his younger brother will be greater than he, and his descendants will become a group of nations.' ²⁰He blessed them that day and said,

'In your[a] name will Israel pronounce this blessing:
"May God make you like Ephraim and Manasseh."'

So he put Ephraim ahead of Manasseh.

²¹Then Israel said to Joseph, 'I am about to die, but God will be with you[b] and take you[c] back to the land of your[d] fathers. ²²And to you I give one more ridge of land[e] than to your brothers, the ridge I took from the Amorites with my sword and my bow.'

Jacob blesses his sons

49 Then Jacob called for his sons and said: 'Gather round so that I can tell you what will happen to you in days to come.

²'Assemble and listen, sons of Jacob;
listen to your father Israel.

³'Reuben, you are my firstborn,
my might, the first sign of my strength,
excelling in honour, excelling in power.
⁴Turbulent as the waters, you will no longer excel,
for you went up onto your father's bed,
onto my couch and defiled it.

⁵'Simeon and Levi are brothers—
their swords[f] are weapons of violence.
⁶Let me not enter their council,
let me not join their assembly,
for they have killed men in their anger
and hamstrung oxen as they pleased.
⁷Cursed be their anger, so fierce,
and their fury, so cruel!
I will scatter them in Jacob
and disperse them in Israel.

⁸'Judah,[g] your brothers will praise you;
your hand will be on the neck of your enemies;
your father's sons will bow down to you.
⁹You are a lion's cub, O Judah;
you return from the prey, my son.
Like a lion he crouches and lies down,
like a lioness—who dares to rouse him?
¹⁰The sceptre will not depart from Judah,
nor the ruler's staff from between his feet,[h]
until he to whom it belongs[i] shall come
and the obedience of the nations be his.
¹¹He will tether his donkey to a vine,
his colt to the choicest branch;
he will wash his garments in wine,
his robes in the blood of grapes.
¹²His eyes will be darker than wine,
his teeth whiter than milk.[j]

¹³'Zebulun will live by the seashore
and become a haven for ships;
his border will extend towards Sidon.

¹⁴'Issachar is a scrawny[k] donkey
lying down among the sheepfolds.[l]
¹⁵When he sees how good is his resting place
and how pleasant is his land,
he will bend his shoulder to the burden
and submit to forced labour.

---

[a] 20 The Hebrew is singular. [b] 21 The Hebrew is plural. [c] 21 The Hebrew is plural. [d] 21 The Hebrew is plural. [e] 22 The Hebrew for *ridge of land* is identical with the place name Shechem. [f] 5 The meaning of the Hebrew for this word is uncertain. [g] 8 *Judah* sounds like and may be derived from the Hebrew for *praise*. [h] 10 Or *from his descendants* [i] 10 Or *to whom tribute belongs*; the meaning of the Hebrew for this phrase is uncertain. [j] 12 Or *will be dull from wine, / his teeth white from milk* [k] 14 Or *strong* [l] 14 Or *the campfires*; or *the saddlebags*

16 'Dan[a] will provide justice for his people
   as one of the tribes of Israel.
17 Dan will be a snake by the roadside,
      a viper along the path,
   that bites the horse's heels
      so that its rider tumbles backwards.

18 'I look for your deliverance, LORD.

19 'Gad[b] will be attacked by a band of raiders,
   but he will attack them at their heels.

20 'Asher's food will be rich;
   he will provide delicacies fit for a king.

21 'Naphtali is a doe set free
   that bears beautiful fawns.[c]

22 'Joseph is a fruitful vine,
   a fruitful vine near a spring,
   whose branches climb over a wall.[d]
23 With bitterness archers attacked him;
   they shot at him with hostility.
24 But his bow remained steady,
   his strong arms stayed[e] supple,
   because of the hand of the Mighty One of Jacob,
   because of the Shepherd, the Rock of Israel,
25 because of your father's God, who helps you,
   because of the Almighty,[f] who blesses you
   with blessings of the heavens above,
      blessings of the deep that lies below,
      blessings of the breast and womb.
26 Your father's blessings are greater
   than the blessings of the ancient mountains,
   than[g] the bounty of the age-old hills.
   Let all these rest on the head of Joseph,
   on the brow of the prince among[h] his brothers.

27 'Benjamin is a ravenous wolf;
   in the morning he devours the prey,
   in the evening he divides the plunder.'

28 All these are the twelve tribes of Israel, and this is what their father said to them when he blessed them, giving each the blessing appropriate to him.

The death of Jacob

29 Then he gave them these instructions: 'I am about to be gathered to my people. Bury me with my fathers in the cave in the field of Ephron the Hittite, 30 the cave in the field of Machpelah, near Mamre in Canaan, which Abraham bought along with the field as a burial place from Ephron the Hittite. 31 There Abraham and his wife Sarah were buried, there Isaac and his wife Rebekah were buried, and there I buried Leah. 32 The field and the cave in it were bought from the Hittites.'[i]

33 When Jacob had finished giving instructions to his sons, he drew his feet up into the bed, breathed his last and was gathered to his people.

50 Joseph threw himself on his father and wept over him and kissed him. 2 Then Joseph directed the doctors in his service to embalm his father Israel. So the doctors embalmed him, 3 taking a full forty days, for that was the time required for embalming. And the Egyptians mourned for him seventy days.

4 When the days of mourning had passed, Joseph said to Pharaoh's court, 'If I have found favour in your eyes, speak to Pharaoh for me. Tell him, 5 "My father made me swear an oath and said, 'I am about to die; bury me in the tomb I dug for myself in the land of Canaan.' Now let me go up and bury my father; then I will return."'

6 Pharaoh said, 'Go up and bury your father, as he made you swear to do.'

7 So Joseph went up to bury his father. All Pharaoh's officials accompanied him—the dignitaries of his court and all the dignitaries of Egypt— 8 besides all the members of Joseph's household and his brothers and those belonging to his father's household. Only their children and their flocks and herds were left in Goshen. 9 Chariots and horsemen[j] also went up with him. It was a very large company.

10 When they reached the threshing-floor of Atad, near the Jordan, they lamented

---

[a] 16 *Dan* here means *he provides justice*. [b] 19 *Gad* sounds like the Hebrew for *attack* and also for *band of raiders*.
[c] 21 Or *free; he utters beautiful words* [d] 22 Or *Joseph is a wild colt, / a wild colt near a spring, / a wild donkey on a terraced hill* [e] 23,24 Or *archers will attack ... will shoot ... will remain ... will stay* [f] 25 Hebrew *Shaddai* [g] 26 Or *of my progenitors, / as great as* [h] 26 Or *of the one separated from* [i] 32 Or *the descendants of Heth* [j] 9 Or *charioteers*

loudly and bitterly; and there Joseph observed a seven-day period of mourning for his father. ¹¹When the Canaanites who lived there saw the mourning at the threshing-floor of Atad, they said, 'The Egyptians are holding a solemn ceremony of mourning.' That is why that place near the Jordan is called Abel Mizraim.*

¹²So Jacob's sons did as he had commanded them: ¹³they carried him to the land of Canaan and buried him in the cave in the field of Machpelah, near Mamre, which Abraham had bought along with the field as a burial place from Ephron the Hittite. ¹⁴After burying his father, Joseph returned to Egypt, together with his brothers and all the others who had gone with him to bury his father.

Joseph reassures his brothers

¹⁵When Joseph's brothers saw that their father was dead, they said, 'What if Joseph holds a grudge against us and pays us back for all the wrongs we did to him?' ¹⁶So they sent word to Joseph, saying, 'Your father left these instructions before he died: ¹⁷"This is what you are to say to Joseph: I ask you to forgive your brothers the sins and the wrongs they committed in treating you so badly." Now please forgive the sins of the servants of the God of your father.' When their message came to him, Joseph wept.

¹⁸His brothers then came and threw themselves down before him. 'We are your slaves,' they said.

¹⁹But Joseph said to them, 'Don't be afraid. Am I in the place of God? ²⁰You intended to harm me, but God intended it for good to accomplish what is now being done, the saving of many lives. ²¹So then, don't be afraid. I will provide for you and your children.' And he reassured them and spoke kindly to them.

The death of Joseph

²²Joseph stayed in Egypt, along with all his father's family. He lived a hundred and ten years ²³and saw the third generation of Ephraim's children. Also the children of Makir son of Manasseh were placed at birth on Joseph's knees.*

²⁴Then Joseph said to his brother Israelites, 'I am about to die. But God will surely come to your aid and take you up out of this land to the land he promised on oath to Abraham, Isaac and Jacob.' ²⁵And Joseph made the Israelites swear an oath and said, 'God will surely come to your aid, and then you must carry my bones up from this place.'

²⁶So Joseph died at the age of a hundred and ten. And after they embalmed him, he was placed in a coffin in Egypt.

---

*11 *Abel Mizraim* means *mourning of the Egyptians*. ᵇ23 That is, were counted as his

Exodus

INTRODUCTION

EXODUS

Author: Moses

When: Probably around 1450 BC to 1400 BC.

Where: Egypt and the wilderness on the way to Canaan.

Did you know? The word Exodus means 'departure'.

Main theme: Genesis ends with Joseph and his family happily settling down in Egypt, but by the time Exodus begins, things have turned sour. The Israelites are living as slaves, oppressed by the Egyptians and working on Pharaoh's building projects. God gives Moses the task of leading the people of Israel in a dramatic exit from Egypt. Once they are free, God tells them how they should live, giving them the Ten Commandments and other laws, as well as detailed instructions about a place of worship.

The Israelites oppressed

1 These are the names of the sons of Israel who went to Egypt with Jacob, each with his family: ²Reuben, Simeon, Levi and Judah; ³Issachar, Zebulun and Benjamin; ⁴Dan and Naphtali; Gad and Asher. ⁵The descendants of Jacob numbered seventy*ᵃ* in all; Joseph was already in Egypt.

⁶Now Joseph and all his brothers and all that generation died, ⁷but the Israelites were exceedingly fruitful; they multiplied greatly, increased in numbers and became so numerous that the land was filled with them.

⁸Then a new king, to whom Joseph meant nothing, came to power in Egypt. ⁹'Look,' he said to his people, 'the Israelites have become far too numerous for us. ¹⁰Come, we must deal shrewdly with them or they will become even more numerous and, if war breaks out, will join our enemies, fight against us and leave the country.'

ᵃ 5 Masoretic Text (see also Gen. 46:27); Dead Sea Scrolls and Septuagint (see also Acts 7:14 and note at Gen. 46:27) *seventy-five*

11So they put slave masters over them to oppress them with forced labour, and they built Pithom and Rameses as store cities for Pharaoh. 12But the more they were oppressed, the more they multiplied and spread; so the Egyptians came to dread the Israelites 13and worked them ruthlessly. 14They made their lives bitter with harsh labour in brick and mortar and with all kinds of work in the fields; in all their harsh labour the Egyptians used them ruthlessly.

15The king of Egypt said to the Hebrew midwives, whose names were Shiphrah and Puah, 16'When you help the Hebrew women in childbirth and observe them on the delivery stool, if it is a boy, kill him; but if it is a girl, let her live.' 17The midwives, however, feared God and did not do what the king of Egypt had told them to do; they let the boys live. 18Then the king of Egypt summoned the midwives and asked them, 'Why have you done this? Why have you let the boys live?'

19The midwives answered Pharaoh, 'Hebrew women are not like Egyptian women; they are vigorous and give birth before the midwives arrive.'

20So God was kind to the midwives and the people increased and became even more numerous. 21And because the midwives feared God, he gave them families of their own.

22Then Pharaoh gave this order to all his people: 'Every Hebrew boy that is born you must throw into the Nile, but let every girl live.'

The birth of Moses

2 Now a man of the house of Levi married a Levite woman, 2and she became pregnant and gave birth to a son. When she saw that he was a fine child, she hid him for three months. 3But when she could hide him no longer, she got a papyrus basket[a] for him and coated it with tar and pitch. Then she placed the child in it and put it among the reeds along the bank of the Nile. 4His sister stood at a distance to see what would happen to him.

5Then Pharaoh's daughter went down to the Nile to bathe, and her attendants were walking along the river-bank. She saw the basket among the reeds and sent her female slave to get it. 6She opened it and saw the baby. He was crying, and she felt sorry for him. 'This is one of the Hebrew babies,' she said.

7Then his sister asked Pharaoh's daughter, 'Shall I go and get one of the Hebrew women to nurse the baby for you?'

8'Yes, go,' she answered. And the girl went and got the baby's mother. 9Pharaoh's daughter said to her, 'Take this baby and nurse him for me, and I will pay you.' So the woman took the baby and nursed him. 10When the child grew older, she took him to Pharaoh's daughter and he became her son. She named him Moses,[b] saying, 'I drew him out of the water.'

Moses flees to Midian

11One day, after Moses had grown up, he went out to where his own people were and watched them at their harsh labour. He saw an Egyptian beating a Hebrew, one of his own people. 12Glancing this way and that and seeing no-one, he killed the Egyptian and hid him in the sand. 13The next day he went out and saw two Hebrews fighting. He

People and Places

Moses
Exodus 2:10

Moses was a prophet who led the people of Israel out of captivity in Egypt, through the wilderness to the edge of the Promised Land. When God first told him what he wanted him to do, Moses was very reluctant, but he became a great leader who built a multitude of oppressed slaves into a united and orderly nation. God revealed the Ten Commandments to Moses in the wilderness.

---

[a] 3 The Hebrew can also mean *ark*, as in Gen. 6:14. [b] 10 *Moses* sounds like the Hebrew for *draw out*.

asked the one in the wrong, 'Why are you hitting your fellow Hebrew?'

¹⁴The man said, 'Who made you ruler and judge over us? Are you thinking of killing me as you killed the Egyptian?' Then Moses was afraid and thought, 'What I did must have become known.'

¹⁵When Pharaoh heard of this, he tried to kill Moses, but Moses fled from Pharaoh and went to live in Midian, where he sat down by a well. ¹⁶Now a priest of Midian had seven daughters, and they came to draw water and fill the troughs to water their father's flock. ¹⁷Some shepherds came along and drove them away, but Moses got up and came to their rescue and watered their flock.

¹⁸When the girls returned to Reuel their father, he asked them, 'Why have you returned so early today?'

¹⁹They answered, 'An Egyptian rescued us from the shepherds. He even drew water for us and watered the flock.'

²⁰'And where is he?' he asked his daughters. 'Why did you leave him? Invite him to have something to eat.'

²¹Moses agreed to stay with the man, who gave his daughter Zipporah to Moses in marriage. ²²Zipporah gave birth to a son, and Moses named him Gershom,^{a} saying, 'I have become a foreigner in a foreign land.'

²³During that long period, the king of Egypt died. The Israelites groaned in their slavery and cried out, and their cry for help because of their slavery went up to God. ²⁴God heard their groaning and he remembered his covenant with Abraham, with Isaac and with Jacob. ²⁵So God looked on the Israelites and was concerned about them.

Moses and the burning bush

3 Now Moses was tending the flock of Jethro his father-in-law, the priest of Midian, and he led the flock to the far side of the wilderness and came to Horeb, the mountain of God. ²There the angel of the LORD appeared to him in flames of fire from within a bush. Moses saw that though the bush was on fire it did not burn up. ³So Moses thought, 'I will go over and see this strange sight—why the bush does not burn up.'

⁴When the LORD saw that he had gone over to look, God called to him from within the bush, 'Moses! Moses!'

And Moses said, 'Here I am.'

⁵'Do not come any closer,' God said. 'Take off your sandals, for the place where you are standing is holy ground.' ⁶Then he said, 'I am the God of your father,^{b} the God of Abraham, the God of Isaac and the God of Jacob.' At this, Moses hid his face, because he was afraid to look at God.

⁷The LORD said, 'I have indeed seen the misery of my people in Egypt. I have heard them crying out because of their slave drivers, and I am concerned about their suffering. ⁸So I have come down to rescue them from the hand of the Egyptians and to bring them up out of that land into a good and spacious land, a land flowing with milk and honey—the home of the Canaanites, Hittites, Amorites, Perizzites, Hivites and Jebusites. ⁹And now the cry of the Israelites has reached me, and I have seen the way the Egyptians are oppressing them. ¹⁰So now, go. I am sending you to Pharaoh to bring my people the Israelites out of Egypt.'

¹¹But Moses said to God, 'Who am I that I should go to Pharaoh and bring the Israelites out of Egypt?'

¹²And God said, 'I will be with you. And this will be the sign to you that it is I who have sent you: when you have brought the people out of Egypt, you^c will worship God on this mountain.'

¹³Moses said to God, 'Suppose I go to the Israelites and say to them, "The God of your fathers has sent me to you," and they ask me, "What is his name?" Then what shall I tell them?'

¹⁴God said to Moses, 'I AM WHO I AM.^{d} This is what you are to say to the Israelites: "I AM has sent me to you."'

¹⁵God also said to Moses, 'Say to the Israelites, "The LORD,^{e} the God of your fathers—the God of Abraham, the God of

---

^{a} 22 *Gershom* sounds like the Hebrew for *a foreigner there*. ^{b} 6 Masoretic Text; Samaritan Pentateuch (see Acts 7:32) *fathers* ^{c} 12 The Hebrew is plural. ^{d} 14 Or *I WILL BE WHAT I WILL BE* ^{e} 15 The Hebrew for LORD sounds like and may be related to the Hebrew for *I AM* in verse 14.

God
Exodus 3:14
God is the Creator and Saviour of the world. God has many names in the Bible, but this name that he told to Moses is the most important one – Yahweh, which probably means 'HE IS', and is translated as LORD in the TNIV.

Isaac and the God of Jacob—has sent me to you."

'This is my name for ever,
the name you shall call me
from generation to generation.

16'Go, assemble the elders of Israel and say to them, "The LORD, the God of your fathers—the God of Abraham, Isaac and Jacob—appeared to me and said: I have watched over you and have seen what has been done to you in Egypt. 17And I have promised to bring you up out of your misery in Egypt into the land of the Canaanites, Hittites, Amorites, Perizzites, Hivites and Jebusites—a land flowing with milk and honey."

18'The elders of Israel will listen to you. Then you and the elders are to go to the king of Egypt and say to him, "The LORD, the God of the Hebrews, has met with us. Let us take a three-day journey into the wilderness to offer sacrifices to the LORD our God." 19But I know that the king of Egypt will not let you go unless a mighty hand compels him. 20So I will stretch out my hand and strike the Egyptians with all the wonders that I will perform among them. After that, he will let you go.

21'And I will make the Egyptians favourably disposed towards this people, so that when you leave you will not go empty-handed. 22Every woman is to ask her neighbour and any woman living in her house for articles of silver and gold and for clothing, which you will put on your sons and daughters. And so you will plunder the Egyptians.'

Signs for Moses

4 Moses answered, 'What if they do not believe me or listen to me and say, "The LORD did not appear to you"?'

2Then the LORD said to him, 'What is that in your hand?'

'A staff,' he replied.

3The LORD said, 'Throw it on the ground.'

Moses threw it on the ground and it became a snake, and he ran from it. 4Then the LORD said to him, 'Reach out your hand and take it by the tail.' So Moses reached out and took hold of the snake and it turned back into a staff in his hand. 5'This,' said the LORD, 'is so that they may believe that the LORD, the God of their fathers—the God of Abraham, the God of Isaac and the God of Jacob—has appeared to you.'

6Then the LORD said, 'Put your hand inside your cloak.' So Moses put his hand into his cloak, and when he took it out, the skin was leprous*ᵃ*—it had become as white as snow.

7'Now put it back into your cloak,' he said. So Moses put his hand back into his cloak, and when he took it out, it was restored, like the rest of his flesh.

8Then the LORD said, 'If they do not believe you or pay attention to the first sign, they may believe the second. 9But if they do not believe these two signs or listen to you, take some water from the Nile and pour it on the dry ground. The water you take from the river will become blood on the ground.'

10Moses said to the LORD, 'Pardon your servant, Lord. I have never been eloquent, neither in the past nor since you have spoken to your servant. I am slow of speech and tongue.'

11The LORD said to him, 'Who gave human beings their mouths? Who makes them deaf or mute? Who gives them sight or makes them blind? Is it not I, the LORD? 12Now go; I will help you speak and will teach you what to say.'

ᵃ 6 The Hebrew word for *leprous* was used for various diseases affecting the skin.

¹³But Moses said, 'Pardon your servant, Lord. Please send someone else.'

¹⁴Then the LORD's anger burned against Moses and he said, 'What about your brother, Aaron the Levite? I know he can speak well. He is already on his way to meet you, and his heart will be glad when he sees you. ¹⁵You shall speak to him and put words in his mouth; I will help both of you speak and will teach you what to do. ¹⁶He will speak to the people for you, and it will be as if he were your mouth and as if you were God to him. ¹⁷But take this staff in your hand so that you can perform the signs with it.'

Moses returns to Egypt

¹⁸Then Moses went back to Jethro his father-in-law and said to him, 'Let me return to my own people in Egypt to see if any of them are still alive.'

Jethro said, 'Go, and I wish you well.'

¹⁹Now the LORD had said to Moses in Midian, 'Go back to Egypt, for all those who wanted to kill you are dead.' ²⁰So Moses took his wife and sons, put them on a donkey and started back to Egypt. And he took the staff of God in his hand.

²¹The LORD said to Moses, 'When you return to Egypt, see that you perform before Pharaoh all the wonders I have given you the power to do. But I will harden his heart so that he will not let the people go. ²²Then say to Pharaoh, "This is what the LORD says: Israel is my firstborn son, ²³and I told you, 'Let my son go, so that he may worship me.' But you refused to let him go; so I will kill your firstborn son."'

²⁴At a lodging place on the way, the LORD met Moses*ᵃ* and was about to kill him. ²⁵But Zipporah took a flint knife, cut off her son's foreskin and touched Moses' feet with it.*ᵇ* 'Surely you are a bridegroom of blood to me,' she said. ²⁶So the LORD let him alone. (At that time she said 'bridegroom of blood', referring to circumcision.)

²⁷The LORD said to Aaron, 'Go into the wilderness to meet Moses.' So he met Moses at the mountain of God and kissed him. ²⁸Then Moses told Aaron everything the LORD had sent him to say, and also about all the signs he had commanded him to perform.

²⁹Moses and Aaron brought together all the elders of the Israelites, ³⁰and Aaron told them everything the LORD had said to Moses. He also performed the signs before the people, ³¹and they believed. And when they heard that the LORD was concerned about them and had seen their misery, they bowed down and worshipped.

Bricks without straw

5 Afterwards Moses and Aaron went to Pharaoh and said, 'This is what the LORD, the God of Israel, says: "Let my people go, so that they may hold a festival to me in the wilderness."'

²Pharaoh said, 'Who is the LORD, that I should obey him and let Israel go? I do not know the LORD and I will not let Israel go.'

³Then they said, 'The God of the Hebrews has met with us. Now let us take a three-day journey into the wilderness to offer sacrifices to the LORD our God, or he may strike us with plagues or with the sword.'

⁴But the king of Egypt said, 'Moses and Aaron, why are you taking the people away from their labour? Get back to your work!' ⁵Then Pharaoh said, 'Look, the people of the land are now numerous, and you are stopping them from working.'

⁶That same day Pharaoh gave this order to the slave drivers and overseers in charge of the people: ⁷'You are no longer to supply the people with straw for making bricks; let them go and gather their own straw. ⁸But require them to make the same number of bricks as before; don't reduce the quota. They are lazy; that is why they are crying out, "Let us go and sacrifice to our God." ⁹Make the work harder for them so that they keep working and pay no attention to lies.'

¹⁰Then the slave drivers and the overseers went out and said to the people, 'This is what Pharaoh says: "I will not give you any more straw. ¹¹Go and get your own straw wherever you can find it, but your work will not be reduced at all."' ¹²So the people scattered all over Egypt to gather stubble to use for straw. ¹³The slave drivers kept

---

ᵃ 24 Hebrew *him* *ᵇ* 25 The meaning of the Hebrew for this clause is uncertain.

pressing them, saying, 'Complete the work required of you for each day, just as when you had straw.' 14And Pharaoh's slave drivers beat the Israelite overseers they had appointed, demanding, 'Why haven't you met your quota of bricks yesterday or today, as before?'

15Then the Israelite overseers went and appealed to Pharaoh: 'Why have you treated your servants this way? 16Your servants are given no straw, yet we are told, "Make bricks!" Your servants are being beaten, but the fault is with your own people.'

17Pharaoh said, 'Lazy, that's what you are—lazy! That is why you keep saying, "Let us go and sacrifice to the LORD." 18Now get to work. You will not be given any straw, yet you must produce your full quota of bricks.'

19The Israelite overseers realised they were in trouble when they were told, 'You are not to reduce the number of bricks required of you for each day.' 20When they left Pharaoh, they found Moses and Aaron waiting to meet them, 21and they said, 'May the LORD look on you and judge you! You have made us obnoxious to Pharaoh and his officials and have put a sword in their hand to kill us.'

God promises deliverance

22Moses returned to the LORD and said, 'Why, Lord, why have you brought trouble on this people? Is this why you sent me? 23Ever since I went to Pharaoh to speak in your name, he has brought trouble on this people, and you have not rescued your people at all.'

6 Then the LORD said to Moses, 'Now you will see what I will do to Pharaoh: because of my mighty hand he will let them go; because of my mighty hand he will drive them out of his country.'

2God also said to Moses, 'I am the LORD. 3I appeared to Abraham, to Isaac and to Jacob as God Almighty,[a] but by my name the LORD[b] I did not make myself known to them.[c] 4I also established my covenant with them to give them the land of Canaan, where they resided as foreigners. 5Moreover, I have heard the groaning of the Israelites, whom the Egyptians are enslaving, and I have remembered my covenant.

6'Therefore, say to the Israelites: "I am the LORD, and I will bring you out from under the yoke of the Egyptians. I will free you from being slaves to them, and I will redeem you with an outstretched arm and with mighty acts of judgment. 7I will take you as my own people, and I will be your God. Then you will know that I am the LORD your God, who brought you out from under the yoke of the Egyptians. 8And I will bring you to the land I swore with uplifted hand to give to Abraham, to Isaac and to Jacob. I will give it to you as a possession. I am the LORD."'

9Moses reported this to the Israelites, but they did not listen to him because of their discouragement and harsh labour.

10Then the LORD said to Moses, 11'Go, tell Pharaoh king of Egypt to let the Israelites go out of his country.'

12But Moses said to the LORD, 'If the Israelites will not listen to me, why would Pharaoh listen to me, since I speak with faltering lips?'[d]

IN OTHER WORDS

Redeem
Exodus 6:6

When you redeem a book token at the local bookshop you exchange your token for the book you want. In the same way, redemption is a kind of trading though not as basic. In the Old Testament, slaves could redeem themselves out of slavery or be redeemed by someone else by means of a payment to the slave's owner. God says here that he will pay the price for setting the Israelite slaves free from Egypt. The New Testament picks up on this image too; Jesus' death paid the price for our sin so we are free and no longer slaves to death (Ephesians 1:7).

---

[a] 3 Hebrew *El-Shaddai* [b] 3 See note at Exodus 3:15. [c] 3 Or *Almighty, and by my name the LORD did I not let myself be known to them?* [d] 12 Hebrew *I am uncircumcised of lips*; also in verse 30

Family record of Moses and Aaron

¹³Now the LORD spoke to Moses and Aaron about the Israelites and Pharaoh king of Egypt, and he commanded them to bring the Israelites out of Egypt.

¹⁴These were the heads of their families:[a]

The sons of Reuben the firstborn son of Israel were Hanok and Pallu, Hezron and Karmi. These were the clans of Reuben.

¹⁵The sons of Simeon were Jemuel, Jamin, Ohad, Jakin, Zohar and Shaul the son of a Canaanite woman. These were the clans of Simeon.

¹⁶These were the names of the sons of Levi according to their records: Gershon, Kohath and Merari. Levi lived 137 years.

¹⁷The sons of Gershon, by clans, were Libni and Shimei.

¹⁸The sons of Kohath were Amram, Izhar, Hebron and Uzziel. Kohath lived 133 years.

¹⁹The sons of Merari were Mahli and Mushi.

These were the clans of Levi according to their records.

²⁰Amram married his father's sister Jochebed, who bore him Aaron and Moses. Amram lived 137 years.

²¹The sons of Izhar were Korah, Nepheg and Zikri.

²²The sons of Uzziel were Mishael, Elzaphan and Sithri.

²³Aaron married Elisheba, daughter of Amminadab and sister of Nahshon, and she bore him Nadab and Abihu, Eleazar and Ithamar.

²⁴The sons of Korah were Assir, Elkanah and Abiasaph. These were the Korahite clans.

²⁵Eleazar son of Aaron married one of the daughters of Putiel, and she bore him Phinehas.

These were the heads of the Levite families, clan by clan.

²⁶It was this Aaron and Moses to whom the LORD said, 'Bring the Israelites out of Egypt by their divisions.' ²⁷They were the ones who spoke to Pharaoh king of Egypt about bringing the Israelites out of Egypt—this same Moses and Aaron.

Aaron to speak for Moses

²⁸Now when the LORD spoke to Moses in Egypt, ²⁹he said to him, 'I am the LORD. Tell Pharaoh king of Egypt everything I tell you.'

³⁰But Moses said to the LORD, 'Since I speak with faltering lips, why would Pharaoh listen to me?'

7 Then the LORD said to Moses, 'See, I have made you like God to Pharaoh, and your brother Aaron will be your prophet. ²You are to say everything I command you, and your brother Aaron is to tell Pharaoh to let the Israelites go out of his country. ³But I will harden Pharaoh's heart, and though I multiply my signs and wonders in Egypt, ⁴he will not listen to you. Then I will lay my hand on Egypt and with mighty acts of judgment I will bring out my divisions, my people the Israelites. ⁵And the Egyptians will know that I am the LORD

People and Places

Aaron
Exodus 7:1
When Moses' nerves got the better of him at the thought of confronting Pharaoh, God allowed him to take along his brother Aaron as his official spokesman. In fact, Moses did go on to do most of the talking and Aaron performed miraculous signs in front of Pharaoh to show how powerful God was. Aaron became the first high priest in Israel's history (Exodus 28).

---

[a] 14 The Hebrew for *families* here and in verse 25 refers to units larger than clans.

when I stretch out my hand against Egypt and bring the Israelites out of it.'

⁶Moses and Aaron did just as the LORD commanded them. ⁷Moses was eighty years old and Aaron eighty-three when they spoke to Pharaoh.

Aaron's staff becomes a snake

⁸The LORD said to Moses and Aaron, ⁹'When Pharaoh says to you, "Perform a miracle," then say to Aaron, "Take your staff and throw it down before Pharaoh," and it will become a snake.'

¹⁰So Moses and Aaron went to Pharaoh and did just as the LORD commanded. Aaron threw his staff down in front of Pharaoh and his officials, and it became a snake. ¹¹Pharaoh then summoned the wise men and sorcerers, and the Egyptian magicians also did the same things by their secret arts: ¹²each one threw down his staff and it became a snake. But Aaron's staff swallowed up their staffs. ¹³Yet Pharaoh's heart became hard and he would not listen to them, just as the LORD had said.

Plagues
Exodus 7:14

God had warned Moses that Pharaoh would need to see God's power before he let the Israelites go, and that's about to happen. The first nine plagues were similar to natural phenomena that happened from time to time – like swarms of frogs or flies – but God made them much worse than usual. The final plague, the death of the firstborn Egyptians, was something that had never been seen before and finally convinced Pharaoh to let the people go.

The plague of blood

¹⁴Then the LORD said to Moses, 'Pharaoh's heart is unyielding; he refuses to let the people go. ¹⁵Go to Pharaoh in the morning as he goes out to the river. Wait on the bank of the Nile to meet him, and take in your hand the staff that was changed into a snake. ¹⁶Then say to him, "The LORD, the God of the Hebrews, has sent me to say to you: let my people go, so that they may worship me in the wilderness. But until now you have not listened. ¹⁷This is what the LORD says: by this you will know that I am the LORD: with the staff that is in my hand I will strike the water of the Nile, and it will be changed into blood. ¹⁸The fish in the Nile will die, and the river will stink; the Egyptians will not be able to drink its water."'

¹⁹The LORD said to Moses, 'Tell Aaron, "Take your staff and stretch out your hand over the waters of Egypt—over the streams and canals, over the ponds and all the reservoirs—and they will turn to blood." Blood will be everywhere in Egypt, even in the wooden buckets and stone jars.'

²⁰Moses and Aaron did just as the LORD had commanded. He raised his staff in the presence of Pharaoh and his officials and struck the water of the Nile, and all the water was changed into blood. ²¹The fish in the Nile died, and the river smelled so bad that the Egyptians could not drink its water. Blood was everywhere in Egypt.

²²But the Egyptian magicians did the same things by their secret arts, and Pharaoh's heart became hard; he would not listen to Moses and Aaron, just as the LORD had said. ²³Instead, he turned and went into his palace, and did not take even this to heart. ²⁴And all the Egyptians dug along the Nile to get drinking water, because they could not drink the water of the river.

The plague of frogs

²⁵Seven days passed after the LORD struck the Nile.*

8 ¹Then the LORD said to Moses, 'Go to Pharaoh and say to him, "This is what the LORD says: let my people go, so that they may worship me. ²If you refuse to let them go, I will send a plague of

---

* 8:1-4 is numbered 7:26-29 in Hebrew texts.

frogs on your whole country. ³The Nile will teem with frogs. They will come up into your palace and your bedroom and onto your bed, into the houses of your officials and on your people, and into your ovens and kneading troughs. ⁴The frogs will come up on you and your people and all your officials." '

*⁵Then the LORD said to Moses, 'Tell Aaron, "Stretch out your hand with your staff over the streams and canals and ponds, and make frogs come up on the land of Egypt." '

⁶So Aaron stretched out his hand over the waters of Egypt, and the frogs came up and covered the land. ⁷But the magicians did the same things by their secret arts; they also made frogs come up on the land of Egypt.

⁸Pharaoh summoned Moses and Aaron and said, 'Pray to the LORD to take the frogs away from me and my people, and I will let your people go to offer sacrifices to the LORD.'

⁹Moses said to Pharaoh, 'I leave to you the honour of setting the time for me to pray for you and your officials and your people that you and your houses may be rid of the frogs, except for those that remain in the Nile.'

¹⁰'Tomorrow,' Pharaoh said.

Moses replied, 'It will be as you say, so that you may know there is no-one like the LORD our God. ¹¹The frogs will leave you and your houses, your officials and your people; they will remain only in the Nile.'

¹²After Moses and Aaron left Pharaoh, Moses cried out to the LORD about the frogs he had brought on Pharaoh. ¹³And the LORD did what Moses asked. The frogs died in the houses, in the courtyards and in the fields. ¹⁴They were piled into heaps, and the land reeked of them. ¹⁵But when Pharaoh saw that there was relief, he hardened his heart and would not listen to Moses and Aaron, just as the LORD had said.

The plague of gnats

¹⁶Then the LORD said to Moses, 'Tell Aaron, "Stretch out your staff and strike the dust of the ground," and throughout the land of Egypt the dust will become gnats.' ¹⁷They did this, and when Aaron stretched out his hand with the staff and struck the dust of the ground, gnats came on people and animals. All the dust throughout the land of Egypt became gnats. ¹⁸But when the magicians tried to produce gnats by their secret arts, they could not.

Since the gnats were on people and animals everywhere, ¹⁹the magicians said to Pharaoh, 'This is the finger of God.' But Pharaoh's heart was hard and he would not listen, just as the LORD had said.

The plague of flies

²⁰Then the LORD said to Moses, 'Get up early in the morning and confront Pharaoh as he goes to the river and say to him, "This is what the LORD says: let my people go, so that they may worship me. ²¹If you do not let my people go, I will send swarms of flies on you and your officials, on your people and into your houses. The houses of the Egyptians will be full of flies; even the ground will be covered with them.

²²' "But on that day I will deal differently with the land of Goshen, where my people live; no swarms of flies will be there, so that you will know that I, the LORD, am in this land. ²³I will make a distinction^a between my people and your people. This sign will occur tomorrow." '

²⁴And the LORD did this. Dense swarms of flies poured into Pharaoh's palace and into the houses of his officials; throughout Egypt the land was ruined by the flies.

²⁵Then Pharaoh summoned Moses and Aaron and said, 'Go, sacrifice to your God here in the land.'

²⁶But Moses said, 'That would not be right. The sacrifices we offer the LORD our God would be detestable to the Egyptians. And if we offer sacrifices that are detestable in their eyes, will they not stone us? ²⁷We must take a three-day journey into the wilderness to offer sacrifices to the LORD our God, as he commands us.'

²⁸Pharaoh said, 'I will let you go to offer sacrifices to the LORD your God in the

---

^{a} 23 Septuagint and Vulgate; Hebrew *will put a deliverance*

* 8:5-32 is numbered 8:1-28 in Hebrew texts.

wilderness, but you must not go very far. Now pray for me.'

29Moses answered, 'As soon as I leave you, I will pray to the LORD, and tomorrow the flies will leave Pharaoh and his officials and his people. Only let Pharaoh be sure that he does not act deceitfully again by not letting the people go to offer sacrifices to the LORD.'

30Then Moses left Pharaoh and prayed to the LORD, 31and the LORD did what Moses asked. The flies left Pharaoh and his officials and his people; not a fly remained. 32But this time also Pharaoh hardened his heart and would not let the people go.

The plague on livestock

9 Then the LORD said to Moses, 'Go to Pharaoh and say to him, "This is what the LORD, the God of the Hebrews, says: 'Let my people go, so that they may worship me.' 2If you refuse to let them go and continue to hold them back, 3the hand of the LORD will bring a terrible plague on your livestock in the field—on your horses, donkeys and camels and on your cattle, sheep and goats. 4But the LORD will make a distinction between the livestock of Israel and that of Egypt, so that no animal belonging to the Israelites will die."'

5The LORD set a time and said, 'Tomorrow the LORD will do this in the land.' 6And the next day the LORD did it: all the livestock of the Egyptians died, but not one animal belonging to the Israelites died. 7Pharaoh investigated and found that not even one of the animals of the Israelites had died. Yet his heart was unyielding and he would not let the people go.

The plague of boils

8Then the LORD said to Moses and Aaron, 'Take handfuls of soot from a furnace and let Moses toss it into the air in the presence of Pharaoh. 9It will become fine dust over the whole land of Egypt, and festering boils will break out on people and animals throughout the land.'

10So they took soot from a furnace and stood before Pharaoh. Moses tossed it into the air, and festering boils broke out on people and animals. 11The magicians could not stand before Moses because of the boils that were on them and on all the Egyptians. 12But the LORD hardened Pharaoh's heart and he would not listen to Moses and Aaron, just as the LORD had said to Moses.

The plague of hail

13Then the LORD said to Moses, 'Get up early in the morning, confront Pharaoh and say to him, "This is what the LORD, the God of the Hebrews, says: let my people go, so that they may worship me, 14or this time I will send the full force of my plagues against you and against your officials and your people, so you may know that there is no-one like me in all the earth. 15For by now I could have stretched out my hand and struck you and your people with a plague that would have wiped you off the earth. 16But I have raised you up[a] for this very purpose, that I might show you my power and that my name might be proclaimed in all the earth. 17You still set yourself against my people and will not let them go. 18Therefore, at this time tomorrow I will send the worst hailstorm that has ever fallen on Egypt, from the day it was founded till now. 19Give an order now to bring your livestock and everything you have in the field to a place of shelter, because the hail will fall on every person and animal that has not been brought in and is still out in the field, and they will die."'

20Those officials of Pharaoh who feared the word of the LORD hurried to bring their slaves and their livestock inside. 21But those who ignored the word of the LORD left their slaves and livestock in the field.

22Then the LORD said to Moses, 'Stretch out your hand towards the sky so that hail will fall all over Egypt—on people and animals and on everything growing in the fields of Egypt.' 23When Moses stretched out his staff towards the sky, the LORD sent thunder and hail, and lightning flashed down to the ground. So the LORD rained hail on the land of Egypt; 24hail fell and lightning flashed back and forth. It was the worst storm in all the land of Egypt since it had become a nation. 25Throughout Egypt

---

[a] 16 Or *have spared you*

hail struck everything in the fields—both people and animals; it beat down everything growing in the fields and stripped every tree. ²⁶The only place it did not hail was the land of Goshen, where the Israelites were.

²⁷Then Pharaoh summoned Moses and Aaron. 'This time I have sinned,' he said to them. 'The LORD is in the right, and I and my people are in the wrong. ²⁸Pray to the LORD, for we have had enough thunder and hail. I will let you go; you don't have to stay any longer.'

²⁹Moses replied, 'When I have gone out of the city, I will spread out my hands in prayer to the LORD. The thunder will stop and there will be no more hail, so you may know that the earth is the LORD's. ³⁰But I know that you and your officials still do not fear the LORD God.'

³¹(The flax and barley were destroyed, since the barley was in the ear and the flax was in bloom. ³²The wheat and spelt, however, were not destroyed, because they ripen later.)

³³Then Moses left Pharaoh and went out of the city. He spread out his hands towards the LORD; the thunder and hail stopped, and the rain no longer poured down on the land. ³⁴When Pharaoh saw that the rain and hail and thunder had stopped, he sinned again: he and his officials hardened their hearts. ³⁵So Pharaoh's heart was hard and he would not let the Israelites go, just as the LORD had said through Moses.

The plague of locusts

10 Then the LORD said to Moses, 'Go to Pharaoh, for I have hardened his heart and the hearts of his officials so that I may perform these signs of mine among them ²that you may tell your children and grandchildren how I dealt harshly with the Egyptians and how I performed my signs among them, and that you may know that I am the LORD.'

³So Moses and Aaron went to Pharaoh and said to him, 'This is what the LORD, the God of the Hebrews, says: "How long will you refuse to humble yourself before me? Let my people go, so that they may worship me. ⁴If you refuse to let them go, I will bring locusts into your country tomorrow. ⁵They will cover the face of the ground so that it cannot be seen. They will devour what little you have left after the hail, including every tree that is growing in your fields. ⁶They will fill your houses and those of all your officials and all the Egyptians—something neither your parents nor your ancestors have ever seen from the day they settled in this land till now."' Then Moses turned and left Pharaoh.

⁷Pharaoh's officials said to him, 'How long will this man be a snare to us? Let the people go, so that they may worship the LORD their God. Do you not yet realise that Egypt is ruined?'

⁸Then Moses and Aaron were brought back to Pharaoh. 'Go, worship the LORD your God,' he said. 'But tell me who will be going.'

⁹Moses answered, 'We will go with our young and our old, with our sons and our daughters, and with our flocks and herds, because we are to celebrate a festival to the LORD.'

¹⁰Pharaoh said, 'The LORD be with you— if I let you go, along with your women and children! Clearly you are bent on evil.ᵃ ¹¹No! Let only the men go and worship the LORD, since that's what you have been asking for.' Then Moses and Aaron were driven out of Pharaoh's presence.

¹²And the LORD said to Moses, 'Stretch out your hand over Egypt so that locusts swarm over the land and devour everything growing in the fields, everything left by the hail.'

¹³So Moses stretched out his staff over Egypt, and the LORD made an east wind blow across the land all that day and all that night. By morning the wind had brought the locusts; ¹⁴they invaded all Egypt and settled down in every area of the country in great numbers. Never before had there been such a plague of locusts, nor will there ever be again. ¹⁵They covered all the ground until it was black. They devoured all that was left after the hail—everything growing in the fields and the fruit on the trees. Nothing green remained on tree or plant in all the land of Egypt.

ᵃ 10 Or *Be careful, trouble is in store for you!*

¹⁶Pharaoh quickly summoned Moses and Aaron and said, 'I have sinned against the LORD your God and against you. ¹⁷Now forgive my sin once more and pray to the LORD your God to take this deadly plague away from me.'

¹⁸Moses then left Pharaoh and prayed to the LORD. ¹⁹And the LORD changed the wind to a very strong west wind, which caught up the locusts and carried them into the Red Sea.*ᵃ* Not a locust was left anywhere in Egypt. ²⁰But the LORD hardened Pharaoh's heart, and he would not let the Israelites go.

The plague of darkness

²¹Then the LORD said to Moses, 'Stretch out your hand towards the sky so that darkness spreads over Egypt—darkness that can be felt.' ²²So Moses stretched out his hand towards the sky, and total darkness covered all Egypt for three days. ²³No-one could see anyone else or move about for three days. Yet all the Israelites had light in the places where they lived.

²⁴Then Pharaoh summoned Moses and said, 'Go, worship the LORD. Even your women and children may go with you; only leave your flocks and herds behind.'

²⁵But Moses said, 'You must allow us to have sacrifices and burnt offerings to present to the LORD our God. ²⁶Our livestock too must go with us; not a hoof is to be left behind. We have to use some of them in worshipping the LORD our God, and until we get there we will not know what we are to use to worship the LORD.'

²⁷But the LORD hardened Pharaoh's heart, and he was not willing to let them go. ²⁸Pharaoh said to Moses, 'Get out of my sight! Make sure you do not appear before me again! The day you see my face you will die.'

²⁹'Just as you say,' Moses replied. 'I will never appear before you again.'

The plague on the firstborn

11 Now the LORD said to Moses, 'I will bring one more plague on Pharaoh and on Egypt. After that, he will let you go from here, and when he does, he will drive you out completely. ²Tell the people that men and women alike are to ask their neighbours for articles of silver and gold.' ³(The LORD made the Egyptians favourably disposed towards the people, and Moses himself was highly regarded in Egypt by Pharaoh's officials and by the people.)

⁴So Moses said, 'This is what the LORD says: "About midnight I will go throughout Egypt. ⁵Every firstborn son in Egypt will die, from the firstborn son of Pharaoh, who sits on the throne, to the firstborn son of the female slave, who is at her hand mill, and all the firstborn of the cattle as well. ⁶There will be loud wailing throughout Egypt—worse than there has ever been or ever will be again. ⁷But among the Israelites not a dog will bark at any person or animal." Then you will know that the LORD makes a distinction between Egypt and Israel. ⁸All these officials of yours will come to me, bowing down before me and saying, "Go, you and all the people who follow you!" After that I will leave.' Then Moses, hot with anger, left Pharaoh.

⁹The LORD had said to Moses, 'Pharaoh will refuse to listen to you—so that my wonders may be multiplied in Egypt.' ¹⁰Moses and Aaron performed all these wonders before Pharaoh, but the LORD hardened Pharaoh's heart, and he would not let the Israelites go out of his country.

The Passover

12 The LORD said to Moses and Aaron in Egypt, ²'This month is to be for you the first month, the first month of your year. ³Tell the whole community of Israel that on the tenth day of this month each man is to take a lamb*ᵇ* for his family, one for each household. ⁴If any household is too small for a whole lamb, they must share one with their nearest neighbour, having taken into account the number of people there are. You are to determine the amount of lamb needed in accordance with what each person will eat. ⁵The animals you choose must be year-old males without defect, and you may take them from the sheep or the goats. ⁶Take care of them until the fourteenth day of the month, when all the

---

ᵃ 19 Or *the Sea of Reeds*   *ᵇ* 3 The Hebrew word can mean *lamb* or *kid*; also in verse 4.

IN OTHER WORDS

Passover
Exodus 12:1

Imagine the drama of this night – cooking a special meal, putting blood on the doorposts of your house and then waiting, with your belongings packed, ready to escape from slavery. It's not something you'd forget in a hurry! And so the Passover became an important festival in the Jewish calendar that is still celebrated today. In Jesus' time Jews would come from all over the world to Jerusalem to remember what happened during the Exodus and to celebrate God's liberation of his people. Jesus celebrated the Passover with his disciples just before he died (Luke 22:15).

---

members of the community of Israel must slaughter them at twilight. 7Then they are to take some of the blood and put it on the sides and tops of the door-frames of the houses where they eat the lambs. 8That same night they are to eat the meat roasted over the fire, along with bitter herbs, and bread made without yeast. 9Do not eat the meat raw or boiled in water, but roast it over a fire—with the head, legs and internal organs. 10Do not leave any of it till morning; if some is left till morning, you must burn it. 11This is how you are to eat it: with your cloak tucked into your belt, your sandals on your feet and your staff in your hand. Eat it in haste; it is the LORD's Passover.

12'On that same night I will pass through Egypt and strike down every firstborn of both people and animals, and I will bring judgment on all the gods of Egypt. I am the LORD. 13The blood will be a sign for you on the houses where you are, and when I see the blood, I will pass over you. No destructive plague will touch you when I strike Egypt.

14'This is a day you are to commemorate; for the generations to come you shall celebrate it as a festival to the LORD—a lasting ordinance. 15For seven days you are to eat bread made without yeast. On the first day remove the yeast from your houses, for whoever eats anything with yeast in it from the first day until the seventh must be cut off from Israel. 16On the first day hold a sacred assembly, and another one on the seventh day. Do no work at all on these days, except to prepare food for everyone to eat; that is all you may do.

17'Celebrate the Festival of Unleavened Bread, because it was on this very day that I brought your divisions out of Egypt. Celebrate this day as a lasting ordinance for the generations to come. 18In the first month you are to eat bread made without yeast, from the evening of the fourteenth day until the evening of the twenty-first day. 19For seven days no yeast is to be found in your houses. And anyone, whether foreigner or native-born, who eats anything with yeast in it must be cut off from the community of Israel. 20Eat nothing made with yeast. Wherever you live, you must eat unleavened bread.'

21Then Moses summoned all the elders of Israel and said to them, 'Go at once and select the animals for your families and slaughter the Passover lamb. 22Take a bunch of hyssop, dip it into the blood in the basin and put some of the blood on the top and on both sides of the door-frame. None of you shall go out of the door of your house until morning. 23When the LORD goes through the land to strike down the Egyptians, he will see the blood on the top and sides of the door-frame and will pass over that doorway, and he will not permit the destroyer to enter your houses and strike you down.

24'Obey these instructions as a lasting ordinance for you and your descendants. 25When you enter the land that the LORD will give you as he promised, observe this ceremony. 26And when your children ask you, "What does this ceremony mean to you?" 27then tell them, "It is the Passover sacrifice to the LORD, who passed over the houses of the Israelites in Egypt and spared our homes when he struck down the Egyptians."' Then the people bowed down and worshipped. 28The Israelites did just what the LORD commanded Moses and Aaron.

²⁹At midnight the LORD struck down all the firstborn in Egypt, from the firstborn of Pharaoh, who sat on the throne, to the firstborn of the prisoner, who was in the dungeon, and the firstborn of all the livestock as well. ³⁰Pharaoh and all his officials and all the Egyptians got up during the night, and there was loud wailing in Egypt, for there was not a house without someone dead.

The exodus

³¹During the night Pharaoh summoned Moses and Aaron and said, 'Up! Leave my people, you and the Israelites! Go, worship the LORD as you have requested. ³²Take your flocks and herds, as you have said, and go. And also bless me.'

³³The Egyptians urged the people to hurry and leave the country. 'For otherwise,' they said, 'we will all die!' ³⁴So the people took their dough before the yeast was added, and carried it on their shoulders in kneading troughs wrapped in clothing. ³⁵The Israelites did as Moses instructed and asked the Egyptians for articles of silver and gold and for clothing. ³⁶The LORD had made the Egyptians favourably disposed towards the people, and they gave them what they asked for; so they plundered the Egyptians.

³⁷The Israelites journeyed from Rameses to Sukkoth. There were about six hundred thousand men on foot, besides women and children. ³⁸Many other people went up with them, and also large droves of livestock, both flocks and herds. ³⁹With the dough the Israelites had brought from Egypt, they baked loaves of unleavened bread. The dough was without yeast because they had been driven out of Egypt and did not have time to prepare food for themselves.

⁴⁰Now the length of time the Israelite people lived in Egypt*ᵃ* was 430 years. ⁴¹At the end of the 430 years, to the very day, all the LORD's divisions left Egypt. ⁴²Because the LORD kept vigil that night to bring them out of Egypt, on this night all the Israelites are to keep vigil to honour the LORD for the generations to come.

Passover restrictions

⁴³The LORD said to Moses and Aaron, 'These are the regulations for the Passover:

'No foreigner is to eat of it. ⁴⁴Any slave you have bought may eat of it after you have circumcised him, ⁴⁵but a temporary resident or a hired worker may not eat of it.

⁴⁶'It must be eaten inside one house; take none of the meat outside the house. Do not break any of the bones. ⁴⁷The whole community of Israel must celebrate it.

⁴⁸'A foreigner residing among you who wants to celebrate the LORD's Passover must have all the males in his household circumcised; then he may take part like one born in the land. No uncircumcised male may eat of it. ⁴⁹The same law applies both to the native-born and to the foreigner residing among you.'

⁵⁰All the Israelites did just what the LORD had commanded Moses and Aaron. ⁵¹And on that very day the LORD brought the Israelites out of Egypt by their divisions.

Consecration of the firstborn

13 The LORD said to Moses, ²'Consecrate to me every firstborn male. The first offspring of every womb among the Israelites belongs to me, whether human or animal.'

³Then Moses said to the people, 'Commemorate this day, the day you came out of Egypt, out of the land of slavery, because the LORD brought you out of it with a mighty hand. Eat nothing containing yeast. ⁴Today, in the month of Aviv, you are leaving. ⁵When the LORD brings you into the land of the Canaanites, Hittites, Amorites, Hivites and Jebusites—the land he swore to your ancestors to give you, a land flowing with milk and honey—you are to observe this ceremony in this month: ⁶for seven days eat bread made without yeast and on the seventh day hold a festival to the LORD. ⁷Eat unleavened bread during those seven days; nothing with yeast in it is to be seen among you, nor shall any yeast be seen anywhere within your borders. ⁸On that

---

ᵃ 40 Masoretic Text; Samaritan Pentateuch and Septuagint *Egypt and Canaan* day tell your children, "I do this because of what the LORD did for me when I came out of Egypt." 9This observance will be for you like a sign on your hand and a reminder on your forehead that this law of the LORD is to be on your lips. For the LORD brought you out of Egypt with his mighty hand. 10You must keep this ordinance at the appointed time year after year.

11'After the LORD brings you into the land of the Canaanites and gives it to you, as he promised on oath to you and your ancestors, 12you are to give over to the LORD the first offspring of every womb. All the firstborn males of your livestock belong to the LORD. 13Redeem with a lamb every firstborn donkey, but if you do not redeem it, break its neck. Redeem every firstborn among your sons.

14'In days to come when your children ask you, "What does this mean?" say to them, "With a mighty hand the LORD brought us out of Egypt, out of the land of slavery. 15When Pharaoh stubbornly refused to let us go, the LORD killed the firstborn of both people and animals in Egypt. This is why I sacrifice to the LORD the first male offspring of every womb and redeem each of my firstborn sons." 16And it will be like a sign on your hand and a symbol on your forehead that the LORD brought us out of Egypt with his mighty hand.'

Crossing the sea

17When Pharaoh let the people go, God did not lead them on the road through the Philistine country, though that was shorter. For God said, 'If they face war, they might change their minds and return to Egypt.' 18So God led the people around by the desert road towards the Red Sea.*a* The Israelites went up out of Egypt ready for battle.

19Moses took the bones of Joseph with him because Joseph had made the Israelites swear an oath. He had said, 'God will surely come to your aid, and then you must carry my bones up with you from this place.'*b*

20After leaving Sukkoth they camped at Etham on the edge of the desert. 21By day the LORD went ahead of them in a pillar of cloud to guide them on their way and by night in a pillar of fire to give them light, so that they could travel by day or night. 22Neither the pillar of cloud by day nor the pillar of fire by night left its place in front of the people.

14 Then the LORD said to Moses, 2'Tell the Israelites to turn back and camp near Pi Hahiroth, between Migdol and the sea. They are to camp by the sea, directly opposite Baal Zephon. 3Pharaoh will think, "The Israelites are wandering around the land in confusion, hemmed in by the desert." 4And I will harden Pharaoh's heart, and he will pursue them. But I will gain glory for myself through Pharaoh and all his army, and the Egyptians will know that I am the LORD.' So the Israelites did this.

5When the king of Egypt was told that the people had fled, Pharaoh and his officials changed their minds about them and said, 'What have we done? We have let the Israelites go and have lost their services!' 6So he had his chariot made ready and took his army with him. 7He took six hundred of the best chariots, along with all the other chariots of Egypt, with officers over all of them. 8The LORD hardened the heart of Pharaoh king of Egypt, so that he pursued the Israelites, who were marching out boldly. 9The Egyptians—all Pharaoh's horses and chariots, horsemen*c* and troops—pursued the Israelites and overtook them as they camped by the sea near Pi Hahiroth, opposite Baal Zephon.

10As Pharaoh approached, the Israelites looked up, and there were the Egyptians, marching after them. They were terrified and cried out to the LORD. 11They said to Moses, 'Was it because there were no graves in Egypt that you brought us to the desert to die? What have you done to us by bringing us out of Egypt? 12Didn't we say to you in Egypt, "Leave us alone; let us serve the Egyptians"? It would have been better for us to serve the Egyptians than to die in the desert!'

13Moses answered the people, 'Do not be afraid. Stand firm and you will see the

---

a 18 Or *the Sea of Reeds*   *b* 19 See Gen. 50:25.   *c* 9 Or *charioteers*; also in verses 17, 18, 23, 26 and 28 deliverance the LORD will bring you today. The Egyptians you see today you will never see again. ¹⁴The LORD will fight for you; you need only to be still.'

¹⁵Then the LORD said to Moses, 'Why are you crying out to me? Tell the Israelites to move on. ¹⁶Raise your staff and stretch out your hand over the sea to divide the water so that the Israelites can go through the sea on dry ground. ¹⁷I will harden the hearts of the Egyptians so that they will go in after them. And I will gain glory through Pharaoh and all his army, through his chariots and his horsemen. ¹⁸The Egyptians will know that I am the LORD when I gain glory through Pharaoh, his chariots and his horsemen.'

¹⁹Then the angel of God, who had been travelling in front of Israel's army, withdrew and went behind them. The pillar of cloud also moved from in front and stood behind them, ²⁰coming between the armies of Egypt and Israel. Throughout the night the cloud brought darkness to the one side and light to the other; so neither went near the other all night long.

²¹Then Moses stretched out his hand over the sea, and all that night the LORD drove the sea back with a strong east wind and turned it into dry land. The waters were divided, ²²and the Israelites went through the sea on dry ground, with a wall of water on their right and on their left.

²³The Egyptians pursued them, and all Pharaoh's horses and chariots and horsemen followed them into the sea. ²⁴During the last watch of the night the LORD looked down from the pillar of fire and cloud at the Egyptian army and threw it into confusion. ²⁵He jammed*ᵃ* the wheels of their chariots so that they had difficulty driving. And the Egyptians said, 'Let's get away from the Israelites! The LORD is fighting for them against Egypt.'

²⁶Then the LORD said to Moses, 'Stretch out your hand over the sea so that the waters may flow back over the Egyptians and their chariots and horsemen.' ²⁷Moses stretched out his hand over the sea, and at daybreak the sea went back to its place. The Egyptians were fleeing towards*ᵇ* it, and the LORD swept them into the sea. ²⁸The water flowed back and covered the chariots and horsemen— the entire army of Pharaoh that had followed the Israelites into the sea. Not one of them survived.

²⁹But the Israelites went through the sea on dry ground, with a wall of water on their right and on their left. ³⁰That day the LORD saved Israel from the hands of the Egyptians, and Israel saw the Egyptians lying dead on the shore. ³¹And when the Israelites saw the great power the LORD displayed against the Egyptians, the people feared the LORD and put their trust in him and in Moses his servant.

The song of Moses and Miriam

15 Then Moses and the Israelites sang this song to the LORD:

'I will sing to the LORD,
   for he is highly exalted.
Both horse and driver
   he has hurled into the sea.

²'The LORD is my strength and my defence*ᶜ*;
   he has become my salvation.
He is my God, and I will praise him,
   my father's God, and I will exalt him.
³The LORD is a warrior;
   the LORD is his name.
⁴Pharaoh's chariots and his army
   he has hurled into the sea.
The best of Pharaoh's officers
   are drowned in the Red Sea.*ᵈ*
⁵The deep waters have covered them;
   they sank to the depths like a stone.
⁶Your right hand, LORD,
   was majestic in power.
Your right hand, LORD,
   shattered the enemy.

⁷'In the greatness of your majesty
   you threw down those who opposed you.
You unleashed your burning anger;
   it consumed them like stubble.
⁸By the blast of your nostrils
   the waters piled up.
The surging waters stood up like a wall;

---

*ᵃ*25 See Samaritan Pentateuch, Septuagint and Syriac; Masoretic Text *removed*   *ᵇ*27 Or *from*   *ᶜ*2 Or *song*   *ᵈ*4 Or *the Sea of Reeds*; also in verse 22

the deep waters congealed in the heart
of the sea.
⁹The enemy boasted,
"I will pursue, I will overtake them.
I will divide the spoils;
I will gorge myself on them.
I will draw my sword
and my hand will destroy them."
¹⁰But you blew with your breath,
and the sea covered them.
They sank like lead
in the mighty waters.
¹¹Who among the gods
is like you, LORD?
Who is like you—
majestic in holiness,
awesome in glory,
working wonders?

¹²'You stretch out your right hand,
and the earth swallows your enemies.
¹³In your unfailing love you will lead
the people you have redeemed.
In your strength you will guide them
to your holy dwelling.
¹⁴The nations will hear and tremble;
anguish will grip the people of
Philistia.
¹⁵The chiefs of Edom will be terrified,
the leaders of Moab will be seized with
trembling,
the people*ᵃ* of Canaan will melt away;
16   terror and dread will fall on them.
By the power of your arm
they will be as still as a stone—
until your people pass by, LORD,
until the people you bought*ᵇ* pass by.
¹⁷You will bring them in and plant them
on the mountain of your inheritance—
the place, LORD, you made for your
dwelling,
the sanctuary, Lord, your hands
established.

¹⁸'The LORD reigns
for ever and ever.'

¹⁹When Pharaoh's horses, chariots and horsemen*ᶜ* went into the sea, the LORD brought the waters of the sea back over them, but the Israelites walked through the sea on dry ground. ²⁰Then Miriam the

People and Places

Miriam
Exodus 15:20
Miriam the prophetess was the sister of Moses and Aaron, and one of the leaders of the people of Israel. She may have been the sister who watched over Moses as a baby in the bulrushes. This song of victory after the Israelites crossed the Red Sea is one of the earliest examples of Hebrew poetry.

prophet, Aaron's sister, took a tambourine in her hand, and all the women followed her, with tambourines and dancing. ²¹Miriam sang to them:

'Sing to the LORD,
    for he is highly exalted.
Both horse and driver
    he has hurled into the sea.'

The waters of Marah and Elim

²²Then Moses led Israel from the Red Sea and they went into the Desert of Shur. For three days they travelled in the desert without finding water. ²³When they came to Marah, they could not drink its water because it was bitter. (That is why the place is called Marah.*ᵈ*) ²⁴So the people grumbled against Moses, saying, 'What are we to drink?'

²⁵Then Moses cried out to the LORD, and the LORD showed him a piece of wood. He threw it into the water, and the water became sweet.

There the LORD issued a ruling and instruction for them and put them to the test. ²⁶He said, 'If you listen carefully to the LORD your God and do what is right in his eyes, if you pay attention to his commands and keep all his decrees, I will not bring on you any of the diseases I brought on the Egyptians, for I am the LORD, who heals you.'

ᵃ 15 Or *rulers*   *ᵇ* 16 Or *created*   *ᶜ* 19 Or *charioteers*   *ᵈ* 23 Marah means *bitter*.

27Then they came to Elim, where there were twelve springs and seventy palm trees, and they camped there near the water.

Manna and quail

16 The whole Israelite community set out from Elim and came to the Desert of Sin, which is between Elim and Sinai, on the fifteenth day of the second month after they had come out of Egypt. 2In the desert the whole community grumbled against Moses and Aaron. 3The Israelites said to them, 'If only we had died by the LORD's hand in Egypt! There we sat round pots of meat and ate all the food we wanted, but you have brought us out into this desert to starve this entire assembly to death.'

4Then the LORD said to Moses, 'I will rain down bread from heaven for you. The people are to go out each day and gather enough for that day. In this way I will test them and see whether they will follow my instructions. 5On the sixth day they are to prepare what they bring in, and that is to be twice as much as they gather on the other days.'

6So Moses and Aaron said to all the Israelites, 'In the evening you will know that it was the LORD who brought you out of Egypt, 7and in the morning you will see the glory of the LORD, because he has heard your grumbling against him. Who are we, that you should grumble against us?' 8Moses also said, 'You will know that it was the LORD when he gives you meat to eat in the evening and all the bread you want in the morning, because he has heard your grumbling against him. Who are we? You are not grumbling against us, but against the LORD.'

9Then Moses told Aaron, 'Say to the entire Israelite community, "Come before the LORD, for he has heard your grumbling."'

10While Aaron was speaking to the whole Israelite community, they looked towards the desert, and there was the glory of the LORD appearing in the cloud.

11The LORD said to Moses, 12'I have heard the grumbling of the Israelites. Tell them, "At twilight you will eat meat, and in the morning you will be filled with bread. Then you will know that I am the LORD your God."'

13That evening quail came and covered the camp, and in the morning there was a layer of dew around the camp. 14When the dew was gone, thin flakes like frost on the ground appeared on the desert floor. 15When the Israelites saw it, they said to each other, 'What is it?' For they did not know what it was.

Moses said to them, 'It is the bread the LORD has given you to eat. 16This is what the LORD has commanded: "Each one is to gather as much as they need. Take an omer^a for each person you have in your tent."'

17The Israelites did as they were told; some gathered much, some little. 18And when they measured it by the omer, the one who gathered much did not have too much, and the one who gathered little did not have too little. Each one had gathered just as much as they needed.

19Then Moses said to them, 'No-one is to keep any of it until morning.'

20However, some of them paid no attention to Moses; they kept part of it until morning, but it was full of maggots and began to smell. So Moses was angry with them.

21Each morning everyone gathered as much as they needed, and when the sun grew hot, it melted away. 22On the sixth day, they gathered twice as much—two omers^b for each person—and the leaders of the community came and reported this to Moses. 23He said to them, 'This is what the LORD commanded: "Tomorrow is to be a day of sabbath rest, a holy sabbath to the LORD. So bake what you want to bake and boil what you want to boil. Save whatever is left and keep it until morning."'

24So they saved it until morning, as Moses commanded, and it did not stink or get maggots in it. 25'Eat it today,' Moses said, 'because today is a sabbath to the LORD. You will not find any of it on the ground today. 26Six days you are to gather it, but on the seventh day, the Sabbath, there will not be any.'

27Nevertheless, some of the people went out on the seventh day to gather it, but they

---

^{a} 16 That is, possibly about 1.3 kilograms; also in verses 18, 32, 33 and 36 ^{b} 22 That is, possibly about 2.7 kilograms found none. ²⁸Then the LORD said to Moses, 'How long will you*ᵃ* refuse to keep my commands and my instructions? ²⁹Bear in mind that the LORD has given you the Sabbath; that is why on the sixth day he gives you bread for two days. Everyone is to stay where they are on the seventh day; no-one is to go out.' ³⁰So the people rested on the seventh day.

³¹The people of Israel called the bread manna.*ᵇ* It was white like coriander seed and tasted like wafers made with honey. ³²Moses said, 'This is what the LORD has commanded: "Take an omer of manna and keep it for the generations to come, so they can see the bread I gave you to eat in the wilderness when I brought you out of Egypt."'

³³So Moses said to Aaron, 'Take a jar and put an omer of manna in it. Then place it before the LORD to be kept for the generations to come.'

³⁴As the LORD commanded Moses, Aaron put the manna with the tablets of the covenant law, that it might be preserved. ³⁵The Israelites ate manna for forty years, until they came to a land that was settled; they ate manna until they reached the border of Canaan.

³⁶(An omer is one tenth of an ephah.)

Water from the rock

17 The whole Israelite community set out from the Desert of Sin, travelling from place to place as the LORD commanded. They camped at Rephidim, but there was no water for the people to drink. ²So they quarrelled with Moses and said, 'Give us water to drink.'

Moses replied, 'Why do you quarrel with me? Why do you put the LORD to the test?'

³But the people were thirsty for water there, and they grumbled against Moses. They said, 'Why did you bring us up out of Egypt to make us and our children and livestock die of thirst?'

⁴Then Moses cried out to the LORD, 'What am I to do with these people? They are almost ready to stone me.'

⁵The LORD answered Moses, 'Go out in front of the people. Take with you some of the elders of Israel and take in your hand the staff with which you struck the Nile, and go. ⁶I will stand there before you by the rock at Horeb. Strike the rock, and water will come out of it for the people to drink.' So Moses did this in the sight of the elders of Israel. ⁷And he called the place Massah*ᶜ* and Meribah*ᵈ* because the Israelites quarrelled and because they tested the LORD saying, 'Is the LORD among us or not?'

The Amalekites defeated

⁸The Amalekites came and attacked the Israelites at Rephidim. ⁹Moses said to Joshua, 'Choose some of our men and go out to fight the Amalekites. Tomorrow I will stand on top of the hill with the staff of God in my hands.'

¹⁰So Joshua fought the Amalekites as Moses had ordered, and Moses, Aaron and Hur went to the top of the hill. ¹¹As long as Moses held up his hands, the Israelites were winning, but whenever he lowered his hands, the Amalekites were winning. ¹²When Moses' hands grew tired, they

making Connections

Names of God
Exodus 17:15

In the ancient world, knowing someone's name was a special privilege that let you in on who they really were. The longer the Israelites walked with God, the more they discovered about his character. Here, Moses gives him a new name – Jehovah Nissi, or 'God is my banner' – because he knows that God is on the side of the Israelites.

---

*ᵃ*28 The Hebrew is plural. *ᵇ*31 *Manna* means *What is it?* (see verse 15). *ᶜ*7 *Massah* means *testing*. *ᵈ*7 *Meribah* means *quarrelling*.

took a stone and put it under him and he sat on it. Aaron and Hur held his hands up—one on one side, one on the other—so that his hands remained steady till sunset. ¹³So Joshua overcame the Amalekite army with the sword.

¹⁴Then the LORD said to Moses, 'Write this on a scroll as something to be remembered and make sure that Joshua hears it, because I will completely blot out the name of Amalek from under heaven.'

¹⁵Moses built an altar and called it The LORD is my Banner. ¹⁶He said, 'Because hands were lifted up against^a the throne of the LORD,^{b} the^c LORD will be at war against the Amalekites from generation to generation.'

Jethro visits Moses

18 Now Jethro, the priest of Midian and father-in-law of Moses, heard of everything God had done for Moses and for his people Israel, and how the LORD had brought Israel out of Egypt.

²After Moses had sent away his wife Zipporah, his father-in-law Jethro received her ³and her two sons. One son was named Gershom,^{d} for Moses said, 'I have become a foreigner in a foreign land'; ⁴and the other was named Eliezer,^{e} for he said, 'My father's God was my helper; he saved me from the sword of Pharaoh.'

⁵Jethro, Moses' father-in-law, together with Moses' sons and wife, came to him in the wilderness, where he was camped near the mountain of God. ⁶Jethro had sent word to him, 'I, your father-in-law Jethro, am coming to you with your wife and her two sons.'

⁷So Moses went out to meet his father-in-law and bowed down and kissed him. They greeted each other and then went into the tent. ⁸Moses told his father-in-law about everything the LORD had done to Pharaoh and the Egyptians for Israel's sake and about all the hardships they had met along the way and how the LORD had saved them.

⁹Jethro was delighted to hear about all the good things the LORD had done for Israel in rescuing them from the hand of the Egyptians. ¹⁰He said, 'Praise be to the LORD, who rescued you from the hand of the Egyptians and of Pharaoh, and who rescued the people from the hand of the Egyptians. ¹¹Now I know that the LORD is greater than all other gods, for he did this to those who had treated Israel arrogantly.' ¹²Then Jethro, Moses' father-in-law, brought a burnt offering and other sacrifices to God, and Aaron came with all the elders of Israel to eat bread with Moses' father-in-law in the presence of God.

¹³The next day Moses took his seat to serve as judge for the people, and they stood round him from morning till evening. ¹⁴When his father-in-law saw all that Moses was doing for the people, he said, 'What is this you are doing for the people? Why do you alone sit as judge, while all these people stand round you from morning till evening?'

¹⁵Moses answered him, 'Because the people come to me to seek God's will. ¹⁶Whenever they have a dispute, it is brought to me, and I decide between the parties and inform them of God's decrees and instructions.'

¹⁷Moses' father-in-law replied, 'What you are doing is not good. ¹⁸You and these people who come to you will only wear yourselves out. The work is too heavy for you; you cannot handle it alone. ¹⁹Listen now to me and I will give you some advice, and may God be with you. You must be the people's representative before God and bring their disputes to him. ²⁰Teach them his decrees and instructions, and show them the way they are to live and how they are to behave. ²¹But select capable men from all the people—men who fear God, trustworthy men who hate dishonest gain—and appoint them as officials over thousands, hundreds, fifties and tens. ²²Let them serve as judges for the people at all times, but let them bring every difficult case to you; the simple cases they can decide themselves. That will make your load lighter, because they will share it with you. ²³If you do this

---

^{a} 16 Or *to* ^{b} 16 The meaning of the Hebrew for this clause is uncertain. ^{c} 16 Or *'Because a hand was against the throne of the LORD, the* ^{d} 3 *Gershom* sounds like the Hebrew for *a foreigner there.* ^{e} 4 *Eliezer* means *my God is helper.*

and God so commands, you will be able to stand the strain, and all these people will go home satisfied.'

24Moses listened to his father-in-law and did everything he said. 25He chose capable men from all Israel and made them leaders of the people, officials over thousands, hundreds, fifties and tens. 26They served as judges for the people at all times. The difficult cases they brought to Moses, but the simple ones they decided themselves.

27Then Moses sent his father-in-law on his way, and Jethro returned to his own country.

At Mount Sinai

19 On [the first day of] the third month after the Israelites left Egypt—on that very day—they came to the Desert of Sinai. 2After they set out from Rephidim, they entered the Desert of Sinai, and Israel camped there in the desert in front of the mountain.

3Then Moses went up to God, and the LORD called to him from the mountain and said, 'This is what you are to say to the house of Jacob and what you are to tell the people of Israel: 4"You yourselves have seen what I did to Egypt, and how I carried you on eagles' wings and brought you to myself. 5Now if you obey me fully and keep my covenant, then out of all nations you will be my treasured possession. Although the whole earth is mine, 6you^a will be for me a kingdom of priests and a holy nation." These are the words you are to speak to the Israelites.'

7So Moses went back and summoned the elders of the people and set before them all the words the LORD had commanded him to speak. 8The people all responded together, 'We will do everything the LORD has said.' So Moses brought their answer back to the LORD.

9The LORD said to Moses, 'I am going to come to you in a dense cloud, so that the people will hear me speaking with you and will always put their trust in you.' Then Moses told the LORD what the people had said.

> **IN OTHER WORDS**
>
> **Consecration**
> Exodus 19:10
> Consecration is the act of setting apart something or someone for God's use. The Israelites were to show that they were God's special people by making themselves clean and dedicating themselves to him.

10And the LORD said to Moses, 'Go to the people and consecrate them today and tomorrow. Make them wash their clothes 11and be ready by the third day, because on that day the LORD will come down on Mount Sinai in the sight of all the people. 12Put limits for the people around the mountain and tell them, "Be careful that you do not approach the mountain or touch the foot of it. Whoever touches the mountain is to be put to death. 13They are to be stoned or shot with arrows; not a hand is to be laid on them. Whether people or animals, they shall not be permitted to live." Only when the ram's horn sounds a long blast may they approach the mountain.'

14After Moses had gone down the mountain to the people, he consecrated them, and they washed their clothes. 15Then he said to the people, 'Prepare yourselves for the third day. Abstain from sexual relations.'

16On the morning of the third day there was thunder and lightning, with a thick cloud over the mountain, and a very loud trumpet blast. Everyone in the camp trembled. 17Then Moses led the people out of the camp to meet with God, and they stood at the foot of the mountain. 18Mount Sinai was covered with smoke, because the LORD descended on it in fire. The smoke billowed up from it like smoke from a furnace, and the whole mountain^b trembled violently. 19As the sound of the trumpet grew louder and louder, Moses spoke and the voice of God answered him.^{c}

---

^{a} 5,6 Or *possession, for the whole earth is mine.* ^{6}You ^{b} 18 Most Hebrew manuscripts; a few Hebrew manuscripts and Septuagint *and all the people* ^{c} 19 Or *and God answered him with thunder*

²⁰The LORD descended to the top of Mount Sinai and called Moses to the top of the mountain. So Moses went up ²¹and the LORD said to him, 'Go down and warn the people so they do not force their way through to see the LORD and many of them perish. ²²Even the priests, who approach the LORD, must consecrate themselves, or the LORD will break out against them.'

²³Moses said to the LORD, 'The people cannot come up Mount Sinai, because you yourself warned us, "Put limits around the mountain and set it apart as holy."'

²⁴The LORD replied, 'Go down and bring Aaron up with you. But the priests and the people must not force their way through to come up to the LORD, or he will break out against them.'

²⁵So Moses went down to the people and told them.

The Ten Commandments

20 And God spoke all these words:

²'I am the LORD your God, who brought you out of Egypt, out of the land of slavery.

³'You shall have no other gods before*ᵃ* me.

⁴'You shall not make for yourself an image in the form of anything in heaven above or on the earth beneath or in the waters below. ⁵You shall not bow down to them or worship them; for I, the LORD your God, am a jealous God, punishing the children for the sin of the parents to the third and fourth generation of those who hate me, ⁶but showing love to a thousand generations of those who love me and keep my commandments.

⁷'You shall not misuse the name of the LORD your God, for the LORD will not hold anyone guiltless who misuses his name.

⁸'Remember the Sabbath day by keeping it holy. ⁹Six days you shall labour and do all your work, ¹⁰but the seventh day is a sabbath to the LORD your God. On it you shall not do any work, neither you, nor your son or daughter, nor your male or female servant, nor your animals, nor any foreigner residing in your towns. ¹¹For in six days the LORD made the heavens and the earth, the sea, and all that is in them, but he rested on the seventh day. Therefore the LORD blessed the Sabbath day and made it holy.

¹²'Honour your father and your mother, so that you may live long in the land the LORD your God is giving you.

¹³'You shall not murder.

¹⁴'You shall not commit adultery.

¹⁵'You shall not steal.

¹⁶'You shall not give false testimony against your neighbour.

¹⁷'You shall not covet your neighbour's house. You shall not covet your neighbour's wife, or his male

---

making Connections

The Ten Commandments
Exodus 20:1

These ten laws were given by God to the Israelites to show them how to live. But they are just as relevant to us today because they have come from God who stays the same throughout time. About one and a half thousand years after God gave these laws, Jesus upheld them in his conversation with an expert in the law (Matthew 22:36). And even now, in the largely non-Christian and non-Jewish West, the Ten Commandments are still the basis for modern-day morality.

ᵃ 3 Or *besides*

or female servant, his ox or donkey, or anything that belongs to your neighbour.'

18 When the people saw the thunder and lightning and heard the trumpet and saw the mountain in smoke, they trembled with fear. They stayed at a distance 19 and said to Moses, 'Speak to us yourself and we will listen. But do not let God speak to us or we will die.'

20 Moses said to the people, 'Do not be afraid. God has come to test you, so that the fear of God will be with you to keep you from sinning.'

21 The people remained at a distance, while Moses approached the thick darkness where God was.

Idols and altars

22 Then the LORD said to Moses, 'Tell the Israelites this: "You have seen for yourselves that I have spoken to you from heaven: 23 do not make any gods to be alongside me; do not make for yourselves gods of silver or gods of gold.

24 ' "Make an altar of earth for me and sacrifice on it your burnt offerings and fellowship offerings, your sheep and goats and your cattle. Wherever I cause my name to be honoured, I will come to you and bless you. 25 If you make an altar of stones for me, do not build it with dressed stones, for you will defile it if you use a tool on it. 26 And do not go up to my altar on steps, lest your nakedness be exposed on it."

21

'These are the laws you are to set before them:

Hebrew servants

2 'If you buy a Hebrew servant, he is to serve you for six years. But in the seventh year, he shall go free, without paying anything. 3 If he comes alone, he is to go free alone; but if he has a wife when he comes, she is to go with him. 4 If his master gives him a wife and she bears him sons or daughters, the woman and her children shall belong to her master, and only the man shall go free.

5 'But if the servant declares, "I love my master and my wife and children and do not want to go free," 6 then his master must take him before the judges.^{a} He shall take him to the door or the door-post and pierce his ear with an awl. Then he will be his servant for life.

7 'If a man sells his daughter as a servant, she is not to go free as male servants do. 8 If she does not please the master who has selected her for himself,^{b} he must let her be redeemed. He has no right to sell her to foreigners, because he has broken faith with her. 9 If he selects her for his son, he must grant her the rights of a daughter. 10 If he marries another woman, he must not deprive the first one of her food, clothing and marital rights. 11 If he does not provide her with these three things, she is to go free, without any payment of money.

Personal injuries

12 'Anyone who strikes someone a fatal blow is to be put to death. 13 However, if it is not done intentionally, but God lets it happen, they are to flee to a place I will designate. 14 But if anyone schemes and kills someone deliberately, that person is to be taken from my altar and put to death.

15 'Anyone who attacks^c their father or mother is to be put to death.

16 'Anyone who kidnaps someone is to be put to death, whether the victim has been sold or is still in the kidnapper's possession.

17 'Anyone who curses their father or mother is to be put to death.

18 'If two people quarrel and one hits the other with a stone or with a fist^d and the victim does not die but is confined to bed, 19 the one who struck the blow will not be held liable if the other can get up and walk around outside with a staff; however, the guilty party must pay the injured person for any loss of time and see that the victim is completely healed.

20 'Anyone who beats their male or female slave with a rod must be punished if the slave dies as a direct result, 21 but they are not to be punished if the slave recovers after a day or two, since the slave is their property.

---

^{a} 6 Or *before God* ^{b} 8 Or *master so that he does not choose her* ^{c} 15 Or *kills* ^{d} 18 Or *with a tool*

22 ′′If people are fighting and a pregnant woman is hit and gives birth prematurely[a] but there is no serious injury, the offender must be fined whatever the woman's husband demands and the court allows. 23But if there is serious injury, you are to take life for life, 24eye for eye, tooth for tooth, hand for hand, foot for foot, 25burn for burn, wound for wound, bruise for bruise.

26′An owner who hits a male or female slave in the eye and destroys it must let the slave go free to compensate for the eye. 27And an owner who knocks out the tooth of a male or female slave must let the slave go free to compensate for the tooth.

28′If a bull gores a man or a woman to death, the bull is to be stoned to death, and its meat must not be eaten. But the owner of the bull will not be held responsible. 29If, however, the bull has had the habit of goring and the owner has been warned but has not kept it penned up and it kills a man or woman, the bull is to be stoned and its owner also is to be put to death. 30However, if payment is demanded, the owner's life may be redeemed by the payment of whatever is demanded. 31This law also applies if the bull gores a son or a daughter. 32If the bull gores a male or female slave, the owner must pay thirty shekels[b] of silver to the master of the slave, and the bull is to be stoned to death.

33′If anyone uncovers a pit or digs one and fails to cover it and an ox or a donkey falls into it, 34the one who opened the pit must pay the owner for the loss and take the dead animal in exchange.

35′If anyone's bull injures the bull of another and it dies, the two parties are to sell the live one and divide both the money and the dead animal equally. 36However, if it was known that the bull had the habit of goring, yet the owner did not keep it penned up, the owner must pay, animal for animal, and take the dead animal in exchange.

Protection of property

22 *′′Whoever steals an ox or a sheep and slaughters it or sells it must pay back five head of cattle for the ox and four sheep for the sheep.

*2′If a thief is caught breaking in and is struck a fatal blow, the defender is not guilty of bloodshed; 3but if it happens[c] after sunrise, the defender is guilty of bloodshed.

′Anyone who steals must certainly make restitution, but if they have nothing, they must be sold to pay for their theft. 4If the stolen animal is found alive in their possession—whether ox or donkey or sheep— they must pay back double.

5′If anyone grazes their livestock in a field or vineyard and lets them stray and they graze in another person's field, restitution must be made from the best of the livestock owner's field and vineyard.

6′If a fire breaks out and spreads into thorn-bushes so that it burns sheaves of corn or standing corn or the whole field, the one who started the fire must make restitution.

7′If anyone gives a neighbour silver or goods for safekeeping and they are stolen from the neighbour's house, the thief, if caught, must pay back double. 8But if the thief is not found, the owner of the house must appear before the judges, and they must[d] determine whether the owner of the house has laid hands on the other person's property. 9In all cases of illegal possession of an ox, a donkey, a sheep, a garment, or any other lost property about which somebody says, "This is mine," both parties are to bring their cases before the judges.[e] The one whom the judges declare[f] guilty must pay back double to the other.

10′If anyone gives a donkey, an ox, a sheep or any other animal to a neighbour for safekeeping and it dies or is injured or is taken away while no-one is looking, 11the issue between them will be settled by the taking of an oath before the LORD that the neighbour did not lay hands on the other person's property. The owner is to accept this, and no restitution is required. 12But if the animal was stolen from the neighbour, restitution must be made to the owner. 13If it was torn to pieces by a wild animal, the

---

[a] 22 Or *and has a miscarriage* [b] 32 That is, about 345 grams [c] 3 Or *if the defender kills the thief* [d] 8 Or *before God, and he will* [e] 9 Or *before God* [f] 9 Or *whom God declares*

* 22:1 is numbered 21:37 in Hebrew texts. * 22:2-31 is numbered 22:1-30 in Hebrew texts.

Exodus 23:9

Sign of the times

Dowry
Exodus 22:16

In the time of the Old Testament, if a man wanted to marry a woman he had to pay a dowry, or bride-price, to her father. This didn't mean that he was buying her – more that he was compensating her father. The woman would no longer be there to help her dad; she would be helping her new husband instead. The dowry could be money, goods, a service or a task.

neighbour shall bring in the remains as evidence and shall not be required to pay for the torn animal.

14'If anyone borrows an animal from a neighbour and it is injured or dies while the owner is not present, restitution must be made. 15But if the owner is with the animal, the borrower will not have to pay. If the animal was hired, the money paid for the hire covers the loss.

Social responsibility

16'If a man seduces a virgin who is not pledged to be married and sleeps with her, he must pay the bride-price, and she shall be his wife. 17If her father absolutely refuses to give her to him, he must still pay the bride-price for virgins.

18'Do not allow a sorceress to live.

19'Anyone who has sexual relations with an animal is to be put to death.

20'Whoever sacrifices to any god other than the LORD must be destroyed.[a]

21'Do not ill-treat or oppress a foreigner, for you were foreigners in Egypt.

22'Do not take advantage of a widow or an orphan. 23If you do and they cry out to me, I will certainly hear their cry. 24My anger will be aroused, and I will kill you with the sword; your wives will become widows and your children fatherless.

25'If you lend money to one of my people among you who is needy, do not treat it like a business deal; charge no interest. 26If you take your neighbour's cloak as a pledge, return it by sunset, 27because that is the only covering they have. What else can they sleep in? When your neighbour cries out to me, I will hear, for I am compassionate.

28'Do not utter blasphemies against God[b] or curse the ruler of your people.

29'Do not hold back offerings from your granaries or your vats.[c]

'You must give me the firstborn of your sons. 30Do the same with your cattle and your sheep. Let them stay with their mothers for seven days, but give them to me on the eighth day.

31'You are to be my holy people. So do not eat the meat of an animal torn by wild beasts; throw it to the dogs.

Laws of justice and mercy

23 'Do not spread false reports. Do not help a guilty person by being a malicious witness.

2'Do not follow the crowd in doing wrong. When you give testimony in a lawsuit, do not pervert justice by siding with the crowd, 3and do not show favouritism to the poor in a lawsuit.

4'If you come across your enemy's ox or donkey wandering off, be sure to return it. 5If you see the donkey of someone who hates you fallen down under its load, do not leave it there; be sure you help your enemy with it.

6'Do not deny justice to your poor people in their lawsuits. 7Have nothing to do with a false charge and do not put an innocent or honest person to death, for I will not acquit the guilty.

8'Do not accept a bribe, for a bribe blinds those who see and twists the words of the righteous.

9'Do not oppress a foreigner; you yourselves know how it feels to be foreigners, because you were foreigners in Egypt.

---

[a] 20 The Hebrew term refers to the irrevocable giving over of things or persons to the LORD, often by totally destroying them. [b] 28 Or *Do not revile the judges* [c] 29 The meaning of the Hebrew for this phrase is uncertain.

Sabbath laws

¹⁰'For six years you are to sow your fields and harvest the crops, ¹¹but during the seventh year let the land lie unploughed and unused. Then the poor among your people may get food from it, and the wild animals may eat what they leave. Do the same with your vineyard and your olive grove.

¹²'Six days do your work, but on the seventh day do not work, so that your ox and your donkey may rest and the slave born in your household, and the foreigner among you as well, may be refreshed.

¹³'Be careful to do everything I have said to you. Do not invoke the names of other gods; do not let them be heard on your lips.

The three annual festivals

¹⁴'Three times a year you are to celebrate a festival to me.

¹⁵'Celebrate the Festival of Unleavened Bread; for seven days eat bread made without yeast, as I commanded you. Do this at the appointed time in the month of Aviv, for in that month you came out of Egypt.

'No-one is to appear before me empty-handed.

¹⁶'Celebrate the Festival of Harvest with the firstfruits of the crops you sow in your field.

'Celebrate the Festival of Ingathering at the end of the year, when you gather in your crops from the field.

¹⁷'Three times a year all the men are to appear before the Sovereign LORD.

¹⁸'Do not offer the blood of a sacrifice to me along with anything containing yeast.

'The fat of my festival offerings must not be kept until morning.

¹⁹'Bring the best of the firstfruits of your soil to the house of the LORD your God.

'Do not cook a young goat in its mother's milk.

God's angel to prepare the way

²⁰'See, I am sending an angel ahead of you to guard you along the way and to bring you to the place I have prepared. ²¹Pay attention to him and listen to what he says. Do not rebel against him; he will not forgive your rebellion, since my Name is in him. ²²If you listen carefully to what he says and do all that I say, I will be an enemy to your enemies and will oppose those who oppose you. ²³My angel will go ahead of you and bring you into the land of the Amorites, Hittites, Perizzites, Canaanites, Hivites and Jebusites, and I will wipe them out. ²⁴Do not bow down before their gods or worship them or follow their practices. You must demolish them and break their sacred stones to pieces. ²⁵Worship the LORD your God, and his blessing will be on your food and water. I will take away disease from among you, ²⁶and none will miscarry or be barren in your land. I will give you a full life span.

²⁷'I will send my terror ahead of you and throw into confusion every nation you encounter. I will make all your enemies turn their backs and run. ²⁸I will send the hornet ahead of you to drive the Hivites, Canaanites and Hittites out of your way. ²⁹But I will not drive them out in a single year, because the land would become desolate and the wild animals too numerous for you. ³⁰Little by little I will drive them out before you, until you have increased enough to take possession of the land.

³¹'I will establish your borders from the Red Sea^a to the Mediterranean Sea,^{b} and from the desert to the River Euphrates. I will give into your hands the people who live in the land, and you will drive them out before you. ³²Do not make a covenant with them or with their gods. ³³Do not let them live in your land or they will cause you to sin against me, because the worship of their gods will certainly be a snare to you.'

The covenant confirmed

24 Then he said to Moses, 'Come up to the LORD, you and Aaron, Nadab and Abihu, and seventy of the elders of Israel. You are to worship at a distance, ²but Moses alone is to approach the LORD; the others must not come near. And the people may not come up with him.'

³When Moses went and told the people all the LORD's words and laws, they responded with one voice, 'Everything the LORD has said we will do.' ⁴Moses then

---

^{a}31 Or the Sea of Reeds ^{b}31 Hebrew to the Sea of the Philistines wrote down everything the LORD had said.

He got up early the next morning and built an altar at the foot of the mountain and set up twelve stone pillars representing the twelve tribes of Israel. 5Then he sent young Israelite men, and they offered burnt offerings and sacrificed young bulls as fellowship offerings to the LORD. 6Moses took half of the blood and put it in bowls, and the other half he splashed against the altar. 7Then he took the Book of the Covenant and read it to the people. They responded, 'We will do everything the LORD has said; we will obey.'

8Moses then took the blood, sprinkled it on the people and said, 'This is the blood of the covenant that the LORD has made with you in accordance with all these words.'

9Moses and Aaron, Nadab and Abihu, and the seventy elders of Israel went up 10and saw the God of Israel. Under his feet was something like a pavement made of lapis lazuli, as bright blue as the sky. 11But God did not raise his hand against these leaders of the Israelites; they saw God, and they ate and drank.

12The LORD said to Moses, 'Come up to me on the mountain and stay here, and I will give you the tablets of stone with the law and commandments I have written for their instruction.'

13Then Moses set out with Joshua his assistant, and Moses went up on the mountain of God. 14He said to the elders, 'Wait here for us until we come back to you. Aaron and Hur are with you, and anyone involved in a dispute can go to them.'

15When Moses went up on the mountain, the cloud covered it, 16and the glory of the LORD settled on Mount Sinai. For six days the cloud covered the mountain, and on the seventh day the LORD called to Moses from within the cloud. 17To the Israelites the glory of the LORD looked like a consuming fire on top of the mountain. 18Then Moses entered the cloud as he went on up the mountain for forty days and forty nights.

Offerings for the tabernacle

25 The LORD said to Moses, 2'Tell the Israelites to bring me an offering. You are to receive the offering for me from everyone whose heart prompts them to give. 3These are the offerings you are to receive from them: gold, silver and bronze; 4blue, purple and scarlet yarn and fine linen; goat hair; 5ram skins dyed red and other durable leather^a; acacia wood; 6olive oil for the light; spices for the anointing oil and for the fragrant incense; 7and onyx stones and other gems to be mounted on the ephod and breastpiece.

8'Then let them make a sanctuary for me, and I will dwell among them. 9Make this tabernacle and all its furnishings exactly like the pattern I will show you.

The ark

10'Let them make an ark^b of acacia wood— two and a half cubits long, a cubit and a half wide, and a cubit and a half high.^{c} 11Overlay it with pure gold, both inside and out, and make a gold moulding around it. 12Cast four gold rings for it and fasten them to its four feet, with two rings on one side and two rings on the other. 13Then make poles of acacia wood and overlay them with gold. 14Insert the poles into the rings on the sides of the ark to carry it. 15The poles are to remain in the rings of this ark; they are not to be removed. 16Then put in the ark the

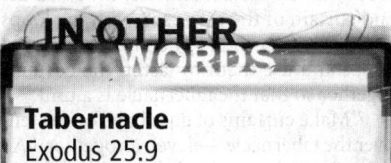

IN OTHER WORDS

Tabernacle
Exodus 25:9

Imagine worshipping God in a tent. That's what the Israelites had to do because they were always on the move and needed to take their place of worship with them. But it was a very special tent, and God told them in great detail what it should be like. It was the home of the Ark of the Covenant, a chest covered in gold which was a symbol of God's presence among them.

---

^{a} 5 Possibly the hides of large aquatic mammals ^{b} 10 That is, a chest ^{c} 10 That is, about 1.1 metres long and 67 centimetres wide and high; also in verse 17 tablets of the covenant law, which I will give you.

17'Make an atonement cover of pure gold—two and a half cubits long and a cubit and a half wide. 18And make two cherubim out of hammered gold at the ends of the cover. 19Make one cherub on one end and the second cherub on the other; make the cherubim of one piece with the cover, at the two ends. 20The cherubim are to have their wings spread upwards, overshadowing the cover with them. The cherubim are to face each other, looking towards the cover. 21Place the cover on top of the ark and put in the ark the tablets of the covenant law that I will give you. 22There, above the cover between the two cherubim that are over the ark of the covenant law, I will meet with you and give you all my commands for the Israelites.

The table

23'Make a table of acacia wood—two cubits long, a cubit wide and a cubit and a half high.[a] 24Overlay it with pure gold and make a gold moulding around it. 25Also make around it a rim a handbreadth[b] wide and put a gold moulding on the rim. 26Make four gold rings for the table and fasten them to the four corners, where the four legs are. 27The rings are to be close to the rim to hold the poles used in carrying the table. 28Make the poles of acacia wood, overlay them with gold and carry the table with them. 29And make its plates and dishes of pure gold, as well as its pitchers and bowls for the pouring out of offerings. 30Put the bread of the Presence on this table to be before me at all times.

The lampstand

31'Make a lampstand of pure gold. Hammer out its base and shaft, and make its flower-like cups, buds and blossoms of one piece with them. 32Six branches are to extend from the sides of the lampstand—three on one side and three on the other. 33Three cups shaped like almond flowers with buds and blossoms are to be on one branch, three on the next branch, and the same for all six branches extending from the lampstand. 34And on the lampstand there are to be four cups shaped like almond flowers with buds and blossoms. 35One bud shall be under the first pair of branches extending from the lampstand, a second bud under the second pair, and a third bud under the third pair—six branches in all. 36The buds and branches shall all be of one piece with the lampstand, hammered out of pure gold.

37'Then make its seven lamps and set them up on it so that they light the space in front of it. 38Its wick trimmers and trays are to be of pure gold. 39A talent[c] of pure gold is to be used for the lampstand and all these accessories. 40See that you make them according to the pattern shown you on the mountain.

The tabernacle

26 'Make the tabernacle with ten curtains of finely twisted linen and blue, purple and scarlet yarn, with cherubim worked into them by skilled hands. 2All the curtains are to be the same size—twenty-eight cubits long and four cubits wide.[d] 3Join five of the curtains together, and do the same with the other five. 4Make loops of blue material along the edge of the end curtain in one set, and do the same with the end curtain in the other set. 5Make fifty loops on one curtain and fifty loops on the end curtain of the other set, with the loops opposite each other. 6Then make fifty gold clasps and use them to fasten the curtains together so that the tabernacle is a unit.

7'Make curtains of goat hair for the tent over the tabernacle—eleven altogether. 8All eleven curtains are to be the same size—thirty cubits long and four cubits wide.[e] 9Join five of the curtains together into one set and the other six into another set. Fold the sixth curtain double at the front of the tent. 10Make fifty loops along the edge of the end curtain in one set and also along the edge of the end curtain in the other set. 11Then make fifty bronze clasps and put them in the loops to fasten the tent together as a unit. 12As for the additional length of the tent curtains, the half curtain that is left

---

[a] 23 That is, about 90 centimetres long, 45 centimetres wide and 67 centimetres high   [b] 25 That is, about 7.5 centimetres   [c] 39 That is, about 34 kilograms   [d] 2 That is, about 13 metres long and 1.8 metres wide   [e] 8 That is, about 13.5 metres long and 1.8 metres wide

over is to hang down at the rear of the tabernacle. 13The tent curtains will be a cubit*[a]* longer on both sides; what is left will hang over the sides of the tabernacle so as to cover it. 14Make for the tent a covering of ram skins dyed red, and over that a covering of other durable leather.[b]

15'Make upright frames of acacia wood for the tabernacle. 16Each frame is to be ten cubits long and a cubit and a half wide,[c] 17with two projections set parallel to each other. Make all the frames of the tabernacle in this way. 18Make twenty frames for the south side of the tabernacle 19and make forty silver bases to go under them—two bases for each frame, one under each projection. 20For the other side, the north side of the tabernacle, make twenty frames 21and forty silver bases—two under each frame. 22Make six frames for the far end, that is, the west end of the tabernacle, 23and make two frames for the corners at the far end. 24At these two corners they must be double from the bottom all the way to the top and fitted into a single ring; both shall be like that. 25So there will be eight frames and sixteen silver bases—two under each frame.

26'Also make crossbars of acacia wood: five for the frames on one side of the tabernacle, 27five for those on the other side, and five for the frames on the west, at the far end of the tabernacle. 28The centre crossbar is to extend from end to end at the middle of the frames. 29Overlay the frames with gold and make gold rings to hold the crossbars. Also overlay the crossbars with gold.

30'Set up the tabernacle according to the plan shown you on the mountain.

31'Make a curtain of blue, purple and scarlet yarn and finely twisted linen, with cherubim worked into it by skilled hands. 32Hang it with gold hooks on four posts of acacia wood overlaid with gold and standing on four silver bases. 33Hang the curtain from the clasps and place the ark of the covenant law behind the curtain. The curtain will separate the Holy Place from the Most Holy Place. 34Put the atonement cover on the ark of the covenant law in the Most Holy Place. 35Place the table outside the curtain on the north side of the tabernacle and put the lampstand opposite it on the south side.

36'For the entrance to the tent make a curtain of blue, purple and scarlet yarn and finely twisted linen—the work of an embroiderer. 37Make gold hooks for this curtain and five posts of acacia wood overlaid with gold. And cast five bronze bases for them.

The altar of burnt offering

27 'Build an altar of acacia wood, three cubits[d] high; it is to be square, five cubits long and five cubits wide.[e] 2Make a horn at each of the four corners, so that the horns and the altar are of one piece, and overlay the altar with bronze. 3Make all its utensils of bronze—its pots to remove the ashes, and its shovels, sprinkling bowls, meat forks and firepans. 4Make a grating for it, a bronze network, and make a bronze ring at each of the four corners of the network. 5Put it under the ledge of the altar so that it is halfway up the altar. 6Make poles of acacia wood for the altar and overlay them with bronze. 7The poles are to be inserted into the rings so they will be on two sides of the altar when it is carried. 8Make the altar hollow, out of boards. It is to be made just as you were shown on the mountain.

The courtyard

9'Make a courtyard for the tabernacle. The south side shall be a hundred cubits[f] long and is to have curtains of finely twisted linen, 10with twenty posts and twenty bronze bases and with silver hooks and bands on the posts. 11The north side shall also be a hundred cubits long and is to have curtains, with twenty posts and twenty bronze bases and with silver hooks and bands on the posts.

12'The west end of the courtyard shall be fifty cubits[g] wide and have curtains, with ten posts and ten bases. 13On the east end, towards the sunrise, the courtyard shall also be fifty cubits wide. 14Curtains fifteen

---

[a] 13 That is, about 45 centimetres   *[b]* 14 Possibly the hides of large aquatic mammals   *[c]* 16 That is, about 4.5 metres long and 67 centimetres wide   *[d]* 1 That is, about 1.4 metres   *[e]* 1 That is, about 2.3 metres long and wide   *[f]* 9 That is, about 45 metres; also in verse 11   *[g]* 12 That is, about 22.5 metres; also in verse 13

cubits[a] long are to be on one side of the entrance, with three posts and three bases, 15and curtains fifteen cubits long are to be on the other side, with three posts and three bases.

16'For the entrance to the courtyard, provide a curtain twenty cubits[b] long, of blue, purple and scarlet yarn and finely twisted linen—the work of an embroiderer—with four posts and four bases. 17All the posts around the courtyard are to have silver bands and hooks, and bronze bases. 18The courtyard shall be a hundred cubits long and fifty cubits wide,[c] with curtains of finely twisted linen five cubits[d] high, and with bronze bases. 19All the other articles used in the service of the tabernacle, whatever their function, including all the tent pegs for it and those for the courtyard, are to be of bronze.

Oil for the lampstand

20'Command the Israelites to bring you clear oil of pressed olives for the light so that the lamps may be kept burning. 21In the tent of meeting, outside the curtain that shields the ark of the covenant law, Aaron and his sons are to keep the lamps burning before the LORD from evening till morning. This is to be a lasting ordinance among the Israelites for the generations to come.

The priestly garments

28 'Let Aaron your brother be brought to you from among the Israelites, with his sons Nadab and Abihu, Eleazar and Ithamar, so that they may serve me as priests. 2Make sacred garments for your brother Aaron to give him dignity and honour. 3Tell all the skilled workers to whom I have given wisdom in such matters that they are to make garments for Aaron, for his consecration, so that he may serve me as priest. 4These are the garments they are to make: a breastpiece, an ephod, a robe, a woven tunic, a turban and a sash. They are to make these sacred garments for your brother Aaron and his sons, so that they may serve me as priests. 5Make them use gold, and blue, purple and scarlet yarn, and fine linen.

The ephod

6'Make the ephod of gold, and of blue, purple and scarlet yarn, and of finely twisted linen—the work of skilled hands. 7It is to have two shoulder pieces attached to two of its corners, so that it can be fastened. 8Its skilfully woven waistband is to be like it—of one piece with the ephod and made with gold, and with blue, purple and scarlet yarn, and with finely twisted linen.

9'Take two onyx stones and engrave on them the names of the sons of Israel 10in the order of their birth—six names on one stone and the remaining six on the other. 11Engrave the names of the sons of Israel on the two stones the way a gem cutter engraves a seal. Then mount the stones in gold filigree settings 12and fasten them on the shoulder pieces of the ephod as memorial stones for the sons of Israel. Aaron is to bear the names on his shoulders as a memorial before the LORD. 13Make gold filigree settings 14and two braided chains of pure gold, like a rope, and attach the chains to the settings.

The breastpiece

15'Fashion a breastpiece for making decisions—the work of skilled hands. Make it like the ephod: of gold, and of blue, purple and scarlet yarn, and of finely twisted linen.

IN OTHER WORDS

Priest
Exodus 28:3

In the Old Testament the priest's job was to represent God to the people and the people to God, a kind of holy go-between. The priest performed all the most important rituals on behalf of the people. In the New Testament, Jesus is described as a high priest, and all believers now have a priestly role to play.

---

[a] 14 That is, about 6.8 metres; also in verse 15   [b] 16 That is, about 9 metres   [c] 18 That is, about 45 metres long and 22.5 metres wide   [d] 18 That is, about 2.3 metres

IN OTHER WORDS

Ephod
Exodus 28:6

As you might expect, high priests had special clothes to wear when they performed their duties. The ephod was rather like a kind of vest worn over a robe. It was made of pure linen with gold, blue, purple and red threads woven into it. On the shoulders of the ephod were two stones engraved with the names of the twelve tribes of Israel, to remind the high priest that he represented them before God.

---

16 It is to be square—a span[a] long and a span wide—and folded double. 17 Then mount four rows of precious stones on it. The first row shall be carnelian, chrysolite and beryl; 18 the second row shall be turquoise, lapis lazuli and emerald; 19 the third row shall be jacinth, agate and amethyst; 20 the fourth row shall be topaz, onyx and jasper.[b] Mount them in gold filigree settings. 21 There are to be twelve stones, one for each of the names of the sons of Israel, each engraved like a seal with the name of one of the twelve tribes.

22 'For the breastpiece make braided chains of pure gold, like a rope. 23 Make two gold rings for it and fasten them to two corners of the breastpiece. 24 Fasten the two gold chains to the rings at the corners of the breastpiece, 25 and the other ends of the chains to the two settings, attaching them to the shoulder pieces of the ephod at the front. 26 Make two gold rings and attach them to the other two corners of the breastpiece on the inside edge next to the ephod. 27 Make two more gold rings and attach them to the bottom of the shoulder pieces on the front of the ephod, close to the seam just above the waistband of the ephod. 28 The rings of the breastpiece are to be tied to the rings of the ephod with blue cord, connecting it to the waistband, so that the breastpiece will not swing out from the ephod.

29 'Whenever Aaron enters the Holy Place, he will bear the names of the sons of Israel over his heart on the breastpiece of decision as a continuing memorial before the LORD. 30 Also put the Urim and the Thummim in the breastpiece, so they may be over Aaron's heart whenever he enters the presence of the LORD. Thus Aaron will always bear the means of making decisions for the Israelites over his heart before the LORD.

Other priestly garments

31 'Make the robe of the ephod entirely of blue cloth, 32 with an opening for the head in its centre. There shall be a woven edge like a collar[c] around this opening, so that it will not tear. 33 Make pomegranates of blue, purple and scarlet yarn around the hem of the robe, with gold bells between them. 34 The gold bells and the pomegranates are to alternate round the hem of the robe. 35 Aaron must wear it when he ministers. The sound of the bells will be heard when he enters the Holy Place before the LORD and when he comes out, so that he will not die.

36 'Make a plate of pure gold and engrave on it as on a seal: HOLY TO THE LORD. 37 Fasten a blue cord to it to attach it to the turban; it is to be on the front of the turban. 38 It will be on Aaron's forehead, and he will bear the guilt involved in the sacred gifts the Israelites consecrate, whatever their gifts may be. It will be on Aaron's forehead continually so that they will be acceptable to the LORD.

39 'Weave the tunic of fine linen and make the turban of fine linen. The sash is to be the work of an embroiderer. 40 Make tunics, sashes and caps for Aaron's sons to give them dignity and honour. 41 After you put these clothes on your brother Aaron and his sons, anoint and ordain them. Consecrate them so they may serve me as priests.

42 'Make linen undergarments as a covering for the body, reaching from the waist to the thigh. 43 Aaron and his sons must

---

[a] 16 That is, about 22.5 centimetres [b] 20 The precise identification of some of these precious stones is uncertain.
[c] 32 The meaning of the Hebrew for this word is uncertain.

wear them whenever they enter the tent of meeting or approach the altar to minister in the Holy Place, so that they will not incur guilt and die.

'This is to be a lasting ordinance for Aaron and his descendants.

Consecration of the priests

29 'This is what you are to do to consecrate them, so that they may serve me as priests: take a young bull and two rams without defect. 2And from the finest wheat flour make round loaves without yeast, thick loaves without yeast and with olive oil mixed in, and thin loaves without yeast and brushed with olive oil. 3Put them in a basket and present them in it—along with the bull and the two rams. 4Then bring Aaron and his sons to the entrance to the tent of meeting and wash them with water. 5Take the garments and dress Aaron with the tunic, the robe of the ephod, the ephod itself and the breastpiece. Fasten the ephod on him by its skilfully woven waistband. 6Put the turban on his head and attach the sacred emblem to the turban. 7Take the anointing oil and anoint him by pouring it on his head. 8Bring his sons and dress them in tunics 9and fasten caps on them. Then tie sashes on Aaron and his sons.[a] The priesthood is theirs by a lasting ordinance. Then you shall ordain Aaron and his sons.

10'Bring the bull to the front of the tent of meeting, and Aaron and his sons shall lay their hands on its head. 11Slaughter it in the LORD's presence at the entrance to the tent of meeting. 12Take some of the bull's blood and put it on the horns of the altar with your finger, and pour out the rest of it at the base of the altar. 13Then take all the fat on the internal organs, the covering of the liver, and both kidneys with the fat on them, and burn them on the altar. 14But burn the bull's flesh and its hide and its intestines outside the camp. It is a sin offering.[b]

15'Take one of the rams, and Aaron and his sons shall lay their hands on its head. 16Slaughter it and take the blood and splash it against the sides of the altar. 17Cut the ram into pieces and wash the internal organs and the legs, putting them with the head and the other pieces. 18Then burn the entire ram on the altar. It is a burnt offering to the LORD, a pleasing aroma, a food offering presented to the LORD.

19'Take the other ram, and Aaron and his sons shall lay their hands on its head. 20Slaughter it, take some of its blood and put it on the lobes of the right ears of Aaron and his sons, on the thumbs of their right hands, and on the big toes of their right feet. Then splash blood against the sides of the altar. 21And take some of the blood on the altar and some of the anointing oil and sprinkle it on Aaron and his garments and on his sons and their garments. Then he and his sons and their garments will be consecrated.

22'Take from this ram the fat, the fat tail, the fat on the internal organs, the covering of the liver, both kidneys with the fat on them, and the right thigh. (This is the ram for the ordination.) 23From the basket of bread made without yeast, which is before the LORD, take one round loaf, one thick loaf with olive oil mixed in, and one thin loaf. 24Put all these in the hands of Aaron and his sons and wave them before the LORD as a wave offering. 25Then take them from their hands and burn them on the altar along with the burnt offering for a pleasing aroma to the LORD, a food offering presented to the LORD. 26After you take the breast of the ram for Aaron's ordination, wave it before the LORD as a wave offering, and it will be your share.

27'Consecrate those parts of the ordination ram that belong to Aaron and his sons: the breast that was waved and the thigh that was presented. 28This is always to be the regular share from the Israelites for Aaron and his sons. It is the contribution the Israelites are to make to the LORD from their fellowship offerings.

29'Aaron's sacred garments will belong to his descendants so that they can be anointed and ordained in them. 30The son who succeeds him as priest and comes to the tent of meeting to minister in the Holy Place is to wear them seven days.

---

[a]9 Hebrew; Septuagint *on them*   [b]14 Or *purification offering*; also in verse 36

IN OTHER WORDS

Atonement
Exodus 29:36

There's a clue to this word's meaning in its spelling. It means 'making at one' – putting things right between God and the human race. Atonement happened through sacrifices in the Old Testament, and through the death and resurrection of Jesus in the New Testament (Romans 3:25).

31'Take the ram for the ordination and cook the meat in a sacred place. 32At the entrance to the tent of meeting, Aaron and his sons are to eat the meat of the ram and the bread that is in the basket. 33They are to eat these offerings by which atonement was made for their ordination and consecration. But no-one else may eat them, because they are sacred. 34And if any of the meat of the ordination ram or any bread is left over till morning, burn it up. It must not be eaten, because it is sacred.

35'Do for Aaron and his sons everything I have commanded you, taking seven days to ordain them. 36Sacrifice a bull each day as a sin offering to make atonement. Purify the altar by making atonement for it, and anoint it to consecrate it. 37For seven days make atonement for the altar and consecrate it. Then the altar will be most holy, and whatever touches it will be holy.

38'This is what you are to offer on the altar regularly each day: two lambs a year old. 39Offer one in the morning and the other at twilight. 40With the first lamb offer a tenth of an ephah^a of the finest flour mixed with a quarter of a hin^b of oil from pressed olives, and a quarter of a hin of wine as a drink offering. 41Sacrifice the other lamb at twilight with the same grain offering and its drink offering as in the morning—a pleasing aroma, a food offering presented to the LORD.

42'For the generations to come this burnt offering is to be made regularly at the entrance to the tent of meeting before the LORD. There I will meet you and speak to you; 43there also I will meet with the Israelites, and the place will be consecrated by my glory.

44'So I will consecrate the tent of meeting and the altar and will consecrate Aaron and his sons to serve me as priests. 45Then I will dwell among the Israelites and be their God. 46They will know that I am the LORD their God, who brought them out of Egypt so that I might dwell among them. I am the LORD their God.

The altar of incense

30 'Make an altar of acacia wood for burning incense. 2It is to be square, a cubit long and a cubit wide, and two cubits high^c—its horns of one piece with it. 3Overlay the top and all the sides and the horns with pure gold, and make a gold moulding around it. 4Make two gold rings for the altar below the moulding—two on each of the opposite sides—to hold the poles used to carry it. 5Make the poles of acacia wood and overlay them with gold. 6Put the altar in front of the curtain that shields the ark of the covenant law—before the atonement cover that is over the tablets of the covenant law—where I will meet with you.

7'Aaron must burn fragrant incense on the altar every morning when he tends the lamps. 8He must burn incense again when he lights the lamps at twilight so that incense will burn regularly before the LORD for the generations to come. 9Do not offer on this altar any other incense or any burnt offering or grain offering, and do not pour a drink offering on it. 10Once a year Aaron shall make atonement on its horns. This annual atonement must be made with the blood of the atoning sin offering^d for the generations to come. It is most holy to the LORD.'

Atonement money

11Then the LORD said to Moses, 12'When you take a census of the Israelites to count them, each one must pay the LORD a ransom

---

^{a}40 That is, probably about 1.5 kilograms ^{b}40 That is, probably about 0.9 litre ^{c}2 That is, about 45 centimetres long and wide and 90 centimetres high ^{d}10 Or *purification offering* for his life at the time he is counted. Then no plague will come on them when you number them. 13Each one who crosses over to those already counted is to give a half shekel,*a* according to the sanctuary shekel, which weighs twenty gerahs. This half shekel is an offering to the LORD. 14All who cross over, those twenty years old or more, are to give an offering to the LORD. 15The rich are not to give more than a half shekel and the poor are not to give less when you make the offering to the LORD to atone for your lives. 16Receive the atonement money from the Israelites and use it for the service of the tent of meeting. It will be a memorial for the Israelites before the LORD, making atonement for your lives.'

Basin for washing

17Then the LORD said to Moses, 18'Make a bronze basin, with its bronze stand, for washing. Place it between the tent of meeting and the altar, and put water in it. 19Aaron and his sons are to wash their hands and feet with water from it. 20Whenever they enter the tent of meeting, they shall wash with water so that they will not die. Also, when they approach the altar to minister by presenting a food offering to the LORD, 21they shall wash their hands and feet so that they will not die. This is to be a lasting ordinance for Aaron and his descendants for the generations to come.'

Anointing oil

22Then the LORD said to Moses, 23'Take the following fine spices: 500 shekels*b* of liquid myrrh, half as much (that is, 250 shekels) of fragrant cinnamon, 250 shekels*c* of fragrant calamus, 24500 shekels of cassia—all according to the sanctuary shekel—and a hin*d* of olive oil. 25Make these into a sacred anointing oil, a fragrant blend, the work of a perfumer. It will be the sacred anointing oil. 26Then use it to anoint the tent of meeting, the ark of the covenant law, 27the table and all its articles, the lampstand and its accessories, the altar of incense, 28the altar of burnt offering and all its utensils, and the basin with its stand. 29You shall consecrate them so they will be most holy, and whatever touches them will be holy.

30'Anoint Aaron and his sons and consecrate them so they may serve me as priests. 31Say to the Israelites, "This is to be my sacred anointing oil for the generations to come. 32Do not pour it on anyone else's body and do not make any other oil using the same formula. It is sacred, and you are to consider it sacred. 33Whoever makes perfume like it and puts it on anyone other than a priest must be cut off from their people." '

Incense

34Then the LORD said to Moses, 'Take fragrant spices—gum resin, onycha and galbanum—and pure frankincense, all in equal amounts, 35and make a fragrant blend of incense, the work of a perfumer. It is to be salted and pure and sacred. 36Grind some of it to powder and place it in front of the ark of the covenant law in the tent of meeting, where I will meet with you. It shall be most holy to you. 37Do not make any incense with this formula for yourselves; consider it holy to the LORD. 38Whoever makes incense like it to enjoy its fragrance must be cut off from their people.'

Bezalel and Oholiab

31 Then the LORD said to Moses, 2'See I have chosen Bezalel son of Uri, the son of Hur, of the tribe of Judah, 3and I have filled him with the Spirit of God, with wisdom, with understanding, with knowledge and with all kinds of skills— 4to make artistic designs for work in gold, silver and bronze, 5to cut and set stones, to work in wood, and to engage in all kinds of crafts. 6Moreover, I have appointed Oholiab son of Ahisamak, of the tribe of Dan, to help him. Also I have given ability to all the skilled workers to make everything I have commanded you: 7the tent of meeting, the ark of the covenant law with the atonement cover on it, and all the other furnishings of the tent— 8the table and its articles, the pure gold lampstand and all its accessories, the altar of incense, 9the altar of burnt offering and all its utensils, the basin with its stand— 10and also the woven garments, both the

---

a 13 That is, about 5.7 grams; also in verse 15   *b* 23 That is, about 5.8 kilograms; also in verse 24   *c* 23 That is, about 2.9 kilograms   *d* 24 That is, probably about 3.6 litres

People and Places

Bezalel
Exodus 31:2

Bezalel has the honour of being the first person in the Bible to be filled with God's Spirit for a special task. And what was that task? Preaching to thousands, destroying lots of God's enemies, healing people from horrible diseases? Actually, he was filled with the Spirit to be an artist – to work with wood, precious metals and jewels in the tabernacle to make it a beautiful and special place in which to worship God.

---

sacred garments for Aaron the priest and the garments for his sons when they serve as priests, 11and the anointing oil and fragrant incense for the Holy Place. They are to make them just as I commanded you.'

The Sabbath

12Then the LORD said to Moses, 13'Say to the Israelites, "You must observe my Sabbaths. This will be a sign between me and you for the generations to come, so that you may know that I am the LORD, who makes you holy.

14 "Observe the Sabbath, because it is holy to you. Anyone who desecrates it is to be put to death; those who do any work on that day must be cut off from their people. 15For six days work is to be done, but the seventh day is a day of sabbath rest, holy to the LORD. Whoever does any work on the Sabbath day is to be put to death. 16The Israelites are to observe the Sabbath, celebrating it for the generations to come as a lasting covenant. 17It will be a sign between me and the Israelites for ever, for in six days the LORD made the heavens and the earth, and on the seventh day he abstained from work and rested."'

18When the LORD finished speaking to Moses on Mount Sinai, he gave him the two tablets of the covenant law, the tablets of stone inscribed by the finger of God.

The golden calf

32 When the people saw that Moses was so long in coming down from the mountain, they gathered round Aaron and said, 'Come, make us gods[a] who will go before us. As for this fellow Moses who brought us up out of Egypt, we don't know what has happened to him.'

2Aaron answered them, 'Take off the gold ear-rings that your wives, your sons and your daughters are wearing, and bring them to me.' 3So all the people took off their ear-rings and brought them to Aaron. 4He took what they handed him and made it into an idol cast in the shape of a calf, fashioning it with a tool. Then they said, 'These are your gods,[b] Israel, who brought you up out of Egypt.'

5When Aaron saw this, he built an altar in front of the calf and announced, 'Tomorrow there will be a festival to the LORD.' 6So the next day the people rose early and sacrificed burnt offerings and presented fellowship offerings. Afterwards they sat down to eat and drink and got up to indulge in revelry.

7Then the LORD said to Moses, 'Go down, because your people, whom you brought up out of Egypt, have become corrupt. 8They have been quick to turn away from what I commanded them and have made themselves an idol cast in the shape of a calf. They have bowed down to it and sacrificed to it and have said, "These are your gods, Israel, who brought you up out of Egypt."

9'I have seen these people,' the LORD said to Moses, 'and they are a stiff-necked people. 10Now leave me alone so that my anger may burn against them and that I may destroy them. Then I will make you into a great nation.'

11But Moses sought the favour of the LORD his God. 'LORD,' he said, 'why should your anger burn against your people, whom you brought out of Egypt with great power and a mighty hand? 12Why should the Egyptians say, "It was with evil intent that

---

[a] 1 Or *a god*; also in verses 23 and 31   [b] 4 Or *This is your god*; also in verse 8

he brought them out, to kill them in the mountains and to wipe them off the face of the earth"? Turn from your fierce anger; relent and do not bring disaster on your people. 13Remember your servants Abraham, Isaac and Israel, to whom you swore by your own self: "I will make your descendants as numerous as the stars in the sky and I will give your descendants all this land I promised them, and it will be their inheritance for ever."' 14Then the LORD relented and did not bring on his people the disaster he had threatened.

15Moses turned and went down the mountain with the two tablets of the covenant law in his hands. They were inscribed on both sides, front and back. 16The tablets were the work of God; the writing was the writing of God, engraved on the tablets.

17When Joshua heard the noise of the people shouting, he said to Moses, 'There is the sound of war in the camp.'

18Moses replied:

'It is not the sound of victory,
 it is not the sound of defeat;
 it is the sound of singing that I hear.'

19When Moses approached the camp and saw the calf and the dancing, his anger burned and he threw the tablets out of his hands, breaking them to pieces at the foot of the mountain. 20And he took the calf they had made and burned it in the fire; then he ground it to powder, scattered it on the water and made the Israelites drink it.

21He said to Aaron, 'What did these people do to you, that you led them into such great sin?'

22'Do not be angry, my lord,' Aaron answered. 'You know how prone these people are to evil. 23They said to me, "Make us gods who will go before us. As for this fellow Moses who brought us up out of Egypt, we don't know what has happened to him." 24So I told them, "Whoever has any gold jewellery, take it off." Then they gave me the gold, and I threw it into the fire, and out came this calf!'

25Moses saw that the people were running wild and that Aaron had let them get out of control and so become a laughingstock to their enemies. 26So he stood at the entrance to the camp and said, 'Whoever is for the LORD, come to me.' And all the Levites rallied to him.

27Then he said to them, 'This is what the LORD, the God of Israel, says: "Each man strap a sword to his side. Go back and forth through the camp from one end to the other, each killing his brother and friend and neighbour."' 28The Levites did as Moses commanded, and that day about three thousand of the people died. 29Then Moses said, 'You have been set apart to the LORD today, for you were against your own sons and brothers, and he has blessed you this day.'

30The next day Moses said to the people, 'You have committed a great sin. But now I will go up to the LORD; perhaps I can make atonement for your sin.'

31So Moses went back to the LORD and said, 'Oh, what a great sin these people have committed! They have made themselves gods of gold. 32But now, please forgive their sin—but if not, then blot me out of the book you have written.'

33The LORD replied to Moses, 'Whoever has sinned against me I will blot out of my book. 34Now go, lead the people to the place I spoke of, and my angel will go before you. However, when the time comes for me to punish, I will punish them for their sin.'

35And the LORD struck the people with a plague because of what they did with the calf Aaron had made.

33

Then the LORD said to Moses, 'Leave this place, you and the people you brought up out of Egypt, and go up to the land I promised on oath to Abraham, Isaac and Jacob, saying, "I will give it to your descendants." 2I will send an angel before you and drive out the Canaanites, Amorites, Hittites, Perizzites, Hivites and Jebusites. 3Go up to the land flowing with milk and honey. But I will not go with you, because you are a stiff-necked people and I might destroy you on the way.'

4When the people heard these distressing words, they began to mourn and no-one put on any ornaments. 5For the LORD had said to Moses, 'Tell the Israelites, "You are a stiff-necked people. If I were to go with you even for a moment, I might destroy you. Now take off your ornaments and I will decide what to do with you."' 6So the Israelites stripped off their ornaments at Mount Horeb.

The tent of meeting

7Now Moses used to take a tent and pitch it outside the camp some distance away, calling it the 'tent of meeting'. Anyone enquiring of the LORD would go to the tent of meeting outside the camp. 8And whenever Moses went out to the tent, all the people rose and stood at the entrances to their tents, watching Moses until he entered the tent. 9As Moses went into the tent, the pillar of cloud would come down and stay at the entrance, while the LORD spoke with Moses. 10Whenever the people saw the pillar of cloud standing at the entrance to the tent, they all stood and worshipped at the entrances to their tents. 11The LORD would speak to Moses face to face, as one speaks to a friend. Then Moses would return to the camp, but his young assistant Joshua son of Nun did not leave the tent.

Moses and the glory of the LORD

12Moses said to the LORD, 'You have been telling me, "Lead these people," but you have not let me know whom you will send with me. You have said, "I know you by name and you have found favour with me." 13If you are pleased with me, teach me your ways so I may know you and continue to find favour with you. Remember that this nation is your people.'

14The LORD replied, 'My Presence will go with you, and I will give you rest.'

15Then Moses said to him, 'If your Presence does not go with us, do not send us up from here. 16How will anyone know that you are pleased with me and with your people unless you go with us? What else will distinguish me and your people from all the other people on the face of the earth?'

17And the LORD said to Moses, 'I will do the very thing you have asked, because I am pleased with you and I know you by name.'

18Then Moses said, 'Now show me your glory.'

19And the LORD said, 'I will cause all my goodness to pass in front of you, and I will proclaim my name, the LORD, in your presence. I will have mercy on whom I will have mercy, and I will have compassion on whom I will have compassion. 20But,' he said, 'you cannot see my face, for no-one may see me and live.'

21Then the LORD said, 'There is a place near me where you may stand on a rock. 22When my glory passes by, I will put you in a cleft in the rock and cover you with my hand until I have passed by. 23Then I will remove my hand and you will see my back; but my face must not be seen.'

The new stone tablets

34 The LORD said to Moses, 'Chisel out two stone tablets like the first ones, and I will write on them the words that were on the first tablets, which you broke. 2Be ready in the morning, and then come up on Mount Sinai. Present yourself to me there on top of the mountain. 3No-one is to come with you or be seen anywhere on the mountain; not even the flocks and herds may graze in front of the mountain.'

4So Moses chiselled out two stone tablets like the first ones and went up Mount Sinai early in the morning, as the LORD had commanded him; and he carried the two stone tablets in his hands. 5Then the LORD came down in the cloud and stood there with him and proclaimed his name,

IN OTHER WORDS

Glory
Exodus 33:18

The word 'glory' in Hebrew comes from another word meaning 'heavy' and originally described the part of a person's character which impresses you the most. In the Bible, 'glory' is often used to describe the presence of God, his power and character, or an event such as Jesus' crucifixion which points to God.

the LORD. 6And he passed in front of Moses, proclaiming, 'The LORD, the LORD, the compassionate and gracious God, slow to anger, abounding in love and faithfulness, 7maintaining love to thousands, and forgiving wickedness, rebellion and sin. Yet he does not leave the guilty unpunished; he punishes the children and their children for the sin of the parents to the third and fourth generation.'

8Moses bowed to the ground at once and worshipped. 9'Lord,' he said, 'if I have found favour in your eyes, then let the Lord go with us. Although this is a stiff-necked people, forgive our wickedness and our sin, and take us as your inheritance.'

10Then the LORD said: 'I am making a covenant with you. Before all your people I will do wonders never before done in any nation in all the world. The people you live among will see how awesome is the work that I, the LORD, will do for you. 11Obey what I command you today. I will drive out before you the Amorites, Canaanites, Hittites, Perizzites, Hivites and Jebusites. 12Be careful not to make a treaty with those who live in the land where you are going, or they will be a snare among you. 13Break down their altars, smash their sacred stones and cut down their Asherah poles.^{a} 14Do not worship any other god, for the LORD, whose name is Jealous, is a jealous God.

15'Be careful not to make a treaty with those who live in the land; for when they prostitute themselves to their gods and sacrifice to them, they will invite you and you will eat their sacrifices. 16And when you choose some of their daughters as wives for your sons and those daughters prostitute themselves to their gods, they will lead your sons to do the same.

17'Do not make any idols.

18'Celebrate the Festival of Unleavened Bread. For seven days eat bread made without yeast, as I commanded you. Do this at the appointed time in the month of Aviv, for in that month you came out of Egypt.

19'The first offspring of every womb belongs to me, including all the firstborn males of your livestock, whether from herd or flock. 20Redeem the firstborn donkey with a lamb, but if you do not redeem it, break its neck. Redeem all your firstborn sons.

'No-one is to appear before me empty-handed.

21'Six days you shall labour, but on the seventh day you shall rest; even during the ploughing season and harvest you must rest.

22'Celebrate the Festival of Weeks with the firstfruits of the wheat harvest, and the Festival of Ingathering at the turn of the year.^{b} 23Three times a year all your men are to appear before the Sovereign LORD, the God of Israel. 24I will drive out nations before you and enlarge your territory, and no-one will covet your land when you go up three times each year to appear before the LORD your God.

25'Do not offer the blood of a sacrifice to me along with anything containing yeast, and do not let any of the sacrifice from the Passover Festival remain until morning.

26'Bring the best of the firstfruits of your soil to the house of the LORD your God.

'Do not cook a young goat in its mother's milk.'

27Then the LORD said to Moses, 'Write down these words, for in accordance with these words I have made a covenant with you and with Israel.' 28Moses was there with the LORD forty days and forty nights without eating bread or drinking water. And he wrote on the tablets the words of the covenant—the Ten Commandments.

The radiant face of Moses

29When Moses came down from Mount Sinai with the two tablets of the covenant law in his hands, he was not aware that his face was radiant because he had spoken with the LORD. 30When Aaron and all the Israelites saw Moses, his face was radiant, and they were afraid to come near him. 31But Moses called to them; so Aaron and all the leaders of the community came back to him, and he spoke to them. 32Afterwards all the Israelites came near him, and he gave them all the commands the LORD had given him on Mount Sinai.

---

^{a}13 That is, wooden symbols of the goddess Asherah ^{b}22 That is, in the autumn

33When Moses finished speaking to them, he put a veil over his face. 34But whenever he entered the LORD's presence to speak with him, he removed the veil until he came out. And when he came out and told the Israelites what he had been commanded, 35they saw that his face was radiant. Then Moses would put the veil back over his face until he went in to speak with the LORD.

Sabbath regulations

35 Moses assembled the whole Israelite community and said to them, 'These are the things the LORD has commanded you to do: 2for six days, work is to be done, but the seventh day shall be your holy day, a day of sabbath rest to the LORD. Whoever does any work on it is to be put to death. 3Do not light a fire in any of your dwellings on the Sabbath day.'

Materials for the tabernacle

4Moses said to the whole Israelite community, 'This is what the LORD has commanded: 5from what you have, take an offering for the LORD. Everyone who is willing is to bring to the LORD an offering of gold, silver and bronze; 6blue, purple and scarlet yarn and fine linen; goat hair; 7ram skins dyed red and other durable leather;[a] acacia wood; 8olive oil for the light; spices for the anointing oil and for the fragrant incense; 9and onyx stones and other gems to be mounted on the ephod and breastpiece.

10'All who are skilled among you are to come and make everything the LORD has commanded: 11the tabernacle with its tent and its covering, clasps, frames, crossbars, posts and bases; 12the ark with its poles and the atonement cover and the curtain that shields it; 13the table with its poles and all its articles and the bread of the Presence; 14the lampstand that is for light with its accessories, lamps and oil for the light; 15the altar of incense with its poles, the anointing oil and the fragrant incense; the curtain for the doorway at the entrance to the tabernacle; 16the altar of burnt offering with its bronze grating, its poles and all its utensils; the bronze basin with its stand; 17the curtains of the courtyard with its posts and bases, and the curtain for the entrance to the courtyard; 18the tent pegs for the tabernacle and for the courtyard, and their ropes; 19the woven garments worn for ministering in the sanctuary—both the sacred garments for Aaron the priest and the garments for his sons when they serve as priests.'

20Then the whole Israelite community withdrew from Moses' presence, 21and everyone who was willing and whose heart moved them came and brought an offering to the LORD for the work on the tent of meeting, for all its service, and for the sacred garments. 22All who were willing, men and women alike, came and brought gold jewellery of all kinds: brooches, ear-rings, rings and ornaments. They all presented their gold as a wave offering to the LORD. 23Everyone who had blue, purple or scarlet yarn or fine linen, or goat hair, ram skins dyed red or other durable leather brought them. 24Those presenting an offering of silver or bronze brought it as an offering to the LORD, and everyone who had acacia wood for any part of the work brought it. 25Every skilled woman spun with her hands and brought what she had spun—blue, purple or scarlet yarn or fine linen. 26And all

---

Sign of the times

Gold jewellery
Exodus 35:22

The Israelites had taken gold jewellery from the Egyptians as they left Egypt and here they passed it on to Moses to help build the temple. The cloth they gave was pretty special too – fine linen was only worn by the wealthiest people, and the colours blue, red and purple were considered to be royal colours because the dyes were so expensive to make.

---

[a] 7 Possibly the hides of large aquatic mammals; also in verse 23

the women who were willing and had the skill spun the goat hair. 27The leaders brought onyx stones and other gems to be mounted on the ephod and breastpiece. 28They also brought spices and olive oil for the light and for the anointing oil and for the fragrant incense. 29All the Israelite men and women who were willing brought to the LORD freewill offerings for all the work the LORD through Moses had commanded them to do.

Bezalel and Oholiab

30Then Moses said to the Israelites, 'See, the LORD has chosen Bezalel son of Uri, the son of Hur, of the tribe of Judah, 31and he has filled him with the Spirit of God, with wisdom, with understanding, with knowledge and with all kinds of skills— 32to make artistic designs for work in gold, silver and bronze, 33to cut and set stones, to work in wood and to engage in all kinds of artistic crafts. 34And he has given both him and Oholiab son of Ahisamak, of the tribe of Dan, the ability to teach others. 35He has filled them with skill to do all kinds of work as engravers, designers, embroiderers in blue, purple and scarlet yarn and fine linen, and weavers—all of them skilled workers and designers. **36** 1So Bezalel, Oholiab and every skilled person to whom the LORD has given skill and ability to know how to carry out all the work of constructing the sanctuary are to do the work just as the LORD has commanded.'

2Then Moses summoned Bezalel and Oholiab and every skilled person to whom the LORD had given ability and who was willing to come and do the work. 3They received from Moses all the offerings the Israelites had brought to carry out the work of constructing the sanctuary. And the people continued to bring freewill offerings morning after morning. 4So all the skilled workers who were doing all the work on the sanctuary left what they were doing 5and said to Moses, 'The people are bringing more than enough for doing the work the LORD commanded to be done.'

6Then Moses gave an order and they sent this word throughout the camp: 'No man or woman is to make anything else as an offering for the sanctuary.' And so the people were restrained from bringing more, 7because what they already had was more than enough to do all the work.

The tabernacle

8All those who were skilled among the workers made the tabernacle with ten curtains of finely twisted linen and blue, purple and scarlet yarn, with cherubim worked into them by expert hands. 9All the curtains were the same size—twenty-eight cubits long and four cubits wide.[a] 10They joined five of the curtains together and did the same with the other five. 11Then they made loops of blue material along the edge of the end curtain in one set, and the same was done with the end curtain in the other set. 12They also made fifty loops on one curtain and fifty loops on the end curtain of the other set, with the loops opposite each other. 13Then they made fifty gold clasps and used them to fasten the two sets of curtains together so that the tabernacle was a unit.

14They made curtains of goat hair for the tent over the tabernacle—eleven altogether. 15All eleven curtains were the same size—thirty cubits long and four cubits wide.[b] 16They joined five of the curtains into one set and the other six into another set. 17Then they made fifty loops along the edge of the end curtain in one set and also along the edge of the end curtain in the other set. 18They made fifty bronze clasps to fasten the tent together as a unit. 19Then they made for the tent a covering of ram skins dyed red, and over that a covering of other durable leather.[c]

20They made upright frames of acacia wood for the tabernacle. 21Each frame was ten cubits long and a cubit and a half wide,[d] 22with two projections set parallel to each other. They made all the frames of the tabernacle in this way. 23They made twenty frames for the south side of the tabernacle 24and made forty silver bases to go under

---

[a] 9 That is, about 13 metres long and 1.8 metres wide [b] 15 That is, about 13.5 metres long and 1.8 metres wide
[c] 19 Possibly the hides of large aquatic mammals [d] 21 That is, about 4.5 metres long and 67 centimetres wide

them—two bases for each frame, one under each projection. 25For the other side, the north side of the tabernacle, they made twenty frames 26and forty silver bases—two under each frame. 27They made six frames for the far end, that is, the west end of the tabernacle, 28and two frames were made for the corners of the tabernacle at the far end. 29At these two corners the frames were double from the bottom all the way to the top and fitted into a single ring; both were made alike. 30So there were eight frames and sixteen silver bases—two under each frame.

31They also made crossbars of acacia wood: five for the frames on one side of the tabernacle, 32five for those on the other side, and five for the frames on the west, at the far end of the tabernacle. 33They made the centre crossbar so that it extended from end to end at the middle of the frames. 34They overlaid the frames with gold and made gold rings to hold the crossbars. They also overlaid the crossbars with gold.

35They made the curtain of blue, purple and scarlet yarn and finely twisted linen, with cherubim worked into it by expert hands. 36They made four posts of acacia wood for it and overlaid them with gold. They made gold hooks for them and cast their four silver bases. 37For the entrance to the tent they made a curtain of blue, purple and scarlet yarn and finely twisted linen— the work of an embroiderer; 38and they made five posts with hooks for them. They overlaid the tops of the posts and their bands with gold and made their five bases of bronze.

The ark

37 Bezalel made the ark of acacia wood—two and a half cubits long, a cubit and a half wide, and a cubit and a half high.^{a} 2He overlaid it with pure gold, both inside and out, and made a gold moulding around it. 3He cast four gold rings for it and fastened them to its four feet, with two rings on one side and two rings on the other. 4Then he made poles of acacia wood and overlaid them with gold. 5And he inserted the poles into the rings on the sides of the ark to carry it.

6He made the atonement cover of pure gold—two and a half cubits long and a cubit and a half wide. 7Then he made two cherubim out of hammered gold at the ends of the cover. 8He made one cherub on one end and the second cherub on the other; at the two ends he made them of one piece with the cover. 9The cherubim had their wings spread upwards, overshadowing the cover with them. The cherubim faced each other, looking towards the cover.

The table

10They^b made the table of acacia wood— two cubits long, a cubit wide and a cubit and a half high.^{c} 11Then they overlaid it with pure gold and made a gold moulding around it. 12They also made around it a rim a handbreadth^d wide and put a gold moulding on the rim. 13They cast four gold rings for the table and fastened them to the four corners, where the four legs were. 14The rings were put close to the rim to hold the poles used in carrying the table. 15The poles for carrying the table were made of acacia wood and were overlaid with gold. 16And they made from pure gold the articles for the table—its plates and dishes and bowls and its pitchers for the pouring out of drink offerings.

The lampstand

17They made the lampstand of pure gold. They hammered out its base and shaft, and made its flowerlike cups, buds and blossoms of one piece with them. 18Six branches extended from the sides of the lampstand—three on one side and three on the other. 19Three cups shaped like almond flowers with buds and blossoms were on one branch, three on the next branch and the same for all six branches extending from the lampstand. 20And on the lampstand were four cups shaped like almond flowers with buds and blossoms. 21One bud was under the first pair of branches extending from the lampstand, a second bud under the second pair, and a third bud

---

^{a} 1 That is, about 1.1 metres long and 67 centimetres wide and high; also in verse 6 ^{b} 10 Or *He*; also in verses 11-29 ^{c} 10 That is, about 90 centimetres long, 45 centimetres wide and 67 centimetres high ^{d} 12 That is, about 7.5 centimetres under the third pair—six branches in all. 22The buds and the branches were all of one piece with the lampstand, hammered out of pure gold.

23They made its seven lamps, as well as its wick trimmers and trays, of pure gold. 24They made the lampstand and all its accessories from one talent[a] of pure gold.

The altar of incense

25They made the altar of incense out of acacia wood. It was square, a cubit long and a cubit wide and two cubits high[b]—its horns of one piece with it. 26They overlaid the top and all the sides and the horns with pure gold, and made a gold moulding around it. 27They made two gold rings below the moulding—two on each of the opposite sides—to hold the poles used to carry it. 28They made the poles of acacia wood and overlaid them with gold.

29They also made the sacred anointing oil and the pure, fragrant incense—the work of a perfumer.

The altar of burnt offering

38 They[c] built the altar of burnt offering of acacia wood, three cubits[d] high; it was square, five cubits long and five cubits wide.[e] 2They made a horn at each of the four corners, so that the horns and the altar were of one piece, and they overlaid the altar with bronze. 3They made all its utensils of bronze—its pots, shovels, sprinkling bowls, meat forks and firepans. 4They made a grating for the altar, a bronze network, to be under its ledge, halfway up the altar. 5They cast bronze rings to hold the poles for the four corners of the bronze grating. 6They made the poles of acacia wood and overlaid them with bronze. 7They inserted the poles into the rings so they would be on the sides of the altar for carrying it. They made it hollow, out of boards.

The basin for washing

8They made the bronze basin and its bronze stand from the mirrors of the women who served at the entrance to the tent of meeting.

The courtyard

9Next they made the courtyard. The south side was a hundred cubits[f] long and had curtains of finely twisted linen, 10with twenty posts and twenty bronze bases, and with silver hooks and bands on the posts. 11The north side was also a hundred cubits long and had twenty posts and twenty bronze bases, with silver hooks and bands on the posts.

12The west end was fifty cubits[g] wide and had curtains, with ten posts and ten bases, with silver hooks and bands on the posts. 13The east end, towards the sunrise, was also fifty cubits wide. 14Curtains fifteen cubits[h] long were on one side of the entrance, with three posts and three bases, 15and curtains fifteen cubits long were on the other side of the entrance to the courtyard, with three posts and three bases. 16All the curtains around the courtyard were of finely twisted linen. 17The bases for the posts were bronze. The hooks and bands on the posts were silver, and their tops were overlaid with silver; so all the posts of the courtyard had silver bands.

18The curtain for the entrance to the courtyard was of blue, purple and scarlet yarn and finely twisted linen—the work of an embroiderer. It was twenty cubits[i] long and, like the curtains of the courtyard, five cubits[j] high, 19with four posts and four bronze bases. Their hooks and bands were

---

IN OTHER WORDS

Altar
Exodus 38:1
An altar was a stone or table where people worshipped or sacrificed offerings to God. Pagan religions had them too.

---

[a] 24 That is, about 34 kilograms [b] 25 That is, about 45 centimetres long and wide and 90 centimetres high [c] 1 Or He; also in verses 2-9 [d] 1 That is, about 1.4 metres [e] 1 That is, about 2.3 metres long and wide [f] 9 That is, about 45 metres [g] 12 That is, about 22.5 metres [h] 14 That is, about 6.8 metres [i] 18 That is, about 9 metres [j] 18 That is, about 2.3 metres

silver, and their tops were overlaid with silver. 20All the tent pegs of the tabernacle and of the surrounding courtyard were bronze.

The materials used

21These are the amounts of the materials used for the tabernacle, the tabernacle of the covenant law, which were recorded at Moses' command by the Levites under the direction of Ithamar son of Aaron, the priest. 22(Bezalel son of Uri, the son of Hur, of the tribe of Judah, made everything the LORD commanded Moses; 23with him was Oholiab son of Ahisamak, of the tribe of Dan—an engraver and designer, and an embroiderer in blue, purple and scarlet yarn and fine linen.) 24The total amount of the gold from the wave offering used for all the work on the sanctuary was 29 talents and 730 shekels,^{a} according to the sanctuary shekel.

25The silver obtained from those of the community who were counted in the census was 100 talents^b and 1,775 shekels,^{c} according to the sanctuary shekel. 26one beka per person, that is, half a shekel,^{d} according to the sanctuary shekel, from everyone who had crossed over to those counted, twenty years old or more, a total of 603,550 men. 27The 100 talents of silver were used to cast the bases for the sanctuary and for the curtain—100 bases from the 100 talents, one talent for each base. 28They used the 1,775 shekels to make the hooks for the posts, to overlay the tops of the posts, and to make their bands.

29The bronze from the wave offering was 70 talents and 2,400 shekels.^{e} 30They used it to make the bases for the entrance to the tent of meeting, the bronze altar with its bronze grating and all its utensils, 31the bases for the surrounding courtyard and those for its entrance and all the tent pegs for the tabernacle and those for the surrounding courtyard.

The priestly garments

39 From the blue, purple and scarlet yarn they made woven garments for ministering in the sanctuary. They also made sacred garments for Aaron, as the LORD commanded Moses.

The ephod

2They^f made the ephod of gold, and of blue, purple and scarlet yarn, and of finely twisted linen. 3They hammered out thin sheets of gold and cut strands to be worked into the blue, purple and scarlet yarn and fine linen—the work of skilled hands. 4They made shoulder pieces for the ephod, which were attached to two of its corners, so that it could be fastened. 5Its skilfully woven waistband was like it—of one piece with the ephod and made with gold, and with blue, purple and scarlet yarn, and with finely twisted linen, as the LORD commanded Moses.

6They mounted the onyx stones in gold filigree settings and engraved them like a seal with the names of the sons of Israel. 7Then they fastened them on the shoulder pieces of the ephod as memorial stones for the sons of Israel, as the LORD commanded Moses.

The breastpiece

8They fashioned the breastpiece—the work of a skilled craftsman. They made it like the ephod: of gold, and of blue, purple and scarlet yarn, and of finely twisted linen. 9It was square—a span^g long and a span wide—and folded double. 10Then they mounted four rows of precious stones on it. The first row was carnelian, chrysolite and beryl; 11the second row was turquoise, lapis lazuli and emerald; 12the third row was jacinth, agate and amethyst; 13the fourth row was topaz, onyx and jasper.^{h} They were mounted in gold filigree settings. 14There were twelve stones, one for each of the names of the sons of Israel, each engraved like a seal with the name of one of the twelve tribes.

---

^{a} 24 The weight of the gold was about 1 metric ton. ^{b} 25 That is, about 3.4 metric tons; also in verse 27 ^{c} 25 That is, about 20 kilograms; also in verse 28 ^{d} 26 That is, about 5.7 grams ^{e} 29 The weight of the bronze was about 2.4 metric tons. ^{f} 2 Or *He*; also in verses 7, 8 and 22 ^{g} 9 That is, about 22.5 centimetres ^{h} 13 The precise identification of some of these precious stones is uncertain.

15For the breastpiece they made braided chains of pure gold, like a rope. 16They made two gold filigree settings and two gold rings, and fastened the rings to two of the corners of the breastpiece. 17They fastened the two gold chains to the rings at the corners of the breastpiece, 18and the other ends of the chains to the two settings, attaching them to the shoulder pieces of the ephod at the front. 19They made two gold rings and attached them to the other two corners of the breastpiece on the inside edge next to the ephod. 20Then they made two more gold rings and attached them to the bottom of the shoulder pieces on the front of the ephod, close to the seam just above the waistband of the ephod. 21They tied the rings of the breastpiece to the rings of the ephod with blue cord, connecting it to the waistband so that the breastpiece would not swing out from the ephod—as the LORD commanded Moses.

Other priestly garments

22They made the robe of the ephod entirely of blue cloth—the work of a weaver—23with an opening in the centre of the robe like the opening of a collar,[a] and a band around this opening, so that it would not tear. 24They made pomegranates of blue, purple and scarlet yarn and finely twisted linen round the hem of the robe. 25And they made bells of pure gold and attached them around the hem between the pomegranates. 26The bells and pomegranates alternated round the hem of the robe to be worn for ministering, as the LORD commanded Moses.

27For Aaron and his sons, they made tunics of fine linen—the work of a weaver—28and the turban of fine linen, the linen caps and the undergarments of finely twisted linen. 29The sash was of finely twisted linen and blue, purple and scarlet yarn—the work of an embroiderer—as the LORD commanded Moses.

30They made the plate, the sacred emblem, out of pure gold and engraved on it, like an inscription on a seal: HOLY TO THE LORD. 31Then they fastened a blue cord to it to attach it to the turban, as the LORD commanded Moses.

Moses inspects the tabernacle

32So all the work on the tabernacle, the tent of meeting, was completed. The Israelites did everything just as the LORD commanded Moses. 33Then they brought the tabernacle to Moses: the tent and all its furnishings, its clasps, frames, crossbars, posts and bases; 34the covering of ram skins dyed red and the covering of other durable leather[b] and the shielding curtain; 35the ark of the covenant law with its poles and the atonement cover; 36the table with all its articles and the bread of the Presence; 37the pure gold lampstand with its row of lamps and all its accessories, and the oil for the light; 38the gold altar, the anointing oil, the fragrant incense, and the curtain for the entrance to the tent; 39the bronze altar with its bronze grating, its poles and all its utensils; the basin with its stand; 40the curtains of the courtyard with its posts and bases, and the curtain for the entrance to the courtyard; the ropes and tent pegs for the courtyard; all the furnishings for the tabernacle, the tent of meeting; 41and the woven garments worn for ministering in the sanctuary, both the sacred garments for Aaron the priest and the garments for his sons when serving as priests.

42The Israelites had done all the work just as the LORD had commanded Moses. 43Moses inspected the work and saw that they had done it just as the LORD had commanded. So Moses blessed them.

Setting up the tabernacle

40 Then the LORD said to Moses: 2'Set up the tabernacle, the tent of meeting, on the first day of the first month. 3Place the ark of the covenant law in it and shield the ark with the curtain. 4Bring in the table and set out what belongs on it. Then bring in the lampstand and set up its lamps. 5Place the gold altar of incense in front of the ark of the covenant law and put the curtain at the entrance to the tabernacle.

6'Place the altar of burnt offering in front of the entrance to the tabernacle, the tent of meeting; 7place the basin between the tent of meeting and the altar and put water in it. 8Set up the courtyard around it

---

[a] 23 The meaning of the Hebrew for this word is uncertain. [b] 34 Possibly the hides of large aquatic mammals

and put the curtain at the entrance to the courtyard.

⁹'Take the anointing oil and anoint the tabernacle and everything in it; consecrate it and all its furnishings, and it will be holy. ¹⁰Then anoint the altar of burnt offering and all its utensils; consecrate the altar, and it will be most holy. ¹¹Anoint the basin and its stand and consecrate them.

¹²'Bring Aaron and his sons to the entrance to the tent of meeting and wash them with water. ¹³Then dress Aaron in the sacred garments, anoint him and consecrate him so that he may serve me as priest. ¹⁴Bring his sons and dress them in tunics. ¹⁵Anoint them just as you anointed their father, so that they may serve me as priests. Their anointing will be to a priesthood that will continue throughout their generations.' ¹⁶Moses did everything just as the LORD commanded him.

¹⁷So the tabernacle was set up on the first day of the first month in the second year. ¹⁸When Moses set up the tabernacle, he put the bases in place, erected the frames, inserted the crossbars and set up the posts. ¹⁹Then he spread the tent over the tabernacle and put the covering over the tent, as the LORD commanded him.

²⁰He took the tablets of the covenant law and placed them in the ark, attached the poles to the ark and put the atonement cover over it. ²¹Then he brought the ark into the tabernacle and hung the shielding curtain and shielded the ark of the covenant law, as the LORD commanded him.

²²Moses placed the table in the tent of meeting on the north side of the tabernacle outside the curtain ²³and set out the bread on it before the LORD, as the LORD commanded him.

²⁴He placed the lampstand in the tent of meeting opposite the table on the south side of the tabernacle ²⁵and set up the lamps before the LORD, as the LORD commanded him.

²⁶Moses placed the gold altar in the tent of meeting in front of the curtain ²⁷and burned fragrant incense on it, as the LORD commanded him.

²⁸Then he put up the curtain at the entrance to the tabernacle. ²⁹He set the altar

making Connections

The cloud of God's glory
Exodus 40:34

The Israelites had seen a cloud as a sign of God's presence before. When they first came out of Egypt, God guided them with a pillar of cloud by day and a pillar of fire by night. Now the cloud rests on the tabernacle to show that God's glory is filling it. And when the cloud lifts they know that it's time to move on.

of burnt offering near the entrance to the tabernacle, the tent of meeting, and offered on it burnt offerings and grain offerings, as the LORD commanded him.

³⁰He placed the basin between the tent of meeting and the altar and put water in it for washing, ³¹and Moses and Aaron and his sons used it to wash their hands and feet. ³²They washed whenever they entered the tent of meeting or approached the altar, as the LORD commanded Moses.

³³Then Moses set up the courtyard around the tabernacle and altar and put up the curtain at the entrance to the courtyard. And so Moses finished the work.

The glory of the LORD

³⁴Then the cloud covered the tent of meeting, and the glory of the LORD filled the tabernacle. ³⁵Moses could not enter the tent of meeting because the cloud had settled on it, and the glory of the LORD filled the tabernacle.

³⁶In all the travels of the Israelites, whenever the cloud lifted from above the tabernacle, they would set out; ³⁷but if the cloud did not lift, they did not set out—until the day it lifted. ³⁸So the cloud of the LORD was over the tabernacle by day, and fire was in the cloud by night, in the sight of all the house of Israel during all their travels.

Leviticus

INTRODUCTION

LEVITICUS

Author: Moses

When: Probably around 1450 BC to 1400 BC.

Where: The people of Israel were camped at Mount Sinai, after their deliverance from Egypt.

Did you know? Leviticus gets its name from the Levites, the Israelite tribe who were priests.

Main theme: Leviticus is a worship manual, full of instructions for how the Israelites were to keep holy and please God. As well as telling them what to do in worship, it explains why they need to worship God – because he loves them, has rescued them and wants to bless them so they will become a nation that reflects God's glory to the nations around them.

The burnt offering

1 The LORD called to Moses and spoke to him from the tent of meeting. He said, ²'Speak to the Israelites and say to them: "When you bring an offering to the LORD, bring as your offering an animal from either the herd or the flock.

³ "'If the offering is a burnt offering from the herd, you are to offer a male without defect. You must present it at the entrance to the tent of meeting so that you may be acceptable to the LORD. ⁴You are to lay your hand on the head of the burnt offering, and it will be accepted on your behalf to make atonement for you. ⁵You are to slaughter the young bull before the LORD, and then Aaron's sons the priests shall bring the blood and splash it against the sides of the altar at the entrance to the tent of meeting. ⁶You are to skin the burnt offering and cut it into pieces. ⁷The sons of Aaron the priest are to put fire on the altar and arrange wood on the fire. ⁸Then Aaron's sons the priests shall arrange the pieces, including the head and the fat, on the wood that is burning on the altar. ⁹You are to wash the internal

organs and the legs with water, and the priest is to burn all of it on the altar. It is a burnt offering, a food offering, an aroma pleasing to the LORD.

¹⁰ "If the offering is a burnt offering from the flock, from either the sheep or the goats, you are to offer a male without defect. ¹¹You are to slaughter it at the north side of the altar before the LORD, and Aaron's sons the priests shall splash its blood against the sides of the altar. ¹²You are to cut it into pieces, and the priest shall arrange them, including the head and the fat, on the wood that is burning on the altar. ¹³You are to wash the internal organs and the legs with water, and the priest is to bring all of them and burn them on the altar. It is a burnt offering, a food offering, an aroma pleasing to the LORD.

¹⁴ "If the offering to the LORD is a burnt offering of birds, you are to offer a dove or a young pigeon. ¹⁵The priest shall bring it to the altar, wring off the head and burn it on the altar; its blood shall be drained out on the side of the altar. ¹⁶He is to remove the crop and the feathers[a] and throw them down east of the altar where the ashes are. ¹⁷He shall tear it open by the wings, not dividing it completely, and then the priest shall burn it on the wood that is burning on the altar. It is a burnt offering, a food offering, an aroma pleasing to the LORD.

The grain offering

2 ' "When anyone brings a grain offering to the LORD, your offering is to be of the finest flour. You are to pour olive oil on it, put incense on it ²and take it to Aaron's sons the priests. The priest shall take a handful of the flour and oil, together with all the incense, and burn this as a memorial[b] portion on the altar, a food offering, an aroma pleasing to the LORD. ³The rest of the grain offering belongs to Aaron and his sons; it is a most holy part of the food offering presented to the LORD.

⁴ "If you bring a grain offering baked in an oven, it is to consist of the finest flour: either thick loaves made without yeast and with olive oil mixed in or thin loaves made without yeast and brushed with olive oil. ⁵If your grain offering is prepared on a griddle, it is to be made of the finest flour mixed with oil, and without yeast. ⁶Crumble it and pour oil on it; it is a grain offering. ⁷If your grain offering is cooked in a pan, it is to be made of the finest flour and some olive oil. ⁸Bring the grain offering made of these things to the LORD; present it to the priest, who shall take it to the altar. ⁹He shall take out the memorial portion from the grain offering and burn it on the altar as a food offering, an aroma pleasing to the LORD. ¹⁰The rest of the grain offering belongs to Aaron and his sons; it is a most holy part of the food offerings presented to the LORD.

¹¹ "Every grain offering you bring to the LORD must be made without yeast, for you are not to burn any yeast or honey in a food offering presented to the LORD. ¹²You may bring them to the LORD as an offering of the firstfruits, but they are not to be offered on the altar as a pleasing aroma. ¹³Season all your grain offerings with salt. Do not leave the salt of the covenant of your God out of your grain offerings; add salt to all your offerings.

¹⁴ "If you bring a grain offering of firstfruits to the LORD, offer crushed heads of new grain roasted in the fire. ¹⁵Put oil and incense on it; it is a grain offering. ¹⁶The priest shall burn the memorial portion of the crushed grain and the oil, together with all the incense, as a food offering presented to the LORD.

The fellowship offering

3 ' "If your offering is a fellowship offering, and you offer an animal from the herd, whether male or female, you are to present before the LORD an animal without defect. ²You are to lay your hand on the head of your offering and slaughter it at the entrance to the tent of meeting. Then Aaron's sons the priests shall splash the blood against the sides of the altar. ³From the fellowship offering you are to bring a food offering to the LORD: the internal organs and all the fat that is connected to them, ⁴both kidneys with the

---

[a] 16 Or *crop with its contents*; the meaning of the Hebrew for this word is uncertain.   [b] 2 Or *representative*; also in verses 9 and 16

> **IN OTHER WORDS**
>
> **Offering**
> Leviticus 3:1
> These different offerings provided a way for sinful people to put things right with God and draw close to him. In the New Testament, the word 'offering' means money given to God as part of worship (2 Corinthians 8:19).

fat on them near the loins, and the long lobe of the liver, which you will remove with the kidneys. ⁵Then Aaron's sons are to burn it on the altar on top of the burnt offering that is lying on the burning wood; it is a food offering, an aroma pleasing to the LORD.

⁶ "If you offer an animal from the flock as a fellowship offering to the LORD, you are to offer a male or female without defect. ⁷If you offer a lamb, you are to present it before the LORD, ⁸lay your hand on its head and slaughter it in front of the tent of meeting. Then Aaron's sons shall splash its blood against the sides of the altar. ⁹From the fellowship offering you are to bring a food offering to the LORD: its fat, the entire fat tail cut off close to the backbone, the internal organs and all the fat that is connected to them, ¹⁰both kidneys with the fat on them near the loins, and the long lobe of the liver, which you will remove with the kidneys. ¹¹The priest shall burn them on the altar as a food offering presented to the LORD.

¹² "If your offering is a goat, you are to present it before the LORD, ¹³lay your hand on its head and slaughter it in front of the tent of meeting. Then Aaron's sons shall splash its blood against the sides of the altar. ¹⁴From what you offer you are to present this food offering to the LORD: the internal organs and all the fat that is connected to them, ¹⁵both kidneys with the fat on them near the loins, and the long lobe of the liver, which you will remove with the kidneys. ¹⁶The priest shall burn them on the altar as a food offering, a pleasing aroma. All the fat is the LORD's.

¹⁷ "'This is a lasting ordinance for the generations to come, wherever you live: you must not eat any fat or any blood.'"

The sin offering

4 The LORD said to Moses, ²'Say to the Israelites: "When anyone sins unintentionally and does what is forbidden in any of the LORD's commands—

³ "'If the anointed priest sins, bringing guilt on the people, he must bring to the LORD a young bull without defect as a sin offering^a for the sin he has committed. ⁴He is to present the bull at the entrance to the tent of meeting before the LORD. He is to lay his hand on its head and slaughter it there before the LORD. ⁵Then the anointed priest shall take some of the bull's blood and carry it into the tent of meeting. ⁶He is to dip his finger into the blood and sprinkle some of it seven times before the LORD, in front of the curtain of the sanctuary. ⁷The priest shall then put some of the blood on the horns of the altar of fragrant incense that is before the LORD in the tent of meeting. The rest of the bull's blood he shall pour out at the base of the altar of burnt offering at the entrance to the tent of meeting. ⁸He shall remove all the fat from the bull of the sin offering—all the fat that is connected to the internal organs, ⁹both kidneys with the fat on them near the loins, and the long lobe of the liver, which he will remove with the kidneys— ¹⁰just as the fat is removed from the ox^b sacrificed as a fellowship offering. Then the priest shall burn them on the altar of burnt offering. ¹¹But the hide of the bull and all its flesh, as well as the head and legs, the internal organs and the intestines— ¹²that is, all the rest of the bull—he must take outside the camp to a place ceremonially clean, where the ashes are thrown, and burn it there in a wood fire on the ash heap.

¹³ "'If the whole Israelite community sins unintentionally and does what is forbidden in any of the LORD's commands, even

---

^{a} 3 Or *purification offering*; here and throughout this chapter ^{b} 10 The Hebrew word can refer to either male or female.

though the community is unaware of the matter, when they realise their guilt ¹⁴and the sin they committed becomes known, the assembly must bring a young bull as a sin offering and present it before the tent of meeting. ¹⁵The elders of the community are to lay their hands on the bull's head before the LORD, and the bull shall be slaughtered before the LORD. ¹⁶Then the anointed priest is to take some of the bull's blood into the tent of meeting. ¹⁷He shall dip his finger into the blood and sprinkle it before the LORD seven times in front of the curtain. ¹⁸He is to put some of the blood on the horns of the altar that is before the LORD in the tent of meeting. The rest of the blood he shall pour out at the base of the altar of burnt offering at the entrance to the tent of meeting. ¹⁹He shall remove all the fat from it and burn it on the altar, ²⁰and do with this bull just as he did with the bull for the sin offering. In this way the priest will make atonement for them, and they will be forgiven. ²¹Then he shall take the bull outside the camp and burn it as he burned the first bull. This is the sin offering for the community.

²²‘ "When a leader sins unintentionally and does what is forbidden in any of the commands of the LORD his God, when he realises his guilt ²³and the sin he has committed becomes known, he must bring as his offering a male goat without defect. ²⁴He is to lay his hand on the goat's head and slaughter it at the place where the burnt offering is slaughtered before the LORD. It is a sin offering. ²⁵Then the priest shall take some of the blood of the sin offering with his finger and put it on the horns of the altar of burnt offering and pour out the rest of the blood at the base of the altar. ²⁶He shall burn all the fat on the altar as he burned the fat of the fellowship offering. In this way the priest will make atonement for the leader's sin, and he will be forgiven.

²⁷‘ "If any member of the community sins unintentionally and does what is forbidden in any of the LORD's commands, when they realise their guilt ²⁸and the sin they have committed becomes known, they must bring as their offering for the sin they committed a female goat without defect. ²⁹They are to lay their hand on the head of the sin offering and slaughter it at the place of the burnt offering. ³⁰Then the priest is to take some of the blood with his finger and put it on the horns of the altar of burnt offering and pour out the rest of the blood at the base of the altar. ³¹They shall remove all the fat, just as the fat is removed from the fellowship offering, and the priest shall burn it on the altar as an aroma pleasing to the LORD. In this way the priest will make atonement for them, and they will be forgiven.

³²‘ "If they bring a lamb as their sin offering, they are to bring a female without defect. ³³They are to lay their hand on its head and slaughter it for a sin offering at the place where the burnt offering is slaughtered. ³⁴Then the priest shall take some of the blood of the sin offering with his finger and put it on the horns of the altar of burnt offering and pour out the rest of the blood at the base of the altar. ³⁵They shall remove all the fat, just as the fat is removed from the lamb of the fellowship offering, and the priest shall burn it on the altar on top of the food offerings presented to the LORD. In this way the priest will make atonement for them for the sin they have committed, and they will be forgiven.

5 ‘ "If anyone sins because they do not speak up when they hear a public charge to testify regarding something they have seen or learned about, they will be held responsible. ²Or if anyone unwittingly touches anything ceremonially unclean— whether the carcass of an unclean animal, wild or domestic, or of any unclean creature that moves along the ground—and they are unaware that they have become unclean, but then they come to realise their guilt; ³or if they touch human uncleanness—anything that would make them unclean— even though they are unaware of it, but then they learn of it and realise their guilt; ⁴or if anyone thoughtlessly takes an oath to do anything, whether good or evil—in any matter one might carelessly swear about— even though they are unaware of it, but then they learn of it and realise their guilt—

⁵when anyone realises their guilt in any of these matters, they must confess in what way they have sinned ⁶and, as a penalty for the sin they have committed, they must bring to the LORD a female lamb or goat from the flock as a sin offering[a]; and the priest shall make atonement for them for their sin.

⁷'"Anyone who cannot afford a lamb is to bring two doves or two young pigeons to the LORD as a penalty for their sin—one for a sin offering and the other for a burnt offering. ⁸They are to bring them to the priest, who shall first offer the one for the sin offering. He is to wring its head from its neck, not dividing it completely, ⁹and is to splash some of the blood of the sin offering against the side of the altar; the rest of the blood must be drained out at the base of the altar. It is a sin offering. ¹⁰The priest shall then offer the other as a burnt offering in the prescribed way and make atonement for them for the sin they have committed, and they will be forgiven.

¹¹'"If, however, they cannot afford two doves or two young pigeons, they are to bring as an offering for their sin a tenth of an ephah[b] of the finest flour for a sin offering. They must not put oil or incense on it, because it is a sin offering. ¹²They are to bring it to the priest, who shall take a handful of it as a memorial[c] portion and burn it on the altar on top of the food offerings presented to the LORD. It is a sin offering. ¹³In this way the priest will make atonement for them for any of these sins they have committed, and they will be forgiven. The rest of the offering will belong to the priest, as in the case of the grain offering."'

The guilt offering

¹⁴The LORD said to Moses: ¹⁵'When anyone is unfaithful to the LORD by sinning unintentionally in regard to any of the LORD's holy things, they are to bring to the LORD as a penalty a ram from the flock, one without defect and of the proper value in silver, according to the sanctuary shekel.[d] It is a guilt offering. ¹⁶They must make restitution for what they have failed to do in regard to the holy things, pay an additional penalty of a fifth of its value and give it all to the priest. The priest will make atonement for them with the ram as a guilt offering, and they will be forgiven.

¹⁷'If anyone sins and does what is forbidden in any of the LORD's commands, even though they do not know it, they are guilty and will be held responsible. ¹⁸They are to bring to the priest as a guilt offering a ram from the flock, one without defect and of the proper value. In this way the priest will make atonement for them for the wrong they have committed unintentionally, and they will be forgiven. ¹⁹It is a guilt offering; they have been guilty of[e] wrongdoing against the LORD.'

6 *The LORD said to Moses: ²'If anyone sins and is unfaithful to the LORD by deceiving a neighbour about something entrusted to them or left in their care or about something stolen, or if they cheat a neighbour, ³or if they find lost property and lie about it, or if they swear falsely about any such sin that people may commit— ⁴when they thus sin and realise their guilt, they must return what they have stolen or taken by extortion, or what was entrusted to them, or the lost property they found, ⁵or whatever it was they swore falsely about. They must make restitution in full, add a fifth of the value to it and give it all to the owner on the day they present their guilt offering. ⁶And as a penalty they must bring to the priest, that is, to the LORD, their guilt offering, a ram from the flock, one without defect and of the proper value. ⁷In this way the priest will make atonement for them before the LORD, and they will be forgiven for any of the things they did that made them guilty.'

The burnt offering

*⁸The LORD said to Moses: ⁹'Give Aaron and his sons this command: "These are the regulations for the burnt offering: the burnt

---

[a] 6 Or *purification offering*; here and throughout this chapter   [b] 11 That is, probably about 1.5 kilograms   [c] 12 Or *representative*   [d] 15 That is, about 11.5 grams   [e] 19 Or *have made full expiation for their*

* 6:1-7 is numbered 5:20-26 in Hebrew texts.   * 6:8-30 is numbered 6:1-23 in Hebrew texts.

Pagan sacrifices
Leviticus 6:8

The pagan nations around the Israelites killed animals as sacrifices too, but they had different ideas about what the sacrifices were for. Some thought that their sacrifices would feed their gods; others thought that they became one with the gods; others thought the sacrifice was like magic and would force their god to do what they wanted. The Israelites knew that their sacrifices were the way that they made amends for what they had done wrong and drew close to God.

---

offering is to remain on the altar hearth throughout the night, till morning, and the fire must be kept burning on the altar. [10]The priest shall then put on his linen clothes, with linen undergarments next to his body, and shall remove the ashes of the burnt offering that the fire has consumed on the altar and place them beside the altar. [11]Then he is to take off these clothes and put on others, and carry the ashes outside the camp to a place that is ceremonially clean. [12]The fire on the altar must be kept burning; it must not go out. Every morning the priest is to add firewood and arrange the burnt offering on the fire and burn the fat of the fellowship offerings on it. [13]The fire must be kept burning on the altar continuously; it must not go out.

The grain offering

[14]"These are the regulations for the grain offering: Aaron's sons are to bring it before the LORD, in front of the altar. [15]The priest is to take a handful of the finest flour and some olive oil, together with all the incense on the grain offering, and burn the memorial[a] portion on the altar as an aroma pleasing to the LORD. [16]Aaron and his sons shall eat the rest of it, but it is to be eaten without yeast in the sanctuary area; they are to eat it in the courtyard of the tent of meeting. [17]It must not be baked with yeast; I have given it as their share of the food offerings presented to me. Like the sin offering[b] and the guilt offering, it is most holy. [18]Any male descendant of Aaron may eat it. For all generations to come it is his perpetual share of the food offerings presented to the LORD. Whatever touches it will become holy."'[c]

[19]The LORD also said to Moses, [20]"This is the offering Aaron and his sons are to bring to the LORD on the day he[d] is anointed: a tenth of an ephah[e] of the finest flour as a regular grain offering, half of it in the morning and half in the evening. [21]It must be prepared with oil on a griddle; bring it well-mixed and present the grain offering broken[f] in pieces as an aroma pleasing to the LORD. [22]The son who is to succeed him as anointed priest shall prepare it. It is the LORD's perpetual share and is to be burned completely. [23]Every grain offering of a priest shall be burned completely; it must not be eaten.'

The sin offering

[24]The LORD said to Moses, [25]'Say to Aaron and his sons: "These are the regulations for the sin offering: the sin offering is to be slaughtered before the LORD in the place where the burnt offering is slaughtered; it is most holy. [26]The priest who offers it shall eat it; it is to be eaten in the sanctuary area, in the courtyard of the tent of meeting. [27]Whatever touches any of the flesh will become holy, and if any of the blood is spattered on a garment, you must wash it in the sanctuary area. [28]The clay pot that the meat is cooked in must be broken; but if it is cooked in a bronze pot, the pot is to be scoured and rinsed with water. [29]Any male in a priest's family may eat it; it is most holy. [30]But any sin offering whose blood is brought into the tent of meeting to make

---

[a] 15 Or representative [b] 17 Or purification offering; also in verses 25 and 30 [c] 18 Or Whoever touches them must be holy; similarly in verse 27 [d] 20 Or each [e] 20 That is, probably about 1.5 kilograms [f] 21 The meaning of the Hebrew for this word is uncertain.

atonement in the Holy Place must not be eaten; it must be burned.

The guilt offering

7 ¹ "'These are the regulations for the guilt offering, which is most holy: ²the guilt offering is to be slaughtered in the place where the burnt offering is slaughtered, and its blood is to be splashed against the sides of the altar. ³All its fat shall be offered: the fat tail and the fat that covers the internal organs, ⁴both kidneys with the fat on them near the loins, and the long lobe of the liver, which is to be removed with the kidneys. ⁵The priest shall burn them on the altar as a food offering presented to the LORD. It is a guilt offering. ⁶Any male in a priest's family may eat it, but it must be eaten in the sanctuary area; it is most holy.

⁷ "'The same law applies to both the sin offering[a] and the guilt offering: they belong to the priest who makes atonement with them. ⁸The priest who offers a burnt offering for anyone may keep its hide for himself. ⁹Every grain offering baked in an oven or cooked in a pan or on a griddle belongs to the priest who offers it, ¹⁰and every grain offering, whether mixed with oil or dry, belongs equally to all the sons of Aaron.

The fellowship offering

¹¹ "'These are the regulations for the fellowship offering anyone may present to the LORD:

¹² "'If they offer it as an expression of thankfulness, then along with this thank-offering they are to offer thick loaves made without yeast and with olive oil mixed in, thin loaves made without yeast and brushed with olive oil, and thick loaves of the finest flour well-kneaded and with olive oil mixed in. ¹³Along with their fellowship offering of thanksgiving they are to present an offering with thick loaves of bread made with yeast. ¹⁴They are to bring one of each kind as an offering, a contribution to the LORD; it belongs to the priest who splashes the blood of the fellowship offering against the altar. ¹⁵The meat of their fellowship offering of thanksgiving must be eaten on the day it is offered; they must leave none of it till morning.

¹⁶ "'If, however, their offering is the result of a vow or is a freewill offering, the sacrifice shall be eaten on the day they offer it, but anything left over may be eaten on the next day. ¹⁷Any meat of the sacrifice left over till the third day must be burned. ¹⁸If any meat of the fellowship offering is eaten on the third day, the one who offered it will not be accepted. It will not be reckoned to their credit, for it has become impure; the person who eats any of it will be held responsible.

¹⁹ "'Meat that touches anything ceremonially unclean must not be eaten; it must be burned. As for other meat, anyone ceremonially clean may eat it. ²⁰But if anyone who is unclean eats any meat of the fellowship offering belonging to the LORD, they must be cut off from their people. ²¹Anyone who touches something unclean—whether human uncleanness or an unclean animal or any unclean creature that moves along the ground[b]—and then eats any of the meat of the fellowship offering belonging to the LORD must be cut off from their people.'"

Eating fat and blood forbidden

²²The LORD said to Moses, ²³'Say to the Israelites: "Do not eat any of the fat of cattle, sheep or goats. ²⁴The fat of an animal found dead or torn by wild animals may be used for any other purpose, but you must not eat it. ²⁵Anyone who eats the fat of an animal from which a food offering may be[c] presented to the LORD must be cut off from their people. ²⁶And wherever you live, you must not eat the blood of any bird or animal. ²⁷Anyone who eats blood must be cut off from their people."'

The priests' share

²⁸The LORD said to Moses, ²⁹'Say to the Israelites: "Anyone who brings a fellowship offering to the LORD is to bring part of it as their sacrifice to the LORD. ³⁰With their own hands they are to present the food offering to the LORD; they are to bring the fat, together with the breast, and wave the breast before the LORD as a wave offering. ³¹The priest shall burn the fat on the altar, but the

---

[a] 7 Or *purification offering*; also in verse 37   [b] 21 A few Hebrew manuscripts, Samaritan Pentateuch, Syriac and Targum (see Lev. 5:2); most Hebrew manuscripts *unclean, detestable thing*   [c] 25 Or *offering is*

breast belongs to Aaron and his sons. ³²You are to give the right thigh of your fellowship offerings to the priest as a contribution. ³³The son of Aaron who offers the blood and the fat of the fellowship offering shall have the right thigh as his share. ³⁴From the fellowship offerings of the Israelites, I have taken the breast that is waved and the thigh that is presented and have given them to Aaron the priest and his sons as their perpetual share from the Israelites."'

³⁵This is the portion of the food offerings presented to the LORD that were allotted to Aaron and his sons on the day they were presented to serve the LORD as priests. ³⁶On the day they were anointed, the LORD commanded that the Israelites give this to them as their perpetual share for the generations to come.

³⁷These, then, are the regulations for the burnt offering, the grain offering, the sin offering, the guilt offering, the ordination offering and the fellowship offering, ³⁸which the LORD gave Moses on Mount Sinai in the Desert of Sinai on the day he commanded the Israelites to bring their offerings to the LORD.

The ordination of Aaron and his sons

8 The LORD said to Moses, ²'Bring Aaron and his sons, their garments, the anointing oil, the bull for the sin offering,ᵃ the two rams and the basket containing bread made without yeast, ³and gather the entire assembly at the entrance to the tent of meeting.' ⁴Moses did as the LORD commanded him, and the assembly gathered at the entrance to the tent of meeting.

⁵Moses said to the assembly, 'This is what the LORD has commanded to be done.' ⁶Then Moses brought Aaron and his sons forward and washed them with water. ⁷He put the tunic on Aaron, tied the sash round him, clothed him with the robe and put the ephod on him. He also fastened the ephod with a decorative waistband, which he tied round him. ⁸He placed the breastpiece on him and put the Urim and Thummim in the breastpiece. ⁹Then he placed the turban on Aaron's head and set the gold plate, the sacred emblem, on the front of it, as the LORD commanded Moses.

¹⁰Then Moses took the anointing oil and anointed the tabernacle and everything in it, and so consecrated them. ¹¹He sprinkled some of the oil on the altar seven times, anointing the altar and all its utensils and the basin with its stand, to consecrate them. ¹²He poured some of the anointing oil on Aaron's head and anointed him to consecrate him. ¹³Then he brought Aaron's sons forward, put tunics on them, tied sashes round them and fastened caps on them, as the LORD commanded Moses.

¹⁴He then presented the bull for the sin offering, and Aaron and his sons laid their hands on its head. ¹⁵Moses slaughtered the bull and took some of the blood, and with his finger he put it on all the horns of the altar to purify the altar. He poured out the rest of the blood at the base of the altar. So he consecrated it to make atonement for it. ¹⁶Moses also took all the fat around the internal organs, the long lobe of the liver, and both kidneys and their fat, and burned it on the altar. ¹⁷But the bull with its hide and its flesh and its intestines he burned outside the camp, as the LORD commanded Moses.

¹⁸He then presented the ram for the burnt offering, and Aaron and his sons laid their hands on its head. ¹⁹Then Moses slaughtered the ram and splashed the blood against the sides of the altar. ²⁰He cut the ram into pieces and burned the head, the

---

> **IN OTHER WORDS**
>
> ### Ordination
> **Leviticus 8:1**
> This special ceremony showed that God had given Aaron the task of being High Priest and that Aaron was willing to take it on and do it with God's help. Ordination of church leaders still happens today, although without the sacrifice of bulls and rams!

ᵃ 2 Or *purification offering*; also in verse 14

pieces and the fat. 21He washed the internal organs and the legs with water and burned the whole ram on the altar. It was a burnt offering, a pleasing aroma, a food offering presented to the LORD, as the LORD commanded Moses.

22He then presented the other ram, the ram for the ordination, and Aaron and his sons laid their hands on its head. 23Moses slaughtered the ram and took some of its blood and put it on the lobe of Aaron's right ear, on the thumb of his right hand and on the big toe of his right foot. 24Moses also brought Aaron's sons forward and put some of the blood on the lobes of their right ears, on the thumbs of their right hands and on the big toes of their right feet. Then he splashed blood against the sides of the altar. 25After that, he took the fat, the fat tail, all the fat around the internal organs, the long lobe of the liver, both kidneys and their fat and the right thigh. 26And from the basket of bread made without yeast, which was before the LORD, he took one thick loaf, one thick loaf with olive oil mixed in, and one thin loaf, and he put these on the fat portions and on the right thigh. 27He put all these in the hands of Aaron and his sons and they waved them before the LORD as a wave offering. 28Then Moses took them from their hands and burned them on the altar on top of the burnt offering as an ordination offering, a pleasing aroma, a food offering presented to the LORD. 29Moses also took the breast, which was his share of the ordination ram, and waved it before the LORD as a wave offering, as the LORD commanded Moses.

30Then Moses took some of the anointing oil and some of the blood from the altar and sprinkled them on Aaron and his garments and on his sons and their garments. So he consecrated Aaron and his garments and his sons and their garments.

31Moses then said to Aaron and his sons, 'Cook the meat at the entrance to the tent of meeting and eat it there with the bread from the basket of ordination offerings, as I was commanded: "Aaron and his sons are to eat it." 32Then burn the rest of the meat and the bread. 33Do not leave the entrance to the tent of meeting for seven days, until the days of your ordination are completed, for your ordination will last seven days. 34What has been done today was commanded by the LORD to make atonement for you. 35You must stay at the entrance to the tent of meeting day and night for seven days and do what the LORD requires, so that you will not die; for that is what I have been commanded.' 36So Aaron and his sons did everything the LORD commanded through Moses.

The priests begin their ministry

9 On the eighth day Moses summoned Aaron and his sons and the elders of Israel. 2He said to Aaron, 'Take a bull calf for your sin offering^a and a ram for your burnt offering, both without defect, and present them before the LORD. 3Then say to the Israelites: "Take a male goat for a sin offering, a calf and a lamb—both a year old and without defect—for a burnt offering, 4and an ox^b and a ram for a fellowship offering to sacrifice before the LORD, together with a grain offering mixed with olive oil. For today the LORD will appear to you." '

5They took the things Moses commanded to the front of the tent of meeting, and the entire assembly came near and stood before the LORD. 6Then Moses said, 'This is what the LORD has commanded you to do, so that the glory of the LORD may appear to you.'

7Moses said to Aaron, 'Come to the altar and sacrifice your sin offering and your burnt offering and make atonement for yourself and the people; sacrifice the offering that is for the people and make atonement for them, as the LORD has commanded.'

8So Aaron came to the altar and slaughtered the calf as a sin offering for himself. 9His sons brought the blood to him, and he dipped his finger into the blood and put it on the horns of the altar; the rest of the blood he poured out at the base of the altar. 10On the altar he burned the fat, the kidneys and the long lobe of the liver from the sin offering, as the LORD commanded Moses;

---

^{a}2 Or *purification offering*; here and throughout this chapter ^{b}4 The Hebrew word can include both male and female; also in verses 18 and 19.

¹¹the flesh and the hide he burned outside the camp.

¹²Then he slaughtered the burnt offering. His sons handed him the blood, and he splashed it against the sides of the altar. ¹³They handed him the burnt offering piece by piece, including the head, and he burned them on the altar. ¹⁴He washed the internal organs and the legs and burned them on top of the burnt offering on the altar.

¹⁵Aaron then brought the offering that was for the people. He took the goat for the people's sin offering and slaughtered it and offered it for a sin offering as he did with the first one.

¹⁶He brought the burnt offering and offered it in the prescribed way. ¹⁷He also brought the grain offering, took a handful of it and burned it on the altar in addition to the morning's burnt offering.

¹⁸He slaughtered the ox and the ram as the fellowship offering for the people. His sons handed him the blood, and he splashed it against the sides of the altar. ¹⁹But the fat portions of the ox and the ram—the fat tail, the layer of fat, the kidneys and the long lobe of the liver— ²⁰these they laid on the breasts, and then Aaron burned the fat on the altar. ²¹Aaron waved the breasts and the right thigh before the LORD as a wave offering, as Moses commanded.

²²Then Aaron lifted his hands towards the people and blessed them. And having sacrificed the sin offering, the burnt offering and the fellowship offering, he stepped down.

²³Moses and Aaron then went into the tent of meeting. When they came out, they blessed the people; and the glory of the LORD appeared to all the people. ²⁴Fire came out from the presence of the LORD and consumed the burnt offering and the fat portions on the altar. And when all the people saw it, they shouted for joy and fell face down.

The death of Nadab and Abihu

10 Aaron's sons Nadab and Abihu took their censers, put fire in them and added incense; and they offered unauthorised fire before the LORD, contrary to his command. ²So fire came out from the presence of the LORD and consumed them, and they died before the LORD. ³Moses then said to Aaron, 'This is what the LORD spoke of when he said:

> "Among those who approach me
> I will be proved holy;
> in the sight of all the people
> I will be honoured."'

Aaron remained silent.

⁴Moses summoned Mishael and Elzaphan, sons of Aaron's uncle Uzziel, and said to them, 'Come here; carry your cousins outside the camp, away from the front of the sanctuary.' ⁵So they came and carried them, still in their tunics, outside the camp, as Moses ordered.

⁶Then Moses said to Aaron and his sons Eleazar and Ithamar, 'Do not let your hair become unkempt*ᵃ* and do not tear your clothes or you will die and the LORD will be angry with the whole community. But your relatives, all the house of Israel, may mourn for those the LORD has destroyed by fire. ⁷Do not leave the entrance to the tent of meeting or you will die, because the LORD's anointing oil is on you.' So they did as Moses said.

⁸Then the LORD said to Aaron, ⁹'You and your sons are not to drink wine or other fermented drink whenever you go into the tent of meeting, or you will die. This is a lasting ordinance for the generations to come, ¹⁰so that you can distinguish between the holy and the common, between the unclean and the clean, ¹¹and so you can teach the Israelites all the decrees the LORD has given them through Moses.'

¹²Moses said to Aaron and his remaining sons, Eleazar and Ithamar, 'Take the grain offering left over from the food offerings prepared without yeast and presented to the LORD and eat it beside the altar, for it is most holy. ¹³Eat it in the sanctuary area, because it is your share and your sons' share of the food offerings presented to the LORD; for so I have been commanded. ¹⁴But you and your sons and your daughters may eat the breast that was waved and the thigh that was presented. Eat them in a ceremonially clean

---

ᵃ 6 Or *Do not uncover your heads*

place; they have been given to you and your children as your share of the Israelites' fellowship offerings. 15The thigh that was presented and the breast that was waved must be brought with the fat portions of the food offerings, to be waved before the LORD as a wave offering. This will be the perpetual share for you and your children, as the LORD has commanded.'

16When Moses enquired about the goat of the sin offering[a] and found that it had been burned, he was angry with Eleazar and Ithamar, Aaron's remaining sons, and asked, 17'Why didn't you eat the sin offering in the sanctuary area? It is most holy; it was given to you to take away the guilt of the community by making atonement for them before the LORD. 18Since its blood was not taken into the Holy Place, you should have eaten the goat in the sanctuary area, as I commanded.'

19Aaron replied to Moses, 'Today they sacrificed their sin offering and their burnt offering before the LORD, but such things as this have happened to me. Would the LORD have been pleased if I had eaten the sin offering today?' 20When Moses heard this, he was satisfied.

Clean and unclean food

11 The LORD said to Moses and Aaron, 2'Say to the Israelites: "Of all the animals that live on land, these are the ones you may eat: 3you may eat any animal that has a divided hoof and that chews the cud.

4' "There are some that only chew the cud or only have a divided hoof, but you must not eat them. The camel, though it chews the cud, does not have a divided hoof; it is ceremonially unclean for you. 5The hyrax, though it chews the cud, does not have a divided hoof; it is unclean for you. 6The hare, though it chews the cud, does not have a divided hoof; it is unclean for you. 7And the pig, though it has a divided hoof, does not chew the cud; it is unclean for you. 8You must not eat their meat or touch their carcasses; they are unclean for you.

9' "Of all the creatures living in the water of the seas and the streams you may eat any that have fins and scales. 10But all creatures in the seas or streams that do not have fins and scales—whether among all the swarming things or among all the other living creatures in the water—you are to regard as unclean. 11And since you are to regard them as unclean, you must not eat their meat; you must regard their carcasses as unclean. 12Anything living in the water that does not have fins and scales is to be regarded as unclean by you.

13' "These are the birds you are to regard as unclean and not eat because they are unclean: the eagle,[b] the vulture, the black vulture, 14the red kite, any kind of black kite, 15any kind of raven, 16the horned owl, the screech owl, the gull, any kind of hawk, 17the little owl, the cormorant, the great owl, 18the white owl, the desert owl, the osprey, 19the stork, any kind of heron, the hoopoe and the bat.

20' "All flying insects that walk on all fours are to be regarded as unclean by you.

Clean and unclean
Leviticus 11:1

The next few chapters of Leviticus spell out what the Israelites are to consider as clean and acceptable to God, and what is unclean and to be avoided. Some foods were unclean, and at certain times people would be unclean. It's not always obvious why some things were clean and others were unclean, but the reason the Israelites should avoid unclean things was because they were to be holy just like God was holy.

---

[a] 16 Or *purification offering*; also in verses 17 and 19   [b] 13 The precise identification of some of the birds, insects and animals in this chapter is uncertain.

²¹There are, however, some flying insects that walk on all fours that you may eat: those that have jointed legs for hopping on the ground. ²²Of these you may eat any kind of locust, cricket, cicada or grasshopper. ²³But all other flying insects that have four legs you are to regard as unclean.

²⁴ "'You will make yourselves unclean by these; whoever touches their carcasses will be unclean till evening. ²⁵Whoever picks up one of their carcasses must wash their clothes, and they will be unclean till evening.

²⁶ "'Every animal that does not have a divided hoof or that does not chew the cud is unclean for you; whoever touches the carcass of any of them will be unclean. ²⁷Of all the animals that walk on all fours, those that walk on their paws are unclean for you; whoever touches their carcasses will be unclean till evening. ²⁸Anyone who picks up their carcasses must wash their clothes, and they will be unclean till evening. These animals are unclean for you.

²⁹ "'Of the animals that move about on the ground, these are unclean for you: the weasel, the rat, any kind of great lizard, ³⁰the gecko, the monitor lizard, the wall lizard, the skink and the chameleon. ³¹Of all those that move along the ground, these are unclean for you. Whoever touches them when they are dead will be unclean till evening. ³²When one of them dies and falls on something, that article, whatever its use, will be unclean, whether it is made of wood, cloth, hide or sackcloth. Put it in water; it will be unclean till evening, and then it will be clean. ³³If one of them falls into a clay pot, everything in it will be unclean, and you must break the pot. ³⁴Any food you are allowed to eat that has come into contact with water from any such pot is unclean, and any liquid that is drunk from such a pot is unclean. ³⁵Anything that one of their carcasses falls on becomes unclean; an oven or cooking pot must be broken up. They are unclean, and you are to regard them as unclean. ³⁶A spring, however, or a cistern for collecting water remains clean, but anyone who touches one of these carcasses is unclean. ³⁷If a carcass falls on any seeds that are to be planted, they remain clean. ³⁸But if water has been put on the seed and a carcass falls on it, it is unclean for you.

³⁹ "'If an animal that you are allowed to eat dies, anyone who touches its carcass will be unclean till evening. ⁴⁰Anyone who eats some of its carcass must wash their clothes, and they will be unclean till evening. Anyone who picks up the carcass must wash their clothes, and they will be unclean till evening.

⁴¹ "'Every creature that moves about on the ground is to be regarded as unclean; it is not to be eaten. ⁴²You are not to eat any creature that moves about on the ground, whether it moves on its belly or walks on all fours or on many feet; it is unclean. ⁴³Do not defile yourselves by any of these creatures. Do not make yourselves unclean by means of them or be made unclean by them. ⁴⁴I am the LORD your God; consecrate yourselves and be holy, because I am holy. Do not make yourselves unclean by any creature that moves about on the ground. ⁴⁵I am the LORD, who brought you up out of Egypt to be your God; therefore be holy, because I am holy.

⁴⁶ "'These are the regulations concerning animals, birds, every living thing that moves in the water and every creature that moves about on the ground. ⁴⁷You must distinguish between the unclean and the clean, between living creatures that may be eaten and those that may not be eaten.'"

Purification after childbirth

12 The LORD said to Moses, ²'Say to the Israelites: "A woman who becomes pregnant and gives birth to a son will be ceremonially unclean for seven days, just as she is unclean during her monthly period. ³On the eighth day the boy is to be circumcised. ⁴Then the woman must wait thirty-three days to be purified from her bleeding. She must not touch anything sacred or go to the sanctuary until the days of her purification are over. ⁵If she gives birth to a daughter, for two weeks the woman will be unclean, as during her period. Then she must wait sixty-six days to be purified from her bleeding.

6 "When the days of her purification for a son or daughter are over, she is to bring to the priest at the entrance to the tent of meeting a year-old lamb for a burnt offering and a young pigeon or a dove for a sin offering.[a] 7 He shall offer them before the LORD to make atonement for her, and then she will be ceremonially clean from her flow of blood.

' "These are the regulations for the woman who gives birth to a boy or a girl. 8 If she cannot afford a lamb, she is to bring two doves or two young pigeons, one for a burnt offering and the other for a sin offering. In this way the priest will make atonement for her, and she will be clean." '

Regulations about defiling skin diseases

13 The LORD said to Moses and Aaron, 2 'When anyone has a swelling or a rash or a shiny spot on their skin that may be a defiling skin disease,[b] they must be brought to Aaron the priest or to one of his sons[c] who is a priest. 3 The priest is to examine the sore on the skin, and if the hair in the sore has turned white and the sore appears to be more than skin deep, it is a defiling skin disease. When the priest examines them, he shall pronounce them ceremonially unclean. 4 If the shiny spot on the skin is white but does not appear to be more than skin deep and the hair in it has not turned white, the priest is to isolate the affected person for seven days. 5 On the seventh day the priest is to examine them, and if he sees that the sore is unchanged and has not spread in the skin, he is to isolate them for another seven days. 6 On the seventh day the priest is to examine them again, and if the sore has faded and has not spread in the skin, the priest shall pronounce them clean; it is only a rash. They must wash their clothes, and they will be clean. 7 But if the rash does spread in their skin after they have shown themselves to the priest to be pronounced clean, they must appear before the priest again. 8 The priest is to examine them, and if the rash has spread in the skin, he shall pronounce them unclean; it is a defiling skin disease.

9 'When anyone has a defiling skin disease, they must be brought to the priest. 10 The priest is to examine them, and if there is a white swelling in the skin that has turned the hair white and if there is raw flesh in the swelling, 11 it is a chronic skin disease and the priest shall pronounce them unclean. He is not to isolate them, because they are already unclean.

12 'If the disease breaks out all over their skin and, so far as the priest can see, it covers all the skin of the affected person from head to foot, 13 the priest is to examine them, and if the disease has covered their whole body, he shall pronounce them clean. Since it has all turned white, they are clean. 14 But whenever raw flesh appears on them, they will be unclean. 15 When the priest sees the raw flesh, he shall pronounce them unclean. The raw flesh is unclean; they have a defiling disease. 16 If the raw flesh changes and turns white, they must go to the priest. 17 The priest is to examine them, and if the sores have turned white, the priest shall pronounce the affected person clean; then they will be clean.

18 'When someone has a boil on their skin and it heals, 19 and in the place where the boil was, a white swelling or reddish-white spot appears, they must present themselves to the priest. 20 The priest is to examine it, and if it appears to be more than skin deep and the hair in it has turned white, the priest shall pronounce them unclean. It is a defiling skin disease that has broken out where the boil was. 21 But if, when the priest examines it, there is no white hair in it and it is not more than skin deep and has faded, then the priest is to isolate them for seven days. 22 If it is spreading in the skin, the priest shall pronounce them unclean; it is a defiling disease. 23 But if the spot is unchanged and has not spread, it is only a scar from the boil, and the priest shall pronounce them clean.

24 'When someone has a burn on their skin and a reddish-white or white spot appears in the raw flesh of the burn, 25 the priest is to examine the spot, and if the hair in it has turned white, and it appears to be

---

[a] 6 Or *purification* offering; also in verse 8   [b] 2 The Hebrew word for *defiling skin disease*, traditionally translated 'leprosy', was used for various diseases affecting the skin; here and throughout verses 3-46.   [c] 2 Or *descendants*

more than skin deep, it is a defiling disease that has broken out in the burn. The priest shall pronounce them unclean; it is a defiling skin disease. 26But if the priest examines it and there is no white hair in the spot and if it is not more than skin deep and has faded, then the priest is to isolate them for seven days. 27On the seventh day the priest is to examine them, and if it is spreading in the skin, the priest shall pronounce them unclean; it is a defiling skin disease. 28If, however, the spot is unchanged and has not spread in the skin but has faded, it is a swelling from the burn, and the priest shall pronounce them clean; it is only a scar from the burn.

29'If a man or woman has a sore on their head or chin, 30the priest is to examine the sore, and if it appears to be more than skin deep and the hair in it is yellow and thin, the priest shall pronounce them unclean; it is a defiling skin disease on the head or chin. 31But if, when the priest examines the sore, it does not seem to be more than skin deep and there is no black hair in it, then the priest is to isolate the affected person for seven days. 32On the seventh day the priest is to examine the sore, and if it has not spread and there is no yellow hair in it and it does not appear to be more than skin deep, 33then the man or woman must shave themselves, except for the affected area, and the priest is to keep them isolated another seven days. 34On the seventh day the priest is to examine the sore, and if it has not spread in the skin and appears to be no more than skin deep, the priest shall pronounce the man or woman clean. They must wash their clothes, and they will be clean. 35But if the sore does spread in the skin after they are pronounced clean, 36the priest is to examine them, and if he finds that the sore has spread in the skin, he does not need to look for yellow hair; they are unclean. 37If, however, the sore is unchanged so far as the priest can see, and if black hair has grown in it, the affected person is healed. They are clean, and the priest shall pronounce them clean.

38'When a man or woman has white spots on the skin, 39the priest is to examine them, and if the spots are dull white, it is a harmless rash that has broken out on the skin; they are clean.

40'A man who has lost his hair and is bald is clean. 41If he has lost his hair from the front of his scalp and has a bald forehead, he is clean. 42But if he has a reddish-white sore on his bald head or forehead, it is a defiling disease breaking out on his head or forehead. 43The priest is to examine him, and if the swollen sore on his bald head or forehead is reddish-white like a defiling skin disease, 44the man is diseased and is unclean. The priest shall pronounce him unclean because of the sore on his head.

45'Anyone with such a defiling disease must wear torn clothes, let their hair be unkempt,[a] cover the lower part of their face and cry out, "Unclean! Unclean!" 46As long as they have the disease they remain unclean. They must live alone; they must live outside the camp.

Regulations about defiling moulds

47'As for any fabric that is spoiled with a defiling mould—any woollen or linen clothing, 48any woven or knitted material of linen or wool, any leather or anything made of leather— 49if the affected area in the fabric, the leather, the woven or knitted material, or any leather article, is greenish or reddish, it is a defiling mould and must be shown to the priest. 50The priest is to examine the affected area and isolate the article for seven days. 51On the seventh day he is to examine it, and if the mould has spread in the fabric, the woven or knitted material, or the leather, whatever its use, it is a persistent defiling mould; the article is unclean. 52He must burn the fabric, the woven or knitted material of wool or linen, or any leather article that has been spoiled, because the defiling mould is persistent; the article must be burned.

53'But if, when the priest examines it, the mould has not spread in the fabric, the woven or knitted material, or the leather article, 54he shall order the spoiled article to be washed. Then he is to isolate it for another seven days. 55After the article has been washed, the priest is to examine it

---

[a] 45 Or *clothes, uncover their head*

again, and if the mould has not changed its appearance, even though it has not spread, it is unclean. Burn it, no matter which side of the fabric has been spoiled. 56If, when the priest examines it, the mould has faded after the article has been washed, he is to tear the spoiled part out of the fabric, the leather, or the woven or knitted material. 57But if it reappears in the fabric, in the woven or knitted material, or in the leather article, it is a spreading mould; whatever has the mould must be burned. 58Any fabric, woven or knitted material, or any leather article that has been washed and is rid of the mould, must be washed again. Then it will be clean.'

59These are the regulations concerning defiling moulds in woollen or linen clothing, woven or knitted material, or any leather article, for pronouncing them clean or unclean.

Making Connections

Hygiene rules
Leviticus 14:1

All these regulations about mould, washing and showing yourself to the priest may seem very fussy, but in a hot country with little water they make a lot of sense. Disease and infections can spread very quickly when lots of people live close together in those conditions. Making sure that people were clean, healthy, and kept away from illness was very wise.

Cleansing from defiling skin diseases

14 The LORD said to Moses, 2'These are the regulations for any diseased person at the time of their ceremonial cleansing, when they are brought to the priest: 3the priest is to go outside the camp and examine them. If they have been healed of their defiling skin disease,^{a} 4the priest shall order that two live clean birds and some cedar wood, scarlet yarn and hyssop be brought for the person to be cleansed. 5Then the priest shall order that one of the birds be killed over fresh water in a clay pot. 6He is then to take the live bird and dip it, together with the cedar wood, the scarlet yarn and the hyssop, into the blood of the bird that was killed over the fresh water. 7Seven times he shall sprinkle the one to be cleansed of the defiling disease, and then pronounce them clean. After that, he is to release the live bird in the open fields.

8'The person to be cleansed must wash their clothes, shave off all their hair and bathe with water; then they will be ceremonially clean. After this they may come into the camp, but they must stay outside their tent for seven days. 9On the seventh day they must shave off all their hair; they must shave their head, their beard, their eyebrows and the rest of their hair. They must wash their clothes and bathe themselves with water, and they will be clean.

10'On the eighth day they must bring two male lambs and one ewe lamb a year old, each without defect, along with three-tenths of an ephah^b of the finest flour mixed with olive oil for a grain offering, and one log^c of oil. 11The priest who pronounces them clean shall present both the one to be cleansed and their offerings before the LORD at the entrance to the tent of meeting.

12'Then the priest is to take one of the male lambs and offer it as a guilt offering, along with the log of oil; he shall wave them before the LORD as a wave offering. 13He is to slaughter the lamb in the sanctuary area where the sin offering^d and the burnt offering are slaughtered. Like the sin offering, the guilt offering belongs to the priest; it is most holy. 14The priest is to take some of the blood of the guilt offering and put it on the lobe of the right ear of the one to be cleansed, on the thumb of their right hand and on the big toe of their right foot. 15The priest shall then take some of the log of oil,

---

^{a} 3 The Hebrew word for *defiling skin disease*, traditionally translated 'leprosy', was used for various diseases affecting the skin; also in verses 7 and 32. ^{b} 10 That is, probably about 5 kilograms ^{c} 10 That is, about 0.3 litre; also in verses 12, 15, 21 and 24 ^{d} 13 Or *purification offering*; also in verses 19, 22 and 31 pour it in the palm of his own left hand, ¹⁶dip his right forefinger into the oil in his palm, and with his finger sprinkle some of it before the LORD seven times. ¹⁷The priest is to put some of the oil remaining in his palm on the lobe of the right ear of the one to be cleansed, on the thumb of their right hand and on the big toe of their right foot, on top of the blood of the guilt offering. ¹⁸The rest of the oil in his palm the priest shall put on the head of the one to be cleansed and make atonement for them before the LORD.

¹⁹'Then the priest is to sacrifice the sin offering and make atonement for the one to be cleansed from their uncleanness. After that, the priest shall slaughter the burnt offering ²⁰and offer it on the altar, together with the grain offering, and make atonement for them, and they will be clean.

²¹'If, however, they are poor and cannot afford these, they must take one male lamb as a guilt offering to be waved to make atonement for them, together with a tenth of an ephah^a of the finest flour mixed with olive oil for a grain offering, a log of oil, ²²and two doves or two young pigeons, which they can afford, one for a sin offering and the other for a burnt offering.

²³'On the eighth day they must bring them for their cleansing to the priest at the entrance to the tent of meeting, before the LORD. ²⁴The priest is to take the lamb for the guilt offering, together with the log of oil, and wave them before the LORD as a wave offering. ²⁵He shall slaughter the lamb for the guilt offering and take some of its blood and put it on the lobe of the right ear of the one to be cleansed, on the thumb of their right hand and on the big toe of their right foot. ²⁶The priest is to pour some of the oil into the palm of his own left hand, ²⁷and with his right forefinger sprinkle some of the oil from his palm seven times before the LORD. ²⁸Some of the oil in his palm he is to put on the same places he put the blood of the guilt offering—on the lobe of the right ear of the one to be cleansed, on the thumb of their right hand and on the big toe of their right foot. ²⁹The rest of the oil in his palm the priest shall put on the head of the one to be cleansed, to make atonement for them before the LORD. ³⁰Then he shall sacrifice the doves or the young pigeons, such as the person can afford, ³¹one as a sin offering and the other as a burnt offering, together with the grain offering. In this way the priest will make atonement before the LORD on behalf of the one to be cleansed.'

³²These are the regulations for anyone who has a defiling skin disease and who cannot afford the usual offerings for their cleansing.

Cleansing from defiling moulds

³³The LORD said to Moses and Aaron, ³⁴'When you enter the land of Canaan, which I am giving you as your possession, and I put a spreading mould in a house in that land, ³⁵the owner of the house must go and tell the priest, "I have seen something that looks like a defiling mould in my house." ³⁶The priest is to order the house to be emptied before he goes in to examine the mould, so that nothing in the house will be pronounced unclean. After this the priest is to go in and inspect the house. ³⁷He is to examine the mould on the walls, and if it has greenish or reddish depressions that appear to be deeper than the surface of the wall, ³⁸the priest shall go out of the doorway of the house and close it up for seven days. ³⁹On the seventh day the priest shall return to inspect the house. If the mould has spread on the walls, ⁴⁰he is to order that the contaminated stones be torn out and thrown into an unclean place outside the town. ⁴¹He must have all the inside walls of the house scraped and the material that is scraped off dumped into an unclean place outside the town. ⁴²Then they are to take other stones to replace these and take new clay and plaster the house.

⁴³'If the defiling mould reappears in the house after the stones have been torn out and the house scraped and plastered, ⁴⁴the priest is to go and examine it and, if the mould has spread in the house, it is a persistent defiling mould; the house is unclean. ⁴⁵It must be torn down—its stones, timbers and all the plaster—and taken out of the town to an unclean place.

---

^{a} 21 That is, probably about 1.5 kilograms

46'Anyone who goes into the house while it is closed up will be unclean till evening. 47Anyone who sleeps or eats in the house must wash their clothes.

48'But if the priest comes to examine it and the mould has not spread after the house has been plastered, he shall pronounce the house clean, because the defiling mould is gone. 49To purify the house he is to take two birds and some cedar wood, scarlet yarn and hyssop. 50He shall kill one of the birds over fresh water in a clay pot. 51Then he is to take the cedar wood, the hyssop, the scarlet yarn and the live bird, dip them into the blood of the dead bird and the fresh water, and sprinkle the house seven times. 52He shall purify the house with the bird's blood, the fresh water, the live bird, the cedar wood, the hyssop and the scarlet yarn. 53Then he is to release the live bird in the open fields outside the town. In this way he will make atonement for the house, and it will be clean.'

54These are the regulations for any defiling skin disease, for a sore, 55for defiling moulds in fabric or in a house, 56and for a swelling, a rash or a shiny spot, 57to determine when something is clean or unclean.

These are the regulations for defiling skin diseases and defiling moulds.

Discharges causing uncleanness

15 The LORD said to Moses and Aaron, 2'Speak to the Israelites and say to them: "When any man has an unusual bodily discharge, such a discharge is unclean. 3Whether it continues flowing from his body or is blocked, it will make him unclean. This is how his discharge will bring about uncleanness:

4' "Any bed the man with a discharge lies on will be unclean, and anything he sits on will be unclean. 5Anyone who touches his bed must wash their clothes and bathe with water, and they will be unclean till evening. 6Whoever sits on anything that the man with a discharge sat on must wash their clothes and bathe with water, and they will be unclean till evening.

7' "Whoever touches the man who has a discharge must wash their clothes and bathe with water, and they will be unclean till evening.

8' "If the man with the discharge spits on anyone who is clean, they must wash their clothes and bathe with water, and they will be unclean till evening.

9' "Everything the man sits on when riding will be unclean, 10and whoever touches any of the things that were under him will be unclean till evening; whoever picks up those things must wash their clothes and bathe with water, and they will be unclean till evening.

11' "Anyone the man with a discharge touches without rinsing his hands with water must wash their clothes and bathe with water, and they will be unclean till evening.

12' "A clay pot that the man touches must be broken, and any wooden article is to be rinsed with water.

13' "When a man is cleansed from his discharge, he is to count seven days for his ceremonial cleansing; he must wash his clothes and bathe himself with fresh water, and he will be clean. 14On the eighth day he must take two doves or two young pigeons and come before the LORD to the entrance to the tent of meeting and give them to the priest. 15The priest is to sacrifice them, the one for a sin offering[a] and the other for a burnt offering. In this way he will make atonement before the LORD for the man because of his discharge.

16' "When a man has an emission of semen, he must bathe his whole body with water, and he will be unclean till evening. 17Any clothing or leather that has semen on it must be washed with water, and it will be unclean till evening. 18When a man has sexual relations with a woman and there is an emission of semen, both of them must bathe with water, and they will be unclean till evening.

19' "When a woman has her regular flow of blood, the impurity of her monthly period will last seven days, and anyone who touches her will be unclean till evening.

---

[a] 15 Or *purification* offering; also in verse 30

20 "'Anything she lies on during her period will be unclean, and anything she sits on will be unclean. 21Anyone who touches her bed will be unclean; they must wash their clothes and bathe with water, and they will be unclean till evening. 22Anyone who touches anything she sits on will be unclean; they must wash their clothes and bathe with water, and they will be unclean till evening. 23Whether it is the bed or anything she was sitting on, anyone who touches it will be unclean till evening.

24 "'If a man has sexual relations with her and her monthly flow touches him, he will be unclean for seven days; any bed he lies on will be unclean.

25 "'When a woman has a discharge of blood for many days at a time other than her monthly period or has a discharge that continues beyond her period, she will be unclean as long as she has the discharge, just as in the days of her period. 26Any bed she lies on while her discharge continues will be unclean, as is her bed during her monthly period, and anything she sits on will be unclean, as during her period. 27Anyone who touches them will be unclean; they must wash their clothes and bathe with water, and they will be unclean till evening. 28 "'When she is cleansed from her discharge, she must count seven days, and after that she will be ceremonially clean. 29On the eighth day she must take two doves or two young pigeons and bring them to the priest at the entrance to the tent of meeting. 30The priest is to sacrifice one for a sin offering and the other for a burnt offering. In this way he will make atonement for her before the LORD for the uncleanness of her discharge.

31 "'You must keep the Israelites separate from things that make them unclean, so they will not die in their uncleanness for defiling my dwelling-place,^{a} which is among them.'"

32These are the regulations for a man with a discharge, for anyone made unclean by an emission of semen, 33for a woman in her monthly period, for a man or a woman with a discharge, and for a man who has sexual relations with a woman who is ceremonially unclean.

IN OTHER WORDS

Day of Atonement
Leviticus 16:1
Although the Israelites regularly made sacrifices for their sins, this was the special day in the year when they focused on getting right with God. Everyone fasted and the High Priest went through elaborate rituals to symbolise the people being made clean from their sin. Towards the end of the ceremony the High Priest would put his hands on a goat and confess all of Israel's sins over it. The goat would then be sent out into the desert to symbolise the sins being taken away by God. That's where we get our word 'scapegoat', meaning someone who takes the blame for things they didn't do.

The Day of Atonement

16 The LORD spoke to Moses after the death of the two sons of Aaron who died when they approached the LORD. 2The LORD said to Moses: 'Tell your brother Aaron that he is not to come whenever he chooses into the Most Holy Place behind the curtain in front of the atonement cover on the ark, or else he will die. For I will appear in the cloud over the atonement cover.

3'This is how Aaron is to enter the Most Holy Place: he must first bring a young bull for a sin offering^b and a ram for a burnt offering. 4He is to put on the sacred linen tunic, with linen undergarments next to his body; he is to tie the linen sash round him and put on the linen turban. These are sacred garments; so he must bathe himself with water before he puts them on. 5From the Israelite community he is to take two male goats for a sin offering and a ram for a burnt offering.

---

^{a} 31 Or *my tabernacle* ^{b} 3 Or *purification offering*; here and throughout this chapter

⁶'Aaron is to offer the bull for his own sin offering to make atonement for himself and his household. ⁷Then he is to take the two goats and present them before the LORD at the entrance to the tent of meeting. ⁸He is to cast lots for the two goats—one lot for the LORD and the other for the scapegoat.[a] ⁹Aaron shall bring the goat whose lot falls to the LORD and sacrifice it for a sin offering. ¹⁰But the goat chosen by lot as the scapegoat shall be presented alive before the LORD to be used for making atonement by sending it into the wilderness as a scapegoat.

¹¹'Aaron shall bring the bull for his own sin offering to make atonement for himself and his household, and he is to slaughter the bull for his own sin offering. ¹²He is to take a censer full of burning coals from the altar before the LORD and two handfuls of finely ground fragrant incense and take them behind the curtain. ¹³He is to put the incense on the fire before the LORD, and the smoke of the incense will conceal the atonement cover above the tablets of the covenant law, so that he will not die. ¹⁴He is to take some of the bull's blood and with his finger sprinkle it on the front of the atonement cover; then he shall sprinkle some of it with his finger seven times before the atonement cover.

¹⁵'He shall then slaughter the goat for the sin offering for the people and take its blood behind the curtain and do with it as he did with the bull's blood: he shall sprinkle it on the atonement cover and in front of it. ¹⁶In this way he will make atonement for the Most Holy Place because of the uncleanness and rebellion of the Israelites, whatever their sins have been. He is to do the same for the tent of meeting, which is among them in the midst of their uncleanness. ¹⁷No-one is to be in the tent of meeting from the time Aaron goes in to make atonement in the Most Holy Place until he comes out, having made atonement for himself, his household and the whole community of Israel.

¹⁸'Then he shall come out to the altar that is before the LORD and make atonement for it. He shall take some of the bull's blood and some of the goat's blood and put it on all the horns of the altar. ¹⁹He shall sprinkle some of the blood on it with his finger seven times to cleanse it and consecrate it from the uncleanness of the Israelites.

²⁰'When Aaron has finished making atonement for the Most Holy Place, the tent of meeting and the altar, he shall bring forward the live goat. ²¹He is to lay both hands on the head of the live goat and confess over it all the wickedness and rebellion of the Israelites—all their sins—and put them on the goat's head. He shall send the goat away into the wilderness in the care of someone appointed for the task. ²²The goat will carry on itself all their sins to a remote place; and the man shall release it in the wilderness.

²³'Then Aaron is to go into the tent of meeting and take off the linen garments he put on before he entered the Most Holy Place, and he is to leave them there. ²⁴He shall bathe himself with water in the sanctuary area and put on his ordinary garments. Then he shall come out and sacrifice the burnt offering for himself and the burnt offering for the people, to make atonement for himself and for the people. ²⁵He shall also burn the fat of the sin offering on the altar.

²⁶'The one who releases the goat as a scapegoat must wash his clothes and bathe himself with water; afterwards he may come into the camp. ²⁷The bull and the goat for the sin offerings, whose blood was brought into the Most Holy Place to make atonement, must be taken outside the camp; their hides, flesh and intestines are to be burned. ²⁸The man who burns them must wash his clothes and bathe himself with water; afterwards he may come into the camp.

²⁹'This is to be a lasting ordinance for you: on the tenth day of the seventh month you must deny yourselves[b] and not do any work—whether native-born or a foreigner residing among you— ³⁰because on this day atonement will be made for you, to cleanse you. Then, before the LORD, you will be clean from all your sins. ³¹It is a day of sabbath rest, and you must deny yourselves; it is a lasting ordinance. ³²The priest who is anointed and ordained to succeed his father

---

[a] 8 The meaning of the Hebrew for this word is uncertain; also in verses 10 and 26. [b] 29 Or *must fast*; also in verse 31

as high priest is to make atonement. He is to put on the sacred linen garments ³³and make atonement for the Most Holy Place, for the tent of meeting and the altar, and for the priests and all the members of the community.

³⁴'This is to be a lasting ordinance for you: atonement is to be made once a year for all the sins of the Israelites.'

And it was done, as the LORD commanded Moses.

Eating blood forbidden

17 The LORD said to Moses, ²'Speak to Aaron and his sons and to all the Israelites and say to them: "This is what the LORD has commanded: ³any Israelite who sacrifices an ox,ᵃ a lamb or a goat in the camp or outside it ⁴instead of bringing it to the entrance to the tent of meeting to present it as an offering to the LORD in front of the tabernacle of the LORD—such people shall be considered guilty of bloodshed; they have shed blood and must be cut off from their people. ⁵This is so that the Israelites will bring to the LORD the sacrifices they are now making in the open fields. They must bring them to the priest, that is, to the LORD, at the entrance to the tent of meeting and sacrifice them as fellowship offerings. ⁶The priest is to splash the blood against the altar of the LORD at the entrance to the tent of meeting and burn the fat as an aroma pleasing to the LORD. ⁷They must no longer offer any of their sacrifices to the goat idolsᵇ to whom they prostitute themselves. This is to be a lasting ordinance for them and for the generations to come."

⁸'Say to them: "Any Israelite or any foreigner residing among them who offers a burnt offering or sacrifice ⁹and does not bring it to the entrance to the tent of meeting to sacrifice it to the LORD must be cut off from their people.

¹⁰' "I will set my face against any Israelite or any foreigner residing among them who eats blood, and I will cut them off from their people. ¹¹For the life of a creature is in the blood, and I have given it to you to make atonement for yourselves on the altar; it is the blood that makes atonement for one's life.ᶜ ¹²Therefore I say to the Israelites, 'None of you may eat blood, nor may any foreigner residing among you eat blood.'

¹³' "Any Israelite or any foreigner residing among you who hunts any animal or bird that may be eaten must drain out the blood and cover it with earth, ¹⁴because the life of every creature is its blood. That is why I have said to the Israelites, 'You must not eat the blood of any creature, because the life of every creature is its blood; anyone who eats it must be cut off.'

¹⁵' "Anyone, whether native-born or foreigner, who eats anything found dead or torn by wild animals must wash their clothes and bathe with water, and they will be ceremonially unclean till evening; then they will be clean. ¹⁶But if they do not wash their clothes and bathe themselves, they will be held responsible."'

Unlawful sexual relations

18 The LORD said to Moses, ²'Speak to the Israelites and say to them: "I am the LORD your God. ³You must not do as they do in Egypt, where you used to live, and you must not do as they do in the land of Canaan, where I am bringing you. Do not follow their practices. ⁴You must obey my

> ### IN OTHER WORDS
>
> **Blood**
> **Leviticus 17:10**
> Blood was the symbol of life for the Israelites and it was shed at all their major festivals. They were to avoid eating blood out of respect for life. It was the shedding of blood in sacrifices that made people right with God. Jesus' blood was shed when he died on the cross; this was the ultimate sacrifice and means that we can be right with God without the need for any more blood being spilt.

ᵃ3 The Hebrew word can include both male and female. ᵇ7 Or *the demons* ᶜ11 Or *atonement by the life in the blood* laws and be careful to follow my decrees. I am the LORD your God. ⁵Keep my decrees and laws, for whoever obeys them will live by them. I am the LORD.

⁶ "No-one is to approach any close relative to have sexual relations. I am the LORD.

⁷ "Do not dishonour your father by having sexual relations with your mother. She is your mother; do not have relations with her.

⁸ "Do not have sexual relations with your father's wife; that would dishonour your father.

⁹ "Do not have sexual relations with your sister, either your father's daughter or your mother's daughter, whether she was born in the same home or elsewhere.

¹⁰ "Do not have sexual relations with your son's daughter or your daughter's daughter; that would dishonour you.

¹¹ "Do not have sexual relations with the daughter of your father's wife, born to your father; she is your sister.

¹² "Do not have sexual relations with your father's sister; she is your father's close relative.

¹³ "Do not have sexual relations with your mother's sister, because she is your mother's close relative.

¹⁴ "Do not dishonour your father's brother by approaching his wife to have sexual relations; she is your aunt.

¹⁵ "Do not have sexual relations with your daughter-in-law. She is your son's wife; do not have relations with her.

¹⁶ "Do not have sexual relations with your brother's wife; that would dishonour your brother.

¹⁷ "Do not have sexual relations with both a woman and her daughter. Do not have sexual relations with either her son's daughter or her daughter's daughter; they are her close relatives. That is wickedness.

¹⁸ "Do not take your wife's sister as a rival wife and have sexual relations with her while your wife is living.

¹⁹ "Do not approach a woman to have sexual relations during the uncleanness of her monthly period.

²⁰ "Do not have sexual relations with your neighbour's wife and defile yourself with her.

²¹ "Do not give any of your children to be sacrificed to Molek, for you must not profane the name of your God. I am the LORD.

²² "Do not have sexual relations with a man as one does with a woman; that is detestable.

²³ "Do not have sexual relations with an animal and defile yourself with it. A woman must not present herself to an animal to have sexual relations with it; that is a perversion.

²⁴ "Do not defile yourselves in any of these ways, because this is how the nations that I am going to drive out before you became defiled. ²⁵Even the land was defiled; so I punished it for its sin, and the land vomited out its inhabitants. ²⁶But you must keep my decrees and my laws. The native-born and the foreigners residing among you must not do any of these detestable things, ²⁷for all these things were done by the people who lived in the land before you, and the land became defiled. ²⁸And if you defile the land, it will vomit you out as it vomited out the nations that were before you.

²⁹ "Everyone who does any of these detestable things—such persons must be cut off from their people. ³⁰Keep my requirements and do not follow any of the detestable customs that were practised before you came and do not defile yourselves with them. I am the LORD your God."'

Various laws

19 The LORD said to Moses, ²'Speak to the entire assembly of Israel and say to them: "Be holy because I, the LORD your God, am holy.

³ "Each of you must respect your mother and father, and you must observe my Sabbaths. I am the LORD your God.

⁴ "Do not turn to idols or make metal gods for yourselves. I am the LORD your God.

⁵ "When you sacrifice a fellowship offering to the LORD, sacrifice it in such a way that it will be accepted on your behalf. ⁶It shall be eaten on the day you sacrifice it

making Connections

Gleaning
Leviticus 19:9

These laws probably saved the lives of people who were poor and had nowhere else to turn. When Ruth and Naomi came back to Bethlehem with nothing, Ruth went gleaning in the field of their distant relative to get some food. Fortunately Boaz had done what the law commanded, otherwise Ruth and Naomi could have starved (Ruth 2:2).

or on the next day; anything left over until the third day must be burned. 7If any of it is eaten on the third day, it is impure and will not be accepted. 8Whoever eats it will be held responsible because they have desecrated what is holy to the LORD; they must be cut off from their people.

9 "When you reap the harvest of your land, do not reap to the very edges of your field or gather the gleanings of your harvest. 10Do not go over your vineyard a second time or pick up the grapes that have fallen. Leave them for the poor and the foreigner. I am the LORD your God.

11 "Do not steal.

' "Do not lie.

' "Do not deceive one another.

12 ' "Do not swear falsely by my name and so profane the name of your God. I am the LORD.

13 "Do not defraud your neighbours or rob them.

' "Do not hold back the wages of a hired worker overnight.

14 ' "Do not curse the deaf or put a stumbling-block in front of the blind, but fear your God. I am the LORD.

15 ' "Do not pervert justice; do not show partiality to the poor or favouritism to the great, but judge your neighbour fairly.

16 ' "Do not go about spreading slander among your people.

' "Do not do anything that endangers your neighbour's life. I am the LORD.

17 ' "Do not hate a fellow Israelite in your heart. Rebuke your neighbour frankly so that you will not share in their guilt.

18 ' "Do not seek revenge or bear a grudge against anyone among your people, but love your neighbour as yourself. I am the LORD.

19 ' "Keep my decrees.

' "Do not mate different kinds of animals.

' "Do not plant your field with two kinds of seed.

' "Do not wear clothing woven of two kinds of material.

20 ' "If a man sleeps with a female slave who is promised to another man but who has not been ransomed or given her freedom, there must be due punishment.[a] Yet they are not to be put to death, because she had not been freed. 21The man, however, must bring a ram to the entrance to the tent of meeting for a guilt offering to the LORD. 22With the ram of the guilt offering the priest is to make atonement for him before the LORD for the sin he has committed, and his sin will be forgiven.

23 ' "When you enter the land and plant any kind of fruit tree, regard its fruit as forbidden.[b] For three years you are to consider it forbidden;[c] it must not be eaten. 24In the fourth year all its fruit will be holy, an offering of praise to the LORD. 25But in the fifth year you may eat its fruit. In this way your harvest will be increased. I am the LORD your God.

26 ' "Do not eat any meat with the blood still in it.

' "Do not practise divination or seek omens.

27 ' "Do not cut the hair at the sides of your head or clip off the edges of your beard.

28 ' "Do not cut your bodies for the dead or put tattoo marks on yourselves. I am the LORD.

29 ' "Do not degrade your daughter by making her a prostitute, or the land will turn

---

[a] 20 Or *be an enquiry* [b] 23 Hebrew *uncircumcised* [c] 23 Hebrew *uncircumcised*

to prostitution and be filled with wickedness.

³⁰ "Observe my Sabbaths and have reverence for my sanctuary. I am the LORD.

³¹ "Do not turn to mediums or seek out spiritists, for you will be defiled by them. I am the LORD your God.

³² "Stand up in the presence of the aged, show respect for the elderly and revere your God. I am the LORD.

³³ "When foreigners reside among you in your land, do not ill-treat them. ³⁴The foreigners residing among you must be treated as your native-born. Love them as yourself, for you were foreigners in Egypt. I am the LORD your God.

³⁵ "Do not use dishonest standards when measuring length, weight or quantity. ³⁶Use honest scales and honest weights, an honest ephah^a and an honest hin.^{b} I am the LORD your God, who brought you out of Egypt.

³⁷ "Keep all my decrees and all my laws and follow them. I am the LORD.'"

Punishments for sin

20 The LORD said to Moses, ²"Say to the Israelites: 'Any Israelite or any foreigner residing in Israel who sacrifices any of his children to Molek is to be put to death. The members of the community are to stone him. ³I myself will set my face against him and will cut him off from his people; for by sacrificing his children to Molek, he has defiled my sanctuary and profaned my holy name. ⁴If the members of the community close their eyes when that man sacrifices one of his children to Molek and if they fail to put him to death, ⁵I myself will set my face against him and his family and will cut them off from their people together with all who follow him in prostituting themselves to Molek.

⁶ "'I will set my face against anyone who turns to mediums and spiritists to prostitute themselves by following them, and I will cut them off from their people.

⁷ "'Consecrate yourselves and be holy, because I am the LORD your God. ⁸Keep my decrees and follow them. I am the LORD, who makes you holy.

⁹ "'Anyone who curses their father or mother is to be put to death. Because they have cursed their father or mother, their blood will be on their own head.

¹⁰ "'If a man commits adultery with another man's wife—with the wife of his neighbour—both the adulterer and the adulteress are to be put to death.

¹¹ "'If a man has sexual relations with his father's wife, he has dishonoured his father. Both the man and the woman are to be put to death; their blood will be on their own heads.

¹² "'If a man has sexual relations with his daughter-in-law, both of them are to be put to death. What they have done is a perversion; their blood will be on their own heads.

¹³ "'If a man has sexual relations with a man as one does with a woman, both of them have done what is detestable. They are to be put to death; their blood will be on their own heads.

¹⁴ "'If a man marries both a woman and her mother, it is wicked. Both he and they must be burned in the fire, so that no wickedness will be among you.

¹⁵ "'If a man has sexual relations with an animal, he is to be put to death, and you must kill the animal.

¹⁶ "'If a woman approaches an animal to have sexual relations with it, kill both the woman and the animal. They are to be put to death; their blood will be on their own heads.

¹⁷ "'If a man marries his sister, the daughter of either his father or his mother, and they have sexual relations, it is a disgrace. They are to be publicly removed from their people. He has dishonoured his sister and will be held responsible.

¹⁸ "'If a man has sexual relations with a woman during her monthly period, he has exposed the source of her flow, and she has also uncovered it. Both of them are to be cut off from their people.

¹⁹ "'Do not have sexual relations with the sister of either your mother or your father,

---

^{a} 36 An ephah was a dry measure having the capacity of about 22 litres. ^{b} 36 A hin was a liquid measure having the capacity of about 3.6 litres.

for that would dishonour a close relative; both of you would be held responsible.

20 "If a man has sexual relations with his aunt, he has dishonoured his uncle. They will be held responsible; they will die childless.

21 "If a man marries his brother's wife, it is an act of impurity; he has dishonoured his brother. They will be childless.

22 "Keep all my decrees and laws and follow them, so that the land where I am bringing you to live may not vomit you out. 23You must not live according to the customs of the nations I am going to drive out before you. Because they did all these things, I abhorred them. 24But I said to you, 'You will possess their land; I will give it to you as an inheritance, a land flowing with milk and honey.' I am the LORD your God, who has set you apart from the nations.

25 "You must therefore make a distinction between clean and unclean animals and between unclean and clean birds. Do not defile yourselves by any animal or bird or anything that moves along the ground—those which I have set apart as unclean for you. 26You are to be holy to me because I, the LORD, am holy, and I have set you apart from the nations to be my own.

27 "A man or woman who is a medium or spiritist among you must be put to death. You are to stone them; their blood will be on their own heads."'

Rules for priests

21 The LORD said to Moses, 'Speak to the priests, the sons of Aaron, and say to them: "A priest must not make himself ceremonially unclean for any of his people who die, 2except for a close relative, such as his mother or father, his son or daughter, his brother, 3or an unmarried sister who is dependent on him since she has no husband—for her he may make himself unclean. 4He must not make himself unclean for people related to him by marriage,[a] and so defile himself.

5 "Priests must not shave their heads or shave off the edges of their beards or cut their bodies. 6They must be holy to their God and must not profane the name of their God. Because they present the food offerings to the LORD, the food of their God, they are to be holy.

7 "They must not marry women defiled by prostitution or divorced from their husbands, because priests are holy to their God. 8Regard them as holy, because they offer up the food of your God. Consider them holy, because I the LORD am holy—I who make you holy.

9 "If a priest's daughter defiles herself by becoming a prostitute, she disgraces her father; she must be burned in the fire.

10 "The high priest, the one among his brothers who has had the anointing oil poured on his head and who has been ordained to wear the priestly garments, must not let his hair become unkempt[b] or tear his clothes. 11He must not enter a place where there is a dead body. He must not make himself unclean, even for his father or mother, 12nor leave the sanctuary of his God or desecrate it, because he has been dedicated by the anointing oil of his God. I am the LORD.

13 "The woman he marries must be a virgin. 14He must not marry a widow, a divorced woman, or a woman defiled by prostitution, but only a virgin from his own

Leaders
Leviticus 21:1

Wow – if you thought it was hard to get into a top university, just look at these requirements for becoming a priest! Priests were to set a good example for the people in every way. They had to make sure they kept themselves holy because they represented God to the people, and God is holy.

---

[a] 4 Or *unclean as a leader among his people*   [b] 10 Or *not uncover his head*

people, 15so that he will not defile his offspring among his people. I am the LORD, who makes him holy."'

16The LORD said to Moses, 17'Say to Aaron: "For the generations to come none of your descendants who has a defect may come near to offer the food of his God. 18No man who has any defect may come near: no man who is blind or lame, disfigured or deformed; 19no man with a crippled foot or hand, 20or who is a hunchback or a dwarf, or who has any eye defect, or who has festering or running sores or damaged testicles. 21No descendant of Aaron the priest who has any defect is to come near to present the food offerings to the LORD. He has a defect; he must not come near to offer the food of his God. 22He may eat the most holy food of his God, as well as the holy food; 23yet because of his defect, he must not go near the curtain or approach the altar, and so desecrate my sanctuary. I am the LORD, who makes them holy."'

24So Moses told this to Aaron and his sons and to all the Israelites.

22 The LORD said to Moses, 2'Tell Aaron and his sons to treat with respect the sacred offerings the Israelites consecrate to me, so that they will not profane my holy name. I am the LORD.

3'Say to them: "For the generations to come, if any of your descendants is ceremonially unclean and yet comes near the sacred offerings that the Israelites consecrate to the LORD, that person must be cut off from my presence. I am the LORD.

4' "If a descendant of Aaron has a defiling skin disease*a* or a bodily discharge, he may not eat the sacred offerings until he is cleansed. He will also be unclean if he touches something defiled by a corpse or by anyone who has an emission of semen, 5or if he touches any crawling thing that makes him unclean, or any person who makes him unclean, whatever the uncleanness may be. 6The one who touches any such thing will be unclean till evening. He must not eat any of the sacred offerings unless he has bathed himself with water. 7When the sun goes down, he will be clean, and after that he may eat the sacred offerings, for they are his food. 8He must not eat anything found dead or torn by wild animals, and so become unclean through it. I am the LORD.

9' "The priests are to perform my service in such a way that they do not become guilty and die for treating it with contempt. I am the LORD, who makes them holy.

10' "No-one outside a priest's family may eat the sacred offering, nor may the guest of a priest or his hired worker eat it. 11But if a priest buys a slave with money, or if slaves are born in his household, they may eat his food. 12If a priest's daughter marries anyone other than a priest, she may not eat any of the sacred contributions. 13But if a priest's daughter becomes a widow or is divorced, yet has no children, and she returns to live in her father's household as in her youth, she may eat of her father's food. No unauthorised person, however, may eat any of it.

14' "Anyone who eats a sacred offering by mistake must make restitution to the priest for the offering and add a fifth of the value to it. 15The priests must not desecrate the sacred offerings the Israelites present to the LORD 16by allowing them to eat the sacred offerings and so bring upon them guilt requiring payment. I am the LORD, who makes them holy."'

Unacceptable sacrifices

17The LORD said to Moses, 18'Speak to Aaron and his sons and to all the Israelites and say to them: "If any of you—whether an Israelite or a foreigner residing in Israel—presents a gift for a burnt offering to the LORD, either to fulfil a vow or as a freewill offering, 19you must present a male without defect from the cattle, sheep or goats in order that it may be accepted on your behalf. 20Do not bring anything with a defect, because it will not be accepted on your behalf. 21When anyone brings from the herd or flock a fellowship offering to the LORD to fulfil a special vow or as a freewill offering, it must be without defect or

---

a 4 The Hebrew word for *defiling skin disease*, traditionally translated 'leprosy', was used for various diseases affecting the skin.

blemish to be acceptable. 22Do not offer to the LORD the blind, the injured or the maimed, or anything with warts or festering or running sores. Do not place any of these on the altar as a food offering presented to the LORD. 23You may, however, present as a freewill offering an ox[a] or a sheep that is deformed or stunted, but it will not be accepted in fulfilment of a vow. 24You must not offer to the LORD an animal whose testicles are bruised, crushed, torn or cut. You must not do this in your own land, 25and you must not accept such animals from the hand of a foreigner and offer them as the food of your God. They will not be accepted on your behalf, because they are deformed and have defects." '

26The LORD said to Moses, 27'When a calf, a lamb or a goat is born, it is to remain with its mother for seven days. From the eighth day on, it will be acceptable as a food offering presented to the LORD. 28Do not slaughter a cow or a sheep and its young on the same day.

29'When you sacrifice a thank-offering to the LORD, sacrifice it in such a way that it will be accepted on your behalf. 30It must be eaten that same day; leave none of it till morning. I am the LORD.

31'Keep my commands and follow them. I am the LORD. 32Do not profane my holy name, for I must be acknowledged as holy by the Israelites. I am the LORD, who made you holy 33and who brought you out of Egypt to be your God. I am the LORD.'

23 The LORD said to Moses, 2'Speak to the Israelites and say to them: "These are my appointed festivals, the appointed festivals of the LORD, which you are to proclaim as sacred assemblies.

The Sabbath

3' "There are six days when you may work, but the seventh day is a day of sabbath rest, a day of sacred assembly. You are not to do any work; wherever you live, it is a sabbath to the LORD.

The Passover and Unleavened Bread

4' "These are the LORD's appointed festivals, the sacred assemblies you are to proclaim at their appointed times: 5the LORD's Passover begins at twilight on the fourteenth day of the first month. 6On the fifteenth day of that month the LORD's Festival of Unleavened Bread begins; for seven days you must eat bread made without yeast. 7On the first day hold a sacred assembly and do not do any of your ordinary work. 8For seven days present a food offering to the LORD. And on the seventh day hold a sacred assembly and do not do any of your ordinary work." '

Firstfruits

9The LORD said to Moses, 10'Speak to the Israelites and say to them: "When you enter the land I am going to give you and you reap its harvest, bring to the priest a sheaf of the first grain you harvest. 11He is to wave the sheaf before the LORD so it will be accepted on your behalf; the priest is to wave it on the day after the Sabbath. 12On the day you wave the sheaf, you must sacrifice as a burnt offering to the LORD a lamb a year old without defect, 13together with its grain offering of one fifth of an ephah[b] of the finest flour mixed with olive oil—a food offering presented to the LORD, a pleasing

---

IN OTHER WORDS

Festival
Leviticus 23:2

These festivals were times of celebration when the Israelites would remember their special relationship with God. The Jews still have three main religious festivals each year: Passover, Pentecost and Tabernacles. These festivals are based on the agricultural year; they reaffirm God's central place in their lives and the importance of receiving God's forgiveness.

---

[a] 23 The Hebrew word can include both male and female.   [b] 13 That is, probably about 3.25 kilograms; also in verse 17

aroma—and its drink offering of a quarter of a hin[a] of wine. 14You must not eat any bread, or roasted or new grain, until the very day you bring this offering to your God. This is to be a lasting ordinance for the generations to come, wherever you live.

Festival of Weeks

15' "From the day after the Sabbath, the day you brought the sheaf of the wave offering, count seven full weeks. 16Count fifty days up to the day after the seventh Sabbath, and then present an offering of new grain to the LORD. 17From wherever you live, bring two loaves made of one fifth of an ephah of the finest flour, baked with yeast, as a wave offering of firstfruits to the LORD. 18Present with this bread seven male lambs, each a year old and without defect, one young bull and two rams. They will be a burnt offering to the LORD, together with their grain offerings and drink offerings—a food offering, an aroma pleasing to the LORD. 19Then sacrifice one male goat for a sin offering[b] and two lambs, each a year old, for a fellowship offering. 20The priest is to wave the two lambs before the LORD as a wave offering, together with the bread of the firstfruits. They are a sacred offering to the LORD for the priest. 21On that same day you are to proclaim a sacred assembly and not do any ordinary work. This is to be a lasting ordinance for the generations to come, wherever you live.

22' "When you reap the harvest of your land, do not reap to the very edges of your field or gather the gleanings of your harvest. Leave them for the poor and for the foreigner residing among you. I am the LORD your God."'

Festival of Trumpets

23The LORD said to Moses, 24'Say to the Israelites: "On the first day of the seventh month you are to have a day of sabbath rest, a sacred assembly commemorated with trumpet blasts. 25Do not do any of your ordinary work, but present a food offering to the LORD."'

Day of Atonement

26The LORD said to Moses, 27'The tenth day of this seventh month is the Day of Atonement. Hold a sacred assembly and deny yourselves,[c] and present a food offering to the LORD. 28Do not do any work on that day, because it is the Day of Atonement, when atonement is made for you before the LORD your God. 29Those who do not deny themselves on that day must be cut off from their people. 30I will destroy from among their people anyone who does any work on that day. 31You shall do no work at all. This is to be a lasting ordinance for the generations to come, wherever you live. 32It is a day of sabbath rest for you, and you must deny yourselves. From the evening of the ninth day of the month until the following evening you are to observe your sabbath.'

Festival of Tabernacles

33The LORD said to Moses, 34'Say to the Israelites: "On the fifteenth day of the seventh month the LORD's Festival of Tabernacles begins, and it lasts for seven days. 35The first day is a sacred assembly; do not do any of your ordinary work. 36For seven days present food offerings to the LORD, and on the eighth day hold a sacred assembly and present a food offering to the LORD. It is the closing special assembly; do not do any of your ordinary work.

37'"These are the LORD's appointed festivals, which you are to proclaim as sacred assemblies for bringing food offerings to the LORD—the burnt offerings and grain offerings, sacrifices and drink offerings required for each day. 38These offerings are in addition to those for the LORD's Sabbaths and[d] in addition to your gifts and whatever you have vowed and all the freewill offerings you give to the LORD.)

39'"So beginning with the fifteenth day of the seventh month, after you have gathered the crops of the land, celebrate the festival to the LORD for seven days; the first day is a day of sabbath rest, and the eighth day also is a day of sabbath rest. 40On the first day you are to take branches from luxuriant trees—from palms, willows and

---

[a] 13 That is, about 0.9 litre [b] 19 Or *purification offering* [c] 27 Or *and fast*; also in verses 29 and 32 [d] 38 Or *These festivals are in addition to the LORD's Sabbaths, and these offerings are*

other leafy trees—and rejoice before the LORD your God for seven days. 41Celebrate this as a festival to the LORD for seven days each year. This is to be a lasting ordinance for the generations to come; celebrate it in the seventh month. 42Live in temporary shelters for seven days: all native-born Israelites are to live in such shelters 43so that your descendants will know that I made the Israelites live in temporary shelters when I brought them out of Egypt. I am the LORD your God."'

44So Moses announced to the Israelites the appointed festivals of the LORD.

Oil and bread set before the LORD

24 The LORD said to Moses, 2'Command the Israelites to bring you clear oil of pressed olives for the light so that the lamps may be kept burning continually. 3Outside the curtain that shields the ark of the covenant law in the tent of meeting, Aaron is to tend the lamps before the LORD from evening till morning, continually. This is to be a lasting ordinance for the generations to come. 4The lamps on the pure gold lampstand before the LORD must be tended continually.

5'Take the finest flour and bake twelve loaves of bread, using one fifth of an ephah*a* for each loaf. 6Arrange them in two piles, six in each pile, on the table of pure gold before the LORD. 7By each pile put some pure incense as a memorial*b* portion to represent the bread and to be a food offering presented to the LORD. 8This bread is to be set out before the LORD regularly, Sabbath after Sabbath, on behalf of the Israelites, as a lasting covenant. 9It belongs to Aaron and his sons, who are to eat it in the sanctuary area, because it is a most holy part of their perpetual share of the food offerings presented to the LORD.'

A blasphemer stoned

10Now the son of an Israelite mother and an Egyptian father went out among the Israelites, and a fight broke out in the camp between him and an Israelite. 11The son of the Israelite woman used the Name blasphemously with a curse; so they brought him to Moses. (His mother's name was Shelomith, the daughter of Dibri the Danite.) 12They put him in custody until the will of the LORD should be made clear to them.

13Then the LORD said to Moses: 14'Take the blasphemer outside the camp. All those who heard him are to lay their hands on his head, and the entire assembly is to stone him. 15Say to the Israelites: "Anyone who curses their God will be held responsible; 16anyone who uses the name of the LORD blasphemously is to be put to death. The entire assembly must stone them. Whether foreigner or native-born, when they use the Name blasphemously they are to be put to death.

17' "Anyone who takes the life of a human being is to be put to death. 18Anyone who takes the life of someone's animal must make restitution—life for life. 19Anyone who injures a neighbour is to be injured in the same manner: 20fracture for fracture, eye for eye, tooth for tooth. The one who has inflicted the injury must suffer the same injury. 21Whoever kills an animal must make restitution, but whoever kills a human being is to be put to death. 22You are to have the same law for the foreigner and the native-born. I am the LORD your God."'

23Then Moses spoke to the Israelites, and they took the blasphemer outside the camp and stoned him. The Israelites did as the LORD commanded Moses.

The sabbath year

25 The LORD said to Moses on Mount Sinai, 2'Speak to the Israelites and say to them: "When you enter the land I am going to give you, the land itself must observe a sabbath to the LORD. 3For six years sow your fields, and for six years prune your vineyards and gather their crops. 4But in the seventh year the land is to have a year of sabbath rest, a sabbath to the LORD. Do not sow your fields or prune your vineyards. 5Do not reap what grows of itself or harvest the grapes of your untended vines. The land is to have a year of rest. 6Whatever the land yields during the sabbath year will be food for you—for yourself, your male and female servants, and the hired worker and

---

a 5 That is, probably about 3.25 kilograms   *b* 7 Or *representative*

> **IN OTHER WORDS**
>
> **Jubilee**
> **Leviticus 25:10**
> The Israelites had so many festivals, it can seem as though life was one long party. Well, the Year of Jubilee was definitely a whole year of celebration, when the people were to act justly, love mercy and be jubilant! People who had got into debt and had sold themselves as slaves were to be set free with their debts cancelled. The Jubilee Year was a chance for everyone to start again and this meant there wouldn't have been big gaps between rich and poor in Israelite society, unlike our own world. This Year of Jubilee inspired the Jubilee campaign for the debts of the poorest countries to be cancelled.

temporary resident who live among you, 7as well as for your livestock and the wild animals in your land. Whatever the land produces may be eaten.

The Year of Jubilee

8 "Count seven sabbath years—seven times seven years—so that the seven sabbath years amount to a period of forty-nine years. 9Then sound the trumpet everywhere on the tenth day of the seventh month; on the Day of Atonement sound the trumpet throughout your land. 10Consecrate the fiftieth year and proclaim liberty throughout the land to all its inhabitants. It shall be a jubilee for you; each of you is to return to your family property and to your own clan. 11The fiftieth year shall be a jubilee for you; do not sow and do not reap what grows of itself or harvest the untended vines. 12For it is a jubilee and is to be holy for you; eat only what is taken directly from the fields.

13 "In this Year of Jubilee everyone is to return to their own property.

14 "If you sell land to any of your own people or buy land from them, do not take advantage of each other. 15You are to buy from your own people on the basis of the number of years since the Jubilee. And they are to sell to you on the basis of the number of years left for harvesting crops. 16When the years are many, you are to increase the price, and when the years are few, you are to decrease the price, because what is really being sold to you is the number of crops. 17Do not take advantage of each other, but fear your God. I am the LORD your God.

18 "Follow my decrees and be careful to obey my laws, and you will live safely in the land. 19Then the land will yield its fruit, and you will eat your fill and live there in safety. 20You may ask, 'What will we eat in the seventh year if we do not plant or harvest our crops?' 21I will send you such a blessing in the sixth year that the land will yield enough for three years. 22While you plant during the eighth year, you will eat from the old crop and will continue to eat from it until the harvest of the ninth year comes in.

23 "The land must not be sold permanently, because the land is mine and you reside in my land as foreigners and strangers. 24Throughout the land that you hold as a possession, you must provide for the redemption of the land.

25 "If anyone among you becomes poor and sells some of their property, their nearest relative is to come and redeem what they have sold. 26If, however, there is no-one to redeem it for them but later on they prosper and acquire sufficient means to redeem it themselves, 27they are to determine the value for the years since they sold it and refund the balance to the one to whom they sold it; they can then go back to their own property. 28But if they do not acquire the means to repay, what was sold will remain in the possession of the buyer until the Year of Jubilee. It will be returned in the Jubilee, and they can then go back to their property.

29 "Anyone who sells a house in a walled city retains the right of redemption a full year after its sale. During that time the seller may redeem it. 30If it is not redeemed before a full year has passed, the house in the walled city shall belong permanently to the buyer and the buyer's descendants. It is not to be

returned in the Jubilee. ³¹But houses in villages without walls round them are to be considered as belonging to the open country. They can be redeemed, and they are to be returned in the Jubilee.

³²' "The Levites always have the right to redeem their houses in the Levitical towns, which they possess. ³³So the property of the Levites is redeemable—that is, a house sold in any town they hold—and is to be returned in the Jubilee, because the houses in the towns of the Levites are their property among the Israelites. ³⁴But the pasture-land belonging to their towns must not be sold; it is their permanent possession.

³⁵' "If any of your own people become poor and are unable to support themselves among you, help them as you would a foreigner and stranger, so that they can continue to live among you. ³⁶Do not take interest or any profit from them, but fear your God, so that your poor neighbours may continue to live among you. ³⁷You must not lend them money at interest or sell them food at a profit. ³⁸I am the LORD your God, who brought you out of Egypt to give you the land of Canaan and to be your God.

³⁹' "If any of your own people become poor and sell themselves to you, do not make them work as slaves. ⁴⁰They are to be treated as hired workers or temporary residents among you; they are to work for you until the Year of Jubilee. ⁴¹Then they and their children are to be released, and they will go back to their own clans and to the property of their ancestors. ⁴²Because the Israelites are my servants, whom I brought out of Egypt, they must not be sold as slaves. ⁴³Do not rule over them ruthlessly, but fear your God.

⁴⁴' "Your male and female slaves are to come from the nations around you; from them you may buy slaves. ⁴⁵You may also buy some of the temporary residents living among you and members of their clans born in your country, and they will become your property. ⁴⁶You can bequeath them to your children as inherited property and can make them slaves for life, but you must not rule over your fellow Israelites ruthlessly.

⁴⁷' "If a foreigner residing among you becomes rich and any of your own people become poor and sell themselves to the foreigner or to a member of the foreigner's clan, ⁴⁸they retain the right of redemption after they have sold themselves. One of their relatives may redeem them: ⁴⁹an uncle or a cousin or any blood-relative in their clan may redeem them. Or if any of them prosper, they may redeem themselves. ⁵⁰They and their buyer are to count the time from the year they sold themselves up to the Year of Jubilee. The price for their release is to be based on the rate paid to a hired worker for that number of years. ⁵¹If many years remain, they must pay for their redemption a larger share of the price paid for them. ⁵²If only a few years remain until the Year of Jubilee, they are to compute that and pay for their redemption accordingly. ⁵³They are to be treated as hired workers from year to year; you must see to it that those to whom they owe service do not rule over them ruthlessly.

⁵⁴' "Even if they are not redeemed in any of these ways, they and their children are to be released in the Year of Jubilee, ⁵⁵for the Israelites belong to me as servants. They are my servants, whom I brought out of Egypt. I am the LORD your God.

Reward for obedience

26 ¹ "Do not make idols or set up an image or a sacred stone for yourselves, and do not place a carved stone in your land to bow down before it. I am the LORD your God.

²' "Observe my Sabbaths and have reverence for my sanctuary. I am the LORD.

³' "If you follow my decrees and are careful to obey my commands, ⁴I will send you rain in its season, and the ground will yield its crops and the trees their fruit. ⁵Your threshing will continue until grape harvest and the grape harvest will continue until planting, and you will eat all the food you want and live in safety in your land.

⁶' "I will grant peace in the land, and you will lie down and no-one will make you afraid. I will remove wild beasts from the land, and the sword will not pass through your country. ⁷You will pursue your enemies, and they will fall by the sword before

you. ⁸Five of you will chase a hundred, and a hundred of you will chase ten thousand, and your enemies will fall by the sword before you.

⁹ "I will look on you with favour and make you fruitful and increase your numbers, and I will keep my covenant with you. ¹⁰You will still be eating last year's harvest when you will have to move it out to make room for the new. ¹¹I will put my dwelling-place*ᵃ* among you, and I will not abhor you. ¹²I will walk among you and be your God, and you will be my people. ¹³I am the LORD your God, who brought you out of Egypt so that you would no longer be slaves to the Egyptians; I broke the bars of your yoke and enabled you to walk with heads held high.

Punishment for disobedience

¹⁴ "But if you will not listen to me and carry out all these commands, ¹⁵and if you reject my decrees and abhor my laws and fail to carry out all my commands and so violate my covenant, ¹⁶then I will do this to you: I will bring on you sudden terror, wasting diseases and fever that will destroy your sight and sap your strength. You will plant seed in vain, because your enemies will eat it. ¹⁷I will set my face against you so that you will be defeated by your enemies; those who hate you will rule over you, and you will flee even when no-one is pursuing you.

¹⁸ "If after all this you will not listen to me, I will punish you for your sins seven times over. ¹⁹I will break down your stubborn pride and make the sky above you like iron and the ground beneath you like bronze. ²⁰Your strength will be spent in vain, because your soil will not yield its crops, nor will the trees of your land yield their fruit.

²¹ "If you remain hostile towards me and refuse to listen to me, I will multiply your afflictions seven times over, as your sins deserve. ²²I will send wild animals against you, and they will rob you of your children, destroy your cattle and make you so few in number that your roads will be deserted.

²³ "If in spite of these things you do not accept my correction but continue to be hostile towards me, ²⁴I myself will be hostile towards you and will afflict you for your sins seven times over. ²⁵And I will bring the sword on you to avenge the breaking of the covenant. When you withdraw into your cities, I will send a plague among you, and you will be given into enemy hands. ²⁶When I cut off your supply of bread, ten women will be able to bake your bread in one oven, and they will dole out the bread by weight. You will eat, but you will not be satisfied.

²⁷ "If in spite of this you still do not listen to me but continue to be hostile towards me, ²⁸then in my anger I will be hostile towards you, and I myself will punish you for your sins seven times over. ²⁹You will eat the flesh of your sons and the flesh of your daughters. ³⁰I will destroy your high places, cut down your incense altars and pile your dead bodies*ᵇ* on the lifeless forms of your idols, and I will abhor you. ³¹I will turn your cities into ruins and lay waste your sanctuaries, and I will take no delight in the pleasing aroma of your offerings. ³²I myself will lay waste the land, so that your enemies who live there will be appalled. ³³I will scatter you among the nations and will draw out my sword and pursue you. Your land will be laid waste, and your cities will lie in ruins. ³⁴Then the land will enjoy its sabbath years all the time that it lies desolate and you are in the country of your enemies; then the land will rest and enjoy its sabbaths. ³⁵All the time that it lies desolate, the land will have the rest it did not have during the sabbaths you lived in it.

³⁶ "As for those of you who are left, I will make their hearts so fearful in the lands of their enemies that the sound of a wind-blown leaf will put them to flight. They will run as though fleeing from the sword, and they will fall, even though no-one is pursuing them. ³⁷They will stumble over one another as though fleeing from the sword, even though no-one is pursuing them. So you will not be able to stand before your enemies. ³⁸You will perish among the nations; the land of your enemies will devour you. ³⁹Those of you who are left will waste away in the lands of their enemies

---

*ᵃ*11 Or *my tabernacle* *ᵇ*30 Or *your funeral offerings*

because of their sins; also because of their ancestors' sins they will waste away.

40' "But if they will confess their sins and the sins of their ancestors—their unfaithfulness and their hostility towards me, 41which made me hostile towards them so that I sent them into the land of their enemies—then when their uncircumcised hearts are humbled and they pay for their sin, 42I will remember my covenant with Jacob and my covenant with Isaac and my covenant with Abraham, and I will remember the land. 43For the land will be deserted by them and will enjoy its sabbaths while it lies desolate without them. They will pay for their sins because they rejected my laws and abhorred my decrees. 44Yet in spite of this, when they are in the land of their enemies, I will not reject them nor abhor them so as to destroy them completely, breaking my covenant with them. I am the LORD their God. 45But for their sake I will remember the covenant with their ancestors whom I brought out of Egypt in the sight of the nations to be their God. I am the LORD.'"

46These are the decrees, the laws and the regulations that the LORD established on Mount Sinai between himself and the Israelites through Moses.

Redeeming what is the LORD's

27 The LORD said to Moses, 2'Speak to the Israelites and say to them: "If anyone makes a special vow to dedicate a person to the LORD by giving the equivalent value, 3set the value of a male between the ages of twenty and sixty at fifty shekels^a of silver, according to the sanctuary shekel;^{b} 4for a female, set her value at thirty shekels;^{c} 5for a person between the ages of five and twenty, set the value of a male at twenty shekels^d and of a female at ten shekels^e; 6for a person between one month and five years, set the value of a male at five shekels^f of silver and that of a female at three shekels^g of silver; 7for a person sixty years old or more, set the value of a male at fifteen shekels^h and of a female at ten shekels. 8If anyone making the vow is too poor to pay the specified amount, the person being dedicated is to be presented to the priest, who will set the value according to what the one making the vow can afford.

9' "If what anyone vowed is an animal that is acceptable as an offering to the LORD, such an animal given to the LORD becomes holy. 10They must not exchange it or substitute a good one for a bad one, or a bad one for a good one; if they should substitute one animal for another, both it and the substitute become holy. 11If what they vowed is a ceremonially unclean animal—one that is not acceptable as an offering to the LORD—the animal must be presented to the priest, 12who will judge its quality as good or bad. Whatever value the priest then sets, that is what it will be. 13If the owner wishes to redeem the animal, a fifth must be added to its value.

14' "If anyone dedicates their house as something holy to the LORD, the priest will judge its quality as good or bad. Whatever value the priest then sets, so it will remain. 15If the one who dedicates their house wishes to redeem it, they must add a fifth to its value, and the house will again become theirs.

16' "If anyone dedicates to the LORD part of their family land, its value is to be set according to the amount of seed required for it—fifty shekels of silver to a homer^i of barley seed. 17If they dedicate a field during the Year of Jubilee, the value that has been set remains. 18But if they dedicate a field after the Jubilee, the priest will determine the value according to the number of years that remain until the next Year of Jubilee, and its set value will be reduced. 19If the one who dedicates the field wishes to redeem it, they must add a fifth to its value, and the field will again become theirs. 20If, however, they do not redeem the field, or if they have sold it to someone else, it can never be redeemed. 21When the field is released in the Jubilee, it will become holy, like a field devoted to the LORD; it will become priestly property.

22' "If anyone dedicates to the LORD a field they have bought, which is not part of

---

^{a}3 That is, about 575 grams; also in verse 16 ^{b}3 That is, about 11.5 grams; also in verse 25 ^{c}4 That is, about 345 grams ^{d}5 That is, about 230 grams ^{e}5 That is, about 115 grams; also in verse 7 ^{f}6 That is, about 55 grams ^{g}6 That is, about 35 grams ^{h}7 That is, about 170 grams ^{i}16 That is, probably about 135 kilograms their family land, 23the priest will determine its value up to the Year of Jubilee, and that person must pay its value on that day as something holy to the LORD. 24In the Year of Jubilee the field will revert to the person from whom it was bought, the one whose land it was. 25Every value is to be set according to the sanctuary shekel, twenty gerahs to the shekel.

26 "No-one, however, may dedicate the firstborn of an animal, since the firstborn already belongs to the LORD; whether an ox[a] or a sheep, it is the LORD's. 27If it is one of the unclean animals, it may be bought back at its set value, adding a fifth of the value to it. If it is not redeemed, it is to be sold at its set value.

28 "But nothing that a person owns and devotes[b] to the LORD—whether a human being or an animal or family land—may be sold or redeemed; everything so devoted is most holy to the LORD.

29 "No-one devoted to destruction[c] may be ransomed; they are to be put to death.

30 "A tithe of everything from the land, whether grain from the soil or fruit from the trees, belongs to the LORD; it is holy to the LORD. 31Whoever would redeem any of their tithe must add a fifth of the value to it. 32Every tithe of the herd and flock—every tenth animal that passes under the shepherd's rod—will be holy to the LORD. 33No-one may pick out the good from the bad or make any substitution. If anyone does make a substitution, both the animal and its substitute become holy and cannot be redeemed.'"

34These are the commands the LORD gave Moses on Mount Sinai for the Israelites.

IN OTHER WORDS

Tithe
Leviticus 27:30
A 'tithe' was a tenth. It was the law for the Israelites to give a tenth of their crops, livestock and any other produce to the temple for worship and sacrifice. Many people today give a tithe to their church or to Christian organisations.

---

[a] 26 The Hebrew word can include both male and female. [b] 28 The Hebrew term refers to the irrevocable giving over of things or persons to the LORD. [c] 29 The Hebrew term refers to the irrevocable giving over of things or persons to the LORD, often by totally destroying them.

Numbers

INTRODUCTION

NUMBERS

Author: Moses

When: Probably around 1450 BC to 1400 BC.

Where: Wandering in the desert between Egypt and Canaan.

Did you know? The people of Israel are counted twice in this book – in chapters 1 and 26 – and that's why the book is called Numbers.

Main theme: Numbers tracks the Israelites as they move through the wilderness on their way to the Promised Land. And what a miserable bunch they are, grumbling about food, water and anything else they can think of! God's patience and Moses' leadership are tested to the limit. The Israelites are afraid to go into the Promised Land, so they don't trust God. As a result, they are sentenced to forty years of aimless wandering. But God doesn't give up on them; he waits for a new generation of Israelites to finish the journey.

The census

1 The LORD spoke to Moses in the tent of meeting in the Desert of Sinai on the first day of the second month of the second year after the Israelites came out of Egypt. He said: 2'Take a census of the whole Israelite community by their clans and families, listing every man by name, one by one. 3You and Aaron are to count according to their divisions all the men in Israel who are twenty years old or more and able to serve in the army. 4One man from each tribe, each of them the head of his family, is to help you. 5These are the names of the men who are to assist you:

from Reuben, Elizur son of Shedeur;
6from Simeon, Shelumiel son of Zurishaddai;
7from Judah, Nahshon son of Amminadab;
8from Issachar, Nethanel son of Zuar;
9from Zebulun, Eliab son of Helon;
10from the sons of Joseph:

from Ephraim, Elishama son of Ammihud;

from Manasseh, Gamaliel son of Pedahzur;

[11] from Benjamin, Abidan son of Gideoni;
[12] from Dan, Ahiezer son of Ammishaddai;
[13] from Asher, Pagiel son of Okran;
[14] from Gad, Eliasaph son of Deuel;
[15] from Naphtali, Ahira son of Enan.'

[16] These were the men appointed from the community, the leaders of their ancestral tribes. They were the heads of the clans of Israel.

[17] Moses and Aaron took these men whose names had been specified, [18] and they called the whole community together on the first day of the second month. The people registered their ancestry by their clans and families, and the men twenty years old or more were listed by name, one by one, [19] as the LORD commanded Moses. And so he counted them in the Desert of Sinai:

[20] From the descendants of Reuben the firstborn son of Israel:

All the men twenty years old or more who were able to serve in the army were listed by name, one by one, according to the records of their clans and families. [21] The number from the tribe of Reuben was 46,500.

[22] From the descendants of Simeon:

All the men twenty years old or more who were able to serve in the army were counted and listed by name, one by one, according to the records of their clans and families. [23] The number from the tribe of Simeon was 59,300.

[24] From the descendants of Gad:

All the men twenty years old or more who were able to serve in the army were listed by name, according to the records of their clans and families. [25] The number from the tribe of Gad was 45,650.

[26] From the descendants of Judah:

All the men twenty years old or more who were able to serve in the army were listed by name, according to the records of their clans and families. [27] The number from the tribe of Judah was 74,600.

[28] From the descendants of Issachar:

All the men twenty years old or more who were able to serve in the army were listed by name, according to the records of their clans and families. [29] The number from the tribe of Issachar was 54,400.

[30] From the descendants of Zebulun:

All the men twenty years old or more who were able to serve in the army were listed by name, according to the records of their clans and families. [31] The number from the tribe of Zebulun was 57,400.

[32] From the sons of Joseph:

From the descendants of Ephraim:

All the men twenty years old or more who were able to serve in the army were listed by name, according to the records of their clans and families. [33] The number from the tribe of Ephraim was 40,500.

[34] From the descendants of Manasseh:

All the men twenty years old or more who were able to serve in the army were listed by name, according to the records of their clans and families. [35] The number from the tribe of Manasseh was 32,200.

[36] From the descendants of Benjamin:

All the men twenty years old or more who were able to serve in the army were listed by name, according to the records of their clans and families. [37] The number from the tribe of Benjamin was 35,400.

[38] From the descendants of Dan:

All the men twenty years old or more who were able to serve in the army were listed by name, according to the records of their clans and families. ³⁹The number from the tribe of Dan was 62,700.

⁴⁰From the descendants of Asher:
All the men twenty years old or more who were able to serve in the army were listed by name, according to the records of their clans and families. ⁴¹The number from the tribe of Asher was 41,500.

⁴²From the descendants of Naphtali:
All the men twenty years old or more who were able to serve in the army were listed by name, according to the records of their clans and families. ⁴³The number from the tribe of Naphtali was 53,400.

⁴⁴These were the men counted by Moses and Aaron and the twelve leaders of Israel, each one representing his family. ⁴⁵All the Israelites twenty years old or more who were able to serve in Israel's army were counted according to their families. ⁴⁶The total number was 603,550.

⁴⁷The ancestral tribe of the Levites, however, was not counted along with the others. ⁴⁸The LORD had said to Moses: ⁴⁹'You must not count the tribe of Levi or include them in the census of the other Israelites. ⁵⁰Instead, appoint the Levites to be in charge of the tabernacle of the covenant law—over all its furnishings and everything belonging to it. They are to carry the tabernacle and all its furnishings; they are to take care of it and camp round it. ⁵¹Whenever the tabernacle is to move, the Levites are to take it down, and whenever the tabernacle is to be set up, the Levites shall do it. Anyone else who approaches it is to be put to death. ⁵²The Israelites are to set up their tents by divisions, each of them in their own camp under their standard. ⁵³The Levites, however, are to set up their tents round the tabernacle of the covenant law so that my wrath will not fall on the Israelite community. The Levites are to be responsible for the care of the tabernacle of the covenant law.'

⁵⁴The Israelites did all this just as the LORD commanded Moses.

People and Places

The twelve tribes of Israel
Numbers 2:1
The twelve tribes of Israel were named after Jacob's twelve sons – mostly. There was no tribe of Levi because his descendants served as priests in the temple. And there was no tribe of Joseph; his sons Ephraim and Manasseh each had a tribe named after them instead.

The arrangement of the tribal camps

2 The LORD said to Moses and Aaron: ²'The Israelites are to camp round the tent of meeting some distance from it, each of them under their standard and holding the banners of their family.'

³On the east, towards the sunrise, the divisions of the camp of Judah are to camp under their standard. The leader of the people of Judah is Nahshon son of Amminadab. ⁴His division numbers 74,600.

⁵The tribe of Issachar will camp next to them. The leader of the people of Issachar is Nethanel son of Zuar. ⁶His division numbers 54,400.

⁷The tribe of Zebulun will be next. The leader of the people of Zebulun is Eliab son of Helon. ⁸His division numbers 57,400.

⁹All the men assigned to the camp of Judah, according to their divisions, number 186,400. They will set out first.

¹⁰On the south will be the divisions of the camp of Reuben under their standard. The leader of the people of Reuben is Elizur son of Shedeur. ¹¹His division numbers 46,500.

¹²The tribe of Simeon will camp next to them. The leader of the people of Simeon is Shelumiel son of Zurishaddai. ¹³His division numbers 59,300.

¹⁴The tribe of Gad will be next. The leader of the people of Gad is Eliasaph son of Deuel.ᵃ ¹⁵His division numbers 45,650.

¹⁶All the men assigned to the camp of Reuben, according to their divisions, number 151,450. They will set out second.

¹⁷Then the tent of meeting and the camp of the Levites will set out in the middle of the camps. They will set out in the same order as they set up camp, each in their own place under their standard.

¹⁸On the west will be the divisions of the camp of Ephraim under their standard. The leader of the people of Ephraim is Elishama son of Ammihud. ¹⁹His division numbers 40,500.

²⁰The tribe of Manasseh will be next to them. The leader of the people of Manasseh is Gamaliel son of Pedahzur. ²¹His division numbers 32,200.

²²The tribe of Benjamin will be next. The leader of the people of Benjamin is Abidan son of Gideoni. ²³His division numbers 35,400.

²⁴All the men assigned to the camp of Ephraim, according to their divisions, number 108,100. They will set out third.

²⁵On the north will be the divisions of the camp of Dan under their standard. The leader of the people of Dan is Ahiezer son of Ammishaddai. ²⁶His division numbers 62,700.

²⁷The tribe of Asher will camp next to them. The leader of the people of Asher is Pagiel son of Okran. ²⁸His division numbers 41,500.

²⁹The tribe of Naphtali will be next. The leader of the people of Naphtali is Ahira son of Enan. ³⁰His division numbers 53,400.

³¹All the men assigned to the camp of Dan number 157,600. They will set out last, under their standards.

³²These are the Israelites, counted according to their families. All the men in the camps, by their divisions, number 603,550. ³³The Levites, however, were not counted along with the other Israelites, as the LORD commanded Moses.

³⁴So the Israelites did everything the LORD commanded Moses; that is the way they camped under their standards, and that is the way they set out, each of them with their clan and family.

The Levites

3 This is the account of the family of Aaron and Moses at the time the LORD spoke to Moses on Mount Sinai.

²The names of the sons of Aaron were Nadab the firstborn and Abihu, Eleazar and Ithamar. ³Those were the names of Aaron's sons, the anointed priests, who were ordained to serve as priests. ⁴Nadab and Abihu, however, died before the LORD when they made an offering with unauthorised fire before him in the Desert of Sinai. They had no sons, so Eleazar and Ithamar served as priests during the lifetime of their father Aaron.

⁵The LORD said to Moses, ⁶'Bring the tribe of Levi and present them to Aaron the priest to assist him. ⁷They are to perform duties for him and for the whole community at the tent of meeting by doing the work of the tabernacle. ⁸They are to take care of all the furnishings of the tent of meeting, fulfilling the obligations of the Israelites by doing the work of the tabernacle. ⁹Give the Levites to Aaron and his sons; they are the

---

ᵃ 14 Many manuscripts of the Masoretic Text, Samaritan Pentateuch and Vulgate (see also Num. 1:14); most manuscripts of the Masoretic Text *Reuel*

Israelites who are to be given wholly to him.[a] 10Appoint Aaron and his sons to serve as priests; anyone else who approaches the sanctuary is to be put to death.'

11The LORD also said to Moses, 12'I have taken the Levites from among the Israelites in place of the first male offspring of every Israelite woman. The Levites are mine, 13for all the firstborn are mine. When I struck down all the firstborn in Egypt, I set apart for myself every firstborn in Israel, whether human or animal. They are to be mine. I am the LORD.'

14The LORD said to Moses in the Desert of Sinai, 15'Count the Levites by their families and clans. Count every male a month old or more.' 16So Moses counted them, as he was commanded by the word of the LORD.

17These were the names of the sons of Levi:
Gershon, Kohath and Merari.
18These were the names of the Gershonite clans:
Libni and Shimei.
19The Kohathite clans:
Amram, Izhar, Hebron and Uzziel.
20The Merarite clans:
Mahli and Mushi.

These were the Levite clans, according to their families.

21To Gershon belonged the clans of the Libnites and Shimeites; these were the Gershonite clans. 22The number of all the males a month old or more who were counted was 7,500. 23The Gershonite clans were to camp on the west, behind the tabernacle. 24The leader of the families of the Gershonites was Eliasaph son of Lael. 25At the tent of meeting the Gershonites were responsible for the care of the tabernacle and tent, its coverings, the curtain at the entrance to the tent of meeting, 26the curtains of the courtyard, the curtain at the entrance to the courtyard surrounding the tabernacle and altar, and the ropes—and everything related to their use.

27To Kohath belonged the clans of the Amramites, Izharites, Hebronites and Uzzielites; these were the Kohathite clans. 28The number of all the males a month old or more was 8,600.[b] The Kohathites were responsible for the care of the sanctuary. 29The Kohathite clans were to camp on the south side of the tabernacle. 30The leader of the families of the Kohathite clans was Elizaphan son of Uzziel. 31They were responsible for the care of the ark, the table, the lampstand, the altars, the articles of the sanctuary used in ministering, the curtain, and everything related to their use. 32The chief leader of the Levites was Eleazar son of Aaron, the priest. He was appointed over those who were responsible for the care of the sanctuary.

33To Merari belonged the clans of the Mahlites and the Mushites; these were the Merarite clans. 34The number of all the males a month old or more who were counted was 6,200. 35The leader of the families of the Merarite clans was Zuriel son of Abihail; they were to camp on the north side of the tabernacle. 36The Merarites were appointed to take care of the frames of the tabernacle, its crossbars, posts, bases, all its equipment, and everything related to their use, 37as well as the posts of the surrounding courtyard with their bases, tent pegs and ropes.

38Moses and Aaron and his sons were to camp to the east of the tabernacle, towards the sunrise, in front of the tent of meeting. They were responsible for the care of the sanctuary on behalf of the Israelites. Anyone else who approached the sanctuary was to be put to death.

39The total number of Levites counted at the LORD's command by Moses and Aaron according to their clans, including every male a month old or more, was 22,000.

40The LORD said to Moses, 'Count all the firstborn Israelite males who are a month old or more and make a list of their names.

---

[a] 9 Most manuscripts of the Masoretic Text; some manuscripts of the Masoretic Text, Samaritan Pentateuch and Septuagint (see also Num. 8:16) *to me*   [b] 28 Hebrew; some Septuagint manuscripts *8,300*

⁴¹Take the Levites for me in place of all the firstborn of the Israelites, and the livestock of the Levites in place of all the firstborn of the livestock of the Israelites. I am the LORD.'

⁴²So Moses counted all the firstborn of the Israelites, as the LORD commanded him. ⁴³The total number of firstborn males a month old or more, listed by name, was 22,273.

⁴⁴The LORD also said to Moses, ⁴⁵'Take the Levites in place of all the firstborn of Israel, and the livestock of the Levites in place of their livestock. The Levites are to be mine. I am the LORD. ⁴⁶To redeem the 273 firstborn Israelites who exceed the number of the Levites, ⁴⁷collect five shekels^a for each one, according to the sanctuary shekel, which weighs twenty gerahs. ⁴⁸Give the money for the redemption of the additional Israelites to Aaron and his sons.'

⁴⁹So Moses collected the redemption money from those who exceeded the number redeemed by the Levites. ⁵⁰From the firstborn of the Israelites he collected silver weighing 1,365 shekels,^{b} according to the sanctuary shekel. ⁵¹Moses gave the redemption money to Aaron and his sons, as he was commanded by the word of the LORD.

The Kohathites

4 The LORD said to Moses and Aaron: ²'Take a census of the Kohathite branch of the Levites by their clans and families. ³Count all the men from thirty to fifty years of age who come to serve in the work at the tent of meeting.

⁴'This is the work of the Kohathites at the tent of meeting: the care of the most holy things. ⁵When the camp is to move, Aaron and his sons are to go in and take down the shielding curtain and put it over the ark of the covenant law. ⁶Then they are to cover the curtain with durable leather,^{c} spread a cloth of solid blue over that and put the poles in place.

⁷'Over the table of the Presence they are to spread a blue cloth and put on it the plates, dishes and bowls, and the jars for drink offerings; the bread that is continually there is to remain on it. ⁸They are to spread a scarlet cloth over them, cover that with durable leather and put the poles in place.

⁹'They are to take a blue cloth and cover the lampstand that is for light, together with its lamps, its wick trimmers and trays, and all its jars for the oil used to supply it. ¹⁰Then they are to wrap it and all its accessories in a covering of durable leather and put it on a carrying frame.

¹¹'Over the gold altar they are to spread a blue cloth and cover that with durable leather and put the poles in place.

¹²'They are to take all the articles used for ministering in the sanctuary, wrap them in a blue cloth, cover that with durable leather and put them on a carrying frame.

¹³'They are to remove the ashes from the bronze altar and spread a purple cloth over it. ¹⁴Then they are to place on it all the utensils used for ministering at the altar, including the firepans, meat forks, shovels and sprinkling bowls. Over it they are to spread a covering of durable leather and put the poles in place.

¹⁵'After Aaron and his sons have finished covering the holy furnishings and all the holy articles, and when the camp is ready to move, only then are the Kohathites to come and do the carrying. But they must not touch the holy things or they will die. The Kohathites are to carry those things that are in the tent of meeting.

¹⁶'Eleazar son of Aaron, the priest, is to have charge of the oil for the light, the fragrant incense, the regular grain offering and the anointing oil. He is to be in charge of the entire tabernacle and everything in it, including its holy furnishings and articles.'

¹⁷The LORD said to Moses and Aaron, ¹⁸'See that the Kohathite tribal clans are not destroyed from among the Levites. ¹⁹So that they may live and not die when they come near the most holy things, do this for them: Aaron and his sons are to go into the sanctuary and assign to each man his work and what he is to carry. ²⁰But the Kohathites must not go in to look at the holy things, even for a moment, or they will die.'

---

^{a} 47 That is, about 55 grams ^{b} 50 That is, about 16 kilograms ^{c} 6 Possibly the hides of dugongs (large aquatic mammals); also elsewhere in this chapter

The Gershonites

21 The LORD said to Moses, 22 "Take a census also of the Gershonites by their families and clans. 23 Count all the men from thirty to fifty years of age who come to serve in the work at the tent of meeting.

24 "This is the service of the Gershonite clans in their carrying and their other work: 25 they are to carry the curtains of the tabernacle, that is, the tent of meeting, its covering and its outer covering of durable leather, the curtains for the entrance to the tent of meeting, 26 the curtains of the courtyard surrounding the tabernacle and altar, the curtain for the entrance to the courtyard, the ropes and all the equipment used in the service of the tent. The Gershonites are to do all that needs to be done with these things. 27 All their service, whether carrying or doing other work, is to be done under the direction of Aaron and his sons. You shall assign to them as their responsibility all they are to carry. 28 This is the service of the Gershonite clans at the tent of meeting. Their duties are to be under the direction of Ithamar son of Aaron, the priest.

The Merarites

29 "Count the Merarites by their clans and families. 30 Count all the men from thirty to fifty years of age who come to serve in the work at the tent of meeting. 31 As part of all their service at the tent, they are to carry the frames of the tabernacle, its crossbars, posts and bases, 32 as well as the posts of the surrounding courtyard with their bases, tent pegs, ropes, all their equipment and everything related to their use. Assign to each man the specific things he is to carry. 33 This is the service of the Merarite clans as they work at the tent of meeting under the direction of Ithamar son of Aaron, the priest.'

The numbering of the Levite clans

34 Moses, Aaron and the leaders of the community counted the Kohathites by their clans and families. 35 All the men from thirty to fifty years of age who came to serve in the work at the tent of meeting, 36 counted by clans, were 2,750. 37 This was the total of all those in the Kohathite clans who served at the tent of meeting. Moses and Aaron counted them according to the LORD's command through Moses.

38 The Gershonites were counted by their clans and families. 39 All the men from thirty to fifty years of age who came to serve in the work at the tent of meeting, 40 counted by their clans and families, were 2,630. 41 This was the total of those in the Gershonite clans who served at the tent of meeting. Moses and Aaron counted them according to the LORD's command.

42 The Merarites were counted by their clans and families. 43 All the men from thirty to fifty years of age who came to serve in the work at the tent of meeting, 44 counted by their clans, were 3,200. 45 This was the total of those in the Merarite clans. Moses and Aaron counted them according to the LORD's command through Moses.

46 So Moses, Aaron and the leaders of Israel counted all the Levites by their clans and families. 47 All the men from thirty to fifty years of age who came to do the work of serving and carrying the tent of meeting 48 numbered 8,580. 49 At the LORD's command through Moses, each was assigned his work and told what to carry.

Thus they were counted, as the LORD commanded Moses.

The purity of the camp

5 The LORD said to Moses, 2 'Command the Israelites to send away from the camp anyone who has a defiling skin disease[a] or a discharge of any kind, or who is ceremonially unclean because of a dead body. 3 Send away male and female alike; send them outside the camp so that they will not defile their camp, where I dwell among them.' 4 The Israelites did so; they sent them outside the camp. They did just as the LORD had instructed Moses.

Restitution for wrongs

5 The LORD said to Moses, 6 'Say to the Israelites: "Any man or woman who wrongs another in any way[b] and so is unfaithful to the LORD is guilty 7 and must confess the sin

---

[a] 2 The Hebrew word for *defiling skin disease*, traditionally translated 'leprosy', was used for various diseases affecting the skin. [b] 6 Or *woman who commits any wrong common to humankind*

they have committed. They must make full restitution for the wrong they have done, add a fifth of the value to it and give it all to the person they have wronged. **8**But if that person has no close relative to whom restitution can be made for the wrong, the restitution belongs to the LORD and must be given to the priest, along with the ram with which atonement is made for the wrongdoer. **9**All the sacred contributions the Israelites bring to a priest will belong to him. **10**All sacred gifts belong to the donors, but what they give to the priest will belong to the priest."'

The test for an unfaithful wife

11Then the LORD said to Moses, **12**'Speak to the Israelites and say to them: "If a man's wife goes astray and is unfaithful to him **13**so that another man has sexual relations with her, and this is hidden from her husband and her impurity is undetected (since there is no witness against her and she has not been caught in the act), **14**and if feelings of jealousy come over her husband and he suspects his wife and she is impure—or if he is jealous and suspects her even though she is not impure— **15**then he is to take his wife to the priest. He must also take an offering of a tenth of an ephah^a of barley flour on her behalf. He must not pour oil on it or put incense on it, because it is a grain offering for jealousy, a reminder-offering to draw attention to wrongdoing.

16' "The priest shall bring her and make her stand before the LORD. **17**Then he shall take some holy water in a clay jar and put some dust from the tabernacle floor into the water. **18**After the priest has made the woman stand before the LORD, he shall loosen her hair and place in her hands the reminder-offering, the grain offering for jealousy, while he himself holds the bitter water that brings a curse. **19**Then the priest shall put the woman under oath and say to her, 'If no other man has had sexual relations with you and you have not gone astray and become impure while married to your husband, may this bitter water that brings a curse not harm you. **20**But if you have gone astray while married to your husband and you have made yourself impure by having sexual relations with a man other than your husband'— **21**here the priest is to put the woman under this curse—'may the LORD cause you to become a curse^b among your people when he makes your womb miscarry and your abdomen swell. **22**May this water that brings a curse enter your body so that your abdomen swells or your womb miscarries.'

' "Then the woman is to say, 'Amen. So be it.'

23' "The priest is to write these curses on a scroll and then wash them off into the bitter water. **24**He shall make the woman drink the bitter water that brings a curse, and this water that brings a curse and causes bitter suffering will enter her. **25**The priest is to take from her hands the grain offering for jealousy, wave it before the LORD and bring it to the altar. **26**The priest is then to take a handful of the grain offering as a memorial^c offering and burn it on the altar; after that, he is to make the woman drink the water. **27**If she has made herself impure and been unfaithful to her husband, this will be the result: when she is made to drink the water that brings a curse and causes bitter suffering, it will enter her, her abdomen will swell and her womb will miscarry, and she will become a curse. **28**If, however, the woman has not made herself impure, but is clean, she will be cleared of guilt and will be able to have children.

29' "This, then, is the law of jealousy when a woman goes astray and makes herself impure while married to her husband, **30**or when feelings of jealousy come over a man because he suspects his wife. The priest is to make her stand before the LORD and is to apply this entire law to her. **31**The husband will be innocent of any wrongdoing, but the woman will bear the consequences of her sin."'

The Nazirite

6 The LORD said to Moses, **2**'Speak to the Israelites and say to them: "If a man or woman wants to make a special vow, a vow

---

^{a} 15 That is, probably about 1.6 kilograms ^{b} 21 That is, may he cause your name to be used in cursing (see Jer. 29:22); or, may others see that you are cursed; similarly in verse 27. ^{c} 26 Or *representative*

making Connections

Nazirite vow
Numbers 6:2

Anyone who wanted to strongly dedicate themselves to God was able to take this vow. They agreed to stay holy by keeping away from certain worldly things like wine and hairdressers! Nazirites grew their hair and didn't shave and they weren't even allowed to drink grape juice or eat grapes or raisins. Samson (Judges 13–16), Samuel (1 Samuel 1–3) and John the Baptist (Luke 1:13–17) were all Nazirites for the whole of their lives; their parents made their vows for them before they were born.

of dedication to the LORD as a Nazirite, ³they must abstain from wine and other fermented drink and must not drink vinegar made from wine or other fermented drink. They must not drink grape juice or eat grapes or raisins. ⁴As long as they remain under their Nazirite vow, they must not eat anything that comes from the grapevine, not even the seeds or skins.

⁵ "During the entire period of the Nazirite's vow, no razor may be used on their head. They must be holy until the period of their dedication to the LORD is over; they must let their hair grow long.

⁶ "Throughout the period of their dedication to the LORD, the Nazirite must not go near a dead body. ⁷Even if their own father or mother or brother or sister dies, they must not make themselves ceremonially unclean on account of them, because the symbol of their dedication to God is on their head. ⁸Throughout the period of their dedication, they are consecrated to the LORD.

⁹ "If someone dies suddenly in the Nazirite's presence, thus defiling the hair that symbolises their dedication, they must shave their head on the seventh day—the day of their cleansing. ¹⁰Then on the eighth day they must bring two doves or two young pigeons to the priest at the entrance to the tent of meeting. ¹¹The priest is to offer one as a sin offering^a and the other as a burnt offering to make atonement for the Nazirite because they sinned by being in the presence of the dead body. That same day they are to consecrate their head again. ¹²They must rededicate themselves to the LORD for the same period of dedication and must bring a year-old male lamb as a guilt offering. The previous days do not count, because they became defiled during their period of dedication.

¹³ "Now this is the law for the Nazirite when the period of their dedication is over. The Nazirite is to be brought to the entrance to the tent of meeting. ¹⁴There they are to present their offerings to the LORD: a year-old male lamb without defect for a burnt offering, a year-old ewe lamb without defect for a sin offering, a ram without defect for a fellowship offering, ¹⁵together with their grain offerings and drink offerings, and a basket of bread made with the finest flour and without yeast—thick loaves with olive oil mixed in, and thin loaves brushed with olive oil.

¹⁶ "The priest is to present the Nazirite before the LORD and make the sin offering and the burnt offering. ¹⁷He is to present the basket of unleavened bread and is to sacrifice the ram as a fellowship offering to the LORD, together with its grain offering and drink offering.

¹⁸ "Then at the entrance to the tent of meeting, the Nazirite must shave off the hair that symbolises their dedication. They are to take the hair and put it in the fire that is under the sacrifice of the fellowship offering.

¹⁹ "After the Nazirite has shaved off the hair that symbolises their dedication, the priest is to place in their hands a boiled shoulder of the ram, and one thick loaf and one thin loaf from the basket, both made

---

^{a} 11 Or *purification offering*; also in verses 14 and 16

Blessing
Numbers 6:24

To bless someone is to declare or wish God's goodness on them, both spiritually and materially. A blessing isn't just nice words; it also has the power to make them happen. Even if someone was blessed by mistake, once the words were spoken they couldn't be taken back.

without yeast. 20The priest shall then wave these before the LORD as a wave offering; they are holy and belong to the priest, together with the breast that was waved and the thigh that was presented. After that, the Nazirite may drink wine.

21' "This is the law of the Nazirite who vows offerings to the LORD in accordance with their dedication, in addition to whatever else they can afford. They must fulfil the vows they have made, according to the law of the Nazirite." '

The priestly blessing

22The LORD said to Moses, 23'Tell Aaron and his sons, "This is how you are to bless the Israelites. Say to them:
24' " 'The LORD bless you
and keep you;
25the LORD make his face shine on you
and be gracious to you;
26the LORD turn his face towards you
and give you peace.' " '

27'So they will put my name on the Israelites, and I will bless them.'

Offerings at the dedication of the tabernacle

7 When Moses finished setting up the tabernacle, he anointed and consecrated it and all its furnishings. He also anointed and consecrated the altar and all its utensils. 2Then the leaders of Israel, the heads of families who were the tribal leaders in charge of those who were counted, made offerings. 3They brought as their gifts before the LORD six covered carts and twelve oxen—an ox from each leader and a cart from every two. These they presented before the tabernacle.

4The LORD said to Moses, 5'Accept these from them, that they may be used in the work at the tent of meeting. Give them to the Levites as each man's work requires.'

6So Moses took the carts and oxen and gave them to the Levites. 7He gave two carts and four oxen to the Gershonites, as their work required, 8and he gave four carts and eight oxen to the Merarites, as their work required. They were all under the direction of Ithamar son of Aaron, the priest. 9But Moses did not give any to the Kohathites, because they were to carry on their shoulders the holy things, for which they were responsible.

10When the altar was anointed, the leaders brought their offerings for its dedication and presented them before the altar. 11For the LORD had said to Moses, 'Each day one leader is to bring his offering for the dedication of the altar.'

12The one who brought his offering on the first day was Nahshon son of Amminadab of the tribe of Judah.

13His offering was one silver plate weighing a hundred and thirty shekels[a] and one silver sprinkling bowl weighing seventy shekels,[b] both according to the sanctuary shekel, each filled with the finest flour mixed with olive oil as a grain offering; 14one gold dish weighing ten shekels,[c] filled with incense; 15one young bull, one ram and one male lamb a year old for a burnt offering; 16one male goat for a sin offering[d]; 17and two oxen, five rams, five male goats and five male lambs a year old to be sacrificed as a fellowship offering. This was the offering of Nahshon son of Amminadab.

---

[a] 13 That is, about 1.5 kilograms; also elsewhere in this chapter [b] 13 That is, about 800 grams; also elsewhere in this chapter [c] 14 That is, about 115 grams; also elsewhere in this chapter [d] 16 Or *purification offering*; also elsewhere in this chapter

¹⁸On the second day Nethanel son of Zuar, the leader of Issachar, brought his offering. ¹⁹The offering he brought was one silver plate weighing a hundred and thirty shekels, and one silver sprinkling bowl weighing seventy shekels, both according to the sanctuary shekel, each filled with the finest flour mixed with olive oil as a grain offering; ²⁰one gold dish weighing ten shekels, filled with incense; ²¹one young bull, one ram and one male lamb a year old for a burnt offering; ²²one male goat for a sin offering; ²³and two oxen, five rams, five male goats and five male lambs a year old to be sacrificed as a fellowship offering. This was the offering of Nethanel son of Zuar.

²⁴On the third day, Eliab son of Helon, the leader of the people of Zebulun, brought his offering.

²⁵His offering was one silver plate weighing a hundred and thirty shekels, and one silver sprinkling bowl weighing seventy shekels, both according to the sanctuary shekel, each filled with the finest flour mixed with olive oil as a grain offering; ²⁶one gold dish weighing ten shekels, filled with incense; ²⁷one young bull, one ram and one male lamb a year old for a burnt offering; ²⁸one male goat for a sin offering; ²⁹and two oxen, five rams, five male goats and five male lambs a year old to be sacrificed as a fellowship offering. This was the offering of Eliab son of Helon.

³⁰On the fourth day Elizur son of Shedeur, the leader of the people of Reuben, brought his offering.

³¹His offering was one silver plate weighing a hundred and thirty shekels, and one silver sprinkling bowl weighing seventy shekels, both according to the sanctuary shekel, each filled with the finest flour mixed with olive oil as a grain offering; ³²one gold dish weighing ten shekels, filled with incense; ³³one young bull, one ram and one male lamb a year old for a burnt offering; ³⁴one male goat for a sin offering; ³⁵and two oxen, five rams, five male goats and five male lambs a year old to be sacrificed as a fellowship offering. This was the offering of Elizur son of Shedeur.

³⁶On the fifth day Shelumiel son of Zurishaddai, the leader of the people of Simeon, brought his offering.

³⁷His offering was one silver plate weighing a hundred and thirty shekels, and one silver sprinkling bowl weighing seventy shekels, both according to the sanctuary shekel, each filled with the finest flour mixed with olive oil as a grain offering; ³⁸one gold dish weighing ten shekels, filled with incense; ³⁹one young bull, one ram and one male lamb a year old for a burnt offering; ⁴⁰one male goat for a sin offering; ⁴¹and two oxen, five rams, five male goats and five male lambs a year old to be sacrificed as a fellowship offering. This was the offering of Shelumiel son of Zurishaddai.

⁴²On the sixth day Eliasaph son of Deuel, the leader of the people of Gad, brought his offering.

⁴³His offering was one silver plate weighing a hundred and thirty shekels, and one silver sprinkling bowl weighing seventy shekels, both according to the sanctuary shekel, each filled with the finest flour mixed with olive oil as a grain offering; ⁴⁴one gold dish weighing ten shekels, filled with incense; ⁴⁵one young bull, one ram and one male lamb a year old for a burnt offering; ⁴⁶one male goat for a sin offering; ⁴⁷and two oxen, five rams, five male goats and five male lambs a year old to be sacrificed as a fellowship offer-

ing. This was the offering of Eliasaph son of Deuel.

⁴⁸On the seventh day Elishama son of Ammihud, the leader of the people of Ephraim, brought his offering.

⁴⁹His offering was one silver plate weighing a hundred and thirty shekels, and one silver sprinkling bowl weighing seventy shekels, both according to the sanctuary shekel, each filled with the finest flour mixed with olive oil as a grain offering; ⁵⁰one gold dish weighing ten shekels, filled with incense; ⁵¹one young bull, one ram and one male lamb a year old for a burnt offering; ⁵²one male goat for a sin offering; ⁵³and two oxen, five rams, five male goats and five male lambs a year old to be sacrificed as a fellowship offering. This was the offering of Elishama son of Ammihud.

⁵⁴On the eighth day Gamaliel son of Pedahzur, the leader of the people of Manasseh, brought his offering.

⁵⁵His offering was one silver plate weighing a hundred and thirty shekels, and one silver sprinkling bowl weighing seventy shekels, both according to the sanctuary shekel, each filled with the finest flour mixed with olive oil as a grain offering; ⁵⁶one gold dish weighing ten shekels, filled with incense; ⁵⁷one young bull, one ram and one male lamb a year old for a burnt offering; ⁵⁸one male goat for a sin offering; ⁵⁹and two oxen, five rams, five male goats and five male lambs a year old to be sacrificed as a fellowship offering. This was the offering of Gamaliel son of Pedahzur.

⁶⁰On the ninth day Abidan son of Gideoni, the leader of the people of Benjamin, brought his offering.

⁶¹His offering was one silver plate weighing a hundred and thirty shekels, and one silver sprinkling bowl weighing seventy shekels, both according to the sanctuary shekel, each filled with the finest flour mixed with olive oil as a grain offering; ⁶²one gold dish weighing ten shekels, filled with incense; ⁶³one young bull, one ram and one male lamb a year old for a burnt offering; ⁶⁴one male goat for a sin offering; ⁶⁵and two oxen, five rams, five male goats and five male lambs a year old to be sacrificed as a fellowship offering. This was the offering of Abidan son of Gideoni.

⁶⁶On the tenth day Ahiezer son of Ammishaddai, the leader of the people of Dan, brought his offering.

⁶⁷His offering was one silver plate weighing a hundred and thirty shekels, and one silver sprinkling bowl weighing seventy shekels, both according to the sanctuary shekel, each filled with the finest flour mixed with olive oil as a grain offering; ⁶⁸one gold dish weighing ten shekels, filled with incense; ⁶⁹one young bull, one ram and one male lamb a year old for a burnt offering; ⁷⁰one male goat for a sin offering; ⁷¹and two oxen, five rams, five male goats and five male lambs a year old to be sacrificed as a fellowship offering. This was the offering of Ahiezer son of Ammishaddai.

⁷²On the eleventh day Pagiel son of Okran, the leader of the people of Asher, brought his offering.

⁷³His offering was one silver plate weighing a hundred and thirty shekels, and one silver sprinkling bowl weighing seventy shekels, both according to the sanctuary shekel, each filled with the finest flour mixed with olive oil as a grain offering; ⁷⁴one gold dish weighing ten shekels, filled with incense; ⁷⁵one young bull, one ram and one male lamb a year old for a burnt offering; ⁷⁶one male goat for a sin offering; ⁷⁷and two

oxen, five rams, five male goats and five male lambs a year old to be sacrificed as a fellowship offering. This was the offering of Pagiel son of Okran.

78 On the twelfth day Ahira son of Enan, the leader of the people of Naphtali, brought his offering.

79 His offering was one silver plate weighing a hundred and thirty shekels, and one silver sprinkling bowl weighing seventy shekels, both according to the sanctuary shekel, each filled with the finest flour mixed with olive oil as a grain offering; 80 one gold dish weighing ten shekels, filled with incense; 81 one young bull, one ram and one male lamb a year old for a burnt offering; 82 one male goat for a sin offering; 83 and two oxen, five rams, five male goats and five male lambs a year old to be sacrificed as a fellowship offering. This was the offering of Ahira son of Enan.

84 These were the offerings of the Israelite leaders for the dedication of the altar when it was anointed: twelve silver plates, twelve silver sprinkling bowls and twelve gold dishes. 85 Each silver plate weighed a hundred and thirty shekels, and each sprinkling bowl seventy shekels. Altogether, the silver dishes weighed two thousand four hundred shekels,[a] according to the sanctuary shekel. 86 The twelve gold dishes filled with incense weighed ten shekels each, according to the sanctuary shekel. Altogether, the gold dishes weighed a hundred and twenty shekels.[b] 87 The total number of animals for the burnt offering came to twelve young bulls, twelve rams and twelve male lambs a year old, together with their grain offering. Twelve male goats were used for the sin offering. 88 The total number of animals for the sacrifice of the fellowship offering came to twenty-four oxen, sixty rams, sixty male goats and sixty male lambs a year old. These were the offerings for the dedication of the altar after it was anointed.

89 When Moses entered the tent of meeting to speak with the LORD, he heard the voice speaking to him from between the two cherubim above the atonement cover on the ark of the covenant law. In this way the LORD spoke to him.

Setting up the lamps

8 The LORD said to Moses, 2 'Speak to Aaron and say to him, "When you set up the lamps, see that all seven light up the area in front of the lampstand."'

3 Aaron did so; he set up the lamps so that they faced forwards on the lampstand, just as the LORD commanded Moses. 4 This is how the lampstand was made: it was made of hammered gold—from its base to its blossoms. The lampstand was made exactly like the pattern the LORD had shown Moses.

The setting apart of the Levites

5 The LORD said to Moses: 6 'Take the Levites from among all the Israelites and make them ceremonially clean. 7 To purify them, do this: sprinkle the water of cleansing on them; then make them shave their whole bodies and wash their clothes. And so they will purify themselves. 8 Make them take a young bull with its grain offering of the finest flour mixed with olive oil; then you are to take a second young bull for a sin offering.[c] 9 Bring the Levites to the front of the tent of meeting and assemble the whole

IN OTHER WORDS

Purification
Numbers 8:7

The Israelites took ritual washing very seriously because they always wanted to be holy. If anything made them unclean, such as touching blood or a dead body, they would go through an act of purification or cleansing to make them clean again. In the New Testament, the blood of Jesus provides purification for sin (Hebrews 1:3).

---

[a] 85 That is, about 28 kilograms   [b] 86 That is, about 1.4 kilograms   [c] 8 Or *purification offering*; also in verse 12

Israelite community. ¹⁰You are to bring the Levites before the LORD, and the Israelites are to lay their hands on them. ¹¹Aaron is to present the Levites before the LORD as a wave offering from the Israelites, so that they may be ready to do the work of the LORD.

¹²'Then the Levites are to lay their hands on the heads of the bulls, using one for a sin offering to the LORD and the other for a burnt offering, to make atonement for the Levites. ¹³Make the Levites stand in front of Aaron and his sons and then present them as a wave offering to the LORD. ¹⁴In this way you are to set the Levites apart from the other Israelites, and the Levites will be mine.

¹⁵'After you have purified the Levites and presented them as a wave offering, they are to come to do their work at the tent of meeting. ¹⁶They are the Israelites who are to be given wholly to me. I have taken them as my own in place of the firstborn, the first male offspring from every Israelite woman. ¹⁷Every firstborn male in Israel, whether human or animal, is mine. When I struck down all the firstborn in Egypt, I set them apart for myself. ¹⁸And I have taken the Levites in place of all the firstborn sons in Israel. ¹⁹From among all the Israelites, I have given the Levites as gifts to Aaron and his sons to do the work at the tent of meeting on behalf of the Israelites and to make atonement for them so that no plague will strike the Israelites when they go near the sanctuary.'

²⁰Moses, Aaron and the whole Israelite community did with the Levites just as the LORD commanded Moses. ²¹The Levites purified themselves and washed their clothes. Then Aaron presented them as a wave offering before the LORD and made atonement for them to purify them. ²²After that, the Levites came to do their work at the tent of meeting under the supervision of Aaron and his sons. They did with the Levites just as the LORD commanded Moses.

²³The LORD said to Moses, ²⁴'This applies to the Levites: men twenty-five years old or more shall come to take part in the work at the tent of meeting, ²⁵but at the age of fifty, they must retire from their usual duties and work no longer. ²⁶They may assist their brothers in performing their duties at the tent of meeting, but they themselves must not do the work. This, then, is how you are to assign the responsibilities of the Levites.'

The Passover

9 The LORD spoke to Moses in the Desert of Sinai in the first month of the second year after they came out of Egypt. He said, ²'Make the Israelites celebrate the Passover at the appointed time. ³Celebrate it at the appointed time, at twilight on the fourteenth day of this month, in accordance with all its rules and regulations.'

⁴So Moses told the Israelites to celebrate the Passover, ⁵and they did so in the Desert of Sinai at twilight on the fourteenth day of the first month. The Israelites did everything just as the LORD commanded Moses.

⁶But some of them could not celebrate the Passover on that day because they were ceremonially unclean on account of a dead body. So they came to Moses and Aaron that same day ⁷and said to Moses, 'We have become unclean because of a dead body, but why should we be kept from presenting the LORD's offering with the other Israelites at the appointed time?'

⁸Moses answered them, 'Wait until I find out what the LORD commands concerning you.'

⁹Then the LORD said to Moses, ¹⁰'Tell the Israelites: "When any of you or your descendants are unclean because of a dead body or are away on a journey, they are still to celebrate the LORD's Passover, ¹¹but they are to do it on the fourteenth day of the second month at twilight. They are to eat the lamb, together with unleavened bread and bitter herbs. ¹²They must not leave any of it till morning or break any of its bones. When they celebrate the Passover, they must follow all the regulations. ¹³But if anyone who is ceremonially clean and not on a journey fails to celebrate the Passover, they must be cut off from their people for not presenting the LORD's offering at the appointed time. They will bear the consequences of their sin.

¹⁴ "A foreigner residing among you is also to celebrate the LORD's Passover in accordance with its rules and regulations.

You must have the same regulations for both the foreigner and the native-born."'

The cloud above the tabernacle

¹⁵On the day the tabernacle, the tent of the covenant law, was set up, the cloud covered it. From evening till morning the cloud above the tabernacle looked like fire. ¹⁶That is how it continued to be; the cloud covered it, and at night it looked like fire. ¹⁷Whenever the cloud lifted from above the tent, the Israelites set out; wherever the cloud settled, the Israelites set up camp. ¹⁸At the LORD's command the Israelites set out, and at his command they set up camp. As long as the cloud stayed over the tabernacle, they remained in camp. ¹⁹When the cloud remained over the tabernacle a long time, the Israelites obeyed the LORD's order and did not set out. ²⁰Sometimes the cloud was over the tabernacle for only a few days; at the LORD's command they would set up camp, and then at his command they would set out. ²¹Sometimes the cloud stayed only from evening till morning, and when it lifted in the morning, they set out. Whether by day or by night, whenever the cloud lifted, they set out. ²²Whether the cloud stayed over the tabernacle for two days or a month or a year, the Israelites would remain in camp and not set out; but when it lifted, they would set out. ²³At the LORD's command they set up camp, and at the LORD's command they set out. They obeyed the LORD's order, in accordance with his command through Moses.

The silver trumpets

10 The LORD said to Moses: ²'Make two trumpets of hammered silver, and use them for calling the community together and for the camps to set out. ³When both are sounded, the whole community is to assemble before you at the entrance to the tent of meeting. ⁴If only one is sounded, the leaders—the heads of the clans of Israel—are to assemble before you. ⁵When a trumpet blast is sounded, the tribes camping on the east are to set out. ⁶At the sounding of a second blast, the camps on the south are to set out. The blast will be the signal for setting out. ⁷To gather the

Silver trumpets
Numbers 10:1
With no phones or emails, how would you communicate with thousands of people? These trumpets made sure that people across the whole Israelite camp knew what God wanted to say to them. Aaron and the priests would blow them at festivals, in battle and to tell the tribes when it was time to set out for the Tent of Meeting.

assembly, blow the trumpets, but not with the signal for setting out.

⁸'The sons of Aaron, the priests, are to blow the trumpets. This is to be a lasting ordinance for you and the generations to come. ⁹When you go into battle in your own land against an enemy who is oppressing you, sound a blast on the trumpets. Then you will be remembered by the LORD your God and rescued from your enemies. ¹⁰Also at your times of rejoicing—your appointed festivals and New Moon feasts—you are to sound the trumpets over your burnt offerings and fellowship offerings, and they will be a memorial for you before your God. I am the LORD your God.'

The Israelites leave Sinai

¹¹On the twentieth day of the second month of the second year, the cloud lifted from above the tabernacle of the covenant law. ¹²Then the Israelites set out from the Desert of Sinai and travelled from place to place until the cloud came to rest in the Desert of Paran. ¹³They set out, this first time, at the LORD's command through Moses.

¹⁴The divisions of the camp of Judah went first, under their standard. Nahshon son of Amminadab was in command. ¹⁵Nethanel son of Zuar was over the

division of the tribe of Issachar, ¹⁶and Eliab son of Helon was over the division of the tribe of Zebulun. ¹⁷Then the tabernacle was taken down, and the Gershonites and Merarites, who carried it, set out.

¹⁸The divisions of the camp of Reuben went next, under their standard. Elizur son of Shedeur was in command. ¹⁹Shelumiel son of Zurishaddai was over the division of the tribe of Simeon, ²⁰and Eliasaph son of Deuel was over the division of the tribe of Gad. ²¹Then the Kohathites set out, carrying the holy things. The tabernacle was to be set up before they arrived.

²²The divisions of the camp of Ephraim went next, under their standard. Elishama son of Ammihud was in command. ²³Gamaliel son of Pedahzur was over the division of the tribe of Manasseh, ²⁴and Abidan son of Gideoni was over the division of the tribe of Benjamin.

²⁵Finally, as the rear guard for all the units, the divisions of the camp of Dan set out under their standard. Ahiezer son of Ammishaddai was in command. ²⁶Pagiel son of Okran was over the division of the tribe of Asher, ²⁷and Ahira son of Enan was over the division of the tribe of Naphtali. ²⁸This was the order of march for the Israelite divisions as they set out.

²⁹Now Moses said to Hobab son of Reuel the Midianite, Moses' father-in-law, 'We are setting out for the place about which the LORD said, "I will give it to you." Come with us and we will treat you well, for the LORD has promised good things to Israel.'

³⁰He answered, 'No, I will not go; I am going back to my own land and my own people.'

³¹But Moses said, 'Please do not leave us. You know where we should camp in the wilderness, and you can be our eyes. ³²If you come with us, we will share with you whatever good things the LORD gives us.'

³³So they set out from the mountain of the LORD and travelled for three days. The ark of the covenant of the LORD went before them during those three days to find them a place to rest. ³⁴The cloud of the LORD was over them by day when they set out from the camp.

³⁵Whenever the ark set out, Moses said,

'Rise up, LORD!
May your enemies be scattered;
may your foes flee before you.'

³⁶Whenever it came to rest, he said,

'Return, LORD,
to the countless thousands of Israel.'

Fire from the LORD

11 Now the people complained about their hardships in the hearing of the LORD, and when he heard them his anger was aroused. Then fire from the LORD burned among them and consumed some of the outskirts of the camp. ²When the people cried out to Moses, he prayed to the LORD and the fire died down. ³So that place was called Taberah,ᵃ because fire from the LORD had burned among them.

Quail from the LORD

⁴The rabble with them began to crave other food, and again the Israelites started wailing and said, 'If only we had meat to eat! ⁵We remember the fish we ate in Egypt at no cost—also the cucumbers, melons, leeks, onions and garlic. ⁶But now we have lost our appetite; we never see anything but this manna!'

⁷The manna was like coriander seed and looked like resin. ⁸The people went around gathering it, and then ground it in a hand-mill or crushed it in a mortar. They cooked it in a pot or made it into loaves. And it tasted like something made with olive oil. ⁹When the dew settled on the camp at night, the manna also came down.

¹⁰Moses heard the people of every family wailing at the entrance to their tents. The LORD became exceedingly angry, and Moses was troubled. ¹¹He asked the LORD, 'Why have you brought this trouble on your servant? What have I done to displease you that you put the burden of all these people on me? ¹²Did I conceive all these people? Did I give them birth? Why do you tell me to carry them in my arms, as a nurse carries an infant, to the land you promised on oath to their ancestors? ¹³Where can I get meat for all these people? They keep wailing to me,

---

ᵃ 3 *Taberah* means *burning*.

"Give us meat to eat!" ¹⁴I cannot carry all these people by myself; the burden is too heavy for me. ¹⁵If this is how you are going to treat me, please go ahead and kill me right now—if I have found favour in your eyes—and do not let me face my own ruin.'

¹⁶The LORD said to Moses: 'Bring me seventy of Israel's elders who are known to you as leaders and officials among the people. Make them come to the tent of meeting, that they may stand there with you. ¹⁷I will come down and speak with you there, and I will take some of the power of the Spirit that is on you and put it on them. They will share the burden of the people with you so that you will not have to carry it alone.

¹⁸'Tell the people: "Consecrate yourselves in preparation for tomorrow, when you will eat meat. The LORD heard you when you wailed, 'If only we had meat to eat! We were better off in Egypt!' Now the LORD will give you meat, and you will eat it. ¹⁹You will not eat it for just one day, or two days, or five, ten or twenty days, ²⁰but for a whole month—until it comes out of your nostrils and you loathe it—because you have rejected the LORD, who is among you, and have wailed before him, saying, 'Why did we ever leave Egypt?'"'

²¹But Moses said, 'Here I am among six hundred thousand men on foot, and you say, "I will give them meat to eat for a whole month!" ²²Would they have enough if flocks and herds were slaughtered for them? Would they have enough if all the fish in the sea were caught for them?'

²³The LORD answered Moses, 'Is the LORD's arm too short? Now you will see whether or not what I say will come true for you.'

²⁴So Moses went out and told the people what the LORD had said. He brought together seventy of their elders and made them stand round the tent. ²⁵Then the LORD came down in the cloud and spoke with him, and he took some of the power of the Spirit that was on him and put it on the seventy elders. When the Spirit rested on them, they prophesied—but did not do so again.

²⁶However, two men, whose names were Eldad and Medad, had remained in the camp. They were listed among the elders, but did not go out to the tent. Yet the Spirit also rested on them, and they prophesied in the camp. ²⁷A young man ran and told Moses, 'Eldad and Medad are prophesying in the camp.'

²⁸Joshua son of Nun, who had been Moses' assistant since youth, spoke up and said, 'Moses, my lord, stop them!'

²⁹But Moses replied, 'Are you jealous for my sake? I wish that all the LORD's people were prophets and that the LORD would put his Spirit on them!' ³⁰Then Moses and the elders of Israel returned to the camp.

³¹Now a wind went out from the LORD and drove quail in from the sea. It scattered them up to two cubits^a deep all around the camp, as far as a day's walk in any direction. ³²All that day and night and all the next day the people went out and gathered quail. No-one gathered less than ten homers.^{b} Then they spread them out all around the camp. ³³But while the meat was still between their teeth and before it could be consumed, the anger of the LORD burned against the people, and he struck them with a severe plague. ³⁴Therefore the place was named Kibroth Hattaavah,^{c} because there they buried the people who had craved other food.

³⁵From Kibroth Hattaavah the people travelled to Hazeroth and stayed there.

Miriam and Aaron oppose Moses

12 Miriam and Aaron began to talk against Moses because of his Cushite wife, for he had married a Cushite. ²'Has the LORD spoken only through Moses?' they asked. 'Hasn't he also spoken through us?' And the LORD heard this.

³(Now Moses was a very humble man, more humble than anyone else on the face of the earth.)

⁴At once the LORD said to Moses, Aaron and Miriam, 'Come out to the tent of meeting, all three of you.' So the three of

---

^{a} 31 That is, about 90 centimetres ^{b} 32 That is, possibly about 1.6 metric tons ^{c} 34 *Kibroth Hattaavah* means *graves of craving*.

them went out. ⁵Then the LORD came down in a pillar of cloud; he stood at the entrance to the tent and summoned Aaron and Miriam. When the two of them stepped forward, ⁶he said, 'Listen to my words:

> 'When there are prophets of the LORD among you,
> I reveal myself to them in visions,
> I speak to them in dreams.
> ⁷But this is not true of my servant Moses;
> he is faithful in all my house.
> ⁸With him I speak face to face,
> clearly and not in riddles;
> he sees the form of the LORD.
> Why then were you not afraid
> to speak against my servant Moses?'

⁹The anger of the LORD burned against them, and he left them.

¹⁰When the cloud lifted from above the tent, Miriam's skin was leprous[a]—it became as white as snow. Aaron turned towards her and saw that she had a defiling skin disease, ¹¹and he said to Moses, 'Please, my lord, I ask you not to hold against us the sin we have so foolishly committed. ¹²Do not let her be like a stillborn infant coming from its mother's womb with its flesh half eaten away.'

¹³So Moses cried out to the LORD, 'Please, God, heal her!'

¹⁴The LORD replied to Moses, 'If her father had spat in her face, would she not have been in disgrace for seven days? Confine her outside the camp for seven days; after that she can be brought back.' ¹⁵So Miriam was confined outside the camp for seven days, and the people did not move on till she was brought back.

¹⁶After that, the people left Hazeroth and camped in the Desert of Paran.

Exploring Canaan

13 The LORD said to Moses, ²'Send some men to explore the land of Canaan, which I am giving to the Israelites. From each ancestral tribe send one of its leaders.'

³So at the LORD's command Moses sent them out from the Desert of Paran. All of them were leaders of the Israelites. ⁴These are their names:

> from the tribe of Reuben, Shammua son of Zakkur;
> ⁵from the tribe of Simeon, Shaphat son of Hori;
> ⁶from the tribe of Judah, Caleb son of Jephunneh;
> ⁷from the tribe of Issachar, Igal son of Joseph;
> ⁸from the tribe of Ephraim, Hoshea son of Nun;
> ⁹from the tribe of Benjamin, Palti son of Raphu;
> ¹⁰from the tribe of Zebulun, Gaddiel son of Sodi;
> ¹¹from the tribe of Manasseh (a tribe of Joseph), Gaddi son of Susi;
> ¹²from the tribe of Dan, Ammiel son of Gemalli;
> ¹³from the tribe of Asher, Sethur son of Michael;
> ¹⁴from the tribe of Naphtali, Nahbi son of Vophsi;
> ¹⁵from the tribe of Gad, Geuel son of Maki.

¹⁶These are the names of the men Moses sent to explore the land. (Moses gave Hoshea son of Nun the name Joshua.)

¹⁷When Moses sent them to explore Canaan, he said, 'Go up through the Negev and on into the hill country. ¹⁸See what the land is like and whether the people who live

---

People and Places

Canaan
Numbers 13:1
Canaan was the Promised Land that God gave to the people of Israel. Lots of it was rocky and mountainous but it also contained good farmland, particularly by the rivers and the coastal plains beside the sea. Today this area includes Israel and some of Syria.

---

[a] 10 The Hebrew for *leprous* was used for various diseases affecting the skin.

there are strong or weak, few or many. ¹⁹What kind of land do they live in? Is it good or bad? What kind of towns do they live in? Are they unwalled or fortified? ²⁰How is the soil? Is it fertile or poor? Are there trees in it or not? Do your best to bring back some of the fruit of the land.' (It was the season for the first ripe grapes.)

²¹So they went up and explored the land from the Desert of Zin as far as Rehob, towards Lebo Hamath. ²²They went up through the Negev and came to Hebron, where Ahiman, Sheshai and Talmai, the descendants of Anak, lived. (Hebron had been built seven years before Zoan in Egypt.) ²³When they reached the Valley of Eshkol,[a] they cut off a branch bearing a single cluster of grapes. Two of them carried it on a pole between them, along with some pomegranates and figs. ²⁴That place was called the Valley of Eshkol because of the cluster of grapes the Israelites cut off there. ²⁵At the end of forty days they returned from exploring the land.

Report on the exploration

²⁶They came back to Moses and Aaron and the whole Israelite community at Kadesh in the Desert of Paran. There they reported to them and to the whole assembly and showed them the fruit of the land. ²⁷They gave Moses this account: 'We went into the land to which you sent us, and it does flow with milk and honey! Here is its fruit. ²⁸But the people who live there are powerful, and the cities are fortified and very large. We even saw descendants of Anak there. ²⁹The Amalekites live in the Negev; the Hittites, Jebusites and Amorites live in the hill country; and the Canaanites live near the sea and along the Jordan.'

³⁰Then Caleb silenced the people before Moses and said, 'We should go up and take possession of the land, for we can certainly do it.'

³¹But the men who had gone up with him said, 'We can't attack those people; they are stronger than we are.' ³²And they spread among the Israelites a bad report about the land they had explored. They said, 'The land we explored devours those living in it. All the people we saw there are of great size. ³³We saw the Nephilim there (the descendants of Anak come from the Nephilim). We seemed like grasshoppers in our own eyes, and we looked the same to them.'

The people rebel

14 That night all the members of the community raised their voices and wept aloud. ²All the Israelites grumbled against Moses and Aaron, and the whole assembly said to them, 'If only we had died in Egypt! Or in this wilderness! ³Why is the LORD bringing us to this land only to let us fall by the sword? Our wives and children will be taken as plunder. Wouldn't it be better for us to go back to Egypt?' ⁴And they said to each other, 'We should choose a leader and go back to Egypt.'

⁵Then Moses and Aaron fell face down in front of the whole Israelite assembly gathered there. ⁶Joshua son of Nun and Caleb son of Jephunneh, who were among those who had explored the land, tore their clothes ⁷and said to the entire Israelite assembly, 'The land we passed through and explored is exceedingly good. ⁸If the LORD is pleased with us, he will lead us into that land, a land flowing with milk and honey, and will give it to us. ⁹Only do not rebel against the LORD. And do not be afraid of the people of the land, because we will devour them. Their protection is gone, but the LORD is with us. Do not be afraid of them.'

¹⁰But the whole assembly talked about stoning them. Then the glory of the LORD appeared at the tent of meeting to all the Israelites. ¹¹The LORD said to Moses, 'How long will these people treat me with contempt? How long will they refuse to believe in me, in spite of all the signs I have performed among them? ¹²I will strike them down with a plague and destroy them, but I will make you into a nation greater and stronger than they.'

¹³Moses said to the LORD, 'Then the Egyptians will hear about it! By your power you brought these people up from among them. ¹⁴And they will tell the inhabitants of this land about it. They have already heard that you, LORD, are with these people and

---

[a] 23 *Eshkol* means *cluster*; also in verse 24.

that you, LORD, have been seen face to face, that your cloud stays over them, and that you go before them in a pillar of cloud by day and a pillar of fire by night. 15If you put these people to death all at once, the nations who have heard this report about you will say, 16"The LORD was not able to bring these people into the land he promised them on oath, so he slaughtered them in the wilderness."

17'Now may the Lord's strength be displayed, just as you have declared: 18"The LORD is slow to anger, abounding in love and forgiving sin and rebellion. Yet he does not leave the guilty unpunished; he punishes the children for the sin of the parents to the third and fourth generation." 19In accordance with your great love, forgive the sin of these people, just as you have pardoned them from the time they left Egypt until now.'

20The LORD replied, 'I have forgiven them, as you asked. 21Nevertheless, as surely as I live and as surely as the glory of the LORD fills the whole earth, 22not one of those who saw my glory and the signs I performed in Egypt and in the wilderness but who disobeyed me and tested me ten times— 23not one of them will ever see the land I promised on oath to their ancestors. No-one who has treated me with contempt will ever see it. 24But because my servant Caleb has a different spirit and follows me wholeheartedly, I will bring him into the land he went to, and his descendants will inherit it. 25Since the Amalekites and Canaanites are living in the valleys, turn back tomorrow and set out towards the desert along the route to the Red Sea.'[a]

26The LORD said to Moses and Aaron: 27'How long will this wicked community grumble against me? I have heard the complaints of these grumbling Israelites. 28So tell them, "As surely as I live, declares the LORD, I will do to you the very thing I heard you say: 29in this wilderness your bodies will fall—every one of you twenty years old or more who was counted in the census and who has grumbled against me. 30Not one of you will enter the land I swore with uplifted hand to make your home, except Caleb son of Jephunneh and Joshua son of Nun. 31As for your children that you said would be taken as plunder, I will bring them in to enjoy the land you have rejected. 32But you—your bodies will fall in this wilderness. 33Your children will be shepherds here for forty years, suffering for your unfaithfulness, until the last of your bodies lies in the wilderness. 34For forty years—one year for each of the forty days you explored the land—you will suffer for your sins and know what it is like to have me against you." 35I, the LORD, have spoken, and I will surely do these things to this whole wicked community, which has banded together against me. They will meet their end in this wilderness; here they will die.'

36So the men Moses had sent to explore the land, who returned and made the whole community grumble against him by spreading a bad report about it— 37these men who were responsible for spreading the bad report about the land were struck down and died of a plague before the LORD. 38Of the men who went to explore the land, only Joshua son of Nun and Caleb son of Jephunneh survived.

39When Moses reported this to all the Israelites, they mourned bitterly. 40Early the next morning they set out for the highest point in the hill country, saying, 'Now we are ready to go up to the land the LORD promised. Surely we have sinned!'

41But Moses said, 'Why are you disobeying the LORD's command? This will not succeed! 42Do not go up, because the LORD is not with you. You will be defeated by your enemies, 43for the Amalekites and Canaanites will face you there. Because you have turned away from the LORD, he will not be with you and you will fall by the sword.'

44Nevertheless, in their presumption they went up towards the highest point in the hill country, though neither Moses nor the ark of the LORD's covenant moved from the camp. 45Then the Amalekites and Canaanites who lived in that hill country came down and attacked them and beat them down all the way to Hormah.

---

[a] 25 Or *the Sea of Reeds*

Supplementary offerings

15 The LORD said to Moses, 2'Speak to the Israelites and say to them: "After you enter the land I am giving you as a home 3and you present to the LORD food offerings from the herd or the flock, as an aroma pleasing to the LORD—whether burnt offerings or sacrifices, for special vows or freewill offerings or festival offerings— 4then the person who brings an offering shall present to the LORD a grain offering of a tenth of an ephah^a of the finest flour mixed with a quarter of a hin^b of olive oil. 5With each lamb for the burnt offering or the sacrifice, prepare a quarter of a hin of wine as a drink offering.

6' "With a ram prepare a grain offering of one fifth of an ephah^c of the finest flour mixed with a third of a hin^d of olive oil, 7and a third of a hin of wine as a drink offering. Offer it as an aroma pleasing to the LORD.

8' "When you prepare a young bull as a burnt offering or sacrifice, for a special vow or a fellowship offering to the LORD, 9bring with the bull a grain offering of three tenths of an ephah^e of the finest flour mixed with half a hin^f of olive oil, 10and also bring half a hin of wine as a drink offering. This will be a food offering, an aroma pleasing to the LORD. 11Each bull or ram, each lamb or young goat, is to be prepared in this manner. 12Do this for each one, for as many as you prepare.

13' "Everyone who is native-born must do these things in this way when they present a food offering as an aroma pleasing to the LORD. 14For the generations to come, whenever a foreigner or anyone else living among you presents a food offering as an aroma pleasing to the LORD, they must do exactly as you do. 15The community is to have the same rules for you and for the foreigner residing among you; this is a lasting ordinance for the generations to come. You and the foreigner shall be the same before the LORD: 16the same laws and regulations will apply both to you and to the foreigner residing among you."'

17The LORD said to Moses, 18'Speak to the Israelites and say to them: "When you enter the land to which I am taking you 19and you eat the food of the land, present a portion as an offering to the LORD. 20Present a loaf from the first of your ground meal and present it as an offering from the threshing-floor. 21Throughout the generations to come you are to give this offering to the LORD from the first of your ground meal.

Offerings for unintentional sins

22' "Now if you as a community unintentionally fail to keep any of these commands the LORD gave Moses— 23any of the LORD's commands to you through him, from the day the LORD gave them and continuing through the generations to come— 24and if this is done unintentionally without the community being aware of it, then the whole community is to offer a young bull for a burnt offering as an aroma pleasing to the LORD, along with its prescribed grain offering and drink offering, and a male goat for a sin offering.^{g} 25The priest is to make atonement for the whole Israelite community, and they will be forgiven, for it was not intentional and they have presented to the LORD for their wrong a food offering and a sin offering. 26The whole Israelite community and the foreigners residing among them will be forgiven, because all the people were involved in the unintentional wrong.

27' "But if just one person sins unintentionally, that person must bring a year-old female goat for a sin offering. 28The priest is to make atonement before the LORD for the one who erred by sinning unintentionally, and when atonement has been made for them, they will be forgiven. 29One and the same law applies to everyone who sins unintentionally, whether a native-born Israelite or a foreigner residing among you.

30' "But anyone who sins defiantly, whether native-born or foreigner, utters blasphemy against the LORD and must be cut off from their people. 31Because they have despised the LORD's word and broken

---

^{a} 4 That is, probably about 1.5 kilograms ^{b} 4 That is, about 0.9 litre; also in verse 5 ^{c} 6 That is, probably about 3.25 kilograms ^{d} 6 That is, about 1.2 litres; also in verse 7 ^{e} 9 That is, probably about 5 kilograms ^{f} 9 That is, about 1.8 litres; also in verse 10 ^{g} 24 Or *purification offering*; also in verses 25 and 27

The Sabbath-breaker put to death

32While the Israelites were in the wilderness, a man was found gathering wood on the Sabbath day. 33Those who found him gathering wood brought him to Moses and Aaron and the whole assembly, 34and they kept him in custody, because it was not clear what should be done to him. 35Then the LORD said to Moses, 'The man must die. The whole assembly must stone him outside the camp.' 36So the assembly took him outside the camp and stoned him to death, as the LORD commanded Moses.

Tassels on garments

37The LORD said to Moses, 38'Speak to the Israelites and say to them: "Throughout the generations to come you are to make tassels on the corners of your garments, with a blue cord on each tassel. 39You will have these tassels to look at and so you will remember all the commands of the LORD, that you may obey them and not prostitute yourselves by chasing after the lusts of your own hearts and eyes. 40Then you will remember to obey all my commands and will be consecrated to your God. 41I am the LORD your God, who brought you out of Egypt to be your God. I am the LORD your God."'

Korah, Dathan and Abiram

16 Korah son of Izhar, the son of Kohath, the son of Levi, and certain Reubenites—Dathan and Abiram, sons of Eliab, and On son of Peleth—became insolent[a] 2and rose up against Moses. With them were 250 Israelite men, well-known community leaders who had been appointed members of the council. 3They came as a group to oppose Moses and Aaron and said to them, 'You have gone too far! The whole community is holy, every one of them, and the LORD is with them. Why then do you set yourselves above the LORD's assembly?'

4When Moses heard this, he fell face down. 5Then he said to Korah and all his followers: 'In the morning the LORD will show who belongs to him and who is holy, and he will make that person come near him. The one he chooses he will cause to come near him. 6You, Korah, and all your followers are to do this: take censers 7and tomorrow put burning coals and incense in them before the LORD. The man the LORD chooses will be the one who is holy. You Levites have gone too far!'

8Moses also said to Korah, 'Now listen, you Levites! 9Isn't it enough for you that the God of Israel has separated you from the rest of the Israelite community and brought you near himself to do the work at the LORD's tabernacle and to stand before the community and minister to them? 10He has brought you and all your fellow Levites near himself, but now you are trying to get the priesthood too. 11It is against the LORD that you and all your followers have banded together. Who is Aaron that you should grumble against him?'

12Then Moses summoned Dathan and Abiram, the sons of Eliab. But they said, 'We will not come! 13Isn't it enough that you have brought us up out of a land flowing with milk and honey to kill us in the wilderness? And now you also want to lord it over us! 14Moreover, you haven't brought us into a land flowing with milk and honey

Sign of the times

Tassels on clothes
Numbers 15:37

Ever written on the back of your hand to remind you to do something? Well, that's what these tassels were for. They weren't a fashion statement; they were there for a purpose. The tassels were to remind the Israelites that they were God's people and were to keep his commandments.

---

[a] 1 Or Peleth—took men

or given us an inheritance of fields and vineyards. Do you want to treat these men like slaves[a]? No, we will not come!'

15Then Moses became very angry and said to the LORD, 'Do not accept their offering. I have not taken so much as a donkey from them, nor have I wronged any of them.'

16Moses said to Korah, 'You and all your followers are to appear before the LORD tomorrow—you and they and Aaron. 17Each one is to take his censer and put incense in it—250 censers in all—and present it before the LORD. You and Aaron are to present your censers also.' 18So each one took his censer, put burning coals and incense in it, and stood with Moses and Aaron at the entrance to the tent of meeting. 19When Korah had gathered all his followers in opposition to them at the entrance to the tent of meeting, the glory of the LORD appeared to the entire assembly. 20The LORD said to Moses and Aaron, 21'Separate yourselves from this assembly so that I can put an end to them at once.'

22But Moses and Aaron fell face down and cried out, 'O God, God of every human spirit, will you be angry with the entire assembly when only one man sins?'

23Then the LORD said to Moses, 24'Say to the assembly, "Move away from the tents of Korah, Dathan and Abiram."'

25Moses got up and went to Dathan and Abiram, and the elders of Israel followed him. 26He warned the assembly, 'Move back from the tents of these wicked men! Do not touch anything belonging to them, or you will be swept away because of all their sins.' 27So they moved away from the tents of Korah, Dathan and Abiram. Dathan and Abiram had come out and were standing with their wives, children and little ones at the entrances to their tents.

28Then Moses said, 'This is how you will know that the LORD has sent me to do all these things and that it was not my idea: 29if these men die a natural death and suffer the common fate of all human beings, then the LORD has not sent me. 30But if the LORD brings about something totally new, and the earth opens its mouth and swallows them, with everything that belongs to them, and they go down alive into the realm of the dead, then you will know that these men have treated the LORD with contempt.'

31As soon as he finished saying all this, the ground under them split apart 32and the earth opened its mouth and swallowed them and their households, and all those associated with Korah, together with their possessions. 33They went down alive into the realm of the dead, with everything they owned; the earth closed over them, and they perished and were gone from the community. 34At their cries, all the Israelites around them fled, shouting, 'The earth is going to swallow us too!'

35And fire came out from the LORD and consumed the 250 men who were offering the incense.

*36The LORD said to Moses, 37'Tell Eleazar son of Aaron, the priest, to remove the censers from the charred remains and scatter the coals some distance away, for the censers are holy— 38the censers of the men who sinned at the cost of their lives. Hammer the censers into sheets to overlay the altar, for they were presented before the LORD and have become holy. Let them be a sign to the Israelites.'

39So Eleazar the priest collected the bronze censers brought by those who had been burned to death, and he had them hammered out to overlay the altar, 40as the LORD directed him through Moses. This was to remind the Israelites that no-one except a descendant of Aaron should come to burn incense before the LORD, or he would become like Korah and his followers.

41The next day the whole Israelite community grumbled against Moses and Aaron. 'You have killed the LORD's people,' they said.

42But when the assembly gathered in opposition to Moses and Aaron and turned towards the tent of meeting, suddenly the cloud covered it and the glory of the LORD appeared. 43Then Moses and Aaron went to the front of the tent of meeting, 44and the

---

[a] 14 Or *to deceive these men*; Hebrew *Will you gouge out the eyes of these men*

* 16:36-50 is numbered 17:1-15 in Hebrew texts.

LORD said to Moses, 45'Get away from this assembly so that I can put an end to them at once.' And they fell face down.

46Then Moses said to Aaron, 'Take your censer and put incense in it, along with burning coals from the altar, and hurry to the assembly to make atonement for them. Wrath has come out from the LORD; the plague has started.' 47So Aaron did as Moses said, and ran into the midst of the assembly. The plague had already started among the people, but Aaron offered the incense and made atonement for them. 48He stood between the living and the dead, and the plague stopped. 49But 14,700 people died from the plague, in addition to those who had died because of Korah. 50Then Aaron returned to Moses at the entrance to the tent of meeting, for the plague had stopped.

The budding of Aaron's staff

17 *The LORD said to Moses, 2'Speak to the Israelites and get twelve staffs from them, one from the leader of each of their ancestral tribes. Write the name of each man on his staff. 3On the staff of Levi write Aaron's name, for there must be one staff for the head of each ancestral tribe. 4Place them in the tent of meeting in front of the ark of the covenant law, where I meet with you. 5The staff belonging to the man I choose will sprout, and I will rid myself of this constant grumbling against you by the Israelites.'

6So Moses spoke to the Israelites, and their leaders gave him twelve staffs, one for the leader of each of their ancestral tribes, and Aaron's staff was among them. 7Moses placed the staffs before the LORD in the tent of the covenant law.

8The next day Moses entered the tent and saw that Aaron's staff, which represented the house of Levi, had not only sprouted but had budded, blossomed and produced almonds. 9Then Moses brought out all the staffs from the LORD's presence to all the Israelites. They looked at them, and each of the leaders took his own staff.

10The LORD said to Moses, 'Put back Aaron's staff in front of the ark of the covenant law, to be kept as a sign to the rebellious. This will put an end to their grumbling against me, so that they will not die.' 11Moses did just as the LORD commanded him.

12The Israelites said to Moses, 'We shall die! We are lost, we are all lost! 13Anyone who even comes near the tabernacle of the LORD will die. Are we all going to die?'

Duties of priests and Levites

18 The LORD said to Aaron, 'You, your sons and your ancestral family are to bear the responsibility for offences connected with the sanctuary, and you and your sons alone are to bear the responsibility for offences connected with the priesthood. 2Bring your fellow Levites from your ancestral tribe to join you and assist you when you and your sons minister before the tent of the covenant law. 3They are to be responsible to you and are to perform all the duties of the tent, but they must not go near the furnishings of the sanctuary or the altar. Otherwise both they and you will die. 4They are to join you and be responsible for the care of the tent of meeting—all the work at the tent—and no-one else may come near where you are.

5'You are to be responsible for the care of the sanctuary and the altar, so that my wrath will not fall on the Israelites again. 6I myself

---

IN OTHER WORDS

Blood
Numbers 18:17

Blood was the symbol of life for the Israelites and it was shed at all their major festivals. They were to avoid eating blood out of respect for life. It was the shedding of blood in sacrifices that made people right with God. Jesus' blood was shed when he died on the cross; this was the ultimate sacrifice and means that we can be right with God without the need for any more blood being spilt.

---

* 17:1-13 is numbered 17:16-28 in Hebrew texts.

have selected your fellow Levites from among the Israelites as a gift to you, dedicated to the LORD to do the work at the tent of meeting. 7But only you and your sons may serve as priests in connection with everything at the altar and inside the curtain. I am giving you the service of the priesthood as a gift. Anyone else who comes near the sanctuary is to be put to death.'

Offerings for priests and Levites

8Then the LORD said to Aaron, 'I myself have put you in charge of the offerings presented to me; all the holy offerings the Israelites give me I give to you and your sons as your portion, your perpetual share. 9You are to have the part of the most holy offerings that is kept from the fire. From all the gifts they bring me as most holy offerings, whether grain or sin[a] or guilt offerings, that part belongs to you and your sons. 10Eat it as something most holy; every male shall eat it. You must regard it as holy.

11'This also is yours: whatever is set aside from the gifts of all the wave offerings of the Israelites. I give this to you and your sons and daughters as your perpetual share. Everyone in your household who is ceremonially clean may eat it.

12'I give you all the finest olive oil and all the finest new wine and grain they give to the LORD as the firstfruits of their harvest. 13All the land's firstfruits that they bring to the LORD will be yours. Everyone in your household who is ceremonially clean may eat it.

14'Everything in Israel that is devoted[b] to the LORD is yours. 15The first offspring of every womb, both human and animal, that is offered to the LORD is yours. But you must redeem every firstborn son and every firstborn male of unclean animals. 16When they are a month old, you must redeem them at the redemption price set at five shekels[c] of silver, according to the sanctuary shekel, which weighs twenty gerahs.

17'But you must not redeem the firstborn of an ox, a sheep or a goat; they are holy. Splash their blood against the altar and burn their fat as a food offering, an aroma pleasing to the LORD. 18Their meat is to be yours, just as the breast of the wave offering and the right thigh are yours. 19Whatever is set aside from the holy offerings the Israelites present to the LORD I give to you and your sons and daughters as your perpetual share. It is an everlasting covenant of salt before the LORD for both you and your offspring.'

20The LORD said to Aaron, 'You will have no inheritance in their land, nor will you have any share among them; I am your share and your inheritance among the Israelites.

21'I give to the Levites all the tithes in Israel as their inheritance in return for the work they do while serving at the tent of meeting. 22From now on the Israelites must not go near the tent of meeting, or they will bear the consequences of their sin and will die. 23It is the Levites who are to do the work at the tent of meeting and bear the responsibility for any offences they commit against it. This is a lasting ordinance for the generations to come. They will receive no inheritance among the Israelites. 24Instead, I give to the Levites as their inheritance the tithes that the Israelites present as an offering to the LORD. That is why I said concerning them: "They will have no inheritance among the Israelites."'

25The LORD said to Moses, 26'Speak to the Levites and say to them: "When you receive from the Israelites the tithe I give you as your inheritance, you must present a tenth of that tithe as the LORD's offering. 27Your offering will be reckoned to you as grain from the threshing-floor or juice from the winepress. 28In this way you also will present an offering to the LORD from all the tithes you receive from the Israelites. From these tithes you must give the LORD's portion to Aaron the priest. 29You must present as the LORD's portion the best and holiest part of everything given to you."'

30'Say to the Levites: "When you present the best part, it will be reckoned to you as the product of the threshing-floor or the winepress. 31You and your households may eat the rest of it anywhere, for it is your wages for your work at the tent of meeting. 32By

---

[a] 9 Or *purification* [b] 14 The Hebrew term refers to the irrevocable giving over of things or persons to the LORD.
[c] 16 That is, about 55 grams

presenting the best part of it you will not be guilty in this matter; then you will not defile the holy offerings of the Israelites, and you will not die.'"

The water of cleansing

19 The LORD said to Moses and Aaron: ²'This is a requirement of the law that the LORD has commanded: tell the Israelites to bring you a red heifer without defect or blemish and that has never been under a yoke. ³Give it to Eleazar the priest; it is to be taken outside the camp and slaughtered in his presence. ⁴Then Eleazar the priest is to take some of its blood on his finger and sprinkle it seven times towards the front of the tent of meeting. ⁵While he watches, the heifer is to be burned—its hide, flesh, blood and intestines. ⁶The priest is to take some cedar wood, hyssop and scarlet wool and throw them onto the burning heifer. ⁷After that, the priest must wash his clothes and bathe himself with water. He may then come into the camp, but he will be ceremonially unclean till evening. ⁸The man who burns it must also wash his clothes and bathe with water, and he too will be unclean till evening.

⁹'A man who is clean shall gather up the ashes of the heifer and put them in a ceremonially clean place outside the camp. They are to be kept by the Israelite community for use in the water of cleansing; it is for purification from sin. ¹⁰The man who gathers up the ashes of the heifer must also wash his clothes, and he too will be unclean till evening. This will be a lasting ordinance both for the Israelites and for the foreigners residing among them.

¹¹'Whoever touches a human corpse will be unclean for seven days. ¹²They must purify themselves with the water on the third day and on the seventh day; then they will be clean. But if they do not purify themselves on the third and seventh days, they will not be clean. ¹³If they fail to purify themselves after touching a human corpse, they defile the LORD's tabernacle. They must be cut off from Israel. Because the water of cleansing has not been sprinkled on them, they are unclean; their uncleanness remains on them.

---

making Connections

Water from the rock
Numbers 20:8

Moses needs to listen more carefully. The people are grumbling again about having no water and so God is about to provide them with some. He tells Moses to speak to the rock and it will produce water. But Moses has been in this situation before, and last time he hit a rock and water came out (Exodus 17:6). For some reason, he doesn't just speak to the rock like God says – he strikes it. And although water comes out anyway, it's a mistake that costs Moses a lot. As a result, God says he can't take the people into the Promised Land.

---

¹⁴'This is the law that applies when a person dies in a tent: anyone who enters the tent and anyone who is in it will be unclean for seven days, ¹⁵and every open container without a lid fastened on it will be unclean.

¹⁶'Anyone out in the open who touches someone who has been killed with a sword or someone who has died a natural death, or anyone who touches a human bone or a grave, will be unclean for seven days.

¹⁷'For the unclean person, put some ashes from the burned purification offering into a jar and pour fresh water over them. ¹⁸Then a man who is ceremonially clean is to take some hyssop, dip it in the water and sprinkle the tent and all the furnishings and the people who were there. He must also sprinkle anyone who has touched a human bone or a grave or anyone who has been killed or anyone who has died a natural death. ¹⁹The man who is clean is to sprinkle those who are unclean on the third and seventh days, and on the seventh day he is to purify them. Those who are being cleansed

must wash their clothes and bathe with water, and that evening they will be clean. 20But if those who are unclean do not purify themselves, they must be cut off from the community, because they have defiled the sanctuary of the LORD. The water of cleansing has not been sprinkled on them, and they are unclean. 21This is a lasting ordinance for them.

'The man who sprinkles the water of cleansing must also wash his clothes, and anyone who touches the water of cleansing will be unclean till evening. 22Anything that an unclean person touches becomes unclean, and anyone who touches it becomes unclean till evening.'

Water from the rock

20 In the first month the whole Israelite community arrived at the Desert of Zin, and they stayed at Kadesh. There Miriam died and was buried.

2Now there was no water for the community, and the people gathered in opposition to Moses and Aaron. 3They quarrelled with Moses and said, 'If only we had died when our brothers fell dead before the LORD! 4Why did you bring the LORD's community into this wilderness, that we and our livestock should die here? 5Why did you bring us up out of Egypt to this terrible place? It has no corn or figs, grapevines or pomegranates. And there is no water to drink!'

6Moses and Aaron went from the assembly to the entrance to the tent of meeting and fell face down, and the glory of the LORD appeared to them. 7The LORD said to Moses, 8'Take the staff, and you and your brother Aaron gather the assembly together. Speak to that rock before their eyes and it will pour out its water. You will bring water out of the rock for the community so that they and their livestock can drink.'

9So Moses took the staff from the LORD's presence, just as he commanded him. 10He and Aaron gathered the assembly together in front of the rock and Moses said to them, 'Listen, you rebels, must we bring you water out of this rock?' 11Then Moses raised his arm and struck the rock twice with his staff. Water gushed out, and the community and their livestock drank.

12But the LORD said to Moses and Aaron, 'Because you did not trust in me enough to honour me as holy in the sight of the Israelites, you will not bring this community into the land I give them.'

13These were the waters of Meribah,[a] where the Israelites quarrelled with the LORD and where he was proved holy among them.

Edom denies Israel passage

14Moses sent messengers from Kadesh to the king of Edom, saying:

> 'This is what your brother Israel says: you know about all the hardships that have come on us. 15Our ancestors went down into Egypt, and we lived there many years. The Egyptians ill-treated us and our ancestors, 16but when we cried out to the LORD, he heard our cry and sent an angel and brought us out of Egypt.

making Connections

Edomites
Numbers 20:14
You may remember that Jacob and Esau were twin brothers who didn't get on (Genesis 27). Well, it seems that their families have inherited that hatred. Jacob was the father of the twelve tribes of Israel, and Esau's descendants are now called the Edomites. Moses asks if the Israelites can go through Edomite territory, but the answer is a very clear NO!

---

[a] 13 *Meribah* means *quarrelling*.

'Now we are here at Kadesh, a town on the edge of your territory. ¹⁷Please let us pass through your country. We will not go through any field or vineyard, or drink water from any well. We will travel along the King's Highway and not turn to the right or to the left until we have passed through your territory.'

¹⁸But Edom answered:

'You may not pass through here; if you try, we will march out and attack you with the sword.'

¹⁹The Israelites replied:

'We will go along the main road, and if we or our livestock drink any of your water, we will pay for it. We only want to pass through on foot—nothing else.'

²⁰Again they answered:

'You may not pass through.'

Then Edom came out against them with a large and powerful army. ²¹Since Edom refused to let them go through their territory, Israel turned away from them.

The death of Aaron

²²The whole Israelite community set out from Kadesh and came to Mount Hor. ²³At Mount Hor, near the border of Edom, the LORD said to Moses and Aaron, ²⁴'Aaron will be gathered to his people. He will not enter the land I give the Israelites, because both of you rebelled against my command at the waters of Meribah. ²⁵Call Aaron and his son Eleazar and take them up Mount Hor. ²⁶Remove Aaron's garments and put them on his son Eleazar, for Aaron will be gathered to his people; he will die there.'

²⁷Moses did as the LORD commanded: they went up Mount Hor in the sight of the whole community. ²⁸Moses removed Aaron's garments and put them on his son Eleazar. And Aaron died there on top of the mountain. Then Moses and Eleazar came down from the mountain, ²⁹and when the whole community learned that Aaron had died, the entire house of Israel mourned for him thirty days.

Arad destroyed

21 When the Canaanite king of Arad, who lived in the Negev, heard that Israel was coming along the road to Atharim, he attacked the Israelites and captured some of them. ²Then Israel made this vow to the LORD: 'If you will deliver these people into our hands, we will totally destroy*ᵃ* their cities.' ³The LORD listened to Israel's plea and gave the Canaanites over to them. They completely destroyed them and their towns; so the place was named Hormah.*ᵇ*

The bronze snake

⁴They travelled from Mount Hor along the route to the Red Sea,*ᶜ* to go round Edom. But the people grew impatient on the way; ⁵they spoke against God and against Moses, and said, 'Why have you brought us up out of Egypt to die in the wilderness? There is no bread! There is no water! And we detest this miserable food!'

making Connections

The bronze snake
Numbers 21:8

Jesus referred to this incident when he was talking to Nicodemus (John 3:1–21). He pointed out that Moses lifted up this snake and everyone who looked at it was saved. Then Jesus said that he would be lifted up, referring to his future death on the cross, so that everyone who believes in him can be saved.

---

*ᵃ*2 The Hebrew term refers to the irrevocable giving over of things or persons to the LORD, often by totally destroying them; also in verse 3.   *ᵇ*3 *Hormah* means *destruction*.   *ᶜ*4 Or *the Sea of Reeds*

⁶Then the LORD sent venomous snakes among them; they bit the people and many Israelites died. ⁷The people came to Moses and said, 'We sinned when we spoke against the LORD and against you. Pray that the LORD will take the snakes away from us.' So Moses prayed for the people.

⁸The LORD said to Moses, 'Make a snake and put it up on a pole; anyone who is bitten can look at it and live.' ⁹So Moses made a bronze snake and put it up on a pole. Then when anyone was bitten by a snake and looked at the bronze snake, they lived.

The journey to Moab

¹⁰The Israelites moved on and camped at Oboth. ¹¹Then they set out from Oboth and camped in Iye Abarim, in the wilderness that faces Moab towards the sunrise. ¹²From there they moved on and camped in the Zered Valley. ¹³They set out from there and camped alongside the Arnon, which is in the wilderness extending into Amorite territory. The Arnon is the border of Moab, between Moab and the Amorites. ¹⁴That is why the Book of the Wars of the LORD says:

'... Zahab[a] in Suphah and the ravines,
    the Arnon ¹⁵and[b] the slopes of the
        ravines
that lead to the settlement of Ar
    and lie along the border of Moab.'

¹⁶From there they continued on to Beer, the well where the LORD said to Moses, 'Gather the people together and I will give them water.'

¹⁷Then Israel sang this song:

'Spring up, O well!
    Sing about it,
¹⁸about the well that the princes dug,
    that the nobles of the people sank—
the nobles with sceptres and staffs.'

Then they went from the wilderness to Mattanah, ¹⁹from Mattanah to Nahaliel, from Nahaliel to Bamoth, ²⁰and from Bamoth to the valley in Moab where the top of Pisgah overlooks the wasteland.

Defeat of Sihon and Og

²¹Israel sent messengers to say to Sihon king of the Amorites:

²²'Let us pass through your country.
    We will not turn aside into any
        field or vineyard, or drink water
        from any well. We will travel along
        the King's Highway until we have
        passed through your territory.'

²³But Sihon would not let Israel pass through his territory. He mustered his entire army and marched out into the wilderness against Israel. When he reached Jahaz, he fought with Israel. ²⁴Israel, however, put him to the sword and took over his land from the Arnon to the Jabbok, but only as far as the Ammonites, because their border was fortified. ²⁵Israel captured all the cities of the Amorites and occupied them, including Heshbon and all its surrounding settlements. ²⁶Heshbon was the city of Sihon king of the Amorites, who had fought against the former king of Moab and had taken from him all his land as far as the Arnon.

²⁷That is why the poets say:

'Come to Heshbon and let it be rebuilt;
    let Sihon's city be restored.

²⁸'Fire went out from Heshbon,
    a blaze from the city of Sihon.
It consumed Ar of Moab,
    the citizens of Arnon's heights.
²⁹Woe to you, Moab!
    You are destroyed, people of
        Chemosh!
He has given up his sons as fugitives
    and his daughters as captives
to Sihon king of the Amorites.

³⁰'But we have overthrown them;
    Heshbon's dominion has been
        destroyed all the way to Dibon.
We have demolished them as far as
        Nophah,
    which extends to Medeba.'

³¹So Israel settled in the land of the Amorites.

---

[a] 14 Septuagint; Hebrew *Waheb*   [b] 14,15 Or *'I have been given from Suphah and the ravines / of the Arnon* ¹⁵*to*

32After Moses had sent spies to Jazer, the Israelites captured its surrounding settlements and drove out the Amorites who were there. 33Then they turned and went up along the road towards Bashan, and Og king of Bashan and his whole army marched out to meet them in battle at Edrei.

34The LORD said to Moses, 'Do not be afraid of him, for I have delivered him into your hands, along with his whole army and his land. Do to him what you did to Sihon king of the Amorites, who reigned in Heshbon.'

35So they struck him down, together with his sons and his whole army, leaving them no survivors. And they took possession of his land.

Balak summons Balaam

22 Then the Israelites travelled to the plains of Moab and camped along the Jordan opposite Jericho.

2Now Balak son of Zippor saw all that Israel had done to the Amorites, 3and Moab was terrified because there were so many people. Indeed, Moab was filled with dread because of the Israelites.

4The Moabites said to the elders of Midian, 'This horde is going to lick up everything around us, as an ox licks up the grass of the field.'

So Balak son of Zippor, who was king of Moab at that time, 5sent messengers to summon Balaam son of Beor, who was at Pethor, near the River Euphrates, in his native land. Balak said:

'A people has come out of Egypt; they cover the face of the land and have settled next to me. 6Now come and put a curse on these people, because they are too powerful for me. Perhaps then I will be able to defeat them and drive them out of the land. For I know that whoever you bless is blessed, and whoever you curse is cursed.'

7The elders of Moab and Midian left, taking with them the fee for divination. When they came to Balaam, they told him what Balak had said.

8'Spend the night here,' Balaam said to them, 'and I will report back to you with the answer the LORD gives me.' So the Moabite officials stayed with him.

9God came to Balaam and asked, 'Who are these men with you?'

10Balaam said to God, 'Balak son of Zippor, king of Moab, sent me this message: 11"A people that has come out of Egypt covers the face of the land. Now come and put a curse on them for me. Perhaps then I will be able to fight them and drive them away."'

12But God said to Balaam, 'Do not go with them. You must not put a curse on those people, because they are blessed.'

13The next morning Balaam got up and said to Balak's officials, 'Go back to your own country, for the LORD has refused to let me go with you.'

14So the Moabite officials returned to Balak and said, 'Balaam refused to come with us.'

15Then Balak sent other officials, more numerous and more distinguished than the first. 16They came to Balaam and said:

'This is what Balak son of Zippor says: do not let anything keep you from coming to me, 17because I will reward you handsomely and do whatever you say. Come and put a curse on these people for me.'

18But Balaam answered them, 'Even if Balak gave me all the silver and gold in his palace, I could not do anything great or small to go beyond the command of the LORD my God. 19Now spend the night here so that I can find out what else the LORD will tell me.'

20That night God came to Balaam and said, 'Since these men have come to summon you, go with them, but do only what I tell you.'

Balaam's donkey

21Balaam got up in the morning, saddled his donkey and went with the Moabite officials. 22But God was very angry when he went, and the angel of the LORD stood in the road to oppose him. Balaam was riding on his donkey, and his two servants were with him. 23When the donkey saw the angel of the LORD standing in the road with a drawn sword in his hand, it turned off the road into a field. Balaam beat it to get it back on the road.

24Then the angel of the LORD stood in a narrow path through the vineyards, with walls on both sides. 25When the donkey saw the angel of the LORD, it pressed close to the wall, crushing Balaam's foot against it. So he beat the donkey again.

26Then the angel of the LORD moved on ahead and stood in a narrow place where there was no room to turn, either to the right or to the left. 27When the donkey saw the angel of the LORD, it lay down under Balaam, and he was angry and beat it with his staff. 28Then the LORD opened the donkey's mouth, and it said to Balaam, 'What have I done to you to make you beat me these three times?'

29Balaam answered the donkey, 'You have made a fool of me! If only I had a sword in my hand, I would kill you here and now.'

30The donkey said to Balaam, 'Am I not your own donkey, which you have always ridden, to this day? Have I been in the habit of doing this to you?'

'No,' he said.

31Then the LORD opened Balaam's eyes, and he saw the angel of the LORD standing in the road with his sword drawn. So he bowed low and fell face down.

32The angel of the LORD asked him, 'Why have you beaten your donkey these three times? I have come here to oppose you because your path is a reckless one before me.'[a] 33The donkey saw me and turned away from me these three times. If it had not turned away, I would certainly have killed you by now, but I would have spared it.'

34Balaam said to the angel of the LORD, 'I have sinned. I did not realise you were standing in the road to oppose me. Now if you are displeased, I will go back.'

35The angel of the LORD said to Balaam, 'Go with the men, but speak only what I tell you.' So Balaam went with Balak's officials.

36When Balak heard that Balaam was coming, he went out to meet him at the Moabite town on the Arnon border, at the edge of his territory. 37Balak said to Balaam, 'Did I not send you an urgent summons? Why didn't you come to me? Am I really not able to reward you?'

38'Well, I have come to you now,' Balaam replied. 'But I can't say whatever I please. I must speak only what God puts in my mouth.'

39Then Balaam went with Balak to Kiriath Huzoth. 40Balak sacrificed cattle and sheep, and gave some to Balaam and the officials who were with him. 41The next morning Balak took Balaam up to Bamoth Baal, and from there he could see the outskirts of the Israelite camp.

Balaam's first message

23 Balaam said, 'Build me seven altars here, and prepare seven bulls and seven rams for me.' 2Balak did as Balaam said, and the two of them offered a bull and a ram on each altar.

3Then Balaam said to Balak, 'Stay here beside your offering while I go aside. Perhaps the LORD will come to meet with me. Whatever he reveals to me I will tell you.' Then he went off to a barren height.

4God met with him, and Balaam said, 'I have prepared seven altars, and on each altar I have offered a bull and a ram.'

5The LORD put a word in Balaam's mouth and said, 'Go back to Balak and give him this word.'

6So he went back to him and found him standing beside his offering, with all the Moabite officials. 7Then Balaam spoke his message:

'Balak brought me from Aram,
  the king of Moab from the eastern
    mountains.
"Come," he said, "curse Jacob for me;
  come, denounce Israel."
8How can I curse
  those whom God has not cursed?
How can I denounce
  those whom the LORD has not
    denounced?
9From the rocky peaks I see them,
  from the heights I view them.
I see people who live apart

---

[a] 32 The meaning of the Hebrew for this clause is uncertain.

Making Connections

Blessing instead of cursing
Numbers 23:11

Balak thinks he's found a deadly secret weapon against the Israelites. He'll get Balaam the prophet to curse them, but his plan seriously backfires. Balaam just can't curse God's chosen people, no matter how hard he tries. He has to do what God says, and ends up blessing them three times instead.

and do not consider themselves one of the nations.
¹⁰Who can count the dust of Jacob
or number the fourth part of Israel?
Let me die the death of the righteous,
and may my final end be like theirs!'

¹¹Balak said to Balaam, 'What have you done to me? I brought you to curse my enemies, but you have done nothing but bless them!'

¹²He answered, 'Must I not speak what the LORD puts in my mouth?'

Balaam's second message

¹³Then Balak said to him, 'Come with me to another place where you can see them; you will not see them all but only the outskirts of their camp. And from there, curse them for me.' ¹⁴So he took him to the field of Zophim on the top of Pisgah, and there he built seven altars and offered a bull and a ram on each altar.

¹⁵Balaam said to Balak, 'Stay here beside your offering while I meet with him over there.'

¹⁶The LORD met with Balaam and put a word in his mouth and said, 'Go back to Balak and give him this word.'

¹⁷So he went to him and found him standing beside his offering, with the Moabite officials. Balak asked him, 'What did the LORD say?'

¹⁸Then he spoke his message:

'Arise, Balak, and listen;
hear me, son of Zippor.
¹⁹God is not human, that he should lie,
not a human being, that he should change his mind.
Does he speak and then not act?
Does he promise and not fulfil?
²⁰I have received a command to bless;
he has blessed, and I cannot change it.

²¹'No misfortune is seen in Jacob,
no misery observed[a] in Israel.
The LORD their God is with them;
the shout of the King is among them.
²²God brought them out of Egypt;
they have the strength of a wild ox.
²³There is no divination against[b] Jacob,
no evil omens against[c] Israel.
It will now be said of Jacob
and of Israel, "See what God has done!"
²⁴The people rise like a lioness;
they rouse themselves like a lion
that does not rest till it devours its prey
and drinks the blood of its victims.'

²⁵Then Balak said to Balaam, 'Neither curse them at all nor bless them at all!'

²⁶Balaam answered, 'Did I not tell you I must do whatever the LORD says?'

Balaam's third message

²⁷Then Balak said to Balaam, 'Come, let me take you to another place. Perhaps it will please God to let you curse them for me from there.' ²⁸And Balak took Balaam to the top of Peor, overlooking the wasteland.

²⁹Balaam said, 'Build me seven altars here, and prepare seven bulls and seven rams for me.' ³⁰Balak did as Balaam had said, and offered a bull and a ram on each altar.

24 Now when Balaam saw that it pleased the LORD to bless Israel, he did not resort to divination as at other times, but turned his face towards the

---

[a] 21 Or *He has not looked on Jacob's offences / or on the wrongs found*   [b] 23 Or *in*   [c] 23 Or *in*

wilderness. ²When Balaam looked out and saw Israel encamped tribe by tribe, the Spirit of God came on him ³and he spoke his message:

> 'The prophecy of Balaam son of Beor,
>   the prophecy of one whose eye sees clearly,
> ⁴the prophecy of one who hears the words of God,
>   who sees a vision from the Almighty,[a]
>   who falls prostrate, and whose eyes are opened:
>
> ⁵'How beautiful are your tents, Jacob,
>   your dwelling-places, Israel!
>
> ⁶'Like valleys they spread out,
>   like gardens beside a river,
> like aloes planted by the LORD,
>   like cedars beside the waters.
> ⁷Water will flow from their buckets;
>   their seed will have abundant water.
>
> 'Their king will be greater than Agag;
>   their kingdom will be exalted.
>
> ⁸'God brought them out of Egypt;
>   they have the strength of a wild ox.
> They devour hostile nations
>   and break their bones in pieces;
>   with their arrows they pierce them.
> ⁹Like a lion they crouch and lie down,
>   like a lioness—who dares to rouse them?
>
> 'May those who bless you be blessed
>   and those who curse you be cursed!'

¹⁰Then Balak's anger burned against Balaam. He struck his hands together and said to him, 'I summoned you to curse my enemies, but you have blessed them these three times. ¹¹Now leave at once and go home! I said I would reward you handsomely, but the LORD has kept you from being rewarded.'

¹²Balaam answered Balak, 'Did I not tell the messengers you sent me, ¹³"Even if Balak gave me all the silver and gold in his palace, I could not do anything of my own accord, good or bad, to go beyond the command of the LORD—and I must say only what the LORD says"? ¹⁴Now I am going back to my people, but come, let me warn you of what this people will do to your people in days to come.'

Balaam's fourth message

¹⁵Then he spoke his message:

> 'The prophecy of Balaam son of Beor,
>   the prophecy of one whose eye sees clearly,
> ¹⁶the prophecy of one who hears the words of God,
>   who has knowledge from the Most High,
>   who sees a vision from the Almighty,
>   who falls prostrate, and whose eyes are opened:
>
> ¹⁷'I see him, but not now;
>   I behold him, but not near.
> A star will come out of Jacob;
>   a sceptre will rise out of Israel.
> He will crush the foreheads of Moab,
>   the skulls[b] of[c] all the people of Sheth.[d]
> ¹⁸Edom will be conquered;
>   Seir, his enemy, will be conquered,
>   but Israel will grow strong.
> ¹⁹A ruler will come out of Jacob
>   and destroy the survivors of the city.'

Balaam's fifth message

²⁰Then Balaam saw Amalek and spoke his message:

> 'Amalek was first among the nations,
>   but they will come to ruin at last.'

Balaam's sixth message

²¹Then he saw the Kenites and spoke his message:

> 'Your dwelling-place is secure,
>   your nest is set in a rock;
> ²²yet you Kenites will be destroyed
>   when Ashur takes you captive.'

Balaam's seventh message

²³Then he spoke his message:

> 'Ah, who can live when God does this?[e]
> ²⁴   Ships will come from the shores of Cyprus;

---

[a] 4 Hebrew *Shaddai*; also in verse 16   [b] 17 Samaritan Pentateuch (see also Jer. 48:45); the meaning of the word in the Masoretic Text is uncertain.   [c] 17 Or possibly *Moab, / batter*   [d] 17 Or *all the noisy boasters*   [e] 23 Masoretic Text; with a different word division of the Hebrew *The people from the islands will gather from the north.*

they will subdue Ashur and Eber,
but they too will come to ruin.'

²⁵Then Balaam got up and returned home, and Balak went his own way.

Moab seduces Israel

25 While Israel was staying in Shittim, the men began to indulge in sexual immorality with Moabite women, ²who invited them to the sacrifices to their gods. The people ate the sacrificial meal and bowed down before these gods. ³So Israel yoked themselves to the Baal of Peor. And the LORD's anger burned against them.

⁴The LORD said to Moses, 'Take all the leaders of these people, kill them and expose them in broad daylight before the LORD, so that the LORD's fierce anger may turn away from Israel.'

⁵So Moses said to Israel's judges, 'Each of you must put to death those of your people who have yoked themselves to the Baal of Peor.'

⁶Then an Israelite man brought into the camp a Midianite woman right before the eyes of Moses and the whole assembly of Israel while they were weeping at the entrance to the tent of meeting. ⁷When Phinehas son of Eleazar, the son of Aaron, the priest, saw this, he left the assembly, took a spear in his hand ⁸and followed the Israelite into the tent. He drove the spear into both of them, right through the Israelite man and into the woman's stomach. Then the plague against the Israelites was stopped; ⁹but those who died in the plague numbered 24,000.

¹⁰The LORD said to Moses, ¹¹'Phinehas son of Eleazar, the son of Aaron, the priest, has turned my anger away from the Israelites. Since he was as zealous for my honour among them as I am, I did not put an end to them in my zeal. ¹²Therefore tell him I am making my covenant of peace with him. ¹³He and his descendants will have a covenant of a lasting priesthood, because he was zealous for the honour of his God and made atonement for the Israelites.'

¹⁴The name of the Israelite who was killed with the Midianite woman was Zimri son of Salu, the leader of a Simeonite family. ¹⁵And the name of the Midianite woman who was put to death was Kozbi daughter of Zur, a tribal chief of a Midianite family.

¹⁶The LORD said to Moses, ¹⁷'Treat the Midianites as enemies and kill them. ¹⁸They treated you as enemies when they deceived you in the Peor incident involving their sister Kozbi, the daughter of a Midianite leader, the woman who was killed when the plague came as a result of that incident.'

The second census

26 After the plague the LORD said to Moses and Eleazar son of Aaron, the priest, ²'Take a census of the whole Israelite community by families—all those twenty years old or more who are able to serve in the army of Israel.' ³So on the plains of Moab by the Jordan opposite Jericho, Moses and Eleazar the priest spoke with them and said, ⁴'Take a census of men twenty years old or more, as the LORD commanded Moses.'

These were the Israelites who came out of Egypt:

⁵The descendants of Reuben, the firstborn son of Israel, were:
    through Hanok, the Hanokite clan;
    through Pallu, the Palluite clan;
⁶through Hezron, the Hezronite clan;
    through Karmi, the Karmite clan.
⁷These were the clans of Reuben; those numbered were 43,730.

⁸The son of Pallu was Eliab, ⁹and the sons of Eliab were Nemuel, Dathan and

People and Places

Baal
Numbers 25:3

Baal was a Canaanite storm god who was thought to bring rain and fertility, producing good harvests and lots of livestock. When the Israelites rebelled against God, they made idols so they could worship Baal.

Abiram. The same Dathan and Abiram were the community officials who rebelled against Moses and Aaron and were among Korah's followers when they rebelled against the LORD. ¹⁰The earth opened its mouth and swallowed them along with Korah, whose followers died when the fire devoured the 250 men. And they served as a warning sign. ¹¹The line of Korah, however, did not die out.

¹²The descendants of Simeon by their clans were:

> through Nemuel, the Nemuelite clan;
> through Jamin, the Jaminite clan;
> through Jakin, the Jakinite clan;
> ¹³through Zerah, the Zerahite clan;
> through Shaul, the Shaulite clan.

¹⁴These were the clans of Simeon; those numbered were 22,200.

¹⁵The descendants of Gad by their clans were:

> through Zephon, the Zephonite clan;
> through Haggi, the Haggite clan;
> through Shuni, the Shunite clan;
> ¹⁶through Ozni, the Oznite clan;
> through Eri, the Erite clan;
> ¹⁷through Arodi,^a the Arodite clan;
> through Areli, the Arelite clan.

¹⁸These were the clans of Gad; those numbered were 40,500.

¹⁹Er and Onan were sons of Judah, but they died in Canaan.

²⁰The descendants of Judah by their clans were:

> through Shelah, the Shelanite clan;
> through Perez, the Perezite clan;
> through Zerah, the Zerahite clan.
> ²¹The descendants of Perez were:
>> through Hezron, the Hezronite clan;
>> through Hamul, the Hamulite clan.

²²These were the clans of Judah; those numbered were 76,500.

²³The descendants of Issachar by their clans were:

> through Tola, the Tolaite clan;
> through Puah, the Puite^b clan;
> ²⁴through Jashub, the Jashubite clan;
> through Shimron, the Shimronite clan.

²⁵These were the clans of Issachar; those numbered were 64,300.

²⁶The descendants of Zebulun by their clans were:

> through Sered, the Seredite clan;
> through Elon, the Elonite clan;
> through Jahleel, the Jahleelite clan.

²⁷These were the clans of Zebulun; those numbered were 60,500.

²⁸The descendants of Joseph by their clans through Manasseh and Ephraim were:

²⁹The descendants of Manasseh:

> through Makir, the Makirite clan (Makir was the father of Gilead);
> through Gilead, the Gileadite clan.

³⁰These were the descendants of Gilead:

> through Iezer, the Iezerite clan;
> through Helek, the Helekite clan;
> ³¹through Asriel, the Asrielite clan;
> through Shechem, the Shechemite clan;
> ³²through Shemida, the Shemidaite clan;
> through Hepher, the Hepherite clan.

³³(Zelophehad son of Hepher had no sons; he had only daughters, whose names were Mahlah, Noah, Hoglah, Milkah and Tirzah.)

³⁴These were the clans of Manasseh; those numbered were 52,700.

³⁵These were the descendants of Ephraim by their clans:

> through Shuthelah, the Shuthelahite clan;
> through Beker, the Bekerite clan;
> through Tahan, the Tahanite clan.

³⁶These were the descendants of Shuthelah:

> through Eran, the Eranite clan.

³⁷These were the clans of Ephraim; those numbered were 32,500.

---

^a 17 Samaritan Pentateuch and Syriac (see also Gen. 46:16); Masoretic Text *Arod*   ^b 23 Samaritan Pentateuch, Septuagint, Vulgate and Syriac (see also 1 Chron. 7:1); Masoretic Text *through Puvah, the Punite*

These were the descendants of Joseph by their clans.

38 The descendants of Benjamin by their clans were:
>through Bela, the Belaite clan;
>through Ashbel, the Ashbelite clan;
>through Ahiram, the Ahiramite clan;
>39 through Shupham,[a] the Shuphamite clan;
>through Hupham, the Huphamite clan.
>40 The descendants of Bela through Ard and Naaman were:
>>through Ard,[b] the Ardite clan;
>>through Naaman, the Naamite clan.

41 These were the clans of Benjamin; those numbered were 45,600.

42 These were the descendants of Dan by their clans:
>through Shuham, the Shuhamite clan.

These were the clans of Dan: 43 all of them were Shuhamite clans; and those numbered were 64,400.

44 The descendants of Asher by their clans were:
>through Imnah, the Imnite clan;
>through Ishvi, the Ishvite clan;
>through Beriah, the Beriite clan;
>45 and through the descendants of Beriah:
>>through Heber, the Heberite clan;
>>through Malkiel, the Malkielite clan.
>46 (Asher had a daughter named Serah.)

47 These were the clans of Asher; those numbered were 53,400.

48 The descendants of Naphtali by their clans were:
>through Jahzeel, the Jahzeelite clan;
>through Guni, the Gunite clan;
>49 through Jezer, the Jezerite clan;
>through Shillem, the Shillemite clan.

50 These were the clans of Naphtali; those numbered were 45,400.

51 The total number of the men of Israel was 601,730.

52 The LORD said to Moses, 53 'The land is to be allotted to them as an inheritance based on the number of names. 54 To a larger group give a larger inheritance, and to a smaller group a smaller one; each is to receive its inheritance according to the number of those listed. 55 Be sure that the land is distributed by lot. What each group inherits will be according to the names for its ancestral tribe. 56 Each inheritance is to be distributed by lot among the larger and smaller groups.'

57 These were the Levites who were counted by their clans:
>through Gershon, the Gershonite clan;
>through Kohath, the Kohathite clan;
>through Merari, the Merarite clan.
>58 These also were Levite clans:
>>the Libnite clan,
>>the Hebronite clan,
>>the Mahlite clan,
>>the Mushite clan,
>>the Korahite clan.
>>(Kohath was the forefather of Amram; 59 the name of Amram's wife was Jochebed, a descendant of Levi, who was born to the Levites[c] in Egypt. To Amram she bore Aaron, Moses and their sister Miriam. 60 Aaron was the father of Nadab and Abihu, Eleazar and Ithamar. 61 But Nadab and Abihu died when they made an offering before the LORD with unauthorised fire.)

62 All the male Levites a month old or more numbered 23,000. They were not counted along with the other Israelites because they received no inheritance among them.

63 These are the men counted by Moses and Eleazar the priest when they counted the Israelites on the plains of Moab by the Jordan opposite Jericho. 64 Not one of them was among those counted by Moses and

---

[a] 39 A few manuscripts of the Masoretic Text, Samaritan Pentateuch, Vulgate and Syriac (see also Septuagint); most manuscripts of the Masoretic Text *Shephupham* [b] 40 Samaritan Pentateuch and Vulgate (see also Septuagint); Masoretic Text does not have *through Ard*. [c] 59 Or *Jochebed, a daughter of Levi, who was born to Levi*

Aaron the priest when they counted the Israelites in the Desert of Sinai. ⁶⁵For the LORD had told those Israelites they would surely die in the wilderness, and not one of them was left except Caleb son of Jephunneh and Joshua son of Nun.

Zelophehad's daughters

27 The daughters of Zelophehad son of Hepher, the son of Gilead, the son of Makir, the son of Manasseh, belonged to the clans of Manasseh son of Joseph. The names of the daughters were Mahlah, Noah, Hoglah, Milkah and Tirzah. They came forward ²and stood before Moses, Eleazar the priest, the leaders and the whole assembly at the entrance to the tent of meeting and said, ³'Our father died in the wilderness. He was not among Korah's followers, who banded together against the LORD, but he died for his own sin and left no sons. ⁴Why should our father's name disappear from his clan because he had no son? Give us property among our father's relatives.'

⁵So Moses brought their case before the LORD, ⁶and the LORD said to him, ⁷'What Zelophehad's daughters are saying is right. You must certainly give them property as an inheritance among their father's relatives and give their father's inheritance to them.

⁸'Say to the Israelites, "If a man dies and leaves no son, give his inheritance to his daughter. ⁹If he has no daughter, give his inheritance to his brothers. ¹⁰If he has no brothers, give his inheritance to his father's brothers. ¹¹If his father had no brothers, give his inheritance to the nearest relative in his clan, that he may possess it. This is to have the force of law for the Israelites, as the LORD commanded Moses."'

Joshua to succeed Moses

¹²Then the LORD said to Moses, 'Go up this mountain in the Abarim Range and see the land I have given the Israelites. ¹³After you have seen it, you too will be gathered to your people, as your brother Aaron was, ¹⁴for when the community rebelled at the waters in the Desert of Zin, both of you disobeyed my command to honour me as holy before their eyes.' (These were the waters of Meribah Kadesh, in the Desert of Zin.)

¹⁵Moses said to the LORD, ¹⁶'May the LORD, the God of every human spirit, appoint someone over this community ¹⁷to go out and come in before them, one who will lead them out and bring them in, so that the LORD's people will not be like sheep without a shepherd.'

¹⁸So the LORD said to Moses, 'Take Joshua son of Nun, a man in whom is the spirit of leadership,[a] and lay your hand on him. ¹⁹Make him stand before Eleazar the priest and the entire assembly and commission him in their presence. ²⁰Give him some of your authority so that the whole Israelite community will obey him. ²¹He is to stand before Eleazar the priest, who will obtain decisions for him by enquiring of the Urim before the LORD. At his command he and the entire community of the Israelites will go out, and at his command they will come in.'

²²Moses did as the LORD commanded him. He took Joshua and made him stand before Eleazar the priest and the whole assembly. ²³Then he laid his hands on him

---

Sign of the times

Zelophehad's daughters
Numbers 27:1

Although it might not seem that fair to us today, men and women were treated quite differently in the Old Testament. A man called Zelophehad had five daughters and no sons. Under the law at the time, when he died his property was to be given to his male relatives, leaving his daughters with nothing. They took their case to Moses and he said that they could inherit from their father, and changed the law so that this would always be the case.

---

[a] 18 Or *the Spirit*

and commissioned him, as the LORD instructed through Moses.

Daily offerings

28 The LORD said to Moses, 2'Give this command to the Israelites and say to them: "Make sure that you present to me at the appointed time my food offerings, as an aroma pleasing to me." 3Say to them: "This is the food offering you are to present to the LORD: two lambs a year old without defect, as a regular burnt offering each day. 4Offer one lamb in the morning and the other at twilight, 5together with a grain offering of a tenth of an ephah[a] of the finest flour mixed with a quarter of a hin[b] of oil from pressed olives. 6This is the regular burnt offering instituted at Mount Sinai as a pleasing aroma, a food offering presented to the LORD. 7The accompanying drink offering is to be a quarter of a hin of fermented drink with each lamb. Pour out the drink offering to the LORD at the sanctuary. 8Offer the second lamb at twilight, along with the same kind of grain offering and drink offering that you offer in the morning. This is a food offering, an aroma pleasing to the LORD.

Sabbath offerings

9' "On the Sabbath day, make an offering of two lambs a year old without defect, together with its drink offering and a grain offering of one fifth of an ephah[c] of the finest flour mixed with olive oil. 10This is the burnt offering for every Sabbath, in addition to the regular burnt offering and its drink offering.

Monthly offerings

11' "On the first of every month, present to the LORD a burnt offering of two young bulls, one ram and seven male lambs a year old, all without defect. 12With each bull there is to be a grain offering of three tenths of an ephah[d] of the finest flour mixed with oil; with the ram, a grain offering of one fifth of an ephah of the finest flour mixed with oil; 13and with each lamb, a grain offering of a tenth of an ephah of the finest flour mixed with oil. This is for a burnt offering, a pleasing aroma, a food offering presented to the LORD. 14With each bull there is to be a drink offering of half a hin[e] of wine; with the ram, a third of a hin;[f] and with each lamb, a quarter of a hin. This is the monthly burnt offering to be made at each new moon during the year. 15Besides the regular burnt offering with its drink offering, one male goat is to be presented to the LORD as a sin offering.[g]

The Passover

16' "On the fourteenth day of the first month the LORD's Passover is to be held. 17On the fifteenth day of this month there is to be a festival; for seven days eat bread made without yeast. 18On the first day hold a sacred assembly and do not do any of your ordinary work. 19Present to the LORD a food offering consisting of a burnt offering of two young bulls, one ram and seven male lambs a year old, all without defect. 20With each bull offer a grain offering of three tenths of an ephah of the finest flour mixed with oil; with the ram, one fifth; 21and with each of the seven lambs, one tenth. 22Include one male goat as a sin offering to make atonement for you. 23Offer these in addition to the regular morning burnt offering. 24In this way present the food offering every day for seven days as an aroma pleasing to the LORD; it is to be offered in addition to the regular burnt offering and its drink offering. 25On the seventh day hold a sacred assembly and do not do any ordinary work.

Festival of Weeks

26' "On the day of firstfruits, when you present to the LORD an offering of new grain during the Festival of Weeks, hold a sacred assembly and do not do any of your ordinary work. 27Present a burnt offering of two young bulls, one ram and seven male lambs a year old as an aroma pleasing to the LORD. 28With each bull there is to be a grain offering of three tenths of an ephah of the finest flour mixed with oil; with the ram, one fifth; 29and with each of the seven lambs, one tenth. 30Include one male goat

---

[a] 5 That is, probably about 1.5 kilograms; also in verses 13, 21 and 29 [b] 5 That is, about 0.9 litre; also in verses 7 and 14
[c] 9 That is, probably about 3.25 kilograms; also in verses 12, 20 and 28 [d] 12 That is, probably about 5 kilograms; also in verses 20 and 28 [e] 14 That is, about 1.8 litres [f] 14 That is, about 1.2 litres [g] 15 Or *purification offering*; also in verse 22

to make atonement for you. ³¹Offer these together with their drink offerings, in addition to the regular burnt offering and its grain offering. Be sure the animals are without defect.

Festival of Trumpets

29 ¹"On the first day of the seventh month hold a sacred assembly and do not do any of your ordinary work. It is a day for you to sound the trumpets. ²As an aroma pleasing to the LORD, offer a burnt offering of one young bull, one ram and seven male lambs a year old, all without defect. ³With the bull offer a grain offering of three tenths of an ephah^a of the finest flour mixed with olive oil; with the ram, one fifth;^{b} ⁴and with each of the seven lambs, one tenth.^{c} ⁵Include one male goat as a sin offering^d to make atonement for you. ⁶These are in addition to the monthly and daily burnt offerings with their grain offerings and drink offerings as specified. They are food offerings presented to the LORD, a pleasing aroma.

Day of Atonement

⁷"On the tenth day of this seventh month hold a sacred assembly. You must deny yourselves^e and do no work. ⁸Present as an aroma pleasing to the LORD a burnt offering of one young bull, one ram and seven male lambs a year old, all without defect. ⁹With the bull offer a grain offering of three tenths of an ephah of the finest flour mixed with olive oil; with the ram, one fifth; ¹⁰and with each of the seven lambs, one tenth. ¹¹Include one male goat as a sin offering, in addition to the sin offering for atonement and the regular burnt offering with its grain offering, and their drink offerings.

Festival of Tabernacles

¹²"On the fifteenth day of the seventh month, hold a sacred assembly and do not do any of your ordinary work. Celebrate a festival to the LORD for seven days. ¹³Present as an aroma pleasing to the LORD a food offering consisting of a burnt offering of thirteen young bulls, two rams and fourteen male lambs a year old, all without defect. ¹⁴With each of the thirteen bulls offer a grain offering of three tenths of an ephah of the finest flour mixed with olive oil; with each of the two rams, one fifth; ¹⁵and with each of the fourteen lambs, one tenth. ¹⁶Include one male goat as a sin offering, in addition to the regular burnt offering with its grain offering and drink offering.

¹⁷"On the second day offer twelve young bulls, two rams and fourteen male lambs a year old, all without defect. ¹⁸With the bulls, rams and lambs, offer their grain offerings and drink offerings according to the number specified. ¹⁹Include one male goat as a sin offering, in addition to the regular burnt offering with its grain offering, and their drink offerings.

²⁰"On the third day offer eleven bulls, two rams and fourteen male lambs a year old, all without defect. ²¹With the bulls, rams and lambs, offer their grain offerings and drink offerings according to the number specified. ²²Include one male goat as a sin offering, in addition to the regular burnt

Festival of Tabernacles
Numbers 29:12

The Festival of Tabernacles was an opportunity for the Israelites to remember the time they had spent wandering in the wilderness. They offered lots of animal sacrifices and had special gatherings on the first and eighth days of the festival. They also had to make and live in shelters of palm and willow trees to remind them that they had to live in tents in the wilderness.

---

^{a}3 That is, probably about 5 kilograms; also in verses 9 and 14 ^{b}3 That is, probably about 3.25 kilograms; also in verses 9 and 14 ^{c}4 That is, probably about 1.5 kilograms; also in verses 10 and 15 ^{d}5 Or *purification offering*; also elsewhere in this chapter ^{e}7 Or *must fast* offering with its grain offering and drink offering.

23'"On the fourth day offer ten bulls, two rams and fourteen male lambs a year old, all without defect. 24With the bulls, rams and lambs, offer their grain offerings and drink offerings according to the number specified. 25Include one male goat as a sin offering, in addition to the regular burnt offering with its grain offering and drink offering.

26'"On the fifth day offer nine bulls, two rams and fourteen male lambs a year old, all without defect. 27With the bulls, rams and lambs, offer their grain offerings and drink offerings according to the number specified. 28Include one male goat as a sin offering, in addition to the regular burnt offering with its grain offering and drink offering.

29'"On the sixth day offer eight bulls, two rams and fourteen male lambs a year old, all without defect. 30With the bulls, rams and lambs, offer their grain offerings and drink offerings according to the number specified. 31Include one male goat as a sin offering, in addition to the regular burnt offering with its grain offering and drink offering.

32'"On the seventh day offer seven bulls, two rams and fourteen male lambs a year old, all without defect. 33With the bulls, rams and lambs, offer their grain offerings and drink offerings according to the number specified. 34Include one male goat as a sin offering, in addition to the regular burnt offering with its grain offering and drink offering.

35'"On the eighth day hold a closing special assembly and do not do any of your ordinary work. 36Present as an aroma pleasing to the LORD a food offering consisting of a burnt offering of one bull, one ram and seven male lambs a year old, all without defect. 37With the bull, the ram and the lambs, offer their grain offerings and drink offerings according to the number specified. 38Include one male goat as a sin offering, in addition to the regular burnt offering with its grain offering and drink offering.

39'"In addition to what you vow and your freewill offerings, offer these to the LORD at your appointed festivals: your burnt offerings, grain offerings, drink offerings and fellowship offerings.'"

*40Moses told the Israelites all that the LORD commanded him.

Vows

30 *Moses said to the heads of the tribes of Israel: 'This is what the LORD commands: 2when a man makes a vow to the LORD or takes an oath to bind himself by a pledge, he must not break his word but must do everything he said.

3'When a young woman still living in her father's household makes a vow to the LORD or binds herself by a pledge 4and her father hears about her vow or pledge but says nothing to her, then all her vows and every pledge by which she bound herself will stand. 5But if her father forbids her when he hears about it, none of her vows or the pledges by which she bound herself will stand; the LORD will release her because her father has forbidden her.

6'If she marries after she makes a vow or after her lips utter a rash promise by which she binds herself 7and her husband hears about it but says nothing to her, then her vows or the pledges by which she bound herself will stand. 8But if her husband forbids her when he hears about it, he nullifies the vow that binds her or the rash promise by which she binds herself, and the LORD will release her.

9'Any vow or obligation taken by a widow or divorced woman will be binding on her.

10'If a woman living with her husband makes a vow or binds herself by a pledge under oath 11and her husband hears about it but says nothing to her and does not forbid her, then all her vows or the pledges by which she bound herself will stand. 12But if her husband nullifies them when he hears about them, then none of the vows or pledges that came from her lips will stand. Her husband has nullified them, and the LORD will release her. 13Her husband may confirm or nullify any vow she makes or any

---

* 29:40 is numbered 30:1 in Hebrew texts.   * 30:1-16 is numbered 30:2-17 in Hebrew texts.

sworn pledge to deny herself.[a] 14But if her husband says nothing to her about it from day to day, then he confirms all her vows or the pledges binding on her. He confirms them by saying nothing to her when he hears about them. 15If, however, he nullifies them some time after he hears about them, then he must bear the consequences of her wrongdoing.'

16These are the regulations the LORD gave Moses concerning relationships between a man and his wife, and between a father and his young daughter still living at home.

Vengeance on the Midianites

31 The LORD said to Moses, 2'Take vengeance on the Midianites for the Israelites. After that, you will be gathered to your people.'

3So Moses said to the people, 'Arm some of your men to go to war against the Midianites so that they may carry out the LORD's vengeance on them. 4Send into battle a thousand men from each of the tribes of Israel.' 5So twelve thousand men armed for battle, a thousand from each tribe, were supplied from the clans of Israel. 6Moses sent them into battle, a thousand from each tribe, along with Phinehas son of Eleazar, the priest, who took with him articles from the sanctuary and the trumpets for signalling.

7They fought against Midian, as the LORD commanded Moses, and killed every man. 8Among their victims were Evi, Rekem, Zur, Hur and Reba—the five kings of Midian. They also killed Balaam son of Beor with the sword. 9The Israelites captured the Midianite women and children and took all the Midianite herds, flocks and goods as plunder. 10They burned all the towns where the Midianites had settled, as well as all their camps. 11They took all the plunder and spoils, including the people and animals, 12and brought the captives, spoils and plunder to Moses and Eleazar the priest and the Israelite assembly at their camp on the plains of Moab, by the Jordan opposite Jericho.

13Moses, Eleazar the priest and all the leaders of the community went to meet them outside the camp. 14Moses was angry with the officers of the army—the commanders of thousands and commanders of hundreds—who returned from the battle.

15'Have you allowed all the women to live?' he asked them. 16'They were the ones who followed Balaam's advice and enticed the Israelites to be unfaithful to the LORD in the Peor incident, so that a plague struck the LORD's people. 17Now kill all the boys. And kill every woman who has slept with a man, 18but save for yourselves every girl who has never slept with a man.

19'Anyone who has killed someone or touched someone who was killed must stay outside the camp seven days. On the third and seventh days you must purify yourselves and your captives. 20Purify every garment as well as everything made of leather, goat hair or wood.'

21Then Eleazar the priest said to the soldiers who had gone into battle, 'This is what is required by the law that the LORD gave Moses: 22gold, silver, bronze, iron, tin, lead 23and anything else that can withstand fire must be put through the fire, and then it will be clean. But it must also be purified with the water of cleansing. And whatever cannot withstand fire must be put through that water. 24On the seventh day wash your clothes and you will be clean. Then you may come into the camp.'

Dividing the spoils

25The LORD said to Moses, 26'You and Eleazar the priest and the family heads of the community are to count all the women and animals that were captured. 27Divide the spoils equally between the soldiers who took part in the battle and the rest of the community. 28From the soldiers who fought in the battle, set apart as tribute for the LORD one out of every five hundred, whether women, cattle, donkeys or sheep. 29Take this tribute from their half share and give it to Eleazar the priest as the LORD's part. 30From the Israelites' half, select one out of every fifty, whether women, cattle, donkeys, sheep or other animals. Give them to the Levites, who are responsible for the

---

[a] 13 Or *to fast*

care of the LORD's tabernacle.' ³¹So Moses and Eleazar the priest did as the LORD commanded Moses.

³²The plunder remaining from the spoils that the soldiers took was 675,000 sheep, ³³72,000 cattle, ³⁴61,000 donkeys ³⁵and 32,000 women who had never slept with a man.

³⁶The half share of those who fought in the battle was:

337,500 sheep, ³⁷of which the tribute for the LORD was 675;

³⁸36,000 cattle, of which the tribute for the LORD was 72;

³⁹30,500 donkeys, of which the tribute for the LORD was 61;

⁴⁰16,000 women, of whom the tribute for the LORD was 32.

⁴¹Moses gave the tribute to Eleazar the priest as the LORD's part, as the LORD commanded Moses.

⁴²The half belonging to the Israelites, which Moses set apart from that of the fighting men— ⁴³the community's half— was 337,500 sheep, ⁴⁴36,000 cattle, ⁴⁵30,500 donkeys ⁴⁶and 16,000 women. ⁴⁷From the Israelites' half, Moses selected one out of every fifty women and animals, as the LORD commanded him, and gave them to the Levites, who were responsible for the care of the LORD's tabernacle.

⁴⁸Then the officers who were over the units of the army—the commanders of thousands and commanders of hundreds— went to Moses ⁴⁹and said to him, 'Your servants have counted the soldiers under our command, and not one is missing. ⁵⁰So we have brought as an offering to the LORD the gold articles each of us acquired— armlets, bracelets, signet rings, ear-rings and necklaces—to make atonement for ourselves before the LORD.'

⁵¹Moses and Eleazar the priest accepted from them the gold—all the handcrafted articles. ⁵²All the gold from the commanders of thousands and commanders of hundreds that Moses and Eleazar presented as a gift to the LORD weighed 16,750 shekels.ᵃ ⁵³Each soldier had taken plunder for himself. ⁵⁴Moses and Eleazar the priest accepted the gold from the commanders of thousands and commanders of hundreds and brought it into the tent of meeting as a memorial for the Israelites before the LORD.

The Transjordan tribes

32 The Reubenites and Gadites, who had very large herds and flocks, saw that the lands of Jazer and Gilead were suitable for livestock. ²So they came to Moses and Eleazar the priest and to the leaders of the community, and said, ³'Ataroth, Dibon, Jazer, Nimrah, Heshbon, Elealeh, Sebam, Nebo and Beon— ⁴the land the LORD subdued before the people of Israel—are suitable for livestock, and your servants have livestock. ⁵If we have found favour in your eyes,' they said, 'let this land be given to your servants as our possession. Do not make us cross the Jordan.'

⁶Moses said to the Gadites and Reubenites, 'Should your own people go to war while you sit here? ⁷Why do you discourage the Israelites from crossing over into the land the LORD has given them? ⁸This is what your fathers did when I sent them from Kadesh Barnea to look over the land. ⁹After they went up to the Valley of Eshkol and viewed the land, they discouraged the Israelites from entering the land the LORD had given them. ¹⁰The LORD's anger was aroused that day and he swore this oath: ¹¹"Because they have not followed me wholeheartedly, not one of those who were twenty years old or more when they came up out of Egypt will see the land I promised on oath to Abraham, Isaac and Jacob— ¹²not one except Caleb son of Jephunneh the Kenizzite and Joshua son of Nun, for they followed the LORD wholeheartedly." ¹³The LORD's anger burned against Israel and he made them wander in the wilderness for forty years, until the whole generation of those who had done evil in his sight was gone.

¹⁴'And here you are, a brood of sinners, standing in the place of your fathers and making the LORD even more angry with Israel. ¹⁵If you turn away from following him, he will again leave all this people in the

---

ᵃ 52 That is, about 190 kilograms

wilderness, and you will be the cause of their destruction.'

16Then they came up to him and said, 'We would like to build pens here for our livestock and cities for our women and children. 17But we will arm ourselves for battle[a] and go ahead of the Israelites until we have brought them to their place. Meanwhile our women and children will live in fortified cities, for protection from the inhabitants of the land. 18We will not return to our homes until all the Israelites have received their inheritance. 19We will not receive any inheritance with them on the other side of the Jordan, because our inheritance has come to us on the east side of the Jordan.'

20Then Moses said to them, 'If you will do this—if you will arm yourselves before the LORD for battle 21and if all of you who are armed cross over the Jordan before the LORD until he has driven his enemies out before him— 22then when the land is subdued before the LORD, you may return and be free from your obligation to the LORD and to Israel. And this land will be your possession before the LORD.

23'But if you fail to do this, you will be sinning against the LORD; and you may be sure that your sin will find you out. 24Build cities for your women and children, and pens for your flocks, but do what you have promised.'

25The Gadites and Reubenites said to Moses, 'We your servants will do as our lord commands. 26Our children and wives, our flocks and herds will remain here in the cities of Gilead. 27But your servants, every man who is armed for battle, will cross over to fight before the LORD, just as our lord says.'

28Then Moses gave orders about them to Eleazar the priest and Joshua son of Nun and to the family heads of the Israelite tribes. 29He said to them, 'If the Gadites and Reubenites, all those armed for battle, cross over the Jordan with you before the LORD, then when the land is subdued before you, you must give them the land of Gilead as their possession. 30But if they do not cross over with you armed, they must accept their possession with you in Canaan.'

31The Gadites and Reubenites answered, 'Your servants will do what the LORD has said. 32We will cross over before the LORD into Canaan armed, but the property we inherit will be on this side of the Jordan.'

33Then Moses gave to the Gadites, the Reubenites and the half-tribe of Manasseh son of Joseph the kingdom of Sihon king of the Amorites and the kingdom of Og king of Bashan—the whole land with its cities and the territory around them.

34The Gadites built up Dibon, Ataroth, Aroer, 35Atroth Shophan, Jazer, Jogbehah, 36Beth Nimrah and Beth Haran as fortified cities, and built pens for their flocks. 37And the Reubenites rebuilt Heshbon, Elealeh and Kiriathaim, 38as well as Nebo and Baal Meon (these names were changed) and Sibmah. They gave names to the cities they rebuilt.

39The descendants of Makir son of Manasseh went to Gilead, captured it and drove out the Amorites who were there. 40So Moses gave Gilead to the Makirites, the descendants of Manasseh, and they settled there. 41Jair, a descendant of Manasseh, captured their settlements and called them Havvoth Jair.[b] 42And Nobah captured Kenath and its surrounding settlements and called it Nobah after himself.

Stages in Israel's journey

33 Here are the stages in the journey of the Israelites when they came out of Egypt by divisions under the leadership of Moses and Aaron. 2At the LORD's command Moses recorded the stages in their journey. This is their journey by stages:

> 3The Israelites set out from Rameses on the fifteenth day of the first month, the day after the Passover. They marched out defiantly in full view of all the Egyptians, 4who were burying all their firstborn, whom the LORD had struck down among them; for the LORD had brought judgment on their gods.

---

[a] 17 Septuagint; Hebrew *will be quick to arm ourselves* [b] 41 Or *them the settlements of Jair*

making Connections

The journey to Canaan
Numbers 33:1

Talk about a bunch of snails! The Israelites took forty years to travel from Egypt to Canaan, a journey that should have taken them eleven days if they had gone straight there. But the problem wasn't that they got lost, or were just incredibly slow. They didn't have enough faith in God, even though he had rescued them from Egypt, and so they were doomed to wander in circles for forty years.

⁵The Israelites left Rameses and camped at Sukkoth.

⁶They left Sukkoth and camped at Etham, on the edge of the desert.

⁷They left Etham, turned back to Pi Hahiroth, to the east of Baal Zephon, and camped near Migdol.

⁸They left Pi Hahiroth[a] and passed through the sea into the desert, and when they had travelled for three days in the Desert of Etham, they camped at Marah.

⁹They left Marah and went to Elim, where there were twelve springs and seventy palm trees, and they camped there.

¹⁰They left Elim and camped by the Red Sea.[b]

¹¹They left the Red Sea and camped in the Desert of Sin.

¹²They left the Desert of Sin and camped at Dophkah.

¹³They left Dophkah and camped at Alush.

¹⁴They left Alush and camped at Rephidim, where there was no water for the people to drink.

¹⁵They left Rephidim and camped in the Desert of Sinai.

¹⁶They left the Desert of Sinai and camped at Kibroth Hattaavah.

¹⁷They left Kibroth Hattaavah and camped at Hazeroth.

¹⁸They left Hazeroth and camped at Rithmah.

¹⁹They left Rithmah and camped at Rimmon Perez.

²⁰They left Rimmon Perez and camped at Libnah.

²¹They left Libnah and camped at Rissah.

²²They left Rissah and camped at Kehelathah.

²³They left Kehelathah and camped at Mount Shepher.

²⁴They left Mount Shepher and camped at Haradah.

²⁵They left Haradah and camped at Makheloth.

²⁶They left Makheloth and camped at Tahath.

²⁷They left Tahath and camped at Terah.

²⁸They left Terah and camped at Mithkah.

²⁹They left Mithkah and camped at Hashmonah.

³⁰They left Hashmonah and camped at Moseroth.

³¹They left Moseroth and camped at Bene Jaakan.

³²They left Bene Jaakan and camped at Hor Haggidgad.

³³They left Hor Haggidgad and camped at Jotbathah.

³⁴They left Jotbathah and camped at Abronah.

³⁵They left Abronah and camped at Ezion Geber.

³⁶They left Ezion Geber and camped at Kadesh, in the Desert of Zin.

---

[a] 8 Many manuscripts of the Masoretic Text, Samaritan Pentateuch and Vulgate; most manuscripts of the Masoretic Text *left from before Hahiroth*   [b] 10 Or *the Sea of Reeds*; also in verse 11

37They left Kadesh and camped at Mount Hor, on the border of Edom. 38At the LORD's command Aaron the priest went up Mount Hor, where he died on the first day of the fifth month of the fortieth year after the Israelites came out of Egypt. 39Aaron was a hundred and twenty-three years old when he died on Mount Hor.

40The Canaanite king of Arad, who lived in the Negev of Canaan, heard that the Israelites were coming.

41They left Mount Hor and camped at Zalmonah.

42They left Zalmonah and camped at Punon.

43They left Punon and camped at Oboth.

44They left Oboth and camped at Iye Abarim, on the border of Moab.

45They left Iye Abarim and camped at Dibon Gad.

46They left Dibon Gad and camped at Almon Diblathaim.

47They left Almon Diblathaim and camped in the mountains of Abarim, near Nebo.

48They left the mountains of Abarim and camped on the plains of Moab by the Jordan opposite Jericho. 49There on the plains of Moab they camped along the Jordan from Beth Jeshimoth to Abel Shittim.

50On the plains of Moab by the Jordan opposite Jericho the LORD said to Moses, 51'Speak to the Israelites and say to them: "When you cross the Jordan into Canaan, 52drive out all the inhabitants of the land before you. Destroy all their carved images and their cast idols, and demolish all their high places. 53Take possession of the land and settle in it, for I have given you the land to possess. 54Distribute the land by lot, according to your clans. To a larger group give a larger inheritance, and to a smaller group a smaller one. Whatever falls to them by lot will be theirs. Distribute it according to your ancestral tribes.

55'"But if you do not drive out the inhabitants of the land, those you allow to remain will become barbs in your eyes and thorns in your sides. They will give you trouble in the land where you will live. 56And then I will do to you what I plan to do to them."'

Boundaries of Canaan

34 The LORD said to Moses, 2'Command the Israelites and say to them: "When you enter Canaan, the land that will be allotted to you as an inheritance is to have these boundaries:

3' "Your southern side will include some of the Desert of Zin along the border of Edom. Your southern boundary will start in the east from the southern end of the Dead Sea, 4cross south of Scorpion Pass, continue on to Zin and go south of Kadesh Barnea. Then it will go to Hazar Addar and over to Azmon, 5where it will turn, join the Wadi of Egypt and end at the Mediterranean Sea.

6' "Your western boundary will be the coast of the Mediterranean Sea. This will be your boundary on the west.

7' "For your northern boundary, run a line from the Mediterranean Sea to Mount Hor 8and from Mount Hor to Lebo Hamath. Then the boundary will go to Zedad, 9continue to Ziphron and end at Hazar Enan. This will be your boundary on the north.

10' "For your eastern boundary, run a line from Hazar Enan to Shepham. 11The boundary will go down from Shepham to Riblah on the east side of Ain and continue along the slopes east of the Sea of Galilee.[a] 12Then the boundary will go down along the Jordan and end at the Dead Sea.

' "This will be your land, with its boundaries on every side."'

13Moses commanded the Israelites: 'Assign this land by lot as an inheritance. The LORD has ordered that it be given to the nine and a half tribes, 14because the families of the tribe of Reuben, the tribe of Gad and the half-tribe of Manasseh have received their inheritance. 15These two and a half tribes

---

[a] 11 Hebrew *Kinnereth*

have received their inheritance east of the Jordan opposite Jericho, towards the sunrise.'

16 The LORD said to Moses, 17 'These are the names of the men who are to assign the land for you as an inheritance: Eleazar the priest and Joshua son of Nun. 18 And appoint one leader from each tribe to help assign the land. 19 These are their names:

Caleb son of Jephunneh,
  from the tribe of Judah;
20 Shemuel son of Ammihud,
  from the tribe of Simeon;
21 Elidad son of Kislon,
  from the tribe of Benjamin;
22 Bukki son of Jogli,
  the leader from the tribe of Dan;
23 Hanniel son of Ephod,
  the leader from the tribe of
  Manasseh son of Joseph;
24 Kemuel son of Shiphtan,
  the leader from the tribe of
  Ephraim son of Joseph;
25 Elizaphan son of Parnak,
  the leader from the tribe of
  Zebulun;
26 Paltiel son of Azzan,
  the leader from the tribe of
  Issachar;
27 Ahihud son of Shelomi,
  the leader from the tribe of Asher;
28 Pedahel son of Ammihud,
  the leader from the tribe of
  Naphtali.'

29 These are the men the LORD commanded to assign the inheritance to the Israelites in the land of Canaan.

Towns for the Levites

35 On the plains of Moab by the Jordan opposite Jericho, the LORD said to Moses, 2 'Command the Israelites to give the Levites towns to live in from the inheritance the Israelites will possess. And give them pasture-lands around the towns. 3 Then they will have towns to live in and pasture-lands for the cattle they own and all their other animals.

4 'The pasture-lands around the towns that you give the Levites will extend a thousand cubits[a] from the town wall. 5 Outside the town, measure two thousand cubits[b] on the east side, two thousand on the south side, two thousand on the west and two thousand on the north, with the town in the centre. They will have this area as pasture-land for the towns.

Cities of refuge

6 'Six of the towns you give the Levites will be cities of refuge, to which a person who has killed someone may flee. In addition, give them forty-two other towns. 7 In all you must give the Levites forty-eight towns, together with their pasture-lands. 8 The towns you give the Levites from the land the Israelites possess are to be given in proportion to the inheritance of each tribe: take many towns from a tribe that has many, but few from one that has few.'

9 Then the LORD said to Moses: 10 'Speak to the Israelites and say to them: "When you cross the Jordan into Canaan, 11 select some towns to be your cities of refuge, to which a person who has killed someone accidentally may flee. 12 They will be places of refuge from the avenger, so that anyone accused of

Cities of refuge
Numbers 35:11

Like modern laws, the Bible makes it clear that there's a difference between murder and manslaughter. Murder is a serious crime because people are made in God's image. In the Old Testament, relatives were allowed to carry out the death penalty in revenge for murder. But sometimes a person might kill someone by accident, which is manslaughter. They were able to run to these cities of refuge for protection until they stood trial.

---

[a] 4 That is, about 450 metres [b] 5 That is, about 900 metres

murder may not die before standing trial before the assembly. ¹³These six towns you give will be your cities of refuge. ¹⁴Give three on this side of the Jordan and three in Canaan as cities of refuge. ¹⁵These six towns will be a place of refuge for Israelites and for foreigners residing among them, so that anyone who has killed another accidentally can flee there.

¹⁶' "If anyone strikes someone a fatal blow with an iron object, that person is a murderer; the murderer is to be put to death. ¹⁷Or if anyone is holding a stone and strikes someone a fatal blow with it, that person is a murderer; the murderer is to be put to death. ¹⁸Or if anyone is holding a wooden object and strikes someone a fatal blow with it, that person is a murderer; the murderer is to be put to death. ¹⁹The avenger of blood shall put the murderer to death; when the avenger comes upon the murderer, the avenger shall put the murderer to death. ²⁰If anyone with malice aforethought pushes another or throws something at them intentionally so that they die ²¹or if out of enmity one person hits another with their fist so that the other dies, that person is to be put to death; that person is a murderer. The avenger of blood shall put the murderer to death when they meet.

²²' "But if without enmity someone suddenly pushes another or throws something at them unintentionally ²³or, without seeing them, drops on them a stone heavy enough to kill them, and they die, then since that other person was not an enemy and no harm was intended, ²⁴the assembly must judge between the accused and the avenger of blood according to these regulations. ²⁵The assembly must protect the one accused of murder from the avenger of blood and send the accused back to the city of refuge to which they fled. The accused must stay there until the death of the high priest, who was anointed with holy oil.

²⁶' "But if the accused ever goes outside the limits of the city of refuge in which refuge was taken ²⁷and the avenger of blood finds that person outside the city, the avenger of blood may kill the accused without being guilty of murder. ²⁸The accused must stay in the city of refuge until the death of the high priest; only after the death of the high priest may an accused person return home.

²⁹' "This is to have the force of law for you throughout the generations to come, wherever you live.

³⁰' "Anyone who kills a person is to be put to death as a murderer only on the testimony of witnesses. But no-one is to be put to death on the testimony of only one witness.

³¹' "Do not accept a ransom for the life of a murderer, who deserves to die. A murderer is to be put to death.

³²' "Do not accept a ransom for anyone who has fled to a city of refuge and so allow them to go back and live on their own land before the death of the high priest.

³³' "Do not pollute the land where you are. Bloodshed pollutes the land, and atonement cannot be made for the land on which blood has been shed, except by the blood of the one who shed it. ³⁴Do not defile the land where you live and where I dwell, for I, the LORD, dwell among the Israelites." '

Inheritance of Zelophehad's daughters

36 The family heads of the clan of Gilead son of Makir, the son of Manasseh, who were from the clans of the descendants of Joseph, came and spoke before Moses and the leaders, the heads of the Israelite families. ²They said, 'When the LORD commanded my lord to give the land as an inheritance to the Israelites by lot, he ordered you to give the inheritance of our brother Zelophehad to his daughters. ³Now suppose they marry men from other Israelite tribes; then their inheritance will be taken from our ancestral inheritance and added to that of the tribe they marry into. And so part of the inheritance allotted to us will be taken away. ⁴When the Year of Jubilee for the Israelites comes, their inheritance will be added to that of the tribe into which they marry, and their property will be taken from the tribal inheritance of our ancestors.'

⁵Then at the LORD's command Moses gave this order to the Israelites: 'What the tribe of the descendants of Joseph is saying is right. ⁶This is what the LORD commands for

Zelophehad's daughters: they may marry anyone they please as long as they marry within their father's tribal clan. ⁷No inheritance in Israel is to pass from one tribe to another, for each of the Israelites shall keep the tribal inheritance of their ancestors. ⁸Every daughter who inherits land in any Israelite tribe must marry someone in her father's tribal clan, so that all Israelites will possess the inheritance of their ancestors. ⁹No inheritance may pass from one tribe to another, for each Israelite tribe is to keep the land it inherits.'

¹⁰So Zelophehad's daughters did as the LORD commanded Moses. ¹¹Zelophehad's daughters—Mahlah, Tirzah, Hoglah, Milkah and Noah—married their cousins on their father's side. ¹²They married within the clans of the descendants of Manasseh son of Joseph, and their inheritance remained in their father's tribe and clan.

¹³These are the commands and regulations the LORD gave through Moses to the Israelites on the plains of Moab by the Jordan opposite Jericho.

Deuteronomy

INTRODUCTION

DEUTERONOMY

Author: Moses

When: Probably around 1450 BC to 1400 BC.

Where: On the edge of Canaan, the Promised Land.

Did you know? The New Testament contains more than eighty quotations from Deuteronomy, which shows what an important book it is.

Main theme: Moses realises that his days as Israel's leader are coming to an end and he knows that God told him he was not allowed to take the people into the Promised Land himself. And so in Deuteronomy we have his farewell speech to the Israelites. Moses knows that they face many new challenges as they move on, so he reminds them of their history and challenges them to stay faithful to God.

The command to leave Horeb

1 These are the words Moses spoke to all Israel in the wilderness east of the Jordan—that is, in the Arabah—opposite Suph, between Paran and Tophel, Laban, Hazeroth and Dizahab. ²(It takes eleven days to go from Horeb to Kadesh Barnea by the Mount Seir road.)

³In the fortieth year, on the first day of the eleventh month, Moses proclaimed to the Israelites all that the LORD had commanded him concerning them. ⁴This was after he had defeated Sihon king of the Amorites, who reigned in Heshbon, and at Edrei had defeated Og king of Bashan, who reigned in Ashtaroth.

⁵East of the Jordan in the territory of Moab, Moses began to expound this law, saying:

⁶The LORD our God said to us at Horeb, 'You have stayed long enough at this mountain. ⁷Break camp and advance into the hill country of the Amorites; go to

all the neighbouring peoples in the Arabah, in the mountains, in the western foothills, in the Negev and along the coast, to the land of the Canaanites and to Lebanon, as far as the great river, the Euphrates. 8See, I have given you this land. Go in and take possession of the land that the LORD swore he would give to your fathers—to Abraham, Isaac and Jacob—and to their descendants after them.'

The appointment of leaders

9At that time I said to you, 'You are too heavy a burden for me to carry alone. 10The LORD your God has increased your numbers so that today you are as many as the stars in the sky. 11May the LORD, the God of your ancestors, increase you a thousand times and bless you as he has promised! 12But how can I bear your problems and your burdens and your disputes all by myself? 13Choose some wise, understanding and respected men from each of your tribes, and I will set them over you.'

14You answered me, 'What you propose to do is good.'

15So I took the leading men of your tribes, wise and respected men, and appointed them to have authority over you—as commanders of thousands, of hundreds, of fifties and of tens and as tribal officials. 16And I charged your judges at that time: hear the disputes between your people and judge fairly, whether the case is between two Israelites or between an Israelite and a foreigner residing among you. 17Do not show partiality in judging; hear both small and great alike. Do not be afraid of anyone, for judgment belongs to God. Bring me any case too hard for you, and I will hear it. 18And at that time I told you everything you were to do.

Spies sent out

19Then, as the LORD our God commanded us, we set out from Horeb and went towards the hill country of the Amorites through all that vast and dreadful wilderness that you have seen, and so we reached Kadesh Barnea. 20Then I said to you, 'You have reached the hill country of the Amorites, which the LORD our God is giving us. 21See, the LORD your God has given you the land. Go up and take possession of it as the LORD, the God of your ancestors, told you. Do not be afraid; do not be discouraged.'

22Then all of you came to me and said, 'Let us send men ahead to spy out the land for us and bring back a report about the route we are to take and the towns we will come to.'

23The idea seemed good to me; so I selected twelve of you, one man from each tribe. 24They left and went up into the hill country, and came to the Valley of Eshkol and explored it. 25Taking with them some of the fruit of the land, they brought it down to us and reported, 'It is a good land that the LORD our God is giving us.'

Rebellion against the LORD

26But you were unwilling to go up; you rebelled against the command of the LORD your God. 27You grumbled in your tents and said, 'The LORD hates us; so he brought us out of Egypt to deliver us into the hands of the Amorites to destroy us. 28Where can we go? Our brothers have made our hearts melt in fear. They say, "The people are stronger and taller than we are; the cities are large, with walls up to the sky. We even saw the Anakites there."'

29Then I said to you, 'Do not be terrified; do not be afraid of them. 30The LORD your God, who is going before you, will fight for you, as he did for you in Egypt, before your very eyes, 31and in the wilderness. There you saw how the LORD your God carried you, as a father carries his son, all the way you went until you reached this place.'

32In spite of this, you did not trust in the LORD your God, 33who went ahead of you on your journey, in fire by night and in a cloud by day, to search out places for you to camp and to show you the way you should go.

34When the LORD heard what you said, he was angry and solemnly swore: 35'No-one from this evil generation shall see the good land I swore to give your ancestors, 36except Caleb son of Jephunneh. He will see it, and I will give him and his descendants the land he set his feet on, because he followed the LORD wholeheartedly.'

37Because of you the LORD became angry with me also and said, 'You shall not enter it, either. ³⁸But your assistant, Joshua son of Nun, will enter it. Encourage him, because he will lead Israel to inherit it. ³⁹And the little ones that you said would be taken captive, your children who do not yet know good from bad—they will enter the land. I will give it to them and they will take possession of it. ⁴⁰But as for you, turn round and set out towards the desert along the route to the Red Sea.'ᵃ

⁴¹Then you replied, 'We have sinned against the LORD. We will go up and fight, as the LORD our God commanded us.' So every one of you put on his weapons, thinking it easy to go up into the hill country.

⁴²But the LORD said to me, 'Tell them, "Do not go up and fight, because I will not be with you. You will be defeated by your enemies."'

⁴³So I told you, but you would not listen. You rebelled against the LORD's command and in your arrogance you marched up into the hill country. ⁴⁴The Amorites who lived in those hills came out against you; they chased you like a swarm of bees and beat you down from Seir all the way to Hormah. ⁴⁵You came back and wept before the LORD, but he paid no attention to your weeping and turned a deaf ear to you. ⁴⁶And so you stayed in Kadesh many days—all the time you spent there.

Wanderings in the wilderness

2 Then we turned back and set out towards the wilderness along the route to the Red Sea,ᵇ as the LORD had directed me. For a long time we made our way around the hill country of Seir.

²Then the LORD said to me, ³'You have made your way around this hill country long enough; now turn north. ⁴Give the people these orders: "You are about to pass through the territory of your relatives the descendants of Esau, who live in Seir. They will be afraid of you, but be very careful. ⁵Do not provoke them to war, for I will not give you any of their land, not even enough to put your foot on. I have given Esau the hill country of Seir as his own. ⁶You are to pay them in silver for the food you eat and the water you drink."'

making Connections

A history lesson
Deuteronomy 2:1

The Israelites who went into the Promised Land weren't the same people who had escaped from Egypt. They were a younger generation but Moses still wants them to keep in mind where they have come from. These first four chapters of Deuteronomy are a short history lesson of their families' time in the wilderness to help them remember God's faithfulness to them, and just how grumpy and rebellious their forefathers were.

⁷The LORD your God has blessed you in all the work of your hands. He has watched over your journey through this vast wilderness. These forty years the LORD your God has been with you, and you have not lacked anything.

⁸So we went on past our relatives the descendants of Esau, who live in Seir. We turned from the Arabah road, which comes up from Elath and Ezion Geber, and travelled along the desert road of Moab.

⁹Then the LORD said to me, 'Do not harass the Moabites or provoke them to war, for I will not give you any part of their land. I have given Ar to the descendants of Lot as a possession.'

¹⁰(The Emites used to live there—a people strong and numerous, and as tall as the Anakites. ¹¹Like the Anakites, they too were considered Rephaites, but the Moabites called them Emites. ¹²Horites used to live in Seir, but the descendants of Esau drove them out. They destroyed the Horites from before them and settled in their place, just as Israel did in the land the LORD gave them as their possession.)

ᵃ 40 Or *the Sea of Reeds*   ᵇ 1 Or *the Sea of Reeds*

13And the LORD said, 'Now get up and cross the Zered Valley.' So we crossed the valley.

14Thirty-eight years passed from the time we left Kadesh Barnea until we crossed the Zered Valley. By then, that entire generation of fighting men had perished from the camp, as the LORD had sworn to them. 15The LORD's hand was against them until he had completely eliminated them from the camp.

16Now when the last of these fighting men among the people had died, 17the LORD said to me, 18"Today you are to pass by the region of Moab at Ar. 19When you come to the Ammonites, do not harass them or provoke them to war, for I will not give you possession of any land belonging to the Ammonites. I have given it as a possession to the descendants of Lot.'

20(That too was considered a land of the Rephaites, who used to live there; but the Ammonites called them Zamzummites. 21They were a people strong and numerous, and as tall as the Anakites. The LORD destroyed them from before the Ammonites, who drove them out and settled in their place. 22The LORD had done the same for the descendants of Esau, who lived in Seir, when he destroyed the Horites from before them. They drove them out and have lived in their place to this day. 23And as for the Avvites who lived in villages as far as Gaza, the Caphtorites coming out from Caphtor[a] destroyed them and settled in their place.)

Defeat of Sihon king of Heshbon

24'Set out now and cross the Arnon Gorge. See, I have given into your hand Sihon the Amorite, king of Heshbon, and his country. Begin to take possession of it and engage him in battle. 25This very day I will begin to put the terror and fear of you on all the nations under heaven. They will hear reports of you and will tremble and be in anguish because of you.'

26From the Desert of Kedemoth I sent messengers to Sihon king of Heshbon offering peace and saying, 27'Let us pass through your country. We will stay on the main road; we will not turn aside to the right or to the left. 28Sell us food to eat and water to drink for their price in silver. Only let us pass through on foot— 29as the descendants of Esau, who live in Seir, and the Moabites, who live in Ar, did for us—until we cross the Jordan into the land the LORD our God is giving us.' 30But Sihon king of Heshbon refused to let us pass through. For the LORD your God had made his spirit stubborn and his heart obstinate in order to give him into your hands, as he has now done.

31The LORD said to me, 'See, I have begun to deliver Sihon and his country over to you. Now begin to conquer and possess his land.'

32When Sihon and all his army came out to meet us in battle at Jahaz, 33the LORD our God delivered him over to us and we struck him down, together with his sons and his whole army. 34At that time we took all his towns and completely destroyed[b] them— men, women and children. We left no survivors. 35But the livestock and the plunder from the towns we had captured we carried off for ourselves. 36From Aroer on the rim of the Arnon Gorge, and from the town in the gorge, even as far as Gilead, not one town was too strong for us. The LORD our God gave us all of them. 37But in accordance with the command of the LORD our God, you did not encroach on any of the land of the Ammonites, neither the land along the course of the Jabbok nor that around the towns in the hills.

Defeat of Og king of Bashan

3 Next we turned and went up along the road towards Bashan, and Og king of Bashan with his whole army marched out to meet us in battle at Edrei. 2The LORD said to me, 'Do not be afraid of him, for I have delivered him into your hands, along with his whole army and his land. Do to him what you did to Sihon king of the Amorites, who reigned in Heshbon.'

3So the LORD our God also gave into our hands Og king of Bashan and all his army.

---

[a] 23 That is, Crete [b] 34 The Hebrew term refers to the irrevocable giving over of things or persons to the LORD, often by totally destroying them.

We struck them down, leaving no survivors. ⁴At that time we took all his cities. There was not one of the sixty cities that we did not take from them—the whole region of Argob, Og's kingdom in Bashan. ⁵All these cities were fortified with high walls and with gates and bars, and there were also a great many unwalled villages. ⁶We completely destroyed*ᵃ* them, as we had done with Sihon king of Heshbon, destroying*ᵇ* every city—men, women and children. ⁷But all the livestock and the plunder from their cities we carried off for ourselves.

⁸So at that time we took from these two kings of the Amorites the territory east of the Jordan, from the Arnon Gorge as far as Mount Hermon. ⁹(Hermon is called Sirion by the Sidonians; the Amorites call it Senir.) ¹⁰We took all the towns on the plateau, and all Gilead, and all Bashan as far as Salekah and Edrei, towns of Og's kingdom in Bashan. ¹¹(Og king of Bashan was the last of the Rephaites. His bed was decorated with iron and was more than nine cubits long and four cubits wide.*ᶜ* It is still in Rabbah of the Ammonites.)

Division of the land

¹²Of the land that we took over at that time, I gave the Reubenites and the Gadites the territory north of Aroer by the Arnon Gorge, including half the hill country of Gilead, together with its towns. ¹³The rest of Gilead and also all of Bashan, the kingdom of Og, I gave to the half-tribe of Manasseh. (The whole region of Argob in Bashan used to be known as a land of the Rephaites. ¹⁴Jair, a descendant of Manasseh, took the whole region of Argob as far as the border of the Geshurites and the Maakathites; it was named after him, so that to this day Bashan is called Havvoth Jair.*ᵈ*) ¹⁵And I gave Gilead to Makir. ¹⁶But to the Reubenites and the Gadites I gave the territory extending from Gilead down to the Arnon Gorge (the middle of the gorge being the border) and out to the River Jabbok, which is the border of the Ammonites. ¹⁷Its western border was the Jordan in the Arabah, from Kinnereth to the Sea of the Arabah (that is, the Dead Sea), below the slopes of Pisgah.

¹⁸I commanded you at that time: 'The LORD your God has given you this land to take possession of it. But all your able-bodied men, armed for battle, must cross over ahead of the other Israelites. ¹⁹However, your wives, your children and your livestock (I know you have much livestock) may stay in the towns I have given you, ²⁰until the LORD gives rest to all your people as he has to you, and they too have taken over the land that the LORD your God is giving them across the Jordan. After that, each of you may go back to the possession I have given you.'

Moses forbidden to cross the Jordan

²¹At that time I commanded Joshua: 'You have seen with your own eyes all that the LORD your God has done to these two kings. The LORD will do the same to all the kingdoms over there where you are going. ²²Do not be afraid of them; the LORD your God himself will fight for you.'

²³At that time I pleaded with the LORD: ²⁴'Sovereign LORD, you have begun to show to your servant your greatness and your strong hand. For what god is there in heaven or on earth who can do the deeds and mighty works you do? ²⁵Let me go over and see the good land beyond the Jordan—that fine hill country and Lebanon.'

²⁶But because of you the LORD was angry with me and would not listen to me. 'That is enough,' the LORD said. 'Do not speak to me any more about this matter. ²⁷Go up to the top of Pisgah and look west and north and south and east. Look at the land with your own eyes, since you are not going to cross this Jordan. ²⁸But commission Joshua, and encourage and strengthen him, for he will lead this people across and will cause them to inherit the land that you will see.' ²⁹So we stayed in the valley near Beth Peor.

Obedience commanded

4 Now, Israel, hear the decrees and laws I am about to teach you. Follow them so that you may live and may go in and take

---

ᵃ 6 The Hebrew term refers to the irrevocable giving over of things or persons to the LORD, often by totally destroying them. *ᵇ* 6 The Hebrew term refers to the irrevocable giving over of things or persons to the LORD, often by totally destroying them. *ᶜ* 11 That is, about 4 metres long and 1.8 metres wide *ᵈ* 14 Or *called the settlements of Jair* possession of the land that the LORD, the God of your ancestors, is giving you. 2Do not add to what I command you and do not subtract from it, but keep the commands of the LORD your God that I give you.

3You saw with your own eyes what the LORD did at Baal Peor. The LORD your God destroyed from among you everyone who followed the Baal of Peor, 4but all of you who held fast to the LORD your God are still alive today.

5See, I have taught you decrees and laws as the LORD my God commanded me, so that you may follow them in the land you are entering to take possession of it. 6Observe them carefully, for this will show your wisdom and understanding to the nations, who will hear about all these decrees and say, 'Surely this great nation is a wise and understanding people.' 7What other nation is so great as to have their gods near them the way the LORD our God is near us whenever we pray to him? 8And what other nation is so great as to have such righteous decrees and laws as this body of laws I am setting before you today?

9Only be careful, and watch yourselves closely so that you do not forget the things your eyes have seen or let them slip from your heart as long as you live. Teach them to your children and to their children after them. 10Remember the day you stood before the LORD your God at Horeb, when he said to me, 'Assemble the people before me to hear my words so that they may learn to revere me as long as they live in the land and may teach them to their children.' 11You came near and stood at the foot of the mountain while it blazed with fire to the very heavens, with black clouds and deep darkness. 12Then the LORD spoke to you out of the fire. You heard the sound of words but saw no form; there was only a voice. 13He declared to you his covenant, the Ten Commandments, which he commanded you to follow and then wrote them on two stone tablets. 14And the LORD directed me at that time to teach you the decrees and laws you are to follow in the land that you are crossing the Jordan to possess.

Idolatry forbidden

15You saw no form of any kind the day the LORD spoke to you at Horeb out of the fire. Therefore watch yourselves very carefully, 16so that you do not become corrupt and make for yourselves an idol, an image of any shape, whether formed like a man or a woman, 17or like any animal on earth or any bird that flies in the air, 18or like any creature that moves along the ground or any fish in the waters below. 19And when you look up to the sky and see the sun, the moon and the stars—all the heavenly array—do not be enticed into bowing down to them and worshipping things the LORD your God has apportioned to all the nations under heaven. 20But as for you, the LORD took you and brought you out of the iron-smelting furnace, out of Egypt, to be the people of his inheritance, as you now are.

21The LORD was angry with me because of you, and he solemnly swore that I would not cross the Jordan and enter the good land the LORD your God is giving you as your inheritance. 22I will die in this land; I will not cross the Jordan; but you are about to cross over and take possession of that good land. 23Be careful not to forget the covenant of the LORD your God that he made with you; do not make for yourselves an idol in the form of anything the LORD your God has forbidden. 24For the LORD your God is a consuming fire, a jealous God.

25After you have had children and grandchildren and have lived in the land a long time—if you then become corrupt and make any kind of idol, doing evil in the eyes of the LORD your God and arousing his anger, 26I call the heavens and the earth as witnesses against you this day that you will quickly perish from the land that you are crossing the Jordan to possess. You will not live there long but will certainly be destroyed. 27The LORD will scatter you among the peoples, and only a few of you will survive among the nations to which the LORD will drive you. 28There you will worship gods of wood and stone made by human hands, which cannot see or hear or eat or smell. 29But if from there you seek the LORD your God, you will find him if you seek him with all your heart and with all your soul. ³⁰When you are in distress and all these things have happened to you, then in later days you will return to the LORD your God and obey him. ³¹For the LORD your God is a merciful God; he will not abandon or destroy you or forget the covenant with your ancestors, which he confirmed to them by oath.

The LORD is God

³²Ask now about the former days, long before your time, from the day God created human beings on the earth; ask from one end of the heavens to the other. Has anything so great as this ever happened, or has anything like it ever been heard of? ³³Has any other people heard the voice of God[a] speaking out of fire, as you have, and lived? ³⁴Has any god ever tried to take for himself one nation out of another nation, by testings, by signs and wonders, by war, by a mighty hand and an outstretched arm, or by great and awesome deeds, like all the things the LORD your God did for you in Egypt before your very eyes?

³⁵You were shown these things so that you might know that the LORD is God; besides him there is no other. ³⁶From heaven he made you hear his voice to discipline you. On earth he showed you his great fire, and you heard his words from out of the fire. ³⁷Because he loved your ancestors and chose their descendants after them, he brought you out of Egypt by his Presence and his great strength, ³⁸to drive out before you nations greater and stronger than you and to bring you into their land to give it to you for your inheritance, as it is today.

³⁹Acknowledge and take to heart this day that the LORD is God in heaven above and on the earth below. There is no other. ⁴⁰Keep his decrees and commands, which I am giving you today, so that it may go well with you and your children after you and that you may live long in the land the LORD your God gives you for all time.

Cities of refuge

⁴¹Then Moses set aside three cities east of the Jordan, ⁴²to which anyone who had killed a person could flee if they had unintentionally killed a neighbour without malice aforethought. They could flee into one of these cities and save their life. ⁴³The cities were these: Bezer in the wilderness plateau, for the Reubenites; Ramoth in Gilead, for the Gadites; and Golan in Bashan, for the Manassites.

Introduction to the law

⁴⁴This is the law Moses set before the Israelites. ⁴⁵These are the stipulations, decrees and laws Moses gave them when they came out of Egypt ⁴⁶and were in the valley near Beth Peor east of the Jordan, in the land of Sihon king of the Amorites, who reigned in Heshbon and was defeated by Moses and the Israelites as they came out of Egypt. ⁴⁷They took possession of his land and the land of Og king of Bashan, the two Amorite kings east of the Jordan. ⁴⁸This land extended from Aroer on the rim of the Arnon Gorge to Mount Sirion[b] (that is, Hermon), ⁴⁹and included all the Arabah east of the Jordan, as far as the Dead Sea,[c] below the slopes of Pisgah.

The Ten Commandments

5 Moses summoned all Israel and said: Hear, Israel, the decrees and the laws I declare in your hearing today. Learn them and be sure to follow them. ²The LORD our God made a covenant with us at Horeb. ³It was not with our ancestors[d] that the LORD made this covenant, but with us, with all of us who are alive here today. ⁴The LORD spoke to you face to face out of the fire on the mountain. ⁵(At that time I stood between the LORD and you to declare to you the word of the LORD, because you were afraid of the fire and did not go up the mountain.) And he said:

⁶'I am the LORD your God, who brought you out of Egypt, out of the land of slavery.

⁷'You shall have no other gods before[e] me.

⁸'You shall not make for yourself an image in the form of anything in heaven above or on the earth beneath or in the waters below.

---

[a] 33 Or *of a god* [b] 48 Syriac (see also Deut. 3:9); Hebrew *Siyon* [c] 49 Hebrew *the Sea of the Arabah* [d] 3 Or *not only with our parents* [e] 7 Or *besides*

9 You shall not bow down to them or worship them; for I, the LORD your God, am a jealous God, punishing the children for the sin of the parents to the third and fourth generation of those who hate me, 10 but showing love to a thousand generations of those who love me and keep my commandments.

11 'You shall not misuse the name of the LORD your God, for the LORD will not hold anyone guiltless who misuses his name.

12 'Observe the Sabbath day by keeping it holy, as the LORD your God has commanded you. 13 Six days you shall labour and do all your work, 14 but the seventh day is a sabbath to the LORD your God. On it you shall not do any work, neither you, nor your son or daughter, nor your male or female servant, nor your ox, your donkey or any of your animals, nor any foreigner residing in your towns, so that your male and female servants may rest, as you do. 15 Remember that you were slaves in Egypt and that the LORD your God brought you out of there with a mighty hand and an outstretched arm. Therefore the LORD your God has commanded you to observe the Sabbath day.

16 'Honour your father and your mother, as the LORD your God has commanded you, so that you may live long and that it may go well with you in the land the LORD your God is giving you.

17 'You shall not murder.

18 'You shall not commit adultery.

19 'You shall not steal.

20 'You shall not give false testimony against your neighbour.

21 'You shall not covet your neighbour's wife. You shall not set your desire on your neighbour's house or land, his male or female servant, his ox or donkey, or anything that belongs to your neighbour.'

22 These are the commandments the LORD proclaimed in a loud voice to your whole assembly there on the mountain from out of the fire, the cloud and the deep darkness; and he added nothing more. Then he wrote them on two stone tablets and gave them to me.

23 When you heard the voice out of the darkness, while the mountain was ablaze with fire, all the leaders of your tribes and your elders came to me. 24 And you said, 'The LORD our God has shown us his glory and his majesty, and we have heard his voice from the fire. Today we have seen that people can live even if God speaks with them. 25 But now, why should we die? This great fire will consume us, and we will die if we hear the voice of the LORD our God any longer. 26 For what mortal has ever heard the voice of the living God speaking out of fire, as we have, and survived? 27 Go near and listen to all that the LORD our God says. Then tell us whatever the LORD our God tells you. We will listen and obey.'

28 The LORD heard you when you spoke to me, and the LORD said to me, 'I have heard what this people said to you. Everything they said was good. 29 Oh, that their hearts would be inclined to fear me and keep all my commands always, so that it might go well with them and their children for ever!

30 'Go, tell them to return to their tents. 31 But you stay here with me so that I may give you all the commands, decrees and laws that you are to teach them to follow in the land I am giving them to possess.'

32 So be careful to do what the LORD your God has commanded you; do not turn aside to the right or to the left. 33 Walk in obedience to all that the LORD your God has commanded you, so that you may live and prosper and prolong your days in the land that you will possess.

Love the LORD your God

6 These are the commands, decrees and laws the LORD your God directed me to teach you to observe in the land that you are crossing the Jordan to possess, 2 so that you, your children and their children after them may fear the LORD your God as long as you live by keeping all his decrees and commands that I give you, and so that you may

making Connections

Shema
Deuteronomy 6:4–9
These verses form the Shema, a confession of faith that has been part of Jewish worship for centuries. Jesus quotes from it in Mark 12:29 when he is asked which is the most important commandment. The Shema stresses the importance of loving God, walking in his ways and remembering his laws.

enjoy long life. ³Hear, Israel, and be careful to obey so that it may go well with you and that you may increase greatly in a land flowing with milk and honey, just as the LORD, the God of your ancestors, promised you.

⁴⁻⁹Hear, O Israel: the LORD our God, the LORD is one.[a] ⁵Love the LORD your God with all your heart and with all your soul and with all your strength. ⁶These commandments that I give you today are to be on your hearts. ⁷Impress them on your children. Talk about them when you sit at home and when you walk along the road, when you lie down and when you get up. ⁸Tie them as symbols on your hands and bind them on your foreheads. ⁹Write them on the doorframes of your houses and on your gates.

¹⁰When the LORD your God brings you into the land he swore to your fathers, to Abraham, Isaac and Jacob, to give you—a land with large, flourishing cities you did not build, ¹¹houses filled with all kinds of good things you did not provide, wells you did not dig, and vineyards and olive groves you did not plant—then when you eat and are satisfied, ¹²be careful that you do not forget the LORD, who brought you out of Egypt, out of the land of slavery.

¹³Fear the LORD your God, serve him only and take your oaths in his name. ¹⁴Do not follow other gods, the gods of the peoples around you; ¹⁵for the LORD your God, who is among you, is a jealous God and his anger will burn against you, and he will destroy you from the face of the land. ¹⁶Do not put the LORD your God to the test as you did at Massah. ¹⁷Be sure to keep the commands of the LORD your God and the stipulations and decrees he has given you. ¹⁸Do what is right and good in the LORD's sight, so that it may go well with you and you may go in and take over the good land that the LORD promised on oath to your ancestors, ¹⁹thrusting out all your enemies before you, as the LORD said.

²⁰In the future, when your children ask you, 'What is the meaning of the stipulations, decrees and laws the LORD our God has commanded you?' ²¹tell them: 'We were slaves of Pharaoh in Egypt, but the LORD brought us out of Egypt with a mighty hand. ²²Before our eyes the LORD sent signs and wonders—great and terrible—on Egypt and Pharaoh and his whole household. ²³But he brought us out from there to bring us in and give us the land that he promised on oath to our ancestors. ²⁴The LORD commanded us to obey all these decrees and to fear the LORD our God, so that we might always prosper and be kept alive, as is the case today. ²⁵And if we are careful to obey all this law before the LORD our God, as he has commanded us, that will be our righteousness.'

Driving out the nations

7 When the LORD your God brings you into the land you are entering to possess and drives out before you many nations—the Hittites, Girgashites, Amorites, Canaanites, Perizzites, Hivites and Jebusites, seven nations larger and stronger than you— ²and when the LORD your God has delivered them over to you and you have defeated them, then you must destroy them totally.[b] Make no treaty with them, and show them no mercy. ³Do not intermarry with them. Do not give your daughters to

---

[a] 4 Or *the LORD our God is one LORD*; or *the LORD is our God, the LORD is one*; or *the LORD is our God, the LORD alone*
[b] 2 The Hebrew term refers to the irrevocable giving over of things or persons to the LORD, often by totally destroying them; also in verse 26.

their sons or take their daughters for your sons, ⁴for they will turn your children away from following me to serve other gods, and the LORD's anger will burn against you and will quickly destroy you. ⁵This is what you are to do to them: break down their altars, smash their sacred stones, cut down their Asherah poles[a] and burn their idols in the fire. ⁶For you are a people holy to the LORD your God. The LORD your God has chosen you out of all the peoples on the face of the earth to be his people, his treasured possession.

⁷The LORD did not set his affection on you and choose you because you were more numerous than other peoples, for you were the fewest of all peoples. ⁸But it was because the LORD loved you and kept the oath he swore to your ancestors that he brought you out with a mighty hand and redeemed you from the land of slavery, from the power of Pharaoh king of Egypt. ⁹Know therefore that the LORD your God is God; he is the faithful God, keeping his covenant of love to a thousand generations of those who love him and keep his commandments. ¹⁰But those who hate him he will repay to their face by destruction; he will not be slow to repay to their face those who hate him.

¹¹Therefore, take care to follow the commands, decrees and laws I give you today.

¹²If you pay attention to these laws and are careful to follow them, then the LORD your God will keep his covenant of love with you, as he swore to your ancestors. ¹³He will love you and bless you and increase your numbers. He will bless the fruit of your womb, the crops of your land—your corn, new wine and oil—the calves of your herds and the lambs of your flocks in the land that he swore to your ancestors to give you. ¹⁴You will be blessed more than any other people; none of your men or women will be childless, nor any of your livestock without young. ¹⁵The LORD will keep you free from every disease. He will not inflict on you the horrible diseases you knew in Egypt, but he will inflict them on all who hate you. ¹⁶You must destroy all the peoples the LORD your God gives over to you. Do not look on them with pity and do not serve their gods, for that will be a snare to you.

¹⁷You may say to yourselves, 'These nations are stronger than we are. How can we drive them out?' ¹⁸But do not be afraid of them; remember well what the LORD your God did to Pharaoh and to all Egypt. ¹⁹You saw with your own eyes the great trials, the signs and wonders, the mighty hand and outstretched arm, with which the LORD your God brought you out. The LORD your God will do the same to all the peoples you now fear. ²⁰Moreover, the LORD your God will send the hornet among them until even the survivors who hide from you have perished. ²¹Do not be terrified by them, for the LORD your God, who is among you, is a great and awesome God. ²²The LORD your God will drive out those nations before you, little by little. You will not be allowed to eliminate them all at once, or the wild animals will multiply around you. ²³But the LORD your God will deliver them over to you, throwing them into great confusion until they are destroyed. ²⁴He will give their kings into your hand, and you will wipe out their names from under heaven. No-one

making Connections

Need for purity
Deuteronomy 7:1
This call for total destruction might seem a bit harsh but there was a good reason behind it. The Canaanites were very immoral and depraved people and it was a question of the Israelites destroying them or being destroyed themselves. God wanted his people to be holy and not to be seduced by the pagan cultures around them.

---

[a] 5 That is, wooden symbols of the goddess Asherah; here and elsewhere in Deuteronomy

will be able to stand up against you; you will destroy them. 25The images of their gods you are to burn in the fire. Do not covet the silver and gold on them, and do not take it for yourselves, or you will be ensnared by it, for it is detestable to the LORD your God. 26Do not bring a detestable thing into your house or you, like it, will be set apart for destruction. Regard it as vile and utterly detest it, for it is set apart for destruction.

Do not forget the LORD

8 Be careful to follow every command I am giving you today, so that you may live and increase and may enter and possess the land that the LORD promised on oath to your ancestors. 2Remember how the LORD your God led you all the way in the wilderness these forty years, to humble and test you in order to know what was in your heart, whether or not you would keep his commands. 3He humbled you, causing you to hunger and then feeding you with manna, which neither you nor your ancestors had known, to teach you that people do not live on bread alone but on every word that comes from the mouth of the LORD. 4Your clothes did not wear out and your feet did not swell during these forty years. 5Know then in your heart that as a man disciplines his son, so the LORD your God disciplines you.

6Observe the commands of the LORD your God, walking in obedience to him and revering him. 7For the LORD your God is bringing you into a good land—a land with streams and pools of water, with springs flowing in the valleys and hills; 8a land with wheat and barley, vines and fig-trees, pomegranates, olive oil and honey; 9a land where bread will not be scarce and you will lack nothing; a land where the rocks are iron and you can dig copper out of the hills.

10When you have eaten and are satisfied, praise the LORD your God for the good land he has given you. 11Be careful that you do not forget the LORD your God, failing to observe his commands, his laws and his decrees that I am giving you this day. 12Otherwise, when you eat and are satisfied, when you build fine houses and settle down, 13and when your herds and flocks grow large and your silver and gold increase and all you have is multiplied, 14then your heart will become proud and you will forget the LORD your God, who brought you out of Egypt, out of the land of slavery. 15He led you through the vast and dreadful wilderness, that thirsty and waterless land, with its venomous snakes and scorpions. He brought you water out of hard rock. 16He gave you manna to eat in the wilderness, something your ancestors had never known, to humble and test you so that in the end it might go well with you. 17You may say to yourself, 'My power and the strength of my hands have produced this wealth for me.' 18But remember the LORD your God, for it is he who gives you the ability to produce wealth, and so confirms his covenant, which he swore to your ancestors, as it is today.

19If you ever forget the LORD your God and follow other gods and worship and bow down to them, I testify against you today that you will surely be destroyed. 20Like the nations the LORD destroyed before you, so you will be destroyed for not obeying the LORD your God.

Not because of Israel's righteousness

9 Hear, Israel: you are now about to cross the Jordan to go in and dispossess nations greater and stronger than you, with large cities that have walls up to the sky. 2The people are strong and tall—Anakites! You know about them and have heard it said: 'Who can stand up against the Anakites?' 3But be assured today that the LORD your God is the one who goes across ahead of you like a devouring fire. He will destroy them; he will subdue them before you. And you will drive them out and annihilate them quickly, as the LORD has promised you.

4After the LORD your God has driven them out before you, do not say to yourself, 'The LORD has brought me here to take possession of this land because of my righteousness.' No, it is on account of the wickedness of these nations that the LORD is going to drive them out before you. 5It is not because of your righteousness or your integrity that you are going in to take possession of their land; but on account of the wickedness of these nations, the LORD your God will drive them out before you, to accomplish what he swore to your fathers, to Abraham, Isaac and Jacob. 6Understand, then, that it is not because of your righteousness that the LORD your God is giving you this good land to possess, for you are a stiff-necked people.

The golden calf

7Remember this and never forget how you aroused the anger of the LORD your God in the wilderness. From the day you left Egypt until you arrived here, you have been rebellious against the LORD. 8At Horeb you aroused the LORD's wrath so that he was angry enough to destroy you. 9When I went up on the mountain to receive the tablets of stone, the tablets of the covenant that the LORD had made with you, I stayed on the mountain for forty days and forty nights; I ate no bread and drank no water. 10The LORD gave me two stone tablets inscribed by the finger of God. On them were all the commandments the LORD proclaimed to you on the mountain out of the fire, on the day of the assembly.

11At the end of the forty days and forty nights, the LORD gave me the two stone tablets, the tablets of the covenant. 12Then the LORD told me, 'Go down from here at once, because your people whom you brought out of Egypt have become corrupt. They have turned away quickly from what I commanded them and have made an idol for themselves.'

13And the LORD said to me, 'I have seen this people, and they are a stiff-necked people indeed! 14Let me alone, so that I may destroy them and blot out their name from under heaven. And I will make you into a nation stronger and more numerous than they.'

15So I turned and went down from the mountain while it was ablaze with fire. And the two tablets of the covenant were in my hands. 16When I looked, I saw that you had sinned against the LORD your God; you had made for yourselves an idol cast in the shape of a calf. You had turned aside quickly from the way that the LORD had commanded you. 17So I took the two tablets and threw them out of my hands, breaking them to pieces before your eyes.

18Then once again I fell prostrate before the LORD for forty days and forty nights; I ate no bread and drank no water, because of all the sin you had committed, doing what was evil in the LORD's sight and so arousing his anger. 19I feared the anger and wrath of the LORD, for he was angry enough with you to destroy you. But again the LORD listened to me. 20And the LORD was angry enough with Aaron to destroy him, but at that time I prayed for Aaron too. 21Also I took that sinful thing of yours, the calf you had made, and burned it in the fire. Then I crushed it and ground it to powder as fine as dust and threw the dust into a stream that flowed down the mountain.

22You also made the LORD angry at Taberah, at Massah and at Kibroth Hattaavah.

23And when the LORD sent you out from Kadesh Barnea, he said, 'Go up and take possession of the land I have given you.' But you rebelled against the command of the LORD your God. You did not trust him or obey him. 24You have been rebellious against the LORD ever since I have known you.

25I lay prostrate before the LORD those forty days and forty nights because the LORD had said he would destroy you. 26I prayed to the LORD and said, 'Sovereign LORD, do not destroy your people, your own inheritance that you redeemed by your great power and brought out of Egypt with a mighty hand. 27Remember your servants Abraham, Isaac and Jacob. Overlook the stubbornness of this people, their wickedness and their sin. 28Otherwise, the country from which you brought us will say, "Because the LORD was not able to take them into the land he had promised them, and because he hated them, he brought them out to put them to death in the wilderness." 29But they are your people, your inheritance that you brought out by your great power and your outstretched arm.'

Tablets like the first ones

10 At that time the LORD said to me, 'Chisel out two stone tablets like the first ones and come up to me on the mountain. Also make a wooden ark.[a] ²I will write on the tablets the words that were on the first tablets, which you broke. Then you are to put them in the ark.'

³So I made the ark out of acacia wood and chiselled out two stone tablets like the first ones, and I went up on the mountain with the two tablets in my hands. ⁴The LORD wrote on these tablets what he had written before, the Ten Commandments he had proclaimed to you on the mountain, out of the fire, on the day of the assembly. And the LORD gave them to me. ⁵Then I came back down the mountain and put the tablets in the ark I had made, as the LORD commanded me, and they are there now.

⁶(The Israelites travelled from the wells of Bene Jaakan to Moserah. There Aaron died and was buried, and Eleazar his son succeeded him as priest. ⁷From there they travelled to Gudgodah and on to Jotbathah, a land with streams of water. ⁸At that time the LORD set apart the tribe of Levi to carry the ark of the covenant of the LORD, to stand before the LORD to minister and to pronounce blessings in his name, as they still do today. ⁹That is why the Levites have no share or inheritance among their fellow Israelites; the LORD is their inheritance, as the LORD your God told them.)

¹⁰Now I had stayed on the mountain for forty days and nights, as I did the first time, and the LORD listened to me at this time also. It was not his will to destroy you. ¹¹'Go,' the LORD said to me, 'and lead the people on their way, so that they may enter and possess the land that I swore to their ancestors to give them.'

Fear the LORD

¹²And now, Israel, what does the LORD your God ask of you but to fear the LORD your God, to walk in obedience to him, to love him, to serve the LORD your God with all your heart and with all your soul, ¹³and to observe the LORD's commands and decrees that I am giving you today for your own good?

¹⁴To the LORD your God belong the heavens, even the highest heavens, the earth and everything in it. ¹⁵Yet the LORD set his affection on your ancestors and loved them,

> **People and Places**
>
> **Levite**
> Deuteronomy 10:8
> Levi was one of Jacob's twelve sons and his descendants were given the job of being priests in the tabernacle, the tent of worship in the wilderness, and later in the temple in Jerusalem. The Levites missed out on being given any land in Canaan, but then they wouldn't have had time to look after it. The other Israelites were told to provide for the Levites through their tithes and offerings.

and he chose you, their descendants, above all the nations—as it is today. ¹⁶Circumcise your hearts, therefore, and do not be stiff-necked any longer. ¹⁷For the LORD your God is God of gods and Lord of lords, the great God, mighty and awesome, who shows no partiality and accepts no bribes. ¹⁸He defends the cause of the fatherless and the widow, and loves the foreigners residing among you, giving them food and clothing. ¹⁹And you are to love those who are foreigners, for you yourselves were foreigners in Egypt. ²⁰Fear the LORD your God and serve him. Hold fast to him and take your oaths in his name. ²¹He is your praise; he is your God, who performed for you those great and awesome wonders you saw with your own eyes. ²²Your ancestors who went down into Egypt were seventy in all, and now the LORD your God has made you as numerous as the stars in the sky.

Love and obey the LORD

11 Love the LORD your God and keep his requirements, his decrees, his laws and his commands always. ²Remember today that your children were not the ones who saw and experienced the discipline of the LORD your God: his majesty, his mighty hand, his outstretched arm; ³the

---

[a] 1 That is, a chest

signs he performed and the things he did in the heart of Egypt, both to Pharaoh king of Egypt and to his whole country; 4what he did to the Egyptian army, to its horses and chariots, how he overwhelmed them with the waters of the Red Sea*a* as they were pursuing you, and how the LORD brought lasting ruin on them. 5It was not your children who saw what he did for you in the wilderness until you arrived at this place, 6and what he did to Dathan and Abiram, sons of Eliab the Reubenite, when the earth opened its mouth right in the middle of all Israel and swallowed them up with their households, their tents and every living thing that belonged to them. 7But it was your own eyes that saw all these great things the LORD has done.

8Observe therefore all the commands I am giving you today, so that you may have the strength to go in and take over the land that you are crossing the Jordan to possess, 9and so that you may live long in the land that the LORD swore to your ancestors to give to them and their descendants, a land flowing with milk and honey. 10The land you are entering to take over is not like the land of Egypt, from which you have come, where you planted your seed and irrigated it by foot as in a vegetable garden. 11But the land you are crossing the Jordan to take possession of is a land of mountains and valleys that drinks rain from heaven. 12It is a land the LORD your God cares for; the eyes of the LORD your God are continually on it from the beginning of the year to its end.

13So if you faithfully obey the commands I am giving you today—to love the LORD your God and to serve him with all your heart and with all your soul— 14then I will send rain on your land in its season, both autumn and spring rains, so that you may gather in your corn, new wine and olive oil. 15I will provide grass in the fields for your cattle, and you will eat and be satisfied.

16Be careful, or you will be enticed to turn away and worship other gods and bow down to them. 17Then the LORD's anger will burn against you, and he will shut the heavens so that it will not rain and the ground will yield no produce, and you will soon perish from the good land the LORD is giving you. 18Fix these words of mine in your hearts and minds; tie them as symbols on your hands and bind them on your foreheads. 19Teach them to your children, talking about them when you sit at home and when you walk along the road, when you lie down and when you get up. 20Write them on the door-frames of your houses and on your gates, 21so that your days and the days of your children may be many in the land that the LORD swore to give your ancestors, as many as the days that the heavens are above the earth.

22If you carefully observe all these commands I am giving you to follow—to love the LORD your God, to walk in obedience to him and to hold fast to him— 23then the LORD will drive out all these nations before you, and you will dispossess nations larger and stronger than you. 24Every place where you set your foot will be yours: your territory will extend from the desert to Lebanon, and from the River Euphrates to the Mediterranean Sea. 25No-one will be able to stand against you. The LORD your God, as he promised you, will put the terror and fear of you on the whole land, wherever you go.

26See, I am setting before you today a blessing and a curse— 27the blessing if you obey the commands of the LORD your God that I am giving you today; 28the curse if you disobey the commands of the LORD your God and turn from the way that I command you today by following other gods, which you have not known. 29When the LORD your God has brought you into the land you are entering to possess, you are to proclaim on Mount Gerizim the blessings, and on Mount Ebal the curses. 30As you know, these mountains are across the Jordan, westward, towards the setting sun, near the great trees of Moreh, in the territory of those Canaanites living in the Arabah in the vicinity of Gilgal. 31You are about to cross the Jordan to enter and take possession of the land the LORD your God is giving you. When you have taken it over and are living there, 32be sure that you obey all the decrees and laws I am setting before you today.

---

a 4 Or the Sea of Reeds

The one place of worship

12 These are the decrees and laws you must be careful to follow in the land that the LORD, the God of your ancestors, has given you to possess—as long as you live in the land. 2Destroy completely all the places on the high mountains, on the hills and under every spreading tree, where the nations you are dispossessing worship their gods. 3Break down their altars, smash their sacred stones and burn their Asherah poles in the fire; cut down the idols of their gods and wipe out their names from those places.

4You must not worship the LORD your God in their way. 5But you are to seek the place the LORD your God will choose from among all your tribes to put his Name there for his dwelling. To that place you must go; 6there bring your burnt offerings and sacrifices, your tithes and special gifts, what you have vowed to give and your freewill offerings, and the firstborn of your herds and flocks. 7There, in the presence of the LORD your God, you and your families shall eat and shall rejoice in everything you have put your hand to, because the LORD your God has blessed you.

8You are not to do as we do here today, everyone doing as they see fit, 9since you have not yet reached the resting place and the inheritance the LORD your God is giving you. 10But you will cross the Jordan and settle in the land the LORD your God is giving you as an inheritance, and he will give you rest from all your enemies around you so that you will live in safety. 11Then to the place the LORD your God will choose as a dwelling for his Name—there you are to bring everything I command you: your burnt offerings and sacrifices, your tithes and special gifts, and all the choice possessions you have vowed to the LORD. 12And there rejoice before the LORD your God—you, your sons and daughters, your male and female servants, and the Levites from your towns who have no land allotted to them or any inheritance of their own. 13Be careful not to sacrifice your burnt offerings anywhere you please. 14Offer them only at the place the LORD will choose in one of your tribes, and there observe everything I command you.

15Nevertheless, you may slaughter your animals in any of your towns and eat as much of the meat as you want, as if it were gazelle or deer, according to the blessing the LORD your God gives you. Both the ceremonially unclean and the clean may eat it. 16But you must not eat the blood; pour it out on the ground like water. 17You must not eat in your own towns the tithe of your corn and new wine and olive oil, or the firstborn of your herds and flocks, or whatever you have vowed to give, or your freewill offerings or special gifts. 18Instead, you are to eat them in the presence of the LORD your God at the place the LORD your God will choose—you, your sons and daughters, your male and female servants, and the Levites from your towns—and you are to rejoice before the LORD your God in everything you put your hand to. 19Be careful not to neglect the Levites as long as you live in your land.

20When the LORD your God has enlarged your territory as he promised you, and you crave meat and say, 'I would like some meat,' then you may eat as much of it as you want. 21If the place where the LORD your God chooses to put his Name is too far away from you, you may slaughter animals from the herds and flocks the LORD has given you, as I have commanded you, and in your own towns you may eat as much of them as you want. 22Eat them as you would gazelle or deer. Both the ceremonially unclean and the clean may eat. 23But be sure you do not eat the blood, because the blood is the life, and you must not eat the life with the meat. 24You must not eat the blood; pour it out on the ground like water. 25Do not eat it, so that it may go well with you and your children after you, because you will be doing what is right in the eyes of the LORD.

26But take your consecrated things and whatever you have vowed to give, and go to the place the LORD will choose. 27Present your burnt offerings on the altar of the LORD your God, both the meat and the blood. The blood of your sacrifices must be poured beside the altar of the LORD your God, but you may eat the meat. 28Be careful to obey

Deuteronomy 12:29

all these regulations I am giving you, so that it may always go well with you and your children after you, because you will be doing what is good and right in the eyes of the LORD your God.

29The LORD your God will cut off before you the nations you are about to invade and dispossess. But when you have driven them out and settled in their land, 30and after they have been destroyed before you, be careful not to be ensnared by enquiring about their gods, saying, 'How do these nations serve their gods? We will do the same.' 31You must not worship the LORD your God in their way, because in worshipping their gods, they do all kinds of detestable things the LORD hates. They even burn their sons and daughters in the fire as sacrifices to their gods.

*32See that you do all I command you; do not add to it or take away from it.

What not to eat
Deuteronomy 14:21

The Israelites were to be a holy people, set apart for God, and this was reflected in what they could and couldn't eat. Some of the guidelines were to do with hygiene and some to allow them to be distinctive. The practice of boiling a goat kid in its mother's milk was a pagan custom. The milk was poured out as a charm to make the land fertile. Not surprising, then, that God told them not to do it!

Worshipping other gods

13 *If a prophet, or one who foretells by dreams, appears among you and announces to you a sign or wonder, 2and if the sign or wonder spoken of takes place, and the prophet says, 'Let us follow other gods' (gods you have not known) 'and let us worship them,' 3you must not listen to the words of that prophet or dreamer. The LORD your God is testing you to find out whether you love him with all your heart and with all your soul. 4It is the LORD your God you must follow, and him you must revere. Keep his commands and obey him; serve him and hold fast to him. 5That prophet or dreamer must be put to death for inciting rebellion against the LORD your God, who brought you out of Egypt and redeemed you from the land of slavery. That prophet or dreamer tried to turn you from the way the LORD your God commanded you to follow. You must purge the evil from among you.

6If your very own brother, or your son or daughter, or the wife you love, or your closest friend secretly entices you, saying, 'Let us go and worship other gods' (gods that neither you nor your ancestors have known, 7gods of the peoples around you, whether near or far, from one end of the land to the other), 8do not yield to them or listen to them. Show them no pity. Do not spare them or shield them. 9You must certainly put them to death. Your hand must be the first in putting them to death, and then the hands of all the people. 10Stone them to death, because they tried to turn you away from the LORD your God, who brought you out of Egypt, out of the land of slavery. 11Then all Israel will hear and be afraid, and no-one among you will do such an evil thing again.

12If you hear it said about one of the towns the LORD your God is giving you to live in 13that wicked people have arisen among you and have led the people of their town astray, saying, 'Let us go and worship other gods' (gods you have not known), 14then you must enquire, probe and investigate it thoroughly. And if it is true and it has been proved that this detestable thing has been done among you, 15you must certainly put to the sword all who live in that

---

a 15 The Hebrew term refers to the irrevocable giving over of things or persons to the LORD, often by totally destroying them.   *b* 17 The Hebrew term refers to the irrevocable giving over of things or persons to the LORD, often by totally destroying them.

* 12:32 is numbered 13:1 in Hebrew texts.   * 13:1-18 is numbered 13:2-19 in Hebrew texts.

town. Destroy it completely,[a] both its people and its livestock. 16Gather all the plunder of the town into the middle of the public square and completely burn the town and all its plunder as a whole burnt offering to the LORD your God. It is to remain a ruin for ever, never to be rebuilt. 17None of those condemned things[b] shall be found in your hands, so that the LORD will turn from his fierce anger; he will show you mercy, have compassion on you, and increase your numbers, as he promised on oath to your ancestors, 18because you obey the LORD your God, keeping all his commands that I am giving you today and doing what is right in his eyes.

Clean and unclean food

14 You are the children of the LORD your God. Do not cut yourselves or shave the front of your heads for the dead, 2for you are a people holy to the LORD your God. Out of all the peoples on the face of the earth, the LORD has chosen you to be his treasured possession.

3Do not eat any detestable thing. 4These are the animals you may eat: the ox, the sheep, the goat, 5the deer, the gazelle, the roe deer, the wild goat, the ibex, the antelope and the mountain sheep.[c] 6You may eat any animal that has a divided hoof and that chews the cud. 7However, of those that chew the cud or that have a divided hoof you may not eat the camel, the hare or the hyrax. Although they chew the cud, they do not have a divided hoof; they are ceremonially unclean for you. 8The pig is also unclean; although it has a divided hoof, it does not chew the cud. You are not to eat their meat or touch their carcasses.

9Of all the creatures living in the water, you may eat any that has fins and scales. 10But anything that does not have fins and scales you may not eat; for you it is unclean.

11You may eat any clean bird. 12But these you may not eat: the eagle, the vulture, the black vulture, 13the red kite, the black kite, any kind of falcon, 14any kind of raven, 15the horned owl, the screech owl, the gull, any kind of hawk, 16the little owl, the great owl, the white owl, 17the desert owl, the osprey, the cormorant, 18the stork, any kind of heron, the hoopoe and the bat.

19All flying insects that swarm are unclean to you; do not eat them. 20But any winged creature that is clean you may eat.

21Do not eat anything you find already dead. You may give it to the foreigners residing in any of your towns, and they may eat it, or you may sell it to any other foreigner. But you are a people holy to the LORD your God.

Do not cook a young goat in its mother's milk.

Tithes

22Be sure to set aside a tenth of all that your fields produce each year. 23Eat the tithe of your corn, new wine and olive oil, and the firstborn of your herds and flocks in the presence of the LORD your God at the place he will choose as a dwelling for his Name, so that you may learn to revere the LORD your God always. 24But if that place is too distant and you have been blessed by the LORD your God and cannot carry your tithe (because

Party time
Deuteronomy 14:22
The Israelites really knew how to party! They were to set aside a tenth of all their produce, take it to the temple and have a huge feast, rejoicing in God's presence. If the temple was too far away, they should sell that produce and take money instead, buying whatever they fancied to eat. But this wasn't an excuse to be greedy; every three years they were to give their tithe to the priests and needy people who lived in the towns.

---

[a] 5 The precise identification of some of the birds and animals in this chapter is uncertain.

the place where the LORD will choose to put his Name is so far away), 25then exchange your tithe for silver, and take the silver with you and go to the place the LORD your God will choose. 26Use the silver to buy whatever you like: cattle, sheep, wine or other fermented drink, or anything you wish. Then you and your household shall eat there in the presence of the LORD your God and rejoice. 27And do not neglect the Levites living in your towns, for they have no land allotted to them or any inheritance of their own.

28At the end of every three years, bring all the tithes of that year's produce and store it in your towns, 29so that the Levites (who have no land allotted to them or any inheritance of their own) and the foreigners, the fatherless and the widows who live in your towns may come and eat and be satisfied, and so that the LORD your God may bless you in all the work of your hands.

The year for cancelling debts

15 At the end of every seven years you must cancel debts. 2This is how it is to be done: every creditor shall cancel any loan they have made to another Israelite. They shall not require payment from anyone among their own people, because the LORD's time for cancelling debts has been proclaimed. 3You may require payment from a foreigner, but you must cancel any debt one of your people owes you. 4However, there need be no poor people among you, for in the land the LORD your God is giving you to possess as your inheritance, he will richly bless you, 5if only you fully obey the LORD your God and are careful to follow all these commands I am giving you today. 6For the LORD your God will bless you as he has promised, and you will lend to many nations but will borrow from none. You will rule over many nations but none will rule over you.

7If anyone is poor among your people in any of the towns of the land that the LORD your God is giving you, do not be hardhearted or tight-fisted towards them. 8Rather, be open-handed and freely lend them whatever they need. 9Be careful not to harbour this wicked thought: 'The seventh year, the year for cancelling debts, is near,' so that you do not show ill will towards the needy among your people and give them nothing. They may then appeal to the LORD against you, and you will be found guilty of sin. 10Give generously to them and do so without a grudging heart; then because of this the LORD your God will bless you in all your work and in everything you put your hand to. 11There will always be poor people in the land. Therefore I command you to be open-handed towards those of your people who are poor and needy in your land.

Freeing servants

12If any of your people, men or women, sell themselves to you and serve you for six years, in the seventh year you must let them go free. 13And when you release them, do not send them away empty-handed. 14Supply them liberally from your flock, your threshing-floor and your winepress. Give to them as the LORD your God has blessed you. 15Remember that you were slaves in Egypt and the LORD your God redeemed you. That is why I give you this command today.

16But if your servant says to you, 'I do not want to leave you,' because he loves you and your family and is well off with you, 17then take an awl and push it through his ear lobe into the door, and he will become your servant for life. Do the same for your female servant.

18Do not consider it a hardship to set your servants free, because their service to you these six years has been worth twice as much as that of a hired hand. And the LORD your God will bless you in everything you do.

The firstborn animals

19Set apart for the LORD your God every firstborn male of your herds and flocks. Do not put the firstborn of your oxen to work, and do not shear the firstborn of your sheep. 20Each year you and your family are to eat them in the presence of the LORD your God at the place he will choose. 21If an animal has a defect, is lame or blind, or has any serious flaw, you must not sacrifice it to the LORD your God. 22You are to eat it in your own towns. Both the ceremonially unclean and the clean may eat it, as if it were gazelle or deer. 23But you must not eat the blood; pour it out on the ground like water.

Passover

16 Observe the month of Aviv and celebrate the Passover of the LORD your God, because in the month of Aviv he brought you out of Egypt by night. 2Sacrifice as the Passover to the LORD your God an animal from your flock or herd at the place the LORD will choose as a dwelling for his Name. 3Do not eat it with bread made with yeast, but for seven days eat unleavened bread, the bread of affliction, because you left Egypt in haste—so that all the days of your life you may remember the time of your departure from Egypt. 4Let no yeast be found in your possession in all your land for seven days. Do not let any of the meat you sacrifice on the evening of the first day remain until morning.

5You must not sacrifice the Passover in any town the LORD your God gives you 6except in the place he will choose as a dwelling for his Name. There you must sacrifice the Passover in the evening, when the sun goes down, on the anniversary[a] of your departure from Egypt. 7Roast it and eat it at the place the LORD your God will choose. Then in the morning return to your tents. 8For six days eat unleavened bread and on the seventh day hold an assembly to the LORD your God and do no work.

Festival of Weeks

9Count seven weeks from the time you begin to put the sickle to the standing corn. 10Then celebrate the Festival of Weeks to the LORD your God by giving a freewill offering in proportion to the blessings the LORD your God has given you. 11And rejoice before the LORD your God at the place he will choose as a dwelling for his Name—you, your sons and daughters, your male and female servants, the Levites in your towns, and the foreigners, the fatherless and the widows living among you. 12Remember that you were slaves in Egypt, and follow carefully these decrees.

Festival of Tabernacles

13Celebrate the Festival of Tabernacles for seven days after you have gathered the produce of your threshing-floor and your winepress. 14Be joyful at your Festival—you, your sons and daughters, your male and female servants, and the Levites, the foreigners, the fatherless and the widows who live in your towns. 15For seven days celebrate the Festival to the LORD your God at the place the LORD will choose. For the LORD your God will bless you in all your harvest and in all the work of your hands, and your joy will be complete.

16Three times a year all your men must appear before the LORD your God at the place he will choose: at the Festival of Unleavened Bread, the Festival of Weeks and the Festival of Tabernacles. No-one should appear before the LORD empty-handed: 17each of you must bring a gift in proportion to the way the LORD your God has blessed you.

Judges

18Appoint judges and officials for each of your tribes in every town the LORD your God is giving you, and they shall judge the people fairly. 19Do not pervert justice or show partiality. Do not accept a bribe, for a bribe blinds the eyes of the wise and twists the words of the righteous. 20Follow justice and justice alone, so that you may live and possess the land the LORD your God is giving you.

Worshipping other gods

21Do not set up any wooden Asherah pole beside the altar you build to the LORD your God, 22and do not erect a sacred stone, for these the LORD your God hates.

17 Do not sacrifice to the LORD your God an ox or a sheep that has any defect or flaw in it, for that would be detestable to him.

2If a man or woman living among you in one of the towns the LORD gives you is found doing evil in the eyes of the LORD your God in violation of his covenant, 3and contrary to my command has worshipped other gods, bowing down to them or to the sun or the moon or the stars in the sky, 4and this has been brought to your attention, then you must investigate it thoroughly. If it is

---
[a] 6 Or down, at the time of day

true and it has been proved that this detestable thing has been done in Israel, ⁵take the man or woman who has done this evil deed to your city gate and stone that person to death. ⁶On the testimony of two or three witnesses a person is to be put to death, but no-one is to be put to death on the testimony of only one witness. ⁷The hands of the witnesses must be the first in putting that person to death, and then the hands of all the people. You must purge the evil from among you.

Law courts

⁸If cases come before your courts that are too difficult for you to judge—whether bloodshed, lawsuits or assaults—take them to the place the LORD your God will choose. ⁹Go to the Levitical priests and to the judge who is in office at that time. Enquire of them and they will give you the verdict. ¹⁰You must act according to the decisions they give you at the place the LORD will choose. Be careful to do everything they instruct you to do. ¹¹Act according to whatever they teach you and the decisions they give you. Do not turn aside from what they tell you, to the right or to the left. ¹²Anyone who shows contempt for the judge or for the priest who stands ministering there to the LORD your God is to be put to death. You must purge the evil from Israel. ¹³All the people will hear and be afraid, and will not be contemptuous again.

The king

¹⁴When you enter the land the LORD your God is giving you and have taken possession of it and settled in it, and you say, 'Let us set a king over us like all the nations around us,' ¹⁵be sure to appoint over you the king the LORD your God chooses. He must be from among your own people. Do not place a foreigner over you, one who is not an Israelite. ¹⁶The king, moreover, must not acquire great numbers of horses for himself or make the people return to Egypt to get more of them, for the LORD has told you, 'You are not to go back that way again.' ¹⁷He must not take many wives, or his heart will be led astray. He must not accumulate large amounts of silver and gold.

¹⁸When he takes the throne of his kingdom, he is to write for himself on a scroll a copy of this law, taken from that of the Levitical priests. ¹⁹It is to be with him, and he is to read it all the days of his life so that he may learn to revere the LORD his God and follow carefully all the words of this law and these decrees ²⁰and not consider himself better than his fellow Israelites and turn from the law to the right or to the left. Then he and his descendants will reign a long time over his kingdom in Israel.

Offerings for priests and Levites

18 The Levitical priests—indeed, the whole tribe of Levi—are to have no land allotted to them or any inheritance with Israel. They shall live on the food offerings presented to the LORD, for that is their inheritance. ²They shall have no inheritance among their fellow Israelites; the LORD is their inheritance, as he promised them.

³This is the share due to the priests from the people who sacrifice a bull or a sheep: the shoulder, the jowls and the internal organs. ⁴You are to give them the firstfruits of your corn, new wine and olive oil, and the first wool from the shearing of your sheep, ⁵for the LORD your God has chosen them and their descendants out of all your tribes to stand and minister in the LORD's name always.

⁶If a Levite moves from one of your towns anywhere in Israel where he is living, and comes in all earnestness to the place the LORD will choose, ⁷he may minister in the name of the LORD his God like all other Levites who serve there in the presence of the LORD. ⁸He is to share equally in their benefits even though he has received money from the sale of family possessions.

Occult practices

⁹When you enter the land the LORD your God is giving you, do not learn to imitate the detestable ways of the nations there. ¹⁰Let no-one be found among you who sacrifices their son or daughter in the fire, who practises divination or sorcery, interprets omens, engages in witchcraft, ¹¹or casts spells, or who is a medium or spiritist or

who consults the dead. 12Anyone who does these things is detestable to the LORD, and because of these detestable practices the LORD your God will drive out those nations before you. 13You must be blameless before the LORD your God.

The prophet

14The nations you will dispossess listen to those who practise sorcery or divination. But as for you, the LORD your God has not permitted you to do so. 15The LORD your God will raise up for you a prophet like me from among you, from your own people. You must listen to him. 16For this is what you asked of the LORD your God at Horeb on the day of the assembly when you said, 'Let us not hear the voice of the LORD our God nor see this great fire any more, or we will die.'

17The LORD said to me: 'What they say is good. 18I will raise up for them a prophet like you from among their people, and I will put my words in his mouth. He will tell them everything I command him. 19I myself will call to account anyone who does not listen to my words that the prophet speaks in my name. 20But a prophet who presumes to speak in my name anything I have not commanded, or a prophet who speaks in the name of other gods, is to be put to death.'

21You may say to yourselves, 'How can we know when a message has not been spoken by the LORD?' 22If what a prophet proclaims in the name of the LORD does not take place or come true, that is a message the LORD has not spoken. That prophet has spoken presumptuously. No-one should be alarmed.

Cities of refuge

19 When the LORD your God has destroyed the nations whose land he is giving you, and when you have driven them out and settled in their towns and houses, 2then set aside for yourselves three cities in the land the LORD your God is giving you to possess. 3Build roads to them and divide into three parts the land the LORD your God is giving you as an inheritance, so that anyone who kills someone else may flee there.

4This is the rule concerning anyone who kills a person and flees there for safety—anyone who kills a neighbour unintentionally, without malice aforethought. 5For instance, a man may go into the forest with his neighbour to cut wood, and as he swings his axe to fell a tree, the head may fly off and hit his neighbour and kill him. That man may flee to one of these cities and save his life. 6Otherwise, the avenger of blood might pursue him in a rage, overtake him if the distance is too great, and kill him even though he is not deserving of death, since he did it to his neighbour without malice aforethought. 7This is why I command you to set aside for yourselves three cities.

8If the LORD your God enlarges your territory, as he promised on oath to your ancestors, and gives you the whole land he promised them, 9because you carefully follow all these laws I command you today—to love the LORD your God and to walk always in obedience to him—then you are to set aside three more cities. 10Do this so that innocent blood will not be shed in your land, which the LORD your God is giving you as your inheritance, and so that you will not be guilty of bloodshed.

11But if out of hate someone lies in wait, assaults and kills a neighbour, and then flees to one of these cities, 12the killer shall be sent for by the town elders, be brought back from the city, and be handed over to the avenger of blood to die. 13Show no pity. You must purge from Israel the guilt of shedding innocent blood, so that it may go well with you.

14Do not move your neighbour's boundary stone set up by your predecessors in the inheritance you receive in the land the LORD your God is giving you to possess.

Witnesses

15One witness is not enough to convict anyone accused of any crime or offence they may have committed. A matter must be established by the testimony of two or three witnesses.

16If a malicious witness takes the stand to accuse someone of a crime, 17the two involved in the dispute must stand in the presence of the LORD before the priests and the judges who are in office at the time.

18The judges must make a thorough investigation, and if the witness proves to be a liar, giving false testimony, 19then do to the false witness as that witness intended to do to the other party. You must purge the evil from among you. 20The rest of the people will hear of this and be afraid, and never again will such an evil thing be done among you. 21Show no pity: life for life, eye for eye, tooth for tooth, hand for hand, foot for foot.

Going to war

20 When you go to war against your enemies and see horses and chariots and an army greater than yours, do not be afraid of them, because the LORD your God, who brought you up out of Egypt, will be with you. 2When you are about to go into battle, the priest shall come forward and address the army. 3He shall say: 'Hear, Israel: today you are going into battle against your enemies. Do not be fainthearted or afraid; do not be terrified or give way to panic before them. 4For the LORD your God is the one who goes with you to fight for you against your enemies to give you victory.'

5The officers shall say to the army: 'Has anyone built a new house and not yet begun to live in it? Let him go home, or he may die in battle and someone else may begin to live in it. 6Has anyone planted a vineyard and not begun to enjoy it? Let him go home, or he may die in battle and someone else enjoy it. 7Has anyone become pledged to a woman and not married her? Let him go home, or he may die in battle and someone else marry her.' 8Then the officers shall add, 'Is anyone afraid or faint-hearted? Let him go home so that the others will not become disheartened too.' 9When the officers have finished speaking to the army, they shall appoint commanders over it.

10When you march up to attack a city, make its people an offer of peace. 11If they accept and open their gates, all the people in it shall be subject to forced labour and shall work for you. 12If they refuse to make peace and they engage you in battle, lay siege to that city. 13When the LORD your God delivers it into your hand, put to the sword all the men in it. 14As for the women, the children, the livestock and everything else in the city, you may take these as plunder for yourselves. And you may use the plunder the LORD your God gives you from your enemies. 15This is how you are to treat all the cities that are at a distance from you and do not belong to the nations nearby.

16However, in the cities of the nations the LORD your God is giving you as an inheritance, do not leave alive anything that breathes. 17Completely destroy*a* them— the Hittites, Amorites, Canaanites, Perizzites, Hivites and Jebusites—as the LORD your God has commanded you. 18Otherwise, they will teach you to follow all the detestable things they do in worshipping their gods, and you will sin against the LORD your God.

19When you lay siege to a city for a long time, fighting against it to capture it, do not destroy its trees by putting an axe to them, because you can eat their fruit. Do not cut them down. Are the trees people, that you should besiege them?*b* 20However, you may cut down trees that you know are not fruit

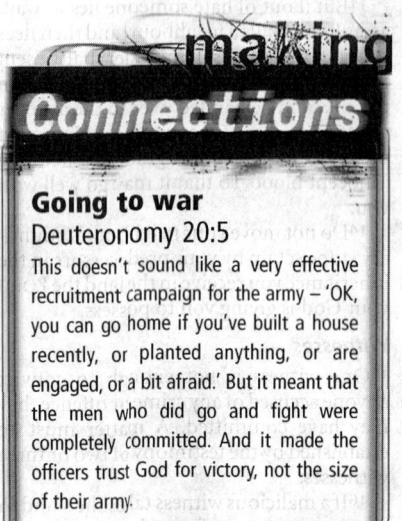

making Connections

Going to war
Deuteronomy 20:5

This doesn't sound like a very effective recruitment campaign for the army – 'OK, you can go home if you've built a house recently, or planted anything, or are engaged, or a bit afraid.' But it meant that the men who did go and fight were completely committed. And it made the officers trust God for victory, not the size of their army.

---

a 17 The Hebrew term refers to the irrevocable giving over of things or persons to the LORD, often by totally destroying them.   *b* 19 Or *down to use in the siege, for the fruit trees are for the benefit of people.*

trees and use them to build siege works until the city at war with you falls.

Atonement for an unsolved murder

21 If someone is found slain, lying in a field in the land the LORD your God is giving you to possess, and it is not known who the killer was, 2your elders and judges shall go out and measure the distance from the body to the neighbouring towns. 3Then the elders of the town nearest the body shall take a heifer that has never been worked and has never worn a yoke 4and lead it down to a valley that has not been ploughed or planted and where there is a flowing stream. There in the valley they are to break the heifer's neck. 5The priests, the sons of Levi, shall step forward, for the LORD your God has chosen them to minister and to pronounce blessings in the name of the LORD and to decide all cases of dispute and assault. 6Then all the elders of the town nearest the body shall wash their hands over the heifer whose neck was broken in the valley, 7and they shall declare: 'Our hands did not shed this blood, nor did our eyes see it done. 8Accept this atonement for your people Israel, whom you have redeemed, LORD, and do not hold your people guilty of the blood of an innocent person.' And the bloodshed will be atoned for. 9So you will purge from yourselves the guilt of shedding innocent blood, since you have done what is right in the eyes of the LORD.

Marrying a captive woman

10When you go to war against your enemies and the LORD your God delivers them into your hands and you take captives, 11if you notice among the captives a beautiful woman and are attracted to her, you may take her as your wife. 12Bring her into your home and make her shave her head, trim her nails 13and put aside the clothes she was wearing when captured. After she has lived in your house and mourned her father and mother for a full month, then you may go to her and be her husband and she shall be your wife. 14If you are not pleased with her, let her go wherever she wishes. You must not sell her or treat her as a slave, since you have dishonoured her.

The right of the firstborn

15If someone has two wives, and he loves one but not the other, and both bear him sons but the firstborn is the son of the wife he does not love, 16when he wills his property to his sons, he must not give the rights of the firstborn to the son of the wife he loves in preference to his actual firstborn, the son of the wife he does not love. 17He must acknowledge the son of his unloved wife as the firstborn by giving him a double share of all he has. That son is the first sign of his father's strength. The right of the firstborn belongs to him.

A rebellious son

18If someone has a stubborn and rebellious son who does not obey his father and mother and will not listen to them when they discipline him, 19his father and mother shall take hold of him and bring him to the elders at the gate of his town. 20They shall say to the elders, 'This son of ours is stubborn and rebellious. He will not obey us. He is a profligate and a drunkard.' 21Then all the men of his town are to stone him to death. You must purge the evil from among you. All Israel will hear of it and be afraid.

Various laws

22If anyone guilty of a capital offence is put to death and their body is exposed on a pole, 23you must not leave the body hanging on the pole overnight. Be sure to bury it that same day, because anyone who is hung on a pole is under God's curse. You must not desecrate the land the LORD your God is giving you as an inheritance.

22 If you see someone else's ox or sheep straying, do not ignore it but be sure to take it back to its owner. 2If the owner does not live near you or if you do not know who owns it, take it home with you and keep it until the owner comes looking for it. Then give it back. 3Do the same if you find someone's donkey or cloak or anything else they have lost. Do not ignore it.

4If you see someone's donkey or ox fallen on the road, do not ignore it. Help the owner to get it to its feet.

5A woman must not wear men's clothing, nor a man wear women's clothing, for the LORD your God detests anyone who does this.

6If you come across a bird's nest beside the road, either in a tree or on the ground, and the mother is sitting on the young or on the eggs, do not take the mother with the young. 7You may take the young, but be sure to let the mother go, so that it may go well with you and you may have a long life.

8When you build a new house, make a parapet around your roof so that you may not bring the guilt of bloodshed on your house if someone falls from the roof.

9Do not plant two kinds of seed in your vineyard; if you do, not only the crops you plant but also the fruit of the vineyard will be defiled.[a]

10Do not plough with an ox and a donkey yoked together.

11Do not wear clothes of wool and linen woven together.

12Make tassels on the four corners of the cloak you wear.

Marriage violations

13If a man takes a wife and, after sleeping with her, dislikes her 14and slanders her and gives her a bad name, saying, 'I married this woman, but when I approached her, I did not find proof of her virginity,' 15then the young woman's father and mother shall bring to the town elders at the gate proof that she was a virgin. 16Her father will say to the elders, 'I gave my daughter in marriage to this man, but he dislikes her. 17Now he has slandered her and said, "I did not find your daughter to be a virgin." But here is the proof of my daughter's virginity.' Then her parents shall display the cloth before the elders of the town, 18and the elders shall take the man and punish him. 19They shall fine him a hundred shekels[b] of silver and give them to the young woman's father, because this man has given an Israelite virgin a bad name. She shall continue to be his wife; he must not divorce her as long as he lives.

20If, however, the charge is true and no proof of the young woman's virginity can be found, 21she shall be brought to the door of her father's house and there the men of her town shall stone her to death. She has done an outrageous thing in Israel by being promiscuous while still in her father's house. You must purge the evil from among you.

22If a man is found sleeping with another man's wife, both the man who slept with her and the woman must die. You must purge the evil from Israel.

23If a man happens to meet in a town a virgin pledged to be married and he sleeps with her, 24you shall take both of them to the gate of that town and stone them to death—the young woman because she was in a town and did not scream for help, and the man because he violated another man's wife. You must purge the evil from among you.

25But if out in the country a man happens to meet a young woman pledged to be married and rapes her, only the man who has done this shall die. 26Do nothing to the woman; she has committed no sin deserving death. This case is like that of someone who attacks and murders a neighbour, 27for the man found the young woman out in the country, and though the betrothed woman screamed, there was no-one to rescue her.

28If a man happens to meet a virgin who is not pledged to be married and rapes her and

---

making Connections

Building regulations
Deuteronomy 22:8
Houses usually had flat roofs that would be used for sleeping and entertaining guests. The Israelites were to take proper safety precautions when they built their houses, to make sure no harm came to their guests.

---

[a]9 Or *be forfeited to the sanctuary* [b]19 That is, about 1.2 kilograms

they are discovered, ²⁹he shall pay her father fifty shekels*ᵃ* of silver. He must marry the young woman, for he has violated her. He can never divorce her as long as he lives.

*³⁰A man is not to marry his father's wife; he must not dishonour his father's bed.

Exclusion from the assembly

23 *No-one who has been emasculated by crushing or cutting may enter the assembly of the LORD.

²No-one born of a forbidden marriage*ᵇ* nor any offspring from such a marriage may enter the assembly of the LORD, not even in the tenth generation.

³No Ammonite or Moabite or any of their descendants may enter the assembly of the LORD, not even in the tenth generation. ⁴For they did not come to meet you with bread and water on your way when you came out of Egypt, and they hired Balaam son of Beor from Pethor in Aram Naharaim*ᶜ* to pronounce a curse on you. ⁵However, the LORD your God would not listen to Balaam but turned the curse into a blessing for you, because the LORD your God loves you. ⁶Do not seek a treaty of friendship with them as long as you live.

⁷Do not despise an Edomite, for the Edomites are related to you. Do not despise an Egyptian, because you resided as foreigners in their country. ⁸The third generation of children born to them may enter the assembly of the LORD.

Uncleanness in the camp

⁹When you set up camp against your enemies, keep away from everything impure. ¹⁰If one of your men is unclean because of a nocturnal emission, he is to go outside the camp and stay there. ¹¹But as evening approaches he is to wash himself, and at sunset he may return to the camp.

¹²Designate a place outside the camp where you can go to relieve yourself. ¹³As part of your equipment have something to dig with, and when you relieve yourself, dig a hole and cover up your excrement. ¹⁴For the LORD your God moves about in your camp to protect you and to deliver your enemies to you. Your camp must be holy, so that he will not see among you anything indecent and turn away from you.

Miscellaneous laws

¹⁵If a slave has taken refuge with you, do not hand them over to their master. ¹⁶Let them live among you wherever they like and in whatever town they choose. Do not oppress them.

¹⁷No Israelite man or woman is to become a shrine-prostitute. ¹⁸You must not bring the earnings of a female prostitute or of a male prostitute*ᵈ* into the house of the LORD your God to pay any vow, because the LORD your God detests them both.

¹⁹Do not charge an Israelite interest, whether on money or food or anything else that may earn interest. ²⁰You may charge a foreigner interest, but not another Israelite, so that the LORD your God may bless you in everything you put your hand to in the land you are entering to possess.

²¹If you make a vow to the LORD your God, do not be slow to pay it, for the LORD your God will certainly demand it of you and you will be guilty of sin. ²²But if you refrain from making a vow, you will not be guilty. ²³Whatever your lips utter you must be sure to do, because you made your vow freely to the LORD your God with your own mouth.

²⁴If you enter your neighbour's vineyard, you may eat all the grapes you want, but do not put any in your basket. ²⁵If you enter your neighbour's cornfield, you may pick the ears with your hands, but you must not put a sickle to the standing corn.

24 If a man marries a woman who becomes displeasing to him because he finds something indecent about her, and he writes her a certificate of divorce, gives it to her and sends her from his house, ²and if after she leaves his house she becomes the wife of another man, ³and her second husband dislikes her and writes her a certificate of divorce, gives it to her and sends her from his house, or if he dies, ⁴then

---

*ᵃ*29 That is, about 575 grams   *ᵇ*2 Or *one of illegitimate birth*   *ᶜ*4 That is, North-west Mesopotamia   *ᵈ*18 Hebrew *of a dog*

* 22:30 is numbered 23:1 in Hebrew texts.   * 23:1-25 is numbered 23:2-26 in Hebrew texts.

her first husband, who divorced her, is not allowed to marry her again after she has been defiled. That would be detestable in the eyes of the LORD. Do not bring sin upon the land the LORD your God is giving you as an inheritance.

⁵If a man has recently married, he must not be sent to war or have any other duty laid on him. For one year he is to be free to stay at home and bring happiness to the wife he has married.

⁶Do not take a pair of millstones—not even the upper one—as security for a debt, because that would be taking a person's livelihood as security.

⁷If someone is caught kidnapping another Israelite and treating or selling that Israelite as a slave, the kidnapper must die. You must purge the evil from among you.

⁸In cases of defiling skin diseases,ᵃ be very careful to do exactly as the Levitical priests instruct you. You must follow carefully what I have commanded them. ⁹Remember what the LORD your God did to Miriam along the way after you came out of Egypt.

¹⁰When you make a loan of any kind to a neighbour, do not go into the neighbour's house to get what is offered to you as a pledge. ¹¹Stay outside and let the neighbour to whom you are making the loan bring the pledge out to you. ¹²If the neighbour is poor, do not go to sleep with that pledge in your possession. ¹³Return the cloak by sunset so that your neighbour may sleep in it. Then you will be thanked, and it will be regarded as a righteous act in the sight of the LORD your God.

¹⁴Do not take advantage of a hired worker who is poor and needy, whether that worker is an Israelite or is a foreigner residing in one of your towns. ¹⁵Pay them their wages each day before sunset, because they are poor and are counting on it. Otherwise they may cry to the LORD against you, and you will be guilty of sin.

¹⁶Parents are not to be put to death for their children, nor children put to death for their parents; each of you will die for your own sin.

Pledges
Deuteronomy 24:17
A pledge was something that was held as security until a promise had been kept. But the Israelites weren't to take advantage of this practice in a way that would harm the poor. A widow would probably only have one cloak, and if someone held it as a pledge, she would have nothing to keep her warm and protected.

¹⁷Do not deprive the foreigner or the fatherless of justice, or take the cloak of the widow as a pledge. ¹⁸Remember that you were slaves in Egypt and the LORD your God redeemed you from there. That is why I command you to do this.

¹⁹When you are harvesting in your field and you overlook a sheaf, do not go back to get it. Leave it for the foreigner, the fatherless and the widow, so that the LORD your God may bless you in all the work of your hands. ²⁰When you beat the olives from your trees, do not go over the branches a second time. Leave what remains for the foreigner, the fatherless and the widow. ²¹When you harvest the grapes in your vineyard, do not go over the vines again. Leave what remains for the foreigner, the fatherless and the widow. ²²Remember that you were slaves in Egypt. That is why I command you to do this.

25 When people have a dispute, they are to take it to court and the judges will decide the case, acquitting the innocent and condemning the guilty. ²If the one who is guilty deserves to be beaten, the judge shall make them lie down and have them flogged in his presence with the number of

---

ᵃ 8 The Hebrew word for *defiling skin diseases*, traditionally translated 'leprosy', was used for various diseases affecting the skin.

lashes the crime deserves, ³but the judge must not impose more than forty lashes. If the guilty party is flogged more than that, your Israelite neighbour will be degraded in your eyes.

⁴Do not muzzle an ox while it is treading out the grain.

⁵If brothers are living together and one of them dies without a son, his widow must not marry outside the family. Her husband's brother shall take her and marry her and fulfil the duty of a brother-in-law to her. ⁶The first son she bears shall carry on the name of the dead brother so that his name will not be blotted out from Israel.

⁷However, if a man does not want to marry his brother's wife, she shall go to the elders at the town gate and say, 'My husband's brother refuses to carry on his brother's name in Israel. He will not fulfil the duty of a brother-in-law to me.' ⁸Then the elders of his town shall summon him and talk to him. If he persists in saying, 'I do not want to marry her,' ⁹his brother's widow shall go up to him in the presence of the elders, take off one of his sandals, spit in his face and say, 'This is what is done to the man who will not build up his brother's family line.' ¹⁰That man's line shall be known in Israel as The Family of the Unsandalled.

¹¹If two men are fighting and the wife of one of them comes to rescue her husband from his assailant, and she reaches out and seizes him by his private parts, ¹²you shall cut off her hand. Show her no pity.

¹³Do not have two differing weights in your bag—one heavy, one light. ¹⁴Do not have two differing measures in your house—one large, one small. ¹⁵You must have accurate and honest weights and measures, so that you may live long in the land the LORD your God is giving you. ¹⁶For the LORD your God detests anyone who does these things, anyone who deals dishonestly.

¹⁷Remember what the Amalekites did to you along the way when you came out of Egypt. ¹⁸When you were weary and worn out, they met you on your journey and attacked all who were lagging behind; they had no fear of God. ¹⁹When the LORD your God gives you rest from all the enemies around you in the land he is giving you to possess as an inheritance, you shall blot out the name of Amalek from under heaven. Do not forget!

Firstfruits and tithes

26 When you have entered the land that the LORD your God is giving you as an inheritance and have taken possession of it and settled in it, ²take some of the firstfruits of all that you produce from the soil of the land that the LORD your God is giving you and put them in a basket. Then go to the place that the LORD your God will choose as a dwelling for his Name ³and say to the priest in office at the time, 'I declare today to the LORD your God that I have come to the land that the LORD swore to our ancestors to give us.' ⁴The priest shall take the basket from your hands and set it down in front of the altar of the LORD your God. ⁵Then you shall declare before the LORD your God: 'My father was a wandering Aramean, and he went down into Egypt with a few people and lived there and became a great nation, powerful and numerous. ⁶But the Egyptians ill-treated us and made us suffer, subjecting us to harsh labour. ⁷Then we cried out to the LORD, the God of our ancestors, and the LORD heard our voice and saw our misery, toil and oppression. ⁸So the LORD brought us out of Egypt with a mighty hand and an outstretched arm, with great terror and with signs and wonders. ⁹He brought us to this place and gave us this land, a land flowing with milk and honey; ¹⁰and now I bring the firstfruits of the soil that you, LORD, have given me.' Place the basket before the LORD your God and bow down before him. ¹¹Then you and the Levites and the foreigners residing among you shall rejoice in all the good things the LORD your God has given to you and your household.

¹²When you have finished setting aside a tenth of all your produce in the third year, the year of the tithe, you shall give it to the Levite, the foreigner, the fatherless and the widow, so that they may eat in your towns and be satisfied. ¹³Then say to the LORD your God: 'I have removed from my house the sacred portion and have given it to the

Levite, the foreigner, the fatherless and the widow, according to all you commanded. I have not turned aside from your commands nor have I forgotten any of them. 14I have not eaten any of the sacred portion while I was in mourning, nor have I removed any of it while I was unclean, nor have I offered any of it to the dead. I have obeyed the LORD my God; I have done everything you commanded me. 15Look down from heaven, your holy dwelling-place, and bless your people Israel and the land you have given us as you promised on oath to our ancestors, a land flowing with milk and honey.'

Follow the LORD's commands

16The LORD your God commands you this day to follow these decrees and laws; carefully observe them with all your heart and with all your soul. 17You have declared this day that the LORD is your God and that you will walk in obedience to him, that you will keep his decrees, commands and laws—that you will listen to him. 18And the LORD has declared this day that you are his people, his treasured possession as he promised, and that you are to keep all his commands. 19He has declared that he will set you in praise, fame and honour high above all the nations he has made and that you will be a people holy to the LORD your God, as he promised.

The altar on Mount Ebal

27 Moses and the elders of Israel commanded the people: 'Keep all these commands that I give you today. 2When you have crossed the Jordan into the land the LORD your God is giving you, set up some large stones and coat them with plaster. 3Write on them all the words of this law when you have crossed over to enter the land the LORD your God is giving you, a land flowing with milk and honey, just as the LORD, the God of your ancestors, promised you. 4And when you have crossed the Jordan, set up these stones on Mount Ebal, as I command you today, and coat them with plaster. 5Build there an altar to the LORD your God, an altar of stones. Do not use any iron tool on them. 6Build the altar of the LORD your God with stones from the field and offer burnt offerings on it to the LORD your God. 7Sacrifice fellowship offerings there, eating them and rejoicing in the presence of the LORD your God. 8And you shall write very clearly all the words of this law on these stones you have set up.'

Curses from Mount Ebal

9Then Moses and the Levitical priests said to all Israel, 'Be silent, Israel, and listen! You have now become the people of the LORD your God. 10Obey the LORD your God and follow his commands and decrees that I give you today.'

11On the same day Moses commanded the people:

12When you have crossed the Jordan, these tribes shall stand on Mount Gerizim to bless the people: Simeon, Levi, Judah, Issachar, Joseph and Benjamin. 13And these tribes shall stand on Mount Ebal to pronounce curses: Reuben, Gad, Asher, Zebulun, Dan and Naphtali.

14The Levites shall recite to all the people of Israel in a loud voice:

> 15'Cursed is anyone who makes an idol—a thing detestable to the LORD, the work of skilled hands—and sets it up in secret.'
> Then all the people shall say, 'Amen!'
> 16'Cursed is anyone who dishonours their father or mother.'
> Then all the people shall say, 'Amen!'
> 17'Cursed is anyone who moves their neighbour's boundary stone.'
> Then all the people shall say, 'Amen!'
> 18'Cursed is anyone who leads the blind astray on the road.'
> Then all the people shall say, 'Amen!'
> 19'Cursed is anyone who withholds justice from the foreigner, the fatherless or the widow.'
> Then all the people shall say, 'Amen!'
> 20'Cursed is anyone who sleeps with his father's wife, for he dishonours his father's bed.'
> Then all the people shall say, 'Amen!'

21 'Cursed is anyone who has sexual relations with any animal.'
Then all the people shall say,
'Amen!'

22 'Cursed is anyone who sleeps with his sister, the daughter of his father or the daughter of his mother.'
Then all the people shall say,
'Amen!'

23 'Cursed is anyone who sleeps with his mother-in-law.'
Then all the people shall say,
'Amen!'

24 'Cursed is anyone who kills their neighbour secretly.'
Then all the people shall say,
'Amen!'

25 'Cursed is anyone who accepts a bribe to kill an innocent person.'
Then all the people shall say,
'Amen!'

26 'Cursed is anyone who does not uphold the words of this law by carrying them out.'
Then all the people shall say,
'Amen!'

Blessings for obedience

28 If you fully obey the LORD your God and carefully follow all his commands that I give you today, the LORD your God will set you high above all the nations on earth. 2 All these blessings will come on you and accompany you if you obey the LORD your God:

3 You will be blessed in the city and blessed in the country.

4 The fruit of your womb will be blessed, and the crops of your land and the young of your livestock—the calves of your herds and the lambs of your flocks.

5 Your basket and your kneading trough will be blessed.

6 You will be blessed when you come in and blessed when you go out.

7 The LORD will grant that the enemies who rise up against you will be defeated before you. They will come at you from one direction but flee from you in seven.

8 The LORD will send a blessing on your barns and on everything you put your hand to. The LORD your God will bless you in the land he is giving you.

9 The LORD will establish you as his holy people, as he promised you on oath, if you keep the commands of the LORD your God and walk in obedience to him. 10 Then all the peoples on earth will see that you are called by the name of the LORD, and they will fear you. 11 The LORD will grant you abundant prosperity—in the fruit of your womb, the young of your livestock and the crops of your ground—in the land he swore to your ancestors to give you.

12 The LORD will open the heavens, the storehouse of his bounty, to send rain on your land in season and to bless all the work of your hands. You will lend to many nations but will borrow from none. 13 The LORD will make you the head, not the tail. If you pay attention to the commands of the LORD your God that I give you this day and carefully follow them, you will always be at the top, never at the bottom. 14 Do not turn aside from any of the commands I give you today, to the right or to the left, following other gods and serving them.

making Connections

Blessing and cursing
Deuteronomy 28:1

The Israelites have a choice to make. Will they follow God and receive his blessing, or disobey God and end up cursed? Put like that it seems an easy choice to make, but again and again they turned their back on God and went their own way.

Curses for disobedience

15However, if you do not obey the LORD your God and do not carefully follow all his commands and decrees I am giving you today, all these curses will come on you and overtake you:

> 16You will be cursed in the city and cursed in the country.
>
> 17Your basket and your kneading trough will be cursed.
>
> 18The fruit of your womb will be cursed, and the crops of your land, and the calves of your herds and the lambs of your flocks.
>
> 19You will be cursed when you come in and cursed when you go out.

20The LORD will send on you curses, confusion and rebuke in everything you put your hand to, until you are destroyed and come to sudden ruin because of the evil you have done in forsaking him.[a] 21The LORD will plague you with diseases until he has destroyed you from the land you are entering to possess. 22The LORD will strike you with wasting disease, with fever and inflammation, with scorching heat and drought, with blight and mildew, which will plague you until you perish. 23The sky over your head will be bronze, the ground beneath you iron. 24The LORD will turn the rain of your country into dust and powder; it will come down from the skies until you are destroyed.

25The LORD will cause you to be defeated before your enemies. You will come at them from one direction but flee from them in seven, and you will become a thing of horror to all the kingdoms on earth. 26Your carcasses will be food for all the birds and the wild animals, and there will be no-one to frighten them away. 27The LORD will afflict you with the boils of Egypt and with tumours, festering sores and the itch, from which you cannot be cured. 28The LORD will afflict you with madness, blindness and confusion of mind. 29At midday you will grope about like a blind person in the dark. You will be unsuccessful in everything you do; day after day you will be oppressed and robbed, with no-one to rescue you.

30You will be pledged to be married to a woman, but another will take her and ravish her. You will build a house, but you will not live in it. You will plant a vineyard, but you will not even begin to enjoy its fruit. 31Your ox will be slaughtered before your eyes, but you will eat none of it. Your donkey will be forcibly taken from you and will not be returned. Your sheep will be given to your enemies, and no-one will rescue them. 32Your sons and daughters will be given to another nation, and you will wear out your eyes watching for them day after day, powerless to lift a hand. 33A people that you do not know will eat what your land and labour produce, and you will have nothing but cruel oppression all your days. 34The sights you see will drive you mad. 35The LORD will afflict your knees and legs with painful boils that cannot be cured, spreading from the soles of your feet to the top of your head.

36The LORD will drive you and the king you set over you to a nation unknown to you or your ancestors. There you will worship other gods, gods of wood and stone. 37You will become a thing of horror, a byword and an object of ridicule among all the peoples where the LORD will drive you.

38You will sow much seed in the field but you will harvest little, because locusts will devour it. 39You will plant vineyards and cultivate them but you will not drink the wine or gather the grapes, because worms will eat them. 40You will have olive trees throughout your country but you will not use the oil, because the olives will drop off. 41You will have sons and daughters but you will not keep them, because they will go into captivity. 42Swarms of locusts will take over all your trees and the crops of your land.

43The foreigners who reside among you will rise above you higher and higher, but you will sink lower and lower. 44They will lend to you, but you will not lend to them. They will be the head, but you will be the tail.

45All these curses will come on you. They will pursue you and overtake you until you are destroyed, because you did not obey the

---

[a] 20 Hebrew *me*

LORD your God and observe the commands and decrees he gave you. 46They will be a sign and a wonder to you and your descendants for ever. 47Because you did not serve the LORD your God joyfully and gladly in the time of prosperity, 48therefore in hunger and thirst, in nakedness and dire poverty, you will serve the enemies the LORD sends against you. He will put an iron yoke on your neck until he has destroyed you.

49The LORD will bring a nation against you from far away, from the ends of the earth, like an eagle swooping down, a nation whose language you will not understand, 50a fierce-looking nation without respect for the old or pity for the young. 51They will devour the young of your livestock and the crops of your land until you are destroyed. They will leave you no corn, new wine or olive oil, nor any calves of your herds or lambs of your flocks until you are ruined. 52They will lay siege to all the cities throughout your land until the high fortified walls in which you trust fall down. They will besiege all the cities throughout the land the LORD your God is giving you.

53Because of the suffering that your enemy will inflict on you during the siege, you will eat the fruit of the womb, the flesh of the sons and daughters the LORD your God has given you. 54Even the most gentle and sensitive man among you will have no compassion on his own brother or the wife he loves or his surviving children, 55and he will not give to one of them any of the flesh of his children that he is eating. It will be all he has left because of the suffering that your enemy will inflict on you during the siege of all your cities. 56The most gentle and sensitive woman among you—so sensitive and gentle that she would not venture to touch the ground with the sole of her foot—will begrudge the husband she loves and her own son or daughter 57the afterbirth from her womb and the children she bears. For in her dire need she intends to eat them secretly because of the suffering your enemy will inflict on you during the siege of your cities.

58If you do not carefully follow all the words of this law, which are written in this book, and do not revere this glorious and awesome name—the LORD your God— 59the LORD will send fearful plagues on you and your descendants, harsh and prolonged disasters, and severe and lingering illnesses. 60He will bring on you all the diseases of Egypt that you dreaded, and they will cling to you. 61The LORD will also bring on you every kind of sickness and disaster not recorded in this Book of the Law, until you are destroyed. 62You who were as numerous as the stars in the sky will be left but few in number, because you did not obey the LORD your God. 63Just as it pleased the LORD to make you prosper and increase in number, so it will please him to ruin and destroy you. You will be uprooted from the land you are entering to possess.

64Then the LORD will scatter you among all nations, from one end of the earth to the other. There you will worship other gods— gods of wood and stone, which neither you nor your ancestors have known. 65Among those nations you will find no repose, no resting place for the sole of your foot. There the LORD will give you an anxious mind, eyes weary with longing, and a despairing heart. 66You will live in constant suspense, filled with dread both night and day, never sure of your life. 67In the morning you will say, 'If only it were evening!' and in the evening, 'If only it were morning!'—because of the terror that will fill your hearts and the sights that your eyes will see. 68The LORD will send you back in ships to Egypt on a journey I said you should never make again. There you will offer yourselves for sale to your enemies as male and female slaves, but no-one will buy you.

Renewal of the covenant

29 *These are the terms of the covenant the LORD commanded Moses to make with the Israelites in Moab, in addition to the covenant he had made with them at Horeb.

*2Moses summoned all the Israelites and said to them:

Your eyes have seen all that the LORD did in Egypt to Pharaoh, to all his officials and to all his land. 3With your own eyes you saw

---

* 29:1 is numbered 28:69 in Hebrew texts.   * 29:2-29 is numbered 29:1-28 in Hebrew texts.

those great trials, those signs and great wonders. 4But to this day the LORD has not given you a mind that understands or eyes that see or ears that hear. 5During the forty years that I led you through the wilderness, your clothes did not wear out, nor did the sandals on your feet. 6You ate no bread and drank no wine or other fermented drink. I did this so that you might know that I am the LORD your God.

7When you reached this place, Sihon king of Heshbon and Og king of Bashan came out to fight against us, but we defeated them. 8We took their land and gave it as an inheritance to the Reubenites, the Gadites and the half-tribe of Manasseh.

9Carefully follow the terms of this covenant, so that you may prosper in everything you do. 10All of you are standing today in the presence of the LORD your God—your leaders and chief men, your elders and officials, and all the other men of Israel, 11together with your children and your wives, and the foreigners living in your camps who chop your wood and carry your water. 12You are standing here in order to enter into a covenant with the LORD your God, a covenant the LORD is making with you this day and sealing with an oath, 13to confirm you this day as his people, that he may be your God as he promised you and as he swore to your fathers, Abraham, Isaac and Jacob. 14I am making this covenant, with its oath, not only with you 15who are standing here with us today in the presence of the LORD our God but also with those who are not here today.

16You yourselves know how we lived in Egypt and how we passed through the countries on the way here. 17You saw among them their detestable images and idols of wood and stone, of silver and gold. 18Make sure there is no man or woman, clan or tribe among you today whose heart turns away from the LORD our God to go and worship the gods of those nations; make sure there is no root among you that produces such bitter poison.

19When such people hear the words of this oath and invoke a blessing on themselves, thinking, 'I will be safe, even though I persist in going my own way,' they will bring disaster on the watered land as well as the dry. 20The LORD will never be willing to forgive them; his wrath and zeal will burn against them. All the curses written in this book will fall on them, and the LORD will blot out their names from under heaven. 21The LORD will single them out from all the tribes of Israel for disaster, according to all the curses of the covenant written in this Book of the Law.

22Your children who follow you in later generations and foreigners who come from distant lands will see the calamities that have fallen on the land and the diseases with which the LORD has afflicted it. 23The whole land will be a burning waste of salt and sulphur—nothing planted, nothing sprouting, no vegetation growing on it. It will be like the destruction of Sodom and Gomorrah, Admah and Zeboyim, which the LORD overthrew in fierce anger. 24All the nations will ask: 'Why has the LORD done this to this land? Why this fierce, burning anger?'

25And the answer will be: 'It is because this people abandoned the covenant of the LORD, the God of their ancestors, the covenant he made with them when he brought them out of Egypt. 26They went off and worshipped other gods and bowed down to them, gods they did not know, gods he had not given them. 27Therefore the LORD's anger burned against this land, so that he brought on it all the curses written in this book. 28In furious anger and in great wrath the LORD uprooted them from their land and thrust them into another land, as it is now.'

29The secret things belong to the LORD our God, but the things revealed belong to us and to our children for ever, that we may follow all the words of this law.

Prosperity after turning to the LORD

30 When all these blessings and curses I have set before you come on you and you take them to heart wherever the LORD your God disperses you among the nations, 2and when you and your children return to the LORD your God and obey him with all your heart and with all your soul according to everything I command you today, 3then the LORD your God will restore your fortunes*a* and have compassion on you and gather you again from all the nations where he scattered you. 4Even if you have been banished to the most distant land under the heavens, from there the LORD your God will gather you and bring you back. 5He will bring you to the land that belonged to your ancestors, and you will take possession of it. He will make you more prosperous and numerous than your ancestors. 6The LORD your God will circumcise your hearts and the hearts of your descendants, so that you may love him with all your heart and with all your soul, and live. 7The LORD your God will put all these curses on your enemies who hate and persecute you. 8You will again obey the LORD and follow all his commands I am giving you today. 9Then the LORD your God will make you most prosperous in all the work of your hands and in the fruit of your womb, the young of your livestock and the crops of your land. The LORD will again delight in you and make you prosperous, just as he delighted in your ancestors, 10if you obey the LORD your God and keep his commands and decrees that are written in this Book of the Law and turn to the LORD your God with all your heart and with all your soul.

The offer of life or death

11Now what I am commanding you today is not too difficult for you or beyond your reach. 12It is not up in heaven, so that you have to ask, 'Who will ascend into heaven to get it and proclaim it to us so that we may obey it?' 13Nor is it beyond the sea, so that you have to ask, 'Who will cross the sea to get it and proclaim it to us so that we may obey it?' 14No, the word is very near you; it is in your mouth and in your heart so that you may obey it.

15See, I set before you today life and prosperity, death and destruction. 16For I command you today to love the LORD your God, to walk in obedience to him, and to keep his commands, decrees and laws; then you will live and increase, and the LORD your God will bless you in the land you are entering to possess.

17But if your heart turns away and you are not obedient, and if you are drawn away to bow down to other gods and worship them, 18I declare to you this day that you will certainly be destroyed. You will not live long in the land you are crossing the Jordan to enter and possess.

19This day I call the heavens and the earth as witnesses against you that I have set before you life and death, blessings and curses. Now choose life, so that you and your children may live 20and that you may love the LORD your God, listen to his voice, and hold fast to him. For the LORD is your life, and he will give you many years in the land he swore to give to your fathers, Abraham, Isaac and Jacob.

Joshua to succeed Moses

31 Then Moses went out and spoke these words to all Israel: 2'I am now a hundred and twenty years old and I am no longer able to lead you. The LORD has said to me, "You shall not cross the Jordan." 3The LORD your God himself will cross over ahead of you. He will destroy these nations before you, and you will take possession of their land. Joshua also will cross over ahead of you, as the LORD said. 4And the LORD will do to them what he did to Sihon and Og, the kings of the Amorites, whom he destroyed along with their land. 5The LORD will deliver them to you, and you must do to them all that I have commanded you. 6Be strong and courageous. Do not be afraid or terrified because of them, for the LORD your God goes with you; he will never leave you nor forsake you.'

7Then Moses summoned Joshua and said to him in the presence of all Israel, 'Be strong and courageous, for you must go with this people into the land that the LORD swore to their ancestors to give them, and you must divide it among them as their inheritance. 8The LORD himself goes before you and will be with you; he will never leave you nor forsake you. Do not be afraid; do not be discouraged.'

---

a 3 Or *will bring you back from captivity*

People and Places

Joshua
Deuteronomy 31:7

Joshua was Moses' successor and the man who led the people of Israel into the Promised Land. He spent a lot of time learning from Moses as he went with him into the mountains to talk to God. He also served in the tabernacle, staying there as Moses' representative when he was busy. He was one of the spies who went into the land of Canaan to see what it was like; he and Caleb were the only ones who said that they could conquer the land with God's help.

The reading of the law

9So Moses wrote down this law and gave it to the priests, the sons of Levi, who carried the ark of the covenant of the LORD, and to all the elders of Israel. 10Then Moses commanded them: 'At the end of every seven years, in the year for cancelling debts, during the Festival of Tabernacles, 11when all Israel comes to appear before the LORD your God at the place he will choose, you shall read this law before them in their hearing. 12Assemble the people—men, women and children, and the foreigners residing in your towns—so that they can listen and learn to fear the LORD your God and follow carefully all the words of this law. 13Their children, who do not know this law, must hear it and learn to fear the LORD your God as long as you live in the land you are crossing the Jordan to possess.'

Israel's rebellion predicted

14The LORD said to Moses, 'Now the day of your death is near. Call Joshua and present yourselves at the tent of meeting, where I will commission him.' So Moses and Joshua came and presented themselves at the tent of meeting.

15Then the LORD appeared at the tent in a pillar of cloud, and the cloud stood over the entrance to the tent. 16And the LORD said to Moses: 'You are going to rest with your ancestors, and these people will soon prostitute themselves to the foreign gods of the land they are entering. They will forsake me and break the covenant I made with them. 17And in that day I will become angry with them and forsake them; I will hide my face from them, and they will be destroyed. Many disasters and calamities will come on them, and in that day they will ask, "Have not these disasters come on us because our God is not with us?" 18And I will certainly hide my face in that day because of all their wickedness in turning to other gods.

19'Now write down this song and teach it to the Israelites and make them sing it, so that it may be a witness for me against them. 20When I have brought them into the land flowing with milk and honey, the land I promised on oath to their ancestors, and when they eat their fill and thrive, they will turn to other gods and worship them, rejecting me and breaking my covenant. 21And when many disasters and calamities come on them, this song will testify against them, because it will not be forgotten by their descendants. I know what they are disposed to do, even before I bring them into the land I promised them on oath.' 22So Moses wrote down this song that day and taught it to the Israelites.

23The LORD gave this command to Joshua son of Nun: 'Be strong and courageous, for you will bring the Israelites into the land I promised them on oath, and I myself will be with you.'

24After Moses finished writing in a book the words of this law from beginning to end, 25he gave this command to the Levites who carried the ark of the covenant of the LORD: 26'Take this Book of the Law and place it beside the ark of the covenant of the LORD your God. There it will remain as a witness against you. 27For I know how rebellious and stiff-necked you are. If you have been rebellious against the LORD while I am still alive and with you, how much more will you rebel after I die! 28Assemble before me all the elders of your tribes and all your

> **IN OTHER WORDS**
>
> **Stiff-necked**
> Deuteronomy 31:27
> This is a great figure of speech meaning people who are obstinate, arrogant and proud. It's taken from stubborn oxen who would turn their shoulders away from the yoke and refuse to follow directions, and it's used quite a few times in the Bible about the Israelites.

officials, so that I can speak these words in their hearing and call the heavens and the earth to testify against them. 29For I know that after my death you are sure to become utterly corrupt and to turn from the way I have commanded you. In days to come, disaster will fall on you because you will do evil in the sight of the LORD and arouse his anger by what your hands have made.'

The song of Moses

30And Moses recited the words of this song from beginning to end in the hearing of the whole assembly of Israel:

32 Listen, you heavens, and I will speak;
   hear, you earth, the words of my mouth.
2Let my teaching fall like rain
   and my words descend like dew,
like showers on new grass,
   like abundant rain on tender plants.

3I will proclaim the name of the LORD.
   Oh, praise the greatness of our God!
4He is the Rock, his works are perfect,
   and all his ways are just.
A faithful God who does no wrong,
   upright and just is he.

5They are corrupt and not his children;
   to their shame they are a warped and crooked generation.
6Is this the way you repay the LORD,
   you foolish and unwise people?
Is he not your Father, your Creator,^{a}
   who made you and formed you?

7Remember the days of old;
   consider the generations long past.
Ask your father and he will tell you,
   your elders, and they will explain to you.
8When the Most High gave the nations their inheritance,
   when he divided all the human race,
he set up boundaries for the peoples
   according to the number of the sons of Israel.^{b}
9For the LORD's portion is his people,
   Jacob his allotted inheritance.

10In a desert land he found him,
   in a barren and howling waste.
He shielded him and cared for him;
   he guarded him as the apple of his eye,
11like an eagle that stirs up its nest
   and hovers over its young,
that spreads its wings to catch them
   and carries them on its pinions.
12The LORD alone led him;
   no foreign god was with him.

> **making Connections**
>
> **God the Rock**
> Deuteronomy 32:4
> At first sight this might not seem a very flattering name for God. But Moses, who wrote these words, had climbed mountains and seen them as he journeyed through the wilderness. His choice of this word symbolises God's strength and stability. God is faithful and can be depended on. He doesn't change and will live forever. He offers protection and shelter.

---
^{a} 6 Or *Father, who bought you* ^{b} 8 Masoretic Text; Dead Sea Scrolls (see also Septuagint) *sons of God*

¹³He made him ride on the heights of the land
  and fed him with the fruit of the fields.
He nourished him with honey from the rock,
  and with oil from the flinty crag,
¹⁴with curds and milk from herd and flock
  and with fattened lambs and goats,
with choice rams of Bashan
  and the finest grains of wheat.
You drank the foaming blood of the grape.

¹⁵Jeshurun[a] grew fat and kicked;
  filled with food, he became heavy and sleek.
He abandoned the God who made him
  and rejected the Rock his Saviour.
¹⁶They made him jealous with their foreign gods
  and angered him with their detestable idols.
¹⁷They sacrificed to demons, which are not God—
  gods they had not known,
  gods that recently appeared,
  gods your ancestors did not fear.
¹⁸You deserted the Rock, who bore you;
  you forgot the God who gave you birth.

¹⁹The LORD saw this and rejected them
  because he was angered by his sons and daughters.
²⁰'I will hide my face from them,' he said,
  'and see what their end will be;
for they are a perverse generation,
  children who are unfaithful.
²¹They made me jealous by what is no god
  and angered me with their worthless idols.
I will make them envious by those who are not a people;
  I will make them angry by a nation that has no understanding.
²²For a fire will be kindled by my wrath,
  one that burns down to the realm of the dead below.
It will devour the earth and its harvests
  and set on fire the foundations of the mountains.

²³'I will heap calamities on them
  and expend my arrows against them.
²⁴I will send wasting famine against them,
  consuming pestilence and deadly plague;
I will send against them the fangs of wild beasts,
  the venom of vipers that glide in the dust.
²⁵In the street the sword will make them childless;
  in their homes terror will reign.
The young men and young women will perish,
  the infants and those with grey hair.
²⁶I said I would scatter them
  and erase their name from human memory,
²⁷but I dreaded the taunt of the enemy,
  lest the adversary misunderstand
and say, "Our hand has triumphed;
  the LORD has not done all this."'

²⁸They are a nation without sense,
  there is no discernment in them.
²⁹If only they were wise and would understand this
  and discern what their end will be!
³⁰How could one man chase a thousand,
  or two put ten thousand to flight,
unless their Rock had sold them,
  unless the LORD had given them up?
³¹For their rock is not like our Rock,
  as even our enemies concede.
³²Their vine comes from the vine of Sodom
  and from the fields of Gomorrah.
Their grapes are filled with poison,
  and their clusters with bitterness.
³³Their wine is the venom of serpents,
  the deadly poison of cobras.

³⁴'Have I not kept this in reserve
  and sealed it in my vaults?
³⁵It is mine to avenge; I will repay.
  In due time their foot will slip;
their day of disaster is near
  and their doom rushes upon them.'

³⁶The LORD will vindicate his people
  and relent concerning his servants
when he sees their strength is gone
  and no-one is left, slave or free.[b]

---

[a] 15 *Jeshurun* means *the upright one,* that is, *Israel.* [b] 36 Or *and they are without a ruler or leader*

37He will say: 'Now where are their gods,
   the rock they took refuge in,
38the gods who ate the fat of their sacrifices
   and drank the wine of their drink
      offerings?
   Let them rise up to help you!
   Let them give you shelter!

39'See now that I myself am He!
   There is no god besides me.
   I put to death and I bring to life,
   I have wounded and I will heal,
   and no-one can deliver out of my hand.
40I lift my hand to heaven and declare:
   as surely as I live for ever,
41when I sharpen my flashing sword
   and my hand grasps it in judgment,
   I will take vengeance on my adversaries
   and repay those who hate me.
42I will make my arrows drunk with blood,
   while my sword devours flesh:
   the blood of the slain and the captives,
   the heads of the enemy leaders.'

43Rejoice, you nations, with his people,[a,b]
   for he will avenge the blood of his
      servants;
   he will take vengeance on his enemies
   and make atonement for his land and
      people.

44Moses came with Joshua[c] son of Nun and spoke all the words of this song in the hearing of the people. 45When Moses had finished reciting all these words to all Israel, 46he said to them, 'Take to heart all the words I have solemnly declared to you this day, so that you may command your children to obey carefully all the words of this law. 47They are not just idle words for you—they are your life. By them you will live long in the land you are crossing the Jordan to possess.'

Moses to die on Mount Nebo

48On that same day the LORD told Moses, 49'Go up into the Abarim Range to Mount Nebo in Moab, opposite Jericho, and view Canaan, the land I am giving the Israelites as their own possession. 50There on the mountain that you have climbed you will die and be gathered to your people, just as your brother Aaron died on Mount Hor and was gathered to his people. 51This is because both of you broke faith with me in the presence of the Israelites at the waters of Meribah Kadesh in the Desert of Zin and because you did not uphold my holiness among the Israelites. 52Therefore, you will see the land only from a distance; you will not enter the land I am giving to the people of Israel.'

Moses blesses the tribes

33 This is the blessing that Moses the man of God pronounced on the Israelites before his death. 2He said:

'The LORD came from Sinai
   and dawned over them from Seir;
   he shone forth from Mount Paran.
He came with[d] myriads of holy ones
   from the south, from his mountain
      slopes.[e]
3Surely it is you who love the people;
   all the holy ones are in your hand.
At your feet they all bow down,
   and from you receive instruction,
4the law that Moses gave us,
   the possession of the assembly of Jacob.
5He was king over Jeshurun[f]
   when the leaders of the people
      assembled,
   along with the tribes of Israel.

6'Let Reuben live and not die,
   nor[g] his people be few.'

7And this he said about Judah:

'Hear, LORD, the cry of Judah;
   bring him to his people.
With his own hands he defends his cause.
   Oh, be his help against his foes!'

8About Levi he said:

'Your Thummim and Urim belong
   to your faithful servant.
You tested him at Massah;
   you contended with him at the waters
      of Meribah.
9He said of his father and mother,
   "I have no regard for them."

---

[a] 43 Or *Make his people rejoice, you nations* [b] 43 Masoretic Text; Dead Sea Scrolls (see also Septuagint) *people, / and let all the angels worship him /* [c] 44 Hebrew *Hoshea*, a variant of *Joshua* [d] 2 Or *from* [e] 2 The meaning of the Hebrew for this phrase is uncertain. [f] 5 *Jeshurun* means *the upright one*, that is, Israel; also in verse 26. [g] 6 Or *but let*

He did not recognise his brothers
or acknowledge his own children,
but he watched over your word
and guarded your covenant.
¹⁰He teaches your precepts to Jacob
and your law to Israel.
He offers incense before you
and whole burnt offerings on your altar.
¹¹Bless all his skills, LORD,
and be pleased with the work of his hands.
Strike down those who rise against him,
his foes till they rise no more.'

¹²About Benjamin he said:

'Let the beloved of the LORD rest secure in him,
for he shields him all day long,
and the one the LORD loves rests between his shoulders.'

¹³About Joseph he said:

'May the LORD bless his land
with the precious dew from heaven above
and with the deep waters that lie below;
¹⁴with the best the sun brings forth
and the finest the moon can yield;
¹⁵with the choicest gifts of the ancient mountains
and the fruitfulness of the everlasting hills;
¹⁶with the best gifts of the earth and its fulness
and the favour of him who dwelt in the burning bush.
Let all these rest on the head of Joseph,
on the brow of the prince among[a] his brothers.
¹⁷In majesty he is like a firstborn bull;
his horns are the horns of a wild ox.
With them he will gore the nations,
even those at the ends of the earth.
Such are the ten thousands of Ephraim;
such are the thousands of Manasseh.'

¹⁸About Zebulun he said:

'Rejoice, Zebulun, in your going out,
and you, Issachar, in your tents.
¹⁹They will summon peoples to the mountain
and there offer the sacrifices of the righteous;
they will feast on the abundance of the seas,
on the treasures hidden in the sand.'

²⁰About Gad he said:

'Blessed is he who enlarges Gad's domain!
Gad lives there like a lion,
tearing at arm or head.
²¹He chose the best land for himself;
the leader's portion was kept for him.
When the heads of the people assembled,
he carried out the LORD's righteous will,
and his judgments concerning Israel.'

²²About Dan he said:

'Dan is a lion's cub,
springing out of Bashan.'

²³About Naphtali he said:

'Naphtali is abounding with the favour of the LORD
and is full of his blessing;
he will inherit southward to the lake.'

²⁴About Asher he said:

'Most blessed of sons is Asher;
let him be favoured by his brothers,
and let him bathe his feet in oil.
²⁵The bolts of your gates will be iron and bronze,
and your strength will equal your days.

²⁶'There is no-one like the God of Jeshurun,
who rides on the heavens to help you
and on the clouds in his majesty.
²⁷The eternal God is your refuge,
and underneath are the everlasting arms.
He will drive out your enemies before you,
saying, "Destroy them!"
²⁸So Israel will live in safety;
Jacob will dwell[b] secure
in a land of grain and new wine,
where the heavens drop dew.
²⁹Blessed are you, Israel!

---

[a] 16 Or *of the one separated from*   [b] 28 Septuagint; Hebrew *Jacob's spring is*

> **IN OTHER WORDS**
>
> **Eternal**
> **Deuteronomy 33:27**
> 'Eternal' means 'existing always', something that lasts forever without an end. God is eternal and so is the life that he offers people who trust him (John 3:16).

Who is like you,
 a people saved by the LORD?
He is your shield and helper
 and your glorious sword.
Your enemies will cower before you,
 and you will tread on their heights.'

The death of Moses

34 Then Moses climbed Mount Nebo from the plains of Moab to the top of Pisgah, opposite Jericho. There the LORD showed him the whole land—from Gilead to Dan, ²all of Naphtali, the territory of Ephraim and Manasseh, all the land of Judah as far as the Mediterranean Sea, ³the Negev and the whole region from the Valley of Jericho, the City of Palms, as far as Zoar. ⁴Then the LORD said to him, 'This is the land I promised on oath to Abraham, Isaac and Jacob when I said, "I will give it to your descendants." I have let you see it with your eyes, but you will not cross over into it.'

⁵And Moses the servant of the LORD died there in Moab, as the LORD had said. ⁶He buried him*ᵃ* in Moab, in the valley opposite Beth Peor, but to this day no-one knows where his grave is. ⁷Moses was a hundred and twenty years old when he died, yet his eyes were not weak nor his strength gone. ⁸The Israelites grieved for Moses in the plains of Moab thirty days, until the time of weeping and mourning was over.

⁹Now Joshua son of Nun was filled with the spirit*ᵇ* of wisdom because Moses had laid his hands on him. So the Israelites listened to him and did what the LORD had commanded Moses.

¹⁰Since then, no prophet has risen in Israel like Moses, whom the LORD knew face to face, ¹¹who did all those signs and wonders the LORD sent him to do in Egypt—to Pharaoh and to all his officials and to his whole land. ¹²For no-one has ever shown the mighty power or performed the awesome deeds that Moses did in the sight of all Israel.

---

*ᵃ*6 Or *He was buried* *ᵇ*9 Or *Spirit*

Joshua

INTRODUCTION

JOSHUA

Author: Joshua wrote most of it.

When: The first twenty-five years in Canaan, probably around 1400 BC to 1375 BC.

Where: Canaan, the Promised Land.

Did you know? The name Joshua means 'the Lord is salvation' and comes from the Hebrew form of the name Jesus.

Main theme: At last, the people of Israel get to enter the Promised Land after so many years wandering in the wilderness. It can't have been easy for Joshua to take over from such a great man as Moses, but he's a strong leader and up to the task. The Israelites drive out the Canaanites and divide up the land between them. But because they don't completely wipe out the pagan religions, they keep getting tempted to worship false gods instead of the one true God.

The LORD commands Joshua

1 After the death of Moses the servant of the LORD, the LORD said to Joshua son of Nun, Moses' assistant: ²'Moses my servant is dead. Now then, you and all these people, get ready to cross the River Jordan into the land I am about to give to them—to the Israelites. ³I will give you every place where you set your foot, as I promised Moses. ⁴Your territory will extend from the desert to Lebanon, and from the great river, the Euphrates—all the Hittite country—to the Mediterranean Sea in the west. ⁵No-one will be able to stand against you all the days of your life. As I was with Moses, so I will be with you; I will never leave you nor forsake you. ⁶Be strong and courageous, because you will lead these people to inherit the land I swore to their ancestors to give them.

⁷'Be strong and very courageous. Be careful to obey all the law my servant Moses gave you; do not turn from it to the right or to the left, that you may be successful wherever you go. ⁸Keep this Book of the

Law always on your lips; meditate on it day and night, so that you may be careful to do everything written in it. Then you will be prosperous and successful. ⁹Have I not commanded you? Be strong and courageous. Do not be afraid; do not be discouraged, for the LORD your God will be with you wherever you go.'

¹⁰So Joshua ordered the officers of the people: ¹¹'Go through the camp and tell the people, "Get your provisions ready. Three days from now you will cross the Jordan here to go in and take possession of the land the LORD your God is giving you for your own."'

¹²But to the Reubenites, the Gadites and the half-tribe of Manasseh, Joshua said, ¹³'Remember the command that Moses the servant of the LORD gave you after he said, "The LORD your God will give you rest by giving you this land." ¹⁴Your wives, your children and your livestock may stay in the land that Moses gave you east of the Jordan, but all your fighting men, ready for battle, must cross over ahead of the other Israelites. You are to help them ¹⁵until the LORD gives them rest, as he has done for you, and until they too have taken possession of the land that the LORD your God is giving them. After that, you may go back and occupy your own land, which Moses the servant of the LORD gave you east of the Jordan towards the sunrise.'

¹⁶Then they answered Joshua, 'Whatever you have commanded us we will do, and wherever you send us we will go. ¹⁷Just as we fully obeyed Moses, so we will obey you. Only may the LORD your God be with you as he was with Moses. ¹⁸Whoever rebels against your word and does not obey it, whatever you may command them, is to be put to death. Only be strong and courageous!'

Rahab and the spies

2 Then Joshua son of Nun secretly sent two spies from Shittim. 'Go, look over the land,' he said, 'especially Jericho.' So they went and entered the house of a prostitute named Rahab and stayed there.

²The king of Jericho was told, 'Look! Some of the Israelites have come here tonight to spy out the land.' ³So the king of Jericho sent this message to Rahab: 'Bring out the men who came to you and entered your house, because they have come to spy out the whole land.'

⁴But the woman had taken the two men and hidden them. She said, 'Yes, the men came to me, but I did not know where they had come from. ⁵At dusk, when it was time to close the city gate, they left. I don't know which way they went. Go after them quickly. You may catch up with them.' ⁶(But she had taken them up to the roof and hidden them under the stalks of flax she had laid out on the roof.) ⁷So the men set out in pursuit of the spies on the road that leads to the fords of the Jordan, and as soon as the pursuers had gone out, the gate was shut.

⁸Before the spies lay down for the night, she went up on the roof ⁹and said to them, 'I know that the LORD has given this land to you and that a great fear of you has fallen on us, so that all who live in this country are melting in fear because of you. ¹⁰We have heard how the LORD dried up the water of the Red Sea[a] for you when you came out of Egypt, and what you did to Sihon and Og, the two kings of the Amorites east of the Jordan, whom you completely destroyed.[b] ¹¹When we heard of it, our hearts sank[c] and everyone's courage failed because of you, for the LORD your God is God in heaven above and on the earth below.

¹²'Now then, please swear to me by the LORD that you will show kindness to my family, because I have shown kindness to you. Give me a sure sign ¹³that you will spare the lives of my father and mother, my brothers and sisters, and all who belong to them—and that you will save us from death.'

¹⁴'Our lives for your lives!' the men assured her. 'If you don't tell what we are doing, we will treat you kindly and faithfully when the LORD gives us the land.'

¹⁵So she let them down by a rope through the window, for the house she lived in was part of the city wall. ¹⁶She said to them, 'Go

---

[a] 10 Or *the Sea of Reeds* [b] 10 The Hebrew term refers to the irrevocable giving over of things or persons to the LORD, often by totally destroying them. [c] 11 Hebrew *melted in fear*

to the hills so that the pursuers will not find you. Hide yourselves there for three days until they return, and then go on your way.'

17Now the men had said to her, 'This oath you made us swear will not be binding on us 18unless, when we enter the land, you have tied this scarlet cord in the window through which you let us down, and unless you have brought your father and mother, your brothers and all your family into your house. 19If any of them go outside your house into the street, their blood will be on their own heads; we will not be responsible. As for those who are in the house with you, their blood will be on our head if a hand is laid on them. 20But if you tell what we are doing, we will be released from the oath you made us swear.'

21'Agreed,' she replied. 'Let it be as you say.' So she sent them away, and they departed. And she tied the scarlet cord in the window.

22When they left, they went into the hills and stayed there three days, until the pursuers had searched all along the road and returned without finding them. 23Then the two men started back. They went down out of the hills, forded the river and came to Joshua son of Nun and told him everything that had happened to them. 24They said to Joshua, 'The LORD has surely given the whole land into our hands; all the people are melting in fear because of us.'

Crossing the Jordan

3 Early in the morning Joshua and all the Israelites set out from Shittim and went to the Jordan, where they camped before crossing over. 2After three days the officers went throughout the camp, 3giving orders to the people: 'When you see the ark of the covenant of the LORD your God, and the Levitical priests carrying it, you are to move out from your positions and follow it. 4Then you will know which way to go, since you have never been this way before. But keep a distance of about two thousand cubits[a] between you and the ark; do not go near it.'

5Joshua told the people, 'Consecrate yourselves, for tomorrow the LORD will do amazing things among you.'

6Joshua said to the priests, 'Take up the ark of the covenant and pass on ahead of the people.' So they took it up and went ahead of them.

7And the LORD said to Joshua, 'Today I will begin to exalt you in the eyes of all Israel, so that they may know that I am with you as I was with Moses. 8Tell the priests who carry the ark of the covenant: "When you reach the edge of the Jordan's waters, go and stand in the river."'

9Joshua said to the Israelites, 'Come here and listen to the words of the LORD your God. 10This is how you will know that the living God is among you and that he will certainly drive out before you the Canaanites, Hittites, Hivites, Perizzites, Girgashites, Amorites and Jebusites. 11See, the ark of the covenant of the Lord of all the earth will go into the Jordan ahead of you. 12Now then, choose twelve men from the tribes of Israel, one from each tribe. 13And as soon as the priests who carry the ark of the LORD—the Lord of all the earth—set foot in the Jordan, its waters flowing downstream will be cut off and stand up in a heap.'

14So when the people broke camp to cross the Jordan, the priests carrying the ark of the covenant went ahead of them. 15Now the Jordan is in flood all during harvest. Yet as soon as the priests who carried the ark reached the Jordan and their feet touched the water's edge, 16the water from upstream stopped flowing. It piled up in a heap a great distance away, at a town called Adam in the vicinity of Zarethan, while the water flowing down to the Sea of the Arabah (that is, the Dead Sea) was completely cut off. So the people crossed over opposite Jericho. 17The priests who carried the ark of the covenant of the LORD stopped in the middle of the Jordan and stood on dry ground, while all Israel passed by until the whole nation had completed the crossing on dry ground.

---

[a] 4 That is, about 900 metres

Sign of the times

Stone memorials
Joshua 4:2

Leaving behind this pile of rocks was a visual and permanent reminder of how God had enabled the Israelites to cross the River Jordan. It was a way of saying 'We were here!', as well as 'God was with us.' Joshua wanted to make sure that the Israelites passed the story on to their children and grandchildren, so that they would never forget God's faithfulness.

4 When the whole nation had finished crossing the Jordan, the LORD said to Joshua, 2'Choose twelve men from among the people, one from each tribe, 3and tell them to take up twelve stones from the middle of the Jordan, from right where the priests are standing, and carry them over with you and put them down at the place where you stay tonight.'

4So Joshua called together the twelve men he had appointed from the Israelites, one from each tribe, 5and said to them, 'Go over before the ark of the LORD your God into the middle of the Jordan. Each of you is to take up a stone on his shoulder, according to the number of the tribes of the Israelites, 6to serve as a sign among you. In the future, when your children ask you, "What do these stones mean?" 7tell them that the flow of the Jordan was cut off before the ark of the covenant of the LORD. When it crossed the Jordan, the waters of the Jordan were cut off. These stones are to be a memorial to the people of Israel for ever.'

8So the Israelites did as Joshua commanded them. They took twelve stones from the middle of the Jordan, according to the number of the tribes of the Israelites, as the LORD had told Joshua; and they carried them over with them to their camp, where they put them down. 9Joshua set up the twelve stones that had been^a in the middle of the Jordan at the spot where the priests who carried the ark of the covenant had stood. And they are there to this day.

10Now the priests who carried the ark remained standing in the middle of the Jordan until everything the LORD had commanded Joshua was done by the people, just as Moses had directed Joshua. The people hurried over, 11and as soon as all of them had crossed, the ark of the LORD and the priests came to the other side while the people watched. 12The men of Reuben, Gad and the half-tribe of Manasseh crossed over, ready for battle, in front of the Israelites, as Moses had directed them. 13About forty thousand armed for battle crossed over before the LORD to the plains of Jericho for war.

14That day the LORD exalted Joshua in the sight of all Israel; and they stood in awe of him all the days of his life, just as they had stood in awe of Moses.

15Then the LORD said to Joshua, 16'Command the priests carrying the ark of the covenant law to come up out of the Jordan.'

17So Joshua commanded the priests, 'Come up out of the Jordan.'

18And the priests came up out of the river carrying the ark of the covenant of the LORD. No sooner had they set their feet on the dry ground than the waters of the Jordan returned to their place and ran in flood as before.

19On the tenth day of the first month the people went up from the Jordan and camped at Gilgal on the eastern border of Jericho. 20And Joshua set up at Gilgal the twelve stones they had taken out of the Jordan. 21He said to the Israelites, 'In the future when your descendants ask their parents, "What do these stones mean?" 22tell them, "Israel crossed the Jordan on dry ground." 23For the LORD your God dried up the Jordan before you until you had crossed over. The LORD your God did to the Jordan what he had done to the Red Sea^b when he dried it up before us until we had crossed over. 24He did this so that all the

---

^{a}9 Or *Joshua also set up twelve stones* ^{b}23 Or *the Sea of Reeds* peoples of the earth might know that the hand of the LORD is powerful and so that you might always fear the LORD your God.'

5 Now when all the Amorite kings west of the Jordan and all the Canaanite kings along the coast heard how the LORD had dried up the Jordan before the Israelites until they[a] had crossed over, their hearts melted in fear and they no longer had the courage to face the Israelites.

Circumcision and passover at Gilgal

2At that time the LORD said to Joshua, 'Make flint knives and circumcise the Israelites again.' 3So Joshua made flint knives and circumcised the Israelites at Gibeath Haaraloth.[b]

4Now this is why he did so: all those who came out of Egypt—all the men of military age—died in the wilderness on the way after leaving Egypt. 5All the people that came out had been circumcised, but all the people born in the wilderness during the journey from Egypt had not. 6The Israelites had moved about in the wilderness for forty years until all the men who were of military age when they left Egypt had died, since they had not obeyed the LORD. For the LORD had sworn to them that they would not see the land that he had solemnly promised their ancestors to give us, a land flowing with milk and honey. 7So he raised up their sons in their place, and these were the ones Joshua circumcised. They were still uncircumcised because they had not been circumcised on the way. 8And after the whole nation had been circumcised, they remained where they were in camp until they were healed.

9Then the LORD said to Joshua, 'Today I have rolled away the reproach of Egypt from you.' So the place has been called Gilgal[c] to this day.

10On the evening of the fourteenth day of the month, while camped at Gilgal on the plains of Jericho, the Israelites celebrated the Passover. 11The day after the Passover, that very day, they ate some of the produce of the land: unleavened bread and roasted grain. 12The manna stopped the day after[d] they ate this food from the land; there was no longer any manna for the Israelites, but that year they ate of the produce of Canaan.

The fall of Jericho

13Now when Joshua was near Jericho, he looked up and saw a man standing in front of him with a drawn sword in his hand. Joshua went up to him and asked, 'Are you for us or for our enemies?'

14'Neither,' he replied, 'but as commander of the army of the LORD I have now come.' Then Joshua fell face down to the ground in reverence, and asked him, 'What message does my Lord[e] have for his servant?'

15The commander of the LORD's army replied, 'Take off your sandals, for the place where you are standing is holy.' And Joshua did so.

6 Now the gates of Jericho were securely barred because of the Israelites. No-one went out and no-one came in.

2Then the LORD said to Joshua, 'See, I have delivered Jericho into your hands, along with its king and its fighting men.

People and Places

Jericho
Joshua 6:1

Jericho is one of the oldest inhabited cities in the world. Several cities have been built on the same site – the one Joshua destroyed was probably the fourth – and lots of archaeological digs have taken place there over the years. This Jericho was built with mud bricks, so most of its remains have been washed away. But it's thought that it had high double walls, each several feet thick. It was certainly a crowded town because people like Rahab had their houses on its walls.

---

[a]1 Another textual tradition *we* [b]3 *Gibeath Haaraloth* means *the hill of foreskins.* [c]9 *Gilgal* sounds like the Hebrew for *roll.* [d]12 Or *the day* [e]14 Or *lord*

³March round the city once with all the armed men. Do this for six days. ⁴Make seven priests carry trumpets of rams' horns in front of the ark. On the seventh day, march round the city seven times, with the priests blowing the trumpets. ⁵When you hear them sound a long blast on the trumpets, make the whole army give a loud shout; then the wall of the city will collapse and the army will go up, everyone straight in.'

⁶So Joshua son of Nun called the priests and said to them, 'Take up the ark of the covenant of the LORD and make seven priests carry trumpets in front of it.' ⁷And he ordered the army, 'Advance! March round the city, with an armed guard going ahead of the ark of the LORD.'

⁸When Joshua had spoken to the people, the seven priests carrying the seven trumpets before the LORD went forward, blowing their trumpets, and the ark of the LORD's covenant followed them. ⁹The armed guard marched ahead of the priests who blew the trumpets, and the rear guard followed the ark. All this time the trumpets were sounding. ¹⁰But Joshua had commanded the army, 'Do not give a war cry, do not raise your voices, do not say a word until the day I tell you to shout. Then shout!' ¹¹So he had the ark of the LORD carried round the city, circling it once. Then the army returned to camp and spent the night there.

¹²Joshua got up early the next morning and the priests took up the ark of the LORD. ¹³The seven priests carrying the seven trumpets went forwards, marching before the ark of the LORD and blowing the trumpets. The armed men went ahead of them and the rear guard followed the ark of the LORD, while the trumpets kept sounding. ¹⁴So on the second day they marched round the city once and returned to the camp. They did this for six days.

¹⁵On the seventh day, they got up at daybreak and marched round the city seven times in the same manner, except that on that day they circled the city seven times. ¹⁶The seventh time round, when the priests sounded the trumpet blast, Joshua commanded the army, 'Shout! For the LORD has given you the city! ¹⁷The city and all that is in it are to be devoted*ᵃ* to the LORD. Only Rahab the prostitute and all who are with her in her house shall be spared, because she hid the spies we sent. ¹⁸But keep away from the devoted things, so that you will not bring about your own destruction by taking any of them. Otherwise you will make the camp of Israel liable to destruction and bring trouble on it. ¹⁹All the silver and gold and the articles of bronze and iron are sacred to the LORD and must go into his treasury.'

²⁰When the trumpets sounded, the army shouted, and at the sound of the trumpet, when the men gave a loud shout, the wall collapsed; so everyone charged straight in, and they took the city. ²¹They devoted the city to the LORD and destroyed with the sword every living thing in it—men and women, young and old, cattle, sheep and donkeys.

²²Joshua said to the two men who had spied out the land, 'Go into the prostitute's house and bring her out and all who belong to her, in accordance with your oath to her.' ²³So the young men who had done the spying went in and brought out Rahab, her father and mother, her brothers and sisters and all who belonged to her. They brought out her entire family and put them in a place outside the camp of Israel.

²⁴Then they burned the whole city and everything in it, but they put the silver and gold and the articles of bronze and iron into the treasury of the LORD's house. ²⁵But Joshua spared Rahab the prostitute, with her family and all who belonged to her, because she hid the men Joshua had sent as spies to Jericho—and she lives among the Israelites to this day.

²⁶At that time Joshua pronounced this solemn oath: 'Cursed before the LORD is anyone who undertakes to rebuild this city, Jericho:

> 'At the cost of his firstborn son
>   he will lay its foundations;
> at the cost of his youngest
>   he will set up its gates.'

ᵃ 17 The Hebrew term refers to the irrevocable giving over of things or persons to the LORD, often by totally destroying them; also in verses 18 and 21.

27So the LORD was with Joshua, and his fame spread throughout the land.

Achan's sin

7 But the Israelites were unfaithful in regard to the devoted things;*a* Achan son of Karmi, the son of Zimri,*b* the son of Zerah, of the tribe of Judah, took some of them. So the LORD's anger burned against Israel.

2Now Joshua sent men from Jericho to Ai,*c* which is near Beth Aven to the east of Bethel, and told them, 'Go up and spy out the region.' So the men went up and spied out Ai.

3When they returned to Joshua, they said, 'Not all the army will have to go up against Ai. Send two or three thousand men to take it and do not weary the whole army, for only a few people live there.' 4So about three thousand went up; but they were routed by the men of Ai, 5who killed about thirty-six of them. They chased the Israelites from the city gate as far as the stone quarries and struck them down on the slopes. At this the hearts of the people melted in fear and became like water.

6Then Joshua tore his clothes and fell face down to the ground before the ark of the LORD, remaining there till evening. The elders of Israel did the same, and sprinkled dust on their heads. 7And Joshua said, 'Ah, Sovereign LORD, why did you ever bring this people across the Jordan to deliver us into the hands of the Amorites to destroy us? If only we had been content to stay on the other side of the Jordan! 8Pardon your servant, Lord. What can I say, now that Israel has been routed by its enemies? 9The Canaanites and the other people of the country will hear about this and they will surround us and wipe out our name from the earth. What then will you do for your own great name?'

10The LORD said to Joshua, 'Stand up! What are you doing down on your face? 11Israel has sinned; they have violated my covenant, which I commanded them to keep. They have taken some of the devoted things; they have stolen, they have lied, they have put them with their own possessions. 12That is why the Israelites cannot stand against their enemies; they turn their backs and run because they have been made liable to destruction. I will not be with you any more unless you destroy whatever among you is devoted to destruction.

13'Go, consecrate the people. Tell them, "Consecrate yourselves in preparation for tomorrow; for this is what the LORD, the God of Israel, says: there are devoted things among you, Israel. You cannot stand against your enemies until you remove them.

14'"In the morning, present yourselves tribe by tribe. The tribe that the LORD chooses shall come forward clan by clan; the clan that the LORD chooses shall come forward family by family; and the family that the LORD chooses shall come forward man by man. 15Whoever is caught with the devoted things shall be destroyed by fire, along with all that belongs to him. He has violated the covenant of the LORD and has done an outrageous thing in Israel!"'

16Early the next morning Joshua made Israel come forward by tribes, and Judah was chosen. 17The clans of Judah came forward, and the Zerahites were chosen. He made the clan of the Zerahites come forward by families, and Zimri was chosen. 18Joshua made his family come forward man by man, and Achan son of Karmi, the son of Zimri, the son of Zerah, of the tribe of Judah, was chosen.

19Then Joshua said to Achan, 'My son, give glory to the LORD, the God of Israel, and honour him. Tell me what you have done; do not hide it from me.'

20Achan replied, 'It is true! I have sinned against the LORD, the God of Israel. This is what I have done: 21when I saw in the plunder a beautiful robe from Babylonia,*d* two hundred shekels*e* of silver and a bar of gold weighing fifty shekels,*f* I coveted them and took them. They are hidden in the ground inside my tent, with the silver underneath.'

22So Joshua sent messengers, and they ran to the tent, and there it was, hidden in

---

a 1 The Hebrew term refers to the irrevocable giving over of things or persons to the LORD, often by totally destroying them; also in verses 11, 12, 13 and 15.   *b* 1 See Septuagint and 1 Chron. 2:6; Hebrew *Zabdi*; also in verses 17 and 18.
c 2 *Ai* means *the ruin*.   *d* 21 Hebrew *Shinar*   *e* 21 That is, about 2.3 kilograms   *f* 21 That is, about 575 grams

his tent, with the silver underneath. 23They took the things from the tent, brought them to Joshua and all the Israelites and spread them out before the LORD.

24Then Joshua, together with all Israel, took Achan son of Zerah, the silver, the robe, the gold bar, his sons and daughters, his cattle, donkeys and sheep, his tent and all that he had, to the Valley of Achor. 25Joshua said, 'Why have you brought this trouble on us? The LORD will bring trouble on you today.'

Then all Israel stoned him, and after they had stoned the rest, they burned them. 26Over Achan they heaped up a large pile of rocks, which remains to this day. Then the LORD turned from his fierce anger. Therefore that place has been called the Valley of Achor[a] ever since.

Ai destroyed

8 Then the LORD said to Joshua, 'Do not be afraid; do not be discouraged. Take the whole army with you, and go up and attack Ai. For I have delivered into your hands the king of Ai, his people, his city and his land. 2You shall do to Ai and its king as you did to Jericho and its king, except that you may carry off their plunder and livestock for yourselves. Set an ambush behind the city.'

3So Joshua and the whole army moved out to attack Ai. He chose thirty thousand of his best fighting men and sent them out at night 4with these orders: 'Listen carefully. You are to set an ambush behind the city. Don't go very far from it. All of you be on the alert. 5I and all those with me will advance on the city, and when the men come out against us, as they did before, we will flee from them. 6They will pursue us until we have lured them away from the city, for they will say, "They are running away from us as they did before." So when we flee from them, 7you are to rise up from ambush and take the city. The LORD your God will give it into your hand. 8When you have taken the city, set it on fire. Do what the LORD has commanded. See to it; you have my orders.'

9Then Joshua sent them off, and they went to the place of ambush and lay in wait between Bethel and Ai, to the west of Ai—but Joshua spent that night with the people.

10Early the next morning Joshua mustered his army, and he and the leaders of Israel marched before them to Ai. 11The entire force that was with him marched up and approached the city and arrived in front of it. They set up camp north of Ai, with the valley between them and the city. 12Joshua had taken about five thousand men and set them in ambush between Bethel and Ai, to the west of the city. 13So the soldiers took up their positions—with the main camp to the north of the city and the ambush to the west of it. That night Joshua went into the valley.

14When the king of Ai saw this, he and all the men of the city hurried out early in the morning to meet Israel in battle at a certain place overlooking the Arabah. But he did not know that an ambush had been set against him behind the city. 15Joshua and all Israel let themselves be driven back before them, and they fled towards the wilderness. 16All the men of Ai were called to pursue them, and they pursued Joshua and were lured away from the city. 17Not a man remained in Ai or Bethel who did not go after Israel. They left the city open and went in pursuit of Israel.

18Then the LORD said to Joshua, 'Hold out towards Ai the javelin that is in your hand, for into your hand I will deliver the city.' So Joshua held out towards the city the javelin that was in his hand. 19As soon as he did this, the men in the ambush rose quickly from their position and rushed forward. They entered the city and captured it and quickly set it on fire.

20The men of Ai looked back and saw the smoke of the city rising against the sky, but they had no chance to escape in any direction; the Israelites who had been fleeing towards the wilderness had turned back against their pursuers. 21For when Joshua and all Israel saw that the ambush had taken the city and that smoke was going up from the city, they turned round and attacked the men of Ai. 22Those in the ambush also came out of the city against them, so that they were caught in the middle, with Israelites on both sides. Israel

---
[a] 26 *Achor* means *trouble.*

cut them down, leaving them neither survivors nor fugitives. 23But they took the king of Ai alive and brought him to Joshua.

24When Israel had finished killing all the men of Ai in the fields and in the wilderness where they had chased them, and when every one of them had been put to the sword, all the Israelites returned to Ai and killed those who were in it. 25Twelve thousand men and women fell that day—all the people of Ai. 26For Joshua did not draw back the hand that held out his javelin until he had destroyed[a] all who lived in Ai. 27But Israel did carry off for themselves the livestock and plunder of this city, as the LORD had instructed Joshua.

28So Joshua burned Ai[b] and made it a permanent heap of ruins, a desolate place to this day. 29He impaled the body of the king of Ai on a pole and left it there until evening. At sunset, Joshua ordered them to take the body from the pole and throw it down at the entrance of the city gate. And they raised a large pile of rocks over it, which remains to this day.

The covenant renewed at Mount Ebal

30Then Joshua built on Mount Ebal an altar to the LORD, the God of Israel, 31as Moses the servant of the LORD had commanded the Israelites. He built it according to what is written in the Book of the Law of Moses—an altar of uncut stones, on which no iron tool had been used. On it they offered to the LORD burnt offerings and sacrificed fellowship offerings. 32There, in the presence of the Israelites, Joshua copied on stones the law of Moses, which he had written. 33All the Israelites, with their elders, officials and judges, were standing on both sides of the ark of the covenant of the LORD, facing the Levitical priests who carried it. Both the foreigners living among them and the native-born were there. Half of the people stood in front of Mount Gerizim and half of them in front of Mount Ebal, as Moses the servant of the LORD had formerly commanded when he gave instructions to bless the people of Israel.

34Afterwards, Joshua read all the words of the law—the blessings and the curses—just as it is written in the Book of the Law. 35There was not a word of all that Moses had commanded that Joshua did not read to the whole assembly of Israel, including the women and children, and the foreigners who lived among them.

The Gibeonite deception

9 Now when all the kings west of the Jordan heard about these things—those in the hill country, in the western foothills, and along the entire coast of the Mediterranean Sea as far as Lebanon (the kings of the Hittites, Amorites, Canaanites, Perizzites, Hivites and Jebusites)— 2they came together to make war against Joshua and Israel.

3However, when the people of Gibeon heard what Joshua had done to Jericho and Ai, 4they resorted to a ruse: they went as a delegation whose donkeys were loaded[c] with worn-out sacks and old wineskins, cracked and mended. 5They put worn and patched sandals on their feet and wore old clothes. All the bread of their food supply was dry and mouldy. 6Then they went to Joshua in the camp at Gilgal and said to him and the Israelites, 'We have come from a distant country; make a treaty with us.'

7The Israelites said to the Hivites, 'But perhaps you live near us, so how can we make a treaty with you?'

8'We are your servants,' they said to Joshua.

But Joshua asked, 'Who are you and where do you come from?'

9They answered: 'Your servants have come from a very distant country because of the fame of the LORD your God. For we have heard reports of him: all that he did in Egypt, 10and all that he did to the two kings of the Amorites east of the Jordan—Sihon king of Heshbon, and Og king of Bashan, who reigned in Ashtaroth. 11And our elders and all those living in our country said to us, "Take provisions for your journey; go and meet them and say to them, 'We are your servants; make a treaty with us.'" 12This

---

[a] 26 The Hebrew term refers to the irrevocable giving over of things or persons to the LORD, often by totally destroying them. [b] 28 *Ai* means *the ruin*. [c] 4 Most Hebrew manuscripts; some Hebrew manuscripts, Vulgate and Syriac (see also Septuagint) *They prepared provisions and loaded their donkeys*

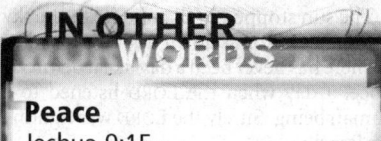

Peace
Joshua 9:15
The Hebrew word for peace is shalom, which means 'a complete wholeness'. It is a much broader and more positive concept than the current use of the word which tends to mean simply 'no war'.

bread of ours was warm when we packed it at home on the day we left to come to you. But now see how dry and mouldy it is. 13And these wineskins that we filled were new, but see how cracked they are. And our clothes and sandals are worn out by the very long journey.'

14The Israelites sampled their provisions but did not enquire of the LORD. 15Then Joshua made a treaty of peace with them to let them live, and the leaders of the assembly ratified it by oath.

16Three days after they made the treaty with the Gibeonites, the Israelites heard that they were neighbours, living near them. 17So the Israelites set out and on the third day came to their cities: Gibeon, Kephirah, Beeroth and Kiriath Jearim. 18But the Israelites did not attack them, because the leaders of the assembly had sworn an oath to them by the LORD, the God of Israel.

The whole assembly grumbled against the leaders, 19but all the leaders answered, 'We have given them our oath by the LORD, the God of Israel, and we cannot touch them now. 20This is what we will do to them: we will let them live, so that God's wrath will not fall on us for breaking the oath we swore to them.' 21They continued, 'Let them live, but let them be woodcutters and water-carriers for the entire community.' So the leaders' promise to them was kept.

22Then Joshua summoned the Gibeonites and said, 'Why did you deceive us by saying, "We live a long way from you," while actually you live near us? 23You are now under a curse: you will never cease to serve as woodcutters and water-carriers for the house of my God.'

24They answered Joshua, 'Your servants were clearly told how the LORD your God had commanded his servant Moses to give you the whole land and to wipe out all its inhabitants from before you. So we feared for our lives because of you, and that is why we did this. 25We are now in your hands. Do to us whatever seems good and right to you.'

26So Joshua saved them from the Israelites, and they did not kill them. 27That day he made the Gibeonites woodcutters and water-carriers for the community and for the altar of the LORD at the place the LORD would choose. And that is what they are to this day.

The sun stands still

10 Now Adoni-Zedek king of Jerusalem heard that Joshua had taken Ai and totally destroyed[a] it, doing to Ai and its king as he had done to Jericho and its king, and that the people of Gibeon had made a treaty of peace with Israel and had become their allies. 2He and his people were very much alarmed at this, because Gibeon was an important city, like one of the royal cities; it was larger than Ai, and all its men were good fighters. 3So Adoni-Zedek king of Jerusalem appealed to Hoham king of Hebron, Piram king of Jarmuth, Japhia king of Lachish and Debir king of Eglon. 4'Come up and help me attack Gibeon,' he said, 'because it has made peace with Joshua and the Israelites.'

5Then the five kings of the Amorites—the kings of Jerusalem, Hebron, Jarmuth, Lachish and Eglon—joined forces. They moved up with all their troops and took up positions against Gibeon and attacked it.

6The Gibeonites then sent word to Joshua in the camp at Gilgal: 'Do not abandon your servants. Come up to us quickly and save us! Help us, because all the Amorite kings from the hill country have joined forces against us.'

7So Joshua marched up from Gilgal with his entire army, including all the best

---

[a] 1 The Hebrew term refers to the irrevocable giving over of things or persons to the LORD, often by totally destroying them; also in verses 28, 35, 37, 39 and 40.

fighting men. ⁸The LORD said to Joshua, 'Do not be afraid of them; I have given them into your hand. Not one of them will be able to withstand you.'

⁹After an all-night march from Gilgal, Joshua took them by surprise. ¹⁰The LORD threw them into confusion before Israel, so Joshua and the Israelites defeated them completely at Gibeon. Israel pursued them along the road going up to Beth Horon and cut them down all the way to Azekah and Makkedah. ¹¹As they fled before Israel on the road down from Beth Horon to Azekah, the LORD hurled large hailstones down on them, and more of them died from the hail than were killed by the swords of the Israelites.

¹²On the day the LORD gave the Amorites over to Israel, Joshua said to the LORD in the presence of Israel:

'Sun, stand still over Gibeon,
    and you, moon, over the Valley of Aijalon.'
¹³So the sun stood still,
    and the moon stopped,
till the nation avenged itself on*ᵃ* its enemies,

as it is written in the Book of Jashar.

The sun stopped in the middle of the sky and delayed going down about a full day. ¹⁴There has never been a day like it before or since, a day when the LORD listened to a human being. Surely the LORD was fighting for Israel!

¹⁵Then Joshua returned with all Israel to the camp at Gilgal.

Five Amorite kings killed

¹⁶Now the five kings had fled and hidden in the cave at Makkedah. ¹⁷When Joshua was told that the five kings had been found hiding in the cave at Makkedah, ¹⁸he said, 'Roll large rocks up to the mouth of the cave, and post some guards there. ¹⁹But don't stop; pursue your enemies! Attack them from the rear and don't let them reach their cities, for the LORD your God has given them into your hand.'

²⁰So Joshua and the Israelites defeated them completely, but a few survivors managed to reach their fortified cities. ²¹The whole army then returned safely to Joshua in the camp at Makkedah, and no-one uttered a word against the Israelites.

²²Joshua said, 'Open the mouth of the cave and bring those five kings out to me.' ²³So they brought the five kings out of the cave—the kings of Jerusalem, Hebron, Jarmuth, Lachish and Eglon. ²⁴When they had brought these kings to Joshua, he summoned all the men of Israel and said to the army commanders who had come with him, 'Come here and put your feet on the necks of these kings.' So they came forward and placed their feet on their necks.

²⁵Joshua said to them, 'Do not be afraid; do not be discouraged. Be strong and courageous. This is what the LORD will do to all the enemies you are going to fight.' ²⁶Then Joshua put the kings to death and exposed their bodies on five poles, and they were left hanging on the poles until evening.

²⁷At sunset Joshua gave the order and they took them down from the poles and threw them into the cave where they had been hiding. At the mouth of the cave they placed large rocks, which are there to this day.

making Connections

When the sun stood still
Joshua 10:12

God created the sun, so it's not surprising that it's under his control. Here he makes the sun stand still when Joshua prays, which shows everyone that God is on Israel's side. And when King Hezekiah asked God to heal him from his illness, God made the sun go backwards as a sign that he had heard Hezekiah and would answer his prayer (Isaiah 38:8).

ᵃ 13 Or nation triumphed over

Southern cities conquered

28 That day Joshua took Makkedah. He put the city and its king to the sword and totally destroyed everyone in it. He left no survivors. And he did to the king of Makkedah as he had done to the king of Jericho.

29 Then Joshua and all Israel with him moved on from Makkedah to Libnah and attacked it. 30 The LORD also gave that city and its king into Israel's hand. The city and everyone in it Joshua put to the sword. He left no survivors there. And he did to its king as he had done to the king of Jericho.

31 Then Joshua and all Israel with him moved on from Libnah to Lachish; he took up positions against it and attacked it. 32 The LORD gave Lachish into Israel's hands, and Joshua took it on the second day. The city and everyone in it he put to the sword, just as he had done to Libnah. 33 Meanwhile, Horam king of Gezer had come up to help Lachish, but Joshua defeated him and his army—until no survivors were left.

34 Then Joshua and all Israel with him moved on from Lachish to Eglon; they took up positions against it and attacked it. 35 They captured it that same day and put it to the sword and totally destroyed everyone in it, just as they had done to Lachish.

36 Then Joshua and all Israel with him went up from Eglon to Hebron and attacked it. 37 They took the city and put it to the sword, together with its king, its villages and everyone in it. They left no survivors. Just as at Eglon, they totally destroyed it and everyone in it.

38 Then Joshua and all Israel with him turned round and attacked Debir. 39 They took the city, its king and its villages, and put them to the sword. Everyone in it they totally destroyed. They left no survivors. They did to Debir and its king as they had done to Libnah and its king and to Hebron.

40 So Joshua subdued the whole region, including the hill country, the Negev, the western foothills and the mountain slopes, together with all their kings. He left no survivors. He totally destroyed all who breathed, just as the LORD, the God of Israel, had commanded. 41 Joshua subdued them from Kadesh Barnea to Gaza and from the whole region of Goshen to Gibeon. 42 All these kings and their lands Joshua conquered in one campaign, because the LORD, the God of Israel, fought for Israel.

43 Then Joshua returned with all Israel to the camp at Gilgal.

Northern kings defeated

11 When Jabin king of Hazor heard of this, he sent word to Jobab king of Madon, to the kings of Shimron and Akshaph, 2 and to the northern kings who were in the mountains, in the Arabah south of Kinnereth, in the western foothills and in Naphoth Dor on the west; 3 to the Canaanites in the east and west; to the Amorites, Hittites, Perizzites and Jebusites in the hill country; and to the Hivites below Hermon in the region of Mizpah. 4 They came out with all their troops and a large number of horses and chariots—a huge army, as numerous as the sand on the seashore. 5 All these kings joined forces and made camp together at the Waters of Merom to fight against Israel.

6 The LORD said to Joshua, 'Do not be afraid of them, because by this time tomorrow I will hand all of them, slain, over to Israel. You are to hamstring their horses and burn their chariots.'

7 So Joshua and his whole army came against them suddenly at the Waters of Merom and attacked them, 8 and the LORD gave them into the hand of Israel. They defeated them and pursued them all the way to Greater Sidon, to Misrephoth Maim, and to the Valley of Mizpah on the east, until no survivors were left. 9 Joshua did to them as the LORD had directed: he hamstrung their horses and burned their chariots.

10 At that time Joshua turned back and captured Hazor and put its king to the sword. (Hazor had been the head of all these kingdoms.) 11 Everyone in it they put to the sword. They totally destroyed[a] them, not sparing anyone that breathed, and he burned Hazor itself.

---

[a] 11 The Hebrew term refers to the irrevocable giving over of things or persons to the LORD, often by totally destroying them; also in verses 12, 20 and 21.

¹²Joshua took all these royal cities and their kings and put them to the sword. He totally destroyed them, as Moses the servant of the LORD had commanded. ¹³Yet Israel did not burn any of the cities built on their mounds—except Hazor, which Joshua burned. ¹⁴The Israelites carried off for themselves all the plunder and livestock of these cities, but all the people they put to the sword until they completely destroyed them, not sparing anyone that breathed. ¹⁵As the LORD commanded his servant Moses, so Moses commanded Joshua, and Joshua did it; he left nothing undone of all that the LORD commanded Moses.

¹⁶So Joshua took this entire land: the hill country, all the Negev, the whole region of Goshen, the western foothills, the Arabah and the mountains of Israel with their foothills, ¹⁷from Mount Halak, which rises towards Seir, to Baal Gad in the Valley of Lebanon below Mount Hermon. He captured all their kings and put them to death. ¹⁸Joshua waged war against all these kings for a long time. ¹⁹Except for the Hivites living in Gibeon, not one city made a treaty of peace with the Israelites, who took them all in battle. ²⁰For it was the LORD himself who hardened their hearts to wage war against Israel, so that he might destroy them totally, exterminating them without mercy, as the LORD had commanded Moses.

²¹At that time Joshua went and destroyed the Anakites from the hill country: from Hebron, Debir and Anab, from all the hill country of Judah, and from all the hill country of Israel. Joshua totally destroyed them and their towns. ²²No Anakites were left in Israelite territory; only in Gaza, Gath and Ashdod did any survive.

²³So Joshua took the entire land, just as the LORD had directed Moses, and he gave it as an inheritance to Israel according to their tribal divisions. Then the land had rest from war.

List of defeated kings

12 These are the kings of the land whom the Israelites had defeated and whose territory they took over east of the Jordan, from the Arnon Gorge to Mount Hermon, including all the eastern side of the Arabah:

²Sihon king of the Amorites, who reigned in Heshbon.

He ruled from Aroer on the rim of the Arnon Gorge—from the middle of the gorge—to the River Jabbok, which is the border of the Ammonites. This included half of Gilead. ³He also ruled over the eastern Arabah from the Sea of Galilee*ᵃ* to the Sea of the Arabah (that is, the Dead Sea), to Beth Jeshimoth, and then southward below the slopes of Pisgah.

⁴And the territory of Og king of Bashan, one of the last of the Rephaites, who reigned in Ashtaroth and Edrei.

⁵He ruled over Mount Hermon, Salekah, all of Bashan to the border of the people of Geshur and Maakah, and half of Gilead to the border of Sihon king of Heshbon.

⁶Moses, the servant of the LORD, and the Israelites conquered them. And Moses the servant of the LORD gave their land to the Reubenites, the Gadites and the half-tribe of Manasseh to be their possession.

⁷These are the kings of the land that Joshua and the Israelites conquered on the west side of the Jordan, from Baal Gad in the Valley of Lebanon to Mount Halak, which rises towards Seir (their lands Joshua gave as an inheritance to the tribes of Israel according to their tribal divisions— ⁸the hill country, the western foothills, the Arabah, the mountain slopes, the wilderness and the Negev—the lands of the Hittites, Amorites, Canaanites, Perizzites, Hivites and Jebusites):

⁹the king of Jericho	one
the king of Ai (near Bethel)	one
¹⁰the king of Jerusalem	one
the king of Hebron	one
¹¹the king of Jarmuth	one
the king of Lachish	one
¹²the king of Eglon	one
the king of Gezer	one

ᵃ 3 Hebrew *Kinnereth*

13the king of Debir	one
the king of Geder	one
14the king of Hormah	one
the king of Arad	one
15the king of Libnah	one
the king of Adullam	one
16the king of Makkedah	one
the king of Bethel	one
17the king of Tappuah	one
the king of Hepher	one
18the king of Aphek	one
the king of Lasharon	one
19the king of Madon	one
the king of Hazor	one
20the king of Shimron Meron	one
the king of Akshaph	one
21the king of Taanach	one
the king of Megiddo	one
22the king of Kedesh	one
the king of Jokneam in Carmel	one
23the king of Dor (in Naphoth Dor)	one
the king of Goyim in Gilgal	one
24the king of Tirzah	one
	thirty-one kings in all.

Land still to be taken

13 When Joshua had grown old, the LORD said to him, 'You are now very old, and there are still very large areas of land to be taken over.

2'This is the land that remains: all the regions of the Philistines and Geshurites, 3from the River Shihor on the east of Egypt to the territory of Ekron on the north, all of it counted as Canaanite though held by the five Philistine rulers in Gaza, Ashdod, Ashkelon, Gath and Ekron; the territory of the Avvites 4on the south; all the land of the Canaanites, from Arah of the Sidonians as far as Aphek and the border of the Amorites; 5the area of Byblos; and all Lebanon to the east, from Baal Gad below Mount Hermon to Lebo Hamath.

6'As for all the inhabitants of the mountain regions from Lebanon to Misrephoth Maim, that is, all the Sidonians, I myself will drive them out before the Israelites. Be sure to allocate this land to Israel for an inheritance, as I have instructed you, 7and divide it as an inheritance among the nine tribes and half of the tribe of Manasseh.'

Division of the land east of the Jordan

8The other half of Manasseh,[a] the Reubenites and the Gadites had received the inheritance that Moses had given them east of the Jordan, as he, the servant of the LORD, had assigned it to them.

>9It extended from Aroer on the rim of the Arnon Gorge, and from the town in the middle of the gorge, and included the whole plateau of Medeba as far as Dibon, 10and all the towns of Sihon king of the Amorites, who ruled in Heshbon, out to the border of the Ammonites. 11It also included Gilead, the territory of the people of Geshur and Maakah, all of Mount Hermon and all Bashan as far as Salekah—12that is, the whole kingdom of Og in Bashan, who had reigned in Ashtaroth and Edrei. (He was the last of the Rephaites.) Moses had defeated them and taken over their land. 13But the Israelites did not drive out the people of Geshur and Maakah, so they continue to live among the Israelites to this day.

14But to the tribe of Levi he gave no inheritance, since the food offerings presented to the LORD, the God of Israel, are their inheritance, as he promised them.

15This is what Moses had given to the tribe of Reuben, according to its clans:

>16The territory from Aroer on the rim of the Arnon Gorge, and from the town in the middle of the gorge, and the whole plateau past Medeba 17to Heshbon and all its

---

[a] 8 Hebrew *With it* (that is, with the other half of Manasseh)

towns on the plateau, including Dibon, Bamoth Baal, Beth Baal Meon, 18Jahaz, Kedemoth, Mephaath, 19Kiriathaim, Sibmah, Zereth Shahar on the hill in the valley, 20Beth Peor, the slopes of Pisgah, and Beth Jeshimoth 21—all the towns on the plateau and the entire realm of Sihon king of the Amorites, who ruled at Heshbon. Moses had defeated him and the Midianite chiefs, Evi, Rekem, Zur, Hur and Reba—princes allied with Sihon—who lived in that country. 22In addition to those slain in battle, the Israelites had put to the sword Balaam son of Beor, who practised divination. 23The boundary of the Reubenites was the bank of the Jordan. These towns and their villages were the inheritance of the Reubenites, according to their clans.

24This is what Moses had given to the tribe of Gad, according to its clans:

25The territory of Jazer, all the towns of Gilead and half the Ammonite country as far as Aroer, near Rabbah; 26and from Heshbon to Ramath Mizpah and Betonim, and from Mahanaim to the territory of Debir; 27and in the valley, Beth Haram, Beth Nimrah, Sukkoth and Zaphon with the rest of the realm of Sihon king of Heshbon (the east side of the Jordan, the territory up to the end of the Sea of Galilee*a*). 28These towns and their villages were the inheritance of the Gadites, according to their clans.

29This is what Moses had given to the half-tribe of Manasseh, that is, to half the family of the descendants of Manasseh, according to its clans:

30The territory extending from Mahanaim and including all of Bashan, the entire realm of Og king of Bashan—all the settlements of Jair in Bashan, sixty towns, 31half of Gilead, and Ashtaroth and Edrei (the royal cities of Og in Bashan). This was for the descendants of Makir son of Manasseh—for half of the sons of Makir, according to their clans.

32This is the inheritance Moses had given when he was in the plains of Moab across the Jordan east of Jericho. 33But to the tribe of Levi, Moses had given no inheritance; the LORD, the God of Israel, is their inheritance, as he promised them.

People and Places

Levite
Joshua 13:14
Levi was one of Jacob's twelve sons and his descendants were given the job of being priests in the tabernacle, the tent of worship in the wilderness, and later in the temple in Jerusalem. The Levites missed out on being given any land in Canaan, but then they wouldn't have had time to look after it. However, they were given towns to live in (Joshua 21:1), and the other Israelites were told to provide for the Levites through their tithes and offerings.

Division of the land west of the Jordan

14 Now these are the areas the Israelites received as an inheritance in the land of Canaan, which Eleazar the priest, Joshua son of Nun and the heads of the tribal clans of Israel allotted to them. 2Their inheritances were assigned by lot to the nine and a half tribes, as the LORD had commanded through Moses. 3Moses had granted the two and a half tribes their inheritance east of the Jordan but had not granted the

---

a 27 Hebrew *Kinnereth*

Levites an inheritance among the rest, ⁴for the sons of Joseph had become two tribes—Manasseh and Ephraim. The Levites received no share of the land but only towns to live in, with pasture-lands for their flocks and herds. ⁵So the Israelites divided the land, just as the LORD had commanded Moses.

Land allotted to Caleb

⁶Now the people of Judah approached Joshua at Gilgal, and Caleb son of Jephunneh the Kenizzite said to him, 'You know what the LORD said to Moses the man of God at Kadesh Barnea about you and me. ⁷I was forty years old when Moses the servant of the LORD sent me from Kadesh Barnea to explore the land. And I brought him back a report according to my convictions, ⁸but the others who went up with me made the hearts of the people sink.*ᵃ* I, however, followed the LORD my God wholeheartedly. ⁹So on that day Moses swore to me, "The land on which your feet have walked will be your inheritance and that of your children for ever, because you have followed the LORD my God wholeheartedly."*ᵇ*

¹⁰'Now then, just as the LORD promised, he has kept me alive for forty-five years since the time he said this to Moses, while Israel moved about in the wilderness. So here I am today, eighty-five years old! ¹¹I am still as strong today as the day Moses sent me out; I'm just as vigorous to go out to battle now as I was then. ¹²Now give me this hill country that the LORD promised me that day. You yourself heard then that the Anakites were there and their cities were large and fortified, but, the LORD helping me, I will drive them out just as he said.'

¹³Then Joshua blessed Caleb son of Jephunneh and gave him Hebron as his inheritance. ¹⁴So Hebron has belonged to Caleb son of Jephunneh the Kenizzite ever since, because he followed the LORD, the God of Israel, wholeheartedly. ¹⁵(Hebron used to be called Kiriath Arba after Arba, who was the greatest man among the Anakites.)

Then the land had rest from war.

Land allotted to Judah

15 The land allotted to the tribe of Judah, according to its clans, extended down to the territory of Edom, to the Desert of Zin in the extreme south.

²Their southern boundary started from the bay at the southern end of the Dead Sea, ³crossed south of Scorpion Pass, continued on to Zin and went over to the south of Kadesh Barnea. Then it ran past Hezron up to Addar and curved around to Karka. ⁴It then passed along to Azmon and joined the Wadi of Egypt, ending at the Mediterranean Sea. This is their*ᶜ* southern boundary.

⁵The eastern boundary is the Dead Sea as far as the mouth of the Jordan.

The northern boundary started from the bay of the sea at the mouth of the Jordan, ⁶went up to Beth Hoglah and continued north of Beth Arabah to the Stone of Bohan son of Reuben. ⁷The boundary then went up to Debir from the Valley of Achor and turned north to Gilgal, which faces the Pass of Adummim south of the gorge. It continued along to the waters of En Shemesh and came out at En Rogel. ⁸Then it ran up the Valley of Ben Hinnom along the southern slope of the Jebusite city (that is, Jerusalem). From there it climbed to the top of the hill west of the Hinnom Valley at the northern end of the Valley of Rephaim. ⁹From the hilltop the boundary headed towards the spring of the waters of Nephtoah, came out at the towns of Mount Ephron and went down towards Baalah (that is, Kiriath Jearim). ¹⁰Then it curved westward from Baalah to Mount Seir, ran along the northern slope of Mount Jearim (that is, Kesalon), continued down to Beth Shemesh and crossed to Timnah. ¹¹It went to

---

*ᵃ*8 Hebrew *melt*   *ᵇ*9 Deut. 1:36   *ᶜ*4 Septuagint; Hebrew *your*

People and Places

Hebron
Joshua 15:13

Hebron is a high town with a rich history. Abram's name was changed to Abraham in Hebron, and it was here that he heard from angels that he would have a son called Isaac. Hebron was a city of refuge, a place that someone could run to for protection if they had killed by accident. And David ruled from Hebron for the first six years of his reign, after which he made Jerusalem his capital city.

---

the northern slope of Ekron, turned toward Shikkeron, passed along to Mount Baalah and reached Jabneel. The boundary ended at the sea.

12 The western boundary is the coastline of the Mediterranean Sea.

These are the boundaries around the people of Judah by their clans.

13 In accordance with the LORD's command to him, Joshua gave to Caleb son of Jephunneh a portion in Judah—Kiriath Arba, that is, Hebron. (Arba was the ancestor of Anak.) 14 From Hebron Caleb drove out the three Anakites—Sheshai, Ahiman and Talmai, the sons of Anak. 15 From there he marched against the people living in Debir (formerly called Kiriath Sepher). 16 And Caleb said, 'I will give my daughter Aksah in marriage to the man who attacks and captures Kiriath Sepher.' 17 Othniel son of Kenaz, Caleb's brother, took it; so Caleb gave his daughter Aksah to him in marriage.

18 One day when she came to Othniel, she urged him[a] to ask her father for a field. When she got off her donkey, Caleb asked her, 'What can I do for you?'

19 She replied, 'Do me a special favour. Since you have given me land in the Negev, give me also springs of water.' So Caleb gave her the upper and lower springs.

20 This is the inheritance of the tribe of Judah, according to its clans:

21 The southernmost towns of the tribe of Judah in the Negev towards the boundary of Edom were:

Kabzeel, Eder, Jagur, 22 Kinah, Dimonah, Adadah, 23 Kedesh, Hazor, Ithnan, 24 Ziph, Telem, Bealoth, 25 Hazor Hadattah, Kerioth Hezron (that is, Hazor), 26 Amam, Shema, Moladah, 27 Hazar Gaddah, Heshmon, Beth Pelet, 28 Hazar Shual, Beersheba, Biziothiah, 29 Baalah, Iyim, Ezem, 30 Eltolad, Kesil, Hormah, 31 Ziklag, Madmannah, Sansannah, 32 Lebaoth, Shilhim, Ain and Rimmon—a total of twenty-nine towns and their villages.

33 In the western foothills:

Eshtaol, Zorah, Ashnah, 34 Zanoah, En Gannim, Tappuah, Enam, 35 Jarmuth, Adullam, Sokoh, Azekah, 36 Shaaraim, Adithaim and Gederah (or Gederothaim)[b]—fourteen towns and their villages.

37 Zenan, Hadashah, Migdal Gad, 38 Dilean, Mizpah, Joktheel, 39 Lachish, Bozkath, Eglon, 40 Kabbon, Lahmas, Kitlish, 41 Gederoth, Beth Dagon, Naamah and Makkedah—sixteen towns and their villages.

42 Libnah, Ether, Ashan, 43 Iphtah, Ashnah, Nezib, 44 Keilah, Akzib and Mareshah—nine towns and their villages.

45 Ekron, with its surrounding settlements and villages; 46 west of Ekron, all that were in the vicinity of Ashdod, together with their villages; 47 Ashdod, its surrounding settlements and villages; and Gaza, its settlements and villages,

---

[a] 18 Hebrew and some Septuagint manuscripts; other Septuagint manuscripts (see also note at Judges 1:14) *Othniel, he urged her* [b] 36 Or *Gederah and Gederothaim*

as far as the Wadi of Egypt and the coastline of the Mediterranean Sea.

⁴⁸In the hill country:

Shamir, Jattir, Sokoh, ⁴⁹Dannah, Kiriath Sannah (that is, Debir), ⁵⁰Anab, Eshtemoh, Anim, ⁵¹Goshen, Holon and Giloh—eleven towns and their villages.

⁵²Arab, Dumah, Eshan, ⁵³Janim, Beth Tappuah, Aphekah, ⁵⁴Humtah, Kiriath Arba (that is, Hebron) and Zior—nine towns and their villages.

⁵⁵Maon, Carmel, Ziph, Juttah, ⁵⁶Jezreel, Jokdeam, Zanoah, ⁵⁷Kain, Gibeah and Timnah—ten towns and their villages.

⁵⁸Halhul, Beth Zur, Gedor, ⁵⁹Maarath, Beth Anoth and Eltekon—six towns and their villages.[a]

⁶⁰Kiriath Baal (that is, Kiriath Jearim) and Rabbah—two towns and their villages.

⁶¹In the wilderness:

Beth Arabah, Middin, Sekakah, ⁶²Nibshan, the City of Salt and En Gedi—six towns and their villages.

⁶³Judah could not dislodge the Jebusites, who were living in Jerusalem; to this day the Jebusites live there with the people of Judah.

Land allotted to Ephraim and Manasseh

16 The land allotted to Joseph began at the Jordan, east of the springs of Jericho, and went up from there through the desert into the hill country of Bethel. ²It went on from Bethel (that is, Luz),[b] crossed over to the territory of the Arkites in Ataroth, ³descended westward to the territory of the Japhletites as far as the region of Lower Beth Horon and on to Gezer, ending at the Mediterranean Sea.

⁴So Manasseh and Ephraim, the descendants of Joseph, received their inheritance.

⁵This was the territory of Ephraim, according to its clans:

The boundary of their inheritance went from Ataroth Addar in the east to Upper Beth Horon ⁶and continued to the Mediterranean Sea. From Mikmethath on the north it curved eastward to Taanath Shiloh, passing by it to Janoah on the east. ⁷Then it went down from Janoah to Ataroth and Naarah, touched Jericho and came out at the Jordan. ⁸From Tappuah the border went west to the Kanah Ravine and ended at the Mediterranean Sea. This was the inheritance of the tribe of the Ephraimites, according to its clans. ⁹It also included all the towns and their villages that were set aside for the Ephraimites within the inheritance of the Manassites.

¹⁰They did not dislodge the Canaanites living in Gezer; to this day the Canaanites live among the people of Ephraim but are required to do forced labour.

17 This was the land allotted to the tribe of Manasseh as Joseph's firstborn, that is, for Makir, Manasseh's firstborn. Makir was the ancestor of the Gileadites, who had received Gilead and Bashan because the Makirites were great soldiers. ²So this land was allotted to the rest of the people of Manasseh—the clans of Abiezer, Helek, Asriel, Shechem, Hepher and Shemida. These are the other male descendants of Manasseh son of Joseph by their clans.

³Now Zelophehad son of Hepher, the son of Gilead, the son of Makir, the son of Manasseh, had no sons but only daughters, whose names were Mahlah, Noah, Hoglah, Milkah and Tirzah. ⁴They went to Eleazar the priest, Joshua son of Nun, and the leaders and said, 'The LORD commanded

---

[a] 59 The Septuagint adds another district of eleven towns, including Tekoa and Ephrathah (Bethlehem). [b] 2 Septuagint; Hebrew *Bethel to Luz*

Moses to give us an inheritance among our relatives.' So Joshua gave them an inheritance along with the brothers of their father, according to the LORD's command. 5Manasseh's share consisted of ten tracts of land besides Gilead and Bashan east of the Jordan, 6because the daughters of the tribe of Manasseh received an inheritance among the sons. The land of Gilead belonged to the rest of the descendants of Manasseh.

7The territory of Manasseh extended from Asher to Mikmethath east of Shechem. The boundary ran southward from there to include the people living at En Tappuah. 8(Manasseh had the land of Tappuah, but Tappuah itself, on the boundary of Manasseh, belonged to the Ephraimites.) 9Then the boundary continued south to the Kanah Ravine. There were towns belonging to Ephraim lying among the towns of Manasseh, but the boundary of Manasseh was the northern side of the ravine and ended at the Mediterranean Sea. 10On the south the land belonged to Ephraim, on the north to Manasseh. The territory of Manasseh reached the Mediterranean Sea and bordered Asher on the north and Issachar on the east.

11Within Issachar and Asher, Manasseh also had Beth Shan, Ibleam and the people of Dor, Endor, Taanach and Megiddo, together with their surrounding settlements (the third in the list is Naphoth^a).

12Yet the Manassites were not able to occupy these towns, for the Canaanites were determined to live in that region. 13However, when the Israelites grew stronger, they subjected the Canaanites to forced labour but did not drive them out completely.

14The people of Joseph said to Joshua, 'Why have you allotted us only one portion of land and one share for an inheritance? We are a numerous people, and the LORD has blessed us abundantly.'

15'If you are so numerous,' Joshua answered, 'and if the hill country of Ephraim is too small for you, go up into the forest and clear land for yourselves there in the land of the Perizzites and Rephaites.'

16The people of Joseph replied, 'The hill country is not enough for us, and all the Canaanites who live in the plain have chariots fitted with iron, both those in Beth Shan and its settlements and those in the Valley of Jezreel.'

17But Joshua said to the house of Joseph—to Ephraim and Manasseh—'You are numerous and very powerful. You will have not only one portion of land allotted to you 18but the forested hill country as well. Clear it, and its farthest limits will be yours; though the Canaanites have chariots fitted with iron and though they are strong, you can drive them out.'

Division of the rest of the land

18 The whole assembly of the Israelites gathered at Shiloh and set up the tent of meeting there. The country was brought under their control, 2but there were still seven Israelite tribes who had not yet received their inheritance.

3 So Joshua said to the Israelites: 'How long will you wait before you begin to take possession of the land that the LORD, the God of your ancestors, has given you? 4Appoint three men from each tribe. I will send them out to make a survey of the land and to write a description of it, according to the inheritance of each. Then they will return to me. 5You are to divide the land into seven parts. Judah is to remain in its territory on the south and the house of Joseph in its territory on the north. 6After you have written descriptions of the seven parts of the land, bring them here to me and I will cast lots for you in the presence of the LORD our God. 7The Levites, however, do not get a portion among you, because the priestly service of the LORD is their inheritance. And Gad, Reuben and the half-tribe of Manasseh have already received their inheritance on the east side of the Jordan.

---

^{a} 11 That is, Naphoth Dor

Moses the servant of the LORD gave it to them.'

8As the men started on their way to map out the land, Joshua instructed them, 'Go and make a survey of the land and write a description of it. Then return to me, and I will cast lots for you here at Shiloh in the presence of the LORD.' 9So they left and went through the land. They wrote its description on a scroll, town by town, in seven parts, and returned to Joshua in the camp at Shiloh. 10Joshua then cast lots for them in Shiloh in the presence of the LORD, and there he distributed the land to the Israelites according to their tribal divisions.

Land allotted to Benjamin

11The first lot came up for the tribe of Benjamin according to its clans. Their allotted territory lay between the tribes of Judah and Joseph:

12On the north side their boundary began at the Jordan, passed the northern slope of Jericho and headed west into the hill country, coming out at the wilderness of Beth Aven. 13From there it crossed to the south slope of Luz (that is, Bethel) and went down to Ataroth Addar on the hill south of Lower Beth Horon.

14From the hill facing Beth Horon on the south the boundary turned south along the western side and came out at Kiriath Baal (that is, Kiriath Jearim), a town of the people of Judah. This was the western side.

15The southern side began at the outskirts of Kiriath Jearim on the west, and the boundary came out at the spring of the waters of Nephtoah. 16The boundary went down to the foot of the hill facing the Valley of Ben Hinnom, north of the Valley of Rephaim. It continued down the Hinnom Valley along the southern slope of the Jebusite city and so to En Rogel. 17It then curved north, went to En Shemesh, continued to Geliloth, which faces the Pass of Adummim, and ran down to the Stone of Bohan son of Reuben. 18It continued to the northern slope of Beth Arabah[a] and on down into the Arabah. 19It then went to the northern slope of Beth Hoglah and came out at the northern bay of the Dead Sea, at the mouth of the Jordan in the south. This was the southern boundary.

20The Jordan formed the boundary on the eastern side.

These were the boundaries that marked out the inheritance of the clans of Benjamin on all sides.

21The tribe of Benjamin, according to its clans, had the following cities:

Jericho, Beth Hoglah, Emek Keziz, 22Beth Arabah, Zemaraim,

making Connections

The tabernacle at Shiloh
Joshua 18:1

After years of being taken with the Israelites on their travels round the wilderness, the tabernacle or Tent of Meeting finds its first permanent home in Shiloh. The Israelites would have gathered here for worship, making Shiloh an important city. The tabernacle containing the Ark of the Covenant stayed here up until Samuel's early years as a priest and prophet. However, the Philistines later captured the ark during a battle and, although it was returned to the Israelites, it never came back to Shiloh (1 Samuel 4:1–11).

---

[a] 18 Septuagint; Hebrew *slope facing the Arabah*

Bethel, 23Avvim, Parah, Ophrah, 24Kephar Ammoni, Ophni and Geba—twelve towns and their villages.

25Gibeon, Ramah, Beeroth, 26Mizpah, Kephirah, Mozah, 27Rekem, Irpeel, Taralah, 28Zelah, Haeleph, the Jebusite city (that is, Jerusalem), Gibeah and Kiriath—fourteen towns and their villages.

This was the inheritance of Benjamin for its clans.

Land allotted to Simeon

19 The second lot came out for the tribe of Simeon according to its clans. Their inheritance lay within the territory of Judah. 2It included:

Beersheba (or Sheba),[a] Moladah, 3Hazar Shual, Balah, Ezem, 4Eltolad, Bethul, Hormah, 5Ziklag, Beth Markaboth, Hazar Susah, 6Beth Lebaoth and Sharuhen—thirteen towns and their villages;

7Ain, Rimmon, Ether and Ashan—four towns and their villages—8and all the villages around these towns as far as Baalath Beer (Ramah in the Negev).

This was the inheritance of the tribe of the Simeonites, according to its clans. 9The inheritance of the Simeonites was taken from the share of Judah, because Judah's portion was more than they needed. So the Simeonites received their inheritance within the territory of Judah.

Land allotted to Zebulun

10The third lot came up for Zebulun according to its clans:

The boundary of their inheritance went as far as Sarid. 11Going west it ran to Maralah, touched Dabbesheth, and extended to the ravine near Jokneam. 12It turned east from Sarid towards the sunrise to the territory of Kisloth Tabor and went on to Daberath and up to Japhia. 13Then it continued eastward to Gath Hepher and Eth Kazin; it came out at Rimmon and turned towards Neah. 14There the boundary went round on the north to Hannathon and ended at the Valley of Iphtah El. 15Included were Kattath, Nahalal, Shimron, Idalah and Bethlehem. There were twelve towns and their villages.

16These towns and their villages were the inheritance of Zebulun, according to its clans.

Land allotted to Issachar

17The fourth lot came out for Issachar according to its clans. 18Their territory included:

Jezreel, Kesulloth, Shunem, 19Hapharaim, Shion, Anaharath, 20Rabbith, Kishion, Ebez, 21 Remeth, En Gannim, En Haddah and Beth Pazzez. 22The boundary touched Tabor, Shahazumah and Beth Shemesh, and ended at the Jordan. There were sixteen towns and their villages.

23These towns and their villages were the inheritance of the tribe of Issachar, according to its clans.

Land allotted to Asher

24The fifth lot came out for the tribe of Asher according to its clans. 25Their territory included:

Helkath, Hali, Beten, Akshaph, 26Allammelek, Amad and Mishal. On the west the boundary touched Carmel and Shihor Libnath. 27It then turned east towards Beth Dagon, touched Zebulun and the Valley of Iphtah El, and went north to Beth Emek and Neiel, passing Kabul on the left. 28It went to Abdon,[b] Rehob, Hammon and Kanah, as far as Greater Sidon. 29The boundary then turned back towards Ramah and went to the

---

[a] 2 Or *Beersheba, Sheba*; 1 Chron. 4:28 does not have *Sheba*. [b] 28 Some Hebrew manuscripts (see also Joshua 21:30); most Hebrew manuscripts *Ebron*

fortified city of Tyre, turned towards Hosah and came out at the Mediterranean Sea in the region of Akzib, ³⁰Ummah, Aphek and Rehob. There were twenty-two towns and their villages.

³¹These towns and their villages were the inheritance of the tribe of Asher, according to its clans.

Land allotted to Naphtali

³²The sixth lot came out for Naphtali according to its clans:

³³Their boundary went from Heleph and the large tree in Zaanannim, passing Adami Nekeb and Jabneel to Lakkum and ending at the Jordan. ³⁴The boundary ran west through Aznoth Tabor and came out at Hukkok. It touched Zebulun on the south, Asher on the west and the Jordan*ᵃ* on the east. ³⁵The fortified cities were Ziddim, Zer, Hammath, Rakkath, Kinnereth, ³⁶Adamah, Ramah, Hazor, ³⁷Kedesh, Edrei, En Hazor, ³⁸Iron, Migdal El, Horem, Beth Anath and Beth Shemesh. There were nineteen towns and their villages.

³⁹These towns and their villages were the inheritance of the tribe of Naphtali, according to its clans.

Land allotted to Dan

⁴⁰The seventh lot came out for the tribe of Dan according to its clans. ⁴¹The territory of their inheritance included:

Zorah, Eshtaol, Ir Shemesh, ⁴²Shaalabbin, Aijalon, Ithlah, ⁴³Elon, Timnah, Ekron, ⁴⁴Eltekeh, Gibbethon, Baalath, ⁴⁵Jehud, Bene Berak, Gath Rimmon, ⁴⁶Me Jarkon and Rakkon, with the area facing Joppa.

⁴⁷(When the territory of the Danites was lost to them, they went up and attacked Leshem, took it, put it to the sword and occupied it. They settled in Leshem and named it Dan after their ancestor.)

⁴⁸These towns and their villages were the inheritance of the tribe of Dan, according to its clans.

Land allotted to Joshua

⁴⁹When they had finished dividing the land into its allotted portions, the Israelites gave Joshua son of Nun an inheritance among them, ⁵⁰as the LORD had commanded. They gave him the town he asked for—Timnath Serah*ᵇ* in the hill country of Ephraim. And he built up the town and settled there.

⁵¹These are the territories that Eleazar the priest, Joshua son of Nun and the heads of the tribal clans of Israel assigned by lot at Shiloh in the presence of the LORD at the entrance to the tent of meeting. And so they finished dividing the land.

Cities of refuge

20 Then the LORD said to Joshua: ²'Tell the Israelites to designate the cities of refuge, as I instructed you through Moses, ³so that anyone who kills a person accidentally and unintentionally may flee

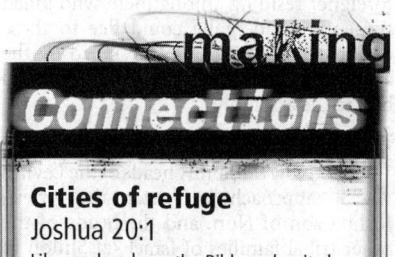

making Connections

Cities of refuge
Joshua 20:1

Like modern laws, the Bible makes it clear that there's a difference between murder and manslaughter. Murder is a serious crime because people are made in God's image. In the Old Testament, relatives were allowed to carry out the death penalty in revenge for murder. But sometimes a person might kill someone by accident, which is manslaughter. They were able to run to these cities of refuge for protection until they stood trial.

ᵃ 34 Septuagint; Hebrew *west, and Judah, the Jordan,*   *ᵇ* 50 Also known as *Timnath Heres* (see Judges 2:9) there and find protection from the avenger of blood. ⁴When they flee to one of these cities, they are to stand in the entrance of the city gate and state their case before the elders of that city. Then the elders are to admit them into their city and give them a place to live with them. ⁵If the avenger of blood pursues them, the elders must not surrender the accused, because they killed their neighbour unintentionally and without malice aforethought. ⁶They are to stay in that city until they have stood trial before the assembly and until the death of the high priest who is serving at that time. Then they may go back to their own home in the town from which they fled.'

⁷So they set apart Kedesh in Galilee in the hill country of Naphtali, Shechem in the hill country of Ephraim, and Kiriath Arba (that is, Hebron) in the hill country of Judah. ⁸East of the Jordan (on the other side from Jericho) they designated Bezer in the wilderness on the plateau in the tribe of Reuben, Ramoth in Gilead in the tribe of Gad, and Golan in Bashan in the tribe of Manasseh. ⁹Any of the Israelites or any foreigner residing among them who killed someone accidentally could flee to these designated cities and not be killed by the avenger of blood prior to standing trial before the assembly.

Towns for the Levites

21 Now the family heads of the Levites approached Eleazar the priest, Joshua son of Nun, and the heads of the other tribal families of Israel ²at Shiloh in Canaan and said to them, 'The LORD commanded through Moses that you give us towns to live in, with pasture-lands for our livestock.' ³So, as the LORD had commanded, the Israelites gave the Levites the following towns and pasture-lands out of their own inheritance:

⁴The first lot came out for the Kohathites, according to their clans. The Levites who were descendants of Aaron the priest were allotted thirteen towns from the tribes of Judah, Simeon and Benjamin. ⁵The rest of Kohath's descendants were allotted ten towns from the clans of the tribes of Ephraim, Dan and half of Manasseh.

⁶The descendants of Gershon were allotted thirteen towns from the clans of the tribes of Issachar, Asher, Naphtali and the half-tribe of Manasseh in Bashan.

⁷The descendants of Merari, according to their clans, received twelve towns from the tribes of Reuben, Gad and Zebulun.

⁸So the Israelites allotted to the Levites these towns and their pasture-lands, as the LORD had commanded through Moses.

⁹From the tribes of Judah and Simeon they allotted the following towns by name ¹⁰(these towns were assigned to the descendants of Aaron who were from the Kohathite clans of the Levites, because the first lot fell to them):

¹¹They gave them Kiriath Arba (that is, Hebron), with its surrounding pasture-land, in the hill country of Judah. (Arba was the ancestor of Anak.) ¹²But the fields and villages around the city they had given to Caleb son of Jephunneh as his possession.

¹³So to the descendants of Aaron the priest they gave Hebron (a city of refuge for one accused of murder), Libnah, ¹⁴Jattir, Eshtemoa, ¹⁵Holon, Debir, ¹⁶Ain, Juttah and Beth Shemesh, together with their pasture-lands—nine towns from these two tribes.

¹⁷And from the tribe of Benjamin they gave them Gibeon, Geba, ¹⁸Anathoth and Almon, together with their pasture-lands—four towns.

¹⁹The total number of towns for the priests, the descendants of Aaron, came to thirteen, together with their pasture-lands.

²⁰The rest of the Kohathite clans of the Levites were allotted towns from the tribe of Ephraim:

²¹In the hill country of Ephraim they were given Shechem (a city of refuge for one accused of murder) and Gezer, ²²Kibzaim and Beth Horon, together with their pasture-lands—four towns.

²³Also from the tribe of Dan they received Eltekeh, Gibbethon, ²⁴Aijalon and Gath Rimmon, together with their pasture-lands—four towns.

²⁵From half the tribe of Manasseh they received Taanach and Gath Rimmon, together with their pasture-lands—two towns. ²⁶All these ten towns and their pasture-lands were given to the rest of the Kohathite clans.

²⁷The Levite clans of the Gershonites were given:

from the half-tribe of Manasseh,
Golan in Bashan (a city of refuge for one accused of murder) and Be Eshterah, together with their pasture-lands—two towns;
²⁸from the tribe of Issachar,
Kishion, Daberath, ²⁹Jarmuth and En Gannim, together with their pasture-lands—four towns;
³⁰from the tribe of Asher,
Mishal, Abdon, ³¹Helkath and Rehob, together with their pasture-lands—four towns;
³²from the tribe of Naphtali,
Kedesh in Galilee (a city of refuge for one accused of murder), Hammoth Dor and Kartan, together with their pasturelands—three towns.

³³The total number of towns of the Gershonite clans came to thirteen, together with their pasture-lands.

³⁴The Merarite clans (the rest of the Levites) were given:

from the tribe of Zebulun,
Jokneam, Kartah, ³⁵Dimnah and Nahalal, together with their pasture-lands—four towns;
³⁶from the tribe of Reuben,
Bezer, Jahaz, ³⁷Kedemoth and Mephaath, together with their pasture-lands—four towns;
³⁸from the tribe of Gad,
Ramoth in Gilead (a city of refuge for one accused of murder), Mahanaim, ³⁹Heshbon and Jazer, together with their pasture-lands—four towns in all.

⁴⁰The total number of towns allotted to the Merarite clans, who were the rest of the Levites, came to twelve.

⁴¹The towns of the Levites in the territory held by the Israelites were forty-eight in all, together with their pasture-lands. ⁴²Each of these towns had pasture-lands surrounding it; this was true for all these towns.

⁴³So the LORD gave Israel all the land he had sworn to give their ancestors, and they took possession of it and settled there. ⁴⁴The LORD gave them rest on every side, just as he had sworn to their ancestors. Not one of their enemies withstood them; the LORD gave all their enemies into their hands. ⁴⁵Not one of all the LORD's good promises to the house of Israel failed; every one was fulfilled.

Eastern tribes return home

22 Then Joshua summoned the Reubenites, the Gadites and the half-tribe of Manasseh ²and said to them, 'You have done all that Moses the servant of the LORD commanded, and you have obeyed me in everything I commanded. ³For a long time now—to this very day—you have not deserted the other Israelites but have carried out the mission the LORD your God gave you. ⁴Now that the LORD your God has given them rest as he promised, return to your homes in the land that Moses the servant of the LORD gave you on the other side of the Jordan. ⁵But be very careful to keep the commandment and the law that Moses the servant of the LORD gave you: to love the LORD your God, to walk in obedience to him, to keep his commands, to hold fast to him and to serve him with all your heart and with all your soul.'

⁶Then Joshua blessed them and sent them away, and they went to their homes. ⁷(To the half-tribe of Manasseh Moses had given land in Bashan, and to the other half of the tribe Joshua gave land on the west side of the Jordan along with the other Israelites.) When Joshua sent them home, he blessed them, ⁸saying, 'Return to your homes with your great wealth—with large herds of livestock, with silver, gold, bronze and

⁹So the Reubenites, the Gadites and the half-tribe of Manasseh left the Israelites at Shiloh in Canaan to return to Gilead, their own land, which they had acquired in accordance with the command of the LORD through Moses.

¹⁰When they came to Geliloth near the Jordan in the land of Canaan, the Reubenites, the Gadites and the half-tribe of Manasseh built an imposing altar there by the Jordan. ¹¹And when the Israelites heard that they had built the altar on the border of Canaan at Geliloth near the Jordan on the Israelite side, ¹²the whole assembly of Israel gathered at Shiloh to go to war against them.

¹³So the Israelites sent Phinehas son of Eleazar, the priest, to the land of Gilead—to Reuben, Gad and the half-tribe of Manasseh. ¹⁴With him they sent ten of the chief men, one from each of the tribes of Israel, each the head of a family division among the Israelite clans.

¹⁵When they went to Gilead—to Reuben, Gad and the half-tribe of Manasseh—they said to them: ¹⁶'The whole assembly of the LORD says: "How could you break faith with the God of Israel like this? How could you turn away from the LORD and build yourselves an altar in rebellion against him now? ¹⁷Was not the sin of Peor enough for us? Up to this very day we have not cleansed ourselves from that sin, even though a plague fell on the community of the LORD! ¹⁸And are you now turning away from the LORD?

'"If you rebel against the LORD today, tomorrow he will be angry with the whole community of Israel. ¹⁹If the land you possess is defiled, come over to the LORD's land, where the LORD's tabernacle stands, and share the land with us. But do not rebel against the LORD or against us by building an altar for yourselves, other than the altar of the LORD our God. ²⁰When Achan son of Zerah was unfaithful in regard to the devoted things,[a] did not wrath come on the whole community of Israel? He was not the only one who died for his sin."'

²¹Then Reuben, Gad and the half-tribe of Manasseh replied to the heads of the clans of Israel: ²²'The Mighty One, God, the LORD! The Mighty One, God, the LORD! He knows! And let Israel know! If this has been in rebellion or disobedience to the LORD, do not spare us this day. ²³If we have built our own altar to turn away from the LORD and to offer burnt offerings and grain offerings, or to sacrifice fellowship offerings on it, may the LORD himself call us to account.

²⁴'No! We did it for fear that some day your descendants might say to ours, "What do you have to do with the LORD, the God of Israel? ²⁵The LORD has made the Jordan a boundary between us and you—you Reubenites and Gadites! You have no share in the LORD." So your descendants might cause ours to stop fearing the LORD.

²⁶'That is why we said, "Let us get ready and build an altar—but not for burnt offerings or sacrifices." ²⁷On the contrary, it is to be a witness between us and you and the generations that follow, that we will worship the LORD at his sanctuary with our burnt offerings, sacrifices and fellowship offerings. Then in the future your descendants will not be able to say to ours, "You have no share in the LORD."

²⁸'And we said, "If they ever say this to us, or to our descendants, we will answer: look at the replica of the LORD's altar, which our people built, not for burnt offerings and sacrifices, but as a witness between us and you."

²⁹'Far be it from us to rebel against the LORD and turn away from him today by building an altar for burnt offerings, grain offerings and sacrifices, other than the altar of the LORD our God that stands before his tabernacle.'

³⁰When Phinehas the priest and the leaders of the community—the heads of the clans of the Israelites—heard what Reuben, Gad and Manasseh had to say, they were pleased. ³¹And Phinehas son of Eleazar, the priest, said to Reuben, Gad and Manasseh, 'Today we know that the LORD is

---

[a] 20 The Hebrew term refers to the irrevocable giving over of things or persons to the LORD, often by totally destroying them.

with us, because you have not been unfaithful to the LORD in this matter. Now you have rescued the Israelites from the LORD's hand.'

32Then Phinehas son of Eleazar, the priest, and the leaders returned to Canaan from their meeting with the Reubenites and Gadites in Gilead and reported to the Israelites. 33They were glad to hear the report and praised God. And they talked no more about going to war against them to devastate the country where the Reubenites and the Gadites lived.

34And the Reubenites and the Gadites gave the altar this name: A Witness Between Us—that the LORD is God.

Joshua's farewell to the leaders

23 After a long time had passed and the LORD had given Israel rest from all their enemies around them, Joshua, by then a very old man, 2summoned all Israel—their elders, leaders, judges and officials—and said to them: 'I am very old. 3You yourselves have seen everything the LORD your God has done to all these nations for your sake; it was the LORD your God who fought for you. 4Remember how I have allotted as an inheritance for your tribes all the land of the nations that remain—the nations I conquered—between the Jordan and the Mediterranean Sea in the west. 5The LORD your God himself will push them out for your sake. He will drive them out before you, and you will take possession of their land, as the LORD your God promised you.

6'Be very strong; be careful to obey all that is written in the Book of the Law of Moses, without turning aside to the right or to the left. 7Do not associate with these nations that remain among you; do not invoke the names of their gods or swear by them. You must not serve them or bow down to them. 8But you are to hold fast to the LORD your God, as you have until now.

9'The LORD has driven out before you great and powerful nations; to this day no-one has been able to withstand you. 10One of you routs a thousand, because the LORD your God fights for you, just as he promised. 11So be very careful to love the LORD your God.

12'But if you turn away and ally yourselves with the survivors of these nations that remain among you and if you intermarry with them and associate with them, 13then you may be sure that the LORD your God will no longer drive out these nations before you. Instead, they will become snares and traps for you, whips on your backs and thorns in your eyes, until you perish from this good land, which the LORD your God has given you.

14'Now I am about to go the way of all the earth. You know with all your heart and soul that not one of all the good promises the LORD your God gave you has failed. Every promise has been fulfilled; not one has failed. 15But just as all the good things the LORD your God has promised you have come to you, so he will bring on you all the evil things he has threatened, until the LORD your God has destroyed you from this good land he has given you. 16If you violate the covenant of the LORD your God, which he commanded you, and go and serve other gods and bow down to them, the LORD's anger will burn against you, and you will quickly perish from the good land he has given you.'

The covenant renewed at Shechem

24 Then Joshua assembled all the tribes of Israel at Shechem. He summoned the elders, leaders, judges and officials of Israel, and they presented themselves before God.

2Joshua said to all the people, 'This is what the LORD, the God of Israel, says: "Long ago your ancestors, including Terah the father of Abraham and Nahor, lived beyond the River Euphrates and worshipped other gods. 3But I took your father Abraham from the land beyond the Euphrates and led him throughout Canaan and gave him many descendants. I gave him Isaac, 4and to Isaac I gave Jacob and Esau. I assigned the hill country of Seir to Esau, but Jacob and his family went down to Egypt.

5' "Then I sent Moses and Aaron, and I afflicted the Egyptians by what I did there, and I brought you out. 6When I brought your people out of Egypt, you came to the sea, and the Egyptians pursued them with chariots and horsemen[a] as far as the Red Sea.[b] 7But they cried to the LORD for help, and he put darkness between you and the Egyptians; he brought the sea over them and covered them. You saw with your own eyes what I did to the Egyptians. Then you lived in the wilderness for a long time.

8'"I brought you to the land of the Amorites who lived east of the Jordan. They fought against you, but I gave them into your hands. I destroyed them from before you, and you took possession of their land. 9When Balak son of Zippor, the king of Moab, prepared to fight against Israel, he sent for Balaam son of Beor to put a curse on you. 10But I would not listen to Balaam, so he blessed you again and again, and I delivered you out of his hand.

11'"Then you crossed the Jordan and came to Jericho. The citizens of Jericho fought against you, as did also the Amorites, Perizzites, Canaanites, Hittites, Girgashites, Hivites and Jebusites, but I gave them into your hands. 12I sent the hornet ahead of you, which drove them out before you— also the two Amorite kings. You did not do it with your own sword and bow. 13So I gave you a land on which you did not toil and cities you did not build; and you live in them and eat from vineyards and olive groves that you did not plant."

14'Now fear the LORD and serve him with all faithfulness. Throw away the gods your ancestors worshipped beyond the River Euphrates and in Egypt, and serve the LORD. 15But if serving the LORD seems undesirable to you, then choose for yourselves this day whom you will serve, whether the gods your ancestors served beyond the Euphrates, or the gods of the Amorites, in whose land you are living. But as for me and my household, we will serve the LORD.'

16Then the people answered, 'Far be it from us to forsake the LORD to serve other gods! 17It was the LORD our God himself who brought us and our parents up out of Egypt, from that land of slavery, and performed those great signs before our eyes. He protected us on our entire journey and among all the nations through which we travelled. 18And the LORD drove out before us all the nations, including the Amorites, who lived in the land. We too will serve the LORD, because he is our God.'

19Joshua said to the people, 'You are not able to serve the LORD. He is a holy God; he is a jealous God. He will not forgive your rebellion and your sins. 20If you forsake the LORD and serve foreign gods, he will turn and bring disaster on you and make an end of you, after he has been good to you.'

21But the people said to Joshua, 'No! We will serve the LORD.'

22Then Joshua said, 'You are witnesses against yourselves that you have chosen to serve the LORD.'

'Yes, we are witnesses,' they replied.

23'Now then,' said Joshua, 'throw away the foreign gods that are among you and yield your hearts to the LORD, the God of Israel.'

24And the people said to Joshua, 'We will serve the LORD our God and obey him.'

25On that day Joshua made a covenant for the people, and there at Shechem he reaffirmed for them decrees and laws. 26And Joshua recorded these things in the Book of the Law of God. Then he took a

making Connections

Joseph's bones
Joshua 24:32

Joseph's bones probably travelled farther after he had died than he did during his lifetime! After years of being carried through the wilderness, they have finally found their resting place in the Promised Land. This was to fulfil the promise that Joseph's brothers made (Genesis 50:25) and Moses carried out (Exodus 13:19), to take his bones with them when they left Egypt.

---

[a]6 Or charioteers [b]6 Or the Sea of Reeds [c]30 Also known as Timnath Heres (see Judges 2:9)

large stone and set it up there under the oak near the holy place of the LORD.

27'See!' he said to all the people. 'This stone will be a witness against us. It has heard all the words the LORD has said to us. It will be a witness against you if you are untrue to your God.'

28Then Joshua dismissed the people, each to their own inheritance.

Buried in the promised land

29After these things, Joshua son of Nun, the servant of the LORD, died at the age of a hundred and ten. 30And they buried him in the land of his inheritance, at Timnath Serah[a] in the hill country of Ephraim, north of Mount Gaash.

31Israel served the LORD throughout the lifetime of Joshua and of the elders who outlived him and who had experienced everything the LORD had done for Israel.

32And Joseph's bones, which the Israelites had brought up from Egypt, were buried at Shechem in the tract of land that Jacob bought for a hundred pieces of silver[b] from the sons of Hamor, the father of Shechem. This became the inheritance of Joseph's descendants.

33And Eleazar son of Aaron died and was buried at Gibeah, which had been allotted to his son Phinehas in the hill country of Ephraim.

---

[a]32 Hebrew *hundred kesitahs*; a kesitah was a unit of money of unknown weight and value.

Judges

INTRODUCTION

JUDGES

Author: Unknown

When: The three hundred years between Joshua's death and the beginning of King Saul's reign, around 1380 BC to 1050 BC.

Where: Canaan, the Promised Land.

Did you know? Judges contains the story of the first left-handed man to get a mention in the Bible, Ehud. And what a great story it is! Read it in chapter 3.

Main theme: One word can sum up this period in the Israelites' history – chaos. After Joshua dies, the people forget the miracles God did for them. There is no strong spiritual leader to take his place, and the people start worshipping false gods which leads to them being taken over by enemy nations. They cry out to God and he sends a judge or deliverer to sort them out. These judges restore order to the land, but inevitably the people go their own way and get into trouble again. Will they never learn?

Israel fights the remaining Canaanites

1 After the death of Joshua, the Israelites asked the LORD, 'Who of us is to go up first to fight against the Canaanites?'

²The LORD answered, 'Judah shall go up; I have given the land into their hands.'

³The men of Judah then said to the Simeonites their fellow Israelites, 'Come up with us into the territory allotted to us, to fight against the Canaanites. We in turn will go with you into yours.' So the Simeonites went with them.

⁴When Judah attacked, the LORD gave the Canaanites and Perizzites into their hands, and they struck down ten thousand men at Bezek. ⁵It was there that they found Adoni-Bezek and fought against him, putting to rout the Canaanites and Perizzites.

⁶Adoni-Bezek fled, but they chased him and caught him, and cut off his thumbs and big toes.

⁷Then Adoni-Bezek said, 'Seventy kings with their thumbs and big toes cut off have picked up scraps under my table. Now God has paid me back for what I did to them.' They brought him to Jerusalem, and he died there.

⁸The men of Judah attacked Jerusalem also and took it. They put the city to the sword and set it on fire.

⁹After that, Judah went down to fight against the Canaanites living in the hill country, the Negev and the western foothills. ¹⁰They advanced against the Canaanites living in Hebron (formerly called Kiriath Arba) and defeated Sheshai, Ahiman and Talmai.

¹¹From there they advanced against the people living in Debir (formerly called Kiriath Sepher). ¹²And Caleb said, 'I will give my daughter Aksah in marriage to the man who attacks and captures Kiriath Sepher.' ¹³Othniel son of Kenaz, Caleb's younger brother, took it; so Caleb gave his daughter Aksah to him in marriage.

¹⁴One day when she came to Othniel, she urged him*ᵃ* to ask her father for a field. When she got off her donkey, Caleb asked her, 'What can I do for you?'

¹⁵She replied, 'Do me a special favour. Since you have given me land in the Negev, give me also springs of water.' So Caleb gave her the upper and lower springs.

¹⁶The descendants of Moses' father-in-law, the Kenite, went up from the City of Palms*ᵇ* with the people of Judah to live among the inhabitants of the Desert of Judah in the Negev near Arad.

¹⁷Then the men of Judah went with the Simeonites their fellow Israelites and attacked the Canaanites living in Zephath, and they totally destroyed*ᶜ* the city. Therefore it was called Hormah.*ᵈ* ¹⁸Judah also took*ᵉ* Gaza, Ashkelon and Ekron—each city with its territory.

¹⁹The LORD was with the men of Judah. They took possession of the hill country, but they were unable to drive the people from the plains, because they had chariots fitted with iron. ²⁰As Moses had promised, Hebron was given to Caleb, who drove from it the three sons of Anak. ²¹The Benjaminites, however, did not drive out the Jebusites, who were living in Jerusalem; to this day the Jebusites live there with the Benjaminites.

²²Now the house of Joseph attacked Bethel, and the LORD was with them. ²³When they sent men to spy out Bethel (formerly called Luz), ²⁴the spies saw a man coming out of the city and they said to him, 'Show us how to get into the city and we will see that you are treated well.' ²⁵So he showed them, and they put the city to the sword but spared the man and his whole family. ²⁶He then went to the land of the Hittites, where he built a city and called it Luz, which is its name to this day.

²⁷But Manasseh did not drive out the people of Beth Shan or Taanach or Dor or Ibleam or Megiddo and their surrounding settlements, for the Canaanites were determined to live in that land. ²⁸When Israel became strong, they pressed the Canaanites into forced labour but never drove them out completely. ²⁹Nor did Ephraim drive out the Canaanites living in Gezer, but the Canaanites continued to live there among them. ³⁰Neither did Zebulun drive out the Canaanites living in Kitron or Nahalol, so these Canaanites lived among them, but Zebulun did subject them to forced labour. ³¹Nor did Asher drive out those living in Akko or Sidon or Ahlab or Akzib or Helbah or Aphek or Rehob. ³²The Asherites lived among the Canaanite inhabitants of the land because they did not drive them out. ³³Neither did Naphtali drive out those living in Beth Shemesh or Beth Anath; but the Naphtalites too lived among the Canaanite inhabitants of the land, and those living in Beth Shemesh and Beth Anath became forced labourers for them. ³⁴The Amorites confined the Danites to the hill country, not allowing them to come down into the plain. ³⁵And the Amorites were determined also to hold out in Mount

---

ᵃ 14 Hebrew; Septuagint and Vulgate *Othniel, he urged her*   *ᵇ* 16 That is, Jericho   *ᶜ* 17 The Hebrew term refers to the irrevocable giving over of things or persons to the LORD, often by totally destroying them.   *ᵈ* 17 *Hormah* means *destruction*.   *ᵉ* 18 Hebrew; Septuagint *Judah did not take*

Heres, Aijalon and Shaalbim, but when the power of the house of Joseph increased, they too were pressed into forced labour. 36The boundary of the Amorites was from Scorpion Pass to Sela and beyond.

The angel of the LORD at Bokim

2 The angel of the LORD went up from Gilgal to Bokim and said, 'I brought you up out of Egypt and led you into the land that I swore to give to your ancestors. I said, "I will never break my covenant with you, 2and you shall not make a covenant with the people of this land, but you shall break down their altars." Yet you have disobeyed me. Why have you done this? 3And I have also said, "I will not drive them out before you; they will become traps for you, and their gods will become snares to you."'

4When the angel of the LORD had spoken these things to all the Israelites, the people wept aloud, 5and they called that place Bokim.*a* There they offered sacrifices to the LORD.

Disobedience and defeat

6After Joshua had dismissed the Israelites, they went to take possession of the land, each to their own inheritance. 7The people served the LORD throughout the lifetime of Joshua and of the elders who outlived him and who had seen all the great things the LORD had done for Israel.

8Joshua son of Nun, the servant of the LORD, died at the age of a hundred and ten. 9And they buried him in the land of his inheritance, at Timnath Heres*b* in the hill country of Ephraim, north of Mount Gaash.

10After that whole generation had been gathered to their ancestors, another generation grew up who knew neither the LORD nor what he had done for Israel. 11Then the Israelites did evil in the eyes of the LORD and served the Baals. 12They forsook the LORD, the God of their ancestors, who had brought them out of Egypt. They followed and worshipped various gods of the peoples around them. They aroused the LORD's anger 13because they forsook him and served Baal and the Ashtoreths. 14In his anger against Israel the LORD gave them into the hands of raiders who plundered them. He sold them into the hands of their enemies all around, whom they were no longer able to resist. 15Whenever Israel went out to fight, the hand of the LORD was against them to defeat them, just as he had sworn to them. They were in great distress.

16Then the LORD raised up judges,*c* who saved them out of the hands of these raiders. 17Yet they would not listen to their judges but prostituted themselves to other gods and worshipped them. Unlike their ancestors, they quickly turned from following the way of their ancestors, the way of obedience to the LORD's commands. 18Whenever the LORD raised up a judge for them, he was with the judge and saved them out of the hands of their enemies as long as the judge lived; for the LORD relented because of their groaning under those who oppressed and afflicted them. 19But when the judge died, the people returned to ways even more corrupt than those of their ancestors, following other gods and serving and worshipping them. They refused to give up their evil practices and stubborn ways.

The judges
Judges 2:16
A judge is someone responsible for administering justice and government. During this period in their history, the Israelites didn't have a king or one strong leader like Moses or Joshua. Instead, every time the Israelites cried out to God, he raised up these military heroes known as judges to lead them out of trouble. The judges were often weak, though, and their success short-lived. The people always went back to idolatry again.

---

*a*5 *Bokim* means *weepers.*   *b*9 Also known as *Timnath Serah* (see Joshua 19:50 and 24:30)   *c*16 Or *leaders*; similarly in verses 17-19

20 Therefore the LORD was very angry with Israel and said, 'Because this nation has violated the covenant I ordained for their ancestors and has not listened to me, 21 I will no longer drive out before them any of the nations Joshua left when he died. 22 I will use them to test Israel and see whether they will keep the way of the LORD and walk in it as their ancestors did.' 23 The LORD had allowed those nations to remain; he did not drive them out at once by giving them into the hands of Joshua.

3 These are the nations the LORD left to test all those Israelites who had not experienced any of the wars in Canaan 2 (he did this only to teach warfare to the descendants of the Israelites who had not had previous battle experience): 3 the five rulers of the Philistines, all the Canaanites, the Sidonians, and the Hivites living in the Lebanon mountains from Mount Baal Hermon to Lebo Hamath. 4 They were left to test the Israelites to see whether they would obey the LORD's commands, which he had given their ancestors through Moses.

5 The Israelites lived among the Canaanites, Hittites, Amorites, Perizzites, Hivites and Jebusites. 6 They took their daughters in marriage and gave their own daughters to their sons, and served their gods.

Othniel

7 The Israelites did evil in the eyes of the LORD; they forgot the LORD their God and served the Baals and the Asherahs. 8 The anger of the LORD burned against Israel so that he sold them into the hands of Cushan-Rishathaim king of Aram Naharaim,[a] to whom the Israelites were subject for eight years. 9 But when they cried out to the LORD, he raised up for them a deliverer, Othniel son of Kenaz, Caleb's younger brother, who saved them. 10 The Spirit of the LORD came on him, so that he became Israel's judge[b] and went to war. The LORD gave Cushan-Rishathaim king of Aram into the hands of Othniel, who overpowered him. 11 So the land had peace for forty years, until Othniel son of Kenaz died.

Ehud

12 Again the Israelites did evil in the eyes of the LORD, and because they did this evil the LORD gave Eglon king of Moab power over Israel. 13 Getting the Ammonites and Amalekites to join him, Eglon came and attacked Israel, and they took possession of the City of Palms.[c] 14 The Israelites were subject to Eglon king of Moab for eighteen years.

15 Again the Israelites cried out to the LORD, and he gave them a deliverer—Ehud, a left-handed man, the son of Gera the Benjaminite. The Israelites sent him with tribute to Eglon king of Moab. 16 Now Ehud had made a double-edged sword about a cubit[d] long, which he strapped to his right thigh under his clothing. 17 He presented the tribute to Eglon king of Moab, who was a very fat man. 18 After Ehud had presented the tribute, he dismissed those who had carried it. 19 But on reaching the stone images near Gilgal he himself went back to Eglon and said, 'Your majesty, I have a secret message for you.'

The king said to his attendants, 'Leave us!' And they all left.

20 Ehud then approached him while he was sitting alone in the upper room of his palace[e] and said, 'I have a message from God for you.' As the king rose from his seat, 21 Ehud reached with his left hand, drew the sword from his right thigh and plunged it into the king's belly. 22 Even the handle sank in after the blade, and his bowels discharged. Ehud did not pull the sword out, and the fat closed in over it. 23 Then Ehud went out to the porch;[f] he shut the doors of the upper room behind him and locked them.

24 After he had gone, the servants came and found the doors of the upper room locked. They said, 'He must be relieving himself in the inner room of the palace.' 25 They waited to the point of embarrassment, but when he did not open the doors of the room, they took a key and unlocked them. There they saw their lord fallen to the floor, dead.

---

[a] 8 That is, North-west Mesopotamia [b] 10 Or *leader* [c] 13 That is, Jericho [d] 16 That is, about 45 centimetres [e] 20 The meaning of the Hebrew for this word is uncertain; also in verse 24. [f] 23 The meaning of the Hebrew for this word is uncertain.

26 While they waited, Ehud got away. He passed by the stone images and escaped to Seirah. 27 When he arrived there, he blew a trumpet in the hill country of Ephraim, and the Israelites went down with him from the hills, with him leading them.

28 'Follow me,' he ordered, 'for the LORD has given Moab, your enemy, into your hands.' So they followed him down and took possession of the fords of the Jordan that led to Moab; they allowed no-one to cross over. 29 At that time they struck down about ten thousand Moabites, all vigorous and strong; not one escaped. 30 That day Moab was made subject to Israel, and the land had peace for eighty years.

Shamgar

31 After Ehud came Shamgar son of Anath, who struck down six hundred Philistines with an ox-goad. He too saved Israel.

Deborah

4 Again the Israelites did evil in the eyes of the LORD, now that Ehud was dead. 2 So the LORD sold them into the hands of Jabin king of Canaan, who reigned in Hazor. Sisera, the commander of his army, was based in Harosheth Haggoyim. 3 Because he had nine hundred chariots fitted with iron and had cruelly oppressed the Israelites for twenty years, they cried to the LORD for help.

4 Now Deborah, a prophet, the wife of Lappidoth, was leading[a] Israel at that time. 5 She held court under the Palm of Deborah between Ramah and Bethel in the hill country of Ephraim, and the Israelites went up to her to have their disputes decided. 6 She sent for Barak son of Abinoam from Kedesh in Naphtali and said to him, 'The LORD, the God of Israel, commands you: "Go, take with you ten thousand men of Naphtali and Zebulun and lead them up to Mount Tabor. 7 I will lead Sisera, the commander of Jabin's army, with his chariots and his troops to the River Kishon and give him into your hands."'

8 Barak said to her, 'If you go with me, I will go; but if you don't go with me, I won't go.'

9 'Certainly I will go with you,' said Deborah. 'But because of the course you are taking, the honour will not be yours, for the LORD will deliver Sisera into the hands of a woman.' So Deborah went with Barak to Kedesh. 10 There Barak summoned Zebulun and Naphtali, and ten thousand men went up under his command. Deborah also went up with him.

11 Now Heber the Kenite had left the other Kenites, the descendants of Hobab, Moses' brother-in-law,[b] and pitched his tent by the great tree in Zaanannim near Kedesh.

12 When they told Sisera that Barak son of Abinoam had gone up to Mount Tabor, 13 Sisera summoned from Harosheth Haggoyim to the River Kishon all his men and his nine hundred chariots fitted with iron.

14 Then Deborah said to Barak, 'Go! This is the day the LORD has given Sisera into your hands. Has not the LORD gone ahead of you?' So Barak went down Mount Tabor, with ten thousand men following him. 15 At Barak's advance, the LORD routed Sisera and all his chariots and army by the sword, and Sisera got down from his chariot and fled on foot.

People and Places

Deborah
Judges 4:4

Deborah was a prophetess, the fifth of Israel's judges and the only one who was female. She told Barak to take 10,000 soldiers and fight Sisera, the leader of Jabin's army who had been terrorising Israel for twenty years. Barak would only go if Deborah went with him, and so the honour of killing Sisera went to a woman, Jael (Judges 4:18–22). Deborah's song in Judges 5 is one of the finest and earliest examples of Hebrew poetry.

---

[a] 4 Traditionally *judging* [b] 11 Or *father-in-law*

¹⁶Barak pursued the chariots and army as far as Harosheth Haggoyim, and all Sisera's troops fell by the sword; not a man was left. ¹⁷Sisera, meanwhile, fled on foot to the tent of Jael, the wife of Heber the Kenite, because there was an alliance between Jabin king of Hazor and the family of Heber the Kenite.

¹⁸Jael went out to meet Sisera and said to him, 'Come, my lord, come right in. Don't be afraid.' So he entered her tent, and she covered him with a blanket.

¹⁹'I'm thirsty,' he said. 'Please give me some water.' She opened a skin of milk, gave him a drink, and covered him up.

²⁰'Stand in the doorway of the tent,' he told her. 'If anyone comes and asks you, "Is there a man in here?" say "No."'

²¹But Jael, Heber's wife, picked up a tent peg and a hammer and went quietly to him while he lay fast asleep, exhausted. She drove the peg through his temple into the ground, and he died.

²²Just then Barak came in pursuit of Sisera, and Jael went out to meet him. 'Come,' she said, 'I will show you the man you're looking for.' So he went in with her, and there lay Sisera with the tent peg through his temple—dead.

²³On that day God subdued Jabin king of Canaan before the Israelites. ²⁴And the hand of the Israelites pressed harder and harder against Jabin king of Canaan until they destroyed him.

The song of Deborah

5 On that day Deborah and Barak son of Abinoam sang this song:

²'When the princes in Israel take the lead,
when the people willingly offer themselves—
praise the LORD!

³'Hear this, you kings! Listen, you rulers!
I, even I, will sing to^a the LORD;
I will praise the LORD, the God of Israel, in song.

⁴'When you, LORD, went out from Seir,
when you marched from the land of Edom,
the earth shook, the heavens poured,
the clouds poured down water.
⁵The mountains quaked before the LORD,
the One of Sinai,
before the LORD, the God of Israel.

⁶'In the days of Shamgar son of Anath,
in the days of Jael, the highways were abandoned;
travellers took to winding paths.
⁷Villagers in Israel would not fight;
they held back until I, Deborah, arose,
until I arose, a mother in Israel.
⁸God chose new leaders
when war came to the city gates,
but not a shield or spear was seen
among forty thousand in Israel.
⁹My heart is with Israel's princes,
with the willing volunteers among the people.
Praise the LORD!

¹⁰'You who ride on white donkeys,
sitting on your saddle blankets,
and you who walk along the road,
consider ¹¹the voice of the singers^b at the watering places.
They recite the victories of the LORD,
the victories of his villagers in Israel.

'Then the people of the LORD
went down to the city gates.
¹²"Wake up, wake up, Deborah!
Wake up, wake up, break out in song!
Arise, Barak!
Take captive your captives, son of Abinoam."

¹³'The remnant of the nobles came down;
the people of the LORD came down to me against the mighty.
¹⁴Some came from Ephraim, whose roots were in Amalek;
Benjamin was with the people who followed you.
From Makir captains came down,
from Zebulun those who bear a commander's^c staff.
¹⁵The princes of Issachar were with Deborah;
yes, Issachar was with Barak,

---

^{a} 3 Or *of* ^{b} 11 The meaning of the Hebrew for this word is uncertain. ^{c} 14 The meaning of the Hebrew for this word is uncertain.

sent under his command into the
    valley.
In the districts of Reuben
    there was much searching of heart.
16Why did you stay among the sheepfolds*a*
    to hear the whistling for the flocks?
In the districts of Reuben
    there was much searching of heart.
17Gilead stayed beyond the Jordan.
    And Dan, why did he linger by the
        ships?
Asher remained on the coast
    and stayed in his coves.
18The people of Zebulun risked their very
        lives;
    so did Naphtali on the terraced fields.

19'Kings came, they fought,
    the kings of Canaan fought.
At Taanach, by the waters of Megiddo,
    they took no plunder of silver.
20From the heavens the stars fought,
    from their courses they fought against
        Sisera.
21The River Kishon swept them away,
    the age-old river, the River Kishon.
March on, my soul; be strong!
22Then thundered the horses' hooves—
    galloping, galloping go his mighty
        steeds.
23"Curse Meroz," said the angel of the
        LORD.
    "Curse its people bitterly,
because they did not come to help the
        LORD,
    to help the LORD against the mighty."

24'Most blessed of women be Jael,
    the wife of Heber the Kenite,
    most blessed of tent-dwelling women.
25He asked for water, and she gave him
        milk;
    in a bowl fit for nobles she brought him
        curdled milk.
26Her hand reached for the tent peg,
    her right hand for the labourer's
        hammer.
She struck Sisera, she crushed his head,
    she shattered and pierced his temple.
27At her feet he sank,
    he fell; there he lay.
At her feet he sank, he fell;
    where he sank, there he fell—dead.

28'Through the window peered Sisera's
        mother;
    behind the lattice she cried out,
    "Why is his chariot so long in coming?
    Why is the clatter of his chariots
        delayed?"
29The wisest of her ladies answer her;
    indeed, she keeps saying to herself,
30"Are they not finding and dividing the
        spoils:
    a woman or two for each man,
    colourful garments as plunder for Sisera,
    colourful garments embroidered,
highly embroidered garments for my
        neck—
all this as plunder?"

31'So may all your enemies perish, O LORD!
    But may all who love you be like the sun
        when it rises in its strength.'

Then the land had peace for forty years.

Gideon

6 The Israelites did evil in the eyes of the LORD, and for seven years he gave them into the hands of the Midianites. 2Because the power of Midian was so oppressive, the Israelites prepared shelters for themselves in mountain clefts, caves and strongholds. 3Whenever the Israelites planted their crops, the Midianites, Amalekites and other eastern peoples invaded the country. 4They camped on the land and ruined the crops all the way to Gaza and did not spare a living thing for Israel, neither sheep nor cattle nor donkeys. 5They came up with their livestock and their tents like swarms of locusts. It was impossible to count them or their camels; they invaded the land to ravage it. 6Midian so impoverished the Israelites that they cried out to the LORD for help.

7When the Israelites cried out to the LORD because of Midian, 8he sent them a prophet, who said, 'This is what the LORD, the God of Israel, says: I brought you up out of Egypt, out of the land of slavery. 9I rescued you from the hand of the Egyptians. And I delivered you from the hand of all

---
a 16 Or *the campfires*; or *the saddlebags*

your oppressors; I drove them out before you and gave you their land. ¹⁰I said to you, "I am the LORD your God; do not worship the gods of the Amorites, in whose land you live." But you have not listened to me.'

¹¹The angel of the LORD came and sat down under the oak in Ophrah that belonged to Joash the Abiezrite, where his son Gideon was threshing wheat in a winepress to keep it from the Midianites. ¹²When the angel of the LORD appeared to Gideon, he said, 'The LORD is with you, mighty warrior.'

¹³'Pardon me, my lord,' Gideon replied, 'but if the LORD is with us, why has all this happened to us? Where are all his wonders that our ancestors told us about when they said, "Did not the LORD bring us up out of Egypt?" But now the LORD has abandoned us and given us into the hand of Midian.'

¹⁴The LORD turned to him and said, 'Go in the strength you have and save Israel out of Midian's hand. Am I not sending you?'

¹⁵'Pardon me, my lord,' Gideon replied, 'but how can I save Israel? My clan is the weakest in Manasseh, and I am the least in my family.'

¹⁶The LORD answered, 'I will be with you, and you will strike down all the Midianites together.'

¹⁷Gideon replied, 'If now I have found favour in your eyes, give me a sign that it is really you talking to me. ¹⁸Please do not go away until I come back and bring my offering and set it before you.'

And the LORD said, 'I will wait until you return.'

¹⁹Gideon went in, prepared a young goat, and from an ephah^a of flour he made bread without yeast. Putting the meat in a basket and its broth in a pot, he brought them out and offered them to him under the oak.

²⁰The angel of God said to him, 'Take the meat and the unleavened bread, place them on this rock, and pour out the broth.' And Gideon did so. ²¹With the tip of the staff that was in his hand, the angel of the LORD touched the meat and the unleavened bread. Fire flared from the rock, consuming

People and Places

Baal and Asherah
Judges 6:25

Baal was a Canaanite storm god who was thought to bring rain and fertility to the land, producing good harvests and lots of livestock. Asherah was the goddess of fertility and her worshippers thought she made the land produce crops and gave them many children. When the Israelites rebelled against God, they made idols so they could worship Baal, and put up sacred poles to worship Asherah.

the meat and the bread. And the angel of the LORD disappeared. ²²When Gideon realised that it was the angel of the LORD, he exclaimed, 'Ah, Sovereign LORD! I have seen the angel of the LORD face to face!'

²³But the LORD said to him, 'Peace! Do not be afraid. You are not going to die.'

²⁴So Gideon built an altar to the LORD there and called it The LORD Is Peace. To this day it stands in Ophrah of the Abiezrites.

²⁵That same night the LORD said to him, 'Take the second bull from your father's herd, the one seven years old.^{b} Tear down your father's altar to Baal and cut down the Asherah pole^c beside it. ²⁶Then build a proper kind of^d altar to the LORD your God on the top of this height. Using the wood of the Asherah pole that you cut down, offer the second^e bull as a burnt offering.'

²⁷So Gideon took ten of his servants and did as the LORD told him. But because he was afraid of his family and the townspeople, he did it at night rather than in the daytime.

²⁸In the morning when the people of the town got up, there was Baal's altar, demolished, with the Asherah pole beside it cut

---

^{a} 19 That is, probably about 16 kilograms ^{b} 25 Or *Take a full-grown, mature bull from your father's herd* ^{c} 25 That is, a wooden symbol of the goddess Asherah; also in verses 26, 28 and 30 ^{d} 26 Or *build with layers of stone an* ^{e} 26 Or *full-grown*; also in verse 28 down and the second bull sacrificed on the newly-built altar!

29They asked each other, 'Who did this?' When they carefully investigated, they were told, 'Gideon son of Joash did it.'

30The people of the town demanded of Joash, 'Bring out your son. He must die, because he has broken down Baal's altar and cut down the Asherah pole beside it.'

31But Joash replied to the hostile crowd around him, 'Are you going to plead Baal's cause? Are you trying to save him? Whoever fights for him shall be put to death by morning! If Baal really is a god, he can defend himself when someone breaks down his altar.' 32So that day they gave Gideon the name Jerub-Baal,[a] saying, 'Let Baal contend with him,' because he broke down Baal's altar.

33Now all the Midianites, Amalekites and other eastern peoples joined forces and crossed over the Jordan and camped in the Valley of Jezreel. 34Then the Spirit of the LORD came on Gideon, and he blew a trumpet, summoning the Abiezrites to follow him. 35He sent messengers throughout Manasseh, calling them to arms, and also into Asher, Zebulun and Naphtali, so that they too went up to meet them.

36Gideon said to God, 'If you will save Israel by my hand as you have promised— 37look, I will place a wool fleece on the threshing-floor. If there is dew only on the fleece and all the ground is dry, then I will know that you will save Israel by my hand, as you said.' 38And that is what happened. Gideon rose early the next day; he squeezed the fleece and wrung out the dew—a bowlful of water.

39Then Gideon said to God, 'Do not be angry with me. Let me make just one more request. Allow me one more test with the fleece, but this time make the fleece dry and let the ground be covered with dew.' 40That night God did so. Only the fleece was dry; all the ground was covered with dew.

Gideon defeats the Midianites

7 Early in the morning, Jerub-Baal (that is, Gideon) and all his men camped at the spring of Harod. The camp of Midian was north of them in the valley near the hill of Moreh. 2The LORD said to Gideon, 'You have too many men. I cannot deliver Midian into their hands, or Israel would boast against me, "My own strength has saved me." 3Now announce to the army, "Anyone who trembles with fear may turn back and leave Mount Gilead."' So twenty-two thousand men left, while ten thousand remained.

4But the LORD said to Gideon, 'There are still too many men. Take them down to the water, and I will sift them out for you there. If I say, "This one shall go with you," he shall go; but if I say, "This one shall not go with you," he shall not go.'

5So Gideon took the men down to the water. There the LORD told him, 'Separate those who lap the water with their tongues like a dog from those who kneel down to drink.' 6Three hundred of them lapped with their hands to their mouths. All the rest got down on their knees to drink.

7The LORD said to Gideon, 'With the three hundred men that lapped I will save you and give the Midianites into your

making Connections

Lapping water
Judges 7:7

The men who lapped the water from their hands would have been able to look around for the enemy while they did so. Those who got down on their knees to drink straight from the water would have been a sitting target if anyone had come up behind them. So the watchful few were allowed to stay while the rest were sent home. Gideon's army has now gone from 32,000 men to just 300. But victory is not about numbers, it's about trusting God.

---

[a] 32 *Jerub-Baal* probably means *let Baal contend*.

hands. Let all the others go, each to his own place.' ⁸So Gideon sent the rest of the Israelites to their tents but kept the three hundred, who took over the provisions and trumpets of the others.

Now the camp of Midian lay below him in the valley. ⁹During that night the LORD said to Gideon, 'Get up, go down against the camp, because I am going to give it into your hands. ¹⁰If you are afraid to attack, go down to the camp with your servant Purah ¹¹and listen to what they are saying. Afterwards, you will be encouraged to attack the camp.' So he and Purah his servant went down to the outposts of the camp. ¹²The Midianites, the Amalekites and all the other eastern peoples had settled in the valley, thick as locusts. Their camels could no more be counted than the sand on the seashore.

¹³Gideon arrived just as a man was telling a friend his dream. 'I had a dream,' he was saying. 'A round loaf of barley bread came tumbling into the Midianite camp. It struck the tent with such force that the tent overturned and collapsed.'

¹⁴His friend responded, 'This can be nothing other than the sword of Gideon son of Joash, the Israelite. God has given the Midianites and the whole camp into his hands.'

¹⁵When Gideon heard the dream and its interpretation, he bowed down and worshipped. He returned to the camp of Israel and called out, 'Get up! The LORD has given the Midianite camp into your hands.' ¹⁶Dividing the three hundred men into three companies, he placed trumpets and empty jars in the hands of all of them, with torches inside.

¹⁷'Watch me,' he told them. 'Follow my lead. When I get to the edge of the camp, do exactly as I do. ¹⁸When I and all who are with me blow our trumpets, then from all round the camp blow yours and shout, "For the LORD and for Gideon."'

¹⁹Gideon and the hundred men with him reached the edge of the camp at the beginning of the middle watch, just after they had changed the guard. They blew their trumpets and broke the jars that were in their hands. ²⁰The three companies blew the trumpets and smashed the jars. Grasping the torches in their left hands and holding in their right hands the trumpets they were to blow, they shouted, 'A sword for the LORD and for Gideon!' ²¹While each man held his position round the camp, all the Midianites ran, crying out as they fled.

²²When the three hundred trumpets sounded, the LORD caused the men throughout the camp to turn on each other with their swords. The army fled to Beth Shittah towards Zererah as far as the border of Abel Meholah near Tabbath. ²³Israelites from Naphtali, Asher and all Manasseh were called out, and they pursued the Midianites. ²⁴Gideon sent messengers throughout the hill country of Ephraim, saying, 'Come down against the Midianites and seize the waters of the Jordan ahead of them as far as Beth Barah.'

So all the men of Ephraim were called out and they seized the waters of the Jordan as far as Beth Barah. ²⁵They also captured two of the Midianite leaders, Oreb and Zeeb. They killed Oreb at the rock of Oreb, and Zeeb at the winepress of Zeeb. They pursued the Midianites and brought the heads of Oreb and Zeeb to Gideon, who was by the Jordan.

Zebah and Zalmunna

8 Now the Ephraimites asked Gideon, 'Why have you treated us like this? Why didn't you call us when you went to fight Midian?' And they challenged him vigorously.

²But he answered them, 'What have I accomplished compared to you? Aren't the gleanings of Ephraim's grapes better than the full grape harvest of Abiezer? ³God gave Oreb and Zeeb, the Midianite leaders, into your hands. What was I able to do compared to you?' At this, their resentment against him subsided.

⁴Gideon and his three hundred men, exhausted yet keeping up the pursuit, came to the Jordan and crossed it. ⁵He said to the men of Sukkoth, 'Give my troops some bread; they are worn out, and I am still pursuing Zebah and Zalmunna, the kings of Midian.'

⁶But the officials of Sukkoth said, 'Do you already have the hands of Zebah and

Zalmunna in your possession? Why should we give bread to your troops?'

7Then Gideon replied, 'Just for that, when the LORD has given Zebah and Zalmunna into my hand, I will tear your flesh with desert thorns and briers.'

8From there he went up to Peniel[a] and made the same request of them, but they answered as the men of Sukkoth had. 9So he said to the men of Peniel, 'When I return in triumph, I will tear down this tower.'

10Now Zebah and Zalmunna were in Karkor with a force of about fifteen thousand men, all that were left of the armies of the eastern peoples; a hundred and twenty thousand swordsmen had fallen. 11Gideon went up by the route of the nomads east of Nobah and Jogbehah and attacked the unsuspecting army. 12Zebah and Zalmunna, the two kings of Midian, fled, but he pursued them and captured them, routing their entire army.

13Gideon son of Joash then returned from the battle by the Pass of Heres. 14He caught a young man of Sukkoth and questioned him, and the young man wrote down for him the names of the seventy-seven officials of Sukkoth, the elders of the town. 15Then Gideon came and said to the men of Sukkoth, 'Here are Zebah and Zalmunna, about whom you taunted me by saying, "Do you already have the hands of Zebah and Zalmunna in your possession? Why should we give bread to your exhausted troops?"' 16He took the elders of the town and taught the men of Sukkoth a lesson by punishing them with desert thorns and briers. 17He also pulled down the tower of Peniel and killed the men of the town.

18Then he asked Zebah and Zalmunna, 'What kind of men did you kill at Tabor?'

'Men like you,' they answered, 'each one with the bearing of a prince.'

19Gideon replied, 'Those were my brothers, the sons of my own mother. As surely as the LORD lives, if you had spared their lives, I would not kill you.' 20Turning to Jether, his eldest son, he said, 'Kill them!' But Jether did not draw his sword, because he was only a boy and was afraid.

21Zebah and Zalmunna said, 'Come, do it yourself. "As is the man, so is his strength."' So Gideon stepped forward and killed them, and took the ornaments off their camels' necks.

Gideon's ephod

22The Israelites said to Gideon, 'Rule over us—you, your son and your grandson—because you have saved us from the hand of Midian.'

23But Gideon told them, 'I will not rule over you, nor will my son rule over you. The LORD will rule over you.' 24And he said, 'I do have one request, that each of you give me an ear-ring from your share of the plunder.' (It was the custom of the Ishmaelites to wear gold ear-rings.)

25They answered, 'We'll be glad to give them.' So they spread out a garment, and each of them threw a ring from his plunder onto it. 26The weight of the gold rings he asked for came to seventeen hundred shekels,[b] not counting the ornaments, the pendants and the purple garments worn by the kings of Midian or the chains that were on their camels' necks. 27Gideon made the

---

making Connections

King Gideon?
Judges 8:23

Gideon rightly turns down the invitation to rule the Israelites and effectively be their king; that was not what God had called him to do. But although he said no, his actions show that perhaps he thought of himself as rather king-like. The gold rings make him as rich as a king, his many wives mean he has a harem like a king, and he even calls his son Abimelek, which means 'my father is king'.

---

[a] 8 Hebrew *Penuel*, a variant of *Peniel*; also in verses 9 and 17   [b] 26 That is, about 20 kilograms

gold into an ephod, which he placed in Ophrah, his town. All Israel prostituted themselves by worshipping it there, and it became a snare to Gideon and his family.

Gideon's death

28Thus Midian was subdued before the Israelites and did not raise its head again. During Gideon's lifetime, the land had peace for forty years.

29Jerub-Baal son of Joash went back home to live. 30He had seventy sons of his own, for he had many wives. 31His concubine, who lived in Shechem, also bore him a son, whom he named Abimelek. 32Gideon son of Joash died at a good old age and was buried in the tomb of his father Joash in Ophrah of the Abiezrites.

33No sooner had Gideon died than the Israelites again prostituted themselves to the Baals. They set up Baal-Berith as their god 34and did not remember the LORD their God, who had rescued them from the hands of all their enemies on every side. 35They also failed to show any loyalty to the family of Jerub-Baal (that is, Gideon) in spite of all the good things he had done for them.

Abimelek

9 Abimelek son of Jerub-Baal went to his mother's brothers in Shechem and said to them and to all his mother's clan, 2'Ask all the citizens of Shechem, "Which is better for you: to have all seventy of Jerub-Baal's sons rule over you, or just one man?" Remember, I am your flesh and blood.'

3When the brothers repeated all this to the citizens of Shechem, they were inclined to follow Abimelek, for they said, 'He is related to us.' 4They gave him seventy shekels*a* of silver from the temple of Baal-Berith, and Abimelek used it to hire reckless scoundrels, who became his followers. 5He went to his father's home in Ophrah and on one stone murdered his seventy brothers, the sons of Jerub-Baal. But Jotham, the youngest son of Jerub-Baal, escaped by hiding. 6Then all the citizens of Shechem and Beth Millo gathered beside the great tree at the pillar in Shechem to crown Abimelek king.

7When Jotham was told about this, he climbed up on the top of Mount Gerizim and shouted to them, 'Listen to me, citizens of Shechem, so that God may listen to you. 8One day the trees went out to anoint a king for themselves. They said to the olive tree, "Be our king."

9'But the olive tree answered, "Should I give up my oil, by which both gods and human beings are honoured, to hold sway over the trees?"

10'Next, the trees said to the fig-tree, "Come and be our king."

11'But the fig-tree replied, "Should I give up my fruit, so good and sweet, to hold sway over the trees?"

12'Then the trees said to the vine, "Come and be our king."

13'But the vine answered, "Should I give up my wine, which cheers both gods and human beings, to hold sway over the trees?"

14'Finally all the trees said to the thorn-bush, "Come and be our king."

15'The thorn-bush said to the trees, "If you really want to anoint me king over you, come and take refuge in my shade; but if not, then let fire come out of the thorn-bush and consume the cedars of Lebanon!"

16'Have you have acted honourably and in good faith by making Abimelek king? Have you been fair to Jerub-Baal and his family? Have you treated him as he deserves? 17Remember that my father fought for you and risked his life to rescue you from the hand of Midian. 18But today you have revolted against my father's family. You have murdered his seventy sons on a single stone and have made Abimelek, the son of his female slave, king over the citizens of Shechem because he is related to you. 19So have you acted honourably and in good faith towards Jerub-Baal and his family today? If you have, may Abimelek be your joy, and may you be his, too! 20But if you have not, let fire come out from Abimelek and consume you, the citizens of Shechem and Beth Millo, and let fire come out from you, the citizens of Shechem and Beth Millo, and consume Abimelek!'

---

a 4 That is, about 800 grams

²¹Then Jotham fled, escaping to Beer, and he lived there because he was afraid of his brother Abimelek.

²²After Abimelek had governed Israel for three years, ²³God stirred up animosity between Abimelek and the citizens of Shechem so that they acted treacherously against Abimelek. ²⁴God did this in order that the crime against Jerub-Baal's seventy sons, the shedding of their blood, might be avenged on their brother Abimelek and on the citizens of Shechem, who had helped him murder his brothers. ²⁵In opposition to him these citizens of Shechem set an ambush on the hilltops to rob everyone who passed by, and this was reported to Abimelek.

²⁶Now Gaal son of Ebed moved with his brothers into Shechem, and its citizens put their confidence in him. ²⁷After they had gone out into the fields and gathered the grapes and trodden them, they held a festival in the temple of their god. While they were eating and drinking, they cursed Abimelek. ²⁸Then Gaal son of Ebed said, 'Who is Abimelek, and who is Shechem, that we should be subject to him? Isn't he Jerub-Baal's son, and isn't Zebul his deputy? Serve the people of Hamor, Shechem's father! Why should we serve Abimelek? ²⁹If only this people were under my command! Then I would get rid of him. I would say to Abimelek, "Call out your whole army!"'[a]

³⁰When Zebul the governor of the city heard what Gaal son of Ebed said, he was very angry. ³¹Under cover he sent messengers to Abimelek, saying, 'Gaal son of Ebed and his relatives have come to Shechem and are stirring up the city against you. ³²Now then, during the night you and your men should come and lie in wait in the fields. ³³In the morning at sunrise, advance against the city. When Gaal and his men come out against you, do whatever your hand finds to do.'

³⁴So Abimelek and all his troops set out by night and took up concealed positions near Shechem in four companies. ³⁵Now Gaal son of Ebed had gone out and was standing at the entrance of the city gate just as Abimelek and his troops came out from their hiding-place.

³⁶When Gaal saw them, he said to Zebul, 'Look, people are coming down from the tops of the mountains!'

Zebul replied, 'You mistake the shadows of the mountains for men.'

³⁷But Gaal spoke up again: 'Look, people are coming down from the central hill,[b] and a company is coming from the direction of the diviners' tree.'

³⁸Then Zebul said to him, 'Where is your big talk now, you who said, "Who is Abimelek that we should be subject to him?" Aren't these the men you ridiculed? Go out and fight them!'

³⁹So Gaal led out[c] the citizens of Shechem and fought Abimelek. ⁴⁰Abimelek chased him all the way to the entrance of the gate, and many fell slain as they fled. ⁴¹Abimelek stayed in Arumah, and Zebul drove Gaal and his relatives out of Shechem.

⁴²The next day the people of Shechem went out to the fields, and this was reported to Abimelek. ⁴³So he took his troops, divided them into three companies and set an ambush in the fields. When he saw the people coming out of the city, he rose to attack them. ⁴⁴Abimelek and the companies with him rushed forward to a position at the entrance of the city gate. Then two companies attacked those in the fields and struck them down. ⁴⁵All that day Abimelek pressed his attack against the city until he had captured it and killed its people. Then he destroyed the city and scattered salt over it.

⁴⁶On hearing this, the citizens in the tower of Shechem went into the stronghold of the temple of El-Berith. ⁴⁷When Abimelek heard that they had assembled there, ⁴⁸he and all his men went up Mount Zalmon. He took an axe and cut off some branches, which he lifted to his shoulders. He ordered the men with him, 'Quick! Do what you have seen me do!' ⁴⁹So all the men cut branches and followed Abimelek. They piled them against the stronghold and set it on fire with the people still inside. So all the people in the tower of Shechem, about a thousand men and women, also died.

⁵⁰Next Abimelek went to Thebez and besieged it and captured it. ⁵¹Inside the city,

---

[a] 29 Septuagint; Hebrew *him.' Then he said to Abimelek, 'Call out your whole army!'*   [b] 37 The Hebrew for this phrase means *the navel of the earth.*   [c] 39 Or *Gaal went out in the sight of*

however, was a strong tower, to which all the men and women—all the people of the city—had fled. They had locked themselves in and climbed up on the tower roof. 52Abimelek went to the tower and attacked it. But as he approached the entrance to the tower to set it on fire, 53a woman dropped an upper millstone on his head and cracked his skull.

54Hurriedly he called to his armour-bearer, 'Draw your sword and kill me, so that they can't say, "A woman killed him."' So his servant ran him through, and he died. 55When the Israelites saw that Abimelek was dead, they went home.

56Thus God repaid the wickedness that Abimelek had done to his father by murdering his seventy brothers. 57God also made the people of Shechem pay for all their wickedness. The curse of Jotham son of Jerub-Baal came on them.

Tola

10 After the time of Abimelek, a man of Issachar named Tola son of Puah, the son of Dodo, rose to save Israel. He lived in Shamir, in the hill country of Ephraim. 2He led[a] Israel for twenty-three years; then he died, and was buried in Shamir.

Jair

3He was followed by Jair of Gilead, who led Israel for twenty-two years. 4He had thirty sons, who rode thirty donkeys. They controlled thirty towns in Gilead, which to this day are called Havvoth Jair.[b] 5When Jair died, he was buried in Kamon.

Jephthah

6Again the Israelites did evil in the eyes of the LORD. They served the Baals and the Ashtoreths, and the gods of Aram, the gods of Sidon, the gods of Moab, the gods of the Ammonites and the gods of the Philistines. And because the Israelites forsook the LORD and no longer served him, 7he became angry with them. He sold them into the hands of the Philistines and the Ammonites, 8who that year shattered and crushed them. For eighteen years they oppressed all the Israelites on the east side of the Jordan in Gilead, the land of the Amorites. 9The Ammonites also crossed the Jordan to fight against Judah, Benjamin and the house of Ephraim; and Israel was in great distress. 10Then the Israelites cried out to the LORD, 'We have sinned against you, forsaking our God and serving the Baals.'

11The LORD replied, 'When the Egyptians, the Amorites, the Ammonites, the Philistines, 12the Sidonians, the Amalekites and the Maonites[c] oppressed you and you cried to me for help, did I not save you from their hands? 13But you have forsaken me and served other gods, so I will no longer save you. 14Go and cry out to the gods you have chosen. Let them save you when you are in trouble!'

15But the Israelites said to the LORD, 'We have sinned. Do with us whatever you think best, but please rescue us now.' 16Then they got rid of the foreign gods among them and served the LORD. And he could bear Israel's misery no longer.

17When the Ammonites were called to arms and camped in Gilead, the Israelites assembled and camped at Mizpah. 18The leaders of the people of Gilead said to each other, 'Whoever will take the lead in attacking the Ammonites will be head over all who live in Gilead.'

11 Jephthah the Gileadite was a mighty warrior. His father was Gilead; his mother was a prostitute. 2Gilead's wife also bore him sons, and when they were grown up, they drove Jephthah away. 'You are not going to get any inheritance in our family,' they said, 'because you are the son of another woman.' 3So Jephthah fled from his brothers and settled in the land of Tob, where a gang of scoundrels gathered around him and followed him.

4Some time later, when the Ammonites were fighting against Israel, 5the elders of Gilead went to get Jephthah from the land of Tob. 6'Come,' they said, 'be our commander, so we can fight the Ammonites.'

---

[a] 2 Traditionally *judged*; also in verse 3 [b] 4 Or *called the settlements of Jair* [c] 12 Hebrew; some Septuagint manuscripts *Midianites*

⁷Jephthah said to them, 'Didn't you hate me and drive me from my father's house? Why do you come to me now, when you're in trouble?'

⁸The elders of Gilead said to him, 'Nevertheless, we are turning to you now; come with us to fight the Ammonites, and you will be head over all of us who live in Gilead.'

⁹Jephthah answered, 'Suppose you take me back to fight the Ammonites and the LORD gives them to me—will I really be your head?'

¹⁰The elders of Gilead replied, 'The LORD is our witness; we will certainly do as you say.' ¹¹So Jephthah went with the elders of Gilead, and the people made him head and commander over them. And he repeated all his words before the LORD in Mizpah.

¹²Then Jephthah sent messengers to the Ammonite king with the question: 'What do you have against me that you have attacked my country?'

¹³The king of the Ammonites answered Jephthah's messengers, 'When Israel came up out of Egypt, they took away my land from the Arnon to the Jabbok, all the way to the Jordan. Now give it back peaceably.'

¹⁴Jephthah sent back messengers to the Ammonite king, ¹⁵saying:

'This is what Jephthah says: Israel did not take the land of Moab or the land of the Ammonites. ¹⁶But when they came up out of Egypt, Israel went through the wilderness to the Red Sea[a] and on to Kadesh. ¹⁷Then Israel sent messengers to the king of Edom, saying, "Give us permission to go through your country," but the king of Edom would not listen. They sent also to the king of Moab, and he refused. So Israel stayed at Kadesh.

¹⁸'Next they travelled through the wilderness, skirted the lands of Edom and Moab, passed along the eastern side of the country of Moab, and camped on the other side of the Arnon. They did not enter the territory of Moab, for the Arnon was its border.

¹⁹'Then Israel sent messengers to Sihon king of the Amorites, who ruled in Heshbon, and said to him, "Let us pass through your country to our own place." ²⁰Sihon, however, did not trust Israel[b] to pass through his territory. He mustered all his army and set up camp at Jahaz and fought with Israel.

²¹'Then the LORD, the God of Israel, gave Sihon and his whole army into Israel's hands, and they defeated them. Israel took over all the land of the Amorites who lived in that country, ²²capturing all of it from the Arnon to the Jabbok and from the desert to the Jordan.

²³'Now since the LORD, the God of Israel, has driven the Amorites out before his people Israel, what right have you to take it over? ²⁴Will you not take what your god Chemosh gives you? Likewise, whatever the LORD our God has given us, we will possess. ²⁵Are you any better than Balak son of Zippor, king of Moab? Did he ever quarrel with Israel or fight with them? ²⁶For three hundred years Israel occupied Heshbon, Aroer, the surrounding settlements and all the towns along the Arnon. Why didn't you retake them during that time? ²⁷I have not wronged you, but you are doing me wrong by waging war against me. Let the LORD, the Judge,[c] decide the dispute this day between the Israelites and the Ammonites.'

²⁸The king of Ammon, however, paid no attention to the message Jephthah sent him.

²⁹Then the Spirit of the LORD came on Jephthah. He crossed Gilead and Manasseh, passed through Mizpah of Gilead, and from there he advanced against the Ammonites. ³⁰And Jephthah made a vow to the LORD: 'If you give the Ammonites into my hands,

---

[a] 16 Or the Sea of Reeds   [b] 20 Or however, would not make an agreement for Israel   [c] 27 Or Ruler

Judges 12:4

IN OTHER WORDS

Syncretism
Judges 11:31

The word 'syncretism' doesn't actually appear in the Bible, but it does accurately describe what is going on in the book of Judges. It means the blending of religions, a pick-and-mix approach where people take what they like from different religions and make up their own. Jephthah defeats the Ammonites in battle and promises to sacrifice to God the first thing that comes out of his house on his return. Unfortunately his daughter runs to meet him, but instead of realising that God hates child sacrifice, he goes ahead and kills her. What a confused man!

³¹whatever comes out of the door of my house to meet me when I return in triumph from the Ammonites will be the LORD's, and I will sacrifice it as a burnt offering.'

³²Then Jephthah went over to fight the Ammonites, and the LORD gave them into his hands. ³³He devastated twenty towns from Aroer to the vicinity of Minnith, as far as Abel Keramim. Thus Israel subdued Ammon.

³⁴When Jephthah returned to his home in Mizpah, who should come out to meet him but his daughter, dancing to the sound of tambourines! She was an only child. Except for her he had neither son nor daughter. ³⁵When he saw her, he tore his clothes and cried, 'Oh! My daughter! You have brought me down and I am devastated. I have made a vow to the LORD that I cannot break.'

³⁶'My father,' she replied, 'you have given your word to the LORD. Do to me just as you promised, now that the LORD has avenged you of your enemies, the Ammonites. ³⁷But grant me this one request,' she said. 'Give me two months to roam the hills and weep with my friends, because I will never marry.'

³⁸'You may go,' he said. And he let her go for two months. She and her friends went into the hills and wept because she would never marry. ³⁹After the two months, she returned to her father, and he did to her as he had vowed. And she was a virgin.

From this comes the Israelite tradition ⁴⁰that each year the young women of Israel go out for four days to commemorate the daughter of Jephthah the Gileadite.

Jephthah and Ephraim

12 The Ephraimite forces were called out, and they crossed over to Zaphon and said to Jephthah, 'Why did you go to fight the Ammonites without calling us to go with you? We're going to burn down your house over your head.'

²Jephthah answered, 'I and my people were engaged in a great struggle with the Ammonites, and although I called, you didn't save me out of their hands. ³When I saw that you wouldn't help, I took my life in my hands and crossed over to fight the Ammonites, and the LORD gave me the victory over them. Now why have you come up today to fight me?'

⁴Jephthah then called together the men of Gilead and fought against Ephraim. The

Accents
Judges 12:4

When you move to a new place, sometimes your accent will be different to those of your new friends. It's one thing to be teased because of the way you pronounce words, but here people's accents got them into serious trouble. People from Ephraim couldn't say 'sh', so they mispronounced the word 'shibboleth' at this test on the River Jordan. And that led to forty-two thousand of them being killed.

Gileadites struck them down because the Ephraimites had said, 'You Gileadites are renegades from Ephraim and Manasseh.' 5The Gileadites captured the fords of the Jordan leading to Ephraim, and whenever a survivor of Ephraim said, 'Let me cross over,' the Gileadites asked him, 'Are you an Ephraimite?' If he replied, 'No,' 6they said, 'All right, say "Shibboleth".' If he said, 'Sibboleth', because he could not pronounce the word correctly, they seized him and killed him at the fords of the Jordan. Forty-two thousand Ephraimites were killed at that time.

7Jephthah led*a* Israel for six years. Then Jephthah the Gileadite died and was buried in a town in Gilead.

Ibzan, Elon and Abdon

8After him, Ibzan of Bethlehem led Israel. 9He had thirty sons and thirty daughters. He gave his daughters away in marriage to those outside his clan, and for his sons he brought in thirty young women as wives from outside his clan. Ibzan led Israel for seven years. 10Then Ibzan died and was buried in Bethlehem.

11After him, Elon the Zebulunite led Israel for ten years. 12Then Elon died and was buried in Aijalon in the land of Zebulun.

13After him, Abdon son of Hillel, from Pirathon, led Israel. 14He had forty sons and thirty grandsons, who rode on seventy donkeys. He led Israel for eight years. 15Then Abdon son of Hillel died and was buried at Pirathon in Ephraim, in the hill country of the Amalekites.

The birth of Samson

13 Again the Israelites did evil in the eyes of the LORD, so the LORD delivered them into the hands of the Philistines for forty years.

2A certain man of Zorah, named Manoah, from the clan of the Danites, had a wife who was childless, unable to give birth. 3The angel of the LORD appeared to her and said, 'You are barren and childless, but you are going to become pregnant and give birth to a son. 4Now see to it that you drink no wine or other fermented drink and that you do not eat anything unclean. 5You will become pregnant and have a son whose head is never to be touched by a razor because the boy is to be a Nazirite, dedicated to God from the womb. He will begin to deliver Israel from the hands of the Philistines.'

6Then the woman went to her husband and told him, 'A man of God came to me. He looked like an angel of God, very awesome. I didn't ask him where he came from, and he didn't tell me his name. 7But he said to me, "You will become pregnant and have a son. Now then, drink no wine or other fermented drink and do not eat anything unclean, because the boy will be a Nazirite of God from the womb until the day of his death."'

8Then Manoah prayed to the LORD: 'Pardon your servant, Lord. I beg you to let the man of God you sent to us come again to teach us how to bring up the boy who is to be born.'

9God heard Manoah, and the angel of God came again to the woman while she was out in the field; but her husband Manoah was not with her. 10The woman hurried to tell her husband, 'He's here! The man who appeared to me the other day!'

11Manoah got up and followed his wife. When he came to the man, he said, 'Are you the man who talked to my wife?'

'I am,' he said.

12So Manoah asked him, 'When your words are fulfilled, what is to be the rule that governs the boy's life and work?'

13The angel of the LORD answered, 'Your wife must do all that I have told her. 14She must not eat anything that comes from the grapevine, nor drink any wine or other fermented drink nor eat anything unclean. She must do everything I have commanded her.'

15Manoah said to the angel of the LORD, 'We would like you to stay until we prepare a young goat for you.'

16The angel of the LORD replied, 'Even though you detain me, I will not eat any of your food. But if you prepare a burnt offering, offer it to the LORD.' (Manoah did not realise that it was the angel of the LORD.)

---

a 7 Traditionally *judged*; also in verses 8–14

17Then Manoah enquired of the angel of the LORD, 'What is your name, so that we may honour you when your word comes true?'

18He replied, 'Why do you ask my name? It is beyond understanding.'[a] 19Then Manoah took a young goat, together with the grain offering, and sacrificed it on a rock to the LORD. And the LORD did an amazing thing while Manoah and his wife watched: 20as the flame blazed up from the altar towards heaven, the angel of the LORD ascended in the flame. Seeing this, Manoah and his wife fell with their faces to the ground. 21When the angel of the LORD did not show himself again to Manoah and his wife, Manoah realised that it was the angel of the LORD.

22'We are doomed to die!' he said to his wife. 'We have seen God!'

23But his wife answered, 'If the LORD had meant to kill us, he would not have accepted a burnt offering and grain offering from our hands, nor shown us all these things or now told us this.'

24The woman gave birth to a boy and named him Samson. He grew and the LORD blessed him, 25and the Spirit of the LORD began to stir him while he was in Mahaneh Dan, between Zorah and Eshtaol.

Samson's marriage

14 Samson went down to Timnah and saw there a young Philistine woman. 2When he returned, he said to his father and mother, 'I have seen a Philistine woman in Timnah; now get her for me as my wife.'

3His father and mother replied, 'Isn't there an acceptable woman among your relatives or among all our people? Must you go to the uncircumcised Philistines to get a wife?'

But Samson said to his father, 'Get her for me. She's the right one for me.' 4(His parents did not know that this was from the LORD, who was seeking an occasion to confront the Philistines; for at that time they were ruling over Israel.)

5Samson went down to Timnah together with his father and mother. As they approached the vineyards of Timnah, suddenly a young lion came roaring towards him. 6The Spirit of the LORD came on him in power so that he tore the lion apart with his bare hands as he might have torn a young goat. But he told neither his father nor his mother what he had done. 7Then he went down and talked with the woman, and he liked her.

8Some time later, when he went back to marry her, he turned aside to look at the lion's carcass, and in it he saw a swarm of bees and some honey. 9He scooped out the honey with his hands and ate as he went along. When he rejoined his parents, he gave them some, and they too ate it. But he did not tell them that he had taken the honey from the lion's carcass.

10Now his father went down to see the woman. And there Samson held a feast, as was customary for young men. 11When the people saw him, they chose thirty men to be his companions.

People and Places

Samson
Judges 14:9

Samson was a funny mixture. His parents had made a Nazirite vow for him when he was a child, which meant that his life was dedicated to God and that he should avoid all products having to do with grapes, and all contact with dead bodies and hairdressers. His long hair was a visible sign of this vow. But he often fell short of the high standards expected of a Nazirite. He took honey from a dead carcass, married a pagan woman, and tried to get revenge instead of leaving it to God. His weakness for women proved to be his downfall when Delilah tricked him into giving her the secret of his strength.

---

[a] 18 Or *is wonderful*

12'Let me tell you a riddle,' Samson said to them. 'If you can give me the answer within the seven days of the feast, I will give you thirty linen garments and thirty sets of clothes. 13If you can't tell me the answer, you must give me thirty linen garments and thirty sets of clothes.'

'Tell us your riddle,' they said. 'Let's hear it.'

14He replied,

'Out of the eater, something to eat;
  out of the strong, something sweet.'

For three days they could not give the answer.

15On the fourth[a] day, they said to Samson's wife, 'Coax your husband into explaining the riddle for us, or we will burn you and your father's household to death. Did you invite us here to steal our property?'

16Then Samson's wife threw herself on him, sobbing, 'You hate me! You don't really love me. You've given my people a riddle, but you haven't told me the answer.'

'I haven't even explained it to my father or mother,' he replied, 'so why should I explain it to you?' 17She cried the whole seven days of the feast. So on the seventh day he finally told her, because she continued to press him. She in turn explained the riddle to her people.

18Before sunset on the seventh day the men of the town said to him,

'What is sweeter than honey?
  What is stronger than a lion?'

Samson said to them,

'If you had not ploughed with my heifer,
  you would not have solved my riddle.'

19Then the Spirit of the LORD came on him in power. He went down to Ashkelon, struck down thirty of their men, stripped them of everything and gave their clothes to those who had explained the riddle. Burning with anger, he returned to his father's home. 20And Samson's wife was given to one of his companions who had attended him at the feast.

Samson's vengeance on the Philistines

15 Later on, at the time of wheat harvest, Samson took a young goat and went to visit his wife. He said, 'I'm going to my wife's room.' But her father would not let him go in.

2'I was so sure you hated her,' he said, 'that I gave her to your companion. Isn't her younger sister more attractive? Take her instead.'

3Samson said to them, 'This time I have a right to get even with the Philistines; I will really harm them.' 4So he went out and caught three hundred foxes and tied them tail to tail in pairs. He then fastened a torch to every pair of tails, 5lit the torches and let the foxes loose in the standing corn of the Philistines. He burned up the shocks and standing corn, together with the vineyards and olive groves.

6When the Philistines asked, 'Who did this?' they were told, 'Samson, the Timnite's son-in-law, because his wife was given to his companion.'

So the Philistines went up and burned her and her father to death. 7Samson said to them, 'Since you've acted like this, I swear that I won't stop until I get my revenge on you.' 8He attacked them viciously and slaughtered many of them. Then he went down and stayed in a cave in the rock of Etam.

9The Philistines went up and camped in Judah, spreading out near Lehi. 10The people of Judah asked, 'Why have you come to fight us?'

'We have come to take Samson prisoner,' they answered, 'to do to him as he did to us.'

11Then three thousand men from Judah went down to the cave in the rock of Etam and said to Samson, 'Don't you realise that the Philistines are rulers over us? What have you done to us?'

He answered, 'I merely did to them what they did to me.'

12They said to him, 'We've come to tie you up and hand you over to the Philistines.'

Samson said, 'Swear to me that you won't kill me yourselves.'

---

[a] 15 Some Septuagint manuscripts and Syriac; Hebrew *seventh*

¹³'Agreed,' they answered. 'We will only tie you up and hand you over to them. We will not kill you.' So they bound him with two new ropes and led him up from the rock. ¹⁴As he approached Lehi, the Philistines came towards him shouting. The Spirit of the LORD came on him in power. The ropes on his arms became like charred flax, and the bindings dropped from his hands. ¹⁵Finding a fresh jaw-bone of a donkey, he grabbed it and struck down a thousand men.

¹⁶Then Samson said,

'With a donkey's jaw-bone
  I have made donkeys of them.ᵃ
With a donkey's jaw-bone
  I have killed a thousand men.'

¹⁷When he finished speaking, he threw away the jaw-bone; and the place was called Ramath Lehi.ᵇ

¹⁸Because he was very thirsty, he cried out to the LORD, 'You have given your servant this great victory. Must I now die of thirst and fall into the hands of the uncircumcised?' ¹⁹Then God opened up the hollow place in Lehi, and water came out of it. When Samson drank, his strength returned and he revived. So the spring was called En Hakkore,ᶜ and it is still there in Lehi.

²⁰Samson ledᵈ Israel for twenty years in the days of the Philistines.

Samson and Delilah

16 One day Samson went to Gaza, where he saw a prostitute. He went in to spend the night with her. ²The people of Gaza were told, 'Samson is here!' So they surrounded the place and lay in wait for him all night at the city gate. They made no move during the night, saying, 'At dawn we'll kill him.'

³But Samson lay there only until the middle of the night. Then he got up and took hold of the doors of the city gate, together with the two posts, and tore them loose, bar and all. He lifted them to his shoulders and carried them to the top of the hill that faces Hebron.

⁴Some time later, he fell in love with a woman in the Valley of Sorek whose name was Delilah. ⁵The rulers of the Philistines went to her and said, 'See if you can lure him into showing you the secret of his great strength and how we can overpower him so that we may tie him up and subdue him. Each one of us will give you eleven hundred shekelsᵉ of silver.'

⁶So Delilah said to Samson, 'Tell me the secret of your great strength and how you can be tied up and subdued.'

⁷Samson answered her, 'If anyone ties me with seven fresh thongsᶠ that have not been dried, I'll become as weak as any other man.'

⁸Then the rulers of the Philistines brought her seven fresh thongs that had not been dried, and she tied him with them. ⁹With men hidden in the room, she called to him, 'Samson, the Philistines are upon you!' But he snapped the thongs as easily as a piece of string snaps when it comes close to a flame. So the secret of his strength was not discovered.

¹⁰Then Delilah said to Samson, 'You have made a fool of me; you lied to me. Come now, tell me how you can be tied.'

¹¹He said, 'If anyone ties me securely with new ropes that have never been used, I'll become as weak as any other man.'

¹²So Delilah took new ropes and tied him with them. Then, with men hidden in the room, she called to him, 'Samson, the Philistines are upon you!' But he snapped the ropes off his arms as if they were threads.

¹³Delilah then said to Samson, 'Until now, you have been making a fool of me and lying to me. Tell me how you can be tied.'

He replied, 'If you weave the seven braids of my head into the fabric ⌊on the loom⌋ and tighten it with the pin, I'll become as weak as any other man.' So while he was sleeping, Delilah took the seven braids of his head, wove them into the fabric ¹⁴andᵍ tightened it with the pin.

ᵃ 16 Or *made a heap or two;* the Hebrew for *donkey* sounds like the Hebrew for *heap*.   ᵇ 17 *Ramath Lehi* means *jaw-bone hill.*   ᶜ 19 *En Hakkore* means *caller's spring.*   ᵈ 20 Traditionally *judged*   ᵉ 5 That is, about 13 kilograms   ᶠ 7 Or *bow-strings;* also in verses 8 and 9   ᵍ 13,14 Some Septuagint manuscripts; Hebrew '⌊I can⌋ *if you weave the seven braids of my head into the fabric ⌊on the loom⌋.' ¹⁴So she*

Again she called to him, 'Samson, the Philistines are upon you!' He awoke from his sleep and pulled up the pin and the loom, with the fabric.

¹⁵Then she said to him, 'How can you say, "I love you," when you won't confide in me? This is the third time you have made a fool of me and haven't told me the secret of your great strength.' ¹⁶With such nagging she prodded him day after day until he was tired to death.

¹⁷So he told her everything. 'No razor has ever been used on my head,' he said, 'because I have been a Nazirite dedicated to God from my mother's womb. If my head were shaved, my strength would leave me, and I would become as weak as any other man.'

¹⁸When Delilah saw that he had told her everything, she sent word to the rulers of the Philistines, 'Come back once more; he has told me everything.' So the rulers of the Philistines returned with the silver in their hands. ¹⁹Having put him to sleep on her lap, she called for someone to shave off the seven braids of his hair, and so began to subdue him.ᵃ And his strength left him.

²⁰Then she called, 'Samson, the Philistines are upon you!'

He awoke from his sleep and thought, 'I'll go out as before and shake myself free.' But he did not know that the LORD had left him.

²¹Then the Philistines seized him, gouged out his eyes and took him down to Gaza. Binding him with bronze shackles, they set him to grinding corn in the prison. ²²But the hair on his head began to grow again after it had been shaved.

The death of Samson

²³Now the rulers of the Philistines assembled to offer a great sacrifice to Dagon their god and to celebrate, saying, 'Our god has delivered Samson, our enemy, into our hands.'

²⁴When the people saw him, they praised their god, saying,

'Our god has delivered our enemy
  into our hands,
the one who laid waste our land
  and multiplied our slain.'

²⁵While they were in high spirits, they shouted, 'Bring out Samson to entertain us.' So they called Samson out of the prison, and he performed for them.

When they stood him among the pillars, ²⁶Samson said to the servant who held his hand, 'Put me where I can feel the pillars that support the temple, so that I may lean against them.' ²⁷Now the temple was crowded with men and women; all the rulers of the Philistines were there, and on the roof were about three thousand men and women watching Samson perform. ²⁸Then Samson prayed to the LORD, 'Sovereign LORD, remember me. Please, God, strengthen me just once more, and let me with one blow get revenge on the Philistines for my two eyes.' ²⁹Then Samson reached towards the two central pillars on which the temple stood. Bracing himself against them, his right hand on the one and his left hand on the other, ³⁰Samson said, 'Let me die with the Philistines!' Then he pushed with all his might, and down came the temple on the rulers and all the people in it. Thus he killed many more when he died than while he lived.

³¹Then his brothers and his father's whole family went down to get him. They brought him back and buried him between Zorah and Eshtaol in the tomb of Manoah his father. He had ledᵇ Israel for twenty years.

Micah's idols

17 Now a man named Micah from the hill country of Ephraim ²said to his mother, 'The eleven hundred shekelsᶜ of silver that were taken from you and about which I heard you utter a curse—I have that silver with me; I took it.'

Then his mother said, 'The LORD bless you, my son!'

³When he returned the eleven hundred shekels of silver to his mother, she said, 'I solemnly consecrate my silver to the LORD for my son to make an image overlaid with silver. I will give it back to you.'

ᵃ 19 Hebrew; some Septuagint manuscripts *and he began to weaken*   ᵇ 31 Traditionally *judged*   ᶜ 2 That is, about 13 kilograms

⁴So after he returned the silver to his mother, she took two hundred shekels[a] of silver and gave them to a silversmith, who used them to make the idol. And it was put in Micah's house.

⁵Now this man Micah had a shrine, and he made an ephod and some household gods and installed one of his sons as his priest. ⁶In those days Israel had no king; everyone did as they saw fit.

⁷A young Levite from Bethlehem in Judah, who had been living within the clan of Judah, ⁸left that town in search of some other place to stay. On his way[b] he came to Micah's house in the hill country of Ephraim.

⁹Micah asked him, 'Where are you from?'

'I'm a Levite from Bethlehem in Judah,' he said, 'and I'm looking for a place to stay.'

¹⁰Then Micah said to him, 'Live with me and be my father and priest, and I'll give you ten shekels[c] of silver a year, your clothes and your food.' ¹¹So the Levite agreed to live with him, and the young man became like one of his sons to him. ¹²Then Micah installed the Levite, and the young man became his priest and lived in his house. ¹³And Micah said, 'Now I know that the LORD will be good to me, since this Levite has become my priest.'

The Danites settle in Laish

18 In those days Israel had no king. And in those days the tribe of the Danites was seeking a place of their own where they might settle, because they had not yet come into an inheritance among the tribes of Israel. ²So the Danites sent five of their leading men from Zorah and Eshtaol to spy out the land and explore it. These men represented all the Danites. They told them, 'Go, explore the land.'

So they entered the hill country of Ephraim and came to the house of Micah, where they spent the night. ³When they were near Micah's house, they recognised the voice of the young Levite; so they turned in there and asked him, 'Who brought you here? What are you doing in this place? Why are you here?'

⁴He told them what Micah had done for him, and said, 'He has hired me and I am his priest.'

⁵Then they said to him, 'Please enquire of God to learn whether our journey will be successful.'

⁶The priest answered them, 'Go in peace. Your journey has the LORD's approval.'

⁷So the five men left and came to Laish, where they saw that the people were living in safety, like the Sidonians, unsuspecting and secure. And since their land lacked nothing, they were prosperous.[d] Also, they lived a long way from the Sidonians and had no relationship with anyone else.[e]

⁸When they returned to Zorah and Eshtaol, the Danites asked them, 'How did you find things?'

⁹They answered, 'Come on, let's attack them! We have seen the land, and it is very good. Aren't you going to do something? Don't hesitate to go there and take it over. ¹⁰When you get there, you will find an unsuspecting people and a spacious land that God has put into your hands, a land that lacks nothing whatever.'

¹¹Then six hundred men of the Danites, armed for battle, set out from Zorah and Eshtaol. ¹²On their way they set up camp near Kiriath Jearim in Judah. This is why the place west of Kiriath Jearim is called Mahaneh Dan[f] to this day. ¹³From there they went on to the hill country of Ephraim and came to Micah's house.

¹⁴Then the five men who had spied out the land of Laish said to their fellow Danites, 'Do you know that one of these houses has an ephod, some household gods and an image overlaid with silver? Now you know what to do.' ¹⁵So they turned in there and went to the house of the young Levite at Micah's place and greeted him. ¹⁶The six hundred Danites, armed for battle, stood at the entrance of the gate. ¹⁷The five men who had spied out the land went inside and took the idol, the ephod and the household gods

---

[a] 4 That is, about 2.3 kilograms [b] 8 Or *To carry on his profession* [c] 10 That is, about 115 grams [d] 7 The meaning of the Hebrew for this clause is uncertain. [e] 7 Hebrew; some Septuagint manuscripts *with the Arameans* [f] 12 *Mahaneh Dan* means *Dan's camp.*

while the priest and the six hundred armed men stood at the entrance of the gate.

18When the five went into Micah's house and took the idol, the ephod and the household gods, the priest said to them, 'What are you doing?'

19They answered him, 'Be quiet! Don't say a word. Come with us, and be our father and priest. Isn't it better that you serve a tribe and clan in Israel as priest rather than just one man's household?' 20The priest was very pleased. He took the ephod, the household gods and the idol and went along with the people. 21Putting their little children, their livestock and their possessions in front of them, they turned away and left.

22When they had gone some distance from Micah's house, the men who lived near Micah were called together and overtook the Danites. 23As they shouted after them, the Danites turned and said to Micah, 'What's the matter with you that you called out your men to fight?'

24He replied, 'You took the gods I made, and my priest, and went away. What else do I have? How can you ask, "What's the matter with you?"'

25The Danites answered, 'Don't argue with us, or some of the men may get angry and attack you, and you and your family will lose your lives.' 26So the Danites went their way, and Micah, seeing that they were too strong for him, turned round and went back home.

27Then they took what Micah had made, and his priest, and went on to Laish, against a peaceful and unsuspecting people. They attacked them with the sword and burned down their city. 28There was no-one to rescue them because they lived a long way from Sidon and had no relationship with anyone else. The city was in a valley near Beth Rehob.

The Danites rebuilt the city and settled there. 29They named it Dan after their ancestor Dan, who was born to Israel—though the city used to be called Laish. 30There the Danites set up for themselves the idol, and Jonathan son of Gershom, the son of Moses,*a* and his sons were priests for the tribe of Dan until the time of the captivity of the land. 31They continued to use the idol Micah had made, all the time the house of God was in Shiloh.

A Levite and his concubine

19 In those days Israel had no king.
Now a Levite who lived in a remote area in the hill country of Ephraim took a concubine from Bethlehem in Judah. 2But she was unfaithful to him. She left him and went back to her parents' home in Bethlehem, Judah. After she had been there for four months, 3her husband went to her to persuade her to return. He had with him his servant and two donkeys. She took him into her parents' home, and when her father saw him, he gladly welcomed him. 4His father-in-law, the woman's father, prevailed on him to stay; so he remained with him three days, eating and drinking, and sleeping there.

5On the fourth day they got up early and he prepared to leave, but the woman's father said to his son-in-law, 'Refresh yourself with something to eat; then you can go.' 6So the two of them sat down to eat and drink together. Afterwards the woman's father said, 'Please stay tonight and enjoy yourself.' 7And when the man got up to go, his father-in-law persuaded him, so he stayed there that night. 8On the morning of the fifth day, when he rose to go, the woman's father said, 'Refresh yourself. Wait till afternoon!' So the two of them ate together.

9Then when the man, with his concubine and his servant, got up to leave, his father-in-law, the woman's father, said, 'Now look, it's almost evening. Spend the night here; the day is nearly over. Stay and enjoy yourself. Early tomorrow morning you can get up and be on your way home.' 10But, unwilling to stay another night, the man left and went towards Jebus (that is, Jerusalem), with his two saddled donkeys and his concubine.

11When they were near Jebus and the day was almost gone, the servant said to his master, 'Come, let's stop at this city of the Jebusites and spend the night.'

---

a 30 An ancient Hebrew scribal tradition, some Septuagint manuscripts and Vulgate; Masoretic Text *Manasseh*

Sign of the times

Hospitality
Judges 19:15

Lots of people travelled from place to place in Bible times. There weren't any hotels or bed and breakfast places to book into, so there were strong expectations that local people would be hospitable and take in travellers. The travellers chose Gibeah because it was an Israelite town and they expected that someone would invite them to stay the night, but they had to wait a long time for it to happen.

12His master replied, 'No. We won't go into any city whose people are not Israelites. We will go on to Gibeah.' 13He added, 'Come, let's try to reach Gibeah or Ramah and spend the night in one of those places.' 14So they went on, and the sun set as they neared Gibeah in Benjamin. 15There they stopped to spend the night. They went and sat in the city square, but no-one took them in for the night.

16That evening an old man from the hill country of Ephraim, who was living in Gibeah (the inhabitants of the place were Benjaminites), came in from his work in the fields. 17When he looked and saw the traveller in the city square, the old man asked, 'Where are you going? Where did you come from?'

18He answered, 'We are on our way from Bethlehem in Judah to a remote area in the hill country of Ephraim where I live. I have been to Bethlehem in Judah and now I am going to the house of the LORD.*a* No-one has taken me in for the night. 19We have both straw and fodder for our donkeys and bread and wine for ourselves your servants—me, the woman and the young man with us. We don't need anything.'

20'You are welcome at my house,' the old man said. 'Let me supply whatever you need. Only don't spend the night in the square.' 21So he took him into his house and fed his donkeys. After they had washed their feet, they had something to eat and drink.

22While they were enjoying themselves, some of the wicked men of the city surrounded the house. Pounding on the door, they shouted to the old man who owned the house, 'Bring out the man who came to your house so we can have sex with him.'

23The owner of the house went outside and said to them, 'No, my friends, don't be so vile. Since this man is my guest, don't do this outrageous thing. 24Look, here is my virgin daughter, and his concubine. I will bring them out to you now, and you can use them and do to them whatever you wish. But as for this man, don't do such an outrageous thing.'

25But the men would not listen to him. So the man took his concubine and sent her outside to them, and they raped her and abused her throughout the night, and at dawn they let her go. 26At daybreak the woman went back to the house where her master was staying, fell down at the door and lay there until daylight.

27When her master got up in the morning and opened the door of the house and stepped out to continue on his way, there lay his concubine, fallen in the doorway of the house, with her hands on the threshold. 28He said to her, 'Get up; let's go.' But there was no answer. Then he put her on his donkey and set out for home.

29When he reached home, he took a knife and cut up his concubine, limb by limb, into twelve parts and sent them into all the areas of Israel. 30Everyone who saw it said, 'Such a thing has never been seen or done, not since the day the Israelites came up out of Egypt. Think about it! Consider it! Tell us what to do!'

The Israelites punish the Benjaminites

20 Then all the Israelites from Dan to Beersheba and from the land of Gilead came out with one accord and

---

a 18 Hebrew, Vulgate, Syriac and Targum; Septuagint *going home* assembled before the LORD in Mizpah. 2The leaders of all the people of the tribes of Israel took their places in the assembly of the people of God, four hundred thousand soldiers armed with swords. 3(The Benjaminites heard that the Israelites had gone up to Mizpah.) Then the Israelites said, 'Tell us how this awful thing happened.'

4So the Levite, the husband of the murdered woman, said, 'I and my concubine came to Gibeah in Benjamin to spend the night. 5During the night the men of Gibeah came after me and surrounded the house, intending to kill me. They raped my concubine, and she died. 6I took my concubine, cut her into pieces and sent one piece to each region of Israel's inheritance, because they committed this lewd and outrageous act in Israel. 7Now, all you Israelites, speak up and give your verdict.'

8All the people rose with one accord, saying, 'None of us will go home. No, not one of us will return to his house. 9But now this is what we'll do to Gibeah: we'll go up against it as the lot directs. 10We'll take ten men out of every hundred from all the tribes of Israel, and a hundred from a thousand, and a thousand from ten thousand, to get provisions for the army. Then, when the army arrives at Gibeah[a] in Benjamin, it can give them what they deserve for this outrageous act done in Israel.' 11So all the Israelites got together and united against the city with one accord.

12The tribes of Israel sent messengers throughout the tribe of Benjamin, saying, 'What about this awful crime that was committed among you? 13Now turn those wicked men of Gibeah over to us so that we may put them to death and purge the evil from Israel.'

But the Benjaminites would not listen to their fellow Israelites. 14From their towns they came together at Gibeah to fight against the Israelites. 15At once the Benjaminites mobilised twenty-six thousand swordsmen from their towns, in addition to seven hundred able young men from those living in Gibeah. 16Among all these soldiers there were seven hundred who were left-handed, each of whom could sling a stone at a hair and not miss.

17Israel, apart from Benjamin, mustered four hundred thousand swordsmen, all of them fighting men.

18The Israelites went up to Bethel[b] and enquired of God. They said, 'Who of us is to go up first to fight against the Benjaminites?'

The LORD replied, 'Judah shall go first.'

19The next morning the Israelites got up and pitched camp near Gibeah. 20The Israelites went out to fight the Benjaminites and took up battle positions against them at Gibeah. 21The Benjaminites came out of Gibeah and cut down twenty-two thousand Israelites on the battlefield that day. 22But the Israelites encouraged one another and again took up their positions where they had stationed themselves on the first day. 23The Israelites went up and wept before the LORD until evening, and they enquired of the LORD. They said, 'Shall we go up again to fight against the Benjaminites, our fellow Israelites?'

The LORD answered, 'Go up against them.'

24Then the Israelites drew near to Benjamin the second day. 25This time, when the Benjaminites came out from Gibeah to oppose them, they cut down another eighteen thousand Israelites, all of them armed with swords.

26Then all the Israelites, the whole army, went up to Bethel, and there they sat weeping before the LORD. They fasted that day until evening and presented burnt offerings and fellowship offerings to the LORD. 27And the Israelites enquired of the LORD. (In those days the ark of the covenant of God was there, 28with Phinehas son of Eleazar, the son of Aaron, ministering before it.) They asked, 'Shall we go up again to fight against the Benjaminites, our fellow Israelites, or not?'

The LORD responded, 'Go, for tomorrow I will give them into your hands.'

29Then Israel set an ambush around Gibeah. 30They set up against the Benjaminites on the third day and took up

---

[a] 10 One Hebrew manuscript; most Hebrew manuscripts *Geba*, a variant of *Gibeah*   [b] 18 Or *to the house of God*; also in verse 26

positions against Gibeah as they had done before. 31The Benjaminites came out to meet them and were drawn away from the city. They began to inflict casualties on the Israelites as before, so that about thirty of them fell in the open field and on the roads—the one leading to Bethel and the other to Gibeah.

32While the Benjaminites were saying, 'We are defeating them as before,' the Israelites were saying, 'Let's retreat and draw them away from the city to the roads.'

33All the men of Israel moved from their places and took up positions at Baal Tamar, and the Israelite ambush charged out of its place on the west[a] of Gibeah.[b] 34Then ten thousand of Israel's able young men made a frontal attack on Gibeah. The fighting was so heavy that the Benjaminites did not realise how near disaster was. 35The LORD defeated Benjamin before Israel, and on that day the Israelites struck down 25,100 Benjaminites, all armed with swords. 36Then the Benjaminites saw that they were beaten.

Now the men of Israel had given way before Benjamin, because they relied on the ambush they had set near Gibeah. 37Those who had been in ambush made a sudden dash into Gibeah, spread out and put the whole city to the sword. 38The Israelites had arranged with the ambush that they should send up a great cloud of smoke from the city, 39and then the Israelites would turn in the battle.

The Benjaminites had begun to inflict casualties on the Israelites (about thirty), and they said, 'We are defeating them as in the first battle.' 40But when the column of smoke began to rise from the city, the Benjaminites turned and saw the smoke of the whole city going up into the sky. 41Then the Israelites turned on them, and the Benjaminites were terrified, because they realised that disaster had come on them. 42So they fled before the Israelites in the direction of the wilderness, but they could not escape the battle. And the Israelites who came out of the towns cut them down there. 43They surrounded the Benjaminites, chased them and easily[c] overran them in the vicinity of Gibeah on the east. 44Eighteen thousand Benjaminites fell, all of them valiant fighters. 45As they turned and fled towards the wilderness to the rock of Rimmon, the Israelites cut down five thousand men along the roads. They kept pressing after the Benjaminites as far as Gidom and struck down two thousand more.

46On that day twenty-five thousand Benjaminite swordsmen fell, all of them valiant fighters. 47But six hundred men turned and fled into the wilderness to the rock of Rimmon, where they stayed for four months. 48The men of Israel went back to Benjamin and put all the towns to the sword, including the animals and everything else they found. All the towns they came across they set on fire.

Wives for the Benjaminites

21 The men of Israel had taken an oath at Mizpah: 'Not one of us will give his daughter in marriage to a Benjaminite.'

2The people went to Bethel,[d] where they sat before God until evening, raising their voices and weeping bitterly. 3'LORD, God of Israel,' they cried, 'why has this happened to Israel? Why should one tribe be missing from Israel today?'

4Early the next day the people built an altar and presented burnt offerings and fellowship offerings.

5Then the Israelites asked, 'Who from all the tribes of Israel has failed to assemble before the LORD?' For they had taken a solemn oath that anyone who failed to assemble before the LORD at Mizpah was to be put to death.

6Now the Israelites grieved for Benjamin, one of their tribes. 'Today one tribe is cut off from Israel,' they said. 7'How can we provide wives for those who are left, since we have taken an oath by the LORD not to give them any of our daughters in marriage?' 8Then they asked, 'Which one of the tribes of Israel failed to assemble before the LORD at Mizpah?' They discovered that no-one from Jabesh Gilead had come to the

---

[a] 33 Some Septuagint manuscripts and Vulgate; the meaning of the Hebrew for this word is uncertain. [b] 33 Hebrew *Geba*, a variant of *Gibeah* [c] 43 The meaning of the Hebrew for this word is uncertain. [d] 2 Or *to the house of God*

camp for the assembly. 9For when they counted the people, they found that none of the people of Jabesh Gilead were there.

10So the assembly sent twelve thousand fighting men with instructions to go to Jabesh Gilead and put to the sword those living there, including the women and children. 11'This is what you are to do,' they said. 'Kill every male and every woman who is not a virgin.' 12They found among the people living in Jabesh Gilead four hundred young women who had never slept with a man, and they took them to the camp at Shiloh in Canaan.

13Then the whole assembly sent an offer of peace to the Benjaminites at the rock of Rimmon. 14So the Benjaminites returned at that time and were given the women of Jabesh Gilead who had been spared. But there were not enough for all of them.

15The people grieved for Benjamin, because the LORD had made a gap in the tribes of Israel. 16And the elders of the assembly said, 'With the women of Benjamin destroyed, how shall we provide wives for the men who are left? 17The Benjaminite survivors must have heirs,' they said, 'so that a tribe of Israel will not be wiped out. 18We can't give them our daughters as wives, since we Israelites have taken this oath: "Cursed be anyone who gives a wife to a Benjaminite." 19But look, there is the annual festival of the LORD in Shiloh, to the north of Bethel, and east of the road that goes from Bethel to Shechem, and to the south of Lebonah.'

20So they instructed the Benjaminites, saying, 'Go and hide in the vineyards 21and watch. When the young women of Shiloh come out to join in the dancing, then rush from the vineyards and each of you seize a wife from the young women of Shiloh and go to the land of Benjamin. 22When their fathers or brothers complain to us, we will say to them, "Do us a kindness by helping them, because we did not get wives for them during the war, and you are innocent, since you did not give your daughters to them."'

23So that is what the Benjaminites did. While the young women were dancing, each man caught one and carried her off to be his wife. Then they returned to their inheritance and rebuilt the towns and settled in them.

24At that time the Israelites left that place and went home to their tribes and clans, each to his own inheritance.

25In those days Israel had no king; everyone did as they saw fit.

Ruth

INTRODUCTION

RUTH

Author: Unknown, possibly the prophet Samuel.

When: These events took place some time during the period of the book of Judges, between 1400 BC and 1050 BC.

Where: Moab and Bethlehem.

Main theme: The name Ruth means 'friendship', and this book tells the story of Ruth's commitment to and friendship with Naomi, her mother-in-law. It shows how God looked after them, first by providing food and then by Ruth meeting her relative Boaz, who becomes her husband. Ruth and Boaz are the great-grandparents of King David; that means they're also part of Jesus' family tree (Matthew 1:5).

Naomi loses her husband and sons

1 In the days when the judges ruled,[a] there was a famine in the land. So a man from Bethlehem in Judah, together with his wife and two sons, went to live for a while in the country of Moab. ²The man's name was Elimelek, his wife's name was Naomi, and the names of his two sons were Mahlon and Kilion. They were Ephrathites from Bethlehem, Judah. And they went to Moab and lived there.

³Now Elimelek, Naomi's husband, died, and she was left with her two sons. ⁴They married Moabite women, one named Orpah and the other Ruth. After they had lived there about ten years, ⁵both Mahlon and Kilion also died, and Naomi was left without her two sons and her husband.

Naomi and Ruth return to Bethlehem

⁶When Naomi heard in Moab that the LORD had come to the aid of his people by providing food for them, she and her daughters-in-law prepared to return home from there. ⁷With her two daughters-in-law she left the place where she had been living and set out on the road that would take them back to the land of Judah.

⁸Then Naomi said to her two daughters-in-law, 'Go back, each of you, to your

---

[a] 1 Traditionally *judged*

mother's home. May the LORD show you kindness, as you have shown kindness to your dead and to me. ⁹May the LORD grant that each of you will find rest in the home of another husband.'

Then she kissed them good-bye and they wept aloud ¹⁰and said to her, 'We will go back with you to your people.'

¹¹But Naomi said, 'Return home, my daughters. Why would you come with me? Am I going to have any more sons, who could become your husbands? ¹²Return home, my daughters; I am too old to have another husband. Even if I thought there was still hope for me—even if I had a husband tonight and then gave birth to sons—¹³would you wait until they grew up? Would you remain unmarried for them? No, my daughters. It is more bitter for me than for you, because the LORD's hand has turned against me!'

¹⁴At this they wept aloud again. Then Orpah kissed her mother-in-law good-bye, but Ruth clung to her.

¹⁵'Look,' said Naomi, 'your sister-in-law is going back to her people and her gods. Go back with her.'

¹⁶But Ruth replied, 'Don't urge me to leave you or to turn back from you. Where you go I will go, and where you stay I will stay. Your people will be my people and your God my God. ¹⁷Where you die I will die, and there I will be buried. May the LORD deal with me, be it ever so severely, if even death separates you and me.' ¹⁸When Naomi realised that Ruth was determined to go with her, she stopped urging her.

¹⁹So the two women went on until they came to Bethlehem. When they arrived in Bethlehem, the whole town was stirred because of them, and the women exclaimed, 'Can this be Naomi?'

²⁰'Don't call me Naomi,'ᵃ she told them. 'Call me Mara,ᵇ because the Almightyᶜ has made my life very bitter. ²¹I went away full, but the LORD has brought me back empty. Why call me Naomi? The LORD has afflictedᵈ me; the Almighty has brought misfortune upon me.'

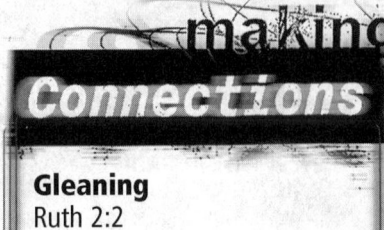

Gleaning
Ruth 2:2

Don't worry – Ruth's not going to get arrested for stealing; what she's doing is perfectly legal. The law said that when the Israelites were harvesting their crops, they should leave a border around the edge of their fields (Leviticus 19:9). This was so people who were poor could help themselves and have something to eat. Fortunately for Ruth, her relative Boaz has done this; otherwise she and Naomi might be very hungry.

²²So Naomi returned from Moab accompanied by Ruth the Moabite, her daughter-in-law, arriving in Bethlehem as the barley harvest was beginning.

Ruth meets Boaz in the cornfield

2 Now Naomi had a relative on her husband's side, a man of standing from the clan of Elimelek, whose name was Boaz.

²And Ruth the Moabite said to Naomi, 'Let me go to the fields and pick up the leftover corn behind anyone in whose eyes I find favour.'

Naomi said to her, 'Go ahead, my daughter.' ³So she went out, entered a field and began to glean behind the harvesters. As it turned out, she found herself working in a field belonging to Boaz, who was from the clan of Elimelek.

⁴Just then Boaz arrived from Bethlehem and greeted the harvesters, 'The LORD be with you!'

'The LORD bless you!' they answered.

⁵Boaz asked the overseer of his harvesters, 'Who does that young woman belong to?'

ᵃ 20 *Naomi* means *pleasant*; also in verse 21. ᵇ 20 *Mara* means *bitter*. ᶜ 20 Hebrew *Shaddai*; also in verse 21
ᵈ 21 Or *has testified against*

⁶The overseer replied, 'She is the Moabite who came back from Moab with Naomi. ⁷She said, "Please let me glean and gather among the sheaves behind the harvesters." She came into the field and has remained here from morning till now, except for a short rest in the shelter.'

⁸So Boaz said to Ruth, 'My daughter, listen to me. Don't go and glean in another field and don't go away from here. Stay here with the women who work for me. ⁹Watch the field where the harvesters are working, and follow along after the women. I have told the men not to lay a hand on you. And whenever you are thirsty, go and get a drink from the water jars the men have filled.'

¹⁰At this, she bowed down with her face to the ground. She asked him, 'Why have I found such favour in your eyes that you notice me—a foreigner?'

¹¹Boaz replied, 'I've been told all about what you have done for your mother-in-law since the death of your husband—how you left your father and mother and your homeland and came to live with a people you did not know before. ¹²May the LORD repay you for what you have done. May you be richly rewarded by the LORD, the God of Israel, under whose wings you have come to take refuge.'

¹³'May I continue to find favour in your eyes, my lord,' she said. 'You have reassured me and have spoken kindly to your servant—though I do not have the standing of one of your servants.'

¹⁴At mealtime Boaz said to her, 'Come over here. Have some bread and dip it in the wine vinegar.'

When she sat down with the harvesters, he offered her some roasted grain. She ate all she wanted and had some left over. ¹⁵As she got up to glean, Boaz gave orders to his men, 'Let her gather among the sheaves and don't reprimand her. ¹⁶Even pull out some stalks for her from the bundles and leave them for her to pick up, and don't rebuke her.'

¹⁷So Ruth gleaned in the field until evening. Then she threshed the barley she had gathered, and it amounted to about an ephah.ᵃ ¹⁸She carried it back to town, and her mother-in-law saw how much she had gathered. Ruth also brought out and gave her what she had left over after she had eaten enough.

¹⁹Her mother-in-law asked her, 'Where did you glean today? Where did you work? Blessed be the man who took notice of you!' Then Ruth told her mother-in-law about the one at whose place she had been working. 'The name of the man I worked with today is Boaz,' she said.

²⁰'The LORD bless him!' Naomi said to her daughter-in-law. 'He has not stopped showing his kindness to the living and the dead.' She added, 'That man is our close relative; he is one of our family guardians.'ᵇ

²¹Then Ruth the Moabite said, 'He even said to me, "Stay with my workers until they finish harvesting all my corn."'

²²Naomi said to Ruth her daughter-in-law, 'It will be good for you, my daughter, to go with the women who work for him, because in someone else's field you might be harmed.'

²³So Ruth stayed close to the women of Boaz to glean until the barley and wheat harvests were finished. And she lived with her mother-in-law.

Ruth and Boaz at the threshing-floor

3 One day Naomi her mother-in-law said to her, 'My daughter, I must find a homeᶜ for you, where you will be well provided for. ²Now Boaz, with whose women you have worked, is a relative of ours. Tonight he will be winnowing barley on the threshing-floor. ³Wash and perfume yourself, and put on your best clothes. Then go down to the threshing-floor, but don't let him know you are there until he has finished eating and drinking. ⁴When he lies down, note the place where he is lying. Then go and uncover his feet and lie down. He will tell you what to do.'

⁵'I will do whatever you say,' Ruth answered. ⁶So she went down to the threshing-floor and did everything her mother-in-law told her to do.

⁷When Boaz had finished eating and drinking and was in good spirits, he went

---

ᵃ 17 That is, probably about 13 kilograms   ᵇ 20 The Hebrew word for *family guardian* is a legal term for one who has the obligation to redeem a relative in serious difficulty (see Lev. 25:25-55).   ᶜ 1 Hebrew *find rest* (see Ruth 1:9) over to lie down at the far end of the grain pile. Ruth approached quietly, uncovered his feet and lay down. 8In the middle of the night something startled the man; he turned—and there was a woman lying at his feet!

9'Who are you?' he asked.

'I am your servant Ruth,' she said. 'Spread the corner of your garment over me, since you are a family guardian.'

10'The LORD bless you, my daughter,' he replied. 'This kindness is greater than that which you showed earlier: you have not run after the younger men, whether rich or poor. 11And now, my daughter, don't be afraid. I will do for you all you ask. All the people of my town know that you are a woman of noble character. 12Although it is true that I am a family guardian, there is another who is more closely related than I. 13Stay here for the night, and in the morning if he wants to do his duty as your family guardian, good; let him redeem you. But if he is not willing, as surely as the LORD lives I will do it. Lie here until morning.'

14So she lay at his feet until morning, but got up before anyone could be recognised; and he said, 'No-one must know that a woman came to the threshing-floor.'

15He also said, 'Bring me the shawl you are wearing and hold it out.' When she did so, he poured into it six measures of barley and put it on her. Then he[a] went back to town.

16When Ruth came to her mother-in-law, Naomi asked, 'How did it go, my daughter?'

Then she told her everything Boaz had done for her 17and added, 'He gave me these six measures of barley, saying, "Don't go back to your mother-in-law empty-handed."'

18Then Naomi said, 'Wait, my daughter, until you find out what happens. For the man will not rest until the matter is settled today.'

Boaz marries Ruth

4 Meanwhile Boaz went up to the town gate and sat down there just as the family guardian he had mentioned came along. Boaz said, 'Come over here, my friend, and sit down.' So he went over and sat down.

2Boaz took ten of the elders of the town and said, 'Sit here,' and they did so. 3Then he said to the family guardian, 'Naomi, who has come back from Moab, is selling the piece of land that belonged to our relative Elimelek. 4I thought I should bring the matter to your attention and suggest that you buy it in the presence of these seated here and in the presence of the elders of my people. If you will redeem it, do so. But if you[b] will not, tell me, so I will know. For no-one has the right to do it except you, and I am next in line.'

'I will redeem it,' he said.

5Then Boaz said, 'On the day you buy the land from Naomi, you also acquire Ruth the Moabite, the[c] dead man's widow, in order to maintain the name of the dead with his property.'

6At this, the family guardian said, 'Then I cannot redeem it because I might endanger my own estate. You redeem it yourself. I cannot do it.'

7(Now in earlier times in Israel, for the redemption and transfer of property to become final, one party took off his sandal and gave it to the other. This was the method of legalising transactions in Israel.)

8So the family guardian said to Boaz, 'Buy it yourself.' And he removed his sandal.

9Then Boaz announced to the elders and all the people, 'Today you are witnesses that I have bought from Naomi all the property of Elimelek, Kilion and Mahlon. 10I have also acquired Ruth the Moabite, Mahlon's widow, as my wife, in order to maintain the name of the dead with his property, so that his name will not disappear from among his family or from his home town. Today you are witnesses!'

11Then the elders and all the people at the gate said, 'We are witnesses. May the LORD make the woman who is coming into your home like Rachel and Leah, who together

---

[a] 15 Most Hebrew manuscripts; many Hebrew manuscripts, Vulgate and Syriac *she* [b] 4 Many Hebrew manuscripts, Septuagint, Vulgate and Syriac; most Hebrew manuscripts *he* [c] 5 Vulgate and Syriac; Hebrew (see also Septuagint) *Naomi and from Ruth the Moabite, you acquire the*

Kinsman-redeemer
Ruth 4:8

Swapping smelly sandals is hardly the most romantic way to start a relationship, is it? But Israelite law was set up to protect the possessions of each tribe. If an Israelite got into trouble and had to sell his land to survive, his nearest male relative, known as the kinsman-redeemer, had the first option to buy it, allowing it to be kept within the family rather than going to a stranger. As Boaz is not Ruth's nearest kinsman, he has to do a deal with the man who is.

built up the house of Israel. May you have standing in Ephrathah and be famous in Bethlehem. ¹²Through the offspring the LORD gives you by this young woman, may your family be like that of Perez, whom Tamar bore to Judah.'

Naomi gains a son

¹³So Boaz took Ruth and she became his wife. When he made love to her, the LORD enabled her to conceive, and she gave birth to a son. ¹⁴The women said to Naomi: 'Praise be to the LORD, who this day has not left you without a family guardian. May he become famous throughout Israel! ¹⁵He will renew your life and sustain you in your old age. For your daughter-in-law, who loves you and who is better to you than seven sons, has given him birth.'

¹⁶Then Naomi took the child in her arms and cared for him. ¹⁷The women living there said, 'Naomi has a son!' And they named him Obed. He was the father of Jesse, the father of David.

The genealogy of David

¹⁸This, then, is the family line of Perez:

Perez was the father of Hezron,
¹⁹Hezron the father of Ram,
Ram the father of Amminadab,
²⁰Amminadab the father of Nahshon,
Nahshon the father of Salmon,[a]
²¹Salmon the father of Boaz,
Boaz the father of Obed,
²²Obed the father of Jesse,
and Jesse the father of David.

---

[a] 20 A few Hebrew manuscripts, some Septuagint manuscripts and Vulgate (see also verse 21 and Septuagint of 1 Chron. 2:11); most Hebrew manuscripts *Salma*

1 Samuel

INTRODUCTION

1 SAMUEL

Author: It's thought that Samuel wrote much of this book, and that Abiathar the priest finished it after Samuel died.

When: Probably from 1100 BC to 1010 BC.

Where: Still in the Promised Land, now known as Israel.

Did you know? Originally 1 and 2 Samuel were one long book. It was split into two when the Hebrew Bible was translated into Greek in the second century BC.

Main theme: This book describes a turning-point in history. Up until now Israel has been a group of tribes, each living on their own land and minding their own business until threats from enemies made them come together to fight. Samuel, under God's leading, sets Israel on the road to being a united kingdom with a king. 1 Samuel tells the story of Samuel, and Saul who was Israel's first king, and introduces David who will have a bigger role in the next book.

The birth of Samuel

1 There was a certain man from Ramathaim, a Zuphite[a] from the hill country of Ephraim, whose name was Elkanah son of Jeroham, the son of Elihu, the son of Tohu, the son of Zuph, an Ephraimite. ²He had two wives; one was called Hannah and the other Peninnah. Peninnah had children, but Hannah had none.

³Year after year this man went up from his town to worship and sacrifice to the LORD Almighty at Shiloh, where Hophni and Phinehas, the two sons of Eli, were priests of the LORD. ⁴Whenever the day came for Elkanah to sacrifice, he would give portions of the meat to his wife Peninnah and to all her sons and daughters. ⁵But to Hannah he gave a double portion because

---

[a] 1 See Septuagint and 1 Chron. 6:26-27,33-35; or *from Ramathaim Zuphim*.

he loved her, and the LORD had closed her womb. 6Because the LORD had closed Hannah's womb, her rival kept provoking her in order to irritate her. 7This went on year after year. Whenever Hannah went up to the house of the LORD, her rival provoked her till she wept and would not eat. 8Her husband Elkanah would say to her, 'Hannah, why are you weeping? Why don't you eat? Why are you downhearted? Don't I mean more to you than ten sons?'

9Once when they had finished eating and drinking in Shiloh, Hannah stood up. Now Eli the priest was sitting on his chair by the doorpost of the LORD's house. 10In her deep anguish Hannah prayed to the LORD, weeping bitterly. 11And she made a vow, saying, 'LORD Almighty, if you will only look on your servant's misery and remember me, and not forget your servant but give her a son, then I will give him to the LORD for all the days of his life, and no razor will ever be used on his head.'

12As she kept on praying to the LORD, Eli observed her mouth. 13Hannah was praying in her heart, and her lips were moving but her voice was not heard. Eli thought she was drunk 14and said to her, 'How long are you going to stay drunk? Put away your wine.'

15'Not so, my lord,' Hannah replied, 'I am a woman who is deeply troubled. I have not been drinking wine or beer; I was pouring out my soul to the LORD. 16Do not take your servant for a wicked woman; I have been praying here out of my great anguish and grief.'

17Eli answered, 'Go in peace, and may the God of Israel grant you what you have asked of him.'

18She said, 'May your servant find favour in your eyes.' Then she went her way and ate something, and her face was no longer downcast.

19Early the next morning they arose and worshipped before the LORD and then went back to their home at Ramah. Elkanah made love to his wife Hannah, and the LORD remembered her. 20So in the course of time Hannah became pregnant and gave birth to a son. She named him Samuel,[a] saying, 'Because I asked the LORD for him.'

Hannah dedicates Samuel

21When Elkanah went up with all his family to offer the annual sacrifice to the LORD and to fulfil his vow, 22Hannah did not go. She said to her husband, 'After the boy is weaned, I will take him and present him before the LORD, and he will live there always.'[b]

23'Do what seems best to you,' her husband Elkanah told her. 'Stay here until you have weaned him; only may the LORD make good his[c] word.' So the woman stayed at home and nursed her son until she had weaned him.

24After he was weaned, she took the boy with her, young as he was, along with a three-year-old bull,[d] an ephah[e] of flour and a skin of wine, and brought him to the house of the LORD at Shiloh. 25When the bull had been sacrificed, they brought the boy to Eli, 26and she said to him, 'Pardon me, my lord. As surely as you live, I am the woman who stood here beside you praying to the LORD. 27I prayed for this child, and the LORD has granted me what I asked of him. 28So now I give him to the LORD. For his whole life he shall be given over to the LORD.' And he worshipped the LORD there.

Hannah's prayer

2 Then Hannah prayed and said:

'My heart rejoices in the LORD;
   in the LORD my horn[f] is lifted high.
My mouth boasts over my enemies,
   for I delight in your deliverance.

2'There is no-one holy like the LORD;
   there is no-one besides you;
   there is no Rock like our God.

3'Do not keep talking so proudly
   or let your mouth speak such arrogance,
for the LORD is a God who knows,
   and by him deeds are weighed.

---

[a] 20 *Samuel* sounds like the Hebrew for *heard by God.*   [b] 22 Masoretic Text; Dead Sea Scrolls *always. I have dedicated him as a Nazirite—all the days of his life.'*   [c] 23 Masoretic Text; Dead Sea Scrolls, Septuagint and Syriac *your*   [d] 24 Dead Sea Scrolls, Septuagint and Syriac; Masoretic Text *with three bulls*   [e] 24 That is, probably about 16 kilograms   [f] 1 *Horn* here symbolises strength; also in verse 10.

4 'The bows of the warriors are broken,
  but those who stumbled are armed with strength.
5 Those who were full hire themselves out for food,
  but those who were hungry are hungry no more.
She who was barren has borne seven children,
  but she who has had many sons pines away.

6 'The LORD brings death and makes alive;
  he brings down to the grave and raises up.
7 The LORD sends poverty and wealth;
  he humbles and he exalts.
8 He raises the poor from the dust
  and lifts the needy from the ash heap;
he seats them with princes
  and makes them inherit a throne of honour.

'For the foundations of the earth are the LORD's;
  on them he has set the world.
9 He will guard the feet of his faithful servants,
  but the wicked will be silenced in the place of darkness.

'It is not by strength that one prevails;
10   those who oppose the LORD will be broken.
The Most High will thunder from heaven;
  the LORD will judge the ends of the earth.

'He will give strength to his king
  and exalt the horn of his anointed.'

11 Then Elkanah went home to Ramah, but the boy ministered before the LORD under Eli the priest.

Eli's wicked sons

12 Eli's sons were scoundrels; they had no regard for the LORD. 13 Now it was the practice of the priests that, whenever any of the people offered a sacrifice, the priest's servant would come with a three-pronged fork in his hand while the meat was being boiled 14 and would plunge the fork into the pan or kettle or cauldron or pot. Whatever the fork brought up the priest would take for himself. This is how they treated all the Israelites who came to Shiloh. 15 But even before the fat was burned, the priest's servant would come and say to the person who was sacrificing, 'Give the priest some meat to roast; he won't accept boiled meat from you, but only raw.'

16 If the person said to him, 'Let the fat be burned first, and then take whatever you want,' the servant would answer, 'No, hand it over now; if you don't, I'll take it by force.'

17 This sin of the young men was very great in the LORD's sight, for they[a] were treating the LORD's offering with contempt.

18 But Samuel was ministering before the LORD—a boy wearing a linen ephod. 19 Each year his mother made him a little robe and took it to him when she went up with her husband to offer the annual sacrifice. 20 Eli would bless Elkanah and his wife, saying, 'May the LORD give you children by this woman to take the place of the one she prayed for and gave to[b] the LORD.' Then they would go home. 21 And the LORD was gracious to Hannah; she gave birth to three sons and two daughters. Meanwhile, the boy Samuel grew up in the presence of the LORD.

22 Now Eli, who was very old, heard about everything his sons were doing to all Israel and how they slept with the women who served at the entrance to the tent of meeting. 23 So he said to them, 'Why do you do such things? I hear from all the people about these wicked deeds of yours. 24 No, my sons; the report I hear spreading among the LORD's people is not good. 25 If anyone sins against another human being, God[c] may mediate for the offender; but if anyone sins against the LORD, who will intercede for them?' His sons, however, did not listen to their father's rebuke, for it was the LORD's will to put them to death.

26 And the boy Samuel continued to grow in stature and in favour with the LORD and with people.

---

[a] 17 Dead Sea Scrolls and Septuagint; Masoretic Text *people* [b] 20 Dead Sea Scrolls; Masoretic Text *and asked from*
[c] 25 Or *the judges*

Prophecy against the house of Eli

27 Now a man of God came to Eli and said to him, 'This is what the LORD says: "Did I not clearly reveal myself to the family of your ancestor when they were in Egypt under Pharaoh? 28 I chose your ancestor out of all the tribes of Israel to be my priest, to go up to my altar, to burn incense, and to wear an ephod in my presence. I also gave your ancestor's family all the food offerings presented by the Israelites. 29 Why do you*a* scorn my sacrifice and offering that I prescribed for my dwelling? Why do you honour your sons more than me by fattening yourselves on the choice parts of every offering made by my people Israel?"

30 'Therefore the LORD, the God of Israel, declares: "I promised that the members of your family would minister before me for ever." But now the LORD declares: "Far be it from me! Those who honour me I will honour, but those who despise me will be disdained. 31 The time is coming when I will cut short your strength and the strength of the members of your family, so that no-one in it will reach old age, 32 and you will see distress in my dwelling. Although good will be done to Israel, no-one in your family line will ever reach old age. 33 Every one of you that I do not cut off from serving at my altar I will spare only to destroy your sight and sap your strength, and all your descendants will die in the prime of life.

34 '"And what happens to your two sons, Hophni and Phinehas, will be a sign to you—they will both die on the same day. 35 I will raise up for myself a faithful priest, who will do according to what is in my heart and mind. I will firmly establish his family line, and he will minister before my anointed one always. 36 Then everyone left in your family line will come and bow down before him for a piece of silver and a loaf of bread and plead, 'Appoint me to some priestly office so that I can have food to eat.'"

The LORD calls Samuel

3 The boy Samuel ministered before the LORD under Eli. In those days the word of the LORD was rare; there were not many visions.

a 29 The Hebrew is plural.

People and Places

Samuel
1 Samuel 3:1

Samuel was the last of the judges and the prophet who anointed Saul to be the first king of Israel. His mother Hannah cried out to God for a baby, and when God answered her prayer she dedicated her first son, Samuel, to God's service. Samuel went to live with Eli the priest and heard God's voice and call on his life when he was very young. He was a better judge than his predecessors but the Israelites still wanted a king like the other nations.

2 One night Eli, whose eyes were becoming so weak that he could barely see, was lying down in his usual place. 3 The lamp of God had not yet gone out, and Samuel was lying down in the house of the LORD, where the ark of God was. 4 Then the LORD called Samuel.

Samuel answered, 'Here I am.' 5 And he ran to Eli and said, 'Here I am; you called me.'

But Eli said, 'I did not call; go back and lie down.' So he went and lay down.

6 Again the LORD called, 'Samuel!' And Samuel got up and went to Eli and said, 'Here I am; you called me.'

'My son,' Eli said, 'I did not call; go back and lie down.'

7 Now Samuel did not yet know the LORD: the word of the LORD had not yet been revealed to him.

8 A third time the LORD called, 'Samuel!' And Samuel got up and went to Eli and said, 'Here I am; you called me.'

Then Eli realised that the LORD was calling the boy. 9 So Eli told Samuel, 'Go and lie down, and if he calls you, say, "Speak, LORD, for your servant is listening."' So Samuel went and lay down in his place.

¹⁰The LORD came and stood there, calling as at the other times, 'Samuel! Samuel!'

Then Samuel said, 'Speak, for your servant is listening.'

¹¹And the LORD said to Samuel: 'See, I am about to do something in Israel that will make the ears of everyone who hears about it tingle. ¹²At that time I will carry out against Eli everything I spoke against his family—from beginning to end. ¹³For I told him that I would judge his family for ever because of the sin he knew about; his sons uttered blasphemies against God,*ᵃ* and he failed to restrain them. ¹⁴Therefore I swore to the house of Eli, "The guilt of Eli's house will never be atoned for by sacrifice or offering."'

¹⁵Samuel lay down until morning and then opened the doors of the house of the LORD. He was afraid to tell Eli the vision, ¹⁶but Eli called him and said, 'Samuel, my son.'

Samuel answered, 'Here I am.'

¹⁷'What was it he said to you?' Eli asked. 'Do not hide it from me. May God deal with you, be it ever so severely, if you hide from me anything he told you.' ¹⁸So Samuel told him everything, hiding nothing from him. Then Eli said, 'He is the LORD; let him do what is good in his eyes.'

¹⁹The LORD was with Samuel as he grew up, and he let none of Samuel's words fall to the ground. ²⁰And all Israel from Dan to Beersheba recognised that Samuel was attested as a prophet of the LORD. ²¹The LORD continued to appear at Shiloh, and there he revealed himself to Samuel through his word.

4 And Samuel's word came to all Israel.

The Philistines capture the ark

Now the Israelites went out to fight against the Philistines. The Israelites camped at Ebenezer, and the Philistines at Aphek. ²The Philistines deployed their forces to meet Israel, and as the battle spread, Israel was defeated by the Philistines, who killed about four thousand of them on the battlefield. ³When the soldiers returned to camp, the elders of Israel asked, 'Why did the LORD bring defeat on us today before the Philistines? Let us bring the ark of the LORD's covenant from Shiloh, so that he may go with us and save us from the hand of our enemies.'

⁴So the people sent men to Shiloh, and they brought back the ark of the covenant of the LORD Almighty, who is enthroned between the cherubim. And Eli's two sons, Hophni and Phinehas, were there with the ark of the covenant of God.

⁵When the ark of the LORD's covenant came into the camp, all Israel raised such a great shout that the ground shook. ⁶Hearing the uproar, the Philistines asked, 'What's all this shouting in the Hebrew camp?'

When they learned that the ark of the LORD had come into the camp, ⁷the Philistines were afraid. 'A god has*ᵇ* come into the camp,' they said. 'We're in trouble! Nothing like this has happened before. ⁸Woe to us! Who will deliver us from the hand of these mighty gods? They are the gods who struck the Egyptians with all kinds of plagues in the wilderness. ⁹Be strong, Philistines! Be men, or you will be subject to the Hebrews, as they have been to you. Be men, and fight!'

¹⁰So the Philistines fought, and the Israelites were defeated and every man fled to his tent. The slaughter was very great; Israel lost thirty thousand foot soldiers. ¹¹The ark of God was captured, and Eli's two sons, Hophni and Phinehas, died.

Death of Eli

¹²That same day a Benjaminite ran from the battle line and went to Shiloh with his clothes torn and dust on his head. ¹³When he arrived, there was Eli sitting on his chair by the side of the road, watching, because his heart feared for the ark of God. When the man entered the town and told what had happened, the whole town sent up a cry.

ᵃ 13 An ancient Hebrew scribal tradition (see also Septuagint); Masoretic Text *sons made themselves contemptible*
ᵇ 7 Or *'Gods have'* (see Septuagint)

14Eli heard the outcry and asked, 'What is the meaning of this uproar?'

The man hurried over to Eli, 15who was ninety-eight years old and whose eyes had failed so that he could not see. 16He told Eli, 'I have just come from the battle line; I fled from it this very day.'

Eli asked, 'What happened, my son?'

17The one who brought the news replied, 'Israel fled before the Philistines, and the army has suffered heavy losses. Also your two sons, Hophni and Phinehas, are dead, and the ark of God has been captured.'

18When he mentioned the ark of God, Eli fell backwards off his chair by the side of the gate. His neck was broken and he died, for he was an old man, and he was heavy. He had led[a] Israel for forty years.

19His daughter-in-law, the wife of Phinehas, was pregnant and near the time of delivery. When she heard the news that the ark of God had been captured and that her father-in-law and her husband were dead, she went into labour and gave birth, but was overcome by her labour pains. 20As she was dying, the women attending her said, 'Don't despair; you have given birth to a son.' But she did not respond or pay any attention.

21She named the boy Ichabod,[b] saying, 'The Glory has departed from Israel'— because of the capture of the ark of God and the deaths of her father-in-law and her husband. 22She said, 'The Glory has departed from Israel, for the ark of God has been captured.'

The ark in Ashdod and Ekron

5 After the Philistines had captured the ark of God, they took it from Ebenezer to Ashdod. 2Then they carried the ark into Dagon's temple and set it beside Dagon. 3When the people of Ashdod rose early the next day, there was Dagon, fallen on his face on the ground before the ark of the LORD! They took Dagon and put him back in his place. 4But the following morning when they rose, there was Dagon, fallen on his face on the ground before the ark of the LORD! His head and hands had been broken off and were lying on the threshold; only his body remained. 5That is why to this day neither the priests of Dagon nor any others who enter Dagon's temple at Ashdod step on the threshold.

6The LORD's hand was heavy on the people of Ashdod and its vicinity; he brought devastation on them and afflicted them with tumours.[c] 7When the people of Ashdod saw what was happening, they said, 'The ark of the god of Israel must not stay here with us, because his hand is heavy on us and on Dagon our god.' 8So they called together all the rulers of the Philistines and asked them, 'What shall we do with the ark of the god of Israel?'

They answered, 'Let the ark of the god of Israel be moved to Gath.' So they moved the ark of the God of Israel.

9But after they had moved it, the LORD's hand was against that city, throwing it into a great panic. He afflicted the people of the city, both young and old, with an outbreak of tumours.[d] 10So they sent the ark of God to Ekron.

As the ark of God was entering Ekron, the people of Ekron cried out, 'They have brought the ark of the god of Israel round to us to kill us and our people.' 11So they called together all the rulers of the Philistines and said, 'Send the ark of the god of Israel away; let it go back to its own place, or it[e] will kill us and our people.' For death had filled the city with panic; God's hand was very heavy on it. 12Those who did not die were afflicted with tumours, and the outcry of the city went up to heaven.

The ark returned to Israel

6 When the ark of the LORD had been in Philistine territory for seven months, 2the Philistines called for the priests and the diviners and said, 'What shall we do with the ark of the LORD? Tell us how we should send it back to its place.'

3They answered, 'If you return the ark of the god of Israel, do not send it back to him without a gift; by all means send a guilt offering to him. Then you will be healed, and you will know why his hand has not been lifted from you.'

---

[a] 18 Traditionally *judged* [b] 21 *Ichabod* means *no glory.* [c] 6 Hebrew; Septuagint and Vulgate *tumours. And rats appeared in their land, and there was death and destruction throughout the city* [d] 9 Or *with tumours in the groin* (see Septuagint) [e] 11 Or *he*

Philistines
1 Samuel 6:1
The Philistines were the sworn enemies of the Israelites. Towards the end of the time of the judges, their increased attacks and their weapons of iron made Israel demand a king so they would be stronger and more united in order to fight back.

⁴The Philistines asked, 'What guilt offering should we send to him?'

They replied, 'Five gold tumours and five gold rats, according to the number of the Philistine rulers, because the same plague has struck both you and your rulers. ⁵Make models of the tumours and of the rats that are destroying the country, and give glory to Israel's god. Perhaps he will lift his hand from you and your gods and your land. ⁶Why do you harden your hearts as the Egyptians and Pharaoh did? When Israel's god dealt harshly with them, did they not send the Israelites out so that they could go on their way?

⁷'Now then, get a new cart ready, with two cows that have calved and have never been yoked. Hitch the cows to the cart, but take their calves away and pen them up. ⁸Take the ark of the LORD and put it on the cart, and in a chest beside it put the gold objects you are sending back to him as a guilt offering. Send it on its way, ⁹but keep watching it. If it goes up to its own territory, towards Beth Shemesh, then the LORD has brought this great disaster on us. But if it does not, then we shall know that it was not his hand that struck us but that it happened to us by chance.'

¹⁰So they did this. They took two such cows and hitched them to the cart and penned up their calves. ¹¹They placed the ark of the LORD on the cart and along with it the chest containing the gold rats and the models of the tumours. ¹²Then the cows went straight up towards Beth Shemesh, keeping on the road and lowing all the way; they did not turn to the right or to the left. The rulers of the Philistines followed them as far as the border of Beth Shemesh.

¹³Now the people of Beth Shemesh were harvesting their wheat in the valley, and when they looked up and saw the ark, they rejoiced at the sight. ¹⁴The cart came to the field of Joshua of Beth Shemesh, and there it stopped beside a large rock. The people chopped up the wood of the cart and sacrificed the cows as a burnt offering to the LORD. ¹⁵The Levites took down the ark of the LORD, together with the chest containing the gold objects, and placed them on the large rock. On that day the people of Beth Shemesh offered burnt offerings and made sacrifices to the LORD. ¹⁶The five rulers of the Philistines saw all this and then returned that same day to Ekron.

¹⁷These are the gold tumours the Philistines sent as a guilt offering to the LORD—one each for Ashdod, Gaza, Ashkelon, Gath and Ekron. ¹⁸And the number of the gold rats was according to the number of Philistine towns belonging to the five rulers—the fortified towns with their country villages. The large rock on which the Levites set the ark of the LORD is a witness to this day in the field of Joshua of Beth Shemesh.

¹⁹But God struck down some of the inhabitants of Beth Shemesh, putting seventy[a] of them to death because they looked into the ark of the LORD. The people mourned because of the heavy blow the LORD had dealt them. ²⁰And the people of Beth Shemesh asked, 'Who can stand in the presence of the LORD, this holy God? To whom will the ark go up from here?'

²¹Then they sent messengers to the people of Kiriath Jearim, saying, 'The Philistines have returned the ark of the LORD. Come down and take it up to your town.'

7 ¹So the men of Kiriath Jearim came and took up the ark of the LORD. They brought it to Abinadab's house on the hill and consecrated Eleazar his son to guard the ark of the LORD. ²The ark remained at

---

[a] 19 A few Hebrew manuscripts; most Hebrew manuscripts and Septuagint *50,070*

Kiriath Jearim a long time—twenty years in all.

Samuel subdues the Philistines at Mizpah

Then all the people of Israel turned back to the LORD. 3So Samuel said to the whole house of Israel, 'If you are returning to the LORD with all your hearts, then rid yourselves of the foreign gods and the Ashtoreths and commit yourselves to the LORD and serve him only, and he will deliver you out of the hand of the Philistines.' 4So the Israelites put away their Baals and Ashtoreths, and served the LORD only.

5Then Samuel said, 'Assemble all Israel at Mizpah, and I will intercede with the LORD for you.' 6When they had assembled at Mizpah, they drew water and poured it out before the LORD. On that day they fasted and there they confessed, 'We have sinned against the LORD.' Now Samuel was serving as leader[a] of Israel at Mizpah.

7When the Philistines heard that Israel had assembled at Mizpah, the rulers of the Philistines came up to attack them. When the Israelites heard of it, they were afraid because of the Philistines. 8They said to Samuel, 'Do not stop crying out to the LORD our God for us, that he may rescue us from the hand of the Philistines.' 9Then Samuel took a suckling lamb and sacrificed it as a whole burnt offering to the LORD. He cried out to the LORD on Israel's behalf, and the LORD answered him.

10While Samuel was sacrificing the burnt offering, the Philistines drew near to engage Israel in battle. But that day the LORD thundered with loud thunder against the Philistines and threw them into such a panic that they were routed before the Israelites. 11The men of Israel rushed out of Mizpah and pursued the Philistines, slaughtering them along the way to a point below Beth Kar.

12Then Samuel took a stone and set it up between Mizpah and Shen. He named it Ebenezer,[b] saying, 'Thus far the LORD has helped us.'

13So the Philistines were subdued and they stopped invading Israel's territory. Throughout Samuel's lifetime, the hand of the LORD was against the Philistines. 14The towns from Ekron to Gath that the Philistines had captured from Israel were restored, and Israel delivered the neighbouring territory from the hands of the Philistines. And there was peace between Israel and the Amorites.

15Samuel continued as Israel's leader all the days of his life. 16From year to year he went on a circuit from Bethel to Gilgal to Mizpah, judging Israel in all those places. 17But he always went back to Ramah, where his home was, and there he also held court for Israel. And he built an altar there to the LORD.

Israel asks for a king

8 When Samuel grew old, he appointed his sons as Israel's leaders.[c] 2The name of his firstborn was Joel and the name of his second was Abijah, and they served at Beersheba. 3But his sons did not follow his ways. They turned aside after dishonest gain and accepted bribes and perverted justice.

4So all the elders of Israel gathered together and came to Samuel at Ramah. 5They said to him, 'You are old, and your sons do not follow your ways; now appoint a king to lead[d] us, such as all the other nations have.'

6But when they said, 'Give us a king to lead us,' this displeased Samuel; so he prayed to the LORD. 7And the LORD told him: 'Listen to all that the people are saying to you; it is not you they have rejected, but they have rejected me as their king. 8As they have done from the day I brought them up out of Egypt until this day, forsaking me and serving other gods, so they are doing to you. 9Now listen to them; but warn them solemnly and let them know what the king who will reign over them will claim as his rights.'

10Samuel told all the words of the LORD to the people who were asking him for a king. 11He said, 'This is what the king who will reign over you will claim as his rights: he will take your sons and make them serve with his chariots and horses, and they will

---

[a] 6 Traditionally *judge*; also in verse 15 [b] 12 *Ebenezer* means *stone of help*. [c] 1 Traditionally *judges* [d] 5 Traditionally *judge*; also in verses 6 and 20

run in front of his chariots. ¹²Some he will assign to be commanders of thousands and commanders of fifties, and others to plough his ground and reap his harvest, and still others to make weapons of war and equipment for his chariots. ¹³He will take your daughters to be perfumers and cooks and bakers. ¹⁴He will take the best of your fields and vineyards and olive groves and give them to his attendants. ¹⁵He will take a tenth of your grain and of your vintage and give it to his officials and attendants. ¹⁶Your male and female servants and the best of your cattle[a] and donkeys he will take for his own use. ¹⁷He will take a tenth of your flocks, and you yourselves will become his slaves. ¹⁸When that day comes, you will cry out for relief from the king you have chosen, but the LORD will not answer you in that day.'

¹⁹But the people refused to listen to Samuel. 'No!' they said. 'We want a king over us. ²⁰Then we shall be like all the other nations, with a king to lead us and to go out before us and fight our battles.'

²¹When Samuel heard all that the people said, he repeated it before the LORD. ²²The LORD answered, 'Listen to them and give them a king.'

Then Samuel said to the Israelites, 'Everyone go back to your own town.'

Samuel anoints Saul

9 There was a Benjaminite, a man of standing, whose name was Kish son of Abiel, the son of Zeror, the son of Bekorath, the son of Aphiah of Benjamin. ²Kish had a son named Saul, as handsome a young man as could be found anywhere in Israel, and he was a head taller than anyone else.

³Now the donkeys belonging to Saul's father Kish were lost, and Kish said to his son Saul, 'Take one of the servants with you and go and look for the donkeys.' ⁴So he passed through the hill country of Ephraim and through the area around Shalisha, but they did not find them. They went on into the district of Shaalim, but the donkeys were not there. Then he passed through the territory of Benjamin, but they did not find them.

People and Places

Saul
1 Samuel 9:2

When Saul first gets mentioned in the Bible, he's looking for his father's lost donkeys, but he soon goes on to more impressive tasks. Anointed by Samuel as the first king of Israel, he's quickly accepted by the people and shows that he is a strong military leader. But he makes several mistakes, taking on the role of priest when he's too impatient to wait for Samuel (1 Samuel 13:8, 9), and sparing the life of the Amalekite king when he should have killed him (1 Samuel 15:3). He couldn't be trusted to do God's will and so, although he remained king until his death, God's Spirit left him.

---

⁵When they reached the district of Zuph, Saul said to the servant who was with him, 'Come, let's go back, or my father will stop thinking about the donkeys and start worrying about us.'

⁶But the servant replied, 'Look, in this town there is a man of God; he is highly respected, and everything he says comes true. Let's go there now. Perhaps he will tell us what way to take.'

⁷Saul said to his servant, 'If we go, what can we give the man? The food in our sacks is gone. We have no gift to take to the man of God. What do we have?'

⁸The servant answered him again. 'Look,' he said, 'I have a quarter of a shekel[b] of silver. I will give it to the man of God so that he will tell us what way to take.' ⁹(Formerly in Israel, if people went to enquire of God, they would say, 'Come, let us go to the seer,' because the prophet of today used to be called a seer.)

---

[a] 16 Septuagint; Hebrew *young men*   [b] 8 That is, about 3 grams

10 'Good,' Saul said to his servant. 'Come, let's go.' So they set out for the town where the man of God was.

11 As they were going up the hill to the town, they met some young women coming out to draw water, and they asked them, 'Is the seer here?'

12 'He is,' they answered. 'He's ahead of you. Hurry now; he has just come to our town today, for the people have a sacrifice at the high place. 13 As soon as you enter the town, you will find him before he goes up to the high place to eat. The people will not begin eating until he comes, because he must bless the sacrifice; afterwards, those who are invited will eat. Go up now; you should find him about this time.'

14 They went up to the town, and as they were entering it, there was Samuel, coming towards them on his way up to the high place.

15 Now the day before Saul came, the LORD had revealed this to Samuel: 16 'About this time tomorrow I will send you a man from the land of Benjamin. Anoint him ruler over my people Israel; he will deliver them from the hand of the Philistines. I have looked on my people, for their cry has reached me.'

17 When Samuel caught sight of Saul, the LORD said to him, 'This is the man I spoke to you about; he will govern my people.'

18 Saul approached Samuel in the gateway and asked, 'Would you please tell me where the seer's house is?'

19 'I am the seer,' Samuel replied. 'Go up ahead of me to the high place, for today you are to eat with me, and in the morning I will send you on your way and tell you all that is in your heart. 20 As for the donkeys you lost three days ago, do not worry about them; they have been found. And to whom is all the desire of Israel turned, if not to you and your whole family line?'

21 Saul answered, 'But am I not a Benjaminite, from the smallest tribe of Israel, and is not my clan the least of all the clans of the tribe of Benjamin? Why do you say such a thing to me?'

22 Then Samuel brought Saul and his servant into the hall and seated them at the head of those who were invited—about thirty in number. 23 Samuel said to the cook, 'Bring the piece of meat I gave you, the one I told you to lay aside.'

24 So the cook took up the thigh with what was on it and set it in front of Saul. Samuel said, 'Here is what has been kept for you. Eat, because it was set aside for you for this occasion from the time I said, "I have invited guests."' And Saul dined with Samuel that day.

25 After they came down from the high place to the town, Samuel talked with Saul on the roof of his house. 26 They rose about daybreak, and Samuel called to Saul on the roof, 'Get ready, and I will send you on your way.' When Saul got ready, he and Samuel went outside together. 27 As they were going down to the edge of the town, Samuel said to Saul, 'Tell the servant to go on ahead of us'—and the servant did so—'but you stay here for a while, so that I may give you a message from God.'

10 Then Samuel took a bottle of olive oil and poured it on Saul's head and kissed him, saying, 'Has not the LORD anointed you ruler over his inheritance?[a] 2 When you leave me today, you will meet two men near Rachel's tomb, at Zelzah on the border of Benjamin. They will say to you, "The donkeys you set out to look for have been found. And now your father has stopped thinking about them and is worried about you. He is asking, 'What shall I do about my son?'"

3 'Then you will go on from there until you reach the great tree of Tabor. Three men going up to God at Bethel will meet you there. One will be carrying three young goats, another three loaves of bread, and another a skin of wine. 4 They will greet you and offer you two loaves of bread, which you will accept from them.

5 'After that you will go to Gibeah of God, where there is a Philistine outpost. As you approach the town, you will meet a

---

[a] 1 Hebrew; Septuagint and Vulgate *over his people Israel? You will reign over the LORD's people and save them from the power of their enemies round about. And this will be a sign to you that the LORD has anointed you ruler over his inheritance:*

procession of prophets coming down from the high place with lyres, tambourines, pipes and harps being played before them, and they will be prophesying. ⁶The Spirit of the LORD will come on you in power, and you will prophesy with them; and you will be changed into a different person. ⁷Once these signs are fulfilled, do whatever your hand finds to do, for God is with you.

⁸'Go down ahead of me to Gilgal. I will surely come down to you to sacrifice burnt offerings and fellowship offerings, but you must wait seven days until I come to you and tell you what you are to do.'

Saul made king

⁹As Saul turned to leave Samuel, God changed Saul's heart, and all these signs were fulfilled that day. ¹⁰When he and his servant arrived at Gibeah, a procession of prophets met him; the Spirit of God came on him in power, and he joined in their prophesying. ¹¹When all those who had formerly known him saw him prophesying with the prophets, they asked each other, 'What is this that has happened to the son of Kish? Is Saul also among the prophets?'

¹²A man who lived there answered, 'And who is their father?' So it became a saying: 'Is Saul also among the prophets?' ¹³After Saul stopped prophesying, he went to the high place.

¹⁴Now Saul's uncle asked him and his servant, 'Where have you been?'

'Looking for the donkeys,' he said. 'But when we saw they were not to be found, we went to Samuel.'

¹⁵Saul's uncle said, 'Tell me what Samuel said to you.'

¹⁶Saul replied, 'He assured us that the donkeys had been found.' But he did not tell his uncle what Samuel had said about the kingship.

¹⁷Samuel summoned the people of Israel to the LORD at Mizpah ¹⁸and said to them, 'This is what the LORD, the God of Israel, says: "I brought Israel up out of Egypt, and I delivered you from the power of Egypt and all the kingdoms that oppressed you." ¹⁹But you have now rejected your God, who saves you out of all your disasters and calamities. And you have said, "No, appoint a king over us." So now present yourselves before the LORD by your tribes and clans.'

²⁰When Samuel had made all Israel come forward by tribes, the tribe of Benjamin was taken by lot. ²¹Then he brought forward the tribe of Benjamin, clan by clan, and Matri's clan was taken. Finally Saul son of Kish was taken. But when they looked for him, he was not to be found. ²²So they enquired further of the LORD, 'Has the man come here yet?'

And the LORD said, 'Yes, he has hidden himself among the supplies.'

²³They ran and brought him out, and as he stood among the people he was a head taller than any of the others. ²⁴Samuel said to all the people, 'Do you see the man the LORD has chosen? There is no-one like him among all the people.'

Then the people shouted, 'Long live the king!'

²⁵Samuel explained to the people the rights and duties of kingship. He wrote them down on a scroll and deposited it before the LORD. Then Samuel dismissed the people to go to their own homes.

²⁶Saul also went to his home in Gibeah, accompanied by valiant men whose hearts God had touched. ²⁷But some scoundrels

Sign of the times

Urim and Thummim
1 Samuel 10:21

Samuel would have chosen the tribe, clan and finally Saul himself using Urim and Thummim. These were small gems or stones that the high priest wore in a pouch on his breastplate. Although no-one knows exactly how they were used, it's thought that the priest would throw them down, a little like dice, and use them to determine God's will.

said, 'How can this fellow save us?' They despised him and brought him no gifts. But Saul kept silent.

Saul rescues the city of Jabesh

11 Nahash[a] the Ammonite went up and besieged Jabesh Gilead. And all the men of Jabesh said to him, 'Make a treaty with us, and we will be subject to you.'

2But Nahash the Ammonite replied, 'I will make a treaty with you only on the condition that I gouge out the right eye of every one of you and so bring disgrace on all Israel.'

3The elders of Jabesh said to him, 'Give us seven days so that we can send messengers throughout Israel; if no-one comes to rescue us, we will surrender to you.'

4When the messengers came to Gibeah of Saul and reported these terms to the people, they all wept aloud. 5Just then Saul was returning from the fields, behind his oxen, and he asked, 'What is wrong with everyone? Why are they weeping?' Then they repeated to him what the men of Jabesh had said.

6When Saul heard their words, the Spirit of God came on him in power, and he burned with anger. 7He took a pair of oxen, cut them into pieces, and sent the pieces by messengers throughout Israel, proclaiming, 'This is what will be done to the oxen of anyone who does not follow Saul and Samuel.' Then the terror of the LORD fell on the people, and they turned out with one accord. 8When Saul mustered them at Bezek, the men of Israel numbered three hundred thousand and those of Judah thirty thousand.

9They told the messengers who had come, 'Say to the men of Jabesh Gilead, "By the time the sun is hot tomorrow, you will be rescued."' When the messengers went and reported this to the men of Jabesh, they were elated. 10They said to the Ammonites, 'Tomorrow we will surrender to you, and you can do to us whatever you like.'

11The next day Saul separated his men into three divisions; during the last watch of the night they broke into the camp of the Ammonites and slaughtered them until the heat of the day. Those who survived were scattered, so that no two of them were left together.

Saul confirmed as king

12The people then said to Samuel, 'Who was it that asked, "Shall Saul reign over us?" Turn these men over to us so that we may put them to death.'

13But Saul said, 'No-one will be put to death today, for this day the LORD has rescued Israel.'

14Then Samuel said to the people, 'Come, let us go to Gilgal and there renew the kingship.' 15So all the people went to Gilgal and made Saul king in the presence of the LORD. There they sacrificed fellowship offerings before the LORD, and Saul and all the Israelites held a great celebration.

Samuel's farewell speech

12 Samuel said to all Israel, 'I have listened to everything you said to me and have set a king over you. 2Now you have a king as your leader. As for me, I am old and grey, and my sons are here with you. I have been your leader from my youth until this day. 3Here I stand. Testify against me in the presence of the LORD and his anointed. Whose ox have I taken? Whose donkey have I taken? Whom have I cheated? Whom have I oppressed? From whose hand have I accepted a bribe to make me shut my eyes? If I have done any of these things, I will make it right.'

4'You have not cheated or oppressed us,' they replied. 'You have not taken anything from anyone's hand.'

5Samuel said to them, 'The LORD is witness against you, and also his anointed is witness this day, that you have not found anything in my hand.'

'We agree,' they said.

6Then Samuel said to the people, 'It is the LORD who appointed Moses and Aaron and brought your ancestors up out of Egypt. 7Now then, stand here, because I am going

---

[a] 1 Masoretic Text; Dead Sea Scrolls *gifts. Now Nahash king of the Ammonites oppressed the Gadites and Reubenites severely. He gouged out all their right eyes and struck terror and dread in Israel. Not a man remained among the Israelites beyond the Jordan whose right eye was not gouged out by Nahash king of the Ammonites, except that seven thousand men fled from the Ammonites and entered Jabesh Gilead. About a month later,* 1Nahash

to confront you with evidence before the LORD as to all the righteous acts performed by the LORD for you and your ancestors.

8'After Jacob entered Egypt, they cried to the LORD for help, and the LORD sent Moses and Aaron, who brought your ancestors out of Egypt and settled them in this place.

9'But they forgot the LORD their God; so he sold them into the hands of Sisera, the commander of the army of Hazor, and into the hands of the Philistines and the king of Moab, who fought against them. 10They cried out to the LORD and said, "We have sinned; we have forsaken the LORD and served the Baals and the Ashtoreths. But now deliver us from the hands of our enemies, and we will serve you." 11Then the LORD sent Jerub-Baal,[a] Barak,[b] Jephthah and Samuel,[c] and he delivered you from the hands of your enemies all around you, so that you lived in safety.

12'But when you saw that Nahash king of the Ammonites was moving against you, you said to me, "No, we want a king to rule over us"—even though the LORD your God was your king. 13Now here is the king you have chosen, the one you asked for; see, the LORD has set a king over you. 14If you fear the LORD and serve and obey him and do not rebel against his commands, and if both you and the king who reigns over you follow the LORD your God—good! 15But if you do not obey the LORD, and if you rebel against his commands, his hand will be against you, as it was against your ancestors.

16'Now then, stand still and see this great thing the LORD is about to do before your eyes! 17Is it not wheat harvest now? I will call on the LORD to send thunder and rain. And you will realise what an evil thing you did in the eyes of the LORD when you asked for a king.'

18Then Samuel called on the LORD, and that same day the LORD sent thunder and rain. So all the people stood in awe of the LORD and of Samuel.

19The people all said to Samuel, 'Pray to the LORD your God for your servants so that we will not die, for we have added to all our other sins the evil of asking for a king.'

20'Do not be afraid,' Samuel replied. 'You have done all this evil; yet do not turn away from the LORD, but serve the LORD with all your heart. 21Do not turn away after useless idols. They can do you no good, nor can they rescue you, because they are useless. 22For the sake of his great name the LORD will not reject his people, because the LORD was pleased to make you his own. 23As for me, far be it from me that I should sin against the LORD by failing to pray for you. And I will teach you the way that is good and right. 24But be sure to fear the LORD and serve him faithfully with all your heart; consider what great things he has done for you. 25Yet if you persist in doing evil, both you and your king will perish.'

Samuel rebukes Saul

13 Saul was thirty[d] years old when he became king, and he reigned over Israel for forty-[e] two years.

2Saul chose three thousand men from Israel; two thousand were with him at Michmash and in the hill country of Bethel, and a thousand were with Jonathan at Gibeah in Benjamin. The rest he sent back to their homes.

3Jonathan attacked the Philistine outpost at Geba, and the Philistines heard about it. Then Saul had the trumpet blown throughout the land and said, 'Let the Hebrews hear!' 4So all Israel heard the news: 'Saul has attacked the Philistine outpost, and now Israel has become obnoxious to the Philistines.' And the people were summoned to join Saul at Gilgal.

5The Philistines assembled to fight Israel, with three thousand[f] chariots, six thousand charioteers, and soldiers as numerous as the sand on the seashore. They went up and camped at Michmash, east of Beth Aven. 6When the Israelites saw that their situation was critical and that their army was hard pressed, they hid in caves and thickets, among the rocks, and in pits and

---

[a] 11 Also called *Gideon* [b] 11 Some Septuagint manuscripts and Syriac; Hebrew *Bedan* [c] 11 Hebrew; some Septuagint manuscripts and Syriac *Samson* [d] 1 A few late manuscripts of the Septuagint; Hebrew does not have *thirty*. [e] 1 Probable reading of the original Hebrew text (see Acts 13:21); Masoretic Text does not have *forty-*. [f] 5 Some Septuagint manuscripts and Syriac; Hebrew *thirty thousand*

cisterns. 7Some Hebrews even crossed the Jordan to the land of Gad and Gilead.

Saul remained at Gilgal, and all the troops with him were quaking with fear. 8He waited for seven days, the time set by Samuel; but Samuel did not come to Gilgal, and Saul's men began to scatter. 9So he said, 'Bring me the burnt offering and the fellowship offerings.' And Saul offered up the burnt offering. 10Just as he finished making the offering, Samuel arrived, and Saul went out to greet him.

11'What have you done?' asked Samuel.

Saul replied, 'When I saw that the men were scattering, and that you did not come at the set time, and that the Philistines were assembling at Michmash, 12I thought, "Now the Philistines will come down against me at Gilgal, and I have not sought the LORD's favour." So I felt compelled to offer the burnt offering.'

13'You have done a foolish thing,' Samuel said. 'You have not kept the command the LORD your God gave you; if you had, he would have established your kingdom over Israel for all time. 14But now your kingdom will not endure; the LORD has sought out a man after his own heart and appointed him ruler of his people, because you have not kept the LORD's command.'

15Then Samuel left Gilgal*a* and went up to Gibeah in Benjamin, and Saul counted the men who were with him. They numbered about six hundred.

Israel without weapons

16Saul and his son Jonathan and the men with them were staying in Gibeah*b* of Benjamin, while the Philistines camped at Michmash. 17Raiding parties went out from the Philistine camp in three detachments. One turned towards Ophrah in the vicinity of Shual, 18another towards Beth Horon, and the third towards the borderland overlooking the Valley of Zeboyim facing the wilderness.

19Not a blacksmith could be found in the whole land of Israel, because the Philistines had said, 'Otherwise the Hebrews will make swords or spears!' 20So all Israel went down

Sign of the times

Iron
1 Samuel 13:19
The Philistines had a monopoly on iron which put them at a great advantage. Iron weapons were much stronger and more deadly than anything else around at the time. To stop the Israelites making weapons, the Philistines had banned all blacksmiths from Israel. The Israelites had iron tools and farming implements but had to go over to the Philistines to get them sharpened.

to the Philistines to have their ploughshares, mattocks, axes and sickles*c* sharpened. 21The price was two-thirds of a shekel*d* for sharpening ploughshares and mattocks, and a third of a shekel*e* for sharpening forks and axes and for repointing goads.

22So on the day of the battle not a soldier with Saul and Jonathan had a sword or spear in his hand; only Saul and his son Jonathan had them.

Jonathan attacks the Philistines

14 23Now a detachment of Philistines had gone out to the pass at Michmash. 1One day Jonathan son of Saul said to his young armour-bearer, 'Come, let's go over to the Philistine outpost on the other side.' But he did not tell his father.

2Saul was staying on the outskirts of Gibeah under a pomegranate tree in Migron. With him were about six hundred men, 3among whom was Ahijah, who was wearing an ephod. He was a son of Ichabod's brother Ahitub son of Phinehas, the son of Eli, the LORD's priest in Shiloh. No-one was aware that Jonathan had left.

---

a 15 Hebrew; Septuagint *Gilgal and went his way; the rest of the people went after Saul to meet the army, and they went out of Gilgal*   *b* 16 Two Hebrew manuscripts; most Hebrew manuscripts *Geba*, a variant of *Gibeah*   *c* 20 Septuagint; Hebrew *ploughshares*   *d* 21 That is, about 8 grams   *e* 21 That is, about 4 grams

⁴On each side of the pass that Jonathan intended to cross to reach the Philistine outpost was a cliff; one was called Bozez and the other Seneh. ⁵One cliff stood to the north towards Michmash, the other to the south towards Geba.

⁶Jonathan said to his young armour-bearer, 'Come, let's go over to the outpost of those uncircumcised fellows. Perhaps the LORD will act on our behalf. Nothing can hinder the LORD from saving, whether by many or by few.'

⁷'Do all that you have in mind,' his armour-bearer said. 'Go ahead; I am with you heart and soul.'

⁸Jonathan said, 'Come on, then; we will cross over towards them and let them see us. ⁹If they say to us, "Wait there until we come to you," we will stay where we are and not go up to them. ¹⁰But if they say, "Come up to us," we will climb up, because that will be our sign that the LORD has given them into our hands.'

¹¹So both of them showed themselves to the Philistine outpost. 'Look!' said the Philistines. 'The Hebrews are crawling out of the holes they were hiding in.' ¹²The men of the outpost shouted to Jonathan and his armour-bearer, 'Come up to us and we'll teach you a lesson.'

So Jonathan said to his armour-bearer, 'Climb up after me; the LORD has given them into the hand of Israel.'

¹³Jonathan climbed up, using his hands and feet, with his armour-bearer right behind him. The Philistines fell before Jonathan, and his armour-bearer followed and killed behind him. ¹⁴In that first attack Jonathan and his armour-bearer killed some twenty men in an area of about half an acre.[a]

Israel routs the Philistines

¹⁵Then panic struck the whole army—those in the camp and field, and those in the outposts and raiding parties—and the ground shook. It was a panic sent by God.[b]

¹⁶Saul's lookouts at Gibeah in Benjamin saw the army melting away in all directions. ¹⁷Then Saul said to the men who were with him, 'Muster the forces and see who has left us.' When they did, it was Jonathan and his armour-bearer who were not there.

¹⁸Saul said to Ahijah, 'Bring the ark of God.' (At that time it was with the Israelites.)[c] ¹⁹While Saul was talking to the priest, the tumult in the Philistine camp increased more and more. So Saul said to the priest, 'Withdraw your hand.'

²⁰Then Saul and all his men assembled and went to the battle. They found the Philistines in total confusion, striking each other with their swords. ²¹Those Hebrews who had previously been with the Philistines and had gone up with them to their camp went over to the Israelites who were with Saul and Jonathan. ²²When all the Israelites who had hidden in the hill country of Ephraim heard that the Philistines were on the run, they joined the battle in hot pursuit. ²³So on that day the LORD saved Israel, and the battle moved on beyond Beth Aven.

Jonathan eats honey

²⁴Now the Israelites were in distress that day, because Saul had bound the people under an oath, saying, 'Cursed be anyone who eats food before evening comes, before I have avenged myself on my enemies!' So none of the troops tasted food.

²⁵The entire army entered the woods, and there was honey on the ground. ²⁶When they went into the woods, they saw the honey oozing out; yet no-one put his hand to his mouth, because they feared the oath. ²⁷But Jonathan had not heard that his father had bound the people with the oath, so he reached out the end of the staff that was in his hand and dipped it into the honeycomb. He raised his hand to his mouth, and his eyes brightened.[d] ²⁸Then one of the soldiers told him, 'Your father bound the army under a strict oath, saying, "Cursed be anyone who eats food today!" That is why the men are faint.'

²⁹Jonathan said, 'My father has made trouble for the country. See how my eyes brightened[e] when I tasted a little of this honey. ³⁰How much better it would have

---

[a] 14 Or about 2,000 square metres [b] 15 Or a terrible panic [c] 18 Hebrew; Septuagint 'Bring the ephod.' (At that time he wore the ephod before the Israelites.) [d] 27 Or his strength was renewed [e] 29 Or my strength was renewed

been if the men had eaten today some of the plunder they took from their enemies. Would not the slaughter of the Philistines have been even greater?'

31 That day, after the Israelites had struck down the Philistines from Michmash to Aijalon, they were exhausted. 32 They pounced on the plunder and, taking sheep, cattle and calves, they butchered them on the ground and ate them, together with the blood. 33 Then someone said to Saul, 'Look, the men are sinning against the LORD by eating meat that has blood in it.'

'You have broken faith,' he said. 'Roll a large stone over here at once.' 34 Then he said, 'Go out among the men and tell them, "Each of you bring me your cattle and sheep, and slaughter them here and eat them. Do not sin against the LORD by eating meat with blood still in it." '

So everyone brought his ox that night and slaughtered it there. 35 Then Saul built an altar to the LORD; it was the first time he had done this.

36 Saul said, 'Let us go down and pursue the Philistines by night and plunder them till dawn, and let us not leave one of them alive.'

'Do whatever seems best to you,' they replied.

But the priest said, 'Let us enquire of God here.'

37 So Saul asked God, 'Shall I go down and pursue the Philistines? Will you give them into Israel's hand?' But God did not answer him that day.

38 Saul therefore said, 'Come here, all you who are leaders of the army, and let us find out what sin has been committed today. 39 As surely as the LORD who rescues Israel lives, even if it lies with my son Jonathan, he must die.' But not one of them said a word.

40 Saul then said to all the Israelites, 'You stand over there; I and Jonathan my son will stand over here.'

'Do what seems best to you,' they replied.

41 Then Saul prayed to the LORD, the God of Israel, 'Why have you not answered your servant today? If the fault is in me or my son Jonathan, respond with Urim, but if the men of Israel are at fault,[a] respond with Thummim.' Jonathan and Saul were taken by lot, and the men were cleared. 42 Saul said, 'Cast the lot between me and Jonathan my son.' And Jonathan was taken.

43 Then Saul said to Jonathan, 'Tell me what you have done.'

So Jonathan told him, 'I tasted a little honey with the end of my staff. And now I must die!'

44 Saul said, 'May God deal with me, be it ever so severely, if you do not die, Jonathan.'

45 But the men said to Saul, 'Should Jonathan die—he who has brought about this great deliverance in Israel? Never! As surely as the LORD lives, not a hair of his head shall fall to the ground, for he did this today with God's help.' So the men rescued Jonathan, and he was not put to death.

46 Then Saul stopped pursuing the Philistines, and they withdrew to their own land.

47 After Saul had assumed rule over Israel, he fought against their enemies on every side: Moab, the Ammonites, Edom, the kings[b] of Zobah, and the Philistines. Wherever he turned, he inflicted punishment on them.[c] 48 He fought valiantly and defeated the Amalekites, delivering Israel from the hands of those who had plundered them.

Saul's family

49 Saul's sons were Jonathan, Ishvi and Malki-Shua. The name of his elder daughter was Merab, and that of the younger was Michal. 50 His wife's name was Ahinoam daughter of Ahimaaz. The name of the commander of Saul's army was Abner son of Ner, and Ner was Saul's uncle. 51 Saul's father Kish and Abner's father Ner were sons of Abiel.

52 All the days of Saul there was bitter war with the Philistines, and whenever Saul saw a mighty or brave man, he took him into his service.

The LORD rejects Saul as king

15 Samuel said to Saul, 'I am the one the LORD sent to anoint you king over his people Israel; so listen now to the message from the LORD. 2 This is what the

---

[a] 41 Septuagint; Hebrew does not have 'Why... at fault. [b] 47 Masoretic Text; Dead Sea Scrolls and Septuagint *king* [c] 47 Hebrew; Septuagint *he was victorious*

Lord Almighty says: "I will punish the Amalekites for what they did to Israel when they waylaid them as they came up from Egypt. ³Now go, attack the Amalekites and totally destroy*ᵃ* all that belongs to them. Do not spare them; put to death men and women, children and infants, cattle and sheep, camels and donkeys."'

⁴So Saul summoned the men and mustered them at Telaim—two hundred thousand foot soldiers and ten thousand from Judah. ⁵Saul went to the city of Amalek and set an ambush in the ravine. ⁶Then he said to the Kenites, 'Go away, leave the Amalekites so that I do not destroy you along with them; for you showed kindness to all the Israelites when they came up out of Egypt.' So the Kenites moved away from the Amalekites.

⁷Then Saul attacked the Amalekites all the way from Havilah to Shur, near the eastern border of Egypt. ⁸He took Agag king of the Amalekites alive, and all his people he totally destroyed with the sword. ⁹But Saul and the army spared Agag and the best of the sheep and cattle, the fat calves*ᵇ* and lambs—everything that was good. These they were unwilling to destroy completely, but everything that was despised and weak they totally destroyed.

¹⁰Then the word of the Lord came to Samuel: ¹¹'I regret that I have made Saul king, because he has turned away from me and has not carried out my instructions.' Samuel was angry, and he cried out to the Lord all that night.

¹²Early in the morning Samuel got up and went to meet Saul, but he was told, 'Saul has gone to Carmel. There he has set up a monument in his own honour and has turned and gone on down to Gilgal.'

¹³When Samuel reached him, Saul said, 'The Lord bless you! I have carried out the Lord's instructions.'

¹⁴But Samuel said, 'What then is this bleating of sheep in my ears? What is this lowing of cattle that I hear?'

¹⁵Saul answered, 'The soldiers brought them from the Amalekites; they spared the best of the sheep and cattle to sacrifice to the Lord your God, but we totally destroyed the rest.'

¹⁶'Enough!' Samuel said to Saul. 'Let me tell you what the Lord said to me last night.'

'Tell me,' Saul replied.

¹⁷Samuel said, 'Although you were once small in your own eyes, did you not become the head of the tribes of Israel? The Lord anointed you king over Israel. ¹⁸And he sent you on a mission, saying, "Go and completely destroy those wicked people, the Amalekites; make war on them until you have wiped them out." ¹⁹Why did you not obey the Lord? Why did you pounce on the plunder and do evil in the eyes of the Lord?'

²⁰'But I did obey the Lord,' Saul said. 'I went on the mission the Lord assigned me. I completely destroyed the Amalekites and brought back Agag their king. ²¹The soldiers took sheep and cattle from the plunder, the best of what was devoted to God, in order to sacrifice them to the Lord your God at Gilgal.'

²²But Samuel replied:

'Does the Lord delight in burnt offerings and sacrifices
as much as in obeying the Lord?
To obey is better than sacrifice,
and to heed is better than the fat of rams.
²³For rebellion is like the sin of divination,
and arrogance like the evil of idolatry.
Because you have rejected the word of the Lord,
he has rejected you as king.'

²⁴Then Saul said to Samuel, 'I have sinned. I violated the Lord's command and your instructions. I was afraid of the men and so I gave in to them. ²⁵Now I beg you, forgive my sin and come back with me, so that I may worship the Lord.'

²⁶But Samuel said to him, 'I will not go back with you. You have rejected the word of the Lord, and the Lord has rejected you as king over Israel!'

²⁷As Samuel turned to leave, Saul caught hold of the hem of his robe, and it tore. ²⁸Samuel said to him, 'The Lord has torn the kingdom of Israel from you today and

---

ᵃ 3 The Hebrew term refers to the irrevocable giving of things or persons to the Lord, often by totally destroying them; also in verses 8, 9, 15, 18, 20 and 21.   *ᵇ* 9 Or *the grown bulls*; the meaning of the Hebrew for this phrase is uncertain.

has given it to one of your neighbours—to one better than you. ²⁹He who is the Glory of Israel does not lie or change his mind; for he is not a human being, that he should change his mind.'

³⁰Saul replied, 'I have sinned. But please honour me before the elders of my people and before Israel; come back with me, so that I may worship the LORD your God.' ³¹So Samuel went back with Saul, and Saul worshipped the LORD.

³²Then Samuel said, 'Bring me Agag king of the Amalekites.'

Agag came to him in chains.*ᵃ* And he thought, 'Surely the bitterness of death is past.'

³³But Samuel said,

'As your sword has made women childless,
 so will your mother be childless among women.'

And Samuel put Agag to death before the LORD at Gilgal.

³⁴Then Samuel left for Ramah, but Saul went up to his home in Gibeah of Saul. ³⁵Until the day Samuel died, he did not go to see Saul again, though Samuel mourned for him. And the LORD regretted that he had made Saul king over Israel.

Samuel anoints David

16 The LORD said to Samuel, 'How long will you mourn for Saul, since I have rejected him as king over Israel? Fill your horn with oil and be on your way; I am sending you to Jesse of Bethlehem. I have chosen one of his sons to be king.'

²But Samuel said, 'How can I go? If Saul hears about it, he will kill me.'

The LORD said, 'Take a heifer with you and say, "I have come to sacrifice to the LORD." ³Invite Jesse to the sacrifice, and I will show you what to do. You are to anoint for me the one I indicate.'

⁴Samuel did what the LORD said. When he arrived at Bethlehem, the elders of the town trembled when they met him. They asked, 'Do you come in peace?'

⁵Samuel replied, 'Yes, in peace; I have come to sacrifice to the LORD. Consecrate yourselves and come to the sacrifice with me.' Then he consecrated Jesse and his sons and invited them to the sacrifice.

⁶When they arrived, Samuel saw Eliab and thought, 'Surely the LORD's anointed stands here before the LORD.'

⁷But the LORD said to Samuel, 'Do not consider his appearance or his height, for I have rejected him. The LORD does not look at the things human beings look at. People look at the outward appearance, but the LORD looks at the heart.'

⁸Then Jesse called Abinadab and made him pass in front of Samuel. But Samuel said, 'The LORD has not chosen this one either.' ⁹Jesse then made Shammah pass by, but Samuel said, 'Nor has the LORD chosen this one.' ¹⁰Jesse made seven of his sons pass before Samuel, but Samuel said to him, 'The LORD has not chosen these.' ¹¹So he asked Jesse, 'Are these all the sons you have?'

'There is still the youngest,' Jesse answered. 'He is tending the sheep.'

Samuel said, 'Send for him; we will not sit down until he arrives.'

¹²So he sent and had him brought in. He was glowing with health and had a fine appearance and handsome features.

Then the LORD said, 'Rise and anoint him; this is the one.'

¹³So Samuel took the horn of oil and anointed him in the presence of his brothers, and from that day on the Spirit of the LORD came on David in power. Samuel then went to Ramah.

David in Saul's service

¹⁴Now the Spirit of the LORD had departed from Saul, and an evil*ᵇ* spirit from the LORD tormented him.

¹⁵Saul's attendants said to him, 'See, an evil spirit from God is tormenting you. ¹⁶Let our lord command his servants here to search for someone who can play the lyre. He will play when the evil spirit from God comes on you, and you will feel better.'

¹⁷So Saul said to his attendants, 'Find someone who plays well and bring him to me.'

¹⁸One of the servants answered, 'I have seen a son of Jesse of Bethlehem who knows

---

ᵃ 32 The meaning of the Hebrew for this phrase is uncertain.   *ᵇ 14* Or *harmful*; also in verses 15, 16 and 23

People and Places

David
1 Samuel 16:13

David was hardly the most likely candidate to be king. His dad didn't even bother to include him when Samuel arrived at their house to worship God. But David was a man after God's own heart (1 Samuel 13:14) and the right person to succeed Saul as king. He is known for his defeat of Goliath, his many beautiful psalms and his strong leadership of the people of Israel. However, he also made many mistakes, most notably his adultery with Bathsheba and the way he tried to cover it up. God promised David a kingdom that would have no end, and this was fulfilled in Jesus who is referred to as 'the Son of David'.

how to play the lyre. He is a brave man and a warrior. He speaks well and is a fine-looking man. And the LORD is with him.'

19Then Saul sent messengers to Jesse and said, 'Send me your son David, who is with the sheep.' 20So Jesse took a donkey loaded with bread, a skin of wine and a young goat and sent them with his son David to Saul.

21David came to Saul and entered his service. Saul liked him very much, and David became one of his armour-bearers. 22Then Saul sent word to Jesse, saying, 'Allow David to remain in my service, for I am pleased with him.'

23Whenever the spirit from God came on Saul, David would take up his lyre and play. Then relief would come to Saul; he would feel better, and the evil spirit would leave him.

David and Goliath

17 Now the Philistines gathered their forces for war and assembled at Sokoh in Judah. They pitched camp at Ephes Dammim, between Sokoh and Azekah. 2Saul and the Israelites assembled and camped in the Valley of Elah and drew up their battle line to meet the Philistines. 3The Philistines occupied one hill and the Israelites another, with the valley between them.

4A champion named Goliath, who was from Gath, came out of the Philistine camp. His height was six cubits and a span.^a 5He had a bronze helmet on his head and wore a coat of scale armour of bronze weighing five thousand shekels;^b 6on his legs he wore bronze greaves, and a bronze javelin was slung on his back. 7His spear shaft was like a weaver's rod, and its iron point weighed six hundred shekels.^c His shield-bearer went ahead of him.

8Goliath stood and shouted to the ranks of Israel, 'Why do you come out and line up for battle? Am I not a Philistine, and are you not the servants of Saul? Choose a man and let him come down to me. 9If he is able to fight and kill me, we will become your subjects; but if I overcome him and kill him, you will become our subjects and serve us.' 10Then the Philistine said, 'This day I defy

Making Connections

Music
1 Samuel 16:18

Music was a significant part of Israelite culture. It was played on important occasions such as festivals, worship services and funerals as well as during everyday life. David probably played the lyre to pass the time while he looked after the sheep. David's lyre would have been like a modern harp but smaller and with fewer strings.

---

^a4 That is, about 2.9 metres ^b5 That is, about 57 kilograms ^c7 That is, about 6.9 kilograms

the armies of Israel! Give me a man and let us fight each other.' ¹¹On hearing the Philistine's words, Saul and all the Israelites were dismayed and terrified.

¹²Now David was the son of an Ephrathite named Jesse, who was from Bethlehem in Judah. Jesse had eight sons, and in Saul's time he was very old. ¹³Jesse's three eldest sons had followed Saul to the war: the firstborn was Eliab; the second, Abinadab; and the third, Shammah. ¹⁴David was the youngest. The three eldest followed Saul, ¹⁵but David went back and forth from Saul to tend his father's sheep at Bethlehem.

¹⁶For forty days the Philistine came forward every morning and evening and took his stand.

¹⁷Now Jesse said to his son David, 'Take this ephah^a of roasted grain and these ten loaves of bread for your brothers and hurry to their camp. ¹⁸Take along these ten cheeses to the commander of their unit. See how your brothers are and bring back some assurance^b from them. ¹⁹They are with Saul and all the men of Israel in the Valley of Elah, fighting against the Philistines.'

²⁰Early in the morning David left the flock in the care of a shepherd, loaded up and set out, as Jesse had directed. He reached the camp as the army was going out to its battle positions, shouting the war cry. ²¹Israel and the Philistines were drawing up their lines facing each other. ²²David left his things with the keeper of supplies, ran to the battle lines and asked his brothers how they were. ²³As he was talking with them, Goliath, the Philistine champion from Gath, stepped out from his lines and shouted his usual defiance, and David heard it. ²⁴Whenever the Israelites saw the man, they all fled from him in great fear.

²⁵Now the Israelites had been saying, 'Do you see how this man keeps coming out? He comes out to defy Israel. The king will give great wealth to the man who kills him. He will also give him his daughter in marriage and will exempt his family line from taxes in Israel.'

²⁶David asked those standing near him, 'What will be done for the man who kills this Philistine and removes this disgrace from Israel? Who is this uncircumcised Philistine that he should defy the armies of the living God?'

²⁷They repeated to him what they had been saying and told him, 'This is what will be done for the man who kills him.'

²⁸When Eliab, David's eldest brother, heard him speaking with the men, he burned with anger at him and asked, 'Why have you come down here? And with whom did you leave those few sheep in the wilderness? I know how conceited you are and how wicked your heart is; you came down only to watch the battle.'

²⁹'Now what have I done?' said David. 'Can't I even speak?' ³⁰He then turned away to someone else and brought up the same matter, and the men answered him as before. ³¹What David said was overheard and reported to Saul, and Saul sent for him.

³²David said to Saul, 'Let no-one lose heart on account of this Philistine; your servant will go and fight him.'

³³Saul replied, 'You are not able to go out against this Philistine and fight him; you are little more than a boy, and he has been a warrior from his youth.'

³⁴But David said to Saul, 'Your servant has been keeping his father's sheep. When a lion or a bear came and carried off a sheep from the flock, ³⁵I went after it, struck it and rescued the sheep from its mouth. When it

Sign of the times

Shepherd
1 Samuel 17:34
It was traditional that the youngest boy in a family became the shepherd; older sons would start by looking after the sheep, but as they grew up they would move onto ploughing, sowing and harvesting crops.

---

^{a} 17 That is, probably about 16 kilograms ^{b} 18 Or *some token*; or *some pledge* of *spoils* turned on me, I seized it by its hair, struck it and killed it. ³⁶Your servant has killed both the lion and the bear; this uncircumcised Philistine will be like one of them, because he has defied the armies of the living God. ³⁷The LORD who rescued me from the paw of the lion and the paw of the bear will rescue me from the hand of this Philistine.'

Saul said to David, 'Go, and the LORD be with you.'

³⁸Then Saul dressed David in his own tunic. He put a coat of armour on him and a bronze helmet on his head. ³⁹David fastened on his sword over the tunic and tried walking around, because he was not used to them.

'I cannot go in these,' he said to Saul, 'because I am not used to them.' So he took them off. ⁴⁰Then he took his staff in his hand, chose five smooth stones from the stream, put them in the pouch of his shepherd's bag and, with his sling in his hand, approached the Philistine.

⁴¹Meanwhile, the Philistine, with his shield-bearer in front of him, kept coming closer to David. ⁴²He looked David over and saw that he was little more than a boy, glowing with health and handsome, and he despised him. ⁴³He said to David, 'Am I a dog, that you come at me with sticks?' And the Philistine cursed David by his gods. ⁴⁴'Come here,' he said, 'and I'll give your flesh to the birds and the wild animals!'

⁴⁵David said to the Philistine, 'You come against me with sword and spear and javelin, but I come against you in the name of the LORD Almighty, the God of the armies of Israel, whom you have defied. ⁴⁶This day the LORD will deliver you into my hands, and I'll strike you down and cut off your head. This very day I will give the carcasses of the Philistine army to the birds and the wild animals, and the whole world will know that there is a God in Israel. ⁴⁷All those gathered here will know that it is not by sword or spear that the LORD saves; for the battle is the LORD's, and he will give all of you into our hands.'

⁴⁸As the Philistine moved closer to attack him, David ran quickly towards the battle line to meet him. ⁴⁹Reaching into his bag

Sign of the times

Sling
1 Samuel 17:49
A shepherd would use his sling against wild animals or robbers but it could also be used to direct the sheep where he wanted them to go. If a sheep was lagging behind or going off in the wrong direction, he would throw a stone to land next to it that would startle it into going the right way.

and taking out a stone, he slung it and struck the Philistine on the forehead. The stone sank into his forehead, and he fell face down on the ground.

⁵⁰So David triumphed over the Philistine with a sling and a stone; without a sword in his hand he struck down the Philistine and killed him.

⁵¹David ran and stood over him. He took hold of the Philistine's sword and drew it from the sheath. After he killed him, he cut off his head with the sword.

When the Philistines saw that their hero was dead, they turned and ran. ⁵²Then the men of Israel and Judah surged forward with a shout and pursued the Philistines to the entrance of Gath[a] and to the gates of Ekron. Their dead were strewn along the Shaaraim road to Gath and Ekron. ⁵³When the Israelites returned from chasing the Philistines, they plundered their camp.

⁵⁴David took the Philistine's head and brought it to Jerusalem; he put the Philistine's weapons in his own tent.

⁵⁵As Saul watched David going out to meet the Philistine, he said to Abner, commander of the army, 'Abner, whose son is that young man?'

Abner replied, 'As surely as you live, Your Majesty, I don't know.'

⁵⁶The king said, 'Find out whose son this young man is.'

---

[a] 52 Some Septuagint manuscripts; Hebrew *of a valley*

⁵⁷As soon as David returned from killing the Philistine, Abner took him and brought him before Saul, with David still holding the Philistine's head.

⁵⁸'Whose son are you, young man?' Saul asked him.

David said, 'I am the son of your servant Jesse of Bethlehem.'

Saul's growing fear of David

18 After David had finished talking with Saul, Jonathan became one in spirit with David, and he loved him as himself. ²From that day Saul kept David with him and did not let him return home to his family. ³And Jonathan made a covenant with David because he loved him as himself. ⁴Jonathan took off the robe he was wearing and gave it to David, along with his tunic, and even his sword, his bow and his belt.

⁵Whatever mission Saul sent him on, David was so successful that Saul gave him a high rank in the army. This pleased all the troops, and Saul's officers as well.

⁶When the men were returning home after David had killed the Philistine, the women came out from all the towns of Israel to meet King Saul with singing and dancing, with joyful songs and with tambourines and lyres. ⁷As they danced, they sang:

'Saul has slain his thousands,
  and David his tens of thousands.'

⁸Saul was very angry; this refrain displeased him greatly. 'They have credited David with tens of thousands,' he thought, 'but me with only thousands. What more can he get but the kingdom?' ⁹And from that time on Saul kept a close eye on David.

¹⁰The next day an evil[a] spirit from God came forcefully on Saul. He was prophesying in his house, while David was playing the lyre, as he usually did. Saul had a spear in his hand ¹¹and he hurled it, saying to himself, 'I'll pin David to the wall.' But David eluded him twice.

¹²Saul was afraid of David, because the LORD was with David but had departed from Saul. ¹³So he sent David away from him and gave him command over a thousand men, and David led the troops in their campaigns. ¹⁴In everything he did he had great success, because the LORD was with him. ¹⁵When Saul saw how successful he was, he was afraid of him. ¹⁶But all Israel and Judah loved David, because he led them in their campaigns.

¹⁷Saul said to David, 'Here is my elder daughter Merab. I will give her to you in marriage; only serve me bravely and fight the battles of the LORD.' For Saul said to himself, 'I will not raise a hand against him. Let the Philistines do that!'

¹⁸But David said to Saul, 'Who am I, and what is my family or my clan in Israel, that I should become the king's son-in-law?' ¹⁹So[b] when the time came for Merab, Saul's daughter, to be given to David, she was given in marriage to Adriel of Meholah.

²⁰Now Saul's daughter Michal was in love with David, and when they told Saul about it, he was pleased. ²¹'I will give her to him,' he thought, 'so that she may be a snare to him and so that the hand of the Philistines may be against him.' So Saul said to David, 'Now you have a second opportunity to become my son-in-law.'

²²Then Saul ordered his attendants: 'Speak to David privately and say, "Look, the king likes you, and his attendants all love you; now become his son-in-law."'

²³They repeated these words to David. But David said, 'Do you think it is a small matter to become the king's son-in-law? I'm only a poor man and little known.'

²⁴When Saul's servants told him what David had said, ²⁵Saul replied, 'Say to David, "The king wants no other price for the bride than a hundred Philistine foreskins, to take revenge on his enemies."' Saul's plan was for David to fall by the hands of the Philistines.

²⁶When the attendants told David these things, he was pleased to become the king's son-in-law. So before the allotted time elapsed, ²⁷David took his men with him and went out and killed two hundred Philistines and brought back their foreskins. They counted out the full number to the king so that David might become the king's son-in-law. Then Saul gave him his daughter Michal in marriage.

---

[a] 10 Or *harmful* [b] 19 Or *However,*

28When Saul realised that the LORD was with David and that his daughter Michal loved David, 29Saul became still more afraid of him, and he remained his enemy for the rest of his days.

30The Philistine commanders continued to go out to battle, and as often as they did, David met with more success than the rest of Saul's officers, and his name became well known.

Saul tries to kill David

19 Saul told his son Jonathan and all the attendants to kill David. But Jonathan had taken a great liking to David 2and warned him, 'My father Saul is looking for a chance to kill you. Be on your guard tomorrow morning; go into hiding and stay there. 3I will go out and stand with my father in the field where you are. I'll speak to him about you and will tell you what I find out.'

4Jonathan spoke well of David to Saul his father and said to him, 'Let not the king do wrong to his servant David; he has not wronged you, and what he has done has benefited you greatly. 5He took his life in his hands when he killed the Philistine. The LORD won a great victory for all Israel, and you saw it and were glad. Why then would you do wrong to an innocent man like David by killing him for no reason?'

6Saul listened to Jonathan and took this oath: 'As surely as the LORD lives, David will not be put to death.'

7So Jonathan called David and told him the whole conversation. He brought him to Saul, and David was with Saul as before.

8Once more war broke out, and David went out and fought the Philistines. He struck them with such force that they fled before him.

9But an evil*[a]* spirit from the LORD came on Saul as he was sitting in his house with his spear in his hand. While David was playing the lyre, 10Saul tried to pin him to the wall with his spear, but David eluded him as Saul drove the spear into the wall. That night David made good his escape.

11Saul sent men to David's house to watch it and to kill him in the morning. But Michal, David's wife, warned him, 'If you don't run for your life tonight, tomorrow you'll be killed.' 12So Michal let David down through a window, and he fled and escaped. 13Then Michal took an idol and laid it on the bed, covering it with a garment and putting some goats' hair at the head.

14When Saul sent the men to capture David, Michal said, 'He is ill.'

15Then Saul sent the men back to see David and told them, 'Bring him up to me in his bed so that I may kill him.' 16But when the men entered, there was the idol in the bed, and at the head was some goats' hair.

17Saul said to Michal, 'Why did you deceive me like this and send my enemy away so that he escaped?'

Michal told him, 'He said to me, "Let me get away. Why should I kill you?"'

18When David had fled and made his escape, he went to Samuel at Ramah and told him all that Saul had done to him. Then he and Samuel went to Naioth and stayed there. 19Word came to Saul: 'David is in Naioth at Ramah'; 20so he sent men to capture him. But when they saw a group of prophets prophesying, with Samuel standing there as their leader, the Spirit of God came on Saul's men, and they also prophesied. 21Saul was told about it, and he sent more men, and they prophesied too. Saul sent men a third time, and they also prophesied. 22Finally, he himself left for Ramah and went to the great cistern at Seku. And he asked, 'Where are Samuel and David?'

'Over in Naioth at Ramah,' they said.

23So Saul went to Naioth at Ramah. But the Spirit of God came even on him, and he walked along prophesying until he came to Naioth. 24He stripped off his garments, and he too prophesied in Samuel's presence. He lay naked all that day and all that night. This is why people say, 'Is Saul also among the prophets?'

David and Jonathan

20 Then David fled from Naioth at Ramah and went to Jonathan and asked, 'What have I done? What is my crime? How have I wronged your father, that he is trying to take my life?'

---

*a*9 Or *harmful*

> ## People and Places
>
> ### Jonathan
> **1 Samuel 20:1**
>
> By rights, Jonathan should have been the next king, not David, because he was Saul's son. But far from being jealous of David, he recognised that God's will was more important. Jonathan was a great soldier and a brave leader in battle, but he's best known for his friendship with David. He warned David when Saul was plotting to take his life, he encouraged David when he was in danger and he spoke up for David when Saul was against him.

2'Never!' Jonathan replied. 'You are not going to die! Look, my father doesn't do anything, great or small, without letting me know. Why should he hide this from me? It isn't so!'

3But David took an oath and said, 'Your father knows very well that I have found favour in your eyes, and he has said to himself, "Jonathan must not know this or he will be grieved." Yet as surely as the LORD lives and as you live, there is only a step between me and death.'

4Jonathan said to David, 'Whatever you want me to do, I'll do for you.'

5So David said, 'Look, tomorrow is the New Moon feast, and I am supposed to dine with the king; but let me go and hide in the field until the evening of the day after tomorrow. 6If your father misses me at all, tell him, "David earnestly asked my permission to hurry to Bethlehem, his home town, because an annual sacrifice is being made there for his whole clan." 7If he says, "Very well," then your servant is safe. But if he loses his temper, you can be sure that he is determined to harm me. 8As for you, show kindness to your servant, for you have brought him into a covenant with you before the LORD. If I am guilty, then kill me yourself! Why hand me over to your father?'

9'Never!' Jonathan said. 'If I had the least inkling that my father was determined to harm you, wouldn't I tell you?'

10David asked, 'Who will tell me if your father answers you harshly?'

11'Come,' Jonathan said, 'let's go out into the field.' So they went there together.

12Then Jonathan said to David, 'I swear by the LORD, the God of Israel, that I will surely sound out my father by this time the day after tomorrow! If he is favourably disposed towards you, will I not send you word and let you know? 13But if my father intends to harm you, may the LORD deal with me, be it ever so severely, if I do not let you know and send you away in peace. May the LORD be with you as he has been with my father. 14But show me unfailing kindness like the LORD's kindness as long as I live, so that I may not be killed, 15and do not ever cut off your kindness from my family—not even when the LORD has cut off every one of David's enemies from the face of the earth.'

16So Jonathan made a covenant with the house of David, saying, 'May the LORD call David's enemies to account.' 17And Jonathan made David reaffirm his oath out of love for him, because he loved him as he loved himself.

18Then Jonathan said to David, 'Tomorrow is the New Moon feast. You will be missed, because your seat will be empty. 19The day after tomorrow, towards evening, go to the place where you hid when this trouble began, and wait by the stone Ezel. 20I will shoot three arrows to the side of it, as though I were shooting at a target. 21Then I will send a boy and say, "Go, find the arrows." If I say to him, "Look, the arrows are on this side of you; bring them here," then come, because, as surely as the LORD lives, you are safe; there is no danger. 22But if I say to the boy, "Look, the arrows are beyond you," then you must go, because the LORD has sent you away. 23And about the matter you and I discussed—remember, the LORD is witness between you and me for ever.'

24So David hid in the field, and when the New Moon feast came, the king sat down to eat. ²⁵He sat in his customary place by the wall, opposite Jonathan,ᵃ and Abner sat next to Saul, but David's place was empty. ²⁶Saul said nothing that day, for he thought, 'Something must have happened to David to make him ceremonially unclean—surely he is unclean.' ²⁷But the next day, the second day of the month, David's place was empty again. Then Saul said to his son Jonathan, 'Why hasn't the son of Jesse come to the meal, either yesterday or today?'

²⁸Jonathan answered, 'David earnestly asked me for permission to go to Bethlehem. ²⁹He said, "Let me go, because our family is observing a sacrifice in the town and my brother has ordered me to be there. If I have found favour in your eyes, let me go to see my brothers." That is why he has not come to the king's table.'

³⁰Saul's anger flared up at Jonathan and he said to him, 'You son of a perverse and rebellious woman! Don't I know that you have sided with the son of Jesse to your own shame and to the shame of the mother who bore you? ³¹As long as the son of Jesse lives on this earth, neither you nor your kingdom will be established. Now send someone to bring him to me, for he must die!'

³²'Why should he be put to death? What has he done?' Jonathan asked his father. ³³But Saul hurled his spear at him to kill him. Then Jonathan knew that his father intended to kill David.

³⁴Jonathan got up from the table in fierce anger; on that second day of the feast he did not eat, because he was grieved at his father's shameful treatment of David.

³⁵In the morning Jonathan went out to the field for his meeting with David. He had a small boy with him, ³⁶and he said to the boy, 'Run and find the arrows I shoot.' As the boy ran, he shot an arrow beyond him. ³⁷When the boy came to the place where Jonathan's arrow had fallen, Jonathan called out after him, 'Isn't the arrow beyond you?' ³⁸Then he shouted, 'Hurry! Go quickly! Don't stop!' The boy picked up the arrow and returned to his master. ³⁹(The boy knew nothing about all this; only Jonathan and David knew.) ⁴⁰Then Jonathan gave his weapons to the boy and said, 'Go, carry them back to town.'

⁴¹After the boy had gone, David got up from the south side of the stone and bowed down before Jonathan three times, with his face to the ground. Then they kissed each other and wept together—but David wept the most.

⁴²Jonathan said to David, 'Go in peace, for we have sworn friendship with each other in the name of the LORD, saying, "The LORD is witness between you and me, and between your descendants and my descendants for ever."' *Then David left, and Jonathan went back to the town.

David at Nob

21 *David went to Nob, to Ahimelek the priest. Ahimelek trembled when he met him, and asked, 'Why are you alone? Why is no-one with you?'

²David answered Ahimelek the priest, 'The king sent me on a mission and said to me, "No-one is to know anything about the mission I am sending you on." As for my

Consecrated bread
1 Samuel 21:4

Every week, consecrated bread was set out in the place of worship as a way of thanking God for providing bread for the people to eat. At the end of the week, the priests would eat the bread but nobody else was allowed to touch it. Ahimelek makes an exception for David and lets him and his men eat the bread. Jesus refers to this example when he's criticised by the Pharisees for picking grain on the Sabbath (Matthew 12:1).

ᵃ 25 Septuagint; Hebrew *wall. Jonathan arose*

* This sentence (20:42b) is numbered 21:1 in Hebrew texts.+1   * 21:1-15 is numbered 21:2-16 in Hebrew texts.

men, I have told them to meet me at a certain place. ³Now then, what have you to hand? Give me five loaves of bread, or whatever you can find.'

⁴But the priest answered David, 'I don't have any ordinary bread to hand; however, there is some consecrated bread here—provided the men have kept themselves from women.'

⁵David replied, 'Indeed women have been kept from us, as usual whenever[a] I set out. The men's bodies are holy even on missions that are not holy. How much more so today!' ⁶So the priest gave him the consecrated bread, since there was no bread there except the bread of the Presence that had been removed from before the LORD and replaced by hot bread on the day it was taken away.

⁷Now one of Saul's servants was there that day, detained before the LORD; he was Doeg the Edomite, Saul's chief shepherd.

⁸David asked Ahimelek, 'Don't you have a spear or sword here? I haven't brought my sword or any other weapon, because the king's mission was urgent.'

⁹The priest replied, 'The sword of Goliath the Philistine, whom you killed in the Valley of Elah, is here; it is wrapped in a cloth behind the ephod. If you want it, take it; there is no sword here but that one.'

David said, 'There is none like it; give it to me.'

David at Gath

¹⁰That day David fled from Saul and went to Achish king of Gath. ¹¹But the servants of Achish said to him, 'Isn't this David, the king of the land? Isn't he the one they sing about in their dances:

> '"Saul has slain his thousands,
> and David his tens of thousands"?'

¹²David took these words to heart and was very much afraid of Achish king of Gath. ¹³So he feigned insanity in their presence; and while he was in their hands he acted like a madman, making marks on the doors of the gate and letting saliva run down his beard.

¹⁴Achish said to his servants, 'Look at the man! He is insane! Why bring him to me? ¹⁵Am I so short of madmen that you have to bring this fellow here to carry on like this in front of me? Must this man come into my house?'

David at Adullam and Mizpah

22 David left Gath and escaped to the cave of Adullam. When his brothers and his father's household heard about it, they went down to him there. ²All those who were in distress or in debt or discontented gathered round him, and he became their commander. About four hundred men were with him.

³From there David went to Mizpah in Moab and said to the king of Moab, 'Would you let my father and mother come and stay with you until I learn what God will do for me?' ⁴So he left them with the king of Moab, and they stayed with him as long as David was in the stronghold.

⁵But the prophet Gad said to David, 'Do not stay in the stronghold. Go into the land of Judah.' So David left and went to the forest of Hereth.

Saul kills the priests of Nob

⁶Now Saul heard that David and his men had been discovered. And Saul was seated, spear in hand, under the tamarisk tree on the hill at Gibeah, with all his officials standing at his side. ⁷He said to them, 'Listen, men of Benjamin! Will the son of Jesse give all of you fields and vineyards? Will he make all of you commanders of thousands and commanders of hundreds? ⁸Is that why you have all conspired against me? No-one tells me when my son makes a covenant with the son of Jesse. None of you is concerned about me or tells me that my son has incited my servant to lie in wait for me, as he does today.'

⁹But Doeg the Edomite, who was standing with Saul's officials, said, 'I saw the son of Jesse come to Ahimelek son of Ahitub at Nob. ¹⁰Ahimelek enquired of the LORD for him; he also gave him provisions and the sword of Goliath the Philistine.'

---

[a] 5 Or *from us in the past few days since*

11Then the king sent for the priest Ahimelek son of Ahitub and all the men of his family, who were the priests at Nob, and they all came to the king. **12**Saul said, 'Listen now, son of Ahitub.'

'Yes, my lord,' he answered.

13Saul said to him, 'Why have you conspired against me, you and the son of Jesse, giving him bread and a sword and enquiring of God for him, so that he has rebelled against me and lies in wait for me, as he does today?'

14Ahimelek answered the king, 'Who of all your servants is as loyal as David, the king's son-in-law, captain of your bodyguard and highly respected in your household? **15**Was that day the first time I enquired of God for him? Of course not! Let not the king accuse your servant or any of his father's family, for your servant knows nothing at all about this whole affair.'

16But the king said, 'You shall surely die, Ahimelek, you and your whole family.'

17Then the king ordered the guards at his side: 'Turn and kill the priests of the LORD, because they too have sided with David. They knew he was fleeing, yet they did not tell me.'

But the king's officials were unwilling to raise a hand to strike the priests of the LORD.

18The king then ordered Doeg, 'You turn and strike down the priests.' So Doeg the Edomite turned and struck them down. That day he killed eighty-five men who wore the linen ephod. **19**He also put to the sword Nob, the town of the priests, with its men and women, its children and infants, and its cattle, donkeys and sheep.

20But one son of Ahimelek son of Ahitub, named Abiathar, escaped and fled to join David. **21**He told David that Saul had killed the priests of the LORD. **22**Then David said to Abiathar, 'That day, when Doeg the Edomite was there, I knew he would be sure to tell Saul. I am responsible for the death of your whole family. **23**Stay with me; don't be afraid. The man who wants to take your life is trying to kill me too. You will be safe with me.'

David saves Keilah

23 When David was told, 'Look, the Philistines are fighting against Keilah and are looting the threshing-floors,' **2**he enquired of the LORD, saying, 'Shall I go and attack these Philistines?'

The LORD answered him, 'Go, attack the Philistines and save Keilah.'

3But David's men said to him, 'Here in Judah we are afraid. How much more, then, if we go to Keilah against the Philistine forces!'

4Once again David enquired of the LORD, and the LORD answered him, 'Go down to Keilah, for I am going to give the Philistines into your hand.' **5**So David and his men went to Keilah, fought the Philistines and carried off their livestock. He inflicted heavy losses on the Philistines and saved the people of Keilah. **6**(Now Abiathar son of Ahimelek had brought the ephod down with him when he fled to David at Keilah.)

Saul pursues David

7Saul was told that David had gone to Keilah, and he said, 'God has delivered him into my hands, for David has imprisoned himself by entering a town with gates and bars.' **8**And Saul called up all his forces for battle, to go down to Keilah to besiege David and his men.

9When David learned that Saul was plotting against him, he said to Abiathar the priest, 'Bring the ephod.' **10**David said, 'LORD, God of Israel, your servant has heard definitely that Saul plans to come to Keilah and destroy the town on account of me. **11**Will the citizens of Keilah surrender me to him? Will Saul come down, as your servant has heard? LORD, God of Israel, tell your servant.'

And the LORD said, 'He will.'

12Again David asked, 'Will the citizens of Keilah surrender me and my men to Saul?'

And the LORD said, 'They will.'

13So David and his men, about six hundred in number, left Keilah and kept moving from place to place. When Saul was told that David had escaped from Keilah, he did not go there.

14David stayed in the wilderness strongholds and in the hills of the Desert of Ziph. Day after day Saul searched for him, but God did not give David into his hands.

15While David was at Horesh in the Desert of Ziph, he learned that Saul had come out to take his life. 16And Saul's son Jonathan went to David at Horesh and helped him to find strength in God. 17'Don't be afraid,' he said. 'My father Saul will not lay a hand on you. You shall be king over Israel, and I will be second to you. Even my father Saul knows this.' 18The two of them made a covenant before the LORD. Then Jonathan went home, but David remained at Horesh.

19The Ziphites went up to Saul at Gibeah and said, 'Is not David hiding among us in the strongholds at Horesh, on the hill of Hakilah, south of Jeshimon? 20Now, Your Majesty, come down whenever it pleases you to do so, and we will be responsible for giving him into your hands.'

21Saul replied, 'The LORD bless you for your concern for me. 22Go and get more information. Find out where David usually goes and who has seen him there. They tell me he is very crafty. 23Find out about all the hiding-places he uses and come back to me with definite information. Then I will go with you; if he is in the area, I will track him down among all the clans of Judah.'

24So they set out and went to Ziph ahead of Saul. Now David and his men were in the Desert of Maon, in the Arabah south of Jeshimon. 25Saul and his men began the search, and when David was told about it, he went down to the rock and stayed in the Desert of Maon. When Saul heard this, he went into the Desert of Maon in pursuit of David.

26Saul was going along one side of the mountain, and David and his men were on the other side, hurrying to get away from Saul. As Saul and his forces were closing in on David and his men to capture them, 27a messenger came to Saul, saying, 'Come quickly! The Philistines are raiding the land.' 28Then Saul broke off his pursuit of David and went to meet the Philistines. That is why they call this place Sela Hammahlekoth.[a] *29And David went up from there and lived in the strongholds of En Gedi.

David spares Saul's life

24 *After Saul returned from pursuing the Philistines, he was told, 'David is in the Desert of En Gedi.' 2So Saul took three thousand able young men from all Israel and set out to look for David and his men near the Crags of the Wild Goats.

3He came to the sheepfolds along the way; a cave was there, and Saul went in to relieve himself. David and his men were far back in the cave. 4The men said, 'This is the day the LORD spoke of when he said[b] to you, "I will give your enemy into your hands for you to deal with as you wish."' Then David crept up unnoticed and cut off a corner of Saul's robe.

5Afterwards, David was conscience-stricken for having cut off a corner of his robe. 6He said to his men, 'The LORD forbid that I should do such a thing to my master, the LORD's anointed, or lay my hand on him; for he is the anointed of the LORD.' 7With these words David sharply rebuked his men and did not allow them to attack Saul. And Saul left the cave and went his way.

IN OTHER WORDS

Anointed
1 Samuel 24:6

The word 'anoint' literally means 'to pour'. Saul had been anointed by Samuel by having oil poured on his head (1 Samuel 10:1). This was to show that he was set apart by God to be king of Israel and belonged to God. Even though he's trying to kill David and David knows he will be king after him, Saul still needs to be respected as special to God.

---

[a] 28 *Sela Hammahlekoth* means *rock of parting*.   [b] 4 Or *'Today the LORD is saying*

* 23:29 is numbered 24:1 in Hebrew texts.   * 24:1-22 is numbered 24:2-23 in Hebrew texts.

8Then David went out of the cave and called out to Saul, 'My lord the king!' When Saul looked behind him, David bowed down and prostrated himself with his face to the ground. 9He said to Saul, 'Why do you listen when men say, "David is bent on harming you"? 10This day you have seen with your own eyes how the LORD gave you into my hands in the cave. Some urged me to kill you, but I spared you; I said, "I will not lay my hand on my lord, because he is the LORD's anointed." 11See, my father, look at this piece of your robe in my hand! I cut off the corner of your robe but did not kill you. See that there is nothing in my hand to indicate that I am guilty of wrongdoing or rebellion. I have not wronged you, but you are hunting me down to take my life. 12May the LORD judge between you and me. And may the LORD avenge the wrongs you have done to me, but my hand will not touch you. 13As the old saying goes, "From evildoers come evil deeds," so my hand will not touch you.

14'Against whom has the king of Israel come out? Whom are you pursuing? A dead dog? A flea? 15May the LORD be our judge and decide between us. May he consider my cause and uphold it; may he vindicate me by delivering me from your hand.'

16When David finished saying this, Saul asked, 'Is that your voice, David my son?' And he wept aloud. 17'You are more righteous than I,' he said. 'You have treated me well, but I have treated you badly. 18You have just now told me about the good you did to me; the LORD gave me into your hands, but you did not kill me. 19When a man finds his enemy, does he let him get away unharmed? May the LORD reward you well for the way you treated me today. 20I know that you will surely be king and that the kingdom of Israel will be established in your hands. 21Now swear to me by the LORD that you will not kill off my descendants or wipe out my name from my father's family.'

22So David gave his oath to Saul. Then Saul returned home, but David and his men went up to the stronghold.

David, Nabal and Abigail

25 Now Samuel died, and all Israel assembled and mourned for him; and they buried him at his home in Ramah. Then David moved down into the Desert of Paran.*a*

2A certain man in Maon, who had property there at Carmel, was very wealthy. He had a thousand goats and three thousand sheep, which he was shearing in Carmel. 3His name was Nabal and his wife's name was Abigail. She was an intelligent and beautiful woman, but her husband was surly and mean in his dealings—he was a Calebite.

4While David was in the wilderness, he heard that Nabal was shearing sheep. 5So he sent ten young men and said to them, 'Go up to Nabal at Carmel and greet him in my name. 6Say to him: "Long life to you! Good health to you and your household! And good health to all that is yours!

7' "Now I hear that it is sheep-shearing time. When your shepherds were with us,

Hospitality
1 Samuel 25:8

Lots of people travelled from place to place in Bible times. There weren't any hotels or bed and breakfast places to book into, so there were strong expectations that local people would be hospitable and take in travellers. David picked a good time too, as during sheep-shearing farmers were expected to be extra generous as a way of thanking God for his blessings. Nabal lived up to his name, which means 'empty person', and refused to help. Fortunately his wife, Abigail, had more sense.

---

a 1 Hebrew and some Septuagint manuscripts; other Septuagint manuscripts *Maon* we did not ill-treat them, and the whole time they were at Carmel nothing of theirs was missing. 8Ask your own servants and they will tell you. Therefore be favourable towards my men, since we come at a festive time. Please give your servants and your son David whatever you can find for them."'

9When David's men arrived, they gave Nabal this message in David's name. Then they waited.

10Nabal answered David's servants, 'Who is this David? Who is this son of Jesse? Many servants are breaking away from their masters these days. 11Why should I take my bread and water, and the meat I have slaughtered for my shearers, and give it to men coming from who knows where?'

12David's men turned round and went back. When they arrived, they reported every word. 13David said to his men, 'Each of you strap on your sword!' So they did, and David strapped his on as well. About four hundred men went up with David, while two hundred stayed with the supplies.

14One of the servants told Abigail, Nabal's wife, 'David sent messengers from the wilderness to give our master his greetings, but he hurled insults at them. 15Yet these men were very good to us. They did not ill-treat us, and the whole time we were out in the fields near them nothing was missing. 16Night and day they were a wall around us the whole time we were herding our sheep near them. 17Now think it over and see what you can do, because disaster is hanging over our master and his whole household. He is such a wicked man that no-one can talk to him.'

18Abigail acted quickly. She took two hundred loaves of bread, two skins of wine, five dressed sheep, five seahs*ᵃ* of roasted grain, a hundred cakes of raisins and two hundred cakes of pressed figs, and loaded them on donkeys. 19Then she told her servants, 'Go on ahead; I'll follow you.' But she did not tell her husband Nabal.

20As she came riding her donkey into a mountain ravine, there were David and his men descending towards her, and she met them. 21David had just said, 'It's been useless—all my watching over this fellow's property in the wilderness so that nothing of his was missing. He has paid me back evil for good. 22May God deal with David,*ᵇ* be it ever so severely, if by morning I leave alive one male of all who belong to him!'

23When Abigail saw David, she quickly got off her donkey and bowed down before David with her face to the ground. 24She fell at his feet and said: 'Pardon your servant, my lord, and let me speak to you; hear what your servant has to say. 25Please pay no attention, my lord, to that wicked man Nabal. He is just like his name—his name means Fool, and folly goes with him. And as for me, your servant, I did not see the men my lord sent. 26And now, my lord, as surely as the LORD your God lives and as you live, since the LORD has kept you from bloodshed and from avenging yourself with your own hands, may your enemies and all who are intent on harming my lord be like Nabal. 27And let this gift, which your servant has brought to my lord, be given to the men who follow you.

28'Please forgive your servant's presumption. The LORD your God will certainly make a lasting dynasty for my lord, because you fight the LORD's battles, and no wrongdoing will be found in you as long as you live. 29Even though someone is pursuing you to take your life, the life of my lord will be bound securely in the bundle of the living by the LORD your God, but the lives of your enemies he will hurl away as from the pocket of a sling. 30When the LORD has fulfilled for my lord every good thing he promised concerning him and has appointed him ruler over Israel, 31my lord will not have on his conscience the staggering burden of needless bloodshed or of having avenged himself. And when the LORD your God has brought my lord success, remember your servant.'

32David said to Abigail, 'Praise be to the LORD, the God of Israel, who has sent you today to meet me. 33May you be blessed for your good judgment and for keeping me from bloodshed this day and from avenging myself with my own hands. 34Otherwise, as

---

ᵃ 18 That is, probably about 27 kilograms   *ᵇ* 22 Some Septuagint manuscripts; Hebrew *with David's enemies* surely as the LORD, the God of Israel, lives, who has kept me from harming you, if you had not come quickly to meet me, not one male belonging to Nabal would have been left alive by daybreak.'

35 Then David accepted from her hand what she had brought to him and said, 'Go home in peace. I have heard your words and granted your request.'

36 When Abigail went to Nabal, he was in the house holding a banquet like that of a king. He was in high spirits and very drunk. So she told him nothing at all until daybreak. 37 Then in the morning, when Nabal was sober, his wife told him all these things, and his heart failed him and he became like a stone. 38 About ten days later, the LORD struck Nabal and he died.

39 When David heard that Nabal was dead, he said, 'Praise be to the LORD, who has upheld my cause against Nabal for treating me with contempt. He has kept his servant from doing wrong and has brought Nabal's wrongdoing down on his own head.'

Then David sent word to Abigail, asking her to become his wife. 40 His servants went to Carmel and said to Abigail, 'David has sent us to you to take you to become his wife.'

41 She bowed down with her face to the ground and said, 'I am your servant and am ready to serve you and wash the feet of my lord's servants.' 42 Abigail quickly got on a donkey and, attended by her five female servants, went with David's messengers and became his wife. 43 David had also married Ahinoam of Jezreel, and they both were his wives. 44 But Saul had given his daughter Michal, David's wife, to Paltiel[a] son of Laish, who was from Gallim.

David again spares Saul's life

26 The Ziphites went to Saul at Gibeah and said, 'Is not David hiding on the hill of Hakilah, which faces Jeshimon?'

2 So Saul went down to the Desert of Ziph, with his three thousand able young Israelites, to search there for David. 3 Saul made his camp beside the road on the hill of Hakilah facing Jeshimon, but David stayed in the wilderness. When he saw that Saul had followed him there, 4 he sent out scouts and learned that Saul had definitely arrived.

5 Then David set out and went to the place where Saul had camped. He saw where Saul and Abner son of Ner, the commander of the army, had lain down. Saul was lying inside the camp, with the army camped around him.

6 David then asked Ahimelek the Hittite and Abishai son of Zeruiah, Joab's brother, 'Who will go down into the camp with me to Saul?'

'I'll go with you,' said Abishai.

7 So David and Abishai went to the army by night, and there was Saul, lying asleep inside the camp with his spear stuck in the ground near his head. Abner and the soldiers were lying round him.

8 Abishai said to David, 'Today God has given your enemy into your hands. Now let me pin him to the ground with one thrust of the spear; I won't strike him twice.'

9 But David said to Abishai, 'Don't destroy him! Who can lay a hand on the LORD's anointed and be guiltless? 10 As surely as the LORD lives,' he said, 'the LORD himself will strike him, or his time will come and he will die, or he will go into battle and perish. 11 But the LORD forbid that I should lay a hand on the LORD's anointed. Now get the spear and water jug that are near his head, and let's go.'

12 So David took the spear and water jug near Saul's head, and they left. No-one saw or knew about it, nor did anyone wake up. They were all sleeping, because the LORD had put them into a deep sleep.

13 Then David crossed over to the other side and stood on top of the hill some distance away; there was a wide space between them. 14 He called out to the army and to Abner son of Ner, 'Aren't you going to answer me, Abner?'

Abner replied, 'Who are you who calls to the king?'

15 David said, 'You're a man, aren't you? And who is like you in Israel? Why didn't you guard your lord the king? Someone

---

[a] 44 Hebrew *Palti*, a variant of *Paltiel*

came to destroy your lord the king. ¹⁶What you have done is not good. As surely as the LORD lives, you and your men must die, because you did not guard your master, the LORD's anointed. Look around you. Where are the king's spear and water jug that were near his head?'

¹⁷Saul recognised David's voice and said, 'Is that your voice, David my son?'

David replied, 'Yes it is, my lord the king.' ¹⁸And he added, 'Why is my lord pursuing his servant? What have I done, and what wrong am I guilty of? ¹⁹Now let my lord the king listen to his servant's words. If the LORD has incited you against me, then may he accept an offering. If, however, people have done it, may they be cursed before the LORD! They have driven me today from my share in the LORD's inheritance and have said, "Go, serve other gods." ²⁰Now do not let my blood fall to the ground far from the presence of the LORD. The king of Israel has come out to look for a flea—as one hunts a partridge in the mountains.'

²¹Then Saul said, 'I have sinned. Come back, David my son. Because you considered my life precious today, I will not try to harm you again. Surely I have acted like a fool and have been terribly wrong.'

²²'Here is the king's spear,' David answered. 'Let one of your servants come over and get it. ²³The LORD rewards every man for his righteousness and faithfulness. The LORD gave you into my hands today, but I would not lay a hand on the LORD's anointed. ²⁴As surely as I valued your life today, so may the LORD value my life and deliver me from all trouble.'

²⁵Then Saul said to David, 'May you be blessed, David my son; you will do great things and surely triumph.'

So David went on his way, and Saul returned home.

David among the Philistines

27 But David thought to himself, 'One of these days I shall be destroyed by the hand of Saul. The best thing I can do is to escape to the land of the Philistines. Then Saul will give up searching for me anywhere in Israel, and I will slip out of his hand.'

²So David and the six hundred men with him left and went over to Achish son of Maok king of Gath. ³David and his men settled in Gath with Achish. Each man had his family with him, and David had his two wives: Ahinoam of Jezreel and Abigail of Carmel, the widow of Nabal. ⁴When Saul was told that David had fled to Gath, he no longer searched for him.

⁵Then David said to Achish, 'If I have found favour in your eyes, let a place be assigned to me in one of the country towns, that I may live there. Why should your servant live in the royal city with you?'

⁶So on that day Achish gave him Ziklag, and it has belonged to the kings of Judah ever since. ⁷David lived in Philistine territory for a year and four months.

⁸Now David and his men went up and raided the Geshurites, the Girzites and the Amalekites. (From ancient times these peoples had lived in the land extending to Shur and Egypt.) ⁹Whenever David attacked an area, he did not leave a man or woman alive, but took sheep and cattle, donkeys and camels, and clothes. Then he returned to Achish.

¹⁰When Achish asked, 'Where did you go raiding today?' David would say, 'Against the Negev of Judah' or 'Against the Negev of Jerahmeel' or 'Against the Negev of the Kenites.' ¹¹He did not leave a man or woman alive to be brought to Gath, for he thought, 'They might inform on us and say, "This is what David did." ' And such was his practice as long as he lived in Philistine territory. ¹²Achish trusted David and said to himself, 'He has become so obnoxious to his people, the Israelites, that he will be my servant for life.'

28 In those days the Philistines gathered their forces to fight against Israel. Achish said to David, 'You must understand that you and your men will accompany me in the army.'

²David said, 'Then you will see for yourself what your servant can do.'

Achish replied, 'Very well, I will make you my bodyguard for life.'

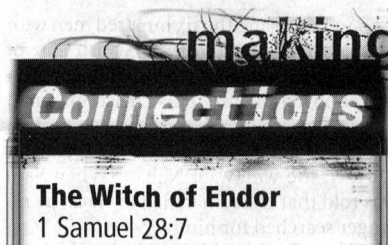

making Connections

The Witch of Endor
1 Samuel 28:7

The Bible warns strongly against mediums and witchcraft, so why does it seem to work for Saul here? In fact, it's God who calls back Samuel in spirit form to speak God's word to Saul. It's not something that the medium can do by herself. Her fright when she sees Samuel's spirit shows that it wasn't something she was used to!

Saul and the medium at Endor

3 Now Samuel was dead, and all Israel had mourned for him and buried him in his own town of Ramah. Saul had expelled the mediums and spiritists from the land.

4 The Philistines assembled and came and set up camp at Shunem, while Saul gathered all Israel and set up camp at Gilboa. 5 When Saul saw the Philistine army, he was afraid; terror filled his heart. 6 He enquired of the LORD, but the LORD did not answer him by dreams or Urim or prophets. 7 Saul then said to his attendants, 'Find me a woman who is a medium, so that I may go and enquire of her.'

'There is one in Endor,' they said.

8 So Saul disguised himself, putting on other clothes, and at night he and two men went to the woman. 'Consult a spirit for me,' he said, 'and bring up for me the one I name.'

9 But the woman said to him, 'Surely you know what Saul has done. He has cut off the mediums and spiritists from the land. Why have you set a trap for my life to bring about my death?'

10 Saul swore to her by the LORD, 'As surely as the LORD lives, you will not be punished for this.'

11 Then the woman asked, 'Whom shall I bring up for you?'

'Bring up Samuel,' he said.

12 When the woman saw Samuel, she cried out at the top of her voice and said to Saul, 'Why have you deceived me? You are Saul!'

13 The king said to her, 'Don't be afraid. What do you see?'

The woman said, 'I see a ghostly figure[a] coming up out of the earth.'

14 'What does he look like?' he asked.

'An old man wearing a robe is coming up,' she said.

Then Saul knew it was Samuel, and he bowed down and prostrated himself with his face to the ground.

15 Samuel said to Saul, 'Why have you disturbed me by bringing me up?'

'I am in great distress,' Saul said. 'The Philistines are fighting against me, and God has departed from me. He no longer answers me, either by prophets or by dreams. So I have called on you to tell me what to do.'

16 Samuel said, 'Why do you consult me, now that the LORD has departed from you and become your enemy? 17 The LORD has done what he predicted through me. The LORD has torn the kingdom out of your hands and given it to one of your neighbours—to David. 18 Because you did not obey the LORD or carry out his fierce wrath against the Amalekites, the LORD has done this to you today. 19 The LORD will deliver both Israel and you into the hands of the Philistines, and tomorrow you and your sons will be with me. The LORD will also give the army of Israel into the hands of the Philistines.'

20 Immediately Saul fell full length on the ground, filled with fear because of Samuel's words. His strength was gone, for he had eaten nothing all that day and all that night.

21 When the woman came to Saul and saw that he was greatly shaken, she said, 'Look, your servant has obeyed you. I took my life in my hands and did what you told me to do. 22 Now please listen to your servant and let me give you some food so that you may eat and have the strength to go on your way.'

---

[a] 13 Or *see spirits*; or *see gods*

23He refused and said, 'I will not eat.'

But his men joined the woman in urging him, and he listened to them. He got up from the ground and sat on the couch.

24The woman had a fattened calf at the house, which she slaughtered at once. She took some flour, kneaded it and baked bread without yeast. 25Then she set it before Saul and his men, and they ate. That same night they got up and left.

Achish sends David back to Ziklag

29 The Philistines gathered all their forces at Aphek, and Israel camped by the spring in Jezreel. 2As the Philistine rulers marched with their units of hundreds and thousands, David and his men were marching at the rear with Achish. 3The commanders of the Philistines asked, 'What about these Hebrews?'

Achish replied, 'Is this not David, who was an officer of Saul king of Israel? He has already been with me for over a year, and from the day he left Saul until now, I have found no fault in him.'

4But the Philistine commanders were angry with Achish and said, 'Send the man back, that he may return to the place you assigned him. He must not go with us into battle, or he will turn against us during the fighting. How better could he regain his master's favour than by taking the heads of our own men? 5Isn't this the David they sang about in their dances:

' "Saul has slain his thousands,
  and David his tens of thousands"?'

6So Achish called David and said to him, 'As surely as the LORD lives, you have been reliable, and I would be pleased for you to serve with me in the army. From the day you came to me until today, I have found no fault in you, but the rulers don't approve of you. 7Now turn back and go in peace; do nothing to displease the Philistine rulers.'

8'But what have I done?' asked David. 'What have you found against your servant from the day I came to you until now? Why can't I go and fight against the enemies of my lord the king?'

9Achish answered, 'I know that you have been as pleasing in my eyes as an angel of God; nevertheless, the Philistine commanders have said, "He must not go up with us into battle." 10Now get up early, along with your master's servants who have come with you, and leave in the morning as soon as it is light.'

11So David and his men got up early in the morning to go back to the land of the Philistines, and the Philistines went up to Jezreel.

David destroys the Amalekites

30 David and his men reached Ziklag on the third day. Now the Amalekites had raided the Negev and Ziklag. They had attacked Ziklag and burned it, 2and had taken captive the women who were in it, both young and old. They killed none of them, but carried them off as they went on their way.

3When David and his men reached Ziklag, they found it destroyed by fire and their wives and sons and daughters taken captive. 4So David and his men wept aloud until they had no strength left to weep. 5David's two wives had been captured— Ahinoam of Jezreel and Abigail, the widow of Nabal of Carmel. 6David was greatly distressed because the men were talking of stoning him; each one was bitter in spirit because of his sons and daughters. But David found strength in the LORD his God.

7Then David said to Abiathar the priest, the son of Ahimelek, 'Bring me the ephod.' Abiathar brought it to him, 8and David enquired of the LORD, 'Shall I pursue this raiding party? Will I overtake them?'

'Pursue them,' he answered. 'You will certainly overtake them and succeed in the rescue.'

9David and the six hundred men with him came to the Besor Valley, where some stayed behind. 10Two hundred of them were too exhausted to cross the valley, but David and the other four hundred continued the pursuit.

11They found an Egyptian in a field and brought him to David. They gave him water to drink and food to eat— 12part of a cake of pressed figs and two cakes of raisins. He ate and was revived, for he had not eaten any food or drunk any water for three days and three nights.

¹³David asked him, 'Who do you belong to? Where do you come from?'

He said, 'I am an Egyptian, the slave of an Amalekite. My master abandoned me when I became ill three days ago. ¹⁴We raided the Negev of the Kerethites, some territory belonging to Judah and the Negev of Caleb. And we burned Ziklag.'

¹⁵David asked him, 'Can you lead me down to this raiding party?'

He answered, 'Swear to me before God that you will not kill me or hand me over to my master, and I will take you down to them.'

¹⁶He led David down, and there they were, scattered over the countryside, eating, drinking and revelling because of the great amount of plunder they had taken from the land of the Philistines and from Judah. ¹⁷David fought them from dusk until the evening of the next day, and none of them got away, except four hundred young men who rode off on camels and fled. ¹⁸David recovered everything the Amalekites had taken, including his two wives. ¹⁹Nothing was missing: young or old, boy or girl, plunder or anything else they had taken. David brought everything back. ²⁰He took all the flocks and herds, and his men drove them ahead of the other livestock, saying, 'This is David's plunder.'

²¹Then David came to the two hundred men who had been too exhausted to follow him and who were left behind at the Besor Valley. They came out to meet David and the men with him. As David and his men approached, he asked them how they were. ²²But all the evil men and troublemakers among David's followers said, 'Because they did not go out with us, we will not share with them the plunder we recovered. However, each man may take his wife and children and go.'

²³David replied, 'No, my brothers, you must not do that with what the LORD has given us. He has protected us and delivered into our hands the raiding party that came against us. ²⁴Who will listen to what you say? The share of the man who stayed with the supplies is to be the same as that of him who went down to the battle. All shall share alike.' ²⁵David made this a statute and ordinance for Israel from that day to this.

²⁶When David reached Ziklag, he sent some of the plunder to the elders of Judah, who were his friends, saying, 'Here is a gift for you from the plunder of the LORD's enemies.'

²⁷David sent it to those who were in Bethel, Ramoth Negev and Jattir; ²⁸to those in Aroer, Siphmoth, Eshtemoa ²⁹and Rakal; to those in the towns of the Jerahmeelites and the Kenites; ³⁰to those in Hormah, Bor Ashan, Athak ³¹and Hebron; and to those in all the other places where he and his men had roamed.

Saul takes his life

31 Now the Philistines fought against Israel; the Israelites fled before them, and many fell dead on Mount Gilboa. ²The Philistines were in hot pursuit of Saul and his sons, and they killed his sons Jonathan, Abinadab and Malki-Shua. ³The fighting grew fierce around Saul, and when the archers overtook him, they wounded him critically.

⁴Saul said to his armour-bearer, 'Draw your sword and run me through, or these uncircumcised fellows will come and run me through and abuse me.'

making Connections

Suicide
1 Samuel 31:4

Saul's servant refused to kill him because he knew that Saul was still God's anointed and anyone who killed him would be punished. Suicide is very rare in the Bible and is only mentioned three other times. The servant killed himself once his master was dead because that was the custom in those times.

But the armour-bearer was terrified and would not do it; so Saul took his own sword and fell on it. ⁵When the armour-bearer saw that Saul was dead, he too fell on his sword and died with him. ⁶So Saul and his three sons and his armour-bearer and all his men died together that same day.

⁷When the Israelites along the valley and those across the Jordan saw that the Israelite army had fled and that Saul and his sons had died, they abandoned their towns and fled. And the Philistines came and occupied them.

⁸The next day, when the Philistines came to strip the dead, they found Saul and his three sons fallen on Mount Gilboa. ⁹They cut off his head and stripped off his armour, and they sent messengers throughout the land of the Philistines to proclaim the news in the temple of their idols and among their people. ¹⁰They put his armour in the temple of the Ashtoreths and fastened his body to the wall of Beth Shan.

¹¹When the people of Jabesh Gilead heard what the Philistines had done to Saul, ¹²all their valiant men marched through the night to Beth Shan. They took down the bodies of Saul and his sons from the wall of Beth Shan and went to Jabesh, where they burned them. ¹³Then they took their bones and buried them under a tamarisk tree at Jabesh, and they fasted seven days.

2 Samuel

INTRODUCTION

2 SAMUEL

Author: Not Samuel, because he had died by the time the events in this book happened. Abiathar the priest might have written this book.

When: The forty years when David was king, around 1010 BC to 971 BC.

Where: Israel.

Main theme: 2 Samuel tells the story of David's reign, his political, spiritual and military triumphs as he drives out the Philistines, unites the people and establishes peaceful relationships with the surrounding nations. But David also makes some serious errors. He commits adultery with Bathsheba and then arranges for her husband to be killed. Confronted with his sin by the prophet Nathan, he repents before God.

David hears of Saul's death

1 After the death of Saul, David returned from striking down the Amalekites and stayed in Ziklag two days. ²On the third day a man arrived from Saul's camp with his clothes torn and dust on his head. When he came to David, he fell to the ground to pay him honour.

³'Where have you come from?' David asked him.

He answered, 'I have escaped from the Israelite camp.'

⁴'What happened?' David asked. 'Tell me.'

'The men fled from the battle,' he replied. 'Many of them fell and died. And Saul and his son Jonathan are dead.'

⁵Then David said to the young man who brought him the report, 'How do you know that Saul and his son Jonathan are dead?'

⁶'I happened to be on Mount Gilboa,' the young man said, 'and there was Saul, leaning on his spear, with the chariots and their drivers in hot pursuit. ⁷When he turned round and saw me, he called out to me, and I said, "What can I do?"

⁸'He asked me, "Who are you?"

'"An Amalekite," I answered.

him down, and he died. ¹⁶For David had said to him, 'Your blood be on your own head. Your own mouth testified against you when you said, "I killed the LORD's anointed."'

David's lament for Saul and Jonathan

¹⁷David took up this lament concerning Saul and his son Jonathan, ¹⁸and he ordered that the people of Judah be taught this lament of the bow (it is written in the Book of Jashar):

¹⁹'A gazelle*ᵃ* lies slain on your heights, Israel.
How the mighty have fallen!

²⁰'Tell it not in Gath,
proclaim it not in the streets of Ashkelon,
lest the daughters of the Philistines be glad,
lest the daughters of the uncircumcised rejoice.

²¹'Mountains of Gilboa,
may you have neither dew nor rain,
may no showers fall on your terraced fields.*ᵇ*
For there the shield of the mighty was despised,
the shield of Saul—no longer rubbed with oil.

²²'From the blood of the slain,
from the flesh of the mighty,
the bow of Jonathan did not turn back,
the sword of Saul did not return unsatisfied.

²³Saul and Jonathan—
in life they were loved and admired,
and in death they were not parted.
They were swifter than eagles,
they were stronger than lions.

²⁴'Daughters of Israel,
weep for Saul,
who clothed you in scarlet and finery,
who adorned your garments with ornaments of gold.

²⁵'How the mighty have fallen in battle!
Jonathan lies slain on your heights.

making Connections

Amalekites
2 Samuel 1:8

Years before, God had told Saul to destroy the Amalekites because they had attacked the Israelites when they came out of Egypt (1 Samuel 15:1–23). Saul almost did what he was told, but spared their king, Agag, and the best of their sheep and cattle. Because of his disobedience, Samuel told him that God rejected him as king. And his disobedience is coming back to haunt him again. Saul has tried to commit suicide and is obviously badly hurt, but the man who finishes him off is an Amalekite, one of the people that Saul should have destroyed.

⁹'Then he said to me, "Stand here by me and kill me! I'm in the throes of death, but I'm still alive."

¹⁰'So I stood beside him and killed him, because I knew that after he had fallen he could not survive. And I took the crown that was on his head and the band on his arm and have brought them here to my lord.'

¹¹Then David and all the men with him took hold of their clothes and tore them. ¹²They mourned and wept and fasted till evening for Saul and his son Jonathan, and for the army of the LORD and the house of Israel, because they had fallen by the sword.

¹³David said to the young man who brought him the report, 'Where are you from?'

'I am the son of a foreigner, an Amalekite,' he answered.

¹⁴David asked him, 'Why weren't you afraid to lift your hand to destroy the LORD's anointed?'

¹⁵Then David called one of his men and said, 'Go, strike him down!' So he struck

---

ᵃ 19 *Gazelle* here symbolises a human dignitary.   *ᵇ* 21 Or / *nor fields that yield grain for offerings*

26 I grieve for you, Jonathan my brother;
  you were very dear to me.
 Your love for me was wonderful,
  more wonderful than that of women.

27 'How the mighty have fallen!
  The weapons of war have perished!'

David anointed king over Judah

2 In the course of time, David enquired of the LORD. 'Shall I go up to one of the towns of Judah?' he asked.

The LORD said, 'Go up.'

David asked, 'Where shall I go?'

'To Hebron,' the LORD answered.

2 So David went up there with his two wives, Ahinoam of Jezreel and Abigail, the widow of Nabal of Carmel. 3 David also took the men who were with him, each with his family, and they settled in Hebron and its towns. 4 Then the men of Judah came to Hebron, and there they anointed David king over the house of Judah.

When David was told that it was the men from Jabesh Gilead who had buried Saul, 5 he sent messengers to them to say to them, 'The LORD bless you for showing this kindness to Saul your master by burying him. 6 May the LORD now show you kindness and faithfulness, and I too will show you the same favour because you have done this. 7 Now then, be strong and brave, for Saul your master is dead, and the house of Judah has anointed me king over them.'

War between the houses of David and Saul

8 Meanwhile, Abner son of Ner, the commander of Saul's army, had taken Ish-Bosheth son of Saul and brought him over to Mahanaim. 9 He made him king over Gilead, Ashuri and Jezreel, and also over Ephraim, Benjamin and all Israel.

10 Ish-Bosheth son of Saul was forty years old when he became king over Israel, and he reigned two years. The house of Judah, however, remained loyal to David. 11 The length of time David was king in Hebron over the house of Judah was seven years and six months.

12 Abner son of Ner, together with the men of Ish-Bosheth son of Saul, left Mahanaim and went to Gibeon. 13 Joab son of Zeruiah and David's men went out and met them at the pool of Gibeon. One group sat down on one side of the pool and one group on the other side.

14 Then Abner said to Joab, 'Let some of the soldiers get up and fight hand to hand in front of us.'

'All right, let them do it,' Joab said.

15 So they stood up and were counted— twelve men for Benjamin and Ish-Bosheth son of Saul, and twelve for David. 16 Then each man grabbed his opponent by the head and thrust his dagger into his opponent's side, and they fell down together. So that place in Gibeon was called Helkath Hazzurim.[a]

17 The battle that day was very fierce, and Abner and the Israelites were defeated by David's men.

18 The three sons of Zeruiah were there: Joab, Abishai and Asahel. Now Asahel was as fleet-footed as a wild gazelle. 19 He chased Abner, turning neither to the right nor to the left as he pursued him. 20 Abner looked behind him and asked, 'Is that you, Asahel?'

'It is,' he answered.

21 Then Abner said to him, 'Turn aside to the right or to the left; take on one of the soldiers and strip him of his weapons.' But Asahel would not stop chasing him.

22 Again Abner warned Asahel, 'Stop chasing me! Why should I strike you down? How could I look your brother Joab in the face?'

23 But Asahel refused to give up the pursuit; so Abner thrust the butt of his spear into Asahel's stomach, and the spear came out through his back. He fell there and died on the spot. And every man stopped when he came to the place where Asahel had fallen and died.

24 But Joab and Abishai pursued Abner, and as the sun was setting, they came to the hill of Ammah, near Giah on the way to the wasteland of Gibeon. 25 Then the men of Benjamin rallied behind Abner. They formed themselves into a group and took their stand on top of a hill.

---

[a] 16 *Helkath Hazzurim* means *field of daggers* or *field of hostilities*.

²⁶Abner called out to Joab, 'Must the sword devour for ever? Don't you realise that this will end in bitterness? How long before you order your men to stop pursuing their fellow Israelites?'

²⁷Joab answered, 'As surely as God lives, if you had not spoken, the men would have continued pursuing them until morning.'

²⁸So Joab blew the trumpet, and everyone came to a halt; they no longer pursued Israel, nor did they fight any more.

²⁹All that night Abner and his men marched through the Arabah. They crossed the Jordan, continued through the morning hours*ᵃ* and came to Mahanaim.

³⁰Then Joab stopped pursuing Abner and assembled the whole army. Besides Asahel, nineteen of David's men were found missing. ³¹But David's men had killed 360 Benjaminites who were with Abner. ³²They took Asahel and buried him in his father's tomb at Bethlehem. Then Joab and his men marched all night and arrived at Hebron by daybreak.

3 The war between the house of Saul and the house of David lasted a long time. David grew stronger and stronger, while the house of Saul grew weaker and weaker.

²Sons were born to David in Hebron:
His firstborn was Amnon the son of Ahinoam of Jezreel;

³his second, Kileab the son of Abigail the widow of Nabal of Carmel;
the third, Absalom the son of Maakah daughter of Talmai king of Geshur;

⁴the fourth, Adonijah the son of Haggith;
the fifth, Shephatiah the son of Abital;

⁵and the sixth, Ithream the son of David's wife Eglah.
These were born to David in Hebron.

Abner goes over to David

⁶During the war between the house of Saul and the house of David, Abner had been strengthening his own position in the house of Saul. ⁷Now Saul had had a concubine named Rizpah daughter of Aiah. And Ish-Bosheth said to Abner, 'Why did you sleep with my father's concubine?'

⁸Abner was very angry because of what Ish-Bosheth said. So he answered, 'Am I a dog's head—on Judah's side? This very day I am loyal to the house of your father Saul and to his family and friends. I haven't handed you over to David. Yet now you accuse me of an offence involving this woman! ⁹May God deal with Abner, be it ever so severely, if I do not do for David what the LORD promised him on oath ¹⁰and transfer the kingdom from the house of Saul and establish David's throne over Israel and Judah from Dan to Beersheba.' ¹¹Ish-Bosheth did not dare to say another word to Abner, because he was afraid of him.

¹²Then Abner sent messengers on his behalf to say to David, 'Whose land is it? Make an agreement with me, and I will help you bring all Israel over to you.'

¹³'Good,' said David. 'I will make an agreement with you. But I demand one thing of you: do not come into my presence unless you bring Michal daughter of Saul when you come to see me.' ¹⁴Then David sent messengers to Ish-Bosheth son of Saul, demanding, 'Give me my wife Michal, whom I betrothed to myself for the price of a hundred Philistine foreskins.'

¹⁵So Ish-Bosheth gave orders and had her taken away from her husband Paltiel son of Laish. ¹⁶Her husband, however, went with her, weeping behind her all the way to Bahurim. Then Abner said to him, 'Go back home!' So he went back.

¹⁷Abner conferred with the elders of Israel and said, 'For some time you have wanted to make David your king. ¹⁸Now do it! For the LORD promised David, "By my servant David I will rescue my people Israel from the hand of the Philistines and from the hand of all their enemies."'

¹⁹Abner also spoke to the Benjaminites in person. Then he went to Hebron to tell David everything that Israel and the whole house of Benjamin wanted to do. ²⁰When Abner, who had twenty men with him, came to David at Hebron, David prepared a feast

---

ᵃ 29 Or See Septuagint; the meaning of the Hebrew for this phrase is uncertain.

for him and his men. 21Then Abner said to David, 'Let me go at once and assemble all Israel for my lord the king, so that they may make a covenant with you, and that you may rule over all that your heart desires.' So David sent Abner away, and he went in peace.

Joab murders Abner

22Just then David's men and Joab returned from a raid and brought with them a great deal of plunder. But Abner was no longer with David in Hebron, because David had sent him away, and he had gone in peace. 23When Joab and all the soldiers with him arrived, he was told that Abner son of Ner had come to the king and that the king had sent him away and that he had gone in peace.

24So Joab went to the king and said, 'What have you done? Look, Abner came to you. Why did you let him go? Now he is gone! 25You know Abner son of Ner; he came to deceive you and observe your movements and find out everything you are doing.'

26Joab then left David and sent messengers after Abner, and they brought him back from the cistern at Sirah. But David did not know it. 27Now when Abner returned to Hebron, Joab took him aside into an inner chamber, as if to speak with him privately. And there, to avenge the blood of his brother Asahel, Joab stabbed him in the stomach, and he died.

28Later, when David heard about this, he said, 'I and my kingdom are for ever innocent before the LORD concerning the blood of Abner son of Ner. 29May his blood fall on the head of Joab and on his whole family! May Joab's family never be without someone who has a running sore or leprosy*a* or who leans on a crutch or who falls by the sword or who lacks food.'

30(Joab and his brother Abishai murdered Abner because he had killed their brother Asahel in the battle of Gibeon.)

31Then David said to Joab and all of Joab's men, 'Tear your clothes and put on sackcloth and walk in mourning in front of Abner.' King David himself walked behind the bier. 32They buried Abner in Hebron, and the king wept aloud at Abner's tomb. All of Joab's men wept also.

33The king sang this lament for Abner:

'Should Abner have died as the lawless die?
34   Your hands were not bound,
    your feet were not fettered.
You fell as one falls before the wicked.'

And all of Joab's men wept over him again.

35Then they all came and urged David to eat something while it was still day; but David took an oath, saying, 'May God deal with me, be it ever so severely, if I taste bread or anything else before the sun sets!'

36All of Joab's men took note and were pleased; indeed, everything the king did pleased them. 37So on that day all of Joab's men and all Israel knew that the king had no part in the murder of Abner son of Ner.

38Then the king said to his men, 'Don't you realise that a great commander has fallen in Israel this day? 39And today, though I am the anointed king, I am weak, and these sons of Zeruiah are too strong for me. May the LORD repay the evildoer according to his evil deeds!'

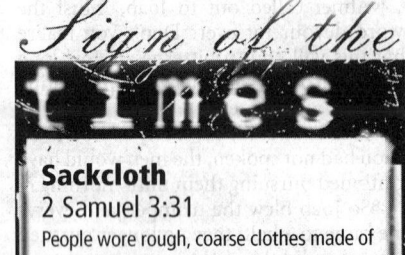

Sign of the times

Sackcloth
2 Samuel 3:31
People wore rough, coarse clothes made of sackcloth as a symbol of mourning or repentance, and would put ashes on their heads. Prophets often wore sackcloth, perhaps to show their brokenness as they delivered their messages of judgment from God.

---

a 29 The Hebrew for *leprosy* was used for various diseases affecting the skin.

Ish-Bosheth murdered

4 When Ish-Bosheth son of Saul heard that Abner had died in Hebron, he lost courage, and all Israel became alarmed. ²Now Saul's son had two leaders of raiding bands. One was named Baanah and the other Rekab; they were sons of Rimmon the Beerothite from the tribe of Benjamin— Beeroth is considered part of Benjamin, ³because the people of Beeroth fled to Gittaim and have resided there as foreigners to this day.

⁴(Jonathan son of Saul had a son who was lame in both feet. He was five years old when the news about Saul and Jonathan came from Jezreel. His nurse picked him up and fled, but as she hurried to leave, he fell and became disabled. His name was Mephibosheth.)

⁵Now Rekab and Baanah, the sons of Rimmon the Beerothite, set out for the house of Ish-Bosheth, and they arrived there in the heat of the day while he was taking his noonday rest. ⁶They went into the inner part of the house as if to get some wheat, and they stabbed him in the stomach. Then Rekab and his brother Baanah slipped away.

⁷They had gone into the house while he was lying on the bed in his bedroom. After they stabbed and killed him, they cut off his head. Taking it with them, they travelled all night by way of the Arabah. ⁸They brought the head of Ish-Bosheth to David at Hebron and said to the king, 'Here is the head of Ish-Bosheth son of Saul, your enemy, who tried to take your life. This day the LORD has avenged my lord the king against Saul and his offspring.'

⁹David answered Rekab and his brother Baanah, the sons of Rimmon the Beerothite, 'As surely as the LORD lives, who has delivered me out of every trouble, ¹⁰when someone told me, "Saul is dead," and thought he was bringing good news, I seized him and put him to death in Ziklag. That was the reward I gave him for his news! ¹¹How much more—when wicked men have killed an innocent man in his own house and on his own bed—should I not now demand his blood from your hand and rid the earth of you!'

¹²So David gave an order to his men, and they killed them. They cut off their hands and feet and hung the bodies by the pool in Hebron. But they took the head of Ish-Bosheth and buried it in Abner's tomb at Hebron.

David becomes king over Israel

5 All the tribes of Israel came to David at Hebron and said, 'We are your own flesh and blood. ²In the past, while Saul was king over us, you were the one who led Israel on their military campaigns. And the LORD said to you, "You shall shepherd my people Israel, and you shall become their ruler."'

³When all the elders of Israel had come to King David at Hebron, the king made a covenant with them at Hebron before the LORD, and they anointed David king over Israel.

⁴David was thirty years old when he became king, and he reigned for forty years. ⁵In Hebron he reigned over Judah for seven years and six months, and in Jerusalem he reigned over all Israel and Judah for thirty-three years.

David conquers Jerusalem

⁶The king and his men marched to Jerusalem to attack the Jebusites, who lived there. The Jebusites said to David, 'You will not get in here; even the blind and the lame can ward you off.' They thought, 'David cannot get in here.' ⁷Nevertheless, David captured the fortress of Zion—which is the City of David.

⁸On that day David had said, 'Anyone who conquers the Jebusites will have to use the water shaft to reach those "lame and blind" who are David's enemies.'[a] That is why they say, 'The "blind and lame" will not enter the palace.'

⁹David then took up residence in the fortress and called it the City of David. He built up the area around it, from the terraces[b] inwards. ¹⁰And he became more and more powerful, because the LORD God Almighty was with him.

---

[a] 8 Or *are hated by David* [b] 9 Or *the Millo*

¹¹Now Hiram king of Tyre sent messengers to David, along with cedar logs and carpenters and stonemasons, and they built a palace for David. ¹²And David knew that the LORD had established him as king over Israel and had exalted his kingdom for the sake of his people Israel.

¹³After he left Hebron, David took more concubines and wives in Jerusalem, and more sons and daughters were born to him. ¹⁴These are the names of the children born to him there: Shammua, Shobab, Nathan, Solomon, ¹⁵Ibhar, Elishua, Nepheg, Japhia, ¹⁶Elishama, Eliada and Eliphelet.

David defeats the Philistines

¹⁷When the Philistines heard that David had been anointed king over Israel, they went up in full force to search for him, but David heard about it and went down to the stronghold. ¹⁸Now the Philistines had come and spread out in the Valley of Rephaim; ¹⁹so David enquired of the LORD, 'Shall I go and attack the Philistines? Will you deliver them into my hands?'

The LORD answered him, 'Go, for I will surely deliver the Philistines into your hands.'

²⁰So David went to Baal Perazim, and there he defeated them. He said, 'As waters break out, the LORD has broken out against my enemies before me.' So that place was called Baal Perazim.[a] ²¹The Philistines abandoned their idols there, and David and his men carried them off.

²²Once more the Philistines came up and spread out in the Valley of Rephaim; ²³so David enquired of the LORD, and he answered, 'Do not go straight up, but circle round behind them and attack them in front of the poplar trees. ²⁴As soon as you hear the sound of marching in the tops of the poplar trees, move quickly, because that will mean the LORD has gone out in front of you to strike the Philistine army.' ²⁵So David did as the LORD commanded him, and he struck down the Philistines all the way from Gibeon[b] to Gezer.

The ark brought to Jerusalem

6 David again brought together all the able young men of Israel—thirty thousand. ²He and all his men went to Baalah[c] in Judah to bring up from there the ark of God, which is called by the Name,[d] the name of the LORD Almighty, who is enthroned between the cherubim on the ark. ³They set the ark of God on a new cart and brought it from the house of Abinadab, which was on the hill. Uzzah and Ahio, sons of Abinadab, were guiding the new cart ⁴with the ark of God on it,[e] and Ahio was walking in front of it. ⁵David and the whole house of Israel were celebrating with all their might before the LORD, with castanets,[f] harps, lyres, tambourines, rattles and cymbals.

⁶When they came to the threshing-floor of Nakon, Uzzah reached out and took hold of the ark of God, because the oxen stumbled. ⁷The LORD's anger burned against Uzzah because of his irreverent act; therefore God struck him down, and he died there beside the ark of God.

⁸Then David was angry because the LORD's wrath had broken out against

IN OTHER WORDS

Ark of the Covenant
2 Samuel 6:3

The Ark of the Covenant was a chest made of acacia wood and overlaid with gold. It had been carried by the Israelites through the wilderness and was the only item of furniture in the innermost room, or Holy of Holies, of the tabernacle. It had a gold mercy seat and two gold statues of cherubim on top of it. Inside were kept the two stone tablets with the Ten Commandments on them.

---

[a] 20 *Baal Perazim* means *the lord who breaks out.* [b] 25 Septuagint (see also 1 Chron. 14:16); Hebrew *Geba* [c] 2 That is, Kiriath Jearim (see 1 Chron. 13:6) [d] 2 Hebrew; Septuagint and Vulgate do not have *the Name.* [e] 3,4 Dead Sea Scrolls and some Septuagint manuscripts; Masoretic Text *cart* ⁴*and they brought it with the ark of God from the house of Abinadab, which was on the hill* [f] 5 Masoretic Text; Dead Sea Scrolls and Septuagint (see also 1 Chron. 13:8) *songs*

Uzzah, and to this day that place is called Perez Uzzah.[a]

9 David was afraid of the LORD that day and said, 'How can the ark of the LORD ever come to me?' 10 He was not willing to take the ark of the LORD to be with him in the City of David. Instead, he took it to the house of Obed-Edom the Gittite. 11 The ark of the LORD remained in the house of Obed-Edom the Gittite for three months, and the LORD blessed him and his entire household.

12 Now King David was told, 'The LORD has blessed the household of Obed-Edom and everything he has, because of the ark of God.' So David went to bring up the ark of God from the house of Obed-Edom to the City of David with rejoicing. 13 When those who were carrying the ark of the LORD had taken six steps, he sacrificed a bull and a fattened calf. 14 Wearing a linen ephod, David was dancing before the LORD with all his might, 15 while he and the entire house of Israel were bringing up the ark of the LORD with shouts and the sound of trumpets.

16 As the ark of the LORD was entering the City of David, Michal daughter of Saul watched from a window. And when she saw King David leaping and dancing before the LORD, she despised him in her heart.

17 They brought the ark of the LORD and set it in its place inside the tent that David had pitched for it, and David sacrificed burnt offerings and fellowship offerings before the LORD. 18 After he had finished sacrificing the burnt offerings and fellowship offerings, he blessed the people in the name of the LORD Almighty. 19 Then he gave a loaf of bread, a cake of dates and a cake of raisins to each person in the whole crowd of Israelites, both men and women. And all the people went to their homes.

20 When David returned home to bless his household, Michal daughter of Saul came out to meet him and said, 'How the king of Israel has distinguished himself today, going around half-naked in full view of the slave girls of his servants as any vulgar fellow would.'

21 David said to Michal, 'It was before the LORD, who chose me rather than your father or anyone from his house when he appointed me ruler over the LORD's people Israel—I will celebrate before the LORD. 22 I will become even more undignified than this, and I will be humiliated in my own eyes. But by these slave girls you spoke of, I will be held in honour.'

23 And Michal daughter of Saul had no children to the day of her death.

God's promise to David

7 After the king was settled in his palace and the LORD had given him rest from all his enemies around him, 2 he said to Nathan the prophet, 'Here I am, living in a house of cedar, while the ark of God remains in a tent.'

3 Nathan replied to the king, 'Whatever you have in mind, go ahead and do it, for the LORD is with you.'

4 But that night the word of the LORD came to Nathan, saying:

> 5 'Go and tell my servant David, "This is what the LORD says: are you the one to build me a house to dwell in? 6 I have not dwelt in a house from the day I brought the Israelites up out of Egypt to this day. I have been moving from place to place with a tent as my dwelling. 7 Wherever I have moved with all the Israelites, did I ever say to any of their rulers whom I commanded to shepherd my people Israel, 'Why have you not built me a house of cedar?' "
>
> 8 'Now then, tell my servant David, "This is what the LORD Almighty says: I took you from the pasture, from tending the flock, and appointed you ruler over my people Israel. 9 I have been with you wherever you have gone, and I have cut off all your enemies from before you. Now I will make your name great, like the names of the greatest men on earth. 10 And I will provide a place for my people Israel and will plant them so that they can have a home of their own and no longer be disturbed. Wicked people shall not oppress them

---

[a] 8 *Perez Uzzah* means *the outbreak against Uzzah*.

any more, as they did at the beginning ¹¹and have done ever since the time I appointed leaders[a] over my people Israel. I will also give you rest from all your enemies.

'"The LORD declares to you that the LORD himself will establish a house for you: ¹²when your days are over and you rest with your ancestors, I will raise up your offspring to succeed you, who will come from your own body, and I will establish his kingdom. ¹³He is the one who will build a house for my Name, and I will establish the throne of his kingdom for ever. ¹⁴I will be his father, and he shall be my son. When he does wrong, I will punish him with a rod wielded by human beings, with floggings inflicted by human hands. ¹⁵But my love will never be taken away from him, as I took it away from Saul, whom I removed from before you. ¹⁶Your house and your kingdom shall endure for ever before me;[b] your throne shall be established for ever."'

¹⁷Nathan reported to David all the words of this entire revelation.

David's prayer

¹⁸Then King David went in and sat before the LORD, and he said:

'Who am I, Sovereign LORD, and what is my family, that you have brought me this far? ¹⁹And as if this were not enough in your sight, Sovereign LORD, you have also spoken about the future of the house of your servant—and this decree, Sovereign LORD, is for a human being![c]

²⁰'What more can David say to you? For you know your servant, Sovereign LORD. ²¹For the sake of your word and according to your will, you have done this great thing and made it known to your servant.

²²'How great you are, Sovereign LORD! There is no-one like you, and there is no God but you, as we have heard with our own ears. ²³And who is like your people Israel—the one nation on earth that God went out to redeem as a people for himself, and to make a name for himself, and to perform great and awesome wonders by driving out nations and their gods from before your people, whom you redeemed from Egypt?[d] ²⁴You have established your people Israel as your very own for ever, and you, LORD, have become their God.

²⁵'And now, LORD God, keep for ever the promise you have made concerning your servant and his house. Do as you promised, ²⁶so that your name will be great for ever. Then people will say, "The LORD Almighty is God over Israel!" And the house of your servant David will be established in your sight.

²⁷'LORD Almighty, God of Israel, you have revealed this to your servant, saying, "I will build a house for you." So your servant has found courage to pray this prayer to you. ²⁸Sovereign LORD, you are God! Your covenant is trustworthy, and you have promised these good things to your servant. ²⁹Now be pleased to bless the house of your servant, that it may continue for ever in your sight; for you, Sovereign LORD, have spoken, and with your blessing the house of your servant will be blessed for ever.'

---

[a] 11 Traditionally *judges* [b] 16 Some Hebrew manuscripts and Septuagint; most Hebrew manuscripts *you* [c] 19 Or *for the human race* [d] 23 See Septuagint and 1 Chron. 17:21; Hebrew *wonders for your land and before your people, whom you redeemed from Egypt, from the nations and their gods.*

David's victories

8 In the course of time, David defeated the Philistines and subdued them, and he took Metheg Ammah from the control of the Philistines.

2 David also defeated the Moabites. He made them lie down on the ground and measured them off with a length of cord. Every two lengths of them were put to death, and the third length was allowed to live. So the Moabites became subject to David and brought him tribute.

3 Moreover, David defeated Hadadezer son of Rehob, king of Zobah, when he went to restore his monument at[a] the River Euphrates. 4 David captured a thousand of his chariots, seven thousand charioteers[b] and twenty thousand foot soldiers. He hamstrung all but a hundred of the chariot horses.

5 When the Arameans of Damascus came to help Hadadezer king of Zobah, David struck down twenty-two thousand of them. 6 He put garrisons in the Aramean kingdom of Damascus, and the Arameans became subject to him and brought tribute. The LORD gave David victory wherever he went.

7 David took the gold shields that belonged to the officers of Hadadezer and brought them to Jerusalem. 8 From Tebah[c] and Berothai, towns that belonged to Hadadezer, King David took a great quantity of bronze.

9 When Tou[d] king of Hamath heard that David had defeated the entire army of Hadadezer, 10 he sent his son Joram[e] to King David to greet him and congratulate him on his victory in battle over Hadadezer, who had been at war with Tou. Joram brought with him articles of silver, of gold and of bronze.

11 King David dedicated these articles to the LORD, as he had done with the silver and gold from all the nations he had subdued: 12 Edom[f] and Moab, the Ammonites and the Philistines, and Amalek. He also dedicated the plunder taken from Hadadezer son of Rehob, king of Zobah.

13 And David became famous after he returned from striking down eighteen thousand Edomites[g] in the Valley of Salt.

14 He put garrisons throughout Edom, and all the Edomites became subject to David. The LORD gave David victory wherever he went.

David's officials

15 David reigned over all Israel, doing what was just and right for all his people. 16 Joab son of Zeruiah was over the army; Jehoshaphat son of Ahilud was recorder; 17 Zadok son of Ahitub and Ahimelek son of Abiathar were priests; Seraiah was secretary; 18 Benaiah son of Jehoiada was over the Kerethites and Pelethites; and David's sons were priests.[h]

David and Mephibosheth

9 David asked, 'Is there anyone still left of the house of Saul to whom I can show kindness for Jonathan's sake?'

2 Now there was a servant of Saul's household named Ziba. They summoned him to appear before David, and the king said to him, 'Are you Ziba?'

'At your service,' he replied.

3 The king asked, 'Is there no-one still left of the house of Saul to whom I can show God's kindness?'

Ziba answered the king, 'There is still a son of Jonathan; he is lame in both feet.'

4 'Where is he?' the king asked.

Ziba answered, 'He is at the house of Makir son of Ammiel in Lo Debar.'

5 So King David had him brought from Lo Debar, from the house of Makir son of Ammiel.

6 When Mephibosheth son of Jonathan, the son of Saul, came to David, he bowed down to pay him honour.

David said, 'Mephibosheth!'

'At your service,' he replied.

7 'Don't be afraid,' David said to him, 'for I will surely show you kindness for the

---

[a] 3 Or *his control along* [b] 4 Septuagint (see also Dead Sea Scrolls and 1 Chron. 18:4); Masoretic Text *captured seventeen hundred of his charioteers* [c] 8 See some Septuagint manuscripts (see also 1 Chron. 18:8); Hebrew *Betah*. [d] 9 Hebrew *Toi*, a variant of *Tou*; also in verse 10 [e] 10 A variant of *Hadoram* [f] 12 Some Hebrew manuscripts, Septuagint and Syriac (see also 1 Chron. 18:11); most Hebrew manuscripts *Aram* [g] 13 A few Hebrew manuscripts, Septuagint and Syriac (see also 1 Chron. 18:12); most Hebrew manuscripts *Aram* (that is, Arameans) [h] 18 Or *were chief officials* (see Septuagint and Targum; see also 1 Chron. 18:17)

sake of your father Jonathan. I will restore to you all the land that belonged to your grandfather Saul, and you will always eat at my table.'

8Mephibosheth bowed down and said, 'What is your servant, that you should notice a dead dog like me?'

9Then the king summoned Ziba, Saul's steward, and said to him, 'I have given your master's grandson everything that belonged to Saul and his family. 10You and your sons and your servants are to farm the land for him and bring in the crops, so that your master's grandson may be provided for. And Mephibosheth, grandson of your master, will always eat at my table.' (Now Ziba had fifteen sons and twenty servants.)

11Then Ziba said to the king, 'Your servant will do whatever my lord the king commands his servant to do.' So Mephibosheth ate at David's*a* table like one of the king's sons.

12Mephibosheth had a young son named Mika, and all the members of Ziba's household were servants of Mephibosheth. 13And Mephibosheth lived in Jerusalem, because he always ate at the king's table; he was lame in both feet.

David defeats the Ammonites

10 In the course of time, the king of the Ammonites died, and his son Hanun succeeded him as king. 2David thought, 'I will show kindness to Hanun son of Nahash, just as his father showed kindness to me.' So David sent a delegation to express his sympathy to Hanun concerning his father.

When David's men came to the land of the Ammonites, 3the Ammonite commanders said to Hanun their lord, 'Do you think David is honouring your father by sending envoys to you to express sympathy? Hasn't David sent them to you only to explore the city and spy it out and overthrow it?' 4So Hanun seized David's envoys, shaved off half of each man's beard, cut off their garments at the buttocks, and sent them away.

5When David was told about this, he sent messengers to meet the men, for they

Beards
2 Samuel 10:4

A beard was a symbol of a man's honour and masculinity. They were shaved only in times of mourning, so to have just half of your beard shaved away would have been extremely embarrassing. But what the Ammonites did to the clothes of David's men made it all doubly humiliating. Showing certain parts of the body was considered shameful; normally it was just prisoners of war who would have their robes cut so short that their buttocks showed.

were greatly humiliated. The king said, 'Stay at Jericho till your beards have grown, and then come back.'

6When the Ammonites realised that they had become obnoxious to David, they hired twenty thousand Aramean foot soldiers from Beth Rehob and Zobah, as well as the king of Maakah with a thousand men, and also twelve thousand men from Tob.

7On hearing this, David sent Joab out with the entire army of fighting men. 8The Ammonites came out and drew up in battle formation at the entrance of their city gate, while the Arameans of Zobah and Rehob and the men of Tob and Maakah were by themselves in the open country.

9Joab saw that there were battle lines in front of him and behind him; so he selected some of the best troops in Israel and deployed them against the Arameans. 10He put the rest of the men under the command of Abishai his brother and deployed them against the Ammonites. 11Joab said, 'If the Arameans are too strong for me, then you are to come to my rescue;

a 11 Septuagint; Hebrew *my*

but if the Ammonites are too strong for you, then I will come to rescue you. 12Be strong, and let us fight bravely for our people and the cities of our God. The LORD will do what is good in his sight.'

13Then Joab and the troops with him advanced to fight the Arameans, and they fled before him. 14When the Ammonites realised that the Arameans were fleeing, they fled before Abishai and went inside the city. So Joab returned from fighting the Ammonites and came to Jerusalem.

15After the Arameans saw that they had been routed by Israel, they regrouped. 16Hadadezer had Arameans brought from beyond the River Euphrates; they went to Helam, with Shobak the commander of Hadadezer's army leading them.

17When David was told of this, he gathered all Israel, crossed the Jordan and went to Helam. The Arameans formed their battle lines to meet David and fought against him. 18But they fled before Israel, and David killed seven hundred of their charioteers and forty thousand of their foot soldiers.[a] He also struck down Shobak the commander of their army, and he died there. 19When all the kings who were vassals of Hadadezer saw that they had been routed by Israel, they made peace with the Israelites and became subject to them.

So the Arameans were afraid to help the Ammonites any more.

David and Bathsheba

11 In the spring, at the time when kings go off to war, David sent Joab out with the king's men and the whole Israelite army. They destroyed the Ammonites and besieged Rabbah. But David remained in Jerusalem.

2One evening David got up from his bed and walked around on the roof of the palace. From the roof he saw a woman washing. The woman was very beautiful, 3and David sent someone to find out about her. The man said, 'She is Bathsheba, the daughter of Eliam and the wife of Uriah the Hittite.' 4Then David sent messengers to get her. She came to him, and he slept with her. (Now she was purifying herself from her monthly uncleanness.) Then she went back home. 5The woman conceived and sent word to David, saying, 'I am pregnant.'

6So David sent this word to Joab: 'Send me Uriah the Hittite.' And Joab sent him to David. 7When Uriah came to him, David asked him how Joab was, how the soldiers were and how the war was going. 8Then David said to Uriah, 'Go down to your house and wash your feet.' So Uriah left the palace, and a gift from the king was sent after him. 9But Uriah slept at the entrance to the palace with all his master's servants and did not go down to his house.

10David was told, 'Uriah did not go home.' So he asked Uriah, 'Haven't you just come from a military campaign? Why didn't you go home?'

11Uriah said to David, 'The ark and Israel and Judah are staying in tents,[b] and my commander Joab and my lord's men are camped in the open country. How could I go to my house to eat and drink and make love to my wife? As surely as you live, I will not do such a thing!'

12Then David said to him, 'Stay here one more day, and tomorrow I will send you back.' So Uriah remained in Jerusalem that day and the next. 13At David's invitation, he ate and drank with him, and David made him drunk. But in the evening Uriah went out to sleep on his mat among his master's servants; he did not go home.

14In the morning David wrote a letter to Joab and sent it with Uriah. 15In it he wrote, 'Put Uriah out in front where the fighting is fiercest. Then withdraw from him so that he will be struck down and die.'

16So while Joab had the city under siege, he put Uriah at a place where he knew the strongest defenders were. 17When the men of the city came out and fought against Joab, some of the men in David's army fell; moreover, Uriah the Hittite died.

18Joab sent David a full account of the battle. 19He instructed the messenger: 'When you have finished giving the king this account of the battle, 20the king's anger may flare up, and he may ask you, "Why did you get so close to the city to fight? Didn't you know they would shoot arrows from the

---

[a] 18 Some Septuagint manuscripts (see also 1 Chron. 19:18); Hebrew *horsemen* [b] 11 Or *staying at Sukkoth*

wall? ²¹Who killed Abimelek son of Jerub-Besheth?*ᵃ* Didn't a woman drop an upper millstone on him from the wall, so that he died in Thebez? Why did you get so close to the wall?" If he asks you this, then say to him, "Moreover, your servant Uriah the Hittite is dead."'

²²The messenger set out, and when he arrived he told David everything Joab had sent him to say. ²³The messenger said to David, 'The men overpowered us and came out against us in the open, but we drove them back to the entrance of the city gate. ²⁴Then the archers shot arrows at your servants from the wall, and some of the king's men died. Moreover, your servant Uriah the Hittite is dead.'

²⁵David told the messenger, 'Say this to Joab: "Don't let this upset you; the sword devours one as well as another. Press the attack against the city and destroy it." Say this to encourage Joab.'

²⁶When Uriah's wife heard that her husband was dead, she mourned for him. ²⁷After the time of mourning was over, David had her brought to his house, and she became his wife and bore him a son. But the thing David had done displeased the LORD.

Nathan rebukes David

12 The LORD sent Nathan to David. When he came to him, he said, 'There were two men in a certain town, one rich and the other poor. ²The rich man had a very large number of sheep and cattle, ³but the poor man had nothing except one little ewe lamb that he had bought. He raised it, and it grew up with him and his children. It shared his food, drank from his cup and even slept in his arms. It was like a daughter to him.

⁴'Now a traveller came to the rich man, but the rich man refrained from taking one of his own sheep or cattle to prepare a meal for the traveller who had come to him. Instead, he took the ewe lamb that belonged to the poor man and prepared it for the one who had come to him.'

⁵David burned with anger against the man and said to Nathan, 'As surely as the LORD lives, the man who did this must die! ⁶He must pay for that lamb four times over, because he did such a thing and had no pity.'

⁷Then Nathan said to David, 'You are the man! This is what the LORD, the God of Israel, says: "I anointed you king over Israel, and I delivered you from the hand of Saul. ⁸I gave your master's house to you, and your master's wives into your arms. I gave you the house of Israel and Judah. And if all this had been too little, I would have given you even more. ⁹Why did you despise the word of the LORD by doing what is evil in his eyes? You struck down Uriah the Hittite with the sword and took his wife to be your own. You killed him with the sword of the Ammonites. ¹⁰Now, therefore, the sword shall never depart from your house, because you despised me and took the wife of Uriah the Hittite to be your own."

¹¹'This is what the LORD says: "Out of your own household I am going to bring calamity on you. Before your very eyes I will take your wives and give them to one who is close to you, and he will sleep with your wives in broad daylight. ¹²You did it in secret, but I will do this thing in broad daylight before all Israel."'

¹³Then David said to Nathan, 'I have sinned against the LORD.'

Nathan replied, 'The LORD has taken away your sin. You are not going to die. ¹⁴But because by doing this you have shown utter contempt for*ᵇ* the LORD, the son born to you will die.'

¹⁵After Nathan had gone home, the LORD struck the child that Uriah's wife had borne to David, and he became ill. ¹⁶David pleaded with God for the child. He fasted and spent the nights lying in sackcloth*ᶜ* on the ground. ¹⁷The elders of his household stood beside him to get him up from the ground, but he refused, and he would not eat any food with them.

¹⁸On the seventh day the child died. David's attendants were afraid to tell him that the child was dead, for they thought, 'While the child was still living, he wouldn't listen to us when we spoke to him. How can

---

ᵃ 21 Also known as *Jerub-Baal* (that is, Gideon)   *ᵇ* 14 An ancient Hebrew scribal tradition; Masoretic Text *for the enemies of*   *ᶜ* 16 Dead Sea Scrolls and Septuagint; Masoretic Text does not have *in sackcloth*.

we now tell him the child is dead? He may do something desperate.'

19David noticed that his attendants were whispering among themselves, and he realised that the child was dead. 'Is the child dead?' he asked.

'Yes,' they replied, 'he is dead.'

20Then David got up from the ground. After he had washed, put on lotions and changed his clothes, he went into the house of the LORD and worshipped. Then he went to his own house, and at his request they served him food, and he ate.

21His attendants asked him, 'Why are you acting in this way? While the child was alive, you fasted and wept, but now that the child is dead, you get up and eat!'

22He answered, 'While the child was still alive, I fasted and wept. I thought, "Who knows? The LORD may be gracious to me and let the child live." 23But now that he is dead, why should I go on fasting? Can I bring him back again? I will go to him, but he will not return to me.'

24Then David comforted his wife Bathsheba, and he went to her and made love to her. She gave birth to a son, and they named him Solomon. The LORD loved him; 25and because the LORD loved him, he sent word through Nathan the prophet to name him Jedidiah.[a]

26Meanwhile Joab fought against Rabbah of the Ammonites and captured the royal citadel. 27Joab then sent messengers to David, saying, 'I have fought against Rabbah and taken its water supply. 28Now muster the rest of the troops and besiege the city and capture it. Otherwise I shall take the city, and it will be named after me.'

29So David mustered the entire army and went to Rabbah, and attacked and captured it. 30David took the crown from their king's[b] head, and it was placed on his own head. It weighed a talent[c] of gold, and it was set with precious stones. David took a great quantity of plunder from the city 31and brought out the people who were there, consigning them to labour with saws and with iron picks and axes, and he made them work at brickmaking.[d] David did this to all

Sign of the times

Crown
2 Samuel 12:30
Metal crowns have been used to signify importance and power for centuries. The practice probably grew from tribal leaders who decorated their turbans or cloth headpieces with jewels and ornaments. Taking someone's crown showed that you were also taking over their power. This crown was incredibly heavy – about 34 kilograms.

the Ammonite towns. Then he and his entire army returned to Jerusalem.

Amnon and Tamar

13 In the course of time, Amnon son of David fell in love with Tamar, the beautiful sister of Absalom son of David.

2Amnon became so obsessed with his sister Tamar that he made himself ill. She was a virgin, and it seemed impossible for him to do anything to her.

3Now Amnon had an advisor named Jonadab son of Shimeah, David's brother. Jonadab was a very shrewd man. 4He asked Amnon, 'Why do you, the king's son, look so haggard morning after morning? Won't you tell me?'

Amnon said to him, 'I'm in love with Tamar, my brother Absalom's sister.'

5'Go to bed and pretend to be ill,' Jonadab said. 'When your father comes to see you, say to him, "I would like my sister Tamar to come and give me something to eat. Let her prepare the food in my sight so that I may watch her and then eat it from her hand."'

6So Amnon lay down and pretended to be ill. When the king came to see him,

---

[a] 25 *Jedidiah* means *loved by the LORD*. [b] 30 Or *from Milkom's* (that is, Molek's) [c] 30 That is, about 34 kilograms
[d] 31 The meaning of the Hebrew for this clause is uncertain.

Amnon said to him, 'I would like my sister Tamar to come and make some special bread in my sight, so that I may eat from her hand.'

7David sent word to Tamar at the palace: 'Go to the house of your brother Amnon and prepare some food for him.' 8So Tamar went to the house of her brother Amnon, who was lying down. She took some dough, kneaded it, made the bread in his sight and baked it. 9Then she took the pan and served him the bread, but he refused to eat.

'Send everyone out of here,' Amnon said. So everyone left him. 10Then Amnon said to Tamar, 'Bring the food here into my bedroom so that I may eat from your hand.' And Tamar took the bread she had prepared and brought it to her brother Amnon in his bedroom. 11But when she took it to him to eat, he grabbed her and said, 'Come to bed with me, my sister.'

12'No, my brother!' she said to him. 'Don't force me! Such a thing should not be done in Israel! Don't do this wicked thing. 13What about me? Where could I get rid of my disgrace? And what about you? You would be like one of the wicked fools in Israel. Please speak to the king; he will not keep me from being married to you.' 14But he refused to listen to her, and since he was stronger than she, he raped her.

15Then Amnon hated her with intense hatred. In fact, he hated her more than he had loved her. Amnon said to her, 'Get up and get out!'

16'No!' she said to him. 'Sending me away would be a greater wrong than what you have already done to me.'

But he refused to listen to her. 17He called his personal servant and said, 'Get this woman out of my sight and bolt the door after her.' 18So his servant put her out and bolted the door after her. She was wearing a richly ornamented*a* robe, for this was the kind of garment the virgin daughters of the king wore. 19Tamar put ashes on her head and tore the ornamented robe she was wearing. She put her hands on her head and went away, weeping aloud as she went.

20Her brother Absalom said to her, 'Has that Amnon, your brother, been with you? Be quiet for now, my sister; he is your brother. Don't take this thing to heart.' And Tamar lived in her brother Absalom's house, a desolate woman.

21When King David heard all this, he was furious. 22And Absalom never spoke to Amnon again; he hated Amnon because he had disgraced his sister Tamar.

Absalom kills Amnon

23Two years later, when Absalom's sheep-shearers were at Baal Hazor near the border of Ephraim, he invited all the king's sons to come there. 24Absalom went to the king and said, 'Your servant has had shearers come. Will the king and his attendants please join me?'

25'No, my son,' the king replied. 'All of us should not go; we would only be a burden to you.' Although Absalom urged him, he still refused to go but gave him his blessing.

26Then Absalom said, 'If not, please let my brother Amnon come with us.'

The king asked him, 'Why should he go with you?' 27But Absalom urged him, so he sent with him Amnon and the rest of the king's sons.

28Absalom ordered his men, 'Listen! When Amnon is in high spirits from drinking wine and I say to you, "Strike Amnon down," then kill him. Don't be afraid. Haven't I given you this order? Be strong and brave.' 29So Absalom's men did to Amnon what Absalom had ordered. Then all the king's sons got up, mounted their mules and fled.

30While they were on their way, the report came to David: 'Absalom has struck down all the king's sons; not one of them is left.' 31The king stood up, tore his clothes and lay down on the ground; and all his attendants stood by with their clothes torn.

32But Jonadab son of Shimeah, David's brother, said, 'My lord should not think that they killed all the princes; only Amnon is dead. This has been Absalom's express intention ever since the day that Amnon raped his sister Tamar. 33My lord the king should not be concerned about the report

---

a 18 The meaning of the Hebrew for this phrase is uncertain; also in verse 19.

that all the king's sons are dead. Only Amnon is dead.'

34Meanwhile, Absalom had fled.

Now the man standing watch looked up and saw many people on the road west of him, coming down the side of the hill. The watchman went and told the king, 'I see men in the direction of Horonaim, on the side of the hill.'[a]

35Jonadab said to the king, 'See, the king's sons have come; it has happened just as your servant said.'

36As he finished speaking, the king's sons came in, wailing loudly. The king, too, and all his attendants wept very bitterly.

37Absalom fled and went to Talmai son of Ammihud, the king of Geshur. But King David mourned many days for his son.

38After Absalom fled and went to Geshur, he stayed there for three years. 39And King David longed to go to Absalom, for he was consoled concerning Amnon's death.

Absalom returns to Jerusalem

14 Joab son of Zeruiah knew that the king's heart longed for Absalom. 2So Joab sent someone to Tekoa and had a wise woman brought from there. He said to her, 'Pretend you are in mourning. Dress in mourning clothes, and don't use any cosmetic lotions. Act like a woman who has spent many days grieving for the dead. 3Then go to the king and speak these words to him.' And Joab put the words in her mouth.

4When the woman from Tekoa went[b] to the king, she fell with her face to the ground to pay him honour, and she said, 'Help me, Your Majesty!'

5The king asked her, 'What is troubling you?'

She said, 'I am a widow; my husband is dead. 6I your servant had two sons. They got into a fight with each other in the field, and no-one was there to separate them. One struck the other and killed him. 7Now the whole clan has risen up against your servant; they say, "Hand over the one who struck his brother down, so that we may put him to death for the life of his brother whom he killed; then we will get rid of the heir as well." They would put out the only burning coal I have left, leaving my husband neither name nor descendant on the face of the earth.'

8The king said to the woman, 'Go home, and I will issue an order on your behalf.'

9But the woman from Tekoa said to him, 'Let my lord the king pardon me and my family, and let the king and his throne be without guilt.'

10The king replied, 'If anyone says anything to you, bring them to me, and they will not bother you again.'

11She said, 'Then let the king invoke the LORD his God to prevent the avenger of blood from adding to the destruction, so that my son shall not be destroyed.'

'As surely as the LORD lives,' he said, 'not one hair of your son's head will fall to the ground.'

12Then the woman said, 'Let your servant speak a word to my lord the king.'

'Speak,' he replied.

13The woman said, 'Why then have you devised a thing like this against the people of God? When the king says this, does he not convict himself, for the king has not brought back his banished son? 14Like water spilled on the ground, which cannot be recovered, so we must die. But that is not what God desires; rather, he devises ways so that a banished person does not remain banished from him.

15'And now I have come to say this to my lord the king because the people have made me afraid. Your servant thought, "I will speak to the king; perhaps he will grant his servant's request. 16Perhaps the king will agree to deliver his servant from the hand of the man who is trying to cut off both me and my son from God's inheritance."

17'And now your servant says, "May the word of my lord the king secure my inheritance, for my lord the king is like an angel of God in discerning good and evil. May the LORD your God be with you."'

18Then the king said to the woman, 'Don't keep from me the answer to what I am going to ask you.'

---

[a] 34 Septuagint; Hebrew does not have this sentence. [b] 4 Many Hebrew manuscripts, Septuagint, Vulgate and Syriac; most Hebrew manuscripts *spoke*

'Let my lord the king speak,' the woman said.

¹⁹The king asked, 'Isn't the hand of Joab with you in all this?'

The woman answered, 'As surely as you live, my lord the king, no-one can turn to the right or to the left from anything my lord the king says. Yes, it was your servant Joab who instructed me to do this and who put all these words into the mouth of your servant. ²⁰Your servant Joab did this to change the present situation. My lord has wisdom like that of an angel of God—he knows everything that happens in the land.'

²¹The king said to Joab, 'Very well, I will do it. Go, bring back the young man Absalom.'

²²Joab fell with his face to the ground to pay him honour, and he blessed the king. Joab said, 'Today your servant knows that he has found favour in your eyes, my lord the king, because the king has granted his servant's request.'

²³Then Joab went to Geshur and brought Absalom back to Jerusalem. ²⁴But the king said, 'He must go to his own house; he must not see my face.' So Absalom went to his own house and did not see the face of the king.

²⁵In all Israel there was not a man so highly praised for his handsome appearance as Absalom. From the top of his head to the sole of his foot there was no blemish in him. ²⁶Whenever he cut the hair of his head—he used to cut his hair once a year because it became too heavy for him—he would weigh it, and its weight was two hundred shekels[a] by the royal standard.

²⁷Three sons and a daughter were born to Absalom. His daughter's name was Tamar, and she became a beautiful woman.

²⁸Absalom lived for two years in Jerusalem without seeing the king's face. ²⁹Then Absalom sent for Joab in order to send him to the king, but Joab refused to come to him. So he sent a second time, but he refused to come. ³⁰Then he said to his servants, 'Look, Joab's field is next to mine, and he has barley there. Go and set it on fire.' So Absalom's servants set the field on fire.

³¹Then Joab did go to Absalom's house, and he said to him, 'Why have your servants set my field on fire?'

³²Absalom said to Joab, 'Look, I sent word to you and said, "Come here so that I can send you to the king to ask, 'Why have I come from Geshur? It would be better for me if I were still there!' " Now then, I want to see the king's face, and if I am guilty of anything, let him put me to death.'

³³So Joab went to the king and told him this. Then the king summoned Absalom, and he came in and bowed down with his face to the ground before the king. And the king kissed Absalom.

Absalom's conspiracy

15 In the course of time, Absalom provided himself with a chariot and horses and with fifty men to run ahead of him. ²He would get up early and stand by the side of the road leading to the city gate. Whenever anyone came with a complaint to be placed before the king for a decision, Absalom would call out to him, 'What town are you from?' He would answer, 'Your servant is from one of the tribes of Israel.' ³Then Absalom would say to him, 'Look, your claims are valid and proper, but there is no representative of the king to hear you.' ⁴And Absalom would add, 'If only I were appointed judge in the land! Then everyone who has a complaint or case could come to me and I would see that they receive justice.'

⁵Also, whenever anyone approached him to bow down before him, Absalom would reach out his hand, take hold of him and kiss him. ⁶Absalom behaved in this way towards all the Israelites who came to the king asking for justice, and so he stole the hearts of the people of Israel.

⁷At the end of four[b] years, Absalom said to the king, 'Let me go to Hebron and fulfil a vow I made to the LORD. ⁸While your servant was living at Geshur in Aram, I made this vow: "If the LORD takes me back to Jerusalem, I will worship the LORD in Hebron." '[c]

⁹The king said to him, 'Go in peace.' So he went to Hebron.

---

[a] 26 That is, about 2.3 kilograms   [b] 7 Some Septuagint manuscripts, Syriac and Josephus; Hebrew *forty*   [c] 8 Some Septuagint manuscripts; Hebrew does not have *in Hebron*.

10Then Absalom sent secret messengers throughout the tribes of Israel to say, 'As soon as you hear the sound of the trumpets, then say, "Absalom is king in Hebron."' 11Two hundred men from Jerusalem had accompanied Absalom. They had been invited as guests and went quite innocently, knowing nothing about the matter. 12While Absalom was offering sacrifices, he also sent for Ahithophel the Gilonite, David's counsellor, to come from Giloh, his home town. And so the conspiracy gained strength, and Absalom's following kept on increasing.

David flees

13A messenger came and told David, 'The hearts of the people of Israel are with Absalom.'

14Then David said to all his officials who were with him in Jerusalem, 'Come! We must flee, or none of us will escape from Absalom. We must leave immediately, or he will move quickly to overtake us and bring ruin on us and put the city to the sword.'

15The king's officials answered him, 'Your servants are ready to do whatever our lord the king chooses.'

16The king set out, with his entire household following him; but he left ten concubines to take care of the palace. 17So the king set out, with all the people following him, and they halted at the edge of the city. 18All his men marched past him, along with all the Kerethites and Pelethites; and all the six hundred Gittites who had accompanied him from Gath marched before the king.

19The king said to Ittai the Gittite, 'Why should you come along with us? Go back and stay with King Absalom. You are a foreigner, an exile from your homeland. 20You came only yesterday. And today shall I make you wander about with us, when I do not know where I am going? Go back, and take your people with you. May the LORD show you kindness and faithfulness.'[a]

21But Ittai replied to the king, 'As surely as the LORD lives, and as my lord the king lives, wherever my lord the king may be, whether it means life or death, there will your servant be.'

22David said to Ittai, 'Go ahead, march on.' So Ittai the Gittite marched on with all his men and the families that were with him.

23The whole countryside wept aloud as all the people passed by. The king also crossed the Kidron Valley, and all the people moved on towards the wilderness.

24Zadok was there, too, and all the Levites who were with him were carrying the ark of the covenant of God. They set down the ark of God, and Abiathar offered sacrifices until all the people had finished leaving the city.

25Then the king said to Zadok, 'Take the ark of God back into the city. If I find favour in the LORD's eyes, he will bring me back and let me see it and his dwelling-place again. 26But if he says, "I am not pleased with you," then I am ready; let him do to me whatever seems good to him.'

27The king also said to Zadok the priest, 'Do you understand? Go back to the city with my blessing. Take your son Ahimaaz with you, and also Abiathar's son Jonathan. You and Abiathar return with your two sons. 28I will wait at the fords in the wilderness until word comes from you to inform me.' 29So Zadok and Abiathar took the ark of God back to Jerusalem and stayed there.

30But David continued up the Mount of Olives, weeping as he went; his head was covered and he was barefoot. All the people with him covered their heads too and were weeping as they went up. 31Now David had been told, 'Ahithophel is among the conspirators with Absalom.' So David prayed, 'LORD, turn Ahithophel's counsel into foolishness.'

32When David arrived at the summit, where people used to worship God, Hushai the Arkite was there to meet him, his robe torn and dust on his head. 33David said to him, 'If you go with me, you will be a burden to me. 34But if you return to the city and say to Absalom, "Your Majesty, I will be your servant; I was your father's servant in the past, but now I will be your servant," then you can help me by frustrating Ahithophel's advice. 35Won't the priests Zadok and Abiathar be there with you? Tell them anything you hear in the king's palace.

---

[a] 20 Septuagint; Hebrew *May kindness and faithfulness be with you*

36Their two sons, Ahimaaz son of Zadok and Jonathan son of Abiathar, are there with them. Send them to me with anything you hear.'

37So Hushai, David's confidant, arrived at Jerusalem as Absalom was entering the city.

David and Ziba

16 When David had gone a short distance beyond the summit, there was Ziba, the steward of Mephibosheth, waiting to meet him. He had a string of donkeys saddled and loaded with two hundred loaves of bread, a hundred cakes of raisins, a hundred cakes of figs and a skin of wine.

2The king asked Ziba, 'Why have you brought these?'

Ziba answered, 'The donkeys are for the king's household to ride on, the bread and fruit are for the men to eat, and the wine is to refresh those who become exhausted in the wilderness.'

3The king then asked, 'Where is your master's grandson?'

Ziba said to him, 'He is staying in Jerusalem, because he thinks, "Today the house of Israel will restore to me my grandfather's kingdom."'

4Then the king said to Ziba, 'All that belonged to Mephibosheth is now yours.'

'I humbly bow,' Ziba said. 'May I find favour in your eyes, my lord the king.'

Shimei curses David

5As King David approached Bahurim, a man from the same clan as Saul's family came out from there. His name was Shimei son of Gera, and he cursed as he came out. 6He pelted David and all the king's officials with stones, though all the troops and the special guard were on David's right and left. 7As he cursed, Shimei said, 'Get out, get out, you murderer, you scoundrel! 8The LORD has repaid you for all the blood you shed in the household of Saul, in whose place you have reigned. The LORD has given the kingdom into the hands of your son Absalom. You have come to ruin because you are a murderer!'

9Then Abishai son of Zeruiah said to the king, 'Why should this dead dog curse my lord the king? Let me go over and cut off his head.'

10But the king said, 'What does this have to do with you, you sons of Zeruiah? If he is cursing because the LORD said to him, "Curse David," who can ask, "Why do you do this?"'

11David then said to Abishai and all his officials, 'My son, who is of my own flesh, is trying to take my life. How much more, then, this Benjaminite! Leave him alone; let him curse, for the LORD has told him to. 12It may be that the LORD will look upon my misery and restore to me his covenant blessing instead of his curse today.'

13So David and his men continued along the road while Shimei was going along the hillside opposite him, cursing as he went and throwing stones at him and showering him with dirt. 14The king and all the people with him arrived at their destination exhausted. And there he refreshed himself.

The advice of Hushai and Ahithophel

15Meanwhile, Absalom and all the men of Israel came to Jerusalem, and Ahithophel was with him. 16Then Hushai the Arkite, David's confidant, went to Absalom and said to him, 'Long live the king! Long live the king!'

17Absalom said to Hushai, 'So this is the love you show your friend? If he's your friend, why didn't you go with him?'

18Hushai said to Absalom, 'No, the one chosen by the LORD, by these people and by all the men of Israel—his I will be, and I will remain with him. 19Furthermore, whom should I serve? Should I not serve the son? Just as I served your father, so I will serve you.'

20Absalom said to Ahithophel, 'Give us your advice. What should we do?'

21Ahithophel answered, 'Sleep with your father's concubines whom he left to take care of the palace. Then all Israel will hear that you have made yourself obnoxious to your father, and the hands of everyone with you will be more resolute.' 22So they pitched a tent for Absalom on the roof, and he slept with his father's concubines in the sight of all Israel.

23Now in those days the advice Ahithophel gave was like that of one who enquires

2 Samuel 17:23

of God. That was how both David and Absalom regarded all of Ahithophel's advice.

17 Ahithophel said to Absalom, 'I would[a] choose twelve thousand men and set out tonight in pursuit of David. 2 I would attack him while he is weary and weak. I would strike him with terror, and then all the people with him will flee. I would strike down only the king 3 and bring all the people back to you. The death of the man you seek will mean the return of all; all the people will be unharmed.' 4 This plan seemed good to Absalom and to all the elders of Israel.

5 But Absalom said, 'Summon also Hushai the Arkite, so that we can hear what he has to say as well.' 6 When Hushai came to him, Absalom said, 'Ahithophel has given this advice. Should we do what he says? If not, give us your opinion.'

7 Hushai replied to Absalom, 'The advice Ahithophel has given is not good this time. 8 You know your father and his men; they are fighters, and as fierce as a wild bear robbed of her cubs. Besides, your father is an experienced fighter; he will not spend the night with the troops. 9 Even now, he is hidden in a cave or some other place. If he should attack your troops first,[b] whoever hears about it will say, "There has been a slaughter among the troops who follow Absalom." 10 Then even the bravest soldier, whose heart is like the heart of a lion, will melt with fear, for all Israel knows that your father is a fighter and that those with him are brave.

11 'So I advise you: let all Israel, from Dan to Beersheba—as numerous as the sand on the seashore—be gathered to you, with you yourself leading them into battle. 12 Then we will attack him wherever he may be found, and we will fall on him as dew settles on the ground. Neither he nor any of his men will be left alive. 13 If he withdraws into a city, then all Israel will bring ropes to that city, and we will drag it down to the valley until not so much as a pebble is left.'

14 Absalom and all the men of Israel said, 'The advice of Hushai the Arkite is better than that of Ahithophel.' For the LORD had determined to frustrate the good advice of Ahithophel in order to bring disaster on Absalom.

15 Hushai told Zadok and Abiathar, the priests, 'Ahithophel has advised Absalom and the elders of Israel to do such and such, but I have advised them to do so and so. 16 Now send a message at once and tell David, "Do not spend the night at the fords in the wilderness; cross over without fail, or the king and all the people with him will be swallowed up."'

17 Jonathan and Ahimaaz were staying at En Rogel. A female servant was to go and inform them, and they were to go and tell King David, for they could not risk being seen entering the city. 18 But a young man saw them and told Absalom. So the two of them left at once and went to the house of a man in Bahurim. He had a well in his courtyard, and they climbed down into it. 19 His wife took a covering and spread it out over the opening of the well and scattered corn over it. No-one knew anything about it.

20 When Absalom's men came to the woman at the house, they asked, 'Where are Ahimaaz and Jonathan?'

The woman answered them, 'They crossed over the brook.'[c] The men searched but found no-one, so they returned to Jerusalem.

21 After they had gone, the two climbed out of the well and went to inform King David. They said to him, 'Set out and cross the river at once; Ahithophel has advised such and such against you.' 22 So David and all the people with him set out and crossed the Jordan. By daybreak, no-one was left who had not crossed the Jordan.

23 When Ahithophel saw that his advice had not been followed, he saddled his donkey and set out for his house in his home town. He put his house in order and then hanged himself. So he died and was buried in his father's tomb.

---

[a] 1 Or *Let me* [b] 9 Or *When some of the men fall at the first attack* [c] 20 Or *'They passed by the sheepfold towards the water.'*

Absalom's death

24 David went to Mahanaim, and Absalom crossed the Jordan with all the men of Israel. 25 Absalom had appointed Amasa over the army in place of Joab. Amasa was the son of Jether,[a] an Ishmaelite[b] who had married Abigal, the daughter of Nahash and sister of Zeruiah the mother of Joab. 26 The Israelites and Absalom camped in the land of Gilead.

27 When David came to Mahanaim, Shobi son of Nahash from Rabbah of the Ammonites, and Makir son of Ammiel from Lo Debar, and Barzillai the Gileadite from Rogelim 28 brought bedding and bowls and articles of pottery. They also brought wheat and barley, flour and roasted grain, beans and lentils,[c] 29 honey and curds, sheep, and cheese from cows' milk for David and his people to eat. For they said, 'The people have become exhausted and hungry and thirsty in the wilderness.'

18 David mustered the men who were with him and appointed over them commanders of thousands and commanders of hundreds. 2 David sent out his troops, a third under the command of Joab, a third under Joab's brother Abishai son of Zeruiah, and a third under Ittai the Gittite. The king told the troops, 'I myself will surely march out with you.'

3 But the men said, 'You must not go out; if we are forced to flee, they won't care about us. Even if half of us die, they won't care; but you are worth ten thousand of us.[d] It would be better now for you to give us support from the city.'

4 The king answered, 'I will do whatever seems best to you.'

So the king stood beside the gate while all his men marched out in units of hundreds and of thousands. 5 The king commanded Joab, Abishai and Ittai, 'Be gentle with the young man Absalom for my sake.' And all the troops heard the king giving orders concerning Absalom to each of the commanders.

6 David's army marched out of the city to fight Israel, and the battle took place in the forest of Ephraim. 7 There Israel's troops were routed by David's men, and the casualties that day were great—twenty thousand men. 8 The battle spread out over the whole countryside, and the forest swallowed up more men that day than the sword.

9 Now Absalom happened to meet David's men. He was riding his mule, and as the mule went under the thick branches of a large oak, Absalom's hair got caught in the tree. He was left hanging in mid-air, while the mule he was riding kept on going.

10 When one of the men saw what had happened, he told Joab, 'I have just seen Absalom hanging in an oak tree.'

11 Joab said to the man who had told him this, 'What! You saw him? Why didn't you strike him to the ground right there? Then I would have had to give you ten shekels[e] of silver and a warrior's belt.'

12 But the man replied, 'Even if a thousand shekels[f] were weighed out into my hands, I would not lay a hand on the king's son. In our hearing the king commanded you and Abishai and Ittai, "Protect the young man Absalom for my sake."[g] 13 And if I had put my life in jeopardy[h]—and nothing is hidden from the king—you would have kept your distance from me.'

14 Joab said, 'I am not going to wait like this for you.' So he took three javelins in his hand and plunged them into Absalom's heart while Absalom was still alive in the oak tree. 15 And ten of Joab's armour-bearers surrounded Absalom, struck him and killed him.

16 Then Joab sounded the trumpet, and the troops stopped pursuing Israel, for Joab halted them. 17 They took Absalom, threw him into a big pit in the forest and piled up a large heap of rocks over him. Meanwhile, all the Israelites fled to their homes.

18 During his life-time Absalom had taken a pillar and erected it in the King's Valley

---

[a] 25 Hebrew *Ithra*, a variant of *Jether*   [b] 25 Some Septuagint manuscripts (see also 1 Chron. 2:17); Hebrew and other Septuagint manuscripts *Israelite*   [c] 28 Most Septuagint manuscripts and Syriac; Hebrew *lentils, and roasted grain*
[d] 3 Two Hebrew manuscripts, some Septuagint manuscripts and Vulgate; most Hebrew manuscripts *care; for now there are ten thousand like us*   [e] 11 That is, about 115 grams   [f] 12 That is, about 11 kilograms   [g] 12 A few Hebrew manuscripts, Septuagint, Vulgate and Syriac; most Hebrew manuscripts may be translated *Absalom, whoever you may be.*   [h] 13 Or *Otherwise, if I had acted treacherously towards him*

Tombs
2 Samuel 18:17
Usually dead bodies were treated with great respect. Families would own tombs where successive generations were laid when they died. These tombs could be natural caves or cut into the hillside. Absalom's body was given a criminal's burial: thrown into a pit and covered in stones.

as a monument to himself, for he thought, 'I have no son to carry on the memory of my name.' He named the pillar after himself, and it is called Absalom's Monument to this day.

David mourns
19Now Ahimaaz son of Zadok said, 'Let me run and take the news to the king that the LORD has vindicated him by delivering him from the hand of his enemies.'

20'You are not the one to take the news today,' Joab told him. 'You may take the news another time, but you must not do so today, because the king's son is dead.'

21Then Joab said to a Cushite, 'Go, tell the king what you have seen.' The Cushite bowed down before Joab and ran off.

22Ahimaaz son of Zadok again said to Joab, 'Come what may, please let me run behind the Cushite.'

But Joab replied, 'My son, why do you want to go? You don't have any news that will bring you a reward.'

23He said, 'Come what may, I want to run.'

So Joab said, 'Run!' Then Ahimaaz ran by way of the plain[a] and outran the Cushite.

24While David was sitting between the inner and outer gates, the watchman went up to the roof of the gateway by the wall. As he looked out, he saw a man running alone. 25The watchman called out to the king and reported it.

The king said, 'If he is alone, he must have good news.' And the runner came closer and closer.

26Then the watchman saw another runner, and he called down to the gatekeeper, 'Look, another man running alone!'

The king said, 'He must be bringing good news, too.'

27The watchman said, 'It seems to me that the first one runs like Ahimaaz son of Zadok.'

'He's a good man,' the king said. 'He comes with good news.'

28Then Ahimaaz called out to the king, 'All is well!' He bowed down before the king with his face to the ground and said, 'Praise be to the LORD your God! He has delivered up those who lifted their hands against my lord the king.'

29The king asked, 'Is the young man Absalom safe?'

Ahimaaz answered, 'I saw great confusion just as Joab was about to send the king's servant and me, your servant, but I don't know what it was.'

30The king said, 'Stand aside and wait here.' So he stepped aside and stood there.

31Then the Cushite arrived and said, 'My lord the king, hear the good news! The LORD has vindicated you today by delivering you from the hand of all who rose up against you.'

32The king asked the Cushite, 'Is the young man Absalom safe?'

The Cushite replied, 'May the enemies of my lord the king and all who rise up to harm you be like that young man.'

*33The king was shaken. He went up to the room over the gateway and wept. As he went, he said: 'O my son Absalom! My son, my son Absalom! If only I had died instead of you—O Absalom, my son, my son!'

19
*Joab was told, 'The king is weeping and mourning for Absalom.'

---

a 23 That is, the plain of the Jordan
* 18:33 is numbered 19:1 in Hebrew texts.   * 19:1-43 is numbered 19:2-44 in Hebrew texts.

²And for the whole army the victory that day was turned into mourning, because on that day the troops heard it said, 'The king is grieving for his son.' ³The men stole into the city that day as men steal in who are ashamed when they flee from battle. ⁴The king covered his face and cried aloud, 'O my son Absalom! O Absalom, my son, my son!'

⁵Then Joab went into the house to the king and said, 'Today you have humiliated all your men, who have just saved your life and the lives of your sons and daughters and the lives of your wives and concubines. ⁶You love those who hate you and hate those who love you. You have made it clear today that the commanders and their men mean nothing to you. I see that you would be pleased if Absalom were alive today and all of us were dead. ⁷Now go out and encourage your men. I swear by the LORD that if you don't go out, not a man will be left with you by nightfall. This will be worse for you than all the calamities that have come on you from your youth till now.'

⁸So the king got up and took his seat in the gateway. When the men were told, 'The king is sitting in the gateway,' they all came before him.

Meanwhile, the Israelites had fled to their homes.

David returns to Jerusalem

⁹Throughout the tribes of Israel, all the people were arguing among themselves, saying, 'The king delivered us from the hand of our enemies; he is the one who rescued us from the hand of the Philistines. But now he has fled the country to escape from Absalom; ¹⁰and Absalom, whom we anointed to rule over us, has died in battle. So why do you say nothing about bringing the king back?'

¹¹King David sent this message to Zadok and Abiathar, the priests: 'Ask the elders of Judah, "Why should you be the last to bring the king back to his palace, since what is being said throughout Israel has reached the king at his quarters? ¹²You are my relatives, my own flesh and blood. So why should you be the last to bring back the king?" ¹³And say to Amasa, "Are you not my own flesh and blood? May God deal with me, be it ever so severely, if you are not the commander of my army for life in place of Joab."'

¹⁴He won over the hearts of the men of Judah so that they were all of one accord. They sent word to the king, 'Return, you and all your men.' ¹⁵Then the king returned and went as far as the Jordan.

Now the men of Judah had come to Gilgal to go out and meet the king and bring him across the Jordan. ¹⁶Shimei son of Gera, the Benjaminite from Bahurim, hurried down with the men of Judah to meet King David. ¹⁷With him were a thousand Benjaminites, along with Ziba, the steward of Saul's household, and his fifteen sons and twenty servants. They rushed to the Jordan, where the king was. ¹⁸They crossed at the ford to take the king's household over and to do whatever he wished.

When Shimei son of Gera crossed the Jordan, he fell prostrate before the king ¹⁹and said to him, 'May my lord not hold me guilty. Do not remember how your servant did wrong on the day my lord the king left Jerusalem. May the king put it out of his mind. ²⁰For I your servant know that I have sinned, but today I have come here as the first of the whole house of Joseph to come down and meet my lord the king.'

²¹Then Abishai son of Zeruiah said, 'Shouldn't Shimei be put to death for this? He cursed the LORD's anointed.'

²²David replied, 'What does this have to do with you, you sons of Zeruiah? What right do you have to interfere? Should anyone be put to death in Israel today? Don't I know that today I am king over Israel?' ²³So the king said to Shimei, 'You shall not die.' And the king promised him on oath.

²⁴Mephibosheth, Saul's grandson, also went down to meet the king. He had not taken care of his feet or trimmed his moustache or washed his clothes from the day the king left until the day he returned safely. ²⁵When he came from Jerusalem to meet the king, the king asked him, 'Why didn't you go with me, Mephibosheth?'

²⁶He said, 'My lord the king, since I your servant am lame, I said, "I will have my donkey saddled and will ride on it, so that I can go with the king." But Ziba my servant

betrayed me. ²⁷And he has slandered your servant to my lord the king. My lord the king is like an angel of God; so do whatever you wish. ²⁸All my grandfather's descendants deserved nothing but death from my lord the king, but you gave your servant a place among those who eat at your table. So what right do I have to make any more appeals to the king?'

²⁹The king said to him, 'Why say more? I order you and Ziba to divide the land.'

³⁰Mephibosheth said to the king, 'Let him take everything, now that my lord the king has returned home safely.'

³¹Barzillai the Gileadite also came down from Rogelim to cross the Jordan with the king and to send him on his way from there. ³²Now Barzillai was very old, eighty years of age. He had provided for the king during his stay in Mahanaim, for he was a very wealthy man. ³³The king said to Barzillai, 'Cross over with me and stay with me in Jerusalem, and I will provide for you.'

³⁴But Barzillai answered the king, 'How many more years shall I live, that I should go up to Jerusalem with the king? ³⁵I am now eighty years old. Can I tell the difference between what is enjoyable and what is not? Can your servant taste what he eats and drinks? Can I still hear the voices of male and female singers? Why should your servant be an added burden to my lord the king? ³⁶Your servant will cross over the Jordan with the king for a short distance, but why should the king reward me in this way? ³⁷Let your servant return, that I may die in my own town near the tomb of my father and mother. But here is your servant Kimham. Let him cross over with my lord the king. Do for him whatever you wish.'

³⁸The king said, 'Kimham shall cross over with me, and I will do for him whatever you wish. And anything you desire from me I will do for you.'

³⁹So all the people crossed the Jordan, and then the king crossed over. The king kissed Barzillai and bade him farewell, and Barzillai returned to his home.

⁴⁰When the king crossed over to Gilgal, Kimham crossed with him. All the troops of Judah and half the troops of Israel had taken the king over.

⁴¹Soon all the men of Israel were coming to the king and saying to him, 'Why did our brothers, the men of Judah, steal the king away and bring him and his household across the Jordan, together with all his men?'

⁴²All the men of Judah answered the men of Israel, 'We did this because the king is closely related to us. Why are you angry about it? Have we eaten any of the king's provisions? Have we taken anything for ourselves?'

⁴³Then the men of Israel answered the men of Judah, 'We have ten shares in the king; so we have a greater claim on David than you have. Why then do you treat us with contempt? Weren't we the first to speak of bringing back our king?'

But the men of Judah responded even more harshly than the men of Israel.

Sheba rebels against David

20 Now a troublemaker named Sheba son of Bikri, a Benjaminite, happened to be there. He sounded the trumpet and shouted,

'We have no share in David,
  no part in Jesse's son!
Everyone to your tents, Israel!'

²So all the men of Israel deserted David to follow Sheba son of Bikri. But the men of Judah stayed by their king all the way from the Jordan to Jerusalem.

³When David returned to his palace in Jerusalem, he took the ten concubines he had left to take care of the palace and put them in a house under guard. He provided for them but had no sexual relations with them. They were kept in confinement till the day of their death, living as widows.

⁴Then the king said to Amasa, 'Summon the men of Judah to come to me within three days, and be here yourself.' ⁵But when Amasa went to summon Judah, he took longer than the time the king had set for him.

⁶David said to Abishai, 'Now Sheba son of Bikri will do us more harm than Absalom did. Take your master's men and pursue him, or he will find fortified cities and

escape from us.'ᵃ ⁷So Joab's men and the Kerethites and Pelethites and all the mighty warriors went out under the command of Abishai. They marched out from Jerusalem to pursue Sheba son of Bikri.

⁸While they were at the great rock in Gibeon, Amasa came to meet them. Joab was wearing his military tunic, and strapped over it at his waist was a belt with a dagger in its sheath. As he stepped forward, it dropped out of its sheath. ⁹Joab said to Amasa, 'How are you, my brother?' Then Joab took Amasa by the beard with his right hand to kiss him. ¹⁰Amasa was not on his guard against the dagger in Joab's hand, and Joab plunged it into his belly, and his intestines spilled out on the ground. Without being stabbed again, Amasa died. Then Joab and his brother Abishai pursued Sheba son of Bikri.

¹¹One of Joab's men stood beside Amasa and said, 'Whoever favours Joab, and whoever is for David, let him follow Joab!' ¹²Amasa lay wallowing in his blood in the middle of the road, and the man saw that all the troops came to a halt there. When he realised that everyone who came up to Amasa stopped, he dragged him from the road into a field and threw a garment over him. ¹³After Amasa had been removed from the road, everyone went on with Joab to pursue Sheba son of Bikri.

¹⁴Sheba passed through all the tribes of Israel to Abel Beth Maakah and through the entire region of the Bikrites,ᵇ who gathered together and followed him. ¹⁵All the troops with Joab came and besieged Sheba in Abel Beth Maakah. They built a siege ramp up to the city, and it stood against the outer fortifications. While they were battering the wall to bring it down, ¹⁶a wise woman called from the city, 'Listen! Listen! Tell Joab to come here so that I can speak to him.' ¹⁷He went towards her, and she asked, 'Are you Joab?'

'I am,' he answered.

She said, 'Listen to what your servant has to say.'

'I'm listening,' he said.

¹⁸She continued, 'Long ago they used to say, "Get your answer at Abel," and that settled it. ¹⁹We are the peaceful and faithful in Israel. You are trying to destroy a city that is a mother in Israel. Why do you want to swallow up the LORD's inheritance?'

²⁰'Far be it from me!' Joab replied, 'Far be it from me to swallow up or destroy! ²¹That is not the case. A man named Sheba son of Bikri, from the hill country of Ephraim, has lifted up his hand against the king, against David. Hand over this one man, and I'll withdraw from the city.'

The woman said to Joab, 'His head will be thrown to you from the wall.'

²²Then the woman went to all the people with her wise advice, and they cut off the head of Sheba son of Bikri and threw it to Joab. So he sounded the trumpet, and his men dispersed from the city, each returning to his home. And Joab went back to the king in Jerusalem.

David's officials

²³Joab was over Israel's entire army; Benaiah son of Jehoiada was over the Kerethites and Pelethites; ²⁴Adoniramᶜ was in charge of forced labour; Jehoshaphat son of Ahilud was recorder; ²⁵Sheva was secretary; Zadok and Abiathar were priests; ²⁶and Ira the Jairiteᵈ was David's priest.

The Gibeonites avenged

21 During the reign of David, there was a famine for three successive years; so David sought the face of the LORD. The LORD said, 'It is on account of Saul and his blood-stained house; it is because he put the Gibeonites to death.'

²The king summoned the Gibeonites and spoke to them. (Now the Gibeonites were not a part of Israel but were survivors of the Amorites; the Israelites had sworn to [spare] them, but Saul in his zeal for Israel and Judah had tried to annihilate them.) ³David asked the Gibeonites, 'What shall I do for you? How shall I make atonement so that you will bless the LORD's inheritance?'

ᵃ 6 Or *and do us serious injury* ᵇ 14 See Septuagint and Vulgate; Hebrew *Berites*. ᶜ 24 Some Septuagint manuscripts (see also 1 Kings 4:6 and 5:14); Hebrew *Adoram* ᵈ 26 Hebrew; some Septuagint manuscripts and Syriac (see also 2 Samuel 23:38) *Ithrite*

People and Places

Gibeonites
2 Samuel 21:1

Joshua had made a covenant with the Gibeonites many years before, granting them protection and allowing them to live (Joshua 9:25–27). Saul broke this covenant when he put the Gibeonites to death; the details of this event aren't given in the Bible. David makes sure that justice is done for the Gibeonites by allowing them to kill some of Saul's descendants.

---

⁴The Gibeonites answered him, 'We have no right to demand silver or gold from Saul or his family, nor do we have the right to put anyone in Israel to death.'

'What do you want me to do for you?' David asked.

⁵They answered the king, 'As for the man who destroyed us and plotted against us so that we have been decimated and have no place anywhere in Israel, ⁶let seven of his male descendants be given to us to be killed and their bodies exposed before the LORD at Gibeah of Saul—the LORD's chosen one.'

So the king said, 'I will give them to you.'

⁷The king spared Mephibosheth son of Jonathan, the son of Saul, because of the oath before the LORD between David and Jonathan son of Saul. ⁸But the king took Armoni and Mephibosheth, the two sons of Aiah's daughter Rizpah, whom she had borne to Saul, together with the five sons of Saul's daughter Merab,ᵃ whom she had borne to Adriel son of Barzillai the Meholathite. ⁹He handed them over to the Gibeonites, who killed them and exposed their bodies on a hill before the LORD. All seven of them fell together; they were put to death during the first days of harvest, just as the barley harvest was beginning.

¹⁰Rizpah daughter of Aiah took sackcloth and spread it out for herself on a rock. From the beginning of the harvest till the rain poured down from the heavens on the bodies, she did not let the birds touch them by day or the wild animals by night. ¹¹When David was told what Aiah's daughter Rizpah, Saul's concubine, had done, ¹²he went and took the bones of Saul and his son Jonathan from the citizens of Jabesh Gilead. (They had stolen their bodies from the public square at Beth Shan, where the Philistines had hung them after they struck Saul down on Gilboa.) ¹³David brought the bones of Saul and his son Jonathan from there, and the bones of those who had been killed and exposed were gathered up.

¹⁴They buried the bones of Saul and his son Jonathan in the tomb of Saul's father Kish, at Zela in Benjamin, and did everything the king commanded. After that, God answered prayer on behalf of the land.

Wars against the Philistines

¹⁵Once again there was a battle between the Philistines and Israel. David went down with his men to fight against the Philistines, and he became exhausted. ¹⁶And Ishbi-Benob, one of the descendants of Rapha, whose bronze spearhead weighed three hundred shekelsᵇ and who was armed with a new ⌊sword⌋, said he would kill David. ¹⁷But Abishai son of Zeruiah came to David's rescue; he struck the Philistine down and killed him. Then David's men swore to him, saying, 'Never again will you go out with us to battle, so that the lamp of Israel will not be extinguished.'

¹⁸In the course of time, there was another battle with the Philistines, at Gob. At that time Sibbekai the Hushathite killed Saph, one of the descendants of Rapha.

¹⁹In another battle with the Philistines at Gob, Elhanan son of Jairᶜ the Bethlehemite killed the brother ofᵈ Goliath the Gittite, who had a spear with a shaft like a weaver's rod.

ᵃ 8 Two Hebrew manuscripts, some Septuagint manuscripts and Syriac (see also 1 Samuel 18:19); most Hebrew and Septuagint manuscripts *Michal* ᵇ 16 That is, about 3.5 kilograms ᶜ 19 See 1 Chron. 20:5; Hebrew *Jaare-Oregim*.
ᵈ 19 See 1 Chron. 20:5; Hebrew does not have *the brother of*.

20In still another battle, which took place at Gath, there was a huge man with six fingers on each hand and six toes on each foot—twenty-four in all. He also was descended from Rapha. 21When he taunted Israel, Jonathan son of Shimeah, David's brother, killed him.

22These four were descendants of Rapha in Gath, and they fell at the hands of David and his men.

David's song of praise

22 David sang to the LORD the words of this song when the LORD delivered him from the hand of all his enemies and from the hand of Saul. 2He said:

'The LORD is my rock, my fortress and my deliverer;
3 my God is my rock, in whom I take refuge,
 my shield[a] and the horn[b] of my salvation.
 He is my stronghold, my refuge and my saviour—
  from violent people you save me.

4'I called to the LORD, who is worthy of praise,
 and have been saved from my enemies.
5The waves of death swirled about me;
 the torrents of destruction overwhelmed me.
6The cords of the grave coiled around me;
 the snares of death confronted me.

7'In my distress I called to the LORD;
 I called out to my God.
 From his temple he heard my voice;
 my cry came to his ears.
8The earth trembled and quaked,
 the foundations of the heavens[c] shook;
 they trembled because he was angry.
9Smoke rose from his nostrils;
 consuming fire came from his mouth,
 burning coals blazed out of it.
10He parted the heavens and came down;
 dark clouds were under his feet.
11He mounted the cherubim and flew;
 he soared[d] on the wings of the wind.
12He made darkness his canopy around him—
 the dark[e] rain clouds of the sky.
13Out of the brightness of his presence bolts of lightning blazed forth.
14The LORD thundered from heaven;
 the voice of the Most High resounded.
15He shot his arrows and scattered the enemy,
 with great bolts of lightning he routed them.
16The valleys of the sea were exposed
 and the foundations of the earth laid bare
 at the rebuke of the LORD,
 at the blast of breath from his nostrils.

17'He reached down from on high and took hold of me;
 he drew me out of deep waters.
18He rescued me from my powerful enemy,
 from my foes, who were too strong for me.
19They confronted me in the day of my disaster,
 but the LORD was my support.
20He brought me out into a spacious place;
 he rescued me because he delighted in me.

21'The LORD has dealt with me according to my righteousness;
 according to the cleanness of my hands he has rewarded me.

making Connections

Psalms
2 Samuel 22:1
David wrote many of the psalms and his song of victory here can be found in a slightly different form in Psalm 18.

---

[a]3 Or *sovereign*   [b]3 *Horn* here symbolises strength.   [c]8 Hebrew; Vulgate and Syriac (see also Psalm 18:7) *mountains*   [d]11 Many Hebrew manuscripts (see also Psalm 18:10); most Hebrew manuscripts *appeared*   [e]12 Septuagint (see also Psalm 18:11); Hebrew *massed*

²²For I have kept the ways of the LORD;
   I am not guilty of turning from my
      God.
²³All his laws are before me;
   I have not turned away from his
      decrees.
²⁴I have been blameless before him
   and have kept myself from sin.
²⁵The LORD has rewarded me according to
      my righteousness,
   according to my cleanness[a] in his sight.

²⁶'To the faithful you show yourself
      faithful,
   to the blameless you show yourself
      blameless,
²⁷to the pure you show yourself pure,
   but to the devious you show yourself
      shrewd.
²⁸You save the humble,
   but your eyes are on the haughty to
      bring them low.
²⁹You, LORD, are my lamp;
   the LORD turns my darkness into light.
³⁰With your help I can advance against a
      troop;[b]
   with my God I can scale a wall.

³¹'As for God, his way is perfect;
   the LORD's word is flawless.
   He shields all who take refuge in him.
³²For who is God besides the LORD?
   And who is the Rock except our God?
³³It is God who arms me with strength[c]
   and keeps my way secure.
³⁴He makes my feet like the feet of a deer
   and causes me to stand on the heights.
³⁵He trains my hands for battle;
   my arms can bend a bow of bronze.
³⁶You make your saving help my shield;
   your help has made[d] me great.
³⁷You provide a broad path for my feet,
   so that my ankles do not give way.

³⁸'I pursued my enemies and crushed them;
   I did not turn back till they were
      destroyed.
³⁹I crushed them completely, and they
      could not rise;
   they fell beneath my feet.

⁴⁰You armed me with strength for battle;
   you humbled my adversaries before
      me.
⁴¹You made my enemies turn their backs in
      flight,
   and I destroyed my foes.
⁴²They cried for help, but there was no-one
      to save them—
   to the LORD, but he did not answer.
⁴³I beat them as fine as the dust of the earth;
   I pounded and trampled them like
      mud in the streets.

⁴⁴'You have delivered me from the attacks
      of the peoples;
   you have preserved me as the head of
      nations.
People I did not know now serve me,
⁴⁵   foreigners cower before me;
   as soon as they hear of me, they obey
      me.
⁴⁶They all lose heart;
   they come trembling[e] from their
      strongholds.

⁴⁷'The LORD lives! Praise be to my Rock!
   Exalted be my God, the Rock, my
      Saviour!
⁴⁸He is the God who avenges me,
   who puts the nations under me,
⁴⁹   who sets me free from my enemies.
You exalted me above my foes;
   from violent people you rescued me.
⁵⁰Therefore I will praise you, LORD, among
      the nations;
   I will sing the praises of your name.

⁵¹'He gives his king great victories;
   he shows unfailing kindness to his
      anointed,
   to David and his descendants for ever.'

David's last words

23 These are the last words of David:

'The inspired utterance of David son of
      Jesse,
   the utterance of the man exalted by the
      Most High,
   the man anointed by the God of Jacob,
   the hero of Israel's songs:

---

[a] 25 Hebrew; Septuagint and Vulgate (see also Psalm 18:24) *to the cleanness of my hands*   [b] 30 Or *can run through a barricade*   [c] 33 Dead Sea Scrolls, some Septuagint manuscripts, Vulgate and Syriac (see also Psalm 18:32); Masoretic Text *who is my strong refuge*   [d] 36 Dead Sea Scrolls; Masoretic Text *shield; I you stoop down to make*   [e] 46 Some Septuagint manuscripts and Vulgate (see also Psalm 18:45); Masoretic Text *they arm themselves*

² 'The Spirit of the LORD spoke through me;
　　his word was on my tongue.
³ The God of Israel spoke,
　　the Rock of Israel said to me:
"When one rules over people in
　　　righteousness,
　when he rules in the fear of God,
⁴ he is like the light of morning at sunrise
　　on a cloudless morning,
　like the brightness after rain
　　that brings grass from the earth."

⁵ 'If my house were not right with God,
　　surely he would not have made with me
　　　an everlasting covenant,
　arranged and secured in every part;
　surely he would not bring to fruition my
　　　salvation
　　and grant me my every desire.
⁶ But evil men are all to be cast aside like
　　　thorns,
　　which are not gathered with the
　　　hand.
⁷ Whoever touches thorns
　　uses a tool of iron or the shaft of a
　　　spear;
　　they are burned up where they lie.'

David's mighty warriors

⁸ These are the names of David's mighty warriors:

Josheb-Basshebeth,[a] a Tahkemonite,[b] was chief of the Three; he raised his spear against eight hundred men, whom he killed[c] in one encounter.

⁹ Next to him was Eleazar son of Dodai the Ahohite. As one of the three mighty warriors, he was with David when they taunted the Philistines gathered ⌊at Pas Dammim⌋[d] for battle. Then the Israelites retreated, ¹⁰ but Eleazar stood his ground and struck down the Philistines till his hand grew tired and froze to the sword. The LORD brought about a great victory that day. The troops returned to Eleazar, but only to strip the dead.

¹¹ Next to him was Shammah son of Agee the Hararite. When the Philistines banded together at a place where there was a field full of lentils, Israel's troops fled from them. ¹² But Shammah took his stand in the middle of the field. He defended it and struck the Philistines down, and the LORD brought about a great victory.

¹³ During harvest time, three of the thirty chief warriors came down to David at the cave of Adullam, while a band of Philistines was encamped in the Valley of Rephaim. ¹⁴ At that time David was in the stronghold, and the Philistine garrison was at Bethlehem. ¹⁵ David longed for water and said, 'Oh, that someone would get me a drink of water from the well near the gate of Bethlehem!' ¹⁶ So the three mighty warriors broke through the Philistine lines, drew water from the well near the gate of Bethlehem and carried it back to David. But he refused to drink it; instead, he poured it out before the LORD. ¹⁷ 'Far be it from me, LORD, to do this!' he said. 'Is it not the blood of men who went at the risk of their lives?' And David would not drink it.

Such were the exploits of the three mighty warriors.

¹⁸ Abishai the brother of Joab son of Zeruiah was chief of the Three.[e] He raised his spear against three hundred men, whom he killed, and so he became as famous as the Three. ¹⁹ Was he not held in greater honour than the Three? He became their commander, even though he was not included among them.

²⁰ Benaiah son of Jehoiada, a valiant fighter from Kabzeel, performed great exploits. He struck down Moab's two mightiest warriors. He also went down into a pit on a snowy day and killed a lion. ²¹ And he struck down a huge Egyptian. Although the Egyptian had a spear in his hand, Benaiah went against him with a club. He snatched the spear from the Egyptian's hand and killed him with his own spear. ²² Such were the exploits of Benaiah son of Jehoiada; he too was as famous as the three mighty warriors. ²³ He was held in greater honour than any of the Thirty, but he was not

---

[a] 8 Hebrew; some Septuagint manuscripts suggest *Ish-Bosheth*, that is, *Esh-Baal* (see also 1 Chron. 11:11 *Jashobeam*).
[b] 8 Probably a variant of *Hakmonite* (see 1 Chron. 11:11)   [c] 8 Some Septuagint manuscripts (see also 1 Chron. 11:11); Hebrew and other Septuagint manuscripts *Three; it was Adino the Eznite who killed eight hundred men*   [d] 9 See 1 Chron. 11:13; Hebrew *gathered there*.   [e] 18 Most Hebrew manuscripts (see also 1 Chron. 11:20); two Hebrew manuscripts and Syriac *Thirty*

included among the Three. And David put him in charge of his bodyguard.

24 Among the Thirty were:
Asahel the brother of Joab,
Elhanan son of Dodo from Bethlehem,
25 Shammah the Harodite,
Elika the Harodite,
26 Helez the Paltite,
Ira son of Ikkesh from Tekoa,
27 Abiezer from Anathoth,
Sibbekai[a] the Hushathite,
28 Zalmon the Ahohite,
Maharai the Netophathite,
29 Heled[b] son of Baanah the Netophathite,
Ithai son of Ribai from Gibeah in Benjamin,
30 Benaiah the Pirathonite,
Hiddai[c] from the ravines of Gaash,
31 Abi-Albon the Arbathite,
Azmaveth the Barhumite,
32 Eliahba the Shaalbonite,
the sons of Jashen,
Jonathan 33 son of[d] Shammah the Hararite,
Ahiam son of Sharar[e] the Hararite,
34 Eliphelet son of Ahasbai the Maakathite,
Eliam son of Ahithophel the Gilonite,
35 Hezro the Carmelite,
Paarai the Arbite,
36 Igal son of Nathan from Zobah,
the son of Hagri,[f]
37 Zelek the Ammonite,
Naharai the Beerothite, the armour-bearer of Joab son of Zeruiah,
38 Ira the Ithrite,
Gareb the Ithrite
39 and Uriah the Hittite.
There were thirty-seven in all.

David enrols the fighting men

24 Again the anger of the LORD burned against Israel, and he incited David against them, saying, 'Go and take a census of Israel and Judah.'

2 So the king said to Joab and the army commanders[g] with him, 'Go throughout the tribes of Israel from Dan to Beersheba and enrol the fighting men, so that I may know how many there are.'

3 But Joab replied to the king, 'May the LORD your God multiply the troops a hundred times over, and may the eyes of my lord the king see it. But why does my lord the king want to do such a thing?'

4 The king's word, however, overruled Joab and the army commanders; so they left the presence of the king to enrol the fighting men of Israel.

5 After crossing the Jordan, they camped near Aroer, south of the town in the gorge, and then went through Gad and on to Jazer. 6 They went to Gilead and the region of Tahtim Hodshi, and on to Dan Jaan and around towards Sidon. 7 Then they went towards the fortress of Tyre and all the towns of the Hivites and Canaanites. Finally, they went on to Beersheba in the Negev of Judah.

8 After they had gone through the entire land, they came back to Jerusalem at the end of nine months and twenty days.

9 Joab reported the number of the fighting men to the king: in Israel there were eight hundred thousand able-bodied men who could handle a sword, and in Judah five hundred thousand.

10 David was conscience-stricken after he had counted the fighting men, and he said to the LORD, 'I have sinned greatly in what I have done. Now, LORD, I beg you, take away the guilt of your servant. I have done a very foolish thing.'

11 Before David got up the next morning, the word of the LORD had come to Gad the prophet, David's seer: 12 'Go and tell David, "This is what the LORD says: I am giving you three options. Choose one of them for me to carry out against you."'

---

[a] 27 Some Septuagint manuscripts (see also 21:18; 1 Chron. 11:29); Hebrew *Mebunnai* [b] 29 Some Hebrew manuscripts and Vulgate (see also 1 Chron. 11:30); most Hebrew manuscripts *Heleb* [c] 30 Hebrew; some Septuagint manuscripts (see also 1 Chron. 11:32) *Hurai* [d] 33 Some Septuagint manuscripts (see also 1 Chron. 11:34); Hebrew does not have *son of*. [e] 33 Hebrew; some Septuagint manuscripts (see also 1 Chron. 11:35) *Sakar* [f] 36 Some Septuagint manuscripts (see also 1 Chron. 11:38); Hebrew *Haggadi* [g] 2 Septuagint (see also verse 4 and 1 Chron. 21:2); Hebrew *Joab the army commander*

making Connections

Araunah's threshing-floor
2 Samuel 24:18
David needs to build an altar and make a sacrifice to God to stop the plague that is killing his people. So he buys this threshing-floor from Araunah, which is the place that the plague has reached. Araunah's threshing-floor was on the mountain where Abraham had taken Isaac to sacrifice him and was the site on which Solomon later built his temple.

13 So Gad went to David and said to him, 'Shall there come on you three[a] years of famine in your land? Or three months of fleeing from your enemies while they pursue you? Or three days of plague in your land? Now then, think it over and decide how I should answer the one who sent me.'

14 David said to Gad, 'I am in deep distress. Let us fall into the hands of the LORD, for his mercy is great; but do not let me fall into human hands.'

15 So the LORD sent a plague on Israel from that morning until the end of the time designated, and seventy thousand of the people from Dan to Beersheba died. 16 When the angel stretched out his hand to destroy Jerusalem, the LORD relented concerning the disaster and said to the angel who was afflicting the people, 'Enough! Withdraw your hand.' The angel of the LORD was then at the threshing-floor of Araunah the Jebusite.

17 When David saw the angel who was striking down the people, he said to the LORD, 'I have sinned; I, the shepherd,[b] have done wrong. These are but sheep. What have they done? Let your hand fall on me and my family.'

David builds an altar

18 On that day Gad went to David and said to him, 'Go up and build an altar to the LORD on the threshing-floor of Araunah the Jebusite.' 19 So David went up, as the LORD had commanded through Gad. 20 When Araunah looked and saw the king and his officials coming towards him, he went out and bowed down before the king with his face to the ground.

21 Araunah said, 'Why has my lord the king come to his servant?'

'To buy your threshing-floor,' David answered, 'so that I can build an altar to the LORD, that the plague on the people may be stopped.'

22 Araunah said to David, 'Let my lord the king take whatever he wishes and offer it up. Here are oxen for the burnt offering, and here are threshing-sledges and ox yokes for the wood. 23 Your Majesty, Araunah[c] gives all this to the king.' Araunah also said to him, 'May the LORD your God accept you.'

24 But the king replied to Araunah, 'No, I insist on paying you for it. I will not sacrifice to the LORD my God burnt offerings that cost me nothing.'

So David bought the threshing-floor and the oxen and paid fifty shekels[d] of silver for them. 25 David built an altar to the LORD there and sacrificed burnt offerings and fellowship offerings. Then the LORD answered his prayer on behalf of the land, and the plague on Israel was stopped.

---

[a] 13 Septuagint (see also 1 Chron. 21:12); Hebrew *seven* [b] 17 Dead Sea Scrolls and Septuagint; Masoretic Text does not have *the shepherd*. [c] 23 Some Hebrew manuscripts and Septuagint; most Hebrew manuscripts *King Araunah*
[d] 24 That is, about 575 grams

1 Kings

INTRODUCTION

1 KINGS

Author: Unknown

When: The two books of Kings cover four hundred years in the history of the people of Israel, from around 970 BC to 587 BC.

Where: Israel.

Did you know? Like 1 and 2 Samuel, 1 and 2 Kings were originally joined together as one book in the Hebrew Bible.

Main theme: As you might expect, this book is all about kings. It continues the history of the people of Israel from the death of David. His son Solomon is the next king of Israel, but after his death the kingdom is split into two. The book follows the parallel histories of the northern kingdom of Israel and the southern kingdom of Judah. The prophet Elijah makes some dramatic appearances too.

Adonijah sets himself up as king

1 When King David was very old, he could not keep warm even when they put covers over him. ²So his attendants said to him, 'Let us look for a young virgin to serve the king and take care of him. She can lie beside him so that our lord the king may keep warm.'

³Then they searched throughout Israel for a beautiful girl and found Abishag, a Shunammite, and brought her to the king. ⁴The girl was very beautiful; she took care of the king and waited on him, but the king had no sexual relations with her.

⁵Now Adonijah, whose mother was Haggith, put himself forward and said, 'I will be king.' So he got chariots and horses*ᵃ* ready, with fifty men to run ahead of him. ⁶(His father had never rebuked him by asking, 'Why do you behave as you do?' He was also very handsome and was born next after Absalom.)

ᵃ 5 Or *charioteers*

7Adonijah conferred with Joab son of Zeruiah and with Abiathar the priest, and they gave him their support. 8But Zadok the priest, Benaiah son of Jehoiada, Nathan the prophet, Shimei and Rei and David's special guard did not join Adonijah.

9Adonijah then sacrificed sheep, cattle and fattened calves at the Stone of Zoheleth near En Rogel. He invited all his brothers, the king's sons, and all the royal officials of Judah, 10but he did not invite Nathan the prophet or Benaiah or the special guard or his brother Solomon.

11Then Nathan asked Bathsheba, Solomon's mother, 'Have you not heard that Adonijah, the son of Haggith, has become king, and our lord David knows nothing about it? 12Now then, let me advise you how you can save your own life and the life of your son Solomon. 13Go in to King David and say to him, "My lord the king, did you not swear to me your servant: 'Surely Solomon your son shall be king after me, and he will sit on my throne'? Why then has Adonijah become king?" 14While you are still there talking to the king, I will come in and add my word to what you have said.'

15So Bathsheba went to see the aged king in his room, where Abishag the Shunammite was attending him. 16Bathsheba bowed down, prostrating herself before the king.

'What is it you want?' the king asked.

17She said to him, 'My lord, you yourself swore to me your servant by the LORD your God: "Solomon your son shall become king after me, and he will sit on my throne." 18But now Adonijah has become king, and you, my lord the king, do not know about it. 19He has sacrificed great numbers of cattle, fattened calves, and sheep, and has invited all the king's sons, Abiathar the priest and Joab the commander of the army, but he has not invited Solomon your servant. 20My lord the king, the eyes of all Israel are on you, to learn from you who will sit on the throne of my lord the king after him. 21Otherwise, as soon as my lord the king is laid to rest with his ancestors, I and my son Solomon will be treated as criminals.'

22While she was still speaking with the king, Nathan the prophet arrived. 23And the king was told, 'Nathan the prophet is here.' So he went before the king and bowed with his face to the ground.

24Nathan said, 'Have you, my lord the king, declared that Adonijah shall be king after you, and that he will sit on your throne? 25Today he has gone down and sacrificed great numbers of cattle, fattened calves, and sheep. He has invited all the king's sons, the commanders of the army and Abiathar the priest. At this very moment they are eating and drinking with him and saying, "Long live King Adonijah!" 26But me your servant, and Zadok the priest, and Benaiah son of Jehoiada, and your servant Solomon he did not invite. 27Is this something my lord the king has done without letting his servants know who should sit on the throne of my lord the king after him?'

David makes Solomon king

28Then King David said, 'Call in Bathsheba.' So she came into the king's presence and stood before him.

29The king then took an oath: 'As surely as the LORD lives, who has delivered me out of every trouble, 30I will surely carry out this very day what I swore to you by the LORD, the God of Israel: Solomon your son shall be king after me, and he will sit on my throne in my place.'

31Then Bathsheba bowed down with her face to the ground, prostrating herself before the king, and said, 'May my lord King David live for ever!'

32King David said, 'Call in Zadok the priest, Nathan the prophet and Benaiah son of Jehoiada.' When they came before the king, 33he said to them: 'Take your lord's servants with you and put Solomon my son on my own mule and take him down to Gihon. 34There shall Zadok the priest and Nathan the prophet anoint him king over Israel. Blow the trumpet and shout, "Long live King Solomon!" 35Then you are to go up with him, and he is to come and sit on my throne and reign in my place. I have appointed him ruler over Israel and Judah.'

36Benaiah son of Jehoiada answered the king, 'Amen! May the LORD, the God of my lord the king, so declare it. 37As the LORD was with my lord the king, so may he be with

Solomon to make his throne even greater than the throne of my lord King David!'

38So Zadok the priest, Nathan the prophet, Benaiah son of Jehoiada, the Kerethites and the Pelethites went down and put Solomon on King David's mule, and they escorted him to Gihon. 39Zadok the priest took the horn of oil from the sacred tent and anointed Solomon. Then they sounded the trumpet and all the people shouted, 'Long live King Solomon!' 40And all the people went up after him, playing pipes and rejoicing greatly, so that the ground shook with the sound.

41Adonijah and all the guests who were with him heard it as they were finishing their feast. On hearing the sound of the trumpet, Joab asked, 'What's the meaning of all the noise in the city?'

42Even as he was speaking, Jonathan son of Abiathar the priest arrived. Adonijah said, 'Come in. A worthy man like you must be bringing good news.'

43'Not at all!' Jonathan answered. 'Our lord King David has made Solomon king. 44The king has sent with him Zadok the priest, Nathan the prophet, Benaiah son of Jehoiada, the Kerethites and the Pelethites, and they have put him on the king's mule, 45and Zadok the priest and Nathan the prophet have anointed him king at Gihon. From there they have gone up cheering, and the city resounds with it. That's the noise you hear. 46Moreover, Solomon has taken his seat on the royal throne. 47Also, the royal officials have come to congratulate our lord King David, saying, "May your God make Solomon's name more famous than yours and his throne greater than yours!" And the king bowed in worship on his bed 48and said, "Praise be to the LORD, the God of Israel, who has allowed my eyes to see a successor on my throne today."'

49At this, all Adonijah's guests rose in alarm and dispersed. 50But Adonijah, in fear of Solomon, went and took hold of the horns of the altar. 51Then Solomon was told, 'Adonijah is afraid of King Solomon and is clinging to the horns of the altar. He says, "Let King Solomon swear to me today that he will not put his servant to death with the sword."'

52Solomon replied, 'If he shows himself to be worthy, not a hair of his head will fall to the ground; but if evil is found in him, he will die.' 53Then King Solomon sent men, and they brought him down from the altar. And Adonijah came and bowed down to King Solomon, and Solomon said, 'Go to your home.'

David's charge to Solomon

2 When the time drew near for David to die, he gave a charge to Solomon his son.

2'I am about to go the way of all the earth,' he said. 'So be strong, act like a man, 3and observe what the LORD your God requires: walk in obedience to him, and keep his decrees and commands, his laws and regulations, as written in the Law of Moses. Do this so that you may prosper in all you do and wherever you go 4and that the LORD may keep his promise to me: "If your descendants watch how they live, and if they walk faithfully before me with all their heart and soul, you will never fail to have a successor on the throne of Israel."

5'Now you yourself know what Joab son of Zeruiah did to me—what he did to the two commanders of Israel's armies, Abner son of Ner and Amasa son of Jether. He killed them, shedding their blood in peacetime as if in battle, and with that blood he

People and Places

Solomon
1 Kings 2:1

Solomon was the son of David. He built the great temple in Jerusalem, something his father had longed to do, and was the first king of Israel to trade profitably with other nations. Solomon was famous for his wisdom and also his love of women. He had many foreign wives who eventually influenced him to turn away from God and worship pagan gods.

stained the belt round his waist and the sandals on his feet. 6Deal with him according to your wisdom, but do not let his grey head go down to the grave in peace.

7'But show kindness to the sons of Barzillai of Gilead and let them be among those who eat at your table. They stood by me when I fled from your brother Absalom.

8'And remember, you have with you Shimei son of Gera, the Benjaminite from Bahurim, who called down bitter curses on me the day I went to Mahanaim. When he came down to meet me at the Jordan, I swore to him by the LORD: "I will not put you to death by the sword." 9But now, do not consider him innocent. You are a man of wisdom; you will know what to do to him. Bring his grey head down to the grave in blood.'

10Then David rested with his ancestors and was buried in the City of David. 11He had reigned for forty years over Israel— seven years in Hebron and thirty-three in Jerusalem. 12So Solomon sat on the throne of his father David, and his rule was firmly established.

Solomon's throne established

13Now Adonijah, the son of Haggith, went to Bathsheba, Solomon's mother. Bathsheba asked him, 'Do you come peacefully?'

He answered, 'Yes, peacefully.' 14Then he added, 'I have something to say to you.'

'You may say it,' she replied.

15'As you know,' he said, 'the kingdom was mine. All Israel looked to me as their king. But things changed, and the kingdom has gone to my brother; for it has come to him from the LORD. 16Now I have one request to make of you. Do not refuse me.'

'You may make it,' she said.

17So he continued, 'Please ask King Solomon—he will not refuse you—to give me Abishag the Shunammite as my wife.'

18'Very well,' Bathsheba replied, 'I will speak to the king for you.'

19When Bathsheba went to King Solomon to speak to him for Adonijah, the king stood up to meet her, bowed down to her and sat down on his throne. He had a throne brought for the king's mother, and she sat down at his right hand.

20'I have one small request to make of you,' she said. 'Do not refuse me.'

The king replied, 'Make it, my mother; I will not refuse you.'

21So she said, 'Let Abishag the Shunammite be given in marriage to your brother Adonijah.'

22King Solomon answered his mother, 'Why do you request Abishag the Shunammite for Adonijah? You might as well request the kingdom for him—after all, he is my older brother—yes, for him and for Abiathar the priest and Joab son of Zeruiah!'

23Then King Solomon swore by the LORD: 'May God deal with me, be it ever so severely, if Adonijah does not pay with his life for this request! 24And now, as surely as the LORD lives—he who has established me securely on the throne of my father David and has founded a dynasty for me as he promised—Adonijah shall be put to death today!' 25So King Solomon gave orders to Benaiah son of Jehoiada, and he struck down Adonijah and he died.

26To Abiathar the priest the king said, 'Go back to your fields in Anathoth. You deserve to die, but I will not put you to death now, because you carried the ark of the Sovereign LORD before my father David and shared all my father's hardships.' 27So Solomon removed Abiathar from the priesthood of the LORD, fulfilling the word the LORD had spoken at Shiloh about the house of Eli.

28When the news reached Joab, who had conspired with Adonijah though not with Absalom, he fled to the tent of the LORD and took hold of the horns of the altar. 29King Solomon was told that Joab had fled to the tent of the LORD and was beside the altar. Then Solomon ordered Benaiah son of Jehoiada, 'Go, strike him down!'

30So Benaiah entered the tent of the LORD and said to Joab, 'The king says, "Come out!"'

But he answered, 'No, I will die here.'

Benaiah reported to the king, 'This is how Joab answered me.'

31Then the king commanded Benaiah, 'Do as he says. Strike him down and bury him, and so clear me and my family line of the guilt of the innocent blood that Joab shed. ³²The LORD will repay him for the blood he shed, because without my father David knowing it he attacked two men and killed them with the sword. Both of them—Abner son of Ner, commander of Israel's army, and Amasa son of Jether, commander of Judah's army—were better men and more upright than he. ³³May the guilt of their blood rest on the head of Joab and his descendants for ever. But on David and his descendants, his house and his throne, may there be the LORD's peace for ever.'

³⁴So Benaiah son of Jehoiada went up and struck down Joab and killed him, and he was buried at his home out in the country. ³⁵The king put Benaiah son of Jehoiada over the army in Joab's position and replaced Abiathar with Zadok the priest.

³⁶Then the king sent for Shimei and said to him, 'Build yourself a house in Jerusalem and live there, but do not go anywhere else. ³⁷The day you leave and cross the Kidron Valley, you can be sure you will die; your blood will be on your own head.'

³⁸Shimei answered the king, 'What you say is good. Your servant will do as my lord the king has said.' And Shimei stayed in Jerusalem for a long time.

³⁹But three years later, two of Shimei's slaves ran off to Achish son of Maakah, king of Gath, and Shimei was told, 'Your slaves are in Gath.' ⁴⁰At this, he saddled his donkey and went to Achish at Gath in search of his slaves. So Shimei went away and brought the slaves back from Gath.

⁴¹When Solomon was told that Shimei had gone from Jerusalem to Gath and had returned, ⁴²the king summoned Shimei and said to him, 'Did I not make you swear by the LORD and warn you, "On the day you leave to go anywhere else, you can be sure you will die"? At that time you said to me, "What you say is good. I will obey." ⁴³Why then did you not keep your oath to the LORD and obey the command I gave you?'

⁴⁴The king also said to Shimei, 'You know in your heart all the wrong you did to my father David. Now the LORD will repay you for your wrongdoing. ⁴⁵But King Solomon will be blessed, and David's throne will remain secure before the LORD for ever.'

⁴⁶Then the king gave the order to Benaiah son of Jehoiada, and he went out and struck Shimei down and he died.

The kingdom was now established in Solomon's hands.

Solomon asks for wisdom

3 Solomon made an alliance with Pharaoh king of Egypt and married his daughter. He brought her to the City of David until he finished building his palace and the temple of the LORD, and the wall around Jerusalem. ²The people, however, were still sacrificing at the high places, because a temple had not yet been built for the Name of the LORD. ³Solomon showed his love for the LORD by walking according to the instructions given him by his father David, except that he offered sacrifices and burned incense on the high places.

⁴The king went to Gibeon to offer sacrifices, for that was the most important high place, and Solomon offered a thousand burnt offerings on that altar. ⁵At Gibeon the LORD appeared to Solomon during the night in a dream, and God said, 'Ask for whatever you want me to give you.'

⁶Solomon answered, 'You have shown great kindness to your servant, my father David, because he was faithful to you and righteous and upright in heart. You have continued this great kindness to him and have given him a son to sit on his throne this very day.

making Connections

High places
1 Kings 3:4
The high places were on hilltops and were dedicated to the worship of pagan gods. They should have been off limits to the people of Israel.

⁷'Now, LORD my God, you have made your servant king in place of my father David. But I am only a little child and do not know how to carry out my duties. ⁸Your servant is here among the people you have chosen, a great people, too numerous to count or number. ⁹So give your servant a discerning heart to govern your people and to distinguish between right and wrong. For who is able to govern this great people of yours?'

¹⁰The Lord was pleased that Solomon had asked for this. ¹¹So God said to him, 'Since you have asked for this and not for long life or wealth for yourself, nor have asked for the death of your enemies but for discernment in administering justice, ¹²I will do what you have asked. I will give you a wise and discerning heart, so that there will never have been anyone like you, nor will there ever be. ¹³Moreover, I will give you what you have not asked for—both wealth and honour—so that in your lifetime you will have no equal among kings. ¹⁴And if you walk in obedience to me and keep my decrees and commands as David your father did, I will give you a long life.' ¹⁵Then Solomon awoke—and he realised it had been a dream.

He returned to Jerusalem, stood before the ark of the Lord's covenant and sacrificed burnt offerings and fellowship offerings. Then he gave a feast for all his court.

A wise ruling

¹⁶Now two prostitutes came to the king and stood before him. ¹⁷One of them said, 'Pardon me, my lord. This woman and I live in the same house. I had a baby while she was there with me. ¹⁸The third day after my child was born, this woman also had a baby. We were alone; there was no-one in the house but the two of us.

¹⁹'During the night this woman's son died because she lay on him. ²⁰So she got up in the middle of the night and took my son from my side while I your servant was asleep. She put him by her breast and put her dead son by my breast. ²¹The next morning, I got up to nurse my son—and he was dead! But when I looked at him closely in the morning light, I saw that it wasn't the son I had borne.'

²²The other woman said, 'No! The living one is my son; the dead one is yours.'

But the first one insisted, 'No! The dead one is yours; the living one is mine.' And so they argued before the king.

²³The king said, 'This one says, "My son is alive and your son is dead," while that one says, "No! Your son is dead and mine is alive."'

²⁴Then the king said, 'Bring me a sword.' So they brought a sword for the king. ²⁵He then gave an order: 'Cut the living child in two and give half to one and half to the other.'

²⁶The woman whose son was alive was deeply moved out of love for her son and said to the king, 'Please, my lord, give her the living baby! Don't kill him!'

But the other said, 'Neither I nor you shall have him. Cut him in two!'

²⁷Then the king gave his ruling: 'Give the living baby to the first woman. Do not kill him; she is his mother.'

²⁸When all Israel heard the verdict the king had given, they held the king in awe, because they saw that he had wisdom from God to administer justice.

Solomon's officials and governors

4 So King Solomon ruled over all Israel. ²And these were his chief officials:

Azariah son of Zadok—the priest;
³Elihoreph and Ahijah, sons of Shisha—secretaries;
Jehoshaphat son of Ahilud—recorder;
⁴Benaiah son of Jehoiada—commander-in-chief;
Zadok and Abiathar—priests;
⁵Azariah son of Nathan—in charge of the district governors;
Zabud son of Nathan—a priest and advisor to the king;
⁶Ahishar—palace administrator;
Adoniram son of Abda—in charge of forced labour.

⁷Solomon had twelve district governors over all Israel, who supplied provisions for the king and the royal household. Each one had to provide supplies for one month in the year. ⁸These are their names:

Ben-Hur—in the hill country of Ephraim;
9Ben-Deker—in Makaz, Shaalbim, Beth Shemesh and Elon Bethhanan;
10Ben-Hesed—in Arubboth (Sokoh and all the land of Hepher were his);
11Ben-Abinadab—in Naphoth Dor (he was married to Taphath daughter of Solomon);
12Baana son of Ahilud—in Taanach and Megiddo, and in all of Beth Shan next to Zarethan below Jezreel, from Beth Shan to Abel Meholah across to Jokmeam;
13Ben-Geber—in Ramoth Gilead (the settlements of Jair son of Manasseh in Gilead were his, as well as the region of Argob in Bashan and its sixty large walled cities with bronze gate bars);
14Ahinadab son of Iddo—in Mahanaim;
15Ahimaaz—in Naphtali (he had married Basemath daughter of Solomon);
16Baana son of Hushai—in Asher and in Aloth;
17Jehoshaphat son of Paruah—in Issachar;
18Shimei son of Ela—in Benjamin;
19Geber son of Uri—in Gilead (the country of Sihon king of the Amorites and the country of Og king of Bashan). He was the only governor over the district.

Solomon's daily provisions

20The people of Judah and Israel were as numerous as the sand on the seashore; they ate, they drank and they were happy. *21And Solomon ruled over all the kingdoms from the River Euphrates to the land of the Philistines, as far as the border of Egypt. These countries brought tribute and were Solomon's subjects all his life.

22Solomon's daily provisions were thirty cors[a] of the finest flour and sixty cors[b] of meal, 23ten head of stall-fed cattle, twenty of pasture-fed cattle and a hundred sheep and goats, as well as deer, gazelles, roebucks and choice fowl. 24For he ruled over all the kingdoms west of the River Euphrates, from Tiphsah to Gaza, and had peace on all sides. 25During Solomon's lifetime Judah and Israel, from Dan to Beersheba, lived in safety, everyone under their own vine and fig-tree.

26Solomon had four[c] thousand stalls for chariot horses, and twelve thousand horses.[d]

27The district governors, each in his month, supplied provisions for King Solomon and all who came to the king's table. They saw to it that nothing was lacking. 28They also brought to the proper place their quotas of barley and straw for the chariot horses and the other horses.

Solomon's wisdom

29God gave Solomon wisdom and very great insight, and a breadth of understanding as measureless as the sand on the seashore. 30Solomon's wisdom was greater than the wisdom of all the people of the East, and greater than all the wisdom of Egypt. 31He was wiser than anyone else, including Ethan the Ezrahite—wiser than Heman, Kalkol and Darda, the sons of Mahol. And his fame spread to all the surrounding nations. 32He spoke three thousand proverbs and his songs numbered a thousand and five. 33He spoke about plant life, from the cedar of Lebanon to the hyssop that grows out of walls. He also spoke about animals and birds, reptiles and fish. 34From all nations people came to listen to Solomon's wisdom, sent by all the kings of the world, who had heard of his wisdom.

Preparations for building the temple

5 *When Hiram king of Tyre heard that Solomon had been anointed king to succeed his father David, he sent his envoys to Solomon, because he had always been on friendly terms with David. 2Solomon sent back this message to Hiram:

---

[a] 22 That is, probably about 5 metric tons [b] 22 That is, probably about 10 metric tons [c] 26 Some Septuagint manuscripts (see also 2 Chron. 9:25); Hebrew *forty* [d] 26 Or *charioteers*

* 4:21-34 is numbered 5:1-14 in Hebrew texts. * 5:1-18 is numbered 5:15-32 in Hebrew texts.

making Connections

Temple
1 Kings 5:5

Many years after the Israelites settled in the Promised Land they built a temple in Jerusalem where the Ark of the Covenant would rest. The first temple built by Solomon was destroyed by the Babylonians. It was rebuilt after the exile (Ezra 3:12), then renovated in a grand manner by Herod around the time of Jesus' birth. This third temple was destroyed in AD 70 as prophesied by Jesus (Matthew 24:2).

3'You know that because of the wars waged against my father David from all sides, he could not build a temple for the Name of the LORD his God until the LORD put his enemies under his feet. 4But now the LORD my God has given me rest on every side, and there is no adversary or disaster. 5I intend, therefore, to build a temple for the Name of the LORD my God, as the LORD told my father David, when he said, "Your son whom I will put on the throne in your place will build the temple for my Name."

6'So give orders that cedars of Lebanon be cut for me. My men will work with yours, and I will pay you for your men whatever wages you set. You know that we have no-one so skilled in felling timber as the Sidonians.'

7When Hiram heard Solomon's message, he was greatly pleased and said, 'Praise be to the LORD today, for he has given David a wise son to rule over this great nation.'

8So Hiram sent word to Solomon:

'I have received the message you sent me and will do all you want in providing the cedar and juniper logs. 9My men will haul them down from Lebanon to the Mediterranean Sea, and I will float them as rafts by sea to the place you specify. There I will separate them and you can take them away. And you are to grant my wish by providing food for my royal household.'

10In this way Hiram kept Solomon supplied with all the cedar and juniper logs he wanted, 11and Solomon gave Hiram twenty thousand cors[a] of wheat as food for his household, in addition to twenty thousand baths[b,c] of pressed olive oil. Solomon continued to do this for Hiram year after year. 12The LORD gave Solomon wisdom, just as he had promised him. There were peaceful relations between Hiram and Solomon, and the two of them made a treaty.

13King Solomon conscripted labourers from all Israel—thirty thousand men. 14He sent them off to Lebanon in shifts of ten thousand a month, so that they spent one month in Lebanon and two months at home. Adoniram was in charge of the forced labour. 15Solomon had seventy thousand carriers and eighty thousand stonecutters in the hills, 16as well as thirty-three hundred[d] overseers who supervised the project and directed the work. 17At the king's command they removed from the quarry large blocks of high-grade stone to provide a foundation of dressed stone for the temple. 18The skilled workers of Solomon and Hiram and those from Byblos cut and prepared the timber and stone for the building of the temple.

Solomon builds the temple

6 In the four hundred and eightieth[e] year after the Israelites came out of Egypt, in the fourth year of Solomon's reign over

---

[a] 11 That is, probably about 3,250 metric tons [b] 11 Septuagint (see also 2 Chron. 2:10); Hebrew *twenty cors*
[c] 11 That is, about 440,000 litres [d] 16 Hebrew; some Septuagint manuscripts (see also 2 Chron. 2:2, 18) *thirty-six hundred* [e] 1 Hebrew; Septuagint *four hundred and fortieth*

Israel, in the month of Ziv, the second month, he began to build the temple of the LORD.

² The temple that King Solomon built for the LORD was sixty cubits long, twenty wide and thirty high.[a] ³ The portico at the front of the main hall of the temple extended the width of the temple, that is twenty cubits,[b] and projected ten cubits[c] from the front of the temple. ⁴ He made narrow windows high up in the temple walls. ⁵ Against the walls of the main hall and inner sanctuary he built a structure around the building, in which there were side rooms. ⁶ The lowest floor was five cubits[d] wide, the middle floor six cubits[e] and the third floor seven.[f] He made offset ledges around the outside of the temple so that nothing would be inserted into the temple walls.

⁷ In building the temple, only blocks dressed at the quarry were used, and no hammer, chisel or any other iron tool was heard at the temple site while it was being built.

⁸ The entrance to the lowest[g] floor was on the south side of the temple; a stairway led up to the middle level and from there to the third. ⁹ So he built the temple and completed it, roofing it with beams and cedar planks. ¹⁰ And he built the side rooms all along the temple. The height of each was five cubits, and they were attached to the temple by beams of cedar.

¹¹ The word of the LORD came to Solomon: ¹² 'As for this temple you are building, if you follow my decrees, observe my laws and keep all my commands and obey them, I will fulfil through you the promise I gave to David your father. ¹³ And I will live among the Israelites and will not abandon my people Israel.'

¹⁴ So Solomon built the temple and completed it. ¹⁵ He lined its interior walls with cedar boards, panelling them from the floor of the temple to the ceiling, and covered the floor of the temple with planks of juniper. ¹⁶ He partitioned off twenty cubits at the rear of the temple with cedar boards from floor to ceiling to form within the temple an inner sanctuary, the Most Holy Place. ¹⁷ The main hall in front of this room was forty cubits[h] long. ¹⁸ The inside of the temple was cedar, carved with gourds and open flowers. Everything was cedar; no stone was to be seen.

¹⁹ He prepared the inner sanctuary within the temple to set the ark of the covenant of the LORD there. ²⁰ The inner sanctuary was twenty cubits long, twenty wide and twenty high. He overlaid the inside with pure gold, and he also overlaid the altar of cedar. ²¹ Solomon covered the inside of the temple with pure gold, and he extended gold chains across the front of the inner sanctuary, which was overlaid with gold. ²² So he overlaid the whole interior with gold. He also overlaid with gold the altar that belonged to the inner sanctuary.

²³ For the inner sanctuary he made a pair of cherubim out of olive wood, each ten cubits high. ²⁴ One wing of the first cherub was five cubits long, and the other wing five cubits — ten cubits from wing tip to wing tip. ²⁵ The second cherub also measured ten cubits, for the two cherubim were identical in size and shape. ²⁶ The height of each cherub was ten cubits. ²⁷ He placed the cherubim inside the innermost room of the temple, with their wings spread out. The wing of one cherub touched one wall, while the wing of the other touched the other wall, and their wings touched each other in the middle of the room. ²⁸ He overlaid the cherubim with gold.

²⁹ On the walls all round the temple, in both the inner and outer rooms, he carved cherubim, palm trees and open flowers. ³⁰ He also covered the floors of both the inner and outer rooms of the temple with gold.

³¹ For the entrance to the inner sanctuary he made doors out of olive wood that were one fifth of the width of the sanctuary. ³² And on the two olive-wood doors he carved cherubim, palm trees and open flowers, and overlaid the cherubim and palm trees with hammered gold. ³³ In the same way, for the entrance to the main hall

---

[a] 2 That is, about 27 metres long, 9 metres wide and 13.5 metres high [b] 3 That is, about 9 metres; also in verses 16 and 20 [c] 3 That is, about 4.5 metres; also in verse 23 [d] 6 That is, about 2.3 metres; also in verses 10 and 24 [e] 6 That is, about 2.7 metres [f] 6 That is, about 3.2 metres [g] 8 Septuagint; Hebrew *middle* [h] 17 That is, about 18 metres

he made doorframes out of olive wood that were one quarter of the width of the hall. 34He also made two doors out of juniper wood, each having two leaves that turned in sockets. 35He carved cherubim, palm trees and open flowers on them and overlaid them with gold hammered evenly over the carvings.

36And he built the inner courtyard of three courses of dressed stone and one course of trimmed cedar beams.

37The foundation of the temple of the LORD was laid in the fourth year, in the month of Ziv. 38In the eleventh year in the month of Bul, the eighth month, the temple was finished in all its details according to its specifications. He had spent seven years building it.

Solomon builds his palace

7 It took Solomon thirteen years, however, to complete the construction of his palace. 2He built the Palace of the Forest of Lebanon a hundred cubits long, fifty wide and thirty high,^{a} with four rows of cedar columns supporting trimmed cedar beams. 3It was roofed with cedar above the beams that rested on the columns—forty-five beams, fifteen to a row. 4Its windows were placed high in sets of three, facing each other. 5All the doorways had rectangular frames; they were in the front part in sets of three, facing each other.^{b}

6He made a colonnade fifty cubits long and thirty wide.^{c} In front of it was a portico, and in front of that were pillars and an overhanging roof.

7He built the throne hall, the Hall of Justice, where he was to judge, and he covered it with cedar from floor to ceiling.^{d} 8And the palace in which he was to live, set farther back, was similar in design. Solomon also made a palace like this hall for Pharaoh's daughter, whom he had married.

9All these structures, from the outside to the great courtyard and from foundation to eaves, were made of blocks of high-grade stone cut to size and trimmed with a saw on their inner and outer faces. 10The foundations were laid with large stones of good quality, some measuring ten cubits^e and some eight.^{f} 11Above were high-grade stones, cut to size, and cedar beams. 12The great courtyard was surrounded by a wall of three courses of dressed stone and one course of trimmed cedar beams, as was the inner courtyard of the temple of the LORD with its portico.

The temple's furnishings

13King Solomon sent to Tyre and brought Huram,^{g} 14whose mother was a widow from the tribe of Naphtali and whose father was from Tyre and a skilled worker in bronze. Huram was filled with wisdom, with understanding and with knowledge to do all kinds of bronze work. He came to King Solomon and did all the work assigned to him.

15He cast two bronze pillars, each eighteen cubits high and twelve cubits in circumference.^{h} 16He also made two capitals of cast bronze to set on the tops of the pillars; each capital was five cubits^i high. 17A network of interwoven chains adorned the capitals on top of the pillars, seven for each capital. 18He made pomegranates in two

making Connections

Bronze
1 Kings 7:14
Bronze is made from copper and tin mixed together. Moulds for the objects to be cast in bronze were made out of clay. The surface of the bronze would then be burnished or polished to make it beautiful.

---

^{a}2 That is, about 45 metres long, 22.5 metres wide and 13.5 metres high ^{b}5 The meaning of the Hebrew for this verse is uncertain. ^{c}6 That is, about 22.5 metres long and 13.5 metres wide ^{d}7 Vulgate and Syriac; Hebrew *floor* ^{e}10 That is, about 4.5 metres; also in verse 23 ^{f}10 That is, about 3.6 metres ^{g}13 Hebrew *Hiram*, a variant of *Huram*; also in verses 40 and 45 ^{h}15 That is, about 8.1 metres high and 5.4 metres in circumference ^{i}16 That is, about 2.3 metres; also in verse 23 rows[a] encircling each network to decorate the capitals on top of the pillars.[b] He did the same for each capital. 19The capitals on top of the pillars in the portico were in the shape of lilies, four cubits[c] high. 20On the capitals of both pillars, above the bowl-shaped part next to the network, were the two hundred pomegranates in rows all around. 21He erected the pillars at the portico of the temple. The pillar to the south he named Jakin[d] and the one to the north Boaz.[e] 22The capitals on top were in the shape of lilies. And so the work on the pillars was completed.

23He made the Sea of cast metal, circular in shape, measuring ten cubits from rim to rim and five cubits high. It took a line of thirty cubits[f] to measure round it. 24Below the rim, gourds encircled it—ten to a cubit. The gourds were cast in two rows in one piece with the Sea.

25The Sea stood on twelve bulls, three facing north, three facing west, three facing south and three facing east. The Sea rested on top of them, and their hindquarters were towards the centre. 26It was a handbreadth[g] in thickness, and its rim was like the rim of a cup, like a lily blossom. It held two thousand baths.[h]

27He also made ten movable stands of bronze; each was four cubits long, four wide and three high.[i] 28This is how the stands were made: they had side panels attached to uprights. 29On the panels between the uprights were lions, bulls and cherubim— and on the uprights as well. Above and below the lions and bulls were wreaths of hammered work. 30Each stand had four bronze wheels with bronze axles, and each had a basin resting on four supports, cast with wreaths on each side. 31On the inside of the stand there was an opening that had a circular frame one cubit[j] deep. This opening was round, and with its basework it measured a cubit and a half.[k] Around its opening there was engraving. The panels of the stands were square, not round. 32The four wheels were under the panels, and the axles of the wheels were attached to the stand. The diameter of each wheel was a cubit and a half. 33The wheels were made like chariot wheels; the axles, rims, spokes and hubs were all of cast metal.

34Each stand had four handles, one on each corner, projecting from the stand. 35At the top of the stand there was a circular band half a cubit[l] deep. The supports and panels were attached to the top of the stand. 36He engraved cherubim, lions and palm trees on the surfaces of the supports and on the panels, in every available space, with wreaths all around. 37This is the way he made the ten stands. They were all cast in the same moulds and were identical in size and shape.

38He then made ten bronze basins, each holding forty baths[m] and measuring four cubits across, one basin to go on each of the ten stands. 39He placed five of the stands on the south side of the temple and five on the north. He placed the Sea on the south side, at the south-east corner of the temple. 40He also made the pots[n] and shovels and sprinkling bowls.

So Huram finished all the work he had undertaken for King Solomon in the temple of the LORD:

41the two pillars;
the two bowl-shaped capitals on top of the pillars;
the two sets of network decorating the two bowl-shaped capitals on top of the pillars;
42the four hundred pomegranates for the two sets of network (two rows of pomegranates for each network decorating the bowl-shaped capitals on top of the pillars);
43the ten stands with their ten basins;
44the Sea and the twelve bulls under it;

---

[a] 18 Two Hebrew manuscripts and Septuagint; most Hebrew manuscripts *made the pillars, and there were two rows*
[b] 18 Many Hebrew manuscripts and Syriac; most Hebrew manuscripts *pomegranates* [c] 19 That is, about 1.8 metres; also in verse 38 [d] 21 *Jakin* probably means *he establishes*. [e] 21 *Boaz* probably means *in him is strength*. [f] 23 That is, about 13.5 metres [g] 26 That is, about 7.5 centimetres [h] 26 That is, about 44,000 litres; the Septuagint does not have this sentence. [i] 27 That is, about 1.8 metres long and wide and 1.4 metres high [j] 31 That is, about 45 centimetres [k] 31 That is, about 67 centimetres; also in verse 32 [l] 35 That is, about 22.5 centimetres [m] 38 That is, about 880 litres [n] 40 Many Hebrew manuscripts, Septuagint, Syriac and Vulgate (see also verse 45 and 2 Chron. 4:11); many other Hebrew manuscripts *basins*

⁴⁵the pots, shovels and sprinkling bowls.

All these objects that Huram made for King Solomon for the temple of the LORD were of burnished bronze. ⁴⁶The king had them cast in clay moulds in the plain of the Jordan between Sukkoth and Zarethan. ⁴⁷Solomon left all these things unweighed, because there were so many; the weight of the bronze was not determined.

⁴⁸Solomon also made all the furnishings that were in the LORD's temple:

the golden altar;
the golden table on which was the bread of the Presence;
⁴⁹the lampstands of pure gold (five on the right and five on the left, in front of the inner sanctuary);
the gold floral work and lamps and tongs;
⁵⁰the pure gold dishes, wick trimmers, sprinkling bowls, dishes and censers;
and the gold sockets for the doors of the innermost room, the Most Holy Place, and also for the doors of the main hall of the temple.

⁵¹When all the work King Solomon had done for the temple of the LORD was finished, he brought in the things his father David had dedicated—the silver and gold and the furnishings—and he placed them in the treasuries of the LORD's temple.

The ark brought to the temple

8 Then King Solomon summoned into his presence at Jerusalem the elders of Israel, all the heads of the tribes and the chiefs of the Israelite families, to bring up the ark of the LORD's covenant from Zion, the City of David. ²All the Israelites came together to King Solomon at the time of the festival in the month of Ethanim, the seventh month.

³When all the elders of Israel had arrived, the priests took up the ark, ⁴and they brought up the ark of the LORD and the tent of meeting and all the sacred furnishings in it. The priests and Levites carried them up, ⁵and King Solomon and the entire assembly of Israel that had gathered about him were before the ark, sacrificing so many sheep and cattle that they could not be recorded or counted.

⁶The priests then brought the ark of the LORD's covenant to its place in the inner sanctuary of the temple, the Most Holy Place, and put it beneath the wings of the cherubim. ⁷The cherubim spread their wings over the place of the ark and overshadowed the ark and its carrying poles. ⁸These poles were so long that their ends could be seen from the Holy Place in front of the inner sanctuary, but not from outside the Holy Place; and they are still there today. ⁹There was nothing in the ark except the two stone tablets that Moses had placed in it at Horeb, where the LORD made a covenant with the Israelites after they came out of Egypt.

¹⁰When the priests withdrew from the Holy Place, the cloud filled the temple of the LORD. ¹¹And the priests could not perform their service because of the cloud, for the glory of the LORD filled his temple.

¹²Then Solomon said, 'The LORD has said that he would dwell in a dark cloud; ¹³I have indeed built a magnificent temple for you, a place for you to dwell for ever.'

making Connections

Festival of Tabernacles
1 Kings 8:2

This festival was the Festival of Tabernacles which was an opportunity for the Israelites to remember the time they had spent wandering in the wilderness. They offered lots of animal sacrifices and had special gatherings on the first and eighth days of the festival. They also had to make and live in shelters of palm and willow trees to remind them that they had to live in tents in the wilderness.

[14]While the whole assembly of Israel was standing there, the king turned round and blessed them. [15]Then he said:

> 'Praise be to the LORD, the God of Israel, who with his own hand has fulfilled what he promised with his own mouth to my father David. For he said, [16]"Since the day I brought my people Israel out of Egypt, I have not chosen a city in any tribe of Israel to have a temple built that my Name might be there, but I have chosen David to rule my people Israel."
>
> [17]'My father David had it in his heart to build a temple for the Name of the LORD, the God of Israel. [18]But the LORD said to my father David, "You did well to have it in your heart to build a temple for my Name. [19]Nevertheless, you are not the one to build the temple, but your son, who is your own flesh and blood—he is the one who will build the temple for my Name."
>
> [20]'The LORD has kept the promise he made: I have succeeded David my father and now I sit on the throne of Israel, just as the LORD promised, and I have built the temple for the Name of the LORD, the God of Israel. [21]I have provided a place there for the ark, in which is the covenant of the LORD that he made with our ancestors when he brought them out of Egypt.'

Solomon's prayer of dedication

[22]Then Solomon stood before the altar of the LORD in front of the whole assembly of Israel, spread out his hands towards heaven [23]and said:

> 'LORD, the God of Israel, there is no God like you in heaven above or on earth below—you who keep your covenant of love with your servants who continue wholeheartedly in your way. [24]You have kept your promise to your servant David my father; with your mouth you have promised and with your hand you have fulfilled it—as it is today.
>
> [25]'Now LORD, the God of Israel, keep for your servant David my father the promises you made to him when you said, "You shall never fail to have a successor to sit before me on the throne of Israel, if only your descendants are careful in all they do to walk before me faithfully as you have done." [26]And now, God of Israel, let your word that you promised your servant David my father come true.
>
> [27]'But will God really dwell on earth? The heavens, even the highest heaven, cannot contain you. How much less this temple I have built! [28]Yet give attention to your servant's prayer and his plea for mercy, LORD my God. Hear the cry and the prayer that your servant is praying in your presence this day. [29]May your eyes be open towards this temple night and day, this place of which you said, "My Name shall be there," so that you will hear the prayer your servant prays towards this place. [30]Hear the supplication of your servant and of your people Israel when they pray towards this place. Hear from heaven, your dwelling-place, and when you hear, forgive.
>
> [31]'When anyone wrongs their neighbour and is required to take an oath and they come and swear the oath before your altar in this temple, [32]then hear from heaven and act. Judge between your servants, condemning the guilty by bringing down on their heads what they have done, and vindicating the innocent by treating them in accordance with their innocence.
>
> [33]'When your people Israel have been defeated by an enemy because they have sinned against

you, and when they turn back to you and give praise to your name, praying and making supplication to you in this temple, ³⁴then hear from heaven and forgive the sin of your people Israel and bring them back to the land you gave to their ancestors.

³⁵'When the heavens are shut up and there is no rain because your people have sinned against you, and when they pray towards this place and give praise to your name and turn from their sin because you have afflicted them, ³⁶then hear from heaven and forgive the sin of your servants, your people Israel. Teach them the right way to live, and send rain on the land you gave your people for an inheritance.

³⁷'When famine or plague comes to the land, or blight or mildew, locusts or grasshoppers, or when an enemy besieges them in any of their cities, whatever disaster or disease may come, ³⁸and when a prayer or plea is made by anyone among your people Israel—being aware of the afflictions of their own hearts, and spreading out their hands towards this temple—³⁹then hear from heaven, your dwelling-place. Forgive and act; deal with everyone according to all they do, since you know their hearts (for you alone know every human heart), ⁴⁰so that they will fear you all the time they live in the land you gave our ancestors.

⁴¹'As for the foreigners who do not belong to your people Israel but have come from a distant land because of your name—⁴²for they will hear of your great name and your mighty hand and your outstretched arm—when they come and pray towards this temple, ⁴³then hear from heaven, your dwelling-place. Do whatever the foreigners ask of you, so that all the peoples of the earth may know your name and fear you, as do your own people Israel, and may know that this house I have built bears your Name.

⁴⁴'When your people go to war against their enemies, wherever you send them, and when they pray to the LORD towards the city you have chosen and the temple I have built for your Name, ⁴⁵then hear from heaven their prayer and their plea, and uphold their cause.

⁴⁶'When they sin against you—for there is no-one who does not sin—and you become angry with them and give them over to their enemies, who take them captive to their own lands, far away or near; ⁴⁷and if they have a change of heart in the land where they are held captive, and repent and plead with you in the land of their captors and say, "We have sinned, we have done wrong, we have acted wickedly"; ⁴⁸and if they turn back to you with all their heart and soul in the land of their enemies who took them captive, and pray to you towards the land you gave their ancestors, towards the city you have chosen and the temple I have built for your Name; ⁴⁹then from heaven, your dwelling-place, hear their prayer and their plea, and uphold their cause. ⁵⁰And forgive your people, who have sinned against you; forgive all the offences they have committed against you, and cause their captors to show them mercy; ⁵¹for they are your people and your inheritance, whom you brought out of Egypt, out of that iron-smelting furnace.

⁵²'May your eyes be open to your servant's plea and to the plea of your people Israel, and may you listen to them whenever they cry out to you. ⁵³For you singled them out from all the nations of the world to be your own

inheritance, just as you declared through your servant Moses when you, Sovereign LORD, brought our ancestors out of Egypt.'

⁵⁴When Solomon had finished all these prayers and supplications to the LORD, he rose from before the altar of the LORD, where he had been kneeling with his hands spread out towards heaven. ⁵⁵He stood and blessed the whole assembly of Israel in a loud voice, saying:

⁵⁶'Praise be to the LORD, who has given rest to his people Israel just as he promised. Not one word has failed of all the good promises he gave through his servant Moses. ⁵⁷May the LORD our God be with us as he was with our ancestors; may he never leave us nor forsake us. ⁵⁸May he turn our hearts to him, to walk in obedience to him and keep the commands, decrees and laws he gave our ancestors. ⁵⁹And may these words of mine, which I have prayed before the LORD, be near to the LORD our God day and night, that he may uphold the cause of his servant and the cause of his people Israel according to each day's need, ⁶⁰so that all the peoples of the earth may know that the LORD is God and that there is no other. ⁶¹And may your hearts be fully committed to the LORD our God, to live by his decrees and obey his commands, as at this time.'

The dedication of the temple

⁶²Then the king and all Israel with him offered sacrifices before the LORD. ⁶³Solomon offered a sacrifice of fellowship offerings to the LORD: twenty-two thousand cattle and a hundred and twenty thousand sheep and goats. So the king and all the Israelites dedicated the temple of the LORD. ⁶⁴On that same day the king consecrated the middle part of the courtyard in front of the temple of the LORD, and there he offered burnt offerings, grain offerings and the fat of the fellowship offerings, because the bronze altar that stood before the LORD was too small to hold the burnt offerings, the grain offerings and the fat of the fellowship offerings.

⁶⁵So Solomon observed the festival at that time, and all Israel with him—a vast assembly, people from Lebo Hamath to the Wadi of Egypt. They celebrated it before the LORD our God for seven days and seven days more, fourteen days in all. ⁶⁶On the following day he sent the people away. They blessed the king and then went home, joyful and glad in heart for all the good things the LORD had done for his servant David and his people Israel.

The LORD appears to Solomon

9 When Solomon had finished building the temple of the LORD and the royal palace, and had achieved all he had desired to do, ²the LORD appeared to him a second time, as he had appeared to him at Gibeon. ³The LORD said to him:

'I have heard the prayer and plea you have made before me; I have consecrated this temple, which you have built, by putting my Name there for ever. My eyes and my heart will always be there.

IN OTHER WORDS

Sacrifice
1 Kings 8:63

A sacrifice is an offering made to God, and is an important idea throughout the Bible. Abraham's near-sacrifice of Isaac (Genesis 22:1–14) and Elijah's sacrifice 'competition' with the prophets of Baal (1 Kings 18:16–39) are good examples of famous sacrifices, but the sacrifice of animals took place every day in the temple in Jerusalem. Jesus' death on the cross was the ultimate sacrifice of atonement that puts things right between God and people (1 John 2:2).

4 'As for you, if you walk before me faithfully with integrity of heart and uprightness, as David your father did, and do all I command and observe my decrees and laws, 5I will establish your royal throne over Israel for ever, as I promised David your father when I said, "You shall never fail to have a successor on the throne of Israel."

6 'But if you[a] or your descendants turn away from me and do not observe the commands and decrees I have given you[b] and go off to serve other gods and worship them, 7then I will cut off Israel from the land I have given them and will reject this temple I have consecrated for my Name. Israel will then become a byword and an object of ridicule among all peoples. 8This temple will become a heap of rubble. All[c] who pass by will be appalled and will scoff and say, "Why has the LORD done such a thing to this land and to this temple?" 9People will answer, "Because they have forsaken the LORD their God, who brought their ancestors out of Egypt, and have embraced other gods, worshipping and serving them—that is why the LORD brought all this disaster on them."'

Solomon's other activities

10At the end of twenty years, during which Solomon built these two buildings—the temple of the LORD and the royal palace— 11King Solomon gave twenty towns in Galilee to Hiram king of Tyre, because Hiram had supplied him with all the cedar and juniper and gold he wanted. 12But when Hiram went from Tyre to see the towns that Solomon had given him, he was not pleased with them. 13'What kind of towns are these you have given me, my brother?' he asked. And he called them the Land of Kabul,[d] a name they have to this day. 14Now Hiram had sent to the king 120 talents[e] of gold.

15Here is the account of the forced labour King Solomon conscripted to build the LORD's temple, his own palace, the terraces,[f] the wall of Jerusalem, and Hazor, Megiddo and Gezer. 16(Pharaoh king of Egypt had attacked and captured Gezer. He had set it on fire. He killed its Canaanite inhabitants and then gave it as a wedding gift to his daughter, Solomon's wife. 17And Solomon rebuilt Gezer.) He built up Lower Beth Horon, 18Baalath, and Tadmor[g] in the desert, within his land, 19as well as all his store cities and the towns for his chariots and for his horses[h]—whatever he desired to build in Jerusalem, in Lebanon and throughout all the territory he ruled.

20There were still people left from the Amorites, Hittites, Perizzites, Hivites and Jebusites (these peoples were not Israelites). 21Solomon conscripted the descendants of all these peoples remaining in the land— whom the Israelites could not exterminate[i]—to serve as slave labour, as it is to this day. 22But Solomon did not make slaves of any of the Israelites; they were his fighting men, his government officials, his officers, his captains, and the commanders of his chariots and charioteers. 23They were also the chief officials in charge of Solomon's projects—550 officials supervising those who did the work.

24After Pharaoh's daughter had come up from the City of David to the palace Solomon had built for her, he constructed the terraces.

25Three times a year Solomon sacrificed burnt offerings and fellowship offerings on the altar he had built for the LORD, burning incense before the LORD along with them, and so fulfilled the temple obligations.

26King Solomon also built ships at Ezion Geber, which is near Elath in Edom, on the shore of the Red Sea.[j] 27And Hiram sent his

---

[a] 6 The Hebrew is plural.   [b] 6 The Hebrew is plural.   [c] 8 See some Septuagint manuscripts, Old Latin, Syriac, Arabic and Targum; Hebrew *And though this temple is now imposing, all*   [d] 13 *Kabul* sounds like the Hebrew for *good-for-nothing*.   [e] 14 That is, about 4 metric tons   [f] 15 Or *the Millo*; also in verse 24   [g] 18 The Hebrew may also be read *Tamar*.   [h] 19 Or *charioteers*   [i] 21 The Hebrew term refers to the irrevocable giving over of things or persons to the LORD, often by totally destroying them.   [j] 26 Or *the Sea of Reeds*

servants—sailors who knew the sea—to serve in the fleet with Solomon's servants. 28They sailed to Ophir and brought back 420 talents[a] of gold, which they delivered to King Solomon.

The queen of Sheba visits Solomon

10 When the queen of Sheba heard about the fame of Solomon and his relationship to the LORD, she came to test Solomon with hard questions. 2Arriving at Jerusalem with a very great caravan—with camels carrying spices, large quantities of gold, and precious stones—she came to Solomon and talked with him about all that she had on her mind. 3Solomon answered all her questions; nothing was too hard for the king to explain to her. 4When the queen of Sheba saw all the wisdom of Solomon and the palace he had built, 5the food on his table, the seating of his officials, the attending servants in their robes, his cupbearers, and the burnt offerings he made at[b] the temple of the LORD, she was overwhelmed.

6She said to the king, 'The report I heard in my own country about your achievements and your wisdom is true. 7But I did not believe these things until I came and saw with my own eyes. Indeed, not even half was told me; in wisdom and wealth you have far exceeded the report I heard. 8How happy your people must be! How happy your officials, who continually stand before you and hear your wisdom! 9Praise be to the LORD your God, who has delighted in you and placed you on the throne of Israel. Because of the LORD's eternal love for Israel, he has made you king to maintain justice and righteousness.'

10And she gave the king 120 talents[c] of gold, large quantities of spices, and precious stones. Never again were so many spices brought in as those the queen of Sheba gave to King Solomon.

11(Hiram's ships brought gold from Ophir; and from there they brought great cargoes of almug-wood[d] and precious stones. 12The king used the almug-wood to make supports[e] for the temple of the LORD and for the royal palace, and to make harps and lyres for the musicians. So much almug-wood has never been imported or seen since that day.)

13King Solomon gave the queen of Sheba all she desired and asked for, besides what he had given her out of his royal bounty. Then she left and returned with her retinue to her own country.

Solomon's splendour

14The weight of the gold that Solomon received yearly was 666 talents,[f] 15not including the revenues from merchants and traders and from all the Arabian kings and the governors of the territories.

16King Solomon made two hundred large shields of hammered gold; six hundred shekels[g] of gold went into each shield. 17He also made three hundred small shields of hammered gold, with three minas[h] of gold in each shield. The king put them in the Palace of the Forest of Lebanon.

18Then the king made a great throne inlaid with ivory and overlaid with fine gold. 19The throne had six steps, and its back had a rounded top. On both sides of

People and Places

Queen of Sheba
1 Kings 10:1
Sheba was a mountainous country in south-west Arabia. It was a strong commercial power because it had many important trade routes through its land. The queen of Sheba may have wanted to talk trade with Solomon as well as checking out his wisdom, to make sure that her caravans of camels could move through the territory under Solomon's control.

---

[a] 28 That is, about 14 metric tons [b] 5 Or *the ascent by which he went up to* [c] 10 That is, about 4 metric tons [d] 11 Probably a variant of *algum-wood*; also in verse 12 [e] 12 The meaning of the Hebrew for this word is uncertain. [f] 14 That is, about 23 metric tons [g] 16 That is, about 6.9 kilograms; also in verse 29 [h] 17 That is, about 1.7 kilograms; or perhaps reference is to double minas, that is, about 3.5 kilograms.

the seat were armrests, with a lion standing beside each of them. 20Twelve lions stood on the six steps, one at either end of each step. Nothing like it had ever been made for any other kingdom. 21All King Solomon's goblets were gold, and all the household articles in the Palace of the Forest of Lebanon were pure gold. Nothing was made of silver, because silver was considered of little value in Solomon's days. 22The king had a fleet of trading ships[a] at sea along with the ships of Hiram. Once every three years it returned carrying gold, silver and ivory, and apes and baboons.

23King Solomon was greater in riches and wisdom than all the other kings of the earth. 24The whole world sought audience with Solomon to hear the wisdom God had put in his heart. 25Year after year, everyone who came brought a gift—articles of silver and gold, robes, weapons and spices, and horses and mules.

26Solomon accumulated chariots and horses; he had fourteen hundred chariots and twelve thousand horses,[b] which he kept in the chariot cities and also with him in Jerusalem. 27The king made silver as common in Jerusalem as stones, and cedar as plentiful as sycamore-fig trees in the foothills. 28Solomon's horses were imported from Egypt and from Kue[c]—the royal merchants purchased them from Kue at the current price. 29They imported a chariot from Egypt for six hundred shekels of silver, and a horse for a hundred and fifty.[d] They also exported them to all the kings of the Hittites and of the Arameans.

Solomon's wives

11 King Solomon, however, loved many foreign women besides Pharaoh's daughter—Moabites, Ammonites, Edomites, Sidonians and Hittites. 2They were from nations about which the LORD had told the Israelites, 'You must not intermarry with them, because they will surely turn your hearts after their gods.' Nevertheless, Solomon held fast to them in love. 3He had seven hundred wives of royal birth and three hundred concubines, and his wives led him astray. 4As Solomon grew old, his wives turned his heart after other gods, and his heart was not fully devoted to the LORD his God, as the heart of David his father had been. 5He followed Ashtoreth the goddess of the Sidonians, and Molek the detestable god of the Ammonites. 6So Solomon did evil in the eyes of the LORD; he did not follow the LORD completely, as David his father had done.

7On a hill east of Jerusalem, Solomon built a high place for Chemosh the detestable god of Moab, and for Molek the detestable god of the Ammonites. 8He did the same for all his foreign wives, who burned incense and offered sacrifices to their gods.

9The LORD became angry with Solomon because his heart had turned away from the LORD, the God of Israel, who had appeared to him twice. 10Although he had forbidden Solomon to follow other gods, Solomon did not keep the LORD's command. 11So the LORD said to Solomon, 'Since this is your attitude and you have not kept my covenant and my decrees, which I commanded you, I will most certainly tear the kingdom away from you and give it to one of your subordinates. 12Nevertheless, for the sake of David your father, I will not do it during your lifetime. I will tear it out of the hand of your son. 13Yet I will not tear the whole kingdom from him, but will give him one tribe for the sake of David my servant and for the sake of Jerusalem, which I have chosen.'

Solomon's adversaries

14Then the LORD raised up against Solomon an adversary, Hadad the Edomite, from the royal line of Edom. 15Earlier when David was fighting with Edom, Joab the commander of the army, who had gone up to bury the dead, had struck down all the men in Edom. 16Joab and all the Israelites stayed there for six months, until they had destroyed all the men in Edom. 17But Hadad, still only a boy, fled to Egypt with some Edomite officials who had served his father. 18They set out from Midian and went to Paran. Then taking people from Paran with them, they went to Egypt, to Pharaoh king

---

[a] 22 Hebrew of ships of Tarshish [b] 26 Or charioteers [c] 28 Probably Cilicia [d] 29 That is, about 1.7 kilograms

of Egypt, who gave Hadad a house and land and provided him with food.

19Pharaoh was so pleased with Hadad that he gave him a sister of his own wife, Queen Tahpenes, in marriage. 20The sister of Tahpenes bore him a son named Genubath, whom Tahpenes brought up in the royal palace. There Genubath lived with Pharaoh's own children.

21While he was in Egypt, Hadad heard that David rested with his ancestors and that Joab the commander of the army was also dead. Then Hadad said to Pharaoh, 'Let me go, so that I may return to my own country.'

22'What have you lacked here that you want to go back to your own country?' Pharaoh asked.

'Nothing,' Hadad replied, 'but do let me go!'

23And God raised up against Solomon another adversary, Rezon son of Eliada, who had fled from his master, Hadadezer king of Zobah. 24When David destroyed Zobah's army, Rezon gathered a band of men around him and became their leader; they went to Damascus, where they settled and took control. 25Rezon was Israel's adversary as long as Solomon lived, adding to the trouble caused by Hadad. So Rezon ruled in Aram and was hostile towards Israel.

Jeroboam rebels against Solomon

26Also, Jeroboam son of Nebat rebelled against the king. He was one of Solomon's officials, an Ephraimite from Zeredah, and his mother was a widow named Zeruah.

27Here is the account of how he rebelled against the king: Solomon had built the terraces[a] and had filled in the gap in the wall of the city of David his father. 28Now Jeroboam was a man of standing, and when Solomon saw how well the young man did his work, he put him in charge of the whole labour force of the house of Joseph.

29About that time Jeroboam was going out of Jerusalem, and Ahijah the prophet of Shiloh met him on the way, wearing a new cloak. The two of them were alone out in the country, 30and Ahijah took hold of the new cloak he was wearing and tore it into twelve pieces. 31Then he said to Jeroboam, 'Take ten pieces for yourself, for this is what the LORD, the God of Israel, says: "See, I am going to tear the kingdom out of Solomon's hand and give you ten tribes. 32But for the sake of my servant David and the city of Jerusalem, which I have chosen out of all the tribes of Israel, he will have one tribe. 33I will do this because they have[b] forsaken me and worshipped Ashtoreth the goddess of the Sidonians, Chemosh the god of the Moabites, and Molek the god of the Ammonites, and have not walked in obedience to me, nor done what is right in my eyes, nor kept my decrees and laws as David, Solomon's father, did.

34" "But I will not take the whole kingdom out of Solomon's hand; I have made him ruler all the days of his life for the sake of David my servant, whom I chose and who obeyed my commands and decrees. 35I will take the kingdom from his son's hands and give you ten tribes. 36I will give one tribe to his son so that David my servant may always have a lamp before me in Jerusalem, the city where I chose to put my Name. 37However, as for you, I will take you, and you will rule over all that your heart desires; you will be king over Israel. 38If you do whatever I command you and walk in obedience to me and do what is right in my eyes by obeying my decrees and commands, as David my servant did, I will be with you. I will build you a dynasty as enduring as the one I built for David and will give Israel to you. 39I will humble David's descendants because of this, but not for ever." '

40Solomon tried to kill Jeroboam, but Jeroboam fled to Egypt, to Shishak the king, and stayed there until Solomon's death.

Solomon's death

41As for the other events of Solomon's reign—all he did and the wisdom he displayed—are they not written in the book of the annals of Solomon? 42Solomon reigned in Jerusalem over all Israel for forty years. 43Then he rested with his ancestors and was buried in the city of David his father. And Rehoboam his son succeeded him as king.

---

[a] 27 Or *the Millo* [b] 33 Hebrew; Septuagint, Vulgate and Syriac *because he has*

Israel rebels against Rehoboam

12 Rehoboam went to Shechem, for all Israel had gone there to make him king. ²When Jeroboam son of Nebat heard this (he was still in Egypt, where he had fled from King Solomon), he returned from[a] Egypt. ³So they sent for Jeroboam, and he and the whole assembly of Israel went to Rehoboam and said to him: ⁴'Your father put a heavy yoke on us, but now lighten the harsh labour and the heavy yoke he put on us, and we will serve you.'

⁵Rehoboam answered, 'Go away for three days and then come back to me.' So the people went away.

⁶Then King Rehoboam consulted the elders who had served his father Solomon during his lifetime. 'How would you advise me to answer these people?' he asked.

⁷They replied, 'If today you will be a servant to these people and serve them and give them a favourable answer, they will always be your servants.'

⁸But Rehoboam rejected the advice the elders gave him and consulted the young men who had grown up with him and were serving him. ⁹He asked them, 'What is your advice? How should we answer these people who say to me, "Lighten the yoke your father put on us"?'

¹⁰The young men who had grown up with him replied, 'These people have said to you, "Your father put a heavy yoke on us, but make our yoke lighter." Now tell them, "My little finger is thicker than my father's waist. ¹¹My father laid on you a heavy yoke; I will make it even heavier. My father scourged you with whips; I will scourge you with scorpions."'

¹²Three days later Jeroboam and all the people returned to Rehoboam, as the king had said, 'Come back to me in three days.' ¹³The king answered the people harshly. Rejecting the advice given him by the elders, ¹⁴he followed the advice of the young men and said, 'My father made your yoke heavy; I will make it even heavier. My father scourged you with whips; I will scourge you with scorpions.' ¹⁵So the king did not listen to the people, for this turn of events was from the LORD, to fulfil the word the LORD had spoken to Jeroboam son of Nebat through Ahijah the Shilonite.

¹⁶When all Israel saw that the king refused to listen to them, they answered the king:

'What share do we have in David,
 what part in Jesse's son?
To your tents, Israel!
 Look after your own house, David!'

So the Israelites went home. ¹⁷But as for the Israelites who were living in the towns of Judah, Rehoboam still ruled over them.

¹⁸King Rehoboam sent out Adoniram,[b] who was in charge of forced labour, but all Israel stoned him to death. King Rehoboam, however, managed to get into his chariot and escape to Jerusalem. ¹⁹So Israel has been in rebellion against the house of David to this day.

²⁰When all the Israelites heard that Jeroboam had returned, they sent and called him to the assembly and made him king over all Israel. Only the tribe of Judah remained loyal to the house of David.

²¹When Rehoboam arrived in Jerusalem, he mustered the whole house of Judah and the tribe of Benjamin—a hundred and eighty thousand able young men—to

People and Places

Israel and Judah
1 Kings 12:20

When Solomon died, his son Rehoboam became king, and during his reign the ten northern tribes of Israel declared independence and set up their own nation under the rule of Jeroboam. They called their new kingdom Israel, which can be a bit confusing because previously the name Israel applied to all twelve tribes. The two tribes left in the south became known as Judah.

---

[a] 2 Or *he remained in* [b] 18 Some Septuagint manuscripts and Syriac (see also 1 Kings 4:6 and 5:14); Hebrew *Adoram*

make war against the house of Israel and to regain the kingdom for Rehoboam son of Solomon. 22But this word of God came to Shemaiah the man of God: 23'Say to Rehoboam son of Solomon king of Judah, to the whole house of Judah and Benjamin, and to the rest of the people, 24"This is what the LORD says: do not go up to fight against your brothers, the Israelites. Go home, every one of you, for this is my doing."' So they obeyed the word of the LORD and went home again, as the LORD had ordered.

Golden calves at Bethel and Dan

25Then Jeroboam fortified Shechem in the hill country of Ephraim and lived there. From there he went out and built up Peniel.*a*

26Jeroboam thought to himself, 'The kingdom is now likely to revert to the house of David. 27If these people go up to offer sacrifices at the temple of the LORD in Jerusalem, they will again give their allegiance to their lord, Rehoboam king of Judah. They will kill me and return to King Rehoboam.'

28After seeking advice, the king made two golden calves. He said to the people, 'It is too much for you to go up to Jerusalem. Here are your gods, Israel, who brought you up out of Egypt.' 29One he set up in Bethel, and the other in Dan. 30And this thing became a sin; the people came to worship the one at Bethel and went as far as Dan to worship the other.*b*

31Jeroboam built shrines on high places and appointed priests from all sorts of people, even though they were not Levites. 32He instituted a festival on the fifteenth day of the eighth month, like the festival held in Judah, and offered sacrifices on the altar. This he did in Bethel, sacrificing to the calves he had made. And at Bethel he also installed priests at the high places he had made. 33On the fifteenth day of the eighth month, a month of his own choosing, he offered sacrifices on the altar he had built at Bethel. So he instituted the festival for the Israelites and went up to the altar to make offerings.

The man of God from Judah

13 By the word of the LORD a man of God came from Judah to Bethel, as Jeroboam was standing by the altar to make an offering. 2He cried out against the altar by the word of the LORD: 'Altar, altar! This is what the LORD says: "A son named Josiah will be born to the house of David. On you he will sacrifice the priests of the high places who make offerings here, and human bones will be burned on you."' 3That same day the man of God gave a sign: 'This is the sign the LORD has declared: the altar will be split apart and the ashes on it will be poured out.'

4When King Jeroboam heard what the man of God cried out against the altar at Bethel, he stretched out his hand from the altar and said, 'Seize him!' But the hand he stretched out towards the man shrivelled up, so that he could not pull it back. 5Also, the altar was split apart and its ashes poured out according to the sign given by the man of God by the word of the LORD.

6Then the king said to the man of God, 'Intercede with the LORD your God and pray for me that my hand may be restored.' So the man of God interceded with the LORD, and the king's hand was restored and became as it was before.

7The king said to the man of God, 'Come home with me for a meal, and I will give you a gift.'

8But the man of God answered the king, 'Even if you were to give me half your possessions, I would not go with you, nor would I eat bread or drink water here. 9For I was commanded by the word of the LORD: "You must not eat bread or drink water or return by the way you came."' 10So he took another road and did not return by the way he had come to Bethel.

11Now there was a certain old prophet living in Bethel, whose sons came and told him all that the man of God had done there that day. They also told their father what he had said to the king. 12Their father asked them, 'Which way did he go?' And his sons showed him which road the man of God from Judah had taken. 13So he said to his sons, 'Saddle the donkey for me.' And when

---

a 25 Hebrew *Penuel*, a variant of *Peniel*   *b* 30 Probable reading of the original Hebrew text; Masoretic Text *people went to the one as far as Dan* they had saddled the donkey for him, he mounted it ¹⁴and rode after the man of God. He found him sitting under an oak tree and asked, 'Are you the man of God who came from Judah?'

'I am,' he replied.

¹⁵So the prophet said to him, 'Come home with me and eat.'

¹⁶The man of God said, 'I cannot turn back and go with you, nor can I eat bread or drink water with you in this place. ¹⁷I have been told by the word of the LORD: "You must not eat bread or drink water there or return by the way you came."'

¹⁸The old prophet answered, 'I too am a prophet, as you are. And an angel said to me by the word of the LORD: "Bring him back with you to your house so that he may eat bread and drink water."' (But he was lying to him.) ¹⁹So the man of God returned with him and ate and drank in his house.

²⁰While they were sitting at the table, the word of the LORD came to the old prophet who had brought him back. ²¹He cried out to the man of God who had come from Judah, 'This is what the LORD says: "You have defied the word of the LORD and have not kept the command the LORD your God gave you. ²²You came back and ate bread and drank water in the place where he told you not to eat or drink. Therefore your body will not be buried in the tomb of your ancestors."'

²³When the man of God had finished eating and drinking, the prophet who had brought him back saddled his donkey for him. ²⁴As he went on his way, a lion met him on the road and killed him, and his body was left lying on the road, with both the donkey and the lion standing beside it. ²⁵Some people who passed by saw the body lying there, with the lion standing beside the body, and they went and reported it in the city where the old prophet lived.

²⁶When the prophet who had brought him back from his journey heard of it, he said, 'It is the man of God who defied the word of the LORD. The LORD has given him over to the lion, which has mauled him and killed him, as the word of the LORD had warned him.'

²⁷The prophet said to his sons, 'Saddle the donkey for me,' and they did so. ²⁸Then he went out and found the body lying on the road, with the donkey and the lion standing beside it. The lion had neither eaten the body nor mauled the donkey. ²⁹So the prophet picked up the body of the man of God, laid it on the donkey, and brought it back to his own city to mourn for him and bury him. ³⁰Then he laid the body in his own tomb, and they mourned over him and said, 'Alas, my brother!'

³¹After burying him, he said to his sons, 'When I die, bury me in the grave where the man of God is buried; lay my bones beside his bones. ³²For the message he declared by the word of the LORD against the altar in Bethel and against all the shrines on the high places in the towns of Samaria will certainly come true.'

³³Even after this, Jeroboam did not change his evil ways, but once more appointed priests for the high places from all sorts of people. Anyone who wanted to become a priest he consecrated for the high places. ³⁴This was the sin of the house of Jeroboam that led to its downfall and to its destruction from the face of the earth.

Ahijah's prophecy against Jeroboam

14 At that time Abijah son of Jeroboam became ill, ²and Jeroboam said to his wife, 'Go, disguise yourself, so that you won't be recognised as the wife of Jeroboam. Then go to Shiloh. Ahijah the prophet is there—the one who told me I would be king over this people. ³Take ten loaves of bread with you, some cakes and a jar of honey, and go to him. He will tell you what will happen to the boy.' ⁴So Jeroboam's wife did what he said and went to Ahijah's house in Shiloh.

Now Ahijah could not see; his sight was gone because of his age. ⁵But the LORD had told Ahijah, 'Jeroboam's wife is coming to ask you about her son, for he is ill, and you are to give her such and such an answer. When she arrives, she will pretend to be someone else.'

⁶So when Ahijah heard the sound of her footsteps at the door, he said, 'Come in, wife of Jeroboam. Why this pretence? I have been sent to you with bad news. ⁷Go, tell

Dogs
1 Kings 14:11
This was a particularly horrible way to end your life. Dogs were considered to be 'unclean' because they fed on dead animals. And it was shameful not to be given a proper burial.

Jeroboam that this is what the LORD, the God of Israel, says: "I raised you up from among the people and appointed you ruler over my people Israel. 8I tore the kingdom away from the house of David and gave it to you, but you have not been like my servant David, who kept my commands and followed me with all his heart, doing only what was right in my eyes. 9You have done more evil than all who lived before you. You have made for yourself other gods, idols made of metal; you have aroused my anger and thrust me behind your back.

10' "Because of this, I am going to bring disaster on the house of Jeroboam. I will cut off from Jeroboam every last male in Israel—slave or free.[a] I will burn up the house of Jeroboam as one burns dung, until it is all gone. 11Dogs will eat those belonging to Jeroboam who die in the city, and the birds will feed on those who die in the country. The LORD has spoken!'

12'As for you, go back home. When you set foot in your city, the boy will die. 13All Israel will mourn for him and bury him. He is the only one belonging to Jeroboam who will be buried, because he is the only one in the house of Jeroboam in whom the LORD, the God of Israel, has found anything good.

14'The LORD will raise up for himself a king over Israel who will cut off the family of Jeroboam. Even now this is beginning to happen.[b] 15And the LORD will strike Israel, so that it will be like a reed swaying in the water. He will uproot Israel from this good land that he gave to their ancestors and scatter them beyond the River Euphrates, because they aroused the LORD's anger by making Asherah poles.[c] 16And he will give Israel up because of the sins Jeroboam has committed and has caused Israel to commit.'

17Then Jeroboam's wife got up and left and went to Tirzah. As soon as she stepped over the threshold of the house, the boy died. 18They buried him, and all Israel mourned for him, as the LORD had said through his servant the prophet Ahijah.

19The other events of Jeroboam's reign, his wars and how he ruled, are written in the book of the annals of the kings of Israel. 20He reigned for twenty-two years and then rested with his ancestors. And Nadab his son succeeded him as king.

Rehoboam king of Judah

21Rehoboam son of Solomon was king in Judah. He was forty-one years old when he became king, and he reigned for seventeen years in Jerusalem, the city the LORD had chosen out of all the tribes of Israel in which to put his Name. His mother's name was Naamah; she was an Ammonite.

22Judah did evil in the eyes of the LORD. By the sins they committed they stirred up his jealous anger more than those who were before them had done. 23They also set up for themselves high places, sacred stones and Asherah poles on every high hill and under every spreading tree. 24There were even male shrine-prostitutes in the land; the people engaged in all the detestable practices of the nations the LORD had driven out before the Israelites.

25In the fifth year of King Rehoboam, Shishak king of Egypt attacked Jerusalem. 26He carried off the treasures of the temple of the LORD and the treasures of the royal palace. He took everything, including all the gold shields Solomon had made. 27So King Rehoboam made bronze shields to replace

---

[a] 10 Or *Israel—every ruler or leader* [b] 14 The meaning of the Hebrew for this sentence is uncertain. [c] 15 That is, wooden symbols of the goddess Asherah; here and elsewhere in 1 Kings

them and assigned these to the commanders of the guard on duty at the entrance to the royal palace. 28Whenever the king went to the LORD's temple, the guards bore the shields, and afterwards they returned them to the guardroom.

29As for the other events of Rehoboam's reign, and all he did, are they not written in the book of the annals of the kings of Judah? 30There was continual warfare between Rehoboam and Jeroboam. 31And Rehoboam rested with his ancestors and was buried with them in the City of David. His mother's name was Naamah; she was an Ammonite. And Abijah*a* his son succeeded him as king.

Abijah king of Judah

15 In the eighteenth year of the reign of Jeroboam son of Nebat, Abijah*b* became king of Judah, 2and he reigned in Jerusalem for three years. His mother's name was Maakah daughter of Abishalom.*c*

3He committed all the sins his father had done before him; his heart was not fully devoted to the LORD his God, as the heart of David his forefather had been. 4Nevertheless, for David's sake the LORD his God gave him a lamp in Jerusalem by raising up a son to succeed him and by making Jerusalem strong. 5For David had done what was right in the eyes of the LORD and had not failed to keep any of the LORD's commands all the days of his life—except in the case of Uriah the Hittite.

6There was war between Abijah*d* and Jeroboam throughout Abijah's lifetime. 7As for the other events of Abijah's reign, and all he did, are they not written in the book of the annals of the kings of Judah? There was war between Abijah and Jeroboam. 8And Abijah rested with his ancestors and was buried in the City of David. And Asa his son succeeded him as king.

Asa king of Judah

9In the twentieth year of Jeroboam king of Israel, Asa became king of Judah, 10and he reigned in Jerusalem for forty-one years. His grandmother's name was Maakah daughter of Abishalom.

11Asa did what was right in the eyes of the LORD, as his father David had done. 12He expelled the male shrine-prostitutes from the land and got rid of all the idols his ancestors had made. 13He even deposed his grandmother Maakah from her position as queen mother, because she had made a repulsive image for the worship of Asherah. Asa cut it down and burned it in the Kidron Valley. 14Although he did not remove the high places, Asa's heart was fully committed to the LORD all his life. 15He brought into the temple of the LORD the silver and gold and the articles that he and his father had dedicated.

16There was war between Asa and Baasha king of Israel throughout their reigns. 17Baasha king of Israel went up against Judah and fortified Ramah to prevent anyone from leaving or entering the territory of Asa king of Judah.

18Asa then took all the silver and gold that was left in the treasuries of the LORD's temple and of his own palace. He entrusted it to his officials and sent them to Ben-Hadad son of Tabrimmon, the son of Hezion, the king of Aram, who was ruling in Damascus. 19'Let there be a treaty between me and you,' he said, 'as there was between my father and your father. See, I am sending you a gift of silver and gold. Now break your treaty with Baasha king of Israel so that he will withdraw from me.'

20Ben-Hadad agreed with King Asa and sent the commanders of his forces against the towns of Israel. He conquered Ijon, Dan, Abel Beth Maakah and all Kinnereth in addition to Naphtali. 21When Baasha heard this, he stopped building Ramah and withdrew to Tirzah. 22Then King Asa issued an order to all Judah—no-one was exempt—and they carried away from Ramah the stones and timber Baasha had been using there. With them King Asa built up Geba in Benjamin, and also Mizpah.

23As for all the other events of Asa's reign, all his achievements, all he did and the cities

---

a 31 Some Hebrew manuscripts and Septuagint (see also 2 Chron. 12:16); most Hebrew manuscripts *Abijam*   *b* 1 Some Hebrew manuscripts and Septuagint (see also 2 Chron. 12:16); most Hebrew manuscripts *Abijam*; also in verses 7 and 8   *c* 2 A variant of *Absalom*; also in verse 10   *d* 6 Some Hebrew manuscripts and Syriac *Abijah* (that is, Abijah); most Hebrew manuscripts *Rehoboam* he built, are they not written in the book of the annals of the kings of Judah? In his old age, however, his feet became diseased. 24Then Asa rested with his ancestors and was buried with them in the city of his father David. And Jehoshaphat his son succeeded him as king.

Nadab king of Israel

25Nadab son of Jeroboam became king of Israel in the second year of Asa king of Judah, and he reigned over Israel for two years. 26He did evil in the eyes of the LORD, following the ways of his father and committing the same sin his father had caused Israel to commit.

27Baasha son of Ahijah of the house of Issachar plotted against him, and he struck him down at Gibbethon, a Philistine town, while Nadab and all Israel were besieging it. 28Baasha killed Nadab in the third year of Asa king of Judah and succeeded him as king.

29As soon as he began to reign, he killed Jeroboam's whole family. He did not leave Jeroboam anyone that breathed, but destroyed them all, according to the word of the LORD given through his servant Ahijah the Shilonite. 30This happened because of the sins Jeroboam had committed and had caused Israel to commit, and because he aroused the anger of the LORD, the God of Israel.

31As for the other events of Nadab's reign, and all he did, are they not written in the book of the annals of the kings of Israel? 32There was war between Asa and Baasha king of Israel throughout their reigns.

Baasha king of Israel

33In the third year of Asa king of Judah, Baasha son of Ahijah became king of all Israel in Tirzah, and he reigned for twenty-four years. 34He did evil in the eyes of the LORD, following the ways of Jeroboam and committing the same sin Jeroboam had caused Israel to commit.

16 Then the word of the LORD came to Jehu son of Hanani concerning Baasha: 2'I lifted you up from the dust and appointed you ruler over my people Israel, but you followed the ways of Jeroboam and caused my people Israel to sin and to arouse my anger by their sins. 3So I am about to wipe out Baasha and his house, and I will make your house like that of Jeroboam son of Nebat. 4Dogs will eat those belonging to Baasha who die in the city, and birds will feed on those who die in the country.'

5As for the other events of Baasha's reign, what he did and his achievements, are they not written in the book of the annals of the kings of Israel? 6Baasha rested with his ancestors and was buried in Tirzah. And Elah his son succeeded him as king.

7Moreover, the word of the LORD came through the prophet Jehu son of Hanani to Baasha and his house, because of all the evil he had done in the eyes of the LORD, arousing his anger by the things he did, becoming like the house of Jeroboam—and also because he destroyed it.

Elah king of Israel

8In the twenty-sixth year of Asa king of Judah, Elah son of Baasha became king of Israel, and he reigned in Tirzah for two years.

9Zimri, one of his officials, who had command of half his chariots, plotted against him. Elah was in Tirzah at the time, getting drunk in the home of Arza, who was in charge of the palace at Tirzah. 10Zimri came in, struck him down and killed him in the twenty-seventh year of Asa king of Judah. Then he succeeded him as king.

11As soon as he began to reign and was seated on the throne, he killed off Baasha's whole family. He did not spare a single male, whether relative or friend. 12So Zimri destroyed the whole family of Baasha, in accordance with the word of the LORD spoken against Baasha through the prophet Jehu— 13because of all the sins Baasha and his son Elah had committed and had caused Israel to commit, so that they aroused the anger of the LORD, the God of Israel, by their worthless idols.

14As for the other events of Elah's reign, and all he did, are they not written in the book of the annals of the kings of Israel?

Zimri king of Israel

15 In the twenty-seventh year of Asa king of Judah, Zimri reigned in Tirzah for seven days. The army was encamped near Gibbethon, a Philistine town. 16 When the Israelites in the camp heard that Zimri had plotted against the king and murdered him, they proclaimed Omri, the commander of the army, king over Israel that very day there in the camp. 17 Then Omri and all the Israelites with him withdrew from Gibbethon and laid siege to Tirzah. 18 When Zimri saw that the city was taken, he went into the citadel of the royal palace and set the palace on fire around him. So he died, 19 because of the sins he had committed, doing evil in the eyes of the LORD and following the ways of Jeroboam and committing the same sin Jeroboam had caused Israel to commit.

20 As for the other events of Zimri's reign, and the rebellion he carried out, are they not written in the book of the annals of the kings of Israel?

Omri king of Israel

21 Then the people of Israel were split into two factions; half supported Tibni son of Ginath for king, and the other half supported Omri. 22 But Omri's followers proved stronger than those of Tibni son of Ginath. So Tibni died and Omri became king.

23 In the thirty-first year of Asa king of Judah, Omri became king of Israel, and he reigned for twelve years, six of them in Tirzah. 24 He bought the hill of Samaria from Shemer for two talents[a] of silver and built a city on the hill, calling it Samaria, after Shemer, the name of the former owner of the hill.

25 But Omri did evil in the eyes of the LORD and sinned more than all those before him. 26 He followed completely the ways of Jeroboam son of Nebat, committing the same sin Jeroboam had caused Israel to commit, so that they aroused the anger of the LORD, the God of Israel, by their worthless idols.

27 As for the other events of Omri's reign, what he did and the things he achieved, are they not written in the book of the annals of the kings of Israel? 28 Omri rested with his ancestors and was buried in Samaria. And Ahab his son succeeded him as king.

Ahab becomes king of Israel

29 In the thirty-eighth year of Asa king of Judah, Ahab son of Omri became king of Israel, and he reigned in Samaria over Israel for twenty-two years. 30 Ahab son of Omri did more evil in the eyes of the LORD than any of those before him. 31 He not only considered it trivial to commit the sins of Jeroboam son of Nebat, but he also married Jezebel daughter of Ethbaal king of the Sidonians, and began to serve Baal and worship him. 32 He set up an altar for Baal in the temple of Baal that he built in Samaria. 33 Ahab also made an Asherah pole and did more to arouse the anger of the LORD, the God of Israel, than did all the kings of Israel before him.

34 In Ahab's time, Hiel of Bethel rebuilt Jericho. He laid its foundations at the cost of his firstborn son Abiram, and he set up its gates at the cost of his youngest son Segub, in accordance with the word of the LORD spoken by Joshua son of Nun.

Elijah fed by ravens

17 Now Elijah the Tishbite, from Tishbe[b] in Gilead, said to Ahab, 'As the LORD, the God of Israel, lives, whom

People and Places

Elijah
1 Kings 17:1
Elijah was a prophet who was used by God to stand against the worship of Baal in Israel. He also opposed the sin and injustices of several kings and queens in Egypt. He performed miracles and had a dramatic showdown with the prophets of Baal on Mount Carmel, showing them very decisively how powerful God is.

---

[a] 24 That is, about 68 kilograms [b] 1 Or *Tishbite, of the settlers*

I serve, there will be neither dew nor rain in the next few years except at my word.'

²Then the word of the LORD came to Elijah: ³'Leave here, turn eastward and hide in the Kerith Ravine, east of the Jordan. ⁴You will drink from the brook, and I have instructed the ravens to supply you with food there.'

⁵So he did what the LORD had told him. He went to the Kerith Ravine, east of the Jordan, and stayed there. ⁶The ravens brought him bread and meat in the morning and bread and meat in the evening, and he drank from the brook.

The widow at Zarephath

⁷Some time later the brook dried up because there had been no rain in the land. ⁸Then the word of the LORD came to him: ⁹'Go at once to Zarephath in the region of Sidon and stay there. I have instructed a widow there to supply you with food.' ¹⁰So he went to Zarephath. When he came to the town gate, a widow was there gathering sticks. He called to her and asked, 'Would you bring me a little water in a jar so I may have a drink?' ¹¹As she was going to get it, he called, 'And bring me, please, a piece of bread.'

¹²'As surely as the LORD your God lives,' she replied, 'I don't have any bread—only a handful of flour in a jar and a little olive oil in a jug. I am gathering a few sticks to take home and make a meal for myself and my son, that we may eat it—and die.'

¹³Elijah said to her, 'Don't be afraid. Go home and do as you have said. But first make a small loaf of bread for me from what you have and bring it to me, and then make something for yourself and your son. ¹⁴For this is what the LORD, the God of Israel, says: "The jar of flour will not be used up and the jug of oil will not run dry until the day the LORD sends rain on the land."'

¹⁵She went away and did as Elijah had told her. So there was food every day for Elijah and for the woman and her family. ¹⁶For the jar of flour was not used up and the jug of oil did not run dry, in keeping with the word of the LORD spoken by Elijah.

¹⁷Some time later the son of the woman who owned the house became ill. He grew worse and worse, and finally stopped breathing. ¹⁸She said to Elijah, 'What do you have against me, man of God? Did you come to remind me of my sin and kill my son?'

¹⁹'Give me your son,' Elijah replied. He took him from her arms, carried him to the upper room where he was staying, and laid him on his bed. ²⁰Then he cried out to the LORD, 'LORD my God, have you brought tragedy even on this widow I am staying with, by causing her son to die?' ²¹Then he stretched himself out on the boy three times and cried out to the LORD, 'LORD my God, let this boy's life return to him!'

²²The LORD heard Elijah's cry, and the boy's life returned to him, and he lived. ²³Elijah picked up the child and carried him down from the room into the house. He gave him to his mother and said, 'Look, your son is alive!'

²⁴Then the woman said to Elijah, 'Now I know that you are a man of God and that the word of the LORD from your mouth is the truth.'

Elijah and Obadiah

18 After a long time, in the third year, the word of the LORD came to Elijah: 'Go and present yourself to Ahab, and I will send rain on the land.' ²So Elijah went to present himself to Ahab.

Now the famine was severe in Samaria, ³and Ahab had summoned Obadiah, who was in charge of his palace. (Obadiah was a devout believer in the LORD. ⁴While Jezebel was killing off the LORD's prophets, Obadiah had taken a hundred prophets and hidden them in two caves, fifty in each, and had supplied them with food and water.) ⁵Ahab had said to Obadiah, 'Go through the land to all the springs and valleys. Maybe we can find some grass to keep the horses and mules alive so we will not have to kill any of our animals.' ⁶So they divided the land they were to cover, Ahab going in one direction and Obadiah in another.

⁷As Obadiah was walking along, Elijah met him. Obadiah recognised him, bowed down to the ground, and said, 'Is it really you, my lord Elijah?'

⁸'Yes,' he replied. 'Go tell your master, "Elijah is here."'

People and Places

Jezebel
1 Kings 18:4

Jezebel was the original wicked queen. Married to Ahab who was king of Israel, she was the real power behind the throne. She introduced Baal worship to the city where she lived, Jezreel, and persecuted the prophets of God. After Ahab was killed in battle, she reigned for another ten years through her two sons Ahaziah and Joram.

9'What have I done wrong,' asked Obadiah, 'that you are handing your servant over to Ahab to be put to death? 10As surely as the LORD your God lives, there is not a nation or kingdom where my master has not sent someone to look for you. And whenever a nation or kingdom claimed you were not there, he made them swear they could not find you. 11But now you tell me to go to my master and say, "Elijah is here." 12I don't know where the Spirit of the LORD may carry you when I leave you. If I go and tell Ahab and he doesn't find you, he will kill me. Yet I your servant have worshipped the LORD since my youth. 13Haven't you heard, my lord, what I did while Jezebel was killing the prophets of the LORD? I hid a hundred of the LORD's prophets in two caves, fifty in each, and supplied them with food and water. 14And now you tell me to go to my master and say, "Elijah is here." He will kill me!'

15Elijah said, 'As the LORD Almighty lives, whom I serve, I will surely present myself to Ahab today.'

Elijah on Mount Carmel

16So Obadiah went to meet Ahab and told him, and Ahab went to meet Elijah. 17When he saw Elijah, he said to him, 'Is that you, you troubler of Israel?'

18'I have not made trouble for Israel,' Elijah replied. 'But you and your father's family have. You have abandoned the LORD's commands and have followed the Baals. 19Now summon the people from all over Israel to meet me on Mount Carmel. And bring the four hundred and fifty prophets of Baal and the four hundred prophets of Asherah, who eat at Jezebel's table.'

20So Ahab sent word throughout all Israel and assembled the prophets on Mount Carmel. 21Elijah went before the people and said, 'How long will you waver between two opinions? If the LORD is God, follow him; but if Baal is God, follow him.'

But the people said nothing.

22Then Elijah said to them, 'I am the only one of the LORD's prophets left, but Baal has four hundred and fifty prophets. 23Get two bulls for us. Let Baal's prophets choose one for themselves, and let them cut it into pieces and put it on the wood but not set fire to it. I will prepare the other bull and put it on the wood but not set fire to it. 24Then you call on the name of your god, and I will call on the name of the LORD. The god who answers by fire—he is God.'

Then all the people said, 'What you say is good.'

25Elijah said to the prophets of Baal, 'Choose one of the bulls and prepare it first, since there are so many of you. Call on the name of your god, but do not light the fire.' 26So they took the bull that was given to them and prepared it.

Then they called on the name of Baal from morning till noon. 'Baal, answer us!' they shouted. But there was no response; no-one answered. And they danced around the altar they had made.

27At noon Elijah began to taunt them. 'Shout louder!' he said. 'Surely he is a god! Perhaps he is deep in thought, or busy, or travelling. Maybe he is sleeping and must be awakened.' 28So they shouted louder and slashed themselves with swords and spears, as was their custom, until their blood flowed. 29Midday passed, and they continued their frantic prophesying until the time for the evening sacrifice. But there was no response, no-one answered, no-one paid attention.

30Then Elijah said to all the people, 'Come here to me.' They came to him, and he repaired the altar of the LORD, which had been torn down. ³¹Elijah took twelve stones, one for each of the tribes descended from Jacob, to whom the word of the LORD had come, saying, 'Your name shall be Israel.' ³²With the stones he built an altar in the name of the LORD, and he dug a trench round it large enough to hold two seahs[a] of seed. ³³He arranged the wood, cut the bull into pieces and laid it on the wood. Then he said to them, 'Fill four large jars with water and pour it on the offering and on the wood.'

³⁴'Do it again,' he said, and they did it again.

'Do it a third time,' he ordered, and they did it the third time. ³⁵The water ran down around the altar and even filled the trench.

³⁶At the time of sacrifice, the prophet Elijah stepped forward and prayed: 'LORD, the God of Abraham, Isaac and Israel, let it be known today that you are God in Israel and that I am your servant and have done all these things at your command. ³⁷Answer me, LORD, answer me, so these people will know that you, LORD, are God, and that you are turning their hearts back again.'

³⁸Then the fire of the LORD fell and burned up the sacrifice, the wood, the stones and the soil, and also licked up the water in the trench.

³⁹When all the people saw this, they fell prostrate and cried, 'The LORD—he is God! The LORD—he is God!'

⁴⁰Then Elijah commanded them, 'Seize the prophets of Baal. Don't let anyone get away!' They seized them, and Elijah had them brought down to the Kishon Valley and slaughtered there.

⁴¹And Elijah said to Ahab, 'Go, eat and drink, for there is the sound of heavy rain.' ⁴²So Ahab went off to eat and drink, but Elijah climbed to the top of Carmel, bent down to the ground and put his face between his knees.

⁴³'Go and look towards the sea,' he told his servant. And he went up and looked.

'There is nothing there,' he said.

Seven times Elijah said, 'Go back.'

⁴⁴The seventh time the servant reported, 'A cloud as small as a man's hand is rising from the sea.'

So Elijah said, 'Go and tell Ahab, "Hitch up your chariot and go down before the rain stops you."'

⁴⁵Meanwhile, the sky grew black with clouds, the wind rose, a heavy rainstorm came on and Ahab rode off to Jezreel. ⁴⁶The power of the LORD came on Elijah and, tucking his cloak into his belt, he ran ahead of Ahab all the way to Jezreel.

Elijah flees to Horeb

19 Now Ahab told Jezebel everything Elijah had done and how he had killed all the prophets with the sword. ²So Jezebel sent a messenger to Elijah to say, 'May the gods deal with me, be it ever so severely, if by this time tomorrow I do not make your life like that of one of them.'

³Elijah was afraid[b] and ran for his life. When he came to Beersheba in Judah, he left his servant there, ⁴while he himself went a day's journey into the wilderness. He came to a broom bush, sat down under it and prayed that he might die. 'I have had enough, LORD,' he said. 'Take my life; I am no better than my ancestors.' ⁵Then he lay down under the tree and fell asleep.

All at once an angel touched him and said, 'Get up and eat.' ⁶He looked around, and there by his head was some bread baked over hot coals, and a jar of water. He ate and drank and then lay down again.

⁷The angel of the LORD came back a second time and touched him and said, 'Get up and eat, for the journey is too much for you.' ⁸So he got up and ate and drank. Strengthened by that food, he travelled for forty days and forty nights until he reached Horeb, the mountain of God. ⁹There he went into a cave and spent the night.

The LORD appears to Elijah

And the word of the LORD came to him: 'What are you doing here, Elijah?'

¹⁰He replied, 'I have been very zealous for the LORD God Almighty. The Israelites have rejected your covenant, torn down your altars, and put your prophets to death with

---

[a] 32 That is, probably about 11 kilograms   [b] 3 Or *Elijah saw*

making Connections

Forty days and forty nights
1 Kings 19:8

Although Elijah may have spent exactly forty days and nights travelling to Horeb, sometimes the number forty is used symbolically in the Bible to mean a long but limited period of time. Forty is also the number of days it rained during the flood (Genesis 7:4), the number of days Moses stayed on Mount Sinai (Exodus 24:18), the number of years the Israelites wandered in the desert (Deuteronomy 2:7) and the number of days that Jesus fasted in the desert (Matthew 4:2).

---

the sword. I am the only one left, and now they are trying to kill me too.'

¹¹The LORD said, 'Go out and stand on the mountain in the presence of the LORD, for the LORD is about to pass by.'

Then a great and powerful wind tore the mountains apart and shattered the rocks before the LORD, but the LORD was not in the wind. After the wind there was an earthquake, but the LORD was not in the earthquake. ¹²After the earthquake came a fire, but the LORD was not in the fire. And after the fire came a gentle whisper. ¹³When Elijah heard it, he pulled his cloak over his face and went out and stood at the mouth of the cave.

Then a voice said to him, 'What are you doing here, Elijah?'

¹⁴He replied, 'I have been very zealous for the LORD God Almighty. The Israelites have rejected your covenant, torn down your altars, and put your prophets to death with the sword. I am the only one left, and now they are trying to kill me too.'

¹⁵The LORD said to him, 'Go back the way you came, and go to the Desert of Damascus. When you get there, anoint Hazael king over Aram. ¹⁶Also, anoint Jehu son of Nimshi king over Israel, and anoint Elisha son of Shaphat from Abel Meholah to succeed you as prophet. ¹⁷Jehu will put to death any who escape the sword of Hazael, and Elisha will put to death any who escape the sword of Jehu. ¹⁸Yet I reserve seven thousand in Israel—all whose knees have not bowed down to Baal and whose mouths have not kissed him.'

The call of Elisha

¹⁹So Elijah went from there and found Elisha son of Shaphat. He was ploughing with twelve yoke of oxen, and he himself was driving the twelfth pair. Elijah went up to him and threw his cloak around him. ²⁰Elisha then left his oxen and ran after Elijah. 'Let me kiss my father and mother good-bye,' he said, 'and then I will come with you.'

'Go back,' Elijah replied. 'What have I done to you?'

People and Places

Elisha
1 Kings 19:21

Elisha succeeded Elijah as a prophet when Elijah's time on earth was finished. He asked for a double portion of Elijah's spirit, and if the number of miracles he performed is anything to go by then he must have received it, as twice as many of his miracles are recorded. Among many other miracles, he helped a widow pay her debts through a bottle of oil that didn't run out (2 Kings 4:1–7), and he brought a child back to life (2 Kings 4:17–37). He also advised kings and was not afraid to criticise them when necessary.

²¹So Elisha left him and went back. He took his yoke of oxen and slaughtered them. He burned the ploughing equipment to cook the meat and gave it to the people, and they ate. Then he set out to follow Elijah and became his servant.

Ben-Hadad attacks Samaria

20 Now Ben-Hadad king of Aram mustered his entire army. Accompanied by thirty-two kings with their horses and chariots, he went up and besieged Samaria and attacked it. ²He sent messengers into the city to Ahab king of Israel, saying, 'This is what Ben-Hadad says: ³"Your silver and gold are mine, and the best of your wives and children are mine."'

⁴The king of Israel answered, 'Just as you say, my lord the king. I and all I have are yours.'

⁵The messengers came again and said, 'This is what Ben-Hadad says: "I sent to demand your silver and gold, your wives and your children. ⁶But about this time tomorrow I am going to send my officials to search your palace and the houses of your officials. They will seize everything you value and carry it away."'

⁷The king of Israel summoned all the elders of the land and said to them, 'See how this man is looking for trouble! When he sent for my wives and my children, my silver and my gold, I did not refuse him.'

⁸The elders and the people all answered, 'Don't listen to him or agree to his demands.'

⁹So he replied to Ben-Hadad's messengers, 'Tell my lord the king, "Your servant will do all you demanded the first time, but this demand I cannot meet."' They left and took the answer back to Ben-Hadad.

¹⁰Then Ben-Hadad sent another message to Ahab: 'May the gods deal with me, be it ever so severely, if enough dust remains in Samaria to give each of my men a handful.'

¹¹The king of Israel answered, 'Tell him: "One who puts on his armour should not boast like one who takes it off."'

¹²Ben-Hadad heard this message while he and the kings were drinking in their tents,[a] and he ordered his men: 'Prepare to attack.' So they prepared to attack the city.

Ahab defeats Ben-Hadad

¹³Meanwhile a prophet came to Ahab king of Israel and announced, 'This is what the LORD says: "Do you see this vast army? I will give it into your hand today, and then you will know that I am the LORD."'

¹⁴'But who will do this?' asked Ahab.

The prophet replied, 'This is what the LORD says: "The junior officers under the provincial commanders will do it."'

'And who will start the battle?' he asked.

The prophet answered, 'You will.'

¹⁵So Ahab summoned the 232 junior officers under the provincial commanders. Then he assembled the rest of the Israelites, 7,000 in all. ¹⁶They set out at noon while Ben-Hadad and the 32 kings allied with him were in their tents getting drunk. ¹⁷The junior officers under the provincial commanders went out first.

Now Ben-Hadad had dispatched scouts, who reported, 'Men are advancing from Samaria.'

¹⁸He said, 'If they have come out for peace, take them alive; if they have come out for war, take them alive.'

¹⁹The junior officers under the provincial commanders marched out of the city with the army behind them ²⁰and each one struck down his opponent. At that, the Arameans fled, with the Israelites in pursuit. But Ben-Hadad king of Aram escaped on horseback with some of his horsemen. ²¹The king of Israel advanced and overpowered the horses and chariots and inflicted heavy losses on the Arameans.

²²Afterwards, the prophet came to the king of Israel and said, 'Strengthen your position and see what must be done, because next spring the king of Aram will attack you again.'

²³Meanwhile, the officials of the king of Aram advised him, 'Their gods are gods of the hills. That is why they were too strong for us. But if we fight them on the plains, surely we will be stronger than they. ²⁴Do this: remove all the kings from their commands and replace them with other officers.

---

[a] 12 Or *in Sukkoth*; also in verse 16

25 You must also raise an army like the one you lost—horse for horse and chariot for chariot—so we can fight Israel on the plains. Then surely we will be stronger than they.' He agreed with them and acted accordingly.

26 The next spring Ben-Hadad mustered the Arameans and went up to Aphek to fight against Israel. 27 When the Israelites were also mustered and given provisions, they marched out to meet them. The Israelites camped opposite them like two small flocks of goats, while the Arameans covered the countryside.

28 The man of God came up and told the king of Israel, 'This is what the LORD says: "Because the Arameans think the LORD is a god of the hills and not a god of the valleys, I will deliver this vast army into your hands, and you will know that I am the LORD."'

29 For seven days they camped opposite each other, and on the seventh day the battle was joined. The Israelites inflicted a hundred thousand casualties on the Aramean foot soldiers in one day. 30 The rest of them escaped to the city of Aphek, where the wall collapsed on twenty-seven thousand of them. And Ben-Hadad fled to the city and hid in an inner room.

31 His officials said to him, 'Look, we have heard that the kings of the house of Israel are merciful. Let us go to the king of Israel with sackcloth round our waists and ropes round our heads. Perhaps he will spare your life.'

32 Wearing sackcloth round their waists and ropes round their heads, they went to the king of Israel and said, 'Your servant Ben-Hadad says: "Please let me live."'

The king answered, 'Is he still alive? He is an old ally.'

33 The men took this as a good sign and were quick to pick up his word. 'Yes, your old ally Ben-Hadad!' they said.

'Go and get him,' the king said. When Ben-Hadad came out, Ahab brought him up into his chariot.

34 'I will return the cities my father took from your father,' Ben-Hadad offered. 'You may set up your own market areas in Damascus, as my father did in Samaria.'

[Ahab said,] 'On the basis of a treaty I will set you free.' So he made a treaty with him, and let him go.

A prophet condemns Ahab

35 By the word of the LORD one of the company of the prophets said to his companion, 'Strike me with your weapon,' but he refused.

36 So the prophet said, 'Because you have not obeyed the LORD, as soon as you leave me a lion will kill you.' And after the man went away, a lion found him and killed him.

37 The prophet found another man and said, 'Strike me, please.' So the man struck him and wounded him. 38 Then the prophet went and stood by the road waiting for the king. He disguised himself with his headband down over his eyes. 39 As the king passed by, the prophet called out to him, 'Your servant went into the thick of the battle, and someone came to me with a captive and said, "Guard this man. If he is missing, it will be your life for his life, or you must pay a talent*a* of silver." 40 While your servant was busy here and there, the man disappeared.'

'That is your sentence,' the king of Israel said. 'You have pronounced it yourself.'

41 Then the prophet quickly removed the headband from his eyes, and the king of Israel recognised him as one of the prophets. 42 He said to the king, 'This is what the LORD says: "You have set free a man I had determined should die.*b* Therefore it is your life for his life, your people for his people."'

43 Sullen and angry, the king of Israel went to his palace in Samaria.

Naboth's vineyard

21 Some time later there was an incident involving a vineyard belonging to Naboth the Jezreelite. The vineyard was in Jezreel, close to the palace of Ahab king of Samaria. 2 Ahab said to Naboth, 'Let me have your vineyard to use for a vegetable garden, since it is close to my palace. In exchange I will give you a better vineyard or, if you prefer, I will pay you whatever it is worth.'

---

a 39 That is, about 34 kilograms   *b* 42 The Hebrew term refers to the irrevocable giving over of things or persons to the LORD, often by totally destroying them.

³But Naboth replied, 'The LORD forbid that I should give you the inheritance of my ancestors.'

⁴So Ahab went home, sullen and angry because Naboth the Jezreelite had said, 'I will not give you the inheritance of my ancestors.' He lay on his bed sulking and refused to eat.

⁵His wife Jezebel came in and asked him, 'Why are you so sullen? Why won't you eat?'

⁶He answered her, 'Because I said to Naboth the Jezreelite, "Sell me your vineyard; or if you prefer, I will give you another vineyard in its place." But he said, "I will not give you my vineyard." '

⁷Jezebel his wife said, 'Is this how you act as king over Israel? Get up and eat! Cheer up. I'll get you the vineyard of Naboth the Jezreelite.'

⁸So she wrote letters in Ahab's name, placed his seal on them, and sent them to the elders and nobles who lived in Naboth's city with him. ⁹In those letters she wrote:

> 'Proclaim a day of fasting and give Naboth a prominent seat among the people. ¹⁰But put two scoundrels opposite him and get them to bring charges that he has cursed both God and the king. Then take him out and stone him to death.'

¹¹So the elders and nobles who lived in Naboth's city did as Jezebel directed in the letters she had written to them. ¹²They proclaimed a fast and seated Naboth in a prominent place among the people. ¹³Then two scoundrels came and sat opposite him and brought charges against Naboth before the people, saying, 'Naboth has cursed both God and the king.' So they took him outside the city and stoned him to death. ¹⁴Then they sent word to Jezebel: 'Naboth has been stoned to death.'

¹⁵As soon as Jezebel heard that Naboth had been stoned to death, she said to Ahab, 'Get up and take possession of the vineyard of Naboth the Jezreelite that he refused to sell you. He is no longer alive, but dead.' ¹⁶When Ahab heard that Naboth was dead, he got up and went down to take possession of Naboth's vineyard.

¹⁷Then the word of the LORD came to Elijah the Tishbite: ¹⁸'Go down to meet Ahab king of Israel, who rules in Samaria. He is now in Naboth's vineyard, where he has gone to take possession of it. ¹⁹Say to him, "This is what the LORD says: have you not murdered a man and seized his property?" Then say to him, "This is what the LORD says: in the place where dogs licked up Naboth's blood, dogs will lick up your blood—yes, yours!" '

²⁰Ahab said to Elijah, 'So you have found me, my enemy!'

'I have found you,' he answered, 'because you have sold yourself to do evil in the eyes of the LORD. ²¹He says, "I am going to bring disaster on you. I will wipe out your descendants and cut off from Ahab every last male in Israel—slave or free.^{a} ²²I will make your house like that of Jeroboam son of Nebat and that of Baasha son of Ahijah, because you have aroused my anger and have caused Israel to sin."

²³'And also concerning Jezebel the LORD says: "Dogs will devour Jezebel by the wall of^b Jezreel."

²⁴'Dogs will eat those belonging to Ahab who die in the city, and the birds will feed on those who die in the country.'

²⁵(There was never anyone like Ahab, who sold himself to do evil in the eyes of the LORD, urged on by Jezebel his wife. ²⁶He behaved in the vilest manner by going after idols, like the Amorites the LORD drove out before Israel.)

²⁷When Ahab heard these words, he tore his clothes, put on sackcloth and fasted. He lay in sackcloth and went around meekly.

²⁸Then the word of the LORD came to Elijah the Tishbite: ²⁹'Have you noticed how Ahab has humbled himself before me? Because he has humbled himself, I will not bring this disaster in his day, but I will bring it on his house in the days of his son.'

Micaiah prophesies against Ahab

22 For three years there was no war between Aram and Israel. ²But in

---

^{a} 21 Or *Israel—every ruler or leader* ^{b} 23 Most Hebrew manuscripts; a few Hebrew manuscripts, Vulgate and Syriac (see also 2 Kings 9:26) *the plot of ground at* the third year Jehoshaphat king of Judah went down to see the king of Israel. ³The king of Israel had said to his officials, 'Don't you know that Ramoth Gilead belongs to us and yet we are doing nothing to retake it from the king of Aram?'

⁴So he asked Jehoshaphat, 'Will you go with me to fight against Ramoth Gilead?'

Jehoshaphat replied to the king of Israel, 'I am as you are, my people as your people, my horses as your horses.' ⁵But Jehoshaphat also said to the king of Israel, 'First seek the counsel of the LORD.'

⁶So the king of Israel brought together the prophets—about four hundred men—and asked them, 'Shall I go to war against Ramoth Gilead, or shall I refrain?'

'Go,' they answered, 'for the Lord will give it into the king's hand.'

⁷But Jehoshaphat asked, 'Is there no longer a prophet of the LORD here whom we can enquire of?'

⁸The king of Israel answered Jehoshaphat, 'There is still one through whom we can enquire of the LORD, but I hate him because he never prophesies anything good about me, but always bad. He is Micaiah son of Imlah.'

'The king should not say such a thing,' Jehoshaphat replied.

⁹So the king of Israel called one of his officials and said, 'Bring Micaiah son of Imlah at once.'

¹⁰Dressed in their royal robes, the king of Israel and Jehoshaphat king of Judah were sitting on their thrones at the threshing-floor by the entrance of the gate of Samaria, with all the prophets prophesying before them. ¹¹Now Zedekiah son of Kenaanah had made iron horns and he declared, 'This is what the LORD says: "With these you will gore the Arameans until they are destroyed."'

¹²All the other prophets were prophesying the same thing. 'Attack Ramoth Gilead and be victorious,' they said, 'for the LORD will give it into the king's hand.'

¹³The messenger who had gone to summon Micaiah said to him, 'Look, the other prophets without exception are predicting success for the king. Let your word agree with theirs, and speak favourably.'

¹⁴But Micaiah said, 'As surely as the LORD lives, I can tell him only what the LORD tells me.'

¹⁵When he arrived, the king asked him, 'Micaiah, shall we go to war against Ramoth Gilead, or not?'

'Attack and be victorious,' he answered, 'for the LORD will give it into the king's hand.'

¹⁶The king said to him, 'How many times must I make you swear to tell me nothing but the truth in the name of the LORD?'

¹⁷Then Micaiah answered, 'I saw all Israel scattered on the hills like sheep without a shepherd, and the LORD said, "These people have no master. Let each one go home in peace."'

¹⁸The king of Israel said to Jehoshaphat, 'Didn't I tell you that he never prophesies anything good about me, but only bad?'

¹⁹Micaiah continued, 'Therefore hear the word of the LORD: I saw the LORD sitting on his throne with all the host of heaven standing round him on his right and on his left. ²⁰And the LORD said, "Who will entice Ahab into attacking Ramoth Gilead and going to his death there?"

'One suggested this, and another that. ²¹Finally, a spirit came forward, stood before the LORD and said, "I will entice him."

²²' "By what means?" the LORD asked.

'"I will go out and be a lying spirit in the mouths of all his prophets," he said.

'"You will succeed in enticing him," said the LORD. "Go and do it."

²³'So now the LORD has put a lying spirit in the mouths of all these prophets of yours. The LORD has decreed disaster for you.'

²⁴Then Zedekiah son of Kenaanah went up and slapped Micaiah in the face. 'Which way did the spirit from^a the LORD go when he went from me to speak to you?' he asked.

²⁵Micaiah replied, 'You will find out on the day you go to hide in an inner room.'

²⁶The king of Israel then ordered, 'Take Micaiah and send him back to Amon the ruler of the city and to Joash the king's son ²⁷and say, "This is what the king says: put

---

^a 24 Or Spirit of

this fellow in prison and give him nothing but bread and water until I return safely."'

28Micaiah declared, 'If you ever return safely, the LORD has not spoken through me.' Then he added, 'Mark my words, all you people!'

Ahab killed at Ramoth Gilead

29So the king of Israel and Jehoshaphat king of Judah went up to Ramoth Gilead. 30The king of Israel said to Jehoshaphat, 'I will enter the battle in disguise, but you wear your royal robes.' So the king of Israel disguised himself and went into battle.

31Now the king of Aram had ordered his thirty-two chariot commanders, 'Do not fight with anyone, small or great, except the king of Israel.' 32When the chariot commanders saw Jehoshaphat, they thought, 'Surely this is the king of Israel.' So they turned to attack him, but when Jehoshaphat cried out, 33the chariot commanders saw that he was not the king of Israel and stopped pursuing him.

34But someone drew his bow at random and hit the king of Israel between the breastplate and the scale armour. The king told his chariot driver, 'Wheel around and get me out of the fighting. I've been wounded.' 35All day long the battle raged, and the king was propped up in his chariot facing the Arameans. The blood from his wound ran onto the floor of the chariot, and that evening he died. 36As the sun was setting, a cry spread through the army: 'Everyone to your own town; everyone to your land!'

37So the king died and was brought to Samaria, and they buried him there. 38They washed the chariot at a pool in Samaria (where the prostitutes bathed),[a] and the dogs licked up his blood, as the word of the LORD had declared.

39As for the other events of Ahab's reign, including all he did, the palace he built and inlaid with ivory, and the cities he fortified, are they not written in the book of the annals of the kings of Israel? 40Ahab rested with his ancestors. And Ahaziah his son succeeded him as king.

Jehoshaphat king of Judah

41Jehoshaphat son of Asa became king of Judah in the fourth year of Ahab king of Israel. 42Jehoshaphat was thirty-five years old when he became king, and he reigned in Jerusalem for twenty-five years. His mother's name was Azubah daughter of Shilhi. 43In everything he followed the ways of his father Asa and did not stray from them; he did what was right in the eyes of the LORD. *The high places, however, were not removed, and the people continued to offer sacrifices and burn incense there. *44Jehoshaphat was also at peace with the king of Israel.

45As for the other events of Jehoshaphat's reign, the things he achieved and his military exploits, are they not written in the book of the annals of the kings of Judah? 46He rid the land of the rest of the male shrine-prostitutes who remained there even after the reign of his father Asa. 47There was then no king in Edom; a provincial governor ruled.

48Now Jehoshaphat built a fleet of trading ships[b] to go to Ophir for gold, but they never set sail—they were wrecked at Ezion Geber. 49At that time Ahaziah son of Ahab said to Jehoshaphat, 'Let my men sail with yours,' but Jehoshaphat refused.

50Then Jehoshaphat rested with his ancestors and was buried with them in the city of David his father. And Jehoram his son succeeded him as king.

Ahaziah king of Israel

51Ahaziah son of Ahab became king of Israel in Samaria in the seventeenth year of Jehoshaphat king of Judah, and he reigned over Israel for two years. 52He did evil in the eyes of the LORD, because he followed the ways of his father and mother and of Jeroboam son of Nebat, who caused Israel to sin. 53He served and worshipped Baal and aroused the anger of the LORD, the God of Israel, just as his father had done.

---

[a] 38 Or *Samaria and cleaned the weapons* [b] 48 Hebrew *of ships of Tarshish*

* This sentence (22:43b) is numbered 22:44 in Hebrew texts. * 22:44-53 is numbered 22:45-54 in Hebrew texts.

2 Kings

INTRODUCTION

2 KINGS

Author: Unknown

When: The two books of Kings cover four hundred years in the history of the people of Israel, from around 970 BC to 587 BC.

Where: The two kingdoms of Israel and Judah.

Main theme: The exploits of the kings of Israel and Judah continue. Some of them were faithful to God, but the most common summary of their reigns is, 'He did evil in the sight of the Lord.' God sends prophets to call his people back to him, but they refuse to come. Eventually Israel is invaded by the Assyrians in 722 BC and Judah falls to the Babylonians in 587 BC.

The LORD's judgment on Ahaziah

1 After Ahab's death, Moab rebelled against Israel. 2Now Ahaziah had fallen through the lattice of his upper room in Samaria and injured himself. So he sent messengers, saying to them, 'Go and consult Baal-Zebub, the god of Ekron, to see if I will recover from this injury.'

3But the angel of the LORD said to Elijah the Tishbite, 'Go up and meet the messengers of the king of Samaria and ask them, "Is it because there is no God in Israel that you are going off to consult Baal-Zebub, the god of Ekron?" 4Therefore this is what the LORD says: "You will not leave the bed you are lying on. You will certainly die!"' So Elijah went.

5When the messengers returned to the king, he asked them, 'Why have you come back?'

6'A man came to meet us,' they replied. 'And he said to us, "Go back to the king who sent you and tell him, 'This is what the LORD says: is it because there is no God in Israel that you are sending messengers to consult Baal-Zebub, the god of Ekron? Therefore you will not leave the bed you are lying on. You will certainly die!'"'

7The king asked them, 'What kind of man was it who came to meet you and told you this?'

⁸They replied, 'He had a garment of hair*ᵃ* and had a leather belt round his waist.'

The king said, 'That was Elijah the Tishbite.'

⁹Then he sent to Elijah a captain with his company of fifty men. The captain went up to Elijah, who was sitting on the top of a hill, and said to him, 'Man of God, the king says, "Come down!"'

¹⁰Elijah answered the captain, 'If I am a man of God, may fire come down from heaven and consume you and your fifty men!' Then the fire fell from heaven and consumed the captain and his men.

¹¹At this the king sent to Elijah another captain with his fifty men. The captain said to him, 'Man of God, this is what the king says, "Come down at once!"'

¹²'If I am a man of God,' Elijah replied, 'may fire come down from heaven and consume you and your fifty men!' Then the fire of God fell from heaven and consumed him and his fifty men.

¹³So the king sent a third captain with his fifty men. This third captain went up and fell on his knees before Elijah. 'Man of God,' he begged, 'please have respect for my life and the lives of these fifty men, your servants! ¹⁴See, fire has fallen from heaven and consumed the first two captains and all their men. But now have respect for my life!'

¹⁵The angel of the LORD said to Elijah, 'Go down with him; do not be afraid of him.' So Elijah got up and went down with him to the king.

¹⁶He told the king, 'This is what the LORD says: is it because there is no God in Israel for you to consult that you have sent messengers to consult Baal-Zebub, the god of Ekron? Because you have done this, you will never leave the bed you are lying on. You will certainly die!' ¹⁷So he died, according to the word of the LORD that Elijah had spoken.

Because Ahaziah had no son, Joram*ᵇ* succeeded him as king in the second year of Jehoram son of Jehoshaphat king of Judah. ¹⁸As for all the other events of Ahaziah's reign, and what he did, are they not written in the book of the annals of the kings of Israel?

Elijah taken up to heaven

2 When the LORD was about to take Elijah up to heaven in a whirlwind, Elijah and Elisha were on their way from Gilgal. ²Elijah said to Elisha, 'Stay here; the LORD has sent me to Bethel.'

But Elisha said, 'As surely as the LORD lives and as you live, I will not leave you.' So they went down to Bethel.

³The company of the prophets at Bethel came out to Elisha and asked, 'Do you know that the LORD is going to take your master from you today?'

'Yes, I know,' Elisha replied, 'so be quiet.'

⁴Then Elijah said to him, 'Stay here, Elisha; the LORD has sent me to Jericho.'

And he replied, 'As surely as the LORD lives and as you live, I will not leave you.' So they went to Jericho.

⁵The company of the prophets at Jericho went up to Elisha and asked him, 'Do you know that the LORD is going to take your master from you today?'

'Yes, I know,' he replied, 'so be quiet.'

⁶Then Elijah said to him, 'Stay here; the LORD has sent me to the Jordan.'

And he replied, 'As surely as the LORD lives and as you live, I will not leave you.' So the two of them walked on.

⁷Fifty men from the company of the prophets went and stood at a distance, facing the place where Elijah and Elisha had stopped at the Jordan. ⁸Elijah took his cloak, rolled it up and struck the water with it. The water divided to the right and to the left, and the two of them crossed over on dry ground.

⁹When they had crossed, Elijah said to Elisha, 'Tell me, what can I do for you before I am taken from you?'

'Let me inherit a double portion of your spirit,' Elisha replied.

¹⁰'You have asked a difficult thing,' Elijah said, 'yet if you see me when I am taken from you, it will be yours—otherwise, it will not.'

¹¹As they were walking along and talking together, suddenly a chariot of fire and horses of fire appeared and separated the two of them, and Elijah went up to heaven in a whirlwind. ¹²Elisha saw this and cried out, 'My father! My father! The chariots and

---

ᵃ 8 Or *He was a hairy man*   *ᵇ* 17 Hebrew *Jehoram*, a variant of *Joram* horsemen of Israel!' And Elisha saw him no more. Then he took hold of his garment and tore it in two.

¹³He picked up the cloak that had fallen from Elijah and went back and stood on the bank of the Jordan. ¹⁴Then he took the cloak that had fallen from him and struck the water with it. 'Where now is the LORD, the God of Elijah?' he asked. When he struck the water, it divided to the right and to the left, and he crossed over.

¹⁵The company of the prophets from Jericho, who were watching, said, 'The spirit of Elijah is resting on Elisha.' And they went to meet him and bowed to the ground before him. ¹⁶'Look,' they said, 'we your servants have fifty able men. Let them go and look for your master. Perhaps the Spirit of the LORD has picked him up and set him down on some mountain or in some valley.'

'No,' Elisha replied, 'do not send them.'

¹⁷But they persisted until he was too embarrassed to refuse. So he said, 'Send them.' And they sent fifty men, who searched for three days but did not find him. ¹⁸When they returned to Elisha, who was staying in Jericho, he said to them, 'Didn't I tell you not to go?'

Healing of the water

¹⁹The people of the city said to Elisha, 'Look, our lord, this town is well situated, as you can see, but the water is bad and the land is unproductive.'

²⁰'Bring me a new bowl,' he said, 'and put salt in it.' So they brought it to him.

²¹Then he went out to the spring and threw the salt into it, saying, 'This is what the LORD says: "I have healed this water. Never again will it cause death or make the land unproductive."' ²²And the water has remained pure to this day, according to the word Elisha had spoken.

Elisha is jeered

²³From there Elisha went up to Bethel. As he was walking along the road, some boys came out of the town and jeered at him. 'Get out of here, baldy!' they said. 'Get out of here, baldy!' ²⁴He turned round, looked at them

IN OTHER WORDS

Curse
2 Kings 2:24
A curse was the opposite of a blessing, a wish of evil on a person, nation or thing.

and called down a curse on them in the name of the LORD. Then two bears came out of the woods and mauled forty-two of the boys. ²⁵And he went on to Mount Carmel and from there returned to Samaria.

Moab revolts

3 Joram[a] son of Ahab became king of Israel in Samaria in the eighteenth year of Jehoshaphat king of Judah, and he reigned for twelve years. ²He did evil in the eyes of the LORD, but not as his father and mother had done. He got rid of the sacred stone of Baal that his father had made. ³Nevertheless he clung to the sins of Jeroboam son of Nebat, which he had caused Israel to commit; he did not turn away from them.

⁴Now Mesha king of Moab raised sheep, and he had to pay the king of Israel a tribute of a hundred thousand lambs and the wool of a hundred thousand rams. ⁵But after Ahab died, the king of Moab rebelled against the king of Israel. ⁶So at that time King Joram set out from Samaria and mobilised all Israel. ⁷He also sent this message to Jehoshaphat king of Judah: 'The king of Moab has rebelled against me. Will you go with me to fight against Moab?'

'I will go with you,' he replied. 'I am as you are, my people as your people, my horses as your horses.'

⁸'By what route shall we attack?' he asked.

'Through the Desert of Edom,' he answered.

⁹So the king of Israel set out with the king of Judah and the king of Edom. After a

---

[a] 1 Hebrew *Jehoram*, a variant of *Joram*; also in verse 6

roundabout march of seven days, the army had no more water for themselves or for the animals with them.

¹⁰'What!' exclaimed the king of Israel. 'Has the LORD called us three kings together only to deliver us into the hands of Moab?'

¹¹But Jehoshaphat asked, 'Is there no prophet of the LORD here, through whom we may enquire of the LORD?'

An officer of the king of Israel answered, 'Elisha son of Shaphat is here. He used to pour water on the hands of Elijah.'ᵃ

¹²Jehoshaphat said, 'The word of the LORD is with him.' So the king of Israel and Jehoshaphat and the king of Edom went down to him.

¹³Elisha said to the king of Israel, 'Why do you want to involve me? Go to the prophets of your father and the prophets of your mother.'

'No,' the king of Israel answered, 'because it was the LORD who called us three kings together to deliver us into the hands of Moab.'

¹⁴Elisha said, 'As surely as the LORD Almighty lives, whom I serve, if I did not have respect for the presence of Jehoshaphat king of Judah, I would not pay any attention to you. ¹⁵But now bring me a harpist.'

While the harpist was playing, the hand of the LORD came on Elisha ¹⁶and he said, 'This is what the LORD says: I will fill this valley with pools of water. ¹⁷For this is what the LORD says: you will see neither wind nor rain, yet this valley will be filled with water, and you, your cattle and your other animals will drink. ¹⁸This is an easy thing in the eyes of the LORD; he will also deliver Moab into your hands. ¹⁹You will overthrow every fortified city and every major town. You will cut down every good tree, block up all the springs, and ruin every good field with stones.'

²⁰The next morning, about the time for offering the sacrifice, there it was—water flowing from the direction of Edom! And the land was filled with water.

²¹Now all the Moabites had heard that the kings had come to fight against them; so every man, young and old, who could bear arms was called up and stationed on the border. ²²When they got up early in the morning, the sun was shining on the water. To the Moabites across the way, the water looked red—like blood. ²³'That's blood!' they said. 'Those kings must have fought and slaughtered each other. Now to the plunder, Moab!'

²⁴But when the Moabites came to the camp of Israel, the Israelites rose up and fought them until they fled. And the Israelites invaded the land and slaughtered the Moabites. ²⁵They destroyed the towns, and each man threw a stone on every good field until it was covered. They blocked up all the springs and cut down every good tree. Only Kir Hareseth was left with its stones in place, but men armed with slings surrounded it and attacked it.

²⁶When the king of Moab saw that the battle had gone against him, he took with him seven hundred swordsmen to break through to the king of Edom, but they failed. ²⁷Then he took his firstborn son, who was to succeed him as king, and offered him as a sacrifice on the city wall. The fury against Israel was great; they withdrew and returned to their own land.

The widow's oil

4 The wife of a man from the company of the prophets cried out to Elisha, 'Your servant my husband is dead, and you know that he revered the LORD. But now his creditor is coming to take my two boys as his slaves.'

²Elisha replied to her, 'How can I help you? Tell me, what do you have in your house?'

'Your servant has nothing there at all,' she said, 'except a little olive oil.'

³Elisha said, 'Go round and ask all your neighbours for empty jars. Don't ask for just a few. ⁴Then go inside and shut the door behind you and your sons. Pour oil into all the jars, and as each is filled, put it to one side.'

⁵She left him and shut the door behind her and her sons. They brought the jars to her and she kept pouring. ⁶When all the jars were full, she said to her son, 'Bring me another one.'

ᵃ 11 That is, he was Elijah's personal servant.

But he replied, 'There is not a jar left.' Then the oil stopped flowing.

7She went and told the man of God, and he said, 'Go, sell the oil and pay your debts. You and your sons can live on what is left.'

The Shunammite's son restored to life

8One day Elisha went to Shunem. And a well-to-do woman was there, who urged him to stay for a meal. So whenever he passed by, he stopped there to eat. 9She said to her husband, 'I know that this man who often comes our way is a holy man of God. 10Let's make a small room on the roof and put in it a bed and a table, a chair and a lamp for him. Then he can stay there whenever he comes to us.'

11One day when Elisha came, he went up to his room and lay down there. 12He said to his servant Gehazi, 'Call the Shunammite.' So he called her, and she stood before him. 13Elisha said to him, 'Tell her, "You have gone to all this trouble for us. Now what can be done for you? Can we speak on your behalf to the king or the commander of the army?"'

She replied, 'I have a home among my own people.'

14'What can be done for her?' Elisha asked.

Gehazi said, 'She has no son, and her husband is old.'

15Then Elisha said, 'Call her.' So he called her, and she stood in the doorway. 16'About this time next year,' Elisha said, 'you will hold a son in your arms.'

'No, my lord!' she objected. 'Please, man of God, don't mislead your servant!'

17But the woman became pregnant, and the next year about that same time she gave birth to a son, just as Elisha had told her.

18The child grew, and one day he went out to his father, who was with the reapers. 19He said to his father, 'My head! My head!'

His father told a servant, 'Carry him to his mother.' 20After the servant had lifted him up and carried him to his mother, the boy sat on her lap until noon, and then he died. 21She went up and laid him on the bed of the man of God, then shut the door and went out.

22She called her husband and said, 'Please send me one of the servants and a donkey so I can go to the man of God quickly and return.'

23'Why go to him today?' he asked. 'It's not the New Moon or the Sabbath.'

'That's all right,' she said.

24She saddled the donkey and said to her servant, 'Lead on; don't slow down for me unless I tell you.' 25So she set out and came to the man of God at Mount Carmel.

When he saw her in the distance, the man of God said to his servant Gehazi, 'Look! There's the Shunammite! 26Run to meet her and ask her, "Are you all right? Is your husband all right? Is your child all right?"'

'Everything is all right,' she said.

27When she reached the man of God at the mountain, she took hold of his feet. Gehazi came over to push her away, but the man of God said, 'Leave her alone! She is in bitter distress, but the LORD has hidden it from me and has not told me why.'

28'Did I ask you for a son, my lord?' she said. 'Didn't I tell you, "Don't raise my hopes"?'

29Elisha said to Gehazi, 'Tuck your cloak into your belt, take my staff in your hand and run. Don't greet anyone you meet, and if anyone greets you, do not answer. Lay my staff on the boy's face.'

30But the child's mother said, 'As surely as the LORD lives and as you live, I will not leave you.' So he got up and followed her.

31Gehazi went on ahead and laid the staff on the boy's face, but there was no sound or response. So Gehazi went back to meet Elisha and told him, 'The boy has not awakened.'

32When Elisha reached the house, there was the boy lying dead on his couch. 33He went in, shut the door on the two of them and prayed to the LORD. 34Then he got on the bed and lay on the boy, mouth to mouth, eyes to eyes, hands to hands. As he stretched himself out on him, the boy's body grew warm. 35Elisha turned away and walked back and forth in the room and then got onto the bed and stretched out on him once more. The boy sneezed seven times and opened his eyes.

36Elisha summoned Gehazi and said, 'Call the Shunammite.' And he did. When she came, he said, 'Take your son.' 37She came in, fell at his feet and bowed to the ground. Then she took her son and went out.

Death in the pot

38 Elisha returned to Gilgal and there was a famine in that region. While the company of the prophets was meeting with him, he said to his servant, 'Put on the large pot and cook some stew for this company.'

39 One of them went out into the fields to gather herbs and found a wild vine. He gathered some of its gourds and filled the fold of his cloak. When he returned, he cut them up into the pot of stew, though no-one knew what they were. **40** The stew was poured out for the men, but as they began to eat it, they cried out, 'Man of God, there is death in the pot!' And they could not eat it.

41 Elisha said, 'Get some flour.' He put it into the pot and said, 'Serve it to the people to eat.' And there was nothing harmful in the pot.

Feeding of a hundred

42 A man came from Baal Shalishah, bringing the man of God twenty loaves of barley bread baked from the first ripe corn, along with some ears of new corn. 'Give it to the people to eat,' Elisha said.

43 'How can I set this before a hundred men?' his servant asked.

But Elisha answered, 'Give it to the people to eat. For this is what the LORD says: "They will eat and have some left over."' **44** Then he set it before them, and they ate and had some left over, according to the word of the LORD.

Naaman healed of leprosy

5 Now Naaman was commander of the army of the king of Aram. He was a great man in the sight of his master and highly regarded, because through him the LORD had given victory to Aram. He was a valiant soldier, but he had leprosy.[a]

2 Now bands of raiders from Aram had gone out and had taken captive a young girl from Israel, and she served Naaman's wife. **3** She said to her mistress, 'If only my master would see the prophet who is in Samaria! He would cure him of his leprosy.'

4 Naaman went to his master and told him what the girl from Israel had said. **5** 'By all means, go,' the king of Aram replied. 'I will send a letter to the king of Israel.' So Naaman left, taking with him ten talents[b] of silver, six thousand shekels[c] of gold and ten sets of clothing. **6** The letter that he took to the king of Israel read: 'With this letter I am sending my servant Naaman to you so that you may cure him of his leprosy.'

7 As soon as the king of Israel read the letter, he tore his robes and said, 'Am I God? Can I kill and bring back to life? Why does this fellow send someone to me to be cured of his leprosy? See how he is trying to pick a quarrel with me!'

8 When Elisha the man of God heard that the king of Israel had torn his robes, he sent him this message: 'Why have you torn your robes? Make the man come to me and he will know that there is a prophet in Israel.' **9** So Naaman went with his horses and chariots and stopped at the door of Elisha's house. **10** Elisha sent a messenger to say to him, 'Go, wash yourself seven times in the Jordan, and your flesh will be restored and you will be cleansed.'

11 But Naaman went away angry and said, 'I thought that he would surely come out to me and stand and call on the name of the

People and Places

River Jordan
2 Kings 5:10

The River Jordan is the longest and most important river in Israel. It is fairly shallow and twists and turns through the country from north to south. It runs from several kilometres north of the Sea of Galilee to the Dead Sea.

---

[a] 1 The Hebrew for *leprosy* was used for various diseases affecting the skin; also in verses 3, 6, 7, 11 and 27. [b] 5 That is, about 340 kilograms [c] 5 That is, about 68 kilograms

LORD his God, wave his hand over the spot and cure me of my leprosy. ¹²Are not Abana and Pharpar, the rivers of Damascus, better than all the waters of Israel? Couldn't I wash in them and be cleansed?' So he turned and went off in a rage.

¹³Naaman's servants went to him and said, 'My father, if the prophet had told you to do some great thing, would you not have done it? How much more, then, when he tells you, "Wash and be cleansed"?' ¹⁴So he went down and dipped himself in the Jordan seven times, as the man of God had told him, and his flesh was restored and became clean like that of a young boy.

¹⁵Then Naaman and all his attendants went back to the man of God. He stood before him and said, 'Now I know that there is no God in all the world except in Israel. So please accept a gift from your servant.'

¹⁶The prophet answered, 'As surely as the LORD lives, whom I serve, I will not accept a thing.' And even though Naaman urged him, he refused.

¹⁷'If you will not,' said Naaman, 'please let me, your servant, be given as much earth as a pair of mules can carry, for your servant will never again make burnt offerings and sacrifices to any other god but the LORD. ¹⁸But may the LORD forgive your servant for this one thing: when my master enters the temple of Rimmon to bow down and he is leaning on my arm and I have to bow there also—when I bow down in the temple of Rimmon, may the LORD forgive your servant for this.'

¹⁹'Go in peace,' Elisha said.

After Naaman had travelled some distance, ²⁰Gehazi, the servant of Elisha the man of God, said to himself, 'My master was too easy on Naaman, this Aramean, by not accepting from him what he brought. As surely as the LORD lives, I will run after him and get something from him.'

²¹So Gehazi hurried after Naaman. When Naaman saw him running towards him, he got down from the chariot to meet him. 'Is everything all right?' he asked.

²²'Everything is all right,' Gehazi answered. 'My master sent me to say, "Two young men from the company of the prophets have just come to me from the hill country of Ephraim. Please give them a talent[a] of silver and two sets of clothing."'

²³'By all means, take two talents,' said Naaman. He urged Gehazi to accept them, and then tied up the two talents of silver in two bags, with two sets of clothing. He gave them to two of his servants, and they carried them ahead of Gehazi. ²⁴When Gehazi came to the hill, he took the things from the servants and put them away in the house. He sent the men away and they left.

²⁵When he went in and stood before his master, Elisha asked him, 'Where have you been, Gehazi?'

'Your servant didn't go anywhere,' Gehazi answered.

²⁶But Elisha said to him, 'Was not my spirit with you when the man got down from his chariot to meet you? Is this the time to take money or to accept clothes—or olive groves and vineyards, or flocks and herds, or male and female slaves? ²⁷Naaman's leprosy will cling to you and to your descendants for ever.' Then Gehazi went from Elisha's presence and his skin was leprous—it had become as white as snow.

An axe-head floats

6 The company of the prophets said to Elisha, 'Look, the place where we meet with you is too small for us. ²Let us go to the Jordan, where each of us can get a pole; and let us build a place there for us to meet.'

And he said, 'Go.'

³Then one of them said, 'Won't you please come with your servants?'

'I will,' Elisha replied. ⁴And he went with them.

They went to the Jordan and began to cut down trees. ⁵As one of them was cutting down a tree, the iron axe-head fell into the water. 'Oh no, my lord!' he cried out. 'It was borrowed!'

⁶The man of God asked, 'Where did it fall?' When he showed him the place, Elisha cut a stick and threw it there, and made the iron float. ⁷'Lift it out,' he said. Then the man reached out his hand and took it.

---

[a] 22 That is, about 34 kilograms

Making Connections: Elisha's miracles
2 Kings 6:6

Elisha performed many miracles with God's power for high government officials like Naaman (2 Kings 5), as well as for people who were poor and oppressed. His life shows a marked contrast with the ineffective kings of his time because he followed God and they didn't.

Elisha traps blinded Arameans

8Now the king of Aram was at war with Israel. After conferring with his officers, he said, 'I will set up my camp in such and such a place.'

9The man of God sent word to the king of Israel: 'Beware of passing that place, because the Arameans are going down there.' 10So the king of Israel checked on the place indicated by the man of God. Time and again Elisha warned the king, so that he was on his guard in such places.

11This enraged the king of Aram. He summoned his officers and demanded of them, 'Tell me! Which of us is on the side of the king of Israel?'

12'None of us, my lord the king,' said one of his officers, 'but Elisha, the prophet who is in Israel, tells the king of Israel the very words you speak in your bedroom.'

13'Go, find out where he is,' the king ordered, 'so that I can send men and capture him.' The report came back: 'He is in Dothan.' 14Then he sent horses and chariots and a strong force there. They went by night and surrounded the city.

15When the servant of the man of God got up and went out early the next morning, an army with horses and chariots had surrounded the city. 'Oh no, my lord! What shall we do?' the servant asked.

16'Don't be afraid,' the prophet answered. 'Those who are with us are more than those who are with them.'

17And Elisha prayed, 'Open his eyes, LORD, so that he may see.' Then the LORD opened the servant's eyes, and he looked and saw the hills full of horses and chariots of fire all round Elisha.

18As the enemy came down towards him, Elisha prayed to the LORD, 'Strike this army with blindness.' So he struck them with blindness, as Elisha had asked.

19Elisha told them, 'This is not the road and this is not the city. Follow me, and I will lead you to the man you are looking for.' And he led them to Samaria.

20After they entered the city, Elisha said, 'LORD, open the eyes of these men so that they can see.' Then the LORD opened their eyes and they looked, and there they were, inside Samaria.

21When the king of Israel saw them, he asked Elisha, 'Shall I kill them, my father? Shall I kill them?'

22'Do not kill them,' he answered. 'Would you kill those you have captured with your own sword or bow? Set food and water before them so that they may eat and drink and then go back to their master.' 23So he prepared a great feast for them, and after they had finished eating and drinking, he sent them away, and they returned to their master. So the bands from Aram stopped raiding Israel's territory.

Famine in besieged Samaria

24Some time later, Ben-Hadad king of Aram mobilised his entire army and marched up and laid siege to Samaria. 25There was a great famine in the city; the siege lasted so long that a donkey's head sold for eighty shekels[a] of silver, and a quarter of a cab[b] of seed pods[c] for five shekels.[d]

26As the king of Israel was passing by on the wall, a woman cried to him, 'Help me, my lord the king!'

27The king replied, 'If the LORD does not help you, where can I get help for you? From

---

[a] 25 That is, about 920 grams   [b] 25 That is, possibly about 100 grams   [c] 25 Or of *doves' dung*   [d] 25 That is, about 55 grams

the threshing-floor? From the winepress?' ²⁸Then he asked her, 'What's the matter?'

She answered, 'This woman said to me, "Give up your son so that we may eat him today, and tomorrow we'll eat my son." ²⁹So we cooked my son and ate him. The next day I said to her, "Give up your son so that we may eat him," but she had hidden him.'

³⁰When the king heard the woman's words, he tore his robes. As he went along the wall, the people looked, and they saw that, under his robes, he had sackcloth on his body. ³¹He said, 'May God deal with me, be it ever so severely, if the head of Elisha son of Shaphat remains on his shoulders today!'

³²Now Elisha was sitting in his house, and the elders were sitting with him. The king sent a messenger ahead, but before he arrived, Elisha said to the elders, 'Don't you see how this murderer is sending someone to cut off my head? Look, when the messenger comes, shut the door and hold it shut against him. Is not the sound of his master's footsteps behind him?' ³³While he was still talking to them, the messenger came down to him.

The king said, 'This disaster is from the LORD. Why should I wait for the LORD any longer?'

7 Elisha replied, 'Hear the word of the LORD. This is what the LORD says: about this time tomorrow, a seah^a of the finest flour will sell for a shekel^b and two seahs^c of barley for a shekel at the gate of Samaria.'

²The officer on whose arm the king was leaning said to the man of God, 'Look, even if the LORD should open the floodgates of the heavens, could this happen?'

'You will see it with your own eyes,' answered Elisha, 'but you will not eat any of it!'

The siege lifted

³Now there were four men with leprosy^d at the entrance of the city gate. They said to each other, 'Why stay here until we die? ⁴If we say, "We'll go into the city"—the famine is there, and we will die. And if we stay here, we will die. So let's go over to the camp of the Arameans and surrender. If they spare us, we live; if they kill us, then we die.'

⁵At dusk they got up and went to the camp of the Arameans. When they reached the edge of the camp, no-one was there, ⁶for the Lord had caused the Arameans to hear the sound of chariots and horses and a great army, so that they said to one another, 'Look, the king of Israel has hired the Hittite and Egyptian kings to attack us!' ⁷So they got up and fled in the dusk and abandoned their tents and their horses and donkeys. They left the camp as it was and ran for their lives.

⁸The men who had leprosy reached the edge of the camp, entered one of the tents and ate and drank. Then they took silver, gold and clothes, and went off and hid them. They returned and entered another tent and took some things from it and hid them also.

⁹Then they said to each other, 'What we're doing is not right. This is a day of good news and we are keeping it to ourselves. If we wait until daylight, punishment will overtake us. Let's go at once and report this to the royal palace.'

¹⁰So they went and called out to the city gatekeepers and told them, 'We went into the Aramean camp and no-one was there—not a sound of anyone—only tethered horses and donkeys, and the tents left just as they were.' ¹¹The gatekeepers shouted the news, and it was reported within the palace.

¹²The king got up in the night and said to his officers, 'I will tell you what the Arameans have done to us. They know we are starving; so they have left the camp to hide in the countryside, thinking, "They will surely come out, and then we will take them alive and get into the city."'

¹³One of his officers answered, 'Make some men take five of the horses that are left in the city. Their plight will be like that of all the Israelites left here—yes, they will only be like all these Israelites who are doomed. So let us send them to find out what happened.'

---

^{a}1 That is, probably about 5.5 kilograms; also in verses 16 and 18 ^{b}1 That is, about 11.5 grams; also in verses 16 and 18 ^{c}1 That is, probably about 9 kilograms; also in verses 16 and 18 ^{d}3 The Hebrew for *leprosy* was used for various diseases affecting the skin; also in verse 8.

¹⁴So they selected two chariots with their horses, and the king sent them after the Aramean army. He commanded the drivers, 'Go and find out what has happened.' ¹⁵They followed them as far as the Jordan, and they found the whole road strewn with the clothing and equipment the Arameans had thrown away in their headlong flight. So the messengers returned and reported to the king. ¹⁶Then the people went out and plundered the camp of the Arameans. So a seah of the finest flour sold for a shekel, and two seahs of barley sold for a shekel, as the LORD had said.

¹⁷Now the king had put the officer on whose arm he leaned in charge of the gate, and the people trampled him in the gateway, and he died, just as the man of God had foretold when the king came down to his house. ¹⁸It happened as the man of God had said to the king: 'About this time tomorrow, a seah of the finest flour will sell for a shekel and two seahs of barley for a shekel at the gate of Samaria.'

¹⁹The officer had said to the man of God, 'Look, even if the LORD should open the floodgates of the heavens, could this happen?' The man of God had replied, 'You will see it with your own eyes, but you will not eat any of it!' ²⁰And that is exactly what happened to him, for the people trampled him in the gateway, and he died.

The Shunammite's land restored

8 Now Elisha had said to the woman whose son he had restored to life, 'Go away with your family and stay for a while wherever you can, because the LORD has decreed a famine in the land that will last seven years.' ²The woman proceeded to do as the man of God said. She and her family went away and stayed in the land of the Philistines for seven years.

³At the end of the seven years she came back from the land of the Philistines and went to appeal to the king for her house and land. ⁴The king was talking to Gehazi, the servant of the man of God, and had said, 'Tell me about all the great things Elisha has done.' ⁵Just as Gehazi was telling the king how Elisha had restored the dead to life, the woman whose son Elisha had brought back to life came to appeal to the king for her house and land.

Gehazi said, 'This is the woman, my lord the king, and this is her son whom Elisha restored to life.' ⁶The king asked the woman about it, and she told him.

Then he assigned an official to her case and said to him, 'Give back everything that belonged to her, including all the income from her land from the day she left the country until now.'

Hazael murders Ben-Hadad

⁷Elisha went to Damascus, and Ben-Hadad king of Aram was ill. When the king was told, 'The man of God has come all the way up here,' ⁸he said to Hazael, 'Take a gift with you and go to meet the man of God. Consult the LORD through him; ask him, "Will I recover from this illness?"'

⁹Hazael went to meet Elisha, taking with him as a gift forty camel-loads of all the finest wares of Damascus. He went in and stood before him, and said, 'Your son Ben-Hadad king of Aram has sent me to ask, "Will I recover from this illness?"'

¹⁰Elisha answered, 'Go and say to him, "You will certainly recover." Nevertheless,ᵃ the LORD has revealed to me that he will in fact die.' ¹¹He stared at him with a fixed gaze until Hazael was embarrassed. Then the man of God began to weep.

Sign of the times

Gifts
2 Kings 8:9
It was customary to take a gift to a prophet when you went to ask his advice (1 Kings 14:2–3). It wasn't a bribe, more like a 'thank you' in advance. After all, the prophets had to make a living somehow.

ᵃ 10 The Hebrew may also be read *Go and say, "You will certainly not recover,"* for.

12 'Why is my lord weeping?' asked Hazael.

'Because I know the harm you will do to the Israelites,' he answered. 'You will set fire to their fortified places, kill their young men with the sword, dash their little children to the ground, and rip open their pregnant women.'

13 Hazael said, 'How could your servant, a mere dog, accomplish such a feat?'

'The LORD has shown me that you will become king of Aram,' answered Elisha.

14 Then Hazael left Elisha and returned to his master. When Ben-Hadad asked, 'What did Elisha say to you?' Hazael replied, 'He told me that you would certainly recover.' 15 But the next day he took a thick cloth, soaked it in water and spread it over the king's face, so that he died. Then Hazael succeeded him as king.

Jehoram king of Judah

16 In the fifth year of Joram son of Ahab king of Israel, when Jehoshaphat was king of Judah, Jehoram son of Jehoshaphat began his reign as king of Judah. 17 He was thirty-two years old when he became king, and he reigned in Jerusalem for eight years. 18 He followed the ways of the kings of Israel, as the house of Ahab had done, for he married a daughter of Ahab. He did evil in the eyes of the LORD. 19 Nevertheless, for the sake of his servant David, the LORD was not willing to destroy Judah. He had promised to maintain a lamp for David and his descendants for ever.

20 In the time of Jehoram, Edom rebelled against Judah and set up its own king. 21 So Jehoram[a] went to Zair with all his chariots. The Edomites surrounded him and his chariot commanders, but he rose up and broke through by night; his army, however, fled back home. 22 To this day Edom has been in rebellion against Judah. Libnah revolted at the same time.

23 As for the other events of Jehoram's reign, and all he did, are they not written in the book of the annals of the kings of Judah? 24 Jehoram rested with his ancestors and was buried with them in the City of David. And Ahaziah his son succeeded him as king.

Ahaziah king of Judah

25 In the twelfth year of Joram son of Ahab king of Israel, Ahaziah son of Jehoram king of Judah began to reign. 26 Ahaziah was twenty-two years old when he became king, and he reigned in Jerusalem for one year. His mother's name was Athaliah, a granddaughter of Omri king of Israel. 27 He followed the ways of the house of Ahab and did evil in the eyes of the LORD, as the house of Ahab had done, for he was related by marriage to Ahab's family.

28 Ahaziah went with Joram son of Ahab to war against Hazael king of Aram at Ramoth Gilead. The Arameans wounded Joram; 29 so King Joram returned to Jezreel to recover from the wounds the Arameans had inflicted on him at Ramoth[b] in his battle with Hazael king of Aram.

Then Ahaziah son of Jehoram king of Judah went down to Jezreel to see Joram son of Ahab, because he had been wounded.

Jehu anointed king of Israel

9 The prophet Elisha summoned a man from the company of the prophets and said to him, 'Tuck your cloak into your belt, take this flask of oil with you and go to Ramoth Gilead. 2 When you get there, look for Jehu son of Jehoshaphat, the son of Nimshi. Go to him, get him away from his companions and take him into an inner room. 3 Then take the flask and pour the oil on his head and declare, "This is what the LORD says: I anoint you king over Israel." Then open the door and run; don't delay!'

4 So the young prophet went to Ramoth Gilead. 5 When he arrived, he found the army officers sitting together. 'I have a message for you, commander,' he said.

'For which of us?' asked Jehu.

'For you, commander,' he replied.

6 Jehu got up and went into the house. Then the prophet poured the oil on Jehu's head and declared, 'This is what the LORD, the God of Israel, says: "I anoint you king over the LORD's people Israel. 7 You are to destroy the house of Ahab your master, and I will avenge the blood of my servants the prophets and the blood of all the LORD's servants shed by Jezebel. 8 The whole house

---

[a] 21 Hebrew *Joram*, a variant of *Jehoram*; also in verses 23 and 24   [b] 29 Hebrew *Ramah*, a variant of *Ramoth*

of Ahab will perish. I will cut off from Ahab every last male in Israel—slave or free.[a] 9I will make the house of Ahab like the house of Jeroboam son of Nebat and like the house of Baasha son of Ahijah. 10As for Jezebel, dogs will devour her on the plot of ground at Jezreel, and no-one will bury her."' Then he opened the door and ran.

11When Jehu went out to his fellow officers, one of them asked him, 'Is everything all right? Why did this maniac come to you?'

'You know the man and the sort of things he says,' Jehu replied.

12'That's not true!' they said. 'Tell us.'

Jehu said, 'Here is what he told me: "This is what the LORD says: I anoint you king over Israel."'

13They quickly took their cloaks and spread them under him on the bare steps. Then they blew the trumpet and shouted, 'Jehu is king!'

Jehu kills Joram and Ahaziah

14So Jehu son of Jehoshaphat, the son of Nimshi, conspired against Joram. (Now Joram and all Israel had been defending Ramoth Gilead against Hazael king of Aram, 15but King Joram[b] had returned to Jezreel to recover from the wounds the Arameans had inflicted on him in the battle with Hazael king of Aram.) Jehu said, 'If you desire to make me king, don't let anyone slip out of the city to go and tell the news in Jezreel.' 16Then he got into his chariot and rode to Jezreel, because Joram was resting there and Ahaziah king of Judah had gone down to see him.

17When the lookout standing on the tower in Jezreel saw Jehu's troops approaching, he called out, 'I see some troops coming.'

'Get a horseman,' Joram ordered. 'Send him to meet them and ask, "Do you come in peace?"'

18The horseman rode off to meet Jehu and said, 'This is what the king says: "Do you come in peace?"'

'What do you have to do with peace?' Jehu replied. 'Fall in behind me.'

The lookout reported, 'The messenger has reached them, but he isn't coming back.'

19So the king sent out a second horseman. When he came to them he said, 'This is what the king says: "Do you come in peace?"'

Jehu replied, 'What do you have to do with peace? Fall in behind me.'

20The lookout reported, 'He has reached them, but he isn't coming back either. The driving is like that of Jehu son of Nimshi—he drives like a maniac.'

21'Hitch up my chariot,' Joram ordered. And when it was hitched up, Joram king of Israel and Ahaziah king of Judah rode out, each in his own chariot, to meet Jehu. They met him at the plot of ground that had belonged to Naboth the Jezreelite. 22When Joram saw Jehu he asked, 'Have you come in peace, Jehu?'

'How can there be peace,' Jehu replied, 'as long as all the idolatry and witchcraft of your mother Jezebel abound?'

23Joram turned about and fled, calling out to Ahaziah, 'Treachery, Ahaziah!'

24Then Jehu drew his bow and shot Joram between the shoulders. The arrow pierced his heart and he slumped down in his chariot. 25Jehu said to Bidkar, his chariot officer, 'Pick him up and throw him on the field that belonged to Naboth the Jezreelite. Remember how you and I were riding together in chariots behind Ahab his father when the LORD spoke this prophecy against him: 26"Yesterday I saw the blood of Naboth and the blood of his sons, declares the LORD, and I will surely make you pay for it on this plot of ground, declares the LORD."[c] Now then, pick him up and throw him on that plot, in accordance with the word of the LORD.'

27When Ahaziah king of Judah saw what had happened, he fled up the road to Beth Haggan.[d] Jehu chased him, shouting, 'Kill him too!' They wounded him in his chariot on the way up to Gur near Ibleam, but he escaped to Megiddo and died there. 28His servants took him by chariot to Jerusalem and buried him with his ancestors in his tomb in the City of David. 29(In the

---

[a] 8 Or *Israel—every ruler or leader*   [b] 15 Hebrew *Jehoram*, a variant of *Joram*; also in verses 17 and 21-24   [c] 26 See 1 Kings 21:19.   [d] 27 Or *fled by way of the garden house*

eleventh year of Joram son of Ahab, Ahaziah had become king of Judah.)

Jezebel killed

30Then Jehu went to Jezreel. When Jezebel heard about it, she painted her eyes, arranged her hair and looked out of a window. 31As Jehu entered the gate, she asked, 'Have you come in peace, you Zimri, you murderer of your master?'*a*

32He looked up at the window and called out, 'Who is on my side? Who?' Two or three eunuchs looked down at him. 33'Throw her down!' Jehu said. So they threw her down, and some of her blood spattered the wall and the horses as they trampled her underfoot.

34Jehu went in and ate and drank. 'Take care of that cursed woman,' he said, 'and bury her, for she was a king's daughter.' 35But when they went out to bury her, they found nothing except her skull, her feet and her hands. 36They went back and told Jehu, who said, 'This is the word of the LORD that he spoke through his servant Elijah the Tishbite: on the plot of ground at Jezreel dogs will devour Jezebel's flesh.*b* 37Jezebel's body will be like dung on the ground in the plot at Jezreel, so that no-one will be able to say, "This is Jezebel."'

Ahab's family killed

10 Now there were in Samaria seventy sons of the house of Ahab. So Jehu wrote letters and sent them to Samaria: to the officials of Jezreel,*c* to the elders and to the guardians of Ahab's children. He said, 2'You have your master's sons with you and you have chariots and horses, a fortified city and weapons. Now as soon as this letter reaches you, 3choose the best and most worthy of your master's sons and set him on his father's throne. Then fight for your master's house.'

4But they were terrified and said, 'If two kings could not resist him, how can we?'

5So the palace administrator, the city governor, the elders and the guardians sent this message to Jehu: 'We are your servants and we will do anything you say. We will not

Killing Ahab's family
2 Kings 10:7

It sounds like Ahab had a huge family, but remember that he had more than one wife, and his grandsons as well as his sons would be counted in this total of seventy. A new ruler would kill all the male descendants of the former king so that none of them could make a claim on the throne.

appoint anyone as king; you do whatever you think best.'

6Then Jehu wrote them a second letter, saying, 'If you are on my side and will obey me, take the heads of your master's sons and come to me in Jezreel by this time tomorrow.'

Now the royal princes, seventy of them, were with the leading men of the city, who were bringing them up. 7When the letter arrived, they took the princes and slaughtered all seventy of them. They put their heads in baskets and sent them to Jehu in Jezreel. 8When the messenger arrived, he told Jehu, 'They have brought the heads of the princes.'

Then Jehu ordered, 'Put them in two piles at the entrance of the city gate until morning.'

9The next morning Jehu went out. He stood before all the people and said, 'You are innocent. It was I who conspired against my master and killed him, but who killed all these? 10Know, then, that not a word the LORD has spoken against the house of Ahab will fail. The LORD has done what he announced through his servant Elijah.' 11So Jehu killed everyone in Jezreel who remained of the house of Ahab, as well as all his chief men, his close friends and his priests, leaving him no survivor.

---

*a*31 Or *'Was there peace for Zimri, who murdered his master?'* *b*36 See 1 Kings 21:23. *c*1 Hebrew; some Septuagint manuscripts and Vulgate *of the city*

¹²Jehu then set out and went towards Samaria. At Beth Eked of the Shepherds, ¹³he met some relatives of Ahaziah king of Judah and asked, 'Who are you?'

They said, 'We are relatives of Ahaziah, and we have come down to greet the families of the king and of the queen mother.'

¹⁴'Take them alive!' he ordered. So they took them alive and slaughtered them by the well of Beth Eked—forty-two of them. He left no survivor.

¹⁵After he left there, he came upon Jehonadab son of Rekab, who was on his way to meet him. Jehu greeted him and said, 'Are you in accord with me, as I am with you?'

'I am,' Jehonadab answered.

'If so,' said Jehu, 'give me your hand.' So he did, and Jehu helped him up into the chariot. ¹⁶Jehu said, 'Come with me and see my zeal for the LORD.' Then he made him ride in his chariot.

¹⁷When Jehu came to Samaria, he killed all who were left there of Ahab's family; he destroyed them, according to the word of the LORD spoken to Elijah.

Servants of Baal killed

¹⁸Then Jehu brought all the people together and said to them, 'Ahab served Baal a little; Jehu will serve him much. ¹⁹Now summon all the prophets of Baal, all his servants and all his priests. See that no-one is missing, because I am going to hold a great sacrifice for Baal. Anyone who fails to come will no longer live.' But Jehu was acting deceptively in order to destroy the servants of Baal.

²⁰Jehu said, 'Call an assembly in honour of Baal.' So they proclaimed it. ²¹Then he sent word throughout Israel, and all the servants of Baal came; not one stayed away. They crowded into the temple of Baal until it was full from one end to the other. ²²And Jehu said to the keeper of the wardrobe, 'Bring robes for all the servants of Baal.' So he brought out robes for them.

²³Then Jehu and Jehonadab son of Rekab went into the temple of Baal. Jehu said to the servants of Baal, 'Look around and see that no-one who serves the LORD is here with you—only servants of Baal.' ²⁴So they went in to make sacrifices and burnt offerings. Now Jehu had posted eighty men outside with this warning: 'If one of you lets any of the men I am placing in your hands escape, it will be your life for his life.'

²⁵As soon as Jehu had finished making the burnt offering, he ordered the guards and officers: 'Go in and kill them; let no-one escape.' So they cut them down with the sword. The guards and officers threw the bodies out and then entered the inner shrine of the temple of Baal. ²⁶They brought the sacred stone out of the temple of Baal and burned it. ²⁷They demolished the sacred stone of Baal and tore down the temple of Baal, and people have used it for a latrine to this day.

²⁸So Jehu destroyed Baal worship in Israel. ²⁹However, he did not turn away from the sins of Jeroboam son of Nebat, which he had caused Israel to commit—the worship of the golden calves at Bethel and Dan.

³⁰The LORD said to Jehu, 'Because you have done well in accomplishing what is right in my eyes and have done to the house of Ahab all I had in mind to do, your descendants will sit on the throne of Israel to the fourth generation.' ³¹Yet Jehu was not careful to keep the law of the LORD, the God of Israel, with all his heart. He did not turn away from the sins of Jeroboam, which he had caused Israel to commit.

³²In those days the LORD began to reduce the size of Israel. Hazael overpowered the Israelites throughout their territory ³³east of the Jordan in all the land of Gilead (the region of Gad, Reuben and Manasseh), from Aroer by the Arnon Gorge through Gilead to Bashan.

³⁴As for the other events of Jehu's reign, all he did, and all his achievements, are they not written in the book of the annals of the kings of Israel?

³⁵Jehu rested with his ancestors and was buried in Samaria. And Jehoahaz his son succeeded him as king. ³⁶The time that Jehu reigned over Israel in Samaria was twenty-eight years.

Athaliah and Joash

11 When Athaliah the mother of Ahaziah saw that her son was dead, she proceeded to destroy the whole royal family. ²But Jehosheba, the daughter of King Jehoram[a] and sister of Ahaziah, took Joash son of Ahaziah and stole him away from among the royal princes, who were about to be murdered. She put him and his nurse in a bedroom to hide him from Athaliah; so he was not killed. 3He remained hidden with his nurse at the temple of the LORD for six years while Athaliah ruled the land.

4In the seventh year Jehoiada sent for the commanders of units of a hundred, the Carites and the guards and had them brought to him at the temple of the LORD. He made a covenant with them and put them under oath at the temple of the LORD. Then he showed them the king's son. 5He commanded them, saying, 'This is what you are to do: you who are in the three companies that are going on duty on the Sabbath—a third of you guarding the royal palace, 6a third at the Sur Gate, and a third at the gate behind the guard, who take turns guarding the temple— 7and you who are in the other two companies that normally go off Sabbath duty are all to guard the temple for the king. 8Station yourselves round the king, each of you with weapon in hand. Anyone who approaches your ranks[b] is to be put to death. Stay close to the king wherever he goes.'

9The commanders of units of a hundred did just as Jehoiada the priest ordered. Each one took his men—those who were going on duty on the Sabbath and those who were going off duty—and came to Jehoiada the priest. 10Then he gave the commanders the spears and shields that had belonged to King David and that were in the temple of the LORD. 11The guards, each with weapon in hand, stationed themselves round the king—near the altar and the temple, from the south side to the north side of the temple.

12Jehoiada brought out the king's son and put the crown on him; he presented him with a copy of the covenant and proclaimed him king. They anointed him, and the people clapped their hands and shouted, 'Long live the king!'

13When Athaliah heard the noise made by the guards and the people, she went to the people at the temple of the LORD. 14She looked and there was the king, standing by the pillar, as the custom was. The officers and the trumpeters were beside the king, and all the people of the land were rejoicing and blowing trumpets. Then Athaliah tore her robes and called out, 'Treason! Treason!'

15Jehoiada the priest ordered the commanders of units of a hundred, who were in charge of the troops: 'Bring her out between the ranks[c] and put to the sword anyone who follows her.' For the priest had said, 'She must not be put to death in the temple of the LORD.' 16So they seized her as she reached the place where the horses enter the palace grounds, and there she was put to death.

17Jehoiada then made a covenant between the LORD and the king and people that they would be the LORD's people. He also made a covenant between the king and the people. 18All the people of the land went to the temple of Baal and tore it down. They smashed the altars and idols to pieces and killed Mattan the priest of Baal in front of the altars.

Then Jehoiada the priest posted guards at the temple of the LORD. 19He took with him the commanders of hundreds, the Carites, the guards and all the people of the land, and together they brought the king down from the temple of the LORD and went into the palace, entering by way of the gate of the guards. The king then took his place on the royal throne. 20All the people of the land rejoiced, and the city was calm, because Athaliah had been slain with the sword at the palace.

*21Joash[d] was seven years old when he began his reign.

Joash repairs the temple

12 *In the seventh year of Jehu, Joash[e] became king, and he reigned in Jerusalem for forty years. His mother's name was Zibiah; she was from Beersheba. 2Joash did what was right in the eyes of the

---

[a]2 Hebrew *Joram*, a variant of *Jehoram*   [b]8 Or *approaches the precincts*   [c]15 Or *out from the precincts*   [d]21 Hebrew *Jehoash*, a variant of *Joash*   [e]1 Hebrew *Jehoash*, a variant of *Joash*; also in verses 2, 4, 6, 7 and 18

* 11:21 is numbered 12:1 in Hebrew texts.   * 12:1-21 is numbered 12:2-22 in Hebrew texts.

LORD all the years Jehoiada the priest instructed him. ³The high places, however, were not removed; the people continued to offer sacrifices and burn incense there.

⁴Joash said to the priests, 'Collect all the money that is brought as sacred offerings to the temple of the LORD—the money collected in the census, the money received from personal vows and the money brought voluntarily to the temple. ⁵Let every priest receive the money from one of the treasurers, then use it to repair whatever damage is found in the temple.'

⁶But by the twenty-third year of King Joash the priests still had not repaired the temple. ⁷Therefore King Joash summoned Jehoiada the priest and the other priests and asked them, 'Why aren't you repairing the damage done to the temple? Take no more money from your treasurers, but hand it over for repairing the temple.' ⁸The priests agreed that they would not collect any more money from the people and that they would not repair the temple themselves.

⁹Jehoiada the priest took a chest and bored a hole in its lid. He placed it beside the altar, on the right side as one enters the temple of the LORD. The priests who guarded the entrance put into the chest all the money that was brought to the temple of the LORD. ¹⁰Whenever they saw that there was a large amount of money in the chest, the royal secretary and the high priest came, counted the money that had been brought into the temple of the LORD and put it into bags. ¹¹When the amount had been determined, they gave the money to the men appointed to supervise the work on the temple. With it they paid those who worked on the temple of the LORD—the carpenters and builders, ¹²the masons and stonecutters. They purchased timber and blocks of dressed stone for the repair of the temple of the LORD, and met all the other expenses of restoring the temple.

¹³The money brought into the temple was not spent for making silver basins, wick trimmers, sprinkling bowls, trumpets or any other articles of gold or silver for the temple of the LORD; ¹⁴it was paid to the workers, who used it to repair the temple.

making Connections

Collecting money
2 Kings 12:9
Is this the first piggy bank in Bible times? Who knows, but it was certainly a more effective way of collecting money than expecting the priests to do it. Every man over the age of twenty had to pay taxes for the work of the priests at the temple. On top of this, people would bring some money as part of their offerings and some as a voluntary gift.

¹⁵They did not require an accounting from those to whom they gave the money to pay the workers, because they acted with complete honesty. ¹⁶The money from the guilt offerings and sin offerings[a] was not brought into the temple of the LORD; it belonged to the priests.

¹⁷About this time Hazael king of Aram went up and attacked Gath and captured it. Then he turned to attack Jerusalem. ¹⁸But Joash king of Judah took all the sacred objects dedicated by his predecessors—Jehoshaphat, Jehoram and Ahaziah, the kings of Judah—and the gifts he himself had dedicated and all the gold found in the treasuries of the temple of the LORD and of the royal palace, and he sent them to Hazael king of Aram, who then withdrew from Jerusalem.

¹⁹As for the other events of the reign of Joash, and all he did, are they not written in the book of the annals of the kings of Judah? ²⁰His officials conspired against him and assassinated him at Beth Millo, on the road down to Silla. ²¹The officials who murdered him were Jozabad son of Shimeath and Jehozabad son of Shomer. He died and was buried with his ancestors in the City of

---

[a] 16 Or *purification offerings*

David. And Amaziah his son succeeded him as king.

Jehoahaz king of Israel

13 In the twenty-third year of Joash son of Ahaziah king of Judah, Jehoahaz son of Jehu became king of Israel in Samaria, and he reigned for seventeen years. 2He did evil in the eyes of the LORD by following the sins of Jeroboam son of Nebat, which he had caused Israel to commit, and he did not turn away from them. 3So the LORD's anger burned against Israel, and for a long time he kept them under the power of Hazael king of Aram and Ben-Hadad his son.

4Then Jehoahaz sought the LORD's favour, and the LORD listened to him, for he saw how severely the king of Aram was oppressing Israel. 5The LORD provided a deliverer for Israel, and they escaped from the power of Aram. So the Israelites lived in their own homes as they had before. 6But they did not turn away from the sins of the house of Jeroboam, which he had caused Israel to commit; they continued in them. Also, the Asherah pole[a] remained standing in Samaria.

7Nothing had been left of the army of Jehoahaz except fifty horsemen, ten chariots and ten thousand foot soldiers, for the king of Aram had destroyed the rest and made them like the dust at threshing time.

8As for the other events of the reign of Jehoahaz, all he did and his achievements, are they not written in the book of the annals of the kings of Israel? 9Jehoahaz rested with his ancestors and was buried in Samaria. And Jehoash[b] his son succeeded him as king.

Jehoash king of Israel

10In the thirty-seventh year of Joash king of Judah, Jehoash son of Jehoahaz became king of Israel in Samaria, and he reigned for sixteen years. 11He did evil in the eyes of the LORD and did not turn away from any of the sins of Jeroboam son of Nebat, which he had caused Israel to commit; he continued in them.

12As for the other events of the reign of Jehoash, all he did and his achievements, including his war against Amaziah king of Judah, are they not written in the book of the annals of the kings of Israel? 13Jehoash rested with his ancestors, and Jeroboam succeeded him on the throne. Jehoash was buried in Samaria with the kings of Israel.

14Now Elisha was suffering from the illness from which he died. Jehoash king of Israel went down to see him and wept over him. 'My father! My father!' he cried. 'The chariots and horsemen of Israel!'

15Elisha said, 'Get a bow and some arrows,' and he did so. 16'Take the bow in your hands,' he said to the king of Israel. When he had taken it, Elisha put his hands on the king's hands.

17'Open the east window,' he said, and he opened it. 'Shoot!' Elisha said, and he shot. 'The LORD's arrow of victory, the arrow of victory over Aram!' Elisha declared. 'You will completely destroy the Arameans at Aphek.'

18Then he said, 'Take the arrows,' and the king took them. Elisha told him, 'Strike the ground.' He struck it three times and stopped. 19The man of God was angry with him and said, 'You should have struck the ground five or six times; then you would have defeated Aram and completely destroyed it. But now you will defeat it only three times.'

20Elisha died and was buried.

Now Moabite raiders used to enter the country every spring. 21Once while some Israelites were burying a man, suddenly they saw a band of raiders; so they threw the man's body into Elisha's tomb. When the body touched Elisha's bones, the man came to life and stood up on his feet.

22Hazael king of Aram oppressed Israel throughout the reign of Jehoahaz. 23But the LORD was gracious to them and had compassion and showed concern for them because of his covenant with Abraham, Isaac and Jacob. To this day he has been unwilling to destroy them or banish them from his presence.

---

[a] 6 That is, a wooden symbol of the goddess Asherah; here and elsewhere in 2 Kings   [b] 9 Hebrew *Joash*, a variant of *Jehoash*; also in verses 12-14 and 25

24Hazael king of Aram died, and Ben-Hadad his son succeeded him as king. 25Then Jehoash son of Jehoahaz recaptured from Ben-Hadad son of Hazael the towns he had taken in battle from his father Jehoahaz. Three times Jehoash defeated him, and so he recovered the Israelite towns.

Amaziah king of Judah

14 In the second year of Jehoash*a* son of Jehoahaz king of Israel, Amaziah son of Joash king of Judah began to reign. 2He was twenty-five years old when he became king, and he reigned in Jerusalem for twenty-nine years. His mother's name was Jehoaddan; she was from Jerusalem. 3He did what was right in the eyes of the LORD, but not as his father David had done. In everything he followed the example of his father Joash. 4The high places, however, were not removed; the people continued to offer sacrifices and burn incense there.

5After the kingdom was firmly in his grasp, he executed the officials who had murdered his father the king. 6Yet he did not put the children of the assassins to death, in accordance with what is written in the Book of the Law of Moses where the LORD commanded: 'Parents are not to be put to death for their children, nor children put to death for their parents; each of you will die for your own sin.'*b*

7He was the one who defeated ten thousand Edomites in the Valley of Salt and captured Sela in battle, calling it Joktheel, the name it has to this day.

8Then Amaziah sent messengers to Jehoash son of Jehoahaz, the son of Jehu, king of Israel, with the challenge: 'Come, meet me face to face.'

9But Jehoash king of Israel replied to Amaziah king of Judah: 'A thistle in Lebanon sent a message to a cedar in Lebanon, "Give your daughter to my son in marriage." Then a wild beast in Lebanon came along and trampled the thistle underfoot. 10You have indeed defeated Edom and now you are arrogant. Glory in your victory, but stay at home! Why ask for trouble and cause your own downfall and that of Judah also?'

11Amaziah, however, would not listen, so Jehoash king of Israel attacked. He and Amaziah king of Judah faced each other at Beth Shemesh in Judah. 12Judah was routed by Israel, and every man fled to his home. 13Jehoash king of Israel captured Amaziah king of Judah, the son of Joash, the son of Ahaziah, at Beth Shemesh. Then Jehoash went to Jerusalem and broke down the wall of Jerusalem from the Ephraim Gate to the Corner Gate—a section about four hundred cubits long.*c* 14He took all the gold and silver and all the articles found in the temple of the LORD and in the treasuries of the royal palace. He also took hostages and returned to Samaria.

15As for the other events of the reign of Jehoash, what he did and his achievements, including his war against Amaziah king of Judah, are they not written in the book of the annals of the kings of Israel? 16Jehoash rested with his ancestors and was buried in Samaria with the kings of Israel. And Jeroboam his son succeeded him as king.

17Amaziah son of Joash king of Judah lived for fifteen years after the death of Jehoash son of Jehoahaz king of Israel. 18As

People and Places

Jeroboam II
2 Kings 14:23
Because of God's love for his people, Israel grew stronger under the reign of Jeroboam II even though he was an evil king. Jeroboam I was the first king of Israel. He had made two gold statues of calves and told the people that they represented God, even though this was against one of the Ten Commandments (1 Kings 12:26–30). Jeroboam II continued to encourage the people to worship these statues.

---

a 1 Hebrew *Joash*, a variant of *Jehoash*; also in verses 13, 23 and 27 *b* 6 Deut. 24:16 *c* 13 That is, about 180 metres for the other events of Amaziah's reign, are they not written in the book of the annals of the kings of Judah?

19They conspired against him in Jerusalem, and he fled to Lachish, but they sent men after him to Lachish and killed him there. 20He was brought back by horse and was buried in Jerusalem with his ancestors, in the City of David.

21Then all the people of Judah took Azariah,[a] who was sixteen years old, and made him king in place of his father Amaziah. 22He was the one who rebuilt Elath and restored it to Judah after Amaziah rested with his ancestors.

Jeroboam II king of Israel

23In the fifteenth year of Amaziah son of Joash king of Judah, Jeroboam son of Jehoash king of Israel became king in Samaria, and he reigned for forty-one years. 24He did evil in the eyes of the LORD and did not turn away from any of the sins of Jeroboam son of Nebat, which he had caused Israel to commit. 25He was the one who restored the boundaries of Israel from Lebo Hamath to the Dead Sea,[b] in accordance with the word of the LORD, the God of Israel, spoken through his servant Jonah son of Amittai, the prophet from Gath Hepher.

26The LORD had seen how bitterly everyone in Israel, whether slave or free, was suffering;[c] there was no-one to help them. 27And since the LORD had not said he would blot out the name of Israel from under heaven, he saved them by the hand of Jeroboam son of Jehoash.

28As for the other events of Jeroboam's reign, all he did, and his military achievements, including how he recovered for Israel both Damascus and Hamath, which had belonged to Judah, are they not written in the book of the annals of the kings of Israel? 29Jeroboam rested with his ancestors, the kings of Israel. And Zechariah his son succeeded him as king.

Azariah king of Judah

15 In the twenty-seventh year of Jeroboam king of Israel, Azariah[d] son of Amaziah king of Judah began to reign. 2He was sixteen years old when he became king, and he reigned in Jerusalem for fifty-two years. His mother's name was Jekoliah; she was from Jerusalem. 3He did what was right in the eyes of the LORD, just as his father Amaziah had done. 4The high places, however, were not removed; the people continued to offer sacrifices and burn incense there.

5The LORD afflicted the king with leprosy[e] until the day he died, and he lived in a separate house.[f] Jotham the king's son had charge of the palace and governed the people of the land.

6As for the other events of Azariah's reign, and all he did, are they not written in the book of the annals of the kings of Judah? 7Azariah rested with his ancestors and was buried near them in the City of David. And Jotham his son succeeded him as king.

Zechariah king of Israel

8In the thirty-eighth year of Azariah king of Judah, Zechariah son of Jeroboam became king of Israel in Samaria, and he reigned for six months. 9He did evil in the eyes of the LORD, as his predecessors had done. He did not turn away from the sins of Jeroboam son of Nebat, which he had caused Israel to commit.

10Shallum son of Jabesh conspired against Zechariah. He attacked him in front of the people,[g] assassinated him and succeeded him as king. 11The other events of Zechariah's reign are written in the book of the annals of the kings of Israel. 12So the word of the LORD spoken to Jehu was fulfilled: 'Your descendants will sit on the throne of Israel to the fourth generation.'[h]

Shallum king of Israel

13Shallum son of Jabesh became king in the thirty-ninth year of Uzziah king of Judah, and he reigned in Samaria for one month. 14Then Menahem son of Gadi went from

---

[a] 21 Also called *Uzziah* [b] 25 Hebrew *the Sea of the Arabah* [c] 26 Or *Israel was suffering. They were without a ruler or leader, and* [d] 1 Also called *Uzziah*; also in verses 6, 7, 8, 17, 23 and 27 [e] 5 The Hebrew for *leprosy* was used for various diseases affecting the skin. [f] 5 Or *in a house where he was relieved of responsibilities* [g] 10 Hebrew; some Septuagint manuscripts *in Ibleam* [h] 12 2 Kings 10:30

Tirzah up to Samaria. He attacked Shallum son of Jabesh in Samaria, assassinated him and succeeded him as king.

¹⁵The other events of Shallum's reign, and the conspiracy he led, are written in the book of the annals of the kings of Israel.

¹⁶At that time Menahem, starting out from Tirzah, attacked Tiphsah and everyone in the city and its vicinity, because they refused to open their gates. He sacked Tiphsah and ripped open all the pregnant women.

Menahem king of Israel

¹⁷In the thirty-ninth year of Azariah king of Judah, Menahem son of Gadi became king of Israel, and he reigned in Samaria for ten years. ¹⁸He did evil in the eyes of the LORD. During his entire reign he did not turn away from the sins of Jeroboam son of Nebat, which he had caused Israel to commit.

¹⁹Then Pul[a] king of Assyria invaded the land, and Menahem gave him a thousand talents[b] of silver to gain his support and strengthen his own hold on the kingdom. ²⁰Menahem exacted this money from Israel. Every wealthy person had to contribute fifty shekels[c] of silver to be given to the king of Assyria. So the king of Assyria withdrew and stayed in the land no longer.

²¹As for the other events of Menahem's reign, and all he did, are they not written in the book of the annals of the kings of Israel? ²²Menahem rested with his ancestors. And Pekahiah his son succeeded him as king.

Pekahiah king of Israel

²³In the fiftieth year of Azariah king of Judah, Pekahiah son of Menahem became king of Israel in Samaria, and he reigned for two years. ²⁴Pekahiah did evil in the eyes of the LORD. He did not turn away from the sins of Jeroboam son of Nebat, which he had caused Israel to commit. ²⁵One of his chief officers, Pekah son of Remaliah, conspired against him. Taking fifty Gileadites with him, he assassinated Pekahiah, along with Argob and Arieh, in the citadel of the royal palace at Samaria. So Pekah killed Pekahiah and succeeded him as king.

²⁶The other events of Pekahiah's reign, and all he did, are written in the book of the annals of the kings of Israel.

Pekah king of Israel

²⁷In the fifty-second year of Azariah king of Judah, Pekah son of Remaliah became king of Israel in Samaria, and he reigned for twenty years. ²⁸He did evil in the eyes of the LORD. He did not turn away from the sins of Jeroboam son of Nebat, which he had caused Israel to commit.

²⁹In the time of Pekah king of Israel, Tiglath-Pileser king of Assyria came and took Ijon, Abel Beth Maakah, Janoah, Kedesh and Hazor. He took Gilead and Galilee, including all the land of Naphtali, and deported the people to Assyria. ³⁰Then Hoshea son of Elah conspired against Pekah son of Remaliah. He attacked and assassinated him, and then succeeded him as king in the twentieth year of Jotham son of Uzziah.

³¹As for the other events of Pekah's reign, and all he did, are they not written in the book of the annals of the kings of Israel?

Jotham king of Judah

³²In the second year of Pekah son of Remaliah king of Israel, Jotham son of Uzziah king of Judah began to reign. ³³He was twenty-five years old when he became king, and he reigned in Jerusalem for sixteen years. His mother's name was Jerusha daughter of Zadok. ³⁴He did what was right in the eyes of the LORD, just as his father Uzziah had done. ³⁵The high places, however, were not removed; the people continued to offer sacrifices and burn incense there. Jotham rebuilt the Upper Gate of the temple of the LORD.

³⁶As for the other events of Jotham's reign, and what he did, are they not written in the book of the annals of the kings of Judah? ³⁷(In those days the LORD began to send Rezin king of Aram and Pekah son of Remaliah against Judah.) ³⁸Jotham rested with his ancestors and was buried with them in the City of David, the city of his father. And Ahaz his son succeeded him as king.

---

[a] 19 Also called *Tiglath-Pileser* [b] 19 That is, about 34 metric tons [c] 20 That is, about 575 grams

Ahaz king of Judah

16 In the seventeenth year of Pekah son of Remaliah, Ahaz son of Jotham king of Judah began to reign. ²Ahaz was twenty years old when he became king, and he reigned in Jerusalem for sixteen years. Unlike David his father, he did not do what was right in the eyes of the LORD his God. ³He followed the ways of the kings of Israel and even sacrificed his son in the fire, engaging in the detestable practices of the nations the LORD had driven out before the Israelites. ⁴He offered sacrifices and burned incense at the high places, on the hilltops and under every spreading tree.

⁵Then Rezin king of Aram and Pekah son of Remaliah king of Israel marched up to fight against Jerusalem and besieged Ahaz, but they could not overpower him. ⁶At that time, Rezin king of Aram recovered Elath for Aram by driving out the people of Judah. Edomites then moved into Elath and have lived there to this day.

⁷Ahaz sent messengers to say to Tiglath-Pileser king of Assyria, 'I am your servant and vassal. Come up and save me out of the hand of the king of Aram and of the king of Israel who are attacking me.' ⁸And Ahaz took the silver and gold found in the temple of the LORD and in the treasuries of the royal palace and sent it as a gift to the king of Assyria. ⁹The king of Assyria complied by attacking Damascus and capturing it. He deported its inhabitants to Kir and put Rezin to death.

¹⁰Then King Ahaz went to Damascus to meet Tiglath-Pileser king of Assyria. He saw an altar in Damascus and sent to Uriah the priest a sketch of the altar, with detailed plans for its construction. ¹¹So Uriah the priest built an altar in accordance with all the plans that King Ahaz had sent from Damascus and finished it before King Ahaz returned. ¹²When the king came back from Damascus and saw the altar, he approached it and presented offerings[a] on it. ¹³He offered up his burnt offering and grain offering, poured out his drink offering, and splashed the blood of his fellowship offerings against the altar. ¹⁴The bronze altar that stood before the LORD he brought from the front of the temple—from between the new altar and the temple of the LORD—and put it on the north side of the new altar.

¹⁵King Ahaz then gave these orders to Uriah the priest: 'On the large new altar, offer the morning burnt offering and the evening grain offering, the king's burnt offering and his grain offering, and the burnt offering of all the people of the land, and their grain offering and their drink offering. Splash against this altar the blood of all the burnt offerings and sacrifices. But I will use the bronze altar for seeking guidance.' ¹⁶And Uriah the priest did just as King Ahaz had ordered.

¹⁷King Ahaz cut off the side panels and removed the basins from the movable stands. He removed the Sea from the bronze bulls that supported it and set it on a stone base. ¹⁸He took away the Sabbath canopy[b] that had been built at the temple and removed the royal entrance outside the temple of the LORD, in deference to the king of Assyria.

¹⁹As for the other events of the reign of Ahaz, and what he did, are they not written in the book of the annals of the kings of Judah? ²⁰Ahaz rested with his ancestors and was buried with them in the City of David. And Hezekiah his son succeeded him as king.

Hoshea last king of Israel

17 In the twelfth year of Ahaz king of Judah, Hoshea son of Elah became king of Israel in Samaria, and he reigned for nine years. ²He did evil in the eyes of the LORD, but not like the kings of Israel who preceded him.

³Shalmaneser king of Assyria came up to attack Hoshea, who had been Shalmaneser's vassal and had paid him tribute. ⁴But the king of Assyria discovered that Hoshea was a traitor, for he had sent envoys to So[c] king of Egypt, and he no longer paid tribute to the king of Assyria, as he had done year by year. Therefore Shalmaneser seized him and put him in prison. ⁵The king of Assyria invaded the entire land, marched against Samaria and laid siege to it for three years. ⁶In the ninth year of Hoshea, the king of

---

[a] 12 Or *and went up* [b] 18 Or *the dais of his throne* (see Septuagint) [c] 4 *So* is probably an abbreviation for *Osorkon*.

Assyria captured Samaria and deported the Israelites to Assyria. He settled them in Halah, in Gozan on the River Habor and in the towns of the Medes.

Israel exiled because of sin

⁷All this took place because the Israelites had sinned against the LORD their God, who had brought them up out of Egypt from under the power of Pharaoh king of Egypt. They worshipped other gods ⁸and followed the practices of the nations the LORD had driven out before them, as well as the practices that the kings of Israel had introduced. ⁹The Israelites secretly did things against the LORD their God that were not right. From watchtower to fortified city they built themselves high places in all their towns. ¹⁰They set up sacred stones and Asherah poles on every high hill and under every spreading tree. ¹¹At every high place they burned incense, as the nations whom the LORD had driven out before them had done. They did wicked things that aroused the LORD's anger. ¹²They worshipped idols, though the LORD had said, 'You shall not do this.'ᵃ ¹³The LORD warned Israel and Judah through all his prophets and seers: 'Turn from your evil ways. Observe my commands and decrees, in accordance with the entire Law that I commanded your ancestors to obey and that I delivered to you through my servants the prophets.'

¹⁴But they would not listen and were as stiff-necked as their ancestors, who did not trust in the LORD their God. ¹⁵They rejected his decrees and the covenant he had made with their ancestors and the statutes he had warned them to keep. They followed worthless idols and themselves became worthless. They imitated the nations around them although the LORD had ordered them, 'Do not do as they do.'

¹⁶They forsook all the commands of the LORD their God and made for themselves two idols cast in the shape of calves, and an Asherah pole. They bowed down to all the starry hosts, and they worshipped Baal. ¹⁷They sacrificed their sons and daughters in the fire. They practised divination and sought omens and sold themselves to do evil in the eyes of the LORD, arousing his anger.

¹⁸So the LORD was very angry with Israel and removed them from his presence. Only the tribe of Judah was left, ¹⁹and even Judah did not keep the commands of the LORD their God. They followed the practices Israel had introduced. ²⁰Therefore the LORD rejected all the people of Israel; he afflicted them and gave them into the hands of plunderers, until he thrust them from his presence.

²¹When he tore Israel away from the house of David, they made Jeroboam son of Nebat their king. Jeroboam enticed Israel away from following the LORD and caused them to commit a great sin. ²²The Israelites persisted in all the sins of Jeroboam and did not turn away from them ²³until the LORD removed them from his presence, as he had warned through all his servants the prophets. So the people of Israel were taken from their homeland into exile in Assyria, and they are still there.

Samaria resettled

²⁴The king of Assyria brought people from Babylon, Kuthah, Avva, Hamath and Sepharvaim and settled them in the towns of Samaria to replace the Israelites. They took over Samaria and lived in its towns. ²⁵When they first lived there, they did not worship the LORD; so he sent lions among them and

---

IN OTHER WORDS

Exile
2 Kings 17:23

Exiles are people who live away from their own country, normally because they have been forced to leave. Israel was taken into exile by the Assyrians because of her disobedience. About a hundred and thirty years later, Judah was taken into exile by the Babylonians.

ᵃ 12 Exodus 20:4, 5

they killed some of the people. 26It was reported to the king of Assyria: 'The people you deported and resettled in the towns of Samaria do not know what the god of that country requires. He has sent lions among them, which are killing them off, because the people do not know what he requires.'

27Then the king of Assyria gave this order: 'Make one of the priests you took captive from Samaria go back to live there and teach the people what the god of the land requires.' 28So one of the priests who had been exiled from Samaria came to live in Bethel and taught them how to worship the LORD.

29Nevertheless, each national group made its own gods in the several towns where they settled, and set them up in the shrines the people of Samaria had made at the high places. 30The people from Babylon made Sukkoth Benoth, those from Kuthah made Nergal, and those from Hamath made Ashima; 31the Avvites made Nibhaz and Tartak, and the Sepharvites burned their children in the fire as sacrifices to Adrammelek and Anammelek, the gods of Sepharvaim. 32They worshipped the LORD, but they also appointed all sorts of their own people to officiate for them as priests in the shrines at the high places. 33They worshipped the LORD, but they also served their own gods in accordance with the customs of the nations from which they had been brought.

34To this day they persist in their former practices. They neither worship the LORD nor adhere to the decrees and regulations, the laws and commands that the LORD gave the descendants of Jacob, whom he named Israel. 35When the LORD made a covenant with the Israelites, he commanded them: 'Do not worship any other gods or bow down to them, serve them or sacrifice to them. 36But the LORD, who brought you up out of Egypt with mighty power and outstretched arm, is the one you must worship. To him you shall bow down and to him offer sacrifices. 37You must always be careful to keep the decrees and regulations, the laws and commands he wrote for you. Do not worship other gods. 38Do not forget the covenant I have made with you, and do not worship other gods. 39Rather, worship the LORD your God; it is he who will deliver you from the hand of all your enemies.'

40They would not listen, however, but persisted in their former practices. 41Even while these people were worshipping the LORD, they were serving their idols. To this day their children and grandchildren continue to do as their ancestors did.

Hezekiah king of Judah

18 In the third year of Hoshea son of Elah king of Israel, Hezekiah son of Ahaz king of Judah began to reign. 2He was twenty-five years old when he became king, and he reigned in Jerusalem for twenty-nine years. His mother's name was Abijah[a] daughter of Zechariah. 3He did what was right in the eyes of the LORD, just as his father David had done. 4He removed the high places, smashed the sacred stones and cut down the Asherah poles. He broke into pieces the bronze snake Moses had made, for up to that time the Israelites had been burning incense to it. (It was called Nehushtan.[b])

People and Places

Hezekiah
2 Kings 18:1

Hezekiah was the greatest king of Judah because he got rid of all the pagan high places, idols and altars in the land. He even destroyed the bronze serpent that Moses had made in the wilderness because the people had started to worship it instead of God (Numbers 21:8–9). Hezekiah fell seriously ill and was told by the prophet Isaiah that he was going to die. He cried out to God and God healed him, giving him an amazing sign to show that he would live (2 Kings 20:1–11).

---

[a] 2 Hebrew *Abi*, a variant of *Abijah*   [b] 4 *Nehushtan* sounds like the Hebrew for both *bronze* and *snake*.

5Hezekiah trusted in the LORD, the God of Israel. There was no-one like him among all the kings of Judah, either before him or after him. 6He held fast to the LORD and did not cease to follow him; he kept the commands the LORD had given Moses. 7And the LORD was with him; he was successful in whatever he undertook. He rebelled against the king of Assyria and did not serve him. 8From watchtower to fortified city, he defeated the Philistines, as far as Gaza and its territory.

9In King Hezekiah's fourth year, which was the seventh year of Hoshea son of Elah king of Israel, Shalmaneser king of Assyria marched against Samaria and laid siege to it. 10At the end of three years the Assyrians took it. So Samaria was captured in Hezekiah's sixth year, which was the ninth year of Hoshea king of Israel. 11The king of Assyria deported Israel to Assyria and settled them in Halah, in Gozan on the River Habor, and in towns of the Medes. 12This happened because they had not obeyed the LORD their God, but had violated his covenant—all that Moses the servant of the LORD commanded. They neither listened to the commands nor carried them out.

13In the fourteenth year of King Hezekiah's reign, Sennacherib king of Assyria attacked all the fortified cities of Judah and captured them. 14So Hezekiah king of Judah sent this message to the king of Assyria at Lachish: 'I have done wrong. Withdraw from me, and I will pay whatever you demand of me.' The king of Assyria exacted from Hezekiah king of Judah three hundred talents[a] of silver and thirty talents[b] of gold. 15So Hezekiah gave him all the silver that was found in the temple of the LORD and in the treasuries of the royal palace.

16At this time Hezekiah king of Judah stripped off the gold with which he had covered the doors and doorposts of the temple of the LORD, and gave it to the king of Assyria.

Sennacherib threatens Jerusalem

17The king of Assyria sent his supreme commander, his chief officer and his field commander with a large army, from Lachish to King Hezekiah at Jerusalem. They came up to Jerusalem and stopped at the aqueduct of the Upper Pool, on the road to the Washerman's Field. 18They called for the king; and Eliakim son of Hilkiah the palace administrator, Shebna the secretary, and Joah son of Asaph the recorder went out to them.

19The field commander said to them, 'Tell Hezekiah:

' "This is what the great king, the king of Assyria, says: on what are you basing this confidence of yours? 20You say you have the counsel and the might for war— but you speak only empty words. On whom are you depending, that you rebel against me? 21Look, I know you are depending on Egypt, that splintered reed of a staff, which pierces the hands of anyone who leans on it! Such is Pharaoh king of Egypt to all who depend on him. 22But if you say to me, 'We are depending on the LORD our God'—isn't he the one whose high places and altars Hezekiah removed, saying to Judah and Jerusalem, 'You must worship before this altar in Jerusalem'?

23' "Come now, make a bargain with my master, the king of Assyria: I will give you two thousand horses—if you can put riders on them! 24How can you repulse one officer of the least of my master's officials, even though you are depending on Egypt for chariots and horsemen?[c] 25Furthermore, have I come to attack and destroy this place without word from the LORD? The LORD himself told me to march against this country and destroy it." '

---

[a] 14 That is, about 10 metric tons [b] 14 That is, about one metric ton [c] 24 Or charioteers

26Then Eliakim son of Hilkiah, and Shebna and Joah said to the field commander, 'Please speak to your servants in Aramaic, since we understand it. Don't speak to us in Hebrew in the hearing of the people on the wall.'

27But the commander replied, 'Was it only to your master and you that my master sent me to say these things, and not to the people sitting on the wall—who, like you, will have to eat their own excrement and drink their own urine?'

28Then the commander stood and called out in Hebrew, 'Hear the word of the great king, the king of Assyria! 29This is what the king says: do not let Hezekiah deceive you. He cannot deliver you from my hand. 30Do not let Hezekiah persuade you to trust in the LORD when he says, "The LORD will surely deliver us; this city will not be given into the hand of the king of Assyria."

31'Do not listen to Hezekiah. This is what the king of Assyria says: make peace with me and come out to me. Then every one of you will eat from your own vine and fig-tree and drink water from your own cistern, 32until I come and take you to a land like your own—a land of grain and new wine, a land of bread and vineyards, a land of olive trees and honey. Choose life and not death!

'Do not listen to Hezekiah, for he is misleading you when he says, "The LORD will deliver us." 33Has the god of any nation ever delivered his land from the hand of the king of Assyria? 34Where are the gods of Hamath and Arpad? Where are the gods of Sepharvaim, Hena and Ivvah? Have they rescued Samaria from my hand? 35Who of all the gods of these countries has been able to save his land from me? How then can the LORD deliver Jerusalem from my hand?'

36But the people remained silent and said nothing in reply, because the king had commanded, 'Do not answer him.'

37Then Eliakim son of Hilkiah the palace administrator, Shebna the secretary, and Joah son of Asaph the recorder went to Hezekiah, with their clothes torn, and told him what the field commander had said.

Jerusalem's deliverance foretold

19 When King Hezekiah heard this, he tore his clothes and put on sackcloth and went into the temple of the LORD. 2He sent Eliakim the palace administrator, Shebna the secretary and the leading priests, all wearing sackcloth, to the prophet Isaiah son of Amoz. 3They told him, 'This is what Hezekiah says: this day is a day of distress and rebuke and disgrace, as when children come to the moment of birth and there is no strength to deliver them. 4It may be that the LORD your God will hear all the words of the field commander, whom his master, the king of Assyria, has sent to ridicule the living God, and that he will rebuke him for the words the LORD your God has heard. Therefore pray for the remnant that still survives.'

5When King Hezekiah's officials came to Isaiah, 6Isaiah said to them, 'Tell your master, "This is what the LORD says: do not be afraid of what you have heard—those words with which the underlings of the king of Assyria have uttered blasphemy against me. 7Listen! When he hears a certain report, I will make him want to return to his own country, and there I will have him cut down with the sword."'

8When the field commander heard that the king of Assyria had left Lachish, he withdrew and found the king fighting against Libnah.

9Now Sennacherib received a report that Tirhakah, the king of Cush,[a] was marching out to fight against him. So he again sent messengers to Hezekiah with this word: 10'Say to Hezekiah king of Judah: do not let the god you depend on deceive you when he says, "Jerusalem will not be given into the hands of the king of Assyria." 11Surely you have heard what the kings of Assyria have done to all the countries, destroying them completely. And will you be delivered? 12Did the gods of the nations that were destroyed by my ancestors deliver them—the gods of Gozan, Harran, Rezeph and the people of Eden who were in Tel Assar? 13Where is the king of Hamath or the king of Arpad? Where are the kings of Lair, Sepharvaim, Hena and Ivvah?'

---

[a] 9 That is, the upper Nile region

Isaiah the prophet
2 Kings 19:20

Some of the books in the Old Testament overlap with each other, telling the story of what happened from different viewpoints. Isaiah gets a short mention here and in 2 Chronicles, and has a whole book of his own which gives more details of his prophecies and ministry.

Hezekiah's prayer

¹⁴Hezekiah received the letter from the messengers and read it. Then he went up to the temple of the LORD and spread it out before the LORD. ¹⁵And Hezekiah prayed to the LORD: 'LORD, the God of Israel, enthroned between the cherubim, you alone are God over all the kingdoms of the earth. You have made heaven and earth. ¹⁶Give ear, LORD, and hear; open your eyes, LORD, and see; listen to the words Sennacherib has sent to ridicule the living God.

¹⁷'It is true, LORD, that the Assyrian kings have laid waste these nations and their lands. ¹⁸They have thrown their gods into the fire and destroyed them, for they were not gods but only wood and stone, fashioned by human hands. ¹⁹Now, LORD our God, deliver us from his hand, so that all the kingdoms of the earth may know that you alone, LORD, are God.'

Isaiah prophesies Sennacherib's fall

²⁰Then Isaiah son of Amoz sent a message to Hezekiah: 'This is what the LORD, the God of Israel, says: I have heard your prayer concerning Sennacherib king of Assyria. ²¹This is the word that the LORD has spoken against him:

'"Virgin Daughter Zion
  despises you and mocks you.
Daughter Jerusalem
  tosses her head as you flee.
²²Who is it you have ridiculed and
    blasphemed?
  Against whom have you raised your
    voice
and lifted your eyes in pride?
  Against the Holy One of Israel!
²³By your messengers
  you have ridiculed the Lord.
And you have said,
  'With my many chariots
I have ascended the heights of the
    mountains,
  the utmost heights of Lebanon.
I have cut down its tallest cedars,
  the choicest of its junipers.
I have reached its remotest parts,
  the finest of its forests.
²⁴I have dug wells in foreign lands
  and drunk the water there.
With the soles of my feet
  I have dried up all the streams of
    Egypt.'

²⁵' "Have you not heard?
  Long ago I ordained it.
In days of old I planned it;
  now I have brought it to pass,
that you have turned fortified cities
  into piles of stone.
²⁶Their people, drained of power,
  are dismayed and put to shame.
They are like plants in the field,
  like tender green shoots,
like grass sprouting on the roof,
  scorched before it grows up.

²⁷' "But I know where you are
  and when you come and go
  and how you rage against me.
²⁸Because you rage against me
  and because your insolence has
    reached my ears,
I will put my hook in your nose
  and my bit in your mouth,
and I will make you return
  by the way you came."

²⁹'This will be the sign for you, Hezekiah:

'This year you will eat what grows by
    itself,
  and the second year what springs from
    that.

But in the third year sow and reap,
  plant vineyards and eat their fruit.
30 Once more a remnant of the house of Judah
  will take root below and bear fruit above.
31 For out of Jerusalem will come a remnant,
  and out of Mount Zion a band of survivors.

'The zeal of the LORD Almighty will accomplish this.

32 'Therefore this is what the LORD says concerning the king of Assyria:

'"He will not enter this city
  or shoot an arrow here.
He will not come before it with shield
  or build a siege ramp against it.
33 By the way that he came he will return;
  he will not enter this city,
            declares the LORD.
34 I will defend this city and save it,
  for my sake and for the sake of David my servant."'

35 That night the angel of the LORD went out and put to death a hundred and eighty-five thousand in the Assyrian camp. When the people got up the next morning—there were all the dead bodies! 36 So Sennacherib king of Assyria broke camp and withdrew. He returned to Nineveh and stayed there.

37 One day, while he was worshipping in the temple of his god Nisrok, his sons Adrammelek and Sharezer killed him with the sword, and they escaped to the land of Ararat. And Esarhaddon his son succeeded him as king.

Hezekiah's illness

20 In those days Hezekiah became ill and was at the point of death. The prophet Isaiah son of Amoz went to him and said, 'This is what the LORD says: put your house in order, because you are going to die; you will not recover.'

2 Hezekiah turned his face to the wall and prayed to the LORD, 3 'Remember, LORD, how I have walked before you faithfully and with wholehearted devotion and have done what is good in your eyes.' And Hezekiah wept bitterly.

4 Before Isaiah had left the middle court, the word of the LORD came to him: 5 'Go back and tell Hezekiah, the ruler of my people, "This is what the LORD, the God of your father David, says: I have heard your prayer and seen your tears; I will heal you. On the third day from now you will go up to the temple of the LORD. 6 I will add fifteen years to your life. And I will deliver you and this city from the hand of the king of Assyria. I will defend this city for my sake and for the sake of my servant David."'

7 Then Isaiah said, 'Prepare a poultice of figs.' They did so and applied it to the boil, and he recovered.

8 Hezekiah had asked Isaiah, 'What will be the sign that the LORD will heal me and that I will go up to the temple of the LORD on the third day from now?'

9 Isaiah answered, 'This is the LORD's sign to you that the LORD will do what he has promised: shall the shadow go forward ten steps, or shall it go back ten steps?'

10 'It is a simple matter for the shadow to go forward ten steps,' said Hezekiah. 'Rather, let it go back ten steps.'

11 Then the prophet Isaiah called on the LORD, and the LORD made the shadow go back the ten steps it had gone down on the stairway of Ahaz.

Envoys from Babylon

12 At that time Marduk-Baladan son of Baladan king of Babylon sent Hezekiah letters and a gift, because he had heard of Hezekiah's illness. 13 Hezekiah received the envoys and showed them all that was in his storehouses—the silver, the gold, the spices and the fine oil—his armoury and everything found among his treasures. There was nothing in his palace or in all his kingdom that Hezekiah did not show them.

14 Then Isaiah the prophet went to King Hezekiah and asked, 'What did those men say, and where did they come from?'

'From a distant land,' Hezekiah replied. 'They came from Babylon.'

15 The prophet asked, 'What did they see in your palace?'

'They saw everything in my palace,' Hezekiah said. 'There is nothing among my treasures that I did not show them.'

Hezekiah's pool
2 Kings 20:20
Water was very precious in biblical times and it was important that people had ways to collect and store it. Hezekiah had a tunnel carved out of rock from the Gihon spring to the Siloam reservoir, an amazing feat of engineering. There is an inscription on the tunnel which tells how workmen started at opposite ends with pickaxes and hammers and finally met in the middle.

16 Then Isaiah said to Hezekiah, 'Hear the word of the LORD: 17 the time will surely come when everything in your palace, and all that your predecessors have stored up until this day, will be carried off to Babylon. Nothing will be left, says the LORD. 18 And some of your descendants, your own flesh and blood who will be born to you, will be taken away, and they will become eunuchs in the palace of the king of Babylon.'

19 'The word of the LORD you have spoken is good,' Hezekiah replied. For he thought, 'Will there not be peace and security in my lifetime?'

20 As for the other events of Hezekiah's reign, all his achievements and how he made the pool and the tunnel by which he brought water into the city, are they not written in the book of the annals of the kings of Judah? 21 Hezekiah rested with his ancestors. And Manasseh his son succeeded him as king.

Manasseh king of Judah

21 Manasseh was twelve years old when he became king, and he reigned in Jerusalem for fifty-five years. His mother's name was Hephzibah. 2 He did evil in the eyes of the LORD, following the detestable practices of the nations the LORD had driven out before the Israelites. 3 He rebuilt the high places his father Hezekiah had destroyed; he also erected altars to Baal and made an Asherah pole, as Ahab king of Israel had done. He bowed down to all the starry hosts and worshipped them. 4 He built altars in the temple of the LORD, of which the LORD had said, 'In Jerusalem I will put my Name.' 5 In the two courts of the temple of the LORD, he built altars to all the starry hosts. 6 He sacrificed his own son in the fire, practised divination, sought omens, and consulted mediums and spiritists. He did much evil in the eyes of the LORD, arousing his anger.

7 He took the carved Asherah pole he had made and put it in the temple, of which the LORD had said to David and to his son Solomon, 'In this temple and in Jerusalem, which I have chosen out of all the tribes of Israel, I will put my Name for ever. 8 I will not again make the feet of the Israelites wander from the land I gave their ancestors, if only they will be careful to do everything I commanded them and will keep the whole Law that my servant Moses gave them.' 9 But the people did not listen. Manasseh led them astray, so that they did more evil than the nations the LORD had destroyed before the Israelites.

10 The LORD said through his servants the prophets: 11 'Manasseh king of Judah has committed these detestable sins. He has done more evil than the Amorites who preceded him and has led Judah into sin with his idols. 12 Therefore this is what the LORD, the God of Israel, says: I am going to bring such disaster on Jerusalem and Judah that the ears of everyone who hears of it will tingle. 13 I will stretch out over Jerusalem the measuring line used against Samaria and the plumb-line used against the house of Ahab. I will wipe out Jerusalem as one wipes out a dish, wiping it and turning it upside-down. 14 I will forsake the remnant of my inheritance and give them into the hands of enemies. They will be looted and plundered by all their enemies; 15 they have done evil in my eyes and have aroused my anger from the day their ancestors came out of Egypt until this day.'

16 Moreover, Manasseh also shed so much innocent blood that he filled Jerusalem from end to end—besides the sin that he had caused Judah to commit, so that they did evil in the eyes of the LORD.

17 As for the other events of Manasseh's reign, and all he did, including the sin he committed, are they not written in the book of the annals of the kings of Judah? 18 Manasseh rested with his ancestors and was buried in his palace garden, the garden of Uzza. And Amon his son succeeded him as king.

Amon king of Judah

19 Amon was twenty-two years old when he became king, and he reigned in Jerusalem for two years. His mother's name was Meshullemeth daughter of Haruz; she was from Jotbah. 20 He did evil in the eyes of the LORD, as his father Manasseh had done. 21 He followed completely the ways of his father, worshipping the idols his father had worshipped, and bowing down to them. 22 He forsook the LORD, the God of his ancestors, and did not walk in obedience to him.

23 Amon's officials conspired against him and assassinated the king in his palace. 24 Then the people of the land killed all who had plotted against King Amon, and they made Josiah his son king in his place.

25 As for the other events of Amon's reign, and what he did, are they not written in the book of the annals of the kings of Judah? 26 He was buried in his tomb in the garden of Uzza. And Josiah his son succeeded him as king.

The Book of the Law found

22 Josiah was eight years old when he became king, and he reigned in Jerusalem for thirty-one years. His mother's name was Jedidah daughter of Adaiah; she was from Bozkath. 2 He did what was right in the eyes of the LORD and followed completely the ways of his father David, not turning aside to the right or to the left.

3 In the eighteenth year of his reign, King Josiah sent the secretary, Shaphan son of Azaliah, the son of Meshullam, to the temple of the LORD. He said: 4 'Go up to Hilkiah the high priest and make him get ready the money that has been brought into the temple of the LORD, which the doorkeepers have collected from the people. 5 Make them entrust it to the men appointed to supervise the work on the temple. And make these men pay the workers who repair the temple of the LORD— 6 the carpenters, the builders and the masons. Also make them purchase timber and dressed stone to repair the temple. 7 But they need not account for the money entrusted to them, because they are honest in their dealings.'

8 Hilkiah the high priest said to Shaphan the secretary, 'I have found the Book of the Law in the temple of the LORD.' He gave it to Shaphan, who read it. 9 Then Shaphan the secretary went to the king and reported to him: 'Your officials have paid out the money that was in the temple of the LORD and have entrusted it to the workers and supervisors at the temple.' 10 Then Shaphan the secretary informed the king, 'Hilkiah the priest has given me a book.' And Shaphan read from it in the presence of the king.

11 When the king heard the words of the Book of the Law, he tore his robes. 12 He gave these orders to Hilkiah the priest, Ahikam son of Shaphan, Akbor son of Micaiah, Shaphan the secretary and Asaiah the king's attendant: 13 'Go and enquire of the LORD for me and for the people and for

---

making Connections

The Book of the Law
2 Kings 22:8

It was customary in ancient times to place documents in the foundations of buildings for safekeeping. During the repairs to the temple, the scrolls of the Law of Moses were found. It probably didn't contain the whole five books of the Law because Shaphan read it twice in an afternoon.

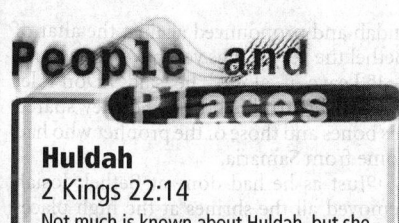

People and Places

Huldah
2 Kings 22:14
Not much is known about Huldah, but she is one of the few female prophets in the Bible. Jeremiah was a prophet at the same time as Huldah, but Josiah consulted her, which shows that she was well respected.

all Judah about what is written in this book that has been found. Great is the LORD's anger that burns against us because those who have gone before us have not obeyed the words of this book; they have not acted in accordance with all that is written there concerning us.'

¹⁴Hilkiah the priest, Ahikam, Akbor, Shaphan and Asaiah went to speak to the prophet Huldah, who was the wife of Shallum son of Tikvah, the son of Harhas, keeper of the wardrobe. She lived in Jerusalem, in the New Quarter.

¹⁵She said to them, 'This is what the LORD, the God of Israel, says: tell the man who sent you to me, ¹⁶"This is what the LORD says: I am going to bring disaster on this place and its people, according to everything written in the book the king of Judah has read. ¹⁷Because they have forsaken me and burned incense to other gods and aroused my anger by all the idols their hands have made,ᵃ my anger will burn against this place and will not be quenched." ¹⁸Tell the king of Judah, who sent you to enquire of the LORD, "This is what the LORD, the God of Israel, says concerning the words you heard: ¹⁹because your heart was responsive and you humbled yourself before the LORD when you heard what I have spoken against this place and its people—that they would become a curseᵇ and be laid waste—and because you tore your robes and wept in my presence, I also have heard you, declares the LORD. ²⁰Therefore I will gather you to your ancestors, and you will be buried in peace. Your eyes will not see all the disaster I am going to bring on this place."'

So they took her answer back to the king.

Josiah renews the covenant

23 Then the king called together all the elders of Judah and Jerusalem. ²He went up to the temple of the LORD with the people of Judah, the inhabitants of Jerusalem, the priests and the prophets—all the people from the least to the greatest. He read in their hearing all the words of the Book of the Covenant, which had been found in the temple of the LORD. ³The king stood by the pillar and renewed the covenant in the presence of the LORD—to follow the LORD and keep his commands, statutes and decrees with all his heart and all his soul, thus confirming the words of the covenant written in this book. Then all the people pledged themselves to the covenant.

⁴The king ordered Hilkiah the high priest, the priests next in rank and the doorkeepers to remove from the temple of the LORD all the articles made for Baal and Asherah and all the starry hosts. He burned them outside Jerusalem in the fields of the Kidron Valley and took the ashes to Bethel. ⁵He did away with the idolatrous priests appointed by the kings of Judah to burn incense on the high places of the towns of Judah and on those around Jerusalem— those who burned incense to Baal, to the sun and moon, to the constellations and to all the starry hosts. ⁶He took the Asherah pole from the temple of the LORD to the Kidron Valley outside Jerusalem and burned it there. He ground it to powder and scattered the dust over the graves of the common people. ⁷He also tore down the quarters of the male shrine-prostitutes that were in the temple of the LORD, the quarters where women did weaving for Asherah.

⁸Josiah brought all the priests from the towns of Judah and desecrated the high places, from Geba to Beersheba, where the priests had burned incense. He broke down

---

ᵃ 17 Or *by everything they have done*   ᵇ 19 That is, their names would be used in cursing (see Jer. 29:22); or, others would see that they are cursed.

the gateway at the entrance of the Gate of Joshua, the city governor, which was on the left of the city gate. 9Although the priests of the high places did not serve at the altar of the LORD in Jerusalem, they ate unleavened bread with their fellow priests.

10He desecrated Topheth, which was in the Valley of Ben Hinnom, so no-one could use it to sacrifice their son or daughter in the fire to Molek. 11He removed from the entrance to the temple of the LORD the horses that the kings of Judah had dedicated to the sun. They were in the court[a] near the room of an official named Nathan-Melek. Josiah then burned the chariots dedicated to the sun.

12He pulled down the altars the kings of Judah had erected on the roof near the upper room of Ahaz, and the altars Manasseh had built in the two courts of the temple of the LORD. He removed them from there, smashed them to pieces and threw the rubble into the Kidron Valley. 13The king also desecrated the high places that were east of Jerusalem on the south of the Hill of Corruption—the ones Solomon king of Israel had built for Ashtoreth the vile goddess of the Sidonians, for Chemosh the vile god of Moab, and for Molek the detestable god of the people of Ammon. 14Josiah smashed the sacred stones and cut down the Asherah poles and covered the sites with human bones.

15Even the altar at Bethel, the high place made by Jeroboam son of Nebat, who had caused Israel to sin—even that altar and high place he demolished. He burned the high place and ground it to powder, and burned the Asherah pole also. 16Then Josiah looked around, and when he saw the tombs that were there on the hillside, he had the bones removed from them and burned on the altar to defile it, in accordance with the word of the LORD proclaimed by the man of God who foretold these things.

17The king asked, 'What is that tombstone I see?'

The people of the city said, 'It marks the tomb of the man of God who came from Judah and pronounced against the altar of Bethel the very things you have done to it.'

18'Leave it alone,' he said. 'Don't let anyone disturb his bones.' So they spared his bones and those of the prophet who had come from Samaria.

19Just as he had done at Bethel, Josiah removed all the shrines at the high places that the kings of Israel had built in the towns of Samaria and that had aroused the LORD's anger. 20Josiah slaughtered all the priests of those high places on the altars and burned human bones on them. Then he went back to Jerusalem.

21The king gave this order to all the people: 'Celebrate the Passover to the LORD your God, as it is written in this Book of the Covenant.' 22Neither in the days of the judges who led Israel nor in the days of the kings of Israel and the kings of Judah had any such Passover been observed. 23But in the eighteenth year of King Josiah, this Passover was celebrated to the LORD in Jerusalem.

24Furthermore, Josiah got rid of the mediums and spiritists, the household gods, the idols and all the other detestable things seen in Judah and Jerusalem. This he did to fulfil the requirements of the law written in the book that Hilkiah the priest had discovered in the temple of the LORD. 25Neither before nor after Josiah was there a king like him who turned to the LORD as he did—with all his heart and with all his soul and with all his strength, in accordance with all the Law of Moses.

26Nevertheless, the LORD did not turn away from the heat of his fierce anger, which burned against Judah because of all that Manasseh had done to arouse his anger. 27So the LORD said, 'I will remove Judah also from my presence as I removed Israel, and I will reject Jerusalem, the city I chose, and this temple, about which I said, "There shall my Name be."[b]'

28As for the other events of Josiah's reign, and all he did, are they not written in the book of the annals of the kings of Judah? 29While Josiah was king, Pharaoh Necho king of Egypt went up to the River Euphrates to help the king of Assyria. King Josiah

---

[a] 11 The meaning of the Hebrew for this word is uncertain.   [b] 27 1 Kings 8:29

marched out to meet him in battle, but Necho faced him and killed him at Megiddo. ³⁰Josiah's servants brought his body in a chariot from Megiddo to Jerusalem and buried him in his own tomb. And the people of the land took Jehoahaz son of Josiah and anointed him and made him king in place of his father.

Jehoahaz king of Judah

³¹Jehoahaz was twenty-three years old when he became king, and he reigned in Jerusalem for three months. His mother's name was Hamutal daughter of Jeremiah; she was from Libnah. ³²He did evil in the eyes of the LORD, just as his predecessors had done. ³³Pharaoh Necho put him in chains at Riblah in the land of Hamath so that he might not reign in Jerusalem, and he imposed on Judah a levy of a hundred talents^a of silver and a talent^b of gold. ³⁴Pharaoh Necho made Eliakim son of Josiah king in place of his father Josiah and changed Eliakim's name to Jehoiakim. But he took Jehoahaz and carried him off to Egypt, and there he died. ³⁵Jehoiakim paid Pharaoh Necho the silver and gold he demanded. In order to do so, he taxed the land and exacted the silver and gold from the people of the land according to their assessments.

Jehoiakim king of Judah

³⁶Jehoiakim was twenty-five years old when he became king, and he reigned in Jerusalem for eleven years. His mother's name was Zebidah daughter of Pedaiah; she was from Rumah. ³⁷And he did evil in the eyes of the LORD, just as his predecessors had done.

24 During Jehoiakim's reign, Nebuchadnezzar king of Babylon invaded the land, and Jehoiakim became his vassal for three years. But then he turned against Nebuchadnezzar and rebelled. ²The LORD sent Babylonian,^{c} Aramean, Moabite and Ammonite raiders against him to destroy Judah, in accordance with the word of the LORD proclaimed by his servants the prophets. ³Surely these things happened to Judah according to the LORD's command, in order to remove them from his presence because of the sins of Manasseh and all he had done, ⁴including the shedding of innocent blood. For he had filled Jerusalem with innocent blood, and the LORD was not willing to forgive.

⁵As for the other events of Jehoiakim's reign, and all he did, are they not written in the book of the annals of the kings of Judah? ⁶Jehoiakim rested with his ancestors. And Jehoiachin his son succeeded him as king.

⁷The king of Egypt did not march out from his own country again, because the king of Babylon had taken all his territory, from the Wadi of Egypt to the River Euphrates.

Jehoiachin king of Judah

⁸Jehoiachin was eighteen years old when he became king, and he reigned in Jerusalem for three months. His mother's name was Nehushta daughter of Elnathan; she was from Jerusalem. ⁹He did evil in the eyes of the LORD, just as his father had done.

¹⁰At that time the officers of Nebuchadnezzar king of Babylon advanced on Jerusalem and laid siege to it, ¹¹and Nebuchadnezzar himself came up to the city while his officers were besieging it. ¹²Jehoiachin king of Judah, his mother, his

---

People and Places

Nebuchadnezzar
2 Kings 24:1

Nebuchadnezzar was the king of Babylon, a man intent on increasing the size of his empire. He took captives from Judah three times, eventually taking over the city of Jerusalem in 586 BC. He had a policy of taking slaves from the lands that he conquered and using them in his ambitious building projects. Nebuchadnezzar also appears in the books of Daniel, Jeremiah, Ezra and Ezekiel.

---

^{a} 33 That is, about 3.4 metric tons ^{b} 33 That is, about 34 kilograms ^{c} 2 Or *Chaldean* attendants, his nobles and his officials all surrendered to him.

In the eighth year of the reign of the king of Babylon, he took Jehoiachin prisoner. 13As the LORD had declared, Nebuchadnezzar removed the treasures from the temple of the LORD and from the royal palace, and cut up the gold articles that Solomon king of Israel had made for the temple of the LORD. 14He carried all Jerusalem into exile: all the officers and fighting men, and all the skilled workers and artisans—a total of ten thousand. Only the poorest people of the land were left.

15Nebuchadnezzar took Jehoiachin captive to Babylon. He also took from Jerusalem to Babylon the king's mother, his wives, his officials and the prominent people of the land. 16The king of Babylon also deported to Babylon the entire force of seven thousand fighting men, strong and fit for war, and a thousand skilled workers and artisans. 17He made Mattaniah, Jehoiachin's uncle, king in his place and changed his name to Zedekiah.

Zedekiah king of Judah

18Zedekiah was twenty-one years old when he became king, and he reigned in Jerusalem for eleven years. His mother's name was Hamutal daughter of Jeremiah; she was from Libnah. 19He did evil in the eyes of the LORD, just as Jehoiakim had done. 20It was because of the LORD's anger that all this happened to Jerusalem and Judah, and in the end he thrust them from his presence.

The fall of Jerusalem

Now Zedekiah rebelled against the king of Babylon.

25 So in the ninth year of Zedekiah's reign, on the tenth day of the tenth month, Nebuchadnezzar king of Babylon marched against Jerusalem with his whole army. He camped outside the city and built siege works all around it. 2The city was kept under siege until the eleventh year of King Zedekiah.

3By the ninth day of the fourth^a month the famine in the city had become so severe that there was no food for the people to eat. 4Then the city wall was broken through, and the whole army fled at night through the gate between the two walls near the king's garden, though the Babylonians^b were surrounding the city. They fled towards the Arabah,^{c} 5but the Babylonian^d army pursued the king and overtook him in the plains of Jericho. All his soldiers were separated from him and scattered, 6and he was captured.

He was taken to the king of Babylon at Riblah, where sentence was pronounced on him. 7They killed the sons of Zedekiah before his eyes. Then they put out his eyes, bound him with bronze shackles and took him to Babylon.

8On the seventh day of the fifth month, in the nineteenth year of Nebuchadnezzar king of Babylon, Nebuzaradan commander of the imperial guard, an official of the king of Babylon, came to Jerusalem. 9He set fire to the temple of the LORD, the royal palace and all the houses of Jerusalem. Every important building he burned down. 10The whole Babylonian army under the commander of the imperial guard broke down the walls around Jerusalem. 11Nebuzaradan the commander of the guard carried into exile the people who remained in the city, along with the rest of the populace and those who had deserted to the king of Babylon. 12But the commander left behind some of the poorest people of the land to work the vineyards and fields.

13The Babylonians broke up the bronze pillars, the movable stands and the bronze Sea that were at the temple of the LORD and they carried the bronze to Babylon. 14They also took away the pots, shovels, wick trimmers, dishes and all the bronze articles used in the temple service. 15The commander of the imperial guard took away the censers and sprinkling bowls—all that were made of pure gold or silver.

16The bronze from the two pillars, the Sea and the movable stands, which Solomon had made for the temple of the LORD, was more than could be weighed. 17Each pillar

---

^{a}3 Probable reading of the original Hebrew text (see Jer. 52:6); Masoretic Text does not have *fourth*. ^{b}4 Or *Chaldeans*; also in verses 13, 25 and 26 ^{c}4 Or *the Jordan Valley* ^{d}5 Or *Chaldean*; also in verses 10 and 24 was eighteen cubits[a] high. The bronze capital on top of one pillar was three cubits[b] high and was decorated with a network and pomegranates of bronze all around. The other pillar, with its network, was similar.

18The commander of the guard took as prisoners Seraiah the chief priest, Zephaniah the priest next in rank and the three doorkeepers. 19Of those still in the city, he took the officer in charge of the fighting men, and five royal advisors. He also took the secretary who was chief officer in charge of conscripting the people of the land and sixty of the conscripts who were found in the city. 20Nebuzaradan the commander took them all and brought them to the king of Babylon at Riblah. 21There at Riblah, in the land of Hamath, the king had them executed.

So Judah went into captivity, away from her land.

22Nebuchadnezzar king of Babylon appointed Gedaliah son of Ahikam, the son of Shaphan, to be over the people he had left behind in Judah. 23When all the army officers and their men heard that the king of Babylon had appointed Gedaliah as governor, they came to Gedaliah at Mizpah—Ishmael son of Nethaniah, Johanan son of Kareah, Seraiah son of Tanhumeth the Netophathite, Jaazaniah the son of the Maakathite, and their men. 24Gedaliah took an oath to reassure them and their men. 'Do not be afraid of the Babylonian officials,' he said. 'Settle down in the land and serve the king of Babylon, and it will go well with you.'

25In the seventh month, however, Ishmael son of Nethaniah, the son of Elishama, who was of royal blood, came with ten men and assassinated Gedaliah and also the men of Judah and the Babylonians who were with him at Mizpah. 26At this, all the people from the least to the greatest, together with the army officers, fled to Egypt for fear of the Babylonians.

Jehoiachin released

27In the thirty-seventh year of the exile of Jehoiachin king of Judah, in the year Awel-Marduk became king of Babylon, he released Jehoiachin king of Judah from prison. He did this on the twenty-seventh day of the twelfth month. 28He spoke kindly to him and gave him a seat of honour higher than those of the other kings who were with him in Babylon. 29So Jehoiachin put aside his prison clothes and for the rest of his life ate regularly at the king's table. 30Day by day the king gave Jehoiachin a regular allowance as long as he lived.

---

[a] 17 That is, about 8.1 metres   [b] 17 That is, about 1.4 metres

1 Chronicles

INTRODUCTION

1 CHRONICLES

Author: Unknown, but it could have been Ezra the priest.

Who to: The Israelites returning to Jerusalem after the exile.

When: 1 Chronicles retells the story of the Israelites from the end of Saul's reign to the death of King David.

Did you know? Ezra the priest may have written four books in the Bible – 1 and 2 Chronicles, Ezra and Nehemiah.

Main theme: Both 1 and 2 Chronicles are books of hope, written to encourage the Israelites as they return to Jerusalem, to remind them of their past and to help them trust God for the future. 1 Chronicles starts with Adam and, after a long list of his descendants, tells the story of King David, focusing on the positive things that he achieved.

Historical records from Adam to Abraham

To Noah's sons

1 Adam, Seth, Enosh, ²Kenan, Mahalalel, Jared, ³Enoch, Methuselah, Lamech, Noah.

⁴The sons of Noah:[a]
  Shem, Ham and Japheth.

The Japhethites

⁵The sons[b] of Japheth:
  Gomer, Magog, Madai, Javan, Tubal, Meshek and Tiras.
⁶The sons of Gomer:
  Ashkenaz, Riphath[c] and Togarmah.
⁷The sons of Javan:
  Elishah, Tarshish, the Kittites and the Rodanites.

---

[a] 4 Septuagint; Hebrew does not have *The sons of Noah*.   [b] 5 *Sons* may mean *descendants* or *successors* or *nations*; also in verses 6-10, 17 and 20.   [c] 6 Many Hebrew manuscripts and Vulgate (see also Septuagint and Gen. 10:3); most Hebrew manuscripts *Diphath*

The Hamites

⁸The sons of Ham:
Cush, Egypt, Put and Canaan.
⁹The sons of Cush:
Seba, Havilah, Sabta, Raamah and Sabteka.
The sons of Raamah:
Sheba and Dedan.
¹⁰Cush was the father[a] of
Nimrod, who became a mighty warrior on earth.
¹¹Egypt was the father of
the Ludites, Anamites, Lehabites, Naphtuhites, ¹²Pathrusites, Kasluhites (from whom the Philistines came) and Caphtorites.
¹³Canaan was the father of
Sidon his firstborn,[b] and of the Hittites, ¹⁴Jebusites, Amorites, Girgashites, ¹⁵Hivites, Arkites, Sinites, ¹⁶Arvadites, Zemarites and Hamathites.

The Semites

¹⁷The sons of Shem:
Elam, Ashur, Arphaxad, Lud and Aram.
The sons of Aram:[c]
Uz, Hul, Gether and Meshek.
¹⁸Arphaxad was the father of Shelah, and Shelah the father of Eber.
¹⁹Two sons were born to Eber:
One was named Peleg,[d] because in his time the earth was divided; his brother was named Joktan.
²⁰Joktan was the father of
Almodad, Sheleph, Hazarmaveth, Jerah, ²¹Hadoram, Uzal, Diklah, ²²Obal,[e] Abimael, Sheba, ²³Ophir, Havilah and Jobab. All these were sons of Joktan.

²⁴Shem, Arphaxad,[f] Shelah,
²⁵Eber, Peleg, Reu,
²⁶Serug, Nahor, Terah
²⁷and Abram (that is, Abraham).

The family of Abraham

²⁸The sons of Abraham:
Isaac and Ishmael.

Descendants of Hagar

²⁹These were their descendants:
Nebaioth the firstborn of Ishmael, Kedar, Adbeel, Mibsam, ³⁰Mishma, Dumah, Massa, Hadad, Tema, ³¹Jetur, Naphish and Kedemah. These were the sons of Ishmael.

Descendants of Keturah

³²The sons born to Keturah, Abraham's concubine:
Zimran, Jokshan, Medan, Midian, Ishbak and Shuah.
The sons of Jokshan:
Sheba and Dedan.
³³The sons of Midian:
Ephah, Epher, Hanok, Abida and Eldaah.
All these were descendants of Keturah.

Descendants of Sarah

³⁴Abraham was the father of Isaac.
The sons of Isaac:
Esau and Israel.

Esau's sons

³⁵The sons of Esau:
Eliphaz, Reuel, Jeush, Jalam and Korah.
³⁶The sons of Eliphaz:
Teman, Omar, Zepho,[g] Gatam and Kenaz;
by Timna: Amalek.[h]
³⁷The sons of Reuel:
Nahath, Zerah, Shammah and Mizzah.

The people of Seir in Edom

³⁸The sons of Seir:
Lotan, Shobal, Zibeon, Anah, Dishon, Ezer and Dishan.

---

[a] 10 *Father* may mean *ancestor* or *predecessor* or *founder*; also in verses 11, 13, 18 and 20. [b] 13 Or *of the Sidonians, the foremost* [c] 17 One Hebrew manuscript and some Septuagint manuscripts (see Gen. 10:23); most Hebrew manuscripts do not have this line. [d] 19 *Peleg* means *division*. [e] 22 Some Hebrew manuscripts and Syriac (see also Gen. 10:28); most Hebrew manuscripts *Ebal* [f] 24 Hebrew; some Septuagint manuscripts *Arphaxad, Cainan* (see also note at Gen. 11:10) [g] 36 Many Hebrew manuscripts, some Septuagint manuscripts and Syriac (see also Gen. 36:11); most Hebrew manuscripts *Zephi* [h] 36 Some Septuagint manuscripts (see also Gen. 36:12); Hebrew *Gatam, Kenaz, Timna and Amalek*

³⁹The sons of Lotan:
  Hori and Homam. Timna was Lotan's sister.
⁴⁰The sons of Shobal:
  Alvan,ᵃ Manahath, Ebal, Shepho and Onam.
The sons of Zibeon:
  Aiah and Anah.
⁴¹The son of Anah:
  Dishon.
The sons of Dishon:
  Hemdan,ᵇ Eshban, Ithran and Keran.
⁴²The sons of Ezer:
  Bilhan, Zaavan and Akan.ᶜ
The sons of Dishan:ᵈ
  Uz and Aran.

The rulers of Edom

⁴³These were the kings who reigned in Edom before any Israelite king reigned:
  Bela son of Beor, whose city was named Dinhabah.
⁴⁴When Bela died, Jobab son of Zerah from Bozrah succeeded him as king.
⁴⁵When Jobab died, Husham from the land of the Temanites succeeded him as king.
⁴⁶When Husham died, Hadad son of Bedad, who defeated Midian in the country of Moab, succeeded him as king. His city was named Avith.
⁴⁷When Hadad died, Samlah from Masrekah succeeded him as king.
⁴⁸When Samlah died, Shaul from Rehoboth on the riverᵉ succeeded him as king.
⁴⁹When Shaul died, Baal-Hanan son of Akbor succeeded him as king.
⁵⁰When Baal-Hanan died, Hadad succeeded him as king. His city was named Pau,ᶠ and his wife's name was Mehetabel daughter of Matred, the daughter of Me-Zahab. ⁵¹Hadad also died.

The chiefs of Edom were:
  Timna, Alvah, Jetheth, ⁵²Oholibamah, Elah, Pinon, ⁵³Kenaz, Teman, Mibzar, ⁵⁴Magdiel and Iram. These were the chiefs of Edom.

Israel's sons

2 These were the sons of Israel:
  Reuben, Simeon, Levi, Judah, Issachar, Zebulun, ²Dan, Joseph, Benjamin, Naphtali, Gad and Asher.

Judah

To Hezron's sons

³The sons of Judah:
  Er, Onan and Shelah. These three were born to him by a Canaanite woman, the daughter of Shua. Er, Judah's firstborn, was wicked in the LORD's sight; so the LORD put him to death. ⁴Judah's daughter-in-law Tamar bore Perez and Zerah to Judah. He had five sons in all.

⁵The sons of Perez:
  Hezron and Hamul.
⁶The sons of Zerah:
  Zimri, Ethan, Heman, Kalkol and Dardaᵍ—five in all.
⁷The son of Karmi:
  Achar,ʰ who brought trouble on Israel by violating the ban on taking devoted things.ⁱ
⁸The son of Ethan:
  Azariah.

ᵃ 40 Many Hebrew manuscripts and some Septuagint manuscripts (see also Gen. 36:23); most Hebrew manuscripts *Alian*   ᵇ 41 Many Hebrew manuscripts and some Septuagint manuscripts (see also Gen. 36:26); most Hebrew manuscripts *Hamran*   ᶜ 42 Many Hebrew and Septuagint manuscripts (see also Gen. 36:27); most Hebrew manuscripts *Zaavan, Jaakan*   ᵈ 42 See Gen. 36:28; Hebrew *Dishon*, a variant of *Dishan*   ᵉ 48 Possibly the Euphrates   ᶠ 50 Many Hebrew manuscripts, some Septuagint manuscripts, Vulgate and Syriac (see also Gen. 36:39); most Hebrew manuscripts *Pai*   ᵍ 6 Many Hebrew manuscripts, some Septuagint manuscripts and Syriac (see also 1 Kings 4:31); most Hebrew manuscripts *Dara*   ʰ 7 *Achar* means *trouble*; *Achar* is called *Achan* in Joshua.   ⁱ 7 The Hebrew term refers to the irrevocable giving over of things or persons to the LORD, often by totally destroying them.

⁹The sons born to Hezron were:
Jerahmeel, Ram and Caleb.[a]

From Ram son of Hezron

¹⁰Ram was the father of
Amminadab, and Amminadab
the father of Nahshon, the leader
of the people of Judah. ¹¹Nahshon
was the father of Salmon,[b] Salmon
the father of Boaz, ¹²Boaz the
father of Obed and Obed the
father of Jesse.

¹³Jesse was the father of
Eliab his firstborn; the second son
was Abinadab, the third Shimea,
¹⁴the fourth Nethanel, the fifth
Raddai, ¹⁵the sixth Ozem and the
seventh David. ¹⁶Their sisters
were Zeruiah and Abigail. Zeruiah's three sons were Abishai,
Joab and Asahel. ¹⁷Abigail was the
mother of Amasa, whose father
was Jether the Ishmaelite.

Caleb son of Hezron

¹⁸Caleb son of Hezron had children by
his wife Azubah (and by Jerioth).
These were her sons: Jesher, Shobab and Ardon. ¹⁹When Azubah
died, Caleb married Ephrath, who
bore him Hur. ²⁰Hur was the
father of Uri, and Uri the father of
Bezalel.

²¹Later, Hezron, when he was sixty
years old, married the daughter of
Makir the father of Gilead. He
made love to her, and she bore
him Segub. ²²Segub was the father
of Jair, who controlled twenty-three towns in Gilead. ²³(But
Geshur and Aram captured Havvoth Jair,[c] as well as Kenath with
its surrounding settlements—sixty towns.) All these were descendants of Makir the father of Gilead.

²⁴After Hezron died in Caleb Ephrathah, Abijah the wife of Hezron
bore him Ashhur the father[d] of
Tekoa.

Jerahmeel son of Hezron

²⁵The sons of Jerahmeel the firstborn
of Hezron:
Ram his firstborn, Bunah, Oren,
Ozem and[e] Ahijah. ²⁶Jerahmeel
had another wife, whose name
was Atarah; she was the mother of
Onam.

²⁷The sons of Ram the firstborn of
Jerahmeel:
Maaz, Jamin and Eker.

²⁸The sons of Onam:
Shammai and Jada.

The sons of Shammai:
Nadab and Abishur.

²⁹Abishur's wife was named Abihail,
who bore him Ahban and Molid.

³⁰The sons of Nadab:
Seled and Appaim. Seled died
without children.

³¹The son of Appaim:
Ishi, who was the father of Sheshan.
Sheshan was the father of Ahlai.

³²The sons of Jada, Shammai's brother:
Jether and Jonathan. Jether died
without children.

³³The sons of Jonathan:
Peleth and Zaza.

These were the descendants of Jerahmeel.

³⁴Sheshan had no sons—only daughters.
He had an Egyptian servant
named Jarha. ³⁵Sheshan gave his
daughter in marriage to his servant Jarha, and she bore him
Attai.

³⁶Attai was the father of Nathan,
Nathan the father of Zabad,
³⁷Zabad the father of Ephlal,
Ephlal the father of Obed,
³⁸Obed the father of Jehu,
Jehu the father of Azariah,
³⁹Azariah the father of Helez,
Helez the father of Eleasah,

---

[a] 9 Hebrew *Kelubai*, a variant of *Caleb*   [b] 11 Septuagint (see also Ruth 4:21); Hebrew *Salma*   [c] 23 Or *captured the settlements of Jair*   [d] 24 *Father* may mean *civic leader* or *military leader*; also in verses 42, 45, 49-52 and possibly elsewhere.   [e] 25 Or *Oren and Ozem, by*

⁴⁰Eleasah the father of Sismai,
Sismai the father of Shallum,
⁴¹Shallum the father of Jekamiah,
and Jekamiah the father of Elishama.

The clans of Caleb

⁴²The sons of Caleb the brother of Jerahmeel:
Mesha his firstborn, who was the father of Ziph, and his son Mareshah,ᵃ who was the father of Hebron.
⁴³The sons of Hebron:
Korah, Tappuah, Rekem and Shema. ⁴⁴Shema was the father of Raham, and Raham the father of Jorkeam. Rekem was the father of Shammai. ⁴⁵The son of Shammai was Maon, and Maon was the father of Beth Zur.
⁴⁶Caleb's concubine Ephah was the mother of Haran, Moza and Gazez. Haran was the father of Gazez.
⁴⁷The sons of Jahdai:
Regem, Jotham, Geshan, Pelet, Ephah and Shaaph.
⁴⁸Caleb's concubine Maakah was the mother of Sheber and Tirhanah. ⁴⁹She also gave birth to Shaaph the father of Madmannah and to Sheva the father of Makbenah and Gibea. Caleb's daughter was Aksah. ⁵⁰These were the descendants of Caleb.

The sons of Hur the firstborn of Ephrathah:
Shobal the father of Kiriath Jearim, ⁵¹Salma the father of Bethlehem, and Hareph the father of Beth Gader.
⁵²The descendants of Shobal the father of Kiriath Jearim were:
Haroeh, half the Manahathites, ⁵³and the clans of Kiriath Jearim: the Ithrites, Puthites, Shumathites and Mishraites. From these descended the Zorathites and Eshtaolites.

⁵⁴The descendants of Salma:
Bethlehem, the Netophathites, Atroth Beth Joab, half the Manahathites, the Zorites, ⁵⁵and the clans of scribesᵇ who lived at Jabez: the Tirathites, Shimeathites and Sucathites. These are the Kenites who came from Hammath, the father of the house of Rekab.ᶜ

The sons of David

3 These were the sons of David born to him in Hebron:
the firstborn was Amnon the son of Ahinoam of Jezreel;
the second, Daniel the son of Abigail of Carmel;
²the third, Absalom the son of Maakah daughter of Talmai king of Geshur;
the fourth, Adonijah the son of Haggith;
³the fifth, Shephatiah the son of Abital;
and the sixth, Ithream, by his wife Eglah.
⁴These six were born to David in Hebron, where he reigned for seven years and six months.

David reigned in Jerusalem for thirty-three years, ⁵and these were the children born to him there:
Shammua,ᵈ Shobab, Nathan and Solomon. These four were by Bathshebaᵉ daughter of Ammiel. ⁶There were also Ibhar, Elishua,ᶠ Eliphelet, ⁷Nogah, Nepheg, Japhia, ⁸Elishama, Eliada and Eliphelet—nine in all. ⁹All these were the sons of David, besides his sons by his concubines. And Tamar was their sister.

The kings of Judah

¹⁰Solomon's son was Rehoboam,
Abijah his son,
Asa his son,

ᵃ 42 The meaning of the Hebrew for this phrase is uncertain.   ᵇ 55 Or *of the Sopherites*   ᶜ 55 Or *father of Beth Rekab*   ᵈ 5 Hebrew *Shimea*, a variant of *Shammua*   ᵉ 5 One Hebrew manuscript and Vulgate (see also Septuagint and 2 Sam. 11:3); most Hebrew manuscripts *Bathshua*   ᶠ 6 Two Hebrew manuscripts (see also 2 Sam. 5:15 and 1 Chron. 14:5); most Hebrew manuscripts *Elishama*

> **IN OTHER WORDS**
>
> **Concubine**
> 1 Chronicles 3:9
> In Bible times, men often had more than one wife. And sometimes they had one or more concubines, a female slave or mistress with whom they would have children.

Jehoshaphat his son,
¹¹Jehoram^a his son,
Ahaziah his son,
Joash his son,
¹²Amaziah his son,
Azariah his son,
Jotham his son,
¹³Ahaz his son,
Hezekiah his son,
Manasseh his son,
¹⁴Amon his son,
Josiah his son.
¹⁵The sons of Josiah:
Johanan the firstborn,
Jehoiakim the second son,
Zedekiah the third,
Shallum the fourth.
¹⁶The successors of Jehoiakim:
Jehoiachin^b his son,
and Zedekiah.

The royal line after the exile

¹⁷The descendants of Jehoiachin the captive:
Shealtiel his son, ¹⁸Malkiram, Pedaiah, Shenazzar, Jekamiah, Hoshama and Nedabiah.
¹⁹The sons of Pedaiah:
Zerubbabel and Shimei.
The sons of Zerubbabel:
Meshullam and Hananiah.
Shelomith was their sister.
²⁰There were also five others:
Hashubah, Ohel, Berekiah, Hasadiah and Jushab-Hesed.

²¹The descendants of Hananiah:
Pelatiah and Jeshaiah, and the sons of Rephaiah, of Arnan, of Obadiah and of Shekaniah.
²²The descendants of Shekaniah:
Shemaiah and his sons:
Hattush, Igal, Bariah, Neariah and Shaphat—six in all.
²³The sons of Neariah:
Elioenai, Hizkiah and Azrikam—three in all.
²⁴The sons of Elioenai:
Hodaviah, Eliashib, Pelaiah, Akkub, Johanan, Delaiah and Anani—seven in all.

Other clans of Judah

4 The descendants of Judah:
Perez, Hezron, Karmi, Hur and Shobal.
²Reaiah son of Shobal was the father of Jahath, and Jahath the father of Ahumai and Lahad. These were the clans of the Zorathites.
³These were the sons^c of Etam:
Jezreel, Ishma and Idbash. Their sister was named Hazzelelponi.
⁴Penuel was the father of Gedor, and Ezer the father of Hushah.
These were the descendants of Hur, the firstborn of Ephrathah and father^d of Bethlehem.
⁵Ashhur the father of Tekoa had two wives, Helah and Naarah.
⁶Naarah bore him Ahuzzam, Hepher, Temeni and Haahashtari. These were the descendants of Naarah.
⁷The sons of Helah:
Zereth, Zohar, Ethnan, ⁸and Koz, who was the father of Anub and Hazzobebah and of the clans of Aharhel son of Harum.

⁹Jabez was more honourable than his brothers. His mother had named him Jabez,^e saying, 'I gave birth to him in pain.' ¹⁰Jabez cried out to the God of Israel, 'Oh, that you would bless me and enlarge my territory! Let your hand be with me, and keep me from harm so that

---

^a 11 Hebrew *Joram*, a variant of *Jehoram* ^b 16 Hebrew *Jeconiah*, a variant of *Jehoiachin*; also in verse 17 ^c 3 Some Septuagint manuscripts (see also Vulgate); Hebrew *father* ^d 4 *Father* may mean *civic leader* or *military leader*; also in verses 12, 14, 17, 18 and possibly elsewhere. ^e 9 *Jabez* sounds like the Hebrew for *pain*.

I will be free from pain.' And God granted his request.

¹¹Kelub, Shuhah's brother, was the father of Mehir, who was the father of Eshton. ¹²Eshton was the father of Beth Rapha, Paseah and Tehinnah the father of Ir Nahash.[a] These were the men of Rekah.

¹³The sons of Kenaz:

Othniel and Seraiah.

The sons of Othniel:

Hathath and Meonothai.[b] ¹⁴Meonothai was the father of Ophrah.

Seraiah was the father of Joab, the father of Ge Harashim.[c] It was called this because its people were skilled workers.

¹⁵The sons of Caleb son of Jephunneh:

Iru, Elah and Naam.

The son of Elah:

Kenaz.

¹⁶The sons of Jehallelel:

Ziph, Ziphah, Tiria and Asarel.

¹⁷The sons of Ezrah:

Jether, Mered, Epher and Jalon.

One of Mered's wives gave birth to Miriam, Shammai and Ishbah the father of Eshtemoa. ¹⁸(His wife from the tribe of Judah gave birth to Jered the father of Gedor, Heber the father of Soko, and Jekuthiel the father of Zanoah.) These were the children of Pharaoh's daughter Bithiah, whom Mered had married.

¹⁹The sons of Hodiah's wife, the sister of Naham:

the father of Keilah the Garmite, and Eshtemoa the Maakathite.

²⁰The sons of Shimon:

Amnon, Rinnah, Ben-Hanan and Tilon.

The descendants of Ishi:

Zoheth and Ben-Zoheth.

²¹The sons of Shelah son of Judah:

Er the father of Lekah, Laadah the father of Mareshah and the clans of the linen workers at Beth Ashbea, ²²Jokim, the men of Kozeba, and Joash and Saraph, who ruled in Moab and Jashubi Lehem. (These records are from ancient times.) ²³They were the potters who lived at Netaim and Gederah; they stayed there and worked for the king.

Simeon

²⁴The descendants of Simeon:

Nemuel, Jamin, Jarib, Zerah and Shaul;

²⁵Shallum was Shaul's son, Mibsam his son and Mishma his son.

²⁶The descendants of Mishma:

Hammuel his son, Zakkur his son and Shimei his son.

²⁷Shimei had sixteen sons and six daughters, but his brothers did not have many children; so their entire clan did not become as numerous as the people of Judah. ²⁸They lived in Beersheba, Moladah, Hazar Shual, ²⁹Bilhah, Ezem, Tolad, ³⁰Bethuel, Hormah, Ziklag, ³¹Beth Markaboth, Hazar Susim, Beth Biri and Shaaraim. These were their towns until the reign of David. ³²Their surrounding villages were Etam, Ain, Rimmon, Token and Ashan—five towns—³³and all the villages around these towns as far as Baalath.[d] These were their settlements. And they kept a genealogical record.

³⁴Meshobab, Jamlech, Joshah son of Amaziah, ³⁵Joel, Jehu son of Joshibiah, the son of Seraiah, the son of Asiel, ³⁶also Elioenai, Jaakobah, Jeshohaiah, Asaiah, Adiel, Jesimiel, Benaiah, ³⁷and Ziza son of Shiphi, the son of Allon, the son of Jedaiah, the son of Shimri, the son of Shemaiah.

³⁸The men listed above by name were leaders of their clans. Their families increased greatly, ³⁹and they went to the outskirts of Gedor to the east of the valley in search of pasture for their flocks. ⁴⁰They found rich, good pasture, and the land was

---

[a] 12 Or *of the city of Nahash*   [b] 13 Some Septuagint manuscripts and Vulgate; Hebrew does not have *and Meonothai*.
[c] 14 *Ge Harashim* means *valley of skilled workers*.   [d] 33 Some Septuagint manuscripts (see also Joshua 19:8); Hebrew *Baal*

spacious, peaceful and quiet. Some Hamites had lived there formerly.

41 The men whose names were listed came in the days of Hezekiah king of Judah. They attacked the Hamites in their dwellings and also the Meunites who were there and completely destroyed[a] them, as is evident to this day. Then they settled in their place, because there was pasture for their flocks. 42 And five hundred of these Simeonites, led by Pelatiah, Neariah, Rephaiah and Uzziel, the sons of Ishi, invaded the hill country of Seir. 43 They killed the remaining Amalekites who had escaped, and they have lived there to this day.

Reuben

5 The sons of Reuben the firstborn of Israel (he was the firstborn, but when he defiled his father's marriage bed, his rights as firstborn were given to the sons of Joseph son of Israel; so he could not be listed in the genealogical record in accordance with his birthright, 2 and though Judah was the strongest of his brothers and a ruler came from him, the rights of the firstborn belonged to Joseph)— 3 the sons of Reuben the firstborn of Israel:

Hanok, Pallu, Hezron and Karmi.

4 The descendants of Joel:

Shemaiah his son, Gog his son, Shimei his son, 5 Micah his son, Reaiah his son, Baal his son,

6 and Beerah his son, whom Tiglath-Pileser[b] king of Assyria took into exile. Beerah was a leader of the Reubenites.

7 Their relatives by clans, listed according to their genealogical records:

Jeiel the chief, Zechariah, 8 and Bela son of Azaz, the son of Shema, the son of Joel. They settled in the area from Aroer to Nebo and Baal Meon. 9 To the east they occupied the land up to the edge of the desert that extends to the River Euphrates, because their livestock had increased in Gilead.

10 During Saul's reign they waged war against the Hagrites, who were defeated at their hands; they occupied the dwellings of the Hagrites throughout the entire region east of Gilead.

Gad

11 The Gadites lived next to them in Bashan, as far as Salekah:

12 Joel was the chief, Shapham the second, then Janai and Shaphat, in Bashan.

13 Their relatives, by families, were:

Michael, Meshullam, Sheba, Jorai, Jakan, Zia and Eber—seven in all.

14 These were the sons of Abihail son of Huri, the son of Jaroah, the son of Gilead, the son of Michael, the son of Jeshishai, the son of Jahdo, the son of Buz.

15 Ahi son of Abdiel, the son of Guni, was head of their family.

16 The Gadites lived in Gilead, in Bashan and its outlying villages, and on all the pasture-lands of Sharon as far as they extended.

17 All these were entered in the genealogical records during the reigns of Jotham king of Judah and Jeroboam king of Israel.

18 The Reubenites, the Gadites and the half-tribe of Manasseh had 44,760 men ready for military service—able-bodied men who could handle shield and sword, who could use a bow, and who were trained for battle. 19 They waged war against the Hagrites, Jetur, Naphish and Nodab. 20 They were helped in fighting them, and God delivered the Hagrites and all their allies into their hands, because they cried out to him during the battle. He answered their prayers, because they trusted in him. 21 They seized the livestock of the Hagrites—fifty thousand camels, two hundred and fifty thousand sheep and two thousand donkeys. They also took one hundred thousand people captive, 22 and many others fell slain, because the battle was

---

[a] 41 The Hebrew term refers to the irrevocable giving over of things or persons to the LORD, often by totally destroying them.   [b] 6 Hebrew *Tilgath-Pilneser*, a variant of *Tiglath-Pileser*; also in verse 26

God's. And they occupied the land until the exile.

The half-tribe of Manasseh

23The people of the half-tribe of Manasseh were numerous; they settled in the land from Bashan to Baal Hermon, that is, to Senir (Mount Hermon).

24These were the heads of their families: Epher, Ishi, Eliel, Azriel, Jeremiah, Hodaviah and Jahdiel. They were brave warriors, famous men, and heads of their families. 25But they were unfaithful to the God of their ancestors and prostituted themselves to the gods of the peoples of the land, whom God had destroyed before them. 26So the God of Israel stirred up the spirit of Pul king of Assyria (that is, Tiglath-Pileser king of Assyria), who took the Reubenites, the Gadites and the half-tribe of Manasseh into exile. He took them to Halah, Habor, Hara and the river of Gozan, where they are to this day.

Levi

6 *The sons of Levi:
Gershon, Kohath and Merari.
2The sons of Kohath:
Amram, Izhar, Hebron and Uzziel.
3The children of Amram:
Aaron, Moses and Miriam.
The sons of Aaron:
Nadab, Abihu, Eleazar and Ithamar.
4Eleazar was the father of Phinehas,
Phinehas the father of Abishua,
5Abishua the father of Bukki,
Bukki the father of Uzzi,
6Uzzi the father of Zerahiah,
Zerahiah the father of Meraioth,
7Meraioth the father of Amariah,
Amariah the father of Ahitub,
8Ahitub the father of Zadok,
Zadok the father of Ahimaaz,
9Ahimaaz the father of Azariah,
Azariah the father of Johanan,
10Johanan the father of Azariah (it was he who served as priest in the temple Solomon built in Jerusalem),
11Azariah the father of Amariah,
Amariah the father of Ahitub,
12Ahitub the father of Zadok,
Zadok the father of Shallum,
13Shallum the father of Hilkiah,
Hilkiah the father of Azariah,
14Azariah the father of Seraiah,
and Seraiah the father of Jozadak.[a]

15Jozadak was deported when the LORD sent Judah and Jerusalem into exile by the hand of Nebuchadnezzar.

*16The sons of Levi:
Gershon,[b] Kohath and Merari.
17These are the names of the sons of Gershon:
Libni and Shimei.
18The sons of Kohath:
Amram, Izhar, Hebron and Uzziel.
19The sons of Merari:
Mahli and Mushi.
These are the clans of the Levites listed according to their fathers:
20of Gershon:
Libni his son, Jahath his son,
Zimmah his son, 21Joah his son,
Iddo his son, Zerah his son
and Jeatherai his son.
22The descendants of Kohath:
Amminadab his son, Korah his son,
Assir his son, 23Elkanah his son,
Ebiasaph his son, Assir his son,
24Tahath his son, Uriel his son,
Uzziah his son and Shaul his son.
25The descendants of Elkanah:
Amasai, Ahimoth,
26Elkanah his son,[c] Zophai his son,
Nahath his son, 27Eliab his son,
Jeroham his son, Elkanah his son
and Samuel his son.[d]
28The sons of Samuel:
Joel[e] the firstborn
and Abijah the second son.

---

[a] 14 Hebrew *Jehozadak*, a variant of *Jozadak*; also in verse 15   [b] 16 Hebrew *Gershom*, a variant of *Gershon*; also in verses 17, 20, 43, 62 and 71   [c] 26 Some Hebrew manuscripts, Septuagint and Syriac; most Hebrew manuscripts *Ahimoth* 26*and Elkanah. The sons of Elkanah:*   [d] 27 Some Septuagint manuscripts (see also 1 Sam. 1:19, 20 and 1 Chron. 6:33, 34); Hebrew does not have *and Samuel his son.*   [e] 28 Some Septuagint manuscripts and Syriac (see also 1 Sam. 8:2 and 1 Chron. 6:33); Hebrew does not have *Joel.*

* 6:1-15 is numbered 5:27-41 in Hebrew texts.   * 6:16-81 is numbered 6:1-66 in Hebrew texts.

Music
1 Chronicles 6:31
Music was a significant part of Israelite culture. It was played on important occasions such as festivals, worship services and funerals as well as during everyday life. David had a love of music and was a very skilled harpist.

29 The descendants of Merari:
Mahli, Libni his son,
Shimei his son, Uzzah his son,
30 Shimea his son, Haggiah his son and Asaiah his son.

The temple musicians

31 These are the men David put in charge of the music in the house of the LORD after the ark came to rest there. 32 They ministered with music before the tabernacle, the tent of meeting, until Solomon built the temple of the LORD in Jerusalem. They performed their duties according to the regulations laid down for them.

33 Here are the men who served, together with their sons:
from the Kohathites:
Heman, the musician,
the son of Joel, the son of Samuel,
34 the son of Elkanah, the son of Jeroham,
the son of Eliel, the son of Toah,
35 the son of Zuph, the son of Elkanah,
the son of Mahath, the son of Amasai,
36 the son of Elkanah, the son of Joel, the son of Azariah, the son of Zephaniah,
37 the son of Tahath, the son of Assir, the son of Ebiasaph, the son of Korah,
38 the son of Izhar, the son of Kohath,
the son of Levi, the son of Israel;
39 and Heman's associate Asaph, who served at his right hand:
Asaph son of Berekiah, the son of Shimea,
40 the son of Michael, the son of Baaseiah,*a*
the son of Malkijah, 41 the son of Ethni,
the son of Zerah, the son of Adaiah,
42 the son of Ethan, the son of Zimmah,
the son of Shimei, 43 the son of Jahath,
the son of Gershon, the son of Levi;
44 and from their associates, the Merarites, at his left hand:
Ethan son of Kishi, the son of Abdi,
the son of Malluk, 45 the son of Hashabiah,
the son of Amaziah, the son of Hilkiah,
46 the son of Amzi, the son of Bani, the son of Shemer, 47 the son of Mahli,
the son of Mushi, the son of Merari,
the son of Levi.

48 Their fellow Levites were assigned to all the other duties of the tabernacle, the house of God. 49 But Aaron and his descendants were the ones who presented offerings on the altar of burnt offering and on the altar of incense in connection with all that was done in the Most Holy Place, making atonement for Israel, in accordance with all that Moses the servant of God had commanded.

50 These were the descendants of Aaron:
Eleazar his son, Phinehas his son, Abishua his son, 51 Bukki his son, Uzzi his son, Zerahiah his son,

---

a 40 Most Hebrew manuscripts; some Hebrew manuscripts, one Septuagint manuscript and Syriac *Maaseiah*

⁵²Meraioth his son, Amariah his son,
Ahitub his son, ⁵³Zadok his son and Ahimaaz his son.

⁵⁴These were the locations of their settlements allotted as their territory (they were assigned to the descendants of Aaron who were from the Kohathite clan, because the first lot was for them):

⁵⁵They were given Hebron in Judah with its surrounding pasture-lands. ⁵⁶But the fields and villages around the city were given to Caleb son of Jephunneh.

⁵⁷So the descendants of Aaron were given Hebron (a city of refuge), and Libnah,[a] Jattir, Eshtemoa, ⁵⁸Hilen, Debir, ⁵⁹Ashan, Juttah[b] and Beth Shemesh, together with their pasture-lands. ⁶⁰And from the tribe of Benjamin they were given Gibeon,[c] Geba, Alemeth and Anathoth, together with their pasture-lands.

The total number of towns distributed among the Kohathite clans came to thirteen.

⁶¹The rest of Kohath's descendants were allotted ten towns from the clans of half the tribe of Manasseh.

⁶²The descendants of Gershon, clan by clan, were allotted thirteen towns from the tribes of Issachar, Asher and Naphtali, and from the part of the tribe of Manasseh that is in Bashan.

⁶³The descendants of Merari, clan by clan, were allotted twelve towns from the tribes of Reuben, Gad and Zebulun.

⁶⁴So the Israelites gave the Levites these towns and their pasture-lands. ⁶⁵From the tribes of Judah, Simeon and Benjamin they allotted the previously named towns.

⁶⁶Some of the Kohathite clans were given as their territory towns from the tribe of Ephraim.

⁶⁷In the hill country of Ephraim they were given Shechem (a city of refuge), and Gezer,[d] ⁶⁸Jokmeam, Beth Horon, ⁶⁹Aijalon and Gath Rimmon, together with their pasture-lands.

⁷⁰And from half the tribe of Manasseh the Israelites gave Aner and Bileam, together with their pasture-lands, to the rest of the Kohathite clans.

⁷¹The Gershonites received the following:
from the clan of the half-tribe of Manasseh
they received Golan in Bashan and also Ashtaroth, together with their pasture-lands;
⁷²from the tribe of Issachar
they received Kedesh, Daberath, ⁷³Ramoth and Anem, together with their pasture-lands;
⁷⁴from the tribe of Asher
they received Mashal, Abdon, ⁷⁵Hukok and Rehob, together with their pasture-lands;
⁷⁶and from the tribe of Naphtali
they received Kedesh in Galilee, Hammon and Kiriathaim, together with their pasture-lands.

⁷⁷The Merarites (the rest of the Levites) received the following:
from the tribe of Zebulun
they received Jokneam, Kartah,[e] Rimmono and Tabor, together with their pasture-lands;
⁷⁸from the tribe of Reuben across the Jordan east of Jericho
they received Bezer in the wilderness, Jahzah, ⁷⁹Kedemoth and Mephaath, together with their pasture-lands;
⁸⁰and from the tribe of Gad
they received Ramoth in Gilead, Mahanaim, ⁸¹Heshbon and Jazer, together with their pasture-lands.

---

[a] 57 See Joshua 21:13; Hebrew *given the cities of refuge: Hebron, Libnah.* [b] 59 Syriac (see also Septuagint and Joshua 21:16); Hebrew does not have *Juttah.* [c] 60 See Joshua 21:17; Hebrew does not have *Gibeon.* [d] 67 See Joshua 21:21; Hebrew *given the cities of refuge: Shechem, Gezer.* [e] 77 See Septuagint and Joshua 21:34; Hebrew does not have *Jokneam, Kartah.*

> **IN OTHER WORDS**
>
> **Genealogy**
> 1 Chronicles 7:2
> A genealogy is a list of a person's ancestors, rather like a family tree. They are important because they allow people to understand their roots and where they have come from. These first nine chapters of 1 Chronicles form the longest genealogy in the Bible, tracing descendants from Adam to the time of Saul.

Issachar

7 The sons of Issachar:
Tola, Puah, Jashub and Shimron—four in all.

²The sons of Tola:
Uzzi, Rephaiah, Jeriel, Jahmai, Ibsam and Samuel—heads of their families. During the reign of David, the descendants of Tola listed as fighting men in their genealogy numbered 22,600.

³The son of Uzzi:
Izrahiah.

The sons of Izrahiah:
Michael, Obadiah, Joel and Ishiah. All five of them were chiefs. ⁴According to their family genealogy, they had 36,000 men ready for battle, for they had many wives and children.

⁵The relatives who were fighting men belonging to all the clans of Issachar, as listed in their genealogy, were 87,000 in all.

Benjamin

⁶Three sons of Benjamin:
Bela, Beker and Jediael.

⁷The sons of Bela:
Ezbon, Uzzi, Uzziel, Jerimoth and Iri, heads of families—five in all. Their genealogical record listed 22,034 fighting men.

⁸The sons of Beker:
Zemirah, Joash, Eliezer, Elioenai, Omri, Jeremoth, Abijah, Anathoth and Alemeth. All these were the sons of Beker. ⁹Their genealogical record listed the heads of families and 20,200 fighting men.

¹⁰The son of Jediael:
Bilhan.

The sons of Bilhan:
Jeush, Benjamin, Ehud, Kenaanah, Zethan, Tarshish and Ahishahar. ¹¹All these sons of Jediael were heads of families. There were 17,200 fighting men ready to go out to war.

¹²The Shuppites and Huppites were the descendants of Ir, and the Hushites^a the descendants of Aher.

Naphtali

¹³The sons of Naphtali:
Jahziel, Guni, Jezer and Shillem^b—the descendants of Bilhah.

Manasseh

¹⁴The descendants of Manasseh:
Asriel was his descendant through his Aramean concubine. She gave birth to Makir the father of Gilead. ¹⁵Makir took a wife from among the Huppites and Shuppites. His sister's name was Maakah.

Another descendant was named Zelophehad, who had only daughters.

¹⁶Makir's wife Maakah gave birth to a son and named him Peresh. His brother was named Sheresh, and his sons were Ulam and Rakem.

¹⁷The son of Ulam:
Bedan.

These were the sons of Gilead son of Makir, the son of Manasseh. ¹⁸His sister Hammoleketh gave birth to Ishhod, Abiezer and Mahlah.

---

^{a} 12 Or *Ir. The sons of Dan:* Hushim, (see Gen. 46:23); Hebrew does not have *The sons of Dan*. ^{b} 13 Some Hebrew and Septuagint manuscripts (see also Gen. 46:24 and Num. 26:49); most Hebrew manuscripts *Shallum*

19 The sons of Shemida were:
Ahian, Shechem, Likhi and Aniam.

Ephraim

20 The descendants of Ephraim:
Shuthelah, Bered his son,
Tahath his son, Eleadah his son,
Tahath his son, 21 Zabad his son
and Shuthelah his son.

Ezer and Elead were killed by the native-born men of Gath, when they went down to seize their livestock. 22 Their father Ephraim mourned for them many days, and his relatives came to comfort him. 23 Then he made love to his wife again, and she became pregnant and gave birth to a son. He named him Beriah,[a] because there had been misfortune in his family. 24 His daughter was Sheerah, who built Lower and Upper Beth Horon as well as Uzzen Sheerah.

25 Rephah was his son, Resheph his son,[b]
Telah his son, Tahan his son,
26 Ladan his son, Ammihud his son,
Elishama his son, 27 Nun his son
and Joshua his son.

28 Their lands and settlements included Bethel and its surrounding villages, Naaran to the east, Gezer and its villages to the west, and Shechem and its villages all the way to Ayyah and its villages. 29 Along the borders of Manasseh were Beth Shan, Taanach, Megiddo and Dor, together with their villages. The descendants of Joseph son of Israel lived in these towns.

Asher

30 The sons of Asher:
Imnah, Ishvah, Ishvi and Beriah.
Their sister was Serah.
31 The sons of Beriah:
Heber and Malkiel, who was the father of Birzaith.
32 Heber was the father of Japhlet, Shomer and Hotham and of their sister Shua.
33 The sons of Japhlet:
Pasak, Bimhal and Ashvath.
These were Japhlet's sons.
34 The sons of Shomer:
Ahi, Rohgah,[c] Hubbah and Aram.
35 The sons of his brother Helem:
Zophah, Imna, Shelesh and Amal.
36 The sons of Zophah:
Suah, Harnepher, Shual, Beri, Imrah, 37 Bezer, Hod, Shamma, Shilshah, Ithran[d] and Beera.
38 The sons of Jether:
Jephunneh, Pispah and Ara.
39 The sons of Ulla:
Arah, Hanniel and Rizia.

40 All these were descendants of Asher—heads of families, choice men, brave warriors and outstanding leaders. The number of men ready for battle, as listed in their genealogy, was 26,000.

The genealogy of Saul the Benjaminite

8 Benjamin was the father of Bela his firstborn,
Ashbel the second son, Aharah the third,
2 Nohah the fourth and Rapha the fifth.

3 The sons of Bela were:
Addar, Gera, Abihud,[e] 4 Abishua, Naaman, Ahoah, 5 Gera, Shephuphan and Huram.

6 These were the descendants of Ehud, who were heads of families of those living in Geba and were deported to Manahath:

7 Naaman, Ahijah and Gera, who deported them and who was the father of Uzza and Ahihud.

8 Sons were born to Shaharaim in Moab after he had divorced his wives Hushim and Baara. 9 By his wife Hodesh he had Jobab, Zibia, Mesha, Malkam, 10 Jeuz, Sakia and Mirmah. These were his sons, heads of families. 11 By Hushim he had Abitub and Elpaal.

12 The sons of Elpaal:
Eber, Misham, Shemed (who built Ono and Lod with its surrounding villages), 13 and Beriah

---

[a] 23 *Beriah* sounds like the Hebrew for *misfortune*.   [b] 25 Some Septuagint manuscripts; Hebrew does not have *his son*.   [c] 34 Or *of his brother Shomer: Rohgah*   [d] 37 Possibly a variant of *Jether*   [e] 3 Or *Gera the father of Ehud*

and Shema, who were heads of families of those living in Aijalon and who drove out the inhabitants of Gath.

14 Ahio, Shashak, Jeremoth, 15 Zebadiah, Arad, Eder, 16 Michael, Ishpah and Joha were the sons of Beriah.

17 Zebadiah, Meshullam, Hizki, Heber, 18 Ishmerai, Izliah and Jobab were the sons of Elpaal.

19 Jakim, Zikri, Zabdi, 20 Elienai, Zillethai, Eliel, 21 Adaiah, Beraiah and Shimrath were the sons of Shimei.

22 Ishpan, Eber, Eliel, 23 Abdon, Zikri, Hanan, 24 Hananiah, Elam, Anthothijah, 25 Iphdeiah and Penuel were the sons of Shashak.

26 Shamsherai, Shehariah, Athaliah, 27 Jaareshiah, Elijah and Zikri were the sons of Jeroham.

28 All these were heads of families, chiefs as listed in their genealogy, and they lived in Jerusalem.

29 Jeiel[a] the father[b] of Gibeon lived in Gibeon.

His wife's name was Maakah, 30 and his firstborn son was Abdon, followed by Zur, Kish, Baal, Ner,[c] Nadab, 31 Gedor, Ahio, Zeker 32 and Mikloth, who was the father of Shimeah. They too lived near their relatives in Jerusalem.

33 Ner was the father of Kish, Kish the father of Saul, and Saul the father of Jonathan, Malki-Shua, Abinadab and Esh-Baal.[d]

34 The son of Jonathan:
Merib-Baal,[e] who was the father of Micah.

35 The sons of Micah:
Pithon, Melek, Tarea and Ahaz.

36 Ahaz was the father of Jehoaddah, Jehoaddah was the father of Alemeth, Azmaveth and Zimri, and Zimri was the father of Moza.

37 Moza was the father of Binea; Raphah was his son, Eleasah his son and Azel his son.

38 Azel had six sons, and these were their names:
Azrikam, Bokeru, Ishmael, Sheariah, Obadiah and Hanan. All these were the sons of Azel.

39 The sons of his brother Eshek:
Ulam his firstborn, Jeush the second son and Eliphelet the third. 40 The sons of Ulam were brave warriors who could handle the bow. They had many sons and grandsons—150 in all.

All these were the descendants of Benjamin.

9 All Israel was listed in the genealogies in the book of the kings of Israel and Judah. They were taken captive to Babylon because of their unfaithfulness.

The people in Jerusalem

2 Now the first to resettle on their own property in their own towns were some Israelites, priests, Levites and temple servants.

3 Those from Judah, from Benjamin, and from Ephraim and Manasseh who lived in Jerusalem were:

4 Uthai son of Ammihud, the son of Omri, the son of Imri, the son of Bani, a descendant of Perez son of Judah.

5 Of the Shelanites[f]:
Asaiah the firstborn and his sons.

6 Of the Zerahites:
Jeuel.
The people from Judah numbered 690.

7 Of the Benjaminites:
Sallu son of Meshullam, the son of Hodaviah, the son of Hassenuah;
8 Ibneiah son of Jeroham; Elah son of Uzzi, the son of Mikri; and Meshullam son of Shephatiah, the son of Reuel, the son of Ibnijah.

9 The people from Benjamin, as listed in their genealogy,

---

[a] 29 Some Septuagint manuscripts (see also 1 Chron. 9:35); Hebrew does not have *Jeiel*. [b] 29 *Father* may mean *civic leader* or *military leader*. [c] 30 Some Septuagint manuscripts (see also 1 Chron. 9:36); Hebrew does not have *Ner*. [d] 33 Also known as *Ish-Bosheth* [e] 34 Also known as *Mephibosheth* [f] 5 See Num. 26:20; Hebrew *Shilonites*.

numbered 956. All these men were heads of their families.

¹⁰Of the priests:

Jedaiah; Jehoiarib; Jakin;

¹¹Azariah son of Hilkiah, the son of Meshullam, the son of Zadok, the son of Meraioth, the son of Ahitub, the official in charge of the house of God;

¹²Adaiah son of Jeroham, the son of Pashhur, the son of Malkijah; and Maasai son of Adiel, the son of Jahzerah, the son of Meshullam, the son of Meshillemith, the son of Immer.

¹³The priests, who were heads of families, numbered 1,760. They were able men, responsible for ministering in the house of God.

¹⁴Of the Levites:

Shemaiah son of Hasshub, the son of Azrikam, the son of Hashabiah, a Merarite; ¹⁵Bakbakkar, Heresh, Galal and Mattaniah son of Mika, the son of Zikri, the son of Asaph; ¹⁶Obadiah son of Shemaiah, the son of Galal, the son of Jeduthun; and Berekiah son of Asa, the son of Elkanah, who lived in the villages of the Netophathites.

¹⁷The gatekeepers:

Shallum, Akkub, Talmon, Ahiman and their fellow Levites, Shallum their chief ¹⁸being stationed at the King's Gate on the east, up to the present time. These were the gatekeepers belonging to the camp of the Levites. ¹⁹Shallum son of Kore, the son of Ebiasaph, the son of Korah, and his fellow gatekeepers from his family (the Korahites) were responsible for guarding the thresholds of the tent just as their ancestors had been responsible for guarding the entrance to the dwelling of the LORD. ²⁰In earlier times Phinehas son of Eleazar was the official in charge of the gatekeepers, and the LORD was with him. ²¹Zechariah son of Meshelemiah was the gatekeeper at the entrance to the tent of meeting.

²²Altogether, those chosen to be gatekeepers at the thresholds numbered 212. They were registered by genealogy in their villages. The gatekeepers had been assigned to their positions of trust by David and Samuel the seer. ²³They and their descendants were in charge of guarding the gates of the house of the LORD—the house called the tent of meeting. ²⁴The gatekeepers were on the four sides: east, west, north and south. ²⁵Their fellow Levites in their villages had to come from time to time and share their duties for seven-day periods. ²⁶But the four principal gatekeepers, who were Levites, were entrusted with the responsibility for the rooms and treasuries in the house of God. ²⁷They would spend the night stationed round the house of God, because they had to guard it; and they had charge of the key for opening it each morning.

²⁸Some of them were in charge of the articles used in the temple service; they counted them when they were brought in and when they were taken out. ²⁹Others were assigned to take care of the furnishings and all the other articles of the sanctuary, as well as the special flour and wine, and the oil, incense and spices. ³⁰But some of the priests took care of mixing the spices. ³¹A Levite named Mattithiah, the firstborn son of Shallum the Korahite, was entrusted with the responsibility for baking the offering bread. ³²Some of the Kohathites, their fellow Levites, were in charge of preparing

---

IN OTHER WORDS

Incense
1 Chronicles 9:29

Incense was a sweet-smelling substance that was burned as an offering to God by the priests during worship in the temple. It symbolised the prayers of God's people.

for every Sabbath the bread set out on the table.

33 Those who were musicians, heads of Levite families, stayed in the rooms of the temple and were exempt from other duties because they were responsible for the work day and night.

34 All these were heads of Levite families, chiefs as listed in their genealogy, and they lived in Jerusalem.

The genealogy of Saul

35 Jeiel the father[a] of Gibeon lived in Gibeon.

His wife's name was Maakah, 36 and his firstborn son was Abdon, followed by Zur, Kish, Baal, Ner, Nadab, 37 Gedor, Ahio, Zechariah and Mikloth. 38 Mikloth was the father of Shimeam. They too lived near their relatives in Jerusalem.

39 Ner was the father of Kish, Kish the father of Saul, and Saul the father of Jonathan, Malki-Shua, Abinadab and Esh-Baal.[b]

40 The son of Jonathan:

Merib-Baal,[c] who was the father of Micah.

41 The sons of Micah:

Pithon, Melek, Tahrea and Ahaz.[d]

42 Ahaz was the father of Jadah, Jadah[e] was the father of Alemeth, Azmaveth and Zimri, and Zimri was the father of Moza. 43 Moza was the father of Binea; Rephaiah was his son, Eleasah his son and Azel his son.

44 Azel had six sons, and these were their names:

Azrikam, Bokeru, Ishmael, Sheariah, Obadiah and Hanan. These were the sons of Azel.

Saul takes his life

10 Now the Philistines fought against Israel; the Israelites fled before them, and many fell dead on Mount Gilboa. 2 The Philistines were in hot pursuit of Saul and his sons, and they killed his sons Jonathan, Abinadab and Malki-Shua. 3 The fighting grew fierce around Saul, and when the archers overtook him, they wounded him.

4 Saul said to his armour-bearer, 'Draw your sword and run me through, or these uncircumcised fellows will come and abuse me.'

But his armour-bearer was terrified and would not do it; so Saul took his own sword and fell on it. 5 When the armour-bearer saw that Saul was dead, he too fell on his sword and died. 6 So Saul and his three sons died, and all his house died together.

7 When all the Israelites in the valley saw that the army had fled and that Saul and his sons had died, they abandoned their towns and fled. And the Philistines came and occupied them.

8 The next day, when the Philistines came to strip the dead, they found Saul and his sons fallen on Mount Gilboa. 9 They stripped him and took his head and his armour, and sent messengers throughout the land of the Philistines to proclaim the news among their idols and their people. 10 They put his armour in the temple of their gods and hung up his head in the temple of Dagon.

11 When all the inhabitants of Jabesh Gilead heard what the Philistines had done to Saul, 12 all their valiant men went and took the bodies of Saul and his sons and brought them to Jabesh. Then they buried their bones under the great tree in Jabesh, and they fasted seven days.

13 Saul died because he was unfaithful to the LORD; he did not keep the word of the LORD, and even consulted a medium for guidance, 14 and did not enquire of the LORD. So the LORD put him to death and turned the kingdom over to David son of Jesse.

David becomes king over Israel

11 All Israel came together to David at Hebron and said, 'We are your own flesh and blood. 2 In the past, even while Saul was king, you were the one who led Israel on

---

[a] 35 *Father* may mean *civic leader* or *military leader*.   [b] 39 Also known as *Ish-Bosheth*   [c] 40 Also known as *Mephibosheth*   [d] 41 Vulgate and Syriac (see also Septuagint and 1 Chron. 8:35); Hebrew does not have *and Ahaz*.   [e] 42 Some Hebrew manuscripts and Septuagint (see also 1 Chron. 8:36); most Hebrew manuscripts *Jarah, Jarah*

their military campaigns. And the LORD your God said to you, "You will shepherd my people Israel, and you will become their ruler."'

3When all the elders of Israel had come to King David at Hebron, he made a covenant with them at Hebron before the LORD, and they anointed David king over Israel, as the LORD had promised through Samuel.

David conquers Jerusalem

4David and all the Israelites marched to Jerusalem (that is, Jebus). The Jebusites who lived there 5said to David, 'You will not get in here.' Nevertheless, David captured the fortress of Zion—which is the City of David.

6David had said, 'Whoever leads the attack on the Jebusites will become commander-in-chief.' Joab son of Zeruiah went up first, and so he received the command.

7David then took up residence in the fortress, and so it was called the City of David. 8He built up the city around it, from the terraces[a] to the surrounding wall, while Joab restored the rest of the city. 9And David became more and more powerful, because the LORD Almighty was with him.

David's mighty warriors

10These were the chiefs of David's mighty warriors—they, together with all Israel, gave his kingship strong support to extend it over the whole land, as the LORD had promised— 11this is the list of David's mighty warriors:

Jashobeam,[b] a Hakmonite, was chief of the officers;[c] he raised his spear against three hundred men, whom he killed in one encounter.

12Next to him was Eleazar son of Dodai the Ahohite, one of the three mighty warriors. 13He was with David at Pas Dammim when the Philistines gathered there for battle. At a place where there was a field full of barley, the troops fled from the Philistines. 14But they took their stand in the middle of the field. They defended it and struck the Philistines down, and the LORD brought about a great victory.

15Three of the thirty chiefs came down to David to the rock at the cave of Adullam, while a band of Philistines was encamped in the Valley of Rephaim. 16At that time David was in the stronghold, and the Philistine garrison was at Bethlehem. 17David longed for water and said, 'Oh, that someone would get me a drink of water from the well near the gate of Bethlehem!' 18So the Three broke through the Philistine lines, drew water from the well near the gate of Bethlehem and carried it back to David. But he refused to drink it; instead, he poured it out to the LORD. 19'God forbid that I should do this!' he said. 'Should I drink the blood of these men who went at the risk of their lives?' Because they risked their lives to bring it back, David would not drink it.

Such were the exploits of the three mighty warriors.

20Abishai the brother of Joab was chief of the Three. He raised his spear against three hundred men, whom he killed, and so he became as famous as the Three. 21He was doubly honoured above the Three and became their commander, even though he was not included among them.

22Benaiah son of Jehoiada, a valiant fighter from Kabzeel, performed great exploits. He struck down Moab's two mightiest warriors. He also went down into a pit on a snowy day and killed a lion. 23And he struck down an Egyptian who was five cubits[d] tall. Although the Egyptian had a spear like a weaver's rod in his hand, Benaiah went against him with a club. He snatched the spear from the Egyptian's hand and killed him with his own spear. 24Such were the exploits of Benaiah son of Jehoiada; he too was as famous as the three mighty warriors. 25He was held in greater honour than any of the Thirty, but he was not included among the Three. And David put him in charge of his bodyguard.

26The mighty warriors were:
  Asahel the brother of Joab,
  Elhanan son of Dodo from Bethlehem,
  27Shammoth the Harorite,
  Helez the Pelonite,

---

[a]8 Or the Millo [b]11 Possibly a variant of Jashob-Baal [c]11 Or Thirty; some Septuagint manuscripts Three (see also 2 Sam. 23:8) [d]23 That is, about 2.3 metres

28 Ira son of Ikkesh from Tekoa,
Abiezer from Anathoth,
29 Sibbekai the Hushathite,
Ilai the Ahohite,
30 Maharai the Netophathite,
Heled son of Baanah the Netophathite,
31 Ithai son of Ribai from Gibeah in Benjamin,
Benaiah the Pirathonite,
32 Hurai from the ravines of Gaash,
Abiel the Arbathite,
33 Azmaveth the Baharumite,
Eliahba the Shaalbonite,
34 the sons of Hashem the Gizonite,
Jonathan son of Shagee the Hararite,
35 Ahiam son of Sakar the Hararite,
Eliphal son of Ur,
36 Hepher the Mekerathite,
Ahijah the Pelonite,
37 Hezro the Carmelite,
Naarai son of Ezbai,
38 Joel the brother of Nathan,
Mibhar son of Hagri,
39 Zelek the Ammonite,
Naharai the Berothite, the armour-bearer of Joab son of Zeruiah,
40 Ira the Ithrite,
Gareb the Ithrite,
41 Uriah the Hittite,
Zabad son of Ahlai,
42 Adina son of Shiza the Reubenite, who was chief of the Reubenites, and the thirty with him,
43 Hanan son of Maakah,
Joshaphat the Mithnite,
44 Uzzia the Ashterathite,
Shama and Jeiel the sons of Hotham the Aroerite,
45 Jediael son of Shimri,
his brother Joha the Tizite,
46 Eliel the Mahavite,
Jeribai and Joshaviah the sons of Elnaam,
Ithmah the Moabite,
47 Eliel, Obed and Jaasiel the Mezobaite.

Long-range weapons
1 Chronicles 12:2
Bows and slings were important weapons because they could inflict damage from a distance. Special units within an army would be trained to use these weapons efficiently. Being able to use them both left- and right-handed gave them flexibility and an advantage in combat.

Warriors join David

12 These were the men who came to David at Ziklag, while he was banished from the presence of Saul son of Kish (they were among the warriors who helped him in battle; 2 they were armed with bows and were able to shoot arrows or to sling stones right-handed or left-handed; they were relatives of Saul from the tribe of Benjamin):

3 Ahiezer their chief and Joash the sons of Shemaah the Gibeathite; Jeziel and Pelet the sons of Azmaveth; Berakah, Jehu the Anathothite, 4 and Ishmaiah the Gibeonite, a mighty warrior among the Thirty, who was a leader of the Thirty; *Jeremiah, Jahaziel, Johanan, Jozabad the Gederathite, *5 Eluzai, Jerimoth, Bealiah, Shemariah and Shephatiah the Haruphite; 6 Elkanah, Ishiah, Azarel, Joezer and Jashobeam the Korahites; 7 and Joelah and Zebadiah the sons of Jeroham from Gedor.

8 Some Gadites defected to David at his stronghold in the wilderness. They were brave warriors, ready for battle and able to handle the shield and spear. Their faces were

---

* The last four names (12:4b) are numbered 12:5 in Hebrew texts.   * 12:5-40 is numbered 12:6-41 in Hebrew texts.

the faces of lions, and they were as swift as gazelles in the mountains.

⁹Ezer was the chief,
  Obadiah the second in command,
  Eliab the third,
¹⁰Mishmannah the fourth, Jeremiah the fifth,
¹¹Attai the sixth, Eliel the seventh,
¹²Johanan the eighth, Elzabad the ninth,
¹³Jeremiah the tenth and Makbannai the eleventh.

¹⁴These Gadites were army commanders; the least was a match for a hundred, and the greatest for a thousand. ¹⁵It was they who crossed the Jordan in the first month when it was overflowing all its banks, and they put to flight everyone living in the valleys, to the east and to the west.

¹⁶Other Benjaminites and some men from Judah also came to David in his stronghold. ¹⁷David went out to meet them and said to them, 'If you have come to me in peace to help me, I am ready for you to join me. But if you have come to betray me to my enemies when my hands are free from violence, may the God of our ancestors see it and judge you.'

¹⁸Then the Spirit came on Amasai, chief of the Thirty, and he said:

'We are yours, David!
  We are with you, son of Jesse!
Success, success to you,
  and success to those who help you,
  for your God will help you.'

So David received them and made them leaders of his raiding bands.

¹⁹Some of the tribe of Manasseh defected to David when he went with the Philistines to fight against Saul. (He and his men did not help the Philistines because, after consultation, their rulers sent him away. They said, 'It will cost us our heads if he deserts to his master Saul.') ²⁰When David went to Ziklag, these were the men of Manasseh who defected to him: Adnah, Jozabad, Jediael, Michael, Jozabad, Elihu and Zillethai, leaders of units of a thousand in Manasseh. ²¹They helped David against raiding bands, for all of them were brave warriors, and they were commanders in his army. ²²Day after day men came to help David, until he had a great army, like the army of God.[a]

Others join David at Hebron

²³These are the numbers of the men armed for battle who came to David at Hebron to turn Saul's kingdom over to him, as the LORD had said:
  ²⁴from Judah, carrying shield and spear—6,800 armed for battle;
  ²⁵from Simeon, warriors ready for battle—7,100;
  ²⁶from Levi—4,600, ²⁷including Jehoiada, leader of the family of Aaron with 3,700 men, ²⁸and Zadok, a brave young warrior, with 22 officers from his family;
  ²⁹from Benjamin, Saul's tribe—3,000, most of whom had remained loyal to Saul's house until then;
  ³⁰from Ephraim, brave warriors, famous in their own clans—20,800;
  ³¹from half the tribe of Manasseh, designated by name to come and make David king—18,000;
  ³²from Issachar, men who understood the times and knew what Israel should do—200 chiefs, with all their relatives under their command;
  ³³from Zebulun, experienced soldiers prepared for battle with every type of weapon, to help David with undivided loyalty—50,000;
  ³⁴from Naphtali—1,000 officers, together with 37,000 men carrying shields and spears;
  ³⁵from Dan, ready for battle—28,600;
  ³⁶from Asher, experienced soldiers prepared for battle—40,000;
  ³⁷and from east of the Jordan, from Reuben, Gad, and the half-tribe of Manasseh, armed with every type of weapon—120,000.

³⁸All these were fighting men who volunteered to serve in the ranks. They came to Hebron fully determined to make David king over all Israel. All the rest of the Israelites were also of one mind to make

---

[a] 22 Or *a great and mighty army*

David king. ³⁹The men spent three days there with David, eating and drinking, for their families had supplied provisions for them. ⁴⁰Also, their neighbours from as far away as Issachar, Zebulun and Naphtali came bringing food on donkeys, camels, mules and oxen. There were plentiful supplies of flour, fig cakes, raisin cakes, wine, oil, cattle and sheep, for there was joy in Israel.

Bringing back the ark

13 David conferred with each of his officers, the commanders of thousands and commanders of hundreds. ²He then said to the whole assembly of Israel, 'If it seems good to you and if it is the will of the LORD our God, let us send word far and wide to the rest of our people throughout the territories of Israel, and also to the priests and Levites who are with them in their towns and pasture-lands, to come and join us. ³Let us bring the ark of our God back to us, for we did not enquire of[a] it[b] during the reign of Saul.' ⁴The whole assembly agreed to do this, because it seemed right to all the people.

⁵So David assembled all Israel, from the River Shihor in Egypt to Lebo Hamath, to bring the ark of God from Kiriath Jearim. ⁶David and all Israel went to Baalah of Judah (Kiriath Jearim) to bring up from there the ark of God the LORD, who is enthroned between the cherubim—the ark that is called by the Name.

⁷They moved the ark of God from Abinadab's house on a new cart, with Uzzah and Ahio guiding it. ⁸David and all the Israelites were celebrating with all their might before God, with songs and with harps, lyres, tambourines, cymbals and trumpets.

⁹When they came to the threshing-floor of Kidon, Uzzah reached out his hand to steady the ark, because the oxen stumbled. ¹⁰The LORD's anger burned against Uzzah, and he struck him down because he had put his hand on the ark. So he died there before God.

¹¹Then David was angry because the LORD's wrath had broken out against Uzzah, and to this day that place is called Perez Uzzah.[c]

¹²David was afraid of God that day and asked, 'How can I ever bring the ark of God to me?' ¹³He did not take the ark to be with him in the City of David. Instead, he took it to the house of Obed-Edom the Gittite. ¹⁴The ark of God remained with the family of Obed-Edom in his house for three months, and the LORD blessed his household and everything he had.

making Connections

Place names
1 Chronicles 13:11

Sometimes when a dramatic or significant event happened, the name of the place where it happened would be changed so that people would remember it. Jacob called the place where he wrestled with God Peniel, which means 'face of God', because he saw God face to face there (Genesis 32:30). David calls this place Perez Uzzah, meaning 'outbreak against Uzzah', because it's the place where God's anger broke out against Uzzah.

David's house and family

14 Now Hiram king of Tyre sent messengers to David, along with cedar logs, stonemasons and carpenters to build a palace for him. ²And David knew that the LORD had established him as king over Israel and that his kingdom had been highly exalted for the sake of his people Israel.

³In Jerusalem David took more wives and became the father of more sons and daughters. ⁴These are the names of the chil-dren born to him there: Shammua, Shobab, Nathan, Solomon, ⁵Ibhar,

---

[a]3 Or *we neglected* [b]3 Or *him* [c]11 *Perez Uzzah* means *outbreak against Uzzah.*

Elishua, Elpelet, 6Nogah, Nepheg, Japhia, 7Elishama, Beeliada*ᵃ* and Eliphelet.

David defeats the Philistines

8When the Philistines heard that David had been anointed king over all Israel, they went up in full force to search for him, but David heard about it and went out to meet them. 9Now the Philistines had come and raided the Valley of Rephaim; 10so David enquired of God: 'Shall I go and attack the Philistines? Will you deliver them into my hands?'

The LORD answered him, 'Go, I will deliver them into your hands.'

11So David and his men went up to Baal Perazim, and there he defeated them. He said, 'As waters break out, God has broken out against my enemies by my hand.' So that place was called Baal Perazim.*ᵇ* 12The Philistines had abandoned their gods there, and David gave orders to burn them in the fire.

13Once more the Philistines raided the valley; 14so David enquired of God again, and God answered him, 'Do not go directly after them, but circle round them and attack them in front of the poplar trees. 15As soon as you hear the sound of marching in the tops of the poplar trees, move out to battle, because that will mean God has gone out in front of you to strike the Philistine army.' 16So David did as God commanded him, and they struck down the Philistine army, all the way from Gibeon to Gezer.

17So David's fame spread throughout every land, and the LORD made all the nations fear him.

The ark brought to Jerusalem

15 After David had constructed buildings for himself in the City of David, he prepared a place for the ark of God and pitched a tent for it. 2Then David said, 'No-one but the Levites may carry the ark of God, because the LORD chose them to carry the ark of the LORD and to minister before him for ever.'

3David assembled all Israel in Jerusalem to bring up the ark of the LORD to the place he had prepared for it. 4He called together the descendants of Aaron and the Levites:

5from the descendants of Kohath,
   Uriel the leader and 120 relatives;
6from the descendants of Merari,
   Asaiah the leader and 220 relatives;
7from the descendants of Gershon,*ᶜ*
   Joel the leader and 130 relatives;
8from the descendants of Elizaphan,
   Shemaiah the leader and 200 relatives;
9from the descendants of Hebron,
   Eliel the leader and 80 relatives;
10from the descendants of Uzziel,
   Amminadab the leader and 112 relatives.

11Then David summoned Zadok and Abiathar the priests, and Uriel, Asaiah, Joel, Shemaiah, Eliel and Amminadab the Levites. 12He said to them, 'You are the heads of the Levitical families; you and your fellow Levites are to consecrate yourselves and bring up the ark of the LORD, the God of Israel, to the place I have prepared for it. 13It was because you, the Levites, did not bring it up the first time that the LORD our God broke out in anger against us. We did not enquire of him about how to do it in the prescribed way.' 14So the priests and Levites consecrated themselves in order to bring up the ark of the LORD, the God of Israel. 15And the Levites carried the ark of God with the poles on their shoulders, as Moses had commanded in accordance with the word of the LORD.

16David told the leaders of the Levites to appoint their fellow Levites as musicians to make a joyful sound with musical instruments: lyres, harps and cymbals.

17So the Levites appointed Heman son of Joel; from his relatives, Asaph son of Berekiah; and from their relatives the Merarites, Ethan son of Kushaiah; 18and with them their relatives next in rank: Zechariah,*ᵈ* Jaaziel, Shemiramoth, Jehiel, Unni, Eliab, Benaiah, Maaseiah, Mattithiah, Eliphelehu, Mikneiah, Obed-Edom and Jeiel,*ᵉ* the gatekeepers.

---

*ᵃ*7 A variant of *Eliada*   *ᵇ*11 *Baal Perazim* means *the lord who breaks out.*   *ᶜ*7 Hebrew *Gershom,* a variant of *Gershon*
*ᵈ*18 Three Hebrew manuscripts and most Septuagint manuscripts (see also verse 20 and 1 Chron. 16:5); most Hebrew manuscripts *Zechariah son and* or *Zechariah, Ben and*   *ᵉ*18 Hebrew; Septuagint (see also verse 21) *Jeiel and Azaziah*

¹⁹The musicians Heman, Asaph and Ethan were to sound the bronze cymbals; ²⁰Zechariah, Jaaziel,[a] Shemiramoth, Jehiel, Unni, Eliab, Maaseiah and Benaiah were to play the lyres according to *alamoth*,[b] ²¹and Mattithiah, Eliphelehu, Mikneiah, Obed-Edom, Jeiel and Azaziah were to play the harps, directing according to *sheminith*.[c] ²²Kenaniah the head Levite was in charge of the singing; that was his responsibility because he was skilful at it.

²³Berekiah and Elkanah were to be doorkeepers for the ark. ²⁴Shebaniah, Joshaphat, Nethanel, Amasai, Zechariah, Benaiah and Eliezer the priests were to blow trumpets before the ark of God. Obed-Edom and Jehiah were also to be doorkeepers for the ark.

²⁵So David and the elders of Israel and the commanders of units of a thousand went to bring up the ark of the covenant of the LORD from the house of Obed-Edom, with rejoicing. ²⁶Because God had helped the Levites who were carrying the ark of the covenant of the LORD, seven bulls and seven rams were sacrificed. ²⁷Now David was clothed in a robe of fine linen, as were all the Levites who were carrying the ark, and as were the musicians, and Kenaniah, who was in charge of the singing of the choirs. David also wore a linen ephod. ²⁸So all Israel brought up the ark of the covenant of the LORD with shouts, with the sounding of rams' horns and trumpets, and of cymbals, and the playing of lyres and harps.

²⁹As the ark of the covenant of the LORD was entering the City of David, Michal daughter of Saul watched from a window. And when she saw King David dancing and celebrating, she despised him in her heart.

Ministering before the ark

16 They brought the ark of God and set it inside the tent that David had pitched for it, and they presented burnt offerings and fellowship offerings before God. ²After David had finished sacrificing the burnt offerings and fellowship offerings, he blessed the people in the name of the LORD. ³Then he gave a loaf of bread, a cake of dates and a cake of raisins to each Israelite man and woman.

⁴He appointed some of the Levites to minister before the ark of the LORD, to extol,[d] thank, and praise the LORD, the God of Israel: ⁵Asaph was the chief, and next to him in rank were Zechariah, then Jaaziel,[e] Shemiramoth, Jehiel, Mattithiah, Eliab, Benaiah, Obed-Edom and Jeiel. They were to play the lyres and harps, Asaph was to sound the cymbals, ⁶and Benaiah and Jahaziel the priests were to blow the trumpets regularly before the ark of the covenant of God.

⁷That day David first appointed Asaph and his associates to give praise to the LORD in this manner:

⁸Give praise to the LORD, call on his name;
  make known among the nations what
    he has done.
⁹Sing to him, sing praise to him;
  tell of all his wonderful acts.
¹⁰Glory in his holy name;
  let the hearts of those who seek the
    LORD rejoice.
¹¹Look to the LORD and his strength;
  seek his face always.

¹²Remember the wonders he has done,
  his miracles, and the judgments he
    pronounced,
¹³you his servants, the descendants of Israel,
  his chosen ones, the children of Jacob.

> **Asaph**
> **1 Chronicles 16:5**
> Asaph was possibly one of the first ever worship leaders. He was the leader of three families who were given responsibility for music in the temple. Twelve psalms were written by Asaph and his family, for example Psalm 82.

---

[a] 20 See verse 18; Hebrew *Aziel*, a variant of *Jaaziel*. [b] 20 Probably a musical term [c] 21 Probably a musical term [d] 4 Or *petition*; or *invoke* [e] 5 See 15:18,20; Hebrew *Jeiel*, possibly another name for *Jaaziel*.

¹⁴He is the LORD our God;
his judgments are in all the earth.

¹⁵He remembers[a] his covenant for ever,
the promise he made, for a thousand generations,
¹⁶the covenant he made with Abraham,
the oath he swore to Isaac.
¹⁷He confirmed it to Jacob as a decree,
to Israel as an everlasting covenant:
¹⁸'To you I will give the land of Canaan
as the portion you will inherit.'

¹⁹When they were but few in number,
few indeed, and strangers in it,
²⁰they[b] wandered from nation to nation,
from one kingdom to another.
²¹He allowed no-one to oppress them;
for their sake he rebuked kings:
²²'Do not touch my anointed ones;
do my prophets no harm.'

²³Sing to the LORD, all the earth;
proclaim his salvation day after day.
²⁴Declare his glory among the nations,
his marvellous deeds among all peoples.

²⁵For great is the LORD and most worthy of praise;
he is to be feared above all gods.
²⁶For all the gods of the nations are idols,
but the LORD made the heavens.
²⁷Splendour and majesty are before him;
strength and joy are in his dwelling-place.

²⁸Ascribe to the LORD, all you families of nations,
ascribe to the LORD glory and strength.
²⁹Ascribe to the LORD the glory due to his name;
bring an offering and come before him.
Worship the LORD in the splendour of his[c] holiness.
³⁰ Tremble before him, all the earth!
The world is firmly established; it cannot be moved.

³¹Let the heavens rejoice, let the earth be glad;
let them say among the nations, 'The LORD reigns!'
³²Let the sea resound, and all that is in it;
let the fields be jubilant, and everything in them!
³³Let the trees of the forest sing,
let them sing for joy before the LORD,
for he comes to judge the earth.

³⁴Give thanks to the LORD, for he is good;
his love endures for ever.
³⁵Cry out, 'Save us, God our Saviour;
gather us and deliver us from the nations,
that we may give thanks to your holy name,
and glory in your praise.'
³⁶Praise be to the LORD, the God of Israel,
from everlasting to everlasting.

Then all the people said 'Amen' and 'Praise the LORD.'

³⁷David left Asaph and his associates before the ark of the covenant of the LORD to minister there regularly, according to each day's requirements. ³⁸He also left Obed-Edom and his sixty-eight associates to minister with them. Obed-Edom son of Jeduthun, and also Hosah, were gate-keepers.

³⁹David left Zadok the priest and his fellow priests before the tabernacle of the LORD at the high place in Gibeon ⁴⁰to present burnt offerings to the LORD on the altar of burnt offering regularly, morning and evening, in accordance with everything written in the Law of the LORD, which he had given Israel. ⁴¹With them were Heman and Jeduthun and the rest of those chosen and designated by name to give thanks to the LORD, 'for his love endures for ever.' ⁴²Heman and Jeduthun were responsible for the sounding of the trumpets and cymbals and for the playing of the other instruments for sacred song. The sons of Jeduthun were stationed at the gate.

⁴³Then all the people left to go to their homes, and David returned home to bless his family.

---

[a] 15 Some Septuagint manuscripts (see also Psalm 105:8); Hebrew *Remember*   [b] 18–20 One Hebrew manuscript, Septuagint and Vulgate (see also Psalm 105:12); most Hebrew manuscripts *inherit, / ¹⁹though you are but few in number, / few indeed, and strangers in it.' / ²⁰They*   [c] 29 Or LORD *with the splendour of*

God's promise to David

17 After David was settled in his palace, he said to Nathan the prophet, 'Here I am, living in a house of cedar, while the ark of the covenant of the LORD is under a tent.'

²Nathan replied to David, 'Whatever you have in mind, do it, for God is with you.'

³But that night the word of God came to Nathan, saying:

⁴'Go and tell my servant David, "This is what the LORD says: you are not the one to build me a house to dwell in. ⁵I have not dwelt in a house from the day I brought Israel up out of Egypt to this day. I have moved from one tent site to another, from one dwelling-place to another. ⁶Wherever I have moved with all the Israelites, did I ever say to any of their leaders[a] whom I commanded to shepherd my people, 'Why have you not built me a house of cedar?'"

⁷'Now then, tell my servant David, "This is what the LORD Almighty says: I took you from the pasture, from tending the flock, and appointed you ruler over my people Israel. ⁸I have been with you wherever you have gone, and I have cut off all your enemies from before you. Now I will make your name like the names of the greatest men on earth. ⁹And I will provide a place for my people Israel and will plant them so that they can have a home of their own and no longer be disturbed. Wicked people will not oppress them any more, as they did at the beginning ¹⁰and have done ever since the time I appointed leaders over my people Israel. I will also subdue all your enemies.

'"I declare to you that the LORD will build a house for you: ¹¹when your days are over and you go to be with your ancestors, I will raise up your offspring to succeed you, one of your own sons, and I will establish his kingdom. ¹²He is the one who will build a house for me, and I will establish his throne for ever. ¹³I will be his father, and he will be my son. I will never take my love away from him, as I took it away from your predecessor. ¹⁴I will set him over my house and my kingdom for ever; his throne will be established for ever."'

¹⁵Nathan reported to David all the words of this entire revelation.

David's prayer

¹⁶Then King David went in and sat before the LORD, and he said:

'Who am I, LORD God, and what is my family, that you have brought me this far? ¹⁷And as if this were not enough in your sight, my God, you have spoken about the future of the house of your servant. You, LORD God, have looked on me as though I were the most exalted of men.

¹⁸'What more can David say to you for honouring your servant? For you know your servant, ¹⁹LORD. For the sake of your servant and according to your will, you have done this great thing and made known all these great promises.

²⁰'There is no-one like you, LORD, and there is no God but you, as we have heard with our own ears. ²¹And who is like your people Israel—the one nation on earth whose God went out to redeem a people for himself, and to make a name for yourself, and to perform great and awesome wonders by driving out nations from before your people, whom you redeemed from Egypt? ²²You made your people Israel your very own for ever, and you, LORD, have become their God.

---

[a] 6 Traditionally *judges*; also in verse 10

²³'And now, LORD, let the promise you have made concerning your servant and his house be established for ever. Do as you promised, ²⁴so that it will be established and that your name will be great for ever. Then people will say, "The LORD Almighty, the God over Israel, is Israel's God!" And the house of your servant David will be established before you.

²⁵'You, my God, have revealed to your servant that you will build a house for him. So your servant has found courage to pray to you. ²⁶You, LORD, are God! You have promised these good things to your servant. ²⁷Now you have been pleased to bless the house of your servant, that it may continue for ever in your sight; for you, LORD, have blessed it, and it will be blessed for ever.'

David's victories

18 In the course of time, David defeated the Philistines and subdued them, and he took Gath and its surrounding villages from the control of the Philistines.

²David also defeated the Moabites, and they became subject to him and brought him tribute.

³Moreover, David defeated Hadadezer king of Zobah, in the vicinity of Hamath, when he went to set up his monument at[a] the River Euphrates. ⁴David captured a thousand of his chariots, seven thousand charioteers and twenty thousand foot soldiers. He hamstrung all but a hundred of the chariot horses.

⁵When the Arameans of Damascus came to help Hadadezer king of Zobah, David struck down twenty-two thousand of them. ⁶He put garrisons in the Aramean kingdom of Damascus, and the Arameans became subject to him and brought him tribute. The LORD gave David victory wherever he went.

⁷David took the gold shields carried by the officers of Hadadezer and brought them to Jerusalem. ⁸From Tebah[b] and Kun, towns that belonged to Hadadezer, David took a great quantity of bronze, which Solomon used to make the bronze Sea, the pillars and various bronze articles.

⁹When Tou king of Hamath heard that David had defeated the entire army of Hadadezer king of Zobah, ¹⁰he sent his son Hadoram to King David to greet him and congratulate him on his victory in battle over Hadadezer, who had been at war with Tou. Hadoram brought all kinds of articles of gold, of silver and of bronze.

¹¹King David dedicated these articles to the LORD, as he had done with the silver and gold he had taken from all these nations: Edom and Moab, the Ammonites and the Philistines, and Amalek.

¹²Abishai son of Zeruiah struck down eighteen thousand Edomites in the Valley of Salt. ¹³He put garrisons in Edom, and all the Edomites became subject to David. The LORD gave David victory wherever he went.

David's officials

¹⁴David reigned over all Israel, doing what was just and right for all his people. ¹⁵Joab son of Zeruiah was over the army; Jehoshaphat son of Ahilud was recorder; ¹⁶Zadok son of Ahitub and Ahimelek[c] son of Abiathar were priests; Shavsha was secretary; ¹⁷Benaiah son of Jehoiada was over the Kerethites and Pelethites; and David's sons were chief officials at the king's side.

David defeats the Ammonites

19 In the course of time, Nahash king of the Ammonites died, and his son succeeded him as king. ²David thought, 'I will show kindness to Hanun son of Nahash, because his father showed kindness to me.' So David sent a delegation to express his sympathy to Hanun concerning his father.

When David's envoys came to Hanun in the land of the Ammonites to express sympathy to him, ³the Ammonite commanders said to Hanun, 'Do you think David is honouring your father by sending

---

[a] 3 Or *to restore his control over*   [b] 8 Hebrew *Tibhath*, a variant of *Tebah*   [c] 16 Some Hebrew manuscripts, Vulgate and Syriac (see also 2 Sam. 8:17); most Hebrew manuscripts *Abimelek*

envoys to you to express sympathy? Haven't his envoys come to you only to explore and spy out the country and overthrow it?' 4So Hanun seized David's envoys, shaved them, cut off their garments at the buttocks, and sent them away.

5When someone came and told David about the men, he sent messengers to meet them, for they were greatly humiliated. The king said, 'Stay at Jericho till your beards have grown, and then come back.'

6When the Ammonites realised that they had become obnoxious to David, Hanun and the Ammonites sent a thousand talents[a] of silver to hire chariots and charioteers from Aram Naharaim,[b] Aram Maakah and Zobah. 7They hired thirty-two thousand chariots and charioteers, as well as the king of Maakah with his troops, who came and camped near Medeba, while the Ammonites were mustered from their towns and moved out for battle.

8On hearing this, David sent Joab out with the entire army of fighting men. 9The Ammonites came out and drew up in battle formation at the entrance to their city, while the kings who had come were by themselves in the open country.

10Joab saw that there were battle lines in front of him and behind him; so he selected some of the best troops in Israel and deployed them against the Arameans. 11He put the rest of the men under the command of Abishai his brother, and they were deployed against the Ammonites. 12Joab said, 'If the Arameans are too strong for me, then you are to rescue me; but if the Ammonites are too strong for you, then I will rescue you. 13Be strong, and let us fight bravely for our people and the cities of our God. The LORD will do what is good in his sight.'

14Then Joab and the troops with him advanced to fight the Arameans, and they fled before him. 15When the Ammonites realised that the Arameans were fleeing, they too fled before his brother Abishai and went inside the city. So Joab went back to Jerusalem.

16After the Arameans saw that they had been routed by Israel, they sent messengers and had Arameans brought from beyond the River Euphrates, with Shophak the commander of Hadadezer's army leading them.

17When David was told of this, he gathered all Israel and crossed the Jordan; he advanced against them and formed his battle lines opposite them. David formed his lines to meet the Arameans in battle, and they fought against him. 18But they fled before Israel, and David killed seven thousand of their charioteers and forty thousand of their foot soldiers. He also killed Shophak the commander of their army.

19When the vassals of Hadadezer saw that they had been routed by Israel, they made peace with David and became subject to him.

So the Arameans were not willing to help the Ammonites any more.

The capture of Rabbah

20 In the spring, at the time when kings go off to war, Joab led out the armed forces. He laid waste the land of the Ammonites and went to Rabbah and besieged it, but David remained in Jerusalem. Joab attacked Rabbah and left it in ruins. 2David took the crown from the head of their king[c]—its weight was found to be a

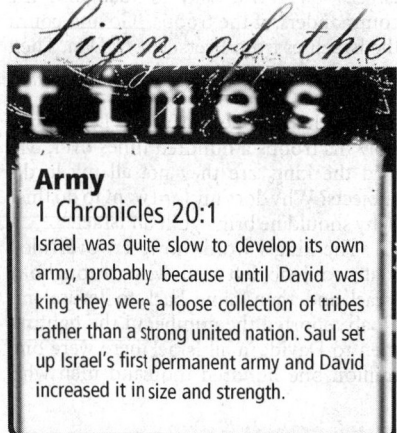

Army
1 Chronicles 20:1
Israel was quite slow to develop its own army, probably because until David was king they were a loose collection of tribes rather than a strong united nation. Saul set up Israel's first permanent army and David increased it in size and strength.

---

[a] 6 That is, about 34 metric tons   [b] 6 That is, North-west Mesopotamia   [c] 2 Or *of Milkom*, that is, Molek

talent[a] of gold, and it was set with precious stones—and it was placed on David's head. He took a great quantity of plunder from the city ³and brought out the people who were there, consigning them to labour with saws and with iron picks and axes. David did this to all the Ammonite towns. Then David and his entire army returned to Jerusalem.

War with the Philistines

⁴In the course of time, war broke out with the Philistines, at Gezer. At that time Sibbekai the Hushathite killed Sippai, one of the descendants of the Rephaites, and the Philistines were subjugated.

⁵In another battle with the Philistines, Elhanan son of Jair killed Lahmi the brother of Goliath the Gittite, who had a spear with a shaft like a weaver's rod.

⁶In still another battle, which took place at Gath, there was a huge man with six fingers on each hand and six toes on each foot—twenty-four in all. He also was descended from Rapha. ⁷When he taunted Israel, Jonathan son of Shimea, David's brother, killed him.

⁸These were descendants of Rapha in Gath, and they fell at the hands of David and his men.

David counts the fighting men

21 Satan rose up against Israel and incited David to take a census of Israel. ²So David said to Joab and the commanders of the troops, 'Go and count the Israelites from Beersheba to Dan. Then report back to me so that I may know how many there are.'

³But Joab replied, 'May the LORD multiply his troops a hundred times over. My lord the king, are they not all my lord's subjects? Why does my lord want to do this? Why should he bring guilt on Israel?'

⁴The king's word, however, overruled Joab; so Joab left and went throughout Israel and then came back to Jerusalem. ⁵Joab reported the number of the fighting men to David: in all Israel there were one million one hundred thousand men who could handle a sword, including four hundred and seventy thousand in Judah.

⁶But Joab did not include Levi and Benjamin in the numbering, because the king's command was repulsive to him. ⁷This command was also evil in the sight of God; so he punished Israel.

⁸Then David said to God, 'I have sinned greatly by doing this. Now, I beg you, take away the guilt of your servant. I have done a very foolish thing.'

⁹The LORD said to Gad, David's seer, ¹⁰'Go and tell David, "This is what the LORD says: I am giving you three options. Choose one of them for me to carry out against you."'

¹¹So Gad went to David and said to him, 'This is what the LORD says: "Take your choice: ¹²three years of famine, three months of being swept away[b] before your enemies, with their swords overtaking you, or three days of the sword of the LORD—days of plague in the land, with the angel of the LORD ravaging every part of Israel." Now then, decide how I should answer the one who sent me.'

¹³David said to Gad, 'I am in deep distress. Let me fall into the hands of the LORD, for his mercy is very great; but do not let me fall into human hands.'

¹⁴So the LORD sent a plague on Israel, and seventy thousand men of Israel fell dead. ¹⁵And God sent an angel to destroy Jerusalem. But as the angel was doing so, the LORD saw it and relented concerning the disaster and said to the angel who was destroying the people, 'Enough! Withdraw your hand.' The angel of the LORD was then standing at the threshing-floor of Araunah[c] the Jebusite.

¹⁶David looked up and saw the angel of the LORD standing between heaven and earth, with a drawn sword in his hand extended over Jerusalem. Then David and the elders, clothed in sackcloth, fell face down.

¹⁷David said to God, 'Was it not I who ordered the fighting men to be counted? I, the shepherd,[d] have sinned and done

---

[a] 2 That is, about 34 kilograms [b] 12 Hebrew; Septuagint and Vulgate (see also 2 Sam. 24:13) *of fleeing* [c] 15 Hebrew *Ornan*, a variant of *Araunah*; also in verses 18-28 [d] 17 Probable reading of the original Hebrew text (see 2 Samuel 24:17 and footnote); Masoretic Text does not have *the shepherd*.

wrong. These are but sheep. What have they done? LORD my God, let your hand fall on me and my family, but do not let this plague remain on your people.'

David builds an altar

18Then the angel of the LORD ordered Gad to tell David to go up and build an altar to the LORD on the threshing-floor of Araunah the Jebusite. 19So David went up in obedience to the word that Gad had spoken in the name of the LORD.

20While Araunah was threshing wheat, he turned and saw the angel; his four sons who were with him hid themselves. 21Then David approached, and when Araunah looked and saw him, he left the threshing-floor and bowed down before David with his face to the ground.

22David said to him, 'Let me have the site of your threshing-floor so that I can build an altar to the LORD, that the plague on the people may be stopped. Sell it to me at the full price.'

23Araunah said to David, 'Take it! Let my lord the king do whatever pleases him. Look, I will give the oxen for the burnt offerings, the threshing-sledges for the wood, and the wheat for the grain offering. I will give all this.'

24But King David replied to Araunah, 'No, I insist on paying the full price. I will not take for the LORD what is yours, or sacrifice a burnt offering that costs me nothing.'

25So David paid Araunah six hundred shekels[a] of gold for the site. 26David built an altar to the LORD there and sacrificed burnt offerings and fellowship offerings. He called on the LORD, and the LORD answered him with fire from heaven on the altar of burnt offering.

27Then the LORD spoke to the angel, and he put his sword back into its sheath. 28At that time, when David saw that the LORD had answered him on the threshing-floor of Araunah the Jebusite, he offered sacrifices there. 29The tabernacle of the LORD, which Moses had made in the wilderness, and the altar of burnt offering were at that time on the high place at Gibeon. 30But David could not go before it to enquire of God, because he was afraid of the sword of the angel of the LORD.

22 Then David said, 'The house of the LORD God is to be here, and also the altar of burnt offering for Israel.'

Preparations for the temple

2So David gave orders to assemble the foreigners residing in Israel, and from among them he appointed stonecutters to prepare dressed stone for building the house of God. 3He provided a large amount of iron to make nails for the doors of the gateways and for the fittings, and more bronze than could be weighed. 4He also provided more cedar logs than could be counted, for the Sidonians and Tyrians had brought large numbers of them to David.

5David said, 'My son Solomon is young and inexperienced, and the house to be built for the LORD should be of great magnificence and fame and splendour in the sight of all the nations. Therefore I will make preparations for it.' So David made extensive preparations before his death.

6Then he called for his son Solomon and charged him to build a house for the LORD, the God of Israel. 7David said to Solomon: 'My son, I had it in my heart to build a house for the Name of the LORD my God. 8But this word of the LORD came to me: "You have shed much blood and have fought many wars. You are not to build a house for my Name, because you have shed much blood on the earth in my sight. 9But you will have a son who will be a man of peace and rest, and I will give him rest from all his enemies on every side. His name will be Solomon,[b] and I will grant Israel peace and quiet during his reign. 10He is the one who will build a house for my Name. He will be my son, and I will be his father. And I will establish the throne of his kingdom over Israel for ever."

11'Now, my son, the LORD be with you, and may you have success and build the house of the LORD your God, as he said you would. 12May the LORD give you discretion and understanding when he puts you in command over Israel, so that you may keep

---

[a] 25 That is, about 6.9 kilograms [b] 9 *Solomon* sounds like and may be derived from the Hebrew for *peace*.

the law of the LORD your God. ¹³Then you will have success if you are careful to observe the decrees and laws that the LORD gave to Moses for Israel. Be strong and courageous. Do not be afraid or discouraged.

¹⁴'I have taken great pains to provide for the temple of the LORD a hundred thousand talents[a] of gold, a million talents[b] of silver, quantities of bronze and iron too great to be weighed, and wood and stone. And you may add to them. ¹⁵You have many workers: stonecutters, masons and carpenters, as well as those skilled in every kind of work ¹⁶in gold and silver, bronze and iron—skilled workers beyond number. Now begin the work, and the LORD be with you.'

¹⁷Then David ordered all the leaders of Israel to help his son Solomon. ¹⁸He said to them, 'Is not the LORD your God with you? And has he not granted you rest on every side? For he has given the inhabitants of the land into my hands, and the land is subject to the LORD and to his people. ¹⁹Now devote your heart and soul to seeking the LORD your God. Begin to build the sanctuary of the LORD God, so that you may bring the ark of the covenant of the LORD and the sacred articles belonging to God into the temple that will be built for the Name of the LORD.'

The Levites

23 When David was old and full of years, he made his son Solomon king over Israel.

²He also gathered together all the leaders of Israel, as well as the priests and Levites. ³The Levites thirty years old or more were counted, and the total number of men was thirty-eight thousand. ⁴David said, 'Of these, twenty-four thousand are to be in charge of the work of the temple of the LORD and six thousand are to be officials and judges. ⁵Four thousand are to be gatekeepers and four thousand are to praise the LORD with the musical instruments I have provided for that purpose.'

⁶David separated the Levites into divisions corresponding to the sons of Levi: Gershon, Kohath and Merari.

Gershonites

⁷Belonging to the Gershonites:
Ladan and Shimei.

⁸The sons of Ladan:
Jehiel the first, Zetham and Joel—three in all.

⁹The sons of Shimei:
Shelomoth, Haziel and Haran—three in all.
These were the heads of the families of Ladan.

¹⁰And the sons of Shimei:
Jahath, Ziza,[c] Jeush and Beriah.
These were the sons of Shimei—four in all.

¹¹Jahath was the first and Ziza the second, but Jeush and Beriah did not have many sons; so they were counted as one family with one assignment.

Kohathites

¹²The sons of Kohath:
Amram, Izhar, Hebron and Uzziel—four in all.

¹³The sons of Amram:
Aaron and Moses.
Aaron was set apart, he and his descendants for ever, to consecrate the most holy things, to offer sacrifices before the LORD, to minister before him and to pronounce blessings in his name for ever. ¹⁴The sons of Moses the man of God were counted as part of the tribe of Levi.

¹⁵The sons of Moses:
Gershom and Eliezer.

¹⁶The descendants of Gershom:
Shubael was the first.

¹⁷The descendants of Eliezer:
Rehabiah was the first.
Eliezer had no other sons, but the sons of Rehabiah were very numerous.

¹⁸The sons of Izhar:
Shelomith was the first.

¹⁹The sons of Hebron:

---

[a] 14 That is, about 3,400 metric tons   [b] 14 That is, about 34,000 metric tons   [c] 10 One Hebrew manuscript, Septuagint and Vulgate (see also verse 11); most Hebrew manuscripts *Zina*

Jeriah the first, Amariah the second, Jahaziel the third and Jekameam the fourth.
²⁰The sons of Uzziel:
Micah the first and Ishiah the second.

Merarites

²¹The sons of Merari:
Mahli and Mushi.
The sons of Mahli:
Eleazar and Kish.
²²Eleazar died without having sons: he had only daughters. Their cousins, the sons of Kish, married them.
²³The sons of Mushi:
Mahli, Eder and Jerimoth—three in all.

²⁴These were the descendants of Levi by their families—the heads of families as they were registered under their names and counted individually, that is, the workers twenty years old or more who served in the temple of the LORD. ²⁵For David had said, 'Since the LORD, the God of Israel, has granted rest to his people and has come to dwell in Jerusalem for ever, ²⁶the Levites no longer need to carry the tabernacle or any of the articles used in its service.' ²⁷According to the last instructions of David, the Levites were counted from those twenty years old or more.

²⁸The duty of the Levites was to help Aaron's descendants in the service of the temple of the LORD: to be in charge of the courtyards, the side rooms, the purification of all sacred things and the performance of other duties at the house of God. ²⁹They were in charge of the bread set out on the table, the special flour for the grain offerings, the thin loaves made without yeast, the baking and the mixing, and all measurements of quantity and size. ³⁰They were also to stand every morning to thank and praise the LORD. They were to do the same in the evening ³¹and whenever burnt offerings were presented to the LORD on the Sabbaths, at the New Moon feasts and at the appointed festivals. They were to serve before the LORD regularly in the proper number and in the way prescribed for them.

³²And so the Levites carried out their responsibilities for the tent of meeting, for the Holy Place and, under their relatives the descendants of Aaron, for the service of the temple of the LORD.

The divisions of priests

24 These were the divisions of the descendants of Aaron:

The sons of Aaron were Nadab, Abihu, Eleazar and Ithamar. ²But Nadab and Abihu died before their father did, and they had no sons; so Eleazar and Ithamar served as the priests. ³With the help of Zadok a descendant of Eleazar and Ahimelek a descendant of Ithamar, David separated them into divisions for their appointed order of ministering. ⁴A larger number of leaders were found among Eleazar's descendants than among Ithamar's, and they were divided accordingly: sixteen heads of families from Eleazar's descendants and eight heads of families from Ithamar's descendants. ⁵They divided them impartially by casting lots, for there were officials of the sanctuary and officials of God among the descendants of both Eleazar and Ithamar.

⁶The scribe Shemaiah son of Nethanel, a Levite, recorded their names in the presence of the king and of the officials: Zadok the priest, Ahimelek son of Abiathar and the heads of families of the priests and of the Levites—one family being taken from Eleazar and then one from Ithamar.

⁷The first lot fell to Jehoiarib,
the second to Jedaiah,
⁸the third to Harim,
the fourth to Seorim,
⁹the fifth to Malkijah,
the sixth to Mijamin,
¹⁰the seventh to Hakkoz,
the eighth to Abijah,
¹¹the ninth to Jeshua,
the tenth to Shekaniah,
¹²the eleventh to Eliashib,
the twelfth to Jakim,
¹³the thirteenth to Huppah,
the fourteenth to Jeshebeab,
¹⁴the fifteenth to Bilgah,
the sixteenth to Immer,
¹⁵the seventeenth to Hezir,

the eighteenth to Happizzez,
16the nineteenth to Pethahiah,
the twentieth to Jehezkel,
17the twenty-first to Jakin,
the twenty-second to Gamul,
18the twenty-third to Delaiah
and the twenty-fourth to Maaziah.

19This was their appointed order of ministering when they entered the temple of the LORD, according to the regulations prescribed for them by their ancestor Aaron, as the LORD, the God of Israel, had commanded him.

The rest of the Levites

20As for the rest of the descendants of Levi:
from the sons of Amram: Shubael;
from the sons of Shubael: Jehdeiah.
21As for Rehabiah, from his sons:
Ishiah was the first.
22From the Izharites: Shelomoth;
from the sons of Shelomoth: Jahath.
23The sons of Hebron: Jeriah the first,[a] Amariah the second, Jahaziel the third and Jekameam the fourth.
24The son of Uzziel: Micah;
from the sons of Micah: Shamir.
25The brother of Micah: Ishiah;
from the sons of Ishiah: Zechariah.
26The sons of Merari: Mahli and Mushi.
The son of Jaaziah: Beno.
27The sons of Merari:
from Jaaziah: Beno, Shoham, Zakkur and Ibri.
28From Mahli: Eleazar, who had no sons.
29From Kish: the son of Kish: Jerahmeel.
30And the sons of Mushi: Mahli, Eder and Jerimoth.

These were the Levites, according to their families. 31They also cast lots, just as their relatives the descendants of Aaron did, in the presence of King David and of Zadok, Ahimelek, and the heads of families of the priests and of the Levites. The families of the eldest brother were treated the same as those of the youngest.

The musicians

Harps and lyres
1 Chronicles 25:1
A harp and a lyre were similar instruments. A lyre was smaller than a harp, and both were smaller than modern harps. A harp could be played by plucking the strings, or by stroking them with a pick, rather like a guitar is played today.

25 David, together with the commanders of the army, set apart some of the sons of Asaph, Heman and Jeduthun for the ministry of prophesying, accompanied by harps, lyres and cymbals. Here is the list of the men who performed this service:

2from the sons of Asaph:
Zakkur, Joseph, Nethaniah and Asarelah. The sons of Asaph were under the supervision of Asaph, who prophesied under the king's supervision.
3As for Jeduthun, from his sons:
Gedaliah, Zeri, Jeshaiah, Shimei,[b] Hashabiah and Mattithiah, six in all, under the supervision of their father Jeduthun, who prophesied, using the harp in thanking and praising the LORD.
4As for Heman, from his sons:
Bukkiah, Mattaniah, Uzziel, Shubael and Jerimoth; Hananiah, Hanani, Eliathah, Giddalti and

---

[a]23 Two Hebrew manuscripts and some Septuagint manuscripts (see also 1 Chron. 23:19); most Hebrew manuscripts *The sons of Jeriah:*   [b]3 One Hebrew manuscript and some Septuagint manuscripts (see also verse 17); most Hebrew manuscripts do not have *Shimei*.

Romamti-Ezer; Joshbekashah, Mallothi, Hothir and Mahazioth. ⁵(All these were sons of Heman the king's seer. They were given to him through the promises of God to exalt him. God gave Heman fourteen sons and three daughters.)

⁶All these men were under the supervision of their father for the music of the temple of the LORD, with cymbals, lyres and harps, for the ministry at the house of God. Asaph, Jeduthun and Heman were under the supervision of the king. ⁷Along with their relatives—all of them trained and skilled in music for the LORD—they numbered 288. ⁸Young and old alike, teacher as well as student, cast lots for their duties.

⁹The first lot, which was for Asaph, fell to Joseph,
his sons and relatives[a] 12[b]
the second to Gedaliah,
him and his relatives and sons, 12
¹⁰the third to Zakkur,
his sons and relatives 12
¹¹the fourth to Izri,[c]
his sons and relatives 12
¹²the fifth to Nethaniah,
his sons and relatives 12
¹³the sixth to Bukkiah,
his sons and relatives 12
¹⁴the seventh to Jesarelah,[d]
his sons and relatives 12
¹⁵the eighth to Jeshaiah,
his sons and relatives 12
¹⁶the ninth to Mattaniah,
his sons and relatives 12
¹⁷the tenth to Shimei,
his sons and relatives 12
¹⁸the eleventh to Azarel,[e]
his sons and relatives 12
¹⁹the twelfth to Hashabiah,
his sons and relatives 12
²⁰the thirteenth to Shubael,
his sons and relatives 12
²¹the fourteenth to Mattithiah,
his sons and relatives 12
²²the fifteenth to Jerimoth,
his sons and relatives 12
²³the sixteenth to Hananiah,
his sons and relatives 12
²⁴the seventeenth to Joshbekashah,
his sons and relatives 12
²⁵the eighteenth to Hanani,
his sons and relatives 12
²⁶the nineteenth to Mallothi,
his sons and relatives 12
²⁷the twentieth to Eliathah,
his sons and relatives 12
²⁸the twenty-first to Hothir,
his sons and relatives 12
²⁹the twenty-second to Giddalti,
his sons and relatives 12
³⁰the twenty-third to Mahazioth,
his sons and relatives 12
³¹the twenty-fourth to Romamti-Ezer,
his sons and relatives. 12

The gatekeepers

26 The divisions of the gatekeepers:

from the Korahites: Meshelemiah son of Kore, one of the sons of Asaph.

²Meshelemiah had sons:
Zechariah the firstborn,
Jediael the second,
Zebadiah the third,
Jathniel the fourth,
³Elam the fifth,
Jehohanan the sixth
and Eliehoenai the seventh.
⁴Obed-Edom also had sons:
Shemaiah the firstborn,
Jehozabad the second,
Joah the third,
Sakar the fourth,
Nethanel the fifth,
⁵Ammiel the sixth,
Issachar the seventh
and Peullethai the eighth.
(For God had blessed Obed-Edom.)

⁶Obed-Edom's son Shemaiah also had sons, who were leaders in their father's family because they

---

[a]9 See Septuagint; Hebrew does not have *his sons and relatives*. [b]9 See the total in verse 7; Hebrew does not have *twelve*. [c]11 A variant of *Zeri* [d]14 A variant of *Asarelah* [e]18 A variant of *Uzziel*

were very capable men. 7The sons of Shemaiah: Othni, Rephael, Obed and Elzabad; his relatives Elihu and Semakiah were also able men. 8All these were descendants of Obed-Edom; they and their sons and their relatives were capable men with the strength to do the work—descendants of Obed-Edom, 62 in all.

9Meshelemiah had sons and relatives, who were able men—18 in all.

10Hosah the Merarite had sons: Shimri the first (although he was not the firstborn, his father had appointed him the first), 11Hilkiah the second, Tabaliah the third and Zechariah the fourth. The sons and relatives of Hosah were 13 in all.

12These divisions of the gatekeepers, through their leaders, had duties for ministering in the temple of the LORD, just as their relatives had. 13Lots were cast for each gate, according to their families, young and old alike.

14The lot for the East Gate fell to Shelemiah.[a] Then lots were cast for his son Zechariah, a wise counsellor, and the lot for the North Gate fell to him. 15The lot for the South Gate fell to Obed-Edom, and the lot for the storehouse fell to his sons. 16The lots for the West Gate and the Shalleketh Gate on the upper road fell to Shuppim and Hosah.

Guard was alongside guard: 17there were six Levites a day on the east, four a day on the north, four a day on the south and two at a time at the storehouse. 18As for the court[b] to the west, there were four at the road and two at the court[c] itself.

19These were the divisions of the gatekeepers who were descendants of Korah and Merari.

The treasurers and other officials

20Their fellow Levites were[d] in charge of the treasuries of the house of God and the treasuries for the dedicated things.

21The descendants of Ladan, who were Gershonites through Ladan and who were heads of families belonging to Ladan the Gershonite, were Jehieli, 22the sons of Jehieli, Zetham and his brother Joel. They were in charge of the treasuries of the temple of the LORD.

23From the Amramites, the Izharites, the Hebronites and the Uzzielites:

24Shubael, a descendant of Gershom son of Moses, was the official in charge of the treasuries. 25His relatives through Eliezer: Rehabiah his son, Jeshaiah his son, Joram his son, Zikri his son and Shelomith his son. 26Shelomith and his relatives were in charge of all the treasuries for the things dedicated by King David, by the heads of families who were the commanders of thousands and commanders of hundreds, and by the other army commanders. 27Some of the plunder taken in battle they dedicated for the repair of the temple of the LORD. 28And everything dedicated by Samuel the seer and by Saul son of Kish, Abner son of Ner and Joab son of Zeruiah, and all the other dedicated things were in the care of Shelomith and his relatives.

29From the Izharites: Kenaniah and his sons were assigned duties away from the temple, as officials and judges over Israel.

30From the Hebronites: Hashabiah and his relatives—seventeen hundred able men—were responsible in Israel west of the Jordan for all the work of the LORD and for the king's service. 31As for the Hebronites, Jeriah was their chief according to the genealogical records of their families. In the fortieth year of David's reign a search was made in the records, and capable men among the Hebronites were found at Jazer in Gilead. 32Jeriah

---

[a] 14 A variant of Meshelemiah   [b] 18 The meaning of the Hebrew for this word is uncertain.   [c] 18 The meaning of the Hebrew for this word is uncertain.   [d] 20 Septuagint; Hebrew As for the Levites, Ahijah was

had two thousand seven hundred relatives, who were able men and heads of families, and King David put them in charge of the Reubenites, the Gadites and the half-tribe of Manasseh for every matter pertaining to God and for the affairs of the king.

Army divisions

27 This is the list of the Israelites—heads of families, commanders of thousands and commanders of hundreds, and their officers, who served the king in all that concerned the army divisions that were on duty month by month throughout the year. Each division consisted of 24,000 men.

2 In charge of the first division, for the first month, was Jashobeam son of Zabdiel. There were 24,000 men in his division. 3 He was a descendant of Perez and chief of all the army officers for the first month.

4 In charge of the division for the second month was Dodai the Ahohite; Mikloth was the leader of his division. There were 24,000 men in his division.

5 The third army commander, for the third month, was Benaiah son of Jehoiada the priest. He was chief and there were 24,000 men in his division. 6 This was the Benaiah who was a mighty warrior among the Thirty and was over the Thirty. His son Ammizabad was in charge of his division.

7 The fourth, for the fourth month, was Asahel the brother of Joab; his son Zebadiah was his successor. There were 24,000 men in his division.

8 The fifth, for the fifth month, was the commander Shamhuth the Izrahite. There were 24,000 men in his division.

9 The sixth, for the sixth month, was Ira the son of Ikkesh the Tekoite. There were 24,000 men in his division.

10 The seventh, for the seventh month, was Helez the Pelonite, an Ephraimite. There were 24,000 men in his division.

11 The eighth, for the eighth month, was Sibbekai the Hushathite, a Zerahite. There were 24,000 men in his division.

12 The ninth, for the ninth month, was Abiezer the Anathothite, a Benjaminite. There were 24,000 men in his division.

13 The tenth, for the tenth month, was Maharai the Netophathite, a Zerahite. There were 24,000 men in his division.

14 The eleventh, for the eleventh month, was Benaiah the Pirathonite, an Ephraimite. There were 24,000 men in his division.

15 The twelfth, for the twelfth month, was Heldai the Netophathite, from the family of Othniel. There were 24,000 men in his division.

Leaders of the tribes

16 The leaders of the tribes of Israel:

over the Reubenites: Eliezer son of Zikri;
over the Simeonites: Shephatiah son of Maakah;
17 over Levi: Hashabiah son of Kemuel;
over Aaron: Zadok;
18 over Judah: Elihu, a brother of David;
over Issachar: Omri son of Michael;
19 over Zebulun: Ishmaiah son of Obadiah;
over Naphtali: Jerimoth son of Azriel;
20 over the Ephraimites: Hoshea son of Azaziah;
over half the tribe of Manasseh: Joel son of Pedaiah;
21 over the half-tribe of Manasseh in Gilead: Iddo son of Zechariah;
over Benjamin: Jaasiel son of Abner;
22 over Dan: Azarel son of Jeroham.

These were the leaders of the tribes of Israel.

23 David did not take the number of the men twenty years old or less, because the LORD had promised to make Israel as numerous as the stars in the sky. 24 Joab son of Zeruiah began to count the men but did not finish. God's wrath came on Israel on account of this numbering, and the

Making Connections

Overseers
1 Chronicles 27:25
With such a large palace and staff, David needed his household to be well organised. Each of these men had responsibility for a different area of palace life and David's property.

number was not entered in the book[a] of the annals of King David.

The king's overseers

25 Azmaveth son of Adiel was in charge of the royal storehouses.

Jonathan son of Uzziah was in charge of the storehouses in the outlying districts, in the towns, the villages and the watchtowers. 26 Ezri son of Kelub was in charge of the workers who farmed the land. 27 Shimei the Ramathite was in charge of the vineyards.

Zabdi the Shiphmite was in charge of the produce of the vineyards for the wine vats. 28 Baal-Hanan the Gederite was in charge of the olive and sycamore-fig trees in the western foothills.

Joash was in charge of the supplies of olive oil. 29 Shitrai the Sharonite was in charge of the herds grazing in Sharon.

Shaphat son of Adlai was in charge of the herds in the valleys. 30 Obil the Ishmaelite was in charge of the camels.

Jehdeiah the Meronothite was in charge of the donkeys. 31 Jaziz the Hagrite was in charge of the flocks.

All these were the officials in charge of King David's property.

32 Jonathan, David's uncle, was a counsellor, a man of insight and a scribe. Jehiel son of Hakmoni took care of the king's sons. 33 Ahithophel was the king's counsellor.

Hushai the Arkite was the king's confidant. 34 Ahithophel was succeeded by Jehoiada son of Benaiah and by Abiathar.

Joab was the commander of the royal army.

David's plans for the temple

28 David summoned all the officials of Israel to assemble at Jerusalem: the officers over the tribes, the commanders of the divisions in the service of the king, the commanders of thousands and commanders of hundreds, and the officials in charge of all the property and livestock belonging to the king and his sons, together with the palace officials, the mighty warriors and all the brave fighting men.

2 King David rose to his feet and said: 'Listen to me, my fellow Israelites, my people. I had it in my heart to build a house as a place of rest for the ark of the covenant of the LORD, for the footstool of our God, and I made plans to build it. 3 But God said to me, "You are not to build a house for my Name, because you are a warrior and have shed blood."

4 'Yet the LORD, the God of Israel, chose me from my whole family to be king over Israel for ever. He chose Judah as leader, and from the house of Judah he chose my family, and from my father's sons he was pleased to make me king over all Israel. 5 Of all my sons—and the LORD has given me many—he has chosen my son Solomon to sit on the throne of the kingdom of the LORD over Israel. 6 He said to me, "Solomon your son is the one who will build my house and my courts, for I have chosen him to be my son, and I will be his father. 7 I will establish his kingdom for ever if he is unswerving in carrying out my commands and laws, as is being done at this time."

8 'So now I charge you in the sight of all Israel and of the assembly of the LORD, and in the hearing of our God: be careful to follow all the commands of the LORD your God, that you may possess this good land

---

[a] 24 Septuagint; Hebrew *number*

and pass it on as an inheritance to your descendants for ever.

9'And you, my son Solomon, acknowledge the God of your father, and serve him with wholehearted devotion and with a willing mind, for the LORD searches every heart and understands every desire and every thought. If you seek him, he will be found by you; but if you forsake him, he will reject you for ever. 10Consider now, for the LORD has chosen you to build a house as the sanctuary. Be strong and do the work.'

11Then David gave his son Solomon the plans for the portico of the temple, its buildings, its storerooms, its upper parts, its inner rooms and the place of atonement. 12He gave him the plans of all that the Spirit had put in his mind for the courts of the temple of the LORD and all the surrounding rooms, for the treasuries of the temple of God and for the treasuries for the dedicated things. 13He gave him instructions for the divisions of the priests and Levites, and for all the work of serving in the temple of the LORD, as well as for all the articles to be used in its service. 14He designated the weight of gold for all the gold articles to be used in various kinds of service, and the weight of silver for all the silver articles to be used in various kinds of service: 15the weight of gold for the gold lampstands and their lamps, with the weight for each lampstand and its lamps; and the weight of silver for each silver lampstand and its lamps, according to the use of each lampstand; 16the weight of gold for each table for consecrated bread; the weight of silver for the silver tables; 17the weight of pure gold for the forks, sprinkling bowls and pitchers; the weight of gold for each gold dish; the weight of silver for each silver dish; 18and the weight of the refined gold for the altar of incense. He also gave him the plan for the chariot, that is, the cherubim of gold that spread their wings and overshadow the ark of the covenant of the LORD.

19'All this,' David said, 'I have in writing as a result of the LORD's hand on me, and he enabled me to understand all the details of the plan.'

20David also said to Solomon his son, 'Be strong and courageous, and do the work. Do not be afraid or discouraged, for the LORD God, my God, is with you. He will not fail you or forsake you until all the work for the service of the temple of the LORD is finished. 21The divisions of the priests and Levites are ready for all the work on the temple of God, and every willing person skilled in any craft will help you in all the work. The officials and all the people will obey your every command.'

Gifts for building the temple

29 Then King David said to the whole assembly: 'My son Solomon, the one whom God has chosen, is young and inexperienced. The task is great, because this palatial structure is not for human beings but for the LORD God. 2With all my resources I have provided for the temple of my God—gold for the gold work, silver for the silver, bronze for the bronze, iron for the iron and wood for the wood, as well as onyx for the settings, turquoise,[a] stones of various colours, and all kinds of fine stone and marble—all of these in large quantities. 3Besides, in my devotion to the temple of my God I now give my personal treasures of gold and silver for the temple of my God, over and above everything I have provided for this holy temple: 4three thousand talents[b] of gold (gold of Ophir) and seven thousand talents[c] of refined silver, for the overlaying of the walls of the buildings, 5for the gold work and the silver work, and for all the work to be done by the skilled workers. Now, who among you is willing to consecrate yourself to the LORD today?'

6Then the leaders of families, the officers of the tribes of Israel, the commanders of thousands and commanders of hundreds, and the officials in charge of the king's work gave willingly. 7They gave towards the work on the temple of God five thousand talents[d] and ten thousand darics[e] of gold, ten thousand talents[f] of silver, eighteen thousand talents[g] of bronze and a hundred

---

[a] 2 The meaning of the Hebrew for this word is uncertain. [b] 4 That is, about 100 metric tons [c] 4 That is, about 235 metric tons [d] 7 That is, about 170 metric tons [e] 7 That is, about 84 kilograms [f] 7 That is, about 340 metric tons [g] 7 That is, about 610 metric tons

thousand talents[a] of iron. 8Anyone who had precious stones gave them to the treasury of the temple of the LORD in the custody of Jehiel the Gershonite. 9The people rejoiced at the willing response of their leaders, for they had given freely and wholeheartedly to the LORD. David the king also rejoiced greatly.

David's prayer

10David praised the LORD in the presence of the whole assembly, saying,

> 'Praise be to you, LORD,
>   the God of our father Israel,
>   from everlasting to everlasting.
> 11Yours, LORD, is the greatness and the power
>   and the glory and the majesty and the splendour,
>   for everything in heaven and earth is yours.
> Yours, LORD, is the kingdom;
>   you are exalted as head over all.
> 12Wealth and honour come from you;
>   you are the ruler of all things.
> In your hands are strength and power
>   to exalt and give strength to all.
> 13Now, our God, we give you thanks,
>   and praise your glorious name.

14'But who am I, and who are my people, that we should be able to give as generously as this? Everything comes from you, and we have given you only what comes from your hand. 15We are foreigners and strangers in your sight, as were all our ancestors. Our days on earth are like a shadow, without hope. 16LORD our God, all this abundance that we have provided for building you a temple for your Holy Name comes from your hand, and all of it belongs to you. 17I know, my God, that you test the heart and are pleased with integrity. All these things have I given willingly and with honest intent. And now I have seen with joy how willingly your people who are here have given to you. 18LORD, the God of our fathers Abraham, Isaac and Israel, keep these desires and thoughts in the hearts of your people for ever, and keep their hearts loyal to you. 19And give my son Solomon the wholehearted devotion to keep your commands, statutes and decrees and to do everything to build the palatial structure for which I have provided.'

20Then David said to the whole assembly, 'Praise the LORD your God.' So they all praised the LORD, the God of their fathers; they bowed down, prostrating themselves before the LORD and the king.

Solomon acknowledged as king

21The next day they made sacrifices to the LORD and presented burnt offerings to him: a thousand bulls, a thousand rams and a thousand male lambs, together with their drink offerings, and other sacrifices in abundance for all Israel. 22They ate and drank with great joy in the presence of the LORD that day.

Then they acknowledged Solomon son of David as king a second time, anointing him before the LORD to be ruler and Zadok to be priest. 23So Solomon sat on the throne of the LORD as king in place of his father David. He prospered and all Israel obeyed him. 24All the officers and mighty warriors, as well as all of King David's sons, pledged their submission to King Solomon.

25The LORD highly exalted Solomon in the sight of all Israel and bestowed on him royal splendour such as no king over Israel ever had before.

The death of David

26David son of Jesse was king over all Israel. 27He ruled over Israel for forty years— seven in Hebron and thirty-three in

---

> **IN OTHER WORDS**
>
> **Joy**
> **1 Chronicles 29:22**
> Joy is a profound kind of happiness. In the Bible, God's people often rejoice at all that he has done for them. Joy is also found in more ordinary things such as having children and working.

---

[a] 7 That is, about 3,400 metric tons

Jerusalem. 28He died at a good old age, having enjoyed long life, wealth and honour. His son Solomon succeeded him as king.

29As for the events of King David's reign, from beginning to end, they are written in the records of Samuel the seer, the records of Nathan the prophet and the records of Gad the seer, 30together with the details of his reign and power, and the circumstances that surrounded him and Israel and the kingdoms of all the other lands.

2 Chronicles

INTRODUCTION

2 CHRONICLES

Author: Unknown, but it could have been Ezra the priest.

Who to: The Israelites returning to Jerusalem after the exile.

When: 2 Chronicles retells the story of the Israelites from King Solomon's reign to their return from exile, a period of over five hundred years.

Did you know? 1 and 2 Chronicles contain many of the same events and people as appear in 1 and 2 Samuel and 1 and 2 Kings, but these books tend to concentrate on the positives and miss out where people made mistakes.

Main theme: Like 1 Chronicles, 2 Chronicles is a book of hope, written to encourage the Israelites as they return to Jerusalem, to remind them of their past and to help them trust God for the future. It starts with Solomon and includes the stories of some of the kings of Judah.

Solomon asks for wisdom

1 Solomon son of David established himself firmly over his kingdom, for the LORD his God was with him and made him exceedingly great.

²Then Solomon spoke to all Israel—to the commanders of thousands and commanders of hundreds, to the judges and to all the leaders in Israel, the heads of families— ³and Solomon and the whole assembly went to the high place at Gibeon, for God's tent of meeting was there, which Moses the LORD's servant had made in the wilderness. ⁴Now David had brought up the ark of God from Kiriath Jearim to the place he had prepared for it, because he had pitched a tent for it in Jerusalem. ⁵But the bronze altar that Bezalel son of Uri, the son of Hur, had made was in Gibeon in front of the tabernacle of the LORD; so Solomon and the assembly enquired of him there. ⁶Solomon went up to the bronze altar before the

LORD in the tent of meeting and offered a thousand burnt offerings on it.

7That night God appeared to Solomon and said to him, 'Ask for whatever you want me to give you.'

8Solomon answered God, 'You have shown great kindness to David my father and have made me king in his place. 9Now, LORD God, let your promise to my father David be confirmed, for you have made me king over a people who are as numerous as the dust of the earth. 10Give me wisdom and knowledge, that I may lead this people, for who is able to govern this great people of yours?'

11God said to Solomon, 'Since this is your heart's desire and you have not asked for wealth, possessions or honour, nor for the death of your enemies, and since you have not asked for a long life but for wisdom and knowledge to govern my people over whom I have made you king, 12therefore wisdom and knowledge will be given you. And I will also give you wealth, possessions and honour, such as no king who was before you ever had and none after you will have.'

13Then Solomon went to Jerusalem from the high place at Gibeon, from before the tent of meeting. And he reigned over Israel.

14Solomon accumulated chariots and horses; he had fourteen hundred chariots and twelve thousand horses,^{a} which he kept in the chariot cities and also with him in Jerusalem. 15The king made silver and gold as common in Jerusalem as stones, and cedar as plentiful as sycamore-fig trees in the foothills. 16Solomon's horses were imported from Egypt and from Kue^b—the royal merchants purchased them from Kue at the current price. 17They imported a chariot from Egypt for six hundred shekels^c of silver, and a horse for a hundred and fifty.^{d} They also exported them to all the kings of the Hittites and of the Arameans.

Preparations for building the temple

2 *Solomon gave orders to build a temple for the Name of the LORD and a royal palace for himself. *2He conscripted 70,000 men as carriers and 80,000 as stonecutters in the hills and 3,600 as supervisors over them.

3Solomon sent this message to Hiram^e king of Tyre:

'Send me cedar logs as you did for my father David when you sent him cedar to build a palace to live in. 4Now I am about to build a temple for the Name of the LORD my God and to dedicate it to him for burning fragrant incense before him, for setting out the consecrated bread regularly, and for making burnt offerings every morning and evening and on the Sabbaths, at the New Moons and at the appointed festivals of the LORD our God. This is a lasting ordinance for Israel.

5'The temple I am going to build will be great, because our God is greater than all other gods. 6But who is able to build a temple for him, since the heavens, even the highest heavens, cannot contain him? Who then am I to build a temple for him, except as a place to burn sacrifices before him?

7'Send me, therefore, a man skilled to work in gold and silver, bronze and iron, and in purple, crimson and blue yarn, and experienced in the art of engraving, to work in Judah and Jerusalem with my skilled workers, whom my father David provided.

8'Send me also cedar, juniper and algum^f logs from Lebanon, for I know that your servants are skilled in cutting timber there. My men shall work with yours 9to provide me with plenty of timber, because the temple I build must be large and magnificent. 10I will give your servants, those who cut the timber, twenty thousand cors^g of ground wheat, twenty thousand cors^h of barley, twenty

---

^{a} 14 Or *charioteers* ^{b} 16 Probably Cilicia ^{c} 17 That is, about 6.9 kilograms ^{d} 17 That is, about 1.7 kilograms
^{e} 3 Hebrew *Huram*, a variant of *Hiram*; also in verses 11 and 12 ^{f} 8 Probably a variant of *almug* ^{g} 10 That is, probably about 3,275 metric tons ^{h} 10 That is, probably about 2,700 metric tons
* 2:1 is numbered 1:18 in Hebrew texts.   * 2:2-18 is numbered 2:1-17 in Hebrew texts.

thousand baths[a] of wine and twenty thousand baths of olive oil.'

11 Hiram king of Tyre replied by letter to Solomon:

'Because the LORD loves his people, he has made you their king.'

12 And Hiram added:

'Praise be to the LORD, the God of Israel, who made heaven and earth! He has given King David a wise son, endowed with intelligence and discernment, who will build a temple for the LORD and a palace for himself.

13 'I am sending you Huram-Abi, a man of great skill, 14 whose mother was from Dan and whose father was from Tyre. He is trained to work in gold and silver, bronze and iron, stone and wood, and with purple and blue and crimson yarn and fine linen. He is experienced in all kinds of engraving and can execute any design given to him. He will work with your skilled workers and with those of my lord, David your father.

15 'Now let my lord send his servants the wheat and barley and the olive oil and wine he promised, 16 and we will cut all the logs from Lebanon that you need and will float them as rafts by sea down to Joppa. You can then take them up to Jerusalem.'

17 Solomon took a census of all the foreigners residing in Israel, after the census his father David had taken; and they were found to be 153,600. 18 He assigned 70,000 of them to be carriers and 80,000 to be stonecutters in the hills, with 3,600 supervisors over them to keep the people working.

Solomon builds the temple

3 Then Solomon began to build the temple of the LORD in Jerusalem on Mount Moriah, where the LORD had appeared to his father David. It was on the threshing-floor of Araunah[b] the Jebusite, the place provided by David. 2 He began building on the second day of the second month in the fourth year of his reign.

3 The foundation Solomon laid for building the temple of God was sixty cubits long and twenty cubits wide[c] (using the cubit of the old standard). 4 The portico at the front of the temple was twenty cubits[d] long across the width of the building and twenty cubits[e] high.

He overlaid the inside with pure gold. 5 He panelled the main hall with juniper and covered it with fine gold and decorated it with palm tree and chain designs. 6 He adorned the temple with precious stones. And the gold he used was gold of Parvaim. 7 He overlaid the ceiling beams, doorframes, walls and doors of the temple with gold, and he carved cherubim on the walls.

8 He built the Most Holy Place, its length corresponding to the width of the temple—twenty cubits long and twenty cubits wide. He overlaid the inside with six hundred talents[f] of fine gold. 9 The gold nails weighed fifty shekels.[g] He also overlaid the upper parts with gold.

10 For the Most Holy Place he made a pair of sculptured cherubim and overlaid them with gold. 11 The total wing-span of the cherubim was twenty cubits. One wing of the first cherub was five cubits[h] long and touched the temple wall, while its other wing, also five cubits long, touched the wing of the other cherub. 12 Similarly one wing of the second cherub was five cubits long and touched the other temple wall, and its other wing, also five cubits long, touched the wing of the first cherub. 13 The wings of these cherubim extended twenty cubits. They stood on their feet, facing the main hall.[i]

---

[a] 10 That is, about 440,000 litres   [b] 1 Hebrew *Ornan*, a variant of *Araunah*   [c] 3 That is, about 27 metres long and 9 metres wide   [d] 4 That is, about 9 metres; also in verses 8, 11 and 13   [e] 4 Some Septuagint and Syriac manuscripts; Hebrew *and a hundred and twenty*   [f] 8 That is, about 20 metric tons   [g] 9 That is, about 575 grams   [h] 11 That is, about 2.3 metres; also in verse 15   [i] 13 Or *facing inwards*

14He made the curtain of blue, purple and crimson yarn and fine linen, with cherubim worked into it.

15For the front of the temple he made two pillars, which totalled thirty-five cubits[a] in length, each with a capital five cubits high. 16He made interwoven chains[b] and put them on top of the pillars. He also made a hundred pomegranates and attached them to the chains. 17He erected the pillars in the front of the temple, one to the south and one to the north. The one to the south he named Jakin[c] and the one to the north Boaz.[d]

The temple's furnishings

4 He made a bronze altar twenty cubits long, twenty cubits wide and ten cubits high.[e] 2He made the Sea of cast metal, circular in shape, measuring ten cubits from rim to rim and five cubits[f] high. It took a line of thirty cubits[g] to measure round it. 3Below the rim, figures of bulls encircled it—ten to a cubit.[h] The bulls were cast in two rows in one piece with the Sea.

4The Sea stood on twelve bulls, three facing north, three facing west, three facing south and three facing east. The Sea rested on top of them, and their hindquarters were towards the centre. 5It was a handbreadth[i] in thickness, and its rim was like the rim of a cup, like a lily blossom. It held three thousand baths.[j]

6He then made ten basins for washing and placed five on the south side and five on the north. In them the things to be used for the burnt offerings were rinsed, but the Sea was to be used by the priests for washing.

7He made ten gold lampstands according to the specifications for them and placed them in the temple, five on the south side and five on the north.

8He made ten tables and placed them in the temple, five on the south side and five on the north. He also made a hundred gold sprinkling bowls.

9He made the courtyard of the priests, and the large court and the doors for the court, and overlaid the doors with bronze.

10He placed the Sea on the south side, at the south-east corner.

11And Huram also made the pots and shovels and sprinkling bowls.

So Huram finished the work he had undertaken for King Solomon in the temple of God:

12the two pillars;
   the two bowl-shaped capitals on top of the pillars;
   the two sets of network decorating the two bowl-shaped capitals on top of the pillars;
13the four hundred pomegranates for the two sets of network (two rows of pomegranates for each network, decorating the bowl-shaped capitals on top of the pillars);
14the stands with their basins;
15the Sea and the twelve bulls under it;
16the pots, shovels, meat forks and all related articles.

All the objects that Huram-Abi made for King Solomon for the temple of the LORD were of polished bronze. 17The king had them cast in clay moulds in the plain of the Jordan between Sukkoth and Zarethan.[k] 18All these things that Solomon made amounted to so much that the weight of the bronze could not be calculated.

19Solomon also made all the furnishings that were in God's temple:

   the golden altar;
   the tables on which was the bread of the Presence;
20the lampstands of pure gold with their lamps, to burn in front of the inner sanctuary as prescribed;
21the gold floral work and lamps and tongs (they were solid gold);
22the pure gold wick trimmers, sprinkling bowls, dishes and censers; and the gold doors of the temple: the inner doors to the Most Holy Place and the doors of the main hall.

---

[a] 15 That is, about 16 metres [b] 16 Or possibly *made chains in the inner sanctuary;* the meaning of the Hebrew for this phrase is uncertain. [c] 17 *Jakin* probably means *he establishes.* [d] 17 *Boaz* probably means *in him is strength.*
[e] 1 That is, about 9 metres long and wide and 4.5 metres high [f] 2 That is, about 2.3 metres [g] 2 That is, about 13.5 metres [h] 3 That is, about 45 centimetres [i] 5 That is, about 7.5 centimetres [j] 5 That is, about 66,000 litres
[k] 17 Hebrew *Zeredatha,* a variant of *Zarethan*

5 When all the work Solomon had done for the temple of the LORD was finished, he brought in the things his father David had dedicated—the silver and gold and all the furnishings—and he placed them in the treasuries of God's temple.

The ark brought to the temple

²Then Solomon summoned to Jerusalem the elders of Israel, all the heads of the tribes and the chiefs of the Israelite families, to bring up the ark of the LORD's covenant from Zion, the City of David. ³And all the Israelites came together to the king at the time of the festival in the seventh month.

⁴When all the elders of Israel had arrived, the Levites took up the ark, ⁵and they brought up the ark and the tent of meeting and all the sacred furnishings in it. The Levitical priests carried them up; ⁶and King Solomon and the entire assembly of Israel that had gathered about him were before the ark, sacrificing so many sheep and cattle that they could not be recorded or counted.

⁷The priests then brought the ark of the LORD's covenant to its place in the inner sanctuary of the temple, the Most Holy Place, and put it beneath the wings of the cherubim. ⁸The cherubim spread their wings over the place of the ark and covered the ark and its carrying poles. ⁹These poles were so long that their ends, extending from the ark, could be seen from in front of the inner sanctuary, but not from outside the Holy Place; and they are still there today. ¹⁰There was nothing in the ark except the two tablets that Moses had placed in it at Horeb, where the LORD made a covenant with the Israelites after they came out of Egypt.

¹¹The priests then withdrew from the Holy Place. All the priests who were there had consecrated themselves, regardless of their divisions. ¹²All the Levites who were musicians—Asaph, Heman, Jeduthun and their sons and relatives—stood on the east side of the altar, dressed in fine linen and playing cymbals, harps and lyres. They were accompanied by 120 priests sounding trumpets. ¹³The trumpeters and musicians joined in unison to give praise and thanks to the LORD. Accompanied by trumpets, cymbals and other instruments, the singers raised their voices in praise to the LORD and sang:

'He is good;
  his love endures for ever.'

Then the temple of the LORD was filled with the cloud, ¹⁴and the priests could not perform their service because of the cloud, for the glory of the LORD filled the temple of God.

6 Then Solomon said, 'The LORD has said that he would dwell in a dark cloud; ²I have built a magnificent temple for you, a place for you to dwell for ever.'

³While the whole assembly of Israel was standing there, the king turned round and blessed them. ⁴Then he said:

'Praise be to the LORD, the God of Israel, who with his hands has fulfilled what he promised with his mouth to my father David. For he said, ⁵"Since the day I brought my people out of Egypt, I have not chosen a city in any tribe of Israel to have a temple built so that my Name might be there, nor have I chosen anyone to be ruler over my people Israel. ⁶But now I have chosen Jerusalem for my Name to be there, and I have chosen David to rule my people Israel."

⁷'My father David had it in his heart to build a temple for the Name of the LORD, the God of Israel. ⁸But the LORD said to my father David, "You did well to have it in your heart to build a temple for my Name. ⁹Nevertheless,

IN OTHER WORDS

Cherubim
2 Chronicles 5:7
The cherubim are winged angelic beings. They are often praising and worshipping God when mentioned in the Bible.

you are not the one to build the temple, but your son, who is your own flesh and blood—he is the one who will build the temple for my Name."

¹⁰'The LORD has kept the promise he made. I have succeeded David my father and now I sit on the throne of Israel, just as the LORD promised, and I have built the temple for the Name of the LORD, the God of Israel. ¹¹There I have placed the ark, in which is the covenant of the LORD that he made with the people of Israel.'

Solomon's prayer of dedication

¹²Then Solomon stood before the altar of the LORD in front of the whole assembly of Israel and spread out his hands. ¹³Now he had made a bronze platform, five cubits long, five cubits wide and three cubits high,[a] and had placed it in the centre of the outer court. He stood on the platform and then knelt down before the whole assembly of Israel and spread out his hands towards heaven. ¹⁴He said:

'LORD, the God of Israel, there is no God like you in heaven or on earth—you who keep your covenant of love with your servants who continue wholeheartedly in your way. ¹⁵You have kept your promise to your servant David my father; with your mouth you have promised and with your hand you have fulfilled it—as it is today.

¹⁶'Now LORD, the God of Israel, keep for your servant David my father the promises you made to him when you said, "You shall never fail to have a successor to sit before me on the throne of Israel, if only your descendants are careful in all they do to walk before me according to my law, as you have done." ¹⁷And now, LORD, the God of Israel, let your word that you promised your servant David come true.

¹⁸'But will God really dwell on earth with human beings? The heavens, even the highest heavens, cannot contain you. How much less this temple that I have built! ¹⁹Yet, LORD my God, give attention to your servant's prayer and his plea for mercy. Hear the cry and the prayer that your servant is praying in your presence. ²⁰May your eyes be open towards this temple day and night, this place of which you said you would put your Name there. May you hear the prayer your servant prays towards this place. ²¹Hear the supplications of your servant and of your people Israel when they pray towards this place. Hear from heaven, your dwelling-place; and when you hear, forgive.

²²'When anyone wrongs their neighbour and is required to take an oath and they come and swear the oath before your altar in this temple, ²³then hear from heaven and act. Judge between your servants, condemning the guilty and bringing down on their heads what they have done, and vindicating the innocent by treating them in accordance with their innocence.

²⁴'When your people Israel have been defeated by an enemy because they have sinned against you and when they turn back and give praise to your name, praying and making supplication before you in this temple, ²⁵then hear from heaven and forgive the sin of your people Israel and bring them back to the land that you gave to them and their ancestors.

²⁶'When the heavens are shut up and there is no rain because your people have sinned against you, and when they pray towards this place and give praise to your name and turn from their sin because you have afflicted them,

---

[a] 13 That is, about 2.3 metres long and wide and 1.4 metres high

27then hear from heaven and forgive the sin of your servants, your people Israel. Teach them the right way to live, and send rain on the land that you gave your people for an inheritance.

28'When famine or plague comes to the land, or blight or mildew, locusts or grasshoppers, or when enemies besiege them in any of their cities, whatever disaster or disease may come, 29and when a prayer or plea is made by anyone among your people Israel—being aware of their afflictions and pains, and spreading out their hands towards this temple— 30then hear from heaven, your dwelling-place. Forgive, and deal with everyone according to all they do, since you know their hearts (for you alone know the human heart), 31so that they will fear you and walk in obedience to you all the time they live in the land that you gave our ancestors.

32'As for foreigners who do not belong to your people Israel but have come from a distant land because of your great name and your mighty hand and your outstretched arm—when they come and pray towards this temple, 33then hear from heaven, your dwelling-place. Do whatever the foreigner asks of you, so that all the peoples of the earth may know your name and fear you, as do your own people Israel, and may know that this house that I have built bears your Name.

34'When your people go to war against their enemies, wherever you send them, and when they pray to you towards this city you have chosen and the temple I have built for your Name, 35then hear from heaven their prayer and their plea, and uphold their cause.

36'When they sin against you—for there is no-one who does not sin—and you become angry with them and give them over to the enemy, who takes them captive to a land far away or near; 37and if they have a change of heart in the land where they are held captive, and repent and plead with you in the land of their captivity and say, "We have sinned, we have done wrong and acted wickedly"; 38and if they turn back to you with all their heart and soul in the land of their captivity where they were taken, and pray towards the land that you gave their ancestors, towards the city you have chosen and towards the temple that I have built for your Name; 39then from heaven, your dwelling-place, hear their prayer and their pleas, and uphold their cause. And forgive your people, who have sinned against you.

40'Now, my God, may your eyes be open and your ears attentive to the prayers offered in this place.

41'Now arise, LORD God, and come to your resting place, you and the ark of your might.
May your priests, LORD God, be clothed with salvation, may your faithful people rejoice in your goodness.
42LORD God, do not reject your anointed one.
Remember the great love promised to David your servant.'

The dedication of the temple

7 When Solomon finished praying, fire came down from heaven and consumed the burnt offering and the sacrifices, and the glory of the LORD filled the temple. 2The priests could not enter the temple of the LORD because the glory of the LORD filled it. 3When all the Israelites saw the fire coming down and the glory of the LORD above the temple, they knelt on the pavement with their faces to the ground, and they worshipped and gave thanks to the LORD, saying,

> 'He is good;
> his love endures for ever.'

4Then the king and all the people offered sacrifices before the LORD. 5And King Solomon offered a sacrifice of twenty-two thousand head of cattle and a hundred and twenty thousand sheep and goats. So the king and all the people dedicated the temple of God. 6The priests took up their positions, as did the Levites with the LORD's musical instruments, which King David had made for praising the LORD and which were used when he gave thanks, saying, 'His love endures for ever.' Opposite the Levites, the priests blew their trumpets, and all the Israelites were standing.

7Solomon consecrated the middle part of the courtyard in front of the temple of the LORD, and there he offered burnt offerings and the fat of the fellowship offerings, because the bronze altar he had made could not hold the burnt offerings, the grain offerings and the fat portions.

8So Solomon observed the festival at that time for seven days, and all Israel with him—a vast assembly, people from Lebo Hamath to the Wadi of Egypt. 9On the eighth day they held an assembly, for they had celebrated the dedication of the altar for seven days and the festival for seven days more. 10On the twenty-third day of the seventh month he sent the people to their homes, joyful and glad in heart for the good things the LORD had done for David and Solomon and for his people Israel.

The LORD appears to Solomon

11When Solomon had finished the temple of the LORD and the royal palace, and had succeeded in carrying out all he had in mind to do in the temple of the LORD and in his own palace, 12the LORD appeared to him at night and said:

> 'I have heard your prayer and
> have chosen this place for myself
> as a temple for sacrifices.
>
> 13'When I shut up the heavens
> so that there is no rain, or

IN OTHER WORDS

Prayer
2 Chronicles 7:14

Prayer is communication with God and can take many forms – talking, listening to God, worshipping, shouting, singing, fasting and so on. If you have ever spoken to God or heard from him you have prayed. Jesus also prayed to God and taught the disciples the Lord's Prayer (Matthew 6:9–13).

---

command locusts to devour the land or send a plague among my people, 14if my people, who are called by my name, will humble themselves and pray and seek my face and turn from their wicked ways, then I will hear from heaven, and I will forgive their sin and will heal their land. 15Now my eyes will be open and my ears attentive to the prayers offered in this place. 16I have chosen and consecrated this temple so that my Name may be there for ever. My eyes and my heart will always be there.

17'As for you, if you walk before me faithfully as David your father did, and do all I command, and observe my decrees and laws, 18I will establish your royal throne, as I covenanted with David your father when I said, "You shall never fail to have a successor to rule over Israel."

19'But if you*a* turn away and forsake the decrees and commands I have given you*b* and go off to serve other gods and worship them, 20then I will uproot Israel from my land, which I have given them, and will reject this temple which I have consecrated for my Name. I will make it a byword and an object of ridicule

---

a 19 The Hebrew is plural.   *b* 19 The Hebrew is plural.

among all peoples. ²¹This temple will become a heap of rubble. All[a] who pass by will be appalled and say, "Why has the LORD done such a thing to this land and to this temple?" ²²People will answer, "Because they have forsaken the LORD, the God of their ancestors, who brought them out of Egypt, and have embraced other gods, worshipping and serving them—that is why he brought all this disaster on them."'

Solomon's other activities

8 At the end of twenty years, during which Solomon built the temple of the LORD and his own palace, ²Solomon rebuilt the villages that Hiram[b] had given him, and settled Israelites in them. ³Solomon then went to Hamath Zobah and captured it. ⁴He also built up Tadmor in the desert and all the store cities he had built in Hamath. ⁵He rebuilt Upper Beth Horon and Lower Beth Horon as fortified cities, with walls and with gates and bars, ⁶as well as Baalath and all his store cities, and all the cities for his chariots and for his horses[c]—whatever he desired to build in Jerusalem, in Lebanon and throughout all the territory that he ruled.

⁷There were still people left from the Hittites, Amorites, Perizzites, Hivites and Jebusites (these people were not Israelites). ⁸Solomon conscripted the descendants of all these people remaining in the land—whom the Israelites had not destroyed—to serve as slave labour, as it is to this day. ⁹But Solomon did not make slaves of the Israelites for his work; they were his fighting men, commanders of his captains, and commanders of his chariots and charioteers. ¹⁰They were also King Solomon's chief officials—two hundred and fifty officials supervising the men.

¹¹Solomon brought Pharaoh's daughter up from the City of David to the palace he had built for her, for he said, 'My wife must not live in the palace of David king of Israel, because the places the ark of the LORD has entered are holy.'

¹²On the altar of the LORD that he had built in front of the portico, Solomon sacrificed burnt offerings to the LORD, ¹³according to the daily requirement for offerings commanded by Moses for the Sabbaths, the New Moons and the three annual festivals—the Festival of Unleavened Bread, the Festival of Weeks and the Festival of Tabernacles. ¹⁴In keeping with the ordinance of his father David, he appointed the divisions of the priests for their duties and the Levites to lead the praise and to assist the priests according to each day's requirement. He also appointed the gatekeepers by divisions for the various gates, because this was what David the man of God had ordered. ¹⁵They did not deviate from the king's commands to the priests or to the Levites in any matter, including that of the treasuries.

¹⁶All Solomon's work was carried out, from the day the foundation of the temple of the LORD was laid until its completion. So the temple of the LORD was finished.

¹⁷Then Solomon went to Ezion Geber and Elath on the coast of Edom. ¹⁸And Hiram sent him ships commanded by his own officers, sailors who knew the sea. These, with Solomon's servants, sailed to Ophir and brought back four hundred and fifty talents[d] of gold, which they delivered to King Solomon.

The queen of Sheba visits Solomon

9 When the queen of Sheba heard of Solomon's fame, she came to Jerusalem to test him with hard questions. Arriving with a very great caravan—with camels carrying spices, large quantities of gold, and precious stones—she came to Solomon and talked with him about all she had on her mind. ²Solomon answered all her questions; nothing was too hard for him to explain to her. ³When the queen of Sheba saw the wisdom of Solomon, as well as the palace he had built, ⁴the food on his table, the seating of his officials, the attending

---

[a] 21 See some Septuagint manuscripts, Old Latin, Syriac, Arabic and Targum; Hebrew *And though this temple is now so imposing, all*   [b] 2 Hebrew *Huram*, a variant of *Hiram*; also in verse 18   [c] 6 Or *charioteers*   [d] 18 That is, about 15 metric tons

Camels
2 Chronicles 9:1

Camels were ideal animals for Palestine and the countries around it. They are well suited to harsh desert life, able to carry large loads and manage on very little water. Their tough feet can cope with walking on rocks and hot sand. Their bushy eyebrows and their ability to tightly close their lips and nostrils help them to cope with sandstorms. Large herds of camels were a sign of great wealth.

servants in their robes, the cupbearers in their robes and the burnt offerings he made at[a] the temple of the LORD, she was overwhelmed.

5 She said to the king, 'The report I heard in my own country about your achievements and your wisdom is true. 6 But I did not believe what they said until I came and saw with my own eyes. Indeed, not even half the greatness of your wisdom was told me; you have far exceeded the report I heard. 7 How happy your people must be! How happy your officials, who continually stand before you and hear your wisdom! 8 Praise be to the LORD your God, who has delighted in you and placed you on his throne as king to rule for the LORD your God. Because of the love of your God for Israel and his desire to uphold them for ever, he has made you king over them, to maintain justice and righteousness.'

9 Then she gave the king 120 talents[b] of gold, large quantities of spices, and precious stones. There had never been such spices as those the queen of Sheba gave to King Solomon.

10 (The servants of Hiram and the servants of Solomon brought gold from Ophir; they also brought algum-wood[c] and precious stones. 11 The king used the algum-wood to make steps for the temple of the LORD and for the royal palace, and to make harps and lyres for the musicians. Nothing like them had ever been seen in Judah.)

12 King Solomon gave the queen of Sheba all she desired and asked for; he gave her more than she had brought to him. Then she left and returned with her retinue to her own country.

Solomon's splendour

13 The weight of the gold that Solomon received yearly was 666 talents,[d] 14 not including the revenues brought in by merchants and traders. Also all the kings of Arabia and the governors of the territories brought gold and silver to Solomon.

15 King Solomon made two hundred large shields of hammered gold; six hundred shekels[e] of hammered gold went into each shield. 16 He also made three hundred small shields of hammered gold, with three hundred shekels[f] of gold in each shield. The king put them in the Palace of the Forest of Lebanon.

17 Then the king made a great throne inlaid with ivory and overlaid with pure gold. 18 The throne had six steps, and a footstool of gold was attached to it. On both sides of the seat were armrests, with a lion standing beside each of them. 19 Twelve lions stood on the six steps, one at either end of each step. Nothing like it had ever been made for any other kingdom. 20 All King Solomon's goblets were gold, and all the household articles in the Palace of the Forest of Lebanon were pure gold. Nothing was made of silver, because silver was considered of little value in Solomon's day. 21 The king had a fleet of trading ships[g] manned by Hiram's[h] servants. Once every three years it returned, carrying gold, silver and ivory, and apes and baboons.

22 King Solomon was greater in riches and wisdom than all the other kings of the earth. 23 All the kings of the earth sought audience

---

[a] 4 Or *and the ascent by which he went up to* [b] 9 That is, about 4 metric tons [c] 10 Probably a variant of *almug-wood* [d] 13 That is, about 23 metric tons [e] 15 That is, about 6.9 kilograms [f] 16 That is, about 3.5 kilograms [g] 21 Hebrew *of ships that could go to Tarshish* [h] 21 Hebrew *Huram*, a variant of *Hiram*

with Solomon to hear the wisdom God had put in his heart. 24Year after year, everyone who came brought a gift—articles of silver and gold, and robes, weapons and spices, and horses and mules.

25Solomon had four thousand stalls for horses and chariots, and twelve thousand horses,[a] which he kept in the chariot cities and also with him in Jerusalem. 26He ruled over all the kings from the River Euphrates to the land of the Philistines, as far as the border of Egypt. 27The king made silver as common in Jerusalem as stones, and cedar as plentiful as sycamore-fig trees in the foothills. 28Solomon's horses were imported from Egypt and from all other countries.

Solomon's death

29As for the other events of Solomon's reign, from beginning to end, are they not written in the records of Nathan the prophet, in the prophecy of Ahijah the Shilonite and in the visions of Iddo the seer concerning Jeroboam son of Nebat? 30Solomon reigned in Jerusalem over all Israel for forty years. 31Then he rested with his ancestors and was buried in the city of David his father. And Rehoboam his son succeeded him as king.

Israel rebels against Rehoboam

10 Rehoboam went to Shechem, for all Israel had gone there to make him king. 2When Jeroboam son of Nebat heard this (he was in Egypt, where he had fled from King Solomon), he returned from Egypt. 3So they sent for Jeroboam, and he and all Israel went to Rehoboam and said to him: 4'Your father put a heavy yoke on us, but now lighten the harsh labour and the heavy yoke he put on us, and we will serve you.'

5Rehoboam answered, 'Come back to me in three days.' So the people went away.

6Then King Rehoboam consulted the elders who had served his father Solomon during his lifetime. 'How would you advise me to answer these people?' he asked.

7They replied, 'If you will be kind to these people and please them and give them a favourable answer, they will always be your servants.'

8But Rehoboam rejected the advice the elders gave him and consulted the young men who had grown up with him and were serving him. 9He asked them, 'What is your advice? How should we answer these people who say to me, "Lighten the yoke your father put on us"?'

10The young men who had grown up with him replied, 'The people have said to you, "Your father put a heavy yoke on us, but make our yoke lighter." Now tell them, "My little finger is thicker than my father's waist. 11My father laid on you a heavy yoke; I will make it even heavier. My father scourged you with whips; I will scourge you with scorpions."'

12Three days later Jeroboam and all the people returned to Rehoboam, as the king had said, 'Come back to me in three days.' 13The king answered them harshly. Rejecting the advice of the elders, 14he followed the advice of the young men and said, 'My father made your yoke heavy; I will make it even heavier. My father scourged you with whips; I will scourge you with scorpions.' 15So the king did not listen to the people, for this turn of events was from God, to fulfil the word that the LORD had spoken to Jeroboam son of Nebat through Ahijah the Shilonite.

16When all Israel saw that the king refused to listen to them, they answered the king:

'What share do we have in David,
    what part in Jesse's son?
To your tents, Israel!
    Look after your own house, David!'

So all the Israelites went home. 17But as for the Israelites who were living in the towns of Judah, Rehoboam still ruled over them.

18King Rehoboam sent out Adoniram,[b] who was in charge of forced labour, but the Israelites stoned him to death. King Rehoboam, however, managed to get into his chariot and escape to Jerusalem. 19So Israel has been in rebellion against the house of David to this day.

---

[a] 25 Or *charioteers* [b] 18 Hebrew *Hadoram*, a variant of *Adoniram*

11 When Rehoboam arrived in Jerusalem, he mustered the house of Judah and Benjamin—a hundred and eighty thousand able young men—to make war against Israel and to regain the kingdom for Rehoboam.

2But this word of the LORD came to Shemaiah the man of God: 3'Say to Rehoboam son of Solomon king of Judah and to all Israel in Judah and Benjamin, 4"This is what the LORD says: do not go up to fight against your fellow Israelites. Go home, every one of you, for this is my doing."' So they obeyed the words of the LORD and turned back from marching against Jeroboam.

Rehoboam fortifies Judah

5Rehoboam lived in Jerusalem and built up towns for defence in Judah: 6Bethlehem, Etam, Tekoa, 7Beth Zur, Soko, Adullam, 8Gath, Mareshah, Ziph, 9Adoraim, Lachish, Azekah, 10Zorah, Aijalon and Hebron. These were fortified cities in Judah and Benjamin. 11He strengthened their defences and put commanders in them, with supplies of food, olive oil and wine. 12He put shields and spears in all the cities, and made them very strong. So Judah and Benjamin were his.

13The priests and Levites from all their districts throughout Israel sided with him. 14The Levites even abandoned their pasture-lands and property and came to Judah and Jerusalem, because Jeroboam and his sons had rejected them as priests of the LORD 15when he appointed his own priests for the high places and for the goat and calf idols he had made. 16Those from every tribe of Israel who set their hearts on seeking the LORD, the God of Israel, followed the Levites to Jerusalem to offer sacrifices to the LORD, the God of their ancestors. 17They strengthened the kingdom of Judah and supported Rehoboam son of Solomon for three years, following the ways of David and Solomon during this time.

Rehoboam's family

18Rehoboam married Mahalath, who was the daughter of David's son Jerimoth and of Abihail, the daughter of Jesse's son Eliab. 19She bore him sons: Jeush, Shemariah and Zaham. 20Then he married Maakah daughter of Absalom, who bore him Abijah, Attai, Ziza and Shelomith. 21Rehoboam loved Maakah daughter of Absalom more than any of his other wives and concubines. In all he had eighteen wives and sixty concubines, twenty-eight sons and sixty daughters.

22Rehoboam appointed Abijah son of Maakah as crown prince among his brothers, in order to make him king. 23He acted wisely, dispersing some of his sons throughout the districts of Judah and Benjamin, and to all the fortified cities. He gave them abundant provisions and took many wives for them.

Shishak attacks Jerusalem

12 After Rehoboam's position as king was established and he had become strong, he and all Israel[a] with him abandoned the law of the LORD. 2Because they had been unfaithful to the LORD, Shishak king of Egypt attacked Jerusalem in the fifth year of King Rehoboam. 3With twelve hundred chariots and sixty thousand horsemen and the innumerable troops of Libyans, Sukkites and Cushites[b] that came with him from Egypt, 4he captured the fortified cities of Judah and came as far as Jerusalem.

5Then the prophet Shemaiah came to Rehoboam and to the leaders of Judah who had assembled in Jerusalem for fear of Shishak, and he said to them, 'This is what the LORD says: "You have abandoned me; therefore I now abandon you to Shishak."'

6The leaders of Israel and the king humbled themselves and said, 'The LORD is just.'

7When the LORD saw that they humbled themselves, this word of the LORD came to Shemaiah: 'Since they have humbled themselves, I will not destroy them but will soon give them deliverance. My wrath will not be poured out on Jerusalem through Shishak. 8They will, however, become subject to him, so that they may learn the difference between serving me and serving the kings of other lands.'

---

[a] 1 That is, Judah, as frequently in 2 Chronicles [b] 3 That is, people from the upper Nile region

9When Shishak king of Egypt attacked Jerusalem, he carried off the treasures of the temple of the LORD and the treasures of the royal palace. He took everything, including the gold shields that Solomon had made. 10So King Rehoboam made bronze shields to replace them and assigned these to the commanders of the guard on duty at the entrance to the royal palace. 11Whenever the king went to the LORD's temple, the guards went with him, bearing the shields, and afterwards they returned them to the guardroom.

12Because Rehoboam humbled himself, the LORD's anger turned from him, and he was not totally destroyed. Indeed, there was some good in Judah.

13King Rehoboam established himself firmly in Jerusalem and continued as king. He was forty-one years old when he became king, and he reigned for seventeen years in Jerusalem, the city the LORD had chosen out of all the tribes of Israel in which to put his Name. His mother's name was Naamah; she was an Ammonite. 14He did evil because he had not set his heart on seeking the LORD.

15As for the events of Rehoboam's reign, from beginning to end, are they not written in the records of Shemaiah the prophet and of Iddo the seer that deal with genealogies? There was continual warfare between Rehoboam and Jeroboam. 16Rehoboam rested with his ancestors and was buried in the City of David. And Abijah his son succeeded him as king.

Abijah king of Judah

13 In the eighteenth year of the reign of Jeroboam, Abijah became king of Judah, 2and he reigned in Jerusalem for three years. His mother's name was Maakah,^a a daughter^b of Uriel of Gibeah.

There was war between Abijah and Jeroboam. 3Abijah went into battle with an army of four hundred thousand able fighting men, and Jeroboam drew up a battle line against him with eight hundred thousand able troops.

4Abijah stood on Mount Zemaraim, in the hill country of Ephraim, and said, 'Jeroboam and all Israel, listen to me! 5Don't you know that the LORD, the God of Israel, has given the kingship of Israel to David and his descendants for ever by a covenant of salt? 6Yet Jeroboam son of Nebat, an official of Solomon son of David, rebelled against his master. 7Some worthless scoundrels gathered around him and opposed Rehoboam son of Solomon when he was young and indecisive and not strong enough to resist them.

8'And now you plan to resist the kingdom of the LORD, which is in the hands of David's descendants. You are indeed a vast army and have with you the golden calves that Jeroboam made to be your gods. 9But didn't you drive out the priests of the LORD, the sons of Aaron, and the Levites, and make priests of your own as the peoples of other lands do? Whoever comes to consecrate himself with a young bull and seven rams may become a priest of what are not gods.

10'As for us, the LORD is our God, and we have not forsaken him. The priests who serve the LORD are sons of Aaron, and the Levites assist them. 11Every morning and evening they present burnt offerings and fragrant incense to the LORD. They set out the bread on the ceremonially clean table and light the lamps on the gold lampstand every evening. We are observing the requirements of the LORD our God. But you have forsaken him. 12God is with us; he is our leader. His priests with their trumpets will sound the battle cry against you. People of Israel, do not fight against the LORD, the God of your ancestors, for you will not succeed.'

13Now Jeroboam had sent troops round to the rear, so that while he was in front of Judah the ambush was behind them. 14Judah turned and saw that they were being attacked at both front and rear. Then they cried out to the LORD. The priests blew their trumpets 15and the men of Judah raised the battle cry. At the sound of their battle cry, God routed Jeroboam and all Israel before Abijah and Judah. 16The Israelites fled before Judah, and God delivered them into their hands. 17Abijah and his troops

---

^a 2 Most Septuagint manuscripts and Syriac (see also 2 Chron. 11:20 and 1 Kings 15:2); Hebrew *Micaiah* ^b 2 Or *granddaughter*

inflicted heavy losses on them, so that there were five hundred thousand casualties among Israel's able men. 18The Israelites were subdued on that occasion, and the men of Judah were victorious because they relied on the LORD, the God of their ancestors.

19Abijah pursued Jeroboam and took from him the towns of Bethel, Jeshanah and Ephron, with their surrounding villages. 20Jeroboam did not regain power during the time of Abijah. And the LORD struck him down and he died.

21But Abijah grew in strength. He married fourteen wives and had twenty-two sons and sixteen daughters.

22The other events of Abijah's reign, what he did and what he said, are written in the annotations of the prophet Iddo.

14 *And Abijah rested with his ancestors and was buried in the City of David. Asa his son succeeded him as king, and in his days the country was at peace for ten years.

Asa king of Judah

*2Asa did what was good and right in the eyes of the LORD his God. 3He removed the foreign altars and the high places, smashed the sacred stones and cut down the Asherah poles.*a* 4He commanded Judah to seek the LORD, the God of their ancestors, and to obey his laws and commands. 5He removed the high places and incense altars in every town in Judah, and the kingdom was at peace under him. 6He built up the fortified cities of Judah, since the land was at peace. No-one was at war with him during those years, for the LORD gave him rest.

7'Let us build up these towns,' he said to Judah, 'and put walls round them, with towers, gates and bars. The land is still ours, because we have sought the LORD our God; we sought him and he has given us rest on every side.' So they built and prospered.

8Asa had an army of three hundred thousand men from Judah, equipped with large shields and with spears, and two

Sign of the times

Chariots
2 Chronicles 14:9
In battle, a chariot would usually carry two soldiers, the driver and a skilled archer. Only wealthier nations were able to set up and maintain a chariot force. Solomon was the first Israelite king to develop a chariot corps in his army (1 Kings 4:26).

hundred and eighty thousand from Benjamin, armed with small shields and with bows. All these were brave fighting men.

9Zerah the Cushite marched out against them with an army of thousands upon thousands and three hundred chariots, and came as far as Mareshah. 10Asa went out to meet him, and they took up battle positions in the Valley of Zephathah near Mareshah.

11Then Asa called to the LORD his God and said, 'LORD, there is no-one like you to help the powerless against the mighty. Help us, LORD our God, for we rely on you, and in your name we have come against this vast army. LORD, you are our God; do not let mere mortals prevail against you.'

12The LORD struck down the Cushites before Asa and Judah. The Cushites fled, 13and Asa and his army pursued them as far as Gerar. Such a great number of Cushites fell that they could not recover; they were crushed before the LORD and his forces. The men of Judah carried off a large amount of plunder. 14They destroyed all the villages around Gerar, for the terror of the LORD had fallen on them. They plundered all these villages, since there was much booty there. 15They also attacked the camps of the herders and carried off droves of sheep and goats and camels. Then they returned to Jerusalem.

---

a 3 That is, wooden symbols of the goddess Asherah; here and elsewhere in 2 Chronicles
* 14:1 is numbered 13:23 in Hebrew texts.   * 14:2-15 is numbered 14:1-14 in Hebrew texts.

Asa's reform

15 The Spirit of God came on Azariah son of Oded. ²He went out to meet Asa and said to him, 'Listen to me, Asa and all Judah and Benjamin. The LORD is with you when you are with him. If you seek him, he will be found by you, but if you forsake him, he will forsake you. ³For a long time Israel was without the true God, without a priest to teach and without the law. ⁴But in their distress they turned to the LORD, the God of Israel, and sought him, and he was found by them. ⁵In those days it was not safe to travel about, for all the inhabitants of the lands were in great turmoil. ⁶One nation was being crushed by another and one city by another, because God was troubling them with every kind of distress. ⁷But as for you, be strong and do not give up, for your work will be rewarded.'

⁸When Asa heard these words and the prophecy of Azariah son of[a] Oded the prophet, he took courage. He removed the detestable idols from the whole land of Judah and Benjamin and from the towns he had captured in the hills of Ephraim. He repaired the altar of the LORD that was in front of the portico of the LORD's temple.

⁹Then he assembled all Judah and Benjamin and the people from Ephraim, Manasseh and Simeon who had settled among them, for large numbers had come over to him from Israel when they saw that the LORD his God was with him.

¹⁰They assembled at Jerusalem in the third month of the fifteenth year of Asa's reign. ¹¹At that time they sacrificed to the LORD seven hundred head of cattle and seven thousand sheep and goats from the plunder they had brought back. ¹²They entered into a covenant to seek the LORD, the God of their ancestors, with all their heart and soul. ¹³All who would not seek the LORD, the God of Israel, were to be put to death, whether small or great, man or woman. ¹⁴They took an oath to the LORD with loud acclamation, with shouting and with trumpets and horns. ¹⁵All Judah rejoiced about the oath because they had sworn it wholeheartedly. They sought God eagerly, and he was found by them. So the LORD gave them rest on every side.

¹⁶King Asa also deposed his grandmother Maakah from her position as queen mother, because she had made a repulsive image for the worship of Asherah. Asa cut it down, broke it up and burned it in the Kidron Valley. ¹⁷Although he did not remove the high places from Israel, Asa's heart was fully committed [to the LORD] all his life. ¹⁸He brought into the temple of God the silver and gold and the articles that he and his father had dedicated.

¹⁹There was no more war until the thirty-fifth year of Asa's reign.

Asa's last years

16 In the thirty-sixth year of Asa's reign Baasha king of Israel went up against Judah and fortified Ramah to prevent anyone from leaving or entering the territory of Asa king of Judah.

²Asa then took the silver and gold out of the treasuries of the LORD's temple and of his own palace and sent it to Ben-Hadad king of Aram, who was ruling in Damascus. ³'Let there be a treaty between me and you,' he said, 'as there was between my father and your father. See, I am sending you silver and gold. Now break your treaty with Baasha king of Israel so that he will withdraw from me.'

⁴Ben-Hadad agreed with King Asa and sent the commanders of his forces against the towns of Israel. They conquered Ijon, Dan, Abel Maim[b] and all the store cities of Naphtali. ⁵When Baasha heard this, he stopped building Ramah and abandoned his work. ⁶Then King Asa brought all the men of Judah, and they carried away from Ramah the stones and timber Baasha had been using. With them he built up Geba and Mizpah.

⁷At that time Hanani the seer came to Asa king of Judah and said to him: 'Because you relied on the king of Aram and not on the LORD your God, the army of the king of Aram has escaped from your hand. ⁸Were not the Cushites[c] and Libyans a mighty army with great numbers of chariots and

---

[a] 8 Vulgate and Syriac (see also Septuagint and verse 1); Hebrew does not have *Azariah son of*. [b] 4 Also known as *Abel Beth Maakah* [c] 8 That is, people from the upper Nile region

horsemen[a]? Yet when you relied on the LORD, he delivered them into your hand. 9For the eyes of the LORD range throughout the earth to strengthen those whose hearts are fully committed to him. You have done a foolish thing, and from now on you will be at war.'

10Asa was angry with the seer because of this; he was so enraged that he put him in prison. At the same time Asa brutally oppressed some of the people.

11The events of Asa's reign, from beginning to end, are written in the book of the kings of Judah and Israel. 12In the thirty-ninth year of his reign Asa was afflicted with a disease in his feet. Though his disease was severe, even in his illness he did not seek help from the LORD, but only from the doctors. 13Then in the forty-first year of his reign Asa died and rested with his ancestors. 14They buried him in the tomb that he had cut out for himself in the City of David. They laid him on a bier covered with spices and various blended perfumes, and they made a huge fire in his honour.

Jehoshaphat king of Judah

17 Jehoshaphat his son succeeded him as king and strengthened himself against Israel. 2He stationed troops in all the fortified cities of Judah and put garrisons in Judah and in the towns of Ephraim that his father Asa had captured.

3The LORD was with Jehoshaphat because he followed the ways of his father David before him. He did not consult the Baals 4but sought the God of his father and followed his commands rather than the practices of Israel. 5The LORD established the kingdom under his control; and all Judah brought gifts to Jehoshaphat, so that he had great wealth and honour. 6His heart was devoted to the ways of the LORD; furthermore, he removed the high places and the Asherah poles from Judah.

7In the third year of his reign he sent his officials Ben-Hail, Obadiah, Zechariah, Nethanel and Micaiah to teach in the towns of Judah. 8With them were certain Levites—Shemaiah, Nethaniah, Zebadiah, Asahel, Shemiramoth, Jehonathan, Adonijah, Tobijah and Tob-Adonijah—and the priests Elishama and Jehoram. 9They taught throughout Judah, taking with them the Book of the Law of the LORD; they went round to all the towns of Judah and taught the people.

10The fear of the LORD fell on all the kingdoms of the lands surrounding Judah, so that they did not make war with Jehoshaphat. 11Some Philistines brought Jehoshaphat gifts and silver as tribute, and the Arabs brought him flocks: seven thousand seven hundred rams and seven thousand seven hundred goats.

12Jehoshaphat became more and more powerful; he built forts and store cities in Judah 13and had large supplies in the towns of Judah. He also kept experienced fighting men in Jerusalem. 14Their enrolment by families was as follows:

> from Judah, commanders of units of 1,000:
> Adnah the commander, with 300,000 fighting men;
> 15next, Jehohanan the commander, with 280,000;
> 16next, Amasiah son of Zikri, who volunteered himself for the service of the LORD, with 200,000.
> 17From Benjamin:
> Eliada, a valiant soldier, with 200,000 men armed with bows and shields;
> 18next, Jehozabad, with 180,000 men armed for battle.

19These were the men who served the king, besides those he stationed in the fortified cities throughout Judah.

Micaiah prophesies against Ahab

18 Now Jehoshaphat had great wealth and honour, and he allied himself with Ahab by marriage. 2Some years later he went down to see Ahab in Samaria. Ahab slaughtered many sheep and cattle for him and the people with him and urged him to attack Ramoth Gilead. 3Ahab king of Israel asked Jehoshaphat king of Judah, 'Will you go with me against Ramoth Gilead?'

---

*a*8 Or *charioteers*

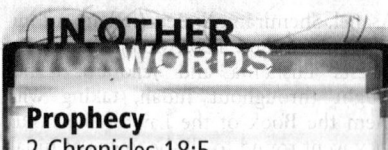

IN OTHER WORDS

Prophecy
2 Chronicles 18:5
A prophet is someone who speaks for God, who receives and delivers messages for him. When God speaks to his people through a prophet it is called prophecy. Sometimes a prophecy tells what God is going to do in the future. Sometimes it is instruction and advice for the present.

Jehoshaphat replied, 'I am as you are, and my people as your people; we will join you in the war.' 4But Jehoshaphat also said to the king of Israel, 'First seek the counsel of the LORD.'

5So the king of Israel brought together the prophets—four hundred men—and asked them, 'Shall we go to war against Ramoth Gilead, or shall I not?'

'Go,' they answered, 'for God will give it into the king's hand.'

6But Jehoshaphat asked, 'Is there no longer a prophet of the LORD here whom we can enquire of?'

7The king of Israel answered Jehoshaphat, 'There is still one through whom we can enquire of the LORD, but I hate him because he never prophesies anything good about me, but always bad. He is Micaiah son of Imlah.'

'The king should not say such a thing,' Jehoshaphat replied.

8So the king of Israel called one of his officials and said, 'Bring Micaiah son of Imlah at once.'

9Dressed in their royal robes, the king of Israel and Jehoshaphat king of Judah were sitting on their thrones at the threshing-floor by the entrance of the gate of Samaria, with all the prophets prophesying before them. 10Now Zedekiah son of Kenaanah had made iron horns, and he declared, 'This is what the LORD says: "With these you will gore the Arameans until they are destroyed."'

11All the other prophets were prophesying the same thing. 'Attack Ramoth Gilead and be victorious,' they said, 'for the LORD will give it into the king's hand.'

12The messenger who had gone to summon Micaiah said to him, 'Look, the other prophets without exception are predicting success for the king. Let your word agree with theirs, and speak favourably.'

13But Micaiah said, 'As surely as the LORD lives, I can tell him only what my God says.'

14When he arrived, the king asked him, 'Micaiah, shall we go to war against Ramoth Gilead, or shall I not?'

'Attack and be victorious,' he answered, 'for they will be given into your hand.'

15The king said to him, 'How many times must I make you swear to tell me nothing but the truth in the name of the LORD?'

16Then Micaiah answered, 'I saw all Israel scattered on the hills like sheep without a shepherd, and the LORD said, "These people have no master. Let each one go home in peace."'

17The king of Israel said to Jehoshaphat, 'Didn't I tell you that he never prophesies anything good about me, but only bad?'

18Micaiah continued, 'Therefore hear the word of the LORD: I saw the LORD sitting on his throne with all the host of heaven standing on his right and on his left. 19And the LORD said, "Who will entice Ahab king of Israel into attacking Ramoth Gilead and going to his death there?"

'One suggested this, and another that. 20Finally, a spirit came forward, stood before the LORD and said, "I will entice him."

'"By what means?" the LORD asked.

21'"I will go and be a lying spirit in the mouths of all his prophets," he said.

'"You will succeed in enticing him," said the LORD. "Go and do it."

22'So now the LORD has put a lying spirit in the mouths of these prophets of yours. The LORD has decreed disaster for you.'

23Then Zedekiah son of Kenaanah went up and slapped Micaiah in the face. 'Which way did the spirit from[a] the LORD go when he went from me to speak to you?' he asked. 24Micaiah replied, 'You will find out on the day you go to hide in an inner room.'

25The king of Israel then ordered, 'Take Micaiah and send him back to Amon the ruler of the city and to Joash the king's son, 26and say, "This is what the king says: put this fellow in prison and give him nothing but bread and water until I return safely."'

27Micaiah declared, 'If you ever return safely, the LORD has not spoken through me.' Then he added, 'Mark my words, all you people!'

Ahab killed at Ramoth Gilead

28So the king of Israel and Jehoshaphat king of Judah went up to Ramoth Gilead. 29The king of Israel said to Jehoshaphat, 'I will enter the battle in disguise, but you wear your royal robes.' So the king of Israel disguised himself and went into battle.

30Now the king of Aram had ordered his chariot commanders, 'Do not fight with anyone, small or great, except the king of Israel.' 31When the chariot commanders saw Jehoshaphat, they thought, 'This is the king of Israel.' So they turned to attack him, but Jehoshaphat cried out, and the LORD helped him. God drew them away from him, 32for when the chariot commanders saw that he was not the king of Israel, they stopped pursuing him.

33But someone drew his bow at random and hit the king of Israel between the breastplate and the scale armour. The king told the chariot driver, 'Wheel round and get me out of the fighting. I've been wounded.' 34All day long the battle raged, and the king of Israel propped himself up in his chariot facing the Arameans until evening. Then at sunset he died.

19 When Jehoshaphat king of Judah returned safely to his palace in Jerusalem, 2Jehu the seer, the son of Hanani, went out to meet him and said to the king, 'Should you help the wicked and love[b] those who hate the LORD? Because of this, the wrath of the LORD is on you. 3There is, however, some good in you, for you have rid the land of the Asherah poles and have set your heart on seeking God.'

Jehoshaphat appoints judges

4Jehoshaphat lived in Jerusalem, and he went out again among the people from Beersheba to the hill country of Ephraim and turned them back to the LORD, the God of their ancestors. 5He appointed judges in the land, in each of the fortified cities of Judah. 6He told them, 'Consider carefully what you do, because you are not judging for mere mortals but for the LORD, who is with you whenever you give a verdict. 7Now let the fear of the LORD be on you. Judge carefully, for with the LORD our God there is no injustice or partiality or bribery.'

8In Jerusalem also, Jehoshaphat appointed some of the Levites, priests and heads of Israelite families to administer the law of the LORD and to settle disputes. And they lived in Jerusalem. 9He gave them these orders: 'You must serve faithfully and wholeheartedly in the fear of the LORD. 10In every case that comes before you from your people who live in the cities—whether bloodshed or other concerns of the law, commands, decrees or regulations—you are to warn them not to sin against the LORD; otherwise his wrath will come on you and your people. Do this, and you will not sin.

11'Amariah the chief priest will be over you in any matter concerning the LORD, and Zebadiah son of Ishmael, the leader of the tribe of Judah, will be over you in any matter concerning the king, and the Levites will serve as officials before you. Act with courage, and may the LORD be with those who do well.'

Jehoshaphat defeats Moab and Ammon

20 After this, the Moabites and Ammonites with some of the Meunites[c] came to make war on Jehoshaphat.

2Some people came and told Jehoshaphat, 'A vast army is coming against you from Edom,[d] from the other side of the Dead Sea. It is already in Hazezon Tamar' (that is, En Gedi). 3Alarmed, Jehoshaphat

---

[a] 23 Or *Spirit of*   [b] 2 Or *and make alliances with*   [c] 1 Some Septuagint manuscripts; Hebrew *Ammonites*   [d] 2 One Hebrew manuscript; most Hebrew manuscripts, Septuagint and Vulgate *Aram*

resolved to enquire of the LORD, and he proclaimed a fast for all Judah. ⁴The people of Judah came together to seek help from the LORD; indeed, they came from every town in Judah to seek him.

⁵Then Jehoshaphat stood up in the assembly of Judah and Jerusalem at the temple of the LORD in the front of the new courtyard ⁶and said:

'LORD, the God of our ancestors, are you not the God who is in heaven? You rule over all the kingdoms of the nations. Power and might are in your hand, and no-one can withstand you. ⁷Our God, did you not drive out the inhabitants of this land before your people Israel and give it for ever to the descendants of Abraham your friend? ⁸They have lived in it and have built in it a sanctuary for your Name, saying, ⁹"If calamity comes upon us, whether the sword of judgment, or plague or famine, we will stand in your presence before this temple that bears your Name and will cry out to you in our distress, and you will hear us and save us."

¹⁰'But now here are men from Ammon, Moab and Mount Seir, whose territory you would not allow Israel to invade when they came from Egypt; so they turned away from them and did not destroy them. ¹¹See how they are repaying us by coming to drive us out of the possession you gave us as an inheritance. ¹²Our God, will you not judge them? For we have no power to face this vast army that is attacking us. We do not know what to do, but our eyes are on you.'

¹³All the men of Judah, with their wives and children and little ones, stood there before the LORD.

¹⁴Then the Spirit of the LORD came on Jahaziel son of Zechariah, the son of Benaiah, the son of Jeiel, the son of Mattaniah, a Levite and descendant of Asaph, as he stood in the assembly.

¹⁵He said: 'Listen, King Jehoshaphat and all who live in Judah and Jerusalem! This is what the LORD says to you: "Do not be afraid or discouraged because of this vast army. For the battle is not yours, but God's. ¹⁶Tomorrow march down against them. They will be climbing up by the Pass of Ziz, and you will find them at the end of the gorge in the Desert of Jeruel. ¹⁷You will not have to fight this battle. Take up your positions; stand firm and see the deliverance the LORD will give you, Judah and Jerusalem. Do not be afraid; do not be discouraged. Go out to face them tomorrow, and the LORD will be with you."'

¹⁸Jehoshaphat bowed down with his face to the ground, and all the people of Judah and Jerusalem fell down in worship before the LORD. ¹⁹Then some Levites from the Kohathites and Korahites stood up and praised the LORD, the God of Israel, with a very loud voice.

²⁰Early in the morning they left for the Desert of Tekoa. As they set out, Jehoshaphat stood and said, 'Listen to me, Judah and people of Jerusalem! Have faith in the LORD your God and you will be upheld; have faith in his prophets and you will be successful.' ²¹After consulting the people, Jehoshaphat appointed men to sing to the LORD and to praise him for the splendour of his[a] holiness as they went out at the head of the army, saying:

'Give thanks to the LORD,
for his love endures for ever.'

²²As they began to sing and praise, the LORD set ambushes against the men of Ammon and Moab and Mount Seir who were invading Judah, and they were defeated. ²³The Ammonites and Moabites rose up against the men from Mount Seir to destroy and annihilate them. After they finished slaughtering the men from Seir, they helped to destroy one another.

²⁴When the men of Judah came to the place that overlooks the desert and looked towards the vast army, they saw only dead bodies lying on the ground; no-one had

---

[a] 21 Or *him with the splendour of*

IN OTHER WORDS

High places
2 Chronicles 20:33
The high places were on hilltops and were dedicated to the worship of pagan gods. They should have been off limits to the people of Israel.

---

escaped. 25So Jehoshaphat and his men went to carry off their plunder, and they found among them a great amount of equipment and clothing[a] and also articles of value—more than they could take away. There was so much plunder that it took three days to collect it. 26On the fourth day they assembled in the Valley of Berakah, where they praised the LORD. This is why it is called the Valley of Berakah[b] to this day.

27Then, led by Jehoshaphat, all the men of Judah and Jerusalem returned joyfully to Jerusalem, for the LORD had given them cause to rejoice over their enemies. 28They entered Jerusalem and went to the temple of the LORD with harps and lyres and trumpets.

29The fear of God came on all the surrounding kingdoms when they heard how the LORD had fought against the enemies of Israel. 30And the kingdom of Jehoshaphat was at peace, for his God had given him rest on every side.

The end of Jehoshaphat's reign

31So Jehoshaphat reigned over Judah. He was thirty-five years old when he became king of Judah, and he reigned in Jerusalem for twenty-five years. His mother's name was Azubah daughter of Shilhi. 32He followed the ways of his father Asa and did not stray from them; he did what was right in the eyes of the LORD. 33The high places, however, were not removed, and the people still had not set their hearts on the God of their ancestors.

34The other events of Jehoshaphat's reign, from beginning to end, are written in the annals of Jehu son of Hanani, which are recorded in the book of the kings of Israel.

35Later, Jehoshaphat king of Judah made an alliance with Ahaziah king of Israel, whose ways were wicked. 36He agreed with him to construct a fleet of trading ships.[c] After these were built at Ezion Geber, 37Eliezer son of Dodavahu of Mareshah prophesied against Jehoshaphat, saying, 'Because you have made an alliance with Ahaziah, the LORD will destroy what you have made.' The ships were wrecked and were not able to set sail to trade.[d]

21

Then Jehoshaphat rested with his ancestors and was buried with them in the City of David. And Jehoram his son succeeded him as king. 2Jehoram's brothers, the sons of Jehoshaphat, were Azariah, Jehiel, Zechariah, Azariahu, Michael and Shephatiah. All these were sons of Jehoshaphat king of Israel.[e] 3Their father had given them many gifts of silver and gold and articles of value, as well as fortified cities in Judah, but he had given the kingdom to Jehoram because he was his firstborn son.

Jehoram king of Judah

4When Jehoram established himself firmly over his father's kingdom, he put all his brothers to the sword along with some of the officials of Israel. 5Jehoram was thirty-two years old when he became king, and he reigned in Jerusalem for eight years. 6He followed the ways of the kings of Israel, as the house of Ahab had done, for he married a daughter of Ahab. He did evil in the eyes of the LORD. 7Nevertheless, because of the covenant the LORD had made with David, the LORD was not willing to destroy the house of David. He had promised to maintain a lamp for him and his descendants for ever.

8In the time of Jehoram, Edom rebelled against Judah and set up its own king. 9So Jehoram went there with his officers and all his chariots. The Edomites surrounded him

---

[a] 25 Some Hebrew manuscripts and Vulgate; most Hebrew manuscripts *corpses*   [b] 26 *Berakah* means *praise*.
[c] 36 Hebrew *of ships that could go to Tarshish*   [d] 37 Hebrew *sail for Tarshish*   [e] 2 That is, Judah, as frequently in 2 Chronicles

and his chariot commanders, but he rose up and broke through by night. ¹⁰To this day Edom has been in rebellion against Judah.

Libnah revolted at the same time, because Jehoram had forsaken the LORD, the God of his ancestors. ¹¹He had also built high places on the hills of Judah and had caused the people of Jerusalem to prostitute themselves and had led Judah astray.

¹²Jehoram received a letter from Elijah the prophet, which said:

> 'This is what the LORD, the God of your father David, says: "You have not followed the ways of your father Jehoshaphat or of Asa king of Judah. ¹³But you have followed the ways of the kings of Israel, and you have led Judah and the people of Jerusalem to prostitute themselves, just as the house of Ahab did. You have also murdered your own brothers, members of your own family, men who were better than you. ¹⁴So now the LORD is about to strike your people, your sons, your wives and everything that is yours, with a heavy blow. ¹⁵You yourself will be very ill with a lingering disease of the bowels, until the disease causes your bowels to come out."'

¹⁶The LORD aroused against Jehoram the hostility of the Philistines and of the Arabs who lived near the Cushites. ¹⁷They attacked Judah, invaded it and carried off all the goods found in the king's palace, together with his sons and wives. Not a son was left to him except Ahaziah,[a] the youngest.

¹⁸After all this, the LORD afflicted Jehoram with an incurable disease of the bowels. ¹⁹In the course of time, at the end of the second year, his bowels came out because of the disease, and he died in great pain. His people made no funeral fire in his honour, as they had for his predecessors.

²⁰Jehoram was thirty-two years old when he became king, and he reigned in Jerusalem for eight years. He passed away, to no-one's regret, and was buried in the City of David, but not in the tombs of the kings.

Ahaziah king of Judah

22 The people of Jerusalem made Ahaziah, Jehoram's youngest son, king in his place, since the raiders, who came with the Arabs into the camp, had killed all the older sons. So Ahaziah son of Jehoram king of Judah began to reign.

²Ahaziah was twenty-two[b] years old when he became king, and he reigned in Jerusalem for one year. His mother's name was Athaliah, a granddaughter of Omri.

³He too followed the ways of the house of Ahab, for his mother encouraged him to act wickedly. ⁴He did evil in the eyes of the LORD, as the house of Ahab had done, for after his father's death they became his advisors, to his undoing. ⁵He also followed their counsel when he went with Joram[c] son of Ahab king of Israel to war against Hazael king of Aram at Ramoth Gilead. The Arameans wounded Joram; ⁶so he returned to Jezreel to recover from the wounds they had inflicted on him at Ramoth[d] in his battle with Hazael king of Aram.

Then Ahaziah[e] son of Jehoram king of Judah went down to Jezreel to see Joram son of Ahab because he had been wounded.

⁷Through Ahaziah's visit to Joram, God brought about Ahaziah's downfall. When Ahaziah arrived, he went out with Joram to meet Jehu son of Nimshi, whom the LORD had anointed to destroy the house of Ahab. ⁸While Jehu was executing judgment on the house of Ahab, he found the officials of Judah and the sons of Ahaziah's relatives, who had been attending Ahaziah, and he killed them. ⁹He then went in search of Ahaziah, and his men captured him while he was hiding in Samaria. He was brought to Jehu and put to death. They buried him, for they said, 'He was a son of Jehoshaphat, who sought the LORD with all his heart.' So there

---

[a] 17 Hebrew *Jehoahaz*, a variant of *Ahaziah* [b] 2 Some Septuagint manuscripts and Syriac (see also 2 Kings 8:26); Hebrew *forty-two* [c] 5 Hebrew *Jehoram*, a variant of *Joram*; also in verses 6 and 7 [d] 6 Hebrew *Ramah*, a variant of *Ramoth* [e] 6 Some Hebrew manuscripts, Septuagint, Vulgate and Syriac (see also 2 Kings 8:29); most Hebrew manuscripts *Azariah*

was no-one in the house of Ahaziah powerful enough to retain the kingdom.

Athaliah and Joash

¹⁰When Athaliah the mother of Ahaziah saw that her son was dead, she proceeded to destroy the whole royal family of the house of Judah. ¹¹But Jehosheba,ᵃ the daughter of King Jehoram, took Joash son of Ahaziah and stole him away from among the royal princes who were about to be murdered and put him and his nurse in a bedroom. Because Jehosheba,ᵇ the daughter of King Jehoram and wife of the priest Jehoiada, was Ahaziah's sister, she hid the child from Athaliah so that she could not kill him. ¹²He remained hidden with them at the temple of God for six years while Athaliah ruled the land.

23 In the seventh year Jehoiada showed his strength. He made a covenant with the commanders of units of a hundred: Azariah son of Jeroham, Ishmael son of Jehohanan, Azariah son of Obed, Maaseiah son of Adaiah, and Elishaphat son of Zikri. ²They went throughout Judah and gathered the Levites and the heads of Israelite families from all the towns. When they came to Jerusalem, ³the whole assembly made a covenant with the king at the temple of God.

Jehoiada said to them, 'The king's son shall reign, as the LORD promised concerning the descendants of David. ⁴Now this is what you are to do: a third of you priests and Levites who are going on duty on the Sabbath are to keep watch at the doors, ⁵a third of you at the royal palace and a third at the Foundation Gate, and all the others are to be in the courtyards of the temple of the LORD. ⁶No-one is to enter the temple of the LORD except the priests and Levites on duty; they may enter because they are consecrated, but all the others are to observe the LORD's command not to enter.ᶜ ⁷The Levites are to station themselves round the king, each with weapon in hand. Anyone who enters the temple is to be put to death. Stay close to the king wherever he goes.'

⁸The Levites and all the men of Judah did just as Jehoiada the priest ordered. Each one took his men—those who were going on duty on the Sabbath and those who were going off duty—for Jehoiada the priest had not released any of the divisions. ⁹Then he gave the commanders of units of a hundred the spears and the large and small shields that had belonged to King David and that were in the temple of God. ¹⁰He stationed all the men, each with his weapon in his hand, round the king—near the altar and the temple, from the south side to the north side of the temple.

¹¹Jehoiada and his sons brought out the king's son and put the crown on him; they presented him with a copy of the covenant and proclaimed him king. They anointed him and shouted, 'Long live the king!'

¹²When Athaliah heard the noise of the people running and cheering the king, she went to them at the temple of the LORD. ¹³She looked, and there was the king, standing by his pillar at the entrance. The officers and the trumpeters were beside the king, and all the people of the land were rejoicing and blowing trumpets, and musicians with their instruments were leading the praises. Then Athaliah tore her robes and shouted, 'Treason! Treason!'

¹⁴Jehoiada the priest sent out the commanders of units of a hundred, who were in charge of the troops, and said to them: 'Bring her out between the ranksᵈ and put to the sword anyone who follows her.' For the priest had said, 'Do not put her to death at the temple of the LORD.' ¹⁵So they seized her as she reached the entrance of the Horse Gate on the palace grounds, and there they put her to death.

¹⁶Jehoiada then made a covenant that he, the people and the kingᵉ would be the LORD's people. ¹⁷All the people went to the temple of Baal and tore it down. They smashed the altars and idols and killed Mattan the priest of Baal in front of the altars.

¹⁸Then Jehoiada placed the oversight of the temple of the LORD in the hands of the

---

ᵃ 11 Hebrew *Jehoshabeath*, a variant of *Jehosheba*   ᵇ 11 Hebrew *Jehoshabeath*, a variant of *Jehosheba*   ᶜ 6 Or *are to stand guard where the LORD has assigned them*   ᵈ 14 Or *out from the precincts*   ᵉ 16 Or *covenant between* [*the LORD*] *and the people and the king that they* (see 2 Kings 11:17)

Levitical priests, to whom David had made assignments in the temple, to present the burnt offerings of the LORD as written in the Law of Moses, with rejoicing and singing, as David had ordered. 19He also stationed gatekeepers at the gates of the LORD's temple so that no-one who was in any way unclean might enter.

20He took with him the commanders of hundreds, the nobles, the rulers of the people and all the people of the land and brought the king down from the temple of the LORD. They went into the palace through the Upper Gate and seated the king on the royal throne. 21All the people of the land rejoiced, and the city was calm, because Athaliah had been slain with the sword.

Joash repairs the temple

24 Joash was seven years old when he became king, and he reigned in Jerusalem for forty years. His mother's name was Zibiah; she was from Beersheba. 2Joash did what was right in the eyes of the LORD all the years of Jehoiada the priest. 3Jehoiada chose two wives for him, and he had sons and daughters.

4Some time later Joash decided to restore the temple of the LORD. 5He called together the priests and Levites and said to them, 'Go to the towns of Judah and collect the money due annually from all Israel, to repair the temple of your God. Do it now.' But the Levites did not act at once.

6Therefore the king summoned Jehoiada the chief priest and said to him, 'Why haven't you required the Levites to bring in from Judah and Jerusalem the tax imposed by Moses the servant of the LORD and by the assembly of Israel for the tent of the covenant law?'

7Now the sons of that wicked woman Athaliah had broken into the temple of God and had used even its sacred objects for the Baals.

8At the king's command, a chest was made and placed outside, at the gate of the temple of the LORD. 9A proclamation was then issued in Judah and Jerusalem that they should bring to the LORD the tax that Moses the servant of God had required of Israel in the wilderness. 10All the officials

Old age
2 Chronicles 24:15
Living to an old age was seen as God's reward for having led a faithful and godly life.

and all the people brought their contributions gladly, dropping them into the chest until it was full. 11Whenever the chest was brought in by the Levites to the king's officials and they saw that there was a large amount of money, the royal secretary and the officer of the chief priest would come and empty the chest and carry it back to its place. They did this regularly and collected a great amount of money. 12The king and Jehoiada gave it to those who carried out the work required for the temple of the LORD. They hired masons and carpenters to restore the LORD's temple, and also workers in iron and bronze to repair the temple.

13The men in charge of the work were diligent, and the repairs progressed under them. They rebuilt the temple of God according to its original design and reinforced it. 14When they had finished, they brought the rest of the money to the king and Jehoiada, and with it were made articles for the LORD's temple: articles for the service and for the burnt offerings, and also dishes and other objects of gold and silver. As long as Jehoiada lived, burnt offerings were presented continually in the temple of the LORD.

15Now Jehoiada was old and full of years, and he died at the age of a hundred and thirty. 16He was buried with the kings in the City of David, because of the good he had done in Israel for God and his temple.

The wickedness of Joash

17After the death of Jehoiada, the officials of Judah came and paid homage to the king, and he listened to them. ¹⁸They abandoned the temple of the LORD, the God of their ancestors, and worshipped Asherah poles and idols. Because of their guilt, God's anger came on Judah and Jerusalem. ¹⁹Although the LORD sent prophets to the people to bring them back to him, and though they testified against them, they would not listen.

²⁰Then the Spirit of God came on Zechariah son of Jehoiada the priest. He stood before the people and said, 'This is what God says: "Why do you disobey the LORD's commands? You will not prosper. Because you have forsaken the LORD, he has forsaken you."'

²¹But they plotted against him, and by order of the king they stoned him to death in the courtyard of the LORD's temple. ²²King Joash did not remember the kindness Zechariah's father Jehoiada had shown him but killed his son, who said as he lay dying, 'May the LORD see this and call you to account.'

²³At the turn of the year,^{a} the army of Aram marched against Joash; it invaded Judah and Jerusalem and killed all the leaders of the people. They sent all the plunder to their king in Damascus. ²⁴Although the Aramean army had come with only a few men, the LORD delivered into their hands a much larger army. Because Judah had forsaken the LORD, the God of their ancestors, judgment was executed on Joash. ²⁵When the Arameans withdrew, they left Joash severely wounded. His officials conspired against him for murdering the son of Jehoiada the priest, and they killed him in his bed. So he died and was buried in the City of David, but not in the tombs of the kings.

²⁶Those who conspired against him were Zabad,^{b} son of Shimeath an Ammonite woman, and Jehozabad, son of Shimrith^c a Moabite woman. ²⁷The account of his sons, the many prophecies about him, and the record of the restoration of the temple of God are written in the annotations on the book of the kings. And Amaziah his son succeeded him as king.

Amaziah king of Judah

25 Amaziah was twenty-five years old when he became king, and he reigned in Jerusalem for twenty-nine years. His mother's name was Jehoaddan; she was from Jerusalem. ²He did what was right in the eyes of the LORD, but not wholeheartedly. ³After the kingdom was firmly in his control, he executed the officials who had murdered his father the king. ⁴Yet he did not put their children to death, but acted in accordance with what is written in the Law, in the Book of Moses, where the LORD commanded: 'Parents shall not be put to death for their children, nor children be put to death for their parents; each of you will die for your own sin.'^{d}

⁵Amaziah called the people of Judah together and assigned them according to their families to commanders of thousands and commanders of hundreds for all Judah and Benjamin. He then mustered those twenty years old or more and found that there were three hundred thousand men fit for military service, able to handle the spear and shield. ⁶He also hired a hundred thousand fighting men from Israel for a hundred talents^e of silver.

⁷But a man of God came to him and said, 'Your Majesty, these troops from Israel must not march with you, for the LORD is not with Israel—not with any of the people of Ephraim. ⁸Even if you go and fight courageously in battle, God will overthrow you before the enemy, for God has the power to help or to overthrow.'

⁹Amaziah asked the man of God, 'But what about the hundred talents I paid for these Israelite troops?'

The man of God replied, 'The LORD can give you much more than that.'

¹⁰So Amaziah dismissed the troops who had come to him from Ephraim and sent them home. They were furious with Judah and left for home in a great rage.

¹¹Amaziah then marshalled his strength and led his army to the Valley of Salt, where he killed ten thousand men of Seir. ¹²The army of Judah also captured ten thousand men alive, took them to the top of a cliff and

---

^{a} 23 Probably in the spring ^{b} 26 A variant of *Jozabad* ^{c} 26 A variant of *Shomer* ^{d} 4 Deut. 24:16 ^{e} 6 That is, about 3.4 metric tons; also in verse 9 threw them down so that all were dashed to pieces.

13 Meanwhile the troops that Amaziah had sent back and had not allowed to take part in the war raided towns belonging to Judah from Samaria to Beth Horon. They killed three thousand people and carried off great quantities of plunder.

14 When Amaziah returned from slaughtering the Edomites, he brought back the gods of the people of Seir. He set them up as his own gods, bowed down to them and burned sacrifices to them. 15 The anger of the LORD burned against Amaziah, and he sent a prophet to him, who said, 'Why do you consult this people's gods, which could not save their own people from your hand?'

16 While he was still speaking, the king said to him, 'Have we appointed you an advisor to the king? Stop! Why be struck down?'

So the prophet stopped but said, 'I know that God has determined to destroy you, because you have done this and have not listened to my counsel.'

17 After Amaziah king of Judah consulted his advisors, he sent this challenge to Jehoash[a] son of Jehoahaz, the son of Jehu, king of Israel: 'Come, meet me face to face.'

18 But Jehoash king of Israel replied to Amaziah king of Judah, 'A thistle in Lebanon sent a message to a cedar in Lebanon, "Give your daughter to my son in marriage." Then a wild beast in Lebanon came along and trampled the thistle underfoot. 19 You say to yourself that you have defeated Edom, and now you are arrogant and proud. But stay at home! Why ask for trouble and cause your own downfall and that of Judah also?'

20 Amaziah, however, would not listen, for God so worked that he might deliver them into the hands of Jehoash, because they sought the gods of Edom. 21 So Jehoash king of Israel attacked. He and Amaziah king of Judah faced each other at Beth Shemesh in Judah. 22 Judah was routed by Israel, and every man fled to his home. 23 Jehoash king of Israel captured Amaziah king of Judah, the son of Joash, the son of Ahaziah,[b] at Beth Shemesh. Then Jehoash brought him to Jerusalem and broke down the wall of Jerusalem from the Ephraim Gate to the Corner Gate—a section about four hundred cubits[c] long. 24 He took all the gold and silver and all the articles found in the temple of God that had been in the care of Obed-Edom, together with the palace treasures and the hostages, and returned to Samaria.

25 Amaziah son of Joash king of Judah lived for fifteen years after the death of Jehoash son of Jehoahaz king of Israel. 26 As for the other events of Amaziah's reign, from beginning to end, are they not written in the book of the kings of Judah and Israel? 27 From the time that Amaziah turned away from following the LORD, they conspired against him in Jerusalem and he fled to Lachish, but they sent men after him to Lachish and killed him there. 28 He was brought back by horse and was buried with his ancestors in the City of Judah.[d]

Uzziah king of Judah

26 Then all the people of Judah took Uzziah,[e] who was sixteen years old, and made him king in place of his father Amaziah. 2 He was the one who rebuilt Elath and restored it to Judah after Amaziah rested with his ancestors.

3 Uzziah was sixteen years old when he became king, and he reigned in Jerusalem for fifty-two years. His mother's name was Jekoliah; she was from Jerusalem. 4 He did what was right in the eyes of the LORD, just as his father Amaziah had done. 5 He sought God during the days of Zechariah, who instructed him in the fear[f] of God. As long as he sought the LORD, God gave him success.

6 He went to war against the Philistines and broke down the walls of Gath, Jabneh and Ashdod. He then rebuilt towns near Ashdod and elsewhere among the Philistines. 7 God helped him against the Philistines and against the Arabs who lived in Gur Baal and against the Meunites. 8 The Ammonites brought tribute to Uzziah, and his

---

[a] 17 Hebrew *Joash*, a variant of *Jehoash*; also in verses 18, 21, 23 and 25 [b] 23 Hebrew *Jehoahaz*, a variant of *Ahaziah* [c] 23 That is, about 180 metres [d] 28 Most Hebrew manuscripts; some Hebrew manuscripts, Septuagint, Vulgate and Syriac (see also 2 Kings 14:20) *David* [e] 1 Also called *Azariah* [f] 5 Many Hebrew manuscripts, Septuagint and Syriac; other Hebrew manuscripts *vision*

fame spread as far as the border of Egypt, because he had become very powerful.

⁹Uzziah built towers in Jerusalem at the Corner Gate, at the Valley Gate and at the angle of the wall, and he fortified them. ¹⁰He also built towers in the wilderness and dug many cisterns, because he had much livestock in the foothills and in the plain. He had people working his fields and vineyards in the hills and in the fertile lands, for he loved the soil.

¹¹Uzziah had a well-trained army, ready to go out by divisions according to their numbers as mustered by Jeiel the secretary and Maaseiah the officer under the direction of Hananiah, one of the royal officials. ¹²The total number of family leaders over the fighting men was 2,600. ¹³Under their command was an army of 307,500 men trained for war, a powerful force to support the king against his enemies. ¹⁴Uzziah provided shields, spears, helmets, coats of armour, bows and slingstones for the entire army. ¹⁵In Jerusalem he made devices designed by skilled workers for use on the towers and on the corner defences so that soldiers could shoot arrows and hurl large stones from the walls. His fame spread far and wide, for he was greatly helped until he became powerful.

¹⁶But after Uzziah became powerful, his pride led to his downfall. He was unfaithful to the LORD his God, and entered the temple of the LORD to burn incense on the altar of incense. ¹⁷Azariah the priest with eighty other courageous priests of the LORD followed him in. ¹⁸They confronted King Uzziah and said, 'It is not right for you, Uzziah, to burn incense to the LORD. That is for the priests, the descendants of Aaron, who have been consecrated to burn incense. Leave the sanctuary, for you have been unfaithful; and you will not be honoured by the LORD God.'

¹⁹Uzziah, who had a censer in his hand ready to burn incense, became angry. While he was raging at the priests in their presence before the incense altar in the LORD's temple, leprosy[a] broke out on his forehead.

²⁰When Azariah the chief priest and all the other priests looked at him, they saw that he had leprosy on his forehead, so they hurried him out. Indeed, he himself was eager to leave, because the LORD had afflicted him.

²¹King Uzziah had leprosy until the day he died. He lived in a separate house[b] — leprous, and excluded from the temple of the LORD. Jotham his son had charge of the palace and governed the people of the land.

²²The other events of Uzziah's reign, from beginning to end, are recorded by the prophet Isaiah son of Amoz. ²³Uzziah rested with his ancestors and was buried near them in a cemetery that belonged to the kings, for people said, 'He had leprosy.' And Jotham his son succeeded him as king.

Jotham king of Judah

27 Jotham was twenty-five years old when he became king, and he reigned in Jerusalem for sixteen years. His mother's name was Jerusha daughter of Zadok. ²He did what was right in the eyes of the LORD, just as his father Uzziah had done, but unlike him he did not enter the temple of the LORD. The people, however, continued their corrupt practices. ³Jotham rebuilt the Upper Gate of the temple of the LORD and did extensive work on the wall at the hill of Ophel. ⁴He built towns in the hill country of Judah and forts and towers in the wooded areas.

⁵Jotham made war on the king of the Ammonites and conquered them. That year the Ammonites paid him a hundred talents[c] of silver, ten thousand cors[d] of wheat and ten thousand cors[e] of barley. The Ammonites brought him the same amount also in the second and third years.

⁶Jotham grew powerful because he walked steadfastly before the LORD his God.

⁷The other events in Jotham's reign, including all his wars and the other things he did, are written in the book of the kings of Israel and Judah. ⁸He was twenty-five years old when he became king, and he reigned in Jerusalem for sixteen years. ⁹Jotham rested with his ancestors and was buried in the City

---

[a] 19 The Hebrew for *leprosy* was used for various diseases affecting the skin; also in verses 20, 21 and 23.   [b] 21 Or *in a house where he was relieved of responsibilities*   [c] 5 That is, about 3.4 metric tons   [d] 5 That is, probably about 1,600 metric tons   [e] 5 That is, probably about 1,350 metric tons

Making Connections

Child sacrifice
2 Chronicles 28:3
Child sacrifice was part of the worship of some foreign gods such as Molek. But the Law of Moses strictly banned child sacrifice (Leviticus 20:1–5).

of David. And Ahaz his son succeeded him as king.

Ahaz king of Judah

28 Ahaz was twenty years old when he became king, and he reigned in Jerusalem for sixteen years. Unlike David his father, he did not do what was right in the eyes of the LORD. 2He followed the ways of the kings of Israel and also made idols for worshipping the Baals. 3He burned sacrifices in the Valley of Ben Hinnom and sacrificed his children in the fire, engaging in the detestable practices of the nations that the LORD had driven out before the Israelites. 4He offered sacrifices and burned incense at the high places, on the hilltops and under every spreading tree.

5Therefore the LORD his God delivered him into the hands of the king of Aram. The Arameans defeated him and took many of his people as prisoners and brought them to Damascus.

He was also given into the hands of the king of Israel, who inflicted heavy casualties on him. 6In one day Pekah son of Remaliah killed a hundred and twenty thousand soldiers in Judah—because Judah had forsaken the LORD, the God of their ancestors. 7Zikri, an Ephraimite warrior, killed Maaseiah the king's son, Azrikam the officer in charge of the palace, and Elkanah, second to the king. 8The men of Israel took captive from their fellow Israelites in Judah two hundred thousand wives, sons and daughters. They also took a great deal of plunder, which they carried back to Samaria.

9But a prophet of the LORD named Oded was there, and he went out to meet the army when it returned to Samaria. He said to them, 'Because the LORD, the God of your ancestors, was angry with Judah, he gave them into your hand. But you have slaughtered them in a rage that reaches to heaven. 10And now you intend to make the men and women of Judah and Jerusalem your slaves. But aren't you also guilty of sins against the LORD your God? 11Now listen to me! Send back your fellow Israelites that you have taken as prisoners, for the LORD's fierce anger rests on you.'

12Then some of the leaders in Ephraim—Azariah son of Jehohanan, Berekiah son of Meshillemoth, Jehizkiah son of Shallum, and Amasa son of Hadlai—confronted those who were arriving from the war. 13'You must not bring those prisoners here,' they said, 'or we will be guilty before the LORD. Do you intend to add to our sin and guilt? For our guilt is already great, and his fierce anger rests on Israel.'

14So the soldiers gave up the prisoners and plunder in the presence of the officials and all the assembly. 15The men designated by name took the prisoners, and from the plunder they clothed all who were naked. They provided them with clothes and sandals, food and drink, and healing balm. All those who were weak they put on donkeys. So they took them back to their fellow Israelites at Jericho, the City of Palms, and returned to Samaria.

16At that time King Ahaz sent to the kings[a] of Assyria for help. 17The Edomites had again come and attacked Judah and carried away prisoners, 18while the Philistines had raided towns in the foothills and in the Negev of Judah. They captured and occupied Beth Shemesh, Aijalon and Gederoth, as well as Soko, Timnah and Gimzo, with their surrounding villages. 19The LORD had humbled Judah because of Ahaz king of Israel,[b] for he had promoted wickedness in Judah and had been most

---

[a] 16 Most Hebrew manuscripts; one Hebrew manuscript, Septuagint and Vulgate (see also 2 Kings 16:7) *king*
[b] 19 That is, Judah, as frequently in 2 Chronicles

unfaithful to the LORD. [20]Tiglath-Pileser[a] king of Assyria came to him, but gave him trouble instead of help. [21]Ahaz took some of the things from the temple of the LORD and from the royal palace and from the officials and presented them to the king of Assyria, but that did not help him.

[22]In his time of trouble King Ahaz became even more unfaithful to the LORD. [23]He offered sacrifices to the gods of Damascus, who had defeated him; for he thought, 'Since the gods of the kings of Aram have helped them, I will sacrifice to them so that they will help me.' But they were his downfall and the downfall of all Israel.

[24]Ahaz gathered together the furnishings from the temple of God and cut them in pieces. He shut the doors of the LORD's temple and set up altars at every street corner in Jerusalem. [25]In every town in Judah he built high places to burn sacrifices to other gods and aroused the anger of the LORD, the God of his ancestors.

[26]The other events of his reign and all his ways, from beginning to end, are written in the book of the kings of Judah and Israel. [27]Ahaz rested with his ancestors and was buried in the city of Jerusalem, but he was not placed in the tombs of the kings of Israel. And Hezekiah his son succeeded him as king.

Hezekiah purifies the temple

29 Hezekiah was twenty-five years old when he became king, and he reigned in Jerusalem for twenty-nine years. His mother's name was Abijah daughter of Zechariah. [2]He did what was right in the eyes of the LORD, just as his father David had done.

[3]In the first month of the first year of his reign, he opened the doors of the temple of the LORD and repaired them. [4]He brought in the priests and the Levites, assembled them in the square on the east side [5]and said, 'Listen to me, Levites! Consecrate yourselves now and consecrate the temple of the LORD, the God of your ancestors. Remove all defilement from the sanctuary. [6]Our ancestors were unfaithful; they did evil in the eyes of the LORD our God and forsook him. They turned their faces away from the LORD's dwelling-place and turned their backs on him. [7]They also shut the doors of the portico and put out the lamps. They did not burn incense or present any burnt offerings at the sanctuary to the God of Israel. [8]Therefore, the anger of the LORD has fallen on Judah and Jerusalem; he has made them an object of dread and horror and scorn, as you can see with your own eyes. [9]This is why our ancestors have fallen by the sword and why our sons and daughters and our wives are in captivity. [10]Now I intend to make a covenant with the LORD, the God of Israel, so that his fierce anger will turn away from us. [11]My sons, do not be negligent now, for the LORD has chosen you to stand before him and serve him, to minister before him and to burn incense.'

[12]Then these Levites set to work:
from the Kohathites,
Mahath son of Amasai and Joel son of Azariah;
from the Merarites,
Kish son of Abdi and Azariah son of Jehallelel;
from the Gershonites,
Joah son of Zimmah and Eden son of Joah;
[13]from the descendants of Elizaphan,
Shimri and Jeiel;
from the descendants of Asaph,
Zechariah and Mattaniah;
[14]from the descendants of Heman,
Jehiel and Shimei;
from the descendants of Jeduthun,
Shemaiah and Uzziel.

[15]When they had assembled their fellow Levites and consecrated themselves, they went in to purify the temple of the LORD, as the king had ordered, following the word of the LORD. [16]The priests went into the sanctuary of the LORD to purify it. They brought out to the courtyard of the LORD's temple everything unclean that they found in the temple of the LORD. The Levites took it and carried it out to the Kidron Valley. [17]They began the consecration on the first day of the first month, and by the eighth day of the month they reached the portico of the

---

[a] 20 Hebrew *Tilgath-Pilneser*, a variant of *Tiglath-Pileser*

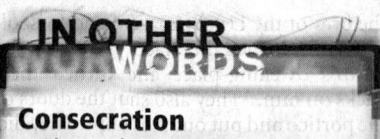

IN OTHER WORDS

Consecration
2 Chronicles 29:17
Consecration is the act of dedicating something or someone for God's use. The temple and its sacred objects had been used for Baal worship by Athaliah, the mother of King Ahaziah of Judah. They needed to be cleansed and then rededicated to the worship of God.

LORD. For eight more days they consecrated the temple of the LORD itself, finishing on the sixteenth day of the first month.

18Then they went in to King Hezekiah and reported: 'We have purified the entire temple of the LORD, the altar of burnt offering with all its utensils, and the table for setting out the consecrated bread, with all its articles. 19We have prepared and consecrated all the articles that King Ahaz removed in his unfaithfulness while he was king. They are now in front of the LORD's altar.'

20Early the next morning King Hezekiah gathered the city officials together and went up to the temple of the LORD. 21They brought seven bulls, seven rams, seven male lambs and seven male goats as a sin offering*a* for the kingdom, for the sanctuary and for Judah. The king commanded the priests, the descendants of Aaron, to offer these on the altar of the LORD. 22So they slaughtered the bulls, and the priests took the blood and splashed it against the altar; next they slaughtered the rams and splashed their blood against the altar; then they slaughtered the lambs and splashed their blood against the altar. 23The goats for the sin offering were brought before the king and the assembly, and they laid their hands on them. 24The priests then slaughtered the goats and presented their blood on the altar for a sin offering to atone for all Israel, because the king had ordered the burnt offering and the sin offering for all Israel.

25He stationed the Levites in the temple of the LORD with cymbals, harps and lyres in the way prescribed by David and Gad the king's seer and Nathan the prophet; this was commanded by the LORD through his prophets. 26So the Levites stood ready with David's instruments, and the priests with their trumpets.

27Hezekiah gave the order to sacrifice the burnt offering on the altar. As the offering began, singing to the LORD began also, accompanied by trumpets and the instruments of David king of Israel. 28The whole assembly bowed in worship, while the musicians played and the trumpets sounded. All this continued until the sacrifice of the burnt offering was completed.

29When the offerings were finished, the king and everyone present with him knelt down and worshipped. 30King Hezekiah and his officials ordered the Levites to praise the LORD with the words of David and of Asaph the seer. So they sang praises with gladness and bowed down and worshipped.

31Then Hezekiah said, 'You have now dedicated yourselves to the LORD. Come and bring sacrifices and thank-offerings to the temple of the LORD.' So the assembly brought sacrifices and thank-offerings, and all whose hearts were willing brought burnt offerings.

32The number of burnt offerings the assembly brought was seventy bulls, a hundred rams and two hundred male lambs—all of them for burnt offerings to the LORD. 33The animals consecrated as sacrifices amounted to six hundred bulls and three thousand sheep and goats. 34The priests, however, were too few to skin all the burnt offerings; so their relatives the Levites helped them until the task was finished and until other priests had been consecrated, for the Levites had been more conscientious in consecrating themselves than the priests had been. 35There were burnt offerings in abundance, together with the fat of the fellowship offerings and the drink offerings that accompanied the burnt offerings.

---

a 21 Or *purification* offering; also in verses 23 and 24

So the service of the temple of the LORD was re-established. 36Hezekiah and all the people rejoiced at what God had brought about for his people, because it was done so quickly.

Hezekiah celebrates the Passover

30 Hezekiah sent word to all Israel and Judah and also wrote letters to Ephraim and Manasseh, inviting them to come to the temple of the LORD in Jerusalem and celebrate the Passover to the LORD, the God of Israel. 2The king and his officials and the whole assembly in Jerusalem decided to celebrate the Passover in the second month. 3They had not been able to celebrate it at the usual time because not enough priests had consecrated themselves and the people had not assembled in Jerusalem. 4The plan seemed right both to the king and to the whole assembly. 5They decided to send a proclamation throughout Israel, from Beersheba to Dan, calling the people to come to Jerusalem and celebrate the Passover to the LORD, the God of Israel. It had not been celebrated in large numbers according to what was written.

6At the king's command, couriers went throughout Israel and Judah with letters from the king and from his officials, which read:

'People of Israel, return to the LORD, the God of Abraham, Isaac and Israel, that he may return to you who are left, who have escaped from the hand of the kings of Assyria. 7Do not be like your parents and your fellow Israelites, who were unfaithful to the LORD, the God of their ancestors, so that he made them an object of horror, as you see. 8Do not be stiff-necked, as your parents were; submit to the LORD. Come to his sanctuary, which he has consecrated for ever. Serve the LORD your God, so that his fierce anger will turn away from you. 9If you return to the LORD, then your fellow Israelites and your children will be shown compassion by their captors and will return to this land, for the LORD your God is gracious and compassionate. He will not turn his face from you if you return to him.'

10The couriers went from town to town in Ephraim and Manasseh, as far as Zebulun, but people scorned and ridiculed them. 11Nevertheless, some from Asher, Manasseh and Zebulun humbled themselves and went to Jerusalem. 12Also in Judah the hand of God was on the people to give them unity of mind to carry out what the king and his officials had ordered, following the word of the LORD.

13A very large crowd of people assembled in Jerusalem to celebrate the Festival of Unleavened Bread in the second month. 14They removed the altars in Jerusalem and cleared away the incense altars and threw them into the Kidron Valley.

15They slaughtered the Passover lamb on the fourteenth day of the second month. The priests and the Levites were ashamed and consecrated themselves and brought burnt offerings to the temple of the LORD. 16Then they took up their usual positions as prescribed in the Law of Moses the man of God. The priests splashed against the altar the blood handed to them by the Levites. 17Since many in the crowd had not consecrated themselves, the Levites had to kill the Passover lambs for all those who were not ceremonially clean and could not consecrate ⌊their lambs⌋ to the LORD. 18Although most of the many people who came from Ephraim, Manasseh, Issachar and Zebulun had not purified themselves, yet they ate the Passover, contrary to what was written. But Hezekiah prayed for them, saying, 'May the LORD, who is good, pardon everyone 19who sets their heart on seeking God—the LORD, the God of their ancestors—even if they are not clean according to the rules of the sanctuary.' 20And the LORD heard Hezekiah and healed the people.

21The Israelites who were present in Jerusalem celebrated the Festival of Unleavened Bread for seven days with great rejoicing, while the Levites and priests praised the LORD every day with resounding instruments dedicated to the LORD.[a]

22 Hezekiah spoke encouragingly to all the Levites, who showed good understanding of the service of the LORD. For the seven days they ate their assigned portion and offered fellowship offerings and praised[b] the LORD, the God of their ancestors.

23 The whole assembly then agreed to celebrate the festival seven more days; so for another seven days they celebrated joyfully. 24 Hezekiah king of Judah provided a thousand bulls and seven thousand sheep and goats for the assembly, and the officials provided them with a thousand bulls and ten thousand sheep and goats. A great number of priests consecrated themselves. 25 The entire assembly of Judah rejoiced, along with the priests and Levites and all who had assembled from Israel, including the foreigners who had come from Israel and also those who resided in Judah. 26 There was great joy in Jerusalem, for since the days of Solomon son of David king of Israel there had been nothing like this in Jerusalem. 27 The priests and the Levites stood to bless the people, and God heard them, for their prayer reached heaven, his holy dwelling-place.

31

When all this had ended, the Israelites who were there went out to the towns of Judah, smashed the sacred stones and cut down the Asherah poles. They destroyed the high places and the altars throughout Judah and Benjamin and in Ephraim and Manasseh. After they had destroyed all of them, the Israelites returned to their own towns and to their own property.

Contributions for worship

2 Hezekiah assigned the priests and Levites to divisions—each of them according to their duties as priests or Levites—to offer burnt offerings and fellowship offerings, to minister, to give thanks and to sing praises at the gates of the LORD's dwelling. 3 The king contributed from his own possessions for the morning and evening burnt offerings and for the burnt offerings on the Sabbaths, at the New Moons and at the appointed festivals as written in the Law of the LORD. 4 He ordered the people living in Jerusalem to give the portion due to the priests and Levites so that they could devote themselves to the Law of the LORD. 5 As soon as the order went out, the Israelites generously gave the firstfruits of their grain, new wine, oil and honey and all that the fields produced. They brought a great amount, a tithe of everything. 6 The people of Israel and Judah who lived in the towns of Judah also brought a tithe of their herds and flocks and a tithe of the holy things dedicated to the LORD their God, and they piled them in heaps. 7 They began doing this in the third month and finished in the seventh month. 8 When Hezekiah and his officials came and saw the heaps, they praised the LORD and blessed his people Israel.

9 Hezekiah asked the priests and Levites about the heaps; 10 and Azariah the chief priest, from the family of Zadok, answered, 'Since the people began to bring their contributions to the temple of the LORD, we have had enough to eat and plenty to spare, because the LORD has blessed his people, and this great amount is left over.'

11 Hezekiah gave orders to prepare storerooms in the temple of the LORD, and this was done. 12 Then they faithfully brought in

IN OTHER WORDS

Firstfruits
2 Chronicles 31:5
The firstborn of the animals and the first crops and vegetables to be harvested from the fields were known as the firstfruits, and the Israelites thought of these as belonging to God. They were offered to God on the Feast of Firstfruits, which was part of the Pentecost celebrations.

---

[a] 21 Or *priests sang to the LORD every day, accompanied by the LORD's instruments of praise.* [b] 22 Or *and confessed their sins to*

the contributions, tithes and dedicated gifts. Konaniah, a Levite, was the overseer in charge of these things, and his brother Shimei was next in rank. 13Jehiel, Azaziah, Nahath, Asahel, Jerimoth, Jozabad, Eliel, Ismakiah, Mahath and Benaiah were assistants of Konaniah and Shimei his brother. All these served by appointment of King Hezekiah and Azariah the official in charge of the temple of God.

14Kore son of Imnah the Levite, keeper of the East Gate, was in charge of the freewill offerings given to God, distributing the contributions made to the LORD and also the consecrated gifts. 15Eden, Miniamin, Jeshua, Shemaiah, Amariah and Shekaniah assisted him faithfully in the towns of the priests, distributing to their fellow priests according to their divisions, old and young alike.

16In addition, they distributed to the males three years old or more whose names were in the genealogical records—all who would enter the temple of the LORD to perform the daily duties of their various tasks, according to their responsibilities and their divisions. 17And they distributed to the priests enrolled by their families in the genealogical records and likewise to the Levites twenty years old or more, according to their responsibilities and their divisions. 18They included all the little ones, the wives, and the sons and daughters of the whole community listed in these genealogical records. For they were faithful in consecrating themselves.

19As for the priests, the descendants of Aaron, who lived on the farm lands around their towns or in any other towns, men were designated by name to distribute portions to every male among them and to all who were recorded in the genealogies of the Levites.

20This is what Hezekiah did throughout Judah, doing what was good and right and faithful before the LORD his God. 21In everything that he undertook in the service of God's temple and in obedience to the law and the commands, he sought his God and worked wholeheartedly. And so he prospered.

Sennacherib threatens Jerusalem

32 After all that Hezekiah had so faithfully done, Sennacherib king of Assyria came and invaded Judah. He laid siege to the fortified cities, thinking to conquer them for himself. 2When Hezekiah saw that Sennacherib had come and that he intended to make war on Jerusalem, 3he consulted with his officials and military staff about blocking off the water from the springs outside the city, and they helped him. 4A large force assembled and blocked all the springs and the stream that flowed through the land. 'Why should the kings^a of Assyria come and find plenty of water?' they said. 5Then he worked hard repairing all the broken sections of the wall and building towers on it. He built another wall outside that one and reinforced the terraces^b of the City of David. He also made large numbers of weapons and shields.

6He appointed military officers over the people and assembled them before him in the square at the city gate and encouraged them with these words: 7'Be strong and courageous. Do not be afraid or discouraged because of the king of Assyria and the vast army with him, for there is a greater power with us than with him. 8With him is only the arm of flesh, but with us is the LORD our God to help us and to fight our battles.' And the people gained confidence from what Hezekiah the king of Judah said.

9Later, when Sennacherib king of Assyria and all his forces were laying siege to Lachish, he sent his officers to Jerusalem with this message for Hezekiah king of Judah and for all the people of Judah who were there:

> 10'This is what Sennacherib king of Assyria says: on what are you basing your confidence, that you remain in Jerusalem under siege? 11When Hezekiah says, "The LORD our God will save us from the hand of the king of Assyria," he is misleading you, to let you die of hunger and thirst. 12Did not Hezekiah himself remove this god's high places and

---

^{a}4 Hebrew; Septuagint and Syriac *king* ^{b}5 Or *the Millo*

> **IN OTHER WORDS**
>
> **Hebrew**
> **2 Chronicles 32:18**
> 'The Hebrews' is the name of the Jewish people in the Old Testament. They are also known as the Israelites. Hebrew is the language that was spoken by the Jews during the time that the Old Testament was written.

altars, saying to Judah and Jerusalem, "You must worship before one altar and burn sacrifices on it"?

13 'Do you not know what I and my predecessors have done to all the peoples of the other lands? Were the gods of those nations ever able to deliver their land from my hand? 14 Who of all the gods of these nations that my predecessors destroyed has been able to save his people from me? How then can your god deliver you from my hand? 15 Now do not let Hezekiah deceive you and mislead you like this. Do not believe him, for no god of any nation or kingdom has been able to deliver his people from my hand or the hand of my predecessors. How much less will your god deliver you from my hand!'

16 Sennacherib's officers spoke further against the LORD God and against his servant Hezekiah. 17 The king also wrote letters ridiculing the LORD, the God of Israel, and saying this against him: 'Just as the gods of the peoples of the other lands did not rescue their people from my hand, so the god of Hezekiah will not rescue his people from my hand.' 18 Then they called out in Hebrew to the people of Jerusalem who were on the wall, to terrify them and make them afraid in order to capture the city. 19 They spoke about the God of Jerusalem as they did about the gods of the other peoples of the world—the work of human hands.

20 King Hezekiah and the prophet Isaiah son of Amoz cried out in prayer to heaven about this. 21 And the LORD sent an angel, who annihilated all the fighting men and the commanders and officers in the camp of the Assyrian king. So he withdrew to his own land in disgrace. And when he went into the temple of his god, some of his sons cut him down with the sword.

22 So the LORD saved Hezekiah and the people of Jerusalem from the hand of Sennacherib king of Assyria and from the hand of all others. He took care of them[a] on every side. 23 Many brought offerings to Jerusalem for the LORD and valuable gifts for Hezekiah king of Judah. From then on he was highly regarded by all the nations.

Hezekiah's pride, success and death

24 In those days Hezekiah became ill and was at the point of death. He prayed to the LORD, who answered him and gave him a miraculous sign. 25 But Hezekiah's heart was proud and he did not respond to the kindness shown him; therefore the LORD's wrath was on him and on Judah and Jerusalem. 26 Then Hezekiah repented of the pride of his heart, as did the people of Jerusalem; therefore the LORD's wrath did not come on them during the days of Hezekiah.

27 Hezekiah had very great wealth and honour, and he made treasuries for his silver and gold and for his precious stones, spices, shields and all kinds of valuables. 28 He also made buildings to store the harvest of grain, new wine and olive oil; and he made stalls for various kinds of cattle, and pens for the flocks. 29 He built villages and acquired great numbers of flocks and herds, for God had given him very great riches.

30 It was Hezekiah who blocked the upper outlet of the Gihon spring and channelled the water down to the west side of the City of David. He succeeded in everything he undertook. 31 But when envoys were sent

---

[a] 22 Hebrew; Septuagint and Vulgate *He gave them rest*

by the rulers of Babylon to ask him about the miraculous sign that had occurred in the land, God left him to test him and to know everything that was in his heart.

32The other events of Hezekiah's reign and his acts of devotion are written in the vision of the prophet Isaiah son of Amoz in the book of the kings of Judah and Israel. 33Hezekiah rested with his ancestors and was buried on the hill where the tombs of David's descendants are. All Judah and the people of Jerusalem honoured him when he died. And Manasseh his son succeeded him as king.

Manasseh king of Judah

33 Manasseh was twelve years old when he became king, and he reigned in Jerusalem for fifty-five years. 2He did evil in the eyes of the LORD, following the detestable practices of the nations the LORD had driven out before the Israelites. 3He rebuilt the high places his father Hezekiah had demolished; he also erected altars to the Baals and made Asherah poles. He bowed down to all the starry hosts and worshipped them. 4He built altars in the temple of the LORD, of which the LORD had said, 'My Name will remain in Jerusalem for ever.' 5In both courts of the temple of the LORD, he built altars to all the starry hosts. 6He sacrificed his children in the fire in the Valley of Ben Hinnom, practised divination and witchcraft, sought omens, and consulted mediums and spiritists. He did much evil in the eyes of the LORD, arousing his anger.

7He took the image he had made and put it in God's temple, of which God had said to David and to his son Solomon, 'In this temple and in Jerusalem, which I have chosen out of all the tribes of Israel, I will put my Name for ever. 8I will not again make the feet of the Israelites leave the land I assigned to your ancestors, if only they will be careful to do everything that I commanded them concerning all the laws, decrees and regulations given through Moses.' 9But Manasseh led Judah and the people of Jerusalem astray, so that they did more evil than the nations the LORD had destroyed before the Israelites.

10The LORD spoke to Manasseh and his people, but they paid no attention. 11So the LORD brought against them the army commanders of the king of Assyria, who took Manasseh prisoner, put a hook in his nose, bound him with bronze shackles and took him to Babylon. 12In his distress he sought the favour of the LORD his God and humbled himself greatly before the God of his ancestors. 13And when he prayed to him, the LORD was moved by his entreaty and listened to his plea; so he brought him back to Jerusalem and to his kingdom. Then Manasseh knew that the LORD is God.

14Afterwards he rebuilt the outer wall of the City of David, west of the Gihon spring in the valley, as far as the entrance of the Fish Gate and encircling the hill of Ophel; he also made it much higher. He stationed military commanders in all the fortified cities in Judah.

15He got rid of the foreign gods and removed the image from the temple of the LORD, as well as all the altars he had built on the temple hill and in Jerusalem; and he threw them out of the city. 16Then he restored the altar of the LORD and sacrificed fellowship offerings and thank-offerings on it, and told Judah to serve the LORD, the God of Israel. 17The people, however, continued to sacrifice at the high places, but only to the LORD their God.

18The other events of Manasseh's reign, including his prayer to his God and the words the seers spoke to him in the name of the LORD, the God of Israel, are written in the annals of the kings of Israel.[a] 19His prayer and how God was moved by his entreaty, as well as all his sins and unfaithfulness, and the sites where he built high places and set up Asherah poles and idols before he humbled himself—all these are written in the records of the seers.[b] 20Manasseh rested with his ancestors and was buried in his palace. And Amon his son succeeded him as king.

---

[a] 18 That is, Judah, as frequently in 2 Chronicles   [b] 19 One Hebrew manuscript and Septuagint; most Hebrew manuscripts *of Hozai*

Amon king of Judah

21 Amon was twenty-two years old when he became king, and he reigned in Jerusalem for two years. 22 He did evil in the eyes of the LORD, as his father Manasseh had done. Amon worshipped and offered sacrifices to all the idols Manasseh had made. 23 But unlike his father Manasseh, he did not humble himself before the LORD; Amon increased his guilt.

24 Amon's officials conspired against him and assassinated him in his palace. 25 Then the people of the land killed all who had plotted against King Amon, and they made Josiah his son king in his place.

Josiah's reforms

34 Josiah was eight years old when he became king, and he reigned in Jerusalem for thirty-one years. 2 He did what was right in the eyes of the LORD and followed the ways of his father David, not turning aside to the right or to the left.

3 In the eighth year of his reign, while he was still young, he began to seek the God of his father David. In his twelfth year he began to purge Judah and Jerusalem of high places, Asherah poles and idols. 4 Under his direction the altars of the Baals were torn down; he cut to pieces the incense altars that were above them, and smashed the Asherah poles and the idols. These he broke to pieces and scattered over the graves of those who had sacrificed to them. 5 He burned the bones of the priests on their altars, and so he purged Judah and Jerusalem. 6 In the towns of Manasseh, Ephraim and Simeon, as far as Naphtali, and in the ruins around them, 7 he tore down the altars and the Asherah poles and crushed the idols to powder and cut to pieces all the incense altars throughout Israel. Then he went back to Jerusalem.

8 In the eighteenth year of Josiah's reign, to purify the land and the temple, he sent Shaphan son of Azaliah and Maaseiah the ruler of the city, with Joah son of Joahaz, the recorder, to repair the temple of the LORD his God.

9 They went to Hilkiah the high priest and gave him the money that had been brought into the temple of God, which the Levites who were the gatekeepers had collected from the people of Manasseh, Ephraim and the entire remnant of Israel and from all the people of Judah and Benjamin and the inhabitants of Jerusalem. 10 Then they entrusted it to the men appointed to supervise the work on the LORD's temple. These men paid the workers who repaired and restored the temple. 11 They also gave money to the carpenters and builders to purchase dressed stone, and timber for joists and beams for the buildings that the kings of Judah had allowed to fall into ruin.

12 The workers did their work faithfully. Over them to direct them were Jahath and Obadiah, Levites descended from Merari, and Zechariah and Meshullam, descended from Kohath. The Levites—all who were skilled in playing musical instruments— 13 had charge of the labourers and supervised all the workers from job to job. Some of the Levites were secretaries, scribes and gatekeepers.

The Book of the Law found

14 While they were bringing out the money that had been taken into the temple of the LORD, Hilkiah the priest found the Book of the Law of the LORD that had been given through Moses. 15 Hilkiah said to Shaphan the secretary, 'I have found the Book of the Law in the temple of the LORD.' He gave it to Shaphan.

16 Then Shaphan took the book to the king and reported to him: 'Your officials are doing everything that has been committed to them. 17 They have paid out the money that was in the temple of the LORD and have entrusted it to the supervisors and workers.' 18 Then Shaphan the secretary informed the king, 'Hilkiah the priest has given me a book.' And Shaphan read from it in the presence of the king.

19 When the king heard the words of the Law, he tore his robes. 20 He gave these orders to Hilkiah, Ahikam son of Shaphan, Abdon son of Micah,[a] Shaphan the secretary and Asaiah the king's attendant: 21 'Go and enquire of the LORD for me and for the remnant in Israel and Judah about what is

---

[a] 20 Also called *Akbor son of Micaiah*

Sign of the times

Tearing robes
2 Chronicles 34:19

In ancient times, people had very visible ways to show their grief or repentance. They would tear their robes, then put on sackcloth and put dust or ashes on their head. This would often be accompanied by loud weeping and wailing.

written in this book that has been found. Great is the LORD's anger that is poured out on us because those who have gone before us have not kept the word of the LORD; they have not acted in accordance with all that is written in this book.'

22 Hilkiah and those the king had sent with him[a] went to speak to the prophet Huldah, who was the wife of Shallum son of Tokhath,[b] the son of Hasrah,[c] keeper of the wardrobe. She lived in Jerusalem, in the New Quarter.

23 She said to them, 'This is what the LORD, the God of Israel, says: tell the man who sent you to me, 24 "This is what the LORD says: I am going to bring disaster on this place and its people—all the curses written in the book that has been read in the presence of the king of Judah. 25 Because they have forsaken me and burned incense to other gods and aroused my anger by all that their hands have made,[d] my anger will be poured out on this place and will not be quenched." 26 Tell the king of Judah, who sent you to enquire of the LORD, "This is what the LORD, the God of Israel, says concerning the words you heard: 27 because your heart was responsive and you humbled yourself before God when you heard what he spoke against this place and its people, and because you humbled yourself before me and tore your robes and wept in my presence, I have heard you, declares the LORD. 28 Now I will gather you to your ancestors, and you will be buried in peace. Your eyes will not see all the disaster I am going to bring on this place and on those who live here."'

So they took her answer back to the king.

29 Then the king called together all the elders of Judah and Jerusalem. 30 He went up to the temple of the LORD with the people of Judah, the inhabitants of Jerusalem, the priests and the Levites—all the people from the least to the greatest. He read in their hearing all the words of the Book of the Covenant, which had been found in the temple of the LORD. 31 The king stood by his pillar and renewed the covenant in the presence of the LORD—to follow the LORD and keep his commands, statutes and decrees with all his heart and all his soul, and to obey the words of the covenant written in this book.

32 Then he made everyone in Jerusalem and Benjamin pledge themselves to it; the people of Jerusalem did this in accordance with the covenant of God, the God of their ancestors.

33 Josiah removed all the detestable idols from all the territory belonging to the Israelites, and he made all who were present in Israel serve the LORD their God. As long as he lived, they did not fail to follow the LORD, the God of their ancestors.

Josiah celebrates the Passover

35 Josiah celebrated the Passover to the LORD in Jerusalem, and the Passover lamb was slaughtered on the fourteenth day of the first month. 2 He appointed the priests to their duties and encouraged them in the service of the LORD's temple. 3 He said to the Levites, who instructed all Israel and who had been consecrated to the LORD: 'Put the sacred ark in the temple that Solomon son of David king of Israel built. It is not to be carried about on your shoulders. Now serve the LORD your God and his people Israel. 4 Prepare yourselves by families in your divisions, according to the instructions

---

[a] 22 One Hebrew manuscript, Vulgate and Syriac; most Hebrew manuscripts do not have *had sent with him*. [b] 22 Also called *Tikvah* [c] 22 Also called *Harhas* [d] 25 Or *by everything they have done*

written by David king of Israel and by his son Solomon.

⁵'Stand in the holy place with a group of Levites for each sub-division of the families of your fellow Israelites, the lay people. ⁶Slaughter the Passover lambs, consecrate yourselves and prepare the lambs for your fellow Israelites, doing what the LORD commanded through Moses.'

⁷Josiah provided for all the lay people who were there a total of thirty thousand lambs and goats for the Passover offerings, and also three thousand cattle—all from the king's own possessions.

⁸His officials also contributed voluntarily to the people and the priests and Levites. Hilkiah, Zechariah and Jehiel, the officials in charge of God's temple, gave the priests two thousand six hundred Passover offerings and three hundred cattle. ⁹Also Konaniah along with Shemaiah and Nethanel, his brothers, and Hashabiah, Jeiel and Jozabad, the leaders of the Levites, provided five thousand Passover offerings and five hundred head of cattle for the Levites.

¹⁰The service was arranged and the priests stood in their places with the Levites in their divisions as the king had ordered. ¹¹The Passover lambs were slaughtered, and the priests splashed against the altar the blood handed to them, while the Levites skinned the animals. ¹²They set aside the burnt offerings to give them to the subdivisions of the families of the people to offer to the LORD, as it is written in the Book of Moses. They did the same with the cattle. ¹³They roasted the Passover animals over the fire as prescribed, and boiled the holy offerings in pots, cauldrons and pans and served them quickly to all the people. ¹⁴After this, they made preparations for themselves and for the priests, because the priests, the descendants of Aaron, were sacrificing the burnt offerings and the fat portions until nightfall. So the Levites made preparations for themselves and for the Aaronic priests.

¹⁵The musicians, the descendants of Asaph, were in the places prescribed by David, Asaph, Heman and Jeduthun the king's seer. The gatekeepers at each gate did not need to leave their posts, because their fellow Levites made the preparations for them.

¹⁶So at that time the entire service of the LORD was carried out for the celebration of the Passover and the offering of burnt offerings on the altar of the LORD, as King Josiah had ordered. ¹⁷The Israelites who were present celebrated the Passover at that time and observed the Festival of Unleavened Bread for seven days. ¹⁸The Passover had not been observed like this in Israel since the days of the prophet Samuel; and none of the kings of Israel had ever celebrated such a Passover as did Josiah, with the priests, the Levites and all Judah and Israel who were there with the people of Jerusalem. ¹⁹This Passover was celebrated in the eighteenth year of Josiah's reign.

The death of Josiah

²⁰After all this, when Josiah had set the temple in order, Necho king of Egypt went up to fight at Carchemish on the Euphrates, and Josiah marched out to meet him in battle. ²¹But Necho sent messengers to him saying, 'What quarrel is there, king of Judah, between you and me? It is not you I am attacking at this time, but the house with which I am at war. God has told me to hurry; so stop opposing God, who is with me, or he will destroy you.'

²²Josiah, however, would not turn away from him, but disguised himself to engage him in battle. He would not listen to what Necho had said at God's command but went to fight him on the plain of Megiddo.

²³Archers shot King Josiah, and he told his officers, 'Take me away; I am badly wounded.' ²⁴So they took him out of his chariot, put him in his other chariot and brought him to Jerusalem, where he died. He was buried in the tombs of his ancestors, and all Judah and Jerusalem mourned for him.

²⁵Jeremiah composed laments for Josiah, and to this day all the male and female singers commemorate Josiah in the laments. These became a tradition in Israel and are written in the Laments.

²⁶The other events of Josiah's reign and his acts of devotion in accordance with what is written in the Law of the LORD— ²⁷all the

events, from beginning to end, are written in the book of the kings of Israel and Judah.

36 ¹And the people of the land took Jehoahaz son of Josiah and made him king in Jerusalem in place of his father.

Jehoahaz king of Judah

²Jehoahaz[a] was twenty-three years old when he became king, and he reigned in Jerusalem for three months. ³The king of Egypt dethroned him in Jerusalem and imposed on Judah a levy of a hundred talents[b] of silver and a talent[c] of gold. ⁴The king of Egypt made Eliakim, a brother of Jehoahaz, king over Judah and Jerusalem and changed Eliakim's name to Jehoiakim. But Necho took Eliakim's brother Jehoahaz and carried him off to Egypt.

Jehoiakim king of Judah

⁵Jehoiakim was twenty-five years old when he became king, and he reigned in Jerusalem for eleven years. He did evil in the eyes of the LORD his God. ⁶Nebuchadnezzar king of Babylon attacked him and bound him with bronze shackles to take him to Babylon. ⁷Nebuchadnezzar also took to Babylon articles from the temple of the LORD and put them in his temple[d] there.

⁸The other events of Jehoiakim's reign, the detestable things he did and all that was found against him, are written in the book of the kings of Israel and Judah. And Jehoiachin his son succeeded him as king.

Jehoiachin king of Judah

⁹Jehoiachin was eighteen[e] years old when he became king, and he reigned in Jerusalem for three months and ten days. He did evil in the eyes of the LORD. ¹⁰In the spring, King Nebuchadnezzar sent for him and brought him to Babylon, together with articles of value from the temple of the LORD, and he made Jehoiachin's uncle,[f] Zedekiah, king over Judah and Jerusalem.

Zedekiah king of Judah

¹¹Zedekiah was twenty-one years old when he became king, and he reigned in Jerusalem for eleven years. ¹²He did evil in the eyes of the LORD his God and did not humble himself before Jeremiah the prophet, who spoke the word of the LORD. ¹³He also rebelled against King Nebuchadnezzar, who had made him take an oath in God's name. He became stiff-necked and hardened his heart and would not turn to the LORD, the God of Israel. ¹⁴Furthermore, all the leaders of the priests and the people became more and more unfaithful, following all the detestable practices of the nations and defiling the temple of the LORD, which he had consecrated in Jerusalem.

The fall of Jerusalem

¹⁵The LORD, the God of their ancestors, sent word to them through his messengers again and again, because he had pity on his people and on his dwelling-place. ¹⁶But they mocked God's messengers, despised his words and scoffed at his prophets until the wrath of the LORD was aroused against his people and there was no remedy. ¹⁷He brought up against them the king of the Babylonians,[g] who killed their young men with the sword in the sanctuary, and spared neither young man nor young woman, the

---

> **IN OTHER WORDS**
>
> **Sabbath rest**
> **2 Chronicles 36:21**
>
> God created the world in six days and rested on the seventh day, setting the example of how people were to live. The Sabbath is the practice of having one day a week as a day of rest and worship and working for the other six days. In Leviticus 25:2, God tells the people that, when they enter the Promised Land, the land must have a sabbath rest too. They are to plant crops for six years and in the seventh year let the land lie fallow, trusting God to provide for them.

---

[a] 2 Hebrew *Joahaz*, a variant of *Jehoahaz*; also in verse 4   [b] 3 That is, about 3.4 metric tons   [c] 3 That is, about 34 kilograms   [d] 7 Or *palace*   [e] 9 One Hebrew manuscript, some Septuagint manuscripts and Syriac (see also 2 Kings 24:8); most Hebrew manuscripts *eight*   [f] 10 Hebrew *brother*, that is, relative (see 2 Kings 24:17)   [g] 17 Or *Chaldeans*

elderly or the aged. God gave them all into the hands of Nebuchadnezzar. ⁱ⁸He carried to Babylon all the articles from the temple of God, both large and small, and the treasures of the LORD's temple and the treasures of the king and his officials. ¹⁹They set fire to God's temple and broke down the wall of Jerusalem; they burned all the palaces and destroyed everything of value there.

²⁰He carried into exile to Babylon the remnant who escaped from the sword, and they became servants to him and his successors until the kingdom of Persia came to power. ²¹The land enjoyed its sabbath rests; all the time of its desolation it rested, until the seventy years were completed in fulfilment of the word of the LORD spoken by Jeremiah.

²²In the first year of Cyrus king of Persia, in order to fulfil the word of the LORD spoken by Jeremiah, the LORD moved the heart of Cyrus king of Persia to make a proclamation throughout his realm and also to put it in writing:

²³'This is what Cyrus king of Persia says:
> '"The LORD, the God of heaven, has given me all the kingdoms of the earth and he has appointed me to build a temple for him at Jerusalem in Judah. Any of his people among you—may the LORD their God be with them, and let them go up."'

Ezra

INTRODUCTION

EZRA

Author: Ezra the priest

When: The exiles returned to Jerusalem in two stages. The first people went home around 525 BC. Ezra arrived around eighty years later with another wave of exiles.

Where: Jerusalem.

Did you know? The first three verses of Ezra are the same as the last three verses of 2 Chronicles, possibly showing that they belonged together in the original version.

Main theme: Ezra begins by telling how the exiles returned to Jerusalem and rebuilt the temple. His mission when he goes home some time later is to encourage the people to rebuild their relationship with God. He reads the Book of the Law to them which sparks off a great revival of faith in God.

Cyrus helps the exiles to return

1 In the first year of Cyrus king of Persia, in order to fulfil the word of the LORD spoken by Jeremiah, the LORD moved the heart of Cyrus king of Persia to make a proclamation throughout his realm and also to put it in writing:

²'This is what Cyrus king of Persia says:

'"The LORD, the God of heaven, has given me all the kingdoms of the earth and he has appointed me to build a temple for him at Jerusalem in Judah. ³Any of his people among you—may their God be with them, and let them go up to Jerusalem in Judah and build the temple of the LORD, the God of Israel, the God who is in Jerusalem. ⁴And in any locality where survivors may now be living, the people are to provide

People and Places

Cyrus
Ezra 1:2

When the Babylonians invaded Judah, they took the people into exile. For years, the people of Judah lived and worked in Babylon and were ruled by its kings. But around fifty years after the exile, the Babylonians were defeated by the Persian Empire, whose king was Cyrus. The Persians had a different attitude to the nations they ruled over. They allowed them to stay in their own countries and put a governor in place to rule over them. They also allowed them to practice their own religions. So, now that Cyrus is in charge of what was the Babylonian Empire, he says that the Israelites can go back home, and they can rebuild the temple.

them with silver and gold, with goods and livestock, and with freewill offerings for the temple of God in Jerusalem."'

5 Then the family heads of Judah and Benjamin, and the priests and Levites—everyone whose heart God had moved—prepared to go up and build the house of the LORD in Jerusalem. 6 All their neighbours assisted them with articles of silver and gold, with goods and livestock, and with valuable gifts, in addition to all the freewill offerings.

7 Moreover, King Cyrus brought out the articles belonging to the temple of the LORD, which Nebuchadnezzar had carried away from Jerusalem and had placed in the temple of his god.[a] 8 Cyrus king of Persia had them brought by Mithredath the treasurer, who counted them out to Sheshbazzar the prince of Judah.

9 This was the inventory:

gold dishes	30
silver dishes	1,000
silver pans[b]	29
10 gold bowls	30
matching silver bowls	410
other articles	1,000

11 In all, there were 5,400 articles of gold and of silver. Sheshbazzar brought all these along with the exiles when they came up from Babylon to Jerusalem.

The list of the exiles who returned

2 Now these are the people of the province who came up from the captivity of the exiles, whom Nebuchadnezzar king of Babylon had taken captive to Babylon (they returned to Jerusalem and Judah, all to their own towns, 2 in company with Zerubbabel, Joshua, Nehemiah, Seraiah, Reelaiah, Mordecai, Bilshan, Mispar, Bigvai, Rehum and Baanah):

The list of the men of the people of Israel:

3 the descendants of Parosh	2,172
4 of Shephatiah	372
5 of Arah	775
6 of Pahath-Moab (through the line of Jeshua and Joab)	2,812
7 of Elam	1,254
8 of Zattu	945
9 of Zakkai	760
10 of Bani	642
11 of Bebai	623
12 of Azgad	1,222
13 of Adonikam	666
14 of Bigvai	2,056
15 of Adin	454
16 of Ater (through Hezekiah)	98
17 of Bezai	323
18 of Jorah	112
19 of Hashum	223
20 of Gibbar	95
21 the men of Bethlehem	123
22 of Netophah	56
23 of Anathoth	128
24 of Azmaveth	42

---

[a] 7 Or *gods* [b] 9 The meaning of the Hebrew for this word is uncertain. [c] 25 See Septuagint (see also Neh. 7:29); Hebrew *Kiriath Arim*.

25 of Kiriath Jearim,[a] Kephirah
and Beeroth — 743
26 of Ramah and Geba — 621
27 of Mikmash — 122
28 of Bethel and Ai — 223
29 of Nebo — 52
30 of Magbish — 156
31 of the other Elam — 1,254
32 of Harim — 320
33 of Lod, Hadid and Ono — 725
34 of Jericho — 345
35 of Senaah — 3,630

36 The priests:

the descendants of Jedaiah
(through the family of Jeshua) — 973
37 of Immer — 1,052
38 of Pashhur — 1,247
39 of Harim — 1,017

40 The Levites:

the descendants of Jeshua and
Kadmiel (of the line of Hodaviah) — 74

41 The musicians:

the descendants of Asaph — 128

42 The gatekeepers of the temple:

the descendants of
Shallum, Ater, Talmon,
Akkub, Hatita and Shobai — 139

43 The temple servants:

the descendants of
Ziha, Hasupha, Tabbaoth,
44 Keros, Siaha, Padon,
45 Lebanah, Hagabah, Akkub,
46 Hagab, Shalmai, Hanan,
47 Giddel, Gahar, Reaiah,
48 Rezin, Nekoda, Gazzam,
49 Uzza, Paseah, Besai,
50 Asnah, Meunim, Nephussim,
51 Bakbuk, Hakupha, Harhur,
52 Bazluth, Mehida, Harsha,
53 Barkos, Sisera, Temah,
54 Neziah and Hatipha

55 The descendants of the servants of
Solomon:

the descendants of
Sotai, Hassophereth, Peruda,
56 Jaala, Darkon, Giddel,
57 Shephatiah, Hattil,
Pokereth-Hazzebaim and Ami

58 The temple servants and the
descendants of the servants of
Solomon — 392

59 The following came up from
the towns of Tel Melah, Tel Harsha, Kerub, Addon and Immer,
but they could not show that their
families were descended from Israel:

60 The descendants of
Delaiah, Tobiah and Nekoda — 652

61 And from among the priests:

The descendants of
Hobaiah, Hakkoz and Barzillai (a
man who had married a daughter of
Barzillai the Gileadite and was called
by that name).

62 These searched for their family records, but they could not find
them and so were excluded from
the priesthood as unclean. 63 The
governor ordered them not to eat
any of the most sacred food until
there was a priest ministering with
the Urim and Thummim.

64 The whole company numbered 42,360, 65 besides their
7,337 male and female slaves;
and they also had 200 male and
female singers. 66 They had 736
horses, 245 mules, 67 435 camels
and 6,720 donkeys.

68 When they arrived at the house of the
LORD in Jerusalem, some of the heads of the
families gave freewill offerings towards the
rebuilding of the house of God on its site.
69 According to their ability they gave to the
treasury for this work 61,000 darics[b] of gold,
5,000 minas[c] of silver and 100 priestly
garments.

70 The priests, the Levites, the musicians,
the gatekeepers and the temple servants

---

[a] 69 That is, about 500 kilograms   [b] 69 That is, about 2.8 metric tons

settled in their own towns, along with some of the other people, and the rest of the Israelites settled in their towns.

Rebuilding the altar

3 When the seventh month came and the Israelites had settled in their towns, the people assembled with one accord in Jerusalem. ²Then Joshua son of Jozadak and his fellow priests and Zerubbabel son of Shealtiel and his associates began to build the altar of the God of Israel to sacrifice burnt offerings on it, in accordance with what is written in the Law of Moses the man of God. ³Despite their fear of the peoples around them, they built the altar on its foundation and sacrificed burnt offerings on it to the LORD, both the morning and evening sacrifices. ⁴Then in accordance with what is written, they celebrated the Festival of Tabernacles with the required number of burnt offerings prescribed for each day. ⁵After that, they presented the regular burnt offerings, the New Moon sacrifices and the sacrifices for all the appointed sacred festivals of the LORD, as well as those brought as freewill offerings to the LORD. ⁶On the first day of the seventh month they began to offer burnt offerings to the LORD, though the foundation of the LORD's temple had not yet been laid.

Rebuilding the temple

⁷Then they gave money to the masons and carpenters, and gave food and drink and olive oil to the people of Sidon and Tyre, so that they would bring cedar logs by sea from Lebanon to Joppa, as authorised by Cyrus king of Persia.

⁸In the second month of the second year after their arrival at the house of God in Jerusalem, Zerubbabel son of Shealtiel, Joshua son of Jozadak and the rest of the people (the priests and the Levites and all who had returned from the captivity to Jerusalem) began the work, appointing Levites twenty years old and older to supervise the building of the house of the LORD. ⁹Joshua and his sons and brothers and Kadmiel and his sons (descendants of Hodaviah*ᵃ*) and the sons of Henadad and their sons and brothers—all Levites—joined together in supervising those working on the house of God.

¹⁰When the builders laid the foundation of the temple of the LORD, the priests in their vestments and with trumpets, and the Levites (the sons of Asaph) with cymbals, took their places to praise the LORD, as prescribed by David king of Israel. ¹¹With praise and thanksgiving they sang to the LORD:

'He is good;
 his love towards Israel endures for
 ever.'

And all the people gave a great shout of praise to the LORD, because the foundation of the house of the LORD was laid. ¹²But many of the older priests and Levites and family heads, who had seen the former temple, wept aloud when they saw the foundation of this temple being laid, while many others shouted for joy. ¹³No-one could distinguish the sound of the shouts of joy from the sound of weeping, because the people made so much noise. And the sound was heard far away.

Temple
Ezra 3:12
When the Israelites finally settled in the Promised Land they built a temple in Jerusalem where the Ark of the Covenant would rest. The first temple built by Solomon (1 Kings 5:5) was destroyed by the Babylonians. Ezra oversaw its rebuilding after the exile, then it was rebuilt again in a grand manner by Herod around the time of Jesus' birth. This third temple was destroyed in AD 70 as prophesied by Jesus (Matthew 24:2).

---

*ᵃ*9 Hebrew *Yehudah*, probably a variant of *Hodaviah*

Opposition to the rebuilding

4 When the enemies of Judah and Benjamin heard that the exiles were building a temple for the LORD, the God of Israel, ²they came to Zerubbabel and to the heads of the families and said, 'Let us help you build because, like you, we seek your God and have been sacrificing to him since the time of Esarhaddon king of Assyria, who brought us here.'

³But Zerubbabel, Joshua and the rest of the heads of the families of Israel answered, 'You have no part with us in building a temple to our God. We alone will build it for the LORD, the God of Israel, as King Cyrus, the king of Persia, commanded us.'

⁴Then the peoples around them set out to discourage the people of Judah and make them afraid to go on building.[a] ⁵They bribed officials to work against them and frustrate their plans during the entire reign of Cyrus king of Persia and down to the reign of Darius king of Persia.

Later opposition under Xerxes and Artaxerxes

⁶At the beginning of the reign of Xerxes,[b] they lodged an accusation against the people of Judah and Jerusalem.

⁷And in the days of Artaxerxes king of Persia, Bishlam, Mithredath, Tabeel and the rest of his associates wrote a letter to Artaxerxes. The letter was written in Aramaic script and in the Aramaic language.[c,d]

⁸Rehum the commanding officer and Shimshai the secretary wrote a letter against Jerusalem to Artaxerxes the king as follows:

⁹Rehum the commanding officer and Shimshai the secretary, together with the rest of their associates—the judges, officials and administrators over the people from Persia, Uruk and Babylon, the Elamites of Susa, ¹⁰and the other people whom the great and honourable Ashurbanipal deported and settled in the city of Samaria and elsewhere in Trans-Euphrates.

¹¹(This is a copy of the letter they sent him.)

To King Artaxerxes,

From your servants, the men of Trans-Euphrates:

¹²The king should know that the people who came up to us from you have gone to Jerusalem and are rebuilding that rebellious and wicked city. They are restoring the walls and repairing the foundations.

¹³Furthermore, the king should know that if this city is built and its walls are restored, no more taxes, tribute or duty will be paid, and eventually the royal revenues will suffer.[e] ¹⁴Now since we are under obligation to the palace and it is not proper for us to see the king dishonoured, we are sending this message to inform the king, ¹⁵so that a search may be made in the archives of your predecessors. In these records you will find that this city is a rebellious city, troublesome to kings and provinces, a place with a long history of sedition. That is why this city was destroyed. ¹⁶We inform the king that if this city is built and its walls are restored, you will be left with nothing in Trans-Euphrates.

¹⁷The king sent this reply:

To Rehum the commanding officer, Shimshai the secretary and the rest of their associates living in Samaria and elsewhere in Trans-Euphrates:

Greetings.

¹⁸The letter you sent us has been read and translated in my presence. ¹⁹I issued an order and a search was made, and it was found that this city has a long history of revolt against kings and has been a

---

[a] 4 Or *and troubled them as they built*   [b] 6 Hebrew *Ahasuerus*   [c] 7 Or *written in Aramaic and translated*   [d] 7 The text of Ezra 4:8-6:18 is in Aramaic.   [e] 13 The meaning of the Aramaic for this clause is uncertain.

place of rebellion and sedition. ²⁰Jerusalem has had powerful kings ruling over the whole of Trans-Euphrates, and taxes, tribute and duty were paid to them. ²¹Now issue an order to these people to stop work, so that this city will not be rebuilt until I so order. ²²Be careful not to neglect this matter. Why let this threat grow, to the detriment of the royal interests?

²³As soon as the copy of the letter of King Artaxerxes was read to Rehum and Shimshai the secretary and their associates, they went immediately to the Jews in Jerusalem and compelled them by force to stop.

²⁴Thus the work on the house of God in Jerusalem came to a standstill until the second year of the reign of Darius king of Persia.

Tattenai's letter to Darius

5 Now Haggai the prophet and Zechariah the prophet, a descendant of Iddo, prophesied to the Jews in Judah and Jerusalem in the name of the God of Israel, who was over them. ²Then Zerubbabel son of Shealtiel and Joshua son of Jozadak set to work to rebuild the house of God in Jerusalem. And the prophets of God were with them, supporting them.

³At that time Tattenai, governor of Trans-Euphrates, and Shethar-Bozenai and their associates went to them and asked, 'Who authorised you to rebuild this temple and to finish it?' ⁴They[a] also asked, 'What are the names of those who are constructing this building?' ⁵But the eye of their God was watching over the elders of the Jews, and they were not stopped until a report could go to Darius and his written reply be received.

⁶This is a copy of the letter that Tattenai, governor of Trans-Euphrates, and Shethar-Bozenai and their associates, the officials of Trans-Euphrates, sent to King Darius. ⁷The report they sent him read as follows:

To King Darius:

Cordial greetings.

⁸The king should know that we went to the district of Judah, to the temple of the great God. The people are building it with large stones and placing the timbers in the walls. The work is being carried on with diligence and is making rapid progress under their direction.

⁹We questioned the elders and asked them, 'Who authorised you to rebuild this temple and to finish it?' ¹⁰We also asked them their names, so that we could write down the names of their leaders for your information.

¹¹This is the answer they gave us:

'We are the servants of the God of heaven and earth, and we are rebuilding the temple that was built many years ago, one that a great king of Israel built and finished. ¹²But because our ancestors angered the God of heaven, he gave them into the hands of Nebuchadnezzar the Chaldean, king of Babylon, who destroyed this temple and deported the people to Babylon.

¹³'However, in the first year of Cyrus king of Babylon, King Cyrus issued a decree to rebuild this house of God. ¹⁴He even removed from the temple[b] of Babylon the gold and silver articles of the house of God, which Nebuchadnezzar had taken from the temple in Jerusalem and brought to the temple[c] in Babylon. Then King Cyrus gave them to a man named Sheshbazzar, whom he had appointed governor, ¹⁵and he told him, "Take these articles and go and deposit them in the temple in Jerusalem. And rebuild the house of God on its site."

---

[a] 4 See Septuagint; Aramaic We   [b] 14 Or palace   [c] 14 Or palace

16'So this Sheshbazzar came and laid the foundations of the house of God in Jerusalem. From that day to the present it has been under construction but is not yet finished.'

17Now if it pleases the king, let a search be made in the royal archives of Babylon to see if King Cyrus did in fact issue a decree to rebuild this house of God in Jerusalem. Then let the king send us his decision in this matter.

The decree of Darius

6 King Darius then issued an order, and they searched in the archives stored in the treasury at Babylon. 2A scroll was found in the citadel of Ecbatana in the province of Media, and this was written on it:

Memorandum:

3In the first year of King Cyrus, the king issued a decree concerning the temple of God in Jerusalem:

Let the temple be rebuilt as a place to present sacrifices, and let its foundations be laid. It is to be sixty cubits^a high and sixty cubits wide, 4with three courses of large stones and one of timber. The costs are to be paid by the royal treasury. 5Also, the gold and silver articles of the house of God, which Nebuchadnezzar took from the temple in Jerusalem and brought to Babylon, are to be returned to their places in the temple in Jerusalem; they are to be deposited in the house of God.

6Now then, Tattenai, governor of Trans-Euphrates, and Shethar-Bozenai and you other officials of that province, stay away from there. 7Do not interfere with the work on this temple of God. Let the governor of the Jews and the Jewish elders rebuild this house of God on its site.

8Moreover, I hereby decree what you are to do for these elders of the Jews in the construction of this house of God:

Their expenses are to be fully paid out of the royal treasury, from the revenues of Trans-Euphrates, so that the work will not stop. 9Whatever is needed—young bulls, rams, male lambs for burnt offerings to the God of heaven, and wheat, salt, wine and olive oil, as requested by the priests in Jerusalem—must be given them daily without fail, 10so that they may offer sacrifices pleasing to the God of heaven and pray for the well-being of the king and his sons.

11Furthermore, I decree that if anyone defies this edict, a beam is to be pulled from their house and they are to be impaled on it. And for this crime their house is to be made a pile of rubble. 12May God, who has caused his Name to dwell there, overthrow any king or people who lifts a hand to change this decree or to destroy this temple in Jerusalem.

People and Places

Darius
Ezra 6:1

Darius was king of Persia after Cyrus and he made sure that the Israelites kept rebuilding the temple in Jerusalem. He even gave them the money to do it. Darius liked to get things done. During his time as king, he built a network of roads, set up a postal system and developed trade.

---

^{a} 3 That is, about 27 metres

I Darius have decreed it. Let it be carried out with diligence.

Completion and dedication of the temple

13 Then, because of the decree King Darius had sent, Tattenai, governor of Trans-Euphrates, and Shethar-Bozenai and their associates carried it out with diligence. 14 So the elders of the Jews continued to build and prosper under the preaching of Haggai the prophet and Zechariah, a descendant of Iddo. They finished building the temple according to the command of the God of Israel and the decrees of Cyrus, Darius and Artaxerxes, kings of Persia. 15 The temple was completed on the third day of the month Adar, in the sixth year of the reign of King Darius. 16 Then the people of Israel—the priests, the Levites and the rest of the exiles—celebrated the dedication of the house of God with joy. 17 For the dedication of this house of God they offered a hundred bulls, two hundred rams, four hundred male lambs and, as a sin offering*a* for all Israel, twelve male goats, one for each of the tribes of Israel. 18 And they installed the priests in their divisions and the Levites in their groups for the service of God at Jerusalem, according to what is written in the Book of Moses.

The Passover

19 On the fourteenth day of the first month, the exiles celebrated the Passover. 20 The priests and Levites had purified themselves and were all ceremonially clean. The Levites slaughtered the Passover lamb for all the exiles, for their relatives the priests and for themselves. 21 So the Israelites who had returned from the exile ate it, together with all who had separated themselves from the unclean practices of their Gentile neighbours in order to seek the LORD, the God of Israel. 22 For seven days they celebrated with joy the Festival of Unleavened Bread, because the LORD had filled them with joy by changing the attitude of the king of Assyria so that he assisted them in the work on the house of God, the God of Israel.

a 17 Or *purification* offering

People and Places

Ezra
Ezra 7:1

Ezra was a priest and a skilled scribe and teacher of the law. He could trace his descendants back to Aaron, the first high priest of Israel. Ezra would have been trained in the knowledge of the law when he was in captivity in Babylon. It was his job to copy, interpret and teach the Books of the Law, making sure that the people understood how to worship God and live in his ways.

Ezra comes to Jerusalem

7 After these things, during the reign of Artaxerxes king of Persia, Ezra son of Seraiah, the son of Azariah, the son of Hilkiah, 2 the son of Shallum, the son of Zadok, the son of Ahitub, 3 the son of Amariah, the son of Azariah, the son of Meraioth, 4 the son of Zerahiah, the son of Uzzi, the son of Bukki, 5 the son of Abishua, the son of Phinehas, the son of Eleazar, the son of Aaron the chief priest— 6 this Ezra came up from Babylon. He was a teacher well versed in the Law of Moses, which the LORD, the God of Israel, had given. The king had granted him everything he asked, for the hand of the LORD his God was on him. 7 Some of the Israelites, including priests, Levites, musicians, gatekeepers and temple servants, also came up to Jerusalem in the seventh year of King Artaxerxes.

8 Ezra arrived in Jerusalem in the fifth month of the seventh year of the king. 9 He had begun his journey from Babylon on the first day of the first month, and he arrived in Jerusalem on the first day of the fifth month, for the gracious hand of his God was on him. 10 For Ezra had devoted himself to the study and observance of the Law of the

LORD, and to teaching its decrees and laws in Israel.

King Artaxerxes' letter to Ezra

11This is a copy of the letter King Artaxerxes had given to Ezra the priest, a teacher of the Law, a man learned in matters concerning the commands and decrees of the LORD for Israel:

12[a]Artaxerxes, king of kings,

> To Ezra the priest, teacher of the Law of the God of heaven:
>
> Greetings.
>
> 13Now I decree that any of the Israelites in my kingdom, including priests and Levites, who volunteer to go to Jerusalem with you, may go. 14You are sent by the king and his seven advisors to inquire about Judah and Jerusalem with regard to the Law of your God, which is in your hand. 15Moreover, you are to take with you the silver and gold that the king and his advisors have freely given to the God of Israel, whose dwelling is in Jerusalem, 16together with all the silver and gold you may obtain from the province of Babylon, as well as the freewill offerings of the people and priests for the temple of their God in Jerusalem. 17With this money be sure to buy bulls, rams and male lambs, together with their grain offerings and drink offerings, and sacrifice them on the altar of the temple of your God in Jerusalem. 18You and your fellow Israelites may then do whatever seems best with the rest of the silver and gold, in accordance with the will of your God. 19Deliver to the God of Jerusalem all the articles entrusted to you for worship in the temple of your God. 20And anything else needed for the temple of your God that you are responsible to supply, you may provide from the royal treasury.
>
> 21Now I, King Artaxerxes, decree that all the treasurers of Trans-Euphrates are to provide with diligence whatever Ezra the priest, the teacher of the Law of the God of heaven, may ask of you— 22up to a hundred talents[b] of silver, a hundred cors[c] of wheat, a hundred baths[d] of wine, a hundred baths of olive oil, and salt without limit. 23Whatever the God of heaven has prescribed, let it be done with diligence for the temple of the God of heaven. Why should his wrath fall on the realm of the king and of his sons? 24You are also to know that you have no authority to impose taxes, tribute or duty on any of the priests, Levites, musicians, gatekeepers, temple servants or other workers at this house of God.
>
> 25And you, Ezra, in accordance with the wisdom of your God, which you possess, appoint magistrates and judges to administer justice to all the people of Trans-Euphrates—all who know the laws of your God. And you are to teach any who do not know them. 26Whoever does not obey the law of your God and the law of the king must surely be punished by death, banishment, confiscation of property, or imprisonment.

27Praise be to the LORD, the God of our ancestors, who has put it into the king's heart to bring honour to the house of the LORD in Jerusalem in this way 28and who has extended his good favour to me before the king and his advisors and all the king's powerful officials. Because the hand of the LORD my God was on me, I took courage and gathered leaders from Israel to go up with me.

---

[a] 12 The text of Ezra 7:12-26 is in Aramaic. [b] 22 That is, about 3.4 metric tons [c] 22 That is, probably about 16 metric tons [d] 22 That is, about 2,200 litres

List of the family heads returning with Ezra

8 These are the family heads and those registered with them who came up with me from Babylon during the reign of King Artaxerxes:

2of the descendants of Phinehas, Gershom;
of the descendants of Ithamar, Daniel;
of the descendants of David, Hattush 3of the descendants of Shekaniah;

of the descendants of Parosh, Zechariah, and with him were registered 150 men;
4of the descendants of Pahath-Moab, Eliehoenai son of Zerahiah, and with him 200 men;
5of the descendants of Zattu,[a] Shekaniah son of Jahaziel, and with him 300 men;
6of the descendants of Adin, Ebed son of Jonathan, and with him 50 men;
7of the descendants of Elam, Jeshaiah son of Athaliah, and with him 70 men;
8of the descendants of Shephatiah, Zebadiah son of Michael, and with him 80 men;
9of the descendants of Joab, Obadiah son of Jehiel, and with him 218 men;
10of the descendants of Bani,[b] Shelomith son of Josiphiah, and with him 160 men;
11of the descendants of Bebai, Zechariah son of Bebai, and with him 28 men;
12of the descendants of Azgad, Johanan son of Hakkatan, and with him 110 men;
13of the descendants of Adonikam, the last ones, whose names were Eliphelet, Jeuel and Shemaiah, and with them 60 men;
14of the descendants of Bigvai, Uthai and Zakkur, and with them 70 men.

The return to Jerusalem

15I assembled them at the canal that flows towards Ahava, and we camped there three days. When I checked among the people and the priests, I found no Levites there. 16So I summoned Eliezer, Ariel, Shemaiah, Elnathan, Jarib, Elnathan, Nathan, Zechariah and Meshullam, who were leaders, and Joiarib and Elnathan, who were men of learning, 17and I ordered them to go to Iddo, the leader in Kasiphia. I told them what to say to Iddo and his associates, the temple servants in Kasiphia, so that they might bring attendants to us for the house of our God. 18Because the gracious hand of our God was on us, they brought us Sherebiah, a capable man, from the descendants of Mahli son of Levi, the son of Israel, and Sherebiah's sons and brothers, 18 in all; 19and Hashabiah, together with Jeshaiah from the descendants of Merari, and his brothers and nephews, 20 men in all. 20They also brought 220 of the temple servants—a body that David and the officials had established to assist the Levites. All were registered by name.

21There, by the Ahava Canal, I proclaimed a fast, so that we might humble ourselves before our God and ask him for a safe journey for us and our children, with all our possessions. 22I was ashamed to ask the king for soldiers and horsemen to protect us from enemies on the road, because we had told the king, 'The gracious hand of our God is on everyone who looks to him, but his great anger is against all who forsake him.' 23So we fasted and petitioned our God about this, and he answered our prayer.

24Then I set apart twelve of the leading priests, namely, Sherebiah, Hashabiah and ten of their brothers, 25and I weighed out to them the offering of silver and gold and the articles that the king, his advisors, his officials and all Israel present there had donated for the house of our God. 26I weighed out to them 650 talents[c] of silver, silver articles weighing 100 talents,[d] 100 talents[e] of gold, 2720 bowls of gold valued at 1,000 darics,[f] and two fine articles of polished bronze, as precious as gold.

---

[a] 5 Some Septuagint manuscripts (also 1 Esdras 8:32); Hebrew does not have *Zattu*. [b] 10 Some Septuagint manuscripts (also 1 Esdras 8:36); Hebrew does not have *Bani*. [c] 26 That is, about 22 metric tons [d] 26 That is, about 3.4 metric tons [e] 26 That is, about 3.4 metric tons [f] 27 That is, about 8.4 kilograms

28 I said to them, 'You as well as these articles are consecrated to the LORD. The silver and gold are a freewill offering to the LORD, the God of your ancestors. 29 Guard them carefully until you weigh them out in the chambers of the house of the LORD in Jerusalem before the leading priests and the Levites and the family heads of Israel.' 30 Then the priests and Levites received the silver and gold and sacred articles that had been weighed out to be taken to the house of our God in Jerusalem.

31 On the twelfth day of the first month we set out from the Ahava Canal to go to Jerusalem. The hand of our God was on us, and he protected us from enemies and bandits along the way. 32 So we arrived in Jerusalem, where we rested three days.

33 On the fourth day, in the house of our God, we weighed out the silver and gold and the sacred articles into the hands of Meremoth son of Uriah, the priest. Eleazar son of Phinehas was with him, and so were the Levites Jozabad son of Jeshua and Noadiah son of Binnui. 34 Everything was accounted for by number and weight, and the entire weight was recorded at that time.

35 Then the exiles who had returned from captivity sacrificed burnt offerings to the God of Israel: twelve bulls for all Israel, ninety-six rams, seventy-seven male lambs and, as a sin offering,*a* twelve male goats. All this was a burnt offering to the LORD. 36 They also delivered the king's orders to the royal satraps and to the governors of Trans-Euphrates who then gave assistance to the people and to the house of God.

Ezra's prayer about intermarriage

9 After these things had been done, the leaders came to me and said, 'The people of Israel, including the priests and the Levites, have not kept themselves separate from the neighbouring peoples with their detestable practices, like those of the Canaanites, Hittites, Perizzites, Jebusites, Ammonites, Moabites, Egyptians and Amorites. 2 They have taken some of their daughters as wives for themselves and their sons, and have mingled the holy race with the peoples around them. And the leaders and officials have led the way in this unfaithfulness.'

Tearing robes
Ezra 9:3
In ancient times, people had very visible ways to show their grief or repentance. They would tear their robes, then put on sackcloth and put dust or ashes on their head. This would often be accompanied by loud weeping and wailing.

3 When I heard this, I tore my tunic and cloak, pulled hair from my head and beard and sat down appalled. 4 Then everyone who trembled at the words of the God of Israel gathered round me because of this unfaithfulness of the exiles. And I sat there appalled until the evening sacrifice.

5 Then, at the evening sacrifice, I rose from my self-abasement, with my tunic and cloak torn, and fell on my knees with my hands spread out to the LORD my God 6 and prayed:

'I am too ashamed and disgraced, my God, to lift up my face to you, because our sins are higher than our heads and our guilt has reached to the heavens. 7 From the days of our ancestors until now, our guilt has been great. Because of our sins, we and our kings and our priests have been subjected to the sword and captivity, to pillage and humiliation at the hand of foreign kings, as it is today.

8 'But now, for a brief moment, the LORD our God has been gracious in leaving us a remnant and giving us a firm place*b* in his sanctuary, and so our God gives light to our eyes and a little relief

---

a 35 Or *purification offering*   *b* 8 Or *a foothold*

in our bondage. 9Though we are slaves, our God has not forsaken us in our bondage. He has shown us kindness in the sight of the kings of Persia: he has granted us new life to rebuild the house of our God and repair its ruins, and he has given us a wall of protection in Judah and Jerusalem.

10'But now, our God, what can we say after this? For we have forsaken the commands 11you gave through your servants the prophets when you said: "The land you are entering to possess is a land polluted by the corruption of its peoples. By their detestable practices they have filled it with their impurity from one end to the other. 12Therefore, do not give your daughters in marriage to their sons or take their daughters for your sons. Do not seek a treaty of friendship with them at any time, that you may be strong and eat the good things of the land and leave it to your children as an everlasting inheritance."

13'What has happened to us is a result of our evil deeds and our great guilt, and yet, our God, you have punished us less than our sins have deserved and have given us a remnant like this. 14Shall we then break your commands again and intermarry with the peoples who commit such detestable practices? Would you not be angry enough with us to destroy us, leaving us no remnant or survivor? 15LORD, the God of Israel, you are righteous! We are left this day as a remnant. Here we are before you in our guilt, though because of it not one of us can stand in your presence.'

The people's confession of sin

10 While Ezra was praying and confessing, weeping and throwing himself down before the house of God, a large crowd of Israelites—men, women and children—gathered round him. They too wept bitterly. 2Then Shekaniah son of Jehiel, one of the descendants of Elam, said to Ezra, 'We have been unfaithful to our God by marrying foreign women from the peoples around us. But in spite of this, there is still hope for Israel. 3Now let us make a covenant before our God to send away all these women and their children, in accordance with the counsel of my lord and of those who fear the commands of our God. Let it be done according to the Law. 4Rise up; this matter is in your hands. We will support you, so take courage and do it.'

5So Ezra rose up and put the leading priests and Levites and all Israel under oath to do what had been suggested. And they took the oath. 6Then Ezra withdrew from before the house of God and went to the room of Jehohanan son of Eliashib. While he was there, he ate no food and drank no water, because he continued to mourn over the unfaithfulness of the exiles.

7A proclamation was then issued throughout Judah and Jerusalem for all the exiles to assemble in Jerusalem. 8Anyone who failed to appear within three days would forfeit all his property, in accordance with the decision of the officials and elders, and would himself be expelled from the assembly of the exiles.

9Within the three days, all the men of Judah and Benjamin had gathered in Jerusalem. And on the twentieth day of the ninth month, all the people were sitting in the square before the house of God, greatly distressed by the occasion and because of the rain. 10Then Ezra the priest stood up and said to them, 'You have been unfaithful; you have married foreign women, adding to Israel's guilt. 11Now honour[a] the LORD, the God of your ancestors, and do his will. Separate yourselves from the peoples around you and from your foreign wives.'

12The whole assembly responded with a loud voice: 'You are right! We must do as you say. 13But there are many people here and it is the rainy season; so we cannot stand outside. Besides, this matter cannot be

---

[a] 11 Or *Now make confession to*

taken care of in a day or two, because we have sinned greatly in this thing. ¹⁴Let our officials act for the whole assembly. Then let everyone in our towns who has married a foreign woman come at a set time, along with the elders and judges of each town, until the fierce anger of our God in this matter is turned away from us.' ¹⁵Only Jonathan son of Asahel and Jahzeiah son of Tikvah, supported by Meshullam and Shabbethai the Levite, opposed this.

¹⁶So the exiles did as was proposed. Ezra the priest selected men who were family heads, one from each family division, and all of them designated by name. On the first day of the tenth month they sat down to investigate the cases, ¹⁷and by the first day of the first month they finished dealing with all the men who had married foreign women.

Those guilty of intermarriage

¹⁸Among the descendants of the priests, the following had married foreign women:

From the descendants of Joshua son of Jozadak, and his brothers: Maaseiah, Eliezer, Jarib and Gedaliah. ¹⁹(They all gave their hands in pledge to put away their wives, and for their guilt they each presented a ram from the flock as a guilt offering.)

²⁰From the descendants of Immer:
Hanani and Zebadiah.

²¹From the descendants of Harim:
Maaseiah, Elijah, Shemaiah, Jehiel and Uzziah.

²²From the descendants of Pashhur:
Elioenai, Maaseiah, Ishmael, Nethanel, Jozabad and Elasah.

²³Among the Levites:
Jozabad, Shimei, Kelaiah (that is Kelita), Pethahiah, Judah and Eliezer.

²⁴From the musicians:
Eliashib.
From the gatekeepers:
Shallum, Telem and Uri.

²⁵And among the other Israelites:

From the descendants of Parosh:
Ramiah, Izziah, Malkijah, Mijamin, Eleazar, Malkijah and Benaiah.

²⁶From the descendants of Elam:
Mattaniah, Zechariah, Jehiel, Abdi, Jeremoth and Elijah.

²⁷From the descendants of Zattu:
Elioenai, Eliashib, Mattaniah, Jeremoth, Zabad and Aziza.

²⁸From the descendants of Bebai:
Jehohanan, Hananiah, Zabbai and Athlai.

²⁹From the descendants of Bani:
Meshullam, Malluk, Adaiah, Jashub, Sheal and Jeremoth.

³⁰From the descendants of Pahath-Moab:
Adna, Kelal, Benaiah, Maaseiah, Mattaniah, Bezalel, Binnui and Manasseh.

³¹From the descendants of Harim:
Eliezer, Ishijah, Malkijah, Shemaiah, Shimeon, ³²Benjamin, Malluk and Shemariah.

³³From the descendants of Hashum:
Mattenai, Mattattah, Zabad, Eliphelet, Jeremai, Manasseh and Shimei.

³⁴From the descendants of Bani:
Maadai, Amram, Uel, ³⁵Benaiah, Bedeiah, Keluhi, ³⁶Vaniah, Meremoth, Eliashib, ³⁷Mattaniah, Mattenai and Jaasu.

³⁸From the descendants of Binnui:[a]
Shimei, ³⁹Shelemiah, Nathan, Adaiah, ⁴⁰MaKnadebai, Shashai, Sharai, ⁴¹Azarel, Shelemiah, Shemariah, ⁴²Shallum, Amariah and Joseph.

⁴³From the descendants of Nebo:
Jeiel, Mattithiah, Zabad, Zebina, Jaddai, Joel and Benaiah.

⁴⁴All these had married foreign women, and some of them had children by these wives.[b]

---

[a] 37,38 See Septuagint (also 1 Esdras 9:34); Hebrew *Jaasu* ³⁸*and Bani and Binnui.* [b] 44 Or *and they sent them away with their children*

Nehemiah

INTRODUCTION

NEHEMIAH

Author: Probably Ezra the priest.

When: Nehemiah served in Israel about a hundred years after the exiles first returned to Jerusalem, around 445 BC.

Where: Jerusalem.

Did you know? Ezra arrived back in Jerusalem about thirteen years before Nehemiah.

Main theme: Nehemiah is cupbearer to the king of Persia when he hears that the exiles who had returned to Jerusalem are in a bad way. He gets permission to go to Jerusalem himself and organises the rebuilding of the wall around the city. His life is a great example of godly leadership and prayer.

Nehemiah's prayer

1 The words of Nehemiah son of Hakaliah:

In the month of Kislev in the twentieth year, while I was in the citadel of Susa, ²Hanani, one of my brothers, came from Judah with some other men, and I questioned them about the Jewish remnant that had survived the exile, and also about Jerusalem.

³They said to me, 'Those who survived the exile and are back in the province are in great trouble and disgrace. The wall of Jerusalem is broken down, and its gates have been burned with fire.'

⁴When I heard these things, I sat down and wept. For some days I mourned and fasted and prayed before the God of heaven. ⁵Then I said:

'LORD, the God of heaven, the great and awesome God, who keeps his covenant of love with those who love him and keep his commandments, ⁶let your ear be attentive and your eyes open to hear the prayer your servant is praying before you day and night for your servants, the people of Israel. I confess the sins we Israelites, including myself and my ancestral family, have committed against you. 7We have acted very wickedly towards you. We have not obeyed the commands, decrees and laws you gave your servant Moses.

8'Remember the instruction you gave your servant Moses, saying, "If you are unfaithful, I will scatter you among the nations, 9but if you return to me and obey my commands, then even if your exiled people are at the farthest horizon, I will gather them from there and bring them to the place I have chosen as a dwelling for my Name."

10'They are your servants and your people, whom you redeemed by your great strength and your mighty hand. 11Lord, let your ear be attentive to the prayer of this your servant and to the prayer of your servants who delight in revering your name. Give your servant success today by granting him favour in the presence of this man.'

I was cupbearer to the king.

Artaxerxes sends Nehemiah to Jerusalem

2 In the month of Nisan in the twentieth year of King Artaxerxes, when wine was brought for him, I took the wine and gave it to the king. I had not been sad in his presence before, 2so the king asked me, 'Why does your face look so sad when you are not ill? This can be nothing but sadness of heart.'

I was very much afraid, 3but I said to the king, 'May the king live for ever! Why should my face not look sad when the city where my ancestors are buried lies in ruins, and its gates have been destroyed by fire?'

4The king said to me, 'What is it you want?'

Then I prayed to the God of heaven, 5and I answered the king, 'If it pleases the king

People and Places

Nehemiah
Nehemiah 2:1
As cupbearer to the king, Nehemiah was more than just a waiter. It was his job to taste the king's food and drink to check that it wasn't poisoned. It was an important position, shown by the fact that Nehemiah could talk openly with the king.

and if your servant has found favour in his sight, let him send me to the city in Judah where my ancestors are buried so that I can rebuild it.'

6Then the king, with the queen sitting beside him, asked me, 'How long will your journey take, and when will you get back?' It pleased the king to send me; so I set a time.

7I also said to him, 'If it pleases the king, may I have letters to the governors of Trans-Euphrates, so that they will provide me safe-conduct until I arrive in Judah? 8And may I have a letter to Asaph, keeper of the royal park, so he will give me timber to make beams for the gates of the citadel by the temple and for the city wall and for the residence I will occupy?' And because the gracious hand of my God was on me, the king granted my requests. 9So I went to the governors of Trans-Euphrates and gave them the king's letters. The king had also sent army officers and cavalry with me.

10When Sanballat the Horonite and Tobiah the Ammonite official heard about this, they were very much disturbed that someone had come to promote the welfare of the Israelites.

Nehemiah inspects Jerusalem's walls

11I went to Jerusalem, and after staying there three days 12I set out during the night with a few others. I had not told anyone what my God had put in my heart to do for Jerusalem. There were no mounts with me except the one I was riding on.

City walls
Nehemiah 2:13
The way to tell a city from a town or village in ancient times was whether it had walls around it for defence. City walls were usually huge, between six and nine metres thick.

13 By night I went out through the Valley Gate towards the Jackal[a] Well and the Dung Gate, examining the walls of Jerusalem, which had been broken down, and its gates, which had been destroyed by fire. 14 Then I moved on towards the Fountain Gate and the King's Pool, but there was not enough room for my mount to get through; 15 so I went up the valley by night, examining the wall. Finally, I turned back and re-entered through the Valley Gate. 16 The officials did not know where I had gone or what I was doing, because as yet I had said nothing to the Jews or the priests or nobles or officials or any others who would be doing the work.

17 Then I said to them, 'You see the trouble we are in: Jerusalem lies in ruins, and its gates have been burned with fire. Come, let us rebuild the wall of Jerusalem, and we will no longer be in disgrace.' 18 I also told them about the gracious hand of my God on me and what the king had said to me.

They replied, 'Let us start rebuilding.' So they began this good work.

19 But when Sanballat the Horonite, Tobiah the Ammonite official and Geshem the Arab heard about it, they mocked and ridiculed us. 'What is this you are doing?' they asked. 'Are you rebelling against the king?'

20 I answered them by saying, 'The God of heaven will give us success. We his servants will start rebuilding, but as for you, you have no share in Jerusalem or any claim or historic right to it.'

Builders of the wall

3 Eliashib the high priest and his fellow priests went to work and rebuilt the Sheep Gate. They dedicated it and set its doors in place, building as far as the Tower of the Hundred, which they dedicated, and as far as the Tower of Hananel. 2 The men of Jericho built the adjoining section, and Zakkur son of Imri built next to them.

3 The Fish Gate was rebuilt by the sons of Hassenaah. They laid its beams and put its doors and bolts and bars in place. 4 Meremoth son of Uriah, the son of Hakkoz, repaired the next section. Next to him Meshullam son of Berekiah, the son of Meshezabel, made repairs, and next to him Zadok son of Baana also made repairs. 5 The next section was repaired by the men of Tekoa, but their nobles would not put their shoulders to the work under their supervisors.[b]

6 The Jeshanah[c] Gate was repaired by Joiada son of Paseah and Meshullam son of Besodeiah. They laid its beams and put its doors with their bolts and bars in place. 7 Next to them, repairs were made by men from Gibeon and Mizpah—Melatiah of Gibeon and Jadon of Meronoth—places under the authority of the governor of Trans-Euphrates. 8 Uzziel son of Harhaiah, one of the goldsmiths, repaired the next section; and Hananiah, one of the perfume-makers, made repairs next to that. They restored Jerusalem as far as the Broad Wall. 9 Rephaiah son of Hur, ruler of a half-district of Jerusalem, repaired the next section. 10 Adjoining this, Jedaiah son of Harumaph made repairs opposite his house, and Hattush son of Hashabneiah made repairs next to him. 11 Malkijah son of Harim and Hasshub son of Pahath-Moab repaired another section and the Tower of the Ovens. 12 Shallum son of Hallohesh, ruler of a half-district of Jerusalem, repaired the next section with the help of his daughters.

---

[a] 13 Or Serpent or fig   [b] 5 Or their Lord or the governor   [c] 6 Or Old

¹³The Valley Gate was repaired by Hanun and the residents of Zanoah. They rebuilt it and put its doors with their bolts and bars in place. They also repaired a thousand cubits[a] of the wall as far as the Dung Gate.

¹⁴The Dung Gate was repaired by Malkijah son of Rekab, ruler of the district of Beth Hakkerem. He rebuilt it and put its doors with their bolts and bars in place.

¹⁵The Fountain Gate was repaired by Shallun son of Kol-Hozeh, ruler of the district of Mizpah. He rebuilt it, roofing it over and putting its doors and bolts and bars in place. He also repaired the wall of the Pool of Siloam,[b] by the King's Garden, as far as the steps going down from the City of David. ¹⁶Beyond him, Nehemiah son of Azbuk, ruler of a half-district of Beth Zur, made repairs up to a point opposite the tombs[c] of David, as far as the artificial pool and the House of the Heroes.

¹⁷Next to him, the repairs were made by the Levites under Rehum son of Bani. Beside him, Hashabiah, ruler of half the district of Keilah, carried out repairs for his district. ¹⁸Next to him, the repairs were made by their neighbours under Binnui[d] son of Henadad, ruler of the other half-district of Keilah. ¹⁹Next to him, Ezer son of Jeshua, ruler of Mizpah, repaired another section, from a point facing the ascent to the armoury as far as the angle of the wall. ²⁰Next to him, Baruch son of Zabbai zealously repaired another section, from the angle to the entrance of the house of Eliashib the high priest. ²¹Next to him, Meremoth son of Uriah, the son of Hakkoz, repaired another section, from the entrance of Eliashib's house to the end of it.

²²The repairs next to him were made by the priests from the surrounding region. ²³Beyond them, Benjamin and Hasshub made repairs in front of their house; and next to them, Azariah son of Maaseiah, the son of Ananiah, made repairs beside his house. ²⁴Next to him, Binnui son of Henadad repaired another section, from Azariah's house to the angle and the corner, ²⁵and Palal son of Uzai worked opposite the angle and the tower projecting from the upper palace near the court of the guard. Next to him, Pedaiah son of Parosh ²⁶and the temple servants living on the hill of Ophel made repairs up to a point opposite the Water Gate towards the east and the projecting tower. ²⁷Next to them, the men of Tekoa repaired another section, from the great projecting tower to the wall of Ophel.

²⁸Above the Horse Gate, the priests made repairs, each in front of his own house. ²⁹Next to them, Zadok son of Immer made repairs opposite his house. Next to him, Shemaiah son of Shekaniah, the guard at the East Gate, made repairs. ³⁰Next to him, Hananiah son of Shelemiah, and Hanun, the sixth son of Zalaph, repaired another section. Next to them, Meshullam son of Berekiah made repairs opposite his living quarters. ³¹Next to him, Malkijah, one of the goldsmiths, made repairs as far as the house of the temple servants and the merchants, opposite the Inspection Gate, and as far as the room above the corner; ³²and between the room above the corner and the Sheep Gate the goldsmiths and merchants made repairs.

Opposition to the rebuilding

4 *When Sanballat heard that we were rebuilding the wall, he became angry and was greatly incensed. He ridiculed the Jews, ²and in the presence of his associates and the army of Samaria, he said, 'What are those feeble Jews doing? Will they restore their wall? Will they offer sacrifices? Will they finish in a day? Can they bring the stones back to life from those heaps of rubble—burned as they are?'

³Tobiah the Ammonite, who was at his side, said, 'What they are building—even a fox climbing up on it would break down their wall of stones!'

⁴Hear us, our God, for we are despised. Turn their insults back on their own heads. Give them over as plunder in a land of

---

[a] 13 That is, about 450 metres   [b] 15 Hebrew *Shelah*, a variant of *Shiloah,* that is, Siloam   [c] 16 Hebrew; Septuagint, some Vulgate manuscripts and Syriac *tomb*   [d] 18 Two Hebrew manuscripts and Syriac (see also Septuagint and verse 24); most Hebrew manuscripts *Bavvai*

* 4:1-6 is numbered 3:33-38 in Hebrew texts.

captivity. ⁵Do not cover up their guilt or blot out their sins from your sight, for they have thrown insults in the face of[a] the builders.

⁶So we rebuilt the wall till all of it reached half its height, for the people worked with all their heart.

*⁷But when Sanballat, Tobiah, the Arabs, the Ammonites and the people of Ashdod heard that the repairs to Jerusalem's walls had gone ahead and that the gaps were being closed, they were very angry. ⁸They all plotted together to come and fight against Jerusalem and stir up trouble against it. ⁹But we prayed to our God and posted a guard day and night to meet this threat.

¹⁰Meanwhile, the people in Judah said, 'The strength of the labourers is giving out, and there is so much rubble that we cannot rebuild the wall.'

¹¹Also our enemies said, 'Before they know it or see us, we will be right there among them and will kill them and put an end to the work.'

¹²Then the Jews who lived near them came and told us ten times over, 'Wherever you turn, they will attack us.'

¹³Therefore I stationed some of the people behind the lowest points of the wall at the exposed places, posting them by families, with their swords, spears and bows. ¹⁴After I looked things over, I stood up and said to the nobles, the officials and the rest of the people, 'Don't be afraid of them. Remember the Lord, who is great and awesome, and fight for your people, your sons and your daughters, your wives and your homes.'

¹⁵When our enemies heard that we were aware of their plot and that God had frustrated it, we all returned to the wall, each to our work.

¹⁶From that day on, half of my men did the work, while the other half were equipped with spears, shields, bows and armour. The officers posted themselves behind all the people of Judah ¹⁷who were building the wall. Those who carried materials did their work with one hand and held a weapon in the other, ¹⁸and each of the builders wore his sword at his side as he worked. But the man who sounded the trumpet stayed with me.

¹⁹Then I said to the nobles, the officials and the rest of the people, 'The work is extensive and spread out, and we are widely separated from each other along the wall. ²⁰Wherever you hear the sound of the trumpet, join us there. Our God will fight for us!'

²¹So we continued the work with half the men holding spears, from the first light of dawn till the stars came out. ²²At that time I also said to the people, 'Let every man and his helper stay inside Jerusalem at night, so that they can serve us as guards by night and as workers by day.' ²³Neither I nor my brothers nor my men nor the guards with me took off our clothes; each had his weapon, even when he went for water.[b]

Nehemiah helps the poor

5 Now the men and their wives raised a great outcry against their fellow Jews. ²Some were saying, 'We and our sons and daughters are numerous; in order for us to eat and stay alive, we must get grain.'

³Others were saying, 'We are mortgaging our fields, our vineyards and our homes to get grain during the famine.'

⁴Still others were saying, 'We have had to borrow money to pay the king's tax on our fields and vineyards. ⁵Although we are of the same flesh and blood as the rest of our people and though our children are as good as theirs, yet we have to subject our sons and daughters to slavery. Some of our daughters have already been enslaved, but we are powerless, because our fields and our vineyards belong to others.'

⁶When I heard their outcry and these charges, I was very angry. ⁷I pondered them in my mind and then accused the nobles and officials. I told them, 'You are charging your own people interest!' So I called together a large meeting to deal with them ⁸and said: 'As far as possible, we have bought back our fellow Jews who were sold to the Gentiles. Now you are selling your own people, only

---

[a] 5 Or *have aroused your anger before*   [b] 23 The meaning of the Hebrew for this clause is uncertain.

* 4:7-23 is numbered 4:1-17 in Hebrew texts.

for them to be sold back to us!' They kept quiet, because they could find nothing to say.

⁹So I continued, 'What you are doing is not right. Shouldn't you walk in the fear of our God to avoid the reproach of our Gentile enemies? ¹⁰I and my brothers and my men are also lending the people money and grain. But let us stop charging interest! ¹¹Give back to them immediately their fields, vineyards, olive groves and houses, and also the interest you are charging them—one per cent of the money, grain, new wine and olive oil.'

¹²'We will give it back,' they said. 'And we will not demand anything more from them. We will do as you say.'

Then I summoned the priests and made the nobles and officials take an oath to do what they had promised. ¹³I also shook out the folds of my robe and said, 'In this way may God shake out of their houses and possessions anyone who does not keep this promise. So may such a person be shaken out and emptied!'

At this the whole assembly said, 'Amen,' and praised the LORD. And the people did as they had promised.

¹⁴Moreover, from the twentieth year of King Artaxerxes, when I was appointed to be their governor in the land of Judah, until his thirty-second year—twelve years—neither I nor my brothers ate the food allotted to the governor. ¹⁵But the earlier governors—those preceding me—placed a heavy burden on the people and took forty shekels[a] of silver from them in addition to food and wine. Their assistants also lorded it over the people. But out of reverence for God I did not act like that. ¹⁶Instead, I devoted myself to the work on this wall. All my men were assembled there for the work; we[b] did not acquire any land.

¹⁷Furthermore, a hundred and fifty Jews and officials ate at my table, as well as those who came to us from the surrounding nations. ¹⁸Each day one ox, six choice sheep and some poultry were prepared for me, and every ten days an abundant supply of wine of all kinds. In spite of all this, I never demanded the food allotted to the governor, because the demands were heavy on these people.

¹⁹Remember me with favour, my God, for all I have done for these people.

Further opposition to the rebuilding

6 When word came to Sanballat, Tobiah, Geshem the Arab and the rest of our enemies that I had rebuilt the wall and not a gap was left in it—though up to that time I had not set the doors in the gates— ²Sanballat and Geshem sent me this message: 'Come, let us meet together in one of the villages[c] on the plain of Ono.'

But they were scheming to harm me; ³so I sent messengers to them with this reply: 'I am carrying on a great project and cannot go down. Why should the work stop while I leave it and go down to you?' ⁴Four times they sent me the same message, and each time I gave them the same answer.

⁵Then, the fifth time, Sanballat sent his assistant to me with the same message, and in his hand was an unsealed letter ⁶in which was written:

> 'It is reported among the nations—and Geshem[d] says it is true—that you and the Jews are plotting to revolt, and therefore you are building the wall. Moreover, according to these reports you are about to become their king ⁷and have even appointed prophets to make this proclamation about you in Jerusalem: "There is a king in Judah!" Now this report will get back to the king; so come, let us meet together.'

⁸I sent him this reply: 'Nothing like what you are saying is happening; you are just making it up out of your head.'

⁹They were all trying to frighten us, thinking, 'Their hands will get too weak for the work, and it will not be completed.'

But I prayed, 'Now strengthen my hands.'

¹⁰One day I went to the house of Shemaiah son of Delaiah, the son of Mehetabel, who was shut in at his home. He said,

---

[a] 15 That is, about 460 grams [b] 16 Most Hebrew manuscripts; some Hebrew manuscripts, Septuagint, Vulgate and Syriac *I* [c] 2 Or *in Kephirim* [d] 6 Hebrew *Gashmu*, a variant of *Geshem*

'Let us meet in the house of God, inside the temple, and let us close the temple doors, because some people are coming to kill you—by night they are coming to kill you.'

11 But I said, 'Should someone like me run away? Or should one like me go into the temple to save his life? I will not go!' 12 I realised that God had not sent him, but that he had prophesied against me because Tobiah and Sanballat had hired him. 13 He had been hired to intimidate me so that I would commit a sin by doing this, and then they would give me a bad name to discredit me.

14 Remember Tobiah and Sanballat, my God, because of what they have done; remember also the prophet Noadiah and how she and the rest of the prophets have been trying to intimidate me. 15 So the wall was completed on the twenty-fifth of Elul, in fifty-two days.

Opposition to the completed wall

16 When all our enemies heard about this, all the surrounding nations were afraid and lost their self-confidence, because they realised that this work had been done with the help of our God.

17 Also, in those days the nobles of Judah were sending many letters to Tobiah, and replies from Tobiah kept coming to them. 18 For many in Judah were under oath to him, since he was son-in-law to Shekaniah son of Arah, and his son Jehohanan had married the daughter of Meshullam son of Berekiah. 19 Moreover, they kept reporting to me his good deeds and then telling him what I said. And Tobiah sent letters to intimidate me.

7 After the wall had been rebuilt and I had set the doors in place, the gatekeepers, the musicians and the Levites were appointed. 2 I put in charge of Jerusalem my brother Hanani, along with Hananiah the commander of the citadel, because he was trustworthy and feared God more than most people do. 3 I said to them, 'The gates of Jerusalem are not to be opened until the sun is hot. While the gatekeepers are still on duty, make them shut the doors and bar them. Also appoint residents of Jerusalem as guards, some at their posts and some near their own houses.'

The list of the exiles who returned

4 Now the city was large and spacious, but there were few people in it, and the houses had not yet been rebuilt. 5 So my God put it into my heart to assemble the nobles, the officials and the common people for registration by families. I found the genealogical record of those who had been the first to return. This is what I found written there:

> 6 These are the people of the province who came up from the captivity of the exiles whom Nebuchadnezzar king of Babylon had taken captive (they returned to Jerusalem and Judah, each to his own town, 7 in company with Zerubbabel, Joshua, Nehemiah, Azariah, Raamiah, Nahamani, Mordecai, Bilshan, Mispereth, Bigvai, Nehum and Baanah):

The list of the men of Israel:

8 the descendants of Parosh	2,172
9 of Shephatiah	372
10 of Arah	652
11 of Pahath-Moab (through the line of Joshua and Joab)	2,818
12 of Elam	1,254
13 of Zattu	845
14 of Zakkai	760
15 of Binnui	648
16 of Bebai	628
17 of Azgad	2,322
18 of Adonikam	667
19 of Bigvai	2,067
20 of Adin	655
21 of Ater (through Hezekiah)	98
22 of Hashum	328
23 of Bezai	324
24 of Hariph	112
25 of Gibeon	95
26 the men of Bethlehem and Netophah	188
27 of Anathoth	128
28 of Beth Azmaveth	42
29 of Kiriath Jearim, Kephirah and Beeroth	743
30 of Ramah and Geba	621

31of Mikmash	122
32of Bethel and Ai	123
33of the other Nebo	52
34of the other Elam	1,254
35of Harim	320
36of Jericho	345
37of Lod, Hadid and Ono	721
38of Senaah	3,930

39The priests:

the descendants of Jedaiah (through the family of Jeshua)	973
40of Immer	1,052
41of Pashhur	1,247
42of Harim	1,017

43The Levites:

the descendants of Jeshua (through Kadmiel through the line of Hodaviah)	74

44The musicians:

the descendants of Asaph	148

45The gatekeepers:

the descendants of Shallum, Ater, Talmon, Akkub, Hatita and Shobai	138

46The temple servants:

the descendants of
Ziha, Hasupha, Tabbaoth,
47Keros, Sia, Padon,
48Lebana, Hagaba, Shalmai,
49Hanan, Giddel, Gahar,
50Reaiah, Rezin, Nekoda,
51Gazzam, Uzza, Paseah,
52Besai, Meunim, Nephussim,
53Bakbuk, Hakupha, Harhur,
54Bazluth, Mehida, Harsha,
55Barkos, Sisera, Temah,
56Neziah and Hatipha

57The descendants of the servants of Solomon:

the descendants of
Sotai, Sophereth, Perida,
58Jaala, Darkon, Giddel,
59Shephatiah, Hattil,
Pokereth-Hazzebaim and Amon

60The temple servants and the descendants of the servants of Solomon	392

61The following came up from the towns of Tel Melah, Tel Harsha, Kerub, Addon and Immer, but they could not show that their families were descended from Israel:

62the descendants of Delaiah, Tobiah and Nekoda	642

63And from among the priests:

the descendants of Hobaiah, Hakkoz and Barzillai (a man who had married a daughter of Barzillai the Gileadite and was called by that name).

64These searched for their family records, but they could not find them and so were excluded from the priesthood as unclean. 65The governor, therefore, ordered them not to eat any of the most sacred food until there should be a priest ministering with the Urim and Thummim.

66The whole company numbered 42,360, 67besides their 7,337 male and female slaves; and they also had 245 male and female singers. 68There were 736 horses, 245 mules,[a] 69435 camels and 6,720 donkeys.

70Some of the heads of the families contributed to the work. The governor gave to the treasury 1,000 darics[b] of gold, 50 bowls and 530 garments for priests. 71Some of the heads of the families gave to the treasury for the work 20,000 darics[c] of gold and 2,200 minas[d] of silver. 72The total given by the rest of the people was 20,000 darics of gold, 2,000 minas[e] of silver and 67 garments for priests.

73The priests, the Levites, the gatekeepers, the musicians and the temple servants, along with certain of the people

---

[a] 68 Some Hebrew manuscripts (see also Ezra 2:66); most Hebrew manuscripts do not have this verse.   [b] 70 That is, about 8.5 kilograms   [c] 71 That is, about 170 kilograms; also in verse 72   [d] 71 That is, about 1.2 metric tons   [e] 72 That is, about 1.1 metric tons

and the rest of the Israelites, settled in their own towns.

Ezra reads the Law

8 When the seventh month came and the Israelites had settled in their towns, ¹all the people assembled with one accord in the square before the Water Gate. They told Ezra the teacher of the Law to bring out the Book of the Law of Moses, which the LORD had commanded for Israel.

²So on the first day of the seventh month Ezra the priest brought the Law before the assembly, which was made up of men and women and all who were able to understand. ³He read it aloud from daybreak till noon as he faced the square before the Water Gate in the presence of the men, women and others who could understand. And all the people listened attentively to the Book of the Law.

⁴Ezra the teacher of the Law stood on a high wooden platform built for the occasion. Beside him on his right stood Mattithiah, Shema, Anaiah, Uriah, Hilkiah and Maaseiah; and on his left were Pedaiah, Mishael, Malkijah, Hashum, Hashbaddanah, Zechariah and Meshullam.

⁵Ezra opened the book. All the people could see him because he was standing above them; and as he opened it, the people all stood up. ⁶Ezra praised the LORD, the great God; and all the people lifted their hands and responded, 'Amen! Amen!' Then they bowed down and worshipped the LORD with their faces to the ground.

⁷The Levites—Jeshua, Bani, Sherebiah, Jamin, Akkub, Shabbethai, Hodiah, Maaseiah, Kelita, Azariah, Jozabad, Hanan and Pelaiah—instructed the people in the Law while the people were standing there. ⁸They read from the Book of the Law of God, making it clear*ᵃ* and giving the meaning so that the people understood what was being read.

⁹Then Nehemiah the governor, Ezra the priest and teacher of the Law, and the Levites who were instructing the people said to them all, 'This day is holy to the LORD your God. Do not mourn or weep.' For all the people had been weeping as they listened to the words of the Law.

¹⁰Nehemiah said, 'Go and enjoy choice food and sweet drinks, and send some to those who have nothing prepared. This day is holy to our Lord. Do not grieve, for the joy of the LORD is your strength.'

¹¹The Levites calmed all the people, saying, 'Be still, for this is a holy day. Do not grieve.'

¹²Then all the people went away to eat and drink, to send portions of food and to celebrate with great joy, because they now understood the words that had been made known to them.

¹³On the second day of the month, the heads of all the families, along with the priests and the Levites, gathered round Ezra the teacher of the Law to give attention to the words of the Law. ¹⁴They found written in the Law, which the LORD had commanded through Moses, that the Israelites were to live in temporary shelters during the festival of the seventh month ¹⁵and that they should proclaim this word and spread it throughout their towns and in Jerusalem: 'Go out into the hill country and bring back

---

making Connections

The Book of the Law
Nehemiah 8:1
Having rebuilt the wall and resettled in their towns, it was time for the Israelites to return to their worship of God. The Law was written in Hebrew, which the people no longer understood, so the Levites would have been translating it into Aramaic and explaining it as they read. Hearing the law had a dramatic effect on the people as they realised that they had not kept it for a long time.

ᵃ 8 Or *God, translating it*

branches from olive and wild olive trees, and from myrtles, palms and other leafy trees, to make temporary shelters'—as it is written.[a]

16 So the people went out and brought back branches and built themselves temporary shelters on their own roofs, in their courtyards, in the courts of the house of God and in the square by the Water Gate and the one by the Gate of Ephraim. 17 The whole company that had returned from exile built temporary shelters and lived in them. From the days of Joshua son of Nun until that day, the Israelites had not celebrated it like this. And their joy was very great.

18 Day after day, from the first day to the last, Ezra read from the Book of the Law of God. They celebrated the festival for seven days, and on the eighth day, in accordance with the regulation, there was an assembly.

The Israelites confess their sins

9 On the twenty-fourth day of the same month, the Israelites gathered together, fasting and wearing sackcloth and putting dust on their heads. 2 Those of Israelite descent had separated themselves from all foreigners. They stood in their places and confessed their sins and the sins of their ancestors. 3 They stood where they were and read from the Book of the Law of the LORD their God for a quarter of the day, and spent another quarter in confession and in worshipping the LORD their God. 4 Standing on the stairs of the Levites were Jeshua, Bani, Kadmiel, Shebaniah, Bunni, Sherebiah, Bani and Kenani. They cried out with loud voices to the LORD their God. 5 And the Levites—Jeshua, Kadmiel, Bani, Hashabneiah, Sherebiah, Hodiah, Shebaniah and Pethahiah—said: 'Stand up and praise the LORD your God, who is from everlasting to everlasting.[b]'

'Blessed be your glorious name,
and may it be exalted above all blessing and praise. 6 You alone are the LORD. You made the heavens, even the highest heavens, and all their starry host, the earth and all that is on it, the seas and all that is in them. You give life to everything, and the multitudes of heaven worship you.

7 'You are the LORD God, who chose Abram and brought him out of Ur of the Chaldeans and named him Abraham. 8 You found his heart faithful to you, and you made a covenant with him to give to his descendants the land of the Canaanites, Hittites, Amorites, Perizzites, Jebusites and Girgashites. You have kept your promise because you are righteous.

9 'You saw the suffering of our ancestors in Egypt; you heard their cry at the Red Sea.[c] 10 You sent signs and wonders against Pharaoh, against all his officials and all the people of his land, for you knew how arrogantly the Egyptians treated them. You made a name for yourself, which remains to this day. 11 You divided the sea before them, so that they passed through it on dry ground, but you hurled their pursuers into the depths, like a stone into mighty waters. 12 By day you led them with a pillar of cloud, and by night with a pillar of fire to give them light on the way they were to take.

13 'You came down on Mount Sinai; you spoke to them from heaven. You gave them regulations and laws that are just and right, and decrees and commands that are good. 14 You made known to them your holy Sabbath and gave them commands, decrees and laws through your servant Moses. 15 In their hunger you gave them bread from heaven and in their thirst you brought them water from the rock; you told them to go in and take possession of the land you had sworn with uplifted hand to give them.

---

[a] 15 See Lev. 23: 37-40. [b] 5 Or *God for ever and ever* [c] 9 Or *the Sea of Reeds*

¹⁶'But they, our ancestors, became arrogant and stiff-necked, and did not obey your commands. ¹⁷They refused to listen and failed to remember the miracles you performed among them. They became stiff-necked and in their rebellion appointed a leader in order to return to their slavery. But you are a forgiving God, gracious and compassionate, slow to anger and abounding in love. Therefore you did not desert them, ¹⁸even when they cast for themselves an image of a calf and said, "This is your god, who brought you up out of Egypt," or when they committed awful blasphemies.

¹⁹'Because of your great compassion you did not abandon them in the wilderness. By day the pillar of cloud did not cease to guide them on their path, nor the pillar of fire by night to shine on the way they were to take. ²⁰You gave your good Spirit to instruct them. You did not withhold your manna from their mouths, and you gave them water for their thirst. ²¹For forty years you sustained them in the wilderness; they lacked nothing, their clothes did not wear out nor did their feet become swollen.

²²'You gave them kingdoms and nations, allotting to them even the remotest frontiers. They took over the country of Sihon[a] king of Heshbon and the country of Og king of Bashan. ²³You made their children as numerous as the stars in the sky, and you brought them into the land that you told their parents to enter and possess. ²⁴Their children went in and took possession of the land. You subdued before them the Canaanites, who lived in the land; you gave the Canaanites into their hands, along with their kings and the peoples of the land, to deal with them as they pleased. ²⁵They captured fortified cities and fertile land; they took possession of houses filled with all kinds of good things, wells already dug, vineyards, olive groves and fruit trees in abundance. They ate to the full and were well-nourished; they revelled in your great goodness.

²⁶'But they were disobedient and rebelled against you; they put your law behind their backs. They killed your prophets, who had warned them in order to turn them back to you; they committed awful blasphemies. ²⁷So you delivered them into the hands of their enemies, who oppressed them. But when they were oppressed they cried out to you. From heaven you heard them, and in your great compassion you gave them deliverers, who rescued them from the hand of their enemies.

²⁸'But as soon as they were at rest, they again did what was evil in your sight. Then you abandoned them to the hand of their enemies so that they ruled over them. And when they cried out to you again, you heard from heaven, and in your compassion you delivered them time after time.

²⁹'You warned them in order to turn them back to your law, but they became arrogant and disobeyed your commands. They sinned against your ordinances, of which you said, "Whoever obeys them will live by them." Stubbornly they turned their backs on you, became stiff-necked and refused to listen. ³⁰For many years you were patient with them. By your Spirit you warned them through your prophets. Yet they paid no attention, so you gave them into the hands of the

---

[a] 22 One Hebrew manuscript and Septuagint; most Hebrew manuscripts *Sihon, that is, the country of the*

neighbouring peoples. 31But in your great mercy you did not put an end to them or abandon them, for you are a gracious and merciful God.

32'Now therefore, our God, the great God, mighty and awesome, who keeps his covenant of love, do not let all this hardship seem trifling in your eyes—the hardship that has come on us, on our kings and leaders, on our priests and prophets, on our ancestors and all your people, from the days of the kings of Assyria until today. 33In all that has happened to us, you have remained righteous; you have acted faithfully, while we acted wickedly. 34Our kings, our leaders, our priests and our ancestors did not follow your law; they did not pay attention to your commands or the statutes you warned them to keep. 35Even while they were in their kingdom, enjoying your great goodness to them in the spacious and fertile land you gave them, they did not serve you or turn from their evil ways.

36'But see, we are slaves today, slaves in the land you gave our ancestors so that they could eat its fruit and the other good things it produces. 37Because of our sins, its abundant harvest goes to the kings you have placed over us. They rule over our bodies and our cattle as they please. We are in great distress.

The agreement of the people

*38'In view of all this, we are making a binding agreement, putting it in writing, and our leaders, our Levites and our priests are affixing their seals to it.'

10 *Those who sealed it were:

Nehemiah the governor, the son of Hakaliah.

Zedekiah, 2Seraiah, Azariah, Jeremiah, 3Pashhur, Amariah, Malkijah, 4Hattush, Shebaniah, Malluk, 5Harim, Meremoth, Obadiah, 6Daniel, Ginnethon, Baruch, 7Meshullam, Abijah, Mijamin, 8Maaziah, Bilgai and Shemaiah. These were the priests.

9The Levites:

Jeshua son of Azaniah, Binnui of the sons of Henadad, Kadmiel, 10and their associates: Shebaniah, Hodiah, Kelita, Pelaiah, Hanan, 11Mika, Rehob, Hashabiah, 12Zakkur, Sherebiah, Shebaniah, 13Hodiah, Bani and Beninu.

14The leaders of the people:

Parosh, Pahath-Moab, Elam, Zattu, Bani, 15Bunni, Azgad, Bebai, 16Adonijah, Bigvai, Adin, 17Ater, Hezekiah, Azzur, 18Hodiah, Hashum, Bezai, 19Hariph, Anathoth, Nebai, 20Magpiash, Meshullam, Hezir, 21Meshezabel, Zadok, Jaddua, 22Pelatiah, Hanan, Anaiah, 23Hoshea, Hananiah, Hasshub, 24Hallohesh, Pilha, Shobek, 25Rehum, Hashabnah, Maaseiah, 26Ahiah, Hanan, Anan, 27Malluk, Harim and Baanah.

28'The rest of the people— priests, Levites, gatekeepers, musicians, temple servants and all who separated themselves from the neighbouring peoples for the sake of the Law of God, together with their wives and all their sons and daughters who are able to understand— 29all these now join their fellow Israelites the nobles, and bind themselves with a curse and an oath to follow the Law of God given through Moses the servant of God and to obey carefully all the commands,

* 9:38 is numbered 10:1 in Hebrew texts.   * 10:1-39 is numbered 10:2-40 in Hebrew texts.

regulations and decrees of the LORD our Lord.

30 'We promise not to give our daughters in marriage to the peoples around us or take their daughters for our sons.

31 'When the neighbouring peoples bring merchandise or grain to sell on the Sabbath, we will not buy from them on the Sabbath or on any holy day. Every seventh year we will forgo working the land and will cancel all debts.

32 'We assume the responsibility for carrying out the commands to give a third of a shekel[a] each year for the service of the house of our God: 33 for the bread set out on the table; for the regular grain offerings and burnt offerings; for the offerings on the Sabbaths, at the New Moon feasts and at the appointed festivals; for the holy offerings; for sin offerings[b] to make atonement for Israel; and for all the duties of the house of our God.

34 'We—the priests, the Levites and the people—have cast lots to determine when each of our families is to bring to the house of our God at set times each year a contribution of wood to burn on the altar of the LORD our God, as it is written in the Law.

35 'We also assume responsibility for bringing to the house of the LORD each year the firstfruits of our crops and of every fruit tree.

36 'As it is also written in the Law, we will bring the firstborn of our sons and of our cattle, of our herds and of our flocks to the house of our God, to the priests ministering there.

37 'Moreover, we will bring to the storerooms of the house of our God, to the priests, the first of our ground meal, of our ⌊grain⌋ offerings, of the fruit of all our trees and of our new wine and olive oil. And we will bring a tithe of our crops to the Levites, for it is the Levites who collect the tithes in all the towns where we work. 38 A priest descended from Aaron is to accompany the Levites when they receive the tithes, and the Levites are to bring a tenth of the tithes up to the house of our God, to the storerooms of the treasury. 39 The people of Israel, including the Levites, are to bring their contributions of grain, new wine and olive oil to the storerooms where the articles for the sanctuary and for the ministering priests, the gatekeepers and the musicians are also kept.

'We will not neglect the house of our God.'

The new residents of Jerusalem

11 Now the leaders of the people settled in Jerusalem. The rest of the people cast lots to bring one out of every ten of them to live in Jerusalem, the holy city, while the remaining nine were to stay in their own towns. 2 The people commended all who volunteered to live in Jerusalem.

3 These are the provincial leaders who settled in Jerusalem (now some Israelites, priests, Levites, temple servants and descendants of Solomon's servants lived in the towns of Judah, each of them on their own property in the various towns, 4 while other people from both Judah and Benjamin lived in Jerusalem):

From the descendants of Judah:

> Athaiah son of Uzziah, the son of Zechariah, the son of Amariah, the son of Shephatiah, the son of Mahalalel, a descendant of Perez; 5 and Maaseiah son of Baruch, the son of Kol-Hozeh, the son of Hazaiah, the son of Adaiah, the son of Joiarib, the son of Zechariah, a descendant of Shelah. 6 The descendants of Perez who lived in

---

[a] 32 That is, about 4 grams   [b] 33 Or *purification offerings*

Sign of the times

Casting lots
Nehemiah 11:1

Lots were thrown on the ground by a priest or official to help them make decisions. It was a similar process to throwing dice, except that people believed that God guided the outcome and it was a way of finding out his will. Although lots are mentioned many times in the Old Testament and a few in the New Testament, no-one now knows what they actually looked like.

Jerusalem totalled 468 men of standing.

⁷From the descendants of Benjamin:

Sallu son of Meshullam, the son of Joed, the son of Pedaiah, the son of Kolaiah, the son of Maaseiah, the son of Ithiel, the son of Jeshaiah, ⁸and his followers, Gabbai and Sallai—928 men. ⁹Joel son of Zikri was their chief officer, and Judah son of Hassenuah was over the New Quarter of the city.

¹⁰From the priests:

Jedaiah; the son of Joiarib; Jakin; ¹¹Seraiah son of Hilkiah, the son of Meshullam, the son of Zadok, the son of Meraioth, the son of Ahitub, the official in charge of the house of God, ¹²and their associates, who carried on work for the temple—822 men; Adaiah son of Jeroham, the son of Pelaliah, the son of Amzi, the son of Zechariah, the son of Pashhur, the son of Malkijah, ¹³and his associates, who were heads of families—242 men; Amashsai son of Azarel, the son of Ahzai, the son of Meshillemoth, the son of Immer, ¹⁴and his[a] associates, who were men of standing—128. Their chief officer was Zabdiel son of Haggedolim.

¹⁵From the Levites:

Shemaiah son of Hasshub, the son of Azrikam, the son of Hashabiah, the son of Bunni; ¹⁶Shabbethai and Jozabad, two of the heads of the Levites, who had charge of the outside work of the house of God; ¹⁷Mattaniah son of Mika, the son of Zabdi, the son of Asaph, the director who led in thanksgiving and prayer; Bakbukiah, second among his associates; and Abda son of Shammua, the son of Galal, the son of Jeduthun. ¹⁸The Levites in the holy city totalled 284.

¹⁹The gatekeepers:

Akkub, Talmon and their associates, who kept watch at the gates—172 men.

²⁰The rest of the Israelites, with the priests and Levites, were in all the towns of Judah, each of them on their ancestral property.
²¹The temple servants lived on the hill of Ophel, and Ziha and Gishpa were in charge of them.
²²The chief officer of the Levites in Jerusalem was Uzzi son of Bani, the son of Hashabiah, the son of Mattaniah, the son of Mika. Uzzi was one of Asaph's descendants, who were the musicians responsible for the service of the house of God. ²³The musicians were under the king's orders, which regulated their daily activity.
²⁴Pethahiah son of Meshezabel, one of the descendants of Zerah son of Judah, was the king's agent in all affairs relating to the people.
²⁵As for the villages with their fields, some of the people of Judah lived in Kiriath

---

[a] 14 Most Septuagint manuscripts; Hebrew *their*

Arba and its surrounding settlements, in Dibon and its settlements, in Jekabzeel and its villages, 26in Jeshua, in Moladah, in Beth Pelet, 27in Hazar Shual, in Beersheba and its settlements, 28in Ziklag, in Mekonah and its settlements, 29in En Rimmon, in Zorah, in Jarmuth, 30Zanoah, Adullam and their villages, in Lachish and its fields, and in Azekah and its settlements. So they were living all the way from Beersheba to the Valley of Hinnom.

31The descendants of the Benjaminites from Geba lived in Mikmash, Aija, Bethel and its settlements, 32in Anathoth, Nob and Ananiah, 33in Hazor, Ramah and Gittaim, 34in Hadid, Zeboim and Neballat, 35in Lod and Ono, and in the Valley of the Skilled Workers.

36Some of the divisions of the Levites of Judah settled in Benjamin.

Priests and Levites

12 These were the priests and Levites who returned with Zerubbabel son of Shealtiel and with Joshua:

Seraiah, Jeremiah, Ezra,
2Amariah, Malluk, Hattush,
3Shekaniah, Rehum, Meremoth,
4Iddo, Ginnethon,[a] Abijah,
5Mijamin,[b] Moadiah, Bilgah,
6Shemaiah, Joiarib, Jedaiah,
7Sallu, Amok, Hilkiah and Jedaiah.

These were the leaders of the priests and their associates in the days of Joshua.

8The Levites were Jeshua, Binnui, Kadmiel, Sherebiah, Judah, and also Mattaniah, who, together with his associates, was in charge of the songs of thanksgiving. 9Bakbukiah and Unni, their associates, stood opposite them in the services.

10Joshua was the father of Joiakim, Joiakim the father of Eliashib, Eliashib the father of Joiada, 11Joiada the father of Jonathan, and Jonathan the father of Jaddua.

12In the days of Joiakim, these were the heads of the priestly families:

of Seraiah's family, Meraiah;
of Jeremiah's, Hananiah;
13of Ezra's, Meshullam;
of Amariah's, Jehohanan;
14of Malluk's, Jonathan;
of Shekaniah's,[c] Joseph;
15of Harim's, Adna;
of Meremoth's,[d] Helkai;
16of Iddo's, Zechariah;
of Ginnethon's, Meshullam;
17of Abijah's, Zikri;
of Miniamin's and of Moadiah's, Piltai;
18of Bilgah's, Shammua;
of Shemaiah's, Jehonathan;
19of Joiarib's, Mattenai;
of Jedaiah's, Uzzi;
20of Sallu's, Kallai;
of Amok's, Eber;
21of Hilkiah's, Hashabiah;
of Jedaiah's, Nethanel.

22The family heads of the Levites in the days of Eliashib, Joiada, Johanan and Jaddua, as well as those of the priests, were recorded in the reign of Darius the Persian. 23The family heads among the descendants of Levi up to the time of Johanan son of Eliashib were recorded in the book of the annals. 24And the leaders of the Levites were Hashabiah, Sherebiah, Jeshua son of Kadmiel, and their associates, who stood opposite them to give praise and thanksgiving, one section responding to the other, as prescribed by David the man of God.

25Mattaniah, Bakbukiah, Obadiah, Meshullam, Talmon and Akkub were gatekeepers who guarded the storerooms at the gates. 26They served in the days of Joiakim son of Joshua, the son of Jozadak, and in the days of Nehemiah the governor and of Ezra the priest, the teacher of the Law.

Dedication of the wall of Jerusalem

27At the dedication of the wall of Jerusalem, the Levites were sought out from where they lived and were brought to Jerusalem to celebrate joyfully the dedication with songs of thanksgiving and with the music of cymbals, harps and lyres. 28The musicians also were brought together from the region around Jerusalem—from the villages of the Netophathites, 29from Beth Gilgal, and from the area of Geba and Azmaveth, for

---

[a]4 Many Hebrew manuscripts and Vulgate (see also Neh. 12:16); most Hebrew manuscripts *Ginnethoi* [b]5 A variant of *Miniamin* [c]14 Very many Hebrew manuscripts, some Septuagint manuscripts and Syriac (see also Neh. 12:3); most Hebrew manuscripts *Shebaniah's* [d]15 Some Septuagint manuscripts (see also Neh. 12:3); Hebrew *Meraioth's*

the musicians had built villages for themselves around Jerusalem. 30When the priests and Levites had purified themselves ceremonially, they purified the people, the gates and the wall.

31I had the leaders of Judah go up on top of[a] the wall. I also assigned two large choirs to give thanks. One was to proceed on top of[b] the wall to the right, towards the Dung Gate. 32Hoshaiah and half the leaders of Judah followed them, 33along with Azariah, Ezra, Meshullam, 34Judah, Benjamin, Shemaiah, Jeremiah, 35as well as some priests with trumpets, and also Zechariah son of Jonathan, the son of Shemaiah, the son of Mattaniah, the son of Micaiah, the son of Zakkur, the son of Asaph, 36and his associates—Shemaiah, Azarel, Milalai, Gilalai, Maai, Nethanel, Judah and Hanani—with musical instruments ⌊prescribed by⌋ David the man of God. Ezra the teacher of the Law led the procession. 37At the Fountain Gate they continued directly up the steps of the City of David on the ascent to the wall and passed above the site of David's palace to the Water Gate on the east.

38The second choir proceeded in the opposite direction. I followed them on top of[c] the wall, together with half the people—past the Tower of the Ovens to the Broad Wall, 39over the Gate of Ephraim, the Jeshanah[d] Gate, the Fish Gate, the Tower of Hananel and the Tower of the Hundred, as far as the Sheep Gate. At the Gate of the Guard they stopped.

40The two choirs that gave thanks then took their places in the house of God; so did I, together with half the officials, 41as well as the priests—Eliakim, Maaseiah, Miniamin, Micaiah, Elioenai, Zechariah and Hananiah with their trumpets— 42and also Maaseiah, Shemaiah, Eleazar, Uzzi, Jehohanan, Malkijah, Elam and Ezer. The choirs sang under the direction of Jezrahiah. 43And on that day they offered great sacrifices, rejoicing because God had given them great joy. The women and children also rejoiced. The sound of rejoicing in Jerusalem could be heard far away.

44At that time men were appointed to be in charge of the storerooms for the contributions, firstfruits and tithes. From the fields around the towns they were to bring into the storerooms the portions required by the Law for the priests and the Levites, for Judah was pleased with the ministering priests and Levites. 45They performed the service of their God and the service of purification, as did also the musicians and gatekeepers, according to the commands of David and his son Solomon. 46For long ago, in the days of David and Asaph, there had been directors for the musicians and for the songs of praise and thanksgiving to God. 47So in the days of Zerubbabel and of Nehemiah, all Israel contributed the daily portions for the musicians and the gatekeepers. They also set aside the portion for the other Levites, and the Levites set aside the portion for the descendants of Aaron.

Nehemiah's final reforms

13 On that day the Book of Moses was read aloud in the hearing of the people and there it was found written that no Ammonite or Moabite should ever be admitted into the assembly of God, 2because they had not met the Israelites with food and water but had hired Balaam to call a curse down on them. (Our God, however, turned the curse into a blessing.) 3When the people heard this law, they excluded from Israel all who were of foreign descent.

4Before this, Eliashib the priest had been put in charge of the storerooms of the house of our God. He was closely associated with Tobiah, 5and he had provided him with a large room formerly used to store the grain offerings and incense and temple articles, and also the tithes of grain, new wine and olive oil prescribed for the Levites, musicians and gatekeepers, as well as the contributions for the priests.

6But while all this was going on, I was not in Jerusalem, for in the thirty-second year of Artaxerxes king of Babylon I had returned to the king. Some time later I asked his permission 7and came back to Jerusalem. Here I learned about the evil thing Eliashib had done in providing Tobiah a room in the courts of the house of God. 8I was greatly

---

[a] 31 Or *go alongside* [b] 31 Or *proceed alongside* [c] 38 Or *them alongside* [d] 39 Or *Old*

displeased and threw all Tobiah's household goods out of the room. ⁹I gave orders to purify the rooms, and then I put back into them the equipment of the house of God, with the grain offerings and the incense.

¹⁰I also learned that the portions assigned to the Levites had not been given to them, and that all the Levites and musicians responsible for the service had gone back to their own fields. ¹¹So I rebuked the officials and asked them, 'Why is the house of God neglected?' Then I called them together and stationed them at their posts.

¹²All Judah brought the tithes of grain, new wine and olive oil into the storerooms. ¹³I put Shelemiah the priest, Zadok the scribe, and a Levite named Pedaiah in charge of the storerooms and made Hanan son of Zakkur, the son of Mattaniah, their assistant, because they were considered trustworthy. They were made responsible for distributing the supplies to their fellow Levites.

¹⁴Remember me for this, my God, and do not blot out what I have so faithfully done for the house of my God and its services.

¹⁵In those days I saw people in Judah treading winepresses on the Sabbath and bringing in grain and loading it on donkeys, together with wine, grapes, figs and all other kinds of loads. And they were bringing all this into Jerusalem on the Sabbath. Therefore I warned them against selling food on that day. ¹⁶People from Tyre who lived in Jerusalem were bringing in fish and all kinds of merchandise and selling them in Jerusalem on the Sabbath to the people of Judah. ¹⁷I rebuked the nobles of Judah and said to them, 'What is this wicked thing you are doing—desecrating the Sabbath day? ¹⁸Didn't your ancestors do the same things, so that our God brought all this calamity on us and on this city? Now you are stirring up more wrath against Israel by desecrating the Sabbath.'

¹⁹When evening shadows fell on the gates of Jerusalem before the Sabbath, I ordered the doors to be shut and not opened until the Sabbath was over. I stationed some of my own men at the gates so that no load could be brought in on the Sabbath day. ²⁰Once or twice the merchants and sellers of all kinds of goods spent the night outside Jerusalem. ²¹But I warned them and said, 'Why do you spend the night by the wall? If you do this again, I will lay hands on you.' From that time on they no longer came on the Sabbath. ²²Then I commanded the Levites to purify themselves and go and guard the gates in order to keep the Sabbath day holy.

Remember me for this also, my God, and show mercy to me according to your great love.

²³Moreover, in those days I saw men of Judah who had married women from Ashdod, Ammon and Moab. ²⁴Half of their children spoke the language of Ashdod or the language of one of the other peoples, and did not know how to speak the language of Judah. ²⁵I rebuked them and called curses down on them. I beat some of them and pulled out their hair. I made them take an oath in God's name and said: 'You are not to give your daughters in marriage to their sons, nor are you to take their daughters in marriage for your sons or for yourselves. ²⁶Was it not because of marriages like these that Solomon king of Israel sinned? Among the many nations there was no king like him. He was loved by his God,

---

IN OTHER WORDS

Sabbath
Nehemiah 13:15

God created the world in six days and rested on the seventh day, setting the example of how people were to live. The Sabbath is the practice of having one day a week as a day of rest and worship and working for the other six days. In Leviticus 25:2, God tells the people that, when they enter the Promised Land, the land must have a sabbath rest too. They are to plant crops for six years and in the seventh year let the land lie fallow, trusting God to provide for them.

and God made him king over all Israel, but even he was led into sin by foreign women. ²⁷Must we hear now that you too are doing all this terrible wickedness and are being unfaithful to our God by marrying foreign women?'

²⁸One of the sons of Joiada son of Eliashib the high priest was son-in-law to Sanballat the Horonite. And I drove him away from me.

²⁹Remember them, my God, because they defiled the priestly office and the covenant of the priesthood and of the Levites.

³⁰So I purified the priests and the Levites of everything foreign, and assigned them duties, each to his own task. ³¹I also made provision for contributions of wood at designated times, and for the firstfruits.

Remember me with favour, my God.

Esther

INTRODUCTION

ESTHER

Author: Unknown

When: The events happen during the reign of King Xerxes, some time in the twenty years from 485 BC.

Where: Susa, the capital city of the Persian Empire.

Did you know? The book of Esther is unusual in that it doesn't mention the name of God. But even though God is not mentioned, his leading and directing of events is clearly seen.

Main theme: This is the story of how Esther's courage and quick thinking saved the Jewish people from tragedy. Chosen by Xerxes, the king of Persia, to be his queen, Esther is in an ideal position to save her people from the deadly plot by Haman.

Queen Vashti deposed

1 This is what happened during the time of Xerxes,[a] the Xerxes who ruled over 127 provinces stretching from India to Cush[b]: 2at that time King Xerxes reigned from his royal throne in the citadel of Susa, 3and in the third year of his reign he gave a banquet for all his nobles and officials. The military leaders of Persia and Media, the princes, and the nobles of the provinces were present.

4For a full 180 days he displayed the vast wealth of his kingdom and the splendour and glory of his majesty. 5When these days were over, the king gave a banquet, lasting seven days, in the enclosed garden of the king's palace, for all the people from the least to the greatest who were in the citadel of Susa. 6The garden had hangings of white and blue linen, fastened with cords of white linen and purple material to silver rings on marble pillars. There were couches of gold and silver on a mosaic pavement of porphyry, marble, mother-of-pearl and other costly stones. 7Wine was served in goblets of gold, each one different from the other, and

---

[a] 1 Hebrew *Ahasuerus*; here and throughout Esther [b] 1 That is, the upper Nile region

the royal wine was abundant, in keeping with the king's liberality. ⁸By the king's command each guest was allowed to drink without restriction, for the king instructed all the wine stewards to serve each man what he wished.

⁹Queen Vashti also gave a banquet for the women in the royal palace of King Xerxes.

¹⁰On the seventh day, when King Xerxes was in high spirits from wine, he commanded the seven eunuchs who served him—Mehuman, Biztha, Harbona, Bigtha, Abagtha, Zethar and Karkas— ¹¹to bring before him Queen Vashti, wearing her royal crown, in order to display her beauty to the people and nobles, for she was lovely to look at. ¹²But when the attendants delivered the king's command, Queen Vashti refused to come. Then the king became furious and burned with anger.

¹³Since it was customary for the king to consult experts in matters of law and justice, he spoke with the wise men who understood the times ¹⁴and were closest to the king—Karshena, Shethar, Admatha, Tarshish, Meres, Marsena and Memukan, the seven nobles of Persia and Media who had special access to the king and were highest in the kingdom.

¹⁵'According to law, what must be done to Queen Vashti?' he asked. 'She has not obeyed the command of King Xerxes that the eunuchs have taken to her.'

¹⁶Then Memukan replied in the presence of the king and the nobles, 'Queen Vashti has done wrong, not only against the king but also against all the nobles and the peoples of all the provinces of King Xerxes. ¹⁷For the queen's conduct will become known to all the women, and so they will despise their husbands and say, "King Xerxes commanded Queen Vashti to be brought before him, but she would not come." ¹⁸This very day the Persian and Median women of the nobility who have heard about the queen's conduct will respond to all the king's nobles in the same way. There will be no end of disrespect and discord.

¹⁹'Therefore, if it pleases the king, let him issue a royal decree and let it be written in the laws of Persia and Media, which cannot be repealed, that Vashti is never again to enter the presence of King Xerxes. Also let the king give her royal position to someone else who is better than she. ²⁰Then when the king's edict is proclaimed throughout all his vast realm, all the women will respect their husbands, from the least to the greatest.'

²¹The king and his nobles were pleased with this advice, so the king did as Memukan proposed. ²²He sent dispatches to all parts of the kingdom, to each province in its own script and to each people in their own language, proclaiming that every man should be ruler over his own household, using his native tongue.

Esther made queen

2 Later when King Xerxes' fury had subsided, he remembered Vashti and what she had done and what he had decreed about her. ²Then the king's personal attendants proposed, 'Let a search be made for beautiful young virgins for the king. ³Let the king appoint commissioners in every province of his realm to bring all these beautiful young women into the harem at the citadel of Susa. Let them be placed under the care of Hegai, the king's eunuch, who is in charge of the women; and let beauty treatments be given to them. ⁴Then let the young woman who pleases the king be queen instead of Vashti.' This advice appealed to the king, and he followed it.

⁵Now there was in the citadel of Susa a Jew of the tribe of Benjamin, named Mordecai son of Jair, the son of Shimei, the son of Kish, ⁶who had been carried into exile from Jerusalem by Nebuchadnezzar king of Babylon, among those taken captive with Jehoiachin[a] king of Judah. ⁷Mordecai had a cousin named Hadassah, whom he had brought up because she had neither father nor mother. This young woman, who was also known as Esther, had a lovely figure and was beautiful. Mordecai had taken her as his own daughter when her father and mother died.

---

[a] 6 Hebrew *Jeconiah*, a variant of *Jehoiachin*

People and Places

Esther
Esther 2:7

At the time of this book, the Jewish people were scattered throughout the ancient world. They had been taken into exile by the Babylonians about a hundred years before. The Persians had defeated the Babylonians and allowed the exiles to return home, but Esther's family must have decided to stay in Persia instead of returning to Jerusalem. She was obviously a very beautiful young woman, and she was also courageous, willing to risk her life for her people. Her name means 'a star'.

8When the king's order and edict had been proclaimed, many young women were brought to the citadel of Susa and put under the care of Hegai. Esther also was taken to the king's palace and entrusted to Hegai, who had charge of the harem. 9She pleased him and won his favour. Immediately he provided her with her beauty treatments and special food. He assigned to her seven female attendants selected from the king's palace and moved her and her attendants into the best place in the harem.

10Esther had not revealed her nationality and family background, because Mordecai had forbidden her to do so. 11Every day he walked to and fro near the courtyard of the harem to find out how Esther was and what was happening to her.

12Before a young woman's turn came to go in to King Xerxes, she had to complete twelve months of beauty treatments prescribed for the women, six months with oil of myrrh and six with perfumes and cosmetics. 13And this is how she would go to the king: anything she wanted was given to her to take with her from the harem to the king's palace. 14In the evening she would go there and in the morning return to another part of the harem to the care of Shaashgaz, the king's eunuch who was in charge of the concubines. She would not return to the king unless he was pleased with her and summoned her by name.

15When the turn came for Esther (the young woman Mordecai had adopted, the daughter of his uncle Abihail) to go to the king, she asked for nothing other than what Hegai, the king's eunuch who was in charge of the harem, suggested. And Esther won the favour of everyone who saw her. 16She was taken to King Xerxes in the royal residence in the tenth month, the month of Tebeth, in the seventh year of his reign.

17Now the king was attracted to Esther more than to any of the other women, and she won his favour and approval more than any of the other virgins. So he set a royal crown on her head and made her queen instead of Vashti. 18And the king gave a great banquet, Esther's banquet, for all his nobles and officials. He proclaimed a holiday throughout the provinces and distributed gifts with royal liberality.

Mordecai uncovers a conspiracy

19When the virgins were assembled a second time, Mordecai was sitting at the king's gate. 20But Esther had kept secret her family background and nationality just as Mordecai had told her to do, for she continued to follow Mordecai's instructions as she had done when he was bringing her up.

21During the time Mordecai was sitting at the king's gate, Bigthana[a] and Teresh, two of the king's officers who guarded the doorway, became angry and conspired to assassinate King Xerxes. 22But Mordecai found out about the plot and told Queen Esther, who in turn reported it to the king, giving credit to Mordecai. 23And when the report was investigated and found to be true, the two officials were impaled on poles. All this was recorded in the book of the annals in the presence of the king.

---

[a] 21 Hebrew *Bigthan*, a variant of *Bigthana*

Sign of the times

Beauty treatments
Esther 2:12
One way of measuring a king's importance and wealth was to see how many concubines he had and how beautiful they were. The beauty treatments described in these verses show that Xerxes was a powerful man. Oil would be rubbed into the skin to make it soft and smooth. Cosmetics were made from seeds, leaves and other natural products.

Haman's plot to destroy the Jews

3 After these events, King Xerxes honoured Haman son of Hammedatha, the Agagite, elevating him and giving him a seat of honour higher than that of all the other nobles. 2All the royal officials at the king's gate knelt down and paid honour to Haman, for the king had commanded this concerning him. But Mordecai would not kneel down or pay him honour.

3Then the royal officials at the king's gate asked Mordecai, 'Why do you disobey the king's command?' 4Day after day they spoke to him but he refused to comply. Therefore they told Haman about it to see whether Mordecai's behaviour would be tolerated, for he had told them he was a Jew.

5When Haman saw that Mordecai would not kneel down or pay him honour, he was enraged. 6Yet having learned who Mordecai's people were, he scorned the idea of killing only Mordecai. Instead Haman looked for a way to destroy all Mordecai's people, the Jews, throughout the whole kingdom of Xerxes.

7In the twelfth year of King Xerxes, in the first month, the month of Nisan, the *pur* (that is, the lot) was cast in the presence of Haman to select a day and month. And the lot fell on[a] the twelfth month, the month of Adar.

8Then Haman said to King Xerxes, 'There is a certain people dispersed among the peoples in all the provinces of your kingdom who keep themselves separate. Their customs are different from those of all other people, and they do not obey the king's laws; it is not in the king's best interest to tolerate them. 9If it pleases the king, let a decree be issued to destroy them, and I will give ten thousand talents[b] of silver to the king's administrators for the royal treasury.'

10So the king took his signet ring from his finger and gave it to Haman son of Hammedatha, the Agagite, the enemy of the Jews. 11'Keep the money,' the king said to Haman, 'and do with the people as you please.'

12Then on the thirteenth day of the first month the royal secretaries were summoned. They wrote out in the script of each province and in the language of each people all Haman's orders to the king's satraps, the governors of the various provinces and the nobles of the various peoples. These were written in the name of King Xerxes himself and sealed with his own ring. 13Dispatches were sent by couriers to all the king's provinces with the order to destroy, kill and annihilate all the Jews—young and old, women and children—on a single day, the thirteenth day of the twelfth month, the month of Adar, and to plunder their goods. 14A copy of the text of the edict was to be issued as law in every province and made known to the people of every nationality so that they would be ready for that day.

15The couriers went out, spurred on by the king's command, and the edict was issued in the citadel of Susa. The king and Haman sat down to drink, but the city of Susa was bewildered.

Mordecai persuades Esther to help

4 When Mordecai learned of all that had been done, he tore his clothes, put on sackcloth and ashes, and went out into the city, wailing loudly and bitterly. 2But he went only as far as the king's gate, because no-one clothed in sackcloth was allowed to

---

[a] 7 Septuagint; Hebrew does not have *And the lot fell on.*   [b] 9 That is, about 335 metric tons

enter it. ³In every province to which the edict and order of the king came, there was great mourning among the Jews, with fasting, weeping and wailing. Many lay in sackcloth and ashes.

⁴When Esther's eunuchs and female attendants came and told her about Mordecai, she was in great distress. She sent clothes for him to put on instead of his sackcloth, but he would not accept them. ⁵Then Esther summoned Hathak, one of the king's eunuchs assigned to attend her, and ordered him to find out what was troubling Mordecai and why.

⁶So Hathak went out to Mordecai in the open square of the city in front of the king's gate. ⁷Mordecai told him everything that had happened to him, including the exact amount of money Haman had promised to pay into the royal treasury for the destruction of the Jews. ⁸He also gave him a copy of the text of the edict for their annihilation, which had been published in Susa, to show to Esther and explain it to her, and he told him to instruct her to go into the king's presence to beg for mercy and plead with him for her people.

⁹Hathak went back and reported to Esther what Mordecai had said. ¹⁰Then she instructed him to say to Mordecai, ¹¹'All the king's officials and the people of the royal provinces know that for any man or woman who approaches the king in the inner court without being summoned the king has but one law: that they be put to death unless the king extends the gold sceptre to them and spares their lives. But thirty days have passed since I was called to go to the king.'

¹²When Esther's words were reported to Mordecai, ¹³he sent back this answer: 'Do not think that because you are in the king's house you alone of all the Jews will escape. ¹⁴For if you remain silent at this time, relief and deliverance for the Jews will arise from another place, but you and your father's family will perish. And who knows but that you have come to royal position for such a time as this?'

¹⁵Then Esther sent this reply to Mordecai: ¹⁶'Go, gather together all the Jews who are in Susa, and fast for me. Do not eat or drink for three days, night or day. I and my attendants will fast as you do. When this is done, I will go to the king, even though it is against the law. And if I perish, I perish.'

¹⁷So Mordecai went away and carried out all of Esther's instructions.

Esther's request to the king

5 On the third day Esther put on her royal robes and stood in the inner court of the palace, in front of the king's hall. The king was sitting on his royal throne in the hall, facing the entrance. ²When he saw Queen Esther standing in the court, he was pleased with her and held out to her the gold sceptre that was in his hand. So Esther approached and touched the tip of the sceptre.

³Then the king asked, 'What is it, Queen Esther? What is your request? Even up to half the kingdom, it will be given you.'

⁴'If it pleases the king,' replied Esther, 'let the king, together with Haman, come today to a banquet I have prepared for him.'

⁵'Bring Haman at once,' the king said, 'so that we may do what Esther asks.'

So the king and Haman went to the banquet Esther had prepared. ⁶As they were drinking wine, the king again asked Esther, 'Now what is your petition? It will be given you. And what is your request? Even up to half the kingdom, it will be granted.'

⁷Esther replied, 'My petition and my request is this: ⁸If the king regards me with favour and if it pleases the king to grant my petition and fulfil my request, let the king and Haman come tomorrow to the banquet I will prepare for them. Then I will answer the king's question.'

IN OTHER WORDS

Fasting
Esther 4:16

Fasting in the Bible usually involves giving up food for a period of time, often to focus on God because of some special request, or to show him that he is worth any sacrifice.

Haman's rage against Mordecai

9Haman went out that day happy and in high spirits. But when he saw Mordecai at the king's gate and observed that he neither rose nor showed fear in his presence, he was filled with rage against Mordecai. 10Nevertheless, Haman restrained himself and went home.

Calling together his friends and Zeresh, his wife, 11Haman boasted to them about his vast wealth, his many sons, and all the ways the king had honoured him and how he had elevated him above the other nobles and officials. 12'And that's not all,' Haman added. 'I'm the only person Queen Esther invited to accompany the king to the banquet she gave. And she has invited me along with the king tomorrow. 13But all this gives me no satisfaction as long as I see that Jew Mordecai sitting at the king's gate.'

14His wife Zeresh and all his friends said to him, 'Let a pole be set up, reaching to a height of fifty cubits,*a*and ask the king in the morning to have Mordecai impaled on it. Then go with the king to the banquet and enjoy yourself.' This suggestion delighted Haman, and he had the pole set up.

Mordecai honoured

6 That night the king could not sleep; so he ordered the book of the chronicles, the record of his reign, to be brought in and read to him. 2It was found recorded there that Mordecai had exposed Bigthana and Teresh, two of the king's officers who guarded the doorway, who had conspired to assassinate King Xerxes.

3'What honour and recognition has Mordecai received for this?' the king asked.

'Nothing has been done for him,' his attendants answered.

4The king said, 'Who is in the court?' Now Haman had just entered the outer court of the palace to speak to the king about impaling Mordecai on the pole he had set up for him.

5His attendants answered, 'Haman is standing in the court.'

'Bring him in,' the king ordered.

Royal robe
Esther 6:8
To be allowed to wear the king's robe would have been a great honour, showing everyone that you had found favour with the king. A horse was a symbol of royal authority too.

6When Haman entered, the king asked him, 'What should be done for the man the king delights to honour?'

Now Haman thought to himself, 'Who is there that the king would rather honour than me?' 7So he answered the king, 'For the man the king delights to honour, 8let them bring a royal robe the king has worn and a horse the king has ridden, one with a royal crest placed on its head. 9Then let the robe and horse be entrusted to one of the king's most noble princes. Let them robe the man the king delights to honour, and lead him on the horse through the city streets, proclaiming before him, "This is what is done for the man the king delights to honour!"'

10'Go at once,' the king commanded Haman. 'Get the robe and the horse and do just as you have suggested for Mordecai the Jew, who sits at the king's gate. Do not neglect anything you have recommended.'

11So Haman got the robe and the horse. He robed Mordecai, and led him on horseback through the city streets, proclaiming before him, 'This is what is done for the man the king delights to honour!'

12Afterwards Mordecai returned to the king's gate. But Haman rushed home, with his head covered in grief, 13and told Zeresh his wife and all his friends everything that had happened to him.

His advisors and his wife Zeresh said to him, 'Since Mordecai, before whom your

---

a 14 That is, about 22.5 metres

downfall has started, is of Jewish origin, you cannot stand against him—you will surely come to ruin!' ¹⁴While they were still talking with him, the king's eunuchs arrived and hurried Haman away to the banquet Esther had prepared.

Haman impaled

7 So the king and Haman went to Queen Esther's banquet, ²and as they were drinking wine on the second day, the king again asked, 'Queen Esther, what is your petition? It will be given you. What is your request? Even up to half the kingdom, it will be granted.'

³Then Queen Esther answered, 'If I have found favour with you, Your Majesty, and if it pleases you, grant me my life—this is my petition. And spare my people—this is my request. ⁴For I and my people have been sold to be destroyed, killed and annihilated. If we had merely been sold as male and female slaves, I would have kept quiet, because no such distress would justify disturbing the king.ᵃ'

⁵King Xerxes asked Queen Esther, 'Who is he? Where is he—the man who has dared to do such a thing?'

⁶Esther said, 'An adversary and enemy! This vile Haman!'

Then Haman was terrified before the king and queen. ⁷The king got up in a rage, left his wine and went out into the palace garden. But Haman, realising that the king had already decided his fate, stayed behind to beg Queen Esther for his life.

⁸Just as the king returned from the palace garden to the banqueting hall, Haman was falling on the couch where Esther was reclining.

The king exclaimed, 'Will he even molest the queen while she is with me in the house?'

As soon as the word left the king's mouth, they covered Haman's face. ⁹Then Harbona, one of the eunuchs attending the king, said, 'A pole reaching to a height of fifty cubitsᵇ stands by Haman's house. He had it set up for Mordecai, who spoke up to help the king.'

Sceptre
Esther 8:4
A sceptre is the official staff of a ruler and symbolises his or her authority and power.

The king said, 'Impale him on it!' ¹⁰So they impaled Haman on the pole he had set up for Mordecai. Then the king's fury subsided.

The king's edict on behalf of the Jews

8 That same day King Xerxes gave Queen Esther the estate of Haman, the enemy of the Jews. And Mordecai came into the presence of the king, for Esther had told how he was related to her. ²The king took off his signet ring, which he had reclaimed from Haman, and presented it to Mordecai. And Esther appointed him over Haman's estate.

³Esther again pleaded with the king, falling at his feet and weeping. She begged him to put an end to the evil plan of Haman the Agagite, which he had devised against the Jews. ⁴Then the king extended the gold sceptre to Esther and she arose and stood before him.

⁵'If it pleases the king,' she said, 'and if he regards me with favour and thinks it the right thing to do, and if he is pleased with me, let an order be written overruling the dispatches that Haman son of Hammedatha, the Agagite, devised and wrote to destroy the Jews in all the king's provinces. ⁶For how can I bear to see disaster fall on my people? How can I bear to see the destruction of my family?'

⁷King Xerxes replied to Queen Esther and to Mordecai the Jew, 'Because Haman attacked the Jews, I have given his estate to Esther, and they have impaled him on the pole he set up. ⁸Now write another decree in the king's name on behalf of the Jews as seems best to you, and seal it with the king's

---

ᵃ 4 Or *quiet, but the compensation our adversary offers cannot be compared with the loss the king would suffer*
ᵇ 9 That is, about 22.5 metres

signet ring—for no document written in the king's name and sealed with his ring can be revoked.'

⁹At once the royal secretaries were summoned—on the twenty-third day of the third month, the month of Sivan. They wrote out all Mordecai's orders to the Jews, and to the satraps, governors and nobles of the 127 provinces stretching from India to Cush.ᵃ These orders were written in the script of each province and the language of each people and also to the Jews in their own script and language. ¹⁰Mordecai wrote in the name of King Xerxes, sealed the dispatches with the king's signet ring, and sent them by mounted couriers, who rode fast horses especially bred for the king.

¹¹The king's edict granted the Jews in every city the right to assemble and protect themselves; to destroy, kill and annihilate the armed men of any nationality or province who might attack them and their women and children,ᵇ and to plunder the property of their enemies. ¹²The day appointed for the Jews to do this in all the provinces of King Xerxes was the thirteenth day of the twelfth month, the month of Adar. ¹³A copy of the text of the edict was to be issued as law in every province and made known to the people of every nationality so that the Jews would be ready on that day to avenge themselves on their enemies.

¹⁴The couriers, riding the royal horses, went out, spurred on by the king's command, and the edict was issued in the citadel of Susa.

The triumph of the Jews

¹⁵When Mordecai left the king's presence, he was wearing royal garments of blue and white, a large crown of gold and a purple robe of fine linen. And the city of Susa held a joyous celebration. ¹⁶For the Jews it was a time of happiness and joy, gladness and honour. ¹⁷In every province and in every city to which the edict of the king came, there was joy and gladness among the Jews, with feasting and celebrating. And many people of other nationalities became Jews because fear of the Jews had seized them.

9 On the thirteenth day of the twelfth month, the month of Adar, the edict commanded by the king was to be carried out. On this day the enemies of the Jews had hoped to overpower them, but now the tables were turned and the Jews got the upper hand over those who hated them. ²The Jews assembled in their cities in all the provinces of King Xerxes to attack those seeking their destruction. No-one could stand against them, because the people of all the other nationalities were afraid of them. ³And all the nobles of the provinces, the satraps, the governors and the king's administrators helped the Jews, because fear of Mordecai had seized them. ⁴Mordecai was prominent in the palace; his reputation spread throughout the provinces, and he became more and more powerful.

⁵The Jews struck down all their enemies with the sword, killing and destroying them, and they did what they pleased to those who hated them. ⁶In the citadel of Susa, the Jews killed and destroyed five hundred men. ⁷They also killed Parshandatha, Dalphon, Aspatha, ⁸Poratha, Adalia, Aridatha, ⁹Parmashta, Arisai, Aridai and Vaizatha, ¹⁰the ten sons of Haman son of Hammedatha, the enemy of the Jews. But they did not lay their hands on the plunder.

¹¹The number of those killed in the citadel of Susa was reported to the king that same day. ¹²The king said to Queen Esther, 'The Jews have killed and destroyed five hundred men and the ten sons of Haman in the citadel of Susa. What have they done in the rest of the king's provinces? Now what is your petition? It will be given you. What is your request? It will also be granted.'

¹³'If it pleases the king,' Esther answered, 'give the Jews in Susa permission to carry out this day's edict tomorrow also, and let Haman's ten sons be impaled on poles.'

¹⁴So the king commanded that this be done. An edict was issued in Susa, and they impaled the ten sons of Haman. ¹⁵The Jews in Susa came together on the fourteenth day of the month of Adar, and they put to death in Susa three hundred men, but they did not lay their hands on the plunder.

ᵃ9 That is, the upper Nile region   ᵇ11 Or *province, together with their women and children, who might attack them;*

making Connections

Purim
Esther 9:18

This celebration became the festival of Purim, an annual Jewish holiday to remember how God used Esther and Mordecai to save the Jewish people from Haman's plot. It was given its name from the Hebrew word purim, which means 'lots', referring to the lots that Haman cast to determine on which day he should carry out his plot.

---

16 Meanwhile, the remainder of the Jews who were in the king's provinces also assembled to protect themselves and get relief from their enemies. They killed seventy-five thousand of them but did not lay their hands on the plunder. 17 This happened on the thirteenth day of the month of Adar, and on the fourteenth they rested and made it a day of feasting and joy.

18 The Jews in Susa, however, had assembled on the thirteenth and fourteenth, and then on the fifteenth they rested and made it a day of feasting and joy.

19 That is why rural Jews—those living in villages—observe the fourteenth of the month of Adar as a day of joy and feasting, a day for giving presents to each other.

Purim established

20 Mordecai recorded these events, and he sent letters to all the Jews throughout the provinces of King Xerxes, near and far, 21 that they should celebrate annually the fourteenth and fifteenth days of the month of Adar 22 as the time when the Jews got relief from their enemies, and as the month when their sorrow was turned into joy and their mourning into a day of celebration. He wrote to them to observe the days as days of feasting and joy and giving presents of food to one another and gifts to the poor.

23 So the Jews agreed to continue the celebration they had begun, doing what Mordecai had written to them. 24 For Haman son of Hammedatha, the Agagite, the enemy of all the Jews, had plotted against the Jews to destroy them and had cast the *pur* (that is, the lot) for their ruin and destruction. 25 But when the plot came to the king's attention,[a] he issued written orders that the evil scheme Haman had devised against the Jews should come back on to his own head, and that he and his sons should be impaled on poles. 26 (Therefore these days were called Purim, from the word *pur*.) Because of everything written in this letter and because of what they had seen and what had happened to them, 27 the Jews took it on themselves to establish the custom that they and their descendants and all who join them should without fail observe these two days every year, in the way prescribed and at the time appointed. 28 These days should be remembered and observed in every generation by every family, and in every province and in every city. And these days of Purim should never cease to be celebrated by the Jews, nor should the memory of them die out among their descendants.

29 So Queen Esther, daughter of Abihail, along with Mordecai the Jew, wrote with full authority to confirm this second letter concerning Purim. 30 And Mordecai sent letters to all the Jews in the 127 provinces of Xerxes' kingdom—words of goodwill and assurance— 31 to establish these days of Purim at their designated times, as Mordecai the Jew and Queen Esther had decreed for them, and as they had established for themselves and their descendants in regard to their times of fasting and lamentation. 32 Esther's decree confirmed these regulations about Purim, and it was written down in the records.

The greatness of Mordecai

10 King Xerxes imposed tribute throughout the empire, to its distant shores. 2 And all his acts of power and

---

[a] 25 Or *when Esther came before the king*

might, together with a full account of the greatness of Mordecai to which the king had raised him, are they not written in the book of the annals of the kings of Media and Persia? ³Mordecai the Jew was second in rank to King Xerxes, pre-eminent among the Jews, and held in high esteem by his many fellow Jews, because he worked for the good of his people and spoke up for the welfare of all the Jews.

Job

INTRODUCTION

JOB

Author: Unknown

When: It's thought that Job lived around the same time as Abraham.

Where: The land of Uz, probably a region in Edom.

Did you know? Much of the book of Job is written in the form of a dramatic poem.

Main theme: The book of Job tackles the question that people have been asking for centuries: why do people suffer? His friends give their view, that suffering is always a punishment from God for sin. But Job is not convinced because he says he hasn't done anything to deserve the hard time he is having. Job learns to trust God even though he can't understand why he is suffering.

Prologue

1 In the land of Uz there lived a man whose name was Job. This man was blameless and upright; he feared God and shunned evil. 2He had seven sons and three daughters, 3and he owned seven thousand sheep, three thousand camels, five hundred yoke of oxen and five hundred donkeys, and had a large number of servants. He was the greatest man among all the people of the East.

4His sons used to hold feasts in their homes on their birthdays, and they would invite their three sisters to eat and drink with them. 5When a period of feasting had run its course, Job would make arrangements for them to be purified. Early in the morning he would sacrifice a burnt offering for each of them, thinking, 'Perhaps my children have sinned and cursed God in their hearts.' This was Job's regular custom.

6One day the angels*ᵃ* came to present themselves before the LORD, and Satan*ᵇ* also came with them. 7The LORD said to Satan, 'Where have you come from?'

---

*ᵃ*6 Hebrew *the sons of God*   *ᵇ*6 Hebrew *satan* means *adversary*.

Satan answered the LORD, 'From roaming through the earth and going to and fro in it.'

⁸Then the LORD said to Satan, 'Have you considered my servant Job? There is no-one on earth like him; he is blameless and upright, a man who fears God and shuns evil.'

⁹'Does Job fear God for nothing?' Satan replied. ¹⁰'Have you not put a hedge around him and his household and everything he has? You have blessed the work of his hands, so that his flocks and herds are spread throughout the land. ¹¹But now stretch out your hand and strike everything he has, and he will surely curse you to your face.'

¹²The LORD said to Satan, 'Very well, then, everything he has is in your power, but on the man himself do not lay a finger.'

Then Satan went out from the presence of the LORD.

¹³One day when Job's sons and daughters were feasting and drinking wine at the eldest brother's house, ¹⁴a messenger came to Job and said, 'The oxen were ploughing and the donkeys were grazing nearby, ¹⁵and the Sabeans attacked and made off with them. They put the servants to the sword, and I am the only one who has escaped to tell you!'

¹⁶While he was still speaking, another messenger came and said, 'The fire of God fell from the sky and burned up the sheep and the servants, and I am the only one who has escaped to tell you!'

¹⁷While he was still speaking, another messenger came and said, 'The Chaldeans formed three raiding parties and swept down on your camels and made off with them. They put the servants to the sword, and I am the only one who has escaped to tell you!'

¹⁸While he was still speaking, yet another messenger came and said, 'Your sons and daughters were feasting and drinking wine at the eldest brother's house, ¹⁹when suddenly a mighty wind swept in from the desert and struck the four corners of the house. It collapsed on them and they are dead, and I am the only one who has escaped to tell you!'

²⁰At this, Job got up and tore his robe and shaved his head. Then he fell to the ground in worship ²¹and said:

'Naked I came from my mother's womb,
  and naked I shall depart.ᵃ
The LORD gave and the LORD has taken
    away;
  may the name of the LORD be praised.'

²²In all this, Job did not sin by charging God with wrongdoing.

2 On another day the angelsᵇ came to present themselves before the LORD, and Satan also came with them to present himself before him. ²And the LORD said to Satan, 'Where have you come from?'

Satan answered the LORD, 'From roaming through the earth and going to and fro in it.'

³Then the LORD said to Satan, 'Have you considered my servant Job? There is no-one on earth like him; he is blameless and upright, a man who fears God and shuns evil. And he still maintains his integrity, though you incited me against him to ruin him without any reason.'

⁴'Skin for skin!' Satan replied. 'A man will give all he has for his own life. ⁵But now stretch out your hand and strike his flesh and bones, and he will surely curse you to your face.'

⁶The LORD said to Satan, 'Very well, then, he is in your hands; but you must spare his life.'

⁷So Satan went out from the presence of the LORD and afflicted Job with painful sores from the soles of his feet to the crown of his head. ⁸Then Job took a piece of broken pottery and scraped himself with it as he sat among the ashes.

⁹His wife said to him, 'Are you still maintaining your integrity? Curse God and die!'

¹⁰He replied, 'You are talking like a foolishᶜ woman. Shall we accept good from God, and not trouble?'

In all this, Job did not sin in what he said.

ᵃ 21 Or *shall return there*   ᵇ 1 Hebrew *the sons of God*   ᶜ 10 The Hebrew word rendered *foolish* denotes moral deficiency.

¹¹When Job's three friends, Eliphaz the Temanite, Bildad the Shuhite and Zophar the Naamathite, heard about all the troubles that had come upon him, they set out from their homes and met together by agreement to go and sympathise with him and comfort him. ¹²When they saw him from a distance, they could hardly recognise him; they began to weep aloud, and they tore their robes and sprinkled dust on their heads. ¹³Then they sat on the ground with him for seven days and seven nights. No-one said a word to him, because they saw how great his suffering was.

Job speaks

3 After this, Job opened his mouth and cursed the day of his birth. ²He said:

³'May the day of my birth perish,
  and the night that said, "A boy is
    conceived!"
⁴That day—may it turn to darkness;
  may God above not care about it;
  may no light shine on it.
  ⁵May gloom and utter darkness claim it
    once more;
  may a cloud settle over it;
  may blackness overwhelm it.
⁶That night—may thick darkness seize it;
  may it not be included among the days
    of the year
  nor be entered in any of the months.
⁷May that night be barren;
  may no shout of joy be heard in it.
⁸May those who curse days*ᵃ* curse that day,
  those who are ready to rouse Leviathan.
⁹May its morning stars become dark;
  may it wait for daylight in vain
  and not see the first rays of dawn,
¹⁰for it did not shut the doors of the womb
    on me
  to hide trouble from my eyes.

¹¹'Why did I not perish at birth,
  and die as I came from the womb?
¹²Why were there knees to receive me
  and breasts that I might be nursed?
¹³For now I would be lying down in peace;
  I would be asleep and at rest
¹⁴with kings and rulers of the earth,
  who built for themselves places now
    lying in ruins,
¹⁵with princes who had gold,
  who filled their houses with silver.
¹⁶Or why was I not hidden away in the
    ground like a stillborn child,
  like an infant who never saw the light of
    day?
¹⁷There the wicked cease from turmoil,
  and there the weary are at rest.
¹⁸Captives also enjoy their ease;
  they no longer hear the slave driver's
    shout.
¹⁹The small and the great are there,
  and the slaves are freed from their
    owners.

²⁰'Why is light given to those in misery,
  and life to the bitter of soul,
²¹to those who long for death that does not
    come,
  who search for it more than for hidden
    treasure,
²²who are filled with gladness
  and rejoice when they reach the grave?
²³Why is life given to a man
  whose way is hidden,
  whom God has hedged in?
²⁴For sighing has become my daily food;
  my groans pour out like water.
²⁵What I feared has come upon me;
  what I dreaded has happened to me.
²⁶I have no peace, no quietness;
  I have no rest, but only turmoil.'

making Connections

Hebrew poetry
Job 3:1
Hebrew poetry doesn't rhyme. It arranges thoughts rather than words, sometimes putting similar thoughts in adjacent lines, sometimes contrasting ones. It is very rhythmic, although this doesn't come across in the translations that we read.

---
*ᵃ*8 Or *the sea*

Eliphaz

4 Then Eliphaz the Temanite replied:

2'If someone ventures a word with you, will you be impatient?
But who can keep from speaking?
3Think how you have instructed many,
how you have strengthened feeble hands.
4Your words have supported those who stumbled;
you have strengthened faltering knees.
5But now trouble comes to you, and you are discouraged;
it strikes you, and you are dismayed.
6Should not your piety be your confidence
and your blameless ways your hope?

7'Consider now: who, being innocent, has ever perished?
Where were the upright ever destroyed?
8As I have observed, those who plough evil
and those who sow trouble reap it.
9At the breath of God they perish;
at the blast of his anger they are no more.
10The lions may roar and growl,
yet the teeth of the great lions are broken.
11The lion perishes for lack of prey,
and the cubs of the lioness are scattered.

12'A word was secretly brought to me,
my ears caught a whisper of it.
13Amid disquieting dreams in the night,
when deep sleep falls on people,
14fear and trembling seized me
and made all my bones shake.
15A spirit glided past my face,
and the hair on my body stood on end.
16It stopped,
but I could not tell what it was.
A form stood before my eyes,
and I heard a hushed voice:
17"Can a mortal be more righteous than God?
Can human beings be more pure than their Maker?
18If God places no trust in his servants,
if he charges his angels with error,
19how much more those who live in houses of clay,
whose foundations are in the dust,
who are crushed more readily than a moth!
20Between dawn and dusk they are broken to pieces;
unnoticed, they perish for ever.
21Are not the cords of their tent pulled up,
so that they die without wisdom?"

5 'Call if you will, but who will answer you?
To which of the holy ones will you turn?
2Resentment kills a fool,
and envy slays the simple.
3I myself have seen a fool taking root,
but suddenly his house was cursed.
4His children are far from safety,
crushed in court without a defender.
5The hungry consume his harvest,
taking it even from among thorns,
and the thirsty pant after his wealth.
6For hardship does not spring from the soil,
nor does trouble sprout from the ground.
7Yet human beings are born to trouble
as surely as sparks fly upwards.

8'But if I were you, I would appeal to God;
I would lay my cause before him.

making Connections

Sparks fly upwards
Job 5:7
If you have ever sat outside and watched a fire, you will understand the image that Eliphaz uses. As the flames leap and dance, sparks fly up into the air – they have no choice in the matter.

⁹He performs wonders that cannot be fathomed,
   miracles that cannot be counted.
¹⁰He bestows rain on the earth;
   he sends water on the countryside.
¹¹The lowly he sets on high,
   and those who mourn are lifted to safety.
¹²He thwarts the plans of the crafty,
   so that their hands achieve no success.
¹³He catches the wise in their craftiness,
   and the schemes of the wily are swept away.
¹⁴Darkness comes upon them in the daytime;
   at noon they grope as in the night.
¹⁵He saves the needy from the sword in their mouth;
   he saves them from the clutches of the powerful.
¹⁶So the poor have hope,
   and injustice shuts its mouth.

¹⁷'Blessed are those whom God corrects;
   so do not despise the discipline of the Almighty.'[a]
¹⁸For he wounds, but he also binds up;
   he injures, but his hands also heal.
¹⁹From six calamities he will rescue you;
   in seven no harm will touch you.
²⁰In famine he will deliver you from death,
   and in battle from the stroke of the sword.
²¹You will be protected from the lash of the tongue,
   and need not fear when destruction comes.
²²You will laugh at destruction and famine,
   and need not fear the wild animals.
²³For you will have a covenant with the stones of the field,
   and the wild animals will be at peace with you.
²⁴You will know that your tent is secure;
   you will take stock of your property and find nothing missing.
²⁵You will know that your children will be many,
   and your descendants like the grass of the earth.
²⁶You will come to the grave in full vigour,
   like sheaves gathered in season.

²⁷'We have examined this, and it is true.
   So hear it and apply it to yourself.'

Job

6

Then Job replied:

²'If only my anguish could be weighed
   and all my misery be placed on the scales!
³It would surely outweigh the sand of the seas—
   no wonder my words have been impetuous.
⁴The arrows of the Almighty are in me,
   my spirit drinks in their poison;
   God's terrors are marshalled against me.
⁵Does a wild donkey bray when it has grass,
   or an ox bellow when it has fodder?
⁶Is tasteless food eaten without salt,
   or is there flavour in the sap of the mallow[b]?
⁷I refuse to touch it;
   such food makes me ill.

⁸'Oh, that I might have my request,
   that God would grant what I hope for,
⁹that God would be willing to crush me,
   to let loose his hand and cut off my life!
¹⁰Then I would still have this consolation—
   my joy in unrelenting pain—
   that I had not denied the words of the Holy One.

¹¹'What strength do I have, that I should still hope?
   What prospects, that I should be patient?
¹²Do I have the strength of stone?
   Is my flesh bronze?
¹³Do I have any power to help myself,
   now that success has been driven from me?

¹⁴'Anyone who withholds kindness from a friend
   forsakes the fear of the Almighty.
¹⁵But my brothers are as undependable as intermittent streams,
   as the streams that overflow
¹⁶when darkened by thawing ice
   and swollen with melting snow,
¹⁷but that cease to flow in the dry season,

---

[a] 17 Hebrew *Shaddai*; here and throughout Job   [b] 6 The meaning of the Hebrew for this phrase is uncertain.

> **IN OTHER WORDS**
>
> **Caravan**
> Job 6:18
> A caravan was a company of people travelling together with camels or donkeys. Merchants travelled in caravans along the trade routes that ran through the ancient world.

and in the heat vanish from their channels.
¹⁸Caravans turn aside from their routes;
 they go off into the wasteland and perish.
¹⁹The caravans of Tema look for water,
 the travelling merchants of Sheba look in hope.
²⁰They are distressed, because they had been confident;
 they arrive there, only to be disappointed.
²¹Now you too have proved to be of no help;
 you see something dreadful and are afraid.
²²Have I ever said, "Give something on my behalf,
 pay a ransom for me from your wealth,
²³deliver me from the hand of the enemy,
 rescue me from the clutches of the ruthless"?

²⁴"Teach me, and I will be quiet;
 show me where I have been wrong.
²⁵How painful are honest words!
 But what do your arguments prove?
²⁶Do you mean to correct what I say,
 and treat my desperate words as wind?
²⁷You would even cast lots for the fatherless
 and barter away your friend.

²⁸'But now be so kind as to look at me.
 Would I lie to your face?
²⁹Relent, do not be unjust;
 reconsider, for my integrity is at stake."^a
³⁰Is there any wickedness on my lips?
 Can my mouth not discern malice?

7 'Do not mortals have hard service on earth?
 Are not their days like those of hired labourers?
²Like a slave longing for the evening shadows,
 or a hired labourer waiting to be paid,
³so I have been allotted months of futility,
 and nights of misery have been assigned to me.
⁴When I lie down I think, "How long before I get up?"
 The night drags on, and I toss and turn until dawn.
⁵My body is clothed with worms and scabs,
 my skin is broken and festering.

⁶'My days are swifter than a weaver's shuttle,
 and they come to an end without hope.
⁷Remember, O God, that my life is but a breath;
 my eyes will never see happiness again.
⁸The eye that now sees me will see me no longer;
 you will look for me, but I will be no more.
⁹As a cloud vanishes and is gone,
 so those who go down to the grave do not return.
¹⁰They will never come to their homes again;
 their places will know them no more.

¹¹'Therefore I will not keep silent;
 I will speak out in the anguish of my spirit,
 I will complain in the bitterness of my soul.
¹²Am I the sea, or the monster of the deep,
 that you put me under guard?
¹³When I think my bed will comfort me
 and my couch will ease my complaint,
¹⁴even then you frighten me with dreams
 and terrify me with visions,
¹⁵so that I prefer strangling and death,
 rather than this body of mine.
¹⁶I despise my life; I would not live for ever.
 Let me alone; my days have no meaning.

---

^a 29 Or *my righteousness still stands*

17'What are human beings that you make so much of them,
that you give them so much attention,
18that you examine them every morning
and test them every moment?
19Will you never look away from me,
or let me alone even for an instant?
20If I have sinned, what have I done to you,
you who watch over us all?
Why have you made me your target?
Have I become a burden to you?[a]
21Why do you not pardon my offences
and forgive my sins?
For I shall soon lie down in the dust;
you will search for me, but I shall be no more.'

Bildad

8 Then Bildad the Shuhite replied:

2'How long will you say such things?
Your words are a blustering wind.
3Does God pervert justice?
Does the Almighty pervert what is right?
4When your children sinned against him,
he gave them over to the penalty of their sin.
5But if you will seek God earnestly
and plead with the Almighty,
6if you are pure and upright,
even now he will rouse himself on your behalf
and restore you to your prosperous state.
7Your beginnings will seem humble,
so prosperous will your future be.

8'Ask the former generations
and find out what their ancestors learned,
9for we were born only yesterday and know nothing,
and our days on earth are but a shadow.
10Will they not instruct you and tell you?
Will they not bring forth words from their understanding?
11Can papyrus grow tall where there is no marsh?
Can reeds thrive without water?
12While still growing and uncut,
they wither more quickly than grass.
13Such is the destiny of all who forget God;
so perishes the hope of the godless.
14What they trust in is fragile[b];
what they rely on is a spider's web.
15They lean on the web, but it gives way;
they cling to it, but it does not hold.
16They are like a well-watered plant in the sunshine,
spreading its shoots over the garden;
17it entwines its roots round a pile of rocks
and looks for a place among the stones.
18But when it is torn from its spot,
that place disowns it and says, "I never saw you."
19Surely its life withers away,
and[c] from the soil other plants grow.

20'Surely God does not reject the blameless
or strengthen the hands of evildoers.
21He will yet fill your mouth with laughter
and your lips with shouts of joy.
22Your enemies will be clothed in shame,
and the tents of the wicked will be no more.'

Job

9 Then Job replied:

2'Indeed, I know that this is true.
But how can mere mortals prove their innocence before God?
3Though they wished to dispute with him,
they could not answer him once in a thousand times.
4His wisdom is profound, his power is vast.
Who has resisted him and come out unscathed?
5He moves mountains without their knowing it
and overturns them in his anger.
6He shakes the earth from its place
and makes its pillars tremble.
7He speaks to the sun and it does not shine;
he seals off the light of the stars.
8He alone stretches out the heavens
and treads on the waves of the sea.
9He is the Maker of the Bear[d] and Orion,

---

[a] 20 A few manuscripts of the Masoretic Text, an ancient Hebrew scribal tradition and Septuagint; most manuscripts of the Masoretic Text *I have become a burden to myself.* [b] 14 The meaning of the Hebrew for this word is uncertain. [c] 19 Or *Surely all the joy it has I is that* [d] 9 Or *of Leo*

the Pleiades and the constellations of
  the south.
¹⁰He performs wonders that cannot be
    fathomed,
  miracles that cannot be counted.
¹¹When he passes me, I cannot see him;
  when he goes by, I cannot perceive
    him.
¹²If he snatches away, who can stop him?
  Who can say to him, "What are you
    doing?"
¹³God does not restrain his anger;
  even the cohorts of Rahab cowered at
    his feet.

¹⁴'How then can I dispute with him?
  How can I find words to argue with
    him?
¹⁵Though I were innocent, I could not
    answer him;
  I could only plead with my Judge for
    mercy.
¹⁶Even if I summoned him and he
    responded,
  I do not believe he would give me a
    hearing.
¹⁷He would crush me with a storm
  and multiply my wounds for no
    reason.
¹⁸He would not let me catch my breath
  but would overwhelm me with misery.
¹⁹If it is a matter of strength, he is mighty!
  And if it is a matter of justice, who can
    challenge him^a?
²⁰Even if I were innocent, my mouth would
    condemn me;
  if I were blameless, it would pronounce
    me guilty.

²¹'Although I am blameless,
  I have no concern for myself;
  I despise my own life.
²²It is all the same; that is why I say,
  "He destroys both the blameless and
    the wicked."
²³When a scourge brings sudden death,
  he mocks the despair of the innocent.
²⁴When a land falls into the hands of the
    wicked,
  he blindfolds its judges.
  If it is not he, then who is it?

making Connections

Soap
Job 9:30
No-one knows what kind of soap people used in biblical times. It may have come from plants or from a mineral called 'lye' that was mixed with oil. 'Slime' was another name for bitumen, a black sticky substance that was used to waterproof boats or as mortar between bricks.

²⁵'My days are swifter than a runner;
  they fly away without a glimpse of joy.
²⁶They skim past like boats of papyrus,
  like eagles swooping down on their
    prey.
²⁷If I say, "I will forget my complaint,
  I will change my expression, and
    smile,"
²⁸I still dread all my sufferings,
  for I know you will not hold me
    innocent.
²⁹Since I am already found guilty,
  why should I struggle in vain?
³⁰Even if I washed myself with soap
  and my hands with cleansing powder,
³¹you would plunge me into a slime pit
  so that even my clothes would detest
    me.

³²'He is not a mere mortal like me that I
    might answer him,
  that we might confront each other in
    court.
³³If only there were someone to arbitrate
    between us,
  to lay a hand on us both,
³⁴someone to remove God's rod from me,
  so that his terror would frighten me no
    more.
³⁵Then I would speak up without fear of
    him,
  but as it now stands with me, I cannot.

---

^a 19 See Septuagint; Hebrew *me*.

10 ¹'I loathe my very life;
therefore I will give free rein to my complaint
and speak out in the bitterness of my soul.
²I say to God: do not declare me guilty,
but tell me what charges you have against me.
³Does it please you to oppress me,
to spurn the work of your hands,
while you smile on the plans of the wicked?
⁴Do you have eyes of flesh?
Do you see as a mortal sees?
⁵Are your days like those of a mortal
or your years like those of a human being,
⁶that you must search out my faults
and probe after my sin—
⁷though you know that I am not guilty
and that no-one can rescue me from your hand?

⁸'Your hands shaped me and made me.
Will you now turn and destroy me?
⁹Remember that you moulded me like clay.
Will you now turn me to dust again?
¹⁰Did you not pour me out like milk
and curdle me like cheese,
¹¹clothe me with skin and flesh
and knit me together with bones and sinews?
¹²You gave me life and showed me kindness,
and in your providence watched over my spirit.

¹³'But this is what you concealed in your heart,
and I know that this was in your mind:
¹⁴if I sinned, you would be watching me
and would not let my offence go unpunished.
¹⁵If I am guilty—woe to me!
Even if I am innocent, I cannot lift my head,
for I am full of shame
and drowned in*ᵃ* my affliction.
¹⁶If I hold my head high, you stalk me like a lion
and again display your awesome power against me.
¹⁷You bring new witnesses against me
and increase your anger towards me;
your forces come against me wave upon wave.

¹⁸'Why then did you bring me out of the womb?
I wish I had died before any eye saw me.
¹⁹If only I had never come into being,
or had been carried straight from the womb to the grave!
²⁰Are not my few days almost over?
Turn away from me so that I can have a moment's joy
²¹before I go to the place of no return,
to the land of gloom and utter darkness,
²²to the land of deepest night,
of utter darkness and disorder,
where even the light is like darkness.'

Zophar

11 Then Zophar the Naamathite replied:

²'Are all these words to go unanswered?
Is this talker to be vindicated?
³Will your idle talk reduce others to silence?
Will no-one rebuke you when you mock?
⁴You say to God, "My beliefs are flawless
and I am pure in your sight."
⁵Oh, how I wish that God would speak,
that he would open his lips against you
⁶and disclose to you the secrets of wisdom,
for true wisdom has two sides.
Know this: God has even forgotten some of your sin.

⁷'Can you fathom the mysteries of God?
Can you probe the limits of the Almighty?
⁸They are higher than the heavens above—
what can you do?
They are deeper than the depths below—what can you know?
⁹Their measure is longer than the earth
and wider than the sea.

ᵃ 15 Or *and aware of*

¹⁰'If he comes along and confines you in prison
  and convenes a court, who can oppose him?
¹¹Surely he recognises deceivers;
  and when he sees evil, does he not take note?
¹²But the witless can no more become wise
  than a wild donkey's colt can be born a human being.[a]

¹³'Yet if you devote your heart to him
  and stretch out your hands to him,
¹⁴if you put away the sin that is in your hand
  and allow no evil to dwell in your tent,
¹⁵then, free of fault, you will lift up your face;
  you will stand firm and without fear.
¹⁶You will surely forget your trouble,
  recalling it only as waters gone by.
¹⁷Life will be brighter than noonday,
  and darkness will become like morning.
¹⁸You will be secure, because there is hope;
  you will look about you and take your rest in safety.
¹⁹You will lie down, with no-one to make you afraid,
  and many will court your favour.
²⁰But the eyes of the wicked will fail,
  and escape will elude them;
  their hope will become a dying gasp.'

Job

12 Then Job replied:

²'Doubtless you are the people,
  and wisdom will die with you!
³But I have a mind as well as you;
  I am not inferior to you.
  Who does not know all these things?

⁴'I have become a laughing-stock to my friends,
  though I called on God and he answered—
  a mere laughing-stock, though righteous and blameless!
⁵Those who are at ease have contempt for misfortune
  as the fate of those whose feet are slipping.
⁶The tents of marauders are undisturbed,
  and those who provoke God are secure—
  those who God has in his hand.[b]

⁷'But ask the animals, and they will teach you,
  or the birds in the sky, and they will tell you;
⁸or speak to the earth, and it will teach you,
  or let the fish in the sea inform you.
⁹Which of all these does not know
  that the hand of the LORD has done this?
¹⁰In his hand is the life of every creature
  and the breath of every human being.
¹¹Does not the ear test words
  as the tongue tastes food?
¹²Is not wisdom found among the aged?
  Does not long life bring understanding?

¹³'To God belong wisdom and power;
  counsel and understanding are his.
¹⁴What he tears down cannot be rebuilt;
  those he imprisons cannot be released.
¹⁵If he holds back the waters, there is drought;
  if he lets them loose, they devastate the land.
¹⁶To him belong strength and insight;
  both deceived and deceiver are his.
¹⁷He leads rulers away stripped
  and makes fools of judges.
¹⁸He takes off the shackles put on by kings
  and ties a loincloth[c] round their waist.
¹⁹He leads priests away stripped
  and overthrows officials long established.
²⁰He silences the lips of trusted advisors
  and takes away the discernment of elders.
²¹He pours contempt on nobles
  and disarms the mighty.
²²He reveals the deep things of darkness
  and brings utter darkness into the light.
²³He makes nations great, and destroys them;

---

[a] 12 Or *wild donkey can be born tame*   [b] 6 Or *those whose god is in their own hand*   [c] 18 Or *shackles of kings / and ties a belt*

he enlarges nations, and disperses them.
24He deprives the leaders of the earth of their reason;
  he makes them wander in a trackless waste.
25They grope in darkness with no light;
  he makes them stagger like drunkards.

13

'My eyes have seen all this,
  my ears have heard and understood it.
2What you know, I also know;
  I am not inferior to you.
3But I desire to speak to the Almighty
  and to argue my case with God.
4You, however, smear me with lies;
  you are worthless healers, all of you!
5If only you would be altogether silent!
  For you, that would be wisdom.
6Hear now my argument;
  listen to the pleas of my lips.
7Will you speak wickedly on God's behalf?
  Will you speak deceitfully for him?
8Will you show him partiality?
  Will you argue the case for God?
9Would it turn out well if he examined you?
  Could you deceive him as you might deceive mortals?
10He would surely call you to account
  if you secretly showed partiality.
11Would not his splendour terrify you?
  Would not the dread of him fall on you?
12Your maxims are proverbs of ashes;
  your defences are defences of clay.

13'Keep silent and let me speak;
  then let come to me what may.
14Why do I put myself in jeopardy
  and take my life in my hands?
15Though he slay me, yet will I hope in him;
  I will surely^a defend my ways to his face.
16Indeed, this will turn out for my deliverance,
  for no godless person would dare come before him!
17Listen carefully to what I say;
  let my words ring in your ears.
18Now that I have prepared my case,
  I know I will be vindicated.
19Can anyone bring charges against me?
  If so, I will be silent and die.

20'Only grant me these two things, God,
  and then I will not hide from you:
21withdraw your hand far from me,
  and stop frightening me with your terrors.
22Then summon me and I will answer,
  or let me speak, and you reply to me.
23How many wrongs and sins have I committed?
  Show me my offence and my sin.
24Why do you hide your face
  and consider me your enemy?
25Will you torment a wind-blown leaf?
  Will you chase after dry chaff?
26For you write down bitter things against me
  and make me reap the sins of my youth.
27You fasten my feet in shackles;
  you keep close watch on all my paths
  by putting marks on the soles of my feet.

28'So humans waste away like something rotten,
  like a garment eaten by moths.

14

'Mortals, born of woman,
  are of few days and full of trouble.
2They spring up like flowers and wither away;
  like fleeting shadows, they do not endure.
3Do you fix your eye on such as these?
  Will you bring them^b before you for judgment?
4Who can bring what is pure from the impure?
  No-one!
5The days of mortals are determined;
  you have decreed the number of their months
  and have set limits they cannot exceed.
6So look away from us and leave us alone,
  till we have put in our time like hired labourers.

7'At least there is hope for a tree:
  if it is cut down, it will sprout again,
  and its new shoots will not fail.

---

^{a} 15 Or *He will surely slay me; I have no hope — / yet I will* ^{b} 3 Septuagint, Vulgate and Syriac; Hebrew *me*

⁸Its roots may grow old in the ground
  and its stump die in the soil,
⁹yet at the scent of water it will bud
  and put forth shoots like a plant.
¹⁰But human beings die and are laid low;
  they breathe their last and are no more.
¹¹As the water of a lake dries up
  or a river bed becomes parched and dry,
¹²so they lie down and do not rise;
  till the heavens are no more, they will not awake
  or be roused from their sleep.

¹³'If only you would hide me in the grave
  and conceal me till your anger has passed!
 If only you would set me a time
  and then remember me!
¹⁴If someone dies, will they live again?
  All the days of my hard service
  I will wait for my renewal*ᵃ* to come.
¹⁵You will call and I will answer you;
  you will long for the creature your hands have made.
¹⁶Surely then you will count my steps
  but not keep track of my sin.
¹⁷My offences will be sealed up in a bag;
  you will cover over my sin.

¹⁸'But as a mountain erodes and crumbles
  and as a rock is moved from its place,
¹⁹as water wears away stones
  and torrents wash away the soil,
  so you destroy everyone's hope.
²⁰You overpower them once for all, and they are gone;
  you change their countenance and send them away.
²¹If their children are honoured, they do not know it;
  if their children are brought low, they do not see it.
²²They feel but the pain of their own bodies
  and mourn only for themselves.'

Eliphaz

15 Then Eliphaz the Temanite replied:

Grey hair
Job 15:10
Wisdom was thought to come with experience, so people who were older and had lived a long life were seen as important sources of wisdom.

²'Would the wise answer with empty notions
  or fill their bellies with the hot east wind?
³Would they argue with useless words,
  with speeches that have no value?
⁴But you even undermine piety
  and hinder devotion to God.
⁵Your sin prompts your mouth;
  you adopt the tongue of the crafty.
⁶Your own mouth condemns you, not mine;
  your own lips testify against you.

⁷'Are you the first man ever born?
  Were you brought forth before the hills?
⁸Do you listen in on God's council?
  Do you have a monoploy on wisdom?
⁹What do you know that we do not know?
  What insights do you have that we do not have?
¹⁰The grey-haired and the aged are on our side,
  men even older than your father.
¹¹Are God's consolations not enough for you,
  words spoken gently to you?
¹²Why has your heart carried you away,
  and why do your eyes flash,
¹³so that you vent your rage against God
  and pour out such words from your mouth?

ᵃ 14 Or *release*

¹⁴'What are mortals, that they could be pure,
  or those born of woman, that they could be righteous?
¹⁵If God places no trust in his holy ones,
  if even the heavens are not pure in his eyes,
¹⁶how much less mortals, who are vile and corrupt,
  who drink up evil like water!

¹⁷'Listen to me and I will explain to you;
  let me tell you what I have seen,
¹⁸what the wise have declared,
  hiding nothing received from their ancestors
¹⁹(to whom alone the land was given
  when no foreigners moved among them):
²⁰all their days the wicked suffer torment,
  the ruthless through all the years stored up for them.
²¹Terrifying sounds fill their ears;
  when all seems well, marauders attack them.
²²They despair of escaping the realm of darkness;
  they are marked for the sword.
²³They wander about for food like vultures;
  they know the day of darkness is at hand.
²⁴Distress and anguish fill them with terror;
  troubles overwhelm them, like a king poised to attack,
²⁵because they shake their fists at God
  and vaunt themselves against the Almighty,
²⁶defiantly charging against him
  with thick, strong shields.

²⁷'Though their faces are covered with fat
  and their waists bulge with flesh,
²⁸they will inhabit ruined towns
  and houses where no-one lives,
  houses crumbling to rubble.
²⁹They will no longer be rich and their wealth will not endure,
  nor will their possessions spread over the land.
³⁰They will not escape the darkness;
  a flame will wither their shoots,
  and the breath of God's mouth will carry them away.
³¹Let them not deceive themselves by trusting what is worthless,
  for they will get nothing in return.
³²Before their time they will wither,
  and their branches will not flourish.
³³They will be like a vine stripped of its unripe grapes,
  like an olive tree shedding its blossoms.
³⁴For the company of the godless will be barren,
  and fire will consume the tents of those who love bribes.
³⁵They conceive trouble and give birth to evil;
  their womb fashions deceit.'

Job

16

Then Job replied:

²'I have heard many things like these;
  you are miserable comforters, all of you!
³Will your long-winded speeches never end?
  What ails you that you keep on arguing?
⁴I also could speak like you,
  if you were in my place;
  I could make fine speeches against you
  and shake my head at you.
⁵But my mouth would encourage you;
  comfort from my lips would bring you relief.

⁶'Yet if I speak, my pain is not relieved;
  and if I refrain, it does not go away.
⁷Surely, God, you have worn me out;
  you have devastated my entire household.
⁸You have shrivelled me up—and it has become a witness;
  my gauntness rises up and testifies against me.
⁹God assails me and tears me in his anger
  and gnashes his teeth at me;
  my opponent fastens on me his piercing eyes.
¹⁰People open their mouths to jeer at me;
  they strike my cheek in scorn
  and unite together against me.
¹¹God has turned me over to the ungodly
  and thrown me into the clutches of the wicked.

¹²All was well with me, but he shattered me;
   he seized me by the neck and crushed
      me.
He has made me his target;
¹³   his archers surround me.
Without pity, he pierces my kidneys
   and spills my gall on the ground.
¹⁴Again and again he bursts upon me;
   he rushes at me like a warrior.

¹⁵'I have sewed sackcloth over my skin
   and buried my brow in the dust.
¹⁶My face is red with weeping,
   dark shadows ring my eyes;
¹⁷yet my hands have been free of violence
   and my prayer is pure.

¹⁸'Earth, do not cover my blood;
   may my cry never be laid to rest!
¹⁹Even now my witness is in heaven;
   my advocate is on high.
²⁰My intercessor is my friend[a]
   as my eyes pour out tears to God;
²¹on behalf of a human being he pleads with
      God
   as one pleads for a friend.

²²'Only a few years will pass
   before I take the path of no return.

17

¹My spirit is broken,
   my days are cut short,
   the grave awaits me.
²Surely mockers surround me;
   my eyes must dwell on their hostility.

³'Give me, O God, the pledge you demand.
   Who else will put up security for me?
⁴You have closed their minds to
      understanding;
   therefore you will not let them
      triumph.

⁵If people denounce their friends for
      reward,
   the eyes of their children will fail.

⁶'God has made me a byword to everyone,
   a man in whose face people spit.
⁷My eyes have grown dim with grief;
   my whole frame is but a shadow.
⁸The upright are appalled at this;
   the innocent are aroused against the
      ungodly.
⁹Nevertheless, the righteous will hold to
      their ways,
   and those with clean hands will grow
      stronger.

¹⁰'But come on, all of you, try again!
   I will not find a wise man among you.
¹¹My days have passed, my plans are
      shattered.
   Yet the desires of my heart
¹²turn night into day;
   in the face of the darkness light is near.
¹³If the only home I hope for is the grave,
   if I spread out my bed in the realm of
      darkness,
¹⁴if I say to corruption, "You are my
      father,"
   and to the worm, "My mother" or "My
      sister",
¹⁵where then is my hope—
   who can see any hope for me?
¹⁶Will it go down to the gates of death?
   Will we descend together into the dust?'

Bildad

18
Then Bildad the Shuhite replied:

²'When will you end these speeches?
   Be sensible, and then we can talk.
³Why are we regarded as cattle
   and considered stupid in your sight?
⁴You who tear yourself to pieces in your
      anger,
   is the earth to be abandoned for your
      sake?
   Or must the rocks be moved from their
      place?

⁵'The lamp of a wicked man is snuffed out;
   the flame of his fire stops burning.
⁶The light in his tent becomes dark;
   the lamp beside him goes out.

IN OTHER WORDS

Spirit
Job 17:1
The spirit of a person is the part that responds to God and connects with him.

---

[a] 20 Or *My friends treat me with scorn*

⁷The vigour of his step is weakened;
  his own schemes throw him down.
⁸His feet thrust him into a net;
  he wanders into its mesh.
⁹A trap seizes him by the heel;
  a snare holds him fast.
¹⁰A noose is hidden for him on the ground;
  a trap lies in his path.
¹¹Terrors startle him on every side
  and dog his every step.
¹²Calamity is hungry for him;
  disaster is ready for him when he falls.
¹³It eats away parts of his skin;
  death's firstborn devours his limbs.
¹⁴He is torn from the security of his tent
  and marched off to the king of terrors.
¹⁵Fire resides[a] in his tent;
  burning sulphur is scattered over his dwelling.
¹⁶His roots dry up below
  and his branches wither above.
¹⁷The memory of him perishes from the earth;
  he has no name in the land.
¹⁸He is driven from light into the realm of darkness
  and is banished from the world.
¹⁹He has no offspring or descendants among his people,
  no survivor where once he lived.
²⁰People of the west are appalled at his fate;
  those of the east are seized with horror.
²¹Surely such is the dwelling of an evil man;
  such is the place of one who knows not God.'

Job

19

Then Job replied:

²'How long will you torment me
  and crush me with words?
³Ten times now you have reproached me;
  shamelessly you attack me.
⁴If it is true that I have gone astray,
  my error remains my concern alone.
⁵If indeed you would exalt yourselves above me
  and use my humiliation against me,
⁶then know that God has wronged me
  and drawn his net around me.

⁷'Though I cry, "Violence!" I get no response;
  though I call for help, there is no justice.
⁸He has blocked my way so that I cannot pass;
  he has shrouded my paths in darkness.
⁹He has stripped me of my honour
  and removed the crown from my head.
¹⁰He tears me down on every side till I am gone;
  he uproots my hope like a tree.
¹¹His anger burns against me;
  he counts me among his enemies.
¹²His troops advance in force;
  they build a siege ramp against me
  and encamp around my tent.

¹³'He has alienated my family from me;
  my acquaintances are completely estranged from me.
¹⁴My relatives have gone away;
  my friends have forgotten me.
¹⁵My guests and my female servants count me a foreigner;
  they look upon me as a stranger.
¹⁶I summon my servant, but he does not answer,
  though I beg him with my own mouth.
¹⁷My breath is offensive to my wife;
  I am loathsome to my own family.
¹⁸Even the little boys scorn me;
  when I appear, they ridicule me.
¹⁹All my intimate friends detest me;
  those I love have turned against me.
²⁰I am nothing but skin and bones;
  I have escaped only by the skin of my teeth.[b]

²¹'Have pity on me, my friends, have pity,
  for the hand of God has struck me.
²²Why do you pursue me as God does?
  Will you never get enough of my flesh?

²³'Oh, that my words were recorded,
  that they were written on a scroll,
²⁴that they were inscribed with an iron tool on[c] lead,
  or engraved in rock for ever!
²⁵I know that my redeemer[d] lives,
  and that in the end he will stand on the earth.[e]

---

[a] 15 Or *Nothing he had remains*   [b] 20 Or *only by my gums*   [c] 24 Or *and*   [d] 25 Or *vindicator*   [e] 25 Or *on my grave*

²⁶And after my skin has been destroyed,
yet*ᵃ* in*ᵇ* my flesh I will see God;
²⁷I myself will see him
with my own eyes—I, and not another.
How my heart yearns within me!

²⁸'If you say, "How we will hound him,
since the root of the trouble lies in him,"*ᶜ*'
²⁹you should fear the sword yourselves;
for wrath will bring punishment by the sword,
and then you will know that there is judgment.*ᵈ*'

Zophar

20 Then Zophar the Naamathite replied:

²'My troubled thoughts prompt me to answer
because I am greatly disturbed.
³I hear a rebuke that dishonours me,
and my understanding inspires me to reply.

⁴'Surely you know how it has been from of old,
ever since people were*ᵉ* placed on the earth,
⁵that the mirth of the wicked is brief,
the joy of the godless lasts but a moment.
⁶Though his pride reaches to the heavens
and his head touches the clouds,
⁷he will perish for ever, like his own dung;
those who have seen him will say, "Where is he?"
⁸Like a dream he flies away, no more to be found,
banished like a vision of the night.
⁹The eye that saw him will not see him again;
his place will look on him no more.
¹⁰His children must make amends to the poor;
his own hands must give back his wealth.
¹¹The youthful vigour that fills his bones
will lie with him in the dust.

¹²'Though evil is sweet in his mouth
and he hides it under his tongue,
¹³though he cannot bear to let it go
and lets it linger in his mouth,
¹⁴yet his food will turn sour in his stomach;
it will become the venom of serpents within him.
¹⁵He will spit out the riches he swallowed;
God will make his stomach vomit them up.
¹⁶He will suck the poison of serpents;
the fangs of an adder will kill him.
¹⁷He will not enjoy the streams,
the rivers flowing with honey and cream.
¹⁸What he toiled for he must give back uneaten;
he will not enjoy the profit from his trading.
¹⁹For he has oppressed the poor and left them destitute;
he has seized houses he did not build.

²⁰'Surely he will have no respite from his craving;
he cannot save himself by his treasure.
²¹Nothing is left for him to devour;
his prosperity will not endure.
²²In the midst of his plenty, distress will overtake him;
the full force of misery will come upon him.
²³When he has filled his belly,
God will vent his burning anger against him
and rain down his blows on him.
²⁴Though he flees from an iron weapon,
a bronze-tipped arrow pierces him.
²⁵He pulls it out of his back,
the gleaming point out of his liver.
Terrors will come over him;
²⁶　total darkness lies in wait for his treasures.
A fire unfanned will consume him
and devour what is left in his tent.
²⁷The heavens will expose his guilt;
the earth will rise up against him.
²⁸A flood will carry off his house,
rushing waters*ᶠ* on the day of God's wrath.

ᵃ 26 Or *And after I awake, / though this [body] has been destroyed, / then*　*ᵇ* 26 Or *destroyed, / apart from*　*ᶜ* 28 Many Hebrew manuscripts, Septuagint and Vulgate; most Hebrew manuscripts *me*　*ᵈ* 29 Or *sword, / that you may come to know the Almighty*　*ᵉ* 4 Or *since Adam was*　*ᶠ* 28 Or *The possessions in his house will be carried off, / washed away*

29 Such is the fate God allots the wicked,
   the heritage appointed for them by
       God.'

Job

21

Then Job replied:

2 'Listen carefully to my words;
   let this be the consolation you give me.
3 Bear with me while I speak,
   and after I have spoken, mock on.

4 'Is my complaint directed to a human
       being?
   Why should I not be impatient?
5 Look at me and be appalled;
   clap your hand over your mouth.
6 When I think about this, I am terrified;
   trembling seizes my body.
7 Why do the wicked live on,
   growing old and increasing in power?
8 They see their children established
       around them,
   their offspring before their eyes.
9 Their homes are safe and free from fear;
   the rod of God is not on them.
10 Their bulls never fail to breed;
   their cows calve and do not miscarry.
11 They send forth their children as a flock;
   their little ones dance about.
12 They sing to the music of tambourine and
       lyre;
   they make merry to the sound of the
       pipe.
13 They spend their years in prosperity
   and go down to the grave in peace.^{a}
14 Yet they say to God, "Leave us alone!
   We have no desire to know your ways.
15 Who is the Almighty, that we should serve
       him?
   What would we gain by praying to
       him?"
16 But their prosperity is not in their own
       hands,
   so I stand aloof from the counsel of the
       wicked.

17 'Yet how often is the lamp of the wicked
       snuffed out?
   How often does calamity come upon
       them,
   the fate God allots in his anger?

18 How often are they like straw before the
       wind,
   like chaff swept away by a gale?
19 ⌊It is said,⌋ "God stores up the
       punishment of the wicked for
       their children."
   Let him repay the wicked, so that they
       themselves will experience it!
20 Let their own eyes see their destruction;
   let them drink of the wrath of the
       Almighty.
21 For what do they care about the families
       they leave behind
   when their allotted months come to an
       end?

22 'Can anyone teach knowledge to God,
   since he judges even the highest?
23 One person dies in full vigour,
   completely secure and at ease,
24 well nourished in body^b
   bones rich with marrow.
25 Another dies in bitterness of soul,
   never having enjoyed anything good.
26 Side by side they lie in the dust,
   and worms cover them both.

27 'I know full well what you are thinking,
   the schemes by which you would
       wrong me.
28 You say, "Where now is the house of the
       great,
   the tents where the wicked lived?"
29 Have you never questioned those who
       travel?
   Have you paid no regard to their
       accounts—
30 that the wicked are spared from the day of
       calamity,
   that they are delivered from^c the day of
       wrath?
31 Who denounces their conduct to their
       face?
   Who repays them for what they have
       done?
32 They are carried to the grave,
   and watch is kept over their
       tombs.
33 The soil in the valley is sweet to them;
   everyone follows after them,

---

^{a} 13 Or *in an instant* ^{b} 24 The meaning of the Hebrew for this word is uncertain. ^{c} 30 Or *are reserved for the day of calamity, / that they are brought forth to*

and a countless throng goes[a] before
them.

³⁴'So how can you console me with your
nonsense?
Nothing is left of your answers but
falsehood!'

Eliphaz

22 Then Eliphaz the Temanite replied:

²'Can a human being be of benefit to God?
Can even the wise benefit him?
³What pleasure would it give the Almighty
if you were righteous?
What would he gain if your ways were
blameless?

⁴'Is it for your piety that he rebukes you
and brings charges against you?
⁵Is not your wickedness great?
Are not your sins endless?
⁶You demanded security from your
relatives for no reason;
you stripped people of their clothing,
leaving them naked.
⁷You gave no water to the weary
and you withheld food from the
hungry,
⁸though you were a powerful man, owning
land—
an honoured man, living on it.
⁹And you sent widows away empty-
handed
and broke the strength of the fatherless.
¹⁰That is why snares are all around you,
why sudden peril terrifies you,
¹¹why it is so dark that you cannot see,
and why a flood of water covers you.

¹²'Is not God in the heights of heaven?
And see how lofty are the highest stars!
¹³Yet you say, "What does God know?
Does he judge through such darkness?
¹⁴Thick clouds veil him, so he does not see
us
as he goes about in the vaulted
heavens."

¹⁵Will you keep to the old path
that the wicked have trod?
¹⁶They were carried off before their time,

Making Connections

Heights of heaven
Job 22:12
People in ancient times thought that the earth was flat and the sky was a dome above it held up by the mountains. God is described here as being very distant, living beyond even the furthest stars.

their foundations washed away by a
flood.
¹⁷They said to God, "Leave us alone!
What can the Almighty do to us?"
¹⁸Yet it was he who filled their houses with
good things,
so I stand aloof from the counsel of the
wicked.
¹⁹'The righteous see their ruin and rejoice;
the innocent mock them, saying,
²⁰"Surely our foes are destroyed,
and fire devours their wealth."

²¹'Submit to God and be at peace with him;
in this way prosperity will come to you.
²²Accept instruction from his mouth
and lay up his words in your heart.
²³If you return to the Almighty, you will be
restored:
if you remove wickedness far from
your tent
²⁴and assign your nuggets to the dust,
your gold of Ophir to the rocks in the
ravines,
²⁵then the Almighty will be your gold,
the choicest silver for you.
²⁶Surely then you will find delight in the
Almighty
and will lift up your face to God.
²⁷You will pray to him, and he will hear you,
and you will fulfil your vows.
²⁸What you decide on will be done,
and light will shine on your ways.

---

a 33 Or *them, as a countless throng went*

²⁹When people are brought low and you say, "Lift them up!"
    then he will save the downcast.
³⁰He will deliver even one who is not innocent,
    who will be delivered through the cleanness of your hands.'

Job

23 Then Job replied:

²'Even today my complaint is bitter;
    his hand[a] is heavy in spite of[b] my groaning.
³If only I knew where to find him;
    if only I could go to his dwelling!
⁴I would state my case before him
    and fill my mouth with arguments.
⁵I would find out what he would answer me,
    and consider what he would say to me.
⁶Would he vigorously oppose me with great power?
    No, he would not press charges against me.
⁷There the upright can establish their innocence before him,
    and there I would be delivered for ever from my judge.

⁸'But if I go to the east, he is not there;
    if I go to the west, I do not find him.
⁹When he is at work in the north, I do not see him;
    when he turns to the south, I catch no glimpse of him.
¹⁰But he knows the way that I take;
    when he has tested me, I shall come forth as gold.
¹¹My feet have closely followed his steps;
    I have kept to his way without turning aside.
¹²I have not departed from the commands of his lips;
    I have treasured the words of his mouth more than my daily bread.

¹³'But he stands alone, and who can oppose him?
    He does whatever he pleases.
¹⁴He carries out his decree against me,
    and many such plans he still has in store.
¹⁵That is why I am terrified before him;
    when I think of all this, I fear him.
¹⁶God has made my heart faint;
    the Almighty has terrified me.
¹⁷Yet I am not silenced by the darkness,
    by the thick darkness that covers my face.

24 'Why does the Almighty not set times for judgment?
    Why must those who know him look in vain for such days?
²There are those who move boundary stones;
    they pasture flocks they have stolen.
³They drive away the orphan's donkey
    and take the widow's ox in pledge.
⁴They thrust the needy from the path
    and force all the poor of the land into hiding.
⁵Like wild donkeys in the desert,
    the poor go about their labour of foraging food;
    the wasteland provides food for their children.
⁶They gather fodder in the fields
    and glean in the vineyards of the wicked.
⁷Lacking clothes, they spend the night naked;
    they have nothing to cover themselves in the cold.
⁸They are drenched by mountain rains
    and hug the rocks for lack of shelter.
⁹The fatherless child is snatched from the breast;
    the infant of the poor is seized for a debt.
¹⁰Lacking clothes, they go about naked;
    they carry the sheaves, but still go hungry.
¹¹They crush olives among the terraces[c];
    they tread the winepresses, yet suffer thirst.
¹²The groans of the dying rise from the city,
    and the souls of the wounded cry out for help.

---

[a] 2 Septuagint and Syriac; Hebrew *the hand on me*   [b] 2 Or *heavy on me in*   [c] 11 The meaning of the Hebrew for this word is uncertain.

But God charges no-one with wrongdoing.

13 'There are those who rebel against the light,
    who do not know its ways
    or stay in its paths.
14 When daylight is gone, the murderer rises up,
    kills the poor and needy,
    and in the night steals forth like a thief.
15 The eye of the adulterer watches for dusk;
    he thinks, "No eye will see me,"
    and he keeps his face concealed.
16 In the dark, thieves break into houses,
    but by day they shut themselves in;
    they want nothing to do with the light.
17 For all of them, midnight is their morning;
    they make friends with the terrors of darkness.

18 'Yet they are foam on the surface of the water;
    their portion of the land is cursed,
    so that no-one goes to the vineyards.
19 As heat and drought snatch away the melted snow,
    so the grave snatches away those who have sinned.
20 The womb forgets them,
    the worm feasts on them;
    the wicked are no longer remembered
    but are broken like a tree.
21 They prey on the barren and childless woman,
    and to the widow show no kindness.
22 But God drags away the mighty by his power;
    though they become established, they have no assurance of life.
23 He may let them rest in a feeling of security,
    but his eyes are on their ways.
24 For a little while they are exalted, and then they are gone;
    they are brought low and gathered up like all others;
    they are cut off like ears of corn.

25 'If this is not so, who can prove me false
    and reduce my words to nothing?'

Bildad

25 Then Bildad the Shuhite replied:

2 'Dominion and awe belong to God;
    he establishes order in the heights of heaven.
3 Can his forces be numbered?
    On whom does his light not rise?
4 How then can a mortal be righteous before God?
    How can one born of woman be pure?
5 If even the moon is not bright
    and the stars are not pure in his eyes,
6 how much less a mortal, who is but a maggot—
    a human being, who is only a worm!'

Job

26 Then Job replied:

2 'How you have helped the powerless!
    How you have saved the arm that is feeble!
3 What advice you have offered to one without wisdom!
    And what great insight you have displayed!
4 Who has helped you utter these words?
    And whose spirit spoke from your mouth?

5 'The dead are in deep anguish,
    those beneath the waters and all that live in them.
6 Death is naked before God;
    Destruction[a] lies uncovered.
7 He spreads out the northern ⌊skies⌋ over empty space;
    he suspends the earth over nothing.
8 He wraps up the waters in his clouds,
    yet the clouds do not burst under their weight.
9 He covers the face of the full moon,
    spreading his clouds over it.
10 He marks out the horizon on the face of the waters
    for a boundary between light and darkness.
11 The pillars of the heavens quake,
    aghast at his rebuke.
12 By his power he churned up the sea;

---

[a] 6 Hebrew *Abaddon*

by his wisdom he cut Rahab to pieces.
¹³By his breath the skies became fair;
   his hand pierced the gliding serpent.
¹⁴And these are but the outer fringe of his works;
   how faint the whisper we hear of him!
   Who then can understand the thunder of his power?'

Job's final word to his friends

27 And Job continued his discourse:

²'As surely as God lives, who has denied me justice,
   the Almighty, who has made my life bitter,
³as long as I have life within me,
   the breath of God in my nostrils,
⁴my lips will not say anything wicked,
   and my tongue will not utter lies.
⁵I will never admit you are in the right;
   till I die, I will not deny my integrity.
⁶I will maintain my innocence and never let go of it;
   my conscience will not reproach me as long as I live.

⁷'May my enemies be like the wicked,
   my adversaries like the unjust!
⁸For what hope have the godless when they are cut off,
   when God takes away their life?
⁹Does God listen to their cry
   when distress comes upon them?
¹⁰Will they find delight in the Almighty?
   Will they call on God at all times?

¹¹'I will teach you about the power of God;
   the ways of the Almighty I will not conceal.
¹²You have all seen this yourselves.
   Why then this meaningless talk?

¹³'Here is the fate God allots to the wicked,
   the heritage a ruthless man receives from the Almighty:
¹⁴However many his children, their fate is the sword;
   his offspring will never have enough to eat.
¹⁵The plague will bury those who survive him,
   and their widows will not weep for them.
¹⁶Though he heaps up silver like dust
   and clothes like piles of clay,
¹⁷what he lays up the righteous will wear,
   and the innocent will divide his silver.
¹⁸The house he builds is like a moth's cocoon,
   like a hut made by a watchman.
¹⁹He lies down wealthy, but will do so no more;
   when he opens his eyes, all is gone.
²⁰Terrors overtake him like a flood;
   a tempest snatches him away in the night.
²¹The east wind carries him off, and he is gone;
   it sweeps him out of his place.
²²It hurls itself against him without mercy
   as he flees headlong from its power.
²³It claps its hands in derision
   and hisses them out of their place.'

Interlude: where wisdom is found

28 There is a mine for silver
   and a place where gold is refined.
²Iron is taken from the earth,
   and copper is smelted from ore.
³Miners put an end to the darkness;
   they search out the farthest recesses
   for ore in the blackest darkness.
⁴Far from human dwellings they cut a shaft,
   in places untouched by human feet;
   far from other people they dangle and sway.
⁵The earth, from which food comes,
   is transformed below as by fire;
⁶lapis lazuli comes from its rocks,
   and its dust contains nuggets of gold.

IN OTHER WORDS

Smelting
Job 28:2
Smelting is another name for refining, the process of heating metal until it is liquid and then removing all its impurities.

⁷No bird of prey knows that hidden path,
   no falcon's eye has seen it.
⁸Proud beasts do not set foot on it,
   and no lion prowls there.
⁹The miners' hands assault the flinty rock
   and lay bare the roots of the mountains.
¹⁰They tunnel through the rock;
   their eyes see all its treasures.
¹¹They search[a] the sources of the rivers
   and bring hidden things to light.

¹²But where can wisdom be found?
   Where does understanding dwell?
¹³No mortal comprehends its worth;
   it cannot be found in the land of the living.
¹⁴The deep says, 'It is not in me';
   the sea says, 'It is not with me.'
¹⁵It cannot be bought with the finest gold,
   nor can its price be weighed out in silver.
¹⁶It cannot be bought with the gold of Ophir,
   with precious onyx or lapis lazuli.
¹⁷Neither gold nor crystal can compare with it,
   nor can it be had for jewels of gold.
¹⁸Coral and jasper are not worthy of mention;
   the price of wisdom is beyond rubies.
¹⁹The topaz of Cush cannot compare with it;
   it cannot be bought with pure gold.

²⁰Where then does wisdom come from?
   Where does understanding dwell?
²¹It is hidden from the eyes of every living thing,
   concealed even from the birds in the sky.
²²Destruction[b] and Death say,
   'Only a rumour of it has reached our ears.'
²³God understands the way to it
   and he alone knows where it dwells,
²⁴for he views the ends of the earth
   and sees everything under the heavens.
²⁵When he established the force of the wind
   and measured out the waters,
²⁶when he made a decree for the rain
   and a path for the thunderstorm,
²⁷then he looked at wisdom and appraised it;
   he confirmed it and tested it.
²⁸And he said to the human race,
   'The fear of the Lord—that is wisdom,
   and to shun evil is understanding.'

Job's final defence

29

Job continued his discourse:

²'How I long for the months gone by,
   for the days when God watched over me,
³when his lamp shone on my head
   and by his light I walked through darkness!
⁴Oh, for the days when I was in my prime,
   when God's intimate friendship blessed my house,
⁵when the Almighty was still with me
   and my children were around me,
⁶when my path was drenched with cream
   and the rock poured out for me streams of olive oil.

⁷'When I went to the gate of the city
   and took my seat in the public square,
⁸the young men saw me and stepped aside
   and the old men rose to their feet;
⁹the chief men refrained from speaking
   and covered their mouths with their hands;
¹⁰the voices of the nobles were hushed,
   and their tongues stuck to the roof of their mouths.
¹¹Whoever heard me spoke well of me,
   and those who saw me commended me,
¹²because I rescued the poor who cried for help,
   and the fatherless who had none to assist them.
¹³Those who were dying blessed me;
   I made the widow's heart sing.
¹⁴I put on righteousness as my clothing;
   justice was my robe and my turban.
¹⁵I was eyes to the blind
   and feet to the lame.
¹⁶I was a father to the needy;
   I took up the case of the stranger.
¹⁷I broke the fangs of the wicked

---

[a] 11 Septuagint, Aquila and Vulgate; Hebrew *They dam up*   [b] 22 Hebrew *Abaddon*

and snatched the victims from their teeth.

18 'I thought, "I shall die in my own house,
my days as numerous as the grains of sand.
19 My roots will reach to the water,
and the dew will lie all night on my branches.
20 My glory will remain fresh in me,
the bow ever new in my hand."

21 'People listened to me expectantly,
waiting in silence for my counsel.
22 After I had spoken, they spoke no more;
my words fell gently on their ears.
23 They waited for me as for showers
and drank in my words as the spring rain.
24 When I smiled at them, they scarcely believed it;
the light of my face was precious to them.[a]
25 I chose the way for them and sat as their chief;
I dwelt as a king among his troops;
I was like one who comforts mourners.

30

'But now they mock me,
men younger than I,
whose fathers I would have disdained
to put with my sheep dogs.
2 Of what use was the strength of their hands to me,
since their vigour had gone from them?
3 Haggard from want and hunger,
they roamed[b] the parched land
in desolate wastelands at night.
4 In the brush they gathered salt herbs,
and their food[c] was the root of the broom bush.
5 They were banished from human society,
shouted at as if they were thieves.
6 They were forced to live in the dry stream beds,
among the rocks and in holes in the ground.
7 They brayed among the bushes
and huddled in the undergrowth.
8 A base and nameless brood,
they were driven out of the land.

making Connections

Salt herbs
Job 30:4

'Salt herbs' is another name for the plant mallow which has thick juicy leaves and small purple flowers. Mallow grows in dry, salty regions. Its leaves are sour and so it was only eaten by the poor who were desperate for food.

9 'And now those young men mock me in song;
I have become a byword among them.
10 They detest me and keep their distance;
they do not hesitate to spit in my face.
11 Now that God has unstrung my bow and afflicted me,
they throw off restraint in my presence.
12 On my right the tribe[d] attacks;
they lay snares for my feet,
they build their siege ramps against me.
13 They break up my road;
they succeed in destroying me.
"No-one can help him," they say
14 They advance as through a gaping breach;
amid the ruins they come rolling in.
15 Terrors overwhelm me;
my dignity is driven away as by the wind,
my safety vanishes like a cloud.

16 'And now my life ebbs away;
days of suffering grip me.
17 Night pierces my bones;
my gnawing pains never rest.
18 In his great power [God] becomes like clothing to me[e];
he binds me like the neck of my garment.
19 He throws me into the mud,
and I am reduced to dust and ashes.

---

[a] 24 The meaning of the Hebrew for this clause is uncertain. [b] 3 Or *gnawed* [c] 4 Or *fuel* [d] 12 The meaning of the Hebrew for this word is uncertain. [e] 18 Hebrew; Septuagint [*God*] *grasps my clothing*

²⁰'I cry out to you, God, but you do not answer;
  I stand up, but you merely look at me.
²¹You turn on me ruthlessly;
  with the might of your hand you attack me.
²²You snatch me up and drive me before the wind;
  you toss me about in the storm.
²³I know you will bring me down to death,
  to the place appointed for all the living.

²⁴'Surely no-one lays a hand on those who are crushed
  when they cry for help in their distress.
²⁵Have I not wept for those in trouble?
  Has not my soul grieved for the poor?
²⁶Yet when I hoped for good, evil came;
  when I looked for light, then came darkness.
²⁷The churning inside me never stops;
  days of suffering confront me.
²⁸I go about blackened, but not by the sun;
  I stand up in the assembly and cry for help.
²⁹I have become a brother of jackals,
  a companion of owls.
³⁰My skin grows black and peels;
  my body burns with fever.
³¹My lyre is tuned to mourning,
  and my pipe to the sound of wailing.

31

'I made a covenant with my eyes
  not to look lustfully at a virgin.
²For what is our lot from God above,
  our heritage from the Almighty on high?
³Is it not ruin for the wicked,
  disaster for those who do wrong?
⁴Does he not see my ways
  and count my every step?

⁵'If I have walked with falsehood
  or my foot has hurried after deceit—
⁶let God weigh me in honest scales
  and he will know that I am blameless—
⁷if my steps have turned from the path,
  if my heart has been led by my eyes,
  or if my hands have been defiled,
⁸then may others eat what I have sown,
  and may my crops be uprooted.

⁹'If my heart has been enticed by a woman,
  or if I have lurked at my neighbour's door,
¹⁰then may my wife grind another man's corn,
  and may other men sleep with her.
¹¹For that would have been wicked,
  a sin to be judged.
¹²It is a fire that burns to Destruction;^{a}
  it would have uprooted my harvest.

¹³'If I have denied justice to any of my servants,
  whether male or female,
  when they had a grievance against me,
¹⁴what will I do when God confronts me?
  What will I answer when called to account?
¹⁵Did not he who made me in the womb make them?
  Did not the same one form us both within our mothers?

¹⁶'If I have denied the desires of the poor
  or let the eyes of the widow grow weary,
¹⁷if I have kept my bread to myself,
  not sharing it with the fatherless—
¹⁸but from my youth I reared them as a father would,
  and from my birth I guided the widow—
¹⁹if I have seen anyone perishing for lack of clothing,
  or the needy without garments,
²⁰and their hearts did not bless me
  for warming them with the fleece from my sheep,
²¹if I have raised my hand against the fatherless,
  knowing that I had influence in court,
²²then let my arm fall from the shoulder,
  let it be broken off at the joint.
²³For I dreaded destruction from God,
  and for fear of his splendour I could not do such things.

²⁴'If I have put my trust in gold
  or said to pure gold, "You are my security,"
²⁵if I have rejoiced over my great wealth,
  the fortune my hands had gained,

---

^{a} 12 Hebrew *Abaddon*

26 if I have regarded the sun in its radiance
   or the moon moving in splendour,
27 so that my heart was secretly enticed
   and my hand offered them a kiss of homage,
28 then these also would be sins to be judged,
   for I would have been unfaithful to God on high.

29 'If I have rejoiced at my enemies' misfortune
   or gloated over the trouble that came to them—
30 I have not allowed my mouth to sin
   by invoking a curse against their life—
31 if those of my household have never said,
   "Who has not been filled with Job's meat?"—
32 but no stranger had to spend the night in the street,
   for my door was always open to the traveller—
33 if I have concealed my sin as people do,[a]
   by hiding my guilt in my heart
34 because I so feared the crowd
   and so dreaded the contempt of the clans
   that I kept silent and would not go outside—

35 ('Oh, that I had someone to hear me!
   I sign now my defence—let the Almighty answer me;
   let my accuser put his indictment in writing.
36 Surely I would wear it on my shoulder,
   I would put it on like a crown.
37 I would give him an account of my every step;
   I would present it to him as to a ruler.)—

38 'if my land cries out against me
   and all its furrows are wet with tears,
39 if I have devoured its yield without payment
   or broken the spirit of its tenants,
40 then let briers come up instead of wheat
   and stinkweed instead of barley.'

The words of Job are ended.

Elihu

32 So these three men stopped answering Job, because he was righteous in his own eyes. 2But Elihu son of Barakel the Buzite, of the family of Ram, became very angry with Job for justifying himself rather than God. 3He was also angry with the three friends, because they had found no way to refute Job, and yet had condemned him.[b] 4Now Elihu had waited before speaking to Job because they were older than he. 5But when he saw that the three men had nothing more to say, his anger was aroused.

6So Elihu son of Barakel the Buzite said:

'I am young in years,
   and you are old;
that is why I was fearful,
   not daring to tell you what I know.
7 I thought, "Age should speak;
   advanced years should teach wisdom."
8 But it is the spirit[c] in mortals,
   the breath of the Almighty, that gives them understanding.
9 It is not only the old[d] who are wise,
   not only the aged who understand what is right.

10 'Therefore I say: listen to me;
   I too will tell you what I know.
11 I waited while you spoke,
   I listened to your reasoning;
   while you were searching for words,
12   I gave you my full attention.
   But not one of you has proved Job wrong;
   none of you has answered his arguments.
13 Do not say, "We have found wisdom;
   let God refute him, not a mere mortal."
14 But Job has not marshalled his words against me,
   and I will not answer him with your arguments.

15 'They are dismayed and have no more to say;
   words have failed them.
16 Must I wait, now that they are silent,
   now that they stand there with no reply?

---

a 33 Or *as Adam did*   *b* 3 Masoretic Text; an ancient Hebrew scribal tradition *Job, and so had condemned God*   *c* 8 Or *Spirit*; also in verse 18   *d* 9 Or *many*; or *great*

17I too will have my say;
  I too will tell what I know.
18For I am full of words,
  and the spirit within me compels me;
19inside I am like bottled-up wine,
  like new wineskins ready to burst.
20I must speak and find relief;
  I must open my lips and reply.
21I will show no partiality,
  nor will I flatter anyone;
22for if I were skilled in flattery,
  my Maker would soon take me away.

33

'But now, Job, listen to my words;
  pay attention to everything I say.
2I am about to open my mouth;
  my words are on the tip of my tongue.
3My words come from an upright heart;
  my lips sincerely speak what I know.
4The Spirit of God has made me;
  the breath of the Almighty gives me life.
5Answer me then, if you can;
  stand up and argue your case before me.
6I am the same as you; in God's sight;
  I too am a piece of clay.
7No fear of me should alarm you,
  nor should my hand be heavy on you.

8'But you have said in my hearing—
  I heard the very words—
9"I am pure, I have done no wrong;
  I am clean and free from sin.
10Yet God has found fault with me;
  he considers me his enemy.
11He fastens my feet in shackles;
  he keeps close watch on all my paths."

12'But I tell you, in this you are not right,
  for God is greater than any mortal.
13Why do you complain to him
  that he responds to no-one's words[a]?
14For God does speak—now one way, now another—
  though no-one perceives it.
15In a dream, in a vision of the night,
  when deep sleep falls on people
  as they slumber in their beds,
16he may speak in their ears
  and terrify them with warnings,
17to turn them from wrongdoing
  and keep them from pride,
18to preserve them from the pit,
  their lives from perishing by the sword.[b]
19'Or they may be chastened on a bed of pain
  with constant distress in their bones,
20so that their bodies find food repulsive
  and their souls loathe the choicest meal.
21Their flesh wastes away to nothing,
  and their bones, once hidden, now stick out.
22They draw near to the pit,
  and their lives to the messengers of death.[c]
23'Yet if there is an angel at their side
  a messenger, one out of a thousand,
  sent to tell them how to be upright,
24and he is gracious to them and says to God,
  "Spare them from going down to the pit;
  I have found a ransom for them—
25let their flesh be renewed like a child's;
  let them be restored as in the days of their youth"—
26then they can pray to God and find favour with him,
  they will see God's face and shout for joy;
  he will restore them to full well-being.
27And they will go to others and say,
  "We have sinned, and we have perverted what is right,
  but we did not get what we deserved.

IN OTHER WORDS

Pit
Job 33:28
A pit is a deep hole in the ground, either natural or one that has been dug out. 'The pit' was another name for Sheol, the place where dead spirits were thought to live.

---

[a] 13 Or that he does not answer for any of his actions [b] 18 Or from crossing the river [c] 22 Or to the place of the dead

28God has delivered us from going down to the pit,
and we shall live to enjoy the light of life."

29'God does all these things to people—
twice, even three times—
30to turn them back from the pit,
that the light of life may shine on them.

31'Pay attention, Job, and listen to me;
be silent, and I will speak.
32If you have anything to say, answer me;
speak up, for I want to vindicate you.
33But if not, then listen to me;
be silent, and I will teach you wisdom.'

34

Then Elihu said:

2'Hear my words, you wise men;
listen to me, you men of learning.
3For the ear tests words
as the tongue tastes food.
4Let us discern for ourselves what is right;
let us learn together what is good.

5'Job says, "I am innocent,
but God denies me justice.
6Although I am right,
I am considered a liar;
although I am guiltless,
his arrow inflicts an incurable wound."
7Is there anyone like Job,
who drinks scorn like water?
8He keeps company with evildoers;
he associates with the wicked.
9For he says, "There is no profit
in trying to please God."

10'So listen to me, you men of understanding.
Far be it from God to do evil,
from the Almighty to do wrong.
11He repays everyone for what they have done;
he brings on them what their conduct deserves.
12It is unthinkable that God would do wrong,
that the Almighty would pervert justice.
13Who appointed him over the earth?
Who put him in charge of the whole world?
14If it were his intention
and he withdrew his spirit[a] and breath,
15all people would perish together
and would return to the dust.

16'If you have understanding, hear this;
listen to what I say.
17Can one who hates justice govern?
Will you condemn the just and mighty One?
18Is he not the One who says to kings, "You are worthless,"
and to nobles, "You are wicked,"
19who shows no partiality to princes
and does not favour the rich over the poor,
for they are all the work of his hands?
20They die in an instant, in the middle of the night;
the people are shaken and they pass away;
the mighty are removed without human hand.

21'His eyes are on the ways of mortals;
he sees their every step.
22There is no deep shadow, no utter darkness,
where evildoers can hide.
23God has no need to examine men further,
that they should come before him for judgment.
24Without enquiry he shatters the mighty
and sets up others in their place.
25Because he takes note of their deeds,
he overthrows them in the night and they are crushed.
26He punishes them for their wickedness
where everyone can see them,
27because they turned from following him
and had no regard for any of his ways.
28They caused the cry of the poor to come before him,
so that he heard the cry of the needy.
29But if he remains silent, who can condemn him?
If he hides his face, who can see him?
Yet he is over individual and nation alike,
30   to keep the godless from ruling,
from laying snares for the people.

---

[a] 14 Or *Spirit*

31 'Suppose someone says to God,
  "I am guilty but will offend no more.
32 Teach me what I cannot see;
  if I have done wrong, I will not do so again."
33 Should God then reward you on your terms,
  when you refuse to repent?
 You must decide, not I;
  so tell me what you know.

34 'Men of understanding declare,
  wise men who hear me say to me,
35 "Job speaks without knowledge;
  his words lack insight."
36 Oh, that Job might be tested to the utmost
  for answering like a wicked man!
37 To his sin he adds rebellion;
  scornfully he claps his hands among us
  and multiplies his words against God.'

35

Then Elihu said:

2 'Do you think this is just?
  You say, "I am in the right, not God."
3 Yet you ask him, "What profit is it to me,[a]
  and what do I gain by not sinning?"

4 'I would like to reply to you
  and to your friends with you.
5 Look up at the heavens and see;
  gaze at the clouds so high above you.
6 If you sin, how does that affect him?
  If your sins are many, what does that do to him?
7 If you are righteous, what do you give to him,
  or what does he receive from your hand?
8 Your wickedness only affects human beings like yourself,
  and your righteousness only members of the human race.

9 'People cry out under a load of oppression;
  they plead for relief from the arm of the powerful.
10 But no-one says, "Where is God my Maker,
  who gives songs in the night,
11 who teaches us more than he teaches[b] the beasts of the earth
  and makes us wiser than[c] the birds in the sky?"
12 He does not answer when people cry out
  because of the arrogance of the wicked.
13 Indeed, God does not listen to their empty plea;
  the Almighty pays no attention to it.
14 How much less, then, will he listen
  when you say that you do not see him,
 that your case is before him
  and you must wait for him,
15 and further, that his anger never punishes
  and he does not take the least notice of wickedness.[d]
16 So Job opens his mouth with empty talk;
  without knowledge he multiplies words.'

36

Elihu continued:

2 'Bear with me a little longer and I will show you
  that there is more to be said on God's behalf.
3 I get my knowledge from afar;
  I will ascribe justice to my Maker.
4 Be assured that my words are not false;
  one who has perfect knowledge is with you.

5 'God is mighty, but despises no-one;
  he is mighty, and firm in his purpose.
6 He does not keep the wicked alive
  but gives the afflicted their rights.
7 He does not take his eyes off the righteous;
  he enthrones them with kings
  and exalts them for ever.
8 But if people are bound in chains,
  held fast by cords of affliction,
9 he tells them what they have done—
  that they have sinned arrogantly.
10 He makes them listen to correction
  and commands them to repent of their evil.
11 If they obey and serve him,
  they will spend the rest of their days in prosperity
  and their years in contentment.

---

[a] 3 Or *you* [b] 10,11 Or *night, / 11who teaches us by* [c] 11 Or *us wise by* [d] 15 Symmachus, Theodotion and Vulgate; the meaning of the Hebrew for this word is uncertain.

¹²But if they do not listen,
　they will perish by the sword[a]
　and die without knowledge.

¹³'The godless in heart harbour resentment;
　even when he fetters them, they do not cry for help.
¹⁴They die in their youth,
　among male prostitutes of the shrines.
¹⁵But those who suffer he delivers in their suffering;
　he speaks to them in their affliction.

¹⁶'He is wooing you from the jaws of distress
　to a spacious place free from restriction,
　to the comfort of your table laden with choice food.
¹⁷But now you are laden with the judgment due to the wicked;
　judgment and justice have taken hold of you.
¹⁸Be careful that no-one entices you by riches;
　do not let a large bribe turn you aside.
¹⁹Would your wealth or even all your mighty efforts
　sustain you so you would not be in distress?
²⁰Do not long for the night,
　to drag people away from their homes.[b]
²¹Beware of turning to evil,
　which you seem to prefer to affliction.

²²'God is exalted in his power.
　Who is a teacher like him?
²³Who has prescribed his ways for him,
　or said to him, "You have done wrong"?
²⁴Remember to extol his work,
　which people have praised in song.
²⁵All human beings have seen it;
　mortals gaze on it from afar.
²⁶How great is God—beyond our understanding!
　The number of his years is past finding out.

²⁷'He draws up the drops of water,
　which distil as rain to the streams[c];
²⁸the clouds pour down their moisture
　and abundant showers fall on the human race.
²⁹Who can understand how he spreads out the clouds,
　how he thunders from his pavilion?
³⁰See how he scatters his lightning about him,
　bathing the depths of the sea.
³¹This is the way he governs[d] the nations
　and provides food in abundance.
³²He fills his hands with lightning
　and commands it to strike its mark.
³³His thunder announces the coming storm;
　even the cattle make known its approach.[e]

37

'At this my heart pounds
　and leaps from its place.
²Listen! Listen to the roar of his voice,
　to the rumbling that comes from his mouth.
³He unleashes his lightning beneath the whole heaven
　and sends it to the ends of the earth.
⁴After that comes the sound of his roar;
　he thunders with his majestic voice.
When his voice resounds,
　he holds nothing back.
⁵God's voice thunders in marvellous ways;
　he does great things beyond our understanding.
⁶He says to the snow, "Fall on the earth,"
　and to the rain shower, "Be a mighty downpour."
⁷So that everyone he has made may know his work,
　he stops all mortals from their labour.[f]
⁸The animals take cover;
　they remain in their dens.
⁹The tempest comes out from its chamber,
　the cold from the driving winds.
¹⁰The breath of God produces ice,
　and the broad waters become frozen.
¹¹He loads the clouds with moisture;
　he scatters his lightning through them.
¹²At his direction they swirl around
　over the face of the whole earth
　to do whatever he commands them.

---

[a] 12 Or *will cross the river*　[b] 20 The meaning of the Hebrew for verses 18-20 is uncertain.　[c] 27 Or *distil from the mist as rain*　[d] 31 Or *nourishes*　[e] 33 Or *announces his coming— / the One zealous against evil*　[f] 7 Or *work, / he fills all mortals with fear by his power*

¹³He brings the clouds to punish people,
    or to water his earth and show his love.
¹⁴'Listen to this, Job;
    stop and consider God's wonders.
¹⁵Do you know how God controls the clouds
    and makes his lightning flash?
¹⁶Do you know how the clouds hang poised,
    those wonders of him who is perfect in knowledge?
¹⁷You who swelter in your clothes
    when the land lies hushed under the south wind,
¹⁸can you join him in spreading out the skies,
    hard as a mirror of cast bronze?

¹⁹'Tell us what we should say to him;
    we cannot draw up our case because of our darkness.
²⁰Should he be told that I want to speak?
    Would anyone ask to be swallowed up?
²¹Now no-one can look at the sun,
    bright as it is in the skies
    after the wind has swept them clean.
²²Out of the north he comes in golden splendour;
    God comes in awesome majesty.
²³The Almighty is beyond our reach and exalted in power;
    in his justice and great righteousness, he does not oppress.
²⁴Therefore, people revere him,
    for does he not have regard for all the wise in heart?'ᵃ

The LORD speaks

38 Then the LORD spoke to Job out of the storm. He said:

²'Who is this that obscures my plans
    with words without knowledge?
³Prepare to defend yourself;
    I will question you,
    and you shall answer me.

⁴'Where were you when I laid the earth's foundation?
    Tell me, if you understand.

making Connections

Star
Job 38:7
The word 'star' can be used as a figure of speech for angels, so morning stars singing together is a poetic image of angels worshipping God.

⁵Who marked off its dimensions? Surely you know!
    Who stretched a measuring line across it?
⁶On what were its footings set,
    or who laid its cornerstone—
⁷while the morning stars sang together
    and all the angelsᵇ shouted for joy?

⁸'Who shut up the sea behind doors
    when it burst forth from the womb,
⁹when I made the clouds its garment
    and wrapped it in thick darkness,
¹⁰when I fixed limits for it
    and set its doors and bars in place,
¹¹when I said, "This far you may come and no farther;
    here is where your proud waves halt"?

¹²'Have you ever given orders to the morning,
    or shown the dawn its place,
¹³that it might take the earth by the edges
    and shake the wicked out of it?
¹⁴The earth takes shape like clay under a seal;
    its features stand out like those of a garment.
¹⁵The wicked are denied their light,
    and their upraised arm is broken.

¹⁶'Have you journeyed to the springs of the sea
    or walked in the recesses of the deep?
¹⁷Have the gates of death been shown to you?

ᵃ 24 Or *for he does not have regard for any who think they are wise.*   ᵇ 7 Hebrew *the sons of God*

Have you seen the gates of the deepest
  darkness?
¹⁸Have you comprehended the vast
  expanses of the earth?
  Tell me, if you know all this.

¹⁹'What is the way to the abode of light?
  And where does darkness reside?
²⁰Can you take them to their places?
  Do you know the paths to their
    dwellings?
²¹Surely you know, for you were already
    born!
  You have lived so many years!

²²'Have you entered the storehouses of the
    snow
  or seen the storehouses of the hail,
²³which I reserve for times of trouble,
  for days of war and battle?
²⁴What is the way to the place where the
    lightning is dispersed,
  or the place where the east winds are
    scattered over the earth?
²⁵Who cuts a channel for the torrents of
    rain,
  and a path for the thunderstorm,
²⁶to water a land where no-one lives,
  an uninhabited desert,
²⁷to satisfy a desolate wasteland
  and make it sprout with grass?
²⁸Does the rain have a father?
  Who fathers the drops of dew?
²⁹From whose womb comes the ice?
  Who gives birth to the frost from the
    heavens
³⁰when the waters become hard as stone,
  when the surface of the deep is frozen?

³¹'Can you bind the chains^a of the Pleiades?
  Can you loosen Orion's belt?
³²Can you bring forth the constellations in
    their seasons^b
  or lead out the Bear^c with its cubs?
³³Do you know the laws of the heavens?
  Can you set up ⌊God's^d⌋ dominion
    over the earth?

³⁴'Can you raise your voice to the clouds
  and cover yourself with a flood of
    water?

³⁵Do you send the lightning bolts on their
    way?
  Do they report to you, "Here we are"?
³⁶Who gives the ibis wisdom ⌊about the
    flooding of the Nile⌋,
  or gives the cockerel understanding ⌊of
    when to crow⌋?^{e}
³⁷Who has the wisdom to count the clouds?
  Who can tip over the water jars of the
    heavens
³⁸when the dust becomes hard
  and the clods of earth stick together?

³⁹'Do you hunt the prey for the lioness
  and satisfy the hunger of the lions
⁴⁰when they crouch in their dens
  or lie in wait in a thicket?
⁴¹Who provides food for the raven
  when its young cry out to God
  and wander about for lack of food?

39

'Do you know when the mountain
  goats give birth?
  Do you watch when the doe bears her
    fawn?
²Do you count the months till they bear?
  Do you know the time they give birth?
³They crouch down and bring forth their
    young;
  their labour pains are ended.
⁴Their young thrive and grow strong in the
    wilds;
  they leave and do not return.

⁵'Who let the wild donkey go free?
  Who untied its ropes?
⁶I gave it the wasteland as its home,
  the salt flats as its habitat.
⁷It laughs at the commotion in the town;
  it does not hear a driver's shout.
⁸It ranges the hills for its pasture
  and searches for any green thing.

⁹'Will the wild ox consent to serve you?
  Will it stay by your manger at night?
¹⁰Can you hold it to the furrow with a
    harness?
  Will it till the valleys behind you?
¹¹Will you rely on it for its great strength?
  Will you leave your heavy work to it?
¹²Can you trust it to haul in your corn
  and bring it to your threshing-floor?

---

^{a} 31 Septuagint; Hebrew *beauty* ^{b} 32 Or *the morning star in its season* ^{c} 32 Or *out Leo* ^{d} 33 Or *his*; or *their*
^{e} 36 The meaning of the Hebrew for this verse is uncertain.

¹³'The wings of the ostrich flap joyfully,
though they cannot compare
with the wings and feathers of the
stork.
¹⁴She lays her eggs on the ground
and lets them warm in the sand,
¹⁵unmindful that a foot may crush them,
that some wild animal may trample
them.
¹⁶She treats her young harshly, as if they
were not hers;
she cares not that her labour was in
vain,
¹⁷for God did not endow her with wisdom
or give her a share of good sense.
¹⁸Yet when she spreads her feathers to run,
she laughs at horse and rider.

¹⁹'Do you give the horse its strength
or clothe its neck with a flowing mane?
²⁰Do you make it leap like a locust,
striking terror with its proud snorting?
²¹It paws fiercely, rejoicing in its strength,
and charges into the fray.
²²It laughs at fear, afraid of nothing;
it does not shy away from the sword.
²³The quiver rattles against its side,
along with the flashing spear and
lance.
²⁴In frenzied excitement it eats up the
ground;
it cannot stand still when the trumpet
sounds.
²⁵At the blast of the trumpet it snorts,
"Aha!"
It catches the scent of battle from afar,
the shout of commanders and the
battle cry.

²⁶'Does the hawk take flight by your
wisdom
and spread its wings towards the
south?
²⁷Does the eagle soar at your command
and build its nest on high?
²⁸It dwells on a cliff and stays there at night;
a rocky crag is its stronghold.
²⁹From there it looks for food;
its eyes detect it from afar.
³⁰Its young ones feast on blood,
and where the slain are, there it is.'

40 The LORD said to Job:

²'Will the one who contends with the
Almighty correct him?
Let him who accuses God answer him!'

³Then Job answered the LORD:

⁴'I am unworthy—how can I reply to you?
I put my hand over my mouth.
⁵I spoke once, but I have no answer—
twice, but I will say no more.'

⁶Then the LORD spoke to Job out of the storm:

⁷'Prepare to defend yourself;
I will question you,
and you shall answer me.

⁸'Would you discredit my justice?
Would you condemn me to justify
yourself?
⁹Do you have an arm like God's,
and can your voice thunder like his?
¹⁰Then adorn yourself with glory and
splendour,
and clothe yourself in honour and
majesty.
¹¹Unleash the fury of your wrath,
look at all who are proud and bring
them,
¹²look at all who are proud and humble
them,
crush the wicked where they stand.
¹³Bury them all in the dust together;
shroud their faces in the grave.
¹⁴Then I myself will admit to you
that your own right hand can save you.

¹⁵'Look at the behemoth,ᵃ
which I made along with you
and which feeds on grass like an ox.
¹⁶What strength it has in its loins,
what power in the muscles of its belly!
¹⁷Its tail sways like a cedar;
the sinews of its thighs are close-knit.
¹⁸Its bones are tubes of bronze,
its limbs like rods of iron.
¹⁹It ranks first among the works of God,
yet its Maker can approach it with his
sword.
²⁰The hills bring it their produce,
and all the wild animals play nearby.

ᵃ 15 Possibly the hippopotamus or the elephant

²¹Under the lotus plant it lies,
   hidden among the reeds in the marsh.
²²The lotuses conceal it in their shadow;
   the poplars by the stream surround it.
²³A raging river does not alarm it;
   it is secure, though the Jordan should surge against its mouth.
²⁴Can anyone capture it by the eyes,
   or trap it and pierce its nose?

41

*"Can you pull in the leviathan[a] with a fishhook
   or tie down its tongue with a rope?
²Can you put a cord through its nose
   or pierce its jaw with a hook?
³Will it keep begging you for mercy?
   Will it speak to you with gentle words?
⁴Will it make an agreement with you
   for you to take it as your slave for life?
⁵Can you make a pet of it like a bird
   or put it on a leash for the young women in your house?
⁶Will traders barter for it?
   Will they divide it up among the merchants?
⁷Can you fill its hide with harpoons
   or its head with fishing spears?
⁸If you lay a hand on it,
   you will remember the struggle and never do it again!
*⁹Any hope of subduing it is false;
   the mere sight of it is overpowering.
¹⁰No-one is fierce enough to rouse it.
   Who then is able to stand against me?
¹¹Who has a claim against me that I must pay?
   Everything under heaven belongs to me.

¹²'I will not fail to speak of Leviathan's limbs,
   its strength and its graceful form.
¹³Who can strip off its outer coat?
   Who can penetrate its double coat of armour?[b]
¹⁴Who dares open the doors of its mouth,
   ringed about with its fearsome teeth?
¹⁵Its back has[c] rows of shields
   tightly sealed together;
¹⁶each is so close to the next
   that no air can pass between.
¹⁷They are joined fast to one another;
   they cling together and cannot be parted.
¹⁸Its snorting throws out flashes of light;
   its eyes are like the rays of dawn.
¹⁹Flames stream from its mouth;
   sparks of fire shoot out.
²⁰Smoke pours from its nostrils
   as from a boiling pot over burning reeds.
²¹Its breath sets coals ablaze,
   and flames dart from its mouth.
²²Strength resides in its neck;
   dismay goes before it.
²³The folds of its flesh are tightly joined;
   they are firm and immovable.
²⁴Its chest is hard as rock,
   hard as a lower millstone.
²⁵When it rises up, the mighty are terrified;
   they retreat before its thrashing.
²⁶The sword that reaches it has no effect,
   nor does the spear or the dart or the javelin.
²⁷Iron it treats like straw
   and bronze like rotten wood.
²⁸Arrows do not make it flee;
   slingstones are like chaff to it.
²⁹A club seems to it but a piece of straw;
   it laughs at the rattling of the lance.
³⁰Its undersides are jagged potsherds,
   leaving a trail in the mud like a threshing-sledge.
³¹It makes the depths churn like a boiling cauldron

IN OTHER WORDS

Leviathan
Job 41:1

The leviathan is a mythical sea monster whose name means 'twisted one'. Sometimes he seems to represent Satan himself.

---

[a] 1 Possibly the crocodile   [b] 13 Septuagint; Hebrew *double bridle*   [c] 15 Or *Its pride is its*

* 41:1-8 is numbered 40:25-32 in Hebrew texts.   * 41:9-34 is numbered 41:1-26 in Hebrew texts.

and stirs up the sea like a pot of ointment.
³²It leaves a glistening wake behind it;
  one would think the deep had white hair.
³³Nothing on earth is its equal—
  a creature without fear.
³⁴It looks down on all that are haughty;
  it is king over all that are proud.'

Job

42

Then Job replied to the LORD:

²'I know that you can do all things;
  no purpose of yours can be thwarted.
³You asked, "Who is this that obscures my plans without knowledge?"
Surely I spoke of things I did not understand,
  things too wonderful for me to know.

⁴'You said, "Listen now, and I will speak;
  I will question you,
  and you shall answer me."
⁵My ears had heard of you
  but now my eyes have seen you.
⁶Therefore I despise myself
  and repent in dust and ashes.'

Epilogue

⁷After the LORD had said these things to Job, he said to Eliphaz the Temanite, 'I am angry with you and your two friends, because you have not spoken of me what is right, as my servant Job has. ⁸So now take seven bulls and seven rams and go to my servant Job and sacrifice a burnt offering for yourselves. My servant Job will pray for you, and I will accept his prayer and not deal with you according to your folly. You have not spoken of me what is right, as my servant Job has.' ⁹So Eliphaz the Temanite, Bildad the Shuhite and Zophar the Naamathite did what the LORD told them; and the LORD accepted Job's prayer.

¹⁰After Job had prayed for his friends, the LORD restored his fortunes and gave him twice as much as he had before. ¹¹All his brothers and sisters and everyone who had known him before came and ate with him in his house. They comforted and consoled him over all the trouble the LORD had brought on him, and each one gave him a piece of silver*ᵃ* and a gold ring.

¹²The LORD blessed the latter part of Job's life more than the former part. He had fourteen thousand sheep, six thousand camels, a thousand yoke of oxen and a thousand donkeys. ¹³And he also had seven sons and three daughters. ¹⁴The first daughter he named Jemimah, the second Keziah and the third Keren-Happuch. ¹⁵Nowhere in all the land were there found women as beautiful as Job's daughters, and their father granted them an inheritance along with their brothers.

¹⁶After this, Job lived a hundred and forty years; he saw his children and their children to the fourth generation. ¹⁷And so he died, old and full of years.

ᵃ 11 Hebrew *him a kesitah*; a kesitah was a unit of money of unknown weight and value.

Psalms

INTRODUCTION

PSALMS

Author: David wrote many of the psalms. Other authors include Moses, Solomon, Asaph and the sons of Korah.

When: Over a long period of time, from Moses to the exile.

Did you know? The original Hebrew manuscripts divide the book of Psalms into five sections, each of which closes with a brief prayer of praise.

Main theme: The psalms are a collection of prayers, poems and hymns to be used in worship to God. Parts of the book were used as a hymnbook in the temple in ancient Israel. A wide range of human emotions are expressed in the psalms from joy to fear, from despair to hope, showing that we can be honest with God about how we feel. Above all, the psalms show us more of who God is and the ways in which we can respond to him.

BOOK I

Psalms 1–41

Psalm 1

¹Blessed are those
  who do not walk in step with the wicked
or stand in the way that sinners take
  or sit in the company of mockers,
²but who delight in the law of the LORD
  and meditate on his law day and night.
³They are like a tree planted by streams of water,
  which yields its fruit in season
and whose leaf does not wither—
  whatever they do prospers.

⁴Not so the wicked!
  They are like chaff
  that the wind blows away.
⁵Therefore the wicked will not stand in the judgment,
  nor sinners in the assembly of the righteous.

IN OTHER WORDS

Heaven
Psalms 2:4

The word 'heaven' is first used in the Bible to describe everything above the earth and what we call the sky (Genesis 1:1,8), but it also describes the place where God lives, his home. The main biblical view of heaven is that it is the spiritual dimension of the universe.

6For the LORD watches over the way of the righteous,
 but the way of the wicked will be destroyed.

Psalm 2

1Why do the nations conspire[a]
 and the peoples plot in vain?
2The kings of the earth rise up
 and the rulers band together
against the LORD and against his anointed, saying,
3'Let us break their chains
 and throw off their shackles.'

4The One enthroned in heaven laughs;
 the Lord scoffs at them.
5He rebukes them in his anger
 and terrifies them in his wrath, saying,
6'I have installed my king
 on Zion, my holy mountain.'

7I will proclaim the LORD's decree:

he said to me, 'You are my son;
 today I have become your father.
8Ask me,
 and I will make the nations your inheritance,
 the ends of the earth your possession.
9You will break them with a rod of iron[b]
 you will dash them to pieces like pottery.'

10Therefore, you kings, be wise;
 be warned, you rulers of the earth.
11Serve the LORD with fear
 and celebrate his rule with trembling.
12Kiss his son, or he will be angry
 and you and your ways will be destroyed,
for his wrath can flare up in a moment.
 Blessed are all who take refuge in him.

Psalm 3

A psalm of David. When he fled from his son Absalom.

*1LORD, how many are my foes!
 How many rise up against me!
2Many are saying of me,
 'God will not deliver him.'[c]

3But you, LORD, are a shield around me,
 my glory, the one who lifts my head high.
4I call out to the LORD,
 and he answers me from his holy mountain.

5I lie down and sleep;
 I wake again, because the LORD sustains me.
6I will not fear though tens of thousands
 assail me on every side.

7Arise, LORD!
 Deliver me, my God!
Strike all my enemies on the jaw;
 break the teeth of the wicked.

8From the LORD comes deliverance.
 May your blessing be on your people.

IN OTHER WORDS

Deliverance
Psalms 3:8

When God's people are suffering from oppression, they cry out to him for rescue or deliverance, longing to be set free. This term is also used to describe someone's release from demonic forces.

---

[a] 1 Hebrew; Septuagint *rage* [b] 9 Or *will rule them with an iron sceptre* (see Septuagint and Syriac) [c] 2 The Hebrew has *Selah* (a word of uncertain meaning) here and at the end of verses 4 and 8.

* 3:1-8 is numbered 3:2-9 in Hebrew texts.

Psalm 4

For the director of music. With stringed instruments. A psalm of David.

*¹Answer me when I call to you,
  my righteous God.
Give me relief from my distress;
  have mercy on me and hear my prayer.

²How long will you men turn my glory into shame?
  How long will you love delusions and seek false gods?[a,b]
³Know that the LORD has set apart his faithful servant for himself;
  the LORD hears when I call to him.

⁴Tremble and[c] do not sin;
  when you are on your beds,
  search your hearts and be silent.
⁵Offer the sacrifices of the righteous
  and trust in the LORD.

⁶Many, LORD, are asking, 'Who will bring us prosperity?'
  Let the light of your face shine on us.
⁷Fill my heart with joy
  when their grain and new wine abound.

⁸In peace I will lie down and sleep,
  for you alone, LORD,
  make me dwell in safety.

Psalm 5

For the director of music. For pipes. A psalm of David.

*¹Listen to my words, LORD,
  consider my lament.
²Hear my cry for help,
  my King and my God,
  for to you I pray.

³In the morning, LORD, you hear my voice;
  in the morning I lay my requests before you
  and wait expectantly.
⁴For you are not a God who is pleased with wickedness;
  with you, evil people are not welcome.
⁵The arrogant cannot stand
  in your presence.
You hate all who do wrong;
⁶ you destroy those who tell lies.
The bloodthirsty and deceitful
  you, LORD, detest.
⁷But I, by your great love,
  can come into your house;
in reverence I bow down
  towards your holy temple.

⁸Lead me, LORD, in your righteousness
  because of my enemies—
  make your way straight before me.
⁹Not a word from their mouth can be trusted;
  their heart is filled with malice.
Their throat is an open grave;
  with their tongues they tell lies.
¹⁰Declare them guilty, O God!
  Let their intrigues be their downfall.
Banish them for their many sins,
  for they have rebelled against you.
¹¹But let all who take refuge in you be glad;
  let them ever sing for joy.
Spread your protection over them,
  that those who love your name may rejoice in you.

¹²Surely, LORD, you bless the righteous;
  you surround them with your favour as with a shield.

Psalm 6

For the director of music. With stringed instruments. According to sheminith.[d]
A psalm of David.

*¹LORD, do not rebuke me in your anger
  or discipline me in your wrath.
²Have mercy on me, LORD, for I am faint;
  heal me, LORD, for my bones are in agony.
³My soul is in deep anguish.
  How long, LORD, how long?

⁴Turn, LORD, and deliver me;
  save me because of your unfailing love.
⁵Among the dead no-one proclaims your name.
  Who praises you from his grave?

---

a 2 Or *seek lies*   *b* 2 The Hebrew has *Selah* (a word of uncertain meaning) here and at the end of verse 4.   *c* 4 Or *In your anger* (see Septuagint)   *d* Title: Probably a musical term

* 4:1-8 is numbered 4:2-9 in Hebrew texts.   * 5:1-12 is numbered 5:2-13 in Hebrew texts.   * 6:1-10 is numbered 6:2-11 in Hebrew texts.

⁶I am worn out from my groaning.
  All night long I flood my bed with weeping
  and drench my couch with tears.
⁷My eyes grow weak with sorrow;
  they fail because of all my foes.

⁸Away from me, all you who do evil,
  for the LORD has heard my weeping.
⁹The LORD has heard my cry for mercy;
  the LORD accepts my prayer.
¹⁰All my enemies will be overwhelmed with shame and anguish;
  they will turn back and suddenly be put to shame.

Psalm 7

A shiggaion^a of David, which he sang to the LORD concerning Cush, a Benjaminite.

*¹LORD my God, I take refuge in you;
  save and deliver me from all who pursue me,
²or they will tear me apart like a lion
  and rip me to pieces with no-one to rescue me.

³LORD my God, if I have done this
  and there is guilt on my hands—
⁴if I have repaid my ally with evil
  or without cause have robbed my foe—
⁵then let my enemy pursue and overtake me;
  let him trample my life to the ground
  and make me sleep in the dust.^b

⁶Arise, LORD, in your anger;
  rise up against the rage of my enemies.
  Awake, my God; decree justice.
⁷Let the assembled peoples gather round you,
  while you sit enthroned over them on high.
⁸ Let the LORD judge the peoples.
  Vindicate me, LORD, according to my righteousness,
    according to my integrity, O Most High.
⁹Bring to an end the violence of the wicked
  and make the righteous secure—
you, the righteous God
  who probes minds and hearts.

> ### IN OTHER WORDS
>
> **Judge**
> Psalms 7:8
> A judge is someone responsible for administering justice and government. God is the supreme judge because he is the creator of the world and is holy and righteous. Jesus is also described as a judge in the New Testament (John 5:27).

¹⁰My shield^c is God Most High,
  who saves the upright in heart.
¹¹God is a righteous judge,
  a God who displays his wrath every day.
¹²If he does not relent,
  he^d will sharpen his sword;
  he will bend and string his bow.
¹³He has prepared his deadly weapons;
  he makes ready his flaming arrows.

¹⁴Those who are pregnant with evil
  conceive trouble and give birth to disillusionment.
¹⁵Those who dig a hole and scoop it out
  fall into the pit they have made.
¹⁶The trouble they cause recoils on them;
  their violence comes down on their own heads.

¹⁷I will give thanks to the LORD because of his righteousness;
  I will sing the praises of the name of the LORD Most High.

Psalm 8

For the director of music. According to gittith.^e A psalm of David.

*¹LORD, our Lord,
  how majestic is your name in all the earth!

You have set your glory
  above the heavens.

---

^a Title: Probably a literary or musical term   ^b 5 The Hebrew has *Selah* (a word of uncertain meaning) here.   ^c 10 Or *sovereign*   ^d 12 Or *If anyone does not repent, I God*   ^e Title: Probably a musical term

* 7:1-17 is numbered 7:2-18 in Hebrew texts.   * 8:1-9 is numbered 8:2-10 in Hebrew texts.

²Through the praise of children and infants
you have established a stronghold against your enemies,
to silence the foe and the avenger.
³When I consider your heavens,
the work of your fingers,
the moon and the stars,
which you have set in place,
⁴what are mere mortals that you are mindful of them,
human beings that you care for them?[a]

⁵You have made them[b] a little lower than the heavenly beings[c]
and crowned them[d] with glory and honour.
⁶You made them rulers over the works of your hands;
you put everything under their[e] feet:
⁷all flocks and herds,
and the animals of the wild,
⁸the birds in the sky,
and the fish in the sea,
all that swim the paths of the seas.

⁹LORD, our Lord,
how majestic is your name in all the earth!

Psalm 9[f]

For the director of music. To the tune of 'The Death of the Son'. A psalm of David.

*¹I will praise you, LORD, with all my heart;
I will tell of all your wonderful deeds.
²I will be glad and rejoice in you;
I will sing the praises of your name, O Most High.

³My enemies turn back;
they stumble and perish before you.
⁴For you have upheld my right and my cause;
sitting enthroned as the righteous judge.
⁵You have rebuked the nations and destroyed the wicked;
you have blotted out their name for ever and ever.
⁶Endless ruin has overtaken my enemies,
you have uprooted their cities;
even the memory of them has perished.

⁷The LORD reigns for ever;
he has established his throne for judgment.
⁸He rules the world in righteousness
and judges the peoples with equity.
⁹The LORD is a refuge for the oppressed,
a stronghold in times of trouble.
¹⁰Those who know your name trust in you,
for you, LORD, have never forsaken those who seek you.

¹¹Sing the praises of the LORD, enthroned in Zion;
proclaim among the nations what he has done.
¹²For he who avenges blood remembers;
he does not ignore the cries of the afflicted.

¹³LORD, see how my enemies persecute me!
Have mercy and lift me up from the gates of death,

People and Places

Zion
Psalms 9:11

The meaning of the name 'Zion' has changed through the Bible. Zion was a city that David captured in battle and which he called the City of David. When Solomon built the temple in Jerusalem, 'Zion' also came to mean the temple and its surrounding area. Soon it was being used as a name for the city of Jerusalem, the land of Judah and the people of Israel as a whole.

---

[a] 4 Or *what is a human being that you are mindful of him, I a son of man that you care for him?* [b] 5 Or *him* [c] 5 Or *than God* [d] 5 Or *him* [e] 6 Or *made him ruler...;/...his* [f] Psalms 9 and 10 may originally have been a single acrostic poem in which alternating lines began with the successive letters of the Hebrew alphabet. In the Septuagint they constitute one psalm.

* 9:1-20 is numbered 9:2-21 in Hebrew texts.

¹⁴that I may declare your praises
  in the gates of Daughter Zion,
  and there rejoice in your salvation.

¹⁵The nations have fallen into the pit they have dug;
  their feet are caught in the net they have hidden.
¹⁶The LORD is known by his acts of justice;
  the wicked are ensnared by the work of their hands.[a]
¹⁷The wicked go down to the realm of the dead,
  all the nations that forget God.
¹⁸But God will never forget the needy;
  the hope of the afflicted will never perish.

¹⁹Arise, LORD, do not let mortals triumph;
  let the nations be judged in your presence.
²⁰Strike them with terror, LORD;
  let the nations know they are only mortals.

Psalm 10[b]

¹Why, LORD, do you stand far off?
  Why do you hide yourself in times of trouble?

²In their arrogance the wicked hunt down the weak,
  catching them in the schemes they devise.
³They boast about the cravings of their hearts;
  they bless the greedy and revile the LORD.
⁴In their pride the wicked do not seek him;
  in all their thoughts there is no room for God.
⁵Their ways are always prosperous;
  your laws are rejected by[c] them;
  they sneer at all their enemies.
⁶They say to themselves, 'Nothing will ever shake us.'
  They swear, 'No-one will ever do us harm.'

⁷Their mouths are full of lies and threats;
  trouble and evil are under their tongues.
⁸They lie in wait near the villages;
  from ambush they murder the innocent.
  Their eyes watch in secret for their victims;
9 like a lion in cover they lie in wait.
  They lie in wait to catch the helpless;
  they catch the helpless and drag them off in their nets.
¹⁰⌊The innocent⌋ are crushed, they collapse;
  they fall victim to superior strength.
¹¹The wicked say to themselves, 'God will never notice;
  he covers his face and never sees.'

¹²Arise, LORD! Lift up your hand, O God.
  Do not forget the helpless.
¹³Why do the wicked revile God?
  Why do they say to themselves,
  'He won't call us to account'?
¹⁴But you, God, see the trouble of the afflicted;
  you consider their grief and take it in hand.
  The victims commit themselves to you;
  you are the helper of the fatherless.
¹⁵Break the arms of the wicked and the evildoers;
  call them to account for their wickedness
  that would not otherwise be found out.

¹⁶The LORD is King for ever and ever;
  the nations will perish from his land.
¹⁷You, LORD, hear the desire of the afflicted;
  you encourage them, and you listen to their cry,
¹⁸defending the fatherless and the oppressed,
  so that mere earthly mortals
  will never again strike terror.

Psalm 11

For the director of music. Of David.

¹In the LORD I take refuge.
  How then can you say to me:
  'Flee like a bird to your mountain.

---

[a] 16 The Hebrew has *Higgaion* and *Selah* (words of uncertain meaning) here; *Selah* occurs also at the end of verse 20.
[b] Psalms 9 and 10 may originally have been a single acrostic poem in which alternating lines began with the successive letters of the Hebrew alphabet. In the Septuagint they constitute one psalm.   [c] 5 See Septuagint; Hebrew *I / they are haughty, and your laws are far from*

2For look, the wicked bend their bows;
  they set their arrows against the strings
 to shoot from the shadows
  at the upright in heart.
3When the foundations are being
    destroyed,
  what can the righteous do?'

4The LORD is in his holy temple;
  the LORD is on his heavenly throne.
 He observes everyone on earth;
  his eyes examine them.
5The LORD examines the righteous,
  but the wicked, those who love
    violence,
  he hates with a passion.
6On the wicked he will rain
  fiery coals and burning sulphur;
  a scorching wind will be their lot.

7For the LORD is righteous,
  he loves justice;
  the upright will see his face.

Psalm 12

For the director of music. According to sheminith.[a] A psalm of David.

*1Help, LORD, for no-one is faithful any
    more;
  those who are loyal have vanished from
    the human race.
2Everyone lies to their neighbour;
  they flatter with their lips
  but harbour deception in their hearts.

3May the LORD silence all flattering lips
  and every boastful tongue—
4those who say,
 'By our tongues we will prevail;
  our own lips will defend us—who is
    lord over us?'

5'Because the poor are plundered and the
    needy groan,
  I will now arise,' says the LORD.
 'I will protect them from those who
    malign them.'
6And the words of the LORD are flawless,
  like silver purified in a crucible,
  like gold[b] refined seven times.

7You, LORD, will keep the needy safe
  and will protect us for ever from the
    wicked,
8who freely strut about
  while depravity is honoured by the
    human race.

Psalm 13

For the director of music. A psalm of David.

*1How long, LORD? Will you forget me for
    ever?
  How long will you hide your face from
    me?
2How long must I wrestle with my
    thoughts
  and day after day have sorrow in my
    heart?
  How long will my enemy triumph over
    me?

3Look on me and answer, LORD my God.
  Give light to my eyes, or I will sleep in
    death,
4and my enemy will say, 'I have overcome
    him,'
  and my foes will rejoice when I fall.

5But I trust in your unfailing love;
  my heart rejoices in your salvation.
6I will sing the LORD's praise,
  for he has been good to me.

Psalm 14

For the director of music. Of David.

1Fools[c] say in their hearts,
  'There is no God.'
 They are corrupt, their deeds are vile;
  there is no-one who does good.

2The LORD looks down from heaven
  on the human race
 to see if there are any who understand,
  any who seek God.
3All have turned away, all have become
    corrupt;
  there is no-one who does good,
  not even one.

4Do all these evildoers know nothing?

---

a Title: Probably a musical term *b* 6 Probable reading of the original Hebrew text; Masoretic Text *earth* *c* 1 The Hebrew words rendered *fool* in Psalms denote one who is morally deficient.

* 12:1-8 is numbered 12:2-9 in Hebrew texts.   * 13:1-6 is numbered 13:2-6 in Hebrew texts.

They devour my people as though eating bread;
    they never call on the LORD.
⁵But there they are, overwhelmed with dread,
    for God is present in the company of the righteous.
⁶You evildoers frustrate the plans of the poor,
    but the LORD is their refuge.

⁷Oh, that salvation for Israel would come out of Zion!
    When the LORD restores his people,
    let Jacob rejoice and Israel be glad!

Psalm 15

A psalm of David.

¹LORD, who may dwell in your sanctuary?
    Who may live on your holy mountain?

²Those whose way of life is blameless,
    who do what is righteous,
    who speak the truth from their hearts;
³who have no slander on their tongues,
    who do their neighbours no wrong,
    who cast no slur on others;
⁴who despise those whose ways are vile
    but honour whoever fears the LORD;
    who keep their oaths even when it hurts;
⁵who lend money to the poor without interest
    and do not accept bribes against the innocent.

Whoever does these things
    will never be shaken.

Psalm 16

A miktam^a of David.

¹Keep me safe, my God,
    for in you I take refuge.

²I say to the LORD, 'You are my Lord;
    apart from you I have no good thing.'
³I say of the godly who are in the land,
    'They are the noble people
    in whom is all my delight.'
⁴Those who run after other gods
    will suffer more and more.

making Connections

Shivviti
Psalms 16:8
Shivviti is the first Hebrew word of Psalm 16:8 and means 'I have set'. Plaques containing this whole verse were often put up in synagogues in front of people praying.

I will not pour out their libations of blood
    or take up their names on my lips.

⁵LORD, you have assigned me my portion and my cup;
    you have made my lot secure.
⁶The boundary lines have fallen for me in pleasant places;
    surely I have a delightful inheritance.

⁷I will praise the LORD, who counsels me;
    even at night my heart instructs me.
⁸I keep my eyes always on the LORD.
    With him at my right hand, I shall not be shaken.

⁹Therefore my heart is glad and my tongue rejoices;
    my body also will rest secure,
¹⁰because you will not abandon me to the realm of the dead,
    nor will you let your faithful^b one see decay.
¹¹You make known to me the path of life;
    you will fill me with joy in your presence,
    with eternal pleasures at your right hand.

Psalm 17

A prayer of David.

¹Hear me, LORD, my plea is just;
    listen to my cry.
Hear my prayer—
    it does not rise from deceitful lips.

---

^a Title: Probably a literary or musical term   ^b 10 Or *holy*

2Let my vindication come from you;
　may your eyes see what is right.

3Though you probe my heart,
　though you examine me at night and
　　test me,
　you will find that I have planned no evil;
　my mouth has not transgressed.
4Though people tried to bribe me,
　I have kept myself from the ways of the
　　violent
　through what your lips have
　　commanded.
5My steps have held to your paths;
　my feet have not stumbled.

6I call on you, my God, for you will answer
　　me;
　turn your ear to me and hear my
　　prayer.
7Show me the wonders of your great love,
　you who save by your right hand
　those who take refuge in you from their
　　foes.

8Keep me as the apple of your eye;
　hide me in the shadow of your wings
9from the wicked who are out to destroy
　　me,
　from my mortal enemies who
　　surround me.

10They close up their callous hearts,
　and their mouths speak with
　　arrogance.
11They have tracked me down, they now
　　surround me,
　with eyes alert, to throw me to the
　　ground.
12They are like a lion hungry for prey,
　like a fierce lion crouching in cover.

13Rise up, LORD, confront them, bring them
　　down;
　with your sword rescue me from the
　　wicked.
14By your hand save me from such people,
　　LORD,
　from those of this world whose reward
　　is in this life.
　May what you have stored up for the
　　wicked fill their bellies;
　may their children gorge themselves on
　　it,
　may there be leftovers for their little
　　ones.

15As for me, I shall be vindicated and shall
　　see your face;
　when I awake, I shall be satisfied with
　　seeing your likeness.

Psalm 18

For the director of music. Of David the servant of the LORD. He sang to the LORD the words of this song when the LORD delivered him from the hand of all his enemies and from the hand of Saul. He said:

*1I love you, LORD, my strength.

2The LORD is my rock, my fortress and my
　　deliverer;
　my God is my rock, in whom I take
　　refuge,
　my shield^a and the horn^b of my
　　salvation, my stronghold.

3I called to the LORD, who is worthy of
　　praise,
　and I have been saved from my
　　enemies.
4The cords of death entangled me;
　the torrents of destruction
　　overwhelmed me.
5The cords of the grave coiled around me;
　the snares of death confronted me.

6In my distress I called to the LORD;
　I cried to my God for help.
　From his temple he heard my voice;
　my cry came before him, into his ears.
7The earth trembled and quaked,
　and the foundations of the mountains
　　shook;
　they trembled because he was angry.
8Smoke rose from his nostrils;
　consuming fire came from his mouth,
　burning coals blazed out of it.
9He parted the heavens and came down;
　dark clouds were under his feet.
10He mounted the cherubim and flew;
　he soared on the wings of the wind.
11He made darkness his covering, his
　　canopy around him—
　the dark rain clouds of the sky.

---

^{a} 2 Or *sovereign*　^{b} 2 *Horn* here symbolises strength.
* 18:1-50 is numbered 18:2-51 in Hebrew texts.

¹²Out of the brightness of his presence
    clouds advanced,
  with hailstones and bolts of lightning.
¹³The LORD thundered from heaven;
    the voice of the Most High resounded.[a]
¹⁴He shot his arrows and scattered the
        enemy,
    with great bolts of lightning he routed
        them.
¹⁵The valleys of the sea were exposed
    and the foundations of the earth laid
        bare
  at your rebuke, LORD,
    at the blast of breath from your
        nostrils.

¹⁶He reached down from on high and took
        hold of me;
    he drew me out of deep waters.
¹⁷He rescued me from my powerful enemy,
    from my foes, who were too strong for
        me.
¹⁸They confronted me in the day of my
        disaster,
    but the LORD was my support.
¹⁹He brought me out into a spacious place;
    he rescued me because he delighted in
        me.

²⁰The LORD has dealt with me according to
        my righteousness;
    according to the cleanness of my hands
        he has rewarded me.
²¹For I have kept the ways of the LORD;
    I am not guilty of turning from my
        God.
²²All his laws are before me;
    I have not turned away from his
        decrees.
²³I have been blameless before him
    and have kept myself from sin.
²⁴The LORD has rewarded me according to
        my righteousness,
    according to the cleanness of my hands
        in his sight.

²⁵To the faithful you show yourself faithful,
    to the blameless you show yourself
        blameless,
²⁶to the pure you show yourself pure,
    but to the devious you show yourself
        shrewd.
²⁷You save the humble
    but bring low those whose eyes are
        haughty.
²⁸You, LORD, keep my lamp burning;
    my God turns my darkness into light.
²⁹With your help I can advance against a
        troop;[b]
    with my God I can scale a wall.

³⁰As for God, his way is perfect:
    the LORD's word is flawless;
    he shields all who take refuge in him.
³¹For who is God besides the LORD?
    And who is the Rock except our God?
³²It is God who arms me with strength
    and keeps my way secure.
³³He makes my feet like the feet of a deer;
    he causes me to stand on the heights.
³⁴He trains my hands for battle;
    my arms can bend a bow of bronze.
³⁵You make your saving help my shield,
    and your right hand sustains me;
    your help has made me great.
³⁶You provide a broad path for my feet,
    so that my ankles do not give way.

³⁷I pursued my enemies and overtook
        them;
    I did not turn back till they were
        destroyed.
³⁸I crushed them so that they could not rise;
    they fell beneath my feet.
³⁹You armed me with strength for battle;
    you humbled my adversaries before
        me.
⁴⁰You made my enemies turn their backs in
        flight,
    and I destroyed my foes.
⁴¹They cried for help, but there was no-one
        to save them—
    to the LORD, but he did not answer.
⁴²I beat them as fine as windblown dust;
    I trampled them[c] like mud in the
        streets.

⁴³You have delivered me from the attacks of
        the people;
    you have made me the head of nations.
    People I did not know now serve me,

---

[a] 13 Some Hebrew manuscripts and Septuagint (see also 2 Samuel 22:14); most Hebrew manuscripts *resounded, / amid hailstones and bolts of lightning*   [b] 29 Or *can run through a barricade*   [c] 42 Many Hebrew manuscripts, Septuagint, Syriac and Targum (see also 2 Samuel 22:43); Masoretic Text *I poured them out*

IN OTHER WORDS

Saviour
Psalms 18:46

A 'saviour' is someone who rescues others from evil, danger or destruction. God is described as a saviour, and at times in Israel's history he sent human deliverers to rescue his people. In the New Testament the title 'Saviour' is given to both God the Father and Jesus his son. Jesus is called 'the saviour of all people' in 1 Timothy 4:10.

44 foreigners cower before me;
   as soon as they hear of me, they obey me.
45 They all lose heart;
   they come trembling from their strongholds.

46 The LORD lives! Praise be to my Rock!
   Exalted be God my Saviour!
47 He is the God who avenges me,
   who subdues nations under me,
48 who saves me from my enemies.
   You exalted me above my foes;
   from violent people you rescued me.
49 Therefore I will praise you, LORD, among the nations;
   I will sing the praises of your name.

50 He gives his king great victories;
   he shows unfailing love to his anointed,
   to David and to his descendants for ever.

Psalm 19

For the director of music. A psalm of David.

*1 The heavens declare the glory of God;
   the skies proclaim the work of his hands.
2 Day after day they pour forth speech;
   night after night they display knowledge.
3 They have no speech, they use no words;
   no sound is heard from them.
4 Yet their voice[a] goes out into all the earth,
   their words to the ends of the world.
In the heavens he has pitched a tent for the sun,
5   which is like a bridegroom coming out of his chamber,
    like a champion rejoicing to run his course.
6 It rises at one end of the heavens
   and makes its circuit to the other;
   nothing is deprived of its warmth.

7 The law of the LORD is perfect,
   refreshing the soul.
  The statutes of the LORD are trustworthy,
   making wise the simple.
8 The precepts of the LORD are right,
   giving joy to the heart.
  The commands of the LORD are radiant,
   giving light to the eyes.
9 The fear of the LORD is pure,
   enduring for ever.
  The ordinances of the LORD are sure,
   and all of them are righteous.

10 They are more precious than gold,
    than much pure gold;
   they are sweeter than honey,
    than honey from the honeycomb.
11 By them your servant is warned;
   in keeping them there is great reward.
12 But who can discern their own errors?
   Forgive my hidden faults.
13 Keep your servant also from wilful sins;
   may they not rule over me.
   Then I will be blameless,
   innocent of great transgression.

14 May these words of my mouth and this meditation of my heart
   be pleasing in your sight,
   LORD, my Rock and my Redeemer.

Psalm 20

For the director of music. A psalm of David.

*1 May the LORD answer you when you are in distress;
   may the name of the God of Jacob protect you.

---

[a] 4 Septuagint, Jerome and Syriac; Hebrew *line*

* 19:1-14 is numbered 19:2-15 in Hebrew texts.   * 20:1-9 is numbered 20:2-10 in Hebrew texts.

²May he send you help from the sanctuary
and grant you support from Zion.
³May he remember all your sacrifices
and accept your burnt offerings.ᵃ
⁴May he give you the desire of your heart
and make all your plans succeed.
⁵May we shout for joy over your victory
and lift up our banners in the name of
our God.

May the LORD grant all your requests.

⁶Now this I know:
The LORD gives victory to his anointed.
He answers him from his heavenly
sanctuary
with the victorious power of his right
hand.
⁷Some trust in chariots and some in horses,
but we trust in the name of the LORD
our God.
⁸They are brought to their knees and fall,
but we rise up and stand firm.
⁹LORD, give victory to the king!
Answer us when we call!

Psalm 21

For the director of music. A psalm of David.

*¹The king rejoices in your strength, LORD.
How great is his joy in the victories you
give!
²You have granted him his heart's desire
and have not withheld the request of
his lips.ᵇ
³You came to greet him with rich blessings
and placed a crown of pure gold on his
head.
⁴He asked you for life, and you gave it to
him—
length of days, for ever and ever.
⁵Through the victories you gave, his glory
is great;
you have bestowed on him splendour
and majesty.
⁶Surely you have granted him unending
blessings
and made him glad with the joy of your
presence.
⁷For the king trusts in the LORD;

through the unfailing love of the Most
High
he will not be shaken.

⁸Your hand will lay hold on all your
enemies;
your right hand will seize your foes.
⁹When you appear for battle,
you will burn them up as in a blazing
furnace.
The LORD will swallow them up in his
wrath,
and his fire will consume them.
¹⁰You will destroy their descendants from
the earth,
their posterity from the human race.
¹¹Though they plot evil against you
and devise wicked schemes, they
cannot succeed.
¹²You will make them turn their backs
when you aim at them with drawn
bow.

¹³Be exalted in your strength, LORD;
we will sing and praise your might.

Psalm 22

*For the director of music. To the tune of
'The Doe of the Morning'. A psalm of
David.*

*¹My God, my God, why have you forsaken
me?
Why are you so far from saving me,
so far from the words of my groaning?
²My God, I cry out by day, but you do not
answer,
by night, but I find no rest.ᶜ

³Yet you are enthroned as the Holy One;
you are the praiseᵈ of Israel.
⁴In you our ancestors put their trust;
they trusted and you delivered them.
⁵They cried to you and were saved;
in you they trusted and were not
disappointed.

⁶But I am a worm, not a human being;
I am scorned by everyone, despised by
the people.
⁷All who see me mock me;
they hurl insults, shaking their heads.

ᵃ 3 The Hebrew has *Selah* (a word of uncertain meaning) here.   ᵇ 2 The Hebrew has *Selah* (a word of uncertain meaning) here.   ᶜ 2 Or *night, and am not silent*   ᵈ 3 Or *Yet you are holy, I enthroned on the praises*

* 21:1-13 is numbered 21:2-14 in Hebrew texts.   * 22:1-31 is numbered 22:2-32 in Hebrew texts.

8'He trusts in the LORD,' they say,
   'let the LORD rescue him.
Let him deliver him,
   since he delights in him.'

9Yet you brought me out of the womb;
   you made me feel secure on my
      mother's breast.
10From birth I was cast on you;
   from my mother's womb you have
      been my God.
11Do not be far from me,
   for trouble is near
   and there is no-one to help.

12Many bulls surround me;
   strong bulls of Bashan encircle me.
13Roaring lions that tear their prey
   open their mouths wide against me.
14I am poured out like water,
   and all my bones are out of joint.
My heart has turned to wax;
   it has melted within me.
15My mouth^a is dried up like a potsherd,
   and my tongue sticks to the roof of my
      mouth;
you lay me^b in the dust of death.
16Dogs surround me,
   a pack of villains encircles me;
   they pierce^c my hands and my feet.
17All my bones are on display;
   people stare and gloat over me.
18They divide my clothes among them
   and cast lots for my garment.

19But you, LORD, do not be far from me.
   You are my strength; come quickly to
      help me.
20Deliver me from the sword,
   my precious life from the power of the
      dogs.
21Rescue me from the mouth of the lions;
   save me from the horns of the wild
      oxen.

22I will declare your name to my people;
   in the assembly I will praise you.
23You who fear the LORD, praise him!
   All you descendants of Jacob, honour
      him!
Revere him,
   all you descendants of Israel!
24For he has not despised or scorned
   the suffering of the afflicted one;
he has not hidden his face from him
   but has listened to his cry for help.

25From you comes the theme of my praise
   in the great assembly;
before those who fear you^d I will fulfil
   my vows.
26The poor will eat and be satisfied;
   those who seek the LORD will praise
      him—
may your hearts live for ever!
27All the ends of the earth
   will remember and turn to the LORD,
and all the families of the nations
   will bow down before him,
28for dominion belongs to the LORD
   and he rules over the nations.

29All the rich of the earth will feast and
      worship;
   all who go down to the dust will kneel
      before him—
those who cannot keep themselves
   alive.
30Posterity will serve him;
   future generations will be told about
      the Lord.
31They will proclaim his righteousness,
   declaring to a people yet unborn:
   he has done it!

Psalm 23

A psalm of David.

1The LORD is my shepherd, I lack nothing.
2 He makes me lie down in green
      pastures,
he leads me beside quiet waters,
3 he refreshes my soul.
He guides me along the right paths
   for his name's sake.
4Even though I walk
   through the darkest valley,^{e}
I will fear no evil,
   for you are with me;
your rod and your staff,
   they comfort me.

---

^{a}15 Probable reading of the original Hebrew text; Masoretic Text *strength* ^{b}15 Or *mouth; / I am laid* ^{c}16 Some Hebrew manuscripts, Septuagint and Syriac; most Hebrew manuscripts *me, / like a lion* ^{d}25 Hebrew *him* ^{e}4 Or *the valley of the shadow of death*

⁵You prepare a table before me
  in the presence of my enemies.
You anoint my head with oil;
  my cup overflows.
⁶Surely your goodness and love will follow me
  all the days of my life,
and I will dwell in the house of the LORD
  for ever.

Psalm 24

Of David. A psalm.

¹The earth is the LORD's, and everything in it,
  the world, and all who live in it;
²for he founded it on the seas
  and established it on the waters.

³Who may ascend the mountain of the LORD?
  Who may stand in his holy place?
⁴Those who have clean hands and a pure heart,
  who do not put their trust in an idol
  or swear by a false god.ᵃ

⁵They will receive blessing from the LORD
  and vindication from God their Saviour.
⁶Such is the generation of those who seek him,
  who seek your face, God of Jacob.ᵇ,ᶜ

⁷Lift up your heads, you gates;
  be lifted up, you ancient doors,
  that the King of glory may come in.
⁸Who is this King of glory?
  The LORD strong and mighty,
  the LORD mighty in battle.
⁹Lift up your heads, you gates;
  lift them up, you ancient doors,
  that the King of glory may come in.
¹⁰Who is he, this King of glory?
  The LORD Almighty—
  he is the King of glory.

Psalm 25ᵈ

Of David.

¹In you, LORD my God,
  I put my trust.

²I trust in you;
  do not let me be put to shame,
  nor let my enemies triumph over me.
³No-one who hopes in you
  will ever be put to shame,
but shame will come on those
  who are treacherous without cause.

⁴Show me your ways, LORD,
  teach me your paths.
⁵Guide me in your truth and teach me,
  for you are God my Saviour,
  and my hope is in you all day long.
⁶Remember, LORD, your great mercy and love,
  for they are from of old.
⁷Do not remember the sins of my youth
  and my rebellious ways;
according to your love remember me,
  for you, LORD, are good.

⁸Good and upright is the LORD;
  therefore he instructs sinners in his ways.
⁹He guides the humble in what is right
  and teaches them his way.
¹⁰All the ways of the LORD are loving and faithful
  towards those who keep the demands of his covenant.
¹¹For the sake of your name, LORD,
  forgive my iniquity, though it is great.

¹²Who, then, are those who fear the LORD?
  He will instruct them in the ways they should choose.
¹³They will spend their days in prosperity,
  and their descendants will inherit the land.
¹⁴The LORD confides in those who fear him;
  he makes his covenant known to them.
¹⁵My eyes are ever on the LORD,
  for only he will release my feet from the snare.

¹⁶Turn to me and be gracious to me,
  for I am lonely and afflicted.
¹⁷Relieve the troubles of my heart
  and free me from my anguish.
¹⁸Look on my affliction and my distress
  and take away all my sins.

ᵃ 4 Or *swear falsely* ᵇ 6 Two Hebrew manuscripts and Syriac (see also Septuagint); most Hebrew manuscripts *face, Jacob* ᶜ 6 The Hebrew has *Selah* (a word of uncertain meaning) here and at the end of verse 10. ᵈ This psalm is an acrostic poem, the verses of which begin with the successive letters of the Hebrew alphabet.

19See how numerous are my enemies
and how fiercely they hate me!

20Guard my life and rescue me;
do not let me be put to shame,
for I take refuge in you.
21May integrity and uprightness protect me,
because my hope, LORD,[a] is in you.

22Redeem Israel, O God,
from all their troubles!

Psalm 26

Of David.

1Vindicate me, LORD,
for I have led a blameless life;
I have trusted in the LORD
and have not faltered.
2Test me, LORD, and try me,
examine my heart and my mind;
3for I have always been mindful of your unfailing love
and have lived in reliance on your faithfulness.

4I do not sit with the deceitful,
nor do I associate with hypocrites.
5I abhor the assembly of evildoers
and refuse to sit with the wicked.
6I wash my hands in innocence,
and go about your altar, LORD,
7proclaiming aloud your praise
and telling of all your wonderful deeds.

8LORD, I love the house where you live,
the place where your glory dwells.
9Do not take away my soul along with sinners,
my life with those who are bloodthirsty,
10in whose hands are wicked schemes,
whose right hands are full of bribes.
11I lead a blameless life;
redeem me and be merciful to me.

12My feet stand on level ground;
in the great congregation I will praise the LORD.

Psalm 27

Of David.

1The LORD is my light and my salvation—
whom shall I fear?
The LORD is the stronghold of my life—
of whom shall I be afraid?

2When the wicked advance against me
to devour[b] me,
it is my enemies and my foes
who will stumble and fall.
3Though an army besiege me,
my heart will not fear;
though war break out against me,
even then I will be confident.

4One thing I ask from the LORD,
this only do I seek:
that I may dwell in the house of the LORD
all the days of my life,
to gaze on the beauty of the LORD
and to seek him in his temple.
5For in the day of trouble
he will keep me safe in his dwelling;
he will hide me in the shelter of his tabernacle
and set me high upon a rock.

6Then my head will be exalted
above the enemies who surround me;
at his tabernacle I will sacrifice with shouts of joy;
I will sing and make music to the LORD.

7Hear my voice when I call, LORD;
be merciful to me and answer me.
8My heart says of you, 'Seek his face!'
Your face, LORD, I will seek.
9Do not hide your face from me,
do not turn your servant away in anger;
you have been my helper.
Do not reject me or forsake me,
God my Saviour.
10Though my father and mother forsake me,
the LORD will receive me.
11Teach me your way, LORD;
lead me in a straight path
because of my oppressors.
12Do not hand me over to the desire of my foes,
for false witnesses rise up against me,
spouting malicious accusations.

13I remain confident of this:
I will see the goodness of the LORD
in the land of the living.

---

[a]21 Septuagint; Hebrew does not have LORD.   [b]2 Or *slander*

¹⁴Wait for the LORD;
be strong and take heart
and wait for the LORD.

Psalm 28

Of David.

¹To you, LORD, I call;
you are my Rock,
do not turn a deaf ear to me.
For if you remain silent,
I shall be like those who go down to the pit.
²Hear my cry for mercy
as I call to you for help,
as I lift up my hands
towards your Most Holy Place.

³Do not drag me away with the wicked,
with those who do evil,
who speak cordially with their neighbours
but harbour malice in their hearts.
⁴Repay them for their deeds
and for their evil work;
repay them for what their hands have done
and bring back on them what they deserve.

⁵Because they have no regard for the deeds of the LORD
and what his hands have done,
he will tear them down
and never build them up again.

⁶Praise be to the LORD,
for he has heard my cry for mercy.
⁷The LORD is my strength and my shield;
my heart trusts in him, and he helps me.
My heart leaps for joy,
and with my song I praise him.

⁸The LORD is the strength of his people,
a fortress of salvation for his anointed one.
⁹Save your people and bless your inheritance;
be their shepherd and carry them for ever.

Psalm 29

A psalm of David.

¹Ascribe to the LORD, you heavenly beings,
ascribe to the LORD glory and strength.
²Ascribe to the LORD the glory due to his name;
worship the LORD in the splendour of his[a] holiness.

³The voice of the LORD is over the waters;
the God of glory thunders,
the LORD thunders over the mighty waters.
⁴The voice of the LORD is powerful;
the voice of the LORD is majestic.
⁵The voice of the LORD breaks the cedars;
the LORD breaks in pieces the cedars of Lebanon.
⁶He makes Lebanon leap like a calf,
Sirion[b] like a young wild ox.
⁷The voice of the LORD strikes
with flashes of lightning.
⁸The voice of the LORD shakes the desert;
the LORD shakes the Desert of Kadesh.
⁹The voice of the LORD twists the oaks[c]
and strips the forests bare.
And in his temple all cry, 'Glory!'

¹⁰The LORD sits enthroned over the flood;
the LORD is enthroned as King for ever.
¹¹The LORD gives strength to his people;
the LORD blesses his people with peace.

Psalm 30

A psalm. A song. For the dedication of the temple.[d] Of David.

*¹I will exalt you, LORD,
for you lifted me out of the depths
and did not let my enemies gloat over me.
²LORD my God, I called to you for help,
and you healed me.
³You, LORD, brought me up from the realm of the dead;
you spared me from going down to the pit.

⁴Sing the praises of the LORD, you his faithful people;
praise his holy name.

---

[a] 2 Or *LORD with the splendour of* [b] 6 That is, Mount Hermon [c] 9 Or *LORD makes the deer give birth* [d] Title: Or *palace*

* 30:1-12 is numbered 30:2-13 in Hebrew texts.

IN OTHER WORDS

Exalt
Psalms 30:1
To exalt is to praise someone or put them in a high position, to acknowledge that something or someone is great.

⁵For his anger lasts only a moment,
  but his favour lasts a lifetime;
weeping may remain for a night,
  but rejoicing comes in the morning.

⁶When I felt secure, I said,
  'I shall never be shaken.'
⁷LORD, when you favoured me,
  you made my royal mountain[a] stand firm;
but when you hid your face,
  I was dismayed.

⁸To you, LORD, I called;
  to the Lord I cried for mercy:
⁹'What is gained if I am silenced,
  if I go down to the pit?
Will the dust praise you?
  Will it proclaim your faithfulness?
¹⁰Hear, LORD, and be merciful to me;
  LORD, be my help.'

¹¹You turned my wailing into dancing;
  you removed my sackcloth and clothed me with joy,
¹²that my heart may sing your praises and not be silent.
  LORD my God, I will praise you for ever.

Psalm 31

For the director of music. A psalm of David.

*¹In you, LORD, I have taken refuge;
  let me never be put to shame;
  deliver me in your righteousness.
²Turn your ear to me,
  come quickly to my rescue;
be my rock of refuge,
  a strong fortress to save me.
³Since you are my rock and my fortress,
  for the sake of your name lead and guide me.
⁴Keep me free from the trap that is set for me,
  for you are my refuge.
⁵Into your hands I commit my spirit;
  redeem me, LORD, my faithful God.

⁶I hate those who cling to worthless idols;
  as for me, I trust in the LORD.
⁷I will be glad and rejoice in your love,
  for you saw my affliction
  and knew the anguish of my soul.
⁸You have not given me into the hands of the enemy
  but have set my feet in a spacious place.

⁹Be merciful to me, LORD, for I am in distress;
  my eyes grow weak with sorrow,
  my soul and body with grief.
¹⁰My life is consumed by anguish
  and my years by groaning;
my strength fails because of my affliction,[b]
  and my bones grow weak.
¹¹Because of all my enemies,
  I am the utter contempt of my neighbours;
I am a dread to my friends—
  those who see me on the street flee from me.
¹²I am forgotten as though I were dead;
  I have become like broken pottery.
¹³For I hear many whispering,
  'Terror on every side!'
They conspire against me
  and plot to take my life.

¹⁴But I trust in you, LORD;
  I say, 'You are my God.'
¹⁵My times are in your hands;
  deliver me from the hands of my enemies,
  from those who pursue me.
¹⁶Let your face shine on your servant;
  save me in your unfailing love.
¹⁷Let me not be put to shame, LORD,
  for I have cried out to you;

---

[a] 7 That is, Mount Zion [b] 10 Or *guilt*
* 31:1-24 is numbered 31:2-25 in Hebrew texts.

but let the wicked be put to shame
and be silent in the realm of the dead.
18Let their lying lips be silenced,
for with pride and contempt
they speak arrogantly against the righteous.

19How great is your goodness,
which you have stored up for those who fear you,
which you bestow in the sight of all
on those who take refuge in you.
20In the shelter of your presence you hide them
from all human intrigues;
you keep them safe in your dwelling
from accusing tongues.

21Praise be to the LORD,
for he showed me the wonders of his love
when I was in a city under siege.
22In my alarm I said,
'I am cut off from your sight!'
Yet you heard my cry for mercy
when I called to you for help.

23Love the LORD, all his faithful people!
The LORD preserves those who are true to him,
but the proud he pays back in full.
24Be strong and take heart,
all you who hope in the LORD.

Psalm 32

Of David. A maskil.*[a]*

1Blessed are those
whose transgressions are forgiven,
whose sins are covered.
2Blessed are those
whose sin the LORD does not count against them
and in whose spirit is no deceit.

3When I kept silent,
my bones wasted away
through my groaning all day long.
4For day and night
your hand was heavy on me;
my strength was sapped
as in the heat of summer.*[b]*

5Then I acknowledged my sin to you
and did not cover up my iniquity.
I said, 'I will confess
my transgressions to the LORD.'
And you forgave
the guilt of my sin.

6Therefore let all the faithful pray to you
while you may be found;
surely the rising of the mighty waters
will not reach them.
7You are my hiding-place;
you will protect me from trouble
and surround me with songs of deliverance.

8I will instruct you and teach you in the way you should go;
I will counsel you with my loving eye on you.
9Do not be like the horse or the mule,
which have no understanding
but must be controlled by bit and bridle
or they will not come to you.
10Many are the woes of the wicked,
but the LORD's unfailing love
surrounds those who trust in him.

11Rejoice in the LORD and be glad, you righteous;
sing, all you who are upright in heart!

Psalm 33

1Sing joyfully to the LORD, you righteous;
it is fitting for the upright to praise him.
2Praise the LORD with the harp;
make music to him on the ten-stringed lyre.
3Sing to him a new song;
play skilfully, and shout for joy.

4For the word of the LORD is right and true;
he is faithful in all he does.
5The LORD loves righteousness and justice;
the earth is full of his unfailing love.

6By the word of the LORD the heavens were made,
their starry host by the breath of his mouth.
7He gathers the waters of the sea into jars;*[c]*
he puts the deep into storehouses.
8Let all the earth fear the LORD;

---

[a] Title: Probably a literary or musical term   *[b]* 4 The Hebrew has *Selah* (a word of uncertain meaning) here and at the end of verses 5 and 7.   *[c]* 7 Or *sea as into a heap*

let all the people of the world revere
him.
⁹For he spoke, and it came to be;
he commanded, and it stood firm.

¹⁰The LORD foils the plans of the nations;
he thwarts the purposes of the peoples.
¹¹But the plans of the LORD stand firm for
ever,
the purposes of his heart through all
generations.

¹²Blessed is the nation whose God is the
LORD,
the people he chose for his inheritance.
¹³From heaven the LORD looks down
and sees all humankind;
¹⁴from his dwelling-place he watches
all who live on earth—
¹⁵he who forms the hearts of all,
who considers everything they do.

¹⁶No king is saved by the size of his army;
no warrior escapes by his great
strength.
¹⁷A horse is a vain hope for deliverance;
despite all its great strength it cannot
save.
¹⁸But the eyes of the LORD are on those who
fear him,
on those whose hope is in his unfailing
love,
¹⁹to deliver them from death
and keep them alive in famine.

²⁰We wait in hope for the LORD;
he is our help and our shield.
²¹In him our hearts rejoice,
for we trust in his holy name.
²²May your unfailing love be with us, LORD,
even as we put our hope in you.

Psalm 34[a]

Of David. When he pretended to be insane before Abimelek, who drove him away, and he left.

*¹I will extol the LORD at all times;
his praise will always be on my lips.
²I will glory in the LORD;
let the afflicted hear and rejoice.
³Glorify the LORD with me:
let us exalt his name together.

> **IN OTHER WORDS**
>
> **Glorify**
> Psalms 34:3
> If you glorify someone you give them honour and worship, you make them more splendid and you revel in their beauty. In the New Testament, Jesus says just before he dies that it is time for him to be glorified, for people to see who he really is (John 12:23).

⁴I sought the LORD, and he answered me;
he delivered me from all my fears.
⁵Those who look to him are radiant;
their faces are never covered with
shame.
⁶This poor man called, and the LORD heard
him;
he saved him out of all his troubles.
⁷The angel of the LORD encamps around
those who fear him,
and he delivers them.

⁸Taste and see that the LORD is good;
blessed are those who take refuge in
him.
⁹Fear the LORD, you his holy people,
for those who fear him lack nothing.
¹⁰The lions may grow weak and hungry,
but those who seek the LORD lack no
good thing.
¹¹Come, my children, listen to me;
I will teach you the fear of the LORD.
¹²Whoever of you loves life
and desires to see many good days,
¹³keep your tongue from evil
and your lips from telling lies.
¹⁴Turn from evil and do good;
seek peace and pursue it.

¹⁵The eyes of the LORD are on the righteous
and his ears are attentive to their cry.
¹⁶The face of the LORD is against those who
do evil,
to blot out their name from the earth.

---

[a] This psalm is an acrostic poem, the verses of which begin with the successive letters of the Hebrew alphabet.
* 34:1-22 is numbered 34:2-23 in Hebrew texts.

17 The righteous cry out, and the LORD hears them;
   he delivers them from all their troubles.
18 The LORD is close to the broken-hearted
   and saves those who are crushed in spirit.

19 The righteous may have many troubles,
   but the LORD delivers them from them all;
20 he protects all their bones,
   not one of them will be broken.

21 Evil will slay the wicked;
   the foes of the righteous will be condemned.
22 The LORD redeems his servants;
   no-one who takes refuge in him will be condemned.

Psalm 35

Of David.

1 Contend, LORD, with those who contend with me;
   fight against those who fight against me.
2 Take up shield and armour;
   arise and come to my aid.
3 Brandish spear and javelin[a]
   against those who pursue me.
   Say to me,
   'I am your salvation.'

4 May those who seek my life
   be disgraced and put to shame;
   may those who plot my ruin
   be turned back in dismay.
5 May they be like chaff before the wind,
   with the angel of the LORD driving them away;
6 may their path be dark and slippery,
   with the angel of the LORD pursuing them.

7 Since they hid their net for me without cause
   and without cause dug a pit for me,
8 may ruin overtake them by surprise—
   may the net they hid entangle them,
   may they fall into the pit, to their ruin.
9 Then my soul will rejoice in the LORD
   and delight in his salvation.
10 My whole being will exclaim,
   'Who is like you, LORD?
   You rescue the poor from those too strong for them,
   the poor and needy from those who rob them.'

11 Ruthless witnesses come forward;
   they question me on things I know nothing about.
12 They repay me evil for good
   and leave me like one bereaved.
13 Yet when they were ill, I put on sackcloth
   and humbled myself with fasting.
   When my prayers returned to me unanswered,
14   I went about mourning
   as though for my friend or brother.
   I bowed my head in grief
   as though weeping for my mother.
15 But when I stumbled, they gathered in glee;
   assailants gathered against me without my knowledge.
   They slandered me without ceasing.
16 Like the ungodly they maliciously mocked;[b]
   they gnashed their teeth at me.

17 How long, Lord, will you look on?
   Rescue me from their ravages,
   my precious life from these lions.
18 I will give you thanks in the great assembly;
   among the throngs I will praise you.
19 Do not let those gloat over me
   who are my enemies without cause;
   do not let those who hate me without reason
   maliciously wink the eye.
20 They do not speak peaceably,
   but devise false accusations
   against those who live quietly in the land.
21 They sneer at me and say, 'Aha! Aha!
   With our own eyes we have seen it.'

22 LORD, you have seen this; do not be silent.
   Do not be far from me, Lord.
23 Awake, and rise to my defence!
   Contend for me, my God and Lord.

---

a 3 Or *and block the way*   *b* 16 Septuagint; Hebrew may mean *ungodly circle of mockers*.

24 Vindicate me in your righteousness,
   LORD my God;
   do not let them gloat over me.
25 Do not let them think, 'Aha, just what we wanted!'
   or say, 'We have swallowed him up.'

26 May all who gloat over my distress
   be put to shame and confusion;
   may all who exalt themselves over me
   be clothed with shame and disgrace.
27 May those who delight in my vindication
   shout for joy and gladness;
   may they always say, 'The LORD be exalted,
   who delights in the well-being of his servant.'

28 My tongue will proclaim your righteousness,
   your praises all day long.

Psalm 36

For the director of music. Of David the servant of the LORD.

*1 I have a message from God in my heart
   concerning the sinfulness of the wicked:[a]
   there is no fear of God
   before their eyes.

2 In their own eyes they flatter themselves
   too much to detect or hate their sin.
3 The words of their mouths are wicked and deceitful;
   they have ceased to be wise and to do good.
4 Even on their beds they plot evil;
   they commit themselves to a sinful course
   and do not reject what is wrong.

5 Your love, LORD, reaches to the heavens,
   your faithfulness to the skies.
6 Your righteousness is like the highest mountains,
   your justice like the great deep.
   You, LORD, preserve both people and animals.
7 How priceless is your unfailing love, O God!
   People take refuge in the shadow of your wings.
8 They feast in the abundance of your house;
   you give them drink from your river of delights.
9 For with you is the fountain of life;
   in your light we see light.

10 Continue your love to those who know you,
   your righteousness to the upright in heart.
11 May the foot of the proud not come against me,
   nor the hand of the wicked drive me away.
12 See how the evildoers lie fallen—
   thrown down, not able to rise!

Psalm 37[b]

Of David.

1 Do not fret because of those who are evil
   or be envious of those who do wrong;
2 for like the grass they will soon wither,
   like green plants they will soon die away.

3 Trust in the LORD and do good;
   dwell in the land and enjoy safe pasture.
4 Take delight in the LORD
   and he will give you the desires of your heart.

5 Commit your way to the LORD;
   trust in him and he will do this:
6 he will make your righteous reward shine like the dawn,
   your vindication like the noonday sun.

7 Be still before the LORD
   and wait patiently for him;
   do not fret when people succeed in their ways,
   when they carry out their wicked schemes.

8 Refrain from anger and turn from wrath;
   do not fret—it leads only to evil.
9 For those who are evil will be destroyed,

---

[a] 1 Or *A message from God: the transgression of the wicked / resides in their hearts.*   [b] This psalm is an acrostic poem, the stanzas of which begin with the successive letters of the Hebrew alphabet.

* 36:1-12 is numbered 36:2-13 in Hebrew texts.

> **IN OTHER WORDS**
>
> **Meek**
> Psalms 37:11
> Meekness is not the same as weakness; it suggests a humble ability to survive life's ups and downs with an even temper. It is used to describe Jesus (2 Corinthians 10:1), and Jesus said that the meek were blessed and would inherit the earth (Matthew 5:5).

but those who hope in the LORD will
    inherit the land.
10 A little while, and the wicked will be no
        more;
    though you look for them, they will not
        be found.
11 But the meek will inherit the land
    and enjoy peace and prosperity.

12 The wicked plot against the righteous
    and gnash their teeth at them;
13 but the Lord laughs at the wicked,
    for he knows their day is coming.

14 The wicked draw the sword
    and bend the bow
to bring down the poor and needy,
    to slay those whose ways are upright.
15 But their swords will pierce their own
        hearts,
    and their bows will be broken.

16 Better the little that the righteous have
    than the wealth of many wicked;
17 for the power of the wicked will be
        broken,
    but the LORD upholds the righteous.

18 The blameless spend their days under the
        LORD's care,
    and their inheritance will endure for
        ever.
19 In times of disaster they will not wither;
    in days of famine they will enjoy plenty.
20 But the wicked will perish:
    though the LORD's enemies are like the
        flowers of the field,
    they will be consumed, they will go up
        in smoke.

21 The wicked borrow and do not repay,
    but the righteous give generously;
22 those the LORD blesses will inherit the
        land,
    but those he curses will be destroyed.

23 The LORD makes firm the steps
    of those who delight in him;
24 though they stumble, they will not fall,
    for the LORD upholds them with his
        hand.

25 I was young and now I am old,
    yet I have never seen the righteous
        forsaken
    or their children begging bread.
26 They are always generous and lend freely;
    their children will be a blessing.[a]

27 Turn from evil and do good;
    then you will dwell in the land for ever.
28 For the LORD loves the just
    and will not forsake his faithful ones.

Wrongdoers will be completely
        destroyed[b];
    the offspring of the wicked will
        perish.
29 The righteous will inherit the land
    and dwell in it for ever.

30 The mouths of the righteous utter
        wisdom,
    and their tongues speak what is just.
31 The law of their God is in their hearts;
    their feet do not slip.

32 The wicked lie in wait for the righteous,
    seeking their very lives;
33 but the LORD will not leave them in their
        power
    or let them be condemned when
        brought to trial.

34 Hope in the LORD
    and keep his way.
He will exalt you to inherit the land;
    when the wicked are destroyed, you
        will see it.

---

[a] 26 Or *freely; / the names of their children will be used in blessings* (see Gen. 48:20); or *freely; / others will see that their children are blessed*   [b] 28 See Septuagint; Hebrew *They will be protected for ever*

35 I have seen the wicked and ruthless
flourishing like a luxuriant native tree,
36 but they soon passed away and were no more;
though I looked for them, they could not be found.
37 Consider the blameless, observe the upright;
a future awaits those who seek peace.[a]
38 But all sinners will be destroyed;
there will be no future[b] for the wicked.

39 The salvation of the righteous comes from the LORD;
he is their stronghold in time of trouble.
40 The LORD helps them and delivers them;
he delivers them from the wicked and saves them,
because they take refuge in him.

Psalm 38

A psalm of David. A petition.

*1 LORD, do not rebuke me in your anger
or discipline me in your wrath.
2 Your arrows have pierced me,
and your hand has come down on me.
3 Because of your wrath there is no health in my body;
there is no soundness in my bones because of my sin.
4 My guilt has overwhelmed me
like a burden too heavy to bear.

5 My wounds fester and are loathsome
because of my sinful folly.
6 I am bowed down and brought very low;
all day long I go about mourning.
7 My back is filled with searing pain;
there is no health in my body.
8 I am feeble and utterly crushed;
I groan in anguish of heart.

9 All my longings lie open before you, Lord:
my sighing is not hidden from you.
10 My heart pounds, my strength fails me;
even the light has gone from my eyes.
11 My friends and companions avoid me because of my wounds;
my neighbours stay far away.
12 Those who seek my life set their traps,
those who would harm me talk of my ruin;
all day long they scheme and lie.

13 I am like the deaf, who cannot hear,
like the mute, who cannot speak;
14 I have become like one who does not hear,
whose mouth can offer no reply.
15 LORD, I wait for you;
you will answer, Lord my God.
16 For I said, 'Do not let them gloat
or exalt themselves over me when my feet slip.'

17 For I am about to fall,
and my pain is ever with me.
18 I confess my iniquity;
I am troubled by my sin.
19 Many have become my enemies without cause[c];
those who hate me without reason are numerous.
20 Those who repay my good with evil
lodge accusations against me,
though I seek only to do what is good.

21 LORD, do not forsake me;
do not be far from me, my God.
22 Come quickly to help me,
my Lord and my Saviour.

Psalm 39

For the director of music. For Jeduthun. A psalm of David.

*1 I said, 'I will watch my ways
and keep my tongue from sin;
I will put a muzzle on my mouth
while in the presence of the wicked.'
2 So I remained utterly silent,
not even saying anything good.
But my anguish increased;
3   my heart grew hot within me.
While I meditated, the fire burned;
then I spoke with my tongue:

4 'Show me, LORD, my life's end
and the number of my days;
let me know how fleeting my life is.
5 You have made my days a mere handbreadth;

---

[a] 37 Or *those who seek peace will have posterity*   [b] 38 Or *posterity*   [c] 19 One Dead Sea Scrolls manuscript; Masoretic Text *my vigorous enemies*

* 38:1-22 is numbered 38:2-23 in Hebrew texts.   * 39:1-13 is numbered 39:2-14 in Hebrew texts.

the span of my years is as nothing
before you.
Everyone is but a breath,
even those who seem secure.*ᵃ*

⁶'Surely everyone goes around like a mere
phantom;
in vain they rush about, heaping up
wealth
without knowing whose it will finally
be.

⁷'But now, Lord, what do I look for?
My hope is in you.
⁸Save me from all my transgressions;
do not make me the scorn of fools.
⁹I was silent; I would not open my mouth,
for you are the one who has done this.
¹⁰Remove your scourge from me;
I am overcome by the blow of your
hand.
¹¹When you rebuke and discipline people
for their sins,
you consume their wealth like a
moth—
surely everyone is but a breath.

¹²'Hear my prayer, LORD,
listen to my cry for help;
do not be deaf to my weeping.
I dwell with you as a foreigner,
a stranger, as all my ancestors were.
¹³Look away from me, that I may enjoy life
again
before I depart and am no more.'

Psalm 40

*For the director of music. Of David.
A psalm.*

*¹I waited patiently for the LORD;
he turned to me and heard my cry.
²He lifted me out of the slimy pit,
out of the mud and mire;
he set my feet on a rock
and gave me a firm place to stand.
³He put a new song in my mouth,
a hymn of praise to our God.
Many will see and fear the LORD
and put their trust in him.

⁴Blessed are those
who make the LORD their trust,
who do not look to the proud,
to those who turn aside to false gods.*ᵇ*
⁵Many, LORD my God,
are the wonders you have done,
the things you planned for us.
None can compare with you;
were I to speak and tell of your deeds,
they would be too many to declare.

⁶Sacrifice and offering you did not
desire—
but my ears you have opened*ᶜ*—
burnt offerings and sin offerings*ᵈ* you
did not require.
⁷Then I said, 'Here I am, I have come—
it is written about me in the scroll.*ᵉ*
⁸I desire to do your will, my God;
your law is within my heart.'

⁹I proclaim your saving acts in the great
assembly;
I do not seal my lips, LORD,
as you know.
¹⁰I do not hide your righteousness in my
heart;
I speak of your faithfulness and your
saving help.
I do not conceal your love and your
faithfulness
from the great assembly.

¹¹Do not withhold your mercy from me,
LORD;
may your love and faithfulness always
protect me.
¹²For troubles without number surround
me;
my sins have overtaken me, and I
cannot see.
They are more than the hairs of my head,
and my heart fails within me.
¹³Be pleased to save me, LORD;
come quickly, LORD, to help me.

¹⁴May all who seek to take my life
be put to shame and confusion;
may all who desire my ruin
be turned back in disgrace.

ᵃ 5 The Hebrew has *Selah* (a word of uncertain meaning) here and at the end of verse 11.   *ᵇ* 4 Or *to lies*   *ᶜ* 6 Hebrew; some Septuagint manuscripts *but a body you have prepared for me*   *ᵈ* 6 Or *purification offerings*   *ᵉ* 7 Or *come I with the scroll written for me*

* 40:1-17 is numbered 40:2-18 in Hebrew texts.

15 May those who say to me, 'Aha! Aha!'
    be appalled at their own shame.
16 But may all who seek you
    rejoice and be glad in you;
  may those who long for your saving help
      always say,
    'The LORD is great!'

17 But as for me, I am poor and needy;
    may the Lord think of me.
  You are my help and my deliverer;
    you are my God, do not delay.

Psalm 41

For the director of music. A psalm of David.

*1 Blessed are those who have regard for the weak;
    the LORD delivers them in times of trouble.
2 The LORD protects and preserves them—
    they are counted among the blessed in the land—
  he does not give them over to the desire of their foes.
3 The LORD sustains them on their sick-bed
    and restores them from their bed of illness.

4 I said, 'Have mercy on me, LORD;
    heal me, for I have sinned against you.'
5 My enemies say of me in malice,
    'When will he die and his name perish?'
6 Whenever they come to see me,
    they speak falsely, while their hearts gather slander;
  then they go out and spread it abroad.

7 All my enemies whisper together against me;
    they imagine the worst for me, saying,
8 'A vile disease has beset him;
    he will never get up from the place where he lies.'
9 Even my close friend,
    someone I trusted,
  one who shared my bread,
    has lifted up his heel against me.

10 But may you have mercy on me, LORD;
    raise me up, that I may repay them.
11 I know that you are pleased with me,
    for my enemy does not triumph over me.
12 In my integrity you uphold me
    and set me in your presence for ever.
13 Praise be to the LORD, the God of Israel,
    from everlasting to everlasting.
  Amen and Amen.

BOOK II

Psalms 42–72

Psalm 42[a]

For the director of music. A maskil[b] of the Sons of Korah.

*1 As the deer pants for streams of water,
    so my soul pants for you, my God.
2 My soul thirsts for God, for the living God.
    When can I go and meet with God?
3 My tears have been my food
    day and night,
  while people say to me all day long,
    'Where is your God?'
4 These things I remember
    as I pour out my soul:
  how I used to go to the house of God
    under the protection of the Mighty One[c]
  with shouts of joy and praise
    among the festive throng.

5 Why, my soul, are you downcast?
    Why so disturbed within me?
  Put your hope in God,
    for I will yet praise him,
    my Saviour and my God.

6 My soul is downcast within me;
    therefore I will remember you
  from the land of the Jordan,
    the heights of Hermon—from Mount Mizar.
7 Deep calls to deep
    in the roar of your waterfalls;
  all your waves and breakers
    have swept over me.

8 By day the LORD directs his love,
    at night his song is with me—
    a prayer to the God of my life.

---

[a] In many Hebrew manuscripts Psalms 42 and 43 constitute one psalm. [b] Title: Probably a literary or musical term [c] 4 See Septuagint and Syriac; the meaning of the Hebrew for this line is uncertain.

* 41:1-13 is numbered 41:2-14 in Hebrew texts.   * 42:1-11 is numbered 42:2-12 in Hebrew texts.

⁹I say to God my Rock,
  'Why have you forgotten me?
Why must I go about mourning,
  oppressed by the enemy?'
¹⁰My bones suffer mortal agony
  as my foes taunt me,
saying to me all day long,
  'Where is your God?'

¹¹Why, my soul, are you downcast?
  Why so disturbed within me?
Put your hope in God,
  for I will yet praise him,
  my Saviour and my God.

Psalm 43[a]

¹Vindicate me, my God,
  and plead my cause
  against an unfaithful nation.
Rescue me from those who are
  deceitful and wicked.
²You are God my stronghold.
  Why have you rejected me?
Why must I go about mourning,
  oppressed by the enemy?
³Send me your light and your faithful care,
  let them lead me;
let them bring me to your holy mountain,
  to the place where you dwell.
⁴Then I will go to the altar of God,
  to God, my joy and my delight.
I will praise you with the lyre,
  O God, my God.

⁵Why, my soul, are you downcast?
  Why so disturbed within me?
Put your hope in God,
  for I will yet praise him,
  my Saviour and my God.

Psalm 44

For the director of music. Of the Sons of Korah. A maskil.[b]

*¹We have heard it with our ears, O God;
  our ancestors have told us
what you did in their days,
  in days long ago.
²With your hand you drove out the nations
  and planted our ancestors;
you crushed the peoples
  and made our ancestors flourish.
³It was not by their sword that they won the land,
  nor did their arm bring them victory;
it was your right hand, your arm,
  and the light of your face, for you loved them.

⁴You are my King and my God,
  who decrees[c] victories for Jacob.
⁵Through you we push back our enemies;
  through your name we trample our foes.
⁶I put no trust in my bow,
  my sword does not bring me victory;
⁷but you give us victory over our enemies,
  you put our adversaries to shame.
⁸In God we make our boast all day long,
  and we will praise your name for ever.[d]

⁹But now you have rejected and humbled us;
  you no longer go out with our armies.
¹⁰You made us retreat before the enemy,
  and our adversaries have plundered us.
¹¹You gave us up to be devoured like sheep
  and have scattered us among the nations.
¹²You sold your people for a pittance,
  gaining nothing from their sale.

¹³You have made us a reproach to our neighbours,
  the scorn and derision of those around us.
¹⁴You have made us a byword among the nations;
  the peoples shake their heads at us.
¹⁵I live in disgrace all day long,
  and my face is covered with shame
¹⁶at the taunts of those who reproach and revile me,
  because of the enemy, who is bent on revenge.

¹⁷All this came upon us,
  though we had not forgotten you;
  we had not been false to your covenant.
¹⁸Our hearts had not turned back;

---

[a] In many Hebrew manuscripts Psalms 42 and 43 constitute one psalm.   [b] Title: Probably a literary or musical term   [c] 4 Septuagint, Aquila and Syriac; Hebrew *King, O God; I command*   [d] 8 The Hebrew has *Selah* (a word of uncertain meaning) here.

* 44:1-26 is numbered 44:2-27 in Hebrew texts.

our feet had not strayed from your path.
¹⁹But you crushed us and made us a haunt for jackals;
you covered us over with deep darkness.

²⁰If we had forgotten the name of our God
or spread out our hands to a foreign god,
²¹would not God have discovered it,
since he knows the secrets of the heart?
²²Yet for your sake we face death all day long;
we are considered as sheep to be slaughtered.

²³Awake, Lord! Why do you sleep?
Rouse yourself! Do not reject us for ever.
²⁴Why do you hide your face
and forget our misery and oppression?

²⁵We are brought down to the dust;
our bodies cling to the ground.
²⁶Rise up and help us;
redeem us because of your unfailing love.

Psalm 45

For the director of music. To the tune of 'Lilies'. Of the Sons of Korah. A maskil.^a A wedding song.

*¹My heart is stirred by a noble theme
as I recite my verses for the king;
my tongue is the pen of a skilful writer.

²You are the most excellent of men
and your lips have been anointed with grace,
since God has blessed you for ever.

³Gird your sword on your side, you mighty one;
clothe yourself with splendour and majesty.
⁴In your majesty ride forth victoriously
in the cause of truth, humility and justice;
let your right hand achieve awesome deeds.

> **Sign of the times**
>
> **Luxury**
> **Psalms 45:8**
> No expense was spared for the king's wedding. Myrrh, aloes and cassia were all types of perfume, expensive and luxurious because they were imported from other lands. Ivory too was a luxury, and gold from Ophir was considered to be the very best.

⁵Let your sharp arrows pierce the hearts of the king's enemies;
let the nations fall beneath your feet.
⁶Your throne, O God,^b will last for ever and ever;
a sceptre of justice will be the sceptre of your kingdom.
⁷You love righteousness and hate wickedness;
therefore God, your God, has set you above your companions
by anointing you with the oil of joy.
⁸All your robes are fragrant with myrrh and aloes and cassia;
from palaces adorned with ivory
the music of the strings makes you glad.
⁹Daughters of kings are among your honoured women;
at your right hand is the royal bride in gold of Ophir.

¹⁰Listen, daughter, and pay careful attention:
forget your people and your father's house.
¹¹Let the king be enthralled by your beauty;
honour him, for he is your lord.
¹²The city of Tyre will come with a gift,^c
people of wealth will seek your favour.

---

^a Title: Probably a literary or musical term   ^b 6 Here the king is addressed as God's representative.   ^c 12 Or *A Tyrian robe is among the gifts*

* 45:1-17 is numbered 45:2-18 in Hebrew texts.

13 All glorious is the princess within her chamber;
 her gown is interwoven with gold.
14 In embroidered garments she is led to the king;
 her virgin companions follow her—
 those brought to be with her.
15 Led in with joy and gladness,
 they enter the palace of the king.

16 Your sons will take the place of your fathers;
 you will make them princes throughout the land.

17 I will perpetuate your memory through all generations;
 therefore the nations will praise you for ever and ever.

Psalm 46

For the director of music. Of the Sons of Korah. According to alamoth.[a] *A song.*

*1 God is our refuge and strength,
 an ever-present help in trouble.
2 Therefore we will not fear, though the earth give way
 and the mountains fall into the heart of the sea,
3 though its waters roar and foam
 and the mountains quake with their surging.[b]

4 There is a river whose streams make glad the city of God,
 the holy place where the Most High dwells.
5 God is within her, she will not fall;
 God will help her at break of day.
6 Nations are in uproar, kingdoms fall;
 he lifts his voice, the earth melts.

7 The LORD Almighty is with us;
 the God of Jacob is our fortress.

8 Come and see what the LORD has done,
 the desolations he has brought on the earth.
9 He makes wars cease
 to the ends of the earth.
 He breaks the bow and shatters the spear;
 he burns the shields[c] with fire.
10 'Be still, and know that I am God;
 I will be exalted among the nations,
 I will be exalted in the earth.'

11 The LORD Almighty is with us;
 the God of Jacob is our fortress.

Psalm 47

For the director of music. Of the Sons of Korah. A psalm.

*1 Clap your hands, all you nations;
 shout to God with cries of joy.

2 For the LORD Most High is awesome,
 the great King over all the earth.
3 He subdued nations under us,
 peoples under our feet.
4 He chose our inheritance for us,
 the pride of Jacob, whom he loved.[d]

5 God has ascended amid shouts of joy,
 the LORD amid the sounding of trumpets.
6 Sing praises to God, sing praises;
 sing praises to our King, sing praises.
7 For God is the King of all the earth;
 sing to him a psalm of praise.

8 God reigns over the nations;
 God is seated on his holy throne.
9 The nobles of the nations assemble
 as the people of the God of Abraham,
 for the kings[e] of the earth belong to God;
 he is greatly exalted.

Psalm 48

A song. A psalm of the Sons of Korah.

*1 Great is the LORD, and most worthy of praise,
 in the city of our God, his holy mountain.

2 Beautiful in its loftiness,
 the joy of the whole earth,
 like the heights of Zaphon[f] is Mount Zion,
 the city of the Great King.

---

[a] Title: Probably a musical term [b] 3 The Hebrew has *Selah* (a word of uncertain meaning) here and at the end of verses 7 and 11. [c] 9 Or *chariots* [d] 4 The Hebrew has *Selah* (a word of uncertain meaning) here. [e] 9 Or *shields* [f] 2 *Zaphon* was the most sacred mountain of the Canaanites.

* 46:1-11 is numbered 46:2-12 in Hebrew texts. * 47:1-9 is numbered 47:2-10 in Hebrew texts. * 48:1-14 is numbered 48:2-15 in Hebrew texts.

3God is in her citadels;
 he has shown himself to be her fortress.

4When the kings joined forces,
 when they advanced together,
5they saw her and were astounded;
 they fled in terror.
6Trembling seized them there,
 pain like that of a woman in labour.
7You destroyed them like ships of Tarshish
 shattered by an east wind.

8As we have heard,
 so we have seen
 in the city of the LORD Almighty,
 in the city of our God:
 God makes her secure
 for ever.[a]

9Within your temple, O God,
 we meditate on your unfailing love.
10Like your name, O God,
 your praise reaches to the ends of the earth;
 your right hand is filled with righteousness.
11Mount Zion rejoices,
 the villages of Judah are glad
 because of your judgments.

12Walk about Zion, go round her,
 count her towers,
13consider well her ramparts,
 view her citadels,
 that you may tell of them
 to the next generation.

14For this God is our God for ever and ever;
 he will be our guide even to the end.

Psalm 49

For the director of music. Of the Sons of Korah. A psalm.

*1Hear this, all you peoples;
 listen, all who live in this world,
2both low and high,
 rich and poor alike:
3my mouth will speak words of wisdom;
 the meditation of my heart will give you understanding.
4I will turn my ear to a proverb;
 with the harp I will expound my riddle:

5Why should I fear when evil days come,
 when wicked deceivers surround me—
6those who trust in their wealth
 and boast of their great riches?
7No-one can redeem the life of another
 or give to God a sufficient ransom—
8the ransom for a life is costly,
 no payment is ever enough—
9so that someone should live on for ever
 and not see decay.

10For all can see that the wise die,
 that the foolish and the senseless also perish,
 leaving their wealth to others.
11Their tombs will remain their houses[b] for ever,
 their dwellings for endless generations,
 though they had[c] named lands after themselves.

12Human beings, despite their wealth, do not endure;
 they are like the beasts that perish.

13This is the fate of those who trust in themselves,
 and of their followers, who approve their sayings.[d]
14They are like sheep and are destined to die;
 death will be their shepherd
 (but the upright will prevail over them
 in the morning).
 Their forms will decay in the grave,
 far from their princely mansions.
15But God will redeem me from the realm of the dead;
 he will surely take me to himself.

16Do not be overawed when others grow rich,
 when the splendour of their houses increases;
17for they will take nothing with them when they die,
 their splendour will not descend with them.
18Though while they live they count themselves blessed—

---

[a] 8 The Hebrew has *Selah* (a word of uncertain meaning) here. *their houses will remain*   [c] 11 Or *generations, / for they have* meaning) here and at the end of verse 15.

[b] 11 Septuagint and Syriac; Hebrew *In their thoughts*

[d] 13 The Hebrew has *Selah* (a word of uncertain meaning)

*49:1-20 is numbered 49:2-21 in Hebrew texts.

and people praise you when you prosper—
19they will join those who have gone before them,
who will never again see the light of life.

20Human beings who have wealth but lack understanding
are like the beasts that perish.

Psalm 50

A psalm of Asaph.

1The Mighty One, God, the LORD,
speaks and summons the earth
from the rising of the sun to where it sets.
2From Zion, perfect in beauty,
God shines forth.
3Our God comes
and will not be silent;
a fire devours before him,
and around him a tempest rages.
4He summons the heavens above,
and the earth, that he may judge his people:
5'Gather to me this consecrated people,
who made a covenant with me by sacrifice.'
6And the heavens proclaim his righteousness,
for he is a God of justice.[a,b]

7'Listen, my people, and I will speak;
I will testify against you, Israel:
I am God, your God.
8I bring no charges against you concerning your sacrifices
or concerning your burnt offerings,
which are ever before me.
9I have no need of a bull from your stall
or of goats from your pens,
10for every animal of the forest is mine,
and the cattle on a thousand hills.
11I know every bird in the mountains,
and the creatures of the field are mine.
12If I were hungry I would not tell you,
for the world is mine, and all that is in it.
13Do I eat the flesh of bulls
or drink the blood of goats?
14Sacrifice thank-offerings to God,
fulfil your vows to the Most High,
15and call on me in the day of trouble;
I will deliver you, and you will honour me.'

16But to the wicked, God says:

'What right have you to recite my laws
or take my covenant on your lips?
17You hate my instruction
and cast my words behind you.
18When you see thieves, you join with them;
you throw in your lot with adulterers.
19You use your mouth for evil
and harness your tongue to deceit.
20You sit and testify against your brother
and slander your own mother's son.
21When you did these things and I kept silent,
you thought I was exactly[c] like you.
But I now bring you to court
and set my accusations before you.

22'Consider this, you who forget God,
or I will tear you to pieces, with no-one to rescue:
23those who sacrifice thank-offerings honour me,
and to the blameless[d] I will show my salvation.'

Psalm 51

For the director of music. A psalm of David. When the prophet Nathan came to him after David had committed adultery with Bathsheba.

*1Have mercy on me, O God,
according to your unfailing love;
according to your great compassion
blot out my transgressions.
2Wash away all my iniquity
and cleanse me from my sin.

3For I know my transgressions,
and my sin is always before me.
4Against you, you only, have I sinned
and done what is evil in your sight;
so you are right in your verdict
and justified when you judge.

---

[a] 6 With a different word division of the Hebrew; Masoretic Text *for God himself is judge* [b] 6 The Hebrew has *Selah* (a word of uncertain meaning) here. [c] 21 Or *thought the 'I AM' was* [d] 23 Probable reading of the original Hebrew text; the meaning of the Masoretic Text for this phrase is uncertain.

* 51:1-19 is numbered 51:3-21 in Hebrew texts.

> **IN OTHER WORDS**
>
> **Mercy**
> Psalms 51:1
>
> An important attribute of God's character, mercy is God's ability to override his desire for justice and forgive our wrongdoing. Jesus' death is the means by which God demonstrates his mercy to us. And Christians in turn are urged to be merciful to each other.

⁵Surely I was sinful at birth,
  sinful from the time my mother conceived me.
⁶Yet you desired faithfulness even in the womb;
  you taught me wisdom in that secret place.
⁷Cleanse me with hyssop, and I shall be clean;
  wash me, and I shall be whiter than snow.
⁸Let me hear joy and gladness;
  let the bones you have crushed rejoice.
⁹Hide your face from my sins
  and blot out all my iniquity.

¹⁰Create in me a pure heart, O God,
  and renew a steadfast spirit within me.
¹¹Do not cast me from your presence
  or take your Holy Spirit from me.
¹²Restore to me the joy of your salvation
  and grant me a willing spirit, to sustain me.
¹³Then I will teach transgressors your ways,
  and sinners will turn back to you.
¹⁴Deliver me from bloodguilt, O God,
  you who are God my Saviour,
  and my tongue will sing of your righteousness.
¹⁵Open my lips, Lord,
  and my mouth will declare your praise.
¹⁶You do not delight in sacrifice, or I would bring it;
  you do not take pleasure in burnt offerings.
¹⁷My sacrifice, O God, is*ᵃ* a broken spirit;
  a broken and contrite heart
  you, God, will not despise.

¹⁸May it please you to prosper Zion,
  to build up the walls of Jerusalem.
¹⁹Then you will delight in the sacrifices of the righteous,
  in burnt offerings offered whole;
  then bulls will be offered on your altar.

Psalm 52

*For the director of music. A maskil*ᵇ *of David. When Doeg the Edomite had gone to Saul and told him: 'David has gone to the house of Ahimelek.'*

*¹Why do you boast of evil, you mighty hero?
  Why do you boast all day long,
  you who are a disgrace in the eyes of God?
²You who practise deceit,
  your tongue plots destruction;
  it is like a sharpened razor.
³You love evil rather than good,
  falsehood rather than speaking the truth.*ᶜ
⁴You love every harmful word,
  you deceitful tongue!

⁵Surely God will bring you down to everlasting ruin:
  he will snatch you up and pluck you from your tent;
  he will uproot you from the land of the living.
⁶The righteous will see and fear;
  they will laugh at you, saying,
⁷'Here now is the one
  who did not make God his stronghold
  but trusted in his great wealth
  and grew strong by destroying others!'

⁸But I am like an olive tree
  flourishing in the house of God;

ᵃ 17 Or *The sacrifices of God are*   ᵇ Title: Probably a literary or musical term   ᶜ 3 The Hebrew has *Selah* (a word of uncertain meaning) here and at the end of verse 5.

*52:1-9 is numbered 52:3-11 in Hebrew texts.

> **IN OTHER WORDS**
>
> ### Praise
> Psalms 52:9
>
> 'Praise' means 'to express admiration', to show how wonderful and fantastic something or someone is. We can praise God through songs, words that we say, things that we do and through the way we live our lives.

I trust in God's unfailing love
    for ever and ever.
9 For what you have done I will always praise you
    in the presence of your faithful people.
And I will hope in your name,
    for your name is good.

Psalm 53

For the director of music. According to mahalath.^{a} A maskil^b of David.

*1 Fools say in their hearts,
    'There is no God.'
They are corrupt, and their ways are vile;
    there is no-one who does good.

2 God looks down from heaven
    on the human race
to see if there are any who understand,
    any who seek God.
3 Everyone has turned away, all have become corrupt;
    there is no-one who does good,
    not even one.

4 Do all these evildoers know nothing?

They devour my people as though eating bread;
    they never call on God.
5 But there they are, overwhelmed with dread,
    where there was nothing to dread.

God scattered the bones of those who attacked you;
    you put them to shame, for God despised them.

6 Oh, that salvation for Israel would come out of Zion!
When God restores his people,
    let Jacob rejoice and Israel be glad!

Psalm 54

For the director of music. With stringed instruments. A maskil^c of David. When the Ziphites had gone to Saul and said, 'Is not David hiding among us?'

*1 Save me, O God, by your name;
    vindicate me by your might.
2 Hear my prayer, O God;
    listen to the words of my mouth.

3 Arrogant foes are attacking me;
    ruthless people seek my life—
    people without regard for God.^{d}

4 Surely God is my help;
    the Lord is the one who sustains me.

5 Let evil recoil on those who slander me;
    in your faithfulness destroy them.

6 I will sacrifice a freewill offering to you;
    I will praise your name, LORD, for it is good.
7 You have delivered me from all my troubles,
    and my eyes have looked in triumph on my foes.

Psalm 55

For the director of music. With stringed instruments. A maskil^e of David.

*1 Listen to my prayer, O God,
    do not ignore my plea;
2   hear me and answer me.

My thoughts trouble me and I am distraught
3   because of what my enemy is saying,
    because of the threats of the wicked;
for they bring down suffering on me
    and assail me in their anger.

---

^{a} Title: Probably a musical term ^{b} Title: Probably a literary or musical term ^{c} Title: Probably a literary or musical term ^{d} 3 The Hebrew has *Selah* (a word of uncertain meaning) here. ^{e} Title: Probably a literary or musical term

* 53:1-6 is numbered 53:2-7 in Hebrew texts.   * 54:1-7 is numbered 54:3-9 in Hebrew texts.   * 55:1-23 is numbered 55:2-24 in Hebrew texts.

⁴My heart is in anguish within me;
   the terrors of death have fallen on me.
⁵Fear and trembling have beset me;
   horror has overwhelmed me.
⁶I said, 'Oh, that I had the wings of a dove!
   I would fly away and be at rest.
⁷I would flee far away
   and stay in the desert[a];
⁸I would hurry to my place of shelter,
   far from the tempest and storm.'

⁹Lord, confuse the wicked, confound their words,
   for I see violence and strife in the city.
¹⁰Day and night they prowl about on its walls;
   malice and abuse are within it.
¹¹Destructive forces are at work in the city;
   threats and lies never leave its streets.

¹²If an enemy were insulting me,
   I could endure it;
  if a foe were rising against me,
   I could hide.
¹³But it is you, one like myself,
   my companion, my close friend,
¹⁴with whom I once enjoyed sweet fellowship
   at the house of God,
  as we walked about
   among the worshippers.

¹⁵Let death take my enemies by surprise;
   let them go down alive to the realm of the dead,
  for evil finds lodging among them.

¹⁶As for me, I call to God,
   and the LORD saves me.
¹⁷Evening, morning and noon
   I cry out in distress,
   and he hears my voice.
¹⁸He rescues me unharmed
   from the battle waged against me,
   even though many oppose me.
¹⁹God, who is enthroned from of old,
   who does not change—
  he will hear them and humble them,
   because they have no fear of God.

²⁰My companion attacks his friends;
   he violates his covenant.
²¹His talk is smooth as butter,
   yet war is in his heart;
  his words are more soothing than oil,
   yet they are drawn swords.

²²Cast your cares on the LORD
   and he will sustain you;
  he will never let
   the righteous be shaken.
²³But you, God, will bring down the wicked
   into the pit of decay;
  the bloodthirsty and deceitful
   will not live out half their days.

But as for me, I trust in you.

Psalm 56

For the director of music. To the tune of 'A Dove on Distant Oaks'. Of David. A miktam.[b] When the Philistines had seized him in Gath.

*¹Be merciful to me, my God,
   for my enemies are in hot pursuit;
   all day long they press their attack.
²My adversaries pursue me all day long;
   in their pride many are attacking me.

³When I am afraid, I put my trust in you.
⁴ In God, whose word I praise—
  in God I trust and am not afraid.
   What can mere mortals do to me?

⁵All day long they twist my words;
   all their schemes are for my ruin.
⁶They conspire, they lurk,
   they watch my steps,
   hoping to take my life.
⁷Because of their wickedness do not[c] let them escape;
   in your anger, God, bring the nations down.

⁸Record my misery;
   list my tears on your scroll[d]—
   are they not in your record?
⁹Then my enemies will turn back
   when I call for help.
  By this I will know that God is for me.
¹⁰In God, whose word I praise,
   in the LORD, whose word I praise—

---

[a] 7 The Hebrew has *Selah* (a word of uncertain meaning) here and in the middle of verse 19.   [b] Title: Probably a literary or musical term   [c] 7 Probable reading of the original Hebrew text; Masoretic Text does not have *do not*.   [d] 8 Or *misery; I put my tears in your wineskin*

*56:1-13 is numbered 56:2-14 in Hebrew texts.

¹¹in God I trust and am not afraid.
What can mere human beings do to me?

¹²I am under vows to you, my God;
I will present my thank-offerings to you.
¹³For you have delivered me from death
and my feet from stumbling,
that I may walk before God
in the light of life.

Psalm 57

For the director of music. To the tune of 'Do Not Destroy'. Of David. A miktam.[a]
When he had fled from Saul into the cave.

*¹Have mercy on me, my God, have mercy on me,
for in you I take refuge.
I will take refuge in the shadow of your wings
until the disaster has passed.

²I cry out to God Most High,
to God, who vindicates me.
³He sends from heaven and saves me,
rebuking those who hotly pursue me—[b]
God sends forth his love and his faithfulness.

⁴I am in the midst of lions;
I am forced to dwell among man-eating beasts,
whose teeth are spears and arrows,
whose tongues are sharp swords.

⁵Be exalted, O God, above the heavens;
let your glory be over all the earth.

⁶They spread a net for my feet—
I was bowed down in distress.
They dug a pit in my path—
but they have fallen into it themselves.

⁷My heart, O God, is steadfast,
my heart is steadfast;
I will sing and make music.
⁸Awake, my soul!
Awake, harp and lyre!
I will awaken the dawn.

⁹I will praise you, Lord, among the nations;
I will sing of you among the peoples.
¹⁰For great is your love, reaching to the heavens;
your faithfulness reaches to the skies.

¹¹Be exalted, O God, above the heavens;
let your glory be over all the earth.

Psalm 58

For the director of music. To the tune of 'Do Not Destroy'. Of David. A miktam.[c]

*¹Do you rulers indeed speak justly?
Do you judge people with equity?
²No, in your heart you devise injustice,
and your hands mete out violence on the earth.

³Even from birth the wicked go astray;
from the womb they are wayward, spreading lies.
⁴Their venom is like the venom of a snake,
like that of a cobra that has stopped its ears,
⁵that will not heed the tune of the charmer,
however skilful the enchanter may be.

⁶Break the teeth in their mouths, O God;
LORD, tear out the fangs of those lions!
⁷Let them vanish like water that flows away;
when they draw the bow, let their arrows fall short.
⁸May they be like a slug that melts away as it moves along,
like a stillborn child that never sees the sun.

⁹Before your pots can feel the heat of the thorns—
whether they be green or dry—the wicked will be swept away.[d]
¹⁰The righteous will be glad when they are avenged,
when they dip their feet in the blood of the wicked.
¹¹Then people will say,
'Surely the righteous still are rewarded;
surely there is a God who judges the earth.'

---

[a] Title: Probably a literary or musical term   [b] 3 The Hebrew has *Selah* (a word of uncertain meaning) here and at the end of verse 6.   [c] Title: Probably a literary or musical term   [d] 9 The meaning of the Hebrew for this verse is uncertain.

* 57:1-11 is numbered 57:2-12 in Hebrew texts.   * 58:1-11 is numbered 58:2-12 in Hebrew texts.

Psalm 59

For the director of music. To the tune of 'Do Not Destroy'. Of David. A miktam.[a] When Saul had sent men to watch David's house in order to kill him.

*1 Deliver me from my enemies, O God;
   be my fortress against those who are attacking me.
2 Deliver me from evildoers
   and save me from those who are after my blood.

3 See how they lie in wait for me!
   Powerful people conspire against me
   for no offence or sin of mine, LORD.
4 I have done no wrong, yet they are ready to attack me.
   Arise to help me; look on my plight!
5 You, LORD God Almighty,
   you who are the God of Israel,
   rouse yourself to punish all the nations;
   show no mercy to wicked traitors.[b]

6 They return at evening,
   snarling like dogs,
   and prowl about the city.
7 See what they spew from their mouths—
   the words from their lips are sharp as swords,
   and they think, 'Who can hear us?'
8 But you laugh at them, LORD;
   you scoff at all those nations.

9 You are my strength, I watch for you;
   you, God, are my fortress,
10 my God on whom I can rely.

God will go before me
   and will let me gloat over those who slander me.
11 But do not kill them, Lord our shield,[c]
   or my people will forget.
In your might uproot them
   and bring them down.
12 For the sins of their mouths,
   for the words of their lips,
   let them be caught in their pride.
For the curses and lies they utter,
13   consume them in wrath,
     consume them till they are no more.
Then it will be known to the ends of the earth
   that God rules over Jacob.

14 They return at evening,
   snarling like dogs,
   and prowl about the city.
15 They wander about for food
   and howl if not satisfied.
16 But I will sing of your strength,
   in the morning I will sing of your love;
for you are my fortress,
   my refuge in times of trouble.

17 You are my strength, I sing praise to you;
   you, God, are my fortress,
   my God on whom I can rely.

Psalm 60

For the director of music. To the tune of 'The Lily of the Covenant'. A miktam[d] of David. For teaching. When he fought Aram Naharaim[e] and Aram Zobah,[f] and when Joab returned and struck down twelve thousand Edomites in the Valley of Salt.

*1 You have rejected us, God, and burst upon us;
   you have been angry—now restore us!
2 You have shaken the land and torn it open;
   mend its fractures, for it is quaking.
3 You have shown your people desperate times;
   you have given us wine that makes us stagger.
4 But for those who fear you, you have raised a banner
   to be unfurled against the bow.[g]

5 Save us and help us with your right hand,
   that those you love may be delivered.
6 God has spoken from his sanctuary:
   'In triumph I will parcel out Shechem
   and measure off the Valley of Sukkoth.
7 Gilead is mine, and Manasseh is mine;
   Ephraim is my helmet,
   Judah is my sceptre.

---

[a] Title: Probably a literary or musical term [b] 5 The Hebrew has *Selah* (a word of uncertain meaning) here and at the end of verse 13. [c] 11 Or *sovereign* [d] Title: Probably a literary or musical term [e] Title: That is, Arameans of North-west Mesopotamia [f] Title: That is, Arameans of central Syria [g] 4 The Hebrew has *Selah* (a word of uncertain meaning) here.

* 59:1-17 is numbered 59:2-18 in Hebrew texts.   * 60:1-12 is numbered 60:3-14 in Hebrew texts.

⁸Moab is my washbasin,
  on Edom I toss my sandal;
  over Philistia I shout in triumph.'

⁹Who will bring me to the fortified city?
  Who will lead me to Edom?
¹⁰Is it not you, God, you who have now rejected us
  and no longer go out with our armies?
¹¹Give us aid against the enemy,
  for human help is worthless.
¹²With God we shall gain the victory,
  and he will trample down our enemies.

Psalm 61

For the director of music. With stringed instruments. Of David.

*¹Hear my cry, O God;
  listen to my prayer.

²From the ends of the earth I call to you,
  I call as my heart grows faint;
  lead me to the rock that is higher than I.
³For you have been my refuge,
  a strong tower against the foe.

⁴I long to dwell in your tent for ever
  and take refuge in the shelter of your wings.ᵃ
⁵For you, God, have heard my vows;
  you have given me the heritage of those who fear your name.

⁶Increase the days of the king's life,
  his years for many generations.
⁷May he be enthroned in God's presence for ever;
  appoint your love and faithfulness to protect him.

⁸Then I will ever sing in praise of your name
  and fulfil my vows day after day.

Psalm 62

For the director of music. For Jeduthun. A psalm of David.

*¹Truly my soul finds rest in God;
  my salvation comes from him.

> **IN OTHER WORDS**
>
> **Soul**
> **Psalms 62:1**
> The word 'soul' refers to your inner life, the place from which your emotions come and which is the centre of your personality. It is the essence of who you are.

²Truly he is my rock and my salvation;
  he is my fortress, I shall never be shaken.

³How long will you assault me?
  Would all of you throw me down—
  this leaning wall, this tottering fence?
⁴Surely they intend to topple me from my lofty place;
  they take delight in lies.
With their mouths they bless,
  but in their hearts they curse.ᵇ

⁵Yes, my soul, find rest in God;
  my hope comes from him.
⁶Truly he is my rock and my salvation;
  he is my fortress, I shall not be shaken.
⁷My salvation and my honour depend on God;ᶜ
  he is my mighty rock, my refuge.
⁸Trust in him at all times, you people;
  pour out your hearts to him,
  for God is our refuge.

⁹Surely the lowborn are but a breath,
  the highborn are but a lie.
If weighed on a balance, they are nothing;
  together they are only a breath.
¹⁰Do not trust in extortion
  or put vain hope in stolen goods;
  though your riches increase,
  do not set your heart on them.

¹¹One thing God has spoken,
  two things I have heard:
'Power belongs to you, God,
¹² and with you, Lord, is unfailing love';
  and, 'You reward everyone
  according to what they have done.'

ᵃ 4 The Hebrew has *Selah* (a word of uncertain meaning) here.   ᵇ 4 The Hebrew has *Selah* (a word of uncertain meaning) here and at the end of verse 8.   ᶜ 7 Or *I God Most High is my salvation and my honour*

* 61:1-8 is numbered 61:2-9 in Hebrew texts.   * 62:1-12 is numbered 62:2-13 in Hebrew texts.

Psalm 63

A psalm of David. When he was in the Desert of Judah.

*1You, God, are my God,
   earnestly I seek you;
 I thirst for you,
   my whole being longs for you,
 in a dry and parched land
   where there is no water.

2I have seen you in the sanctuary
   and beheld your power and your glory.
3Because your love is better than life,
   my lips will glorify you.
4I will praise you as long as I live,
   and in your name I will lift up my hands.
5I will be satisfied as with the richest of foods;
   with singing lips my mouth will praise you.

6On my bed I remember you;
   I think of you through the watches of the night.
7Because you are my help,
   I sing in the shadow of your wings.
8I cling to you;
   your right hand upholds me.

9Those who seek my life will be destroyed;
   they will go down to the depths of the earth.
10They will be given over to the sword
   and become food for jackals.

11But the king will rejoice in God;
   all who swear by God will glory in him,
   while the mouths of liars will be silenced.

Psalm 64

For the director of music. A psalm of David.

*1Hear me, my God, as I voice my complaint;
   protect my life from the threat of the enemy.

2Hide me from the conspiracy of the wicked,
   from the plots of evildoers.
3They sharpen their tongues like swords
   and aim cruel words like deadly arrows.
4They shoot from ambush at the innocent;
   they shoot suddenly, without fear.

5They encourage each other in evil plans,
   they talk about hiding their snares;
   they say, 'Who will see it?'*a*
6They plot injustice and say,
   'We have devised a perfect plan!'
   Surely the human mind and heart are cunning.

7But God will shoot them with his arrows;
   they will suddenly be struck down.
8He will turn their own tongues against them
   and bring them to ruin;
   all who see them will shake their heads in scorn.

9All people will fear;
   they will proclaim the works of God
   and ponder what he has done.

10The righteous will rejoice in the LORD
   and take refuge in him;
   all the upright in heart will glory in him!

Psalm 65

For the director of music. A psalm of David. A song.

*1Praise awaits*b* you, our God, in Zion;
   to you our vows will be fulfilled.
2You who answer prayer,
   to you all people will come.
3When we were overwhelmed by sins,
   you forgave*c* our transgressions.
4Blessed are those you choose
   and bring near to live in your courts!
 We are filled with the good things of your house,
   of your holy temple.

5You answer us with awesome and righteous deeds,
   God our Saviour,
 the hope of all the ends of the earth
   and of the farthest seas,

---

a 5 Or *us*   *b* 1 Or *befits*; the meaning of the Hebrew for this word is uncertain.   *c* 3 Or *made atonement for*

* 63:1-11 is numbered 63:2-12 in Hebrew texts.   * 64:1-10 is numbered 64:2-11 in Hebrew texts.   * 65:1-13 is numbered 65:2-14 in Hebrew texts.

⁶who formed the mountains by your power,
   having armed yourself with strength,
⁷who stilled the roaring of the seas,
   the roaring of their waves,
   and the turmoil of the nations.
⁸The whole earth is filled with awe at your wonders;
   where morning dawns, where evening fades,
   you call forth songs of joy.

⁹You care for the land and water it;
   you enrich it abundantly.
The streams of God are filled with water
   to provide the people with corn,
   for so you have ordained it.ᵃ
¹⁰You drench its furrows and level its ridges;
   you soften it with showers and bless its crops.
¹¹You crown the year with your bounty,
   and your carts overflow with abundance.
¹²The grasslands of the wilderness overflow;
   the hills are clothed with gladness.
¹³The meadows are covered with flocks
   and the valleys are mantled with corn;
   they shout for joy and sing.

Psalm 66

For the director of music. A song. A psalm.

¹ Shout for joy to God, all the earth!
²   Sing the glory of his name;
   make his praise glorious.
³Say to God, 'How awesome are your deeds!
   So great is your power
   that your enemies cringe before you.
⁴All the earth bows down to you;
   they sing praise to you,
   they sing the praises of your name.'ᵇ

⁵Come and see what God has done,
   his awesome deeds for humankind!
⁶He turned the sea into dry land,
   they passed through the waters on foot—
   come, let us rejoice in him.

⁷He rules for ever by his power,
   his eyes watch the nations—
   let not the rebellious rise up against him.

⁸Praise our God, all peoples,
   let the sound of his praise be heard;
⁹he has preserved our lives
   and kept our feet from slipping.
¹⁰For you, God, tested us;
   you refined us like silver.
¹¹You brought us into prison
   and laid burdens on our backs.
¹²You let people ride over our heads;
   we went through fire and water,
   but you brought us to a place of abundance.

¹³I will come to your temple with burnt offerings
   and fulfil my vows to you—
¹⁴vows my lips promised and my mouth spoke
   when I was in trouble.
¹⁵I will sacrifice fat animals to you
   and an offering of rams;
   I will offer bulls and goats.

¹⁶Come and hear, all you who fear God;
   let me tell you what he has done for me.
¹⁷I cried out to him with my mouth;
   his praise was on my tongue.
¹⁸If I had cherished sin in my heart,
   the Lord would not have listened;
¹⁹but God has surely listened
   and has heard my prayer.
²⁰Praise be to God,
   who has not rejected my prayer
   or withheld his love from me!

Psalm 67

For the director of music. With stringed instruments. A psalm. A song.

*¹May God be gracious to us and bless us
   and make his face shine on us—ᶜ
²so that your ways may be known on earth,
   your salvation among all nations.

³May the peoples praise you, God;
   may all the peoples praise you.

ᵃ 9 Or *for that is how you prepare the land*   ᵇ 4 The Hebrew has *Selah* (a word of uncertain meaning) here and at the end of verses 7 and 15.   ᶜ 1 The Hebrew has *Selah* (a word of uncertain meaning) here and at the end of verse 4.

* 67:1-7 is numbered 67:2-8 in Hebrew texts.

⁴May the nations be glad and sing for joy,
　for you rule the peoples with equity
　and guide the nations of the earth.
⁵May the peoples praise you, God;
　may all the peoples praise you.

⁶The land yields its harvest;
　God, our God, blesses us.
⁷May God bless us still,
　so that all the ends of the earth will fear him.

Psalm 68

*For the director of music. Of David.
A psalm. A song.**

*¹May God arise, may his enemies be scattered;
　may his foes flee before him.
²May you blow them away like smoke—
　as wax melts before the fire,
　may the wicked perish before God.
³But may the righteous be glad
　and rejoice before God;
　may they be happy and joyful.

⁴Sing to God, sing in praise of his name,
　extol him who rides on the clouds*ᵃ*;
　rejoice before him—his name is the LORD.

⁵A father to the fatherless, a defender of widows,
　is God in his holy dwelling.
⁶God sets the lonely in families,*ᵇ*
　he leads out the prisoners with singing;
　but the rebellious live in a sun-scorched land.

⁷When you, God, went out before your people,
　when you marched through the wilderness,*ᶜ*
⁸the earth shook, the heavens poured down rain,
　before God, the One of Sinai,
　before God, the God of Israel.
⁹You gave abundant showers, O God;
　you refreshed your weary inheritance.
¹⁰Your people settled in it,
　and from your bounty, God, you provided for the poor.

¹¹The Lord announced the word,
　and great was the company of those who proclaimed it:
¹²'Kings and armies flee in haste;
　every household shares in the plunder.
¹³Even while you sleep among the sheepfolds,*ᵈ*
　the wings of my dove are sheathed with silver,
　its feathers with shining gold.'
¹⁴When the Almighty*ᵉ* scattered the kings in the land,
　it was like snow fallen on Mount Zalmon.

¹⁵Mount Bashan, majestic mountain,
　Mount Bashan, rugged mountain,
¹⁶why gaze in envy, you rugged mountain,
　at the mountain where God chooses to reign,
　where the LORD himself will dwell for ever?
¹⁷The chariots of God are tens of thousands
　and thousands of thousands;
　the Lord has come from Sinai into his sanctuary.*ᶠ*

making Connections

Riding on the clouds
Psalms 68:4

The Canaanites had a storm god called Baal who they believed brought rain to make their crops grow. This psalm recognises that God has power over the weather; he is the one who 'rides the clouds' or, in other words, brings much-needed rain.

---

*ᵃ*4 Or *name, I prepare the way for him who rides through the deserts*　*ᵇ*6 Or *the desolate in a homeland*　*ᶜ*7 The Hebrew has *Selah* (a word of uncertain meaning) here and at the end of verses 19 and 32.　*ᵈ*13 Or *the campfires;* or *the saddlebags*　*ᵉ*14 Hebrew *Shaddai*　*ᶠ*17 Probable reading of the original Hebrew text; Masoretic Text *Lord is among them at Sinai in holiness*

* 68:1-35 is numbered 68:2-36 in Hebrew texts.　　* 68:1-35 is numbered 68:2-36 in Hebrew texts.

18When you ascended on high,
  you took many captives;
  you received gifts from people,
  even from^a the rebellious—
    that you,^{b} LORD God, might dwell
      there.

19Praise be to the Lord, to God our Saviour,
  who daily bears our burdens.
20Our God is a God who saves;
  from the Sovereign LORD comes escape
    from death.
21Surely God will crush the heads of his
    enemies,
  the hairy crowns of those who go on in
    their sins.
22The Lord says, 'I will bring them from
    Bashan;
  I will bring them from the depths of the
    sea,
23that your feet may wade in the blood of
    your foes,
  while the tongues of your dogs have
    their share.'

24Your procession, God, has come into
    view,
  the procession of my God and King
    into the sanctuary.
25In front are the singers, after them the
    musicians;
  with them are the young women
    playing the tambourines.
26Praise God in the great congregation;
  praise the LORD in the assembly of
    Israel.
27There is the little tribe of Benjamin,
    leading them,
  there the great throng of Judah's
    princes,
  and there the princes of Zebulun and of
    Naphtali.

28Summon your power, God;^{c}
  show us your strength, our God, as you
    have done before.
29Because of your temple at Jerusalem
  kings will bring you gifts.
30Rebuke the beast among the reeds,
  the herd of bulls among the calves of
    the nations.

Humbled, may it bring bars of silver.
  Scatter the nations who delight in war.
31Envoys will come from Egypt;
  Cush^d will submit herself to God.

32Sing to God, you kingdoms of the earth,
  sing praise to the Lord,
33to him who rides the ancient skies above,
  who thunders with mighty voice.
34Proclaim the power of God,
  whose majesty is over Israel,
  whose power is in the skies.
35You, God, are awesome in your
    sanctuary;
  the God of Israel gives power and
    strength to his people.

Praise be to God!

Psalm 69

*For the director of music. To the tune of
'Lilies'. Of David.*

*1Save me, O God,
  for the waters have come up to my
    neck.
2I sink in the miry depths,
  where there is no foothold.
I have come into the deep waters;
  the floods engulf me.
3I am worn out calling for help;
  my throat is parched.
My eyes fail,
  looking for my God.
4Those who hate me without reason
  outnumber the hairs of my head;
many are my enemies without cause,
  those who seek to destroy me.
I am forced to restore
  what I did not steal.

5You, God, know my folly;
  my guilt is not hidden from you.

6Lord, the LORD Almighty,
  may those who hope in you
    not be disgraced because of me;
God of Israel,
  may those who seek you
    not be put to shame because of me.
7For I endure scorn for your sake,
  and shame covers my face.

---

^{a} 18 Or *gifts for people, / even* ^{b} 18 Or *they* ^{c} 28 Many Hebrew manuscripts, Septuagint and Syriac; most Hebrew manuscripts *Your God has summoned power for you* ^{d} 31 That is, the upper Nile region

* 69:1-36 is numbered 69:2-37 in Hebrew texts.

8 I am a foreigner to my own family,
  a stranger to my own mother's children;
9 for zeal for your house consumes me,
  and the insults of those who insult you fall on me.
10 When I weep and fast,
  I must endure scorn;
11 when I put on sackcloth,
  people make sport of me.
12 Those who sit at the gate mock me,
  and I am the song of the drunkards.

13 But I pray to you, LORD,
  in the time of your favour;
 in your great love, O God,
  answer me with your sure salvation.
14 Rescue me from the mire,
  do not let me sink;
 deliver me from those who hate me,
  from the deep waters.
15 Do not let the floodwaters engulf me
  or the depths swallow me up
  or the pit close its mouth over me.

16 Answer me, LORD, out of the goodness of your love;
  in your great mercy turn to me.
17 Do not hide your face from your servant;
  answer me quickly, for I am in trouble.
18 Come near and rescue me;
  redeem me because of my foes.

19 You know how I am scorned, disgraced and shamed;
  all my enemies are before you.
20 Scorn has broken my heart
  and has left me helpless;
 I looked for sympathy, but there was none,
  for comforters, but I found none.
21 They put gall in my food
  and gave me vinegar for my thirst.

22 May the table set before them become a snare;
  may it become retribution and^a a trap.
23 May their eyes be darkened so that they cannot see,
  and their backs be bent for ever.
24 Pour out your wrath on them;
  let your fierce anger overtake them.

25 May their place be deserted;
  let there be no-one to dwell in their tents.
26 For they persecute those you wound
  and talk about the pain of those you hurt.
27 Charge them with crime upon crime;
  do not let them share in your salvation.
28 May they be blotted out of the book of life
  and not be listed with the righteous.

29 But as for me, afflicted and in pain—
  may your salvation, God, protect me.

30 I will praise God's name in song
  and glorify him with thanksgiving.
31 This will please the LORD more than an ox,
  more than a bull with its horns and hooves.
32 The poor will see and be glad—
  you who seek God, may your hearts live!
33 The LORD hears the needy
  and does not despise his captive people.

34 Let heaven and earth praise him,
  the seas and all that move in them,
35 for God will save Zion
  and rebuild the cities of Judah.
 Then people will settle there and possess it;
36 the children of his servants will inherit it,
  and those who love his name will dwell there.

Psalm 70

For the director of music. Of David. A petition.

*1 Hasten, O God, to save me;
  come quickly, LORD, to help me.

2 May those who seek my life
  be put to shame and confusion;
 may all who desire my ruin
  be turned back in disgrace.
3 May those who say to me, 'Aha! Aha!'
  turn back because of their shame.
4 But may all who seek you
  rejoice and be glad in you;

---

^{a} 22 Or *snare / and their fellowship become*

* 70:1-5 is numbered 70:2-6 in Hebrew texts.

may those who long for your saving help
always say,
'The LORD is great!'

⁵But as for me, I am poor and needy;
come quickly to me, O God.
You are my help and my deliverer;
LORD, do not delay.

Psalm 71

¹In you, LORD, I have taken refuge;
let me never be put to shame.
²In your righteousness, rescue me and
deliver me;
turn your ear to me and save me.
³Be my rock of refuge,
to which I can always go;
give the command to save me,
for you are my rock and my fortress.
⁴Deliver me, my God, from the hand of the
wicked,
from the grasp of those who are evil
and cruel.

⁵For you have been my hope, Sovereign
LORD,
my confidence since my youth.
⁶From my birth I have relied on you;
you brought me forth from my
mother's womb.
I will ever praise you.
⁷I have become like a portent to many,
but you are my strong refuge.
⁸My mouth is filled with your praise,
declaring your splendour all day long.

⁹Do not cast me away when I am old;
do not forsake me when my strength is
gone.
¹⁰For my enemies speak against me;
those who wait to kill me conspire
together.
¹¹They say, 'God has forsaken him;
pursue him and seize him,
for no-one will rescue him.'
¹²Do not be far from me, my God;
come quickly, God, to help me.
¹³May my accusers perish in shame;
may those who want to harm me
be covered with scorn and disgrace.

¹⁴As for me, I shall always have hope;
I will praise you more and more.

¹⁵My mouth will tell of your righteous
deeds,
of your saving acts all day long—
though I know not how to relate them
all.
¹⁶I will come and proclaim your mighty
acts, Sovereign LORD;
I will proclaim your righteous deeds,
yours alone.
¹⁷Since my youth, God, you have taught
me,
and to this day I declare your
marvellous deeds.
¹⁸Even when I am old and grey,
do not forsake me, my God,
till I declare your power to the next
generation,
your mighty acts to all who are to
come.

¹⁹Your righteousness, God, reaches to the
skies,
you who have done great things.
Who is like you, God?
²⁰Though you have made me see troubles,
many and bitter,
you will restore my life again;
from the depths of the earth
you will again bring me up.
²¹You will increase my honour
and comfort me once more.

²²I will praise you with the harp
for your faithfulness, my God;
I will sing praise to you with the lyre,
Holy One of Israel.

IN OTHER WORDS

Hope
Psalms 71:5

We often use the word 'hope' to express a vague wish that things will turn out right: 'I hope it doesn't rain tomorrow', or 'I hope the bus arrives soon.' But the hope that is talked about in the Bible is a confident expectation that God will act. Hope enables you to keep going even in the face of hardship and doubt.

²³My lips will shout for joy
    when I sing praise to you—
  I, whom you have redeemed.
²⁴My tongue will tell of your righteous acts
    all day long,
  for those who wanted to harm me
    have been put to shame and confusion.

Psalm 72

Of Solomon.

¹Endow the king with your justice, O God,
    the royal son with your righteousness.
²May he judge your people in righteousness,
    your afflicted ones with justice.

³May the mountains bring prosperity to the people,
    the hills the fruit of righteousness.
⁴May he defend the afflicted among the people
    and save the children of the needy;
    may he crush the oppressor.
⁵May he endure[a] as long as the sun,
    as long as the moon, through all generations.
⁶May he be like rain falling on a mown field,
    like showers watering the earth.
⁷In his days may the righteous flourish
    and prosperity abound till the moon is no more.

⁸May he rule from sea to sea
    and from the River[b] to the ends of the earth.
⁹May the desert tribes bow before him
    and his enemies lick the dust.
¹⁰May the kings of Tarshish and of distant shores
    bring tribute to him.
  May the kings of Sheba and Seba
    present him with gifts.
¹¹May all kings bow down to him
    and all nations serve him.

¹²For he will deliver the needy who cry out,
    the afflicted who have no-one to help.
¹³He will take pity on the weak and the needy
    and save the needy from death.
¹⁴He will rescue them from oppression and violence,
    for precious is their blood in his sight.

¹⁵Long may he live!
    May gold from Sheba be given to him.
  May people ever pray for him
    and bless him all day long.
¹⁶May corn abound throughout the land;
    on the tops of the hills may it sway.
  May the crops flourish like Lebanon
    and thrive[c] like the grass of the field.
¹⁷May his name endure for ever;
    may it continue as long as the sun.

  Then all nations will be blessed through him,[d]
    and they will call him blessed.

¹⁸Praise be to the LORD God, the God of Israel,
    who alone does marvellous deeds.
¹⁹Praise be to his glorious name for ever;
    may the whole earth be filled with his glory.
        Amen and Amen.

²⁰This concludes the prayers of David son of Jesse.

BOOK III

Psalms 73–89

Psalm 73

A psalm of Asaph.

¹Surely God is good to Israel,
    to those who are pure in heart.

²But as for me, my feet had almost slipped;
    I had nearly lost my foothold.
³For I envied the arrogant
    when I saw the prosperity of the wicked.

⁴They have no struggles;
    their bodies are healthy and strong.[e]
⁵They are free from common human burdens;
    they are not plagued by human ills.
⁶Therefore pride is their necklace;
    they clothe themselves with violence.

---

[a] 5 Septuagint; Hebrew *You will be feared* [b] 8 That is, the Euphrates [c] 16 Probable reading of the original Hebrew text; Masoretic Text *Lebanon, / from the city* [d] 17 Or *will use his name in blessings* (see Gen. 48:20) [e] 4 With a different word division of the Hebrew; Masoretic Text *struggles at their death; / their bodies are healthy*

7 From their callous hearts comes iniquity;[a]
  the evil conceits of their minds know
    no limits.
8 They scoff, and speak with malice;
  with arrogance they threaten
    oppression.
9 Their mouths lay claim to heaven,
  and their tongues take possession of
    the earth.
10 Therefore their people turn to them
  and drink up waters in abundance.[b]
11 They say, 'How would God know?
  Does the Most High know anything?'

12 This is what the wicked are like—
  always free of care, they go on amassing
    wealth.

13 Surely in vain I have kept my heart pure
  and have washed my hands in
    innocence.
14 All day long I have been afflicted,
  and every morning brings new
    punishments.

15 If I had spoken out like that,
  I would have betrayed your children.
16 When I tried to understand all this,
  it troubled me deeply
17 till I entered the sanctuary of God;
  then I understood their final destiny.

18 Surely you place them on slippery
    ground;
  you cast them down to ruin.
19 How suddenly are they destroyed,
  completely swept away by terrors!
20 They are like a dream when one awakes;
  when you arise, Lord,
  you will despise them as fantasies.

21 When my heart was grieved
  and my spirit embittered,
22 I was senseless and ignorant;
  I was a brute beast before you.

23 Yet I am always with you;
  you hold me by my right hand.
24 You guide me with your counsel,
  and afterwards you will take me into
    glory.
25 Whom have I in heaven but you?
  And earth has nothing I desire besides
    you.
26 My flesh and my heart may fail,
  but God is the strength of my heart
  and my portion for ever.

27 Those who are far from you will perish;
  you destroy all who are unfaithful to
    you.
28 But as for me, it is good to be near God.
  I have made the Sovereign LORD my
    refuge;
  I will tell of all your deeds.

Psalm 74

A maskil[c] of Asaph.

1 O God, why have you rejected us for ever?
  Why does your anger smoulder against
    the sheep of your pasture?
2 Remember the people you purchased
    long ago,
  the tribe of your inheritance, whom
    you redeemed—
  Mount Zion, where you dwelt.
3 Turn your steps towards these everlasting
    ruins,
  all this destruction the enemy has
    brought on the sanctuary.

4 Your foes roared in the place where you
    met with us;
  they set up their standards as signs.
5 They behaved like men wielding axes
  to cut through a thicket of trees.
6 They smashed all the carved panelling
  with their axes and hatchets.
7 They burned your sanctuary to the
    ground;
  they defiled the dwelling-place of your
    Name.
8 They said in their hearts, 'We will crush
    them completely!'
  They burned every place where God
    was worshipped in the land.

9 We are given no signs from God;
  no prophets are left,
  and none of us knows how long this
    will be.
10 How long will the enemy mock you, God?
  Will the foe revile your name for ever?

---

[a] 7 Syriac (see also Septuagint); Hebrew *Their eyes bulge with fat* [b] 10 The meaning of the Hebrew for this verse is uncertain. [c] Title: Probably a literary or musical term

11Why do you hold back your hand, your
   right hand?
  Take it from the folds of your garment
   and destroy them!

12But God is my King from long ago;
  he brings salvation on the earth.

13It was you who split open the sea by your
   power;
  you broke the heads of the monster in
   the waters.
14It was you who crushed the heads of
   Leviathan
  and gave it as food to the creatures of
   the desert.
15It was you who opened up springs and
   streams;
  you dried up the ever-flowing rivers.
16The day is yours, and yours also the night;
  you established the sun and moon.
17It was you who set all the boundaries of
   the earth;
  you made both summer and winter.

18Remember how the enemy has mocked
   you, LORD,
  how foolish people have reviled your
   name.
19Do not hand over the life of your dove to
   wild beasts;
  do not forget the lives of your afflicted
   people for ever.
20Have regard for your covenant,
  because haunts of violence fill the dark
   places of the land.
21Do not let the oppressed retreat in
   disgrace;
  may the poor and needy praise your
   name.
22Rise up, O God, and defend your cause;
  remember how fools mock you all day
   long.
23Do not ignore the clamour of your
   adversaries,
  the uproar of your enemies, which rises
   continually.

Psalm 75

*For the director of music. To the tune of
'Do Not Destroy'. A psalm of Asaph. A song.*

*1We praise you, God,
  we praise you, for your Name is near;
  people tell of your wonderful deeds.

2You say, 'I choose the appointed time;
  it is I who judge with equity.
3When the earth and all its people quake,
  it is I who hold its pillars firm.^{a}
4To the arrogant I say, "Boast no more,"
  and to the wicked, "Do not lift up your
   horns.^{b}
5Do not lift your horns against heaven;
  do not speak with outstretched neck."'

6No-one from the east or the west
  or from the desert can exalt themselves.
7It is God who judges:
  he brings one down, he exalts another.
8In the hand of the LORD is a cup
  full of foaming wine mixed with spices;
  he pours it out, and all the wicked of the
   earth
  drink it down to its very dregs.

9As for me, I will declare this for ever;
  I will sing praise to the God of Jacob,
10who says, 'I will cut off the horns of all the
   wicked,
  but the horns of the righteous shall be
   lifted up.'

Psalm 76

*For the director of music. With stringed
instruments. A psalm of Asaph. A song.*

*1God is renowned in Judah;
  in Israel his name is great.
2His tent is in Salem,
  his dwelling-place in Zion.
3There he broke the flashing arrows,
  the shields and the swords, the
   weapons of war.^{c}

4You are resplendent with light,
  more majestic than mountains rich
   with game.
5The valiant lie plundered,
  they sleep their last sleep;

---

^{a}3 The Hebrew has *Selah* (a word of uncertain meaning) here. ^{b}4 *Horns* here symbolise strength; also in verses 5 and 10. ^{c}3 The Hebrew has *Selah* (a word of uncertain meaning) here and at the end of verse 9.

*75:1-10 is numbered 75:2-11 in Hebrew texts. *76:1-12 is numbered 76:2-13 in Hebrew texts.

not one of the warriors
    can lift his hands.
⁶At your rebuke, God of Jacob,
    both horse and chariot lie still.

⁷It is you alone who are to be feared.
    Who can stand before you when you are angry?
⁸From heaven you pronounced judgment,
    and the land feared and was quiet—
⁹when you, God, rose up to judge,
    to save all the afflicted of the land.
¹⁰Surely your wrath against human beings brings you praise,
    and the survivors of your wrath are restrained.[a]

¹¹Make vows to the LORD your God and fulfil them;
    let all the neighbouring lands
    bring gifts to the One to be feared.
¹²He breaks the spirit of rulers;
    he is feared by the kings of the earth.

Psalm 77

For the director of music. For Jeduthun. Of Asaph. A psalm.

*¹I cried out to God for help;
    I cried out to God to hear me.
²When I was in distress, I sought the Lord;
    at night I stretched out untiring hands,
    and I would not be comforted.

³I remembered you, God, and I groaned;
    I meditated, and my spirit grew faint.[b]
⁴You kept my eyes from closing;
    I was too troubled to speak.
⁵I thought about the former days,
    the years of long ago;
⁶I remembered my songs in the night.
    My heart meditated and my spirit asked:

⁷'Will the Lord reject for ever?
    Will he never show his favour again?
⁸Has his unfailing love vanished for ever?
    Has his promise failed for all time?
⁹Has God forgotten to be merciful?
    Has he in anger withheld his compassion?'

IN OTHER WORDS

Miracle
Psalms 77:14

A miracle is something that doesn't conform to the normal laws of nature, like a healing or a dramatic weather change that has no ordinary explanation. God is into miracles; Jesus performed many miracles during his life (Mark 6:2), and so did his disciples once they had received the Holy Spirit.

¹⁰Then I thought, 'To this I will appeal:
    the years when the Most High stretched out his right hand.
¹¹I will remember the deeds of the LORD;
    yes, I will remember your miracles of long ago.
¹²I will consider all your works
    and meditate on all your mighty deeds.'

¹³Your ways, God, are holy.
    What god is as great as our God?
¹⁴You are the God who performs miracles;
    you display your power among the peoples.
¹⁵With your mighty arm you redeemed your people,
    the descendants of Jacob and Joseph.

¹⁶The waters saw you, God,
    the waters saw you and writhed;
    the very depths were convulsed.
¹⁷The clouds poured down water,
    the heavens resounded with thunder;
    your arrows flashed back and forth.
¹⁸Your thunder was heard in the whirlwind,
    your lightning lit up the world;
    the earth trembled and quaked.
¹⁹Your path led through the sea,
    your way through the mighty waters,
    though your footprints were not seen.

²⁰You led your people like a flock
    by the hand of Moses and Aaron.

---

[a] 10 Or *Surely human wrath brings you praise, I and with the remainder of wrath you arm yourself*   [b] 3 The Hebrew has *Selah* (a word of uncertain meaning) here and at the end of verses 9 and 15.

* 77:1-20 is numbered 77:2-21 in Hebrew texts.

Psalm 78

A maskil[a] of Asaph.

¹My people, hear my teaching;
   listen to the words of my mouth.
²I will open my mouth with a parable;
   I will teach you lessons from the past—
³things we have heard and known,
   things our ancestors have told us.
⁴We will not hide them from their descendants;
   we will tell the next generation
the praiseworthy deeds of the LORD,
   his power, and the wonders he has done.

⁵He decreed statutes for Jacob
   and established the law in Israel,
which he commanded our ancestors
   to teach their children,
⁶so that the next generation would know them,
   even the children yet to be born,
   and they in turn would tell their children.
⁷Then they would put their trust in God
   and would not forget his deeds
   but would keep his commands.
⁸They would not be like their ancestors—
   a stubborn and rebellious generation,
whose hearts were not loyal to God,
   whose spirits were not faithful to him.

⁹The men of Ephraim, though armed with bows,
   turned back on the day of battle;
¹⁰they did not keep God's covenant
   and refused to live by his law.
¹¹They forgot what he had done,
   the wonders he had shown them.
¹²He did miracles in the sight of their ancestors
   in the land of Egypt, in the region of Zoan.
¹³He divided the sea and led them through;
   he made the water stand up like a wall.
¹⁴He guided them with the cloud by day
   and with light from the fire all night.
¹⁵He split the rocks in the wilderness
   and gave them water as abundant as the seas;
¹⁶he brought streams out of a rocky crag
   and made water flow down like rivers.

¹⁷But they continued to sin against him,
   rebelling in the wilderness against the Most High.
¹⁸They wilfully put God to the test
   by demanding the food they craved.
¹⁹They spoke against God;
   they said, 'Can God really
   spread a table in the wilderness?
²⁰True, he struck the rock,
   and water gushed out,
   streams flowed abundantly,
but can he also give us bread?
   Can he supply meat for his people?'
²¹When the LORD heard them, he was furious;
   his fire broke out against Jacob,
   and his wrath rose against Israel,
²²for they did not believe in God
   or trust in his deliverance.
²³Yet he gave a command to the skies above
   and opened the doors of the heavens;
²⁴he rained down manna for the people to eat,
   he gave them the grain of heaven.
²⁵Human beings ate the bread of angels;
   he sent them all the food they could eat.
²⁶He let loose the east wind from the heavens
   and by his power made the south wind blow.
²⁷He rained meat down on them like dust,
   birds like sand on the seashore.
²⁸He made them come down inside their camp,
   all around their tents.
²⁹They ate till they were gorged—
   he had given them what they craved.
³⁰But before they turned from what they craved,
   even while the food was still in their mouths,
³¹God's anger rose against them;
   he put to death the sturdiest among them,
   cutting down the young men of Israel.

³²In spite of all this, they kept on sinning;
   in spite of his wonders, they did not believe.
³³So he ended their days in futility
   and their years in terror.

---
[a] Title: Probably a literary or musical term

34 Whenever God slew them, they would seek him;
   they eagerly turned to him again.
35 They remembered that God was their Rock,
   that God Most High was their Redeemer.
36 But then they would flatter him with their mouths,
   lying to him with their tongues;
37 their hearts were not loyal to him,
   they were not faithful to his covenant.
38 Yet he was merciful;
   he forgave their iniquities
   and did not destroy them.
 Time after time he restrained his anger
   and did not stir up his full wrath.
39 He remembered that they were but flesh,
   a passing breeze that does not return.

40 How often they rebelled against him in the wilderness
   and grieved him in the wasteland!
41 Again and again they put God to the test;
   they vexed the Holy One of Israel.
42 They did not remember his power—
   the day he redeemed them from the oppressor,
43 the day he displayed his signs in Egypt,
   his wonders in the region of Zoan.
44 He turned their river into blood;
   they could not drink from their streams.
45 He sent swarms of flies that devoured them,
   and frogs that devastated them.
46 He gave their crops to the grasshopper,
   their produce to the locust.
47 He destroyed their vines with hail
   and their sycamore-figs with sleet.
48 He gave over their cattle to the hail,
   their livestock to bolts of lightning.
49 He unleashed against them his hot anger,
   his wrath, indignation and hostility—
   a band of destroying angels.
50 He prepared a path for his anger;
   he did not spare them from death
   but gave them over to the plague.
51 He struck down all the firstborn of Egypt,
   the firstfruits of manhood in the tents of Ham.
52 But he brought his people out like a flock;
   he led them like sheep through the wilderness.
53 He guided them safely, so they were unafraid;
   but the sea engulfed their enemies.
54 And so he brought them to the border of his holy land,
   to the hill country his right hand had taken.
55 He drove out nations before them
   and allotted their lands to them as an inheritance;
   he settled the tribes of Israel in their homes.

56 But they put God to the test
   and rebelled against the Most High;
   they did not keep his statutes.
57 Like their ancestors they were disloyal and faithless,
   as unreliable as a faulty bow.
58 They angered him with their high places;
   they aroused his jealousy with their idols.
59 When God heard them, he was furious;
   he rejected Israel completely.
60 He abandoned the tabernacle of Shiloh,
   the tent he had set up among mortals.
61 He sent the ark of his might into captivity,
   his splendour into the hands of the enemy.
62 He gave his people over to the sword;
   he was furious with his inheritance.
63 Fire consumed their young men,
   and their young women had no wedding songs;
64 their priests were put to the sword,
   and their widows could not weep.

65 Then the Lord awoke as from sleep,
   as a warrior wakes from the stupor of wine.
66 He beat back his enemies;
   he put them to everlasting shame.
67 Then he rejected the tents of Joseph,
   he did not choose the tribe of Ephraim;
68 but he chose the tribe of Judah,
   Mount Zion, which he loved.
69 He built his sanctuary like the heights,
   like the earth that he established for ever.
70 He chose David his servant
   and took him from the sheepfolds;

⁷¹from tending the sheep he brought him
to be the shepherd of his people Jacob,
of Israel his inheritance.
⁷²And David shepherded them with
integrity of heart;
with skilful hands he led them.

Psalm 79

A psalm of Asaph.

¹O God, the nations have invaded your
inheritance;
they have defiled your holy temple,
they have reduced Jerusalem to rubble.
²They have left the dead bodies of your
servants
as food for the birds of the sky,
the flesh of your own people for the
wild animals.
³They have poured out blood like water
all around Jerusalem,
and there is no-one to bury the dead.
⁴We are objects of contempt to our
neighbours,
of scorn and derision to those around
us.

⁵How long, LORD? Will you be angry for
ever?
How long will your jealousy burn like
fire?
⁶Pour out your wrath on the nations
that do not acknowledge you,
on the kingdoms
that do not call on your name;
⁷for they have devoured Jacob
and devastated his homeland.

⁸Do not hold against us the sins of past
generations;
may your mercy come quickly to meet
us,
for we are in desperate need.
⁹Help us, God our Saviour,
for the glory of your name;
deliver us and forgive our sins
for your name's sake.
¹⁰Why should the nations say,
'Where is their God?'

Before our eyes, make known among the
nations

> ### Sign of the times
>
> **Seven**
> Psalms 79:12
> The number seven was a sacred number to the Israelites. It symbolised perfection or completion. So asking God to pay back reproach seven times over was a way of making sure that the neighbours got their full dose of punishment.

that you avenge the outpoured blood
of your servants.
¹¹May the groans of the prisoners come
before you;
with your strong arm preserve those
condemned to die.
¹²Pay back into the laps of our neighbours
seven times
the contempt they have hurled at you,
Lord.
¹³Then we your people, the sheep of your
pasture,
will praise you for ever;
from generation to generation
we will proclaim your praise.

Psalm 80

*For the director of music. To the tune of
'The Lilies of the Covenant'. Of Asaph.
A psalm.*

*¹Hear us, Shepherd of Israel,
you who lead Joseph like a flock.
You who sit enthroned between the
cherubim,
shine forth ²before Ephraim,
Benjamin and Manasseh.
Awaken your might;
come and save us.

³Restore us, O God;
make your face shine on us,
that we may be saved.

---

* 80:1-19 is numbered 80:2-20 in Hebrew texts.

⁴How long, LORD God Almighty,
　　will your anger smoulder
　　against the prayers of your people?
⁵You have fed them with the bread of tears;
　　you have made them drink tears by the bowlful.
⁶You have made us an object of derision[a] to our neighbours,
　　and our enemies mock us.

⁷Restore us, God Almighty;
　　make your face shine on us,
　　that we may be saved.

⁸You transplanted a vine from Egypt;
　　you drove out the nations and planted it.
⁹You cleared the ground for it,
　　and it took root and filled the land.
¹⁰The mountains were covered with its shade,
　　the mighty cedars with its branches.
¹¹Its branches reached as far as the Sea,[b]
　　its shoots as far as the River.[c]

¹²Why have you broken down its walls
　　so that all who pass by pick its grapes?
¹³Boars from the forest ravage it
　　and wild animals feed on it.
¹⁴Return to us, God Almighty!
　　Look down from heaven and see!
　Watch over this vine,
15　　the root your right hand has planted,
　　the son[d] you have raised up for yourself.

¹⁶Your vine is cut down, it is burned with fire;
　　at your rebuke your people perish.
¹⁷Let your hand rest on the man at your right hand,
　　the son of man you have raised up for yourself.
¹⁸Then we will not turn away from you;
　　revive us, and we will call on your name.

¹⁹Restore us, LORD God Almighty;
　　make your face shine on us,
　　that we may be saved.

Psalm 81

For the director of music. According to gittith.[e] Of Asaph.

*¹Sing for joy to God our strength;
　　shout aloud to the God of Jacob!
²Begin the music, strike the tambourine,
　　play the melodious harp and lyre.

³Sound the ram's horn at the New Moon,
　　and when the moon is full, on the day of our Feast;
⁴this is a decree for Israel,
　　an ordinance of the God of Jacob.
⁵When God went out against Egypt,
　　he established it as a statute for Joseph.

I heard an unknown voice say:

⁶'I removed the burden from their shoulders;
　　their hands were set free from the basket.
⁷In your distress you called and I rescued you,
　　I answered you out of a thundercloud;
　　I tested you at the waters of Meribah.[f]
⁸Hear me, my people, and I will warn you—
　　if you would only listen to me, Israel!
⁹You shall have no foreign god among you;
　　you shall not worship any god other than me.
¹⁰I am the LORD your God,
　　who brought you up out of Egypt.
Open wide your mouth and I will fill it.

¹¹'But my people would not listen to me;
　　Israel would not submit to me.
¹²So I gave them over to their stubborn hearts
　　to follow their own devices.

¹³'If my people would only listen to me,
　　if Israel would only follow my ways,
¹⁴how quickly I would subdue their enemies
　　and turn my hand against their foes!
¹⁵Those who hate the LORD would cringe before him,

---

a 6 Probable reading of the original Hebrew text; Masoretic Text *contention*　　*b* 11 Probably the Mediterranean　　*c* 11 That is, the Euphrates　　*d* 15 Or *branch*　　*e* Title: Probably a musical term　　*f* 7 The Hebrew has *Selah* (a word of uncertain meaning) here.

* 81:1-16 is numbered 81:2-17 in Hebrew texts.

and their punishment would last for
 ever.
16But you would be fed with the finest of
 wheat;
 with honey from the rock I would
 satisfy you.'

Psalm 82

A psalm of Asaph.

1God presides in the great assembly;
 he gives judgment among the 'gods':
2'How long will you[a] defend the unjust
 and show partiality to the wicked?[b]
3Defend the weak and the fatherless;
 uphold the cause of the poor and the
 oppressed.
4Rescue the weak and the needy;
 deliver them from the hand of the
 wicked.

5'The "gods" know nothing, they
 understand nothing.
 They walk about in darkness;
 all the foundations of the earth are
 shaken.

6'I said, "You are 'gods';
 you are all sons of the Most High."
7But you will die like mere mortals;
 you will fall like every other ruler.'

8Rise up, O God, judge the earth,
 for all the nations are your inheritance.

Psalm 83

A song. A psalm of Asaph.

*1O God, do not remain silent;
 do not turn a deaf ear,
 do not stand aloof, O God.
2See how your enemies growl,
 how your foes rear their heads.
3With cunning they conspire against your
 people;
 they plot against those you cherish.
4'Come,' they say, 'let us destroy them as a
 nation,
 so that Israel's name is remembered no
 more.'

5With one mind they plot together;
 they form an alliance against you—
6the tents of Edom and the Ishmaelites,
 of Moab and the Hagrites,
7Byblos, Ammon and Amalek,
 Philistia, with the people of Tyre.
8Even Assyria has joined them
 to reinforce Lot's descendants.[c]

9Do to them as you did to Midian,
 as you did to Sisera and Jabin at the
 River Kishon,
10who perished at Endor
 and became like dung on the ground.
11Make their nobles like Oreb and Zeeb,
 all their princes like Zebah and
 Zalmunna,
12who said, 'Let us take possession
 of the pasture-lands of God.'

13Make them like tumble-weed, my God,
 like chaff before the wind.
14As fire consumes the forest
 or a flame sets the mountains ablaze,
15so pursue them with your tempest
 and terrify them with your storm.
16Cover their faces with shame, LORD,
 so that they will seek your name.

17May they ever be ashamed and dismayed;
 may they perish in disgrace.
18Let them know that you, whose name is
 the LORD—
 that you alone are the Most High over
 all the earth.

Psalm 84

*For the director of music. According to
gittith.[d] Of the Sons of Korah. A psalm.*

*1How lovely is your dwelling-place,
 LORD Almighty!
2My soul yearns, even faints,
 for the courts of the LORD;
 my heart and my flesh cry out
 for the living God.
3Even the sparrow has found a home,
 and the swallow a nest for herself,
 where she may have her young—
 a place near your altar,
 LORD Almighty, my King and my God.

---

[a] 2 The Hebrew is plural.   [b] 2 The Hebrew has *Selah* (a word of uncertain meaning) here.   [c] 8 The Hebrew has *Selah* (a word of uncertain meaning) here.   [d] Title: Probably a musical term

* 83:1-18 is numbered 83:2-19 in Hebrew texts.   * 84:1-12 is numbered 84:2-13 in Hebrew texts.

Sign of the times

Doorkeeper
Psalms 84:10

A doorkeeper or porter guarded the entrance to a city, temple or a rich man's house to make sure the wrong people didn't get in. It was quite a lowly job, but the psalmist says he would take it just for the privilege of being in God's house.

⁴Blessed are those who dwell in your house;
    they are ever praising you.*ᵃ*

⁵Blessed are those whose strength is in you,
    whose hearts are set on pilgrimage.
⁶As they pass through the Valley of Baka,
    they make it a place of springs;
    the autumn rains also cover it with pools.*ᵇ*
⁷They go from strength to strength,
    till each appears before God in Zion.

⁸Hear my prayer, LORD God Almighty;
    listen to me, God of Jacob.
⁹Look on our shield,*ᶜ* O God;
    look with favour on your anointed one.

¹⁰Better is one day in your courts
    than a thousand elsewhere;
I would rather be a doorkeeper in the house of my God
    than dwell in the tents of the wicked.
¹¹For the LORD God is a sun and shield;
    the LORD bestows favour and honour;
no good thing does he withhold
    from those whose way of life is blameless.
¹²LORD Almighty,
    blessed are those who trust in you.

Psalm 85

For the director of music. Of the Sons of Korah. A psalm.

*¹You, LORD, showed favour to your land;
    you restored the fortunes of Jacob.
²You forgave the iniquity of your people
    and covered all their sins.*ᵈ*
³You set aside all your wrath
    and turned from your fierce anger.

⁴Restore us again, God our Saviour,
    and put away your displeasure towards us.
⁵Will you be angry with us for ever?
    Will you prolong your anger through all generations?
⁶Will you not revive us again,
    that your people may rejoice in you?
⁷Show us your unfailing love, LORD,
    and grant us your salvation.

⁸I will listen to what God the LORD says;
    he promises peace to his people, his faithful servants—
but let them not turn to folly.
⁹Surely his salvation is near those who fear him,
    that his glory may dwell in our land.

¹⁰Love and faithfulness meet together;
    righteousness and peace kiss each other.
¹¹Faithfulness springs forth from the earth,
    and righteousness looks down from heaven.
¹²The LORD will indeed give what is good,
    and our land will yield its harvest.
¹³Righteousness goes before him
    and prepares the way for his steps.

Psalm 86

A prayer of David.

¹Hear me, LORD, and answer me,
    for I am poor and needy.
²Guard my life, for I am faithful to you;
    save your servant who trusts in you.
You are my God; ³have mercy on me, Lord,
    for I call to you all day long.

ᵃ 4 The Hebrew has *Selah* (a word of uncertain meaning) here and at the end of verse 8. *ᵇ* 6 Or *blessings* *ᶜ* 9 Or *sovereign* *ᵈ* 2 The Hebrew has *Selah* (a word of uncertain meaning) here.

* 85:1-13 is numbered 85:2-14 in Hebrew texts.

⁴Bring joy to your servant, Lord,
  for I put my trust in you.

⁵You, Lord, are forgiving and good,
  abounding in love to all who call to
    you.
⁶Hear my prayer, LORD;
  listen to my cry for mercy.
⁷When I am in distress, I call to you,
  because you answer me.

⁸Among the gods there is none like you,
    Lord;
  no deeds can compare with yours.
⁹All the nations you have made
  will come and worship before you,
    Lord;
  they will bring glory to your name.
¹⁰For you are great and do marvellous
    deeds;
  you alone are God.

¹¹Teach me your way, LORD,
    that I may rely on your faithfulness;
  give me an undivided heart,
    that I may fear your name.
¹²I will praise you, Lord my God, with all my
    heart;
  I will glorify your name for ever.
¹³For great is your love towards me;
  you have delivered me from the depths,
    from the realm of the dead.

¹⁴Arrogant foes are attacking me, O God;
  a band of ruthless people seeks my life—
    they have no regard for you.
¹⁵But you, Lord, are a compassionate and
    gracious God,
  slow to anger, abounding in love and
    faithfulness.
¹⁶Turn to me and have mercy on me;
  show your strength on behalf of your
    servant
  and save the son of a woman
    who served you before me.
¹⁷Give me a sign of your goodness,
    that my enemies may see it and be put
      to shame,
  for you, LORD, have helped me and
    comforted me.

Psalm 87

Of the Sons of Korah. A psalm. A song.

¹He has founded his city on the holy
    mountain.
²The LORD loves the gates of Zion
  more than all the other dwellings of
    Jacob.
³Glorious things are said of you,
  city of God:ᵃ
⁴'I will record Rahabᵇ and Babylon
  among those who acknowledge
    me—
Philistia too, and Tyre, along with
    Cushᶜ—
  and will say, "This one was born in
    Zion."'ᵈ
⁵Indeed, of Zion it will be said,
  'This one and that one were born in
    her,
  and the Most High himself will
    establish her.'
⁶The LORD will write in the register of the
    peoples:
  'This one was born in Zion.'

⁷As they make music they will sing,
  'All my fountains are in you.'

Psalm 88

*A song. A psalm of the Sons of Korah. For
the director of music. According to* mahalath leannoth.ᵉ *A maskil*ᶠ *of Heman the
Ezrahite.*

*¹LORD, you are the God who saves me;
  day and night I cry out to you.
²May my prayer come before you;
  turn your ear to my cry.

³I am overwhelmed with troubles
  and my life draws near to death.
⁴I am counted among those who go down
    to the pit;
  I am like one without strength.
⁵I am set apart with the dead,
  like the slain who lie in the grave,
  whom you remember no more,
  who are cut off from your care.

ᵃ 3 The Hebrew has *Selah* (a word of uncertain meaning) here and at the end of verse 6.   ᵇ 4 A poetic name for Egypt
ᶜ 4 That is, the upper Nile region   ᵈ 4 Or *'I will record concerning those who acknowledge me: / "This one was born in Zion." / I hear this, Rahab and Babylon, / and you too, Philistia, Tyre and Cush.'*   ᵉ Title: Possibly a tune, 'The Suffering of Affliction'   ᶠ Title: Probably a literary or musical term

* 88:1-18 is numbered 88:2-19 in Hebrew texts.

⁶You have put me in the lowest pit,
in the darkest depths.
⁷Your wrath lies heavily on me;
you have overwhelmed me with all
your waves.ᵃ
⁸You have taken from me my closest
friends
and have made me repulsive to them.
I am confined and cannot escape;
⁹ my eyes are dim with grief.

I call to you, LORD, every day;
I spread out my hands to you.
¹⁰Do you show your wonders to the dead?
Do their spirits rise up and praise you?
¹¹Is your love declared in the grave,
your faithfulness in Destruction?ᵇ
¹²Are your wonders known in the place of
darkness,
or your righteous deeds in the land of
oblivion?

¹³But I cry to you for help, LORD;
in the morning my prayer comes
before you.
¹⁴Why, LORD, do you reject me
and hide your face from me?

¹⁵From my youth I have suffered and been
close to death;
I have borne your terrors and am in
despair.
¹⁶Your wrath has swept over me;
your terrors have destroyed me.
¹⁷All day long they surround me like a
flood;
they have completely engulfed me.
¹⁸You have taken from me friend and
neighbour—
darkness is my closest friend.

Psalm 89

A maskilᶜ of Ethan the Ezrahite.

*¹I will sing of the LORD's great love for ever;
with my mouth I will make your
faithfulness known
through all generations.
²I will declare that your love stands firm for
ever,

Rahab
Psalms 89:10
Rahab was probably an ancient sea monster that represented the power of the ocean. Rahab gets a mention in Isaiah 51:9 as well.

that you have established your
faithfulness in heaven itself.
³You said, 'I have made a covenant with my
chosen one,
I have sworn to David my servant,
⁴"I will establish your line for ever
and make your throne firm through all
generations."'ᵈ

⁵The heavens praise your wonders, LORD,
your faithfulness too, in the assembly
of the holy ones.
⁶For who in the skies above can compare
with the LORD?
Who is like the LORD among the
heavenly beings?
⁷In the council of the holy ones God is
greatly feared;
he is more awesome than all who
surround him.
⁸Who is like you, LORD God Almighty?
You, LORD, are mighty, and your
faithfulness surrounds you.

⁹You rule over the surging sea;
when its waves mount up, you still
them.
¹⁰You crushed Rahab like one of the slain;
with your strong arm you scattered
your enemies.
¹¹The heavens are yours, and yours also the
earth;

ᵃ7 The Hebrew has *Selah* (a word of uncertain meaning) here and at the end of verse 10.   ᵇ11 Hebrew *Abaddon*
ᶜTitle: Probably a literary or musical term   ᵈ4 The Hebrew has *Selah* (a word of uncertain meaning) here and at the end of verses 37, 45 and 48.

* 89:1-52 is numbered 89:2-53 in Hebrew texts.

you founded the world and all that is in it.
¹²You created the north and the south;
Tabor and Hermon sing for joy at your name.
¹³Your arm is endued with power;
your hand is strong, your right hand exalted.

¹⁴Righteousness and justice are the foundation of your throne;
love and faithfulness go before you.
¹⁵Blessed are those who have learned to acclaim you,
who walk in the light of your presence, LORD.
¹⁶They rejoice in your name all day long;
they exult in your righteousness.
¹⁷For you are their glory and strength,
and by your favour you exalt our horn.[a]
¹⁸Indeed, our shield[b] belongs to the LORD,
our king to the Holy One of Israel.

¹⁹Once you spoke in a vision,
to your faithful people you said:
'I have bestowed strength on a warrior;
I have raised up a young man from among the people.
²⁰I have found David my servant;
with my sacred oil I have anointed him.
²¹My hand will sustain him;
surely my arm will strengthen him.
²²No enemy will get the better of him;
no wicked person will oppress him.
²³I will crush his foes before him
and strike down his adversaries.
²⁴My faithful love will be with him,
and through my name his horn[c] will be exalted.
²⁵I will set his hand over the sea,
his right hand over the rivers.
²⁶He will call out to me, "You are my Father,
my God, the Rock my Saviour."
²⁷And I will appoint him to be my firstborn,
the most exalted of the kings of the earth.
²⁸I will maintain my love to him for ever,
and my covenant with him will never fail.
²⁹I will establish his line for ever,
his throne as long as the heavens endure.

³⁰'If his sons forsake my law
and do not follow my statutes,
³¹if they violate my decrees
and fail to keep my commands,
³²I will punish their sin with the rod,
their iniquity with flogging;
³³but I will not take my love from him,
nor will I ever betray my faithfulness.
³⁴I will not violate my covenant
or alter what my lips have uttered.
³⁵Once for all, I have sworn by my holiness—
and I will not lie to David—
³⁶that his line will continue for ever
and his throne endure before me like the sun;
³⁷it will be established for ever like the moon,
the faithful witness in the sky.'

³⁸But you have rejected, you have spurned,
you have been very angry with your anointed one.
³⁹You have renounced the covenant with your servant
and have defiled his crown in the dust.
⁴⁰You have broken through all his walls
and reduced his strongholds to ruins.
⁴¹All who pass by have plundered him;
he has become the scorn of his neighbours.
⁴²You have exalted the right hand of his foes;
you have made all his enemies rejoice.
⁴³Indeed, you have turned back the edge of his sword
and have not supported him in battle.
⁴⁴You have put an end to his splendour
and cast his throne to the ground.
⁴⁵You have cut short the days of his youth;
you have covered him with a mantle of shame.

⁴⁶How long, LORD? Will you hide yourself for ever?
How long will your wrath burn like fire?
⁴⁷Remember how fleeting is my life.

---

[a] 17 *Horn* here symbolises strong one.   [b] 18 Or *sovereign*   [c] 24 *Horn* here symbolises strength.

For what futility you have created all
  humanity!
⁴⁸Who can live and not see death,
  or who can escape the power of the
    grave?
⁴⁹Lord, where is your former great love,
  which in your faithfulness you swore to
    David?
⁵⁰Remember, Lord, how your servant has[a]
  been mocked,
  how I bear in my heart the taunts of all
    the nations,
⁵¹the taunts with which your enemies,
  LORD, have mocked,
  with which they have mocked every
    step of your anointed one.

⁵²Praise be to the LORD for ever!
  Amen and Amen.

BOOK IV

Psalms 90–106

Psalm 90

A prayer of Moses the man of God.

¹Lord, you have been our dwelling-place
  throughout all generations.
²Before the mountains were born
  or you brought forth the whole world,
  from everlasting to everlasting you are
    God.

³You turn people back to dust,
  saying, 'Return to dust, you mortals.'
⁴A thousand years in your sight
  are like a day that has just gone by,
  or like a watch in the night.
⁵Yet you sweep people away in the sleep of
    death—
  they are like the new grass of the
    morning:
⁶in the morning it springs up new,
  but by evening it is dry and withered.

⁷We are consumed by your anger
  and terrified by your indignation.
⁸You have set our iniquities before you,
  our secret sins in the light of your
    presence.
⁹All our days pass away under your wrath;
  we finish our years with a moan.

¹⁰Our days may come to seventy years,
  or eighty, if our strength endures;
  yet the best of them are but trouble and
    sorrow,
  for they quickly pass, and we fly away.
¹¹If only we knew the power of your anger!
  Your wrath is as great as the fear that is
    your due.
¹²Teach us to number our days,
  that we may gain a heart of wisdom.

¹³Relent, LORD! How long will it be?
  Have compassion on your servants.
¹⁴Satisfy us in the morning with your
    unfailing love,
  that we may sing for joy and be glad all
    our days.
¹⁵Make us glad for as many days as you have
    afflicted us,
  for as many years as we have seen
    trouble.
¹⁶May your deeds be shown to your
    servants,
  your splendour to their children.

¹⁷May the favour[b] of the Lord our God rest
    on us;
  establish the work of our hands for
    us—
  yes, establish the work of our hands.

Psalm 91

¹Whoever dwells in the shelter of the Most
    High
  will rest in the shadow of the
    Almighty.[c]
²They say of the LORD, 'He is my refuge and
    my fortress,
  my God, in whom I trust.'

³Surely he will save you
  from the fowler's snare
  and from the deadly pestilence.
⁴He will cover you with his feathers,
  and under his wings you will find
    refuge;
  his faithfulness will be your shield and
    rampart.
⁵You will not fear the terror of night,
  nor the arrow that flies by day,
⁶nor the pestilence that stalks in the
    darkness,
  nor the plague that destroys at midday.

---

[a] 50 Or *your servants have* [b] 17 Or *beauty* [c] 1 Hebrew *Shaddai*

7A thousand may fall at your side,
   ten thousand at your right hand,
   but it will not come near you.
8You will only observe with your eyes
   and see the punishment of the wicked.

9If you say, 'The LORD is my refuge,'
   and you make the Most High your
      dwelling,
10no harm will overtake you,
   no disaster will come near your tent.
11For he will command his angels
      concerning you
   to guard you in all your ways;
12they will lift you up in their hands,
   so that you will not strike your foot
      against a stone.
13You will tread on the lion and the cobra;
   you will trample the great lion and the
      serpent.

14'Because they love me,' says the LORD, 'I
      will rescue them;
   I will protect them, for they
      acknowledge my name.
15They will call on me, and I will answer
      them;
   I will be with them in trouble,
   I will deliver them and honour them.
16With long life I will satisfy them
   and show them my salvation.'

Psalm 92

A psalm. A song. For the Sabbath day.

*1It is good to praise the LORD
   and make music to your name, O Most
      High,
2proclaiming your love in the morning
   and your faithfulness at night,
3to the music of the ten-stringed lyre
   and the melody of the harp.

4For you make me glad by your deeds,
      LORD;
   I sing for joy at what your hands have
      done.
5How great are your works, LORD,
   how profound your thoughts!
6Senseless people do not know,
   fools do not understand,

making Connections

Cedar of Lebanon
Psalms 92:12
Trees are used as symbols of God's people several times in the psalms (Psalm 1:3 and Psalm 52:8). Someone who has a firm grounding in God's word and who regularly feeds on God through prayer and Bible reading is like a healthy tree beside a stream. Cedar trees had a fragrant, strong wood that was ideal for building houses, temples and ships. Lebanon was well known for its cedar forests.

7that though the wicked spring up like
      grass
   and all evildoers flourish,
   they will be destroyed for ever.

8But you, LORD, are for ever exalted.

9For surely your enemies, LORD,
   surely your enemies will perish;
   all evildoers will be scattered.
10You have exalted my horn[a] like that of a
      wild ox;
   fine oils have been poured on me.
11My eyes have seen the defeat of my
      adversaries;
   my ears have heard the rout of my
      wicked foes.

12The righteous will flourish like a palm
      tree,
   they will grow like a cedar of
      Lebanon;
13planted in the house of the LORD,
   they will flourish in the courts of our
      God.
14They will still bear fruit in old age,
   they will stay fresh and green,

---

[a] 10 *Horn* here symbolises strength.

* 92:1-15 is numbered 92:2-16 in Hebrew texts.

15 proclaiming, 'The LORD is upright;
he is my Rock, and there is no
wickedness in him.'

Psalm 93

1 The LORD reigns, he is robed in majesty;
the LORD is robed in majesty and
armed with strength;
indeed, the world is established, firm
and secure.
2 Your throne was established long ago;
you are from all eternity.

3 The seas have lifted up, LORD,
the seas have lifted up their voice;
the seas have lifted up their pounding
waves.
4 Mightier than the thunder of the great
waters,
mightier than the breakers of the sea—
the LORD on high is mighty.

5 Your statutes, LORD, stand firm;
holiness adorns your house
for endless days.

Psalm 94

1 The LORD is a God who avenges.
O God who avenges, shine forth.
2 Rise up, Judge of the earth;
pay back to the proud what they
deserve.
3 How long, LORD, will the wicked,
how long will the wicked be jubilant?

4 They pour out arrogant words;
all the evildoers are full of boasting.
5 They crush your people, LORD;
they oppress your inheritance.
6 They slay the widow and the foreigner;
they murder the fatherless.
7 They say, 'The LORD does not see;
the God of Jacob takes no notice.'

8 Take notice, you senseless ones among the
people;
you fools, when will you become wise?
9 Does he who fashioned the ear not hear?
Does he who formed the eye not see?
10 Does he who disciplines nations not
punish?
Does he who teaches human beings
lack knowledge?
11 The LORD knows all human plans;
he knows that they are futile.

12 Blessed are those you discipline, LORD,
those you teach from your law;
13 you grant them relief from days of
trouble,
till a pit is dug for the wicked.
14 For the LORD will not reject his people;
he will never forsake his inheritance.
15 Judgment will again be founded on
righteousness,
and all the upright in heart will follow
it.

16 Who will rise up for me against the
wicked?
Who will take a stand for me against
evildoers?
17 Unless the LORD had given me help,
I would soon have dwelt in the silence
of death.
18 When I said, 'My foot is slipping,'
your unfailing love, LORD, supported
me.
19 When anxiety was great within me,
your consolation brought me joy.

20 Can a corrupt throne be allied with you—
a throne that brings on misery by its
decrees?
21 The wicked band together against the
righteous
and condemn the innocent to death.
22 But the LORD has become my fortress,
and my God the rock in whom I take
refuge.
23 He will repay them for their sins
and destroy them for their wickedness;
the LORD our God will destroy them.

Psalm 95

1 Come, let us sing for joy to the LORD;
let us shout aloud to the Rock of our
salvation.
2 Let us come before him with thanksgiving
and extol him with music and song.

3 For the LORD is the great God,
the great King above all gods.
4 In his hand are the depths of the earth,
and the mountain peaks belong to
him.
5 The sea is his, for he made it,
and his hands formed the dry land.

6 Come, let us bow down in worship,
let us kneel before the LORD our Maker;

7 for he is our God
   and we are the people of his pasture,
   the flock under his care.

Today, if only you would hear his voice,
8 'Do not harden your hearts as you did at Meribah,[a]
   as you did that day at Massah[b] in the wilderness,
9 where your ancestors tested me;
   they tried me, though they had seen what I did.
10 For forty years I was angry with that generation;
   I said, "They are a people whose hearts go astray,
   and they have not known my ways."
11 So I declared on oath in my anger,
   "They shall never enter my rest." '

Psalm 96

1 Sing to the LORD a new song;
   sing to the LORD, all the earth.
2 Sing to the LORD, praise his name;
   proclaim his salvation day after day.
3 Declare his glory among the nations,
   his marvellous deeds among all peoples.

4 For great is the LORD and most worthy of praise;
   he is to be feared above all gods.
5 For all the gods of the nations are idols,
   but the LORD made the heavens.
6 Splendour and majesty are before him;
   strength and glory are in his sanctuary.

7 Ascribe to the LORD, all you families of nations,
   ascribe to the LORD glory and strength.
8 Ascribe to the LORD the glory due to his name;
   bring an offering and come into his courts.
9 Worship the LORD in the splendour of his[c] holiness;
   tremble before him, all the earth.
10 Say among the nations, 'The LORD reigns.'
   The world is firmly established, it cannot be moved;
   he will judge the peoples with equity.

11 Let the heavens rejoice, let the earth be glad;
   let the sea resound, and all that is in it.
12 Let the fields be jubilant, and everything in them;
   let all the trees of the forest sing for joy.
13 Let all creation rejoice before the LORD,
   for he comes,
   he comes to judge the earth.
   He will judge the world in righteousness
   and the peoples in his faithfulness.

Psalm 97

1 The LORD reigns, let the earth be glad;
   let the distant shores rejoice.
2 Clouds and thick darkness surround him;
   righteousness and justice are the foundation of his throne.
3 Fire goes before him
   and consumes his foes on every side.
4 His lightning lights up the world;
   the earth sees and trembles.
5 The mountains melt like wax before the LORD,
   before the Lord of all the earth.
6 The heavens proclaim his righteousness,
   and all peoples see his glory.

7 All who worship images are put to shame,
   those who boast in idols—
   worship him, all you gods!

8 Zion hears and rejoices
   and the villages of Judah are glad
   because of your judgments, LORD.
9 For you, LORD, are the Most High over all the earth;
   you are exalted far above all gods.
10 Let those who love the LORD hate evil,
   for he guards the lives of his faithful ones
   and delivers them from the hand of the wicked.
11 Light shines[d] on the righteous
   and joy on the upright in heart.
12 Rejoice in the LORD, you who are righteous,
   and praise his holy name.

---

[a] 8 *Meribah* means *quarrelling*. [b] 8 *Massah* means *testing*. [c] 9 Or *LORD with the splendour of* [d] 11 One Hebrew manuscript and ancient versions (see also 112:4); most Hebrew manuscripts *Light is sown*

Psalm 98

A psalm.

¹Sing to the LORD a new song,
   for he has done marvellous things;
 his right hand and his holy arm
   have worked salvation for him.
²The LORD has made his salvation known
   and revealed his righteousness to the
      nations.
³He has remembered his love
   and his faithfulness to the house of
      Israel;
 all the ends of the earth have seen
   the salvation of our God.

⁴Shout for joy to the LORD, all the earth,
   burst into jubilant song with music;
⁵make music to the LORD with the harp,
   with the harp and the sound of singing,
⁶with trumpets and the blast of the ram's
      horn—
   shout for joy before the LORD, the King.

⁷Let the sea resound, and everything in it,
   the world, and all who live in it.
⁸Let the rivers clap their hands,
   let the mountains sing together for joy;
⁹let them sing before the LORD,
   for he comes to judge the earth.
 He will judge the world in righteousness
   and the peoples with equity.

Psalm 99

¹The LORD reigns,
   let the nations tremble;
 he sits enthroned between the cherubim,
   let the earth shake.
²Great is the LORD in Zion;
   he is exalted over all the nations.
³Let them praise your great and awesome
      name—
   he is holy.

⁴The King is mighty, he loves justice—
   you have established equity;
 in Jacob you have done
   what is just and right.
⁵Exalt the LORD our God
   and worship at his footstool;
   he is holy.

⁶Moses and Aaron were among his priests,
 Samuel was among those who called on
      his name;
 they called on the LORD
   and he answered them.
⁷He spoke to them from the pillar of cloud;
   they kept his statutes and the decrees he
      gave them.

⁸LORD our God,
   you answered them;
 you were to Israel a forgiving God,
   though you punished their misdeeds.*ᵃ*
⁹Exalt the LORD our God
   and worship at his holy mountain,
   for the LORD our God is holy.

Psalm 100

A psalm. For giving grateful praise.

¹Shout for joy to the LORD, all the earth.
² Worship the LORD with gladness;
   come before him with joyful songs.
³Know that the LORD is God.
   It is he who made us, and we are his;*ᵇ*
 we are his people, the sheep of his
      pasture.

⁴Enter his gates with thanksgiving
   and his courts with praise;
   give thanks to him and praise his name.
⁵For the LORD is good and his love endures
      for ever;
   his faithfulness continues through all
      generations.

Psalm 101

Of David. A psalm.

¹I will sing of your love and justice;
   to you, LORD, I will sing praise.
²I will be careful to lead a blameless life—
   when will you come to me?

 I will conduct the affairs of my house
   with a blameless heart.
³I will not look with approval
   on anything that is vile.

 I hate what faithless people do;
   I will have no part in it.
⁴The perverse of heart shall be far from me;
   I will have nothing to do with what is
      evil.

ᵃ 8 Or *God, I an avenger of the wrongs done to them*   *ᵇ* 3 Or *and not we ourselves*

IN OTHER WORDS

Justice
Psalms 101:1

The main use of the word 'justice' in the Bible refers to the honest practice of the law so that God's people could rely on their legal system. God also demands justice from individuals, particularly in relation to the poor. Justice is seen as one of God's most important attributes.

5 Whoever slanders their neighbour in secret,
  I will put to silence;
 whoever has haughty eyes and a proud heart,
  I will not endure.

6 My eyes will be on the faithful in the land,
  that they may dwell with me;
 those whose way of life is blameless
  will minister to me.

7 No-one who practises deceit
  will dwell in my house;
 no-one who speaks falsely
  will stand in my presence.

8 Every morning I will put to silence
  all the wicked in the land;
 I will cut off every evildoer
  from the city of the LORD.

Psalm 102

A prayer of an afflicted person who has grown weak and pours out a lament before the LORD.

*1 Hear my prayer, LORD;
  let my cry for help come to you.
2 Do not hide your face from me
  when I am in distress.
 Turn your ear to me;
  when I call, answer me quickly.

3 For my days vanish like smoke;
  my bones burn like glowing embers.
4 My heart is blighted and withered like grass;
  I forget to eat my food.
5 In my distress I groan aloud
  and am reduced to skin and bones.
6 I am like a desert owl,
  like an owl among the ruins.
7 I lie awake; I have become
  like a bird alone on a roof.
8 All day long my enemies taunt me;
  those who rail against me use my name as a curse.
9 For I eat ashes as my food
  and mingle my drink with tears
10 because of your great wrath,
  for you have taken me up and thrown me aside.
11 My days are like the evening shadow;
  I wither away like grass.

12 But you, LORD, sit enthroned for ever;
  your renown endures through all generations.
13 You will arise and have compassion on Zion,
  for it is time to show favour to her;
  the appointed time has come.
14 For her stones are dear to your servants;
  her very dust moves them to pity.
15 The nations will fear the name of the LORD,
  all the kings of the earth will revere your glory.
16 For the LORD will rebuild Zion
  and appear in his glory.
17 He will respond to the prayer of the destitute;
  he will not despise their plea.

18 Let this be written for a future generation,
  that a people not yet created may praise the LORD:
19 'The LORD looked down from his sanctuary on high,
  from heaven he viewed the earth,
20 to hear the groans of the prisoners
  and release those condemned to death.'
21 So the name of the LORD will be declared in Zion
  and his praise in Jerusalem

---

* 102:1-28 is numbered 102:2-29 in Hebrew texts.

22 when the peoples and the kingdoms
assemble to worship the LORD.

23 In the course of my life[a] he broke my strength;
he cut short my days.
24 So I said:
'Do not take me away, my God, in the midst of my days;
your years go on through all generations.
25 In the beginning you laid the foundations of the earth,
and the heavens are the work of your hands.
26 They will perish, but you remain;
they will all wear out like a garment.
Like clothing you will change them
and they will be discarded.
27 But you remain the same,
and your years will never end.
28 The children of your servants will live in your presence;
their descendants will be established before you.'

Psalm 103

Of David.

1 Praise the LORD, my soul;
all my inmost being, praise his holy name.
2 Praise the LORD, my soul,
and forget not all his benefits—
3 who forgives all your sins
and heals all your diseases,
4 who redeems your life from the pit
and crowns you with love and compassion,
5 who satisfies your desires with good things
so that your youth is renewed like the eagle's.

6 The LORD works righteousness
and justice for all the oppressed.

7 He made known his ways to Moses,
his deeds to the people of Israel:
8 the LORD is compassionate and gracious,
slow to anger, abounding in love.
9 He will not always accuse,
nor will he harbour his anger for ever;
10 he does not treat us as our sins deserve
or repay us according to our iniquities.
11 For as high as the heavens are above the earth,
so great is his love for those who fear him;
12 as far as the east is from the west,
so far has he removed our transgressions from us.

13 As a father has compassion on his children,
so the LORD has compassion on those who fear him;
14 for he knows how we are formed,
he remembers that we are dust.
15 As for mortals, their days are like grass,
they flourish like a flower of the field;
16 the wind blows over it and it is gone,
and its place remembers it no more.
17 But from everlasting to everlasting
the LORD's love is with those who fear him,
and his righteousness with their children's children—
18 with those who keep his covenant
and remember to obey his precepts.

19 The LORD has established his throne in heaven,
and his kingdom rules over all.

20 Praise the LORD, you his angels,
you mighty ones who do his bidding,
who obey his word.
21 Praise the LORD, all his heavenly hosts,
you his servants who do his will.

IN OTHER WORDS

Forgive
Psalms 103:3

To forgive is to pardon someone or to let them off from being punished for doing wrong. Forgiveness is two-sided: God forgives us when we repent of our sins, and we need to forgive others just as God has forgiven us.

---

[a] 23 Or *By his power*

22 Praise the Lord, all his works
everywhere in his dominion.

Praise the Lord, my soul.

Psalm 104

1 Praise the Lord, my soul.

Lord my God, you are very great;
you are clothed with splendour and majesty.

2 The Lord wraps himself in light as with a garment;
he stretches out the heavens like a tent
3 and lays the beams of his upper chambers on their waters.
He makes the clouds his chariot
and rides on the wings of the wind.
4 He makes winds his messengers,[a]
flames of fire his servants.

5 He set the earth on its foundations;
it can never be moved.
6 You covered it with the deep as with a garment;
the waters stood above the mountains.
7 But at your rebuke the waters fled,
at the sound of your thunder they took to flight;
8 they flowed over the mountains,
they went down into the valleys,
to the place you assigned for them.
9 You set a boundary they cannot cross;
never again will they cover the earth.

10 He makes springs pour water into the ravines;
it flows between the mountains.
11 They give water to all the beasts of the field;
the wild donkeys quench their thirst.
12 The birds of the sky nest by the waters;
they sing among the branches.
13 He waters the mountains from his upper chambers;
the land is satisfied by the fruit of his work.
14 He makes grass grow for the cattle,
and plants for people to cultivate—
bringing forth food from the earth:
15 wine that gladdens human hearts,
oil to make their faces shine,
and bread that sustains their hearts.

16 The trees of the Lord are well watered,
the cedars of Lebanon that he planted.
17 There the birds make their nests;
the stork has its home in the junipers.
18 The high mountains belong to the wild goats;
the crags are a refuge for the hyrax.

19 He made the moon to mark the seasons,
and the sun knows when to go down.
20 You bring darkness, it becomes night,
and all the beasts of the forest prowl.
21 The lions roar for their prey
and seek their food from God.
22 The sun rises, and they steal away;
they return and lie down in their dens.
23 Then people go out to their work,
to their labour until evening.

24 How many are your works, Lord!
In wisdom you made them all;
the earth is full of your creatures.
25 There is the sea, vast and spacious,
teeming with creatures beyond number—
living things both large and small.
26 There the ships go to and fro,
and the leviathan, which you formed to frolic there.

27 All creatures look to you
to give them their food at the proper time.
28 When you give it to them,
they gather it up;
when you open your hand,
they are satisfied with good things.
29 When you hide your face,
they are terrified;
when you take away their breath,
they die and return to the dust.
30 When you send your Spirit,
they are created,
and you renew the face of the ground.

31 May the glory of the Lord endure for ever;
may the Lord rejoice in his works—
32 he who looks at the earth, and it trembles,
who touches the mountains, and they smoke.

---

[a] 4 Or *angels*

making Connections

A history lesson
Psalms 105

This is a history lesson in the form of a song! It was really important for God's people to remember their past and how God had been faithful to them for centuries. Psalms like this one tell the story of the Israelites' escape from Egypt so that future generations won't forget what God is like.

33I will sing to the LORD all my life;
  I will sing praise to my God as long as I live.
34May my meditation be pleasing to him,
  as I rejoice in the LORD.
35But may sinners vanish from the earth
  and the wicked be no more.

Praise the LORD, my soul.

Praise the LORD.[a]

Psalm 105

1Give praise to the LORD, call on his name;
  make known among the nations what he has done.
2Sing of him, sing his praises;
  tell of all his wonderful acts.
3Glory in his holy name;
  let the hearts of those who seek the LORD rejoice.
4Look to the LORD and his strength;
  seek his face always.

5Remember the wonders he has done,
  his miracles, and the judgments he pronounced,
6you his servants, the descendants of Abraham,
  his chosen ones, the children of Jacob.
7He is the LORD our God;
  his judgments are in all the earth.

8He remembers his covenant for ever,
  the promise he made, for a thousand generations,
9the covenant he made with Abraham,
  the oath he swore to Isaac.
10He confirmed it to Jacob as a decree,
  to Israel as an everlasting covenant:
11'To you I will give the land of Canaan
  as the portion you will inherit.'

12When they were but few in number,
  few indeed, and strangers in it,
13they wandered from nation to nation,
  from one kingdom to another.
14He allowed no-one to oppress them;
  for their sake he rebuked kings:
15'Do not touch my anointed ones;
  do my prophets no harm.'

16He called down famine on the land
  and destroyed all their supplies of food;
17and he sent a man before them—
  Joseph, sold as a slave.
18They bruised his feet with shackles,
  his neck was put in irons,
19till what he foretold came to pass,
  till the word of the LORD proved him true.
20The king sent and released him,
  the ruler of peoples set him free.
21He made him master of his household,
  ruler over all he possessed,
22to instruct his princes as he pleased
  and teach his elders wisdom.

23Then Israel entered Egypt;
  Jacob resided as a foreigner in the land of Ham.
24The LORD made his people very fruitful;
  he made them too numerous for their foes,
25whose hearts he turned to hate his people,
  to conspire against his servants.
26He sent Moses his servant,
  and Aaron, whom he had chosen.
27They performed his signs among them,
  his wonders in the land of Ham.
28He sent darkness and made the land dark—
  for had they not rebelled against his words?
29He turned their waters into blood,
  causing their fish to die.

---

[a] 35 Hebrew *Hallelu Yah*; in the Septuagint this line stands at the beginning of Psalm 105.

30Their land teemed with frogs,
which went up into the bedrooms of their rulers.
31He spoke, and there came swarms of flies,
and gnats throughout their country.
32He turned their rain into hail,
with lightning throughout their land;
33he struck down their vines and fig-trees
and shattered the trees of their country.
34He spoke, and the locusts came,
grasshoppers without number;
35they ate up every green thing in their land,
ate up the produce of their soil.
36Then he struck down all the firstborn in their land,
the firstfruits of all their manhood.
37He brought out Israel, laden with silver and gold,
and from among their tribes no-one faltered.
38Egypt was glad when they left,
because dread of Israel had fallen on them.

39He spread out a cloud as a covering,
and a fire to give light at night.
40They asked, and he brought them quail;
he fed them well with the bread of heaven.
41He opened the rock, and water gushed out;
it flowed like a river in the desert.

42For he remembered his holy promise
given to his servant Abraham.
43He brought out his people with rejoicing,
his chosen ones with shouts of joy;
44he gave them the lands of the nations,
and they fell heir to what others had toiled for—
45that they might keep his precepts
and observe his laws.

Praise the LORD.[a]

Psalm 106

1Praise the LORD.[b]

Give thanks to the LORD, for he is good;
his love endures for ever.

2Who can proclaim the mighty acts of the LORD
or fully declare his praise?

3Blessed are those who act justly,
who always do what is right.

4Remember me, LORD, when you show favour to your people,
come to my aid when you save them,
5that I may enjoy the prosperity of your chosen ones,
that I may share in the joy of your nation
and join your inheritance in giving praise.

6We have sinned, even as our ancestors did;
we have done wrong and acted wickedly.
7When our ancestors were in Egypt,
they gave no thought to your miracles;
they did not remember your many kindnesses,
and they rebelled by the sea, the Red Sea.[c]
8Yet he saved them for his name's sake,
to make his mighty power known.
9He rebuked the Red Sea, and it dried up;
he led them through the depths as through a desert.
10He saved them from the hand of the foe;
from the hand of the enemy he redeemed them.
11The waters covered their adversaries;
not one of them survived.
12Then they believed his promises
and sang his praise.

13But they soon forgot what he had done
and did not wait for his plan to unfold.
14In the desert they gave in to their craving;
in the wilderness they put God to the test.
15So he gave them what they asked for,
but sent a wasting disease among them.

16In the camp they grew envious of Moses
and of Aaron, who was consecrated to the LORD.
17The earth opened up and swallowed Dathan;
it buried the company of Abiram.
18Fire blazed among their followers;
a flame consumed the wicked.

---

[a]45 Hebrew *Hallelu Yah* [b]1 Hebrew *Hallelu Yah*; also in verse 48 [c]7 Or *the Sea of Reeds*; also in verses 9 and 22

¹⁹At Horeb they made a calf
  and worshipped an idol cast from metal.
²⁰They exchanged their glorious God
  for an image of a bull, which eats grass.
²¹They forgot the God who saved them,
  who had done great things in Egypt,
²²miracles in the land of Ham
  and awesome deeds by the Red Sea.
²³So he said he would destroy them—
  had not Moses, his chosen one,
 stood in the breach before him
  to keep his wrath from destroying them.

²⁴Then they despised the pleasant land;
  they did not believe his promise.
²⁵They grumbled in their tents
  and did not obey the LORD.
²⁶So he swore to them with uplifted hand
  that he would make them fall in the wilderness,
²⁷make their descendants fall among the nations
  and scatter them throughout the lands.

²⁸They yoked themselves to the Baal of Peor
  and ate sacrifices offered to lifeless gods;
²⁹they aroused the LORD's anger by their wicked deeds,
  and a plague broke out among them.
³⁰But Phinehas stood up and intervened,
  and the plague was checked.
³¹This was credited to him as righteousness
  for endless generations to come.
³²By the waters of Meribah they angered the LORD,
  and trouble came to Moses because of them;
³³for they rebelled against the Spirit of God,
  and rash words came from Moses' lips.*a*

³⁴They did not destroy the peoples
  as the LORD had commanded them,
³⁵but they mingled with the nations
  and adopted their customs.
³⁶They worshipped their idols,
  which became a snare to them.
³⁷They sacrificed their sons
  and their daughters to demons.
³⁸They shed innocent blood,
  the blood of their sons and daughters,
 whom they sacrificed to the idols of Canaan,
  and the land was desecrated by their blood.
³⁹They defiled themselves by what they did;
  by their deeds they prostituted themselves.

⁴⁰Therefore the LORD was angry with his people
  and abhorred his inheritance.
⁴¹He gave them into the hands of the nations,
  and their foes ruled over them.
⁴²Their enemies oppressed them
  and subjected them to their power.
⁴³Many times he delivered them,
  but they were bent on rebellion
  and they wasted away in their sin.
⁴⁴Yet he took note of their distress
  when he heard their cry;
⁴⁵for their sake he remembered his covenant
  and out of his great love he relented.
⁴⁶He caused all who held them captive
  to show them mercy.

⁴⁷Save us, LORD our God,
  and gather us from the nations,
 that we may give thanks to your holy name
  and glory in your praise.

⁴⁸Praise be to the LORD, the God of Israel,
  from everlasting to everlasting.

Let all the people say, 'Amen!'

Praise the LORD.

BOOK V

Psalms 107–150

Psalm 107

¹Give thanks to the LORD, for he is good;
  his love endures for ever.

²Let the redeemed of the LORD tell their story—
  those he redeemed from the hand of the foe,

---

a 33 Or *against his spirit, / and rash words came from his lips*

Making Connections

Returning from exile
Psalms 107:3

This psalm was probably written after the Israelites had been in exile. They had been sent not only to Babylon, but to other nations as well, which is why they are being gathered from the east, west, north and south.

³those he gathered from the lands,
from east and west, from north and south.[a]

⁴Some wandered in desert wastelands,
finding no way to a city where they could settle.
⁵They were hungry and thirsty,
and their lives ebbed away.
⁶Then they cried out to the LORD in their trouble,
and he delivered them from their distress.
⁷He led them by a straight way
to a city where they could settle.
⁸Let them give thanks to the LORD for his unfailing love
and his wonderful deeds for the human race,
⁹for he satisfies the thirsty
and fills the hungry with good things.

¹⁰Some sat in darkness, in utter darkness,
prisoners suffering in iron chains,
¹¹because they rebelled against God's commands
and despised the plans of the Most High.
¹²So he subjected them to bitter labour;
they stumbled, and there was no-one to help.
¹³Then they cried to the LORD in their trouble,
and he saved them from their distress.
¹⁴He brought them out of darkness, the utter darkness,
and broke away their chains.
¹⁵Let them give thanks to the LORD for his unfailing love
and his wonderful deeds for the human race,
¹⁶for he breaks down gates of bronze
and cuts through bars of iron.

¹⁷Some became fools through their rebellious ways
and suffered affliction because of their iniquities.
¹⁸They loathed all food
and drew near the gates of death.
¹⁹Then they cried to the LORD in their trouble,
and he saved them from their distress.
²⁰He sent out his word and healed them;
he rescued them from the grave.
²¹Let them give thanks to the LORD for his unfailing love
and his wonderful deeds for the human race,
²²Let them sacrifice thank-offerings
and tell of his works with songs of joy.

²³Some went out on the sea in ships;
they were merchants on the mighty waters.
²⁴They saw the works of the LORD,
his wonderful deeds in the deep.
²⁵For he spoke and stirred up a tempest
that lifted high the waves.
²⁶They mounted up to the heavens and went down to the depths;
in their peril their courage melted away.
²⁷They reeled and staggered like drunkards;
they were at their wits' end.
²⁸Then they cried out to the LORD in their trouble,
and he brought them out of their distress.
²⁹He stilled the storm to a whisper;
the waves of the sea[b] were hushed.
³⁰They were glad when it grew calm,
and he guided them to their desired haven.

---

[a] 3 Hebrew *north and the sea*   [b] 29 Dead Sea Scrolls; Masoretic Text / *their waves*

31Let them give thanks to the LORD for his unfailing love
and his wonderful deeds for the human race.
32Let them exalt him in the assembly of the people
and praise him in the council of the elders.

33He turned rivers into a desert,
flowing springs into thirsty ground,
34and fruitful land into a salt waste,
because of the wickedness of those who lived there.
35He turned the desert into pools of water
and the parched ground into flowing springs;
36there he brought the hungry to live,
and they founded a city where they could settle.
37They sowed fields and planted vineyards
that yielded a fruitful harvest;
38he blessed them, and their numbers greatly increased,
and he did not let their herds diminish.

39Then their numbers decreased, and they were humbled
by oppression, calamity and sorrow;
40he who pours contempt on nobles
made them wander in a trackless waste.
41But he lifted the needy out of their affliction
and increased their families like flocks.
42The upright see and rejoice,
but all the wicked shut their mouths.

43Let all who are wise heed these things
and ponder the loving deeds of the LORD.

Psalm 108

A song. A psalm of David.

*1My heart, O God, is steadfast;
I will sing and make music with all my soul.
2Awake, harp and lyre!
I will awaken the dawn.
3I will praise you, LORD, among the nations;
I will sing of you among the peoples.

4For great is your love, higher than the heavens;
your faithfulness reaches to the skies.
5Be exalted, O God, above the heavens;
let your glory be over all the earth.

6Save us and help us with your right hand,
that those you love may be delivered.
7God has spoken from his sanctuary:
'In triumph I will parcel out Shechem
and measure off the Valley of Sukkoth.
8Gilead is mine, Manasseh is mine;
Ephraim is my helmet,
Judah is my sceptre.
9Moab is my washbasin,
on Edom I toss my sandal;
over Philistia I shout in triumph.'

10Who will bring me to the fortified city?
Who will lead me to Edom?
11Is it not you, God, you who have rejected us
and no longer go out with our armies?
12Give us aid against the enemy,
for human help is worthless.
13With God we shall gain the victory,
and he will trample down our enemies.

Psalm 109

For the director of music. Of David. A psalm.

1My God, whom I praise,
do not remain silent,
2for people who are wicked and deceitful
have opened their mouths against me;
they have spoken against me with lying tongues.
3With words of hatred they surround me;
they attack me without cause.
4In return for my friendship they accuse me,
but I am a man of prayer.
5They repay me evil for good,
and hatred for my friendship.

6Appoint someone evil to oppose my enemy;
let an accuser stand at his right hand.
7When he is tried, let him be found guilty,
and may his prayers condemn him.

---

* 108:1-13 is numbered 108:2-14 in Hebrew texts.

8 May his days be few;
   may another take his place of leadership.
9 May his children be fatherless
   and his wife a widow.
10 May his children be wandering beggars;
   may they be driven[a] from their ruined homes.
11 May a creditor seize all he has;
   may strangers plunder the fruits of his labour.
12 May no-one extend kindness to him
   or take pity on his fatherless children.
13 May his descendants be cut off,
   their names blotted out from the next generation.
14 May the iniquity of his fathers be remembered before the LORD;
   may the sin of his mother never be blotted out.
15 May their sins always remain before the LORD,
   that he may blot out their name from the earth.
16 For he never thought of doing a kindness,
   but hounded to death the poor
   and the needy and the broken-hearted.
17 He loved to pronounce a curse—
   may it come on him.
   He found no pleasure in blessing—
   may it be far from him.
18 He wore cursing as his garment;
   it entered into his body like water,
   into his bones like oil.
19 May it be like a cloak wrapped about him,
   like a belt tied for ever round him.
20 May this be the LORD's payment to my accusers,
   to those who speak evil of me.
21 But you, Sovereign LORD,
   help me for your name's sake;
   out of the goodness of your love, deliver me.
22 For I am poor and needy,
   and my heart is wounded within me.
23 I fade away like an evening shadow;
   I am shaken off like a locust.
24 My knees give way from fasting;
   my body is thin and gaunt.
25 I am an object of scorn to my accusers;
   when they see me, they shake their heads.
26 Help me, LORD my God;
   save me according to your unfailing love.
27 Let them know that it is your hand,
   that you, LORD, have done it.
28 While they curse, may you bless;
   may those who attack me be put to shame,
   but may your servant rejoice.
29 May my accusers be clothed with disgrace
   and wrapped in shame as in a cloak.
30 With my mouth I will greatly extol the LORD;
   in the great throng of worshippers I will praise him.
31 For he stands at the right hand of the needy,
   to save their lives from those who would condemn them.

Psalm 110

Of David. A psalm.

1 The LORD says to my lord:[b]
'Sit at my right hand
until I make your enemies
a footstool for your feet.'

Sign of the times

Right hand
Psalms 110:1
The right hand is significant because it's the side associated with power and authority. Jesus says that he will be seen sitting at the right hand of God (Matthew 26:64). Footstools were often used with a throne and some ancient ones have been found with pictures of defeated enemies carved into them.

---

[a] 10 Septuagint; Hebrew *sought* [b] 1 Or *Lord*

²The LORD will extend your mighty sceptre
  from Zion, saying,
  'Rule in the midst of your enemies.'
³Your troops will be willing
  on your day of battle.
 Arrayed in holy splendour,
  your young men will come to you
  like dew from the morning's womb.[a]

⁴The LORD has sworn
  and will not change his mind:
 'You are a priest for ever,
  in the order of Melchizedek.'

⁵The Lord is at your right hand[b];
  he will crush kings on the day of his
    wrath.
⁶He will judge nations, heaping up the
    dead
  and crushing the rulers of the whole
    earth.
⁷He will drink from a brook along the way;[c]
  and so he will lift up his head.

Psalm 111[d]

¹Praise the LORD.[e]

 I will extol the LORD with all my heart
  in the council of the upright and in the
    assembly.

²Great are the works of the LORD;
  they are pondered by all who delight in
    them.
³Glorious and majestic are his deeds,
  and his righteousness endures for ever.
⁴He has caused his wonders to be
    remembered;
  the LORD is gracious and
    compassionate.
⁵He provides food for those who fear him;
  he remembers his covenant for ever.
⁶He has shown his people the power of his
    works,
  giving them the lands of other nations.
⁷The works of his hands are faithful and
    just;
  all his precepts are trustworthy.
⁸They are established for ever and ever,
  enacted in faithfulness and
    uprightness.

⁹He provided redemption for his people;
  he ordained his covenant for ever—
  holy and awesome is his name.

¹⁰The fear of the LORD is the beginning of
    wisdom;
  all who follow his precepts have good
    understanding.
 To him belongs eternal praise.

Psalm 112[f]

¹Praise the LORD.[g]

 Blessed are those who fear the LORD,
  who find great delight in his
    commands.

²Their children will be mighty in the land;
  the generation of the upright will be
    blessed.
³Wealth and riches are in their houses,
  and their righteousness endures for
    ever.
⁴Even in darkness light dawns for the
    upright,
  for those who are gracious and
    compassionate and righteous.
⁵Good will come to those who are
    generous and lend freely,
  who conduct their affairs with justice.

⁶Surely the righteous will never be shaken;
  they will be remembered for ever.
⁷They will have no fear of bad news;
  their hearts are steadfast, trusting in
    the LORD.
⁸Their hearts are secure, they will have no
    fear;
  in the end they will look in triumph on
    their foes.
⁹They have scattered abroad their gifts to
    the poor,
  their righteousness endures for ever;
  their horn[h] will be lifted high in
    honour.

¹⁰The wicked will see and be vexed,
  they will gnash their teeth and waste
    away;
  the longings of the wicked will come to
    nothing.

---

[a] 3 The meaning of the Hebrew for this sentence is uncertain. [b] 5 Or *My lord is at your right hand*, LORD [c] 7 The meaning of the Hebrew for this clause is uncertain. [d] This psalm is an acrostic poem, the lines of which begin with the successive letters of the Hebrew alphabet. [e] 1 Hebrew *Hallelu Yah* [f] This psalm is an acrostic poem, the lines of which begin with the successive letters of the Hebrew alphabet. [g] 1 Hebrew *Hallelu Yah* [h] 9 *Horn* here symbolises dignity.

Psalm 113

1 Praise the LORD.[a]

Praise the LORD, you his servants;
  praise the name of the LORD.
2 Let the name of the LORD be praised,
  both now and for evermore.
3 From the rising of the sun to the place where it sets,
  the name of the LORD is to be praised.

4 The LORD is exalted over all the nations,
  his glory above the heavens.
5 Who is like the LORD our God,
  the One who sits enthroned on high,
6 who stoops down to look
  on the heavens and the earth?

7 He raises the poor from the dust
  and lifts the needy from the ash heap;
8 he seats them with princes,
  with the princes of his people.
9 He settles the childless woman in her home
  as a happy mother of children.

Praise the LORD.

Psalm 114

1 When Israel came out of Egypt,
  the house of Jacob from a people of foreign tongue,
2 Judah became God's sanctuary,
  Israel his dominion.

3 The sea looked and fled,
  the Jordan turned back;
4 the mountains leaped like rams,
  the hills like lambs.

5 Why was it, sea, that you fled?
  Why, Jordan, did you turn back?
6 Why, mountains, did you leap like rams,
  you hills, like lambs?

7 Tremble, earth, at the presence of the Lord,
  at the presence of the God of Jacob,
8 who turned the rock into a pool,
  the hard rock into springs of water.

Psalm 115

1 Not to us, LORD, not to us
  but to your name be the glory,
  because of your love and faithfulness.

2 Why do the nations say,
  'Where is their God?'
3 Our God is in heaven;
  he does whatever pleases him.
4 But their idols are silver and gold,
  made by human hands.
5 They have mouths, but cannot speak,
  eyes, but cannot see.
6 They have ears, but cannot hear,
  noses, but cannot smell.
7 They have hands, but cannot feel,
  feet, but cannot walk,
  nor can they utter a sound with their throats.
8 Those who make them will be like them,
  and so will all who trust in them.

9 House of Israel, trust in the LORD—
  he is their help and shield.
10 House of Aaron, trust in the LORD—
  he is their help and shield.
11 You who fear him, trust in the LORD—
  he is their help and shield.

12 The LORD remembers us and will bless us:
  he will bless the house of Israel,
  he will bless the house of Aaron,
13 he will bless those who fear the LORD—
  small and great alike.

14 May the LORD cause you to increase,
  both you and your children.
15 May you be blessed by the LORD,
  the Maker of heaven and earth.

16 The highest heavens belong to the LORD,
  but the earth he has given to the human race.
17 It is not the dead who praise the LORD,
  those who go down to the place of silence;
18 it is we who extol the LORD,
  both now and for evermore.

Praise the LORD.[b]

Psalm 116

1 I love the LORD, for he heard my voice;
  he heard my cry for mercy.

---

[a] 1 Hebrew *Hallelu Yah*; also in verse 9   [b] 18 Hebrew *Hallelu Yah*

²Because he turned his ear to me,
 I will call on him as long as I live.

³The cords of death entangled me,
 the anguish of the grave came over me;
 I was overcome by distress and sorrow.
⁴Then I called on the name of the LORD:
 'LORD, save me!'

⁵The LORD is gracious and righteous;
 our God is full of compassion.
⁶The LORD protects the unwary;
 when I was brought low, he saved me.

⁷Return to your rest, my soul,
 for the LORD has been good to you.

⁸For you, LORD, have delivered me from death,
 my eyes from tears,
 my feet from stumbling,
⁹that I may walk before the LORD
 in the land of the living.

¹⁰I trusted in the LORD when I said,
 'I am greatly afflicted';
¹¹in my alarm I said,
 'Everyone is a liar.'

¹²What shall I return to the LORD
 for all his goodness to me?
¹³I will lift up the cup of salvation
 and call on the name of the LORD.
¹⁴I will fulfil my vows to the LORD
 in the presence of all his people.

¹⁵Precious in the sight of the LORD
 is the death of those faithful to him.
¹⁶Truly I am your servant, LORD;
 I am your servant, as was my mother before me;
 you have loosed my bonds of affliction.

¹⁷I will sacrifice a thank-offering to you
 and call on the name of the LORD.
¹⁸I will fulfil my vows to the LORD
 in the presence of all his people,
¹⁹in the courts of the house of the LORD—
 in your midst, Jerusalem.

Praise the LORD.ᵃ

Psalm 117

¹Praise the LORD, all you nations;
 extol him, all you peoples.

²For great is his love towards us,
 and the faithfulness of the LORD
 endures for ever.

Praise the LORD.ᵇ

Psalm 118

¹Give thanks to the LORD, for he is good;
 his love endures for ever.

²Let Israel say:
 'His love endures for ever.'
³Let the house of Aaron say:
 'His love endures for ever.'
⁴Let those who fear the LORD say:
 'His love endures for ever.'

⁵When hard pressed, I cried to the LORD;
 he brought me into a spacious place.
⁶The LORD is with me; I will not be afraid.
 What can human beings do to me?
⁷The LORD is with me; he is my helper.
 I look in triumph on my enemies.

⁸It is better to take refuge in the LORD
 than to trust in human beings.
⁹It is better to take refuge in the LORD
 than to trust in princes.

¹⁰All the nations surrounded me,
 but in the name of the LORD I cut them down.
¹¹They surrounded me on every side,
 but in the name of the LORD I cut them down.
¹²They swarmed around me like bees,
 but they were consumed as quickly as burning thorns;
 in the name of the LORD I cut them down.
¹³I was pushed back and about to fall,
 but the LORD helped me.
¹⁴The LORD is my strength and my defenceᶜ;
 he has become my salvation.

¹⁵Shouts of joy and victory
 resound in the tents of the righteous:
 'The LORD's right hand has done mighty things!
¹⁶ The LORD's right hand is lifted high;
 the LORD's right hand has done mighty things!'
¹⁷I will not die but live,
 and will proclaim what the LORD has done.

ᵃ 19 Hebrew *Hallelu Yah*   ᵇ 2 Hebrew *Hallelu Yah*   ᶜ 14 Or *song*

¹⁸The LORD has chastened me severely,
  but he has not given me over to death.
¹⁹Open for me the gates of the righteous;
  I will enter and give thanks to the LORD.
²⁰This is the gate of the LORD
  through which the righteous may enter.
²¹I will give you thanks, for you answered me;
  you have become my salvation.

²²The stone the builders rejected
  has become the cornerstone;
²³the LORD has done this,
  and it is marvellous in our eyes.
²⁴The LORD has done it this very day;
  let us rejoice today and be glad.

²⁵LORD, save us!
  LORD, grant us success!

²⁶Blessed is he who comes in the name of the LORD.
  From the house of the LORD we bless you.[a]
²⁷The LORD is God,
  and he has made his light shine on us.
With boughs in hand, join in the festal procession
  up[b] to the horns of the altar.

²⁸You are my God, and I will praise you;
  you are my God, and I will exalt you.

²⁹Give thanks to the LORD, for he is good;
  his love endures for ever.

Psalm 119[c]

א Aleph

¹Blessed are those whose ways are blameless,
  who walk according to the law of the LORD.
²Blessed are those who keep his statutes
  and seek him with all their heart—
³they do no wrong
  but follow his ways.
⁴You have laid down precepts
  that are to be fully obeyed.
⁵Oh, that my ways were steadfast
  in obeying your decrees!
⁶Then I would not be put to shame
  when I consider all your commands.

Acrostic psalm
Psalms 119:1
This is the longest psalm in the Bible but that's not the only reason it's remarkable. It's an acrostic psalm; there are eight verses for each letter of the Hebrew alphabet, and every verse starts with that letter. It was perhaps the psalmist's way of showing that God's law was relevant to every part of life, 'from A to Z', as well as an easy way to memorise the psalm.

⁷I will praise you with an upright heart
  as I learn your righteous laws.
⁸I will obey your decrees;
  do not utterly forsake me.

ב Beth

⁹How can those who are young keep their way pure?
  By living according to your word.
¹⁰I seek you with all my heart;
  do not let me stray from your commands.
¹¹I have hidden your word in my heart
  that I might not sin against you.
¹²Praise be to you, LORD;
  teach me your decrees.
¹³With my lips I recount
  all the laws that come from your mouth.
¹⁴I rejoice in following your statutes
  as one rejoices in great riches.
¹⁵I meditate on your precepts
  and consider your ways.
¹⁶I delight in your decrees;
  I will not neglect your word.

ג Gimel

¹⁷Be good to your servant while I live,
  that I may obey your word.

---

[a] 26 The Hebrew is plural. [b] 27 Or *Bind the festal sacrifice with ropes / and take it* [c] This psalm is an acrostic poem; the verses of each stanza begin with the same letter of the Hebrew alphabet.

18Open my eyes that I may see
   wonderful things in your law.
19I am a stranger on earth;
   do not hide your commands from me.
20My soul is consumed with longing
   for your laws at all times.
21You rebuke the arrogant, who are accursed,
   those who stray from your commands.
22Remove from me scorn and contempt,
   for I keep your statutes.
23Though rulers sit together and slander me,
   your servant will meditate on your decrees.
24Your statutes are my delight;
   they are my counsellors.

ד Daleth

25I am laid low in the dust;
   preserve my life according to your word.
26I gave an account of my ways and you answered me;
   teach me your decrees.
27Cause me to understand the way of your precepts,
   that I may meditate on your wonderful deeds.
28My soul is weary with sorrow;
   strengthen me according to your word.
29Keep me from deceitful ways;
   be gracious to me and teach me your law.
30I have chosen the way of faithfulness;
   I have set my heart on your laws.
31I hold fast to your statutes, LORD;
   do not let me be put to shame.
32I run in the path of your commands,
   for you have set my heart free.

ה He

33Teach me, LORD, the way of your decrees,
   that I may follow it to the end.[a]
34Give me understanding, so that I may keep your law
   and obey it with all my heart.
35Direct me in the path of your commands,
   for there I find delight.

> **IN OTHER WORDS**
>
> **Law**
> Psalms 119:44
>
> 'The Law' refers to the commands and guidelines that Moses received from God and passed onto the people of Israel in the Old Testament. Far from being restrictive, the psalmist delights in the law as something that brings freedom. In the New Testament, Jesus came to fulfil the law, not do away with it. Just keeping the law is not enough; Jesus says that what matters is our motivation, or what's in our hearts (Matthew 5:17).

36Turn my heart towards your statutes
   and not towards selfish gain.
37Turn my eyes away from worthless things;
   preserve my life according to your word.[b]
38Fulfil your promise to your servant,
   so that you may be feared.
39Take away the disgrace I dread,
   for your laws are good.
40How I long for your precepts!
   In your righteousness preserve my life.

ו Waw

41May your unfailing love come to me, LORD,
   your salvation, according to your promise;
42then I can answer anyone who taunts me,
   for I trust in your word.
43Never take your word of truth from my mouth,
   for I have put my hope in your laws.
44I will always obey your law,
   for ever and ever.
45I will walk about in freedom,
   for I have sought out your precepts.
46I will speak of your statutes before kings
   and will not be put to shame,

---

[a] 33 Or *follow it for its reward* [b] 37 Two manuscripts of the Masoretic Text and Dead Sea Scrolls; most manuscripts of the Masoretic Text *life in your way*

⁴⁷for I delight in your commands
  because I love them.
⁴⁸I reach out for your commands, which I love,
  that I may meditate on your decrees.

ז Zayin

⁴⁹Remember your word to your servant,
  for you have given me hope.
⁵⁰My comfort in my suffering is this:
  your promise preserves my life.
⁵¹The arrogant mock me unmercifully,
  but I do not turn from your law.
⁵²I remember, LORD, your ancient laws,
  and I find comfort in them.
⁵³Indignation grips me because of the wicked,
  who have forsaken your law.
⁵⁴Your decrees are the theme of my song
  wherever I lodge.
⁵⁵In the night, LORD, I remember your name,
  that I may keep your law.
⁵⁶This has been my practice:
  I obey your precepts.

ח Heth

⁵⁷You are my portion, LORD;
  I have promised to obey your words.
⁵⁸I have sought your face with all my heart;
  be gracious to me according to your promise.
⁵⁹I have considered my ways
  and have turned my steps to your statutes.
⁶⁰I will hasten and not delay
  to obey your commands.
⁶¹Though the wicked bind me with ropes,
  I will not forget your law.
⁶²At midnight I rise to give you thanks
  for your righteous laws.
⁶³I am a friend to all who fear you,
  to all who follow your precepts.
⁶⁴The earth is filled with your love, LORD;
  teach me your decrees.

ט Teth

⁶⁵Do good to your servant
  according to your word, LORD.
⁶⁶Teach me knowledge and good judgment,
  for I trust your commands.
⁶⁷Before I was afflicted I went astray,
  but now I obey your word.
⁶⁸You are good, and what you do is good;
  teach me your decrees.
⁶⁹Though the arrogant have smeared me with lies,
  I keep your precepts with all my heart.
⁷⁰Their hearts are callous and unfeeling,
  but I delight in your law.
⁷¹It was good for me to be afflicted
  so that I might learn your decrees.
⁷²The law from your mouth is more precious to me
  than thousands of pieces of silver and gold.

י Yodh

⁷³Your hands made me and formed me;
  give me understanding to learn your commands.
⁷⁴May those who fear you rejoice when they see me,
  for I have put my hope in your word.
⁷⁵I know, LORD, that your laws are righteous,
  and that in faithfulness you have afflicted me.
⁷⁶May your unfailing love be my comfort,
  according to your promise to your servant.
⁷⁷Let your compassion come to me that I may live,
  for your law is my delight.
⁷⁸May the arrogant be put to shame for wronging me without cause;
  but I will meditate on your precepts.
⁷⁹May those who fear you turn to me,
  those who understand your statutes.
⁸⁰May my heart be blameless towards your decrees,
  that I may not be put to shame.

כ Kaph

⁸¹My soul faints with longing for your salvation,
  but I have put my hope in your word.
⁸²My eyes fail, looking for your promise;
  I say, 'When will you comfort me?'
⁸³Though I am like a wineskin in the smoke,
  I do not forget your decrees.
⁸⁴How long must your servant wait?
  When will you punish my persecutors?
⁸⁵The arrogant dig pits to trap me,
  contrary to your law.

⁸⁶All your commands are trustworthy;
  help me, for I am being persecuted
    without cause.
⁸⁷They almost wiped me from the earth,
  but I have not forsaken your precepts.
⁸⁸In your unfailing love preserve my life,
  that I may obey the statutes of your
    mouth.

ל Lamedh

⁸⁹Your word, LORD, is eternal;
  it stands firm in the heavens.
⁹⁰Your faithfulness continues through all
    generations;
  you established the earth, and it
    endures.
⁹¹Your laws endure to this day,
  for all things serve you.
⁹²If your law had not been my delight,
  I would have perished in my affliction.
⁹³I will never forget your precepts,
  for by them you have preserved my
    life.
⁹⁴Save me, for I am yours;
  I have sought out your precepts.
⁹⁵The wicked are waiting to destroy me,
  but I will ponder your statutes.
⁹⁶To all perfection I see a limit,
  but your commands are boundless.

מ Mem

⁹⁷Oh, how I love your law!
  I meditate on it all day long.
⁹⁸Your commands are always with me
  and make me wiser than my enemies.
⁹⁹I have more insight than all my teachers,
  for I meditate on your statutes.
¹⁰⁰I have more understanding than the
    elders,
  for I obey your precepts.
¹⁰¹I have kept my feet from every evil path
  so that I might obey your word.
¹⁰²I have not departed from your laws,
  for you yourself have taught me.
¹⁰³How sweet are your words to my taste,
  sweeter than honey to my mouth!
¹⁰⁴I gain understanding from your
    precepts;
  therefore I hate every wrong path.

נ Nun

¹⁰⁵Your word is a lamp to my feet
  and a light for my path.
¹⁰⁶I have taken an oath and confirmed it,
  that I will follow your righteous laws.
¹⁰⁷I have suffered much;
  preserve my life, LORD, according to
    your word.
¹⁰⁸Accept, LORD, the willing praise of my
    mouth,
  and teach me your laws.
¹⁰⁹Though I constantly take my life in my
    hands,
  I will not forget your law.
¹¹⁰The wicked have set a snare for me,
  but I have not strayed from your
    precepts.
¹¹¹Your statutes are my heritage for ever;
  they are the joy of my heart.
¹¹²My heart is set on keeping your decrees
  to the very end.ᵃ

ס Samekh

¹¹³I hate double-minded people,
  but I love your law.
¹¹⁴You are my refuge and my shield;
  I have put my hope in your word.
¹¹⁵Away from me, you evildoers,
  that I may keep the commands of my
    God!
¹¹⁶Sustain me according to your promise,
    and I shall live;
  do not let my hopes be dashed.
¹¹⁷Uphold me, and I shall be delivered;
  I shall always have regard for your
    decrees.
¹¹⁸You reject all who stray from your
    decrees,
  for their delusions come to nothing.
¹¹⁹All the wicked of the earth you discard
    like dross;
  therefore I love your statutes.
¹²⁰My flesh trembles in fear of you;
  I stand in awe of your laws.

ע Ayin

¹²¹I have done what is righteous and just;
  do not leave me to my oppressors.
¹²²Ensure your servant's well-being;
  do not let the arrogant oppress me.

ᵃ 112 Or *I for their enduring reward*

123My eyes fail, looking for your salvation,
  looking for your righteous promise.
124Deal with your servant according to your love
  and teach me your decrees.
125I am your servant; give me discernment
  that I may understand your statutes.
126It is time for you to act, LORD;
  your law is being broken.
127Because I love your commands
  more than gold, more than pure gold,
128and because I consider all your precepts right,
  I hate every wrong path.

פ Pe

129Your statutes are wonderful;
  therefore I obey them.
130The unfolding of your words gives light;
  it gives understanding to the simple.
131I open my mouth and pant,
  longing for your commands.
132Turn to me and have mercy on me,
  as you always do to those who love your name.
133Direct my footsteps according to your word;
  let no sin rule over me.
134Redeem me from human oppression,
  that I may obey your precepts.
135Make your face shine on your servant
  and teach me your decrees.
136Streams of tears flow from my eyes,
  for your law is not obeyed.

צ Tsadhe

137You are righteous, LORD,
  and your laws are right.
138The statutes you have laid down are righteous;
  they are fully trustworthy.
139My zeal wears me out,
  for my enemies ignore your words.
140Your promises have been thoroughly tested,
  and your servant loves them.
141Though I am lowly and despised,
  I do not forget your precepts.
142Your righteousness is everlasting
  and your law is true.
143Trouble and distress have come upon me,
  but your commands give me delight.
144Your statutes are always righteous;
  give me understanding that I may live.

ק Qoph

145I call with all my heart; answer me, LORD,
  and I will obey your decrees.
146I call out to you; save me
  and I will keep your statutes.
147I rise before dawn and cry for help;
  I have put my hope in your word.
148My eyes stay open through the watches of the night,
  that I may meditate on your promises.
149Hear my voice in accordance with your love;
  preserve my life, LORD, according to your laws.
150Those who devise wicked schemes are near,
  but they are far from your law.
151Yet you are near, LORD,
  and all your commands are true.
152Long ago I learned from your statutes
  that you established them to last forever.

ר Resh

153Look on my suffering and deliver me,
  for I have not forgotten your law.
154Defend my cause and redeem me;
  preserve my life according to your promise.
155Salvation is far from the wicked,
  for they do not seek out your decrees.
156Your compassion, LORD, is great;
  preserve my life according to your laws.
157Many are the foes who persecute me,
  but I have not turned from your statutes.
158I look on the faithless with loathing,
  for they do not obey your word.
159See how I love your precepts;
  preserve my life, LORD, in accordance with your love.
160All your words are true;
  all your righteous laws are eternal.

ש Sin and Shin

161Rulers persecute me without cause,
  but my heart trembles at your word.

¹⁶²I rejoice in your promise
  like one who finds great spoil.
¹⁶³I hate and detest falsehood
  but I love your law.
¹⁶⁴Seven times a day I praise you
  for your righteous laws.
¹⁶⁵Great peace have those who love your law,
  and nothing can make them stumble.
¹⁶⁶I wait for your salvation, LORD,
  and I follow your commands.
¹⁶⁷I obey your statutes,
  for I love them greatly.
¹⁶⁸I obey your precepts and your statutes,
  for all my ways are known to you.

ת Taw

¹⁶⁹May my cry come before you, LORD;
  give me understanding according to your word.
¹⁷⁰May my supplication come before you;
  deliver me according to your promise.
¹⁷¹May my lips overflow with praise,
  for you teach me your decrees.
¹⁷²May my tongue sing of your word,
  for all your commands are righteous.
¹⁷³May your hand be ready to help me,
  for I have chosen your precepts.
¹⁷⁴I long for your salvation, LORD,
  and your law gives me delight.
¹⁷⁵Let me live that I may praise you,
  and may your laws sustain me.
¹⁷⁶I have strayed like a lost sheep.
  Seek your servant,
  for I have not forgotten your commands.

Psalm 120

A song of ascents.

¹I call on the LORD in my distress,
  and he answers me.
²Save me, LORD,
  from lying lips
  and from deceitful tongues.

³What will he do to you,
  and what more besides,
  you deceitful tongue?
⁴He will punish you with a warrior's sharp arrows,
  with burning coals of the broom bush.

> ### Sign of the times
>
> **Song of ascents**
> Psalms 120:1
>
> The Israelites would go to Jerusalem for the three main festivals every year. Jerusalem was built on hills and the temple was built on Mount Zion. Psalms 120–134 are called 'songs of ascents' and would probably have been sung by the worshippers as they made their way to the temple.

⁵Woe to me that I dwell in Meshek,
  that I live among the tents of Kedar!
⁶Too long have I lived
  among those who hate peace.
⁷I am for peace;
  but when I speak, they are for war.

Psalm 121

A song of ascents.

¹I lift up my eyes to the mountains—
  where does my help come from?
²My help comes from the LORD,
  the Maker of heaven and earth.

³He will not let your foot slip—
  he who watches over you will not slumber;
⁴indeed, he who watches over Israel
  will neither slumber nor sleep.

⁵The LORD watches over you—
  the LORD is your shade at your right hand;
⁶the sun will not harm you by day,
  nor the moon by night.

⁷The LORD will keep you from all harm—
  he will watch over your life;
⁸the LORD will watch over your coming and going
  both now and for evermore.

Psalm 122

A song of ascents. Of David.

¹I rejoiced with those who said to me,
  'Let us go to the house of the LORD.'
²Our feet are standing
  in your gates, Jerusalem.

³Jerusalem is built like a city
  that is closely compacted together.
⁴That is where the tribes go up—
  the tribes of the LORD—
to praise the name of the LORD
  according to the statute given to Israel.
⁵There stand the thrones for judgment,
  the thrones of the house of David.

⁶Pray for the peace of Jerusalem:
  'May those who love you be secure.
⁷May there be peace within your walls
  and security within your citadels.'
⁸For the sake of my friends and of all the people,
  I will say, 'Peace be within you.'
⁹For the sake of the house of the LORD our God,
  I will seek your prosperity.

Psalm 123

A song of ascents.

¹I lift up my eyes to you,
  to you who sit enthroned in heaven.
²As the eyes of slaves look to the hand of their master,
  as the eyes of a female slave look to the hand of her mistress,
so our eyes look to the LORD our God,
  till he shows us his mercy.

³Have mercy on us, LORD, have mercy on us,
  for we have endured no end of contempt.
⁴We have endured no end
  of ridicule from the arrogant,
  of contempt from the proud.

Psalm 124

A song of ascents. Of David.

¹If the LORD had not been on our side—
  let Israel say—
²if the LORD had not been on our side
  when people attacked us,
³they would have swallowed us alive
  when their anger flared against us;
⁴the flood would have engulfed us,
  the torrent would have swept over us,
⁵the raging waters
  would have swept us away.

⁶Praise be to the LORD,
  who has not let us be torn by their teeth.
⁷We have escaped like a bird
  from the fowler's snare;
the snare has been broken,
  and we have escaped.
⁸Our help is in the name of the LORD,
  the Maker of heaven and earth.

Psalm 125

A song of ascents.

¹Those who trust in the LORD are like Mount Zion,
  which cannot be shaken but endures for ever.
²As the mountains surround Jerusalem,
  so the LORD surrounds his people
  both now and for evermore.

³The sceptre of the wicked will not remain
  over the land allotted to the righteous,
for then the righteous might use
  their hands to do evil.

⁴LORD, do good to those who are good,
  to those who are upright in heart.
⁵But those who turn to crooked ways
  the LORD will banish with the evildoers.

Peace be on Israel.

Psalm 126

A song of ascents.

¹When the LORD restored the fortunes of[a] Zion,
  we were like those who dreamed.[b]
²Our mouths were filled with laughter,
  our tongues with songs of joy.
Then it was said among the nations,
  'The LORD has done great things for them.'
³The LORD has done great things for us,
  and we are filled with joy.

---

[a] 1 Or LORD brought back the captives to [b] 1 Or those restored to health

⁴Restore our fortunes,ᵃ LORD,
  like streams in the Negev.
⁵Those who sow with tears
  will reap with songs of joy.
⁶Those who go out weeping,
  carrying seed to sow,
will return with songs of joy,
  carrying sheaves with them.

Psalm 127

A song of ascents. Of Solomon.

¹Unless the LORD builds the house,
  the builders labour in vain.
Unless the LORD watches over the city,
  the guards stand watch in vain.
²In vain you rise early
  and stay up late,
toiling for food to eat—
  for he grants sleep toᵇ those he loves.

³Children are a heritage from the LORD,
  offspring a reward from him.
⁴Like arrows in the hands of a warrior
  are children born in one's youth.
⁵Blessed is the man
  whose quiver is full of them.
They will not be put to shame
  when they contend with their
    opponents in court.

Psalm 128

A song of ascents.

¹Blessed are all who fear the LORD,
  who walk in obedience to him.
²You will eat the fruit of your labour;
  blessings and prosperity will be yours.
³Your wife will be like a fruitful vine
  within your house;
your children will be like olive shoots
  round your table.
⁴Yes, this will be the blessing
  for the man who fears the LORD.

⁵May the LORD bless you from Zion;
  may you see the prosperity of
    Jerusalem
  all the days of your life.
⁶May you live to see your children's
    children—
  peace be on Israel.

Psalm 129

A song of ascents.

¹'They have greatly oppressed me from my
    youth,'
  let Israel say;
²'they have greatly oppressed me from my
    youth,
  but they have not gained the victory
    over me.
³Ploughmen have ploughed my back
  and made their furrows long.
⁴But the LORD is righteous;
  he has cut me free from the cords of the
    wicked.'

⁵May all who hate Zion
  be turned back in shame.
⁶May they be like grass on the roof,
  which withers before it can grow;
⁷reapers cannot fill their hands with it,
  nor those who gather fill their arms.
⁸May those who pass by not say to them,
  'The blessing of the LORD be on you;
  we bless you in the name of the LORD.'

Psalm 130

A song of ascents.

¹Out of the depths I cry to you, LORD;
² Lord, hear my voice.
Let your ears be attentive
  to my cry for mercy.

³If you, LORD, kept a record of sins,
  Lord, who could stand?
⁴But with you there is forgiveness,
  so that we can, with reverence, serve
    you.

⁵I wait for the LORD, my whole being waits,
  and in his word I put my hope.
⁶I wait for the Lord
  more than watchmen wait for the
    morning,
  more than watchmen wait for the
    morning.

⁷Israel, put your hope in the LORD,
  for with the LORD is unfailing love
  and with him is full redemption.
⁸He himself will redeem Israel
  from all their sins.

ᵃ 4 Or *Bring back our captives*   ᵇ 2 Or *eat— / for while they sleep he provides for*

Psalm 131

A song of ascents. Of David.

¹My heart is not proud, LORD,
  my eyes are not haughty;
I do not concern myself with great
    matters
  or things too wonderful for me.
²But I have calmed myself
  and quietened my ambitions.
I am like a weaned child with its mother;
  like a weaned child I am content.

³Israel, put your hope in the LORD
  both now and for evermore.

Psalm 132

A song of ascents.

¹LORD, remember David
  and all his self-denial.

²He swore an oath to the LORD
  and made a vow to the Mighty One of
    Jacob:
³'I will not enter my house
  or go to my bed,
⁴I will allow no sleep to my eyes
  or slumber to my eyelids,
⁵till I find a place for the LORD,
  a dwelling for the Mighty One of
    Jacob.'

⁶We heard it in Ephrathah,
  we came upon it in the fields of
    Jaar:*ᵃ*
⁷'Let us go to his dwelling-place,
  let us worship at his footstool, saying,
⁸"Arise, LORD, and come to your resting
    place,
  you and the ark of your might.
⁹May your priests be clothed with your
    righteousness;
  may your faithful people sing for joy." '

¹⁰For the sake of your servant David,
  do not reject your anointed one.

¹¹The LORD swore an oath to David,
  a sure oath that he will not revoke:
'One of your own descendants
  I will place on your throne.
¹²If your sons keep my covenant
  and the statutes I teach them,
then their sons shall sit
  on your throne for ever and ever.'

¹³For the LORD has chosen Zion,
  he has desired it for his dwelling,
    saying,
¹⁴'This is my resting place for ever and ever;
  here I will sit enthroned, for I have
    desired it.
¹⁵I will bless her with abundant provisions;
  her poor I will satisfy with food.
¹⁶I will clothe her priests with salvation,
  and her faithful people shall ever sing
    for joy.

¹⁷'Here I will make a horn*ᵇ* grow for David
  and set up a lamp for my anointed one.
¹⁸I will clothe his enemies with shame,
  but his head shall be adorned with a
    resplendent crown.'

Psalm 133

A song of ascents. Of David.

¹How good and pleasant it is
  when God's people live together in
    unity!

²It is like precious oil poured on the head,
  running down on the beard,
  running down on Aaron's beard,
  down on the collar of his robe.
³It is as if the dew of Hermon
  were falling on Mount Zion.
For there the LORD bestows his blessing,
  even life for evermore.

Sign of the times

Anointing oil
Psalms 133:2

Olive oil was used to anoint Aaron as the first high priest. It was poured on his head, and the image of it running down onto his beard and robes speaks of generosity and blessing.

---

*ᵃ*6 Or *heard of it in Ephrathah, / we found it in the fields of Jearim.* (See 1 Chron. 13:5,6) (and no quotation marks around verses 7-9)   *ᵇ*17 *Horn* here symbolises strong one, that is, king.

Psalm 134

A song of ascents.

¹Praise the LORD, all you servants of the LORD
who minister by night in the house of the LORD.
²Lift up your hands in the sanctuary
and praise the LORD.

³May the LORD bless you from Zion,
he who is the Maker of heaven and earth.

Psalm 135

¹Praise the LORD.[a]

Praise the name of the LORD;
praise him, you servants of the LORD,
²you who minister in the house of the LORD,
in the courts of the house of our God.

³Praise the LORD, for the LORD is good;
sing praise to his name, for that is pleasant.
⁴For the LORD has chosen Jacob to be his own,
Israel to be his treasured possession.

⁵I know that the LORD is great,
that our Lord is greater than all gods.
⁶The LORD does whatever pleases him,
in the heavens and on the earth,
in the seas and all their depths.
⁷He makes clouds rise from the ends of the earth;
he sends lightning with the rain
and brings out the wind from his storehouses.

⁸He struck down the firstborn of Egypt,
the firstborn of people and animals.
⁹He sent his signs and wonders into your midst, Egypt,
against Pharaoh and all his servants.
¹⁰He struck down many nations
and killed mighty kings—
¹¹Sihon king of the Amorites,
Og king of Bashan,
and all the kings of Canaan—
¹²and he gave their land as an inheritance,
an inheritance to his people Israel.

¹³Your name, LORD, endures for ever,
your renown, LORD, through all generations.
¹⁴For the LORD will vindicate his people
and relent concerning his servants.

¹⁵The idols of the nations are silver and gold,
made by human hands.
¹⁶They have mouths, but cannot speak,
eyes, but cannot see.
¹⁷They have ears, but cannot hear,
nor is there breath in their mouths.
¹⁸Those who make them will be like them,
and so will all who trust in them.

¹⁹House of Israel, praise the LORD;
house of Aaron, praise the LORD;
²⁰house of Levi, praise the LORD;
you who fear him, praise the LORD.
²¹Praise be to the LORD from Zion,
to him who dwells in Jerusalem.

Praise the LORD.

Psalm 136

¹Give thanks to the LORD, for he is good.
His love endures for ever.
²Give thanks to the God of gods.
His love endures for ever.
³Give thanks to the Lord of lords:
His love endures for ever.

⁴to him who alone does great wonders,
His love endures for ever.
⁵who by his understanding made the heavens,
His love endures for ever.
⁶who spread out the earth upon the waters,
His love endures for ever.
⁷who made the great lights—
His love endures for ever.
⁸the sun to govern the day,
His love endures for ever.
⁹the moon and stars to govern the night;
His love endures for ever.

¹⁰to him who struck down the firstborn of Egypt
His love endures for ever.
¹¹and brought Israel out from among them
His love endures for ever.
¹²with a mighty hand and outstretched arm;
His love endures for ever.

---

[a] 1 Hebrew *Hallelu Yah*; also in verses 3 and 21

¹³to him who divided the Red Sea[a] asunder
His love endures for ever.
¹⁴and brought Israel through the midst of it,
His love endures for ever.
¹⁵but swept Pharaoh and his army into the Red Sea;
His love endures for ever.

¹⁶to him who led his people through the wilderness;
His love endures for ever.

¹⁷to him who struck down great kings,
His love endures for ever.
¹⁸and killed mighty kings—
His love endures for ever.
¹⁹Sihon king of the Amorites
His love endures for ever.
²⁰and Og king of Bashan—
His love endures for ever.
²¹and gave their land as an inheritance,
His love endures for ever.
²²an inheritance to his servant Israel.
His love endures for ever.

²³He remembered us in our low estate
His love endures for ever.
²⁴and freed us from our enemies.
His love endures for ever.
²⁵He gives food to every creature.
His love endures for ever.

²⁶Give thanks to the God of heaven.
His love endures for ever.

Psalm 137

¹By the rivers of Babylon we sat and wept
when we remembered Zion.
²There on the poplars
we hung our harps,
³for there our captors asked us for songs,
our tormentors demanded songs of joy;
they said, 'Sing us one of the songs of Zion!'

⁴How can we sing the songs of the LORD
while in a foreign land?
⁵If I forget you, Jerusalem,
may my right hand forget its skill.
⁶May my tongue cling to the roof of my mouth
if I do not remember you,
if I do not consider Jerusalem
my highest joy.

⁷Remember, LORD, what the Edomites did
on the day Jerusalem fell.
'Tear it down,' they cried,
'tear it down to its foundations!'
⁸Daughter Babylon, doomed to destruction,
happy are those who repay you
according to what you have done to us.
⁹Happy are those who seize your infants
and dash them against the rocks.

Psalm 138

Of David.

¹I will praise you, LORD, with all my heart;
before the 'gods' I will sing your praise.
²I will bow down towards your holy temple
and will praise your name
for your unfailing love and your faithfulness,
for you have so exalted your solemn decree
that it surpasses your fame.
³When I called, you answered me;
you greatly emboldened me.

⁴May all the kings of the earth praise you, LORD,
when they hear what you have decreed.
⁵May they sing of the ways of the LORD,
for the glory of the LORD is great.

⁶Though the LORD is exalted, he looks kindly on the lowly,
but he takes notice of the proud from afar.
⁷Though I walk in the midst of trouble,
you preserve my life.
You stretch out your hand against the anger of my foes;
with your right hand you save me.
⁸The LORD will vindicate me;
your love, LORD, endures for ever—
do not abandon the works of your hands.

Psalm 139

For the director of music. Of David. A psalm.

¹You have searched me, LORD,
and you know me.

---

[a] 13 Or *the Sea of Reeds*; also in verse 15

²You know when I sit and when I rise;
 you perceive my thoughts from afar.
³You discern my going out and my lying down;
 you are familiar with all my ways.
⁴Before a word is on my tongue
 you, LORD, know it completely.
⁵You hem me in behind and before,
 and you lay your hand upon me.
⁶Such knowledge is too wonderful for me,
 too lofty for me to attain.

⁷Where can I go from your Spirit?
 Where can I flee from your presence?
⁸If I go up to the heavens, you are there;
 if I make my bed in the depths, you are there.
⁹If I rise on the wings of the dawn,
 if I settle on the far side of the sea,
¹⁰even there your hand will guide me,
 your right hand will hold me fast.
¹¹If I say, 'Surely the darkness will hide me
 and the light become night around me,'
¹²even the darkness will not be dark to you;
 the night will shine like the day,
 for darkness is as light to you.

¹³For you created my inmost being;
 you knit me together in my mother's womb.
¹⁴I praise you because I am fearfully and wonderfully made;
 your works are wonderful,
 I know that full well.
¹⁵My frame was not hidden from you
 when I was made in the secret place.
 When I was woven together in the depths of the earth,
¹⁶ your eyes saw my unformed body.
 All the days ordained for me
 were written in your book
 before one of them came to be.
¹⁷How precious to me are your thoughts,[a] God!
 How vast is the sum of them!
¹⁸Were I to count them,
 they would outnumber the grains of sand—
 when I awake, I am still with you.

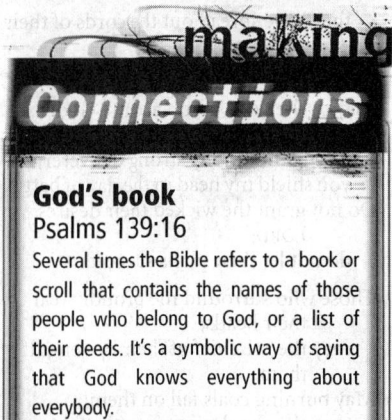

God's book
Psalms 139:16
Several times the Bible refers to a book or scroll that contains the names of those people who belong to God, or a list of their deeds. It's a symbolic way of saying that God knows everything about everybody.

¹⁹If only you, God, would slay the wicked!
 Away from me, you who are bloodthirsty!
²⁰They speak of you with evil intent;
 your adversaries misuse your name.
²¹Do I not hate those who hate you, LORD,
 and abhor those who are in rebellion against you?
²²I have nothing but hatred for them;
 I count them my enemies.
²³Search me, God, and know my heart;
 test me and know my anxious thoughts.
²⁴See if there is any offensive way in me,
 and lead me in the way everlasting.

Psalm 140

For the director of music. A psalm of David.

*¹Rescue me, LORD, from evildoers;
 protect me from the violent,
²who devise evil plans in their hearts
 and stir up war every day.
³They make their tongues as sharp as a serpent's;
 the poison of vipers is on their lips.[b]

⁴Keep me safe, LORD, from the hands of the wicked;
 protect me from the violent,
 who devise ways to trip my feet.
⁵The arrogant have hidden a snare for me;

---

[a] 17 Or *precious are your thoughts concerning me* at the end of verses 5 and 8. [b] 3 The Hebrew has *Selah* (a word of uncertain meaning) here and

* 140:1-13 is numbered 140:2-14 in Hebrew texts.

they have spread out the cords of their net
and have set traps for me along my path.
⁶I say to the LORD, 'You are my God.'
Hear, LORD, my cry for mercy.
⁷Sovereign LORD, my strong deliverer,
you shield my head in the day of battle.
⁸Do not grant the wicked their desires, LORD;
do not let their plans succeed.

⁹Those who surround me proudly rear their heads;
may the mischief of their lips engulf them.
¹⁰May burning coals fall on them;
may they be thrown into the fire,
into miry pits, never to rise.
¹¹May slanderers not be established in the land;
may disaster hunt down the violent.

¹²I know that the LORD secures justice for the poor
and upholds the cause of the needy.
¹³Surely the righteous will praise your name,
and the upright will live in your presence.

Psalm 141

A psalm of David.

¹I call to you, LORD, come quickly to me;
hear me when I call to you.
²May my prayer be set before you like incense;
may the lifting up of my hands be like the evening sacrifice.

³Set a guard over my mouth, LORD;
keep watch over the door of my lips.
⁴Do not let my heart be drawn to what is evil
so that I take part in wicked deeds
along with those who are evildoers;
do not let me eat of their delicacies.

⁵Let a righteous man strike me—that is a kindness;
let him rebuke me—that is oil on my head.
My head will not refuse it,
for my prayer will still be against the deeds of evildoers.

⁶Their rulers will be thrown down from the cliffs,
and the wicked will learn that my words were well spoken.
⁷They will say, 'As one ploughs and breaks up the earth,
so our bones have been scattered at the mouth of the grave.'

⁸But my eyes are fixed on you, Sovereign LORD;
in you I take refuge—do not give me over to death.
⁹Keep me safe from the traps set by evildoers,
from the snares they have laid for me.
¹⁰Let the wicked fall into their own nets,
while I pass by in safety.

Psalm 142

A maskil[a] of David. When he was in the cave. A prayer.

*¹I cry aloud to the LORD;
I lift up my voice to the LORD for mercy.
²I pour out before him my complaint;
before him I tell my trouble.

³When my spirit grows faint within me,
it is you who watch over my way.
In the path where I walk
people have hidden a snare for me.
⁴Look and see, there is no-one at my right hand;
no-one is concerned for me.
I have no refuge;
no-one cares for my life.

⁵I cry to you, LORD;
I say, 'You are my refuge,
my portion in the land of the living.'

⁶Listen to my cry,
for I am in desperate need;
rescue me from those who pursue me,
for they are too strong for me.

---

[a] Title: Probably a literary or musical term

* 142:1-7 is numbered 142:2-8 in Hebrew texts.

⁷Set me free from my prison,
    that I may praise your name.
Then the righteous will gather about me
    because of your goodness to me.

Psalm 143

A psalm of David.

¹LORD, hear my prayer,
    listen to my cry for mercy;
in your faithfulness and righteousness
    come to my relief.
²Do not bring your servant into judgment,
    for no-one living is righteous before you.
³The enemy pursues me,
    he crushes me to the ground;
he makes me dwell in the darkness
    like those long dead.
⁴So my spirit grows faint within me;
    my heart within me is dismayed.
⁵I remember the days of long ago;
    I meditate on all your works
    and consider what your hands have done.
⁶I spread out my hands to you;
    I thirst for you like a parched land.ᵃ

⁷Answer me quickly, LORD;
    my spirit fails.
Do not hide your face from me
    or I will be like those who go down to the pit.
⁸Let the morning bring me word of your unfailing love,
    for I have put my trust in you.
Show me the way I should go,
    for to you I entrust my life.
⁹Rescue me from my enemies, LORD,
    for I hide myself in you.
¹⁰Teach me to do your will,
    for you are my God;
may your good Spirit
    lead me on level ground.

¹¹For your name's sake, LORD, preserve my life;
    in your righteousness, bring me out of trouble.
¹²In your unfailing love, silence my enemies;
    destroy all my foes,
    for I am your servant.

Psalm 144

Of David.

¹Praise be to the LORD my Rock,
    who trains my hands for war,
    my fingers for battle.
²He is my loving God and my fortress,
    my stronghold and my deliverer,
my shield, in whom I take refuge,
    who subdues peoplesᵇ under me.

³LORD, what are human beings that you care for them,
    mere mortals that you think of them?
⁴They are like a breath;
    their days are like a fleeting shadow.

⁵Part your heavens, LORD, and come down;
    touch the mountains, so that they smoke.
⁶Send forth lightning and scatter the enemy;
    shoot your arrows and rout them.
⁷Reach down your hand from on high;
    deliver me and rescue me
from the mighty waters,
    from the hands of foreigners
⁸whose mouths are full of lies,
    whose right hands are deceitful.

⁹I will sing a new song to you, my God;
    on the ten-stringed lyre I will make music to you,
¹⁰to the One who gives victory to kings,
    who delivers his servant David.

From the deadly sword ¹¹deliver me;
    rescue me from the hands of foreigners
whose mouths are full of lies,
    whose right hands are deceitful.

¹²Then our sons in their youth
    will be like well-nurtured plants,
and our daughters will be like pillars
    carved to adorn a palace.
¹³Our barns will be filled
    with every kind of provision.
Our sheep will increase by thousands,
    by tens of thousands in our fields;

ᵃ 6 The Hebrew has *Selah* (a word of uncertain meaning) here.   ᵇ 2 Many manuscripts of the Masoretic Text, Dead Sea Scrolls, Aquila, Jerome and Syriac; most manuscripts of the Masoretic Text *subdues my people*

14 our oxen will draw heavy loads.[a]
There will be no breaching of walls,
no going into captivity,
no cry of distress in our streets.
15 Blessed is the people of whom this is true;
blessed is the people whose God is the LORD.

Psalm 145[b]

A psalm of praise. Of David.

1 I will exalt you, my God the King;
I will praise your name for ever and ever.
2 Every day I will praise you
and extol your name for ever and ever.

3 Great is the LORD and most worthy of praise;
his greatness no-one can fathom.
4 One generation commends your works to another;
they tell of your mighty acts.
5 They speak of the glorious splendour of your majesty—
and I will meditate on your wonderful works.[c]
6 They tell of the power of your awesome works—
and I will proclaim your great deeds.
7 They celebrate your abundant goodness
and joyfully sing of your righteousness.

8 The LORD is gracious and compassionate,
slow to anger and rich in love.

9 The LORD is good to all;
he has compassion on all he has made.
10 All your works praise you, LORD;
your faithful people extol you.
11 They tell of the glory of your kingdom
and speak of your might,
12 so that all people may know of your mighty acts
and the glorious splendour of your kingdom.
13 Your kingdom is an everlasting kingdom,
and your dominion endures through all generations.

The LORD is trustworthy in all he promises
and faithful in all he does.[d]
14 The LORD upholds all who fall
and lifts up all who are bowed down.
15 The eyes of all look to you,
and you give them their food at the proper time.
16 You open your hand
and satisfy the desires of every living thing.

17 The LORD is righteous in all his ways
and faithful in all he does.
18 The LORD is near to all who call on him,
to all who call on him in truth.
19 He fulfils the desires of those who fear him;
he hears their cry and saves them.
20 The LORD watches over all who love him,
but all the wicked he will destroy.

21 My mouth will speak in praise of the LORD.
Let every creature praise his holy name for ever and ever.

Psalm 146

1 Praise the LORD.[e]

Praise the LORD, my soul.

2 I will praise the LORD all my life;
I will sing praise to my God as long as I live.

IN OTHER WORDS

Righteous
Psalms 145:17
Being righteous includes both doing the right things and having right relationships and attitudes. It is most often used to describe God's character and activity in the world, but Christians are also called to be righteous in their actions and relationships.

---

[a] 14 Or *our chieftains will be firmly established* [b] This psalm is an acrostic poem, the verses of which (including verse 13b) begin with the successive letters of the Hebrew alphabet. [c] 5 Dead Sea Scrolls and Syriac (see also Septuagint); Masoretic Text *On the glorious splendour of your majesty / and on your wonderful works I will meditate* [d] 13 One manuscript of the Masoretic Text, Dead Sea Scrolls and Syriac (see also Septuagint); most manuscripts of the Masoretic Text do not have the last two lines of verse 13. [e] 1 Hebrew *Hallelu Yah*; also in verse 10

³Do not put your trust in princes,
  in human beings, who cannot save.
⁴When their spirit departs, they return to the ground;
  on that very day their plans come to nothing.
⁵Blessed are those whose help is the God of Jacob,
  whose hope is in the LORD their God.

⁶He is the Maker of heaven and earth,
  the sea, and everything in them—
  he remains faithful for ever.
⁷He upholds the cause of the oppressed
  and gives food to the hungry.
The LORD sets prisoners free,
⁸ the LORD gives sight to the blind,
  the LORD lifts up those who are bowed down,
  the LORD loves the righteous.
⁹The LORD watches over the foreigner
  and sustains the fatherless and the widow,
  but he frustrates the ways of the wicked.

¹⁰The LORD reigns for ever,
  your God, O Zion, for all generations.

Praise the LORD.

Psalm 147

¹Praise the LORD.[a]

How good it is to sing praises to our God,
  how pleasant and fitting to praise him!

²The LORD builds up Jerusalem;
  he gathers the exiles of Israel.
³He heals the broken-hearted
  and binds up their wounds.
⁴He determines the number of the stars
  and calls them each by name.
⁵Great is our Lord and mighty in power;
  his understanding has no limit.
⁶The LORD sustains the humble
  but casts the wicked to the ground.

⁷Sing to the LORD with grateful praise;
  make music to our God on the harp.

⁸He covers the sky with clouds;
  he supplies the earth with rain
  and makes grass grow on the hills.
⁹He provides food for the cattle
  and for the young ravens when they call.

¹⁰His pleasure is not in the strength of the horse,
  nor his delight in the power of human legs;
¹¹the LORD delights in those who fear him,
  who put their hope in his unfailing love.

¹²Extol the LORD, Jerusalem;
  praise your God, Zion.

¹³He strengthens the bars of your gates
  and blesses your people within you.
¹⁴He grants peace to your borders
  and satisfies you with the finest of wheat.

¹⁵He sends his command to the earth;
  his word runs swiftly.
¹⁶He spreads the snow like wool
  and scatters the frost like ashes.
¹⁷He hurls down hail like pebbles.
  Who can withstand his icy blast?
¹⁸He sends his word and melts them;
  he stirs up his breezes, and the waters flow.

¹⁹He has revealed his word to Jacob,
  his laws and decrees to Israel.
²⁰He has done this for no other nation;
  they do not know his laws.[b]

Praise the LORD.

Psalm 148

¹Praise the LORD.[c]

Praise the LORD from the heavens;
  praise him in the heights above.
²Praise him, all his angels;
  praise him, all his heavenly hosts.
³Praise him, sun and moon;
  praise him, all you shining stars.
⁴Praise him, you highest heavens
  and you waters above the skies.

⁵Let them praise the name of the LORD,
  for at his command they were created,
⁶and he established them for ever and ever—

---

[a] 1 Hebrew *Hallelu Yah*; also in verse 20   [b] 20 Masoretic Text; Dead Sea Scrolls and Septuagint / *he has not made his laws known to them*   [c] 1 Hebrew *Hallelu Yah*; also in verse 14

he issued a decree that will never pass away.

⁷Praise the LORD from the earth,
you great sea creatures and all ocean depths,
⁸lightning and hail, snow and clouds,
stormy winds that do his bidding,
⁹you mountains and all hills,
fruit trees and all cedars,
¹⁰wild animals and all cattle,
small creatures and flying birds,
¹¹kings of the earth and all nations,
you princes and all rulers on earth,
¹²young men and women,
old men and children.

¹³Let them praise the name of the LORD,
for his name alone is exalted;
his splendour is above the earth and the heavens.
¹⁴And he has raised up for his people a horn,ᵃ
the praise of all his faithful servants,
of Israel, the people close to his heart.

Praise the LORD.

Psalm 149

¹Praise the LORD.ᵇ

Sing to the LORD a new song,
his praise in the assembly of his faithful people.
²Let Israel rejoice in their Maker;
let the people of Zion be glad in their King.
³Let them praise his name with dancing
and make music to him with tambourine and harp.
⁴For the LORD takes delight in his people;
he crowns the humble with victory.
⁵Let his faithful people rejoice in this honour
and sing for joy on their beds.

> **IN OTHER WORDS**
>
> **Sanctuary**
> Psalms 150:1
> A sanctuary is a holy place set apart for the worship of God or as a refuge from danger.

⁶May the praise of God be in their mouths
and a double-edged sword in their hands,
⁷to inflict vengeance on the nations
and punishment on the peoples,
⁸to bind their kings with fetters,
their nobles with shackles of iron,
⁹to carry out the sentence written against them—
this is the glory of all his faithful people.

Praise the LORD.

Psalm 150

¹Praise the LORD.ᶜ

Praise God in his sanctuary;
praise him in his mighty heavens.
²Praise him for his acts of power;
praise him for his surpassing greatness.
³Praise him with the sounding of the trumpet,
praise him with the harp and lyre,
⁴praise him with tambourine and dancing,
praise him with the strings and pipe,
⁵praise him with the clash of cymbals,
praise him with resounding cymbals.

⁶Let everything that has breath praise the LORD.

Praise the LORD.

ᵃ 14 *Horn* here symbolises strength.   ᵇ 1 Hebrew *Hallelu Yah*; also in verse 9   ᶜ 1 Hebrew *Hallelu Yah*; also in verse 6

Proverbs

INTRODUCTION

PROVERBS

Author: Solomon wrote most of this book. Other writers include Agur (30:1) and King Lemuel (31:1).

Who to: Solomon addresses one of his sons, whose name was Rehoboam.

When: Solomon reigned from 971 BC to 931 BC. Chapters 25 to 29 were added in around 720 BC, after his death.

Did you know? The first six verses of chapter 1 are actually the title of the book, the longest title of any Old Testament book.

Main theme: The book of Proverbs contains wisdom and instructions on how to live life well. Many ancient cultures had proverbs like these, but this book is unique in one important aspect; it points people towards God, saying that the best way to live is to worship God and to live in his way. Proverbs is a very practical book, giving advice on how to choose friends, the value of hard work and how to stop arguments, among other things.

1

Purpose and theme

The proverbs of Solomon son of David, king of Israel:

²for gaining wisdom and instruction;
  for understanding words of insight;
³for receiving instruction in prudent
    behaviour,
  doing what is right and just and fair;
⁴for giving prudence to those who are
    simple,*ᵃ*
  knowledge and discretion to the
    young—
⁵let the wise listen and add to their
    learning,

ᵃ 4 The Hebrew word rendered *simple* in Proverbs denotes a person who is gullible, without moral direction and inclined to evil.

and let the discerning get guidance—
⁶for understanding proverbs and parables,
the sayings and riddles of the wise.ᵃ

⁷The fear of the LORD is the beginning of knowledge,
but fools[b] despise wisdom and instruction.

Prologue: exhortations to embrace wisdom

Warning against the invitation of sinful men

⁸Listen, my son, to your father's instruction
and do not forsake your mother's teaching.
⁹They are a garland to grace your head
and a chain to adorn your neck.

¹⁰My son, if sinful men entice you,
do not give in to them.
¹¹If they say, 'Come along with us;
let's lie in wait for innocent blood,
let's ambush some harmless soul;
¹²let's swallow them alive, like the grave,
and whole, like those who go down to the pit;
¹³we will get all sorts of valuable things
and fill our houses with plunder;
¹⁴cast lots with us;
we will all share the loot'—
¹⁵my son, do not go along with them,
do not set foot on their paths;
¹⁶for their feet rush into evil,
they are swift to shed blood.
¹⁷How useless to spread a net
where every bird can see it!
¹⁸These men lie in wait for their own blood;
they ambush only themselves!
¹⁹Such are the paths of all who go after ill-gotten gain;
it takes away the life of those who get it.

Wisdom's rebuke

²⁰Out in the open wisdom calls aloud,
she raises her voice in the public square;
²¹on top of the wallᶜ she cries out,
at the city gate she makes her speech:

²²'How long will you who are simple love your simple ways?
How long will mockers delight in mockery
and fools hate knowledge?
²³Repent at my rebuke!
Then I will pour out my thoughts to you,
I will make known to you my teachings.
²⁴But since you refuse to listen when I call
and no-one pays attention when I stretch out my hand,
²⁵since you disregard all my advice
and do not accept my rebuke,
²⁶I in turn will laugh when disaster strikes you;
I will mock when calamity overtakes you—
²⁷when calamity overtakes you like a storm,
when disaster sweeps over you like a whirlwind,
when distress and trouble overwhelm you.

²⁸'Then they will call to me but I will not answer;
they will look for me but will not find me,
²⁹since they hated knowledge
and did not choose to fear the LORD.
³⁰Since they would not accept my advice
and spurned my rebuke,
³¹they will eat the fruit of their ways
and be filled with the fruit of their schemes.
³²For the waywardness of the simple will kill them,
and the complacency of fools will destroy them;
³³but whoever listens to me will live in safety
and be at ease, without fear of harm.'

Moral benefits of wisdom

2 My son, if you accept my words
and store up my commands within you,
²turning your ear to wisdom
and applying your heart to understanding—

ᵃ6 Or *understanding a proverb, namely, a parable, / and the sayings of the wise, their riddles*   ᵇ7 The Hebrew words rendered *fool* in Proverbs, and often elsewhere in the Old Testament, denote a person who is morally deficient.
ᶜ21 Septuagint; Hebrew / *at noisy street corners*

³indeed, if you call out for insight
  and cry aloud for understanding,
⁴and if you look for it as for silver
  and search for it as for hidden treasure,
⁵then you will understand the fear of the LORD
  and find the knowledge of God.
⁶For the LORD gives wisdom;
  from his mouth come knowledge and understanding.
⁷He holds success in store for the upright,
  he is a shield to those whose way of life is blameless,
⁸for he guards the course of the just
  and protects the way of his faithful ones.

⁹Then you will understand what is right and just
  and fair—every good path.
¹⁰For wisdom will enter your heart,
  and knowledge will be pleasant to your soul.
¹¹Discretion will protect you,
  and understanding will guard you.

¹²Wisdom will save you from the ways of wicked men,
  from men whose words are perverse,
¹³who have left the straight paths
  to walk in dark ways,
¹⁴who delight in doing wrong
  and rejoice in the perverseness of evil,
¹⁵whose paths are crooked
  and who are devious in their ways.

¹⁶Wisdom will save you also from the adulterous woman,
  from the wayward woman with her seductive words,
¹⁷who has left the partner of her youth
  and ignored the covenant she made before God.ᵃ
¹⁸Surely her house leads down to death
  and her paths to the spirits of the dead.
¹⁹None who go to her return
  or attain the paths of life.

²⁰Thus you will walk in the ways of the just
  and keep to the paths of the righteous.
²¹For the upright will live in the land,
  and the blameless will remain in it;
²²but the wicked will be cut off from the land,
  and the unfaithful will be torn from it.

Wisdom bestows well-being

3 My son, do not forget my teaching,
  but keep my commands in your heart,
²for they will prolong your life many years
  and bring you peace and prosperity.

³Let love and faithfulness never leave you;
  bind them round your neck,
  write them on the tablet of your heart.
⁴Then you will win favour and a good name
  in the sight of God and humankind.

⁵Trust in the LORD with all your heart
  and lean not on your own understanding;
⁶in all your ways submit to him,
  and he will make your paths straight.ᵇ

⁷Do not be wise in your own eyes;
  fear the LORD and shun evil.
⁸This will bring health to your body
  and nourishment to your bones.

⁹Honour the LORD with your wealth,
  with the firstfruits of all your crops;
¹⁰then your barns will be filled to overflowing,
  and your vats will brim over with new wine.

¹¹My son, do not despise the LORD's discipline,
  and do not resent his rebuke,
¹²because the LORD disciplines those he loves,
  as a father the son he delights in.ᶜ

¹³Blessed are those who find wisdom,
  those who gain understanding,
¹⁴for she is more profitable than silver
  and yields better returns than gold.
¹⁵She is more precious than rubies;
  nothing you desire can compare with her.
¹⁶Long life is in her right hand;
  in her left hand are riches and honour.
¹⁷Her ways are pleasant ways,
  and all her paths are peace.

ᵃ 17 Or *covenant of her God*   ᵇ 6 Or *will direct your paths.*   ᶜ 12 Hebrew; Septuagint *I and he chastens everyone he accepts as his child*

18She is a tree of life to those who take hold of her;
  those who hold her fast will be blessed.

19By wisdom the LORD laid the earth's foundations,
  by understanding he set the heavens in place;
20by his knowledge the deeps were divided,
  and the clouds let drop the dew.

21My son, do not let wisdom and understanding out of your sight,
  preserve sound judgment and discretion;
22they will be life for you,
  an ornament to grace your neck.
23Then you will go on your way in safety,
  and your foot will not stumble.
24When you lie down, you will not be afraid;
  when you lie down, your sleep will be sweet.
25Have no fear of sudden disaster
  or of the ruin that overtakes the wicked,
26for the LORD will be at your side
  and will keep your foot from being snared.

27Do not withhold good from those to whom it is due,
  when it is in your power to act.
28Do not say to your neighbour,
  'Come back tomorrow and I'll give it to you'—
  when you already have it with you.
29Do not plot harm against your neighbour,
  who lives trustfully near you.
30Do not accuse anyone for no reason—
  when they have done you no harm.

31Do not envy the violent
  or choose any of their ways.
32For the LORD detests the perverse
  but takes the upright into his confidence.
33The LORD's curse is on the house of the wicked,
  but he blesses the home of the righteous.
34He mocks proud mockers
  but shows favour to the humble and oppressed.
35The wise inherit honour,
  but fools get only shame.

Get wisdom at any cost

4 Listen, my sons, to a father's instruction;
  pay attention and gain understanding.
2I give you sound learning,
  so do not forsake my teaching.
3For I too was a son to my father,
  still tender, and cherished by my mother.
4Then he taught me, and he said to me,
  'Take hold of my words with all your heart;
  keep my commands, and you will live.
5Get wisdom, get understanding;
  do not forget my words or turn away from them.
6Do not forsake wisdom, and she will protect you;
  love her, and she will watch over you.
7The beginning of wisdom is this: get*a* wisdom.
  Though it cost all you have,*b* get understanding.
8Cherish her, and she will exalt you;
  embrace her, and she will honour you.
9She will give you a garland to grace your head
  and present you with a glorious crown.'

10Listen, my son, accept what I say,
  and the years of your life will be many.
11I instruct you in the way of wisdom
  and lead you along straight paths.
12When you walk, your steps will not be hampered;
  when you run, you will not stumble.
13Hold on to instruction, do not let it go;
  guard it well, for it is your life.
14Do not set foot on the path of the wicked
  or walk in the way of evildoers.
15Avoid it, do not travel on it;
  turn from it and go on your way.
16For they cannot rest until they do evil;
  they are robbed of sleep till they make someone stumble.

---

a 7 Or *Wisdom is supreme; therefore get*   *b* 7 Or *Whatever else you get*

17They eat the bread of wickedness
and drink the wine of violence.

18The path of the righteous is like the morning sun,
shining ever brighter till the full light of day.
19But the way of the wicked is like deep darkness;
they do not know what makes them stumble.

20My son, pay attention to what I say;
turn your ear to my words.
21Do not let them out of your sight,
keep them within your heart;
22for they are life to those who find them
and health to one's whole body.
23Above all else, guard your heart,
for everything you do flows from it.
24Keep your mouth free of perversity;
keep corrupt talk far from your lips.
25Let your eyes look straight ahead;
fix your gaze directly before you.
26Give careful thought to the[a] paths for your feet
and be steadfast in all your ways.
27Do not turn to the right or the left;
keep your foot from evil.

Warning against adultery

5 My son, pay attention to my wisdom,
turn your ear to my words of insight,
2that you may maintain discretion
and your lips may preserve knowledge.
3For the lips of the adulterous woman drip honey,
and her speech is smoother than oil;
4but in the end she is bitter as gall,
sharp as a double-edged sword.
5Her feet go down to death;
her steps lead straight to the grave.
6She gives no thought to the way of life;
her paths wander aimlessly, but she does not know it.

7Now then, my sons, listen to me;
do not turn aside from what I say.
8Keep to a path far from her,
do not go near the door of her house,
9lest you lose your honour to others
and your dignity[b] to one who is cruel,

> **IN OTHER WORDS**
>
> **Rejoice**
> Proverbs 5:18
> To rejoice literally means 'to take joy in something'. In the Bible, people are encouraged to 'rejoice in the Lord' (Joel 2:23), and we're told that God rejoices over us (Zephaniah 3:17).

10lest strangers feast on your wealth
and your toil enrich the house of another.
11At the end of your life you will groan,
when your flesh and body are spent.
12You will say, 'How I hated discipline!
How my heart spurned correction!
13I would not obey my teachers
or turn my ear to my instructors.
14And I was soon in serious trouble
in the assembly of God's people.'

15Drink water from your own cistern,
running water from your own well.
16Should your springs overflow in the streets,
your streams of water in the public squares?
17Let them be yours alone,
never to be shared with strangers.
18May your fountain be blessed,
and may you rejoice in the wife of your youth.
19A loving doe, a graceful deer—
may her breasts satisfy you always,
may you ever be intoxicated with her love.
20Why, my son, be intoxicated with another man's wife?
Why embrace the bosom of a wayward woman?

21For your ways are in full view of the LORD,
and he examines all your paths.
22The evil deeds of the wicked ensnare them;
the cords of their sins hold them fast.

---

[a] 26 Or *Make level*   [b] 9 Or *years*

23 For lack of discipline they will die,
　led astray by their own great folly.

Warnings against folly

6 My son, if you have put up security for your neighbour,
　if you have shaken hands in pledge for a stranger,
2 you have been trapped by what you said,
　ensnared by the words of your mouth.
3 So do this, my son, to free yourself,
　since you have fallen into your neighbour's hands:
　go—to the point of exhaustion—[a]
　and give your neighbour no rest!
4 Allow no sleep to your eyes,
　no slumber to your eyelids.
5 Free yourself, like a gazelle from the hand of the hunter,
　like a bird from the snare of the fowler.

6 Go to the ant, you sluggard;
　consider its ways and be wise!
7 It has no commander,
　no overseer or ruler,
8 yet it stores its provisions in summer
　and gathers its food at harvest.

9 How long will you lie there, you sluggard?
　When will you get up from your sleep?
10 A little sleep, a little slumber,
　a little folding of the hands to rest—
11 and poverty will come on you like a thief
　and scarcity like an armed man.

12 Troublemakers and villains,
　who go about with corrupt mouths,
13 　who wink maliciously with their eyes,
　signal with their feet
　and motion with their fingers,
14 　who plot evil with deceit in their hearts—
　they always stir up dissension.
15 Therefore disaster will overtake them in an instant;
　they will suddenly be destroyed—without remedy.

16 There are six things the LORD hates,
　seven that are detestable to him:
17 　haughty eyes,
　a lying tongue,
　hands that shed innocent blood,
18 　a heart that devises wicked schemes,
　feet that are quick to rush into evil,
19 　a false witness who pours out lies
　and a person who stirs up dissension in the community.

Warning against adultery

20 My son, keep your father's command
　and do not forsake your mother's teaching.
21 Bind them always on your heart;
　fasten them round your neck.
22 When you walk, they will guide you;
　when you sleep, they will watch over you;
　when you awake, they will speak to you.
23 For this command is a lamp,
　this teaching is a light,
　and correction and instruction are the way to life,
24 keeping you from your neighbour's wife,
　from the smooth talk of a wayward woman.

25 Do not lust in your heart after her beauty
　or let her captivate you with her eyes.
26 For a prostitute can be had for a loaf of bread,
　but another man's wife preys on your very life.
27 Can a man scoop fire into his lap
　without his clothes being burned?
28 Can a man walk on hot coals
　without his feet being scorched?
29 So is he who sleeps with another man's wife;
　no-one who touches her will go unpunished.

30 People do not despise a thief if he steals
　to satisfy his hunger when he is starving.
31 Yet if he is caught, he must pay sevenfold,
　though it costs him all the wealth of his house.
32 But a man who commits adultery has no sense;
　whoever does so destroys himself.

---

[a] 3 Or *Go and humble yourself,*

33 Blows and disgrace are his lot,
and his shame will never be wiped away.
34 For jealousy arouses a husband's fury,
and he will show no mercy when he takes revenge.
35 He will not accept any compensation;
he will refuse a bribe, however great it is.

Warning against the adulterous woman

7 My son, keep my words
and store up my commands within you.
2 Keep my commands and you will live;
guard my teachings as the apple of your eye.
3 Bind them on your fingers;
write them on the tablet of your heart.
4 Say to wisdom, 'You are my sister,'
and to insight, 'You are my relative.'
5 They will keep you from the adulterous woman,
from the wayward woman with her seductive words.

6 At the window of my house
I looked down through the lattice.
7 I saw among the simple,
I noticed among the young men,
a youth who had no sense.
8 He was going down the street near her corner,
walking along in the direction of her house
9 at twilight, as the day was fading,
as the dark of night set in.

10 Then out came a woman to meet him,
dressed like a prostitute and with crafty intent.
11 (She is unruly and defiant,
her feet never stay at home;
12 now in the street, now in the squares,
at every corner she lurks.)
13 She took hold of him and kissed him
and with a brazen face she said:

14 'Today I fulfilled my vows,
and I have food from my fellowship offering at home.
15 So I came out to meet you;
I looked for you and have found you!
16 I have covered my bed
with coloured linens from Egypt.
17 I have perfumed my bed
with myrrh, aloes and cinnamon.
18 Come, let's drink deep of love till morning;
let's enjoy ourselves with love!
19 My husband is not at home;
he has gone on a long journey.
20 He took his purse filled with money
and will not be home till full moon.'

21 With persuasive words she led him astray;
she seduced him with her smooth talk.
22 All at once he followed her
like an ox going to the slaughter,
like a deer*a* stepping into a noose*b*
23 till an arrow pierces his liver,
like a bird darting into a snare,
little knowing it will cost him his life.

24 Now then, my sons, listen to me;
pay attention to what I say.
25 Do not let your heart turn to her ways
or stray into her paths.
26 Many are the victims she has brought down;
her slain are a mighty throng.
27 Her house is a highway to the grave,
leading down to the chambers of death.

Wisdom's call

8 Does not wisdom call out?
Does not understanding raise her voice?
2 At the highest point along the way,
where the paths meet, she takes her stand;
3 beside the gate leading into the city,
at the entrance, she cries aloud:
4 'To you, O people, I call out;
I raise my voice to all humanity.
5 You who are simple, gain prudence;
you who are foolish, set your hearts on it.*c*
6 Listen, for I have trustworthy things to say;
I open my lips to speak what is right.
7 My mouth speaks what is true,
for my lips detest wickedness.

---

a 22 Syriac (see also Septuagint); Hebrew *fool*   *b* 22 The meaning of the Hebrew for this line is uncertain.
c 5 Septuagint; Hebrew *foolish, instruct your minds*

Making Connections

Wisdom
Proverbs 8:1

In this passage wisdom is described as a woman. She calls out from three of the three busiest places in the city – the heights where worship places were set up; the crossroads where paths met and travellers and traders would talk and do business; and the city gates where trials took place and deals were struck.

8 All the words of my mouth are just;
  none of them is crooked or perverse.
9 To the discerning all of them are right;
  they are upright to those who have found knowledge.
10 Choose my instruction instead of silver,
  knowledge rather than choice gold,
11 for wisdom is more precious than rubies,
  and nothing you desire can compare with her.

12 'I, wisdom, dwell together with prudence;
  I possess knowledge and discretion.
13 To fear the LORD is to hate evil;
  I hate pride and arrogance,
  evil behaviour and perverse speech.
14 Counsel and sound judgment are mine;
  I have insight, I have power.
15 By me kings reign
  and rulers issue decrees that are just;
16 by me princes govern,
  and nobles—all who rule on earth.[a]
17 I love those who love me,
  and those who seek me find me.
18 With me are riches and honour,
  enduring wealth and prosperity.
19 My fruit is better than fine gold;
  what I yield surpasses choice silver.
20 I walk in the way of righteousness,
  along the paths of justice,
21 bestowing a rich inheritance on those who love me
  and making their treasuries full.

22 'The LORD brought me forth as the first of his works,[b,c]
  before his deeds of old;
23 I was formed long ages ago,
  at the very beginning, when the world came to be.
24 When there were no oceans, I was given birth,
  when there were no springs abounding with water;
25 before the mountains were settled in place,
  before the hills, I was given birth,
26 before he made the world or its fields
  or any of the dust of the earth.
27 I was there when he set the heavens in place,
  when he marked out the horizon on the face of the deep,
28 when he established the clouds above
  and fixed securely the fountains of the deep,
29 when he gave the sea its boundary
  so that the waters would not overstep his command,
  and when he marked out the foundations of the earth.
30 Then I was constantly[d] at his side.
  I was filled with delight day after day,
  rejoicing always in his presence,
31 rejoicing in his whole world
  and delighting in the human race.

32 'Now then, my children, listen to me;
  blessed are those who keep my ways.
33 Listen to my instruction and be wise;
  do not disregard it.
34 Blessed are those who listen to me,
  watching daily at my doors,
  waiting at my doorway.
35 For those who find me find life
  and receive favour from the LORD.
36 But those who fail to find me harm themselves;
  all who hate me love death.'

---

[a] 16 Some Hebrew manuscripts and Septuagint; other Hebrew manuscripts *all righteous rulers* [b] 22 Or *way;* or *dominion* [c] 22 Or *The LORD possessed me at the beginning of his work;* or *The LORD brought me forth at the beginning of his work* [d] 30 Or *was the master worker;* or *was a little child*

Invitations of wisdom and folly

9 Wisdom has built her house;
  she has set up[a] its seven pillars.
2 She has prepared her meat and mixed her wine;
  she has also set her table.
3 She has sent out her servants, and she calls
  from the highest point of the city,
4 'Let all who are simple come to my house!'
  To those who have no sense she says,
5 'Come, eat my food
  and drink the wine I have mixed.
6 Leave your simple ways and you will live;
  walk in the way of insight.'

7 Whoever corrects a mocker invites insults;
  whoever rebukes the wicked incurs abuse.
8 Do not rebuke mockers or they will hate you;
  rebuke the wise and they will love you.
9 Instruct the wise and they will be wiser still;
  teach the righteous and they will add to their learning.

10 The fear of the LORD is the beginning of wisdom,
  and knowledge of the Holy One is understanding.
11 For through wisdom[b] your days will be many,
  and years will be added to your life.
12 If you are wise, your wisdom will reward you;
  if you are a mocker, you alone will suffer.

13 Folly is an unruly woman;
  she is simple and knows nothing.
14 She sits at the door of her house,
  on a seat at the highest point of the city,
15 calling out to those who pass by,
  who go straight on their way,
16 'Let all who are simple come to my house!'
  To those who have no sense she says,
17 'Stolen water is sweet;
  food eaten in secret is delicious!'
18 But little do they know that the dead are there,
  that her guests are deep in the realm of the dead.

Proverbs of Solomon

10 The proverbs of Solomon:

Wise children bring joy to their father,
  but foolish children bring grief to their mother.

2 Ill-gotten treasures have no lasting value,
  but righteousness delivers from death.

3 The LORD does not let the righteous go hungry,
  but he thwarts the craving of the wicked.

4 Lazy hands make for poverty,
  but diligent hands bring wealth.

5 He who gathers crops in summer is a prudent son,
  but he who sleeps during harvest is a disgraceful son.

6 Blessings crown the head of the righteous,
  but violence overwhelms the mouth of the wicked.[c]

7 The name of the righteous is used in blessings,[d]
  but the name of the wicked will rot.

8 The wise in heart accept commands,
  but a chattering fool comes to ruin.

9 Whoever walks in integrity walks securely,
  but whoever takes crooked paths will be found out.

10 Whoever winks maliciously causes grief,
  and a chattering fool comes to ruin.

11 The mouth of the righteous is a fountain of life,
  but the mouth of the wicked conceals violence.

12 Hatred stirs up dissension,
  but love covers over all wrongs.

---

[a] 1 Septuagint, Syriac and Targum; Hebrew *has hewn out* [b] 11 Septuagint, Syriac and Targum; Hebrew *me* [c] 6 Or *but the mouth of the wicked conceals violence* [d] 7 See Gen. 48:20.

¹³Wisdom is found on the lips of the discerning,
but a rod is for the back of one who has no sense.

¹⁴The wise store up knowledge,
but the mouth of a fool invites ruin.

¹⁵The wealth of the rich is their fortified city,
but poverty is the ruin of the poor.

¹⁶The wages of the righteous is life,
but the earnings of the wicked are sin and death.

¹⁷Whoever heeds discipline shows the way to life,
but whoever ignores correction leads others astray.

¹⁸Whoever conceals hatred with lying lips and spreads slander is a fool.

¹⁹Sin is not ended by multiplying words,
but the prudent hold their tongues.

²⁰The tongue of the righteous is choice silver,
but the heart of the wicked is of little value.

²¹The lips of the righteous nourish many,
but fools die for lack of sense.

²²The blessing of the LORD brings wealth,
without painful toil for it.

²³Fools find pleasure in wicked schemes,
but those who have understanding delight in wisdom.

²⁴What the wicked dread will overtake them;
what the righteous desire will be granted.

²⁵When the storm has swept by, the wicked are gone,
but the righteous stand firm for ever.

²⁶As vinegar to the teeth and smoke to the eyes,
so are sluggards to those who send them.

²⁷The fear of the LORD adds length to life,
but the years of the wicked are cut short.

²⁸The prospect of the righteous is joy,
but the hopes of the wicked come to nothing.

²⁹The way of the LORD is a refuge for the blameless,
but it is the ruin of those who do evil.

³⁰The righteous will never be uprooted,
but the wicked will not remain in the land.

³¹From the mouth of the righteous comes the fruit of wisdom,
but a perverse tongue will be silenced.

³²The lips of the righteous know what finds favour,
but the mouth of the wicked only what is perverse.

11

The LORD detests dishonest scales,
but accurate weights find favour with him.

²When pride comes, then comes disgrace,
but with humility comes wisdom.

³The integrity of the upright guides them,
but the unfaithful are destroyed by their duplicity.

⁴Wealth is worthless in the day of wrath,
but righteousness delivers from death.

⁵The righteousness of the blameless makes their paths straight,
but the wicked are brought down by their own wickedness.

⁶The righteousness of the upright delivers them,
but the unfaithful are trapped by evil desires.

⁷Hopes placed in mortals die with them;
all the promise of[a] their power comes to nothing.

⁸The righteous are rescued from trouble,
and it falls on the wicked instead.

⁹With their mouths the godless destroy their neighbours,

---

[a] 7 Two Hebrew manuscripts; most Hebrew manuscripts, Vulgate, Syriac and Targum *When the wicked die, their hope perishes; / all they expected from*

Sign of the times

Accurate scales
Proverbs 11:1

Why should God get excited about something like accurate weights? Well, in the markets traders would sometimes use false weights to trick people. Instead of getting what they had asked and paid for, people would end up with less because a false weight had been used that was lighter than it was supposed to be. This proverb is a way of saying that God hates deceit and hypocrisy, but he loves truth.

but through knowledge the righteous escape.

10 When the righteous prosper, the city rejoices;
 when the wicked perish, there are shouts of joy.

11 Through the blessing of the upright a city is exalted,
 but by the mouth of the wicked it is destroyed.

12 Those who have no sense deride their neighbours,
 but those who have understanding hold their tongues.

13 Gossips betray a confidence,
 but the trustworthy keep a secret.

14 For lack of guidance a nation falls,
 but victory is won through many advisors.

15 Whoever puts up security for a stranger will surely suffer,
 but whoever refuses to shake hands in pledge is safe.

16 A kind-hearted woman gains honour,
 but ruthless men gain only wealth.

17 Those who are kind benefit themselves,
 but the cruel bring ruin on themselves.

18 The wicked earn deceptive wages,
 but those who sow righteousness reap a sure reward.

19 Truly the righteous attain life,
 but those who pursue evil go to their death.

20 The LORD detests those whose hearts are perverse,
 but he delights in those whose ways are blameless.

21 Be sure of this: the wicked will not go unpunished,
 but those who are righteous will go free.

22 Like a gold ring in a pig's snout
 is a beautiful woman who shows no discretion.

23 The desire of the righteous ends only in good,
 but the hope of the wicked only in wrath.

24 One person gives freely, yet gains even more;
 another withholds unduly, but comes to poverty.

25 A generous person will prosper;
 whoever refreshes others will be refreshed.

26 People curse those who hoard grain,
 but they pray God's blessing on those who are willing to sell.

27 Whoever seeks good finds favour,
 but evil comes to those who search for it.

28 Those who trust in their riches will fall,
 but the righteous will thrive like a green leaf.

29 Those who bring ruin on their families will inherit only wind,
 and the fool will be servant to the wise.

30 The fruit of the righteous is a tree of life,
 and those who win souls are wise.

31 If the righteous receive their due on earth,
how much more the ungodly and the sinner!

12

Whoever loves discipline loves knowledge,
but whoever hates correction is stupid.

2 Good people obtain favour from the LORD,
but he condemns those who devise wicked schemes.

3 No-one can be established through wickedness,
but the righteous cannot be uprooted.

4 A wife of noble character is her husband's crown,
but a disgraceful wife is like decay in his bones.

5 The plans of the righteous are just,
but the advice of the wicked is deceitful.

6 The words of the wicked lie in wait for blood,
but the speech of the upright rescues them.

7 The wicked are overthrown and are no more,
but the house of the righteous stands firm.

8 People are praised according to their prudence,
and those with warped minds are despised.

9 Better to be a nobody and yet have a servant
than pretend to be somebody and have no food.

10 The righteous care for the needs of their animals,
but the kindest acts of the wicked are cruel.

11 Those who work their land will have abundant food,
but those who chase fantasies have no sense.

> **IN OTHER WORDS**
>
> **Evil**
> Proverbs 12:13
> Is evil just the absence of good or is it something more active? The Bible's teaching on the existence of Satan certainly implies that there is an active force in the world today which is evil.

12 The wicked desire the plunder[a] of evildoers,
but the root of the righteous flourishes.

13 Evildoers are trapped by their sinful talk,
and so the innocent escape trouble.

14 From the fruit of their lips people are filled with good things,
and the work of their hands brings them reward.

15 The way of fools seems right to them,
but the wise listen to advice.

16 Fools show their annoyance at once,
but the prudent overlook an insult.

17 An honest witness tells the truth,
but a false witness tells lies.

18 The words of the reckless pierce like swords,
but the tongue of the wise brings healing.

19 Truthful lips endure for ever,
but a lying tongue lasts only a moment.

20 Deceit is in the hearts of those who plot evil,
but those who promote peace have joy.

21 No harm overtakes the righteous,
but the wicked have their fill of trouble.

22 The LORD detests lying lips,
but he delights in people who are trustworthy.

---

[a] 12 Or *stronghold*

²³The prudent keep their knowledge to themselves,
 but a fool's heart blurts out folly.

²⁴Diligent hands will rule,
 but laziness ends in forced labour.

²⁵Anxiety weighs down the heart,
 but a kind word cheers it up.

²⁶The righteous choose their friends carefully,
 but the way of the wicked leads them astray.

²⁷The lazy do not roast[a] any game,
 but the diligent feed on the riches of the hunt.

²⁸In the way of righteousness there is life;
 along that path is immortality.

13

A wise child heeds a parent's instruction,
 but a mocker does not respond to rebukes.

²From the fruit of their lips people enjoy good things,
 but the unfaithful have an appetite for violence.

³Those who guard their lips preserve their lives,
 but those who speak rashly will come to ruin.

⁴A sluggard's appetite is never filled,
 but the desires of the diligent are fully satisfied.

⁵The righteous hate what is false,
 but the wicked make themselves obnoxious
 and are filled with shame.

⁶Righteousness guards the person of integrity,
 but wickedness overthrows the sinner.

⁷One person pretends to be rich, yet has nothing;
 another pretends to be poor, yet has great wealth.

⁸The rich may be able to ransom their lives,
 but the poor cannot respond to threatening rebukes.

⁹The light of the righteous shines brightly,
 but the lamp of the wicked is snuffed out.

¹⁰Where there is strife, there is pride,
 but wisdom is found in those who take advice.

¹¹Dishonest money dwindles away,
 but whoever gathers money little by little makes it grow.

¹²Hope deferred makes the heart sick,
 but a longing fulfilled is a tree of life.

¹³Whoever scorns instruction will pay for it,
 but whoever respects a command is rewarded.

¹⁴The teaching of the wise is a fountain of life,
 turning a person from the snares of death.

¹⁵Good judgment wins favour,
 but the way of the unfaithful leads to their destruction.[b]

¹⁶All who are prudent act with[c] knowledge,
 but fools expose their folly.

¹⁷A wicked messenger falls into trouble,
 but a trustworthy envoy brings healing.

¹⁸Whoever disregards discipline comes to poverty and shame,
 but whoever heeds correction is honoured.

¹⁹A longing fulfilled is sweet to the soul,
 but fools detest turning from evil.

²⁰Walk with the wise and become wise,
 for a companion of fools suffers harm.

²¹Trouble pursues the sinner,
 but the righteous are rewarded with good things.

²²Good people leave an inheritance for their children's children,

---

[a] 27 The meaning of the Hebrew for this word is uncertain.   [b] 15 Septuagint and Syriac; the meaning of the Hebrew for this phrase is uncertain.   [c] 16 Or *prudent protect themselves through*

but a sinner's wealth is stored up for the righteous.

23 An unploughed field produces food for the poor,
but injustice sweeps it away.

24 Those who spare the rod hate their children,
but those who love them are careful to discipline them.

25 The righteous eat to their hearts' content,
but the stomach of the wicked goes hungry.

14
The wise woman builds her house,
but with her own hands the foolish one tears hers down.

2 Whoever fears the LORD walks uprightly,
but those who despise him are devious in their ways.

3 A fool's mouth lashes out with pride,
but the lips of the wise protect them.

4 Where there are no oxen, the manger is empty,
but from the strength of an ox come abundant harvests.

5 An honest witness does not deceive,
but a false witness pours out lies.

6 The mocker seeks wisdom and finds none,
but knowledge comes easily to the discerning.

7 Stay away from the foolish,
for you will not find knowledge on their lips.

8 The wisdom of the prudent is to give thought to their ways,
but the folly of fools is deception.

9 Fools mock at making amends for sin,
but goodwill is found among the upright.

10 Each heart knows its own bitterness,
and no-one else can share its joy.

11 The house of the wicked will be destroyed,
but the tent of the upright will flourish.

12 There is a way that appears to be right,
but in the end it leads to death.

13 Even in laughter the heart may ache,
and rejoicing may end in grief.

14 The faithless will be fully repaid for their ways,
and the good rewarded for theirs.

15 The simple believe anything,
but the prudent give thought to their steps.

16 The wise fear the LORD and shun evil,
but a fool is hotheaded and yet feels secure.

17 The quick-tempered do foolish things,
and those who devise evil schemes are hated.

18 The simple inherit folly,
but the prudent are crowned with knowledge.

19 Evildoers will bow down in the presence of the good,
and the wicked at the gates of the righteous.

20 The poor are shunned even by their neighbours,
but the rich have many friends.

21 It is a sin to despise one's neighbour,
but blessed are those who are kind to the needy.

22 Do not those who plot evil go astray?
But those who plan what is good find*a* love and faithfulness.

23 All hard work brings a profit,
but mere talk leads only to poverty.

24 The wealth of the wise is their crown,
but the folly of fools yields folly.

25 A truthful witness saves lives,
but a false witness is deceitful.

26 Those who fear the LORD have a secure fortress,
and for their children it will be a refuge.

---

a 22 Or *show*

27The fear of the LORD is a fountain of life,
   turning a person from the snares of death.

28A large population is a king's glory,
   but without subjects a prince is ruined.

29Those who are patient have great understanding,
   but the quick-tempered display folly.

30A heart at peace gives life to the body,
   but envy rots the bones.

31Whoever oppresses the poor shows contempt for their Maker,
   but whoever is kind to the needy honours God.

32When calamity comes, the wicked are brought down,
   but even in death the righteous seek refuge in God.

33Wisdom reposes in the heart of the discerning
   and even among fools she lets herself be known.[a]

34Righteousness exalts a nation,
   but sin condemns any people.

35A king delights in a wise servant,
   but a shameful servant arouses his fury.

15

A gentle answer turns away wrath,
   but a harsh word stirs up anger.

2The tongue of the wise adorns knowledge,
   but the mouth of the fool gushes folly.

3The eyes of the LORD are everywhere,
   keeping watch on the wicked and the good.

4The soothing tongue is a tree of life,
   but a perverse tongue crushes the spirit.

5A fool spurns a parent's discipline,
   but whoever heeds correction shows prudence.

6The house of the righteous contains great treasure,
   but the income of the wicked brings ruin.

> **IN OTHER WORDS**
>
> **Heart**
> Proverbs 15:11
> When the Bible refers to the heart in a verse like this, it isn't talking about the pump that circulates blood through your body. The heart is the central core of a person, where thoughts, feeling and decisions come from.

7The lips of the wise spread knowledge,
   but the hearts of fools are not upright.

8The LORD detests the sacrifice of the wicked,
   but the prayer of the upright pleases him.

9The LORD detests the way of the wicked,
   but he loves those who pursue righteousness.

10Stern discipline awaits those who leave the path;
   those who hate correction will die.

11Death and Destruction[b] lie open before the LORD—
   how much more do human hearts!

12Mockers resent correction,
   so they avoid the wise.

13A happy heart makes the face cheerful,
   but heartache crushes the spirit.

14The discerning heart seeks knowledge,
   but the mouth of a fool feeds on folly.

15All the days of the oppressed are wretched,
   but the cheerful heart has a continual feast.

16Better a little with the fear of the LORD
   than great wealth with turmoil.

17Better a dish of vegetables with love
   than a fattened calf with hatred.

---

[a] 33 Hebrew; Septuagint and Syriac / *but in the heart of fools she is not known*   [b] 11 Hebrew *Abaddon*

¹⁸The hot-tempered stir up dissension,
but those who are patient calm a quarrel.

¹⁹The way of the sluggard is blocked with thorns,
but the path of the upright is a highway.

²⁰Wise children bring joy to their father,
but foolish children despise their mother.

²¹Folly brings joy to those who have no sense,
but those who have understanding keep a straight course.

²²Plans fail for lack of counsel,
but with many advisors they succeed.

²³A person finds joy in giving an apt reply—
and how good is a timely word!

²⁴The path of life leads upwards for the prudent
to keep them from going down to the realm of the dead.

²⁵The LORD tears down the house of the proud,
but he sets the widow's boundary stones in place.

²⁶The LORD detests the thoughts of the wicked,
but gracious words are pure in his sight.

²⁷The greedy bring ruin to their housholds,
but those who hate bribes will live.

²⁸The heart of the righteous weighs its answers,
but the mouth of the wicked gushes evil.

²⁹The LORD is far from the wicked,
but he hears the prayer of the righteous.

³⁰Light in a messenger's eyes brings joy to the heart,
and good news gives health to the bones.

³¹Whoever heeds life-giving correction
will be at home among the wise.

³²Those who disregard discipline despise themselves,
but those who heed correction gain understanding.

³³Wisdom's instruction is to fear the LORD,
and humility comes before honour.

16

To human beings belong the plans of the heart,
but from the LORD comes the proper answer of the tongue.

²People may think all their ways are pure,
but motives are weighed by the LORD.

³Commit to the LORD whatever you do,
and he will establish your plans.

⁴The LORD works out everything to its proper end—
even the wicked for a day of disaster.

⁵The LORD detests all the proud of heart.
Be sure of this: they will not go unpunished.

⁶Through love and faithfulness sin is atoned for;
through the fear of the LORD evil is avoided.

⁷When the LORD takes pleasure in anyone's way,
he causes their enemies to make peace with them.

⁸Better a little with righteousness
than much gain with injustice.

⁹In their hearts human beings plan their course,
but the LORD establishes their steps.

¹⁰The lips of a king speak as an oracle,
and his mouth does not betray justice.

¹¹Honest scales and balances belong to the LORD;
all the weights in the bag are of his making.

¹²Kings detest wrongdoing,
for a throne is established through righteousness.

¹³Kings take pleasure in honest lips;
they value persons who speak what is right.

¹⁴A king's wrath is a messenger of death,
but the wise will appease it.

15 When a king's face brightens, it means life;
   his favour is like a rain cloud in spring.

16 How much better to get wisdom than gold,
   to get insight rather than silver!

17 The highway of the upright avoids evil;
   those who guard their ways preserve their lives.

18 Pride goes before destruction,
   a haughty spirit before a fall.

19 Better to be lowly in spirit along with the oppressed
   than to share plunder with the proud.

20 Those who give heed to instruction prosper,[a]
   and blessed are those who trust in the LORD.

21 The wise in heart are called discerning,
   and gracious words promote instruction.[b]

22 Prudence is a fountain of life to the prudent,
   but folly brings punishment to fools.

23 The hearts of the wise make their mouths prudent,
   and their lips promote instruction.[c]

24 Gracious words are a honeycomb,
   sweet to the soul and healing to the bones.

25 There is a way that appears to be right,
   but in the end it leads to death.

26 The appetite of labourers works for them;
   their hunger drives them on.

27 Scoundrels plot evil,
   and on their lips it is like a scorching fire.

28 The perverse stir up dissension,
   and gossips separate close friends.

29 The violent entice their neighbours
   and lead them down a path that is not good.

30 Those who wink with their eyes are plotting perversity;
   those who purse their lips are bent on evil.

31 Grey hair is a crown of splendour;
   it is attained in the way of righteousness.

32 Better a patient person than a warrior,
   those with self-control than those who take a city.

33 The lot is cast into the lap,
   but its every decision is from the LORD.

17 Better a dry crust with peace and quiet
   than a house full of feasting, with strife.

2 A prudent servant will rule over a disgraceful son,
   and will share the inheritance as one of the family.

3 The crucible for silver and the furnace for gold,
   but the LORD tests the heart.

Sign of the times

Furnace
Proverbs 17:3

A furnace was used to refine gold and get rid of all its impurities. Gold would be melted in the furnace at incredibly high temperatures. Once the gold was liquid, it was easy to collect and remove the dirt or impurities because they were different weights. The pure gold would then be allowed to solidify again. God tests the thoughts and actions of his people in a similar way.

---

[a] 20 Or *who speak prudently find what is good* [b] 21 Or *words make a person persuasive* [c] 23 Or *prudent / and make their lips persuasive*

⁴A wicked person listens to deceitful lips;
  a liar pays attention to a destructive tongue.

⁵Whoever mocks the poor shows contempt for their Maker;
  whoever gloats over disaster will not go unpunished.

⁶Children's children are a crown to the aged,
  and parents are the pride of their children.

⁷Eloquent lips are unsuited to a godless fool—
  how much worse lying lips to a ruler!

⁸A bribe is seen as a charm by those who give it;
  they think success will come at every turn.

⁹Whoever would foster love covers over an offence,
  but whoever repeats the matter separates close friends.

¹⁰A rebuke impresses a discerning person more than a hundred lashes a fool.

¹¹Evildoers foster rebellion against God;
  the messenger of death will be sent against them.

¹²Better to meet a bear robbed of her cubs than a fool bent on folly.

¹³Evil will never leave the house
  of one who pays back evil for good.

¹⁴Starting a quarrel is like breaching a dam;
  so drop the matter before a dispute breaks out.

¹⁵Acquitting the guilty and condemning the innocent—
  the LORD detests them both.

¹⁶Why should fools have money in hand to buy wisdom,
  when they are not able to understand it?

¹⁷A friend loves at all times,
  and a brother is born for a time of adversity.

¹⁸One who has no sense shakes hands in pledge
  and puts up security for a neighbour.

¹⁹Whoever loves a quarrel loves sin;
  whoever builds a high gate invites destruction.

²⁰One whose heart is corrupt does not prosper;
  one whose tongue is perverse falls into trouble.

²¹To have a fool for a child brings grief;
  there is no joy for the parent of a godless fool.

²²A cheerful heart is good medicine,
  but a crushed spirit dries up the bones.

²³The wicked accept bribes in secret
  to pervert the course of justice.

²⁴A discerning person keeps wisdom in view,
  but a fool's eyes wander to the ends of the earth.

²⁵Foolish children bring grief to their father
  and bitterness to the mother who bore them.

²⁶If imposing a fine on the innocent is not good,
  surely to flog honest officials is not right.

²⁷Those who have knowledge use words with restraint,
  and those who have understanding are even-tempered.

²⁸Even fools are thought wise if they keep silent,
  and discerning if they hold their tongues.

18

An unfriendly person pursues selfish ends
  and against all sound judgment starts quarrels.

²Fools find no pleasure in understanding
  but delight in airing their own opinions.

³When wickedness comes, so does contempt,
  and with shame comes reproach.

⁴The words of the mouth are deep waters,
  but the fountain of wisdom is a rushing stream.

⁵It is not good to be partial to the wicked
  and so deprive the innocent of justice.

⁶The lips of fools bring them strife,
  and their mouths invite a beating.

⁷The mouths of fools are their undoing,
  and their lips are a snare to their very lives.

⁸The words of a gossip are like choice morsels;
  they go down to the inmost parts.

⁹One who is slack in his work
  is a close relative of one who destroys.

¹⁰The name of the LORD is a fortified tower;
  the righteous run to it and are safe.

¹¹The wealth of the rich is their fortified city;
  they imagine it a wall too high to scale.

¹²Before a downfall the heart is haughty,
  but humility comes before honour.

¹³To answer before listening—
  that is folly and shame.

¹⁴The human spirit can endure in times of illness,
  but a crushed spirit who can bear?

¹⁵The heart of the discerning acquires knowledge,
  for the ears of the wise seek it out.

¹⁶A gift opens the way
  and ushers the giver into the presence of the great.

¹⁷In a lawsuit the first to speak seems right,
  until someone comes forward and cross-examines.

¹⁸Casting the lot settles disputes
  and keeps strong opponents apart.

¹⁹A brother wronged is more unyielding than a fortified city;
  disputes are like the barred gates of a citadel.

²⁰From the fruit of their mouths people's stomachs are filled;
  with the harvest of their lips they are satisfied.

²¹The tongue has the power of life and death,
  and those who love it will eat its fruit.

²²He who finds a wife finds what is good
  and receives favour from the LORD.

²³The poor plead for mercy,
  but the rich answer harshly.

²⁴One who has unreliable friends soon comes to ruin,
  but there is a friend who sticks closer than a brother.

19

Better the poor whose way of life is blameless
  than a fool whose lips are perverse.

²Desire without knowledge is not good—
  how much more will hasty feet miss the way!

³One's own folly leads to ruin,
  yet the heart rages against the LORD.

⁴Wealth attracts many friends,
  but even the closest friends of the poor desert them.

⁵A false witness will not go unpunished,
  and whoever pours out lies will not go free.

⁶Many curry favour with a ruler,
  and everyone is the friend of one who gives gifts.

⁷The poor are shunned by all their relatives—
  how much more do their friends avoid them!
  Though they pursue them with pleading,
  they are nowhere to be found.[a]

⁸Those who get wisdom love their own lives;
  those who cherish understanding will soon prosper.

⁹A false witness will not go unpunished,
  and whoever pours out lies will perish.

---

[a] 7 The meaning of the Hebrew for this sentence is uncertain.

¹⁰It is not fitting for a fool to live in luxury—
  how much worse for a slave to rule over
    princes!

¹¹A person's wisdom yields patience;
  it is to one's glory to overlook an
    offence.

¹²A king's rage is like the roar of a lion,
  but his favour is like dew on the
    grass.

¹³A foolish child is a father's ruin,
  and a quarrelsome wife is like
    the constant dripping of a leaky
      roof.

¹⁴Houses and wealth are inherited from
    parents,
  but a prudent wife is from the LORD.

¹⁵Laziness brings on deep sleep,
  and the shiftless go hungry.

¹⁶Those who obey instructions preserve
    their lives,
  but those who are contemptuous of
    their ways will die.

¹⁷Those who are kind to the poor lend to the
    LORD,
  and he will reward them for what they
    have done.

¹⁸Discipline your children, for in that there
    is hope;
  do not be a willing party to their
    death.

¹⁹The hot-tempered must pay the penalty;
  rescue them, and you will have to do it
    again.

²⁰Listen to advice and accept discipline,
  and at the end you will be counted
    among the wise.

²¹Many are the plans in a human heart,
  but it is the LORD's purpose that
    prevails.

²²What a person desires is unfailing love;ᵃ
  better to be poor than a liar.

²³The fear of the LORD leads to life;
  then one rests content, untouched by
    trouble.

> **IN OTHER WORDS**
>
> **Sluggard**
> **Proverbs 19:24**
> A sluggard is someone who is really, really lazy. Proverbs often warns about the dangers of being lazy and the wisdom of being hard-working.

²⁴Sluggards bury their hands in the dish
  and will not even bring them back to
    their mouths!

²⁵Flog a mocker, and the simple will learn
    prudence;
  rebuke the discerning, and they will
    gain knowledge.

²⁶Whoever robs their father and drives out
    their mother
  is a child who brings shame and
    disgrace.

²⁷Stop listening to instruction, my child,
  and you will stray from the words of
    knowledge.

²⁸A corrupt witness mocks at justice,
  and the mouth of the wicked gulps
    down evil.

²⁹Penalties are prepared for mockers,
  and beatings for the backs of fools.

20 Wine is a mocker and beer a
    brawler;
  whoever is led astray by them is not
    wise.

²A king's wrath strikes terror like the roar
    of a lion;
  those who anger him forfeit their lives.

³It is to one's honour to avoid strife,
  but every fool is quick to quarrel.

⁴Sluggards do not plough in season;
  so at harvest time they look but find
    nothing.

ᵃ 22 Or *Greed is a person's shame*

⁵The purposes of the human heart are deep waters,
 but those who have insight draw them out.

⁶Many claim to have unfailing love,
 but a faithful person who can find?

⁷The righteous lead blameless lives;
 blessed are their children after them.

⁸When a king sits on his throne to judge,
 he winnows out all evil with his eyes.

⁹Who can say, 'I have kept my heart pure;
 I am clean and without sin'?

¹⁰Differing weights and differing measures—
 the LORD detests them both.

¹¹Even small children are known by their actions,
 so is their conduct really pure and upright?

¹²Ears that hear and eyes that see—
 the LORD has made them both.

¹³Do not love sleep or you will grow poor;
 stay awake and you will have food to spare.

¹⁴'It's no good, it's no good!' says the buyer—
 then goes off and boasts about the purchase.

¹⁵Gold there is, and rubies in abundance,
 but lips that speak knowledge are a rare jewel.

¹⁶Take the garment of one who puts up security for a stranger;
 hold it in pledge if it is done for an outsider.

¹⁷Food gained by fraud tastes sweet,
 but one ends up with a mouth full of gravel.

¹⁸Plans are established by seeking advice;
 so if you wage war, obtain guidance.

¹⁹A gossip betrays a confidence;
 so avoid anyone who talks too much.

²⁰If you curse your father or mother,
 your lamp will be snuffed out in pitch darkness.

²¹An inheritance claimed too soon
 will not be blessed at the end.

²²Do not say, 'I'll pay you back for this wrong!'
 Wait for the LORD, and he will avenge you.

²³The LORD detests differing weights,
 and dishonest scales do not please him.

²⁴A person's steps are directed by the LORD.
 How then can anyone understand their own way?

²⁵It is a trap to dedicate something rashly
 and only later to consider one's vows.

²⁶A wise king winnows out the wicked;
 he drives the threshing wheel over them.

²⁷The human spirit is[a] the lamp of the LORD
 that sheds light on one's inmost being.

²⁸Love and faithfulness keep a king safe;
 through love his throne is made secure.

²⁹The glory of young men is their strength,
 grey hair the splendour of the old.

³⁰Blows and wounds cleanse away evil,
 and beatings purge the inmost being.

21

In the LORD's hand the king's heart is a stream of water
 that he channels towards all who please him.

²People may think all their ways are right,
 but the LORD weighs the heart.

³To do what is right and just
 is more acceptable to the LORD than sacrifice.

⁴Haughty eyes and a proud heart—
 the unploughed field of the wicked—
 produce sin.

⁵The plans of the diligent lead to profit
 as surely as haste leads to poverty.

---

[a] 27 Or *A person's words are*

⁶A fortune made by a lying tongue
is a fleeting vapour and a deadly snare.ᵃ

⁷The violence of the wicked will drag them away,
for they refuse to do what is right.

⁸The way of the guilty is devious,
but the conduct of the innocent is upright.

⁹Better to live on a corner of the roof
than share a house with a quarrelsome wife.

¹⁰The wicked crave evil;
their neighbours get no mercy from them.

¹¹When a mocker is punished, the simple gain wisdom;
by paying attention to the wise they get knowledge.

¹²The Righteous Oneᵇ takes note of the house of the wicked
and brings the wicked to ruin.

¹³Those who shut their ears to the cry of the poor
will also cry out and not be answered.

¹⁴A gift given in secret soothes anger,
and a bribe concealed in the cloak pacifies great wrath.

¹⁵When justice is done, it brings joy to the righteous
but terror to evildoers.

¹⁶Whoever strays from the path of prudence
comes to rest in the company of the dead.

¹⁷Whoever loves pleasure will become poor;
whoever loves wine and oil will never be rich.

¹⁸The wicked become a ransom for the righteous,
and the unfaithful for the upright.

¹⁹Better to live in a desert
than with a quarrelsome and nagging wife.

²⁰The wise store up choice food and oil,
but fools gulp theirs down.

²¹Whoever pursues righteousness and love
finds life, prosperityᶜ and honour.

²²One who is wise can go up against the city of the mighty
and pull down the stronghold in which they trust.

²³Those who guard their mouths and their tongues
keep themselves from calamity.

²⁴The proud and arrogant—'Mocker' is their name;
they behave with insolent fury.

²⁵The craving of sluggards will be the death of them,
because their hands refuse to work.

²⁶All day long they crave for more,
but the righteous give without sparing.

²⁷The sacrifice of the wicked is detestable—
how much more so when brought with evil intent!

²⁸Those who give false witness will perish,
but a careful listener will testify successfully.

²⁹The wicked put up a bold front,
but the upright give thought to their ways.

³⁰There is no wisdom, no insight, no plan
that can succeed against the LORD.

³¹The horse is made ready for the day of battle,
but victory rests with the LORD.

22

A good name is more desirable than great riches;
to be esteemed is better than silver or gold.

²Rich and poor have this in common:
the LORD is the Maker of them all.

³The prudent see danger and take refuge,
but the simple keep going and pay the penalty.

ᵃ 6 Some Hebrew manuscripts, Septuagint and Vulgate; most Hebrew manuscripts *vapour for those who seek death*
ᵇ 12 Or *The righteous person*   ᶜ 21 Or *righteousness*

⁴Humility is the fear of the LORD;
  its wages are riches and honour and life.

⁵In the paths of the wicked are snares and pitfalls,
  but those who would preserve their life stay far from them.

⁶Start children off on the way they should go,
  and even when they are old they will not turn from it.

⁷The rich rule over the poor,
  and the borrower is slave to the lender.

⁸Those who sow injustice reap calamity,
  and the rod they wield in fury will be broken.

⁹The generous will themselves be blessed,
  for they share their food with the poor.

¹⁰Drive out the mocker, and out goes strife;
  quarrels and insults are ended.

¹¹One who loves a pure heart and who speaks with grace
  will have the king for a friend.

¹²The eyes of the LORD keep watch over knowledge,
  but he frustrates the words of the unfaithful.

¹³The sluggard says, 'There's a lion outside! I'll be killed in the public square!'

¹⁴The mouth of an adulterous woman is a deep pit;
  a man who is under the LORD's wrath falls into it.

¹⁵Folly is bound up in the heart of a child,
  but the rod of discipline will drive it far away.

¹⁶Those who oppress the poor to increase their wealth
  and those who give gifts to the rich—
  both come to poverty.

Thirty sayings of the wise

Saying 1

¹⁷Pay attention and turn your ear to the sayings of the wise;
  apply your heart to what I teach,
¹⁸for it is pleasing when you keep them in your heart
  and have all of them ready on your lips.
¹⁹So that your trust may be in the LORD,
  I teach you today, even you.
²⁰Have I not written thirty sayings for you,
  sayings of counsel and knowledge,
²¹teaching you to be honest and to speak the truth,
  so that you bring back truthful reports to those you serve?

Saying 2

²²Do not exploit the poor because they are poor
  and do not crush the needy in court,
²³for the LORD will take up their case
  and will exact life for life.

Saying 3

²⁴Do not make friends with the hot-tempered,
  do not associate with those who are easily angered,
²⁵or you may learn their ways
  and get yourself ensnared.

Saying 4

²⁶Do not be one who shakes hands in pledge
  or puts up security for debts;
²⁷if you lack the means to pay,
  your very bed will be snatched from under you.

Sign of the times

Boundary stone
Proverbs 22:28

Land had been allocated to the Israelites according to their tribes when they arrived in Canaan, the Promised Land. Rather than fences or walls running around the edge of each tribe's allocation, boundary stones were set up every so often to show whose land was whose.

Saying 5

28 Do not move an ancient boundary stone
set up by your ancestors.

Saying 6

29 Do you see those who are skilled in their work?
They will serve before kings;
they will not serve before officials of low rank.

Saying 7

23 When you sit to dine with a ruler,
note well what[a] is before you,
2 and put a knife to your throat
if you are given to gluttony.
3 Do not crave his delicacies,
for that food is deceptive.

Saying 8

4 Do not wear yourself out to get rich;
do not trust your own cleverness.
5 Cast but a glance at riches, and they are gone,
for they will surely sprout wings
and fly off to the sky like an eagle.

Saying 9

6 Do not eat the food of a stingy host,
do not crave his delicacies;
7 for he is the kind of person
who is always thinking about the cost.[b]
'Eat and drink,' he says to you,
but his heart is not with you.
8 You will vomit up the little you have eaten
and will have wasted your compliments.

Saying 10

9 Do not speak to fools,
for they will scorn your prudent words.

Saying 11

10 Do not move an ancient boundary stone
or encroach on the fields of the fatherless,
11 for their Defender is strong;
he will take up their case against you.

Saying 12

12 Apply your heart to instruction
and your ears to words of knowledge.

Saying 13

13 Do not withhold discipline from children;
if you punish them with the rod, they will not die.
14 Punish them with the rod
and save them from death.

Saying 14

15 My son, if your heart is wise,
then my heart will be glad indeed;
16 my inmost being will rejoice
when your lips speak what is right.

Saying 15

17 Do not let your heart envy sinners,
but always be zealous for the fear of the LORD.
18 There is surely a future hope for you,
and your hope will not be cut off.

Saying 16

19 Listen, my son, and be wise,
and set your heart on the right path:
20 do not join those who drink too much wine
or gorge themselves on meat,
21 for drunkards and gluttons become poor,
and drowsiness clothes them in rags.

Saying 17

22 Listen to your father, who gave you life,
and do not despise your mother when she is old.
23 Buy the truth and do not sell it—
wisdom, instruction and insight as well.
24 The father of a righteous child has great joy;
a man who fathers a wise son rejoices in him.
25 May your father and mother rejoice;
may she who gave you birth be joyful!

---

[a] 1 Or *who*   [b] 7 Or *for as he thinks within himself, I so he is; or for as he puts on a feast, I so he is*

Saying 18

26My son, give me your heart
 and let your eyes delight in my ways,
27for an adulterous woman is a deep pit
 and a wayward wife is a narrow well.
28Like a bandit she lies in wait,
 and multiplies the unfaithful among men.

Saying 19

29Who has woe? Who has sorrow?
 Who has strife? Who has complaints?
 Who has needless bruises? Who has bloodshot eyes?
30Those who linger over wine,
 who go to sample bowls of mixed wine.
31Do not gaze at wine when it is red,
 when it sparkles in the cup,
 when it goes down smoothly!
32In the end it bites like a snake
 and poisons like a viper.
33Your eyes will see strange sights
 and your mind imagine confusing things.
34You will be like one sleeping on the high seas,
 lying on top of the rigging.
35'They hit me,' you will say, 'but I'm not hurt!
 They beat me, but I don't feel it!
 When will I wake up
 so I can find another drink?'

Saying 20

24 Do not envy the wicked,
 do not desire their company;
2for their hearts plot violence,
 and their lips talk about making trouble.

Saying 21

3By wisdom a house is built,
 and through understanding it is established;
4through knowledge its rooms are filled with rare and beautiful treasures.

Saying 22

5The wise prevail through great power,
 and those who have knowledge muster their strength.
6Surely you need guidance to wage war,
 and victory is won through many advisors.

Saying 23

7Wisdom is too high for fools;
 in the assembly at the gate they must not open their mouths.

Saying 24

8Whoever plots evil
 will be known as a schemer.
9The schemes of folly are sin,
 and people detest a mocker.

Saying 25

10If you falter in a time of trouble,
 how small is your strength!
11Rescue those being led away to death;
 hold back those staggering towards slaughter.
12If you say, 'But we knew nothing about this,'
 does not he who weighs the heart perceive it?
 Does not he who guards your life know it?
 Will he not repay everyone according to what they have done?

Saying 26

13Eat honey, my son, for it is good;
 honey from the comb is sweet to your taste.
14Know also that wisdom is like honey for you:
 if you find it, there is a future hope for you,
 and your hope will not be cut off.

Saying 27

15Do not lurk like a thief near the house of the righteous,
 do not plunder their dwelling-place;
16for though the righteous fall seven times, they rise again,
 but the wicked stumble when calamity strikes.

Saying 28

17Do not gloat when your enemies fall;
 when they stumble, do not let your heart rejoice,

18or the LORD will see and disapprove
and turn his wrath away from them.

Saying 29

19Do not fret because of evildoers
or be envious of the wicked,
20for the evildoer has no future hope,
and the lamp of the wicked will be snuffed out.

Saying 30

21Fear the LORD and the king, my son,
and do not join with rebellious officials,
22for those two will send sudden destruction on them,
and who knows what calamities they can bring?

Further sayings of the wise

23These also are sayings of the wise:
To show partiality in judging is not good:
24whoever says to the guilty, 'You are innocent,'
will be cursed by peoples and denounced by nations.
25But it will go well with those who convict the guilty,
and rich blessing will come on them.

26An honest answer
is like a kiss on the lips.

27Put your outdoor work in order
and get your fields ready;
after that, build your house.

28Do not testify against your neighbour without cause—
would you use your lips to mislead?
29Do not say, 'I'll do to them as they have done to me;
I'll pay them back for what they did.'

30I went past the field of a sluggard,
past the vineyard of someone who has no sense;
31thorns had come up everywhere,
the ground was covered with weeds,
and the stone wall was in ruins.

32I applied my heart to what I observed
and learned a lesson from what I saw:
33a little sleep, a little slumber,
a little folding of the hands to rest—
34and poverty will come on you like a thief
and scarcity like an armed man.

More proverbs of Solomon

25 These are more proverbs of Solomon, compiled by the men of Hezekiah king of Judah:

2It is the glory of God to conceal a matter;
to search out a matter is the glory of kings.
3As the heavens are high and the earth is deep,
so the hearts of kings are unsearchable.

4Remove the dross from the silver,
and a silversmith can produce a vessel;
5remove wicked officials from the king's presence,
and his throne will be established through righteousness.

6Do not exalt yourself in the king's presence,
and do not claim a place among his great men;
7it is better for him to say to you, 'Come up here,'
than for him to humiliate you before his nobles.

What you have seen with your eyes
8 do not bring[a] hastily to court,
for what will you do in the end
if your neighbour puts you to shame?

9If you take your neighbour to court,
do not betray another's confidence,
10or the one who hears it may shame you
and the charge against you will stand.

11Like apples[b] of gold in settings of silver
is a ruling rightly given.
12Like an ear-ring of gold or an ornament of fine gold
is the rebuke of a wise judge to a listening ear.

---

[a] 7, 8 Or *nobles / on whom you had set your eyes. / 8Do not go* [b] 11 Or possibly *apricots*

¹³Like a snow-cooled drink at harvest time
  is a trustworthy messenger to the one who sends him;
  he refreshes the spirit of his master.
¹⁴Like clouds and wind without rain
  is one who boasts of gifts never given.
¹⁵Through patience a ruler can be persuaded,
  and a gentle tongue can break a bone.
¹⁶If you find honey, eat just enough—
  too much of it, and you will vomit.
¹⁷Seldom set foot in your neighbour's house—
  too much of you, and you will be hated.
¹⁸Like a club or a sword or a sharp arrow
  is one who gives false testimony against a neighbour.
¹⁹Like a broken tooth or a lame foot
  is reliance on the unfaithful in a time of trouble.
²⁰Like one who takes away a garment on a cold day,
  or like vinegar poured on a wound,
  is one who sings songs to a heavy heart.
²¹If your enemy is hungry, give him food to eat;
  if he is thirsty, give him water to drink.
²²In doing this, you will heap burning coals on his head,
  and the Lord will reward you.
²³Like a north wind that brings unexpected rain
  is a sly tongue—which provokes a horrified look.
²⁴Better to live on a corner of the roof
  than share a house with a quarrelsome wife.
²⁵Like cold water to a weary soul
  is good news from a distant land.
²⁶Like a muddied spring or a polluted well
  are the righteous who give way to the wicked.
²⁷It is not good to eat too much honey,
  nor is it honourable to search out matters that are too deep.
²⁸Like a city whose walls are broken through
  is a person who lacks self-control.

Sign of the times

Burning coals
Proverbs 25:22

In ancient Egypt, there was a custom that someone who had done something wrong was made to carry a bowl of hot coals on their head to show that they were sorry. Doing the opposite of what's expected and treating your enemy well should have a similar result – making people sorry for what they have done wrong.

---

26 Like snow in summer or rain in harvest,
  honour is not fitting for a fool.
²Like a fluttering sparrow or a darting swallow,
  an undeserved curse does not come to rest.
³A whip for the horse, a bridle for the donkey,
  and a rod for the backs of fools!
⁴Do not answer fools according to their folly,
  or you yourself will be just like them.
⁵Answer fools according to their folly,
  or they will be wise in their own eyes.
⁶To send a message by the hands of a fool
  is like cutting off one's feet or drinking poison.
⁷Like the useless legs of one who is lame
  is a proverb in the mouth of a fool.
⁸Like tying a stone in a sling
  is the giving of honour to a fool.
⁹Like a thorn-bush in a drunkard's hand
  is a proverb in the mouth of a fool.
¹⁰Like an archer who wounds at random
  is one who hires a fool or any passer-by.
¹¹As a dog returns to its vomit,
  so fools repeat their folly.
¹²Do you see people who are wise in their own eyes?

There is more hope for fools than for them.

¹³A sluggard says, 'There's a lion in the road,
a fierce lion roaming the streets!'
¹⁴As a door turns on its hinges,
so a sluggard turns on the bed.
¹⁵Sluggards bury their hands in the dish
and are too lazy to bring them back to their mouths.
¹⁶Sluggards are wiser in their own eyes
than seven people who answer discreetly.

¹⁷Like one who grabs a stray dog by the ears
is someone who rushes into a quarrel not their own.

¹⁸Like a maniac shooting
flaming arrows of death
¹⁹is one who deceives a neighbour
and says, 'I was only joking!'

²⁰Without wood a fire goes out;
without a gossip a quarrel dies down.
²¹As charcoal to embers and as wood to fire,
so is a quarrelsome person for kindling strife.
²²The words of a gossip are like choice morsels;
they go down to the inmost parts.

²³Like a coating of silver dross on earthenware
are fervent[a] lips with an evil heart.
²⁴Enemies disguise themselves with their lips,
but in their hearts they harbour deceit.
²⁵Though their speech is charming, do not believe them,
for seven abominations fill their hearts.
²⁶Their malice may be concealed by deception,
but their wickedness will be exposed in the assembly.
²⁷If anyone digs a pit, they themselves will fall into it;
if anyone rolls a stone, it will roll back on them.
²⁸A lying tongue hates those it hurts,
and a flattering mouth works ruin.

27

Do not boast about tomorrow,
for you do not know what a day may bring.

²Let someone else praise you, and not your own mouth;
an outsider, and not your own lips.

³Stone is heavy and sand a burden,
but a fool's provocation is heavier than both.

⁴Anger is cruel and fury overwhelming,
but who can stand before jealousy?

⁵Better is open rebuke
than hidden love.
⁶Wounds from a friend can be trusted,
but an enemy multiplies kisses.

⁷One who is full loathes honey from the comb,
but to the hungry even what is bitter tastes sweet.

⁸Like a bird that flees its nest
is anyone who flees from home.

⁹Perfume and incense bring joy to the heart,
and the pleasantness of a friend springs from their heartfelt advice.

¹⁰Do not forsake your friend or a friend of your family,
and do not go to your relative's house when disaster strikes you—
better a neighbour nearby than a relative far away.

¹¹Be wise, my child, and bring joy to my heart;
then I can answer anyone who treats me with contempt.

¹²The prudent see danger and take refuge,
but the simple keep going and pay the penalty.

¹³Take the garment of one who puts up security for a stranger;
hold it in pledge if it is done for an outsider.

¹⁴If anyone loudly blesses a neighbour early in the morning,
it will be taken as a curse.

---

[a] 23 Hebrew; Septuagint *smooth*

¹⁵A quarrelsome wife is like the dripping of a leaky roof in a rainstorm;
¹⁶restraining her is like restraining the wind or grasping oil with the hand.

¹⁷As iron sharpens iron,
so one person sharpens another.

¹⁸Those who guard a fig-tree will eat its fruit,
and those who protect their masters will be honoured.

¹⁹As water reflects the face,
so one's life reflects the heart.[a]

²⁰Death and Destruction[b] are never satisfied,
and neither are human eyes.

²¹The crucible for silver and the furnace for gold,
but people are tested by their praise.

²²Though you grind fools in a mortar,
grinding them like grain with a pestle,
you will not remove their folly from them.

²³Be sure you know the condition of your flocks,
give careful attention to your herds;
²⁴for riches do not endure for ever,
and a crown is not secure for all generations.
²⁵When the hay is removed and new growth appears
and the grass from the hills is gathered in,
²⁶the lambs will provide you with clothing,
and the goats with the price of a field.
²⁷You will have plenty of goats' milk to feed your family
and to nourish your women servants.

28

The wicked flee though no-one pursues,
but the righteous are as bold as a lion.

²When a country is rebellious, it has many rulers,
but a ruler with discernment and knowledge maintains order.

IN OTHER WORDS

Discernment
Proverbs 28:11
Discernment is the ability to tell the difference between good and bad, between truth and lies. Discernment is a gift of the Holy Spirit (1 Corinthians 12:7–11).

³A ruler[c] who oppresses the poor
is like driving rain that leaves no crops.

⁴Those who forsake instruction praise the wicked,
but those who heed it resist them.

⁵Evildoers do not understand what is right,
but those who seek the LORD understand it fully.

⁶Better the poor whose way of life is blameless
than the rich whose ways are perverse.

⁷Those who heed instruction are discerning children,
but companions of gluttons disgrace their parents.

⁸Whoever increases wealth by taking interest or profit from the poor
amasses it for another, who will be kind to the poor.

⁹If anyone turns a deaf ear to my instruction,
even their prayers are detestable.

¹⁰Those who lead the upright along an evil path
will fall into their own trap,
but the blameless will receive a good inheritance.

¹¹The rich are wise in their own eyes;
one who is poor and discerning sees how deluded they are.

¹²When the righteous triumph, there is great elation;

---

[a] 19 Or *so others reflect your heart back to you* [b] 20 Hebrew *Abaddon* [c] 3 Or *A poor person*

but when the wicked rise to power,
people go into hiding.

13 Those who conceal their sins do not prosper,
but those who confess and renounce them find mercy.

14 Blessed are those who always tremble before God,
but those who harden their hearts fall into trouble.

15 Like a roaring lion or a charging bear
is a wicked ruler over a helpless people.

16 A tyrannical ruler practises extortion,
but one who hates ill-gotten gain will enjoy a long reign.

17 Anyone tormented by the guilt of murder will seek refuge in the grave;
let no-one hold them back.

18 Those whose way of life is blameless are kept safe,
but those whose ways are perverse will fall into the pit.[a]

19 Those who work their land will have abundant food,
but those who chase fantasies will have their fill of poverty.

20 A faithful person will be richly blessed,
but one eager to get rich will not go unpunished.

21 To show partiality is not good—
yet a person will do wrong for a piece of bread.

22 The stingy are eager to get rich
and are unaware that poverty awaits them.

23 Whoever rebukes a person will in the end gain favour
rather than one who has a flattering tongue.

24 Whoever robs their father or mother
and says, 'It's not wrong,'
is partner to one who destroys.

25 The greedy stir up dissension,
but those who trust in the LORD will prosper.

26 Those who trust in themselves are fools,
but those who walk in wisdom are kept safe.

27 Those who give to the poor will lack nothing,
but those who close their eyes to them receive many curses.

28 When the wicked rise to power, people go into hiding;
but when the wicked perish, the righteous thrive.

29

Whoever remains stiff-necked after many rebukes
will suddenly be destroyed—without remedy.

2 When the righteous thrive, the people rejoice;
when the wicked rule, the people groan.

3 A man who loves wisdom brings joy to his father,
but a companion of prostitutes squanders his wealth.

4 By justice a king gives a country stability,
but those who are greedy for[b] bribes tear it down.

5 Those who flatter their neighbours
are spreading nets for their feet.

6 Evildoers are snared by their own sin,
but the righteous shout for joy and are glad.

7 The righteous care about justice for the poor,
but the wicked have no such concern.

8 Mockers stir up a city,
but the wise turn away anger.

9 If a wise person goes to court with a fool,
the fool rages and scoffs, and there is no peace.

10 The bloodthirsty hate people of integrity
and seek to kill the upright.

---

[a] 18 Syriac (see Septuagint); Hebrew *into one*   [b] 4 Or *who give*

¹¹Fools give full vent to their rage,
  but the wise bring calm in the end.

¹²If a ruler listens to lies,
  all his officials become wicked.

¹³The poor and the oppressor have this in common:
  the LORD gives sight to the eyes of both.

¹⁴If a king judges the poor with fairness,
  his throne will be established for ever.

¹⁵A rod and a reprimand impart wisdom,
  but children left to themselves disgrace their mother.

¹⁶When the wicked thrive, so does sin,
  but the righteous will see their downfall.

¹⁷Discipline your children, and they will give you peace;
  they will bring you the delights you desire.

¹⁸Where there is no revelation, people cast off restraint;
  but blessed are those who heed wisdom's instruction.

¹⁹Servants cannot be corrected by mere words;
  though they understand, they will not respond.

²⁰Do you see someone who speaks in haste?
  There is more hope for a fool than for them.

²¹A servant pampered from youth
  will turn out to be insolent.

²²An angry person stirs up dissension,
  and a hot-tempered person commits many sins.

²³Pride brings a person low,
  but the lowly in spirit gain honour.

²⁴The accomplices of thieves are their own enemies;
  they are put under oath and dare not testify.

²⁵To fear anyone will prove to be a snare,
  but whoever trusts in the LORD is kept safe.

> **IN OTHER WORDS**
>
> **Revelation**
> **Proverbs 29:18**
> The word 'revelation' is based on the word 'reveal'. It means making something known. Our knowledge of God is revealed to us by him. The last book in the Bible is called Revelation, and is the account of a vision that John saw about the future.

²⁶Many seek an audience with a ruler,
  but it is from the LORD that one gets justice.

²⁷The righteous detest the dishonest;
  the wicked detest the upright.

Sayings of Agur

30 The sayings of Agur son of Jakeh—
  an inspired utterance.

This man's utterance to Ithiel:

'I am weary, God,
  but I can prevail.ᵃ
²Surely I am only a brute, not a man;
  I do not have human understanding.
³I have not learned wisdom,
  nor have I attained to the knowledge of the Holy One.
⁴Who has gone up to heaven and come down?
  Whose hands have gathered up the wind?
  Who has wrapped up the waters in a cloak?
  Who has established all the ends of the earth?
  What is his name, and what is the name of his son?
  Surely you know!

⁵'Every word of God is flawless;
  he is a shield to those who take refuge in him.

ᵃ 1 With a different word division of the Hebrew; Masoretic Text *utterance to Ithiel, I to Ithiel and Ukal:*

6 Do not add to his words,
  or he will rebuke you and prove you a liar.

7 'Two things I ask of you, LORD;
  do not refuse me before I die:
8 keep falsehood and lies far from me;
  give me neither poverty nor riches,
  but give me only my daily bread.
9 Otherwise, I may have too much and disown you
  and say, "Who is the LORD?"
  Or I may become poor and steal,
  and so dishonour the name of my God.

10 'Do not slander servants to their master,
  or they will curse you, and you will pay for it.

11 'There are those who curse their fathers
  and do not bless their mothers;
12 those who are pure in their own eyes
  and yet are not cleansed of their filth;
13 those whose eyes are ever so haughty,
  whose glances are so disdainful;
14 those whose teeth are swords
  and whose jaws are set with knives
  to devour the poor from the earth
  and the needy from among the human race.

15 'The leech has two daughters.
  "Give! Give!" they cry.

'There are three things that are never satisfied,
  four that never say, "Enough!":
16 the grave, the barren womb,
  land, which is never satisfied with water,
  and fire, which never says, "Enough!"

17 'The eye that mocks a father,
  that scorns an aged mother,
  will be pecked out by the ravens of the valley,
  will be eaten by the vultures.

18 'There are three things that are too amazing for me,
  four that I do not understand:
19 the way of an eagle in the sky,
  the way of a snake on a rock,
  the way of a ship on the high seas,
  and the way of a man with a young woman.

20 'This is the way of an adulterous woman:
  she eats and wipes her mouth
  and says, "I've done nothing wrong."

21 'Under three things the earth trembles,
  under four it cannot bear up:
22 a servant who becomes king,
  a godless fool who gets plenty to eat,
23 a contemptible woman who gets married,
  and a servant who displaces her mistress.

24 'Four things on earth are small,
  yet they are extremely wise:
25 ants are creatures of little strength,
  yet they store up their food in the summer;
26 hyraxes are creatures of little power,
  yet they make their home in the crags;
27 locusts have no king,
  yet they advance together in ranks;
28 a lizard can be caught with the hand,
  yet it is found in kings' palaces.

29 'There are three things that are stately in their stride,
  four that move with stately bearing:
30 a lion, mighty among beasts,
  who retreats before nothing;
31 a strutting cock, a he-goat,
  and a king secure against revolt.^{a}

32 'If you play the fool and exalt yourself,
  or if you plan evil,
  clap your hand over your mouth!
33 For as churning cream produces butter,
  and as twisting the nose produces blood,
  so stirring up anger produces strife.'

Sayings of King Lemuel

31 The sayings of King Lemuel—an inspired utterance his mother taught him.

2 Listen, my son! Listen, son of my womb!
  Listen, my son, the answer to my prayers!
3 Do not spend your strength^b on women,
  your vigour on those who ruin kings.

---

^{a} 31 The meaning of the Hebrew for this phrase is uncertain. ^{b} 3 Or *wealth*

⁴It is not for kings, Lemuel—
  it is not for kings to drink wine,
  not for rulers to crave beer,
⁵lest they drink and forget what has been decreed,
  and deprive all the oppressed of their rights.
⁶Let beer be for those who are perishing,
  wine for those who are in anguish!
⁷Let them drink and forget their poverty
  and remember their misery no more.

⁸Speak up for those who cannot speak for themselves,
  for the rights of all who are destitute.
⁹Speak up and judge fairly;
  defend the rights of the poor and needy.

Epilogue: the wife of noble character

¹⁰ ᵃA wife of noble character who can find?
  She is worth far more than rubies.
¹¹Her husband has full confidence in her
  and lacks nothing of value.
¹²She brings him good, not harm,
  all the days of her life.
¹³She selects wool and flax
  and works with eager hands.
¹⁴She is like the merchant ships,
  bringing her food from afar.
¹⁵She gets up while it is still night;
  she provides food for her family
  and portions for her women servants.
¹⁶She considers a field and buys it;
  out of her earnings she plants a vineyard.
¹⁷She sets about her work vigorously;
  her arms are strong for her tasks.
¹⁸She sees that her trading is profitable,
  and her lamp does not go out at night.
¹⁹In her hand she holds the distaff
  and grasps the spindle with her fingers.
²⁰She opens her arms to the poor
  and extends her hands to the needy.
²¹When it snows, she has no fear for her household;
  for all of them are clothed in scarlet.
²²She makes coverings for her bed;
  she is clothed in fine linen and purple.
²³Her husband is respected at the city gate,
  where he takes his seat among the elders of the land.
²⁴She makes linen garments and sells them,
  and supplies the merchants with sashes.
²⁵She is clothed with strength and dignity;
  she can laugh at the days to come.
²⁶She speaks with wisdom,
  and faithful instruction is on her tongue.
²⁷She watches over the affairs of her household
  and does not eat the bread of idleness.
²⁸Her children arise and call her blessed;
  her husband also, and he praises her:
²⁹'Many women do noble things,
  but you surpass them all.'
³⁰Charm is deceptive, and beauty is fleeting;
  but a woman who fears the LORD is to be praised.
³¹Honour her for all that her hands have done,
  and let her works bring her praise at the city gate.

ᵃ 10 Verses 10-31 are an acrostic poem, the verses of which begin with the successive letters of the Hebrew alphabet.

Ecclesiastes

INTRODUCTION

ECCLESIASTES

Author: Solomon

When: During his reign of forty years from 971 BC to 931 BC.

Did you know? Ecclesiastes is one of the 'Wisdom' books in the Old Testament that wrestle with the meaning of life. The others are Job, Proverbs and some of the Psalms.

Main theme: Ecclesiastes doesn't exactly start on a cheerful note. By verse 2, Solomon has decided that everything in life is meaningless, if you look at it from a human perspective. But don't worry; there are some positive thoughts in here too. Basically, Solomon is saying that fame, wealth, happiness, hard work and popularity won't bring lasting satisfaction, but following God will. And remember that life is to be enjoyed (Ecclesiastes 3:12,13).

Everything is meaningless

1 The words of the Teacher,[a] son of David, king of Jerusalem:

2'Meaningless! Meaningless!'
  says the Teacher.
'Utterly meaningless!
  Everything is meaningless.'

3What does anyone gain from all their labours
  at which they toil under the sun?
4Generations come and generations go,
  but the earth remains for ever.
5The sun rises and the sun sets,
  and hurries back to where it rises.
6The wind blows to the south
  and turns to the north;
round and round it goes,
  ever returning on its course.
7All streams flow into the sea,
  yet the sea is never full.
To the place the streams come from,
  there they return again.

---

[a] 1 Or *the leader of the assembly*; also in verses 2 and 12

making Connections

Elohim
Ecclesiastes 1:13
The only name used for God in the book of Ecclesiastes is Elohim in Hebrew, the name of God found in the creation story (Genesis 1:1–2:4). The more usual name for God throughout the Old Testament is Yahweh, which is written LORD in this Bible.

8All things are wearisome,
   more than one can say.
The eye never has enough of seeing,
   nor the ear its fill of hearing.
9What has been will be again,
   what has been done will be done again;
   there is nothing new under the sun.
10Is there anything of which one can say,
   'Look! This is something new'?
It was here already, long ago;
   it was here before our time.
11There is no remembrance of people of old,
   and even those who are yet to come
will not be remembered
   by those who follow them.

Wisdom is meaningless

12I, the Teacher, was king over Israel in Jerusalem. 13I applied my mind to study and to explore by wisdom all that is done under the heavens. What a heavy burden God has laid on the human race! 14I have seen all the things that are done under the sun; all of them are meaningless, a chasing after the wind.

15What is crooked cannot be straightened;
   what is lacking cannot be counted.

16I said to myself, 'Look, I have grown and increased in wisdom more than anyone who has ruled over Jerusalem before me; I have experienced much of wisdom and knowledge.' 17Then I applied myself to the understanding of wisdom, and also of madness and folly, but I learned that this, too, is a chasing after the wind.

18For with much wisdom comes much sorrow;
   the more knowledge, the more grief.

Pleasures are meaningless

2 I said to myself, 'Come now, I will test you with pleasure to find out what is good.' But that also proved to be meaningless. 2'Laughter,' I said, 'is madness. And what does pleasure accomplish?' 3I tried cheering myself with wine, and embracing folly—my mind still guiding me with wisdom. I wanted to see what was good for people to do under the heavens during the few days of their lives.

4I undertook great projects: I built houses for myself and planted vineyards. 5I made gardens and parks and planted all kinds of fruit trees in them. 6I made reservoirs to water groves of flourishing trees. 7I bought male and female slaves and had other slaves who were born in my house. I also owned more herds and flocks than anyone in Jerusalem before me. 8I amassed silver and gold for myself, and the treasure of kings and provinces. I acquired male and female singers, and a harem[a] as well—the delights of a man's heart. 9I became greater by far than anyone in Jerusalem before me. In all this my wisdom stayed with me.

10I denied myself nothing my eyes desired;
   I refused my heart no pleasure.
My heart took delight in all my labour,
   and this was the reward for all my toil.
11Yet when I surveyed all that my hands had done
   and what I had toiled to achieve,
everything was meaningless, a chasing after the wind;
   nothing was gained under the sun.

Wisdom and folly are meaningless

12Then I turned my thoughts to consider wisdom,
   and also madness and folly.

---

[a] 8 The meaning of the Hebrew for this phrase is uncertain.

What more can the king's successor do
  than what has already been done?
13 I saw that wisdom is better than folly,
  just as light is better than darkness.
14 The wise have eyes in their heads,
  while fools walk in the darkness;
 but I came to realise
  that the same fate overtakes them both.

15 Then I said to myself,

'The fate of the fool will overtake me also.
  What then do I gain by being wise?'
I said to myself,
  'This too is meaningless.'
16 For the wise, like the fool, will not be long
    remembered;
  the days have already come when both
    have been forgotten.
Like the fool, the wise too must die!

Toil is meaningless

17 So I hated life, because the work that is done under the sun was grievous to me. All of it is meaningless, a chasing after the wind. 18 I hated all the things I had toiled for under the sun, because I must leave them to the one who comes after me. 19 And who knows whether that person will be wise or foolish? Yet they will have control over all the toil into which I have poured my effort and skill under the sun. This too is meaningless. 20 So my heart began to despair over all my toilsome labour under the sun. 21 For people may labour with wisdom, knowledge and skill, and then they must leave all they own to others who have not toiled for it. This too is meaningless and a great misfortune. 22 What do people get for all the toil and anxious striving with which they labour under the sun? 23 All their days their work is grief and pain; even at night their minds do not rest. This too is meaningless.

24 People can do nothing better than to eat and drink and find satisfaction in their toil. This too, I see, is from the hand of God, 25 for without him, who can eat or find enjoyment? 26 To the person who pleases him, God gives wisdom, knowledge and happiness, but to the sinner he gives the task of gathering and storing up wealth to hand it over to the one who pleases God. This too is meaningless, a chasing after the wind.

A time for everything

3 There is a time for everything,
  and a season for every activity under
    the heavens:

2 a time to be born and a time to die,
   a time to plant and a time to uproot,
3 a time to kill and a time to heal,
   a time to tear down and a time to build,
4 a time to weep and a time to laugh,
   a time to mourn and a time to dance,
5 a time to scatter stones and a time to
     gather them,
   a time to embrace and a time to refrain,
6 a time to search and a time to give up,
   a time to keep and a time to throw
     away,
7 a time to tear and a time to mend,
   a time to be silent and a time to speak,
8 a time to love and a time to hate,
   a time for war and a time for peace.

9 What do workers gain from their toil? 10 I have seen the burden God has laid on the human race. 11 He has made everything beautiful in its time. He has also set eternity in the human heart; yet no-one can fathom what God has done from beginning to end. 12 I know that there is nothing better for people than to be happy and to do good while they live. 13 That each of them may eat and drink, and find satisfaction in all their toil—this is the gift of God. 14 I know that everything God does will endure for ever; nothing can be added to it and nothing taken from it. God does it so that people will fear him.

15 Whatever is has already been,
  and what will be has been before;
  and God will call the past to account.[a]

16 And I saw something else under the sun:

In the place of judgment—wickedness
    was there,
  in the place of justice—wickedness was
    there.

17 I said to myself,

---

[a] 15 Or *God calls back the past*

'God will bring into judgment
both the righteous and the wicked,
for there will be a time for every activity,
a time to judge every deed.'

18I also said to myself, 'As for human beings, God tests them so that they may see that they are like the animals. 19Surely the fate of human beings is like that of the animals; the same fate awaits them both: as one dies, so dies the other. All have the same breath;[a] the human race has no advantage over animals. Everything is meaningless. 20All go to the same place; all come from dust, and to dust all return. 21Who knows if the human spirit rises upwards, and if the spirit of the animal goes down into the earth?'

22So I saw that there is nothing better for people than to enjoy their work, because that is their lot. For who can bring them to see what will happen after them?

Oppression, toil, friendlessness

4 Again I looked and saw all the oppression that was taking place under the sun:

I saw the tears of the oppressed—
and they have no comforter;
power was on the side of their
oppressors—
and they have no comforter.
2And I declared that the dead,
who had already died,
are happier than the living,
who are still alive.
3But better than both
is the one who has not yet been,
who has not seen the evil
that is done under the sun.

4And I saw that all toil and all achievement spring from one person's envy of another. This too is meaningless, a chasing after the wind.

5Fools fold their hands
and ruin themselves.
6Better one handful with tranquillity
than two handfuls with toil
and chasing after the wind.

Making Connections

Chasing after wind
Ecclesiastes 4:4
This is a great example of a pointless activity. Why chase after the wind, because you can never catch it, control it or change it?

7Again I saw something meaningless under the sun:

8There was a man all alone;
he had neither son nor brother.
There was no end to his toil,
yet his eyes were not content with his
wealth.
'For whom am I toiling,' he asked,
'and why am I depriving myself of
enjoyment?'
This too is meaningless—
a miserable business!

9Two are better than one,
because they have a good return for
their labour:
10if they fall down,
they can help each other up.
But pity those who fall
and have no-one to help them up!
11Also, if two lie down together, they will
keep warm.
But how can one keep warm alone?
12Though one may be overpowered,
two can defend themselves.
A cord of three strands is not quickly
broken.

Advancement is meaningless

13Better a poor but wise youth than an old but foolish king who no longer knows how to heed a warning. 14The youth may have come from prison to the kingship, or he may have been born in poverty within his kingdom. 15I saw that all who lived and

---

[a] 19 Or *spirit*

walked under the sun followed the youth, the king's successor. ¹⁶There was no end to all the people who were before them. But those who came later were not pleased with the successor. This too is meaningless, a chasing after the wind.

Fulfil your vow to God

5 *Guard your steps when you go to the house of God. Go near to listen rather than to offer the sacrifice of fools, who do not know that they do wrong.

*²Do not be quick with your mouth,
  do not be hasty in your heart
  to utter anything before God.
God is in heaven
  and you are on earth,
  so let your words be few.
³A dream comes when there are many cares,
  and many words mark the speech of a fool.

⁴When you make a vow to God, do not delay to fulfil it. He has no pleasure in fools; fulfil your vow. ⁵It is better not to make a vow than to make one and not fulfil it. ⁶Do not let your mouth lead you into sin. And do not protest to the [temple] messenger, 'My vow was a mistake.' Why should God be angry at what you say and destroy the work of your hands? ⁷Much dreaming and many words are meaningless. Therefore fear God.

Riches are meaningless

⁸If you see the poor oppressed in a district, and justice and rights denied, do not be surprised at such things; for one official is eyed by a higher one, and over them both are others higher still. ⁹The increase from the land is taken by all; the king himself profits from the fields.

¹⁰Those who love money never have enough;
  those who love wealth are never satisfied with their income.
This too is meaningless.

¹¹As goods increase,
  so do those who consume them.
And what benefit are they to the owners
  except to feast their eyes on them?

¹²The sleep of labourers is sweet,
  whether they eat little or much,
but the abundance of the rich
  permits them no sleep.

¹³I have seen a grievous evil under the sun:
  wealth hoarded to the harm of its owners,
¹⁴ or wealth lost through some misfortune,
so that when they have children
  there is nothing left for them to inherit.
¹⁵Everyone comes naked from their mother's womb,
  and as everyone comes, so they depart.
They take nothing from their toil
  that they can carry in their hands.

¹⁶This too is a grievous evil:

As everyone comes, so they depart,
  and what do they gain,
  since they toil for the wind?
¹⁷All their days they eat in darkness,
  with great frustration, affliction and anger.

¹⁸This is what I have observed to be good: that it is appropriate for people to eat, to drink and to find satisfaction in their toilsome labour under the sun during the few days of life God has given them—for this is their lot. ¹⁹Moreover, when God gives people wealth and possessions, and the ability to enjoy them, to accept their lot and be happy in their toil—this is a gift of God. ²⁰They seldom reflect on the days of their lives, because God keeps them occupied with gladness of heart.

6 I have seen another evil under the sun, and it weighs heavily on the human race: ²God gives some people wealth, possessions and honour, so that they lack nothing their hearts desire, but God does not grant the ability to enjoy them, and strangers enjoy them instead. This is meaningless, a grievous evil.

³A man may have a hundred children and live many years; yet no matter how long he lives, if he cannot enjoy his prosperity and does not receive proper burial, I say that a stillborn child is better off than he. ⁴It comes without meaning, it departs in darkness, and in darkness its name is

---

* 5:1 is numbered 4:17 in Hebrew texts.   * 5:2-20 is numbered 5:1-19 in Hebrew texts.

shrouded. ⁵Though it never saw the sun or knew anything, it has more rest than does that man— ⁶even if he lives a thousand years twice over but fails to enjoy his prosperity. Do not all go to the same place?

⁷Everyone's toil is for the mouth,
    yet the appetite is never satisfied.
⁸What advantage have the wise over fools?
    What do the poor gain
      by knowing how to conduct
        themselves before others?
⁹Better what the eye sees
    than the roving of the appetite.
This too is meaningless,
    a chasing after the wind.

¹⁰Whatever exists has already been named,
    and what humanity is has been known;
no-one can contend
    with someone who is stronger.
¹¹The more the words,
    the less the meaning,
    and how does that profit anyone?

¹²For who knows what is good for people in life, during the few and meaningless days they pass through like a shadow? Who can tell them what will happen under the sun after they are gone?

Wisdom

7 A good name is better than fine perfume,
    and the day of death better than the day of birth.
²It is better to go to a house of mourning
    than to go to a house of feasting,
for death is the destiny of everyone;
    the living should take this to heart.
³Frustration is better than laughter,
    because a sad face is good for the heart.
⁴The heart of the wise is in the house of mourning,
    but the heart of fools is in the house of pleasure.
⁵It is better to heed the rebuke of a wise person
    than to listen to the song of fools.
⁶Like the crackling of thorns under the pot,
    so is the laughter of fools.
This too is meaningless.

⁷Extortion turns the wise into fools,
    and a bribe corrupts the heart.

> **IN OTHER WORDS**
>
> ### Wisdom
> **Ecclesiastes 7:11**
> Wisdom is the ability to use knowledge in the right way. So it's not about learning lots of facts and information, it's about choosing how that knowledge affects the way you live.

⁸The end of a matter is better than its beginning,
    and patience is better than pride.
⁹Do not be quickly provoked in your spirit,
    for anger resides in the lap of fools.

¹⁰Do not say, 'Why were the old days better than these?'
    For it is not wise to ask such questions.

¹¹Wisdom, like an inheritance, is a good thing
    and benefits those who see the sun.
¹²Wisdom is a shelter
    as money is a shelter,
but the advantage of knowledge is this:
    wisdom preserves the life of its possessor.

¹³Consider what God has done:

Who can straighten
    what he has made crooked?
¹⁴When times are good, be happy;
    but when times are bad, consider:
God has made the one
    as well as the other.
Therefore, you cannot discover
    anything about your future.

¹⁵In this meaningless life of mine I have seen both of these:

the righteous perishing in their righteousness,
    and the wicked living long in their wickedness.
¹⁶Do not be over-righteous,
    neither be overwise—

why destroy yourself?
¹⁷Do not be overwicked,
and do not be a fool—
why die before your time?
¹⁸It is good to grasp the one
and not let go of the other.
Whoever fears God will avoid all
⌊extremes⌋.*a*

¹⁹Wisdom makes one wise person more
powerful
than ten rulers in a city.

²⁰Indeed, there is no-one on earth who is
righteous,
no-one who does what is right and
never sins.

²¹Do not pay attention to every word
people say,
or you may hear your servant cursing
you—
²²for you know in your heart
that many times you yourself have
cursed others.

²³All this I tested by wisdom and I said,

'I am determined to be wise'—
but this was beyond me.
²⁴Whatever exists is far off and most
profound—
who can discover it?
²⁵So I turned my mind to understand,
to investigate and to search out
wisdom and the scheme of things
and to understand the stupidity of
wickedness
and the madness of folly.

²⁶I find more bitter than death
the woman who is a snare,
whose heart is a trap
and whose hands are chains.
The man who pleases God will escape her,
but the sinner she will ensnare.

²⁷'Look,' says the Teacher,*b* 'this is what I
have discovered:

'Adding one thing to another to discover
the scheme of things—
28   while I was still searching
but not finding—

I found one ⌊upright⌋ man among a
thousand,
but not one ⌊upright⌋ woman among
them all.
²⁹This only have I found:
God created humanity upright,
but they have gone in search of many
schemes.'

8

Who is like the wise?
Who knows the explanation of things?
Wisdom brightens the face
and changes its hard appearance.

Obey the king

²Obey the king's command, I say, because you took an oath before God. ³Do not be in a hurry to leave the king's presence. Do not stand up for a bad cause, for he will do whatever he pleases. ⁴Since a king's word is supreme, who can say to him, 'What are you doing?'

⁵Whoever obeys his command will come
to no harm,
and the wise heart will know the proper
time and procedure.
⁶For there is a proper time and procedure
for every matter,
though a person may be weighed down
by misery.

⁷Since no-one knows the future,
who can say what is to come?
⁸As no-one has power over the wind to
contain it,
so*c* no-one has power over the time of
their death.
As no-one is discharged in time of war,
so wickedness will not release those
who practise it.

⁹All this I saw, as I applied my mind to everything done under the sun. There is a time when a man lords it over others to his own*d* hurt. ¹⁰Then too, I saw the wicked buried—those who used to come and go from the holy place and receive praise*e* in the city where they did this. This too is meaningless.

---

a 18 Or *will follow them both*   *b* 27 Or *the leader of the assembly*   *c* 8 Or *over the human spirit to retain it, I and so*
d 9 Or *to their*   *e* 10 Some Hebrew manuscripts and Septuagint (Aquila); most Hebrew manuscripts *and are forgotten*

¹¹When the sentence for a crime is not quickly carried out, people's hearts are filled with schemes to do wrong. ¹²Although a wicked person who commits a hundred crimes may live a long time, I know that it will go better with those who fear God, who are reverent before him. ¹³Yet because the wicked do not fear God, it will not go well with them, and their days will not lengthen like a shadow.

¹⁴There is something else meaningless that occurs on earth: the righteous who get what the wicked deserve, and the wicked who get what the righteous deserve. This too, I say, is meaningless. ¹⁵So I commend the enjoyment of life, because there is nothing better for people under the sun than to eat and drink and be glad. Then joy will accompany them in their toil all the days of the life God has given them under the sun.

¹⁶When I applied my mind to know wisdom and to observe the labour that is done on earth—people getting no sleep day or night—¹⁷then I saw all that God has done. No-one can comprehend what goes on under the sun. People toil to search it out, but no one can discover its meaning. Even if the wise claim they know, they cannot really comprehend it.

A common destiny for all

9 So I reflected on all this and concluded that the righteous and the wise and what they do are in God's hands, but no-one knows whether love or hate awaits them. ²All share a common destiny—the righteous and the wicked, the good and the bad,ᵃ the clean and the unclean, those who offer sacrifices and those who do not.

As it is with the good,
   so with the sinful;
as it is with those who take oaths,
   so with those who are afraid to take
     them.

³This is the evil in everything that happens under the sun: the same destiny overtakes all. The hearts of people, moreover, are full of evil and there is madness in their hearts while they live, and afterwards they join the dead. ⁴Anyone who is among the living has hopeᵇ—even a live dog is better off than a dead lion!

⁵For the living know that they will die,
   but the dead know nothing;
they have no further reward,
   and even their name is forgotten.
⁶Their love, their hate
   and their jealousy have long since
     vanished;
never again will they have a part
   in anything that happens under the
     sun.

⁷Go, eat your food with gladness, and drink your wine with a joyful heart, for God has already approved what you do. ⁸Always be clothed in white, and always anoint your head with oil. ⁹Enjoy life with your wife, whom you love, all the days of this meaningless life that God has given you under the sun—all your meaningless days. For this is your lot in life and in your toilsome labour under the sun. ¹⁰Whatever your hand finds to do, do it with all your might, for in the realm of the dead, where you are going, there is neither working nor planning nor knowledge nor wisdom.

¹¹I have seen something else under the sun:

The race is not to the swift
   or the battle to the strong,
nor does food come to the wise
   or wealth to the brilliant
   or favour to the learned;
but time and chance happen to them all.

¹²Moreover, no-one knows when their hour will come:

As fish are caught in a cruel net,
   or birds are taken in a snare,
so people are trapped by evil times
   that fall unexpectedly upon them.

Wisdom better than folly

¹³I also saw under the sun this example of wisdom that greatly impressed me: ¹⁴there was once a small city with only a few people in it. And a powerful king came against it,

---

ᵃ 2 Septuagint (Aquila), Vulgate and Syriac; Hebrew does not have *and the bad*.   ᵇ 4 Or *What then is to be chosen? With all who live, there is hope* surrounded it and built huge siege works against it. ¹⁵Now there lived in that city a man poor but wise, and he saved the city by his wisdom. But nobody remembered that poor man. ¹⁶So I said, 'Wisdom is better than strength.' But the poor man's wisdom is despised, and his words are no longer heeded.

¹⁷The quiet words of the wise are more to be heeded
than the shouts of a ruler of fools.
¹⁸Wisdom is better than weapons of war,
but one sinner destroys much good.

10
As dead flies give perfume a bad smell,
so a little folly outweighs wisdom and honour.
²The heart of the wise inclines to the right,
but the heart of the fool to the left.
³Even as fools walk along the road,
they lack sense
and show everyone how stupid they are.
⁴If a ruler's anger rises against you,
do not leave your post;
calmness can lay great offences to rest.

⁵There is an evil I have seen under the sun,
the sort of error that arises from a ruler:
⁶fools are put in many high positions,
while the rich occupy the low ones.
⁷I have seen slaves on horseback,
while princes go on foot like slaves.

⁸Whoever digs a pit may fall into it;
whoever breaks through a wall may be bitten by a snake.
⁹Whoever quarries stones may be injured by them;
whoever splits logs may be endangered by them.

¹⁰If the axe is dull
and its edge unsharpened,
more strength is needed,
but skill will bring success.

¹¹If a snake bites before it is charmed,
the charmer receives no fee.

¹²Words from the mouth of the wise are gracious,
but fools are consumed by their own lips.
¹³At the beginning their words are folly;
at the end they are wicked madness—
¹⁴ and fools multiply words.

No-one knows what is coming—
who can tell them what will happen after them?

¹⁵The toil of fools wearies them;
they do not know the way to town.

¹⁶Woe to the land whose king was a servant*a*
and whose princes feast in the morning.
¹⁷Blessed is the land whose king is of noble birth
and whose princes eat at a proper time—
for strength and not for drunkenness.

¹⁸Through laziness, the rafters sag;
because of idle hands, the house leaks.

¹⁹A feast is made for laughter,
wine makes life merry,
and money is the answer for everything.

Sign of the times

Snake charming
Ecclesiastes 10:11

Snake charming was quite common in the ancient world. Snake charmers would tame poisonous cobras and use them to perform tricks. The word for 'charmer' means 'controller of the tongue'. Charmers would use their voices to control the snakes. By charming the snakes, they also had control of the snakes' tongues, which is where people thought the poison came from.

---

a 16 Or *king is a child*

20 Do not revile the king even in your thoughts,
or curse the rich in your bedroom,
because a bird in the sky may carry your words,
and a bird on the wing may report what you say.

Invest in many ventures

11 Ship your grain across the sea;
after many days you may receive a return.
2 Invest in seven ventures, yes, in eight;
you do not know what disaster may come upon the land.
3 If clouds are full of water,
they pour rain on the earth.
Whether a tree falls to the south or to the north,
in the place where it falls, there it will lie.
4 Whoever watches the wind will not plant;
whoever looks at the clouds will not reap.
5 As you do not know the path of the wind,
or how the body is formed^a in a mother's womb,
so you cannot understand the work of God,
the Maker of all things.
6 Sow your seed in the morning,
and at evening let your hands not be idle,
for you do not know which will succeed,
whether this or that,
or whether both will do equally well.

Remember your Creator while young

7 Light is sweet,
and it pleases the eyes to see the sun.
8 However many years anyone may live,
let them enjoy them all.
But let them remember the days of darkness,
for there will be many.
Everything to come is meaningless.

9 You who are young, be happy while you are young,
and let your hearts give you joy in the days of your youth.
Follow the ways of your heart
and whatever your eyes see,
but know that for all these things
God will bring you into judgment.
10 So then, banish anxiety from your heart
and cast off the troubles of your body,
for youth and vigour are meaningless.

12 Remember your Creator
in the days of your youth,
before the days of trouble come
and the years approach when you will say,
'I find no pleasure in them'—
2 before the sun and the light
and the moon and the stars grow dark,
and the clouds return after the rain;
3 when the keepers of the house tremble,
and the strong men stoop,
when the grinders cease because they are few,
and those looking through the windows grow dim;
4 when the doors to the street are closed
and the sound of grinding fades;
when people rise up at the sound of birds,
but all their songs grow faint;
5 when people are afraid of heights
and of dangers in the streets;
when the almond tree blossoms
and the grasshopper drags itself along
and desire no longer is stirred.
Then people go to their eternal home
and mourners go about the streets.

6 Remember him—before the silver cord is severed,
and the golden bowl is broken;
before the pitcher is shattered at the spring,
and the wheel broken at the well,
7 and the dust returns to the ground it came from,
and the spirit returns to God who gave it.

8 'Meaningless! Meaningless!' says the Teacher.^{b}
'Everything is meaningless!'

---

^{a} 5 Or *know how life* (or *the spirit*) *I enters the body being formed* ^{b} 8 Or *the leader of the assembly*; also in verses 9 and 10

The conclusion of the matter

⁹Not only was the Teacher wise, but also he imparted knowledge to the people. He pondered and searched out and set in order many proverbs. ¹⁰The Teacher searched to find just the right words, and what he wrote was upright and true.

¹¹The words of the wise are like goads, their collected sayings like firmly embedded nails—given by one shepherd.*ᵃ* ¹²Be warned, my son, of anything in addition to them.

Of making many books there is no end, and much study wearies the body.

¹³Now all has been heard;
here is the conclusion of the matter:
fear God and keep his commandments,
for this is the [duty] of every human being.
¹⁴For God will bring every deed into judgment,
including every hidden thing,
whether it is good or evil.

ᵃ 11 Or *Shepherd*

Song of Songs

INTRODUCTION

SONG OF SONGS

Author: Solomon

When: Probably written early in his reign, around 965 BC.

Where: Solomon was King of Israel.

Main theme: You may not expect to read much about romance and sexuality in the Bible, but in this book you'll find beautiful descriptions of both. This song is a celebration of the love between a man and a woman and has three voices in it: King Solomon the 'He', a Shulamite woman who is the 'She', and their friends. There is a lot of debate about the meaning of this unusual book. Some people think it should be understood literally as a healthy expression of love; other people say it is more symbolic and is about God's love for his people. Perhaps both ideas are present.

1 Solomon's Song of Songs.

She[a]

2Let him kiss me with the kisses of his mouth—
 for your love is more delightful than wine.
3Pleasing is the fragrance of your perfumes;
 your name is like perfume poured out.
 No wonder the young women love you!
4Take me away with you—let us hurry!
 Let the king bring me into his chambers.

Friends

We rejoice and delight in you;[b]
 we will praise your love more than wine.

---

[a] 2 The main male and female speakers (identified primarily on the basis of the gender of the relevant Hebrew forms) are indicated by the captions He and She respectively. The words of others are marked Friends. In some instances the divisions and their captions are debatable.   [b] 4 The Hebrew is masculine singular.

She

How right they are to adore you!

5 Dark am I, yet lovely,
 daughters of Jerusalem,
 dark like the tents of Kedar,
 like the tent curtains of Solomon.[a]
6 Do not stare at me because I am dark,
 because I am darkened by the sun.
 My mother's sons were angry with me
 and made me take care of the
 vineyards;
 my own vineyard I had to neglect.
7 Tell me, you whom I love,
 where you graze your flock
 and where you rest your sheep at
 midday.
 Why should I be like a veiled woman
 beside the flocks of your friends?

Friends

8 If you do not know, most beautiful of
 women,
 follow the tracks of the sheep
 and graze your young goats
 by the tents of the shepherds.

He

9 I liken you, my darling, to a mare
 among Pharaoh's chariot horses.
10 Your cheeks are beautiful with ear-rings,
 your neck with strings of jewels.
11 We will make you ear-rings of gold,
 studded with silver.

She

12 While the king was at his table,
 my perfume spread its fragrance.
13 My beloved is to me a sachet of myrrh
 resting between my breasts.
14 My beloved is to me a cluster of henna
 blossoms
 from the vineyards of En Gedi.

He

15 How beautiful you are, my darling!
 Oh, how beautiful!
 Your eyes are doves.

She

16 How handsome you are, my beloved!
 Oh, how charming!
 And our bed is verdant.

He

17 The beams of our house are cedars;
 our rafters are firs.

She[b]

2 I am a rose[c] of Sharon,
 a lily of the valleys.

He

2 Like a lily among thorns
 is my darling among the young
 women.

She

3 Like an apple[d] tree among the trees of the
 forest
 is my beloved among the young
 men.
 I delight to sit in his shade,
 and his fruit is sweet to my taste.
4 Let him lead me to the banqueting hall,
 and let his banner over me be love.
5 Strengthen me with raisins,
 refresh me with apples,
 for I am faint with love.
6 His left arm is under my head,
 and his right arm embraces me.
7 Daughters of Jerusalem, I charge you
 by the gazelles and by the does of the
 field:
 do not arouse or awaken love
 until it so desires.

8 Listen! My beloved!
 Look! Here he comes,
 leaping across the mountains,
 bounding over the hills.
9 My beloved is like a gazelle or a young
 stag.
 Look! There he stands behind our
 wall,
 gazing through the windows,
 peering through the lattice.
10 My beloved spoke and said to me,
 'Arise, my darling,
 my beautiful one, come with me.
11 See! The winter is past;
 the rains are over and gone.
12 Flowers appear on the earth;
 the season of singing has come,

---

[a] 5 Or *Salma* [b] 1 Or *He* [c] 1 Probably a member of the crocus family [d] 3 Or possibly *apricot*; here and elsewhere in Song of Songs

the cooing of doves
　　is heard in our land.
¹³The fig-tree forms its early fruit;
　　the blossoming vines spread their
　　　　fragrance.
Arise, come, my darling;
　　my beautiful one, come with me.'

He

¹⁴My dove in the clefts of the rock,
　　in the hiding-places on the
　　　　mountainside,
show me your face,
　　let me hear your voice;
for your voice is sweet,
　　and your face is lovely.
¹⁵Catch for us the foxes,
　　the little foxes
that ruin the vineyards,
　　our vineyards that are in bloom.

She

¹⁶My beloved is mine and I am his;
　　he browses among the lilies.
¹⁷Until the day breaks
　　and the shadows flee,
turn, my beloved,
　　and be like a gazelle
or like a young stag
　　on the rugged hills.[a]

3 All night long on my bed
　　I looked for the one my heart loves;
　　I looked for him but did not find him.
²I will get up now and go about the city,
　　through its streets and squares;
　　I will search for the one my heart loves.
So I looked for him but did not find
　　him.
³The watchmen found me
　　as they made their rounds in the city.
'Have you seen the one my heart loves?'
⁴Scarcely had I passed them
　　when I found the one my heart loves.
I held him and would not let him go
　　till I had brought him to my mother's
　　　　house,
to the room of the one who conceived
　　me.
⁵Daughters of Jerusalem, I charge you

by the gazelles and by the does of the
　　field:
do not arouse or awaken love
　　until it so desires.

⁶Who is this coming up from the
　　wilderness
like a column of smoke,
perfumed with myrrh and incense
　　made from all the spices of the
　　　　merchant?
⁷Look! It is Solomon's carriage,
　　escorted by sixty warriors,
　　the noblest of Israel,
⁸all of them wearing the sword,
　　all experienced in battle,
each with his sword at his side,
　　prepared for the terrors of the night.
⁹King Solomon made for himself the
　　carriage;
　　he made it of wood from Lebanon.
¹⁰Its posts he made of silver,
　　its base of gold.
Its seat was upholstered with purple,
　　its interior inlaid with love.
Daughters of Jerusalem, ¹¹come out,
　　and look, you daughters of Zion.
Look[b] on King Solomon wearing a crown,
　　the crown with which his mother
　　　　crowned him
on the day of his wedding,
　　the day his heart rejoiced.

He

4 How beautiful you are, my darling!
　　Oh, how beautiful!
Your eyes behind your veil are doves.
Your hair is like a flock of goats
　　descending from the hills of Gilead.
²Your teeth are like a flock of sheep just
　　shorn,
　　coming up from the washing.
Each has its twin;
　　not one of them is alone.
³Your lips are like a scarlet ribbon;
　　your mouth is lovely.
Your temples behind your veil
　　are like the halves of a pomegranate.
⁴Your neck is like the tower of David,
　　built with courses of stone;[c]
on it hang a thousand shields,

---

[a] 17 Or *the hills of Bether*　　[b] 10,11 Or *interior lovingly inlaid / by the daughters of Jerusalem. / ¹¹Come out, you daughters of Zion, / and look*　　[c] 4 The meaning of the Hebrew for this phrase is uncertain.

making Connections

Poetic language
Song of Songs 4:1
How would you feel if someone said your hair was like goats and your neck was like a tower? These might not sound like great compliments to us, but they did make sense to people in Solomon's time. The rippling effect of a flock of goats moving down a mountainside would have been seen as very beautiful. A tower on a city wall would be seen as strong and noble. Just don't try these same words out on your girlfriend or boyfriend!

all of them shields of warriors.
⁵Your breasts are like two fawns,
  like twin fawns of a gazelle
  that browse among the lilies.
⁶Until the day breaks
  and the shadows flee,
 I will go to the mountain of myrrh
  and to the hill of incense.
⁷All beautiful you are, my darling;
  there is no flaw in you.

⁸Come with me from Lebanon, my bride,
  come with me from Lebanon.
Descend from the crest of Amana,
  from the top of Senir, the summit of Hermon,
from the lions' dens
  and the mountain haunts of leopards.
⁹You have stolen my heart, my sister, my bride;
  you have stolen my heart
with one glance of your eyes,
  with one jewel of your necklace.
¹⁰How delightful is your love, my sister, my bride!
  How much more pleasing is your love than wine,
and the fragrance of your perfume
  more than any spice!
¹¹Your lips drop sweetness as the honeycomb, my bride;
  milk and honey are under your tongue.
The fragrance of your garments
  is like the fragrance of Lebanon.
¹²You are a garden locked up, my sister, my bride;
  you are a spring enclosed, a sealed fountain.
¹³Your plants are an orchard of pomegranates
  with choice fruits,
  with henna and nard,
¹⁴ nard and saffron,
  calamus and cinnamon,
  with every kind of incense tree,
  with myrrh and aloes
  and all the finest spices.
¹⁵You are*ᵃ* a garden fountain,
  a well of flowing water
  streaming down from Lebanon.

She
¹⁶Awake, north wind,
  and come, south wind!
Blow on my garden,
  that its fragrance may spread abroad.
Let my beloved come into his garden
  and taste its choice fruits.

He
5 I have come into my garden, my sister, my bride;
  I have gathered my myrrh with my spice.
I have eaten my honeycomb and my honey;
  I have drunk my wine and my milk.

Friends
Eat, friends, and drink;
  drink your fill of love.

She
²I slept but my heart was awake.
  Listen! My beloved is knocking:
'Open to me, my sister, my darling,
  my dove, my flawless one.

ᵃ 15 Or *I am* (spoken by *She*)

Making Connections

Spices
Song of Songs 4:14

Spices were an expensive luxury in Solomon's time as most of them had to be imported from countries like Syria, and even from Asia and Africa. Henna was used as a dye and the sweet-smelling flowers of the henna plant were worn by women in small bags around their necks. Nard was used in a perfumed ointment, and spices like myrrh and calamus would have been used to make anointing oil.

My head is drenched with dew,
    my hair with the dampness of the night.'
³I have taken off my robe—
    must I put it on again?
I have washed my feet—
    must I soil them again?
⁴My beloved thrust his hand through the latch-opening;
    my heart began to pound for him.
⁵I arose to open for my beloved,
    and my hands dripped with myrrh,
my fingers with flowing myrrh,
    on the handles of the bolt.
⁶I opened for my beloved,
    but my beloved had left; he was gone.
My heart sank at his departure.*a*
I looked for him but did not find him.
    I called him but he did not answer.
⁷The watchmen found me
    as they made their rounds in the city.
They beat me, they bruised me;
    they took away my cloak,
those watchmen of the walls!
⁸Daughters of Jerusalem, I charge you—
    if you find my beloved,
what will you tell him?
    Tell him I am faint with love.

Friends

⁹How is your beloved better than others,
    most beautiful of women?
How is your beloved better than others,
    that you so charge us?

She

¹⁰My beloved is radiant and ruddy,
    outstanding among ten thousand.
¹¹His head is purest gold;
    his hair is wavy
    and black as a raven.
¹²His eyes are like doves
    by the water streams,
washed in milk,
    mounted like jewels.
¹³His cheeks are like beds of spice
    yielding perfume.
His lips are like lilies
    dripping with myrrh.
¹⁴His arms are rods of gold
    set with topaz.
His body is like polished ivory
    decorated with lapis lazuli.
¹⁵His legs are pillars of marble
    set on bases of pure gold.
His appearance is like Lebanon,
    choice as its cedars.
¹⁶His mouth is sweetness itself;
    he is altogether lovely.
This is my beloved, this is my friend,
    daughters of Jerusalem.

Friends

6 Where has your beloved gone,
    most beautiful of women?
Which way did your beloved turn,
    that we may look for him with you?

She

²My beloved has gone down to his garden,
    to the beds of spices,
to browse in the gardens
    and to gather lilies.
³I am my beloved's and my beloved is mine;
    he browses among the lilies.

He

⁴You are as beautiful as Tirzah, my darling,
    as lovely as Jerusalem,

---

a 6 Or *heart had gone out to him when he spoke*

as majestic as troops with banners.
⁵Turn your eyes from me;
   they overwhelm me.
Your hair is like a flock of goats
   descending from Gilead.
⁶Your teeth are like a flock of sheep
   coming up from the washing.
Each has its twin,
   not one of them is missing.
⁷Your temples behind your veil
   are like the halves of a pomegranate.
⁸Sixty queens there may be,
   and eighty concubines,
   and virgins beyond number;
⁹but my dove, my perfect one, is unique,
   the only daughter of her mother,
   the favourite of the one who bore her.
The young women saw her and called her blessed;
   the queens and concubines praised her.

Friends

¹⁰Who is this that appears like the dawn,
   fair as the moon, bright as the sun,
   majestic as the stars in procession?

He

¹¹I went down to the grove of nut trees
   to look at the new growth in the valley,
to see if the vines had budded
   or the pomegranates were in bloom.
¹²Before I realised it,
   my desire set me among the royal
      chariots of my people.ᵃ

Friends

*¹³Come back, come back, O Shulammite;
   come back, come back, that we may
      gaze on you!

He

Why would you gaze on the Shulammite
   as on the dance of Mahanaim?

7 *How beautiful your sandalled feet,
   O prince's daughter!
Your graceful legs are like jewels,
   the work of an artist's hands.
²Your navel is a rounded goblet
   that never lacks blended wine.
Your waist is a mound of wheat
   encircled by lilies.
³Your breasts are like two fawns,
   like twin fawns of a gazelle.
⁴Your neck is like an ivory tower.
Your eyes are the pools of Heshbon
   by the gate of Bath Rabbim.
Your nose is like the tower of Lebanon
   looking towards Damascus.
⁵Your head crowns you like Mount Carmel.
Your hair is like royal tapestry;
   the king is held captive by its tresses.
⁶How beautiful you are and how pleasing,
   my love, with your delights!
⁷Your stature is like that of the palm,
   and your breasts like clusters of fruit.
⁸I said, 'I will climb the palm tree;
   I will take hold of its fruit.'
May your breasts be like clusters of grapes
      on the vine,
   the fragrance of your breath like
      apples,
9   and your mouth like the best wine.

She

May the wine go straight to my beloved,
   flowing gently over lips and teeth.ᵇ
¹⁰I belong to my beloved,
   and his desire is for me.
¹¹Come, my beloved, let us go to the countryside,
   let us spend the night in the villages.ᶜ
¹²Let us go early to the vineyards
   to see if the vines have budded,
   if their blossoms have opened,
   and if the pomegranates are in bloom—
      there I will give you my love.
¹³The mandrakes send out their fragrance,
   and at our door is every delicacy,
   both new and old,
      that I have stored up for you, my beloved.

8 If only you were to me like a brother,
   who was nursed at my mother's breasts!
Then, if I found you outside,

ᵃ 12 Or *among the chariots of Amminadab*; or *among the chariots of the people of the prince*   ᵇ 9 Septuagint, Aquila, Vulgate and Syriac; Hebrew *lips of sleepers*   ᶜ 11 Or *the henna bushes*

* 6:13 is numbered 7:1 in Hebrew texts.   * 7:1-13 is numbered 7:2-14 in Hebrew texts.

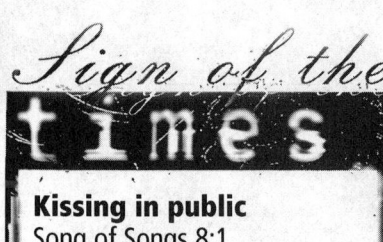

Sign of the times

Kissing in public
Song of Songs 8:1
A woman could kiss her brother in public, but it was considered shameful for two people who were not related to kiss in front of others.

   I would kiss you,
     and no-one would despise me.
 ²I would lead you
     and bring you to my mother's house—
     she who has taught me.
   I would give you spiced wine to drink,
     the nectar of my pomegranates.
 ³His left arm is under my head
     and his right arm embraces me.
 ⁴Daughters of Jerusalem, I charge you:
     do not arouse or awaken love
     until it so desires.

Friends

 ⁵Who is this coming up from the
     wilderness
     leaning on her beloved?

She

   Under the apple tree I roused you;
     there your mother conceived you,
     there she who was in labour gave you
     birth.
 ⁶Place me like a seal over your heart,
     like a seal on your arm;
   for love is as strong as death,
     its jealousy^a unyielding as the grave.
   It burns like blazing fire,
     like a mighty flame.^b
 ⁷Many waters cannot quench love;
     rivers cannot sweep it away.
   If one were to give
     all the wealth of one's house for love,
     it^c would be utterly scorned.

Friends

 ⁸We have a little sister,
     and her breasts are not yet grown.
   What shall we do for our sister
     on the day she is spoken for?
 ⁹If she is a wall,
     we will build towers of silver on her.
   If she is a door,
     we will enclose her with panels of
     cedar.

She

 ¹⁰I am a wall,
     and my breasts are like towers.
   Thus I have become in his eyes
     like one bringing contentment.
 ¹¹Solomon had a vineyard in Baal Hamon;
     he let out his vineyard to tenants.
   Each was to bring for its fruit
     a thousand shekels^d of silver.
 ¹²But my own vineyard is mine to give;
     the thousand shekels are for you,
     Solomon,
   and two hundred^e are for those who
     tend its fruit.

He

 ¹³You who dwell in the gardens
     with friends in attendance,
     let me hear your voice!

She

 ¹⁴Come away, my beloved,
     and be like a gazelle
   or like a young stag
     on the spice-laden mountains.

^a 6 Or *ardour* ^b 6 Or *fire, I like the very flame of the LORD* ^c 7 Or *he* ^d 11 That is, about 11.5 kilograms; also in verse 12 ^e 12 That is, about 2.3 kilograms

Isaiah

INTRODUCTION

ISAIAH

Author: Isaiah

Who to: The people of Judah and Jerusalem.

When: Probably around 700 BC.

Where: Isaiah lived in Jerusalem.

Did you know? The book of Isaiah is split into two distinct parts. It has sixty-six chapters in all, thirty-nine chapters in the first part and twenty-seven in the second – just like the number of books in the Bible as a whole and in the Old and New Testaments.

Main theme: Isaiah gives lots of insight into the nature of God, probably more than any other book in the Old Testament. In the first part of his book, Isaiah talks about the judgment that is going to come on Judah because of their sin and rebellion, but among his strong words are some beautiful poems of hope and comfort. The second part of Isaiah is full of comfort for Judah once they have suffered God's judgment, and a promise that they will be restored. Isaiah also points to the future as he foresees the coming of Jesus.

1 The vision concerning Judah and Jerusalem that Isaiah son of Amoz saw during the reigns of Uzziah, Jotham, Ahaz and Hezekiah, kings of Judah.

A rebellious nation

2Hear me, you heavens! Listen, earth!
  For the LORD has spoken:
'I reared children and brought them up,
  but they have rebelled against me.
3The ox knows its master,
  the donkey its owner's manger,
but Israel does not know,
  my people do not understand.'

⁴Ah, sinful nation,
　a people whose guilt is great,
a brood of evildoers,
　children given to corruption!
They have forsaken the LORD;
　they have spurned the Holy One of
　　Israel
and turned their backs on him.

⁵Why should you be beaten any more?
　Why do you persist in rebellion?
Your whole head is injured,
　your whole heart afflicted.
⁶From the sole of your foot to the top of
　　your head
　there is no soundness—
only wounds and bruises
　and open sores,
not cleansed or bandaged
　or soothed with oil.

⁷Your country is desolate,
　your cities burned with fire;
your fields are being stripped by
　　foreigners
　right before you,
laid waste as when overthrown by
　　strangers.
⁸Daughter Zion is left
　like a shelter in a vineyard,
like a hut in a field of melons,
　like a city under siege.
⁹Unless the LORD Almighty
　had left us some survivors,
we would have become like Sodom,
　we would have been like Gomorrah.

¹⁰Hear the word of the LORD,
　you rulers of Sodom;
listen to the instruction of our God,
　you people of Gomorrah!
¹¹'The multitude of your sacrifices—
　what are they to me?' says the LORD.
'I have more than enough of burnt
　　offerings,
　of rams and the fat of fattened animals;
I have no pleasure
　in the blood of bulls and lambs and
　　goats.
¹²When you come to appear before me,
　who has asked this of you,
　this trampling of my courts?
¹³Stop bringing meaningless offerings!
　Your incense is detestable to me.
New Moons, Sabbaths and
　　convocations—
　I cannot bear your evil assemblies.
¹⁴Your New Moon feasts and your
　　appointed festivals
I hate with all my being.
They have become a burden to me;
　I am weary of bearing them.
¹⁵When you spread out your hands in
　　prayer,
　I will hide my eyes from you;
even if you offer many prayers,
　I will not listen.
Your hands are full of blood;
16　wash and make yourselves clean.
Take your evil deeds
　out of my sight!
Stop doing wrong,
17　learn to do right!
Seek justice,
　encourage the oppressed.[a]
Defend the cause of the fatherless,
　plead the case of the widow.

¹⁸'Come now, let us reason together,'
　says the LORD.
'Though your sins are like scarlet,
　they shall be as white as snow;
though they are red as crimson,
　they shall be like wool.
¹⁹If you are willing and obedient,
　you will eat the best from the land;
²⁰but if you resist and rebel,
　you will be devoured by the sword.'
For the mouth of the LORD has spoken.

²¹See how the faithful city
　has become a prostitute!
She once was full of justice;
　righteousness used to dwell in her—
　but now murderers!
²²Your silver has become dross,
　your choice wine is diluted with water.
²³Your rulers are rebels,
　companions of thieves;
they all love bribes
　and chase after gifts.
They do not defend the cause of the
　　fatherless;
　the widow's case does not come before
　　them.

---

[a] 17 Or *justice, I rebuke the oppressor*

²⁴Therefore the Lord, the LORD Almighty,
  the Mighty One of Israel, declares:
'Ah, I will vent my wrath on my foes
  and avenge myself on my enemies.
²⁵I will turn my hand against you;
  I will thoroughly purge away your dross
  and remove all your impurities.
²⁶I will restore your judges as in days of old,
  your rulers as at the beginning.
Afterwards you will be called
  the City of Righteousness,
  the Faithful City.'

²⁷Zion will be delivered with justice,
  her penitent ones with righteousness.
²⁸But rebels and sinners will both be broken,
  and those who forsake the LORD will perish.

²⁹'You will be ashamed because of the sacred oaks
  in which you have delighted;
you will be disgraced because of the gardens
  that you have chosen.
³⁰You will be like an oak with fading leaves,
  like a garden without water.
³¹The mighty man will become tinder
  and his work a spark;
both will burn together,
  with no-one to quench the fire.'

The mountain of the LORD

2 This is what Isaiah son of Amoz saw concerning Judah and Jerusalem:

²In the last days

the mountain of the LORD's temple will be established
  as the highest of the mountains;
it will be exalted above the hills,
  and all nations will stream to it.

³Many peoples will come and say,

'Come, let us go up to the mountain of the LORD,
  to the house of the God of Jacob.
He will teach us his ways,
  so that we may walk in his paths.'
The law will go out from Zion,
  the word of the LORD from Jerusalem.
⁴He will judge between the nations
  and will settle disputes for many peoples.
They will beat their swords into ploughshares
  and their spears into pruning hooks.
Nation will not take up sword against nation,
  nor will they train for war any more.

⁵Come, house of Jacob,
  let us walk in the light of the LORD.

The day of the LORD

⁶You have abandoned your people,
  the house of Jacob.
They are full of superstitions from the East;
  they practise divination like the Philistines
  and clasp hands with pagans.
⁷Their land is full of silver and gold;
  there is no end to their treasures.
Their land is full of horses;
  there is no end to the chariots.
⁸Their land is full of idols;
  they bow down to the work of their hands,
  to what their fingers have made.

---

making Connections

Swords into ploughshares
Isaiah 2:4

In the past, the Philistines had stopped the Israelites from having blacksmiths in their land in case they made weapons (1 Samuel 13:9). But Isaiah sees a time coming when there will be no need for weapons because there will be no war. Swords will be made into ploughs – instead of being used for weapons of war, metal will be made into tools to bring about fruitfulness.

⁹So people will be brought low
and everyone humbled—
do not forgive them.ᵃ

¹⁰Go into the rocks, hide in the ground
from the fearful presence of the LORD
and the splendour of his majesty!
¹¹The eyes of the arrogant will be humbled
and human pride brought low;
the LORD alone will be exalted in that day.

¹²The LORD Almighty has a day in store
for all the proud and lofty,
for all that is exalted
(and they will be humbled),
¹³for all the cedars of Lebanon, tall and lofty,
and all the oaks of Bashan,
¹⁴for all the towering mountains
and all the high hills,
¹⁵for every lofty tower
and every fortified wall,
¹⁶for every trading shipᵇ
and every stately vessel.

¹⁷The arrogance of all people will be brought low
and human pride humbled;
the LORD alone will be exalted in that day,
¹⁸ and the idols will totally disappear.

¹⁹People will flee to caves in the rocks
and to holes in the ground
from the fearful presence of the LORD
and the splendour of his majesty,
when he rises to shake the earth.
²⁰In that day people will throw away
to the moles and bats
their idols of silver and idols of gold,
which they made to worship.
²¹They will flee to caverns in the rocks
and to the overhanging crags
from the fearful presence of the LORD
and the splendour of his majesty,
when he rises to shake the earth.

²²Stop trusting in human beings,
who have but a breath in their nostrils.
Why hold them in esteem?

Judgment on Jerusalem and Judah

3 See now, the Lord,
the LORD Almighty,
is about to take from Jerusalem and Judah
both supply and support:
all supplies of food and all supplies of water,
² the hero and the warrior,

the judge and the prophet,
the diviner and the elder,
³the captain of fifty and the person of rank,
the counsellor, skilled worker and
clever enchanter.

⁴I will make mere youths their officials;
children will govern them.
⁵People will oppress each other—
one against another, neighbour against neighbour.
The young will rise up against the old,
the nobody against the honoured.

⁶A man will seize one of his brothers
in his father's house, and say,
'You have a cloak, you be our leader;
take charge of this heap of ruins!'
⁷But in that day he will cry out,
'I have no remedy.
I have no food or clothing in my house;
do not make me the leader of the people.'

⁸Jerusalem staggers,
Judah is falling;
their words and deeds are against the LORD,
defying his glorious presence.
⁹The look on their faces testifies against them;
they parade their sin like Sodom;
they do not hide it.
Woe to them!
They have brought disaster upon themselves.

¹⁰Tell the righteous it will be well with them,
for they will enjoy the fruit of their deeds.
¹¹Woe to the wicked!
Disaster is upon them!
They will be paid back
for what their hands have done.

¹²Youths oppress my people,
women rule over them.
My people, your guides lead you astray;
they turn you from the path.

ᵃ 9 Or *not raise them up* ᵇ 16 Hebrew *every ship of Tarshish*

¹³The LORD takes his place in court;
  he rises to judge the people.
¹⁴The LORD enters into judgment
    against the elders and leaders of his people:
'It is you who have ruined my vineyard;
  the plunder from the poor is in your houses.
¹⁵What do you mean by crushing my people
    and grinding the faces of the poor?'
  declares the Lord, the LORD Almighty.

¹⁶The LORD says,
'The women of Zion are haughty,
  walking along with outstretched necks,
    flirting with their eyes,
  tripping along with mincing steps,
    with ornaments jingling on their ankles.
¹⁷Therefore the Lord will bring sores on the heads of the women of Zion;
  the LORD will make their scalps bald.'

¹⁸In that day the Lord will snatch away their finery: the bangles and headbands and crescent necklaces, ¹⁹the ear-rings and bracelets and veils, ²⁰the head-dresses and ankle chains and sashes, the perfume bottles and charms, ²¹the signet rings and nose rings, ²²the fine robes and the capes and cloaks, the purses ²³and mirrors, and the linen garments and tiaras and shawls.

²⁴Instead of fragrance there will be a stench;
    instead of a sash, a rope;
  instead of well-dressed hair, baldness;
    instead of fine clothing, sackcloth;
    instead of beauty, branding.
²⁵Your men will fall by the sword,
  your warriors in battle.
²⁶The gates of Zion will lament and mourn;
  destitute, she will sit on the ground.

4 In that day seven women
    will take hold of one man
  and say, 'We will eat our own food
    and provide our own clothes;
  only let us be called by your name.
    Take away our disgrace!'

The Branch of the LORD

²In that day the Branch of the LORD will be beautiful and glorious, and the fruit of the land will be the pride and glory of the survivors in Israel. ³Those who are left in Zion, who remain in Jerusalem, will be called holy, all who are recorded among the living in Jerusalem. ⁴The Lord will wash away the filth of the women of Zion; he will cleanse the bloodstains from Jerusalem by a spirit^a of judgment and a spirit^b of fire. ⁵Then the LORD will create over all of Mount Zion and over those who assemble there a cloud of smoke by day and a glow of flaming fire by night; over everything the glory^c will be a canopy. ⁶It will be a shelter and shade from the heat of the day, and a refuge and hiding-place from the storm and rain.

The song of the vineyard

5 I will sing for the one I love
    a song about his vineyard:
  my loved one had a vineyard
    on a fertile hillside.
²He dug it up and cleared it of stones
    and planted it with the choicest vines.
  He built a watchtower in it
    and cut out a winepress as well.

Vineyards
Isaiah 5:1
A landowner with a vineyard always needed lots of labourers to help look after it (Matthew 20:1). Vineyards were usually on stony hillsides and had hedges or walls around them to protect them from wild animals. Often a tower would be built and a watchman would keep a lookout for robbers.

---

^{a}4 Or the Spirit ^{b}4 Or the Spirit ^{c}5 Or over all the glory there

Then he looked for a crop of good grapes,
　but it yielded only bad fruit.

3 'Now you dwellers in Jerusalem and
　　people of Judah,
　judge between me and my vineyard.
4 What more could have been done for my
　　vineyard
　than I have done for it?
　When I looked for good grapes,
　　why did it yield only bad?
5 Now I will tell you
　　what I am going to do to my vineyard:
　I will take away its hedge,
　　and it will be destroyed;
　I will break down its wall,
　　and it will be trampled.
6 I will make it a wasteland,
　　neither pruned nor cultivated,
　　and briers and thorns will grow there.
　I will command the clouds
　　not to rain on it.'

7 The vineyard of the LORD Almighty
　　is the house of Israel,
　and the people of Judah
　　are the vines he delighted in.
　And he looked for justice, but saw
　　bloodshed;
　　for righteousness, but heard cries of
　　　distress.

Woes and judgments

8 Woe to you who add house to house
　　and join field to field
　till no space is left
　　and you live alone in the land.

9 The LORD Almighty has declared in my
　　hearing:

'Surely the great houses will become
　desolate,
　the fine mansions left without
　　occupants.
10 A ten-acre vineyard[a] will produce only a
　　bath[b] of wine,
　　a homer[c] of seed only an ephah[d] of
　　　grain.'
11 Woe to those who rise early in the
　　morning

to run after their drinks,
who stay up late at night
　till they are inflamed with wine.
12 They have harps and lyres at their
　　banquets,
　pipes and tambourines and wine,
　but they have no regard for the deeds of
　　the LORD,
　no respect for the work of his hands.
13 Therefore my people will go into exile
　　for lack of understanding;
　those of high rank will die of hunger
　　and the common people will be
　　　parched with thirst.
14 Therefore the grave enlarges its appetite
　　and opens wide its mouth;
　into it will descend their nobles and
　　masses
　　with all their brawlers and revellers.
15 So people will be brought low
　　and everyone humbled,
　　the eyes of the arrogant humbled.
16 But the LORD Almighty will be exalted by
　　his justice,
　　and the holy God will be proved holy by
　　　his righteous acts.
17 Then sheep will graze as in their own
　　pasture;
　lambs will feed[e] among the ruins of the
　　rich.

18 Woe to those who draw sin along with
　　cords of deceit,
　　and wickedness as with cart ropes,
19 to those who say, 'Let God hurry;
　　let him hasten his work
　　so that we may see it.
　The plan of the Holy One of Israel—
　　let it approach, let it come into view,
　　so that we may know it.'

20 Woe to those who call evil good
　　and good evil,
　who put darkness for light
　　and light for darkness,
　who put bitter for sweet
　　and sweet for bitter.

21 Woe to those who are wise in their own
　　eyes
　　and clever in their own sight.

---

[a] 10 Or *a vineyard of four hectares*   [b] 10 That is, about 22 litres   [c] 10 That is, probably about 160 kilograms
[d] 10 That is, probably about 16 kilograms   [e] 17 Septuagint; Hebrew / *strangers will eat*

Isaiah 5:22

22Woe to those who are heroes at drinking wine
   and champions at mixing drinks,
23who acquit the guilty for a bribe,
   but deny justice to the innocent.
24Therefore, as tongues of fire lick up straw
   and as dry grass sinks down in the flames,
so their roots will decay
   and their flowers blow away like dust;
for they have rejected the law of the LORD Almighty
   and spurned the word of the Holy One of Israel.
25Therefore the LORD's anger burns against his people;
   his hand is raised and he strikes them down.
The mountains shake,
   and the dead bodies are like refuse in the streets.

Yet for all this, his anger is not turned away,
   his hand is still upraised.

26He lifts up a banner for the distant nations,
   he whistles for those at the ends of the earth.
Here they come,
   swiftly and speedily!
27Not one of them grows tired or stumbles,
   not one slumbers or sleeps;
not a belt is loosened at the waist,
   not a sandal thong is broken.
28Their arrows are sharp,
   all their bows are strung;
their horses' hooves seem like flint,
   their chariot wheels like a whirlwind.
29Their roar is like that of the lion,
   they roar like young lions;
they growl as they seize their prey
   and carry it off with no-one to rescue.
30In that day they will roar over it
   like the roaring of the sea.
And if one looks at the land,
   there is only darkness and distress;
   even the sun will be darkened by clouds.

Isaiah's commission

6 In the year that King Uzziah died, I saw the Lord seated on a throne, high and exalted, and the train of his robe filled the temple. 2Above him were seraphs, each with six wings: with two wings they covered their faces, with two they covered their feet, and with two they were flying. 3And they were calling to one another:

'Holy, holy, holy is the LORD Almighty;
   the whole earth is full of his glory.'

4At the sound of their voices the doorposts and thresholds shook and the temple was filled with smoke.

5'Woe to me!' I cried. 'I am ruined! For I am a man of unclean lips, and I live among a people of unclean lips, and my eyes have seen the King, the LORD Almighty.'

6Then one of the seraphs flew to me with a live coal in his hand, which he had taken with tongs from the altar. 7With it he touched my mouth and said, 'See, this has touched your lips; your guilt is taken away and your sin atoned for.'

8Then I heard the voice of the Lord saying, 'Whom shall I send? And who will go for us?'

And I said, 'Here am I. Send me!'
9He said, 'Go and tell this people:

'"Be ever hearing, but never understanding;
   be ever seeing, but never perceiving."
10Make the heart of this people calloused;
   make their ears dull
   and close their eyes.[a]
Otherwise they might see with their eyes,
   hear with their ears,
   understand with their hearts,
and turn and be healed.'

11Then I said, 'For how long, Lord?'
And he answered:

'Until the cities lie ruined
   and without inhabitant,
until the houses are left deserted
   and the fields ruined and ravaged,
12until the LORD has sent everyone far away
   and the land is utterly forsaken.

---

[a] 9, 10 Hebrew; Septuagint ' "You will be ever hearing, but never understanding; / you will be ever seeing, but never perceiving." / 10This people's heart has become calloused; / they hardly hear with their ears, / and they have closed their eyes.

¹³And though a tenth remains in the land,
it will again be laid waste.
But as the terebinth and oak
leave stumps when they are cut down,
so the holy seed will be the stump in the
land.'

The sign of Immanuel

7 When Ahaz son of Jotham, the son of Uzziah, was king of Judah, King Rezin of Aram and Pekah son of Remaliah king of Israel marched up to fight against Jerusalem, but they could not overpower it.

²Now the house of David was told, 'Aram has allied itself with*ᵃ* Ephraim'; so the hearts of Ahaz and his people were shaken, as the trees of the forest are shaken by the wind.

³Then the LORD said to Isaiah, 'Go out, you and your son Shear-Jashub,*ᵇ* to meet Ahaz at the end of the aqueduct of the Upper Pool, on the road to the Launderer's Field. ⁴Say to him, "Be careful, keep calm and don't be afraid. Do not lose heart because of these two smouldering stubs of firewood—because of the fierce anger of Rezin and Aram and of the son of Remaliah. ⁵Aram, Ephraim and Remaliah's son have plotted your ruin, saying, ⁶'Let us invade Judah; let us tear it apart and divide it among ourselves, and make the son of Tabeel king over it.' ⁷Yet this is what the Sovereign LORD says:

' "It will not take place,
it will not happen,
⁸for the head of Aram is Damascus,
and the head of Damascus is only
Rezin.
Within sixty-five years
Ephraim will be too shattered to be a
people.
⁹The head of Ephraim is Samaria,
and the head of Samaria is only
Remaliah's son.
If you do not stand firm in your faith,
you will not stand at all." '

¹⁰Again the LORD spoke to Ahaz, ¹¹'Ask the LORD your God for a sign, whether in the deepest depths or in the highest heights.'

> **Immanuel**
> **Isaiah 7:14**
> The name Immanuel means 'God with us', and is a name for Jesus. Matthew refers to this verse in Isaiah when he talks about how Jesus' birth fulfilled the prophecies about him (Matthew 1:23).

¹²But Ahaz said, 'I will not ask; I will not put the LORD to the test.'

¹³Then Isaiah said, 'Hear now, you house of David! Is it not enough to try the patience of human beings? Will you try the patience of my God also? ¹⁴Therefore the Lord himself will give you*ᶜ* a sign: the virgin*ᵈ* will conceive and give birth to a son, and*ᵉ* will call him Immanuel.*ᶠ* ¹⁵He will be eating curds and honey when he knows enough to reject the wrong and choose the right, ¹⁶for before the boy knows enough to reject the wrong and choose the right, the land of the two kings you dread will be laid waste. ¹⁷The LORD will bring on you and on your people and on the house of your father a time unlike any since Ephraim broke away from Judah—he will bring the king of Assyria.'

Assyria, the LORD's instrument

¹⁸In that day the LORD will whistle for flies from the Nile delta in Egypt and for bees from the land of Assyria. ¹⁹They will all come and settle in the steep ravines and in the crevices in the rocks, on all the thornbushes and at all the water holes. ²⁰In that day the Lord will use a razor hired from beyond the River Euphrates—the king of Assyria—to shave your head and the hair of your legs, and to take off your beards also. ²¹In that day, a person will keep alive a young cow and two goats. ²²And because of the abundance of the milk they give, there will be curds to eat. All who remain in the land will eat curds and honey. ²³In that day,

---

ᵃ 2 Or *has set up camp in*   *ᵇ* 3 *Shear-Jashub* means *a remnant will return.*   *ᶜ* 14 The Hebrew is plural.   *ᵈ* 14 Or *young woman*   *ᵉ* 14 Masoretic Text; Dead Sea Scrolls *and he* or *and they*   *ᶠ* 14 *Immanuel* means *God with us.*

in every place where there were a thousand vines worth a thousand silver shekels,*ᵃ* there will be only briers and thorns. 24Hunters will go there with bow and arrow, for the land will be covered with briers and thorns. 25As for all the hills once cultivated by the hoe, you will no longer go there for fear of the briers and thorns; they will become places where cattle are turned loose and where sheep run.

Isaiah and his children as signs

8 The LORD said to me, 'Take a large scroll and write on it with an ordinary pen: Maher-Shalal-Hash-Baz.'*ᵇ* 2So I called in Uriah the priest and Zechariah son of Jeberekiah as reliable witnesses for me. 3Then I made love to the prophetess, and she conceived and gave birth to a son. And the LORD said to me, 'Name him Maher-Shalal-Hash-Baz. 4Before the boy knows how to say "My father" or "My mother", the wealth of Damascus and the plunder of Samaria will be carried off by the king of Assyria.'

5The LORD spoke to me again:

6'Because this people has rejected
 the gently flowing waters of Shiloah
and rejoices over Rezin
 and the son of Remaliah,
7therefore the Lord is about to bring
 against them
the mighty floodwaters of the
 Euphrates—
the king of Assyria with all his pomp.
It will overflow all its channels,
 run over all its banks
8and sweep on into Judah, swirling over it,
 passing through it and reaching up to
 the neck.
Its outspread wings will cover the breadth
 of your land,
Immanuel!'*ᶜ*

9Raise the war cry,*ᵈ* you nations, and be
 shattered!
Listen, all you distant lands.
Prepare for battle, and be shattered!
Prepare for battle, and be shattered!

10Devise your strategy, but it will be
 thwarted;
propose your plan, but it will not stand,
 for God is with us.*ᵉ*

11This is what the LORD says to me with his strong hand upon me, warning me not to follow the way of this people:

12'Do not call conspiracy
 everything this people calls a
 conspiracy;
do not fear what they fear,
 and do not dread it.
13The LORD Almighty is the one you are to
 regard as holy,
he is the one you are to fear,
he is the one you are to dread.
14He will be a holy place;
 for both houses of Israel he will be
a stone that causes people to stumble
 and a rock that makes them fall.
And for the people of Jerusalem he will be
 a trap and a snare.
15Many of them will stumble;
 they will fall and be broken,
 they will be snared and captured.'

16Bind up this testimony of warning
 and seal up God's instruction among
 my disciples.
17I will wait for the LORD,
 who is hiding his face from the house of
 Jacob.
I will put my trust in him.

18Here am I, and the children the LORD has given me. We are signs and symbols in Israel from the LORD Almighty, who dwells on Mount Zion.

The darkness turns to light

19When someone tells you to consult mediums and spiritists, who whisper and mutter, should not a people enquire of their God? Why consult the dead on behalf of the living? 20Consult God's instruction and the testimony of warning. If anyone does not speak according to this word, they have no light of dawn. 21Distressed and hungry, they will roam through the land; when they are famished, they will become

---

*ᵃ*23 That is, about 11.5 kilograms   *ᵇ*1 *Maher-Shalal-Hash-Baz* means *quick to the plunder, swift to the spoil*; also in verse 3.   *ᶜ*8 *Immanuel* means *God with us.*   *ᵈ*9 Or *Do your worst*   *ᵉ*10 Hebrew *Immanuel* enraged and, looking upwards, will curse their king and their God. ²²Then they will look towards the earth and see only distress and darkness and fearful gloom, and they will be thrust into utter darkness.

9

*Nevertheless, there will be no more gloom for those who were in distress. In the past he humbled the land of Zebulun and the land of Naphtali, but in the future he will honour Galilee of the nations, by the Way of the Sea, beyond the Jordan—

*²The people walking in darkness
    have seen a great light;
on those living in the land of deep
    darkness
    a light has dawned.
³You have enlarged the nation
    and increased their joy;
they rejoice before you
    as people rejoice at the harvest,
as soldiers rejoice
    when dividing the plunder.
⁴For as in the day of Midian's defeat,
    you have shattered
the yoke that burdens them,
    the bar across their shoulders,
    the rod of their oppressor.
⁵Every warrior's boot used in battle
    and every garment rolled in blood
will be destined for burning,
    will be fuel for the fire.
⁶For to us a child is born,
    to us a son is given,
    and the government will be on his
        shoulders.
And he will be called
    Wonderful Counsellor, Mighty God,
    Everlasting Father, Prince of Peace.
⁷Of the increase of his government and
    peace
there will be no end.
He will reign on David's throne
    and over his kingdom,
establishing and upholding it
    with justice and righteousness
    from that time on and for ever.
The zeal of the LORD Almighty
    will accomplish this.

The LORD's anger against Israel

⁸The Lord has sent a message against
    Jacob;
    it will fall on Israel.
⁹All the people will know it—
    Ephraim and the inhabitants of
    Samaria—
who say with pride
    and arrogance of heart,
¹⁰'The bricks have fallen down,
    but we will rebuild with dressed stone;
the fig-trees have been felled,
    but we will replace them with cedars.'
¹¹But the LORD has strengthened Rezin's
    foes against them
    and has spurred their enemies on.
¹²Arameans from the east and Philistines
    from the west
have devoured Israel with open
    mouth.

Yet for all this, his anger is not turned
    away,
    his hand is still upraised.

¹³But the people have not returned to him
    who struck them,
    nor have they sought the LORD
        Almighty.
¹⁴So the LORD will cut off from Israel both
    head and tail,
    both palm branch and reed in a single
        day;
¹⁵the elders and dignitaries are the head,
    the prophets who teach lies are the tail.
¹⁶Those who guide this people mislead
    them,
    and those who are guided are led
        astray.
¹⁷Therefore the Lord will take no pleasure
    in the young men,
    nor will he pity the fatherless and
        widows,
for everyone is ungodly and wicked,
    every mouth speaks folly.

Yet for all this, his anger is not turned
    away,
    his hand is still upraised.

¹⁸Surely wickedness burns like a fire;
    it consumes briers and thorns,
    it sets the forest thickets ablaze,

---

* 9:1 is numbered 8:23 in Hebrew texts.   * 9:2-21 is numbered 9:1-20 in Hebrew texts.

so that it rolls upwards in a column of smoke.
¹⁹By the wrath of the LORD Almighty
the land will be scorched
and the people will be fuel for the fire;
they will not spare each other.
²⁰On the right they will devour,
but still be hungry;
on the left they will eat,
but not be satisfied.
They will all feed on the flesh of their own offspring:[a]
²¹ Manasseh will feed on Ephraim, and Ephraim on Manasseh;
together they will turn against Judah.

Yet for all this, his anger is not turned away,
his hand is still upraised.

10
Woe to those who make unjust laws,
to those who issue oppressive decrees,
²to deprive the poor of their rights
and withhold justice from the oppressed of my people,
making widows their prey
and robbing the fatherless.
³What will you do on the day of reckoning,
when disaster comes from afar?
To whom will you run for help?
Where will you leave your riches?
⁴Nothing will remain but to cringe among the captives
or fall among the slain.

Yet for all this, his anger is not turned away,
his hand is still upraised.

God's judgment on Assyria

⁵'Woe to the Assyrian, the rod of my anger,
in whose hand is the club of my wrath!
⁶I send him against a godless nation,
I dispatch him against a people who anger me,
to seize loot and snatch plunder,
and to trample them down like mud in the streets.
⁷But this is not what he intends,
this is not what he has in mind;
his purpose is to destroy,
to put an end to many nations.
⁸"Are not my commanders all kings?" he says.
⁹ "Has not Kalno fared like Carchemish?
Is not Hamath like Arpad,
and Samaria like Damascus?
¹⁰As my hand seized the kingdoms of the idols,
kingdoms whose images excelled those of Jerusalem and Samaria—
¹¹shall I not deal with Jerusalem and her images
as I dealt with Samaria and her idols?"'

¹²When the Lord has finished all his work against Mount Zion and Jerusalem, he will say, 'I will punish the king of Assyria for the wilful pride of his heart and the haughty look in his eyes. ¹³For he says:

' "By the strength of my hand I have done this,
and by my wisdom, because I have understanding.
I removed the boundaries of nations,
I plundered their treasures;
like a mighty one I subdued[b] their kings.
¹⁴As one reaches into a nest,
so my hand reached for the wealth of the nations;
as people gather abandoned eggs,
so I gathered all the countries;
not one flapped a wing,
or opened its mouth to chirp."'

¹⁵Does the axe raise itself above the one who swings it,
or the saw boast against the one who uses it?
As if a rod were to wield the person who lifts it up,
or a club brandish one who is not wood!
¹⁶Therefore, the Lord, the LORD Almighty,
will send a wasting disease upon his sturdy warriors;
under his pomp a fire will be kindled
like a blazing flame.
¹⁷The Light of Israel will become a fire,
their Holy One a flame;

---
[a] 20 Or *arm* [b] 13 Or *treasures; / I subdued the mighty,*

IN OTHER WORDS

Remnant
Isaiah 10:20

A remnant is a bit that is left over, and the word is often used in relation to spare cloth. In the Bible, 'the remnant' refers to the part of a nation or community that is left behind after a judgment or disaster. The remnant survives and from it grows a new community.

---

in a single day it will burn and consume
  his thorns and his briers.
¹⁸The splendour of his forests and fertile fields
  it will completely destroy,
  as when those who are ill waste away.
¹⁹And the remaining trees of his forests will be so few
  that a child could write them down.

The remnant of Israel

²⁰In that day the remnant of Israel,
  the survivors of the house of Jacob,
  will no longer rely on him
  who struck them down
but will truly rely on the LORD,
  the Holy One of Israel.
²¹A remnant will return,^a a remnant of Jacob
  will return to the Mighty God.
²²Though your people be like the sand by the sea, Israel,
  only a remnant will return.
Destruction has been decreed,
  overwhelming and righteous.
²³The Lord, the LORD Almighty, will carry out
  the destruction decreed upon the whole land.

²⁴Therefore, this is what the Lord, the LORD Almighty, says:

'My people who live in Zion,
  do not be afraid of the Assyrians,
who beat you with a rod
  and lift up a club against you, as Egypt did.
²⁵Very soon my anger against you will end
  and my wrath will be directed to their destruction.'

²⁶The LORD Almighty will lash them with a whip,
  as when he struck down Midian at the rock of Oreb;
and he will raise his staff over the waters,
  as he did in Egypt.
²⁷In that day their burden will be lifted from your shoulders,
  their yoke from your neck;
the yoke will be broken
  because you have grown so fat.^b

²⁸They enter Aiath;
  they pass through Migron;
  they store supplies at Michmash.
²⁹They go over the pass, and say,
  'We will camp overnight at Geba.'
Ramah trembles;
  Gibeah of Saul flees.
³⁰Cry out, Daughter Gallim!
Listen, Laishah!
Poor Anathoth!
³¹Madmenah is in flight;
  the people of Gebim take cover.
³²This day they will halt at Nob;
  they will shake their fist
at the mount of Daughter Zion,
  at the hill of Jerusalem.

³³See, the Lord, the LORD Almighty,
  will lop off the boughs with great power.
The lofty trees will be felled,
  the tall ones will be brought low.
³⁴He will cut down the forest thickets with an axe;
  Lebanon will fall before the Mighty One.

The branch from Jesse

11 A shoot will come up from the stump of Jesse;
  from his roots a Branch will bear fruit.
²The Spirit of the LORD will rest on him—

---

^a 21 Hebrew *shear-jashub*; also in verse 22   ^b 27 Hebrew; Septuagint *broken / from your shoulders*

People and Places

Jesse
Isaiah 11:1

Jesse was the father of David who became a great king. Jesus came from David's family and he is the shoot from the stump of Jesse that this passage talks about. Paul refers to Isaiah 11:10 when he talks about the Old Testament prophecies that Jesus fulfilled (Romans 15:12).

---

the Spirit of wisdom and of understanding,
the Spirit of counsel and of might,
the Spirit of the knowledge and fear of the LORD—
³and he will delight in the fear of the LORD.

He will not judge by what he sees with his eyes,
or decide by what he hears with his ears;
⁴but with righteousness he will judge the needy,
with justice he will give decisions for the poor of the earth.
He will strike the earth with the rod of his mouth;
with the breath of his lips he will slay the wicked.
⁵Righteousness will be his belt
and faithfulness the sash round his waist.

⁶The wolf will live with the lamb,
the leopard will lie down with the goat,
the calf and the lion and the yearling[a] together;
and a little child will lead them.
⁷The cow will feed with the bear,
their young will lie down together,
and the lion will eat straw like the ox.
⁸Infants will play near the hole of the cobra;
young children will put their hands into the viper's nest.
⁹They will neither harm nor destroy
on all my holy mountain,
for the earth will be filled with the knowledge of the LORD
as the waters cover the sea.

¹⁰In that day the Root of Jesse will stand as a banner for the peoples; the nations will rally to him, and his resting place will be glorious. ¹¹In that day the Lord will reach out his hand a second time to reclaim the surviving remnant of his people from Assyria, from Lower Egypt, from Upper Egypt, from Cush,[b] from Elam, from Babylonia,[c] from Hamath and from the islands of the Mediterranean.

¹²He will raise a banner for the nations
and gather the exiles of Israel;
he will assemble the scattered people of Judah
from the four quarters of the earth.
¹³Ephraim's jealousy will vanish,
and Judah's enemies[d] will be destroyed;
Ephraim will not be jealous of Judah,
nor Judah hostile towards Ephraim.
¹⁴They will swoop down on the slopes of Philistia to the west;
together they will plunder the people to the east.
They will lay hands on Edom and Moab,
and the Ammonites will be subject to them.
¹⁵The LORD will dry up
the gulf of the Egyptian sea;
with a scorching wind he will sweep his hand
over the River Euphrates.
He will break it up into seven streams
so that anyone can cross over in sandals.
¹⁶There will be a highway for the remnant of his people
that is left from Assyria,
as there was for Israel
when they came up from Egypt.

---

[a] 6 Hebrew; Septuagint *lion will feed* [b] 11 That is, the upper Nile region [c] 11 Hebrew *Shinar* [d] 13 Or *hostility*

Songs of praise

12 In that day you will say:

'I will praise you, LORD.
Although you were angry with me,
your anger has turned away
and you have comforted me.
² Surely God is my salvation;
I will trust and not be afraid.
The LORD, the LORD, is my strength and my defence[a];
he has become my salvation.'
³ With joy you will draw water
from the wells of salvation.

⁴ In that day you will say:

'Give praise to the LORD, call on his name;
make known among the nations what he has done,
and proclaim that his name is exalted.
⁵ Sing to the LORD, for he has done glorious things;
let this be known to all the world.
⁶ Shout aloud and sing for joy, people of Zion,
for great is the Holy One of Israel among you.'

A prophecy against Babylon

13 A prophecy concerning Babylon that Isaiah son of Amoz saw:

² Raise a banner on a bare hilltop,
shout to them;
beckon to them
to enter the gates of the nobles.
³ I have commanded my holy ones;
I have summoned my warriors to carry out my wrath—
those who rejoice in my triumph.

⁴ Listen, a noise on the mountains,
like that of a great multitude!
Listen, an uproar among the kingdoms,
like nations massing together!
The LORD Almighty is mustering
an army for war.
⁵ They come from faraway lands,
from the ends of the heavens—
the LORD and the weapons of his wrath—
to destroy the whole country.

⁶ Wail, for the day of the LORD is near;
it will come like destruction from the Almighty.[b]
⁷ Because of this, all hands will go limp,
every man's heart will melt.
⁸ Terror will seize them,
pain and anguish will grip them;
they will writhe like a woman in labour.
They will look aghast at each other,
their faces aflame.

⁹ See, the day of the LORD is coming
—a cruel day, with wrath and fierce anger—
to make the land desolate
and destroy the sinners within it.
¹⁰ The stars of heaven and their constellations
will not show their light.
The rising sun will be darkened
and the moon will not give its light.
¹¹ I will punish the world for its evil,
the wicked for their sins.
I will put an end to the arrogance of the haughty
and will humble the pride of the ruthless.
¹² I will make people scarcer than pure gold,
more rare than the gold of Ophir.
¹³ Therefore I will make the heavens tremble;
and the earth will shake from its place
at the wrath of the LORD Almighty,
in the day of his burning anger.

¹⁴ Like a hunted gazelle,
like sheep without a shepherd,
they will all return to their own people,
they will flee to their native land.
¹⁵ Whoever is captured will be thrust through;
all who are caught will fall by the sword.
¹⁶ Their infants will be dashed to pieces before their eyes;
their houses will be looted and their wives ravished.

¹⁷ See, I will stir up against them the Medes,
who do not care for silver
and have no delight in gold.
¹⁸ Their bows will strike down the young men;
they will have no mercy on infants

---

[a] 2 Or *song* [b] 6 Hebrew *Shaddai*

nor will they look with compassion on
    children.
¹⁹Babylon, the jewel of kingdoms,
    the pride and glory of the
        Babylonians,ᵃ
will be overthrown by God
    like Sodom and Gomorrah.
²⁰She will never be inhabited
    or lived in through all generations;
there no nomads will pitch their tents,
    there no shepherds will rest their
        flocks.
²¹But desert creatures will lie there,
    jackals will fill her houses;
there the owls will dwell,
    and there the wild goats will leap about.
²²Hyenas will inhabit her strongholds,
    jackals her luxurious palaces.
Her time is at hand,
    and her days will not be prolonged.

making Connections

Morning star
Isaiah 14:12

Isaiah describes here the downfall of the king of Babylon, but some people see this as a description of Satan who used to be an angel in heaven but who rebelled against God and was thrown out. The Latin word for 'morning star' is Lucifer, which is another name for Satan.

14 The LORD will have compassion
        on Jacob;
    once again he will choose Israel
        and will settle them in their own land.
Foreigners will join them
    and unite with the house of Jacob.
²Nations will take them
    and bring them to their own place.
And the house of Israel will take
        possession of the nations
    and make them male and female
        servants in the LORD's land.
They will make captives of their captors
    and rule over their oppressors.

³On the day the LORD gives you relief from your suffering and turmoil and from the harsh labour forced on you, ⁴you will take up this taunt against the king of Babylon:

How the oppressor has come to an end!
    How his furyᵇ has ended!
⁵The LORD has broken the rod of the
        wicked,
    the sceptre of the rulers,
⁶which in anger struck down peoples
    with unceasing blows,
and in fury subdued nations
    with relentless aggression.

⁷All the lands are at rest and at peace;
    they break into singing.
⁸Even the junipers and the cedars of
        Lebanon
    exult over you and say,
'Now that you have been laid low,
    no-one comes to cut us down.'

⁹The realm of the dead below is all astir
    to meet you at your coming;
it rouses the spirits of the departed to
        greet you—
    all those who were leaders in the
        world;
it makes them rise from their thrones—
    all those who were kings over the
        nations.
¹⁰They will all respond,
    they will say to you,
'You also have become weak, as we are;
    you have become like us.'
¹¹All your pomp has been brought down to
        the grave,
    along with the noise of your harps;
maggots are spread out beneath you
    and worms cover you.

¹²How you have fallen from heaven,
    morning star, son of the dawn!
You have been cast down to the earth,
    you who once laid low the nations!

ᵃ19 Or *Chaldeans* ᵇ4 Dead Sea Scrolls, Septuagint and Syriac; the meaning of the word in the Masoretic Text is uncertain.

¹³You said in your heart,
  'I will ascend to heaven;
I will raise my throne
  above the stars of God;
I will sit enthroned on the mount of assembly,
  on the utmost heights of Mount Zaphon.ᵃ
¹⁴I will ascend above the tops of the clouds;
  I will make myself like the Most High.'
¹⁵But you are brought down to the realm of the dead,
  to the depths of the pit.

¹⁶Those who see you stare at you,
  they ponder your fate:
'Is this the man who shook the earth
  and made kingdoms tremble,
¹⁷the man who made the world a wilderness,
  who overthrew its cities
  and would not let his captives go home?'

¹⁸All the kings of the nations lie in state,
  each in his own tomb.
¹⁹But you are cast out of your tomb
  like a rejected branch;
you are covered with the slain,
  with those pierced by the sword,
  those who descend to the stones of the pit.
Like a corpse trampled underfoot,
²⁰ you will not join them in burial,
for you have destroyed your land
  and killed your people.

Let the offspring of the wicked
  never be mentioned again.
²¹Prepare a place to slaughter his children
  for the sins of their ancestors;
they are not to rise to inherit the land
  and cover the earth with their cities.

²²'I will rise up against them,'
  declares the LORD Almighty.
'I will wipe out Babylon's name and survivors,
  her offspring and descendants,'
    declares the LORD.
²³'I will turn her into a place for owls
  and into swampland;
I will sweep her with the broom of destruction,'
  declares the LORD Almighty.

²⁴The LORD Almighty has sworn,

'Surely, as I have planned, so it will be,
  and as I have purposed, so it will happen.
²⁵I will crush the Assyrian in my land;
  on my mountains I will trample him down.
His yoke will be taken from my people,
  and his burden removed from their shoulders.'

²⁶This is the plan determined for the whole world;
  this is the hand stretched out over all nations.
²⁷For the LORD Almighty has purposed, and who can thwart him?
  His hand is stretched out, and who can turn it back?

A prophecy against the Philistines

²⁸This prophecy came in the year King Ahaz died:

²⁹Do not rejoice, all you Philistines,
  that the rod that struck you is broken;
from the root of that snake will spring up a viper,
  its fruit will be a darting, venomous serpent.
³⁰The poorest of the poor will find pasture,
  and the needy will lie down in safety.
But your root I will destroy by famine;
  it will slay your survivors.

³¹Wail, you gate! Howl, you city!
  Melt away, all you Philistines!
A cloud of smoke comes from the north,
  and there is not a straggler in its ranks.
³²What answer shall be given
  to the envoys of that nation?
'The LORD has established Zion,
  and in her his afflicted people will find refuge.'

A prophecy against Moab

15 A prophecy concerning Moab:

Ar in Moab is ruined,
  destroyed in a night!

ᵃ 13 Or *of the north*; Zaphon was the most sacred mountain of the Canaanites.

Kir in Moab is ruined,
　destroyed in a night!
²Dibon goes up to its temple,
　to its high places to weep;
Moab wails over Nebo and Medeba.
Every head is shaved
　and every beard cut off.
³In the streets they wear sackcloth;
　on the roofs and in the public squares
they all wail,
　prostrate with weeping.
⁴Heshbon and Elealeh cry out,
　their voices are heard all the way to Jahaz.
Therefore the armed men of Moab cry out,
　and their hearts are faint.

⁵My heart cries out over Moab;
　her fugitives flee as far as Zoar,
　as far as Eglath Shelishiyah.
They go up the hill to Luhith,
　weeping as they go;
on the road to Horonaim
　they lament their destruction.
⁶The waters of Nimrim are dried up
　and the grass is withered;
the vegetation is gone
　and nothing green is left.
⁷So the wealth they have acquired and stored up
　they carry away over the Ravine of the Poplars.
⁸Their outcry echoes along the border of Moab;
　their wailing reaches as far as Eglaim,
　their lamentation as far as Beer Elim.
⁹The waters of Dimon*ᵃ* are full of blood,
　but I will bring still more upon Dimon*ᵇ*—
a lion upon the fugitives of Moab
　and upon those who remain in the land.

16

Send lambs as tribute
　to the ruler of the land,
from Sela, across the desert,
　to the mount of Daughter Zion.
²Like fluttering birds
　pushed from the nest,
so are the women of Moab
　at the fords of the Arnon.

³'Make up your mind,' Moab says.
　'Render a decision.
Make your shadow like night—
　at high noon.
Hide the fugitives,
　do not betray the refugees.
⁴Let the Moabite fugitives stay with you;
　be their shelter from the destroyer.'

The oppressor will come to an end,
　and destruction will cease;
the aggressor will vanish from the land.
⁵In love a throne will be established;
　in faithfulness a man will sit on it—
　one from the house*ᶜ* of David—
one who in judging seeks justice
　and speeds the cause of righteousness.

⁶We have heard of Moab's pride—
　her overweening pride and conceit,
　her pride and her insolence—
　but her boasts are empty.
⁷Therefore the Moabites wail,
　they wail together for Moab.
Lament and grieve
　for the raisin cakes of Kir Hareseth.
⁸The fields of Heshbon wither,
　the vines of Sibmah also.
The rulers of the nations
　have trampled down the choicest vines,
which once reached Jazer
　and spread towards the desert.
Their shoots spread out
　and went as far as the sea.*ᵈ*
⁹So I weep, as Jazer weeps,
　for the vines of Sibmah.
Heshbon and Elealeh,
　I drench you with tears!
The shouts of joy over your ripened fruit
　and over your harvests have been stilled.
¹⁰Joy and gladness are taken away from the orchards;
　no-one sings or shouts in the vineyards;
no-one treads out wine at the presses,
　for I have put an end to the shouting.

ᵃ 9 *Dimon*, a wordplay on Dibon (see verse 2) sounds like the Hebrew for *blood*.　*ᵇ* 9 *Dimon*, a wordplay on Dibon (see verse 2) sounds like the Hebrew for *blood*.　*ᶜ* 5 Hebrew *tent*　*ᵈ* 8 Probably the Dead Sea

¹¹My heart laments for Moab like a harp,
  my inmost being for Kir Haresheth.
¹²When Moab appears at her high place,
  she only wears herself out;
when she goes to her shrine to pray,
  it is to no avail.

¹³This is the word the LORD has already spoken concerning Moab. ¹⁴But now the LORD says: 'Within three years, as a servant bound by contract would count them, Moab's splendour and all her many people will be despised, and her survivors will be very few and feeble.'

A prophecy against Damascus

17 A prophecy concerning Damascus:

'See, Damascus will no longer be a city
  but will become a heap of ruins.
²The cities of Aroer will be deserted
  and left to flocks, which will lie down,
  with no-one to make them afraid.
³The fortified city will disappear from Ephraim,
  and royal power from Damascus;
the remnant of Aram will be
  like the glory of the Israelites,'
    declares the LORD Almighty.

⁴'In that day the glory of Jacob will fade;
  the fat of his body will waste away.
⁵It will be as when reapers harvest the standing corn,
  gathering the corn in their arms—
as when someone gleans ears of corn
  in the Valley of Rephaim.
⁶Yet some gleanings will remain,
  as when an olive tree is beaten,
leaving two or three olives on the topmost branches,
  four or five on the fruitful boughs,'
    declares the LORD,
    the God of Israel.

⁷In that day people will look to their Maker
  and turn their eyes to the Holy One of Israel.
⁸They will not look to the altars,
  the work of their hands,
and they will have no regard for the Asherah poles*ᵃ*
and the incense altars their fingers have made.

⁹In that day their strong cities, which they left because of the Israelites, will be like places abandoned to thickets and undergrowth. And all will be desolation.
¹⁰You have forgotten God your Saviour;
  you have not remembered the Rock,
  your fortress.
Therefore, though you set out the finest plants
  and plant imported vines,
¹¹though on the day you set them out, you make them grow,
  and on the morning when you plant them, you bring them to bud,
yet the harvest will be as nothing
  in the day of disease and incurable pain.

¹²Woe to the many nations that rage—
  they rage like the raging sea!
Woe to the peoples who roar—
  they roar like the roaring of great waters!
¹³Although the peoples roar like the roar of surging waters,
  when he rebukes them they flee far away,
driven before the wind like chaff on the hills,
  like tumble-weed before a gale.
¹⁴In the evening, sudden terror!
  Before the morning, they are gone!
This is the portion of those who loot us,
  the lot of those who plunder us.

A prophecy against Cush

18 Woe to the land of whirring wings*ᵇ*
  along the rivers of Cush,*ᶜ*
²which sends envoys by sea
  in papyrus boats over the water.

Go, swift messengers,
to a people tall and smooth-skinned,
  to a people feared far and wide,
an aggressive nation of strange speech,
  whose land is divided by rivers.

³All you people of the world,
  you who live on the earth,

---

*ᵃ*8 That is, wooden symbols of the goddess Asherah *ᵇ*1 Or *of locusts* *ᶜ*1 That is, the upper Nile region

when a banner is raised on the mountains,
   you will see it,
and when a trumpet sounds,
   you will hear it.
⁴This is what the LORD says to me:
   'I will remain quiet and will look on from my dwelling-place,
like shimmering heat in the sunshine,
   like a cloud of dew in the heat of harvest.'
⁵For, before the harvest, when the blossom is gone
   and the flower becomes a ripening grape,
he will cut off the shoots with pruning knives,
   and cut down and take away the spreading branches.
⁶They will all be left to the mountain birds of prey
   and to the wild animals;
the birds will feed on them all summer,
   the wild animals all winter.

⁷At that time gifts will be brought to the LORD Almighty

from a people tall and smooth-skinned,
   from a people feared far and wide,
an aggressive nation of strange speech,
   whose land is divided by rivers—

the gifts will be brought to Mount Zion, the place of the Name of the LORD Almighty.

A prophecy against Egypt

19 A prophecy concerning Egypt:

See, the LORD rides on a swift cloud
   and is coming to Egypt.
The idols of Egypt tremble before him,
   and the hearts of the Egyptians melt within them.

²'I will stir up Egyptian against Egyptian—
   brother will fight against brother,
   neighbour against neighbour,
   city against city,
   kingdom against kingdom.
³The Egyptians will lose heart,
   and I will bring their plans to nothing;
they will consult the idols and the spirits of the dead,
   the mediums and the spiritists.

The Nile
Isaiah 19:5
The River Nile was essential to the well-being of the land of Egypt. Every year during the rainy season, the Nile would flood and fertilise the crops growing along its banks. A year without floods meant the crops would fail and there would be famine.

⁴I will hand the Egyptians over
   to the power of a cruel master,
and a fierce king will rule over them,'
   declares the Lord, the LORD Almighty.

⁵The waters of the river will dry up,
   and the river bed will be parched and dry.
⁶The canals will stink;
   the streams of Egypt will dwindle and dry up.
The reeds and rushes will wither,
⁷   also the plants along the Nile,
   at the mouth of the river.
Every sown field along the Nile
   will become parched, will blow away and be no more.
⁸Those who fish will groan and lament,
   all who cast hooks into the Nile;
those who throw nets on the water
   will pine away.
⁹Those who work with combed flax will despair,
   the weavers of fine linen will lose hope.
¹⁰The workers in cloth will be dejected,
   and all the wage earners will be sick at heart.

¹¹The officials of Zoan are nothing but fools;
   the wise counsellors of Pharaoh give senseless advice.

How can you say to Pharaoh,
'I am one of the wise men,
a disciple of the ancient kings'?

12 Where are your wise men now?
Let them show you and make known
what the LORD Almighty
has planned against Egypt.
13 The officials of Zoan have become fools,
the leaders of Memphis are deceived;
the cornerstones of her peoples
have led Egypt astray.
14 The LORD has poured into them
a spirit of dizziness;
they make Egypt stagger in all that she does,
as drunkards stagger around in their vomit.
15 There is nothing Egypt can do—
head or tail, palm branch or reed.

16 In that day the Egyptians will become weaklings. They will shudder with fear at the uplifted hand that the LORD Almighty raises against them. 17 And the land of Judah will bring terror to the Egyptians; everyone to whom Judah is mentioned will be terrified, because of what the LORD Almighty is planning against them.

18 In that day five cities in Egypt will speak the language of Canaan and swear allegiance to the LORD Almighty. One of them will be called the City of the Sun.^a

19 In that day there will be an altar to the LORD in the heart of Egypt, and a monument to the LORD at its border. 20 It will be a sign and witness to the LORD Almighty in the land of Egypt. When they cry out to the LORD because of their oppressors, he will send them a saviour and defender, and he will rescue them. 21 So the LORD will make himself known to the Egyptians, and in that day they will acknowledge the LORD. They will worship with sacrifices and grain offerings; they will make vows to the LORD and keep them. 22 The LORD will strike Egypt with a plague; he will strike them and heal them. They will turn to the LORD, and he will respond to their pleas and heal them.

23 In that day there will be a highway from Egypt to Assyria. The Assyrians will go to Egypt and the Egyptians to Assyria. The Egyptians and Assyrians will worship together. 24 In that day Israel will be the third, along with Egypt and Assyria, a blessing^b on the earth. 25 The LORD Almighty will bless them, saying, 'Blessed be Egypt my people, Assyria my handiwork, and Israel my inheritance.'

A prophecy against Egypt and Cush

20 In the year that the supreme commander, sent by Sargon king of Assyria, came to Ashdod and attacked and captured it— 2 at that time the LORD spoke through Isaiah son of Amoz. He said to him, 'Take off the sackcloth from your body and the sandals from your feet.' And he did so, going around stripped and barefoot.

3 Then the LORD said, 'Just as my servant Isaiah has gone stripped and barefoot for three years, as a sign and portent against Egypt and Cush,^c 4 so the king of Assyria will lead away stripped and barefoot the Egyptian captives and Cushite exiles, young and old, with buttocks bared—to Egypt's shame. 5 Those who trusted in Cush and boasted in Egypt will be dismayed and put to shame. 6 In that day the people who live on this coast will say, "See what has

Sign of the times

Sandals
Isaiah 20:2
Only the poorest people did not have sandals, so being forced to take off your sandals and go around barefoot was a big embarrassment.

---

^a 18 Some manuscripts of the Masoretic Text, Dead Sea Scrolls, Symmachus and Vulgate; most manuscripts of the Masoretic Text *the City of Destruction*   ^b 24 Or *Assyria, whose names will be used in blessings* (see Gen. 48:20); or *Assyria, who will be seen by others as blessed*   ^c 3 That is, the upper Nile region; also in verse 5

happened to those we relied on, those we fled to for help and deliverance from the king of Assyria! How then can we escape?"'

A prophecy against Babylon

21 A prophecy concerning the Desert by the Sea:

Like whirlwinds sweeping through the southland,
    an invader comes from the desert,
    from a land of terror.

²A dire vision has been shown to me:
    the traitor betrays, the looter takes loot.
Elam, attack! Media, lay siege!
    I will bring to an end all the groaning she caused.

³At this my body is racked with pain,
    pangs seize me, like those of a woman in labour;
I am staggered by what I hear,
    I am bewildered by what I see.
⁴My heart falters,
    fear makes me tremble;
the twilight I longed for
    has become a horror to me.

⁵They set the tables,
    they spread the rugs,
    they eat, they drink!
Get up, you officers,
    oil the shields!

⁶This is what the Lord says to me:

'Go, post a lookout
    and let him report what he sees.
⁷When he sees chariots
    with teams of horses,
riders on donkeys
    or riders on camels,
let him be alert,
    fully alert.'

⁸And the lookout[a] shouted,

'Day after day, my lord, I stand on the watchtower;
    every night I stay at my post.
⁹Look, here comes a man in a chariot
    with a team of horses.
And he gives back the answer:

"Babylon has fallen, has fallen!
All the images of its gods
    lie shattered on the ground!"'

¹⁰My people who are crushed on the threshing-floor,
    I tell you what I have heard
from the LORD Almighty,
    from the God of Israel.

A prophecy against Edom

¹¹A prophecy concerning Dumah:[b]

Someone calls to me from Seir,
    'Watchman, what is left of the night?
    Watchman, what is left of the night?'
¹²The watchman replies,
    'Morning is coming, but also the night.
If you would ask, then ask;
    and come back yet again.'

A prophecy against Arabia

¹³A prophecy concerning Arabia:

You caravans of Dedanites,
    who camp in the thickets of Arabia,
¹⁴   bring water for the thirsty;
you who live in Tema,
    bring food for the fugitives.
¹⁵They flee from the sword,
    from the drawn sword,
from the bent bow
    and from the heat of battle.

¹⁶This is what the Lord says to me: 'Within one year, as a servant bound by contract would count it, all the splendour of Kedar will come to an end. ¹⁷The survivors of the archers, the warriors of Kedar, will be few.' The LORD, the God of Israel, has spoken.

A prophecy about Jerusalem

22 A prophecy concerning the Valley of Vision:

What troubles you now,
    that you have all gone up on the roofs,
²you town so full of commotion,
    you city of tumult and revelry?
Your slain were not killed by the sword,
    nor did they die in battle.
³All your leaders have fled together;

---

[a] 8 Dead Sea Scrolls and Syriac; Masoretic Text *A lion*   [b] 11 *Dumah*, a word play on *Edom*, means *silence* or *stillness*.

they have been captured without using the bow.
All you who were caught were taken prisoner together,
having fled while the enemy was still far away.
4Therefore I said, 'Turn away from me; let me weep bitterly.
Do not try to console me
over the destruction of my people.'

5The Lord, the LORD Almighty, has a day
of tumult and trampling and terror
in the Valley of Vision,
a day of battering down walls
and of crying out to the mountains.
6Elam takes up the quiver,
with her charioteers and horses;
Kir uncovers the shield.
7Your choicest valleys are full of chariots,
and horsemen are posted at the city gates.

8The Lord stripped away the defences of Judah,
and you looked in that day
to the weapons in the Palace of the Forest.
9You saw that the City of David
had many breaches in its defences;
you stored up water
in the Lower Pool.
10You counted the buildings in Jerusalem
and tore down houses to strengthen the wall.
11You built a reservoir between the two walls
for the water of the Old Pool,
but you did not look to the One who made it,
or have regard for the One who planned it long ago.

12The Lord, the LORD Almighty,
called you on that day
to weep and to wail,
to tear out your hair and put on sackcloth.
13But see, there is joy and revelry,
slaughtering of cattle and killing of sheep,
eating of meat and drinking of wine!
'Let us eat and drink,' you say,
'for tomorrow we die!'

14The LORD Almighty has revealed this in my hearing: 'Till your dying day this sin will not be atoned for,' says the Lord, the LORD Almighty.

15This is what the Lord, the LORD Almighty, says:

'Go, say to this steward,
to Shebna, who is in charge of the palace:
16what are you doing here and who gave you permission
to cut out a grave for yourself here,
hewing your grave on the height
and chiselling your resting place in the rock?

17'Beware, the LORD is about to take firm hold of you
and hurl you away, you mighty man.
18He will roll you up tightly like a ball
and throw you into a large country.
There you will die
and there the chariots you were so proud of
will become a disgrace to your master's house.
19I will depose you from your office,
and you will be ousted from your position.

20'In that day I will summon my servant, Eliakim son of Hilkiah. 21I will clothe him with your robe and fasten your sash around him and hand your authority over to him. He will be a father to those who live in Jerusalem and to the house of Judah. 22I will place on his shoulder the key to the house of David; what he opens no-one can shut, and what he shuts no-one can open. 23I will drive him like a peg into a firm place; he will become a seat*a* of honour for the house of his father. 24All the glory of his family will hang on him: its offspring and offshoots—all its lesser vessels, from the bowls to all the jars.

25'In that day,' declares the LORD Almighty, 'the peg driven into the firm place will give way; it will be sheared off and

---

*a*23 Or *throne*

will fall, and the load hanging on it will be cut down.' The LORD has spoken.

A prophecy against Tyre

23 A prophecy concerning Tyre:

Wail, you ships of Tarshish!
For Tyre is destroyed
and left without house or harbour.
From the land of Cyprus
word has come to them.

2 Be silent, you people of the island
and you merchants of Sidon,
whom the seafarers have enriched.
3 On the great waters
came the grain of the Shihor;
the harvest of the Nile[a] was the revenue of Tyre,
and she became the market-place of the nations.

4 Be ashamed, Sidon, and you fortress of the sea,
for the sea has spoken:
'I have neither been in labour nor given birth;
I have neither reared sons nor brought up daughters.'
5 When word comes to Egypt,
they will be in anguish at the report from Tyre.

6 Cross over to Tarshish;
wail, you people of the island.
7 Is this your city of revelry,
the old, old city,
whose feet have taken her
to settle in far-off lands?
8 Who planned this against Tyre,
the bestower of crowns,
whose merchants are princes,
whose traders are renowned in the earth?
9 The LORD Almighty planned it,
to bring down her pride in all her splendour
and to humble all who are renowned on the earth.

10 Till[b] your land as they do along the Nile,
Daughter Tarshish,
for you no longer have a harbour.
11 The LORD has stretched out his hand over the sea
and made its kingdoms tremble.
He has given an order concerning Phoenicia
that her fortresses be destroyed.
12 He said, 'No more of your revelling,
Virgin Daughter Sidon, now crushed!

'Up, cross over to Cyprus;
even there you will find no rest.'
13 Look at the land of the Babylonians,[c]
this people that is now of no account!
The Assyrians have made it
a place for desert creatures;
they raised up their siege towers,
they stripped its fortresses bare
and turned it into a ruin.

14 Wail, you ships of Tarshish;
your fortress is destroyed!

15 At that time Tyre will be forgotten for seventy years, the span of a king's life. But at the end of these seventy years, it will happen to Tyre as in the song of the prostitute:

16 'Take up a harp, walk through the city,
you forgotten prostitute;
play the harp well, sing many a song,
so that you will be remembered.'

17 At the end of seventy years, the LORD will deal with Tyre. She will return to her lucrative prostitution and will ply her trade with all the kingdoms on the face of the earth. 18 Yet her profit and her earnings will be set apart for the LORD; they will not be stored up or hoarded. Her profits will go to those who live before the LORD, for abundant food and fine clothes.

The LORD's devastation of the earth

24 See, the LORD is going to lay waste the earth
and devastate it;
he will ruin its face
and scatter its inhabitants—
2 it will be the same
for priest as for people,

---

[a] 2, 3 Masoretic Text; Dead Sea Scrolls *Sidon, / who cross over the sea; / your envoys* 3*are on the great waters. / The grain of the Shihor, / the harvest of the Nile,*   [b] 10 Dead Sea Scrolls and some Septuagint manuscripts; Masoretic Text *Go through*   [c] 13 Or *Chaldeans*

Celebration at harvest
Isaiah 24:7
Forget the tins of baked beans and unwanted marrows that often end up at our traditional harvest festival services; the Israelites knew how to celebrate in style. Harvest was a time for music, songs, wine and feasting. But if there's no harvest then there's nothing to celebrate.

for master as for his servant,
for mistress as for her servant,
for seller as for buyer,
for borrower as for lender,
for debtor as for creditor.
³The earth will be completely laid waste
and totally plundered.
The LORD has spoken
this word.

⁴The earth dries up and withers,
the world languishes and withers,
the heavens languish with the earth.
⁵The earth is defiled by its people;
they have disobeyed the laws,
violated the statutes
and broken the everlasting covenant.
⁶Therefore a curse consumes the earth;
its people must bear their guilt.
Therefore earth's inhabitants are burned up,
and very few are left.
⁷The new wine dries up and the vine withers;
all the merrymakers groan.
⁸The gaiety of the tambourines is stilled,
the noise of the revellers has stopped,
the joyful harp is silent.
⁹No longer do they drink wine with a song;
the beer is bitter to its drinkers.
¹⁰The ruined city lies desolate;
the entrance to every house is barred.
¹¹In the streets they cry out for wine;
all joy turns to gloom,
all gaiety is banished from the earth.
¹²The city is left in ruins,
its gate is battered to pieces.
¹³So will it be on the earth
and among the nations,
as when an olive tree is beaten,
or as when gleanings are left after the grape harvest.

¹⁴They raise their voices, they shout for joy;
from the west they acclaim the LORD's majesty.
¹⁵Therefore in the east give glory to the LORD;
exalt the name of the LORD, the God of Israel,
in the islands of the sea.
¹⁶From the ends of the earth we hear singing:
'Glory to the Righteous One.'

But I said, 'I waste away, I waste away!
Woe to me!
The treacherous betray!
With treachery the treacherous betray!'
¹⁷Terror and pit and snare await you,
people of the earth.
¹⁸Whoever flees at the sound of terror
will fall into a pit;
whoever climbs out of the pit
will be caught in a snare.

The floodgates of the heavens are opened,
the foundations of the earth shake.
¹⁹The earth is broken up,
the earth is split asunder,
the earth is violently shaken.
²⁰The earth reels like a drunkard,
it sways like a hut in the wind;
so heavy upon it is the guilt of its rebellion
that it falls—never to rise again.
²¹In that day the LORD will punish
the powers in the heavens above
and the kings on the earth below.
²²They will be herded together
like prisoners bound in a dungeon;
they will be shut up in prison
and be punished[a] after many days.

---

[a] 22 Or *released*

²³The moon will be dismayed,
 the sun ashamed;
for the LORD Almighty will reign
 on Mount Zion and in Jerusalem,
 and before its elders—with great glory.

Praise to the LORD

25 LORD, you are my God;
 I will exalt you and praise your name,
for in perfect faithfulness
 you have done wonderful things,
 things planned long ago.
²You have made the city a heap of rubble,
 the fortified town a ruin,
 the foreigners' stronghold a city no more;
 it will never be rebuilt.
³Therefore strong peoples will honour you;
 cities of ruthless nations will revere you.
⁴You have been a refuge for the poor,
 a refuge for the needy in their distress,
 a shelter from the storm
 and a shade from the heat.
For the breath of the ruthless
 is like a storm driving against a wall
⁵ and like the heat of the desert.
You silence the uproar of foreigners;
 as heat is reduced by the shadow of a cloud,
 so the song of the ruthless is stilled.

⁶On this mountain the LORD Almighty will prepare
 a feast of rich food for all peoples,
a banquet of aged wine—
 the best of meats and the finest of wines.
⁷On this mountain he will destroy
 the shroud that enfolds all peoples,
 the sheet that covers all nations;
⁸ he will swallow up death for ever.
The Sovereign LORD will wipe away the tears
 from all faces;
he will remove his people's disgrace
 from all the earth.
             The LORD has spoken.

⁹In that day they will say,
'Surely this is our God;
 we trusted in him, and he saved us.
This is the LORD, we trusted in him;
 let us rejoice and be glad in his salvation.'

¹⁰The hand of the LORD will rest on this mountain;
 but Moab will be trampled in their land
 as straw is trampled down in the manure.
¹¹They will stretch out their hands in it,
 as swimmers stretch out their hands to swim.
God will bring down their pride
 despite the cleverness[a] of their hands.
¹²He will bring down your high fortified walls
 and lay them low;
he will bring them down to the ground,
 to the very dust.

A song of praise

26 In that day this song will be sung in the land of Judah:

We have a strong city;
 God makes salvation
 its walls and ramparts.
²Open the gates
 that the righteous nation may enter,
 the nation that keeps faith.
³You will keep in perfect peace
 those whose minds are steadfast,
 because they trust in you.
⁴Trust in the LORD for ever,
 for the LORD, the LORD, is the Rock eternal.
⁵He humbles those who dwell on high,
 he lays the lofty city low;
he levels it to the ground
 and casts it down to the dust.
⁶Feet trample it down—
 the feet of the oppressed,
 the footsteps of the poor.

⁷The path of the righteous is level;
 you, the Upright One, make the way of the righteous smooth.
⁸Yes, LORD, walking in the way of your laws,[b]
 we wait for you;

---

[a] 11 The meaning of the Hebrew for this word is uncertain. [b] 8 Or *judgments*

your name and renown
   are the desire of our hearts.
9My soul yearns for you in the night;
   in the morning my spirit longs for you.
When your judgments come upon the earth,
   the people of the world learn righteousness.
10But when grace is shown to the wicked,
   they do not learn righteousness;
even in a land of uprightness they go on doing evil
   and do not regard the majesty of the LORD.
11LORD, your hand is lifted high,
   but they do not see it.
Let them see your zeal for your people and be put to shame;
   let the fire reserved for your enemies consume them.

12LORD, you establish peace for us;
   all that we have accomplished you have done for us.
13LORD our God, other lords besides you have ruled over us,
   but your name alone do we honour.
14They are now dead, they live no more;
   their spirits do not rise.
You punished them and brought them to ruin;
   you wiped out all memory of them.
15You have enlarged the nation, LORD;
   you have enlarged the nation.
You have gained glory for yourself;
   you have extended all the borders of the land.

16LORD, they came to you in their distress;
   when you disciplined them,
   they could barely whisper a prayer.[a]
17As a pregnant woman about to give birth
   writhes and cries out in her pain,
   so were we in your presence, LORD.
18We were with child, we writhed in pain,
   but we gave birth to wind.
We have not brought salvation to the earth,
   and the people of the world have not been reborn.[b]

19But your dead will live, LORD;
   their bodies will rise—
let those who dwell in the dust
   wake up and shout for joy—
your dew is like the dew of the morning;
   you will make it fall on the spirits of the dead.

20Go, my people, enter your rooms
   and shut the doors behind you;
hide yourselves for a little while
   until his wrath has passed by.
21See, the LORD is coming out of his dwelling
   to punish the people of the earth for their sins.
The earth will disclose the blood shed on it;
   the earth will conceal its slain no longer.

Deliverance of Israel

27 In that day,

the LORD will punish with his sword—
   his fierce, great and powerful sword—
Leviathan the gliding serpent,
   Leviathan the coiling serpent;
he will slay the monster of the sea.
2In that day—

'Sing about a fruitful vineyard:
3   I, the LORD, watch over it;
   I water it continually.
I guard it day and night
   so that no-one may harm it.
4   I am not angry.
If only there were briers and thorns confronting me!
   I would march against them in battle;
   I would set them all on fire.
5Or else let them come to me for refuge;
   let them make peace with me,
   yes, let them make peace with me.'

6In days to come Jacob will take root,
   Israel will bud and blossom
   and fill all the world with fruit.

7Has ⌊the LORD⌋ struck her
   as he struck down those who struck her?
Has she been killed
   as those were killed who killed her?

---

[a] 16 The meaning of the Hebrew for this clause is uncertain.   [b] 18 Or *have not fallen*

⁸By warfare[a] and exile you contend with her—
with his fierce blast he drives her out,
as on a day the east wind blows.
⁹By this, then, will Jacob's guilt be atoned for,
and this will be the full fruit of the removal of his sin:
when he makes all the altar stones
to be like limestone crushed to pieces,
no Asherah poles[b] or incense altars will be left standing.
¹⁰The fortified city stands desolate,
an abandoned settlement, forsaken like the wilderness;
there the calves graze,
there they lie down;
they strip its branches bare.
¹¹When its twigs are dry, they are broken off
and women come and make fires with them.
For this is a people without understanding;
so their Maker has no compassion on them,
and their Creator shows them no favour.

¹²In that day the LORD will thresh from the flowing Euphrates to the Wadi of Egypt, and you, Israel, will be gathered up one by one. ¹³And in that day a great trumpet will sound. Those who were perishing in Assyria and those who were exiled in Egypt will come and worship the LORD on the holy mountain in Jerusalem.

Woe to the leaders of Ephraim and Judah

28 Woe to that wreath, the pride of Ephraim's drunkards,
to the fading flower, his glorious beauty,
set on the head of a fertile valley—
to that city, the pride of those laid low by wine!
²See, the Lord has one who is powerful and strong.
Like a hailstorm and a destructive wind,
like a driving rain and a flooding downpour,
he will throw it forcefully to the ground.
³That wreath, the pride of Ephraim's drunkards,
will be trampled underfoot.
⁴That fading flower, his glorious beauty,
set on the head of a fertile valley,
will be like figs ripe before harvest—
as soon as people see them and take them in hand,
they swallow them.

⁵In that day the LORD Almighty
will be a glorious crown,
a beautiful wreath
for the remnant of his people.
⁶He will be a spirit of justice
to those who sit in judgment,
a source of strength
to those who turn back the battle at the gate.

⁷And these also stagger from wine
and reel from beer:
priests and prophets stagger from beer
and are befuddled with wine;
they reel from beer,
they stagger when seeing visions,
they stumble when rendering decisions.
⁸All the tables are covered with vomit
and there is not a spot without filth.

⁹'Who is it he is trying to teach?
To whom is he explaining his message?
To children weaned from their milk,
to those just taken from the breast?
¹⁰For it is:
do this, do that,
a rule for this, a rule for that;[c]
a little here, a little there.'

¹¹Very well then, with foreign lips and strange tongues
God will speak to this people,
¹²to whom he said,
'This is the resting-place, let the weary rest';

---

[a] 8 See Septuagint; the meaning of the Hebrew for this word is uncertain.   [b] 9 That is, wooden symbols of the goddess Asherah   [c] 10 Hebrew *sav lasav sav lasav / kav lakav kav lakav* (probably meaningless sounds mimicking the prophet's words); also in verse 13

Plumb-line
Isaiah 28:17
A plumb-line is a small heavy weight on the end of a cord or a piece of string that is used to measure whether a wall is truly vertical.

and, 'This is the place of repose'—
but they would not listen.
13 So then, the word of the LORD to them will become:
do this, do that,
a rule for this, a rule for that;
a little here, a little there—
so that as they go they will fall backwards;
they will be injured and snared and captured.

14 Therefore hear the word of the LORD, you scoffers
who rule this people in Jerusalem.
15 You boast, 'We have entered into a covenant with death,
with the realm of the dead we have made an agreement.
When an overwhelming scourge sweeps by,
it cannot touch us,
for we have made a lie our refuge
and falsehood[a] our hiding-place.'

16 So this is what the Sovereign LORD says:

'See, I lay a stone in Zion, a tested stone,
a precious cornerstone for a sure foundation;
the one who relies on it
will never be stricken with panic.
17 I will make justice the measuring line
and righteousness the plumb-line;
hail will sweep away your refuge, the lie,
and water will overflow your hiding-place.
18 Your covenant with death will be annulled;
your agreement with the realm of the dead will not stand.
When the overwhelming scourge sweeps by,
you will be beaten down by it.
19 As often as it comes it will carry you away;
morning after morning, by day and by night,
it will sweep through.'

The understanding of this message
will bring sheer terror.
20 The bed is too short to stretch out on,
the blanket too narrow to wrap around you.
21 The LORD will rise up as he did at Mount Perazim,
he will rouse himself as in the Valley of Gibeon—
to do his work, his strange work,
and perform his task, his alien task.
22 Now stop your mocking,
or your chains will become heavier;
the Lord, the LORD Almighty, has told me
of the destruction decreed against the whole land.

23 Listen and hear my voice;
pay attention and hear what I say.
24 When farmers plough for planting, do they plough continually?
Do they keep on breaking up and working the soil?
25 When they have levelled the surface,
do they not sow caraway and scatter cummin?
Do they not plant wheat in its place,[b]
barley in its plot,[c]
and spelt in its field?
26 Their God instructs them
and teaches them the right way.

27 Caraway is not threshed with a sledge,
nor is a cartwheel rolled over cummin;
caraway is beaten out with a rod,
and cummin with a stick.
28 Grain must be ground to make bread;
so one does not go on threshing it for ever.
The wheels of a threshing-cart may be rolled over it,
but one does not use horses to grind grain.

---

[a] 15 Or *false gods* [b] 25 The meaning of the Hebrew for this word is uncertain. [c] 25 The meaning of the Hebrew for this word is uncertain.

29All this also comes from the LORD Almighty,
whose plan is wonderful,
whose wisdom is magnificent.

Woe to David's city

29 Woe to you, Ariel, Ariel,
the city where David settled!
Add year to year
and let your cycle of festivals go on.
2Yet I will besiege Ariel;
she will mourn and lament,
she will be to me like an altar hearth.[a]
3I will encamp against you on all sides;
I will encircle you with towers
and set up my siege works against you.
4Brought low, you will speak from the ground;
your speech will mumble out of the dust.
Your voice will come ghostlike from the earth;
out of the dust your speech will whisper.

5But your many enemies will become like fine dust,
the ruthless hordes like blown chaff.
Suddenly, in an instant,
6   the LORD Almighty will come
with thunder and earthquake and great noise,
with whirlwind and tempest and flames of a devouring fire.
7Then the hordes of all the nations that fight against Ariel,
that attack her and her fortress and besiege her,
will be as it is with a dream,
with a vision in the night—
8as when hungry people dream they are eating,
but they awaken, and their hunger remains;
as when thirsty people dream they are drinking,
but they awaken faint, with their thirst unquenched.
So will it be with the hordes of all the nations
that fight against Mount Zion.

9Be stunned and amazed,
blind yourselves and be sightless;
be drunk, but not from wine,
stagger, but not from beer.
10The LORD has brought over you a deep sleep:
he has sealed your eyes (the prophets);
he has covered your heads (the seers).

11For you this whole vision is nothing but words sealed in a scroll. And if you give the scroll to someone who can read, and say, 'Read this, please,' they will answer, 'I can't; it is sealed.' 12Or if you give the scroll to someone who cannot read, and say, 'Read this, please,' they will answer, 'I don't know how to read.'

13The Lord says:

'These people come near to me with their mouth
and honour me with their lips,
but their hearts are far from me.
Their worship of me
is based on merely human rules they have been taught.[b]
14Therefore once more I will astound these people
with wonder upon wonder;
the wisdom of the wise will perish,
the intelligence of the intelligent will vanish.'
15Woe to those who go to great depths
to hide their plans from the LORD,
who do their work in darkness and think,
'Who sees us? Who will know?'
16You turn things upside down,
as if the potter were thought to be like the clay!
Shall what is formed say to the one who formed it,
'You did not make me'?
Can the pot say to the potter,
'You know nothing'?

17In a very short time, will not Lebanon be turned into a fertile field
and the fertile field seem like a forest?
18In that day the deaf will hear the words of the scroll,

---

[a] 2 The Hebrew for *altar hearth* sounds like the Hebrew for *Ariel*.   [b] 13 Hebrew; Septuagint *They worship me in vain; / their teachings are merely human rules*

and out of gloom and darkness
  the eyes of the blind will see.
¹⁹Once more the humble will rejoice in the LORD;
  the needy will rejoice in the Holy One of Israel.
²⁰The ruthless will vanish,
  the mockers will disappear,
  and all who have an eye for evil will be cut down—
²¹those who with a word make someone out to be guilty,
  who ensnare the defender in court
  and with false testimony deprive the innocent of justice.

²²Therefore this is what the LORD, who redeemed Abraham, says to the house of Jacob:

'No longer will Jacob be ashamed;
  no longer will their faces grow pale.
²³When they see among them their children,
  the work of my hands,
  they will keep my name holy;
  they will acknowledge the holiness of the Holy One of Jacob,
  and will stand in awe of the God of Israel.
²⁴Those who are wayward in spirit will gain understanding;
  those who complain will accept instruction.'

Woe to the obstinate nation

30 'Woe to the obstinate children,'
  declares the LORD,
'to those who carry out plans that are not mine,
  forming an alliance, but not by my Spirit,
  heaping sin upon sin;
²who go down to Egypt
  without consulting me;
  who look for help to Pharaoh's protection,
  to Egypt's shade for refuge.
³But Pharaoh's protection will be to your shame,
  Egypt's shade will bring you disgrace.
⁴Though they have officials in Zoan
  and their envoys have arrived in Hanes,
⁵everyone will be put to shame
  because of a people useless to them,
  who bring neither help nor advantage,
  but only shame and disgrace.'

⁶A prophecy concerning the animals of the Negev:

Through a land of hardship and distress,
  of lions and lionesses,
  of adders and darting snakes,
  the envoys carry their riches on donkeys' backs,
  their treasures on the humps of camels,
to that unprofitable nation,
⁷ to Egypt, whose help is utterly useless.
Therefore I call her
  Rahab the Do-Nothing.

⁸Go now, write it on a tablet for them,
  inscribe it on a scroll,
that for the days to come
  it may be an everlasting witness.
⁹For these are rebellious people, deceitful children,
  children unwilling to listen to the LORD's instruction.
¹⁰They say to the seers,
  'See no more visions!'
and to the prophets,
  'Give us no more visions of what is right!
Tell us pleasant things,
  prophesy illusions.
¹¹Leave this way,
  get off this path,
and stop confronting us
  with the Holy One of Israel!'

¹²Therefore, this is what the Holy One of Israel says:

'Because you have rejected this message,
  relied on oppression
  and depended on deceit,
¹³this sin will become for you
  like a high wall, cracked and bulging,
  that collapses suddenly, in an instant.
¹⁴It will break in pieces like pottery,
  shattered so mercilessly
  that among its pieces not a fragment will be found
  for taking coals from a hearth
  or scooping water out of a cistern.'

¹⁵This is what the Sovereign LORD, the Holy One of Israel, says:

'In repentance and rest is your salvation,
 in quietness and trust is your strength,
 but you would have none of it.
¹⁶You said, "No, we will flee on horses."
 Therefore you will flee!
You said, "We will ride off on swift horses."
 Therefore your pursuers will be swift!
¹⁷A thousand will flee
 at the threat of one;
at the threat of five
 you will all flee away,
till you are left
 like a flagstaff on a mountaintop,
 like a banner on a hill.'

¹⁸Yet the LORD longs to be gracious to you;
 therefore he will rise up to show you compassion.
For the LORD is a God of justice.
 Blessed are all who wait for him!

¹⁹People of Zion, who live in Jerusalem, you will weep no more. How gracious he will be when you cry for help! As soon as he hears, he will answer you. ²⁰Although the Lord gives you the bread of adversity and the water of affliction, your teachers will be hidden no more; with your own eyes you will see them. ²¹Whether you turn to the right or to the left, your ears will hear a voice behind you, saying, 'This is the way; walk in it.' ²²Then you will desecrate your idols overlaid with silver and your images covered with gold; you will throw them away like a menstrual cloth and say to them, 'Away with you!'

²³He will also send you rain for the seed you sow in the ground, and the food that comes from the land will be rich and plentiful. In that day your cattle will graze in broad meadows. ²⁴The oxen and donkeys that work the soil will eat fodder and mash, spread out with fork and shovel. ²⁵In the day of great slaughter, when the towers fall, streams of water will flow on every high mountain and every lofty hill. ²⁶The moon will shine like the sun, and the sunlight will be seven times brighter, like the light of seven full days, when the LORD binds up the bruises of his people and heals the wounds he inflicted.

²⁷See, the Name of the LORD comes from afar,
 with burning anger and dense clouds of smoke;
his lips are full of wrath,
 and his tongue is a consuming fire.
²⁸His breath is like a rushing torrent,
 rising up to the neck.
He shakes the nations in the sieve of destruction;
 he places in the jaws of the peoples
 a bit that leads them astray.
²⁹And you will sing
 as on the night you celebrate a holy festival;
your hearts will rejoice
 as when people playing pipes go up
 to the mountain of the LORD,
 to the Rock of Israel.
³⁰The LORD will cause people to hear his majestic voice
 and will make them see his arm coming down
with raging anger and consuming fire,
 with cloudburst, thunderstorm and hail.
³¹The voice of the LORD will shatter Assyria;
 with his rod he will strike them down.
³²Every stroke the LORD lays on them
 with his punishing club
will be to the music of tambourines and harps,
 as he fights them in battle with the blows of his arm.
³³Topheth has long been prepared;
 it has been made ready for the king.
Its fire pit has been made deep and wide,
 with an abundance of fire and wood;
the breath of the LORD,
 like a stream of burning sulphur,
 sets it ablaze.

Woe to those who rely on Egypt

31 Woe to those who go down to Egypt for help,
 who rely on horses,
who trust in the multitude of their chariots
 and in the great strength of their horsemen,

but do not look to the Holy One of Israel,
  or seek help from the LORD.
²Yet he too is wise and can bring disaster;
  he does not take back his words.
He will rise up against the house of the wicked,
  against those who help evildoers.
³But the Egyptians are mortals and not God;
  their horses are flesh and not spirit.
When the LORD stretches out his hand,
  those who help will stumble,
  those who are helped will fall;
  all will perish together.

⁴This is what the LORD says to me:

'As a lion growls,
  a great lion over its prey—
and though a whole band of shepherds
  is called together against it,
it is not frightened by their shouts
  or disturbed by their clamour—
so the LORD Almighty will come down
  to do battle on Mount Zion and on its heights.
⁵Like birds hovering overhead,
  the LORD Almighty will shield Jerusalem;
he will shield it and deliver it,
  he will "pass over" it and will rescue it.'

⁶Return, you Israelites, to the One you have so greatly revolted against. ⁷For in that day every one of you will reject the idols of silver and gold your sinful hands have made. ⁸'Assyria will fall by no human sword;
  a sword, not of mortals, will devour them.
They will flee before the sword
  and their young men will be put to forced labour.
⁹Their stronghold will fall because of terror;
  at the sight of the battle standard their commanders will panic,'
declares the LORD,
  whose fire is in Zion,
  whose furnace is in Jerusalem.

The kingdom of righteousness

32 See, a king will reign in righteousness
  and rulers will rule with justice.
²Each one will be like a shelter from the wind
  and a refuge from the storm,
like streams of water in the desert
  and the shadow of a great rock in a thirsty land.
³Then the eyes of those who see will no longer be closed,
  and the ears of those who hear will listen.
⁴The fearful heart will know and understand,
  and the stammering tongue will be fluent and clear.
⁵No longer will the fool be called noble
  nor the scoundrel be highly respected.
⁶For fools speak folly,
  their hearts are bent on evil:
they practise ungodliness
  and spread error concerning the LORD;
the hungry they leave empty
  and from the thirsty they withhold water.
⁷Scoundrels use wicked methods,
  they make up evil schemes
to destroy the poor with lies,
  even when the plea of the needy is just.
⁸But the noble make noble plans,
  and by noble deeds they stand.

The women of Jerusalem

⁹You women who are so complacent,
  rise up and listen to me;
you daughters who feel secure,
  hear what I have to say!
¹⁰In little more than a year
  you who feel secure will tremble;
the grape harvest will fail,
  and the harvest of fruit will not come.
¹¹Tremble, you complacent women;
  shudder, you daughters who feel secure!
Strip off your clothes,
  put sackcloth round your waists.
¹²Beat your breasts for the pleasant fields,
  for the fruitful vines
¹³and for the land of my people,
  a land overgrown with thorns and briers—
yes, mourn for all houses of merriment
  and for this city of revelry.

¹⁴The fortress will be abandoned,
  the noisy city deserted;
 citadel and watchtower will become a
    wasteland for ever,
  the delight of donkeys, a pasture for
    flocks,
¹⁵till the Spirit is poured on us from on
    high,
  and the desert becomes a fertile field,
  and the fertile field seems like a forest.
¹⁶The LORD's justice will dwell in the desert,
  his righteousness live in the fertile field.
¹⁷The fruit of that righteousness will be
    peace;
  its effect will be quietness and
    confidence for ever.
¹⁸My people will live in peaceful dwelling-
    places,
  in secure homes,
  in undisturbed places of rest.
¹⁹Though hail flattens the forest
  and the city is levelled completely,
²⁰how blessed you will be,
  sowing your seed by every stream,
  and letting your cattle and donkeys
    range free.

Distress and help

33 Woe to you, destroyer,
  you who have not been destroyed!
 Woe to you, betrayer,
  you who have not been betrayed!
 When you stop destroying,
  you will be destroyed;
 when you stop betraying,
  you will be betrayed.

²LORD, be gracious to us;
  we long for you.
 Be our strength every morning,
  our salvation in time of distress.
³At the uproar of your army, the peoples
    flee;
  when you rise up, the nations scatter.
⁴Their plunder is harvested as by young
    locusts;
  like a swarm of locusts people pounce
    on it.

⁵The LORD is exalted, for he dwells on high;
 he will fill Zion with his justice and
    righteousness.
⁶He will be the sure foundation for your
    times,
  a rich store of salvation and wisdom
    and knowledge;
  the fear of the LORD is the key to this
    treasure.^a

⁷Look, their brave men cry aloud in the
    streets;
  the envoys of peace weep bitterly.
⁸The highways are deserted,
  no travellers are on the roads.
 The treaty is broken,
  its witnesses^b are despised,
  no-one is respected.
⁹The land dries up and wastes away,
  Lebanon is ashamed and withers;
 Sharon is like the Arabah,
  and Bashan and Carmel drop their
    leaves.

¹⁰'Now will I arise,' says the LORD.
  'Now will I be exalted;
  now will I be lifted up.
¹¹You conceive chaff,
  you give birth to straw;
  your breath is a fire that consumes you.
¹²The peoples will be burned as if to lime;
  like cut thorn-bushes they will be set
    ablaze.'

¹³You who are far away, hear what I have
    done;
  you who are near, acknowledge my
    power!
¹⁴The sinners in Zion are terrified;
  trembling grips the godless:
 'Who of us can dwell with the consuming
    fire?
  Who of us can dwell with everlasting
    burning?'
¹⁵Those who walk righteously
  and speak what is right,
 who reject gain from extortion
  and keep their hands from accepting
    bribes,
 who stop their ears against plots of
    murder
  and shut their eyes against
    contemplating evil—
¹⁶they are the ones who will dwell on the
    heights,

---
^a 6 Or *is a treasure from him*   ^b 8 Dead Sea Scrolls; Masoretic Text / *the cities*

whose refuge will be the mountain fortress.
Their bread will be supplied,
and water will not fail them.

17 Your eyes will see the king in his beauty
and view a land that stretches afar.
18 In your thoughts you will ponder the former terror:
'Where is that chief officer?
Where is the one who took the revenue?
Where is the officer in charge of the towers?'
19 You will see those arrogant people no more,
people whose speech is obscure,
whose language is strange and incomprehensible.

20 Look on Zion, the city of our festivals;
your eyes will see Jerusalem,
a peaceful abode, a tent that will not be moved;
its stakes will never be pulled up,
nor any of its ropes broken.
21 There the LORD will be our Mighty One.
It will be like a place of broad rivers and streams.
No galley with oars will ride them,
no mighty ship will sail them.
22 For the LORD is our judge,
the LORD is our lawgiver,
the LORD is our king;
it is he who will save us.

23 Your rigging hangs loose:
the mast is not held secure,
the sail is not spread.
Then an abundance of spoils will be divided
and even the lame will carry off plunder.
24 No-one living in Zion will say, 'I am ill';
and the sins of those who dwell there will be forgiven.

Judgment against the nations

34 Come near, you nations, and listen;
pay attention, you peoples!
Let the earth hear, and all that is in it,
the world, and all that comes out of it!
2 The LORD is angry with all nations;
his wrath is on all their armies.
He will totally destroy[a] them,
he will give them over to slaughter.
3 Their slain will be thrown out,
their dead bodies will send up a stench;
the mountains will be soaked with their blood.
4 All the stars in the sky will be dissolved
and the heavens rolled up like a scroll;
all the starry host will fall
like withered leaves from the vine,
like shrivelled figs from the fig-tree.

5 My sword has drunk its fill in the heavens;
see, it descends in judgment on Edom,
the people I have totally destroyed.
6 The sword of the LORD is bathed in blood,
it is covered with fat—
the blood of lambs and goats,
fat from the kidneys of rams.
For the LORD has a sacrifice in Bozrah
and a great slaughter in Edom.
7 And the wild oxen will fall with them,
the bull calves and the great bulls.
Their land will be drenched with blood,
and the dust will be soaked with fat.

8 For the LORD has a day of vengeance,
a year of retribution, to uphold Zion's cause.
9 Edom's streams will be turned into pitch,
her dust into burning sulphur;
her land will become blazing pitch!
10 It will not be quenched night or day;
its smoke will rise for ever.
From generation to generation it will lie desolate;
no-one will ever pass through it again.
11 The desert owl[b] and screech owl[c] will possess it;
the great owl[d] and the raven will nest there.
God will stretch out over Edom
the measuring line of chaos
and the plumb-line of desolation.
12 Her nobles will have nothing there to be called a kingdom,
all her princes will vanish away.

---

[a] 2 The Hebrew term refers to the irrevocable giving over of things or persons to the LORD, often by totally destroying them; also in verse 5. [b] 11 The precise identification of these birds is uncertain. [c] 11 The precise identification of these birds is uncertain. [d] 11 The precise identification of these birds is uncertain.

¹³Thorns will overrun her citadels,
  nettles and brambles her strongholds.
She will become a haunt for jackals,
  a home for owls.
¹⁴Desert creatures will meet with hyenas,
  and wild goats will bleat to each other;
there the night creatures will also lie down
  and find for themselves places of rest.
¹⁵The owl will nest there and lay eggs,
  she will hatch them, and care for her
    young
  under the shadow of her wings;
there also the falcons will gather,
  each with its mate.

¹⁶Look in the scroll of the LORD and read:

None of these will be missing,
  not one will lack her mate.
For it is his mouth that has given the
    order,
  and his Spirit will gather them
    together.
¹⁷He allots their portions;
  his hand distributes them by measure.
They will possess it for ever
  and dwell there from generation to
    generation.

Joy of the redeemed

35 The desert and the parched land
  will be glad;
  the wilderness will rejoice and
    blossom.
Like the crocus, ²it will burst into bloom;
  it will rejoice greatly and shout for joy.
The glory of Lebanon will be given to it,
  the splendour of Carmel and Sharon;
they will see the glory of the LORD,
  the splendour of our God.

³Strengthen the feeble hands,
  steady the knees that give way;
⁴say to those with fearful hearts,
  'Be strong, do not fear;
your God will come,
  he will come with vengeance;
with divine retribution
  he will come to save you.'

⁵Then will the eyes of the blind be opened
  and the ears of the deaf unstopped.
⁶Then will the lame leap like a deer,
  and the mute tongue shout for joy.
Water will gush forth in the wilderness
  and streams in the desert.
⁷The burning sand will become a pool,
  the thirsty ground bubbling springs.
In the haunts where jackals once lay,
  grass and reeds and papyrus will grow.

⁸And a highway will be there;
  it will be called the Way of Holiness;
  it will be for those who walk on that
    Way.
The unclean will not journey on it;
  wicked fools will not go about on it.
⁹No lion will be there,
  nor any ravenous beast;
  they will not be found there.
But only the redeemed will walk there,
¹⁰ and those the LORD has rescued will
    return.
They will enter Zion with singing;
  everlasting joy will crown their heads.
Gladness and joy will overtake them,
  and sorrow and sighing will flee away.

IN OTHER WORDS

Divine
Isaiah 35:4
The word 'divine' means 'holy' or 'of God'.

Sennacherib threatens Jerusalem

36 In the fourteenth year of King Hezekiah's reign, Sennacherib king of Assyria attacked all the fortified cities of Judah and captured them. ²Then the king of Assyria sent his field commander with a large army from Lachish to King Hezekiah at Jerusalem. When the commander stopped at the aqueduct of the Upper Pool, on the road to the Launderer's Field, ³Eliakim son of Hilkiah the palace administrator, Shebna the secretary, and Joah son of Asaph the recorder went out to him.

⁴The field commander said to them, 'Tell Hezekiah:

'"This is what the great king, the king of Assyria, says: on what are you basing this confidence of yours? ⁵You say you have counsel and might for war—but you speak only empty words. On whom are you depending, that you rebel against me? 6Look, I know you are depending on Egypt, that splintered reed of a staff, which pierces the hand of anyone who leans on it! Such is Pharaoh king of Egypt to all who depend on him. 7But if you say to me, 'We are depending on the LORD our God'—isn't he the one whose high places and altars Hezekiah removed, saying to Judah and Jerusalem, 'You must worship before this altar'?

8' "Come now, make a bargain with my master, the king of Assyria: I will give you two thousand horses—if you can put riders on them! 9How then can you repulse one officer of the least of my master's officials, even though you are depending on Egypt for chariots and horsemen[a]? 10Furthermore, have I come to attack and destroy this land without the LORD? The LORD himself told me to march against this country and destroy it." '

11Then Eliakim, Shebna and Joah said to the field commander, 'Please speak to your servants in Aramaic, since we understand it. Don't speak to us in Hebrew in the hearing of the people on the wall.'

12But the commander replied, 'Was it only to your master and you that my master sent me to say these things, and not to the people sitting on the wall—who, like you, will have to eat their own excrement and drink their own urine?'

13Then the commander stood and called out in Hebrew, 'Hear the words of the great king, the king of Assyria! 14This is what the king says: do not let Hezekiah deceive you. He cannot deliver you! 15Do not let Hezekiah persuade you to trust in the LORD when he says, "The LORD will surely deliver us; this city will not be given into the hand of the king of Assyria."

16'Do not listen to Hezekiah. This is what the king of Assyria says: make peace with me and come out to me. Then every one of you will eat from your own vine and fig-tree and drink water from your own cistern, 17until I come and take you to a land like your own—a land of corn and new wine, a land of bread and vineyards.

18'Do not let Hezekiah mislead you when he says, "The LORD will deliver us." Have the gods of any nations ever delivered their lands from the hand of the king of Assyria? 19Where are the gods of Hamath and Arpad? Where are the gods of Sepharvaim? Have they rescued Samaria from my hand? 20Who of all the gods of these countries have been able to save their lands from me? How then can the LORD deliver Jerusalem from my hand?'

21But the people remained silent and said nothing in reply, because the king had commanded, 'Do not answer him.'

22Then Eliakim son of Hilkiah the palace administrator, Shebna the secretary and Joah son of Asaph the recorder went to Hezekiah, with their clothes torn, and told him what the field commander had said.

Jerusalem's deliverance foretold

37 When King Hezekiah heard this, he tore his clothes and put on sackcloth and went into the temple of the LORD. 2He sent Eliakim the palace administrator, Shebna the secretary, and the leading priests, all wearing sackcloth, to the prophet Isaiah son of Amoz. 3They told him, 'This is what Hezekiah says: this day is a day of distress and rebuke and disgrace, as when children come to the moment of birth and there is no strength to deliver them. 4It may be that the LORD your God will hear the words of the field commander, whom his master, the king of Assyria, has sent to ridicule the living God, and that he will rebuke him for the words the LORD your God has heard. Therefore pray for the remnant that still survives.'

5When King Hezekiah's officials came to Isaiah, 6Isaiah said to them, 'Tell your master, "This is what the LORD says: do not be afraid of what you have heard—those

---

[a] 9 Or *charioteers*

words with which the underlings of the king of Assyria have blasphemed me. 7Listen! When he hears a certain report, I will make him want to return to his own country, and there I will have him cut down with the sword."'

8When the field commander heard that the king of Assyria had left Lachish, he withdrew and found the king fighting against Libnah.

9Now Sennacherib received a report that Tirhakah, the king of Cush,[a] was marching out to fight against him. When he heard it, he sent messengers to Hezekiah with this word: 10'Say to Hezekiah king of Judah: do not let the god you depend on deceive you when he says, "Jerusalem will not be given into the hands of the king of Assyria." 11Surely you have heard what the kings of Assyria have done to all the countries, destroying them completely. And will you be delivered? 12Did the gods of the nations that were destroyed by my ancestors deliver them—the gods of Gozan, Harran, Rezeph and the people of Eden who were in Tel Assar? 13Where is the king of Hamath or the king of Arpad? Where are the kings of Lair, Sepharvaim, Hena and Ivvah?'

Hezekiah's prayer

14Hezekiah received the letter from the messengers and read it. Then he went up to the temple of the LORD and spread it out before the LORD. 15And Hezekiah prayed to the LORD: 16'LORD Almighty, the God of Israel, enthroned between the cherubim, you alone are God over all the kingdoms of the earth. You have made heaven and earth. 17Give ear, LORD, and hear; open your eyes, LORD, and see; listen to all the words Sennacherib has sent to ridicule the living God.

18'It is true, LORD, that the Assyrian kings have laid waste all these peoples and their lands. 19They have thrown their gods into the fire and destroyed them, for they were not gods but only wood and stone, fashioned by human hands. 20Now, LORD our God, deliver us from his hand, so that all the kingdoms of the earth may know that you, LORD, are the only God.[b]

Sennacherib's fall

21Then Isaiah son of Amoz sent a message to Hezekiah: 'This is what the LORD, the God of Israel, says: because you have prayed to me concerning Sennacherib king of Assyria, 22this is the word the LORD has spoken against him:

'Virgin Daughter Zion
    despises and mocks you.
Daughter Jerusalem
    tosses her head as you flee.
23Who is it you have ridiculed and
    blasphemed?
Against whom have you raised your
    voice
and lifted your eyes in pride?
    Against the Holy One of Israel!
24By your messengers
    you have ridiculed the Lord.
And you have said,
    "With my many chariots
I have ascended the heights of the
    mountains,
    the utmost heights of Lebanon.
I have cut down its tallest cedars,
    the choicest of its junipers.
I have reached its remotest heights,
    the finest of its forests.
25I have dug wells in foreign lands[c]
    and drunk the water there.
With the soles of my feet
    I have dried up all the streams of
    Egypt."

26'Have you not heard?
    Long ago I ordained it.
In days of old I planned it;
    now I have brought it to pass,
that you have turned fortified cities
    into piles of stone.
27Their people, drained of power,
    are dismayed and put to shame.
They are like plants in the field,
    like tender green shoots,
like grass sprouting on the roof,
    scorched[d] before it grows up.

---

[a] 9 That is, the upper Nile region   [b] 20 Dead Sea Scrolls (see also 2 Kings 19:19); Masoretic Text *you alone are the LORD*   [c] 25 Dead Sea Scrolls (see also 2 Kings 19:24); Masoretic Text does not have *in foreign lands*.   [d] 27 Some manuscripts of the Masoretic Text, Dead Sea Scrolls and some Septuagint manuscripts (see also 2 Kings 19:26); most manuscripts of the Masoretic Text *roof / and terraced fields*

²⁸'But I know where you are
    and when you come and go
    and how you rage against me.
²⁹Because you rage against me
    and because your insolence has
        reached my ears,
I will put my hook in your nose
    and my bit in your mouth,
and I will make you return
    by the way you came.

³⁰'This will be the sign for you, Hezekiah:

'This year you will eat what grows by itself,
    and the second year what springs from
        that.
But in the third year sow and reap,
    plant vineyards and eat their fruit.
³¹Once more a remnant of the house of
        Judah
    will take root below and bear fruit
        above.
³²For out of Jerusalem will come a remnant,
    and out of Mount Zion a band of
        survivors.
The zeal of the LORD Almighty
    will accomplish this.

³³'Therefore this is what the LORD says concerning the king of Assyria:

'He will not enter this city
    or shoot an arrow here.
He will not come before it with shield
    or build a siege ramp against it.
³⁴By the way that he came he will return;
    he will not enter this city,'
                    declares the LORD.
³⁵'I will defend this city and save it,
    for my sake and for the sake of David
        my servant!'

³⁶Then the angel of the LORD went out and put to death a hundred and eighty-five thousand in the Assyrian camp. When the people got up the next morning—there were all the dead bodies! ³⁷So Sennacherib king of Assyria broke camp and withdrew. He returned to Nineveh and stayed there.

³⁸One day, while he was worshipping in the temple of his god Nisrok, his sons Adrammelek and Sharezer killed him with the sword, and they escaped to the land of Ararat. And Esarhaddon his son succeeded him as king.

Hezekiah's illness

38 In those days Hezekiah became ill and was at the point of death. The prophet Isaiah son of Amoz went to him and said, 'This is what the LORD says: put your house in order, because you are going to die; you will not recover.'

²Hezekiah turned his face to the wall and prayed to the LORD, ³'Remember, LORD, how I have walked before you faithfully and with wholehearted devotion and have done what is good in your eyes.' And Hezekiah wept bitterly.

⁴Then the word of the LORD came to Isaiah: ⁵'Go and tell Hezekiah, "This is what the LORD, the God of your father David, says: I have heard your prayer and seen your tears; I will add fifteen years to your life. ⁶And I will deliver you and this city from the hand of the king of Assyria. I will defend this city.

⁷ "This is the LORD's sign to you that the LORD will do what he has promised: ⁸I will make the shadow cast by the sun go back the ten steps it has gone down on the stairway of Ahaz." ' So the sunlight went back the ten steps it had gone down.

⁹A writing of Hezekiah king of Judah after his illness and recovery:

¹⁰I said, 'In the prime of my life
    must I go through the gates of death
    and be robbed of the rest of my years?'
¹¹I said, 'I will not again see the LORD,
    the LORD, in the land of the living;
no longer will I look on my fellow
        mortals,
    or be with those who now dwell in this
        world.
¹²Like a shepherd's tent my house
    has been pulled down and taken from
        me.
Like a weaver I have rolled up my life,
    and he has cut me off from the loom;
    day and night you made an end of
        me.
¹³I waited patiently till dawn,
    but like a lion he broke all my bones;
    day and night you made an end of
        me.
¹⁴I cried like a swift or thrush,
    I moaned like a mourning dove.

making Connections

When the sun went backwards
Isaiah 38:8

God created the sun, so it's not surprising that it's under his control. There are two occasions in the Bible where God interrupts the sun's normal pattern for his purposes. When King Hezekiah asks God to heal him from his illness, God makes the sun go backwards as a sign that he has heard Hezekiah and will answer his prayer. And God made the sun stand still when Joshua prayed during a battle with the Amorites, which showed everyone that God was on Israel's side (Joshua 10:12).

My eyes grew weak as I looked to the heavens.
  I am being threatened; Lord, come to my aid!'
15But what can I say?
  He has spoken to me, and he himself has done this.
I will walk humbly all my years
  because of this anguish of my soul.
16Lord, by such things people live;
  and my spirit finds life in them too.
You restored me to health
  and let me live.
17Surely it was for my benefit
  that I suffered such anguish.
In your love you kept me
  from the pit of destruction;
you have put all my sins
  behind your back.
18For the grave cannot praise you,
  death cannot sing your praise;
those who go down to the pit
  cannot hope for your faithfulness.
19The living, the living—they praise you,
  as I am doing today;
parents tell their children
  about your faithfulness.
20The LORD will save me,
  and we will sing with stringed instruments
all the days of our lives
  in the temple of the LORD.

21Isaiah had said, 'Prepare a poultice of figs and apply it to the boil, and he will recover.'
22Hezekiah had asked, 'What will be the sign that I will go up to the temple of the LORD?'

Envoys from Babylon

39 At that time Marduk-Baladan son of Baladan king of Babylon sent Hezekiah letters and a gift, because he had heard of his illness and recovery. 2Hezekiah received the envoys gladly and showed them what was in his storehouses—the silver, the gold, the spices, the fine olive oil—his entire armoury and everything found among his treasures. There was nothing in his palace or in all his kingdom that Hezekiah did not show them.

3Then Isaiah the prophet went to King Hezekiah and asked, 'What did those men say, and where did they come from?'
'From a distant land,' Hezekiah replied. 'They came to me from Babylon.'
4The prophet asked, 'What did they see in your palace?'
'They saw everything in my palace,' Hezekiah said. 'There is nothing among my treasures that I did not show them.'
5Then Isaiah said to Hezekiah, 'Hear the word of the LORD Almighty: 6the time will surely come when everything in your palace, and all that your predecessors have stored up until this day, will be carried off to Babylon. Nothing will be left, says the LORD. 7And some of your descendants, your own flesh and blood who will be born to you, will be taken away, and they will become eunuchs in the palace of the king of Babylon.'
8'The word of the LORD you have spoken is good,' Hezekiah replied. For he thought, 'There will be peace and security in my lifetime.'

Comfort for God's people

40 Comfort, comfort my people,
  says your God.
2 Speak tenderly to Jerusalem,
  and proclaim to her
that her hard service has been completed,
  that her sin has been paid for,
that she has received from the LORD's hand
  double for all her sins.

3 A voice of one calling:

'In the wilderness prepare
  the way for the LORD;[a]
make straight in the desert
  a highway for our God.[b]
4 Every valley shall be raised up,
  every mountain and hill made low;
the rough ground shall become level,
  the rugged places a plain.
5 And the glory of the LORD will be revealed,
  and all people will see it together.
    For the mouth of the LORD has spoken.'

6 A voice says, 'Cry out.'
  And I said, 'What shall I cry?'

'All people are like grass,
  and all human faithfulness is like the flowers of the field.
7 The grass withers and the flowers fall,
  because the breath of the LORD blows on them.
  Surely the people are grass.
8 The grass withers and the flowers fall,
  but the word of our God endures for ever.'

9 You who bring good news to Zion,
  go up on a high mountain.
You who bring good news to Jerusalem,[c]
  lift up your voice with a shout,
lift it up, do not be afraid;
  say to the towns of Judah,
  'Here is your God!'
10 See, the Sovereign LORD comes with power,
  and his arm rules for him.
See, his reward is with him,
  and his recompense accompanies him.
11 He tends his flock like a shepherd:
  he gathers the lambs in his arms
and carries them close to his heart;
  he gently leads those that have young.

12 Who has measured the waters in the hollow of his hand,
  or with the breadth of his hand marked off the heavens?
Who has held the dust of the earth in a basket,
  or weighed the mountains on the scales and the hills in a balance?
13 Who can fathom the Spirit[d] of the LORD,
  or instruct the LORD as his counsellor?
14 Whom did the LORD consult to enlighten him,
  and who taught him the right way?
Who was it that taught him knowledge,
  or showed him the path of understanding?

15 Surely the nations are like a drop in a bucket;
  they are regarded as dust on the scales;
he weighs the islands as though they were fine dust.
16 Lebanon is not sufficient for altar fires,
  nor its animals enough for burnt offerings.
17 Before him all the nations are as nothing;
  they are regarded by him as worthless and less than nothing.

18 With whom, then, will you compare God?
  To what image will you liken him?
19 As for an idol, a metalworker casts it,
  and a goldsmith overlays it with gold and fashions silver chains for it.
20 People too poor to present such an offering
  select wood that will not rot.
They look for a skilled worker
  to set up an idol that will not topple.

21 Do you not know?
  Have you not heard?
Has it not been told you from the beginning?

---

[a] 3 Or *A voice of one calling in the wilderness: /* 'Prepare the way for the LORD   [b] 3 Hebrew; Septuagint *make straight the paths of our God*   [c] 9 Or *Zion, bringer of good news, / go up on a high mountain. / Jerusalem, bringer of good news*   [d] 13 Or *mind*

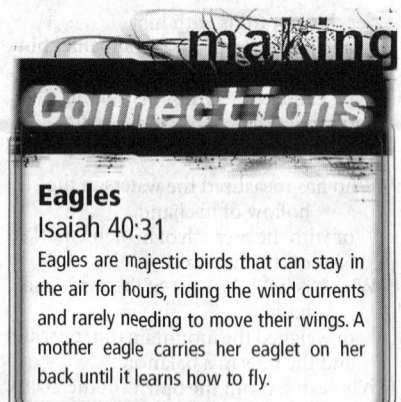

Making Connections

Eagles
Isaiah 40:31
Eagles are majestic birds that can stay in the air for hours, riding the wind currents and rarely needing to move their wings. A mother eagle carries her eaglet on her back until it learns how to fly.

Have you not understood since the earth was founded?
22 He sits enthroned above the circle of the earth,
and its people are like grasshoppers.
He stretches out the heavens like a canopy,
and spreads them out like a tent to live in.
23 He brings princes to naught
and reduces the rulers of this world to nothing.
24 No sooner are they planted,
no sooner are they sown,
no sooner do they take root in the ground,
than he blows on them and they wither,
and a whirlwind sweeps them away like chaff.
25 'To whom will you compare me?
Or who is my equal?' says the Holy One.
26 Lift up your eyes and look to the heavens:
who created all these?
He who brings out the starry host one by one,
and calls them each by name.
Because of his great power and mighty strength,
not one of them is missing.
27 Why do you complain, Jacob?
Why do you say, Israel,
'My way is hidden from the LORD;
my cause is disregarded by my God'?
28 Do you not know?
Have you not heard?
The LORD is the everlasting God,
the Creator of the ends of the earth.
He will not grow tired or weary,
and his understanding no-one can fathom.
29 He gives strength to the weary
and increases the power of the weak.
30 Even youths grow tired and weary,
and young men stumble and fall;
31 but those who hope in the LORD
will renew their strength.
They will soar on wings like eagles;
they will run and not grow weary,
they will walk and not be faint.

The helper of Israel

41 'Be silent before me, you islands!
Let the nations renew their strength!
Let them come forward and speak;
let us meet together at the place of judgment.

2 'Who has stirred up one from the east,
calling him in righteousness to his service?[a]
He hands nations over to him
and subdues kings before him.
He turns them to dust with his sword,
to wind-blown chaff with his bow.
3 He pursues them and moves on unscathed,
by a path his feet have not travelled before.
4 Who has done this and carried it through,
calling forth the generations from the beginning?
I, the LORD—with the first of them
and with the last—I am he.'

5 The islands have seen it and fear;
the ends of the earth tremble.
They approach and come forward;
6 they help each other
and say to their companions, 'Be strong!'
7 The metalworker encourages the goldsmith,

---

[a] 2 Or *east, / whom* victory meets at every step

and the one who smooths with the hammer
spurs on the one who strikes the anvil.
One says of the welding, 'It is good.'
The other nails down the idol so that it will not topple.

⁸'But you, Israel, my servant,
Jacob, whom I have chosen,
you descendants of Abraham my friend,
⁹I took you from the ends of the earth,
from its farthest corners I called you.
I said, "You are my servant";
I have chosen you and have not rejected you.
¹⁰So do not fear, for I am with you;
do not be dismayed, for I am your God.
I will strengthen you and help you;
I will uphold you with my righteous right hand.

¹¹'All who rage against you
will surely be ashamed and disgraced;
those who oppose you
will be as nothing and perish.
¹²Though you search for your enemies,
you will not find them.
Those who wage war against you
will be as nothing at all.
¹³For I am the LORD your God
who takes hold of your right hand
and says to you, Do not fear;
I will help you.
¹⁴Do not be afraid, you worm Jacob,
little Israel, do not fear,
for I myself will help you,' declares the LORD,
your Redeemer, the Holy One of Israel.
¹⁵'See, I will make you into a threshing-sledge,
new and sharp, with many teeth.
You will thresh the mountains and crush them,
and reduce the hills to chaff.
¹⁶You will winnow them, the wind will pick them up,
and a gale will blow them away.
But you will rejoice in the LORD
and glory in the Holy One of Israel.

¹⁷'The poor and needy search for water,
but there is none;
their tongues are parched with thirst.
But I the LORD will answer them;
I, the God of Israel, will not forsake them.
¹⁸I will make rivers flow on barren heights,
and springs within the valleys.
I will turn the desert into pools of water,
and the parched ground into springs.
¹⁹I will put in the desert
the cedar and the acacia, the myrtle and the olive.
I will set junipers in the wasteland,
the fir and the cypress together,
²⁰so that people may see and know,
may consider and understand,
that the hand of the LORD has done this,
that the Holy One of Israel has created it.

²¹'Present your case,' says the LORD.
'Set forth your arguments,' says Jacob's King.
²²'Tell us, you idols,
what is going to happen.
Tell us what the former things were,
so that we may consider them
and know their final outcome.
Or declare to us the things to come,
²³ tell us what the future holds,
so that we may know you are gods.
Do something, whether good or bad,
so that we will be dismayed and filled with fear.
²⁴But you are less than nothing
and you can do nothing;
those who choose you are detestable.

²⁵'I have stirred up one from the north, and he comes—
one from the rising sun who calls on my name.
He treads on rulers as if they were mortar,
as if he were a potter treading the clay.
²⁶Who told of this from the beginning, so that we could know,
or beforehand, so that we could say, "He was right"?
No-one told of this,
no-one foretold it,
no-one heard any words from you.
²⁷I was the first to tell Zion, "Look, here they are!"
I gave to Jerusalem a messenger of good news.

28 I look but there is no-one—
 no-one among the gods to give counsel,
 no-one to give answer when I ask them.
29 See, they are all false!
 Their deeds amount to nothing;
 their images are but wind and confusion.

The servant of the LORD

42 'Here is my servant, whom I uphold,
 my chosen one in whom I delight;
 I will put my Spirit on him,
 and he will bring justice to the nations.
2 He will not shout or cry out,
 or raise his voice in the streets.
3 A bruised reed he will not break,
 and a smouldering wick he will not snuff out.
 In faithfulness he will bring forth justice;
4 he will not falter or be discouraged
 till he establishes justice on earth.
 In his teaching the islands will put their hope.'

5 This is what God the LORD says—
 he who created the heavens and stretched them out,
 who spread out the earth with all that springs from it,
 who gives breath to its people,
 and life to those who walk on it:
6 'I, the LORD, have called you in righteousness;
 I will take hold of your hand.
 I will keep you and will make you
 to be a covenant for the people
 and a light for the Gentiles,
7 to open eyes that are blind,
 to free captives from prison
 and to release from the dungeon those who sit in darkness.

8 'I am the LORD; that is my name!
 I will not yield my glory to another
 or my praise to idols.
9 See, the former things have taken place,
 and new things I declare;
 before they spring into being
 I announce them to you.'

Song of praise to the LORD

10 Sing to the LORD a new song,
 his praise from the ends of the earth,
 you who go down to the sea, and all that is in it,
 you islands, and all who live in them.
11 Let the wilderness and its towns raise their voices;
 let the settlements where Kedar lives rejoice.
 Let the people of Sela sing for joy;
 let them shout from the mountaintops.
12 Let them give glory to the LORD
 and proclaim his praise in the islands.
13 The LORD will march out like a champion,
 like a warrior he will stir up his zeal;
 with a shout he will raise the battle cry
 and will triumph over his enemies.

14 'For a long time I have kept silent,
 I have been quiet and held myself back.
 But now, like a woman in childbirth,
 I cry out, I gasp and pant.
15 I will lay waste the mountains and hills
 and dry up all their vegetation;
 I will turn rivers into islands
 and dry up the pools.

Making Connections

Servant songs
Isaiah 42:1

This is the first of four 'servant songs' in Isaiah. The servant will bring justice to the nations and lead Israel back to God. The servant will be a light to other nations so that people will recognise who God is, and the servant will need to suffer in order to get his work done. Some people think the servant is a reference to Israel itself; other people see the servant as a prophecy about Jesus, showing what his life and work will be like. The other 'servant songs' are in Isaiah 49:1–6, 50:4–11 and 52:13–53:12.

16 I will lead the blind by ways they have not known,
   along unfamiliar paths I will guide them;
I will turn the darkness into light before them
   and make the rough places smooth.
These are the things I will do;
   I will not forsake them.
17 But those who trust in idols,
   who say to images, "You are our gods,"
   will be turned back in utter shame.

Israel blind and deaf

18 'Hear, you deaf;
   look, you blind, and see!
19 Who is blind but my servant,
   and deaf like the messenger I send?
Who is blind like the one in covenant with me,
   blind like the servant of the LORD?
20 You have seen many things, but have paid no attention;
   your ears are open, but you hear nothing.'
21 It pleased the LORD
   for the sake of his righteousness
   to make his law great and glorious.
22 But this is a people plundered and looted,
   all of them trapped in pits
   or hidden away in prisons.
They have become plunder,
   with no-one to rescue them;
they have been made loot,
   with no-one to say, 'Send them back.'

23 Which of you will listen to this
   or pay close attention in time to come?
24 Who handed Jacob over to become loot,
   and Israel to the plunderers?
Was it not the LORD,
   against whom we have sinned?
For they would not follow his ways;
   they did not obey his law.
25 So he poured out on them his burning anger,
   the violence of war.
It enveloped them in flames, yet they did not understand;
   it consumed them, but they did not take it to heart.

Israel's only Saviour

43 But now, this is what the LORD says—
he who created you, Jacob,
he who formed you, Israel:
'Do not fear, for I have redeemed you;
   I have summoned you by name; you are mine.
2 When you pass through the waters,
   I will be with you;
and when you pass through the rivers,
   they will not sweep over you.
When you walk through the fire,
   you will not be burned;
   the flames will not set you ablaze.
3 For I am the LORD your God,
   the Holy One of Israel, your Saviour;
I give Egypt for your ransom,
   Cush*a* and Seba in your stead.
4 Since you are precious and honoured in my sight,
   and because I love you,
I will give nations in exchange for you,
   and peoples in exchange for your life.
5 Do not be afraid, for I am with you;
   I will bring your children from the east
   and gather you from the west.
6 I will say to the north, "Give them up!"
   and to the south, "Do not hold them back."
Bring my sons from afar
   and my daughters from the ends of the earth—
7 everyone who is called by my name,
   whom I created for my glory,
   whom I formed and made.'

8 Lead out those who have eyes but are blind,
   who have ears but are deaf.
9 All the nations gather together
   and the peoples assemble.
Which of their gods foretold this
   and proclaimed to us the former things?
Let them bring in their witnesses to prove they were right,
   so that others may hear and say, 'It is true.'
10 'You are my witnesses,' declares the LORD,
   'and my servant whom I have chosen,

---

a 3 That is, the upper Nile region

so that you may know and believe me
    and understand that I am he.
Before me no god was formed,
    nor will there be one after me.
¹¹I, even I, am the LORD,
    and apart from me there is no saviour.
¹²I have revealed and saved and
        proclaimed—
    I, and not some foreign god among you.
You are my witnesses,' declares the LORD,
    'that I am God.
¹³ Yes, and from ancient days I am he.
No-one can deliver out of my hand.
    When I act, who can reverse it?'

God's mercy and Israel's unfaithfulness

¹⁴This is what the LORD says—
    your Redeemer, the Holy One of Israel:
'For your sake I will send to Babylon
    and bring down as fugitives all the
        Babylonians,^a
    in the ships in which they took pride.
¹⁵I am the LORD, your Holy One,
    Israel's Creator, your King.'

¹⁶This is what the LORD says—
    he who made a way through the sea,
    a path through the mighty waters,
¹⁷who drew out the chariots and horses,
    the army and reinforcements together,
and they lay there, never to rise again,
    extinguished, snuffed out like a wick:
¹⁸'Forget the former things;
    do not dwell on the past.
¹⁹See, I am doing a new thing!
    Now it springs up; do you not perceive
        it?
I am making a way in the wilderness
    and streams in the wasteland.
²⁰The wild animals honour me,
    the jackals and the owls,
because I provide water in the wilderness
    and streams in the wasteland,
to give drink to my people, my chosen,
²¹ the people I formed for myself
    that they may proclaim my praise.

²²'Yet you have not called on me, Jacob,
    you have not wearied yourselves for^b
        me, Israel.
²³You have not brought me sheep for burnt
        offerings,
    nor honoured me with your
        sacrifices.
I have not burdened you with grain
        offerings
    nor wearied you with demands for
        incense.
²⁴You have not bought any fragrant
        calamus for me,
    or lavished on me the fat of your
        sacrifices.
But you have burdened me with your sins
    and wearied me with your offences.

²⁵'I, even I, am he who blots out
    your transgressions, for my own sake,
    and remembers your sins no more.
²⁶Review the past for me,
    let us argue the matter together;
    state the case for your innocence.
²⁷Your first father sinned;
    those I sent to teach you rebelled
        against me.
²⁸So I disgraced the dignitaries of your
        temple;
    I consigned Jacob to destruction^c
    and Israel to scorn.

Israel the chosen

44 'But now listen, Jacob, my servant,
    Israel, whom I have chosen.
²This is what the LORD says—
    he who made you, who formed you in
        the womb,
    and who will help you:
do not be afraid, Jacob, my servant,
    Jeshurun,^d whom I have chosen.
³For I will pour water on the thirsty land,
    and streams on the dry ground;
I will pour out my Spirit on your
        offspring,
    and my blessing on your descendants.
⁴They will spring up like grass in a
        meadow,
    like poplar trees by flowing streams.
⁵Some will say, "I belong to the LORD";
    others will call themselves by the name
        of Jacob;

---

^a 14 Or *Chaldeans* ^b 22 Or *Jacob; I surely you have grown weary of* ^c 28 The Hebrew term refers to the irrevocable giving over of things or persons to the LORD, often by totally destroying them. ^d 2 *Jeshurun* means *the upright one*, that is, Israel.

still others will write on their hand, "The
   LORD's",
and will take the name Israel.

The LORD, not idols

6'This is what the LORD says—
   Israel's King and Redeemer, the LORD
      Almighty:
I am the first and I am the last;
   apart from me there is no God.
7Who then is like me? Let them proclaim it.
   Let them declare and lay out before me
what has happened since I established my
      ancient people,
   and what is yet to come—
   yes, let them foretell what will come.
8Do not tremble, do not be afraid.
   Did I not proclaim this and foretell it
      long ago?
You are my witnesses. Is there any God
      besides me?
   No, there is no other Rock; I know not
      one.'

9All who make idols are nothing,
   and the things they treasure are
      worthless.
Those who would speak up for them are
      blind;
   they are ignorant, to their own shame.
10Who shapes a god and casts an idol,
   which can profit nothing?
11People like that will be put to shame;
   skilled workers are only human beings.
Let them all come together and take their
      stand;
   they will be brought down to terror and
      shame.

12The blacksmith takes a tool
   and works with it in the coals;
he shapes an idol with hammers,
   he forges it with the might of his arm.
He gets hungry and loses his strength;
   he drinks no water and grows faint.
13The carpenter measures with a line
   and makes an outline with a marker;
he roughs it out with chisels
   and marks it with compasses.
He shapes it in human form,
   human form in all its glory,
   that it may dwell in a shrine.
14He cut down cedars,
   or perhaps took a cypress or oak.
He let it grow among the trees of the
      forest,
   or planted a pine, and the rain made it
      grow.
15It is used as fuel for burning;
   some of it he takes and warms himself,
   he kindles a fire and bakes bread.
But he also fashions a god and worships it;
   he makes an idol and bows down to it.
16Half of the wood he burns in the fire;
   over it he prepares his meal,
   he roasts his meat and eats his fill.
He also warms himself and says,
   'Ah! I am warm; I see the fire.'
17From the rest he makes a god, his idol;
   he bows down to it and worships.
He prays to it and says,
   'Save me! You are my god!'
18They know nothing, they understand
      nothing;
   their eyes are plastered over so that they
      cannot see,
   and their minds closed so that they
      cannot understand.
19No-one stops to think,
   no-one has the knowledge or
      understanding to say,
'Half of it I used for fuel;
   I even baked bread over its coals,
   I roasted meat and I ate.
Shall I make a detestable thing from what
      is left?
   Shall I bow down to a block of wood?'
20Such people feed on ashes, a deluded
      heart misleads them;
   they cannot save themselves, or say,
   'Is not this thing in my right hand a
      lie?'

21'Remember these things, Jacob,
   for you, Israel, are my servant.
I have made you, you are my servant;
   Israel, I will not forget you.
22I have swept away your offences like a
      cloud,
   your sins like the morning mist.
Return to me,
   for I have redeemed you.'

23Sing for joy, you heavens, for the LORD
      has done this;
   shout aloud, you earth beneath.
Burst into song, you mountains,

you forests and all your trees,
for the LORD has redeemed Jacob,
he displays his glory in Israel.

Jerusalem to be inhabited

24'This is what the LORD says—
your Redeemer, who formed you in the womb:

I am the LORD,
who has made all things,
who alone stretched out the heavens,
who spread out the earth by myself,

25who foils the signs of false prophets
and makes fools of diviners,
who overthrows the learning of the wise
and turns it into nonsense,

26who carries out the words of his servants
and fulfils the predictions of his messengers,

who says of Jerusalem, "It shall be inhabited,"
of the towns of Judah, "They shall be rebuilt,"
and of their ruins, "I will restore them,"

27who says to the watery deep, "Be dry,
and I will dry up your streams,"

28who says of Cyrus, "He is my shepherd
and will accomplish all that I please";
he will say of Jerusalem, "Let it be rebuilt,"
and of the temple, "Let its foundations be laid."'

45

'This is what the LORD says to his anointed,
to Cyrus, whose right hand I take hold of
to subdue nations before him
and to strip kings of their armour,
to open doors before him
so that gates will not be shut:
2I will go before you
and will level the mountains;[a]
I will break down gates of bronze
and cut through bars of iron.
3I will give you the treasures of darkness,
riches stored in secret places,
so that you may know that I am the LORD,

> ### IN OTHER WORDS
>
> ### Anointed
> ### Isaiah 45:1
>
> The Jews were looking forward to a messiah (meaning 'anointed one') who was anointed by God to deliver and redeem his people. The Old Testament contains lots of prophecies about the coming of such a figure; the New Testament sees that expectation fulfilled in Jesus.

the God of Israel, who summons you by name.
4For the sake of Jacob my servant,
of Israel my chosen,
I summon you by name
and bestow on you a title of honour,
though you do not acknowledge me.
5I am the LORD, and there is no other;
apart from me there is no God.
I will strengthen you,
though you have not acknowledged me,
6so that from the rising of the sun
to the place of its setting
people may know there is none besides me.
I am the LORD, and there is no other.
7I form the light and create darkness,
I bring prosperity and create disaster;
I, the LORD, do all these things.

8'You heavens above, rain down my righteousness;
let the clouds shower it down.
Let the earth open wide,
let salvation spring up,
let righteousness flourish with it;
I, the LORD, have created it.

9'Woe to those who quarrel with their Maker,
those who are nothing but potsherds
among the potsherds on the ground.
Does the clay say to the potter,
"What are you making?"

---

[a] 2 Dead Sea Scrolls and Septuagint; the meaning of the word in the Masoretic Text is uncertain.

Does your work say,
"The potter has no hands"?
¹⁰Woe to those who say to their father,
"What have you begotten?"
or to their mother,
"What have you brought to birth?"

¹¹'This is what the LORD says—
the Holy One of Israel, and its Maker:
concerning things to come,
do you question me about my children,
or give me orders about the work of my hands?
¹²It is I who made the earth
and created human beings on it.
My own hands stretched out the heavens;
I marshalled their starry hosts.
¹³I will raise up Cyrus[a] in my righteousness:
I will make all his ways straight.
He will rebuild my city
and set my exiles free,
but not for a price or reward,
says the LORD Almighty.'

¹⁴This is what the LORD says:

'The products of Egypt and the merchandise of Cush,[b]
and those tall Sabeans—
they will come over to you
and will be yours;
they will trudge behind you,
coming over to you in chains.
They will bow down before you
and plead with you, saying,
"Surely God is with you, and there is no other;
there is no other god."'

¹⁵Truly you are a God who has been hiding himself,
the God and Saviour of Israel.
¹⁶All the makers of idols will be put to shame and disgraced;
they will go off into disgrace together.
¹⁷But Israel will be saved by the LORD
with an everlasting salvation;
you will never be put to shame or disgraced,
to ages everlasting.

¹⁸For this is what the LORD says—
he who created the heavens,
he is God;
he who fashioned and made the earth,
he founded it;
he did not create it to be empty,
but formed it to be inhabited—
he says:
'I am the LORD,
and there is no other.
¹⁹I have not spoken in secret,
from somewhere in a land of darkness;
I have not said to Jacob's descendants,
"Seek me in vain."
I, the LORD, speak the truth;
I declare what is right.

²⁰'Gather together and come;
assemble, you fugitives from the nations.
Ignorant are those who carry about idols of wood,
who pray to gods that cannot save.
²¹Declare what is to be, present it—
let them take counsel together.
Who foretold this long ago,
who declared it from the distant past?
Was it not I, the LORD?
And there is no God apart from me,
a righteous God and a Saviour;
there is none but me.

²²'Turn to me and be saved,
all you ends of the earth;
for I am God, and there is no other.
²³By myself I have sworn,
my mouth has uttered in all integrity
a word that will not be revoked:
before me every knee will bow;
by me every tongue will swear.
²⁴They will say of me, "In the LORD alone are deliverance and strength."'
All who have raged against him
will come to him and be put to shame.
²⁵But all the descendants of Israel
will find deliverance in the LORD
and will make their boast in him.

Gods of Babylon

46 Bel bows down, Nebo stoops low;
their idols are borne by beasts of burden.[c]
The images that are carried about are burdensome,
a burden for the weary.

---

[a] 13 Hebrew *him*   [b] 14 That is, the upper Nile region   [c] 1 Or *are but beasts and cattle*

²They stoop and bow down together;
  unable to rescue the burden,
  they themselves go off into captivity.

³'Listen to me, house of Jacob,
  all the remnant of the house of Israel,
you whom I have upheld since your birth,
  and have carried since you were born.
⁴Even to your old age and grey hairs
  I am he, I am he who will sustain you.
I have made you and I will carry you;
  I will sustain you and I will rescue you.

⁵'With whom will you compare me or
    count me equal?
  To whom will you liken me that we
    may be compared?
⁶Some pour out gold from their bags
  and weigh out silver on the scales;
they hire a goldsmith to make it into a
    god,
  and they bow down and worship it.
⁷They lift it to their shoulders and carry it;
  they set it up in its place, and there it
    stands.
  From that spot it cannot move.
Though people cry out to it, it does not
    answer;
  it cannot save them from their
    troubles.

⁸'Remember this, keep it in mind,
  take it to heart, you rebels.
⁹Remember the former things, those of
    long ago;
  I am God, and there is no other;
  I am God, and there is none like me.
¹⁰I make known the end from the
    beginning,
  from ancient times, what is still to
    come.
I say, "My purpose will stand,
  and I will do all that I please."
¹¹From the east I summon a bird of prey;
  from a far-off land, a man to fulfil my
    purpose.
What I have said, that I will bring about;
  what I have planned, that I will do.
¹²Listen to me, you stubborn-hearted,
  you who are now far from my
    righteousness.

¹³I am bringing my righteousness near,
  it is not far away;
  and my salvation will not be delayed.
I will grant salvation to Zion,
  my splendour to Israel.

The fall of Babylon

47 'Go down, sit in the dust,
  Virgin Daughter Babylon;
sit on the ground without a throne,
  queen city of the Babylonians.ᵃ
No more will you be called
  tender or delicate.
²Take millstones and grind flour;
  take off your veil.
Lift up your skirts, bare your legs,
  and wade through the streams.
³Your nakedness will be exposed
  and your shame uncovered.
I will take vengeance;
  I will spare no-one.'

⁴Our Redeemer—the LORD Almighty is
    his name—
  is the Holy One of Israel.

⁵'Sit in silence, go into darkness,
  queen city of the Babylonians;
no more will you be called
  queen of kingdoms.
⁶I was angry with my people
  and desecrated my inheritance;
I gave them into your hand,
  and you showed them no mercy.
Even on the aged
  you laid a very heavy yoke.
⁷You said, "I am for ever—
  the eternal queen!"
But you did not consider these things
  or reflect on what might happen.

⁸'Now then, listen, you lover of pleasure,
  lounging in your security
and saying to yourself,
  "I am, and there is none besides me.
I will never be a widow
  or suffer the loss of children."
⁹Both of these will overtake you
  in a moment, on a single day:
  loss of children and widowhood.
They will come upon you in full measure,
  in spite of your many sorceries
  and all your potent spells.

ᵃ 1 Or *Chaldeans*; also in verse 5

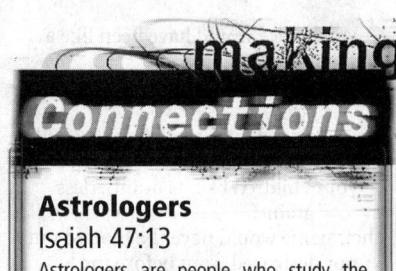

making Connections

Astrologers
Isaiah 47:13

Astrologers are people who study the stars, planets, sun and moon in the belief that they influence what happens to people on the earth. Astrology attempts to predict the future based on what is happening in the night sky.

---

¹⁰You have trusted in your wickedness
　and have said, "No-one sees me."
Your wisdom and knowledge mislead you
　when you say to yourself,
　"I am, and there is none besides me."
¹¹Disaster will come upon you,
　and you will not know how to conjure it away.
A calamity will fall upon you
　that you cannot ward off with a ransom;
a catastrophe you cannot foresee
　will suddenly come upon you.

¹²'Keep on, then, with your magic spells
　and with your many sorceries,
　which you have laboured at since childhood.
Perhaps you will succeed,
　perhaps you will cause terror.
¹³All the counsel you have received has only worn you out!
　Let your astrologers come forward,
those stargazers who make predictions month by month,
　let them save you from what is coming upon you.
¹⁴Surely they are like stubble;
　the fire will burn them up.
They cannot even save themselves
　from the power of the flame.
Here are no coals to warm anyone;
　here is no fire to sit by.

¹⁵That is all they can do for you—
　these you have dealt with
　and laboured with since childhood.
All of them go on in their error;
　there is not one that can save you.

Stubborn Israel

48 'Listen to this, house of Jacob,
　you who are called by the name of Israel
and come from the line of Judah,
you who take oaths in the name of the LORD
　and invoke the God of Israel—
　but not in truth or righteousness—
²you who call yourselves citizens of the holy city
　and claim to rely on the God of Israel—
　the LORD Almighty is his name:
³I foretold the former things long ago,
　my mouth announced them and I made them known;
　then suddenly I acted, and they came to pass.
⁴For I knew how stubborn you were;
　the sinews of your neck were iron,
　your forehead was bronze.
⁵Therefore I told you these things long ago;
　before they happened I announced them to you
so that you could not say,
　"My images brought them about;
　my wooden image and metal god ordained them."
⁶You have heard these things; look at them all.
　Will you not admit them?

'From now on I will tell you of new things,
　of hidden things unknown to you.
⁷They are created now, and not long ago;
　you have not heard of them before today.
So you cannot say,
　"Yes, I knew of them."
⁸You have neither heard nor understood;
　from of old your ears have not been open.
Well do I know how treacherous you are;
　you were called a rebel from birth.
⁹For my own name's sake I delay my wrath;

for the sake of my praise I hold it back from you,
so as not to destroy you completely.
¹⁰See, I have refined you, though not as silver;
I have tested you in the furnace of affliction.
¹¹For my own sake, for my own sake, I do this.
How can I let myself be defamed?
I will not yield my glory to another.

Israel freed

¹²'Listen to me, Jacob,
Israel, whom I have called:
I am he;
I am the first and I am the last.
¹³My own hand laid the foundations of the earth,
and my right hand spread out the heavens;
when I summon them,
they all stand up together.

¹⁴'Come together, all of you, and listen:
which of the idols has foretold these things?
The LORD's chosen ally
will carry out his purpose against Babylon;
his arm will be against the Babylonians.*ᵃ*

¹⁵I, even I, have spoken;
yes, I have called him.
I will bring him,
and he will succeed in his mission.

¹⁶'Come near me and listen to this:

'From the first announcement I have not spoken in secret;
at the time it happens, I am there.'

And now the Sovereign LORD has sent me, endowed with his Spirit.

¹⁷This is what the LORD says—
your Redeemer, the Holy One of Israel:
'I am the LORD your God,
who teaches you what is best for you,
who directs you in the way you should go.
¹⁸If only you had paid attention to my commands,
your peace would have been like a river,
your well-being like the waves of the sea.
¹⁹Your descendants would have been like the sand,
your children like its numberless grains;
their name would never be blotted out
nor destroyed from before me.'

²⁰Leave Babylon,
flee from the Babylonians!
Announce this with shouts of joy
and proclaim it.
Send it out to the ends of the earth;
say, 'The LORD has redeemed his servant Jacob.'
²¹They did not thirst when he led them through the deserts;
he made water flow for them from the rock;
he split the rock
and water gushed out.

²²'There is no peace,' says the LORD, 'for the wicked.'

The servant of the LORD

49 Listen to me, you islands;
hear this, you distant nations:
before I was born the LORD called me;
from my birth he has made mention of my name.
²He made my mouth like a sharpened sword,
in the shadow of his hand he hid me;
he made me into a polished arrow
and concealed me in his quiver.
³He said to me, 'You are my servant,
Israel, in whom I will display my splendour.'
⁴But I said, 'I have laboured in vain;
I have spent my strength for nothing at all.
Yet what is due to me is in the LORD's hand,
and my reward is with my God.'

⁵And now the LORD says—
he who formed me in the womb to be his servant

ᵃ 14 Or *Chaldeans*; also in verse 20

to bring Jacob back to him
and gather Israel to himself,
for I am^a honoured in the eyes of the LORD
and my God has been my strength—
⁶he says:

'It is too small a thing for you to be my servant
to restore the tribes of Jacob
and bring back those of Israel I have kept.
I will also make you a light for the Gentiles,
that my salvation may reach to the ends of the earth.'

⁷This is what the LORD says—
the Redeemer and Holy One of Israel—
to him who was despised and abhorred by the nation,
to the servant of rulers:
'Kings will see you and stand up,
princes will see and bow down,
because of the LORD, who is faithful,
the Holy One of Israel, who has chosen you.'

Restoration of Israel

⁸This is what the LORD says:

'In the time of my favour I will answer you,
and in the day of salvation I will help you;
I will keep you and will make you
to be a covenant for the people,
to restore the land
and to reassign its desolate inheritances,
⁹to say to the captives, "Come out,"
and to those in darkness, "Be free!"

'They will feed beside the roads
and find pasture on every barren hill.
¹⁰They will neither hunger nor thirst,
nor will the desert heat or the sun beat down on them.
He who has compassion on them will guide them
and lead them beside springs of water.
¹¹I will turn all my mountains into roads,
and my highways will be raised up.
¹²See, they will come from afar—
some from the north, some from the west,
some from the region of Aswan.'^b

¹³Shout for joy, you heavens;
rejoice, you earth;
burst into song, you mountains!
For the LORD comforts his people
and will have compassion on his afflicted ones.

¹⁴But Zion said, 'The LORD has forsaken me,
the Lord has forgotten me.'

¹⁵'Can a mother forget the baby at her breast
and have no compassion on the child she has borne?
Though she may forget,
I will not forget you!
¹⁶See, I have engraved you on the palms of my hands;
your walls are ever before me.
¹⁷Your children hasten back,
and those who laid you waste depart from you.
¹⁸Lift up your eyes and look around;
all your children gather and come to you.
As surely as I live,' declares the LORD,
'you will wear them all as ornaments;
you will put them on, like a bride.

¹⁹'Though you were ruined and made desolate
and your land laid waste,
now you will be too small for your people,
and those who devoured you will be far away.
²⁰The children born during your bereavement
will yet say in your hearing,
"This place is too small for us;
give us more space to live in."
²¹Then you will say in your heart,
"Who bore me these?
I was bereaved and barren;
I was exiled and rejected.

---

^a 5 Or *him, I but Israel would not be gathered; I yet I will be*   ^b 12 Dead Sea Scrolls; Masoretic Text *Sinim*

> Who brought these up?
> I was left all alone,
> but these—where have they come from?"'

²²This is what the Sovereign Lord says:

> 'See, I will beckon to the nations,
> I will lift up my banner to the peoples;
> they will bring your sons in their arms
> and carry your daughters on their hips.
> ²³Kings will be your foster fathers,
> and their queens your nursing mothers.
> They will bow down before you with their faces to the ground;
> they will lick the dust at your feet.
> Then you will know that I am the Lord;
> those who hope in me will not be disappointed.'

²⁴Can plunder be taken from warriors,
or captives be rescued from the fierce?[a]

²⁵But this is what the Lord says:

> 'Yes, captives will be taken from warriors,
> and plunder retrieved from the fierce;
> I will contend with those who contend with you,
> and your children I will save.
> ²⁶I will make your oppressors eat their own flesh;
> they will be drunk on their own blood, as with wine.
> Then the whole human race will know
> that I, the Lord, am your Saviour,
> your Redeemer, the Mighty One of Jacob.'

Israel's sin and the servant's obedience

50 This is what the Lord says:

> 'Where is your mother's certificate of divorce
> with which I sent her away?
> Or to which of my creditors
> did I sell you?
> Because of your sins you were sold;
> because of your transgressions your mother was sent away.
> ²When I came, why was there no-one?
> When I called, why was there no-one to answer?

Certificate of divorce
Isaiah 50:1
The Law of Moses allowed a man to divorce his wife in some cases (Deuteronomy 24:1–4). The man would give his wife a certificate of divorce which would allow her to remarry.

> Was my arm too short to deliver you?
> Do I lack the strength to rescue you?
> By a mere rebuke I dry up the sea,
> I turn rivers into a desert;
> their fish rot for lack of water
> and die of thirst.
> ³I clothe the heavens with darkness
> and make sackcloth its covering.'

⁴The Sovereign Lord has given me an instructed tongue,
to know the word that sustains the weary.
He wakens me morning by morning,
wakens my ear to listen like one being taught.
⁵The Sovereign Lord has opened my ears;
I have not been rebellious,
I have not turned away.
⁶I offered my back to those who beat me,
my cheeks to those who pulled out my beard;
I did not hide my face
from mocking and spitting.
⁷Because the Sovereign Lord helps me,
I will not be disgraced.
Therefore have I set my face like flint,
and I know I will not be put to shame.
⁸He who vindicates me is near.
Who then will bring charges against me?
Let us face each other!
Who are my accusers?
Let them confront me!

---

[a] 24 Dead Sea Scrolls, Vulgate and Syriac (see also Septuagint and verse 25); Masoretic Text *righteous*

⁹It is the Sovereign LORD who helps me.
  Who will condemn me?
 They will all wear out like a garment;
  the moths will eat them up.

¹⁰Who among you fears the LORD
  and obeys the word of his servant?
 Let those who walk in the dark,
  who have no light,
 trust in the name of the LORD
  and rely on their God.
¹¹But now, all you who light fires
  and provide yourselves with flaming torches,
 go, walk in the light of your fires
  and of the torches you have set ablaze.
 This is what you shall receive from my hand:
  you will lie down in torment.

Everlasting salvation for Zion

51 'Listen to me, you who pursue righteousness
  and who seek the LORD:
 look to the rock from which you were cut
  and to the quarry from which you were hewn;
 ²look to Abraham, your father,
  and to Sarah, who gave you birth.
 When I called him he was only one man,
  and I blessed him and made him many.
 ³The LORD will surely comfort Zion
  and will look with compassion on all her ruins;
 he will make her deserts like Eden,
  her wastelands like the garden of the LORD.
 Joy and gladness will be found in her,
  thanksgiving and the sound of singing.

⁴'Listen to me, my people;
  hear me, my nation:
 instruction will go out from me;
  my justice will become a light to the nations.
 ⁵My righteousness draws near speedily,
  my salvation is on the way,
  and my arm will bring justice to the nations.
 The islands will look to me
  and wait in hope for my arm.
 ⁶Lift up your eyes to the heavens,
  look at the earth beneath;
 the heavens will vanish like smoke,
  the earth will wear out like a garment
  and its inhabitants die like flies.
 But my salvation will last for ever,
  my righteousness will never fail.

⁷'Hear me, you who know what is right,
  you people who have taken my instruction to heart:
 do not fear the reproach of mere mortals
  or be terrified by their insults.
 ⁸For the moth will eat them up like a garment;
  the worm will devour them like wool.
 But my righteousness will last for ever,
  my salvation through all generations.'

⁹Awake, awake, arm of the LORD,
  clothe yourself with strength!
 Awake, as in days gone by,
  as in generations of old.
 Was it not you who cut Rahab to pieces,
  who pierced that monster through?
¹⁰Was it not you who dried up the sea,
  the waters of the great deep,
 who made a road in the depths of the sea
  so that the redeemed might cross over?
¹¹Those the LORD has rescued will return.
  They will enter Zion with singing;
  everlasting joy will crown their heads.
 Gladness and joy will overtake them,
  and sorrow and sighing will flee away.

¹²'I, even I, am he who comforts you.
  Who are you that you fear mere mortals,
  human beings, who are but grass,
¹³that you forget the LORD your Maker,
  who stretched out the heavens
  and laid the foundations of the earth,
 that you live in constant terror every day
  because of the wrath of the oppressor,
  who is bent on destruction?
 For where is the wrath of the oppressor?
¹⁴ The cowering prisoners will soon be set free;
  they will not die in their dungeon,
  nor will they lack bread.
¹⁵For I am the LORD your God,
  who stirs up the sea so that its waves roar—
  the LORD Almighty is his name.
¹⁶I have put my words in your mouth

The cup of the LORD's wrath

17 Awake, awake!
  Rise up, Jerusalem,
you who have drunk from the hand of the
    LORD
  the cup of his wrath,
you who have drained to its dregs
  the goblet that makes people stagger.
18 Among all the children she bore
  there was none to guide her;
among all the children she brought up
  there was none to take her by the hand.
19 These double calamities have come upon
    you—
  who can comfort you?—
ruin and destruction, famine and
    sword—
  who can[a] console you?
20 Your children have fainted;
  they lie at every street corner,
  like antelope caught in a net.
They are filled with the wrath of the LORD,
  with the rebuke of your God.
21 Therefore hear this, you afflicted one,
  made drunk, but not with wine.
22 This is what your Sovereign LORD says,
  your God, who defends his people:
'See, I have taken out of your hand
  the cup that made you stagger;
from that cup, the goblet of my wrath,
  you will never drink again.
23 I will put it into the hands of your
    tormentors,
  who said to you,
"Fall prostrate that we may walk on
    you."
And you made your back like the ground,
  like a street to be walked on.'

52

Awake, awake, Zion,
  clothe yourself with strength!
Put on your garments of splendour,
  Jerusalem, the holy city.
The uncircumcised and defiled
  will not enter you again.
2 Shake off your dust;
  rise up, sit enthroned, Jerusalem.
Free yourself from the chains on your
    neck,
  Daughter Zion, now a captive.

3 For this is what the LORD says:

'You were sold for nothing,
  and without money you will be
    redeemed.'

4 For this is what the Sovereign LORD
says:

'At first my people went down to Egypt to
    live;
lately, Assyria has oppressed them.

5 'And now what do I have here?' declares
the LORD.

'For my people have been taken away for
    nothing,
  and those who rule them mock,'[b]
            declares the LORD.
'And all day long
  my name is constantly blasphemed.
6 Therefore my people will know my name;
  therefore in that day they will know
  that it is I who foretold it.
  Yes, it is I.'

7 How beautiful on the mountains
  are the feet of those who bring good
    news,
who proclaim peace,
  who bring good tidings,
  who proclaim salvation,
who say to Zion,
  'Your God reigns!'
8 Listen! Your watchmen lift up their
    voices;
  together they shout for joy.
When the LORD returns to Zion,
  they will see it with their own eyes.
9 Burst into songs of joy together,
  you ruins of Jerusalem,
for the LORD has comforted his people,
  he has redeemed Jerusalem.

---

[a] 19 Dead Sea Scrolls, Septuagint, Vulgate and Syriac; Masoretic Text *how can I*   [b] 5 Dead Sea Scrolls and Vulgate; Masoretic Text *wail*

¹⁰The Lord will lay bare his holy arm
in the sight of all the nations,
and all the ends of the earth will see
the salvation of our God.

¹¹Depart, depart, go out from there!
Touch no unclean thing!
Come out from it and be pure,
you who carry the articles of the Lord's
house.
¹²But you will not leave in haste
or go in flight;
for the Lord will go before you,
the God of Israel will be your rear
guard.

The suffering and glory of the servant

¹³See, my servant will act wisely;[a]
he will be raised and lifted up and
highly exalted.
¹⁴Just as there were many who were
appalled at him[b]—
his appearance was so disfigured
beyond that of any human being
and his form marred beyond human
likeness—
¹⁵so he will sprinkle many nations,[c]
and kings will shut their mouths
because of him.
For what they were not told, they will see,
and what they have not heard, they will
understand.

53

Who has believed our message
and to whom has the arm of the
Lord been revealed?
²He grew up before him like a tender shoot,
and like a root out of dry ground.
He had no beauty or majesty to attract us
to him,
nothing in his appearance that we
should desire him.
³He was despised and rejected by others,
a man of suffering, and familiar with
pain.
Like one from whom people hide their
faces
he was despised, and we held him in
low esteem.

> **IN OTHER WORDS**
>
> **Transgression**
> Isaiah 53:8
>
> 'Transgression' is another word for sin or wrongdoing, but transgression is a deliberate breaking of the law rather than an accidental one. In the Old Testament, the Hebrew word that is most often translated as 'transgression' means 'rebellion'.

⁴Surely he took up our pain
and bore our suffering,
yet we considered him punished by God,
stricken by him, and afflicted.
⁵But he was pierced for our transgressions,
he was crushed for our iniquities;
the punishment that brought us peace
was on him,
and by his wounds we are healed.
⁶We all, like sheep, have gone astray,
each of us has turned to our own way;
and the Lord has laid on him
the iniquity of us all.

⁷He was oppressed and afflicted,
yet he did not open his mouth;
he was led like a lamb to the slaughter,
and as a sheep before its shearers is
silent,
so he did not open his mouth.
⁸By oppression[d] and judgment he was
taken away.
Yet who of his generation protested?
For he was cut off from the land of the
living;
for the transgression of my people he
was punished.[e]
⁹He was assigned a grave with the wicked,
and with the rich in his death,
though he had done no violence,
nor was any deceit in his mouth.

¹⁰Yet it was the Lord's will to crush him and
cause him to suffer,
and though the Lord makes[f] his life an
offering for sin,

---

[a] 13 Or *will prosper* [b] 14 Hebrew *you* [c] 15 Or *so will many nations be amazed at him* (see also Septuagint) [d] 8 Or *From arrest* [e] 8 Or *generation considered / that he was cut off from the land of the living, / that he was punished for the transgression of my people?* [f] 10 Hebrew *though you make*

he will see his offspring and prolong his days,
and the will of the LORD will prosper in his hand.
11 After he has suffered,
he will see the light of life[a] and be satisfied;[b]
by his knowledge[c] my righteous servant will justify many,
and he will bear their iniquities.
12 Therefore I will give him a portion among the great,[d]
and he will divide the spoils with the strong,[e]
because he poured out his life unto death,
and was numbered with the transgressors.
For he bore the sin of many,
and made intercession for the transgressors.

The future glory of Zion

54 'Sing, barren woman,
you who never bore a child;
burst into song, shout for joy,
you who were never in labour;
because more are the children of the desolate woman
than of her who has a husband,'
says the LORD.
2 'Enlarge the place of your tent,
stretch your tent curtains wide,
do not hold back;
lengthen your cords,
strengthen your stakes.
3 For you will spread out to the right and to the left;
your descendants will dispossess nations
and settle in their desolate cities.

4 'Do not be afraid; you will not be put to shame.
Do not fear disgrace; you will not be humiliated.
You will forget the shame of your youth
and remember no more the reproach of your widowhood.
5 For your Maker is your husband—
the LORD Almighty is his name—
the Holy One of Israel is your Redeemer;
he is called the God of all the earth.
6 The LORD will call you back
as if you were a wife deserted and distressed in spirit—
a wife who married young,
only to be rejected,' says your God.
7 'For a brief moment I abandoned you,
but with deep compassion I will bring you back.
8 In a surge of anger
I hid my face from you for a moment,
but with everlasting kindness
I will have compassion on you,'
says the LORD your Redeemer.

9 'To me this is like the days of Noah,
when I swore that the waters of Noah would never again cover the earth.
So now I have sworn not to be angry with you,
never to rebuke you again.
10 Though the mountains be shaken
and the hills be removed,
yet my unfailing love for you will not be shaken
nor my covenant of peace be removed,'
says the LORD, who has compassion on you.

11 'Afflicted city, lashed by storms and not comforted,
I will rebuild you with stones of turquoise,[f]
your foundations with lapis lazuli.
12 I will make your battlements of rubies,
your gates of sparkling jewels,
and all your walls of precious stones.
13 All your children will be taught by the LORD,
and great will be their peace.
14 In righteousness you will be established:
tyranny will be far from you;
you will have nothing to fear.
Terror will be far removed;
it will not come near you.
15 If anyone does attack you, it will not be my doing;
whoever attacks you will surrender to you.

---

[a] 11 Dead Sea Scrolls (see also Septuagint); Masoretic Text does not have *the light of life*. [b] 11 Or (with Masoretic Text) *11 He will see the fruit of his suffering / and will be satisfied* [c] 11 Or *by knowledge of him* [d] 12 Or *many* [e] 12 Or *numerous* [f] 11 The meaning of the Hebrew for this word is uncertain.

Making Connections

Blacksmith
Isaiah 54:16

A blacksmith would melt iron over a fire and then pour it into a mould and allow it to cool. Once the metal had cooled it could be pounded into shape. Blacksmiths made weapons as well as tools for use in the home and on the farm.

16 'See, it is I who created the blacksmith
who fans the coals into flame
and forges a weapon fit for its work.
And it is I who have created the destroyer to work havoc;
17 no weapon forged against you will prevail,
and you will refute every tongue that accuses you.
This is the heritage of the servants of the LORD,
and this is their vindication from me,'
declares the LORD.

Invitation to the thirsty

55 'Come, all you who are thirsty,
come to the waters;
and you who have no money,
come, buy and eat!
Come, buy wine and milk
without money and without cost.
2 Why spend money on what is not bread,
and your labour on what does not satisfy?
Listen, listen to me, and eat what is good,
and you will delight in the richest of fare.
3 Give ear and come to me;
listen, that you may live.
I will make an everlasting covenant with you,
my faithful love promised to David.
4 See, I have made him a witness to the peoples,
a ruler and commander of the peoples.
5 Surely you will summon nations you know not,
and nations you do not know will come running to you,
because of the LORD your God,
the Holy One of Israel,
for he has endowed you with splendour.'

6 Seek the LORD while he may be found;
call on him while he is near.
7 Let the wicked forsake their ways
and the unrighteous their thoughts.
Let them turn to the LORD, and he will have mercy on them,
and to our God, for he will freely pardon.

8 'For my thoughts are not your thoughts,
neither are your ways my ways,'
declares the LORD.
9 'As the heavens are higher than the earth,
so are my ways higher than your ways
and my thoughts than your thoughts.
10 As the rain and the snow
come down from heaven,
and do not return to it
without watering the earth
and making it bud and flourish,
so that it yields seed for the sower and bread for the eater,
11 so is my word that goes out from my mouth:
it will not return to me empty,
but will accomplish what I desire
and achieve the purpose for which I sent it.
12 You will go out in joy
and be led forth in peace;
the mountains and hills
will burst into song before you,
and all the trees of the field
will clap their hands.
13 Instead of the thorn-bush will grow the juniper,
and instead of briers the myrtle will grow.
This will be for the LORD's renown,
for an everlasting sign,
that will endure for ever.'

Salvation for others

56 This is what the LORD says:

'Maintain justice
  and do what is right,
for my salvation is close at hand
  and my righteousness will soon be revealed.
²Blessed are those who do this—
  who hold it fast,
those who keep the Sabbath without desecrating it,
  and keep their hands from doing any evil.'

³Let no foreigners who have bound themselves to the LORD say,
  'The LORD will surely exclude me from his people.'
And let no eunuch complain,
  'I am only a dry tree.'

⁴For this is what the LORD says:

'To the eunuchs who keep my Sabbaths,
  who choose what pleases me
  and hold fast to my covenant—
⁵to them I will give within my temple and its walls
  a memorial and a name
  better than sons and daughters;
I will give them an everlasting name
  that will endure for ever.
⁶And foreigners who bind themselves to the LORD
  to minister to him,
to love the name of the LORD,
  and to be his servants,
all who keep the Sabbath without desecrating it
  and who hold fast to my covenant—
⁷these I will bring to my holy mountain
  and give them joy in my house of prayer.
Their burnt offerings and sacrifices
  will be accepted on my altar;
for my house will be called
  a house of prayer for all nations.'
⁸The Sovereign LORD declares—
  he who gathers the exiles of Israel:
'I will gather still others to them
  besides those already gathered.'

God's accusation against the wicked

⁹Come, all you beasts of the field,
  come and devour, all you beasts of the forest!
¹⁰Israel's watchmen are blind,
  they all lack knowledge;
they are all mute dogs,
  they cannot bark;
they lie around and dream,
  they love to sleep.
¹¹They are dogs with mighty appetites;
  they never have enough.
They are shepherds who lack understanding;
  they all turn to their own way,
  they seek their own gain.
¹²'Come,' each one cries, 'let me get wine!
  Let us drink our fill of beer!
And tomorrow will be like today,
  or even far better.'

57 The righteous perish,
  and no-one takes it to heart;
the devout are taken away,
  and no-one understands
that the righteous are taken away
  to be spared from evil.
²Those who walk uprightly
  enter into peace;
they find rest as they lie in death.

³'But you—come here, you children of a sorceress,
  you offspring of adulterers and prostitutes!
⁴Whom are you mocking?
  At whom do you sneer
  and stick out your tongue?
Are you not a brood of rebels,
  the offspring of liars?
⁵You burn with lust among the oaks
  and under every spreading tree;
you sacrifice your children in the ravines
  and under the overhanging crags.
⁶The idols among the smooth stones of the ravines are your portion;
  they, they are your lot.
Yes, to them you have poured out drink offerings
  and offered grain offerings.
In view of all this, should I relent?

7 You have made your bed on a high and
    lofty hill;
  there you went up to offer your
    sacrifices.
8 Behind your doors and your doorposts
    you have put your pagan symbols.
  Forsaking me, you uncovered your bed,
    you climbed into it and opened it wide;
  you made a pact with those whose beds
      you love,
    and you looked on their nakedness.
9 You went to Molek*a* with olive oil
    and increased your perfumes.
  You sent your ambassadors*b* far away;
    you descended to the very realm of the
      dead!
10 You wearied yourself by such going
      about,
    but you would not say, "It is hopeless."
  You found renewal of your strength,
    and so you did not faint.

11 'Whom have you so dreaded and feared
    that you have not been true to me,
  and have neither remembered me
    nor taken this to heart?
  Is it not because I have long been silent
    that you do not fear me?
12 I will expose your righteousness and your
      works,
    and they will not benefit you.
13 When you cry out for help,
    let your collection of idols save you!
  The wind will carry all of them off,
    a mere breath will blow them away.
  But whoever takes refuge in me
    will inherit the land
    and possess my holy mountain.'

Comfort for the contrite

14 And it will be said:

  'Build up, build up, prepare the road!
    Remove the obstacles out of the way of
      my people.'
15 For this is what the high and exalted One
      says—
    he who lives for ever, whose name is
      holy:
  'I live in a high and holy place,
    but also with those who are contrite
      and lowly in spirit,
  to revive the spirit of the lowly
    and to revive the heart of the contrite.
16 I will not accuse them for ever,
    nor will I always be angry,
  for then they would faint away because of
      me—
    the very people I have created.
17 I was enraged by their sinful greed;
    I punished them, and hid my face in
      anger,
    yet they kept on in their wilful ways.
18 I have seen their ways, but I will heal them;
    I will guide them and restore comfort
      to them,
19 creating praise on the lips of the
      mourners in Israel.
  Peace, peace, to those far and near,'
    says the LORD. 'And I will heal them.'
20 But the wicked are like the tossing sea,
    which cannot rest,
    whose waves cast up mire and mud.
21 'There is no peace,' says my God, 'for the
      wicked.'

True fasting

58 'Shout it aloud, do not hold back.
      Raise your voice like a trumpet.
  Declare to my people their rebellion
    and to the house of Jacob their sins.
2 For day after day they seek me out;
    they seem eager to know my ways,
  as if they were a nation that does what is
      right
    and has not forsaken the commands of
      its God.
  They ask me for just decisions
    and seem eager for God to come near
      them.
3 "Why have we fasted," they say,
    "and you have not seen it?
  Why have we humbled ourselves,
    and you have not noticed?"

  'Yet on the day of your fasting, you do as
      you please
    and exploit all your workers.
4 Your fasting ends in quarrelling and strife,
    and in striking each other with wicked
      fists.
  You cannot fast as you do today

---

a 9 Or *to the king*   *b* 9 Or *idols*

> **IN OTHER WORDS**
>
> **Fasting**
> **Isaiah 58:3**
> Fasting in the Bible usually involves giving up food for a period of time, often to focus on God for some special request, or to show him that he is worth any sacrifice.

and expect your voice to be heard on high.
5 Is this the kind of fast I have chosen,
  only a day for people to humble themselves?
Is it only for bowing one's head like a reed
  and for lying in sackcloth and ashes?
Is that what you call a fast,
  a day acceptable to the LORD?

6 'Is not this the kind of fasting I have chosen:
to loose the chains of injustice
  and untie the cords of the yoke,
to set the oppressed free
  and break every yoke?
7 Is it not to share your food with the hungry
  and to provide the poor wanderer with shelter—
when you see the naked, to clothe them,
  and not to turn away from your own flesh and blood?
8 Then your light will break forth like the dawn,
  and your healing will quickly appear;
then your righteousness[a] will go before you,
  and the glory of the LORD will be your rear guard.
9 Then you will call, and the LORD will answer;
  you will cry for help, and he will say: here am I.

'If you do away with the yoke of oppression,
  with the pointing finger and malicious talk,
10 and if you spend yourselves on behalf of the hungry
  and satisfy the needs of the oppressed,
then your light will rise in the darkness,
  and your night will become like the noonday.
11 The LORD will guide you always;
  he will satisfy your needs in a sun-scorched land
  and will strengthen your frame.
You will be like a well-watered garden,
  like a spring whose waters never fail.
12 Your people will rebuild the ancient ruins
  and will raise up the age-old foundations;
you will be called Repairer of Broken Walls,
  Restorer of Streets with Dwellings.

13 'If you keep your feet from breaking the Sabbath
  and from doing as you please on my holy day,
if you call the Sabbath a delight
  and the LORD's holy day honourable,
and if you honour it by not going your own way
  and not doing as you please or speaking idle words,
14 then you will find your joy in the LORD,
  and I will cause you to ride in triumph on the heights of the land
  and to feast on the inheritance of your father Jacob.'
For the mouth of the LORD has spoken.

Sin, confession and redemption

59 Surely the arm of the LORD is not too short to save,
  nor his ear too dull to hear.
2 But your iniquities have separated you from your God;
  your sins have hidden his face from you, so that he will not hear.
3 For your hands are stained with blood,
  your fingers with guilt.
Your lips have spoken falsely,
  and your tongue mutters wicked things.

---

[a] 8 Or *your righteous One*

⁴No-one calls for justice;
no-one pleads their case with integrity.
They rely on empty arguments, they utter lies;
they conceive trouble and give birth to evil.
⁵They hatch the eggs of vipers
and spin a spider's web.
Whoever eats their eggs will die,
and when one is broken, an adder is hatched.
⁶Their cobwebs are useless for clothing;
they cannot cover themselves with what they make.
Their deeds are evil deeds,
and acts of violence are in their hands.
⁷Their feet rush into sin;
they are swift to shed innocent blood.
They pursue evil schemes;
acts of violence mark their ways.
⁸The way of peace they do not know;
there is no justice in their paths.
They have turned them into crooked roads;
no-one who walks along them will know peace.

⁹So justice is far from us,
and righteousness does not reach us.
We look for light, but all is darkness;
for brightness, but we walk in deep shadows.
¹⁰Like the blind we grope along the wall,
feeling our way like people without eyes.
At midday we stumble as if it were twilight;
among the strong, we are like the dead.
¹¹We all growl like bears;
we moan mournfully like doves.
We look for justice, but find none;
for deliverance, but it is far away.

¹²For our offences are many in your sight,
and our sins testify against us.
Our offences are ever with us,
and we acknowledge our iniquities:
¹³rebellion and treachery against the LORD,
turning our backs on our God,
inciting revolt and oppression,
uttering lies our hearts have conceived.
¹⁴So justice is driven back,
and righteousness stands at a distance;
truth has stumbled in the streets,
honesty cannot enter.
¹⁵Truth is nowhere to be found,
and whoever shuns evil becomes a prey.

The LORD looked and was displeased
that there was no justice.
¹⁶He saw that there was no-one,
he was appalled that there was no-one to intervene;
so his own arm achieved salvation for him,
and his own righteousness sustained him.
¹⁷He put on righteousness as his breastplate,
and the helmet of salvation on his head;
he put on the garments of vengeance
and wrapped himself in zeal as in a cloak.
¹⁸According to what they have done,
so will he repay
wrath to his enemies
and retribution to his foes;
he will repay the islands their due.
¹⁹From the west, people will fear the name of the LORD,
and from the rising of the sun, they will revere his glory.
For he will come like a pent-up flood
that the breath of the LORD drives along.[a]

²⁰'The Redeemer will come to Zion,
to those in Jacob who repent of their sins,'

declares the LORD.

²¹'As for me, this is my covenant with them,' says the LORD. 'My Spirit, who is on you, and my words that I have put in your mouth will not depart from your mouth, or from the mouths of your children, or from the mouths of their descendants from this time on and for ever,' says the LORD.

The glory of Zion

60 'Arise, shine, for your light has come,
and the glory of the LORD rises upon you.

---

[a] 19 Or *When enemies come in like a flood, / the Spirit of the LORD will put them to flight*

²See, darkness covers the earth
  and thick darkness is over the peoples,
but the LORD rises upon you
  and his glory appears over you.
³Nations will come to your light,
  and kings to the brightness of your dawn.

⁴'Lift up your eyes and look about you:
  all assemble and come to you;
your sons come from afar,
  and your daughters are carried on the hip.
⁵Then you will look and be radiant,
  your heart will throb and swell with joy;
the wealth on the seas will be brought to you,
  to you the riches of the nations will come.
⁶Herds of camels will cover your land,
  young camels of Midian and Ephah.
And all from Sheba will come,
  bearing gold and incense
and proclaiming the praise of the LORD.
⁷All Kedar's flocks will be gathered to you,
  the rams of Nebaioth will serve you;
they will be accepted as offerings on my altar,
  and I will adorn my glorious temple.

⁸'Who are these that fly along like clouds,
  like doves to their nests?
⁹Surely the islands look to me;
  in the lead are the ships of Tarshish,^{a}
bringing your children from afar,
  with their silver and gold,
to the honour of the LORD your God,
  the Holy One of Israel,
for he has endowed you with splendour.

¹⁰'Foreigners will rebuild your walls,
  and their kings will serve you.
Though in anger I struck you,
  in favour I will show you compassion.
¹¹Your gates will always stand open,
  they will never be shut, day or night,
so that people may bring you the wealth of the nations—
  their kings led in triumphal procession.
¹²For the nation or kingdom that will not serve you will perish;
  it will be utterly ruined.

¹³'The glory of Lebanon will come to you,
  the juniper, the fir and the cypress together,
to adorn my sanctuary;
  and I will glorify the place for my feet.
¹⁴The children of your oppressors will come bowing before you;
  all who despise you will bow down at your feet
and will call you the City of the LORD,
  Zion of the Holy One of Israel.

¹⁵'Although you have been forsaken and hated,
  with no-one travelling through,
I will make you the everlasting pride
  and the joy of all generations.
¹⁶You will drink the milk of nations
  and be nursed at royal breasts.
Then you will know that I, the LORD, am your Saviour,
  your Redeemer, the Mighty One of Jacob.
¹⁷Instead of bronze I will bring you gold,
  and silver in place of iron.
Instead of wood I will bring you bronze,
  and iron in place of stones.
I will make peace your governor
  and well-being your ruler.
¹⁸No longer will violence be heard in your land,
  nor ruin or destruction within your borders,
but you will call your walls Salvation
  and your gates Praise.
¹⁹The sun will no more be your light by day,
  nor will the brightness of the moon shine on you,
for the LORD will be your everlasting light,
  and your God will be your glory.
²⁰Your sun will never set again,
  and your moon will wane no more;
the LORD will be your everlasting light,
  and your days of sorrow will end.
²¹Then will all your people be righteous
  and they will possess the land for ever.

---

^{a} 9 Or *the trading ships*

They are the shoot I have planted,
   the work of my hands,
   for the display of my splendour.
22The least of you will become a thousand,
   the smallest a mighty nation.
I am the LORD;
   in its time I will do this swiftly.'

The year of the LORD's favour

61 The Spirit of the Sovereign LORD is on me,
   because the LORD has anointed me
   to proclaim good news to the poor.
He has sent me to bind up the broken-hearted,
   to proclaim freedom for the captives
   and release from darkness for the prisoners,*a*
2to proclaim the year of the LORD's favour
   and the day of vengeance of our God,
to comfort all who mourn,
3   and provide for those who grieve in Zion—
to bestow on them a crown of beauty
   instead of ashes,
the oil of joy
   instead of mourning,
and a garment of praise
   instead of a spirit of despair.
They will be called mighty oaks,
   a planting of the LORD
   for the display of his splendour.

4They will rebuild the ancient ruins
   and restore the places long devastated;
they will renew the ruined cities
   that have been devastated for generations.
5Strangers will shepherd your flocks;
   foreigners will work your fields and vineyards.
6And you will be called priests of the LORD,
   you will be named ministers of our God.
You will feed on the wealth of nations,
   and in their riches you will boast.

7Instead of your shame
   you will receive a double portion,
and instead of disgrace
   you will rejoice in your inheritance.
And so you will inherit a double portion in your land,
   and everlasting joy will be yours.

8'For I, the LORD, love justice;
   I hate robbery and wrongdoing.
In my faithfulness I will reward my people
   and make an everlasting covenant with them.
9Their descendants will be known among the nations
   and their offspring among the peoples.
All who see them will acknowledge
   that they are a people the LORD has blessed.'

10I delight greatly in the LORD;
   my soul rejoices in my God.
For he has clothed me with garments of salvation
   and arrayed me in a robe of his righteousness,
as a bridegroom adorns his head like a priest,
   and as a bride adorns herself with her jewels.
11For as the soil makes the young plant come up
   and a garden causes seeds to grow,
so the Sovereign LORD will make righteousness
   and praise spring up before all nations.

A prophecy about Jesus
Isaiah 61:1–2

When Jesus started his ministry, he went to the synagogue in Nazareth where he had been brought up (Luke 4:16–21). He stood up and read these words aloud from the scroll of Isaiah, and then he said that he was the one who would make them come true.

---

a 1 Hebrew; Septuagint *the blind*

Zion's new name

62 For Zion's sake I will not keep silent,
for Jerusalem's sake I will not remain quiet,
till her vindication shines out like the dawn,
her salvation like a blazing torch.
²The nations will see your vindication,
and all kings your glory;
you will be called by a new name
that the mouth of the LORD will bestow.
³You will be a crown of splendour in the LORD's hand,
a royal diadem in the hand of your God.
⁴No longer will they call you Deserted,
or name your land Desolate.
But you will be called Hephzibah,[a]
and your land Beulah;[b]
for the LORD will take delight in you,
and your land will be married.
⁵As a young man marries a young woman,
so will your Builder marry you;
as a bridegroom rejoices over his bride,
so will your God rejoice over you.

⁶I have posted watchmen on your walls, Jerusalem;
they will never be silent day or night.
You who call on the LORD,
give yourselves no rest,
⁷and give him no rest till he establishes Jerusalem
and makes her the praise of the earth.

⁸The LORD has sworn by his right hand
and by his mighty arm:
'Never again will I give your grain
as food for your enemies,
and never again will foreigners drink the new wine
for which you have toiled;
⁹but those who harvest it will eat it
and praise the LORD,
and those who gather the grapes will drink it
in the courts of my sanctuary.'

¹⁰Pass through, pass through the gates!
Prepare the way for the people.
Build up, build up the highway!
Remove the stones.
Raise a banner for the nations.

¹¹The LORD has made proclamation
to the ends of the earth:
'Say to Daughter Zion,
"See, your Saviour comes!
See, his reward is with him,
and his recompense accompanies him."'
¹²They will be called the Holy People,
the Redeemed of the LORD;
and you will be called Sought After,
the City No Longer Deserted.

God's day of vengeance and redemption

63 Who is this coming from Edom,
from Bozrah, with his garments stained crimson?
Who is this, robed in splendour,
striding forward in the greatness of his strength?

'It is I, speaking in righteousness,
mighty to save.'

²Why are your garments red,
like those of one treading the winepress?

³'I have trodden the winepress alone;
from the nations no-one was with me.
I trampled them in my anger
and trod them down in my wrath;
their blood spattered my garments,
and I stained all my clothing.
⁴It was for me the day of vengeance;
the year for me to redeem had come.
⁵I looked, but there was no-one to help,
I was appalled that no-one gave support;
so my own arm achieved salvation for me,
and my own wrath sustained me.
⁶I trampled the nations in my anger;
in my wrath I made them drunk
and poured their blood on the ground.'

Praise and prayer

⁷I will tell of the kindnesses of the LORD,
the deeds for which he is to be praised,

---

[a] 4 *Hephzibah* means *my delight is in her.* [b] 4 *Beulah* means *married.*

according to all the LORD has done for
us—
yes, the many good things he has done
for the house of Israel,
according to his compassion and many
kindnesses.
8He said, 'Surely they are my people,
children who will be true to me';
and so he became their Saviour.
9In all their distress he too was distressed,
and the angel of his presence saved
them.^{a}
In his love and mercy he redeemed them;
he lifted them up and carried them
all the days of old.
10Yet they rebelled
and grieved his Holy Spirit.
So he turned and became their enemy
and he himself fought against them.

11Then his people recalled^b the days of old,
the days of Moses and his people—
where is he who brought them through
the sea,
with the shepherd of his flock?
Where is he who set
his Holy Spirit among them,
12who sent his glorious arm of power
to be at Moses' right hand,
who divided the waters before them,
to gain for himself everlasting renown,
13who led them through the depths?
Like a horse in open country,
they did not stumble;
14like cattle that go down to the plain,
they were given rest by the Spirit of the
LORD.
This is how you guided your people
to make for yourself a glorious name.

15Look down from heaven and see,
from your lofty throne, holy and
glorious.
Where are your zeal and your might?
Your tenderness and compassion are
withheld from us.
16But you are our Father,
though Abraham does not know us
or Israel acknowledge us;
you, LORD, are our Father,
our Redeemer from of old is your
name.
17Why, LORD, do you make us wander from
your ways
and harden our hearts so we do not
revere you?
Return for the sake of your servants,
the tribes that are your inheritance.
18For a little while your people possessed
your holy place,
but now our enemies have trampled
down your sanctuary.
19We are yours from of old;
but you have not ruled over them,
they have not been called^c by your
name.

64
*Oh, that you would rend the
heavens and come down,
that the mountains would tremble
before you!
*2As when fire sets twigs ablaze
and causes water to boil,
come down to make your name known to
your enemies
and cause the nations to quake before
you!
3For when you did awesome things that we
did not expect,
you came down, and the mountains
trembled before you.
4Since ancient times no-one has heard,
no ear has perceived,
no eye has seen any God besides you,
who acts on behalf of those who wait
for him.
5You come to the help of those who gladly
do right,
who remember your ways.
But when we continued to sin against
them,
you were angry.
How then can we be saved?
6All of us have become like one who is
unclean,
and all our righteous acts are like filthy
rags;
we all shrivel up like a leaf,

---

^{a} 9 Or *Saviour* ^{9}*in their distress. / It was no envoy or angel / but his own presence that saved them* ^{b} 11 Or *But may he recall* ^{c} 19 Or *We are like those you have never ruled, / like those never called*

* 64:1 is numbered 63:19b in Hebrew texts.   * 64:2-12 is numbered 64:1-11 in Hebrew texts.

and like the wind our sins sweep us
  away.
⁷No-one calls on your name
  or strives to lay hold of you;
for you have hidden your face from us
  and have given us over to*ᵃ* our sins.

⁸Yet you, LORD, are our Father.
  We are the clay, you are the potter;
  we are all the work of your hand.
⁹Do not be angry beyond measure, LORD;
  do not remember our sins for ever.
Oh, look upon us we pray,
  for we are all your people.
¹⁰Your sacred cities have become a
    wasteland;
  even Zion is a wasteland, Jerusalem a
    desolation.
¹¹Our holy and glorious temple, where our
    ancestors praised you,
  has been burned with fire,
  and all that we treasured lies in ruins.
¹²After all this, LORD, will you hold yourself
    back?
  Will you keep silent and punish us
    beyond measure?

Judgment and salvation

65 'I revealed myself to those who
did not ask for me;
  I was found by those who did not seek
    me.
To a nation that did not call on my name,
  I said, "Here am I, here am I."
²All day long I have held out my hands
  to an obstinate people,
who walk in ways not good,
  pursuing their own imaginations—
³a people who continually provoke me
    to my very face,
  offering sacrifices in gardens
  and burning incense on altars of brick;
⁴who sit among the graves
  and spend their nights keeping secret
    vigil;
who eat the flesh of pigs,
  and whose pots hold broth of impure
    meat;
⁵who say, "Keep away; don't come near
    me,
  for I am too sacred for you!"

Such people are smoke in my nostrils,
  a fire that keeps burning all day.

⁶'See, it stands written before me;
  I will not keep silent but will pay back in
    full;
  I will pay it back into their laps—
⁷both your sins and the sins of your
    ancestors,'
  says the LORD.
'Because they burned sacrifices on the
    mountains
  and defied me on the hills,
I will measure into their laps
  the full payment for their former
    deeds.'

⁸This is what the LORD says:

'As when juice is still found in a cluster of
    grapes
  and people say, "Don't destroy it,
    there is still a blessing in it,"
so will I do on behalf of my servants;
  I will not destroy them all.
⁹I will bring forth descendants from Jacob,
  and from Judah those who will possess
    my mountains;
my chosen people will inherit them,
  and there will my servants live.
¹⁰Sharon will become a pasture for flocks,
  and the Valley of Achor a resting place
    for herds,
  for my people who seek me.

¹¹'But as for you who forsake the LORD
  and forget my holy mountain,
who spread a table for Fortune
  and fill bowls of mixed wine for
    Destiny,
¹²I will destine you for the sword,
  and all of you will fall in the slaughter;
for I called but you did not answer,
  I spoke but you did not listen.
You did evil in my sight
  and chose what displeases me.'

¹³Therefore this is what the Sovereign
LORD says:

'My servants will eat,
  but you will go hungry;
my servants will drink,
  but you will go thirsty;

ᵃ 7 Septuagint, Syriac and Targum; Hebrew *have made us melt because of*

making Connections

New heavens and new earth
Isaiah 65:17

Isaiah looks forward to a future time when the heavens and earth will be renewed to the state that God originally intended. All evil, sickness and conflict will be destroyed and there will be peace and prosperity for all. John also looked forward to this time in Revelation 21:1.

my servants will rejoice,
  but you will be put to shame.
¹⁴My servants will sing
  out of the joy of their hearts,
but you will cry out
  from anguish of heart
  and wail in brokenness of spirit.
¹⁵You will leave your name
  for my chosen ones to use in their curses;
the Sovereign LORD will put you to death,
  but to his servants he will give another name.
¹⁶Whoever invokes a blessing in the land
  will do so by the one true God;
whoever takes an oath in the land
  will swear by the one true God.
For the past troubles will be forgotten
  and hidden from my eyes.

New heavens and a new earth

¹⁷'See, I will create
  new heavens and a new earth.
The former things will not be remembered,
  nor will they come to mind.
¹⁸But be glad and rejoice for ever
  in what I will create,
for I will create Jerusalem to be a delight
  and its people a joy.
¹⁹I will rejoice over Jerusalem
  and take delight in my people;
the sound of weeping and of crying
  will be heard in it no more.
²⁰'Never again will there be in it
  infants who live but a few days,
  or older people who do not live out their years;
those who die at a hundred
  will be thought mere youths;
those who fail to reach[a] a hundred
  will be considered accursed.
²¹They will build houses and dwell in them;
  they will plant vineyards and eat their fruit.
²²No longer will they build houses and
    others live in them,
  or plant and others eat.
For as the days of a tree,
  so will be the days of my people;
my chosen ones will long enjoy
  the work of their hands.
²³They will not labour in vain,
  nor will they bear children doomed to misfortune;
for they will be a people blessed by the LORD,
  they and their descendants with them.
²⁴Before they call I will answer;
  while they are still speaking I will hear.
²⁵The wolf and the lamb will feed together,
  and the lion will eat straw like the ox,
  but dust will be the serpent's food.
They will neither harm nor destroy
  on all my holy mountain,'
says the LORD.

Judgment and hope

66 This is what the LORD says:

'Heaven is my throne,
  and the earth is my footstool.
Where is the house you will build for me?
  Where will my resting place be?
²Has not my hand made all these things,
  and so they came into being?'
declares the LORD.

'These are the ones I look on with favour:
  those who are humble and contrite in spirit,
  and who tremble at my word.

---

[a] 20 Or youths; / sinners who reach

³But whoever sacrifices a bull
   is like one who kills a human being,
and whoever offers a lamb
   is like one who breaks a dog's neck;
whoever makes a grain offering
   is like one who presents pig's blood,
and whoever burns memorial incense
   is like one who worships an idol.
They have chosen their own ways,
   and they delight in their abominations;
⁴so I also will choose harsh treatment for them
   and will bring on them what they dread.
For when I called, no-one answered,
   when I spoke, no-one listened.
They did evil in my sight
   and chose what displeases me.'

⁵Hear the word of the LORD,
   you who tremble at his word;
'Your own people who hate you,
   and exclude you because of my name, have said,
"Let the LORD be glorified,
   that we may see your joy!"
Yet they will be put to shame.
⁶Hear that uproar from the city,
   hear that noise from the temple!
It is the sound of the LORD
   repaying his enemies all they deserve.

⁷'Before she goes into labour,
   she gives birth;
before the pains come upon her,
   she delivers a child.
⁸Who has ever heard of such things?
   Who has ever seen things like this?
Can a country be born in a day
   or a nation be brought forth in a moment?
Yet no sooner is Zion in labour
   than she gives birth to her children.
⁹Do I bring to the moment of birth
   and not give delivery?' says the LORD.
'Do I close up the womb
   when I bring to delivery?' says your God.
¹⁰'Rejoice with Jerusalem and be glad for her,
   all you who love her;
rejoice greatly with her,
   all you who mourn over her.
¹¹For you will feed and be satisfied
   at her comforting breasts;
you will drink deeply
   and delight in her overflowing abundance.'

¹²For this is what the LORD says:

'I will extend peace to her like a river,
   and the wealth of nations like a flooding stream;
you will feed and be carried on her arm
   and dandled on her knees.
¹³As a mother comforts her child,
   so will I comfort you;
and you will be comforted over Jerusalem.'

¹⁴When you see this, your heart will rejoice
   and you will flourish like grass;
the hand of the LORD will be made known to his servants,
   but his fury will be shown to his foes.
¹⁵See, the LORD is coming with fire,
   and his chariots are like a whirlwind;
he will bring down his anger with fury,
   and his rebuke with flames of fire.
¹⁶For with fire and with his sword
   the LORD will execute judgment on all people,
and many will be those slain by the LORD.

¹⁷'Those who consecrate and purify themselves to go into the gardens, following one who is among those who eat the flesh of pigs, rats and other unclean things—they will meet their end together with the one they follow,' declares the LORD.

¹⁸'And I, because of what they have planned and done, am about to come[a] and gather the people of all nations and languages, and they will come and see my glory.

¹⁹'I will set a sign among them, and I will send some of those who survive to the nations—to Tarshish, to the Libyans[b] and Lydians (famous as archers), to Tubal and Greece, and to the distant islands that have not heard of my fame or seen my glory. They

---

[a] 18 The meaning of the Hebrew for this clause is uncertain. [b] 19 Some Septuagint manuscripts *Put* (Libyans); Hebrew *Pul*

will proclaim my glory among the nations. ²⁰And they will bring all your people, from all the nations, to my holy mountain in Jerusalem as an offering to the LORD—on horses, in chariots and wagons, and on mules and camels,' says the LORD. 'They will bring them, as the Israelites bring their grain offerings, to the temple of the LORD in ceremonially clean vessels. ²¹And I will select some of them also to be priests and Levites,' says the LORD.

²²'As the new heavens and the new earth that I make will endure before me,' declares the LORD, 'so will your name and descendants endure. ²³From one New Moon to another and from one Sabbath to another, all people will come and bow down before me,' says the LORD. ²⁴'And they will go out and look on the dead bodies of those who rebelled against me; their worm will not die, nor will their fire be quenched, and they will be loathsome to the whole human race.'

Jeremiah

INTRODUCTION

JEREMIAH

Author: Jeremiah

Who to: The people of Judah.

When: Baruch the scribe probably put the book in its final form just after Jeremiah died, around 585 BC.

Did you know? Jeremiah's first attempt at writing this book ended up in the fire when King Jehoiakim decided he didn't like what Jeremiah was saying (Jeremiah 36:1–28). So Jeremiah started again.

Main theme: Jeremiah warns the people of Judah that trouble is coming. After years of rejecting God and worshipping false idols, they will be taken into captivity when the Babylonians invade Judah. The people of Judah refuse to listen and they are taken into exile just as Jeremiah said. The chapters in Jeremiah aren't arranged in the order that things happened, so it can be a difficult book to follow and understand. Through it all, Jeremiah has an unshakeable faith in God and confidence that God will restore Judah in the future.

1 The words of Jeremiah son of Hilkiah, one of the priests at Anathoth in the territory of Benjamin. ²The word of the LORD came to him in the thirteenth year of the reign of Josiah son of Amon king of Judah, ³and through the reign of Jehoiakim son of Josiah king of Judah, down to the fifth month of the eleventh year of Zedekiah son of Josiah king of Judah, when the people of Jerusalem went into exile.

The call of Jeremiah

⁴The word of the LORD came to me, saying,

⁵'Before I formed you in the womb I knew[a] you,

---
[a] 5 Or *chose*

before you were born I set you apart;
I appointed you as a prophet to the
nations.'

⁶'Ah, Sovereign LORD,' I said, 'I do not know how to speak; I am too young.'

⁷But the LORD said to me, 'Do not say, "I am too young." You must go to everyone I send you to and say whatever I command you. ⁸Do not be afraid of them, for I am with you and will rescue you,' declares the LORD.

⁹Then the LORD reached out his hand and touched my mouth and said to me, 'I have put my words in your mouth. ¹⁰See, today I appoint you over nations and kingdoms to uproot and tear down, to destroy and overthrow, to build and to plant.'

¹¹The word of the LORD came to me: 'What do you see, Jeremiah?'

'I see the branch of an almond tree,' I replied.

¹²The LORD said to me, 'You have seen correctly, for I am watching*ᵃ* to see that my word is fulfilled.'

¹³The word of the LORD came to me again: 'What do you see?'

'I see a pot that is boiling,' I answered. 'It is tilting towards us from the north.'

¹⁴The LORD said to me, 'From the north disaster will be poured out on all who live in the land. ¹⁵I am about to summon all the peoples of the northern kingdoms,' declares the LORD.

'Their kings will come and set up their thrones
  in the entrance of the gates of Jerusalem;
they will come against all her surrounding walls
  and against all the towns of Judah.
¹⁶I will pronounce my judgments on my people
  because of their wickedness in forsaking me,
in burning incense to other gods
  and in worshipping what their hands have made.

¹⁷'Get yourself ready! Stand up and say to them whatever I command you. Do not be terrified by them, or I will terrify you before them. ¹⁸Today I have made you a fortified city, an iron pillar and a bronze wall to stand against the whole land—against the kings of Judah, its officials, its priests and the people of the land. ¹⁹They will fight against you but will not overcome you, for I am with you and will rescue you,' declares the LORD.

Israel forsakes God

2 The word of the LORD came to me: ²'Go and proclaim in the hearing of Jerusalem:

'This is what the LORD says:

'"I remember the devotion of your youth,
  how as a bride you loved me
and followed me through the wilderness,
  through a land not sown.
³Israel was holy to the LORD,
  the firstfruits of his harvest;
all who devoured her were held guilty,
  and disaster overtook them,"'
          declares the LORD.

⁴Hear the word of the LORD, house of Jacob,
  all you clans of the house of Israel.

⁵This is what the LORD says:

'What fault did your ancestors find in me,
  that they strayed so far from me?
They followed worthless idols
  and became worthless themselves.
⁶They did not ask, "Where is the LORD,
  who brought us up out of Egypt
and led us through the barren wilderness,
  through a land of deserts and ravines,
a land of drought and utter darkness,
  a land where no-one travels and no-one lives?"
⁷I brought you into a fertile land
  to eat its fruit and rich produce.
But you came and defiled my land
  and made my inheritance detestable.
⁸The priests did not ask,
  "Where is the LORD?"
Those who deal with the law did not know me;
  the leaders rebelled against me.
The prophets prophesied by Baal,
  following worthless idols.

ᵃ 12 The Hebrew for *watching* sounds like the Hebrew for *almond tree*.

> **IN OTHER WORDS**
>
> **Cisterns**
> **Jeremiah 2:13**
> A cistern is an underground tank used to catch and store rainwater. Most rain falls during the winter in Israel so it was important that people were able to store water for use during the summer months.

⁹'Therefore I bring charges against you again,'
>declares the LORD.
'And I will bring charges against your children's children.
¹⁰Cross over to the coasts of Cyprus and look,
send to Kedar[a] and observe closely;
see if there has ever been anything like this:
¹¹has a nation ever changed its gods?
(Yet they are not gods at all.)
But my people have exchanged their glorious God
for worthless idols.
¹²Be appalled at this, you heavens,
and shudder with great horror,'
>declares the LORD.
¹³'My people have committed two sins:
They have forsaken me,
the spring of living water,
and have dug their own cisterns,
broken cisterns that cannot hold water.
¹⁴Is Israel a servant, a slave by birth?
Why then has he become plunder?
¹⁵Lions have roared;
they have growled at him.
They have laid waste his land;
his towns are burned and deserted.
¹⁶Also, the men of Memphis and Tahpanhes
have cracked your skull.
¹⁷Have you not brought this on yourselves
by forsaking the LORD your God
when he led you in the way?
¹⁸Now why go to Egypt
to drink water from the Nile?[b]
And why go to Assyria
to drink water from the Euphrates?
¹⁹Your wickedness will punish you;
your backsliding will rebuke you.
Consider then and realise
how evil and bitter it is for you
when you forsake the LORD your God
and have no awe of me,'
>declares the Lord,
>the LORD Almighty.

²⁰'Long ago you broke off your yoke
and tore off your bonds;
you said, "I will not serve you!"
Indeed, on every high hill
and under every spreading tree
you lay down as a prostitute.
²¹I had planted you like a choice vine
of sound and reliable stock.
How then did you turn against me
into a corrupt, wild vine?
²²Although you wash yourself with soap
and use an abundance of cleansing powder,
the stain of your guilt is still before me,'
>declares the Sovereign LORD.
²³'How can you say, "I am not defiled;
I have not run after the Baals"?
See how you behaved in the valley;
consider what you have done.
You are a swift she-camel
running here and there,
²⁴a wild donkey accustomed to the desert,
sniffing the wind in her craving—
in her heat who can restrain her?
Any males that pursue her need not tire themselves;
at mating time they will find her.
²⁵Do not run until your feet are bare
and your throat is dry.
But you said, "It's no use!
I love foreign gods,
and I must go after them."

²⁶'As a thief is disgraced when he is caught,
so the house of Israel is disgraced—
they, their kings and their officials,
their priests and their prophets,
²⁷They say to wood, "You are my father,"
and to stone, "You gave me birth."

---

[a] 10 In the Syro-Arabian desert   [b] 18 Hebrew *Shihor*; that is, a branch of the Nile

They have turned their backs to me
and not their faces;
yet when they are in trouble, they say,
"Come and save us!"
²⁸Where then are the gods you made for
yourselves?
Let them come if they can save you
when you are in trouble!
For you, Judah, have as many gods
as you have towns.

²⁹'Why do you bring charges against me?
You have all rebelled against me,'
declares the LORD.
³⁰'In vain I punished your people;
they did not respond to correction.
Your sword has devoured your prophets
like a ravenous lion.

³¹'You of this generation, consider the
word of the LORD:

'Have I been a desert to Israel
or a land of great darkness?
Why do my people say, "We are free to
roam;
we will come to you no more"?
³²Does a young woman forget her jewellery,
a bride her wedding ornaments?
Yet my people have forgotten me,
days without number.
³³How skilled you are at pursuing love!
Even the worst of women can learn
from your ways.
³⁴On your clothes is found
the lifeblood of the innocent poor,
though you did not catch them
breaking in.
Yet in spite of all this
35   you say, "I am innocent;
he is not angry with me."
But I will pass judgment on you
because you say, "I have not sinned."
³⁶Why do you go about so much,
changing your ways?
You will be disappointed by Egypt
as you were by Assyria.
³⁷You will also leave that place
with your hands on your head,
for the LORD has rejected those you trust;
you will not be helped by them.

3 'If a man divorces his wife
and she leaves him and marries
another man,
should he return to her again?
Would not the land be completely
defiled?
But you have lived as a prostitute with
many lovers—
would you now return to me?'
declares the LORD.
²'Look up to the barren heights and see.
Is there any place where you have not
been ravished?
By the roadside you sat waiting for lovers,
sat like a nomad in the desert.
You have defiled the land
with your prostitution and
wickedness.
³Therefore the showers have been
withheld,
and no spring rains have fallen.
Yet you have the brazen look of a prostitute;
you refuse to blush with shame.
⁴Have you not just called to me:
"My Father, my friend from my youth,
⁵will you always be angry?
Will your wrath continue for ever?"
This is how you talk,
but you do all the evil you can.'

People and Places

Israel and Judah
Jeremiah 3:6

When Solomon died, his son Rehoboam became king, and during his reign the ten northern tribes of Israel declared independence and set up their own nation under the rule of Jeroboam (1 Kings 12). They called their new kingdom Israel, which can be a bit confusing because previously the name Israel applied to all twelve tribes. The two tribes left in the south became known as Judah.

Unfaithful Israel

⁶During the reign of King Josiah, the LORD said to me, 'Have you seen what faithless Israel has done? She has gone up on every high hill and under every spreading tree and has committed adultery there. ⁷I thought that after she had done all this she would return to me but she did not, and her unfaithful sister Judah saw it. ⁸I gave faithless Israel her certificate of divorce and sent her away because of all her adulteries. Yet I saw that her unfaithful sister Judah had no fear; she also went out and committed adultery. ⁹Because Israel's immorality mattered so little to her, she defiled the land and committed adultery with stone and wood. ¹⁰In spite of all this, her unfaithful sister Judah did not return to me with all her heart, but only in pretence,' declares the LORD.

¹¹The LORD said to me, 'Faithless Israel is more righteous than unfaithful Judah. ¹²Go, proclaim this message towards the north:

'"Return, faithless Israel," declares the LORD,
"I will frown on you no longer,
for I am faithful," declares the LORD,
"I will not be angry for ever.
¹³Only acknowledge your guilt—
you have rebelled against the LORD your God,
you have scattered your favours to foreign gods
under every spreading tree,
and have not obeyed me,"'
declares the LORD.

¹⁴'Return, faithless people,' declares the LORD, 'for I am your husband. I will choose you—one from a town and two from a clan—and bring you to Zion. ¹⁵Then I will give you shepherds after my own heart, who will lead you with knowledge and understanding. ¹⁶In those days, when your numbers have increased greatly in the land,' declares the LORD, 'people will no longer say, "The ark of the covenant of the LORD." It will never enter their minds or be remembered; it will not be missed, nor will another one be made. ¹⁷At that time they will call Jerusalem The Throne of the LORD, and all nations will gather in Jerusalem to honour the name of the LORD. No longer will they follow the stubbornness of their evil hearts. ¹⁸In those days the house of Judah will join the house of Israel, and together they will come from a northern land to the land I gave your ancestors as an inheritance.

¹⁹'I myself said,

'"How gladly would I treat you like my children
and give you a pleasant land,
the most beautiful inheritance of any nation."
I thought you would call me "Father"
and not turn away from following me.
²⁰But like a woman unfaithful to her husband,
so you, house of Israel, have been unfaithful to me,'
declares the LORD.

²¹A cry is heard on the barren heights,
the weeping and pleading of the people of Israel,
because they have perverted their ways
and have forgotten the LORD their God.

²²'Return, faithless people;
I will cure you of backsliding.'

'Yes, we will come to you,
for you are the LORD our God.
²³Surely the [idolatrous] commotion on the hills
and mountains is a deception;
surely in the LORD our God
is the salvation of Israel.
²⁴From our youth shameful gods have consumed
the fruits of our ancestors' labour—
their flocks and herds,
their sons and daughters.
²⁵Let us lie down in our shame,
and let our disgrace cover us.
We have sinned against the LORD our God,
both we and our ancestors;
from our youth till this day
we have not obeyed the LORD our God.'

4 'If you, Israel, will return,
　　then return to me,'
　　　　　　　　　declares the LORD.
'If you put your detestable idols out of my
　　sight
　　and no longer go astray,
²and if in a truthful, just and righteous way
　　you swear, "As surely as the LORD
　　lives,"
　then the nations will invoke blessings by
　　him
　　and in him they will boast.'

³This is what the LORD says to the people
of Judah and to Jerusalem:

'Break up your unploughed ground
　　and do not sow among thorns.
⁴Circumcise yourselves to the LORD,
　　circumcise your hearts,
　you people of Judah and inhabitants of
　　Jerusalem,
　or my wrath will flare up and burn like fire
　because of the evil you have done—
　　burn with no-one to quench it.

Disaster from the north

⁵'Announce in Judah and proclaim in
　　Jerusalem and say:
　　"Sound the trumpet throughout the
　　　land!"
　Cry aloud and say:
　　"Gather together!
　　Let us flee to the fortified cities!"
⁶Raise the signal to go to Zion!
　　Flee for safety without delay!
　For I am bringing disaster from the north,
　　even terrible destruction.'

⁷A lion has come out of his lair;
　　a destroyer of nations has set out.
　He has left his place
　　to lay waste your land.
　Your towns will lie in ruins
　　without inhabitant.
⁸So put on sackcloth,
　　lament and wail,
　for the fierce anger of the LORD
　　has not turned away from us.

⁹'In that day,' declares the LORD,
　'the king and the officials will lose
　　heart,
　the priests will be horrified,
　　and the prophets will be appalled.'

¹⁰Then I said, 'Ah, Sovereign LORD, how completely you have deceived this people and Jerusalem by saying, "You will have peace," when the sword is at our throats.'

¹¹At that time this people and Jerusalem will be told, 'A scorching wind from the barren heights in the desert blows towards my people, but not to winnow or cleanse; ¹²a wind too strong for that comes from me.*ᵃ* Now I pronounce my judgments against them.'

¹³Look! He advances like the clouds,
　　his chariots come like a whirlwind,
　his horses are swifter than eagles.
　　Woe to us! We are ruined!
¹⁴Jerusalem, wash the evil from your heart
　　and be saved.
　　How long will you harbour wicked
　　　thoughts?
¹⁵A voice is announcing from Dan,
　　proclaiming disaster from the hills of
　　　Ephraim.
¹⁶'Tell this to the nations,
　　proclaim concerning Jerusalem:
　"A besieging army is coming from a
　　distant land,
　　raising a war cry against the cities of
　　　Judah.
¹⁷They surround her like people guarding a
　　field,
　　because she has rebelled against me,"'
　　　　　　　　　declares the LORD.
¹⁸'Your own conduct and actions
　　have brought this on you.
　This is your punishment.
　　How bitter it is!
　　How it pierces to the heart!'

¹⁹Oh, my anguish, my anguish!
　　I writhe in pain.
　Oh, the agony of my heart!
　　My heart pounds within me,
　　I cannot keep silent.
　For I have heard the sound of the
　　trumpet;
　　I have heard the battle cry.
²⁰Disaster follows disaster;
　　the whole land lies in ruins.

ᵃ 12 Or *comes at my command*

In an instant my tents are destroyed,
  my shelter in a moment.
21How long must I see the battle standard
  and hear the sound of the trumpet?

22'My people are fools;
  they do not know me.
They are senseless children;
  they have no understanding.
They are skilled in doing evil;
  they know not how to do good.'

23I looked at the earth,
  and it was formless and empty;
and at the heavens,
  and their light was gone.
24I looked at the mountains,
  and they were quaking;
  all the hills were swaying.
25I looked, and there were no people;
  every bird in the sky had flown away.
26I looked, and the fruitful land was a desert;
  all its towns lay in ruins
  before the LORD, before his fierce anger.

27This is what the LORD says:

'The whole land will be ruined,
  though I will not destroy it completely.
28Therefore the earth will mourn
  and the heavens above grow dark,
because I have spoken and will not relent,
  I have decided and will not turn back.'

29At the sound of horsemen and archers
  every town takes to flight.
Some go into the thickets;
  some climb up among the rocks.
All the towns are deserted;
  no-one lives in them.

30What are you doing, you devastated one?
  Why dress yourself in scarlet
  and put on jewels of gold?
Why colour your eyes with paint?
  You adorn yourself in vain.
Your lovers despise you;
  they seek your life.

31I hear a cry as of a woman in labour,
  a groan as of one bearing her first
    child—
the cry of Daughter Zion gasping for
    breath,
  stretching out her hands and saying,
'Alas! I am fainting;
  my life is given over to murderers.'

Not one is upright

5 'Go up and down the streets of
   Jerusalem,
  look around and consider,
  search through her squares.
If you can find but one person
  who deals honestly and seeks the truth,
  I will forgive this city.
2Although they say, "As surely as the LORD
    lives,"
  still they are swearing falsely.'

3LORD, do not your eyes look for truth?
  You struck them, but they felt no pain;
  you crushed them but they refused
    correction.
They made their faces harder than stone
  and refused to repent.
4I thought, 'These are only the poor;
  they are foolish,
for they do not know the way of the LORD,
  the requirements of their God.
5So I will go to the leaders
  and speak to them;
surely they know the way of the LORD,
  the requirements of their God.'
But with one accord they too had broken
    off the yoke
  and torn off the bonds.
6Therefore a lion from the forest will attack
    them,
  a wolf from the desert will ravage them,
a leopard will lie in wait near their towns
  to tear to pieces any who venture out,
for their rebellion is great
  and their backslidings many.

7'Why should I forgive you?
  Your children have forsaken me
  and sworn by gods that are not gods.
I supplied all their needs,
  yet they committed adultery
  and thronged to the houses of
    prostitutes.
8They are well-fed, lusty stallions,
  each neighing for another man's wife.
9Should I not punish them for this?'
  declares the LORD.
'Should I not avenge myself
  on such a nation as this?

10'Go through her vineyards and ravage
    them,
  but do not destroy them completely.

Strip off her branches,
>for these people do not belong to the LORD.

11 The house of Israel and the house of Judah
have been utterly unfaithful to me,'
>>declares the LORD.

12 They have lied about the LORD;
>they said, 'He will do nothing!
No harm will come to us;
>we will never see sword or famine.
13 The prophets are but wind
>and the word is not in them;
so let what they say be done to them.'

14 Therefore this is what the LORD God Almighty says:

'Because the people have spoken these words,
>I will make my words in your mouth a fire
and these people the wood it consumes.
15 House of Israel,' declares the LORD,
>'I am bringing a distant nation against you—
an ancient and enduring nation,
>a people whose language you do not know,
>>whose speech you do not understand.
16 Their quivers are like an open grave;
>all of them are mighty warriors.
17 They will devour your harvests and food,
>devour your sons and daughters;
they will devour your flocks and herds,
>devour your vines and fig trees.
With the sword they will destroy
>the fortified cities in which you trust.

18 'Yet even in those days,' declares the LORD, 'I will not destroy you completely. 19 And when the people ask, "Why has the LORD our God done all this to us?" you will tell them, "As you have forsaken me and served foreign gods in your own land, so now you will serve foreigners in a land not your own."

20 'Announce this to the house of Jacob
>and proclaim it in Judah:
21 hear this, you foolish and senseless people,
>who have eyes but do not see,
>who have ears but do not hear:
22 should you not fear me?' declares the LORD.
>'Should you not tremble in my presence?
I made the sand a boundary for the sea,
>an everlasting barrier it cannot cross.
The waves may roll, but they cannot prevail;
>they may roar, but they cannot cross it.
23 But these people have stubborn and rebellious hearts;
>they have turned aside and gone away.
24 They do not say to themselves,
>"Let us fear the LORD our God,
who gives autumn and spring rains in season,
>who assures us of the regular weeks of harvest."
25 Your wrongdoings have kept these away;
>your sins have deprived you of good.

26 'Among my people are the wicked
>who lie in wait like those who snare birds
and like those who set traps to catch people.
27 Like cages full of birds,
>their houses are full of deceit;
they have become rich and powerful
28 >and have grown fat and sleek.
Their evil deeds have no limit;
>they do not seek justice.
They do not promote the case of the fatherless;
>they do not defend the just cause of the poor.
29 Should I not punish them for this?' declares the LORD.
>'Should I not avenge myself
on such a nation as this?

30 'A horrible and shocking thing
>has happened in the land:
31 the prophets prophesy lies,
>the priests rule by their own authority,
and my people love it this way.
>But what will you do in the end?

Jerusalem under siege

6 'Flee for safety, people of Benjamin!
Flee from Jerusalem!
Sound the trumpet in Tekoa!
>Raise the signal over Beth Hakkerem!

> **IN OTHER WORDS**
>
> ### Siege ramps
> **Jeremiah 6:6**
> Jerusalem was surrounded by a wall which made it more difficult to invade. An enemy would need to lay siege to the city, surrounding it with soldiers and cutting off its supply lines in an attempt to make the people surrender. Siege ramps would have enabled the enemy to get over the wall at a strategic point during the siege.

For disaster looms out of the north,
  even terrible destruction.
2I will destroy Daughter Zion,
  so beautiful and delicate.
3Shepherds with their flocks will come against her;
  they will pitch their tents round her,
  each of them tending their own portion.'

4'Prepare for battle against her!
  Arise, let us attack at noon!
But, alas, the daylight is fading,
  and the shadows of evening grow long.
5So arise, let us attack at night
  and destroy her fortresses!'

6This is what the LORD Almighty says:

'Cut down the trees
  and build siege ramps against Jerusalem.
This city must be punished;
  it is filled with oppression.
7As a well pours out its water,
  so she pours out her wickedness.
Violence and destruction resound in her;
  her sickness and wounds are ever before me.
8Take warning, Jerusalem,
  or I will turn away from you
and make your land desolate
  so that no-one can live in it.'

9This is what the LORD Almighty says:

'Let them glean the remnant of Israel
  as thoroughly as a vine;
pass your hand over the branches again,
  like one gathering grapes.'

10To whom can I speak and give warning?
  Who will listen to me?
Their ears are closed[a]
  so that they cannot hear.
The word of the LORD is offensive to them;
  they find no pleasure in it.
11But I am full of the wrath of the LORD,
  and I cannot hold it in.

'Pour it out on the children in the street
  and on the youths gathered together;
both husband and wife will be caught in it,
  and the old, those weighed down with years.
12Their houses will be turned over to others,
  together with their fields and their wives,
when I stretch out my hand
  against those who live in the land,'
    declares the LORD.
13'From the least to the greatest,
  all are greedy for gain;
prophets and priests alike,
  all practise deceit.
14They dress the wound of my people
  as though it were not serious.
"Peace, peace," they say,
  when there is no peace.
15Are they ashamed of their detestable conduct?
  No, they have no shame at all;
  they do not even know how to blush.
So they will fall among the fallen;
  they will be brought down when I punish them,'
    says the LORD.

16This is what the LORD says:

'Stand at the crossroads and look;
  ask for the ancient paths,
ask where the good way is, and walk in it,
  and you will find rest for your souls.
But you said, "We will not walk in it."
17I appointed watchmen over you and said,

---

[a] 10 Hebrew *uncircumcised*

"Listen to the sound of the trumpet!"
But you said, "We will not listen."
¹⁸Therefore hear, you nations;
 you who are witnesses,
 observe what will happen to them.
¹⁹Hear, you earth:
 I am bringing disaster on this people,
 the fruit of their schemes,
because they have not listened to my words
 and have rejected my law.
²⁰What do I care about incense from Sheba
 or sweet calamus from a distant land?
Your burnt offerings are not acceptable;
 your sacrifices do not please me.'

²¹Therefore this is what the LORD says:

'I will put obstacles before this people.
Parents and children alike will stumble over them;
neighbours and friends will perish.'

²²This is what the LORD says:

'Look, an army is coming
 from the land of the north;
a great nation is being stirred up
 from the ends of the earth.
²³They are armed with bow and spear;
 they are cruel and show no mercy.
They sound like the roaring sea
 as they ride on their horses;
they come like men in battle formation
 to attack you, Daughter Zion.'

²⁴We have heard reports about them,
 and our hands hang limp.
Anguish has gripped us,
 pain like that of a woman in labour.
²⁵Do not go out to the fields
 or walk on the roads,
for the enemy has a sword,
 and there is terror on every side.
²⁶Put on sackcloth, my people,
 and roll in ashes;
mourn with bitter wailing
 as for an only son,
for suddenly the destroyer
 will come upon us.

²⁷'I have made you a tester of metals
 and my people the ore,
that you may observe
 and test their ways.

²⁸They are all hardened rebels,
 going about to slander.
They are bronze and iron;
 they all act corruptly.
²⁹The bellows blow fiercely
 to burn away the lead with fire,
but the refining goes on in vain;
 the wicked are not purged out.
³⁰They are called rejected silver,
 because the LORD has rejected them.'

False religion worthless

7 This is the word that came to Jeremiah from the LORD: ²'Stand at the gate of the LORD's house and there proclaim this message:

'"Hear the word of the LORD, all you people of Judah who come through these gates to worship the LORD. ³This is what the LORD Almighty, the God of Israel, says: reform your ways and your actions, and I will let you live in this place. ⁴Do not trust in deceptive words and say, 'This is the temple of the LORD, the temple of the LORD, the temple of the LORD!' ⁵If you really change your ways and your actions and deal with each other justly, ⁶if you do not oppress the foreigner, the fatherless or the widow and do not shed innocent blood in this place, and if you do not follow other gods to your own harm, ⁷then I will let you live in this place, in the land I gave to your ancestors for ever and ever. ⁸But look, you are trusting in deceptive words that are worthless.

⁹'"Will you steal and murder, commit adultery and perjury,*ᵃ* burn incense to Baal and follow other gods you have not known, ¹⁰and then come and stand before me in this house, which bears my Name, and say, 'We are safe'—safe to do all these detestable things? ¹¹Has this house, which bears my Name, become a den of robbers to you? But I have been watching! declares the LORD.

¹²'"Go now to the place in Shiloh where I first made a dwelling for my Name, and see what I did to it because of the wickedness of my people Israel. ¹³While you were doing all these things, declares the LORD, I spoke to you again and again, but you did not listen; I called you, but you did not answer. ¹⁴Therefore, what I did to Shiloh I will now do to the

---

ᵃ 9 Or *and swear by false gods*

house that bears my Name, the temple you trust in, the place I gave to you and your ancestors. ¹⁵I will thrust you from my presence, just as I did all your fellow Israelites, the people of Ephraim."

¹⁶'So do not pray for this people nor offer any plea or petition for them; do not plead with me, for I will not listen to you. ¹⁷Do you not see what they are doing in the towns of Judah and in the streets of Jerusalem? ¹⁸The children gather wood, the fathers light the fire, and the women knead the dough and make cakes to offer to the Queen of Heaven. They pour out drink offerings to other gods to arouse my anger. ¹⁹But am I the one they are provoking? declares the LORD. Are they not rather harming themselves, to their own shame?

²⁰' "Therefore this is what the Sovereign LORD says: my anger and my wrath will be poured out on this place—on people and animals, on the trees of the field and on the crops of your land—and it will burn and not be quenched.

²¹' "This is what the LORD Almighty, the God of Israel, says: go ahead, add your burnt offerings to your other sacrifices and eat the meat yourselves! ²²For when I brought your ancestors out of Egypt and spoke to them, I did not just give them commands about burnt offerings and sacrifices, ²³but I gave them this command: obey me, and I will be your God and you will be my people. Walk in obedience to all I command you, that it may go well with you. ²⁴But they did not listen or pay attention; instead, they followed the stubborn inclinations of their evil hearts. They went backwards and not forwards. ²⁵From the time your ancestors left Egypt until now, day after day, again and again I sent you my servants the prophets. ²⁶But they did not listen to me or pay attention. They were stiff-necked and did more evil than their ancestors."

²⁷'When you tell them all this, they will not listen to you; when you call to them, they will not answer. ²⁸Therefore say to them, "This is the nation that has not obeyed the LORD its God or responded to correction. Truth has perished; it has vanished from their lips.

²⁹' "Cut off your hair and throw it away; take up a lament on the barren heights, for the LORD has rejected and abandoned this generation that is under his wrath.

The valley of slaughter

³⁰' "The people of Judah have done evil in my eyes, declares the LORD. They have set up their detestable idols in the house that bears my Name and have defiled it. ³¹They have built the high places of Topheth in the Valley of Ben Hinnom to burn their sons and daughters in the fire—something I did not command, nor did it enter my mind. ³²So beware, the days are coming, declares the LORD, when people will no longer call it Topheth or the Valley of Ben Hinnom, but the Valley of Slaughter, for they will bury the dead in Topheth until there is no more room. ³³Then the carcasses of this people will become food for the birds and the wild animals, and there will be no-one to frighten them away. ³⁴I will bring an end to the sounds of joy and gladness and to the voices of bride and bridegroom in the towns of Judah and the streets of Jerusalem, for the land will become desolate.

8 ' "At that time, declares the LORD, the bones of the kings and officials of Judah, the bones of the priests and prophets, and the bones of the people of Jerusalem will be removed from their graves. ²They will be exposed to the sun and the moon and all the stars of the heavens, which they have loved and served and which they have followed and consulted and worshipped. They will not be gathered up or buried, but will be like dung lying on the ground. ³Wherever I banish them, all the survivors of this evil nation will prefer death to life, declares the LORD Almighty."

Sin and punishment

⁴'Say to them, "This is what the LORD says:

' "When people fall down, do they not get up?
When people turn away, do they not return?
⁵Why then have these people turned away?

Why does Jerusalem always turn away?
They cling to deceit;
  they refuse to return.
⁶I have listened attentively,
  but they do not say what is right.
None of them repent of their wickedness,
  saying, 'What have I done?'
They each pursue their own course
  like a horse charging into battle.
⁷Even the stork in the sky
  knows her appointed seasons,
and the dove, the swift and the thrush
  observe the time of their migration.
But my people do not know
  the requirements of the LORD.

⁸ "'How can you say, "We are wise,
  for we have the law of the LORD,"
when actually the lying pen of the scribes
  has handled it falsely?
⁹The wise will be put to shame;
  they will be dismayed and trapped.
Since they have rejected the word of the LORD,
  what kind of wisdom do they have?
¹⁰Therefore I will give their wives to other men
  and their fields to new owners.
From the least to the greatest,
  all are greedy for gain;
prophets and priests alike,
  all practise deceit.
¹¹They dress the wound of my people
  as though it were not serious.
'Peace, peace,' they say,
  when there is no peace.
¹²Are they ashamed of their detestable conduct?
  No, they have no shame at all;
  they do not even know how to blush.
So they will fall among the fallen;
  they will be brought down when they are punished,
               says the LORD.

¹³ "'I will take away their harvest,
               declares the LORD.
There will be no grapes on the vine.
There will be no figs on the tree,
  and their leaves will wither.
What I have given them
  will be taken from them."' ᵃ

¹⁴Why are we sitting here?
  Gather together!
Let us flee to the fortified cities
  and perish there!
For the LORD our God has doomed us to perish
  and given us poisoned water to drink,
  because we have sinned against him.
¹⁵We hoped for peace
  but no good has come,
for a time of healing
  but there is only terror.
¹⁶The snorting of the enemy's horses
  is heard from Dan;
at the neighing of their stallions
  the whole land trembles.
They have come to devour
  the land and everything in it,
  the city and all who live there.

¹⁷'See, I will send venomous snakes among you,
  vipers that cannot be charmed,
  and they will bite you,'
               declares the LORD.

¹⁸You who are my Comforterᵇ in sorrow,
  my heart is faint within me.
¹⁹Listen to the cry of my people
  from a land far away:
'Is the LORD not in Zion?
  Is her King no longer there?'

'Why have they aroused my anger with their images,
  with their worthless foreign idols?'

²⁰'The harvest is past,
  the summer has ended,
  and we are not saved.'

²¹Since my people are crushed, I am crushed;
  I mourn, and horror grips me.
²²Is there no balm in Gilead?
  Is there no physician there?
Why then is there no healing
  for the wound of my people?

ᵃ 13 The meaning of the Hebrew for this sentence is uncertain.   ᵇ 18 The meaning of the Hebrew for this word is uncertain.

Making Connections

Balm of Gilead
Jeremiah 8:22
The balm of Gilead was an aromatic gum or resin which was used for medicinal purposes, to soothe and to heal.

9 *¹Oh, that my head were a spring of water
and my eyes a fountain of tears!
I would weep day and night
for the slain of my people.
*²Oh, that I had in the desert
a lodging place for travellers,
so that I might leave my people
and go away from them;
for they are all adulterers,
a crowd of unfaithful people.

³'They make ready their tongue
like a bow, to shoot lies;
it is not by truth
that they triumph*ᵃ* in the land.
They go from one sin to another;
they do not acknowledge me,'
declares the LORD.
⁴'Beware of your friends;
do not trust any of your people.
For every one of them is a deceiver,*ᵇ*
and every friend a slanderer.
⁵Friend deceives friend,
and no-one speaks the truth.
They have taught their tongues to lie;
they weary themselves with sinning.
⁶You*ᶜ* live in the midst of deception;
in their deceit they refuse to
acknowledge me,'
declares the LORD.

⁷Therefore this is what the LORD Almighty says:

'See, I will refine and test them,
for what else can I do
because of the sin of my people?
⁸Their tongue is a deadly arrow;
it speaks deceitfully.
With their mouths they all speak cordially
to their neighbours,
but in their hearts they set traps for
them.
⁹Should I not punish them for this?'
declares the LORD.
'Should I not avenge myself
on such a nation as this?'

¹⁰I will weep and wail for the mountains
and take up a lament concerning the
wilderness grasslands.
They are desolate and untravelled,
and the lowing of cattle is not heard.
The birds have all fled
and the animals are gone.

¹¹'I will make Jerusalem a heap of ruins,
a haunt of jackals;
and I will lay waste the towns of Judah
so that no-one can live there.'

¹²Who is wise enough to understand this? Who has been instructed by the LORD and can explain it? Why has the land been ruined and laid waste like a desert that no-one can cross?

¹³The LORD said, 'It is because they have forsaken my law, which I set before them; they have not obeyed me or followed my law. ¹⁴Instead, they have followed the stubbornness of their hearts; they have followed the Baals, as their ancestors taught them.' ¹⁵Therefore, this is what the LORD Almighty, the God of Israel, says: 'See, I will make this people eat bitter food and drink poisoned water. ¹⁶I will scatter them among nations that neither they nor their ancestors have known, and I will pursue them with the sword until I have made an end of them.'

¹⁷This is what the LORD Almighty says:

'Consider now! Call for the wailing
women to come;
send for the most skilful of them.

---

*ᵃ*3 Or *lies; / they are not valiant for truth*   *ᵇ*4 Or *a deceiving Jacob*   *ᶜ*6 That is, Jeremiah (the Hebrew is singular)
* 9:1 is numbered 8:23 in Hebrew texts.   * 9:2-26 is numbered 9:1-25 in Hebrew texts.

¹⁸Let them come quickly
    and wail over us
till our eyes overflow with tears
    and water streams from our eyelids.
¹⁹The sound of wailing is heard from Zion:
    "How ruined we are!
    How great is our shame!
We must leave our land
    because our houses are in ruins."'

²⁰Now, you women, hear the word of the
    LORD;
    open your ears to the words of his
        mouth.
Teach your daughters how to wail;
    teach one another a lament.
²¹Death has climbed in through our
        windows
    and has entered our fortresses;
it has removed the children from the
        streets
    and the youths from the public
        squares.

²²Say, 'This is what the LORD declares:

'"Dead bodies will lie
    like dung on the open field,
like cut corn behind the reaper,
    with no-one to gather them."'

²³This is what the LORD says:

'Let not the wise boast of their wisdom
    or the strong boast of their strength
    or the rich boast of their riches,
²⁴but let those who boast boast about this:
    that they understand and know me,
    that I am the LORD, who exercises
        kindness,
    justice and righteousness on earth,
    for in these I delight,'
                            declares the LORD.

²⁵'The days are coming,' declares the LORD, 'when I will punish all who are circumcised only in the flesh— ²⁶Egypt, Judah, Edom, Ammon, Moab and all who live in the wilderness in distant places.[a] For all these nations are really uncircumcised, and even the whole house of Israel is uncircumcised in heart.'

God and idols

10 Hear what the LORD says to you, house of Israel. ²This is what the LORD says:

'Do not learn the ways of the nations
    or be terrified by signs in the sky,
    though the nations are terrified by
        them.
³For the practices of the peoples are
        worthless;
    they cut a tree out of the forest,
    and a skilled worker shapes it with a
        chisel.
⁴They adorn it with silver and gold;
    they fasten it with hammer and nails
    so that it will not totter.
⁵Like a scarecrow in a melon patch,
    their idols cannot speak;
they must be carried
    because they cannot walk.
Do not fear them;
    they can do no harm
    nor can they do any good.'

⁶No-one is like you, LORD;
    you are great,
    and your name is mighty in power.
⁷Who should not fear you,
    King of the nations?
    This is your due.
Among all the wise rulers of the nations
    and in all their kingdoms,
    there is no-one like you.

⁸They are all senseless and foolish;
    they are taught by worthless wooden
        idols.
⁹Hammered silver is brought from
        Tarshish
    and gold from Uphaz.
What the goldsmith and engraver have
        made
    is then dressed in blue and purple—
    all made by skilled workers.
¹⁰But the LORD is the true God;
    he is the living God, the eternal King.
When he is angry, the earth trembles;
    the nations cannot endure his wrath.

¹¹'Tell them this: "These gods, who did not make the heavens and the earth, will

---

[a] 26 Or *wilderness and who clip the hair by their foreheads*

perish from the earth and from under the heavens."'[a]

12But God made the earth by his power;
    he founded the world by his wisdom
    and stretched out the heavens by his understanding.
13When he thunders, the waters in the heavens roar;
    he makes clouds rise from the ends of the earth.
He sends lightning with the rain
    and brings out the wind from his storehouses.

14Everyone is senseless and without knowledge;
    all goldsmiths are shamed by their idols.
Their images are a fraud;
    they have no breath in them.
15They are worthless, the objects of mockery;
    when their judgment comes, they will perish.
16He who is the Portion of Jacob is not like these,
    for he is the Maker of all things,
including Israel, the tribe of his inheritance—
    the LORD Almighty is his name.

Coming destruction

17Gather up your belongings to leave the land,
    you who live under siege.
18For this is what the LORD says:
    'At this time I will hurl out
    those who live in this land;
I will bring distress on them
    so that they may be captured.'

19Woe to me because of my injury!
    My wound is incurable!
Yet I said to myself,
    'This is my sickness, and I must endure it.'
20My tent is destroyed;
    all its ropes are snapped.
My children are gone from me and are no more;
    no-one is left now to pitch my tent
    or to set up my shelter.

21The shepherds are senseless
    and do not enquire of the LORD;
so they do not prosper
    and all their flock is scattered.
22Listen! The report is coming—
    a great commotion from the land of the north!
It will make the towns of Judah desolate,
    a haunt of jackals.

Jeremiah's prayer

23LORD, I know that people's lives are not their own;
    it is not for them to direct their steps.
24Discipline me, LORD, but only in due measure—
    not in your anger,
    or you will reduce me to nothing.
25Pour out your wrath on the nations
    that do not acknowledge you,
    on the peoples who do not call on your name.
For they have devoured Jacob;
    they have devoured him completely
    and destroyed his homeland.

The covenant is broken

11 This is the word that came to Jeremiah from the LORD: 2'Listen to the terms of this covenant and tell them to the people of Judah and to those who live in Jerusalem. 3Tell them that this is what the LORD, the God of Israel, says: "Cursed is everyone who does not obey the terms of this covenant— 4the terms I commanded your ancestors when I brought them out of Egypt, out of the iron-smelting furnace." I said, "Obey me and do everything I command you, and you will be my people, and I will be your God. 5Then I will fulfil the oath I swore to your ancestors, to give them a land flowing with milk and honey"—the land you possess today.'

I answered, 'Amen, LORD.'

6The LORD said to me, 'Proclaim all these words in the towns of Judah and in the streets of Jerusalem: "Listen to the terms of this covenant and follow them. 7From the time I brought your ancestors up from Egypt until today, I warned them again and again, saying, 'Obey me.' 8But they did not

---

[a] 11 The text of this verse is in Aramaic.

listen or pay attention; instead, they followed the stubbornness of their evil hearts. So I brought on them all the curses of the covenant I had commanded them to follow but that they did not keep."'

⁹Then the LORD said to me, 'There is a conspiracy among the people of Judah and those who live in Jerusalem. ¹⁰They have returned to the sins of their ancestors, who refused to listen to my words. They have followed other gods to serve them. Both the house of Israel and the house of Judah have broken the covenant I made with their ancestors. ¹¹Therefore this is what the LORD says: "I will bring on them a disaster they cannot escape. Although they cry out to me, I will not listen to them. ¹²The towns of Judah and the people of Jerusalem will go and cry out to the gods to whom they burn incense, but they will not help them at all when disaster strikes. ¹³You, Judah, have as many gods as you have towns; and the altars you have set up to burn incense to that shameful god Baal are as many as the streets of Jerusalem."

¹⁴'Do not pray for this people or offer any plea or petition for them, because I will not listen when they call to me in the time of their distress.

¹⁵'What is my beloved doing in my temple
    as she, with many others, works out her evil schemes?
Can consecrated meat avert your punishment?
When you engage in your wickedness,
    then you rejoice.'[a]

¹⁶The LORD called you a thriving olive tree
    with fruit beautiful in form.
But with the roar of a mighty storm
    he will set it on fire,
    and its branches will be broken.

¹⁷The LORD Almighty, who planted you, has decreed disaster for you, because the house of Israel and the house of Judah have done evil and aroused my anger by burning incense to Baal.

Plot against Jeremiah

¹⁸Because the LORD revealed their plot to me, I knew it, for at that time he showed me what they were doing. ¹⁹I had been like a gentle lamb led to the slaughter; I did not realise that they had plotted against me, saying,

'Let us destroy the tree and its fruit;
    let us cut him off from the land of the living,
    that his name be remembered no more.'

²⁰But you, LORD Almighty, who judge righteously
    and test the heart and mind,
let me see your vengeance on them,
    for to you I have committed my cause.

²¹'Therefore this is what the LORD says about the people of Anathoth who are seeking your life and saying, "Do not prophesy in the name of the LORD or you will die by our hands"— ²²therefore this is what the LORD Almighty says: "I will punish them. Their young men will die by the sword, their sons and daughters by famine. ²³Not even a remnant will be left to them, because I will bring disaster on the people of Anathoth in the year of their punishment."'

Jeremiah's complaint

12 You are always righteous, LORD,
    when I bring a case before you.
Yet I would speak with you about your justice:
    why does the way of the wicked prosper?
    Why do all the faithless live at ease?
²You have planted them, and they have taken root;
    they grow and bear fruit.
You are always on their lips
    but far from their hearts.
³Yet you know me, LORD;
    you see me and test my thoughts about you.
Drag them off like sheep to be butchered!
    Set them apart for the day of slaughter!
⁴How long will the land lie parched
    and the grass in every field be withered?
Because those who live in it are wicked,
    the animals and birds have perished.
Moreover, the people are saying,
    'He will not see what happens to us.'

---

[a] 15 Or *Could consecrated meat avert your punishment? / Then you would rejoice*

God's answer

5 'If you have raced with people on foot
    and they have worn you out,
  how can you compete with horses?
If you stumble[a] in safe country,
  how will you manage in the thickets by[b] the Jordan?
6 Your relatives, members of your own family,
    even they have betrayed you;
  they have raised a loud cry against you.
Do not trust them,
  though they speak well of you.

7 'I will forsake my house,
    abandon my inheritance;
  I will give the one I love
    into the hands of her enemies.
8 My inheritance has become to me
    like a lion in the forest.
  She roars at me;
    therefore I hate her.
9 Has not my inheritance become to me
    like a speckled bird of prey
  that other birds of prey surround and attack?
  Go and gather all the wild beasts;
    bring them to devour.
10 Many shepherds will ruin my vineyard
    and trample down my field;
  they will turn my pleasant field
    into a desolate wasteland.
11 It will be made a wasteland,
    parched and desolate before me;
  the whole land will be laid waste
    because there is no-one who cares.
12 Over all the barren heights in the desert
    destroyers will swarm,
  for the sword of the LORD will devour
    from one end of the land to the other;
    no-one will be safe.
13 They will sow wheat but reap thorns;
    they will wear themselves out but gain nothing.
  They will bear the shame of their harvest
    because of the LORD's fierce anger.'

14 This is what the LORD says: 'As for all my wicked neighbours who seize the inheritance I gave to my people Israel, I will uproot them from their lands and I will uproot the house of Judah from among them. 15 But after I uproot them, I will again have compassion and will bring each of them back to their own inheritance and their own country. 16 And if they learn well the ways of my people and swear by my name, saying, "As surely as the LORD lives"—even as they once taught my people to swear by Baal—then they will be established among my people. 17 But if any nation does not listen, I will completely uproot and destroy it,' declares the LORD.

A linen belt

13 This is what the LORD said to me: 'Go and buy a linen belt and put it round your waist, but do not let it touch water.' 2 So I bought a belt, as the LORD directed, and put it round my waist.

3 Then the word of the LORD came to me a second time: 4 'Take the belt you bought and are wearing round your waist, and go now to Perath[c] and hide it there in a crevice in the rocks.' 5 So I went and hid it at Perath, as the LORD told me.

6 Many days later the LORD said to me, 'Go now to Perath and get the belt I told you to hide there.' 7 So I went to Perath and dug

Linen belt
Jeremiah 13:1
Jeremiah often did symbolic things to get his message across. Here he wears a new white linen belt around his waist, which symbolised how God's people could be clean and close to him. Then he put the belt in a gap in some rocks and, not surprisingly, many days later it was ruined. This showed what would happen to the people of Judah if they went away from God.

---

[a] 5 Or *you feel secure only* [b] 5 Or *the flooding of* [c] 4 Or possibly *to the Euphrates*; similarly in verses 5-7

up the belt and took it from the place where I had hidden it, but now it was ruined and completely useless.

⁸Then the word of the LORD came to me: ⁹'This is what the LORD says: "In the same way I will ruin the pride of Judah and the great pride of Jerusalem. ¹⁰These wicked people, who refuse to listen to my words, who follow the stubbornness of their hearts and go after other gods to serve and worship them, will be like this belt—completely useless! ¹¹For as a belt is bound round the waist, so I bound the whole house of Israel and the whole house of Judah to me," declares the LORD, "to be my people for my renown and praise and honour. But they have not listened."

Wineskins

¹²'Say to them: "This is what the LORD, the God of Israel, says: every wineskin should be filled with wine." And if they say to you, "Don't we know that every wineskin should be filled with wine?" ¹³then tell them, "This is what the LORD says: I am going to fill with drunkenness all who live in this land, including the kings who sit on David's throne, the priests, the prophets and all those living in Jerusalem. ¹⁴I will smash them one against the other, parents and children alike, declares the LORD. I will allow no pity or mercy or compassion to keep me from destroying them."'

Threat of captivity

¹⁵Hear and pay attention,
  do not be arrogant,
    for the LORD has spoken.
¹⁶Give glory to the LORD your God
    before he brings the darkness,
  before your feet stumble
    on the darkening hills.
  You hope for light,
    but he will turn it to utter darkness
    and change it to deep gloom.
¹⁷If you do not listen,
    I will weep in secret
      because of your pride;
  my eyes will weep bitterly,
    overflowing with tears,
  because the LORD's flock will be taken captive.

¹⁸Say to the king and to the queen mother,
  'Come down from your thrones,
  for your glorious crowns
    will fall from your heads.'
¹⁹The cities in the Negev will be shut up,
    and there will be no-one to open them.
  All Judah will be carried into exile,
    carried completely away.

²⁰Look up and see
    those who are coming from the north.
  Where is the flock that was entrusted to you,
    the sheep of which you boasted?
²¹What will you say when ⌊the LORD⌋ sets over you
    those you cultivated as your special allies?
  Will not pain grip you
    like that of a woman in labour?
²²And if you ask yourself,
    'Why has this happened to me?'—
  it is because of your many sins
    that your skirts have been torn off
    and your body ill-treated.
²³Can an Ethiopian*ᵃ* change his skin
    or a leopard its spots?
  Neither can you do good
    who are accustomed to doing evil.

²⁴'I will scatter you like chaff
    driven by the desert wind.
²⁵This is your lot,
    the portion I have decreed for you,'
      declares the LORD,
  'because you have forgotten me
    and trusted in false gods.
²⁶I will pull up your skirts over your face
    that your shame may be seen—
²⁷your adulteries and lustful neighings,
    your shameless prostitution!
  I have seen your detestable acts
    on the hills and in the fields.
  Woe to you, Jerusalem!
    How long will you be unclean?'

Drought, famine, sword

14 This is the word of the LORD that came to Jeremiah concerning the drought:

ᵃ 23 Hebrew *Cushite* (probably a person from the upper Nile region)

²'Judah mourns,
  her cities languish;
they wail for the land,
  and a cry goes up from Jerusalem.
³The nobles send their servants for water;
  they go to the cisterns
  but find no water.
They return with their jars unfilled;
  dismayed and despairing,
  they cover their heads.
⁴The ground is cracked
  because there is no rain in the land;
the farmers are dismayed
  and cover their heads.
⁵Even the doe in the field
  deserts her newborn fawn
  because there is no grass.
⁶Wild donkeys stand on the barren heights
  and pant like jackals;
their eyes fail
  for lack of food.'

⁷Although our sins testify against us,
  do something, LORD, for the sake of
    your name.
For our backsliding is great;
  we have sinned against you.
⁸You who are the hope of Israel,
  its Saviour in times of distress,
why are you like a stranger in the land,
  like a traveller who stays only a night?
⁹Why are you like someone taken by
    surprise,
  like a warrior powerless to save?
You are among us, LORD,
  and we bear your name;
  do not forsake us!

¹⁰This is what the LORD says about this people:

'They greatly love to wander;
  they do not restrain their feet.
So the LORD does not accept them;
  he will now remember their
    wickedness
  and punish them for their sins.'

¹¹Then the LORD said to me, 'Do not pray for the well-being of this people. ¹²Although they fast, I will not listen to their cry; though they offer burnt offerings and grain offerings, I will not accept them. Instead, I will destroy them with the sword, famine and plague.'

¹³But I said, 'Ah, Sovereign LORD, the prophets keep telling them, "You will not see the sword or suffer famine. Indeed, I will give you lasting peace in this place."'

¹⁴Then the LORD said to me, 'The prophets are prophesying lies in my name. I have not sent them or appointed them or spoken to them. They are prophesying to you false visions, divinations, idolatries[a] and the delusions of their own minds. ¹⁵Therefore, this is what the LORD says about the prophets who are prophesying in my name: I did not send them, yet they are saying, "No sword or famine will touch this land." Those same prophets will perish by sword and famine. ¹⁶And the people they are prophesying to will be thrown out into the streets of Jerusalem because of the famine and sword. There will be no-one to bury them, their wives, their sons and their daughters. I will pour out on them the calamity they deserve.

¹⁷'Speak this word to them:

'"Let my eyes overflow with tears
  night and day without ceasing;
for the Virgin Daughter, my people,
  has suffered a grievous wound,
  a crushing blow.
¹⁸If I go into the country,
  I see those slain by the sword;
if I go into the city,
  I see the ravages of famine.
Both prophet and priest
  have gone to a land they know not."'

¹⁹Have you rejected Judah completely?
  Do you despise Zion?
Why have you afflicted us
  so that we cannot be healed?
We hoped for peace
  but no good has come,
for a time of healing
  but there is only terror.
²⁰We acknowledge our wickedness, LORD,
  and the guilt of our ancestors;
  we have indeed sinned against you.
²¹For the sake of your name do not despise
    us;
  do not dishonour your glorious throne.

---

[a] 14 Or *visions, worthless divinations*

Remember your covenant with us
and do not break it.
²²Do any of the worthless idols of the
nations bring rain?
Do the skies themselves send down
showers?
No, it is you, LORD our God.
Therefore our hope is in you,
for you are the one who does all
this.

15 Then the LORD said to me: 'Even if Moses and Samuel were to stand before me, my heart would not go out to this people. Send them away from my presence! Let them go! ²And if they ask you, "Where shall we go?" tell them, "This is what the LORD says:

'"Those destined for death, to death;
those for the sword, to the sword;
those for starvation, to starvation;
those for captivity, to captivity."

³'I will send four kinds of destroyers against them,' declares the LORD, 'the sword to kill and the dogs to drag away and the birds and the wild animals to devour and destroy. ⁴I will make them abhorrent to all the kingdoms of the earth because of what Manasseh son of Hezekiah king of Judah did in Jerusalem.

⁵'Who will have pity on you, Jerusalem?
Who will mourn for you?
Who will stop to ask how you are?
⁶You have rejected me,' declares the
LORD.
'You keep on backsliding.
So I will lay hands on you and destroy
you;
I am tired of holding back.
⁷I will winnow them with a winnowing
fork
at the city gates of the land.
I will bring bereavement and destruction
on my people,
for they have not changed their ways.
⁸I will make their widows more numerous
than the sand of the sea.
At midday I will bring a destroyer
against the mothers of their young
men;
suddenly I will bring down on them
anguish and terror.
⁹The mother of seven will grow faint
and breathe her last.
Her sun will set while it is still day;
she will be disgraced and humiliated.
I will put the survivors to the sword
before their enemies,'
declares the LORD.

¹⁰Alas, my mother, that you gave me birth,
a man with whom the whole land
strives and contends!
I have neither lent nor borrowed,
yet everyone curses me.

¹¹The LORD said,

'Surely I will deliver you for a good
purpose;
surely I will make your enemies plead
with you
in times of disaster and times of
distress.

¹²'Can anyone break iron—
iron from the north—or bronze?

¹³'Your wealth and your treasures
I will give as plunder, without charge,
because of all your sins
throughout your country.
¹⁴I will enslave you to your enemies
in*a* a land you do not know,
for my anger will kindle a fire
that will burn against you.'

¹⁵LORD, you understand;
remember me and care for me.
Avenge me on my persecutors.
You are long-suffering—do not take me
away;
think of how I suffer reproach for your
sake.
¹⁶When your words came, I ate them;
they were my joy and my heart's
delight,
for I bear your name,
LORD God Almighty.
¹⁷I never sat in the company of revellers,
never made merry with them;

---

a 14 Some Hebrew manuscripts, Septuagint and Syriac (see also Jer. 17:4); most Hebrew manuscripts *I will cause your enemies to bring you / into*

> **IN OTHER WORDS**
>
> ### Repent
> **Jeremiah 15:19**
>
> 'To repent' means literally 'to turn around' or 'to change one's mind', which leads to a change in behaviour. In the Bible, the word 'repent' specifically means turning away from sin.

I sat alone because your hand was on me
   and you had filled me with
      indignation.
18 Why is my pain unending
   and my wound grievous and
      incurable?
You are to me like a deceptive brook,
   like a spring that fails.

19 Therefore this is what the LORD says:

'If you repent, I will restore you
   that you may serve me;
if you utter worthy, not worthless, words,
   you will be my spokesman.
Let this people turn to you,
   but you must not turn to them.
20 I will make you a wall to this people,
   a fortified wall of bronze;
they will fight against you
   but will not overcome you,
for I am with you
   to rescue and save you,'
                     declares the LORD.
21 'I will save you from the hands of the
      wicked
   and deliver you from the grasp of the
      cruel.'

Day of disaster

16 Then the word of the LORD came to me: 2 'You must not marry and have sons or daughters in this place.' 3 For this is what the LORD says about the sons and daughters born in this land and about the women who are their mothers and the men who are their fathers: 4 'They will die of deadly diseases. They will not be mourned or buried but will be like dung lying on the ground. They will perish by sword and famine, and their dead bodies will become food for the birds and the wild animals.'

5 For this is what the LORD says: 'Do not enter a house where there is a funeral meal; do not go to mourn or show sympathy, because I have withdrawn my blessing, my love and my pity from this people,' declares the LORD. 6 'Both high and low will die in this land. They will not be buried or mourned, nor will people cut themselves or shave their heads for them. 7 No-one will offer food to comfort those who mourn for the dead—not even for a father or a mother—nor will anyone give them a drink to console them.

8 'And do not enter a house where there is feasting and sit down to eat and drink. 9 For this is what the LORD Almighty, the God of Israel, says: before your eyes and in your days I will bring an end to the sounds of joy and gladness and to the voices of bride and bridegroom in this place.

10 'When you tell these people all this and they ask you, "Why has the LORD decreed such a great disaster against us? What wrong have we done? What sin have we committed against the LORD our God?" 11 then say to them, "It is because your ancestors forsook me," declares the LORD, "and followed other gods and served and worshipped them. They forsook me and did not keep my law. 12 But you have behaved more wickedly than your ancestors. See how all of you are following the stubbornness of your evil hearts instead of obeying me. 13 So I will throw you out of this land into a land neither you nor your ancestors have known, and there you will serve other gods day and night, for I will show you no favour."

14 'However, the days are coming,' declares the LORD, 'when people will no longer say, "As surely as the LORD lives, who brought the Israelites up out of Egypt," 15 but they will say, "As surely as the LORD lives, who brought the Israelites up out of the land of the north and out of all the countries where he had banished them." For I will restore them to the land I gave to their ancestors.

16 'But now I will send for many fishermen,' declares the LORD, 'and they will catch

them. After that I will send for many hunters, and they will hunt them down on every mountain and hill and from the crevices of the rocks. ¹⁷My eyes are on all their ways; they are not hidden from me, nor is their sin concealed from my eyes. ¹⁸I will repay them double for their wickedness and their sin, because they have defiled my land with the lifeless forms of their vile images and have filled my inheritance with their detestable idols.'

¹⁹LORD, my strength and my fortress,
   my refuge in time of distress,
to you the nations will come
   from the ends of the earth and say,
'Our ancestors possessed nothing but false gods,
   worthless idols that did them no good.
²⁰Do people make their own gods?
   Yes, but they are not gods!'

²¹'Therefore I will teach them—
   this time I will teach them
   my power and might.
Then they will know
   that my name is the LORD.

17
'Judah's sin is engraved with an iron tool,
   inscribed with a flint point,
on the tablets of their hearts
   and on the horns of their altars.
²Even their children remember
   their altars and Asherah poles*ᵃ*
beside the spreading trees
   and on the high hills.
³My mountain in the land
   and your*ᵇ* wealth and all your treasures
I will give away as plunder,
   together with your high places,
   because of sin throughout your country.
⁴Through your own fault you will lose
   the inheritance I gave you.
I will enslave you to your enemies
   in a land you do not know,
for you have kindled my anger,
   and it will burn for ever.'

⁵This is what the LORD says:

'Cursed are those who trust in mortals,
   who depend on flesh for their strength
   and whose hearts turn away from the LORD.
⁶They will be like a bush in the wastelands;
   they will not see prosperity when it comes.
They will dwell in the parched places of the desert,
   in a salt land where no-one lives.

⁷'But blessed are those who trust in the LORD,
   whose confidence is in him.
⁸They will be like a tree planted by the water
   that sends out its roots by the stream.
It does not fear when heat comes;
   its leaves are always green.
It has no worries in a year of drought
   and never fails to bear fruit.'

⁹The heart is deceitful above all things
   and beyond cure.
   Who can understand it?

¹⁰'I the LORD search the heart
   and examine the mind,
to reward everyone according to their conduct,
   according to what their deeds deserve.'

¹¹Like a partridge that hatches eggs it did not lay
   are those who gain riches by unjust means.
When their lives are half gone, their riches will desert them,
   and in the end they will prove to be fools.

¹²A glorious throne, exalted from the beginning,
   is the place of our sanctuary.
¹³LORD, you are the hope of Israel;
   all who forsake you will be put to shame.
Those who turn away from you will be written in the dust
   because they have forsaken the LORD,
   the spring of living water.

ᵃ 2 That is, wooden symbols of the goddess Asherah   ᵇ 2, 3 Or hills | ³and the mountains of the land. | Your

¹⁴Heal me, LORD, and I shall be healed;
  save me and I shall be saved,
  for you are the one I praise.
¹⁵They keep saying to me,
  'Where is the word of the LORD?
  Let it now be fulfilled!'
¹⁶I have not run away from being your shepherd;
  you know I have not desired the day of despair.
  What passes my lips is open before you.
¹⁷Do not be a terror to me;
  you are my refuge in the day of disaster.
¹⁸Let my persecutors be put to shame,
  but keep me from shame;
  let them be terrified,
  but keep me from terror.
  Bring on them the day of disaster;
  destroy them with double destruction.

Keeping the Sabbath holy

¹⁹This is what the LORD said to me: 'Go and stand at the gate of the people, through which the kings of Judah go in and out; stand also at all the other gates of Jerusalem. ²⁰Say to them, "Hear the word of the LORD, you kings of Judah and all people of Judah and everyone living in Jerusalem who come through these gates. ²¹This is what the LORD says: be careful not to carry a load on the Sabbath day or bring it through the gates of Jerusalem. ²²Do not bring a load out of your houses or do any work on the Sabbath, but keep the Sabbath day holy, as I commanded your ancestors. ²³Yet they did not listen or pay attention; they were stiff-necked and would not listen or respond to discipline. ²⁴But if you are careful to obey me, declares the LORD, and bring no load through the gates of this city on the Sabbath, but keep the Sabbath day holy by not doing any work on it, ²⁵then kings who sit on David's throne will come through the gates of this city with their officials. They and their officials will come riding in chariots and on horses, accompanied by the men of Judah and those living in Jerusalem, and this city will be inhabited for ever. ²⁶People will come from the towns of Judah and the villages around Jerusalem, from the territory of Benjamin and the western foothills, from the hill country and the Negev, bringing burnt offerings and sacrifices, grain offerings and incense, and bringing thank-offerings to the house of the LORD. ²⁷But if you do not obey me to keep the Sabbath day holy by not carrying any load as you come through the gates of Jerusalem on the Sabbath day, then I will kindle an unquenchable fire in the gates of Jerusalem that will consume her fortresses."'

At the potter's house

18 This is the word that came to Jeremiah from the LORD: ²'Go down to the potter's house, and there I will give you my message.' ³So I went down to the potter's house, and I saw him working at the wheel. ⁴But the pot he was shaping from the clay was marred in his hands; so the potter formed it into another pot, shaping it as seemed best to him.

⁵Then the word of the LORD came to me. ⁶He said, 'Can I not do with you, house of Israel, as this potter does?' declares the LORD. 'Like clay in the hand of the potter, so are you in my hand, house of Israel. ⁷If at any time I announce that a nation or kingdom is to be uprooted, torn down and destroyed, ⁸and if that nation I warned repents of its evil, then I will relent and not inflict on it the disaster I had planned. ⁹And if at another time I announce that a nation or kingdom is to be built up and planted,

making Connections

Clay pottery
Jeremiah 18:1
Clay was a common material, used for bricks, seals and writing tablets as well as pots, utensils, lamps and dishes. Clay is a very flexible material and can be moulded into all kinds of shapes. Clay pottery is one of the longest lasting materials ever made. Although clay pots break easily, the fragments last for centuries, giving clues as to how people lived.

¹⁰and if it does evil in my sight and does not obey me, then I will reconsider the good I had intended to do for it.

¹¹'Now therefore say to the people of Judah and those living in Jerusalem, "This is what the LORD says: look! I am preparing a disaster for you and devising a plan against you. So turn from your evil ways, each one of you, and reform your ways and your actions." ¹²But they will reply, "It's no use. We will continue with our own plans; we will all follow the stubbornness of our evil hearts."'

¹³Therefore this is what the LORD says:

'Enquire among the nations:
  who has ever heard anything like this?
A most horrible thing has been done
  by Virgin Israel.
¹⁴Does the snow of Lebanon
  ever vanish from its rocky slopes?
Do its cool waters from distant sources
  ever cease to flow?^{a}
¹⁵Yet my people have forgotten me;
  they burn incense to worthless idols,
which made them stumble in their ways,
  in the ancient paths.
They made them walk in byways,
  on roads not built up.
¹⁶Their land will be an object of horror
  and of lasting scorn;
all who pass by will be appalled
  and will shake their heads.
¹⁷Like a wind from the east,
  I will scatter them before their enemies;
I will show them my back and not my face
  in the day of their disaster.'

¹⁸They said, 'Come, let's make plans against Jeremiah; for the teaching of the law by the priest will not cease, nor will counsel from the wise, nor the word from the prophets. So come, let's attack him with our tongues and pay no attention to anything he says.'

¹⁹Listen to me, LORD;
  hear what my accusers are saying!
²⁰Should good be repaid with evil?
  Yet they have dug a pit for me.
Remember that I stood before you
  and spoke on their behalf
  to turn your wrath away from them.
²¹So give their children over to famine;
  hand them over to the power of the sword.
Let their wives be made childless and widows;
  let their men be put to death,
  their young men slain by the sword in battle.
²²Let a cry be heard from their houses
  when you suddenly bring invaders against them,
for they have dug a pit to capture me
  and have hidden snares for my feet.
²³But you, LORD, know
  all their plots to kill me.
Do not forgive their crimes
  or blot out their sins from your sight.
Let them be overthrown before you;
  deal with them in the time of your anger.

19 This is what the LORD says: 'Go and buy a clay jar from a potter. Take along some of the elders of the people and of the priests ²and go out to the Valley of Ben Hinnom, near the entrance of the Potsherd Gate. There proclaim the words I tell you, ³and say, "Hear the word of the LORD, you kings of Judah and people of Jerusalem. This is what the LORD Almighty, the God of Israel, says: listen! I am going to bring a disaster on this place that will make the ears of everyone who hears of it tingle. ⁴For they have forsaken me and made this a place of foreign gods; they have burned incense in it to gods that neither they nor their ancestors nor the kings of Judah ever knew, and they have filled this place with the blood of the innocent. ⁵They have built the high places of Baal to burn their children in the fire as offerings to Baal—something I did not command or mention, nor did it enter my mind. ⁶So beware, the days are coming, declares the LORD, when people will no longer call this place Topheth or the Valley of Ben Hinnom, but the Valley of Slaughter.

⁷ "'In this place I will ruin^b the plans of Judah and Jerusalem. I will make them fall by the sword before their enemies, at the

---

^{a} 14 The meaning of the Hebrew for this sentence is uncertain (see verses 1 and 10). ^{b} 7 The Hebrew for *ruin* sounds like the Hebrew for *jar* hands of those who seek their lives, and I will give their carcasses as food to the birds and the wild animals. 8I will devastate this city and make it an object of horror and scorn; all who pass by will be appalled and will scoff because of all its wounds. 9I will make them eat the flesh of their sons and daughters, and they will eat one another's flesh because their enemies will press the siege so hard against them to destroy them."

10'Then break the jar while those who go with you are watching, 11and say to them, "This is what the LORD Almighty says: I will smash this nation and this city just as this potter's jar is smashed and cannot be repaired. They will bury the dead in Topheth until there is no more room. 12This is what I will do to this place and to those who live here, declares the LORD. I will make this city like Topheth. 13The houses in Jerusalem and those of the kings of Judah will be defiled like this place, Topheth—all the houses where they burned incense on the roofs to all the starry hosts and poured out drink offerings to other gods."'

14Jeremiah then returned from Topheth, where the LORD had sent him to prophesy, and stood in the court of the LORD's temple and said to all the people, 15'This is what the LORD Almighty, the God of Israel, says: "Listen! I am going to bring on this city and all the villages around it every disaster I pronounced against them, because they were stiff-necked and would not listen to my words."'

Jeremiah and Pashhur

20 When the priest Pashhur son of Immer, the official in charge of the temple of the LORD, heard Jeremiah prophesying these things, 2he had Jeremiah the prophet beaten and put in the stocks at the Upper Gate of Benjamin at the LORD's temple. 3The next day, when Pashhur released him from the stocks, Jeremiah said to him, 'The LORD's name for you is not Pashhur, but Terror on Every Side. 4For this is what the LORD says: "I will make you a terror to yourself and to all your friends; with your own eyes you will see them fall by the sword of their enemies. I will give all Judah into the hands of the king of Babylon, who will carry them away to Babylon or put them to the sword. 5I will deliver all the wealth of this city into the hands of their enemies—all its products, all its valuables and all the treasures of the kings of Judah. They will take it away as plunder and carry it off to Babylon. 6And you, Pashhur, and all who live in your house will go into exile to Babylon. There you will die and be buried, you and all your friends to whom you have prophesied lies."'

Jeremiah's complaint

7You deceived^a me, LORD, and I was deceived;^{b}
  you overpowered me and prevailed.
I am ridiculed all day long;
  everyone mocks me.
8Whenever I speak, I cry out
  proclaiming violence and destruction.
So the word of the LORD has brought me
  insult and reproach all day long.
9But if I say, 'I will not mention his word
  or speak any more in his name,'
his word is in my heart like a fire,
  a fire shut up in my bones.
I am weary of holding it in;
  indeed, I cannot.
10I hear many whispering,
  'Terror on every side!
  Denounce him! Let's denounce him!'
All my friends
  are waiting for me to slip, saying,
'Perhaps he will be deceived;
  then we will prevail over him
  and take our revenge on him.'

11But the LORD is with me like a mighty warrior;
  so my persecutors will stumble and not prevail.
They will fail and be thoroughly disgraced;
  their dishonour will never be forgotten.
12LORD Almighty, you who examine the righteous
  and probe the heart and mind,
let me see your vengeance on them,
  for to you I have committed my cause.

---

^{a}7 Or *persuaded* ^{b}7 Or *persuaded*

¹³Sing to the LORD!
 Give praise to the LORD!
He rescues the life of the needy
 from the hands of the wicked.

¹⁴Cursed be the day I was born!
 May the day my mother bore me not be
  blessed!
¹⁵Cursed be the man who brought my
  father the news,
 who made him very glad, saying,
 'A child is born to you—a son!'
¹⁶May that man be like the towns
  the LORD overthrew without pity.
 May he hear wailing in the morning,
  a battle cry at noon.
¹⁷For he did not kill me in the womb,
 with my mother as my grave,
  her womb enlarged for ever.
¹⁸Why did I ever come out of the womb
 to see trouble and sorrow
  and to end my days in shame?

God rejects Zedekiah's request

21 The word came to Jeremiah from the LORD when King Zedekiah sent to him Pashhur son of Malkijah and the priest Zephaniah son of Maaseiah. They said: ²'Enquire now of the LORD for us because Nebuchadnezzar[a] king of Babylon is attacking us. Perhaps the LORD will perform wonders for us as in times past so that he will withdraw from us.'

³But Jeremiah answered them, 'Tell Zedekiah, ⁴"This is what the LORD, the God of Israel, says: I am about to turn against you the weapons of war that are in your hands, which you are using to fight the king of Babylon and the Babylonians[b] who are outside the wall besieging you. And I will gather them inside this city. ⁵I myself will fight against you with an outstretched hand and a mighty arm in furious anger and in great wrath. ⁶I will strike down those who live in this city—both people and animals—and they will die of a terrible plague. ⁷After that, declares the LORD, I will give Zedekiah king of Judah, his officials and the people in this city who survive the plague, sword and famine, into the hands of Nebuchadnezzar king of Babylon and to their enemies who seek their lives. He will put them to the sword; he will show them no mercy or pity or compassion."

⁸'Furthermore, tell the people, "This is what the LORD says: see, I am setting before you the way of life and the way of death. ⁹Whoever stays in this city will die by the sword, famine or plague. But whoever goes out and surrenders to the Babylonians who are besieging you will live; they will escape with their lives. ¹⁰I have determined to do this city harm and not good, declares the LORD. It will be given into the hands of the king of Babylon, and he will destroy it with fire."

¹¹'Moreover, say to the royal house of Judah, "Hear the word of the LORD. ¹²This is what the LORD says to you, house of David:

'"Administer justice every morning;
 rescue from the hands of their
  oppressors
those who have been robbed,
 or my wrath will break out and burn like
  fire
because of the evil you have done—
 burn with no-one to quench it.
¹³I am against you, Jerusalem,
 you who live above this valley
  on the rocky plateau, declares the
   LORD—
you who say, 'Who can come against us?
 Who can enter our refuge?'
¹⁴I will punish you as your deeds deserve,
  declares the LORD.
I will kindle a fire in your forests
 that will consume everything around
  you."'

Judgment against wicked kings

22 This is what the LORD says: 'Go down to the palace of the king of Judah and proclaim this message there: ²"Hear the word of the LORD to you, king of Judah, you who sit on David's throne—you, your officials and your people who come through these gates. ³This is what the LORD says: do what is just and right. Rescue from the hands of their oppressors those who have been robbed. Do no wrong or

---

[a] 2 Hebrew *Nebuchadrezzar*, of which *Nebuchadnezzar* is a variant; here and often in Jeremiah and Ezekiel [b] 4 Or *Chaldeans*; also in verse 9

Gilead
Jeremiah 22:6
Gilead was the name of a mountainous region east of the River Jordan. It always had lots of rainfall each year and so was covered in thick forests.

violence to the foreigner, the fatherless or the widow, and do not shed innocent blood in this place. ⁴For if you are careful to carry out these commands, then kings who sit on David's throne will come through the gates of this palace, riding in chariots and on horses, accompanied by their officials and their people. ⁵But if you do not obey these commands, declares the LORD, I swear by myself that this palace will become a ruin."'

⁶For this is what the LORD says about the palace of the king of Judah:

'Though you are like Gilead to me,
  like the summit of Lebanon,
I will surely make you like a wasteland,
  like towns not inhabited.
⁷I will send destroyers against you,
  each man with his weapons,
and they will cut up your fine cedar beams
  and throw them into the fire.

⁸'People from many nations will pass by this city and will ask one another, "Why has the LORD done such a thing to this great city?" ⁹And the answer will be: "Because they have forsaken the covenant of the LORD their God and have worshipped and served other gods."'

¹⁰Do not weep for the dead ⌊king⌋ or
  mourn his loss;
    rather, weep bitterly for him who is
    exiled,
because he will never return
  nor see his native land again.

¹¹For this is what the LORD says about Shallum*a* son of Josiah, who succeeded his father as king of Judah but has gone from this place: 'He will never return. ¹²He will die in the place where they have led him captive; he will not see this land again.'

¹³'Woe to him who builds his palace by
    unrighteousness,
  his upper rooms by injustice,
making his subjects work for nothing,
  not paying them for their labour.
¹⁴He says, "I will build myself a great palace
  with spacious upper rooms."
So he makes large windows in it,
  panels it with cedar
  and decorates it in red.

¹⁵'Does it make you a king
  to have more and more cedar?
Did not your father have food and drink?
  He did what was right and just,
  so all went well with him.
¹⁶He defended the cause of the poor and
    needy,
  and so all went well.
Is that not what it means to know me?'
  declares the LORD.
¹⁷'But your eyes and your heart
  are set only on dishonest gain,
on shedding innocent blood
  and on oppression and extortion.'

¹⁸Therefore this is what the LORD says about Jehoiakim son of Josiah king of Judah:

'They will not mourn for him:
  "Alas, my brother! Alas, my sister!"
They will not mourn for him:
  "Alas, my master! Alas, his splendour!"
¹⁹He will have the burial of a donkey—
  dragged away and thrown
  outside the gates of Jerusalem.

²⁰'Go up to Lebanon and cry out,
  let your voice be heard in Bashan,
cry out from Abarim,
  for all your allies are crushed.
²¹I warned you when you felt secure,
  but you said, "I will not listen!"
This has been your way from your youth;
  you have not obeyed me.
²²The wind will drive all your shepherds
    away,
  and your allies will go into exile.

---
a 11 Also called *Jehoahaz*

Then you will be ashamed and disgraced
because of all your wickedness.
23You who live in "Lebanon",[a]
who are nestled in cedar buildings,
how you will groan when pangs come
upon you,
pain like that of a woman in labour!

24'As surely as I live,' declares the LORD, 'even if you, Jehoiachin[b] son of Jehoiakim king of Judah, were a signet ring on my right hand, I would still pull you off. 25I will deliver you into the hands of those who seek your life, those you fear—Nebuchadnezzar king of Babylon and the Babylonians.[c] 26I will hurl you and the mother who gave you birth into another country, where neither of you was born, and there you both will die. 27You will never come back to the land you long to return to.'

28Is this man Jehoiachin a despised, broken pot,
an object no-one wants?
Why will he and his children be hurled out,
cast into a land they do not know?
29O land, land, land,
hear the word of the LORD!
30This is what the LORD says:
'Record this man as if childless,
a man who will not prosper in his lifetime,
for none of his offspring will prosper,
none will sit on the throne of David
or rule any more in Judah.'

The righteous Branch

23 'Woe to the shepherds who are destroying and scattering the sheep of my pasture!' declares the LORD. 2Therefore this is what the LORD, the God of Israel, says to the shepherds who tend my people: 'Because you have scattered my flock and driven them away and have not bestowed care on them, I will bestow punishment on you for the evil you have done,' declares the LORD. 3'I myself will gather the remnant of my flock out of all the countries where I have driven them and will bring them back to their pasture, where they will be fruitful and increase in number. 4I will place shepherds over them who will tend them, and they will no longer be afraid or terrified, nor will any be missing,' declares the LORD.

Shepherds
Jeremiah 23:1
A shepherd invested a lot of care and time into his flock; after all, his sheep were his livelihood. He would provide his flock with water and food, would know which sheep were his, and would risk his life to protect them if necessary. Compare that to the shepherds described in these verses.

5'The days are coming,' declares the LORD,
'when I will raise up for David[d] a righteous Branch,
a King who will reign wisely
and do what is just and right in the land.
6In his days Judah will be saved
and Israel will live in safety.
This is the name by which he will be called:
The LORD Our Righteous Saviour.

7'So then, the days are coming,' declares the LORD, 'when people will no longer say, "As surely as the LORD lives, who brought the Israelites up out of Egypt," 8but they will say, "As surely as the LORD lives, who brought the descendants of Israel up out of the land of the north and out of all the countries where he had banished them." Then they will live in their own land.'

Lying prophets

9Concerning the prophets:

My heart is broken within me;
all my bones tremble.

---

[a] 23 That is, the palace in Jerusalem (see 1 Kings 7:2) [b] 24 Hebrew *Koniah*, a variant of *Jehoiachin*; also in verse 28
[c] 25 Or *Chaldeans* [d] 5 Or *up from David's line*

I am like a drunken man,
 like one overcome by wine,
because of the LORD
 and his holy words.

¹⁰The land is full of adulterers;
 because of the curse[a] the land lies parched
 and the pastures in the wilderness are withered.
The ⌊prophets⌋ follow an evil course
 and use their power unjustly.

¹¹'Both prophet and priest are godless;
 even in my temple I find their wickedness,'
　　　　　　　　　　declares the LORD.
¹²'Therefore their path will become slippery;
 they will be banished to darkness
 and there they will fall.
I will bring disaster on them
 in the year they are punished,'
　　　　　　　　　　declares the LORD.

¹³'Among the prophets of Samaria
 I saw this repulsive thing:
they prophesied by Baal
 and led my people Israel astray.
¹⁴And among the prophets of Jerusalem
 I have seen something horrible:
they commit adultery and live a lie.
They strengthen the hands of evildoers,
 so that none of them turn from their wickedness.
They are all like Sodom to me;
 the people of Jerusalem are like Gomorrah.'

¹⁵Therefore, this is what the LORD Almighty says concerning the prophets:

'I will make them eat bitter food
 and drink poisoned water,
because from the prophets of Jerusalem
 ungodliness has spread throughout the land.'

¹⁶This is what the LORD Almighty says:

'Do not listen to what the prophets are prophesying to you;
 they fill you with false hopes.
They speak visions from their own minds,
 not from the mouth of the LORD.
¹⁷They keep saying to those who despise me,
 "The LORD says: you will have peace."
And to all who follow the stubbornness of their hearts
 they say, "No harm will come to you."
¹⁸But which of them has stood in the council of the LORD
 to see or to hear his word?
Who has listened and heard his word?
¹⁹See, the storm of the LORD
 will burst out in wrath,
a whirlwind swirling down
 on the heads of the wicked.
²⁰The anger of the LORD will not turn back
 until he fully accomplishes
 the purposes of his heart.
In days to come
 you will understand it clearly.
²¹I did not send these prophets,
 yet they have run with their message;
I did not speak to them,
 yet they have prophesied.
²²But if they had stood in my council,
 they would have proclaimed my words to my people
and would have turned them from their evil ways
 and from their evil deeds.

²³'Am I only a God nearby,'
　　　　　　　　　　declares the LORD,
'and not a God far away?
²⁴Who can hide in secret places
 so that I cannot see them?'
　　　　　　　　　　declares the LORD.
'Do not I fill heaven and earth?'
　　　　　　　　　　declares the LORD.

²⁵'I have heard what the prophets say who prophesy lies in my name. They say, "I had a dream! I had a dream!" ²⁶How long will this continue in the hearts of these lying prophets, who prophesy the delusions of their own minds? ²⁷They think the dreams they tell one another will make my people forget my name, just as their ancestors forgot my name through Baal worship. ²⁸Let the prophets who have dreams tell their dreams, but let the one who has my word speak it faithfully. For what has straw

---
[a] 10 Or *because of these things*

to do with grain?' declares the LORD. ²⁹'Is not my word like fire,' declares the LORD, 'and like a hammer that breaks a rock in pieces?

³⁰'Therefore,' declares the LORD, 'I am against the prophets who steal from one another words supposedly from me. ³¹Yes,' declares the LORD, 'I am against the prophets who wag their own tongues and yet declare, "The LORD declares." ³²Indeed, I am against those who prophesy false dreams,' declares the LORD. 'They tell them and lead my people astray with their reckless lies, yet I did not send or appoint them. They do not benefit these people in the least,' declares the LORD.

False prophecy

³³'When these people, or a prophet or a priest, ask you, "What is the message from the LORD?" say to them, "What message? I will forsake you, declares the LORD." ³⁴If a prophet or a priest or anyone else claims, "This is a message from the LORD," I will punish them and their households. ³⁵This is what each of you keeps saying to your friends and other Israelites: "What is the LORD's answer?" or "What has the LORD spoken?" ³⁶But you must not mention "a message from the LORD" again, because everyone's own word becomes a message from God. So you distort the words of the living God, the LORD Almighty, our God. ³⁷This is what you keep saying to a prophet: "What is the LORD's answer to you?" or "What has the LORD spoken?" ³⁸Although you claim, "This is a message from the LORD," this is what the LORD says: you used the words, "This is a message from the LORD," even though I told you that you must not claim, "This is a message from the LORD." ³⁹Therefore, I will surely forget you and cast you out of my presence along with the city I gave to you and your ancestors. ⁴⁰I will bring on you everlasting disgrace—everlasting shame that will not be forgotten.'

Two baskets of figs

24 After Jehoiachin[a] son of Jehoiakim king of Judah and the officials, the artisans and the other skilled workers of Judah were carried into exile from Jerusalem to Babylon by Nebuchadnezzar king of Babylon, the LORD showed me two baskets of figs placed in front of the temple of the LORD. ²One basket had very good figs, like those that ripen early; the other basket had very bad figs, so bad that they could not be eaten.

³Then the LORD asked me, 'What do you see, Jeremiah?'

'Figs,' I answered. 'The good ones are very good, but the bad ones are so bad that they cannot be eaten.'

⁴Then the word of the LORD came to me: ⁵'This is what the LORD, the God of Israel, says: "Like these good figs, I regard as good the exiles from Judah, whom I sent away from this place to the land of the Babylonians.[b] ⁶My eyes will watch over them for their good, and I will bring them back to this land. I will build them up and not tear them down; I will plant them and not uproot them. ⁷I will give them a heart to know me, that I am the LORD. They will be my people, and I will be their God, for they will return to me with all their heart.

⁸' "But like the bad figs, which are so bad that they cannot be eaten," says the LORD, "so will I deal with Zedekiah king of Judah, his officials and the survivors from Jerusalem, whether they remain in this land or live in Egypt. ⁹I will make them abhorrent and an offence to all the kingdoms of the earth, a reproach and a byword, a curse[c] and an object of ridicule, wherever I banish them. ¹⁰I will send the sword, famine and plague against them until they are destroyed from the land I gave to them and their ancestors." '

Seventy years of captivity

25 The word came to Jeremiah concerning all the people of Judah in the fourth year of Jehoiakim son of Josiah king of Judah, which was the first year of Nebuchadnezzar king of Babylon. ²So Jeremiah the prophet said to all the people of Judah and to all those living in Jerusalem: ³for twenty-three years—from the thirteenth year of Josiah son of Amon king of

---

[a] 1 Hebrew *Jeconiah*, a variant of *Jehoiachin*   [b] 5 Or *Chaldeans*   [c] 9 That is, their names will be used in cursing (see Jer. 29:22); or, others will see that they are cursed.

Judah until this very day—the word of the LORD has come to me and I have spoken to you again and again, but you have not listened.

4And though the LORD has sent all his servants the prophets to you again and again, you have not listened or paid any attention. 5They said, 'Turn now, each of you, from your evil ways and your evil practices, and you can stay in the land the LORD gave to you and your ancestors for ever and ever. 6Do not follow other gods to serve and worship them; do not arouse my anger with what your hands have made. Then I will not harm you.'

7'But you did not listen to me,' declares the LORD, 'and you have aroused my anger with what your hands have made, and you have brought harm to yourselves.'

8Therefore the LORD Almighty says this: 'Because you have not listened to my words, 9I will summon all the peoples of the north and my servant Nebuchadnezzar king of Babylon,' declares the LORD, 'and I will bring them against this land and its inhabitants and against all the surrounding nations. I will completely destroy[a] them and make them an object of horror and scorn, and an everlasting ruin. 10I will banish from them the sounds of joy and gladness, the voices of bride and bridegroom, the sound of millstones and the light of the lamp. 11This whole country will become a desolate wasteland, and these nations will serve the king of Babylon for seventy years.

12'But when the seventy years are fulfilled, I will punish the king of Babylon and his nation, the land of the Babylonians,[b] for their guilt,' declares the LORD, 'and will make it desolate for ever. 13I will bring on that land all the things I have spoken against it, all that are written in this book and prophesied by Jeremiah against all the nations. 14They themselves will be enslaved by many nations and great kings; I will repay them according to their deeds and the work of their hands.'

The cup of God's wrath

15This is what the LORD, the God of Israel, said to me: 'Take from my hand this cup filled with the wine of my wrath and make all the nations to whom I send you drink it. 16When they drink it, they will stagger and go mad because of the sword I will send among them.'

17So I took the cup from the LORD's hand and made all the nations to whom he sent me drink it: 18Jerusalem and the towns of Judah, its kings and officials, to make them a ruin and an object of horror and scorn, a curse[c]—as they are today; 19Pharaoh king of Egypt, his attendants, his officials and all his people, 20and all the foreign people there; all the kings of Uz; all the kings of the Philistines (those of Ashkelon, Gaza, Ekron, and the people left at Ashdod); 21Edom, Moab and Ammon; 22all the kings of Tyre and Sidon; the kings of the coastlands across the sea; 23Dedan, Tema, Buz and all who are in distant places;[d] 24all the kings of Arabia and all the kings of the foreign people who live in the wilderness; 25all the kings of Zimri, Elam and Media; 26and all the kings of the north, near and far, one after the other—all the kingdoms on the face of the earth. And after all of them, the king of Sheshak[e] will drink it too.

27'Then tell them, "This is what the LORD Almighty, the God of Israel, says: drink, get drunk and vomit, and fall to rise no more because of the sword I will send among you." 28But if they refuse to take the cup from your hand and drink, tell them, "This is what the LORD Almighty says: you must drink it! 29See, I am beginning to bring disaster on the city that bears my Name, and will you indeed go unpunished? You will not go unpunished, for I am calling down a sword on all who live on the earth, declares the LORD Almighty."

30'Now prophesy all these words against them and say to them:

'"The LORD will roar from on high;
he will thunder from his holy dwelling
and roar mightily against his land.

---

[a] 9 The Hebrew term refers to the irrevocable giving over of things or persons to the LORD, often by totally destroying them.   [b] 12 Or Chaldeans   [c] 18 That is, their names to be used in cursing (see Jer. 29:22); or, to be seen by others as cursed   [d] 23 Or who clip the hair by their foreheads   [e] 26 Sheshak is a cryptogram for Babylon.

He will shout like those who tread the
   grapes,
   shout against all who live on the earth.
^{31}The tumult will resound to the ends of the
   earth,
   for the LORD will bring charges against
      the nations;
he will bring judgment on all humankind
   and put the wicked to the sword,"'
                              declares the LORD.

^{32}This is what the LORD Almighty says:

'Look! Disaster is spreading
   from nation to nation;
a mighty storm is rising
   from the ends of the earth.'

^{33}At that time those slain by the LORD will be everywhere—from one end of the earth to the other. They will not be mourned or gathered up or buried, but will be like dung lying on the ground.

^{34}Weep and wail, you shepherds;
   roll in the dust, you leaders of the flock.
For your time to be slaughtered has come;
   you will fall like the best of the rams.^{a}
^{35}The shepherds will have nowhere to flee,
   the leaders of the flock no place to
      escape.
^{36}Hear the cry of the shepherds,
   the wailing of the leaders of the flock,
   for the LORD is destroying their
      pasture.
^{37}The peaceful meadows will be laid waste
   because of the fierce anger of the LORD.
^{38}Like a lion he will leave his lair,
   and their land will become desolate
because of the sword^{b} of the oppressor
   and because of the LORD's fierce anger.

Jeremiah threatened with death

26 Early in the reign of Jehoiakim son of Josiah king of Judah, this word came from the LORD: ^{2}'This is what the LORD says: stand in the courtyard of the LORD's house and speak to all the people of the towns of Judah who come to worship in the house of the LORD. Tell them everything I command you; do not omit a word. ^{3}Perhaps they will listen and each will turn from their evil ways. Then I will relent and not inflict on them the disaster I was planning because of the evil they have done. ^{4}Say to them, "This is what the LORD says: if you do not listen to me and follow my law, which I have set before you, ^{5}and if you do not listen to the words of my servants the prophets, whom I have sent to you again and again (though you have not listened), ^{6}then I will make this house like Shiloh and this city a curse^{c} among all the nations of the earth."'

^{7}The priests, the prophets and all the people heard Jeremiah speak these words in the house of the LORD. ^{8}But as soon as Jeremiah finished telling all the people everything the LORD had commanded him to say, the priests, the prophets and all the people seized him and said, 'You must die! ^{9}Why do you prophesy in the LORD's name that this house will be like Shiloh and this city will be desolate and deserted?' And all the people crowded around Jeremiah in the house of the LORD.

> ## People and Places
>
> ### Shiloh
> **Jeremiah 26:6**
> Shiloh used to be a very important town in Israel. It was the place where the tabernacle was given its first permanent home after the people of Israel entered the Promised Land. The people of Israel went there to worship God during the time of the judges, making it a busy and significant place. But when the Ark of the Covenant was moved to another city, Shiloh became less important. Once Jerusalem was established as the capital city and the site of the temple, there was no longer a reason to visit Shiloh.

---

^{a} 34 Septuagint; Hebrew *fall and be shattered like fine pottery* ^{b} 38 Some Hebrew manuscripts and Septuagint (see also Jer. 46:16 and 50:16); most Hebrew manuscripts *anger* ^{c} 6 That is, their names will be used in cursing (see Jer. 29:22); or, others will see that they are cursed.

10When the officials of Judah heard about these things, they went up from the royal palace to the house of the LORD and took their places at the entrance of the New Gate of the LORD's house. 11Then the priests and the prophets said to the officials and all the people, 'This man should be sentenced to death because he has prophesied against this city. You have heard it with your own ears!'

12Then Jeremiah said to all the officials and all the people: 'The LORD sent me to prophesy against this house and this city all the things you have heard. 13Now reform your ways and your actions and obey the LORD your God. Then the LORD will relent and not bring the disaster he has pronounced against you. 14As for me, I am in your hands; do with me whatever you think is good and right. 15Be assured, however, that if you put me to death, you will bring the guilt of innocent blood on yourselves and on this city and on those who live in it, for in truth the LORD has sent me to you to speak all these words in your hearing.'

16Then the officials and all the people said to the priests and the prophets, 'This man should not be sentenced to death! He has spoken to us in the name of the LORD our God.'

17Some of the elders of the land stepped forward and said to the entire assembly of people, 18'Micah of Moresheth prophesied in the days of Hezekiah king of Judah. He told all the people of Judah, "This is what the LORD Almighty says:

> '"Zion will be ploughed like a field,
>   Jerusalem will become a heap of rubble,
> the temple hill a mound overgrown with thickets."'*a*

19'Did Hezekiah king of Judah or anyone else in Judah put him to death? Did not Hezekiah fear the LORD and seek his favour? And did not the LORD relent, so that he did not bring the disaster he pronounced against them? We are about to bring a terrible disaster on ourselves!'

20(Now Uriah son of Shemaiah from Kiriath Jearim was another man who prophesied in the name of the LORD; he prophesied the same things against this city and this land as Jeremiah did. 21When King Jehoiakim and all his officers and officials heard his words, the king sought to put him to death. But Uriah heard of it and fled in fear to Egypt. 22King Jehoiakim, however, sent Elnathan son of Akbor to Egypt, along with some other men. 23They brought Uriah out of Egypt and took him to King Jehoiakim, who had him struck down with a sword and his body thrown into the burial place of the common people.)

24Furthermore, Ahikam son of Shaphan supported Jeremiah, and so he was not handed over to the people to be put to death.

Judah to serve Nebuchadnezzar

27 Early in the reign of Zedekiah*b* son of Josiah king of Judah, this word came to Jeremiah from the LORD: 2this is what the LORD said to me: 'Make a yoke out of straps and crossbars and put it on your neck. 3Then send word to the kings of Edom, Moab, Ammon, Tyre and Sidon through the envoys who have come to Jerusalem to Zedekiah king of Judah. 4Give them a message for their masters and say, "This is what the LORD Almighty, the God of Israel, says: 'Tell this to your masters:

making Connections

Yoke
Jeremiah 27:2
A yoke was a type of harness which connected a pair of oxen to a plough. It was usually a wooden beam shaped to fit over the necks of two animals and held in place with a wooden peg.

---

a 18 Micah 3:12   *b* 1 A few Hebrew manuscripts and Syriac (see also Jer. 27:3, 12 and 28:1); most Hebrew manuscripts *Jehoiakim* (most Septuagint manuscripts do not have this verse.)

5with my great power and outstretched arm I made the earth and its people and the animals that are on it, and I give it to anyone I please. 6Now I will give all your countries into the hands of my servant Nebuchadnezzar king of Babylon; I will make even the wild animals subject to him. 7All nations will serve him and his son and his grandson until the time for his land comes; then many nations and great kings will subjugate him.

8' "If, however, any nation or kingdom will not serve Nebuchadnezzar king of Babylon or bow its neck under his yoke, I will punish that nation with the sword, famine and plague, declares the LORD, until I destroy it by his hand. 9So do not listen to your prophets, your diviners, your interpreters of dreams, your mediums or your sorcerers who tell you, "You will not serve the king of Babylon." 10They prophesy lies to you that will only serve to remove you far from your lands; I will banish you and you will perish. 11But if any nation will bow its neck under the yoke of the king of Babylon and serve him, I will let that nation remain in its own land to till it and to live there, declares the LORD.'"

12I gave the same message to Zedekiah king of Judah. I said, 'Bow your neck under the yoke of the king of Babylon; serve him and his people, and you will live. 13Why will you and your people die by the sword, famine and plague with which the LORD has threatened any nation that will not serve the king of Babylon? 14Do not listen to the words of the prophets who say to you, "You will not serve the king of Babylon," for they are prophesying lies to you. 15"I have not sent them," declares the LORD. "They are prophesying lies in my name. Therefore, I will banish you and you will perish, both you and the prophets who prophesy to you."'

16Then I said to the priests and all these people, 'This is what the LORD says: do not listen to the prophets who say, "Very soon now the articles from the LORD's house will be brought back from Babylon." They are prophesying lies to you. 17Do not listen to them. Serve the king of Babylon, and you will live. Why should this city become a ruin? 18If they are prophets and have the word of the LORD, let them plead with the LORD Almighty that the articles which remain in the house of the LORD and in the palace of the king of Judah and in Jerusalem will not be taken to Babylon. 19For this is what the LORD Almighty says about the pillars, the Sea, the movable stands and the other articles that are left in this city, 20which Nebuchadnezzar king of Babylon did not take away when he carried Jehoiachin[a] son of Jehoiakim king of Judah into exile from Jerusalem to Babylon, along with all the nobles of Judah and Jerusalem— 21yes, this is what the LORD Almighty, the God of Israel, says about the things that are left in the house of the LORD and in the palace of the king of Judah and in Jerusalem: 22"They will be taken to Babylon and there they will remain until the day I come for them," declares the LORD. "Then I will bring them back and restore them to this place."'

The false prophet Hananiah

28 In the fifth month of that same year, the fourth year, early in the reign of Zedekiah king of Judah, the prophet Hananiah son of Azzur, who was from Gibeon, said to me in the house of the LORD in the presence of the priests and all the people: 2'This is what the LORD Almighty, the God of Israel, says: "I will break the yoke of the king of Babylon. 3Within two years I will bring back to this place all the articles of the LORD's house that Nebuchadnezzar king of Babylon removed from here and took to Babylon. 4I will also bring back to this place Jehoiachin son of Jehoiakim king of Judah and all the other exiles from Judah who went to Babylon," declares the LORD, "for I will break the yoke of the king of Babylon."'

5Then the prophet Jeremiah replied to the prophet Hananiah before the priests and all the people who were standing in the house of the LORD. 6He said, 'Amen! May the LORD do so! May the LORD fulfil the words you have prophesied by bringing the articles of the LORD's house and all the exiles back to this place from Babylon.

---

[a] 20 Hebrew *Jeconiah*, a variant of *Jehoiachin*; also in 28:4 and 29:2

⁷Nevertheless, listen to what I have to say in your hearing and in the hearing of all the people: ⁸from early times the prophets who preceded you and me have prophesied war, disaster and plague against many countries and great kingdoms. ⁹But the prophet who prophesies peace will be recognised as one truly sent by the LORD only if his prediction comes true.'

¹⁰Then the prophet Hananiah took the yoke off the neck of the prophet Jeremiah and broke it, ¹¹and he said before all the people, 'This is what the LORD says: "In the same way I will break the yoke of Nebuchadnezzar king of Babylon off the neck of all the nations within two years."' At this, the prophet Jeremiah went on his way.

¹²After the prophet Hananiah had broken the yoke off the neck of the prophet Jeremiah, the word of the LORD came to Jeremiah: ¹³'Go and tell Hananiah, "This is what the LORD says: you have broken a wooden yoke, but in its place you will get a yoke of iron. ¹⁴This is what the LORD Almighty, the God of Israel, says: I will put an iron yoke on the necks of all these nations to make them serve Nebuchadnezzar king of Babylon, and they will serve him. I will even give him control over the wild animals."'

¹⁵Then the prophet Jeremiah said to Hananiah the prophet, 'Listen, Hananiah! The LORD has not sent you, yet you have persuaded this nation to trust in lies. ¹⁶Therefore, this is what the LORD says: "I am about to remove you from the face of the earth. This very year you are going to die, because you have preached rebellion against the LORD."'

¹⁷In the seventh month of that same year, Hananiah the prophet died.

A letter to the exiles

29 This is the text of the letter that the prophet Jeremiah sent from Jerusalem to the surviving elders among the exiles and to the priests, the prophets and all the other people Nebuchadnezzar had carried into exile from Jerusalem to Babylon. ²(This was after King Jehoiachin and the queen mother, the court officials and the leaders of Judah and Jerusalem, the artisans and the other skilled workers had gone into exile from Jerusalem.) ³He entrusted the letter to Elasah son of Shaphan and to Gemariah son of Hilkiah, whom Zedekiah king of Judah sent to King Nebuchadnezzar in Babylon. It said:

⁴This is what the LORD Almighty, the God of Israel, says to all those I carried into exile from Jerusalem to Babylon: ⁵'Build houses and settle down; plant gardens and eat what they produce. ⁶Marry and have sons and daughters; find wives for your sons and give your daughters in marriage, so that they too may have sons and daughters. Increase in number there; do not decrease. ⁷Also, seek the peace and prosperity of the city to which I have carried you into exile. Pray to the LORD for it, because if it prospers, you too will prosper.' ⁸Yes, this is what the LORD Almighty, the God of Israel, says: 'Do not let the prophets and diviners among you deceive you. Do not listen to the dreams you encourage them to have. ⁹They are prophesying lies to you in my name. I have not sent them,' declares the LORD.

¹⁰This is what the LORD says: 'When seventy years are completed for Babylon, I will come to you and fulfil my good promise to bring you back to this place. ¹¹For I know the plans I have for you,' declares the LORD, 'plans to prosper you and not to harm you, plans to give you hope and a future. ¹²Then you will call on me and come and pray to me, and I will listen to you. ¹³You will seek me and find me when you seek me with all your heart. ¹⁴I will be found by you,' declares the LORD, 'and will bring you back from captivity.ᵃ I will gather you from all the nations and places where I

ᵃ 14 Or *will restore your fortunes*

have banished you,' declares the LORD, 'and will bring you back to the place from which I carried you into exile.'

15You may say, 'The LORD has raised up prophets for us in Babylon,' 16but this is what the LORD says about the king who sits on David's throne and all the people who remain in this city, your fellow citizens who did not go with you into exile— 17yes, this is what the LORD Almighty says: 'I will send the sword, famine and plague against them and I will make them like figs that are so bad that they cannot be eaten. 18I will pursue them with the sword, famine and plague and will make them abhorrent to all the kingdoms of the earth, a curse[a] and an object of horror, of scorn and reproach, among all the nations where I drive them. 19For they have not listened to my words,' declares the LORD, 'words that I sent to them again and again by my servants the prophets. And you exiles have not listened either,' declares the LORD.

20Therefore, hear the word of the LORD, all you exiles whom I have sent away from Jerusalem to Babylon. 21This is what the LORD Almighty, the God of Israel, says about Ahab son of Kolaiah and Zedekiah son of Maaseiah, who are prophesying lies to you in my name: 'I will deliver them into the hands of Nebuchadnezzar king of Babylon, and he will put them to death before your very eyes. 22Because of them, all the exiles from Judah who are in Babylon will use this curse: "May the LORD treat you like Zedekiah and Ahab, whom the king of Babylon burned in the fire." 23For they have done outrageous things in Israel; they have committed adultery with their neighbours' wives, and in my name they have uttered lies— which I did not authorise. I know it and am a witness to it,' declares the LORD.

Message to Shemaiah

24Tell Shemaiah the Nehelamite, 25'This is what the LORD Almighty, the God of Israel, says: you sent letters in your own name to all the people in Jerusalem, to the priest Zephaniah son of Maaseiah, and to all the other priests. You said to Zephaniah, 26"The LORD has appointed you priest in place of Jehoiada to be in charge of the house of the LORD; you should put any crazy person who acts like a prophet into the stocks and neck-irons. 27So why have you not reprimanded Jeremiah from Anathoth, who poses as a prophet among you? 28He has sent this message to us in Babylon: it will be a long time. Therefore build houses and settle down; plant gardens and eat what they produce."'

29Zephaniah the priest, however, read the letter to Jeremiah the prophet. 30Then the word of the LORD came to Jeremiah: 31'Send this message to all the exiles: "This is what the LORD says about Shemaiah the Nehelamite: because Shemaiah has prophesied to you, even though I did not send him, and has persuaded you to trust in lies, 32this is what the LORD says: I will surely punish Shemaiah the Nehelamite and his descendants. He will have no-one left among this people, nor will he see the good things I will do for my people, declares the LORD, because he has preached rebellion against me."'

Restoration of Israel

30 This is the word that came to Jeremiah from the LORD: 2'This is what the LORD, the God of Israel, says: "Write in a book all the words I have spoken to you. 3The days are coming," declares the LORD, "when I will bring my people Israel and Judah back from captivity[b] and restore them to the land I gave to their ancestors to possess," says the LORD.'

---

[a] 18 That is, their names will be used in cursing (see Jer. 29:22); or, others will see that they are cursed.   [b] 3 Or *will restore the fortunes of my people Israel and Judah*

Scrolls
Jeremiah 30:2
Jeremiah would have written his words on a papyrus scroll. The stalks from the papyrus plant were soaked, laid across each other and then pounded with a mallet to make them join together. Ink was made from soot mixed with water and tree sap.

⁴These are the words the LORD spoke concerning Israel and Judah: ⁵'This is what the LORD says:

'"Cries of fear are heard—
terror, not peace.
⁶Ask and see:
can a man bear children?
Then why do I see every strong man
with his hands on his stomach like a woman in labour,
every face turned deathly pale?
⁷How awful that day will be!
None will be like it.
It will be a time of trouble for Jacob,
but he will be saved out of it.

⁸'"In that day," declares the LORD Almighty,
"I will break the yoke off their necks
and will tear off their bonds;
no longer will foreigners enslave them.
⁹Instead, they will serve the LORD their God
and David their king,
whom I will raise up for them.

¹⁰'"So do not be afraid, Jacob my servant;
do not be dismayed, Israel,"
declares the LORD.
"I will surely save you out of a distant place,
your descendants from the land of their exile.
Jacob will again have peace and security,
and no-one will make him afraid.
¹¹I am with you and will save you,"
declares the LORD.
"Though I completely destroy all the nations
among which I scatter you,
I will not completely destroy you.
I will discipline you but only in due measure;
I will not let you go entirely unpunished."

¹²'This is what the LORD says:

'"Your wound is incurable,
your injury beyond healing.
¹³There is no-one to plead your cause,
no remedy for your sore,
no healing for you.
¹⁴All your allies have forgotten you;
they care nothing for you.
I have struck you as an enemy would
and punished you as would the cruel,
because your guilt is so great
and your sins so many.
¹⁵Why do you cry out over your wound,
your pain that has no cure?
Because of your great guilt and many sins
I have done these things to you.

¹⁶'"But all who devour you will be devoured;
all your enemies will go into exile.
Those who plunder you will be plundered;
all who make spoil of you I will despoil.
¹⁷But I will restore you to health
and heal your wounds,"
declares the LORD,
"because you are called an outcast,
Zion for whom no-one cares."

¹⁸'This is what the LORD says:

'"I will restore the fortunes of Jacob's tents
and have compassion on his dwellings;
the city will be rebuilt on her ruins,
and the palace will stand in its proper place.
¹⁹From them will come songs of thanksgiving
and the sound of rejoicing.

I will add to their numbers,
    and they will not be decreased;
I will bring them honour,
    and they will not be disdained.
20 Their children will be as in days of old,
    and their community will be established before me;
I will punish all who oppress them.
21 Their leader will be one of their own;
    their ruler will arise from among them.
I will bring him near and he will come close to me—
    for who is he who will devote himself to be close to me?"
               declares the LORD.
22 ' "So you will be my people,
    and I will be your God." '

23 See, the storm of the LORD
    will burst out in wrath,
a driving wind swirling down
    on the heads of the wicked.
24 The fierce anger of the LORD will not turn back
    until he fully accomplishes
    the purposes of his heart.
In days to come
    you will understand this.

31

'At that time,' declares the LORD, 'I will be the God of all the families of Israel, and they will be my people.'

2 This is what the LORD says:

'The people who survive the sword
    will find favour in the wilderness;
I will come to give rest to Israel.'

3 The LORD appeared to us in the past,[a] saying:

'I have loved you with an everlasting love;
    I have drawn you with unfailing kindness.
4 I will build you up again,
    and you, Virgin Israel, will be rebuilt.
Again you will take up your tambourines
    and go out to dance with the joyful.
5 Again you will plant vineyards
    on the hills of Samaria;
the farmers will plant them
    and enjoy their fruit.
6 There will be a day when watchmen cry out
    on the hills of Ephraim,
"Come, let us go up to Zion,
    to the LORD our God." '

7 This is what the LORD says:

'Sing with joy for Jacob;
    shout for the foremost of the nations.
Make your praises heard, and say,
    "LORD, save your people,
    the remnant of Israel."
8 See, I will bring them from the land of the north
    and gather them from the ends of the earth.
Among them will be the blind and the lame,
    expectant mothers and women in labour;
a great throng will return.
9 They will come with weeping;
    they will pray as I bring them back.
I will lead them beside streams of water
    on a level path where they will not stumble,
because I am Israel's father,
    and Ephraim is my firstborn son.

10 'Hear the word of the LORD, you nations;
    proclaim it in distant coastlands:
"He who scattered Israel will gather them
    and will watch over his flock like a shepherd."
11 For the LORD will deliver Jacob
    and redeem them from the hand of those stronger than they.
12 They will come and shout for joy on the heights of Zion;
    they will rejoice in the bounty of the LORD—
the grain, the new wine and the olive oil,
    the young of the flocks and herds.
They will be like a well-watered garden,
    and they will sorrow no more.
13 Then young women will dance and be glad,
    young men and old as well.
I will turn their mourning into gladness;
    I will give them comfort and joy instead of sorrow.

---

[a] 3 Or LORD has appeared to us from afar

People and Places

Rachel
Jeremiah 31:15
Rachel was one of Jacob's wives and her two sons were Joseph and Benjamin. She was buried near Ramah, a town which was now on the border between the two kingdoms of Judah and Israel.

14 I will satisfy the priests with abundance,
and my people will be filled with my bounty,'
    declares the LORD.

15 This is what the LORD says:

'A voice is heard in Ramah,
    mourning and great weeping,
Rachel weeping for her children
    and refusing to be comforted,
    because they are no more.'

16 This is what the LORD says:

'Restrain your voice from weeping
    and your eyes from tears,
for your work will be rewarded,'
    declares the LORD.
'They will return from the land of the enemy.
17 So there is hope for your descendants,'
    declares the LORD.
'Your children will return to their own land.

18 'I have surely heard Ephraim's moaning:
"You disciplined me like an unruly calf,
    and I have been disciplined.
Restore me, and I will return,
    because you are the LORD my God.
19 After I strayed,
    I repented;
after I came to understand,
    I beat my breast.
I was ashamed and humiliated
because I bore the disgrace of my youth."
20 Is not Ephraim my dear son,
    the child in whom I delight?
Though I often speak against him,
    I still remember him.
Therefore my heart yearns for him;
    I have great compassion for him,'
    declares the LORD.

21 'Set up road signs;
    put up guideposts.
Take note of the highway,
    the road that you take.
Return, Virgin Israel,
    return to your towns.
22 How long will you wander,
    unfaithful Daughter Israel?
The LORD will create a new thing on earth—
    the woman will return to[a] the man.'

23 This is what the LORD Almighty, the God of Israel, says: 'When I bring them back from captivity,[b] the people in the land of Judah and in its towns will once again use these words: "The LORD bless you, you prosperous city, you sacred mountain." 24 People will live together in Judah and all its towns—farmers and those who move about with their flocks. 25 I will refresh the weary and satisfy the faint.'

26 At this I awoke and looked around. My sleep had been pleasant to me.

27 'The days are coming,' declares the LORD, 'when I will plant the house of Israel and the house of Judah with the offspring of people and of animals. 28 Just as I watched over them to uproot and tear down, and to overthrow, destroy and bring disaster, so I will watch over them to build and to plant,' declares the LORD. 29 'In those days people will no longer say,

"The parents have eaten sour grapes,
    and the children's teeth are set on edge."

30 Instead, everyone will die for their own sin; whoever eats sour grapes—their own teeth will be set on edge.

31 'The days are coming,' declares the LORD, 'when I will make a new covenant

---

[a] 22 Or will protect   [b] 23 Or I restore their fortunes

with the house of Israel
and with the house of Judah.
³²It will not be like the covenant
I made with their ancestors
when I took them by the hand
to lead them out of Egypt,
because they broke my covenant,
though I was a husband to[a] them,'[b]
declares the LORD.
³³'This is the covenant that I will make with
the house of Israel
after that time,' declares the LORD.
'I will put my law in their minds
and write it on their hearts.
I will be their God,
and they will be my people.
³⁴No longer will they teach their
neighbours,
or say to one another, "Know the
LORD,"
because they will all know me,
from the least of them to the greatest,'
declares the LORD.
'For I will forgive their wickedness
and will remember their sins no more.'

³⁵This is what the LORD says,

he who appoints the sun
to shine by day,
who decrees the moon and stars
to shine by night,
who stirs up the sea
so that its waves roar—
the LORD Almighty is his name:
³⁶'Only if these decrees vanish from my
sight,'
declares the LORD,
'will the descendants of Israel ever cease
to be a nation before me.'

³⁷This is what the LORD says:

'Only if the heavens above can be
measured
and the foundations of the earth below
be searched out
will I reject all the descendants of Israel
because of all they have done,'
declares the LORD.

³⁸'The days are coming,' declares the LORD, 'when this city will be rebuilt for me from the Tower of Hananel to the Corner Gate. ³⁹The measuring line will stretch from there straight to the hill of Gareb and then turn to Goah. ⁴⁰The whole valley where dead bodies and ashes are thrown, and all the terraces out to the Kidron Valley on the east as far as the corner of the Horse Gate, will be holy to the LORD. The city will never again be uprooted or demolished.'

Jeremiah buys a field

32 This is the word that came to Jeremiah from the LORD in the tenth year of Zedekiah king of Judah, which was the eighteenth year of Nebuchadnezzar. ²The army of the king of Babylon was then besieging Jerusalem, and Jeremiah the prophet was confined in the courtyard of the guard in the royal palace of Judah.

³Now Zedekiah king of Judah had imprisoned him there, saying, 'Why do you prophesy as you do? You say, "This is what the LORD says: I am about to give this city into the hands of the king of Babylon, and he will capture it. ⁴Zedekiah king of Judah will not escape the Babylonians[c] but will certainly be given into the hands of the king of Babylon, and will speak with him face to face and see him with his own eyes. ⁵He will take Zedekiah to Babylon, where he will remain until I deal with him, declares the LORD. If you fight against the Babylonians, you will not succeed."'

⁶Jeremiah said, 'The word of the LORD came to me: ⁷Hanamel son of Shallum your uncle is going to come to you and say, "Buy my field at Anathoth, because as nearest relative it is your right and duty to buy it."

⁸'Then, just as the LORD had said, my cousin Hanamel came to me in the courtyard of the guard and said, "Buy my field at Anathoth in the territory of Benjamin. Since it is your right to redeem it and possess it, buy it for yourself."

'I knew that this was the word of the LORD; ⁹so I bought the field at Anathoth from my cousin Hanamel and weighed out for him seventeen shekels[d] of silver. ¹⁰I signed and sealed the deed, had it witnessed, and weighed out the silver on the scales. ¹¹I

---

[a] 32 Hebrew; Septuagint and Syriac *covenant, I and I turned away from* [b] 32 Or *was their master* [c] 4 Or *Chaldeans*; also in verses 5, 24, 25, 28, 29 and 43 [d] 9 That is, about 200 grams

making Connections

Buying a field
Jeremiah 32:9

People must have thought Jeremiah was mad. He had been predicting for years that the Babylonians would take over Jerusalem, and yet here he is buying some land just before it's about to happen. That land would be worthless once the Babylonians arrived. But this was another of Jeremiah's symbolic acts showing his hope for the future. He's looking beyond the years of captivity to a time when Judah will be restored and people will once again worship God in the temple.

took the deed of purchase—the sealed copy containing the terms and conditions, as well as the unsealed copy— 12and I gave this deed to Baruch son of Neriah, the son of Mahseiah, in the presence of my cousin Hanamel and of the witnesses who had signed the deed and of all the Jews sitting in the courtyard of the guard.

13'In their presence I gave Baruch these instructions: 14"This is what the LORD Almighty, the God of Israel, says: take these documents, both the sealed and unsealed copies of the deed of purchase, and put them in a clay jar so that they will last a long time. 15For this is what the LORD Almighty, the God of Israel, says: houses, fields and vineyards will again be bought in this land."

16'After I had given the deed of purchase to Baruch son of Neriah, I prayed to the LORD:

17'Ah, Sovereign LORD, you have made the heavens and the earth by your great power and outstretched arm. Nothing is too hard for you. 18You show love to thousands but bring the punishment for the parents' sins into the laps of their children after them. Great and mighty God, whose name is the LORD Almighty, 19great are your purposes and mighty are your deeds. Your eyes are open to the ways of all; you reward everyone according to their conduct and as their deeds deserve. 20You performed signs and wonders in Egypt and have continued them to this day, both in Israel and among all nations, and have gained the renown that is still yours. 21You brought your people Israel out of Egypt with signs and wonders, by a mighty hand and an outstretched arm and with great terror. 22You gave them this land you had sworn to give to their ancestors, a land flowing with milk and honey. 23They came in and took possession of it, but they did not obey you or follow your law; they did not do what you commanded them to do. So you brought all this disaster on them.

24'See how the siege ramps are built up to take the city. Because of the sword, famine and plague, the city will be given into the hands of the Babylonians who are attacking it. What you said has happened, as you now see. 25And though the city will be given into the hands of the Babylonians, you, Sovereign LORD, say to me, "Buy the field with silver and have the transaction witnessed."'

26Then the word of the LORD came to Jeremiah: 27'I am the LORD, the God of the whole human race. Is anything too hard for me? 28Therefore, this is what the LORD says: I am about to give this city into the hands of the Babylonians and to Nebuchadnezzar king of Babylon, who will capture it. 29The Babylonians who are attacking this city will come in and set it on fire; they will burn it down, along with the houses where the people aroused my anger by burning incense on the roofs to Baal and by pouring out drink offerings to other gods.

30'The people of Israel and Judah have done nothing but evil in my sight from their youth; indeed, the people of Israel have done nothing but arouse my anger with what their hands have made, declares the LORD. 31From the day it was built until now, this city has so aroused my anger and wrath that I must remove it from my sight. 32The people of Israel and Judah have provoked me by all the evil they have done—they, their kings and officials, their priests and prophets, the people of Judah and those living in Jerusalem. 33They turned their backs to me and not their faces; though I taught them again and again, they would not listen or respond to discipline. 34They set up their vile images in the house that bears my Name and defiled it. 35They built high places for Baal in the Valley of Ben Hinnom to sacrifice their sons and daughters to Molek, though I never commanded—nor did it enter my mind—that they should do such a detestable thing and so make Judah sin.

36'You are saying about this city, "By the sword, famine and plague it will be given into the hands of the king of Babylon"; but this is what the LORD, the God of Israel, says: 37I will surely gather them from all the lands where I banish them in my furious anger and great wrath; I will bring them back to this place and let them live in safety. 38They will be my people, and I will be their God. 39I will give them singleness of heart and action, so that they will always fear me and that all will then go well for them and for their children after them. 40I will make an everlasting covenant with them: I will never stop doing good to them, and I will inspire them to fear me, so that they will never turn away from me. 41I will rejoice in doing them good and will assuredly plant them in this land with all my heart and soul.

42'This is what the LORD says: as I have brought all this great calamity on this people, so I will give them all the prosperity I have promised them. 43Once more fields will be bought in this land of which you say, "It is a desolate waste, without people or animals, for it has been given into the hands of the Babylonians." 44Fields will be bought for silver, and deeds will be signed, sealed and witnessed in the territory of Benjamin, in the villages around Jerusalem, in the towns of Judah and in the towns of the hill country, of the western foothills and of the Negev, because I will restore their fortunes,[a] declares the LORD.'

Promise of restoration

33 While Jeremiah was still confined in the courtyard of the guard, the word of the LORD came to him a second time: 2'This is what the LORD says, he who made the earth, the LORD who formed it and established it—the LORD is his name: 3"Call to me and I will answer you and tell you great and unsearchable things you do not know." 4For this is what the LORD, the God of Israel, says about the houses in this city and the royal palaces of Judah that have been torn down to be used against the siege ramps and the sword 5in the fight with the Babylonians:[b] "They will be filled with the dead bodies of the people I will slay in my anger and wrath. I will hide my face from this city because of all its wickedness.

6' "Nevertheless, I will bring health and healing to it; I will heal my people and will let them enjoy abundant peace and security. 7I will bring Judah and Israel back from captivity[c] and will rebuild them as they were before. 8I will cleanse them from all the sin they have committed against me and will forgive all their sins of rebellion against me. 9Then this city will bring me renown, joy, praise and honour before all nations on earth that hear of all the good things I do for it; and they will be in awe and will tremble at the abundant prosperity and peace I provide for it."

10'This is what the LORD says: "You say about this place, 'It is a desolate waste, without people or animals.' Yet in the towns of Judah and the streets of Jerusalem that are deserted, inhabited by neither people nor animals, there will be heard once more 11the sounds of joy and gladness, the voices of bride and bridegroom, and the voices of

---

[a] 44 Or *will bring them back from captivity*   [b] 5 Or *Chaldeans*   [c] 7 Or *will restore the fortunes of Judah and Israel*

those who bring thank-offerings to the house of the LORD, saying,

> 'Give thanks to the LORD Almighty,
> for the LORD is good;
> his love endures for ever.'

For I will restore the fortunes of the land as they were before," says the LORD.

¹²'This is what the LORD Almighty says: "In this place, desolate and without people or animals—in all its towns there will again be pastures for shepherds to rest their flocks. ¹³In the towns of the hill country, of the western foothills and of the Negev, in the territory of Benjamin, in the villages around Jerusalem and in the towns of Judah, flocks will again pass under the hand of the one who counts them," says the LORD.

¹⁴' "The days are coming," declares the LORD, "when I will fulfil the good promise I made to the house of Israel and to the house of Judah.

¹⁵' "In those days and at that time
> I will make a righteous Branch sprout from David's line;
> he will do what is just and right in the land.
¹⁶In those days Judah will be saved
> and Jerusalem will live in safety.
> This is the name by which it^a will be called:
> The LORD Our Righteous Saviour."

¹⁷For this is what the LORD says: "David will never fail to have a man to sit on the throne of the house of Israel, ¹⁸nor will the Levitical priests ever fail to have a man to stand before me continually to offer burnt offerings, to burn grain offerings and to present sacrifices." '

¹⁹The word of the LORD came to Jeremiah: ²⁰'This is what the LORD says: "If you can break my covenant with the day and my covenant with the night, so that day and night no longer come at their appointed time, ²¹then my covenant with David my servant—and my covenant with the Levites who are priests ministering before me—can be broken and David will no longer have a descendant to reign on his throne. ²²I will make the descendants of David my servant and the Levites who minister before me as countless as the stars in the sky and as measureless as the sand on the seashore." '

²³The word of the LORD came to Jeremiah: ²⁴'Have you not noticed that these people are saying, "The LORD has rejected the two kingdoms^b he chose"? So they despise my people and no longer regard them as a nation. ²⁵This is what the LORD says: "If I have not made my covenant with day and night and established the laws of heaven and earth, ²⁶then I will reject the descendants of Jacob and David my servant and will not choose one of his sons to rule over the descendants of Abraham, Isaac and Jacob. For I will restore their fortunes^c and have compassion on them." '

Warning to Zedekiah

34 While Nebuchadnezzar king of Babylon and all his army and all the kingdoms and peoples in the empire he ruled were fighting against Jerusalem and all its surrounding towns, this word came to Jeremiah from the LORD: ²'This is what the LORD, the God of Israel, says: go to Zedekiah king of Judah and tell him, "This is what the LORD says: I am about to give this city into the hands of the king of Babylon, and he will burn it down. ³You will not escape from his grasp but will surely be captured and given into his hands. You will see the king of Babylon with your own eyes, and he will speak with you face to face. And you will go to Babylon.

⁴' "Yet hear the LORD's promise to you, Zedekiah king of Judah. This is what the LORD says concerning you: you will not die by the sword; ⁵you will die peacefully. As people made a funeral fire in honour of your ancestors, the former kings who preceded you, so they will make a fire in your honour and lament, 'Alas, master!' I myself make this promise, declares the LORD." '

⁶Then Jeremiah the prophet told all this to Zedekiah king of Judah, in Jerusalem, ⁷while the army of the king of Babylon was fighting against Jerusalem and the other cities of Judah that were still holding out—

---

^{a} 16 Or he ^{b} 24 Or families ^{c} 26 Or *will bring them back from captivity*

Lachish and Azekah. These were the only fortified cities left in Judah.

Freedom for slaves

8The word came to Jeremiah from the LORD after King Zedekiah had made a covenant with all the people in Jerusalem to proclaim freedom for the slaves. 9Everyone was to free their Hebrew slaves, both male and female; no-one was to hold another Jew in bondage. 10So all the officials and people who entered into this covenant agreed that they would free their male and female slaves and no longer hold them in bondage. They agreed, and set them free. 11But afterwards they changed their minds and took back the slaves they had freed and enslaved them again.

12Then the word of the LORD came to Jeremiah: 13'This is what the LORD, the God of Israel, says: I made a covenant with your ancestors when I brought them out of Egypt, out of the land of slavery. I said, 14"Every seventh year each of you must free any other Hebrews who have sold themselves to you. After they have served you for six years, you must let them go free."[a] Your ancestors, however, did not listen to me or pay attention to me. 15Recently you repented and did what is right in my sight: each of you proclaimed freedom to your own people. You even made a covenant before me in the house that bears my Name. 16But now you have turned round and profaned my name; each of you has taken back the male and female slaves you had set free to go where they wished. You have forced them to become your slaves again.

17'Therefore, this is what the LORD says: you have not obeyed me; you have not proclaimed freedom to your own people. So I now proclaim "freedom" for you, declares the LORD—"freedom" to fall by the sword, plague and famine. I will make you abhorrent to all the kingdoms of the earth. 18Those who have violated my covenant and have not fulfilled the terms of the covenant they made before me, I will treat like the calf they cut in two and then walked between its pieces. 19The leaders of Judah and Jerusalem, the court officials, the priests and all the people of the land who walked between the pieces of the calf, 20I will deliver into the hands of their enemies who seek their lives. Their dead bodies will become food for the birds and the wild animals.

21'I will deliver Zedekiah king of Judah and his officials into the hands of their enemies who seek their lives, to the army of the king of Babylon, which has withdrawn from you. 22I am going to give the order, declares the LORD, and I will bring them back to this city. They will fight against it, take it and burn it down. And I will lay waste the towns of Judah so that no-one can live there.'

The Rekabites

35 This is the word that came to Jeremiah from the LORD during the reign of Jehoiakim son of Josiah king of Judah: 2'Go to the Rekabite family and invite them to come to one of the side rooms of the house of the LORD and give them wine to drink.'

3So I went to get Jaazaniah son of Jeremiah, the son of Habazziniah, and his brothers and all his sons—the whole family of the Rekabites. 4I brought them into the house of the LORD, into the room of the sons of Hanan son of Igdaliah the man of God. It was next to the room of the officials, which was over that of Maaseiah son of Shallum the door-keeper. 5Then I set bowls full of wine and some cups before the members of the Rekabite family and said to them, 'Drink some wine.'

6But they replied, 'We do not drink wine, because our ancestor Jehonadab[b] son of Rekab gave us this command: "Neither you nor your descendants must ever drink wine. 7Also you must never build houses, sow seed or plant vineyards; you must never have any of these things, but must always live in tents. Then you will live a long time in the land where you are nomads." 8We have obeyed everything our ancestor Jehonadab son of Rekab commanded us. Neither we nor our wives nor our sons and daughters have ever drunk wine 9or built houses to live in or had vineyards, fields or crops. 10We have lived in tents and have fully obeyed

---

[a] 14 Deut. 15:12 [b] 6 Hebrew *Jonadab*, a variant of *Jehonadab*; here and often in this chapter

everything our ancestor Jehonadab commanded us. ¹¹But when Nebuchadnezzar king of Babylon invaded this land, we said, "Come, we must go to Jerusalem to escape the Babylonian[a] and Aramean armies." So we have remained in Jerusalem.'

¹²Then the word of the LORD came to Jeremiah, saying: ¹³'This is what the LORD Almighty, the God of Israel, says: go and tell the people of Judah and those living in Jerusalem, "Will you not learn a lesson and obey my words?" declares the LORD. ¹⁴"Jehonadab son of Rekab ordered his descendants not to drink wine and this command has been kept. To this day they do not drink wine, because they obey their ancestor's command. But I have spoken to you again and again, yet you have not obeyed me. ¹⁵Again and again I sent all my servants the prophets to you. They said, 'Each of you must turn from your wicked ways and reform your actions; do not follow other gods to serve them. Then you shall live in the land I have given to you and your ancestors.' But you have not paid attention or listened to me. ¹⁶The descendants of Jehonadab son of Rekab have carried out the command their ancestor gave them, but these people have not obeyed me."

¹⁷'Therefore, this is what the LORD God Almighty, the God of Israel, says: "Listen! I am going to bring on Judah and on everyone living in Jerusalem every disaster I pronounced against them. I spoke to them, but they did not listen; I called to them, but they did not answer."'

¹⁸Then Jeremiah said to the family of the Rekabites, 'This is what the LORD Almighty, the God of Israel, says: "You have obeyed the command of your ancestor Jehonadab and have followed all his instructions and have done everything he ordered." ¹⁹Therefore, this is what the LORD Almighty, the God of Israel, says: "Jehonadab son of Rekab shall never fail to have a descendant to serve me."'

Jehoiakim burns Jeremiah's scroll

36 In the fourth year of Jehoiakim son of Josiah king of Judah, this word came to Jeremiah from the LORD: ²'Take a

making Connections

Scribe
Jeremiah 36:4
A scribe was a man who wrote down what someone else dictated to him. Paul probably dictated his letters in the New Testament too (Romans 16:22).

scroll and write on it all the words I have spoken to you concerning Israel, Judah and all the other nations from the time I began speaking to you in the reign of Josiah till now. ³Perhaps when the people of Judah hear about every disaster I plan to inflict on them, they will each turn from their wicked ways; then I will forgive their wickedness and their sin.'

⁴So Jeremiah called Baruch son of Neriah, and while Jeremiah dictated all the words the LORD had spoken to him, Baruch wrote them on the scroll. ⁵Then Jeremiah told Baruch, 'I am restricted; I am not allowed to go to the LORD's temple. ⁶So you go to the house of the LORD on a day of fasting and read to the people from the scroll the words of the LORD that you wrote as I dictated. Read them to all the people of Judah who come in from their towns. ⁷Perhaps they will bring their petition before the LORD, and will all turn from their wicked ways, for the anger and wrath pronounced against this people by the LORD are great.'

⁸Baruch son of Neriah did everything Jeremiah the prophet told him to do; at the LORD's temple he read the words of the LORD from the scroll. ⁹In the ninth month of the fifth year of Jehoiakim son of Josiah king of Judah, a time of fasting before the LORD was proclaimed for all the people in Jerusalem and those who had come from the towns of Judah. ¹⁰From the room of Gemariah son of Shaphan the secretary,

---

[a] 11 Or *Chaldean*

which was in the upper courtyard at the entrance of the New Gate of the temple, Baruch read to all the people at the LORD's temple the words of Jeremiah from the scroll.

11When Micaiah son of Gemariah, the son of Shaphan, heard all the words of the LORD from the scroll, 12he went down to the secretary's room in the royal palace, where all the officials were sitting: Elishama the secretary, Delaiah son of Shemaiah, Elnathan son of Akbor, Gemariah son of Shaphan, Zedekiah son of Hananiah, and all the other officials. 13After Micaiah told them everything he had heard Baruch read to the people from the scroll, 14all the officials sent Jehudi son of Nethaniah, the son of Shelemiah, the son of Cushi, to say to Baruch, 'Bring the scroll from which you have read to the people and come.' So Baruch son of Neriah went to them with the scroll in his hand. 15They said to him, 'Sit down, please, and read it to us.'

So Baruch read it to them. 16When they heard all these words, they looked at each other in fear and said to Baruch, 'We must report all these words to the king.' 17Then they asked Baruch, 'Tell us, how did you come to write all this? Did Jeremiah dictate it?'

18'Yes,' Baruch replied, 'he dictated all these words to me, and I wrote them in ink on the scroll.'

19Then the officials said to Baruch, 'You and Jeremiah, go and hide. Don't let anyone know where you are.'

20After they put the scroll in the room of Elishama the secretary, they went to the king in the courtyard and reported everything to him. 21The king sent Jehudi to get the scroll, and Jehudi brought it from the room of Elishama the secretary and read it to the king and all the officials standing beside him. 22It was the ninth month and the king was sitting in the winter apartment, with a fire burning in the brazier in front of him. 23Whenever Jehudi had read three or four columns of the scroll, the king cut them off with a scribe's knife and threw them into the brazier, until the entire scroll was burned in the fire. 24The king and all his attendants who heard all these words showed no fear, nor did they tear their clothes. 25Even though Elnathan, Delaiah and Gemariah urged the king not to burn the scroll, he would not listen to them. 26Instead, the king commanded Jerahmeel, a son of the king, Seraiah son of Azriel and Shelemiah son of Abdeel to arrest Baruch the scribe and Jeremiah the prophet. But the LORD had hidden them.

27After the king burned the scroll containing the words that Baruch had written at Jeremiah's dictation, the word of the LORD came to Jeremiah: 28'Take another scroll and write on it all the words that were on the first scroll, which Jehoiakim king of Judah burned up. 29Also tell Jehoiakim king of Judah, "This is what the LORD says: you burned that scroll and said, 'Why did you write on it that the king of Babylon would certainly come and destroy this land and wipe from it both people and animals?' 30Therefore, this is what the LORD says about Jehoiakim king of Judah: he will have no-one to sit on the throne of David; his body will be thrown out and exposed to the heat by day and the frost by night. 31I will punish him and his children and his attendants for their wickedness; I will bring on them and those living in Jerusalem and the people of Judah every disaster I pronounced against them, because they have not listened."'

32So Jeremiah took another scroll and gave it to the scribe Baruch son of Neriah, and as Jeremiah dictated, Baruch wrote on it all the words of the scroll that Jehoiakim king of Judah had burned in the fire. And many similar words were added to them.

Jeremiah in prison

37 Zedekiah son of Josiah was made king of Judah by Nebuchadnezzar king of Babylon; he reigned in place of Jehoiachin[a] son of Jehoiakim. 2Neither he nor his attendants nor the people of the land paid any attention to the words the LORD had spoken through Jeremiah the prophet.

3King Zedekiah, however, sent Jehukal son of Shelemiah with the priest Zephaniah son of Maaseiah to Jeremiah the prophet

---

[a] 1 Hebrew *Koniah*, a variant of *Jehoiachin*

with this message: 'Please pray to the LORD our God for us.'

⁴Now Jeremiah was free to come and go among the people, for he had not yet been put in prison. ⁵Pharaoh's army had marched out of Egypt, and when the Babylonians[a] who were besieging Jerusalem heard the report about them, they withdrew from Jerusalem.

⁶Then the word of the LORD came to Jeremiah the prophet: ⁷'This is what the LORD, the God of Israel, says: tell the king of Judah, who sent you to enquire of me, "Pharaoh's army, which has marched out to support you, will go back to its own land, to Egypt. ⁸Then the Babylonians will return and attack this city; they will capture it and burn it down."

⁹'This is what the LORD says: do not deceive yourselves, thinking, "The Babylonians will surely leave us." They will not! ¹⁰Even if you were to defeat the entire Babylonian[b] army that is attacking you and only wounded men were left in their tents, they would come out and burn this city down.'

¹¹After the Babylonian army had withdrawn from Jerusalem because of Pharaoh's army, ¹²Jeremiah started to leave the city to go to the territory of Benjamin to get his share of the property among the people there. ¹³But when he reached the Benjamin Gate, the captain of the guard, whose name was Irijah son of Shelemiah, the son of Hananiah, arrested him and said, 'You are deserting to the Babylonians!'

¹⁴'That's not true!' Jeremiah said. 'I am not deserting to the Babylonians.' But Irijah would not listen to him; instead, he arrested Jeremiah and brought him to the officials. ¹⁵They were angry with Jeremiah and had him beaten and imprisoned in the house of Jonathan the secretary, which they had made into a prison.

¹⁶Jeremiah was put into a vaulted cell in a dungeon, where he remained a long time. ¹⁷Then King Zedekiah sent for him and had him brought to the palace, where he asked him privately, 'Is there any word from the LORD?'

'Yes,' Jeremiah replied, 'you will be delivered into the hands of the king of Babylon.'

¹⁸Then Jeremiah said to King Zedekiah, 'What crime have I committed against you or your attendants or this people, that you have put me in prison? ¹⁹Where are your prophets who prophesied to you, "The king of Babylon will not attack you or this land"? ²⁰But now, my lord the king, please listen. Let me bring my petition before you: do not send me back to the house of Jonathan the secretary, or I shall die there.'

²¹King Zedekiah then gave orders for Jeremiah to be placed in the courtyard of the guard and given a loaf of bread from the street of the bakers each day until all the bread in the city was gone. So Jeremiah remained in the courtyard of the guard.

Jeremiah thrown into a cistern

38 Shephatiah son of Mattan, Gedaliah son of Pashhur, Jehukal[c] son of Shelemiah, and Pashhur son of Malkijah heard what Jeremiah was telling all the people when he said, ²'This is what the LORD says: "Whoever stays in this city will die by the sword, famine or plague, but whoever goes over to the Babylonians[d] will live. They will escape with their lives; they will live." ³And this is what the LORD says: "This city will certainly be given into the hands of the army of the king of Babylon, who will capture it."'

⁴Then the officials said to the king, 'This man should be put to death. He is discouraging the soldiers who are left in this city, as well as all the people, by the things he is saying to them. This man is not seeking the good of these people but their ruin.'

⁵'He is in your hands,' King Zedekiah answered. 'The king can do nothing to oppose you.'

⁶So they took Jeremiah and put him into the cistern of Malkijah, the king's son, which was in the courtyard of the guard. They lowered Jeremiah by ropes into the cistern; it had no water in it, only mud, and Jeremiah sank down into the mud.

---

[a] 5 Or *Chaldeans*; also in verses 8, 9, 13 and 14   [b] 10 Or *Chaldean*; also in verse 11   [c] 1 Hebrew *Jukal*, a variant of *Jehukal*   [d] 2 Or *Chaldeans*; also in verses 18, 19 and 23

7But Ebed-Melek, a Cushite,[a] an official[b] in the royal palace, heard that they had put Jeremiah into the cistern. While the king was sitting in the Benjamin Gate, 8Ebed-Melek went out of the palace and said to him, 9'My lord the king, these men have acted wickedly in all they have done to Jeremiah the prophet. They have thrown him into a cistern, where he will starve to death when there is no longer any bread in the city.'

10Then the king commanded Ebed-Melek the Cushite, 'Take thirty men from here with you and lift Jeremiah the prophet out of the cistern before he dies.'

11So Ebed-Melek took the men with him and went to a room under the treasury in the palace. He took some old rags and worn-out clothes from there and let them down with ropes to Jeremiah in the cistern. 12Ebed-Melek the Cushite said to Jeremiah, 'Put these old rags and worn-out clothes under your arms to pad the ropes.' Jeremiah did so, 13and they pulled him up with the ropes and lifted him out of the cistern. And Jeremiah remained in the courtyard of the guard.

Zedekiah questions Jeremiah again

14Then King Zedekiah sent for Jeremiah the prophet and had him brought to the third entrance to the temple of the LORD. 'I am going to ask you something,' the king said to Jeremiah. 'Do not hide anything from me.'

15Jeremiah said to Zedekiah, 'If I give you an answer, will you not kill me? Even if I did give you counsel, you would not listen to me.'

16But King Zedekiah swore this oath secretly to Jeremiah: 'As surely as the LORD lives, who has given us breath, I will neither kill you nor hand you over to those who are seeking your life.'

17Then Jeremiah said to Zedekiah, 'This is what the LORD God Almighty, the God of Israel, says: "If you surrender to the officers of the king of Babylon, your life will be spared and this city will not be burned down; you and your family will live. 18But if you will not surrender to the officers of the king of Babylon, this city will be given into the hands of the Babylonians and they will burn it down; you yourself will not escape from them."'

19King Zedekiah said to Jeremiah, 'I am afraid of the Jews who have gone over to the Babylonians, for the Babylonians may hand me over to them and they will ill-treat me.'

20'They will not hand you over,' Jeremiah replied. 'Obey the LORD by doing what I tell you. Then it will go well with you, and your life will be spared. 21But if you refuse to surrender, this is what the LORD has revealed to me: 22all the women left in the palace of the king of Judah will be brought out to the officials of the king of Babylon. Those women will say to you:

> '"They misled you and overcame you—
> those trusted friends of yours.
> Your feet are sunk in the mud;
> your friends have deserted you."

23'All your wives and children will be brought out to the Babylonians. You yourself will not escape from their hands but will be captured by the king of Babylon; and this city will[c] be burned down.'

24Then Zedekiah said to Jeremiah, 'Do not let anyone know about this conversation, or you may die. 25If the officials hear that I talked with you, and they come to you and say, "Tell us what you said to the king and what the king said to you; do not hide it from us or we will kill you," 26then tell them, "I was pleading with the king not to send me back to Jonathan's house to die there."'

27All the officials did come to Jeremiah and question him, and he told them everything the king had ordered him to say. So they said no more to him, for no-one had heard his conversation with the king.

28And Jeremiah remained in the courtyard of the guard until the day Jerusalem was captured.

The fall of Jerusalem

39 This is how Jerusalem was taken: 1in the ninth year of Zedekiah king of Judah, in the tenth month, Nebuchadnezzar king of Babylon marched against Jerusalem with his whole army and laid

---

[a] 7 Probably from the upper Nile region   [b] 7 Or *a eunuch*   [c] 23 Or *and you will cause this city to*

siege to it. ²And on the ninth day of the fourth month of Zedekiah's eleventh year, the city wall was broken through. ³Then all the officials of the king of Babylon came and took seats in the Middle Gate: Nergal-Sharezer of Samgar, Nebo-Sarsekim[a] a chief officer, Nergal-Sharezer a high official and all the other officials of the king of Babylon. ⁴When Zedekiah king of Judah and all the soldiers saw them, they fled; they left the city at night by way of the king's garden, through the gate between the two walls, and headed towards the Arabah.[b]

⁵But the Babylonian[c] army pursued them and overtook Zedekiah in the plains of Jericho. They captured him and took him to Nebuchadnezzar king of Babylon at Riblah in the land of Hamath, where he pronounced sentence on him. ⁶There at Riblah the king of Babylon slaughtered the sons of Zedekiah before his eyes and also killed all the nobles of Judah. ⁷Then he put out Zedekiah's eyes and bound him with bronze shackles to take him to Babylon.

⁸The Babylonians[d] set fire to the royal palace and the houses of the people and broke down the walls of Jerusalem. ⁹Nebuzaradan commander of the imperial guard carried into exile to Babylon the people who remained in the city, along with those who had gone over to him, and the rest of the people. ¹⁰But Nebuzaradan the commander of the guard left behind in the land of Judah some of the poor people, who owned nothing; and at that time he gave them vineyards and fields.

¹¹Now Nebuchadnezzar king of Babylon had given these orders about Jeremiah through Nebuzaradan commander of the imperial guard: ¹²'Take him and look after him; don't harm him but do for him whatever he asks.' ¹³So Nebuzaradan the commander of the guard, Nebushazban a chief officer, Nergal-Sharezer a high official and all the other officers of the king of Babylon ¹⁴sent and had Jeremiah taken out of the courtyard of the guard. They handed him over to Gedaliah son of Ahikam, the son of Shaphan, to take him back to his home. So he remained among his own people.

¹⁵While Jeremiah had been confined in the courtyard of the guard, the word of the LORD came to him: ¹⁶'Go and tell Ebed-Melek the Cushite, "This is what the LORD Almighty, the God of Israel, says: I am about to fulfil my words against this city—words concerning disaster, not prosperity. At that time they will be fulfilled before your eyes. ¹⁷But I will rescue you on that day, declares the LORD; you will not be given into the hands of those you fear. ¹⁸I will save you; you will not fall by the sword but will escape with your life, because you trust in me, declares the LORD."'

Jeremiah freed

40 The word came to Jeremiah from the LORD after Nebuzaradan commander of the imperial guard had released him at Ramah. He had found Jeremiah bound in chains among all the captives from Jerusalem and Judah who were being carried into exile to Babylon. ²When the commander of the guard found Jeremiah, he said to him, 'The LORD your God decreed this disaster for this place. ³And now the LORD has brought it about; he has done just as he said he would. All this happened because you people sinned against the LORD and did not obey him. ⁴But today I am freeing you from the chains on your wrists. Come with me to Babylon, if you like, and I will look after you; but if you do not want to, then don't come. Look, the whole country lies before you; go wherever you please.' ⁵However, before Jeremiah turned to go,[e] Nebuzaradan added, 'Go back to Gedaliah son of Ahikam, the son of Shaphan, whom the king of Babylon has appointed over the towns of Judah, and live with him among the people, or go anywhere else you please.'

Then the commander gave him provisions and a present and let him go. ⁶So Jeremiah went to Gedaliah son of Ahikam at Mizpah and stayed with him among the people who were left behind in the land.

Gedaliah assassinated

⁷When all the army officers and their men who were still in the open country heard that the king of Babylon had appointed

---

[a] 3 Or *Nergal-Sharezer, Samgar-Nebo, Sarsekim* [b] 4 Or *the Jordan Valley* [c] 5 Or *Chaldean* [d] 8 Or *Chaldeans*
[e] 5 Or *Jeremiah answered*

IN OTHER WORDS

Jew
Jeremiah 40:11
'The Jews' is another name for the Israelites from the Old Testament. People from the kingdom of Judah began to be called Jews in the period 800–600 BC, and so did people from other nations who followed their religion.

Gedaliah son of Ahikam as governor over the land and had put him in charge of the men, women and children who were the poorest in the land and who had not been carried into exile to Babylon, 8they came to Gedaliah at Mizpah—Ishmael son of Nethaniah, Johanan and Jonathan the sons of Kareah, Seraiah son of Tanhumeth, the sons of Ephai the Netophathite, and Jaazaniah*a* the son of the Maakathite, and their men. 9Gedaliah son of Ahikam, the son of Shaphan, took an oath to reassure them and their men. 'Do not be afraid to serve the Babylonians,'*b* he said. 'Settle down in the land and serve the king of Babylon, and it will go well with you. 10I myself will stay in Mizpah to represent you before the Babylonians who come to us, but you are to harvest the wine, summer fruit and olive oil, and put them in your storage jars, and live in the towns you have taken over.'

11When all the Jews in Moab, Ammon, Edom and all the other countries heard that the king of Babylon had left a remnant in Judah and had appointed Gedaliah son of Ahikam, the son of Shaphan, as governor over them, 12they all came back to the land of Judah, to Gedaliah at Mizpah, from all the countries where they had been scattered. And they harvested an abundance of wine and summer fruit.

13Johanan son of Kareah and all the army officers still in the open country came to Gedaliah at Mizpah 14and said to him, 'Don't you know that Baalis king of the Ammonites has sent Ishmael son of Nethaniah to take your life?' But Gedaliah son of Ahikam did not believe them.

15Then Johanan son of Kareah said privately to Gedaliah in Mizpah, 'Let me go and kill Ishmael son of Nethaniah, and no-one will know it. Why should he take your life and cause all the Jews who are gathered around you to be scattered and the remnant of Judah to perish?'

16But Gedaliah son of Ahikam said to Johanan son of Kareah, 'Don't do such a thing! What you are saying about Ishmael is not true.'

41 In the seventh month Ishmael son of Nethaniah, the son of Elishama, who was of royal blood and had been one of the king's officers, came with ten men to Gedaliah son of Ahikam at Mizpah. While they were eating together there, 2Ishmael son of Nethaniah and the ten men who were with him got up and struck down Gedaliah son of Ahikam, the son of Shaphan, with the sword, killing the one whom the king of Babylon had appointed as governor over the land. 3Ishmael also killed all the men of Judah who were with Gedaliah at Mizpah, as well as the Babylonian*c* soldiers who were there.

4The day after Gedaliah's assassination, before anyone knew about it, 5eighty men who had shaved off their beards, torn their clothes and cut themselves came from Shechem, Shiloh and Samaria, bringing grain offerings and incense with them to the house of the LORD. 6Ishmael son of Nethaniah went out from Mizpah to meet them, weeping as he went. When he met them, he said, 'Come to Gedaliah son of Ahikam.' 7When they went into the city, Ishmael son of Nethaniah and the men who were with him slaughtered them and threw them into a cistern. 8But ten of them said to Ishmael, 'Don't kill us! We have wheat and barley, olive oil and honey, hidden in a field.' So he let them alone and did not kill them with the others. 9Now the cistern where he threw all the bodies of the men he had killed along with Gedaliah was the one King Asa had made as part of his defence

---

*a*8 Hebrew *Jezaniah*, a variant of *Jaazaniah* *b*9 Or *Chaldeans*; also in verse 10 *c*3 Or *Chaldean* against Baasha king of Israel. Ishmael son of Nethaniah filled it with the dead.

10 Ishmael made captives of all the rest of the people who were in Mizpah—the king's daughters along with all the others who were left there, over whom Nebuzaradan commander of the imperial guard had appointed Gedaliah son of Ahikam. Ishmael son of Nethaniah took them captive and set out to cross over to the Ammonites.

11 When Johanan son of Kareah and all the army officers who were with him heard about all the crimes Ishmael son of Nethaniah had committed, 12 they took all their men and went to fight Ishmael son of Nethaniah. They caught up with him near the great pool in Gibeon. 13 When all the people Ishmael had with him saw Johanan son of Kareah and the army officers who were with him, they were glad. 14 All the people Ishmael had taken captive at Mizpah turned and went over to Johanan son of Kareah. 15 But Ishmael son of Nethaniah and eight of his men escaped from Johanan and fled to the Ammonites.

Flight to Egypt

16 Then Johanan son of Kareah and all the army officers who were with him led away all the people of Mizpah who had survived, whom Johanan had recovered from Ishmael son of Nethaniah after Ishmael had assassinated Gedaliah son of Ahikam—the soldiers, women, children and court officials he had recovered from Gibeon. 17 And they went on, stopping at Geruth Kimham near Bethlehem on their way to Egypt 18 to escape the Babylonians.*a* They were afraid of them because Ishmael son of Nethaniah had killed Gedaliah son of Ahikam, whom the king of Babylon had appointed as governor over the land.

42 Then all the army officers, including Johanan son of Kareah and Jezaniah*b* son of Hoshaiah, and all the people from the least to the greatest approached 2 Jeremiah the prophet and said to him, 'Please hear our petition and pray to the LORD your God for this entire remnant. For as you now see, though we were once many, now only a few are left. 3 Pray that the LORD your God will tell us where we should go and what we should do.'

4 'I have heard you,' replied Jeremiah the prophet. 'I will certainly pray to the LORD your God as you have requested; I will tell you everything the LORD says and will keep nothing back from you.'

5 Then they said to Jeremiah, 'May the LORD be a true and faithful witness against us if we do not act in accordance with everything the LORD your God sends you to tell us. 6 Whether it is favourable or unfavourable, we will obey the LORD our God, to whom we are sending you, so that it will go well with us, for we will obey the LORD our God.'

7 Ten days later the word of the LORD came to Jeremiah. 8 So he called together Johanan son of Kareah and all the army officers who were with him and all the people from the least to the greatest. 9 He said to them, 'This is what the LORD, the God of Israel, to whom you sent me to present your petition, says: 10 "If you stay in this land, I will build you up and not tear you down; I will plant you and not uproot you, for I have relented concerning the disaster I have inflicted on you. 11 Do not be afraid of the king of Babylon, whom you now fear. Do not be afraid of him, declares the LORD, for I am with you and will save you and deliver you from his hands. 12 I will show you compassion so that he will have compassion on you and restore you to your land."

13 'However, if you say, "We will not stay in this land," and so disobey the LORD your God, 14 and if you say, "No, we will go and live in Egypt, where we will not see war or hear the trumpet or be hungry for bread," 15 then hear the word of the LORD, you remnant of Judah. This is what the LORD Almighty, the God of Israel, says: "If you are determined to go to Egypt and you do go to settle there, 16 then the sword you fear will overtake you there, and the famine you dread will follow you into Egypt, and there you will die. 17 Indeed, all who are determined to go to Egypt to settle there will die by the sword, famine and plague; not one of

---

a 18 Or *Chaldeans* *b* 1 Hebrew; Septuagint (see also 43:2) *Azariah* them will survive or escape the disaster I will bring on them." ¹⁸This is what the LORD Almighty, the God of Israel, says: "As my anger and wrath have been poured out on those who lived in Jerusalem, so will my wrath be poured out on you when you go to Egypt. You will be a curse^a and an object of horror, a curse^b and an object of reproach; you will never see this place again."

¹⁹'Remnant of Judah, the LORD has told you, "Do not go to Egypt." Be sure of this: I warn you today ²⁰that you made a fatal mistake when you sent me to the LORD your God and said, "Pray to the LORD our God for us; tell us everything he says and we will do it." ²¹I have told you today, but you still have not obeyed the LORD your God in all he sent me to tell you. ²²So now, be sure of this: you will die by the sword, famine and plague in the place where you want to go to settle.'

43 When Jeremiah had finished telling the people all the words of the LORD their God—everything the LORD had sent him to tell them— ²Azariah son of Hoshaiah and Johanan son of Kareah and all the arrogant men said to Jeremiah, 'You are lying! The LORD our God has not sent you to say, "You must not go to Egypt to settle there." ³But Baruch son of Neriah is inciting you against us to hand us over to the Babylonians,^{c} so that they may kill us or carry us into exile to Babylon.'

⁴So Johanan son of Kareah and all the army officers and all the people disobeyed the LORD's command to stay in the land of Judah. ⁵Instead, Johanan son of Kareah and all the army officers led away all the remnant of Judah who had come back to live in the land of Judah from all the nations where they had been scattered. ⁶They also led away all those whom Nebuzaradan commander of the imperial guard had left with Gedaliah son of Ahikam, the son of Shaphan—the men, the women, the children and the king's daughters. And they took Jeremiah the prophet and Baruch son of Neriah along with them. ⁷So they entered Egypt in disobedience to the LORD and went as far as Tahpanhes.

⁸In Tahpanhes the word of the LORD came to Jeremiah: ⁹'While the Jews are watching, take some large stones with you and bury them in clay in the brick pavement at the entrance to Pharaoh's palace in Tahpanhes. ¹⁰Then say to them, "This is what the LORD Almighty, the God of Israel, says: I will send for my servant Nebuchadnezzar king of Babylon, and I will set his throne over these stones I have buried here; he will spread his royal canopy above them. ¹¹He will come and attack Egypt, bringing death to those destined for death, captivity to those destined for captivity, and the sword to those destined for the sword. ¹²He will set fire to the temples of the gods of Egypt; he will burn their temples and take their gods captive. As a shepherd picks his garment clean of lice, so he will pick Egypt clean and depart. ¹³There in the temple of the sun^d in Egypt he will demolish the sacred pillars and will burn down the temples of the gods of Egypt."'

Disaster because of idolatry

44 This word came to Jeremiah concerning all the Jews living in Lower Egypt—in Migdol, Tahpanhes and Memphis—and in Upper Egypt: ²'This is what the LORD Almighty, the God of Israel, says: you saw the great disaster I brought on Jerusalem and on all the towns of Judah. Today they lie deserted and in ruins ³because of the evil they have done. They aroused my anger by burning incense to and worshipping other gods that neither they nor you nor your ancestors ever knew. ⁴Again and again I sent my servants the prophets, who said, "Do not do this detestable thing that I hate!" ⁵But they did not listen or pay attention; they did not turn from their wickedness or stop burning incense to other gods. ⁶Therefore, my fierce anger was poured out; it raged against the towns of Judah and the streets of Jerusalem and made them the desolate ruins they are today.

---

^{a} 18 That is, your name will be used in cursing (see Jer. 29:22); or, others will see that you are cursed. ^{b} 18 That is, your name will be used in cursing (see Jer. 29:22); or, others will see that you are cursed. ^{c} 3 Or *Chaldeans* ^{d} 13 Or *in Heliopolis*

⁷'Now this is what the LORD God Almighty, the God of Israel, says: why bring such great disaster on yourselves by cutting off from Judah the men and women, the children and infants, and so leave yourselves without a remnant? ⁸Why arouse my anger with what your hands have made, burning incense to other gods in Egypt, where you have come to live? You will destroy yourselves and make yourselves a curse*ᵃ* and an object of reproach among all the nations on earth. ⁹Have you forgotten the wickedness committed by your ancestors and by the kings and queens of Judah and the wickedness committed by you and your wives in the land of Judah and the streets of Jerusalem? ¹⁰To this day they have not humbled themselves or shown reverence, nor have they followed my law and the decrees I set before you and your ancestors.

¹¹'Therefore, this is what the LORD Almighty, the God of Israel, says: I am determined to bring disaster on you and to destroy all Judah. ¹²I will take away the remnant of Judah who were determined to go to Egypt to settle there. They will all perish in Egypt; they will fall by the sword or die from famine. From the least to the greatest, they will die by sword or famine. They will become a curse and an object of horror, a curse and an object of reproach. ¹³I will punish those who live in Egypt with the sword, famine and plague, as I punished Jerusalem. ¹⁴None of the remnant of Judah who have gone to live in Egypt will escape or survive to return to the land of Judah, to which they long to return and live; none will return except a few fugitives.'

¹⁵Then all the men who knew that their wives were burning incense to other gods, along with all the women who were present—a large assembly—and all the people living in Lower and Upper Egypt, said to Jeremiah, ¹⁶'We will not listen to the message you have spoken to us in the name of the LORD! ¹⁷We will certainly do everything we said we would: we will burn incense to the Queen of Heaven and will pour out drink offerings to her just as we

Worship of the Queen of Heaven
Jeremiah 44:17

'The Queen of Heaven' is another name for the Canaanite goddess Astarte, goddess of the moon and fertility. Cakes were offered to her (Jeremiah 7:18), as well as wine and incense.

and our ancestors, our kings and our officials did in the towns of Judah and in the streets of Jerusalem. At that time we had plenty of food and were well off and suffered no harm. ¹⁸But ever since we stopped burning incense to the Queen of Heaven and pouring out drink offerings to her, we have had nothing and have been perishing by sword and famine.'

¹⁹The women added, 'When we burned incense to the Queen of Heaven and poured out drink offerings to her, did not our husbands know that we were making cakes impressed with her image and pouring out drink offerings to her?'

²⁰Then Jeremiah said to all the people, both men and women, who were answering him, ²¹'Did not the LORD remember and call to mind the incense burned in the towns of Judah and the streets of Jerusalem by you and your ancestors, your kings and your officials and the people of the land? ²²When the LORD could no longer endure your wicked actions and the detestable things you did, your land became a curse and a desolate waste without inhabitants, as it is today. ²³Because you have burned incense and have sinned against the LORD and have not obeyed him or followed his law or his decrees or his stipulations, this disaster has come upon you, as you now see.'

ᵃ 8 That is, your name will be used in cursing (see Jer. 29:22); or, others will see that you are cursed; also in verse 12; similarly in verse 22.

24Then Jeremiah said to all the people, including the women, 'Hear the word of the LORD, all you people of Judah in Egypt. 25This is what the LORD Almighty, the God of Israel, says: you and your wives have done what you said you would do when you promised, "We will certainly carry out the vows we made to burn incense and pour out drink offerings to the Queen of Heaven."

'Go ahead then, do what you promised! Keep your vows! 26But hear the word of the LORD, all you Jews living in Egypt: "I swear by my great name," says the LORD, "that no-one from Judah living anywhere in Egypt shall ever again invoke my name or swear, 'As surely as the Sovereign LORD lives.' 27For I am watching over them for harm, not for good; the Jews in Egypt will perish by sword and famine until they are all destroyed. 28Those who escape the sword and return to the land of Judah from Egypt will be very few. Then the whole remnant of Judah who came to live in Egypt will know whose word will stand—mine or theirs.

29' "This will be the sign to you that I will punish you in this place," declares the LORD, "so that you will know that my threats of harm against you will surely stand." 30This is what the LORD says: "I am going to deliver Pharaoh Hophra king of Egypt into the hands of his enemies who seek his life, just as I gave Zedekiah king of Judah into the hands of Nebuchadnezzar king of Babylon, the enemy who was seeking his life." '

A message to Baruch

45 When Baruch son of Neriah wrote on a scroll the words Jeremiah the prophet dictated in the fourth year of Jehoiakim son of Josiah king of Judah, Jeremiah said this to Baruch: 2'This is what the LORD, the God of Israel, says to you, Baruch: 3you said, "Woe to me! The LORD has added sorrow to my pain; I am worn out with groaning and find no rest." 4But the LORD has told me to say to you, "This is what the LORD says: I will overthrow what I have built and uproot what I have planted, throughout the earth. 5Should you then seek great things for yourself? Do not seek them. For I will bring disaster on all people, declares the LORD, but wherever you go I will let you escape with your life." '

A message about Egypt

46 This is the word of the LORD that came to Jeremiah the prophet concerning the nations:

2Concerning Egypt:

This is the message against the army of Pharaoh Necho king of Egypt, which was defeated at Carchemish on the River Euphrates by Nebuchadnezzar king of Babylon in the fourth year of Jehoiakim son of Josiah king of Judah:

3'Prepare your shields, both large and small,
   and march out for battle!
4Harness the horses,
   mount the steeds!
Take up your positions
   with helmets on!
Polish your spears,
   put on your armour!
5What do I see?
   They are terrified,
they are retreating,
   their warriors are defeated.
They flee in haste
   without looking back,
and there is terror on every side,'
               declares the LORD.
6'The swift cannot flee
   nor the strong escape.
In the north by the River Euphrates
   they stumble and fall.

7'Who is this that rises like the Nile,
   like rivers of surging waters?
8Egypt rises like the Nile,
   like rivers of surging waters.
She says, "I will rise and cover the earth;
   I will destroy cities and their people."
9Charge, you horses!
   Drive furiously, you charioteers!
March on, you warriors—men of Cush[a]
   and Put who carry shields,
   men of Lydia who draw the bow.
10But that day belongs to the Lord, the
   LORD Almighty—

---

[a] 9 That is, the upper Nile region

a day of vengeance, for vengeance on
  his foes.
The sword will devour till it is satisfied,
  till it has quenched its thirst with
    blood.
For the Lord, the LORD Almighty, will
    offer sacrifice
  in the land of the north by the River
    Euphrates.

11 'Go up to Gilead and get balm,
  Virgin Daughter Egypt.
But you multiply remedies in vain;
  there is no healing for you.
12 The nations will hear of your shame;
  your cries will fill the earth.
One warrior will stumble over another;
  both will fall down together.'

13 This is the message the LORD spoke to Jeremiah the prophet about the coming of Nebuchadnezzar king of Babylon to attack Egypt:

14 'Announce this in Egypt, and proclaim it
    in Migdol;
  proclaim it also in Memphis and
    Tahpanhes:
"Take up your positions and get ready,
  for the sword devours those around
    you."
15 Why will your warriors be laid low?
  They cannot stand, for the LORD will
    push them down.
16 They will stumble repeatedly;
  they will fall over each other.
They will say, "Get up, let us go back
  to our own people and our native
    lands,
  away from the sword of the oppressor."
17 There they will exclaim,
  "Pharaoh king of Egypt is only a loud
    noise;
  he has missed his opportunity."

18 'As surely as I live,' declares the King,
  whose name is the LORD Almighty,
'one will come who is like Tabor among
    the mountains,
  like Carmel by the sea.
19 Pack your belongings for exile,
  you who live in Egypt,
for Memphis will be laid waste
  and lie in ruins without inhabitant.

20 'Egypt is a beautiful heifer,
  but a gadfly is coming
    against her from the north.
21 The mercenaries in her ranks
  are like fattened calves.
They too will turn and flee together,
  they will not stand their ground,
for the day of disaster is coming upon
    them,
  the time for them to be punished.
22 Egypt will hiss like a fleeing serpent
  as the enemy advances in force;
they will come against her with
    axes,
  like those who cut down trees.
23 They will chop down her forest,'
            declares the LORD,
  'dense though it be.
They are more numerous than locusts,
  they cannot be counted.
24 Daughter Egypt will be put to shame,
  given into the hands of the people of
    the north.'

25 The LORD Almighty, the God of Israel, says: 'I am about to bring punishment on Amon god of Thebes, on Pharaoh, on Egypt and her gods and her kings, and on those who rely on Pharaoh. 26 I will give them into the hands of those who seek their lives—Nebuchadnezzar king of Babylon and his officers. Later, however, Egypt will be inhabited as in times past,' declares the LORD.

27 'Do not be afraid, Jacob my servant;
  do not be dismayed, Israel.
I will surely save you out of a distant place,
  your descendants from the land of
    their exile.
Jacob will again have peace and
    security,
  and no-one will make him afraid.
28 Do not be afraid, Jacob my servant,
  for I am with you,' declares the LORD.
'Though I completely destroy all the
    nations
  among which I scatter you,
  I will not completely destroy you.
I will discipline you but only in due
    measure;
  I will not let you go entirely
    unpunished.'

A message about the Philistines

47 This is the word of the LORD that came to Jeremiah the prophet concerning the Philistines before Pharaoh attacked Gaza:

²This is what the LORD says:

'See how the waters are rising in the north;
 they will become an overflowing torrent.
They will overflow the land and everything in it,
 the towns and those who live in them.
The people will cry out;
 all who dwell in the land will wail
³at the sound of the hooves of galloping steeds,
 at the noise of enemy chariots
 and the rumble of their wheels.
Parents will not turn to help their children;
 their hands will hang limp.
⁴For the day has come
 to destroy all the Philistines
and to remove all survivors
 who could help Tyre and Sidon.
The LORD is about to destroy the Philistines,
 the remnant from the coasts of Caphtor.ᵃ
⁵Gaza will shave her head in mourning;
 Ashkelon will be silenced.
You remnant on the plain,
 how long will you cut yourselves?

⁶ '"Ah, sword of the LORD," ⌊you cry,⌋
 "how long till you rest?
Return to your sheath;
 cease and be still."
⁷But how can it rest
 when the LORD has commanded it,
when he has ordered it
 to attack Ashkelon and the coast?'

A message about Moab

48 Concerning Moab:

This is what the LORD Almighty, the God of Israel, says:

> ### People and Places
>
> **Moab**
> Jeremiah 48:1
> Moab was a neighbouring country to Israel, situated to the east across the Dead Sea. Moab's history was intertwined with that of Israel; Moab oppressed Israel during the time of the judges (Judges 3:12–30), and David conquered Moab during his reign (2 Samuel 8:2).

'Woe to Nebo, for it will be ruined.
 Kiriathaim will be disgraced and captured;
 the strongholdᵇ will be disgraced and shattered.
²Moab will be praised no more;
 in Heshbonᶜ people will plot her downfall:
 "Come, let us put an end to that nation."
You, the people of Madmen,ᵈ will also be silenced;
 the sword will pursue you.
³Cries of anguish arise from Horonaim,
 cries of great havoc and destruction.
⁴Moab will be broken;
 her little ones will cry out.ᵉ
⁵They go up the hill to Luhith,
 weeping bitterly as they go;
on the road down to Horonaim
 anguished cries over the destruction are heard.
⁶Flee! Run for your lives;
 become like a bushᶠ in the desert.
⁷Since you trust in your deeds and riches,
 you too will be taken captive,
and Chemosh will go into exile,
 together with his priests and officials.
⁸The destroyer will come against every town,
 and not a town will escape.

ᵃ 4 That is, Crete ᵇ 1 Or *captured; I Misgab* ᶜ 2 The Hebrew for *Heshbon* sounds like the Hebrew for *plot*. ᵈ 2 The name of the Moabite town Madmen sounds like the Hebrew for *be silenced*. ᵉ 4 Hebrew; Septuagint */ proclaim it to Zoar* ᶠ 6 Or *like Aroer*

The valley will be ruined
  and the plateau destroyed,
  because the LORD has spoken.
⁹Put salt on Moab,
  for she will be laid waste;ᵃ
  her towns will become desolate,
  with no-one to live in them.

¹⁰'A curse on those who are lax in doing the
    LORD's work!
  A curse on those who keep their swords
    from bloodshed!

¹¹'Moab has been at rest from youth,
  like wine left on its dregs,
  not poured from one jar to another—
    she has not gone into exile.
  So she tastes as she did,
    and her aroma is unchanged.

¹²But days are coming,'
    declares the LORD,
  'when I will send people who pour from
    jars,
  and they will pour her out;
  they will empty her jars
    and smash her jugs.

¹³Then Moab will be ashamed of Chemosh,
  as the house of Israel was ashamed
    when they trusted in Bethel.

¹⁴'How can you say, "We are warriors,
    men valiant in battle"?

¹⁵Moab will be destroyed and her towns
    invaded;
  her finest young men will go down in
    the slaughter,'
    declares the King, whose name is the
      LORD Almighty.

¹⁶'The fall of Moab is at hand;
  her calamity will come quickly.

¹⁷Mourn for her, all who live around her,
  all who know her fame;
  say, "How broken is the mighty sceptre,
    how broken the glorious staff!"

¹⁸'Come down from your glory
  and sit on the parched ground,
  you inhabitants of Daughter Dibon,
  for Moab's destroyer
    will come up against you
    and ruin your fortified cities.

¹⁹Stand by the road and watch,
  you who live in Aroer.
  Ask the man fleeing and the woman
    escaping,
  ask them, "What has happened?"

²⁰Moab is disgraced, for she is shattered.
  Wail and cry out!
  Announce by the Arnon
    that Moab is destroyed.

²¹Judgment has come to the plateau—
  to Holon, Jahzah and Mephaath,
²² to Dibon, Nebo and Beth Diblathaim,
²³ to Kiriathaim, Beth Gamul and Beth
    Meon,
²⁴ to Kerioth and Bozrah—
  to all the towns of Moab, far and near.

²⁵Moab's hornᵇ is cut off;
  her arm is broken,'
    declares the LORD.

²⁶'Make her drunk,
  for she has defied the LORD.
  Let Moab wallow in her vomit;
  let her be an object of ridicule.

²⁷Was not Israel the object of your ridicule?
  Was she caught among thieves,
  that you shake your head in scorn
    whenever you speak of her?

²⁸Abandon your towns and dwell among
    the rocks,
  you who live in Moab.
  Be like a dove that makes its nest
    at the mouth of a cave.

²⁹'We have heard of Moab's pride—
  her overweening pride and conceit,
  her pride and arrogance
    and the haughtiness of her heart.

³⁰I know her insolence but it is futile,'
    declares the LORD,
  'and her boasts accomplish nothing.

³¹Therefore I wail over Moab,
  for all Moab I cry out,
  I moan for the people of Kir Hareseth.

³²I weep for you, as Jazer weeps,
  you vines of Sibmah.
  Your branches spread as far as the seaᶜ;
    they reached as far asᵈ Jazer.
  The destroyer has fallen
    on your ripened fruit and grapes.

³³Joy and gladness are gone
  from the orchards and fields of Moab.

ᵃ 9 Or *Give wings to Moab, / for she will fly away* ᵇ 25 *Horn* here symbolises strength. ᶜ 32 Probably the Dead Sea
ᵈ 32 Two Hebrew manuscripts and Septuagint; most Hebrew manuscripts *as far as the Sea of*

I have stopped the flow of wine from the presses;
  no-one treads them with shouts of joy.
Although there are shouts,
  they are not shouts of joy.

³⁴'The sound of their cry rises
  from Heshbon to Elealeh and Jahaz,
from Zoar as far as Horonaim and Eglath Shelishiyah,
  for even the waters of Nimrim are dried up.
³⁵In Moab I will put an end
  to those who make offerings on the high places
and burn incense to their gods,'
  declares the LORD.
³⁶'So my heart laments for Moab like the music of a pipe;
  it laments like a pipe for the people of Kir Hareseth.
The wealth they acquired is gone.
³⁷Every head is shaved
  and every beard cut off;
every hand is slashed
  and every waist is covered with sackcloth.
³⁸On all the roofs in Moab
  and in the public squares
there is nothing but mourning,
  for I have broken Moab
  like a jar that no-one wants,'
  declares the LORD.
³⁹'How shattered she is! How they wail!
  How Moab turns her back in shame!
Moab has become an object of ridicule,
  an object of horror to all those around her.'

⁴⁰This is what the LORD says:

'Look! An eagle is swooping down,
  spreading its wings over Moab.
⁴¹Kerioth^a will be captured
  and the strongholds taken.
In that day the hearts of Moab's warriors
  will be like the heart of a woman in labour.
⁴²Moab will be destroyed as a nation
  because she defied the LORD.
⁴³Terror and pit and snare await you,
  you people of Moab,'
  declares the LORD.

⁴⁴'Whoever flees from the terror
  will fall into a pit,
whoever climbs out of the pit
  will be caught in a snare;
for I will bring on Moab
  the year of her punishment,'
  declares the LORD.

⁴⁵'In the shadow of Heshbon
  the fugitives stand helpless,
for a fire has gone out from Heshbon,
  a blaze from the midst of Sihon;
it burns the foreheads of Moab,
  the skulls of the noisy boasters.
⁴⁶Woe to you, Moab!
  The people of Chemosh are destroyed;
your sons are taken into exile
  and your daughters into captivity.

⁴⁷'Yet I will restore the fortunes of Moab
  in days to come,'
  declares the LORD.

Here ends the judgment on Moab.

A message about Ammon

49

Concerning the Ammonites:

This is what the LORD says:

'Has Israel no children?
  Has she no heirs?
Why then has Molek^b taken possession of Gad?
  Why do his people live in its towns?
²But the days are coming,'
  declares the LORD,
'when I will sound the battle cry
  against Rabbah of the Ammonites;
it will become a mound of ruins,
  and its surrounding villages will be set on fire.
Then Israel will drive out
  those who drove her out,'
  says the LORD.
³'Wail, Heshbon, for Ai is destroyed!
  Cry out, you inhabitants of Rabbah!
Put on sackcloth and mourn;
  rush here and there inside the walls,
for Molek will go into exile,
  together with his priests and officials.
⁴Why do you boast of your valleys,
  boast of your valleys so fruitful?

---

^a 41 Or *The cities* ^b 1 Or *their king*; also in verse 3

Unfaithful Daughter Ammon,
you trust in your riches and say,
"Who will attack me?"
⁵I will bring terror on you
from all those around you,'
declares the Lord,
the LORD Almighty.
'Every one of you will be driven away,
and no-one will gather the fugitives.

⁶'Yet afterwards, I will restore the fortunes
of the Ammonites,'
declares the LORD.

A message about Edom

⁷Concerning Edom:

This is what the LORD Almighty says:

'Is there no longer wisdom in Teman?
Has counsel perished from the
prudent?
Has their wisdom decayed?
⁸Turn and flee, hide in deep caves,
you who live in Dedan,
for I will bring disaster on Esau
at the time when I punish him.
⁹If grape-pickers came to you,
would they not leave a few grapes?
If thieves came during the night,
would they not steal only as much as
they wanted?
¹⁰But I will strip Esau bare;
I will uncover his hiding-places,
so that he cannot conceal himself.
His armed men are destroyed,
also his allies and neighbours,
so there is no-one to say,
¹¹"Leave your fatherless children; I will
keep them alive.
Your widows too can depend on
me."'

¹²This is what the LORD says: 'If those who do not deserve to drink the cup must drink it, why should you go unpunished? You will not go unpunished, but must drink it. ¹³I swear by myself,' declares the LORD, 'that Bozrah will become a ruin and a curse,ᵃ an object of horror and reproach; and all its towns will be in ruins for ever.'

¹⁴I have heard a message from the LORD;
an envoy was sent to the nations to say,

> **People and Places**
>
> **Edom**
> Jeremiah 49:7
> Edom was another name for Esau, the brother of Jacob. The Israelites were descended from Jacob and the Edomites were descended from his brother Esau, so they shared some common history. But by the time of Jeremiah there was no love lost between them. Edom had tried to invade Judah in the past (2 Chronicles 20:2), and Judah in turn had controlled Edom for a while (2 Kings 8:20).

'Assemble yourselves to attack it!
Rise up for battle!'

¹⁵'Now I will make you small among the
nations,
despised among the peoples.
¹⁶The terror you inspire
and the pride of your heart have
deceived you,
you who live in the clefts of the rocks,
who occupy the heights of the hill.
Though you build your nest as high as the
eagle's,
from there I will bring you down,'
declares the LORD.
¹⁷'Edom will become an object of horror;
all who pass by will be appalled and will
scoff
because of all its wounds.
¹⁸As Sodom and Gomorrah were
overthrown,
along with their neighbouring towns,'
says the LORD,
'so no-one will live there;
no-one will dwell in it.

¹⁹'Like a lion coming up from Jordan's
thickets
to a rich pasture-land,

ᵃ 13 That is, its name will be used in cursing (see Jer. 29:22); or, others will see that it is cursed.

I will chase Edom from its land in an instant.
> Who is the chosen one I will appoint for this?
> Who is like me and who can challenge me?
> And what shepherd can stand against me?'

20Therefore, hear what the LORD has planned against Edom,
what he has purposed against those who live in Teman:
the young of the flock will be dragged away;
their pasture will be appalled at their fate.
21At the sound of their fall the earth will tremble;
their cry will resound to the Red Sea.[a]
22Look! An eagle will soar and swoop down,
spreading its wings over Bozrah.
In that day the hearts of Edom's warriors will be like the heart of a woman in labour.

A message about Damascus

23Concerning Damascus:

'Hamath and Arpad are dismayed,
for they have heard bad news.
They are disheartened,
troubled like[b] the restless sea.
24Damascus has become feeble,
she has turned to flee
and panic has gripped her;
anguish and pain have seized her,
pain like that of a woman in labour.
25Why has the city of renown not been abandoned,
the town in which I delight?
26Surely, her young men will fall in the streets;
all her soldiers will be silenced in that day,'
> declares the LORD Almighty.
27'I will set fire to the walls of Damascus;
it will consume the fortresses of Ben-Hadad.'

A message about Kedar and Hazor

28Concerning Kedar and the kingdoms of Hazor, which Nebuchadnezzar king of Babylon attacked:

This is what the LORD says:

'Arise, and attack Kedar
and destroy the people of the East.
29Their tents and their flocks will be taken;
their shelters will be carried off
with all their goods and camels.
People will shout to them,
"Terror on every side!"

30'Flee quickly away!
Stay in deep caves, you who live in Hazor,'
> declares the LORD.
'Nebuchadnezzar king of Babylon has plotted against you;
he has devised a plan against you.

31'Arise and attack a nation at ease,
which lives in confidence,'
> declares the LORD,
'a nation that has neither gates nor bars;
its people live far from danger.
32Their camels will become plunder,
and their large herds will be booty.
I will scatter to the winds those who are in distant places[c]
and will bring disaster on them from every side,'
> declares the LORD.
33'Hazor will become a haunt of jackals,
a desolate place for ever.
No-one will live there;
no-one will dwell in it.'

A message about Elam

34This is the word of the LORD that came to Jeremiah the prophet concerning Elam, early in the reign of Zedekiah king of Judah:

35This is what the LORD Almighty says:

'See, I will break the bow of Elam,
the mainstay of their might.
36I will bring against Elam the four winds
from the four quarters of the heavens;
I will scatter them to the four winds,
and there will not be a nation
where Elam's exiles do not go.

---

[a] 21 Or *the Sea of Reeds* [b] 23 Hebrew *on* or *by* [c] 32 Or *who clip the hair by their foreheads*

⁣³⁷'I will shatter Elam before their foes,
  before those who seek their lives;
I will bring disaster on them,
  even my fierce anger,'
            declares the LORD.
'I will pursue them with the sword
  until I have made an end of them.
³⁸I will set my throne in Elam
  and destroy her king and officials,'
            declares the LORD.

³⁹'Yet I will restore the fortunes of Elam
  in days to come,'
            declares the LORD.

A message about Babylon

50 This is the word the LORD spoke through Jeremiah the prophet concerning Babylon and the land of the Babylonians:*ᵃ*

²'Announce and proclaim among the
    nations,
  lift up a banner and proclaim it;
  keep nothing back, but say,
"Babylon will be captured;
  Bel will be put to shame,
  Marduk filled with terror.
Her images will be put to shame
  and her idols filled with terror."

³A nation from the north will attack her
  and lay waste her land.
No-one will live in it;
  both people and animals will flee away.

⁴'In those days, at that time,'
            declares the LORD,
'the people of Israel and the people of
    Judah together
  will go in tears to seek the LORD their
    God.
⁵They will ask the way to Zion
  and turn their faces towards it.
They will come and bind themselves to
    the LORD
  in an everlasting covenant
  that will not be forgotten.

⁶'My people have been lost sheep;
  their shepherds have led them astray
  and caused them to roam on the
    mountains.
They wandered over mountain and hill
  and forgot their own resting place.
⁷Whoever found them devoured them;
  their enemies said, "We are not guilty,
  for they sinned against the LORD, their
    verdant pasture,
  the LORD, the hope of their ancestors."

⁸'Flee out of Babylon;
  leave the land of the Babylonians,
  and be like the goats that lead the flock.
⁹For I will stir up and bring against
    Babylon
  an alliance of great nations from the
    land of the north.
They will take up their positions against
    her,
  and from the north she will be
    captured.
Their arrows will be like skilled warriors
  who do not return empty-handed.
¹⁰So Babylonia*ᵇ* will be plundered;
  all who plunder her will have their fill,'
            declares the LORD.

¹¹'Because you rejoice and are glad,
  you who pillage my inheritance,
because you frolic like a heifer threshing
    corn
  and neigh like stallions,
¹²your mother will be greatly ashamed;
  she who gave you birth will be
    disgraced.
She will be the least of the nations—
  a wilderness, a dry land, a desert.
¹³Because of the LORD's anger she will not
    be inhabited
  but will be completely desolate.
All who pass Babylon will be appalled;
  they will scoff because of all her
    wounds.

¹⁴'Take up your positions round Babylon,
  all you who draw the bow.
Shoot at her! Spare no arrows,
  for she has sinned against the LORD.
¹⁵Shout against her on every side!
  She surrenders, her towers fall,
  her walls are torn down.
Since this is the vengeance of the LORD,
  take vengeance on her;
  do to her as she has done to others.

ᵃ 1 Or *Chaldeans;* also in verses 8, 25, 35 and 45   *ᵇ* 10 Or *Chaldea*

¹⁶Cut off from Babylon the sowers,
  and the reapers with their sickles at harvest.
Because of the sword of the oppressor
  let everyone return to their own people,
  let everyone flee to their own land.

¹⁷'Israel is a scattered flock
  that lions have chased away.
The first to devour them
  was the king of Assyria;
the last to crush their bones
  was Nebuchadnezzar king of Babylon.'

¹⁸Therefore this is what the LORD Almighty, the God of Israel, says:

'I will punish the king of Babylon and his land
  as I punished the king of Assyria.
¹⁹But I will bring Israel back to their own pasture,
  and they will graze on Carmel and Bashan;
their appetite will be satisfied
  on the hills of Ephraim and Gilead.
²⁰In those days, at that time,'
  declares the LORD,
'search will be made for Israel's guilt,
  but there will be none,
and for the sins of Judah,
  but none will be found,
  for I will forgive the remnant I spare.

²¹'Attack the land of Merathaim
  and those who live in Pekod.
Pursue, kill and completely destroy*ᵃ* them,'
                              declares the LORD.
'Do everything I have commanded you.
²²The noise of battle is in the land,
  the noise of great destruction!
²³How broken and shattered
  is the hammer of the whole earth!
How desolate is Babylon
  among the nations!
²⁴I set a trap for you, Babylon,
  and you were caught before you knew it;
you were found and captured
  because you opposed the LORD.
²⁵The LORD has opened his arsenal
  and brought out the weapons of his wrath,
for the Sovereign LORD Almighty has work to do
  in the land of the Babylonians.
²⁶Come against her from afar.
  Break open her granaries;
  pile her up like heaps of grain.
Completely destroy her
  and leave her no remnant.
²⁷Kill all her young bulls;
  let them go down to the slaughter!
Woe to them! For their day has come,
  the time for them to be punished.
²⁸Listen to the fugitives and refugees from Babylon
  declaring in Zion
how the LORD our God has taken vengeance,
  vengeance for his temple.

²⁹'Summon archers against Babylon,
  all those who draw the bow.
Encamp all round her;
  let no-one escape.
Repay her for her deeds;
  do to her as she has done.
For she defied the LORD,
  the Holy One of Israel.
³⁰Therefore, her young men will fall in the streets;
  all her soldiers will be silenced in that day,'
                              declares the LORD.
³¹'See, I am against you, you arrogant one,'
  declares the Lord, the LORD Almighty,
'for your day has come,
  the time for you to be punished.
³²The arrogant one will stumble and fall
  and no-one will help her up;
I will kindle a fire in her towns
  that will consume all who are around her.'

³³This is what the LORD Almighty says:

'The people of Israel are oppressed,
  and the people of Judah as well.
All their captors hold them fast,
  refusing to let them go.
³⁴Yet their Redeemer is strong;
  the LORD Almighty is his name.

ᵃ 21 The Hebrew term refers to the irrevocable giving over of things or persons to the LORD, often by totally destroying them; also in verse 26.

Hyenas
Jeremiah 50:39
The hyena is a member of the dog family which runs down its prey and eats it with its powerful jaws. Hyenas are scavengers who will eat the carcasses of dead animals. The Israelites hated them for this reason, because it made them 'unclean' animals.

He will vigorously defend their cause
  so that he may bring rest to their land,
  but unrest to those who live in Babylon.

35 'A sword against the Babylonians!'
    declares the LORD—
  'against those who live in Babylon
    and against her officials and wise counsellors!
36 A sword against her false prophets!
    They will become fools.
  A sword against her warriors!
    They will be filled with terror.
37 A sword against her horses and chariots
    and all the foreigners in her ranks!
    They will become weaklings.
  A sword against her treasures!
    They will be plundered.
38 A drought on[a] her waters!
    They will dry up.
  For it is a land of idols,
    idols that will go mad with terror.

39 'So desert creatures and hyenas will live there,
    and there the owl will dwell.
  It will never again be inhabited
    or lived in from generation to generation.
40 As I overthrew Sodom and Gomorrah
    along with their neighbouring towns,'
        declares the LORD,
  'so no-one will live there;
    no-one will dwell in it.

41 'Look! An army is coming from the north;
    a great nation and many kings
    are being stirred up from the ends of the earth.
42 They are armed with bows and spears;
    they are cruel and without mercy.
  They sound like the roaring sea
    as they ride on their horses;
  they come like men in battle formation
    to attack you, Daughter Babylon.
43 The king of Babylon has heard reports about them,
    and his hands hang limp.
  Anguish has gripped him,
    pain like that of a woman in labour.
44 Like a lion coming up from Jordan's thickets
    to a rich pasture-land,
  I will chase Babylon from its land in an instant.
  Who is the chosen one I will appoint for this?
  Who is like me and who can challenge me?
  And what shepherd can stand against me?'

45 Therefore, hear what the LORD has planned against Babylon,
  what he has purposed against the land of the Babylonians:
  the young of the flock will be dragged away;
    their pasture will be appalled at their fate.
46 At the sound of Babylon's capture the earth will tremble;
    its cry will resound among the nations.

51

This is what the LORD says:

'See, I will stir up the spirit of a destroyer
  against Babylon and the people of Leb Kamai.[b]
2 I will send foreigners to Babylon
  to winnow her and to devastate her land;

---

[a] 38 Or *A sword against*   [b] 1 *Leb Kamai* is a cryptogram for Chaldea, that is, Babylonia.

they will oppose her on every side
  in the day of her disaster.
³Let not the archer string his bow,
  nor let him put on his armour.
Do not spare her young men;
  completely destroy^a her army.
⁴They will fall down slain in Babylon,^{b}
  fatally wounded in her streets.
⁵For Israel and Judah have not been forsaken
  by their God, the LORD Almighty,
though their land^c is full of guilt
  before the Holy One of Israel.

⁶'Flee from Babylon!
  Run for your lives!
  Do not be destroyed because of her sins.
It is time for the LORD's vengeance;
  he will repay her what she deserves.
⁷Babylon was a gold cup in the LORD's hand;
  she made the whole earth drunk.
The nations drank her wine;
  therefore they have now gone mad.
⁸Babylon will suddenly fall and be broken.
  Wail over her!
Get balm for her pain;
  perhaps she can be healed.

⁹' "We would have healed Babylon,
  but she cannot be healed;
let us leave her and each go to our own land,
  for her judgment reaches to the skies,
  it rises as high as the heavens."

¹⁰' "The LORD has vindicated us;
  come, let us tell in Zion
  what the LORD our God has done."

¹¹'Sharpen the arrows,
  take up the shields!
The LORD has stirred up the kings of the Medes,
  because his purpose is to destroy Babylon.
The LORD will take vengeance,
  vengeance for his temple.
¹²Lift up a banner against the walls of Babylon!
  Reinforce the guard,
  station the watchmen,
  prepare an ambush!
The LORD will carry out his purpose,
  his decree against the people of Babylon.

¹³You who live by many waters
  and are rich in treasures,
your end has come,
  the time for you to be destroyed.
¹⁴The LORD Almighty has sworn by himself:
  I will surely fill you with troops, as with a swarm of locusts,
  and they will shout in triumph over you.

¹⁵'He made the earth by his power;
  he founded the world by his wisdom
  and stretched out the heavens by his understanding.
¹⁶When he thunders, the waters in the heavens roar;
  he makes clouds rise from the ends of the earth.
He sends lightning with the rain
  and brings out the wind from his storehouses.

¹⁷'Everyone is senseless and without knowledge;
  all goldsmiths are shamed by their idols.
Their images are a fraud;
  they have no breath in them.
¹⁸They are worthless, the objects of mockery;
  when their judgment comes, they will perish.
¹⁹He who is the Portion of Jacob is not like these,
  for he is the Maker of all things,
including the tribe of his inheritance—
  the LORD Almighty is his name.

²⁰'You are my war club,
  my weapon for battle—
with you I shatter nations,
  with you I destroy kingdoms,
²¹with you I shatter horse and rider,
  with you I shatter chariot and driver,
²²with you I shatter man and woman,
  with you I shatter old man and youth,

---

^{a} 3 The Hebrew term refers to the irrevocable giving over of things or persons to the LORD, often by totally destroying them. ^{b} 4 Or *Chaldea* ^{c} 5 Or *Almighty, I and the land* [*of the Babylonians*]

with you I shatter young man and
young woman,
²³with you I shatter shepherd and flock,
with you I shatter farmer and oxen,
with you I shatter governors and
officials.

²⁴'Before your eyes I will repay Babylon and all who live in Babylonia[a] for all the wrong they have done in Zion,' declares the LORD.

²⁵'I am against you, you destroying
mountain,
you who destroy the whole earth,'
declares the LORD.
'I will stretch out my hand against you,
roll you off the cliffs,
and make you a burnt-out mountain.
²⁶No rock will be taken from you for a
cornerstone,
nor any stone for a foundation,
for you will be desolate for ever,'
declares the LORD.

²⁷'Lift up a banner in the land!
Blow the trumpet among the nations!
Prepare the nations for battle against her;
summon against her these kingdoms:
Ararat, Minni and Ashkenaz.
Appoint a commander against her;
send up horses like a swarm of locusts.
²⁸Prepare the nations for battle against
her—
the kings of the Medes,
their governors and all their officials,
and all the countries they rule.
²⁹The land trembles and writhes,
for the LORD's purposes against
Babylon stand—
to lay waste the land of Babylon
so that no-one will live there.
³⁰Babylon's warriors have stopped
fighting;
they remain in their strongholds.
Their strength is exhausted;
they have become weaklings.
Her dwellings are set on fire;
the bars of her gates are broken.
³¹One courier follows another
and messenger follows messenger
to announce to the king of Babylon
that his entire city is captured,
³²the river crossings seized,
the marshes set on fire,
and the soldiers terrified.'

³³This is what the LORD Almighty, the God of Israel, says:

'Daughter Babylon is like a threshing-
floor
at the time it is trampled;
the time to harvest her will soon come.'

³⁴'Nebuchadnezzar king of Babylon has
devoured us,
he has thrown us into confusion,
he has made us an empty jar.
Like a serpent he has swallowed us
and filled his stomach with our
delicacies,
and then has spewed us out.
³⁵May the violence done to our flesh[b] be on
Babylon,'
say the inhabitants of Zion.
'May our blood be on those who live in
Babylonia,'
says Jerusalem.

³⁶Therefore, this is what the LORD says:

'See, I will defend your cause
and avenge you;
I will dry up her sea
and make her springs dry.
³⁷Babylon will be a heap of ruins,
a haunt of jackals,
an object of horror and scorn,
a place where no-one lives.
³⁸Her people all roar like young lions,
they growl like lion cubs.
³⁹But while they are aroused,
I will set out a feast for them
and make them drunk,
so that they shout with laughter—
then sleep for ever and not awake,'
declares the LORD.

⁴⁰'I will bring them down
like lambs to the slaughter,
like rams and goats.

⁴¹'How Sheshak[c] will be captured,
the boast of the whole earth seized!
How desolate Babylon will be
among the nations!
⁴²The sea will rise over Babylon;
its roaring waves will cover her.

---

[a] 24 Or *Chaldea*; also in verse 35   [b] 35 Or *done to us and to our children*   [c] 41 *Sheshak* is a cryptogram for Babylon.

⁴³Her towns will be desolate,
  a dry and desert land,
a land where no-one lives,
  through which no-one travels.
⁴⁴I will punish Bel in Babylon
  and make him spew out what he has swallowed.
The nations will no longer stream to him.
And the wall of Babylon will fall.

⁴⁵'Come out of her, my people!
  Run for your lives!
  Run from the fierce anger of the LORD.
⁴⁶Do not lose heart or be afraid
  when rumours are heard in the land;
one rumour comes this year, another the next,
  rumours of violence in the land
  and of ruler against ruler.
⁴⁷For the time will surely come
  when I will punish the idols of Babylon;
her whole land will be disgraced
  and her slain will all lie fallen within her.
⁴⁸Then heaven and earth and all that is in them
  will shout for joy over Babylon,
for out of the north
  destroyers will attack her,'
            declares the LORD.

⁴⁹'Babylon must fall because of Israel's slain,
  just as the slain in all the earth
  have fallen because of Babylon.
⁵⁰You who have escaped the sword,
  leave and do not linger!
Remember the LORD in a distant land,
  and call to mind Jerusalem.'

⁵¹'We are disgraced,
  for we have been insulted
  and shame covers our faces,
because foreigners have entered
  the holy places of the LORD's house.'

⁵²'But days are coming,' declares the LORD,
  'when I will punish her idols,
and throughout her land
  the wounded will groan.
⁵³Even if Babylon reaches the sky
  and fortifies her lofty stronghold,
  I will send destroyers against her,'
            declares the LORD.

⁵⁴'The sound of a cry comes from Babylon,
  the sound of great destruction
  from the land of the Babylonians.ᵃ
⁵⁵The LORD will destroy Babylon;
  he will silence her noisy din.
Waves of enemies will rage like great waters;
  the roar of their voices will resound.
⁵⁶A destroyer will come against Babylon;
  her warriors will be captured,
  and their bows will be broken.
For the LORD is a God of retribution;
  he will repay in full.
⁵⁷I will make her officials and wise counsellors drunk,
  her governors, officers and warriors as well;
they will sleep for ever and not awake,'
  declares the King, whose name is the LORD Almighty.

⁵⁸This is what the LORD Almighty says:

'Babylon's thick wall will be levelled
  and her high gates set on fire;
the peoples exhaust themselves for nothing,
  the nations' labour is only fuel for the flames.'

⁵⁹This is the message Jeremiah the prophet gave to the staff officer Seraiah son of Neriah, the son of Mahseiah, when he went to Babylon with Zedekiah king of Judah in the fourth year of his reign. ⁶⁰Jeremiah had written on a scroll about all the disasters that would come upon Babylon—all that had been recorded concerning Babylon. ⁶¹He said to Seraiah, 'When you get to Babylon, see that you read all these words aloud. ⁶²Then say, "LORD, you have said you will destroy this place, so that neither people nor animals will live in it; it will be desolate for ever." ⁶³When you finish reading this scroll, tie a stone to it and throw it into the Euphrates. ⁶⁴Then say, "So will Babylon sink to rise no more because of the disaster I will bring on her. And her people will fall."'

The words of Jeremiah end here.

ᵃ54 Or Chaldeans

making Connections

Jeremiah's last prophetic act
Jeremiah 51:64

A papyrus scroll thrown into the river would quickly disintegrate. This would illustrate Jeremiah's point very well – that the Babylonians would face destruction in the future from which they would never recover.

The fall of Jerusalem

52 Zedekiah was twenty-one years old when he became king, and he reigned in Jerusalem for eleven years. His mother's name was Hamutal daughter of Jeremiah; she was from Libnah. ²He did evil in the eyes of the LORD, just as Jehoiakim had done. ³It was because of the LORD's anger that all this happened to Jerusalem and Judah, and in the end he thrust them from his presence.

Now Zedekiah rebelled against the king of Babylon.

⁴So in the ninth year of Zedekiah's reign, on the tenth day of the tenth month, Nebuchadnezzar king of Babylon marched against Jerusalem with his whole army. They camped outside the city and built siege works all around it. ⁵The city was kept under siege until the eleventh year of King Zedekiah.

⁶By the ninth day of the fourth month the famine in the city had become so severe that there was no food for the people to eat. ⁷Then the city wall was broken through, and the whole army fled. They left the city at night through the gate between the two walls near the king's garden, though the Babylonians*ᵃ* were surrounding the city. They fled towards the Arabah,*ᵇ* ⁸but the Babylonian*ᶜ* army pursued King Zedekiah and overtook him in the plains of Jericho. All his soldiers were separated from him and scattered, ⁹and he was captured.

He was taken to the king of Babylon at Riblah in the land of Hamath, where he pronounced sentence on him. ¹⁰There at Riblah the king of Babylon killed the sons of Zedekiah before his eyes; he also killed all the officials of Judah. ¹¹Then he put out Zedekiah's eyes, bound him with bronze shackles and took him to Babylon, where he put him in prison till the day of his death.

¹²On the tenth day of the fifth month, in the nineteenth year of Nebuchadnezzar king of Babylon, Nebuzaradan commander of the imperial guard, who served the king of Babylon, came to Jerusalem. ¹³He set fire to the temple of the LORD, the royal palace and all the houses of Jerusalem. Every important building he burned down. ¹⁴The whole Babylonian army, under the commander of the imperial guard, broke down all the walls around Jerusalem. ¹⁵Nebuzaradan the commander of the guard carried into exile some of the poorest people and those who remained in the city, along with the rest of the skilled workers*ᵈ* and those who had deserted to the king of Babylon. ¹⁶But Nebuzaradan left behind the rest of the poorest people of the land to work the vineyards and fields.

¹⁷The Babylonians broke up the bronze pillars, the movable stands and the bronze Sea that were at the temple of the LORD and they carried all the bronze to Babylon. ¹⁸They also took away the pots, shovels, wick trimmers, sprinkling bowls, dishes and all the bronze articles used in the temple service. ¹⁹The commander of the imperial guard took away the basins, censers, sprinkling bowls, pots, lampstands, dishes and bowls used for drink offerings—all that were made of pure gold or silver.

²⁰The bronze from the two pillars, the Sea and the twelve bronze bulls under it, and the movable stands, which King Solomon had made for the temple of the LORD, was more than could be weighed. ²¹Each pillar was eighteen cubits high and twelve cubits in

---

ᵃ 7 Or *Chaldeans;* also in verse 17   *ᵇ* 7 Or *the Jordan Valley*   *ᶜ* 8 Or *Chaldean;* also in verse 14   *ᵈ* 15 Or *the populace* circumference;^{a} each was four fingers thick, and hollow. 22The bronze capital on the top of one pillar was five cubits^b high and was decorated with a network and pomegranates of bronze all around. The other pillar, with its pomegranates, was similar. 23There were ninety-six pomegranates on the sides; the total number of pomegranates above the surrounding network was a hundred.

24The commander of the guard took as prisoners Seraiah the chief priest, Zephaniah the priest next in rank and the three doorkeepers. 25Of those still in the city, he took the officer in charge of the fighting men, and seven royal advisors. He also took the secretary who was chief officer in charge of conscripting the people of the land, sixty of whom were found in the city. 26Nebuzaradan the commander took them all and brought them to the king of Babylon at Riblah. 27There at Riblah, in the land of Hamath, the king had them executed.

So Judah went into captivity, away from her land. 28This is the number of the people Nebuchadnezzar carried into exile:

in the seventh year, 3,023 Jews;
29in Nebuchadnezzar's eighteenth year,
832 people from Jerusalem;
30in his twenty-third year,
745 Jews taken into exile by Nebuzaradan
the commander of the imperial guard.
There were 4,600 people in all.

Jehoiachin released

31In the thirty-seventh year of the exile of Jehoiachin king of Judah, in the year Awel-Marduk became king of Babylon, on the twenty-fifth day of the twelfth month, he released Jehoiachin king of Judah and freed him from prison. 32He spoke kindly to him and gave him a seat of honour higher than those of the other kings who were with him in Babylon. 33So Jehoiachin put aside his prison clothes and for the rest of his life ate regularly at the king's table. 34Day by day the king of Babylon gave Jehoiachin a regular allowance as long as he lived, till the day of his death.

---

^{a}21 That is, about 8.1 metres high and 5.4 metres in circumference ^{b}22 That is, about 2.3 metres

Lamentations

INTRODUCTION

LAMENTATIONS

Author: Jeremiah the prophet

When: Probably just after 586 BC, when Jerusalem was destroyed and the temple burned.

Where: Written in Jerusalem. The most important people in the city were taken into captivity in Babylon, but Jeremiah was allowed to stay in Jerusalem.

Did you know? Lamentations contains five poems, one in each chapter. The first four are 'acrostics' with each verse beginning with a letter of the Hebrew alphabet. The fourth poem has three verses for every letter.

Main theme: Jeremiah is really upset that Jerusalem has been destroyed and lets everyone know how he feels. Jerusalem was Judah's capital city but, more importantly, it was the home of the temple, the place of God's presence where people worshipped him.

1[a] How deserted lies the city,
   once so full of people!
How like a widow is she,
   who once was great among the nations!
She who was queen among the provinces
   has now become a slave.

2 Bitterly she weeps at night,
   tears are on her cheeks.
Among all her lovers
   there is none to comfort her.
All her friends have betrayed her;
   they have become her enemies.

3 After affliction and harsh labour,
   Judah has gone into exile.
She dwells among the nations;
   she finds no resting place.
All who pursue her have overtaken her
   in the midst of her distress.

---

[a] This chapter is an acrostic poem, the verses of which begin with the successive letters of the Hebrew alphabet.

⁴The roads to Zion mourn,
> for no-one comes to her appointed festivals.
> All her gateways are desolate,
> her priests groan,
> her young women grieve,
> and she is in bitter anguish.

⁵Her foes have become her masters;
> her enemies are at ease.
> The LORD has brought her grief
> because of her many sins.
> Her children have gone into exile,
> captive before the foe.

⁶All the splendour has departed
> from Daughter Zion.
> Her princes are like deer
> that find no pasture;
> in weakness they have fled
> before the pursuer.

⁷In the days of her affliction and wandering
> Jerusalem remembers all the treasures
> that were hers in days of old.
> When her people fell into enemy hands,
> there was no-one to help her.
> Her enemies looked at her
> and laughed at her destruction.

⁸Jerusalem has sinned greatly
> and so has become unclean.
> All who honoured her despise her,
> for they have seen her nakedness;
> she herself groans
> and turns away.

⁹Her filthiness clung to her skirts;
> she did not consider her future.
> Her fall was astounding;
> there was none to comfort her.
> 'Look, LORD, on my affliction,
> for the enemy has triumphed.'

¹⁰The enemy laid hands
> on all her treasures;
> she saw pagan nations
> enter her sanctuary—
> those you had forbidden
> to enter your assembly.

¹¹All her people groan
> as they search for bread;
> they barter their treasures for food
> to keep themselves alive.
> 'Look, LORD, and consider,
> for I am despised.'

¹²'Is it nothing to you, all you who pass by?
> Look around and see.
> Is any suffering like my suffering
> that was inflicted on me,
> that the LORD brought on me
> in the day of his fierce anger?

¹³'From on high he sent fire,
> sent it down into my bones.
> He spread a net for my feet
> and turned me back.
> He made me desolate,
> faint all the day long.

¹⁴'My sins have been bound into a yoke;ᵃ
> by his hands they were woven together.
> They have been hung on my neck,
> and the Lord has sapped my strength.
> He has given me into the hands
> of those I cannot withstand.

¹⁵'The Lord has rejected
> all the warriors in my midst;
> he has summoned an army against me
> toᵇ crush my young men.
> In his winepress the Lord has trampled
> Virgin Daughter Judah.

¹⁶'This is why I weep
> and my eyes overflow with tears.
> No-one is near to comfort me,
> no-one to restore my spirit.
> My children are destitute
> because the enemy has prevailed.'

¹⁷Zion stretches out her hands,
> but there is no-one to comfort her.
> The LORD has decreed for Jacob
> that his neighbours become his foes;
> Jerusalem has become
> an unclean thing among them.

¹⁸'The LORD is righteous,
> yet I rebelled against his command.
> Listen, all you peoples;
> look on my suffering.
> My young men and young women
> have gone into exile.

¹⁹'I called to my allies
> but they betrayed me.

ᵃ 14 Most Hebrew manuscripts; many Hebrew manuscripts and Septuagint *He kept watch over my sins* ᵇ 15 Or *has set a time for me / when he will*

My priests and my elders
  perished in the city
while they searched for food
  to keep themselves alive.

²⁰'See, LORD, how distressed I am!
  I am in torment within,
and in my heart I am disturbed,
  for I have been most rebellious.
Outside, the sword bereaves;
  inside, there is only death.

²¹'People have heard my groaning,
  but there is no-one to comfort me.
All my enemies have heard of my distress;
  they rejoice at what you have done.
May you bring the day you have announced
  so that they may become like me.

²²'Let all their wickedness come before you;
  deal with them
as you have dealt with me
  because of all my sins.
My groans are many
  and my heart is faint.'

Horn
Lamentations 2:3
Some animals, such as oxen or rams, have horns that they use to fight, so a horn came to symbolise power and strength.

2 ^a How the Lord has covered Daughter Zion
  with the cloud of his anger!^b
He has hurled down the splendour of Israel
  from heaven to earth;
he has not remembered his footstool
  in the day of his anger.

²Without pity the Lord has swallowed up
  all the dwellings of Jacob;
in his wrath he has torn down
  the strongholds of Daughter Judah.
He has brought her kingdom and its princes
  down to the ground in dishonour.

³In fierce anger he has cut off
  every horn^c of Israel.
He has withdrawn his right hand
  at the approach of the enemy.
He has burned in Jacob like a flaming fire
  that consumes everything around it.

⁴Like an enemy he has strung his bow;
  his right hand is ready.
Like a foe he has slain
  all who were pleasing to the eye;
he has poured out his wrath like fire
  on the tent of Daughter Zion.

⁵The Lord is like an enemy;
  he has swallowed up Israel.
He has swallowed up all her palaces
  and destroyed her strongholds.
He has multiplied mourning and lamentation
  for Daughter Judah.

⁶He has laid waste his dwelling like a garden;
  he has destroyed his place of meeting.
The LORD has made Zion forget
  her appointed festivals and her Sabbaths;
in his fierce anger he has spurned
  both king and priest.

⁷The Lord has rejected his altar
  and abandoned his sanctuary.
He has given the walls of her palaces
  into the hands of the enemy;
they have raised a shout in the house of the LORD
  as on the day of an appointed festival.

⁸The LORD determined to tear down
  the wall around Daughter Zion.
He stretched out a measuring line

---

^a This chapter is an acrostic poem, the verses of which begin with the successive letters of the Hebrew alphabet. ^b 1 Or *How the Lord in his anger / has treated Daughter Zion with contempt!* ^c 3 Or *off / all the strength*; or *every king*; *horn* here symbolises strength.

and did not withhold his hand from
 destroying.
He made ramparts and walls lament;
 together they wasted away.

9 Her gates have sunk into the ground;
 their bars he has broken and destroyed.
Her king and her princes are exiled
 among the nations,
the law is no more,
and her prophets no longer find
 visions from the LORD.

10 The elders of Daughter Zion
 sit on the ground in silence;
they have sprinkled dust on their heads
 and put on sackcloth.
The young women of Jerusalem
 have bowed their heads to the ground.

11 My eyes fail from weeping,
 I am in torment within;
my heart is poured out on the ground
 because my people are destroyed,
because children and infants faint
 in the streets of the city.

12 They say to their mothers,
 'Where is bread and wine?'
as they faint like the wounded
 in the streets of the city,
as their lives ebb away
 in their mothers' arms.

13 What can I say for you?
 With what can I compare you,
 Daughter Jerusalem?
To what can I liken you,
 that I may comfort you,
 Virgin Daughter Zion?
Your wound is as deep as the sea.
 Who can heal you?

14 The visions of your prophets
 were false and worthless;
they did not expose your sin
 to ward off your captivity.
The prophecies they gave you
 were false and misleading.

15 All who pass your way
 clap their hands at you;
they scoff and shake their heads
 at Daughter Jerusalem:
'Is this the city that was called
 the perfection of beauty,
 the joy of the whole earth?'

16 All your enemies open their mouths
 wide against you;
they scoff and gnash their teeth
 and say, 'We have swallowed her up.
This is the day we have waited for;
 we have lived to see it.'

17 The LORD has done what he planned;
 he has fulfilled his word,
 which he decreed long ago.
He has overthrown you without pity,
 he has let the enemy gloat over you,
 he has exalted the horn^a of your foes.

18 The hearts of the people
 cry out to the Lord.
You walls of Daughter Zion,
 let your tears flow like a river
 day and night;
give yourself no relief,
 your eyes no rest.

19 Arise, cry out in the night,
 as the watches of the night begin;
pour out your heart like water
 in the presence of the Lord.
Lift up your hands to him
 for the lives of your children,
who faint from hunger
 at every street corner.

20 'Look, LORD, and consider:
 whom have you ever treated like this?
Should women eat their offspring,
 the children they have cared for?
Should priest and prophet be killed
 in the sanctuary of the Lord?

21 'Young and old lie together
 in the dust of the streets;
my young men and young women
 have fallen by the sword.
You have slain them in the day of your
 anger;
 you have slaughtered them without
 pity.

22 'As you summon to a feast day,
 so you summoned against me terrors
 on every side.

---

^{a} 17 *Horn* here symbolises strength.

In the day of the LORD's anger
   no-one escaped or survived;
those I cared for and reared
   my enemy has destroyed.'

3[a] I am one who has seen affliction
   by the rod of the LORD's wrath.
²He has driven me away and made me walk
   in darkness rather than light;
³indeed, he has turned his hand against me
   again and again, all day long.

⁴He has made my skin and my flesh grow old
   and has broken my bones.
⁵He has besieged me and surrounded me
   with bitterness and hardship.
⁶He has made me dwell in darkness
   like those long dead.

⁷He has walled me in so that I cannot escape;
   he has weighed me down with chains.
⁸Even when I call out or cry for help,
   he shuts out my prayer.
⁹He has barred my way with blocks of stone;
   he has made my paths crooked.

¹⁰Like a bear lying in wait,
   like a lion in hiding,
¹¹he dragged me from the path and mangled me
   and left me without help.
¹²He drew his bow
   and made me the target for his arrows.

¹³He pierced my heart
   with arrows from his quiver.
¹⁴I became the laughing-stock of all my people;
   they mock me in song all day long.
¹⁵He has filled me with bitter herbs
   and sated me with gall.

¹⁶He has broken my teeth with gravel;
   he has trampled me in the dust.
¹⁷I have been deprived of peace;
   I have forgotten what prosperity is.
¹⁸So I say, 'My splendour is gone
   and all that I had hoped from the LORD.'

---

making Connections

Bitter herbs
Lamentations 3:15
The Israelites ate bitter herbs during the Passover celebrations to help them remember their bitter experience as slaves in Egypt.

---

¹⁹I remember my affliction and my wandering,
   the bitterness and the gall.
²⁰I well remember them,
   and my soul is downcast within me.
²¹Yet this I call to mind
   and therefore I have hope:

²²Because of the LORD's great love we are not consumed,
   for his compassions never fail.
²³They are new every morning;
   great is your faithfulness.
²⁴I say to myself, 'The LORD is my portion;
   therefore I will wait for him.'

²⁵The LORD is good to those whose hope is in him,
   to the one who seeks him;
²⁶it is good to wait quietly
   for the salvation of the LORD.
²⁷It is good for people to bear the yoke
   while they are young.

²⁸Let them sit alone in silence,
   for the LORD has laid it on them.
²⁹Let them bury their faces in the dust—
   there may yet be hope.
³⁰Let them offer their cheeks to one who would strike them,
   and let them be filled with disgrace.

³¹For people are not cast off
   by the Lord for ever.

---

[a] This chapter is an acrostic poem; the verses of each stanza begin with the successive letters of the Hebrew alphabet, and the verses within each stanza begin with the same letter.

³²Though he brings grief, he will show compassion,
  so great is his unfailing love.
³³For he does not willingly bring affliction
  or grief to any human being.

³⁴To crush underfoot
  all prisoners in the land,
³⁵to deny people their rights
  before the Most High,
³⁶to deprive them of justice—
  would not the Lord see such things?

³⁷Who can speak and have it happen
  if the Lord has not decreed it?
³⁸Is it not from the mouth of the Most High
  that both calamities and good things come?
³⁹Why should the living complain
  when punished for their sins?

⁴⁰Let us examine our ways and test them,
  and let us return to the LORD.
⁴¹Let us lift up our hearts and our hands
  to God in heaven, and say:
⁴²'We have sinned and rebelled
  and you have not forgiven.

⁴³'You have covered yourself with anger
  and pursued us;
  you have slain without pity.
⁴⁴You have covered yourself with a cloud
  so that no prayer can get through.
⁴⁵You have made us scum and refuse
  among the nations.

⁴⁶'All our enemies have opened their mouths
  wide against us.
⁴⁷We have suffered terror and pitfalls,
  ruin and destruction.'

⁴⁸Streams of tears flow from my eyes
  because my people are destroyed.

⁴⁹My eyes will flow unceasingly,
  without relief,
⁵⁰until the LORD looks down
  from heaven and sees.
⁵¹What I see brings grief to my soul
  because of all the women of my city.

⁵²Those who were my enemies without cause
  hunted me like a bird.
⁵³They tried to end my life in a pit
  and threw stones at me;
⁵⁴the waters closed over my head,
  and I thought I was about to perish.

⁵⁵I called on your name, LORD,
  from the depths of the pit.
⁵⁶You heard my plea: 'Do not close your ears
  to my cry for relief.'
⁵⁷You came near when I called you,
  and you said, 'Do not fear.'

⁵⁸You, Lord, took up my case;
  you redeemed my life.
⁵⁹LORD, you have seen the wrong done to me.
  Uphold my cause!
⁶⁰You have seen the depth of their vengeance,
  all their plots against me.

⁶¹LORD, you have heard their insults,
  all their plots against me—
⁶²what my enemies whisper and mutter
  against me all day long.
⁶³Look at them! Sitting or standing,
  they mock me in their songs.

⁶⁴Pay them back what they deserve, LORD,
  for what their hands have done.
⁶⁵Put a veil over their hearts,
  and may your curse be on them!
⁶⁶Pursue them in anger and destroy them
  from under the heavens of the LORD.

4 ᵃ How the gold has lost its lustre,
  the fine gold become dull!
The sacred gems are scattered
  at every street corner.

²How the precious children of Zion,
  once worth their weight in gold,
are now considered as pots of clay,
  the work of a potter's hands!

³Even jackals offer their breasts
  to nurse their young,
but my people have become heartless
  like ostriches in the desert.

⁴Because of thirst the infant's tongue
  sticks to the roof of its mouth;
the children beg for bread,
  but no-one gives it to them.

ᵃ This chapter is an acrostic poem, the verses of which begin with the successive letters of the Hebrew alphabet.

⁵Those who once ate delicacies
   are destitute in the streets.
Those nurtured in purple
   now lie on ash heaps.

⁶The punishment of my people
   is greater than that of Sodom,
which was overthrown in a moment
   without a hand turned to help her.

⁷Their princes were brighter than snow
   and whiter than milk,
their bodies more ruddy than rubies,
   their appearance like lapis lazuli.

⁸But now they are blacker than soot;
   they are not recognised in the streets.
Their skin has shrivelled on their bones;
   it has become as dry as a stick.

⁹Those killed by the sword are better off
   than those who die of famine;
racked with hunger, they waste away
   for lack of food from the field.

¹⁰With their own hands compassionate
      women
   have cooked their own children,
who became their food
   when my people were destroyed.

¹¹The LORD has given full vent to his wrath;
   he has poured out his fierce anger.
He kindled a fire in Zion
   that consumed her foundations.

¹²The kings of the earth did not believe,
   nor did any of the peoples of the world,
that enemies and foes could enter
   the gates of Jerusalem.

¹³But it happened because of the sins of her
      prophets
   and the iniquities of her priests,
who shed within her
   the blood of the righteous.

¹⁴Now they grope through the streets
   as if they were blind.
They are so defiled with blood
   that no-one dares to touch their
      garments.

¹⁵'Go away! You are unclean!' people cry to
      them.
   'Away! Away! Don't touch us!'
When they flee and wander about,
   people among the nations say,
   'They can stay here no longer.'

¹⁶The LORD himself has scattered them;
   he no longer watches over them.
The priests are shown no honour,
   the elders no favour.

¹⁷Moreover, our eyes failed,
   looking in vain for help;
from our towers we watched
   for a nation that could not save us.

¹⁸People stalked us at every step,
   so we could not walk in our streets.
Our end was near, our days were
      numbered,
   for our end had come.

¹⁹Our pursuers were swifter
   than eagles in the sky;
they chased us over the mountains
   and lay in wait for us in the desert.

²⁰The LORD's anointed, our very life breath,
   was caught in their traps.
We thought that under his shadow
   we would live among the nations.

²¹Rejoice and be glad, Daughter Edom,
   you who live in the land of Uz.
But to you also the cup will be passed;
   you will be drunk and stripped naked.

²²Your punishment will end, Daughter
      Zion;
   he will not prolong your exile.
But he will punish your sin, Daughter
      Edom,
   and expose your wickedness.

5

Remember, LORD, what has happened
      to us;
   look, and see our disgrace.
²Our inheritance has been turned over to
      strangers,
   our homes to foreigners.
³We have become fatherless,
   our mothers are widows.
⁴We must buy the water we drink;
   our wood can be had only at a price.
⁵Those who pursue us are at our heels;
   we are weary and find no rest.
⁶We submitted to Egypt and Assyria
   to get enough bread.

7 Our parents sinned and are no more,
   and we bear their punishment.
8 Slaves rule over us,
   and there is none to free us from their hands.
9 We get our bread at the risk of our lives
   because of the sword in the desert.
10 Our skin is hot as an oven,
   feverish from hunger.
11 Women have been ravished in Zion,
   and virgins in the towns of Judah.
12 Princes have been hung up by their hands;
   elders are shown no respect.
13 Young men toil at the millstones;
   boys stagger under loads of wood.
14 The elders are gone from the city gate;
   the young men have stopped their music.
15 Joy is gone from our hearts;
   our dancing has turned to mourning.
16 The crown has fallen from our head.
   Woe to us, for we have sinned!
17 Because of this our hearts are faint;
   because of these things our eyes grow dim
18 for Mount Zion, which lies desolate,
   with jackals prowling over it.

19 You, LORD, reign for ever;
   your throne endures from generation to generation.
20 Why do you always forget us?
   Why do you forsake us so long?
21 Restore us to yourself, LORD, that we may return;
   renew our days as of old
22 unless you have utterly rejected us
   and are angry with us beyond measure.

Ezekiel

INTRODUCTION

EZEKIEL

Author: Ezekiel

Who to: The people of Judah in captivity in Babylon.

When: Ezekiel prophesied for about twenty years from around 593 BC.

Where: Ezekiel was held captive in Babylon.

Did you know? The Babylonians took people captive from Jerusalem in three stages. Daniel was among the first to be taken in about 605 BC. Ezekiel went in the next stage around 597 BC, and then Jerusalem was destroyed in 586 BC and the rest of the people were taken into captivity.

Main theme: In captivity in Babylon, Ezekiel writes about God's judgment on Judah and the surrounding nations and about the future blessing of God's people. He includes dramatic visions given to him by God and uses vibrant and symbolic language.

Ezekiel's inaugural vision

1 In my thirtieth year, in the fourth month on the fifth day, while I was among the exiles by the River Kebar, the heavens were opened and I saw visions of God.

²On the fifth of the month—it was the fifth year of the exile of King Jehoiachin— ³the word of the LORD came to Ezekiel the priest, the son of Buzi, by the River Kebar in the land of the Babylonians.*a* There the hand of the LORD was on him.

⁴I looked, and I saw a violent storm coming out of the north—an immense cloud with flashing lightning and surrounded by brilliant light. The centre of

---
a 3 Or *Chaldeans*

the fire looked like glowing metal, 5and in the fire was what looked like four living creatures. In appearance their form was human, 6but each of them had four faces and four wings. 7Their legs were straight; their feet were like those of a calf and gleamed like burnished bronze. 8Under their wings on their four sides they had human hands. All four of them had faces and wings, 9and the wings of one touched the wings of another. Each one went straight ahead; they did not turn as they moved.

10Their faces looked like this: each of the four had the face of a human being, and on the right side each had the face of a lion, and on the left the face of an ox; each also had the face of an eagle. 11Such were their faces. They each had two wings spreading out upwards, each wing touching that of the creature on either side; and each had two other wings covering its body. 12Each one went straight ahead. Wherever the spirit would go, they would go, without turning as they went. 13The appearance of the living creatures was like burning coals of fire or like torches. Fire moved back and forth among the creatures; it was bright, and lightning flashed out of it. 14The creatures sped back and forth like flashes of lightning.

15As I looked at the living creatures, I saw a wheel on the ground beside each creature with its four faces. 16This was the appearance and structure of the wheels: they sparkled like topaz, and all four looked alike. Each appeared to be made like a wheel intersecting a wheel. 17As they moved, they would go in any one of the four directions the creatures faced; the wheels did not change direction as the creatures went. 18Their rims were high and awesome, and all four rims were full of eyes all around.

19When the living creatures moved, the wheels beside them moved; and when the living creatures rose from the ground, the wheels also rose. 20Wherever the spirit would go, they would go, and the wheels would rise along with them, because the spirit of the living creatures was in the wheels. 21When the creatures moved, they also moved; when the creatures stood still, they also stood still; and when the creatures rose from the ground, the wheels rose along with them, because the spirit of the living creatures was in the wheels.

22Spread out above the heads of the living creatures was what looked something like a vault, sparkling like crystal, and awesome. 23Under the vault their wings were stretched out one towards the other, and each had two wings covering its body. 24When the creatures moved, I heard the sound of their wings, like the roar of rushing waters, like the voice of the Almighty,*a* like the tumult of an army. When they stood still, they lowered their wings.

25Then there came a voice from above the vault over their heads as they stood with lowered wings. 26Above the vault over their heads was what looked like a throne of lapis lazuli, and high above on the throne was a figure like that of a man. 27I saw that from what appeared to be his waist up he looked like glowing metal, as if full of fire, and that from there down he looked like fire; and brilliant light surrounded him. 28Like the appearance of a rainbow in the clouds on a rainy day, so was the radiance around him.

This was the appearance of the likeness of the glory of the LORD. When I saw it, I fell face down, and I heard the voice of one speaking.

IN OTHER WORDS

Glory
Ezekiel 1:28

The word 'glory' in Hebrew comes from another word meaning 'heavy' and originally described the part of a person's character which impresses you the most. In the Bible, 'glory' is often used to describe the presence of God, his power and character, or an event such as Jesus' crucifixion which points to God.

---

a 24 Hebrew *Shaddai*

Ezekiel's call to be a prophet

2 He said to me, 'Son of man,[a] stand up on your feet and I will speak to you.' ²As he spoke, the Spirit came into me and raised me to my feet, and I heard him speaking to me.

³He said: 'Son of man, I am sending you to the Israelites, to a rebellious nation that has rebelled against me; they and their ancestors have been in revolt against me to this very day. ⁴The people to whom I am sending you are obstinate and stubborn. Say to them, "This is what the Sovereign LORD says." ⁵And whether they listen or fail to listen—for they are a rebellious house—they will know that a prophet has been among them. ⁶And you, son of man, do not be afraid of them or their words. Do not be afraid, though briers and thorns are all around you and you live among scorpions. Do not be afraid of what they say or be terrified by them, though they are a rebellious house. ⁷You must speak my words to them, whether they listen or fail to listen, for they are rebellious. ⁸But you, son of man, listen to what I say to you. Do not rebel like that rebellious house; open your mouth and eat what I give you.'

⁹Then I looked, and I saw a hand stretched out to me. In it was a scroll, ¹⁰which he unrolled before me. On both sides of it were written words of lament and mourning and woe.

3 And he said to me, 'Son of man, eat what is before you, eat this scroll; then go and speak to the house of Israel.' ²So I opened my mouth, and he gave me the scroll to eat.

³Then he said to me, 'Son of man, eat this scroll I am giving you and fill your stomach with it.' So I ate it, and it tasted as sweet as honey in my mouth.

⁴He then said to me: 'Son of man, go now to the house of Israel and speak my words to them. ⁵You are not being sent to a people of obscure speech and strange language, but to the house of Israel— ⁶not to many peoples of obscure speech and strange language, whose words you cannot understand. Surely if I had sent you to them, they would have listened to you. ⁷But the house of Israel is not willing to listen to you because they are not willing to listen to me, for the whole house of Israel is hardened and obstinate. ⁸But I will make you as unyielding and hardened as they are. ⁹I will make your forehead like the hardest stone, harder than flint. Do not be afraid of them or terrified by them, though they are a rebellious house.'

¹⁰And he said to me, 'Son of man, listen carefully and take to heart all the words I speak to you. ¹¹Go now to your people in exile and speak to them. Say to them, "This is what the Sovereign LORD says," whether they listen or fail to listen.'

¹²Then the Spirit lifted me up, and I heard behind me a loud rumbling sound as the glory of the LORD rose from the place where it was standing.[b] ¹³It was the sound of the wings of the living creatures brushing against each other and the sound of the wheels beside them, a loud rumbling sound. ¹⁴The Spirit then lifted me up and took me away, and I went in bitterness and in the anger of my spirit, with the strong hand of the LORD on me. ¹⁵I came to the exiles who lived at Tel Aviv near the River Kebar. And there, where they were living, I sat among them for seven days—deeply distressed.

Ezekiel's task as watchman

¹⁶At the end of seven days the word of the LORD came to me: ¹⁷'Son of man, I have made you a watchman for the house of Israel; so hear the word I speak and give them warning from me. ¹⁸When I say to the wicked, "You will surely die," and you do not warn them or speak out to dissuade them from their evil ways in order to save their lives, those wicked people will die for[c] their sins, and I will hold you accountable for their blood. ¹⁹But if you do warn the wicked and they do not turn from their wickedness or from their evil ways, they will die for their sins; but you will have saved yourself.

---

[a] 1 The Hebrew phrase *ben adam* means *human being*. The phrase *son of man* is retained as a form of address here and throughout Ezekiel because of its traditional associations. [b] 12 Probable reading of the original Hebrew text; Masoretic Text *sound—may the glory of the LORD be praised from his place* [c] 18 Or *in*; also in verses 19 and 20

20'Again, when the righteous turn from their righteousness and do evil, and I put a stumbling-block before them, they will die. Since you did not warn them, they will die for their sins. The righteous things they did will not be remembered, and I will hold you accountable for their blood. 21But if you do warn the righteous not to sin and they do not sin, they will surely live because they took warning, and you will have saved yourself.'

22The hand of the LORD was on me there, and he said to me, 'Get up and go out to the plain, and there I will speak to you.' 23So I got up and went out to the plain. And the glory of the LORD was standing there, like the glory I had seen by the River Kebar, and I fell face down.

24Then the Spirit came into me and raised me to my feet. He spoke to me and said: 'Go, shut yourself inside your house. 25And you, son of man, they will tie with ropes; you will be bound so that you cannot go out among the people. 26I will make your tongue stick to the roof of your mouth so that you will be silent and unable to rebuke them, for they are a rebellious house. 27But when I speak to you, I will open your mouth and you shall say to them, "This is what the Sovereign LORD says." Whoever will listen let them listen, and whoever will refuse let them refuse; for they are a rebellious house.

Siege of Jerusalem symbolised

4 'Now, son of man, take a block of clay, put it in front of you and draw the city of Jerusalem on it. 2Then lay siege to it: erect siege works against it, build a ramp up to it, set up camps against it and put battering-rams around it. 3Then take an iron pan, place it as an iron wall between you and the city and turn your face towards it. It will be under siege, and you shall besiege it. This will be a sign to the house of Israel.

4'Then lie on your left side and put the sin of the house of Israel upon yourself.[a] You are to bear their sin for the number of days you lie on your side. 5I have assigned you the same number of days as the years of their sin. So for 390 days you will bear the sin of the house of Israel.

Making Connections

Symbolic acts
Ezekiel 4:1

Ezekiel makes sure people take notice of his message by acting out Israel and Judah's punishment. Lying next to a picture of the city of Jerusalem under siege for more than a year, he is to eat bread made from a mixture of grains. The only time bread would be made in this way was during a famine when there was not enough of one grain on its own to make bread. Ezekiel draws the line at cooking over a fire of human excrement because it would make him unclean, so God relents and allows him to use cow manure instead.

6'After you have finished this, lie down again, this time on your right side, and bear the sin of the house of Judah. I have assigned you 40 days, a day for each year. 7Turn your face towards the siege of Jerusalem and with bared arm prophesy against her. 8I will tie you up with ropes so that you cannot turn from one side to the other until you have finished the days of your siege.

9'Take wheat and barley, beans and lentils, millet and spelt; put them in a storage jar and use them to make bread for yourself. You are to eat it during the 390 days you lie on your side. 10Weigh out twenty shekels[b] of food to eat each day and eat it at set times. 11Also measure out a sixth of a hin[c] of water and drink it at set times. 12Eat the food as you would a loaf of barley bread; bake it in the sight of the people, using human excrement for fuel.' 13The LORD said, 'In this way the people of Israel will eat defiled food among the nations where I will drive them.'

---

[a] 4 Or *upon your side*   [b] 10 That is, about 230 grams   [c] 11 That is, about 0.6 litre

14Then I said, 'Not so, Sovereign LORD! I have never defiled myself. From my youth until now I have never eaten anything found dead or torn by wild animals. No impure meat has ever entered my mouth.'

15'Very well,' he said, 'I will let you bake your bread over cow dung instead of human excrement.'

16He then said to me: 'Son of man, I am about to cut off the food supply in Jerusalem. The people will eat rationed food in anxiety and drink rationed water in despair, 17for food and water will be scarce. They will be appalled at the sight of each other and will waste away because of[a] their sin.

God's razor of judgment

5 'Now, son of man, take a sharp sword and use it as a barber's razor to shave your head and your beard. Then take a set of scales and divide up the hair. 2When the days of your siege come to an end, burn a third of the hair inside the city. Take a third and strike it with the sword all around the city. And scatter a third to the wind. For I will pursue them with drawn sword. 3But take a few hairs and tuck them away in the folds of your garment. 4Again, take a few of these and throw them into the fire and burn them up. A fire will spread from there to the whole house of Israel.

5'This is what the Sovereign LORD says: this is Jerusalem, which I have set in the centre of the nations, with countries all around her. 6Yet in her wickedness she has rebelled against my laws and decrees more than the nations and countries around her. She has rejected my laws and has not followed my decrees.

7'Therefore this is what the Sovereign LORD says: you have been more unruly than the nations around you and have not followed my decrees or kept my laws. You have not even[b] conformed to the standards of the nations around you.

8'Therefore this is what the Sovereign LORD says: I myself am against you, Jerusalem, and I will inflict punishment on you in the sight of the nations. 9Because of all your detestable idols, I will do to you what I have never done before and will never do again. 10Therefore in your midst parents will eat their children, and children will eat their parents. I will inflict punishment on you and will scatter all your survivors to the winds. 11Therefore as surely as I live, declares the Sovereign LORD, because you have defiled my sanctuary with all your vile images and detestable practices, I myself will shave you; I will not look on you with pity or spare you. 12A third of your people will die of the plague or perish by famine inside you; a third will fall by the sword outside your walls; and a third I will scatter to the winds and pursue with drawn sword.

13'Then my anger will cease and my wrath against them will subside, and I will be avenged. And when I have spent my wrath on them, they will know that I the LORD have spoken in my zeal.

14'I will make you a ruin and a reproach among the nations around you, in the sight of all who pass by. 15You will be a reproach and a taunt, a warning and an object of horror to the nations around you when I inflict punishment on you in anger and in wrath and with stinging rebuke. I the LORD have spoken. 16When I shoot at you with my deadly and destructive arrows of famine, I will shoot to destroy you. I will bring more and more famine upon you and cut off your supply of food. 17I will send famine and wild beasts against you, and they will leave you childless. Plague and bloodshed will sweep through you, and I will bring the sword against you. I the LORD have spoken.'

Doom for the mountains of Israel

6 The word of the LORD came to me: 2'Son of man, set your face against the mountains of Israel; prophesy against them 3and say: "You mountains of Israel, hear the word of the Sovereign LORD. This is what the Sovereign LORD says to the mountains and hills, to the ravines and valleys: I am about to bring a sword against you, and I will destroy your high places. 4Your altars will be demolished and your incense altars will be smashed; and I will slay your people in front of your idols. 5I will lay the dead bodies of the Israelites in front of their idols, and I will scatter your bones around your

---

[a] 17 Or *away in* [b] 7 Most Hebrew manuscripts; some Hebrew manuscripts and Syriac *You have*

altars. ⁶Wherever you live, the towns will be laid waste and the high places demolished, so that your altars will be laid waste and devastated, your idols smashed and ruined, your incense altars broken down, and what you have made wiped out. ⁷Your people will fall slain among you, and you will know that I am the LORD.

⁸' "But I will spare some, for some of you will escape the sword when you are scattered among the lands and nations. ⁹Then in the nations where they have been carried captive, those who escape will remember me— how I have been grieved by their adulterous hearts, which have turned away from me, and by their eyes, which have lusted after their idols. They will loathe themselves for the evil they have done and for all their detestable practices. ¹⁰And they will know that I am the LORD; I did not threaten in vain to bring this calamity on them.

¹¹' "This is what the Sovereign LORD says: strike your hands together and stamp your feet and cry out 'Alas!' because of all the wicked and detestable practices of the house of Israel, for they will fall by the sword, famine and plague. ¹²Those who are far away will die of the plague, and those who are near will fall by the sword, and those who survive and are spared will die of famine. So will I spend my wrath on them. ¹³And they will know that I am the LORD, when their people lie slain among their idols around their altars, on every high hill and on all the mountaintops, under every spreading tree and every leafy oak—places where they offered fragrant incense to all their idols. ¹⁴And I will stretch out my hand against them and make the land a desolate waste from the desert to Diblah*ᵃ*—wherever they live. Then they will know that I am the LORD.' "

The end has come

7 The word of the LORD came to me: ²'Son of man, this is what the Sovereign LORD says to the land of Israel:

' "The end! The end has come
    upon the four corners of the land!
³The end is now upon you,
    and I will unleash my anger against you.
I will judge you according to your conduct
    and repay you for all your detestable practices.
⁴I will not look on you with pity;
    I will not spare you.
I will surely repay you for your conduct
    and for the detestable practices among you.

' "Then you will know that I am the LORD."

⁵'This is what the Sovereign LORD says:

' "Disaster! Unheard-of*ᵇ* disaster!
    See, it comes!
⁶The end has come!
    The end has come!
It has roused itself against you.
    See, it comes!
⁷Doom has come upon you,
    upon you who dwell in the land.
The time has come! The day is near!
    There is panic, not joy, on the mountains.
⁸I am about to pour out my wrath on you
    and spend my anger against you.
I will judge you according to your conduct
    and repay you for all your detestable practices.
⁹I will not look on you with pity;
    I will not spare you.
I will repay you for your conduct
    and for the detestable practices among you.

' "Then you will know that it is I the LORD who strikes you.

¹⁰' "See, the day!
    See, it comes!
Doom has burst forth,
    the rod has budded,
    arrogance has blossomed!
¹¹Violence has arisen,*ᶜ*
    a rod to punish the wicked.
None of the people will be left,
    none of that crowd—
none of their wealth,
    nothing of value.

ᵃ 14 Most Hebrew manuscripts; a few Hebrew manuscripts *Riblah*   *ᵇ* 5 Most Hebrew manuscripts; some Hebrew manuscripts and Syriac *Disaster after*   *ᶜ* 11 Or *The violent one has become*

¹²The time has come!
  The day has arrived!
  Let not the buyer rejoice
    nor the seller grieve,
  for my wrath is on the whole crowd.
¹³The sellers will not recover
    the property they have sold—
    as long as both buyers and sellers live.
  For the vision concerning the whole crowd
    will not be reversed.
  Because of their sins, not one of them
    will preserve their life.

¹⁴' "They have blown the trumpet,
    they have made all things ready,
  but no-one will go into battle,
    for my wrath is on the whole crowd.
¹⁵Outside is the sword;
    inside are plague and famine.
  Those in the country
    will die by the sword;
  those in the city
    will be devoured by famine and plague.
¹⁶The fugitives who escape
    will flee to the mountains.
  Like doves of the valleys,
    they will all moan,
    each for their own sins.
¹⁷Every hand will go limp;
    every knee will be wet with urine.
¹⁸They will put on sackcloth
    and be clothed with terror.
  Every face will be covered with shame,
    and every head will be shaved.

¹⁹' "They will throw their silver into the streets,
    and their gold will be treated as a thing unclean.
  Their silver and gold
    will not be able to deliver them
    in the day of the LORD's wrath.
  It will not satisfy their hunger
    or fill their stomachs,
  for it has caused them to stumble into sin.
²⁰They took pride in their beautiful jewellery
    and used it to make their detestable idols.
  They made it into vile images;
    therefore I will make it a thing unclean for them.
²¹I will give their wealth as plunder to foreigners
    and as loot to the wicked of the earth,
    who will defile it.
²²I will turn my face away from the people,
    and robbers will desecrate the place I treasure.
  They will enter it
    and will defile it.

²³' "Prepare chains!
  For the land is full of bloodshed,
    and the city is full of violence.
²⁴I will bring the most wicked of nations
    to take possession of their houses.
  I will put an end to the pride of the mighty,
    and their sanctuaries will be desecrated.
²⁵When terror comes,
    they will seek peace in vain.
²⁶Calamity upon calamity will come,
    and rumour upon rumour.
  They will go searching for a vision from the prophet,
    priestly instruction in the law will cease,
    the counsel of the elders will come to an end.
²⁷The king will mourn,
    the prince will be clothed with despair,
    and the hands of the people of the land will tremble.
  I will deal with them according to their conduct,
    and by their own standards I will judge them.

' "Then they will know that I am the LORD." '

Idolatry in the temple

8 In the sixth year, in the sixth month on the fifth day, while I was sitting in my house and the elders of Judah were sitting before me, the hand of the Sovereign LORD came on me there. ²I looked, and I saw a figure like that of a man.[a] From what appeared to be his waist down he was like fire, and from there up his appearance was

---

[a] 2 Or *saw a fiery figure*

as bright as glowing metal. ³He stretched out what looked like a hand and took me by the hair of my head. The Spirit lifted me up between earth and heaven and in visions of God he took me to Jerusalem, to the entrance of the north gate of the inner court, where the idol that provokes to jealousy stood. ⁴And there before me was the glory of the God of Israel, as in the vision I had seen in the plain.

⁵Then he said to me, 'Son of man, look towards the north.' So I looked, and in the entrance north of the gate of the altar I saw this idol of jealousy.

⁶And he said to me, 'Son of man, do you see what they are doing—the utterly detestable things the house of Israel is doing here, things that will drive me far from my sanctuary? But you will see things that are even more detestable.'

⁷Then he brought me to the entrance to the court. I looked, and I saw a hole in the wall. ⁸He said to me, 'Son of man, now dig into the wall.' So I dug into the wall and saw a doorway there.

⁹And he said to me, 'Go in and see the wicked and detestable things they are doing here.' ¹⁰So I went in and looked, and I saw portrayed all over the walls all kinds of crawling things and unclean animals and all the idols of the house of Israel. ¹¹In front of them stood seventy elders of the house of Israel, and Jaazaniah son of Shaphan was standing among them. Each had a censer in his hand, and a fragrant cloud of incense was rising.

¹²He said to me, 'Son of man, have you seen what the elders of the house of Israel are doing in the darkness, each at the shrine of his own idol? They say, "The LORD does not see us; the LORD has forsaken the land."'
¹³Again, he said, 'You will see them doing things that are even more detestable.'

¹⁴Then he brought me to the entrance of the north gate of the house of the LORD, and I saw women sitting there, mourning the god Tammuz. ¹⁵He said to me, 'Do you see this, son of man? You will see things that are even more detestable than this.'

¹⁶He then brought me into the inner court of the house of the LORD, and there at the entrance to the temple, between the portico and the altar, were about twenty-five men. With their backs towards the temple of the LORD and their faces towards the east, they were bowing down to the sun in the east.

¹⁷He said to me, 'Have you seen this, son of man? Is it a trivial matter for the house of Judah to do the detestable things they are doing here? Must they also fill the land with violence and continually arouse my anger? Look at them putting the branch to their nose! ¹⁸Therefore I will deal with them in anger; I will not look on them with pity or spare them. Although they shout in my ears, I will not listen to them.'

Judgment on the idolaters

9 Then I heard him call out in a loud voice, 'Bring near those who are appointed to execute judgment on the city, each with weapon in hand.' ²And I saw six men coming from the direction of the upper gate, which faces north, each with a deadly weapon in his hand. With them was a man clothed in linen who had a writing kit at his side. They came in and stood beside the bronze altar.

³Now the glory of the God of Israel went up from above the cherubim, where it had been, and moved to the threshold of the temple. Then the LORD called to the man clothed in linen who had the writing kit at his side ⁴and said to him, 'Go throughout the city of Jerusalem and put a mark on the foreheads of those who grieve and lament over all the detestable things that are done in it.'

⁵As I listened, he said to the others, 'Follow him through the city and kill, without showing pity or compassion. ⁶Slaughter the old men, the young men

IN OTHER WORDS

Cherubim
Ezekiel 9:3
The cherubim are winged angelic beings. They are often praising and worshipping God when mentioned in the Bible.

and women, the mothers and children, but do not touch anyone who has the mark. Begin at my sanctuary.' So they began with the old men who were in front of the temple.

7Then he said to them, 'Defile the temple and fill the courts with the slain. Go!' So they went out and began killing throughout the city. 8While they were killing and I was left alone, I fell face down, crying out, 'Ah, Sovereign LORD! Are you going to destroy the entire remnant of Israel in this outpouring of your wrath on Jerusalem?'

9He answered me, 'The sin of the house of Israel and Judah is exceedingly great; the land is full of bloodshed and the city is full of injustice. They say, "The LORD has forsaken the land; the LORD does not see." 10So I will not look on them with pity or spare them, but I will bring down on their own heads what they have done.'

11Then the man in linen with the writing kit at his side brought back word, saying, 'I have done as you commanded.'

God's glory departs from the temple

10 I looked, and I saw the likeness of a throne of lapis lazuli above the vault that was over the heads of the cherubim. 2The LORD said to the man clothed in linen, 'Go in among the wheels beneath the cherubim. Fill your hands with burning coals from among the cherubim and scatter them over the city.' And as I watched, he went in.

3Now the cherubim were standing on the south side of the temple when the man went in, and a cloud filled the inner court. 4Then the glory of the LORD rose from above the cherubim and moved to the threshold of the temple. The cloud filled the temple, and the court was full of the radiance of the glory of the LORD. 5The sound of the wings of the cherubim could be heard as far away as the outer court, like the voice of God Almighty*a* when he speaks.

6When the LORD commanded the man in linen, 'Take fire from among the wheels, from among the cherubim,' the man went in and stood beside a wheel. 7Then one of the cherubim reached out his hand to the fire that was among them. He took up some of it and put it into the hands of the man in linen, who took it and went out. 8(Under the wings of the cherubim could be seen what looked like human hands.)

9I looked, and I saw beside the cherubim four wheels, one beside each of the cherubim; the wheels sparkled like topaz. 10As for their appearance, the four of them looked alike; each was like a wheel intersecting a wheel. 11As they moved, they would go in any one of the four directions the cherubim faced; the wheels did not turn about*b* as the cherubim went. The cherubim went in whatever direction the head faced, without turning as they went. 12Their entire bodies, including their backs, their hands and their wings, were completely full of eyes, as were their four wheels. 13I heard the wheels being called 'the whirling wheels'. 14Each of the cherubim had four faces: one face was that of a cherub, the second the face of a human being, the third the face of a lion, and the fourth the face of an eagle.

15Then the cherubim rose upward. These were the living creatures I had seen by the River Kebar. 16When the cherubim moved, the wheels beside them moved; and when the cherubim spread their wings to rise from the ground, the wheels did not leave their side. 17When the cherubim stood still, they also stood still; and when the cherubim rose, they rose with them, because the spirit of the living creatures was in them.

18Then the glory of the LORD departed from over the threshold of the temple and stopped above the cherubim. 19While I watched, the cherubim spread their wings and rose from the ground, and as they went, the wheels went with them. They stopped at the entrance of the east gate of the LORD's house, and the glory of the God of Israel was above them.

20These were the living creatures I had seen beneath the God of Israel by the River Kebar, and I realised that they were cherubim. 21Each had four faces and four wings, and under their wings was what looked like human hands. 22Their faces had the same appearance as those I had seen by the River Kebar. Each one went straight ahead.

*a*5 Hebrew *El-Shaddai* *b*11 Or *aside*

God's sure judgment on Jerusalem

11 Then the Spirit lifted me up and brought me to the gate of the house of the LORD that faces east. There at the entrance of the gate were twenty-five men, and I saw among them Jaazaniah son of Azzur and Pelatiah son of Benaiah, leaders of the people. ²The LORD said to me, 'Son of man, these are the men who are plotting evil and giving wicked advice in this city. ³They say, "Haven't our houses been recently rebuilt? This city is a pot, and we are the meat in it." ⁴Therefore prophesy against them; prophesy, son of man.'

⁵Then the Spirit of the LORD came on me, and he told me to say: 'This is what the LORD says: that is what you are saying, house of Israel, but I know what is going through your mind. ⁶You have killed many people in this city and filled its streets with the dead.

⁷'Therefore this is what the Sovereign LORD says: the bodies you have thrown there are the meat and this city is the pot, but I will drive you out of it. ⁸You fear the sword, and the sword is what I will bring against you, declares the Sovereign LORD. ⁹I will drive you out of the city and deliver you into the hands of foreigners and inflict punishment on you. ¹⁰You will fall by the sword, and I will execute judgment on you at the borders of Israel. Then you will know that I am the LORD. ¹¹This city will not be a pot for you, nor will you be the meat in it; I will execute judgment on you at the borders of Israel. ¹²And you will know that I am the LORD, for you have not followed my decrees or kept my laws but have conformed to the standards of the nations around you.'

¹³Now as I was prophesying, Pelatiah son of Benaiah died. Then I fell face down and cried out in a loud voice, 'Ah, Sovereign LORD! Will you completely destroy the remnant of Israel?'

The promise of Israel's return

¹⁴The word of the LORD came to me: ¹⁵'Son of man, the people of Jerusalem have said of your fellow exiles and the whole house of Israel,[a] "They are far away from the LORD; this land was given to us as our possession."

¹⁶'Therefore say: "This is what the Sovereign LORD says: although I sent them far away among the nations and scattered them among the countries, yet for a little while I have been a sanctuary for them in the countries where they have gone."

¹⁷'Therefore say: "This is what the Sovereign LORD says: I will gather you from the nations and bring you back from the countries where you have been scattered, and I will give you back the land of Israel again."

¹⁸'They will return to it and remove all its vile images and detestable idols. ¹⁹I will give them an undivided heart and put a new spirit in them; I will remove from them their heart of stone and give them a heart of flesh. ²⁰Then they will follow my decrees and be careful to keep my laws. They will be my people, and I will be their God. ²¹But as for those whose hearts are devoted to their vile images and detestable idols, I will bring down on their own heads what they have done, declares the Sovereign LORD.'

²²Then the cherubim, with the wheels beside them, spread their wings, and the glory of the God of Israel was above them. ²³The glory of the LORD went up from within the city and stopped above the mountain east of it. ²⁴The Spirit lifted me up and brought me to the exiles in Babylonia[b] in the vision given by the Spirit of God.

Then the vision I had seen went up from me, ²⁵and I told the exiles everything the LORD had shown me.

The exile symbolised

12 The word of the LORD came to me: ²'Son of man, you are living among a rebellious people. They have eyes to see but do not see and ears to hear but do not hear, for they are a rebellious people.

³'Therefore, son of man, pack your belongings for exile and in the daytime, as they watch, set out and go from where you are to another place. Perhaps they will understand, though they are a rebellious

---

[a] 15 Or *said of your brothers—your brothers who are your blood-relatives and the whole house of Israel—*   [b] 24 Or *Chaldea*

Digging through walls
Ezekiel 12:7
Most houses in Babylon were built with bricks made of mud that had been dried in the sun. It would have been fairly easy to dig a hole through these bricks.

house. ⁴During the daytime, while they watch, bring out your belongings packed for exile. Then in the evening, while they are watching, go out like those who go into exile. ⁵While they watch, dig through the wall and take your belongings out through it. ⁶Put them on your shoulder as they are watching and carry them out at dusk. Cover your face so that you cannot see the land, for I have made you a sign to the house of Israel.'

⁷So I did as I was commanded. During the day I brought out my things packed for exile. Then in the evening I dug through the wall with my hands. I took my belongings out at dusk, carrying them on my shoulders while they watched.

⁸In the morning the word of the LORD came to me: ⁹'Son of man, did not that rebellious house of Israel ask you, "What are you doing?"

¹⁰'Say to them, "This is what the Sovereign LORD says: this prophecy concerns the prince in Jerusalem and the whole house of Israel who are there." ¹¹Say to them, "I am a sign to you."

'As I have done, so it will be done to them. They will go into exile as captives.

¹²'The prince among them will put his things on his shoulder at dusk and leave, and a hole will be dug in the wall for him to go through. He will cover his face so that he cannot see the land. ¹³I will spread my net for him, and he will be caught in my snare; I will bring him to Babylonia, the land of the Chaldeans, but he will not see it, and there he will die. ¹⁴I will scatter to the winds all those around him—his staff and all his troops—and I will pursue them with drawn sword.

¹⁵'They will know that I am the LORD, when I disperse them among the nations and scatter them through the countries. ¹⁶But I will spare a few of them from the sword, famine and plague, so that in the nations where they go they may acknowledge all their detestable practices. Then they will know that I am the LORD.'

¹⁷The word of the LORD came to me: ¹⁸'Son of man, tremble as you eat your food, and shudder in fear as you drink your water. ¹⁹Say to the people of the land: "This is what the Sovereign LORD says about those living in Jerusalem and in the land of Israel: they will eat their food in anxiety and drink their water in despair, for their land will be stripped of everything in it because of the violence of all who live there. ²⁰The inhabited towns will be laid waste and the land will be desolate. Then you will know that I am the LORD."'

There will be no delay

²¹The word of the LORD came to me: ²²'Son of man, what is this proverb you have in the land of Israel: "The days go by and every vision comes to nothing"? ²³Say to them, "This is what the Sovereign LORD says: I am going to put an end to this proverb, and they will no longer quote it in Israel." Say to them, "The days are near when every vision will be fulfilled. ²⁴For there will be no more false visions or flattering divinations among the people of Israel. ²⁵But I the LORD will speak what I will, and it shall be fulfilled without delay. For in your days, you rebellious house, I will fulfil whatever I say, declares the Sovereign LORD."'

²⁶The word of the LORD came to me: ²⁷'Son of man, the house of Israel is saying, "The vision he sees is for many years from now, and he prophesies about the distant future."

²⁸'Therefore say to them, "This is what the Sovereign LORD says: none of my words will be delayed any longer; whatever I say will be fulfilled, declares the Sovereign LORD."'

False prophets condemned

13 The word of the LORD came to me: 2'Son of man, prophesy against the prophets of Israel who are now prophesying. Say to those who prophesy out of their own imagination: "Hear the word of the LORD! 3This is what the Sovereign LORD says: woe to the foolish[a] prophets who follow their own spirit and have seen nothing! 4Your prophets, Israel, are like jackals among ruins. 5You have not gone up to the breaches in the wall to repair it for the house of Israel so that it will stand firm in the battle on the day of the LORD. 6Their visions are false and their divinations a lie. Even though the LORD has not sent them, they say, 'The LORD declares', and expect him to fulfil their words. 7Have you not seen false visions and uttered lying divinations when you say, 'The LORD declares', though I have not spoken?

8' "Therefore this is what the Sovereign LORD says: because of your false words and lying visions, I am against you, declares the Sovereign LORD. 9My hand will be against the prophets who see false visions and utter lying divinations. They will not belong to the council of my people or be listed in the records of the house of Israel, nor will they enter the land of Israel. Then you will know that I am the Sovereign LORD.

10' "Because they lead my people astray, saying, 'Peace', when there is no peace, and because, when a flimsy wall is built, they cover it with whitewash, 11therefore tell those who cover it with whitewash that it is going to fall. Rain will come in torrents, and I will send hailstones hurtling down, and violent winds will burst forth. 12When the wall collapses, will people not ask you, 'Where is the whitewash you covered it with?'

13' "Therefore this is what the Sovereign LORD says: in my wrath I will unleash a violent wind, and in my anger hailstones and torrents of rain will fall with destructive fury. 14I will tear down the wall you have covered with whitewash and will level it to the ground so that its foundation will be laid bare. When it[b] falls, you will be destroyed in it; and you will know that I am the LORD. 15So I will spend my wrath against the wall and against those who covered it with whitewash. I will say to you, 'The wall is gone and so are those who whitewashed it, 16those prophets of Israel who prophesied to Jerusalem and saw visions of peace for her when there was no peace, declares the Sovereign LORD."'

17'Now, son of man, set your face against the daughters of your people who prophesy out of their own imagination. Prophesy against them 18and say, "This is what the Sovereign LORD says: woe to the women who sew magic charms on all their wrists and make veils of various lengths for their heads in order to ensnare people. Will you ensnare the lives of my people but preserve your own? 19You have profaned me among my people for a few handfuls of barley and scraps of bread. By lying to my people, who listen to lies, you have killed those who should not have died and have spared those who should not live.

20' "Therefore this is what the Sovereign LORD says: I am against your magic charms with which you ensnare people like birds and I will tear them from your arms; I will set free the people that you ensnare like birds. 21I will tear off your veils and save my people from your hands, and they will no longer fall prey to your power. Then you will know that I am the LORD. 22Because you disheartened the righteous with your lies, when I had brought them no grief, and because you encouraged the wicked not to turn from their evil ways and so save their lives, 23therefore you will no longer see false visions or practise divination. I will save my people from your hands. And then you will know that I am the LORD."'

Idolaters condemned

14 Some of the elders of Israel came to me and sat down in front of me. 2Then the word of the LORD came to me: 3'Son of man, these men have set up idols in their hearts and put wicked stumbling-blocks before their faces. Should I let them enquire of me at all? 4Therefore speak to them and tell them, "This is what the Sovereign LORD says: when any of the

---

[a] 3 Or *wicked* [b] 14 Or *the city*

Israelites set up idols in their hearts and put a wicked stumbling-block before their faces and then go to a prophet, I the LORD will answer them myself in keeping with their great idolatry. ⁵I will do this to recapture the hearts of the people of Israel, who have all deserted me for their idols."

⁶'Therefore say to the house of Israel, 'This is what the Sovereign LORD says: repent! Turn from your idols and renounce all your detestable practices!

⁷'"When any of the Israelites or any foreigner residing in Israel separate themselves from me and set up idols in their hearts and put a wicked stumbling-block before their faces and then go to a prophet to enquire of me, I the LORD will answer them myself. ⁸I will set my face against them and make them an example and a byword. I will remove them from my people. Then you will know that I am the LORD.

⁹'"And if the prophet is enticed to utter a prophecy, I the LORD have enticed that prophet, and I will stretch out my hand against him and destroy him from among my people Israel. ¹⁰They will bear their guilt—the prophet will be as guilty as the one who consults him. ¹¹Then the people of Israel will no longer stray from me, nor will they defile themselves any more with all their sins. They will be my people, and I will be their God, declares the Sovereign LORD."'

Jerusalem's judgment inescapable

¹²The word of the LORD came to me: ¹³'Son of man, if a country sins against me by being unfaithful and I stretch out my hand against it to cut off its food supply and send famine upon it and kill its people and their animals, ¹⁴even if these three men—Noah, Daniel*ᵃ* and Job—were in it, they could save only themselves by their righteousness, declares the Sovereign LORD.

¹⁵'Or if I send wild beasts through that country and they leave it childless and it becomes desolate so that no-one can pass through it because of the beasts, ¹⁶as surely as I live, declares the Sovereign LORD, even if these three men were in it, they could not save their own sons or daughters. They alone would be saved, but the land would be desolate.

¹⁷'Or if I bring a sword against that country and say, "Let the sword pass throughout the land," and I kill its people and their animals, ¹⁸as surely as I live, declares the Sovereign LORD, even if these three men were in it, they could not save their own sons or daughters. They alone would be saved.

¹⁹'Or if I send a plague into that land and pour out my wrath on it through bloodshed, killing its people and their animals, ²⁰as surely as I live, declares the Sovereign LORD, even if Noah, Daniel and Job were in it, they could save neither son nor daughter. They would save only themselves by their righteousness.

²¹'For this is what the Sovereign LORD says: how much worse will it be when I send against Jerusalem my four dreadful judgments—sword and famine and wild beasts and plague—to kill its men and their animals! ²²Yet there will be some survivors—sons and daughters who will be brought out of it. They will come to you, and when you see their conduct and their actions, you will be consoled regarding the disaster I have brought on Jerusalem—every disaster I have brought on it. ²³You will be consoled when you see their conduct and their actions, for you will know that I have done nothing in it without cause, declares the Sovereign LORD.'

Jerusalem as a useless vine

15 The word of the LORD came to me: ²'Son of man, how is the wood of a vine different from that of a branch from any of the trees in the forest? ³Is wood ever taken from it to make anything useful? Do they make pegs from it to hang things on? ⁴And after it is thrown on the fire as fuel and the fire burns both ends and chars the middle, is it then useful for anything? ⁵If it was not useful for anything when it was whole, how much less can it be made into something useful when the fire has burned it and it is charred?

⁶'Therefore this is what the Sovereign LORD says: as I have given the wood of the

---

ᵃ 14 Or *Danel*, a man of renown in ancient literature; also in verse 20

Rituals at birth
Ezekiel 16:4

A midwife would help women give birth to their children. She would cut the umbilical cord, wash the baby, rub it with salt and then wrap it snugly in cloth. The salt may have toughened the skin of babies and helped to prevent infection.

vine among the trees of the forest as fuel for the fire, so will I treat the people living in Jerusalem. ⁷I will set my face against them. Although they have come out of the fire, the fire will yet consume them. And when I set my face against them, you will know that I am the LORD. ⁸I will make the land desolate because they have been unfaithful, declares the Sovereign LORD.'

Jerusalem as an adulterous wife

16 The word of the LORD came to me: ²'Son of man, confront Jerusalem with her detestable practices ³and say, "This is what the Sovereign LORD says to Jerusalem: your ancestry and birth were in the land of the Canaanites; your father was an Amorite and your mother a Hittite. ⁴On the day you were born your cord was not cut, nor were you washed with water to make you clean, nor were you rubbed with salt or wrapped in cloths. ⁵No-one looked on you with pity or had compassion enough to do any of these things for you. Rather, you were thrown out into the open field, for on the day you were born you were despised.

⁶ "Then I passed by and saw you kicking about in your blood, and as you lay there in your blood I said to you, 'Live!'ᵃ ⁷I made you grow like a plant of the field. You grew and developed and entered puberty. Your breasts had formed and your hair had grown, yet you were stark naked.

⁸ "Later I passed by, and when I looked at you and saw that you were old enough for love, I spread the corner of my garment over you and covered your nakedness. I gave you my solemn oath and entered into a covenant with you, declares the Sovereign LORD, and you became mine.

⁹ "I bathed you with water and washed the blood from you and put ointments on you. ¹⁰I clothed you with an embroidered dress and put sandals of fine leather on you. I dressed you in fine linen and covered you with costly garments. ¹¹I adorned you with jewellery: I put bracelets on your arms and a necklace round your neck, ¹²and I put a ring on your nose, ear-rings on your ears and a beautiful crown on your head. ¹³So you were adorned with gold and silver; your clothes were of fine linen and costly fabric and embroidered cloth. Your food was honey, olive oil and the finest flour. You became very beautiful and rose to be a queen. ¹⁴And your fame spread among the nations on account of your beauty, because the splendour I had given you made your beauty perfect, declares the Sovereign LORD.

¹⁵ "But you trusted in your beauty and used your fame to become a prostitute. You lavished your favours on anyone who passed by and your beauty became his. ¹⁶You took some of your garments to make gaudy high places, where you carried on your prostitution. You went to him, and he possessed your beauty.ᵇ ¹⁷You also took the

Prostitute
Ezekiel 16:15

A prostitute is someone who has sex in return for money. When the Israelites turned away from God and worshipped other gods, they were likened to prostitutes.

ᵃ 6 A few Hebrew manuscripts, Septuagint and Syriac; most Hebrew manuscripts repeat the last clause.   ᵇ 16 The meaning of the Hebrew for this sentence is uncertain.

fine jewellery I gave you, the jewellery made of my gold and silver, and you made for yourself male idols and engaged in prostitution with them. 18And you took your embroidered clothes to put on them, and you offered my oil and incense before them. 19Also the food I provided for you—the flour, olive oil and honey I gave you to eat—you offered as fragrant incense before them. That is what happened, declares the Sovereign LORD.

20' "And you took your sons and daughters whom you bore to me and sacrificed them as food to the idols. Was your prostitution not enough? 21You slaughtered my children and sacrificed them to the idols. 22In all your detestable practices and your prostitution you did not remember the days of your youth, when you were naked and bare, kicking about in your blood.

23' "Woe! Woe to you, declares the Sovereign LORD. In addition to all your other wickedness, 24you built a mound for yourself and made a lofty shrine in every public square. 25At every street corner you built your lofty shrines and degraded your beauty, spreading your legs with increasing promiscuity to anyone who passed by. 26You engaged in prostitution with the Egyptians, your neighbours with large genitals, and aroused my anger with your increasing promiscuity. 27So I stretched out my hand against you and reduced your territory; I gave you over to the greed of your enemies, the daughters of the Philistines, who were shocked by your lewd conduct. 28You engaged in prostitution with the Assyrians too, because you were insatiable; and even after that, you still were not satisfied. 29Then you increased your promiscuity to include Babylonia,[a] a land of merchants, but even with this you were not satisfied.

30' "I am filled with fury against you,[b] declares the Sovereign LORD, when you do all these things, acting like a brazen prostitute! 31When you built your mounds at every street corner and made your lofty shrines in every public square, you were unlike a prostitute, because you scorned payment.

32' "You adulterous wife! You prefer strangers to your own husband! 33All prostitutes receive gifts, but you give gifts to all your lovers, bribing them to come to you from everywhere for your illicit favours. 34So in your prostitution you are the opposite of others; no-one runs after you for your favours. You are the very opposite, for you give payment and none is given to you.

35' "Therefore, you prostitute, hear the word of the LORD! 36This is what the Sovereign LORD says: because you poured out your lust and exposed your nakedness in your promiscuity with your lovers, and because of all your detestable idols, and because you gave them your children's blood, 37therefore I am going to gather all your lovers, with whom you found pleasure, those you loved as well as those you hated. I will gather them against you from all around and will strip you in front of them, and they will see all your nakedness. 38I will sentence you to the punishment of women who commit adultery and who shed blood; I will bring on you the blood vengeance of my wrath and jealous anger. 39Then I will deliver you into the hands of your lovers, and they will tear down your mounds and destroy your lofty shrines. They will strip you of your clothes and take your fine jewellery and leave you naked and bare. 40They will bring a mob against you, who will stone you and hack you to pieces with their swords. 41They will burn down your houses and inflict punishment on you in the sight of many women. I will put a stop to your prostitution, and you will no longer pay your lovers. 42Then my wrath against you will subside and my jealous anger will turn away from you; I will be calm and no longer angry.

43' "Because you did not remember the days of your youth but enraged me with all these things, I will surely bring down on your head what you have done, declares the Sovereign LORD. Did you not add lewdness to all your other detestable practices?

---

[a] 29 Or *Chaldea* [b] 30 Or *How feverish is your heart,*

⁴⁴' "Everyone who quotes proverbs will quote this proverb about you: 'Like mother, like daughter.' ⁴⁵You are a true daughter of your mother, who despised her husband and her children; and you are a true sister of your sisters, who despised their husbands and their children. Your mother was a Hittite and your father an Amorite. ⁴⁶Your elder sister was Samaria, who lived to the north of you with her daughters; and your younger sister, who lived to the south of you with her daughters, was Sodom. ⁴⁷You not only followed their ways and copied their detestable practices, but in all your ways you soon became more depraved than they. ⁴⁸As surely as I live, declares the Sovereign LORD, your sister Sodom and her daughters never did what you and your daughters have done.

⁴⁹' "Now this was the sin of your sister Sodom: she and her daughters were arrogant, overfed and unconcerned; they did not help the poor and needy. ⁵⁰They were haughty and did detestable things before me. Therefore I did away with them as you have seen. ⁵¹Samaria did not commit half the sins you did. You have done more detestable things than they, and have made your sisters seem righteous by all these things you have done. ⁵²Bear your disgrace, for you have furnished some justification for your sisters. Because your sins were more vile than theirs, they appear more righteous than you. So then, be ashamed and bear your disgrace, for you have made your sisters appear righteous.

⁵³' "However, I will restore the fortunes of Sodom and her daughters and of Samaria and her daughters, and your fortunes along with them, ⁵⁴so that you may bear your disgrace and be ashamed of all you have done in giving them comfort. ⁵⁵And your sisters, Sodom with her daughters and Samaria with her daughters, will return to what they were before; and you and your daughters will return to what you were before. ⁵⁶You would not even mention your sister Sodom in the day of your pride, ⁵⁷before your wickedness was uncovered. Even so, you are now scorned by the daughters of Edom^a and all her neighbours and the daughters of the Philistines—all those around you who despise you. ⁵⁸You will bear the consequences of your lewdness and your detestable practices, declares the LORD.

⁵⁹' "This is what the Sovereign LORD says: I will deal with you as you deserve, because you have despised my oath by breaking the covenant. ⁶⁰Yet I will remember the covenant I made with you in the days of your youth, and I will establish an everlasting covenant with you. ⁶¹Then you will remember your ways and be ashamed when you receive your sisters, both those who are older than you and those who are younger. I will give them to you as daughters, but not on the basis of my covenant with you. ⁶²So I will establish my covenant with you, and you will know that I am the LORD. ⁶³Then, when I make atonement for you for all you have done, you will remember and be ashamed and never again open your mouth because of your humiliation, declares the Sovereign LORD.'"

Two eagles and a vine

17 The word of the LORD came to me: ²'Son of man, set forth an allegory and tell it to the house of Israel as a parable. ³Say to them, "This is what the Sovereign LORD says: a great eagle with powerful wings, long feathers and full plumage of varied colours came to Lebanon. Taking hold of the top of a cedar, ⁴he broke off its topmost shoot and carried it away to a land of merchants, where he planted it in a city of traders.

⁵' "He took one of the seedlings of the land and put it in fertile soil. He planted it like a willow by abundant water, ⁶and it sprouted and became a low, spreading vine. Its branches turned towards him, but its roots remained under it. So it became a vine and produced branches and put out leafy boughs.

⁷' "But there was another great eagle with powerful wings and full plumage. The vine now sent out its roots towards him from the plot where it was planted and stretched out its branches to him for water. ⁸It had been planted in good soil by

---

^{a} 57 Many Hebrew manuscripts and Syriac; most Hebrew manuscripts, Septuagint and Vulgate *Aram* abundant water so that it would produce branches, bear fruit and become a splendid vine."

9'Say to them, "This is what the Sovereign LORD says: will it thrive? Will it not be uprooted and stripped of its fruit so that it withers? All its new growth will wither. It will not take a strong arm or many people to pull it up by the roots. 10It has been planted, but will it thrive? Will it not wither completely when the east wind strikes it—wither away in the plot where it grew?"'

11Then the word of the LORD came to me: 12'Say to this rebellious house, "Do you not know what these things mean?" Say to them: "The king of Babylon went to Jerusalem and carried off her king and her nobles, bringing them back with him to Babylon. 13Then he took a member of the royal family and made a treaty with him, putting him under oath. He also carried away the leading men of the land, 14so that the kingdom would be brought low, unable to rise again, surviving only by keeping his treaty. 15But the king rebelled against him by sending his envoys to Egypt to get horses and a large army. Will he succeed? Will he who does such things escape? Will he break the treaty and yet escape?

16' "As surely as I live, declares the Sovereign LORD, he shall die in Babylon, in the land of the king who put him on the throne, whose oath he despised and whose treaty he broke. 17Pharaoh with his mighty army and great horde will be of no help to him in war, when ramps are built and siege works erected to destroy many lives. 18He despised the oath by breaking the covenant. Because he had given his hand in pledge and yet did all these things, he shall not escape.

19' "Therefore this is what the Sovereign LORD says: as surely as I live, I will bring down on his head my oath that he despised and my covenant that he broke. 20I will spread my net for him, and he will be caught in my snare. I will bring him to Babylon and execute judgment on him there because he was unfaithful to me. 21All his choice troops will fall by the sword, and the survivors will be scattered to the winds. Then you will know that I the LORD have spoken.

22' "This is what the Sovereign LORD says: I myself will take a shoot from the very top of a cedar and plant it; I will break off a tender sprig from its topmost shoots and plant it on a high and lofty mountain. 23On the mountain heights of Israel I will plant it; it will produce branches and bear fruit and become a splendid cedar. Birds of every kind will nest in it; they will find shelter in the shade of its branches. 24All the trees of the forest will know that I the LORD bring down the tall tree and make the low tree grow tall. I dry up the green tree and make the dry tree flourish.

'"I the LORD have spoken, and I will do it."'

The one who sins will die

18 The word of the LORD came to me: 2'What do you people mean by quoting this proverb about the land of Israel:

'"The parents eat sour grapes,
  and the children's teeth are set on edge"?

3'As surely as I live, declares the Sovereign LORD, you will no longer quote this proverb in Israel. 4For everyone belongs to me, the parent as well as the child—both alike belong to me. The one who sins is the one who will die.
5'Suppose there is a righteous man
  who does what is just and right.

Eating sour grapes
Ezekiel 18:2
This was a popular saying, meaning that children suffered because of what their parents did. The Israelites who quoted it were trying to blame their misfortune on their ancestors instead of recognising their own responsibility to walk in God's ways.

⁶He does not eat at the mountain shrines
  or look to the idols of the house of
    Israel.
He does not defile his neighbour's wife
  or have sexual relations with a woman
    during her period.
⁷He does not oppress anyone,
  but returns what he took in pledge for a
    loan.
He does not commit robbery,
  but gives his food to the hungry
  and provides clothing for the naked.
⁸He does not lend to them at interest
  or take a profit from them.
He withholds his hand from doing wrong
  and judges fairly between two parties.
⁹He follows my decrees
  and faithfully keeps my laws.
That man is righteous;
  he will surely live,
            declares the Sovereign LORD.

¹⁰'Suppose he has a violent son, who sheds blood or does any of these other things*ᵃ* ¹¹(though the father has done none of them):

'He eats at the mountain shrines.
He defiles his neighbour's wife.
¹²He oppresses the poor and needy.
He commits robbery.
He does not return what he took in pledge.
He looks to the idols.
He does detestable things.
¹³He lends at interest and takes a profit.

Will such a man live? He will not! Because he has done all these detestable things, he is to be put to death; his blood will be on his own head.

¹⁴'But suppose this son has a son who sees all the sins his father commits, and though he sees them, he does not do such things:

¹⁵'He does not eat at the mountain shrines
  or look to the idols of the house of
    Israel.
He does not defile his neighbour's wife.
¹⁶He does not oppress anyone
  or require a pledge for a loan.
He does not commit robbery,
  but gives his food to the hungry
  and provides clothing for the naked.
¹⁷He withholds his hand from ill-treating
    the poor
  and takes no interest or profit from
    them.
He keeps my laws and follows my decrees.

He will not die for his father's sin; he will surely live. ¹⁸But his father will die for his own sin, because he practised extortion, robbed his brother and did what was wrong among his people.

¹⁹'Yet you ask, "Why does the son not share the guilt of his father?" Since the son has done what is just and right and has been careful to keep all my decrees, he will surely live. ²⁰The one who sins is the one who will die. The child will not share the guilt of the parent, nor will the parent share the guilt of the child. The righteousness of the righteous will be credited to them, and the wickedness of the wicked will be charged against them.

²¹'But if the wicked turn away from all the sins they have committed and keep all my decrees and do what is just and right, they will surely live; they will not die. ²²None of the offences they have committed will be remembered against them. Because of the righteous things they have done, they will live. ²³Do I take any pleasure in the death of the wicked? declares the Sovereign LORD. Rather, am I not pleased when they turn from their ways and live?

²⁴'But if the righteous turn from their righteousness and commit sin and do the same detestable things the wicked do, will they live? None of the righteous things they have done will be remembered. Because of the unfaithfulness they are guilty of and because of the sins they have committed, they will die.

²⁵'Yet you say, "The way of the Lord is not just." Hear, house of Israel: is my way unjust? Is it not your ways that are unjust? ²⁶If the righteous turn from their righteousness and commit sin, they will die for it; because of the sin they have committed they will die. ²⁷But if the wicked turn away from the wickedness they have committed and do what is just and right, they will save their lives. ²⁸Because they consider all the

---

ᵃ 10 Or *things to a brother*

offences they have committed and turn away from them, they will surely live; they will not die. ²⁹Yet the house of Israel says, "The way of the Lord is not just." Are my ways unjust, house of Israel? Is it not your ways that are unjust?

³⁰'Therefore, house of Israel, I will judge each of you according to your own ways, declares the Sovereign LORD. Repent! Turn away from all your offences; then sin will not be your downfall. ³¹Rid yourselves of all the offences you have committed, and get a new heart and a new spirit. Why will you die, house of Israel? ³²For I take no pleasure in the death of anyone, declares the Sovereign LORD. Repent and live!

A lament over Israel's princes

19 'Take up a lament concerning the princes of Israel ²and say:

'"What a lioness was your mother
     among the lions!
She lay down among them
     and reared her cubs.
³She brought up one of her cubs,
     and he became a strong lion.
He learned to tear the prey
     and he devoured people.
⁴The nations heard about him,
     and he was trapped in their pit.
They led him with hooks
     to the land of Egypt.

⁵'"When she saw her hope unfulfilled,
     her expectation gone,
she took another of her cubs
     and made him a strong lion.
⁶He prowled among the lions,
     for he was now a strong lion.
He learned to tear the prey
     and he devoured people.
⁷He broke down[a] their strongholds
     and devastated their towns.
The land and all who were in it
     were terrified by his roaring.
⁸Then the nations came against him,
     those from regions round about.
They spread their net for him,
     and he was trapped in their pit.
⁹With hooks they pulled him into a cage
     and brought him to the king of
          Babylon.
They put him in prison,
     so his roar was heard no longer
          on the mountains of Israel.

¹⁰'"Your mother was like a vine in your
          vineyard[b]
     planted by the water;
it was fruitful and full of branches
     because of abundant water.
¹¹Its branches were strong,
     fit for a ruler's sceptre.
It towered high
     above the thick foliage,
conspicuous for its height
     and for its many branches.
¹²But it was uprooted in fury
     and thrown to the ground.
The east wind made it shrivel,
     it was stripped of its fruit;
its strong branches withered
     and fire consumed them.
¹³Now it is planted in the desert,
     in a dry and thirsty land.
¹⁴Fire spread from one of its main[c] branches
     and consumed its fruit.
No strong branch is left on it
     fit for a ruler's sceptre."

'This is a lament and is to be used as a lament.'

Rebellious Israel purged

20 In the seventh year, in the fifth month on the tenth day, some of the elders of Israel came to enquire of the LORD, and they sat down in front of me.

²Then the word of the LORD came to me: ³'Son of man, speak to the elders of Israel and say to them, "This is what the Sovereign LORD says: have you come to enquire of me? As surely as I live, I will not let you enquire of me, declares the Sovereign LORD."

⁴'Will you judge them? Will you judge them, son of man? Then confront them with the detestable practices of their ancestors ⁵and say to them: "This is what the Sovereign LORD says: on the day I chose Israel, I swore with uplifted hand to the descendants of the house of Jacob and revealed myself to

---

[a] 7 Targum (see Septuagint); Hebrew *He knew*   [b] 10 Two Hebrew manuscripts; most Hebrew manuscripts *your blood*
[c] 14 Or *from under its*

them in Egypt. With uplifted hand I said to them, 'I am the LORD your God.' 6On that day I swore to them that I would bring them out of Egypt into a land I had searched out for them, a land flowing with milk and honey, the most beautiful of all lands. 7And I said to them, 'Each of you, get rid of the vile images you have set your eyes on, and do not defile yourselves with the idols of Egypt. I am the LORD your God.'

8' "But they rebelled against me and would not listen to me; they did not get rid of the vile images they had set their eyes on, nor did they forsake the idols of Egypt. So I said I would pour out my wrath on them and spend my anger against them in Egypt. 9But for the sake of my name, I brought them out of Egypt. I did it to keep my name from being profaned in the eyes of the nations among whom they lived and in whose sight I had revealed myself to the Israelites. 10Therefore I led them out of Egypt and brought them into the wilderness. 11I gave them my decrees and made known to them my laws, through which people will live if they obey them. 12Also I gave them my Sabbaths as a sign between us, so they would know that I the LORD made them holy.

13' "Yet the people of Israel rebelled against me in the wilderness. They did not follow my decrees but rejected my laws—through which people will live if they obey them—and they utterly desecrated my Sabbaths. So I said I would pour out my wrath on them and destroy them in the wilderness. 14But for the sake of my name I did what would keep it from being profaned in the eyes of the nations in whose sight I had brought them out. 15Also with uplifted hand I swore to them in the wilderness that I would not bring them into the land I had given them—a land flowing with milk and honey, the most beautiful of all lands— 16because they rejected my laws and did not follow my decrees and desecrated my Sabbaths. For their hearts were devoted to their idols. 17Yet I looked on them with pity and did not destroy them or put an end to them in the wilderness. 18I said to their children in the wilderness, 'Do not follow the statutes of your parents or keep their laws or defile yourselves with their idols. 19I am the LORD your God; follow my decrees and be careful to keep my laws. 20Keep my Sabbaths holy, that they may be a sign between us. Then you will know that I am the LORD your God.'

21' "But the children rebelled against me: they did not follow my decrees, they were not careful to keep my laws, of which I said, 'Whoever obeys them will live by them,' and they desecrated my Sabbaths. So I said I would pour out my wrath on them and spend my anger against them in the wilderness. 22But I withheld my hand, and for the sake of my name I did what would keep it from being profaned in the eyes of the nations in whose sight I had brought them out. 23Also with uplifted hand I swore to them in the wilderness that I would disperse them among the nations and scatter them through the countries, 24because they had not obeyed my laws but had rejected my decrees and desecrated my Sabbaths, and their eyes lusted after their parents' idols. 25So I gave them other statutes that were not good and laws through which they could not live; 26I defiled them through their gifts—the sacrifice of every firstborn—that I might fill them with horror so that they would know that I am the LORD."

27'Therefore, son of man, speak to the people of Israel and say to them, "This is what the Sovereign LORD says: in this also your ancestors blasphemed me by being unfaithful to me: 28when I brought them into the land I had sworn to give them and they saw any high hill or any leafy tree, there they offered their sacrifices, made offerings that aroused my anger, presented their fragrant incense and poured out their drink offerings. 29Then I said to them: what is this high place you go to?" ' (It is called Bamah*a* to this day.)

Rebellious Israel renewed

30'Therefore say to the house of Israel: "This is what the Sovereign LORD says: will you defile yourselves the way your ancestors did and lust after their vile images? 31When you offer your gifts—the sacrifice of your

---

a 29 *Bamah* means *high place*.

children in the fire—you continue to defile yourselves with all your idols to this day. Am I to let you enquire of me, house of Israel? As surely as I live, declares the Sovereign LORD, I will not let you enquire of me.

32 "You say, 'We want to be like the nations, like the peoples of the world, who serve wood and stone.' But what you have in mind will never happen. 33As surely as I live, declares the Sovereign LORD, I will reign over you with a mighty hand and an outstretched arm and with outpoured wrath. 34I will bring you from the nations and gather you from the countries where you have been scattered—with a mighty hand and an outstretched arm and with outpoured wrath. 35I will bring you into the wilderness of the nations and there, face to face, I will execute judgment upon you. 36As I judged your ancestors in the wilderness of the land of Egypt, so I will judge you, declares the Sovereign LORD. 37I will take note of you as you pass under my rod, and I will bring you into the bond of the covenant. 38I will purge you of those who revolt and rebel against me. Although I will bring them out of the land where they are living, yet they will not enter the land of Israel. Then you will know that I am the LORD.

39 "As for you, house of Israel, this is what the Sovereign LORD says: go and serve your idols, every one of you! But afterwards you will surely listen to me and no longer profane my holy name with your gifts and idols. 40For on my holy mountain, the high mountain of Israel, declares the Sovereign LORD, there in the land the entire house of Israel will serve me, and there I will accept them. There I will require your offerings and your choice gifts,*a* along with all your holy sacrifices. 41I will accept you as fragrant incense when I bring you out from the nations and gather you from the countries where you have been scattered, and I will be proved holy through you in the sight of the nations. 42Then you will know that I am the LORD, when I bring you into the land of Israel, the land I had sworn with uplifted hand to give to your ancestors.

> **Profanity and Blasphemy**
> Ezekiel 20:39
> When a person dishonours or offends God through their words or their actions, they commit blasphemy. In the New Testament, blasphemy includes insulting God's people (Matthew 12:31).

43There you will remember your conduct and all the actions by which you have defiled yourselves, and you will loathe yourselves for all the evil you have done. 44You will know that I am the LORD, when I deal with you for my name's sake and not according to your evil ways and your corrupt practices, house of Israel, declares the Sovereign LORD."'

Prophecy against the south

*45The word of the LORD came to me: 46'Son of man, set your face towards the south; preach against the south and prophesy against the forest of the southland. 47Say to the southern forest: "Hear the word of the LORD. This is what the Sovereign LORD says: I am about to set fire to you, and it will consume all your trees, both green and dry. The blazing flame will not be quenched, and every face from south to north will be scorched by it. 48Everyone will see that I the LORD have kindled it; it will not be quenched."'

49Then I said, 'Ah, Sovereign LORD! They are saying of me, "Isn't he just telling parables?"'

Babylon as God's sword of judgment

21 *The word of the LORD came to me: 2'Son of man, set your face against Jerusalem and preach against the sanctuary. Prophesy against the land of Israel 3and say to her: "This is what the LORD says: I am against you. I will draw my sword from its

---

a 40 Or *and the gifts of your firstfruits*

* 20:45-49 is numbered 21:1-5 in Hebrew texts.   * 21:1-32 is numbered 21:6-37 in Hebrew texts.

sheath and cut off from you both the righteous and the wicked. ⁴Because I am going to cut off the righteous and the wicked, my sword will be unsheathed against everyone from south to north. ⁵Then all people will know that I the LORD have drawn my sword from its sheath; it will not return again."

⁶'Therefore groan, son of man! Groan before them with broken heart and bitter grief. ⁷And when they ask you, "Why are you groaning?" you shall say, "Because of the news that is coming. Every heart will melt and every hand go limp; every spirit will become faint and every knee be wet with urine." It is coming! It will surely take place, declares the Sovereign LORD.'

⁸The word of the LORD came to me: ⁹'Son of man, prophesy and say, "This is what the Lord says:

'"A sword, a sword,
　sharpened and polished—
¹⁰sharpened for the slaughter,
　polished to flash like lightning!

'"Shall we rejoice in the sceptre of my royal son? The sword despises every such stick.

¹¹'"The sword is appointed to be polished,
　to be grasped with the hand;
it is sharpened and polished,
　made ready for the hand of the
　　slayer.
¹²Cry out and wail, son of man,
　for it is against my people;
it is against all the princes of Israel.
They are thrown to the sword
　along with my people.
Therefore beat your breast.

¹³'"Testing will surely come. And what if even the sceptre, which the sword despises, does not continue? declares the Sovereign LORD."

¹⁴'So then, son of man, prophesy
　and strike your hands together.
Let the sword strike twice,
　even three times.
It is a sword for slaughter—
　a sword for great slaughter,
　　closing in on them from every side.
¹⁵So that hearts may melt
　and the fallen be many,
I have stationed the sword for slaughter[a]
　at all their gates.
Oh! It is made to flash like lightning,
　it is grasped for slaughter.
¹⁶Slash to the right, you sword,
　then to the left,
wherever your blade is turned.
¹⁷I too will strike my hands together,
　and my wrath will subside.
I the LORD have spoken.'

¹⁸The word of the LORD came to me: ¹⁹'Son of man, mark out two roads for the sword of the king of Babylon to take, both starting from the same country. Make a signpost where the road branches off to the city. ²⁰Mark out one road for the sword to come against Rabbah of the Ammonites and another against Judah and fortified Jerusalem. ²¹For the king of Babylon will stop at the fork in the road, at the junction of the two roads, to seek an omen: he will cast lots with arrows, he will consult his idols, he will examine the liver. ²²Into his right hand will come the lot for Jerusalem, where he is to set up battering-rams, to give the command to slaughter, to sound the battle cry, to set battering-rams against the gates, to build a ramp and to erect siege works. ²³It will seem like a false omen to those who have sworn allegiance to him, but he will remind them of their guilt and take them captive.

²⁴'Therefore this is what the Sovereign LORD says: "Because you people have brought to mind your guilt by your open rebellion, revealing your sins in all that you do—because you have done this, you will be taken captive.

²⁵'"You profane and wicked prince of Israel, whose day has come, whose time of punishment has reached its climax, ²⁶this is what the Sovereign LORD says: take off the turban, remove the crown. It will not be as it was: The lowly will be exalted and the exalted will be brought low. ²⁷A ruin! A ruin! I will make it a ruin! The crown will not be restored until he to whom it rightfully belongs shall come; to him I will give it."

---

[a] 15 Septuagint; the meaning of the Hebrew for this word is uncertain.

28'And you, son of man, prophesy and say, "This is what the Sovereign LORD says about the Ammonites and their insults:

'"A sword, a sword,
  drawn for the slaughter,
polished to consume
  and to flash like lightning!
29Despite false visions concerning you
  and lying divinations about you,
it will be laid on the necks
  of the wicked who are to be slain,
whose day has come,
  whose time of punishment has reached
    its climax.

30'"Let the sword return to its sheath.
  In the place where you were created,
in the land of your ancestry,
  I will judge you.
31I will pour out my wrath on you
  and breathe out my fiery anger against
    you;
I will deliver you into the hands of brutal
    men,
  men skilled in destruction.
32You will be fuel for the fire,
  your blood will be shed in your land,
you will be remembered no more;
  for I the LORD have spoken."'"

Judgment on Jerusalem's sins

22 The word of the LORD came to me: 2'Son of man, will you judge her? Will you judge this city of bloodshed? Then confront her with all her detestable practices 3and say: "This is what the Sovereign LORD says: you city that brings on herself doom by shedding blood in her midst and defiles herself by making idols, 4you have become guilty because of the blood you have shed and have become defiled by the idols you have made. You have brought your days to a close, and the end of your years has come. Therefore I will make you an object of scorn to the nations and a laughing-stock to all the countries. 5Those who are near and those who are far away will mock you, you infamous city, full of turmoil.

6'"See how each of the princes of Israel who are in you uses his power to shed blood. 7In you they have treated father and mother with contempt; in you they have oppressed the foreigner and ill-treated the fatherless and the widow. 8You have despised my holy things and desecrated my Sabbaths. 9In you are slanderers who are bent on shedding blood; in you are those who eat at the mountain shrines and commit lewd acts. 10In you are those who dishonour their father's bed; in you are those who violate women during their period, when they are ceremonially unclean. 11In you one man commits a detestable offence with his neighbour's wife, another shamefully defiles his daughter-in-law, and another violates his sister, his own father's daughter. 12In you are people who accept bribes to shed blood; you take interest and make a profit from the poor. You extort unjust gain from your neighbours. And you have forgotten me, declares the Sovereign LORD.

13'"I will surely strike my hands together at the unjust gain you have made and at the blood you have shed in your midst. 14Will your courage endure or your hands be strong in the day I deal with you? I the LORD have spoken, and I will do it. 15I will disperse you among the nations and scatter you through the countries; and I will put an end to your uncleanness. 16When you have been defiled[a] in the eyes of the nations, you will know that I am the LORD."'

17Then the word of the LORD came to me: 18'Son of man, the house of Israel has become dross to me; all of them are the

---

IN OTHER WORDS

Dross
Ezekiel 22:18
To refine metal, you heat it until it is liquid. The impurities can then be separated off and the pure metal used for weapons, tools, ornaments or utensils. 'Dross' is the name for the impurities left behind once the pure metal has been poured off.

---

[a] 16 Or *When I have allotted you your inheritance*

copper, tin, iron and lead left inside a furnace. They are but the dross of silver. ¹⁹Therefore this is what the Sovereign LORD says: "Because you have all become dross, I will gather you into Jerusalem. ²⁰As silver, copper, iron, lead and tin are gathered into a furnace to be melted with a fiery blast, so will I gather you in my anger and my wrath and put you inside the city and melt you. ²¹I will gather you and I will blow on you with my fiery wrath, and you will be melted inside her. ²²As silver is melted in a furnace, so you will be melted inside her, and you will know that I the LORD have poured out my wrath on you."'

²³Again the word of the LORD came to me: ²⁴'Son of man, say to the land, "You are a land that has not been cleansed or rained on in the day of wrath." ²⁵There is a conspiracy of her princes[a] within her like a roaring lion tearing its prey; they devour people, take treasures and precious things and make many widows within her. ²⁶Her priests do violence to my law and profane my holy things; they do not distinguish between the holy and the common; they teach that there is no difference between the unclean and the clean; and they shut their eyes to the keeping of my Sabbaths, so that I am profaned among them. ²⁷Her officials within her are like wolves tearing their prey; they shed blood and kill people to make unjust gain. ²⁸Her prophets whitewash these deeds for them by false visions and lying divinations. They say, "This is what the Sovereign LORD says"—when the LORD has not spoken. ²⁹The people of the land practise extortion and commit robbery; they oppress the poor and needy and ill-treat the foreigner, denying them justice.

³⁰'I looked for someone among them who would build up the wall and stand before me in the gap on behalf of the land so that I would not have to destroy it, but I found no-one. ³¹So I will pour out my wrath on them and consume them with my fiery anger, bringing down on their own heads all they have done, declares the Sovereign LORD.'

Two adulterous sisters

23 The word of the LORD came to me: ²'Son of man, there were two women, daughters of the same mother. ³They became prostitutes in Egypt, engaging in prostitution from their youth. In that land their breasts were fondled and their virgin bosoms caressed. ⁴The elder one was named Oholah, and her sister was Oholibah. They were mine and gave birth to sons and daughters. Oholah is Samaria, and Oholibah is Jerusalem.

⁵'Oholah engaged in prostitution while she was still mine; and she lusted after her lovers, the Assyrians—warriors ⁶clothed in blue, governors and commanders, all of them handsome young men, and mounted horsemen. ⁷She gave herself as a prostitute to all the elite of the Assyrians and defiled herself with all the idols of everyone she lusted after. ⁸She did not give up the prostitution she began in Egypt, when during her youth men slept with her, caressed her virgin bosom and poured out their lust on her.

⁹'Therefore I delivered her into the hands of her lovers, the Assyrians, for whom she lusted. ¹⁰They stripped her naked, took away her sons and daughters and killed her with the sword. She became a byword among women, and punishment was inflicted on her.

¹¹'Her sister Oholibah saw this, yet in her lust and prostitution she was more depraved than her sister. ¹²She too lusted after the Assyrians—governors and commanders, warriors in full dress, mounted horsemen, all handsome young men. ¹³I saw that she too defiled herself; both of them went the same way.

¹⁴'But she carried her prostitution still further. She saw men portrayed on a wall, figures of Chaldeans[b] portrayed in red, ¹⁵with belts round their waists and flowing turbans on their heads; all of them looked like Babylonian chariot officers, natives of Chaldea.[c] ¹⁶As soon as she saw them, she lusted after them and sent messengers to them in Chaldea. ¹⁷Then the Babylonians came to her, to the bed of love, and in their lust they defiled her. After she had been

---

[a] 25 Septuagint; Hebrew *prophets*   [b] 14 Or *Babylonians*   [c] 15 Or *Babylonia*; also in verse 16

defiled by them, she turned away from them in disgust. ¹⁸When she carried on her prostitution openly and exposed her nakedness, I turned away from her in disgust, just as I had turned away from her sister. ¹⁹Yet she became more and more promiscuous as she recalled the days of her youth, when she was a prostitute in Egypt. ²⁰There she lusted after her lovers, whose genitals were like those of donkeys and whose emission was like that of horses. ²¹So you longed for the lewdness of your youth, when in Egypt your bosom was caressed and your young breasts fondled.[a]

²²'Therefore, Oholibah, this is what the Sovereign LORD says: I will stir up your lovers against you, those you turned away from in disgust, and I will bring them against you from every side— ²³the Babylonians and all the Chaldeans, the men of Pekod and Shoa and Koa, and all the Assyrians with them, handsome young men, all of them governors and commanders, chariot officers and men of high rank, all mounted on horses. ²⁴They will come against you with weapons,[b] chariots and wagons and with a throng of people; they will take up positions against you on every side with large and small shields and with helmets. I will turn you over to them for punishment, and they will punish you according to their standards. ²⁵I will direct my jealous anger against you, and they will deal with you in fury. They will cut off your noses and your ears, and those of you who are left will fall by the sword. They will take away your sons and daughters, and those of you who are left will be consumed by fire. ²⁶They will also strip you of your clothes and take your fine jewellery. ²⁷So I will put a stop to the lewdness and prostitution you began in Egypt. You will not look on these things with longing or remember Egypt any more.

²⁸'For this is what the Sovereign LORD says: I am about to deliver you into the hands of those you hate, to those you turned away from in disgust. ²⁹They will deal with you in hatred and take away everything you have worked for. They will leave you stark naked, and the shame of your prostitution will be exposed. Your lewdness and promiscuity ³⁰have brought this on you, because you lusted after the nations and defiled yourself with their idols. ³¹You have gone the way of your sister; so I will put her cup into your hand.

³²'This is what the Sovereign LORD says:

'You will drink your sister's cup,
 a cup large and deep;
it will bring scorn and derision,
 for it holds so much.
³³You will be filled with drunkenness and sorrow,
 the cup of ruin and desolation,
 the cup of your sister Samaria.
³⁴You will drink it and drain it dry
 and chew on its pieces—
 and you will tear your breasts.

I have spoken, declares the Sovereign LORD.

³⁵'Therefore this is what the Sovereign LORD says: since you have forgotten me and thrust me behind your back, you must bear the consequences of your lewdness and prostitution.'

³⁶The LORD said to me: 'Son of man, will you judge Oholah and Oholibah? Then confront them with their detestable practices, ³⁷for they have committed adultery and blood is on their hands. They committed adultery with their idols; they even sacrificed their children, whom they bore to me, as food for them. ³⁸They have also done this to me: at that same time they defiled my sanctuary and desecrated my Sabbaths. ³⁹On the very day they sacrificed their children to their idols, they entered my sanctuary and desecrated it. That is what they did in my house.

⁴⁰'They even sent messengers for men who came from far away, and when they arrived you bathed yourself for them, painted your eyes and put on your jewellery. ⁴¹You sat on an elegant couch, with a table spread before it on which you had placed the incense and olive oil that belonged to me.

⁴²'The noise of a carefree crowd was around her; drunkards were brought from

---

[a] 21 Syriac (see also verse 3); Hebrew *caressed because of your young breasts*   [b] 24 The meaning of the Hebrew for this word is uncertain.

the desert along with men from the rabble, and they put bracelets on the arms of the woman and her sister and beautiful crowns on their heads. 43Then I said about the one worn out by adultery, "Now let them use her as a prostitute, for that is all she is." 44And they slept with her. As men sleep with a prostitute, so they slept with those lewd women, Oholah and Oholibah. 45But righteous judges will sentence them to the punishment of women who commit adultery and shed blood, because they are adulterous and blood is on their hands.

46'This is what the Sovereign LORD says: bring a mob against them and give them over to terror and plunder. 47The mob will stone them and cut them down with their swords; they will kill their sons and daughters and burn down their houses.

48'So I will put an end to lewdness in the land, that all women may take warning and not imitate you. 49You will suffer the penalty for your lewdness and bear the consequences of your sins of idolatry. Then you will know that I am the Sovereign LORD.'

Jerusalem as a cooking pot

24 In the ninth year, in the tenth month on the tenth day, the word of the LORD came to me: 2'Son of man, record this date, this very date, because the king of Babylon has laid siege to Jerusalem this very day. 3Tell this rebellious house a parable and say to them: "This is what the Sovereign LORD says:

'"Put on the cooking pot; put it on
 and pour water into it.
4Put into it the pieces of meat,
 all the choice pieces—the leg and the
  shoulder.
Fill it with the best of these bones;
5 take the pick of the flock.
Pile wood beneath it for the bones;
 bring it to the boil
 and cook the bones in it.

6'"For this is what the Sovereign LORD says:

'"Woe to the city of bloodshed,
 to the pot now encrusted,
 whose deposit will not go away!
Take the meat out piece by piece
 in whatever order it comes.

7'"For the blood she shed is in her midst:
 she poured it on the bare rock;
 she did not pour it on the ground,
 where the dust would cover it.
8To stir up wrath and take revenge
 I put her blood on the bare rock,
 so that it would not be covered.

9'"Therefore this is what the Sovereign LORD says:

'"Woe to the city of bloodshed!
 I, too, will pile the wood high.
10So heap on the wood
 and kindle the fire.
Cook the meat well,
 mixing in the spices;
 and let the bones be charred.
11Then set the empty pot on the coals
 till it becomes hot and its copper glows,
 so that its impurities may be melted
 and its deposit burned away.
12It has frustrated all efforts;
 its heavy deposit has not been
  removed,
 not even by fire.

13'"Now your impurity is lewdness. Because I tried to cleanse you but you would not be cleansed from your impurity, you will not be clean again until my wrath against you has subsided.

14'"I the LORD have spoken. The time has come for me to act. I will not hold back; I will not have pity, nor will I relent. You will be judged according to your conduct and your actions, declares the Sovereign LORD."'

Ezekiel's wife dies

15The word of the LORD came to me: 16'Son of man, with one blow I am about to take away from you the delight of your eyes. Yet do not lament or weep or shed any tears. 17Groan quietly; do not mourn for the dead. Keep your turban fastened and your sandals on your feet; do not cover your moustache and beard or eat the customary food [of mourners].'

18So I spoke to the people in the morning, and in the evening my wife died. The next morning I did as I had been commanded.

Sign of the times

Mourning rituals
Ezekiel 24:17

When someone died, there were certain rituals that their family and friends would follow in order to mourn for them properly. People would uncover their heads and take off their sandals. They would wail and cry loudly, especially during the funeral procession.

19 Then the people asked me, 'Won't you tell us what these things have to do with us? Why are you acting like this?'

20 So I said to them, 'The word of the LORD came to me: 21 say to the house of Israel, "This is what the Sovereign LORD says: I am about to desecrate my sanctuary—the stronghold in which you take pride, the delight of your eyes, the object of your affection. The sons and daughters you left behind will fall by the sword. 22 And you will do as I have done. You will not cover your moustache and beard or eat the customary food [of mourners]. 23 You will keep your turbans on your heads and your sandals on your feet. You will not mourn or weep but will waste away because of[a] your sins and groan among yourselves. 24 Ezekiel will be a sign to you; you will do just as he has done. When this happens, you will know that I am the Sovereign LORD."

25 'And you, son of man, on the day I take away their stronghold, their joy and glory, the delight of their eyes, their heart's desire, and their sons and daughters as well— 26 on that day a fugitive will come to tell you the news. 27 At that time your mouth will be opened; you will speak with him and will no longer be silent. So you will be a sign to them, and they will know that I am the LORD.'

A prophecy against Ammon

25 The word of the LORD came to me: 2'Son of man, set your face against the Ammonites and prophesy against them. 3 Say to them, "Hear the word of the Sovereign LORD. This is what the Sovereign LORD says: because you said 'Aha!' over my sanctuary when it was desecrated and over the land of Israel when it was laid waste and over the people of Judah when they went into exile, 4 therefore I am going to give you to the people of the East as a possession. They will set up their camps and pitch their tents among you; they will eat your fruit and drink your milk. 5 I will turn Rabbah into a pasture for camels and Ammon into a resting place for sheep. Then you will know that I am the LORD. 6 For this is what the Sovereign LORD says: because you have clapped your hands and stamped your feet, rejoicing with all the malice of your heart against the land of Israel, 7 therefore I will stretch out my hand against you and give you as plunder to the nations. I will wipe you out from among the nations and exterminate you from the countries. I will destroy you, and you will know that I am the LORD."'

A prophecy against Moab

8 'This is what the Sovereign LORD says: "Because Moab and Seir said, 'Look, the house of Judah has become like all the other nations,' 9 therefore I will expose the flank of Moab, beginning at its frontier towns— Beth Jeshimoth, Baal Meon and Kiriathaim—the glory of that land. 10 I will give Moab along with the Ammonites to the people of the East as a possession, so that the Ammonites will not be remembered among the nations; 11 and I will inflict punishment on Moab. Then they will know that I am the LORD."'

A prophecy against Edom

12 'This is what the Sovereign LORD says: "Because Edom took revenge on the house of Judah and became very guilty by doing so, 13 therefore this is what the Sovereign LORD says: I will stretch out my hand against Edom and kill its people and their animals. I

---
[a] 23 Or away in

will lay it waste, and from Teman to Dedan they will fall by the sword. ¹⁴I will take vengeance on Edom by the hand of my people Israel, and they will deal with Edom in accordance with my anger and my wrath; they will know my vengeance, declares the Sovereign LORD."'

A prophecy against Philistia

¹⁵'This is what the Sovereign LORD says: "Because the Philistines acted in vengeance and took revenge with malice in their hearts, and with ancient hostility sought to destroy Judah, ¹⁶therefore this is what the Sovereign LORD says: I am about to stretch out my hand against the Philistines, and I will wipe out the Kerethites and destroy those remaining along the coast. ¹⁷I will carry out great vengeance on them and punish them in my wrath. Then they will know that I am the LORD, when I take vengeance on them."'

A prophecy against Tyre

26 In the eleventh month of the twelfth[a] year, on the first day of the month, the word of the LORD came to me: ²'Son of man, because Tyre has said of Jerusalem, "Aha! The gate to the nations is broken, and its doors have swung open to me; now that she lies in ruins I will prosper," ³therefore this is what the Sovereign LORD says: I am against you, Tyre, and I will bring many nations against you, like the sea casting up its waves. ⁴They will destroy the walls of Tyre and pull down her towers; I will scrape away her rubble and make her a bare rock. ⁵Out in the sea she will become a place to spread fishing nets, for I have spoken, declares the Sovereign LORD. She will become plunder for the nations, ⁶and her settlements on the mainland will be ravaged by the sword. Then they will know that I am the LORD.

⁷'For this is what the Sovereign LORD says: from the north I am going to bring against Tyre Nebuchadnezzar[b] king of Babylon, king of kings, with horses and chariots, with horsemen and a great army. ⁸He will ravage your settlements on the mainland with the sword; he will set up siege works against you, build a ramp up to your walls and raise his shields against you. ⁹He will direct the blows of his battering-rams against your walls and demolish your towers with his weapons. ¹⁰His horses will be so many that they will cover you with dust. Your walls will tremble at the noise of the war horses, wagons and chariots when he enters your gates as men enter a city whose walls have been broken through. ¹¹The hooves of his horses will trample all your streets; he will kill your people with the sword, and your strong pillars will fall to the ground. ¹²They will plunder your wealth and loot your merchandise; they will break down your walls and demolish your fine houses and throw your stones, timber and rubble into the sea. ¹³I will put an end to your noisy songs, and the music of your harps will be heard no more. ¹⁴I will make you a bare rock, and you will become a place to spread fishing nets. You will never be rebuilt, for I the LORD have spoken, declares the Sovereign LORD.

¹⁵'This is what the Sovereign LORD says to Tyre: will not the coastlands tremble at the sound of your fall, when the wounded groan and the slaughter takes place in you? ¹⁶Then all the princes of the coast will step down from their thrones and lay aside their robes and take off their embroidered garments. Clothed with terror, they will sit on the ground, trembling every moment, appalled at you. ¹⁷Then they will take up a lament concerning you and say to you:

'"How you are destroyed, city of renown,
  peopled by men of the sea!
You were a power on the seas,
  you and your citizens;
you put your terror
  on all who lived there.
¹⁸Now the coastlands tremble
  on the day of your fall;
the islands in the sea
  are terrified at your collapse."

¹⁹'This is what the Sovereign LORD says: when I make you a desolate city, like cities no longer inhabited, and when I bring the ocean depths over you and its vast waters

---

[a] 1 Probable reading of the original Hebrew text; Masoretic Text does not have *month of the twelfth*. [b] 7 Hebrew *Nebuchadrezzar*, of which *Nebuchadnezzar* is a variant; here and often in Ezekiel and Jeremiah

cover you, ²⁰then I will bring you down with those who go down to the pit, to the people of long ago. I will make you dwell in the earth below, as in ancient ruins, with those who go down to the pit, and you will not return or take your place[a] in the land of the living. ²¹I will bring you to a horrible end and you will be no more. You will be sought, but you will never again be found, declares the Sovereign LORD.'

A lament over Tyre

27 The word of the LORD came to me: ²'Son of man, take up a lament concerning Tyre. ³Say to Tyre, situated at the gateway to the sea, merchant of peoples on many coasts, "This is what the Sovereign LORD says:

' "You say, Tyre,
'I am perfect in beauty.'
⁴Your domain was on the high seas;
  your builders brought your beauty to perfection.
⁵They made all your timbers
  of juniper from Senir;[b]
they took a cedar from Lebanon
  to make a mast for you.
⁶Of oaks from Bashan
  they made your oars;
of cypress wood[c] from the coasts of Cyprus
  they made your deck, inlaid with ivory.
⁷Fine embroidered linen from Egypt was your sail
  and served as your banner;
your awnings were of blue and purple
  from the coasts of Elishah.
⁸Men of Sidon and Arvad were your oarsmen;
  your skilled men, Tyre, were aboard as your sailors.
⁹Veteran craftsmen of Byblos were on board
  as shipwrights to caulk your seams.
All the ships of the sea and their sailors
  came alongside to trade for your wares.
¹⁰' "Men of Persia, Lydia and Put
  served as soldiers in your army.

Purple fabric
Ezekiel 27:16
Tyre was famous for the purple dye that was made from shellfish found along the coast. Two hundred and fifty thousand shellfish were needed to make one ounce of dye, so it was expensive and highly sought after. Royal robes were purple and so were the hangings and curtains in the temple.

They hung their shields and helmets on your walls,
  bringing you splendour.
¹¹Men of Arvad and Helek
  guarded your walls on every side;
men of Gammad
  were in your towers.
They hung their shields around your walls;
  they brought your beauty to perfection.

¹²' "Tarshish did business with you because of your great wealth of goods; they exchanged silver, iron, tin and lead for your merchandise.

¹³' "Greece, Tubal and Meshek did business with you; they traded human beings and articles of bronze for your wares.

¹⁴' "Men of Beth Togarmah exchanged chariot horses, cavalry horses and mules for your merchandise.

¹⁵' "The men of Rhodes[d] traded with you, and many coastlands were your customers; they paid you with ivory tusks and ebony.

¹⁶' "Aram[e] did business with you because of your many products; they exchanged turquoise, purple fabric, embroidered

---

[a] 20 Septuagint; Hebrew *return, and I will give glory*   [b] 5 That is, Mount Hermon   [c] 6 Targum; the Masoretic Text has a different division of the consonants.   [d] 15 Septuagint; Hebrew *Dedan*   [e] 16 Most Hebrew manuscripts; some Hebrew manuscripts and Syriac *Edom*

work, fine linen, coral and rubies for your merchandise.

17 ' "Judah and Israel traded with you; they exchanged wheat from Minnith and confections,[a] honey, olive oil and balm for your wares.

18 ' "Damascus did business with you because of your many products and great wealth of goods. They offered wine from Helbon, wool from Zahar 19 and casks of wine from Izal in exchange for your wares: wrought iron, cassia and calamus.

20 ' "Dedan traded in saddle blankets with you.

21 ' "Arabia and all the princes of Kedar were your customers; they did business with you in lambs, rams and goats.

22 ' "The merchants of Sheba and Raamah traded with you; for your merchandise they exchanged the finest of all kinds of spices and precious stones, and gold.

23 ' "Harran, Kanneh and Eden and merchants of Sheba, Ashur and Kilmad traded with you. 24 In your market-place they traded with you beautiful garments, blue fabric, embroidered work and multicoloured rugs with cords twisted and tightly knotted.

25 ' "The ships of Tarshish serve
    as carriers for your wares.
You are filled with heavy cargo
    as you sail the sea.
26 Your oarsmen take you
    out to the high seas.
But the east wind will break you to pieces
    far out at sea.
27 Your wealth, merchandise and wares,
    your mariners, sailors and shipwrights,
your merchants and all your soldiers,
    and everyone else on board
will sink into the heart of the sea
    on the day of your shipwreck.
28 The shorelands will quake
    when your sailors cry out.
29 All who handle the oars
    will abandon their ships;
the mariners and all the sailors
    will stand on the shore.
30 They will raise their voice
    and cry bitterly over you;

they will sprinkle dust on their heads
    and roll in ashes.
31 They will shave their heads because of you
    and will put on sackcloth.
They will weep over you with anguish of
        soul
    and with bitter mourning.
32 As they wail and mourn over you,
    they will take up a lament concerning
        you:
'Who was ever silenced like Tyre,
    surrounded by the sea?'
33 When your merchandise went out on the
        seas,
    you satisfied many nations;
with your great wealth and your wares
    you enriched the kings of the earth.
34 Now you are shattered by the sea
    in the depths of the waters;
your wares and all your company
    have gone down with you.
35 All who live in the coastlands
    are appalled at you;
their kings shudder with horror
    and their faces are distorted with fear.
36 The merchants among the nations scoff at
        you;
    you have come to a horrible end
    and will be no more.'"

A prophecy against the king of Tyre

28 The word of the LORD came to me: 2 'Son of man, say to the ruler of Tyre, "This is what the Sovereign LORD says:

' "In the pride of your heart
    you say, 'I am a god;
I sit on the throne of a god
    in the heart of the seas.'
But you are a mortal and not a god,
    though you think you are as wise as a
        god.
3 Are you wiser than Daniel?[b]
    Is no secret hidden from you?
4 By your wisdom and understanding
    you have gained wealth for yourself
and amassed gold and silver
    in your treasuries.
5 By your great skill in trading
    you have increased your wealth,
and because of your wealth
    your heart has grown proud.

---

[a] 17 The meaning of the Hebrew for this word is uncertain.   [b] 3 Or *Danel*, a man of renown in ancient literature

6 ' "Therefore this is what the Sovereign LORD says:

' "Because you think you are wise,
  as wise as a god,
7 I am going to bring foreigners against you,
  the most ruthless of nations;
they will draw their swords against your beauty and wisdom
  and pierce your shining splendour.
8 They will bring you down to the pit,
  and you will die a violent death
  in the heart of the seas.
9 Will you then say, 'I am a god,'
  in the presence of those who kill you?
You will be but a mortal, not a god,
  in the hands of those who slay you.
10 You will die the death of the uncircumcised
  at the hands of foreigners.

I have spoken, declares the Sovereign LORD." '

11 The word of the LORD came to me: 12 'Son of man, take up a lament concerning the king of Tyre and say to him: "This is what the Sovereign LORD says:

' "You were the seal of perfection,
  full of wisdom and perfect in beauty.
13 You were in Eden,
  the garden of God;
every precious stone adorned you:
  carnelian, chrysolite and emerald,
  topaz, onyx and jasper,
  lapis lazuli, turquoise and beryl.*a*
Your settings and mountings*b* were made of gold;
  on the day you were created they were prepared.
14 You were anointed as a guardian cherub,
  for so I ordained you.
You were on the holy mount of God;
  you walked among the fiery stones.
15 You were blameless in your ways
  from the day you were created
  till wickedness was found in you.
16 Through your widespread trade
  you were filled with violence,
  and you sinned.
So I drove you in disgrace from the mount of God,
  and I expelled you, guardian cherub,
  from among the fiery stones.
17 Your heart became proud
  on account of your beauty,
and you corrupted your wisdom
  because of your splendour.
So I threw you to the earth;
  I made a spectacle of you before kings.
18 By your many sins and dishonest trade
  you have desecrated your sanctuaries.
So I made a fire come out from you,
  and it consumed you,
and I reduced you to ashes on the ground
  in the sight of all who were watching.
19 All the nations who knew you
  are appalled at you;
you have come to a horrible end
  and will be no more." ' "

A prophecy against Sidon

20 The word of the LORD came to me: 21 'Son of man, set your face against Sidon; prophesy against her 22 and say: "This is what the Sovereign LORD says:

' "I am against you, Sidon,
  and among you I will display my glory.
You will know that I am the LORD,
  when I inflict punishment on you
  and within you am proved to be holy.
23 I will send a plague upon you
  and make blood flow in your streets.
The slain will fall within you,
  with the sword against you on every side.
Then you will know that I am the LORD.

24 ' "No longer will the people of Israel have malicious neighbours who are painful briers and sharp thorns. Then they will know that I am the Sovereign LORD.

25 ' "This is what the Sovereign LORD says: when I gather the people of Israel from the nations where they have been scattered, I will be proved holy through them in the sight of the nations. Then they will live in their own land, which I gave to my servant Jacob. 26 They will live there in safety and will build houses and plant vineyards; they

---

a 13 The precise identification of some of these precious stones is uncertain.   *b* 13 The meaning of the Hebrew for this phrase is uncertain.

will live in safety when I inflict punishment on all their neighbours who maligned them. Then they will know that I am the LORD their God."'

A prophecy against Egypt

Judgment on Pharaoh

29 In the tenth year, in the tenth month on the twelfth day, the word of the LORD came to me: ²'Son of man, set your face against Pharaoh king of Egypt and prophesy against him and against all Egypt. ³Speak to him and say: "This is what the Sovereign LORD says:

'"I am against you, Pharaoh king of Egypt,
  you great monster lying among your streams.
You say, 'The Nile belongs to me;
  I made it for myself.'
⁴But I will put hooks in your jaws
  and make the fish of your streams stick to your scales.
I will pull you out from among your streams,
  with all the fish sticking to your scales.
⁵I will leave you in the desert,
  you and all the fish of your streams.
You will fall on the open field
  and not be gathered or picked up.
I will give you as food
  to the beasts of the earth and the birds of the sky.

⁶Then all who live in Egypt will know that I am the LORD.

'"You have been a staff of reed for the house of Israel. ⁷When they grasped you with their hands, you splintered and you tore open their shoulders; when they leaned on you, you broke and their backs were wrenched.[a]

⁸'"Therefore this is what the Sovereign LORD says: I will bring a sword against you and kill your people and their animals. ⁹Egypt will become a desolate wasteland. Then they will know that I am the LORD.

'"Because you said, 'The Nile is mine; I made it,' ¹⁰therefore I am against you and against your streams, and I will make the land of Egypt a ruin and a desolate waste from Migdol to Aswan, as far as the border of Cush.[b] ¹¹No foot will pass through it, neither people nor animals; no-one will live there for forty years. ¹²I will make the land of Egypt desolate among devastated lands, and her cities will lie desolate for forty years among ruined cities. And I will disperse the Egyptians among the nations and scatter them through the countries.

¹³'"Yet this is what the Sovereign LORD says: at the end of forty years I will gather the Egyptians from the nations where they were scattered. ¹⁴I will bring them back from captivity and return them to Upper Egypt, the land of their ancestry. There they will be a lowly kingdom. ¹⁵It will be the lowliest of kingdoms and will never again exalt itself above the other nations. I will make it so weak that it will never again rule over the nations. ¹⁶Egypt will no longer be a source of confidence for the people of Israel but will be a reminder of their sin in turning to her for help. Then they will know that I am the Sovereign LORD."'

Nebuchadnezzar's reward

¹⁷In the twenty-seventh year, in the first month on the first day, the word of the LORD came to me: ¹⁸'Son of man, Nebuchadnezzar king of Babylon drove his army in a hard campaign against Tyre; every head was rubbed bare and every shoulder made raw. Yet he and his army got no reward from the campaign he led against Tyre. ¹⁹Therefore this is what the Sovereign LORD says: I am going to give Egypt to Nebuchadnezzar king of Babylon, and he will carry off its wealth. He will loot and plunder the land as pay for his army. ²⁰I have given him Egypt as a reward for his efforts because he and his army did it for me, declares the Sovereign LORD.

²¹'On that day I will make a horn[c] grow for the house of Israel, and I will open your mouth among them. Then they will know that I am the LORD.'

---

[a] 7 Syriac (see also Septuagint and Vulgate); Hebrew *and you caused their backs to stand*   [b] 10 That is, the upper Nile region   [c] 21 *Horn* here symbolises strength.

A lament over Egypt

30 The word of the LORD came to me: ²"Son of man, prophesy and say: 'This is what the Sovereign LORD says:

"'Wail and say,
  'Alas for that day!'
³For the day is near,
  the day of the LORD is near—
a day of clouds,
  a time of doom for the nations.
⁴A sword will come against Egypt,
  and anguish will come upon Cush.*ᵃ*
When the slain fall in Egypt,
  her wealth will be carried away
  and her foundations torn down.

⁵Cush and Libya, Lydia and all Arabia, Kub and the people of the covenant land will fall by the sword along with Egypt.

⁶"This is what the LORD says:

"'The allies of Egypt will fall
  and her proud strength will fail.
From Migdol to Aswan
  they will fall by the sword within her,
    declares the Sovereign LORD.
⁷"'They will be desolate
  among desolate lands,
and their cities will lie
  among ruined cities.
⁸Then they will know that I am the LORD,
  when I set fire to Egypt
  and all her helpers are crushed.

⁹"'On that day messengers will go out from me in ships to frighten Cush out of her complacency. Anguish will take hold of them on the day of Egypt's doom, for it is sure to come.

¹⁰"'This is what the Sovereign LORD says:

"'I will put an end to the hordes of Egypt
  by the hand of Nebuchadnezzar king of Babylon.
¹¹He and his army—the most ruthless of nations—
  will be brought in to destroy the land.
They will draw their swords against Egypt
  and fill the land with the slain.
¹²I will dry up the waters of the Nile
  and sell the land to an evil nation;
by the hand of foreigners
  I will lay waste the land and everything in it.

I the LORD have spoken.

¹³"This is what the Sovereign LORD says:

"'I will destroy the idols
  and put an end to the images in Memphis.
No longer will there be a prince in Egypt,
  and I will spread fear throughout the land.
¹⁴I will lay waste Upper Egypt,
  set fire to Zoan
  and inflict punishment on Thebes.
¹⁵I will pour out my wrath on Pelusium,
  the stronghold of Egypt,
  and wipe out the hordes of Thebes.
¹⁶I will set fire to Egypt;
  Pelusium will writhe in agony.
Thebes will be taken by storm;
  Memphis will be in constant distress.
¹⁷The young men of Heliopolis and Bubastis
  will fall by the sword,
  and the cities themselves will go into captivity.
¹⁸Dark will be the day at Tahpanhes
  when I break the yoke of Egypt;
  there her proud strength will come to an end.
She will be covered with clouds,
  and her villages will go into captivity.
¹⁹So I will inflict punishment on Egypt,
  and they will know that I am the LORD."'

Pharaoh's arms are broken

²⁰In the eleventh year, in the first month on the seventh day, the word of the LORD came to me: ²¹'Son of man, I have broken the arm of Pharaoh king of Egypt. It has not been bound up to be healed or put in a splint so that it may become strong enough to hold a sword. ²²Therefore this is what the Sovereign LORD says: I am against Pharaoh king of Egypt. I will break both his arms, the good arm as well as the broken one, and make the sword fall from his hand. ²³I will disperse the Egyptians among the nations and scatter

---

ᵃ 4 That is, the upper Nile region; also in verses 5 and 9

> **People and Places**
>
> **Pharaoh**
> Ezekiel 30:21
> The king of Egypt was given the title pharaoh, a term probably meaning 'the great house' or 'the great double house'. The Egyptians believed that the pharaoh was a god, the incarnation of the god Horus and the son of the god Ra. The pharaoh was in complete control of the land; his word was law.

them through the countries. 24I will strengthen the arms of the king of Babylon and put my sword in his hand, but I will break the arms of Pharaoh, and he will groan before him like someone mortally wounded. 25I will strengthen the arms of the king of Babylon, but the arms of Pharaoh will fall limp. Then they will know that I am the LORD, when I put my sword into the hand of the king of Babylon and he brandishes it against Egypt. 26I will disperse the Egyptians among the nations and scatter them through the countries. Then they will know that I am the LORD.'

Pharaoh as a felled cedar of Lebanon

31 In the eleventh year, in the third month on the first day, the word of the LORD came to me: 2'Son of man, say to Pharaoh king of Egypt and to his hordes:

' "Who can be compared with you in majesty?
3Consider Assyria, once a cedar in Lebanon,
   with beautiful branches
      overshadowing the forest;
   it towered on high,
      its top above the thick foliage.
4The waters nourished it,
   deep springs made it grow tall;
   their streams flowed
      all around its base
   and sent their channels
      to all the trees of the field.
5So it towered higher
      than all the trees of the field;
   its boughs increased
      and its branches grew long,
      spreading because of abundant waters.
6All the birds of the sky
      nested in its boughs,
   all the wild animals
      gave birth under its branches;
   all the great nations
      lived in its shade.
7It was majestic in beauty,
      with its spreading boughs,
   for its roots went down
      to abundant waters.
8The cedars in the garden of God
      could not rival it,
   nor could the junipers
      equal its boughs,
   nor could the plane trees
      compare with its branches—
   no tree in the garden of God
      could match its beauty.
9I made it beautiful
      with abundant branches,
   the envy of all the trees of Eden
      in the garden of God.

10' "Therefore this is what the Sovereign LORD says: because the great cedar towered over the thick foliage, and because it was proud of its height, 11I gave it into the hands of the ruler of the nations, for him to deal with according to its wickedness. I cast it aside, 12and the most ruthless of foreign nations cut it down and left it. Its boughs fell on the mountains and in all the valleys; its branches lay broken in all the ravines of the land. All the nations of the earth came out from under its shade and left it. 13All the birds settled on the fallen tree, and all the wild animals lived among its branches. 14Therefore no other trees by the waters are ever to tower proudly on high, lifting their tops above the thick foliage. No other trees so well-watered are ever to reach such a height; they are all destined for death, for the earth below, among mortals who go down to the realm of the dead.

15' "This is what the Sovereign LORD says: on the day it was brought down to the realm of the dead I covered the deep springs with mourning for it; I held back its streams, and its abundant waters were restrained. Because of it I clothed Lebanon with gloom, and all the trees of the field withered away. ⁱ⁶I made the nations tremble at the sound of its fall when I brought it down to the realm of the dead to be with those who go down to the pit. Then all the trees of Eden, the choicest and best of Lebanon, the well-watered trees, were consoled in the earth below. ¹⁷They too, like the great cedar, had gone down to the realm of the dead, to those killed by the sword, along with the armed men who lived in its shade among the nations.

¹⁸ "Which of the trees of Eden can be compared with you in splendour and majesty? Yet you, too, will be brought down with the trees of Eden to the earth below; you will lie among the uncircumcised, with those killed by the sword.

'"This is Pharaoh and all his hordes, declares the Sovereign LORD.'"

A lament over Pharaoh

32 In the twelfth year, in the twelfth month on the first day, the word of the LORD came to me: ²'Son of man, take up a lament concerning Pharaoh king of Egypt and say to him:

'"You are like a lion among the nations;
  you are like a monster in the seas
thrashing about in your streams,
  churning the water with your feet
  and muddying the streams.

³' "This is what the Sovereign LORD says:

'"With a great throng of people
  I will cast my net over you,
  and they will haul you up in my net.
⁴I will throw you on the land
  and hurl you on the open field.
I will let all the birds of the sky settle on
    you
  and all the wild animals gorge
    themselves on you.
⁵I will spread your flesh on the mountains
  and fill the valleys with your remains.
⁶I will drench the land with your flowing
    blood
  all the way to the mountains,
  and the ravines will be filled with your
    flesh.
⁷When I snuff you out, I will cover the
    heavens
  and darken their stars;
I will cover the sun with a cloud,
  and the moon will not give its light.
⁸All the shining lights in the heavens
  I will darken over you;
I will bring darkness over your land,
          declares the Sovereign LORD.
⁹I will trouble the hearts of many peoples
  when I bring about your destruction
    among the nations,
  among*ᵃ* lands you have not known.
¹⁰I will cause many peoples to be appalled at
    you,
  and their kings will shudder with
    horror because of you
  when I brandish my sword before
    them.
On the day of your downfall
  each of them will tremble
  every moment for his life.

¹¹' "For this is what the Sovereign LORD says:

'"The sword of the king of Babylon
  will come against you.
¹²I will cause your hordes to fall
  by the swords of mighty men—
  the most ruthless of all nations.
They will shatter the pride of Egypt,
  and all her hordes will be overthrown.
¹³I will destroy all her cattle
  from beside abundant waters
no longer to be stirred by human feet
  or muddied by the hooves of cattle.
¹⁴Then I will let her waters settle
  and make her streams flow like oil,
          declares the Sovereign LORD.
¹⁵When I make Egypt desolate
  and strip the land of everything in it,
when I strike down all who live there,
  then they will know that I am the
    LORD."

---

*ᵃ*9 Hebrew; Septuagint *bring you into captivity among the nations,* / *to*

16'This is the lament they will chant for her. The daughters of the nations will chant it; for Egypt and all her hordes they will chant it, declares the Sovereign LORD.'

Egypt's descent into the realm of the dead

17In the twelfth year, on the fifteenth day of the month, the word of the LORD came to me: 18'Son of man, wail for the hordes of Egypt and consign to the earth below both her and the daughters of mighty nations, along with those who go down to the pit. 19Say to them, "Are you more favoured than others? Go down and be laid among the uncircumcised." 20They will fall among those killed by the sword. The sword is drawn; let her be dragged off with all her hordes. 21From within the realm of the dead the mighty leaders will say of Egypt and her allies, "They have come down and they lie with the uncircumcised, with those killed by the sword."

22'Assyria is there with her whole army; she is surrounded by the graves of all her slain, all who have fallen by the sword. 23Their graves are in the depths of the pit and her army lies around her grave. All who had spread terror in the land of the living are slain, fallen by the sword.

24'Elam is there, with all her hordes around her grave. All of them are slain, fallen by the sword. All who had spread terror in the land of the living went down uncircumcised to the earth below. They bear their shame with those who go down to the pit. 25A bed is made for her among the slain, with all her hordes around her grave. All of them are uncircumcised, killed by the sword. Because their terror had spread in the land of the living, they bear their shame with those who go down to the pit; they are laid among the slain.

26'Meshek and Tubal are there, with all their hordes around their graves. All of them are uncircumcised, killed by the sword because they spread their terror in the land of the living. 27But they do not lie with the fallen warriors of old,[a] who went down to the realm of the dead with their weapons of war—their swords placed under their heads and their shields[b] resting on their bones—though these warriors also had terrorised the land of the living.

28'You too, Pharaoh, will be broken and will lie among the uncircumcised, with those killed by the sword.

29'Edom is there, her kings and all her princes; despite their power, they are laid with those killed by the sword. They lie with the uncircumcised, with those who go down to the pit.

30'All the princes of the north and all the Sidonians are there; they went down with the slain in disgrace despite the terror caused by their power. They lie uncircumcised with those killed by the sword and bear their shame with those who go down to the pit.

31'Pharaoh—he and all his army—will see them and he will be consoled for all his hordes that were killed by the sword, declares the Sovereign LORD. 32Although I allowed him to spread terror in the land of the living, Pharaoh and all his hordes will be laid among the uncircumcised, with those killed by the sword, declares the Sovereign LORD.'

Renewal of Ezekiel's call as watchman

33 The word of the LORD came to me: 2'Son of man, speak to your people and say to them: "When I bring the sword against a land, and the people of the land choose one of their men and make him their watchman, 3and he sees the sword coming against the land and blows the trumpet to warn the people, 4then if anyone hears the trumpet but does not heed the warning and the sword comes and takes their life, their blood will be on their own head. 5Since they heard the sound of the trumpet but did not heed the warning, their blood will be on their own head. If they had heeded the warning, they would have saved themselves. 6But if the watchman sees the sword coming and does not blow the trumpet to warn the people and the sword comes and takes someone's life, that person's life will be taken because

---

[a] 27 Septuagint; Hebrew *warriors who were uncircumcised* Masoretic Text *punishment*   [b] 27 Probable reading of the original Hebrew text;

Watchman
Ezekiel 33:2

Because of the dangers of being raided, cities, villages and even farms would have watchmen. Their job was to look out for anything suspicious or hostile and to warn people of any coming danger. Watchmen would usually be up on the city wall or in a watchtower, to enable them to see threats in plenty of time.

of their sin, but I will hold the watchman accountable for their blood."

7'Son of man, I have made you a watchman for the house of Israel; so hear the word I speak and give them warning from me. 8When I say to the wicked, "You wicked people, you will surely die," and you do not speak out to dissuade them from their ways, those wicked people will die for[a] their sins, and I will hold you accountable for their blood. 9But if you do warn the wicked to turn from their ways and they do not do so, they will die for their sins, though you yourself will be saved.

10'Son of man, say to the house of Israel, "This is what you are saying: 'Our offences and sins weigh us down, and we are wasting away because of[b] them. How then can we live?'" 11Say to them, "As surely as I live, declares the Sovereign LORD, I take no pleasure in the death of the wicked, but rather that they turn from their ways and live. Turn! Turn from your evil ways! Why will you die, house of Israel?"

12'Therefore, son of man, say to your people, "If someone who is righteous disobeys, that person's former righteousness will count for nothing. And if someone who is wicked repents, that person's former wickedness will not bring condemnation. The righteous, if they sin, will not be allowed to live because of their former righteousness." 13If I tell the righteous that they will surely live, but then they trust in their righteousness and do evil, none of the righteous things they have done will be remembered; they will die for the evil they have done. 14And if I say to the wicked, "You will surely die," but they then turn away from their sins and do what is just and right— 15if they give back what they took in pledge for a loan, return what they have stolen, follow the decrees that give life, and do no evil, they will surely live; they will not die. 16None of the sins they have committed will be remembered against them. They have done what is just and right; they will surely live.

17'Yet your people say, "The way of the Lord is not just." But it is their way that is not just. 18If the righteous turn from their righteousness and do evil, they will die for it. 19And if the wicked turn away from their wickedness and do what is just and right, they will live by doing so. 20Yet you say, house of Israel, "The way of the Lord is not just." But I will judge each of you according to your own ways.'

Jerusalem's fall explained

21In the twelfth year of our exile, in the tenth month on the fifth day, a man who had escaped from Jerusalem came to me and said, 'The city has fallen!' 22Now the evening before the man arrived, the hand of the LORD was on me, and he opened my mouth before the man came to me in the morning. So my mouth was opened and I was no longer silent.

23Then the word of the LORD came to me: 24'Son of man, the people living in those ruins in the land of Israel are saying, "Abraham was only one man, yet he possessed the land. But we are many; surely the land has been given to us as our possession." 25Therefore say to them, "This is what the Sovereign LORD says: since you eat meat with the blood still in it and look to your idols and shed blood, should you then possess the land? 26You rely on your sword, you do detestable

---

[a] 8 Or in; also in verse 9   [b] 10 Or away in

things, and each of you defiles his neighbour's wife. Should you then possess the land?"

²⁷'Say this to them: "This is what the Sovereign LORD says: as surely as I live, those who are left in the ruins will fall by the sword, those out in the country I will give to the wild animals to be devoured, and those in strongholds and caves will die of a plague. ²⁸I will make the land a desolate waste, and her proud strength will come to an end, and the mountains of Israel will become desolate so that no-one will cross them. ²⁹Then they will know that I am the LORD, when I have made the land a desolate waste because of all the detestable things they have done."

³⁰'As for you, son of man, your people are talking together about you by the walls and at the doors of the houses, saying to each other, "Come and hear the message that has come from the LORD." ³¹My people come to you, as they usually do, and sit before you to hear your words, but they do not put them into practice. Their mouths speak of love, but their hearts are greedy for unjust gain. ³²Indeed, to them you are nothing more than one who sings love songs with a beautiful voice and plays an instrument well, for they hear your words but do not put them into practice.

³³'When all this comes true—and it surely will—then they will know that a prophet has been among them.'

The LORD will be Israel's shepherd

34 The word of the LORD came to me: ²'Son of man, prophesy against the shepherds of Israel; prophesy and say to them: "This is what the Sovereign LORD says: woe to you shepherds of Israel who only take care of yourselves! Should not shepherds take care of the flock? ³You eat the curds, clothe yourselves with the wool and slaughter the choice animals, but you do not take care of the flock. ⁴You have not strengthened the weak or healed those who are ill or bound up the injured. You have not brought back the strays or searched for the lost. You have ruled them harshly and brutally. ⁵So they were scattered because there was no shepherd, and when they were scattered they became food for all the wild animals. ⁶My sheep wandered over all the mountains and on every high hill. They were scattered over the whole earth, and no-one searched or looked for them.

⁷' "Therefore, you shepherds, hear the word of the LORD: ⁸as surely as I live, declares the Sovereign LORD, because my flock lacks a shepherd and so has been plundered and has become food for all the wild animals, and because my shepherds did not search for my flock but cared for themselves rather than for my flock, ⁹therefore, you shepherds, hear the word of the LORD: ¹⁰this is what the Sovereign LORD says: I am against the shepherds and will hold them accountable for my flock. I will remove them from tending the flock so that the shepherds can no longer feed themselves. I will rescue my flock from their mouths, and it will no longer be food for them.

¹¹' "For this is what the Sovereign LORD says: I myself will search for my sheep and look after them. ¹²As shepherds look after their scattered flocks when they are with them, so will I look after my sheep. I will rescue them from all the places where they were scattered on a day of clouds and darkness. ¹³I will bring them out from the nations and gather them from the countries, and I will bring them into their own land. I will pasture them on the mountains of Israel, in the ravines and in all the settlements in the land. ¹⁴I will tend them in a good pasture, and the mountain heights of Israel will be their grazing land. There they will lie down in good grazing land, and there they will feed in a rich pasture on the mountains of Israel. ¹⁵I myself will tend my sheep and make them lie down, declares the Sovereign LORD. ¹⁶I will search for the lost and bring back the strays. I will bind up the injured and strengthen the weak, but the sleek and the strong I will destroy. I will shepherd the flock with justice.

¹⁷' "As for you, my flock, this is what the Sovereign LORD says: I will judge between one sheep and another, and between rams and goats. ¹⁸Is it not enough for you to feed on the good pasture? Must you also trample the rest of your pasture with your feet? Is it not enough for you to drink clear water?

Must you also muddy the rest with your feet? ¹⁹Must my flock feed on what you have trampled and drink what you have muddied with your feet?

²⁰'"Therefore this is what the Sovereign LORD says to them: see, I myself will judge between the fat sheep and the lean sheep. ²¹Because you shove with flank and shoulder, butting all the weak sheep with your horns until you have driven them away, ²²I will save my flock, and they will no longer be plundered. I will judge between one sheep and another. ²³I will place over them one shepherd, my servant David, and he will tend them; he will tend them and be their shepherd. ²⁴I the LORD will be their God, and my servant David will be prince among them. I the LORD have spoken.

²⁵'"I will make a covenant of peace with them and rid the land of savage beasts so that they may live in the wilderness and sleep in the forests in safety. ²⁶I will make them and the places surrounding my hill a blessing.ᵃ I will send down showers in season; there will be showers of blessing. ²⁷The trees will yield their fruit and the ground will yield its crops; the people will be secure in their land. They will know that I am the LORD, when I break the bars of their yoke and rescue them from the hands of those who enslaved them. ²⁸They will no longer be plundered by the nations, nor will wild animals devour them. They will live in safety, and no-one will make them afraid. ²⁹I will provide for them a land renowned for its crops, and they will no longer be victims of famine in the land or bear the scorn of the nations. ³⁰Then they will know that I, the LORD their God, am with them and that they, the house of Israel, are my people, declares the Sovereign LORD. ³¹You are my sheep, the sheep of my pasture, and I am your God, declares the Sovereign LORD."'

A prophecy against Edom

35 The word of the LORD came to me: ²'Son of man, set your face against Mount Seir; prophesy against it ³and say: "This is what the Sovereign LORD says: I am against you, Mount Seir, and I will stretch out my hand against you and make you a desolate waste. ⁴I will turn your towns into ruins and you will be desolate. Then you will know that I am the LORD.

⁵'"Because you harboured an ancient hostility and delivered the Israelites over to the sword at the time of their calamity, the time their punishment reached its climax, ⁶therefore as surely as I live, declares the Sovereign LORD, I will give you over to bloodshed and it will pursue you. Since you did not hate bloodshed, bloodshed will pursue you. ⁷I will make Mount Seir a desolate waste and cut off from it all who come and go. ⁸I will fill your mountains with the slain; those killed by the sword will fall on your hills and in your valleys and in all your ravines. ⁹I will make you desolate for ever; your towns will not be inhabited. Then you will know that I am the LORD.

¹⁰'"Because you have said, 'These two nations and countries will be ours and we will take possession of them,' even though I the LORD was there, ¹¹therefore as surely as I live, declares the Sovereign LORD, I will treat you in accordance with the anger and jealousy you showed in your hatred of them and I will make myself known among them when I judge you. ¹²Then you will know that I the LORD have heard all the contemptible things you have said against the mountains of Israel. You said, 'They have been laid waste and have been given over to us to devour.' ¹³You boasted against me and spoke against me without restraint, and I heard it. ¹⁴This is what the Sovereign LORD says: while the whole earth rejoices, I will make you desolate. ¹⁵Because you rejoiced when the inheritance of the house of Israel became desolate, that is how I will treat you. You will be desolate, Mount Seir, you and all of Edom. Then they will know that I am the LORD."'

Hope for the mountains of Israel

36 'Son of man, prophesy to the mountains of Israel and say, "Mountains of Israel, hear the word of the LORD. ²This is what the Sovereign LORD

ᵃ 26 Or *I will cause them and the places surrounding my hill to be named in blessings* (see Gen. 48:20); or *I will cause them and the places surrounding my hill to be seen as blessed* says: the enemy said of you, 'Aha! The ancient heights have become our possession.' " ³Therefore prophesy and say, "This is what the Sovereign LORD says: because they ravaged and crushed you from every side so that you became the possession of the rest of the nations and the object of people's malicious talk and slander, ⁴therefore, mountains of Israel, hear the word of the Sovereign LORD: this is what the Sovereign LORD says to the mountains and hills, to the ravines and valleys, to the desolate ruins and the deserted towns that have been plundered and ridiculed by the rest of the nations around you— ⁵this is what the Sovereign LORD says: in my burning zeal I have spoken against the rest of the nations, and against Edom, for with glee and with malice in their hearts they made my land their own possession so that they might plunder its pasture-land." ⁶Therefore prophesy concerning the land of Israel and say to the mountains and hills, to the ravines and valleys: "This is what the Sovereign LORD says: I speak in my jealous wrath because you have suffered the scorn of the nations. ⁷Therefore this is what the Sovereign LORD says: I swear with uplifted hand that the nations around you will also suffer scorn.

⁸ "But you, mountains of Israel, will produce branches and fruit for my people Israel, for they will soon come home. ⁹I am concerned for you and will look on you with favour; you will be ploughed and sown, ¹⁰and I will multiply the number of people living on you, even the whole house of Israel. The towns will be inhabited and the ruins rebuilt. ¹¹I will increase the number of people and animals living on you, and they will be fruitful and become numerous. I will settle people on you as in the past and will make you prosper more than before. Then you will know that I am the LORD. ¹²I will cause people, my people Israel, to live on you. They will possess you, and you will be their inheritance; you will never again deprive them of their children.

¹³' "This is what the Sovereign LORD says: because some say to you, 'You devour your people and deprive your nation of its children,' ¹⁴therefore you will no longer devour people or make your nation childless, declares the Sovereign LORD. ¹⁵No longer will I make you hear the taunts of the nations, and no longer will you suffer the scorn of the peoples or cause your nation to fall, declares the Sovereign LORD." '

Israel's restoration assured

¹⁶Again the word of the LORD came to me: ¹⁷'Son of man, when the people of Israel were living in their own land, they defiled it by their conduct and their actions. Their conduct was like a woman's monthly uncleanness in my sight. ¹⁸So I poured out my wrath on them because they had shed blood in the land and because they had defiled it with their idols. ¹⁹I dispersed them among the nations, and they were scattered through the countries; I judged them according to their conduct and their actions. ²⁰And wherever they went among the nations they profaned my holy name, for it was said of them, "These are the LORD's people, and yet they had to leave his land." ²¹I had concern for my holy name, which the house of Israel profaned among the nations where they had gone.

²²'Therefore say to the house of Israel, "This is what the Sovereign LORD says: it is not for your sake, house of Israel, that I am going to do these things, but for the sake of my holy name, which you have profaned among the nations where you have gone. ²³I will show the holiness of my great name, which has been profaned among the nations, the name you have profaned among them. Then the nations will know that I am the LORD, declares the Sovereign LORD, when I am proved holy through you before their eyes.

²⁴' "For I will take you out of the nations; I will gather you from all the countries and bring you back into your own land. ²⁵I will sprinkle clean water on you, and you will be clean; I will cleanse you from all your impurities and from all your idols. ²⁶I will give you a new heart and put a new spirit in you; I will remove from you your heart of stone and give you a heart of flesh. ²⁷And I will put my Spirit in you and move you to follow my decrees and be careful to keep my laws. ²⁸Then you will live in the land I gave your ancestors; you will be my people, and I

will be your God. ²⁹I will save you from all your uncleanness. I will call for the corn and make it plentiful and will not bring famine upon you. ³⁰I will increase the fruit of the trees and the crops of the field, so that you will no longer suffer disgrace among the nations because of famine. ³¹Then you will remember your evil ways and wicked deeds, and you will loathe yourselves for your sins and detestable practices. ³²I want you to know that I am not doing this for your sake, declares the Sovereign LORD. Be ashamed and disgraced for your conduct, house of Israel!

³³'"This is what the Sovereign LORD says: on the day I cleanse you from all your sins, I will resettle your towns, and the ruins will be rebuilt. ³⁴The desolate land will be cultivated instead of lying desolate in the sight of all who pass through it. ³⁵They will say, 'This land that was laid waste has become like the garden of Eden; the cities that were lying in ruins, desolate and destroyed, are now fortified and inhabited.' ³⁶Then the nations around you that remain will know that I the LORD have rebuilt what was destroyed and have replanted what was desolate. I the LORD have spoken, and I will do it."

³⁷'This is what the Sovereign LORD says: once again I will yield to the plea of the house of Israel and do this for them: I will make their people as numerous as sheep, ³⁸as numerous as the flocks for offerings at Jerusalem during her appointed festivals. So will the ruined cities be filled with flocks of people. Then they will know that I am the LORD.'

The valley of dry bones

37 The hand of the LORD was on me, and he brought me out by the Spirit of the LORD and set me in the middle of a valley; it was full of bones. ²He led me to and fro among them, and I saw a great many bones on the floor of the valley, bones that were very dry. ³He asked me, 'Son of man, can these bones live?'

I said, 'Sovereign LORD, you alone know.'

⁴Then he said to me, 'Prophesy to these bones and say to them, "Dry bones, hear the word of the LORD! ⁵This is what the Sovereign LORD says to these bones: I will make breath^a enter you, and you will come to life. ⁶I will attach tendons to you and make flesh come upon you and cover you with skin; I will put breath in you, and you will come to life. Then you will know that I am the LORD."'

⁷So I prophesied as I was commanded. And as I was prophesying, there was a noise, a rattling sound, and the bones came together, bone to bone. ⁸I looked, and tendons and flesh appeared on them and skin covered them, but there was no breath in them.

⁹Then he said to me, 'Prophesy to the breath; prophesy, son of man, and say to it, "This is what the Sovereign LORD says: come, breath, from the four winds and breathe into these slain, that they may live."' ¹⁰So I prophesied as he commanded me, and breath entered them; they came to life and stood up on their feet—a vast army.

¹¹Then he said to me: 'Son of man, these bones are the whole house of Israel. They say, "Our bones are dried up and our hope is gone; we are cut off." ¹²Therefore prophesy and say to them: "This is what the Sovereign LORD says: my people, I am going to open your graves and bring you up from them; I will bring you back to the land of Israel. ¹³Then you, my people, will know that I am the LORD, when I open your graves and bring you up from them. ¹⁴I will put my Spirit in you and you will live, and I will

making Connections

Breath
Ezekiel 37:1
The Hebrew word ruach can mean 'breath', 'wind' or 'spirit'. In this vision of dry bones coming back to life, all three meanings are used.

---

^{a} 5 The Hebrew for this word can also mean *wind* or *spirit* (see verses 6-14).

settle you in your own land. Then you will know that I the LORD have spoken, and I have done it, declares the LORD."'

One nation under one king

15 The word of the LORD came to me: 16'Son of man, take a stick of wood and write on it, "Belonging to Judah and the Israelites associated with him." Then take another stick of wood, and write on it, "Belonging to Joseph (that is, to Ephraim) and all the house of Israel associated with him." 17 Join them together into one stick so that they will become one in your hand.

18'When your people ask you, "Won't you tell us what you mean by this?" 19 say to them, "This is what the Sovereign LORD says: I am going to take the stick of Joseph—which is in Ephraim's hand—and of the Israelite tribes associated with him, and join it to Judah's stick. I will make them into a single stick of wood, and they will become one in my hand." 20 Hold before their eyes the sticks you have written on 21 and say to them, "This is what the Sovereign LORD says: I will take the Israelites out of the nations where they have gone. I will gather them from all around and bring them back into their own land. 22 I will make them one nation in the land, on the mountains of Israel. There will be one king over all of them and they will never again be two nations or be divided into two kingdoms. 23 They will no longer defile themselves with their idols and vile images or with any of their offences, for I will save them from all their sinful backsliding,^{a} and I will cleanse them. They will be my people, and I will be their God.

24' "My servant David will be king over them, and they will all have one shepherd. They will follow my laws and be careful to keep my decrees. 25 They will live in the land I gave to my servant Jacob, the land where your ancestors lived. They and their children and their children's children will live there for ever, and David my servant will be their prince for ever. 26 I will make a covenant of peace with them; it will be an everlasting covenant. I will establish them and increase their numbers, and I will put my sanctuary among them for ever. 27 My dwelling-place will be with them; I will be their God, and they will be my people. 28 Then the nations will know that I the LORD make Israel holy, when my sanctuary is among them for ever."'

The LORD's great victory over the nations

38 The word of the LORD came to me: 2'Son of man, set your face against Gog, of the land of Magog, the chief prince of^b Meshek and Tubal; prophesy against him 3 and say: "This is what the Sovereign LORD says: I am against you, Gog, chief prince of^c Meshek and Tubal. 4 I will turn you around, put hooks in your jaws and bring you out with your whole army—your horses, your horsemen fully armed, and a great horde with large and small shields, all of them brandishing their swords. 5 Persia, Cush^d and Put will be with them, all with shields and helmets, 6 also Gomer with all its troops, and Beth Togarmah from the far north with all its troops—the many nations with you.

7' "Get ready; be prepared, you and all the hordes gathered about you, and take command of them. 8 After many days you will be called to arms. In future years you will invade a land that has recovered from war, whose people were gathered from many nations to the mountains of Israel, which had long been desolate. They had been brought out from the nations, and now all of them live in safety. 9 You and all your troops and the many nations with you will go up, advancing like a storm; you will be like a cloud covering the land.

10' "This is what the Sovereign LORD says: on that day thoughts will come into your mind and you will devise an evil scheme. 11 You will say, 'I will invade a land of unwalled villages; I will attack a peaceful and unsuspecting people—all of them living without walls and without gates and bars. 12 I will plunder and loot and turn my hand against the resettled ruins and the people gathered from the nations, rich in livestock and goods, living at the centre of

---

^{a} 23 Many Hebrew manuscripts (see also Septuagint); most Hebrew manuscripts *all their dwelling-places where they sinned* ^{b} 2 Or *the prince of Rosh,* ^{c} 3 Or *Gog, prince of Rosh,* ^{d} 5 That is, the upper Nile region the land.'[a] ¹³Sheba and Dedan and the merchants of Tarshish and all her villages[b] will say to you, 'Have you come to plunder? Have you gathered your hordes to loot, to carry off silver and gold, to take away livestock and goods and to seize much plunder?'"

¹⁴'Therefore, son of man, prophesy and say to Gog: "This is what the Sovereign LORD says: in that day, when my people Israel are living in safety, will you not take notice of it? ¹⁵You will come from your place in the far north, you and many nations with you, all of them riding on horses, a great horde, a mighty army. ¹⁶You will advance against my people Israel like a cloud that covers the land. In days to come, Gog, I will bring you against my land, so that the nations may know me when I am proved holy through you before their eyes.

¹⁷'"This is what the Sovereign LORD says: you are the one I spoke of in former days by my servants the prophets of Israel. At that time they prophesied for years that I would bring you against them. ¹⁸This is what will happen in that day: when Gog attacks the land of Israel, my hot anger will be aroused, declares the Sovereign LORD. ¹⁹In my zeal and fiery wrath I declare that at that time there shall be a great earthquake in the land of Israel. ²⁰The fish in the sea, the birds in the sky, the beasts of the field, every creature that moves along the ground, and all the people on the face of the earth will tremble at my presence. The mountains will be overturned, the cliffs will crumble and every wall will fall to the ground. ²¹I will summon a sword against Gog on all my mountains, declares the Sovereign LORD. Every man's sword will be against his fellow. ²²I will execute judgment on him with plague and bloodshed; I will pour down torrents of rain, hailstones and burning sulphur on him and on his troops and on the many nations with him. ²³And so I will show my greatness and my holiness, and I will make myself known in the sight of many nations. Then they will know that I am the LORD."

39 'Son of man, prophesy against Gog and say: "This is what the Sovereign LORD says: I am against you, Gog, chief prince of[c] Meshek and Tubal. ²I will turn you around and drag you along. I will bring you from the far north and send you against the mountains of Israel. ³Then I will strike your bow from your left hand and make your arrows drop from your right hand. ⁴On the mountains of Israel you will fall, you and all your troops and the nations with you. I will give you as food to all kinds of carrion birds and to the wild animals. ⁵You will fall in the open field, for I have spoken, declares the Sovereign LORD. ⁶I will send fire on Magog and on those who live in safety in the coastlands, and they will know that I am the LORD.

⁷'"I will make known my holy name among my people Israel. I will no longer let my holy name be profaned, and the nations will know that I the LORD am the Holy One in Israel. ⁸It is coming! It will surely take place, declares the Sovereign LORD. This is the day I have spoken of.

⁹'"Then those who live in the towns of Israel will go out and use the weapons for fuel and burn them up—the small and large shields, the bows and arrows, the war clubs and spears. For seven years they will use them for fuel. ¹⁰They will not need to gather wood from the fields or cut it from the forests, because they will use the weapons for fuel. And they will plunder those who plundered them and loot those who looted them, declares the Sovereign LORD.

¹¹'"On that day I will give Gog a burial place in Israel, in the valley of those who travel east of the Sea. It will block the way of travellers, because Gog and all his hordes will be buried there. So it will be called the Valley of Hamon Gog.[d]

¹²'"For seven months the house of Israel will be burying them in order to cleanse the land. ¹³All the people of the land will bury them, and the day I display my glory will be a memorable day for them, declares the Sovereign LORD. ¹⁴People will be continually employed in cleansing the land. They will spread out across the land and, along

---

[a] 12 The Hebrew for this phrase means *the navel of the earth*.   [b] 13 Or *her strong lions*   [c] 1 Or *Gog, prince of Rosh*,
[d] 11 *Hamon Gog* means *hordes of Gog*.

Sign of the times

Burying bodies
Ezekiel 39:12

The Law of Moses said that touching a dead body made you ritually unclean. The blood of dead bodies could make the whole land unclean (Numbers 35:33), and so it was important for the Israelites to bury all the bodies in order to cleanse the land again.

with others, they will bury any bodies that are lying on the ground.

'"After the seven months they will carry out a more detailed search. 15As they go through the land, anyone who sees a human bone will leave a marker beside it until the gravediggers bury it in the Valley of Hamon Gog, 16near a town called Hamonah.^{a} And so they will cleanse the land."

17'Son of man, this is what the Sovereign LORD says: call out to every kind of bird and all the wild animals: "Assemble and come together from all around to the sacrifice I am preparing for you, the great sacrifice on the mountains of Israel. There you will eat flesh and drink blood. 18You will eat the flesh of mighty men and drink the blood of the princes of the earth as if they were rams and lambs, goats and bulls—all of them fattened animals from Bashan. 19At the sacrifice I am preparing for you, you will eat fat till you are glutted and drink blood till you are drunk. 20At my table you will eat your fill of horses and riders, mighty men and soldiers of every kind," declares the Sovereign LORD.

21'I will display my glory among the nations, and all the nations will see the punishment I inflict and the hand I lay on them. 22From that day forward the house of Israel will know that I am the LORD their God. 23And the nations will know that the people of Israel went into exile for their sin, because they were unfaithful to me. So I hid my face from them and handed them over to their enemies, and they all fell by the sword. 24I dealt with them according to their uncleanness and their offences, and I hid my face from them.

25'Therefore this is what the Sovereign LORD says: I will now restore the fortunes of Jacob^b and will have compassion on all the people of Israel, and I will be zealous for my holy name. 26They will forget their shame and all the unfaithfulness they showed towards me when they lived in safety in their land with no-one to make them afraid. 27When I have brought them back from the nations and have gathered them from the countries of their enemies, I will be proved holy through them in the sight of many nations. 28Then they will know that I am the LORD their God, for though I sent them into exile among the nations, I will gather them to their own land, not leaving any behind. 29I will no longer hide my face from them, for I will pour out my Spirit on the house of Israel, declares the Sovereign LORD.'

The temple area restored

40 In the twenty-fifth year of our exile, at the beginning of the year, on the tenth of the month, in the fourteenth year after the fall of the city—on that very day the hand of the LORD was on me and he took me there. 2In visions of God he took me to the land of Israel and set me on a very high mountain, on whose south side were some buildings that looked like a city. 3He took me there, and I saw a man whose appearance was like bronze; he was standing in the gateway with a linen cord and a measuring rod in his hand. 4The man said to me, 'Son of man, look carefully and listen closely and pay attention to everything I am going to show you, for that is why you have been brought here. Tell the house of Israel everything you see.'

The east gate to the outer court

5I saw a wall completely surrounding the temple area. The length of the measuring

---

^{a}16 Hamonah means horde. ^{b}25 Or now bring Jacob back from captivity

IN OTHER WORDS

Cubit
Ezekiel 40:5

A cubit was a measurement of length and was about 45cm, the distance between the elbow and the fingertip. To confuse matters, there were obviously different sizes of cubit. Ezekiel refers to a 'long cubit' which was bigger than a standard cubit!

rod in the man's hand was six long cubits,[a] each of which was a cubit and a handbreadth. He measured the wall; it was one measuring rod thick and one rod high.

6Then he went to the east gate. He climbed its steps and measured the threshold of the gate; it was one rod deep. 7The alcoves for the guards were one rod long and one rod wide, and the projecting walls between the alcoves were five cubits[b] thick. And the threshold of the gate next to the portico facing the temple was one rod deep.

8Then he measured the portico of the gateway; 9it[c] was eight cubits[d] deep and its jambs were two cubits[e] thick. The portico of the gateway faced the temple.

10Inside the east gate were three alcoves on each side; the three had the same measurements, and the faces of the projecting walls on each side had the same measurements. 11Then he measured the width of the entrance of the gateway; it was ten cubits and its length was thirteen cubits.[f] 12In front of each alcove was a wall one cubit high, and the alcoves were six cubits square. 13Then he measured the gateway from the top of the rear wall of one alcove to the top of the opposite one; the distance was twenty-five cubits[g] from one parapet opening to the opposite one. 14He measured along the faces of the projecting walls all around the inside of the gateway—sixty cubits.[h] The measurement was up to the portico[i] facing the courtyard.[j] 15The distance from the entrance of the gateway to the far end of its portico was fifty cubits.[k] 16The alcoves and the projecting walls inside the gateway were surmounted by narrow parapet openings all round, as was the portico; the openings all round faced inward. The faces of the projecting walls were decorated with palm trees.

The outer court

17Then he brought me into the outer court. There I saw some rooms and a pavement that had been constructed all round the court; there were thirty rooms along the pavement. 18It abutted the sides of the gateways and was as wide as they were long; this was the lower pavement. 19Then he measured the distance from the inside of the lower gateway to the outside of the inner court; it was a hundred cubits[l] on the east side as well as on the north.

The north gate

20Then he measured the length and width of the north gate, leading into the outer court. 21Its alcoves—three on each side—its projecting walls and its portico had the same measurements as those of the first gateway. It was fifty cubits long and twenty-five cubits wide. 22Its openings, its portico and its palm tree decorations had the same measurements as those of the gate facing east. Seven steps led up to it, with its portico opposite them. 23There was a gate to the inner court facing the north gate, just as there was on the east. He measured from one gate to the opposite one; it was a hundred cubits.

The south gate

24Then he led me to the south side and I saw the south gate. He measured its jambs and

---

[a] 5 That is, about 3.1 metres; also in verse 12. The long cubit of about 52 centimetres is the basic unit of measurement of length throughout Ezekiel 40-48. [b] 7 That is, about 2.6 metres; also in verse 48 [c] 8, 9 Many Hebrew manuscripts, Septuagint, Vulgate and Syriac; most Hebrew manuscripts *gateway facing the temple; it was one rod deep.* 9Then *he measured the portico of the gateway; it* [d] 9 That is, about 4.2 metres [e] 9 That is, about 1 metre [f] 11 That is, about 5.2 metres wide and 6.8 metres long [g] 13 That is, about 13 metres; also in verses 21, 25, 29, 30, 33 and 36 [h] 14 That is, about 31 metres [i] 14 Septuagint; Hebrew *projecting wall* [j] 14 The meaning of the Hebrew for this verse is uncertain. [k] 15 That is, about 26 metres; also in verses 21, 25, 29, 33 and 36 [l] 19 That is, about 52 metres; also in verses 23, 27 and 47

its portico, and they had the same measurements as the others. ²⁵The gateway and its portico had narrow openings all round, like the openings of the others. It was fifty cubits long and twenty-five cubits wide. ²⁶Seven steps led up to it, with its portico opposite them; it had palm tree decorations on the faces of the projecting walls on each side. ²⁷The inner court also had a gate facing south, and he measured from this gate to the outer gate on the south side; it was a hundred cubits.

The gates to the inner court

²⁸Then he brought me into the inner court through the south gate, and he measured the south gate; it had the same measurements as the others. ²⁹Its alcoves, its projecting walls and its portico had the same measurements as the others. The gateway and its portico had openings all round. It was fifty cubits long and twenty-five cubits wide. ³⁰(The porticoes of the gateways around the inner court were twenty-five cubits wide and five cubits deep.) ³¹Its portico faced the outer court; palm trees decorated its jambs, and eight steps led up to it.

³²Then he brought me to the inner court on the east side, and he measured the gateway; it had the same measurements as the others. ³³Its alcoves, its projecting walls and its portico had the same measurements as the others. The gateway and its portico had openings all round. It was fifty cubits long and twenty-five cubits wide. ³⁴Its portico faced the outer court; palm trees decorated the jambs on either side, and eight steps led up to it.

³⁵Then he brought me to the north gate and measured it. It had the same measurements as the others, ³⁶as did its alcoves, its projecting walls and its portico, and it had openings all round. It was fifty cubits long and twenty-five cubits wide. ³⁷Its portico*ᵃ* faced the outer court; palm trees decorated the jambs on either side, and eight steps led up to it.

The rooms for preparing sacrifices

³⁸A room with a doorway was by the portico in each of the inner gateways, where the burnt offerings were washed. ³⁹In the portico of the gateway were two tables on each side, on which the burnt offerings, sin offerings*ᵇ* and guilt offerings were slaughtered. ⁴⁰By the outside wall of the portico of the gateway, near the steps at the entrance of the north gateway were two tables, and on the other side of the steps were two tables. ⁴¹So there were four tables on one side of the gateway and four on the other—eight tables in all—on which the sacrifices were slaughtered. ⁴²There were also four tables of dressed stone for the burnt offerings, each a cubit and a half long, a cubit and a half wide and a cubit high.*ᶜ* On them were placed the utensils for slaughtering the burnt offerings and the other sacrifices. ⁴³And double-pronged hooks, each a handbreadth*ᵈ* long, were attached to the wall all round. The tables were for the flesh of the offerings.

The rooms for the priests

⁴⁴Outside the inner gate, within the inner court, were two rooms, one*ᵉ* at the side of the north gate and facing south, and another at the side of the south*ᶠ* gate and facing north. ⁴⁵He said to me, 'The room facing south is for the priests who guard the temple, ⁴⁶and the room facing north is for the priests who guard the altar. These are the sons of Zadok, who are the only Levites who may draw near to the LORD to minister before him.'

⁴⁷Then he measured the court: it was square—a hundred cubits long and a hundred cubits wide. And the altar was in front of the temple.

The new temple

⁴⁸He brought me to the portico of the temple and measured the jambs of the portico; they were five cubits wide on either side. The width of the entrance was fourteen cubits*ᵍ* and its projecting walls were*ʰ* three cubits*ⁱ* wide on either side. ⁴⁹The

---

ᵃ 37 Septuagint (see also verses 31 and 34); Hebrew *jambs* *ᵇ* 39 Or *purification offerings* *ᶜ* 42 That is, about 78 centimetres long and wide and 52 centimetres high *ᵈ* 43 That is, about 9 centimetres *ᵉ* 44 Septuagint; Hebrew *were rooms for singers, which were* *ᶠ* 44 Septuagint; Hebrew *east* *ᵍ* 48 That is, about 7.3 metres *ʰ* 48 Septuagint; Hebrew *entrance was* *ⁱ* 48 That is, about 1.5 metres

making Connections

Inner sanctuary
Ezekiel 41:3

The inner sanctuary was the most holy place in the temple and was where the Ark of the Covenant was kept to symbolise God's presence. Ezekiel doesn't go with the man into this inner sanctuary because only the high priest was allowed in there once a year.

portico was twenty cubits*a* wide, and twelve*b* cubits*c* from front to back. It was reached by a flight of stairs,*d* and there were pillars on each side of the jambs.

41

Then the man brought me to the main hall and measured the jambs; the width of the jambs was six cubits*e* on each side.*f* **2** The entrance was ten cubits*g* wide, and the projecting walls on each side of it were five cubits*h* wide. He also measured the main hall; it was forty cubits long and twenty cubits wide.*i*

3 Then he went into the inner sanctuary and measured the jambs of the entrance; each was two cubits*j* wide. The entrance was six cubits wide, and the projecting walls on each side of it were seven cubits*k* wide. **4** And he measured the length of the inner sanctuary; it was twenty cubits, and its width was twenty cubits across the end of the main hall. He said to me, 'This is the Most Holy Place.'

5 Then he measured the wall of the temple; it was six cubits thick, and each side room round the temple was four cubits*l* wide. **6** The side rooms were on three levels, one above another, thirty on each level. There were ledges all round the wall of the temple to serve as supports for the side rooms, so that the supports were not inserted into the wall of the temple. **7** The side rooms all round the temple were wider at each successive level. The structure surrounding the temple was built in ascending stages, so that the rooms widened as one went upwards. A stairway went up from the lowest floor to the top floor through the middle floor.

8 I saw that the temple had a raised base all round it, forming the foundation of the side rooms. It was the length of the rod, six long cubits. **9** The outer wall of the side rooms was five cubits thick. The open area between the side rooms of the temple **10** and the ⌊priests'⌋ rooms was twenty cubits wide all round the temple. **11** There were entrances to the side rooms from the open area, one on the north and another on the south; and the base adjoining the open area was five cubits wide all round.

12 The building facing the temple courtyard on the west side was seventy cubits*m* wide. The wall of the building was five cubits thick all round, and its length was ninety cubits.*n*

13 Then he measured the temple; it was a hundred cubits*o* long, and the temple courtyard and the building with its walls were also a hundred cubits long. **14** The width of the temple courtyard on the east, including the front of the temple, was a hundred cubits.

15 Then he measured the length of the building facing the courtyard at the rear of the temple, including its galleries on each side; it was a hundred cubits.

The main hall, the inner sanctuary and the portico facing the court, **16** as well as the thresholds and the narrow windows and galleries round the three of them—everything beyond and including the threshold was covered with wood. The floor, the wall up to the windows, and the windows were

---

a 49 That is, about 10.4 metres   *b* 49 Septuagint; Hebrew *eleven*   *c* 49 That is, about 6.2 metres   *d* 49 Hebrew; Septuagint *Ten steps led up to it*   *e* 1 That is, about 3.1 metres; also in verses 3, 5 and 8   *f* 1 One Hebrew manuscript and Septuagint; most Hebrew manuscripts *side, the width of the tent*   *g* 2 That is, about 5.2 metres   *h* 2 That is, about 2.6 metres; also in verses 9, 11 and 12   *i* 2 That is, about 21 metres long and 10.4 metres wide   *j* 3 That is, about 1 metre; also in verse 22   *k* 3 That is, about 3.6 metres   *l* 5 That is, about about 2.1 metres   *m* 12 That is, about 36 metres   *n* 12 That is, about 47 metres   *o* 13 That is, about 52 metres; also in verses 14 and 15 covered. 17In the space above the outside of the entrance to the inner sanctuary and on the walls at regular intervals all round the inner and outer sanctuary 18were carved cherubim and palm trees. Palm trees alternated with cherubim. Each cherub had two faces: 19the face of a human being towards the palm tree on one side and the face of a lion towards the palm tree on the other. They were carved all round the whole temple. 20From the floor to the area above the entrance, cherubim and palm trees were carved on the wall of the main hall.

21The main hall had a rectangular doorframe, and the one at the front of the Most Holy Place was similar. 22There was a wooden altar three cubits^a high and two cubits square;^{b} its corners, its base^c and its sides were of wood. The man said to me, 'This is the table that is before the LORD.' 23Both the main hall and the Most Holy Place had double doors. 24Each door had two leaves—two hinged leaves for each door. 25And on the doors of the main hall were carved cherubim and palm trees like those carved on the walls, and there was a wooden overhang on the front of the portico. 26On the side walls of the portico were narrow windows with palm trees carved on each side. The side rooms of the temple also had overhangs.

The rooms for the priests

42 Then the man led me northward into the outer court and brought me to the rooms opposite the temple courtyard and opposite the outer wall on the north side. 2The building whose door faced north was a hundred cubits long and fifty cubits^d wide. 3Both in the section twenty cubits^e from the inner court and in the section opposite the pavement of the outer court, gallery faced gallery at the three levels. 4In front of the rooms was an inner passageway ten cubits wide and a hundred cubits^f long^g. Their doors were on the north. 5Now the upper rooms were narrower, for the galleries took more space from them than from the rooms on the lower and middle floors of the building. 6The rooms on the top floor had no pillars, as the courts had; so they were smaller in floor space than those on the lower and middle floors. 7There was an outer wall parallel to the rooms and the outer court; it extended in front of the rooms for fifty cubits. 8While the row of rooms on the side next to the outer court was fifty cubits long, the row on the side nearest the sanctuary was a hundred cubits long. 9The lower rooms had an entrance on the east side as one enters them from the outer court.

10On the south side^h along the length of the wall of the outer court, adjoining the temple courtyard and opposite the outer wall, were rooms 11with a passageway in front of them. These were like the rooms on the north; they had the same length and width, with similar exits and dimensions. Similar to the doorways on the north 12were the doorways of the rooms on the south. There was a doorway at the beginning of the passageway that was parallel to the corresponding wall extending eastward, by which one enters the rooms.

13Then he said to me, 'The north and south rooms facing the temple courtyard are the priests' rooms, where the priests who approach the LORD will eat the most holy offerings. There they will put the most holy offerings—the grain offerings, the sin offerings^i and the guilt offerings—for the place is holy. 14Once the priests enter the holy precincts, they are not to go into the outer court until they leave behind the garments in which they minister, for these are holy. They are to put on other clothes before they go near the places that are for the people.'

15When he had finished measuring what was inside the temple area, he led me out by the east gate and measured the area all around: 16he measured the east side with the measuring rod; it was five hundred cubits.^{j,k} 17He measured the north side; it was five hundred cubits^l by the measuring

---

^{a}22 That is, about 1.5 metres ^{b}22 Septuagint; Hebrew *long* ^{c}22 Septuagint; Hebrew *length* ^{d}2 That is, about 52 metres long and 26 metres wide ^{e}3 That is, 10.4 metres ^{f}4 Septuagint and Syriac; Hebrew *and one cubit* ^{g}4 That is, about 5.2 metres wide and 52 metres long ^{h}10 Septuagint; Hebrew *Eastward* ^{i}13 Or *purification offerings* ^{j}16 See Septuagint of verse 17; Hebrew *rods*; also in verses 18 and 19. ^{k}16 Five hundred cubits equals about 260 metres; also in verses 17, 18 and 19. ^{l}17 Septuagint; Hebrew *rods* rod. ¹⁸He measured the south side; it was five hundred cubits by the measuring rod. ¹⁹Then he turned to the west side and measured; it was five hundred cubits by the measuring rod. ²⁰So he measured the area on all four sides. It had a wall round it, five hundred cubits long and five hundred cubits wide, to separate the holy from the common.

God's glory returns to the temple

43 Then the man brought me to the gate facing east, ²and I saw the glory of the God of Israel coming from the east. His voice was like the roar of rushing waters, and the land was radiant with his glory. ³The vision I saw was like the vision I had seen when he[a] came to destroy the city and like the visions I had seen by the River Kebar, and I fell face down. ⁴The glory of the LORD entered the temple through the gate facing east. ⁵Then the Spirit lifted me up and brought me into the inner court, and the glory of the LORD filled the temple.

⁶While the man was standing beside me, I heard someone speaking to me from inside the temple. ⁷He said: 'Son of man, this is the place of my throne and the place for the soles of my feet. This is where I will live among the Israelites for ever. The house of Israel will never again defile my holy name—neither they nor their kings—by their prostitution and the funeral offerings[b] for their kings at their death.[c] ⁸When they placed their threshold next to my threshold and their doorposts beside my doorposts, with only a wall between us and me, they defiled my holy name by their detestable practices. So I destroyed them in my anger. ⁹Now let them put away from me their prostitution and the funeral offerings for their kings, and I will live among them for ever.

¹⁰'Son of man, describe the temple to the people of Israel, that they may be ashamed of their sins. Let them consider its perfection, ¹¹and if they are ashamed of all they have done, make known to them the design of the temple—its arrangement, its exits and entrances—its whole design and all its regulations[d] and laws. Write these down before them so that they may be faithful to its design and follow all its regulations.

¹²'This is the law of the temple: all the surrounding area on top of the mountain will be most holy. Such is the law of the temple.

The great altar restored

¹³'These are the measurements of the altar in long cubits,[e] that cubit being a cubit and a handbreadth: its gutter is a cubit deep and a cubit wide, with a kerb of one span[f] around the edge. And this is the height of the altar: ¹⁴from the gutter on the ground up to the lower ledge that goes round the altar it is two cubits high, and the ledge is a cubit wide.[g] From this lower ledge to the upper ledge that goes round the altar it is four cubits high, and that ledge is also a cubit wide.[h] ¹⁵Above that, the altar hearth is four cubits high, and four horns project upwards from the hearth. ¹⁶The altar hearth is square, twelve cubits[i] long and twelve cubits wide. ¹⁷The upper ledge also is square, fourteen cubits[j] long and fourteen cubits wide. All round the altar is a gutter of one cubit with a kerb of half a cubit.[k] The steps of the altar face east.'

¹⁸Then he said to me, 'Son of man, this is what the Sovereign LORD says: these will be the regulations for sacrificing burnt offerings and splashing blood against the altar when it is built: ¹⁹you are to give a young bull as a sin offering[l] to the Levitical priests of the family of Zadok, who come near to minister before me, declares the Sovereign LORD. ²⁰You are to take some of its blood and put it on the four horns of the altar and on the four corners of the upper ledge and all round the rim, and so purify the altar and make atonement for it. ²¹You are to take the bull for the sin offering and burn it in the

---

[a] 3 Some Hebrew manuscripts and Vulgate; most Hebrew manuscripts *I*   [b] 7 Or *the memorial monuments*; also in verse 9   [c] 7 Or *their high places*   [d] 11 Some Hebrew manuscripts and Septuagint; most Hebrew manuscripts *regulations and its whole design*   [e] 13 That is, about about 52 centimetres; also in verses 14 and 17. The long cubit is the basic unit for linear measurement throughout Ezekiel 40-48.   [f] 13 That is, about 26 centimetres   [g] 14 That is, about 104 centimetres high and 52 centimetres wide   [h] 14 That is, about 2.1 metres high and 52 centimetres wide   [i] 16 That is, about 6.2 metres   [j] 17 That is, about 7.3 metres   [k] 17 That is, about 26 centimetres   [l] 19 Or *purification offering*; also in verses 21, 22 and 25

IN OTHER WORDS

Atonement
Ezekiel 43:20

There's a clue to this word's meaning in its spelling. It means 'making at one' – putting things right between God and the human race. Atonement happened through sacrifices in the Old Testament, and through the death and resurrection of Jesus in the New Testament (Romans 3:25).

---

designated part of the temple area outside the sanctuary.

22'On the second day you are to offer a male goat without defect for a sin offering, and the altar is to be purified as it was purified with the bull. 23When you have finished purifying it, you are to offer a young bull and a ram from the flock, both without defect. 24You are to offer them before the LORD, and the priests are to sprinkle salt on them and sacrifice them as a burnt offering to the LORD.

25'For seven days you are to provide a male goat daily for a sin offering; you are also to provide a young bull and a ram from the flock, both without defect. 26For seven days they are to make atonement for the altar and cleanse it; thus they will dedicate it. 27At the end of these days, from the eighth day on, the priests are to present your burnt offerings and fellowship offerings on the altar. Then I will accept you, declares the Sovereign LORD.'

The priesthood restored

44 Then the man brought me back to the outer gate of the sanctuary, the one facing east, and it was shut. 2The LORD said to me, 'This gate is to remain shut. It must not be opened; no-one may enter through it. It is to remain shut because the LORD, the God of Israel, has entered through it. 3The prince himself is the only one who may sit inside the gateway to eat in the presence of the LORD. He is to enter by way of the portico of the gateway and go out the same way.'

4Then the man brought me by way of the north gate to the front of the temple. I looked and saw the glory of the LORD filling the temple of the LORD, and I fell face down.

5The LORD said to me, 'Son of man, look carefully, listen closely and give attention to everything I tell you concerning all the regulations and instructions regarding the temple of the LORD. Give attention to the entrance to the temple and all the exits of the sanctuary. 6Say to the rebellious house of Israel, "This is what the Sovereign LORD says: enough of your detestable practices, house of Israel! 7In addition to all your other detestable practices, you brought foreigners uncircumcised in heart and flesh into my sanctuary, desecrating my temple while you offered me food, fat and blood, and you broke my covenant. 8Instead of carrying out your duty in regard to my holy things, you put others in charge of my sanctuary. 9This is what the Sovereign LORD says: no foreigner uncircumcised in heart and flesh is to enter my sanctuary, not even the foreigners who live among the Israelites.

10' "The Levites who went far from me when Israel went astray and who wandered from me after their idols must bear the consequences of their sin. 11They may serve in my sanctuary, having charge of the gates of the temple and serving in it; they may slaughter the burnt offerings and sacrifices for the people and stand before the people and serve them. 12But because they served them in the presence of their idols and made the house of Israel fall into sin, therefore I have sworn with uplifted hand that they must bear the consequences of their sin, declares the Sovereign LORD. 13They are not to come near to serve me as priests or come near any of my holy things or my most holy offerings; they must bear the shame of their detestable practices. 14And I will appoint them to guard the temple for all the work that is to be done in it.

15' "But the Levitical priests, who are descendants of Zadok and who guarded my sanctuary when the Israelites went astray from me, are to come near to minister before me; they are to stand before me to offer sacrifices of fat and blood, declares the Sovereign LORD. 16They alone are to enter my sanctuary; they alone are to come near my table to minister before me and serve me as guards.

17 "When they enter the gates of the inner court, they are to wear linen clothes; they must not wear any woollen garment while ministering at the gates of the inner court or inside the temple. 18They are to wear linen turbans on their heads and linen undergarments round their waists. They must not wear anything that makes them perspire. 19When they go out into the outer court where the people are, they are to take off the clothes they have been ministering in and leave them in the sacred rooms, and put on other clothes, so that the people are not consecrated through contact with their garments.

20 "They must not shave their heads or let their hair grow long, but they are to keep the hair of their heads trimmed. 21No priest is to drink wine when he enters the inner court. 22They must not marry widows or divorced women; they may marry only virgins of Israelite descent or widows of priests. 23They are to teach my people the difference between the holy and the common and show them how to distinguish between the unclean and the clean.

24 "In any dispute, the priests are to serve as judges and decide it according to my ordinances. They are to keep my laws and my decrees for all my appointed festivals, and they are to keep my Sabbaths holy.

25 "A priest must not defile himself by going near a dead person; however, if the dead person was his father or mother, son or daughter, brother or unmarried sister, then he may defile himself. 26After he is cleansed, he must wait seven days. 27On the day he goes into the inner court of the sanctuary to minister in the sanctuary, he is to offer a sin offering[a] for himself, declares the Sovereign LORD.

28 "I am to be the only inheritance the priests have. You are to give them no possession in Israel; I will be their possession. 29They will eat the grain offerings, the sin offerings and the guilt offerings; and everything in Israel devoted[b] to the LORD will belong to them. 30The best of all the firstfruits and of all your special gifts will belong to the priests. You are to give them the first portion of your ground meal so that a blessing may rest on your household. 31The priests must not eat anything, whether bird or animal, found dead or torn by wild animals.

Israel fully restored

45 "When you allot the land as an inheritance, you are to present to the LORD a portion of the land as a sacred district, 25,000 cubits[c] long and 20,000[d] cubits[e] wide; the entire area will be holy. 2Of this, a section 500 cubits[f] square is to be for the sanctuary, with 50 cubits[g] around it for open land. 3In the sacred district, measure off a section 25,000 cubits long and 10,000 cubits[h] wide. In it will be the sanctuary, the Most Holy Place. 4It will be the sacred portion of the land for the priests, who minister in the sanctuary and who draw near to minister before the LORD. It will be a place for their houses as well as a holy place for the sanctuary. 5An area 25,000 cubits long and 10,000 cubits wide will belong to the Levites, who serve in the temple, as their possession for towns to live in.[i]

6 "You are to give the city as its property an area 5,000 cubits[j] wide and 25,000 cubits long, adjoining the sacred portion; it will belong to the whole house of Israel.

7 "The prince will have the land bordering each side of the area formed by the sacred district and the property of the city. It will extend westward from the west side and eastward from the east side, running lengthwise from the western to the eastern border parallel to one of the tribal portions. 8This land will be his possession in Israel. And my princes will no longer oppress my people but will allow the house of Israel to possess the land according to their tribes.

---

[a] 27 Or *purification offering*; also in verse 29 [b] 29 The Hebrew term refers to the irrevocable giving over of things or persons to the LORD. [c] 1 That is, about 8 miles or about 13 kilometres; also in verses 3, 5 and 6 [d] 1 Septuagint (see also verses 3 and 5 and 48:9); Hebrew *10,000* [e] 1 That is, about 6 1/2 miles or about 10 kilometres [f] 2 That is, about 260 metres [g] 2 That is, about 26 metres [h] 3 That is, about 3 miles or about 5.2 kilometres; also in verse 5 [i] 5 Septuagint; Hebrew *temple; they will have as their possession 20 rooms* [j] 6 That is, about 1 2/3 miles or about 2.6 kilometres

Accurate scales
Ezekiel 45:10

Why should God stress the need for accurate weights? Well, in the markets traders would sometimes use false weights to trick people. Instead of getting what they had asked and paid for, people would end up with less because a false weight had been used that was lighter than it was supposed to be. This verse is a way of saying that God hates deceit and hypocrisy, but he loves truth.

9 "'This is what the Sovereign LORD says: you have gone far enough, princes of Israel! Give up your violence and oppression and do what is just and right. Stop dispossessing my people, declares the Sovereign LORD. 10You are to use accurate scales, an accurate ephah[a] and an accurate bath.[b] 11The ephah and the bath are to be the same size, the bath containing a tenth of a homer and the ephah a tenth of a homer; the homer is to be the standard measure for both. 12The shekel[c] is to consist of twenty gerahs. Twenty shekels plus twenty-five shekels plus fifteen shekels equal one mina.[d]

13 "'This is the special gift you are to offer: a sixth of an ephah[e] from each homer of wheat and a sixth of an ephah[f] from each homer of barley. 14The prescribed portion of olive oil, measured by the bath,[g] is a tenth of a bath from each cor (which consists of ten baths or one homer, for ten baths are equivalent to a homer). 15Also one sheep is to be taken from every flock of two hundred from the well-watered pastures of Israel. These will be used for the grain offerings, burnt offerings and fellowship offerings to make atonement for the people, declares the Sovereign LORD. 16All the people of the land will be required to give this special offering to the prince in Israel. 17It will be the duty of the prince to provide the burnt offerings, grain offerings and drink offerings at the festivals, the New Moons and the Sabbaths—at all the appointed festivals of the house of Israel. He will provide the sin offerings,[h] grain offerings, burnt offerings and fellowship offerings to make atonement for the house of Israel.

18 "'This is what the Sovereign LORD says: in the first month on the first day you are to take a young bull without defect and purify the sanctuary. 19The priest is to take some of the blood of the sin offering and put it on the doorposts of the temple, on the four corners of the upper ledge of the altar and on the gateposts of the inner court. 20You are to do the same on the seventh day of the month for anyone who sins unintentionally or through ignorance; so you are to make atonement for the temple.

21 "'In the first month on the fourteenth day you are to observe the Passover, a festival lasting seven days, during which you shall eat bread made without yeast. 22On that day the prince is to provide a bull as a sin offering for himself and for all the people of the land. 23Every day during the seven days of the Festival he is to provide seven bulls and seven rams without defect as a burnt offering to the LORD, and a male goat for a sin offering. 24He is to provide as a grain offering an ephah for each bull and an ephah for each ram, along with a hin[i] of olive oil for each ephah.

25 "'During the seven days of the Festival, which begins in the seventh month on the fifteenth day, he is to make the same provision for sin offerings, burnt offerings, grain offerings and oil.

46

"'This is what the Sovereign LORD says: the gate of the inner court facing east is to be shut on the six working

---

[a] 10 An ephah was a dry measure of capacity of about 22 litres. [b] 10 A bath was a liquid measure of capacity of about 22 litres. [c] 12 A shekel weighed about 11.5 grams. [d] 12 That is, 60 shekels; the common mina was 50 shekels. Sixty shekels were about 680 grams. [e] 13 That is, probably about 2.75 kilograms [f] 13 That is, probably about 2.25 kilograms [g] 14 That is, about 2.2 litres [h] 17 Or *purification offerings*; also in verses 19, 22, 23 and 25 [i] 24 That is, about 3.6 litres

days, but on the Sabbath day and on the day of the New Moon it is to be opened. ²The prince is to enter from the outside through the portico of the gateway and stand by the gatepost. The priests are to sacrifice his burnt offering and his fellowship offerings. He is to bow down in worship at the threshold of the gateway and then go out, but the gate will not be shut until evening. ³On the Sabbaths and New Moons the people of the land are to worship in the presence of the LORD at the entrance of that gateway. ⁴The burnt offering the prince brings to the LORD on the Sabbath day is to be six male lambs and a ram, all without defect. ⁵The grain offering given with the ram is to be an ephah,^{a} and the grain offering with the lambs is to be as much as he pleases, along with a hin^b of olive oil for each ephah. ⁶On the day of the New Moon he is to offer a young bull, six lambs and a ram, all without defect. ⁷He is to provide as a grain offering one ephah with the bull, one ephah with the ram, and with the lambs as much as he wants to give, along with a hin of oil for each ephah. ⁸When the prince enters, he is to go in through the portico of the gateway, and he is to come out the same way.

⁹ "When the people of the land come before the LORD at the appointed festivals, whoever enters by the north gate to worship is to go out by the south gate; and whoever enters by the south gate is to go out by the north gate. No-one is to return through the gate by which he entered, but each is to go out by the opposite gate. ¹⁰The prince is to be among them, going in when they go in and going out when they go out. ¹¹At the feasts and the appointed festivals, the grain offering is to be an ephah with a bull, an ephah with a ram, and with the lambs as much as he pleases, along with a hin of oil for each ephah.

¹² "When the prince provides a freewill offering to the LORD—whether a burnt offering or fellowship offerings—the gate facing east is to be opened for him. He shall offer his burnt offering or his fellowship offerings as he does on the Sabbath day. Then he shall go out, and after he has gone out, the gate will be shut.

¹³ "Every day you are to provide a year-old lamb without defect for a burnt offering to the LORD; morning by morning you shall provide it. ¹⁴You are also to provide with it morning by morning a grain offering, consisting of a sixth of an ephah^c with a third of a hin^d of oil to moisten the flour. The presenting of this grain offering to the LORD is a lasting ordinance. ¹⁵So the lamb and the grain offering and the oil shall be provided morning by morning for a regular burnt offering.

¹⁶ "This is what the Sovereign LORD says: if the prince makes a gift from his inheritance to one of his sons, it will also belong to his descendants; it is to be their property by inheritance. ¹⁷If, however, he makes a gift from his inheritance to one of his servants, the servant may keep it until the year of freedom; then it will revert to the prince. His inheritance belongs to his sons only; it is theirs. ¹⁸The prince must not take any of the inheritance of the people, driving them off their property. He is to give his sons their inheritance out of his own property, so that not one of my people will be separated from their property.' "

¹⁹Then the man brought me through the entrance at the side of the gate to the sacred rooms facing north, which belonged to the priests, and showed me a place at the western end. ²⁰He said to me, 'This is the place where the priests are to cook the guilt offering and the sin offering^e and bake the grain offering, to avoid bringing them into the outer court and consecrating the people.'

²¹He then brought me to the outer court and led me round to its four corners, and I saw in each corner another court. ²²In the four corners of the outer court were enclosed^f courts, forty cubits long and thirty cubits wide;^{g} each of the courts in the four corners was the same size. ²³Around the inside of each of the four courts was a ledge of stone, with places for fire built all round under the ledge. ²⁴He said to me, 'These are

---

^{a}5 That is, probably about 16 kilograms; also in verses 7 and 11 ^{b}5 That is, about 3.6 litres; also in verses 7 and 11 ^{c}14 That is, probably about 2.75 kilograms ^{d}14 That is, about 1.2 litres ^{e}20 Or *purification offering* ^{f}22 The meaning of the Hebrew for this word is uncertain. ^{g}22 That is, about 21 metres long and 16 metres wide

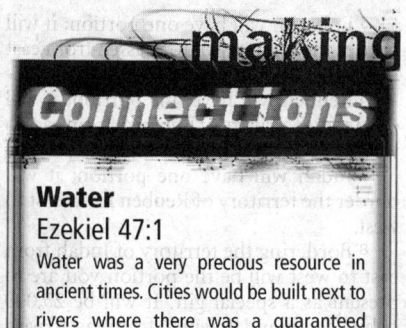

Water
Ezekiel 47:1

Water was a very precious resource in ancient times. Cities would be built next to rivers where there was a guaranteed supply of water. In other areas, where water was scarce, people would build cisterns to store it or dig wells to gain access to it. Water brought life and fruitfulness. People literally couldn't live without it.

the kitchens where those who minister at the temple are to cook the sacrifices of the people.'

The river from the temple

47 The man brought me back to the entrance to the temple, and I saw water coming out from under the threshold of the temple towards the east (for the temple faced east). The water was coming down from under the south side of the temple, south of the altar. ²He then brought me out through the north gate and led me round the outside to the outer gate facing east, and the water was trickling from the south side.

³As the man went eastward with a measuring line in his hand, he measured off a thousand cubits[a] and then led me through water that was ankle-deep. ⁴He measured off another thousand cubits and led me through water that was knee-deep. He measured off another thousand and led me through water that was up to the waist. ⁵He measured off another thousand, but now it was a river that I could not cross, because the water had risen and was deep enough to swim in—a river that no-one could cross. ⁶He asked me, 'Son of man, do you see this?'

Then he led me back to the bank of the river. ⁷When I arrived there, I saw a great number of trees on each side of the river. ⁸He said to me, 'This water flows towards the eastern region and goes down into the Arabah,[b] where it enters the Dead Sea. When it empties into the sea, the salty water there becomes fresh. ⁹Swarms of living creatures will live wherever the river flows. There will be large numbers of fish, because this water flows there and makes the salt water fresh; so where the river flows everything will live. ¹⁰People will fish along the shore; from En Gedi to En Eglaim there will be places for spreading nets. The fish will be of many kinds—like the fish of the Mediterranean Sea. ¹¹But the swamps and marshes will not become fresh; they will be left for salt. ¹²Fruit trees of all kinds will grow on both banks of the river. Their leaves will not wither, nor will their fruit fail. Every month they will bear fruit, because the water from the sanctuary flows to them. Their fruit will serve for food and their leaves for healing.'

The boundaries of the land

¹³This is what the Sovereign LORD says: 'These are the boundaries of the land that you will divide among the twelve tribes of Israel as their inheritance, with two portions for Joseph. ¹⁴You are to divide it equally among them. Because I swore with uplifted hand to give it to your ancestors, this land will become your inheritance.

¹⁵'This is to be the boundary of the land:

'On the north side it will run from the Mediterranean Sea by the Hethlon road past Lebo Hamath to Zedad, ¹⁶Berothah[c] and Sibraim (which lies on the border between Damascus and Hamath), as far as Hazer Hattikon, which is on the border of Hauran. ¹⁷The boundary will extend from the sea to Hazar Enan,[d] along the northern border of Damascus, with the border

---

[a] 3 That is, about 520 metres [b] 8 Or *the Jordan Valley* [c] 15,16 See Septuagint and Ezekiel 48:1; Hebrew *road to go into Zedad,* ¹⁶*Hamath, Berothah.* [d] 17 Hebrew *Enon,* a variant of *Enan*

of Hamath to the north. This will be the northern boundary.

18'On the east side the boundary will run between Hauran and Damascus, along the Jordan between Gilead and the land of Israel, to the Dead Sea and as far as Tamar.*a* This will be the eastern boundary.

19'On the south side it will run from Tamar as far as the waters of Meribah Kadesh, then along the Wadi of Egypt to the Mediterranean Sea. This will be the southern boundary.

20'On the west side, the Mediterranean Sea will be the boundary to a point opposite Lebo Hamath. This will be the western boundary.

21'You are to distribute this land among yourselves according to the tribes of Israel. 22You are to allot it as an inheritance for yourselves and for the foreigners residing among you and who have children. You are to consider them as native-born Israelites; along with you they are to be allotted an inheritance among the tribes of Israel. 23In whatever tribe foreigners reside, there you are to give them their inheritance,' declares the Sovereign LORD.

The division of the land

48 'These are the tribes, listed by name: at the northern frontier, Dan will have one portion; it will follow the Hethlon road to Lebo Hamath; Hazar Enan and the northern border of Damascus next to Hamath will be part of its border from the east side to the west side.

2'Asher will have one portion; it will border the territory of Dan from east to west.

3'Naphtali will have one portion; it will border the territory of Asher from east to west.

4'Manasseh will have one portion; it will border the territory of Naphtali from east to west.

5'Ephraim will have one portion; it will border the territory of Manasseh from east to west.

6'Reuben will have one portion; it will border the territory of Ephraim from east to west.

7'Judah will have one portion; it will border the territory of Reuben from east to west.

8'Bordering the territory of Judah from east to west will be the portion you are to present as a special gift. It will be 25,000 cubits*b* wide, and its length from east to west will equal one of the tribal portions; the sanctuary will be in the centre of it.

9'The special portion you are to offer to the LORD will be 25,000 cubits long and 10,000 cubits*c* wide. 10This will be the sacred portion for the priests. It will be 25,000 cubits long on the north side, 10,000 cubits wide on the west side, 10,000 cubits wide on the east side and 25,000 cubits long on the south side. In the centre of it will be the sanctuary of the LORD. 11This will be for the consecrated priests, the Zadokites, who were faithful in serving me and did not go astray as the Levites did when the Israelites went astray. 12It will be a special gift to them from the sacred portion of the land, a most holy portion, bordering the territory of the Levites.

13'Alongside the territory of the priests, the Levites will be allotted a portion of land 25,000 cubits long and 10,000 cubits wide. Its total length will be 25,000 cubits and its width 10,000 cubits. 14They must not sell or exchange any of it. This is the best of the land and must not pass into other hands, because it is holy to the LORD.

15'The remaining area, 5,000 cubits*d* wide and 25,000 cubits long, will be for the common use of the city, for houses and for pasture-land. The city will be in the centre of it 16and will have these measurements: the north side 4,500 cubits,*e* the south side 4,500 cubits, the east side 4,500 cubits, and the west side 4,500 cubits. 17The pasture-land for the city will be 250 cubits*f* on the north, 250 cubits on the south, 250 cubits on the

---

a 18 See Syriac; Hebrew *Israel. You will measure to the Dead Sea.* *b* 8 That is, about 8 miles or about 13 kilometres; also in verses 9, 10, 13, 15, 20 and 21   *c* 9 That is, about 3 miles or about 5.2 kilometres; also in verses 10, 13 and 18
d 15 That is, about 1 2/3 miles or about 2.6 kilometres   *e* 16 That is, about 1 1/2 miles or about 2.4 kilometres; also in verses 30, 32, 33 and 34   *f* 17 That is, about 130 metres

east, and 250 cubits on the west. 18What remains of the area, bordering on the sacred portion and running the length of it, will be 10,000 cubits on the east side and 10,000 cubits on the west side. Its produce will supply food for the workers of the city. 19The workers from the city who farm it will come from all the tribes of Israel. 20The entire portion will be a square, 25,000 cubits on each side. As a special gift you will set aside the sacred portion, along with the property of the city.

21'What remains on both sides of the area formed by the sacred portion and the property of the city will belong to the prince. It will extend eastward from the 25,000 cubits of the sacred portion to the eastern border, and westward from the 25,000 cubits to the western border. Both these areas running the length of the tribal portions will belong to the prince, and the sacred portion with the temple sanctuary will be in the centre of them. 22So the property of the Levites and the property of the city will lie in the centre of the area that belongs to the prince. The area belonging to the prince will lie between the border of Judah and the border of Benjamin.

23'As for the rest of the tribes: Benjamin will have one portion; it will extend from the east side to the west side.

24'Simeon will have one portion; it will border the territory of Benjamin from east to west.

25'Issachar will have one portion; it will border the territory of Simeon from east to west.

26'Zebulun will have one portion; it will border the territory of Issachar from east to west.

27'Gad will have one portion; it will border the territory of Zebulun from east to west.

28'The southern boundary of Gad will run south from Tamar to the waters of Meribah Kadesh, then along the Wadi of Egypt to the Mediterranean Sea.

29'This is the land you are to allot as an inheritance to the tribes of Israel, and these will be their portions,' declares the Sovereign LORD.

The gates of the new city

30'These will be the exits of the city: beginning on the north side, which is 4,500 cubits long, 31the gates of the city will be named after the tribes of Israel. The three gates on the north side will be the gate of Reuben, the gate of Judah and the gate of Levi.

32'On the east side, which is 4,500 cubits long, will be three gates: the gate of Joseph, the gate of Benjamin and the gate of Dan.

33'On the south side, which measures 4,500 cubits, will be three gates: the gate of Simeon, the gate of Issachar and the gate of Zebulun.

34'On the west side, which is 4,500 cubits long, will be three gates: the gate of Gad, the gate of Asher and the gate of Naphtali.

35'The distance all around will be 18,000 cubits.[a]

'And the name of the city from that time on will be:

THE LORD IS THERE.'

---

[a] 35 That is, about 6 miles or about 9.4 kilometres

Daniel

INTRODUCTION

DANIEL

Author: Daniel

When: Daniel was taken into captivity in 605 BC.

Where: Daniel lived in Babylon for more than fifty years.

Did you know? While Daniel was held captive in Babylon, the Medes and Persians invaded and defeated the Babylonians. So Daniel continued as a servant in the court of the Persian king.

Main theme: Daniel shows how it is possible to be faithful to God in the middle of a pagan and alien culture. He and his friends stuck to their decision to worship God and saw how God blessed them and stood by them. Several chapters of Daniel are full of his visions about the future. Some of these events have now happened and some are about the end of time.

Daniel's training in Babylon

1 In the third year of the reign of Jehoiakim king of Judah, Nebuchadnezzar king of Babylon came to Jerusalem and besieged it. 2And the Lord delivered Jehoiakim king of Judah into his hand, along with some of the articles from the temple of God. These he carried off to the temple of his god in Babylonia[a] and put in the treasure-house of his god.

3Then the king ordered Ashpenaz, chief of his court officials, to bring into the king's service some of the Israelites from the royal family and the nobility— 4young men without any physical defect, handsome, showing aptitude for every kind of learning, well informed, quick to understand, and qualified to serve in the king's palace. He was to teach them the language and literature of the Babylonians.[b] 5The king assigned them a daily amount of food and wine from the king's table. They were to be trained for three years, and after that they were to enter the king's service.

[a] 2 Hebrew *Shinar*   [b] 4 Or *Chaldeans*

People and Places

Daniel
Daniel 1:6

Daniel was a Jew who was taken from Jerusalem in 605 BC when Nebuchadnezzar besieged the city and took some people back to Babylon. He became a leading official in the Babylonian empire, and later under the kings of Persia. He was a skilful interpreter of dreams and a prophet to whom God gave dreams and visions about events in the future and the end of the world.

---

6 Among those who were chosen were some from Judah: Daniel, Hananiah, Mishael and Azariah. 7 The chief official gave them new names: to Daniel, the name Belteshazzar; to Hananiah, Shadrach; to Mishael, Meshach; and to Azariah, Abednego.

8 But Daniel resolved not to defile himself with the royal food and wine, and he asked the chief official for permission not to defile himself in this way. 9 Now God had caused the official to show favour and compassion to Daniel, 10 but the official told Daniel, 'I am afraid of my lord the king, who has assigned your^a food and drink. Why should he see you looking worse than the other young men of your age? The king would then have my head because of you.'

11 Daniel then said to the guard whom the chief official had appointed over Daniel, Hananiah, Mishael and Azariah, 12 'Please test your servants for ten days: give us nothing but vegetables to eat and water to drink. 13 Then compare our appearance with that of the young men who eat the royal food, and treat your servants in accordance with what you see.' 14 So he agreed to this and tested them for ten days.

15 At the end of the ten days they looked healthier and better nourished than any of the young men who ate the royal food. 16 So the guard took away their choice food and the wine they were to drink and gave them vegetables instead.

17 To these four young men God gave knowledge and understanding of all kinds of literature and learning. And Daniel could understand visions and dreams of all kinds.

18 At the end of the time set by the king to bring them into his service, the chief official presented them to Nebuchadnezzar. 19 The king talked with them, and he found none equal to Daniel, Hananiah, Mishael and Azariah; so they entered the king's service. 20 In every matter of wisdom and understanding about which the king questioned them, he found them ten times better than all the magicians and enchanters in his whole kingdom.

21 And Daniel remained there until the first year of King Cyrus.

Nebuchadnezzar's dream

2 In the second year of his reign, Nebuchadnezzar had dreams; his mind was troubled and he could not sleep. 2 So the king summoned the magicians, enchanters, sorcerers and astrologers^b to tell him what he had dreamed. When they came in and stood before the king, 3 he said to them, 'I have had a dream that troubles me and I want to know what it means.'^{c}

4 Then the astrologers answered the king,^{d} 'May the king live for ever! Tell your servants the dream, and we will interpret it.'

5 The king replied to the astrologers, 'This is what I have firmly decided: if you do not tell me what my dream was and interpret it, I will have you cut into pieces and your houses turned into piles of rubble. 6 But if you tell me the dream and explain it, you will receive from me gifts and rewards and great honour. So tell me the dream and interpret it for me.'

7 Once more they replied, 'Let the king tell his servants the dream, and we will interpret it.'

---

^{a} 10 The Hebrew for *your* and *you* in this verse is plural. ^{b} 2 Or *Chaldeans*; also in verses 4, 5 and 10 ^{c} 3 Or *was*
^{d} 4 At this point the Hebrew text has *in Aramaic*, indicating that the text from here to the end of chapter 7 is in Aramaic.

⁸Then the king answered, 'I am certain that you are trying to gain time, because you realise that this is what I have firmly decided: ⁹if you do not tell me the dream, there is only one penalty for you. You have conspired to tell me misleading and wicked things, hoping the situation will change. So then, tell me the dream, and I will know that you can interpret it for me.'

¹⁰The astrologers answered the king, 'There is not a person on earth who can do what the king asks! No king, however great and mighty, has ever asked such a thing of any magician or enchanter or astrologer. ¹¹What the king asks is too difficult. No-one can reveal it to the king except the gods, and they do not live among human beings.'

¹²This made the king so angry and furious that he ordered the execution of all the wise men of Babylon. ¹³So the decree was issued to put the wise men to death, and men were sent to look for Daniel and his friends to put them to death.

¹⁴When Arioch, the commander of the king's guard, had gone out to put to death the wise men of Babylon, Daniel spoke to him with wisdom and tact. ¹⁵He asked the king's officer, 'Why did the king issue such a harsh decree?' Arioch then explained the matter to Daniel. ¹⁶At this, Daniel went in to the king and asked for time, so that he might interpret the dream for him.

¹⁷Then Daniel returned to his house and explained the matter to his friends Hananiah, Mishael and Azariah. ¹⁸He urged them to plead for mercy from the God of heaven concerning this mystery, so that he and his friends might not be executed with the rest of the wise men of Babylon. ¹⁹During the night the mystery was revealed to Daniel in a vision. Then Daniel praised the God of heaven ²⁰and said:

'Praise be to the name of God for ever and ever;
  wisdom and power are his.
²¹He changes times and seasons;
  he deposes kings and raises up others.
He gives wisdom to the wise
  and knowledge to the discerning.
²²He reveals deep and hidden things;
  he knows what lies in darkness,
  and light dwells with him.
²³I thank and praise you, God of my ancestors:
  you have given me wisdom and power,
  you have made known to me what we asked of you,
  you have made known to us the dream of the king.'

Daniel interprets the dream

²⁴Then Daniel went to Arioch, whom the king had appointed to execute the wise men of Babylon, and said to him, 'Do not execute the wise men of Babylon. Take me to the king, and I will interpret his dream for him.'

²⁵Arioch took Daniel to the king at once and said, 'I have found a man among the exiles from Judah who can tell the king what his dream means.'

²⁶The king asked Daniel (also called Belteshazzar), 'Are you able to tell me what I saw in my dream and interpret it?'

²⁷Daniel replied, 'No wise man, enchanter, magician or diviner can explain to the king the mystery he has asked about, ²⁸but there is a God in heaven who reveals mysteries. He has shown King Nebuchadnezzar what will happen in days to come. Your dream and the visions that passed through your mind as you were lying in bed are these:

²⁹'As Your Majesty was lying there, your mind turned to things to come, and the revealer of mysteries showed you what is going to happen. ³⁰As for me, this mystery has been revealed to me, not because I have greater wisdom than anyone else alive, but so that Your Majesty may know the interpretation and that you may understand what went through your mind.

³¹'Your Majesty looked, and there before you stood a large statue—an enormous, dazzling statue, awesome in appearance. ³²The head of the statue was made of pure gold, its chest and arms of silver, its belly and thighs of bronze, ³³its legs of iron, its feet partly of iron and partly of baked clay. ³⁴While you were watching, a rock was cut out, but not by human hands. It struck the statue on its feet of iron and clay and smashed them. ³⁵Then the iron, the clay, the bronze, the silver and the gold were all broken to pieces and became like chaff on a threshing-floor in the summer. The wind

swept them away without leaving a trace. But the rock that struck the statue became a huge mountain and filled the whole earth.

36'This was the dream, and now we will interpret it to the king. 37Your Majesty, you are the king of kings. The God of heaven has given you dominion and power and might and glory; 38in your hands he has placed all people everywhere and the beasts of the field and the birds in the sky. Wherever they live, he has made you ruler over them all. You are that head of gold.

39'After you, another kingdom will arise, inferior to yours. Next, a third kingdom, one of bronze, will rule over the whole earth. 40Finally, there will be a fourth kingdom, strong as iron—for iron breaks and smashes everything—and as iron breaks things to pieces, so it will crush and break all the others. 41Just as you saw that the feet and toes were partly of baked clay and partly of iron, so this will be a divided kingdom; yet it will have some of the strength of iron in it, even as you saw iron mixed with clay. 42As the toes were partly iron and partly clay, so this kingdom will be partly strong and partly brittle. 43And just as you saw the iron mixed with baked clay, so the people will be a mixture and will not remain united, any more than iron mixes with clay.

44'In the time of those kings, the God of heaven will set up a kingdom that will never be destroyed, nor will it be left to another people. It will crush all those kingdoms and bring them to an end, but it will itself endure for ever. 45This is the meaning of the vision of the rock cut out of a mountain, but not by human hands—a rock that broke the iron, the bronze, the clay, the silver and the gold to pieces.

'The great God has shown the king what will take place in the future. The dream is true and its interpretation is trustworthy.'

46Then King Nebuchadnezzar fell prostrate before Daniel and paid him honour and ordered that an offering and incense be presented to him. 47The king said to Daniel, 'Surely your God is the God of gods and the Lord of kings and a revealer of mysteries, for you were able to reveal this mystery.'

48Then the king placed Daniel in a high position and lavished many gifts on him. He made him ruler over the entire province of Babylon and placed him in charge of all its wise men. 49Moreover, at Daniel's request the king appointed Shadrach, Meshach and Abednego chief ministers over the province of Babylon, while Daniel himself remained at the royal court.

The image of gold and the blazing furnace

3 King Nebuchadnezzar made an image of gold, sixty cubits high and six cubits wide,[a] and set it up on the plain of Dura in the province of Babylon. 2He then summoned the satraps, prefects, governors, advisors, treasurers, judges, magistrates and all the other provincial officials to come to the dedication of the image he had set up. 3So the satraps, prefects, governors, advisors, treasurers, judges, magistrates and all the other provincial officials assembled for the dedication of the image that King Nebuchadnezzar had set up, and they stood before it.

4Then the herald loudly proclaimed, 'Nations and peoples of every language, this is what you are commanded to do: 5as soon as you hear the sound of the horn, flute, zither, lyre, harp, pipe and all kinds of music, you must fall down and worship the image of gold that King Nebuchadnezzar has set up. 6Whoever does not fall down and worship will immediately be thrown into a blazing furnace.'

7Therefore, as soon as they heard the sound of the horn, flute, zither, lyre, harp and all kinds of music, all the nations and peoples of every language fell down and worshipped the image of gold that King Nebuchadnezzar had set up.

8At this time some astrologers[b] came forward and denounced the Jews. 9They said to King Nebuchadnezzar, 'May the king live for ever! 10Your Majesty has issued a decree that everyone who hears the sound of the horn, flute, zither, lyre, harp, pipe and all kinds of music must fall down and worship the image of gold, 11and that whoever does not fall down and worship will be thrown into a blazing furnace. 12But

---

[a] 1 That is, about 27 metres high and 2.7 metres wide   [b] 8 Or *Chaldeans*

there are some Jews whom you have set over the affairs of the province of Babylon—Shadrach, Meshach and Abednego—who pay no attention to you, Your Majesty. They neither serve your gods nor worship the image of gold you have set up.'

¹³Furious with rage, Nebuchadnezzar summoned Shadrach, Meshach and Abednego. So these men were brought before the king, ¹⁴and Nebuchadnezzar said to them, 'Is it true, Shadrach, Meshach and Abednego, that you do not serve my gods or worship the image of gold I have set up? ¹⁵Now when you hear the sound of the horn, flute, zither, lyre, harp, pipe and all kinds of music, if you are ready to fall down and worship the image I made, very good. But if you do not worship it, you will be thrown immediately into a blazing furnace. Then what god will be able to rescue you from my hand?'

¹⁶Shadrach, Meshach and Abednego replied to him, 'King Nebuchadnezzar, we do not need to defend ourselves before you in this matter. ¹⁷If the God we serve is able to deliver us, then he will deliver us from the blazing furnace and from Your Majesty's hand. ¹⁸But even if he does not, we want you to know, Your Majesty, that we will not serve your gods or worship the image of gold you have set up.'

¹⁹Then Nebuchadnezzar was furious with Shadrach, Meshach and Abednego, and his attitude towards them changed. He ordered the furnace to be heated seven times hotter than usual ²⁰and commanded some of the strongest soldiers in his army to tie up Shadrach, Meshach and Abednego and throw them into the blazing furnace. ²¹So these men, wearing their robes, trousers, turbans and other clothes, were bound and thrown into the blazing furnace. ²²The king's command was so urgent and the furnace so hot that the flames of the fire killed the soldiers who took up Shadrach, Meshach and Abednego, ²³and these three men, firmly tied, fell into the blazing furnace.

²⁴Then King Nebuchadnezzar leaped to his feet in amazement and asked his advisors, 'Weren't there three men that we tied up and threw into the fire?'

They replied, 'Certainly, Your Majesty.'

²⁵He said, 'Look! I see four men walking around in the fire, unbound and unharmed, and the fourth looks like a son of the gods.'

²⁶Nebuchadnezzar then approached the opening of the blazing furnace and shouted, 'Shadrach, Meshach and Abednego, servants of the Most High God, come out! Come here!'

So Shadrach, Meshach and Abednego came out of the fire, ²⁷and the satraps, prefects, governors and royal advisors crowded around them. They saw that the fire had not harmed their bodies, nor was a hair of their heads singed; their robes were not scorched, and there was no smell of fire on them.

²⁸Then Nebuchadnezzar said, 'Praise be to the God of Shadrach, Meshach and Abednego, who has sent his angel and rescued his servants! They trusted in him and defied the king's command and were willing to give up their lives rather than serve or worship any god except their own God. ²⁹Therefore I decree that the people of any nation or language who say anything against the God of Shadrach, Meshach and Abednego be cut into pieces and their houses be turned into piles of rubble, for no other god can save in this way.'

³⁰Then the king promoted Shadrach, Meshach and Abednego in the province of Babylon.

Nebuchadnezzar's dream of a tree

4 *King Nebuchadnezzar,

To the nations and peoples of every language, who live in all the earth:

May you prosper greatly!

²It is my pleasure to tell you about the miraculous signs and wonders that the Most High God has performed for me.

³How great are his signs,
how mighty his wonders!

---

* 4:1-3 is numbered 3:31-33 in Aramaic texts.

Sign of the times

How to start a letter
Daniel 4:1

This is a rather ambitious opening to a letter, addressing it to everyone in the whole world! But this was a common introduction to an official letter like this which was designed to give it more importance.

His kingdom is an eternal kingdom;
his dominion endures from generation to generation.

*⁴I, Nebuchadnezzar, was at home in my palace, contented and prosperous. ⁵I had a dream that made me afraid. As I was lying in bed, the images and visions that passed through my mind terrified me. ⁶So I commanded that all the wise men of Babylon be brought before me to interpret the dream for me. ⁷When the magicians, enchanters, astrologers[a] and diviners came, I told them the dream, but they could not interpret it for me. ⁸Finally, Daniel came into my presence and I told him the dream. (He is called Belteshazzar, after the name of my god, and the spirit of the holy gods is in him.)

⁹I said, 'Belteshazzar, chief of the magicians, I know that the spirit of the holy gods is in you, and no mystery is too difficult for you. Here is my dream; interpret it for me. ¹⁰These are the visions I saw while lying in bed: I looked, and there before me stood a tree in the middle of the land. Its height was enormous. ¹¹The tree grew large and strong and its top touched the sky; it was visible to the ends of the earth. ¹²Its leaves were beautiful, its fruit abundant, and on it was food for all. Under it the wild animals found shelter, and the birds lived in its branches; from it every creature was fed.

¹³'In the visions I saw while lying in bed, I looked, and there before me was a holy one, a messenger,[b] coming down from heaven. ¹⁴He called in a loud voice: "Cut down the tree and trim off its branches; strip off its leaves and scatter its fruit. Let the animals flee from under it and the birds from its branches. ¹⁵But let the stump and its roots, bound with iron and bronze, remain in the ground, in the grass of the field.

'"Let him be drenched with the dew of heaven, and let him live with the animals among the plants of the earth. ¹⁶Let his mind be changed from that of a human being and let him be given the mind of an animal, till seven times[c] pass by for him.

¹⁷'"The decision is announced by messengers, the holy ones declare the verdict, so that the living may know that the Most High is sovereign over the kingdoms on earth and gives them to anyone he wishes and sets over them the lowliest of people."

¹⁸'This is the dream that I, King Nebuchadnezzar, had. Now, Belteshazzar, tell me what it means, for none of the wise men in my kingdom can interpret it for me. But you can, because the spirit of the holy gods is in you.'

Daniel interprets the dream

¹⁹Then Daniel (also called Belteshazzar) was greatly perplexed

---

[a] 7 Or *Chaldeans*   [b] 13 Or *watchman*; also in verses 17 and 23   [c] 16 Or *years*; also in verses 23, 25 and 32

* 4:4-37 is numbered 4:1-34 in Aramaic texts.

for a time, and his thoughts terrified him. So the king said, 'Belteshazzar, do not let the dream or its meaning alarm you.'

Belteshazzar answered, 'My lord, if only the dream applied to your enemies and its meaning to your adversaries! 20The tree you saw, which grew large and strong, with its top touching the sky, visible to the whole earth, 21with beautiful leaves and abundant fruit, providing food for all, giving shelter to the wild animals, and having nesting places in its branches for the birds— 22Your Majesty, you are that tree! You have become great and strong; your greatness has grown until it reaches the sky, and your dominion extends to distant parts of the earth.

23'Your Majesty saw a holy one, a messenger, coming down from heaven and saying, "Cut down the tree and destroy it, but leave the stump, bound with iron and bronze, in the grass of the field, while its roots remain in the ground. Let him be drenched with the dew of heaven; let him live with the wild animals, until seven times pass by for him."

24'This is the interpretation, Your Majesty, and this is the decree the Most High has issued against my lord the king: 25you will be driven away from people and will live with the wild animals; you will eat grass like the ox and be drenched with the dew of heaven. Seven times will pass by for you until you acknowledge that the Most High is sovereign over the kingdoms on earth and gives them to anyone he wishes. 26The command to leave the stump of the tree with its roots means that your kingdom will be restored to you when you acknowledge that Heaven rules. 27Therefore, Your Majesty, be pleased to accept my advice: renounce your sins by doing what is right, and your wickedness by being kind to the oppressed. It may be that then your prosperity will continue.'

The dream is fulfilled

28All this happened to King Nebuchadnezzar. 29Twelve months later, as the king was walking on the roof of the royal palace of Babylon, 30he said, 'Is not this the great Babylon I have built as the royal residence, by my mighty power and for the glory of my majesty?'

31Even as the words were on his lips, a voice came from heaven, 'This is what is decreed for you, King Nebuchadnezzar: your royal authority has been taken from you. 32You will be driven away from people and will live with the wild animals; you will eat grass like the ox. Seven times will pass by for you until you acknowledge that the Most High is sovereign over the kingdoms on earth and gives them to anyone he wishes.'

Palace of Babylon
Daniel 4:30

Nebuchadnezzar rebuilt the city of Babylon during his reign, using the people that he had taken into captivity as slaves on his many building projects. He created a huge palace and temple in honour of the city's god, Marduk. This was protected by a double wall which was so wide that a chariot pulled by four horses could ride along the top.

33Immediately what had been said about Nebuchadnezzar was fulfilled. He was driven away from people and ate grass like the ox. His body was drenched with the dew of heaven until his hair grew like the feathers of an eagle and his nails like the claws of a bird.

34At the end of that time, I, Nebuchadnezzar, raised my eyes towards heaven, and my sanity was restored. Then I praised the Most High; I honoured and glorified him who lives for ever.

> His dominion is an eternal dominion;
> his kingdom endures from generation to generation.
> 35 All the peoples of the earth are regarded as nothing.
> He does as he pleases with the powers of heaven and the peoples of the earth.
> No-one can hold back his hand
> or say to him: 'What have you done?'

36At the same time that my sanity was restored, my honour and splendour were returned to me for the glory of my kingdom. My advisors and nobles sought me out, and I was restored to my throne and became even greater than before. 37Now I, Nebuchadnezzar, praise and exalt and glorify the King of heaven, because everything he does is right and all his ways are just. And those who walk in pride he is able to humble.

The writing on the wall

5 King Belshazzar gave a great banquet for a thousand of his nobles and drank wine with them. 2While Belshazzar was drinking his wine, he gave orders to bring in the gold and silver goblets that Nebuchadnezzar his father[a] had taken from the temple in Jerusalem, so that the king and his nobles, his wives and his concubines might drink from them. 3So they brought in the gold goblets that had been taken from the temple of God in Jerusalem, and the king and his nobles, his wives and his concubines drank from them. 4As they drank the wine, they praised the gods of gold and silver, of bronze, iron, wood and stone.

5Suddenly the fingers of a human hand appeared and wrote on the plaster of the wall, near the lampstand in the royal palace. The king watched the hand as it wrote. 6His face turned pale and he was so frightened that his legs became weak and his knees were knocking.

7The king summoned the enchanters, astrologers[b] and diviners. Then he said to these wise men of Babylon, 'Whoever reads this writing and tells me what it means will be clothed in purple and have a gold chain placed round his neck, and he will be made the third highest ruler in the kingdom.'

8Then all the king's wise men came in, but they could not read the writing or tell the king what it meant. 9So King Belshazzar became even more terrified and his face grew more pale. His nobles were baffled.

10The queen,[c] hearing the voices of the king and his nobles, came into the banqueting hall. 'May the king live for ever!' she said. 'Don't be alarmed! Don't look so pale! 11There is a man in your kingdom who has the spirit of the holy gods in him. In the time of your father he was found to have insight and intelligence and wisdom like that of the gods. Your father, King Nebuchadnezzar, appointed him chief of the magicians, enchanters, astrologers and diviners. 12He did this because Daniel, whom the king called Belteshazzar, was found to have a keen mind and knowledge and understanding, and also the ability to interpret dreams, explain riddles and solve difficult problems. Call for Daniel, and he will tell you what the writing means.'

13So Daniel was brought before the king, and the king said to him, 'Are you Daniel, one of the exiles my father the king brought from Judah? 14I have heard that the spirit of the gods is in you and that you have insight, intelligence and outstanding wisdom.

---

[a] 2 Or *ancestor*; or *predecessor*; also in verses 11, 13 and 18   [b] 7 Or *Chaldeans*; also in verse 11   [c] 10 Or *queen mother*

15The wise men and enchanters were brought before me to read this writing and tell me what it means, but they could not explain it. 16Now I have heard that you are able to give interpretations and to solve difficult problems. If you can read this writing and tell me what it means, you will be clothed in purple and have a gold chain placed round your neck, and you will be made the third highest ruler in the kingdom.'

17Then Daniel answered the king, 'You may keep your gifts for yourself and give your rewards to someone else. Nevertheless, I will read the writing for the king and tell him what it means.

18'Your Majesty, the Most High God gave your father Nebuchadnezzar sovereignty and greatness and glory and splendour. 19Because of the high position he gave him, all the nations and peoples of every language dreaded and feared him. Those the king wanted to put to death, he put to death; those he wanted to spare, he spared; those he wanted to promote, he promoted; and those he wanted to humble, he humbled. 20But when his heart became arrogant and hardened with pride, he was deposed from his royal throne and stripped of his glory. 21He was driven away from people and given the mind of an animal; he lived with the wild donkeys and ate grass like the ox; and his body was drenched with the dew of heaven, until he acknowledged that the Most High God is sovereign over the kingdoms on earth and sets over them anyone he wishes.

22'But you, Belshazzar, his son,[a] have not humbled yourself, though you knew all this. 23Instead, you have set yourself up against the Lord of heaven. You had the goblets from his temple brought to you, and you and your nobles, your wives and your concubines drank wine from them. You praised the gods of silver and gold, of bronze, iron, wood and stone, which cannot see or hear or understand. But you did not honour the God who holds in his hand your life and all your ways. 24Therefore he sent the hand that wrote the inscription.

25'This is the inscription that was written:

MENE, MENE, TEKEL, PARSIN

26'This is what these words mean:

Mene[b]: God has numbered the days of your reign and brought it to an end.

27*Tekel*[c]: You have been weighed on the scales and found wanting.

28*Peres*[d]: Your kingdom is divided and given to the Medes and Persians.'

29Then at Belshazzar's command, Daniel was clothed in purple, a gold chain was placed round his neck, and he was proclaimed the third highest ruler in the kingdom.

30That very night Belshazzar, king of the Babylonians,[e] was slain, *31and Darius the Mede took over the kingdom, at the age of sixty-two.

Daniel in the den of lions

6 *It pleased Darius to appoint 120 satraps to rule throughout the kingdom, 2with three chief ministers over them, one of whom was Daniel. The satraps were made accountable to them so that the king might not suffer loss. 3Now Daniel so distinguished himself among the chief ministers and the satraps by his exceptional qualities that the king planned to set him over the whole kingdom. 4At this, the chief ministers and the satraps tried to find grounds for charges against Daniel in his conduct of government affairs, but they were unable to do so. They could find no corruption in him, because he was trustworthy and neither corrupt nor negligent. 5Finally these men said, 'We will never find any basis for charges against this man Daniel unless it has something to do with the law of his God.'

6So these chief ministers and satraps went as a group to the king and said: 'May King Darius live for ever! 7The royal ministers, prefects, satraps, advisors and

---

[a] 22 Or *descendant*; or *successor* [b] 26 *Mene* can mean *numbered* or *mina* (a unit of money). [c] 27 *Tekel* can mean *weighed* or *shekel*. [d] 28 *Peres* (the singular of *Parsin*) can mean *divided* or *Persia* or *a half mina* or *a half shekel*. [e] 30 Or *Chaldeans*

* 5:31 is numbered 6:1 in Aramaic texts.   * 6:1-28 is numbered 6:2-29 in Aramaic texts.

> **People and Places**
>
> **Medes and Persians**
> Daniel 6:12
>
> Media was an ancient country which conquered, made alliances with and was defeated by many different nations throughout its history. Media was defeated by Persia in the time of King Cyrus, but because Media was an important country the dual name of 'the Medes and Persians' was used. Once a law was made in Media, it could not be changed, even by the king.

governors have all agreed that the king should issue an edict and enforce the decree that anyone who prays to any god or human being during the next thirty days, except to you, Your Majesty, shall be thrown into the lions' den. 8Now, Your Majesty, issue the decree and put it in writing so that it cannot be altered—in accordance with the law of the Medes and Persians, which cannot be repealed.' 9So King Darius put the decree in writing.

10Now when Daniel learned that the decree had been published, he went home to his upstairs room where the windows opened towards Jerusalem. Three times a day he got down on his knees and prayed, giving thanks to his God, just as he had done before. 11Then these men went as a group and found Daniel praying and asking God for help. 12So they went to the king and spoke to him about his royal decree: 'Did you not publish a decree that during the next thirty days anyone who prays to any god or human being except to you, Your Majesty, would be thrown into the lions' den?'

The king answered, 'The decree stands—in accordance with the law of the Medes and Persians, which cannot be repealed.'

13Then they said to the king, 'Daniel, who is one of the exiles from Judah, pays no attention to you, Your Majesty, or to the decree you put in writing. He still prays three times a day.' 14When the king heard this, he was greatly distressed; he was determined to rescue Daniel and made every effort until sunset to save him.

15Then the men went as a group to King Darius and said to him, 'Remember, Your Majesty, that according to the law of the Medes and Persians no decree or edict that the king issues can be changed.'

16So the king gave the order, and they brought Daniel and threw him into the lions' den. The king said to Daniel, 'May your God, whom you serve continually, rescue you!'

17A stone was brought and placed over the mouth of the den, and the king sealed it with his own signet ring and with the rings of his nobles, so that Daniel's situation might not be changed. 18Then the king returned to his palace and spent the night without eating and without any entertainment being brought to him. And he could not sleep.

19At the first light of dawn, the king got up and hurried to the lions' den. 20When he came near the den, he called to Daniel in an anguished voice, 'Daniel, servant of the living God, has your God, whom you serve continually, been able to rescue you from the lions?'

21Daniel answered, 'May the king live for ever! 22My God sent his angel, and he shut the mouths of the lions. They have not hurt me, because I was found innocent in his sight. Nor have I ever done any wrong before you, Your Majesty.'

23The king was overjoyed and gave orders to lift Daniel out of the den. And when Daniel was lifted from the den, no wound was found on him, because he had trusted in his God.

24At the king's command, the men who had falsely accused Daniel were brought in and thrown into the lions' den, along with their wives and children. And before they reached the floor of the den, the lions overpowered them and crushed all their bones.

25Then King Darius wrote to all the nations and peoples of every language in all the earth:

> 'May you prosper greatly!

26'I issue a decree that in every part of my kingdom people must fear and reverence the God of Daniel.

> 'For he is the living God
> and he endures for ever;
> his kingdom will not be destroyed,
> his dominion will never end.
> 27He rescues and he saves;
> he performs signs and wonders
> in the heavens and on the earth.
> He has rescued Daniel
> from the power of the lions.'

28So Daniel prospered during the reign of Darius and the reign of Cyrus[a] the Persian.

Daniel's dream of four beasts

7 In the first year of Belshazzar king of Babylon, Daniel had a dream, and visions passed through his mind as he was lying in bed. He wrote down the substance of his dream.

2Daniel said: 'In my vision at night I looked, and there before me were the four winds of heaven churning up the great sea. 3Four great beasts, each different from the others, came up out of the sea.

4'The first was like a lion, and it had the wings of an eagle. I watched until its wings were torn off and it was lifted from the ground so that it stood on two feet like a human being, and a human mind was given to it.

5'And there before me was a second beast, which looked like a bear. It was raised up on one of its sides, and it had three ribs in its mouth between its teeth. It was told, "Get up and eat your fill of flesh!"

6'After that, I looked, and there before me was another beast, one that looked like a leopard. And on its back it had four wings like those of a bird. This beast had four heads, and it was given authority to rule.

7'After that, in my vision at night I looked, and there before me was a fourth beast—terrifying and frightening and very powerful. It had large iron teeth; it crushed and devoured its victims and trampled underfoot whatever was left. It was different from all the former beasts, and it had ten horns.

8'While I was thinking about the horns, there before me was another horn, a little one, which came up among them; and three of the first horns were uprooted before it. This horn had eyes like the eyes of a human being and a mouth that spoke boastfully.

9'As I looked,

> 'thrones were set in place,
> and the Ancient of Days took his seat.
> His clothing was as white as snow;
> the hair of his head was white like wool.
> His throne was flaming with fire,
> and its wheels were all ablaze.
> 10A river of fire was flowing,
> coming out from before him.
> Thousands upon thousands attended him;
> ten thousand times ten thousand stood before him.
> The court was seated,
> and the books were opened.

11'Then I continued to watch because of the boastful words the horn was speaking. I kept looking until the beast was slain and its body destroyed and thrown into the blazing fire. 12(The other beasts had been stripped of their authority, but were allowed to live for a period of time.)

13'In my vision at night I looked, and there before me was one like a son of man,[b] coming with the clouds of heaven. He approached the Ancient of Days and was led into his presence. 14He was given authority, glory and sovereign power; all nations and peoples of every language worshipped him. His dominion is an everlasting dominion that will not pass away, and his kingdom is one that will never be destroyed.

The interpretation of the dream

15'I, Daniel, was troubled in spirit, and the visions that passed through my mind disturbed me. 16I approached one of those

---

[a] 28 Or *Darius, that is, the reign of Cyrus* [b] 13 The Aramaic phrase *bar enash* means *human being*. The phrase *son of man* is retained as a form of address here because of its traditional associations.

> **People and Places**
>
> **Son of Man**
> Daniel 7:13
>
> Daniel uses this term to describe the Messiah who will come in judgment and with authority. It is Jesus' favourite way of referring to himself in the New Testament (Luke 6:5). It also means just 'man', and so when Jesus uses it as a title for himself, it emphasises his servant role and his humanity.

standing there and asked him the meaning of all this.

'So he told me and gave me the interpretation of these things: 17"The four great beasts are four kings that will rise from the earth. 18But the holy people of the Most High will receive the kingdom and will possess it for ever—yes, for ever and ever."

19'Then I wanted to know the meaning of the fourth beast, which was different from all the others and most terrifying, with its iron teeth and bronze claws—the beast that crushed and devoured its victims and trampled underfoot whatever was left. 20I also wanted to know about the ten horns on its head and about the other horn that came up, before which three of them fell—the horn that looked more imposing than the others and that had eyes and a mouth that spoke boastfully. 21As I watched, this horn was waging war against the holy people and defeating them, 22until the Ancient of Days came and pronounced judgment in favour of the holy people of the Most High, and the time came when they possessed the kingdom.

23'He gave me this explanation: "The fourth beast is a fourth kingdom that will appear on earth. It will be different from all the other kingdoms and will devour the whole earth, trampling it down and crushing it. 24The ten horns are ten kings who will come from this kingdom. After them another king will arise, different from the earlier ones; he will subdue three kings. 25He will speak against the Most High and oppress his holy people and try to change the set times and the laws. The holy people will be delivered into his hands for a time, times and half a time.^{a}

26' "But the court will sit, and his power will be taken away and completely destroyed for ever. 27Then the sovereignty, power and greatness of all the kingdoms under heaven will be handed over to the holy people of the Most High. His kingdom will be an everlasting kingdom, and all rulers will worship and obey him."

28'This is the end of the matter. I, Daniel, was deeply troubled by my thoughts, and my face turned pale, but I kept the matter to myself.'

Daniel's vision of a ram and a goat

8 In the third year of King Belshazzar's reign, I, Daniel, had a vision, after the one that had already appeared to me. 2In my vision I saw myself in the citadel of Susa in the province of Elam; in the vision I was beside the Ulai Canal. 3I looked up, and there before me was a ram with two horns, standing beside the canal, and the horns were long. One of the horns was longer than the other but grew up later. 4I watched the ram as it charged towards the west and the north and the south. No animal could stand against it, and none could rescue from its power. It did as it pleased and became great.

5As I was thinking about this, suddenly a goat with a prominent horn between its eyes came from the west, crossing the whole earth without touching the ground. 6It came towards the two-horned ram I had seen standing beside the canal and charged at it in great rage. 7I saw it attack the ram furiously, striking the ram and shattering its two horns. The ram was powerless to stand against it; the goat knocked it to the ground and trampled on it, and none could rescue the ram from its power. 8The goat became very great, but at the height of its power the large horn was broken off, and in its place

---

^{a} 25 Or *for a year, two years and half a year*

four prominent horns grew up towards the four winds of heaven.

9 Out of one of them came another horn, which started small but grew in power to the south and to the east and towards the Beautiful Land. 10 It grew until it reached the host of the heavens, and it threw some of the starry host down to the earth and trampled on them. 11 It set itself up to be as great as the commander of the army of the LORD; it took away the daily sacrifice from the LORD, and his sanctuary was thrown down. 12 Because of rebellion, the LORD's people[a] and the daily sacrifice were given over to it. It prospered in everything it did, and truth was thrown to the ground.

13 Then I heard a holy one speaking, and another holy one said to him, 'How long will it take for the vision to be fulfilled—the vision concerning the daily sacrifice, the rebellion that causes desolation, the surrender of the sanctuary and the trampling underfoot of the LORD's people?'

14 He said to me, 'It will take 2,300 evenings and mornings; then the sanctuary will be reconsecrated.'

The interpretation of the vision

15 While I, Daniel, was watching the vision and trying to understand it, there before me stood one who looked like a man. 16 And I heard a man's voice from the Ulai calling, 'Gabriel, tell this man the meaning of the vision.'

17 As he came near the place where I was standing, I was terrified and fell prostrate. 'Son of man,'[b] he said to me, 'understand that the vision concerns the time of the end.'

18 While he was speaking to me, I was in a deep sleep, with my face to the ground. Then he touched me and raised me to my feet.

19 He said: 'I am going to tell you what will happen later in the time of wrath, because the vision concerns the appointed time of the end.[c] 20 The two-horned ram that you saw represents the kings of Media and Persia. 21 The shaggy goat is the king of Greece, and the large horn between its eyes is the first king. 22 The four horns that replaced the one that was broken off represent four kingdoms that will emerge from his nation but will not have the same power.

23 'In the latter part of their reign, when rebels have become completely wicked, a fierce-looking king, a master of intrigue, will arise. 24 He will become very strong, but not by his own power. He will cause astounding devastation and will succeed in whatever he does. He will destroy the mighty warriors, the holy people. 25 He will cause deceit to prosper, and he will consider himself superior. When they feel secure, he will destroy many and take his stand against the Prince of princes. Yet he will be destroyed, but not by human power.

26 'The vision of the evenings and mornings that has been given you is true, but seal up the vision, for it concerns the distant future.'

27 I, Daniel, was worn out. I lay exhausted for several days. Then I got up and went about the king's business. I was appalled by the vision; it was beyond understanding.

Daniel's prayer

9 In the first year of Darius son of Xerxes[d] (a Mede by descent), who was made ruler over the Babylonian[e] kingdom— 2 in the first year of his reign, I, Daniel, understood from the Scriptures, according to the word of the LORD given to

Scripture
Daniel 9:2
The word 'scripture' literally means 'writings', but it is used exclusively in the Bible to mean writings that have special authority because they are inspired by God. Daniel would have had parts of the Old Testament as his scriptures.

---

[a] 12 Or *rebellion, the armies* [b] 17 The Hebrew phrase *ben adam* means *human being*. The phrase *son of man* is retained as a form of address here because of its traditional associations. [c] 19 Or *because the end will be at the appointed time* [d] 1 Hebrew *Ahasuerus* [e] 1 Or *Chaldean*

Jeremiah the prophet, that the desolation of Jerusalem would last seventy years. ³So I turned to the Lord God and pleaded with him in prayer and petition, in fasting, and in sackcloth and ashes.

⁴I prayed to the LORD my God and confessed:

'Lord, the great and awesome God, who keeps his covenant of love with those who love him and keep his commandments, ⁵we have sinned and done wrong. We have been wicked and have rebelled; we have turned away from your commands and laws. ⁶We have not listened to your servants the prophets, who spoke in your name to our kings, our princes and our ancestors, and to all the people of the land.

⁷'Lord, you are righteous, but this day we are covered with shame—the people of Judah and Jerusalem and all Israel, both near and far, in all the countries where you have scattered us because of our unfaithfulness to you. ⁸We and our kings, our princes and our ancestors are covered with shame, LORD, because we have sinned against you. ⁹The Lord our God is merciful and forgiving, even though we have rebelled against him; ¹⁰we have not obeyed the LORD our God or kept the laws he gave us through his servants the prophets. ¹¹All Israel has transgressed your law and turned away, refusing to obey you.

'Therefore the curses and sworn judgments written in the Law of Moses, the servant of God, have been poured out on us, because we have sinned against you. ¹²You have fulfilled the words spoken against us and against our rulers by bringing on us great disaster. Under the whole heaven nothing has ever been done like what has been done to Jerusalem. ¹³Just as it is written in the Law of Moses, all this disaster has come on us, yet we have not sought the favour of the LORD our God by turning from our sins and giving attention to your truth. ¹⁴The LORD did not hesitate to bring the disaster on us, for the LORD our God is righteous in everything he does; yet we have not obeyed him.

¹⁵'Now, Lord our God, who brought your people out of Egypt with a mighty hand and who made for yourself a name that endures to this day, we have sinned, we have done wrong. ¹⁶Lord, in keeping with all your righteous acts, turn away your anger and your wrath from Jerusalem, your city, your holy hill. Our sins and the iniquities of our ancestors have made Jerusalem and your people an object of scorn to all those around us.

¹⁷'Now, our God, hear the prayers and petitions of your servant. For your sake, Lord, look with favour on your desolate sanctuary. ¹⁸Give ear, our God, and hear; open your eyes and see the desolation of the city that bears your Name. We do not make requests of you because we are righteous, but because of your great mercy. ¹⁹Lord, listen! Lord, forgive! Lord, hear and act! For your sake, my God, do not delay, because your city and your people bear your Name.'

The seventy 'sevens'

²⁰While I was speaking and praying, confessing my sin and the sin of my people Israel and making my request to the LORD my God for his holy hill— ²¹while I was still in prayer, Gabriel, the man I had seen in the earlier vision, came to me in swift flight about the time of the evening sacrifice. ²²He instructed me and said to me, 'Daniel, I have now come to give you insight and understanding. ²³As soon as you began to pray, a word went out, which I have come to tell

you, for you are highly esteemed. Therefore, consider the word and understand the vision:

24 'Seventy "sevens"[a] are decreed for your people and your holy city to finish[b] transgression, to put an end to sin, to atone for wickedness, to bring in everlasting righteousness, to seal up vision and prophecy and to anoint the Most Holy Place.[c]

25 'Know and understand this: from the time the word goes out to restore and rebuild Jerusalem until the Anointed One,[d] the ruler, comes, there will be seven "sevens", and sixty-two "sevens". It will be rebuilt with streets and a trench, but in times of trouble. 26 After the sixty-two "sevens", the Anointed One will be put to death and will have nothing.[e] The people of the ruler who will come will destroy the city and the sanctuary. The end will come like a flood: war will continue until the end, and desolations have been decreed. 27 He will confirm a covenant with many for one "seven".[f] In the middle of the "seven"[g] he will put an end to sacrifice and offering. And at the temple[h] he will set up an abomination that causes desolation, until the end that is decreed is poured out on him.[i],[j]

Daniel's vision of a man

10 In the third year of Cyrus king of Persia, a revelation was given to Daniel (who was called Belteshazzar). Its message was true and it concerned a great war.[k] The understanding of the message came to him in a vision.

2 At that time I, Daniel, mourned for three weeks. 3 I ate no choice food; no meat or wine touched my lips; and I used no lotions at all until the three weeks were over.

4 On the twenty-fourth day of the first month, as I was standing on the bank of the great river, the Tigris, 5 I looked up and there before me was a man dressed in linen, with a belt of fine gold from Uphaz round his waist. 6 His body was like topaz, his face like lightning, his eyes like flaming torches, his arms and legs like the gleam of burnished bronze, and his voice like the sound of a multitude.

7 I, Daniel, was the only one who saw the vision; those who were with me did not see it, but such terror overwhelmed them that they fled and hid themselves. 8 So I was left alone, gazing at this great vision; I had no strength left, my face turned deathly pale and I was helpless. 9 Then I heard him speaking, and as I listened to him, I fell into a deep sleep, my face to the ground.

10 A hand touched me and set me trembling on my hands and knees. 11 He said, 'Daniel, you who are highly esteemed, consider carefully the words I am about to speak to you, and stand up, for I have now been sent to you.' And when he said this to me, I stood up trembling.

12 Then he continued, 'Do not be afraid, Daniel. Since the first day that you set your mind to gain understanding and to humble yourself before your God, your words were heard, and I have come in response to them. 13 But the prince of the Persian kingdom resisted me twenty-one days. Then Michael, one of the chief princes, came to help me, because I was detained there with the king of Persia. 14 Now I have come to explain to you what will happen to your people in the future, for the vision concerns a time yet to come.'

15 While he was saying this to me, I bowed with my face towards the ground and was speechless. 16 Then one who looked like a man[l] touched my lips, and I opened my mouth and began to speak. I said to the one standing before me, 'I am overcome with anguish because of the vision, my lord, and I feel very weak. 17 How can I, your servant, talk with you, my lord? My strength is gone and I can hardly breathe.'

18 Again the one who looked like a man touched me and gave me strength. 19 'Do not be afraid, you who are highly esteemed,' he said. 'Peace! Be strong now; be strong.'

---

[a] 24 Or "weeks"; also in verses 25 and 26   [b] 24 Or restrain   [c] 24 Or the most holy One   [d] 25 Or an anointed one; also in verse 26   [e] 26 Or death and will have no-one; or death, but not for himself   [f] 27 Or "week"   [g] 27 Or "week"   [h] 27 Septuagint and Theodotion; Hebrew wing   [i] 27 Or it   [j] 27 Or And one who causes desolation will come upon the wing of the abominable [temple], until the end that is decreed is poured out on the desolated [city]   [k] 1 Or trial and burdensome   [l] 16 Most manuscripts of the Masoretic Text; one manuscript of the Masoretic Text, Dead Sea Scrolls and Septuagint Then something that looked like a human hand

When he spoke to me, I was strengthened and said, 'Speak, my lord, since you have given me strength.'

20So he said, 'Do you know why I have come to you? Soon I will return to fight against the prince of Persia, and when I go, the prince of Greece will come; 21but first I will tell you what is written in the Book of Truth. (No-one supports me against them except Michael, your prince. 1And in the first year of Darius the Mede, I took my stand to support and protect him.)

The kings of the south and the north

2'Now then, I tell you the truth: three more kings will arise in Persia, and then a fourth, who will be far richer than all the others. When he has gained power by his wealth, he will stir up everyone against the kingdom of Greece. 3Then a mighty king will arise, who will rule with great power and do as he pleases. 4After he has arisen, his empire will be broken up and parcelled out towards the four winds of heaven. It will not go to his descendants, nor will it have the power he exercised, because his empire will be uprooted and given to others.

5'The king of the South will become strong, but one of his commanders will become even stronger than he and will rule his own kingdom with great power. 6After some years, they will become allies. The daughter of the king of the South will go to the king of the North to make an alliance, but she will not retain her power, and he and his power[a] will not last. In those days she will be betrayed, together with her royal escort and her father[b] and the one who supported her.

7'Someone from within her family will arise to take her place. He will attack the forces of the king of the North and enter his fortress; he will fight against them and be victorious. 8He will also seize their gods, their metal images and their valuable articles of silver and gold and carry them off to Egypt. For some years he will leave the king of the North alone. 9Then the king of the North will invade the realm of the king of the South but will retreat to his own country. 10His sons will prepare for war and assemble a great army, which will sweep on like an irresistible flood and carry the battle as far as his fortress.

11'Then the king of the South will march out in a rage and fight against the king of the North, who will raise a large army, but it will be defeated. 12When the army is carried off, the king of the South will be filled with pride and will slaughter many thousands, yet he will not remain triumphant. 13For the king of the North will muster another army, larger than the first; and after several years, he will advance with a huge army fully equipped.

14'In those times many will rise against the king of the South. Those who are violent among your own people will rebel in fulfilment of the vision, but without success. 15Then the king of the North will come and build up siege ramps and will capture a fortified city. The forces of the South will be powerless to resist; even their best troops will not have the strength to stand. 16The invader will do as he pleases; no-one will be able to stand against him. He will establish himself in the Beautiful Land and will have the power to destroy it. 17He will determine to come with the might of his entire kingdom and will make an alliance with the king of the South. And he will give him a daughter in marriage in order to overthrow the kingdom, but his plans[c] will not succeed or help him. 18Then he will turn his attention to the coastlands and will take many of them, but a commander will put an end to his insolence and will turn his insolence back on him. 19After this, he will turn back towards the fortresses of his own country but will stumble and fall, to be seen no more.

20'His successor will send out a tax collector to maintain the royal splendour. In a few years, however, he will be destroyed, yet not in anger or in battle.

21'He will be succeeded by a contemptible person who has not been given the honour of royalty. He will invade the kingdom when its people feel secure, and he will seize it through intrigue. 22Then an overwhelming army will be swept away

---

[a] 6 Or *offspring*   [b] 6 Or *child* (see Vulgate and Syriac)   [c] 17 Or *but she*

before him; both it and a prince of the covenant will be destroyed. 23After coming to an agreement with him, he will act deceitfully, and with only a few people he will rise to power. 24When the richest provinces feel secure, he will invade them and will achieve what neither his fathers nor his forefathers did. He will distribute plunder, loot and wealth among his followers. He will plot the overthrow of fortresses—but only for a time.

25'With a large army he will stir up his strength and courage against the king of the South. The king of the South will wage war with a large and very powerful army, but he will not be able to stand because of the plots devised against him. 26Those who eat from the king's provisions will try to destroy him; his army will be swept away, and many will fall in battle. 27The two kings, with their hearts bent on evil, will sit at the same table and lie to each other, but to no avail, because an end will still come at the appointed time. 28The king of the North will return to his own country with great wealth, but his heart will be set against the holy covenant. He will take action against it and then return to his own country.

29'At the appointed time he will invade the South again, but this time the outcome will be different from what it was before. 30Ships of the western coastlands will oppose him, and he will lose heart. Then he will turn back and vent his fury against the holy covenant. He will return and show favour to those who forsake the holy covenant.

31'His armed forces will rise up to desecrate the temple fortress and will abolish the daily sacrifice. Then they will set up the abomination that causes desolation. 32With flattery he will corrupt those who have violated the covenant, but the people who know their God will firmly resist him.

33'Those who are wise will instruct many, though for a time they will fall by the sword or be burned or captured or plundered. 34When they fall, they will receive a little help, and many who are not sincere will join them. 35Some of the wise will stumble, so that they may be refined, purified and made spotless until the time of the end, for it will still come at the appointed time.

The king who exalts himself

36'The king will do as he pleases. He will exalt and magnify himself above every god and will say unheard-of things against the God of gods. He will be successful until the time of wrath is completed, for what has been determined must take place. 37He will show no regard for the gods of his ancestors or for the one desired by women, nor will he regard any god, but will exalt himself above them all. 38Instead of them, he will honour a god of fortresses; a god unknown to his ancestors he will honour with gold and silver, with precious stones and costly gifts. 39He will attack the mightiest fortresses with the help of a foreign god and will greatly honour those who acknowledge him. He will make them rulers over many people and will distribute the land at a price.[a]

40'At the time of the end the king of the South will engage him in battle, and the king of the North will storm out against him with chariots and cavalry and a great fleet of ships. He will invade many countries and sweep through them like a flood. 41He will also invade the Beautiful Land. Many countries will fall, but Edom, Moab and the leaders of Ammon will be delivered from his hand. 42He will extend his power over many countries; Egypt will not escape. 43He will gain control of the treasures of gold and silver and all the riches of Egypt, with the Libyans and Cushites[b] in submission. 44But reports from the east and the north will alarm him, and he will set out in a great rage to destroy and annihilate many. 45He will pitch his royal tents between the seas at[c] the beautiful holy mountain. Yet he will come to his end, and no-one will help him.

The end times

12 'At that time Michael, the great prince who protects your people, will arise. There will be a time of distress such as has not happened from the beginning of nations until then. But at that time

---

[a] 39 Or *land for a reward*   [b] 43 That is, people from the upper Nile region   [c] 45 Or *the sea and*

People and Places

Michael
Daniel 12:1

Michael was an archangel who served as a guardian or prince over the nation of Israel. Revelation tells how Michael and his angels fought with Satan in heaven before Satan was thrown out (Revelation 12:7).

your people—everyone whose name is found written in the book—will be delivered. ²Multitudes who sleep in the dust of the earth will awake: some to everlasting life, others to shame and everlasting contempt. ³Those who are wise*ᵃ* will shine like the brightness of the heavens, and those who lead many to righteousness, like the stars for ever and ever. ⁴But you, Daniel, close up and seal the words of the scroll until the time of the end. Many will go here and there to increase knowledge.'

⁵Then I, Daniel, looked, and there before me stood two others, one on this bank of the river and one on the opposite bank. ⁶One of them said to the man clothed in linen, who was above the waters of the river, 'How long will it be before these astonishing things are fulfilled?'

⁷The man clothed in linen, who was above the waters of the river, lifted his right hand and his left hand towards heaven, and I heard him swear by him who lives for ever, saying, 'It will be for a time, times and half a time.*ᵇ* When the power of the holy people has been finally broken, all these things will be completed.'

⁸I heard, but I did not understand. So I asked, 'My lord, what will the outcome of all this be?'

⁹He replied, 'Go your way, Daniel, because the words are closed up and sealed until the time of the end. ¹⁰Many will be purified, made spotless and refined, but the wicked will continue to be wicked. None of the wicked will understand, but those who are wise will understand.

¹¹'From the time that the daily sacrifice is abolished and the abomination that causes desolation is set up, there will be 1,290 days. ¹²Blessed is the one who waits for and reaches the end of the 1,335 days.

¹³'As for you, go your way till the end. You will rest, and then at the end of the days you will rise to receive your allotted inheritance.'

---

*ᵃ*3 Or *who impart wisdom*   *ᵇ*7 Or *a year, two years and half a year*

Hosea

INTRODUCTION

HOSEA

Author: Hosea

When: The kings that Hosea mentions in the first verse of his book reigned for about forty years between them, from around 755 BC to 715 BC.

Where: Hosea lived in the northern kingdom of Israel.

Main theme: The book of Hosea is full of God's unchanging love for his people in spite of their sin and rebellion. Hosea tells the story of his own unfaithful wife, Gomer, and how she leaves Hosea and their children. He goes after her and brings her back home, a tender picture of how God doesn't give up on Israel but keeps on loving them.

1 The word of the LORD that came to Hosea son of Beeri during the reigns of Uzziah, Jotham, Ahaz and Hezekiah, kings of Judah, and during the reign of Jeroboam son of Joash king of Israel:

Hosea's wife and children

2When the LORD began to speak through Hosea, the LORD said to him, 'Go, marry a promiscuous woman and have children with her, for like an adulterous wife this land is guilty of unfaithfulness to the LORD.' 3So he married Gomer daughter of Diblaim, and she conceived and bore him a son.

4Then the LORD said to Hosea, 'Call him Jezreel, because I will soon punish the house of Jehu for the massacre at Jezreel, and I will put an end to the kingdom of Israel. 5In that day I will break Israel's bow in the Valley of Jezreel.'

6Gomer conceived again and gave birth to a daughter. Then the LORD said to Hosea, 'Call her Lo-Ruhamah (which means "not loved"), for I will no longer show love to the house of Israel, that I should at all forgive them. 7Yet I will show love to the house of Judah; and I will save them—not by bow, sword or battle, or by horses and horsemen, but by the LORD their God.'

8After she had weaned Lo-Ruhamah, Gomer had another son. 9Then the LORD

Sign of the times

Names
Hosea 1:6

People in the Bible were very conscious of the meaning of names, believing that there was a link between a person's name and their nature. Hosea's daughter was called Lo-Ruhamah, which means 'not loved', and his son was called Lo-Ammi, which means 'not my people'. Hosea wasn't being cruel to his children by giving them those names; he was reflecting how God felt about the people of Israel.

---

said, 'Call him Lo-Ammi (which means "not my people"), for you are not my people, and I am not your God.[a]

*10'Yet the Israelites will be like the sand on the seashore, which cannot be measured or counted. In the place where it was said to them, "You are not my people", they will be called "children of the living God". 11The people of Judah and the people of Israel will come together; they will appoint one leader and will come up out of the land, for great will be the day of Jezreel.

2 *'Say of your brothers, "My people", and of your sisters, "My loved one".

Israel punished and restored

2'Rebuke your mother, rebuke her,
  for she is not my wife,
  and I am not her husband.
Let her remove the adulterous look from her face
  and the unfaithfulness from between her breasts.
3Otherwise I will strip her naked
  and make her as bare as on the day she was born;
I will make her like a desert,
  turn her into a parched land,
  and slay her with thirst.
4I will not show my love to her children,
  because they are the children of adultery.
5Their mother has been unfaithful
  and has conceived them in disgrace.
She said, "I will go after my lovers,
  who give me my food and my water,
  my wool and my linen, my olive oil and my drink."
6Therefore I will block her path with thornbushes;
  I will wall her in so that she cannot find her way.
7She will chase after her lovers but not catch them;
  she will look for them but not find them.
Then she will say,
  "I will go back to my husband as at first,
  for then I was better off than now."
8She has not acknowledged that I was the one
  who gave her the grain, the new wine and oil,
  who lavished on her the silver and gold—
  which they used for Baal.
9'Therefore I will take away my corn when it ripens,
  and my new wine when it is ready.
I will take back my wool and my linen,
  intended to cover her nakedness.
10So now I will expose her lewdness
  before the eyes of her lovers;
  no-one will take her out of my hands.
11I will stop all her celebrations:
  her yearly festivals, her New Moons,
  her Sabbath days—all her appointed festivals.
12I will ruin her vines and her fig-trees,
  which she said were her pay from her lovers;
I will make them a thicket,
  and wild animals will devour them.
13I will punish her for the days
  she burned incense to the Baals;
  she decked herself with rings and jewellery,

---

[a] 9 Or your I AM

* 1:10-11 is numbered 2:1-2 in Hebrew texts.   * 2:1-23 is numbered 2:3-25 in Hebrew texts.

and went after her lovers,
but me she forgot,'
>declares the LORD.

¹⁴'Therefore I am now going to allure her;
I will lead her into the wilderness
and speak tenderly to her.
¹⁵There I will give her back her vineyards,
and will make the Valley of Achor*a* a
door of hope.
There she will respond*b* as in the days of
her youth,
as in the day she came up out of Egypt.

¹⁶'In that day,' declares the LORD,
'you will call me "my husband";
you will no longer call me "my
master".'*c*
¹⁷I will remove the names of the Baals from
her lips;
no longer will their names be invoked.
¹⁸In that day I will make a covenant for
them
with the beasts of the field, the birds in
the sky
and the creatures that move along the
ground.
Bow and sword and battle
I will abolish from the land,
so that all may lie down in safety.
¹⁹I will betroth you to me for ever;
I will betroth you in*d* righteousness and
justice,
in*e* love and compassion.
²⁰I will betroth you in faithfulness,
and you will acknowledge the LORD.

²¹'In that day I will respond,'
declares the LORD—
'I will respond to the skies,
and they will respond to the earth;
²²and the earth will respond to the grain,
the new wine and the olive oil,
and they will respond to Jezreel.*f*
²³I will plant her for myself in the land;
I will show my love to the one I called
"Not my loved one".*g*
I will say to those called "Not my
people",*h* "You are my people";
and they will say, "You are my God."'

Hosea's reconciliation with his wife

3 The LORD said to me, 'Go, show your love to your wife again, though she is loved by another and is an adulteress. Love her as the LORD loves the Israelites, though they turn to other gods and love the sacred raisin cakes.'

²So I bought her for fifteen shekels*i* of silver and about a homer and a lethek*j* of barley. ³Then I told her, 'You are to live with me for many days; you must not be a prostitute or be intimate with any man, and I will behave the same way towards you.'

⁴For the Israelites will live for many days without king or prince, without sacrifice or sacred stones, without ephod or household gods. ⁵Afterwards the Israelites will return and seek the LORD their God and David their king. They will come trembling to the LORD and to his blessings in the last days.

The charge against Israel

4 Hear the word of the LORD, you Israelites,
because the LORD has a charge to bring
against you who live in the land:
'There is no faithfulness, no love,
no acknowledgment of God in the
land.
²There is only cursing,*k* lying and murder,
stealing and adultery;
they break all bounds,
and bloodshed follows bloodshed.
³Because of this the land dries up,
and all who live in it waste away;
the beasts of the field, the birds in the sky
and the fish in the sea are swept away.

⁴'But let no-one bring a charge,
let no-one accuse another,
for your people are like those
who bring charges against a priest.
⁵You stumble day and night,
and the prophets stumble with you.
So I will destroy your mother—
⁶ my people are destroyed from lack of
knowledge.

'Because you have rejected knowledge,
I also reject you as my priests;

---

a 15 *Achor* means *trouble*. *b* 15 Or *sing* *c* 16 Hebrew *baal* *d* 19 Or *with*; also in verse 20 *e* 19 Or *with* *f* 22 *Jezreel* means *God plants*. *g* 23 Hebrew *Lo-Ruhamah* (see 1:6) *h* 23 Hebrew *Lo-Ammi* (see 1:9) *i* 2 That is, about 170 grams *j* 2 A homer and a lethek possibly weighed about 195 kilograms. *k* 2 That is, to pronounce a curse on

because you have ignored the law of your God,
I also will ignore your children.
⁷The more the priests increased,
the more they sinned against me;
they exchanged their glorious God*ᵃ* for something disgraceful.
⁸They feed on the sins of my people
and relish their wickedness.
⁹And it will be: like people, like priests.
I will punish both of them for their ways
and repay them for their deeds.

¹⁰'They will eat but not have enough;
they will engage in prostitution but not increase,
because they have deserted the LORD
to give themselves ¹¹to prostitution;
old wine and new wine
take away their understanding.
¹²My people consult a wooden idol
and are answered by a stick of wood.
A spirit of prostitution leads them astray;
they are unfaithful to their God.
¹³They sacrifice on the mountaintops
and burn offerings on the hills,
under oak, poplar and terebinth,
where the shade is pleasant.
Therefore your daughters turn to prostitution
and your daughters-in-law to adultery.

¹⁴'I will not punish your daughters
when they turn to prostitution,
nor your daughters-in-law
when they commit adultery,
because the men themselves consort with harlots
and sacrifice with shrine-prostitutes—
a people without understanding will come to ruin!

¹⁵'Though you, Israel, commit adultery,
do not let Judah become guilty.

'Do not go to Gilgal;
do not go up to Beth Aven.*ᵇ*
And do not swear, "As surely as the LORD lives!"

¹⁶The Israelites are stubborn,
like a stubborn heifer.
How then can the LORD pasture them
like lambs in a meadow?
¹⁷Ephraim is joined to idols;
leave him alone!
¹⁸Even when their drinks are gone,
they continue their prostitution;
their rulers dearly love shameful ways.
¹⁹A whirlwind will sweep them away,
and their sacrifices will bring them shame.

Judgment against Israel

5 'Hear this, you priests!
Pay attention, you Israelites!
Listen, royal house!
This judgment is against you:
you have been a snare at Mizpah,
a net spread out on Tabor.
²The rebels are deep in slaughter.
I will discipline all of them.
³I know all about Ephraim;
Israel is not hidden from me.
Ephraim, you have now turned to prostitution;
Israel is corrupt.

⁴'Their deeds do not permit them
to return to their God.
A spirit of prostitution is in their heart;
they do not acknowledge the LORD.
⁵Israel's arrogance testifies against them;
the Israelites, even Ephraim, stumble in their sin;
Judah also stumbles with them.
⁶When they go with their flocks and herds
to seek the LORD,
they will not find him;
he has withdrawn himself from them.
⁷They are unfaithful to the LORD;
they give birth to illegitimate children.
When they celebrate their New Moon feasts,
he will devour*ᶜ* their fields.

⁸'Sound the trumpet in Gibeah,
the horn in Ramah.
Raise the battle cry in Beth Aven;*ᵈ*
lead on, Benjamin.

---

*ᵃ*7 Syriac (see also an ancient Hebrew scribal tradition); Masoretic Text *I will exchange their glory*   *ᵇ*15 *Beth Aven* means *house of wickedness* (a derogatory name for Bethel, which means *house of God*).   *ᶜ*7 Or *Now their New Moon feasts I will devour them and*   *ᵈ*8 *Beth Aven* means *house of wickedness* (a derogatory name for Bethel, which means *house of God*).

> **IN OTHER WORDS**
>
> **Wrath**
> Hosea 5:10
> 'Wrath' is another word for 'anger', and is used to describe both human anger and God's anger.

⁹Ephraim will be laid waste
  on the day of reckoning.
Among the tribes of Israel
  I proclaim what is certain.
¹⁰Judah's leaders are like those
  who move boundary stones.
I will pour out my wrath on them
  like a flood of water.
¹¹Ephraim is oppressed,
  trampled in judgment,
  intent on pursuing idols.*[a]*
¹²I am like a moth to Ephraim,
  like rot to the people of Judah.
¹³'When Ephraim saw his sickness,
  and Judah his sores,
then Ephraim turned to Assyria,
  and sent to the great king for help.
But he is not able to cure you,
  not able to heal your sores.
¹⁴For I will be like a lion to Ephraim,
  like a great lion to Judah.
I will tear them to pieces and go away;
  I will carry them off, with no-one to rescue them.
¹⁵Then I will return to my lair
  until they have borne their guilt
  and seek my face—
in their misery
  they will earnestly seek me.'

Israel unrepentant

6 'Come, let us return to the LORD.
  He has torn us to pieces
  but he will heal us;
he has injured us
  but he will bind up our wounds.
²After two days he will revive us;
  on the third day he will restore us,
  that we may live in his presence.
³Let us acknowledge the LORD;
  let us press on to acknowledge him.
As surely as the sun rises,
  he will appear;
he will come to us like the winter rains,
  like the spring rains that water the earth.'

⁴'What can I do with you, Ephraim?
  What can I do with you, Judah?
Your love is like the morning mist,
  like the early dew that disappears.
⁵Therefore I cut you in pieces with my prophets,
  I killed you with the words of my mouth—
then my judgments go forth like the sun.*[b]*
⁶For I desire mercy, not sacrifice,
  and acknowledgment of God rather than burnt offerings.
⁷As at Adam,*[c]* they have broken the covenant;
  they were unfaithful to me there.
⁸Gilead is a city of wicked people,
  stained with footprints of blood.
⁹As marauders lie in ambush for a victim,
  so do bands of priests;
they murder on the road to Shechem,
  carrying out their wicked schemes.
¹⁰I have seen a horrible thing
  in the house of Israel.

> **People and Places**
>
> **Ephraim**
> Hosea 5:14
> Ephraim was Joseph's son and his descendants were one of the twelve tribes of Israel who settled in the Promised Land. The tribe of Ephraim was large and influential in Israel; sometimes the name Ephraim was used for Israel because of its size and its leadership role.

---

[a] 11 The meaning of the Hebrew for this word is uncertain.   [b] 5 The meaning of the Hebrew for this line is uncertain.
[c] 7 Or *Like Adam*; or *Like human beings*

There Ephraim is given to prostitution
and Israel is defiled.

¹¹'Also for you, Judah,
a harvest is appointed.

'Whenever I would restore the fortunes of my people,

7 ¹whenever I would heal Israel,
the sins of Ephraim are exposed
and the crimes of Samaria revealed.
They practise deceit,
thieves break into houses,
bandits rob in the streets;
²but they do not realise
that I remember all their evil deeds.
Their sins engulf them;
they are always before me.

³'They delight the king with their wickedness,
the princes with their lies.
⁴They are all adulterers,
burning like an oven
whose fire the baker need not stir
from the kneading of the dough till it rises.
⁵On the day of the festival of our king
the princes become inflamed with wine,
and he joins hands with the mockers.
⁶Their hearts are like an oven;
they approach him with intrigue.
Their passion smoulders all night;
in the morning it blazes like a flaming fire.
⁷All of them are hot as an oven;
they devour their rulers.
All their kings fall,
and none of them calls on me.

⁸'Ephraim mixes with the nations;
Ephraim is a flat loaf not turned over.
⁹Foreigners sap his strength,
but he does not realise it.
His hair is sprinkled with grey,
but he does not notice.
¹⁰Israel's arrogance testifies against him,
but despite all this
he does not return to the LORD his God
or search for him.

¹¹'Ephraim is like a dove,
easily deceived and senseless—
now calling to Egypt,
now turning to Assyria.
¹²When they go, I will throw my net over them;
I will pull them down like the birds in the sky.
When I hear them flocking together,
I will catch them.
¹³Woe to them,
because they have strayed from me!
Destruction to them,
because they have rebelled against me!
I long to redeem them
but they speak about me falsely.
¹⁴They do not cry out to me from their hearts
but wail on their beds.
They slash themselves,[a] appealing to their gods
for grain and new wine,
but they turn away from me.
¹⁵I trained them and strengthened their arms,
but they plot evil against me.
¹⁶They do not turn to the Most High;
they are like a faulty bow.
Their leaders will fall by the sword
because of their insolent words.
For this they will be ridiculed
in the land of Egypt.

Israel to reap the whirlwind

8 'Put the trumpet to your lips!
An eagle is over the house of the LORD
because the people have broken my covenant
and rebelled against my law.
²Israel cries out to me,
"Our God, we acknowledge you!"
³But Israel has rejected what is good;
an enemy will pursue him.
⁴They set up kings without my consent;
they choose princes without my approval.
With their silver and gold
they make idols for themselves
to their own destruction.
⁵Throw out your calf-idol, Samaria!
My anger burns against them.
How long will they be incapable of purity?

---

[a] 14 Some Hebrew manuscripts and Septuagint; most Hebrew manuscripts *They gather together*

6 They are from Israel!
This calf—a metalworker has made it;
  it is not God.
It will be broken in pieces,
  that calf of Samaria.

7 'They sow the wind
  and reap the whirlwind.
The stalk has no head;
  it will produce no flour.
Were it to yield grain,
  foreigners would swallow it up.
8 Israel is swallowed up;
  now she is among the nations
  like something no-one wants.
9 For they have gone up to Assyria
  like a wild donkey wandering alone.
Ephraim has sold herself to lovers.
10 Although they have sold themselves
  among the nations,
  I will now gather them together.
They will begin to waste away
  under the oppression of the mighty
  king.

11 'Though Ephraim built many altars for
  sin offerings,
these have become altars for sinning.
12 I wrote for them the many things of my
  law,
but they regarded them as something
  foreign.
13 Though they offer sacrifices as gifts to me,
  and though they eat the meat,
  the LORD is not pleased with them.
Now he will remember their wickedness
  and punish their sins:
  they will return to Egypt.
14 Israel has forgotten his Maker
  and built palaces;
Judah has fortified many towns.
But I will send fire on their cities
  that will consume their fortresses.'

Punishment for Israel

9 Do not rejoice, Israel;
  do not be jubilant like the other
  nations.
For you have been unfaithful to your
  God;
you love the wages of a prostitute
  at every threshing-floor.
2 Threshing-floors and winepresses will
  not feed the people;
the new wine will fail them.
3 They will not remain in the LORD's land;
Ephraim will return to Egypt
  and eat unclean food in Assyria.
4 They will not pour out wine offerings to
  the LORD,
nor will their sacrifices please him.
Such sacrifices will be to them like the
  bread of mourners;
all who eat them will be unclean.
This food will be for themselves;
  it will not come into the temple of the
  LORD.

5 What will you do on the day of your
  appointed festivals,
on the festal days of the LORD?
6 Even if they escape from destruction,
Egypt will gather them,
  and Memphis will bury them.
Their treasures of silver will be taken over
  by briers,
  and thorns will overrun their tents.
7 The days of punishment are coming,
  the days of reckoning are at hand.
Let Israel know this.
Because your sins are so many
  and your hostility so great,
the prophet is considered a fool,
  anyone who is inspired a maniac.
8 The prophet, along with my God,
  is the watchman over Ephraim,[a]
yet snares await him on all his paths,
  and hostility in the house of his God.
9 They have sunk deep into corruption,
  as in the days of Gibeah.
God will remember their wickedness
  and punish them for their sins.

10 'When I found Israel,
  it was like finding grapes in the
  desert;
when I saw your ancestors,
  it was like seeing the early fruit on the
  fig-tree.
But when they came to Baal Peor,
  they consecrated themselves to that
  shameful idol
  and became as vile as the thing they
  loved.

---

[a] 8 Or *The prophet is the watchman over Ephraim, / the people of my God*

¹¹Ephraim's glory will fly away like a bird—
    no birth, no pregnancy, no conception.
¹²Even if they bring up children,
    I will bereave them of every one.
Woe to them
    when I turn away from them!
¹³I have seen Ephraim, like Tyre,
    planted in a pleasant place.
But Ephraim will bring out
    their children to the slayer.'

¹⁴Give them, LORD—
    what will you give them?
Give them wombs that miscarry
    and breasts that are dry.

¹⁵'Because of all their wickedness in Gilgal,
    I hated them there.
Because of their sinful deeds,
    I will drive them out of my house.
I will no longer love them;
    all their leaders are rebellious.
¹⁶Ephraim is blighted,
    their root is withered,
    they yield no fruit.
Even if they bear children,
    I will slay their cherished offspring.'

¹⁷My God will reject them
    because they have not obeyed him;
    they will be wanderers among the nations.

10

Israel was a spreading vine;
    he brought forth fruit for himself.
As his fruit increased,
    he built more altars;
as his land prospered,
    he adorned his sacred stones.
²Their heart is deceitful,
    and now they must bear their guilt.
The LORD will demolish their altars
    and destroy their sacred stones.

³Then they will say, 'We have no king
    because we did not revere the LORD.
But even if we had a king,
    what could he do for us?'
⁴They make many promises,
    take false oaths
    and make agreements;
therefore lawsuits spring up
    like poisonous weeds in a ploughed field.
⁵The people who live in Samaria fear
    for the calf-idol of Beth Aven.ᵃ
Its people will mourn over it,
    and so will its idolatrous priests,
those who had rejoiced over its splendour,
    because it is taken from them into exile.
⁶It will be carried to Assyria
    as tribute for the great king.
Ephraim will be disgraced;
    Israel will be ashamed of its foreign alliances.
⁷Samaria's king will be destroyed,
    swept away like a twig on the surface of the waters.
⁸The high places of wickednessᵇ will be destroyed—
    it is the sin of Israel.
Thorns and thistles will grow up
    and cover their altars.
Then they will say to the mountains,
    'Cover us!'
    and to the hills, 'Fall on us!'

⁹'Since the days of Gibeah, you have sinned, Israel,
    and there you have remained.ᶜ

making Connections

Vines
Hosea 10:1

Vines grew well in the soil and climate of Palestine, but it was a lot of work to look after them. Every year the vines would be pruned, and any branches that were not producing fruit were cut off. Grapes were harvested in September and October with much celebration. Here, Israel is likened to a vine. Jesus calls himself the true vine in John 15:1.

ᵃ5 *Beth Aven* means *house of wickedness* (a derogatory name for Bethel, which means *house of God*). ᵇ8 Hebrew *aven*, a reference to Beth Aven (a derogatory name for Bethel); see verse 5. ᶜ9 Or *there a stand was taken*

Will not war again overtake
    the evildoers in Gibeah?
[10]When I please, I will punish them;
    nations will be gathered against them
    to put them in bonds for their double sin.
[11]Ephraim is a trained heifer
    that loves to thresh;
so I will put a yoke
    on her fair neck.
I will drive Ephraim,
    Judah must plough,
    and Jacob must break up the ground.
[12]Sow for yourselves righteousness,
    reap the fruit of unfailing love,
and break up your unploughed ground;
    for it is time to seek the LORD,
until he comes
    and showers his righteousness on you.
[13]But you have planted wickedness,
    you have reaped evil,
    you have eaten the fruit of deception.
Because you have depended on your own strength
    and on your many warriors,
[14]the roar of battle will rise against your people,
    so that all your fortresses will be devastated—
as Shalman devastated Beth Arbel on the day of battle,
    when mothers were dashed to the ground with their children.
[15]So will it happen to you, Bethel,
    because your wickedness is great.
When that day dawns,
    the king of Israel will be completely destroyed.

God's love for Israel

11 'When Israel was a child, I loved him,
    and out of Egypt I called my son.
[2]But the more they were called,
    the more they went away from me.[a]
They sacrificed to the Baals
    and they burned incense to images.
[3]It was I who taught Ephraim to walk,
    taking them by the arms;
but they did not realise
    it was I who healed them.
[4]I led them with cords of human kindness,
    with ties of love.
To them I was like one who lifts
    a little child to the cheek,
    and I bent down to feed them.

[5]'Will they not return to Egypt
    and will not Assyria rule over them
    because they refuse to repent?
[6]Swords will flash in their cities,
    will destroy the bars of their gates
    and put an end to their plans.
[7]My people are determined to turn from me.
    Even though they call me God Most High,
    I will by no means exalt them.

[8]'How can I give you up, Ephraim?
    How can I hand you over, Israel?
How can I treat you like Admah?
    How can I make you like Zeboyim?
My heart is changed within me;
    all my compassion is aroused.
[9]I will not carry out my fierce anger,
    nor will I devastate Ephraim again.
For I am God, and not a human being—
    the Holy One among you.
    I will not come against their cities.
[10]They will follow the LORD;
    he will roar like a lion.
When he roars,
    his children will come trembling from the west.
[11]They will come trembling
    like birds from Egypt,
    like doves from Assyria.
I will settle them in their homes,'
    declares the LORD.

Israel's sin

*[12]Ephraim has surrounded me with lies,
    the house of Israel with deceit.
And Judah is unruly against God,
    even against the faithful Holy One.

12 *[1]Ephraim feeds on the wind;
    he pursues the east wind all day
    and multiplies lies and violence.

---

[a] 2 Septuagint; Hebrew *them*

* 11:12 is numbered 12:1 in Hebrew texts.   * 12:1-14 is numbered 12:2-15 in Hebrew texts.

He makes a treaty with Assyria
and sends olive oil to Egypt.
²The LORD has a charge to bring against Judah;
he will punish Jacob[a] according to his ways
and repay him according to his deeds.
³In the womb he grasped his brother's heel;
as a man he struggled with God.
⁴He struggled with the angel and overcame him;
he wept and begged for his favour.
He found him at Bethel
and talked with him there—
⁵the LORD God Almighty,
the LORD is his name!
⁶But you must return to your God;
maintain love and justice,
and wait for your God always.

⁷The merchants use dishonest scales;
they love to defraud.
⁸Ephraim boasts,
'I am very rich; I have become wealthy.
With all my wealth they will not find in me
any iniquity or sin.'

⁹'I have been the LORD your God
ever since you came out of Egypt;
I will make you live in tents again,
as in the days of your appointed festivals.
¹⁰I spoke to the prophets,
gave them many visions
and told parables through them.'

¹¹Is Gilead wicked?
Its people are worthless!
Do they sacrifice bulls in Gilgal?
Their altars will be like piles of stones on a ploughed field.
¹²Jacob fled to the country of Aram;[b]
Israel served to get a wife,
and to pay for her he tended sheep.
¹³The LORD used a prophet to bring Israel up from Egypt,
by a prophet he cared for him.
¹⁴But Ephraim has aroused his bitter anger;
his Lord will leave on him the guilt of his bloodshed
and will repay him for his contempt.

The LORD's anger against Israel

13 When Ephraim spoke, people trembled;
he was exalted in Israel.
But he became guilty of Baal worship and died.
²Now they sin more and more;
they make idols for themselves from their silver,
cleverly fashioned images,
all of them the work of skilled hands.
It is said of them,
'They offer human sacrifices!
They kiss[c] calf-idols!'
³Therefore they will be like the morning mist,
like the early dew that disappears,
like chaff swirling from a threshing-floor,
like smoke escaping through a window.

⁴'But I have been the LORD your God
ever since you came out of Egypt.
You shall acknowledge no God but me,
no Saviour except me.
⁵I cared for you in the wilderness,
in the land of burning heat.
⁶When I fed them, they were satisfied;
when they were satisfied, they became proud;
then they forgot me.
⁷So I will come upon them like a lion,
like a leopard I will lurk by the path.
⁸Like a bear robbed of her cubs,
I will attack them and rip them open;
like a lion I will devour them—
a wild animal will tear them apart.

⁹'You are destroyed, Israel,
because you are against me, against your helper.
¹⁰Where is your king, that he may save you?
Where are your rulers in all your towns,
of whom you said,
"Give me a king and princes"?
¹¹So in my anger I gave you a king,
and in my wrath I took him away.
¹²The guilt of Ephraim is stored up,
his sins are kept on record.

---

[a] 2 *Jacob* means *he grasps the heel*, a Hebrew idiom for *he takes advantage of* or *he deceives*.   [b] 12 That is, North-west Mesopotamia   [c] 2 Or '*Men who sacrifice / kiss*

¹³Pains as of a woman in childbirth come to him,
> but he is a child without wisdom;
when the time arrives,
> he does not come to the opening of the womb.

¹⁴'I will deliver them from the power of the grave;
> I will redeem them from death.
Where, O death, are your plagues?
> Where, O grave, is your destruction?

'I will have no compassion,
¹⁵ even though he thrives among his brothers.
An east wind from the LORD will come,
> blowing in from the desert;
his spring will fail
> and his well dry up.
His storehouse will be plundered
> of all its treasures.
*¹⁶The people of Samaria must bear their guilt,
> because they have rebelled against their God.
They will fall by the sword;
> their little ones will be dashed to the ground,
> their pregnant women ripped open.'

Repentance to bring blessing

14 *'Return, Israel, to the LORD your God.
> Your sins have been your downfall!
²Take words with you
and return to the LORD.
Say to him:
'Forgive all our sins
and receive us graciously,
> that we may offer the fruit of our lips.^{a}
³Assyria cannot save us;
> we will not mount war-horses.
We will never again say "Our gods"
> to what our own hands have made,
for in you the fatherless find compassion.'

> ## IN OTHER WORDS
>
> ### Repent
> **Hosea 14:1**
> This call to return to the Lord is a call for repentance. 'To repent' means literally 'to turn around' or 'to change one's mind', which leads to a change in behaviour. In the Bible, the word 'repent' specifically means turning away from sin.

⁴'I will heal their waywardness
> and love them freely,
for my anger has turned away from them.
⁵I will be like the dew to Israel;
> he will blossom like a lily.
Like a cedar of Lebanon
> he will send down his roots;
⁶ his young shoots will grow.

His splendour will be like an olive tree,
> his fragrance like a cedar of Lebanon.
⁷People will dwell again in his shade;
> they will flourish like the corn,
they will blossom like the vine—
> Israel's fame will be like the wine of Lebanon.

⁸Ephraim, what more have I^b to do with idols?
> I will answer him and care for him.
I am like a flourishing juniper;
> your fruitfulness comes from me.'

⁹Who is wise? Let them realise these things.
> Who is discerning? Let them understand.
The ways of the LORD are right;
> the righteous walk in them,
> but the rebellious stumble in them.

---
^{a}2 Or *offer our lips as sacrifices of bulls* ^{b}8 Or Hebrew; Septuagint *What more has Ephraim*
* 13:16 is numbered 14:1 in Hebrew texts. * 14:1-9 is numbered 14:2-10 in Hebrew texts.

Joel

INTRODUCTION

JOEL

Author: Joel

When: Unknown. In fact very little is known about Joel, other than that he was the son of Pethuel. He doesn't mention any kings or historical events that might give a clue to when he wrote his book.

Did you know? The name Joel means 'the Lord is God'.

Main theme: Joel warns his readers to repent of their sins and turn back to God. He describes the devastation that has been left by a great swarm of locusts and explains that that would be nothing compared to what God could do in his judgment. But of course, those who do turn back to God will be restored and blessed.

1 The word of the LORD that came to Joel son of Pethuel.

An invasion of locusts

²Hear this, you elders;
 listen, all who live in the land.
Has anything like this ever happened in your days
 or in the days of your ancestors?
³Tell it to your children,
 and let your children tell it to their children,
 and their children to the next generation.
⁴What the locust swarm has left
 the great locusts have eaten;
what the great locusts have left
 the young locusts have eaten;
what the young locusts have left
 other locusts[a] have eaten.

⁵Wake up, you drunkards, and weep!
 Wail, all you drinkers of wine;
wail because of the new wine,
 for it has been snatched from your lips.
⁶A nation has invaded my land,
 a mighty army without number;
it has the teeth of a lion,
 the fangs of a lioness.
⁷It has laid waste my vines
 and ruined my fig-trees.

---
[a] 4 The precise meaning of the four Hebrew words used here for locusts is uncertain.

Making Connections

Locusts
Joel 1:4

A locust is a type of grasshopper and, although it is a relatively small insect, it can do great damage when it is part of a swarm. A cloud of millions of locusts will descend on one place and eat every plant in sight. It's very difficult to stop a swarm of locusts.

It has stripped off their bark
   and thrown it away,
   leaving their branches white.

⁸Mourn like a virgin in sackcloth
   grieving for the betrothed of her youth.
⁹Grain offerings and drink offerings
   are cut off from the house of the LORD.
The priests are in mourning,
   those who minister before the LORD.
¹⁰The fields are ruined,
   the ground is dried up;
the grain is destroyed,
   the new wine is dried up,
   the olive oil fails.

¹¹Despair, you farmers,
   wail, you vine growers;
grieve for the wheat and the barley,
   because the harvest of the field is destroyed.
¹²The vine is dried up
   and the fig-tree is withered;
the pomegranate, the palm and the apple*ᵃ* tree—
   all the trees of the field—are dried up.
Surely the people's joy
   is withered away.

A call to lamentation

¹³Put on sackcloth, you priests, and mourn;
   wail, you who minister before the altar.
Come, spend the night in sackcloth,
   you who minister before my God;
for the grain offerings and drink offerings
   are withheld from the house of your God.

¹⁴Declare a holy fast;
   call a sacred assembly.
Summon the elders
   and all who live in the land
to the house of the LORD your God,
   and cry out to the LORD.

¹⁵Alas for that day!
   For the day of the LORD is near;
   it will come like destruction from the Almighty.*ᵇ*

¹⁶Has not the food been cut off
   before our very eyes—
joy and gladness
   from the house of our God?
¹⁷The seeds are shrivelled
   beneath the clods.*ᶜ*
The storehouses are in ruins,
   the granaries have been broken down,
   for the grain has dried up.
¹⁸How the cattle moan!
   The herds mill about
because they have no pasture;
   even the flocks of sheep are suffering.

¹⁹To you, LORD, I call,
   for fire has devoured the pastures in the wilderness
and flames have burned up all the trees of the field.
²⁰Even the wild animals pant for you;
   the streams of water have dried up
   and fire has devoured the pastures in the wilderness.

An army of locusts

2 Blow the trumpet in Zion;
   sound the alarm on my holy hill.

Let all who live in the land tremble,
   for the day of the LORD is coming.
It is close at hand—
² a day of darkness and gloom,
   a day of clouds and blackness.
Like dawn spreading across the mountains
   a large and mighty army comes,

ᵃ 12 Or possibly *apricot* *ᵇ* 15 Hebrew *Shaddai* *ᶜ* 17 The meaning of the Hebrew for this word is uncertain.

such as never was of old
   nor ever will be in ages to come.
³Before them fire devours,
   behind them a flame blazes.
Before them the land is like the garden of Eden,
   behind them, a desert waste—
   nothing escapes them.
⁴They have the appearance of horses;
   they gallop along like cavalry.
⁵With a noise like that of chariots
   they leap over the mountaintops,
like a crackling fire consuming stubble,
   like a mighty army drawn up for battle.
⁶At the sight of them, nations are in anguish;
   every face turns pale.
⁷They charge like warriors;
   they scale walls like soldiers.
They all march in line,
   not swerving from their course.
⁸They do not jostle each other;
   each marches straight ahead.
They plunge through defences
   without breaking ranks.
⁹They rush upon the city;
   they run along the wall.
They climb into the houses;
   like thieves they enter through the windows.

¹⁰Before them the earth shakes,
   the heavens tremble,
the sun and moon are darkened,
   and the stars no longer shine.
¹¹The LORD thunders
   at the head of his army;
his forces are beyond number,
   and mighty is the army that obeys his command.
The day of the LORD is great;
   it is dreadful.
Who can endure it?

Rend your heart

¹²'Even now,' declares the LORD,
   'return to me with all your heart,
   with fasting and weeping and mourning.'
¹³Rend your heart
   and not your garments.
Return to the LORD your God,
   for he is gracious and compassionate,
slow to anger and abounding in love,
   and he relents from sending calamity.
¹⁴Who knows? He may turn and relent
   and leave behind a blessing—
grain offerings and drink offerings
   for the LORD your God.

¹⁵Blow the trumpet in Zion,
   declare a holy fast,
   call a sacred assembly.
¹⁶Gather the people,
   consecrate the assembly;
bring together the elders,
   gather the children,
   those nursing at the breast.
Let the bridegroom leave his room
   and the bride her chamber.
¹⁷Let the priests, who minister before the LORD,
   weep between the portico and the altar.
Let them say, 'Spare your people, LORD.
   Do not make your inheritance an object of scorn,
   a byword among the nations.
Why should they say among the peoples,
   "Where is their God?"'

The LORD's answer

¹⁸Then the LORD was jealous for his land
   and took pity on his people.

¹⁹The LORD replied*ᵃ* to them:

'I am sending you grain, new wine and olive oil,
   enough to satisfy you fully;
never again will I make you
   an object of scorn to the nations.

²⁰'I will drive the northern horde far from you,
   pushing it into a parched and barren land;
its eastern ranks will drown in the Dead Sea
   and its western ranks in the Mediterranean Sea.
And its stench will go up;
   its smell will rise.'

ᵃ 18, 19 Or LORD will be jealous . . . / and take pity . . . / ¹⁹The LORD will reply

Surely he has done great things!
21 Do not be afraid, land of Judah;
be glad and rejoice.
Surely the LORD has done great things!
22 Do not be afraid, you wild animals,
for the pastures in the wilderness are becoming green.
The trees are bearing their fruit;
the fig-tree and the vine yield their riches.
23 Be glad, people of Zion,
rejoice in the LORD your God,
for he has given you
the autumn rains in righteousness.
He sends you abundant showers,
both autumn and spring rains, as before.
24 The threshing-floors will be filled with grain;
the vats will overflow with new wine and oil.

25 'I will repay you for the years the locusts have eaten—
the great locust and the young locust,
the other locusts and the locust swarm[a]—
my great army that I sent among you.
26 You will have plenty to eat, until you are full,
and you will praise the name of the LORD your God,
who has worked wonders for you;
never again will my people be shamed.
27 Then you will know that I am in Israel,
that I am the LORD your God,
and that there is no other;
never again will my people be shamed.

The day of the LORD

*28 'And afterwards,
I will pour out my Spirit on all people.
Your sons and daughters will prophesy,
your old men will dream dreams,
your young men will see visions.
29 Even on my servants, both men and women,
I will pour out my Spirit in those days.

> **IN OTHER WORDS**
>
> **Deliverance**
> Joel 2:32
> When God's people are suffering from oppression, they cry out to him for rescue or deliverance, longing to be set free. This term is also used to describe someone's release from demonic forces.

30 I will show wonders in the heavens
and on the earth,
blood and fire and billows of smoke.
31 The sun will be turned to darkness
and the moon to blood
before the coming of the great and dreadful day of the LORD.
32 And everyone who calls
on the name of the LORD will be saved;
for on Mount Zion and in Jerusalem
there will be deliverance,
as the LORD has said,
even among the survivors
whom the LORD calls.

The nations judged

3 *'In those days and at that time,
when I restore the fortunes of Judah and Jerusalem,
2 I will gather all nations
and bring them down to the Valley of Jehoshaphat.[b]
There I will enter into judgment against them
concerning my inheritance, my people Israel,
for they scattered my people among the nations
and divided up my land.
3 They cast lots for my people
and traded boys for prostitutes;
they sold girls for wine
that they might drink.

4 'Now what have you against me, Tyre and Sidon and all you regions of Philistia?

---

[a] 25 The precise meaning of the four Hebrew words used here for locusts is uncertain.   [b] 2 *Jehoshaphat* means *the LORD judges*; also in verse 12.

* 2:28-32 is numbered 3:1-5 in Hebrew texts.   * 3:1-21 is numbered 4:1-21 in Hebrew texts.

Are you repaying me for something I have done? If you are paying me back, I will swiftly and speedily return on your own heads what you have done. ⁵For you took my silver and my gold and carried off my finest treasures to your temples.ᵃ ⁶You sold the people of Judah and Jerusalem to the Greeks, that you might send them far from their homeland.

⁷'See, I am going to rouse them out of the places to which you sold them, and I will return on your own heads what you have done. ⁸I will sell your sons and daughters to the people of Judah, and they will sell them to the Sabeans, a nation far away.' The LORD has spoken.

⁹Proclaim this among the nations:
  prepare for war!
Rouse the warriors!
  Let all the fighting men draw near and attack.
¹⁰Beat your ploughshares into swords
  and your pruning hooks into spears.
Let the weakling say,
  'I am strong!'
¹¹Come quickly, all you nations from every side,
  and assemble there.

Bring down your warriors, LORD!

¹²'Let the nations be roused;
  let them advance into the Valley of Jehoshaphat,
for there I will sit
  to judge all the nations on every side.
¹³Swing the sickle,
  for the harvest is ripe.
Come, trample the grapes,
  for the winepress is full
  and the vats overflow—
so great is their wickedness!'

¹⁴Multitudes, multitudes
  in the valley of decision!
For the day of the LORD is near
  in the valley of decision.
¹⁵The sun and moon will be darkened,
  and the stars no longer shine.
¹⁶The LORD will roar from Zion
  and thunder from Jerusalem;
  the earth and the heavens will tremble.
But the LORD will be a refuge for his people,
  a stronghold for the people of Israel.

Blessings for God's people

¹⁷'Then you will know that I, the LORD your God,
  dwell in Zion, my holy hill.
Jerusalem will be holy;
  never again will foreigners invade her.

¹⁸'In that day the mountains will drip new wine,
  and the hills will flow with milk;
  all the ravines of Judah will run with water.
A fountain will flow out of the LORD's house
  and will water the valley of acacias.ᵇ
¹⁹But Egypt will be desolate,
  Edom a desert waste,
because of violence done to the people of Judah,
  in whose land they shed innocent blood.
²⁰Judah will be inhabited for ever
  and Jerusalem through all generations.
²¹Shall I leave their innocent blood unpunished?
  No, I will not.'

  The LORD dwells in Zion!

ᵃ 5 Or *palaces* ᵇ 18 Or *Valley of Shittim*

Amos

INTRODUCTION

AMOS

Author: Amos

Who to: Both Judah and Israel.

When: During the reigns of King Uzziah of Judah and King Jeroboam of Israel, around 760 BC.

Where: Amos lived in Tekoa, a village near Jerusalem in Judah.

Did you know? Amos was a shepherd who also looked after sycamore fruit (Amos 7:14).

Main theme: Justice is the main theme of the book of Amos. He sees the people living in luxury with no concern for the poor and he reminds them that justice is far more important than going through the motions of worship. Amos is also a book of judgment – against the surrounding nations, against Judah, and most harshly against Israel for rejecting the one true God in order to worship false gods.

1 The words of Amos, one of the shepherds of Tekoa—the vision he saw concerning Israel two years before the earthquake, when Uzziah was king of Judah and Jeroboam son of Jehoash[a] was king of Israel.

²He said:

'The LORD roars from Zion
 and thunders from Jerusalem;
the pastures of the shepherds dry up,
 and the top of Carmel withers.'

Judgment on Israel's neighbours

³This is what the LORD says:

'For three sins of Damascus,
 even for four, I will not turn back ⌊my wrath⌋.

---

[a] 1 Hebrew *Joash*, a variant of *Jehoash*

making Connections

Dramatic announcements
Amos 1:3

At award ceremonies the winners are often announced in reverse order, allowing a nice build-up of tension to see who has won the top prize. Amos uses a similar dramatic effect when he talks about God's judgment. He starts with places that are far away and people who are distant ethnic relations, and circles in to pronounce God's longest judgment on his own people, Israel.

Because she threshed Gilead
  with sledges having iron teeth,
⁴I will send fire on the house of Hazael
  that will consume the fortresses of Ben-Hadad.
⁵I will break down the gate of Damascus;
  I will destroy the king who is in^a the Valley of Aven^b
and the one who holds the sceptre in Beth Eden.
  The people of Aram will go into exile to Kir,'
                                    says the LORD.

⁶This is what the LORD says:

'For three sins of Gaza,
  even for four, I will not turn back ⌊my wrath⌋.
Because she took captive whole communities
  and sold them to Edom,
⁷I will send fire on the walls of Gaza
  that will consume her fortresses.
⁸I will destroy the king^c of Ashdod
  and the one who holds the sceptre in Ashkelon.

I will turn my hand against Ekron,
  till the last of the Philistines are dead,'
                         says the Sovereign LORD.

⁹This is what the LORD says:

'For three sins of Tyre,
  even for four, I will not turn back ⌊my wrath⌋.
Because she sold whole communities of captives to Edom,
  disregarding a treaty of brotherhood,
¹⁰I will send fire on the walls of Tyre
  that will consume her fortresses.'

¹¹This is what the LORD says:

'For three sins of Edom,
  even for four, I will not turn back ⌊my wrath⌋.
Because he pursued his brother with a sword
  and slaughtered the women of the land,
because his anger raged continually
  and his fury flamed unchecked,
¹²I will send fire on Teman
  that will consume the fortresses of Bozrah.'

¹³This is what the LORD says:

'For three sins of Ammon,
  even for four, I will not turn back ⌊my wrath⌋.
Because he ripped open the pregnant women of Gilead
  in order to extend his borders,
¹⁴I will set fire to the walls of Rabbah
  that will consume her fortresses
amid war cries on the day of battle,
  amid violent winds on a stormy day.
¹⁵Their king^d will go into exile,
  he and his officials together,'
                                    says the LORD.

2 This is what the LORD says:

'For three sins of Moab,
  even for four, I will not turn back ⌊my wrath⌋.
Because he burned to lime
  the bones of Edom's king,

---

^{a} 5 Or *the inhabitants of* ^{b} 5 *Aven* means *wickedness*. ^{c} 8 Or *inhabitants* ^{d} 15 Or /*Molek*

> **IN OTHER WORDS**
>
> **Justice**
> Amos 2:7
> The main use of the word 'justice' in the Bible refers to the honest practice of the law so that God's people could rely on their legal system. God also demands justice from individuals, particularly in relation to the poor. Justice is seen as one of God's most important attributes.

²I will send fire on Moab
 that will consume the fortresses of Kerioth.ᵃ
Moab will go down in great tumult
 amid war cries and the blast of the trumpet.
³I will destroy her ruler
 and kill all her officials with him,'
     says the LORD.

⁴This is what the LORD says:

'For three sins of Judah,
 even for four, I will not turn back ⌊my wrath⌋.
Because they have rejected the law of the LORD
 and have not kept his decrees,
because they have been led astray by false gods,ᵇ
 the godsᶜ their ancestors followed,
⁵I will send fire on Judah
 that will consume the fortresses of Jerusalem.'

Judgment on Israel

⁶This is what the LORD says:

'For three sins of Israel,
 even for four, I will not turn back ⌊my wrath⌋.
They sell the innocent for silver,
 and the needy for a pair of sandals.
⁷They trample on the heads of the poor
 as on the dust of the ground
 and deny justice to the oppressed.
Father and son use the same girl
 and so profane my holy name.
⁸They lie down beside every altar
 on garments taken in pledge.
In the house of their god
 they drink wine taken as fines.

⁹'Yet I destroyed the Amorites before them,
 though they were tall as the cedars
 and strong as the oaks.
I destroyed their fruit above
 and their roots below.
¹⁰I brought you up out of Egypt
 and led you for forty years in the wilderness
 to give you the land of the Amorites.

¹¹'I also raised up prophets from among your children
 and Nazirites from among your youths.
Is this not true, people of Israel?'
     declares the LORD.
¹²'But you made the Nazirites drink wine
 and commanded the prophets not to prophesy.

¹³'Now then, I will crush you
 as a cart crushes when loaded with grain.
¹⁴The swift will not escape,
 the strong will not muster their strength,
 and the warrior will not save his life.
¹⁵The archer will not stand his ground,
 the fleet-footed soldier will not get away,
 and the horseman will not save his life.
¹⁶Even the bravest warriors
 will flee naked on that day,'
     declares the LORD.

Witnesses summoned against Israel

3 Hear this word, people of Israel, the word the LORD has spoken against you—against the whole family I brought up out of Egypt:

²'You only have I chosen
 of all the families of the earth;
therefore I will punish you
 for all your sins.'

ᵃ 2 Or *of her cities* ᵇ 4 Or *by lies* ᶜ 4 Or *lies*

³Do two walk together
  unless they have agreed to do so?
⁴Does a lion roar in the thicket
  when it has no prey?
Does it growl in its den
  when it has caught nothing?
⁵Does a bird swoop down to a trap on the ground
  when no bait is there?
Does a trap spring up from the ground
  if it has not caught anything?
⁶When a trumpet sounds in a city,
  do not the people tremble?
When disaster comes to a city,
  has not the LORD caused it?

⁷Surely the Sovereign LORD does nothing
  without revealing his plan
  to his servants the prophets.

⁸The lion has roared—
  who will not fear?
The Sovereign LORD has spoken—
  who can but prophesy?

⁹Proclaim to the fortresses of Ashdod
  and to the fortresses of Egypt:
'Assemble yourselves on the mountains of Samaria;
  see the great unrest within her
  and the oppression among her people.'

¹⁰'They do not know how to do right,'
        declares the LORD,
  'who store up in their fortresses
  what they have plundered and looted.'

¹¹Therefore this is what the Sovereign LORD says:

'An enemy will overrun your land,
  pull down your strongholds
  and plunder your fortresses.'

¹²This is what the LORD says:

'As a shepherd saves from the lion's mouth
  only two leg bones or a piece of an ear,
so will the Israelites be saved,
  those who sit in Samaria
  on the edge of their beds
  and in Damascus on their couches.'ᵃ

¹³'Hear this and testify against the house of Jacob,' declares the Lord, the LORD God Almighty.
¹⁴'On the day I punish Israel for her sins,
  I will destroy the altars of Bethel;
the horns of the altar will be cut off
  and fall to the ground.
¹⁵I will tear down the winter house
  along with the summer house;
the houses adorned with ivory will be destroyed
  and the mansions will be demolished,'
        declares the LORD.

Israel has not returned to God

4 Hear this word, you cows of Bashan on Mount Samaria,
  you women who oppress the poor
  and crush the needy
and say to your husbands, 'Bring us some drinks!'
²The Sovereign LORD has sworn by his holiness:

'The time will surely come
when you will be taken away with hooks,
  the last of you with fishhooks.ᵇ
³You will each go straight out
  through breaches in the wall,
  and you will be cast out towards Harmon,'ᶜ
        declares the LORD.
⁴'Go to Bethel and sin;
  go to Gilgal and sin yet more.
Bring your sacrifices every morning,
  your tithes every three years.ᵈ
⁵Burn leavened bread as a thank-offering
  and brag about your freewill offerings—
boast about them, you Israelites,
  for this is what you love to do,'
        declares the Sovereign LORD.

⁶'I gave you empty stomachs in every city
  and lack of bread in every town,
  yet you have not returned to me,'
        declares the LORD.

⁷'I also withheld rain from you
  when the harvest was still three months away.

ᵃ 12 Or *Israelites living in Samaria be saved, / with only the head of a bed / and a piece of fabric from a couch*   ᵇ 2 Or *away in baskets, / the last of you in fish baskets*   ᶜ 3 Masoretic Text; with a different word division of the Hebrew (see Septuagint) *out, you mountain of oppression*   ᵈ 4 Or *days*

I sent rain on one town,
   but withheld it from another.
One field had rain;
   another had none and dried up.
⁸People staggered from town to town for water
   but did not get enough to drink,
   yet you have not returned to me,'
         declares the LORD.

⁹'Many times I struck your gardens and vineyards,
   destroying them with blight and mildew.
Locusts devoured your fig and olive trees,
   yet you have not returned to me,'
         declares the LORD.

¹⁰'I sent plagues among you
   as I did to Egypt.
I killed your young men with the sword,
   along with your captured horses.
I filled your nostrils with the stench of your camps,
   yet you have not returned to me,'
         declares the LORD.

¹¹'I overthrew some of you
   as I overthrew Sodom and Gomorrah.
You were like a burning stick snatched from the fire,
   yet you have not returned to me,'
         declares the LORD.

¹²'Therefore this is what I will do to you, Israel,
   and because I will do this to you, Israel,
   prepare to meet your God.'

¹³He who forms the mountains,
   who creates the wind,
   and who reveals his thoughts to mortals,
who turns dawn to darkness,
   and treads on the heights of the earth—
   the LORD God Almighty is his name.

A lament and call to repentance

5 Hear this word, house of Israel, this lament I take up concerning you:

²'Fallen is Virgin Israel,
   never to rise again,
deserted in her own land,
   with no-one to lift her up.'

³This is what the Sovereign LORD says to the house of Israel:

'Your city that marches out a thousand strong
   will have only a hundred left;
your town that marches out a hundred strong
   will have only ten left.'

⁴This is what the LORD says to the house of Israel:

'Seek me and live;
⁵   do not seek Bethel,
   do not go to Gilgal,
      do not journey to Beersheba.
For Gilgal will surely go into exile,
   and Bethel will be reduced to nothing.'ᵃ
⁶Seek the LORD and live,
   or he will sweep through the house of Joseph like a fire;
it will devour them,
   and Bethel will have no-one to quench it.

⁷There are those who turn justice into bitterness
   and cast righteousness to the ground.

⁸He who made the Pleiades and Orion,
   who turns midnight into dawn
   and darkens day into night,
who calls for the waters of the sea
   and pours them out over the face of the land—
   the LORD is his name.
⁹He flashes destruction on the stronghold
   and brings the fortified city to ruin.

¹⁰There are those who hate the one who reproves in court
   and detest the one who tells the truth.

¹¹You levy a straw tax on the poor
   and impose a tax on their grain.
Therefore, though you have built stone mansions,
   you will not live in them;
though you have planted lush vineyards,
   you will not drink their wine.
¹²For I know how many are your offences
   and how great your sins.

ᵃ 5 Hebrew *aven*, a reference to Beth Aven (a derogatory name for Bethel); see Hosea 4:15.

IN OTHER WORDS

Religion
Amos 5:21

The word 'religion' describes activities such as worship, ritual, prayer and morality by which people express their belief in God. The term is sometimes used negatively in the Bible because of the belief that religious activity will never earn us salvation. Only God's activity can save.

There are those who oppress the innocent
    and take bribes
    and deprive the poor of justice in the courts.
13 Therefore the prudent keep quiet in such times,
    for the times are evil.

14 Seek good, not evil,
    that you may live.
Then the LORD God Almighty will be with you,
    just as you say he is.
15 Hate evil, love good;
    maintain justice in the courts.
Perhaps the LORD God Almighty will have mercy
    on the remnant of Joseph.

16 Therefore this is what the Lord, the LORD God Almighty, says:

'There will be wailing in all the streets
    and cries of anguish in every public square.
The farmers will be summoned to weep
    and the mourners to wail.
17 There will be wailing in all the vineyards,
    for I will pass through your midst,'
        says the LORD.

The day of the LORD

18 Woe to you who long
    for the day of the LORD!
Why do you long for the day of the LORD?
    That day will be darkness, not light.
19 It will be as though a man fled from a lion
    only to meet a bear,
as though he entered his house
    and rested his hand on the wall
    only to have a snake bite him.
20 Will not the day of the LORD be darkness, not light—
    pitch-dark, without a ray of brightness?

21 'I hate, I despise your religious festivals;
    I cannot stand your assemblies.
22 Even though you bring me burnt offerings and grain offerings,
    I will not accept them.
Though you bring choice fellowship offerings,
    I will have no regard for them.
23 Away with the noise of your songs!
    I will not listen to the music of your harps.
24 But let justice roll on like a river,
    righteousness like a never-failing stream!

25 'Did you bring me sacrifices and offerings
    for forty years in the wilderness, house of Israel?
26 You have lifted up the shrine of your king,
    the pedestal of your idols,
    the star of your god—[a]
    which you made for yourselves.
27 Therefore I will send you into exile
    beyond Damascus,'
        says the LORD, whose name is God Almighty.

Woe to the complacent

6 Woe to you who are complacent in Zion,
    and to you who feel secure on Mount Samaria,
you notable men of the foremost nation,
    to whom the people of Israel come!
2 Go to Kalneh and look at it;
    go from there to great Hamath,
    and then go down to Gath in Philistia.
Are they better off than your two kingdoms?

---

[a] 26 Or *lifted up Sakkuth your king / and Kaiwan your idols, / your star-gods*; Septuagint *lifted up the shrine of Molek / and the star of your god Rephan, / their idols*

Is their land larger than yours?
³You put off the evil day
 and bring near a reign of terror.
⁴You lie on beds inlaid with ivory
 and lounge on your couches.
 You dine on choice lambs
 and fattened calves.
⁵You strum away on your harps like David
 and improvise on musical instruments.
⁶You drink wine by the bowlful
 and use the finest lotions,
 but you do not grieve over the ruin of Joseph.
⁷Therefore you will be among the first to go into exile;
 your feasting and lounging will end.

The LORD abhors the pride of Israel

⁸The Sovereign LORD has sworn by himself—the LORD God Almighty declares:

'I abhor the pride of Jacob
 and detest his fortresses;
I will deliver up the city
 and everything in it.'

⁹If ten people are left in one house, they too will die. ¹⁰And if the relative who comes to carry the bodies out of the house to burn them[a] asks anyone who might be hiding there, 'Is anyone else with you?' and he says, 'No,' then he will go on to say, 'Hush! We must not mention the name of the LORD.'

¹¹For the LORD has given the command,
 and he will smash the great house into pieces
 and the small house into bits.

¹²Do horses run on the rocky crags?
 Does one plough the sea[b] with oxen?
But you have turned justice into poison
 and the fruit of righteousness into bitterness—
¹³you who rejoice in the conquest of Lo Debar[c]
 and say, 'Did we not take Karnaim[d] by our own strength?'

¹⁴For the LORD God Almighty declares,
 'I will stir up a nation against you,
 house of Israel,
that will oppress you all the way
 from Lebo Hamath to the valley of the Arabah.'

Locusts, fire and a plumb-line

7 This is what the Sovereign LORD showed me: he was preparing swarms of locusts after the king's share had been harvested and just as the late crops were coming up. ²When they had stripped the land clean, I cried out, 'Sovereign LORD, forgive! How can Jacob survive? He is so small!'

³So the LORD relented.

'This will not happen,' the LORD said.

⁴This is what the Sovereign LORD showed me: the Sovereign LORD was calling for judgment by fire; it dried up the great deep and devoured the land. ⁵Then I cried out, 'Sovereign LORD, I beg you, stop! How can Jacob survive? He is so small!'

⁶So the LORD relented.

'This will not happen either,' the Sovereign LORD said.

⁷This is what he showed me: the Lord was standing by a wall that had been built true to plumb,[e] with a plumb-line[f] in his hand. ⁸And the LORD asked me, 'What do you see, Amos?'

'A plumb-line,' I replied.

Then the Lord said, 'Look, I am setting a plumb-line among my people Israel; I will spare them no longer.

⁹'The high places of Isaac will be destroyed

Plumb-line
Amos 7:7
A plumb-line is a small heavy weight on the end of a cord or a piece of string that is used to measure whether a wall is truly vertical.

---

[a] 10 Or *to make a funeral fire in honour of the dead* [b] 12 With a different word division of the Hebrew; Masoretic Text *plough there* [c] 13 *Lo Debar* means *nothing*. [d] 13 *Karnaim* means *horns*; *horn* here symbolises strength. [e] 7 The meaning of the Hebrew for this phrase is uncertain. [f] 7 The meaning of the Hebrew for this phrase is uncertain; also in verse 8.

and the sanctuaries of Israel will be ruined;
with my sword I will rise against the house of Jeroboam.'

Amos and Amaziah

10 Then Amaziah the priest of Bethel sent a message to Jeroboam king of Israel: 'Amos is raising a conspiracy against you in the very heart of Israel. The land cannot bear all his words. 11 For this is what Amos is saying:

> '"Jeroboam will die by the sword,
> and Israel will surely go into exile,
> away from their native land."'

12 Then Amaziah said to Amos, 'Get out, you seer! Go back to the land of Judah. Earn your bread there and do your prophesying there. 13 Don't prophesy any more at Bethel, because this is the king's sanctuary and the temple of the kingdom.'

14 Amos answered Amaziah, 'I was neither a prophet nor the disciple of a prophet, but I was a shepherd, and I also took care of sycamore-fig trees. 15 But the LORD took me from tending the flock and said to me, "Go, prophesy to my people Israel." 16 Now then, hear the word of the LORD. You say,

> '"Do not prophesy against Israel,
> and stop preaching against the house of Isaac."

17 'Therefore this is what the LORD says:

> '"Your wife will become a prostitute in the city,
> and your sons and daughters will fall by the sword.
> Your land will be measured and divided up,
> and you yourself will die in a pagan[a] country.
> And Israel will surely go into exile,
> away from their native land."'

A basket of ripe fruit

8 This is what the Sovereign LORD showed me: a basket of ripe fruit. 2 'What do you see, Amos?' he asked.

'A basket of ripe fruit,' I answered.

Then the LORD said to me, 'The time is ripe for my people Israel; I will spare them no longer.

3 'In that day,' declares the Sovereign LORD, 'the songs in the temple will turn to wailing.[b] Many, many bodies—flung everywhere! Silence!'

4 Hear this, you who trample the needy
and do away with the poor of the land,

5 saying,

'When will the New Moon be over
that we may sell grain,
and the Sabbath be ended
that we may market wheat?'—
skimping on the measure,
boosting the price
and cheating with dishonest scales,
6 buying the poor with silver
and the needy for a pair of sandals,
selling even the sweepings with the wheat.

7 The LORD has sworn by himself, the Pride of Jacob: 'I will never forget anything they have done.

8 'Will not the land tremble for this,
and all who live in it mourn?
The whole land will rise like the Nile;
it will be stirred up and then sink
like the river of Egypt.

9 'In that day,' declares the Sovereign LORD,

'I will make the sun go down at noon
and darken the earth in broad daylight.
10 I will turn your religious festivals into mourning
and all your singing into weeping.
I will make all of you wear sackcloth
and shave your heads.
I will make that time like mourning for an only son
and the end of it like a bitter day.

11 'The days are coming,' declares the Sovereign LORD,

'when I will send a famine through the land—
not a famine of food or a thirst for water,

---

[a] 17 Hebrew *an unclean* [b] 3 Or *'the temple singers will wail*

but a famine of hearing the words of
  the LORD.
¹²People will stagger from sea to sea
  and wander from north to east,
searching for the word of the LORD,
  but they will not find it.

¹³'In that day

'the lovely young women and strong
    young men
  will faint because of thirst.
¹⁴Those who swear by the sin of Samaria—
  who say, "As surely as your god lives,
    Dan",
  or, "As surely as the god^a of Beersheba
    lives"—
  they will fall, never to rise again.'

Israel to be destroyed

9 I saw the Lord standing by the altar,
and he said:

'Strike the tops of the pillars
    so that the thresholds shake.
Bring them down on the heads of all the
    people;
  those who are left I will kill with the
    sword.
Not one will get away,
  none will escape.
²Though they dig down to the depths
    below,
  from there my hand will take them.
Though they climb up to the heavens
    above,
  from there I will bring them down.
³Though they hide themselves on the top
    of Carmel,
  there I will hunt them down and seize
    them.
Though they hide from my eyes at the
    bottom of the sea,
  there I will command the serpent to
    bite them.
⁴Though they are driven into exile by their
    enemies,
  there I will command the sword to slay
    them.

'I will fix my eyes on them
  for evil and not for good.'

⁵The Lord, the LORD Almighty—
he touches the earth and it melts,
  and all who live in it mourn;
the whole land rises like the Nile,
  then sinks like the river of Egypt;
⁶he builds his lofty palace^b in the heavens
  and sets its foundation^c on the earth;
he calls for the waters of the sea
  and pours them out over the face of the
    land—
  the LORD is his name.

⁷'Are not you Israelites
  the same to me as the Cushites?'^{d}
      declares the LORD.
'Did I not bring Israel up from Egypt,
  the Philistines from Caphtor^e
  and the Arameans from Kir?

⁸'Surely the eyes of the Sovereign LORD
  are on the sinful kingdom.
I will destroy it
  from the face of the earth.
Yet I will not totally destroy
  the house of Jacob,'
      declares the LORD.
⁹'For I will give the command,
  and I will shake the house of Israel
    among all the nations
as grain is shaken in a sieve,
  and not a pebble will reach the ground.
¹⁰All the sinners among my people
  will die by the sword,
all those who say,
  "Disaster will not overtake or meet
    us."

Israel's restoration

¹¹'In that day

I will restore David's fallen shelter—
  I will repair its broken walls
  and restore its ruins—
  and will rebuild it as it used to be,
¹²so that they may possess the remnant of
    Edom
  and all the nations that bear my name,'^{f}
      declares the LORD,
        who will do these things.

---

^{a} 14 Hebrew *the way* ^{b} 6 The meaning of the Hebrew for this phrase is uncertain. ^{c} 6 The meaning of the Hebrew for this word is uncertain. ^{d} 7 That is, people from the upper Nile region ^{e} 7 That is, Crete ^{f} 12 Hebrew; Septuagint *so that the remnant of people / and all the nations that bear my name may seek* [*the Lord*]

¹³'The days are coming,' declares the LORD,

> 'when the reaper will be overtaken by the one who ploughs
> and the planter by the one treading grapes.
> New wine will drip from the mountains and flow from all the hills,
> ¹⁴ and I will bring my people Israel back from exile.[a]
>
> 'They will rebuild the ruined cities and live in them.
> They will plant vineyards and drink their wine;
> they will make gardens and eat their fruit.
> ¹⁵I will plant Israel in their own land, never again to be uprooted
> from the land I have given them,'
>
> says the LORD your God.

---

[a] 14 Or *will restore the fortunes of my people Israel*

Obadiah

INTRODUCTION

Obadiah

Author: Obadiah

When: Probably written just after 586 BC when Jerusalem was destroyed by the Babylonians.

Where: After Jerusalem was destroyed, many of its citizens were taken to Babylon, although some stayed in the city.

Did you know? This is the shortest book in the Old Testament, just twenty-one verses.

Main theme: Obadiah has a message from God against the people of Edom. The Edomites mocked God's people when Jerusalem was under siege, and then joined in the destruction and looting of the city. As a result, says Obadiah, Edom will be destroyed, but Judah will be blessed and will return to her land.

¹The vision of Obadiah.

This is what the Sovereign LORD says about Edom—

We have heard a message from the LORD:
　an envoy was sent to the nations to say,
'Rise, let us go against her for battle'—

²'See, I will make you small among the nations;
　you will be utterly despised.
³The pride of your heart has deceived you,
　you who live in the clefts of the rocks*ᵃ*
and make your home on the heights,
you who say to yourself,
　"Who can bring me down to the ground?"
⁴Though you soar like the eagle
　and make your nest among the stars,
　from there I will bring you down,'
　　　　　　　declares the LORD.
⁵'If thieves came to you,
　if robbers in the night—
oh, what a disaster awaits you—
　would they not steal only as much as they wanted?

ᵃ 3 Or *of Sela*

People and Places

Edom
Obadiah 1:8

Edom was another name for Esau, the brother of Jacob. The Israelites were descended from Jacob and the Edomites were descended from his brother Esau, so they shared some common history. But there was no love lost between them.

If grape pickers came to you,
  would they not leave a few grapes?
⁶But how Esau will be ransacked,
  his hidden treasures pillaged!
⁷All your allies will force you to the border;
  your friends will deceive and overpower you;
those who eat your bread will set a trap for you,*ᵃ*
  but you will not detect it.

⁸'In that day,' declares the LORD,
  'will I not destroy the wise in Edom,
  people of understanding in the mountains of Esau?
⁹Your warriors, Teman, will be terrified,
  and everyone in Esau's mountains
    will be cut down in the slaughter.
¹⁰Because of the violence against your brother Jacob,
  you will be covered with shame;
  you will be destroyed for ever.
¹¹On the day you stood aloof
  while strangers carried off his wealth
and foreigners entered his gates
  and cast lots for Jerusalem,
  you were like one of them.
¹²You should not gloat over your brother
  in the day of his misfortune,
nor rejoice over the people of Judah
  in the day of their destruction,
nor boast so much
  in the day of their trouble.
¹³You should not march through the gates of my people
  in the day of their disaster,
nor gloat over them in their calamity
  in the day of their disaster,
nor seize their wealth
  in the day of their disaster.
¹⁴You should not wait at the crossroads
  to cut down their fugitives,
nor hand over their survivors
  in the day of their trouble.

¹⁵'The day of the LORD is near
  for all nations.
As you have done, it will be done to you;
  your deeds will return upon your own head.
¹⁶Just as you drank on my holy hill,
  so all the nations will drink continually;
they will drink and drink
  and be as if they had never been.
¹⁷But on Mount Zion will be deliverance;
  it will be holy,
and the house of Jacob
  will possess its inheritance.
¹⁸The house of Jacob will be a fire
  and the house of Joseph a flame;
the house of Esau will be stubble,
  and they will set it on fire and consume it.
There will be no survivors
  from the house of Esau.'
            The LORD has spoken.

¹⁹People from the Negev will occupy
  the mountains of Esau,
and people from the foothills will possess
  the land of the Philistines.
They will occupy the fields of Ephraim and Samaria,
  and Benjamin will possess Gilead.
²⁰This company of Israelite exiles who are in Canaan
  will possess ⌊the land⌋ as far as Zarephath;
the exiles from Jerusalem who are in Sepharad
  will possess the towns of the Negev.
²¹Deliverers will go up on*ᵇ* Mount Zion
  to govern the mountains of Esau.
And the kingdom will be the LORD's.

ᵃ 7 The meaning of the Hebrew for this clause is uncertain.   *ᵇ* 21 Or *from*

Jonah

INTRODUCTION

JONAH

Author: Jonah

When: Probably around 760 BC.

Where: Nineveh was the capital of the Assyrian empire.

Did you know? Jonah also makes an appearance in 2 Kings 14:25.

Main theme: The book of Jonah shows that God's love is for all people, even for pagans and Gentiles as well as for his own chosen people, the Israelites. Jonah was a very reluctant and sulky prophet but God still used him.

Jonah flees from the LORD

1 The word of the LORD came to Jonah son of Amittai: ²'Go to the great city Nineveh and preach against it, because its wickedness has come up before me.'

³But Jonah ran away from the LORD and headed for Tarshish. He went down to Joppa, where he found a ship bound for that port. After paying the fare, he went aboard and sailed for Tarshish to flee from the LORD.

⁴Then the LORD sent a great wind on the sea, and such a violent storm arose that the ship threatened to break up. ⁵All the sailors were afraid and each cried out to his own god. And they threw the cargo into the sea to lighten the ship.

But Jonah had gone below deck, where he lay down and fell into a deep sleep. ⁶The captain went to him and said, 'How can you sleep? Get up and call on your god! Maybe he will take notice of us so that we will not perish.'

⁷Then the sailors said to each other, 'Come, let us cast lots to find out who is responsible for this calamity.' They cast lots and the lot fell on Jonah. ⁸So they asked him, 'Tell us, who is responsible for making all this trouble for us? What kind of work do you do? Where do you come from? What is your country? From what people are you?'

⁹He answered, 'I am a Hebrew and I worship the LORD, the God of heaven, who made the sea and the dry land.'

¹⁰This terrified them and they asked, 'What have you done?' (They knew he was running away from the LORD, because he had already told them so.)

People and Places

Tarshish
Jonah 1:3

The city of Tarshish is probably now Tartessus in southern Spain, near Gibraltar. It was literally in the opposite direction to Nineveh, so there is no doubt that Jonah was trying to run away!

---

¹¹The sea was getting rougher and rougher. So they asked him, 'What should we do to you to make the sea calm down for us?'

¹²'Pick me up and throw me into the sea,' he replied, 'and it will become calm. I know that it is my fault that this great storm has come upon you.'

¹³Instead, the men did their best to row back to land. But they could not, for the sea grew even wilder than before. ¹⁴Then they cried out to the LORD, 'Please, LORD, do not let us die for taking this man's life. Do not hold us accountable for killing an innocent man, for you, LORD, have done as you pleased.' ¹⁵Then they took Jonah and threw him overboard, and the raging sea grew calm. ¹⁶At this the men greatly feared the LORD, and they offered a sacrifice to the LORD and made vows to him.

*¹⁷Now the LORD provided a huge fish to swallow Jonah, and Jonah was in the belly of the fish three days and three nights.

Jonah's prayer

2 *From inside the fish Jonah prayed to the LORD his God. ²He said:

'In my distress I called to the LORD,
  and he answered me.
From deep in the realm of the dead I called for help,
  and you listened to my cry.
³You hurled me into the deep,
  into the very heart of the seas,
  and the currents swirled about me;
all your waves and breakers
  swept over me.
⁴I said, "I have been banished
  from your sight;
yet I will look again
  towards your holy temple."
⁵The engulfing waters threatened me,ᵃ
  the deep surrounded me;
seaweed was wrapped around my head.
⁶To the roots of the mountains I sank down;
  the earth beneath barred me in for ever.
But you, LORD my God,
  brought my life up from the pit.

⁷'When my life was ebbing away,
  I remembered you, LORD,
and my prayer rose to you,
  to your holy temple.

⁸'Those who cling to worthless idols
  forfeit God's love for them.
⁹But I, with shouts of grateful praise,
  will sacrifice to you.
What I have vowed I will make good.
  I will say, "Salvation comes from the LORD."'

¹⁰And the LORD commanded the fish, and it vomited Jonah onto dry land.

Jonah goes to Nineveh

3 Then the word of the LORD came to Jonah a second time: ²'Go to the great city of Nineveh and proclaim to it the message I give you.'

³Jonah obeyed the word of the LORD and went to Nineveh. Now Nineveh was a very large city; it took three days to go through it. ⁴Jonah began by going a day's journey into the city, proclaiming, 'Forty more days and Nineveh will be overthrown.' ⁵The Ninevites believed God. They declared a fast, and all of them, from the greatest to the least, put on sackcloth.

⁶When the news reached the king of Nineveh, he rose from his throne, took off his royal robes, covered himself with sackcloth and sat down in the dust. ⁷Then he issued a proclamation in Nineveh:

ᵃ 5 Or *waters were at my throat*

* 1:17 is numbered 2:1 in Hebrew texts.   * 2:1-10 is numbered 2:2-11 in Hebrew texts.

'By the decree of the king and his nobles:

> Do not let people or animals, herds or flocks, taste anything; do not let them eat or drink. 8But let people and animals be covered with sackcloth. Let everyone call urgently on God. Let them give up their evil ways and their violence. 9Who knows? God may yet relent and with compassion turn from his fierce anger so that we will not perish.'

10When God saw what they did and how they turned from their evil ways, he relented and did not bring on them the destruction he had threatened.

Jonah's anger at the LORD's compassion

4 But to Jonah this seemed very wrong, and he became angry. 2He prayed to the LORD, 'Isn't this what I said, LORD, when I was still at home? That is what I tried to forestall by fleeing to Tarshish. I knew that you are a gracious and compassionate God, slow to anger and abounding in love, a God who relents from sending calamity. 3Now, LORD, take away my life, for it is better for me to die than to live.'

4But the LORD replied, 'Is it right for you to be angry?'

5Jonah went out and sat down at a place east of the city. There he made himself a shelter, sat in its shade and waited to see what would happen to the city. 6Then the LORD God provided a gourd[a] and made it grow up over Jonah to give shade for his head to ease his discomfort, and Jonah was very happy about the gourd. 7But at dawn the next day God provided a worm, which chewed the gourd so that it withered. 8When the sun rose, God provided a scorching east wind, and the sun blazed on Jonah's head so that he grew faint. He wanted to die, and said, 'It would be better for me to die than to live.'

9But God said to Jonah, 'Is it right for you to be angry about the gourd?'

'It is,' he said. 'And I'm so angry I wish I were dead.'

10But the LORD said, 'You have been concerned about this gourd, though you did not tend it or make it grow. It sprang up overnight and died overnight. 11And should I not have concern for the great city Nineveh, in which there are more than a hundred and twenty thousand people who cannot tell their right hand from their left— and also many animals?'

---

[a] 6 The precise identification of this plant is uncertain; also in verses 7, 9 and 10.

Micah

INTRODUCTION

MICAH

Author: Micah

Who to: The people of Jerusalem and Samaria.

When: The kings that Micah mentions in his opening verse reigned from around 750 BC to around 687 BC.

Where: Micah lived in Judah.

Did you know? Micah clearly predicts the coming of the Messiah and says that he will be born in Bethlehem.

Main theme: Micah is a champion of the oppressed. He speaks out against wealthy people who take the land of the poor, and attacks dishonest merchants who cheat the poor. Like many of the prophets, he warns the people of God's judgment if they do not turn back to him, and emphasises the reality of God's love.

1 The word of the LORD that came to Micah of Moresheth during the reigns of Jotham, Ahaz and Hezekiah, kings of Judah—the vision he saw concerning Samaria and Jerusalem.

²Hear, you peoples, all of you,
 listen, earth and all who live in it,
that the Sovereign LORD may witness against you,
 the Lord from his holy temple.

Judgment against Samaria and Jerusalem

³Look! The LORD is coming from his dwelling-place;
 he comes down and treads on the heights of the earth.
⁴The mountains melt beneath him
 and the valleys split apart,
like wax before the fire,
 like water rushing down a slope.
⁵All this is because of Jacob's transgression,
 because of the sins of the house of Israel.

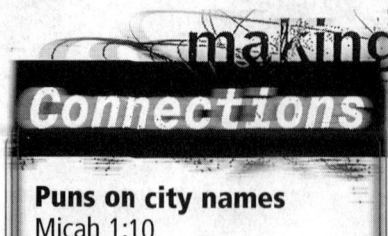

Puns on city names
Micah 1:10

Micah uses some great puns on city names to drive his message home. 'In Beth Ophrah, roll in the dust,' he says, when the name Beth Ophrah means 'house of dust'. Perhaps today he'd say something like, 'You'll see war in Warsaw. You'll run for cover in Iran.'

What is Jacob's transgression?
　Is it not Samaria?
What is Judah's high place?
　Is it not Jerusalem?

⁶'Therefore I will make Samaria a heap of rubble,
　a place for planting vineyards.
I will pour her stones into the valley
　and lay bare her foundations.
⁷All her idols will be broken to pieces;
　all her temple gifts will be burned with fire;
I will destroy all her images.
Since she gathered her gifts from the wages of prostitutes,
　as the wages of prostitutes they will again be used.'

Weeping and mourning

⁸Because of this I will weep and wail;
　I will go about barefoot and naked.
I will howl like a jackal
　and moan like an owl.
⁹For Samaria's wound is incurable;
　it has come to Judah.
It has reached the very gate of my people,
　even to Jerusalem itself.

¹⁰Tell it not in Gath;[a]
　weep not at all.
In Beth Ophrah[b]
　roll in the dust.
¹¹Pass on in nakedness and shame,
　you who live in Shaphir.[c]
Those who live in Zaanan[d]
　will not come out.
Beth Ezel is in mourning;
　its protection is taken from you.
¹²Those who live in Maroth[e] writhe in pain,
　waiting for relief,
because disaster has come from the LORD,
　even to the gate of Jerusalem.
¹³You who live in Lachish,[f]
　harness the team to the chariot.
You were the beginning of sin
　to Daughter Zion,
for the transgressions of Israel
　were found in you.
¹⁴Therefore you will give parting gifts
　to Moresheth Gath.
The town of Akzib[g] will prove deceptive
　to the kings of Israel.
¹⁵I will bring a conqueror against you
　who live in Mareshah.[h]
The nobles of Israel
　will flee to Adullam.
¹⁶Shave your head in mourning
　for the children in whom you delight;
make yourself as bald as the vulture,
　for they will go from you into exile.

Human plans and God's plans

2 Woe to those who plan iniquity,
　to those who plot evil on their beds!
At morning's light they carry it out
　because it is in their power to do it.
²They covet fields and seize them,
　and houses, and take them.
They defraud people of their homes,
　they rob them of their inheritance.

³Therefore, the LORD says:

'I am planning disaster against this people,
　from which you cannot save yourselves.

---

[a] 10 *Gath* sounds like the Hebrew for *tell*. [b] 10 *Beth Ophrah* means *house of dust*. [c] 11 *Shaphir* means *pleasant*.
[d] 11 *Zaanan* sounds like the Hebrew for *come out*. [e] 12 *Maroth* sounds like the Hebrew for *bitter*. [f] 13 *Lachish* sounds like the Hebrew for *team*. [g] 14 *Akzib* means *deception*. [h] 15 *Mareshah* sounds like the Hebrew for *conqueror*.

Iniquity
Micah 2:1
'Iniquity' is another word for 'sin'.

You will no longer walk proudly,
  for it will be a time of calamity.
⁴In that day people will ridicule you;
  they will taunt you with this mournful song:
"We are utterly ruined;
  my people's possession is divided up.
He takes it from me!
  He assigns our fields to traitors." '

⁵Therefore you will have no-one in the assembly of the LORD
  to divide the land by lot.

False prophets

⁶'Do not prophesy,' their prophets say.
  'Do not prophesy about these things;
  disgrace will not overtake us.'
⁷House of Jacob, should it be said,
  'Does the LORD become*ᵃ* impatient?
  Does he do such things?'

'Do not my words do good
  to those whose ways are upright?
⁸Lately my people have risen up
  like an enemy.
You strip off the rich robe
  from those who pass by without a care,
  like men returning from battle.
⁹You drive the women of my people
  from their pleasant homes.
You take away my blessing
  from their children for ever.
¹⁰Get up, go away!
  For this is not your resting place,
because it is defiled,
  it is ruined, beyond all remedy.
¹¹If liars and deceivers come and say,
    "We will prophesy for you plenty of wine and beer,"
  they would be just the prophets for this people!

Deliverance promised

¹²'I will surely gather all of you, Jacob;
  I will surely bring together the remnant of Israel.
I will bring them together like sheep in a sheepfold,
  like a flock in its pasture;
  the place will throng with people.
¹³One who breaks open the way will go up before them;
  they will break through the gate and go out.
Their King will pass through before them,
  the LORD at their head.'

Leaders and prophets rebuked

3 Then I said,

'Listen, you leaders of Jacob,
  you rulers of the house of Israel.
Should you not know justice,
 ² you who hate good and love evil;
who tear the skin from my people
  and the flesh from their bones;
³who eat my people's flesh,
  strip off their skin
  and break their bones in pieces;
who chop them up like meat for the pan,
  like flesh for the pot?'

⁴Then they will cry out to the LORD,
  but he will not answer them.
At that time he will hide his face from them
  because of the evil they have done.

⁵This is what the LORD says:

'As for the prophets
  who lead my people astray,
if you feed them,
  they proclaim "peace";
if you do not,
  they prepare to wage war against you.
⁶Therefore night will come over you, without visions,
  and darkness, without divination.
The sun will set for the prophets,
  and the day will go dark for them.
⁷The seers will be ashamed
  and the diviners disgraced.
They will all cover their faces
  because there is no answer from God.'

ᵃ 7 Or *Is the Spirit of the* LORD

⁸But as for me, I am filled with power,
  with the Spirit of the LORD,
  and with justice and might,
to declare to Jacob his transgression,
  to Israel his sin.

⁹Hear this, you leaders of the house of Jacob,
  you rulers of the house of Israel,
who despise justice
  and distort all that is right;
¹⁰who build Zion with bloodshed,
  and Jerusalem with wickedness.
¹¹Her leaders judge for a bribe,
  her priests teach for a price,
  and her prophets tell fortunes for money.
Yet they lean upon the LORD and say,
  'Is not the LORD among us?
  No disaster will come upon us.'
¹²Therefore because of you,
  Zion will be ploughed like a field,
  Jerusalem will become a heap of rubble,
  the temple hill a mound overgrown with thickets.

The mountain of the LORD

4 In the last days

the mountain of the LORD's temple will be established
  as chief among the mountains;
it will be raised above the hills,
  and peoples will stream to it.

²Many nations will come and say,

'Come, let us go up to the mountain of the LORD,
  to the house of the God of Jacob.
He will teach us his ways,
  so that we may walk in his paths.'
The law will go out from Zion,
  the word of the LORD from Jerusalem.
³He will judge between many peoples
  and will settle disputes for strong nations far and wide.
They will beat their swords into ploughshares
  and their spears into pruning hooks.
Nation will not take up sword against nation,
  nor will they train for war any more.

⁴Everyone will sit under their own vine
  and under their own fig-tree,
  and no-one will make them afraid,
  for the LORD Almighty has spoken.
⁵All the nations may walk
  in the name of their gods;
we will walk in the name of the LORD
  our God for ever and ever.

The LORD's plan

⁶'In that day,' declares the LORD,

'I will gather the lame;
  I will assemble the exiles
  and those I have brought to grief.
⁷I will make the lame a remnant,
  those driven away a strong nation.
The LORD will rule over them in Mount Zion
  from that day and for ever.
⁸As for you, watchtower of the flock,
  stronghold*ᵃ* of Daughter Zion,
the former dominion will be restored to you;
  kingship will come to Daughter Jerusalem.'

⁹Why do you now cry aloud—
  have you no king?*ᵇ*
Has your ruler*ᶜ* perished,
  that pain seizes you like that of a woman in labour?
¹⁰Writhe in agony, Daughter Zion,
  like a woman in labour,
for now you must leave the city
  to camp in the open field.
You will go to Babylon;
  there you will be rescued.
There the LORD will redeem you
  out of the hand of your enemies.

¹¹But now many nations
  are gathered against you.
They say, 'Let her be defiled,
  let our eyes gloat over Zion!'
¹²But they do not know
  the thoughts of the LORD;
they do not understand his plan,
  he who gathers them like sheaves to the threshing-floor.
¹³'Rise and thresh, Daughter Zion,
  for I will give you horns of iron;
  I will give you hooves of bronze,

---

*ᵃ*8 Or *hill*   *ᵇ*9 Or *King*   *ᶜ*9 Or *Ruler*

and you will break to pieces many
  nations.'
You will devote their ill-gotten gains to
  the LORD,
  their wealth to the Lord of all the earth.

A promised ruler from Bethlehem

5 *Marshal your troops now, city of troops,
  for a siege is laid against us.
They will strike Israel's ruler
  on the cheek with a rod.

*²'But you, Bethlehem Ephrathah,
  though you are small among the clans*ᵃ* of Judah,
out of you will come for me
  one who will be ruler over Israel,
whose origins are from of old,
  from ancient times.'

³Therefore Israel will be abandoned
  until the time when she who is in labour gives birth
and the rest of his brothers return
  to join the Israelites.

⁴He will stand and shepherd his flock
  in the strength of the LORD,
  in the majesty of the name of the LORD his God.
And they will live securely, for then his greatness
  will reach to the ends of the earth.

⁵And he will be our peace
  when the Assyrians invade our land
  and march through our fortresses.
We will raise against them seven shepherds,
  even eight commanders,
⁶who will rule*ᵇ* the land of Assyria with the sword,
  the land of Nimrod with drawn sword.*ᶜ*
He will deliver us from the Assyrians
  when they invade our land
  and march into our borders.

⁷The remnant of Jacob will be
  in the midst of many peoples
like dew from the LORD,
  like showers on the grass,

> ### People and Places
>
> **Bethlehem**
> Micah 5:2
> The Christmas carol calls Bethlehem a 'little town', but a lot has happened there throughout history. Rachel, Jacob's wife, was buried there (Genesis 35:19), and it's where most of the action in the book of Ruth takes place. David was anointed king at Bethlehem where his family lived (1 Samuel 16:4), and so it is known as the City of David. And Micah says there is more to come, a new ruler will be born here. Can you guess who it is? (See Luke 2:4.)

which do not wait for mortals
  or depend on any human being.
⁸The remnant of Jacob will be among the nations,
  in the midst of many peoples,
like a lion among the beasts of the forest,
  like a young lion among flocks of sheep,
which mauls and mangles as it goes,
  and no-one can rescue.
⁹Your hand will be lifted up in triumph
  over your enemies,
  and all your foes will be destroyed.

¹⁰'In that day,' declares the LORD,

'I will destroy your horses from among you
  and demolish your chariots.
¹¹I will destroy the cities of your land
  and tear down all your strongholds.
¹²I will destroy your witchcraft
  and you will no longer cast spells.
¹³I will destroy your idols
  and your sacred stones from among you;
you will no longer bow down
  to the work of your hands.

---

*ᵃ*2 Or *rulers* *ᵇ*6 Or *crush* *ᶜ*6 Or *Nimrod in its gates*

* 5:1 is numbered 4:14 in Hebrew texts.   * 5:2-15 is numbered 5:1-14 in Hebrew texts.

¹⁴I will uproot from among you your
    Asherah poles[a]
  when I demolish your cities.
¹⁵I will take vengeance in anger and wrath
  on the nations that have not obeyed
    me.'

The Lord's case against Israel

6 Listen to what the Lord says:

'Stand up, plead my case before the
    mountains;
  let the hills hear what you have to say.

²'Hear, you mountains, the Lord's
    accusation;
  listen, you everlasting foundations of
    the earth.
For the Lord has a case against his people;
  he is lodging a charge against Israel.

³'My people, what have I done to you?
  How have I burdened you? Answer me.
⁴I brought you up out of Egypt
  and redeemed you from the land of
    slavery.
I sent Moses to lead you,
  also Aaron and Miriam.
⁵My people, remember
  what Balak king of Moab plotted
  and what Balaam son of Beor
    answered.
Remember your journey from Shittim to
    Gilgal,
  that you may know the righteous acts
    of the Lord.'

⁶With what shall I come before the Lord
  and bow down before the exalted God?
Shall I come before him with burnt
    offerings,
  with calves a year old?
⁷Will the Lord be pleased with thousands
    of rams,
  with ten thousand rivers of oil?
Shall I offer my firstborn for my
    transgression,
  the fruit of my body for the sin of my
    soul?
⁸He has shown all you people what is good.

> ## IN OTHER WORDS
>
> **Mercy**
> Micah 6:8
> An important attribute of God's character, mercy is God's ability to override his desire for justice and forgive our wrongdoing. Jesus' death is the means by which God demonstrates his mercy to us. And Christians in turn are urged to be merciful to each other.

And what does the Lord require of
    you?
To act justly and to love mercy
  and to walk humbly[b] with your God.

Israel's guilt and punishment

⁹Listen! The Lord is calling to the city—
  and to fear your name is wisdom—
    'Heed the rod and the One who
      appointed it.[c]
¹⁰Am I still to forget your ill-gotten
    treasures, you wicked house,
  and the short ephah,[d] which is
    accursed?
¹¹Shall I acquit a person with dishonest
    scales,
  with a bag of false weights?
¹²Her rich people are violent;
  her inhabitants are liars
  and their tongues speak deceitfully.
¹³Therefore, I have begun to destroy you,
  to ruin[e] you because of your sins.
¹⁴You will eat but not be satisfied;
  your stomach will still be empty.[f]
You will store up but save nothing,
  because what you save[g] I will give to the
    sword.
¹⁵You will plant but not harvest;
  you will press olives but not use the oil
    on yourselves,
  you will crush grapes but not drink the
    wine.

---

[a] 14 That is, wooden symbols of the goddess Asherah   [b] 8 Or *prudently*   [c] 9 The meaning of the Hebrew for this line is uncertain.   [d] 10 An ephah was a dry measure.   [e] 13 Or *Therefore, I will make you ill and destroy you; / I will ruin*   [f] 14 The meaning of the Hebrew for this word is uncertain.   [g] 14 Or *You will press towards birth but not give birth, / and what you bring to birth*

16 You have observed the statutes of Omri
 and all the practices of Ahab's house;
 you have followed their traditions.
Therefore I will give you over to ruin
 and your people to derision;
 you will bear the scorn of the nations.'[a]

Israel's misery

7 What misery is mine!
 I am like one who gathers summer fruit
 at the gleaning of the vineyard;
there is no cluster of grapes to eat,
 none of the early figs that I crave.
2 The faithful have been swept from the land;
 not one upright person remains.
Everyone lies in wait to shed blood;
 they hunt each other with nets.
3 Both hands are skilled in doing evil;
 the ruler demands gifts,
the judge accepts bribes,
 the powerful dictate what they desire—
 they all conspire together.
4 The best of them is like a brier,
 the most upright worse than a thorn hedge.
The day of your watchmen has come,
 the day God visits you.
 Now is the time of their confusion.
5 Do not trust a neighbour;
 put no confidence in a friend.
Even with the woman who lies in your embrace
 be careful of your words.
6 For a son dishonours his father,
 a daughter rises up against her mother,
a daughter-in-law against her mother-in-law—
 your enemies are the members of your own household.

7 But as for me, I watch in hope for the LORD,
 I wait for God my Saviour;
 my God will hear me.

Israel will rise

8 Do not gloat over me, my enemy!
 Though I have fallen, I will rise.
Though I sit in darkness,
 the LORD will be my light.
9 Because I have sinned against him,
 I will bear the LORD's wrath,
until he pleads my case
 and establishes my right.
He will bring me out into the light;
 I will see his righteousness.
10 Then my enemy will see it
 and will be covered with shame,
she who said to me,
 'Where is the LORD your God?'
My eyes will see her downfall;
 even now she will be trampled underfoot
 like mire in the streets.

11 The day for building your walls will come,
 the day for extending your boundaries.
12 In that day people will come to you
 from Assyria and the cities of Egypt,
even from Egypt to the Euphrates
 and from sea to sea
 and from mountain to mountain.
13 The earth will become desolate because of its inhabitants,
 as the result of their deeds.

Prayer and praise

14 Shepherd your people with your staff,
 the flock of your inheritance,
which lives by itself in a forest,
 in fertile pasture-lands.[b]
Let them feed in Bashan and Gilead
 as in days long ago.

15 'As in the days when you came out of Egypt,
 I will show them my wonders.'

16 Nations will see and be ashamed,
 deprived of all their power.
They will put their hands over their mouths
 and their ears will become deaf.
17 They will lick dust like a snake,
 like creatures that crawl on the ground.
They will come trembling out of their dens;
 they will turn in fear to the LORD our God
 and will be afraid of you.

---

[a] 16 Septuagint; Hebrew *scorn due to my people*   [b] 14 Or *in the middle of Carmel*

18Who is a God like you,
  who pardons sin and forgives the
    transgression
  of the remnant of his inheritance?
You do not stay angry for ever
  but delight to show mercy.
19You will again have compassion on us;
  you will tread our sins underfoot
  and hurl all our iniquities into the
    depths of the sea.
20You will be faithful to Jacob,
  and show love to Abraham,
as you pledged on oath to our ancestors
  in days long ago.

Nahum

INTRODUCTION

NAHUM

Author: Nahum

When: Nineveh was destroyed around 612 BC, so this book was probably written just before that.

Where: Nahum is called 'an Elkoshite', but no-one is sure where Elkosh was.

Main theme: This is a rant against the city of Nineveh. Nahum contrasts the power and goodness of God with the evil that the Assyrians have done. He talks about the coming destruction of Assyria and its capital city Nineveh.

1 A prophecy concerning Nineveh. The book of the vision of Nahum the Elkoshite.

The LORD's anger against Nineveh

²The LORD is a jealous and avenging God;
  the LORD takes vengeance and is filled with wrath.
The LORD takes vengeance on his foes
  and vents his wrath against his enemies.
³The LORD is slow to anger but great in power;
  the LORD will not leave the guilty unpunished.
His way is in the whirlwind and the storm,
  and clouds are the dust of his feet.
⁴He rebukes the sea and dries it up;
  he makes all the rivers run dry.
Bashan and Carmel wither
  and the blossoms of Lebanon fade.
⁵The mountains quake before him
  and the hills melt away.
The earth trembles at his presence,
  the world and all who live in it.
⁶Who can withstand his indignation?
  Who can endure his fierce anger?
His wrath is poured out like fire;
  the rocks are shattered before him.

⁷The LORD is good,
  a refuge in times of trouble.
He cares for those who trust in him,
⁸ but with an overwhelming flood
  he will make an end of Nineveh;
  he will pursue his foes into darkness.

⁹Whatever they plot against the LORD
  he[a] will bring to an end;
  trouble will not come a second time.
¹⁰They will be entangled among thorns
  and drunk from their wine;
  they will be consumed like dry
    stubble.[b]
¹¹From you, Nineveh, has one come forth
  who plots evil against the LORD
  and devises wicked plans.

¹²This is what the LORD says:

'Although they have allies and are
    numerous,
  they will be destroyed and pass away.
Although I have afflicted you, Judah,
  I will afflict you no more.
¹³Now I will break their yoke from your
    neck
  and tear your shackles away.'

¹⁴The LORD has given a command
    concerning you, Nineveh:
  'You will have no descendants to bear
    your name.
I will destroy the images and idols
  that are in the temple of your gods.
I will prepare your grave,
  for you are vile.'

*¹⁵Look, there on the mountains,
  the feet of one who brings good news,
  who proclaims peace!
Celebrate your festivals, Judah,
  and fulfil your vows.
No more will the wicked invade you;
  they will be completely destroyed.

Nineveh to fall

2 *An attacker advances against you,
    Nineveh.
  Guard the fortress,
  watch the road,
  brace yourselves,
  marshal all your strength!

²The LORD will restore the splendour of
    Jacob
  like the splendour of Israel,
though destroyers have laid them waste
  and have ruined their vines.

³The shields of the soldiers are red;
  the warriors are clad in scarlet.
The metal on the chariots flashes
  on the day they are made ready;
  the spears of juniper are
    brandished.[c]
⁴The chariots storm through the streets,
  rushing back and forth through the
    squares.
They look like flaming torches;
  they dart about like lightning.

⁵Nineveh summons her picked troops,
  yet they stumble on their way.
They dash to the city wall;
  the protective shield is put in place.
⁶The river gates are thrown open
  and the palace collapses.
⁷It is decreed[d] that Nineveh
  be exiled and carried away.
Her female slaves moan like doves
  and beat on their breasts.
⁸Nineveh is like a pool
  whose water is draining away.
'Stop! Stop!' they cry,
  but no-one turns back.
⁹Plunder the silver!
  Plunder the gold!
The supply is endless,
  the wealth from all its treasures!
¹⁰She is pillaged, plundered, stripped!
  Hearts melt, knees give way,
  bodies tremble, every face grows pale.

¹¹Where now is the lions' den,
  the place where they fed their young,
where the lion and lioness went,
  and the cubs, with nothing to fear?
¹²The lion killed enough for his cubs
  and strangled the prey for his mate,
filling his lairs with the kill
  and his dens with the prey.

¹³'I am against you,'
  declares the LORD Almighty.
'I will burn up your chariots in smoke,

---

[a]9 Or *What do you foes plot against the LORD? / He*   [b]10 The meaning of the Hebrew for this verse is uncertain.
[c]3 Hebrew; Septuagint and Syriac *ready; / the horsemen rush to and fro.*   [d]7 The meaning of the Hebrew for this word is uncertain.

* 1:15 is numbered 2:1 in Hebrew texts.   * 2:1-13 is numbered 2:2-14 in Hebrew texts.

People and Places

Nineveh
Nahum 3:1

Earlier in history, Jonah had visited Nineveh and challenged the people to repent, which they did (Jonah 3:5). But this time God's judgment was not turned back. Nineveh was destroyed in 612 BC, just as Nahum had prophesied.

and the sword will devour your young lions.
I will leave you no prey on the earth.
The voices of your messengers
  will no longer be heard.'

Woe to Nineveh

3 Woe to the city of blood,
    full of lies,
  full of plunder,
    never without victims!
² The crack of whips,
    the clatter of wheels,
  galloping horses
    and jolting chariots!
³ Charging cavalry,
    flashing swords
    and glittering spears!
  Many casualties,
    piles of dead,
  bodies without number,
    people stumbling over the corpses—
⁴ all because of the wanton lust of a prostitute,
    alluring, the mistress of sorceries,
  who enslaved nations by her prostitution
    and peoples by her witchcraft.

⁵ 'I am against you,' declares the LORD Almighty.
  'I will lift your skirts over your face.
  I will show the nations your nakedness
    and the kingdoms your shame.
⁶ I will pelt you with filth,
    I will treat you with contempt
    and make you a spectacle.
⁷ All who see you will flee from you and say,
    "Nineveh is in ruins—who will mourn for her?"
  Where can I find anyone to comfort you?'

⁸ Are you better than Thebes,
    situated on the Nile,
    with water around her?
  The river was her defence,
    the waters her wall.
⁹ Cush*ᵃ* and Egypt were her boundless strength;
  Put and Libya were among her allies.
¹⁰ Yet she was taken captive
    and went into exile.
  Her infants were dashed to pieces
    at every street corner.
  Lots were cast for her nobles,
    and all her great men were put in chains.
¹¹ You too will become drunk;
    you will go into hiding
    and seek refuge from the enemy.

¹² All your fortresses are like fig-trees
    with their first ripe fruit;
  when they are shaken,
    the figs fall into the mouth of the eater.
¹³ Look at your troops—
    they are all weaklings.
  The gates of your land
    are wide open to your enemies;
  fire has consumed the bars of your gates.

¹⁴ Draw water for the siege,
    strengthen your defences!
  Work the clay,
    tread the mortar,
    repair the brickwork!
¹⁵ There the fire will consume you;
    the sword will cut you down—
    and it will devour you like a swarm of locusts.
  Multiply like grasshoppers,
    multiply like locusts!
¹⁶ You have increased the number of your merchants

ᵃ 9 That is, the upper Nile region

till they are more than the stars in the sky,
but like locusts they strip the land
and then fly away.
¹⁷Your guards are like locusts,
your officials like swarms of locusts
that settle in the walls on a cold day—
but when the sun appears they fly away,
and no-one knows where.

¹⁸King of Assyria, your shepherds*ᵃ* slumber;
your nobles lie down to rest.
Your people are scattered on the mountains
with no-one to gather them.
¹⁹Nothing can heal you;
your wound is fatal.
All who hear the news about you
clap their hands at your fall,
for who has not felt
your endless cruelty?

ᵃ 18 That is, rulers

Habakkuk

INTRODUCTION

HABAKKUK

Author: Habakkuk

When: Probably written some time before the destruction of Jerusalem, around 600 BC.

Where: Very little is known about Habakkuk apart from his name.

Main theme: Habakkuk starts his book on a despairing note, aware of injustice and violence around him and feeling that God isn't doing anything about it. He questions God, who answers and assures him that he will judge people for their sin, and that he will act with justice and mercy. Habakkuk ends with a beautiful psalm of praise to God.

1 The prophecy that Habakkuk the prophet received.

Habakkuk's complaint

²How long, LORD, must I call for help,
  but you do not listen?
Or cry out to you, 'Violence!'
  but you do not save?
³Why do you make me look at injustice?
  Why do you tolerate wrongdoing?
Destruction and violence are before me;
  there is strife, and conflict abounds.
⁴Therefore the law is paralysed,
  and justice never prevails.
The wicked hem in the righteous,
  so that justice is perverted.

The LORD's answer

⁵'Look at the nations and watch—
  and be utterly amazed.
For I am going to do something in your days
  that you would not believe,
  even if you were told.
⁶I am raising up the Babylonians,[a]
  that ruthless and impetuous people,
who sweep across the whole earth
  to seize dwellings not their own.
⁷They are a feared and dreaded people;
  they are a law to themselves
  and promote their own honour.
⁸Their horses are swifter than leopards,
  fiercer than wolves at dusk.

[a] 6 Or *Chaldeans*

People and Places

Babylonians
Habakkuk 1:6

Babylon was a city that would now be in modern Iraq. It was the capital city of the empire of Babylonia. The Babylonians were a dominant power who were always a big enemy of Israel and who eventually invaded Judah and sent nearly all the Israelites into exile. They were sometimes known as the Chaldeans. In the New Testament, 'Babylon' signifies the world in opposition to God (Revelation 14:8).

Their cavalry gallops headlong;
　　their horsemen come from afar.
They fly like a vulture swooping to devour;
9　they all come bent on violence.
　Their hordes[a] advance like a desert wind
　　and gather prisoners like sand.
10 They mock kings
　　and scoff at rulers.
　They laugh at all fortified cities;
　　by building earthen ramps they capture them.
11 Then they sweep past like the wind and go on—
　　guilty people, whose own strength is their god.'

Habakkuk's second complaint

12 LORD, are you not from everlasting?
　　My God, my Holy One, you[b] will never die.
　You, LORD, have appointed them to execute judgment;
　　you, my Rock, have ordained them to punish.
13 Your eyes are too pure to look on evil;
　　you cannot tolerate wrongdoing.
　Why then do you tolerate the treacherous?
　　Why are you silent while the wicked swallow up those more righteous than themselves?
14 You have made people like the fish in the sea,
　　like the sea creatures that have no ruler.
15 The wicked foe pulls all of them up with hooks,
　　he catches them in his net,
　he gathers them up in his drag-net;
　　and so he rejoices and is glad.
16 Therefore he sacrifices to his net
　　and burns incense to his drag-net,
　for by his net he lives in luxury
　　and enjoys the choicest food.
17 Is he to keep on emptying his net,
　　destroying nations without mercy?

2 I will stand at my watch
　　and station myself on the ramparts;
　I will look to see what he will say to me,
　　and what answer I am to give to this complaint.[c]

The LORD's answer

2 Then the LORD replied:

'Write down the revelation
　and make it plain on tablets
　so that a herald[d] may run with it.
3 For the revelation awaits an appointed time;
　it speaks of the end
　and will not prove false.
Though it linger, wait for it;
　it[e] will certainly come
　and will not delay.

4 'See, he is puffed up;
　his desires are not upright—
　but the righteous will live by their faithfulness[f]—
5 indeed, wine betrays him;
　he is arrogant and never at rest.
Because he is as greedy as the grave
　and like death is never satisfied,
he gathers to himself all the nations
　and takes captive all the peoples.

---

[a] 9 The meaning of the Hebrew for this word is uncertain.　[b] 12 An ancient Hebrew scribal tradition; Masoretic Text *we*　[c] 1 Or *and what to answer when I am rebuked*　[d] 2 Or *so that whoever reads it*　[e] 3 Or *Though he linger, wait for him; / he*　[f] 4 Or *faith*

⁶'Will not all of them taunt him with ridicule and scorn, saying,

' "Woe to him who piles up stolen goods
and makes himself wealthy by extortion!
How long must this go on?"
⁷Will not your creditors suddenly arise?
Will they not wake up and make you tremble?
Then you will become their prey.
⁸Because you have plundered many nations,
the peoples who are left will plunder you.
For you have shed human blood;
you have destroyed lands and cities
and everyone in them.

⁹'Woe to him who builds his house by unjust gain,
setting his nest on high
to escape the clutches of ruin!
¹⁰You have plotted the ruin of many peoples,
shaming your own house and forfeiting your life.
¹¹The stones of the wall will cry out,
and the beams of the woodwork will echo it.

¹²'Woe to him who builds a city with bloodshed
and establishes a town by injustice!
¹³Has not the LORD Almighty determined
that the people's labour is only fuel for the fire,
that the nations exhaust themselves for nothing?
¹⁴For the earth will be filled with the knowledge of the glory of the LORD
as the waters cover the sea.

¹⁵'Woe to him who gives drink to his neighbours,
pouring it from the wineskin till they are drunk,
so that he can gaze on their naked bodies!
¹⁶You will be filled with shame instead of glory.
Now it is your turn! Drink and let your nakedness be exposed!ᵃ
The cup from the LORD's right hand is coming round to you,
and disgrace will cover your glory.
¹⁷The violence you have done to Lebanon will overwhelm you,
and your destruction of animals will terrify you.
For you have shed human blood;
you have destroyed lands and cities
and everyone in them.

¹⁸'Of what value is an idol that someone has carved?
Or an image that teaches lies?
For those who make them trust in their own creations;
they make idols that cannot speak.
¹⁹Woe to him who says to wood, "Come to life!"
Or to lifeless stone, "Wake up!"
Can it give guidance?
It is covered with gold and silver;
there is no breath in it.'

²⁰The LORD is in his holy temple;
let all the earth be silent before him.

Habakkuk's prayer

3 A prayer of Habakkuk the prophet. On *shigionoth*.ᵇ

²LORD, I have heard of your fame;
I stand in awe of your deeds, LORD.
Renew them in our day,
in our time make them known;
in wrath remember mercy.

³God came from Teman,
the Holy One from Mount Paran.ᶜ
His glory covered the heavens
and his praise filled the earth.
⁴His splendour was like the sunrise;
rays flashed from his hand,
where his power was hidden.
⁵Plague went before him;
pestilence followed his steps.
⁶He stood, and shook the earth;

ᵃ 16 Masoretic Text; Dead Sea Scrolls, Aquila, Vulgate and Syriac (see also Septuagint) *and stagger*   ᵇ 1 Probably a literary or musical term   ᶜ 3 The Hebrew has *Selah* (a word of uncertain meaning) here and at the middle of verse 9 and at the end of verse 13.

> **IN OTHER WORDS**
>
> **Threshing**
> Habakkuk 3:12
> Threshing was the process of separating the grain from its stalk. A farmer would beat small amounts of grain by hand, or use a machine drawn by animals for larger amounts.

he looked, and made the nations tremble.
The ancient mountains crumbled
 and the age-old hills collapsed—
but he marches on for ever.
⁷I saw the tents of Cushan in distress,
 the dwellings of Midian in anguish.

⁸Were you angry with the rivers, LORD?
 Was your wrath against the streams?
Did you rage against the sea
 when you rode your horses
 and your chariots to victory?
⁹You uncovered your bow,
 you called for many arrows.
You split the earth with rivers;
¹⁰ the mountains saw you and writhed.
Torrents of water swept by;
 the deep roared
 and lifted its waves on high.
¹¹Sun and moon stood still in the heavens
 at the glint of your flying arrows,
 at the lightning of your flashing spear.

¹²In wrath you strode through the earth
 and in anger you threshed the nations.
¹³You came out to deliver your people,
 to save your anointed one.
You crushed the leader of the land of wickedness,
 you stripped him from head to foot.
¹⁴With his own spear you pierced his head
 when his warriors stormed out to scatter us,
gloating as though about to devour
 the wretched who were in hiding.
¹⁵You trampled the sea with your horses,
 churning the great waters.

¹⁶I heard and my heart pounded,
 my lips quivered at the sound;
decay crept into my bones,
 and my legs trembled.
Yet I will wait patiently for the day of calamity
 to come on the nation invading us.
¹⁷Though the fig-tree does not bud
 and there are no grapes on the vines,
though the olive crop fails
 and the fields produce no food,
though there are no sheep in the sheepfold
 and no cattle in the stalls,
¹⁸yet I will rejoice in the LORD,
 I will be joyful in God my Saviour.

¹⁹The Sovereign LORD is my strength;
 he makes my feet like the feet of a deer,
 he enables me to tread on the heights.

For the director of music. On my stringed instruments.

Zephaniah

INTRODUCTION

Zephaniah

Author: Zephaniah

Who to: The people of Judah.

When: Zephaniah was a prophet during the reign of Josiah the king of Judah, from about 641 BC to 609 BC.

Where: Zephaniah lived in Judah.

Did you know? Zephaniah lived at the same time as Jeremiah the prophet. He was the great-great-grandson of King Hezekiah of Judah, a king who was known for his faithfulness to God (2 Kings 18–20).

Main theme: Zephaniah tells it like it is. He speaks graphically about the judgment that will come on Judah because of the people's rebellion and injustice. But it's not all doom and gloom. God will keep safe a small group of people who will stay faithful to him.

1 The word of the LORD that came to Zephaniah son of Cushi, the son of Gedaliah, the son of Amariah, the son of Hezekiah, during the reign of Josiah son of Amon king of Judah:

Judgment on the whole earth in the day of the LORD

²'I will sweep away everything
　from the face of the earth,'
　　　　　　　　declares the LORD.

³'I will sweep away both people and
　　animals;
I will sweep away the birds in the sky
　and the fish in the sea—
and the idols that cause the wicked to
　　stumble.'[a]

'When I destroy all people
　on the face of the earth,'
　　　　　　　　declares the LORD,
⁴'I will stretch out my hand against Judah
　and against all who live in Jerusalem.

---

[a] 3 The meaning of the Hebrew for this line is uncertain.

I will destroy every remnant of Baal worship in this place,
every remembrance of the idolatrous priests—
⁵those who bow down on the roofs
to worship the starry host,
those who bow down and swear by the LORD
and who also swear by Molek,[a]
⁶those who turn back from following the LORD
and neither seek the LORD nor enquire of him.'

⁷Be silent before the Sovereign LORD,
for the day of the LORD is near.
The LORD has prepared a sacrifice;
he has consecrated those he has invited.

⁸'On the day of the LORD's sacrifice
I will punish the officials
and the king's sons
and all those clad
in foreign clothes.
⁹On that day I will punish
all who avoid stepping on the threshold,[b]
who fill the temple of their gods
with violence and deceit.

¹⁰'On that day,'
declares the LORD,
'a cry will go up from the Fish Gate,
wailing from the New Quarter,
and a loud crash from the hills.
¹¹Wail, you who live in the market district;[c]
all your merchants will be wiped out,
all who trade with[d] silver will be destroyed.

¹²At that time I will search Jerusalem with lamps
and punish those who are complacent,
who are like wine left on its dregs,
who think, "The LORD will do nothing, either good or bad."
¹³Their wealth will be plundered,
their houses demolished.
Though they build houses,
they will not live in them;
though they plant vineyards,
they will not drink the wine.'

¹⁴The great day of the LORD is near—
near and coming quickly.
The cry on the day of the LORD is bitter;
the Mighty Warrior shouts his battle cry.
¹⁵That day will be a day of wrath—
a day of distress and anguish,
a day of trouble and ruin,
a day of darkness and gloom,
a day of clouds and blackness—
¹⁶ a day of trumpet and battle cry
against the fortified cities
and against the corner towers.

¹⁷'I will bring such distress on all people
that they will grope about like those who are blind,
because they have sinned against the LORD.
Their blood will be poured out like dust
and their entrails like dung.
¹⁸Neither their silver nor their gold
will be able to save them
on the day of the LORD's wrath.'

In the fire of his jealousy
the whole earth will be consumed,
for he will make a sudden end
of all who live on the earth.

Judah and Jerusalem judged along with the nations

Judah summoned to repent

2 Gather together, gather yourselves together,
you shameful nation,
²before the decree takes effect
and that day passes like windblown chaff,
before the LORD's fierce anger
comes upon you,
before the day of the LORD's wrath
comes upon you.
³Seek the LORD, all you humble of the land,
you who do what he commands.
Seek righteousness, seek humility;
perhaps you will be sheltered
on the day of the LORD's anger.

---

a 5 Hebrew *Malkam*   *b* 9 See 1 Samuel 5:5.   *c* 11 Or *the Mortar*   *d* 11 Or *in*

IN OTHER WORDS

Righteous
Zephaniah 2:3
Being righteous includes both doing the right things and having right relationships and attitudes. It is most often used to describe God's character and activity in the world, but Christians are also called to be righteous in their actions and relationships.

Philistia
4 Gaza will be abandoned
  and Ashkelon left in ruins.
At midday Ashdod will be emptied
  and Ekron uprooted.
5 Woe to you who live by the sea,
  you Kerethite people;
the word of the LORD is against you,
  Canaan, land of the Philistines.
He says, 'I will destroy you,
  and none will be left.'
6 The land by the sea will become pastures
  having wells for shepherds
  and sheepfolds for flocks.
7 That land will belong
  to the remnant of the house of Judah;
  there they will find pasture.
In the evening they will lie down
  in the houses of Ashkelon.
The LORD their God will care for them;
  he will restore their fortunes.[a]

Moab and Ammon
8 'I have heard the insults of Moab
  and the taunts of the Ammonites,
who insulted my people
  and made threats against their land.
9 Therefore, as surely as I live,'
  declares the LORD Almighty,
  the God of Israel,
'surely Moab will become like Sodom,
  the Ammonites like Gomorrah—
a place of weeds and salt pits,
  a wasteland for ever.
The remnant of my people will plunder them;
  the survivors of my nation will inherit their land.'
10 This is what they will get in return for their pride,
  for insulting and mocking
  the people of the LORD Almighty.
11 The LORD will be awesome to them
  when he destroys all the gods of the earth.
Distant nations will bow down to him,
  all of them in their own lands.

Cush
12 'You Cushites,[b] too,
  will be slain by my sword.'

Assyria
13 He will stretch out his hand against the north
  and destroy Assyria,
leaving Nineveh utterly desolate
  and dry as the desert.
14 Flocks and herds will lie down there,
  creatures of every kind.
The desert owl and the screech owl
  will roost on her columns.
Their hooting will echo through the windows,
  rubble will fill the doorways,
  the beams of cedar will be exposed.
15 This is the city of revelry
  that lived in safety.
She said to herself,
  'I am the one! And there is none besides me.'
What a ruin she has become,
  a lair for wild beasts!
All who pass by her scoff
  and shake their fists.

Jerusalem
3 Woe to the city of oppressors,
  rebellious and defiled!
2 She obeys no-one,
  she accepts no correction.
She does not trust in the LORD,
  she does not draw near to her God.
3 Her officials within her
  are roaring lions;

---

[a] 7 Or *will bring back their captives* [b] 12 That is, people from the upper Nile region

her rulers are evening wolves,
  who leave nothing for the morning.
4 Her prophets are unprincipled;
  they cannot be trusted.
Her priests profane the sanctuary
  and do violence to the law.
5 The LORD within her is righteous;
  he does no wrong.
Morning by morning he dispenses his justice,
  and every new day he does not fail,
  yet the unrighteous know no shame.

Jerusalem remains unrepentant

6 'I have destroyed nations;
  their strongholds are demolished.
I have left their streets deserted,
  with no-one passing through.
Their cities are laid waste;
  they are deserted and empty.
7 Of Jerusalem I thought,
  "Surely you will fear me
  and accept correction!"
Then her place of refuge[a] would not be destroyed,
  nor all my punishments come upon[b] her.
But they were still eager
  to act corruptly in all they did.
8 Therefore wait for me,'
  declares the LORD,
'for the day I will stand up to testify.[c]
I have decided to assemble the nations,
  to gather the kingdoms
and to pour out my wrath on them—
  all my fierce anger.
The whole world will be consumed
  by the fire of my jealous anger.

Restoration of Israel's remnant

9 'Then I will purify the lips of the peoples,
  that all of them may call on the name of the LORD
  and serve him shoulder to shoulder.
10 From beyond the rivers of Cush[d]
  my worshippers, my scattered people,
  will bring me offerings.
11 On that day you, Jerusalem, will not be put to shame

IN OTHER WORDS

Remnant
Zephaniah 3:12
A remnant is a bit that is left over, and the word is often used in relation to spare cloth. In the Bible, 'the remnant' refers to the part of a nation or community that is left behind after a judgment or disaster. The remnant survives and from it grows a new community.

---

for all the wrongs you have done to me,
because I will remove from you
  those who revel in your glory.
Never again will you be haughty
  on my holy hill.
12 But I will leave within you
  the meek and humble.
The remnant of Israel
  will trust in the name of the LORD.
13 They will do no wrong;
  they will tell no lies.
A deceitful tongue
  will not be found in their mouths.
They will eat and lie down
  and no-one will make them afraid.'

14 Sing, Daughter Zion;
  shout aloud, Israel!
Be glad and rejoice with all your heart,
  Daughter Jerusalem!
15 The LORD has taken away your punishment,
  he has turned back your enemy.
The LORD, the King of Israel, is with you;
  never again will you fear any harm.
16 On that day
  they will say to Jerusalem,
'Do not fear, Zion;
  do not let your hands hang limp.
17 The LORD your God is with you,
  the Mighty Warrior who saves.
He will take great delight in you;
  in his love he will no longer rebuke you,
  but will rejoice over you with singing.'

---

[a] 7 Or *her sanctuary* [b] 7 Or *all those I appointed over* [c] 8 Septuagint and Syriac; Hebrew *will rise up to plunder*
[d] 10 That is, the upper Nile region

¹⁸'I will remove from you
 all who mourn over the loss of your
  appointed festivals,
 which is a burden and reproach for
  you.
¹⁹At that time I will deal
 with all who oppressed you.
I will rescue the lame;
 I will gather the exiles.
I will give them praise and honour
 in every land where they have suffered
  shame.
²⁰At that time I will gather you;
 at that time I will bring you home.
I will give you honour and praise
 among all the peoples of the earth
when I restore your fortunes*[a]*
 before your very eyes,'
                              says the LORD.

---

[a] 20 Or *I bring back your captives*

Haggai

INTRODUCTION

HAGGAI

Author: Haggai

Who to: The people of Judah.

When: Haggai gave his prophecy in the second year of King Darius of Persia which was 520 BC.

Where: The people of Judah were back in Jerusalem having been in exile in Babylon for fifty years.

Did you know? Haggai was a prophet at the same time as Zechariah. His name means 'festive'.

Main theme: When the people first returned to Judah they started rebuilding the temple, but they ran out of steam and got discouraged. Haggai encourages them to get building again, reminding them how important it is to worship God and be faithful to him.

A call to build the house of the LORD

1 In the second year of King Darius, on the first day of the sixth month, the word of the LORD came through the prophet Haggai to Zerubbabel son of Shealtiel, governor of Judah, and to Joshua[a] son of Jozadak,[b] the high priest:

2This is what the LORD Almighty says: 'These people say, "The time has not yet come to rebuild the LORD's house." '

3Then the word of the LORD came through the prophet Haggai: 4'Is it a time for you yourselves to be living in your panelled houses, while this house remains a ruin?'

5Now this is what the LORD Almighty says: 'Give careful thought to your ways. 6You have planted much, but have harvested little. You eat, but never have enough. You drink, but never have your fill. You put

---

[a] 1 A variant of *Jeshua*; here and elsewhere in Haggai [b] 1 Hebrew *Jehozadak*, a variant of *Jozadak*; also in verses 12 and 14

on clothes, but are not warm. You earn wages, only to put them in a purse with holes in it.'

7This is what the LORD Almighty says: 'Give careful thought to your ways. 8Go up into the mountains and bring down timber and build the house, so that I may take pleasure in it and be honoured,' says the LORD. 9'You expected much, but see, it turned out to be little. What you brought home, I blew away. Why?' declares the LORD Almighty. 'Because of my house, which remains a ruin, while each of you is busy with his own house. 10Therefore, because of you the heavens have withheld their dew and the earth its crops. 11I called for a drought on the fields and the mountains, on the grain, the new wine, the olive oil and everything else the ground produces, on people and livestock, and on all the labour of your hands.'

12Then Zerubbabel son of Shealtiel, Joshua son of Jozadak, the high priest, and the whole remnant of the people obeyed the voice of the LORD their God and the message of the prophet Haggai, because the LORD their God had sent him. And the people feared the LORD.

13Then Haggai, the LORD's messenger, gave this message of the LORD to the people: 'I am with you,' declares the LORD. 14So the LORD stirred up the spirit of Zerubbabel son of Shealtiel, governor of Judah, and the spirit of Joshua son of Jozadak, the high priest, and the spirit of the whole remnant of the people. They came and began to work on the house of the LORD Almighty, their God, 15on the twenty-fourth day of the sixth month.

The promised glory of the new house

2 In the second year of King Darius, 1on the twenty-first day of the seventh month, the word of the LORD came through the prophet Haggai: 2'Speak to Zerubbabel son of Shealtiel, governor of Judah, to Joshua son of Jozadak,[a] the high priest, and to the remnant of the people. Ask them, 3"Who of you is left who saw this house in its former glory? How does it look to you now? Does it not seem to you like nothing? 4But now be strong, Zerubbabel," declares the LORD. "Be strong, Joshua son of Jozadak, the high priest. Be strong, all you people of the land," declares the LORD, "and work. For I am with you," declares the LORD Almighty. 5"This is what I covenanted with you when you came out of Egypt. And my Spirit remains among you. Do not fear."

6'This is what the LORD Almighty says: "In a little while I will once more shake the heavens and the earth, the sea and the dry land. 7I will shake all nations, and what is desired by all nations will come, and I will fill this house with glory," says the LORD Almighty. 8"The silver is mine and the gold is mine," declares the LORD Almighty. 9"The glory of this present house will be greater than the glory of the former house," says the LORD Almighty. "And in this place I will grant peace," declares the LORD Almighty.'

Blessings for a defiled people

10On the twenty-fourth day of the ninth month, in the second year of Darius, the word of the LORD came to the prophet Haggai: 11'This is what the LORD Almighty says: "Ask the priests what the law says: 12ifa person carries consecrated meat in the fold of his garment, and that fold touches some bread or stew, some wine, olive oil or other food, does it become consecrated?"'

The priests answered, 'No.'

13Then Haggai said, 'If a person defiled by contact with a dead body touches one of these things, does it become defiled?'

'Yes,' the priests replied, 'it becomes defiled.'

14Then Haggai said, '"So it is with this people and this nation in my sight," declares the LORD. "Whatever they do and whatever they offer there is defiled.

15'"Now give careful thought to this from this day on[b]—consider how things were before one stone was laid on another in the LORD's temple. 16When anyone came to a heap of twenty measures, there were only ten. When anyone went to a wine vat to draw fifty measures, there were only twenty. 17I struck all the work of your hands with

---

[a] 2 Hebrew *Jehozadak*, a variant of *Jozadak*; also in verse 4   [b] 15 Or *to the days past*

blight, mildew and hail, yet you did not return to me," declares the LORD. 18"From this day on, from this twenty-fourth day of the ninth month, give careful thought to the day when the foundation of the LORD's temple was laid. Give careful thought: 19is there yet any seed left in the barn? Until now, the vine and the fig tree, the pomegranate and the olive tree have not borne fruit.

' "From this day on I will bless you." '

Zerubbabel the LORD's signet ring

20The word of the LORD came to Haggai a second time on the twenty-fourth day of the month: 21'Tell Zerubbabel governor of Judah that I am going to shake the heavens and the earth. 22I will overturn royal thrones and shatter the power of the foreign kingdoms. I will overthrow chariots and their drivers; horses and their riders will fall, each by the sword of his comrade.

Sign of the times

Signet ring
Haggai 2:23
A signet ring was used to seal a document, rather as we would use a signature today.

23' "On that day," declares the LORD Almighty, "I will take you, my servant Zerubbabel son of Shealtiel," declares the LORD, "and I will make you like my signet ring, for I have chosen you," declares the LORD Almighty.'

Zechariah

INTRODUCTION

ZECHARIAH

Author: Zechariah

Who to: The people of Judah.

When: Zechariah's first prophecy is in the second year of the reign of King Darius, 520 BC. Other prophecies come later.

Where: The people of Judah were back in Jerusalem having been in exile in Babylon for fifty years.

Main theme: Zechariah encourages the people to continue to rebuild the temple, and tells them about eight visions he has seen in the night that convince him this is the right thing to do. He looks forward to God's promises for the future, particularly the Messiah. In fact the Messiah is specifically mentioned eight times in just fourteen chapters.

A call to return to the LORD

1 In the eighth month of the second year of Darius, the word of the LORD came to the prophet Zechariah son of Berekiah, the son of Iddo:

² 'The LORD was very angry with your ancestors. ³Therefore tell the people: this is what the LORD Almighty says: "Return to me," declares the LORD Almighty, "and I will return to you," says the LORD Almighty. ⁴Do not be like your ancestors, to whom the earlier prophets proclaimed: this is what the LORD Almighty says: "Turn from your evil ways and your evil practices." But they would not listen or pay attention to me, declares the LORD. ⁵Where are your ancestors now? And the prophets, do they live for ever? ⁶But did not my words and my decrees, which I commanded my servants the prophets, overtake your ancestors?

'Then they repented and said, "The LORD Almighty has done to us what our ways and practices deserve, just as he determined to do."'

The man among the myrtle trees

7 On the twenty-fourth day of the eleventh month, the month of Shebat, in the second year of Darius, the word of the LORD came to the prophet Zechariah son of Berekiah, the son of Iddo.

8 During the night I had a vision, and there before me was a man mounted on a red horse. He was standing among the myrtle trees in a ravine. Behind him were red, brown and white horses.

9 I asked, 'What are these, my lord?'
The angel who was talking with me answered, 'I will show you what they are.'

10 Then the man standing among the myrtle trees explained, 'They are the ones the LORD has sent to go throughout the earth.'

11 And they reported to the angel of the LORD who was standing among the myrtle trees, 'We have gone throughout the earth and found the whole world at rest and in peace.'

12 Then the angel of the LORD said, 'LORD Almighty, how long will you withhold mercy from Jerusalem and from the towns of Judah, which you have been angry with these seventy years?' 13 So the LORD spoke kind and comforting words to the angel who talked with me.

14 Then the angel who was speaking to me said, 'Proclaim this word: this is what the LORD Almighty says: "I am very jealous for Jerusalem and Zion, 15 and I am very angry with the nations that feel secure. I was only a little angry, but they added to the calamity."

16 "Therefore, this is what the LORD says: "I will return to Jerusalem with mercy, and there my house will be rebuilt. And the measuring line will be stretched out over Jerusalem," declares the LORD Almighty.

17 'Proclaim further: this is what the LORD Almighty says: "My towns will again overflow with prosperity, and the LORD will again comfort Zion and choose Jerusalem."'

Four horns and four craftsmen

*18 Then I looked up, and there before me were four horns. 19 I asked the angel who was speaking to me, 'What are these?'

He answered me, 'These are the horns that scattered Judah, Israel and Jerusalem.'

20 Then the LORD showed me four craftsmen. 21 I asked, 'What are these coming to do?'

He answered, 'These are the horns that scattered Judah so its people could not raise their heads, but the craftsmen have come to terrify them and throw down these horns of the nations who lifted up their horns against the land of Judah to scatter its people.'

A man with a measuring line

2 *Then I looked up, and there before me was a man with a measuring line in his hand. 2 I asked, 'Where are you going?'

He answered me, 'To measure Jerusalem, to find out how wide and how long it is.'

3 While the angel who was speaking to me was leaving, another angel came to meet him 4 and said to him: 'Run, tell that young man, "Jerusalem will be a city without walls because of the great number of people and animals in it. 5 And I myself will be a wall of fire around it," declares the LORD, "and I will be its glory within."

6 'Come! Come! Flee from the land of the north,' declares the LORD, 'for I have scattered you to the four winds of heaven,' declares the LORD.

7 'Come, Zion! Escape, you who live in Daughter Babylon!' 8 For this is what the LORD Almighty says: 'After the Glorious One has sent me against the nations that have plundered you—for whoever touches you touches the apple of his eye— 9 I will surely raise my hand against them so that their slaves will plunder them.*a* Then you will know that the LORD Almighty has sent me.

10 'Shout and be glad, Daughter Zion. For I am coming, and I will live among you,' declares the LORD. 11 'Many nations will be joined with the LORD in that day and will become my people. I will live among you and you will know that the LORD Almighty has sent me to you. 12 The LORD will inherit Judah as his portion in the holy land and will

---

a 8, 9 Or *says after... eye:* 9'I... *plunder them.*'

* 1:18-21 is numbered 2:1-4 in Hebrew texts.   * 2:1-13 is numbered 2:5-17 in Hebrew texts.

again choose Jerusalem. ¹³Be still before the LORD, all people, because he has roused himself from his holy dwelling.'

Clean garments for the high priest

3 Then he showed me Joshua[a] the high priest standing before the angel of the LORD, and Satan[b] standing at his right side to accuse him. ²The LORD said to Satan, 'The LORD rebuke you, Satan! The LORD, who has chosen Jerusalem, rebuke you! Is not this man a burning stick snatched from the fire?'

³Now Joshua was dressed in filthy clothes as he stood before the angel. ⁴The angel said to those who were standing before him, 'Take off his filthy clothes.'

Then he said to Joshua, 'See, I have taken away your sin, and I will put fine garments on you.'

⁵Then I said, 'Put a clean turban on his head.' So they put a clean turban on his head and clothed him, while the angel of the LORD stood by.

⁶The angel of the LORD gave this charge to Joshua: ⁷'This is what the LORD Almighty says: "If you will walk in obedience to me and keep my requirements, then you will govern my house and have charge of my courts, and I will give you a place among these standing here.

⁸"Listen, High Priest Joshua, you and your associates seated before you, you who are symbolic of things to come: I am going to bring my servant, the Branch. ⁹See, the stone I have set in front of Joshua! There are seven eyes[c] on that one stone, and I will engrave an inscription on it," says the LORD Almighty, "and I will remove the sin of this land in a single day.

¹⁰"In that day each of you will invite your neighbour to sit under your vine and fig-tree," declares the LORD Almighty.'

The gold lampstand and the two olive trees

4 Then the angel who talked with me returned and wakened me, as one is wakened from sleep. ²He asked me, 'What do you see?'

Lampstand
Zechariah 4:2
This seven-branched lampstand is called a menorah and is an ancient symbol for the Jewish people. Moses was told to make one for the tabernacle in the wilderness (Exodus 25:31–40), and Solomon made ten of them for the temple (1 Kings 7:49).

I answered, 'I see a solid gold lampstand with a bowl at the top and seven lamps on it, with seven channels to the lamps. ³Also there are two olive trees by it, one on the right of the bowl and the other on its left.'

⁴I asked the angel who talked with me, 'What are these, my lord?'

⁵He answered, 'Do you not know what these are?'

'No, my lord,' I replied.

⁶So he said to me, 'This is the word of the LORD to Zerubbabel: "Not by might nor by power, but by my Spirit," says the LORD Almighty.

⁷'What are you, mighty mountain? Before Zerubbabel you will become level ground. Then he will bring out the capstone to shouts of "God bless it! God bless it!"'

⁸Then the word of the LORD came to me: ⁹'The hands of Zerubbabel have laid the foundation of this temple; his hands will also complete it. Then you will know that the LORD Almighty has sent me to you.

¹⁰'Who dares despise the day of small things, since the seven eyes of the LORD that range throughout the earth will rejoice when they see the chosen capstone[d] in the hand of Zerubbabel?'

¹¹Then I asked the angel, 'What are these two olive trees on the right and the left of the lampstand?'

---

[a] 1 A variant of *Jeshua*; here and elsewhere in Zechariah   [b] 1 Hebrew *satan* means *adversary*.   [c] 9 Or *facets*   [d] 10 Or *the plumb-line*

12 Again I asked him, 'What are these two olive branches beside the two gold pipes that pour out golden oil?'

13 He replied, 'Do you not know what these are?'

'No, my lord,' I said.

14 So he said, 'These are the two who are anointed to[a] serve the Lord of all the earth.'

The flying scroll

5 I looked again, and there before me was a flying scroll.

2 He asked me, 'What do you see?'

I answered, 'I see a flying scroll, twenty cubits long and ten cubits wide.'[b]

3 And he said to me, 'This is the curse that is going out over the whole land; for according to what it says on one side, every thief will be banished, and according to what it says on the other, everyone who swears falsely will be banished. 4 The LORD Almighty declares, "I will send it out, and it will enter the house of the thief and the house of anyone who swears falsely by my name. It will remain in that house and destroy it completely, both its timbers and its stones."'

The woman in a basket

5 Then the angel who was speaking to me came forward and said to me, 'Look up and see what this is that is appearing.'

6 I asked, 'What is it?'

He replied, 'It is a basket.' And he added, 'This is the iniquity[c] of the people throughout the land.'

7 Then the cover of lead was raised, and there in the basket sat a woman! 8 He said, 'This is wickedness,' and he pushed her back into the basket and pushed the lead cover down over its mouth.

9 Then I looked up—and there before me were two women, with the wind in their wings! They had wings like those of a stork, and they lifted up the basket between heaven and earth.

10 'Where are they taking the basket?' I asked the angel who was speaking to me.

11 He replied, 'To the country of Babylonia[d] to build a house for it. When it is ready, the basket will be set there in its place.'

Four chariots

6 I looked up again, and there before me were four chariots coming out from between two mountains—mountains of bronze. 2 The first chariot had red horses, the second black, 3 the third white, and the fourth dappled—all of them powerful. 4 I asked the angel who was speaking to me, 'What are these, my lord?'

5 The angel answered me, 'These are the four spirits[e] of heaven, going out from standing in the presence of the Lord of the whole world. 6 The one with the black horses is going towards the north country, the one with the white horses towards the west,[f] and the one with the dappled horses towards the south.'

7 When the powerful horses went out, they were straining to go throughout the earth. And he said, 'Go throughout the earth!' So they went throughout the earth.

8 Then he called to me, 'Look, those going towards the north country have given my Spirit[g] rest in the land of the north.'

A crown for Joshua

9 The word of the LORD came to me: 10 'Take ⌊silver and gold⌋ from the exiles Heldai, Tobijah and Jedaiah, who have arrived from Babylon. Go the same day to the house of Josiah son of Zephaniah. 11 Take the silver and gold and make a crown, and set it on the head of the high priest, Joshua son of Jozadak.[h] 12 Tell him this is what the LORD Almighty says: "Here is the man whose name is the Branch, and he will branch out from his place and build the temple of the LORD. 13 It is he who will build the temple of the LORD, and he will be clothed with majesty and will sit and rule on his throne. And he[i] will be a priest on his throne. And there will be harmony between the two." 14 The crown will be given to Heldai,[j] Tobijah, Jedaiah and Hen[k] son of Zephaniah as a memorial in the temple of the LORD. 15 Those who are far away will come and help to build the temple of the

---

[a] 14 Or *two who bring oil and* [b] 2 That is, about 9 metres long and 4.5 metres wide [c] 6 Or *appearance* [d] 11 Hebrew *Shinar* [e] 5 Or *winds* [f] 6 Or *horses after them* [g] 8 Or *spirit* [h] 11 Hebrew *Jehozadak*, a variant of *Jozadak* [i] 13 Or *there* [j] 14 Syriac; Hebrew *Helem* [k] 14 Or *and the gracious one, the*

LORD, and you will know that the LORD Almighty has sent me to you. This will happen if you diligently obey the LORD your God.'

Justice and mercy, not fasting

7 In the fourth year of King Darius, the word of the LORD came to Zechariah on the fourth day of the ninth month, the month of Kislev. 2The people of Bethel had sent Sharezer and Regem-Melek, together with their men, to entreat the LORD 3by asking the priests of the house of the LORD Almighty and the prophets, 'Should I mourn and fast in the fifth month, as I have done for so many years?'

4Then the word of the LORD Almighty came to me: 5'Ask all the people of the land and the priests, "When you fasted and mourned in the fifth and seventh months for the past seventy years, was it really for me that you fasted? 6And when you were eating and drinking, were you not just feasting for yourselves? 7Are these not the words the LORD proclaimed through the earlier prophets when Jerusalem and its surrounding towns were at rest and prosperous, and the Negev and the western foothills were settled?"'

People and Places

Jerusalem
Zechariah 8:3

Jerusalem is an ancient city, perhaps five thousand years old. It was captured by David when he became king, and he turned it into the capital city of the kingdom of Israel. Much of the drama of the Bible focuses around this city, which had theological significance as the location of God's temple and the place for sacrificial worship. Today, Jerusalem is a significant place for Jews, Christians and Muslims.

8And the word of the LORD came again to Zechariah: 9'This is what the LORD Almighty said: "Administer true justice; show mercy and compassion to one another. 10Do not oppress the widow or the fatherless, the foreigner or the poor. Do not plot evil against each other."

11'But they refused to pay attention; stubbornly they turned their backs and covered their ears. 12They made their hearts as hard as flint and would not listen to the law or to the words that the LORD Almighty had sent by his Spirit through the earlier prophets. So the LORD Almighty was very angry.

13' "When I called, they did not listen; so when they called, I would not listen," says the LORD Almighty. 14"I scattered them with a whirlwind among all the nations, where they were strangers. The land they left behind them was so desolate that no-one travelled through it. This is how they made the pleasant land desolate." '

The LORD promises to bless Jerusalem

8 The word of the LORD Almighty came to me.

2This is what the LORD Almighty says: 'I am very jealous for Zion; I am burning with jealousy for her.'

3This is what the LORD says: 'I will return to Zion and dwell in Jerusalem. Then Jerusalem will be called the City of Truth, and the mountain of the LORD Almighty will be called the Holy Mountain.'

4This is what the LORD Almighty says: 'Once again men and women of ripe old age will sit in the streets of Jerusalem, each of them with walking-stick in hand because of their age. 5The city streets will be filled with boys and girls playing there.'

6This is what the LORD Almighty says: 'It may seem marvellous to the remnant of this people at that time, but will it seem marvellous to me?' declares the LORD Almighty.

7This is what the LORD Almighty says: 'I will save my people from the countries of the east and the west. 8I will bring them back to live in Jerusalem; they will be my people, and I will be faithful and righteous to them as their God.'

⁹This is what the LORD Almighty says: 'Now hear these words, "Let your hands be strong so that the temple may be built." This is also what the prophets said who were present when the foundation was laid for the house of the LORD Almighty. ¹⁰Before that time there were no wages for people or animals. People could not go about their business safely because of conflicts, since I had turned them all against each other. ¹¹But now I will not deal with the remnant of this people as I did in the past,' declares the LORD Almighty.

¹²'The seed will grow well, the vine will yield its fruit, the ground will produce its crops, and the heavens will drop their dew. I will give all these things as an inheritance to the remnant of this people. ¹³Just as you, Judah and Israel, have been a curse[a] among the nations, so I will save you, and you will be a blessing.[b] Do not be afraid, but let your hands be strong.'

¹⁴This is what the LORD Almighty says: 'Just as I had determined to bring disaster on you and showed no pity when your ancestors angered me,' says the LORD Almighty, ¹⁵'so now I have determined to do good again to Jerusalem and Judah. Do not be afraid. ¹⁶These are the things you are to do: Speak the truth to each other, and render true and sound judgment in your courts; ¹⁷do not plot evil against each other, and do not love to swear falsely. I hate all this,' declares the LORD.

¹⁸The word of the LORD Almighty came to me.

¹⁹This is what the LORD Almighty says: 'The fasts of the fourth, fifth, seventh and tenth months will become joyful and glad occasions and happy festivals for Judah. Therefore love truth and peace.'

²⁰This is what the LORD Almighty says: 'Many peoples and the inhabitants of many cities will yet come, ²¹and the inhabitants of one city will go to another and say, "Let us go at once to entreat the LORD and seek the LORD Almighty. I myself am going." ²²And many peoples and powerful nations will come to Jerusalem to seek the LORD Almighty and to entreat him.'

²³This is what the LORD Almighty says: 'In those days ten people from all languages and nations will take firm hold of one Jew by the hem of his robe and say, "Let us go with you, because we have heard that God is with you."'

Judgment on Israel's enemies

9 A prophecy:

The word of the LORD is against the land of Hadrak
  and will come to rest on Damascus—
for the eyes of all people and all the tribes of Israel
  are on the LORD—[c]
²and on Hamath too, which borders on it,
  and on Tyre and Sidon, though they are very skilful.
³Tyre has built herself a stronghold;
  she has heaped up silver like dust,
  and gold like the dirt of the streets.
⁴But the Lord will take away her possessions
  and destroy her power on the sea,
  and she will be consumed by fire.
⁵Ashkelon will see it and fear;
  Gaza will writhe in agony,
  and Ekron too, for her hope will wither.
Gaza will lose her king
  and Ashkelon will be deserted.
⁶A mongrel people will occupy Ashdod,
  and I will put an end to the pride of the Philistines.
⁷I will take the blood from their mouths,
  the forbidden food from between their teeth.
Those who are left will belong to our God
  and become a clan in Judah,
  and Ekron will be like the Jebusites.
⁸But I will encamp at my temple
  to guard it against marauding forces.
Never again will an oppressor overrun my people,
  for now I am keeping watch.

---

[a] 13 That is, your name has been used in cursing (see Jer. 29:23); or, you have been regarded as under a curse. [b] 13 Or and your name will be used in blessings (see Gen. 48:20); or and you will be seen as blessed [c] 1 Or Damascus. / For the eye of the LORD is on all people, / as well as on the tribes of Israel.

A king on a donkey
Zechariah 9:9
A king would usually travel on a horse or in a chariot, not on a humble donkey. Matthew quotes this verse in his Gospel when Jesus rides into Jerusalem on a donkey (Matthew 21:5).

The coming of Zion's king

9 Rejoice greatly, Daughter Zion!
  Shout, Daughter Jerusalem!
See, your king comes to you,
  righteous and having salvation,
lowly and riding on a donkey,
  on a colt, the foal of a donkey.
10 I will take away the chariots from Ephraim
  and the war horses from Jerusalem,
  and the battle-bow will be broken.
He will proclaim peace to the nations.
  His rule will extend from sea to sea
  and from the River[a] to the ends of the earth.
11 As for you, because of the blood of my covenant with you,
  I will free your prisoners from the waterless pit.
12 Return to your fortress, you prisoners of hope;
  even now I announce that I will restore twice as much to you.
13 I will bend Judah as I bend my bow
  and fill it with Ephraim.
I will rouse your sons, Zion,
  against your sons, Greece,
  and make you like a warrior's sword.

The LORD will appear

14 Then the LORD will appear over them;
  his arrow will flash like lightning.
The Sovereign LORD will sound the trumpet;
  he will march in the storms of the south,
15   and the LORD Almighty will shield them.
They will destroy
  and overcome with slingstones.
They will drink and roar as with wine;
  they will be full like a bowl
  used for sprinkling[b] the corners of the altar.
16 The LORD their God will save his people on that day
  as a shepherd saves his flock.
They will sparkle in his land
  like jewels in a crown.
17 How attractive and beautiful they will be!
  Grain will make the young men thrive,
  and new wine the young women.

The LORD will care for Judah

10 Ask the LORD for rain in the springtime;
  it is the LORD who sends the thunderstorms.
He gives showers of rain to all people,
  and plants of the field to everyone.
2 The idols speak deceitfully,
  diviners see visions that lie;
they tell dreams that are false,
  they give comfort in vain.
Therefore the people wander like sheep
  oppressed for lack of a shepherd.

3 'My anger burns against the shepherds,
  and I will punish the leaders;
for the LORD Almighty will care
  for his flock, the house of Judah,
  and make them like a proud horse in battle.
4 From Judah will come the cornerstone,
  from him the tent peg,
from him the battle-bow,
  from him every ruler.
5 Together they[c] will be like mighty warriors in battle
  trampling their enemy into the mud of the streets.
They will fight because the LORD is with them,

---

[a] 10 That is, the Euphrates   [b] 15 Or bowl, / like   [c] 4, 5 Or ruler, all of them together. / 5 They

and they will put the enemy horsemen to shame.

6 'I will strengthen the house of Judah
and save the house of Joseph.
I will restore them
because I have compassion on them.
They will be as though
I had not rejected them,
for I am the LORD their God
and I will answer them.
7 The Ephraimites will become like mighty warriors,
and their hearts will be glad as with wine.
Their children will see it and be joyful;
their hearts will rejoice in the LORD.
8 I will signal for them
and gather them in.
Surely I will redeem them;
they will be as numerous as before.
9 Though I scatter them among the peoples,
yet in distant lands they will remember me.
They and their children will survive,
and they will return.
10 I will bring them back from Egypt
and gather them from Assyria.
I will bring them to Gilead and Lebanon,
and there will not be room enough for them.
11 They will pass through the sea of trouble;
the surging sea will be subdued
and all the depths of the Nile will dry up.
Assyria's pride will be brought down
and Egypt's sceptre will pass away.
12 I will strengthen them in the LORD
and in his name they will live securely,'
declares the LORD.

11

Open your doors, Lebanon,
so that fire may devour your cedars!
2 Wail, you juniper, for the cedar has fallen;
the stately trees are ruined!
Wail, oaks of Bashan;
the dense forest has been cut down!
3 Listen to the wail of the shepherds;
their rich pastures are destroyed!
Listen to the roar of the lions;
the lush thicket of the Jordan is ruined!

Two shepherds

4 This is what the LORD my God says: 'Shepherd the flock marked for slaughter. 5 Their buyers slaughter them and go unpunished. Those who sell them say, "Praise the LORD, I am rich!" Their own shepherds do not spare them. 6 For I will no longer have pity on the people of the land,' declares the LORD. 'I will give everyone into the hands of their neighbours and their king. They will devastate the land, and I will not rescue them from their hands.'

7 So I shepherded the flock marked for slaughter, particularly the oppressed of the flock. Then I took two staffs and called one Favour and the other Union, and I shepherded the flock. 8 In one month I got rid of the three shepherds.

The flock detested me, and I grew weary of them 9 and said, 'I will not be your shepherd. Let the dying die, and the perishing perish. Let those who are left eat one another's flesh.'

10 Then I took my staff called Favour and broke it, revoking the covenant I had made with all the nations. 11 It was revoked on that day, and so the oppressed of the flock who were watching me knew it was the word of the LORD.

12 I told them, 'If you think it best, give me my pay; but if not, keep it.' So they paid me thirty pieces of silver.

13 And the LORD said to me, 'Throw it to the potter'—the handsome price at which they valued me! So I took the thirty pieces of silver and threw them to the potter at the house of the LORD.

14 Then I broke my second staff called Union, breaking the family bond between Judah and Israel.

15 Then the LORD said to me, 'Take again the equipment of a foolish shepherd. 16 For I am going to raise up a shepherd over the land who will not care for the lost, or seek the young, or heal the injured, or feed the healthy, but will eat the meat of the choice sheep, tearing off their hooves.

17 'Woe to the worthless shepherd,
who deserts the flock!

Making Connections

Thirty pieces of silver
Zechariah 11:13

Thirty pieces of silver was the price of a common slave according to Exodus 21:32. Judas betrayed Jesus for thirty pieces of silver. When he tried to return the money, the chief priests used it to buy a potter's field as a burial place for foreign people (Matthew 27:5–7).

> May the sword strike his arm and his right eye!
> May his arm be completely withered, his right eye totally blinded!'

Jerusalem's enemies to be destroyed

12 A prophecy: the word of the LORD concerning Israel.

The LORD, who stretches out the heavens, who lays the foundation of the earth, and who forms the spirit in human beings, declares: ²'I am going to make Jerusalem a cup that sends all the surrounding peoples reeling. Judah will be besieged as well as Jerusalem. ³On that day, when all the nations of the earth are gathered against her, I will make Jerusalem an immovable rock for all the nations. All who try to move it will injure themselves. ⁴On that day I will strike every horse with panic and its rider with madness,' declares the LORD. 'I will keep a watchful eye over the house of Judah, but I will blind all the horses of the nations. ⁵Then the clans of Judah will say in their hearts, "The people of Jerusalem are strong, because the LORD Almighty is their God."

⁶'On that day I will make the clans of Judah like a brazier in a woodpile, like a flaming torch among sheaves. They will consume right and left all the surrounding peoples, but Jerusalem will remain intact in her place.

⁷'The LORD will save the dwellings of Judah first, so that the honour of the house of David and of Jerusalem's inhabitants may not be greater than that of Judah. ⁸On that day the LORD will shield those who live in Jerusalem, so that the feeblest among them will be like David, and the house of David will be like God, like the angel of the LORD going before them. ⁹On that day I will set out to destroy all the nations that attack Jerusalem.

Mourning for the one they pierced

¹⁰'And I will pour out on the house of David and the inhabitants of Jerusalem a spirit*ᵃ* of grace and supplication. They will look on*ᵇ* me, the one they have pierced, and they will mourn for him as one mourns for an only child, and grieve bitterly for him as one grieves for a firstborn son. ¹¹On that day the weeping in Jerusalem will be great, like the weeping of Hadad Rimmon in the plain of Megiddo. ¹²The land will mourn, each clan by itself, with their wives by themselves: the clan of the house of David and their wives, the clan of the house of Nathan and their wives, ¹³the clan of the house of Levi and their wives, the clan of Shimei and their wives, ¹⁴and all the rest of the clans and their wives.

Cleansing from sin

13 'On that day a fountain will be opened to the house of David and the inhabitants of Jerusalem, to cleanse them from sin and impurity.

²'On that day, I will banish the names of the idols from the land, and they will be remembered no more,' declares the LORD Almighty. 'I will remove both the prophets and the spirit of impurity from the land. ³And if some still prophesy, their fathers and mothers, to whom they were born, will say to them, "You must die, because you have told lies in the LORD's name." When they prophesy, their own parents will stab them.

⁴'On that day the prophets will all be ashamed of their prophetic visions. They

---

ᵃ 10 Or *the Spirit* *ᵇ* 10 Or *to*

will not put on a prophet's garment of hair in order to deceive. 5Every one of them will say, "I am not a prophet. I am a farmer; the land has been my livelihood since my youth.*ᵃ*" 6If someone asks, "What are these wounds on your body?"*ᵇ* they will answer, "The wounds I was given at the house of my friends."

The shepherd struck, the sheep scattered

7'Awake, sword, against my shepherd,
 against the man who is close to me!'
declares the LORD Almighty.
'Strike the shepherd,
 and the sheep will be scattered,
 and I will turn my hand against the
  little ones.
8In the whole land,' declares the LORD,
'two-thirds will be struck down and
  perish;
 yet one-third will be left in it.
9This third I will bring into the fire;
 I will refine them like silver
 and test them like gold.
They will call on my name
 and I will answer them;
I will say, "They are my people,"
 and they will say, "The LORD is our
  God."'

The LORD comes and reigns

14 A day of the LORD is coming, Jerusalem, when your possessions will be plundered and divided up within your very walls.

2I will gather all the nations to Jerusalem to fight against it; the city will be captured, the houses ransacked, and the women ravished. Half of the city will go into exile, but the rest of the people will not be taken from the city. 3Then the LORD will go out and fight against those nations, as he fights on a day of battle. 4On that day his feet will stand on the Mount of Olives, east of Jerusalem, and the Mount of Olives will be split in two from east to west, forming a great valley, with half of the mountain moving north and half moving south. 5You will flee by my mountain valley, for it will extend to Azel. You will flee as you fled from the earthquake*ᶜ* in the days of Uzziah king of Judah. Then the LORD my God will come, and all the holy ones with him.

6On that day there will be no sunlight, no cold, frosty darkness. 7It will be a unique day—a day known only to the LORD—with no distinction between day and night. When evening comes, there will be light.

8On that day living water will flow out from Jerusalem, half of it east to the Dead Sea and half of it west to the Mediterranean Sea, in summer and in winter.

9The LORD will be king over the whole earth. On that day there will be one LORD, and his name the only name.

10The whole land, from Geba to Rimmon, south of Jerusalem, will become like the Arabah. But Jerusalem will be raised up high from the Benjamin Gate to the site of the First Gate, to the Corner Gate, and from the Tower of Hananel to the royal winepresses, and will remain in its place. 11It will be inhabited; never again will it be destroyed. Jerusalem will be secure.

12This is the plague with which the LORD will strike all the nations that fought against Jerusalem: their flesh will rot while they are still standing on their feet, their eyes will rot in their sockets, and their tongues will rot in their mouths. 13On that day people will be stricken by the LORD with great panic. They will seize each other by the hand and attack one another. 14Judah too will fight at Jerusalem. The wealth of all the surrounding nations will be collected—great quantities of gold and silver and clothing. 15A similar plague will strike the horses and mules, the camels and donkeys, and all the animals in those camps.

16Then the survivors from all the nations that have attacked Jerusalem will go up year after year to worship the King, the LORD Almighty, and to celebrate the Festival of Tabernacles. 17If any of the peoples of the earth do not go up to Jerusalem to worship the King, the LORD Almighty, they will have no rain. 18If the Egyptian people do not go up and take part, they will have no rain. The LORD*ᵈ* will bring on them the plague he

---

ᵃ 5 Or *farmer; a man sold me in my youth*   *ᵇ* 6 Or *wounds between your hands*   *ᶜ* 5 Or *⁵My mountain valley will be blocked and will extend to Azel. It will be blocked as it was blocked because of the earthquake*   *ᵈ* 18 Or *part, then the* LORD inflicts on the nations that do not go up to celebrate the Festival of Tabernacles. ¹⁹This will be the punishment of Egypt and the punishment of all the nations that do not go up to celebrate the Festival of Tabernacles.

²⁰On that day HOLY TO THE LORD will be inscribed on the bells of the horses, and the cooking pots in the LORD's house will be like the sacred bowls in front of the altar. ²¹Every pot in Jerusalem and Judah will be holy to the LORD Almighty, and all who come to sacrifice will take some of the pots and cook in them. And on that day there will no longer be a Canaanite[a] in the house of the LORD Almighty.

---

[a] 21 Or *merchant*

Malachi

INTRODUCTION

MALACHI

Author: Malachi

Who to: The people of Israel.

When: Probably about a hundred years after the people of Israel returned from exile, around 450 BC.

Did you know? After the book of Malachi, there is a silence of four hundred years before Jesus is born.

Main theme: Reading Malachi is like eavesdropping on a conversation between God and the people of Israel. Malachi highlights how shallow Israel's worship has become. They are trying to get away with sacrificing imperfect animals and not giving their full tithe to God. Malachi encourages them to get it right and reminds them of God's love for them.

1 A prophecy: the word of the LORD to Israel through Malachi.[a]

Israel doubts God's love

2'I have loved you,' says the LORD.

'But you ask, "How have you loved us?"'

'Was not Esau Jacob's brother?' declares the LORD. 'Yet I have loved Jacob, 3but Esau I have hated, and I have turned his hill country into a wasteland and left his inheritance to the desert jackals.'

4Edom may say, 'Though we have been crushed, we will rebuild the ruins.'

But this is what the LORD Almighty says: 'They may build, but I will demolish. They will be called the Wicked Land, a people always under the wrath of the LORD. 5You will see it with your own eyes and say, "Great is the LORD—even beyond the borders of Israel!"'

---

[a] 1 *Malachi* means *my messenger*.

Breaking covenant through blemished sacrifices

6'A son honours his father, and slaves honour their master. If I am a father, where is the honour due to me? If I am a master, where is the respect due to me?' says the LORD Almighty.

'It is you priests who show contempt for my name.

'But you ask, "How have we shown contempt for your name?"

7'By offering defiled food on my altar.

'But you ask, "How have we defiled you?"

'By saying that the LORD's table is contemptible. 8When you offer blind animals for sacrifice, is that not wrong? When you sacrifice lame or diseased animals, is that not wrong? Try offering them to your governor! Would he be pleased with you? Would he accept you?' says the LORD Almighty.

9'Now implore God to be gracious to us. With such offerings from your hands, will he accept you?'—says the LORD Almighty.

10'Oh, that one of you would shut the temple doors, so that you would not light useless fires on my altar! I am not pleased with you,' says the LORD Almighty, 'and I will accept no offering from your hands. 11My name will be great among the nations, from where the sun rises to where it sets. In every place incense and pure offerings will be brought to me, because my name will be great among the nations,' says the LORD Almighty.

12'But you profane it by saying, "The Lord's table is defiled," and, "Its food is contemptible." 13And you say, "What a burden!" and you sniff at it contemptuously,' says the LORD Almighty.

'When you bring injured, lame or diseased animals and offer them as sacrifices, should I accept them from your hands?' says the LORD. 14'Cursed is the cheat who has an acceptable male in his flock and vows to give it, but then sacrifices a blemished animal to the Lord. For I am a great king,' says the LORD Almighty, 'and my name is to be feared among the nations.

Additional warning to the priests

2 'And now, you priests, this warning is for you. 2If you do not listen, and if you do not resolve to honour my name,' says the LORD Almighty, 'I will send a curse on you, and I will curse your blessings. Yes, I have already cursed them, because you have not resolved to honour me.

3'Because of you I will rebuke your descendants;[a] I will smear on your faces the dung from your festival sacrifices, and you will be carried off with it. 4And you will know that I have sent you this warning so that my covenant with Levi may continue,' says the LORD Almighty. 5'My covenant was with him, a covenant of life and peace, and I gave them to him; this called for reverence and he revered me and stood in awe of my name. 6True instruction was in his mouth and nothing false was found on his lips. He walked with me in peace and uprightness, and turned many from sin.

7'For the lips of a priest ought to preserve knowledge, because he is the messenger of the LORD Almighty and people seek instruction from his mouth. 8But you have turned from the way and by your teaching have caused many to stumble; you have violated the covenant with Levi,' says the LORD Almighty. 9'So I have caused you to be despised and humiliated before all the people, because you have not followed my ways but have shown partiality in matters of the law.'

Breaking covenant through divorce

10Do we not all have one Father?[b] Did not one God create us? Why do we profane the covenant of our ancestors by being unfaithful to one another?

11Judah has been unfaithful. A detestable thing has been committed in Israel and in Jerusalem: Judah has desecrated the sanctuary the LORD loves by marrying women who worship a foreign god. 12If anyone does this, whoever he may be, may the LORD remove him from the tents of Jacob[c]—even though he brings an offering to the LORD Almighty.

---

[a] 3 Or *will blight your corn*   [b] 10 Or *father*   [c] 12 Or 12*May the LORD remove from the tents of Jacob anyone who gives testimony on behalf of the man who does this*

¹³Another thing you do: you flood the LORD's altar with tears. You weep and wail because he no longer looks with favour on your offerings or accepts them with pleasure from your hands. ¹⁴You ask, 'Why?' It is because the LORD is the witness between you and the wife of your youth. You have been unfaithful to her, though she is your partner, the wife of your marriage covenant.

¹⁵Has not the LORD made the two of you one? You belong to him in body and spirit. And why has he made you one? Because he was seeking godly offspring.*ᵃ* So be on your guard, and do not be unfaithful to the wife of your youth.

¹⁶'I hate divorce,' says the LORD God of Israel, 'and I hate it when people clothe themselves with injustice,' says the LORD Almighty.

So be on your guard, and do not be unfaithful.

Breaking covenant through injustice

¹⁷You have wearied the LORD with your words.

'How have we wearied him?' you ask.

By saying, 'All who do evil are good in the eyes of the LORD, and he is pleased with them' or 'Where is the God of justice?'

3 'I will send my messenger, who will prepare the way before me. Then suddenly the Lord you are seeking will come to his temple; the messenger of the covenant, whom you desire, will come,' says the LORD Almighty.

²But who can endure the day of his coming? Who can stand when he appears? For he will be like a refiner's fire or a launderer's soap. ³He will sit as a refiner and purifier of silver; he will purify the Levites and refine them like gold and silver. Then the LORD will have men who will bring offerings in righteousness, ⁴and the offerings of Judah and Jerusalem will be acceptable to the LORD, as in days gone by, as in former years.

⁵'So I will come to put you on trial. I will be quick to testify against sorcerers, adulterers and perjurers, against those who defraud labourers of their wages, who oppress the widows and the fatherless, and deprive the foreigners among you of justice, but do not fear me,' says the LORD Almighty.

Breaking covenant by withholding tithes

⁶'I the LORD do not change. So you, the descendants of Jacob, are not destroyed. ⁷Ever since the time of your ancestors you have turned away from my decrees and have not kept them. Return to me, and I will return to you,' says the LORD Almighty.

'But you ask, "How are we to return?"'

⁸'Will a mere mortal rob God? Yet you rob me.

'But you ask, "How are we robbing you?"'

'In tithes and offerings. ⁹You are under a curse—your whole nation—because you are robbing me. ¹⁰Bring the whole tithe into the storehouse, that there may be food in my house. Test me in this,' says the LORD Almighty, 'and see if I will not throw open the floodgates of heaven and pour out so much blessing that there will not be room enough to store it. ¹¹I will prevent pests from devouring your crops, and the vines in your fields will not drop their fruit before it is ripe,' says the LORD Almighty. ¹²'Then all the nations will call you blessed, for yours will be a delightful land,' says the LORD Almighty.

> **Sign of the times**
>
> **Refining**
> Malachi 3:2
>
> To get rid of the impurities in metal and to make it stronger, it was refined in a furnace. It would be melted until it was a liquid. The impurities could then be separated off, and the pure metal was poured into a mould and allowed to cool.

ᵃ 15 The meaning of the Hebrew for the first part of this verse is uncertain.

> **IN OTHER WORDS**
>
> **Tithe**
> Malachi 3:10
> A 'tithe' was a tenth. It was the law for the Israelites to give a tenth of their crops, livestock and any other produce to the temple for worship and sacrifice. Many people today give a tithe to their church or to Christian organisations.

Israel speaks arrogantly against God

13'You have spoken arrogantly against me,' says the LORD.

'Yet you ask, "What have we said against you?"

14'You have said, "It is futile to serve God. What do we gain by carrying out his requirements and going about like mourners before the LORD Almighty? 15But now we call the arrogant blessed. Certainly evildoers prosper, and even when they put God to the test, they get away with it."'

The faithful remnant

16Then those who feared the LORD talked with each other, and the LORD listened and heard. A scroll of remembrance was written in his presence concerning those who feared the LORD and honoured his name.

17'On the day when I act,' says the LORD Almighty, 'they will be my treasured possession. I will spare them, just as a father has compassion and spares his son who serves him. 18And you will again see the distinction between the righteous and the wicked, between those who serve God and those who do not.

Judgment and covenant renewal

4 *'Surely the day is coming; it will burn like a furnace. All the arrogant and every evildoer will be stubble, and that day that is coming will set them on fire,' says the LORD Almighty. 'Not a root or a branch will be left to them. 2But for you who revere my name, the sun of righteousness will rise with healing in its rays. And you will go out and frolic like well-fed calves. 3Then you will trample on the wicked; they will be ashes under the soles of your feet on the day when I act,' says the LORD Almighty.

4'Remember the law of my servant Moses, the decrees and laws I gave him at Horeb for all Israel.

5'See, I will send the prophet Elijah to you before that great and dreadful day of the LORD comes. 6He will turn the hearts of the parents to their children, and the hearts of the children to their parents; or else I will come and strike the land with total destruction.'

---

* 4:1-6 is numbered 3:19-24 in Hebrew texts.

The New Testament

Matthew

INTRODUCTION

Matthew

Author: Unknown, thought to be based on sayings collected by Matthew the tax collector, one of Jesus' disciples (Matthew 9:9).

Who to: Written for a Jewish audience.

When: It covers the events of Jesus' life, from 4 BC to AD 30. It was probably written in the 50s or 60s AD.

Where: Judea

Did you know? Matthew, Mark and Luke are called the Synoptic Gospels because they are quite similar in the language they use, the events they include and the order in which they tell the story.

Main theme: The Gospel of Matthew was written to convince Jewish readers that Jesus is the Messiah. It starts with Jesus' family tree showing that he is descended from Abraham. Matthew talks a lot about the kingdom of heaven, the reign of God over the whole universe and over every part of our lives.

The genealogy of Jesus the Messiah

1 This is the genealogy[a] of Jesus the Messiah[b] the son of David, the son of Abraham:

2 Abraham was the father of Isaac,
  Isaac the father of Jacob,
  Jacob the father of Judah and his brothers,
3 Judah the father of Perez and Zerah, whose mother was Tamar,
  Perez the father of Hezron,
  Hezron the father of Ram,
4 Ram the father of Amminadab,
  Amminadab the father of Nahshon,
  Nahshon the father of Salmon,
5 Salmon the father of Boaz, whose mother was Rahab,
  Boaz the father of Obed, whose mother was Ruth,
  Obed the father of Jesse,
6 and Jesse the father of King David.

---

[a] 1 Or *is an account of the origin* [b] 1 Or *Jesus Christ. Messiah* (Hebrew) and *Christ* (Greek) both mean *Anointed One*; also in verse 18.

David was the father of Solomon,
   whose mother had been Uriah's wife,
7 Solomon the father of Rehoboam,
   Rehoboam the father of Abijah,
   Abijah the father of Asa,
8 Asa the father of Jehoshaphat,
   Jehoshaphat the father of Jehoram,
   Jehoram the father of Uzziah,
9 Uzziah the father of Jotham,
   Jotham the father of Ahaz,
   Ahaz the father of Hezekiah,
10 Hezekiah the father of Manasseh,
   Manasseh the father of Amon,
   Amon the father of Josiah,
11 and Josiah the father of Jeconiah[a] and his brothers at the time of the exile to Babylon.

12 After the exile to Babylon:
   Jeconiah was the father of Shealtiel,
   Shealtiel the father of Zerubbabel,
13 Zerubbabel the father of Abiud,
   Abiud the father of Eliakim,
   Eliakim the father of Azor,
14 Azor the father of Zadok,
   Zadok the father of Akim,
   Akim the father of Eliud,
15 Eliud the father of Eleazar,
   Eleazar the father of Matthan,
   Matthan the father of Jacob,
16 and Jacob the father of Joseph, the husband of Mary, and Mary was the mother of Jesus who is called the Messiah.

17 Thus there were fourteen generations in all from Abraham to David, fourteen from David to the exile to Babylon, and fourteen from the exile to the Messiah.

Joseph accepts Jesus as his son

18 This is how the birth of Jesus the Messiah came about[b]: his mother Mary was pledged to be married to Joseph, but before they came together, she was found to be pregnant through the Holy Spirit. 19 Because Joseph her husband was a righteous man and did not want to expose her to public disgrace, he had in mind to divorce her quietly.

20 But after he had considered this, an angel of the Lord appeared to him in a dream and said, 'Joseph son of David, do not be afraid to take Mary home as your wife, because what is conceived in her is from the Holy Spirit. 21 She will give birth to a son, and you are to give him the name Jesus,[c] because he will save his people from their sins.'

22 All this took place to fulfil what the Lord had said through the prophet: 23 'The virgin will conceive and give birth to a son, and they will call him Immanuel'[d] (which means 'God with us').

24 When Joseph woke up, he did what the angel of the Lord had commanded him and took Mary home as his wife. 25 But he had no union with her until she gave birth to a son. And he gave him the name Jesus.

The Magi visit the Messiah

2 After Jesus was born in Bethlehem in Judea, during the time of King Herod, Magi[e] from the east came to Jerusalem 2 and asked, 'Where is the one who has been born king of the Jews? We saw his star when it rose and have come to worship him.'

People and Places

Mary
Matthew 1:18

Girls got married when they were very young at this time, and so Mary was probably a teenager when the angel Gabriel appeared to her and told her that she was to have a baby who would be God's Son. She willingly accepted this calling from God even though it nearly led to Joseph leaving her. Mary was present at Jesus' first miracle and at his death on the cross.

---

[a] 11 That is, Jehoiachin; also in verse 12   [b] 18 Or *The origin of Jesus the Messiah was like this*   [c] 21 *Jesus* is the Greek form of *Joshua*, which means *the LORD saves*.   [d] 23 Isaiah 7:14   [e] 1 Traditionally *wise men*

People and Places

Herod
Matthew 2:1

Actually there were several King Herods in the first century. They were puppet kings under the Roman Empire. Herod the Great was king of Judah when Jesus was born. His son Herod Antipas ruled over Galilee when Jesus was an adult.

3When King Herod heard this he was disturbed, and all Jerusalem with him. 4When he had called together all the people's chief priests and teachers of the law, he asked them where the Messiah was to be born. 5'In Bethlehem in Judea,' they replied, 'for this is what the prophet has written:

6' "But you, Bethlehem, in the land of Judah,
　are by no means least among the rulers of Judah;
for out of you will come a ruler
　who will shepherd my people Israel."*a*'

7Then Herod called the Magi secretly and found out from them the exact time the star had appeared. 8He sent them to Bethlehem and said, 'Go and make a careful search for the child. As soon as you find him, report to me, so that I too may go and worship him.'

9After they had heard the king, they went on their way, and the star they had seen when it rose went ahead of them until it stopped over the place where the child was. 10When they saw the star, they were overjoyed. 11On coming to the house, they saw the child with his mother Mary, and they bowed down and worshipped him. Then they opened their treasures and presented him with gifts of gold, frankincense and myrrh. 12And having been warned in a dream not to go back to Herod, they returned to their country by another route.

The escape to Egypt

13When they had gone, an angel of the Lord appeared to Joseph in a dream. 'Get up,' he said, 'take the child and his mother and escape to Egypt. Stay there until I tell you, for Herod is going to search for the child to kill him.'

14So he got up, took the child and his mother during the night and left for Egypt, 15where he stayed until the death of Herod. And so was fulfilled what the Lord had said through the prophet: 'Out of Egypt I called my son.'*b*

16When Herod realised that he had been outwitted by the Magi, he was furious, and he gave orders to kill all the boys in Bethlehem and its vicinity who were two years old and under, in accordance with the time he had learned from the Magi. 17Then what was said through the prophet Jeremiah was fulfilled:

18'A voice is heard in Ramah,
　weeping and great mourning,
Rachel weeping for her children
　and refusing to be comforted,
because they are no more.'*c*

The return to Nazareth

19After Herod died, an angel of the Lord appeared in a dream to Joseph in Egypt 20and said, 'Get up, take the child and his mother and go to the land of Israel, for those who were trying to take the child's life are dead.'

21So he got up, took the child and his mother and went to the land of Israel. 22But when he heard that Archelaus was reigning in Judea in place of his father Herod, he was afraid to go there. Having been warned in a dream, he withdrew to the district of Galilee, 23and he went and lived in a town called Nazareth. So was fulfilled what was said through the prophets: 'He will be called a Nazarene.'

John the Baptist prepares the way

3 In those days John the Baptist came, preaching in the wilderness of Judea 2and saying, 'Repent, for the kingdom of heaven has come near.' 3This is he who was spoken of through the prophet Isaiah:

---

*a*6 Micah 5:2,4　*b*15 Hosea 11:1　*c*18 Jer. 31:15

'A voice of one calling in the wilderness,
"Prepare the way for the Lord,
    make straight paths for him."'[a]

4 John's clothes were made of camel's hair, and he had a leather belt round his waist. His food was locusts and wild honey. 5 People went out to him from Jerusalem and all Judea and the whole region of the Jordan. 6 Confessing their sins, they were baptised by him in the River Jordan.

7 But when he saw many of the Pharisees and Sadducees coming to where he was baptising, he said to them: 'You brood of vipers! Who warned you to flee from the coming wrath? 8 Produce fruit in keeping with repentance. 9 And do not think you can say to yourselves, "We have Abraham as our father." I tell you that out of these stones God can raise up children for Abraham. 10 The axe has been laid to the root of the trees, and every tree that does not produce good fruit will be cut down and thrown into the fire.

11 'I baptise you with[b] water for repentance. But after me comes one who is more powerful than I, whose sandals I am not worthy to carry. He will baptise you with[c] the Holy Spirit and fire. 12 His winnowing fork is in his hand, and he will clear his threshing-floor, gathering his wheat into the barn and burning up the chaff with unquenchable fire.'

The baptism of Jesus

13 Then Jesus came from Galilee to the Jordan to be baptised by John. 14 But John tried to deter him, saying, 'I need to be baptised by you, and do you come to me?'

15 Jesus replied, 'Let it be so now; it is proper for us to do this to fulfil all righteousness.' Then John consented.

16 As soon as Jesus was baptised, he went up out of the water. At that moment heaven was opened, and he saw the Spirit of God descending like a dove and alighting on him. 17 And a voice from heaven said, 'This is my Son, whom I love; with him I am well pleased.'

People and Places

Satan
Matthew 4:1

Also known as the devil, the prince of evil or Beelzebub, Satan is the great opponent of God and people. The word satan means 'adversary', and Jesus saw Satan as his true enemy.

Jesus is tested in the wilderness

4 Then Jesus was led by the Spirit into the wilderness to be tempted[d] by the devil. 2 After fasting for forty days and forty nights, he was hungry. 3 The tempter came to him and said, 'If you are the Son of God, tell these stones to become bread.'

4 Jesus answered, 'It is written: "People do not live on bread alone, but on every word that comes from the mouth of God."'[e]

5 Then the devil took him to the holy city and set him on the highest point of the temple. 6 'If you are the Son of God,' he said, 'throw yourself down. For it is written:

"He will command his angels concerning you,
    and they will lift you up in their hands,
so that you will not strike your foot
    against a stone."'[f]

7 Jesus answered him, 'It is also written: "Do not put the Lord your God to the test."'[g]

8 Again, the devil took him to a very high mountain and showed him all the kingdoms of the world and their splendour. 9 'All this I will give you,' he said, 'if you will bow down and worship me.'

10 Jesus said to him, 'Away from me, Satan! For it is written: "Worship the Lord your God, and serve him only."'[h]

11 Then the devil left him, and angels came and attended him.

---

[a] 3 Isaiah 40:3 [b] 11 Or in [c] 11 Or in [d] 1 The Greek for tempted can also mean tested. [e] 4 Deut. 8:3
[f] 6 Psalm 91:11,12 [g] 7 Deut. 6:16 [h] 10 Deut. 6:13

Jesus begins to preach

¹²When Jesus heard that John had been put in prison, he withdrew to Galilee. ¹³Leaving Nazareth, he went and lived in Capernaum, which was by the lake in the area of Zebulun and Naphtali— ¹⁴to fulfil what was said through the prophet Isaiah:

¹⁵'Land of Zebulun and land of Naphtali,
   the Way of the Sea, beyond the Jordan,
   Galilee of the Gentiles—
¹⁶the people living in darkness
   have seen a great light;
 on those living in the land of the shadow
      of death
   a light has dawned.'[a]

¹⁷From that time on Jesus began to preach, 'Repent, for the kingdom of heaven has come near.'

Jesus calls his first disciples

¹⁸As Jesus was walking beside the Sea of Galilee, he saw two brothers, Simon called Peter and his brother Andrew. They were casting a net into the lake, for they were fishermen. ¹⁹'Come, follow me,' Jesus said, 'and I will send you out to fish for people.' ²⁰At once they left their nets and followed him.

²¹Going on from there, he saw two other brothers, James son of Zebedee and his brother John. They were in a boat with their father Zebedee, preparing their nets. Jesus called them, ²²and immediately they left the boat and their father and followed him.

Jesus heals the sick

²³Jesus went throughout Galilee, teaching in their synagogues, proclaiming the good news of the kingdom, and healing every disease and illness among the people. ²⁴News about him spread all over Syria, and people brought to him all who were ill with various diseases, those suffering severe pain, the demon-possessed, those having seizures, and the paralysed; and he healed them. ²⁵Large crowds from Galilee, the Decapolis,[b] Jerusalem, Judea and the region across the Jordan followed him.

Introduction to the Sermon on the Mount

5 Now when Jesus saw the crowds, he went up on a mountainside and sat down. His disciples came to him, ²and he began to teach them.

The Beatitudes

He said:

³'Blessed are the poor in spirit,
   for theirs is the kingdom of heaven.
⁴Blessed are those who mourn,
   for they will be comforted.
⁵Blessed are the meek,
   for they will inherit the earth.
⁶Blessed are those who hunger and thirst
      for righteousness,
   for they will be filled.
⁷Blessed are the merciful,
   for they will be shown mercy.
⁸Blessed are the pure in heart,
   for they will see God.
⁹Blessed are the peacemakers,
   for they will be called children of God.
¹⁰Blessed are those who are persecuted
      because of righteousness,
   for theirs is the kingdom of heaven.

¹¹'Blessed are you when people insult you, persecute you and falsely say all kinds of evil against you because of me. ¹²Rejoice and be glad, because great is your reward in heaven, for in the same way they persecuted the prophets who were before you.

Salt and light

¹³'You are the salt of the earth. But if the salt loses its saltiness, how can it be made salty again? It is no longer good for anything, except to be thrown out and trampled underfoot.

¹⁴'You are the light of the world. A city on a hill cannot be hidden. ¹⁵Neither do people light a lamp and put it under a bowl. Instead they put it on its stand, and it gives light to everyone in the house. ¹⁶In the same way, let your light shine before others, that they may see your good deeds and glorify your Father in heaven.

The fulfilment of the law

¹⁷'Do not think that I have come to abolish the Law or the Prophets; I have not come to

---

[a] 16 Isaiah 9:1,2   [b] 25 That is, the Ten Cities

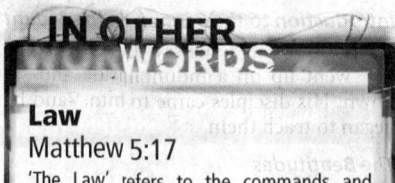

IN OTHER WORDS

Law
Matthew 5:17
'The Law' refers to the commands and guidelines that Moses received from God and passed onto the people of Israel in the Old Testament. Jesus came to fulfil the law, not do away with it. Just keeping the law is not enough; Jesus says that what matters is our motivation, or what's in our hearts.

abolish them but to fulfil them. 18Truly I tell you, until heaven and earth disappear, not the smallest letter, not the least stroke of a pen, will by any means disappear from the Law until everything is accomplished. 19Anyone who sets aside one of the least of these commands and teaches others accordingly will be called least in the kingdom of heaven, but whoever practises and teaches these commands will be called great in the kingdom of heaven. 20For I tell you that unless your righteousness surpasses that of the Pharisees and the teachers of the law, you will certainly not enter the kingdom of heaven.

Murder

21'You have heard that it was said to the people long ago, "You shall not murder,[a] and anyone who murders will be subject to judgment." 22But I tell you that anyone who is angry with a brother or sister[b] will be subject to judgment. Again, anyone who says to a brother or sister, "Raca,"[c] is answerable to the Sanhedrin. And anyone who says, "You fool!" will be in danger of the fire of hell.

23'Therefore, if you are offering your gift at the altar and there remember that your brother or sister has something against you, 24leave your gift there in front of the altar. First go and be reconciled to that person; then come and offer your gift.

25'Settle matters quickly with your adversary who is taking you to court. Do it while you are still together on the way, or your adversary may hand you over to the judge, and the judge may hand you over to the officer, and you may be thrown into prison. 26Truly I tell you, you will not get out until you have paid the last penny.

Adultery

27'You have heard that it was said, "You shall not commit adultery."[d] 28But I tell you that anyone who looks at a woman lustfully has already committed adultery with her in his heart. 29If your right eye causes you to stumble, gouge it out and throw it away. It is better for you to lose one part of your body than for your whole body to be thrown into hell. 30And if your right hand causes you to stumble, cut it off and throw it away. It is better for you to lose one part of your body than for your whole body to go into hell.

Divorce

31'It has been said, "Anyone who divorces his wife must give her a certificate of divorce."[e] 32But I tell you that anyone who divorces his wife, except for sexual immorality, causes her to become an adulteress, and anyone who marries the divorced woman commits adultery.

Oaths

33'Again, you have heard that it was said to the people long ago, "Do not break your oath, but fulfil to the Lord the oaths you have made." 34But I tell you, do not swear an oath at all: either by heaven, for it is God's throne; 35or by the earth, for it is his footstool; or by Jerusalem, for it is the city of the Great King. 36And do not swear by your head, for you cannot make even one hair white or black. 37All you need to say is simply "Yes," or "No"; anything beyond this comes from the evil one.[f]

Eye for eye

38'You have heard that it was said, "Eye for eye, and tooth for tooth."[g] 39But I tell you, do not resist an evil person. If anyone slaps you on the right cheek, turn to them the

---

[a] 21 Exodus 20:13 [b] 22 Some manuscripts *brother or sister without cause* [c] 22 An Aramaic term of contempt
[d] 27 Exodus 20:14 [e] 31 Deut. 24:1 [f] 37 Or *from evil* [g] 38 Exodus 21:24; Lev. 24:20; Deut. 19:21

other cheek also. ⁴⁰And if anyone wants to sue you and take your shirt, hand over your coat as well. ⁴¹If anyone forces you to go one mile, go with them two miles. ⁴²Give to the one who asks you, and do not turn away from the one who wants to borrow from you.

Love for enemies

⁴³'You have heard that it was said, "Love your neighbour*ᵃ* and hate your enemy." ⁴⁴But I tell you, love your enemies and pray for those who persecute you, ⁴⁵that you may be children of your Father in heaven. He causes his sun to rise on the evil and the good, and sends rain on the righteous and the unrighteous. ⁴⁶If you love those who love you, what reward will you get? Are not even the tax collectors doing that? ⁴⁷And if you greet only your own people, what are you doing more than others? Do not even pagans do that? ⁴⁸Be perfect, therefore, as your heavenly Father is perfect.

Giving to the needy

6 'Be careful not to do your "acts of righteousness" in front of others, to be seen by them. If you do, you will have no reward from your Father in heaven.

²'So when you give to the needy, do not announce it with trumpets, as the hypocrites do in the synagogues and on the streets, to be honoured by others. Truly I tell you, they have received their reward in full. ³But when you give to the needy, do not let your left hand know what your right hand is doing, ⁴so that your giving may be in secret. Then your Father, who sees what is done in secret, will reward you.

Prayer

⁵'And when you pray, do not be like the hypocrites, for they love to pray standing in the synagogues and on the street corners to be seen by others. Truly I tell you, they have received their reward in full. ⁶But when you pray, go into your room, close the door and pray to your Father, who is unseen. Then your Father, who sees what is done in secret, will reward you. ⁷And when you pray, do not keep on babbling like pagans, for they

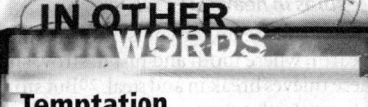

IN OTHER WORDS

Temptation
Matthew 6:13
The word 'temptation' means a test or a trial. In the Bible there are examples of both God and Satan testing the faith of believers, but for different reasons. Satan wants people to fail and to turn away from God. God wants people to grow in their faith in him (1 Corinthians 10:13).

think they will be heard because of their many words. ⁸Do not be like them, for your Father knows what you need before you ask him.

⁹'This, then, is how you should pray:

'"Our Father in heaven,
    hallowed be your name,
¹⁰your kingdom come,
    your will be done,
        on earth as it is in heaven.
¹¹Give us today our daily bread.
¹²And forgive us our debts,
    as we also have forgiven our debtors.
¹³And lead us not into temptation,*ᵇ*
    but deliver us from the evil one.*ᶜ*"

¹⁴For if you forgive others when they sin against you, your heavenly Father will also forgive you. ¹⁵But if you do not forgive others their sins, your Father will not forgive your sins.

Fasting

¹⁶'When you fast, do not look sombre as the hypocrites do, for they disfigure their faces to show others they are fasting. Truly I tell you, they have received their reward in full. ¹⁷But when you fast, put oil on your head and wash your face, ¹⁸so that it will not be obvious to others that you are fasting, but only to your Father, who is unseen; and your Father, who sees what is done in secret, will reward you.

ᵃ 43 Lev. 19:18   *ᵇ* 13 The Greek for *temptation* can also mean *testing*.   *ᶜ* 13 Or *from evil*; some late manuscripts *one, / for yours is the kingdom and the power and the glory for ever. Amen.*

Treasures in heaven

19'Do not store up for yourselves treasures on earth, where moth and rust destroy, and where thieves break in and steal. 20But store up for yourselves treasures in heaven, where moth and rust do not destroy, and where thieves do not break in and steal. 21For where your treasure is, there your heart will be also.

22'The eye is the lamp of the body. If your eyes are healthy,[a] your whole body will be full of light. 23But if your eyes are unhealthy,[b] your whole body will be full of darkness. If then the light within you is darkness, how great is that darkness!

24'No-one can serve two masters. Either you will hate the one and love the other, or you will be devoted to the one and despise the other. You cannot serve both God and Money.

Do not worry

25'Therefore I tell you, do not worry about your life, what you will eat or drink; or about your body, what you will wear. Is not life more important than food, and the body more important than clothes? 26Look at the birds of the air; they do not sow or reap or store away in barns, and yet your heavenly Father feeds them. Are you not much more valuable than they? 27Can any one of you by worrying add a single hour to your life[c]?

28'And why do you worry about clothes? See how the flowers of the field grow. They do not labour or spin. 29Yet I tell you that not even Solomon in all his splendour was dressed like one of these. 30If that is how God clothes the grass of the field, which is here today and tomorrow is thrown into the fire, will he not much more clothe you—you of little faith? 31So do not worry, saying, "What shall we eat?" or "What shall we drink?" or "What shall we wear?" 32For the pagans run after all these things, and your heavenly Father knows that you need them. 33But seek first his kingdom and his righteousness, and all these things will be given to you as well. 34Therefore do not worry about tomorrow, for tomorrow will worry about itself. Each day has enough trouble of its own.

Judging others

7 'Do not judge, or you too will be judged. 2For in the same way as you judge others, you will be judged, and with the measure you use, it will be measured to you.

3'Why do you look at the speck of sawdust in someone else's eye and pay no attention to the plank in your own eye? 4How can you say, "Let me take the speck out of your eye," when all the time there is a plank in your own eye? 5You hypocrite, first take the plank out of your own eye, and then you will see clearly to remove the speck from the other person's eye.

6'Do not give dogs what is sacred; do not throw your pearls to pigs. If you do, they may trample them under their feet, and then turn and tear you to pieces.

Ask, seek, knock

7'Ask and it will be given to you; seek and you will find; knock and the door will be opened to you. 8For everyone who asks receives; those who seek find; and to those who knock, the door will be opened.

9'Which of you, if your son asks for bread, will give him a stone? 10Or if he asks for a fish, will give him a snake? 11If you, then, though you are evil, know how to give good gifts to your children, how much more will your Father in heaven give good gifts to those who ask him! 12So in everything, do to others what you would have them do to you, for this sums up the Law and the Prophets.

The narrow and wide gates

13'Enter through the narrow gate. For wide is the gate and broad is the road that leads to destruction, and many enter through it. 14But small is the gate and narrow the road that leads to life, and only a few find it.

True and false prophets

15'Watch out for false prophets. They come to you in sheep's clothing, but inwardly they are ferocious wolves. 16By their fruit you will recognise them. Do people pick grapes

---

[a] 22 The Greek for *healthy* here implies *generous*. [b] 23 The Greek for *unhealthy* here implies *stingy*. [c] 27 Or *single cubit to your height*

from thorn-bushes, or figs from thistles? 17Likewise, every good tree bears good fruit, but a bad tree bears bad fruit. 18A good tree cannot bear bad fruit, and a bad tree cannot bear good fruit. 19Every tree that does not bear good fruit is cut down and thrown into the fire. 20Thus, by their fruit you will recognise them.

True and false disciples

21'Not everyone who says to me, "Lord, Lord," will enter the kingdom of heaven, but only those who do the will of my Father who is in heaven. 22Many will say to me on that day, "Lord, Lord, did we not prophesy in your name and in your name drive out demons and in your name perform many miracles?" 23Then I will tell them plainly, "I never knew you. Away from me, you evildoers!"

The wise and foolish builders

24'Therefore everyone who hears these words of mine and puts them into practice is like a wise man who built his house on the rock. 25The rain came down, the streams rose, and the winds blew and beat against that house; yet it did not fall, because it had its foundation on the rock. 26But everyone who hears these words of mine and does not put them into practice is like a foolish man who built his house on sand. 27The rain came down, the streams rose, and the winds blew and beat against that house, and it fell with a great crash.'

28When Jesus had finished saying these things, the crowds were amazed at his teaching, 29because he taught as one who had authority, and not as their teachers of the law.

Jesus heals a man with leprosy

8 When Jesus came down from the mountainside, large crowds followed him. 2A man with leprosy*ᵃ* came and knelt before him and said, 'Lord, if you are willing, you can make me clean.'

3Jesus reached out his hand and touched the man. 'I am willing,' he said. 'Be clean!' Immediately he was cleansed of his leprosy. 4Then Jesus said to him, 'See that you don't

Sign of the times

Leprosy
Matthew 8:2
In the first century, the word translated here as 'leprosy' was used for several different kinds of skin diseases. People with these diseases were considered 'unclean', and had to keep their distance from everyone else. In order to be allowed to live as part of the community again, someone who had had leprosy had to show themselves to the priest who would examine them and decide whether they were clean.

tell anyone. But go, show yourself to the priest and offer the gift Moses commanded, as a testimony to them.'

The faith of the centurion

5When Jesus had entered Capernaum, a centurion came to him, asking for help. 6'Lord,' he said, 'my servant lies at home paralysed, suffering terribly.'

7Jesus said to him, 'Shall I come and heal him?'

8The centurion replied, 'Lord, I do not deserve to have you come under my roof. But just say the word, and my servant will be healed. 9For I myself am a man under authority, with soldiers under me. I tell this one, "Go," and he goes; and that one, "Come," and he comes. I say to my servant, "Do this," and he does it.'

10When Jesus heard this, he was amazed and said to those following him, 'Truly I tell you, I have not found anyone in Israel with such great faith. 11I say to you that many will come from the east and the west, and will take their places at the feast with Abraham, Isaac and Jacob in the kingdom of heaven. 12But the subjects of the kingdom will be

---

ᵃ 2 The Greek word traditionally translated *leprosy* was used for various diseases affecting the skin.

thrown outside, into the darkness, where there will be weeping and gnashing of teeth.'

¹³Then Jesus said to the centurion, 'Go! Let it be done just as you believed it would.' And his servant was healed at that very hour.

Jesus heals many

¹⁴When Jesus came into Peter's house, he saw Peter's mother-in-law lying in bed with a fever. ¹⁵He touched her hand and the fever left her, and she got up and began to wait on him.

¹⁶When evening came, many who were demon-possessed were brought to him, and he drove out the spirits with a word and healed all who were ill. ¹⁷This was to fulfil what was spoken through the prophet Isaiah:

'He took up our infirmities
  and bore our diseases.'ᵃ

The cost of following Jesus

¹⁸When Jesus saw the crowd around him, he gave orders to cross to the other side of the lake. ¹⁹Then a teacher of the law came to him and said, 'Teacher, I will follow you wherever you go.'

²⁰Jesus replied, 'Foxes have holes and birds have nests, but the Son of Man has nowhere to lay his head.'

²¹Another disciple said to him, 'Lord, first let me go and bury my father.'

²²But Jesus told him, 'Follow me, and let the dead bury their own dead.'

Jesus calms the storm

²³Then he got into the boat and his disciples followed him. ²⁴Suddenly a furious storm came up on the lake, so that the waves swept over the boat. But Jesus was sleeping. ²⁵The disciples went and woke him, saying, 'Lord, save us! We're going to drown!'

²⁶He replied, 'You of little faith, why are you so afraid?' Then he got up and rebuked the winds and the waves, and it was completely calm.

²⁷The men were amazed and asked, 'What kind of man is this? Even the winds and the waves obey him!'

Jesus restores two demon-possessed men

²⁸When he arrived at the other side in the region of the Gadarenes,ᵇ two demon-possessed men coming from the tombs met him. They were so violent that no-one could pass that way. ²⁹'What do you want with us, Son of God?' they shouted. 'Have you come here to torture us before the appointed time?'

³⁰Some distance from them a large herd of pigs was feeding. ³¹The demons begged Jesus, 'If you drive us out, send us into the herd of pigs.'

³²He said to them, 'Go!' So they came out and went into the pigs, and the whole herd rushed down the steep bank into the lake and died in the water. ³³Those tending the pigs ran off, went into the town and reported all this, including what had happened to the demon-possessed men. ³⁴Then the whole town went out to meet Jesus. And when they saw him, they pleaded with him to leave their region.

Jesus forgives and heals a paralysed man

9 Jesus stepped into a boat, crossed over and came to his own town. ²Some men brought to him a paralysed man, lying on a mat. When Jesus saw their faith, he said to the man, 'Take heart, son; your sins are forgiven.'

³At this, some of the teachers of the law said to themselves, 'This fellow is blaspheming!'

⁴Knowing their thoughts, Jesus said, 'Why do you entertain evil thoughts in your hearts? ⁵Which is easier: to say, "Your sins are forgiven," or to say, "Get up and walk"? ⁶But I want you to know that the Son of Man has authority on earth to forgive sins.' So he said to the paralysed man, 'Get up, take your mat and go home.' ⁷Then the man got up and went home. ⁸When the crowd saw this, they were filled with awe; and they praised God, who had given such authority to human beings.

The calling of Matthew

⁹As Jesus went on from there, he saw a man named Matthew sitting at the tax collector's

---

ᵃ 17 Isaiah 53:4 (see Septuagint) ᵇ 28 Some manuscripts *Gergesenes*; other manuscripts *Gerasenes*

People and Places

Pharisee
Matthew 9:11

The Pharisees were a religious and political party in first-century Israel. They were known for teaching that people should stick very strictly to the law and this brought them into conflict with Jesus, who criticised them for their lack of compassion.

booth. 'Follow me,' he told him, and Matthew got up and followed him.

10While Jesus was having dinner at Matthew's house, many tax collectors and sinners came and ate with him and his disciples. 11When the Pharisees saw this, they asked his disciples, 'Why does your teacher eat with tax collectors and sinners?'

12On hearing this, Jesus said, 'It is not the healthy who need a doctor, but those who are ill. 13But go and learn what this means: "I desire mercy, not sacrifice."[a] For I have not come to call the righteous, but sinners.'

Jesus questioned about fasting

14Then John's disciples came and asked him, 'How is it that we and the Pharisees fast often, but your disciples do not fast?'

15Jesus answered, 'How can the guests of the bridegroom mourn while he is with them? The time will come when the bridegroom will be taken from them; then they will fast.

16'No-one sews a patch of unshrunk cloth on an old garment, for the patch will pull away from the garment, making the tear worse. 17Neither do people pour new wine into old wineskins. If they do, the skins will burst; the wine will run out, and the wineskins will be ruined. No, they pour new wine into new wineskins, and both are preserved.'

Jesus raises a dead girl and heals a sick woman

18While he was saying this, a synagogue leader came and knelt before him and said, 'My daughter has just died. But come and put your hand on her, and she will live.' 19Jesus got up and went with him, and so did his disciples.

20Just then a woman who had been subject to bleeding for twelve years came up behind him and touched the edge of his cloak. 21She said to herself, 'If I only touch his cloak, I will be healed.'

22Jesus turned and saw her. 'Take heart, daughter,' he said, 'your faith has healed you.' And the woman was healed from that moment.

23When Jesus entered the synagogue leader's house and saw the noisy crowd and the people playing pipes, 24he said, 'Go away. The girl is not dead but asleep.' But they laughed at him. 25After the crowd had been put outside, he went in and took the girl by the hand, and she got up. 26News of this spread through all that region.

Jesus heals the blind and the mute

27As Jesus went on from there, two blind men followed him, calling out, 'Have mercy on us, Son of David!'

Sign of the times

Mourners
Matthew 9:23

At any funeral, there would be professional mourners as well as friends and family who were genuinely sad. These people were paid to turn up, sing funeral songs, play instruments and generally weep and wail to show how much the person was missed.

---

[a] 13 Hosea 6:6

28When he had gone indoors, the blind men came to him, and he asked them, 'Do you believe that I am able to do this?'

'Yes, Lord,' they replied.

29Then he touched their eyes and said, 'According to your faith let it be done to you'; 30and their sight was restored. Jesus warned them sternly, 'See that no-one knows about this.' 31But they went out and spread the news about him all over that region.

32While they were going out, a man who was demon-possessed and could not talk was brought to Jesus. 33And when the demon was driven out, the man who had been mute spoke. The crowd was amazed and said, 'Nothing like this has ever been seen in Israel.'

34But the Pharisees said, 'It is by the prince of demons that he drives out demons.'

The workers are few

35Jesus went through all the towns and villages, teaching in their synagogues, proclaiming the good news of the kingdom and healing every disease and illness. 36When he saw the crowds, he had compassion on them, because they were harassed and helpless, like sheep without a shepherd. 37Then he said to his disciples, 'The harvest is plentiful but the workers are few. 38Ask the Lord of the harvest, therefore, to send out workers into his harvest field.'

Jesus sends out the Twelve

10 Jesus called his twelve disciples to him and gave them authority to drive out evil[a] spirits and to heal every disease and illness.

2These are the names of the twelve apostles: first, Simon (who is called Peter) and his brother Andrew; James son of Zebedee, and his brother John; 3Philip and Bartholomew; Thomas and Matthew the tax collector; James son of Alphaeus, and Thaddaeus; 4Simon the Zealot and Judas Iscariot, who betrayed him.

5These twelve Jesus sent out with the following instructions: 'Do not go among the Gentiles or enter any town of the Samaritans. 6Go rather to the lost sheep of Israel. 7As you go, proclaim this message: "The kingdom of heaven has come near." 8Heal those who are ill, raise the dead, cleanse those who have leprosy,[b] drive out demons. Freely you have received, freely give.

9'Do not get any gold or silver or copper to take with you in your belts— 10no bag for the journey or extra shirt or sandals or a staff, for workers are worth their keep. 11Whatever town or village you enter, search for some worthy person there and stay at that person's house until you leave. 12As you enter the home, give it your greeting. 13If the home is deserving, let your peace rest on it; if it is not, let your peace return to you. 14If anyone will not welcome you or listen to your words, shake the dust off your feet when you leave that home or town. 15Truly I tell you, it will be more bearable for Sodom and Gomorrah on the day of judgment than for that town.

16'I am sending you out like sheep among wolves. Therefore be as shrewd as snakes and as innocent as doves. 17Be on your guard; you will be handed over to the local councils and be flogged in the synagogues. 18On my account you will be brought before governors and kings as witnesses to them and to the Gentiles. 19But when they arrest you, do not worry about what to say or how to say it. At that time you will be given what to say, 20for it will not be you

IN OTHER WORDS

Healing
Matthew 10:1

To heal someone means to make them physically and spiritually well. The Bible is full of stories of people being supernaturally healed by God. Some people have the gift of healing, but it is still God rather than them who performs the healing.

---

[a] 1 Greek *unclean* [b] 8 The Greek word traditionally translated *leprosy* was used for various diseases affecting the skin.

speaking, but the Spirit of your Father speaking through you.

21'Brother will betray brother to death, and a father his child; children will rebel against their parents and have them put to death. 22Everyone will hate you because of me, but those who stand firm to the end will be saved. 23When you are persecuted in one place, flee to another. Truly I tell you, you will not finish going through the towns of Israel before the Son of Man comes.

24'Students are not above their teacher, nor servants above their master. 25It is enough for students to be like their teacher, and servants like their master. If the head of the house has been called Beelzebul, how much more the members of his household!

26'So do not be afraid of them. There is nothing concealed that will not be disclosed, or hidden that will not be made known. 27What I tell you in the dark, speak in the daylight; what is whispered in your ear, proclaim from the roofs. 28Do not be afraid of those who kill the body but cannot kill the soul. Rather, be afraid of the One who can destroy both soul and body in hell. 29Are not two sparrows sold for a penny? Yet not one of them will fall to the ground outside your Father's care.^{a} 30And even the very hairs of your head are all numbered. 31So don't be afraid; you are worth more than many sparrows.

32'Whoever publicly acknowledges me I will also acknowledge before my Father in heaven. 33But whoever publicly disowns me I will disown before my Father in heaven.

34'Do not suppose that I have come to bring peace to the earth. I did not come to bring peace, but a sword. 35For I have come to turn

> "'a man against his father,
>   a daughter against her mother,
> a daughter-in-law against her mother-in-law—
> 36   your enemies will be the members of your own household."^{b}

37'Anyone who loves their father or mother more than me is not worthy of me; anyone who loves a son or daughter more than me is not worthy of me. 38Whoever does not take up their cross and follow me is not worthy of me. 39Whoever finds their life will lose it, and whoever loses their life for my sake will find it.

40'Anyone who welcomes you welcomes me, and anyone who welcomes me welcomes the one who sent me. 41Whoever welcomes someone known to be a prophet will receive a prophet's reward, and whoever welcomes someone known to be righteous will receive a righteous person's reward. 42And if anyone gives even a cup of cold water to one of these little ones who is known to be my disciple, truly I tell you, that person will certainly be rewarded.'

Jesus and John the Baptist

11 After Jesus had finished instructing his twelve disciples, he went on from there to teach and preach in the towns of Galilee.^{c}

2When John heard in prison what the Messiah was doing, he sent his disciples 3to ask him, 'Are you the one who was to come, or should we expect someone else?'

4Jesus replied, 'Go back and report to John what you hear and see: 5the blind receive sight, the lame walk, those who have leprosy^d are cleansed, the deaf hear, the dead are raised, and the good news is proclaimed to the poor. 6Blessed is anyone who does not stumble on account of me.'

7As John's disciples were leaving, Jesus began to speak to the crowd about John: 'What did you go out into the wilderness to see? A reed swayed by the wind? 8If not, what did you go out to see? A man dressed in fine clothes? No, those who wear fine clothes are in kings' palaces. 9Then what did you go out to see? A prophet? Yes, I tell you, and more than a prophet. 10This is the one about whom it is written:

> "'I will send my messenger ahead of you,
>   who will prepare your way before you."'^{e}

11Truly I tell you, among those born of women there has not risen anyone greater than John the Baptist; yet whoever is least in the kingdom of heaven is greater than he.

---

^{a} 29 Or *will*; or *knowledge* ^{b} 36 Micah 7:6 ^{c} 1 Greek *in their towns* ^{d} 5 The Greek word traditionally translated *leprosy* was used for various diseases affecting the skin. ^{e} 10 Mal. 3:1

12 From the days of John the Baptist until now, the kingdom of heaven has been subjected to violence,*a* and violent people have been raiding it. 13 For all the Prophets and the Law prophesied until John. 14 And if you are willing to accept it, he is the Elijah who was to come. 15 Whoever has ears, let them hear.

16 'To what can I compare this generation? They are like children sitting in the market-places and calling out to others:

17 ' "We played the pipe for you,
   and you did not dance;
  we sang a dirge,
   and you did not mourn."

18 For John came neither eating nor drinking, and they say, "He has a demon." 19 The Son of Man came eating and drinking, and they say, "Here is a glutton and a drunkard, a friend of tax collectors and sinners." But wisdom is proved right by her actions.'

Woe on unrepentant towns

20 Then Jesus began to denounce the towns in which most of his miracles had been performed, because they did not repent. 21 'Woe to you, Chorazin! Woe to you, Bethsaida! If the miracles that were performed in you had been performed in Tyre and Sidon, they would have repented long ago in sackcloth and ashes. 22 But I tell you, it will be more bearable for Tyre and Sidon on the day of judgment than for you. 23 And you, Capernaum, will you be lifted up to the skies? No, you will go down to the depths.*b* If the miracles that were performed in you had been performed in Sodom, it would have remained to this day. 24 But I tell you that it will be more bearable for Sodom on the day of judgment than for you.'

The Father revealed in the Son

25 At that time Jesus said, 'I praise you, Father, Lord of heaven and earth, because you have hidden these things from the wise and learned, and revealed them to little children. 26 Yes, Father, for this was your good pleasure. 27 All things have been committed to me by my Father. No-one knows the Son except the Father, and no-one knows the Father except the Son and those to whom the Son chooses to reveal him.

28 'Come to me, all you who are weary and burdened, and I will give you rest. 29 Take my yoke upon you and learn from me, for I am gentle and humble in heart, and you will find rest for your souls. 30 For my yoke is easy and my burden is light.'

Jesus is Lord of the Sabbath

12 At that time Jesus went through the cornfields on the Sabbath. His disciples were hungry and began to pick some ears of corn and eat them. 2 When the Pharisees saw this, they said to him, 'Look! Your disciples are doing what is unlawful on the Sabbath.'

3 He answered, 'Haven't you read what David did when he and his companions were hungry? 4 He entered the house of God, and he and his companions ate the consecrated bread—which was not lawful for them to do, but only for the priests. 5 Or haven't you read in the Law that the priests on Sabbath duty in the temple desecrate the Sabbath and yet are innocent? 6 I tell you that one*c* greater than the temple is here. 7 If

Eating bread on the Sabbath
Matthew 12:1
The Sabbath is the Jewish day of rest which starts at sunset on Friday and ends at sunset on Saturday. The Pharisees were upset that Jesus and his disciples had picked some grain on the Sabbath. They said this was work, which was forbidden. But Jesus had a good role model to point to. David and his friends had eaten consecrated bread which technically they shouldn't have done (1 Samuel 21:1–6).

---

a 12 Or *been forcefully advancing* *b* 23 Greek *to Hades* *c* 6 Or *something* you had known what these words mean, "I desire mercy, not sacrifice,"*a* you would not have condemned the innocent. 8For the Son of Man is Lord of the Sabbath.'

9Going on from that place, he went into their synagogue, 10and a man with a shrivelled hand was there. Looking for a reason to accuse Jesus, they asked him, 'Is it lawful to heal on the Sabbath?'

11He said to them, 'If any of you has a sheep and it falls into a pit on the Sabbath, will you not take hold of it and lift it out? 12How much more valuable is a human being than a sheep! Therefore it is lawful to do good on the Sabbath.'

13Then he said to the man, 'Stretch out your hand.' So he stretched it out and it was completely restored, just as sound as the other. 14But the Pharisees went out and plotted how they might kill Jesus.

God's chosen servant

15Aware of this, Jesus withdrew from that place. A large crowd followed him, and he healed all who were ill. 16He warned them not to tell others about him. 17This was to fulfil what was spoken through the prophet Isaiah:

18'Here is my servant whom I have chosen,
　　the one I love, in whom I delight;
　I will put my Spirit on him,
　　and he will proclaim justice to the
　　　nations.
19He will not quarrel or cry out;
　　no-one will hear his voice in the streets.
20A bruised reed he will not break,
　　and a smouldering wick he will not
　　　snuff out,
till he leads justice to victory.
21　In his name the nations will put their
　　　hope.'*b*

Jesus and Beelzebul

22Then they brought him a demon-possessed man who was blind and mute, and Jesus healed him, so that he could both talk and see. 23All the people were astonished and said, 'Could this be the Son of David?'

24But when the Pharisees heard this, they said, 'It is only by Beelzebul, the prince of demons, that this fellow drives out demons.'

25Jesus knew their thoughts and said to them, 'Every kingdom divided against itself will be ruined, and every city or household divided against itself will not stand. 26If Satan drives out Satan, he is divided against himself. How then can his kingdom stand? 27And if I drive out demons by Beelzebul, by whom do your people drive them out? So then, they will be your judges. 28But if it is by the Spirit of God that I drive out demons, then the kingdom of God has come upon you.

29'Or again, how can anyone enter a strong man's house and carry off his possessions without first tying up the strong man? Then his house can be plundered.

30'Whoever is not with me is against me, and whoever does not gather with me scatters. 31And so I tell you, people will be forgiven every sin and blasphemy. But blasphemy against the Spirit will not be forgiven. 32Anyone who speaks a word against the Son of Man will be forgiven, but anyone who speaks against the Holy Spirit will not be forgiven, either in this age or in the age to come.

33'Make a tree good and its fruit will be good, or make a tree bad and its fruit will be bad, for a tree is recognised by its fruit. 34You brood of vipers, how can you who are evil say anything good? For out of the overflow of the heart the mouth speaks. 35Good people bring good things out of the good stored up in them, and evil people bring evil things out of the evil stored up in them. 36But I tell you that people will have to give account on the day of judgment for every empty word they have spoken. 37For by your words you will be acquitted, and by your words you will be condemned.'

The sign of Jonah

38Then some of the Pharisees and teachers of the law said to him, 'Teacher, we want to see a sign from you.'

39He answered, 'A wicked and adulterous generation asks for a sign! But none will be given it except the sign of the prophet Jonah. 40For as Jonah was three days and three

---

a 7 Hosea 6:6　　*b* 21 Isaiah 42:1-4

nights in the belly of a huge fish, so the Son of Man will be three days and three nights in the heart of the earth. 41The people of Nineveh will stand up at the judgment with this generation and condemn it; for they repented at the preaching of Jonah, and now one[a] greater than Jonah is here. 42The Queen of the South will rise at the judgment with this generation and condemn it; for she came from the ends of the earth to listen to Solomon's wisdom, and now one greater than Solomon is here.

43'When an evil[b] spirit comes out of anyone, it goes through arid places seeking rest and does not find it. 44Then it says, "I will return to the house I left." When it arrives, it finds the house unoccupied, swept clean and put in order. 45Then it goes and takes with it seven other spirits more wicked than itself, and they go in and live there. And the final condition of that person is worse than the first. That is how it will be with this wicked generation.'

Jesus' mother and brothers

46While Jesus was still talking to the crowd, his mother and brothers stood outside, wanting to speak to him. 47Someone told him, 'Your mother and brothers are standing outside, wanting to speak to you.'

48He replied to him, 'Who is my mother, and who are my brothers?' 49Pointing to his disciples, he said, 'Here are my mother and my brothers. 50For whoever does the will of my Father in heaven is my brother and sister and mother.'

The parable of the sower

13 That same day Jesus went out of the house and sat by the lake. 2Such large crowds gathered round him that he got into a boat and sat in it, while all the people stood on the shore. 3Then he told them many things in parables, saying: 'A farmer went out to sow his seed. 4As he was scattering the seed, some fell along the path, and the birds came and ate it up. 5Some fell on rocky places, where it did not have much soil. It sprang up quickly, because the soil was shallow. 6But when the sun came up, the plants were scorched, and they withered because they had no root. 7Other seed fell among thorns, which grew up and choked the plants. 8Still other seed fell on good soil, where it produced a crop—a hundred, sixty or thirty times what was sown. 9Whoever has ears, let them hear.'

10The disciples came to him and asked, 'Why do you speak to the people in parables?'

11He replied, 'The knowledge of the secrets of the kingdom of heaven has been given to you, but not to them. 12Those who have will be given more, and they will have an abundance. As for those who do not have, even what they have will be taken from them. 13This is why I speak to them in parables:

'Though seeing, they do not see;
  though hearing, they do not hear or understand.

14In them is fulfilled the prophecy of Isaiah:

' "You will be ever hearing but never understanding;
  you will be ever seeing but never perceiving.
15For this people's heart has become calloused;
  they hardly hear with their ears,
  and they have closed their eyes.
Otherwise they might see with their eyes,
  hear with their ears,
  understand with their hearts
and turn, and I would heal them." '[c]

16But blessed are your eyes because they see, and your ears because they hear. 17Truly I tell you, many prophets and righteous people longed to see what you see but did not see it, and to hear what you hear but did not hear it.

18'Listen then to what the parable of the sower means: 19when people hear the message about the kingdom and do not understand it, the evil one comes and snatches away what was sown in their hearts. This is the seed sown along the path. 20The seed falling on rocky ground refers to people who hear the word and at once receive it with joy. 21But since they have no root, they last only a short time.

---

[a] 41 Or *something*; also in verse 42 [b] 43 Greek *unclean* [c] 15 Isaiah 6:9,10 (see Septuagint)

When trouble or persecution comes because of the word, they quickly fall away. 22The seed falling among the thorns refers to people who hear the word, but the worries of this life and the deceitfulness of wealth choke the word, making it unfruitful. 23But the seed falling on good soil refers to people who hear the word and understand it. They produce a crop, yielding a hundred, sixty or thirty times what was sown.'

The parable of the weeds

24Jesus told them another parable: 'The kingdom of heaven is like a man who sowed good seed in his field. 25But while everyone was sleeping, his enemy came and sowed weeds among the wheat, and went away. 26When the wheat sprouted and formed ears, then the weeds also appeared.

27'The owner's servants came to him and said, "Sir, didn't you sow good seed in your field? Where then did the weeds come from?"

28' "An enemy did this," he replied.

'The servants asked him, "Do you want us to go and pull them up?"

29' "No," he answered, "because while you are pulling up the weeds, you may uproot the wheat with them. 30Let both grow together until the harvest. At that time I will tell the harvesters: first collect the weeds and tie them in bundles to be burned; then gather the wheat and bring it into my barn." '

The parables of the mustard seed and the yeast

31He told them another parable: 'The kingdom of heaven is like a mustard seed, which a man took and planted in his field. 32Though it is the smallest of all seeds, yet when it grows, it is the largest of garden plants and becomes a tree, so that the birds come and perch in its branches.'

33He told them still another parable: 'The kingdom of heaven is like yeast that a woman took and mixed into about thirty kilograms of flour until it worked all through the dough.'

making Connections

Mustard seeds
Matthew 13:31
The mustard plant produces tiny black seeds, one of the smallest seeds known in Jesus' day. The seeds were used to flavour food, to keep it fresh and to produce oil. Mustard plants grew wild along the side of the roads in Palestine and could grow to a height of almost five metres.

34Jesus spoke all these things to the crowd in parables; he did not say anything to them without using a parable. 35So was fulfilled what was spoken through the prophet:

'I will open my mouth in parables,
I will utter things hidden since the creation of the world.'[a]

The parable of the weeds explained

36Then he left the crowd and went into the house. His disciples came to him and said, 'Explain to us the parable of the weeds in the field.'

37He answered, 'The one who sowed the good seed is the Son of Man. 38The field is the world, and the good seed stands for the people of the kingdom. The weeds are the people of the evil one, 39and the enemy who sows them is the devil. The harvest is the end of the age, and the harvesters are angels.

40'As the weeds are pulled up and burned in the fire, so it will be at the end of the age. 41The Son of Man will send out his angels, and they will weed out of his kingdom everything that causes sin and all who do evil. 42They will throw them into the blazing furnace, where there will be weeping and gnashing of teeth. 43Then the righteous will shine like the sun in the kingdom of their Father. Whoever has ears, let them hear.

---

[a] 35 Psalm 78:2

The parables of the hidden treasure and the pearl

44'The kingdom of heaven is like treasure hidden in a field. When a man found it, he hid it again, and then in his joy went and sold all he had and bought that field.

45'Again, the kingdom of heaven is like a merchant looking for fine pearls. 46When he found one of great value, he went away and sold everything he had and bought it.

The parable of the net

47'Once again, the kingdom of heaven is like a net that was let down into the lake and caught all kinds of fish. 48When it was full, the fishermen pulled it up on the shore. Then they sat down and collected the good fish in baskets, but threw the bad away. 49This is how it will be at the end of the age. The angels will come and separate the wicked from the righteous 50and throw them into the blazing furnace, where there will be weeping and gnashing of teeth.

51'Have you understood all these things?' Jesus asked.

'Yes,' they replied.

52He said to them, 'Therefore every teacher of the law who has been instructed about the kingdom of heaven is like the owner of a house who brings out of his storeroom new treasures as well as old.'

A prophet without honour

53When Jesus had finished these parables, he moved on from there. 54Coming to his home town, he began teaching the people in their synagogue, and they were amazed. 'Where did this man get this wisdom and these miraculous powers?' they asked. 55'Isn't this the carpenter's son? Isn't his mother's name Mary, and aren't his brothers James, Joseph, Simon and Judas? 56Aren't all his sisters with us? Where then did this man get all these things?' 57And they took offence at him.

But Jesus said to them, 'Only in their own towns and in their own homes are prophets without honour.'

58And he did not do many miracles there because of their lack of faith.

John the Baptist beheaded

14 At that time Herod the tetrarch heard the reports about Jesus, 2and he said to his attendants, 'This is John the Baptist; he has risen from the dead! That is why miraculous powers are at work in him.'

3Now Herod had arrested John and bound him and put him in prison because of Herodias, his brother Philip's wife, 4for John had been saying to him: 'It is not lawful for you to have her.' 5Herod wanted to kill John, but he was afraid of the people, because they considered him a prophet.

6On Herod's birthday the daughter of Herodias danced for them and pleased Herod so much 7that he promised with an oath to give her whatever she asked. 8Prompted by her mother, she said, 'Give me here on a dish the head of John the Baptist.' 9The king was distressed, but because of his oaths and his dinner guests, he ordered that her request be granted 10and had John beheaded in the prison. 11His head was brought in on a dish and given to the girl, who carried it to her mother. 12John's disciples came and took his body and buried it. Then they went and told Jesus.

Jesus feeds the five thousand

13When Jesus heard what had happened, he withdrew by boat privately to a solitary place. Hearing of this, the crowds followed him on foot from the towns. 14When Jesus landed and saw a large crowd, he had compassion on them and healed those who were ill.

15As evening approached, the disciples came to him and said, 'This is a remote place, and it's already getting late. Send the crowds away, so that they can go to the villages and buy themselves some food.'

16Jesus replied, 'They do not need to go away. You give them something to eat.'

17'We have here only five loaves of bread and two fish,' they answered.

18'Bring them here to me,' he said. 19And he told the people to sit down on the grass. Taking the five loaves and the two fish and looking up to heaven, he gave thanks and broke the loaves. Then he gave them to the disciples, and the disciples gave them to the people. 20They all ate and were satisfied, and the disciples picked up twelve basketfuls of broken pieces that were left over. 21The number of those who ate was about five thousand men, besides women and children.

Jesus walks on the water

22Immediately Jesus made the disciples get into the boat and go on ahead of him to the other side, while he dismissed the crowd. 23After he had dismissed them, he went up on a mountainside by himself to pray. When evening came, he was there alone, 24but the boat was already a considerable distance from land, buffeted by the waves because the wind was against it.

25Shortly before dawn Jesus went out to them, walking on the lake. 26When the disciples saw him walking on the lake, they were terrified. 'It's a ghost,' they said, and cried out in fear.

27But Jesus immediately said to them: 'Take courage! It is I. Don't be afraid.'

28'Lord, if it's you,' Peter replied, 'tell me to come to you on the water.'

29'Come,' he said.

Then Peter got down out of the boat, walked on the water and came towards Jesus. 30But when he saw the wind, he was afraid and, beginning to sink, cried out, 'Lord, save me!'

31Immediately Jesus reached out his hand and caught him. 'You of little faith,' he said, 'why did you doubt?'

32And when they climbed into the boat, the wind died down. 33Then those who were in the boat worshipped him, saying, 'Truly you are the Son of God.'

34When they had crossed over, they landed at Gennesaret. 35And when the men of that place recognised Jesus, they sent word to all the surrounding country. People brought all who were ill to him 36and begged him to let those who were ill just touch the edge of his cloak, and all who touched him were healed.

That which defiles

15 Then some Pharisees and teachers of the law came to Jesus from Jerusalem and asked, 2'Why do your disciples break the tradition of the elders? They don't wash their hands before they eat!'

3Jesus replied, 'And why do you break the command of God for the sake of your tradition? 4For God said, "Honour your father and mother"[a] and "Anyone who curses their father or mother is to be put to death."[b] 5But you say that if anyone declares that what might have been used to help their father or mother is "devoted to God," 6they are not to "honour their father or mother" with it. Thus you nullify the word of God for the sake of your tradition. 7You hypocrites! Isaiah was right when he prophesied about you:

8'"These people honour me with their lips,
    but their hearts are far from me.
9They worship me in vain;
    their teachings are merely human rules."'[c]

10Jesus called the crowd to him and said, 'Listen and understand. 11What goes into your mouth does not defile you, but what comes out of your mouth, that is what defiles you.'

12Then the disciples came to him and asked, 'Do you know that the Pharisees were offended when they heard this?'

13He replied, 'Every plant that my heavenly Father has not planted will be pulled up by the roots. 14Leave them; they are blind guides.[d] If the blind lead the blind, both will fall into a pit.'

15Peter said, 'Explain the parable to us.'

16'Are you still so dull?' Jesus asked them. 17'Don't you see that whatever enters the mouth goes into the stomach and then out of the body? 18But the things that come out of the mouth come from the heart, and these defile you. 19For out of the heart come evil thoughts, murder, adultery, sexual immorality, theft, false testimony, slander. 20These are what defile you; but eating with unwashed hands does not defile you.'

---

[a]4 Exodus 20:12; Deut. 5:16   [b]4 Exodus 21:17; Lev. 20:9   [c]9 Isaiah 29:13   [d]14 Some manuscripts *blind guides of the blind*

The faith of a Canaanite woman

21Leaving that place, Jesus withdrew to the region of Tyre and Sidon. 22A Canaanite woman from that vicinity came to him, crying out, 'Lord, Son of David, have mercy on me! My daughter is demon-possessed and suffering terribly.'

23Jesus did not answer a word. So his disciples came to him and urged him, 'Send her away, for she keeps crying out after us.'

24He answered, 'I was sent only to the lost sheep of Israel.'

25The woman came and knelt before him. 'Lord, help me!' she said.

26He replied, 'It is not right to take the children's bread and toss it to the dogs.'

27'Yes it is, Lord,' she said. 'Even the dogs eat the crumbs that fall from their master's table.'

28Then Jesus said to her, 'Woman,^{a} you have great faith! Your request is granted.' And her daughter was healed from that very hour.

Jesus feeds the four thousand

29Jesus left there and went along the Sea of Galilee. Then he went up on a mountainside and sat down. 30Great crowds came to him, bringing the lame, the blind, the crippled, the mute and many others, and laid them at his feet; and he healed them. 31The people were amazed when they saw the mute speaking, the crippled made well, the lame walking and the blind seeing. And they praised the God of Israel.

32Jesus called his disciples to him and said, 'I have compassion for these people; they have already been with me three days and have nothing to eat. I do not want to send them away hungry, or they may collapse on the way.'

33His disciples answered, 'Where could we get enough bread in this remote place to feed such a crowd?'

34'How many loaves do you have?' Jesus asked.

'Seven,' they replied, 'and a few small fish.'

35He told the crowd to sit down on the ground. 36Then he took the seven loaves and the fish, and when he had given thanks, he broke them and gave them to the disciples, and they in turn to the people. 37They all ate and were satisfied. Afterwards the disciples picked up seven basketfuls of broken pieces that were left over. 38The number of those who ate was four thousand men, besides women and children. 39After Jesus had sent the crowd away, he got into the boat and went to the vicinity of Magadan.

The demand for a sign

16 The Pharisees and Sadducees came to Jesus and tested him by asking him to show them a sign from heaven.

2He replied,^{b} 'When evening comes, you say, "It will be fair weather, for the sky is red," 3and in the morning, "Today it will be stormy, for the sky is red and overcast." You know how to interpret the appearance of the sky, but you cannot interpret the signs of the times. 4A wicked and adulterous generation looks for a sign, but none will be given it except the sign of Jonah.' Jesus then left them and went away.

The yeast of the Pharisees and Sadducees

5When they went across the lake, the disciples forgot to take bread. 6'Be careful,' Jesus said to them. 'Be on your guard against the yeast of the Pharisees and Sadducees.'

7They discussed this among themselves and said, 'It is because we didn't bring any bread.'

8Aware of their discussion, Jesus asked, 'You of little faith, why are you talking among yourselves about having no bread? 9Do you still not understand? Don't you remember the five loaves for the five thousand, and how many basketfuls you gathered? 10Or the seven loaves for the four thousand, and how many basketfuls you gathered? 11How is it you don't understand that I was not talking to you about bread? But be on your guard against the yeast of the Pharisees and Sadducees.' 12Then they understood that he was not telling them to guard against the yeast used in bread, but

---

^{a} 28 The Greek for *Woman* does not denote any disrespect. ^{b} 2 Some early manuscripts do not have the rest of verse 2 and all of verse 3.

against the teaching of the Pharisees and Sadducees.

Peter declares that Jesus is the Messiah

13 When Jesus came to the region of Caesarea Philippi, he asked his disciples, 'Who do people say the Son of Man is?'

14 They replied, 'Some say John the Baptist; others say Elijah; and still others, Jeremiah or one of the prophets.'

15 'But what about you?' he asked. 'Who do you say I am?'

16 Simon Peter answered, 'You are the Messiah, the Son of the living God.'

17 Jesus replied, 'Blessed are you, Simon son of Jonah, for this was not revealed to you by flesh and blood, but by my Father in heaven. 18 And I tell you that you are Peter,[a] and on this rock I will build my church, and the gates of death[b] will not overcome it. 19 I will give you the keys of the kingdom of heaven; whatever you bind on earth will be[c] bound in heaven, and whatever you loose on earth will be[d] loosed in heaven.' 20 Then he ordered his disciples not to tell anyone that he was the Messiah.

Jesus predicts his death

21 From that time on Jesus began to explain to his disciples that he must go to Jerusalem and suffer many things at the hands of the elders, the chief priests and the teachers of the law, and that he must be killed and on the third day be raised to life.

22 Peter took him aside and began to rebuke him. 'Never, Lord!' he said. 'This shall never happen to you!'

23 Jesus turned and said to Peter, 'Get behind me, Satan! You are a stumbling-block to me; you do not have in mind the concerns of God, but merely human concerns.'

24 Then Jesus said to his disciples, 'Whoever wants to be my disciple must deny themselves and take up their cross and follow me. 25 For whoever wants to save their life[e] will lose it, but whoever loses their life for me will find it. 26 What good will it be for you to gain the whole world, yet forfeit your soul? Or what can you give in exchange for your soul? 27 For the Son of Man is going to come in his Father's glory with his angels, and then he will reward everyone according to what they have done.

28 'Truly I tell you, some who are standing here will not taste death before they see the Son of Man coming in his kingdom.'

The transfiguration

17 After six days Jesus took with him Peter, James and John the brother of James, and led them up a high mountain by themselves. 2 There he was transfigured before them. His face shone like the sun, and his clothes became as white as the light. 3 Just then there appeared before them Moses and Elijah, talking with Jesus.

4 Peter said to Jesus, 'Lord, it is good for us to be here. If you wish, I will put up three shelters—one for you, one for Moses and one for Elijah.'

5 While he was still speaking, a bright cloud covered them, and a voice from the cloud said, 'This is my Son, whom I love; with him I am well pleased. Listen to him!'

6 When the disciples heard this, they fell face down to the ground, terrified. 7 But Jesus came and touched them. 'Get up,' he said. 'Don't be afraid.' 8 When they looked up, they saw no-one except Jesus.

9 As they were coming down the mountain, Jesus instructed them, 'Don't tell anyone what you have seen, until the Son of Man has been raised from the dead.'

10 The disciples asked him, 'Why then do the teachers of the law say that Elijah must come first?'

11 Jesus replied, 'To be sure, Elijah comes and will restore all things. 12 But I tell you, Elijah has already come, and they did not recognise him, but have done to him everything they wished. In the same way the Son of Man is going to suffer at their hands.' 13 Then the disciples understood that he was talking to them about John the Baptist.

Jesus heals a demon-possessed boy

14 When they came to the crowd, a man approached Jesus and knelt before him. 15 'Lord, have mercy on my son,' he said. 'He has seizures and is suffering greatly. He

---

[a] 18 The Greek for *Peter* means *rock*. [b] 18 Greek *Hades* [c] 19 Or *will have been* [d] 19 Or *will have been* [e] 25 The Greek word means either *life* or *soul*; also in verse 26.

often falls into the fire or into the water. 16I brought him to your disciples, but they could not heal him.'

17'You unbelieving and perverse generation,' Jesus replied, 'how long shall I stay with you? How long shall I put up with you? Bring the boy here to me.' 18Jesus rebuked the demon, and it came out of the boy, and he was healed from that moment.

19Then the disciples came to Jesus in private and asked, 'Why couldn't we drive it out?'

20(21)He replied, 'Because you have so little faith. Truly I tell you, if you have faith as small as a mustard seed, you can say to this mountain, "Move from here to there," and it will move. Nothing will be impossible for you.'

Jesus predicts his death a second time

22When they came together in Galilee, he said to them, 'The Son of Man is going to be delivered over to human hands. 23He will be killed, and on the third day he will be raised to life.' And the disciples were filled with grief.

The temple tax

24After Jesus and his disciples arrived in Capernaum, the collectors of the two-drachma temple tax came to Peter and asked, 'Doesn't your teacher pay the temple tax?'

25'Yes, he does,' he replied.

When Peter came into the house, Jesus was the first to speak. 'What do you think, Simon?' he asked. 'From whom do the kings of the earth collect duty and taxes—from their own children or from others?'

26'From others,' Peter answered.

'Then the children are exempt,' Jesus said to him. 27'But so that we may not cause offence, go to the lake and throw out your line. Take the first fish you catch; open its mouth and you will find a four-drachma coin. Take it and give it to them for my tax and yours.'

The greatest in the kingdom of heaven

18 At that time the disciples came to Jesus and asked, 'Who, then, is the greatest in the kingdom of heaven?'

2He called a little child, whom he placed among them. 3And he said: 'Truly I tell you, unless you change and become like little children, you will never enter the kingdom of heaven. 4Therefore, whoever takes a humble place—becoming like this child—is the greatest in the kingdom of heaven. 5And whoever welcomes one such child in my name welcomes me.

Causing to stumble

6'If anyone causes one of these little ones—those who believe in me—to stumble, it would be better for them if a large millstone were hung round their neck and they were drowned in the depths of the sea. 7Woe to the world because of the things that cause people to stumble! Such things must come, but woe to the person through whom they come! 8If your hand or your foot causes you to stumble, cut it off and throw it away. It is better for you to enter life maimed or crippled than to have two hands or two feet and be thrown into eternal fire. 9And if your eye causes you to stumble, gouge it out and throw it away. It is better for you to enter life with one eye than to have two eyes and be thrown into the fire of hell.

The parable of the wandering sheep

10(11)'See that you do not despise one of these little ones. For I tell you that their angels in heaven always see the face of my Father in heaven.

Sign of the times

Temple tax
Matthew 17:24

Moses put in place this temple tax (Exodus 30:11–16). Every Jewish male over the age of twenty had to pay half a shekel in Jewish money which was two drachmas in Greek coins. That was about the amount that a labourer got paid for working two days.

¹²'What do you think? If a man owns a hundred sheep, and one of them wanders away, will he not leave the ninety-nine on the hills and go to look for the one that wandered off? ¹³And if he finds it, truly I tell you, he is happier about that one sheep than about the ninety-nine that did not wander off. ¹⁴In the same way your Father in heaven is not willing that any of these little ones should perish.

Dealing with sin in the church

¹⁵'If a brother or sister sins,ᵃ go and point out the fault, just between the two of you. If they listen to you, you have won them over. ¹⁶But if they will not listen, take one or two others along, so that "every matter may be established by the testimony of two or three witnesses."ᵇ ¹⁷If they still refuse to listen, tell it to the church; and if they refuse to listen even to the church, treat them as you would a pagan or a tax collector.

¹⁸'Truly I tell you, whatever you bind on earth will beᶜ bound in heaven, and whatever you loose on earth will beᵈ loosed in heaven.

¹⁹'Again, truly I tell you that if two of you on earth agree about anything you ask for, it will be done for you by my Father in heaven. ²⁰For where two or three come together in my name, there am I with them.'

The parable of the unmerciful servant

²¹Then Peter came to Jesus and asked, 'Lord, how many times shall I forgive someone who sins against me? Up to seven times?'

²²Jesus answered, 'I tell you, not seven times, but seventy-seven times.ᵉ

²³'Therefore, the kingdom of heaven is like a king who wanted to settle accounts with his servants. ²⁴As he began the settlement, a man who owed him ten thousand bags of goldᶠ was brought to him. ²⁵Since he was not able to pay, the master ordered that he and his wife and his children and all that he had be sold to repay the debt.

²⁶'The servant fell on his knees before him. "Be patient with me," he begged, "and I will pay back everything." ²⁷The servant's master took pity on him, cancelled the debt and let him go.

²⁸'But when that servant went out, he found one of his fellow-servants who owed him a hundred silver coins.ᵍ He grabbed him and began to choke him. "Pay back what you owe me!" he demanded.

²⁹'His fellow-servant fell to his knees and begged him, "Be patient with me, and I will pay you back."

³⁰'But he refused. Instead, he went off and had the man thrown into prison until he could pay the debt. ³¹When the other servants saw what had happened, they were greatly distressed and went and told their master everything that had happened.

³²'Then the master called the servant in. "You wicked servant," he said, "I cancelled all that debt of yours because you begged me to. ³³Shouldn't you have had mercy on your fellow-servant just as I had on you?" ³⁴In anger his master handed him over to the jailers to be tortured, until he should pay back all he owed.

³⁵'This is how my heavenly Father will treat each of you unless you forgive a brother or sister from your heart.'

Divorce

19 When Jesus had finished saying these things, he left Galilee and went into the region of Judea to the other side of the Jordan. ²Large crowds followed him, and he healed them there.

³Some Pharisees came to him to test him. They asked, 'Is it lawful for a man to divorce his wife for any and every reason?'

⁴'Haven't you read,' he replied, 'that at the beginning the Creator "made them male and female,"ʰ ⁵and said, "For this reason a man will leave his father and mother and be united to his wife, and the two will become one flesh"ⁱ? ⁶So they are no longer two, but one. Therefore what God has joined together, let no-one separate.'

⁷'Why then,' they asked, 'did Moses command that a man give his wife a certificate of divorce and send her away?'

ᵃ 15 Some manuscripts *sins against you*   ᵇ 16 Deut. 19:15   ᶜ 18 Or *will have been*   ᵈ 18 Or *will have been*   ᵉ 22 Or *seventy times seven*   ᶠ 24 Greek *ten thousand talents*; a talent was worth about 20 years of a day labourer's wages.   ᵍ 28 Greek *a hundred denarii*; a denarius was the daily wage of a day labourer (see Matt. 20:2).   ʰ 4 Gen. 1:27   ⁱ 5 Gen. 2:24

8 Jesus replied, 'Moses permitted you to divorce your wives because your hearts were hard. But it was not this way from the beginning. 9 I tell you that anyone who divorces his wife, except for sexual immorality, and marries another woman commits adultery.'

10 The disciples said to him, 'If this is the situation between a husband and wife, it is better not to marry.'

11 Jesus replied, 'Not everyone can accept this word, but only those to whom it has been given. 12 For some are eunuchs because they were born that way; others have been made eunuchs; and others have renounced marriage[a] because of the kingdom of heaven. The one who can accept this should accept it.'

The little children and Jesus

13 Then people brought little children to Jesus for him to place his hands on them and pray for them. But the disciples rebuked them.

14 Jesus said, 'Let the little children come to me, and do not hinder them, for the kingdom of heaven belongs to such as these.' 15 When he had placed his hands on them, he went on from there.

The rich and the kingdom of God

16 Just then a man came up to Jesus and asked, 'Teacher, what good thing must I do to get eternal life?'

17 'Why do you ask me about what is good?' Jesus replied. 'There is only One who is good. If you want to enter life, keep the commandments.'

18 'Which ones?' he enquired.

Jesus replied, '"You shall not murder, you shall not commit adultery, you shall not steal, you shall not give false testimony, 19 honour your father and mother,"[b] and "love your neighbour as yourself."[c]'

20 'All these I have kept,' the young man said. 'What do I still lack?'

21 Jesus answered, 'If you want to be perfect, go, sell your possessions and give to the poor, and you will have treasure in heaven. Then come, follow me.'

22 When the young man heard this, he went away sad, because he had great wealth.

23 Then Jesus said to his disciples, 'Truly I tell you, it is hard for the rich to enter the kingdom of heaven. 24 Again I tell you, it is easier for a camel to go through the eye of a needle than for the rich to enter the kingdom of God.'

25 When the disciples heard this, they were greatly astonished and asked, 'Who then can be saved?'

26 Jesus looked at them and said, 'With human beings this is impossible, but with God all things are possible.'

27 Peter answered him, 'We have left everything to follow you! What then will there be for us?'

28 Jesus said to them, 'Truly I tell you, at the renewal of all things, when the Son of Man sits on his glorious throne, you who have followed me will also sit on twelve thrones, judging the twelve tribes of Israel. 29 And everyone who has left houses or brothers or sisters or father or mother or wife[d] or children or fields for my sake will receive a hundred times as much and will inherit eternal life. 30 But many who are first will be last, and many who are last will be first.

The parable of the workers in the vineyard

20 'For the kingdom of heaven is like a landowner who went out early in the morning to hire workers for his vineyard. 2 He agreed to pay them a denarius for the day and sent them into his vineyard.

3 'About nine in the morning he went out and saw others standing in the market-place doing nothing. 4 He told them, "You also go and work in my vineyard, and I will pay you whatever is right." 5 So they went.

'He went out again about noon and about three in the afternoon and did the same thing. 6 About five in the afternoon he went out and found still others standing around. He asked them, "Why have you been standing here all day long doing nothing?"

7 '"Because no-one has hired us," they answered.

---

[a] 12 Or *have made themselves eunuchs* [b] 19 Exodus 20:12-16; Deut. 5:16-20 [c] 19 Lev. 19:18 [d] 29 Some manuscripts *do not have* or wife.

'He said to them, "You also go and work in my vineyard."

8'When evening came, the owner of the vineyard said to his supervisor, "Call the workers and pay them their wages, beginning with the last ones hired and going on to the first."

9'The workers who were hired about five in the afternoon came and each received a denarius. 10So when those came who were hired first, they expected to receive more. But each one of them also received a denarius. 11When they received it, they began to grumble against the landowner. 12"These men who were hired last worked only one hour," they said, "and you have made them equal to us who have borne the burden of the work and the heat of the day."

13'But he answered one of them, "Friend, I am not being unfair to you. Didn't you agree to work for a denarius? 14Take your pay and go. I want to give the one who was hired last the same as I gave you. 15Don't I have the right to do what I want with my own money? Or are you envious because I am generous?"

16'So the last will be first, and the first will be last.'

Jesus predicts his death a third time

17Now Jesus was going up to Jerusalem. On the way, he took the Twelve aside and said to them, 18'We are going up to Jerusalem, and the Son of Man will be delivered over to the chief priests and the teachers of the law. They will condemn him to death 19and will hand him over to the Gentiles to be mocked and flogged and crucified. On the third day he will be raised to life!'

A mother's request

20Then the mother of Zebedee's sons came to Jesus with her sons and, kneeling down, asked a favour of him.

21'What is it you want?' he asked.

She said, 'Grant that one of these two sons of mine may sit at your right and the other at your left in your kingdom.'

22'You don't know what you are asking,' Jesus said to them. 'Can you drink the cup I am going to drink?'

making Connections

Vineyards
Matthew 20:1
A landowner with a vineyard always needed lots of labourers to help look after it. Vineyards were usually on stony hillsides and had hedges or walls around them to protect them from wild animals. Often a tower would be built and a watchman would keep a lookout for robbers (Isaiah 5:1).

'We can,' they answered.

23Jesus said to them, 'You will indeed drink from my cup, but to sit at my right or left is not for me to grant. These places belong to those for whom they have been prepared by my Father.'

24When the ten heard about this, they were indignant with the two brothers. 25Jesus called them together and said, 'You know that the rulers of the Gentiles lord it over them, and their high officials exercise authority over them. 26Not so with you. Instead, whoever wants to become great among you must be your servant, 27and whoever wants to be first must be your slave— 28just as the Son of Man did not come to be served, but to serve, and to give his life as a ransom for many.'

Two blind men receive sight

29As Jesus and his disciples were leaving Jericho, a large crowd followed him. 30Two blind men were sitting by the roadside, and when they heard that Jesus was passing by, they shouted, 'Lord, Son of David, have mercy on us!'

31The crowd rebuked them and told them to be quiet, but they shouted all the louder, 'Lord, Son of David, have mercy on us!'

32 Jesus stopped and called them. 'What do you want me to do for you?' he asked.

33 'Lord,' they answered, 'we want our sight.'

34 Jesus had compassion on them and touched their eyes. Immediately they received their sight and followed him.

Jesus comes to Jerusalem as king

21 As they approached Jerusalem and came to Bethphage on the Mount of Olives, Jesus sent two disciples, 2 saying to them, 'Go to the village ahead of you, and at once you will find a donkey tied there, with her colt by her. Untie them and bring them to me. 3 If anyone says anything to you, say that the Lord needs them, and he will send them right away.'

4 This took place to fulfil what was spoken through the prophet:

5 'Say to Daughter Zion,
"See, your king comes to you,
gentle and riding on a donkey,
and on a colt, the foal of a donkey."'^a

6 The disciples went and did as Jesus had instructed them. 7 They brought the donkey and the colt and placed their cloaks on them for Jesus to sit on. 8 A very large crowd spread their cloaks on the road, while others cut branches from the trees and spread them on the road. 9 The crowds that went ahead of him and those that followed shouted,

'Hosanna^b to the Son of David!'

'Blessed is he who comes in the name of the Lord!'^c

'Hosanna^d in the highest heaven!'

10 When Jesus entered Jerusalem, the whole city was stirred and asked, 'Who is this?'

11 The crowds answered, 'This is Jesus, the prophet from Nazareth in Galilee.'

Jesus at the temple

12 Jesus entered the temple courts and drove out all who were buying and selling there. He overturned the tables of the money-changers and the benches of those selling doves. 13 'It is written,' he said to them,

IN OTHER WORDS

Hosanna
Matthew 21:9
Hosanna is a Hebrew word meaning 'save us'. Originally it was a prayer asking for God's help, but by this time it was a shout of joy or welcome. It has become a word in its own right like 'Hallelujah'.

'"My house will be called a house of prayer,"^e but you are making it "a den of robbers."'^f

14 The blind and the lame came to him at the temple, and he healed them. 15 But when the chief priests and the teachers of the law saw the wonderful things he did and the children shouting in the temple courts, 'Hosanna to the Son of David,' they were indignant.

16 'Do you hear what these children are saying?' they asked him.

'Yes,' replied Jesus, 'have you never read,

'"From the lips of children and infants
you have ordained praise"^g?'

17 And he left them and went out of the city to Bethany, where he spent the night.

Jesus curses a fig-tree

18 Early in the morning, as he was on his way back to the city, he was hungry. 19 Seeing a fig-tree by the road, he went up to it but found nothing on it except leaves. Then he said to it, 'May you never bear fruit again!' Immediately the tree withered.

20 When the disciples saw this, they were amazed. 'How did the fig-tree wither so quickly?' they asked.

21 Jesus replied, 'Truly I tell you, if you have faith and do not doubt, not only can you do what was done to the fig-tree, but also you can say to this mountain, "Go, throw yourself into the sea," and it will be

---

^a 5 Zech. 9:9   ^b 9 A Hebrew expression meaning 'Save!' which became an exclamation of praise; also in verse 15
^c 9 Psalm 118:25,26   ^d 9 A Hebrew expression meaning 'Save!' which became an exclamation of praise; also in verse 15
^e 13 Isaiah 56:7   ^f 13 Jer. 7:11   ^g 16 Psalm 8:2 (see Septuagint)

done. ²²If you believe, you will receive whatever you ask for in prayer.'

The authority of Jesus questioned

²³Jesus entered the temple courts, and, while he was teaching, the chief priests and the elders of the people came to him. 'By what authority are you doing these things?' they asked. 'And who gave you this authority?'

²⁴Jesus replied, 'I will also ask you one question. If you answer me, I will tell you by what authority I am doing these things. ²⁵John's baptism—where did it come from? Was it from heaven, or of human origin?'

They discussed it among themselves and said, 'If we say, "From heaven", he will ask, "Then why didn't you believe him?" ²⁶But if we say, "Of human origin"—we are afraid of the people, for they all hold that John was a prophet.'

²⁷So they answered Jesus, 'We don't know.'

Then he said, 'Neither will I tell you by what authority I am doing these things.

The parable of the two sons

²⁸'What do you think? There was a man who had two sons. He went to the first and said, "Son, go and work today in the vineyard."

²⁹'"I will not," he answered, but later he changed his mind and went.

³⁰'Then the father went to the other son and said the same thing. He answered, "I will, sir," but he did not go.

³¹'Which of the two did what his father wanted?'

'The first,' they answered.

Jesus said to them, 'Truly I tell you, the tax collectors and the prostitutes are entering the kingdom of God ahead of you. ³²For John came to you to show you the way of righteousness, and you did not believe him, but the tax collectors and the prostitutes did. And even after you saw this, you did not repent and believe him.

The parable of the tenants

³³'Listen to another parable: there was a landowner who planted a vineyard. He put a wall round it, dug a winepress in it and built a watchtower. Then he rented the vineyard to some farmers and moved to another place. ³⁴When the harvest time approached, he sent his servants to the tenants to collect his fruit.

³⁵'The tenants seized his servants; they beat one, killed another, and stoned a third. ³⁶Then he sent other servants to them, more than the first time, and the tenants treated them in the same way. ³⁷Last of all, he sent his son to them. "They will respect my son," he said.

³⁸'But when the tenants saw the son, they said to each other, "This is the heir. Come, let's kill him and take his inheritance." ³⁹So they took him and threw him out of the vineyard and killed him.

⁴⁰'Therefore, when the owner of the vineyard comes, what will he do to those tenants?'

⁴¹'He will bring those wretches to a wretched end,' they replied, 'and he will rent the vineyard to other tenants, who will give him his share of the crop at harvest time.'

⁴²Jesus said to them, 'Have you never read in the Scriptures:

'"The stone the builders rejected
  has become the cornerstone;
the Lord has done this,
  and it is marvellous in our eyes"[a]?

⁴³'Therefore I tell you that the kingdom of God will be taken away from you and given to a people who will produce its fruit. ⁴⁴Anyone who falls on this stone will be broken to pieces, but anyone on whom it falls will be crushed.'[b]

⁴⁵When the chief priests and the Pharisees heard Jesus' parables, they knew he was talking about them. ⁴⁶They looked for a way to arrest him, but they were afraid of the crowd because the people held that he was a prophet.

The parable of the wedding banquet

22 Jesus spoke to them again in parables, saying: ²'The kingdom of heaven is like a king who prepared a wedding banquet for his son. ³He sent his

---

[a] 42 Psalm 118:22,23 [b] 44 Some manuscripts do not have verse 44.

> **Weddings**
> Matthew 22:2
> Weddings were very elaborate celebrations that could last a whole week. Both the bride and groom would dress up in beautiful clothes and ornaments. The bridegroom would lead a procession of his friends and family to the bride's house where he would receive her from her parents. He then led everyone back to his house for a banquet. It wasn't just a family affair though; the whole community took part in the music, dancing and poetry to celebrate.

servants to those who had been invited to the banquet to tell them to come, but they refused to come.

4'Then he sent some more servants and said, "Tell those who have been invited that I have prepared my dinner: my oxen and fattened cattle have been slaughtered, and everything is ready. Come to the wedding banquet."

5'But they paid no attention and went off—one to his field, another to his business. 6The rest seized his servants, ill-treated them and killed them. 7The king was enraged. He sent his army and destroyed those murderers and burned their city.

8'Then he said to his servants, "The wedding banquet is ready, but those I invited did not deserve to come. 9Go to the street corners and invite to the banquet anyone you find." 10So the servants went out into the streets and gathered all the people they could find, the bad as well as the good, and the wedding hall was filled with guests.

11'But when the king came in to see the guests, he noticed a man there who was not wearing wedding clothes. 12"Friend," he asked, "how did you get in here without wedding clothes?" The man was speechless.

13'Then the king told the attendants, "Tie him hand and foot, and throw him outside, into the darkness, where there will be weeping and gnashing of teeth.

14'For many are invited, but few are chosen.'

Paying the poll-tax to Caesar

15Then the Pharisees went out and laid plans to trap him in his words. 16They sent their disciples to him along with the Herodians. 'Teacher,' they said, 'we know that you are a man of integrity and that you teach the way of God in accordance with the truth. You aren't swayed by others, because you pay no attention to who they are. 17Tell us then, what is your opinion? Is it right to pay the poll-tax[a] to Caesar or not?'

18But Jesus, knowing their evil intent, said, 'You hypocrites, why are you trying to trap me? 19Show me the coin used for paying the tax.' They brought him a denarius, 20and he asked them, 'Whose image is this? And whose inscription?'

21'Caesar's,' they replied.

Then he said to them, 'Give back to Caesar what is Caesar's, and to God what is God's.'

22When they heard this, they were amazed. So they left him and went away.

Marriage at the resurrection

23That same day the Sadducees, who say there is no resurrection, came to him with a question. 24'Teacher,' they said, 'Moses told us that if a man dies without having children, his brother must marry the widow and raise up offspring for him. 25Now there were seven brothers among us. The first one married and died, and since he had no children, he left his wife to his brother. 26The same thing happened to the second and third brother, right on down to the seventh. 27Finally, the woman died. 28Now then, at the resurrection, whose wife will she

---

[a] 17 The poll-tax was a special tax levied on subject peoples, not on Roman citizens.

The Ten Commandments
Matthew 22:36

The Law that this expert is referring to is the Ten Commandments and the other commands that God gave to the Israelites through Moses in the Old Testament (Exodus 20:1–17). About one and a half thousand years after God first gave those laws, Jesus shows that they are still important in his time, and they are just as relevant today because they come from God who stays the same throughout history. Even now, in the largely non-Christian and non-Jewish West, the Ten Commandments are still the basis for modern-day morality.

---

be of the seven, since all of them were married to her?'

29Jesus replied, 'You are in error because you do not know the Scriptures or the power of God. 30At the resurrection people will neither marry nor be given in marriage; they will be like the angels in heaven. 31But about the resurrection of the dead—have you not read what God said to you, 32"I am the God of Abraham, the God of Isaac, and the God of Jacob"[a]? He is not the God of the dead but of the living.'

33When the crowds heard this, they were astonished at his teaching.

The greatest commandment

34Hearing that Jesus had silenced the Sadducees, the Pharisees got together. 35One of them, an expert in the law, tested him with this question: 36'Teacher, which is the greatest commandment in the Law?'

37Jesus replied: '"Love the Lord your God with all your heart and with all your soul and with all your mind."[b] 38This is the first and greatest commandment. 39And the second is like it: "Love your neighbour as yourself."[c] 40All the Law and the Prophets hang on these two commandments.'

Whose son is the Messiah?

41While the Pharisees were gathered together, Jesus asked them, 42'What do you think about the Messiah? Whose son is he?'

'The son of David,' they replied.

43He said to them, 'How is it then that David, speaking by the Spirit, calls him "Lord"? For he says,

44' "The Lord said to my Lord:
  'Sit at my right hand
  until I put your enemies
    under your feet.' "[d]

45If then David calls him "Lord", how can he be his son?' 46No-one could say a word in reply, and from that day on no-one dared to ask him any more questions.

A warning against hypocrisy

23 Then Jesus said to the crowds and to his disciples: 2'The teachers of the law and the Pharisees sit in Moses' seat. 3So you must be careful to do everything they tell you. But do not do what they do, for they do not practise what they preach. 4They tie up heavy, cumbersome loads and put them on other people's shoulders, but they themselves are not willing to lift a finger to move them.

5'Everything they do is done for people to see: They make their phylacteries[e] wide and the tassels on their garments long; 6they love the place of honour at banquets and the most important seats in the synagogues; 7they love to be greeted with respect in the market-places and to have people call them "Rabbi".

8'But you are not to be called "Rabbi", for you have only one Master and you are all brothers. 9And do not call anyone on earth "father", for you have one Father, and he is in heaven. 10Nor are you to be called "teacher", for you have one Teacher, the

---

[a]32 Exodus 3:6 [b]37 Deut. 6:5 [c]39 Lev. 19:18 [d]44 Psalm 110:1 [e]5 That is, boxes containing Scripture verses, worn on forehead and arm

Messiah. ¹¹The greatest among you will be your servant. ¹²For those who exalt themselves will be humbled, and those who humble themselves will be exalted.

Seven woes on the teachers of the law and the Pharisees

¹³⁽¹⁴⁾'Woe to you, teachers of the law and Pharisees, you hypocrites! You shut the door of the kingdom of heaven in people's faces. You yourselves do not enter, nor will you let those enter who are trying to.

¹⁵'Woe to you, teachers of the law and Pharisees, you hypocrites! You travel over land and sea to win a single convert, and then you make that convert twice as much a child of hell as you are.

¹⁶'Woe to you, blind guides! You say, "If anyone swears by the temple, it means nothing; but whoever swears by the gold of the temple is bound by the oath." ¹⁷You blind fools! Which is greater: the gold, or the temple that makes the gold sacred? ¹⁸You also say, "If anyone swears by the altar, it means nothing; but whoever swears by the gift on the altar is bound by the oath." ¹⁹You blind men! Which is greater: the gift, or the altar that makes the gift sacred? ²⁰Therefore, anyone who swears by the altar swears by it and by everything on it. ²¹And anyone who swears by the temple swears by it and by the one who dwells in it. ²²And anyone who swears by heaven swears by God's throne and by the one who sits on it.

²³'Woe to you, teachers of the law and Pharisees, you hypocrites! You give a tenth of your spices—mint, dill and cumin. But you have neglected the more important matters of the law—justice, mercy and faithfulness. You should have practised the latter, without neglecting the former. ²⁴You blind guides! You strain out a gnat but swallow a camel.

²⁵'Woe to you, teachers of the law and Pharisees, you hypocrites! You clean the outside of the cup and dish, but inside they are full of greed and self-indulgence. ²⁶Blind Pharisee! First clean the inside of the cup and dish, and then the outside also will be clean.

²⁷'Woe to you, teachers of the law and Pharisees, you hypocrites! You are like whitewashed tombs, which look beautiful on the outside but on the inside are full of the bones of the dead and everything unclean. ²⁸In the same way, on the outside you appear to people as righteous but on the inside you are full of hypocrisy and wickedness.

²⁹'Woe to you, teachers of the law and Pharisees, you hypocrites! You build tombs for the prophets and decorate the graves of the righteous. ³⁰And you say, "If we had lived in the days of our ancestors, we would not have taken part with them in shedding the blood of the prophets." ³¹So you testify against yourselves that you are the descendants of those who murdered the prophets. ³²Fill up, then, the measure of the sin of your ancestors!

³³'You snakes! You brood of vipers! How will you escape being condemned to hell? ³⁴Therefore I am sending you prophets and sages and teachers. Some of them you will kill and crucify; others you will flog in your synagogues and pursue from town to town. ³⁵And so upon you will come all the righteous blood that has been shed on earth, from the blood of righteous Abel to the blood of Zechariah son of Berekiah, whom you murdered between the temple and the altar. ³⁶Truly I tell you, all this will come upon this generation.

³⁷'Jerusalem, Jerusalem, you who kill the prophets and stone those sent to you, how often I have longed to gather your children together, as a hen gathers her chicks under her wings, and you were not willing. ³⁸Look, your house is left to you desolate. ³⁹For I tell you, you will not see me again until you say, "Blessed is he who comes in the name of the Lord."[a]

The destruction of the temple and signs of the end times

24 Jesus left the temple and was walking away when his disciples came up to him to call his attention to its buildings. ²'Do you see all these things?' he asked. 'Truly I tell you, not one stone here

---

[a] 39 Psalm 118:26

making Connections

The destruction of the temple
Matthew 24:1

The temple had been renovated by Herod in Jerusalem. It was huge; the foundations were nearly one and a half kilometres around the base and some of the blocks of stone were about ten metres long. Jesus' prediction came true in AD 70 when the Romans invaded Jerusalem and destroyed the temple.

will be left on another; every one will be thrown down.'

3As Jesus was sitting on the Mount of Olives, the disciples came to him privately. 'Tell us,' they said, 'when will this happen, and what will be the sign of your coming and of the end of the age?'

4Jesus answered: 'Watch out that no-one deceives you. 5For many will come in my name, claiming, "I am the Messiah," and will deceive many. 6You will hear of wars and rumours of wars, but see to it that you are not alarmed. Such things must happen, but the end is still to come. 7Nation will rise against nation, and kingdom against kingdom. There will be famines and earthquakes in various places. 8All these are the beginning of birth-pains.

9'Then you will be handed over to be persecuted and put to death, and you will be hated by all nations because of me. 10At that time many will turn away from the faith and will betray and hate each other, 11and many false prophets will appear and deceive many people. 12Because of the increase of wickedness, the love of most will grow cold, 13but whoever stands firm to the end will be saved. 14And this gospel of the kingdom will be preached in the whole world as a testimony to all nations, and then the end will come.

15'So when you see standing in the holy place "the abomination that causes desolation,"[a] spoken of through the prophet Daniel—let the reader understand— 16then let those who are in Judea flee to the mountains. 17Let no-one on the housetop go down to take anything out of the house. 18Let no-one in the field go back to get their cloak. 19How dreadful it will be in those days for pregnant women and nursing mothers! 20Pray that your flight will not take place in winter or on the Sabbath. 21For then there will be great distress, unequalled from the beginning of the world until now—and never to be equalled again.

22'If those days had not been cut short, no-one would survive, but for the sake of the elect those days will be shortened. 23At that time if anyone says to you, "Look, here is the Messiah!" or, "There he is!" do not believe it. 24For false messiahs and false prophets will appear and perform great signs and wonders to deceive, if possible, even the elect. 25See, I have told you ahead of time.

26'So if anyone tells you, "There he is, out in the desert," do not go out; or, "Here he is, in the inner rooms," do not believe it. 27For as lightning that comes from the east is visible even in the west, so will be the coming of the Son of Man. 28Wherever there is a carcass, there the vultures will gather.

29'Immediately after the distress of those days

' "the sun will be darkened,
  and the moon will not give its light;
the stars will fall from the sky,
  and the heavenly bodies will be shaken."[b]

30'At that time the sign of the Son of Man will appear in the sky, and all the peoples of the earth[c] will mourn. They will see the Son of Man coming on the clouds of the sky, with power and great glory. 31And he will send his angels with a loud trumpet call, and they will gather his elect from the four

---

[a] 15 Daniel 9:27; 11:31; 12:11   [b] 29 Isaiah 13:10; 34:4   [c] 30 Or *the tribes of the land*

winds, from one end of the heavens to the other.

32'Now learn this lesson from the fig-tree: as soon as its twigs become tender and its leaves come out, you know that summer is near. 33Even so, when you see all these things, you know that it[a] is near, right at the door. 34Truly I tell you, this generation will certainly not pass away until all these things have happened. 35Heaven and earth will pass away, but my words will never pass away.

The day and hour unknown

36'But about that day or hour no-one knows, not even the angels in heaven, nor the Son,[b] but only the Father. 37As it was in the days of Noah, so it will be at the coming of the Son of Man. 38For in the days before the flood, people were eating and drinking, marrying and giving in marriage, up to the day Noah entered the ark; 39and they knew nothing about what would happen until the flood came and took them all away. That is how it will be at the coming of the Son of Man. 40Two men will be in the field; one will be taken and the other left. 41Two women will be grinding with a hand mill; one will be taken and the other left.

42'Therefore keep watch, because you do not know on what day your Lord will come. 43But understand this: if the owner of the house had known at what time of night the thief was coming, he would have kept watch and would not have let his house be broken into. 44So you also must be ready, because the Son of Man will come at an hour when you do not expect him.

45'Who then is the faithful and wise servant, whom the master has put in charge of the servants in his household to give them their food at the proper time? 46It will be good for that servant whose master finds him doing so when he returns. 47Truly I tell you, he will put him in charge of all his possessions. 48But suppose that servant is wicked and says to himself, "My master is staying away a long time," 49and he then begins to beat his fellow-servants and to eat and drink with drunkards. 50The master of that servant will come on a day when he does not expect him and at an hour he is not aware of. 51He will cut him to pieces and assign him a place with the hypocrites, where there will be weeping and gnashing of teeth.

The parable of the ten virgins

25 'At that time the kingdom of heaven will be like ten virgins who took their lamps and went out to meet the bridegroom. 2Five of them were foolish and five were wise. 3The foolish ones took their lamps but did not take any oil with them. 4The wise, however, took oil in jars along with their lamps. 5The bridegroom was a long time in coming, and they all became drowsy and fell asleep.

6'At midnight the cry rang out: "Here's the bridegroom! Come out to meet him!"

7'Then all the virgins woke up and trimmed their lamps. 8The foolish ones said to the wise, "Give us some of your oil; our lamps are going out."

9'"No," they replied, "there may not be enough for both us and you. Instead, go to those who sell oil and buy some for yourselves."

10'But while they were on their way to buy the oil, the bridegroom arrived. The virgins who were ready went in with him to the wedding banquet. And the door was shut.

11'Later the others also came. "Sir! Sir!" they said. "Open the door for us!"

12'But he replied, "Truly I tell you, I don't know you."

13'Therefore keep watch, because you do not know the day or the hour.

The parable of the bags of gold

14'Again, it will be like a man going on a journey, who called his servants and entrusted his wealth to them. 15To one he gave five bags of gold, to another two bags, and to another one bag,[c] each according to his ability. Then he went on his journey. 16The man who had received five bags of gold went at once and put his money to work and gained five bags more. 17So also, the one with two bags of gold gained two more. 18But the man who had received one bag

---

[a] 33 Or he [b] 36 Some manuscripts do not have *nor the Son*. [c] 15 Greek *five talents ... two talents ... one talent*; also throughout this parable; a talent was worth about 20 years of a day labourer's wage.

went off, dug a hole in the ground and hid his master's money.

19'After a long time the master of those servants returned and settled accounts with them. 20The man who had received five bags of gold brought the other five. "Master," he said, "you entrusted me with five bags of gold. See, I have gained five more."

21'His master replied, "Well done, good and faithful servant! You have been faithful with a few things; I will put you in charge of many things. Come and share your master's happiness!"

22'The man with two bags of gold also came. "Master," he said, "you entrusted me with two bags of gold; see, I have gained two more."

23'His master replied, "Well done, good and faithful servant! You have been faithful with a few things; I will put you in charge of many things. Come and share your master's happiness!"

24'Then the man who had received one bag of gold came. "Master," he said, "I knew that you are a hard man, harvesting where you have not sown and gathering where you have not scattered seed. 25So I was afraid and went out and hid your gold in the ground. See, here is what belongs to you."

26'His master replied, "You wicked, lazy servant! So you knew that I harvest where I have not sown and gather where I have not scattered seed? 27Well then, you should have put my money on deposit with the bankers, so that when I returned I would have received it back with interest.

28' "Take the bag of gold from him and give it to the one who has ten bags. 29For those who have will be given more, and they will have an abundance. As for those who do not have, even what they have will be taken from them. 30And throw that worthless servant outside, into the darkness, where there will be weeping and gnashing of teeth."

The sheep and the goats

31'When the Son of Man comes in his glory, and all the angels with him, he will sit on his glorious throne. 32All the nations will be gathered before him, and he will separate the people one from another as a shepherd separates the sheep from the goats. 33He will put the sheep on his right and the goats on his left.

34'Then the King will say to those on his right, "Come, you who are blessed by my Father; take your inheritance, the kingdom prepared for you since the creation of the world. 35For I was hungry and you gave me something to eat, I was thirsty and you gave me something to drink, I was a stranger and you invited me in, 36I needed clothes and you clothed me, I was ill and you looked after me, I was in prison and you came to visit me."

37'Then the righteous will answer him, "Lord, when did we see you hungry and feed you, or thirsty and give you something to drink? 38When did we see you a stranger and invite you in, or needing clothes and clothe you? 39When did we see you ill or in prison and go to visit you?"

40'The King will reply, "Truly I tell you, whatever you did for one of the least of these brothers and sisters of mine, you did for me."

41'Then he will say to those on his left, "Depart from me, you who are cursed, into the eternal fire prepared for the devil and his angels. 42For I was hungry and you gave me nothing to eat, I was thirsty and you gave me nothing to drink, 43I was a stranger and you did not invite me in, I needed clothes and you did not clothe me, I was ill and in prison and you did not look after me."

44'They also will answer, "Lord, when did we see you hungry or thirsty or a stranger or needing clothes or ill or in prison, and did not help you?"

45'He will reply, "Truly I tell you, whatever you did not do for one of the least of these, you did not do for me."

46'Then they will go away to eternal punishment, but the righteous to eternal life.'

The plot against Jesus

26 When Jesus had finished saying all these things, he said to his disciples, 2'As you know, the Passover is two days away—and the Son of Man will be handed over to be crucified.'

3Then the chief priests and the elders of the people assembled in the palace of the high priest, whose name was Caiaphas, 4and they plotted to arrest Jesus in some sly way and kill him. 5'But not during the Feast,' they said, 'or there may be a riot among the people.'

Jesus anointed at Bethany

6While Jesus was in Bethany in the home of Simon the Leper, 7a woman came to him with an alabaster jar of very expensive perfume, which she poured on his head as he was reclining at the table.

8When the disciples saw this, they were indignant. 'Why this waste?' they asked. 9'This perfume could have been sold at a high price and the money given to the poor.'

10Aware of this, Jesus said to them, 'Why are you bothering this woman? She has done a beautiful thing to me. 11The poor you will always have with you,^{a} but you will not always have me. 12When she poured this perfume on my body, she did it to prepare me for burial. 13Truly I tell you, wherever this gospel is preached throughout the world, what she has done will also be told, in memory of her.'

Judas agrees to betray Jesus

14Then one of the Twelve—the one called Judas Iscariot—went to the chief priests 15and asked, 'What are you willing to give me if I deliver him over to you?' So they counted out for him thirty pieces of silver. 16From then on Judas watched for an opportunity to hand him over.

The Last Supper

17On the first day of the Feast of Unleavened Bread, the disciples came to Jesus and asked, 'Where do you want us to make preparations for you to eat the Passover?'

18He replied, 'Go into the city to a certain man and tell him, "The Teacher says: my appointed time is near. I am going to celebrate the Passover with my disciples at your house."' 19So the disciples did as Jesus had directed them and prepared the Passover.

20When evening came, Jesus was reclining at the table with the Twelve. 21And while they were eating, he said, 'Truly I tell you, one of you will betray me.'

22They were very sad and began to say to him one after the other, 'Surely not I, Lord?'

23Jesus replied, 'The one who has dipped his hand into the bowl with me will betray me. 24The Son of Man will go just as it is written about him. But woe to that man who betrays the Son of Man! It would be better for him if he had not been born.'

25Then Judas, the one who would betray him, said, 'Surely not I, Rabbi?'

Jesus answered, 'You have said so.'

26While they were eating, Jesus took bread, and when he had given thanks, he broke it and gave it to his disciples, saying, 'Take and eat; this is my body.'

27Then he took the cup, and when he had given thanks, he gave it to them, saying, 'Drink from it, all of you. 28This is my blood of the^b covenant, which is poured out for many for the forgiveness of sins. 29I tell you, I will not drink of this fruit of the vine from now on until that day when I drink it new with you in my Father's kingdom.'

30When they had sung a hymn, they went out to the Mount of Olives.

People and Places

Judas Iscariot
Matthew 26:14

Judas was the disciples' treasurer, so he had responsibility for their money. He came from Kerioth in southern Judah and was the only one of the disciples not from Galilee. During the week of the Passover festival, he went to the chief priests and offered to betray Jesus for a reward. It's hard to understand why he did this, but it's clear that he regretted it. He tried to return the money and then went and hanged himself.

---

^{a} 11 See Deut. 15:11. ^{b} 28 Some manuscripts *the new*

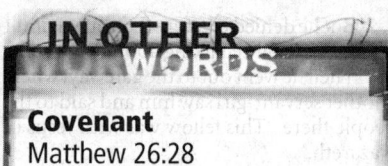

IN OTHER WORDS

Covenant
Matthew 26:28
A covenant is a special agreement or a contract showing a close relationship between two parties. In the Old Testament, God made a covenant with Abraham (Genesis 15:18), and a covenant with the nation of Israel (Genesis 35:9–12). When Jesus shares the Last Supper with the disciples he says that he has put in place a new covenant.

Jesus predicts Peter's denial

31 Then Jesus told them, 'This very night you will all fall away on account of me, for it is written:

' "I will strike the shepherd,
    and the sheep of the flock will be scattered." '*a*

32 But after I have risen, I will go ahead of you into Galilee.'

33 Peter replied, 'Even if all fall away on account of you, I never will.'

34 'Truly I tell you,' Jesus answered, 'this very night, before the cock crows, you will disown me three times.'

35 But Peter declared, 'Even if I have to die with you, I will never disown you.' And all the other disciples said the same.

Gethsemane

36 Then Jesus went with his disciples to a place called Gethsemane, and he said to them, 'Sit here while I go over there and pray.' 37 He took Peter and the two sons of Zebedee along with him, and he began to be sorrowful and troubled. 38 Then he said to them, 'My soul is overwhelmed with sorrow to the point of death. Stay here and keep watch with me.'

39 Going a little farther, he fell with his face to the ground and prayed, 'My Father, if it is possible, may this cup be taken from me. Yet not as I will, but as you will.'

40 Then he returned to his disciples and found them sleeping. 'Couldn't you men keep watch with me for one hour?' he asked Peter. 41 'Watch and pray so that you will not fall into temptation. The spirit is willing, but the flesh is weak.'

42 He went away a second time and prayed, 'My Father, if it is not possible for this cup to be taken away unless I drink it, may your will be done.'

43 When he came back, he again found them sleeping, because their eyes were heavy. 44 So he left them and went away once more and prayed the third time, saying the same thing.

45 Then he returned to the disciples and said to them, 'Are you still sleeping and resting? Look, the hour is near, and the Son of Man is delivered into the hands of sinners. 46 Rise! Let us go! Here comes my betrayer!'

Jesus arrested

47 While he was still speaking, Judas, one of the Twelve, arrived. With him was a large crowd armed with swords and clubs, sent from the chief priests and the elders of the people. 48 Now the betrayer had arranged a signal with them: 'The one I kiss is the man; arrest him.' 49 Going at once to Jesus, Judas said, 'Greetings, Rabbi!' and kissed him.

50 Jesus replied, 'Friend, do what you came for.'*b*

Then the men stepped forward, seized Jesus and arrested him. 51 With that, one of Jesus' companions reached for his sword, drew it out and struck the servant of the high priest, cutting off his ear.

52 'Put your sword back in its place,' Jesus said to him, 'for all who draw the sword will die by the sword. 53 Do you think I cannot call on my Father, and he will at once put at my disposal more than twelve legions of angels? 54 But how then would the Scriptures be fulfilled that say it must happen in this way?'

55 In that hour Jesus said to the crowd, 'Am I leading a rebellion, that you have come out with swords and clubs to capture

---

a 31 Zech. 13:7   *b* 50 Or *'Friend, why have you come?'*

me? Every day I sat in the temple courts teaching, and you did not arrest me. 56But this has all taken place that the writings of the prophets might be fulfilled.' Then all the disciples deserted him and fled.

Jesus before the Sanhedrin

57Those who had arrested Jesus took him to Caiaphas the high priest, where the teachers of the law and the elders had assembled. 58But Peter followed him at a distance, right up to the courtyard of the high priest. He entered and sat down with the guards to see the outcome.

59The chief priests and the whole Sanhedrin were looking for false evidence against Jesus so that they could put him to death. 60But they did not find any, though many false witnesses came forward.

Finally two came forward 61and declared, 'This fellow said, "I am able to destroy the temple of God and rebuild it in three days."'

62Then the high priest stood up and said to Jesus, 'Are you not going to answer? What is this testimony that these men are bringing against you?' 63But Jesus remained silent.

The high priest said to him, 'I charge you under oath by the living God: Tell us if you are the Messiah, the Son of God.'

64'You have said so,' Jesus replied. 'But I say to all of you: from now on you will see the Son of Man sitting at the right hand of the Mighty One and coming on the clouds of heaven.'[a]

65Then the high priest tore his clothes and said, 'He has spoken blasphemy! Why do we need any more witnesses? Look, now you have heard the blasphemy. 66What do you think?'

'He is worthy of death,' they answered.

67Then they spat in his face and struck him with their fists. Others slapped him 68and said, 'Prophesy to us, Messiah. Who hit you?'

Peter disowns Jesus

69Now Peter was sitting out in the courtyard, and a servant-girl came to him. 'You also were with Jesus of Galilee,' she said.

70But he denied it before them all. 'I don't know what you're talking about,' he said.

71Then he went out to the gateway, where another servant-girl saw him and said to the people there, 'This fellow was with Jesus of Nazareth.'

72He denied it again, with an oath: 'I don't know the man!'

73After a little while, those standing there went up to Peter and said, 'Surely you are one of them; your accent gives you away.'

74Then he began to call down curses, and he swore to them, 'I don't know the man!'

Immediately a cock crowed. 75Then Peter remembered the word Jesus had spoken: 'Before the cock crows, you will disown me three times.' And he went outside and wept bitterly.

Judas hangs himself

27 Early in the morning, all the chief priests and the elders of the people came to the decision to put Jesus to death. 2They bound him, led him away and handed him over to Pilate the governor.

3When Judas, who had betrayed him, saw that Jesus was condemned, he was seized with remorse and returned the thirty pieces of silver to the chief priests and the elders. 4'I have sinned,' he said, 'for I have betrayed innocent blood.'

'What is that to us?' they replied. 'That's your responsibility.'

5So Judas threw the money into the temple and left. Then he went away and hanged himself.

6The chief priests picked up the coins and said, 'It is against the law to put this into the treasury, since it is blood money.' 7So they decided to use the money to buy the potter's field as a burial place for foreigners. 8That is why it has been called the Field of Blood to this day. 9Then what was spoken by Jeremiah the prophet was fulfilled: 'They took the thirty pieces of silver, the price set on him by the people of Israel, 10and they used them to buy the potter's field, as the Lord commanded me.'[b]

---

[a] 64 See Psalm 110:1; Daniel 7:13. [b] 10 See Zech. 11:12,13; Jer. 19:1-13; 32:6-9.

People and Places

Pilate
Matthew 27:2

Pontius Pilate was the Roman ruler in charge of Judea. The Jews weren't allowed to execute anyone without approval from the Roman authorities, which is why they brought Jesus to Pilate. Pilate seemed convinced that Jesus hadn't done anything worthy of the death penalty, and tried to set him free. But when the Jews insisted on Jesus' crucifixion, he gave in to them rather than damaging his reputation and career.

Jesus before Pilate

11Meanwhile Jesus stood before the governor, and the governor asked him, 'Are you the king of the Jews?'

'You have said so,' Jesus replied.

12When he was accused by the chief priests and the elders, he gave no answer. 13Then Pilate asked him, 'Don't you hear the testimony they are bringing against you?' 14But Jesus made no reply, not even to a single charge—to the great amazement of the governor.

15Now it was the governor's custom at the Feast to release a prisoner chosen by the crowd. 16At that time they had a well-known prisoner whose name was Jesus[a] Barabbas. 17So when the crowd had gathered, Pilate asked them, 'Which one do you want me to release to you: Jesus Barabbas, or Jesus who is called the Messiah?' 18For he knew it was out of envy that they had handed Jesus over to him.

19While Pilate was sitting on the judge's seat, his wife sent him this message: 'Don't have anything to do with that innocent man, for I have suffered a great deal today in a dream because of him.'

20But the chief priests and the elders persuaded the crowd to ask for Barabbas and to have Jesus executed.

21'Which of the two do you want me to release to you?' asked the governor.

'Barabbas,' they answered.

22'What shall I do, then, with Jesus who is called the Messiah?' Pilate asked.

They all answered, 'Crucify him!'

23'Why? What crime has he committed?' asked Pilate.

But they shouted all the louder, 'Crucify him!'

24When Pilate saw that he was getting nowhere, but that instead an uproar was starting, he took water and washed his hands in front of the crowd. 'I am innocent of this man's blood,' he said. 'It is your responsibility!'

25All the people answered, 'His blood is on us and on our children!'

26Then he released Barabbas to them. But he had Jesus flogged, and handed him over to be crucified.

The soldiers mock Jesus

27Then the governor's soldiers took Jesus into the Praetorium and gathered the whole company of soldiers round him. 28They stripped him and put a scarlet robe on him, 29and then twisted together a crown of thorns and set it on his head. They put a staff in his right hand as a sceptre. Then they knelt in front of him and mocked him. 'Hail, king of the Jews!' they said. 30They spat on him, and took the staff and struck him on the head again and again. 31After they had mocked him, they took off the robe and put his own clothes on him. Then they led him away to crucify him.

The crucifixion of Jesus

32As they were going out, they met a man from Cyrene, named Simon, and they forced him to carry the cross. 33They came to a place called Golgotha (which means 'the place of the skull'). 34There they offered Jesus wine to drink, mixed with gall; but after tasting it, he refused to drink it. 35When they had crucified him, they divided up his clothes by casting lots. 36And

---

[a] 16 Many manuscripts do not have *Jesus*; also in verse 17.

IN OTHER WORDS

Cross
Matthew 27:32

The cross was a horrific way of executing a criminal. After being severely beaten with leather lashes, the victim would usually have to carry the crossbeam to the execution site where the upright stake was already in place. Death was caused by suffocation or exhaustion after a long period of agonising pain. After the Roman emperor Constantine became a Christian, the cross became a sacred symbol and its use as a means of execution was stopped. The cross is central to the Christian faith.

---

sitting down, they kept watch over him there. 37Above his head they placed the written charge against him: THIS IS JESUS, THE KING OF THE JEWS.

38Two rebels were crucified with him, one on his right and one on his left. 39Those who passed by hurled insults at him, shaking their heads 40and saying, 'You who are going to destroy the temple and build it in three days, save yourself! Come down from the cross, if you are the Son of God!'

41In the same way the chief priests, the teachers of the law and the elders mocked him. 42'He saved others,' they said, 'but he can't save himself! He's the king of Israel! Let him come down now from the cross, and we will believe in him. 43He trusts in God. Let God rescue him now if he wants him, for he said, "I am the Son of God."' 44In the same way the rebels who were crucified with him also heaped insults on him.

The death of Jesus

45From noon until three in the afternoon darkness came over all the land. 46About three in the afternoon Jesus cried out in a loud voice, 'Eli, Eli,[a] lema sabachthani?' (which means 'My God, my God, why have you forsaken me?').[b]

47When some of those standing there heard this, they said, 'He's calling Elijah.' 48Immediately one of them ran and got a sponge. He filled it with wine vinegar, put it on a staff, and offered it to Jesus to drink. 49The rest said, 'Now leave him alone. Let's see if Elijah comes to save him.'

50And when Jesus had cried out again in a loud voice, he gave up his spirit.

51At that moment the curtain of the temple was torn in two from top to bottom. The earth shook, the rocks split 52and the tombs broke open. The bodies of many holy people who had died were raised to life. 53They came out of the tombs after Jesus' resurrection and[c] went into the holy city and appeared to many people.

54When the centurion and those with him who were guarding Jesus saw the earthquake and all that had happened, they were terrified, and exclaimed, 'Surely he was the Son of God!'

55Many women were there, watching from a distance. They had followed Jesus from Galilee to care for his needs. 56Among them were Mary Magdalene, Mary the mother of James and Joseph,[d] and the mother of Zebedee's sons.

The burial of Jesus

57As evening approached, there came a rich man from Arimathea, named Joseph, who had himself become a disciple of Jesus. 58Going to Pilate, he asked for Jesus' body, and Pilate ordered that it be given to him. 59Joseph took the body, wrapped it in a clean linen cloth, 60and placed it in his own new tomb that he had cut out of the rock. He rolled a big stone in front of the entrance to the tomb and went away. 61Mary Magdalene and the other Mary were sitting there opposite the tomb.

The guard at the tomb

62The next day, the one after Preparation Day, the chief priests and the Pharisees went to Pilate. 63'Sir,' they said, 'we remember

---

[a] 46 Some manuscripts *Eloi, Eloi* [b] 46 Psalm 22:1 [c] 53 Or *tombs, and after Jesus' resurrection they* [d] 56 Greek *Joses*, a variant of *Joseph*

that while he was still alive that deceiver said, "After three days I will rise again." 64So give the order for the tomb to be made secure until the third day. Otherwise, his disciples may come and steal the body and tell the people that he has been raised from the dead. This last deception will be worse than the first.'

65'Take a guard,' Pilate answered. 'Go, make the tomb as secure as you know how.' 66So they went and made the tomb secure by putting a seal on the stone and posting the guard.

Jesus has risen

28 After the Sabbath, at dawn on the first day of the week, Mary Magdalene and the other Mary went to look at the tomb.

2There was a violent earthquake, for an angel of the Lord came down from heaven and, going to the tomb, rolled back the stone and sat on it. 3His appearance was like lightning, and his clothes were white as snow. 4The guards were so afraid of him that they shook and became like dead men.

5The angel said to the women, 'Do not be afraid, for I know that you are looking for Jesus, who was crucified. 6He is not here; he has risen, just as he said. Come and see the place where he lay. 7Then go quickly and tell his disciples: "He has risen from the dead and is going ahead of you into Galilee. There you will see him." Now I have told you.'

8So the women hurried away from the tomb, afraid yet filled with joy, and ran to tell his disciples. 9Suddenly Jesus met them. 'Greetings,' he said. They came to him, clasped his feet and worshipped him. 10Then Jesus said to them, 'Do not be afraid. Go and tell my brothers to go to Galilee; there they will see me.'

The guards' report

11While the women were on their way, some of the guards went into the city and reported to the chief priests everything that had happened. 12When the chief priests had met with the elders and devised a plan, they gave the soldiers a large sum of money, 13telling them, 'You are to say, "His disciples came during the night and stole him away while we were asleep." 14If this report gets to the governor, we will satisfy him and keep you out of trouble.' 15So the soldiers took the money and did as they were instructed. And this story has been widely circulated among the Jews to this very day.

The great commission

16Then the eleven disciples went to Galilee, to the mountain where Jesus had told them to go. 17When they saw him, they worshipped him; but some doubted. 18Then Jesus came to them and said, 'All authority in heaven and on earth has been given to me. 19Therefore go and make disciples of all nations, baptising them in[a] the name of the Father and of the Son and of the Holy Spirit, 20and teaching them to obey everything I have commanded you. And surely I am with you always, to the very end of the age.'

> **People and Places**
>
> **Trinity**
> **Matthew 28:19**
> Although the word 'Trinity' doesn't appear in the Bible, the idea that God is one and three is very much part of the New Testament's teaching. The three persons that make up the Trinity are God the Father, Jesus who is God the Son, and the Holy Spirit.

---

a 19 Or *into*; see Acts 8:16; 19:5; Romans 6:3; 1 Cor. 1:13; 10:2; Gal. 3:27.

Mark

INTRODUCTION

Mark

Author: Mark, thought to be the John Mark who is mentioned in Acts 12:12 and who went with Paul and Barnabas on their first missionary journey.

Who to: Written for a Gentile audience, in particular the Romans.

When: It covers the events of Jesus' life, from about AD 27–30. It may have been the first Gospel to be written, probably between the early 50s and early 60s.

Where: Judea

Did you know? This is the shortest Gospel. Mark explains lots of things for people who don't have a Jewish background, so it's easy to understand too.

Main theme: Mark's Gospel is full of action, telling us more about what Jesus did than what he said. Right from the start of his Gospel (1:1), Mark wants his readers to know that Jesus is God's Son. But he also shows that Jesus is human, experiencing lots of different emotions and encountering difficulties on his journey to the cross.

John the Baptist prepares the way

1 The beginning of the good news about Jesus the Messiah,[a,b] ²as it is written in Isaiah the prophet:

'I will send my messenger ahead of you,
    who will prepare your way'[c]—
³'a voice of one calling in the wilderness,
    "Prepare the way for the Lord,
    make straight paths for him." '[d]

⁴And so John the Baptist appeared in the wilderness, preaching a baptism of repentance for the forgiveness of sins. ⁵The whole Judean countryside and all the people of Jerusalem went out to him. Confessing their

---
[a] 1 Or *Jesus Christ*. *Messiah* (Hebrew) and *Christ* (Greek) both mean *Anointed One*.   [b] 1 Many manuscripts *Messiah, the Son of God*   [c] 2 Mal. 3:1   [d] 3 Isaiah 40:3

> **IN OTHER WORDS**
>
> **Kingdom of God**
> **Mark 1:15**
> The kingdom of God is the place where God rules, where evil is destroyed, justice is everywhere and people are blessed. In Jesus' parables the kingdom starts small, like a mustard seed, or yeast, or a pearl, and then spreads (Matthew 13:31–46). When Jesus began his ministry, he said that the kingdom of God was among the people, but we won't fully see God's rule on earth until Jesus comes again. Sometimes the Gospels refer to 'the kingdom of heaven' – it's the same thing.

sins, they were baptised by him in the River Jordan. 6John wore clothing made of camel's hair, with a leather belt round his waist, and he ate locusts and wild honey. 7And this was his message: 'After me comes the one more powerful than I, the thongs of whose sandals I am not worthy to stoop down and untie. 8I baptise you with[a] water, but he will baptise you with[b] the Holy Spirit.'

The baptism and testing of Jesus

9At that time Jesus came from Nazareth in Galilee and was baptised by John in the Jordan. 10Just as Jesus was coming up out of the water, he saw heaven being torn open and the Spirit descending on him like a dove. 11And a voice came from heaven: 'You are my Son, whom I love; with you I am well pleased.'

12At once the Spirit sent him out into the wilderness, 13and he was in the wilderness for forty days, being tempted[c] by Satan. He was with the wild animals, and angels attended him.

Jesus announces the good news

14After John was put in prison, Jesus went into Galilee, proclaiming the good news of God. 15'The time has come,' he said. 'The kingdom of God has come near. Repent and believe the good news!'

Jesus calls his first disciples

16As Jesus walked beside the Sea of Galilee, he saw Simon and his brother Andrew casting a net into the lake, for they were fishermen. 17'Come, follow me,' Jesus said, 'and I will send you out to fish for people.' 18At once they left their nets and followed him.

19When he had gone a little farther, he saw James son of Zebedee and his brother John in a boat, preparing their nets. 20Without delay he called them, and they left their father Zebedee in the boat with the hired men and followed him.

Jesus drives out an evil spirit

21They went to Capernaum, and when the Sabbath came, Jesus went into the synagogue and began to teach. 22The people were amazed at his teaching, because he taught them as one who had authority, not as the teachers of the law. 23Just then a man in their synagogue who was possessed by an evil[d] spirit cried out, 24'What do you want with us, Jesus of Nazareth? Have you come to destroy us? I know who you are—the Holy One of God!'

25'Be quiet!' said Jesus sternly. 'Come out of him!' 26The evil spirit shook the man violently and came out of him with a shriek.

27The people were all so amazed that they asked each other, 'What is this? A new teaching—and with authority! He even gives orders to evil spirits and they obey him.' 28News about him spread quickly over the whole region of Galilee.

Jesus heals many

29As soon as they left the synagogue, they went with James and John to the home of Simon and Andrew. 30Simon's mother-in-law was in bed with a fever, and they immediately told Jesus about her. 31So he went to her, took her hand and helped her up. The fever left her and she began to wait on them.

32That evening after sunset the people brought to Jesus all who were ill and

---

[a] 8 Or *in* [b] 8 Or *in* [c] 13 The Greek for *tempted* can also mean *tested*. [d] 23 Greek *unclean*; also in verses 26 and 27

demon-possessed. 33The whole town gathered at the door, 34and Jesus healed many who had various diseases. He also drove out many demons, but he would not let the demons speak because they knew who he was.

Jesus prays in a solitary place

35Very early in the morning, while it was still dark, Jesus got up, left the house and went off to a solitary place, where he prayed. 36Simon and his companions went to look for him, 37and when they found him, they exclaimed: 'Everyone is looking for you!'

38Jesus replied, 'Let us go somewhere else—to the nearby villages—so that I can preach there also. That is why I have come.' 39So he travelled throughout Galilee, preaching in their synagogues and driving out demons.

Jesus heals a man with leprosy

40A man with leprosy[a] came to him and begged him on his knees, 'If you are willing, you can make me clean.'

41Jesus was indignant.[b] He reached out his hand and touched the man. 'I am willing,' he said. 'Be clean!' 42Immediately the leprosy left him and he was cleansed.

43Jesus sent him away at once with a strong warning: 44'See that you don't tell this to anyone. But go, show yourself to the priest and offer the sacrifices that Moses commanded for your cleansing, as a testimony to them.' 45Instead he went out and began to talk freely, spreading the news. As a result, Jesus could no longer enter a town openly but stayed outside in lonely places. Yet the people still came to him from everywhere.

Jesus forgives and heals a paralysed man

2 A few days later, when Jesus again entered Capernaum, the people heard that he had come home. 2They gathered in such large numbers that there was no room left, not even outside the door, and he preached the word to them. 3Some men came, bringing to him a paralysed man, carried by four of them. 4Since they could not get him to Jesus because of the crowd, they made an opening in the roof above Jesus by digging through it and then lowered the mat the man was lying on. 5When Jesus saw their faith, he said to the paralysed man, 'Son, your sins are forgiven.'

6Now some teachers of the law were sitting there, thinking to themselves, 7'Why does this fellow talk like that? He's blaspheming! Who can forgive sins but God alone?'

8Immediately Jesus knew in his spirit that this was what they were thinking in their hearts, and he said to them, 'Why are you thinking these things? 9Which is easier: to say to this paralysed man, "Your sins are forgiven," or to say, "Get up, take your mat and walk"? 10But I want you to know that the Son of Man has authority on earth to forgive sins.' So he said to the man, 11'I tell you, get up, take your mat and go home.' 12He got up, took his mat and walked out in full view of them all. This amazed everyone and they praised God, saying, 'We have never seen anything like this!'

Jesus calls Levi and eats with sinners

13Once again Jesus went out beside the lake. A large crowd came to him, and he began to teach them. 14As he walked along, he saw Levi son of Alphaeus sitting at the tax collector's booth. 'Follow me,' Jesus told him, and Levi got up and followed him.

15While Jesus was having dinner at Levi's house, many tax collectors and sinners were eating with him and his disciples, for there were many who followed him. 16When the teachers of the law who were Pharisees saw him eating with the sinners and tax collectors, they asked his disciples: 'Why does he eat with tax collectors and sinners?'

17On hearing this, Jesus said to them, 'It is not the healthy who need a doctor, but those who are ill. I have not come to call the righteous, but sinners.'

Jesus questioned about fasting

18Now John's disciples and the Pharisees were fasting. Some people came and asked Jesus, 'How is it that John's disciples and the disciples of the Pharisees are fasting, but yours are not?'

---

[a] 40 The Greek word traditionally translated *leprosy* was used for various diseases affecting the skin. [b] 41 Many manuscripts *Jesus was filled with compassion*

Bride of Christ
Mark 2:20
One of the ways the church is described in the New Testament is as 'the bride of Christ', with Jesus as the bridegroom (Ephesians 5:25–33). It shows how much Jesus loves the church.

19 Jesus answered, 'How can the guests of the bridegroom fast while he is with them? They cannot, so long as they have him with them. 20 But the time will come when the bridegroom will be taken from them, and on that day they will fast.

21 'No-one sews a patch of unshrunk cloth on an old garment. If they do, the new piece will pull away from the old, making the tear worse. 22 And people do not pour new wine into old wineskins. If they do, the wine will burst the skins, and both the wine and the wineskins will be ruined. No, they pour new wine into new wineskins.'

Jesus is Lord of the Sabbath

23 One Sabbath Jesus was going through the cornfields, and as his disciples walked along, they began to pick some ears of corn. 24 The Pharisees said to him, 'Look, why are they doing what is unlawful on the Sabbath?'

25 He answered, 'Have you never read what David did when he and his companions were hungry and in need? 26 In the days of Abiathar the high priest, he entered the house of God and ate the consecrated bread, which is lawful only for priests to eat. And he also gave some to his companions.'

27 Then he said to them, 'The Sabbath was made for people, not people for the Sabbath. 28 So the Son of Man is Lord even of the Sabbath.'

Jesus heals on the Sabbath

3 Another time Jesus went into the synagogue, and a man with a shrivelled hand was there. 2 Some of them were looking for a reason to accuse Jesus, so they watched him closely to see if he would heal him on the Sabbath. 3 Jesus said to the man with the shrivelled hand, 'Stand up in front of everyone.'

4 Then Jesus asked them, 'Which is lawful on the Sabbath: to do good or to do evil, to save life or to kill?' But they remained silent.

5 He looked around at them in anger and, deeply distressed at their stubborn hearts, said to the man, 'Stretch out your hand.' He stretched it out, and his hand was completely restored. 6 Then the Pharisees went out and began to plot with the Herodians how they might kill Jesus.

Crowds follow Jesus

7 Jesus withdrew with his disciples to the lake, and a large crowd from Galilee followed. 8 When they heard all he was doing, many people came to him from Judea, Jerusalem, Idumea, and the regions across the Jordan and around Tyre and Sidon. 9 Because of the crowd he told his disciples to have a small boat ready for him, to keep the people from crowding him. 10 For he had healed many, so that those with diseases were pushing forward to touch him. 11 Whenever the evil[a] spirits saw him, they fell down before him and cried out, 'You are the Son of God.' 12 But he gave them strict orders not to tell others about him.

Jesus appoints the Twelve

13 Jesus went up on a mountainside and called to him those he wanted, and they came to him. 14 He appointed twelve[b] that they might be with him and that he might send them out to preach 15 and to have authority to drive out demons. 16 These are the twelve he appointed: Simon (to whom he gave the name Peter); 17 James son of Zebedee and his brother John (to them he gave the name Boanerges, which means 'sons of thunder'), 18 Andrew, Philip, Bartholomew, Matthew, Thomas, James son of Alphaeus, Thaddaeus, Simon the Zealot 19 and Judas Iscariot, who betrayed him.

---

[a] 11 Greek *unclean*; also in verse 30 [b] 14 Some manuscripts *twelve—designating them apostles—*

Jesus accused by his family and by teachers of the law

20Then Jesus entered a house, and again a crowd gathered, so that he and his disciples were not even able to eat. 21When his family[a] heard about this, they went to take charge of him, for they said, 'He is out of his mind.'

22And the teachers of the law who came down from Jerusalem said, 'He is possessed by Beelzebul! By the prince of demons he is driving out demons.'

23So Jesus called them over to him and began to speak to them in parables: 'How can Satan drive out Satan? 24If a kingdom is divided against itself, that kingdom cannot stand. 25If a house is divided against itself, that house cannot stand. 26And if Satan opposes himself and is divided, he cannot stand; his end has come. 27In fact, no-one can enter a strong man's house without first tying him up. Then he can plunder the strong man's house. 28Truly I tell you, people will be forgiven all their sins and all the blasphemies they utter. 29But whoever blasphemes against the Holy Spirit will never be forgiven, but is guilty of an eternal sin.'

30He said this because they were saying, 'He has an evil spirit.'

31Then Jesus' mother and brothers arrived. Standing outside, they sent someone in to call him. 32A crowd was sitting round him, and they told him, 'Your mother and brothers are outside looking for you.'

33'Who are my mother and my brothers?' he asked.

34Then he looked at those seated in a circle round him and said, 'Here are my mother and my brothers! 35Whoever does God's will is my brother and sister and mother.'

The parable of the sower

4 Again Jesus began to teach by the lake. The crowd that gathered round him was so large that he got into a boat and sat in it out on the lake, while all the people were along the shore at the water's edge. 2He taught them many things by parables, and in his teaching said: 3'Listen! A farmer went out to sow his seed. 4As he was scattering the seed, some fell along the path, and the birds came and ate it up. 5Some fell on rocky places, where it did not have much soil. It sprang up quickly, because the soil was shallow. 6But when the sun came up, the plants were scorched, and they withered because they had no root. 7Other seed fell among thorns, which grew up and choked the plants, so that they did not bear grain. 8Still other seed fell on good soil. It came up, grew and produced a crop, some multiplying thirty, some sixty, some a hundred times.'

9Then Jesus said, 'Whoever has ears to hear, let them hear.'

10When he was alone, the Twelve and the others around him asked him about the parables. 11He told them, 'The secret of the kingdom of God has been given to you. But to those on the outside everything is said in parables 12so that,

'"they may be ever seeing but never perceiving,
and ever hearing but never understanding;
otherwise they might turn and be forgiven!"'[b]

13Then Jesus said to them, 'Don't you understand this parable? How then will you understand any parable? 14The farmer sows the word. 15Some people are like seed along the path, where the word is sown. As soon as they hear it, Satan comes and takes away the word that was sown in them. 16Others, like seed sown on rocky places, hear the word and at once receive it with joy. 17But since they have no root, they last only a short time. When trouble or persecution comes because of the word, they quickly fall away. 18Still others, like seed sown among thorns, hear the word; 19but the worries of this life, the deceitfulness of wealth and the desires for other things come in and choke the word, making it unfruitful. 20Others, like seed sown on good soil, hear the word, accept it, and produce a crop—some thirty, some sixty, some a hundred times what was sown.'

---

[a] 21 Or *his associates* [b] 12 Isaiah 6:9,10

Sign of the times

Lamps
Mark 4:21
People lit their houses with oil-burning lamps. These were usually made of pottery and often had a spout for the wick, and a handle so they could be carried. Lamps with a single wick would burn for two to four hours.

A lamp on a stand

21He said to them, 'Do you bring in a lamp to put it under a bowl or a bed? Instead, don't you put it on its stand? 22For whatever is hidden is meant to be disclosed, and whatever is concealed is meant to be brought out into the open. 23If anyone has ears to hear, let them hear.'

24'Consider carefully what you hear,' he continued. 'With the measure you use, it will be measured to you—and even more. 25Those who have will be given more; as for those who do not have, even what they have will be taken from them.'

The parable of the growing seed

26He also said, 'This is what the kingdom of God is like. A man scatters seed on the ground. 27Night and day, whether he sleeps or gets up, the seed sprouts and grows, though he does not know how. 28All by itself the soil produces corn—first the stalk, then the ear, then the full grain in the ear. 29As soon as the corn is ripe, he puts the sickle to it, because the harvest has come.'

The parable of the mustard seed

30Again he said, 'What shall we say the kingdom of God is like, or what parable shall we use to describe it? 31It is like a mustard seed, which is the smallest of all seeds on earth. 32Yet when planted, it grows and becomes the largest of all garden plants, with such big branches that the birds can perch in its shade.'

33With many similar parables Jesus spoke the word to them, as much as they could understand. 34He did not say anything to them without using a parable. But when he was alone with his own disciples, he explained everything.

Jesus calms the storm

35That day when evening came, he said to his disciples, 'Let us go over to the other side.' 36Leaving the crowd behind, they took him along, just as he was, in the boat. There were also other boats with him. 37A furious squall came up, and the waves broke over the boat, so that it was nearly swamped. 38Jesus was in the stern, sleeping on a cushion. The disciples woke him and said to him, 'Teacher, don't you care if we drown?'

39He got up, rebuked the wind and said to the waves, 'Quiet! Be still!' Then the wind died down and it was completely calm.

40He said to his disciples, 'Why are you so afraid? Do you still have no faith?'

41They were terrified and asked each other, 'Who is this? Even the wind and the waves obey him!'

Jesus restores a demon-possessed man

5 They went across the lake to the region of the Gerasenes.[a] 2When Jesus got out of the boat, a man with an evil[b] spirit came from the tombs to meet him. 3This man lived in the tombs, and no-one could bind him anymore, not even with a chain. 4For he had often been chained hand and foot, but he tore the chains apart and broke the irons on his feet. No-one was strong enough to subdue him. 5Night and day among the tombs and in the hills he would cry out and cut himself with stones.

6When he saw Jesus from a distance, he ran and fell on his knees in front of him. 7He shouted at the top of his voice, 'What do you want with me, Jesus, Son of the Most High God? In God's name don't torture me!' 8For Jesus had said to him, 'Come out of this man, you evil spirit!'

---

[a]1 Some manuscripts *Gadarenes*; other manuscripts *Gergesenes* [b]2 Greek *unclean*; also in verses 8 and 13

making Connections

Pigs
Mark 5:11

The Jews considered pigs to be unclean animals and they would never have been pig farmers themselves. So the region of the Gerasenes must have been a place where lots of Gentiles lived and few Jews.

9Then Jesus asked him, 'What is your name?'

'My name is Legion,' he replied, 'for we are many.' 10And he begged Jesus again and again not to send them out of the area.

11A large herd of pigs was feeding on the nearby hillside. 12The demons begged Jesus, 'Send us among the pigs; allow us to go into them.' 13He gave them permission, and the evil spirits came out and went into the pigs. The herd, about two thousand in number, rushed down the steep bank into the lake and were drowned.

14Those tending the pigs ran off and reported this in the town and countryside, and the people went out to see what had happened. 15When they came to Jesus, they saw the man who had been possessed by the legion of demons, sitting there, dressed and in his right mind; and they were afraid. 16Those who had seen it told the people what had happened to the demon-possessed man—and told about the pigs as well. 17Then the people began to plead with Jesus to leave their region.

18As Jesus was getting into the boat, the man who had been demon-possessed begged to go with him. 19Jesus did not let him, but said, 'Go home to your own people and tell them how much the Lord has done for you, and how he has had mercy on you.' 20So the man went away and began to tell in the Decapolis[a] how much Jesus had done for him. And all the people were amazed.

Jesus raises a dead girl and heals a sick woman

21When Jesus had again crossed over by boat to the other side of the lake, a large crowd gathered round him while he was by the lake. 22Then one of the synagogue leaders, named Jairus, came, and when he saw Jesus, he fell at his feet. 23He pleaded earnestly with him, 'My little daughter is dying. Please come and put your hands on her so that she will be healed and live.' 24So Jesus went with him.

A large crowd followed and pressed round him. 25And a woman was there who had been subject to bleeding for twelve years. 26She had suffered a great deal under the care of many doctors and had spent all she had, yet instead of getting better she grew worse. 27When she heard about Jesus, she came up behind him in the crowd and touched his cloak, 28because she thought, 'If I just touch his clothes, I will be healed.' 29Immediately her bleeding stopped and she felt in her body that she was freed from her suffering.

30At once Jesus realised that power had gone out from him. He turned round in the crowd and asked, 'Who touched my clothes?'

31'You see the people crowding against you,' his disciples answered, 'and yet you can ask, "Who touched me?"'

32But Jesus kept looking around to see who had done it. 33Then the woman, knowing what had happened to her, came and fell at his feet and, trembling with fear, told him the whole truth. 34He said to her, 'Daughter, your faith has healed you. Go in peace and be freed from your suffering.'

35While Jesus was still speaking, some people came from the house of Jairus, the synagogue leader. 'Your daughter is dead,' they said. 'Why bother the teacher anymore?'

36Overhearing[b] what they said, Jesus told him, 'Don't be afraid; just believe.'

37He did not let anyone follow him except Peter, James and John the brother of James. 38When they came to the home of the synagogue leader, Jesus saw a commotion, with people crying and wailing loudly.

---

[a]20 That is, the Ten Cities [b]36 Or *Ignoring*

³⁹He went in and said to them, 'Why all this commotion and wailing? The child is not dead but asleep.' ⁴⁰But they laughed at him.

After he put them all out, he took the child's father and mother and the disciples who were with him, and went in where the child was. ⁴¹He took her by the hand and said to her, *'Talitha koum!'* (which means 'Little girl, I say to you, get up!'). ⁴²Immediately the girl stood up and began to walk around (she was twelve years old). At this they were completely astonished. ⁴³He gave strict orders not to let anyone know about this, and told them to give her something to eat.

A prophet without honour

6 Jesus left there and went to his home town, accompanied by his disciples. ²When the Sabbath came, he began to teach in the synagogue, and many who heard him were amazed.

'Where did this man get these things?' they asked. 'What's this wisdom that has been given him? What are these remarkable miracles he is performing? ³Isn't this the carpenter? Isn't this Mary's son and the brother of James, Joseph,[a] Judas and Simon? Aren't his sisters here with us?' And they took offence at him.

⁴Jesus said to them, 'Only in their own towns, among their relatives and in their own homes are prophets without honour.' ⁵He could not do any miracles there, except lay his hands on a few people who were ill and heal them. ⁶He was amazed at their lack of faith.

Jesus sends out the Twelve

Then Jesus went around teaching from village to village. ⁷Calling the Twelve to him, he began to send them out two by two and gave them authority over evil[b] spirits.

⁸These were his instructions: 'Take nothing for the journey except a staff—no bread, no bag, no money in your belts. ⁹Wear sandals but not an extra shirt. ¹⁰Whenever you enter a house, stay there until you leave that town. ¹¹And if any place will not welcome you or listen to you, shake the dust off your feet when you leave, as a testimony against them.'

¹²They went out and preached that people should repent. ¹³They drove out many demons and anointed with oil many people who were ill and healed them.

John the Baptist beheaded

¹⁴King Herod heard about this, for Jesus' name had become well known. Some were saying,[c] 'John the Baptist has been raised from the dead, and that is why miraculous powers are at work in him.'

¹⁵Others said, 'He is Elijah.'

And still others claimed, 'He is a prophet, like one of the prophets of long ago.'

¹⁶But when Herod heard this, he said, 'John, whom I beheaded, has been raised from the dead!'

¹⁷For Herod himself had given orders to have John arrested, and he had him bound and put in prison. He did this because of Herodias, his brother Philip's wife, whom he had married. ¹⁸For John had been saying to Herod, 'It is not lawful for you to have your brother's wife.' ¹⁹So Herodias nursed a grudge against John and wanted to kill him. But she was not able to, ²⁰because Herod feared John and protected him, knowing him to be a righteous and holy man. When Herod heard John, he was greatly puzzled[d]; yet he liked to listen to him.

²¹Finally the opportune time came. On his birthday Herod gave a banquet for his high officials and military commanders and the leading men of Galilee. ²²When the daughter of[e] Herodias came in and danced, she pleased Herod and his dinner guests.

The king said to the girl, 'Ask me for anything you want, and I'll give it to you.' ²³And he promised her with an oath, 'Whatever you ask I will give you, up to half my kingdom.'

²⁴She went out and said to her mother, 'What shall I ask for?'

'The head of John the Baptist,' she answered.

---

[a] 3 Greek *Joses*, a variant of *Joseph* [b] 7 Greek *unclean* [c] 14 Some early manuscripts *He was saying* [d] 20 Some early manuscripts *he did many things* [e] 22 Some early manuscripts *When his daughter*

Making oaths
Mark 6:26
An oath was a solemn statement that was made when someone promised to do something. Oaths were taken very seriously, especially by rulers, and people would not go back on what they had promised to do under oath.

²⁵At once the girl hurried in to the king with the request: 'I want you to give me right now the head of John the Baptist on a dish.'

²⁶The king was greatly distressed, but because of his oaths and his dinner guests, he did not want to refuse her. ²⁷So he immediately sent an executioner with orders to bring John's head. The man went, beheaded John in the prison, ²⁸and brought back his head on a dish. He presented it to the girl, and she gave it to her mother. ²⁹On hearing of this, John's disciples came and took his body and laid it in a tomb.

Jesus feeds the five thousand

³⁰The apostles gathered round Jesus and reported to him all they had done and taught. ³¹Then, because so many people were coming and going that they did not even have a chance to eat, he said to them, 'Come with me by yourselves to a quiet place and get some rest.'

³²So they went away by themselves in a boat to a solitary place. ³³But many who saw them leaving recognised them and ran on foot from all the towns and got there ahead of them. ³⁴When Jesus landed and saw a large crowd, he had compassion on them, because they were like sheep without a shepherd. So he began teaching them many things.

³⁵By this time it was late in the day, so his disciples came to him. 'This is a remote place,' they said, 'and it's already very late. ³⁶Send the people away so that they can go to the surrounding countryside and villages and buy themselves something to eat.'

³⁷But he answered, 'You give them something to eat.'

They said to him, 'That would take almost a year's wages[a]! Are we to go and spend that much on bread and give it to them to eat?'

³⁸'How many loaves do you have?' he asked. 'Go and see.'

When they found out, they said, 'Five—and two fish.'

³⁹Then Jesus told them to make all the people sit down in groups on the green grass. ⁴⁰So they sat down in groups of hundreds and fifties. ⁴¹Taking the five loaves and the two fish and looking up to heaven, he gave thanks and broke the loaves. Then he gave them to his disciples to set before the people. He also divided the two fish among them all. ⁴²They all ate and were satisfied, ⁴³and the disciples picked up twelve basketfuls of broken pieces of bread and fish. ⁴⁴The number of the men who had eaten was five thousand.

Jesus walks on the water

⁴⁵Immediately Jesus made his disciples get into the boat and go on ahead of him to Bethsaida, while he dismissed the crowd. ⁴⁶After leaving them, he went up on a mountainside to pray.

⁴⁷When evening came, the boat was in the middle of the lake, and he was alone on land. ⁴⁸He saw the disciples straining at the oars, because the wind was against them. Shortly before dawn he went out to them, walking on the lake. He was about to pass by them, ⁴⁹but when they saw him walking on the lake, they thought he was a ghost. They cried out, ⁵⁰because they all saw him and were terrified.

Immediately he spoke to them and said, 'Take courage! It is I. Don't be afraid.' ⁵¹Then he climbed into the boat with them, and the wind died down. They were completely amazed, ⁵²for they had not

---

[a] 37 Greek *take two hundred denarii*

understood about the loaves; their hearts were hardened.

53When they had crossed over, they landed at Gennesaret and anchored there. 54As soon as they got out of the boat, people recognised Jesus. 55They ran throughout that whole region and carried those who were ill on mats to wherever they heard he was. 56And wherever he went—into villages, towns or countryside—they placed those who were ill in the market-places. They begged him to let them touch even the edge of his cloak, and all who touched him were healed.

That which defiles

7 The Pharisees and some of the teachers of the law who had come from Jerusalem gathered round Jesus 2and saw some of his disciples eating food with hands that were defiled, that is, unwashed. 3(The Pharisees and all the Jews do not eat unless they give their hands a ceremonial washing, holding to the tradition of the elders. 4When they come from the market-place they do not eat unless they wash. And they observe many other traditions, such as the washing of cups, pitchers and kettles.*ᵃ*)

5So the Pharisees and teachers of the law asked Jesus, 'Why don't your disciples live according to the tradition of the elders instead of eating their food with defiled hands?'

6He replied, 'Isaiah was right when he prophesied about you hypocrites; as it is written:

'"These people honour me with their lips,
    but their hearts are far from me.
7They worship me in vain;
    their teachings are merely human
      rules."*ᵇ*

8You have let go of the commands of God and are holding on to human traditions.'

9And he continued, 'You have a fine way of setting aside the commands of God in order to observe*ᶜ* your own traditions! 10For Moses said, "Honour your father and mother,"*ᵈ* and, "Anyone who curses their father or mother is to be put to death."*ᵉ* 11But you say that if anyone declares that what might have been used to help their father or mother is Corban (that is, devoted to God)— 12then you no longer let them do anything for their father or mother. 13Thus you nullify the word of God by your tradition that you have handed down. And you do many things like that.'

14Again Jesus called the crowd to him and said, 'Listen to me, everyone, and understand this. 15(16)Nothing outside you can defile you by going into you. Rather, it is what comes out of you that defiles you.'

17After he had left the crowd and entered the house, his disciples asked him about this parable. 18'Are you so dull?' he asked. 'Don't you see that nothing that enters you from the outside can defile you? 19For it doesn't go into your heart but into your stomach, and then out of your body.' (In saying this, Jesus declared all foods clean.)

20He went on: 'What comes out of you is what defiles you. 21For from within, out of your hearts, come evil thoughts, sexual immorality, theft, murder, 22adultery, greed, malice, deceit, lewdness, envy, slander, arrogance and folly. 23All these evils come from inside and defile you.'

Jesus honours a Syro-Phoenician woman's faith

24Jesus left that place and went to the vicinity of Tyre.*ᶠ* He entered a house and did not want anyone to know it; yet he could not keep his presence secret. 25In fact, as soon as she heard about him, a woman whose little daughter was possessed by an evil*ᵍ* spirit came and fell at his feet. 26The woman was a Greek, born in Syrian Phoenicia. She begged Jesus to drive the demon out of her daughter.

27'First let the children eat all they want,' he told her, 'for it is not right to take the children's bread and toss it to the dogs.'

28'Lord,' she replied, 'even the dogs under the table eat the children's crumbs.'

29Then he told her, 'For such a reply, you may go; the demon has left your daughter.'

---

*ᵃ*4 Some early manuscripts *pitchers, kettles and dining couches* *ᵇ*6,7 Isaiah 29:13 *ᶜ*9 Some manuscripts *set up* *ᵈ*10 Exodus 20:12; Deut. 5:16 *ᵉ*10 Exodus 21:17; Lev. 20:9 *ᶠ*24 Many early manuscripts *Tyre and Sidon* *ᵍ*25 Greek *unclean*

30 She went home and found her child lying on the bed, and the demon gone.

Jesus heals a deaf and mute man

31 Then Jesus left the vicinity of Tyre and went through Sidon, down to the Sea of Galilee and into the region of the Decapolis.[a] 32 There some people brought to him a man who was deaf and could hardly talk, and they begged Jesus to place his hand on him.

33 After he took him aside, away from the crowd, Jesus put his fingers into the man's ears. Then he spat and touched the man's tongue. 34 He looked up to heaven and with a deep sigh said to him, *'Ephphatha!'* (which means 'Be opened!'). 35 At this, the man's ears were opened, his tongue was loosed and he began to speak plainly.

36 Jesus commanded them not to tell anyone. But the more he did so, the more they kept talking about it. 37 People were overwhelmed with amazement. 'He has done everything well,' they said. 'He even makes the deaf hear and the mute speak.'

Jesus feeds the four thousand

8 During those days another large crowd gathered. Since they had nothing to eat, Jesus called his disciples to him and said, 2 'I have compassion for these people; they have already been with me three days and have nothing to eat. 3 If I send them home hungry, they will collapse on the way, because some of them have come a long distance.'

4 His disciples answered, 'But where in this remote place can anyone get enough bread to feed them?'

5 'How many loaves do you have?' Jesus asked.

'Seven,' they replied.

6 He told the crowd to sit down on the ground. When he had taken the seven loaves and given thanks, he broke them and gave them to his disciples to set before the people, and they did so. 7 They had a few small fish as well; he gave thanks for them also and told the disciples to distribute them. 8 The people ate and were satisfied. Afterwards the disciples picked up seven basketfuls of broken pieces that were left over. 9 About four thousand were present. And having sent them away, 10 he got into the boat with his disciples and went to the region of Dalmanutha.

11 The Pharisees came and began to question Jesus. To test him, they asked him for a sign from heaven. 12 He sighed deeply and said, 'Why does this generation ask for a sign? Truly I tell you, no sign will be given to it.' 13 Then he left them, got back into the boat and crossed to the other side.

The yeast of the Pharisees and Herod

14 The disciples had forgotten to bring bread, except for one loaf they had with them in the boat. 15 'Be careful,' Jesus warned them. 'Watch out for the yeast of the Pharisees and that of Herod.'

16 They discussed this with one another and said, 'It is because we have no bread.'

17 Aware of their discussion, Jesus asked them: 'Why are you talking about having no bread? Do you still not see or understand? Are your hearts hardened? 18 Do you have eyes but fail to see, and ears but fail to hear? And don't you remember? 19 When I broke the five loaves for the five thousand, how many basketfuls of pieces did you pick up?'

'Twelve,' they replied.

People and Places

Christ
Mark 8:29

Christ was the Greek word for the Messiah or 'anointed one'. The Jews were looking forward to a Messiah who would defeat their enemies and then rule over them, bringing peace and prosperity. Priests, kings and prophets were anointed with oil in the Old Testament to show they were set apart for their important work. Jesus was anointed with the Holy Spirit in a unique way for the work he came to do.

---

[a] 31 That is, the Ten Cities

²⁰'And when I broke the seven loaves for the four thousand, how many basketfuls of pieces did you pick up?'

They answered, 'Seven.'

²¹He said to them, 'Do you still not understand?'

Jesus heals a blind man at Bethsaida

²²They came to Bethsaida, and some people brought a blind man and begged Jesus to touch him. ²³He took the blind man by the hand and led him outside the village. When he had spat on the man's eyes and put his hands on him, Jesus asked, 'Do you see anything?'

²⁴He looked up and said, 'I see people; they look like trees walking around.'

²⁵Once more Jesus put his hands on the man's eyes. Then his eyes were opened, his sight was restored, and he saw everything clearly. ²⁶Jesus sent him home, saying, 'Don't even go into^a the village.'

Peter declares that Jesus is the Messiah

²⁷Jesus and his disciples went on to the villages around Caesarea Philippi. On the way he asked them, 'Who do people say I am?'

²⁸They replied, 'Some say John the Baptist; others say Elijah; and still others, one of the prophets.'

²⁹'But what about you?' he asked. 'Who do you say I am?'

Peter answered, 'You are the Messiah.'

³⁰Jesus warned them not to tell anyone about him.

Jesus predicts his death

³¹He then began to teach them that the Son of Man must suffer many things and be rejected by the elders, the chief priests and the teachers of the law, and that he must be killed and after three days rise again. ³²He spoke plainly about this, and Peter took him aside and began to rebuke him.

³³But when Jesus turned and looked at his disciples, he rebuked Peter. 'Get behind me, Satan!' he said. 'You do not have in mind the concerns of God, but merely human concerns.'

The way of the cross

³⁴Then he called the crowd to him along with his disciples and said: 'Whoever wants to be my disciple must deny themselves and take up their cross and follow me. ³⁵For whoever wants to save their life^b will lose it, but whoever loses their life for me and for the gospel will save it. ³⁶What good is it for you to gain the whole world, yet forfeit your soul? ³⁷Or what can you give in exchange for your soul? ³⁸If any of you are ashamed of me and my words in this adulterous and sinful generation, the Son of Man will be ashamed of you when he comes in his Father's glory with the holy angels.'

9 And he said to them, 'Truly I tell you, some who are standing here will not taste death before they see that the kingdom of God has come with power.'

The transfiguration

²After six days Jesus took Peter, James and John with him and led them up a high mountain, where they were all alone. There he was transfigured before them. ³His clothes became dazzling white, whiter than anyone in the world could bleach them. ⁴And there appeared before them Elijah and Moses, who were talking with Jesus.

⁵Peter said to Jesus, 'Rabbi, it is good for us to be here. Let us put up three shelters— one for you, one for Moses and one for Elijah.' ⁶(He did not know what to say, they were so frightened.)

⁷Then a cloud appeared and covered them, and a voice came from the cloud: 'This is my Son, whom I love. Listen to him!'

⁸Suddenly, when they looked around, they no longer saw anyone with them except Jesus.

⁹As they were coming down the mountain, Jesus gave them orders not to tell anyone what they had seen until the Son of Man had risen from the dead. ¹⁰They kept the matter to themselves, discussing what 'rising from the dead' meant.

¹¹And they asked him, 'Why do the teachers of the law say that Elijah must come first?'

---

^{a} 26 Some manuscripts *go and tell anyone in* ^{b} 35 The Greek word means either *life* or *soul*; also in verses 36 and 37.

Rabbi
Mark 9:5
The word rabbi is Hebrew for 'teacher', and it's a title of honour and respect. The rabbi was normally the person who taught the law, so when the disciples call Jesus 'Rabbi' they are likening him to other preachers, who often travelled around teaching people as they went.

12 Jesus replied, 'To be sure, Elijah does come first, and restores all things. Why then is it written that the Son of Man must suffer much and be rejected? 13 But I tell you, Elijah has come, and they have done to him everything they wished, just as it is written about him.'

Jesus heals a boy possessed by an evil spirit

14 When they came to the other disciples, they saw a large crowd around them and the teachers of the law arguing with them. 15 As soon as all the people saw Jesus, they were overwhelmed with wonder and ran to greet him.

16 'What are you arguing with them about?' he asked.

17 A man in the crowd answered, 'Teacher, I brought you my son, who is possessed by a spirit that has robbed him of speech. 18 Whenever it seizes him, it throws him to the ground. He foams at the mouth, gnashes his teeth and becomes rigid. I asked your disciples to drive out the spirit, but they could not.'

19 'You unbelieving generation,' Jesus replied, 'how long shall I stay with you? How long shall I put up with you? Bring the boy to me.'

20 So they brought him. When the spirit saw Jesus, it immediately threw the boy into a convulsion. He fell to the ground and rolled around, foaming at the mouth.

21 Jesus asked the boy's father, 'How long has he been like this?'

'From childhood,' he answered. 22 'It has often thrown him into fire or water to kill him. But if you can do anything, take pity on us and help us.'

23 ' "If you can"?' said Jesus. 'Everything is possible for one who believes.'

24 Immediately the boy's father exclaimed, 'I do believe; help me overcome my unbelief!'

25 When Jesus saw that a crowd was running to the scene, he rebuked the evil[a] spirit. 'You deaf and mute spirit,' he said, 'I command you, come out of him and never enter him again.'

26 The spirit shrieked, convulsed him violently and came out. The boy looked so much like a corpse that many said, 'He's dead.' 27 But Jesus took him by the hand and lifted him to his feet, and he stood up.

28 After Jesus had gone indoors, his disciples asked him privately, 'Why couldn't we drive it out?'

29 He replied, 'This kind can come out only by prayer.[b]'

Jesus predicts his death a second time

30 They left that place and passed through Galilee. Jesus did not want anyone to know where they were, 31 because he was teaching his disciples. He said to them, 'The Son of Man is going to be delivered over to human hands. He will be killed, and after three days he will rise.' 32 But they did not understand what he meant and were afraid to ask him about it.

33 They came to Capernaum. When he was in the house, he asked them, 'What were you arguing about on the road?' 34 But they kept quiet because on the way they had argued about who was the greatest.

35 Sitting down, Jesus called the Twelve and said, 'Anyone who wants to be first must be the very last, and the servant of all.'

36 He took a little child whom he placed among them. Taking the child in his arms, he said to them, 37 'Whoever welcomes one of these little children in my name welcomes me; and whoever welcomes me does not welcome me but the one who sent me.'

[a] 25 Greek *unclean* [b] 29 Some manuscripts *prayer and fasting*

Whoever is not against us is for us

38'Teacher,' said John, 'we saw someone driving out demons in your name and we told him to stop, because he was not one of us.'

39'Do not stop him,' Jesus said. 'No-one who does a miracle in my name can in the next moment say anything bad about me, 40for whoever is not against us is for us. 41Truly I tell you, anyone who gives you a cup of water in my name because you belong to the Messiah will certainly be rewarded.

Causing to stumble

42'If anyone causes one of these little ones—those who believe in me—to stumble, it would be better for them if a large millstone were hung round their neck and they were thrown into the sea. 43(44)If your hand causes you to stumble, cut it off. It is better for you to enter life maimed than with two hands to go into hell, where the fire never goes out. 45(46)And if your foot causes you to stumble, cut it off. It is better for you to enter life crippled than to have two feet and be thrown into hell. 47And if your eye causes you to stumble, pluck it out. It is better for you to enter the kingdom of God with one eye than to have two eyes and be thrown into hell, 48where

' "their worm does not die,
 and the fire is not quenched." *a*

49Everyone will be salted with fire.

50'Salt is good, but if it loses its saltiness, how can you make it salty again? Have salt in yourselves, and be at peace with each other.'

Divorce

10 Jesus then left that place and went into the region of Judea and across the Jordan. Again crowds of people came to him, and as was his custom, he taught them.

2Some Pharisees came and tested him by asking, 'Is it lawful for a man to divorce his wife?'

3'What did Moses command you?' he replied.

4They said, 'Moses permitted a man to write a certificate of divorce and send her away.'

5'It was because your hearts were hard that Moses wrote you this law,' Jesus replied. 6'But at the beginning of creation God "made them male and female". *b* 7"For this reason a man will leave his father and mother and be united to his wife, *c* 8and the two will become one flesh." *d* So they are no longer two, but one. 9Therefore what God has joined together, let no-one separate.'

10When they were in the house again, the disciples asked Jesus about this. 11He answered, 'Anyone who divorces his wife and marries another woman commits adultery against her. 12And if she divorces her husband and marries another man, she commits adultery.'

The little children and Jesus

13People were bringing little children to Jesus for him to place his hands on them, but the disciples rebuked them. 14When Jesus saw this, he was indignant. He said to them, 'Let the little children come to me, and do not hinder them, for the kingdom of God belongs to such as these. 15Truly I tell you, anyone who will not receive the kingdom of God like a little child will never enter it.' 16And he took the children in his arms, placed his hands on them and blessed them.

The rich and the kingdom of God

17As Jesus started on his way, a man ran up to him and fell on his knees before him. 'Good teacher,' he asked, 'what must I do to inherit eternal life?'

18'Why do you call me good?' Jesus answered. 'No-one is good—except God alone. 19You know the commandments: "You shall not murder, you shall not commit adultery, you shall not steal, you shall not give false testimony, you shall not defraud, honour your father and mother." *e* '

---

a 48 Isaiah 66:24   *b* 6 Gen. 1:27   *c* 7 Some early manuscripts do not have *and be united to his wife.*   *d* 8 Gen. 2:24
e 19 Exodus 20:12-16; Deut. 5:16-20

making Connections

The camel and the eye of the needle
Mark 10:25

Pause for a moment and picture a camel, loaded up with goods and baggage, next to a needle. Can you imagine the look on the camel's face at the suggestion that it should go through the tiny eye of the needle? This great figure of speech from Jesus would no doubt have made people laugh, and illustrated his point very well.

20'Teacher,' he declared, 'all these I have kept since I was a boy.'

21Jesus looked at him and loved him. 'One thing you lack,' he said. 'Go, sell everything you have and give to the poor, and you will have treasure in heaven. Then come, follow me.'

22At this the man's face fell. He went away sad, because he had great wealth.

23Jesus looked round and said to his disciples, 'How hard it is for the rich to enter the kingdom of God!'

24The disciples were amazed at his words. But Jesus said again, 'Children, how hard it is[a] to enter the kingdom of God! 25It is easier for a camel to go through the eye of a needle than for the rich to enter the kingdom of God.'

26The disciples were even more amazed, and said to each other, 'Who then can be saved?'

27Jesus looked at them and said, 'With human beings this is impossible, but not with God; all things are possible with God.'

28Then Peter spoke up, 'We have left everything to follow you!'

29'Truly I tell you,' Jesus replied, 'no-one who has left home or brothers or sisters or mother or father or children or fields for me and the gospel 30will fail to receive a hundred times as much in this present age: homes, brothers, sisters, mothers, children and fields—along with persecutions—and in the age to come eternal life. 31But many who are first will be last, and the last first.'

Jesus predicts his death a third time

32They were on their way up to Jerusalem, with Jesus leading the way, and the disciples were astonished, while those who followed were afraid. Again he took the Twelve aside and told them what was going to happen to him. 33'We are going up to Jerusalem,' he said, 'and the Son of Man will be delivered over to the chief priests and the teachers of the law. They will condemn him to death and will hand him over to the Gentiles, 34who will mock him and spit on him, flog him and kill him. Three days later he will rise.'

The request of James and John

35Then James and John, the sons of Zebedee, came to him. 'Teacher,' they said, 'we want you to do for us whatever we ask.'

36'What do you want me to do for you?' he asked.

37They replied, 'Let one of us sit at your right and the other at your left in your glory.'

38'You don't know what you are asking,' Jesus said. 'Can you drink the cup I drink or be baptised with the baptism I am baptised with?'

39'We can,' they answered.

Jesus said to them, 'You will drink the cup I drink and be baptised with the baptism I am baptised with, 40but to sit at my right or left is not for me to grant. These places belong to those for whom they have been prepared.'

41When the ten heard about this, they became indignant with James and John. 42Jesus called them together and said, 'You know that those who are regarded as rulers of the Gentiles lord it over them, and their high officials exercise authority over them. 43Not so with you. Instead, whoever wants to become great among you must be your

---

[a] 24 Some manuscripts *is for those who trust in riches*

servant, ⁴⁴and whoever wants to be first must be slave of all. ⁴⁵For even the Son of Man did not come to be served, but to serve, and to give his life as a ransom for many.'

Blind Bartimaeus receives his sight

⁴⁶Then they came to Jericho. As Jesus and his disciples, together with a large crowd, were leaving the city, a blind man, Bartimaeus (which means 'son of Timaeus'), was sitting by the roadside begging. ⁴⁷When he heard that it was Jesus of Nazareth, he began to shout, 'Jesus, Son of David, have mercy on me!'

⁴⁸Many rebuked him and told him to be quiet, but he shouted all the more, 'Son of David, have mercy on me!'

⁴⁹Jesus stopped and said, 'Call him.'

So they called to the blind man, 'Cheer up! On your feet! He's calling you.' ⁵⁰Throwing his cloak aside, he jumped to his feet and came to Jesus.

⁵¹'What do you want me to do for you?' Jesus asked him.

The blind man said, 'Rabbi, I want to see.'

⁵²'Go,' said Jesus, 'your faith has healed you.' Immediately he received his sight and followed Jesus along the road.

Jesus comes to Jerusalem as king

11 As they approached Jerusalem and came to Bethphage and Bethany at the Mount of Olives, Jesus sent two of his disciples, ²saying to them, 'Go to the village ahead of you, and just as you enter it, you will find a colt tied there, which no-one has ever ridden. Untie it and bring it here. ³If anyone asks you, "Why are you doing this?" say, "The Lord needs it and will send it back here shortly."'

⁴They went and found a colt outside in the street, tied at a doorway. As they untied it, ⁵some people standing there asked, 'What are you doing, untying that colt?' ⁶They answered as Jesus had told them to, and the people let them go. ⁷When they brought the colt to Jesus and threw their cloaks over it, he sat on it. ⁸Many people spread their cloaks on the road, while others spread branches they had cut in the fields. ⁹Those who went ahead and those who followed shouted,

'Hosanna!ᵃ'

'Blessed is he who comes in the name of the Lord!'ᵇ

¹⁰'Blessed is the coming kingdom of our father David!'

'Hosanna in the highest heaven!'

¹¹Jesus entered Jerusalem and went into the temple courts. He looked around at everything, but since it was already late, he went out to Bethany with the Twelve.

Jesus curses a fig-tree and clears the temple courts

¹²The next day as they were leaving Bethany, Jesus was hungry. ¹³Seeing in the distance a fig-tree in leaf, he went to find out if it had any fruit. When he reached it, he found nothing but leaves, because it was not the season for figs. ¹⁴Then he said to the tree, 'May no-one ever eat fruit from you again.' And his disciples heard him say it.

¹⁵On reaching Jerusalem, Jesus entered the temple courts and began driving out those who were buying and selling there. He

Money changers
Mark 11:15
People came to Jerusalem for special festivals like the Passover. As part of their worship they would sacrifice animals, so many traders set up animal pens in the outer courts of the temple. People also needed a special kind of money to pay their temple tax, which is why the money changers also did good business.

ᵃ9 A Hebrew expression meaning 'Save!' which became an exclamation of praise; also in verse 10   ᵇ9 Psalm 118:25,26 overturned the tables of the money-changers and the benches of those selling doves, 16and would not allow anyone to carry merchandise through the temple courts. 17And as he taught them, he said, 'Is it not written: "My house will be called a house of prayer for all nations"[a]? But you have made it "a den of robbers".[b]'

18The chief priests and the teachers of the law heard this and began looking for a way to kill him, for they feared him, because the whole crowd was amazed at his teaching.

19When evening came, Jesus and his disciples[c] went out of the city.

20In the morning, as they went along, they saw the fig-tree withered from the roots. 21Peter remembered and said to Jesus, 'Rabbi, look! The fig-tree you cursed has withered!'

22'Have faith in God,' Jesus answered. 23'Truly[d] I tell you, if you say to this mountain, "Go, throw yourself into the sea," and do not doubt in your heart but believe that what you say will happen, it will be done for you. 24Therefore I tell you, whatever you ask for in prayer, believe that you have received it, and it will be yours. 25(26)And when you stand praying, if you hold anything against anyone, forgive them, so that your Father in heaven may forgive you your sins.'

The authority of Jesus questioned

27They arrived again in Jerusalem, and while Jesus was walking in the temple courts, the chief priests, the teachers of the law and the elders came to him. 28'By what authority are you doing these things?' they asked. 'And who gave you authority to do this?'

29Jesus replied, 'I will ask you one question. Answer me, and I will tell you by what authority I am doing these things. 30John's baptism—was it from heaven, or of human origin? Tell me!'

31They discussed it among themselves and said, 'If we say, "From heaven", he will ask, "Then why didn't you believe him?" 32But if we say, "Of human origin"....' (They feared the people, for everyone held that John really was a prophet.)

33So they answered Jesus, 'We don't know.'

Jesus said, 'Neither will I tell you by what authority I am doing these things.'

The parable of the tenants

12 Jesus then began to speak to them in parables: 'A man planted a vineyard. He put a wall round it, dug a pit for the winepress and built a watchtower. Then he rented the vineyard to some farmers and moved to another place. 2At harvest time he sent a servant to the tenants to collect from them some of the fruit of the vineyard. 3But they seized him, beat him and sent him away empty-handed. 4Then he sent another servant to them; they struck this man on the head and treated him shamefully. 5He sent still another, and that one they killed. He sent many others; some of them they beat, others they killed.

6'He had one left to send, a son, whom he loved. He sent him last of all, saying, "They will respect my son."

7'But the tenants said to one another, "This is the heir. Come, let's kill him, and the inheritance will be ours." 8So they took him and killed him, and threw him out of the vineyard.

9'What then will the owner of the vineyard do? He will come and kill those tenants and give the vineyard to others. 10Haven't you read this passage of Scripture:

'"The stone the builders rejected
  has become the cornerstone;
11the Lord has done this,
  and it is marvellous in our eyes"[e]?'

12Then the chief priests, the teachers of the law and the elders looked for a way to arrest him because they knew he had spoken the parable against them. But they were afraid of the crowd; so they left him and went away.

Paying the poll-tax to Caesar

13Later they sent some of the Pharisees and Herodians to Jesus to catch him in his words. 14They came to him and said,

---

[a] 17 Isaiah 56:7   [b] 17 Jer. 7:11   [c] 19 Some early manuscripts *came, Jesus*   [d] 22,23 Some early manuscripts *'If you have faith in God,' Jesus answered, 23'truly*   [e] 11 Psalm 118:22,23

Sign of the times

Roman occupation
Mark 12:16

The Roman Empire controlled most of the known world during New Testament times. Judea, the area where Jesus lived, became subject to Rome in 63 BC, and the Roman occupation continued for the whole of New Testament times. The Jews were allowed to practice their own religion and build synagogues, and they had some limited power over their own affairs (Mark 14:36).

'Teacher, we know that you are a man of integrity. You aren't swayed by others, because you pay no attention to who they are; but you teach the way of God in accordance with the truth. Is it right to pay the poll-tax[a] to Caesar or not? 15Should we pay or shouldn't we?'

But Jesus knew their hypocrisy. 'Why are you trying to trap me?' he asked. 'Bring me a denarius and let me look at it.' 16They brought the coin, and he asked them, 'Whose image is this? And whose inscription?'

'Caesar's,' they replied.

17Then Jesus said to them, 'Give back to Caesar what is Caesar's and to God what is God's.'

And they were amazed at him.

Marriage at the resurrection

18Then the Sadducees, who say there is no resurrection, came to him with a question. 19'Teacher,' they said, 'Moses wrote for us that if a man's brother dies and leaves a wife but no children, the man must marry the widow and raise up offspring for his brother. 20Now there were seven brothers. The first one married and died without leaving any children. 21The second one married the widow, but he also died, leaving no child. It was the same with the third. 22In fact, none of the seven left any children. Last of all, the woman died too. 23At the resurrection[b] whose wife will she be, since the seven were married to her?'

24Jesus replied, 'Are you not in error because you do not know the Scriptures or the power of God? 25When the dead rise, they will neither marry nor be given in marriage; they will be like the angels in heaven. 26Now about the dead rising—have you not read in the Book of Moses, in the account of the burning bush, how God said to him, "I am the God of Abraham, the God of Isaac, and the God of Jacob"[c]? 27He is not the God of the dead, but of the living. You are badly mistaken!'

The greatest commandment

28One of the teachers of the law came and heard them debating. Noticing that Jesus had given them a good answer, he asked him, 'Of all the commandments, which is the most important?'

29'The most important one,' answered Jesus, 'is this: "Hear, O Israel: the Lord our God, the Lord is one.[d] 30Love the Lord your God with all your heart and with all your soul and with all your mind and with all your strength."[e] 31The second is this: "Love your neighbour as yourself."[f] There is no commandment greater than these.'

32'Well said, teacher,' the man replied. 'You are right in saying that God is one and there is no other but him. 33To love him with all your heart, with all your understanding and with all your strength, and to love your neighbour as yourself is more important than all burnt offerings and sacrifices.'

34When Jesus saw that he had answered wisely, he said to him, 'You are not far from the kingdom of God.' And from then on no-one dared ask him any more questions.

---

[a] 14 The poll-tax was a special tax levied on subject peoples, not on Roman citizens. [b] 23 Some manuscripts *resurrection, when people rise from the dead,* [c] 26 Exodus 3:6 [d] 29 Or *the Lord our God is one Lord* [e] 30 Deut. 6:4,5 [f] 31 Lev. 19:18

Whose son is the Messiah?

35 While Jesus was teaching in the temple courts, he asked, 'Why do the teachers of the law say that the Messiah is the son of David? 36 David himself, speaking by the Holy Spirit, declared:

'"The Lord said to my Lord:
'Sit at my right hand
until I put your enemies
under your feet.'"*a*

37 David himself calls him "Lord". How then can he be his son?'

The large crowd listened to him with delight.

Warning against the teachers of the law

38 As he taught, Jesus said, 'Watch out for the teachers of the law. They like to walk around in flowing robes and be greeted with respect in the market-places, 39 and have the most important seats in the synagogues and the places of honour at banquets. 40 They devour widows' houses and for a show make lengthy prayers. These men will be punished most severely.'

The widow's offering

41 Jesus sat down opposite the place where the offerings were put and watched the crowd putting their money into the temple treasury. Many rich people threw in large amounts. 42 But a poor widow came and put in two very small copper coins, worth only a fraction of a penny.

43 Calling his disciples to him, Jesus said, 'Truly I tell you, this poor widow has put more into the treasury than all the others. 44 They all gave out of their wealth; but she, out of her poverty, put in everything—all she had to live on.'

The destruction of the temple and signs of the end times

13 As Jesus was leaving the temple, one of his disciples said to him, 'Look, Teacher! What massive stones! What magnificent buildings!'

2 'Do you see all these great buildings?' replied Jesus. 'Not one stone here will be left on another; every one will be thrown down.'

3 As Jesus was sitting on the Mount of Olives opposite the temple, Peter, James, John and Andrew asked him privately, 4 'Tell us, when will these things happen? And what will be the sign that they are all about to be fulfilled?'

5 Jesus said to them: 'Watch out that no-one deceives you. 6 Many will come in my name, claiming, "I am he," and will deceive many. 7 When you hear of wars and rumours of wars, do not be alarmed. Such things must happen, but the end is still to come. 8 Nation will rise against nation, and kingdom against kingdom. There will be earthquakes in various places, and famines. These are the beginning of birth-pains.

9 'You must be on your guard. You will be handed over to the local councils and flogged in the synagogues. On account of me you will stand before governors and kings as witnesses to them. 10 And the gospel must first be preached to all nations. 11 Whenever you are arrested and brought to trial, do not worry beforehand about what to say. Just say whatever is given you at the time, for it is not you speaking, but the Holy Spirit.

12 'Brother will betray brother to death, and a father his child. Children will rebel against their parents and have them put to death. 13 Everyone will hate you because of me, but those who stand firm to the end will be saved.

14 'When you see "the abomination that causes desolation"*b* standing where it*c* does not belong—let the reader understand—then let those who are in Judea flee to the mountains. 15 Let no-one on the housetop go down or enter the house to take anything out. 16 Let no-one in the field go back to get their cloak. 17 How dreadful it will be in those days for pregnant women and nursing mothers! 18 Pray that this will not take place in winter, 19 because those will be days of distress unequalled from the beginning, when God created the world, until now—and never to be equalled again.

20 'If the Lord had not cut short those days, no-one would survive. But for the sake of the elect, whom he has chosen, he has shortened them. 21 At that time if anyone

---

a 36 Psalm 110:1 *b* 14 Daniel 9:27; 11:31; 12:11 *c* 14 Or *he* says to you, "Look, here is the Messiah!" or, "Look, there he is!" do not believe it. 22For false messiahs and false prophets will appear and perform signs and wonders to deceive, if possible, even the elect. 23So be on your guard; I have told you everything in advance.

24'But in those days, following that distress,

' "the sun will be darkened,
 and the moon will not give its light;
25the stars will fall from the sky,
 and the heavenly bodies will be shaken." [a]

26'At that time people will see the Son of Man coming in clouds with great power and glory. 27And he will send his angels and gather his elect from the four winds, from the ends of the earth to the ends of the heavens.

28'Now learn this lesson from the fig-tree: as soon as its twigs get tender and its leaves come out, you know that summer is near. 29Even so, when you see these things happening, you know that it[b] is near, right at the door. 30Truly I tell you, this generation will certainly not pass away until all these things have happened. 31Heaven and earth will pass away, but my words will never pass away.

The day and hour unknown

32'But about that day or hour no-one knows, not even the angels in heaven, nor the Son, but only the Father. 33Be on guard! Be alert[c]! You do not know when that time will come. 34It's like a man going away: he leaves his house and puts his servants in charge, each with an assigned task, and tells the one at the door to keep watch.

35'Therefore keep watch because you do not know when the owner of the house will come back—whether in the evening, or at midnight, or when the cock crows, or at dawn. 36If he comes suddenly, do not let him find you sleeping. 37What I say to you, I say to everyone: "Watch!" '

Jesus anointed at Bethany

14 Now the Passover and the Feast of Unleavened Bread were only two days away, and the chief priests and the teachers of the law were looking for some sly way to arrest Jesus and kill him. 2'But not during the Feast,' they said, 'or the people may riot.'

3While he was in Bethany, reclining at the table in the home of Simon the Leper, a woman came with an alabaster jar of very expensive perfume, made of pure nard. She broke the jar and poured the perfume on his head.

4Some of those present were saying indignantly to one another, 'Why this waste of perfume? 5It could have been sold for more than a year's wages[d] and the money given to the poor.' And they rebuked her harshly.

6'Leave her alone,' said Jesus. 'Why are you bothering her? She has done a beautiful thing to me. 7The poor you will always have with you,[e] and you can help them any time you want. But you will not always have me. 8She did what she could. She poured perfume on my body beforehand to prepare for my burial. 9Truly I tell you, wherever the gospel is preached throughout the world, what she has done will also be told, in memory of her.'

10Then Judas Iscariot, one of the Twelve, went to the chief priests to betray Jesus to them. 11They were delighted to hear this and promised to give him money. So he watched for an opportunity to hand him over.

The Last Supper

12On the first day of the Feast of Unleavened Bread, when it was customary to sacrifice the Passover lamb, Jesus' disciples asked him, 'Where do you want us to go and make preparations for you to eat the Passover?'

13So he sent two of his disciples, telling them, 'Go into the city, and a man carrying a jar of water will meet you. Follow him. 14Say to the owner of the house he enters, "The Teacher asks: where is my guest room, where I may eat the Passover with my

---

[a] 25 Isaiah 13:10; 34:4 [b] 29 Or he [c] 33 Some manuscripts alert and pray [d] 5 Greek than three hundred denarii [e] 7 See Deut. 15:11.

IN OTHER WORDS

The Last Supper
Mark 14:12
In the last days of his life, Jesus ate a Passover meal with his disciples and encouraged them to remember him and his death every time they had the meal. Also known as the Lord's Supper, this is what we now call Holy Communion or the Eucharist.

disciples?" ¹⁵He will show you a large room upstairs, furnished and ready. Make preparations for us there.'

¹⁶The disciples left, went into the city and found things just as Jesus had told them. So they prepared the Passover.

¹⁷When evening came, Jesus arrived with the Twelve. ¹⁸While they were reclining at the table eating, he said, 'Truly I tell you, one of you will betray me—one who is eating with me.'

¹⁹They were saddened, and one by one they said to him, 'Surely not I?'

²⁰'It is one of the Twelve,' he replied, 'one who dips bread into the bowl with me. ²¹The Son of Man will go just as it is written about him. But woe to that man who betrays the Son of Man! It would be better for him if he had not been born.'

²²While they were eating, Jesus took bread, and when he had given thanks, he broke it and gave it to his disciples, saying, 'Take it; this is my body.'

²³Then he took the cup, and when he had given thanks, he gave it to them, and they all drank from it.

²⁴'This is my blood of the^a covenant, which is poured out for many,' he said to them. ²⁵'Truly I tell you, I will not drink again of the fruit of the vine until that day when I drink it new in the kingdom of God.'

²⁶When they had sung a hymn, they went out to the Mount of Olives.

Jesus predicts Peter's denial

²⁷'You will all fall away,' Jesus told them, 'for it is written:

'"I will strike the shepherd,
and the sheep will be scattered."^{b}

²⁸But after I have risen, I will go ahead of you into Galilee.'

²⁹Peter declared, 'Even if all fall away, I will not.'

³⁰'Truly I tell you,' Jesus answered, 'today—yes, tonight—before the cock crows twice^c you yourself will disown me three times.'

³¹But Peter insisted emphatically, 'Even if I have to die with you, I will never disown you.' And all the others said the same.

Gethsemane

³²They went to a place called Gethsemane, and Jesus said to his disciples, 'Sit here while I pray.' ³³He took Peter, James and John along with him, and he began to be deeply distressed and troubled. ³⁴'My soul is overwhelmed with sorrow to the point of death,' he said to them. 'Stay here and keep watch.'

³⁵Going a little farther, he fell to the ground and prayed that if possible the hour might pass from him. ³⁶'Abba,^{d} Father,' he said, 'everything is possible for you. Take this cup from me. Yet not what I will, but what you will.'

³⁷Then he returned to his disciples and found them sleeping. 'Simon,' he said to Peter, 'are you asleep? Could you not keep watch for one hour? ³⁸Watch and pray so that you will not fall into temptation. The spirit is willing, but the flesh is weak.'

³⁹Once more he went away and prayed the same thing. ⁴⁰When he came back, he again found them sleeping, because their eyes were heavy. They did not know what to say to him.

⁴¹Returning the third time, he said to them, 'Are you still sleeping and resting? Enough! The hour has come. Look, the Son of Man is delivered into the hands of sinners. ⁴²Rise! Let us go! Here comes my betrayer!'

---

^{a}24 Some manuscripts *the new* ^{b}27 Zech. 13:7 ^{c}30 Some early manuscripts do not have *twice*. ^{d}36 Aramaic for *Father*

IN OTHER WORDS

Abba
Mark 14:36
Aramaic was the common language spoken in Israel during Jesus' time, and Abba means 'Daddy' in Aramaic. It shows how close Jesus was to his Father, and how close we can be too (Romans 8:15).

Jesus arrested

43 Just as he was speaking, Judas, one of the Twelve, appeared. With him was a crowd armed with swords and clubs, sent from the chief priests, the teachers of the law, and the elders. 44 Now the betrayer had arranged a signal with them: 'The one I kiss is the man; arrest him and lead him away under guard.' 45 Going at once to Jesus, Judas said, 'Rabbi!' and kissed him. 46 The men seized Jesus and arrested him. 47 Then one of those standing near drew his sword and struck the servant of the high priest, cutting off his ear.

48 'Am I leading a rebellion,' said Jesus, 'that you have come out with swords and clubs to capture me? 49 Every day I was with you, teaching in the temple courts, and you did not arrest me. But the Scriptures must be fulfilled.' 50 Then everyone deserted him and fled.

51 A young man, wearing nothing but a linen garment, was following Jesus. When they seized him, 52 he fled naked, leaving his garment behind.

Jesus before the Sanhedrin

53 They took Jesus to the high priest, and all the chief priests, the elders and the teachers of the law came together. 54 Peter followed him at a distance, right into the courtyard of the high priest. There he sat with the guards and warmed himself at the fire.

55 The chief priests and the whole Sanhedrin were looking for evidence against Jesus so that they could put him to death, but they did not find any. 56 Many testified falsely against him, but their statements did not agree.

57 Then some stood up and gave this false testimony against him: 58 'We heard him say, "I will destroy this temple made with human hands and in three days will build another, not made with hands."' 59 Yet even then their testimony did not agree.

60 Then the high priest stood up before them and asked Jesus, 'Are you not going to answer? What is this testimony that these men are bringing against you?' 61 But Jesus remained silent and gave no answer.

Again the high priest asked him, 'Are you the Messiah, the Son of the Blessed One?'

62 'I am,' said Jesus. 'And you will see the Son of Man sitting at the right hand of the Mighty One and coming on the clouds of heaven.'

63 The high priest tore his clothes. 'Why do we need any more witnesses?' he asked. 64 'You have heard the blasphemy. What do you think?'

They all condemned him as worthy of death. 65 Then some began to spit at him; they blindfolded him, struck him with their fists, and said, 'Prophesy!' And the guards took him and beat him.

Peter disowns Jesus

66 While Peter was below in the courtyard, one of the servant-girls of the high priest came by. 67 When she saw Peter warming himself, she looked closely at him.

'You also were with that Nazarene, Jesus,' she said.

68 But he denied it. 'I don't know or understand what you're talking about,' he said, and went out into the entrance.[a]

69 When the servant-girl saw him there, she said again to those standing round them, 'This fellow is one of them.' 70 Again he denied it.

After a little while, those standing near said to Peter, 'Surely you are one of them, for you are a Galilean.'

71 He began to call down curses, and he swore to them, 'I don't know this man you're talking about.'

---

[a] 68 Some early manuscripts *entrance and the cock crowed*

People and Places

Sanhedrin
Mark 15:1

The Sanhedrin was the highest ruling body among the Jewish people at the time of Jesus, and was led by the high priest. It was given limited power by the Romans to make rulings about some religious, civil and criminal matters.

⁷²Immediately the cock crowed the second time.ᵃ Then Peter remembered the word Jesus had spoken to him: 'Before the cock crows twiceᵇ you will disown me three times.' And he broke down and wept.

Jesus before Pilate

15 Very early in the morning, the chief priests, with the elders, the teachers of the law and the whole Sanhedrin, reached a decision. They bound Jesus, led him away and handed him over to Pilate.

²'Are you the king of the Jews?' asked Pilate.

'You have said so,' Jesus replied.

³The chief priests accused him of many things. ⁴So again Pilate asked him, 'Aren't you going to answer? See how many things they are accusing you of.'

⁵But Jesus still made no reply, and Pilate was amazed.

⁶Now it was the custom at the Feast to release a prisoner whom the people requested. ⁷A man called Barabbas was in prison with the rebels who had committed murder in the uprising. ⁸The crowd came up and asked Pilate to do for them what he usually did.

⁹'Do you want me to release to you the king of the Jews?' asked Pilate, ¹⁰knowing it was out of envy that the chief priests had handed Jesus over to him. ¹¹But the chief priests stirred up the crowd to get Pilate to release Barabbas instead.

¹²'What shall I do, then, with the one you call the king of the Jews?' Pilate asked them.

¹³'Crucify him!' they shouted.

¹⁴'Why? What crime has he committed?' asked Pilate.

But they shouted all the louder, 'Crucify him!'

¹⁵Wanting to satisfy the crowd, Pilate released Barabbas to them. He had Jesus flogged, and handed him over to be crucified.

The soldiers mock Jesus

¹⁶The soldiers led Jesus away into the palace (that is, the Praetorium) and called together the whole company of soldiers. ¹⁷They put a purple robe on him, then twisted together a crown of thorns and set it on him. ¹⁸And they began to call out to him, 'Hail, king of the Jews!' ¹⁹Again and again they struck him on the head with a staff and spat on him. Falling on their knees, they paid homage to him. ²⁰And when they had mocked him, they took off the purple robe and put his own clothes on him. Then they led him out to crucify him.

The crucifixion of Jesus

²¹A certain man from Cyrene, Simon, the father of Alexander and Rufus, was passing by on his way in from the country, and they forced him to carry the cross. ²²They brought Jesus to the place called Golgotha (which means 'the place of the skull'). ²³Then they offered him wine mixed with myrrh, but he did not take it. ²⁴And they crucified him. Dividing up his clothes, they cast lots to see what each would get.

²⁵It was nine in the morning when they crucified him. ²⁶The written notice of the charge against him read: THE KING OF THE JEWS. ²⁷⁽²⁸⁾They crucified two rebels with him, one on his right and one on his left. ²⁹Those who passed by hurled insults at him, shaking their heads and saying, 'So! You who are going to destroy the temple and build it in three days, ³⁰come down from the cross and save yourself!'

³¹In the same way the chief priests and the teachers of the law mocked him among themselves. 'He saved others,' they said,

---

ᵃ72 Some early manuscripts do not have *the second time*. ᵇ72 Some early manuscripts do not have *twice*.

'but he can't save himself! 32Let this Messiah, this king of Israel, come down now from the cross, that we may see and believe.' Those crucified with him also heaped insults on him.

The death of Jesus

33At noon, darkness came over the whole land until three in the afternoon. 34And at three in the afternoon Jesus cried out in a loud voice, *'Eloi, Eloi, lema sabachthani?'* (which means 'My God, my God, why have you forsaken me?').*a*

35When some of those standing near heard this, they said, 'Listen, he's calling Elijah.'

36Someone ran, filled a sponge with wine vinegar, put it on a staff, and offered it to Jesus to drink. 'Now leave him alone. Let's see if Elijah comes to take him down,' he said.

37With a loud cry, Jesus breathed his last.

38The curtain of the temple was torn in two from top to bottom. 39And when the centurion, who stood there in front of Jesus, saw how he died,*b* he said, 'Surely this man was the Son of God!'

40Some women were watching from a distance. Among them were Mary Magdalene, Mary the mother of James the younger and of Joseph,*c* and Salome. 41In Galilee these women had followed him and cared for his needs. Many other women who had come up with him to Jerusalem were also there.

The burial of Jesus

42It was Preparation Day (that is, the day before the Sabbath). So as evening approached, 43Joseph of Arimathea, a prominent member of the Council, who was himself waiting for the kingdom of God, went boldly to Pilate and asked for Jesus' body. 44Pilate was surprised to hear that he was already dead. Summoning the centurion, he asked him if Jesus had already died. 45When he learned from the centurion that it was so, he gave the body to Joseph. 46So Joseph bought some linen cloth, took down the body, wrapped it in the linen, and placed it in a tomb cut out of rock. Then he rolled a stone against the entrance of the tomb. 47Mary Magdalene and Mary the mother of Joseph saw where he was laid.

Jesus has risen

16 When the Sabbath was over, Mary Magdalene, Mary the mother of James, and Salome bought spices so that they might go to anoint Jesus' body. 2Very early on the first day of the week, just after sunrise, they were on their way to the tomb 3and they asked each other, 'Who will roll the stone away from the entrance of the tomb?'

4But when they looked up, they saw that the stone, which was very large, had been rolled away. 5As they entered the tomb, they saw a young man dressed in a white robe sitting on the right side, and they were alarmed.

6'Don't be alarmed,' he said. 'You are looking for Jesus the Nazarene, who was crucified. He has risen! He is not here. See the place where they laid him. 7But go, tell his disciples and Peter, "He is going ahead of you into Galilee. There you will see him, just as he told you." '

8Trembling and bewildered, the women went out and fled from the tomb. They said nothing to anyone, because they were afraid.

(The earliest manuscripts and some other ancient witnesses do not have Mark 16:9-20.)

9When Jesus rose early on the first day of the week, he appeared first to Mary Magdalene, out of whom he had driven seven demons. 10She went and told those who had been with him and who were mourning and weeping. 11When they heard that Jesus was alive and that she had seen him, they did not believe it.

12Afterwards Jesus appeared in a different form to two of them while they were walking in the country. 13These returned and reported it to the rest; but they did not believe them either.

14Later Jesus appeared to the Eleven as they were eating; he rebuked them for their lack of faith and

---

a 34 Psalm 22:1 *b* 39 Some manuscripts *saw that he died with such a cry* *c* 40 Greek *Joses*, a variant of *Joseph*; also in verse 47

> **IN OTHER WORDS**
>
> **Taken up**
> Mark 16:19
> Forty days after Jesus rose from the dead, he returned to heaven to be with his Father and to establish his kingdom. This dramatic departure is known as 'the ascension'.

their stubborn refusal to believe those who had seen him after he had risen.

¹⁵He said to them, 'Go into all the world and preach the gospel to all creation. ¹⁶Whoever believes and is baptised will be saved, but whoever does not believe will be condemned. ¹⁷And these signs will accompany those who believe: in my name they will drive out demons; they will speak in new tongues; ¹⁸they will pick up snakes with their hands; and when they drink deadly poison, it will not hurt them at all; they will place their hands on people who are ill, and they will get well.'

¹⁹After the Lord Jesus had spoken to them, he was taken up into heaven and he sat at the right hand of God. ²⁰Then the disciples went out and preached everywhere, and the Lord worked with them and confirmed his word by the signs that accompanied it.

Luke

INTRODUCTION

Luke

Author: Luke, a doctor who also wrote Acts.

Who to: Theophilus, whose name means 'lover of God'.

When: It covers the events of Jesus' life, from 4 BC to AD 30. It was probably written in the 60s AD.

Where: Judea

Did you know? The early church adopted symbols for the Gospels – Matthew was a lion, Mark was an ox, Luke was a man and John was an eagle.

Main theme: Luke was a Gentile and he wrote his Gospel for Gentiles, people who weren't Jews. He tells lots of vivid stories about Jesus and was much more interested in people than in ideas. He shows that Jesus came for everyone, not just the Jews.

Introduction

1 Many have undertaken to draw up an account of the things that have been fulfilled[a] among us, 2just as they were handed down to us by those who from the first were eye witnesses and servants of the word. 3With this in mind, since I myself have carefully investigated everything from the beginning, I too decided to write an orderly account for you, most excellent Theophilus, 4so that you may know the certainty of the things you have been taught.

The birth of John the Baptist foretold

5In the time of Herod king of Judea there was a priest named Zechariah, who belonged to the priestly division of Abijah; his wife Elizabeth was also a descendant of Aaron. 6Both of them were righteous in the sight of God, observing all the Lord's commands and decrees blamelessly. 7But they were childless because Elizabeth was not able to conceive, and they were both well advanced in years.

[a] 1 Or *been surely believed*

IN OTHER WORDS

Angel
Luke 1:26

An angel is a messenger of God. Angels appear to be special envoys who God sometimes uses to communicate with people. They must have been scary to meet because often the first thing they say is, 'Don't be afraid!'

8Once when Zechariah's division was on duty and he was serving as priest before God, 9he was chosen by lot, according to the custom of the priesthood, to go into the temple of the Lord and burn incense. 10And when the time for the burning of incense came, all the assembled worshippers were praying outside.

11Then an angel of the Lord appeared to him, standing at the right side of the altar of incense. 12When Zechariah saw him, he was startled and was gripped with fear. 13But the angel said to him: 'Do not be afraid, Zechariah; your prayer has been heard. Your wife Elizabeth will bear you a son, and you are to call him John. 14He will be a joy and delight to you, and many will rejoice because of his birth, 15for he will be great in the sight of the Lord. He is never to take wine or other fermented drink, and he will be filled with the Holy Spirit even before he is born. 16Many of the people of Israel will he bring back to the Lord their God. 17And he will go on before the Lord, in the spirit and power of Elijah, to turn the hearts of the parents to their children and the disobedient to the wisdom of the righteous—to make ready a people prepared for the Lord.'

18Zechariah asked the angel, 'How can I be sure of this? I am an old man and my wife is well on in years.'

19The angel said to him, 'I am Gabriel. I stand in the presence of God, and I have been sent to speak to you and to tell you this good news. 20And now you will be silent and not able to speak until the day this happens, because you did not believe my words, which will come true at their appointed time.'

21Meanwhile, the people were waiting for Zechariah and wondering why he stayed so long in the temple. 22When he came out, he could not speak to them. They realised he had seen a vision in the temple, for he kept making signs to them but remained unable to speak.

23When his time of service was completed, he returned home. 24After this his wife Elizabeth became pregnant and for five months remained in seclusion. 25'The Lord has done this for me,' she said. 'In these days he has shown his favour and taken away my disgrace among the people.'

The birth of Jesus foretold

26In the sixth month of Elizabeth's pregnancy, God sent the angel Gabriel to Nazareth, a town in Galilee, 27to a virgin pledged to be married to a man named Joseph, a descendant of David. The virgin's name was Mary. 28The angel went to her and said, 'Greetings, you who are highly favoured! The Lord is with you.'

29Mary was greatly troubled at his words and wondered what kind of greeting this might be. 30But the angel said to her, 'Do not be afraid, Mary, you have found favour with God. 31You will conceive and give birth to a son, and you are to call him Jesus. 32He will be great and will be called the Son of the Most High. The Lord God will give him the throne of his father David, 33and he will reign over the house of Jacob for ever; his kingdom will never end.'

34'How will this be,' Mary asked the angel, 'since I am a virgin?'

35The angel answered, 'The Holy Spirit will come on you, and the power of the Most High will overshadow you. So the holy one to be born will be called*a* the Son of God. 36Even Elizabeth your relative is going to have a child in her old age, and she who was said to be unable to conceive is in her sixth month. 37For no word from God will ever fail.'

---

a 35 Or *So the child to be born will be called holy,*

38'I am the Lord's servant,' Mary answered. 'May it be to me according to your word.' Then the angel left her.

Mary visits Elizabeth

39At that time Mary got ready and hurried to a town in the hill country of Judea, **40**where she entered Zechariah's home and greeted Elizabeth. **41**When Elizabeth heard Mary's greeting, the baby leaped in her womb, and Elizabeth was filled with the Holy Spirit. **42**In a loud voice she exclaimed: 'Blessed are you among women, and blessed is the child you will bear! **43**But why am I so favoured, that the mother of my Lord should come to me? **44**As soon as the sound of your greeting reached my ears, the baby in my womb leaped for joy. **45**Blessed is she who has believed that the Lord would fulfil his promises to her!'

Mary's song

46And Mary said:

'My soul glorifies the Lord
47   and my spirit rejoices in God my Saviour,
48for he has been mindful
   of the humble state of his servant.
   From now on all generations will call me blessed,
49   for the Mighty One has done great things for me—
   holy is his name.
50His mercy extends to those who fear him,
   from generation to generation.
51He has performed mighty deeds with his arm;
   he has scattered those who are proud in their inmost thoughts.
52He has brought down rulers from their thrones
   but has lifted up the humble.
53He has filled the hungry with good things
   but has sent the rich away empty.
54He has helped his servant Israel,
   remembering to be merciful
55to Abraham and his descendants for ever,
   just as he promised our ancestors.'

56Mary stayed with Elizabeth for about three months and then returned home.

The birth of John the Baptist

57When it was time for Elizabeth to have her baby, she gave birth to a son. **58**Her neighbours and relatives heard that the Lord had shown her great mercy, and they shared her joy.

59On the eighth day they came to circumcise the child, and they were going to name him after his father Zechariah, **60**but his mother spoke up and said, 'No! He is to be called John.'

61They said to her, 'There is no-one among your relatives who has that name.'

62Then they made signs to his father, to find out what he would like to name the child. **63**He asked for a writing tablet, and to everyone's astonishment he wrote, 'His name is John.' **64**Immediately his mouth was opened and his tongue was loosed, and he began to speak, praising God. **65**The neighbours were all filled with awe, and throughout the hill country of Judea people were talking about all these things. **66**Everyone who heard this wondered about it, asking, 'What then is this child going to be?' For the Lord's hand was with him.

Zechariah's song

67His father Zechariah was filled with the Holy Spirit and prophesied:

68'Praise be to the Lord, the God of Israel,
   because he has come to his people and redeemed them.
69He has raised up a horn*a* of salvation for us
   in the house of his servant David
70(as he said through his holy prophets of long ago),
71salvation from our enemies
   and from the hand of all who hate us—
72to show mercy to our ancestors
   and to remember his holy covenant,
73   the oath he swore to our father Abraham:
74to rescue us from the hand of our enemies,
   and to enable us to serve him without fear
75   in holiness and righteousness before him all our days.

---

a 69 *Horn* here symbolises a strong king.

⁷⁶And you, my child, will be called a
prophet of the Most High;
for you will go on before the Lord to
prepare the way for him,
⁷⁷to give his people the knowledge of
salvation
through the forgiveness of their sins,
⁷⁸because of the tender mercy of our God,
by which the rising sun will come to us
from heaven
⁷⁹to shine on those living in darkness
and in the shadow of death,
to guide our feet into the path of peace.'

⁸⁰And the child grew and became strong in spirit*a*; and he lived in the wilderness until he appeared publicly to Israel.

The birth of Jesus

2 In those days Caesar Augustus issued a decree that a census should be taken of the entire Roman world. ²(This was the first census that took place while Quirinius was governor of Syria.) ³And everyone went to their own town to register.

⁴So Joseph also went up from the town of Nazareth in Galilee to Judea, to Bethlehem the town of David, because he belonged to the house and line of David. ⁵He went there to register with Mary, who was pledged to be married to him and was expecting a child. ⁶While they were there, the time came for the baby to be born, ⁷and she gave birth to her firstborn, a son. She wrapped him in cloths and placed him in a manger, because there was no guest room available for them.

The shepherds and the angels

⁸And there were shepherds living out in the fields near by, keeping watch over their flocks at night. ⁹An angel of the Lord appeared to them, and the glory of the Lord shone around them, and they were terrified. ¹⁰But the angel said to them, 'Do not be afraid. I bring you good news of great joy that will be for all the people. ¹¹Today in the town of David a Saviour has been born to you; he is the Messiah, the Lord. ¹²This will be a sign to you: you will find a baby wrapped in cloths and lying in a manger.'

¹³Suddenly a great company of the heavenly host appeared with the angel, praising God and saying,

¹⁴'Glory to God in the highest heaven,
and on earth peace to those on whom
his favour rests.'

¹⁵When the angels had left them and gone into heaven, the shepherds said to one another, 'Let's go to Bethlehem and see this thing that has happened, which the Lord has told us about.'

People and Places

Bethlehem
Luke 2:4

The Christmas carol calls Bethlehem a 'little town', but a lot has happened there throughout history. Rachel, Jacob's wife, was buried there (Genesis 35:19), and it's where most of the action in the book of Ruth takes place. David was anointed king at Bethlehem where his family lived (1 Samuel 16:4), and so it is known as the City of David. Because Joseph was descended from David, he and Mary had to go back to Bethlehem for the census, and that's where Jesus was born.

People and Places

Caesar Augustus
Luke 2:1

Augustus means 'holy' or 'sacred', and it was a title of honour given to the first Roman emperor, Octavian, who was then known as Caesar Augustus. He was the ruler of the Roman Empire when Jesus was born.

---

a 80 Or *in the Spirit*

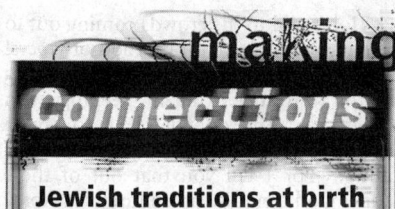

Making Connections

Jewish traditions at birth
Luke 2:21

After a Jewish woman gave birth, she was considered ritually unclean. If she had a son, she had to stay at home for seven days, and then on the eighth day the baby boy would be circumcised to show that he belonged to God. The mother would stay at home for another thirty days and then offer a sacrifice to make her clean again.

16So they hurried off and found Mary and Joseph, and the baby, who was lying in the manger. 17When they had seen him, they spread the word concerning what had been told them about this child, 18and all who heard it were amazed at what the shepherds said to them. 19But Mary treasured up all these things and pondered them in her heart. 20The shepherds returned, glorifying and praising God for all the things they had heard and seen, which were just as they had been told.

Jesus presented in the temple

21On the eighth day, when it was time to circumcise the child, he was named Jesus, the name the angel had given him before he was conceived.

22When the time came for the purification rites required by the Law of Moses, Joseph and Mary took him to Jerusalem to present him to the Lord 23(as it is written in the Law of the Lord, 'Every firstborn male is to be consecrated to the Lord'[a]), 24and to offer a sacrifice in keeping with what is said in the Law of the Lord: 'a pair of doves or two young pigeons'.[b]

25Now there was a man in Jerusalem called Simeon, who was righteous and devout. He was waiting for the consolation of Israel, and the Holy Spirit was on him. 26It had been revealed to him by the Holy Spirit that he would not die before he had seen the Lord's Messiah. 27Moved by the Spirit, he went into the temple courts. When the parents brought in the child Jesus to do for him what the custom of the Law required, 28Simeon took him in his arms and praised God, saying:

29'Sovereign Lord, as you have promised,
  you may now dismiss[c] your servant in peace.
30For my eyes have seen your salvation,
31 which you have prepared in the sight of all nations:
32a light for revelation to the Gentiles,
  and the glory of your people Israel.'

33The child's father and mother marvelled at what was said about him. 34Then Simeon blessed them and said to Mary, his mother: 'This child is destined to cause the falling and rising of many in Israel, and to be a sign that will be spoken against, 35so that the thoughts of many hearts will be revealed. And a sword will pierce your own soul too.'

36There was also a prophet, Anna, the daughter of Phanuel, of the tribe of Asher. She was very old; she had lived with her husband seven years after her marriage, 37and then had been a widow for eighty-four years.[d] She never left the temple but worshipped night and day, fasting and praying. 38Coming up to them at that very moment, she gave thanks to God and spoke about the child to all who were looking forward to the redemption of Jerusalem.

39When Joseph and Mary had done everything required by the Law of the Lord, they returned to Galilee to their own town of Nazareth. 40And the child grew and became strong; he was filled with wisdom, and the grace of God was on him.

The boy Jesus at the temple

41Every year Jesus' parents went to Jerusalem for the Feast of the Passover. 42When he was twelve years old, they went up to the

---

[a] 23 Exodus 13:2,12 [b] 24 Lev. 12:8 [c] 29 Or *promised, I now dismiss* [d] 37 Or *then was a widow until she was eighty-four*

Feast, according to the custom. 43After the Feast was over, while his parents were returning home, the boy Jesus stayed behind in Jerusalem, but they were unaware of it. 44Thinking he was in their company, they travelled on for a day. Then they began looking for him among their relatives and friends. 45When they did not find him, they went back to Jerusalem to look for him. 46After three days they found him in the temple courts, sitting among the teachers, listening to them and asking them questions. 47Everyone who heard him was amazed at his understanding and his answers. 48When his parents saw him, they were astonished. His mother said to him, 'Son, why have you treated us like this? Your father and I have been anxiously searching for you.'

49'Why were you searching for me?' he asked. 'Didn't you know I had to be in my Father's house?'[a] 50But they did not understand what he was saying to them.

51Then he went down to Nazareth with them and was obedient to them. But his mother treasured all these things in her heart. 52And as Jesus grew up, he increased in wisdom and in favour with God and people.

John the Baptist prepares the way

3 In the fifteenth year of the reign of Tiberius Caesar—when Pontius Pilate was governor of Judea, Herod tetrarch of Galilee, his brother Philip tetrarch of Iturea and Traconitis, and Lysanias tetrarch of Abilene— 2during the high-priesthood of Annas and Caiaphas, the word of God came to John son of Zechariah in the wilderness. 3He went into all the country around the Jordan, preaching a baptism of repentance for the forgiveness of sins. 4As it is written in the book of the words of Isaiah the prophet:

'A voice of one calling in the wilderness,
"Prepare the way for the Lord,
  make straight paths for him.
5Every valley shall be filled in,
  every mountain and hill made low.
The crooked roads shall become straight,
  the rough ways smooth.
6And all people will see God's salvation."'[b]

7John said to the crowds coming out to be baptised by him, 'You brood of vipers! Who warned you to flee from the coming wrath? 8Produce fruit in keeping with repentance. And do not begin to say to yourselves, "We have Abraham as our father." For I tell you that out of these stones God can raise up children for Abraham. 9The axe has been laid to the root of the trees, and every tree that does not produce good fruit will be cut down and thrown into the fire.'

10'What should we do then?' the crowd asked.

11John answered, 'Anyone who has two shirts should share with the one who has none, and anyone who has food should do the same.'

12Even tax collectors came to be baptised. 'Teacher,' they asked, 'what should we do?'

13'Don't collect any more than you are required to,' he told them.

14Then some soldiers asked him, 'And what should we do?'

He replied, 'Don't extort money and don't accuse people falsely—be content with your pay.'

15The people were waiting expectantly and were all wondering in their hearts if John might possibly be the Messiah. 16John answered them all, 'I baptise you with[c] water. But one who is more powerful than I will come, the thongs of whose sandals I am not worthy to untie. He will baptise you with[d] the Holy Spirit and fire. 17His winnowing fork is in his hand to clear his threshing-floor and to gather the wheat into his barn, but he will burn up the chaff with unquenchable fire.' 18And with many other words John exhorted the people and proclaimed the good news to them.

19But when John rebuked Herod the tetrarch because of his marriage to Herodias, his brother's wife, and all the other evil things he had done, 20Herod added this to them all: he locked John up in prison.

The baptism and genealogy of Jesus

21When all the people were being baptised, Jesus was baptised too. And as he was praying, heaven was opened 22and the Holy

---

[a] 49 Or *be about my Father's business* [b] 6 Isaiah 40:3-5 [c] 16 Or *in* [d] 16 Or *in*

Spirit descended on him in bodily form like a dove. And a voice came from heaven: 'You are my Son, whom I love; with you I am well pleased.'

23Now Jesus himself was about thirty years old when he began his ministry. He was the son, so it was thought, of Joseph,

the son of Heli, 24the son of Matthat,
the son of Levi, the son of Melki,
the son of Jannai, the son of Joseph,
25the son of Mattathias, the son of Amos,
the son of Nahum, the son of Esli,
the son of Naggai, 26the son of Maath,
the son of Mattathias, the son of Semein,
the son of Josek, the son of Joda,
27the son of Joanan, the son of Rhesa,
the son of Zerubbabel, the son of Shealtiel,
the son of Neri, 28the son of Melki,
the son of Addi, the son of Cosam,
the son of Elmadam, the son of Er,
29the son of Joshua, the son of Eliezer,
the son of Jorim, the son of Matthat,
the son of Levi, 30the son of Simeon,
the son of Judah, the son of Joseph,
the son of Jonam, the son of Eliakim,
31the son of Melea, the son of Menna,
the son of Mattatha, the son of Nathan,
the son of David, 32the son of Jesse,
the son of Obed, the son of Boaz,
the son of Salmon,^{a} the son of Nahshon,
33the son of Amminadab, the son of Ram,^{b}
the son of Hezron, the son of Perez,
the son of Judah, 34the son of Jacob,
the son of Isaac, the son of Abraham,
the son of Terah, the son of Nahor,
35the son of Serug, the son of Reu,
the son of Peleg, the son of Eber,
the son of Shelah, 36the son of Cainan,
the son of Arphaxad, the son of Shem,
the son of Noah, the son of Lamech,
37the son of Methuselah, the son of Enoch,
the son of Jared, the son of Mahalalel,
the son of Kenan, 38the son of Enosh,
the son of Seth, the son of Adam,
the son of God.

Jesus is tested in the wilderness

4 Jesus, full of the Holy Spirit, left the Jordan and was led by the Spirit into the wilderness, 2where for forty days he was tempted^c by the devil. He ate nothing during those days, and at the end of them he was hungry.

3The devil said to him, 'If you are the Son of God, tell this stone to become bread.'

4Jesus answered, 'It is written: "People do not live on bread alone."^{d}'

5The devil led him up to a high place and showed him in an instant all the kingdoms of the world. 6And he said to him, 'I will give you all their authority and splendour; it has been given to me, and I can give it to anyone I want to. 7If you worship me, it will all be yours.'

8Jesus answered, 'It is written: "Worship the Lord your God and serve him only."^{e}'

9The devil led him to Jerusalem and had him stand on the highest point of the temple. 'If you are the Son of God,' he said, 'throw yourself down from here. 10For it is written:

'"He will command his angels concerning you
to guard you carefully;
11they will lift you up in their hands,
so that you will not strike your foot against a stone."^{f}'

12Jesus answered, 'It is said: "Do not put the Lord your God to the test."^{g}'

13When the devil had finished all this tempting, he left him until an opportune time.

Jesus rejected at Nazareth

14Jesus returned to Galilee in the power of the Spirit, and news about him spread through the whole countryside. 15He was

---

^{a}32 Some early manuscripts *Sala* ^{b}33 Some manuscripts *Amminadab, the son of Admin, the son of Arni*; other manuscripts vary widely. ^{c}2 The Greek for *tempted* can also mean *tested*. ^{d}4 Deut. 8:3 ^{e}8 Deut. 6:13
^{f}11 Psalm 91:11,12 ^{g}12 Deut. 6:16

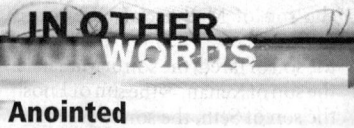

IN OTHER WORDS

Anointed
Luke 4:18
The word 'anoint' literally means 'to pour'. In the Old Testament, priests, kings and prophets were anointed by having oil poured on their heads. This was to show that they were set apart by God for a special task.

teaching in their synagogues, and everyone praised him.

16He went to Nazareth, where he had been brought up, and on the Sabbath day he went into the synagogue, as was his custom. He stood up to read, 17and the scroll of the prophet Isaiah was handed to him. Unrolling it, he found the place where it is written:

18'The Spirit of the Lord is on me,
  because he has anointed me
    to proclaim good news to the poor.
He has sent me to proclaim freedom for
    the prisoners
  and recovery of sight for the blind,
to set the oppressed free,
19 to proclaim the year of the Lord's
    favour.'[a]

20Then he rolled up the scroll, gave it back to the attendant and sat down. The eyes of everyone in the synagogue were fastened on him. 21He began by saying to them, 'Today this scripture is fulfilled in your hearing.'

22All spoke well of him and were amazed at the gracious words that came from his lips. 'Isn't this Joseph's son?' they asked.

23Jesus said to them, 'Surely you will quote this proverb to me: "Physician, heal yourself!" And you will tell me, "Do here in your home town what we have heard that you did in Capernaum."'

24'Truly I tell you,' he continued, 'prophets are not accepted in their home towns. 25I assure you that there were many widows in Israel in Elijah's time, when the sky was shut for three and a half years and there was a severe famine throughout the land. 26Yet Elijah was not sent to any of them, but to a widow in Zarephath in the region of Sidon. 27And there were many in Israel with leprosy[b] in the time of Elisha the prophet, yet not one of them was cleansed—only Naaman the Syrian.'

28All the people in the synagogue were furious when they heard this. 29They got up, drove him out of the town, and took him to the brow of the hill on which the town was built, in order to throw him off the cliff. 30But he walked right through the crowd and went on his way.

Jesus drives out an evil spirit

31Then he went down to Capernaum, a town in Galilee, and on the Sabbath he taught the people. 32They were amazed at his teaching, because his words had authority.

33In the synagogue there was a man possessed by a demon, an evil[c] spirit. He cried out at the top of his voice, 34'Go away! What do you want with us, Jesus of Nazareth? Have you come to destroy us? I know who you are—the Holy One of God!'

35'Be quiet!' Jesus said sternly. 'Come out of him!' Then the demon threw the man down before them all and came out without injuring him.

36All the people were amazed and said to each other, 'What words these are! With authority and power he gives orders to evil spirits and they come out!' 37And the news about him spread throughout the surrounding area.

Jesus heals many

38Jesus left the synagogue and went to the home of Simon. Now Simon's mother-in-law was suffering from a high fever, and they asked Jesus to help her. 39So he bent over her and rebuked the fever, and it left her. She got up at once and began to wait on them.

40At sunset, the people brought to Jesus all who had various kinds of illness, and laying his hands on each one, he healed

---

[a] 19 Isaiah 61:1,2 (see Septuagint); Isaiah 58:6   [b] 27 The Greek word traditionally translated *leprosy* was used for various diseases affecting the skin.   [c] 33 Greek *unclean*; also in verse 36

them. 41Moreover, demons came out of many people, shouting, 'You are the Son of God!' But he rebuked them and would not allow them to speak, because they knew he was the Messiah.

42At daybreak, Jesus went out to a solitary place. The people were looking for him and when they came to where he was, they tried to keep him from leaving them. 43But he said, 'I must proclaim the good news of the kingdom of God to the other towns also, because that is why I was sent.' 44And he kept on preaching in the synagogues of Judea.

Jesus calls his first disciples

5 One day as Jesus was standing by the Lake of Gennesaret,^{a} the people were crowding round him and listening to the word of God. 2He saw at the water's edge two boats, left there by the fishermen, who were washing their nets. 3He got into one of the boats, the one belonging to Simon, and asked him to put out a little from the shore. Then he sat down and taught the people from the boat.

4When he had finished speaking, he said to Simon, 'Put out into deep water, and let down the nets for a catch.'

5Simon answered, 'Master, we've worked hard all night and haven't caught anything. But because you say so, I will let down the nets.'

6When they had done so, they caught such a large number of fish that their nets began to break. 7So they signalled to their partners in the other boat to come and help them, and they came and filled both boats so full that they began to sink.

8When Simon Peter saw this, he fell at Jesus' knees and said, 'Go away from me, Lord; I am a sinful man!' 9For he and all his companions were astonished at the catch of fish they had taken, 10and so were James and John, the sons of Zebedee, Simon's partners.

Then Jesus said to Simon, 'Don't be afraid; from now on you will fish for people.' 11So they pulled their boats up on shore, left everything and followed him.

Jesus heals a man with leprosy

12While Jesus was in one of the towns, a man came along who was covered with leprosy.^{b} When he saw Jesus, he fell with his face to the ground and begged him, 'Lord, if you are willing, you can make me clean.'

13Jesus reached out his hand and touched the man. 'I am willing,' he said. 'Be clean!' And immediately the leprosy left him.

14Then Jesus ordered him, 'Don't tell anyone, but go, show yourself to the priest and offer the sacrifices that Moses commanded for your cleansing, as a testimony to them.'

15Yet the news about him spread all the more, so that crowds of people came to hear him and to be healed of their illnesses. 16But Jesus often withdrew to lonely places and prayed.

Jesus forgives and heals a paralysed man

17One day Jesus was teaching, and Pharisees and teachers of the law were sitting there. They had come from every village of Galilee and from Judea and Jerusalem. And the power of the Lord was with Jesus to heal those who were ill. 18Some men came carrying a paralysed man on a mat and tried to take him into the house to lay him before Jesus. 19When they could not find a way to do this because of the crowd, they went up on the roof and lowered him on his mat through the tiles into the middle of the crowd, right in front of Jesus.

20When Jesus saw their faith, he said, 'Friend, your sins are forgiven.'

21The Pharisees and the teachers of the law began thinking to themselves, 'Who is this fellow who speaks blasphemy? Who can forgive sins but God alone?'

22Jesus knew what they were thinking and asked, 'Why are you thinking these things in your hearts? 23Which is easier: to say, "Your sins are forgiven," or to say, "Get up and walk"? 24But I want you to know that the Son of Man has authority on earth to forgive sins.' So he said to the paralysed man, 'I tell you, get up, take your mat and go home.' 25Immediately he stood up in front of them, took what he had been lying on and

---

^{a} 1 That is, Sea of Galilee ^{b} 12 The Greek word traditionally translated *leprosy* was used for various diseases affecting the skin.

Disciple
Luke 5:33

Each rabbi, or teacher, would have his own set of disciples, people who followed his teaching. Jesus had twelve disciples while he was on earth, as well as lots of other followers. People who follow Jesus today are still sometimes called disciples.

went home praising God. 26Everyone was amazed and gave praise to God. They were filled with awe and said, 'We have seen remarkable things today.'

Jesus calls Levi and eats with sinners

27After this, Jesus went out and saw a tax collector by the name of Levi sitting at his tax booth. 'Follow me,' Jesus said to him, 28and Levi got up, left everything and followed him.

29Then Levi held a great banquet for Jesus at his house, and a large crowd of tax collectors and others were eating with them. 30But the Pharisees and the teachers of the law who belonged to their sect complained to his disciples, 'Why do you eat and drink with tax collectors and sinners?'

31Jesus answered them, 'It is not the healthy who need a doctor, but those who are ill. 32I have not come to call the righteous, but sinners to repentance.'

Jesus questioned about fasting

33They said to him, 'John's disciples often fast and pray, and so do the disciples of the Pharisees, but yours go on eating and drinking.'

34Jesus answered, 'Can you make the friends of the bridegroom fast while he is with them? 35But the time will come when the bridegroom will be taken from them; in those days they will fast.'

36He told them this parable: 'No-one tears a piece out of a new garment to patch an old one. If they do, they will have torn the new garment, and the patch from the new will not match the old. 37And people do not pour new wine into old wineskins. If they do, the new wine will burst the skins; the wine will run out and the wineskins will be ruined. 38No, new wine must be poured into new wineskins. 39And none of you, after drinking old wine, wants the new, for you say, "The old is better."'

Jesus is Lord of the Sabbath

6 One Sabbath Jesus was going through the cornfields, and his disciples began to pick some ears of corn, rub them in their hands and eat the grain. 2Some of the Pharisees asked, 'Why are you doing what is unlawful on the Sabbath?'

3Jesus answered them, 'Have you never read what David did when he and his companions were hungry? 4He entered the house of God, and taking the consecrated bread, he ate what is lawful only for priests to eat. And he also gave some to his companions.' 5Then Jesus said to them, 'The Son of Man is Lord of the Sabbath.'

6On another Sabbath he went into the synagogue and was teaching, and a man was there whose right hand was shrivelled. 7The Pharisees and the teachers of the law were looking for a reason to accuse Jesus, so they watched him closely to see if he would heal on the Sabbath. 8But Jesus knew what they were thinking and said to the man with the shrivelled hand, 'Get up and stand in front of everyone.' So he got up and stood there.

Son of Man
Luke 6:5

Daniel used this term first to describe the Messiah who would come in judgment and with authority (Daniel 7:13). It is Jesus' favourite way of referring to himself. It also means just 'man', and so when Jesus uses it as a title for himself, it emphasises his servant role and his humanity.

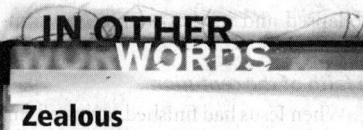

IN OTHER WORDS

Zealous
Luke 6:15
To say that 'zealous' means 'keen' is a bit of an understatement! In Jesus' time, the Zealots were a terrorist group who were trying to overthrow the Romans. They were willing to fight to the death for Jewish independence.

9 Then Jesus said to them, 'I ask you, which is lawful on the Sabbath: to do good or to do evil, to save life or to destroy it?' 10 He looked round at them all, and then said to the man, 'Stretch out your hand.' He did so, and his hand was completely restored. 11 But the Pharisees and the teachers of the law were furious and began to discuss with one another what they might do to Jesus.

The twelve apostles

12 One of those days Jesus went out to a mountainside to pray, and spent the night praying to God. 13 When morning came, he called his disciples to him and chose twelve of them, whom he also designated apostles: 14 Simon (whom he named Peter), his brother Andrew, James, John, Philip, Bartholomew, 15 Matthew, Thomas, James son of Alphaeus, Simon who was called the Zealot, 16 Judas son of James, and Judas Iscariot, who became a traitor.

Blessings and woes

17 He went down with them and stood on a level place. A large crowd of his disciples was there and a great number of people from all over Judea, from Jerusalem, and from the coastal region around Tyre and Sidon, 18 who had come to hear him and to be healed of their diseases. Those troubled by evil[a] spirits were cured, 19 and the people all tried to touch him, because power was coming from him and healing them all.

20 Looking at his disciples, he said:

'Blessed are you who are poor,
  for yours is the kingdom of God.
21 Blessed are you who hunger now,
  for you will be satisfied.
Blessed are you who weep now,
  for you will laugh.
22 Blessed are you when people hate you,
  when they exclude you and insult you
    and reject your name as evil,
  because of the Son of Man.

23 'Rejoice in that day and leap for joy, because great is your reward in heaven. For that is how their ancestors treated the prophets.

24 'But woe to you who are rich,
  for you have already received your
    comfort.
25 Woe to you who are well fed now,
  for you will go hungry.
Woe to you who laugh now,
  for you will mourn and weep.
26 Woe to you when everyone speaks well of
    you,
  for that is how their ancestors treated
    the false prophets.

Love for enemies

27 'But to you who are listening I say: love your enemies, do good to those who hate you, 28 bless those who curse you, pray for those who ill-treat you. 29 If someone slaps you on one cheek, turn the other also. If someone takes your coat, do not withhold your shirt. 30 Give to everyone who asks you, and if anyone takes what belongs to you, do not demand it back. 31 Do to others as you would have them do to you.

32 'If you love those who love you, what credit is that to you? Even sinners love those who love them. 33 And if you do good to those who are good to you, what credit is that to you? Even sinners do that. 34 And if you lend to those from whom you expect repayment, what credit is that to you? Even sinners lend to sinners, expecting to be repaid in full. 35 But love your enemies, do good to them, and lend to them without expecting to get anything back. Then your reward will be great, and you will be

---
[a] 18 Greek *unclean*

children of the Most High, because he is kind to the ungrateful and wicked. 36Be merciful, just as your Father is merciful.

Judging others

37'Do not judge, and you will not be judged. Do not condemn, and you will not be condemned. Forgive, and you will be forgiven. 38Give, and it will be given to you. A good measure, pressed down, shaken together and running over, will be poured into your lap. For with the measure you use, it will be measured to you.'

39He also told them this parable: 'Can the blind lead the blind? Will they not both fall into a pit? 40Students are not above their teacher, but all who are fully trained will be like their teacher.

41'Why do you look at the speck of sawdust in someone else's eye and pay no attention to the plank in your own eye? 42How can you say, "Friend, let me take the speck out of your eye," when you yourself fail to see the plank in your own eye? You hypocrite, first take the plank out of your eye, and then you will see clearly to remove the speck from the other person's eye.

A tree and its fruit

43'No good tree bears bad fruit, nor does a bad tree bear good fruit. 44Each tree is recognised by its own fruit. People do not pick figs from thorn-bushes, or grapes from briers. 45Good people bring good things out of the good stored up in their heart, and evil people bring evil things out of the evil stored up in their heart. For out of the overflow of the heart the mouth speaks.

The wise and foolish builders

46'Why do you call me, "Lord, Lord," and do not do what I say? 47As for those who come to me and hear my words and put them into practice, I will show you what they are like. 48They are like a man building a house, who dug down deep and laid the foundation on rock. When the flood came, the torrent struck that house but could not shake it, because it was well built. 49But those who hear my words and do not put them into practice are like a man who built a house on the ground without a foundation. The moment the torrent struck that house, it collapsed and its destruction was complete.'

The faith of the centurion

7 When Jesus had finished saying all this to the people who were listening, he entered Capernaum. 2There a centurion's servant, whom his master valued highly, was ill and about to die. 3The centurion heard of Jesus and sent some elders of the Jews to him, asking him to come and heal his servant. 4When they came to Jesus, they pleaded earnestly with him, 'This man deserves to have you do this, 5because he loves our nation and has built our synagogue.' 6So Jesus went with them.

He was not far from the house when the centurion sent friends to say to him: 'Lord, don't trouble yourself, for I do not deserve to have you come under my roof. 7That is why I did not even consider myself worthy to come to you. But say the word, and my servant will be healed. 8For I myself am a man under authority, with soldiers under me. I tell this one, "Go", and he goes; and that one, "Come", and he comes. I say to my servant, "Do this", and he does it.'

9When Jesus heard this, he was amazed at him, and turning to the crowd following him, he said, 'I tell you, I have not found such great faith even in Israel.' 10Then the men who had been sent returned to the house and found the servant well.

Jesus raises a widow's son

11Soon afterwards, Jesus went to a town called Nain, and his disciples and a large crowd went along with him. 12As he approached the town gate, a dead person was being carried out—the only son of his mother, and she was a widow. And a large crowd from the town was with her. 13When the Lord saw her, his heart went out to her and he said, 'Don't cry.'

14Then he went up and touched the bier they were carrying him on, and the bearers stood still. He said, 'Young man, I say to you, get up!' 15The dead man sat up and began to talk, and Jesus gave him back to his mother.

16They were all filled with awe and praised God. 'A great prophet has appeared among us,' they said. 'God has come to help his people.' 17This news about Jesus spread throughout Judea and the surrounding country.

Jesus and John the Baptist

18John's disciples told him about all these things. Calling two of them, 19he sent them to the Lord to ask, 'Are you the one who was to come, or should we expect someone else?'

20When the men came to Jesus, they said, 'John the Baptist sent us to you to ask, "Are you the one who was to come, or should we expect someone else?"'

21At that very time Jesus cured many who had diseases, illnesses and evil spirits, and gave sight to many who were blind. 22So he replied to the messengers, 'Go back and report to John what you have seen and heard: the blind receive sight, the lame walk, those who have leprosy[a] are cleansed, the deaf hear, the dead are raised, and the good news is proclaimed to the poor. 23Blessed is anyone who does not stumble on account of me.'

24After John's messengers left, Jesus began to speak to the crowd about John: 'What did you go out into the wilderness to see? A reed swayed by the wind? 25If not, what did you go out to see? A man dressed in fine clothes? No, those who wear expensive clothes and indulge in luxury are in palaces. 26But what did you go out to see? A prophet? Yes, I tell you, and more than a prophet. 27This is the one about whom it is written:

'"I will send my messenger ahead of you,
    who will prepare your way before
        you."[b]

28I tell you, among those born of women there is no-one greater than John; yet the one who is least in the kingdom of God is greater than he.'

29(All the people, even the tax collectors, when they heard Jesus' words, acknowledged that God's way was right, because they had been baptised by John. 30But the Pharisees and the experts in the law rejected God's purpose for themselves, because they had not been baptised by John.)

31Jesus went on to say, 'To what, then, can I compare the people of this generation? What are they like? 32They are like children sitting in the market-place and calling out to each other:

'"We played the pipe for you,
    and you did not dance;
we sang a dirge,
    and you did not cry."

33For John the Baptist came neither eating bread nor drinking wine, and you say, "He has a demon." 34The Son of Man came eating and drinking, and you say, "Here is a glutton and a drunkard, a friend of tax collectors and sinners." 35But wisdom is proved right by all her children.'

Jesus anointed by a sinful woman

36When one of the Pharisees invited Jesus to have dinner with him, he went to the Pharisee's house and reclined at the table. 37A woman in that town who lived a sinful life learned that Jesus was eating at the Pharisee's house, so she came there with an alabaster jar of perfume. 38As she stood behind him at his feet weeping, she began to wet his feet with her tears. Then she wiped them with her hair, kissed them and poured perfume on them.

39When the Pharisee who had invited him saw this, he said to himself, 'If this man were a prophet, he would know who is touching him and what kind of woman she is—that she is a sinner.'

40Jesus answered him, 'Simon, I have something to tell you.'

'Tell me, teacher,' he said.

41'Two people owed money to a certain money-lender. One owed him five hundred denarii,[c] and the other fifty. 42Neither of them had the money to pay him back, so he forgave the debts of both. Now which of them will love him more?'

43Simon replied, 'I suppose the one who had the bigger debt forgiven.'

'You have judged correctly,' Jesus said.

44Then he turned towards the woman and said to Simon, 'Do you see this woman? I came into your house. You did not give me

---

[a] 22 The Greek word traditionally translated *leprosy* was used for various diseases affecting the skin. [b] 27 Mal. 3:1
[c] 41 A denarius was the daily wage of a day labourer (see Matt. 20:2).

any water for my feet, but she wet my feet with her tears and wiped them with her hair. ⁴⁵You did not give me a kiss, but this woman, from the time I entered, has not stopped kissing my feet. ⁴⁶You did not put oil on my head, but she has poured perfume on my feet. ⁴⁷Therefore, I tell you, her many sins have been forgiven—as her great love has shown. But whoever has been forgiven little loves little.'

⁴⁸Then Jesus said to her, 'Your sins are forgiven.'

⁴⁹The other guests began to say among themselves, 'Who is this who even forgives sins?'

⁵⁰Jesus said to the woman, 'Your faith has saved you; go in peace.'

The parable of the sower

8 After this, Jesus travelled about from one town and village to another, proclaiming the good news of the kingdom of God. The Twelve were with him, ²and also some women who had been cured of evil spirits and diseases: Mary (called Magdalene) from whom seven demons had come out; ³Joanna the wife of Chuza, the manager of Herod's household; Susanna; and many others. These women were helping to support them out of their own means.

⁴While a large crowd was gathering and people were coming to Jesus from town after town, he told this parable: ⁵'A farmer went out to sow his seed. As he was scattering the seed, some fell along the path; it was trampled on, and the birds ate it up. ⁶Some fell on rock, and when it came up, the plants withered because they had no moisture. ⁷Other seed fell among thorns, which grew up with it and choked the plants. ⁸Still other seed fell on good soil. It came up and yielded a crop, a hundred times more than was sown.'

When he said this, he called out, 'Whoever has ears to hear, let them hear.'

⁹His disciples asked him what this parable meant. ¹⁰He said, 'The knowledge of the secrets of the kingdom of God has been given to you, but to others I speak in parables, so that,

'"though seeing, they may not see;
though hearing, they may not
understand."'[a]

¹¹'This is the meaning of the parable: the seed is the word of God. ¹²Those along the path are the ones who hear, and then the devil comes and takes away the word from their hearts, so that they may not believe and be saved. ¹³Those on the rock are the ones who receive the word with joy when they hear it, but they have no root. They believe for a while, but in the time of testing they fall away. ¹⁴The seed that fell among thorns stands for those who hear, but as they go on their way they are choked by life's worries, riches and pleasures, and they do not mature. ¹⁵But the seed on good soil stands for those with a noble and good heart, who hear the word, retain it, and by persevering produce a crop.

A lamp on a stand

¹⁶'No-one lights a lamp and hides it in a clay jar or puts it under a bed. Instead, they put it on a stand, so that those who come in can see the light. ¹⁷For there is nothing hidden that will not be disclosed, and nothing concealed that will not be known or brought out into the open. ¹⁸Therefore consider carefully how you listen. Those who have will be given more; as for those who do not have, even what they think they have will be taken from them.'

Jesus' mother and brothers

¹⁹Now Jesus' mother and brothers came to see him, but they were not able to get near him because of the crowd. ²⁰Someone told him, 'Your mother and brothers are standing outside, wanting to see you.'

²¹He replied, 'My mother and brothers are those who hear God's word and put it into practice.'

Jesus calms the storm

²²One day Jesus said to his disciples, 'Let us go over to the other side of the lake.' So they got into a boat and set out. ²³As they sailed, he fell asleep. A squall came down on the lake, so that the boat was being swamped, and they were in great danger.

---

[a] 10 Isaiah 6:9

24The disciples went and woke him, saying, 'Master, Master, we're going to drown!'

He got up and rebuked the wind and the raging waters; the storm subsided, and all was calm. 25'Where is your faith?' he asked his disciples.

In fear and amazement they asked one another, 'Who is this? He commands even the winds and the water, and they obey him.'

Jesus restores a demon-possessed man

26They sailed to the region of the Gerasenes,[a] which is across the lake from Galilee. 27When Jesus stepped ashore, he was met by a demon-possessed man from the town. For a long time this man had not worn clothes or lived in a house, but had lived in the tombs. 28When he saw Jesus, he cried out and fell at his feet, shouting at the top of his voice, 'What do you want with me, Jesus, Son of the Most High God? I beg you, don't torture me!' 29For Jesus had commanded the evil[b] spirit to come out of the man. Many times it had seized him, and though he was chained hand and foot and kept under guard, he had broken his chains and had been driven by the demon into solitary places.

30Jesus asked him, 'What is your name?'

'Legion,' he replied, because many demons had gone into him. 31And they begged Jesus repeatedly not to order them to go into the Abyss.

32A large herd of pigs was feeding there on the hillside. The demons begged Jesus to let them go into the pigs, and he gave them permission. 33When the demons came out of the man, they went into the pigs, and the herd rushed down the steep bank into the lake and was drowned.

34When those tending the pigs saw what had happened, they ran off and reported this in the town and countryside, 35and the people went out to see what had happened. When they came to Jesus, they found the man from whom the demons had gone out, sitting at Jesus' feet, dressed and in his right mind; and they were afraid. 36Those who had seen it told the people how the demon-possessed man had been cured. 37Then all the people of the region of the Gerasenes asked Jesus to leave them, because they were overcome with fear. So he got into the boat and left.

38The man from whom the demons had gone out begged to go with him, but Jesus sent him away, saying, 39'Return home and tell how much God has done for you.' So the man went away and told all over the town how much Jesus had done for him.

Jesus raises a dead girl and heals a sick woman

40Now when Jesus returned, a crowd welcomed him, for they were all expecting him. 41Then a man named Jairus, a synagogue leader, came and fell at Jesus' feet, pleading with him to come to his house 42because his only daughter, a girl of about twelve, was dying.

As Jesus was on his way, the crowds almost crushed him. 43And a woman was there who had been subject to bleeding for twelve years,[c] but no-one could heal her. 44She came up behind him and touched the edge of his cloak, and immediately her bleeding stopped.

45'Who touched me?' Jesus asked.

When they all denied it, Peter said, 'Master, the people are crowding and pressing against you.'

46But Jesus said, 'Someone touched me; I know that power has gone out from me.'

47Then the woman, seeing that she could not go unnoticed, came trembling and fell at his feet. In the presence of all the people, she told why she had touched him and how she had been instantly healed. 48Then he said to her, 'Daughter, your faith has healed you. Go in peace.'

49While Jesus was still speaking, someone came from the house of Jairus, the synagogue leader. 'Your daughter is dead,' he said. 'Don't bother the teacher anymore.'

50Hearing this, Jesus said to Jairus, 'Don't be afraid; just believe, and she will be healed.'

---

[a] 26 Some manuscripts *Gadarenes*; other manuscripts *Gergesenes*; also in verse 37   [b] 29 Greek *unclean*   [c] 43 Many manuscripts *years, and she had spent all she had on doctors*

⁵¹When he arrived at the house of Jairus, he did not let anyone go in with him except Peter, John and James, and the child's father and mother. ⁵²Meanwhile, all the people were wailing and mourning for her. 'Stop wailing,' Jesus said. 'She is not dead but asleep.'

⁵³They laughed at him, knowing that she was dead. ⁵⁴But he took her by the hand and said, 'My child, get up!' ⁵⁵Her spirit returned, and at once she stood up. Then Jesus told them to give her something to eat. ⁵⁶Her parents were astonished, but he ordered them not to tell anyone what had happened.

Jesus sends out the Twelve

9 When Jesus had called the Twelve together, he gave them power and authority to drive out all demons and to cure diseases, ²and he sent them out to proclaim the kingdom of God and to heal those who were ill. ³He told them: 'Take nothing for the journey—no staff, no bag, no bread, no money, no extra shirt. ⁴Whatever house you enter, stay there until you leave that town. ⁵If people do not welcome you, shake the dust off your feet when you leave their town, as a testimony against them.' ⁶So they set out and went from village to village, proclaiming the good news and healing people everywhere.

⁷Now Herod the tetrarch heard about all that was going on. And he was perplexed because some were saying that John had been raised from the dead, ⁸others that Elijah had appeared, and still others that one of the prophets of long ago had come back to life. ⁹But Herod said, 'I beheaded John. Who, then, is this I hear such things about?' And he tried to see him.

Jesus feeds the five thousand

¹⁰When the apostles returned, they reported to Jesus what they had done. Then he took them with him and they withdrew by themselves to a town called Bethsaida, ¹¹but the crowds learned about it and followed him. He welcomed them and spoke to them about the kingdom of God, and healed those who needed healing.

¹²Late in the afternoon the Twelve came to him and said, 'Send the crowd away so they can go to the surrounding villages and countryside and find food and lodging, because we are in a remote place here.'

¹³He replied, 'You give them something to eat.'

They answered, 'We have only five loaves of bread and two fish—unless we go and buy food for all this crowd.' ¹⁴(About five thousand men were there.)

But he said to his disciples, 'Make them sit down in groups of about fifty each.' ¹⁵The disciples did so, and everyone sat down. ¹⁶Taking the five loaves and the two fish and looking up to heaven, he gave thanks and broke them. Then he gave them to the disciples to set before the people. ¹⁷They all ate and were satisfied, and the disciples picked up twelve basketfuls of broken pieces that were left over.

Peter declares that Jesus is the Messiah

¹⁸Once when Jesus was praying in private and his disciples were with him, he asked them, 'Who do the crowds say I am?'

¹⁹They replied, 'Some say John the Baptist; others say Elijah; and still others, that one of the prophets of long ago has come back to life.'

²⁰'But what about you?' he asked. 'Who do you say I am?'

Peter answered, 'God's Messiah.'

Jesus predicts his death

²¹Jesus strictly warned them not to tell this to anyone. ²²And he said, 'The Son of Man must suffer many things and be rejected by the elders, the chief priests and the teachers of the law, and he must be killed and on the third day be raised to life.'

²³Then he said to them all: 'Whoever wants to be my disciple must deny themselves and take up their cross daily and follow me. ²⁴For whoever wants to save their life will lose it, but whoever loses their life for me will save it. ²⁵What good is it for you to gain the whole world, and yet lose or forfeit your very self? ²⁶If any of you are ashamed of me and my words, the Son of Man will be ashamed of you when he comes in his glory and in the glory of the Father and of the holy angels.

27'Truly I tell you, some who are standing here will not taste death before they see the kingdom of God.'

The transfiguration

28About eight days after Jesus said this, he took Peter, John and James with him and went up onto a mountain to pray. 29As he was praying, the appearance of his face changed, and his clothes became as bright as a flash of lightning. 30Two men, Moses and Elijah, 31appeared in glorious splendour, talking with Jesus. They spoke about his departure,[a] which he was about to bring to fulfilment at Jerusalem. 32Peter and his companions were very sleepy, but when they became fully awake, they saw his glory and the two men standing with him. 33As the men were leaving Jesus, Peter said to him, 'Master, it is good for us to be here. Let us put up three shelters—one for you, one for Moses and one for Elijah.' (He did not know what he was saying.)

34While he was speaking, a cloud appeared and covered them, and they were afraid as they entered the cloud. 35A voice came from the cloud, saying, 'This is my Son, whom I have chosen; listen to him.' 36When the voice had spoken, they found that Jesus was alone. The disciples kept this to themselves and did not tell anyone at that time what they had seen.

Jesus heals a demon-possessed boy

37The next day, when they came down from the mountain, a large crowd met him. 38A man in the crowd called out, 'Teacher, I beg you to look at my son, for he is my only child. 39A spirit seizes him and he suddenly screams; it throws him into convulsions so that he foams at the mouth. It scarcely ever leaves him and is destroying him. 40I begged your disciples to drive it out, but they could not.'

41'You unbelieving and perverse generation,' Jesus replied, 'how long shall I stay with you and put up with you? Bring your son here.'

42Even while the boy was coming, the demon threw him to the ground in a convulsion. But Jesus rebuked the evil[b] spirit, healed the boy and gave him back to his father. 43And they were all amazed at the greatness of God.

Jesus predicts his death a second time

While everyone was marvelling at all that Jesus did, he said to his disciples, 44'Listen carefully to what I am about to tell you: the Son of Man is going to be delivered over to human hands.' 45But they did not understand what this meant. It was hidden from them, so that they did not grasp it, and they were afraid to ask him about it.

46An argument started among the disciples as to which of them would be the greatest. 47Jesus, knowing their thoughts, took a little child and made him stand beside him. 48Then he said to them, 'Whoever welcomes this little child in my name welcomes me; and whoever welcomes me welcomes the one who sent me. For whoever is least among you all is the greatest.'

49'Master,' said John, 'we saw someone driving out demons in your name and we tried to stop him, because he is not one of us.'

50'Do not stop him,' Jesus said, 'for whoever is not against you is for you.'

Samaritan opposition

51As the time approached for him to be taken up to heaven, Jesus resolutely set out for Jerusalem. 52And he sent messengers on ahead, who went into a Samaritan village to get things ready for him; 53but the people there did not welcome him, because he was heading for Jerusalem. 54When the disciples James and John saw this, they asked, 'Lord, do you want us to call fire down from heaven to destroy them[c]?' 55But Jesus turned and rebuked them. 56Then he and his disciples went to another village.

The cost of following Jesus

57As they were walking along the road, a man said to him, 'I will follow you wherever you go.'

58Jesus replied, 'Foxes have holes and birds have nests, but the Son of Man has nowhere to lay his head.'

59He said to another man, 'Follow me.'

---

[a] 31 Greek *exodus* [b] 42 Greek *unclean* [c] 54 Some manuscripts *them, just as Elijah did*

But he replied, 'Lord, first let me go and bury my father.'

60Jesus said to him, 'Let the dead bury their own dead, but you go and proclaim the kingdom of God.'

61Still another said, 'I will follow you, Lord; but first let me go back and say goodbye to my family.'

62Jesus replied, 'No-one who puts a hand to the plough and looks back is fit for service in the kingdom of God.'

Jesus sends out the seventy-two

10 After this the Lord appointed seventy-two[a] others and sent them two by two ahead of him to every town and place where he was about to go. 2He told them, 'The harvest is plentiful, but the workers are few. Ask the Lord of the harvest, therefore, to send out workers into his harvest field. 3Go! I am sending you out like lambs among wolves. 4Do not take a purse or bag or sandals; and do not greet anyone on the road.

5'When you enter a house, first say, "Peace to this house." 6If the head of the house loves peace, your peace will rest on that house; if not, it will return to you. 7Stay there, eating and drinking whatever they give you, for workers deserve their wages. Do not move around from house to house.

8'When you enter a town and are welcomed, eat what is set before you. 9Heal those there who are ill and tell them, "The kingdom of God has come near to you." 10But when you enter a town and are not welcomed, go into its streets and say, 11"Even the dust of your town we wipe from our feet as a warning to you. Yet be sure of this: the kingdom of God has come near." 12I tell you, it will be more bearable on that day for Sodom than for that town.

13'Woe to you, Chorazin! Woe to you, Bethsaida! For if the miracles that were performed in you had been performed in Tyre and Sidon, they would have repented long ago, sitting in sackcloth and ashes. 14But it will be more bearable for Tyre and Sidon at the judgment than for you. 15And you, Capernaum, will you be lifted up to the skies? No, you will go down to the depths.[b]

16'Whoever listens to you listens to me; whoever rejects you rejects me; but whoever rejects me rejects him who sent me.'

17The seventy-two returned with joy and said, 'Lord, even the demons submit to us in your name.'

18He replied, 'I saw Satan fall like lightning from heaven. 19I have given you authority to trample on snakes and scorpions and to overcome all the power of the enemy; nothing will harm you. 20However, do not rejoice that the spirits submit to you, but rejoice that your names are written in heaven.'

21At that time Jesus, full of joy through the Holy Spirit, said, 'I praise you, Father, Lord of heaven and earth, because you have hidden these things from the wise and learned, and revealed them to little children. Yes, Father, for this was your good pleasure.

22'All things have been committed to me by my Father. No-one knows who the Son is except the Father, and no-one knows who the Father is except the Son and those to whom the Son chooses to reveal him.'

23Then he turned to his disciples and said privately, 'Blessed are the eyes that see what you see. 24For I tell you that many prophets and kings wanted to see what you see but did not see it, and to hear what you hear but did not hear it.'

The parable of the good Samaritan

25On one occasion an expert in the law stood up to test Jesus. 'Teacher,' he asked, 'what must I do to inherit eternal life?'

26'What is written in the Law?' he replied. 'How do you read it?'

27He answered, '"Love the Lord your God with all your heart and with all your soul and with all your strength and with all your mind"[c]; and, "Love your neighbour as yourself."[d]'

28'You have answered correctly,' Jesus replied. 'Do this and you will live.'

29But he wanted to justify himself, so he asked Jesus, 'And who is my neighbour?'

30In reply Jesus said: 'A man was going down from Jerusalem to Jericho, when he fell into the hands of robbers. They stripped him of his clothes, beat him and went away,

---

[a] 1 Some manuscripts *seventy*; also in verse 17   [b] 15 Greek *to Hades*   [c] 27 Deut. 6:5   [d] 27 Lev. 19:18

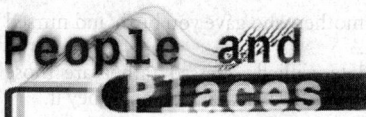

People and Places

Samaritan
Luke 10:33

At the time of Jesus, Samaria was a region, as well as the name of a town in central Israel which had once been the capital of the northern kingdom of Israel. There was a lot of rivalry between the Jews and the Samaritans. The Jews looked down on the Samaritans because they had married outside their ethnic group.

leaving him half-dead. 31A priest happened to be going down the same road, and when he saw the man, he passed by on the other side. 32So too, a Levite, when he came to the place and saw him, passed by on the other side. 33But a Samaritan, as he travelled, came where the man was; and when he saw him, he took pity on him. 34He went to him and bandaged his wounds, pouring on oil and wine. Then he put the man on his own donkey, brought him to an inn and took care of him. 35The next day he took out two denarii^a and gave them to the innkeeper. "Look after him," he said, "and when I return, I will reimburse you for any extra expense you may have."

36'Which of these three do you think was a neighbour to the man who fell into the hands of robbers?'

37The expert in the law replied, 'The one who had mercy on him.'

Jesus told him, 'Go and do likewise.'

At the home of Martha and Mary

38As Jesus and his disciples were on their way, he came to a village where a woman named Martha opened her home to him. 39She had a sister called Mary, who sat at the Lord's feet listening to what he said. 40But Martha was distracted by all the preparations that had to be made. She came to him and asked, 'Lord, don't you care that my sister has left me to do the work by myself? Tell her to help me!'

41'Martha, Martha,' the Lord answered, 'you are worried and upset about many things, 42but few things are needed—or indeed only one.^{b} Mary has chosen what is better, and it will not be taken away from her.'

Jesus' teaching on prayer

11 One day Jesus was praying in a certain place. When he finished, one of his disciples said to him, 'Lord, teach us to pray, just as John taught his disciples.'

2He said to them, 'When you pray, say:

'"Father,^{c}
hallowed be your name,
your kingdom come.^{d}
3Give us each day our daily bread.
4Forgive us our sins,
 for we also forgive everyone who sins against us.^{e}
And lead us not into temptation."'^{f}

5Then Jesus said to them, 'Suppose you have a friend, and you go to him at midnight and say, "Friend, lend me three loaves of bread; 6a friend of mine on a journey has come to me, and I have nothing to set before him." 7And suppose the one inside answers, "Don't bother me. The door is already locked, and my children and I are in bed. I can't get up and give you anything." 8I tell you, even though he will not get up and give you the bread because of friendship, yet because of your shameless audacity^g he will surely get up and give you as much as you need.

9'So I say to you: ask and it will be given to you; seek and you will find; knock and the door will be opened to you. 10For everyone who asks receives; those who seek find; and to those who knock, the door will be opened.

---

^{a}35 A denarius was the daily wage of a day labourer (see Matt. 20:2). ^{b}42 Some manuscripts *but only one thing is needed* ^{c}2 Some manuscripts *Our Father in heaven* ^{d}2 Some manuscripts *come. May your will be done on earth as it is in heaven.* ^{e}4 Greek *everyone who is indebted to us* ^{f}4 Some manuscripts *temptation, but deliver us from the evil one* ^{g}8 Or *yet to preserve his good name*

¹¹'Which of you fathers, if your son asks for[a] a fish, will give him a snake instead? ¹²Or if he asks for an egg, will give him a scorpion? ¹³If you then, though you are evil, know how to give good gifts to your children, how much more will your Father in heaven give the Holy Spirit to those who ask him!'

Jesus and Beelzebul

¹⁴Jesus was driving out a demon that was mute. When the demon left, the man who had been mute spoke, and the crowd was amazed. ¹⁵But some of them said, 'By Beelzebul, the prince of demons, he is driving out demons.' ¹⁶Others tested him by asking for a sign from heaven.

¹⁷Jesus knew their thoughts and said to them: 'Any kingdom divided against itself will be ruined, and a house divided against itself will fall. ¹⁸If Satan is divided against himself, how can his kingdom stand? I say this because you claim that I drive out demons by Beelzebul. ¹⁹Now if I drive out demons by Beelzebul, by whom do your followers drive them out? So then, they will be your judges. ²⁰But if I drive out demons by the finger of God, then the kingdom of God has come upon you.

²¹'When a strong man, fully armed, guards his own house, his possessions are safe. ²²But when someone stronger attacks and overpowers him, he takes away the armour in which the man trusted and divides up his plunder.

²³'Whoever is not with me is against me, and whoever does not gather with me scatters.

²⁴'When an evil[b] spirit comes out of anyone, it goes through arid places seeking rest and does not find it. Then it says, "I will return to the house I left." ²⁵When it arrives, it finds the house swept clean and put in order. ²⁶Then it goes and takes seven other spirits more wicked than itself, and they go in and live there. And the final condition of that person is worse than the first.'

²⁷As Jesus was saying these things, a woman in the crowd called out, 'Blessed is the mother who gave you birth and nursed you.'

²⁸He replied, 'Blessed rather are those who hear the word of God and obey it.'

The sign of Jonah

²⁹As the crowds increased, Jesus said, 'This is a wicked generation. It asks for a sign, but none will be given it except the sign of Jonah. ³⁰For as Jonah was a sign to the Ninevites, so also will the Son of Man be to this generation. ³¹The Queen of the South will rise at the judgment with the people of this generation and condemn them, for she came from the ends of the earth to listen to Solomon's wisdom; and now one[c] greater than Solomon is here. ³²The people of Nineveh will stand up at the judgment with this generation and condemn it, for they repented at the preaching of Jonah; and now one greater than Jonah is here.

The lamp of the body

³³'None of you lights a lamp and puts it in a place where it will be hidden, or under a bowl. Instead you put it on its stand, so that those who come in may see the light. ³⁴Your eye is the lamp of your body. When your eyes are healthy,[d] your whole body also is full of light. But when they are unhealthy,[e] your body also is full of darkness. ³⁵See to it, then, that the light within you is not darkness. ³⁶Therefore, if your whole body is full of light, and no part of it dark, it will be just as full of light as when a lamp shines its light on you.'

Woes on the Pharisees and the experts in the law

³⁷When Jesus had finished speaking, a Pharisee invited him to eat with him; so he went in and reclined at the table. ³⁸But the Pharisee was surprised when he noticed that Jesus did not first wash before the meal.

³⁹Then the Lord said to him, 'Now then, you Pharisees clean the outside of the cup and dish, but inside you are full of greed and wickedness. ⁴⁰You foolish people! Did not the one who made the outside make the inside also? ⁴¹But now as for what is inside

---

[a] 11 Some manuscripts *for bread, will give him a stone? Or if he asks for*   [b] 24 Greek *unclean*   [c] 31 Or *something*; also in verse 32   [d] 34 The Greek for *healthy* here implies *generous*.   [e] 34 The Greek for *unhealthy* here implies *stingy*.

Reclining at table
Luke 11:37
The Greeks and Romans used to lie on couches around tables while they ate. They would lie on their left side and eat their food with their right hand. Jewish people often followed this custom too.

you—be generous to the poor, and everything will be clean for you.

42'Woe to you Pharisees, because you give God a tenth of your mint, rue and all other kinds of garden herbs, but you neglect justice and the love of God. You should have practised the latter without leaving the former undone.

43'Woe to you Pharisees, because you love the most important seats in the synagogues and respectful greetings in the market-places.

44'Woe to you, because you are like unmarked graves, which people walk over without knowing it.'

45One of the experts in the law answered him, 'Teacher, when you say these things, you insult us also.'

46Jesus replied, 'And you experts in the law, woe to you, because you load people down with burdens they can hardly carry, and you yourselves will not lift one finger to help them.

47'Woe to you, because you build tombs for the prophets, and it was your ancestors who killed them. 48So you testify that you approve of what your ancestors did; they killed the prophets, and you build their tombs. 49Because of this, God in his wisdom said, "I will send them prophets and apostles, some of whom they will kill and others they will persecute." 50Therefore this generation will be held responsible for the blood of all the prophets that has been shed since the beginning of the world, 51from the blood of Abel to the blood of Zechariah, who was killed between the altar and the sanctuary. Yes, I tell you, this generation will be held responsible for it all.

52'Woe to you experts in the law, because you have taken away the key to knowledge. You yourselves have not entered, and you have hindered those who were entering.'

53When Jesus went outside, the Pharisees and the teachers of the law began to oppose him fiercely and to besiege him with questions, 54waiting to catch him in something he might say.

Warnings and encouragements

12 Meanwhile, when a crowd of many thousands had gathered, so that they were trampling on one another, Jesus began to speak first to his disciples, saying: 'Be^a on your guard against the yeast of the Pharisees, which is hypocrisy. 2There is nothing concealed that will not be disclosed, or hidden that will not be made known. 3What you have said in the dark will be heard in the daylight, and what you have whispered in the ear in the inner rooms will be proclaimed from the roofs.

4'I tell you, my friends, do not be afraid of those who kill the body and after that can do no more. 5But I will show you whom you should fear: fear him who, after your body has been killed, has authority to throw you into hell. Yes, I tell you, fear him. 6Are not five sparrows sold for two pennies? Yet not one of them is forgotten by God. 7Indeed, the very hairs of your head are all numbered. Don't be afraid; you are worth more than many sparrows.

8'I tell you, whoever publicly acknowledges me, the Son of Man will also acknowledge before the angels of God. 9But whoever publicly disowns me will be disowned before the angels of God. 10And everyone who speaks a word against the Son of Man will be forgiven, but anyone who blasphemes against the Holy Spirit will not be forgiven.

11'When you are brought before synagogues, rulers and authorities, do not worry

---

^{a} 1 Or *speak to his disciples, saying: 'First of all, be* about how you will defend yourselves or what you will say, 12for the Holy Spirit will teach you at that time what you should say.'

The parable of the rich fool

13Someone in the crowd said to him, 'Teacher, tell my brother to divide the inheritance with me.'

14Jesus replied, 'Man, who appointed me a judge or an arbiter between you?' 15Then he said to them, 'Watch out! Be on your guard against all kinds of greed; life does not consist in an abundance of possessions.'

16And he told them this parable: 'The ground of a certain rich man yielded an abundant harvest. 17He thought to himself, "What shall I do? I have no place to store my crops."

18'Then he said, "This is what I'll do. I will tear down my barns and build bigger ones, and there I will store my surplus grain. 19And I'll say to myself, 'You have plenty of grain laid up for many years. Take life easy; eat, drink and be merry.'"

20'But God said to him, "You fool! This very night your life will be demanded from you. Then who will get what you have prepared for yourself?"

21'This is how it will be with those who store up things for themselves but are not rich towards God.'

Do not worry

22Then Jesus said to his disciples: 'Therefore I tell you, do not worry about your life, what you will eat; or about your body, what you will wear. 23Life is more than food, and the body more than clothes. 24Consider the ravens: they do not sow or reap, they have no storeroom or barn; yet God feeds them. And how much more valuable you are than birds! 25Who of you by worrying can add a single hour to your life*a*? 26Since you cannot do this very little thing, why do you worry about the rest?

27'Consider how the wild flowers grow. They do not labour or spin. Yet I tell you, not even Solomon in all his splendour was dressed like one of these. 28If that is how God clothes the grass of the field, which is here today, and tomorrow is thrown into the fire, how much more will he clothe you—you of little faith! 29And do not set your heart on what you will eat or drink; do not worry about it. 30For the pagan world runs after all such things, and your Father knows that you need them. 31But seek his kingdom, and these things will be given to you as well.

32'Do not be afraid, little flock, for your Father has been pleased to give you the kingdom. 33Sell your possessions and give to the poor. Provide purses for yourselves that will not wear out, a treasure in heaven that will never fail, where no thief comes near and no moth destroys. 34For where your treasure is, there your heart will be also.

Watchfulness

35'Be dressed ready for service and keep your lamps burning, 36like servants waiting for their master to return from a wedding banquet, so that when he comes and knocks they can immediately open the door for him. 37It will be good for those servants whose master finds them watching when he comes. Truly I tell you, he will dress himself to serve, will make them recline at the table and will come and wait on them. 38It will be good for those servants whose master finds them ready, even if he comes in the middle of the night or towards daybreak. 39But understand this: if the owner of the house

making Connections

Slaves
Luke 12:37
The word that is translated as 'servant' in the New Testament actually means 'slave'. Slaves were owned and controlled by their masters; they weren't just employed to do a job.

---

a 25 Or *single cubit* to your height

had known at what hour the thief was coming, he would not have let his house be broken into. 40You also must be ready, because the Son of Man will come at an hour when you do not expect him.'

41Peter asked, 'Lord, are you telling this parable to us, or to everyone?'

42The Lord answered, 'Who then is the faithful and wise manager, whom the master puts in charge of his servants to give them their food allowance at the proper time? 43It will be good for that servant whom the master finds doing so when he returns. 44Truly I tell you, he will put him in charge of all his possessions. 45But suppose the servant says to himself, "My master is taking a long time in coming," and he then begins to beat the other servants, both men and women, and to eat and drink and get drunk. 46The master of that servant will come on a day when he does not expect him and at an hour he is not aware of. He will cut him to pieces and assign him a place with the unbelievers.

47'The servant who knows the master's will and does not get ready or does not do what the master wants will be beaten with many blows. 48But the one who does not know and does things deserving punishment will be beaten with few blows. From everyone who has been given much, much will be demanded; and from the one who has been entrusted with much, much more will be asked.

Not peace but division

49'I have come to bring fire on the earth, and how I wish it were already kindled! 50But I have a baptism to undergo, and what constraint I am under until it is completed! 51Do you think I came to bring peace on earth? No, I tell you, but division. 52From now on there will be five in one family divided against each other, three against two and two against three. 53They will be divided, father against son and son against father, mother against daughter and daughter against mother, mother-in-law against daughter-in-law and daughter-in-law against mother-in-law.'

Interpreting the times

54He said to the crowd: 'When you see a cloud rising in the west, immediately you say, "It's going to rain," and it does. 55And when the south wind blows, you say, "It's going to be hot," and it is. 56Hypocrites! You know how to interpret the appearance of the earth and the sky. How is it that you don't know how to interpret this present time?

57'Why don't you judge for yourselves what is right? 58As you are going with your adversary to the magistrate, try hard to be reconciled on the way, or your adversary may drag you off to the judge, and the judge turn you over to the officer, and the officer throw you into prison. 59I tell you, you will not get out until you have paid the last penny.'

Repent or perish

13 Now there were some present at that time who told Jesus about the Galileans whose blood Pilate had mixed with their sacrifices. 2Jesus answered, 'Do you think that these Galileans were worse sinners than all the other Galileans because they suffered this way? 3I tell you, no! But unless you repent, you too will all perish. 4Or those eighteen who died when the tower in Siloam fell on them—do you think they were more guilty than all the others living in Jerusalem? 5I tell you, no! But unless you repent, you too will all perish.'

6Then he told this parable: 'A man had a fig-tree growing in his vineyard, and he went to look for fruit on it but did not find any. 7So he said to the man who took care of the vineyard, "For three years now I've been coming to look for fruit on this fig-tree and haven't found any. Cut it down! Why should it use up the soil?"

8' "Sir," the man replied, "leave it alone for one more year, and I'll dig round it and fertilise it. 9If it bears fruit next year, fine! If not, then cut it down."'

Jesus heals a crippled woman on the Sabbath

10On a Sabbath Jesus was teaching in one of the synagogues, 11and a woman was there who had been crippled by a spirit for eighteen years. She was bent over and could not straighten up at all. 12When Jesus saw her, he called her forward and said to her, 'Woman,[a] you are set free from your infirmity.' 13Then he put his hands on her, and immediately she straightened up and praised God.

14Indignant because Jesus had healed on the Sabbath, the synagogue leader said to the people, 'There are six days for work. So come and be healed on those days, not on the Sabbath.'

15The Lord answered him, 'You hypocrites! Doesn't each of you on the Sabbath untie your ox or donkey from the stall and lead it out to give it water? 16Then should not this woman, a daughter of Abraham, whom Satan has kept bound for eighteen long years, be set free on the Sabbath day from what bound her?'

17When he said this, all his opponents were humiliated, but the people were delighted with all the wonderful things he was doing.

The parables of the mustard seed and the yeast

18Then Jesus asked, 'What is the kingdom of God like? What shall I compare it to? 19It is like a mustard seed, which a man took and planted in his garden. It grew and became a tree, and the birds perched in its branches.'

20Again he asked, 'What shall I compare the kingdom of God to? 21It is like yeast that a woman took and mixed into about thirty kilograms of flour until it worked all through the dough.'

The narrow door

22Then Jesus went through the towns and villages, teaching as he made his way to Jerusalem. 23Someone asked him, 'Lord, are only a few people going to be saved?'

He said to them, 24'Make every effort to enter through the narrow door, because many, I tell you, will try to enter and will not be able to. 25Once the owner of the house gets up and closes the door, you will stand outside knocking and pleading, "Sir, open the door for us."

'But he will answer, "I don't know you or where you come from."

26'Then you will say, "We ate and drank with you, and you taught in our streets."

27'But he will reply, "I don't know you or where you come from. Away from me, all you evildoers!"

28'There will be weeping there, and gnashing of teeth, when you see Abraham, Isaac and Jacob and all the prophets in the kingdom of God, but you yourselves thrown out. 29People will come from east and west and north and south, and will take their places at the feast in the kingdom of God. 30Indeed there are those who are last who will be first, and first who will be last.'

Jesus' sorrow for Jerusalem

31At that time some Pharisees came to Jesus and said to him, 'Leave this place and go somewhere else. Herod wants to kill you.'

32He replied, 'Go and tell that fox, "I will keep on driving out demons and healing people today and tomorrow, and on the third day I will reach my goal." 33In any case, I must press on today and tomorrow and the next day—for surely no prophet can die outside Jerusalem!

34'Jerusalem, Jerusalem, you who kill the prophets and stone those sent to you, how often I have longed to gather your children together, as a hen gathers her chicks under her wings, and you were not willing. 35Look, your house is left to you desolate. I tell you, you will not see me again until you say, "Blessed is he who comes in the name of the Lord."[b]'

Jesus at a Pharisee's house

14 One Sabbath, when Jesus went to eat in the house of a prominent Pharisee, he was being carefully watched. 2There in front of him was a man suffering from abnormal swelling of his body. 3Jesus asked the Pharisees and experts in the law, 'Is it lawful to heal on the Sabbath or not?' 4But they remained silent. So taking hold of the man, he healed him and sent him on his way.

5Then he asked them, 'If one of you has a child[c] or an ox that falls into a well on the Sabbath day, will you not immediately pull it out?' 6And they had nothing to say.

---

[a] 12 The Greek for *Woman* does not denote any disrespect. [b] 35 Psalm 118:26 [c] 5 Some manuscripts *donkey*

IN OTHER WORDS

Parable
Luke 14:7

The Greek word for 'parable' means 'something put alongside', and so a parable is a story that uses one thing to explain something else. Jesus is well known for his parables where he takes a situation that is familiar to his listeners and uses it to explain a truth about his kingdom. Parables are also found in the Old Testament (2 Samuel 12:1–4).

7When he noticed how the guests picked the places of honour at the table, he told them this parable: 8'When someone invites you to a wedding feast, do not take the place of honour, for a person more distinguished than you may have been invited. 9If so, the host who invited both of you will come and say to you, "Give this person your seat." Then, humiliated, you will have to take the least important place. 10But when you are invited, take the lowest place, so that when your host comes, he will say to you, "Friend, move up to a better place." Then you will be honoured in the presence of all the other guests. 11For all those who exalt themselves will be humbled, and those who humble themselves will be exalted.'

12Then Jesus said to his host, 'When you give a luncheon or dinner, do not invite your friends, your brothers or sisters, your relatives, or your rich neighbours; if you do, they may invite you back and so you will be repaid. 13But when you give a banquet, invite the poor, the crippled, the lame, the blind, 14and you will be blessed. Although they cannot repay you, you will be repaid at the resurrection of the righteous.'

The parable of the great banquet

15When one of those at the table with him heard this, he said to Jesus, 'Blessed are those who will eat at the feast in the kingdom of God.'

16Jesus replied: 'A certain man was preparing a great banquet and invited many guests. 17At the time of the banquet he sent his servant to tell those who had been invited, "Come, for everything is now ready."

18'But they all alike began to make excuses. The first said, "I have just bought a field, and I must go and see it. Please excuse me."

19'Another said, "I have just bought five yoke of oxen, and I'm on my way to try them out. Please excuse me."

20'Still another said, "I have just got married, so I can't come."

21'The servant came back and reported this to his master. Then the owner of the house became angry and ordered his servant, "Go out quickly into the streets and alleys of the town and bring in the poor, the crippled, the blind and the lame."

22' "Sir," the servant said, "what you ordered has been done, but there is still room."

23'Then the master told his servant, "Go out to the roads and country lanes and compel them to come in, so that my house will be full. 24I tell you, not one of those who were invited will get a taste of my banquet." '

The cost of being a disciple

25Large crowds were travelling with Jesus, and turning to them he said: 26'If anyone comes to me and does not hate father and mother, wife and children, brothers and sisters—yes, even life itself—such a person cannot be my disciple. 27And whoever does not carry their cross and follow me cannot be my disciple.

28'Suppose one of you wants to build a tower. Won't you first sit down and estimate the cost to see if you have enough money to complete it? 29For if you lay the foundation and are not able to finish it, everyone who sees it will ridicule you, 30saying, "This person began to build and wasn't able to finish."

31'Or suppose a king is about to go to war against another king. Won't he first sit down and consider whether he is able with ten thousand men to oppose the one coming against him with twenty thousand? 32If he is not able, he will send a delegation while the other is still a long way off and will ask for terms of peace. 33In the same way, those of you who do not give up everything you have cannot be my disciples.

34'Salt is good, but if it loses its saltiness, how can it be made salty again? 35It is fit neither for the soil nor for the manure heap; it is thrown out.

'Whoever has ears to hear, let them hear.'

The parable of the lost sheep

15 Now the tax collectors and sinners were all gathering round to hear Jesus. 2But the Pharisees and the teachers of the law muttered, 'This man welcomes sinners, and eats with them.'

3Then Jesus told them this parable: 4'Suppose one of you has a hundred sheep and loses one of them. Doesn't he leave the ninety-nine in the open country and go after the lost sheep until he finds it? 5And when he finds it, he joyfully puts it on his shoulders 6and goes home. Then he calls his friends and neighbours together and says, "Rejoice with me; I have found my lost sheep." 7I tell you that in the same way there will be more rejoicing in heaven over one sinner who repents than over ninety-nine righteous people who do not need to repent.

The parable of the lost coin

8'Or suppose a woman has ten silver coins[a] and loses one. Doesn't she light a lamp, sweep the house and search carefully until she finds it? 9And when she finds it, she calls her friends and neighbours together and says, "Rejoice with me; I have found my lost coin." 10In the same way, I tell you, there is rejoicing in the presence of the angels of God over one sinner who repents.'

The parable of the lost son

11Jesus continued: 'There was a man who had two sons. 12The younger one said to his father, "Father, give me my share of the estate." So he divided his property between them.

13'Not long after that, the younger son got together all he had, set off for a distant country and there squandered his wealth in wild living. 14After he had spent everything, there was a severe famine in that whole country, and he began to be in need. 15So he went and hired himself out to a citizen of that country, who sent him to his fields to feed pigs. 16He longed to fill his stomach with the pods that the pigs were eating, but no-one gave him anything.

17'When he came to his senses, he said, "How many of my father's hired servants have food to spare, and here I am starving to death! 18I will set out and go back to my father and say to him: Father, I have sinned against heaven and against you. 19I am no longer worthy to be called your son; make me like one of your hired servants." 20So he got up and went to his father.

'But while he was still a long way off, his father saw him and was filled with compassion for him; he ran to his son, threw his arms round him and kissed him.

21'The son said to him, "Father, I have sinned against heaven and against you. I am no longer worthy to be called your son."

22'But the father said to his servants, "Quick! Bring the best robe and put it on him. Put a ring on his finger and sandals on his feet. 23Bring the fattened calf and kill it. Let's have a feast and celebrate. 24For this son of mine was dead and is alive again; he was lost and is found." So they began to celebrate.

Sign of the times

Belonging to a family
Luke 15:22
The father in this story welcomes his younger son back into the family. The ring that he gave him showed that the son had an important place in the family. Putting sandals on his feet showed that he was a son and not a servant, as servants didn't wear sandals.

---

[a] 8 Greek *ten drachmas*, each worth about a day's wages

25'Meanwhile, the elder son was in the field. When he came near the house, he heard music and dancing. 26So he called one of the servants and asked him what was going on. 27"Your brother has come," he replied, "and your father has killed the fattened calf because he has him back safe and sound."

28'The elder brother became angry and refused to go in. So his father went out and pleaded with him. 29But he answered his father, "Look! All these years I've been slaving for you and never disobeyed your orders. Yet you never gave me even a young goat so I could celebrate with my friends. 30But when this son of yours who has squandered your property with prostitutes comes home, you kill the fattened calf for him!"

31' "My son," the father said, "you are always with me, and everything I have is yours. 32But we had to celebrate and be glad, because this brother of yours was dead and is alive again; he was lost and is found." '

The parable of the shrewd manager

16 Jesus told his disciples: 'There was a rich man whose manager was accused of wasting his possessions. 2So he called him in and asked him, "What is this I hear about you? Give an account of your management, because you cannot be manager any longer."

3'The manager said to himself, "What shall I do now? My master is taking away my job. I'm not strong enough to dig, and I'm ashamed to beg— 4I know what I'll do so that, when I lose my job here, people will welcome me into their houses."

5'So he called in each one of his master's debtors. He asked the first, "How much do you owe my master?"

6' "Three thousand litres of olive oil," he replied.

'The manager told him, "Take your bill, sit down quickly, and make it fifteen hundred."

7'Then he asked the second, "And how much do you owe?"

' "Thirty tons of wheat," he replied.

'He told him, "Take your bill and make it twenty-four."

8'The master commended the dishonest manager because he had acted shrewdly. For the people of this world are more shrewd in dealing with their own kind than are the people of the light. 9I tell you, use worldly wealth to gain friends for yourselves, so that when it is gone, you will be welcomed into eternal dwellings.

10'Whoever can be trusted with very little can also be trusted with much, and whoever is dishonest with very little will also be dishonest with much. 11So if you have not been trustworthy in handling worldly wealth, who will trust you with true riches? 12And if you have not been trustworthy with someone else's property, who will give you property of your own?

13'No-one can serve two masters. Either you will hate the one and love the other, or you will be devoted to the one and despise the other. You cannot serve both God and Money.'

14The Pharisees, who loved money, heard all this and were sneering at Jesus. 15He said to them, 'You are the ones who justify yourselves in the eyes of others, but God knows your hearts. What people value highly is detestable in God's sight.

Additional teachings

16'The Law and the Prophets were proclaimed until John. Since that time, the good news of the kingdom of God is being preached, and people are forcing their way into it. 17It is easier for heaven and earth to disappear than for the least stroke of a pen to drop out of the Law.

18'Anyone who divorces his wife and marries another woman commits adultery, and the man who marries a divorced woman commits adultery.

The rich man and Lazarus

19'There was a rich man who was dressed in purple and fine linen and lived in luxury every day. 20At his gate was laid a beggar named Lazarus, covered with sores 21and longing to eat what fell from the rich man's table. Even the dogs came and licked his sores.

22'The time came when the beggar died and the angels carried him to Abraham's side. The rich man also died and was buried.

23In Hades, where he was in torment, he looked up and saw Abraham far away, with Lazarus by his side. 24So he called to him, "Father Abraham, have pity on me and send Lazarus to dip the tip of his finger in water and cool my tongue, because I am in agony in this fire."

25'But Abraham replied, "Son, remember that in your lifetime you received your good things, while Lazarus received bad things, but now he is comforted here and you are in agony. 26And besides all this, between us and you a great chasm has been set in place, so that those who want to go from here to you cannot, nor can anyone cross over from there to us."

27'He answered, "Then I beg you, father, send Lazarus to my family, 28for I have five brothers. Let him warn them, so that they will not also come to this place of torment."

29'Abraham replied, "They have Moses and the Prophets; let them listen to them."

30'"No, father Abraham," he said, "but if someone from the dead goes to them, they will repent."

31'He said to him, "If they do not listen to Moses and the Prophets, they will not be convinced even if someone rises from the dead."'

Sin, faith, duty

17 Jesus said to his disciples: 'Things that cause people to stumble are bound to come, but woe to anyone through whom they come. 2It would be better for you to be thrown into the sea with a millstone tied round your neck than for you to cause one of these little ones to stumble. 3So watch yourselves.

'If a brother or sister sins against you, rebuke them; and if they repent, forgive them. 4Even if they sin against you seven times in a day and seven times come back to you saying "I repent," you must forgive them.'

5The apostles said to the Lord, 'Increase our faith!'

6He replied, 'If you have faith as small as a mustard seed, you can say to this mulberry tree, "Be uprooted and planted in the sea," and it will obey you.

7'Suppose one of you has a servant ploughing or looking after the sheep. Will he say to the servant when he comes in from the field, "Come along now and sit down to eat"? 8Won't he rather say, "Prepare my supper, get yourself ready and wait on me while I eat and drink; after that you may eat and drink"? 9Will he thank the servant because he did what he was told to do? 10So you also, when you have done everything you were told to do, should say, "We are unworthy servants; we have only done our duty."'

Jesus heals ten men with leprosy

11Now on his way to Jerusalem, Jesus travelled along the border between Samaria and Galilee. 12As he was going into a village, ten men who had leprosy^a met him. They stood at a distance 13and called out in a loud voice, 'Jesus, Master, have pity on us!'

14When he saw them, he said, 'Go, show yourselves to the priests.' And as they went, they were cleansed.

15One of them, when he saw he was healed, came back, praising God in a loud voice. 16He threw himself at Jesus' feet and thanked him—and he was a Samaritan.

17Jesus asked, 'Were not all ten cleansed? Where are the other nine? 18Was no-one found to return and give praise to God except this foreigner?' 19Then he said to him, 'Rise and go; your faith has made you well.'

The coming of the kingdom of God

20Once, having been asked by the Pharisees when the kingdom of God would come, Jesus replied, 'The coming of the kingdom of God is not something that can be observed, 21nor will people say, "Here it is," or "There it is," because the kingdom of God is in your midst.'^{b}

22Then he said to his disciples, 'The time is coming when you will long to see one of the days of the Son of Man, but you will not see it. 23People will tell you, "There he is!" or "Here he is!" Do not go running off after them. 24For the Son of Man in his day^c will

---

^{a} 12 The Greek word traditionally translated *leprosy* was used for various diseases affecting the skin. ^{b} 21 Or *is within you* ^{c} 24 Some manuscripts do not have *in his day*.

be like the lightning, which flashes and lights up the sky from one end to the other. 25But first he must suffer many things and be rejected by this generation.

26'Just as it was in the days of Noah, so also will it be in the days of the Son of Man. 27People were eating, drinking, marrying and being given in marriage up to the day Noah entered the ark. Then the flood came and destroyed them all.

28'It was the same in the days of Lot. People were eating and drinking, buying and selling, planting and building. 29But the day Lot left Sodom, fire and sulphur rained down from heaven and destroyed them all.

30'It will be just like this on the day the Son of Man is revealed. 31On that day no-one who is on the housetop, with possessions inside, should go down to get them. Likewise, no-one in the field should go back for anything. 32Remember Lot's wife! 33Whoever tries to keep their life will lose it, and whoever loses their life will preserve it. 34I tell you, on that night two people will be in one bed; one will be taken and the other left. 35(36)Two women will be grinding corn together; one will be taken and the other left.'

37'Where, Lord?' they asked.

He replied, 'Where there is a dead body, there the vultures will gather.'

The parable of the persistent widow

18 Then Jesus told his disciples a parable to show them that they should always pray and not give up. 2He said: 'In a certain town there was a judge who neither feared God nor cared what people thought. 3And there was a widow in that town who kept coming to him with the plea, "Grant me justice against my adversary."

4'For some time he refused. But finally he said to himself, "Even though I don't fear God or care what people think, 5yet because this widow keeps bothering me, I will see that she gets justice, so that she won't eventually come and attack me!"'

6And the Lord said, 'Listen to what the unjust judge says. 7And will not God bring about justice for his chosen ones, who cry out to him day and night? Will he keep putting them off? 8I tell you, he will see that they get justice, and quickly. However, when the Son of Man comes, will he find faith on the earth?'

The parable of the Pharisee and the tax collector

9To some who were confident of their own righteousness and looked down on everyone else, Jesus told this parable: 10'Two men went up to the temple to pray, one a Pharisee and the other a tax collector. 11The Pharisee stood by himself and prayed: "God, I thank you that I am not like other people—robbers, evildoers, adulterers—or even like this tax collector. 12I fast twice a week and give a tenth of all I get."

13'But the tax collector stood at a distance. He would not even look up to heaven, but beat his breast and said, "God, have mercy on me, a sinner."

14'I tell you that this man, rather than the other, went home justified before God. For all those who exalt themselves will be humbled, and those who humble themselves will be exalted.'

The little children and Jesus

15People were also bringing babies to Jesus for him to place his hands on them. When the disciples saw this, they rebuked them. 16But Jesus called the children to him and said, 'Let the little children come to me, and do not hinder them, for the kingdom of God belongs to such as these. 17Truly I tell you, anyone who will not receive the kingdom of God like a little child will never enter it.'

The rich and the kingdom of God

18A certain ruler asked him, 'Good teacher, what must I do to inherit eternal life?'

19'Why do you call me good?' Jesus answered. 'No-one is good—except God alone. 20You know the commandments: "You shall not commit adultery, you shall not murder, you shall not steal, you shall not give false testimony, honour your father and mother."[a]'

21'All these I have kept since I was a boy,' he said.

---

[a] 20 Exodus 20:12-16; Deut. 5:16-20

22When Jesus heard this, he said to him, 'You still lack one thing. Sell everything you have and give to the poor, and you will have treasure in heaven. Then come, follow me.'

23When he heard this, he became very sad, because he was very wealthy. 24Jesus looked at him and said, 'How hard it is for the rich to enter the kingdom of God! 25Indeed, it is easier for a camel to go through the eye of a needle than for the rich to enter the kingdom of God.'

26Those who heard this asked, 'Who then can be saved?'

27Jesus replied, 'What is impossible with human beings is possible with God.'

28Peter said to him, 'We have left all we had to follow you!'

29'Truly I tell you,' Jesus said to them, 'no-one who has left home or wife or brothers or sisters or parents or children for the sake of the kingdom of God 30will fail to receive many times as much in this age, and in the age to come eternal life.'

Jesus predicts his death a third time

31Jesus took the Twelve aside and told them, 'We are going up to Jerusalem, and everything that is written by the prophets about the Son of Man will be fulfilled. 32He will be handed over to the Gentiles. They will mock him, insult him and spit on him; 33they will flog him and kill him. On the third day he will rise again.'

34The disciples did not understand any of this. Its meaning was hidden from them, and they did not know what he was talking about.

A blind beggar receives his sight

35As Jesus approached Jericho, a blind man was sitting by the roadside begging. 36When he heard the crowd going by, he asked what was happening. 37They told him, 'Jesus of Nazareth is passing by.'

38He called out, 'Jesus, Son of David, have mercy on me!'

39Those who led the way rebuked him and told him to be quiet, but he shouted all the more, 'Son of David, have mercy on me!'

40Jesus stopped and ordered the man to be brought to him. When he came near, Jesus asked him, 41'What do you want me to do for you?'

People and Places

David
Luke 18:38
David was one of the greatest kings of Israel. He was described as a man after God's own heart and is known for his defeat of Goliath, his many beautiful psalms and his strong leadership of the people of Israel. However, he also made many mistakes, most notably his adultery with Bathsheba and the way he tried to cover it up. God promised David a kingdom that would have no end, and this was fulfilled in Jesus, who is referred to as 'the Son of David'.

'Lord, I want to see,' he replied.

42Jesus said to him, 'Receive your sight; your faith has healed you.' 43Immediately he received his sight and followed Jesus, praising God. When all the people saw it, they also praised God.

Zacchaeus the tax collector

19 Jesus entered Jericho and was passing through. 2A man was there by the name of Zacchaeus; he was a chief tax collector and was wealthy. 3He wanted to see who Jesus was, but because he was short he could not see over the crowd. 4So he ran ahead and climbed a sycamore-fig tree to see him, since Jesus was coming that way.

5When Jesus reached the spot, he looked up and said to him, 'Zacchaeus, come down immediately. I must stay at your house today.' 6So he came down at once and welcomed him gladly.

7All the people saw this and began to mutter, 'He has gone to be the guest of a "sinner".'

8But Zacchaeus stood up and said to the Lord, 'Look, Lord! Here and now I give half of my possessions to the poor, and if I have cheated anybody out of anything, I will pay back four times the amount.'

⁹Jesus said to him, 'Today salvation has come to this house, because this man, too, is a son of Abraham. ¹⁰For the Son of Man came to seek and to save what was lost.'

The parable of the ten minas

¹¹While they were listening to this, he went on to tell them a parable, because he was near Jerusalem and the people thought that the kingdom of God was going to appear at once. ¹²He said: 'A man of noble birth went to a distant country to have himself appointed king and then to return. ¹³So he called ten of his servants and gave them ten minas.[a] "Put this money to work," he said, "until I come back."

¹⁴'But his subjects hated him and sent a delegation after him to say, "We don't want this man to be our king."

¹⁵'He was made king, however, and returned home. Then he sent for the servants to whom he had given the money, in order to find out what they had gained with it.

¹⁶'The first one came and said, "Sir, your mina has earned ten more."

¹⁷' "Well done, my good servant!" his master replied. "Because you have been trustworthy in a very small matter, take charge of ten cities."

¹⁸'The second came and said, "Sir, your mina has earned five more."

¹⁹'His master answered, "You take charge of five cities."

²⁰'Then another servant came and said, "Sir, here is your mina; I have kept it laid away in a piece of cloth. ²¹I was afraid of you, because you are a hard man. You take out what you did not put in and reap what you did not sow."

²²'His master replied, "I will judge you by your own words, you wicked servant! You knew, did you, that I am a hard man, taking out what I did not put in, and reaping what I did not sow? ²³Why then didn't you put my money on deposit, so that when I came back, I could have collected it with interest?"

²⁴'Then he said to those standing by, "Take his mina away from him and give it to the one who has ten minas."

²⁵' "Sir," they said, "he already has ten!"

²⁶'He replied, "I tell you that to everyone who has, more will be given, but as for those who have nothing, even what they have will be taken away. ²⁷But those enemies of mine who did not want me to be a king over them—bring them here and kill them in front of me." '

Jesus comes to Jerusalem as king

²⁸After Jesus had said this, he went on ahead, going up to Jerusalem. ²⁹As he approached Bethphage and Bethany at the hill called the Mount of Olives, he sent two of his disciples, saying to them, ³⁰'Go to the village ahead of you, and as you enter it, you will find a colt tied there, which no-one has ever ridden. Untie it and bring it here. ³¹If anyone asks you, "Why are you untying it?" say, "The Lord needs it." '

³²Those who were sent ahead went and found it just as he had told them. ³³As they were untying the colt, its owners asked them, 'Why are you untying the colt?'

³⁴They replied, 'The Lord needs it.'

³⁵They brought it to Jesus, threw their cloaks on the colt and put Jesus on it. ³⁶As he went along, people spread their cloaks on the road.

Sign of the times

Money
Luke 19:11

Both Greek and Roman coins were in circulation in Palestine in Jesus' time. The basic Greek coin was a drachma, and was the amount a labourer would earn for a day's work. The mina was worth 100 drachmas, so was a fair amount of money, just over three months' salary.

---

[a] 13 A mina was about three months' wages.

37When he came near the place where the road goes down the Mount of Olives, the whole crowd of disciples began joyfully to praise God in loud voices for all the miracles they had seen:

38'Blessed is the king who comes in the name of the Lord!'[a]

'Peace in heaven and glory in the highest!'

39Some of the Pharisees in the crowd said to Jesus, 'Teacher, rebuke your disciples!'

40'I tell you,' he replied, 'if they keep quiet, the stones will cry out.'

41As he approached Jerusalem and saw the city, he wept over it **42**and said, 'If you, even you, had only known on this day what would bring you peace—but now it is hidden from your eyes. **43**The days will come on you when your enemies will build an embankment against you and encircle you and hem you in on every side. **44**They will dash you to the ground, you and the children within your walls. They will not leave one stone on another, because you did not recognise the time of God's coming to you.'

Jesus at the temple

45When Jesus entered the temple courts, he began to drive out those who were selling. **46**'It is written,' he said to them, ' "My house will be a house of prayer"[b]; but you have made it "a den of robbers".'[c]

47Every day he was teaching at the temple. But the chief priests, the teachers of the law and the leaders among the people were trying to kill him. **48**Yet they could not find any way to do it, because all the people hung on his words.

The authority of Jesus questioned

20 One day as Jesus was teaching the people in the temple courts and proclaiming the good news, the chief priests and the teachers of the law, together with the elders, came up to him. **2**'Tell us by what authority you are doing these things,' they said. 'Who gave you this authority?'

3He replied, 'I will also ask you a question. Tell me, **4**John's baptism—was it from heaven, or of human origin?'

5They discussed it among themselves and said, 'If we say, "From heaven", he will ask, "Why didn't you believe him?" **6**But if we say, "Of human origin", all the people will stone us, because they are persuaded that John was a prophet.'

7So they answered, 'We don't know where it was from.'

8Jesus said, 'Neither will I tell you by what authority I am doing these things.'

The parable of the tenants

9He went on to tell the people this parable: 'A man planted a vineyard, rented it to some farmers and went away for a long time. **10**At harvest time he sent a servant to the tenants so they would give him some of the fruit of the vineyard. But the tenants beat him and sent him away empty-handed. **11**He sent another servant, but that one also they beat and treated shamefully and sent away empty-handed. **12**He sent still a third, and they wounded him and threw him out.

13'Then the owner of the vineyard said, "What shall I do? I will send my son, whom I love; perhaps they will respect him."

14'But when the tenants saw him, they talked the matter over. "This is the heir," they said. "Let's kill him, and the inheritance will be ours." **15**So they threw him out of the vineyard and killed him.

'What then will the owner of the vineyard do to them? **16**He will come and kill those tenants and give the vineyard to others.'

When the people heard this, they said, 'God forbid!'

17Jesus looked directly at them and asked, 'Then what is the meaning of that which is written:

' "The stone the builders rejected
has become the cornerstone"[d]?

18Everyone who falls on that stone will be broken to pieces, but anyone on whom it falls will be crushed.'

19The teachers of the law and the chief priests looked for a way to arrest him immediately, because they knew he had spoken this parable against them. But they were afraid of the people.

---

[a] 38 Psalm 118:26 [b] 46 Isaiah 56:7 [c] 46 Jer. 7:11 [d] 17 Psalm 118:22

Paying taxes to Caesar

20Keeping a close watch on him, they sent spies, who pretended to be sincere. They hoped to catch Jesus in something he said so that they might hand him over to the power and authority of the governor. 21So the spies questioned him: 'Teacher, we know that you speak and teach what is right, and that you do not show partiality but teach the way of God in accordance with the truth. 22Is it right for us to pay taxes to Caesar or not?'

23He saw through their duplicity and said to them, 24'Show me a denarius. Whose image and inscription are on it?'

'Caesar's,' they replied.

25He said to them, 'Then give back to Caesar what is Caesar's, and to God what is God's.'

26They were unable to trap him in what he had said there in public. And astonished by his answer, they became silent.

The resurrection and marriage

27Some of the Sadducees, who say there is no resurrection, came to Jesus with a question. 28'Teacher,' they said, 'Moses wrote for us that if a man's brother dies and leaves a wife but no children, the man must marry the widow and raise up offspring for his brother. 29Now there were seven brothers. The first one married a woman and died childless. 30The second 31and then the third married her, and in the same way the seven died, leaving no children. 32Finally, the woman died too. 33Now then, at the resurrection whose wife will she be, since the seven were married to her?'

34Jesus replied, 'The people of this age marry and are given in marriage. 35But those who are considered worthy of taking part in the age to come and in the resurrection from the dead will neither marry nor be given in marriage, 36and they can no longer die; for they are like the angels. They are God's children, since they are children of the resurrection. 37But in the account of the burning bush, even Moses showed that the dead rise, for he calls the Lord "the God of Abraham, and the God of Isaac, and the God of Jacob".[a] 38He is not the God of the dead, but of the living, for to him all are alive.'

39Some of the teachers of the law responded, 'Well said, teacher!' 40And noone dared to ask him any more questions.

Whose son is the Messiah?

41Then Jesus said to them, 'Why is it said that the Messiah is the son of David? 42David himself declares in the Book of Psalms:

'"The Lord said to my Lord:
  'Sit at my right hand
43until I make your enemies
  a footstool for your feet.'"[b]

44'David calls him "Lord". How then can he be his son?'

Warning against the teachers of the law

45While all the people were listening, Jesus said to his disciples, 46'Beware of the teachers of the law. They like to walk around in flowing robes and love to be greeted with respect in the market-places and have the most important seats in the synagogues and the places of honour at banquets. 47They devour widows' houses and for a show make lengthy prayers. These men will be punished most severely.'

> **People and Places**
>
> **Sadducees**
> Luke 20:27
> The Sadducees were a group of Jewish leaders who took the original Law of Moses very seriously and didn't believe in the resurrection of the dead. They were a powerful group of men who came from the leading families in Israel. They liked to make fun of their opponents by trying to show that their beliefs were ridiculous.

---

[a] 37 Exodus 3:6 [b] 43 Psalm 110:1

The widow's offering

21 As Jesus looked up, he saw the rich putting their gifts into the temple treasury. ²He also saw a poor widow put in two very small copper coins. ³'Truly I tell you,' he said, 'this poor widow has put in more than all the others. ⁴All these people gave their gifts out of their wealth; but she out of her poverty put in all she had to live on.'

The destruction of the temple and signs of the end times

⁵Some of his disciples were remarking about how the temple was adorned with beautiful stones and with gifts dedicated to God. But Jesus said, ⁶'As for what you see here, the time will come when not one stone will be left on another; every one of them will be thrown down.'

⁷'Teacher,' they asked, 'when will these things happen? And what will be the sign that they are about to take place?'

⁸He replied: 'Watch out that you are not deceived. For many will come in my name, claiming, "I am he," and "The time is near." Do not follow them. ⁹When you hear of wars and uprisings, do not be frightened. These things must happen first, but the end will not come right away.'

¹⁰Then he said to them: 'Nation will rise against nation, and kingdom against kingdom. ¹¹There will be great earthquakes, famines and pestilences in various places, and fearful events and great signs from heaven.

¹²'But before all this, they will lay hands on you and persecute you. They will deliver you to synagogues and prisons, and you will be brought before kings and governors, and all on account of my name. ¹³And so you will bear testimony to me. ¹⁴But make up your mind not to worry beforehand how you will defend yourselves. ¹⁵For I will give you words and wisdom that none of your adversaries will be able to resist or contradict. ¹⁶You will be betrayed even by parents, brothers, sisters, relatives and friends, and they will put some of you to death. ¹⁷Everyone will hate you because of me. ¹⁸But not a hair of your head will perish. ¹⁹Stand firm, and you will win life.

²⁰'When you see Jerusalem being surrounded by armies, you will know that its desolation is near. ²¹Then let those who are in Judea flee to the mountains, let those in the city get out, and let those in the country not enter the city. ²²For this is the time of punishment in fulfilment of all that has been written. ²³How dreadful it will be in those days for pregnant women and nursing mothers! There will be great distress in the land and wrath against this people. ²⁴They will fall by the sword and will be taken as prisoners to all the nations. Jerusalem will be trampled on by the Gentiles until the times of the Gentiles are fulfilled.

²⁵'There will be signs in the sun, moon and stars. On the earth, nations will be in anguish and perplexity at the roaring and tossing of the sea. ²⁶People will faint from terror, apprehensive of what is coming on the world, for the heavenly bodies will be shaken. ²⁷At that time they will see the Son of Man coming in a cloud with power and great glory. ²⁸When these things begin to take place, stand up and lift up your heads, because your redemption is drawing near.'

²⁹He told them this parable: 'Look at the fig-tree and all the trees. ³⁰When they sprout leaves, you can see for yourselves and know that summer is near. ³¹Even so, when you see these things happening, you know that the kingdom of God is near.

³²'Truly I tell you, this generation will certainly not pass away until all these things have happened. ³³Heaven and earth will pass away, but my words will never pass away.

³⁴'Be careful, or your hearts will be weighed down with dissipation, drunkenness and the anxieties of life, and that day will close on you suddenly like a trap. ³⁵For it will come on all those who live on the face of the whole earth. ³⁶Be always on the watch, and pray that you may be able to escape all that is about to happen, and that you may be able to stand before the Son of Man.'

³⁷Each day Jesus was teaching at the temple, and each evening he went out to spend the night on the hill called the Mount of Olives, ³⁸and all the people came early in the morning to hear him at the temple.

Judas agrees to betray Jesus

22 Now the Feast of Unleavened Bread, called the Passover, was approaching, ²and the chief priests and the teachers of the law were looking for some way to get rid of Jesus, for they were afraid of the people. ³Then Satan entered Judas, called Iscariot, one of the Twelve. ⁴And Judas went to the chief priests and the officers of the temple guard and discussed with them how he might betray Jesus. ⁵They were delighted and agreed to give him money. ⁶He consented, and watched for an opportunity to hand Jesus over to them when no crowd was present.

The Last Supper

⁷Then came the day of Unleavened Bread on which the Passover lamb had to be sacrificed. ⁸Jesus sent Peter and John, saying, 'Go and make preparations for us to eat the Passover.'

⁹'Where do you want us to prepare for it?' they asked.

¹⁰He replied, 'As you enter the city, a man carrying a jar of water will meet you. Follow him to the house that he enters, ¹¹and say to the owner of the house, "The Teacher asks: where is the guest room, where I may eat the Passover with my disciples?" ¹²He will show you a large room upstairs, all furnished. Make preparations there.'

¹³They left and found things just as Jesus had told them. So they prepared the Passover.

¹⁴When the hour came, Jesus and his apostles reclined at the table. ¹⁵And he said to them, 'I have eagerly desired to eat this Passover with you before I suffer. ¹⁶For I tell you, I will not eat it again until it finds fulfilment in the kingdom of God.'

¹⁷After taking the cup, he gave thanks and said, 'Take this and divide it among you. ¹⁸For I tell you I will not drink again of the fruit of the vine until the kingdom of God comes.'

¹⁹And he took bread, gave thanks and broke it, and gave it to them, saying, 'This is my body given for you; do this in remembrance of me.'

²⁰In the same way, after the supper he took the cup, saying, 'This cup is the new covenant in my blood, which is poured out for you. ²¹But the hand of him who is going to betray me is with mine on the table. ²²The Son of Man will go as it has been decreed. But woe to that man who betrays him!' ²³They began to question among themselves which of them it might be who would do this.

²⁴A dispute also arose among them as to which of them was considered to be greatest. ²⁵Jesus said to them, 'The kings of the Gentiles lord it over them; and those who exercise authority over them call themselves Benefactors. ²⁶But you are not to be like that. Instead, the greatest among you should be like the youngest, and the one who rules like the one who serves. ²⁷For who is greater, the one who is at the table or the one who serves? Is it not the one who is at the table? But I am among you as one who serves. ²⁸You are those who have stood by me in my trials. ²⁹And I confer on you a kingdom, just as my Father conferred one on me, ³⁰so that you may eat and drink at my table in my kingdom and sit on thrones, judging the twelve tribes of Israel.

IN OTHER WORDS

Passover
Luke 22:15
The Passover celebrates one of the most dramatic nights in human history – when the Israelites cooked a special meal, put blood on the doorposts of their houses and then waited, with their belongings packed, for God to deliver them from slavery (Exodus 12:1). The Passover became an important festival in the Jewish calendar that is still celebrated today. In Jesus' time, Jews would come from all over the world to Jerusalem to remember what happened during the Exodus and to celebrate God's liberation of his people.

31'Simon, Simon, Satan has asked to sift all of you as wheat. 32But I have prayed for you, Simon, that your faith may not fail. And when you have turned back, strengthen your brothers.'

33But he replied, 'Lord, I am ready to go with you to prison and to death.'

34Jesus answered, 'I tell you, Peter, before the cock crows today, you will deny three times that you know me.'

35Then Jesus asked them, 'When I sent you without purse, bag or sandals, did you lack anything?'

'Nothing,' they answered.

36He said to them, 'But now if you have a purse, take it, and also a bag; and if you don't have a sword, sell your cloak and buy one. 37It is written: "And he was numbered with the transgressors"[a]; and I tell you that this must be fulfilled in me. Yes, what is written about me is reaching its fulfilment.'

38The disciples said, 'See, Lord, here are two swords.'

'That is enough,' he replied.

Jesus prays on the Mount of Olives

39Jesus went out as usual to the Mount of Olives, and his disciples followed him. 40On reaching the place, he said to them, 'Pray that you will not fall into temptation.' 41He withdrew about a stone's throw beyond them, knelt down and prayed, 42'Father, if you are willing, take this cup from me; yet not my will, but yours be done.' 43An angel from heaven appeared to him and strengthened him. 44And being in anguish, he prayed more earnestly, and his sweat was like drops of blood falling to the ground.[b]

45When he rose from prayer and went back to the disciples, he found them asleep, exhausted from sorrow. 46'Why are you sleeping?' he asked them. 'Get up and pray so that you will not fall into temptation.'

Jesus arrested

47While he was still speaking a crowd came up, and the man who was called Judas, one of the Twelve, was leading them. He approached Jesus to kiss him, 48but Jesus asked him, 'Judas, are you betraying the Son of Man with a kiss?'

49When Jesus' followers saw what was going to happen, they said, 'Lord, should we strike with our swords?' 50And one of them struck the servant of the high priest, cutting off his right ear.

51But Jesus answered, 'No more of this!' And he touched the man's ear and healed him.

52Then Jesus said to the chief priests, the officers of the temple guard, and the elders, who had come for him, 'Am I leading a rebellion, that you have come with swords and clubs? 53Every day I was with you in the temple courts, and you did not lay a hand on me. But this is your hour—when darkness reigns.'

Peter disowns Jesus

54Then seizing him, they led him away and took him into the house of the high priest. Peter followed at a distance. 55And when some there had kindled a fire in the middle of the courtyard and had sat down together, Peter sat down with them. 56A servant-girl saw him seated there in the firelight. She looked closely at him and said, 'This man was with him.'

57But he denied it. 'Woman,[c] I don't know him,' he said.

58A little later someone else saw him and said, 'You also are one of them.'

'Man, I am not!' Peter replied.

59About an hour later another asserted, 'Certainly this fellow was with him, for he is a Galilean.'

60Peter replied, 'Man, I don't know what you're talking about!' Just as he was speaking, the cock crowed. 61The Lord turned and looked straight at Peter. Then Peter remembered the word the Lord had spoken to him: 'Before the cock crows today, you will disown me three times.' 62And he went outside and wept bitterly.

The guards mock Jesus

63The men who were guarding Jesus began mocking and beating him. 64They blindfolded him and demanded, 'Prophesy! Who hit you?' 65And they said many other insulting things to him.

---

[a] 37 Isaiah 53:12   [b] 43,44 Some early manuscripts do not have verses 43 and 44.   [c] 57 The Greek for *Woman* does not denote any disrespect.

Jesus before Pilate and Herod

66At daybreak the council of the elders of the people, both the chief priests and the teachers of the law, met together, and Jesus was led before them. 67'If you are the Messiah,' they said, 'tell us.'

Jesus answered, 'If I tell you, you will not believe me, 68and if I asked you, you would not answer. 69But from now on, the Son of Man will be seated at the right hand of the mighty God.'

70They all asked, 'Are you then the Son of God?'

He replied, 'You say that I am.'

71Then they said, 'Why do we need any more testimony? We have heard it from his own lips.'

23 Then the whole assembly rose and led him off to Pilate. 2And they began to accuse him, saying, 'We have found this man subverting our nation. He opposes payment of taxes to Caesar and claims to be Messiah, a king.'

3So Pilate asked Jesus, 'Are you the king of the Jews?'

'You have said so,' Jesus replied.

4Then Pilate announced to the chief priests and the crowd, 'I find no basis for a charge against this man.'

5But they insisted, 'He stirs up the people all over Judea by his teaching. He started in Galilee and has come all the way here.'

6On hearing this, Pilate asked if the man was a Galilean. 7When he learned that Jesus was under Herod's jurisdiction, he sent him to Herod, who was also in Jerusalem at that time.

8When Herod saw Jesus, he was greatly pleased, because for a long time he had been wanting to see him. From what he had heard about him, he hoped to see him perform a sign of some sort. 9He plied him with many questions, but Jesus gave him no answer. 10The chief priests and the teachers of the law were standing there, vehemently accusing him. 11Then Herod and his soldiers ridiculed and mocked him. Dressing him in an elegant robe, they sent him back to Pilate. 12That day Herod and Pilate became friends—before this they had been enemies.

13Pilate called together the chief priests, the rulers and the people, 14and said to them, 'You brought me this man as one who was inciting the people to rebellion. I have examined him in your presence and have found no basis for your charges against him. 15Neither has Herod, for he sent him back to us; as you can see, he has done nothing to deserve death. 16(17)Therefore, I will punish him and then release him.'

18With one voice they cried out, 'Away with this man! Release Barabbas to us!' 19(Barabbas had been thrown into prison for an insurrection in the city, and for murder.)

20Wanting to release Jesus, Pilate appealed to them again. 21But they kept shouting, 'Crucify him! Crucify him!'

22For the third time he spoke to them: 'Why? What crime has this man committed? I have found in him no grounds for the death penalty. Therefore I will have him punished and then release him.'

23But with loud shouts they insistently demanded that he be crucified, and their shouts prevailed. 24So Pilate decided to grant their demand. 25He released the man who had been thrown into prison for insurrection and murder, the one they asked for, and surrendered Jesus to their will.

The crucifixion of Jesus

26As the soldiers led him away, they seized Simon from Cyrene, who was on his way in from the country, and put the cross on him and made him carry it behind Jesus. 27A large number of people followed him, including women who mourned and wailed for him. 28Jesus turned and said to them, 'Daughters of Jerusalem, do not weep for me; weep for yourselves and for your children. 29For the time will come when you will say, "Blessed are the childless women, the wombs that never bore and the breasts that never nursed!" 30Then

' "they will say to the mountains, 'Fall on us!'
and to the hills 'Cover us!' " [a]

---

[a] 30 Hosea 10:8

31'For if people do these things when the tree is green, what will happen when it is dry?'

32Two other men, both criminals, were also led out with him to be executed. 33When they came to the place called the Skull, they crucified him there, along with the criminals—one on his right, the other on his left. 34Jesus said, 'Father, forgive them, for they do not know what they are doing.'[a] And they divided up his clothes by casting lots.

35The people stood watching, and the rulers even sneered at him. They said, 'He saved others; let him save himself if he is God's Messiah, the Chosen One.'

36The soldiers also came up and mocked him. They offered him wine vinegar 37and said, 'If you are the king of the Jews, save yourself.'

38There was a written notice above him, which read: THIS IS THE KING OF THE JEWS.

39One of the criminals who hung there hurled insults at him: 'Aren't you the Messiah? Save yourself and us!'

40But the other criminal rebuked him. 'Don't you fear God,' he said, 'since you are under the same sentence? 41We are punished justly, for we are getting what our deeds deserve. But this man has done nothing wrong.'

42Then he said, 'Jesus, remember me when you come into your kingdom.[b]'

43Jesus answered him, 'Truly I tell you, today you will be with me in paradise.'

The death of Jesus

44It was now about noon, and darkness came over the whole land until three in the afternoon, 45for the sun stopped shining. And the curtain of the temple was torn in two. 46Jesus called out with a loud voice, 'Father, into your hands I commit my spirit.'[c] When he had said this, he breathed his last.

47The centurion, seeing what had happened, praised God and said, 'Surely this was a righteous man.' 48When all the people who had gathered to witness this sight saw what took place, they beat their breasts and went away. 49But all those who knew him, including the women who had followed him from Galilee, stood at a distance, watching these things.

The burial of Jesus

50Now there was a man named Joseph, a member of the Council, a good and upright man, 51who had not consented to their decision and action. He came from the Judean town of Arimathea, and he himself was waiting for the kingdom of God. 52Going to Pilate, he asked for Jesus' body. 53Then he took it down, wrapped it in linen cloth and placed it in a tomb cut in the rock, one in which no-one had yet been laid. 54It was Preparation Day, and the Sabbath was about to begin.

55The women who had come with Jesus from Galilee followed Joseph and saw the tomb and how his body was laid in it. 56Then they went home and prepared spices and perfumes. But they rested on the Sabbath in obedience to the commandment.

Jesus has risen

24 On the first day of the week, very early in the morning, the women took the spices they had prepared and went to the tomb. 2They found the stone rolled away from the tomb, 3but when they entered, they did not find the body of the Lord Jesus. 4While they were wondering

> **IN OTHER WORDS**
>
> **Paradise**
> **Luke 23:43**
>
> 'Paradise' is a word that originally came from Persia and was used to describe a wooded park or a garden with fruit trees. The Jews called the Garden of Eden 'paradise', and it is now used as a descriptive word for heaven (Revelation 2:7).

---

[a] 34 Some early manuscripts do not have this sentence.   [b] 42 Some manuscripts *come with your kingly power*
[c] 46 Psalm 31:5

about this, suddenly two men in clothes that gleamed like lightning stood beside them. 5In their fright the women bowed down with their faces to the ground, but the men said to them, 'Why do you look for the living among the dead? 6He is not here; he has risen! Remember how he told you, while he was still with you in Galilee: 7"The Son of Man must be delivered over to the hands of sinners, be crucified and on the third day be raised again."' 8Then they remembered his words.

9When they came back from the tomb, they told all these things to the Eleven and to all the others. 10It was Mary Magdalene, Joanna, Mary the mother of James, and the others with them who told this to the apostles. 11But they did not believe the women, because their words seemed to them like nonsense. 12Peter, however, got up and ran to the tomb. Bending over, he saw the strips of linen lying by themselves, and he went away, wondering to himself what had happened.

On the road to Emmaus

13Now that same day two of them were going to a village called Emmaus, about seven miles[a] from Jerusalem. 14They were talking with each other about everything that had happened. 15As they talked and discussed these things with each other, Jesus himself came up and walked along with them; 16but they were kept from recognising him.

17He asked them, 'What are you discussing together as you walk along?'

They stood still, their faces downcast. 18One of them, named Cleopas, asked him, 'Are you only a visitor to Jerusalem and do not know the things that have happened there in these days?'

19'What things?' he asked.

'About Jesus of Nazareth,' they replied. 'He was a prophet, powerful in word and deed before God and all the people. 20The chief priests and our rulers handed him over to be sentenced to death, and they crucified him; 21but we had hoped that he was the one who was going to redeem Israel. And what is more, it is the third day since all this took place. 22In addition, some of our women amazed us. They went to the tomb early this morning 23but didn't find his body. They came and told us that they had seen a vision of angels, who said he was alive. 24Then some of our companions went to the tomb and found it just as the women had said, but him they did not see.'

25He said to them, 'How foolish you are, and how slow to believe all that the prophets have spoken! 26Did not the Messiah have to suffer these things and then enter his glory?' 27And beginning with Moses and all the Prophets, he explained to them what was said in all the Scriptures concerning himself.

28As they approached the village to which they were going, Jesus continued on as if he were going further. 29But they urged him strongly, 'Stay with us, for it is nearly evening; the day is almost over.' So he went in to stay with them.

30When he was at the table with them, he took bread, gave thanks, broke it and began to give it to them. 31Then their eyes were opened and they recognised him, and he disappeared from their sight. 32They asked each other, 'Were not our hearts burning within us while he talked with us on the road and opened the Scriptures to us?'

33They got up and returned at once to Jerusalem. There they found the Eleven and those with them, assembled together 34and saying, 'It is true! The Lord has risen and has appeared to Simon.' 35Then the two told what had happened on the way, and how Jesus was recognised by them when he broke the bread.

Jesus appears to the disciples

36While they were still talking about this, Jesus himself stood among them and said to them, 'Peace be with you.'

37They were startled and frightened, thinking they saw a ghost. 38He said to them, 'Why are you troubled, and why do doubts rise in your minds? 39Look at my hands and my feet. It is I myself! Touch me and see; a ghost does not have flesh and bones, as you see I have.'

---

[a] 13 Or about 11 kilometres

⁴⁰When he had said this, he showed them his hands and feet. ⁴¹And while they still did not believe it because of joy and amazement, he asked them, 'Do you have anything here to eat?' ⁴²They gave him a piece of broiled fish, ⁴³and he took it and ate it in their presence.

⁴⁴He said to them, 'This is what I told you while I was still with you: everything must be fulfilled that is written about me in the Law of Moses, the Prophets and the Psalms.'

⁴⁵Then he opened their minds so they could understand the Scriptures. ⁴⁶He told them, 'This is what is written: the Messiah will suffer and rise from the dead on the third day, ⁴⁷and repentance for the forgiveness of sins will be preached in his name to all nations, beginning at Jerusalem. ⁴⁸You are witnesses of these things. ⁴⁹I am going to send you what my Father has promised; but stay in the city until you have been clothed with power from on high.'

The ascension of Jesus

⁵⁰When he had led them out to the vicinity of Bethany, he lifted up his hands and blessed them. ⁵¹While he was blessing them, he left them and was taken up into heaven. ⁵²Then they worshipped him and returned to Jerusalem with great joy. ⁵³And they stayed continually at the temple, praising God.

John

INTRODUCTION

John

Author: John, the disciple of Jesus.

When: It covers the events of Jesus' life, from about AD 27–30. It was probably written towards the end of the first century AD.

Where: Ephesus or Judea.

Did you know? There are virtually no parables in the Gospel of John.

Main theme: John's Gospel goes beyond the facts and events that you find in the first three Gospels. He wants people to understand deeper spiritual truths about Jesus. John uses symbols such as bread, water and light to reveal aspects of Jesus' character. He talks about Jesus' unique relationship with his Father. Above all, he wants people to believe in Jesus, to have an active trust in him (John 20:31).

The Word became flesh

1 In the beginning was the Word, and the Word was with God, and the Word was God. ²He was with God in the beginning. ³Through him all things were made; without him nothing was made that has been made. ⁴In him was life, and that life was the light of all people. ⁵The light shines in the darkness, and the darkness has not overcome[a] it.

⁶There was a man sent from God whose name was John. ⁷He came as a witness to testify concerning that light, so that through him all might believe. ⁸He himself was not the light; he came only as a witness to the light.

⁹The true light that gives light to everyone was coming into the world. ¹⁰He was in the world, and though the world was made through him, the world did not recognise him. ¹¹He came to that which was his own, but his own did not receive him. ¹²Yet to all who did receive him, to those who believed in his name, he gave the right to become children of God— ¹³children born not of natural descent, nor of human decision or a husband's will, but born of God.

¹⁴The Word became flesh and made his dwelling among us. We have seen his glory, the glory of the one and only ⌊Son⌋, who came from the Father, full of grace and truth.

---

[a] 5 Or *understood*

> **IN OTHER WORDS**
>
> **Children of God**
> John 1:12
> People who believe in God are given the right to become children of God, to call God 'Father', and to try to live like him.

15(John testified concerning him. He cried out, saying, 'This is he of whom I said, "He who comes after me has surpassed me because he was before me."') 16Out of his fulness we have all received grace in place of grace already given. 17For the law was given through Moses; grace and truth came through Jesus Christ. 18No-one has ever seen God, but the one and only [Son], who is himself God and[a] is in the closest relationship with the Father, has made him known.

John the Baptist denies being the Messiah

19Now this was John's testimony when the Jewish leaders in Jerusalem sent priests and Levites to ask him who he was. 20He did not fail to confess, but confessed freely, 'I am not the Messiah.'

21They asked him, 'Then who are you? Are you Elijah?'

He said, 'I am not.'

'Are you the Prophet?'

He answered, 'No.'

22Finally they said, 'Who are you? Give us an answer to take back to those who sent us. What do you say about yourself?'

23John replied in the words of Isaiah the prophet, 'I am the voice of one calling in the wilderness, "Make straight the way for the Lord."'[b]

24Now the Pharisees who had been sent 25questioned him, 'Why then do you baptise if you are not the Messiah, nor Elijah, nor the Prophet?'

26'I baptise with[c] water,' John replied, 'but among you stands one you do not know. 27He is the one who comes after me, the thongs of whose sandals I am not worthy to untie.'

28This all happened at Bethany on the other side of the Jordan, where John was baptising.

John's testimony about Jesus

29The next day John saw Jesus coming towards him and said, 'Look, the Lamb of God, who takes away the sin of the world! 30This is the one I meant when I said, "A man who comes after me has surpassed me because he was before me." 31I myself did not know him, but the reason I came baptising with water was that he might be revealed to Israel.'

32Then John gave this testimony: 'I saw the Spirit come down from heaven as a dove and remain on him. 33And I myself did not know him, but the one who sent me to baptise with water told me, "The man on whom you see the Spirit come down and remain is the one who will baptise with the Holy Spirit." 34I have seen and I testify that this is God's Chosen One.'[d]

John's disciples follow Jesus

35The next day John was there again with two of his disciples. 36When he saw Jesus

> **IN OTHER WORDS**
>
> **Lamb**
> John 1:29
> In the Old Testament, a young sheep was a good sacrifice to God. Jesus was called the 'Lamb of God' by John the Baptist, because he was to be the ultimate sacrifice that would mean all sin could be forgiven and people could be right with God. After Jesus' resurrection, the church used the image of the lamb to symbolise his death as an atonement for sin.

---

[a] 18 Some manuscripts *but the only Son, who* [b] 23 Isaiah 40:3 [c] 26 Or *in*; also in verses 31 and 33 (twice) [d] 34 See Isaiah 42:1; many manuscripts *is the Son of God*.

passing by, he said, 'Look, the Lamb of God!'

37When the two disciples heard him say this, they followed Jesus. 38Turning round, Jesus saw them following and asked, 'What do you want?'

They said, 'Rabbi' (which means 'Teacher'), 'where are you staying?'

39'Come,' he replied, 'and you will see.'

So they went and saw where he was staying, and they spent that day with him. It was about four in the afternoon.

40Andrew, Simon Peter's brother, was one of the two who heard what John had said and who had followed Jesus. 41The first thing Andrew did was to find his brother Simon and tell him, 'We have found the Messiah' (that is, the Christ). 42And he brought him to Jesus.

Jesus looked at him and said, 'You are Simon son of John. You will be called Cephas' (which, when translated, is Peter[a]).

Jesus calls Philip and Nathanael

43The next day Jesus decided to leave for Galilee. Finding Philip, he said to him, 'Follow me.'

44Philip, like Andrew and Peter, was from the town of Bethsaida. 45Philip found Nathanael and told him, 'We have found the one Moses wrote about in the Law, and about whom the prophets also wrote— Jesus of Nazareth, the son of Joseph.'

46'Nazareth! Can anything good come from there?' Nathanael asked.

'Come and see,' said Philip.

47When Jesus saw Nathanael approaching, he said of him, 'Here truly is an Israelite in whom there is no deceit.'

48'How do you know me?' Nathanael asked.

Jesus answered, 'I saw you while you were still under the fig-tree before Philip called you.'

49Then Nathanael declared, 'Rabbi, you are the Son of God; you are the king of Israel.'

50Jesus said, 'You believe[b] because I told you I saw you under the fig-tree. You will see greater things than that.' 51He then added, 'Very truly I tell you,[c] you[d] will see "heaven open, and the angels of God ascending and descending on"[e] the Son of Man.'

Jesus changes water into wine

2 On the third day a wedding took place at Cana in Galilee. Jesus' mother was there, 2and Jesus and his disciples had also been invited to the wedding. 3When the wine was gone, Jesus' mother said to him, 'They have no more wine.'

4'Woman,[f] why do you involve me?' Jesus replied. 'My hour has not yet come.'

5His mother said to the servants, 'Do whatever he tells you.'

6Nearby stood six stone water jars, the kind used by the Jews for ceremonial washing, each holding from eighty to a hundred and twenty litres.

7Jesus said to the servants, 'Fill the jars with water'; so they filled them to the brim.

8Then he told them, 'Now draw some out and take it to the master of the banquet.'

They did so, 9and the master of the banquet tasted the water that had been turned into wine. He did not realise where it had come from, though the servants who had drawn the water knew. Then he called the bridegroom aside 10and said, 'Everyone brings out the choice wine first and then the cheaper wine after the guests have had too much to drink; but you have saved the best till now.'

11What Jesus did here in Cana of Galilee was the first of the signs through which he revealed his glory; and his disciples put their faith in him.

12After this he went down to Capernaum with his mother and brothers and his disciples. There they stayed for a few days.

Jesus clears the temple courts

13When it was almost time for the Jewish Passover, Jesus went up to Jerusalem. 14In the temple courts he found people selling cattle, sheep and doves, and others sitting at tables exchanging money. 15So he made a whip out of cords, and drove all from the temple courts, both sheep and cattle; he scattered the coins of the money-changers and overturned their tables. 16To those who

---

[a] 42 *Cephas* (Aramaic) and *Peter* (Greek) both mean *rock*. [b] 50 Or *Do you believe . . . ?* [c] 51 The Greek is plural. [d] 51 The Greek is plural. [e] 51 Gen. 28:12 [f] 4 The Greek for *Woman* does not denote any disrespect.

making Connections

Temple
John 2:19
When the Israelites finally settled in the Promised Land they built a temple in Jerusalem where the Ark of the Covenant would rest. The first temple built by Solomon (1 Kings 5:5) was destroyed by the Babylonians. It was rebuilt after the exile (Ezra 3:12), then renovated in a grand manner by Herod around the time of Jesus' birth. This temple was destroyed in AD 70 as prophesied by Jesus (Matthew 24:2).

sold doves he said, 'Get these out of here! Stop turning my Father's house into a market!' 17His disciples remembered that it is written: 'Zeal for your house will consume me.'[a]

18The Jews then responded to him, 'What sign can you show us to prove your authority to do all this?'

19Jesus answered them, 'Destroy this temple, and I will raise it again in three days.'

20They replied, 'It has taken forty-six years to build this temple, and you are going to raise it in three days?' 21But the temple he had spoken of was his body. 22After he was raised from the dead, his disciples recalled what he had said. Then they believed the Scripture and the words that Jesus had spoken.

23Now while he was in Jerusalem at the Passover Feast, many people saw the signs he was performing and believed in his name.[b] 24But Jesus would not entrust himself to them, for he knew all people. 25He did not need human testimony about them, for he knew what was in them.

Jesus teaches Nicodemus

3 Now there was a Pharisee, a man named Nicodemus who was a member of the Jewish ruling council. 2He came to Jesus at night and said, 'Rabbi, we know that you are a teacher who has come from God. For no-one could perform the signs you are doing if God were not with him.'

3Jesus replied, 'Very truly I tell you, no-one can see the kingdom of God without being born again.'[c]

4'How can anyone be born when they are old?' Nicodemus asked. 'Surely they cannot enter a second time into their mother's womb to be born!'

5Jesus answered, 'Very truly I tell you, no-one can enter the kingdom of God without being born of water and the Spirit. 6Flesh gives birth to flesh, but the Spirit[d] gives birth to spirit. 7You should not be surprised at my saying, "You[e] must be born again." 8The wind blows wherever it pleases. You hear its sound, but you cannot tell where it comes from or where it is going. So it is with everyone born of the Spirit.'[f]

9'How can this be?' Nicodemus asked.

10'You are Israel's teacher,' said Jesus, 'and do you not understand these things? 11Very truly I tell you, we speak of what we know, and we testify to what we have seen, but still you people do not accept our testimony. 12I have spoken to you of earthly things and you do not believe; how then will you believe if I speak of heavenly things? 13No-one has ever gone into heaven except the one who came from heaven—the Son of Man.[g] 14Just as Moses lifted up the snake in the wilderness, so the Son of Man must be lifted up,[h] 15that everyone who believes may have eternal life in him.'[i]

16For God so loved the world that he gave his one and only Son, that whoever believes in him shall not perish but have eternal life. 17For God did not send his Son into the world to condemn the world, but to save the world through him. 18Whoever believes in him is not condemned, but whoever does not believe stands condemned already because they have not believed in the name of

---

[a] 17 Psalm 69:9 [b] 23 Or *in him* [c] 3 The Greek for *again* also means *from above*; also in verse 7. [d] 6 Or *but spirit*
[e] 7 The Greek is plural. [f] 8 The Greek for *Spirit* is the same as that for *wind*. [g] 13 Some manuscripts *Man, who is in heaven* [h] 14 The Greek for *lifted up* also means *exalted*. [i] 15 Some interpreters end the quotation with verse 21.

IN OTHER WORDS

Love
John 3:16
Surely 'love' doesn't need much explanation? Well, when the first Christians tried to describe the love that God had for them and they had for each other, they used their Greek word agape. In most instances in the New Testament, it is this special word which describes God's sacrificial love for us and Christians' love for each other. Love is perhaps the most important aspect of God's character as revealed in the Bible.

God's one and only Son. 19This is the verdict: light has come into the world, but people loved darkness instead of light because their deeds were evil. 20All those who do evil hate the light, and will not come into the light for fear that their deeds will be exposed. 21But those who live by the truth come into the light, so that it may be seen plainly that what they have done has been done in the sight of God.

John testifies again about Jesus

22After this, Jesus and his disciples went out into the Judean countryside, where he spent some time with them, and baptised. 23Now John also was baptising at Aenon near Salim, because there was plenty of water, and people were coming and being baptised. 24(This was before John was put in prison.) 25An argument developed between some of John's disciples and a certain Jew over the matter of ceremonial washing. 26They came to John and said to him, 'Rabbi, that man who was with you on the other side of the Jordan—the one you testified about—look, he is baptising, and everyone is going to him.'

27To this John replied, 'A person can receive only what is given from heaven. 28You yourselves can testify that I said, "I am not the Messiah but am sent ahead of him." 29The bride belongs to the bridegroom. The friend who attends the bridegroom waits and listens for him, and is full of joy when he hears the bridegroom's voice. That joy is mine, and it is now complete. 30He must become greater; I must become less.'[a]

31The one who comes from above is above all; the one who is from the earth belongs to the earth, and speaks as one from the earth. The one who comes from heaven is above all. 32He testifies to what he has seen and heard, but no-one accepts his testimony. 33The person who has accepted it has certified that God is truthful. 34For the one whom God has sent speaks the words of God, for God[b] gives the Spirit without limit. 35The Father loves the Son and has placed everything in his hands. 36Whoever believes in the Son has eternal life, but whoever rejects the Son will not see life, for God's wrath remains on them.

Jesus talks with a Samaritan woman

4 Now Jesus learned that the Pharisees had heard that he was gaining and baptising more disciples than John— 2although in fact it was not Jesus who baptised, but his disciples. 3So he left Judea and went back once more to Galilee.

4Now he had to go through Samaria. 5So he came to a town in Samaria called Sychar, near the plot of ground Jacob had given to his son Joseph. 6Jacob's well was there, and Jesus, tired as he was from the journey, sat down by the well. It was about noon.

7When a Samaritan woman came to draw water, Jesus said to her, 'Will you give me a drink?' 8(His disciples had gone into the town to buy food.)

9The Samaritan woman said to him, 'You are a Jew and I am a Samaritan woman. How can you ask me for a drink?' (For Jews do not associate with Samaritans.[c])

10Jesus answered her, 'If you knew the gift of God and who it is that asks you for a drink, you would have asked him and he would have given you living water.'

---

[a] 30 Some interpreters end the quotation with verse 36. [b] 34 Greek he [c] 9 Or do not use dishes Samaritans have used

11'Sir,' the woman said, 'you have nothing to draw with and the well is deep. Where can you get this living water? 12Are you greater than our father Jacob, who gave us the well and drank from it himself, as did also his sons and his flocks and herds?'

13Jesus answered, 'Everyone who drinks this water will be thirsty again, 14but those who drink the water I give them will never thirst. Indeed, the water I give them will become in them a spring of water welling up to eternal life.'

15The woman said to him, 'Sir, give me this water so that I won't get thirsty and have to keep coming here to draw water.'

16He told her, 'Go, call your husband and come back.'

17'I have no husband,' she replied.

Jesus said to her, 'You are right when you say you have no husband. 18The fact is, you have had five husbands, and the man you now have is not your husband. What you have just said is quite true.'

19'Sir,' the woman said, 'I can see that you are a prophet. 20Our ancestors worshipped on this mountain, but you Jews claim that the place where we must worship is in Jerusalem.'

21'Woman,'*a* Jesus replied, 'believe me, a time is coming when you will worship the Father neither on this mountain nor in Jerusalem. 22You Samaritans worship what you do not know; we worship what we do know, for salvation is from the Jews. 23Yet a time is coming and has now come when the true worshippers will worship the Father in the Spirit and in truth, for they are the kind of worshippers the Father seeks. 24God is spirit, and his worshippers must worship in the Spirit and in truth.'

25The woman said, 'I know that Messiah' (called Christ) 'is coming. When he comes, he will explain everything to us.'

26Then Jesus declared, 'I, the one speaking to you—I am he.'

The disciples rejoin Jesus

27Just then his disciples returned and were surprised to find him talking with a woman. But no-one asked, 'What do you want?' or 'Why are you talking with her?'

28Then, leaving her water jar, the woman went back to the town and said to the people, 29'Come, see a man who told me everything I've ever done. Could this be the Messiah?' 30They came out of the town and made their way towards him.

31Meanwhile his disciples urged him, 'Rabbi, eat something.'

32But he said to them, 'I have food to eat that you know nothing about.'

33Then his disciples said to each other, 'Could someone have brought him food?'

34'My food,' said Jesus, 'is to do the will of him who sent me and to finish his work. 35Don't you have a saying, "It's still four months until harvest"? I tell you, open your eyes and look at the fields! They are ripe for harvest. 36Even now those who reap draw their wages, even now they harvest the crop for eternal life, so that the sower and the reaper may be glad together. 37Thus the saying "One sows and another reaps" is true. 38I sent you to reap what you have not worked for. Others have done the hard work, and you have reaped the benefits of their labour.'

Many Samaritans believe

39Many of the Samaritans from that town believed in him because of the woman's testimony, 'He told me everything I've ever done.' 40So when the Samaritans came to him, they urged him to stay with them, and he stayed two days. 41And because of his words many more became believers.

42They said to the woman, 'We no longer believe just because of what you said; now we have heard for ourselves, and we know that this man really is the Saviour of the world.'

Jesus heals the official's son

43After the two days he left for Galilee. 44(Now Jesus himself had pointed out that prophets have no honour in their own country.) 45When he arrived in Galilee, the Galileans welcomed him. They had seen all that he had done in Jerusalem at the Passover Feast, for they also had been there.

46Once more he visited Cana in Galilee, where he had turned the water into wine.

---

a 21 The Greek for *Woman* does not denote any disrespect.

And there was a certain royal official whose son lay ill at Capernaum. ⁴⁷When this man heard that Jesus had arrived in Galilee from Judea, he went to him and begged him to come and heal his son, who was close to death.

⁴⁸'Unless you people see signs and wonders,' Jesus told him, 'you will never believe.'

⁴⁹The royal official said, 'Sir, come down before my child dies.'

⁵⁰'Go,' Jesus replied, 'your son will live.'

The man took Jesus at his word and departed. ⁵¹While he was still on the way, his servants met him with the news that his boy was living. ⁵²When he enquired as to the time when his son got better, they said to him, 'Yesterday, at one in the afternoon, the fever left him.'

⁵³Then the father realised that this was the exact time at which Jesus had said to him, 'Your son will live.' So he and his whole household believed.

⁵⁴This is the second sign Jesus performed after coming from Judea to Galilee.

The healing at the pool

5 Some time later, Jesus went up to Jerusalem for one of the Jewish festivals. ²Now there is in Jerusalem near the Sheep Gate a pool, which in Aramaic is called Bethesda*ᵃ* and which is surrounded by five covered colonnades. ³⁽⁴⁾Here a great number of disabled people used to lie—the blind, the lame, the paralysed.*ᵇ* ⁵One who was there had been an invalid for thirty-eight years. ⁶When Jesus saw him lying there and learned that he had been in this condition for a long time, he asked him, 'Do you want to get well?'

⁷'Sir,' the invalid replied, 'I have no-one to help me into the pool when the water is stirred. While I am trying to get in, someone else goes down ahead of me.'

⁸Then Jesus said to him, 'Get up! Pick up your mat and walk.' ⁹At once the man was cured; he picked up his mat and walked.

The day on which this took place was a Sabbath, ¹⁰and so the Jewish leaders said to

Work on the Sabbath
John 5:10
After God created the world, he rested in the seventh day, the Sabbath. The Jewish law said that people could not work on the Sabbath, and they had lots of laws about what constituted work. Carrying a load of any kind was considered to be work, even if you had just been healed and it was your mat that you were carrying!

the man who had been healed, 'It is the Sabbath; the law forbids you to carry your mat.'

¹¹But he replied, 'The man who made me well said to me, "Pick up your mat and walk."'

¹²So they asked him, 'Who is this fellow who told you to pick it up and walk?'

¹³The man who was healed had no idea who it was, for Jesus had slipped away into the crowd that was there.

¹⁴Later Jesus found him at the temple and said to him, 'See, you are well again. Stop sinning or something worse may happen to you.' ¹⁵The man went away and told the Jewish leaders that it was Jesus who had made him well.

The authority of the Son

¹⁶So, because Jesus was doing these things on the Sabbath, the Jewish leaders began to persecute him. ¹⁷In his defence Jesus said to them, 'My Father is always at his work to this very day, and I too am working.' ¹⁸For this reason they tried all the more to kill him; not only was he breaking the Sabbath,

---

ᵃ 2 Some manuscripts *Bethzatha*; other manuscripts *Bethsaida*   *ᵇ* 3 Some later manuscripts and some ancient witnesses, wholly or in part, *paralysed—and they waited for the moving of the waters. ⁴From time to time an angel of the Lord would come down and stir up the waters. The first person into the pool after each such disturbance would be cured of whatever disease they had.*

but he was even calling God his own Father, making himself equal with God.

19 Jesus gave them this answer: 'Very truly I tell you, the Son can do nothing by himself; he can do only what he sees his Father doing, because whatever the Father does the Son also does. 20 For the Father loves the Son and shows him all he does. Yes, and he will show him even greater works than these, so that you will be amazed. 21 For just as the Father raises the dead and gives them life, even so the Son gives life to whom he is pleased to give it. 22 Moreover, the Father judges no-one, but has entrusted all judgment to the Son, 23 that all may honour the Son just as they honour the Father. Whoever does not honour the Son does not honour the Father, who sent him.

24 'Very truly I tell you, whoever hears my word and believes him who sent me has eternal life and will not be judged but has crossed over from death to life. 25 Very truly I tell you, a time is coming and has now come when the dead will hear the voice of the Son of God and those who hear will live. 26 For as the Father has life in himself, so he has granted the Son also to have life in himself. 27 And he has given him authority to judge because he is the Son of Man.

28 'Do not be amazed at this, for a time is coming when all who are in their graves will hear his voice 29 and come out—those who have done what is good will rise to live, and those who have done what is evil will rise to be condemned. 30 By myself I can do nothing; I judge only as I hear, and my judgment is just, for I seek not to please myself but him who sent me.

Testimonies about Jesus

31 'If I testify about myself, my testimony is not true. 32 There is another who testifies in my favour, and I know that his testimony about me is true.

33 'You have sent to John and he has testified to the truth. 34 Not that I accept human testimony; but I mention it that you may be saved. 35 John was a lamp that burned and gave light, and you chose for a time to enjoy his light.

36 'I have testimony weightier than that of John. For the works that the Father has given me to finish—the very works that I am doing—testify that the Father has sent me. 37 And the Father who sent me has himself testified concerning me. You have never heard his voice nor seen his form, 38 nor does his word dwell in you, for you do not believe the one he sent. 39 You study[a] the Scriptures diligently because you think that in them you possess eternal life. These are the very Scriptures that testify about me, 40 yet you refuse to come to me to have life.

41 'I do not accept glory from human beings, 42 but I know you. I know that you do not have the love of God in your hearts. 43 I have come in my Father's name, and you do not accept me; but if someone else comes in his own name, you will accept him. 44 How can you believe since you accept glory from one another but do not seek the glory that comes from the only God[b]?

45 'But do not think I will accuse you before the Father. Your accuser is Moses, on whom your hopes are set. 46 If you believed Moses, you would believe me, for he wrote about me. 47 But since you do not believe what he wrote, how are you going to believe what I say?'

Jesus feeds the five thousand

6 Some time after this, Jesus crossed to the far shore of the Sea of Galilee (that is, the Sea of Tiberias), 2 and a great crowd of people followed him because they saw the signs he had performed by healing those who were ill. 3 Then Jesus went up on a mountainside and sat down with his disciples. 4 The Jewish Passover Feast was near.

5 When Jesus looked up and saw a great crowd coming towards him, he said to Philip, 'Where shall we buy bread for these people to eat?' 6 He asked this only to test him, for he already had in mind what he was going to do.

7 Philip answered him, 'It would take almost a year's wages[c] to buy enough bread for each one to have a bite!'

8 Another of his disciples, Andrew, Simon Peter's brother, spoke up, 9 'Here is a boy with five small barley loaves and two

---

[a] 39 Or *Study*   [b] 44 Some early manuscripts *the Only One*   [c] 7 Greek *two hundred denarii*

small fish, but how far will they go among so many?'

¹⁰Jesus said, 'Make the people sit down.' There was plenty of grass in that place, and they sat down (about five thousand men were there). ¹¹Jesus then took the loaves, gave thanks, and distributed to those who were seated as much as they wanted. He did the same with the fish.

¹²When they had all had enough to eat, he said to his disciples, 'Gather the pieces that are left over. Let nothing be wasted.' ¹³So they gathered them and filled twelve baskets with the pieces of the five barley loaves left over by those who had eaten.

¹⁴After the people saw the sign Jesus performed, they began to say, 'Surely this is the Prophet who is to come into the world.' ¹⁵Jesus, knowing that they intended to come and make him king by force, withdrew again to a mountain by himself.

Jesus walks on the water

¹⁶When evening came, his disciples went down to the lake, ¹⁷where they got into a boat and set off across the lake for Capernaum. By now it was dark, and Jesus had not yet joined them. ¹⁸A strong wind was blowing and the waters grew rough. ¹⁹When they had rowed about three or three and a half miles,[a] they saw Jesus approaching the boat, walking on the water; and they were frightened. ²⁰But he said to them, 'It is I; don't be afraid.' ²¹Then they were willing to take him into the boat, and immediately the boat reached the shore where they were heading.

²²The next day the crowd that had stayed on the opposite shore of the lake realised that only one boat had been there, and that Jesus had not entered it with his disciples, but that they had gone away alone. ²³Then some boats from Tiberias landed near the place where the people had eaten the bread after the Lord had given thanks. ²⁴Once the crowd realised that neither Jesus nor his disciples were there, they got into the boats and went to Capernaum in search of Jesus.

Jesus the bread of life

²⁵When they found him on the other side of the lake, they asked him, 'Rabbi, when did you get here?'

²⁶Jesus answered, 'Very truly I tell you, you are looking for me, not because you saw the signs I performed but because you ate the loaves and had your fill. ²⁷Do not work for food that spoils, but for food that endures to eternal life, which the Son of Man will give you. On him God the Father has placed his seal of approval.'

²⁸Then they asked him, 'What must we do to do the works God requires?'

²⁹Jesus answered, 'The work of God is this: to believe in the one he has sent.'

³⁰So they asked him, 'What sign then will you give that we may see it and believe you? What will you do? ³¹Our ancestors ate the manna in the wilderness; as it is written: "He gave them bread from heaven to eat."[b]'

³²Jesus said to them, 'Very truly I tell you, it is not Moses who has given you the bread from heaven, but it is my Father who gives you the true bread from heaven. ³³For the bread of God is the bread that comes down from heaven and gives life to the world.'

³⁴'Sir,' they said, 'always give us this bread.'

³⁵Then Jesus declared, 'I am the bread of life. Whoever comes to me will never go hungry, and whoever believes in me will never be thirsty. ³⁶But as I told you, you have seen me and still you do not believe. ³⁷All whom the Father gives me will come to me, and whoever comes to me I will never drive away. ³⁸For I have come down from heaven not to do my will but to do the will of him who sent me. ³⁹And this is the will of him who sent me, that I shall lose none of all those he has given me, but raise them up at the last day. ⁴⁰For my Father's will is that everyone who looks to the Son and believes in him shall have eternal life, and I will raise them up at the last day.'

⁴¹At this the Jews there began to grumble about him because he said, 'I am the bread that came down from heaven.' ⁴²They said, 'Is this not Jesus, the son of Joseph, whose father and mother we know? How can he now say, "I came down from heaven"?'

---

[a] 19 Or about 5 or 6 kilometres   [b] 31 Exodus 16:4; Neh. 9:15; Psalm 78:24,25

making Connections

'I am' statements
John 6:35

This is the first of several announcements in John's Gospel where Jesus describes himself with a statement beginning with 'I am'. Jesus says he is the bread of life (6:35); the light of the world (8:12 and 9:5); the gate (10:7, 9); the good shepherd (10:11, 14); the resurrection and the life (11:25); the way, the truth and the life (14:6); and the true vine (15:1, 5). When Moses met God at the burning bush, he asked what God's name was and God said, 'I am who I am'. When Jesus uses the words 'I am', he is declaring his divinity, that he is God.

43'Stop grumbling among yourselves,' Jesus answered. 44'No-one can come to me unless the Father who sent me draws them, and I will raise them up at the last day. 45It is written in the Prophets: "They will all be taught by God."[a] Everyone who has heard the Father and learned from him comes to me. 46No-one has seen the Father except the one who is from God; only he has seen the Father. 47Very truly I tell you, whoever believes has eternal life. 48I am the bread of life. 49Your ancestors ate the manna in the wilderness, yet they died. 50But here is the bread that comes down from heaven, which people may eat and not die. 51I am the living bread that came down from heaven. Whoever eats of this bread will live for ever. This bread is my flesh, which I will give for the life of the world.'

52Then the Jews began to argue sharply among themselves, 'How can this man give us his flesh to eat?'

53Jesus said to them, 'Very truly I tell you, unless you eat the flesh of the Son of Man and drink his blood, you have no life in you. 54Whoever eats my flesh and drinks my blood has eternal life, and I will raise them up at the last day. 55For my flesh is real food and my blood is real drink. 56Whoever eats my flesh and drinks my blood remains in me, and I in them. 57Just as the living Father sent me and I live because of the Father, so the one who feeds on me will live because of me. 58This is the bread that came down from heaven. Your ancestors ate manna and died, but whoever feeds on this bread will live for ever.' 59He said this while teaching in the synagogue in Capernaum.

Many disciples desert Jesus

60On hearing it, many of his disciples said, 'This is a hard teaching. Who can accept it?'

61Aware that his disciples were grumbling about this, Jesus said to them, 'Does this offend you? 62Then what if you see the Son of Man ascend to where he was before! 63The Spirit gives life; the flesh counts for nothing. The words I have spoken to you—they are full of the Spirit[b] and life. 64Yet there are some of you who do not believe.' For Jesus had known from the beginning which of them did not believe and who would betray him. 65He went on to say, 'This is why I told you that no-one can come to me unless the Father has enabled them.'

66From this time many of his disciples turned back and no longer followed him.

67'You do not want to leave too, do you?' Jesus asked the Twelve.

68Simon Peter answered him, 'Lord, to whom shall we go? You have the words of eternal life. 69We have come to believe and to know that you are the Holy One of God.'

70Then Jesus replied, 'Have I not chosen you, the Twelve? Yet one of you is a devil!' 71(He meant Judas, the son of Simon Iscariot, who, though one of the Twelve, was later to betray him.)

Jesus goes to the Feast of Tabernacles

7 After this, Jesus went around in Galilee. He did not want[c] to go about in Judea because the Jewish leaders there were

---

[a] 45 Isaiah 54:13   [b] 63 Or *are Spirit;* or *are spirit*   [c] 1 Some manuscripts *not have authority*

looking for a way to kill him. ²But when the Jewish Feast of Tabernacles was near, ³Jesus' brothers said to him, 'Leave Galilee and go to Judea, so that your disciples there may see the works you do. ⁴No-one who wants to become a public figure acts in secret. Since you are doing these things, show yourself to the world.' ⁵For even his own brothers did not believe in him.

⁶Therefore Jesus told them, 'My time is not yet here; for you any time will do. ⁷The world cannot hate you, but it hates me because I testify that its works are evil. ⁸You go to the Feast. I am not^a going up to this Feast, because my time has not yet fully come.' ⁹Having said this, he stayed in Galilee.

¹⁰However, after his brothers had left for the Feast, he went also, not publicly, but in secret. ¹¹Now at the Feast the Jewish leaders were watching for Jesus and asking, 'Where is he?'

¹²Among the crowds there was widespread whispering about him. Some said, 'He is a good man.'

Others replied, 'No, he deceives the people.' ¹³But no-one would say anything publicly about him for fear of the leaders.

Jesus teaches at the Feast

¹⁴Not until halfway through the Feast did Jesus go up to the temple courts and begin to teach. ¹⁵The Jews there were amazed and asked, 'How did this man get such learning without having been taught?'

¹⁶Jesus answered, 'My teaching is not my own. It comes from the one who sent me. ¹⁷Anyone who chooses to do the will of God will find out whether my teaching comes from God or whether I speak on my own. ¹⁸Whoever speaks on their own does so to gain personal glory, but he who seeks the glory of the one who sent him is a man of truth; there is nothing false about him. ¹⁹Has not Moses given you the law? Yet not one of you keeps the law. Why are you trying to kill me?'

²⁰'You are demon-possessed,' the crowd answered. 'Who is trying to kill you?'

²¹Jesus said to them, 'I did one miracle, and you are all amazed. ²²Yet, because Moses gave you circumcision (though actually it did not come from Moses, but from the patriarchs), you circumcise a boy on the Sabbath. ²³Now if a boy can be circumcised on the Sabbath so that the law of Moses may not be broken, why are you angry with me for healing a man's whole body on the Sabbath? ²⁴Stop judging by mere appearances, but instead judge correctly.'

Division over who Jesus is

²⁵At that point some of the people of Jerusalem began to ask, 'Isn't this the man they are trying to kill? ²⁶Here he is, speaking publicly, and they are not saying a word to him. Have the authorities really concluded that he is the Messiah? ²⁷But we know where this man is from; when the Messiah comes, no-one will know where he is from.'

²⁸Then Jesus, still teaching in the temple courts, cried out, 'Yes, you know me, and you know where I am from. I am not here on my own authority, but he who sent me is true. You do not know him, ²⁹but I know him because I am from him and he sent me.'

³⁰At this they tried to seize him, but no-one laid a hand on him, because his hour had not yet come. ³¹Still, many in the crowd put their faith in him. They said, 'When the Messiah comes, will he perform more signs than this man?'

³²The Pharisees heard the crowd whispering such things about him. Then the chief priests and the Pharisees sent temple guards to arrest him.

³³Jesus said, 'I am with you for only a short time, and then I go to the one who sent me. ³⁴You will look for me, but you will not find me; and where I am, you cannot come.'

³⁵The Jews said to one another, 'Where does this man intend to go that we cannot find him? Will he go where our people live scattered among the Greeks, and teach the Greeks? ³⁶What did he mean when he said, "You will look for me, but you will not find me," and "Where I am, you cannot come"?'

³⁷On the last and greatest day of the Feast, Jesus stood and said in a loud voice, 'Let anyone who is thirsty come to me and drink. ³⁸Whoever believes in me, as Scripture has said, rivers of living water will flow from

---

^{a}8 Some manuscripts *not yet*

Water at the festival
John 7:37

The Festival of Tabernacles lasted seven days. Each day a group of priests would go to the Pool of Siloam, a reservoir in the city of Jerusalem, fill a container with water and take it back to the temple. People would follow the priests down to the pool and back again to the temple. During this festival, Jesus said that he was the real source of living water.

within them."[a] 39By this he meant the Spirit, whom those who believed in him were later to receive. Up to that time the Spirit had not been given, since Jesus had not yet been glorified.

40On hearing his words, some of the people said, 'Surely this man is the Prophet.'

41Others said, 'He is the Messiah.'

Still others asked, 'How can the Messiah come from Galilee? 42Does not Scripture say that the Messiah will come from David's descendants and from Bethlehem, the town where David lived?' 43Thus the people were divided because of Jesus. 44Some wanted to seize him, but no-one laid a hand on him.

Unbelief of the Jewish leaders

45Finally the temple guards went back to the chief priests and the Pharisees, who asked them, 'Why didn't you bring him in?'

46'No-one ever spoke the way this man does,' the guards replied.

47'You mean he has deceived you also?' the Pharisees retorted. 48'Have any of the rulers or of the Pharisees believed in him? 49No! But this mob that knows nothing of the law—there is a curse on them.'

50Nicodemus, who had gone to Jesus earlier and who was one of their own number, asked, 51'Does our law condemn a man without first hearing him to find out what he has been doing?'

52They replied, 'Are you from Galilee, too? Look into it, and you will find that a prophet does not come out of Galilee.'

(The earliest manuscripts and many other ancient witnesses do not have John 7:53–8:11.)

8 53Then they all went home, 1but Jesus went to the Mount of Olives.

2At dawn he appeared again in the temple courts, where all the people gathered round him, and he sat down to teach them. 3The teachers of the law and the Pharisees brought in a woman caught in adultery. They made her stand before the group 4and said to Jesus, 'Teacher, this woman was caught in the act of adultery. 5In the Law Moses commanded us to stone such women. Now what do you say?' 6They were using this question as a trap, in order to have a basis for accusing him.

But Jesus bent down and started to write on the ground with his finger. 7When they kept on questioning him, he straightened up and said to them, 'Let any one of you who is without sin be the first to throw a stone at her.' 8Again he stooped down and wrote on the ground.

9At this, those who heard began to go away one at a time, the older ones first, until only Jesus was left, with the woman still standing there. 10Jesus straightened up and asked her, 'Woman,[b] where are they? Has no-one condemned you?'

11'No-one, sir,' she said.

'Then neither do I condemn you,' Jesus declared. 'Go now and leave your life of sin.'

Dispute over Jesus' testimony

12When Jesus spoke again to the people, he said, 'I am the light of the world. Whoever follows me will never walk in darkness, but will have the light of life.'

13The Pharisees challenged him, 'Here you are, appearing as your own witness; your testimony is not valid.'

---

[a] 37,38 Or me. And let anyone drink 38who believes in me.' As Scripture has said, 'Out of him (or them) will flow rivers of living water.'   [b] 10 The Greek for Woman does not denote any disrespect.

making Connections

Law about adultery
John 8:5
According to the Law of Moses, if a man and a woman were caught in adultery they should both be stoned to death (Leviticus 20:10), but the man involved in this case is nowhere to be seen. The witnesses were supposed to be the first ones to throw stones.

¹⁴Jesus answered, 'Even if I testify on my own behalf, my testimony is valid, for I know where I came from and where I am going. But you have no idea where I come from or where I am going. ¹⁵You judge by human standards; I pass judgment on no-one. ¹⁶But if I do judge, my decisions are true, because I am not alone. I stand with the Father, who sent me. ¹⁷In your own Law it is written that the testimony of two witnesses is true. ¹⁸I am one who testifies for myself; my other witness is the Father, who sent me.'

¹⁹Then they asked him, 'Where is your father?'

'You do not know me or my Father,' Jesus replied. 'If you knew me, you would know my Father also.' ²⁰He spoke these words while teaching in the temple courts near the place where the offerings were put. Yet no-one seized him, because his hour had not yet come.

Dispute over who Jesus is

²¹Once more Jesus said to them, 'I am going away, and you will look for me, and you will die in your sin. Where I go, you cannot come.'

²²This made the Jews ask, 'Will he kill himself? Is that why he says, "Where I go, you cannot come"?'

²³But he continued, 'You are from below; I am from above. You are of this world; I am not of this world. ²⁴I told you that you would die in your sins; if you do not believe that I am he, you will indeed die in your sins.'

²⁵'Who are you?' they asked.

'Just what I have been telling you from the beginning,' Jesus replied. ²⁶'I have much to say in judgment of you. But he who sent me is trustworthy, and what I have heard from him I tell the world.'

²⁷They did not understand that he was telling them about his Father. ²⁸So Jesus said, 'When you have lifted up^a the Son of Man, then you will know that I am he and that I do nothing on my own but speak just what the Father has taught me. ²⁹The one who sent me is with me; he has not left me alone, for I always do what pleases him.' ³⁰Even as he spoke, many put their faith in him.

Dispute over whose children Jesus' opponents are

³¹To the Jews who had believed him, Jesus said, 'If you hold to my teaching, you are really my disciples. ³²Then you will know the truth, and the truth will set you free.'

³³They answered him, 'We are Abraham's descendants and have never been slaves of anyone. How can you say that we shall be set free?'

³⁴Jesus replied, 'Very truly I tell you, everyone who sins is a slave to sin. ³⁵Now a

IN OTHER WORDS

Judge
John 8:16
A judge is someone responsible for administering justice and government. God is the supreme judge because he is the creator of the world and is holy and righteous. Here Jesus says that God has passed on to him authority to judge.

---

^{a} 28 The Greek for *lifted up* also means *exalted*.

slave has no permanent place in the family, but a son belongs to it for ever. ³⁶So if the Son sets you free, you will be free indeed. ³⁷I know you are Abraham's descendants. Yet you are looking for a way to kill me, because you have no room for my word. ³⁸I am telling you what I have seen in the Father's presence, and you are doing what you have heard from your father.ᵃ'

³⁹'Abraham is our father,' they answered.

'If you were Abraham's children,' said Jesus, 'then you wouldᵇ do what Abraham did. ⁴⁰As it is, you are looking for a way to kill me, a man who has told you the truth that I heard from God. Abraham did not do such things. ⁴¹You are doing the works of your own father.'

'We are not illegitimate children,' they protested. 'The only Father we have is God himself.'

⁴²Jesus said to them, 'If God were your Father, you would love me, for I came from God and now am here. I have not come on my own; but he sent me. ⁴³Why is my language not clear to you? Because you are unable to hear what I say. ⁴⁴You belong to your father, the devil, and you want to carry out your father's desires. He was a murderer from the beginning, not holding to the truth, for there is no truth in him. When he lies, he speaks his native language, for he is a liar and the father of lies. ⁴⁵Yet because I tell the truth, you do not believe me! ⁴⁶Can any of you prove me guilty of sin? If I am telling the truth, why don't you believe me? ⁴⁷Whoever belongs to God hears what God says. The reason you do not hear is that you do not belong to God.'

Jesus' claims about himself

⁴⁸The Jews answered him, 'Aren't we right in saying that you are a Samaritan and demon-possessed?'

⁴⁹'I am not possessed by a demon,' said Jesus, 'but I honour my Father and you dishonour me. ⁵⁰I am not seeking glory for myself; but there is one who seeks it, and he is the judge. ⁵¹Very truly I tell you, whoever obeys my word will never see death.'

> ## People and Places
>
> **LORD**
> **John 8:58**
>
> Jesus says, 'Before Abraham was born, I am,' and people are so outraged they pick up stones ready to throw at him. Why did he get that reaction? When God spoke to Moses at the burning bush (Exodus 3:14), he revealed his name as 'HE IS', or Yahweh. This was considered such a holy name in late Old Testament times that Jews wouldn't even say it, but instead used the word Adonai, meaning 'my Lord', for God. So when Jesus says, 'I am', he is using God's holy name for himself and effectively saying that he is God. That's why the Jews were so livid. The name Yahweh is written as LORD in this Bible.

⁵²At this they exclaimed, 'Now we know that you are demon-possessed! Abraham died and so did the prophets, yet you say that whoever obeys your word will never taste death. ⁵³Are you greater than our father Abraham? He died, and so did the prophets. Who do you think you are?'

⁵⁴Jesus replied, 'If I glorify myself, my glory means nothing. My Father, whom you claim as your God, is the one who glorifies me. ⁵⁵Though you do not know him, I know him. If I said I did not, I would be a liar like you, but I do know him and obey his word. ⁵⁶Your father Abraham rejoiced at the thought of seeing my day; he saw it and was glad.'

⁵⁷'You are not yet fifty years old,' they said to him, 'and you have seen Abraham!'

⁵⁸'Very truly I tell you,' Jesus answered, 'before Abraham was born, I am!' ⁵⁹At this, they picked up stones to stone him, but Jesus hid himself, slipping away from the temple grounds.

ᵃ 38 Or *presence. Therefore do what you have heard from the Father.* ᵇ 39 Some early manuscripts *'If you are Abraham's children,' said Jesus, 'then*

Jesus heals a man born blind

9 As he went along, he saw a man blind from birth. 2His disciples asked him, 'Rabbi, who sinned, this man or his parents, that he was born blind?'

3'Neither this man nor his parents sinned,' said Jesus, 'but this happened so that the works of God might be displayed in him. 4As long as it is day, we must do the works of him who sent me. Night is coming, when no-one can work. 5While I am in the world, I am the light of the world.'

6Having said this, he spat on the ground, made some mud with the saliva, and put it on the man's eyes. 7'Go,' he told him, 'wash in the Pool of Siloam' (this word means 'Sent'). So the man went and washed, and came home seeing.

8His neighbours and those who had formerly seen him begging asked, 'Isn't this the same man who used to sit and beg?' 9Some claimed that he was.

Others said, 'No, he only looks like him.'
But he himself insisted, 'I am the man.'

10'How then were your eyes opened?' they asked.

11He replied, 'The man they call Jesus made some mud and put it on my eyes. He told me to go to Siloam and wash. So I went and washed, and then I could see.'

12'Where is this man?' they asked him.
'I don't know,' he said.

The Pharisees investigate the healing

13They brought to the Pharisees the man who had been blind. 14Now the day on which Jesus had made the mud and opened the man's eyes was a Sabbath. 15Therefore the Pharisees also asked him how he had received his sight. 'He put mud on my eyes,' the man replied, 'and I washed, and now I see.'

16Some of the Pharisees said, 'This man is not from God, for he does not keep the Sabbath.'

But others asked, 'How can a sinner perform such signs?' So they were divided.

17Then they turned again to the blind man, 'What have you to say about him? It was your eyes he opened.'

The man replied, 'He is a prophet.'

18They still did not believe that he had been blind and had received his sight until they sent for the man's parents. 19'Is this your son?' they asked. 'Is this the one you say was born blind? How is it that now he can see?'

20'We know he is our son,' the parents answered, 'and we know he was born blind. 21But how he can see now, or who opened his eyes, we don't know. Ask him. He is of age; he will speak for himself.' 22His parents said this because they were afraid of the Jewish leaders, who already had decided that anyone who acknowledged that Jesus was the Messiah would be put out of the synagogue. 23That was why his parents said, 'He is of age; ask him.'

24A second time they summoned the man who had been blind. 'Give glory to God and tell the truth' they said. 'We know this man is a sinner.'

25He replied, 'Whether he is a sinner or not, I don't know. One thing I do know. I was blind but now I see!'

26Then they asked him, 'What did he do to you? How did he open your eyes?'

27He answered, 'I have told you already and you did not listen. Why do you want to hear it again? Do you want to become his disciples too?'

28Then they hurled insults at him and said, 'You are this fellow's disciple! We are disciples of Moses! 29We know that God spoke to Moses, but as for this fellow, we don't even know where he comes from.'

30The man answered, 'Now that is remarkable! You don't know where he comes from, yet he opened my eyes. 31We know that God does not listen to sinners. He listens to the godly person who does his will. 32Nobody has ever heard of opening the eyes of a man born blind. 33If this man were not from God, he could do nothing.'

34To this they replied, 'You were steeped in sin at birth; how dare you lecture us!' And they threw him out.

Spiritual blindness

35Jesus heard that they had thrown him out, and when he found him, he said, 'Do you believe in the Son of Man?'

36'Who is he, sir?' the man asked. 'Tell me so that I may believe in him.'

37Jesus said, 'You have now seen him; in fact, he is the one speaking with you.'

38Then the man said, 'Lord, I believe,' and he worshipped him.

39Jesus said,[a] 'For judgment I have come into this world, so that the blind will see and those who see will become blind.'

40Some Pharisees who were with him heard him say this and asked, 'What? Are we blind too?'

41Jesus said, 'If you were blind, you would not be guilty of sin; but now that you claim you can see, your guilt remains.

The good shepherd and his sheep

10 'Very truly I tell you Pharisees, anyone who does not enter the sheepfold by the gate, but climbs in by some other way, is a thief and a robber. 2The one who enters by the gate is the shepherd of the sheep. 3The gatekeeper opens the gate for him, and the sheep listen to his voice. He calls his own sheep by name and leads them out. 4When he has brought out all his own, he goes on ahead of them, and his sheep follow him because they know his voice. 5But they will never follow a stranger; in fact, they will run away from him because they do not recognise a stranger's voice.' 6Jesus used this figure of speech, but the Pharisees did not understand what he was telling them.

7Therefore Jesus said again, 'Very truly I tell you, I am the gate for the sheep. 8All who have come before me are thieves and robbers, but the sheep have not listened to them. 9I am the gate; whoever enters through me will be saved.[b] They will come in and go out, and find pasture. 10The thief comes only to steal and kill and destroy; I have come that they may have life, and have it to the full.

11'I am the good shepherd. The good shepherd lays down his life for the sheep. 12The hired hand is not the shepherd and does not own the sheep. So when he sees the wolf coming, he abandons the sheep and runs away. Then the wolf attacks the flock and scatters it. 13The man runs away because he is a hired hand and cares nothing for the sheep.

14'I am the good shepherd; I know my sheep and my sheep know me— 15just as the Father knows me and I know the Father—and I lay down my life for the sheep. 16I have other sheep that are not of this sheepfold. I must bring them also. They too will listen to my voice, and there shall be one flock and one shepherd. 17The reason my Father loves me is that I lay down my life—only to take it up again. 18No-one takes it from me, but I lay it down of my own accord. I have authority to lay it down and authority to take it up again. This command I received from my Father.'

19The Jews who heard these words were again divided. 20Many of them said, 'He is demon-possessed and raving mad. Why listen to him?'

21But others said, 'These are not the sayings of someone possessed by a demon. Can a demon open the eyes of the blind?'

Further conflict over Jesus' claims

22Then came the Feast of Dedication[c] at Jerusalem. It was winter, 23and Jesus was in the temple courts walking in Solomon's Colonnade. 24The Jews who were there gathered round him, saying, 'How long will you keep us in suspense? If you are the Messiah, tell us plainly.'

25Jesus answered, 'I did tell you, but you do not believe. The works I do in my Father's name testify about me, 26but you do not believe because you are not my sheep. 27My sheep listen to my voice; I know them, and they follow me. 28I give them eternal life, and they shall never perish; no-one will snatch them out of my hand. 29My Father, who has given them to me, is greater than all[d]; no-one can snatch them out of my Father's hand. 30I and the Father are one.'

31Again the Jews picked up stones to stone him, 32but Jesus said to them, 'I have shown you many good works from the Father. For which of these do you stone me?'

33'We are not stoning you for any good work,' they replied, 'but for blasphemy, because you, a mere man, claim to be God.'

---

[a] 38,39 Some early manuscripts do not have verses 38 and 39a. [b] 9 Or *kept safe* [c] 22 That is, Hanukkah [d] 29 Many early manuscripts *What my Father has given me is greater than all*

34Jesus answered them, 'Is it not written in your Law, "I have said you are 'gods'"*a*? 35If he called them "gods", to whom the word of God came—and Scripture cannot be broken— 36what about the one whom the Father set apart as his very own and sent into the world? Why then do you accuse me of blasphemy because I said, "I am God's Son"? 37Do not believe me unless I do the works of my Father. 38But if I do them, even though you do not believe me, believe the works, that you may know and understand that the Father is in me, and I in the Father.' 39Again they tried to seize him, but he escaped their grasp.

40Then Jesus went back across the Jordan to the place where John had been baptising in the early days. Here he stayed 41and many people came to him. They said, 'Though John never performed a sign, all that John said about this man was true.' 42And in that place many believed in Jesus.

The death of Lazarus

11 Now a man named Lazarus was ill. He was from Bethany, the village of Mary and her sister Martha. 2(This Mary, whose brother Lazarus now lay ill, was the same one who poured perfume on the Lord and wiped his feet with her hair.) 3So the sisters sent word to Jesus, 'Lord, the one you love is ill.'

4When he heard this, Jesus said, 'This illness will not end in death. No, it is for God's glory so that God's Son may be glorified through it.' 5Now Jesus loved Martha and her sister and Lazarus. 6So when he heard that Lazarus was ill, he stayed where he was two more days, 7and then he said to his disciples, 'Let us go back to Judea.'

8'But Rabbi,' they said, 'a short while ago the Jews there tried to stone you, and yet you are going back?'

9Jesus answered, 'Are there not twelve hours of daylight? Those who walk in the day-time will not stumble, for they see by this world's light. 10It is when people walk at night that they stumble, for they have no light.'

> ### People and Places
>
> **Martha**
> John 11:20
> Martha was a follower of Jesus, along with her sister Mary and brother Lazarus. She is known for being busy with the housework when Jesus came to visit, while her sister Mary sat at Jesus' feet and listened to him (Luke 10:38–41). But Martha learned from Jesus too. In this story she affirms her faith in him as the Messiah, the Son of God, rather like Peter does in Luke 9:20.

11After he had said this, he went on to tell them, 'Our friend Lazarus has fallen asleep; but I am going there to wake him up.'

12His disciples replied, 'Lord, if he sleeps, he will get better.' 13Jesus had been speaking of his death, but his disciples thought he meant natural sleep.

14So then he told them plainly, 'Lazarus is dead, 15and for your sake I am glad I was not there, so that you may believe. But let us go to him.'

16Then Thomas (also known as Didymus*b*) said to the rest of the disciples, 'Let us also go, that we may die with him.'

Jesus comforts the sisters of Lazarus

17On his arrival, Jesus found that Lazarus had already been in the tomb for four days. 18Now Bethany was less than two miles*c* from Jerusalem, 19and many Jews had come to Martha and Mary to comfort them in the loss of their brother. 20When Martha heard that Jesus was coming, she went out to meet him, but Mary stayed at home.

21'Lord,' Martha said to Jesus, 'if you had been here, my brother would not have died. 22But I know that even now God will give you whatever you ask.'

23Jesus said to her, 'Your brother will rise again.'

---

a 34 Psalm 82:6   *b* 16 *Thomas* (Aramaic) and *Didymus* (Greek) both mean *twin*.   *c* 18 Or about 3 kilometres

24 Martha answered, 'I know he will rise again in the resurrection at the last day.'

25 Jesus said to her, 'I am the resurrection and the life. Anyone who believes in me will live, even though they die; 26 and whoever lives by believing in me will never die. Do you believe this?'

27 'Yes, Lord,' she told him, 'I believe that you are the Messiah, the Son of God, who was to come into the world.'

28 After she had said this, she went back and called her sister Mary aside. 'The Teacher is here,' she said, 'and is asking for you.' 29 When Mary heard this, she got up quickly and went to him. 30 Now Jesus had not yet entered the village, but was still at the place where Martha had met him. 31 When the Jews who had been with Mary in the house, comforting her, noticed how quickly she got up and went out, they followed her, supposing she was going to the tomb to mourn there.

32 When Mary reached the place where Jesus was and saw him, she fell at his feet and said, 'Lord, if you had been here, my brother would not have died.'

33 When Jesus saw her weeping, and the Jews who had come along with her also weeping, he was deeply moved in spirit and troubled. 34 'Where have you laid him?' he asked.

'Come and see, Lord,' they replied.

35 Jesus wept.

36 Then the Jews said, 'See how he loved him!'

37 But some of them said, 'Could not he who opened the eyes of the blind man have kept this man from dying?'

Jesus raises Lazarus from the dead

38 Jesus, once more deeply moved, came to the tomb. It was a cave with a stone laid across the entrance. 39 'Take away the stone,' he said.

'But, Lord,' said Martha, the sister of the dead man, 'by this time there is a bad odour, for he has been there four days.'

40 Then Jesus said, 'Did I not tell you that if you believe, you will see the glory of God?'

41 So they took away the stone. Then Jesus looked up and said, 'Father, I thank you that you have heard me. 42 I knew that you always hear me, but I said this for the benefit of the people standing here, that they may believe that you sent me.'

43 When he had said this, Jesus called in a loud voice, 'Lazarus, come out!' 44 The dead man came out, his hands and feet wrapped with strips of linen, and a cloth round his face.

Jesus said to them, 'Take off the grave clothes and let him go.'

The plot to kill Jesus

45 Therefore many of the Jews who had come to visit Mary, and had seen what Jesus did, put their faith in him. 46 But some of them went to the Pharisees and told them what Jesus had done. 47 Then the chief priests and the Pharisees called a meeting of the Sanhedrin.

'What are we accomplishing?' they asked. 'Here is this man performing many signs. 48 If we let him go on like this, everyone will believe in him, and then the Romans will come and take away both our temple and our nation.'

49 Then one of them, named Caiaphas, who was high priest that year, spoke up, 'You know nothing at all! 50 You do not realise that it is better for you that one man die for the people than that the whole nation perish.'

51 He did not say this on his own, but as high priest that year he prophesied that Jesus would die for the Jewish nation, 52 and not only for that nation but also for the scattered children of God, to bring them together and make them one. 53 So from that day on they plotted to take his life.

54 Therefore Jesus no longer moved about publicly among the Jews. Instead he withdrew to a region near the wilderness, to a village called Ephraim, where he stayed with his disciples.

55 When it was almost time for the Jewish Passover, many went up from the country to Jerusalem for their ceremonial cleansing before the Passover. 56 They kept looking for Jesus, and as they stood in the temple courts they asked one another, 'What do you think? Isn't he coming to the Feast at all?' 57 But the chief priests and the Pharisees had given orders that anyone who found out where Jesus was should report it so that they might arrest him.

Jesus anointed at Bethany

12 Six days before the Passover, Jesus came to Bethany, where Lazarus lived, whom Jesus had raised from the dead. ²Here a dinner was given in Jesus' honour. Martha served, while Lazarus was among those reclining at the table with him. ³Then Mary took about half a litre of pure nard, an expensive perfume; she poured it on Jesus' feet and wiped his feet with her hair. And the house was filled with the fragrance of the perfume.

⁴But one of his disciples, Judas Iscariot, who was later to betray him, objected, ⁵'Why wasn't this perfume sold and the money given to the poor? It was worth a year's wages.ᵃ' ⁶He did not say this because he cared about the poor but because he was a thief; as keeper of the money bag, he used to help himself to what was put into it.

⁷'Leave her alone,' Jesus replied. '⌊It was intended⌋ that she should save this perfume for the day of my burial. ⁸You will always have the poor among you,ᵇ but you will not always have me.'

⁹Meanwhile a large crowd of Jews found out that Jesus was there and came, not only because of him but also to see Lazarus, whom he had raised from the dead. ¹⁰So the chief priests made plans to kill Lazarus as well, ¹¹for on account of him many of the Jews were going over to Jesus and putting their faith in him.

IN OTHER WORDS

Glorify
John 12:23
If you glorify someone you give them honour and worship, you make them more splendid and you revel in their beauty. The psalms have lots of invitations to glorify God (Psalm 34:3).

Jesus comes to Jerusalem as king

¹²The next day the great crowd that had come for the Feast heard that Jesus was on his way to Jerusalem. ¹³They took palm branches and went out to meet him, shouting,

'Hosanna!ᶜ'

'Blessed is he who comes in the name of the Lord!'ᵈ

'Blessed is the king of Israel!'

¹⁴Jesus found a young donkey and sat upon it, as it is written:

¹⁵'Do not be afraid, Daughter Zion;
  see, your king is coming,
  seated on a donkey's colt.'ᵉ

¹⁶At first his disciples did not understand all this. Only after Jesus was glorified did they realise that these things had been written about him and that these things had been done to him.

¹⁷Now the crowd that was with him when he called Lazarus from the tomb and raised him from the dead continued to spread the word. ¹⁸Many people, because they had heard that he had performed this sign, went out to meet him. ¹⁹So the Pharisees said to one another, 'See, this is getting us nowhere. Look how the whole world has gone after him!'

Jesus predicts his death

²⁰Now there were some Greeks among those who went up to worship at the Feast. ²¹They came to Philip, who was from Bethsaida in Galilee, with a request. 'Sir,' they said, 'we would like to see Jesus.' ²²Philip went to tell Andrew; Andrew and Philip in turn told Jesus.

²³Jesus replied, 'The hour has come for the Son of Man to be glorified. ²⁴Very truly I tell you, unless a grain of wheat falls to the ground and dies, it remains only a single seed. But if it dies, it produces many seeds. ²⁵Those who love their life will lose it, while those who hate their life in this world will keep it for eternal life. ²⁶Whoever serves me must follow me; and where I am, my servant

---

ᵃ5 Greek *three hundred denarii* ᵇ8 See Deut. 15:11. ᶜ13 A Hebrew expression meaning 'Save!' which became an exclamation of praise ᵈ13 Psalm 118:25,26 ᵉ15 Zech. 9:9

also will be. My Father will honour the one who serves me.

27'Now my soul is troubled, and what shall I say? "Father, save me from this hour"? No, it was for this very reason I came to this hour. 28Father, glorify your name!'

Then a voice came from heaven, 'I have glorified it, and will glorify it again.' 29The crowd that was there and heard it said it had thundered; others said an angel had spoken to him.

30Jesus said, 'This voice was for your benefit, not mine. 31Now is the time for judgment on this world; now the prince of this world will be driven out. 32And I, when I am lifted up[a] from the earth, will draw all people to myself.' 33He said this to show the kind of death he was going to die.

34The crowd spoke up, 'We have heard from the Law that the Messiah will remain for ever, so how can you say, "The Son of Man must be lifted up"? Who is this "Son of Man"?'

35Then Jesus told them, 'You are going to have the light just a little while longer. Walk while you have the light, before darkness overtakes you. Those who walk in the dark do not know where they are going. 36Put your trust in the light while you have the light, so that you may become children of light.' When he had finished speaking, Jesus left and hid himself from them.

Belief and unbelief among the Jews

37Even after Jesus had performed so many signs in their presence, they still would not believe in him. 38This was to fulfil the word of Isaiah the prophet:

'Lord, who has believed our message
    and to whom has the arm of the Lord
        been revealed?'[b]

39For this reason they could not believe, because, as Isaiah says elsewhere:

40'He has blinded their eyes
    and hardened their hearts,
so they can neither see with their eyes,
    nor understand with their hearts,
        nor turn—and I would heal them.'[c]

41Isaiah said this because he saw Jesus' glory and spoke about him.

42Yet at the same time many even among the leaders believed in him. But because of the Pharisees they would not openly acknowledge their faith for fear they would be put out of the synagogue; 43for they loved human glory more than the glory of God.

44Then Jesus cried out, 'Those who believe in me do not believe in me only, but in the one who sent me. 45When they look at me, they see the one who sent me. 46I have come into the world as a light, so that no-one who believes in me should stay in darkness.

47'As for those who hear my words but do not keep them, I do not judge them. For I did not come to judge the world, but to save the world. 48There is a judge for those who reject me and do not accept my words; the very words I have spoken will condemn them at the last day. 49For I did not speak on my own, but the Father who sent me commanded me to say all that I have spoken. 50I know that his command leads to eternal life. So whatever I say is just what the Father has told me to say.'

Jesus washes his disciples' feet

13 It was just before the Passover Feast. Jesus knew that the hour had come for him to leave this world and go to the Father. Having loved his own who were in the world, he loved them to the end.

2The evening meal was in progress, and the devil had already prompted Judas, the son of Simon Iscariot, to betray Jesus. 3Jesus knew that the Father had put all things under his power, and that he had come from God and was returning to God; 4so he got up from the meal, took off his outer clothing, and wrapped a towel round his waist. 5After that, he poured water into a basin and began to wash his disciples' feet, drying them with the towel that was wrapped round him.

6He came to Simon Peter, who said to him, 'Lord, are you going to wash my feet?'

7Jesus replied, 'You do not realise now what I am doing, but later you will understand.'

---

[a] 32 The Greek for *lifted up* also means *exalted*.   [b] 38 Isaiah 53:1   [c] 40 Isaiah 6:10

Foot washing
John 13:5

Jesus lived in a hot, dusty country where water was precious and there were no power showers. Feet in sandals would get hot, dirty and smelly. When you visited someone's house, it was normal practice for the lowliest servant to wash your feet as a sign of your host's welcome and hospitality. Jesus takes on this role when he washes his disciples' feet at the Last Supper.

8'No,' said Peter, 'you shall never wash my feet.'

Jesus answered, 'Unless I wash you, you have no part with me.'

9'Then, Lord,' Simon Peter replied, 'not just my feet but my hands and my head as well!'

10Jesus answered, 'Those who have had a bath need only to wash their feet; their whole body is clean. And you are clean, though not every one of you.' 11For he knew who was going to betray him, and that was why he said not every one was clean.

12When he had finished washing their feet, he put on his clothes and returned to his place. 'Do you understand what I have done for you?' he asked them. 13'You call me "Teacher" and "Lord", and rightly so, for that is what I am. 14Now that I, your Lord and Teacher, have washed your feet, you also should wash one another's feet. 15I have set you an example that you should do as I have done for you. 16Very truly I tell you, servants are not greater than their master, nor are messengers greater than the one who sent them. 17Now that you know these things, you will be blessed if you do them.

Jesus predicts his betrayal

18'I am not referring to all of you; I know those I have chosen. But this is to fulfil this passage of Scripture: "He who shared my bread has lifted up his heel against me."[a]

19'I am telling you now before it happens, so that when it does happen you will believe that I am who I am. 20Very truly I tell you, whoever accepts anyone I send accepts me; and whoever accepts me accepts the one who sent me.'

21After he had said this, Jesus was troubled in spirit and testified, 'Very truly I tell you, one of you is going to betray me.'

22His disciples stared at one another, at a loss to know which of them he meant. 23One of them, the disciple whom Jesus loved, was reclining next to him. 24Simon Peter motioned to this disciple and said, 'Ask him which one he means.'

25Leaning back against Jesus, he asked him, 'Lord, who is it?'

26Jesus answered, 'It is the one to whom I will give this piece of bread when I have dipped it in the dish.' Then, dipping the piece of bread, he gave it to Judas, the son of Simon Iscariot. 27As soon as Judas took the bread, Satan entered into him.

So Jesus told him, 'What you are about to do, do quickly.' 28But no-one at the meal understood why Jesus said this to him. 29Since Judas had charge of the money, some thought Jesus was telling him to buy what was needed for the Feast, or to give something to the poor. 30As soon as Judas had taken the bread, he went out. And it was night.

Jesus predicts Peter's denial

31When he was gone, Jesus said, 'Now is the Son of Man glorified and God is glorified in him. 32If God is glorified in him,[b] God will glorify the Son in himself, and will glorify him at once.

33'My children, I will be with you only a little longer. You will look for me, and just as I told the Jews, so I tell you now: where I am going, you cannot come.

34'A new command I give you: love one another. As I have loved you, so you must love one another. 35By this everyone will

---

[a] 18 Psalm 41:9 [b] 32 Many early manuscripts do not have *If God is glorified in him.*

know that you are my disciples, if you love one another.'

36Simon Peter asked him, 'Lord, where are you going?'

Jesus replied, 'Where I am going, you cannot follow now, but you will follow later.'

37Peter asked, 'Lord, why can't I follow you now? I will lay down my life for you.'

38Then Jesus answered, 'Will you really lay down your life for me? Very truly I tell you, before the cock crows, you will disown me three times!

Jesus comforts his disciples

14 'Do not let your hearts be troubled. Trust in God[a]; trust also in me. 2My Father's house has plenty of room; if that were not so, would I have told you that I am going there to prepare a place for you? 3And if I go and prepare a place for you, I will come back and take you to be with me that you also may be where I am. 4You know the way to the place where I am going.'

Jesus the way to the Father

5Thomas said to him, 'Lord, we don't know where you are going, so how can we know the way?'

6Jesus answered, 'I am the way and the truth and the life. No-one comes to the Father except through me. 7If you really know me, you will know[b] my Father as well. From now on, you do know him and have seen him.'

8Philip said, 'Lord, show us the Father and that will be enough for us.'

9Jesus answered: 'Don't you know me, Philip, even after I have been among you such a long time? Anyone who has seen me has seen the Father. How can you say, "Show us the Father"? 10Don't you believe that I am in the Father, and that the Father is in me? The words I say to you I do not speak on my own authority. Rather, it is the Father, living in me, who is doing his work. 11Believe me when I say that I am in the Father and the Father is in me; or at least believe on the evidence of the works themselves. 12Very truly I tell you, all who have faith in me will do the works I have been doing, and they will do even greater things than these, because I am going to the Father. 13And I will do whatever you ask in my name, so that the Father may be glorified in the Son. 14You may ask me for anything in my name, and I will do it.

Jesus promises the Holy Spirit

15'If you love me, keep my commands. 16And I will ask the Father, and he will give you another advocate to help you and be with you for ever— 17the Spirit of truth. The world cannot accept him, because it neither sees him nor knows him. But you know him, for he lives with you and will be[c] in you. 18I will not leave you as orphans; I will come to you. 19Before long, the world will not see me any more, but you will see me. Because I live, you also will live. 20On that day you will realise that I am in my Father, and you are in me, and I am in you. 21Whoever has my commands and keeps them is the one who loves me. Anyone who loves me will be loved by my Father, and I too will love them and show myself to them.'

22Then Judas (not Judas Iscariot) said, 'But, Lord, why do you intend to show yourself to us and not to the world?'

23Jesus replied, 'Anyone who loves me will obey my teaching. My Father will love them, and we will come to them and make our home with them. 24Anyone who does not love me will not obey my teaching. These words you hear are not my own; they belong to the Father who sent me.

25'All this I have spoken while still with you. 26But the Advocate, the Holy Spirit, whom the Father will send in my name, will teach you all things and will remind you of everything I have said to you. 27Peace I leave with you; my peace I give you. I do not give to you as the world gives. Do not let your hearts be troubled and do not be afraid.

28'You heard me say, "I am going away and I am coming back to you." If you loved me, you would be glad that I am going to the Father, for the Father is greater than I. 29I have told you now before it happens, so that when it does happen you will believe. 30I

---

[a] 1 Or *You trust in God* [b] 7 Some manuscripts *If you really knew me, you would know* [c] 17 Some early manuscripts *and is*

will not say much more to you, for the prince of this world is coming. He has no hold over me, ³¹but he comes so that the world may learn that I love the Father and do exactly what my Father has commanded me.

'Come now; let us leave.

The vine and the branches

15 ¹'I am the true vine, and my Father is the gardener. ²He cuts off every branch in me that bears no fruit, while every branch that does bear fruit he prunes[a] so that it will be even more fruitful. ³You are already clean because of the word I have spoken to you. ⁴Remain in me, as I also remain in you. No branch can bear fruit by itself; it must remain in the vine. Neither can you bear fruit unless you remain in me.

⁵'I am the vine; you are the branches. If you remain in me and I in you, you will bear much fruit; apart from me you can do nothing. ⁶If you do not remain in me, you are like a branch that is thrown away and withers; such branches are picked up, thrown into the fire and burned. ⁷If you remain in me and my words remain in you, ask whatever you wish, and it will be done for you. ⁸This is to my Father's glory, that you bear much fruit, showing yourselves to be my disciples.

⁹'As the Father has loved me, so have I loved you. Now remain in my love. ¹⁰If you keep my commands, you will remain in my love, just as I have kept my Father's commands and remain in his love. ¹¹I have told you this so that my joy may be in you and that your joy may be complete. ¹²My command is this: love each other as I have loved you. ¹³Greater love has no-one than this: to lay down one's life for one's friends. ¹⁴You are my friends if you do what I command. ¹⁵I no longer call you servants, because servants do not know their master's business. Instead, I have called you friends, for everything that I learned from my Father I have made known to you. ¹⁶You did not choose me, but I chose you and appointed you so that you might go and bear fruit—fruit that will last—and so that whatever

making Connections

Vine
John 15:1
Vines grew well in the soil and climate of Palestine, but it was a lot of work to look after them. Every year the vines would be pruned, and any branches that were not producing fruit were cut off. Grapes were harvested in September and October with much celebration.

you ask in my name the Father will give you. ¹⁷This is my command: love each other.

The world hates the disciples

¹⁸'If the world hates you, keep in mind that it hated me first. ¹⁹If you belonged to the world, it would love you as its own. As it is, you do not belong to the world, but I have chosen you out of the world. That is why the world hates you. ²⁰Remember what I told you: "Servants are not greater than their master."[b] If they persecuted me, they will persecute you also. If they obeyed my teaching, they will obey yours also. ²¹They will treat you this way because of my name, for they do not know the one who sent me. ²²If I had not come and spoken to them, they would not be guilty of sin; but now they have no excuse for their sin. ²³Those who hate me hate my Father as well. ²⁴If I had not done among them the works no-one else did, they would not be guilty of sin. As it is, they have seen, and yet they have hated both me and my Father. ²⁵But this is to fulfil what is written in their Law: "They hated me without reason."[c]

The work of the Holy Spirit

²⁶'When the Advocate comes, whom I will send to you from the Father—the Spirit of truth who goes out from the Father—he will testify about me. ²⁷And you also must

---

[a] 2 The Greek for *he prunes* also means *he cleans*.   [b] 20 John 13:16   [c] 25 Psalms 35:19; 69:4

testify, for you have been with me from the beginning.

16 'All this I have told you so that you will not fall away. ²They will put you out of the synagogue; in fact, the hour is coming when those who kill you will think they are offering a service to God. ³They will do such things because they have not known the Father or me. ⁴I have told you this, so that when their hour comes you will remember that I warned you about them. I did not tell you this from the beginning because I was with you, ⁵but now I am going to him who sent me. None of you asks me, "Where are you going?" ⁶Rather, you are filled with grief because I have said these things. ⁷But very truly I tell you, it is for your good that I am going away. Unless I go away, the Advocate will not come to you; but if I go, I will send him to you. ⁸When he comes, he will prove the world to be in the wrong about sin and righteousness and judgment: ⁹about sin, because people do not believe in me; ¹⁰about righteousness, because I am going to the Father, where you can see me no longer; ¹¹and about judgment, because the prince of this world now stands condemned.

¹²'I have much more to say to you, more than you can now bear. ¹³But when he, the Spirit of truth, comes, he will guide you into all the truth. He will not speak on his own; he will speak only what he hears, and he will tell you what is yet to come. ¹⁴He will glorify me because it is from me that he will receive what he will make known to you. ¹⁵All that belongs to the Father is mine. That is why I said the Spirit will receive from me what he will make known to you.'

The disciples' grief will turn to joy

¹⁶Jesus went on to say, 'In a little while you will see me no more, and then after a little while you will see me.'

¹⁷At this, some of his disciples said to one another, 'What does he mean by saying, "In a little while you will see me no more, and then after a little while you will see me," and "Because I am going to the Father"?' ¹⁸They kept asking, 'What does he mean by "a little while"? We don't understand what he is saying.'

¹⁹Jesus saw that they wanted to ask him about this, so he said to them, 'Are you asking one another what I meant when I said, "In a little while you will see me no more, and then after a little while you will see me"? ²⁰Very truly I tell you, you will weep and mourn while the world rejoices. You will grieve, but your grief will turn to joy. ²¹A woman giving birth to a child has pain because her time has come; but when her baby is born she forgets the anguish because of her joy that a child is born into the world. ²²So with you: now is your time of grief, but I will see you again and you will rejoice, and no-one will take away your joy. ²³In that day you will no longer ask me anything. Very truly I tell you, my Father will give you whatever you ask in my name. ²⁴Until now you have not asked for anything in my name. Ask and you will receive, and your joy will be complete.

²⁵'Though I have been speaking figuratively, a time is coming when I will no longer use this kind of language but will tell you plainly about my Father. ²⁶In that day you will ask in my name. I am not saying that I will ask the Father on your behalf. ²⁷No, the Father himself loves you because you have loved me and have believed that I came from God. ²⁸I came from the Father and entered

People and Places

Holy Spirit
John 16:7

Jesus promises that, when he leaves his disciples, they will receive the Holy Spirit in his place. The Holy Spirit is the third person of the Trinity. The Spirit is seen as having a creative and sustaining role, and was present at the creation of the world, 'hovering over the waters' (Genesis 1:2). The Holy Spirit inspired Scripture (2 Timothy 3:16) and is here today as God's presence with us and in us.

the world; now I am leaving the world and going back to the Father.'

29Then Jesus' disciples said, 'Now you are speaking clearly and without figures of speech. 30Now we can see that you know all things and that you do not even need to have anyone ask you questions. This makes us believe that you came from God.'

31'Do you now believe?' Jesus replied. 32'A time is coming and in fact has come when you will be scattered, each to your own home. You will leave me all alone. Yet I am not alone, for my Father is with me.

33'I have told you these things, so that in me you may have peace. In this world you will have trouble. But take heart! I have overcome the world.'

Jesus prays to be glorified

17 After Jesus said this, he looked towards heaven and prayed:

'Father, the hour has come. Glorify your Son, that your Son may glorify you. 2For you granted him authority over all people that he might give eternal life to all those you have given him. 3Now this is eternal life: that they know you, the only true God, and Jesus Christ, whom you have sent. 4I have brought you glory on earth by finishing the work you gave me to do. 5And now, Father, glorify me in your presence with the glory I had with you before the world began.

Jesus prays for his disciples

6'I have revealed you[a] to those whom you gave me out of the world. They were yours; you gave them to me and they have obeyed your word. 7Now they know that everything you have given me comes from you. 8For I gave them the words you gave me and they accepted them. They knew with certainty that I came from you, and they believed that you sent me. 9I pray for them. I am not praying for the world, but for those you have given me, for they are yours. 10All I have is yours, and all you have is mine. And glory has come to me through them. 11I will remain in the world no longer, but they are still in the world, and I am coming to you. Holy Father, protect them by the power of[b] your name, the name you gave me, so that they may be one as we are one. 12While I was with them, I protected them and kept them safe by[c] that name you gave me. None has been lost except the one doomed to destruction so that Scripture would be fulfilled.

13'I am coming to you now, but I say these things while I am still in the world, so that they may have the full measure of my joy within them. 14I have given them your word and the world has hated them, for they are not of the world any more than I am of the world. 15My prayer is not that you take them out of the world but that you protect them from the evil one. 16They are not of the world, even as I am not of it. 17Sanctify them by[d] the truth; your word is truth. 18As you sent me into the world, I have sent them into the world. 19For them I sanctify myself, that they too may be truly sanctified.

Jesus prays for all believers

20'My prayer is not for them alone. I pray also for those who will believe in me through their message, 21that all of them may be one, Father, just as you are in me and I am in you. May they also be in us so that the world may believe that you have sent me. 22I have given them the glory that you gave me, that they may be one as we are one— 23I in them and you in me—so that they may be brought

---

[a] 6 Greek *your name*; also in verse 26 [b] 11 Or *Father, keep them faithful to* [c] 12 Or *kept them faithful to* [d] 17 Or *them to live in accordance with*

to complete unity. Then the world will know that you sent me and have loved them even as you have loved me.

24 'Father, I want those you have given me to be with me where I am, and to see my glory, the glory you have given me because you loved me before the creation of the world.

25 'Righteous Father, though the world does not know you, I know you, and they know that you have sent me. 26 I have made you known to them, and will continue to make you known in order that the love you have for me may be in them and that I myself may be in them.'

Jesus arrested

18 When he had finished praying, Jesus left with his disciples and crossed the Kidron Valley. On the other side there was a garden, and he and his disciples went into it.

2 Now Judas, who betrayed him, knew the place, because Jesus had often met there with his disciples. 3 So Judas came to the garden, guiding a detachment of soldiers and some officials from the chief priests and the Pharisees. They were carrying torches, lanterns and weapons.

4 Jesus, knowing all that was going to happen to him, went out and asked them, 'Who is it you want?'

5 'Jesus of Nazareth,' they replied.

'I am he,' Jesus said. (And Judas the traitor was standing there with them.) 6 When Jesus said, 'I am he,' they drew back and fell to the ground.

7 Again he asked them, 'Who is it you want?'

'Jesus of Nazareth,' they said.

8 Jesus answered, 'I told you that I am he. If you are looking for me, then let these men go.' 9 This happened so that the words he had spoken would be fulfilled: 'I have not lost one of those you gave me.'[a]

10 Then Simon Peter, who had a sword, drew it and struck the high priest's servant, cutting off his right ear. (The servant's name was Malchus.)

11 Jesus commanded Peter, 'Put your sword away! Shall I not drink the cup the Father has given me?'

12 Then the detachment of soldiers with its commander and the Jewish officials arrested Jesus. They bound him 13 and brought him first to Annas, who was the father-in-law of Caiaphas, the high priest that year. 14 Caiaphas was the one who had advised the Jewish leaders that it would be good if one man died for the people.

Peter's first denial

15 Simon Peter and another disciple were following Jesus. Because this disciple was known to the high priest, he went with Jesus into the high priest's courtyard, 16 but Peter had to wait outside at the door. The other disciple, who was known to the high priest, came back, spoke to the servant-girl on duty there and brought Peter in.

17 'You aren't one of this man's disciples too, are you?' she asked Peter.

He replied, 'I am not.'

18 It was cold, and the servants and officials stood round a fire they had made to keep warm. Peter also was standing with them, warming himself.

The high priest questions Jesus

19 Meanwhile, the high priest questioned Jesus about his disciples and his teaching.

20 'I have spoken openly to the world,' Jesus replied. 'I always taught in synagogues or at the temple, where all the Jews come together. I said nothing in secret. 21 Why question me? Ask those who heard me. Surely they know what I said.'

22 When Jesus said this, one of the officials near by slapped him in the face. 'Is this the way you answer the high priest?' he demanded.

23 'If I said something wrong,' Jesus replied, 'testify as to what is wrong. But if I spoke the truth, why did you strike me?' 24 Then Annas sent him bound to Caiaphas the high priest.

---
a 9 John 6:39

Peter's second and third denials

25Meanwhile, Simon Peter was still standing there warming himself. So they asked him, 'You aren't one of his disciples too, are you?'

He denied it, saying, 'I am not.'

26One of the high priest's servants, a relative of the man whose ear Peter had cut off, challenged him, 'Didn't I see you with him in the garden?' 27Again Peter denied it, and at that moment a cock began to crow.

Jesus before Pilate

28Then the Jewish leaders took Jesus from Caiaphas to the palace of the Roman governor. By now it was early morning, and to avoid ceremonial uncleanness they did not enter the palace, because they wanted to be able to eat the Passover. 29So Pilate came out to them and asked, 'What charges are you bringing against this man?'

30'If he were not a criminal,' they replied, 'we would not have handed him over to you.'

31Pilate said, 'Take him yourselves and judge him by your own law.'

'But we have no right to execute anyone,' they objected. 32This took place to fulfil what Jesus had said about the kind of death he was going to die.

33Pilate then went back inside the palace, summoned Jesus and asked him, 'Are you the king of the Jews?'

34'Is that your own idea,' Jesus asked, 'or did others talk to you about me?'

35'Am I a Jew?' Pilate replied. 'Your own people and chief priests handed you over to me. What is it you have done?'

36Jesus said, 'My kingdom is not of this world. If it were, my servants would fight to prevent my arrest by the Jewish leaders. But now my kingdom is from another place.'

37'You are a king, then!' said Pilate.

Jesus answered, 'You say that I am a king. In fact, the reason I was born and came into the world is to testify to the truth. Everyone on the side of truth listens to me.'

38'What is truth?' retorted Pilate. With this he went out again to the Jews gathered there and said, 'I find no basis for a charge against him. 39But it is your custom for me to release to you one prisoner at the time of the Passover. Do you want me to release "the king of the Jews"?'

40They shouted back, 'No, not him! Give us Barabbas!' Now Barabbas had taken part in an uprising.

Jesus sentenced to be crucified

19 Then Pilate took Jesus and had him flogged. 2The soldiers twisted together a crown of thorns and put it on his head. They clothed him in a purple robe 3and went up to him again and again, saying, 'Hail, king of the Jews!' And they slapped him in the face.

4Once more Pilate came out and said to the Jews, 'Look, I am bringing him out to you to let you know that I find no basis for a charge against him.' 5When Jesus came out wearing the crown of thorns and the purple robe, Pilate said to them, 'Here is the man!'

6As soon as the chief priests and their officials saw him, they shouted, 'Crucify! Crucify!'

But Pilate answered, 'You take him and crucify him. As for me, I find no basis for a charge against him.'

7The Jews insisted, 'We have a law, and according to that law he must die, because he claimed to be the Son of God.'

8When Pilate heard this, he was even more afraid, 9and he went back inside the

making Connections

Right to execute
John 18:31

The Roman authorities gave the Jews a certain amount of control over their own affairs, but they did not have the power to put anyone to death. The Jews needed the Romans to sentence Jesus to death, and that's why Jesus died by crucifixion, the Roman method of execution, rather than the Jewish method of stoning.

palace. 'Where do you come from?' he asked Jesus, but Jesus gave him no answer. ¹⁰'Do you refuse to speak to me?' Pilate said. 'Don't you realise I have power either to free you or to crucify you?'

¹¹Jesus answered, 'You would have no power over me if it were not given to you from above. Therefore the one who handed me over to you is guilty of a greater sin.'

¹²From then on, Pilate tried to set Jesus free, but the Jews kept shouting, 'If you let this man go, you are no friend of Caesar. Anyone who claims to be a king opposes Caesar.'

¹³When Pilate heard this, he brought Jesus out and sat down on the judge's seat at a place known as the Stone Pavement (which in Aramaic is Gabbatha). ¹⁴It was the day of Preparation of the Passover; it was about noon.

'Here is your king,' Pilate said to the Jews.

¹⁵But they shouted, 'Take him away! Take him away! Crucify him!'

'Shall I crucify your king?' Pilate asked.

'We have no king but Caesar,' the chief priests answered.

¹⁶Finally Pilate handed him over to them to be crucified.

The crucifixion of Jesus

So the soldiers took charge of Jesus. ¹⁷Carrying his own cross, he went out to the place of the Skull (which in Aramaic is called Golgotha). ¹⁸Here they crucified him, and with him two others—one on each side and Jesus in the middle.

¹⁹Pilate had a notice prepared and fastened to the cross. It read: JESUS OF NAZARETH, THE KING OF THE JEWS. ²⁰Many of the Jews read this sign, for the place where Jesus was crucified was near the city, and the sign was written in Aramaic, Latin and Greek. ²¹The chief priests of the Jews protested to Pilate, 'Do not write "The King of the Jews", but that this man claimed to be king of the Jews.'

²²Pilate answered, 'What I have written, I have written.'

²³When the soldiers crucified Jesus, they took his clothes, dividing them into four shares, one for each of them, with the undergarment remaining. This garment was seamless, woven in one piece from top to bottom.

²⁴'Let's not tear it,' they said to one another. 'Let's decide by lot who will get it.'

This happened that the scripture might be fulfilled that said,

'They divided my clothes among them
    and cast lots for my garment.'ᵃ

So this is what the soldiers did.

IN OTHER WORDS

Crucifixion
John 19:18

In the Roman Empire, crucifixion was a way of torturing and executing criminals, especially political rebels. The victim was nailed to a wooden cross and left to die. It was a particularly nasty way to kill someone.

Languages
John 19:20

Pilate wrote this sign – that Jesus was the King of the Jews – in the three most common languages of the time. The Romans, who were in charge, spoke Latin, Greek, or both; the Greek language was still popular from the time the Greeks had ruled the area before the Romans; and Aramaic was the language of the ordinary people. Jesus spoke Aramaic, and probably Greek as well.

ᵃ24 Psalm 22:18

25Near the cross of Jesus stood his mother, his mother's sister, Mary the wife of Clopas, and Mary Magdalene. 26When Jesus saw his mother there, and the disciple whom he loved standing near by, he said to her, 'Woman,^{a} here is your son,' 27and to the disciple, 'Here is your mother.' From that time on, this disciple took her into his home.

The death of Jesus

28Later, knowing that everything had now been finished, and so that Scripture would be fulfilled, Jesus said, 'I am thirsty.' 29A jar of wine vinegar was there, so they soaked a sponge in it, put the sponge on a stalk of the hyssop plant, and lifted it to Jesus' lips. 30When he had received the drink, Jesus said, 'It is finished.' With that, he bowed his head and gave up his spirit.

31Now it was the day of Preparation, and the next day was to be a special Sabbath. Because the Jewish leaders did not want the bodies left on the crosses during the Sabbath, they asked Pilate to have the legs broken and the bodies taken down. 32The soldiers therefore came and broke the legs of the first man who had been crucified with Jesus, and then those of the other. 33But when they came to Jesus and found that he was already dead, they did not break his legs. 34Instead, one of the soldiers pierced Jesus' side with a spear, bringing a sudden flow of blood and water. 35The man who saw it has given testimony, and his testimony is true. He knows that he tells the truth, and he testifies so that you also may believe. 36These things happened so that the scripture would be fulfilled: 'Not one of his bones will be broken,'^{b} 37and, as another scripture says, 'They will look on the one they have pierced.'^{c}

The burial of Jesus

38Later, Joseph of Arimathea asked Pilate for the body of Jesus. Now Joseph was a disciple of Jesus, but secretly because he feared the Jewish leaders. With Pilate's permission, he came and took the body away. 39He was accompanied by Nicodemus, the man who earlier had visited Jesus at night. Nicodemus brought a mixture of myrrh and aloes, about thirty-five kilograms. 40Taking Jesus' body, the two of them wrapped it, with the spices, in strips of linen. This was in accordance with Jewish burial customs. 41At the place where Jesus was crucified, there was a garden, and in the garden a new tomb, in which no-one had ever been laid. 42Because it was the Jewish day of Preparation and since the tomb was near by, they laid Jesus there.

> **People and Places**
>
> **Mary Magdalene**
> John 20:1
> Mary Magdalene was a woman who helped to support Jesus and his disciples as they travelled around preaching and healing (Luke 8:2). She became one of Jesus' followers after he had cast seven demons out of her. She was the first person to see Jesus after he rose from the dead and she was given the task of telling the other disciples that she had seen him alive.

The empty tomb

20 Early on the first day of the week, while it was still dark, Mary Magdalene went to the tomb and saw that the stone had been removed from the entrance. 2So she came running to Simon Peter and the other disciple, the one Jesus loved, and said, 'They have taken the Lord out of the tomb, and we don't know where they have put him!'

3So Peter and the other disciple started for the tomb. 4Both were running, but the other disciple outran Peter and reached the tomb first. 5He bent over and looked in at the strips of linen lying there but did not go in. 6Then Simon Peter came along behind him and went straight into the tomb. He

---

^{a} 26 The Greek for *Woman* does not denote any disrespect. ^{b} 36 Exodus 12:46; Num. 9:12; Psalm 34:20
^{c} 37 Zech. 12:10

saw the strips of linen lying there, 7as well as the cloth that had been wrapped round Jesus' head. The cloth was still lying in its place, separate from the linen. 8Finally the other disciple, who had reached the tomb first, also went inside. He saw and believed. 9(They still did not understand from Scripture that Jesus had to rise from the dead.) 10Then the disciples went back to where they were staying.

Jesus appears to Mary Magdalene

11Now Mary stood outside the tomb crying. As she wept, she bent over to look into the tomb 12and saw two angels in white, seated where Jesus' body had been, one at the head and the other at the foot.

13They asked her, 'Woman,[a] why are you crying?'

'They have taken my Lord away,' she said, 'and I don't know where they have put him.' 14At this, she turned round and saw Jesus standing there, but she did not realise that it was Jesus.

15He asked her, 'Woman, why are you crying? Who is it you are looking for?'

Thinking he was the gardener, she said, 'Sir, if you have carried him away, tell me where you have put him, and I will get him.'

16Jesus said to her, 'Mary.'

She turned towards him and cried out in Aramaic, 'Rabboni!' (which means 'Teacher').

17Jesus said, 'Do not hold on to me, for I have not yet ascended to the Father. Go instead to my brothers and tell them, "I am ascending to my Father and your Father, to my God and your God."'

18Mary Magdalene went to the disciples with the news: 'I have seen the Lord!' And she told them that he had said these things to her.

Jesus appears to his disciples

19On the evening of that first day of the week, when the disciples were together, with the doors locked for fear of the Jewish leaders, Jesus came and stood among them and said, 'Peace be with you!' 20After he said this, he showed them his hands and side. The disciples were overjoyed when they saw the Lord.

21Again Jesus said, 'Peace be with you! As the Father has sent me, I am sending you.' 22And with that he breathed on them and said, 'Receive the Holy Spirit. 23If you forgive the sins of anyone, their sins are forgiven; if you do not forgive them, they are not forgiven.'

Jesus appears to Thomas

24Now Thomas (also known as Didymus[b]), one of the Twelve, was not with the disciples when Jesus came. 25So the other disciples told him, 'We have seen the Lord!'

But he said to them, 'Unless I see the nail marks in his hands and put my finger where the nails were, and put my hand into his side, I will not believe.'

26A week later his disciples were in the house again, and Thomas was with them. Though the doors were locked, Jesus came and stood among them and said, 'Peace be with you!' 27Then he said to Thomas, 'Put your finger here; see my hands. Reach out your hand and put it into my side. Stop doubting and believe.'

28Thomas said to him, 'My Lord and my God!'

29Then Jesus told him, 'Because you have seen me, you have believed; blessed are those who have not seen and yet have believed.'

The purpose of John's gospel

30Jesus performed many other signs in the presence of his disciples, which are not recorded in this book. 31But these are written that you may believe[c] that Jesus is the Messiah, the Son of God, and that by believing you may have life in his name.

Jesus and the miraculous catch of fish

21 Afterwards Jesus appeared again to his disciples, by the Sea of Gallilee.[d] It happened this way: 2Simon Peter, Thomas (also known as Didymus[e]), Nathanael from Cana in Galilee, the sons of Zebedee, and two other disciples were together. 3'I'm going out to fish,' Simon Peter told them,

---

[a] 13 The Greek for Woman does not denote any disrespect; also in verse 15. [b] 24 Thomas (Aramaic) and Didymus (Greek) both mean twin. [c] 31 Or may continue to believe [d] 1 Greek Tiberias [e] 2 Thomas (Aramaic) and Didymus (Greek) both mean twin.

and they said, 'We'll go with you.' So they went out and got into the boat, but that night they caught nothing.

⁴Early in the morning, Jesus stood on the shore, but the disciples did not realise that it was Jesus.

⁵He called out to them, 'Friends, haven't you any fish?'

'No,' they answered.

⁶He said, 'Throw your net on the right side of the boat and you will find some.' When they did, they were unable to haul the net in because of the large number of fish.

⁷Then the disciple whom Jesus loved said to Peter, 'It is the Lord!' As soon as Simon Peter heard him say, 'It is the Lord,' he wrapped his outer garment round him (for he had taken it off) and jumped into the water. ⁸The other disciples followed in the boat, towing the net full of fish, for they were not far from shore, about a hundred metres. ⁹When they landed, they saw a fire of burning coals there with fish on it, and some bread.

¹⁰Jesus said to them, 'Bring some of the fish you have just caught.'

¹¹Simon Peter climbed aboard and dragged the net ashore. It was full of large fish, 153, but even with so many the net was not torn. ¹²Jesus said to them, 'Come and have breakfast.' None of the disciples dared ask him, 'Who are you?' They knew it was the Lord. ¹³Jesus came, took the bread and gave it to them, and did the same with the fish. ¹⁴This was now the third time Jesus appeared to his disciples after he was raised from the dead.

Jesus reinstates Peter

¹⁵When they had finished eating, Jesus said to Simon Peter, 'Simon son of John, do you love me more than these?'

'Yes, Lord,' he said, 'you know that I love you.'

Jesus said, 'Feed my lambs.'

¹⁶Again Jesus said, 'Simon son of John, do you love me?'

He answered, 'Yes, Lord, you know that I love you.'

Jesus said, 'Take care of my sheep.'

¹⁷The third time he said to him, 'Simon son of John, do you love me?'

Peter
John 21:15
Originally called Simon, Jesus renamed him Peter, 'the Rock', the first time he met him. Peter was a fisherman who became one of Jesus' best-known disciples. Peter denied knowing Jesus three times while Jesus was on trial (Luke 22:54–62), but here he is given an opportunity to say three times that he does love Jesus. Jesus gives Peter the task of starting the church and, on the day of Pentecost, Peter preaches and three thousand people become Christians (Acts 2:14–41).

Peter was hurt because Jesus asked him the third time, 'Do you love me?' He said, 'Lord, you know all things; you know that I love you.'

Jesus said, 'Feed my sheep. ¹⁸Very truly I tell you, when you were younger you dressed yourself and went where you wanted; but when you are old you will stretch out your hands, and someone else will dress you and lead you where you do not want to go.' ¹⁹Jesus said this to indicate the kind of death by which Peter would glorify God. Then he said to him, 'Follow me!'

²⁰Peter turned and saw that the disciple whom Jesus loved was following them. (This was the one who had leaned back against Jesus at the supper and had said, 'Lord, who is going to betray you?') ²¹When Peter saw him, he asked, 'Lord, what about him?'

²²Jesus answered, 'If I want him to remain alive until I return, what is that to you? You must follow me.' ²³Because of this, the rumour spread among the believers that this disciple would not die. But Jesus did not say that he would not die; he only said, 'If I want him to remain alive until I return, what is that to you?'

John 21:24

24This is the disciple who testifies to these things and who wrote them down. We know that his testimony is true.

25Jesus did many other things as well. If every one of them were written down, I suppose that even the whole world would not have room for the books that would be written.

Acts

INTRODUCTION

Acts

Author: Luke, a doctor who also wrote the Gospel of Luke.

Who to: Theophilus, whose name means 'lover of God'.

When: The events in Acts happened during the thirty years or so after Jesus ascended.

Where: Starting in Jerusalem, Acts then follows Paul's missionary journeys to the countries we now call Syria, Cyprus, Turkey, Greece, Malta and Italy.

Did you know? Luke was very well connected. He mentions ninety-five people from thirty-two countries, fifty-four cities and nine Mediterranean islands.

Main theme: This is the sequel to Luke's Gospel and tells the story of how the church began. The two main characters in it are Peter, one of Jesus' disciples, and Paul, who started out persecuting Christians but then had a dramatic conversion and followed Jesus. The Holy Spirit has a major part to play in directing the growth of the early church.

Jesus taken up into heaven

1 In my former book, Theophilus, I wrote about all that Jesus began to do and to teach ²until the day he was taken up to heaven, after giving instructions through the Holy Spirit to the apostles he had chosen. ³After his suffering, he presented himself to them and gave many convincing proofs that he was alive. He appeared to them over a period of forty days and spoke about the kingdom of God. ⁴On one occasion, while he was eating with them, he gave them this command: 'Do not leave Jerusalem, but wait for the gift my Father promised, which you have heard me speak about. ⁵For John baptised with*a* water, but in a few days you will be baptised with*b* the Holy Spirit.'

a 5 Or *in* *b* 5 Or *in*

6So when they met together, they asked him, 'Lord, are you at this time going to restore the kingdom to Israel?'

7He said to them: 'It is not for you to know the times or dates the Father has set by his own authority. 8But you will receive power when the Holy Spirit comes on you; and you will be my witnesses in Jerusalem, and in all Judea and Samaria, and to the ends of the earth.'

9After he said this, he was taken up before their very eyes, and a cloud hid him from their sight.

10They were looking intently up into the sky as he was going, when suddenly two men dressed in white stood beside them. 11'Men of Galilee,' they said, 'why do you stand here looking into the sky? This same Jesus, who has been taken from you into heaven, will come back in the same way you have seen him go into heaven.'

Matthias chosen to replace Judas

12Then the apostles returned to Jerusalem from the hill called the Mount of Olives, a Sabbath day's walk[a] from the city. 13When they arrived, they went upstairs to the room where they were staying. Those present were Peter, John, James and Andrew; Philip and Thomas, Bartholomew and Matthew; James son of Alphaeus and Simon the Zealot, and Judas son of James. 14They all joined together constantly in prayer, along with the women and Mary the mother of Jesus, and with his brothers.

15In those days Peter stood up among the believers (a group numbering about a hundred and twenty) 16and said, 'Brothers and sisters, the Scripture had to be fulfilled in which the Holy Spirit spoke long ago through David concerning Judas, who served as guide for those who arrested Jesus. 17He was one of our number and shared in our ministry.'

18(With the reward he got for his wickedness, Judas bought a field; there he fell headlong, his body burst open and all his intestines spilled out. 19Everyone in Jerusalem heard about this, so they called that field in their language Akeldama, that is, Field of Blood.)

20'For,' said Peter, 'it is written in the Book of Psalms:

' "May his place be deserted;
  let there be no-one to dwell in it,"[b]

and,

' "May another take his place of
    leadership."'[c]

21Therefore it is necessary to choose one of the men who have been with us the whole time the Lord Jesus went in and out among us, 22beginning from John's baptism to the time when Jesus was taken up from us. For one of these must become a witness with us of his resurrection.'

23So they proposed the names of two men: Joseph called Barsabbas (also known as Justus) and Matthias. 24Then they prayed, 'Lord, you know everyone's heart. Show us which of these two you have chosen 25to take over this apostolic ministry, which Judas left to go where he belongs.' 26Then they cast lots, and the lot fell to Matthias; so he was added to the eleven apostles.

The Holy Spirit comes at Pentecost

2 When the day of Pentecost came, they were all together in one place. 2Suddenly a sound like the blowing of a violent wind came from heaven and filled the whole house where they were sitting. 3They saw what seemed to be tongues of fire that

---

IN OTHER WORDS

Pentecost
Acts 2:1

Pentecost was the equivalent of harvest festival for the Israelites. It is also known as the Festival of Weeks and was first celebrated by the Israelites after they had escaped from Egypt (Leviticus 23:15). It is often called 'the birthday of the church', because God gave the Holy Spirit to the first disciples at this Pentecost celebration.

---

[a] 12 That is, about 5/8 mile or about 1 kilometre   [b] 20 Psalm 69:25   [c] 20 Psalm 109:8

People and Places

Holy Spirit
Acts 2:4

Jesus promises that, when he leaves his disciples, they will receive the Holy Spirit in his place. The Holy Spirit is the third person of the Trinity. The Spirit is seen as having a creative and sustaining role, and was present at the creation of the world, 'hovering over the waters' (Genesis 1:2). The Holy Spirit inspired Scripture (2 Timothy 3:16) and is here today as God's presence with us and in us.

---

separated and came to rest on each of them. ⁴All of them were filled with the Holy Spirit and began to speak in other tongues*ᵃ* as the Spirit enabled them.

⁵Now there were staying in Jerusalem God-fearing Jews from every nation under heaven. ⁶When they heard this sound, a crowd came together in bewilderment, because each one heard their own language being spoken. ⁷Utterly amazed, they asked: 'Aren't all these who are speaking Galileans? ⁸Then how is it that each of us hears them in our native language? ⁹Parthians, Medes and Elamites; residents of Mesopotamia, Judea and Cappadocia, Pontus and Asia,*ᵇ* ¹⁰Phrygia and Pamphylia, Egypt and the parts of Libya near Cyrene; visitors from Rome ¹¹(both Jews and converts to Judaism); Cretans and Arabs—we hear them declaring the wonders of God in our own tongues!' ¹²Amazed and perplexed, they asked one another, 'What does this mean?'

¹³Some, however, made fun of them and said, 'They have had too much wine.'

Peter addresses the crowd

¹⁴Then Peter stood up with the Eleven, raised his voice and addressed the crowd: 'Fellow Jews and all of you who live in Jerusalem, let me explain this to you; listen carefully to what I say. ¹⁵These people are not drunk, as you suppose. It's only nine in the morning! ¹⁶No, this is what was spoken by the prophet Joel:

¹⁷'"In the last days, God says,
  I will pour out my Spirit on all people.
Your sons and daughters will prophesy,
  your young men will see visions,
  your old men will dream dreams.
¹⁸Even on my servants, both men and women,
  I will pour out my Spirit in those days,
  and they will prophesy.
¹⁹I will show wonders in the heaven above
  and signs on the earth below,
  blood and fire and billows of smoke.
²⁰The sun will be turned to darkness
  and the moon to blood
  before the coming of the great and glorious day of the Lord.
²¹And everyone who calls
  on the name of the Lord will be saved."*ᶜ*

²²'People of Israel, listen to this: Jesus of Nazareth was a man accredited by God to you by miracles, wonders and signs, which God did among you through him, as you yourselves know. ²³This man was handed over to you by God's deliberate plan and foreknowledge; and you, with the help of wicked men,*ᵈ* put him to death by nailing him to the cross. ²⁴But God raised him from the dead, freeing him from the agony of death, because it was impossible for death to keep its hold on him. ²⁵David said about him:

'"I saw the Lord always before me.
  Because he is at my right hand,
  I will not be shaken.
²⁶Therefore my heart is glad and my tongue rejoices;
  my body also will rest in hope,
²⁷because you will not abandon me to the realm of the dead,
  you will not let your holy one see decay.
²⁸You have made known to me the paths of life;
  you will fill me with joy in your presence."*ᵉ*

---

*ᵃ*4 Or *languages*; also in verse 11   *ᵇ*9 That is, the Roman province by that name   *ᶜ*21 Joel 2:28-32   *ᵈ*23 Or *of those not having the law* (that is, Gentiles)   *ᵉ*28 Psalm 16:8-11 (see Septuagint)

29'Brothers and sisters, we all know that the patriarch David died and was buried, and his tomb is here to this day. 30But he was a prophet and knew that God had promised him on oath that he would place one of his descendants on his throne. 31Seeing what was to come, he spoke of the resurrection of the Messiah, that he was not abandoned to the realm of the dead, nor did his body see decay. 32God has raised this Jesus to life, and we are all witnesses of the fact. 33Exalted to the right hand of God, he has received from the Father the promised Holy Spirit and has poured out what you now see and hear. 34For David did not ascend to heaven, and yet he said,

' "The Lord said to my Lord:
'Sit at my right hand
35until I make your enemies
a footstool for your feet.' "*a*

36'Therefore let all Israel be assured of this: God has made this Jesus, whom you crucified, both Lord and Messiah.'

37When the people heard this, they were cut to the heart and said to Peter and the other apostles, 'Brothers, what shall we do?'

38Peter replied, 'Repent and be baptised, every one of you, in the name of Jesus Christ for the forgiveness of your sins. And you will receive the gift of the Holy Spirit. 39The promise is for you and your children and for all who are far off—for all whom the Lord our God will call.'

40With many other words he warned them; and he pleaded with them, 'Save yourselves from this corrupt generation.' 41Those who accepted his message were baptised, and about three thousand were added to their number that day.

The fellowship of the believers

42They devoted themselves to the apostles' teaching and to fellowship, to the breaking of bread and to prayer. 43Everyone was filled with awe at the many wonders and signs performed by the apostles. 44All the believers were together and had everything in common. 45They sold property and possessions to give to anyone who had need. 46Every day they continued to meet together in the temple courts. They broke bread in their homes and ate together with glad and sincere hearts, 47praising God and enjoying the favour of all the people. And the Lord added to their number daily those who were being saved.

Peter heals a lame beggar

3 One day Peter and John were going up to the temple at the time of prayer—at three in the afternoon. 2Now a man who was lame from birth was being carried to the temple gate called Beautiful, where he was put every day to beg from those going into the temple courts. 3When he saw Peter and John about to enter, he asked them for money. 4Peter looked straight at him, as did John. Then Peter said, 'Look at us!' 5So the man gave them his attention, expecting to get something from them.

6Then Peter said, 'Silver or gold I do not have, but what I do have I give you. In the name of Jesus Christ of Nazareth, walk.' 7Taking him by the right hand, he helped him up, and instantly the man's feet and ankles became strong. 8He jumped to his feet and began to walk. Then he went with them into the temple courts, walking and jumping, and praising God. 9When all the people saw him walking and praising God, 10they recognised him as the same man who used to sit begging at the temple gate called Beautiful, and they were filled with wonder and amazement at what had happened to him.

Peter speaks to the onlookers

11While the man held on to Peter and John, all the people were astonished and came running to them in the place called Solomon's Colonnade. 12When Peter saw this, he said to them: 'People of Israel, why does this surprise you? Why do you stare at us as if by our own power or godliness we had made this man walk? 13The God of Abraham, Isaac and Jacob, the God of our fathers, has glorified his servant Jesus. You handed him over to be killed, and you disowned him before Pilate, though he had decided to let him go. 14You disowned the Holy and Righteous One and asked that a

---

a 35 Psalm 110:1

murderer be released to you. 15You killed the author of life, but God raised him from the dead. We are witnesses of this. 16By faith in the name of Jesus, this man whom you see and know was made strong. It is Jesus' name and the faith that comes through him that has completely healed him, as you can all see.

17'Now, brothers and sisters, I know that you acted in ignorance, as did your leaders. 18But this is how God fulfilled what he had foretold through all the prophets, saying that his Messiah would suffer. 19Repent, then, and turn to God, so that your sins may be wiped out, that times of refreshing may come from the Lord, 20and that he may send the Messiah, who has been appointed for you—even Jesus. 21Heaven must receive him until the time comes for God to restore everything, as he promised long ago through his holy prophets. 22For Moses said, "The Lord your God will raise up for you a prophet like me from among your own people; you must listen to everything he tells you. 23Anyone who does not listen to him will be completely cut off from their people."[a]

24'Indeed, beginning with Samuel, all the prophets who have spoken have foretold these days. 25And you are heirs of the prophets and of the covenant God made with your fathers. He said to Abraham, "Through your offspring all peoples on earth will be blessed."[b] 26When God raised up his servant, he sent him first to you to bless you by turning each of you from your wicked ways.'

Peter and John before the Sanhedrin

4 The priests and the captain of the temple guard and the Sadducees came up to Peter and John while they were speaking to the people. 2They were greatly disturbed because the apostles were teaching the people, proclaiming in Jesus the resurrection of the dead. 3They seized Peter and John, and because it was evening, they put them in jail until the next day. 4But many who heard the message believed; so the number of men who believed grew to about five thousand.

IN OTHER WORDS

Salvation
Acts 4:12
In the New Testament one of the major images of becoming a Christian is that of being 'saved'. Salvation is the process of being saved from sin and its punishment in order to live for God. Salvation is possible because of the life, death and resurrection of Jesus.

5The next day the rulers, the elders and the teachers of the law met in Jerusalem. 6Annas the high priest was there, and so were Caiaphas, John, Alexander and others of the high priest's family. 7They had Peter and John brought before them and began to question them: 'By what power or what name did you do this?'

8Then Peter, filled with the Holy Spirit, said to them: 'Rulers and elders of the people! 9If we are being called to account today for an act of kindness shown to a man who was lame and are being asked how he was healed, 10then know this, you and all the people of Israel: it is by the name of Jesus Christ of Nazareth, whom you crucified but whom God raised from the dead, that this man stands before you healed. 11Jesus is

'"the stone you builders rejected,
which has become the cornerstone."[c]

12Salvation is found in no-one else, for there is no other name given under heaven by which we must be saved.'

13When they saw the courage of Peter and John and realised that they were unschooled, ordinary men, they were astonished and they took note that these men had been with Jesus. 14But since they could see the man who had been healed standing there with them, there was nothing they could say. 15So they ordered them to withdraw from the Sanhedrin and then conferred together. 16'What are we going to

---

[a] 23 Deut. 18:15,18,19 [b] 25 Gen. 22:18; 26:4 [c] 11 Psalm 118:22

do with these men?' they asked. 'Everyone living in Jerusalem knows they have performed a notable sign, and we cannot deny it. 17But to stop this thing from spreading any further among the people, we must warn them to speak no longer to anyone in this name.'

18Then they called them in again and commanded them not to speak or teach at all in the name of Jesus. 19But Peter and John replied, 'Which is right in God's eyes: to listen to you, or to him? You be the judges! 20As for us, we cannot help speaking about what we have seen and heard.'

21After further threats they let them go. They could not decide how to punish them, because all the people were praising God for what had happened. 22For the man who was miraculously healed was over forty years old.

The believers' prayer

23On their release, Peter and John went back to their own people and reported all that the chief priests and the elders had said to them. 24When they heard this, they raised their voices together in prayer to God. 'Sovereign Lord,' they said, 'you made the heaven and the earth and the sea, and everything in them. 25You spoke by the Holy Spirit through the mouth of your servant, our father David:

' "Why do the nations rage
    and the peoples plot in vain?
26The kings of the earth rise up
    and the rulers band together
against the Lord
    and against his anointed one."$^{a\,"\,b}$

27Indeed Herod and Pontius Pilate met together with the Gentiles and the people of Israel in this city to conspire against your holy servant Jesus, whom you anointed. 28They did what your power and will had decided beforehand should happen. 29Now, Lord, consider their threats and enable your servants to speak your word with great boldness. 30Stretch out your hand to heal and perform signs and wonders through the name of your holy servant Jesus.'

31After they prayed, the place where they were meeting was shaken. And they were all filled with the Holy Spirit and spoke the word of God boldly.

The believers share their possessions

32All the believers were one in heart and mind. No-one claimed that any of their possessions was their own, but they shared everything they had. 33With great power the apostles continued to testify to the resurrection of the Lord Jesus. And God's grace was so powerfully at work in them all 34that there was no needy person among them. For from time to time those who owned land or houses sold them, brought the money from the sales 35and put it at the apostles' feet, and it was distributed to anyone who had need.

36Joseph, a Levite from Cyprus, whom the apostles called Barnabas (which means 'son of encouragement'), 37sold a field he owned and brought the money and put it at the apostles' feet.

Ananias and Sapphira

5 Now a man named Ananias, together with his wife Sapphira, also sold a piece of property. 2With his wife's full knowledge he kept back part of the money for himself, but brought the rest and put it at the apostles' feet.

3Then Peter said, 'Ananias, how is it that Satan has so filled your heart that you have lied to the Holy Spirit and have kept for yourself some of the money you received for the land? 4Didn't it belong to you before it was sold? And after it was sold, wasn't the money at your disposal? What made you think of doing such a thing? You have not lied just to human beings but to God.'

5When Ananias heard this, he fell down and died. And great fear seized all who heard what had happened. 6Then some young men came forward, wrapped up his body, and carried him out and buried him.

7About three hours later his wife came in, not knowing what had happened. 8Peter asked her, 'Tell me, is this the price you and Ananias got for the land?'

'Yes,' she said, 'that is the price.'

---

^{a} 26 That is, Messiah or Christ ^{b} 26 Psalm 2:1,2

9 Peter said to her, 'How could you conspire to test the Spirit of the Lord? Listen! The feet of those who buried your husband are at the door, and they will carry you out also.'

10 At that moment she fell down at his feet and died. Then the young men came in and, finding her dead, carried her out and buried her beside her husband. 11 Great fear seized the whole church and all who heard about these events.

The apostles heal many

12 The apostles performed many signs and wonders among the people. And all the believers used to meet together in Solomon's Colonnade. 13 No-one else dared join them, even though they were highly regarded by the people. 14 Nevertheless, more and more men and women believed in the Lord and were added to their number. 15 As a result, people brought those who were ill into the streets and laid them on beds and mats so that at least Peter's shadow might fall on some of them as he passed by. 16 Crowds gathered also from the towns around Jerusalem, bringing those who were ill and those tormented by evil*a* spirits, and all of them were healed.

The apostles persecuted

17 Then the high priest and all his associates, who were members of the party of the Sadducees, were filled with jealousy. 18 They arrested the apostles and put them in the public jail. 19 But during the night an angel of the Lord opened the doors of the jail and brought them out. 20 'Go, stand in the temple courts,' he said, 'and tell the people all about this new life.'

21 At daybreak they entered the temple courts, as they had been told, and began to teach the people.

When the high priest and his associates arrived, they called together the Sanhedrin—the full assembly of the elders of Israel—and sent to the jail for the apostles. 22 But on arriving at the jail, the officers did not find them there. So they went back and reported, 23 'We found the jail securely locked, with the guards standing at the doors; but when we opened them, we found no-one inside.' 24 On hearing this report, the captain of the temple guard and the chief priests were puzzled, wondering what this might lead to.

25 Then someone came and said, 'Look! The men you put in jail are standing in the temple courts teaching the people.' 26 At that, the captain went with his officers and brought the apostles. They did not use force, because they feared that the people would stone them.

27 The apostles were brought in and made to appear before the Sanhedrin to be questioned by the high priest. 28 'We gave you strict orders not to teach in this name,' he said. 'Yet you have filled Jerusalem with your teaching and are determined to make us guilty of this man's blood.'

29 Peter and the other apostles replied: 'We must obey God rather than human beings! 30 The God of our ancestors raised Jesus from the dead—whom you killed by hanging him on a cross. 31 God exalted him to his own right hand as Prince and Saviour that he might bring Israel to repentance and forgive their sins. 32 We are witnesses of these things, and so is the Holy Spirit, whom God has given to those who obey him.'

33 When they heard this, they were furious and wanted to put them to death. 34 But a Pharisee named Gamaliel, a teacher of the law, who was honoured by all the people, stood up in the Sanhedrin and ordered that the men be put outside for a little while. 35 Then he addressed the Sanhedrin: 'Men of Israel, consider carefully what you intend to do to these men. 36 Some time ago Theudas appeared, claiming to be somebody, and about four hundred men rallied to him. He was killed, all his followers were dispersed, and it all came to nothing. 37 After him, Judas the Galilean appeared in the days of the census and led a band of people in revolt. He too was killed, and all his followers were scattered. 38 Therefore, in the present case I advise you: leave these men alone! Let them go! For if their purpose or activity is of human origin, it will fail. 39 But if it is from God, you will not be able

---

a 16 Greek *unclean*

to stop these men; you will only find yourselves fighting against God.'

⁴⁰His speech persuaded them. They called the apostles in and had them flogged. Then they ordered them not to speak in the name of Jesus, and let them go.

⁴¹The apostles left the Sanhedrin, rejoicing because they had been counted worthy of suffering disgrace for the Name. ⁴²Day after day, in the temple courts and from house to house, they never stopped teaching and proclaiming the good news that Jesus is the Messiah.

The choosing of the seven

6 In those days when the number of disciples was increasing, the Hellenistic Jews[a] among them complained against the Hebraic Jews because their widows were being overlooked in the daily distribution of food. ²So the Twelve gathered all the disciples together and said, 'It would not be right for us to neglect the ministry of the word of God in order to wait on tables. ³Brothers and sisters, choose seven men from among you who are known to be full of the Spirit and wisdom. We will turn this responsibility over to them ⁴and will give our attention to prayer and the ministry of the word.'

⁵This proposal pleased the whole group. They chose Stephen, a man full of faith and of the Holy Spirit; also Philip, Procorus, Nicanor, Timon, Parmenas, and Nicolas from Antioch, a convert to Judaism. ⁶They presented them to the apostles, who prayed and laid their hands on them.

⁷So the word of God spread. The number of disciples in Jerusalem increased rapidly, and a large number of priests became obedient to the faith.

Stephen seized

⁸Now Stephen, a man full of God's grace and power, performed great wonders and signs among the people. ⁹Opposition arose, however, from members of the Synagogue of the Freedmen (as it was called)—Jews of Cyrene and Alexandria as well as the provinces of Cilicia and Asia—who began to argue with Stephen. ¹⁰But they could not

> **People and Places**
>
> **Sanhedrin**
> Acts 6:12
> The Sanhedrin was the highest ruling body among the Jewish people at the time of Jesus, and was led by the high priest. It was given limited power by the Romans to make rulings about some religious, civil and criminal matters.

stand up against the wisdom the Spirit gave him as he spoke.

¹¹Then they secretly persuaded some men to say, 'We have heard Stephen speak blasphemous words against Moses and against God.'

¹²So they stirred up the people and the elders and the teachers of the law. They seized Stephen and brought him before the Sanhedrin. ¹³They produced false witnesses, who testified, 'This fellow never stops speaking against this holy place and against the law. ¹⁴For we have heard him say that this Jesus of Nazareth will destroy this place and change the customs Moses handed down to us.'

¹⁵All who were sitting in the Sanhedrin looked intently at Stephen, and they saw that his face was like the face of an angel.

Stephen's speech to the Sanhedrin

7 Then the high priest asked Stephen, 'Are these charges true?'

²To this he replied: 'Brothers and fathers, listen to me! The God of glory appeared to our father Abraham while he was still in Mesopotamia, before he lived in Harran. ³"Leave your country and your people," God said, "and go to the land I will show you."[b]

⁴'So he left the land of the Chaldeans and settled in Harran. After the death of his father, God sent him to this land where you are now living. ⁵He gave him no inheritance

---

[a] 1 That is, Jews who had adopted the Greek language and culture [b] 3 Gen. 12:1

here, not even enough ground to set his foot on. But God promised him that he and his descendants after him would possess the land, even though at that time Abraham had no child. 6God spoke to him in this way: "For four hundred years your descendants will be strangers in a country not their own, and they will be enslaved and ill-treated. 7But I will punish the nation they serve as slaves," God said, "and afterwards they will come out of that country and worship me in this place."[a] 8Then he gave Abraham the covenant of circumcision. And Abraham became the father of Isaac and circumcised him eight days after his birth. Later Isaac became the father of Jacob, and Jacob became the father of the twelve patriarchs.

9'Because the patriarchs were jealous of Joseph, they sold him as a slave into Egypt. But God was with him 10and rescued him from all his troubles. He gave Joseph wisdom and enabled him to gain the goodwill of Pharaoh king of Egypt. So Pharaoh made him ruler over Egypt and all his palace.

11'Then a famine struck all Egypt and Canaan, bringing great suffering, and our people could not find food. 12When Jacob heard that there was grain in Egypt, he sent our ancestors on their first visit. 13On their second visit, Joseph told his brothers who he was, and Pharaoh learned about Joseph's family. 14After this, Joseph sent for his father Jacob and his whole family, seventy-five in all. 15Then Jacob went down to Egypt, where he and our ancestors died. 16Their bodies were brought back to Shechem and placed in the tomb that Abraham had bought from the sons of Hamor at Shechem for a certain sum of money.

17'As the time drew near for God to fulfil his promise to Abraham, the number of our people in Egypt had greatly increased. 18Then "a new king, to whom Joseph meant nothing, came to power in Egypt".[b] 19He dealt treacherously with our people and oppressed our ancestors by forcing them to throw out their newborn babies so that they would die.

20'At that time Moses was born, and he was no ordinary child.[c] For three months he was cared for in his parents' home. 21When he was placed outside, Pharaoh's daughter took him and brought him up as her own son. 22Moses was educated in all the wisdom of the Egyptians and was powerful in speech and action.

23'When Moses was forty years old, he decided to visit his own people, the Israelites. 24He saw one of them being ill-treated by an Egyptian, so he went to his defence and avenged him by killing the Egyptian. 25Moses thought that his own people would realise that God was using him to rescue them, but they did not. 26The next day Moses came upon two Israelites who were fighting. He tried to reconcile them by saying, "Men, you are brothers; why do you want to hurt each other?"

27'But the man who was ill-treating the other pushed Moses aside and said, "Who made you ruler and judge over us? 28Are you thinking of killing me as you killed the Egyptian yesterday?"[d] 29When Moses heard this, he fled to Midian, where he settled as a foreigner and had two sons.

30'After forty years had passed, an angel appeared to Moses in the flames of a burning bush in the desert near Mount Sinai. 31When he saw this, he was amazed at the sight. As he went over to get a closer look, he heard the Lord say: 32"I am the God of your fathers, the God of Abraham, Isaac and Jacob."[e] Moses trembled with fear and did not dare to look.

33'Then the Lord said to him, "Take off your sandals, for the place where you are standing is holy ground. 34I have indeed seen the oppression of my people in Egypt. I have heard their groaning and have come down to set them free. Now come, I will send you back to Egypt."[f]

35'This is the same Moses they had rejected with the words, "Who made you ruler and judge?" He was sent to be their ruler and deliverer by God himself, through the angel who appeared to him in the bush. 36He led them out of Egypt and performed

---

[a]7 Gen. 15:13,14 [b]18 Exodus 1:8 [c]20 Or *was fair in the sight of God* [d]28 Exodus 2:14 [e]32 Exodus 3:6 [f]34 Exodus 3:5,7,8,10

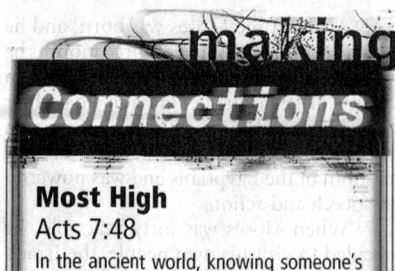

Most High
Acts 7:48

In the ancient world, knowing someone's name was a special privilege that let you in on who they really were. God showed his love for his people by telling them several of his names, each of which revealed something about his character. 'Most High' is a name for God which appears often in the Old Testament (Psalm 92:1). It emphasises the might and power of God.

wonders and signs in Egypt, at the Red Sea and for forty years in the wilderness.

37'This is the Moses who told the Israelites, "God will send you a prophet like me from your own people."*a* 38He was in the assembly in the wilderness, with the angel who spoke to him on Mount Sinai, and with our ancestors; and he received living words to pass on to us.

39'But our ancestors refused to obey him. Instead, they rejected him and in their hearts turned back to Egypt. 40They told Aaron, "Make us gods who will go before us. As for this fellow Moses who led us out of Egypt—we don't know what has happened to him!"*b* 41That was the time they made an idol in the form of a calf. They brought sacrifices to it and revelled in what their own hands had made. 42But God turned away from them and gave them over to the worship of the sun, moon and stars. This agrees with what is written in the book of the prophets:

'"Did you bring me sacrifices and offerings
for forty years in the wilderness, house of Israel?
43You have taken up the tabernacle of Molek
and the star of your god Rephan,
the idols you made to worship.
Therefore I will send you into exile"*c*
beyond Babylon.

44'Our ancestors had the tabernacle of the covenant law with them in the wilderness. It had been made as God directed Moses, according to the pattern he had seen. 45Having received the tabernacle, our ancestors under Joshua brought it with them when they took the land from the nations God drove out before them. It remained in the land until the time of David, 46who enjoyed God's favour and asked that he might provide a dwelling-place for the God of Jacob.*d* 47But it was Solomon who built a house for him.

48'However, the Most High does not live in houses made by human hands. As the prophet says:

49' "Heaven is my throne,
and the earth is my footstool.
What kind of house will you build for me?
says the Lord.
Or where will my resting place be?
50Has not my hand made all these things?"*e*

51'You stiff-necked people! Your hearts and ears are still uncircumcised. You are just like your ancestors: you always resist the Holy Spirit! 52Was there ever a prophet your ancestors did not persecute? They even killed those who predicted the coming of the Righteous One. And now you have betrayed and murdered him— 53you who have received the law that was given through angels but have not obeyed it.'

The stoning of Stephen

54When the members of the Sanhedrin heard this, they were furious and gnashed their teeth at him. 55But Stephen, full of the Holy Spirit, looked up to heaven and saw the glory of God, and Jesus standing at the right hand of God. 56'Look,' he said, 'I see

---

a 37 Deut. 18:15   *b* 40 Exodus 32:1   *c* 43 Amos 5:25-27 (see Septuagint)   *d* 46 Some early manuscripts *the house of Jacob*   *e* 50 Isaiah 66:1,2 heaven open and the Son of Man standing at the right hand of God.'

57At this they covered their ears and, yelling at the top of their voices, they all rushed at him, 58dragged him out of the city and began to stone him. Meanwhile, the witnesses laid their coats at the feet of a young man named Saul.

59While they were stoning him, Stephen prayed, 'Lord Jesus, receive my spirit.' 60Then he fell on his knees and cried out, 'Lord, do not hold this sin against them.' When he had said this, he fell asleep.

8

And Saul approved of their killing him.

The church persecuted and scattered

On that day a great persecution broke out against the church in Jerusalem, and all except the apostles were scattered throughout Judea and Samaria. 2Godly men buried Stephen and mourned deeply for him. 3But Saul began to destroy the church. Going from house to house, he dragged off both men and women and put them in prison.

Philip in Samaria

4Those who had been scattered preached the word wherever they went. 5Philip went down to a city in Samaria and proclaimed the Messiah there. 6When the crowds heard Philip and saw the signs he performed, they all paid close attention to what he said. 7With shrieks, evil^a spirits came out of many, and many who were paralysed or lame were healed. 8So there was great joy in that city.

Simon the sorcerer

9Now for some time a man named Simon had practised sorcery in the city and amazed all the people of Samaria. He boasted that he was someone great, 10and all the people, both high and low, gave him their attention and exclaimed, 'This man is rightly called the Great Power of God.' 11They followed him because he had amazed them for a long time with his sorcery. 12But when they believed Philip as he proclaimed the good news of the kingdom of God and the name of Jesus Christ, they were baptised, both men and women. 13Simon himself believed and was baptised. And he followed Philip everywhere, astonished by the great signs and miracles he saw.

14When the apostles in Jerusalem heard that Samaria had accepted the word of God, they sent Peter and John to Samaria. 15When they arrived, they prayed for the new believers there that they might receive the Holy Spirit, 16because the Holy Spirit had not yet come on any of them; they had simply been baptised into^b the name of the Lord Jesus. 17Then Peter and John placed their hands on them, and they received the Holy Spirit.

18When Simon saw that the Spirit was given at the laying on of the apostles' hands, he offered them money 19and said, 'Give me also this ability so that everyone on whom I lay my hands may receive the Holy Spirit.'

20Peter answered: 'May your money perish with you, because you thought you could buy the gift of God with money! 21You have no part or share in this ministry, because your heart is not right before God. 22Repent of this wickedness and pray to the Lord in the hope that he may forgive you for having such a thought in your heart. 23For I see that you are full of bitterness and captive to sin.'

24Then Simon answered, 'Pray to the Lord for me so that nothing you have said may happen to me.'

25After they had further proclaimed the word of the Lord and testified about Jesus, Peter and John returned to Jerusalem, preaching the gospel in many Samaritan villages.

Philip and the Ethiopian

26Now an angel of the Lord said to Philip, 'Go south to the road—the desert road—that goes down from Jerusalem to Gaza.' 27So he started out, and on his way he met an Ethiopian^c eunuch, an important official in charge of all the treasury of the Kandake (which means 'queen of the Ethiopians'). This man had gone to Jerusalem to worship, 28and on his way home was sitting in his chariot reading the Book of Isaiah the

---

^{a}7 Greek *unclean* ^{b}16 Or *in* ^{c}27 That is, from the southern Nile region prophet. ²⁹The Spirit told Philip, 'Go to that chariot and stay near it.'

³⁰Then Philip ran up to the chariot and heard the man reading Isaiah the prophet. 'Do you understand what you are reading?' Philip asked.

³¹'How can I,' he said, 'unless someone explains it to me?' So he invited Philip to come up and sit with him.

³²This is the passage of Scripture the eunuch was reading:

'He was led like a sheep to the slaughter,
    and as a lamb before its shearer is silent,
    so he did not open his mouth.
³³In his humiliation he was deprived of justice.
    Who can speak of his descendants?
    For his life was taken from the earth.'[a]

³⁴The eunuch asked Philip, 'Tell me, please, who is the prophet talking about, himself or someone else?' ³⁵Then Philip began with that very passage of Scripture and told him the good news about Jesus.

³⁶⁽³⁷⁾As they travelled along the road, they came to some water and the eunuch said, 'Look, here is water. What can stand in the way of my being baptised?'[b] ³⁸And he gave orders to stop the chariot. Then both Philip and the eunuch went down into the water and Philip baptised him. ³⁹When they came up out of the water, the Spirit of the Lord suddenly took Philip away, and the eunuch did not see him again, but went on his way rejoicing. ⁴⁰Philip, however, appeared at Azotus and travelled about, preaching the gospel in all the towns until he reached Caesarea.

Saul's conversion

9 Meanwhile, Saul was still breathing out murderous threats against the Lord's disciples. He went to the high priest ²and asked him for letters to the synagogues in Damascus, so that if he found any there who belonged to the Way, whether men or women, he might take them as prisoners to Jerusalem. ³As he neared Damascus on his journey, suddenly a light from heaven flashed around him. ⁴He fell to the ground

Paul
Acts 9:1

When Paul first makes an appearance in the Bible, he is known as Saul, and has made it his mission to destroy Christians. One dramatic encounter with God later, and his life has turned upside down. Also known as Paul, his mission is to spread the gospel as far as he can. Paul wrote more than half the books in the New Testament, encouraging the early church and its leaders. Paul suffered for his faith, being imprisoned and beaten.

and heard a voice say to him, 'Saul, Saul, why do you persecute me?'

⁵'Who are you, Lord?' Saul asked.

'I am Jesus, whom you are persecuting,' he replied. ⁶'Now get up and go into the city, and you will be told what you must do.'

⁷The men travelling with Saul stood there speechless; they heard the sound but did not see anyone. ⁸Saul got up from the ground, but when he opened his eyes he could see nothing. So they led him by the hand into Damascus. ⁹For three days he was blind, and did not eat or drink anything.

¹⁰In Damascus there was a disciple named Ananias. The Lord called to him in a vision, 'Ananias!'

'Yes, Lord,' he answered.

¹¹The Lord told him, 'Go to the house of Judas on Straight Street and ask for a man from Tarsus named Saul, for he is praying. ¹²In a vision he has seen a man named Ananias come and place his hands on him to restore his sight.'

¹³'Lord,' Ananias answered, 'I have heard many reports about this man and all the harm he has done to your people in Jerusalem. ¹⁴And he has come here with

---

[a] 33 Isaiah 53:7,8 (see Septuagint) [b] 36 Some late manuscripts *baptised?' ³⁷Philip said, 'If you believe with all your heart, you may.' The eunuch answered, 'I believe that Jesus Christ is the Son of God.'*

> **IN OTHER WORDS**
>
> **Synagogue**
> Acts 9:20
>
> As the Jews began to live farther away from the temple in Jerusalem, lots of local places of worship called 'synagogues' began to spring up so that people could continue to learn about the Law of Moses and worship God. The synagogue was also a school for teaching children to read, and sometimes a local court of justice where minor offences would be dealt with.

authority from the chief priests to arrest all who call on your name.'

15But the Lord said to Ananias, 'Go! This man is my chosen instrument to proclaim my name to the Gentiles and their kings and to the people of Israel. 16I will show him how much he must suffer for my name.'

17Then Ananias went to the house and entered it. Placing his hands on Saul, he said, 'Brother Saul, the Lord—Jesus, who appeared to you on the road as you were coming here—has sent me so that you may see again and be filled with the Holy Spirit.' 18Immediately, something like scales fell from Saul's eyes, and he could see again. He got up and was baptised, 19and after taking some food, he regained his strength.

Saul in Damascus and Jerusalem

Saul spent several days with the disciples in Damascus. 20At once he began to preach in the synagogues that Jesus is the Son of God. 21All those who heard him were astonished and asked, 'Isn't he the man who caused havoc in Jerusalem among those who call on this name? And hasn't he come here to take them as prisoners to the chief priests?' 22Yet Saul grew more and more powerful and baffled the Jews living in Damascus by proving that Jesus is the Messiah.

23After many days had gone by, there was a conspiracy among the Jews to kill him, 24but Saul learned of their plan. Day and night they kept close watch on the city gates in order to kill him. 25But his followers took him by night and lowered him in a basket through an opening in the wall.

26When he came to Jerusalem, he tried to join the disciples, but they were all afraid of him, not believing that he really was a disciple. 27But Barnabas took him and brought him to the apostles. He told them how Saul on his journey had seen the Lord and that the Lord had spoken to him, and how in Damascus he had preached fearlessly in the name of Jesus. 28So Saul stayed with them and moved about freely in Jerusalem, speaking boldly in the name of the Lord. 29He talked and debated with the Hellenistic Jews,[a] but they tried to kill him. 30When the believers learned of this, they took him down to Caesarea and sent him off to Tarsus.

31Then the church throughout Judea, Galilee and Samaria enjoyed a time of peace and was strengthened. Living in the fear of the Lord and encouraged by the Holy Spirit, it increased in numbers.

Aeneas and Dorcas

32As Peter travelled about the country, he went to visit the Lord's people who lived in Lydda. 33There he found a man named Aeneas, who was paralysed and had been bedridden for eight years. 34'Aeneas,' Peter said to him, 'Jesus Christ heals you. Get up and roll up your mat.' Immediately Aeneas got up. 35All those who lived in Lydda and Sharon saw him and turned to the Lord.

36In Joppa there was a disciple named Tabitha (in Greek her name is Dorcas); she was always doing good and helping the poor. 37About that time she became ill and died, and her body was washed and placed in an upstairs room. 38Lydda was near Joppa; so when the disciples heard that Peter was in Lydda, they sent two men to him and urged him, 'Please come at once!'

39Peter went with them, and when he arrived he was taken upstairs to the room. All the widows stood round him, crying and

---

[a] 29 That is, Jews who had adopted the Greek language and culture

showing him the robes and other clothing that Dorcas had made while she was still with them.

40 Peter sent them all out of the room; then he got down on his knees and prayed. Turning towards the dead woman, he said, 'Tabitha, get up.' She opened her eyes, and seeing Peter she sat up. 41 He took her by the hand and helped her to her feet. Then he called for the believers, especially the widows, and presented her to them alive. 42 This became known all over Joppa, and many people believed in the Lord. 43 Peter stayed in Joppa for some time with a tanner named Simon.

Cornelius calls for Peter

10 At Caesarea there was a man named Cornelius, a centurion in what was known as the Italian Regiment. 2 He and all his family were devout and God-fearing; he gave generously to those in need and prayed to God regularly. 3 One day at about three in the afternoon he had a vision. He distinctly saw an angel of God, who came to him and said, 'Cornelius!'

4 Cornelius stared at him in fear. 'What is it, Lord?' he asked.

The angel answered, 'Your prayers and gifts to the poor have come up as a memorial offering before God. 5 Now send men to Joppa to bring back a man named Simon who is called Peter. 6 He is staying with Simon the tanner, whose house is by the sea.'

7 When the angel who spoke to him had gone, Cornelius called two of his servants and a devout soldier who was one of his attendants. 8 He told them everything that had happened and sent them to Joppa.

Peter's vision

9 About noon the following day as they were on their journey and approaching the city, Peter went up on the roof to pray. 10 He became hungry and wanted something to eat, and while the meal was being prepared, he fell into a trance. 11 He saw heaven opened and something like a large sheet being let down to earth by its four corners. 12 It contained all kinds of four-footed animals, as well as reptiles and birds. 13 Then a voice told him, 'Get up, Peter. Kill and eat.'

14 'Surely not, Lord!' Peter replied. 'I have never eaten anything impure or unclean.'

15 The voice spoke to him a second time, 'Do not call anything impure that God has made clean.'

16 This happened three times, and immediately the sheet was taken back to heaven.

17 While Peter was wondering about the meaning of the vision, the men sent by Cornelius found out where Simon's house was and stopped at the gate. 18 They called out, asking if Simon who was known as Peter was staying there.

19 While Peter was still thinking about the vision, the Spirit said to him, 'Simon, three[a] men are looking for you. 20 So get up and go downstairs. Do not hesitate to go with them, for I have sent them.'

21 Peter went down and said to the men, 'I'm the one you're looking for. Why have you come?'

---

making Connections

Clean and unclean
Acts 10:12

This must have been such a shocking sight for Peter – more like a nightmare than a daydream. All his life, he'd been told that these animals were unclean and to be avoided, but now God is telling him to eat them! But God wants to make the point that his love is for everyone, not just the Jewish people. When Cornelius' men arrive to invite him back to their master's house, he's ready to go and tell them about Jesus.

---

[a] 19 One early manuscript *two*; other manuscripts do not have the number.

22The men replied, 'We have come from Cornelius the centurion. He is a righteous and God-fearing man, who is respected by all the Jewish people. A holy angel told him to ask you to come to his house so that he could hear what you have to say.' 23Then Peter invited the men into the house to be his guests.

Peter at Cornelius' house

The next day Peter started out with them, and some of the believers from Joppa went along. 24The following day he arrived in Caesarea. Cornelius was expecting them and had called together his relatives and close friends. 25As Peter entered the house, Cornelius met him and fell at his feet in reverence. 26But Peter made him get up. 'Stand up,' he said, 'I am only human myself.'

27While talking with him, Peter went inside and found a large gathering of people. 28He said to them: 'You are well aware that it is against our law for a Jew to associate with Gentiles or visit them. But God has shown me that I should not call anyone impure or unclean. 29So when I was sent for, I came without raising any objection. May I ask why you sent for me?'

30Cornelius answered: 'Three days ago I was in my house praying at this hour, at three in the afternoon. Suddenly a man in shining clothes stood before me 31and said, "Cornelius, God has heard your prayer and remembered your gifts to the poor. 32Send to Joppa for Simon who is called Peter. He is a guest in the home of Simon the tanner, who lives by the sea." 33So I sent for you immediately, and it was good of you to come. Now we are all here in the presence of God to listen to everything the Lord has commanded you to tell us.'

34Then Peter began to speak: 'I now realise how true it is that God does not show favouritism 35but accepts those from every nation who fear him and do what is right. 36You know the message God sent to the people of Israel, announcing the good news of peace through Jesus Christ, who is Lord of all. 37You know what has happened throughout the province of Judea, beginning in Galilee after the baptism that John preached— 38how God anointed Jesus of Nazareth with the Holy Spirit and power, and how he went around doing good and healing all who were under the power of the devil, because God was with him.

39'We are witnesses of everything he did in the country of the Jews and in Jerusalem. They killed him by hanging him on a cross, 40but God raised him from the dead on the third day and caused him to be seen. 41He was not seen by all the people, but by witnesses whom God had already chosen— by us who ate and drank with him after he rose from the dead. 42He commanded us to preach to the people and to testify that he is the one whom God appointed as judge of the living and the dead. 43All the prophets testify about him that everyone who believes in him receives forgiveness of sins through his name.'

44While Peter was still speaking these words, the Holy Spirit came on all who heard the message. 45The circumcised believers who had come with Peter were astonished that the gift of the Holy Spirit had been poured out even on Gentiles. 46For they heard them speaking in tongues[a] and praising God.

Then Peter said, 47'Surely no-one can stand in the way of their being baptised with water. They have received the Holy Spirit just as we have.' 48So he ordered that they be baptised in the name of Jesus Christ. Then they asked Peter to stay with them for a few days.

Peter explains his actions

11 The apostles and the believers throughout Judea heard that the Gentiles also had received the word of God. 2So when Peter went up to Jerusalem, the circumcised believers criticised him 3and said, 'You went into the house of the uncircumcised and ate with them.'

4Starting from the beginning, Peter told them the whole story: 5'I was in the city of Joppa praying, and in a trance I saw a vision. I saw something like a large sheet being let down from heaven by its four corners, and it came down to where I was. 6I looked into it

---

[a] 46 Or other languages

and saw four-footed animals of the earth, wild beasts, reptiles and birds. ⁷Then I heard a voice telling me, "Get up, Peter. Kill and eat."

⁸'I replied, "Surely not, Lord! Nothing impure or unclean has ever entered my mouth."

⁹'The voice spoke from heaven a second time, "Do not call anything impure that God has made clean." ¹⁰This happened three times, and then it was all pulled up to heaven again.

¹¹'Right then three men who had been sent to me from Caesarea stopped at the house where I was staying. ¹²The Spirit told me to have no hesitation about going with them. These six brothers also went with me, and we entered the man's house. ¹³He told us how he had seen an angel appear in his house and say, "Send to Joppa for Simon who is called Peter. ¹⁴He will bring you a message through which you and all your household will be saved."

¹⁵'As I began to speak, the Holy Spirit came on them as he had come on us at the beginning. ¹⁶Then I remembered what the Lord had said: "John baptised with[a] water, but you will be baptised with[b] the Holy Spirit." ¹⁷So if God gave them the same gift he gave us who believed in the Lord Jesus Christ, who was I to think that I could stand in God's way?'

¹⁸When they heard this, they had no further objections and praised God, saying, 'So then, even to Gentiles God has granted repentance that leads to life.'

The church in Antioch

¹⁹Now those who had been scattered by the persecution that broke out when Stephen was killed travelled as far as Phoenicia, Cyprus and Antioch, spreading the word only among Jews. ²⁰Some of them, however, men from Cyprus and Cyrene, went to Antioch and began to speak to Greeks also, telling them the good news about the Lord Jesus. ²¹The Lord's hand was with them, and a great number of people believed and turned to the Lord.

²²News of this reached the ears of the church in Jerusalem, and they sent Barnabas

People and Places

Christian
Acts 11:26
The word 'Christian' means a person who belongs to Jesus. It was first used in Antioch by people outside the church to describe these new followers of Jesus.

to Antioch. ²³When he arrived and saw what the grace of God had done, he was glad and encouraged them all to remain true to the Lord with all their hearts. ²⁴He was a good man, full of the Holy Spirit and faith, and a great number of people were brought to the Lord.

²⁵Then Barnabas went to Tarsus to look for Saul, ²⁶and when he found him, he brought him to Antioch. So for a whole year Barnabas and Saul met with the church and taught great numbers of people. The disciples were called Christians first at Antioch.

²⁷During this time some prophets came down from Jerusalem to Antioch. ²⁸One of them, named Agabus, stood up and through the Spirit predicted that a severe famine would spread over the entire Roman world. (This happened during the reign of Claudius.) ²⁹The disciples, as each one was able, decided to provide help for the believers living in Judea. ³⁰This they did, sending their gift to the elders by Barnabas and Saul.

Peter's miraculous escape from prison

12 It was about this time that King Herod arrested some who belonged to the church, intending to persecute them. ²He had James, the brother of John, put to death with the sword. ³When he saw that this met with approval among the Jews, he proceeded to seize Peter also. This happened during the Feast of Unleavened Bread. ⁴After arresting him, he put him in prison, handing him over to be

---

[a] 16 Or *in* [b] 16 Or *in*

guarded by four squads of four soldiers each. Herod intended to bring him out for public trial after the Passover.

⁵So Peter was kept in prison, but the church was earnestly praying to God for him.

⁶The night before Herod was to bring him to trial, Peter was sleeping between two soldiers, bound with two chains, and sentries stood guard at the entrance. ⁷Suddenly an angel of the Lord appeared and a light shone in the cell. He struck Peter on the side and woke him up. 'Quick, get up!' he said, and the chains fell off Peter's wrists.

⁸Then the angel said to him, 'Put on your clothes and sandals.' And Peter did so. 'Wrap your cloak round you and follow me,' the angel told him. ⁹Peter followed him out of the prison, but he had no idea that what the angel was doing was really happening; he thought he was seeing a vision. ¹⁰They passed the first and second guards and came to the iron gate leading to the city. It opened for them by itself, and they went through it. When they had walked the length of one street, suddenly the angel left him.

¹¹Then Peter came to himself and said, 'Now I know without a doubt that the Lord has sent his angel and rescued me from Herod's clutches and from everything the Jewish people were hoping would happen.'

¹²When this had dawned on him, he went to the house of Mary the mother of John, also called Mark, where many people had gathered and were praying. ¹³Peter knocked at the outer entrance, and a servant named Rhoda came to answer the door. ¹⁴When she recognised Peter's voice, she was so overjoyed she ran back without opening it and exclaimed, 'Peter is at the door!'

¹⁵'You're out of your mind,' they told her. When she kept insisting that it was so, they said, 'It must be his angel.'

¹⁶But Peter kept on knocking, and when they opened the door and saw him, they were astonished. ¹⁷Peter motioned with his hand for them to be quiet and described how the Lord had brought him out of prison. 'Tell James and the other brothers and sisters about this,' he said, and then he left for another place.

¹⁸In the morning, there was no small commotion among the soldiers as to what had become of Peter. ¹⁹After Herod had a thorough search made for him and did not find him, he cross-examined the guards and ordered that they be executed.

Herod's death

Then Herod went from Judea to Caesarea and stayed there. ²⁰He had been quarrelling with the people of Tyre and Sidon; they now joined together and sought an audience with him. Having secured the support of Blastus, a trusted personal servant of the king, they asked for peace, because they depended on the king's country for their food supply.

²¹On the appointed day Herod, wearing his royal robes, sat on his throne and delivered a public address to the people. ²²They shouted, 'This is the voice of a god, not of a mere mortal.' ²³Immediately, because Herod did not give praise to God, an angel of the Lord struck him down, and he was eaten by worms and died.

²⁴But the word of God continued to increase and spread.

Barnabas and Saul sent off

²⁵When Barnabas and Saul had finished their mission, they returned from[a] Jerusalem, taking with them John, also called Mark. ¹Now in the church at Antioch there were prophets and teachers: Barnabas, Simeon called Niger, Lucius of Cyrene, Manaen (who had been brought up with Herod the tetrarch) and Saul. ²While they were worshipping the Lord and fasting, the Holy Spirit said, 'Set apart for me Barnabas and Saul for the work to which I have called them.' ³So after they had fasted and prayed, they placed their hands on them and sent them off.

On Cyprus

⁴The two of them, sent on their way by the Holy Spirit, went down to Seleucia and sailed from there to Cyprus. ⁵When they arrived at Salamis, they proclaimed the

---

[a] 25 Some manuscripts *to*

word of God in the Jewish synagogues. John was with them as their helper.

6They travelled through the whole island until they came to Paphos. There they met a Jewish sorcerer and false prophet named Bar-Jesus, 7who was an attendant of the proconsul, Sergius Paulus. The proconsul, an intelligent man, sent for Barnabas and Saul because he wanted to hear the word of God. 8But Elymas the sorcerer (for that is what his name means) opposed them and tried to turn the proconsul from the faith. 9Then Saul, who was also called Paul, filled with the Holy Spirit, looked straight at Elymas and said, 10'You are a child of the devil and an enemy of everything that is right! You are full of all kinds of deceit and trickery. Will you never stop perverting the right ways of the Lord? 11Now the hand of the Lord is against you. You are going to be blind for a time, not even able to see the light of the sun.'

Immediately mist and darkness came over him, and he groped about, seeking someone to lead him by the hand. 12When the proconsul saw what had happened, he believed, for he was amazed at the teaching about the Lord.

In Pisidian Antioch

13From Paphos, Paul and his companions sailed to Perga in Pamphylia, where John left them to return to Jerusalem. 14From Perga they went on to Pisidian Antioch. On the Sabbath they entered the synagogue and sat down. 15After the reading from the Law and the Prophets, the leaders of the synagogue sent word to them, saying, 'Brothers, if you have a word of exhortation for the people, please speak.'

16Standing up, Paul motioned with his hand and said: 'People of Israel and you Gentiles who worship God, listen to me! 17The God of the people of Israel chose our ancestors; he made the people prosper during their stay in Egypt; with mighty power he led them out of that country; 18for about forty years he endured their conduct[a] in the wilderness; 19and he overthrew seven nations in Canaan, giving their land to his people as their inheritance. 20All this took about 450 years.

'After this, God gave them judges until the time of Samuel the prophet. 21Then the people asked for a king, and he gave them Saul son of Kish, of the tribe of Benjamin, who ruled for forty years. 22After removing Saul, he made David their king. God testified concerning him: "I have found David son of Jesse, a man after my own heart; he will do everything I want him to do."

23'From this man's descendants God has brought to Israel the Saviour Jesus, as he promised. 24Before the coming of Jesus, John preached repentance and baptism to all the people of Israel. 25As John was completing his work, he said: "Who do you suppose I am? I am not the one you are looking for. But there is someone coming after me whose sandals I am not worthy to untie."

26'Brothers and sisters from the children of Abraham and you God-fearing Gentiles, it is to us that this message of salvation has been sent. 27The people of Jerusalem and their rulers did not recognise Jesus, yet in condemning him they fulfilled the words of the prophets that are read every Sabbath. 28Though they found no proper ground for a death sentence, they asked Pilate to have him executed. 29When they had carried out all that was written about him, they took him down from the cross and laid him in a tomb. 30But God raised him from the dead, 31and for many days he was seen by those who had travelled with him from Galilee to Jerusalem. They are now his witnesses to our people.

32'We tell you the good news: what God promised our ancestors 33he has fulfilled for us, their children, by raising up Jesus. As it is written in the second Psalm:

'"You are my son;
today I have become your father."[b]

34God raised him from the dead so that he will never be subject to decay. As God has said,

---

[a] 18 Some manuscripts *he cared for them*   [b] 33 Psalm 2:7

' "I will give you the holy and sure
   blessings promised to David." '[a]

35So it is also stated elsewhere:

' "You will not let your holy one see
   decay." '[b]

36'Now when David had served God's purpose in his own generation, he fell asleep; he was buried with his ancestors and his body decayed. 37But the one whom God raised from the dead did not see decay.

38'Therefore, my brothers and sisters, I want you to know that through Jesus the forgiveness of sins is proclaimed to you. 39Through him everyone who believes is set free from every sin, a justification you were not able to obtain under the law of Moses. 40Take care that what the prophets have said does not happen to you:

41' "Look, you scoffers,
   wonder and perish,
for I am going to do something in your
     days
that you would never believe,
   even if someone told you." '[c]

42As Paul and Barnabas were leaving the synagogue, the people invited them to speak further about these things on the next Sabbath. 43When the congregation was dismissed, many of the Jews and devout converts to Judaism followed Paul and Barnabas, who talked with them and urged them to continue in the grace of God.

44On the next Sabbath almost the whole city gathered to hear the word of the Lord. 45When the Jews saw the crowds, they were filled with jealousy. They began to contradict what Paul was saying and heaped abuse on him.

46Then Paul and Barnabas answered them boldly: 'We had to speak the word of God to you first. Since you reject it and do not consider yourselves worthy of eternal life, we now turn to the Gentiles. 47For this is what the Lord has commanded us:

' "I have made you[d] a light for the
   Gentiles,
that you[e] may bring salvation to the
   ends of the earth." '[f]

48When the Gentiles heard this, they were glad and honoured the word of the Lord; and all who were appointed for eternal life believed.

49The word of the Lord spread through the whole region. 50But the Jewish leaders incited the God-fearing women of high standing and the leading men of the city. They stirred up persecution against Paul and Barnabas, and expelled them from their region. 51So they shook the dust off their feet as a warning to them and went to Iconium. 52And the disciples were filled with joy and with the Holy Spirit.

In Iconium

14 At Iconium Paul and Barnabas went as usual into the Jewish synagogue. There they spoke so effectively that a great number of Jews and Greeks believed. 2But the Jews who refused to believe stirred up the other Gentiles and poisoned their minds against the brothers. 3So Paul and Barnabas spent considerable time there, speaking boldly for the Lord, who confirmed the message of his grace by enabling them to perform signs and wonders. 4The people of the city were divided; some sided with the Jews, others with the apostles. 5There was a plot afoot among both Gentiles and Jews, together with their leaders, to ill-treat them and stone them. 6But they found out about it and fled to the Lycaonian cities of Lystra and Derbe and to the surrounding country, 7where they continued to preach the gospel.

In Lystra and Derbe

8In Lystra there sat a man who was lame. He had been that way from birth and had never walked. 9He listened to Paul as he was speaking. Paul looked directly at him, saw that he had faith to be healed 10and called out, 'Stand up on your feet!' At that, the man jumped up and began to walk.

11When the crowd saw what Paul had done, they shouted in the Lycaonian language, 'The gods have come down to us in

---

[a] 34 Isaiah 55:3   [b] 35 Psalm 16:10 (see Septaugint)   [c] 41 Hab. 1:5   [d] 47 The Greek is singular.   [e] 47 The Greek is singular.   [f] 47 Isaiah 49:6

Sign of the times

Greek gods
Acts 14:12

The ancient Greeks worshipped many gods and goddesses. Zeus was their chief god, who ruled the weather and decided the outcome of battles. Hermes was Zeus' son and was the gods' messenger. The people thought Paul was Hermes because he talked so much.

human form!' 12Barnabas they called Zeus, and Paul they called Hermes because he was the chief speaker. 13The priest of Zeus, whose temple was just outside the city, brought bulls and wreaths to the city gates because he and the crowd wanted to offer sacrifices to them.

14But when the apostles Barnabas and Paul heard of this, they tore their clothes and rushed out into the crowd, shouting: 15'Friends, why are you doing this? We too are only human, like you. We are bringing you good news, telling you to turn from these worthless things to the living God, who made heaven and earth and sea and everything in them. 16In the past, he let all nations go their own way. 17Yet he has not left himself without testimony: he has shown kindness by giving you rain from heaven and crops in their seasons; he provides you with plenty of food and fills your hearts with joy.' 18Even with these words, they had difficulty keeping the crowd from sacrificing to them.

19Then some Jews came from Antioch and Iconium and won the crowd over. They stoned Paul and dragged him outside the city, thinking he was dead. 20But after the disciples had gathered round him, he got up and went back into the city. The next day he and Barnabas left for Derbe.

The return to Antioch in Syria

21They preached the gospel in that city and won a large number of disciples. Then they returned to Lystra, Iconium and Antioch, 22strengthening the disciples and encouraging them to remain true to the faith. 'We must go through many hardships to enter the kingdom of God,' they said. 23Paul and Barnabas appointed elders[a] for them in each church and, with prayer and fasting, committed them to the Lord, in whom they had put their trust. 24After going through Pisidia, they came into Pamphylia, 25and when they had preached the word in Perga, they went down to Attalia.

26From Attalia they sailed back to Antioch, where they had been committed to the grace of God for the work they had now completed. 27On arriving there, they gathered the church together and reported all that God had done through them and how he had opened a door of faith to the Gentiles. 28And they stayed there a long time with the disciples.

The council at Jerusalem

15 Certain individuals came down from Judea to Antioch and were teaching the believers: 'Unless you are circumcised, according to the custom taught by Moses, you cannot be saved.' 2This brought Paul and Barnabas into sharp dispute and debate with them. So Paul and Barnabas were appointed, along with some other believers, to go up to Jerusalem to see the apostles and elders about this question. 3The church sent them on their way, and as they travelled through Phoenicia and Samaria, they told how the Gentiles had been converted. This news made all the believers very glad. 4When they came to Jerusalem, they were welcomed by the church and the apostles and elders, to whom they reported everything God had done through them.

5Then some of the believers who belonged to the party of the Pharisees stood up and said, 'The Gentiles must be circumcised and required to keep the law of Moses.'

6The apostles and elders met to consider this question. 7After much discussion, Peter got up and addressed them: 'Brothers, you

---

[a] 23 Or *Barnabas ordained elders*; or *Barnabas had elders elected*

know that some time ago God made a choice among you that the Gentiles should hear from my lips the message of the gospel and believe. 8God, who knows the heart, showed that he accepted them by giving the Holy Spirit to them, just as he did to us. 9He did not discriminate between us and them, for he purified their hearts by faith. 10Now then, why do you try to test God by putting on the necks of Gentiles a yoke that neither we nor our ancestors have been able to bear? 11No! We believe it is through the grace of our Lord Jesus that we are saved, just as they are.'

12The whole assembly became silent as they listened to Barnabas and Paul telling about the signs and wonders God had done among the Gentiles through them. 13When they finished, James spoke up. 'Brothers,' he said, 'listen to me. 14Simon[a] has described to us how God first intervened to choose a people for his name from the Gentiles. 15The words of the prophets are in agreement with this, as it is written:

16 ' "After this I will return
  and rebuild David's fallen tent.
 Its ruins I will rebuild,
  and I will restore it,
17that the rest of humanity may seek the Lord,
  even all the Gentiles who bear my name,
 says the Lord, who does these things"[b]—
18 things known from long ago.[c]

19'It is my judgment, therefore, that we should not make it difficult for the Gentiles who are turning to God. 20Instead we should write to them, telling them to abstain from food polluted by idols, from sexual immorality, from the meat of strangled animals and from blood. 21For the law of Moses has been preached in every city from the earliest times and is read in the synagogues on every Sabbath.'

The council's letter to Gentile believers

22Then the apostles and elders, with the whole church, decided to choose some of their own men and send them to Antioch with Paul and Barnabas. They chose Judas (called Barsabbas) and Silas, who were leaders among the believers. 23With them they sent the following letter:

Gentile
Acts 15:23
The word 'Gentile' is used in the Bible to describe any people who are not part of the Jewish race.

The apostles and elders, your brothers,

To the Gentile believers in Antioch, Syria and Cilicia:

Greetings.

24We have heard that some went out from us without our authorisation and disturbed you, troubling your minds by what they said. 25So we all agreed to choose some men and send them to you with our dear friends Barnabas and Paul— 26men who have risked their lives for the name of our Lord Jesus Christ. 27Therefore we are sending Judas and Silas to confirm by word of mouth what we are writing. 28It seemed good to the Holy Spirit and to us not to burden you with anything beyond the following requirements: 29You are to abstain from food sacrificed to idols, from blood, from the meat of strangled animals and from sexual immorality. You will do well to avoid these things.

Farewell.

---

[a] 14 Greek *Simeon*, a variant of *Simon*; that is, Peter   [b] 17 Amos 9:11,12 (see Septuagint)   [c] 17,18 Some manuscripts *things"— / 18the Lord's work is known to him from long ago*

30So they were sent off and went down to Antioch, where they gathered the church together and delivered the letter. 31The people read it and were glad for its encouraging message. 32Judas and Silas, who themselves were prophets, said much to encourage and strengthen the believers. 33(34)After spending some time there, they were sent off by the believers with the blessing of peace to return to those who had sent them. 35But Paul and Barnabas remained in Antioch, where they and many others taught and preached the word of the Lord.

Disagreement between Paul and Barnabas

36Some time later Paul said to Barnabas, 'Let us go back and visit the believers in all the towns where we preached the word of the Lord and see how they are doing.' 37Barnabas wanted to take John, also called Mark, with them, 38but Paul did not think it wise to take him, because he had deserted them in Pamphylia and had not continued with them in the work. 39They had such a sharp disagreement that they parted company. Barnabas took Mark and sailed for Cyprus, 40but Paul chose Silas and left, commended by the believers to the grace of the Lord. 41He went through Syria and Cilicia, strengthening the churches.

Timothy joins Paul and Silas

16 Paul came to Derbe and then to Lystra, where a disciple named Timothy lived, whose mother was Jewish and a believer but whose father was a Greek. 2The believers at Lystra and Iconium spoke well of him. 3Paul wanted to take him along on the journey, so he circumcised him because of the Jews who lived in that area, for they all knew that his father was a Greek. 4As they travelled from town to town, they delivered the decisions reached by the apostles and elders in Jerusalem for the people to obey. 5So the churches were strengthened in the faith and grew daily in numbers.

Paul's vision of the man of Macedonia

6Paul and his companions travelled throughout the region of Phrygia and Galatia, having been kept by the Holy Spirit from preaching the word in the province of Asia. 7When they came to the border of Mysia, they tried to enter Bithynia, but the Spirit of Jesus would not allow them to. 8So they passed by Mysia and went down to Troas. 9During the night Paul had a vision of a man of Macedonia standing and begging him, 'Come over to Macedonia and help us.' 10After Paul had seen the vision, we got ready at once to leave for Macedonia, concluding that God had called us to preach the gospel to them.

Lydia's conversion in Philippi

11From Troas we put out to sea and sailed straight for Samothrace, and the next day we went on to Neapolis. 12From there we travelled to Philippi, a Roman colony and the leading city of that district[a] of Macedonia. And we stayed there several days.

13On the Sabbath we went outside the city gate to the river, where we expected to find a place of prayer. We sat down and began to speak to the women who had gathered there. 14One of those listening was a woman from the city of Thyatira named Lydia, a dealer in purple cloth. She was a worshipper of God. The Lord opened her heart to respond to Paul's message. 15When she and the members of her household were baptised, she invited us to her home. 'If you consider me a believer in the Lord,' she said, 'come and stay at my house.' And she persuaded us.

Paul and Silas in prison

16Once when we were going to the place of prayer, we were met by a female slave who had a spirit by which she predicted the future. She earned a great deal of money for her owners by fortune-telling. 17She followed Paul and the rest of us, shouting, 'These men are servants of the Most High God, who are telling you the way to be saved.' 18She kept this up for many days. Finally Paul became so annoyed that he turned round and said to the spirit, 'In the

---

[a] 12 The text and meaning of the Greek for *the leading city of that district* are uncertain.

name of Jesus Christ I command you to come out of her!' At that moment the spirit left her.

19When her owners realised that their hope of making money was gone, they seized Paul and Silas and dragged them into the market-place to face the authorities. 20They brought them before the magistrates and said, 'These men are Jews, and are throwing our city into an uproar 21by advocating customs unlawful for us Romans to accept or practise.'

22The crowd joined in the attack against Paul and Silas, and the magistrates ordered them to be stripped and beaten with rods. 23After they had been severely flogged, they were thrown into prison, and the jailer was commanded to guard them carefully. 24When he received these orders, he put them in the inner cell and fastened their feet in the stocks.

25About midnight Paul and Silas were praying and singing hymns to God, and the other prisoners were listening to them. 26Suddenly there was such a violent earthquake that the foundations of the prison were shaken. At once all the prison doors flew open, and everyone's chains came loose. 27The jailer woke up, and when he saw the prison doors open, he drew his sword and was about to kill himself because he thought the prisoners had escaped. 28But Paul shouted, 'Don't harm yourself! We are all here!'

29The jailer called for lights, rushed in and fell trembling before Paul and Silas. 30He then brought them out and asked, 'Sirs, what must I do to be saved?'

31They replied, 'Believe in the Lord Jesus, and you will be saved—you and your household.' 32Then they spoke the word of the Lord to him and to all the others in his house. 33At that hour of the night the jailer took them and washed their wounds; then immediately he and all his household were baptised. 34The jailer brought them into his house and set a meal before them; he was filled with joy because he had come to believe in God—he and his whole household.

35When it was daylight, the magistrates sent their officers to the jailer with the order: 'Release those men.' 36The jailer told Paul, 'The magistrates have ordered that you and Silas be released. Now you can leave. Go in peace.'

37But Paul said to the officers: 'They beat us publicly without a trial, even though we are Roman citizens, and threw us into prison. And now do they want to get rid of us quietly? No! Let them come themselves and escort us out.'

38The officers reported this to the magistrates, and when they heard that Paul and Silas were Roman citizens, they were alarmed. 39They came to appease them and escorted them from the prison, requesting them to leave the city. 40After Paul and Silas came out of the prison, they went to Lydia's house, where they met with the believers and encouraged them. Then they left.

In Thessalonica

17 When Paul and his companions had passed through Amphipolis and Apollonia, they came to Thessalonica, where there was a Jewish synagogue. 2As was his custom, Paul went into the synagogue, and on three Sabbath days he reasoned with them from the Scriptures, 3explaining and proving that the Messiah had to suffer and rise from the dead. 'This Jesus I am proclaiming to you is the Messiah,' he said. 4Some of the Jews were persuaded and joined Paul and Silas, as did a large number of God-fearing Greeks and not a few prominent women.

5But other Jews were jealous; so they rounded up some bad characters from the market-place, formed a mob and started a riot in the city. They rushed to Jason's house in search of Paul and Silas in order to bring them out to the crowd.[a] 6But when they did not find them, they dragged Jason and some other believers before the city officials, shouting: 'These men who have caused trouble all over the world have now come here, 7and Jason has welcomed them into his house. They are all defying Caesar's decrees, saying that there is another king,

---

[a] 5 Or *the assembly of the people*

one called Jesus.' 8When they heard this, the crowd and the city officials were thrown into turmoil. 9Then they put Jason and the others on bail and let them go.

In Berea

10As soon as it was night, the believers sent Paul and Silas away to Berea. On arriving there, they went to the Jewish synagogue. 11Now the Berean Jews were of more noble character than those in Thessalonica, for they received the message with great eagerness and examined the Scriptures every day to see if what Paul said was true. 12Many of them believed, as did also a number of prominent Greek women and many Greek men.

13But when the Jews in Thessalonica learned that Paul was preaching the word of God at Berea, some of them went there too, agitating the crowds and stirring them up. 14The believers immediately sent Paul to the coast, but Silas and Timothy stayed at Berea. 15Those who escorted Paul brought him to Athens and then left with instructions for Silas and Timothy to join him as soon as possible.

In Athens

16While Paul was waiting for them in Athens, he was greatly distressed to see that the city was full of idols. 17So he reasoned in the synagogue with both Jews and God-fearing Greeks, as well as in the market-place day by day with those who happened to be there. 18A group of Epicurean and Stoic philosophers began to debate with him. Some of them asked, 'What is this babbler trying to say?' Others remarked, 'He seems to be advocating foreign gods.' They said this because Paul was preaching the good news about Jesus and the resurrection. 19Then they took him and brought him to a meeting of the Areopagus, where they said to him, 'May we know what this new teaching is that you are presenting? 20You are bringing some strange ideas to our ears, and we would like to know what they mean.' 21(All the Athenians and the foreigners who lived there spent their time doing nothing but talking about and listening to the latest ideas.)

> **People and Places**
>
> **Philosophers in Athens**
> **Acts 17:18**
> Athens was full of people who liked to talk about ideas. The Epicureans' aim in life was to chase pleasure and avoid pain. The Stoics thought you should just accept what came your way and not get too excited about anything. Both groups found reasons to argue with Paul and they invited him to their council – the Areopagus – to debate some more. But, very cleverly, Paul didn't start by telling them that he thought they were wrong. He found something in their culture to talk about – the altar to 'an unknown god' – and introduced the God he knew to them. Some of them believed and some wanted to find out more.

22Paul then stood up in the meeting of the Areopagus and said: 'People of Athens! I see that in every way you are very religious. 23For as I walked around and looked carefully at your objects of worship, I even found an altar with this inscription: TO AN UNKNOWN GOD. So you are ignorant of the very thing you worship—and this is what I am going to proclaim to you.

24'The God who made the world and everything in it is the Lord of heaven and earth and does not live in temples built by hands. 25And he is not served by human hands, as if he needed anything. Rather, he himself gives everyone life and breath and everything else. 26From one man he made all the nations, that they should inhabit the whole earth; and he marked out their appointed times in history and the boundaries of their lands. 27God did this so that they would seek him and perhaps reach out for him and find him, though he is not far from any one of us. 28"For in him we live and move and have our being."*a* As some of your own poets have said, "We are his offspring."*b*

29'Therefore since we are God's offspring, we should not think that the divine being is like gold or silver or stone—an image made by human design and skill. 30In the past God overlooked such ignorance, but now he commands all people everywhere to repent. 31For he has set a day when he will judge the world with justice by the man he has appointed. He has given proof of this to everyone by raising him from the dead.'

32When they heard about the resurrection of the dead, some of them sneered, but others said, 'We want to hear you again on this subject.' 33At that, Paul left the Council. 34Some of the people became followers of Paul and believed. Among them was Dionysius, a member of the Areopagus, also a woman named Damaris, and a number of others.

In Corinth

18 After this, Paul left Athens and went to Corinth. 2There he met a Jew named Aquila, a native of Pontus, who had recently come from Italy with his wife Priscilla, because Claudius had ordered all Jews to leave Rome. Paul went to see them, 3and because he was a tentmaker as they were, he stayed and worked with them. 4Every Sabbath he reasoned in the synagogue, trying to persuade Jews and Greeks.

5When Silas and Timothy came from Macedonia, Paul devoted himself exclusively to preaching, testifying to the Jews that Jesus was the Messiah. 6But when they opposed Paul and became abusive, he shook out his clothes in protest and said to them, 'Your blood be on your own heads! I am innocent of it. From now on I will go to the Gentiles.'

7Then Paul left the synagogue and went next door to the house of Titius Justus, a worshipper of God. 8Crispus, the synagogue leader, and his entire household believed in the Lord; and many of the Corinthians who heard Paul believed and were baptised.

Sign of the times

Tent making
Acts 18:3
In Paul's time, tents weren't used for holidays – they were used for living in or for storage. Tents would be made of cloth, often made of goats' hair, or animal skins. The skins were soaked, all the hairs were scraped off, and then they were dried. Tents would be made of sections of this leather sewn together.

9One night the Lord spoke to Paul in a vision: 'Do not be afraid; keep on speaking, do not be silent. 10For I am with you, and no-one is going to attack and harm you, because I have many people in this city.' 11So Paul stayed in Corinth for a year and a half, teaching them the word of God.

12While Gallio was proconsul of Achaia, the Jews of Corinth made a united attack on Paul and brought him to the place of judgment. 13'This man,' they charged, 'is persuading the people to worship God in ways contrary to the law.'

14Just as Paul was about to speak, Gallio said to them, 'If you Jews were making a complaint about some misdemeanour or serious crime, it would be reasonable for me to listen to you. 15But since it involves questions about words and names and your own law—settle the matter yourselves. I will not be a judge of such things.' 16So he drove them off. 17Then the crowd there turned on Sosthenes the synagogue leader and beat him in front of the proconsul; and Gallio showed no concern whatever.

Priscilla, Aquila and Apollos

18Paul stayed on in Corinth for some time. Then he left the believers and sailed for Syria, accompanied by Priscilla and Aquila.

---

a 28 From the Cretan philosopher Epimenides   *b* 28 From the Cilician Stoic philosopher Aratus

Before he sailed, he had his hair cut off at Cenchreae because of a vow he had taken. 19They arrived at Ephesus, where Paul left Priscilla and Aquila. He himself went into the synagogue and reasoned with the Jews. 20When they asked him to spend more time with them, he declined. 21But as he left, he promised, 'I will come back if it is God's will.' Then he set sail from Ephesus. 22When he landed at Caesarea, he went up to Jerusalem and greeted the church and then went down to Antioch.

23After spending some time in Antioch, Paul set out from there and travelled from place to place throughout the region of Galatia and Phrygia, strengthening all the disciples.

24Meanwhile a Jew named Apollos, a native of Alexandria, came to Ephesus. He was a learned man, with a thorough knowledge of the Scriptures. 25He had been instructed in the way of the Lord, and he spoke with great fervour[a] and taught about Jesus accurately, though he knew only the baptism of John. 26He began to speak boldly in the synagogue. When Priscilla and Aquila heard him, they invited him to their home and explained to him the way of God more adequately.

27When Apollos wanted to go to Achaia, the believers encouraged him and wrote to the disciples there to welcome him. When he arrived, he was a great help to those who by grace had believed. 28For he vigorously refuted the Jews in public debate, proving from the Scriptures that Jesus was the Messiah.

Paul in Ephesus

19 While Apollos was at Corinth, Paul took the road through the interior and arrived at Ephesus. There he found some disciples 2and asked them, 'Did you receive the Holy Spirit when[b] you believed?'

They answered, 'No, we have not even heard that there is a Holy Spirit.'

3So Paul asked, 'Then what baptism did you receive?'

'John's baptism,' they replied.

4Paul said, 'John's baptism was a baptism of repentance. He told the people to believe in the one coming after him, that is, in Jesus.' 5On hearing this, they were baptised into[c] the name of the Lord Jesus. 6When Paul placed his hands on them, the Holy Spirit came on them, and they spoke in tongues[d] and prophesied. 7There were about twelve men in all.

8Paul entered the synagogue and spoke boldly there for three months, arguing persuasively about the kingdom of God. 9But some of them became obstinate; they refused to believe and publicly maligned the Way. So Paul left them. He took the disciples with him and had discussions daily in the lecture hall of Tyrannus. 10This went on for two years, so that all the Jews and Greeks who lived in the province of Asia heard the word of the Lord.

11God did extraordinary miracles through Paul, 12so that even handkerchiefs and aprons that had touched him were taken to those who were ill, and their illnesses were cured and the evil spirits left them.

13Some Jews who went around driving out evil spirits tried to invoke the name of the Lord Jesus over those who were demon-possessed. They would say, 'In the name of the Jesus whom Paul preaches, I command you to come out.' 14Seven sons of Sceva, a Jewish chief priest, were doing this. 15⌊One day⌋ the evil spirit answered them, 'Jesus I know, and I know about Paul, but who are you?' 16Then the man who had the evil spirit jumped on them and overpowered them all. He gave them such a beating that they ran out of the house naked and bleeding.

17When this became known to the Jews and Greeks living in Ephesus, they were all seized with fear, and the name of the Lord Jesus was held in high honour. 18Many of those who believed now came and openly confessed what they had done. 19A number who had practised sorcery brought their scrolls together and burned them publicly. When they calculated the value of the scrolls, the total came to fifty thousand drachmas.[e] 20In this way the word of the Lord spread widely and grew in power.

---

[a] 25 Or *with fervour in the Spirit* [b] 2 Or *after* [c] 5 Or *in* [d] 6 Or *other languages* [e] 19 A drachma was a silver coin worth about a day's wages.

People and Places

Artemis
Acts 19:24

Artemis was the Greek goddess of hunting and the moon, known as Diana to the Romans. Ephesus was home to the Temple of Diana, one of the seven wonders of the ancient world, and silversmiths there made a good living from selling models of the temple. Paul's preaching about Jesus threatens to destroy their livelihood so it's not surprising that they get upset with him.

21After all this had happened, Paul decided[a] to go to Jerusalem, passing through Macedonia and Achaia. 'After I have been there,' he said, 'I must visit Rome also.' 22He sent two of his helpers, Timothy and Erastus, to Macedonia, while he stayed in the province of Asia a little longer.

The riot in Ephesus

23About that time there arose a great disturbance about the Way. 24A silversmith named Demetrius, who made silver shrines of Artemis, brought in no little business for the skilled workers there. 25He called them together, along with the workers in related trades, and said: 'You know, my friends, that we receive a good income from this business. 26And you see and hear how this fellow Paul has convinced and led astray large numbers of people here in Ephesus and in practically the whole province of Asia. He says that gods made by human hands are no gods at all. 27There is danger not only that our trade will lose its good name, but also that the temple of the great goddess Artemis will be discredited; and the goddess herself, who is worshipped throughout the province of Asia and the world, will be robbed of her divine majesty.'

28When they heard this, they were furious and began shouting: 'Great is Artemis of the Ephesians!' 29Soon the whole city was in an uproar. The people seized Gaius and Aristarchus, Paul's travelling companions from Macedonia, and all of them rushed together into the theatre. 30Paul wanted to appear before the crowd, but the disciples would not let him. 31Even some of the officials of the province, friends of Paul, sent him a message begging him not to venture into the theatre.

32The assembly was in confusion: some were shouting one thing, some another. Most of the people did not even know why they were there. 33The Jews in the crowd pushed Alexander to the front, and they shouted instructions to him. He motioned for silence in order to make a defence before the people. 34But when they realised he was a Jew, they all shouted in unison for about two hours: 'Great is Artemis of the Ephesians!'

35The city clerk quietened the crowd and said: 'People of Ephesus, doesn't all the world know that the city of Ephesus is the guardian of the temple of the great Artemis and of her image, which fell from heaven? 36Therefore, since these facts are undeniable, you ought to calm down and not do anything rash. 37You have brought these men here, though they have neither robbed temples nor uttered blasphemy against our goddess. 38If, then, Demetrius and his associates have a grievance against anybody, the courts are open and there are proconsuls. They can press charges. 39If there is anything further you want to bring up, it must be settled in a legal assembly. 40As it is, we are in danger of being charged with rioting because of what happened today. In that case we would not be able to account for this commotion, since there is no reason for it.' 41After he had said this, he dismissed the assembly.

Through Macedonia and Greece

20 When the uproar had ended, Paul sent for the disciples and, after encouraging them, said good-bye and set out for Macedonia. 2He travelled through

---

[a]21 Or *decided in the Spirit*

that area, speaking many words of encouragement to the people, and finally arrived in Greece, 3where he stayed three months. Because some Jews had plotted against him just as he was about to sail for Syria, he decided to go back through Macedonia. 4He was accompanied by Sopater son of Pyrrhus from Berea, Aristarchus and Secundus from Thessalonica, Gaius from Derbe, Timothy also, and Tychicus and Trophimus from the province of Asia. 5These men went on ahead and waited for us at Troas. 6But we sailed from Philippi after the Feast of Unleavened Bread, and five days later joined the others at Troas, where we stayed seven days.

Eutychus raised from the dead at Troas

7On the first day of the week we came together to break bread. Paul spoke to the people and, because he intended to leave the next day, kept on talking until midnight. 8There were many lamps in the upstairs room where we were meeting. 9Seated in a window was a young man named Eutychus, who was sinking into a deep sleep as Paul talked on and on. When he was sound asleep, he fell to the ground from the third storey and was picked up dead. 10Paul went down, threw himself on the young man and put his arms round him. 'Don't be alarmed,' he said. 'He's alive!' 11Then he went upstairs again and broke bread and ate. After talking until daylight, he left. 12The people took the young man home alive and were greatly comforted.

Paul's farewell to the Ephesian elders

13We went on ahead to the ship and sailed for Assos, where we were going to take Paul aboard. He had made this arrangement because he was going there on foot. 14When he met us at Assos, we took him aboard and went on to Mitylene. 15The next day we set sail from there and arrived off Chios. The day after that we crossed over to Samos, and on the following day arrived at Miletus. 16Paul had decided to sail past Ephesus to avoid spending time in the province of Asia, for he was in a hurry to reach Jerusalem, if possible, by the day of Pentecost.

17From Miletus, Paul sent to Ephesus for the elders of the church. 18When they arrived, he said to them: 'You know how I lived the whole time I was with you, from the first day I came into the province of Asia. 19I served the Lord with great humility and with tears and in the midst of severe testing by the plots of the Jews. 20You know that I have not hesitated to preach anything that would be helpful to you but have taught you publicly and from house to house. 21I have declared to both Jews and Greeks that they must turn to God in repentance and have faith in our Lord Jesus.

22'And now, compelled by the Spirit, I am going to Jerusalem, not knowing what will happen to me there. 23I only know that in every city the Holy Spirit warns me that prison and hardships are facing me. 24However, I consider my life worth nothing to me; my only aim is to finish the race and complete the task the Lord Jesus has given me—the task of testifying to the good news of God's grace.

25'Now I know that none of you among whom I have gone about preaching the kingdom will ever see me again. 26Therefore, I declare to you today that I am innocent of the blood of everyone. 27For I have not hesitated to proclaim to you the whole will of God. 28Keep watch over yourselves and all the flock of which the Holy Spirit has made you overseers. Be shepherds of the church of God,[a] which he bought with his own blood. 29I know that after I leave, savage wolves will come in among you and will not spare the flock. 30Even from your own number some will arise and distort the truth in order to draw away disciples after them. 31So be on your guard! Remember that for three years I never stopped warning each of you night and day with tears.

32'Now I commit you to God and to the word of his grace, which can build you up and give you an inheritance among all those who are sanctified. 33I have not coveted anyone's silver or gold or clothing. 34You yourselves know that these hands of mine have supplied my own needs and the needs of my companions. 35In everything I did, I

---

[a] 28 Many manuscripts *of the Lord*

showed you that by this kind of hard work we must help the weak, remembering the words the Lord Jesus himself said: "It is more blessed to give than to receive."'

36When Paul had finished speaking, he knelt down with all of them and prayed. 37They all wept as they embraced him and kissed him. 38What grieved them most was his statement that they would never see his face again. Then they accompanied him to the ship.

On to Jerusalem

21 After we had torn ourselves away from them, we put out to sea and sailed straight to Kos. The next day we went to Rhodes and from there to Patara. 2We found a ship crossing over to Phoenicia, went on board and set sail. 3After sighting Cyprus and passing to the south of it, we sailed on to Syria. We landed at Tyre, where our ship was to unload its cargo. 4We sought out the disciples there and stayed with them seven days. Through the Spirit they urged Paul not to go on to Jerusalem. 5When it was time to leave, we left and continued on our way. All of them, including wives and children, accompanied us out of the city, and there on the beach we knelt to pray. 6After saying good-bye to each other, we went aboard the ship, and they returned home.

7We continued our voyage from Tyre and landed at Ptolemais, where we greeted the believers and stayed with them for a day. 8Leaving the next day, we reached Caesarea and stayed at the house of Philip the evangelist, one of the Seven. 9He had four unmarried daughters who prophesied.

10After we had been there a number of days, a prophet named Agabus came down from Judea. 11Coming over to us, he took Paul's belt, tied his own hands and feet with it and said, 'The Holy Spirit says, "In this way the Jewish leaders in Jerusalem will bind the owner of this belt and will hand him over to the Gentiles."'

12When we heard this, we and the people there pleaded with Paul not to go up to Jerusalem. 13Then Paul answered, 'Why are you weeping and breaking my heart? I am ready not only to be bound, but also to die in Jerusalem for the name of the Lord Jesus.'

> **IN OTHER WORDS**
>
> **Rites and ritual**
> **Acts 21:24**
> Although the word 'ritual' doesn't appear in the Bible, it is an important idea to understand. Ritual speaks of the connection between the physical and spiritual parts of life which is acknowledged in religious actions or ceremonies. Holy Communion, or the Eucharist, is a ritual or rite, as were Old Testament sacrifices.

14When he would not be dissuaded, we gave up and said, 'The Lord's will be done.'

15After this, we started on our way up to Jerusalem. 16Some of the disciples from Caesarea accompanied us and brought us to the home of Mnason, where we were to stay. He was a man from Cyprus and one of the early disciples.

Paul's arrival at Jerusalem

17When we arrived at Jerusalem, the believers received us warmly. 18The next day Paul and the rest of us went to see James, and all the elders were present. 19Paul greeted them and reported in detail what God had done among the Gentiles through his ministry.

20When they heard this, they praised God. Then they said to Paul: 'You see, brother, how many thousands of Jews have believed, and all of them are zealous for the law. 21They have been informed that you teach all the Jews who live among the Gentiles to turn away from Moses, telling them not to circumcise their children or live according to our customs. 22What shall we do? They will certainly hear that you have come, 23so do what we tell you. There are four men with us who have made a vow. 24Take these men, join in their purification rites and pay their expenses, so that they can have their heads shaved. Then everyone will know there is no truth in these reports about you, but that you yourself are living in obedience to the law. 25As for the Gentile believers, we have written to them our decision that they should abstain from food sacrificed to idols, from blood, from the meat of strangled animals and from sexual immorality.'

26The next day Paul took the men and purified himself along with them. Then he went to the temple to give notice of the date when the days of purification would end and the offering would be made for each of them.

Paul arrested

27When the seven days were nearly over, some Jews from the province of Asia saw Paul at the temple. They stirred up the whole crowd and seized him, 28shouting, 'People of Israel, help us! This is the man who teaches everyone everywhere against our people and our law and this place. And besides, he has brought Greeks into the temple and defiled this holy place.' 29(They had previously seen Trophimus the Ephesian in the city with Paul and assumed that Paul had brought him into the temple.)

30The whole city was aroused, and the people came running from all directions. Seizing Paul, they dragged him from the temple, and immediately the gates were shut. 31While they were trying to kill him, news reached the commander of the Roman troops that the whole city of Jerusalem was in an uproar. 32He at once took some officers and soldiers and ran down to the crowd. When the rioters saw the commander and his soldiers, they stopped beating Paul.

33The commander came up and arrested him and ordered him to be bound with two chains. Then he asked who he was and what he had done. 34Some in the crowd shouted one thing and some another, and since the commander could not get at the truth because of the uproar, he ordered that Paul be taken into the barracks. 35When Paul reached the steps, the violence of the mob was so great he had to be carried by the soldiers. 36The crowd that followed kept shouting, 'Get rid of him!'

Paul speaks to the crowd

37As the soldiers were about to take Paul into the barracks, he asked the commander, 'May I say something to you?'

'Do you speak Greek?' he replied. 38'Aren't you the Egyptian who started a revolt and led four thousand terrorists out into the wilderness some time ago?'

39Paul answered, 'I am a Jew, from Tarsus in Cilicia, a citizen of no ordinary city. Please let me speak to the people.'

40Having received the commander's permission, Paul stood on the steps and motioned to the crowd. When they were all silent, he said to them in Aramaic*a*:

22 1'Brothers and fathers, listen now to my defence.'

2When they heard him speak to them in Aramaic, they became very quiet.

Then Paul said: 3'I am a Jew, born in Tarsus of Cilicia, but brought up in this city. I studied under Gamaliel and was thoroughly trained in the law of our ancestors. I was just as zealous for God as any of you are today. 4I persecuted the followers of this Way to their death, arresting both men and women and throwing them into prison, 5as the high priest and all the Council can themselves testify. I even obtained letters from them to their associates in Damascus, and went there to bring these people as prisoners to Jerusalem to be punished.

6'About noon as I came near Damascus, suddenly a bright light from heaven flashed around me. 7I fell to the ground and heard a voice say to me, "Saul! Saul! Why do you persecute me?"

8' "Who are you, Lord?" I asked.

' "I am Jesus of Nazareth, whom you are persecuting," he replied. 9My companions saw the light, but they did not understand the voice of him who was speaking to me.

10' "What shall I do, Lord?" I asked.

' "Get up," the Lord said, "and go into Damascus. There you will be told all that you have been assigned to do." 11My companions led me by the hand into Damascus, because the brilliance of the light had blinded me.

12'A man named Ananias came to see me. He was a devout observer of the law and

---

a 40 Or possibly *Hebrew*; also in 22:2

highly respected by all the Jews living there. ¹³He stood beside me and said, "Brother Saul, receive your sight!" And at that very moment I was able to see him.

¹⁴'Then he said: "The God of our ancestors has chosen you to know his will and to see the Righteous One and to hear words from his mouth. ¹⁵You will be his witness to all people of what you have seen and heard. ¹⁶And now what are you waiting for? Get up, be baptised and wash your sins away, calling on his name."

¹⁷'When I returned to Jerusalem and was praying at the temple, I fell into a trance ¹⁸and saw the Lord speaking to me. "Quick!" he said. "Leave Jerusalem immediately, because the people here will not accept your testimony about me."

¹⁹' "Lord," I replied, "these people know that I went from one synagogue to another to imprison and beat those who believe in you. ²⁰And when the blood of your martyr[a] Stephen was shed, I stood there giving my approval and guarding the clothes of those who were killing him."

²¹'Then the Lord said to me, "Go; I will send you far away to the Gentiles." '

Paul the Roman citizen

²²The crowd listened to Paul until he said this. Then they raised their voices and shouted, 'Rid the earth of him! He's not fit to live!'

²³As they were shouting and throwing off their cloaks and flinging dust into the air, ²⁴the commander ordered that Paul be taken into the barracks. He directed that he be flogged and interrogated in order to find out why the people were shouting at him like this. ²⁵As they stretched him out to flog him, Paul said to the centurion standing there, 'Is it legal for you to flog a Roman citizen who hasn't even been found guilty?'

²⁶When the centurion heard this, he went to the commander and reported it. 'What are you going to do?' he asked. 'This man is a Roman citizen.'

²⁷The commander went to Paul and asked, 'Tell me, are you a Roman citizen?'

'Yes, I am,' he answered.

Roman citizenship
Acts 22:25
Paul was born a Roman citizen, which means that his father must have been a Roman citizen too. This gave him several rights, including the right to appeal directly to the Roman Emperor. Other rights that Roman citizens held included voting, holding positions of authority and owning property. But they also had to pay taxes and serve in the army if called to do so.

²⁸Then the commander said, 'I had to pay a lot of money for my citizenship.'

'But I was born a citizen,' Paul replied.

²⁹Those who were about to interrogate him withdrew immediately. The commander himself was alarmed when he realised that he had put Paul, a Roman citizen, in chains.

Paul before the Sanhedrin

³⁰The commander wanted to find out exactly why Paul was being accused by the Jews. So the next day he released him and ordered the chief priests and all the members of the Sanhedrin to assemble. Then he brought Paul and set him before them.

23 Paul looked straight at the Sanhedrin and said, 'My brothers, I have fulfilled my duty to God in all good conscience to this day.' ²At this the high priest Ananias ordered those standing near Paul to strike him on the mouth. ³Then Paul said to him, 'God will strike you, you whitewashed wall! You sit there to judge me according to the law, yet you yourself violate the law by commanding that I be struck!'

---
[a] 20 Or *witness*

4 Those who were standing near Paul said, 'How dare you insult God's high priest!'

5 Paul replied, 'Brothers, I did not realise that he was the high priest; for it is written: "Do not speak evil about the ruler of your people."[a]'

6 Then Paul, knowing that some of them were Sadducees and the others Pharisees, called out in the Sanhedrin, 'My brothers, I am a Pharisee, descended from Pharisees. I stand on trial because of the hope of the resurrection of the dead.' 7 When he said this, a dispute broke out between the Pharisees and the Sadducees, and the assembly was divided. 8 (The Sadducees say that there is no resurrection, and that there are neither angels nor spirits, but the Pharisees believe all these things.)

9 There was a great uproar, and some of the teachers of the law who were Pharisees stood up and argued vigorously. 'We find nothing wrong with this man,' they said. 'What if a spirit or an angel has spoken to him?' 10 The dispute became so violent that the commander was afraid Paul would be torn to pieces by them. He ordered the troops to go down and take him away from them by force and bring him into the barracks.

11 The following night the Lord stood near Paul and said, 'Take courage! As you have testified about me in Jerusalem, so you must also testify in Rome.'

The plot to kill Paul

12 The next morning the Jews formed a conspiracy and bound themselves with an oath not to eat or drink until they had killed Paul. 13 More than forty men were involved in this plot. 14 They went to the chief priests and the elders and said, 'We have taken a solemn oath not to eat anything until we have killed Paul. 15 Now then, you and the Sanhedrin petition the commander to bring him before you on the pretext of wanting more accurate information about his case. We are ready to kill him before he gets here.'

16 But when the son of Paul's sister heard of this plot, he went into the barracks and told Paul.

17 Then Paul called one of the centurions and said, 'Take this young man to the commander; he has something to tell him.' 18 So he took him to the commander.

The centurion said, 'Paul, the prisoner, sent for me and asked me to bring this young man to you because he has something to tell you.'

19 The commander took the young man by the hand, drew him aside and asked, 'What is it you want to tell me?'

20 He said: 'The Jews have agreed to ask you to bring Paul before the Sanhedrin tomorrow on the pretext of wanting more accurate information about him. 21 Don't give in to them, because more than forty of them are waiting in ambush for him. They have taken an oath not to eat or drink until they have killed him. They are ready now, waiting for your consent to their request.'

22 The commander dismissed the young man with this warning: 'Don't tell anyone that you have reported this to me.'

Paul transferred to Caesarea

23 Then he called two of his centurions and ordered them, 'Get ready a detachment of two hundred soldiers, seventy horsemen and two hundred spearmen[b] to go to Caesarea at nine tonight. 24 Provide horses for Paul so that he may be taken safely to Governor Felix.'

25 He wrote a letter as follows:

26 Claudius Lysias,

To His Excellency, Governor Felix:

Greetings.

27 This man was seized by the Jews and they were about to kill him, but I came with my troops and rescued him, for I had learned that he is a Roman citizen. 28 I wanted to know why they were accusing him, so I brought him to their Sanhedrin. 29 I found that the accusation had to do with questions about their law, but there was no charge against him that deserved death or imprisonment. 30 When I was informed of a

---

[a] 5 Exodus 22:28 [b] 23 The meaning of the Greek for this word is uncertain.

plot to be carried out against the man, I sent him to you at once. I also ordered his accusers to present to you their case against him.

31 So the soldiers, carrying out their orders, took Paul with them during the night and brought him as far as Antipatris. 32 The next day they let the cavalry go on with him, while they returned to the barracks. 33 When the cavalry arrived in Caesarea, they delivered the letter to the governor and handed Paul over to him. 34 The governor read the letter and asked what province he was from. Learning that he was from Cilicia, 35 he said, 'I will hear your case when your accusers get here.' Then he ordered that Paul be kept under guard in Herod's palace.

Paul's trial before Felix

24 Five days later the high priest Ananias went down to Caesarea with some of the elders and a lawyer named Tertullus, and they brought their charges against Paul before the governor. 2 When Paul was called in, Tertullus presented his case before Felix: 'We have enjoyed a long period of peace under you, and your foresight has brought about reforms in this nation. 3 Everywhere and in every way, most excellent Felix, we acknowledge this with profound gratitude. 4 But in order not to weary you further, I would request that you be kind enough to hear us briefly.

5 'We have found this man to be a troublemaker, stirring up riots among the Jews all over the world. He is a ringleader of the Nazarene sect 6(7) and even tried to desecrate the temple; so we seized him. 8 By examining him yourself you will be able to learn the truth about all these charges we are bringing against him.'

9 The other Jews joined in the accusation, asserting that these things were true.

10 When the governor motioned for him to speak, Paul replied: 'I know that for a number of years you have been a judge over this nation; so I gladly make my defence. 11 You can easily verify that no more than twelve days ago I went up to Jerusalem to worship. 12 My accusers did not find me arguing with anyone at the temple, or stirring up a crowd in the synagogues or anywhere else in the city. 13 And they cannot prove to you the charges they are now making against me. 14 However, I admit that I worship the God of our ancestors as a follower of the Way, which they call a sect. I believe everything that is in accordance with the Law and that is written in the Prophets, 15 and I have the same hope in God as these people themselves have, that there will be a resurrection of both the righteous and the wicked. 16 So I strive always to keep my conscience clear before God and all people.

17 'After an absence of several years, I came to Jerusalem to bring my people gifts for the poor and to present offerings. 18 I was ceremonially clean when they found me in the temple courts doing this. There was no crowd with me, nor was I involved in any disturbance. 19 But there are some Jews from the province of Asia, who ought to be here before you and bring charges if they have anything against me. 20 Or these who are here should state what crime they found in me when I stood before the Sanhedrin— 21 unless it was this one thing I shouted as I stood in their presence: "It is concerning the resurrection of the dead that I am on trial before you today."'

22 Then Felix, who was well acquainted with the Way, adjourned the proceedings. 'When Lysias the commander comes,' he said, 'I will decide your case.' 23 He ordered the centurion to keep Paul under guard but to give him some freedom and permit his friends to take care of his needs.

24 Several days later Felix came with his wife Drusilla, who was Jewish. He sent for Paul and listened to him as he spoke about faith in Christ Jesus. 25 As Paul talked about righteousness, self-control and the judgment to come, Felix was afraid and said, 'That's enough for now! You may leave. When I find it convenient, I will send for you.' 26 At the same time he was hoping that Paul would offer him a bribe, so he sent for him frequently and talked with him.

27 When two years had passed, Felix was succeeded by Porcius Festus, but because Felix wanted to grant a favour to the Jews, he left Paul in prison.

Paul's trial before Festus

25 Three days after arriving in the province, Festus went up from Caesarea to Jerusalem, ²where the chief priests and the Jewish leaders appeared before him and presented the charges against Paul. ³They requested Festus, as a favour to them, to have Paul transferred to Jerusalem, for they were preparing an ambush to kill him along the way. ⁴Festus answered, 'Paul is being held at Caesarea, and I myself am going there soon. ⁵Let some of your leaders come with me, and if the man has done anything wrong, they can press charges against him there.'

⁶After spending eight or ten days with them, Festus went down to Caesarea. The next day he convened the court and ordered that Paul be brought before him. ⁷When Paul came in, the Jews who had come down from Jerusalem stood round him. They brought many serious charges against him, but they could not prove them.

⁸Then Paul made his defence: 'I have done nothing wrong against the Jewish law or against the temple or against Caesar.'

⁹Festus, wishing to do the Jews a favour, said to Paul, 'Are you willing to go up to Jerusalem and stand trial before me there on these charges?'

¹⁰Paul answered: 'I am now standing before Caesar's court, where I ought to be tried. I have not done any wrong to the Jews, as you yourself know very well. ¹¹If, however, I am guilty of doing anything deserving death, I do not refuse to die. But if the charges brought against me by these Jews are not true, no-one has the right to hand me over to them. I appeal to Caesar!'

¹²After Festus had conferred with his council, he declared: 'You have appealed to Caesar. To Caesar you will go!'

Festus consults King Agrippa

¹³A few days later King Agrippa and Bernice arrived at Caesarea to pay their respects to Festus. ¹⁴Since they were spending many days there, Festus discussed Paul's case with the king. He said: 'There is a man here whom Felix left as a prisoner. ¹⁵When I went to Jerusalem, the chief priests and the elders of the Jews brought charges against him and asked that he be condemned.

¹⁶'I told them that it is not the Roman custom to hand over anyone before they have faced their accusers and have had an opportunity to defend themselves against the charges. ¹⁷When they came here with me, I did not delay the case, but convened the court the next day and ordered the man to be brought in. ¹⁸When his accusers got up to speak, they did not charge him with any of the crimes I had expected. ¹⁹Instead, they had some points of dispute with him about their own religion and about a dead man named Jesus whom Paul claimed was alive. ²⁰I was at a loss how to investigate such matters; so I asked if he would be willing to go to Jerusalem and stand trial there on these charges. ²¹But when Paul made his appeal to be held over for the Emperor's decision, I ordered him to be held until I could send him to Caesar.'

²²Then Agrippa said to Festus, 'I would like to hear this man myself.'

He replied, 'Tomorrow you will hear him.'

Paul before Agrippa

²³The next day Agrippa and Bernice came with great pomp and entered the audience room with the high-ranking military officers and the prominent men of the city. At the command of Festus, Paul was brought in. ²⁴Festus said: 'King Agrippa, and all who are present with us, you see this man! The whole Jewish community has petitioned me about him in Jerusalem and here in Caesarea, shouting that he ought not to live any longer. ²⁵I found he had done nothing deserving of death, but because he made his appeal to the Emperor I decided to send him to Rome. ²⁶But I have nothing definite to write to His Majesty about him. Therefore I have brought him before all of you, and especially before you, King Agrippa, so that as a result of this investigation I may have something to write. ²⁷For I think it is unreasonable to send a prisoner on to Rome without specifying the charges against him.'

IN OTHER WORDS

Testify
Acts 26:5

A testimony is evidence given to support facts, for example in a court of law. The two stone tablets that Moses wrote the Ten Commandments on were known as 'the Testimony'. The word 'testimony' has also come to mean a person's story of how they became a Christian, or of what God has done in their life. Here, Paul gives his testimony to King Agrippa.

26 Then Agrippa said to Paul, 'You have permission to speak for yourself.'

So Paul motioned with his hand and began his defence: 2'King Agrippa, I consider myself fortunate to stand before you today as I make my defence against all the accusations of the Jews, 3and especially so because you are well acquainted with all the Jewish customs and controversies. Therefore, I beg you to listen to me patiently.

4'The Jewish people all know the way I have lived ever since I was a child, from the beginning of my life in my own country, and also in Jerusalem. 5They have known me for a long time and can testify, if they are willing, that I conformed to the strictest sect of our religion, living as a Pharisee. 6And now it is because of my hope in what God has promised our ancestors that I am on trial today. 7This is the promise our twelve tribes are hoping to see fulfilled as they earnestly serve God day and night. King Agrippa, it is because of this hope that the Jews are accusing me. 8Why should any of you consider it incredible that God raises the dead?

9'I too was convinced that I ought to do all that was possible to oppose the name of Jesus of Nazareth. 10And that is just what I did in Jerusalem. On the authority of the chief priests I put many of the Lord's people in prison, and when they were put to death, I cast my vote against them. 11Many a time I went from one synagogue to another to have them punished, and I tried to force them to blaspheme. I was so obsessed with persecuting them that I even hunted them down in foreign cities.

12'On one of these journeys I was going to Damascus with the authority and commission of the chief priests. 13About noon, King Agrippa, as I was on the road, I saw a light from heaven, brighter than the sun, blazing around me and my companions. 14We all fell to the ground, and I heard a voice saying to me in Aramaic,[a] "Saul, Saul, why do you persecute me? It is hard for you to kick against the goads."

15'Then I asked, "Who are you, Lord?"

'"I am Jesus, whom you are persecuting," the Lord replied. 16"Now get up and stand on your feet. I have appeared to you to appoint you as a servant and as a witness of what you have seen and will see of me. 17I will rescue you from your own people and from the Gentiles. I am sending you to them 18to open their eyes and turn them from darkness to light, and from the power of Satan to God, so that they may receive forgiveness of sins and a place among those who are sanctified by faith in me."

19'So then, King Agrippa, I was not disobedient to the vision from heaven. 20First to those in Damascus, then to those in Jerusalem and in all Judea, and then to the Gentiles, I preached that they should repent and turn to God and demonstrate their repentance by their deeds. 21That is why some Jews seized me in the temple courts and tried to kill me. 22But God has helped me to this very day; so I stand here and testify to small and great alike. I am saying nothing beyond what the prophets and Moses said would happen— 23that the Messiah would suffer and, as the first to rise from the dead, would bring the message of light to his own people and to the Gentiles.'

24At this point Festus interrupted Paul's defence. 'You are out of your mind, Paul!' he shouted. 'Your great learning is driving you insane.'

---

[a] 14 Or *Hebrew*

25 'I am not insane, most excellent Festus,' Paul replied. 'What I am saying is true and reasonable. 26 The king is familiar with these things, and I can speak freely to him. I am convinced that none of this has escaped his notice, because it was not done in a corner. 27 King Agrippa, do you believe the prophets? I know you do.'

28 Then Agrippa said to Paul, 'Do you think that in such a short time you can persuade me to be a Christian?'

29 Paul replied, 'Short time or long—I pray to God that not only you but all who are listening to me today may become what I am, except for these chains.'

30 The king rose, and with him the governor and Bernice and those sitting with them. 31 After they left the room, they began saying to one another, 'This man is not doing anything that deserves death or imprisonment.'

32 Agrippa said to Festus, 'This man could have been set free if he had not appealed to Caesar.'

Paul sails for Rome

27 When it was decided that we would sail for Italy, Paul and some other prisoners were handed over to a centurion named Julius, who belonged to the Imperial Regiment. 2 We boarded a ship from Adramyttium about to sail for ports along the coast of the province of Asia, and we put out to sea. Aristarchus, a Macedonian from Thessalonica, was with us.

3 The next day we landed at Sidon; and Julius, in kindness to Paul, allowed him to go to his friends so they might provide for his needs. 4 From there we put out to sea again and passed to the lee of Cyprus because the winds were against us. 5 When we had sailed across the open sea off the coast of Cilicia and Pamphylia, we landed at Myra in Lycia. 6 There the centurion found an Alexandrian ship sailing for Italy and put us on board. 7 We made slow headway for many days and had difficulty arriving off Cnidus. When the wind did not allow us to hold our course, we sailed to the lee of Crete, opposite Salmone. 8 We moved along the coast with difficulty and came to a place called Fair Havens, near the town of Lasea.

9 Much time had been lost, and sailing had already become dangerous because by now it was after the Day of Atonement.[a] So Paul warned them, 10 'Men, I can see that our voyage is going to be disastrous and bring great loss to ship and cargo, and to our own lives also.' 11 But the centurion, instead of listening to what Paul said, followed the advice of the pilot and of the owner of the ship. 12 Since the harbour was unsuitable to winter in, the majority decided that we should sail on, hoping to reach Phoenix and winter there. This was a harbour in Crete, facing both south-west and north-west.

The storm

13 When a gentle south wind began to blow, they saw their opportunity; so they weighed anchor and sailed along the shore of Crete. 14 Before very long, a wind of hurricane force, called the 'North-Easter', swept down from the island. 15 The ship was caught by the storm and could not head into the wind; so we gave way to it and were driven along. 16 As we passed to the lee of a small island called Cauda, we were hardly able to make the lifeboat secure, 17 so the men hoisted it aboard. Then they passed ropes under the

Travel by ship
Acts 27:2

In Paul's time, there were no cruise ships or ferries. Ships were used almost exclusively to transport goods or soldiers. Passengers were, however, allowed to travel on merchant ships if there was room after all the cargo had been loaded. Travel by sea was quite risky and so people usually preferred to travel by land.

---

[a] 9 That is, Yom Kippur

ship itself to hold it together. Because they were afraid they would run aground on the sand-bars of Syrtis, they lowered the sea anchor[a] and let the ship be driven along. 18We took such a violent battering from the storm that the next day they began to throw the cargo overboard. 19On the third day, they threw the ship's tackle overboard with their own hands. 20When neither sun nor stars appeared for many days and the storm continued raging, we finally gave up all hope of being saved.

21After they had gone a long time without food, Paul stood up before them and said: 'Men, you should have taken my advice not to sail from Crete; then you would have spared yourselves this damage and loss. 22But now I urge you to keep up your courage, because not one of you will be lost; only the ship will be destroyed. 23Last night an angel of the God whose I am and whom I serve stood beside me 24and said, "Do not be afraid, Paul. You must stand trial before Caesar; and God has graciously given you the lives of all who sail with you." 25So keep up your courage, men, for I have faith in God that it will happen just as he told me. 26Nevertheless, we must run aground on some island.'

The shipwreck

27On the fourteenth night we were still being driven across the Adriatic[b] Sea, when about midnight the sailors sensed they were approaching land. 28They took soundings and found that the water was forty metres deep. A short time later they took soundings again and found it was thirty metres deep. 29Fearing that we would be dashed against the rocks, they dropped four anchors from the stern and prayed for daylight. 30In an attempt to escape from the ship, the sailors let the lifeboat down into the sea, pretending they were going to lower some anchors from the bow. 31Then Paul said to the centurion and the soldiers, 'Unless these men stay with the ship, you cannot be saved.' 32So the soldiers cut the ropes that held the lifeboat and let it drift away.

33Just before dawn Paul urged them all to eat. 'For the last fourteen days,' he said, 'you have been in constant suspense and have gone without food—you haven't eaten anything. 34Now I urge you to take some food. You need it to survive. Not one of you will lose a single hair from his head.' 35After he said this, he took some bread and gave thanks to God in front of them all. Then he broke it and began to eat. 36They were all encouraged and ate some food themselves. 37Altogether there were 276 of us on board. 38When they had eaten as much as they wanted, they lightened the ship by throwing the grain into the sea.

39When daylight came, they did not recognise the land, but they saw a bay with a sandy beach, where they decided to run the ship aground if they could. 40Cutting loose the anchors, they left them in the sea and at the same time untied the ropes that held the rudders. Then they hoisted the foresail to the wind and made for the beach. 41But the ship struck a sand-bar and ran aground. The bow stuck fast and would not move, and the stern was broken to pieces by the pounding of the surf.

42The soldiers planned to kill the prisoners to prevent any of them from swimming away and escaping. 43But the centurion wanted to spare Paul's life and kept them from carrying out their plan. He ordered those who could swim to jump overboard first and get to land. 44The rest were to get there on planks or on other pieces of the ship. In this way everyone reached land safely.

Paul ashore on Malta

28 Once safely on shore, we found out that the island was called Malta. 2The islanders showed us unusual kindness. They built a fire and welcomed us all because it was raining and cold. 3Paul gathered a pile of brushwood and, as he put it on the fire, a viper, driven out by the heat, fastened itself on his hand. 4When the islanders saw the snake hanging from his hand, they said to each other, 'This man must be a murderer; for though he escaped from the sea, the goddess Justice has not allowed him to live.' 5But Paul shook the snake off into the fire and suffered no ill effects. 6The people expected him to swell

---

[a] 17 Or *the sails*   [b] 27 In ancient times the name referred to an area extending well south of Italy.

up or suddenly fall dead; but after waiting a long time and seeing nothing unusual happen to him, they changed their minds and said he was a god.

7There was an estate near by that belonged to Publius, the chief official of the island. He welcomed us to his home and showed us generous hospitality for three days. 8His father was ill in bed, suffering from fever and dysentery. Paul went in to see him and, after prayer, placed his hands on him and healed him. 9When this had happened, the rest of those on the island who were ill came and were cured. 10They honoured us in many ways; and when we were ready to sail, they furnished us with the supplies we needed.

Paul's arrival at Rome

11After three months we put out to sea in a ship that had wintered in the island—it was an Alexandrian ship with the figurehead of the twin gods Castor and Pollux. 12We put in at Syracuse and stayed there three days. 13From there we set sail and arrived at Rhegium. The next day the south wind came up, and on the following day we reached Puteoli. 14There we found some believers who invited us to spend a week with them. And so we came to Rome. 15The believers there had heard that we were coming, and they travelled as far as the Forum of Appius and the Three Taverns to meet us. At the sight of these people Paul thanked God and was encouraged. 16When we got to Rome, Paul was allowed to live by himself, with a soldier to guard him.

Paul preaches at Rome under guard

17Three days later he called together the local Jewish leaders. When they had assembled, Paul said to them: 'My brothers, although I have done nothing against our people or against the customs of our ancestors, I was arrested in Jerusalem and handed over to the Romans. 18They examined me and wanted to release me, because I was not guilty of any crime deserving death. 19The Jews objected, so I was compelled to make an appeal to Caesar. I certainly did not intend to bring any charge against my own people. 20For this reason I have asked to see you and talk with you. It is because of the hope of Israel that I am bound with this chain.'

21They replied, 'We have not received any letters from Judea concerning you, and none of our people who have come from there has reported or said anything bad about you. 22But we want to hear what your views are, for we know that people everywhere are talking against this sect.'

23They arranged to meet Paul on a certain day, and came in even larger numbers to the place where he was staying. He witnessed to them from morning till evening, explaining about the kingdom of God, and from the Law of Moses and from the Prophets he tried to persuade them about Jesus. 24Some were convinced by what he said, but others would not believe. 25They disagreed among themselves and began to leave after Paul had made this final statement: 'The Holy Spirit spoke the truth to your ancestors when he said through Isaiah the prophet:

26' "Go to this people and say,
 'You will be ever hearing but never
  understanding;
 you will be ever seeing but never
  perceiving.'
27For this people's heart has become
  calloused;
 they hardly hear with their ears,
 and they have closed their eyes.
Otherwise they might see with their eyes,
 hear with their ears,
 understand with their hearts
and turn, and I would heal them." *a*

28(29)'Therefore I want you to know that God's salvation has been sent to the Gentiles, and they will listen!'

30For two whole years Paul stayed there in his own rented house and welcomed all who came to see him. 31He proclaimed the kingdom of God and taught about the Lord Jesus Christ—with all boldness and without hindrance!

---

a 27 Isaiah 6:9,10 (see Septuagint)

Romans

INTRODUCTION

Romans

Author: Paul

Who to: Christians in Rome.

When: Probably during Paul's third missionary journey as he made plans to visit Rome, around AD 56.

Where: Rome was the capital city of the Roman Empire and is now the capital of Italy.

Did you know? Paul had never visited Rome when he wrote this letter. He did eventually get there, but as a prisoner.

Main theme: Paul writes confidently about God's power to save people. Everyone, both Jews and Gentiles, needs to be forgiven and put right with God, and that happens through God's grace alone. There is nothing that we can do to earn God's love and forgiveness; all we need is faith.

1 Paul, a servant of Christ Jesus, called to be an apostle and set apart for the gospel of God— ²the gospel he promised beforehand through his prophets in the Holy Scriptures ³regarding his Son, who as to his earthly life*ᵃ* was a descendant of David, ⁴and who through the Spirit of holiness was appointed the Son of God in power*ᵇ* by his resurrection from the dead: Jesus Christ our Lord. ⁵Through him we received grace and apostleship to call all the Gentiles to faith and obedience for his name's sake. ⁶And you also are among those Gentiles who are called to belong to Jesus Christ.

⁷To all in Rome who are loved by God and called to be his holy people:

Grace and peace to you from God our Father and from the Lord Jesus Christ.

Paul's longing to visit Rome

⁸First, I thank my God through Jesus Christ for all of you, because your faith is

---

ᵃ 3 Or *who according to the flesh*   *ᵇ* 4 Or *was declared with power to be the Son of God*

Resurrection
Romans 1:4
'Resurrection' means coming back to life after death. The resurrection of Jesus is of central importance to the Christian faith. Believers in Jesus will one day be raised to life and will be with him forever.

being reported all over the world. 9God, whom I serve in my spirit in preaching the gospel of his Son, is my witness how constantly I remember you 10in my prayers at all times; and I pray that now at last by God's will the way may be opened for me to come to you.

11I long to see you so that I may impart to you some spiritual gift to make you strong— 12that is, that you and I may be mutually encouraged by each other's faith. 13I do not want you to be unaware, brothers and sisters, that I planned many times to come to you (but have been prevented from doing so until now) in order that I might have a harvest among you, just as I have had among the other Gentiles.

14I am a debtor both to Greeks and non-Greeks, both to the wise and the foolish. 15That is why I am so eager to preach the gospel also to you who are in Rome.

16I am not ashamed of the gospel, because it is the power of God that brings salvation to everyone who believes: first to the Jew, then to the Gentile. 17For in the gospel the righteousness of God is revealed—a righteousness that is by faith from first to last,[a] just as it is written: 'The righteous will live by faith.'[b]

God's wrath against sinful humanity

18The wrath of God is being revealed from heaven against all the godlessness and wickedness of human beings who suppress the truth by their wickedness, 19since what may be known about God is plain to them, because God has made it plain to them. 20For since the creation of the world God's invisible qualities—his eternal power and divine nature—have been clearly seen, being understood from what has been made, so that people are without excuse.

21For although they knew God, they neither glorified him as God nor gave thanks to him, but their thinking became futile and their foolish hearts were darkened. 22Although they claimed to be wise, they became fools 23and exchanged the glory of the immortal God for images made to look like mortal human beings and birds and animals and reptiles.

24Therefore God gave them over in the sinful desires of their hearts to sexual impurity for the degrading of their bodies with one another. 25They exchanged the truth about God for a lie, and worshipped and served created things rather than the Creator—who is for ever praised. Amen.

26Because of this, God gave them over to shameful lusts. Even their women exchanged natural sexual relations for unnatural ones. 27In the same way the men also abandoned natural relations with women and were inflamed with lust for one another. Men committed shameful acts with other men, and received in themselves the due penalty for their error.

28Furthermore, just as they did not think it worth while to retain the knowledge of God, so God gave them over to a depraved mind, so that they do what ought not to be done. 29They have become filled with every kind of wickedness, evil, greed and depravity. They are full of envy, murder, strife, deceit and malice. They are gossips, 30slanderers, God-haters, insolent, arrogant and boastful; they invent ways of doing evil; they disobey their parents; 31they have no understanding, no fidelity, no love, no mercy. 32Although they know God's righteous decree that those who do such things deserve death, they not only continue to do these very things but also approve of those who practise them.

God's righteous judgment

2 You, therefore, have no excuse, you who pass judgment on someone else,

---

[a] 17 Or *is from faith to faith* [b] 17 Hab. 2:4

for at whatever point you judge another, you are condemning yourself, because you who pass judgment do the same things. ²Now we know that God's judgment against those who do such things is based on truth. ³So when you, a mere human, pass judgment on them and yet do the same things, do you think you will escape God's judgment? ⁴Or do you show contempt for the riches of his kindness, forbearance and patience, not realising that God's kindness is intended to lead you to repentance?

⁵But because of your stubbornness and your unrepentant heart, you are storing up wrath against yourself for the day of God's wrath, when his righteous judgment will be revealed. ⁶God 'will repay everyone according to what they have done.'[a] ⁷To those who by persistence in doing good seek glory, honour and immortality, he will give eternal life. ⁸But for those who are self-seeking and who reject the truth and follow evil, there will be wrath and anger. ⁹There will be trouble and distress for every human being who does evil: first for the Jew, then for the Gentile; ¹⁰but glory, honour and peace for everyone who does good: first for the Jew, then for the Gentile. ¹¹For God does not show favouritism.

¹²All who sin apart from the law will also perish apart from the law, and all who sin under the law will be judged by the law. ¹³For it is not those who hear the law who are righteous in God's sight, but it is those who obey the law who will be declared righteous. ¹⁴(Indeed, when Gentiles, who do not have the law, do by nature things required by the law, they are a law for themselves, even though they do not have the law. ¹⁵They show that the requirements of the law are written on their hearts, their consciences also bearing witness, and their thoughts now accusing, now even defending them.) ¹⁶This will take place on the day when God judges everyone's secrets through Jesus Christ, as my gospel declares.

The Jews and the law

¹⁷Now you, if you call yourself a Jew; if you rely on the law and boast in God; ¹⁸if you know his will and approve of what is superior because you are instructed by the law; ¹⁹if you are convinced that you are a guide for the blind, a light for those who are in the dark, ²⁰an instructor of the foolish, a teacher of infants, because you have in the law the embodiment of knowledge and truth— ²¹you, then, who teach others, do you not teach yourself? You who preach against stealing, do you steal? ²²You who say that people should not commit adultery, do you commit adultery? You who abhor idols, do you rob temples? ²³You who boast in the law, do you dishonour God by breaking the law? ²⁴As it is written: 'God's name is blasphemed among the Gentiles because of you.'[b]

²⁵Circumcision has value if you observe the law, but if you break the law, you have become as though you had not been circumcised. ²⁶If those who are not circumcised keep the law's requirements, will they not be regarded as though they were circumcised? ²⁷The one who is not circumcised physically and yet obeys the law will condemn you who, even though you have the[c] written code and circumcision, are a law-breaker.

²⁸A person is not a Jew who is one only outwardly, nor is circumcision merely outward and physical. ²⁹No, a person is a Jew who is one inwardly; and circumcision is circumcision of the heart, by the Spirit, not by the written code. Such a person's praise is not from other people, but from God.

God's faithfulness

3 What advantage, then, is there in being a Jew, or what value is there in circumcision? ²Much in every way! First of all, the Jews have been entrusted with the very words of God.

³What if some were unfaithful? Will their unfaithfulness nullify God's faithfulness? ⁴Not at all! Let God be true, and every human being a liar. As it is written:

'So that you may be proved right when
 you speak
 and prevail when you judge.'[d]

---

[a] 6 Psalm 62:12; Prov. 24:12   [b] 24 Isaiah 52:5 (see Septuagint); Ezek. 36:20,22   [c] 27 Or who, by means of a
[d] 4 Psalm 51:4

⁵But if our unrighteousness brings out God's righteousness more clearly, what shall we say? That God is unjust in bringing his wrath on us? (I am using a human argument.) ⁶Certainly not! If that were so, how could God judge the world? ⁷Someone might argue, 'If my falsehood enhances God's truthfulness and so increases his glory, why am I still condemned as a sinner?' ⁸Why not say—as we are being slanderously reported as saying and as some claim that we say—'Let us do evil that good may result'? Their condemnation is just!

No-one is righteous

⁹What shall we conclude then? Do we have any advantage? Not at all! We have already made the charge that Jews and Gentiles alike are all under the power of sin. ¹⁰As it is written:

> 'There is no-one righteous, not even one;
> 11   there is no-one who understands;
>   there is no-one who seeks God.
> ¹²All have turned away,
>   they have together become worthless;
>   there is no-one who does good,
>   not even one.'[a]
> ¹³'Their throats are open graves;
>   their tongues practise deceit.'[b]
> 'The poison of vipers is on their lips.'[c]
> 14   'Their mouths are full of cursing and
>   bitterness.'[d]
> ¹⁵'Their feet are swift to shed blood;
> 16   ruin and misery mark their ways,
> ¹⁷and the way of peace they do not know.'[e]
> 18   'There is no fear of God before their
>   eyes.'[f]

¹⁹Now we know that whatever the law says, it says to those who are under the law, so that every mouth may be silenced and the whole world held accountable to God. ²⁰Therefore no-one will be declared righteous in God's sight by observing the law; rather, through the law we become conscious of our sin.

Righteousness through faith

²¹But now apart from the law the righteousness of God has been made known, to which the Law and the Prophets testify. ²²This righteousness is given through faith in[g] Jesus Christ to all who believe. There is no difference between Jew and Gentile, ²³for all have sinned and fall short of the glory of God, ²⁴and all are justified freely by his grace through the redemption that came by Christ Jesus. ²⁵God presented Christ as a sacrifice of atonement,[h] through the shedding of his blood—to be received by faith. He did this to demonstrate his justice, because in his forbearance he had left the sins committed beforehand unpunished ²⁶—he did it to demonstrate his justice at the present time, so as to be just and the one who justifies those who have faith in Jesus.

²⁷Where, then, is boasting? It is excluded. Because of what law? The law that requires works? No, because of the 'law' that requires faith. ²⁸For we maintain that a person is justified by faith apart from observing the law. ²⁹Is God the God of Jews only? Is he not the God of Gentiles too? Yes, of Gentiles too, ³⁰since there is only one God, who will justify the circumcised by faith and the uncircumcised through that same faith. ³¹Do we, then, nullify the law by this faith? Not at all! Rather, we uphold the law.

Abraham justified by faith

4 What then shall we say that Abraham, the forefather of us Jews, discovered in

---

> **IN OTHER WORDS**
>
> **Atonement**
> Romans 3:25
> There's a clue to this word's meaning in its spelling. It means 'making at one' – putting things right between God and the human race. Atonement happened through sacrifices in the Old Testament (Exodus 29:36), and through the death and resurrection of Jesus in the New Testament.

---

[a] 12 Psalms 14:1-3; 53:1-3; Eccles. 7:20   [b] 13 Psalm 5:9   [c] 13 Psalm 140:3   [d] 14 Psalm 10:7 (see Septuagint)
[e] 17 Isaiah 59:7,8   [f] 18 Psalm 36:1   [g] 22 Or *through the faithfulness of*   [h] 25 The Greek for *sacrifice of atonement* refers to the atonement cover on the ark of the covenant (see Lev. 16:15,16).

this matter? ²If, in fact, Abraham was justified by works, he had something to boast about—but not before God. ³What does Scripture say? 'Abraham believed God, and it was credited to him as righteousness.'[a]

⁴Now to anyone who works, their wages are not credited to them as a gift, but as an obligation. ⁵However, to anyone who does not work but trusts God who justifies the ungodly, their faith is credited as righteousness. ⁶David says the same thing when he speaks of the blessedness of those to whom God credits righteousness apart from works:

⁷'Blessed are those
whose transgressions are forgiven,
whose sins are covered.
⁸Blessed are those
whose sin the Lord will never count
against them.'[b]

⁹Is this blessedness only for the circumcised, or also for the uncircumcised? We have been saying that Abraham's faith was credited to him as righteousness. ¹⁰Under what circumstances was it credited? Was it after he was circumcised, or before? It was not after, but before! ¹¹And he received circumcision as a sign, a seal of the righteousness that he had by faith while he was still uncircumcised. So then, he is the father of all who believe but have not been circumcised, in order that righteousness might be credited to them. ¹²And he is then also the father of the circumcised who not only are circumcised but who also follow in the footsteps of the faith that our father Abraham had before he was circumcised.

¹³It was not through the law that Abraham and his offspring received the promise that he would be heir of the world, but through the righteousness that comes by faith. ¹⁴For if those who depend on the law are heirs, faith means nothing and the promise is worthless, ¹⁵because the law brings wrath. And where there is no law there is no transgression.

¹⁶Therefore, the promise comes by faith, so that it may be by grace and may be guaranteed to all Abraham's offspring—not only to those who are of the law but also to those who have the faith of Abraham. He is the father of us all. ¹⁷As it is written: 'I have made you a father of many nations.'[c] He is our father in the sight of God, in whom he believed—the God who gives life to the dead and calls into being things that were not.

¹⁸Against all hope, Abraham in hope believed and so became the father of many nations, just as it had been said to him, 'So shall your offspring be.'[d] ¹⁹Without weakening in his faith, he faced the fact that his body was as good as dead—since he was about a hundred years old—and that Sarah's womb was also dead. ²⁰Yet he did not waver through unbelief regarding the promise of God, but was strengthened in his faith and gave glory to God, ²¹being fully persuaded that God had power to do what he had promised. ²²This is why 'it was credited to him as righteousness.' ²³The words 'it was credited to him' were written not for him alone, ²⁴but also for us, to whom God will credit righteousness—for us who believe in him who raised Jesus our Lord from the dead. ²⁵He was delivered over to death for our sins and was raised to life for our justification.

Peace and hope

5 Therefore, since we have been justified through faith, we[e] have peace with God through our Lord Jesus Christ, ²through whom we have gained access by faith into

IN OTHER WORDS

Justified
Romans 5:1
Justification is the process by which sinful people are made acceptable to a holy God. It's not through what we do or who we are. We are justified because Jesus died on the cross and took our sin on himself. All we need is faith in Jesus.

---

[a]3 Gen. 15:6; also in verse 22 [b]8 Psalm 32:1,2 [c]17 Gen. 17:5 [d]18 Gen. 15:5 [e]1 Many manuscripts *let us*

this grace in which we now stand. And we[a] boast in the hope of the glory of God. 3Not only so, but we[b] also glory in our sufferings, because we know that suffering produces perseverance; 4perseverance, character; and character, hope. 5And hope does not put us to shame, because God's love has been poured out into our hearts through the Holy Spirit, who has been given to us.

6You see, at just the right time, when we were still powerless, Christ died for the ungodly. 7Very rarely will anyone die for a righteous person, though for a good person someone might possibly dare to die. 8But God demonstrates his own love for us in this: while we were still sinners, Christ died for us.

9Since we have now been justified by his blood, how much more shall we be saved from God's wrath through him! 10For if, while we were God's enemies, we were reconciled to him through the death of his Son, how much more, having been reconciled, shall we be saved through his life! 11Not only is this so, but we also boast in God through our Lord Jesus Christ, through whom we have now received reconciliation.

Death through Adam, life through Christ

12Therefore, just as sin entered the world through one man, and death through sin, and in this way death came to all people, because all sinned—

13To be sure, sin was in the world before the law was given, but sin is not charged against anyone's account where there is no law. 14Nevertheless, death reigned from the time of Adam to the time of Moses, even over those who did not sin by breaking a command, as did Adam, who is a pattern of the one to come.

15But the gift is not like the trespass. For if the many died by the trespass of the one man, how much more did God's grace and the gift that came by the grace of the one man, Jesus Christ, overflow to the many! 16Nor can the gift of God be compared with the result of one man's sin: the judgment followed one sin and brought condemnation, but the gift followed many trespasses and brought justification. 17For if, by the trespass of the one man, death reigned through that one man, how much more will those who receive God's abundant provision of grace and of the gift of righteousness reign in life through the one man, Jesus Christ!

18Consequently, just as one trespass resulted in condemnation for all people, so also one righteous act resulted in justification and life for all. 19For just as through the disobedience of the one man the many were made sinners, so also through the obedience of the one man the many will be made righteous.

20The law was brought in so that the trespass might increase. But where sin increased, grace increased all the more, 21so that, just as sin reigned in death, so also grace might reign through righteousness to bring eternal life through Jesus Christ our Lord.

Dead to sin, alive in Christ

6 What shall we say, then? Shall we go on sinning, so that grace may increase? 2By no means! We are those who have died to sin; how can we live in it any longer? 3Or don't you know that all of us who were baptised into Christ Jesus were baptised into his death? 4We were therefore buried with him through baptism into death in order that, just as Christ was raised from the dead through the glory of the Father, we too may live a new life.

IN OTHER WORDS

Baptism
Romans 6:3
Originally an act of ceremonial cleansing for Jews, baptism was transformed by John the Baptist and is used by the church as a sign of cleansing and salvation that is open to all who believe.

---

[a] 2 Or let us [b] 3 Or let us

5If we have been united with him in a death like his, we will certainly also be united with him in a resurrection like his. 6For we know that our old self was crucified with him so that the body ruled by sin might be done away with,*a* that we should no longer be slaves to sin— 7because anyone who has died has been set free from sin.

8Now if we died with Christ, we believe that we will also live with him. 9For we know that since Christ was raised from the dead, he cannot die again; death no longer has mastery over him. 10The death he died, he died to sin once for all; but the life he lives, he lives to God.

11In the same way, count yourselves dead to sin but alive to God in Christ Jesus. 12Therefore do not let sin reign in your mortal body so that you obey its evil desires. 13Do not offer any part of yourself to sin as an instrument of wickedness, but rather offer yourselves to God as those who have been brought from death to life; and offer every part of yourself to him as an instrument of righteousness. 14For sin shall no longer be your master, because you are not under the law, but under grace.

Slaves to righteousness

15What then? Shall we sin because we are not under the law but under grace? By no means! 16Don't you know that when you offer yourselves to someone as obedient slaves, you are slaves of the one you obey— whether you are slaves to sin, which leads to death, or to obedience, which leads to righteousness? 17But thanks be to God that, though you used to be slaves to sin, you have come to obey from your heart the pattern of teaching that has now claimed your allegiance. 18You have been set free from sin and have become slaves to righteousness.

19I am using an example from everyday life because of your human limitations. Just as you used to offer yourselves as slaves to impurity and to ever-increasing wickedness, so now offer yourselves as slaves to righteousness leading to holiness. 20When you were slaves to sin, you were free from the control of righteousness. 21What benefit did you reap at that time from the things you are now ashamed of? Those things result in death! 22But now that you have been set free from sin and have become slaves of God, the benefit you reap leads to holiness, and the result is eternal life. 23For the wages of sin is death, but the gift of God is eternal life in*b* Christ Jesus our Lord.

Released from the law, bound to Christ

7 Do you not know, brothers and sisters—for I am speaking to those who know the law—that the law has authority over someone only as long as that person lives? 2For example, by law a married woman is bound to her husband as long as he is alive, but if her husband dies, she is released from the law that binds her to him. 3So then, if she marries another man while her husband is still alive, she is called an adulteress. But if her husband dies, she is released from that law and is not an adulteress if she marries another man.

4So, my brothers and sisters, you also died to the law through the body of Christ, that you might belong to another, to him who was raised from the dead, in order that we might bear fruit for God. 5For when we were controlled by our sinful nature,*c* the sinful passions aroused by the law were at work in us, so that we bore fruit for death. 6But now, by dying to what once bound us, we have been released from the law so that we serve in the new way of the Spirit, and not in the old way of the written code.

The law and sin

7What shall we say, then? Is the law sinful? Certainly not! Nevertheless, I would not have known what sin was had it not been for the law. For I would not have known what coveting really was if the law had not said, 'You shall not covet.'*d* 8But sin, seizing the opportunity afforded by the commandment, produced in me every kind of coveting. For apart from the law, sin was dead. 9Once I was alive apart from the law; but when the commandment came, sin sprang to life and I died. 10I found that the very commandment that was intended to bring life actually brought death. 11For sin,

---

a 6 Or *be rendered powerless* *b* 23 Or *through* *c* 5 Or *by the flesh* *d* 7 Exodus 20:17; Deut. 5:21

seizing the opportunity afforded by the commandment, deceived me, and through the commandment put me to death. 12So then, the law is holy, and the commandment is holy, righteous and good.

13Did that which is good, then, become death to me? By no means! Nevertheless, in order that sin might be recognised as sin, it used what is good to bring about my death, so that through the commandment sin might become utterly sinful.

14We know that the law is spiritual; but I am unspiritual, sold as a slave to sin. 15I do not understand what I do. For what I want to do I do not do, but what I hate I do. 16And if I do what I do not want to do, I agree that the law is good. 17As it is, it is no longer I myself who do it, but it is sin living in me. 18I know that good itself does not dwell in me, that is, in my sinful nature.[a] For I have the desire to do what is good, but I cannot carry it out. 19For I do not do the good I want to do, but the evil I do not want to do—this I keep on doing. 20Now if I do what I do not want to do, it is no longer I who do it, but it is sin living in me that does it.

21So I find this law at work: although I want to do good, evil is right there with me. 22For in my inner being I delight in God's law; 23but I see another law at work in me, waging war against the law of my mind and making me a prisoner of the law of sin at work within me. 24What a wretched man I am! Who will rescue me from this body of death? 25Thanks be to God, who delivers me through Jesus Christ our Lord!

So then, I myself in my mind am a slave to God's law, but in my sinful nature[b] a slave to the law of sin.

Life through the Spirit

8 Therefore, there is now no condemnation for those who are in Christ Jesus, 2because through Christ Jesus the law of the Spirit who gives life has set you[c] free from the law of sin and death. 3For what the law was powerless to do because it was weakened by the sinful nature,[d] God did by sending his own Son in the likeness of sinful humanity to be a sin offering.[e] And so he condemned sin in human flesh, 4in order that the righteous requirement of the law might be fully met in us, who do not live according to the sinful nature but according to the Spirit.

5Those who live according to the sinful nature have their minds set on what that nature desires; but those who live in accordance with the Spirit have their minds set on what the Spirit desires. 6The mind controlled by the sinful nature[f] is death, but the mind controlled by the Spirit is life and peace. 7The sinful mind[g] is hostile to God; it does not submit to God's law, nor can it do so. 8Those controlled by the sinful nature cannot please God.

9You, however, are not controlled by the sinful nature but are in the Spirit, if indeed the Spirit of God lives in you. And if anyone does not have the Spirit of Christ, they do not belong to Christ. 10But if Christ is in you, then even though your body is subject to death because of sin, the Spirit gives life[h] because of righteousness. 11And if the Spirit of him who raised Jesus from the dead is living in you, he who raised Christ from the dead will also give life to your mortal bodies because of[i] his Spirit who lives in you.

12Therefore, brothers and sisters, we have an obligation—but it is not to the sinful nature, to live according to it. 13For if you live according to the sinful nature, you will die; but if by the Spirit you put to death the misdeeds of the body, you will live.

14For those who are led by the Spirit of God are the children of God. 15The Spirit you received does not make you slaves, so that you live in fear again; rather, the Spirit you received brought about your adoption to sonship.[j] And by him we cry, 'Abba,[k] Father.' 16The Spirit himself testifies with our spirit that we are God's children. 17Now if we are children, then we are heirs—heirs of God and co-heirs with Christ, if indeed we share in his sufferings in order that we may also share in his glory.

---

[a] 18 Or *my flesh* [b] 25 Or *in the flesh* [c] 2 The Greek is singular; some manuscripts *me* [d] 3 Or *the flesh*; also in verses 4, 5, 8, 9, 12 and 13 [e] 3 Or *humanity, for sin* [f] 6 Or *mind set on the flesh* [g] 7 Or *the mind set on the flesh* [h] 10 Or *you, your body is dead because of sin, yet your spirit is alive* [i] 11 Some manuscripts *bodies through* [j] 15 The Greek word for *adoption to sonship* is a term referring to the full legal standing of an adopted male heir in Roman culture. [k] 15 Aramaic for *Father*

> **IN OTHER WORDS**
>
> **Abba**
> Romans 8:15
> Aramaic was the common language spoken in Israel during Jesus' time, and Abba means 'Daddy' in Aramaic. It shows how close Jesus was to his Father (Mark 14:36), and how close we can be too.

Present suffering and future glory

18I consider that our present sufferings are not worth comparing with the glory that will be revealed in us. 19The creation waits in eager expectation for the children of God to be revealed. 20For the creation was subjected to frustration, not by its own choice, but by the will of the one who subjected it, in hope 21that[a] the creation itself will be liberated from its bondage to decay and brought into the freedom and glory of the children of God.

22We know that the whole creation has been groaning as in the pains of childbirth right up to the present time. 23Not only so, but we ourselves, who have the firstfruits of the Spirit, groan inwardly as we wait eagerly for our adoption, the redemption of our bodies. 24For in this hope we were saved. But hope that is seen is no hope at all. Who hopes for what they already have? 25But if we hope for what we do not yet have, we wait for it patiently.

26In the same way, the Spirit helps us in our weakness. We do not know what we ought to pray for, but the Spirit himself intercedes for us through wordless groans. 27And he who searches our hearts knows the mind of the Spirit, because the Spirit intercedes for God's people in accordance with the will of God.

28And we know that in all things God works for the good of those who love him, who[b] have been called according to his purpose. 29For those God foreknew he also predestined to be conformed to the image of his Son, that he might be the firstborn among many brothers and sisters. 30And those he predestined, he also called; those he called, he also justified; those he justified, he also glorified.

More than conquerors

31What, then, shall we say in response to these things? If God is for us, who can be against us? 32He who did not spare his own Son, but gave him up for us all—how will he not also, along with him, graciously give us all things? 33Who will bring any charge against those whom God has chosen? It is God who justifies. 34Who then can condemn? No-one. Christ Jesus who died—more than that, who was raised to life—is at the right hand of God and is also interceding for us. 35Who shall separate us from the love of Christ? Shall trouble or hardship or persecution or famine or nakedness or danger or sword? 36As it is written:

> 'For your sake we face death all day long;
> we are considered as sheep to be
>   slaughtered.'[c]

37No, in all these things we are more than conquerors through him who loved us. 38For I am convinced that neither death nor life, neither angels nor demons,[d] neither the present nor the future, nor any powers, 39neither height nor depth, nor anything else in all creation, will be able to separate us from the love of God that is in Christ Jesus our Lord.

Paul's anguish over Israel

9 I speak the truth in Christ—I am not lying, my conscience confirms it through the Holy Spirit— 2I have great sorrow and unceasing anguish in my heart. 3For I could wish that I myself were cursed and cut off from Christ for the sake of my people, those of my own race, 4the people of Israel. Theirs is the adoption; theirs the divine glory, the covenants, the receiving of the law, the temple worship and the promises. 5Theirs are the patriarchs, and from them is traced the human ancestry of the

---

[a] 20,21 Or *subjected it in hope.* 21*For* [b] 28 Or *that all things work together for good to those who love God, who;* or *that in all things God works together with those who love him to bring about what is good—with those who*
[c] 36 Psalm 44:22 [d] 38 Or *nor heavenly rulers*

Messiah, who is God over all, for ever praised!*a* Amen.

God's sovereign choice

6It is not as though God's word had failed. For not all who are descended from Israel are Israel. **7**Nor because they are his descendants are they all Abraham's children. On the contrary, 'It is through Isaac that your offspring will be reckoned.'*b* **8**In other words, it is not the natural children who are God's children, but it is the children of the promise who are regarded as Abraham's offspring. **9**For this was how the promise was stated: 'At the appointed time I will return, and Sarah will have a son.'*c*

10Not only that, but Rebekah's children were conceived at the same time by our father Isaac. **11**Yet, before the twins were born or had done anything good or bad—in order that God's purpose in election might stand: **12**not by works but by him who calls—she was told, 'The older will serve the younger.'*d* **13**Just as it is written: 'Jacob I loved, but Esau I hated.'*e*

14What then shall we say? Is God unjust? Not at all! **15**For he says to Moses,

'I will have mercy on whom I have mercy,
  and I will have compassion on whom I have compassion.'*f*

16It does not, therefore, depend on human desire or effort, but on God's mercy. **17**For Scripture says to Pharaoh: 'I raised you up for this very purpose, that I might display my power in you and that my name might be proclaimed in all the earth.'*g* **18**Therefore God has mercy on whom he wants to have mercy, and he hardens whom he wants to harden.

19One of you will say to me: 'Then why does God still blame us? For who is able to resist his will?' **20**But who are you, a mere human being, to talk back to God? 'Shall what is formed say to the one who formed it, "Why did you make me like this?" '*h* **21**Does not the potter have the right to make out of the same lump of clay some pottery for noble purposes and some for disposal of refuse?

22What if God, although choosing to show his wrath and make his power known, bore with great patience the objects of his wrath—prepared for destruction? **23**What if he did this to make the riches of his glory known to the objects of his mercy, whom he prepared in advance for glory— **24**even us, whom he also called, not only from the Jews but also from the Gentiles? **25**As he says in Hosea:

'I will call them "my people" who are not my people;
  and I will call her "my loved one" who is not my loved one,'*i*

26and,

'In the very place where it was said to them,
  "You are not my people,"
 they will be called "children of the living God".'*j*

27Isaiah cries out concerning Israel:

'Though the number of the Israelites be like the sand by the sea,
  only the remnant will be saved.
28For the Lord will carry out
  his sentence on earth with speed and finality.'*k*

29It is just as Isaiah said previously:

'Unless the Lord Almighty
  had left us descendants,
we would have become like Sodom,
  we would have been like Gomorrah.'*l*

Israel's unbelief

30What then shall we say? That the Gentiles, who did not pursue righteousness, have obtained it, a righteousness that is by faith; **31**but the people of Israel, who pursued the law as the way of righteousness, have not attained their goal. **32**Why not? Because they pursued it not by faith but as if it were by works. They stumbled over the 'stumbling stone'. **33**As it is written:

'See, I lay in Zion a stone that causes people to stumble
  and a rock that makes them fall,

---

a 5 Or *Messiah, who is over all. God be for ever praised!* Or *Messiah. God who is over all be for ever praised!*
b 7 Gen. 21:12 *c* 9 Gen. 18:10,14 *d* 12 Gen. 25:23 *e* 13 Mal. 1:2,3 *f* 15 Exodus 33:19 *g* 17 Exodus 9:16
h 20 Isaiah 29:16; 45:9 *i* 25 Hosea 2:23 *j* 26 Hosea 1:10 *k* 28 Isaiah 10:22,23 (see Septuagint) *l* 29 Isaiah 1:9

and the one who believes in him will never be put to shame.'[a]

10 Brothers and sisters, my heart's desire and prayer to God for the Israelites is that they may be saved. 2For I can testify about them that they are zealous for God, but their zeal is not based on knowledge. 3Since they did not know the righteousness of God and sought to establish their own, they did not submit to God's righteousness. 4Christ is the culmination of the law so that there may be righteousness for everyone who believes.

5Moses writes this about the righteousness that is by the law: 'Whoever does these things will live by them.'[b] 6But the righteousness that is by faith says: 'Do not say in your heart, "Who will ascend into heaven?"'[c] (that is, to bring Christ down) 7'or "Who will descend into the deep?"'[d] (that is, to bring Christ up from the dead). 8But what does it say? 'The word is near you; it is in your mouth and in your heart,'[e] that is, the message concerning faith that we proclaim: 9if you declare with your mouth, 'Jesus is Lord,' and believe in your heart that God raised him from the dead, you will be saved. 10For it is with your heart that you believe and are justified, and it is with your mouth that you profess your faith and are saved. 11As Scripture says, 'Anyone who believes in him will never be put to shame.'[f] 12For there is no difference between Jew and Gentile—the same Lord is Lord of all and richly blesses all who call on him, 13for, 'Everyone who calls on the name of the Lord will be saved.'[g]

14How, then, can they call on the one they have not believed in? And how can they believe in the one of whom they have not heard? And how can they hear without someone preaching to them? 15And how can anyone preach unless they are sent? As it is written: 'How beautiful are the feet of those who bring good news!'[h]

16But not all the Israelites accepted the good news. For Isaiah says, 'Lord, who has believed our message?'[i] 17Consequently, faith comes from hearing the message, and the message is heard through the word about Christ. 18But I ask: did they not hear? Of course they did:

'Their voice has gone out into all the earth,
their words to the ends of the world.'[j]

19Again I ask: did Israel not understand? First, Moses says,

'I will make you envious by those who are not a nation;
I will make you angry by a nation that has no understanding.'[k]

20And Isaiah boldly says,

'I was found by those who did not seek me;
I revealed myself to those who did not ask for me.'[l]

21But concerning Israel he says,

'All day long I have held out my hands
to a disobedient and obstinate people.'[m]

The remnant of Israel

11 I ask then: did God reject his people? By no means! I am an Israelite myself, a descendant of Abraham, from the tribe of Benjamin. 2God did not reject his people, whom he foreknew. Don't you know what Scripture says in the passage about Elijah—how he appealed to God against Israel: 3'Lord, they have killed your prophets and torn down your altars; I am the only one left, and they are trying to kill me'[n]? 4And what was God's answer to him? 'I have reserved for myself seven thousand who have not bowed the knee to Baal.'[o] 5So too, at the present time there is a remnant chosen by grace. 6And if by grace, then it cannot be based on works; if it were, grace would no longer be grace.

7What then? What the people of Israel sought so earnestly they did not obtain. The elect among them did, but the others were hardened, 8as it is written:

---

[a] 33 Isaiah 8:14; 28:16   [b] 5 Lev. 18:5   [c] 6 Deut. 30:12   [d] 7 Deut. 30:13   [e] 8 Deut. 30:14   [f] 11 Isaiah 28:16 (see Septuagint)   [g] 13 Joel 2:32   [h] 15 Isaiah 52:7   [i] 16 Isaiah 53:1   [j] 18 Psalm 19:4   [k] 19 Deut. 32:21   [l] 20 Isaiah 65:1   [m] 21 Isaiah 65:2   [n] 3 1 Kings 19:10,14   [o] 4 1 Kings 19:18

'God gave them a spirit of stupor,
  eyes that could not see
  and ears that could not hear,
to this very day.'[a]

⁹And David says:

'May their table become a snare and a trap,
  a stumbling-block and a retribution for them.
¹⁰May their eyes be darkened so they cannot see,
  and their backs be bent for ever.'[b]

Ingrafted branches

¹¹Again I ask: did they stumble so as to fall beyond recovery? Not at all! Rather, because of their transgression, salvation has come to the Gentiles to make Israel envious. ¹²But if their transgression means riches for the world, and their loss means riches for the Gentiles, how much greater riches will their fulness bring!

¹³I am talking to you Gentiles. Inasmuch as I am the apostle to the Gentiles, I make much of my ministry ¹⁴in the hope that I may somehow arouse my own people to envy and save some of them. ¹⁵For if their rejection brought reconciliation to the world, what will their acceptance be but life from the dead? ¹⁶If the part of the dough offered as firstfruits is holy, then the whole batch is holy; if the root is holy, so are the branches.

¹⁷If some of the branches have been broken off, and you, though a wild olive shoot, have been grafted in among the others and now share in the nourishing sap from the olive root, ¹⁸do not consider yourself to be superior to those other branches. If you do, consider this: you do not support the root, but the root supports you. ¹⁹You will say then, 'Branches were broken off so that I could be grafted in.' ²⁰Granted. But they were broken off because of unbelief, and you stand by faith. Do not be arrogant, but tremble. ²¹For if God did not spare the natural branches, he will not spare you either.

²²Consider therefore the kindness and sternness of God: sternness to those who fell, but kindness to you, provided that you continue in his kindness. Otherwise, you also will be cut off. ²³And if they do not persist in unbelief, they will be grafted in, for God is able to graft them in again. ²⁴After all, if you were cut out of an olive tree that is wild by nature, and contrary to nature were grafted into a cultivated olive tree, how much more readily will these, the natural branches, be grafted into their own olive tree!

All Israel will be saved

²⁵I do not want you to be ignorant of this mystery, brothers and sisters, so that you may not think you are superior: Israel has experienced a hardening in part until the full number of the Gentiles has come in, ²⁶and in this way[c] all Israel will be saved. As it is written:

'The deliverer will come from Zion;
  he will turn godlessness away from Jacob.
²⁷And this is[d] my covenant with them
  when I take away their sins.'[e]

making Connections

Grafting
Romans 11:17

To improve the flavour and quality of fruit, gardeners will sometimes graft a branch from one tree onto another. A small cut is made in the bark of the tree, and the branch that is being grafted is inserted into the cut and then bound in place. The tree then accepts the new branch and they grow together as one. In Paul's example, the Jews are the original olive tree and the Gentiles are a branch from a wild olive tree that has been grafted in.

---

[a] 8 Deut. 29:4; Isaiah 29:10   [b] 10 Psalm 69:22,23   [c] 26 Or *and so*   [d] 27 Or *will be*   [e] 27 Isaiah 59:20,21; 27:9 (see Septuagint); Jer. 31:33,34

28As far as the gospel is concerned, they are enemies for your sake; but as far as election is concerned, they are loved on account of the patriarchs, 29for God's gifts and his call are irrevocable. 30Just as you who were at one time disobedient to God have now received mercy as a result of their disobedience, 31so they too have now become disobedient in order that they too may now[a] receive mercy as a result of God's mercy to you. 32For God has bound everyone over to disobedience so that he may have mercy on them all.

Doxology

33Oh, the depth of the riches of the wisdom
  and[b] knowledge of God!
How unsearchable his judgments,
  and his paths beyond tracing out!
34'Who has known the mind of the Lord?
  Or who has been his counsellor?'[c]
35'Who has ever given to God,
  that God should repay them?'[d]
36For from him and through him and to
  him are all things.
To him be the glory for ever! Amen.

A living sacrifice

12 Therefore, I urge you, brothers and sisters, in view of God's mercy, to offer your bodies as a living sacrifice, holy and pleasing to God—this is your true worship. 2Do not conform to the pattern of this world, but be transformed by the renewing of your mind. Then you will be able to test and approve what God's will is— his good, pleasing and perfect will.

Humble service in the body of Christ

3For by the grace given me I say to every one of you: do not think of yourself more highly than you ought, but rather think of yourself with sober judgment, in accordance with the faith God has distributed to each of you. 4For just as each of us has one body with many members, and these members do not all have the same function, 5so in Christ we, though many, form one body, and each member belongs to all the others. 6We have different gifts, according to the grace given to each of us. If your gift is prophesying, then prophesy in accordance with your[e] faith; 7if it is serving, then serve; if it is teaching, then teach; 8if it is to encourage, then give encouragement; if it is giving, then give generously; if it is to lead,[f] do it diligently; if it is to show mercy, do it cheerfully.

Love in action

9Love must be sincere. Hate what is evil; cling to what is good. 10Be devoted to one another in love. Honour one another above yourselves. 11Never be lacking in zeal, but keep your spiritual fervour, serving the Lord. 12Be joyful in hope, patient in affliction, faithful in prayer. 13Share with the Lord's people who are in need. Practise hospitality.

14Bless those who persecute you; bless and do not curse. 15Rejoice with those who rejoice; mourn with those who mourn. 16Live in harmony with one another. Do not be proud, but be willing to associate with people of low position.[g] Do not think you are superior.

17Do not repay anyone evil for evil. Be careful to do what is right in the eyes of everyone. 18If it is possible, as far as it depends on you, live at peace with everyone. 19Do not take revenge, my dear friends, but leave room for God's wrath, for it is written: 'It is mine to avenge; I will repay,'[h] says the Lord. 20On the contrary:

> **IN OTHER WORDS**
>
> **Blessing**
> Romans 12:14
>
> To bless someone is to declare or wish God's goodness on them, both spiritually and materially. A blessing isn't just nice words; it also has the power to make them happen. Even if someone was blessed by mistake, once the words were spoken they couldn't be taken back. Read Numbers 6:24 for a wonderful Old Testament blessing.

---

[a]31 Some manuscripts do not have *now*. [b]33 Or *riches and the wisdom and the* [c]34 Isaiah 40:13 [d]35 Job 41:11 [e]6 Or *the* [f]8 Or *to provide for others* [g]16 Or *willing to do menial work* [h]19 Deut. 32:35

'If your enemy is hungry, feed him;
  if he is thirsty, give him something to drink.
In doing this, you will heap burning coals on his head.'[a]

21 Do not be overcome by evil, but overcome evil with good.

Submission to governing authorities

13 Let everyone be subject to the governing authorities, for there is no authority except that which God has established. The authorities that exist have been established by God. 2 Consequently, whoever rebels against the authority is rebelling against what God has instituted, and those who do so will bring judgment on themselves. 3 For rulers hold no terror for those who do right, but for those who do wrong. Do you want to be free from fear of the one in authority? Then do what is right and you will be commended. 4 For the one in authority is God's servant for your good. But if you do wrong, be afraid, for rulers do not bear the sword for no reason. They are God's servants, agents of wrath to bring punishment on the wrongdoer. 5 Therefore, it is necessary to submit to the authorities, not only because of possible punishment but also as a matter of conscience.

6 This is also why you pay taxes, for the authorities are God's servants, who give their full time to governing. 7 Give to everyone what you owe: if you owe taxes, pay taxes; if revenue, then revenue; if respect, then respect; if honour, then honour.

Love fulfils the law

8 Let no debt remain outstanding, except the continuing debt to love one another, for whoever loves others has fulfilled the law. 9 The commandments, 'You shall not commit adultery,' 'You shall not murder,' 'You shall not steal,' 'You shall not covet,'[b] and whatever other command there may be, are summed up in this one command: 'Love your neighbour as yourself.'[c] 10 Love does no harm to its neighbour. Therefore love is the fulfilment of the law.

The day is near

11 And do this, understanding the present time. The hour has already come for you to wake up from your slumber, because our salvation is nearer now than when we first believed. 12 The night is nearly over; the day is almost here. So let us put aside the deeds of darkness and put on the armour of light. 13 Let us behave decently, as in the daytime, not in carousing and drunkenness, not in sexual immorality and debauchery, not in dissension and jealousy. 14 Rather, clothe yourselves with the Lord Jesus Christ, and do not think about how to gratify the desires of the sinful nature.[d]

The weak and the strong

14 Accept those whose faith is weak, without quarrelling over disputable matters. 2 One person's faith allows them to eat everything, but another person, whose faith is weak, eats only vegetables. 3 The one who eats everything must not treat with contempt the one who does not, and the one who does not eat everything must not judge the one who does, for God has accepted that person. 4 Who are you to judge someone else's servant? To their own master they stand or fall. And they will stand, for the Lord is able to make them stand.

5 Some consider one day more sacred than another; others consider every day alike. Everyone should be fully convinced in their own mind. 6 Those who regard one day as special do so to the Lord. Those who eat meat do so to the Lord, for they give thanks

IN OTHER WORDS

Sacred
Romans 14:5
'Sacred' is another word for 'holy', something that is set apart for a spiritual use.

---

[a] 20 Prov. 25:21,22 [b] 9 Exodus 20:13-15,17; Deut. 5:17-19,21 [c] 9 Lev. 19:18 [d] 14 Or the flesh

to God; and those who abstain do so to the Lord and give thanks to God. 7For we do not live to ourselves alone and we do not die to ourselves alone. 8If we live, we live to the Lord; and if we die, we die to the Lord. So, whether we live or die, we belong to the Lord. 9For this very reason, Christ died and returned to life so that he might be the Lord of both the dead and the living.

10You, then, why do you judge your brother or sister? Or why do you treat your brother or sister with contempt? For we will all stand before God's judgment seat. 11It is written:

'"As surely as I live," says the Lord,
"Every knee will bow before me;
  every tongue will confess to God."' *a*

12So then, we will all give an account of ourselves to God.

13Therefore let us stop passing judgment on one another. Instead, make up your mind not to put any stumbling-block or obstacle in the way of a brother or sister. 14I am convinced, being fully persuaded in the Lord Jesus, that nothing is unclean in itself. But if anyone regards something as unclean, then for that person it is unclean. 15If your brother or sister is distressed because of what you eat, you are no longer acting in love. Do not by your eating destroy your brother or sister for whom Christ died. 16Therefore do not let what you know is good be spoken of as evil. 17For the kingdom of God is not a matter of eating and drinking, but of righteousness, peace and joy in the Holy Spirit, 18because anyone who serves Christ in this way is pleasing to God and receives human approval.

19Let us therefore make every effort to do what leads to peace and to mutual edification. 20Do not destroy the work of God for the sake of food. All food is clean, but it is wrong for a person to eat anything that causes someone else to stumble. 21It is better not to eat meat or drink wine or to do anything else that will cause your brother or sister to fall.

22So whatever you believe about these things keep between yourself and God. Blessed are those who do not condemn themselves by what they approve. 23But those who have doubts are condemned if they eat, because their eating is not from faith; and everything that does not come from faith is sin.

15

We who are strong ought to bear with the failings of the weak and not to please ourselves. 2We should all please our neighbours for their good, to build them up. 3For even Christ did not please himself but, as it is written: 'The insults of those who insult you have fallen on me.' *b* 4For everything that was written in the past was written to teach us, so that through the endurance taught in the Scriptures and the encouragement they provide we might have hope.

5May the God who gives endurance and encouragement give you the same attitude of mind toward each other that Christ Jesus had, 6so that with one mind and one voice you may glorify the God and Father of our Lord Jesus Christ.

7Accept one another, then, just as Christ accepted you, in order to bring praise to God. 8For I tell you that Christ has become a servant of the Jews*c* on behalf of God's truth, so that the promises made to the patriarchs might be confirmed 9and, moreover, that the Gentiles might glorify God for his mercy. As it is written:

'Therefore I will praise you among the
    Gentiles;
  I will sing the praises of your name.' *d*

10Again, it says,

'Rejoice, you Gentiles, with his people.' *e*

11And again,

'Praise the Lord, all you Gentiles;
  let all the peoples extol him.' *f*

12And again, Isaiah says,

'The Root of Jesse will spring up,
  one who will arise to rule over the
    nations;
  in him the Gentiles will hope.' *g*

---

a 11 Isaiah 45:23 *b* 3 Psalm 69:9 *c* 8 Greek *circumcision* *d* 9 2 Samuel 22:50; Psalm 18:49 *e* 10 Deut. 32:43
f 11 Psalm 117:1 *g* 12 Isaiah 11:10 (see Septuagint)

¹³May the God of hope fill you with all joy and peace as you trust in him, so that you may overflow with hope by the power of the Holy Spirit.

Paul the minister to the Gentiles

¹⁴I myself am convinced, my brothers and sisters, that you yourselves are full of goodness, filled with knowledge and competent to instruct one another. ¹⁵Yet I have written to you quite boldly on some points to remind you of them again, because of the grace God gave me ¹⁶to be a minister of Christ Jesus to the Gentiles. He gave me the priestly duty of proclaiming the gospel of God, so that the Gentiles might become an offering acceptable to God, sanctified by the Holy Spirit.

¹⁷Therefore I glory in Christ Jesus in my service to God. ¹⁸I will not venture to speak of anything except what Christ has accomplished through me in leading the Gentiles to obey God by what I have said and done— ¹⁹by the power of signs and wonders, through the power of the Spirit of God. So from Jerusalem all the way round to Illyricum, I have fully proclaimed the gospel of Christ. ²⁰It has always been my ambition to preach the gospel where Christ was not known, so that I would not be building on someone else's foundation. ²¹Rather, as it is written:

> 'Those who were not told about him will see,
> and those who have not heard will understand.'ᵃ

²²This is why I have often been hindered from coming to you.

Paul's plan to visit Rome

²³But now that there is no more place for me to work in these regions, and since I have been longing for many years to visit you, ²⁴I plan to do so when I go to Spain. I hope to see you while passing through and that you will assist me on my journey there, after I have enjoyed your company for a while. ²⁵Now, however, I am on my way to Jerusalem in the service of the Lord's people there. ²⁶For Macedonia and Achaia were pleased to make a contribution for the poor among the Lord's people in Jerusalem. ²⁷They were pleased to do it, and indeed they owe it to them. For if the Gentiles have shared in the Jews' spiritual blessings, they owe it to the Jews to share with them their material blessings. ²⁸So after I have completed this task and have made sure that they have received this fruit, I will go to Spain and visit you on the way. ²⁹I know that when I come to you, I will come in the full measure of the blessing of Christ.

³⁰I urge you, brothers and sisters, by our Lord Jesus Christ and by the love of the Spirit, to join me in my struggle by praying to God for me. ³¹Pray that I may be kept safe from the unbelievers in Judea and that the contribution I take to Jerusalem may be favourably received by the Lord's people there, ³²so that by God's will I may come to you with joy and together with you be refreshed. ³³The God of peace be with you all. Amen.

Personal greetings

16 I commend to you our sister Phoebe, a deaconᵇ of the church in Cenchreae. ²I ask you to receive her in the Lord in a way worthy of his people and to give her any help she may need from you, for she has been the benefactor of many people, including me.

³Greet Priscillaᶜ and Aquila, my fellow-workers in Christ Jesus. ⁴They risked their lives for me. Not only I but all the churches of the Gentiles are grateful to them.

⁵Greet also the church that meets at their house.

IN OTHER WORDS

Convert
Romans 16:5
'To convert' means 'to turn' or 'to return'. A convert is someone who makes a decision to follow Jesus; or, in other words, becomes a Christian.

ᵃ 21 Isaiah 52:15 (see Septuagint)   ᵇ 1 Or *servant*   ᶜ 3 Greek *Prisca*, a variant of *Priscilla*

Greet my dear friend Epenetus, who was the first convert to Christ in the province of Asia.

⁶Greet Mary, who worked very hard for you.

⁷Greet Andronicus and Junia, my fellow Jews who have been in prison with me. They are outstanding among the apostles, and they were in Christ before I was.

⁸Greet Ampliatus, my dear friend in the Lord.

⁹Greet Urbanus, our fellow-worker in Christ, and my dear friend Stachys.

¹⁰Greet Apelles, whose fidelity to Christ has stood the test.

Greet those who belong to the household of Aristobulus.

¹¹Greet Herodion, my fellow Jew.

Greet those in the household of Narcissus who are in the Lord.

¹²Greet Tryphena and Tryphosa, those women who work hard in the Lord.

Greet my dear friend Persis, another woman who has worked very hard in the Lord.

¹³Greet Rufus, chosen in the Lord, and his mother, who has been a mother to me, too.

¹⁴Greet Asyncritus, Phlegon, Hermes, Patrobas, Hermas and the other brothers and sisters with them.

¹⁵Greet Philologus, Julia, Nereus and his sister, and Olympas and all the Lord's people who are with them.

¹⁶Greet one another with a holy kiss.

All the churches of Christ send greetings.

¹⁷I urge you, brothers and sisters, to watch out for those who cause divisions and put obstacles in your way that are contrary to the teaching you have learned. Keep away from them. ¹⁸For such people are not serving our Lord Christ, but their own appetites. By smooth talk and flattery they deceive the minds of naïve people. ¹⁹Everyone has heard about your obedience, so I rejoice because of you; but I want you to be wise about what is good, and innocent about what is evil.

²⁰The God of peace will soon crush Satan under your feet.

The grace of our Lord Jesus be with you.

²¹Timothy, my co-worker, sends his greetings to you, as do Lucius, Jason and Sosipater, my fellow Jews.

²²I, Tertius, who wrote down this letter, greet you in the Lord.

²³(24)Gaius, whose hospitality I and the whole church here enjoy, sends you his greetings.

Erastus, who is the city's director of public works, and our brother Quartus send you their greetings.[a]

²⁵Now to him who is able to establish you in accordance with my gospel, the message I proclaim about Jesus Christ, in keeping with the revelation of the mystery hidden for long ages past, ²⁶but now revealed and made known through the prophetic writings by the command of the eternal God, so that all the Gentiles might come to faith and obedience— ²⁷to the only wise God be glory for ever through Jesus Christ! Amen.

---

[a] 23 Some manuscripts *their greetings.* ²⁴*May the grace of our Lord Jesus Christ be with all of you. Amen.*

1 Corinthians

INTRODUCTION

1 Corinthians

Author: Paul

Who to: Christians in Corinth.

When: Written from Ephesus during Paul's third missionary journey, around AD 56.

Where: Corinth was ancient Greece's most important trade city.

Did you know? This wasn't actually the first letter that Paul wrote to this church (1 Corinthians 5:9), but that one was lost. The Corinthians obviously sent Paul a letter in return with questions that they wanted answered (1 Corinthians 7:1).

Main theme: Paul writes this letter to people who are struggling to know how to live the Christian life surrounded by people who aren't Christians. There were all kinds of divisions in the church which Paul tells them to put right. And then he gives ethical advice on how to do the right thing in issues such as sex, marriage and worship.

1 Paul, called to be an apostle of Christ Jesus by the will of God, and our brother Sosthenes,

2To the church of God in Corinth, to those sanctified in Christ Jesus and called to be his holy people, together with all those everywhere who call on the name of our Lord Jesus Christ—their Lord and ours:

3Grace and peace to you from God our Father and the Lord Jesus Christ.

Thanksgiving

4I always thank my God for you because of his grace given you in Christ Jesus. 5For in him you have been enriched in every way—with all kinds of speech and with all knowledge— 6God thus confirming our testimony about Christ among you. 7Therefore you do not lack any spiritual gift as you eagerly wait for our Lord Jesus Christ to be revealed. 8He will also keep you firm to the end, so that you will be blameless on the day of our Lord Jesus Christ. 9God is faithful, who has called you into fellowship with his Son, Jesus Christ our Lord.

A church divided over leaders

10I appeal to you, brothers and sisters, in the name of our Lord Jesus Christ, that all of you agree with one another in what you say and that there be no divisions among you, but that you be perfectly united in mind and thought. 11My brothers and sisters, some from Chloe's household have informed me that there are quarrels among you. 12What I mean is this: one of you says, 'I follow Paul'; another, 'I follow Apollos'; another, 'I follow Cephas*a*'; still another, 'I follow Christ.'

13Is Christ divided? Was Paul crucified for you? Were you baptised into*b* the name of Paul? 14I thank God that I did not baptise any of you except Crispus and Gaius, 15so no-one can say that you were baptised into my name. 16(Yes, I also baptised the household of Stephanas; beyond that, I don't remember if I baptised anyone else.) 17For Christ did not send me to baptise, but to preach the gospel—not with wisdom and eloquence, lest the cross of Christ be emptied of its power.

Christ crucified is God's power and wisdom

18For the message of the cross is foolishness to those who are perishing, but to us who are being saved it is the power of God. 19For it is written:

'I will destroy the wisdom of the wise;
 the intelligence of the intelligent I will
  frustrate.'*c*

20Where are the wise? Where is the teacher of the law? Where is the philosopher of this age? Has not God made foolish the wisdom of the world? 21For since in the wisdom of God the world through its wisdom did not know him, God was pleased through the foolishness of what was preached to save those who believe. 22Jews demand signs and Greeks look for wisdom, 23but we preach Christ crucified: a stumbling-block to Jews and foolishness to Gentiles, 24but to those whom God has called, both Jews and Greeks, Christ the power of God and the wisdom of God. 25For the foolishness of God is wiser than human wisdom, and the weakness of God is stronger than human strength.

26Brothers and sisters, think of what you were when you were called. Not many of you were wise by human standards; not many were influential; not many were of noble birth. 27But God chose the foolish things of the world to shame the wise; God chose the weak things of the world to shame the strong. 28God chose the lowly things of this world and the despised things—and the things that are not—to nullify the things that are, 29so that no-one may boast before him. 30It is because of him that you are in Christ Jesus, who has become for us wisdom from God—that is, our righteousness, holiness and redemption. 31Therefore, as it is written: 'Let those who boast boast in the Lord.'*d*

2 And so it was with me, brothers and sisters. When I came to you, I did not come with eloquence or human wisdom as I proclaimed to you the testimony about God.*e* 2For I resolved to know nothing while I was with you except Jesus Christ and him crucified. 3I came to you in weakness with great fear and trembling. 4My message and my preaching were not with wise and persuasive words, but with a demonstration of the Spirit's power, 5so that your faith might not rest on human wisdom, but on God's power.

God's wisdom revealed by the Spirit

6We do, however, speak a message of wisdom among the mature, but not the wisdom of this age or of the rulers of this age, who are coming to nothing. 7No, we declare God's wisdom, a mystery that has been hidden and that God destined for our glory before time began. 8None of the rulers of this age understood it, for if they had, they would not have crucified the Lord of glory. 9However, as it is written:

'What no eye has seen,
 what no ear has heard,

---

a 12 That is, Peter *b* 13 Or *in*; also in verse 15 *c* 19 Isaiah 29:14 *d* 31 Jer. 9:24 *e* 1 Some manuscripts *as I proclaimed to you God's mystery*

and what no human mind has
 conceived—
these things God has prepared for
 those who love him'*ᵃ*—

¹⁰for God has revealed them to us by his Spirit.

The Spirit searches all things, even the deep things of God. ¹¹For who knows a person's thoughts except that person's own spirit within? In the same way no-one knows the thoughts of God except the Spirit of God. ¹²We have not received the spirit of the world but the Spirit who is from God, that we may understand what God has freely given us. ¹³This is what we speak, not in words taught us by human wisdom but in words taught by the Spirit, explaining spiritual realities with Spirit-taught words.*ᵇ* ¹⁴The person without the Spirit does not accept the things that come from the Spirit of God but considers them foolishness, and cannot understand them because they are discerned only through the Spirit. ¹⁵The person with the Spirit makes judgments about all things, but such a person is not subject to merely human judgments, ¹⁶for,

'Who has known the mind of the Lord
 so as to instruct him?'*ᶜ*

But we have the mind of Christ.

The church and its leaders

3 Brothers and sisters, I could not address you as spiritual but as worldly—mere infants in Christ. ²I gave you milk, not solid food, for you were not yet ready for it. Indeed, you are still not ready. ³You are still worldly. For since there is jealousy and quarrelling among you, are you not worldly? Are you not acting like mere human beings? ⁴For when one says, 'I follow Paul,' and another, 'I follow Apollos,' are you not mere human beings?

⁵What, after all, is Apollos? And what is Paul? Only servants, through whom you came to believe—as the Lord has assigned to each his task. ⁶I planted the seed, Apollos watered it, but God has been making it grow. ⁷So neither the one who plants nor the one who waters is anything, but only God, who makes things grow. ⁸The one who plants and the one who waters have one purpose, and they will each be rewarded according to their own labour. ⁹For we are God's fellow-workers; you are God's field, God's building.

¹⁰By the grace God has given me, I laid a foundation as a wise builder, and someone else is building on it. But each one should build with care. ¹¹For no-one can lay any foundation other than the one already laid, which is Jesus Christ. ¹²If anyone builds on this foundation using gold, silver, costly stones, wood, hay or straw, ¹³their work will be shown for what it is, because the Day will bring it to light. It will be revealed with fire, and the fire will test the quality of each person's work. ¹⁴If what has been built survives, the builder will receive a reward. ¹⁵If it is burned up, the builder will suffer loss but yet will be saved—even though only as one escaping through the flames.

¹⁶Don't you know that you yourselves are God's temple and that God's Spirit dwells among you? ¹⁷If anyone destroys God's temple, God will destroy that person; for God's temple is sacred, and you together are that temple.

¹⁸Do not deceive yourselves. If any of you think you are wise by the standards of this age, you should become 'fools' so that you may become wise. ¹⁹For the wisdom of this world is foolishness in God's sight. As it is written: 'He catches the wise in their craftiness'*ᵈ*; ²⁰and again, 'The Lord knows that the thoughts of the wise are futile.'*ᵉ* ²¹So then, no more boasting about human leaders! All things are yours, ²²whether Paul or Apollos or Cephas*ᶠ* or the world or life or death or the present or the future—all are yours, ²³and you are of Christ, and Christ is of God.

The nature of true apostleship

4 This, then, is how you ought to regard us: as servants of Christ and as those entrusted with the mysteries God has revealed. ²Now it is required that those who have been given a trust must prove

---

*ᵃ*9 Isaiah 64:4   *ᵇ*13 Or *Spirit, interpreting spiritual truths to those who are spiritual*   *ᶜ*16 Isaiah 40:13   *ᵈ*19 Job 5:13
*ᵉ*20 Psalm 94:11   *ᶠ*22 That is, Peter

faithful. 3I care very little if I am judged by you or by any human court; indeed, I do not even judge myself. 4My conscience is clear, but that does not make me innocent. It is the Lord who judges me. 5Therefore judge nothing before the appointed time; wait till the Lord comes. He will bring to light what is hidden in darkness and will expose the motives of people's hearts. At that time each will receive their praise from God.

6Now, brothers and sisters, I have applied these things to myself and Apollos for your benefit, so that you may learn from us the meaning of the saying, 'Do not go beyond what is written.' Then you will not be puffed up in being a follower of one of us over against the other. 7For who makes you different from anyone else? What do you have that you did not receive? And if you did receive it, why do you boast as though you did not?

8Already you have all you want! Already you have become rich! You have begun to reign—and that without us! How I wish that you really had begun to reign so that we also might reign with you! 9For it seems to me that God has put us apostles on display at the end of the procession, like those condemned to die in the arena. We have been made a spectacle to the whole universe, to angels as well as to human beings. 10We are fools for Christ, but you are so wise in Christ! We are weak, but you are strong! You are honoured, we are dishonoured! 11To this very hour we go hungry and thirsty, we are in rags, we are brutally treated, we are homeless. 12We work hard with our own hands. When we are cursed, we bless; when we are persecuted, we endure it; 13when we are slandered, we answer kindly. We have become the scum of the earth, the garbage of the world—right up to this moment.

Paul's appeal and warning

14I am writing this not to shame you but to warn you as my dear children. 15Even if you had ten thousand guardians in Christ, you do not have many fathers, for in Christ Jesus I became your father through the gospel. 16Therefore I urge you to imitate me. 17For this reason I have sent to you Timothy, my son whom I love, who is faithful in the Lord. He will remind you of my way of life in Christ Jesus, which agrees with what I teach everywhere in every church.

18Some of you have become arrogant, as if I were not coming to you. 19But I will come to you very soon, if the Lord is willing, and then I will find out not only how these arrogant people are talking, but what power they have. 20For the kingdom of God is not a matter of talk but of power. 21What do you prefer? Shall I come to you with a rod of discipline, or shall I come in love and with a gentle spirit?

Dealing with a case of incest

5 It is actually reported that there is sexual immorality among you, and of a kind that even pagans do not tolerate: a man has his father's wife. 2And you are proud! Shouldn't you rather have gone into mourning and have put out of your fellowship the man who has been doing this? 3For my part, even though I am not physically present, I am with you in spirit. As one who is present with you in this way, I have already passed judgment in the name of our Lord Jesus on the one who has been doing this. 4So when you are assembled and I am with you in spirit, and the power of our Lord Jesus is present, 5hand this man over to Satan for the destruction of the sinful nature*a* so that his spirit may be saved on the day of the Lord.

6Your boasting is not good. Don't you know that a little yeast leavens the whole batch of dough? 7Get rid of the old yeast, so that you may be a new unleavened batch— as you really are. For Christ, our Passover lamb, has been sacrificed. 8Therefore let us keep the Festival, not with the old bread leavened with malice and wickedness, but with the unleavened bread of sincerity and truth.

9I wrote to you in my letter not to associate with sexually immoral people— 10not at all meaning the people of this world who are immoral, or the greedy and swindlers, or idolaters. In that case you would have to leave this world. 11But now I am

---

a 5 Or *of his body*; or *of the flesh*

Making Connections

Yeast
1 Corinthians 5:6
Yeast is a simple fungus that is added to flour and water to make dough. A small piece of yeast spreads throughout the whole dough and makes it rise.

writing to you that you must not associate with any who claim to be fellow believers but are sexually immoral or greedy, idolaters or slanderers, drunkards or swindlers. With such persons do not even eat.

12 What business is it of mine to judge those outside the church? Are you not to judge those inside? 13 God will judge those outside. 'Expel the wicked person from among you.'[a]

Lawsuits among believers

6 If any of you has a dispute with another, do you dare to take it before the ungodly for judgment instead of before the Lord's people? 2 Or do you not know that the Lord's people will judge the world? And if you are to judge the world, are you not competent to judge trivial cases? 3 Do you not know that we will judge angels? How much more the things of this life! 4 Therefore, if you have disputes about such matters, do you ask for a ruling from those whose way of life is scorned in the church? 5 I say this to shame you. Is it possible that there is nobody among you wise enough to judge a dispute between believers? 6 But instead, one brother goes to law against another—and this in front of unbelievers!

7 The very fact that you have lawsuits among you means you have been completely defeated already. Why not rather be wronged? Why not rather be cheated? 8 Instead, you yourselves cheat and do wrong, and you do this to your brothers and sisters. 9 Or do you not know that wrongdoers will not inherit the kingdom of God? Do not be deceived: neither the sexually immoral nor idolaters nor adulterers nor male prostitutes nor practising homosexuals 10 nor thieves nor the greedy nor drunkards nor slanderers nor swindlers will inherit the kingdom of God. 11 And that is what some of you were. But you were washed, you were sanctified, you were justified in the name of the Lord Jesus Christ and by the Spirit of our God.

Sexual immorality

12 'I have the right to do anything,' you say—but not everything is beneficial. 'I have the right to do anything'—but I will not be mastered by anything. 13 You say, 'Food for the stomach and the stomach for food, and God will destroy them both.' The body, however, is not meant for sexual immorality but for the Lord, and the Lord for the body. 14 By his power God raised the Lord from the dead, and he will raise us also. 15 Do you not know that your bodies are members of Christ himself? Shall I then take the members of Christ and unite them with a prostitute? Never! 16 Do you not know that he who unites himself with a prostitute is one with her in body? For it is said, 'The two will become one flesh.'[b] 17 But whoever is united with the Lord is one with him in spirit.[c]

18 Flee from sexual immorality. All other sins people commit are outside their bodies, but those who sin sexually sin against their own bodies. 19 Do you not know that your bodies are temples of the Holy Spirit, who is in you, whom you have received from God? You are not your own; 20 you were bought at a price. Therefore honour God with your bodies.

Concerning married life

7 Now for the matters you wrote about: 'It is good for a man not to have sexual relations with a woman.' 2 But since sexual immorality is occurring, each man should have sexual relations with his own wife, and each woman with her own husband. 3 The husband should fulfil his marital duty to his

---

[a] 13 Deut. 13:5; 17:7; 19:19; 21:21; 22:21,24; 24:7   [b] 16 Gen. 2:24   [c] 17 Or *in the Spirit*

wife, and likewise the wife to her husband. ⁴The wife does not have authority over her own body but yields it to her husband. In the same way, the husband does not have authority over his own body but yields it to his wife. ⁵Do not deprive each other except perhaps by mutual consent and for a time, so that you may devote yourselves to prayer. Then come together again so that Satan will not tempt you because of your lack of self-control. ⁶I say this as a concession, not as a command. ⁷I wish that all of you were as I am. But each of you has your own gift from God; one has this gift, another has that.

⁸Now to the unmarried[a] and the widows I say: it is good for them to stay unmarried, as I do. ⁹But if they cannot control themselves, they should marry, for it is better to marry than to burn with passion.

¹⁰To the married I give this command (not I, but the Lord): a wife must not separate from her husband. ¹¹But if she does, she must remain unmarried or else be reconciled to her husband. And a husband must not divorce his wife.

¹²To the rest I say this (I, not the Lord): If any brother has a wife who is not a believer and she is willing to live with him, he must not divorce her. ¹³And if a woman has a husband who is not a believer and he is willing to live with her, she must not divorce him. ¹⁴For the unbelieving husband has been sanctified through his wife, and the unbelieving wife has been sanctified through her believing husband. Otherwise your children would be unclean, but as it is, they are holy.

¹⁵But if the unbeliever leaves, let it be so. The brother or sister is not bound in such circumstances; God has called us to live in peace. ¹⁶How do you know, wife, whether you will save your husband? Or, how do you know, husband, whether you will save your wife?

Concerning change of status

¹⁷Nevertheless, each of you should live as a believer in whatever situation the Lord has assigned to you, just as God has called you. This is the rule I lay down in all the churches. ¹⁸Was a man already circumcised when he was called? He should not become uncircumcised. Was a man uncircumcised when he was called? He should not be circumcised. ¹⁹Circumcision is nothing and uncircumcision is nothing. Keeping God's commands is what counts. ²⁰Each of you should remain in the situation you were in when God called you.

²¹Were you a slave when you were called? Don't let it trouble you—although if you can gain your freedom, do so. ²²For those who were slaves when called to faith in the Lord are the Lord's freed people; similarly, those who were free when called are Christ's slaves. ²³You were bought at a price; do not become slaves of human beings. ²⁴Brothers and sisters, all of you, as responsible to God, should remain in the situation in which God called you.

Concerning the unmarried

²⁵Now about virgins: I have no command from the Lord, but I give a judgment as one who by the Lord's mercy is trustworthy. ²⁶Because of the present crisis, I think that it is good for a man to remain as he is. ²⁷Are you pledged to a woman? Do not seek to be released. Are you free from such a commitment? Do not look for a wife. ²⁸But if you do marry, you have not sinned; and if a virgin marries, she has not sinned. But those who marry will face many troubles in this life, and I want to spare you this.

²⁹What I mean, brothers and sisters, is that the time is short. From now on those who are married should live as if they were not; ³⁰those who mourn, as if they did not; those who are happy, as if they were not; those who buy something, as if it were not theirs to keep; ³¹those who use the things of the world, as if not engrossed in them. For this world in its present form is passing away.

³²I would like you to be free from concern. An unmarried man is concerned about the Lord's affairs—how he can please the Lord. ³³But a married man is concerned about the affairs of this world—how he can please his wife— ³⁴and his interests are divided. An unmarried woman or virgin is

---

[a] 8 Or *widowers*

concerned about the Lord's affairs: her aim is to be devoted to the Lord in both body and spirit. But a married woman is concerned about the affairs of this world—how she can please her husband. 35I am saying this for your own good, not to restrict you, but that you may live in a right way in undivided devotion to the Lord.

36If anyone is worried that he might not be acting honourably towards the virgin he is engaged to, and if she is getting beyond the usual age for marrying[a] and he feels he ought to marry, he should do as he wants. He is not sinning. They should get married. 37But the man who has settled the matter in his own mind, who is under no compulsion but has control over his own will, and who has made up his mind not to marry the virgin—this man also does the right thing. 38So then, he who marries the virgin does right, but he who does not marry her does better.[b]

39A woman is bound to her husband as long as he lives. But if her husband dies, she is free to marry anyone she wishes, but he must belong to the Lord. 40In my judgment, she is happier if she stays as she is—and I think that I too have the Spirit of God.

Concerning food sacrificed to idols

8 Now about food sacrificed to idols: we know that 'We all possess knowledge.' But knowledge puffs up while love builds up. 2Those who think they know something do not yet know as they ought to know. 3But whoever loves God is known by God.[c]

4So then, about eating food sacrificed to idols: we know that 'An idol is nothing at all in the world' and that 'There is no God but one.' 5For even if there are so-called gods, whether in heaven or on earth (as indeed there are many 'gods' and many 'lords'), 6yet for us there is but one God, the Father, from whom all things came and for whom we live; and there is but one Lord, Jesus Christ, through whom all things came and through whom we live.

IN OTHER WORDS

Idol
1 Corinthians 8:4
In the Bible an idol is a statue of a false god, but today the word is used to mean anything that someone holds as the most important thing in their life, more important even than God.

7But not everyone possesses this knowledge. Some people are still so accustomed to idols that when they eat sacrificial food they think of it as having been sacrificed to a god, and since their conscience is weak, it is defiled. 8But food does not bring us near to God; we are no worse if we do not eat, and no better if we do.

9Be careful, however, that the exercise of your rights does not become a stumbling-block to the weak. 10For if anyone with a weak conscience sees you, with all your knowledge, eating in an idol's temple, won't they be emboldened to eat what is sacrificed to idols? 11So this weak brother or sister, for whom Christ died, is destroyed by your knowledge. 12When you sin against them in this way and wound their weak conscience, you sin against Christ. 13Therefore, if what I eat causes my brother or sister to fall into sin, I will never eat meat again, so that I will not cause them to fall.

Paul's rights as an apostle

9 Am I not free? Am I not an apostle? Have I not seen Jesus our Lord? Are you not the result of my work in the Lord? 2Even though I may not be an apostle to others, surely I am to you! For you are the seal of my apostleship in the Lord.

3This is my defence to those who sit in judgment on me. 4Don't we have the right

---

[a] 36 Or *if his (or her) passions are too strong* [b] 36-38 Or 36*If anyone thinks he is not treating his daughter properly, and if she is getting along in years (or if her passions are too strong), and he feels she ought to marry, he should do as he wants. He is not sinning. He should let her get married.* 37*But the man who has settled the matter in his own mind, who is under no compulsion but has control over his own will, and who has made up his mind to keep the virgin unmarried—this man also does the right thing.* 38*So then, he who gives his virgin in marriage does right, but he who does not give her in marriage does better.* [c] 2,3 An early manuscript and another ancient witness *think they have knowledge do not yet know as they ought to know.* 3*But whoever loves truly knows.*

IN OTHER WORDS

Apostle
1 Corinthians 9:1

Apostle is a Greek word which means 'sent one', someone to whom Jesus has given authority for certain tasks. The first apostles were the twelve disciples who Jesus sent out in twos during his ministry to preach and heal like he did (Mark 3:14).

---

to food and drink? 5Don't we have the right to take a believing wife along with us, as do the other apostles and the Lord's brothers and Cephas[a]? 6Or is it only I and Barnabas who don't have the right not to work for a living?

7Who serves as a soldier at his own expense? Who plants a vineyard and does not eat of its grapes? Who tends a flock and does not drink of the milk? 8Do I say this merely on human authority? Doesn't the Law say the same thing? 9For it is written in the Law of Moses: 'Do not muzzle an ox while it is treading out the grain.'[b] Is it about oxen that God is concerned? 10Surely he says this for us, doesn't he? Yes, this was written for us, because when farmers plough and thresh, they should be able to do so in the hope of sharing in the harvest. 11If we have sown spiritual seed among you, is it too much if we reap a material harvest from you? 12If others have this right of support from you, shouldn't we have it all the more?

But we did not use this right. On the contrary, we put up with anything rather than hinder the gospel of Christ.

13Don't you know that those who serve in the temple get their food from the temple, and that those who serve at the altar share in what is offered on the altar? 14In the same way, the Lord has commanded that those who preach the gospel should receive their living from the gospel.

15But I have not used any of these rights. And I am not writing this in the hope that you will do such things for me, for I would rather die than allow anyone to deprive me of this boast. 16For when I preach the gospel, I cannot boast, since I am compelled to preach. Woe to me if I do not preach the gospel! 17If I preach voluntarily, I have a reward; if not voluntarily, I am simply discharging the trust committed to me. 18What then is my reward? Just this: that in preaching the gospel I may offer it free of charge, and so not misuse my rights as a preacher of the gospel.

Paul's use of his freedom

19Though I am free and belong to no-one, I have made myself a slave to everyone, to win as many as possible. 20To the Jews I became like a Jew, to win the Jews. To those under the law I became like one under the law (though I myself am not under the law), so as to win those under the law. 21To those not having the law I became like one not having the law (though I am not free from God's law but am under Christ's law), so as to win those not having the law. 22To the weak I became weak, to win the weak. I have become all things to all people so that by all possible means I might save some. 23I do all this for the sake of the gospel, that I may share in its blessings.

The need for self-discipline

24Do you not know that in a race all the runners run, but only one gets the prize? Run in such a way as to get the prize. 25Everyone who competes in the games goes into strict training. They do it to get a crown that will not last; but we do it to get a crown that will last for ever. 26Therefore I do not run like someone running aimlessly; I do not fight like a boxer beating the air. 27No, I strike a blow to my body and make it my slave so that after I have preached to others, I myself will not be disqualified for the prize.

Warnings from Israel's history

10 For I do not want you to be ignorant of the fact, brothers and sisters, that our ancestors were all under the

---

[a] 5 That is, Peter [b] 9 Deut. 25:4

cloud and that they all passed through the sea. ²They were all baptised into Moses in the cloud and in the sea. ³They all ate the same spiritual food ⁴and drank the same spiritual drink; for they drank from the spiritual rock that accompanied them, and that rock was Christ. ⁵Nevertheless, God was not pleased with most of them; their bodies were scattered over the wilderness.

⁶Now these things occurred as examples to keep us from setting our hearts on evil things as they did. ⁷Do not be idolaters, as some of them were; as it is written: 'The people sat down to eat and drink and got up to indulge in revelry.'ᵃ ⁸We should not commit sexual immorality, as some of them did—and in one day twenty-three thousand of them died. ⁹We should not test Christ,ᵇ as some of them did—and were killed by snakes. ¹⁰And do not grumble, as some of them did—and were killed by the destroying angel.

¹¹These things happened to them as examples and were written down as warnings for us, on whom the culmination of the ages has come. ¹²So, if you think you are standing firm, be careful that you don't fall! ¹³No temptationᶜ has overtaken you except what is common to us all. And God is faithful; he will not let you be temptedᵈ beyond what you can bear. But when you are tempted,ᵉ he will also provide a way out so that you can endure it.

Idol feasts and the Lord's Supper

¹⁴Therefore, my dear friends, flee from idolatry. ¹⁵I speak to sensible people; judge for yourselves what I say. ¹⁶Is not the cup of thanksgiving for which we give thanks a participation in the blood of Christ? And is not the bread that we break a participation in the body of Christ? ¹⁷Because there is one loaf, we, who are many, are one body, for we all partake of the one loaf.

¹⁸Consider the people of Israel: do not those who eat the sacrifices participate in the altar? ¹⁹Do I mean then that food sacrificed to an idol is anything, or that an idol is anything? ²⁰No, but the sacrifices of pagans are offered to demons, not to God, and I do not want you to be participants with demons. ²¹You cannot drink the cup of the Lord and the cup of demons too; you cannot have a part in both the Lord's table and the table of demons. ²²Are we trying to arouse the Lord's jealousy? Are we stronger than he?

The believer's freedom

²³'I have the right to do anything,' you say—but not everything is beneficial. 'I have the right to do anything'—but not everything is constructive. ²⁴No-one should seek their own good, but the good of others.

²⁵Eat anything sold in the meat market without raising questions of conscience, ²⁶for, 'The earth is the Lord's, and everything in it.'ᶠ

²⁷If an unbeliever invites you to a meal and you want to go, eat whatever is put before you without raising questions of conscience. ²⁸But if someone says to you, 'This has been offered in sacrifice,' then do not eat it, both for the sake of the one who told you and for the sake of conscience. ²⁹I am referring to the other person's conscience, not yours. For why is my freedom being judged by another's conscience? ³⁰If I take part in the meal with thankfulness, why am I denounced because of something I thank God for?

³¹So whether you eat or drink or whatever you do, do it all for the glory of God.

> **IN OTHER WORDS**
>
> **Temptation**
> **1 Corinthians 10:13**
> The word 'temptation' means a test or a trial. In the Bible there are examples of both God and Satan testing the faith of believers, but for different reasons. Satan wants people to fail and to turn away from God. God wants people to grow in their faith in him (Matthew 6:13).

ᵃ7 Exodus 32:6   ᵇ9 Some manuscripts *test the Lord*   ᶜ13 The Greek for *temptation* and *tempted* can also mean *testing* and *tested*.   ᵈ13 The Greek for *temptation* and *tempted* can also mean *testing* and *tested*.   ᵉ13 The Greek for *temptation* and *tempted* can also mean *testing* and *tested*.   ᶠ26 Psalm 24:1

32Do not cause anyone to stumble, whether Jews, Greeks or the church of God— 33even as I try to please everyone in every way. For I am not seeking my own good but the good of many, so that they may be saved.

11 1Follow my example, as I follow the example of Christ.

On covering the head in worship

2I praise you for remembering me in everything and for holding to the traditions just as I passed them on to you. 3But I want you to realise that the head of every man is Christ, and the head of the woman is man,[a] and the head of Christ is God. 4Every man who prays or prophesies with his head covered dishonours his head. 5But every woman who prays or prophesies with her head uncovered dishonours her head—it is the same as having her head shaved. 6For if a woman does not cover her head, she might as well have her hair cut off; but if it is a disgrace for a woman to have her hair cut off or her head shaved, then she should cover her head.

7A man ought not to cover his head, since he is the image and glory of God; but woman is the glory of man. 8For man did not come from woman, but woman from man; 9neither was man created for woman, but woman for man. 10It is for this reason that a woman ought to have authority over her own[b] head, because of the angels. 11Nevertheless, in the Lord woman is not independent of man, nor is man independent of woman. 12For as woman came from man, so also man is born of woman. But everything comes from God.

13Judge for yourselves: is it proper for a woman to pray to God with her head uncovered? 14Does not the very nature of things teach you that if a man has long hair, it is a disgrace to him, 15but that if a woman has long hair, it is her glory? For long hair is given to her as a covering. 16If anyone wants to be contentious about this, we have no other practice—nor do the churches of God.

Correcting an abuse of the Lord's Supper

17In the following directives I have no praise for you, for your meetings do more harm than good. 18In the first place, I hear that when you come together as a church, there are divisions among you, and to some extent I believe it. 19No doubt there have to be differences among you to show which of you have God's approval. 20So then, when you come together, it is not the Lord's Supper you eat, 21for when you are eating, some of you go ahead with your own private suppers. As a result, one person remains hungry and another gets drunk. 22Don't you have homes to eat and drink in? Or do you despise the church of God by humiliating those who have nothing? What shall I say to you? Shall I praise you? Certainly not in this matter!

23For I received from the Lord what I also passed on to you: the Lord Jesus, on the night he was betrayed, took bread, 24and when he had given thanks, he broke it and said, 'This is my body, which is for you; do this in remembrance of me.' 25In the same way, after supper he took the cup, saying, 'This cup is the new covenant in my blood; do this, whenever you drink it, in remembrance of me.' 26For whenever you eat this bread and drink this cup, you proclaim the Lord's death until he comes.

27So then, whoever eats the bread or drinks the cup of the Lord in an unworthy manner will be guilty of sinning against the

---

Sign of the times

Hair
1 Corinthians 11:6

Untidy or loose hair was equated with adultery and prostitution in New Testament times. Paul advised Christian women to cover their heads when they were praying in the early church.

---

[a] 3 Or of the wife is her husband   [b] 10 Or have a sign of authority on her

body and blood of the Lord. 28Everyone ought to examine themselves before they eat of the bread and drink of the cup. 29For those who eat and drink without discerning the body of Christ eat and drink judgment on themselves. 30That is why many among you are weak and ill, and a number of you have fallen asleep. 31But if we were more discerning with regard to ourselves, we would not come under such judgment. 32Nevertheless, when we are judged in this way by the Lord, we are being disciplined so that we will not be finally condemned with the world.

33So then, my brothers and sisters, when you gather to eat, you should all eat together. 34Those who are hungry should eat something at home, so that when you meet together it may not result in judgment.

And when I come I will give further instructions.

Concerning spiritual gifts

12 Now about the gifts of the Spirit, brothers and sisters, I do not want you to be uninformed. 2You know that when you were pagans, somehow or other you were influenced and led astray to dumb idols. 3Therefore I want you to know that no-one who is speaking by the Spirit of God says, 'Jesus be cursed,' and no-one can say, 'Jesus is Lord,' except by the Holy Spirit.

4There are different kinds of gifts, but the same Spirit distributes them. 5There are different kinds of service, but the same Lord. 6There are different kinds of working, but in all of them and in everyone it is the same God at work.

7Now to each one the manifestation of the Spirit is given for the common good. 8To one there is given through the Spirit a message of wisdom, to another a message of knowledge by means of the same Spirit, 9to another faith by the same Spirit, to another gifts of healing by that one Spirit, 10to another miraculous powers, to another prophecy, to another distinguishing between spirits, to another speaking in different kinds of tongues,*a* and to still another the interpretation of tongues.*b* 11All these are the work of one and the same Spirit, and he distributes them to each one, just as he determines.

Unity and diversity in the body

12Just as a body, though one, has many parts, but all its many parts form one body, so it is with Christ. 13For we were all baptised by*c* one Spirit so as to form one body—whether Jews or Gentiles, slave or free—and we were all given the one Spirit to drink. 14And so the body is not made up of one part but of many.

15Now if the foot should say, 'Because I am not a hand, I do not belong to the body,' it would not for that reason cease to be part of the body. 16And if the ear should say, 'Because I am not an eye, I do not belong to the body,' it would not for that reason cease to be part of the body. 17If the whole body were an eye, where would the sense of hearing be? If the whole body were an ear, where would the sense of smell be? 18But in fact God has placed the parts in the body, every one of them, just as he wanted them to be. 19If they were all one part, where would the body be? 20As it is, there are many parts, but one body.

21The eye cannot say to the hand, 'I don't need you!' And the head cannot say to the feet, 'I don't need you!' 22On the contrary, those parts of the body that seem to be weaker are indispensable, 23and the parts that we think are less honourable we treat with special honour. And the parts that are unpresentable are treated with special modesty, 24while our presentable parts need no special treatment. But God has put the body together, giving greater honour to the parts that lacked it, 25so that there should be no division in the body, but that its parts should have equal concern for each other. 26If one part suffers, every part suffers with it; if one part is honoured, every part rejoices with it.

27Now you are the body of Christ, and each one of you is a part of it. 28And God has placed in the church first of all apostles, second prophets, third teachers, then miracles, then gifts of healing, of helping, of guidance, and of different kinds of tongues. 29Are all apostles? Are all prophets? Are all

---

a 10 Or *languages*; also in verse 28   *b* 10 Or *languages*; also in verse 28   *c* 13 Or *with*; or *in* teachers? Do all work miracles? ³⁰Do all have gifts of healing? Do all speak in tongues*ᵃ*? Do all interpret? ³¹Now eagerly desire*ᵇ* the greater gifts.

Love is indispensable

And yet I will show you the most excellent way.

13 If I speak in human or angelic tongues,*ᶜ* but do not have love, I am only a resounding gong or a clanging cymbal. ²If I have the gift of prophecy and can fathom all mysteries and all knowledge, and if I have a faith that can move mountains, but do not have love, I am nothing. ³If I give all I possess to the poor and give over my body [to hardship] that I may boast,*ᵈ* but do not have love, I gain nothing.

⁴Love is patient, love is kind. It does not envy, it does not boast, it is not proud. ⁵It does not dishonour others, it is not self-seeking, it is not easily angered, it keeps no record of wrongs. ⁶Love does not delight in evil but rejoices with the truth. ⁷It always protects, always trusts, always hopes, always perseveres.

⁸Love never fails. But where there are prophecies, they will cease; where there are tongues, they will be stilled; where there is knowledge, it will pass away. ⁹For we know in part and we prophesy in part, ¹⁰but when completeness comes, what is in part disappears. ¹¹When I was a child, I talked like a child, I thought like a child, I reasoned like a child. When I became a man, I put the ways of childhood behind me. ¹²For now we see only a reflection as in a mirror; then we shall see face to face. Now I know in part; then I shall know fully, even as I am fully known.

¹³And now these three remain: faith, hope and love. But the greatest of these is love.

Intelligibility in worship

14 Follow the way of love and eagerly desire spiritual gifts, especially the gift of prophecy. ²For those who speak in a tongue*ᵉ* do not speak to other people but to God. Indeed, no-one understands them; they utter mysteries by the Spirit. ³But those

IN OTHER WORDS

Edify
1 Corinthians 14:4
'To edify' literally means 'to build up', as in strengthening believers in their faith.

who prophesy speak to people for their strengthening, encouragement and comfort. ⁴Those who speak in a tongue edify themselves, but those who prophesy edify the church. ⁵I would like every one of you to speak in tongues,*ᶠ* but even more to prophesy. Those who prophesy are greater than those who speak in tongues,*ᵍ* unless they interpret, so that the church may be edified.

⁶Now, brothers and sisters, if I come to you and speak in tongues, what good will I be to you, unless I bring you some revelation or knowledge or prophecy or word of instruction? ⁷Even in the case of lifeless things that make sounds, such as the pipe or harp, how will anyone know what tune is being played unless there is a distinction in the notes? ⁸Again, if the trumpet does not sound a clear call, who will get ready for battle? ⁹So it is with you. Unless you speak intelligible words with your tongue, how will anyone know what you are saying? You will just be speaking into the air. ¹⁰Undoubtedly there are all sorts of languages in the world, yet none of them is without meaning. ¹¹If then I do not grasp the meaning of what someone is saying, I am a foreigner to the speaker, and the speaker is a foreigner to me. ¹²So it is with you. Since you are eager for gifts of the Spirit, try to excel in those that build up the church.

¹³For this reason those who speak in a tongue should pray that they may interpret what they say. ¹⁴For if I pray in a tongue, my spirit prays, but my mind is unfruitful. ¹⁵So what shall I do? I will pray with my spirit, but I will also pray with my understanding; I will sing with my spirit, but I will also sing

---

*ᵃ*30 Or *other languages*   *ᵇ*31 Or *But you are eagerly desiring*   *ᶜ*1 Or *languages*   *ᵈ*3 Some manuscripts *body to the flames*   *ᵉ*2 Or *in another language*; also in verses 4, 13, 14, 19, 26 and 27   *ᶠ*5 Or *in other languages*; also in verses 6, 18, 22, 23 and 39   *ᵍ*5 Or *in other languages*; also in verses 6, 18, 22, 23 and 39

IN OTHER WORDS

Tongues
1 Corinthians 14:13

The Holy Spirit sometimes gives people the ability to 'speak in tongues', meaning in a language that they haven't learned and possibly can't understand themselves. On the day of Pentecost, the disciples were given the ability to speak in other languages that people could understand (Acts 2:4–12). In his letter to the Corinthians, the tongues that Paul talks about are languages given by God which are used to praise him, some of which are human languages (1 Corinthians 13:1). Another gift of the Holy Spirit is 'interpretation', being able to understand what someone who is speaking in tongues is saying.

---

with my understanding. 16Otherwise when you are praising God in the Spirit, how can the others, who are now put in the same situation as an enquirer,[a] say 'Amen' to your thanksgiving, since they do not know what you are saying? 17You are giving thanks well enough, but the others are not edified.

18I thank God that I speak in tongues more than all of you. 19But in the church I would rather speak five intelligible words to instruct others than ten thousand words in a tongue.

20Brothers and sisters, stop thinking like children. In regard to evil be infants, but in your thinking be adults. 21In the Law it is written:

'With other tongues
    and through the lips of foreigners
I will speak to this people,
    but even then they will not listen to me,
        says the Lord.'[b]

22Tongues, then, are a sign, not for believers but for unbelievers; prophecy, however, is not for unbelievers but for believers. 23So if the whole church comes together and everyone speaks in tongues, and enquirers or unbelievers come in, will they not say that you are out of your mind? 24But if an unbeliever or an enquirer comes in while everyone is prophesying, they are convicted of sin and are brought under judgment by all, 25as the secrets of their hearts are laid bare. So they will fall down and worship God, exclaiming, 'God is really among you!'

Good order in worship

26What then shall we say, brothers and sisters? When you come together, each of you has a hymn, or a word of instruction, a revelation, a tongue or an interpretation. Everything must be done so that the church may be built up. 27If anyone speaks in a tongue, two—or at the most three—should speak, one at a time, and someone must interpret. 28If there is no interpreter, the speaker should keep quiet in the church; let them speak to themselves and to God.

29Two or three prophets should speak, and the others should weigh carefully what is said. 30And if a revelation comes to someone who is sitting down, the first speaker should stop. 31For you can all prophesy in turn so that everyone may be instructed and encouraged. 32The spirits of prophets are subject to the control of prophets. 33For God is not a God of disorder but of peace—as in all the congregations of the Lord's people.

34Women should remain silent in the churches. They are not allowed to speak, but must be in submission, as the law says. 35If they want to enquire about something, they should ask their own husbands at home; for it is disgraceful for a woman to speak in the church.[c]

36Or did the word of God originate with you? Or are you the only people it has reached? 37If any think they are prophets or otherwise gifted by the Spirit, let them acknowledge that what I am writing to you

---

[a] 16 The Greek word for *enquirer* is a technical term for someone not fully initiated into a religion; also in verses 23 and 24.   [b] 21 Isaiah 28:11,12   [c] 34,35 In some manuscripts these verses come after verse 40.

is the Lord's command. 38Those who ignore this will themselves be ignored.[a]

39Therefore, my brothers and sisters, be eager to prophesy, and do not forbid speaking in tongues. 40But everything should be done in a fitting and orderly way.

The resurrection of Christ

15 Now, brothers and sisters, I want to remind you of the gospel I preached to you, which you received and on which you have taken your stand. 2By this gospel you are saved, if you hold firmly to the word I preached to you. Otherwise, you have believed in vain.

3For what I received I passed on to you as of first importance[b]: that Christ died for our sins according to the Scriptures, 4that he was buried, that he was raised on the third day according to the Scriptures, 5and that he appeared to Cephas,[c] and then to the Twelve. 6After that, he appeared to more than five hundred of the brothers and sisters at the same time, most of whom are still living, though some have fallen asleep. 7Then he appeared to James, then to all the apostles, 8and last of all he appeared to me also, as to one abnormally born.

9For I am the least of the apostles and do not even deserve to be called an apostle, because I persecuted the church of God. 10But by the grace of God I am what I am, and his grace to me was not without effect. No, I worked harder than all of them—yet not I, but the grace of God that was with me. 11Whether, then, it is I or they, this is what we preach, and this is what you believed.

The resurrection of the dead

12But if it is preached that Christ has been raised from the dead, how can some of you say that there is no resurrection of the dead? 13If there is no resurrection of the dead, then not even Christ has been raised. 14And if Christ has not been raised, our preaching is useless and so is your faith. 15More than that, we are then found to be false witnesses about God, for we have testified about God that he raised Christ from the dead. But he did not raise him if in fact the dead are not raised. 16For if the dead are not raised, then Christ has not been raised either. 17And if Christ has not been raised, your faith is futile; you are still in your sins. 18Then those also who have fallen asleep in Christ are lost. 19If only for this life we have hope in Christ, we are to be pitied more than all others.

20But Christ has indeed been raised from the dead, the firstfruits of those who have fallen asleep. 21For since death came through a human being, the resurrection of the dead comes also through a human being. 22For as in Adam all die, so in Christ all will be made alive. 23But in this order: Christ, the firstfruits; then, when he comes, those who belong to him. 24Then the end will come, when he hands over the kingdom to God the Father after he has destroyed all dominion, authority and power. 25For he must reign until he has put all his enemies under his feet. 26The last enemy to be destroyed is death. 27For he 'has put everything under his feet'.[d] Now when it says that 'everything' has been put under him, it is clear that this does not include God himself, who put everything under Christ. 28When he has done this, then the Son himself will be made subject to him who put everything under him, so that God may be all in all.

29Now if there is no resurrection, what will those do who are baptised for the dead? If the dead are not raised at all, why are people baptised for them? 30And as for us, why do we endanger ourselves every hour? 31I face death every day—yes, just as surely

> **IN OTHER WORDS**
>
> **Resurrection**
> **1 Corinthians 15:12**
> 'Resurrection' means coming back to life after death. The resurrection of Jesus is of central importance to the Christian faith. Believers in Jesus will one day be raised to life and will be with him forever.

---

[a] 38 Some manuscripts *Those who are ignorant of this will be ignorant* [b] 3 Or *you at the first* [c] 5 That is, Peter [d] 27 Psalm 8:6

as I boast about you in Christ Jesus our Lord. ³²If I fought wild beasts in Ephesus with no more than human hopes, what have I gained? If the dead are not raised,

'Let us eat and drink,
for tomorrow we die.'[a]

³³Do not be misled: 'Bad company corrupts good character.'[b] ³⁴Come back to your senses as you ought, and stop sinning; for there are some who are ignorant of God—I say this to your shame.

The resurrection body

³⁵But someone will ask, 'How are the dead raised? With what kind of body will they come?' ³⁶How foolish! What you sow does not come to life unless it dies. ³⁷When you sow, you do not plant the body that will be, but just a seed, perhaps of wheat or of something else. ³⁸But God gives it a body as he has determined, and to each kind of seed he gives its own body. ³⁹All flesh is not the same: human beings have one kind of flesh, animals have another, birds another and fish another. ⁴⁰There are also heavenly bodies and there are earthly bodies; but the splendour of the heavenly bodies is one kind, and the splendour of the earthly bodies is another. ⁴¹The sun has one kind of splendour, the moon another and the stars another; and star differs from star in splendour.

⁴²So will it be with the resurrection of the dead. The body that is sown is perishable, it is raised imperishable; ⁴³it is sown in dishonour, it is raised in glory; it is sown in weakness, it is raised in power; ⁴⁴it is sown a natural body, it is raised a spiritual body.

If there is a natural body, there is also a spiritual body. ⁴⁵So it is written: 'The first Adam became a living being'[c]; the last Adam, a life-giving spirit. ⁴⁶The spiritual did not come first, but the natural, and after that the spiritual. ⁴⁷The first man was of the dust of the earth; the second man is of heaven. ⁴⁸As was the earthly man, so are those who are of the earth; and as is the heavenly man, so also are those who are of heaven. ⁴⁹And just as we have borne the image of the earthly man, so shall we[d] bear the image of the heavenly man.

⁵⁰I declare to you, brothers and sisters, that flesh and blood cannot inherit the kingdom of God, nor does the perishable inherit the imperishable. ⁵¹Listen, I tell you a mystery: we will not all sleep, but we will all be changed— ⁵²in a flash, in the twinkling of an eye, at the last trumpet. For the trumpet will sound, the dead will be raised imperishable, and we will be changed. ⁵³For the perishable must clothe itself with the imperishable, and the mortal with immortality. ⁵⁴When the perishable has been clothed with the imperishable, and the mortal with immortality, then the saying that is written will come true: 'Death has been swallowed up in victory.'[e]

⁵⁵'Where, O death, is your victory?
Where, O death, is your sting?'[f]

⁵⁶The sting of death is sin, and the power of sin is the law. ⁵⁷But thanks be to God! He gives us the victory through our Lord Jesus Christ.

⁵⁸Therefore, my dear brothers and sisters, stand firm. Let nothing move you. Always give yourselves fully to the work of the Lord, because you know that your labour in the Lord is not in vain.

The collection for the Lord's people

16 Now about the collection for the Lord's people: do what I told the Galatian churches to do. ²On the first day of every week, each one of you should set aside a sum of money in keeping with your income, saving it up, so that when I come no collections will have to be made. ³Then, when I arrive, I will give letters of introduction to the men you approve and send them with your gift to Jerusalem. ⁴If it seems advisable for me to go also, they will accompany me.

Personal requests

⁵After I go through Macedonia, I will come to you—for I will be going through Macedonia. ⁶Perhaps I will stay with you for a while, or even spend the winter, so that you

---

[a] 32 Isaiah 22:13 [b] 33 From the Greek poet Menander [c] 45 Gen. 2:7 [d] 49 Some early manuscripts *so let us*
[e] 54 Isaiah 25:8 [f] 55 Hosea 13:14

can help me on my journey, wherever I go. ⁷For I do not want to see you now and make only a passing visit; I hope to spend some time with you, if the Lord permits. ⁸But I will stay on at Ephesus until Pentecost, ⁹because a great door for effective work has opened to me, and there are many who oppose me.

¹⁰When Timothy comes, see to it that he has nothing to fear while he is with you, for he is carrying on the work of the Lord, just as I am. ¹¹No-one, then, should treat him with contempt. Send him on his way in peace so that he may return to me. I am expecting him along with the brothers.

¹²Now about our brother Apollos: I strongly urged him to go to you with the brothers. He was quite unwilling to go now, but he will go when he has the opportunity.

¹³Be on your guard; stand firm in the faith; be courageous; be strong. ¹⁴Do everything in love.

¹⁵You know that the household of Stephanas were the first converts in Achaia, and they have devoted themselves to the service of the Lord's people. I urge you, brothers and sisters, ¹⁶to submit to such as these and to everyone who joins in the work and labours at it. ¹⁷I was glad when Stephanas, Fortunatus and Achaicus arrived, because they have supplied what was lacking from you. ¹⁸For they refreshed my spirit and yours also. Such men deserve recognition.

Final greetings

¹⁹The churches in the province of Asia send you greetings. Aquila and Priscilla[a] greet you warmly in the Lord, and so does the church that meets at their house. ²⁰All the brothers and sisters here send you greetings. Greet one another with a holy kiss.

²¹I, Paul, write this greeting in my own hand.

²²If anyone does not love the Lord, let that person be cursed! Come, Lord[b]!

²³The grace of the Lord Jesus be with you.

²⁴My love to all of you in Christ Jesus. Amen.[c]

---

[a] 19 Greek *Prisca*, a variant of *Priscilla*   [b] 22 The Greek for *Come, Lord* reproduces an Aramaic expression (*Marana tha*) used by early Christians.   [c] 24 Some manuscripts do not have *Amen*.

2 Corinthians

INTRODUCTION

2 Corinthians

Author: Paul

Who to: Christians in Corinth.

When: Written in Macedonia about a year after Paul's first letter to the Corinthians.

Where: Corinth was ancient Greece's most important trade city.

Did you know? You can read how the church in Corinth started in Acts 18:1–18.

Main theme: In this letter Paul talks about what it's like to be a minister. Some people had obviously been spreading rumours about him – that he was not qualified to be a leader and was proud and boastful. He defends his ministry, and encourages the believers to stay true to their faith in Jesus.

1 Paul, an apostle of Christ Jesus by the will of God, and Timothy our brother,

To the church of God in Corinth, together with all his holy people throughout Achaia:

2Grace and peace to you from God our Father and the Lord Jesus Christ.

Praise to the God of all comfort

3Praise be to the God and Father of our Lord Jesus Christ, the Father of compassion and the God of all comfort, 4who comforts us in all our troubles, so that we can comfort those in any trouble with the comfort we ourselves receive from God. 5For just as we share abundantly in the sufferings of Christ, so also our comfort abounds through Christ. 6If we are distressed, it is for your comfort and salvation; if we are comforted, it is for your comfort, which produces in you patient endurance of the same sufferings we suffer. 7And our hope for you is firm, because we know that just as you share in our sufferings, so also you share in our comfort.

8We do not want you to be uninformed, brothers and sisters, about the troubles we experienced in the province of Asia. We were under great pressure, far beyond our ability to endure, so that we despaired of life itself. 9Indeed, we felt we had received the sentence of death. But this happened that we might not rely on ourselves but on God, who raises the dead. 10He has delivered us from such a deadly peril, and he will deliver us again. On him we have set our hope that he will continue to deliver us, 11as you help us by your prayers. Then many will give thanks on our behalf for the gracious favour granted us in answer to the prayers of many.

Paul's change of plans

12Now this is our boast: our conscience testifies that we have conducted ourselves in the world, and especially in our relations with you, with integrity[a] and godly sincerity. We have done so, relying not on worldly wisdom but on God's grace. 13For we do not write to you anything you cannot read or understand. And I hope that, 14as you have understood us in part, you will come to understand fully that you can boast of us just as we will boast of you in the day of the Lord Jesus.

15Because I was confident of this, I wanted to visit you first so that you might benefit twice. 16I wanted to visit you on my way to Macedonia and to come back to you from Macedonia, and then to let you send me on my way to Judea. 17Was I fickle when I intended to do this? Or do I make my plans in a worldly manner so that in the same breath I say both 'Yes, yes' and 'No, no'?

18But as surely as God is faithful, our message to you is not 'Yes' and 'No'. 19For the Son of God, Jesus Christ, who was preached among you by us—by me, Silas[b] and Timothy—was not 'Yes' and 'No', but in him it has always been 'Yes'. 20For no matter how many promises God has made, they are 'Yes' in Christ. And so through him the 'Amen' is spoken by us to the glory of God. 21Now it is God who makes both us and you stand firm in Christ. He anointed us, 22set his seal of ownership on us, and put his Spirit in our hearts as a deposit, guaranteeing what is to come.

23I call God as my witness—and I stake my life on it—that it was in order to spare you that I did not return to Corinth. 24Not that we lord it over your faith, but we work with you for your joy, because it is by faith you stand firm. **2** 1So I made up my mind that I would not make another painful visit to you. 2For if I grieve you, who is left to make me glad but you whom I have grieved? 3I wrote as I did, so that when I came I would not be distressed by those who should have made me rejoice. I had confidence in all of you, that you would all share my joy. 4For I wrote to you out of great distress and anguish of heart and with many tears, not to grieve you but to let you know the depth of my love for you.

Forgiveness for the offender

5If anyone has caused grief, he has not so much grieved me as he has grieved all of you to some extent—not to put it too severely. 6The punishment inflicted on him by the majority is sufficient. 7Now instead, you ought to forgive and comfort him, so that he will not be overwhelmed by excessive sorrow. 8I urge you, therefore, to reaffirm your love for him. 9Another reason I wrote to you was to see if you would stand the test and be obedient in everything. 10Anyone you forgive, I also forgive. And what I have forgiven—if there was anything to forgive—I have forgiven in the sight of Christ for your sake, 11in order that Satan might not outwit us. For we are not unaware of his schemes.

Ministers of the new covenant

12Now when I went to Troas to preach the gospel of Christ and found that the Lord had opened a door for me, 13I still had no peace of mind, because I did not find my brother Titus there. So I said good-bye to them and went on to Macedonia.

14But thanks be to God, who always leads us as captives in Christ's triumphal procession and uses us to spread the aroma of the knowledge of him everywhere. 15For we are to God the pleasing aroma of Christ among those who are being saved and those who are perishing. 16To the one we are an aroma that brings death; to the other, an aroma that brings life. And who is equal to such a task? 17Unlike so many, we do not peddle

---

[a] 12 Many manuscripts *holiness* [b] 19 Greek *Silvanus*, a variant of *Silas*

the word of God for profit. On the contrary, in Christ we speak before God with sincerity, as those sent from God.

3 Are we beginning to commend ourselves again? Or do we need, like some people, letters of recommendation to you or from you? ²You yourselves are our letter, written on our hearts, known and read by everyone. ³You show that you are a letter from Christ, the result of our ministry, written not with ink but with the Spirit of the living God, not on tablets of stone but on tablets of human hearts.

⁴Such confidence we have through Christ before God. ⁵Not that we are competent in ourselves to claim anything for ourselves, but our competence comes from God. ⁶He has made us competent as ministers of a new covenant—not of the letter but of the Spirit; for the letter kills, but the Spirit gives life.

The greater glory of the new covenant

⁷Now if the ministry that brought death, which was engraved in letters on stone, came with glory, so that the Israelites could not look steadily at the face of Moses because of its glory, transitory though it was, ⁸will not the ministry of the Spirit be even more glorious? ⁹If the ministry that brought condemnation was glorious, how much more glorious is the ministry that brings righteousness! ¹⁰For what was glorious has no glory now in comparison with the surpassing glory. ¹¹And if what was transitory came with glory, how much greater is the glory of that which lasts!

¹²Therefore, since we have such a hope, we are very bold. ¹³We are not like Moses, who would put a veil over his face to prevent the Israelites from seeing the end of what was passing away. ¹⁴But their minds were made dull, for to this day the same veil remains when the old covenant is read. It has not been removed, because only in Christ is it taken away. ¹⁵Even to this day when Moses is read, a veil covers their hearts. ¹⁶But whenever anyone turns to the Lord, the veil is taken away. ¹⁷Now the Lord is the Spirit, and where the Spirit of the Lord is, there is freedom. ¹⁸And we all, who with unveiled faces contemplate^a the Lord's glory, are being transformed into his image with ever-increasing glory, which comes from the Lord, who is the Spirit.

Present weakness and resurrection life1

4 Therefore, since through God's mercy we have this ministry, we do not lose heart. ²Rather, we have renounced secret and shameful ways; we do not use deception, nor do we distort the word of God. On the contrary, by setting forth the truth plainly we commend ourselves to everyone's conscience in the sight of God. ³And even if our gospel is veiled, it is veiled to those who are perishing. ⁴The god of this age has blinded the minds of unbelievers, so that they cannot see the light of the gospel that displays the glory of Christ, who is the image of God. ⁵For what we preach is not ourselves, but Jesus Christ as Lord, and ourselves as your servants for Jesus' sake. ⁶For God, who said, 'Let light shine out of darkness,'^{b} made his light shine in our hearts to give us the light of the knowledge of God's glory displayed in the face of Christ.

⁷But we have this treasure in jars of clay to show that this all-surpassing power is from God and not from us. ⁸We are hard pressed on every side, but not crushed; perplexed, but not in despair; ⁹persecuted, but not abandoned; struck down, but not destroyed. ¹⁰We always carry around in our body the death of Jesus, so that the life of Jesus may also be revealed in our body. ¹¹For we who are alive are always being given over to death for Jesus' sake, so that his life may also be revealed in our mortal body. ¹²So then, death is at work in us, but life is at work in you.

¹³It is written: 'I believed; therefore I have spoken.'^{c} Since we have that same spirit of^d faith, we also believe and therefore speak, ¹⁴because we know that the one who raised the Lord Jesus from the dead will also raise us with Jesus and present us with you to himself. ¹⁵All this is for your benefit, so that the grace that is reaching more and more people may cause thanksgiving to overflow to the glory of God.

---

^{a} 18 Or *reflect* ^{b} 6 Gen. 1:3 ^{c} 13 Psalm 116:10 (see Septuagint) ^{d} 13 Or *Spirit-given*

Clay pottery
2 Corinthians 4:7

Clay was a common material, used for bricks, seals and writing tablets as well as pots, utensils, lamps and dishes (Jeremiah 18:1). Clay is a very flexible material and can be moulded into all kinds of shapes. Clay pottery is one of the longest lasting materials ever made. Although clay pots break easily, the fragments last for centuries, giving clues as to how people lived.

16 Therefore we do not lose heart. Though outwardly we are wasting away, yet inwardly we are being renewed day by day. 17 For our light and momentary troubles are achieving for us an eternal glory that far outweighs them all. 18 So we fix our eyes not on what is seen, but on what is unseen, since what is seen is temporary, but what is unseen is eternal.

Awaiting the new body

5 For we know that if the earthly tent we live in is destroyed, we have a building from God, an eternal house in heaven, not built by human hands. 2 Meanwhile we groan, longing to be clothed with our heavenly dwelling, 3 because when we are clothed, we will not be found naked. 4 For while we are in this tent, we groan and are burdened, because we do not wish to be unclothed but to be clothed with our heavenly dwelling, so that what is mortal may be swallowed up by life. 5 Now the one who has fashioned us for this very purpose is God, who has given us the Spirit as a deposit, guaranteeing what is to come.

6 Therefore we are always confident and know that as long as we are at home in the body we are away from the Lord. 7 We live by faith, not by sight. 8 We are confident, I say, and would prefer to be away from the body and at home with the Lord. 9 So we make it our goal to please him, whether we are at home in the body or away from it. 10 For we must all appear before the judgment seat of Christ, that everyone may receive what is due to them for the things done while in the body, whether good or bad.

The ministry of reconciliation

11 Since, then, we know what it is to fear the Lord, we try to persuade people. What we are is plain to God, and I hope it is also plain to your conscience. 12 We are not trying to commend ourselves to you again, but are giving you an opportunity to take pride in us, so that you can answer those who take pride in what is seen rather than in what is in the heart. 13 If we are 'out of our mind,' as some say, it is for God; if we are in our right mind, it is for you. 14 For Christ's love compels us, because we are convinced that one died for all, and therefore all died. 15 And he died for all, that those who live should no longer live for themselves but for him who died for them and was raised again.

16 So from now on we regard no-one from a worldly point of view. Though we once regarded Christ in this way, we do so no longer. 17 Therefore, if anyone is in Christ, the new creation has come: the old has gone, the new is here! 18 All this is from God, who reconciled us to himself through Christ and gave us the ministry of reconciliation: 19 that God was reconciling the world to himself in Christ, not counting people's sins against them. And he has committed to us the message of reconciliation. 20 We are therefore Christ's ambassadors, as though God were making his appeal through us. We implore you on Christ's behalf: be reconciled to God. 21 God made him who had no sin to be sin[a] for us, so that in him we might become the righteousness of God.

6 As God's fellow-workers we urge you not to receive God's grace in vain. 2 For he says,

---

[a] 21 Or *be a sin offering*

'In the time of my favour I heard you,
and in the day of salvation I helped
you.'[a]

I tell you, now is the time of God's favour, now is the day of salvation.

Paul's hardships

3We put no stumbling-block in anyone's path, so that our ministry will not be discredited. 4Rather, as servants of God we commend ourselves in every way: in great endurance; in troubles, hardships and distresses; 5in beatings, imprisonments and riots; in hard work, sleepless nights and hunger; 6in purity, understanding, patience and kindness; in the Holy Spirit and in sincere love; 7in truthful speech and in the power of God; with weapons of righteousness in the right hand and in the left; 8through glory and dishonour, bad report and good report; genuine, yet regarded as impostors; 9known, yet regarded as unknown; dying, and yet we live on; beaten, and yet not killed; 10sorrowful, yet always rejoicing; poor, yet making many rich; having nothing, and yet possessing everything.

11We have spoken freely to you, Corinthians, and opened wide our hearts to you. 12We are not withholding our affection from you, but you are withholding yours from us. 13As a fair exchange—I speak as to my children—open wide your hearts also.

Warning against idolatry

14Do not be yoked together with unbelievers. For what do righteousness and wickedness have in common? Or what fellowship can light have with darkness? 15What harmony is there between Christ and Belial[b]? Or what does a believer have in common with an unbeliever? 16What agreement is there between the temple of God and idols? For we are the temple of the living God. As God has said:

'I will live with them
    and walk among them,
and I will be their God,
    and they will be my people.'[c]

making Connections

Yoke
2 Corinthians 6:14
A yoke was a type of harness which connected a pair of oxen to a plough. It was usually a wooden beam shaped to fit over the necks of two animals and held in place with a wooden peg.

17Therefore,

'Come out from them
    and be separate,
                              says the Lord.
Touch no unclean thing,
    and I will receive you.'[d]

18And,

'I will be a Father to you,
    and you will be my sons and daughters,
        says the Lord Almighty.'[e]

7 Therefore, since we have these promises, dear friends, let us purify ourselves from everything that contaminates body and spirit, perfecting holiness out of reverence for God.

Paul's joy over the church's repentance

2Make room for us in your hearts. We have wronged no-one, we have corrupted no-one, we have exploited no-one. 3I do not say this to condemn you; I have said before that you have such a place in our hearts that we would live or die with you. 4I have spoken to you with great frankness; I take great pride in you. I am greatly encouraged; in all our troubles my joy knows no bounds.

5For when we came into Macedonia, this body of ours had no rest, but we were harassed at every turn—conflicts on the outside, fears within. 6But God, who

---

[a]2 Isaiah 49:8 [b]15 Greek *Beliar*, a variant of *Belial* [c]16 Lev. 26:12; Jer. 32:38; Ezek. 37:27 [d]17 Isaiah 52:11; Ezek. 20:34,41 [e]18 2 Samuel 7:14; 7:8

comforts the downcast, comforted us by the coming of Titus, 7and not only by his coming but also by the comfort you had given him. He told us about your longing for me, your deep sorrow, your ardent concern for me, so that my joy was greater than ever.

8Even if I caused you sorrow by my letter, I do not regret it. Though I did regret it—I see that my letter hurt you, but only for a little while— 9yet now I am happy, not because you were made sorry, but because your sorrow led you to repentance. For you became sorrowful as God intended and so were not harmed in any way by us. 10Godly sorrow brings repentance that leads to salvation and leaves no regret, but worldly sorrow brings death. 11See what this godly sorrow has produced in you: what earnestness, what eagerness to clear yourselves, what indignation, what alarm, what longing, what concern, what readiness to see justice done. At every point you have proved yourselves to be innocent in this matter. 12So even though I wrote to you, it was neither on account of the one who did the wrong nor on account of the injured party, but rather that before God you could see for yourselves how devoted to us you are. 13By all this we are encouraged.

In addition to our own encouragement, we were especially delighted to see how happy Titus was, because his spirit has been refreshed by all of you. 14I had boasted to him about you, and you have not embarrassed me. But just as everything we said to you was true, so our boasting about you to Titus has proved to be true as well. 15And his affection for you is all the greater when he remembers that you were all obedient, receiving him with fear and trembling. 16I am glad I can have complete confidence in you.

The collection for the Lord's people

8 And now, brothers and sisters, we want you to know about the grace that God has given the Macedonian churches. 2In the midst of a very severe trial, their overflowing joy and their extreme poverty welled up in rich generosity. 3For I testify that they gave as much as they were able, and even beyond their ability. Entirely on their own, 4they urgently pleaded with us for the privilege of sharing in this service to the Lord's people. 5And they went beyond our expectations; having given themselves first of all to the Lord, they gave themselves by the will of God also to us. 6So we urged Titus, just as he had earlier made a beginning, to bring also to completion this act of grace on your part. 7But since you excel in everything—in faith, in speech, in knowledge, in complete earnestness and in the love we have kindled in you^a—see that you also excel in this grace of giving.

8I am not commanding you, but I want to test the sincerity of your love by comparing it with the earnestness of others. 9For you know the grace of our Lord Jesus Christ, that though he was rich, yet for your sake he became poor, so that you through his poverty might become rich.

10And here is my judgment about what is best for you in this matter. Last year you were the first not only to give but also to have the desire to do so. 11Now finish the work, so that your eager willingness to do it may be matched by your completion of it, according to your means. 12For if the willingness is there, the gift is acceptable according to what one has, not according to what one does not have.

13Our desire is not that others might be relieved while you are hard pressed, but that there might be equality. 14At the present time your plenty will supply what they need, so that in turn their plenty will supply what you need. The goal is equality, 15as it is written: 'The one who gathered much did not have too much, and the one who gathered little did not have too little.'^{b}

Titus sent to receive the collection

16Thanks be to God, who put into the heart of Titus the same concern I have for you. 17For Titus not only welcomed our appeal, but he is coming to you with much enthusiasm and on his own initiative. 18And we are sending along with him the brother who is praised by all the churches for his service to the gospel. 19What is more, he was

---

^{a} 7 Some manuscripts *and in your love for us* ^{b} 15 Exodus 16:18

IN OTHER WORDS

Offering
2 Corinthians 8:19
In the Old Testament, offerings were sacrifices made to God to enable sinful people to put things right and draw close to him (Leviticus 3:1). Now, the word 'offering' refers to money given to God as part of worship.

chosen by the churches to accompany us as we carry the offering, which we administer in order to honour the Lord himself and to show our eagerness to help. 20We want to avoid any criticism of the way we administer this liberal gift. 21For we are taking pains to do what is right, not only in the eyes of the Lord but also in the eyes of others.

22In addition, we are sending with them our brother who has often proved to us in many ways that he is zealous, and now even more so because of his great confidence in you. 23As for Titus, he is my partner and fellow-worker among you; as for our brothers, they are representatives of the churches and an honour to Christ. 24Therefore show these men the proof of your love and the reason for our pride in you, so that the churches can see it.

9 There is no need for me to write to you about this service to the Lord's people. 2For I know your eagerness to help, and I have been boasting about it to the Macedonians, telling them that since last year you in Achaia were ready to give; and your enthusiasm has stirred most of them to action. 3But I am sending the brothers in order that our boasting about you in this matter should not prove hollow, but that you may be ready, as I said you would be. 4For if any Macedonians come with me and find you unprepared, we—not to say anything about you—would be ashamed of having been so confident. 5So I thought it necessary to urge the brothers to visit you in advance and finish the arrangements for the generous gift you had promised. Then it will be ready as a generous gift, not as one grudgingly given.

Generosity encouraged

6Remember this: whoever sows sparingly will also reap sparingly, and whoever sows generously will also reap generously. 7Each of you should give what you have decided in your heart to give, not reluctantly or under compulsion, for God loves a cheerful giver. 8And God is able to bless you abundantly, so that in all things at all times, having all that you need, you will abound in every good work. 9As it is written:

> 'They have scattered abroad their gifts to the poor;
> their righteousness endures for ever.'[a]

10Now he who supplies seed to the sower and bread for food will also supply and increase your store of seed and will enlarge the harvest of your righteousness. 11You will be made rich in every way so that you can be generous on every occasion, and through us your generosity will result in thanksgiving to God.

12This service that you perform is not only supplying the needs of the Lord's people but is also overflowing in many expressions of thanks to God. 13Because of the service by which you have proved yourselves, people will praise God for the obedience that accompanies your confession of the gospel of Christ, and for your generosity in sharing with them and with everyone else. 14And in their prayers for you their hearts will go out to you, because of the surpassing grace God has given you. 15Thanks be to God for his indescribable gift!

Paul's defence of his ministry

10 By the meekness and gentleness of Christ, I appeal to you—I, Paul, who am 'timid' when face to face with you, but 'bold' towards you when away! 2I beg you that when I come I may not have to be as bold as I expect to be towards some people who think that we live by the standards of

---
[a] 9 Psalm 112:9

this world. 3For though we live in the world, we do not wage war as the world does. 4The weapons we fight with are not the weapons of the world. On the contrary, they have divine power to demolish strongholds. 5We demolish arguments and every pretension that sets itself up against the knowledge of God, and we take captive every thought to make it obedient to Christ. 6And we will be ready to punish every act of disobedience, once your obedience is complete.

7You are judging by appearances.[a] If anyone is confident that they belong to Christ, they should consider again that we belong to Christ just as much as they do. 8So even if I boast somewhat freely about the authority the Lord gave us for building you up rather than tearing you down, I will not be ashamed of it. 9I do not want to seem to be trying to frighten you with my letters. 10For some say, 'His letters are weighty and forceful, but in person he is unimpressive and his speaking amounts to nothing.' 11Such people should realise that what we are in our letters when we are absent, we will be in our actions when we are present.

12We do not dare to classify or compare ourselves with some who commend themselves. When they measure themselves by themselves and compare themselves with themselves, they are not wise. 13We, however, will not boast beyond proper limits, but will confine our boasting to the sphere of service God himself has assigned to us, a sphere that also includes you. 14We are not going too far in our boasting, as would be the case if we had not come to you, for we did get as far as you with the gospel of Christ. 15Neither do we go beyond our limits by boasting of work done by others. Our hope is that, as your faith continues to grow, our sphere of activity among you will greatly expand, 16so that we can preach the gospel in the regions beyond you. For we do not want to boast about work already done in someone else's territory. 17But, 'Let those who boast boast in the Lord.'[b] 18For it is not those who commend themselves who are approved, but those whom the Lord commends.

Paul and the false apostles

11 I hope you will put up with me in a little foolishness. Yes, please put up with me! 2I am jealous for you with a godly jealousy. I promised you to one husband, to Christ, so that I might present you as a pure virgin to him. 3But I am afraid that just as Eve was deceived by the snake's cunning, your minds may somehow be led astray from your sincere and pure devotion to Christ. 4For if someone comes to you and preaches a Jesus other than the Jesus we preached, or if you receive a different spirit from the Spirit you received, or a different gospel from the one you accepted, you put up with it easily enough.

5I do not think I am in the least inferior to those 'super-apostles'.[c] 6I may indeed be untrained as a speaker, but I do have knowledge. We have made this perfectly clear to you in every way. 7Was it a sin for me to lower myself in order to elevate you by preaching the gospel of God to you free of charge? 8I robbed other churches by receiving support from them so as to serve you. 9And when I was with you and needed something, I was not a burden to anyone, for the brothers and sisters who came from Macedonia supplied what I needed. I have kept myself from being a burden to you in any way, and will continue to do so. 10As surely as the truth of Christ is in me, nobody in the regions of Achaia will stop this boasting of mine. 11Why? Because I do not love you? God knows I do!

12And I will keep on doing what I am doing in order to cut the ground from under those who want an opportunity to be considered equal with us in the things they boast about. 13For such persons are false apostles, deceitful workers, masquerading as apostles of Christ. 14And no wonder, for Satan himself masquerades as an angel of light. 15It is not surprising, then, if his servants also masquerade as servants of righteousness. Their end will be what their actions deserve.

Paul boasts about his sufferings

16I repeat: let no-one take me for a fool. But if you do, then tolerate me just as you would

---

[a] 7 Or *Look at the obvious facts* [b] 17 Jer. 9:24 [c] 5 Or *to the most eminent apostles*

a fool, so that I may do a little boasting. ¹⁷In this self-confident boasting I am not talking as the Lord would, but as a fool. ¹⁸Since many are boasting in the way the world does, I too will boast. ¹⁹You gladly put up with fools since you are so wise! ²⁰In fact, you even put up with any who enslave you or exploit you or take advantage of you or push themselves forward or slap you in the face. ²¹To my shame I admit that we were too weak for that!

Whatever anyone else dares to boast about—I am speaking as a fool—I also dare to boast about. ²²Are they Hebrews? So am I. Are they Israelites? So am I. Are they Abraham's descendants? So am I. ²³Are they servants of Christ? (I am out of my mind to talk like this.) I am more. I have worked much harder, been in prison more frequently, been flogged more severely, and been exposed to death again and again. ²⁴Five times I received from the Jews the forty lashes minus one. ²⁵Three times I was beaten with rods, once I was pelted with stones, three times I was shipwrecked, I spent a night and a day in the open sea, ²⁶I have been constantly on the move. I have been in danger from rivers, in danger from bandits, in danger from my own people, in danger from Gentiles; in danger in the city, in danger in the country, in danger at sea; and in danger from false believers. ²⁷I have laboured and toiled and have often gone without sleep; I have known hunger and thirst and have often gone without food; I have been cold and naked. ²⁸Besides everything else, I face daily the pressure of my concern for all the churches. ²⁹Who is weak, and I do not feel weak? Who is led into sin, and I do not inwardly burn?

³⁰If I must boast, I will boast of the things that show my weakness. ³¹The God and Father of the Lord Jesus, who is to be praised for ever, knows that I am not lying. ³²In Damascus the governor under King Aretas had the city of the Damascenes guarded in order to arrest me. ³³But I was lowered in a basket from a window in the wall and slipped through his hands.

Paul's vision and his thorn

12 I must go on boasting. Although there is nothing to be gained, I will go on to visions and revelations from the Lord. ²I know a man in Christ who fourteen years ago was caught up to the third heaven. Whether it was in the body or out of the body I do not know—God knows. ³And I know that this man—whether in the body or apart from the body I do not know, but God knows— ⁴was caught up to paradise and heard inexpressible things, things that no-one is permitted to tell. ⁵I will boast about someone like that, but I will not boast about myself, except about my weaknesses. ⁶Even if I should choose to boast, I would not be a fool, because I would be speaking the truth. But I refrain, so no-one will think more of me than is warranted by what I do or say, ⁷or because of these surpassingly great revelations. Therefore, in order to keep me from becoming conceited, I was given a thorn in my flesh, a messenger of Satan, to torment me. ⁸Three times I pleaded with the Lord to take it away from me. ⁹But he said to me, 'My grace is sufficient for you, for my power is made perfect in weakness.' Therefore I will boast

making Connections

Thorn in the flesh
2 Corinthians 12:7

Nobody knows what Paul's 'thorn in the flesh' actually was, but it was obviously a real pain. The Greek word for thorn can also be used to refer to a stake that someone can be impaled upon! Some people think it might have been a physical weakness or disability, but the troubles and sufferings Paul describes in chapters 11 and 12 were primarily caused by people. It is more probable that someone sent from Satan had the special purpose of making life very difficult for Paul and Paul asked for relief from this.

all the more gladly about my weaknesses, so that Christ's power may rest on me. ¹⁰That is why, for Christ's sake, I delight in weaknesses, in insults, in hardships, in persecutions, in difficulties. For when I am weak, then I am strong.

Paul's concern for the Corinthians

¹¹I have made a fool of myself, but you drove me to it. I ought to have been commended by you, for I am not in the least inferior to the 'super-apostles',[a] even though I am nothing. ¹²I persevered in demonstrating among you the marks of a true apostle, including signs, wonders and miracles. ¹³How were you inferior to the other churches, except that I was never a burden to you? Forgive me this wrong!

¹⁴Now I am ready to visit you for the third time, and I will not be a burden to you, because what I want is not your possessions but you. After all, children should not have to save up for their parents, but parents for their children. ¹⁵So I will very gladly spend for you everything I have and expend myself as well. If I love you more, will you love me less? ¹⁶Be that as it may, I have not been a burden to you. Yet, crafty fellow that I am, I caught you by trickery! ¹⁷Did I exploit you through any of the men I sent to you? ¹⁸I urged Titus to go to you and I sent our brother with him. Titus did not exploit you, did he? Did we not walk in the same footsteps by the same Spirit?

¹⁹Have you been thinking all along that we have been defending ourselves to you? We have been speaking in the sight of God as those in Christ; and everything we do, dear friends, is for your strengthening. ²⁰For I am afraid that when I come I may not find you as I want you to be, and you may not find me as you want me to be. I fear that there may be quarrelling, jealousy, outbursts of anger, factions, slander, gossip, arrogance and disorder. ²¹I am afraid that when I come again my God will humble me before you, and I will be grieved over many who have sinned earlier and have not repented of the impurity, sexual sin and debauchery in which they have indulged.

Final warnings

13 This will be my third visit to you. 'Every matter must be established by the testimony of two or three witnesses.'[b] ²I already gave you a warning when I was with you the second time. I now repeat it while absent: on my return I will not spare those who sinned earlier or any of the others, ³since you are demanding proof that Christ is speaking through me. He is not weak in dealing with you, but is powerful among you. ⁴For to be sure, he was crucified in weakness, yet he lives by God's power. Likewise, we are weak in him, yet by God's power we will live with him in our dealing with you.

⁵Examine yourselves to see whether you are in the faith; test yourselves. Do you not realise that Christ Jesus is in you—unless, of course, you fail the test? ⁶And I trust that you will discover that we have not failed the test. ⁷Now we pray to God that you will not do anything wrong. Not that people will see that we have stood the test but that you will do what is right even though we may seem to have failed. ⁸For we cannot do anything against the truth, but only for the truth. ⁹We are glad whenever we are weak but you are strong; and our prayer is that you may be fully restored. ¹⁰This is why I write these things when I am absent, that when I come I may not have to be harsh in my use of

People and Places

Trinity
2 Corinthians 13:14
Although the word 'Trinity' doesn't appear in the Bible, the idea that God is one and three is very much part of the New Testament's teaching. The three persons that make up the Trinity are God the Father, Jesus who is God the Son, and the Holy Spirit.

---

[a] 11 Or *the most eminent apostles* [b] 1 Deut. 19:15

authority—the authority the Lord gave me for building you up, not for tearing you down.

Final greetings

¹¹Finally, brothers and sisters, rejoice! Strive for full restoration, encourage one another, be of one mind, live in peace. And the God of love and peace will be with you.

¹²Greet one another with a holy kiss. ¹³All God's people here send their greetings.

¹⁴May the grace of the Lord Jesus Christ, and the love of God, and the fellowship of the Holy Spirit be with you all.

Galatians

INTRODUCTION

Galatians

Author: Paul

Who to: Christians in Galatia.

When: Galatians may be Paul's earliest letter, written around AD 48.

Where: Galatia was a region in central Asia Minor, in the country we now call Turkey.

Did you know? On his first missionary journey, Paul preached the gospel in four Galatian cities (Acts 13 and 14) and he returned to the area on his later trips.

Main theme: You can sum up the whole book of Galatians in one word: grace! After Paul had visited the Galatians, other false teachers had come and persuaded them that the gospel Paul had preached wasn't enough for them to be saved. Rubbish, says Paul. You don't need to be circumcised, keep the Sabbath or obey the law to be saved. All you need is faith to receive God's grace.

1 Paul, an apostle—sent not with a human commission nor by human authority, but by Jesus Christ and God the Father, who raised him from the dead— ²and all the brothers and sisters with me,

To the churches in Galatia:

³Grace and peace to you from God our Father and the Lord Jesus Christ, ⁴who gave himself for our sins to rescue us from the present evil age, according to the will of our God and Father, ⁵to whom be glory for ever and ever. Amen.

No other gospel

⁶I am astonished that you are so quickly deserting the one who called you by the grace of Christ and are turning to a different gospel— ⁷which is really no gospel at all. Evidently some people are throwing you into confusion and are trying to pervert the gospel of Christ. ⁸But even if we or an angel from heaven should preach a gospel other than the one we preached to you, let that person be under God's curse! ⁹As we have already said, so now I say again: if anybody is preaching to you a gospel other than what

you accepted, let that person be under God's curse!

¹⁰Am I now trying to win human approval, or God's approval? Or am I trying to please people? If I were still trying to please people, I would not be a servant of Christ.

Paul called by God

¹¹I want you to know, brothers and sisters, that the gospel I preached is not of human origin. ¹²I did not receive it from any human source, nor was I taught it; rather, I received it by revelation from Jesus Christ.

¹³For you have heard of my previous way of life in Judaism, how intensely I persecuted the church of God and tried to destroy it. ¹⁴I was advancing in Judaism beyond many of my own age among my people and was extremely zealous for the traditions of my fathers. ¹⁵But when God, who set me apart from birth[a] and called me by his grace, was pleased ¹⁶to reveal his Son in me so that I might preach him among the Gentiles, my immediate response was not to consult any human being. ¹⁷I did not go up to Jerusalem to see those who were apostles before I was, but I went into Arabia. Later I returned to Damascus.

¹⁸Then after three years, I went up to Jerusalem to get acquainted with Cephas[b] and stayed with him fifteen days. ¹⁹I saw none of the other apostles—only James, the Lord's brother. ²⁰I assure you before God that what I am writing to you is no lie.

²¹Then I went to Syria and Cilicia. ²²I was personally unknown to the churches of Judea that are in Christ. ²³They only heard the report: 'The man who formerly persecuted us is now preaching the faith he once tried to destroy.' ²⁴And they praised God because of me.

Paul accepted by the apostles

2 Then after fourteen years, I went up again to Jerusalem, this time with Barnabas. I took Titus along also. ²I went in response to a revelation and, meeting privately with those esteemed as leaders, I set before them the gospel that I preach among the Gentiles. I wanted to be sure I was not running and had not been running my race in vain. ³Yet not even Titus, who was with me, was compelled to be circumcised, even though he was a Greek. ⁴This matter arose because some false believers had infiltrated our ranks to spy on the freedom we have in Christ Jesus and to make us slaves. ⁵We did not give in to them for a moment, so that the truth of the gospel might remain with you.

⁶As for those who were held in high esteem—whatever they were makes no difference to me; God does not show favouritism—they added nothing to my message. ⁷On the contrary, they saw that I had been entrusted with the task of preaching the gospel to the Gentiles,[c] just as Peter had been to the Jews.[d] ⁸For God, who was at work in Peter as an apostle to the Jews, was also at work in me as an apostle to the Gentiles. ⁹James, Cephas[e] and John, those esteemed as pillars, gave me and Barnabas the right hand of fellowship when they recognised the grace given to me. They agreed that we should go to the Gentiles, and they to the Jews. ¹⁰All they asked was that we should continue to remember the poor, the very thing I had been eager to do all along.

Paul opposes Cephas

¹¹When Cephas came to Antioch, I opposed him to his face, because he stood condemned. ¹²For before certain people came from James, he used to eat with the Gentiles. But when they arrived, he began to draw back and separate himself from the

> **Gentile**
> Galatians 2:7
> The word 'Gentile' is used in the Bible to describe any people who are not part of the Jewish race.

---

[a] 15 Or *from my mother's womb* [b] 18 That is, Peter [c] 7 Greek *uncircumcised* [d] 7 Greek *circumcised*; also in verses 8 and 9 [e] 9 That is, Peter; also in verses 11 and 14

Gentiles because he was afraid of those who belonged to the circumcision group. 13The other Jews joined him in his hypocrisy, so that by their hypocrisy even Barnabas was led astray.

14When I saw that they were not acting in line with the truth of the gospel, I said to Cephas in front of them all, 'You are a Jew, yet you live like a Gentile and not like a Jew. How is it, then, that you force Gentiles to follow Jewish customs?

15'We who are Jews by birth and not sinful Gentiles 16know that a person is not justified by observing the law, but by faith in Jesus Christ. So we, too, have put our faith in Christ Jesus that we may be justified by faith in[a] Christ and not by observing the law, because by observing the law no-one will be justified.

17'But if, in seeking to be justified in Christ, we Jews find ourselves also among the 'sinners', doesn't that mean that Christ promotes sin? Absolutely not! 18If I rebuild what I destroyed, then I really would be a law-breaker.

19'For through the law I died to the law so that I might live for God. 20I have been crucified with Christ and I no longer live, but Christ lives in me. The life I now live in the body, I live by faith in the Son of God, who loved me and gave himself for me. 21I do not set aside the grace of God, for if righteousness could be gained through the law, Christ died for nothing!'[b]

Faith or observance of the law

3 You foolish Galatians! Who has bewitched you? Before your very eyes Jesus Christ was clearly portrayed as crucified. 2I would like to learn just one thing from you: did you receive the Spirit by observing the law, or by believing what you heard? 3Are you so foolish? After beginning with the Spirit, are you now trying to finish by human effort? 4Have you experienced[c] so much in vain—if it really was in vain? 5Does God give you his Spirit and work miracles among you by your observing the law, or by your believing what you heard? 6So also Abraham 'believed God, and it was credited to him as righteousness.'[d]

7Understand, then, that those who have faith are children of Abraham. 8Scripture foresaw that God would justify the Gentiles by faith, and announced the gospel in advance to Abraham: 'All nations will be blessed through you.'[e] 9So those who rely on faith are blessed along with Abraham, the man of faith.

10All who rely on observing the law are under a curse, for it is written: 'Cursed is everyone who does not continue to do everything written in the Book of the Law.'[f] 11Clearly no-one is justified before God by the law, because 'the righteous will live by faith.'[g] 12The law is not based on faith; on the contrary, it says, 'Whoever does these things will live by them.'[h] 13Christ redeemed us from the curse of the law by becoming a curse for us, for it is written: 'Cursed is everyone who is hung on a pole.'[i] 14He redeemed us in order that the blessing given to Abraham might come to the Gentiles through Christ Jesus, so that by faith we might receive the promise of the Spirit.

The law and the promise

15Brothers and sisters, let me take an example from everyday life. Just as no-one can set aside or add to a human covenant that has been duly established, so it is in this case. 16The promises were spoken to Abraham and to his seed. Scripture does not say 'and to seeds', meaning many people, but 'and to your seed',[j] meaning one person, who is Christ. 17What I mean is this: the law, introduced 430 years later, does not set aside the covenant previously established by God and thus do away with the promise. 18For if the inheritance depends on the law, then it no longer depends on the promise; but God in his grace gave it to Abraham through a promise.

19What, then, was the purpose of the law? It was added because of transgressions until the Seed to whom the promise referred had come. The law was given through angels and entrusted to a mediator. 20A mediator,

---

[a] 16 Or *but through the faithfulness of . . . justified on the basis of the faithfulness of* [b] 21 Some interpreters end the quotation after verse 14. [c] 4 Or *suffered* [d] 6 Gen. 15:6 [e] 8 Gen. 12:3; 18:18; 22:18 [f] 10 Deut. 27:26 [g] 11 Hab. 2:4 [h] 12 Lev. 18:5 [i] 13 Deut. 21:23 [j] 16 Gen. 12:7; 13:15; 24:7

however, implies more than one party; but God is one.

21Is the law, therefore, opposed to the promises of God? Absolutely not! For if a law had been given that could impart life, then righteousness would certainly have come by the law. 22But Scripture has locked up everything under the control of sin, so that what was promised, being given through faith in Jesus Christ, might be given to those who believe.

Children of God

23Before the coming of this faith,*a* we were held in custody under the law, locked up until the faith that was to come would be revealed. 24So the law was put in charge of us until Christ came that we might be justified by faith. 25Now that this faith has come, we are no longer under the supervision of the law.

26So in Christ Jesus you are all children of God through faith, 27for all of you who were baptised into Christ have clothed yourselves with Christ. 28There is neither Jew nor Gentile, neither slave nor free, neither male nor female, for you are all one in Christ Jesus. 29If you belong to Christ, then you are Abraham's seed, and heirs according to the promise.

4 What I am saying is that as long as heirs are under age they are no different from slaves, although they own the whole estate. 2They are subject to guardians and trustees until the time set by their fathers. 3So also, when we were under age, we were in slavery under the elemental spiritual forces*b* of the world. 4But when the set time had fully come, God sent his Son, born of a woman, born under the law, 5to redeem those under the law, that we might receive adoption to sonship.*c* 6Because you are his sons, God sent the Spirit of his Son into our hearts, the Spirit who calls out, 'Abba,*d* Father.' 7So you are no longer slaves, but God's children; and since you are his children, he has made you also heirs.

Sign of the times

Guardians and trustees
Galatians 4:2
A guardian had responsibility for looking after a child until he or she was fourteen. A trustee oversaw the finances of a young man until he was twenty-five.

Paul's concern for the Galatians

8Formerly, when you did not know God, you were slaves to those who by nature are not gods. 9But now that you know God—or rather are known by God—how is it that you are turning back to those weak and miserable forces*e*? Do you wish to be enslaved by them all over again? 10You are observing special days and months and seasons and years! 11I fear for you, that somehow I have wasted my efforts on you.

12I plead with you, brothers and sisters, become like me, for I became like you. You have done me no wrong. 13As you know, it was because of an illness that I first preached the gospel to you. 14Even though my illness was a trial to you, you did not treat me with contempt or scorn. Instead, you welcomed me as if I were an angel of God, as if I were Christ Jesus himself. 15What has happened to all your joy? I can testify that, if you could have done so, you would have torn out your eyes and given them to me. 16Have I now become your enemy by telling you the truth?

17Those people are zealous to win you over, but for no good. What they want is to alienate you from us, so that you may have zeal for them. 18It is fine to be zealous, provided the purpose is good, and to be so always, not just when I am with you. 19My dear children, for whom I am again in the pains of childbirth until Christ is formed in

---

a 22,23 Or *through the faithfulness of Jesus....* 23*Before faith came* *b* 3 Or *under the basic principles* *c* 5 The Greek word for *adoption to sonship* is a legal term referring to the full legal standing of an adopted male heir in Roman culture. *d* 6 Aramaic for *Father* *e* 9 Or *principles* you, 20how I wish I could be with you now and change my tone, because I am perplexed about you!

Hagar and Sarah

21Tell me, you who want to be under the law, are you not aware of what the law says? 22For it is written that Abraham had two sons, one by the slave woman and the other by the free woman. 23His son by the slave woman was born as the result of human effort,[a] but his son by the free woman was born as the result of a divine promise.

24I am taking these things figuratively, for the women represent two covenants. One covenant is from Mount Sinai and bears children who are to be slaves: this is Hagar. 25Now Hagar stands for Mount Sinai in Arabia and corresponds to the present city of Jerusalem, because she is in slavery with her children. 26But the Jerusalem that is above is free, and she is our mother. 27For it is written:

'Be glad, barren woman,
  you who never bore a child;
break forth and cry aloud,
  you who were never in labour;
because more are the children of the
    desolate woman
  than of her who has a husband.'[b]

28Now you, brothers and sisters, like Isaac, are children of promise. 29At that time the son born by human effort persecuted the son born by the power of the Spirit. It is the same now. 30But what does Scripture say? 'Get rid of the slave woman and her son, for the slave woman's son will never share in the inheritance with the free woman's son.'[c] 31Therefore, brothers and sisters, we are not children of the slave woman, but of the free woman.

Freedom in Christ

5 It is for freedom that Christ has set us free. Stand firm, then, and do not let yourselves be burdened again by a yoke of slavery.

2Mark my words! I, Paul, tell you that if you let yourselves be circumcised, Christ will be of no value to you at all. 3Again I declare to every man who lets himself be circumcised that he is required to obey the whole law. 4You who are trying to be justified by the law have been alienated from Christ; you have fallen away from grace. 5But by faith we eagerly await through the Spirit the righteousness for which we hope. 6For in Christ Jesus neither circumcision nor uncircumcision has any value. The only thing that counts is faith expressing itself through love.

7You were running a good race. Who cut in on you to keep you from obeying the truth? 8That kind of persuasion does not come from the one who calls you. 9'A little yeast works through the whole batch of dough.' 10I am confident in the Lord that you will take no other view. The one who is throwing you into confusion will have to pay the penalty, whoever that may be. 11Brothers and sisters, if I am still preaching circumcision, why am I still being persecuted? In that case the offence of the cross has been abolished. 12As for those agitators, I wish they would go the whole way and emasculate themselves!

Life by the Spirit

13You, my brothers and sisters, were called to be free. But do not use your freedom to indulge the sinful nature[d]; rather, serve one another humbly in love. 14For the entire law is fulfilled in keeping this one command: 'Love your neighbour as yourself.'[e] 15If you keep on biting and devouring each other, watch out or you will be destroyed by each other.

16So I say, live by the Spirit, and you will not gratify the desires of the sinful nature. 17For the sinful nature desires what is contrary to the Spirit, and the Spirit what is contrary to the sinful nature. They are in conflict with each other, so that you are not to do whatever[f] you want. 18But if you are led by the Spirit, you are not under the law.

19The acts of the sinful nature are obvious: sexual immorality, impurity, debauchery; 20idolatry and witchcraft; hatred, discord, jealousy, fits of rage, selfish ambition, dissensions, factions 21and envy;

---

[a] 23 Or *born according to the flesh*; also in verse 29 [b] 27 Isaiah 54:1 [c] 30 Gen. 21:10 [d] 13 Or *the flesh*; also in verses 16, 17, 19 and 24 [e] 14 Lev. 19:18 [f] 17 Or *you do not do what*

drunkenness, orgies, and the like. I warn you, as I did before, that those who live like this will not inherit the kingdom of God.

22But the fruit of the Spirit is love, joy, peace, patience, kindness, goodness, faithfulness, 23gentleness and self-control. Against such things there is no law. 24Those who belong to Christ Jesus have crucified the sinful nature with its passions and desires. 25Since we live by the Spirit, let us keep in step with the Spirit. 26Let us not become conceited, provoking and envying each other.

Doing good to all

6 Brothers and sisters, if someone is caught in a sin, you who live by the Spirit should restore that person gently. But watch yourselves, or you also may be tempted. 2Carry each other's burdens, and in this way you will fulfil the law of Christ. 3If any of you think you are something when you are nothing, you deceive yourselves. 4Each of you should test your own actions. Then you can take pride in yourself, without comparing yourself to somebody else, 5for each of you should carry your own load. 6Nevertheless, those who receive instruction in the word should share all good things with their instructor.

7Do not be deceived: God cannot be mocked. People reap what they sow. 8Those who sow to please their sinful nature, from that nature^a will reap destruction; those who sow to please the Spirit, from the Spirit will reap eternal life. 9Let us not become weary in doing good, for at the proper time we will reap a harvest if we do not give up. 10Therefore, as we have opportunity, let us do good to all people, especially to those who belong to the family of believers.

Marks of Jesus
Galatians 6:17
The word 'marks' in Greek refers to the way cattle were branded with the mark of their owner. Paul was beaten many times because of his faith, which would have left scars on his body. Those scars are like a brand that shows he belongs to Jesus.

Not circumcision but the new creation

11See what large letters I use as I write to you with my own hand!

12Those who want to impress others by means of the flesh are trying to compel you to be circumcised. The only reason they do this is to avoid being persecuted for the cross of Christ. 13Not even those who are circumcised keep the law, yet they want you to be circumcised that they may boast about your circumcision in the flesh. 14May I never boast except in the cross of our Lord Jesus Christ, through which^b the world has been crucified to me, and I to the world. 15Neither circumcision nor uncircumcision means anything; what counts is the new creation. 16Peace and mercy to all who follow this rule—to^c the Israel of God.

17From now on, let no-one cause me trouble, for I bear on my body the marks of Jesus.

18The grace of our Lord Jesus Christ be with your spirit, brothers and sisters. Amen.

---

^{a} 8 Or their flesh, from the flesh ^{b} 14 Or whom ^{c} 16 Or rule and to

Ephesians

INTRODUCTION

Ephesians

Author: Paul

Who to: Christians in Ephesus.

When: While Paul was in prison in Rome, probably in the early 60s AD.

Where: Ephesus was a large city on the coast of Asia Minor, in the country we now call Turkey.

Did you know? This is one of four letters that Paul wrote from prison. The others are Philippians, Colossians and Philemon.

Main theme: Reading Ephesians is like sitting down to a rich banquet – there's so much in it. Paul talks about the relationship between Jesus who is in heaven and his body, the church, which is on earth. He uses marriage as a picture of how much Jesus loves the church, and encourages Christians to live their lives so they are a credit to Jesus.

1 Paul, an apostle of Christ Jesus by the will of God,

To God's holy people in Ephesus,*a* the faithful in Christ Jesus:

²Grace and peace to you from God our Father and the Lord Jesus Christ.

Praise for spiritual blessings in Christ

³Praise be to the God and Father of our Lord Jesus Christ, who has blessed us in the heavenly realms with every spiritual blessing in Christ. ⁴For he chose us in him before the creation of the world to be holy and blameless in his sight. In love ⁵he*b* predestined us for adoption to sonship*c* through Jesus Christ, in accordance with his pleasure and will— ⁶to the praise of his

---

a 1 Some early manuscripts do not have *in Ephesus*. *b* 4,5 Or *sight in love.* ⁵*He* *c* 5 The Greek word for *adoption to sonship* is a legal term referring to the full legal standing of an adopted male heir in Roman culture.

glorious grace, which he has freely given us in the One he loves. 7In him we have redemption through his blood, the forgiveness of sins, in accordance with the riches of God's grace 8that he lavished on us. With all wisdom and understanding, 9he*a* made known to us the mystery of his will according to his good pleasure, which he purposed in Christ, 10to be put into effect when the times reach their fulfilment—to bring unity to all things in heaven and on earth under Christ.

11In him we were also chosen,*b* having been predestined according to the plan of him who works out everything in conformity with the purpose of his will, 12in order that we, who were the first to put our hope in Christ, might be for the praise of his glory. 13And you also were included in Christ when you heard the word of truth, the gospel of your salvation. When you believed, you were marked in him with a seal, the promised Holy Spirit, 14who is a deposit guaranteeing our inheritance until the redemption of those who are God's possession—to the praise of his glory.

Thanksgiving and prayer

15For this reason, ever since I heard about your faith in the Lord Jesus and your love for all his people, 16I have not stopped giving thanks for you, remembering you in my prayers. 17I keep asking that the God of our Lord Jesus Christ, the glorious Father, may give you the Spirit*c* of wisdom and revelation, so that you may know him better. 18I pray that the eyes of your heart may be enlightened in order that you may know the hope to which he has called you, the riches of his glorious inheritance in his people, 19and his incomparably great power for us who believe. That power is the same as the mighty strength 20he exerted when he raised Christ from the dead and seated him at his right hand in the heavenly realms, 21far above all rule and authority, power and dominion, and every name that can be invoked, not only in the present age but also in the one to come. 22And God placed all things under his feet and appointed him to be head over everything for the church,

> **IN OTHER WORDS**
>
> **Grace**
> **Ephesians 2:5**
> Grace is the undeserved favour of God, his unconditional love for us shown through Jesus dying for us even when we didn't know him.

23which is his body, the fulness of him who fills everything in every way.

Made alive in Christ

2 As for you, you were dead in your transgressions and sins, 2in which you used to live when you followed the ways of this world and of the ruler of the kingdom of the air, the spirit who is now at work in those who are disobedient. 3All of us also lived among them at one time, gratifying the cravings of our sinful nature*d* and following its desires and thoughts. Like the rest, we were by nature deserving of wrath. 4But because of his great love for us, God, who is rich in mercy, 5made us alive with Christ even when we were dead in transgressions—it is by grace you have been saved. 6And God raised us up with Christ and seated us with him in the heavenly realms in Christ Jesus, 7in order that in the coming ages he might show the incomparable riches of his grace, expressed in his kindness to us in Christ Jesus. 8For it is by grace you have been saved, through faith—and this is not from yourselves, it is the gift of God— 9not by works, so that no-one can boast. 10For we are God's handiwork, created in Christ Jesus to do good works, which God prepared in advance for us to do.

Jew and Gentile reconciled through Christ

11Therefore, remember that formerly you who are Gentiles by birth and called 'uncircumcised' by those who call themselves 'the circumcision' (which is done in the body by human hands)— 12remember that at that time you were separate from

---

a 8,9 Or *us with all wisdom and understanding.* 9*And he*   *b* 11 Or *were made heirs*   *c* 17 Or *a spirit*   *d* 3 Or *our flesh*

Christ, excluded from citizenship in Israel and foreigners to the covenants of the promise, without hope and without God in the world. 13But now in Christ Jesus you who once were far away have been brought near by the blood of Christ.

14For he himself is our peace, who has made the two one and has destroyed the barrier, the dividing wall of hostility, 15by setting aside in his flesh the law with its commands and regulations. His purpose was to create in himself one new humanity out of the two, thus making peace, 16and in one body to reconcile both of them to God through the cross, by which he put to death their hostility. 17He came and preached peace to you who were far away and peace to those who were near. 18For through him we both have access to the Father by one Spirit.

19Consequently, you are no longer foreigners and strangers, but fellow-citizens with God's people and also members of his household, 20built on the foundation of the apostles and prophets, with Christ Jesus himself as the chief cornerstone. 21In him the whole building is joined together and rises to become a holy temple in the Lord. 22And in him you too are being built together to become a dwelling in which God lives by his Spirit.

God's marvellous plan for the Gentiles

3 For this reason I, Paul, the prisoner of Christ Jesus for the sake of you Gentiles—

2Surely you have heard about the administration of God's grace that was given to me for you, 3that is, the mystery made known to me by revelation, as I have already written briefly. 4In reading this, then, you will be able to understand my insight into the mystery of Christ, 5which was not made known to people in other generations as it has now been revealed by the Spirit to God's holy apostles and prophets. 6This mystery is that through the gospel the Gentiles are heirs together with Israel, members together of one body, and sharers together in the promise in Christ Jesus.

7I became a servant of this gospel by the gift of God's grace given me through the working of his power. 8Although I am less than the least of all the Lord's people, this grace was given me: to preach to the Gentiles the boundless riches of Christ, 9and to make plain to everyone the administration of this mystery, which for ages past was kept hidden in God, who created all things. 10His intent was that now, through the church, the manifold wisdom of God should be made known to the rulers and authorities in the heavenly realms, 11according to his eternal purpose that he accomplished in Christ Jesus our Lord. 12In him and through faith in him we may approach God with freedom and confidence. 13I ask you, therefore, not to be discouraged because of my sufferings for you, which are your glory.

A prayer for the Ephesians

14For this reason I kneel before the Father, 15from whom every family*a* in heaven and on earth derives its name. 16I pray that out of his glorious riches he may strengthen you with power through his Spirit in your inner being, 17so that Christ may dwell in your hearts through faith. And I pray that you, being rooted and established in love, 18may have power, together with all the Lord's people, to grasp how wide and long and high and deep is the love of Christ, 19and to know this love that surpasses knowledge— that you may be filled to the measure of all the fulness of God.

20Now to him who is able to do immeasurably more than all we ask or imagine, according to his power that is at work within us, 21to him be glory in the church and in Christ Jesus throughout all generations, for ever and ever! Amen.

Unity and maturity in the body of Christ

4 As a prisoner for the Lord, then, I urge you to live a life worthy of the calling you have received. 2Be completely humble and gentle; be patient, bearing with one another in love. 3Make every effort to keep the unity of the Spirit through the bond of peace. 4There is one body and one Spirit, just as you were called to one hope when you were called; 5one Lord, one faith, one

---

a 15 The Greek for *family* (*patria*) is derived from the Greek for *father* (*pater*).

baptism; 6one God and Father of all, who is over all and through all and in all.

7But to each one of us grace has been given as Christ apportioned it. 8This is why it*a* says:

> 'When he ascended on high,
> he took many captives
> and gave gifts to his people.'*b*

9(What does 'he ascended' mean except that he also descended to the lower, earthly regions*c*? 10He who descended is the very one who ascended higher than all the heavens, in order to fill the whole universe.) 11So Christ himself gave the apostles, the prophets, the evangelists, the pastors and teachers, 12to equip his people for works of service, so that the body of Christ may be built up 13until we all reach unity in the faith and in the knowledge of the Son of God and become mature, attaining to the whole measure of the fulness of Christ.

14Then we will no longer be infants, tossed back and forth by the waves, and blown here and there by every wind of teaching and by the cunning and craftiness of people in their deceitful scheming. 15Instead, speaking the truth in love, we will in all things grow up into him who is the head, that is, Christ. 16From him the whole body, joined and held together by every supporting ligament, grows and builds itself up in love, as each part does its work.

Instructions for Christian living

17So I tell you this, and insist on it in the Lord, that you must no longer live as the Gentiles do, in the futility of their thinking. 18They are darkened in their understanding and separated from the life of God because of the ignorance that is in them due to the hardening of their hearts. 19Having lost all sensitivity, they have given themselves over to sensuality so as to indulge in every kind of impurity, and they are full of greed.

20That, however, is not the way of life you learned 21when you heard about Christ and were taught in him in accordance with the truth that is in Jesus. 22You were taught, with regard to your former way of life, to put off your old self, which is being corrupted by its deceitful desires; 23to be made new in the attitude of your minds; 24and to put on the new self, created to be like God in true righteousness and holiness.

25Therefore each of you must put off falsehood and speak truthfully to your neighbour, for we are all members of one body. 26'In your anger do not sin'*d*: do not let the sun go down while you are still angry, 27and do not give the devil a foothold. 28Those who have been stealing must steal no longer, but must work, doing something useful with their own hands, that they may have something to share with those in need.

29Do not let any unwholesome talk come out of your mouths, but only what is helpful for building others up according to their needs, that it may benefit those who listen. 30And do not grieve the Holy Spirit of God, with whom you were sealed for the day of redemption. 31Get rid of all bitterness, rage and anger, brawling and slander, along with every form of malice. 32Be kind and compassionate to one another, forgiving each other, just as in Christ God forgave you.

5 1Follow God's example, therefore, as dearly loved children 2and live a life of love, just as Christ loved us and gave himself up for us as a fragrant offering and sacrifice to God.

3But among you there must not be even a hint of sexual immorality, or of any kind of impurity, or of greed, because these are improper for the Lord's people. 4Nor should there be obscenity, foolish talk or coarse joking, which are out of place, but rather thanksgiving. 5For of this you can be sure: no immoral, impure or greedy person—such a person is an idolater—has any inheritance in the kingdom of Christ and of God.*e* 6Let no-one deceive you with empty words, for because of such things God's wrath comes on those who are disobedient. 7Therefore do not be partners with them.

8For you were once darkness, but now you are light in the Lord. Live as children of light 9(for the fruit of the light consists in all goodness, righteousness and truth) 10and find out what pleases the Lord. 11Have

---

*a*8 Or God   *b*8 Psalm 68:18   *c*9 Or *the depths of the earth*   *d*26 Psalm 4:4 (see Septuagint)   *e*5 Or *kingdom of the Christ and God*

making Connections

Idolatry
Ephesians 5:5

Idolatry is the worship of false idols or gods. Ephesus was dominated by the worship of Artemis, the Greek goddess of hunting, who was also known as Diana by the Romans; so the Ephesian Christians had to live surrounded by idolatry. Idolatry is also having anything other than God as the most important thing in your life.

---

nothing to do with the fruitless deeds of darkness, but rather expose them. 12It is shameful even to mention what the disobedient do in secret. 13But everything exposed by the light becomes visible—and everything that is illuminated becomes a light. 14This is why it is said:

'Wake up, sleeper,
 rise from the dead,
 and Christ will shine on you.'

15Be very careful, then, how you live—not as unwise but as wise, 16making the most of every opportunity, because the days are evil. 17Therefore do not be foolish, but understand what the Lord's will is. 18Do not get drunk on wine, which leads to debauchery. Instead, be filled with the Spirit, 19speaking to one another with psalms, hymns and songs from the Spirit. Sing and make music from your heart to the Lord, 20always giving thanks to God the Father for everything, in the name of our Lord Jesus Christ.

Instructions for Christian households

21Submit to one another out of reverence for Christ.

22Wives, submit yourselves to your own husbands as you do to the Lord. 23For the husband is the head of the wife as Christ is the head of the church, his body, of which he is the Saviour. 24Now as the church submits to Christ, so also wives should submit to their husbands in everything.

25Husbands, love your wives, just as Christ loved the church and gave himself up for her 26to make her holy, cleansing^a her by the washing with water through the word, 27and to present her to himself as a radiant church, without stain or wrinkle or any other blemish, but holy and blameless. 28In this same way, husbands ought to love their wives as their own bodies. He who loves his wife loves himself. 29After all, people have never hated their own bodies, but they feed and care for them, just as Christ does the church— 30for we are members of his body. 31'For this reason a man will leave his father and mother and be united to his wife, and the two will become one flesh.'^{b} 32This is a profound mystery—but I am talking about Christ and the church. 33However, each one of you also must love his wife as he loves himself, and the wife must respect her husband.

6 Children, obey your parents in the Lord, for this is right. 2'Honour your father and mother'—which is the first commandment with a promise— 3'so that it may go well with you and that you may enjoy long life on the earth.'^{c}

4Fathers,^{d} do not exasperate your children; instead, bring them up in the training and instruction of the Lord.

5Slaves, obey your earthly masters with respect and fear, and with sincerity of heart, just as you would obey Christ. 6Obey them not only to win their favour when their eye is on you, but as slaves of Christ, doing the will of God from your heart. 7Serve wholeheartedly, as if you were serving the Lord, not people, 8because you know that the Lord will reward each one of you for whatever good you do, whether you are slave or free.

9And masters, treat your slaves in the same way. Do not threaten them, since you know that he who is both their Master and yours is in heaven, and there is no favouritism with him.

---

^{a}26 Or *having cleansed* ^{b}31 Gen. 2:24 ^{c}3 Deut. 5:16 ^{d}4 Or *Parents*

The armour of God

¹⁰Finally, be strong in the Lord and in his mighty power. ¹¹Put on the full armour of God, so that you can take your stand against the devil's schemes. ¹²For our struggle is not against flesh and blood, but against the rulers, against the authorities, against the powers of this dark world and against the spiritual forces of evil in the heavenly realms. ¹³Therefore put on the full armour of God, so that when the day of evil comes, you may be able to stand your ground, and after you have done everything, to stand. ¹⁴Stand firm then, with the belt of truth buckled round your waist, with the breastplate of righteousness in place, ¹⁵and with your feet fitted with the readiness that comes from the gospel of peace. ¹⁶In addition to all this, take up the shield of faith, with which you can extinguish all the flaming arrows of the evil one. ¹⁷Take the helmet of salvation and the sword of the Spirit, which is the word of God.

¹⁸And pray in the Spirit on all occasions with all kinds of prayers and requests. With this in mind, be alert and always keep on praying for all the Lord's people. ¹⁹Pray also for me, that whenever I speak, words may be given me so that I will fearlessly make known the mystery of the gospel, ²⁰for which I am an ambassador in chains. Pray that I may declare it fearlessly, as I should.

Final greetings

²¹Tychicus, the dear brother and faithful servant in the Lord, will tell you everything, so that you also may know how I am and what I am doing. ²²I am sending him to you for this very purpose, that you may know how we are, and that he may encourage you.

²³Peace to the brothers and sisters, and love with faith from God the Father and the Lord Jesus Christ. ²⁴Grace to all who love our Lord Jesus Christ with an undying love.[a]

---

[a] 24 Or *Grace and immortality to all who love our Lord Jesus Christ.*

Philippians

INTRODUCTION

Philippians

Author: Paul, with greetings from Timothy.

Who to: To Christians in Philippi.

When: While Paul was in prison in Rome, probably the early 60s AD.

Where: Philippi was a city in Macedonia, part of the country that we now call Greece.

Did you know? The church at Philippi was started when Paul was in prison (Acts 16:25–34) and now he's writing to them from prison.

Main theme: The secret of a joyful life, says Paul in this letter, is to have Jesus at the centre of it. And Paul should know. He talks about the hardships that he's suffered as well as the things he could be proud of, but says that the most important thing is to know Jesus. This is a letter full of joy in spite of it being written from prison – Paul mentions joy or says rejoice eighteen times in just four chapters.

1 Paul and Timothy, servants of Christ Jesus,

To all God's holy people in Christ Jesus at Philippi, together with the overseers and deacons:

²Grace and peace to you from God our Father and the Lord Jesus Christ.

Thanksgiving and prayer

³I thank my God every time I remember you. ⁴In all my prayers for all of you, I always pray with joy ⁵because of your partnership in the gospel from the first day until now, ⁶being confident of this, that he who began a good work in you will carry it on to completion until the day of Christ Jesus.

⁷It is right for me to feel this way about all of you, since I have you in my heart and, whether I am in chains or defending and confirming the gospel, all of you share in God's grace with me. ⁸God can testify how I long for all of you with the affection of Christ Jesus.

⁹And this is my prayer: that your love may abound more and more in knowledge

and depth of insight, 10so that you may be able to discern what is best and may be pure and blameless for the day of Christ, 11filled with the fruit of righteousness that comes through Jesus Christ—to the glory and praise of God.

Paul's chains advance the gospel

12Now I want you to know, brothers and sisters, that what has happened to me has actually served to advance the gospel. 13As a result, it has become clear throughout the whole palace guard[a] and to everyone else that I am in chains for Christ. 14And because of my chains, most of the brothers and sisters have become confident in the Lord and dare all the more to proclaim the gospel without fear.

15It is true that some preach Christ out of envy and rivalry, but others out of goodwill. 16The latter do so out of love, knowing that I am put here for the defence of the gospel. 17The former preach Christ out of selfish ambition, not sincerely, supposing that they can stir up trouble for me while I am in chains. 18But what does it matter? The important thing is that in every way, whether from false motives or true, Christ is preached. And because of this I rejoice.

Yes, and I will continue to rejoice, 19for I know that through your prayers and God's provision of the Spirit of Jesus Christ what has happened to me will turn out for my deliverance.[b] 20I eagerly expect and hope that I will in no way be ashamed, but will have sufficient courage so that now as always Christ will be exalted in my body, whether by life or by death. 21For to me, to live is Christ and to die is gain. 22If I am to go on living in the body, this will mean fruitful labour for me. Yet what shall I choose? I do not know! 23I am torn between the two: I desire to depart and be with Christ, which is better by far; 24but it is more necessary for you that I remain in the body. 25Convinced of this, I know that I will remain, and I will continue with all of you for your progress and joy in the faith, 26so that through my being with you again your boasting in Christ Jesus will abound on account of me.

Life worthy of the gospel

27Whatever happens, as citizens of heaven live in a manner worthy of the gospel of Christ. Then, whether I come and see you or only hear about you in my absence, I will know that you stand firm in the one Spirit,[c] striving together with one accord for the faith of the gospel 28without being frightened in any way by those who oppose you. This is a sign to them that they will be destroyed, but that you will be saved—and that by God. 29For it has been granted to you on behalf of Christ not only to believe on him, but also to suffer for him, 30since you are going through the same struggle you saw I had, and now hear that I still have.

Imitating Christ's humility

2 Therefore if you have any encouragement from being united with Christ, if any comfort from his love, if any common sharing in the Spirit, if any tenderness and compassion, 2then make my joy complete by being like-minded, having the same love, being one in spirit and of one mind. 3Do nothing out of selfish ambition or vain conceit. Rather, in humility value others above yourselves, 4not looking to your own interests but each of you to the interests of the others.

5In your relationships with one another, have the same attitude of mind Christ Jesus had:

6who, being in very nature[d] God,
    did not consider equality with God
        something to be used to his own advantage;
7rather, he made himself nothing
    by taking the very nature[e] of a servant,
    being made in human likeness.
8And being found in appearance as a human being,
    he humbled himself
    by becoming obedient to death—
        even death on a cross!

9Therefore God exalted him to the highest place
    and gave him the name that is above every name,

---

[a] 13 Or *whole palace*   [b] 19 Or *vindication; or salvation*   [c] 27 Or *in one spirit*   [d] 6 Or *in the form of*   [e] 7 Or *the form*

¹⁰that at the name of Jesus every knee should bow,
>in heaven and on earth and under the earth,
¹¹and every tongue acknowledge that Jesus Christ is Lord,
>to the glory of God the Father.

Do everything without grumbling

¹²Therefore, my dear friends, as you have always obeyed—not only in my presence, but now much more in my absence—continue to work out your salvation with fear and trembling, ¹³for it is God who works in you to will and to act in order to fulfil his good purpose.

¹⁴Do everything without grumbling or arguing, ¹⁵so that you may become blameless and pure, 'children of God without fault in a warped and crooked generation.'*ᵃ* Then you will shine among them like stars in the sky ¹⁶as you hold firmly to the word of life. And then I will be able to boast on the day of Christ that I did not run or labour in vain. ¹⁷But even if I am being poured out like a drink offering on the sacrifice and service coming from your faith, I am glad and rejoice with all of you. ¹⁸So you too should be glad and rejoice with me.

Timothy and Epaphroditus

¹⁹I hope in the Lord Jesus to send Timothy to you soon, that I also may be cheered when I receive news about you. ²⁰I have no-one else like him, who will show genuine concern for your welfare. ²¹For everyone looks out for their own interests, not those of Jesus Christ. ²²But you know that Timothy has proved himself, because as a son with his father he has served with me in the work of the gospel. ²³I hope, therefore, to send him as soon as I see how things go with me. ²⁴And I am confident in the Lord that I myself will come soon.

²⁵But I think it is necessary to send back to you Epaphroditus, my brother, co-worker and fellow-soldier, who is also your messenger, whom you sent to take care of my needs. ²⁶For he longs for all of you and is distressed because you heard he was ill. ²⁷Indeed he was ill, and almost died. But God had mercy on him, and not on him only but also on me, to spare me sorrow upon sorrow. ²⁸Therefore I am all the more eager to send him, so that when you see him again you may be glad and I may have less anxiety. ²⁹Welcome him in the Lord with great joy, and honour people like him, ³⁰because he almost died for the work of Christ. He risked his life to make up for the help you yourselves could not give me.

No confidence in the flesh

3 Further, my brothers and sisters, rejoice in the Lord! It is no trouble for me to write the same things to you again, and it is a safeguard for you. ²Watch out for those dogs, those evildoers, those mutilators of the flesh. ³For it is we who are the circumcision, we who serve God by his Spirit, who boast in Christ Jesus, and who put no confidence in the flesh— ⁴though I myself have reasons for such confidence.

If others think they have reasons to put confidence in the flesh, I have more: ⁵circumcised on the eighth day, of the people of Israel, of the tribe of Benjamin, a Hebrew of Hebrews; in regard to the law, a Pharisee; ⁶as for zeal, persecuting the church; as for righteousness based on the law, faultless.

⁷But whatever were gains to me I now consider loss for the sake of Christ. ⁸What is more, I consider everything a loss because of the surpassing worth of knowing Christ Jesus my Lord, for whose sake I have lost all things. I consider them garbage, that I may gain Christ ⁹and be found in him, not having a righteousness of my own that

People and Places

Hebrews
Philippians 3:5
'Hebrews' was the name used for the Jewish people in the Old Testament. Hebrew was the language that they spoke.

ᵃ 15 Deut. 32:5

comes from the law, but that which is through faith in[a] Christ—the righteousness that comes from God on the basis of faith. 10I want to know Christ—yes, to know the power of his resurrection and participation in his sufferings, becoming like him in his death, 11and so, somehow, attaining to the resurrection from the dead.

12Not that I have already obtained all this, or have already arrived at my goal, but I press on to take hold of that for which Christ Jesus took hold of me. 13Brothers and sisters, I do not consider myself yet to have taken hold of it. But one thing I do: forgetting what is behind and straining towards what is ahead, 14I press on towards the goal to win the prize for which God has called me heavenwards in Christ Jesus.

Following Paul's example

15All of us, then, who are mature should take such a view of things. And if on some point you think differently, that too God will make clear to you. 16Only let us live up to what we have already attained.

17Join together in following my example, brothers and sisters, and just as you have us as a model, keep your eyes on those who live as we do. 18For, as I have often told you before and now tell you again even with tears, many live as enemies of the cross of Christ. 19Their destiny is destruction, their god is their stomach, and their glory is in their shame. Their mind is set on earthly things. 20But our citizenship is in heaven. And we eagerly await a Saviour from there, the Lord Jesus Christ, 21who, by the power that enables him to bring everything under his control, will transform our lowly bodies so that they will be like his glorious body.

Closing appeal for steadfastness and unity

4 Therefore, my brothers and sisters, you whom I love and long for, my joy and crown, stand firm in the Lord in this way, dear friends!

2I plead with Euodia and I plead with Syntyche to be of the same mind in the Lord. 3Yes, and I ask you, my true companion, help these women since they have contended at my side in the cause of the gospel, along with Clement and the rest of my co-workers, whose names are in the book of life.

Final exhortations

4Rejoice in the Lord always. I will say it again: rejoice! 5Let your gentleness be evident to all. The Lord is near. 6Do not be anxious about anything, but in every situation, by prayer and petition, with thanksgiving, present your requests to God. 7And the peace of God, which transcends all understanding, will guard your hearts and your minds in Christ Jesus.

8Finally, brothers and sisters, whatever is true, whatever is noble, whatever is right, whatever is pure, whatever is lovely, whatever is admirable—if anything is excellent or praiseworthy—think about such things. 9Whatever you have learned or received or heard from me, or seen in me—put it into practice. And the God of peace will be with you.

Thanks for their gifts

10I rejoiced greatly in the Lord that at last you renewed your concern for me. Indeed, you were concerned, but you had no opportunity to show it. 11I am not saying this because I am in need, for I have learned to be content whatever the circumstances. 12I know what it is to be in need, and I know what it is to have plenty. I have learned the secret of being content in any and every situation, whether well fed or hungry, whether living in plenty or in want. 13I can do all this through him who gives me strength.

14Yet it was good of you to share in my troubles. 15Moreover, as you Philippians know, in the early days of your acquaintance with the gospel, when I set out from Macedonia, not one church shared with me in the matter of giving and receiving, except you only; 16for even when I was in Thessalonica, you sent me aid more than once when I was in need. 17Not that I desire your gifts; what I desire is that more be credited to your account. 18I have received full payment and have more than enough. I

---

[a] 9 Or through the faithfulness of

am amply supplied, now that I have received from Epaphroditus the gifts you sent. They are a fragrant offering, an acceptable sacrifice, pleasing to God. 19And my God will meet all your needs according to the riches of his glory in Christ Jesus.

20To our God and Father be glory for ever and ever. Amen.

Final greetings

21Greet all God's people in Christ Jesus. The brothers and sisters who are with me send greetings. 22All the Lord's people here send you greetings, especially those who belong to Caesar's household.

23The grace of the Lord Jesus Christ be with your spirit. Amen.[a]

---

[a] 23 Some manuscripts do not have *Amen*.

Colossians

INTRODUCTION

Colossians

Author: Paul and Timothy

Who to: Christians in Colossae.

When: While Paul was in prison in Rome, probably in the early 60s AD.

Where: Colossae was a city in the Roman province of Asia, in the country that we now call Turkey.

Main theme: The Colossians were in danger of being led astray by false teaching, so Paul reminds them of where their focus should be: on Jesus. He paints a powerful picture of Jesus' role in the creation and redemption of the whole universe. And he also gives practical advice on how a Christian's behaviour should be consistent with their beliefs.

1 Paul, an apostle of Christ Jesus by the will of God, and Timothy our brother,

2To God's holy people in Colossae, the faithful brothers and sisters in Christ:

Grace and peace to you from God our Father.[a]

Thanksgiving and prayer

3We always thank God, the Father of our Lord Jesus Christ, when we pray for you, 4because we have heard of your faith in Christ Jesus and of the love you have for all his people— 5the faith and love that spring from the hope stored up for you in heaven and about which you have already heard in the true word of the gospel 6that has come to you. In the same way, the gospel is bearing fruit and growing throughout the whole world— just as it has been doing among you since the day you heard it and truly understood God's grace. 7You learned it from Epaphras, our dear fellow-servant,[b] who is a faithful minister of Christ on our[c] behalf, 8and who also told us of your love in the Spirit.

9For this reason, since the day we heard about you, we have not stopped praying for

---

[a]2 Some manuscripts *Father and the Lord Jesus Christ* [b]7 Or *slave* [c]7 Some manuscripts *your*

you. We continually ask God to fill you with the knowledge of his will through all the wisdom and understanding that the Spirit gives,[a] 10so that you may live a life worthy of the Lord and please him in every way: bearing fruit in every good work, growing in the knowledge of God, 11being strengthened with all power according to his glorious might so that you may have great endurance and patience, 12and giving joyful thanks to the Father, who has qualified you[b] to share in the inheritance of his people in the kingdom of light. 13For he has rescued us from the dominion of darkness and brought us into the kingdom of the Son he loves, 14in whom we have redemption, the forgiveness of sins.

The supremacy of the Son of God

15The Son is the image of the invisible God, the firstborn over all creation. 16For in him all things were created: things in heaven and on earth, visible and invisible, whether thrones or powers or rulers or authorities; all things have been created through him and for him. 17He is before all things, and in him all things hold together. 18And he is the head of the body, the church; he is the beginning and the firstborn from among the dead, so that in everything he might have the supremacy. 19For God was pleased to have all his fulness dwell in him, 20and through him to reconcile to himself all things, whether things on earth or things in heaven, by making peace through his blood, shed on the cross.

21Once you were alienated from God and were enemies in your minds because of[c] your evil behaviour. 22But now he has reconciled you by Christ's physical body through death to present you holy in his sight, without blemish and free from accusation— 23if you continue in your faith, established and firm, and do not move from the hope held out in the gospel. This is the gospel that you heard and that has been proclaimed to every creature under heaven, and of which I, Paul, have become a servant.

Paul's labour for the church

24Now I rejoice in what I am suffering for you, and I fill up in my flesh what is still lacking in regard to Christ's afflictions, for the sake of his body, which is the church. 25I have become its servant by the commission God gave me to present to you the word of God in its fulness— 26the mystery that has been kept hidden for ages and generations, but is now disclosed to the Lord's people. 27To them God has chosen to make known among the Gentiles the glorious riches of this mystery, which is Christ in you, the hope of glory.

28We proclaim him, admonishing and teaching everyone with all wisdom, so that we may present everyone fully mature in Christ. 29To this end I strenuously contend with all the energy Christ so powerfully works in me.

2 I want you to know how hard I am contending for you and for those at Laodicea, and for all who have not met me personally. 2My goal is that they may be encouraged in heart and united in love, so that they may have the full riches of complete understanding, in order that they may know the mystery of God, namely, Christ, 3in whom are hidden all the treasures of wisdom and knowledge. 4I tell you this so that no-one may deceive you by fine-sounding arguments. 5For though I am absent from you in body, I am present with you in spirit and delight to see how disciplined you are and how firm your faith in Christ is.

Spiritual fulness in Christ

6So then, just as you received Christ Jesus as Lord, continue to live your lives in him, 7rooted and built up in him, strengthened in the faith as you were taught, and overflowing with thankfulness.

8See to it that no-one takes you captive through hollow and deceptive philosophy, which depends on human tradition and the elemental spiritual forces[d] of this world rather than on Christ.

---

[a] 9 Or *all spiritual wisdom and understanding* [b] 12 Some manuscripts *us* [c] 21 Or *minds, as shown by* [d] 8 Or *the basic principles*; also in verse 20

9 For in Christ all the fulness of the Deity lives in bodily form, 10 and in Christ you have been brought to fulness. He is the head over every power and authority. 11 In him you were also circumcised with a circumcision not performed by human hands. Your sinful nature[a] was put off when you were circumcised by[b] Christ, 12 having been buried with him in baptism, in which you were also raised with him through your faith in the working of God, who raised him from the dead.

13 When you were dead in your sins and in the uncircumcision of your sinful nature,[c] God made you[d] alive with Christ. He forgave us all our sins, 14 having cancelled the charge of our legal indebtedness, which stood against us and condemned us; he has taken it away, nailing it to the cross. 15 And having disarmed the powers and authorities, he made a public spectacle of them, triumphing over them by the cross.[e]

Freedom from human rules

16 Therefore do not let anyone judge you by what you eat or drink, or with regard to a religious festival, a New Moon celebration or a Sabbath day. 17 These are a shadow of the things that were to come; the reality, however, is found in Christ. 18 Do not let anyone who delights in false humility and the worship of angels disqualify you. Such people also go into great detail about what they have seen, and their unspiritual minds puff them up with idle notions. 19 They have lost connection with the head, from whom the whole body, supported and held together by its ligaments and sinews, grows as God causes it to grow.

20 Since you died with Christ to the elemental spiritual forces of this world, why, as though you still belonged to the world, do you submit to its rules: 21 'Do not handle! Do not taste! Do not touch!'? 22 These rules, which have to do with things that are all destined to perish with use, are based on merely human commands and teachings. 23 Such regulations indeed have an appearance of wisdom, with their self-imposed worship, their false humility and their harsh treatment of the body, but they lack any value in restraining sensual indulgence.

Living as those made alive in Christ

3 Since, then, you have been raised with Christ, set your hearts on things above, where Christ is seated at the right hand of God. 2 Set your minds on things above, not on earthly things. 3 For you died, and your life is now hidden with Christ in God. 4 When Christ, who is your[f] life, appears, then you also will appear with him in glory.

5 Put to death, therefore, whatever belongs to your earthly nature: sexual immorality, impurity, lust, evil desires and greed, which is idolatry. 6 Because of these, the wrath of God is coming.[g] 7 You used to walk in these ways, in the life you once lived. 8 But now you must also rid yourselves of all such things as these: anger, rage, malice, slander and filthy language from your lips. 9 Do not lie to each other, since you have taken off your old self with its practices 10 and have put on the new self, which is being renewed in knowledge in the image of its Creator. 11 Here there is no Gentile or Jew, circumcised or uncircumcised, barbarian, Scythian, slave or free, but Christ is all, and is in all.

making Connections

People groups
Colossians 3:11

Paul is making the point that Christians need to be united, rather than splitting themselves into separate people groups. A Gentile was someone who was not a Jew; a barbarian was someone who couldn't speak Greek and was considered lower class; Scythians were known for their cruelty. I think he's just about covered everyone in this verse!

---

[a] 11 Or *Your flesh* [b] 11 Or *put off in the circumcision of* [c] 13 Or *your flesh* [d] 13 Some manuscripts *us* [e] 15 Or *them in him* [f] 4 Some manuscripts *our* [g] 6 Some early manuscripts *coming on those who are disobedient*

¹²Therefore, as God's chosen people, holy and dearly loved, clothe yourselves with compassion, kindness, humility, gentleness and patience. ¹³Bear with each other and forgive one another if any of you has a grievance against someone. Forgive as the Lord forgave you. ¹⁴And over all these virtues put on love, which binds them all together in perfect unity.

¹⁵Let the peace of Christ rule in your hearts, since as members of one body you were called to peace. And be thankful. ¹⁶Let the message of Christ dwell among you richly as you teach and admonish one another with all wisdom through psalms, hymns and songs from the Spirit, singing to God with gratitude in your hearts. ¹⁷And whatever you do, whether in word or deed, do it all in the name of the Lord Jesus, giving thanks to God the Father through him.

Instructions for Christian households

¹⁸Wives, submit yourselves to your husbands, as is fitting in the Lord.

¹⁹Husbands, love your wives and do not be harsh with them.

²⁰Children, obey your parents in everything, for this pleases the Lord.

²¹Fathers,*ᵃ* do not embitter your children, or they will become discouraged.

²²Slaves, obey your earthly masters in everything; and do it, not only when their eye is on you and to curry their favour, but with sincerity of heart and reverence for the Lord. ²³Whatever you do, work at it with all your heart, as working for the Lord, not for human masters, ²⁴since you know that you will receive an inheritance from the Lord as a reward. It is the Lord Christ you are serving. ²⁵Those who do wrong will be repaid for their wrongs, and there is no favouritism.

4 Masters, provide your slaves with what is right and fair, because you know that you also have a Master in heaven.

Further instructions

²Devote yourselves to prayer, being watchful and thankful. ³And pray for us, too, that God may open a door for our message, so that we may proclaim the mystery of Christ, for which I am in chains. ⁴Pray that I may proclaim it clearly, as I should. ⁵Be wise in the way you act towards outsiders; make the most of every opportunity. ⁶Let your conversation be always full of grace, seasoned with salt, so that you may know how to answer everyone.

Final greetings

⁷Tychicus will tell you all the news about me. He is a dear brother, a faithful minister and fellow-servant*ᵇ* in the Lord. ⁸I am sending him to you for the express purpose that you may know about our*ᶜ* circumstances and that he may encourage your hearts. ⁹He is coming with Onesimus, our faithful and dear brother, who is one of you. They will tell you everything that is happening here.

¹⁰My fellow-prisoner Aristarchus sends you his greetings, as does Mark, the cousin of Barnabas. (You have received instructions about him; if he comes to you, welcome him.) ¹¹Jesus, who is called Justus, also sends greetings. These are the only Jews*ᵈ* among my fellow-workers for the kingdom of God, and they have proved a comfort to me. ¹²Epaphras, who is one of you and a servant of Christ Jesus, sends greetings. He is always wrestling in prayer for you, that you may stand firm in all the will of God, mature and fully assured. ¹³I vouch for him that he is working hard for you and for those at Laodicea and Hierapolis. ¹⁴Our dear friend Luke, the doctor, and Demas send greetings. ¹⁵Give my greetings to the brothers and sisters at Laodicea, and to Nympha and the church in her house.

¹⁶After this letter has been read to you, see that it is also read in the church of the Laodiceans and that you in turn read the letter from Laodicea.

¹⁷Tell Archippus: 'See to it that you complete the work you have received in the Lord.'

¹⁸I, Paul, write this greeting in my own hand. Remember my chains. Grace be with you.

---

*ᵃ*21 Or *Parents* *ᵇ*7 Or *slave*; also in verse 12 *ᶜ*8 Some manuscripts *that he may know about your* *ᵈ*11 Greek *only ones of the circumcision group*

1 Thessalonians

INTRODUCTION

1 Thessalonians

Author: Paul, with greetings from Silas and Timothy.

Who to: Christians in Thessalonica.

When: Paul probably wrote this letter around AD 50.

Where: Thessalonica was the major seaport of Macedonia, in the country that we now call Greece.

Did you know? You can read about how Paul started the church in Thessalonica in Acts 17:1–9.

Main theme: Paul had to leave the young church in Thessalonica quite suddenly when the local Jews objected to his teaching. So he writes to encourage them in their faith, telling them to live in a way that pleases God. He writes about the second coming of Christ, urging the Thessalonians to be ready whenever it might happen.

1 Paul, Silas[a] and Timothy,

To the church of the Thessalonians in God the Father and the Lord Jesus Christ:

Grace and peace to you.

Thanksgiving for the Thessalonians' faith

2We always thank God for all of you and continually mention you in our prayers. 3We remember before our God and Father your work produced by faith, your labour prompted by love, and your endurance inspired by hope in our Lord Jesus Christ.

4For we know, brothers and sisters loved by God, that he has chosen you, 5because our gospel came to you not simply with words but also with power, with the Holy Spirit and deep conviction. You know how we lived among you for your sake. 6You became imitators of us and of the Lord, for you welcomed the message in the midst of severe suffering with the joy given by the Holy Spirit. 7And so you became a model to all the believers in Macedonia and Achaia. 8The Lord's message rang out from you not only in Macedonia and Achaia—your faith

---

[a] 1 Greek *Silvanus*, a variant of *Silas*

in God has become known everywhere. Therefore we do not need to say anything about it, 9for they themselves report what happened when we visited you. They tell how you turned to God from idols to serve the living and true God, 10and to wait for his Son from heaven, whom he raised from the dead—Jesus, who rescues us from the coming wrath.

Paul's ministry in Thessalonica

2 You know, brothers and sisters, that our visit to you was not without results. 2We had previously suffered and been treated outrageously in Philippi, as you know, but with the help of our God we dared to tell you his gospel in the face of strong opposition. 3For the appeal we make does not spring from error or impure motives, nor are we trying to trick you. 4On the contrary, we speak as those approved by God to be entrusted with the gospel. We are not trying to please people but God, who tests our hearts. 5You know we never used flattery, nor did we put on a mask to cover up greed—God is our witness. 6We were not looking for praise from any human being, not from you or anyone else, even though as apostles of Christ we could have asserted our prerogatives. 7Instead, we were like young children among you.

Just as a nursing mother cares for her children, 8so we cared for you. Because we loved you so much, we were delighted to share with you not only the gospel of God but our lives as well. 9Surely you remember, brothers and sisters, our toil and hardship; we worked night and day in order not to be a burden to anyone while we preached the gospel of God to you.

10You are witnesses, and so is God, of how holy, righteous and blameless we were among you who believed. 11For you know that we dealt with each of you as a father deals with his own children, 12encouraging, comforting and urging you to live lives worthy of God, who calls you into his kingdom and glory.

13And we also thank God continually because, when you received the word of God, which you heard from us, you accepted it not as a human word, but as it actually is, the word of God, which is indeed at work in you who believe. 14For you, brothers and sisters, became imitators of God's churches in Judea, which are in Christ Jesus: you suffered from your fellow Gentiles the same things those churches suffered from the Jews, 15who killed the Lord Jesus and the prophets and also drove us out. They displease God and are hostile to everyone 16in their effort to keep us from speaking to the Gentiles so that they may be saved. In this way they always heap up their sins to the limit. The wrath of God has come upon them at last.[a]

Paul's longing to see the Thessalonians

17But, brothers and sisters, when we were orphaned by being separated from you for a short time (in person, not in thought), out of our intense longing we made every effort to see you. 18For we wanted to come to you—certainly I, Paul, did, again and again—but Satan blocked our way. 19For what is our hope, our joy, or the crown in which we will glory in the presence of our Lord Jesus when he comes? Is it not you? 20Indeed, you are our glory and joy.

3 So when we could stand it no longer, we thought it best to be left by ourselves in Athens. 2We sent Timothy, who is our brother and co-worker in God's service in spreading the gospel of Christ, to strengthen and encourage you in your faith, 3so that no-one would be unsettled by these trials. You know quite well that we are destined for

---

> **IN OTHER WORDS**
>
> **Church**
> **1 Thessalonians 2:14**
> The word in the New Testament that is translated as 'church' means 'the gathering'. So it really is the people and not the building that make the church!

---

[a] 16 Or *them fully*

them. ⁴In fact, when we were with you, we kept telling you that we would be persecuted. And it turned out that way, as you well know. ⁵For this reason, when I could stand it no longer, I sent to find out about your faith. I was afraid that in some way the tempter had tempted you and that our labours might have been in vain.

Timothy's encouraging report

⁶But Timothy has just now come to us from you and has brought good news about your faith and love. He has told us that you always have pleasant memories of us and that you long to see us, just as we also long to see you. ⁷Therefore, brothers and sisters, in all our distress and persecution we were encouraged about you because of your faith. ⁸For now we really live, since you are standing firm in the Lord. ⁹How can we thank God enough for you in return for all the joy we have in the presence of our God because of you? ¹⁰Night and day we pray most earnestly that we may see you again and supply what is lacking in your faith.

¹¹Now may our God and Father himself and our Lord Jesus clear the way for us to come to you. ¹²May the Lord make your love increase and overflow for each other and for everyone else, just as ours does for you. ¹³May he strengthen your hearts so that you will be blameless and holy in the presence of our God and Father when our Lord Jesus comes with all his holy ones.

Living to please God

4 As for other matters, brothers and sisters, we instructed you how to live in order to please God, as in fact you are living. Now we ask you and urge you in the Lord Jesus to do this more and more. ²For you know what instructions we gave you by the authority of the Lord Jesus.

³It is God's will that you should be sanctified: that you should avoid sexual immorality; ⁴that each of you should learn to control your own body^a in a way that is holy and honourable, ⁵not in passionate lust like the pagans, who do not know God; ⁶and that in this matter no-one should wrong or take advantage of a brother or sister. The Lord will punish all those who commit such sins, as we told you and warned you before. ⁷For God did not call us to be impure, but to live a holy life. ⁸Therefore, anyone who rejects this instruction does not reject a human being but God, the very God who gives you his Holy Spirit.

⁹Now about your love for one another we do not need to write to you, for you yourselves have been taught by God to love each other. ¹⁰And in fact, you do love all the brothers and sisters throughout Macedonia. Yet we urge you, dear friends, to do so more and more, ¹¹and to make it your ambition to lead a quiet life: you should mind your own business and work with your hands, just as we told you, ¹²so that your daily life may win the respect of outsiders and so that you will not be dependent on anybody.

Believers who have died

¹³Brothers and sisters, we do not want you to be uninformed about those who sleep in death, so that you do not grieve like the rest, who have no hope. ¹⁴We believe that Jesus died and rose again, and so we believe that God will bring with Jesus those who have fallen asleep in him. ¹⁵According to the Lord's word, we tell you that we who are still alive, who are left till the coming of the Lord, will certainly not precede those who have fallen asleep. ¹⁶For the Lord himself will come down from heaven, with a loud command, with the voice of the archangel and with the trumpet call of God, and the dead in Christ will rise first. ¹⁷After that, we who are still alive and are left will be caught up together with them in the clouds to meet the Lord in the air. And so we will be with the Lord for ever. ¹⁸Therefore encourage one another with these words.

The day of the Lord

5 Now, brothers and sisters, about times and dates we do not need to write to you, ²for you know very well that the day of the Lord will come like a thief in the night. ³While people are saying, 'Peace and safety', destruction will come on them suddenly, as

---

^{a} 4 Or *learn to live with his own wife; or learn to acquire a wife* labour pains on a pregnant woman, and they will not escape.

⁴But you, brothers and sisters, are not in darkness so that this day should surprise you like a thief. ⁵You are all children of the light and children of the day. We do not belong to the night or to the darkness. ⁶So then, let us not be like others, who are asleep, but let us be awake and sober. ⁷For those who sleep, sleep at night, and those who get drunk, get drunk at night. ⁸But since we belong to the day, let us be sober, putting on faith and love as a breastplate, and the hope of salvation as a helmet. ⁹For God did not appoint us to suffer wrath but to receive salvation through our Lord Jesus Christ. ¹⁰He died for us so that, whether we are awake or asleep, we may live together with him. ¹¹Therefore encourage one another and build each other up, just as in fact you are doing.

Final instructions

¹²Now we ask you, brothers and sisters, to acknowledge those who work hard among you, who care for you in the Lord and who admonish you. ¹³Hold them in the highest regard in love because of their work. Live in peace with each other. ¹⁴And we urge you, brothers and sisters, warn those who are idle and disruptive, encourage the disheartened, help the weak, be patient with everyone. ¹⁵Make sure that nobody pays back wrong for wrong, but always strive to do what is good for each other and for everyone else.

¹⁶Rejoice always, ¹⁷pray continually, ¹⁸give thanks in all circumstances; for this is God's will for you in Christ Jesus.

¹⁹Do not put out the Spirit's fire. ²⁰Do not treat prophecies with contempt ²¹but test them all; hold on to what is good, ²²reject whatever is harmful.

²³May God himself, the God of peace, sanctify you through and through. May your whole spirit, soul and body be kept blameless at the coming of our Lord Jesus Christ. ²⁴The one who calls you is faithful, and he will do it.

²⁵Brothers and sisters, pray for us. ²⁶Greet all God's people with a holy kiss. ²⁷I charge you before the Lord to have this letter read to all the brothers and sisters.

²⁸The grace of our Lord Jesus Christ be with you.

2 Thessalonians

INTRODUCTION

2 Thessalonians

Author: Paul, with greetings from Silas and Timothy.

Who to: Christians in Thessalonica.

When: Paul probably wrote this letter around AD 50.

Where: Thessalonica was the major seaport of Macedonia, in the country that we now call Greece.

Main theme: Paul continues with his theme of the second coming of Jesus, clarifying and expanding on his teaching in his first letter. He warns the Thessalonians not to be idle, but to work hard.

1 Paul, Silas[a] and Timothy,

To the church of the Thessalonians in God our Father and the Lord Jesus Christ:

²Grace and peace to you from God the Father and the Lord Jesus Christ.

Thanksgiving and prayer

³We ought always to thank God for you, brothers and sisters, and rightly so, because your faith is growing more and more, and the love all of you have for one another is increasing. ⁴Therefore, among God's churches we boast about your perseverance and faith in all the persecutions and trials you are enduring.

⁵All this is evidence that God's judgment is right, and as a result you will be counted worthy of the kingdom of God, for which you are suffering. ⁶God is just: he will pay back trouble to those who trouble you ⁷and give relief to you who are troubled, and to us as well. This will happen when the Lord Jesus is revealed from heaven in blazing fire with his powerful angels. ⁸He will punish those who do not know God and do not obey the gospel of our Lord Jesus. ⁹They will be punished with everlasting destruction and shut out from the presence of the Lord and from the glory of his might ¹⁰on the day he comes to be glorified in his holy people and to be marvelled at among all those who have believed. This includes you, because you believed our testimony to you.

¹¹With this in mind, we constantly pray for you, that our God may make you worthy of his calling, and that by his power he may bring to fruition your every desire for

---

[a] 1 Greek *Silvanus*, a variant of *Silas*

goodness and your every deed prompted by faith. ¹²We pray this so that the name of our Lord Jesus may be glorified in you, and you in him, according to the grace of our God and the Lord Jesus Christ.ᵃ

The man of lawlessness

2 Concerning the coming of our Lord Jesus Christ and our being gathered to him, we ask you, brothers and sisters, ²not to become easily unsettled or alarmed by the teaching allegedly from us—whether by a prophecy or by word of mouth or by letter—asserting that the day of the Lord has already come. ³Don't let anyone deceive you in any way, for ⌊that day will not come⌋ until the rebellion occurs and the man of lawlessnessᵇ is revealed, the man doomed to destruction. ⁴He will oppose and will exalt himself over everything that is called God or is worshipped, so that he sets himself up in God's temple, proclaiming himself to be God.

⁵Don't you remember that when I was with you I used to tell you these things? ⁶And now you know what is holding him back, so that he may be revealed at the proper time. ⁷For the secret power of lawlessness is already at work; but the one who now holds it back will continue to do so till he is taken out of the way. ⁸And then the lawless one will be revealed, whom the Lord Jesus will overthrow with the breath of his mouth and destroy by the splendour of his coming. ⁹The coming of the lawless one will be in accordance with how Satan works. He will use all sorts of displays of power through signs and wonders that serve the lie, ¹⁰and all the ways that wickedness deceives those who are perishing. They perish because they refused to love the truth and so be saved. ¹¹For this reason God sends them a powerful delusion so that they will believe the lie ¹²and so that all will be condemned who have not believed the truth but have delighted in wickedness.

Stand firm

¹³But we ought always to thank God for you, brothers and sisters loved by the Lord, because God chose you as firstfruitsᶜ to be saved through the sanctifying work of the Spirit and through belief in the truth. ¹⁴He called you to this through our gospel, that you might share in the glory of our Lord Jesus Christ.

¹⁵So then, brothers and sisters, stand firm and hold fast to the teachingsᵈ we passed on to you, whether by word of mouth or by letter.

¹⁶May our Lord Jesus Christ himself and God our Father, who loved us and by his grace gave us eternal encouragement and good hope, ¹⁷encourage your hearts and strengthen you in every good deed and word.

Request for prayer

3 As for other matters, brothers and sisters, pray for us that the message of the Lord may spread rapidly and be honoured, just as it was with you. ²And pray that we may be delivered from wicked and evil people, for not everyone has faith. ³But the Lord is faithful, and he will strengthen you and protect you from the evil one. ⁴We have confidence in the Lord that you are doing and will continue to do the things we command. ⁵May the Lord direct your hearts into God's love and Christ's perseverance.

Paul's job
2 Thessalonians 3:8
Paul worked as a tentmaker on his missionary journeys, making and repairing leather tents. That meant he could provide for himself while he stayed in different towns setting up churches and preaching the gospel (Acts 18:3).

ᵃ12 Or *God and Lord, Jesus Christ* ᵇ3 Some manuscripts *sin* ᶜ13 Some manuscripts *because from the beginning God chose you* ᵈ15 Or *traditions* ᵉ6 Or *tradition*

Warning against idleness

⁶In the name of the Lord Jesus Christ, we command you, brothers and sisters, to keep away from every believer who is idle and disruptive and does not live according to the teaching*ᵃ* you received from us. ⁷For you yourselves know how you ought to follow our example. We were not idle when we were with you, ⁸nor did we eat anyone's food without paying for it. On the contrary, we worked night and day, labouring and toiling so that we would not be a burden to any of you. ⁹We did this, not because we do not have the right to such help, but in order to offer ourselves as a model for you to imitate. ¹⁰For even when we were with you, we gave you this rule: 'Anyone who is unwilling to work shall not eat.'

¹¹We hear that some among you are idle and disruptive. They are not busy; they are busybodies. ¹²Such people we command and urge in the Lord Jesus Christ to settle down and earn the bread they eat. ¹³And as for you, brothers and sisters, never tire of doing what is good.

¹⁴Take special note of those who do not obey our instruction in this letter. Do not associate with them, in order that they may feel ashamed. ¹⁵Yet do not regard them as enemies, but warn them as fellow believers.

Final greetings

¹⁶Now may the Lord of peace himself give you peace at all times and in every way. The Lord be with all of you.

¹⁷I, Paul, write this greeting in my own hand, which is the distinguishing mark in all my letters. This is how I write.

¹⁸The grace of our Lord Jesus Christ be with you all.

1 Timothy

INTRODUCTION

1 Timothy

Author: Paul

Who to: Timothy, a young church leader.

When: Probably written around AD 65.

Where: Timothy was leading a church in Ephesus.

Did you know? You can read about when Paul first met Timothy in Acts 16:1. Timothy is the joint sender of six of Paul's letters.

Main theme: This is the nearest we get in the Bible to an instruction manual on how to run a church. Paul advises Timothy on issues like prayer, worship and what sort of people should be leaders. He warns Timothy to beware of false teaching and encourages him to set a good example even though he is young.

1 Paul, an apostle of Christ Jesus by the command of God our Saviour and of Christ Jesus our hope,

²To Timothy my true son in the faith:

Grace, mercy and peace from God the Father and Christ Jesus our Lord.

Timothy charged to oppose false teachers

³As I urged you when I went into Macedonia, stay there in Ephesus so that you may command certain people not to teach false doctrines any longer ⁴or to devote themselves to myths and endless genealogies. Such things promote controversial speculations rather than advancing God's work—which is by faith. ⁵The goal of this command is love, which comes from a pure heart and a good conscience and a sincere faith. ⁶Some have departed from these and have turned to meaningless talk. ⁷They want to be teachers of the law, but they do not know what they are talking about or what they so confidently affirm.

⁸We know that the law is good if one uses it properly. ⁹We also know that the law is made not for the righteous but for lawbreakers and rebels, the ungodly and sinful, the unholy and irreligious, for those who kill their fathers or mothers, for murderers, ¹⁰for the sexually immoral, for those

practising homosexuality, for slave traders and liars and perjurers. And it is for whatever else is contrary to the sound doctrine 11that conforms to the gospel concerning the glory of the blessed God, which he entrusted to me.

The Lord's grace to Paul

12I thank Christ Jesus our Lord, who has given me strength, that he considered me trustworthy, appointing me to his service. 13Even though I was once a blasphemer and a persecutor and a violent man, I was shown mercy because I acted in ignorance and unbelief. 14The grace of our Lord was poured out on me abundantly, along with the faith and love that are in Christ Jesus.

15Here is a trustworthy saying that deserves full acceptance: Christ Jesus came into the world to save sinners—of whom I am the worst. 16But for that very reason I was shown mercy so that in me, the worst of sinners, Christ Jesus might display his immense patience as an example for those who would believe in him and receive eternal life. 17Now to the King eternal, immortal, invisible, the only God, be honour and glory for ever and ever. Amen.

The charge to Timothy renewed

18Timothy, my son, I am giving you this command in keeping with the prophecies once made about you, so that by recalling them you may fight the battle well, 19holding on to faith and a good conscience, which some have rejected and so have suffered shipwreck with regard to the faith. 20Among them are Hymenaeus and Alexander, whom I have handed over to Satan to be taught not to blaspheme.

Instructions on worship

2 I urge, then, first of all, that petitions, prayers, intercession and thanksgiving be made for everyone— 2for kings and all those in authority, that we may live peaceful and quiet lives in all godliness and holiness. 3This is good, and pleases God our Saviour, 4who wants all people to be saved and to come to a knowledge of the truth. 5For there is one God and one mediator between God and human beings, Christ Jesus, himself human, 6who gave himself as a ransom for all people. This has now been witnessed to at the proper time. 7And for this purpose I was appointed a herald and an apostle—I am telling the truth, I am not lying—and a true and faithful teacher of the Gentiles.

8Therefore I want the men everywhere to pray, lifting up holy hands without anger or disputing. 9I also want the women to dress modestly, with decency and propriety, adorning themselves, not with elaborate hairstyles or gold or pearls or expensive clothes, 10but with good deeds, appropriate for women who profess to worship God.

11A woman^a should learn in quietness and full submission. 12I do not permit a woman to teach or to assume authority over a man;^{b,c} she must be quiet. 13For Adam was formed first, then Eve. 14And Adam was not the one deceived; it was the woman who was deceived and became a sinner. 15But women^d will be saved through childbearing—if they continue in faith, love and holiness with propriety.

Qualifications for overseers and deacons

3 Here is a trustworthy saying: whoever aspires to be an overseer desires a noble

---

> **People and Places**
>
> **Ephesus**
> 1 Timothy 1:3
> Ephesus was a large and important city on the coast of Asia Minor, in the country that we now call Turkey. It was a busy seaport and was the largest city in the province at that time. The Temple of Artemis dominated the city. She was the Greek goddess of hunting and the moon, and was also known by her Roman name, Diana.

---

^{a} 11 Or *wife*; also inverse 12 ^{b} 12 Or *teach a man in a domineering way; or teach or to exercise (or have) authority over a man* ^{c} 12 Or *over her husband* ^{d} 15 Greek *she* task. ²Now the overseer is to be above reproach, faithful to his wife, temperate, self-controlled, respectable, hospitable, able to teach, ³not given to drunkenness, not violent but gentle, not quarrelsome, not a lover of money. ⁴He must manage his own family well and see that his children obey him, and he must do so in a manner worthy of full[a] respect. ⁵(If anyone does not know how to manage his own family, how can he take care of God's church?) ⁶He must not be a recent convert, or he may become conceited and fall under the same judgment as the devil. ⁷He must also have a good reputation with outsiders, so that he will not fall into disgrace and into the devil's trap.

⁸In the same way, deacons are to be worthy of respect, sincere, not indulging in much wine, and not pursuing dishonest gain. ⁹They must keep hold of the deep truths of the faith with a clear conscience. ¹⁰They must first be tested; and then if there is nothing against them, let them serve as deacons.

¹¹In the same way, the women[b] are to be worthy of respect, not malicious talkers but temperate and trustworthy in everything.

¹²A deacon must be faithful to his wife and must manage his children and his household well. ¹³Those who have served well gain an excellent standing and great assurance in their faith in Christ Jesus.

Deacon
1 Timothy 3:8
The word 'deacon' literally means 'a servant'. It was first used to describe those who provided food for the widows in the Jerusalem church, but soon came to refer to a particular position of responsibility in the church.

Reasons for Paul's instructions

¹⁴Although I hope to come to you soon, I am writing to you with these instructions so that, ¹⁵if I am delayed, you will know how people ought to conduct themselves in God's household, which is the church of the living God, the pillar and foundation of the truth. ¹⁶Beyond all question, the mystery from which true godliness springs is great:

> he appeared in a body,
>   was vindicated by the Spirit,[c]
> was seen by angels,
>   was preached among the nations,
> was believed on in the world,
>   was taken up in glory.

4 The Spirit clearly says that in later times some will abandon the faith and follow deceiving spirits and things taught by demons. ²Such teachings come through hypocritical liars, whose consciences have been seared as with a hot iron. ³They forbid people to marry and order them to abstain from certain foods, which God created to be received with thanksgiving by those who believe and who know the truth. ⁴For everything God created is good, and nothing is to be rejected if it is received with thanksgiving, ⁵because it is consecrated by the word of God and prayer.

⁶If you point these things out to the brothers and sisters, you will be a good minister of Christ Jesus, nourished on the truths of the faith and of the good teaching that you have followed. ⁷Have nothing to do with godless myths and old wives' tales; rather, train yourself to be godly. ⁸For physical training is of some value, but godliness has value for all things, holding promise for both the present life and the life to come. ⁹This is a trustworthy saying that deserves full acceptance. ¹⁰That is why we labour and strive, because we have put our hope in the living God, who is the Saviour of all people, and especially of those who believe.

¹¹Command and teach these things. ¹²Don't let anyone look down on you because you are young, but set an example

---

[a] 4 Or *him with proper* [b] 11 Probably women who are deacons, or possibly deacons' wives [c] 16 Or *vindicated in spirit*

IN OTHER WORDS

Doctrine
1 Timothy 4:16
Doctrine is the set of beliefs that we have about who God is, who Jesus is and what the human race is like.

for the believers in speech, in conduct, in love, in faith and in purity. ¹³Until I come, devote yourself to the public reading of Scripture, to preaching and to teaching. ¹⁴Do not neglect your gift, which was given you through prophecy when the body of elders laid their hands on you.

¹⁵Be diligent in these matters; give yourself wholly to them, so that everyone may see your progress. ¹⁶Watch your life and doctrine closely. Persevere in them, because if you do, you will save both yourself and your hearers.

Widows, elders and slaves

5 Do not rebuke an older man harshly, but exhort him as if he were your father. Treat younger men as brothers, ²older women as mothers, and younger women as sisters, with absolute purity.

³Give proper recognition to those widows who are really in need. ⁴But if a widow has children or grandchildren, these should learn first of all to put their religion into practice by caring for their own family and so repaying their parents and grandparents, for this is pleasing to God. ⁵The widow who is really in need and left all alone puts her hope in God and continues night and day to pray and to ask God for help. ⁶But the widow who lives for pleasure is dead even while she lives. ⁷Give the people these instructions, so that no-one may be open to blame. ⁸Anyone who does not provide for their relatives, and especially for their own household, has denied the faith and is worse than an unbeliever.

⁹No widow may be put on the list of widows unless she is over sixty, has been faithful to her husband, ¹⁰and is well known for her good deeds, such as bringing up children, showing hospitality, washing the feet of the Lord's people, helping those in trouble and devoting herself to all kinds of good deeds.

¹¹As for younger widows, do not put them on such a list. For when their sensual desires overcome their dedication to Christ, they want to marry. ¹²Thus they bring judgment on themselves, because they have broken their first pledge. ¹³Besides, they get into the habit of being idle and going about from house to house. And not only do they become idlers, but also busybodies who talk nonsense, saying things they ought not to. ¹⁴So I counsel younger widows to marry, to have children, to manage their homes and to give the enemy no opportunity for slander. ¹⁵Some have in fact already turned away to follow Satan.

¹⁶If any woman who is a believer has widows in her care, she should continue to help them and not let the church be burdened with them, so that the church can help those widows who are really in need.

¹⁷The elders who direct the affairs of the church well are worthy of double honour, especially those whose work is preaching and teaching. ¹⁸For Scripture says, 'Do not muzzle an ox while it is treading out the grain,'ᵃ and 'Workers deserve their wages.'ᵇ ¹⁹Do not entertain an accusation against an elder unless it is brought by two or three witnesses. ²⁰But those elders who are sinning you are to reprove before everyone, so that the others may take warning. ²¹I charge you, in the sight of God and Christ Jesus and the elect angels, to keep these instructions without partiality, and to do nothing out of favouritism.

²²Do not be hasty in the laying on of hands, and do not share in the sins of others. Keep yourself pure.

²³Stop drinking only water, and use a little wine because of your stomach and your frequent illnesses.

²⁴The sins of some are obvious, reaching the place of judgment ahead of them; the sins of others trail behind them. ²⁵In the

---

ᵃ 18 Deut. 25:4 ᵇ 18 Luke 10:7

same way, good deeds are obvious, and even those that are not obvious cannot remain hidden for ever.

6 All who are under the yoke of slavery should consider their masters worthy of full respect, so that God's name and our teaching may not be slandered. ²Those who have believing masters should not show them disrespect just because they are fellow-believers. Instead, they should serve them even better because their masters are dear to them as fellow believers and are devoted to the welfare*ᵃ* of their slaves.

False teachers and the love of money

These are the things you are to teach and insist on. ³If anyone teaches otherwise and does not agree to the sound instruction of our Lord Jesus Christ and to godly teaching, ⁴they are conceited and understand nothing. They have an unhealthy interest in controversies and quarrels about words that result in envy, strife, malicious talk, evil suspicions ⁵and constant friction between people of corrupt mind, who have been robbed of the truth and who think that godliness is a means to financial gain.

⁶But godliness with contentment is great gain. ⁷For we brought nothing into the world, and we can take nothing out of it. ⁸But if we have food and clothing, we will be content with that. ⁹Those who want to get rich fall into temptation and a trap and into many foolish and harmful desires that plunge people into ruin and destruction. ¹⁰For the love of money is a root of all kinds of evil. Some people, eager for money, have wandered from the faith and pierced themselves with many griefs.

Final charge to Timothy

¹¹But you, man of God, flee from all this, and pursue righteousness, godliness, faith, love, endurance and gentleness. ¹²Fight the good fight of the faith. Take hold of the eternal life to which you were called when you made your good confession in the presence of many witnesses. ¹³In the sight of God, who gives life to everything, and of Christ Jesus, who while testifying before Pontius Pilate made the good confession, I charge you ¹⁴to keep this command without spot or blame until the appearing of our Lord Jesus Christ, ¹⁵which God will bring about in his own time—God, the blessed and only Ruler, the King of kings and Lord of lords, ¹⁶who alone is immortal and who lives in unapproachable light, whom no-one has seen or can see. To him be honour and might for ever. Amen.

¹⁷Command those who are rich in this present world not to be arrogant nor to put their hope in wealth, which is so uncertain, but to put their hope in God, who richly provides us with everything for our enjoyment. ¹⁸Command them to do good, to be rich in good deeds, and to be generous and willing to share. ¹⁹In this way they will lay up treasure for themselves as a firm foundation for the coming age, so that they may take hold of the life that is truly life.

²⁰Timothy, guard what has been entrusted to your care. Turn away from godless chatter and the opposing ideas of what is falsely called knowledge, ²¹which some have professed and in so doing have departed from the faith.

Grace be with you all.

---

*ᵃ*2 Or *and benefit from the service*

2 Timothy

INTRODUCTION

2 Timothy

Author: Paul

Who to: Timothy, a young church leader.

When: Probably written around AD 65.

Where: Timothy was leading a church in Ephesus.

Did you know? Paul wrote this letter from Rome where he was imprisoned.

Main theme: Paul encourages Timothy to be strong and keep the faith even in difficult circumstances. He warns him again about the dangers of false teaching. Paul ends his letter on a very personal note. He is aware that he hasn't got much longer to live and asks Timothy to quickly come and be with him.

1 Paul, an apostle of Christ Jesus by the will of God, in keeping with the promise of life that is in Christ Jesus,

2To Timothy, my dear son:

Grace, mercy and peace from God the Father and Christ Jesus our Lord.

Thanksgiving

3I thank God, whom I serve, as my ancestors did, with a clear conscience, as night and day I constantly remember you in my prayers. 4Recalling your tears, I long to see you, so that I may be filled with joy. 5I am reminded of your sincere faith, which first lived in your grandmother Lois and in your mother Eunice and, I am persuaded, now lives in you also.

Appeal for loyalty to Paul and the gospel

6For this reason I remind you to fan into flame the gift of God, which is in you through the laying on of my hands. 7For the Spirit God gave us does not make us timid, but gives us power, love and self-discipline. 8So do not be ashamed of the testimony about our Lord or of me his prisoner. But join with me in suffering for the gospel, by the power of God, 9who has saved us and called us to a holy life—not because of anything we have done but because of his own purpose and grace. This grace was given us in Christ Jesus before the beginning of time, ¹⁰but it has now been revealed through the appearing of our Saviour, Christ Jesus, who has destroyed death and has brought life and immortality to light through the gospel. ¹¹And of this gospel I was appointed a herald and an apostle and a teacher. ¹²That is why I am suffering as I am. Yet this is no cause for shame, because I know whom I have believed, and am convinced that he is able to guard what I have entrusted to him until that day.

¹³What you heard from me, keep as the pattern of sound teaching, with faith and love in Christ Jesus. ¹⁴Guard the good deposit that was entrusted to you—guard it with the help of the Holy Spirit who lives in us.

Examples of disloyalty and loyalty

¹⁵You know that everyone in the province of Asia has deserted me, including Phygelus and Hermogenes.

¹⁶May the Lord show mercy to the household of Onesiphorus, because he often refreshed me and was not ashamed of my chains. ¹⁷On the contrary, when he was in Rome, he searched hard for me until he found me. ¹⁸May the Lord grant that he will find mercy from the Lord on that day! You know very well in how many ways he helped me in Ephesus.

The appeal renewed

2 You then, my son, be strong in the grace that is in Christ Jesus. ²And the things you have heard me say in the presence of many witnesses entrust to reliable people who will also be qualified to teach others. ³Join with me in suffering, like a good soldier of Christ Jesus. ⁴No-one serving as a soldier gets involved in civilian affairs; rather, they try to please their commanding officer. ⁵Similarly, anyone who competes as an athlete does not receive the victor's crown except by competing according to the rules. ⁶The hardworking farmer should be the first to receive a share of the crops. ⁷Reflect on what I am saying, for the Lord will give you insight into all this.

⁸Remember Jesus Christ, raised from the dead, descended from David. This is my gospel, ⁹for which I am suffering even to the point of being chained like a criminal. But God's word is not chained. ¹⁰Therefore I endure everything for the sake of the elect, that they too may obtain the salvation that is in Christ Jesus, with eternal glory.

¹¹Here is a trustworthy saying:

If we died with him,
 we will also live with him;
¹²if we endure,
 we will also reign with him.
If we disown him,
 he will also disown us;
¹³if we are faithless,
 he remains faithful,
 for he cannot disown himself.

Dealing with false teachers

¹⁴Keep reminding God's people of these things. Warn them before God against quarrelling about words; it is of no value, and only ruins those who listen. ¹⁵Do your best to present yourself to God as one approved, a worker who does not need to be ashamed and who correctly handles the word of truth. ¹⁶Avoid godless chatter, because those who indulge in it will become more and more ungodly. ¹⁷Their teaching will spread like gangrene. Among them are Hymenaeus and Philetus, ¹⁸who have departed from the truth. They say that the resurrection has already taken place, and they destroy the faith of some. ¹⁹Nevertheless, God's solid foundation stands firm, sealed with this inscription: 'The Lord knows those who are his,' and, 'Everyone who confesses the name of the Lord must turn away from wickedness.'

²⁰In a large house there are articles not only of gold and silver, but also of wood and clay; some are for noble purposes and some for disposal of refuse. ²¹Those who cleanse themselves from the latter will be instruments for noble purposes, made holy, useful to the Master and prepared to do any good work.

²²Flee the evil desires of youth and pursue righteousness, faith, love and peace, along with those who call on the Lord out of a pure heart. ²³Don't have anything to do with foolish and stupid arguments, because you know they produce quarrels. ²⁴And the Lord's servant must not be quarrelsome but

must be kind to everyone, able to teach, not resentful. 25Opponents must be gently instructed, in the hope that God will grant them repentance leading them to a knowledge of the truth, 26and that they will come to their senses and escape from the trap of the devil, who has taken them captive to do his will.

3 But mark this: there will be terrible times in the last days. 2People will be lovers of themselves, lovers of money, boastful, proud, abusive, disobedient to their parents, ungrateful, unholy, 3without love, unforgiving, slanderous, without self-control, brutal, not lovers of the good, 4treacherous, rash, conceited, lovers of pleasure rather than lovers of God— 5having a form of godliness but denying its power. Have nothing to do with such people.

6They are the kind who worm their way into homes and gain control over gullible women, who are loaded down with sins and are swayed by all kinds of evil desires, 7always learning but never able to come to a knowledge of the truth. 8Just as Jannes and Jambres opposed Moses, so also these teachers oppose the truth. They are men of depraved minds, who, as far as the faith is concerned, are rejected. 9But they will not get very far because, as in the case of those men, their folly will be clear to everyone.

A final charge to Timothy

10You, however, know all about my teaching, my way of life, my purpose, faith, patience, love, endurance, 11persecutions, sufferings—what kinds of things happened to me in Antioch, Iconium and Lystra, the persecutions I endured. Yet the Lord rescued me from all of them. 12In fact, everyone who wants to live a godly life in Christ Jesus will be persecuted, 13while evildoers and impostors will go from bad to worse, deceiving and being deceived. 14But as for you, continue in what you have learned and have become convinced of, because you know those from whom you learned it, 15and how from infancy you have known the Holy Scriptures, which are able to make you wise for salvation through faith in Christ Jesus. 16All Scripture is God-breathed and is useful for teaching, rebuking, correcting and training in righteousness, 17so that all God's people*a* may be thoroughly equipped for every good work.

4 In the presence of God and of Christ Jesus, who will judge the living and the dead, and in view of his appearing and his kingdom, I give you this charge: 2preach the word; be prepared in season and out of season; correct, rebuke and encourage—with great patience and careful instruction. 3For the time will come when people will not put up with sound doctrine. Instead, to suit their own desires, they will gather round them a great number of teachers to say what their itching ears want to hear. 4They will turn their ears away from the truth and turn aside to myths. 5But you, keep your head in all situations, endure hardship, do the work of an evangelist, discharge all the duties of your ministry.

6For I am already being poured out like a drink offering, and the time for my departure is near. 7I have fought the good fight, I have finished the race, I have kept the faith. 8Now there is in store for me the crown of righteousness, which the Lord, the righteous Judge, will award to me on that day—and not only to me, but also to all who have longed for his appearing.

Personal remarks

9Do your best to come to me quickly, 10for Demas, because he loved this world, has deserted me and has gone to Thessalonica. Crescens has gone to Galatia, and Titus to

Evangelist
2 Timothy 4:5
An evangelist is someone who tells other people about the good news of Jesus.

---

a 17 Or *that the servant of God*

Dalmatia. ¹¹Only Luke is with me. Get Mark and bring him with you, because he is helpful to me in my ministry. ¹²I sent Tychicus to Ephesus. ¹³When you come, bring the cloak that I left with Carpus at Troas, and my scrolls, especially the parchments.

¹⁴Alexander the metalworker did me a great deal of harm. The Lord will repay him for what he has done. ¹⁵You too should be on your guard against him, because he strongly opposed our message.

¹⁶At my first defence, no-one came to my support, but everyone deserted me. May it not be held against them. ¹⁷But the Lord stood at my side and gave me strength, so that through me the message might be fully proclaimed and all the Gentiles might hear it. And I was delivered from the lion's mouth. ¹⁸The Lord will rescue me from every evil attack and will bring me safely to his heavenly kingdom. To him be glory for ever and ever. Amen.

Final greetings

¹⁹Greet Priscilla[a] and Aquila and the household of Onesiphorus. ²⁰Erastus stayed in Corinth, and I left Trophimus ill in Miletus. ²¹Do your best to get here before winter. Eubulus greets you, and so do Pudens, Linus, Claudia and all the brothers and sisters.

²²The Lord be with your spirit. Grace be with you all.

---

[a] 19 Greek *Prisca*, a variant of *Priscilla*

Titus

INTRODUCTION

Titus

Author: Paul

Who to: Titus, a man who worked with Paul (2 Corinthians 8:23).

When: Probably written around AD 64–66.

Where: Crete, where Titus was setting up churches.

Did you know? Paul wrote three letters to individuals, Titus and 1 and 2 Timothy. These letters are called the Pastoral Epistles because they talk about how to be a pastor and lead a church.

Main theme: Paul's letter to Titus warns against false teachers and talks about the need for sound doctrine, or teaching about God's truth. It challenges Christians to put their beliefs into action and to do good things.

1 Paul, a servant of God and an apostle of Jesus Christ to further the faith of God's elect and their knowledge of the truth that leads to godliness— 2in the hope of eternal life, which God, who does not lie, promised before the beginning of time, 3and which now at his appointed season he has brought to light through the preaching entrusted to me by the command of God our Saviour,

4To Titus, my true son in our common faith:

Grace and peace from God the Father and Christ Jesus our Saviour.

Appointing elders who love what is good

5The reason I left you in Crete was that you might put in order what was left unfinished and appoint[a] elders in every town, as I directed you. 6An elder must be blameless, faithful to his wife, a man whose children believe and are not open to the charge of being wild and disobedient. 7Since an overseer manages God's household, he must be blameless—not overbearing, not quick-tempered, not given to drunkenness,

---

[a] 5 Or ordain

not violent, not pursuing dishonest gain. ⁸Rather, he must be hospitable, one who loves what is good, who is self-controlled, upright, holy and disciplined. ⁹He must hold firmly to the trustworthy message as it has been taught, so that he can encourage others by sound doctrine and refute those who oppose it.

Rebuking those who fail to do good

¹⁰For there are many rebellious people, full of meaningless talk and deception, especially those of the circumcision group. ¹¹They must be silenced, because they are disrupting whole households by teaching things they ought not to teach—and that for the sake of dishonest gain. ¹²One of Crete's own prophets has said it: 'Cretans are always liars, evil brutes, lazy gluttons.'*ᵃ* ¹³He has surely told the truth! Therefore rebuke them sharply, so that they will be sound in the faith ¹⁴and will pay no attention to Jewish myths or to the merely human commands of those who reject the truth. ¹⁵To the pure, all things are pure, but to those who are corrupted and do not believe, nothing is pure. In fact, both their minds and consciences are corrupted. ¹⁶They claim to know God, but by their actions they deny him. They are detestable, disobedient and unfit for doing anything good.

Doing good for the sake of the gospel

2 You, however, must teach what is appropriate to sound doctrine. ²Teach the older men to be temperate, worthy of respect, self-controlled, and sound in faith, in love and in endurance.

³Likewise, teach the older women to be reverent in the way they live, not to be slanderers or addicted to much wine, but to teach what is good. ⁴Then they can urge the younger women to love their husbands and children, ⁵to be self-controlled and pure, to be busy at home, to be kind, and to be subject to their husbands, so that no-one will malign the word of God.

⁶Similarly, encourage the young men to be self-controlled. ⁷In everything set them an example by doing what is good. In your teaching show integrity, seriousness ⁸and soundness of speech that cannot be condemned, so that those who oppose you may be ashamed because they have nothing bad to say about us.

⁹Teach slaves to be subject to their masters in everything, to try to please them, not to talk back to them, ¹⁰and not to steal from them, but to show that they can be fully trusted, so that in every way they will make the teaching about God our Saviour attractive.

¹¹For the grace of God has appeared that offers salvation to all people. ¹²It teaches us to say 'No' to ungodliness and worldly passions, and to live self-controlled, upright and godly lives in this present age, ¹³while we wait for the blessed hope—the appearing of the glory of our great God and Saviour, Jesus Christ, ¹⁴who gave himself for us to redeem us from all wickedness and to purify for himself a people that are his very own, eager to do what is good.

¹⁵These, then, are the things you should teach. Encourage and rebuke with all authority. Do not let anyone despise you.

Saved in order to do good

3 Remind the people to be subject to rulers and authorities, to be obedient, to be ready to do whatever is good, ²to slander no-one, to be peaceable and considerate, and always to be gentle towards everyone.

³At one time we too were foolish, disobedient, deceived and enslaved by all kinds of passions and pleasures. We lived in malice and envy, being hated and hating one another. ⁴But when the kindness and love of God our Saviour appeared, ⁵he saved us, not because of righteous things we had done, but because of his mercy. He saved us through the washing of rebirth and renewal by the Holy Spirit, ⁶whom he poured out on us generously through Jesus Christ our Saviour, ⁷so that, having been justified by his grace, we might become heirs having the hope of eternal life. ⁸This is a trustworthy saying. And I want you to stress these things, so that those who have trusted in God may be careful to devote themselves to doing

---

ᵃ 12 From the Cretan philosopher Epimenides

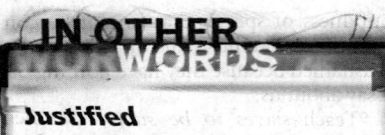

IN OTHER WORDS

Justified
Titus 3:7
Justification is the way in which sinful people are made acceptable to a holy God. It's not through what we do or who we are. We are justified because Jesus died on the cross and took our sin on himself. In other words it's all because of God's grace.

what is good. These things are excellent and profitable for everyone.

⁹But avoid foolish controversies and genealogies and arguments and quarrels about the law, because these are unprofitable and useless. ¹⁰Warn divisive people once, and then warn them a second time. After that, have nothing to do with them. ¹¹You may be sure that such people are warped and sinful; they are self-condemned.

Final remarks

¹²As soon as I send Artemas or Tychicus to you, do your best to come to me at Nicopolis, because I have decided to winter there. ¹³Do everything you can to help Zenas the lawyer and Apollos on their way and see that they have everything they need. ¹⁴Our people must learn to devote themselves to doing what is good, in order to provide for urgent needs and not live unproductive lives.

¹⁵Everyone with me sends you greetings. Greet those who love us in the faith.

Grace be with you all.

Philemon

INTRODUCTION

Philemon

Author: Paul, with greetings from Timothy.

Who to: Philemon, Apphia and Archippus.

When: While Paul was in prison in Rome, probably in the early 60s AD.

Where: Philemon lived in Colossae.

Did you know? This letter to Philemon was probably written at the same time as Paul's letter to the Colossians. Both letters send greetings from the same people (Colossians 4:7–17 and Philemon 23, 24) and were delivered by Tychicus and Onesimus (Colossians 4:7–9).

Main theme: This is the shortest of Paul's letters and the most personal. Paul writes to Philemon to ask him to forgive Onesimus, his slave who had run away, and welcome him back.

---

¹Paul, a prisoner of Christ Jesus, and Timothy our brother,

To Philemon our dear friend and fellow-worker— ²also to Apphia our sister and Archippus our fellow-soldier—and to the church that meets in your home:

³Grace and peace to you[a] from God our Father and the Lord Jesus Christ.

Thanksgiving and prayer

⁴I always thank my God as I remember you in my prayers, ⁵because I hear about your love for all his people and your faith in the Lord Jesus. ⁶I pray that your partnership with us in the faith may be effective in deepening your understanding of every good thing we share for the sake of Christ. ⁷Your love has given me great joy and encouragement, because you, brother, have refreshed the hearts of the Lord's people.

Paul's plea for Onesimus

⁸Therefore, although in Christ I could be bold and order you to do what you ought to do, ⁹yet I prefer to appeal to you on the basis of love. It is as none other than Paul—an old

---

[a] 3 The Greek is plural; also in verses 22 and 25; elsewhere in this letter 'you' is singular.

People and Places

Onesimus
Philemon 10

Onesimus was a slave who ran away from his master, Philemon. While on the run, he met Paul in Rome and became a Christian. Legally, Philemon was allowed to punish a slave for doing something wrong, but Paul appeals to him to welcome Onesimus back as a brother and not a slave. Onesimus' name means 'useless', but Paul says he will now be useful to Philemon.

---

man and now also a prisoner of Christ Jesus— ¹⁰that I appeal to you for my son Onesimus,*ᵃ* who became my son while I was in chains. ¹¹Formerly he was useless to you, but now he has become useful both to you and to me.

¹²I am sending him—who is my very heart—back to you. ¹³I would have liked to keep him with me so that he could take your place in helping me while I am in chains for the gospel. ¹⁴But I did not want to do anything without your consent, so that any favour you do would not seem forced but would be voluntary. ¹⁵Perhaps the reason he was separated from you for a little while was that you might have him back for ever— ¹⁶no longer as a slave, but better than a slave, as a dear brother. He is very dear to me but even dearer to you, both as a fellow-man and as a brother in the Lord.

¹⁷So if you consider me a partner, welcome him as you would welcome me. ¹⁸If he has done you any wrong or owes you anything, charge it to me. ¹⁹I, Paul, am writing this with my own hand. I will pay it back—not to mention that you owe me your very self. ²⁰I do wish, brother, that I may have some benefit from you in the Lord; refresh my heart in Christ. ²¹Confident of your obedience, I write to you, knowing that you will do even more than I ask.

²²And one thing more: prepare a guest room for me, because I hope to be restored to you in answer to your prayers.

²³Epaphras, my fellow-prisoner in Christ Jesus, sends you greetings. ²⁴And so do Mark, Aristarchus, Demas and Luke, my fellow-workers.

²⁵The grace of the Lord Jesus Christ be with your spirit.

ᵃ 10 Onesimus means useful.

Hebrews

INTRODUCTION

Hebrews

Author: Unknown

Who to: Originally written to people with a Jewish background.

When: Before AD 70.

Where: Possibly written from Italy (Hebrews 13:24).

Did you know? Hebrews and 1 John are the only letters in the New Testament that don't start with a greeting from the author.

Main theme: Hebrews shows the relationship between Judaism and Christianity, arguing that Jesus is the Son of God and the Messiah that the Jews were waiting for. It uses lots of quotations and images from the Old Testament that Jewish people would be very familiar with, and shows that Jesus is both better than the Old Testament images and the fulfilment of them. Hebrews encourages its readers to stay true to their new Christian faith.

God's final word: his Son

1 In the past God spoke to our ancestors through the prophets at many times and in various ways, ²but in these last days he has spoken to us by his Son, whom he appointed heir of all things, and through whom also he made the universe. ³The Son is the radiance of God's glory and the exact representation of his being, sustaining all things by his powerful word. After he had provided purification for sins, he sat down at the right hand of the Majesty in heaven. ⁴So he became as much superior to the angels as the name he has inherited is superior to theirs.

The Son superior to angels

⁵For to which of the angels did God ever say,

'You are my Son;
 today I have become your Father'[a]?

Or again,

'I will be his Father,
 and he will be my Son'[b]?

---
[a] 5 Psalm 2:7 [b] 5 2 Samuel 7:14; 1 Chron. 17:13

IN OTHER WORDS

Purification
Hebrews 1:3

In the Old Testament, the Israelites took ritual washing very seriously because they always wanted to be holy. If anything made them unclean, such as touching blood or a dead body, they would go through an act of purification or cleansing to make them clean again (Numbers 8:7). In the New Testament, the blood of Jesus provides purification for sin.

6And again, when God brings his firstborn into the world, he says,

> 'Let all God's angels worship him.'[a]

7In speaking of the angels he says,

> 'He makes his angels spirits,
> and his servants flames of fire.'[b]

8But about the Son he says,

> 'Your throne, O God, will last for ever and ever;
> a sceptre of justice will be the sceptre of your kingdom.
> 9You have loved righteousness and hated wickedness;
> therefore God, your God, has set you above your companions
> by anointing you with the oil of joy.'[c]

10He also says,

> 'In the beginning, Lord, you laid the foundations of the earth,
> and the heavens are the work of your hands.
> 11They will perish, but you remain;
> they will all wear out like a garment.
> 12You will roll them up like a robe;
> like a garment they will be changed.
> But you remain the same,
> and your years will never end.'[d]

13To which of the angels did God ever say,

> 'Sit at my right hand
> until I make your enemies
> a footstool for your feet'[e]?

14Are not all angels ministering spirits sent to serve those who will inherit salvation?

Warning to pay attention

2 We must pay the most careful attention, therefore, to what we have heard, so that we do not drift away. 2For since the message spoken through angels was binding, and every violation and disobedience received its just punishment, 3how shall we escape if we ignore so great a salvation? This salvation, which was first announced by the Lord, was confirmed to us by those who heard him. 4God also testified to it by signs, wonders and various miracles, and by gifts of the Holy Spirit distributed according to his will.

Jesus made like his brothers and sisters

5It is not to angels that he has subjected the world to come, about which we are speaking. 6But there is a place where someone has testified:

> 'What are mere mortals that you are mindful of them,
> human beings that you care for them?
> 7You made them a little lower than the angels;
> you crowned them with glory and honour
> 8 and put everything under their feet.'[f]

In putting everything under them,[g] God left nothing that is not subject to them.[h] Yet at present we do not see everything subject to them.[i] 9But we do see Jesus, who was made lower than the angels for a little while, now crowned with glory and honour because he suffered death, so that by the grace of God he might taste death for everyone.

10In bringing many sons and daughters to glory, it was fitting that God, for whom

---

[a] 6 Deut. 32:43 (see Dead Sea Scrolls and Septuagint) [b] 7 Psalm 104:4 [c] 9 Psalm 45:6,7 [d] 12 Psalm 102:25-27
[e] 13 Psalm 110:1 [f] 6-8 Psalm 8:4-6; or 'What is a human being that you are mindful of him,/ the son of man that you care for him?/ 7You made him lower than the angels for a little while;/ you crowned him with glory and honour/ 8and put everything under his feet.' [g] 8 Or him [h] 8 Or him [i] 8 Or him

and through whom everything exists, should make the pioneer of their salvation perfect through what he suffered. ¹¹Both the one who makes people holy and those who are made holy are of the same family. So Jesus is not ashamed to call them brothers and sisters. ¹²He says,

'I will declare your name to my brothers and sisters;
    in the assembly I will sing your praises.'ᵃ

¹³And again,

'I will put my trust in him.'ᵇ

And again he says,

'Here am I, and the children God has given me.'ᶜ

¹⁴Since the children have flesh and blood, he too shared in their humanity so that by his death he might break the power of him who holds the power of death—that is, the devil— ¹⁵and free those who all their lives were held in slavery by their fear of death. ¹⁶For surely it is not angels he helps, but Abraham's descendants. ¹⁷For this reason he had to be made like his brothers and sisters in every way, in order that he might become a merciful and faithful high priest in service to God, and that he might make atonement for the sins of the people. ¹⁸Because he himself suffered when he was tempted, he is able to help those who are being tempted.

Jesus greater than Moses

3 Therefore, holy brothers and sisters, who share in the heavenly calling, fix your thoughts on Jesus, whom we acknowledge as our apostle and high priest. ²He was faithful to the one who appointed him, just as Moses was faithful in all God's house. ³Jesus has been found worthy of greater honour than Moses, just as the builder of a house has greater honour than the house itself. ⁴For every house is built by someone, but God is the builder of everything. ⁵'Moses was faithful as a servant in all God's house,'ᵈ bearing witness to what would be spoken by God in the future. ⁶But Christ is faithful as the Son over God's house. And we are his house, if indeed we hold firmly to our confidence and the hope in which we glory.

Warning against unbelief

⁷So, as the Holy Spirit says:

'Today, if you hear his voice,
⁸   do not harden your hearts
    as you did in the rebellion,
      during the time of testing in the wilderness,
⁹where your ancestors tested and tried me,
    though for forty years they saw what I did.
¹⁰That is why I was angry with that generation;
    I said, "Their hearts are always going astray,
    and they have not known my ways."
¹¹So I declared on oath in my anger,
    "They shall never enter my rest."'ᵉ

¹²See to it, brothers and sisters, that none of you has a sinful, unbelieving heart that turns away from the living God. ¹³But encourage one another daily, as long as it is called 'Today', so that none of you may be hardened by sin's deceitfulness. ¹⁴We have come to share in Christ, if indeed we hold firmly till the end our original conviction. ¹⁵As has just been said:

'Today, if you hear his voice,
    do not harden your hearts
    as you did in the rebellion.'ᶠ

¹⁶Who were they who heard and rebelled? Were they not all those Moses led out of Egypt? ¹⁷And with whom was he angry for forty years? Was it not with those who sinned, whose bodies perished in the wilderness? ¹⁸And to whom did God swear that they would never enter his rest if not to those who disobeyed? ¹⁹So we see that they were not able to enter, because of their unbelief.

A Sabbath-rest for the people of God

4 Therefore, since the promise of entering his rest still stands, let us be careful that none of you be found to have fallen short of it. ²For we also have had the good news proclaimed to us, just as they did; but

---

ᵃ 12 Psalm 22:22   ᵇ 13 Isaiah 8:17   ᶜ 13 Isaiah 8:18   ᵈ 5 Num. 12:7   ᵉ 11 Psalm 95:7-11   ᶠ 15 Psalm 95:7,8 the message they heard was of no value to them, because they did not share the faith of those who obeyed.[a] 3Now we who have believed enter that rest, just as God has said,

'So I declared on oath in my anger,
"They shall never enter my rest."'[b]

And yet his work has been finished since the creation of the world. 4For somewhere he has spoken about the seventh day in these words: 'On the seventh day God rested from all his work.'[c] 5And again in the passage above he says, 'They shall never enter my rest.'

6Therefore since it still remains for some to enter that rest, and since those who formerly had the good news proclaimed to them did not go in because of their disobedience, 7God again set a certain day, calling it 'Today'. This he did when a long time later he spoke through David, as in the passage already quoted:

'Today, if you hear his voice,
do not harden your hearts.'[d]

8For if Joshua had given them rest, God would not have spoken later about another day. 9There remains, then, a Sabbath-rest for the people of God; 10for those who enter God's rest also rest from their own work, just as God did from his. 11Let us, therefore, make every effort to enter that rest, so that no-one will perish by following their example of disobedience.

12For the word of God is alive and active. Sharper than any double-edged sword, it penetrates even to dividing soul and spirit, joints and marrow; it judges the thoughts and attitudes of the heart. 13Nothing in all creation is hidden from God's sight. Everything is uncovered and laid bare before the eyes of him to whom we must give account.

Jesus the great high priest

14Therefore, since we have a great high priest who has ascended into heaven,[e] Jesus the Son of God, let us hold firmly to the faith we profess. 15For we do not have a high priest who is unable to feel sympathy for our weaknesses, but we have one who has been tempted in every way, just as we are—yet he did not sin. 16Let us then approach God's throne of grace with confidence, so that we may receive mercy and find grace to help us in our time of need.

5 Every high priest is selected from among the people and is appointed to represent them in matters related to God, to offer gifts and sacrifices for sins. 2He is able to deal gently with those who are ignorant and are going astray, since he himself is subject to weakness. 3This is why he has to offer sacrifices for his own sins, as well as for the sins of the people. 4And no-one takes this honour on himself, but he receives it when called by God, just as Aaron was.

5In the same way, Christ did not take on himself the glory of becoming a high priest. But God said to him,

'You are my Son;
today I have become your Father.'[f]

6And he says in another place,

'You are a priest for ever,
in the order of Melchizedek.'[g]

7During the days of Jesus' life on earth, he offered up prayers and petitions with fervent cries and tears to the one who could save him from death, and he was heard because of his reverent submission. 8Son

---

IN OTHER WORDS

Sabbath-rest
Hebrews 4:9
God created the world in six days and rested on the seventh day, setting the example of how people were to live. The Sabbath is the practice of having one day a week as a day of rest and worship and working for the other six days.

---

[a] 2 Some manuscripts *because those who heard did not combine it with faith* [b] 3 Psalm 95:11; also in verse 5
[c] 4 Gen. 2:2 [d] 7 Psalm 95:7,8 [e] 14 Greek *has gone through the heavens* [f] 5 Psalm 2:7 [g] 6 Psalm 110:4

People and Places

Melchizedek
Hebrews 7:1

There's an air of mystery around Melchizedek. He was a king of Salem who met Abraham and gave him bread and wine. In return, Abraham gave him a tithe, a tenth of his possessions (Genesis 14:18–20). And that's all we know about him. Because he was both a king and a priest, he is seen as a model for Jesus, who is the ultimate king and priest.

---

kindred are descended from Abraham. 6This man, however, did not trace his descent from Levi, yet he collected a tenth from Abraham and blessed him who had the promises. 7And without doubt the lesser is blessed by the greater. 8In the one case, the tenth is collected by those who die; but in the other case, by him who is declared to be living. 9One might even say that Levi, who collects the tenth, paid the tenth through Abraham, 10because when Melchizedek met Abraham, Levi was still in the body of his ancestor.

Jesus Like Melchizedek

11If perfection could have been attained through the Levitical priesthood—and indeed the law given to the people established that priesthood—why was there still need for another priest to come, one in the order of Melchizedek, not in the order of Aaron? 12For when the priesthood is changed, the law must be changed also. 13He of whom these things are said belonged to a different tribe, and no-one from that tribe has ever served at the altar. 14For it is clear that our Lord descended from Judah, and in regard to that tribe Moses said nothing about priests. 15And what we have said is even more clear if another priest like Melchizedek appears, 16one who has become a priest not on the basis of a regulation as to his ancestry but on the basis of the power of an indestructible life. 17For it is declared:

'You are a priest for ever,
  in the order of Melchizedek.'[a]

18The former regulation is set aside because it was weak and useless 19(for the law made nothing perfect), and a better hope is introduced, by which we draw near to God.

20And it was not without an oath! Others became priests without any oath, 21but he became a priest with an oath when God said to him:

'The Lord has sworn
  and will not change his mind:
  "You are a priest for ever."'[b]

22Because of this oath, Jesus has become the guarantor of a better covenant.

23Now there have been many of those priests, since death prevented them from continuing in office; 24but because Jesus lives for ever, he has a permanent priesthood. 25Therefore he is able to save completely[c] those who come to God through him, because he always lives to intercede for them.

26Such a high priest truly meets our need—one who is holy, blameless, pure, set apart from sinners, exalted above the heavens. 27Unlike the other high priests, he does not need to offer sacrifices day after day, first for his own sins, and then for the sins of the people. He sacrificed for their sins once for all when he offered himself. 28For the law appoints as high priests men in all their weakness; but the oath, which came after the law, appointed the Son, who has been made perfect for ever.

The high priest of a new covenant

8 Now the main point of what we are saying is this: we do have such a high priest, who sat down at the right hand of the throne of the Majesty in heaven, 2and who serves in the sanctuary, the true tabernacle set up by the Lord, not by a mere human being.

---

[a] 17 Psalm 110:4   [b] 21 Psalm 110:4   [c] 25 Or *for ever*

though he was, he learned obedience from what he suffered 9and, once made perfect, he became the source of eternal salvation for all who obey him 10and was designated by God to be high priest in the order of Melchizedek.

Warning against falling away

11We have much to say about this, but it is hard to make it clear to you because you no longer try to understand. 12In fact, though by this time you ought to be teachers, you need someone to teach you the elementary truths of God's word all over again. You need milk, not solid food! 13Anyone who lives on milk, being still an infant, is not acquainted with the teaching about righteousness. 14But solid food is for the mature, who by constant use have trained themselves to distinguish good from evil.

6 Therefore let us move beyond the elementary teachings about Christ and be taken forward to maturity, not laying again the foundation of repentance from acts that lead to death,[a] and of faith in God, 2instruction about cleansing rites,[b] the laying on of hands, the resurrection of the dead, and eternal judgment. 3And God permitting, we will do so.

4It is impossible for those who have once been enlightened, who have tasted the heavenly gift, who have shared in the Holy Spirit, 5who have tasted the goodness of the word of God and the powers of the coming age 6and who have fallen[c] away, to be brought back to repentance. To their loss they are crucifying the Son of God all over again and subjecting him to public disgrace. 7Land that drinks in the rain often falling on it and that produces a crop useful to those for whom it is farmed receives the blessing of God. 8But land that produces thorns and thistles is worthless and is in danger of being cursed. In the end it will be burned.

9Even though we speak like this, dear friends, we are convinced of better things in *your case—the things that have to do with* salvation. 10God is not unjust; he will not forget your work and the love you have shown him as you have helped his people and continue to help them. 11We want each of you to show this same diligence to the very end, in order to make your hope sure. 12We do not want you to become lazy, but to imitate those who through faith and patience inherit what has been promised.

The certainty of God's promise

13When God made his promise to Abraham, since there was no-one greater for him to swear by, he swore by himself, 14saying, 'I will surely bless you and give you many descendants.'[d] 15And so after waiting patiently, Abraham received what was promised.

16People swear by someone greater than themselves, and the oath confirms what is said and puts an end to all argument. 17Because God wanted to make the unchanging nature of his purpose very clear to the heirs of what was promised, he confirmed it with an oath. 18God did this so that, by two unchangeable things in which it is impossible for God to lie, we who have fled to take hold of the hope set before us may be greatly encouraged. 19We have this hope as an anchor for the soul, firm and secure. It enters the inner sanctuary behind the curtain, 20where our forerunner, Jesus, has entered on our behalf. He has become a high priest for ever, in the order of Melchizedek.

Melchizedek the priest

7 This Melchizedek was king of Salem and priest of God Most High. He met Abraham returning from the defeat of the kings and blessed him, 2and Abraham gave him a tenth of everything. First, the name Melchizedek means 'king of righteousness'; then also, 'king of Salem' means 'king of peace'. 3Without father or mother, without genealogy, without beginning of days or end of life, resembling the Son of God, he remains a priest for ever.

4Just think how great he was: even the patriarch Abraham gave him a tenth of the plunder! 5Now the law requires the descendants of Levi who become priests to collect a tenth from the people—that is, from their kindred—even though their

---

[a] 1 Or *from useless rituals* [b] 2 Or *about baptisms* [c] 6 Or *age,* 6*if they fall* [d] 14 Gen. 22:17

³Every high priest is appointed to offer both gifts and sacrifices, and so it was necessary for this one also to have something to offer. ⁴If he were on earth, he would not be a priest, for there are already priests who offer the gifts prescribed by the law. ⁵They serve at a sanctuary that is a copy and shadow of what is in heaven. This is why Moses was warned when he was about to build the tabernacle: 'See to it that you make everything according to the pattern shown you on the mountain.'ᵃ ⁶But in fact the ministry Jesus has received is as superior to theirs as the covenant of which he is mediator is superior to the old one, since the new covenant is established on better promises.

⁷For if there had been nothing wrong with that first covenant, no place would have been sought for another. ⁸But God found fault with the people and said*ᵇ*:

'The days are coming, declares the Lord,
  when I will make a new covenant
with the house of Israel
  and with the house of Judah.
⁹It will not be like the covenant
  I made with their ancestors
when I took them by the hand
  to lead them out of Egypt,
because they did not remain faithful to
  my covenant,
and I turned away from them,
  declares the Lord.
¹⁰This is the covenant I will establish with
  the house of Israel
after that time, declares the Lord.
I will put my laws in their minds
  and write them on their hearts.
I will be their God,
  and they will be my people.
¹¹No longer will they teach their
  neighbours,
  or say to one another, "Know the
    Lord,"
because they will all know me,
  from the least of them to the greatest.
¹²For I will forgive their wickedness
  and will remember their sins no
    more.'*ᶜ*

¹³By calling this covenant 'new', he has made the first one obsolete; and what is obsolete and outdated will soon disappear.

Worship in the earthly tabernacle

9 Now the first covenant had regulations for worship and also an earthly sanctuary. ²A tabernacle was set up. In its first room were the lampstand and the table with its consecrated bread; this was called the Holy Place. ³Behind the second curtain was a room called the Most Holy Place, ⁴which had the golden altar of incense and the gold-covered ark of the covenant. This ark contained the gold jar of manna, Aaron's staff that had budded, and the stone tablets of the covenant. ⁵Above the ark were the cherubim of the Glory, overshadowing the atonement cover. But we cannot discuss these things in detail now.

⁶When everything had been arranged like this, the priests entered regularly into the outer room to carry on their ministry. ⁷But only the high priest entered the inner room, and that only once a year, and never without blood, which he offered for himself and for the sins the people had committed in ignorance. ⁸The Holy Spirit was showing by this that the way into the Most Holy Place had not yet been disclosed as long as the first tabernacle was still functioning. ⁹This is an illustration for the present time, indicating that the gifts and sacrifices being offered were not able to clear the conscience of the worshipper. ¹⁰They are only a matter of food and drink and various ceremonial washings—external regulations applying until the time of the new order.

The blood of Christ

¹¹But when Christ came as high priest of the good things that are now already here,*ᵈ* he went through the greater and more perfect tabernacle that is not made with human hands, that is to say, is not a part of this creation. ¹²He did not enter by means of the blood of goats and calves; but he entered the Most Holy Place once for all by his own blood, so obtaining*ᵉ* eternal redemption. ¹³The blood of goats and bulls and the ashes of a heifer sprinkled on those who are

---

ᵃ 5 Exodus 25:40 *ᵇ* 8 Some manuscripts may be translated *fault and said to the people*. *ᶜ* 12 Jer. 31:31-34
ᵈ 11 Some early manuscripts *are to come* *ᵉ* 12 Or *blood, having obtained*

ceremonially unclean sanctify them so that they are outwardly clean. 14How much more, then, will the blood of Christ, who through the eternal Spirit offered himself unblemished to God, cleanse our consciences from acts that lead to death,[a] so that we may serve the living God!

15For this reason Christ is the mediator of a new covenant, that those who are called may receive the promised eternal inheritance—now that he has died as a ransom to set them free from the sins committed under the first covenant.

16In the case of a will,[b] it is necessary to prove the death of the one who made it, 17because a will is in force only when somebody has died; it never takes effect while the one who made it is living. 18This is why even the first covenant was not put into effect without blood. 19When Moses had proclaimed every command of the law to all the people, he took the blood of calves, together with water, scarlet wool and branches of hyssop, and sprinkled the scroll and all the people. 20He said, 'This is the blood of the covenant, which God has commanded you to keep.'[c] 21In the same way, he sprinkled with the blood both the tabernacle and everything used in its ceremonies. 22In fact, the law requires that nearly everything be cleansed with blood, and without the shedding of blood there is no forgiveness.

23It was necessary, then, for the copies of the heavenly things to be purified with these sacrifices, but the heavenly things themselves with better sacrifices than these. 24For Christ did not enter a sanctuary made with human hands that was only a copy of the true one; he entered heaven itself, now to appear for us in God's presence. 25Nor did he enter heaven to offer himself again and again, the way the high priest enters the Most Holy Place every year with blood that is not his own. 26Otherwise Christ would have had to suffer many times since the creation of the world. But he has appeared once for all at the culmination of the ages to do away with sin by the sacrifice of himself. 27Just as people are destined to die once, and after that to face judgment, 28so Christ was sacrificed once to take away the sins of many; and he will appear a second time, not to bear sin, but to bring salvation to those who are waiting for him.

Christ's sacrifice once for all

10 The law is only a shadow of the good things that are coming—not the realities themselves. For this reason it can never, by the same sacrifices repeated endlessly year after year, make perfect those who draw near to worship. 2Otherwise, would they not have stopped being offered? For the worshippers would have been cleansed once for all, and would no longer have felt guilty for their sins. 3But those sacrifices are an annual reminder of sins. 4It is impossible for the blood of bulls and goats to take away sins.

5Therefore, when Christ came into the world, he said:

'Sacrifice and offering you did not desire,
  but a body you prepared for me;
6with burnt offerings and sin offerings
  you were not pleased.
7Then I said, "Here I am—it is written
  about me in the scroll—
I have come to do your will, my
  God."'[d]

8First he said, 'Sacrifices and offerings, burnt offerings and sin offerings you did not desire, nor were you pleased with them'— though they were offered in accordance with the law. 9Then he said, 'Here I am, I have come to do your will.' He sets aside the first to establish the second. 10And by that will, we have been made holy through the sacrifice of the body of Jesus Christ once for all.

11Day after day every priest stands and performs his religious duties; again and again he offers the same sacrifices, which can never take away sins. 12But when this priest had offered for all time one sacrifice for sins, he sat down at the right hand of God, 13and since that time he waits for his enemies to be made his footstool. 14For by

---

[a] 14 Or *from useless rituals* [b] 16 Same Greek word as *covenant*; also in verse 17 [c] 20 Exodus 24:8 [d] 7 Psalm 40:6-8 (see Septuagint)

one sacrifice he has made perfect for ever those who are being made holy.

15 The Holy Spirit also testifies to us about this. First he says:

16 'This is the covenant I will make with them
after that time, says the Lord.
I will put my laws in their hearts,
and I will write them on their minds.'*a*

17 Then he adds:

'Their sins and lawless acts
I will remember no more.'*b*

18 And where these have been forgiven, sacrifice for sin is no longer necessary.

A call to persevere in faith

19 Therefore, brothers and sisters, since we have confidence to enter the Most Holy Place by the blood of Jesus, 20 by a new and living way opened for us through the curtain, that is, his body, 21 and since we have a great priest over the house of God, 22 let us draw near to God with a sincere heart in full assurance of faith, having our hearts sprinkled to cleanse us from a guilty conscience and having our bodies washed with pure water. 23 Let us hold unswervingly to the hope we profess, for he who promised is faithful. 24 And let us consider how we may spur one another on towards love and good deeds, 25 not giving up meeting together, as some are in the habit of doing, but encouraging one another—and all the more as you see the Day approaching.

26 If we deliberately keep on sinning after we have received the knowledge of the truth, no sacrifice for sins is left, 27 but only a fearful expectation of judgment and of raging fire that will consume the enemies of God. 28 Anyone who rejected the law of Moses died without mercy on the testimony of two or three witnesses. 29 How much more severely do you think those deserve to be punished who have trampled the Son of God underfoot, who have treated as an unholy thing the blood of the covenant that sanctified them, and who have insulted the Spirit of grace? 30 For we know him who said, 'It is mine to avenge; I will repay,'*c* and again, 'The Lord will judge his people.'*d* 31 It is a dreadful thing to fall into the hands of the living God.

32 Remember those earlier days after you had received the light, when you endured in a great conflict full of suffering.

Most Holy Place
Hebrews 10:19

The Most Holy Place was strictly off limits. It was a room at the heart of the tabernacle that contained the Ark of the Covenant. It was separated from the rest of the tabernacle by a curtain. The high priest was the only person who was allowed to enter the Most Holy Place, and he was only allowed to go in there once a year, on the Day of Atonement. But when Jesus died the curtain in the temple in Jerusalem was torn in two from top to bottom (Matthew 27:51), to show that people could now come directly into God's presence by themselves.

Judgment day
Hebrews 10:27

The Bible clearly speaks of a time when everyone who has lived will come before God and be judged according to their actions and relationship with Jesus. God knows when this day will be (Acts 17:31), but we don't (Matthew 24:36).

---

a 16 Jer. 31:33   *b* 17 Jer. 31:34   *c* 30 Deut. 32:35   *d* 30 Deut. 32:36; Psalm 135:14

33Sometimes you were publicly exposed to insult and persecution; at other times you stood side by side with those who were so treated. 34You suffered along with those in prison and joyfully accepted the confiscation of your property, because you knew that you yourselves had better and lasting possessions. 35So do not throw away your confidence; it will be richly rewarded.

36You need to persevere so that when you have done the will of God, you will receive what he has promised. 37For,

'In just a little while,
he who is coming will come
and will not delay.'^{a}

38And,

'But my righteous one^b will live by faith.
And I take no pleasure
in the one who shrinks back.'^{c}

39But we are not of those who shrink back and are destroyed, but of those who believe and are saved.

Faith in action

11 Now faith is being sure of what we hope for and certain of what we do not see. 2This is what the ancients were commended for.

3By faith we understand that the universe was formed at God's command, so that what is seen was not made out of what was visible.

4By faith Abel brought God a better offering than Cain did. By faith he was commended as righteous, when God spoke well of his offerings. And by faith Abel still speaks, even though he is dead.

5By faith Enoch was taken from this life, so that he did not experience death: 'He could not be found, because God had taken him away.'^{d} For before he was taken, he was commended as one who pleased God. 6And without faith it is impossible to please God, because anyone who comes to him must believe that he exists and that he rewards those who earnestly seek him.

7By faith Noah, when warned about things not yet seen, in holy fear built an ark to save his family. By his faith he condemned the world and became heir of the righteousness that is in keeping with faith.

8By faith Abraham, when called to go to a place he would later receive as his inheritance, obeyed and went, even though he did not know where he was going. 9By faith he made his home in the promised land like a stranger in a foreign country; he lived in tents, as did Isaac and Jacob, who were heirs with him of the same promise. 10For he was looking forward to the city with foundations, whose architect and builder is God. 11And by faith even Sarah, who was past childbearing age, was enabled to bear children because she^e considered him faithful who had made the promise. 12And so from this one man, and he as good as dead, came descendants as numerous as the stars in the sky and as countless as the sand on the seashore.

13All these people were still living by faith when they died. They did not receive the things promised; they only saw them and welcomed them from a distance, admitting that they were foreigners and strangers on earth. 14People who say such things show that they are looking for a country of their own. 15If they had been thinking of the country they had left, they would have had opportunity to return. 16Instead, they were longing for a better country—a heavenly one. Therefore God is not ashamed to be

IN OTHER WORDS

Faith
Hebrews 11:1
Faith is a belief in God or a confident attitude towards him, that affects the way we live. In fact this verse defines faith very well. It's 'being sure of what we hope for and certain of what we do not see'.

---

^{a}37 Isaiah 26:20; Hab. 2:3 ^{b}38 One early manuscript *But the righteous* ^{c}38 Hab. 2:4 (Septuagint) ^{d}5 Gen. 5:24
^{e}11 Or *By faith Abraham, even though he was too old to have children—and Sarah herself was not able to conceive—was enabled to become a father because he*

called their God, for he has prepared a city for them.

17By faith Abraham, when God tested him, offered Isaac as a sacrifice. He who had embraced the promises was about to sacrifice his one and only son, 18even though God had said to him, 'It is through Isaac that your offspring will be reckoned.'[a] 19Abraham reasoned that God could even raise the dead, and so in a manner of speaking he did receive Isaac back from death.

20By faith Isaac blessed Jacob and Esau in regard to their future.

21By faith Jacob, when he was dying, blessed each of Joseph's sons, and worshipped as he leaned on the top of his staff.

22By faith Joseph, when his end was near, spoke about the exodus of the Israelites from Egypt and gave instructions concerning the burial of his bones.

23By faith Moses' parents hid him for three months after he was born, because they saw he was no ordinary child, and they were not afraid of the king's edict.

24By faith Moses, when he had grown up, refused to be known as the son of Pharaoh's daughter. 25He chose to be ill-treated along with the people of God rather than to enjoy the fleeting pleasures of sin. 26He regarded disgrace for the sake of Christ as of greater value than the treasures of Egypt, because he was looking ahead to his reward. 27By faith he left Egypt, not fearing the king's anger; he persevered because he saw him who is invisible. 28By faith he kept the Passover and the application of blood, so that the destroyer of the firstborn would not touch the firstborn of Israel.

29By faith the people passed through the Red Sea as on dry land; but when the Egyptians tried to do so, they were drowned.

30By faith the walls of Jericho fell, after the army had marched round them for seven days.

31By faith the prostitute Rahab, because she welcomed the spies, was not killed with those who were disobedient.[b]

32And what more shall I say? I do not have time to tell about Gideon, Barak, Samson and Jephthah, about David and Samuel and the prophets, 33who through faith conquered kingdoms, administered justice, and gained what was promised; who shut the mouths of lions, 34quenched the fury of the flames, and escaped the edge of the sword; whose weakness was turned to strength; and who became powerful in battle and routed foreign armies. 35Women received back their dead, raised to life again. There were others who were tortured, refusing to be released so that they might gain an even better resurrection. 36Some faced jeers and flogging, and even chains and imprisonment. 37They were put to death by stoning;[c] they were sawn in two; they were killed by the sword. They went about in sheepskins and goatskins, destitute, persecuted and ill-treated— 38the world was not worthy of them. They wandered in deserts and mountains, and in caves and holes in the ground.

39These were all commended for their faith, yet none of them received what had been promised. 40God had planned something better for us so that only together with us would they be made perfect.

12 Therefore, since we are surrounded by such a great cloud of witnesses, let us throw off everything that hinders and the sin that so easily entangles. And let us run with perseverance the race marked out for us, 2fixing our eyes on Jesus, the pioneer and perfecter of faith. For the joy that was set before him he endured the cross, scorning its shame, and sat down at the right hand of the throne of God. 3Consider him who endured such opposition from sinners, so that you will not grow weary and lose heart.

God disciplines his children

4In your struggle against sin, you have not yet resisted to the point of shedding your blood. 5And have you completely forgotten this word of encouragement that addresses you as children? It says,

'My son, do not make light of the Lord's discipline,

---

[a] 18 Gen. 21:12   [b] 31 Or *unbelieving*   [c] 37 Some early manuscripts *stoning; they were put to the test;*

and do not lose heart when he rebukes you,
⁶because the Lord disciplines those he loves,
and he chastens everyone he accepts as his child.'ᵃ

⁷Endure hardship as discipline; God is treating you as his children. For what children are not disciplined by their father? ⁸If you are not disciplined—and everyone undergoes discipline—then you are not legitimate children at all. ⁹Moreover, we have all had parents who disciplined us and we respected them for it. How much more should we submit to the Father of spirits and live! ¹⁰Our parents disciplined us for a little while as they thought best; but God disciplines us for our good, that we may share in his holiness. ¹¹No discipline seems pleasant at the time, but painful. Later on, however, it produces a harvest of righteousness and peace for those who have been trained by it.

¹²Therefore, strengthen your feeble arms and weak knees! ¹³'Make level paths for your feet,'ᵇ so that the lame may not be disabled, but rather healed.

Warning and encouragement

¹⁴Make every effort to live in peace with everyone and to be holy; without holiness no-one will see the Lord. ¹⁵See to it that no-one falls short of the grace of God and that no bitter root grows up to cause trouble and defile many. ¹⁶See that no-one is sexually immoral, or is godless like Esau, who for a single meal sold his inheritance rights as the oldest son. ¹⁷Afterwards, as you know, when he wanted to inherit this blessing, he was rejected. Even though he sought the blessing with tears, he could not change what he had done.

The mountain of fear and the mountain of joy

¹⁸You have not come to a mountain that can be touched and that is burning with fire; to darkness, gloom and storm; ¹⁹to a trumpet blast or to such a voice speaking words that those who heard it begged that no further word be spoken to them,

People and Places

Mount Zion
Hebrews 12:22

The meaning of the name 'Zion' has changed through the Bible. Zion was a city that David captured in battle and which he called the City of David. When Solomon built the temple in Jerusalem, 'Zion' also came to mean the temple and its surrounding area. Soon it was being used as a name for the city of Jerusalem, the land of Judah and the people of Israel as a whole.

²⁰because they could not bear what was commanded: 'If even an animal touches the mountain, it must be stoned to death.'ᶜ ²¹The sight was so terrifying that Moses said, 'I am trembling with fear.'ᵈ

²²But you have come to Mount Zion, to the city of the living God, the heavenly Jerusalem. You have come to thousands upon thousands of angels in joyful assembly, ²³to the church of the firstborn, whose names are written in heaven. You have come to God, the Judge of all, to the spirits of the righteous made perfect, ²⁴to Jesus the mediator of a new covenant, and to the sprinkled blood that speaks a better word than the blood of Abel.

²⁵See to it that you do not refuse him who speaks. If they did not escape when they refused him who warned them on earth, how much less will we, if we turn away from him who warns us from heaven? ²⁶At that time his voice shook the earth, but now he has promised, 'Once more I will shake not only the earth but also the heavens.'ᵉ ²⁷The words 'once more' indicate the removing of what can be shaken—that is, created things—so that what cannot be shaken may remain.

²⁸Therefore, since we are receiving a kingdom that cannot be shaken, let us be

---

ᵃ5,6 Prov. 3:11,12 (see Septuagint) ᵇ13 Prov. 4:26 ᶜ20 Exodus 19:12,13 ᵈ21 See Deut. 9:19. ᵉ26 Haggai 2:6

thankful, and so worship God acceptably with reverence and awe, ²⁹for our 'God is a consuming fire.'ᵃ

Concluding exhortations

13 Keep on loving one another as brothers and sisters. ²Do not forget to show hospitality to strangers, for by so doing some people have shown hospitality to angels without knowing it. ³Continue to remember those in prison as if you were together with them in prison, and those who are ill-treated as if you yourselves were suffering.

⁴Marriage should be honoured by all, and the marriage bed kept pure, for God will judge the adulterer and all the sexually immoral. ⁵Keep your lives free from the love of money and be content with what you have, because God has said,

'Never will I leave you;
    never will I forsake you.'ᵇ

⁶So we say with confidence,

'The Lord is my helper; I will not be afraid.
    What can human beings do to me?'ᶜ

⁷Remember your leaders, who spoke the word of God to you. Consider the outcome of their way of life and imitate their faith. ⁸Jesus Christ is the same yesterday and today and for ever.

⁹Do not be carried away by all kinds of strange teachings. It is good for our hearts to be strengthened by grace, not by the eating of ceremonial foods, which is of no benefit to those who observe such rituals. ¹⁰We have an altar from which those who minister at the tabernacle have no right to eat.

¹¹The high priest carries the blood of animals into the Most Holy Place as a sin offering, but the bodies are burned outside the camp. ¹²And so Jesus also suffered outside the city gate to make the people holy through his own blood. ¹³Let us, then, go to him outside the camp, bearing the disgrace he bore. ¹⁴For here we do not have an enduring city, but we are looking for the city that is to come.

¹⁵Through Jesus, therefore, let us continually offer to God a sacrifice of praise— the fruit of lips that openly profess his name. ¹⁶And do not forget to do good and to share with others, for with such sacrifices God is pleased.

¹⁷Have confidence in your leaders and submit to their authority, because they keep watch over you as those who must give an account. Do this so that their work will be a joy, not a burden, for that would be of no benefit to you.

¹⁸Pray for us. We are sure that we have a clear conscience and desire to live honourably in every way. ¹⁹I particularly urge you to pray so that I may be restored to you soon.

Benediction and final greetings

²⁰Now may the God of peace, who through the blood of the eternal covenant brought back from the dead our Lord Jesus, that great Shepherd of the sheep, ²¹equip you with everything good for doing his will, and may he work in us what is pleasing to him, through Jesus Christ, to whom be glory for ever and ever. Amen.

²²Brothers and sisters, I urge you to bear with my word of exhortation, for in fact I have written to you quite briefly.

²³I want you to know that our brother Timothy has been released. If he arrives soon, I will come with him to see you.

²⁴Greet all your leaders and all the Lord's people. Those from Italy send you their greetings.

²⁵Grace be with you all.

ᵃ 29 Deut. 4:24   ᵇ 5 Deut. 31:6   ᶜ 6 Psalm 118:6,7

James

INTRODUCTION

James

Author: James, thought to be the brother of Jesus.

Who to: Jewish people.

When: This could be the earliest of the New Testament letters, possibly written around AD 45.

Main theme: James says that real faith gets put into action. It's not enough to believe in Jesus. That belief needs to affect the way that we live and, in particular, the way that we treat the poor.

1 James, a servant of God and of the Lord Jesus Christ,

To the twelve tribes scattered among the nations:

Greetings.

Trials and temptations

2Consider it pure joy, my brothers and sisters, whenever you face trials of many kinds, 3because you know that the testing of your faith produces perseverance. 4Let perseverance finish its work so that you may be mature and complete, not lacking anything. 5If any of you lacks wisdom, you should ask God, who gives generously to all without finding fault, and it will be given to you. 6But when you ask, you must believe and not doubt, because the one who doubts is like a wave of the sea, blown and tossed by the wind. 7Those who doubt should not think they will receive anything from the Lord; 8they are double-minded and unstable in all they do.

9Believers in humble circumstances ought to take pride in their high position. 10But the rich should take pride in their humiliation—since they will pass away like a wild flower. 11For the sun rises with scorching heat and withers the plant; its blossom falls and its beauty is destroyed. In the same way, the rich will fade away even while they go about their business.

12Blessed are those who persevere under trial, because when they have stood the test, they will receive the crown of life that God has promised to those who love him.

13When tempted, no-one should say, 'God is tempting me.' For God cannot be tempted by evil, nor does he tempt anyone; 14but each of you is tempted when you are dragged away by your own evil desire and enticed. 15Then, after desire has conceived, it gives birth to sin; and sin, when it is full-grown, gives birth to death.

16Don't be deceived, my dear brothers and sisters. 17Every good and perfect gift is from above, coming down from the Father of the heavenly lights, who does not change like shifting shadows. 18He chose to give us birth through the word of truth, that we might be a kind of firstfruits of all he created.

Listening and doing

19My dear brothers and sisters, take note of this: everyone should be quick to listen, slow to speak and slow to become angry, 20because our anger does not produce the righteousness that God desires. 21Therefore, get rid of all moral filth and the evil that is so prevalent, and humbly accept the word planted in you, which can save you.

22Do not merely listen to the word, and so deceive yourselves. Do what it says. 23Those who listen to the word but do not do what it says are like people who look at their faces in a mirror 24and, after looking at themselves, go away and immediately forget what they look like. 25But those who look intently into the perfect law that gives freedom and continue in it—not forgetting what they have heard but doing it—they will be blessed in what they do.

26Those who consider themselves religious and yet do not keep a tight rein on their tongues deceive themselves, and their religion is worthless. 27Religion that God our Father accepts as pure and faultless is this: to look after orphans and widows in their distress and to keep oneself from being polluted by the world.

Favouritism forbidden

2 My brothers and sisters, believers in our glorious Lord Jesus Christ must not show favouritism. 2Suppose someone comes into your meeting wearing a gold ring and fine clothes, and a poor person in filthy old clothes also comes in. 3If you show special attention to the one wearing fine clothes and say, 'Here's a good seat for you,' but say to the one who is poor, 'You stand there' or 'Sit on the floor by my feet,' 4have you not discriminated among yourselves and become judges with evil thoughts?

5Listen, my dear brothers and sisters: has not God chosen those who are poor in the eyes of the world to be rich in faith and to inherit the kingdom he promised those who love him? 6But you have dishonoured the poor. Is it not the rich who are exploiting you? Are they not the ones who are dragging you into court? 7Are they not the ones who are blaspheming the noble name of him to whom you belong?

8If you really keep the royal law found in Scripture, 'Love your neighbour as yourself,'[a] you are doing right. 9But if you show favouritism, you sin and are convicted by the law as law-breakers. 10For whoever keeps the whole law and yet stumbles at just one point is guilty of breaking all of it. 11For he who said, 'You shall not commit adultery,'[b] also said, 'You shall not murder.'[c] If you do not commit adultery but do commit murder, you have become a law-breaker.

12Speak and act as those who are going to be judged by the law that gives freedom, 13because judgment without mercy will be shown to anyone who has not been merciful. Mercy triumphs over judgment.

Faith and deeds

14What good is it, my brothers and sisters, if people claim to have faith but have no deeds? Can such faith save them? 15Suppose a brother or sister is without clothes and daily food. 16If one of you says to them, 'Go in peace; keep warm and well fed,' but does nothing about their physical needs, what good is it? 17In the same way, faith by itself, if it is not accompanied by action, is dead.

18But someone will say, 'You have faith; I have deeds.'

Show me your faith without deeds, and I will show you my faith by what I do. 19You believe that there is one God. Good! Even the demons believe that—and shudder.

20You foolish person, do you want evidence that faith without deeds is useless[d]? 21Was not our father Abraham considered righteous for what he did when he offered his son Isaac on the altar? 22You see that his faith and his actions were working together, and his faith was made complete by what he

---

[a] 8 Lev. 19:18   [b] 11 Exodus 20:14; Deut. 5:18   [c] 11 Exodus 20:13; Deut. 5:17   [d] 20 Some early manuscripts *dead*

did. 23And the scripture was fulfilled that says, 'Abraham believed God, and it was credited to him as righteousness,'[a] and he was called God's friend. 24You see that people are justified by what they do and not by faith alone.

25In the same way, was not even Rahab the prostitute considered righteous for what she did when she gave lodging to the spies and sent them off in a different direction? 26As the body without the spirit is dead, so faith without deeds is dead.

Taming the tongue

3 Not many of you should presume to be teachers, my brothers and sisters, because you know that we who teach will be judged more strictly. 2We all stumble in many ways. Those who are never at fault in what they say are perfect, able to keep their whole body in check.

3When we put bits into the mouths of horses to make them obey us, we can turn the whole animal. 4Or take ships as an example. Although they are so large and are driven by strong winds, they are steered by a very small rudder wherever the pilot wants to go. 5Likewise, the tongue is a small part of the body, but it makes great boasts. Consider what a great forest is set on fire by a small spark. 6The tongue also is a fire, a world of evil among the parts of the body. It corrupts the whole person, sets the whole course of one's life on fire, and is itself set on fire by hell.

7All kinds of animals, birds, reptiles and sea creatures are being tamed and have been tamed by human beings, 8but no-one can tame the tongue. It is a restless evil, full of deadly poison.

9With the tongue we praise our Lord and Father, and with it we curse human beings, who have been made in God's likeness. 10Out of the same mouth come praise and cursing. My brothers and sisters, this should not be. 11Can both fresh water and salt water flow from the same spring? 12My brothers and sisters, can a fig-tree bear olives, or a grapevine bear figs? Neither can a salt spring produce fresh water.

IN OTHER WORDS

Curse
James 3:9
A curse was the opposite of a blessing, a wish of evil on a person, nation or thing.

Two kinds of wisdom

13Who is wise and understanding among you? Let them show it by their good life, by deeds done in the humility that comes from wisdom. 14But if you harbour bitter envy and selfish ambition in your hearts, do not boast about it or deny the truth. 15Such 'wisdom' does not come down from heaven but is earthly, unspiritual, demonic. 16For where you have envy and selfish ambition, there you find disorder and every evil practice.

17But the wisdom that comes from heaven is first of all pure; then peace-loving, considerate, submissive, full of mercy and good fruit, impartial and sincere. 18Peacemakers who sow in peace reap a harvest of righteousness.

Submit yourselves to God

4 What causes fights and quarrels among you? Don't they come from your desires that battle within you? 2You desire but do not have, so you kill. You covet but you cannot get what you want, so you quarrel and fight. You do not have because you do not ask God. 3When you ask, you do not receive, because you ask with wrong motives, that you may spend what you get on your pleasures.

4You adulterous people, don't you know that friendship with the world means enmity against God? Anyone who chooses to be a friend of the world becomes an enemy of God. 5Or do you think Scripture says without reason that he jealously longs for the spirit he has caused to dwell in us?[b] 6But he gives us more grace. That is why Scripture says:

---

[a] 23 Gen. 15:6 [b] 5 Or that the spirit he caused to dwell in us envies intensely; or that the Spirit he caused to dwell in us longs jealously

'God opposes the proud
but shows favour to the humble and oppressed.'[a]

7Submit yourselves, then, to God. Resist the devil, and he will flee from you. 8Come near to God and he will come near to you. Wash your hands, you sinners, and purify your hearts, you double-minded. 9Grieve, mourn and wail. Change your laughter to mourning and your joy to gloom. 10Humble yourselves before the Lord, and he will lift you up.

11Brothers and sisters, do not slander one another. Anyone who speaks against a brother or sister or judges them speaks against the law and judges it. When you judge the law, you are not keeping it, but sitting in judgment on it. 12There is only one Lawgiver and Judge, the one who is able to save and destroy. But you—who are you to judge your neighbour?

Boasting about tomorrow

13Now listen, you who say, 'Today or tomorrow we will go to this or that city, spend a year there, carry on business and make money.' 14Why, you do not even know what will happen tomorrow. What is your life? You are a mist that appears for a little while and then vanishes. 15Instead, you ought to say, 'If it is the Lord's will, we will live and do this or that.' 16As it is, you boast in your arrogant schemes. All such boasting is evil. 17So then, if you know the good you ought to do and don't do it, you sin.

Warning to rich oppressors

5 Now listen, you rich people, weep and wail because of the misery that is coming on you. 2Your wealth has rotted, and moths have eaten your clothes. 3Your gold and silver are corroded. Their corrosion will testify against you and eat your flesh like fire. You have hoarded wealth in the last days. 4Look! The wages you failed to pay the workers who mowed your fields are crying out against you. The cries of the harvesters have reached the ears of the Lord Almighty. 5You have lived on earth in luxury and self-indulgence. You have fattened yourselves in the day of slaughter.[b] 6You have condemned and murdered the innocent one, who was not opposing you.

Patience in suffering

7Be patient, then, brothers and sisters, until the Lord's coming. See how the farmer waits for the land to yield its valuable crop, patiently waiting for the autumn and spring rains. 8You too, be patient and stand firm, because the Lord's coming is near. 9Don't grumble against one another, brothers and sisters, or you will be judged. The Judge is standing at the door!

10Brothers and sisters, as an example of patience in the face of suffering, take the prophets who spoke in the name of the Lord. 11As you know, we count as blessed those who have persevered. You have heard of Job's perseverance and have seen what the Lord finally brought about. The Lord is full of compassion and mercy.

12Above all, my brothers and sisters, do not swear—not by heaven or by earth or by anything else. All you need to say is a simple 'Yes' or 'No'. Otherwise you will be condemned.

The prayer of faith

13Is anyone among you in trouble? Let them pray. Is anyone happy? Let them sing songs of praise. 14Is anyone among you ill? Let them call the elders of the church to pray over them and anoint them with oil in the name of the Lord. 15And the prayer offered in faith will make them well; the Lord will raise them up. If they have sinned, they will be forgiven. 16Therefore confess your sins to each other and pray for each other so that

IN OTHER WORDS

Perseverance
James 5:11
Perseverance is the ability to keep going even when things get tough.

---

[a] 6 Prov. 3:34 [b] 5 Or *yourselves as in a day of feasting*

you may be healed. The prayer of a righteous person is powerful and effective.

17Elijah was a human being, even as we are. He prayed earnestly that it would not rain, and it did not rain on the land for three and a half years. 18Again he prayed, and the heavens gave rain, and the earth produced its crops.

19My brothers and sisters, if one of you should wander from the truth and someone should bring them back, 20remember this: whoever turns a sinner from the way of error will save them from death and cover over a multitude of sins.

1 Peter

INTRODUCTION

1 Peter

Author: Peter

Who to: Christians everywhere.

When: Probably around AD 65.

Did you know? Peter is the disciple that we learn most about in the Gospels. The first twelve chapters of Acts describe his ministry in the early church.

Main theme: This is a letter about suffering. Peter writes to people who are downhearted because of persecution, to encourage them to keep going in times of difficulty and disappointment. He says that Christians should set a good example by the way that they live, so that people around them will see that God is real.

1

Peter, an apostle of Jesus Christ,

To God's elect, exiles, scattered throughout the provinces of Pontus, Galatia, Cappadocia, Asia and Bithynia, ²who have been chosen according to the foreknowledge of God the Father, through the sanctifying work of the Spirit, to be obedient to Jesus Christ and sprinkled with his blood:

Grace and peace be yours in abundance.

Praise to God for a living hope

³Praise be to the God and Father of our Lord Jesus Christ! In his great mercy he has given us new birth into a living hope through the resurrection of Jesus Christ from the dead, ⁴and into an inheritance that can never perish, spoil or fade. This inheritance is kept in heaven for you, ⁵who through faith are shielded by God's power until the coming of the salvation that is ready to be revealed in the last time. ⁶In all this you greatly rejoice, though now for a little while you may have had to suffer grief in all kinds of trials. ⁷These have come so that your faith—of greater worth than gold, which perishes even though refined by fire—may be proved genuine and may result in praise, glory and honour when Jesus Christ is revealed. ⁸Though you have not seen him, you love him; and even

though you do not see him now, you believe in him and are filled with an inexpressible and glorious joy, ⁹for you are receiving the end result of your faith, the salvation of your souls.

¹⁰Concerning this salvation, the prophets, who spoke of the grace that was to come to you, searched intently and with the greatest care, ¹¹trying to find out the time and circumstances to which the Spirit of Christ in them was pointing when he predicted the sufferings of Christ and the glories that would follow. ¹²It was revealed to them that they were not serving themselves but you, when they spoke of the things that have now been told you by those who have preached the gospel to you by the Holy Spirit sent from heaven. Even angels long to look into these things.

Be holy

¹³Therefore, with minds that are alert and fully sober, set your hope on the grace to be brought to you when Jesus Christ is revealed at his coming. ¹⁴As obedient children, do not conform to the evil desires you had when you lived in ignorance. ¹⁵But just as he who called you is holy, so be holy in all you do; ¹⁶for it is written: 'Be holy, because I am holy.'ᵃ

¹⁷Since you call on a Father who judges each person's work impartially, live out your time as foreigners here in reverent fear. ¹⁸For you know that it was not with perishable things such as silver or gold that you were redeemed from the empty way of life handed down to you from your ancestors, ¹⁹but with the precious blood of Christ, a lamb without blemish or defect. ²⁰He was chosen before the creation of the world, but was revealed in these last times for your sake. ²¹Through him you believe in God, who raised him from the dead and glorified him, and so your faith and hope are in God.

²²Now that you have purified yourselves by obeying the truth so that you have sincere love for each other, love one another deeply, from the heart.ᵇ ²³For you have been born again, not of perishable seed, but of imperishable, through the living and enduring word of God. ²⁴For,

> 'All people are like grass,
>   and all their glory is like the flowers of the field;
> the grass withers and the flowers fall,
> 25 but the word of the Lord endures for ever.'ᶜ

And this is the word that was preached to you.

2 Therefore, rid yourselves of all malice and all deceit, hypocrisy, envy, and slander of every kind. ²Like newborn babies, crave pure spiritual milk, so that by it you may grow up in your salvation, ³now that you have tasted that the Lord is good.

The living Stone and a chosen people

⁴As you come to him, the living Stone—rejected by human beings but chosen by God and precious to him— ⁵you also, like living stones, are being built into a spiritual houseᵈ to be a holy priesthood, offering spiritual sacrifices acceptable to God through Jesus Christ. ⁶For in Scripture it says:

> 'See, I lay a stone in Zion,
>   a chosen and precious cornerstone,

making Connections

Cornerstone
1 Peter 2:6
As you may have guessed, the cornerstone was a stone put at the corner of a building, where two walls came together. The cornerstone provided a strong base for the walls, helping to align them properly and hold the building together.

ᵃ 16 Lev. 11:44,45; 19:2 ᵇ 22 Some early manuscripts *from a pure heart* ᶜ 25 Isaiah 40:6-8 (see Septuagint) ᵈ 5 Or *into a temple of the Spirit*

IN OTHER WORDS

Submit
1 Peter 2:13
To submit to someone is to defer to them, to put yourself under their authority.

and the one who trusts in him
   will never be put to shame.'*a*

7Now to you who believe, this stone is precious. But to those who do not believe,

'The stone the builders rejected
   has become the cornerstone,'*b*

8and,

'A stone that causes people to stumble
   and a rock that makes them fall.'*c*

They stumble because they disobey the message—which is also what they were destined for.

9But you are a chosen people, a royal priesthood, a holy nation, God's special possession, that you may declare the praises of him who called you out of darkness into his wonderful light. 10Once you were not a people, but now you are the people of God; once you had not received mercy, but now you have received mercy.

Living godly lives in a pagan society

11Dear friends, I urge you, as foreigners and exiles, to abstain from sinful desires, which war against your soul. 12Live such good lives among the pagans that, though they accuse you of doing wrong, they may see your good deeds and glorify God on the day he visits us.

13Submit yourselves for the Lord's sake to every human authority: whether to the emperor, as the supreme authority, 14or to governors, who are sent by him to punish those who do wrong and to commend those who do right. 15For it is God's will that by doing good you should silence the ignorant talk of the foolish. 16Live as free people, but do not use your freedom as a cover-up for evil; live as God's slaves. 17Show proper respect to everyone, love your fellow-believers, fear God, honour the emperor.

18Slaves, in reverent fear of God submit yourselves to your masters, not only to those who are good and considerate, but also to those who are harsh. 19For it is commendable if you bear up under the pain of unjust suffering because you are conscious of God. 20But how is it to your credit if you receive a beating for doing wrong and endure it? But if you suffer for doing good and you endure it, this is commendable before God. 21To this you were called, because Christ suffered for you, leaving you an example, that you should follow in his steps.

22'He committed no sin,
   and no deceit was found in his
      mouth.'*d*

23When they hurled their insults at him, he did not retaliate; when he suffered, he made no threats. Instead, he entrusted himself to him who judges justly. 24'He himself bore our sins' in his body on the cross, so that we might die to sins and live for righteousness; 'by his wounds you have been healed.' 25For 'you were like sheep going astray,'*e* but now you have returned to the Shepherd and Overseer of your souls.

3 Wives, in the same way submit yourselves to your own husbands so that, if any of them do not believe the word, they may be won over without words by the behaviour of their wives, 2when they see the purity and reverence of your lives. 3Your beauty should not come from outward adornment, such as elaborate hairstyles and the wearing of gold jewellery and fine clothes. 4Rather, it should be that of your inner self, the unfading beauty of a gentle and quiet spirit, which is of great worth in God's sight. 5For this is the way the holy women of the past who put their hope in God used to adorn themselves. They submitted themselves to their own husbands, 6like Sarah, who obeyed Abraham and called him her lord. You are her daughters

---

a 6 Isaiah 28:16   *b* 7 Psalm 118:22   *c* 8 Isaiah 8:14   *d* 22 Isaiah 53:9   *e* 24,25 Isaiah 53:4,5,6 (see Septuagint) if you do what is right and do not give way to fear.

7 Husbands, in the same way be considerate as you live with your wives, and treat them with respect as the weaker partner and as heirs with you of the gracious gift of life, so that nothing will hinder your prayers.

Suffering for doing good

8 Finally, all of you, be like-minded, be sympathetic, love one another, be compassionate and humble. 9 Do not repay evil with evil or insult with insult. On the contrary, repay evil with blessing, because to this you were called so that you may inherit a blessing. 10 For,

'Whoever among you would love life
  and see good days
must keep your tongue from evil
  and your lips from deceitful speech.
11 Turn from evil and do good;
  seek peace and pursue it.
12 For the eyes of the Lord are on the righteous
  and his ears are attentive to their prayer,
but the face of the Lord is against those who do evil.'[a]

13 Who is going to harm you if you are eager to do good? 14 But even if you should suffer for what is right, you are blessed. 'Do not fear their threats; do not be frightened.'[b] 15 But in your hearts revere Christ as Lord. Always be prepared to give an answer to everyone who asks you to give the reason for the hope that you have. But do this with gentleness and respect, 16 keeping a clear conscience, so that those who speak maliciously against your good behaviour in Christ may be ashamed of their slander. 17 It is better, if it is God's will, to suffer for doing good than for doing evil. 18 For Christ also suffered once for sins, the righteous for the unrighteous, to bring you to God. He was put to death in the body but made alive in the Spirit. 19 In that state[c] he went and made proclamation to the imprisoned spirits— 20 to those who were disobedient long ago when God waited patiently in the days of Noah while the ark was being built. In it only a few people, eight in all, were saved through water, 21 and this water symbolises baptism that now saves you also—not the removal of dirt from the body but the pledge of a clear conscience towards God.[d] It saves you by the resurrection of Jesus Christ, 22 who has gone into heaven and is at God's right hand—with angels, authorities and powers in submission to him.

Living for God

4 Therefore, since Christ suffered in his body, arm yourselves also with the same attitude, because those who have suffered in their bodies have finished with sin. 2 As a result, they do not live the rest of their earthly lives for evil human desires, but rather for the will of God. 3 For you have spent enough time in the past doing what pagans choose to do—living in debauchery, lust, drunkenness, orgies, carousing and detestable idolatry. 4 They are surprised that you do not join them in their reckless, wild living, and they heap abuse on you. 5 But they will have to give account to him who is ready to judge the living and the dead. 6 For this is the reason the gospel was preached even to those who are now dead, so that they might be judged according to human

Sign of the times

Trade guilds
1 Peter 4:3

In many cities, people who wanted to do business would be expected to join a trade guild, an association for traders. Some trade guilds held wild banquets where meat was served that had been sacrificed to idols. This might be what Peter is talking about in these verses.

---

[a] 12 Psalm 34:12-16 [b] 14 Isaiah 8:12 [c] 18,19 Or *alive in the spirit,* 19 *in which also* [d] 21 Or *but an appeal to God for a clear conscience*

standards in regard to the body, but live according to God in regard to the spirit.

7 The end of all things is near. Therefore be alert and of sober mind so that you may pray. 8 Above all, love each other deeply, because love covers over a multitude of sins. 9 Offer hospitality to one another without grumbling. 10 Each of you should use whatever gift you have received to serve others, as faithful stewards of God's grace in its various forms. 11 If you speak, you should do so as one who speaks the very words of God. If you serve, you should do so with the strength God provides, so that in all things God may be praised through Jesus Christ. To him be the glory and the power for ever and ever. Amen.

Suffering for being a Christian

12 Dear friends, do not be surprised at the fiery ordeal that has come on you to test you, as though something strange were happening to you. 13 But rejoice inasmuch as you participate in the sufferings of Christ, so that you may be overjoyed when his glory is revealed. 14 If you are insulted because of the name of Christ, you are blessed, for the Spirit of glory and of God rests on you. 15 If you suffer, it should not be as a murderer or thief or any other kind of criminal, or even as a meddler. 16 However, if you suffer as a Christian, do not be ashamed, but praise God that you bear that name. 17 For it is time for judgment to begin with God's household; and if it begins with us, what will the outcome be for those who do not obey the gospel of God? 18 And,

'If it is hard for the righteous to be saved,
what will become of the ungodly and the sinner?'*a*

19 So then, those who suffer according to God's will should commit themselves to their faithful Creator and continue to do good.

To the elders and the flock

5 To the elders among you, I appeal as a fellow-elder and a witness of Christ's sufferings who also will share in the glory to be revealed: 2 be shepherds of God's flock that is under your care, watching over them—not because you must, but because you are willing, as God wants you to be; not pursuing dishonest gain, but eager to serve; 3 not lording it over those entrusted to you, but being examples to the flock. 4 And when the Chief Shepherd appears, you will receive the crown of glory that will never fade away.

5 In the same way, you who are younger, submit yourselves to your elders. All of you, clothe yourselves with humility towards one another, because,

'God opposes the proud
but shows favour to the humble and oppressed.'*b*

6 Humble yourselves, therefore, under God's mighty hand, that he may lift you up in due time. 7 Cast all your anxiety on him because he cares for you.

8 Be alert and of sober mind. Your enemy the devil prowls around like a roaring lion looking for someone to devour. 9 Resist him, standing firm in the faith, because you know that your fellow-believers throughout the world are undergoing the same kind of sufferings.

10 And the God of all grace, who called you to his eternal glory in Christ, after you have suffered a little while, will himself restore you and make you strong, firm and steadfast. 11 To him be the power for ever and ever. Amen.

Final greetings

12 With the help of Silas,*c* whom I regard as a faithful brother, I have written to you briefly, encouraging you and testifying that this is the true grace of God. Stand fast in it.

13 She who is in Babylon, chosen together with you, sends you her greetings, and so does my son Mark. 14 Greet one another with a kiss of love.

Peace to all of you who are in Christ.

---

a 18 Prov. 11:31 (see Septuagint)   *b* 5 Prov. 3:34   *c* 12 Greek *Silvanus*, a variant of *Silas*

2 Peter

INTRODUCTION

2 Peter

Author: Peter

When: Probably around AD 66.

Did you know? Peter was present at the transfiguration, when Moses and Elijah appeared with Jesus on a mountain (Matthew 17:1–13). Peter refers to this in 2 Peter 1:16–18.

Main theme: Peter has some harsh words to say about false teachers. He talks about the certainty that Jesus will return to earth again, and encourages people to be ready for him.

1 Simon Peter, a servant and apostle of Jesus Christ,

To those who through the righteousness of our God and Saviour Jesus Christ have received a faith as precious as ours:

2 Grace and peace be yours in abundance through the knowledge of God and of Jesus our Lord.

Confirming one's calling and election

3 His divine power has given us everything we need for a godly life through our knowledge of him who called us by his own glory and goodness. 4 Through these he has given us his very great and precious promises, so that through them you may participate in the divine nature, having escaped the corruption in the world caused by evil desires.

5 For this very reason, make every effort to add to your faith goodness; and to goodness, knowledge; 6 and to knowledge, self-control; and to self-control, perseverance; and to perseverance, godliness; 7 and to godliness, mutual affection; and to mutual affection, love. 8 For if you possess these qualities in increasing measure, they will keep you from being ineffective and unproductive in your knowledge of our Lord Jesus Christ. 9 But if any of you do not have them, you are short-sighted and blind, and you have forgotten that you have been cleansed from your past sins.

10 Therefore, my brothers and sisters, make every effort to confirm your calling and election. For if you do these things, you will never stumble, 11 and you will receive a rich welcome into the eternal kingdom of our Lord and Saviour Jesus Christ.

IN OTHER WORDS

Prophecy
2 Peter 1:19

A prophet is someone who speaks for God, who receives and delivers messages for him. When God speaks to his people through a prophet it is called 'prophecy'. Sometimes a prophecy tells what God is going to do in the future. Sometimes it is instruction and advice for the present.

Prophecy of Scripture

12So I will always remind you of these things, even though you know them and are firmly established in the truth you now have. 13I think it is right to refresh your memory as long as I live in the tent of this body, 14because I know that I will soon put it aside, as our Lord Jesus Christ has made clear to me. 15And I will make every effort to see that after my departure you will always be able to remember these things.

16For we did not follow cleverly devised stories when we told you about the coming of our Lord Jesus Christ in power, but we were eye-witnesses of his majesty. 17He received honour and glory from God the Father when the voice came to him from the Majestic Glory, saying, 'This is my Son, whom I love; with him I am well pleased.'[a] 18We ourselves heard this voice that came from heaven when we were with him on the sacred mountain.

19We also have the prophetic message as something completely reliable, and you will do well to pay attention to it, as to a light shining in a dark place, until the day dawns and the morning star rises in your hearts. 20Above all, you must understand that no prophecy of Scripture came about by the prophet's own interpretation of things. 21For prophecy never had its origin in the human will, but prophets, though human, spoke from God as they were carried along by the Holy Spirit.

False teachers and their destruction

2 But there were also false prophets among the people, just as there will be false teachers among you. They will secretly introduce destructive heresies, even denying the sovereign Lord who bought them—bringing swift destruction on themselves. 2Many will follow their depraved conduct and will bring the way of truth into disrepute. 3In their greed these teachers will exploit you with fabricated stories. Their condemnation has long been hanging over them, and their destruction has not been sleeping.

4For if God did not spare angels when they sinned, but sent them to hell,[b] putting them in chains of darkness[c] to be held for judgment; 5if he did not spare the ancient world when he brought the flood on its ungodly people, but protected Noah, a preacher of righteousness, and seven others; 6if he condemned the cities of Sodom and Gomorrah by burning them to ashes, and made them an example of what is going to happen to the ungodly; 7and if he rescued Lot, a righteous man, who was distressed by the depraved conduct of the lawless 8(for that righteous man, living among them day after day, was tormented in his righteous soul by the lawless deeds he saw and heard)— 9if this is so, then the Lord knows how to rescue the godly from trials and to hold the unrighteous for punishment on the day of judgment. 10This is especially true of those who follow the corrupt desire of the sinful nature[d] and despise authority.

Bold and arrogant, they are not afraid to heap abuse on celestial beings; 11yet even angels, although they are stronger and more powerful, do not heap abuse on such beings when bringing judgment on them from[e] the Lord. 12But these people blaspheme in matters they do not understand. They are like unreasoning animals, creatures of instinct, born only to be caught and destroyed, and like animals they too will perish.

13They will be paid back with harm for the harm they have done. Their idea of pleasure is to carouse in broad daylight.

---

[a] 17 Matt. 17:5; Mark 9:7; Luke 9:35   [b] 4 Greek *Tartarus*   [c] 4 Some manuscripts *in gloomy dungeons*   [d] 10 Or *the flesh*   [e] 11 Many manuscripts *beings in the presence of*

They are blots and blemishes, revelling in their pleasures while they feast with you.[a] 14With eyes full of adultery, they never stop sinning; they seduce the unstable; they are experts in greed—an accursed brood! 15They have left the straight way and wandered off to follow the way of Balaam son of Bezer,[b] who loved the wages of wickedness. 16But he was rebuked for his wrongdoing by a donkey—an animal without speech—who spoke with a human voice and restrained the prophet's madness.

17These people are springs without water and mists driven by a storm. Blackest darkness is reserved for them. 18For they mouth empty, boastful words and, by appealing to the lustful desires of sinful human nature, they entice people who are just escaping from those who live in error. 19They promise them freedom, while they themselves are slaves of depravity—for 'people are slaves to whatever has mastered them.' 20If they have escaped the corruption of the world by knowing our Lord and Saviour Jesus Christ and are again entangled in it and are overcome, they are worse off at the end than they were at the beginning. 21It would have been better for them not to have known the way of righteousness, than to have known it and then to turn their backs on the sacred command that was passed on to them. 22Of them the proverbs are true: 'A dog returns to its vomit,'[c] and, 'A sow that is washed returns to her wallowing in the mud.'

The day of the Lord

3 Dear friends, this is now my second letter to you. I have written both of them as reminders to stimulate you to wholesome thinking. 2I want you to recall the words spoken in the past by the holy prophets and the command given by our Lord and Saviour through your apostles.

3Above all, you must understand that in the last days scoffers will come, scoffing and following their own evil desires. 4They will say, 'Where is this "coming" he promised? Ever since our ancestors died, everything goes on as it has since the beginning of creation.' 5But they deliberately forget that long ago by God's word the heavens came into being and the earth was formed out of water and by water. 6By these waters also the world of that time was deluged and destroyed. 7By the same word the present heavens and earth are reserved for fire, being kept for the day of judgment and destruction of the ungodly.

8But do not forget this one thing, dear friends: with the Lord a day is like a thousand years, and a thousand years are like a day. 9The Lord is not slow in keeping his promise, as some understand slowness. Instead he is patient with you, not wanting anyone to perish, but everyone to come to repentance.

10But the day of the Lord will come like a thief. The heavens will disappear with a roar; the elements will be destroyed by fire, and the earth and everything done in it will be laid bare.[d]

11Since everything will be destroyed in this way, what kind of people ought you to be? You ought to live holy and godly lives 12as you look forward to the day of God and speed its coming.[e] That day will bring about the destruction of the heavens by fire, and the elements will melt in the heat. 13But in keeping with his promise we are looking forward to a new heaven and a new earth, where righteousness dwells.

Paul's letters
2 Peter 3:15
Peter's mention of what Paul wrote shows that Paul's letters were being read widely in the early church and were considered to be inspired by God.

---

[a] 13 Some manuscripts *in their love feasts* [b] 15 Greek *Bosor* [c] 22 Prov. 26:11 [d] 10 Some manuscripts *be burned up*
[e] 12 Or *as you wait eagerly for the day of God to come*

¹⁴So then, dear friends, since you are looking forward to this, make every effort to be found spotless, blameless and at peace with him. ¹⁵Bear in mind that our Lord's patience means salvation, just as our dear brother Paul also wrote to you with the wisdom that God gave him. ¹⁶He writes the same way in all his letters, speaking in them of these matters. His letters contain some things that are hard to understand, which ignorant and unstable people distort, as they do the other Scriptures, to their own destruction.

¹⁷Therefore, dear friends, since you have been forewarned, be on your guard so that you may not be carried away by the error of the lawless and fall from your secure position. ¹⁸But grow in the grace and knowledge of our Lord and Saviour Jesus Christ. To him be glory both now and for ever! Amen.

1 John

INTRODUCTION

1 John

Author: John, who also wrote the Gospel of John.

When: Probably written towards the end of the first century AD.

Where: It's thought that John wrote his letters from Ephesus.

Main theme: John writes about love – the love of God for us and the love we need to have towards each other. But love is not just a warm fuzzy feeling. Love is an action, something that we do by keeping God's commands and loving others.

The incarnation of the Word of life

1 That which was from the beginning, which we have heard, which we have seen with our eyes, which we have looked at and our hands have touched—this we proclaim concerning the Word of life. 2The life appeared; we have seen it and testify to it, and we proclaim to you the eternal life, which was with the Father and has appeared to us. 3We proclaim to you what we have seen and heard, so that you also may have fellowship with us. And our fellowship is with the Father and with his Son, Jesus Christ. 4We write this to make our[a] joy complete.

Light and darkness, sin and forgiveness

5This is the message we have heard from him and declare to you: God is light; in him there is no darkness at all. 6If we claim to have fellowship with him and yet walk in the darkness, we lie and do not live out the truth. 7But if we walk in the light, as he is in the light, we have fellowship with one another, and the blood of Jesus, his Son, purifies us from all[b] sin.

8If we claim to be without sin, we deceive ourselves and the truth is not in us. 9If we confess our sins, he is faithful and just and will forgive us our sins and purify us from all unrighteousness. 10If we claim we have not sinned, we make him out to be a liar and his word is not in us.

2 My dear children, I write this to you so that you will not sin. But if anybody does sin, we have an advocate with the Father—Jesus Christ, the Righteous One. 2He is the atoning sacrifice for our sins, and not only for ours but also for the sins of the whole world.

[a] 4 Some manuscripts *your*   [b] 7 Or *every*

Love and hatred for fellow-believers

3 We know that we have come to know him if we keep his commands. 4 Those who say, 'I know him,' but do not do what he commands are liars, and the truth is not in them. 5 But if anyone obeys his word, love for God[a] is truly made complete in them. This is how we know we are in him: 6 whoever claims to live in him must live as Jesus did.

7 Dear friends, I am not writing you a new command but an old one, which you have had since the beginning. This old command is the message you have heard. 8 Yet I am writing you a new command; its truth is seen in him and in you, because the darkness is passing and the true light is already shining.

9 Those who claim to be in the light but hate a fellow-believer are still in the darkness. 10 Those who love their fellow-believers live in the light, and there is nothing in them to make them stumble. 11 But those who hate a fellow-believer are in the darkness and walk around in the darkness; they do not know where they are going, because the darkness has blinded them.

Reasons for writing

12 I am writing to you, dear children,
because your sins have been forgiven
on account of his name.

13 I am writing to you, fathers,
because you know him who is from the beginning.
I am writing to you, young people,
because you have overcome the evil one.

14 I write to you, dear children,
because you know the Father.
I write to you, fathers,
because you know him who is from the beginning.
I write to you, young people,
because you are strong,
and the word of God lives in you,
and you have overcome the evil one.

On not loving the world

15 Do not love the world or anything in the world. If you love the world, love for the Father[b] is not in you. 16 For everything in the world—the cravings of sinful people, the lust of their eyes and their boasting about what they have and do—comes not from the Father but from the world. 17 The world and its desires pass away, but whoever does the will of God lives for ever.

Warnings against denying the Son

18 Dear children, this is the last hour; and as you have heard that the antichrist is coming, even now many antichrists have come. This is how we know it is the last hour. 19 They went out from us, but they did not really belong to us. For if they had belonged to us, they would have remained with us; but their going showed that none of them belonged to us.

20 But you have an anointing from the Holy One, and all of you know the truth.[c] 21 I do not write to you because you do not know the truth, but because you do know it and because no lie comes from the truth. 22 Who is the liar? It is whoever denies that Jesus is the Messiah.[d] Such a person is the antichrist—denying the Father and the Son. 23 No-one who denies the Son has the Father; whoever acknowledges the Son has the Father also.

24 As for you, see that what you have heard from the beginning remains in you. If it

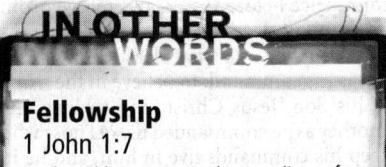

IN OTHER WORDS

Fellowship
1 John 1:7

In the Old Testament, the Israelites often made 'fellowship sacrifices' as a sign of being close to God. In the New Testament, the Greek word 'fellowship' means something like 'sharing in a common life', implying a relationship of mutual commitment.

---

[a] 5 Or *word, God's love*   [b] 15 Or *world, the Father's love*   [c] 20 Some manuscripts *and you know all things*
[d] 22 Greek *Christ*

does, you also will remain in the Son and in the Father. 25And this is what he promised us—eternal life.

26I am writing these things to you about those who are trying to lead you astray. 27As for you, the anointing you received from him remains in you, and you do not need anyone to teach you. But as his anointing teaches you about all things and as that anointing is real, not counterfeit—just as it has taught you, remain in him.

God's children and sin

28And now, dear children, continue in him, so that when he appears we may be confident and unashamed before him at his coming.

29If you know that he is righteous, you know that everyone who does what is right has been born of him.

3 See what great love the Father has lavished on us, that we should be called children of God! And that is what we are! The reason the world does not know us is that it did not know him. 2Dear friends, now we are children of God, and what we will be has not yet been made known. But we know that when Christ appears,[a] we shall be like him, for we shall see him as he is. 3All who have this hope in him purify themselves, just as he is pure.

4Everyone who sins breaks the law; in fact, sin is lawlessness. 5But you know that he appeared so that he might take away our sins. And in him is no sin. 6No-one who lives in him keeps on sinning. No-one who continues to sin has either seen him or known him.

7Dear children, do not let anyone lead you astray. The one who does what is right is righteous, just as he is righteous. 8The one who does what is sinful is of the devil, because the devil has been sinning from the beginning. The reason the Son of God appeared was to destroy the devil's work. 9Those who are born of God will not continue to sin, because God's seed remains in them; they cannot go on sinning, because they have been born of God. 10This is how we know who the children of God are and who the children of the devil are: those who do not do what is right are not God's children; nor are those who do not love their brothers and sisters.

More on love and hatred

11For this is the message you heard from the beginning: we should love one another. 12Do not be like Cain, who belonged to the evil one and murdered his brother. And why did he murder him? Because his own actions were evil and his brother's were righteous. 13Do not be surprised, my brothers and sisters, if the world hates you. 14We know that we have passed from death to life, because we love each other. Anyone who does not love remains in death. 15Anyone who hates a fellow-believer is a murderer, and you know that no murderers have eternal life in them.

16This is how we know what love is: Jesus Christ laid down his life for us. And we ought to lay down our lives for one another. 17If any one of you has material possessions and sees a brother or sister in need but has no pity on them, how can the love of God be in you? 18Dear children, let us not love with words or tongue but with actions and in truth.

19This is how we know that we belong to the truth and how we set our hearts at rest in his presence: 20if our hearts condemn us, we know that God is greater than our hearts, and he knows everything. 21Dear friends, if our hearts do not condemn us, we have confidence before God 22and receive from him anything we ask, because we keep his commands and do what pleases him. 23And this is his command: to believe in the name of his Son, Jesus Christ, and to love one another as he commanded us. 24Those who keep his commands live in him, and he in them. And this is how we know that he lives in us: we know it by the Spirit he gave us.

On denying the incarnation

4 Dear friends, do not believe every spirit, but test the spirits to see whether they are from God, because many false prophets have gone out into the world. 2This is how you can recognise the Spirit of God: every spirit that acknowledges that

---

[a] 2 Or *when it is made known*

Jesus Christ has come in the flesh is from God, 3but every spirit that does not acknowledge Jesus is not from God. This is the spirit of the antichrist, which you have heard is coming and even now is already in the world.

4You, dear children, are from God and have overcome them, because the one who is in you is greater than the one who is in the world. 5They are from the world and therefore speak from the viewpoint of the world, and the world listens to them. 6We are from God, and whoever knows God listens to us; but whoever is not from God does not listen to us. This is how we recognise the Spirit[a] of truth and the spirit of falsehood.

God's love and ours

7Dear friends, let us love one another, for love comes from God. Everyone who loves has been born of God and knows God. 8Whoever does not love does not know God, because God is love. 9This is how God showed his love among us: he sent his one and only Son into the world that we might live through him. 10This is love: not that we loved God, but that he loved us and sent his Son as an atoning sacrifice for our sins. 11Dear friends, since God so loved us, we also ought to love one another. 12No-one has ever seen God; but if we love one another, God lives in us and his love is made complete in us.

13This is how we know that we live in him and he in us: he has given us of his Spirit. 14And we have seen and testify that the Father has sent his Son to be the Saviour of the world. 15If anyone acknowledges that Jesus is the Son of God, God lives in them and they in God. 16And so we know and rely on the love God has for us.

God is love. Whoever lives in love lives in God, and God in them. 17This is how love is made complete among us so that we will have confidence on the day of judgment: in this world we are like Jesus. 18There is no fear in love. But perfect love drives out fear, because fear has to do with punishment. The one who fears is not made perfect in love.

19We love because he first loved us. 20If we say we love God yet hate a brother or sister, we are liars. For if we do not love a fellow-believer, whom we have seen, we cannot love God, whom we have not seen. 21And he has given us this command: those who love God must also love one another.

Faith in the incarnate Son of God

5 Everyone who believes that Jesus is the Messiah is born of God, and everyone who loves the father loves his child as well. 2This is how we know that we love the children of God: by loving God and carrying out his commands. 3In fact, this is love for God: to keep his commands. And his commands are not burdensome, 4for everyone born of God overcomes the world. This is the victory that has overcome the world, even our faith. 5Who is it that overcomes the world? Only the one who believes that Jesus is the Son of God.

6This is the one who came by water and blood—Jesus Christ. He did not come by water only, but by water and blood. And it is the Spirit who testifies, because the Spirit is the truth. 7For there are three that testify: 8the[b] Spirit, the water and the blood; and the three are in agreement. 9We accept human testimony, but God's testimony is greater because it is the testimony of God, which he has given about his Son. 10Whoever believes in the Son of God accepts this testimony. Whoever does not believe God has made him out to be a liar, because they have not believed the testimony God has given about his Son. 11And this is the testimony: God has given us eternal life, and this life is in his Son. 12Whoever has the Son has life; whoever does not have the Son of God does not have life.

Concluding affirmations

13I write these things to you who believe in the name of the Son of God so that you may know that you have eternal life. 14This is the confidence we have in approaching God: that if we ask anything according to his will,

---

[a] 6 Or spirit [b] 7,8 Late manuscripts of the Vulgate *testify in heaven: the Father, the Word and the Holy Spirit, and these three are one. 8And there are three that testify on earth: the* (not found in any Greek manuscript before the fourteenth century)

he hears us. ¹⁵And if we know that he hears us—whatever we ask—we know that we have what we asked of him.

¹⁶If you see any brother or sister commit a sin that does not lead to death, you should pray and God will give them life. I refer to those whose sin does not lead to death. There is a sin that leads to death. I am not saying that you should pray about that. ¹⁷All wrongdoing is sin, and there is sin that does not lead to death.

¹⁸We know that anyone born of God does not continue to sin; the One who was born of God keeps them safe, and the evil one cannot harm them. ¹⁹We know that we are children of God, and that the whole world is under the control of the evil one. ²⁰We know also that the Son of God has come and has given us understanding, so that we may know him who is true. And we are in him who is true by being in his Son Jesus Christ. He is the true God and eternal life.

²¹Dear children, keep yourselves from idols.

2 John

INTRODUCTION

2 John

Author: John, who also wrote the Gospel of John.

Who to: 'The chosen lady and her children'.

When: Probably written towards the end of the first century AD.

Where: It's thought that John wrote his letters from Ephesus.

Did you know? 'The chosen lady and her children' could be a way of referring to the church and all Christians.

Main theme: John writes on a similar theme to his first letter, the need to love one another. He also warns about the dangers of false teaching.

¹The elder,

To the lady chosen by God and to her children, whom I love in the truth—and not I only, but also all who know the truth— ²because of the truth, which lives in us and will be with us for ever:

³Grace, mercy and peace from God the Father and from Jesus Christ, the Father's Son, will be with us in truth and love.

⁴It has given me great joy to find some of your children walking in the truth, just as the Father commanded us. ⁵And now, dear lady, I am not writing you a new command but one we have had from the beginning. I ask that we love one another. ⁶And this is love: that we walk in obedience to his

IN OTHER WORDS

Antichrist
2 John 7

The antichrist is only mentioned by name in John's letters. However, the idea of an antichrist – a person who will oppose Jesus during the last days – is a popular image. John tells us that this person is not Satan, but that he comes by the activity of Satan.

commands. As you have heard from the beginning, his command is that you walk in love.

7 Many deceivers, who do not acknowledge Jesus Christ as coming in the flesh, have gone out into the world. Any such person is the deceiver and the antichrist. 8 Watch out that you do not lose what we[a] have worked for, but that you may be rewarded fully. 9 Anyone who runs ahead and does not continue in the teaching of Christ does not have God; whoever continues in the teaching has both the Father and the Son. 10 If anyone comes to you and does not bring this teaching, do not take them into your house or welcome them. 11 Anyone who welcomes them shares in their wicked work.

12 I have much to write to you, but I do not want to use paper and ink. Instead, I hope to visit you and talk with you face to face, so that our joy may be complete.

13 The children of your sister, who is chosen by God, send their greetings.

---

[a] 8 Some manuscripts *you*

3 John

INTRODUCTION

3 John

Author: John, who also wrote the Gospel of John.

Who to: Gaius.

When: Probably written towards the end of the first century AD.

Where: It's thought that John wrote his letters from Ephesus.

Main theme: This short letter promises Gaius that John will visit him soon. John commends him for his faith, and encourages him to do good.

¹The elder,

To my dear friend Gaius, whom I love in the truth.

²Dear friend, I pray that you may enjoy good health and that all may go well with you, just as you are progressing spiritually. ³It gave me great joy when some believers came and testified to your faithfulness to the truth, telling how you continue to walk in it. ⁴I have no greater joy than to hear that my children are walking in the truth.

⁵Dear friend, you are faithful in what you are doing for the brothers and sisters, even though they are strangers to you. ⁶They have told the church about your love. You will do well to send them on their way in a manner worthy of God. ⁷It was for the sake of the Name that they went out, receiving no help from the pagans. ⁸We ought therefore to show hospitality to such people so that we may work together for the truth.

⁹I wrote to the church, but Diotrephes, who loves to be first, will have nothing to do with us. ¹⁰So when I come, I will call attention to what he is doing, spreading malicious nonsense about us. Not satisfied

IN OTHER WORDS

Church
3 John 9
The word in the New Testament that is translated as 'church' means 'the gathering'. So it really is the people and not the building that make the church!

with that, he refuses to welcome other believers. He also stops those who want to do so and puts them out of the church.

¹¹Dear friend, do not imitate what is evil but what is good. Anyone who does what is good is from God. Anyone who does what is evil has not seen God. ¹²Demetrius is well spoken of by everyone—and even by the truth itself. We also speak well of him, and you know that our testimony is true.

¹³I have much to write to you, but I do not want to do so with pen and ink. ¹⁴I hope to see you soon, and we will talk face to face.

Peace to you. The friends here send their greetings. Greet the friends there by name.

Jude

INTRODUCTION

Jude

Author: Jude

When: Probably written towards the end of the first century AD.

Did you know? Jude is 'the brother of James'. If this is the same man that wrote the letter of James, then because he was Jesus' brother, that would make Jude a brother of Jesus too!

Main theme: Jude launches a stinging attack on false teachers and encourages his readers to stay true to the apostles' teaching.

---

¹Jude, a servant of Jesus Christ and a brother of James,

To those who have been called, who are loved in God the Father and kept for[a] Jesus Christ:

²Mercy, peace and love be yours in abundance.

The sin and doom of ungodly people

³Dear friends, although I was very eager to write to you about the salvation we share, I felt compelled to write and urge you to contend for the faith that the Lord has once for all entrusted to us, his people. ⁴For certain individuals whose condemnation was written about[b] long ago have secretly slipped in among you. They are ungodly people, who pervert the grace of our God into a licence for immorality and deny Jesus Christ our only Sovereign and Lord.

⁵Though you already know all this, I want to remind you that the Lord[c] at one time delivered his people out of Egypt, but later destroyed those who did not believe. ⁶And the angels who did not keep their positions of authority but abandoned their proper dwelling—these he has kept in darkness, bound with everlasting chains for judgment on the great Day. ⁷In a similar way, Sodom and Gomorrah and the surrounding towns gave themselves up to sexual immorality and perversion. They serve as an example of those who suffer the punishment of eternal fire.

⁸In the very same way, on the strength of their dreams these ungodly people pollute their own bodies, reject authority and heap abuse on celestial beings. ⁹But even the archangel Michael, when he was disputing with the devil about the body of Moses, did not himself dare to condemn him for

---

[a] 1 Or *by; or in*   [b] 4 Or *individuals who were marked out for condemnation*   [c] 5 Some early manuscripts *Jesus*

making Connections

Old writings
Jude 9
Don't worry; your Bible isn't missing some bits! This story of Michael and the devil and the quote from Enoch in verses 14 and 15 aren't in the Bible. They were part of old writings that were popular in New Testament times, but which aren't part of Scripture.

slander but said, 'The Lord rebuke you!'[a] 10Yet these people speak abusively against whatever they do not understand; and what things they do understand by instinct, like unreasoning animals—these are the very things that destroy them.

11Woe to them! They have taken the way of Cain; they have rushed for profit into Balaam's error; they have been destroyed in Korah's rebellion.

12These people are blemishes at your love feasts, eating with you without the slightest qualm—shepherds who feed only themselves. They are clouds without rain, blown along by the wind; autumn trees, without fruit and uprooted—twice dead. 13They are wild waves of the sea, foaming up their shame; wandering stars, for whom blackest darkness has been reserved for ever.

14Enoch, the seventh from Adam, prophesied about them: 'See, the Lord is coming with thousands upon thousands of his holy ones 15to judge everyone, and to convict all the ungodly of all the ungodly acts they have done in an ungodly way, and of all the defiant words ungodly sinners have spoken against him.'[b] 16These people are grumblers and fault-finders; they follow their own evil desires; they boast about themselves and flatter others for their own advantage.

A call to persevere

17But, dear friends, remember what the apostles of our Lord Jesus Christ foretold. 18They said to you, 'In the last times there will be scoffers who will follow their own ungodly desires.' 19These are the people who divide you, who follow mere natural instincts and do not have the Spirit.

20But you, dear friends, by building yourselves up in your most holy faith and praying in the Holy Spirit, 21keep yourselves in God's love as you wait for the mercy of our Lord Jesus Christ to bring you to eternal life.

22Be merciful to those who doubt; 23save others by snatching them from the fire; to others show mercy, mixed with fear—hating even the clothing stained by corrupted flesh.[c]

Doxology

24To him who is able to keep you from stumbling and to present you before his glorious presence without fault and with great joy— 25to the only God our Saviour be glory, majesty, power and authority, through Jesus Christ our Lord, before all ages, now and for evermore! Amen.

---

[a]9 Jude is alluding to the Jewish *Testament of Moses* (approximately the first century A.D.). [b]14,15 From the Jewish *First Book of Enoch* (approximately the first century B.C.) [c]22,23 The Greek manuscripts of these verses vary at several points.

Revelation

INTRODUCTION

Revelation

Author: John, who also wrote the Gospel of John and the letters of John.

Who to: 'The seven churches', Christians who were facing trials and persecution.

When: Probably written towards the end of the first century AD.

Where: John was on the island of Patmos when he saw his vision.

Did you know? The original title of this book in Greek was 'Apocalypse', which means 'unveiling', revealing hidden things which are known only to God.

Main theme: John writes about conditions in the seven churches in the world at that time, and the end of the world. He uses symbols, dramatic images and numbers. He describes the battle between good and evil, between God and Satan; God's ultimate and decisive victory over all evil; and God's future kingdom. Many people have tried to interpret Revelation and there are different theories as to what various parts of the vision mean. What is clear is that God is all-powerful and the future is in his hands.

Prologue

1 The revelation from Jesus Christ, which God gave him to show his servants what must soon take place. He made it known by sending his angel to his servant John, ²who testifies to everything he saw—that is, the word of God and the testimony of Jesus Christ. ³Blessed is the one who reads aloud the words of this prophecy, and blessed are those who hear it and take to heart what is written in it, because the time is near.

Greetings and doxology

⁴John,

To the seven churches in the province of Asia:

Grace and peace to you from him who is, and who was, and who is to come, and from the seven spirits[a] before his throne, 5and from Jesus Christ, who is the faithful witness, the firstborn from the dead, and the ruler of the kings of the earth.

To him who loves us and has freed us from our sins by his blood, 6and has made us to be a kingdom and priests to serve his God and Father—to him be glory and power for ever and ever! Amen.

7'Look, he is coming with the clouds,'[b]
and 'every eye will see him,
even those who pierced him';
and all peoples on earth 'will mourn because of him'.[c]
So shall it be! Amen.

8'I am the Alpha and the Omega,' says the Lord God, 'who is, and who was, and who is to come, the Almighty.'

John's vision of Christ

9I, John, your brother and companion in the suffering and kingdom and patient endurance that are ours in Jesus, was on the island of Patmos because of the word of God and the testimony of Jesus. 10On the Lord's Day I was in the Spirit, and I heard behind me a loud voice like a trumpet, 11which said: 'Write on a scroll what you see and send it to the seven churches: to Ephesus, Smyrna, Pergamum, Thyatira, Sardis, Philadelphia and Laodicea.'

12I turned round to see the voice that was speaking to me. And when I turned I saw seven golden lampstands, 13and among the lampstands was someone like a son of man,[d] dressed in a robe reaching down to his feet and with a golden sash round his chest. 14The hair on his head was white like wool, as white as snow, and his eyes were like blazing fire. 15His feet were like bronze glowing in a furnace, and his voice was like the sound of rushing waters. 16In his right hand he held seven stars, and coming out of his mouth was a sharp, double-edged sword. His face was like the sun shining in all its brilliance.

17When I saw him, I fell at his feet as though dead. Then he placed his right hand on me and said: 'Do not be afraid. I am the First and the Last. 18I am the Living One; I was dead, and now look, I am alive for ever and ever! And I hold the keys of death and Hades.

19'Write, therefore, what you have seen: both what is now and what will take place later. 20The mystery of the seven stars that you saw in my right hand and of the seven golden lampstands is this: the seven stars are the angels[e] of the seven churches, and the seven lampstands are the seven churches.

To the church in Ephesus

2 'To the angel[f] of the church in Ephesus write:

These are the words of him who holds the seven stars in his right hand and walks among the seven golden lampstands. 2I know your deeds, your hard work and your perseverance. I know that you cannot tolerate wicked people, that you have tested those who claim to be apostles but are not, and have found them false. 3You have persevered and have endured hardships for my name, and have not grown weary.

4Yet I hold this against you: you have forsaken the love you had at first. 5Consider how far you have fallen! Repent and do the things you did at first. If you do not repent, I will come to you and remove your lampstand from its place. 6But you have this in your favour: you hate the practices of the Nicolaitans, which I also hate.

7Whoever has ears, let them hear what the Spirit says to the churches. To those who are victorious, I will give the right to eat from the tree of life, which is in the paradise of God.

---

[a] 4 That is, the sevenfold Spirit [b] 7 Daniel 7:13 [c] 7 Zech. 12:10 [d] 13 See Daniel 7:13. [e] 20 Or messengers [f] 1 Or messenger; also in verses 8, 12 and 18

IN OTHER WORDS

Paradise
Revelation 2:7
'Paradise' is a word that originally came from Persia and was used to describe a wooded park or a garden with fruit trees. The Jews called the Garden of Eden 'paradise', and it is now used as a descriptive word for heaven (Luke 23:43).

To the church in Smyrna

8"To the angel of the church in Smyrna write:

> These are the words of him who is the First and the Last, who died and came to life again. 9I know your afflictions and your poverty—yet you are rich! I know about the slander of those who say they are Jews and are not, but are a synagogue of Satan. 10Do not be afraid of what you are about to suffer. I tell you, the devil will put some of you in prison to test you, and you will suffer persecution for ten days. Be faithful, even to the point of death, and I will give you life as your victor's crown.
>
> 11Whoever has ears, let them hear what the Spirit says to the churches. Those who are victorious will not be hurt at all by the second death.

To the church in Pergamum

12"To the angel of the church in Pergamum write:

> These are the words of him who has the sharp, double-edged sword. 13I know where you live—where Satan has his throne. Yet you remain true to my name. You did not renounce your faith in me, not even in the days of Antipas, my faithful witness, who was put to death in your city—where Satan lives.
>
> 14Nevertheless, I have a few things against you: there are some among you who hold to the teaching of Balaam, who taught Balak to entice the Israelites to sin so that they ate food sacrificed to idols and committed sexual immorality. 15Likewise, you also have those who hold to the teaching of the Nicolaitans. 16Repent therefore! Otherwise, I will soon come to you and will fight against them with the sword of my mouth.
>
> 17Whoever has ears, let them hear what the Spirit says to the churches. To those who are victorious, I will give some of the hidden manna. I will also give each of them a white stone with a new name written on it, known only to the one who receives it.

To the church in Thyatira

18"To the angel of the church in Thyatira write:

> These are the words of the Son of God, whose eyes are like blazing fire and whose feet are like burnished bronze. 19I know your deeds, your love and faith, your service and perseverance, and that you are now doing more than you did at first.
>
> 20Nevertheless, I have this against you: you tolerate that woman Jezebel, who calls herself a prophet. By her teaching she misleads my servants into sexual immorality and the eating of food sacrificed to idols. 21I have given her time to repent of her immorality, but she is unwilling. 22So I will cast her on a bed of suffering, and I will make those who commit adultery with her suffer intensely, unless they repent of her ways. 23I will strike her children dead. Then all the churches will know that I am he who searches hearts and

minds, and I will repay each of you according to your deeds. 24Now I say to the rest of you in Thyatira, to you who do not hold to her teaching and have not learned Satan's so-called deep secrets, 'I will not impose any other burden on you, 25except to hold on to what you have until I come.'

26To those who are victorious and do my will to the end, I will give authority over the nations— 27they 'will rule them with an iron sceptre and will dash them to pieces like pottery'[a]—just as I have received authority from my Father. 28I will also give them the morning star. 29Whoever has ears, let them hear what the Spirit says to the churches.

To the church in Sardis

3 'To the angel[b] of the church in Sardis write:

These are the words of him who holds the seven spirits[c] of God and the seven stars. I know your deeds; you have a reputation of being alive, but you are dead. 2Wake up! Strengthen what remains and is about to die, for I have found your deeds unfinished in the sight of my God. 3Remember, therefore, what you have received and heard; hold it fast, and repent. But if you do not wake up, I will come like a thief, and you will not know at what time I will come to you.

4Yet you have a few people in Sardis who have not soiled their clothes. They will walk with me, dressed in white, for they are worthy. 5Those who are victorious will, like them, be dressed in white. I will never blot out their names from the book of life, but will acknowledge their names before my Father and his angels. 6Whoever has ears, let them hear what the Spirit says to the churches.

To the church in Philadelphia

7'To the angel of the church in Philadelphia write:

These are the words of him who is holy and true, who holds the key of David. What he opens no-one can shut, and what he shuts no-one can open. 8I know your deeds. See, I have placed before you an open door that no-one can shut. I know that you have little strength, yet you have kept my word and have not denied my name. 9I will make those who are of the synagogue of Satan, who claim to be Jews though they are not, but are liars—I will make them come and fall down at your feet and acknowledge that I have loved you. 10Since you have kept my command to endure patiently, I will also keep you from the hour of trial that is going to come on the whole world to test those who live on the earth.

11I am coming soon. Hold on to what you have, so that no-one will take your crown. 12Those who are victorious I will make pillars in the temple of my God. Never again will they leave it. I will write on them the name of my God and the name of the city of my God, the new Jerusalem, which is coming down out of heaven from my God; and I will also write on them my new name. 13Whoever has ears, let them hear what the Spirit says to the churches.

To the church in Laodicea

14'To the angel of the church in Laodicea write:

These are the words of the Amen, the faithful and true

---

[a] 27 Psalm 2:9 [b] 1 Or *messenger*; also in verses 7 and 14 [c] 1 That is, the sevenfold Spirit

Revelation 4:11

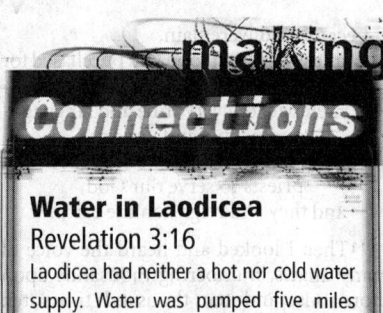

Making Connections

Water in Laodicea
Revelation 3:16
Laodicea had neither a hot nor cold water supply. Water was pumped five miles along an aqueduct from the hot springs of Denizli. By the time it arrived it was lukewarm and poor in quality.

witness, the ruler of God's creation. ¹⁵I know your deeds, that you are neither cold nor hot. I wish you were either one or the other! ¹⁶So, because you are lukewarm—neither hot nor cold—I am about to spit you out of my mouth. ¹⁷You say, 'I am rich; I have acquired wealth and do not need a thing.' But you do not realise that you are wretched, pitiful, poor, blind and naked. ¹⁸I counsel you to buy from me gold refined in the fire, so that you can become rich; and white clothes to wear, so that you can cover your shameful nakedness; and salve to put on your eyes, so that you can see.

¹⁹Those whom I love I rebuke and discipline. So be earnest, and repent. ²⁰Here I am! I stand at the door and knock. If anyone hears my voice and opens the door, I will come in and eat with them, and they with me.

²¹To those who are victorious, I will give the right to sit with me on my throne, just as I was victorious and sat down with my Father on his throne. ²²Whoever has ears, let them hear what the Spirit says to the churches.'

The throne in heaven

4 After this I looked, and there before me was a door standing open in heaven. And the voice I had first heard speaking to me like a trumpet said, 'Come up here, and I will show you what must take place after this.' ²At once I was in the Spirit, and there before me was a throne in heaven with someone sitting on it. ³And the one who sat there had the appearance of jasper and ruby. A rainbow that shone like an emerald encircled the throne. ⁴Surrounding the throne were twenty-four other thrones, and seated on them were twenty-four elders. They were dressed in white and had crowns of gold on their heads. ⁵From the throne came flashes of lightning, rumblings and peals of thunder. Before the throne, seven lamps were blazing. These are the seven spirits[a] of God. ⁶Also before the throne there was what looked like a sea of glass, clear as crystal.

In the centre, round the throne, were four living creatures, and they were covered with eyes, in front and behind. ⁷The first living creature was like a lion, the second was like an ox, the third had a face like a man, the fourth was like a flying eagle. ⁸Each of the four living creatures had six wings and was covered with eyes all round, even under its wings. Day and night they never stop saying:

' "Holy, holy, holy
is the Lord God Almighty," [b]
who was, and is, and is to come.'

⁹Whenever the living creatures give glory, honour and thanks to him who sits on the throne and who lives for ever and ever, ¹⁰the twenty-four elders fall down before him who sits on the throne and worship him who lives for ever and ever. They lay their crowns before the throne and say:

¹¹'You are worthy, our Lord and God,
to receive glory and honour and power,
for you created all things,
and by your will they were created
and have their being.'

---

[a] 5 That is, the sevenfold Spirit [b] 8 Isaiah 6:3

IN OTHER WORDS

Lamb
Revelation 5:6

In the Old Testament, a young sheep was a good sacrifice to God. Jesus was called the 'Lamb of God' by John the Baptist, because he was to be the ultimate sacrifice that would mean all sin could be forgiven and people could be right with God (John 1:29). After Jesus' resurrection, the church used the image of the lamb to symbolise his death as an atonement for sin.

The scroll and the Lamb

5 Then I saw in the right hand of him who sat on the throne a scroll with writing on both sides and sealed with seven seals. 2 And I saw a mighty angel proclaiming in a loud voice, 'Who is worthy to break the seals and open the scroll?' 3 But no-one in heaven or on earth or under the earth could open the scroll or even look inside it. 4 I wept and wept because no-one was found who was worthy to open the scroll or look inside. 5 Then one of the elders said to me, 'Do not weep! See, the Lion of the tribe of Judah, the Root of David, has triumphed. He is able to open the scroll and its seven seals.'

6 Then I saw a Lamb, looking as if it had been slain, standing in the centre before the throne, encircled by the four living creatures and the elders. The Lamb had seven horns and seven eyes, which are the seven spirits[a] of God sent out into all the earth. 7 He went and took the scroll from the right hand of him who sat on the throne. 8 And when he had taken it, the four living creatures and the twenty-four elders fell down before the Lamb. Each one had a harp and they were holding golden bowls full of incense, which are the prayers of God's people. 9 And they sang a new song, saying:

'You are worthy to take the scroll
 and to open its seals,
because you were slain,
 and with your blood you purchased for God
 members of every tribe and language
  and people and nation.
10 You have made them to be a kingdom and
  priests to serve our God,
 and they will reign[b] on the earth.'

11 Then I looked and heard the voice of many angels, numbering thousands upon thousands, and ten thousand times ten thousand. They encircled the throne and the living creatures and the elders. 12 In a loud voice they were saying:

'Worthy is the Lamb, who was slain,
 to receive power and wealth and
  wisdom and strength
 and honour and glory and praise!'

13 Then I heard every creature in heaven and on earth and under the earth and on the sea, and all that is in them, saying:

'To him who sits on the throne and to the
  Lamb
 be praise and honour and glory and
  power,
   for ever and ever!'

14 The four living creatures said, 'Amen', and the elders fell down and worshipped.

The seals

6 I watched as the Lamb opened the first of the seven seals. Then I heard one of the four living creatures say in a voice like thunder, 'Come!' 2 I looked, and there before me was a white horse! Its rider held a bow, and he was given a crown, and he rode out as a conqueror bent on conquest.

3 When the Lamb opened the second seal, I heard the second living creature say, 'Come!' 4 Then another horse came out, a fiery red one. Its rider was given power to take peace from the earth and to make people slay each other. To him was given a large sword.

5 When the Lamb opened the third seal, I heard the third living creature say, 'Come!' I looked, and there before me was a black horse! Its rider was holding a pair of scales in

---

[a] 6 That is, the sevenfold Spirit   [b] 10 Some manuscripts *they reign*

his hand. ⁶Then I heard what sounded like a voice among the four living creatures, saying, 'A kilogram of wheat for a day's wages, and three kilograms of barley for a day's wages, and do not damage the oil and the wine!'

⁷When the Lamb opened the fourth seal, I heard the voice of the fourth living creature say, 'Come!' ⁸I looked, and there before me was a pale horse! Its rider was named Death, and Hades was following close behind him. They were given power over a quarter of the earth to kill by sword, famine and plague, and by the wild beasts of the earth.

⁹When he opened the fifth seal, I saw under the altar the souls of those who had been slain because of the word of God and the testimony they had maintained. ¹⁰They called out in a loud voice, 'How long, Sovereign Lord, holy and true, until you judge the inhabitants of the earth and avenge our blood?' ¹¹Then each of them was given a white robe, and they were told to wait a little longer, until the full number of their fellow-servants and brothers and sisters were killed just as they had been.

¹²I watched as he opened the sixth seal. There was a great earthquake. The sun turned black like sackcloth made of goat hair, the whole moon turned blood red, ¹³and the stars in the sky fell to earth, as figs drop from a fig-tree when shaken by a strong wind. ¹⁴The sky receded like a scroll, rolling up, and every mountain and island was removed from its place.

¹⁵Then the kings of the earth, the princes, the generals, the rich, the mighty, and everyone else, both slave and free, hid in caves and among the rocks of the mountains. ¹⁶They called to the mountains and the rocks, 'Fall on us and hide us*ᵃ* from the face of him who sits on the throne and from the wrath of the Lamb! ¹⁷For the great day of their*ᵇ* wrath has come, and who can withstand it?'

144,000 sealed

7 After this I saw four angels standing at the four corners of the earth, holding back the four winds of the earth to prevent

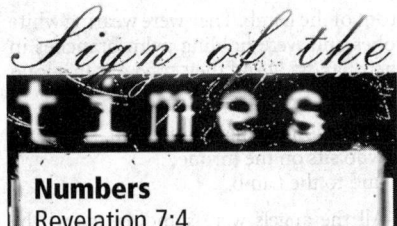

Sign of the times

Numbers
Revelation 7:4
Some numbers had special meanings in the ancient world and so some numbers in the Bible can be understood symbolically. The number 12 was considered to be a symbol of completeness. 144,000 is 12 multiplied by 12 and then multiplied by 1,000. This number represents the complete people of God.

any wind from blowing on the land or on the sea or on any tree. ²Then I saw another angel coming up from the east, having the seal of the living God. He called out in a loud voice to the four angels who had been given power to harm the land and the sea: ³'Do not harm the land or the sea or the trees until we put a seal on the foreheads of the servants of our God.' ⁴Then I heard the number of those who were sealed: 144,000 from all the tribes of Israel.

⁵From the tribe of Judah 12,000 were sealed,
from the tribe of Reuben 12,000,
from the tribe of Gad 12,000,
⁶from the tribe of Asher 12,000,
from the tribe of Naphtali 12,000,
from the tribe of Manasseh 12,000,
⁷from the tribe of Simeon 12,000,
from the tribe of Levi 12,000,
from the tribe of Issachar 12,000,
⁸from the tribe of Zebulun 12,000,
from the tribe of Joseph 12,000,
from the tribe of Benjamin 12,000.

The great multitude in white robes

⁹After this I looked, and there before me was a great multitude that no-one could count, from every nation, tribe, people and language, standing before the throne and in

---

ᵃ 16 See Hosea 10:8. *ᵇ* 17 Some manuscripts *his*

front of the Lamb. They were wearing white robes and were holding palm branches in their hands. 10And they cried out in a loud voice:

'Salvation belongs to our God,
who sits on the throne,
and to the Lamb.'

11All the angels were standing round the throne and round the elders and the four living creatures. They fell down on their faces before the throne and worshipped God, 12saying:

'Amen!
Praise and glory
and wisdom and thanks and honour
and power and strength
be to our God for ever and ever.
Amen!'

13Then one of the elders asked me, 'These in white robes—who are they, and where did they come from?'

14I answered, 'Sir, you know.'

And he said, 'These are they who have come out of the great tribulation; they have washed their robes and made them white in the blood of the Lamb. 15Therefore,

'they are before the throne of God
and serve him day and night in his temple;
and he who sits on the throne
will spread his tent over them.
16"Never again will they hunger;
never again will they thirst.
The sun will not beat down on them,"[a]
nor any scorching heat.
17For the Lamb at the centre before the throne
will be their shepherd;
"he will lead them to springs of living water."[b]
"And God will wipe away every tear from their eyes."[c]

The seventh seal and the golden censer

8 When he opened the seventh seal, there was silence in heaven for about half an hour.

2And I saw the seven angels who stand before God, and seven trumpets were given to them.

3Another angel, who had a golden censer, came and stood at the altar. He was given much incense to offer, with the prayers of all God's people, on the golden altar before the throne. 4The smoke of the incense, together with the prayers of God's people, went up before God from the angel's hand. 5Then the angel took the censer, filled it with fire from the altar, and hurled it on the earth; and there came peals of thunder, rumblings, flashes of lightning and an earthquake.

The trumpets

6Then the seven angels who had the seven trumpets prepared to sound them.

7The first angel sounded his trumpet, and there came hail and fire mixed with blood, and it was hurled down on the earth. A third of the earth was burned up, a third of the trees were burned up, and all the green grass was burned up.

8The second angel sounded his trumpet, and something like a huge mountain, all ablaze, was thrown into the sea. A third of the sea turned into blood, 9a third of the living creatures in the sea died, and a third of the ships were destroyed.

10The third angel sounded his trumpet, and a great star, blazing like a torch, fell from the sky on a third of the rivers and on the springs of water—11the name of the star is Wormwood.[d] A third of the waters turned bitter, and many people died from the waters that had become bitter.

12The fourth angel sounded his trumpet, and a third of the sun was struck, a third of the moon, and a third of the stars, so that a third of them turned dark. A third of the day was without light, and also a third of the night.

13As I watched, I heard an eagle that was flying in mid-air call out in a loud voice: 'Woe! Woe! Woe to the inhabitants of the earth, because of the trumpet blasts about to be sounded by the other three angels!'

---

[a] 16 Isaiah 49:10   [b] 17 Isaiah 49:10   [c] 17 Isaiah 25:8   [d] 11 Wormwood is a bitter substance.

9 The fifth angel sounded his trumpet, and I saw a star that had fallen from the sky to the earth. The star was given the key to the shaft of the Abyss. 2When he opened the Abyss, smoke rose from it like the smoke from a gigantic furnace. The sun and sky were darkened by the smoke from the Abyss. 3And out of the smoke locusts came down on the earth and were given power like that of scorpions of the earth. 4They were told not to harm the grass of the earth or any plant or tree, but only those people who did not have the seal of God on their foreheads. 5They were not allowed to kill them but only to torture them for five months. And the agony they suffered was like that of the sting of a scorpion when it strikes. 6During those days people will seek death but will not find it; they will long to die, but death will elude them.

7The locusts looked like horses prepared for battle. On their heads they wore something like crowns of gold, and their faces resembled human faces. 8Their hair was like women's hair, and their teeth were like lions' teeth. 9They had breastplates like breastplates of iron, and the sound of their wings was like the thundering of many horses and chariots rushing into battle. 10They had tails with stings, like scorpions, and in their tails they had power to torment people for five months. 11They had as king over them the angel of the Abyss, whose name in Hebrew is Abaddon and in Greek is Apollyon (that is, Destroyer).

12The first woe is past; two other woes are yet to come.

13The sixth angel sounded his trumpet, and I heard a voice coming from the four horns of the golden altar that is before God. 14It said to the sixth angel who had the trumpet, 'Release the four angels who are bound at the great river Euphrates.' 15And the four angels who had been kept ready for this very hour and day and month and year were released to kill a third of the world's people. 16The number of the mounted troops was two hundred million. I heard their number.

17The horses and riders I saw in my vision looked like this: their breastplates were fiery red, dark blue, and yellow as sulphur. The heads of the horses resembled the heads of lions, and out of their mouths came fire, smoke and sulphur. 18A third of the people were killed by the three plagues of fire, smoke and sulphur that came out of their mouths. 19The power of the horses was in their mouths and in their tails; for their tails were like snakes, having heads with which they inflict injury.

20The rest of the people who were not killed by these plagues still did not repent of the work of their hands; they did not stop worshipping demons, and idols of gold, silver, bronze, stone and wood—idols that cannot see or hear or walk. 21Nor did they repent of their murders, their magic arts, their sexual immorality or their thefts.

The angel and the little scroll

10 Then I saw another mighty angel coming down from heaven. He was robed in a cloud, with a rainbow above his head; his face was like the sun, and his legs were like fiery pillars. 2He was holding a little scroll, which lay open in his hand. He planted his right foot on the sea and his left foot on the land, 3and he gave a loud shout like the roar of a lion. When he shouted, the voices of the seven thunders spoke. 4And when the seven thunders spoke, I was about to write; but I heard a voice from heaven say, 'Seal up what the seven thunders have said and do not write it down.'

5Then the angel I had seen standing on the sea and on the land raised his right hand to heaven. 6And he swore by him who lives for ever and ever, who created the heavens and all that is in them, the earth and all that is in it, and the sea and all that is in it, and said, 'There will be no more delay! 7But in the days when the seventh angel is about to sound his trumpet, the mystery of God will be accomplished, just as he announced to his servants the prophets.'

8Then the voice that I had heard from heaven spoke to me once more: 'Go, take the scroll that lies open in the hand of the angel who is standing on the sea and on the land.'

9So I went to the angel and asked him to give me the little scroll. He said to me, 'Take it and eat it. It will turn your stomach sour, but "in your mouth it will be as sweet as honey."[a] 10I took the little scroll from the angel's hand and ate it. It tasted as sweet as honey in my mouth, but when I had eaten it, my stomach turned sour. 11Then I was told, 'You must prophesy again about many peoples, nations, languages and kings.'

The two witnesses

11 I was given a reed like a measuring rod and was told, 'Go and measure the temple of God and the altar, with its worshippers. 2But exclude the outer court; do not measure it, because it has been given to the Gentiles. They will trample on the holy city for 42 months. 3And I will appoint my two witnesses, and they will prophesy for 1,260 days, clothed in sackcloth.' 4They are 'the two olive trees' and the two lampstands, and 'they stand before the Lord of the earth.'[b] 5If anyone tries to harm them, fire comes from their mouths and devours their enemies. This is how anyone who wants to harm them must die. 6They have power to shut up the sky so that it will not rain during the time they are prophesying; and they have power to turn the waters into blood and to strike the earth with every kind of plague as often as they want.

7Now when they have finished their testimony, the beast that comes up from the Abyss will attack them, and overpower and kill them. 8Their bodies will lie in the public square of the great city, which is figuratively called Sodom and Egypt, where also their Lord was crucified. 9For three and a half days many from every people, tribe, language and nation will gaze on their bodies and refuse them burial. 10The inhabitants of the earth will gloat over them and will celebrate by sending each other gifts, because these two prophets had tormented those who live on the earth.

11But after the three and a half days the breath[c] of life from God entered them, and they stood on their feet, and terror struck those who saw them. 12Then they heard a loud voice from heaven saying to them, 'Come up here.' And they went up to heaven in a cloud, while their enemies looked on.

13At that very hour there was a severe earthquake and a tenth of the city collapsed. Seven thousand people were killed in the earthquake, and the survivors were terrified and gave glory to the God of heaven.

14The second woe has passed; the third woe is coming soon.

The seventh trumpet

15The seventh angel sounded his trumpet, and there were loud voices in heaven, which said:

'The kingdom of the world has become
   the kingdom of our Lord and of his
      Messiah,
   and he will reign for ever and ever.'

16And the twenty-four elders, who were seated on their thrones before God, fell on their faces and worshipped God, 17saying:

'We give thanks to you, Lord God
      Almighty,
   the One who is and who was,
   because you have taken your great power
      and have begun to reign.
18The nations were angry,
      and your wrath has come.
   The time has come for judging the dead,
      and for rewarding your servants the
         prophets
   and your people who revere your name,
      both great and small—
   and for destroying those who destroy the
      earth.'

19Then God's temple in heaven was opened, and within his temple was seen the ark of his covenant. And there came flashes of lightning, rumblings, peals of thunder, an earthquake and a great hailstorm.

The woman and the dragon

12 A great and wondrous sign appeared in heaven: a woman clothed with the sun, with the moon under her feet and a crown of twelve stars on her head. 2She was pregnant and cried out in pain as she was about to give birth. 3Then another sign appeared in heaven: an enormous red dragon with seven heads and ten horns and seven crowns on its heads. 4Its tail swept a

---

[a] 9 Ezek. 3:3   [b] 4 See Zech. 4:3,11,14.   [c] 11 Or *Spirit* (see Ezek. 37:5,14)

> **People and Places**
>
> **Satan**
> Revelation 12:9
> Also known as the devil, the prince of evil or Beelzebub, Satan is the great opponent of God and people. The word satan means 'adversary', and Jesus saw Satan as his true enemy.

third of the stars out of the sky and flung them to the earth. The dragon stood in front of the woman who was about to give birth, so that it might devour her child the moment he was born. ⁵She gave birth to a son, a male child, who 'will rule all the nations with an iron sceptre.'ᵃ And her child was snatched up to God and to his throne. ⁶The woman fled into the wilderness to a place prepared for her by God, where she might be taken care of for 1,260 days.

⁷And there was war in heaven. Michael and his angels fought against the dragon, and the dragon and his angels fought back. ⁸But he was not strong enough, and they lost their place in heaven. ⁹The great dragon was hurled down—that ancient snake called the devil, or Satan, who leads the whole world astray. He was hurled to the earth, and his angels with him.

¹⁰Then I heard a loud voice in heaven say:

'Now have come the salvation and the power
 and the kingdom of our God,
 and the authority of his Messiah.
For the accuser of our brothers and sisters,
 who accuses them before our God day and night,
 has been hurled down.
¹¹They triumphed over him
 by the blood of the Lamb
 and by the word of their testimony;
they did not love their lives so much
 as to shrink from death.
¹²Therefore rejoice, you heavens
 and you who dwell in them!
But woe to the earth and the sea,
 because the devil has gone down to you!
He is filled with fury,
 because he knows that his time is short.'

¹³When the dragon saw that he had been hurled to the earth, he pursued the woman who had given birth to the male child. ¹⁴The woman was given the two wings of a great eagle, so that she might fly to the place prepared for her in the wilderness, where she would be taken care of for a time, times and half a time, out of the snake's reach. ¹⁵Then from his mouth the snake spewed water like a river, to overtake the woman and sweep her away with the torrent. ¹⁶But the earth helped the woman by opening its mouth and swallowing the river that the dragon had spewed out of his mouth. ¹⁷Then the dragon was enraged at the woman and went off to make war against the rest of her offspring—those who keep God's commands and hold fast their testimony about Jesus.

The beast out of the sea

13 The dragonᵇ stood on the shore of the sea. And I saw a beast coming out of the sea. It had ten horns and seven heads, with ten crowns on its horns, and on each head a blasphemous name. ²The beast I saw resembled a leopard, but had feet like those of a bear and a mouth like that of a lion. The dragon gave the beast his power and his throne and great authority. ³One of the heads of the beast seemed to have had a fatal wound, but the fatal wound had been healed. The whole world was filled with wonder and followed the beast. ⁴People worshipped the dragon because he had given authority to the beast, and they also worshipped the beast and asked, 'Who is like the beast? Who can make war against it?'

⁵The beast was given a mouth to utter proud words and blasphemies and to exercise its authority for forty-two months. ⁶It opened its mouth to utter blasphemy against

---

ᵃ5 Psalm 2:9   ᵇ1 Some manuscripts *And I*

God, and to slander his name and his dwelling-place and those who live in heaven. ⁷It was given power to make war against God's holy people and to conquer them. And it was given authority over every tribe, people, language and nation. ⁸All inhabitants of the earth will worship the beast—all whose names have not been written in the Lamb's book of life, the Lamb who was slain from the creation of the world.*ᵃ*

⁹Whoever has ears, let them hear.

¹⁰'If anyone is to go into captivity,
into captivity they will go.
If anyone is to be killed*ᵇ* with the sword,
with the sword they will be killed.'*ᶜ*

This calls for patient endurance and faithfulness on the part of God's people.

The beast out of the earth

¹¹Then I saw another beast, coming out of the earth. It had two horns like a lamb, but it spoke like a dragon. ¹²It exercised all the authority of the first beast on its behalf, and made the earth and its inhabitants worship the first beast, whose fatal wound had been healed. ¹³And it performed great signs, even causing fire to come down from heaven to the earth in full view of everyone. ¹⁴Because of the signs it was given power to perform on behalf of the first beast, it deceived the inhabitants of the earth. It ordered them to set up an image in honour of the beast who was wounded by the sword and yet lived. ¹⁵It was given power to give breath to the image of the first beast, so that it could speak and cause all who refused to worship the image to be killed. ¹⁶It also forced all people, great and small, rich and poor, free and slave, to receive a mark on their right hands or on their foreheads, ¹⁷so that they could not buy or sell unless they had the mark, which is the name of the beast or the number of its name.

¹⁸This calls for wisdom. Let those who have insight calculate the number of the beast, for it is the number of a man.*ᵈ* That number is 666.

The Lamb and the 144,000

14 Then I looked, and there before me was the Lamb, standing on Mount Zion, and with him 144,000 who had his name and his Father's name written on their foreheads. ²And I heard a sound from heaven like the roar of rushing waters and like a loud peal of thunder. The sound I heard was like that of harpists playing their harps. ³And they sang a new song before the throne and before the four living creatures and the elders. No-one could learn the song except the 144,000 who had been redeemed from the earth. ⁴These are those who did not defile themselves with women, for they remained virgins. They follow the Lamb wherever he goes. They were purchased from among the human race and offered as firstfruits to God and the Lamb. ⁵No lie was found in their mouths; they are blameless.

The three angels

⁶Then I saw another angel flying in mid-air, and he had the eternal gospel to proclaim to those who live on the earth—to every nation, tribe, language and people. ⁷He said in a loud voice, 'Fear God and give him glory, because the hour of his judgment has come. Worship him who made the heavens, the earth, the sea and the springs of water.'

⁸A second angel followed and said, '"Fallen! Fallen is Babylon the Great,"*ᵉ* which made all the nations drink the maddening wine of her adulteries.'

⁹A third angel followed them and said in a loud voice: 'If anyone worships the beast and its image and receives its mark on their forehead or on their hand, ¹⁰they, too, will drink of the wine of God's fury, which has been poured full strength into the cup of his wrath. They will be tormented with burning sulphur in the presence of the holy angels and of the Lamb. ¹¹And the smoke of their torment will rise for ever and ever. There will be no rest day or night for those who worship the beast and its image, or for anyone who receives the mark of its name.'

¹²This calls for patient endurance on the part of the people of God who keep his commands and remain faithful to Jesus.

---

*ᵃ*8 *Or written from the creation of the world in the book of life belonging to the Lamb who was slain*   *ᵇ*10 Some manuscripts *anyone kills*   *ᶜ*10 Jer. 15:2   *ᵈ*18 Or *is humanity's number*   *ᵉ*8 Isaiah 21:9

People and Places

Babylon
Revelation 14:8

Babylon was a city that would now be in modern Iraq. It was the capital city of the empire of Babylonia. The Babylonians were a dominant power who were always a big enemy of Israel and who eventually invaded Judah and sent nearly all the Israelites into exile. In the New Testament, and specifically in this verse, 'Babylon' signifies the world in opposition to God.

---

13 Then I heard a voice from heaven say, 'Write: blessed are the dead who die in the Lord from now on.'

'Yes,' says the Spirit, 'they will rest from their labour, for their deeds will follow them.'

Harvesting the earth and trampling the winepress

14 I looked, and there before me was a white cloud, and seated on the cloud was one like a son of man[a] with a crown of gold on his head and a sharp sickle in his hand. 15 Then another angel came out of the temple and called in a loud voice to him who was sitting on the cloud, 'Take your sickle and reap, because the time to reap has come, for the harvest of the earth is ripe.' 16 So he who was seated on the cloud swung his sickle over the earth, and the earth was harvested.

17 Another angel came out of the temple in heaven, and he too had a sharp sickle. 18 Still another angel, who had charge of the fire, came from the altar and called in a loud voice to him who had the sharp sickle, 'Take your sharp sickle and gather the clusters of grapes from the earth's vine, because its grapes are ripe.' 19 The angel swung his sickle on the earth, gathered its grapes and threw them into the great winepress of God's wrath. 20 They were trampled in the winepress outside the city, and blood flowed out of the press, rising as high as the horses' bridles for a distance of 1,600 stadia.[b]

Seven angels with seven plagues

15 I saw in heaven another great and marvellous sign: seven angels with the seven last plagues—last, because with them God's wrath is completed. 2 And I saw what looked like a sea of glass glowing with fire and, standing beside the sea, those who had been victorious over the beast and its image and over the number of its name. They held harps given them by God 3 and sang the song of God's servant Moses and of the Lamb:

'Great and marvellous are your deeds,
    Lord God Almighty.
Just and true are your ways,
    King of the nations.[c]
4 Who will not fear you, Lord,
    and bring glory to your name?
For you alone are holy.
All nations will come
    and worship before you,
for your righteous acts have been
    revealed.'[d]

5 After this I looked, and I saw in heaven the temple—that is, the tabernacle of the covenant law—and it was opened. 6 Out of the temple came the seven angels with the seven plagues. They were dressed in clean, shining linen and wore golden sashes round their chests. 7 Then one of the four living creatures gave to the seven angels seven golden bowls filled with the wrath of God, who lives for ever and ever. 8 And the temple was filled with smoke from the glory of God and from his power, and no-one could enter the temple until the seven plagues of the seven angels were completed.

The seven bowls of God's wrath

16 Then I heard a loud voice from the temple saying to the seven angels, 'Go, pour out the seven bowls of God's wrath on the earth.'

2 The first angel went and poured out his bowl on the land, and ugly, festering sores

---

[a] 14 See Daniel 7:13.   [b] 20 That is, about 180 miles or about 300 kilometres   [c] 3 Some manuscripts *ages*
[d] 3,4 Phrases in this song are drawn from Psalm 111:2,3; Deut. 32:4; Jer. 10:7; Psalms 86:9; 98:2.

broke out on the people who had the mark of the beast and worshipped its image.

³The second angel poured out his bowl on the sea, and it turned into blood like that of a dead person, and every living thing in the sea died.

⁴The third angel poured out his bowl on the rivers and springs of water, and they became blood. ⁵Then I heard the angel in charge of the waters say:

'You are just in these judgments,
 you who are and who were, the Holy One,
because you have so judged;
⁶for they have shed the blood of your people and your prophets,
 and you have given them blood to drink as they deserve.'

⁷And I heard the altar respond:

'Yes, Lord God Almighty,
 true and just are your judgments.'

⁸The fourth angel poured out his bowl on the sun, and the sun was allowed to scorch people with fire. ⁹They were seared by the intense heat and they cursed the name of God, who had control over these plagues, but they refused to repent and glorify him.

¹⁰The fifth angel poured out his bowl on the throne of the beast, and its kingdom was plunged into darkness. People gnawed their tongues in agony ¹¹and cursed the God of heaven because of their pains and their sores, but they refused to repent of what they had done.

¹²The sixth angel poured out his bowl on the great river Euphrates, and its water was dried up to prepare the way for the kings from the East. ¹³Then I saw three evil[a] spirits that looked like frogs; they came out of the mouth of the dragon, out of the mouth of the beast and out of the mouth of the false prophet. ¹⁴They are demonic spirits that perform signs, and they go out to the kings of the whole world, to gather them for the battle on the great day of God Almighty.

People and Places

Armageddon
Revelation 16:16
The Hebrew form of the name Armageddon probably means 'Hill of Megiddo', which was the site of many battles in ancient times (2 Kings 23:29). Armageddon is the name given in Revelation to the site of the final battle of the world in which God will destroy Satan and his armies.

¹⁵'Look, I come like a thief! Blessed are those who stay awake and keep their clothes on, so that they may not go naked and be shamefully exposed.'

¹⁶Then they gathered the kings together to the place that in Hebrew is called Armageddon.

¹⁷The seventh angel poured out his bowl into the air, and out of the temple came a loud voice from the throne, saying, 'It is done!' ¹⁸Then there came flashes of lightning, rumblings, peals of thunder and a severe earthquake. No earthquake like it has ever occurred since the human race has been on earth, so tremendous was the quake. ¹⁹The great city split into three parts, and the cities of the nations collapsed. God remembered Babylon the Great and gave her the cup filled with the wine of the fury of his wrath. ²⁰Every island fled away and the mountains could not be found. ²¹From the sky huge hailstones, each weighing about forty kilograms fell on people. And they cursed God on account of the plague of hail, because the plague was so terrible.

Babylon, the prostitute on the beast

17 One of the seven angels who had the seven bowls came and said to

---

[a] 13 Greek *unclean*

me, 'Come, I will show you the punishment of the great prostitute, who sits by many waters. ²With her the kings of the earth committed adultery, and the inhabitants of the earth were intoxicated with the wine of her adulteries.'

³Then the angel carried me away in the Spirit into a desert. There I saw a woman sitting on a scarlet beast that was covered with blasphemous names and had seven heads and ten horns. ⁴The woman was dressed in purple and scarlet, and was glittering with gold, precious stones and pearls. She held a golden cup in her hand, filled with abominable things and the filth of her adulteries. ⁵This title was written on her forehead:

MYSTERY
BABYLON THE GREAT
THE MOTHER OF PROSTITUTES
AND OF THE ABOMINATIONS OF THE EARTH.

⁶I saw that the woman was drunk with the blood of God's people, the blood of those who bore testimony to Jesus.

When I saw her, I was greatly astonished. ⁷Then the angel said to me: 'Why are you astonished? I will explain to you the mystery of the woman and of the beast she rides, which has the seven heads and ten horns. ⁸The beast, which you saw, once was, now is not, and will come up out of the Abyss and go to its destruction. The inhabitants of the earth whose names have not been written in the book of life from the creation of the world will be astonished when they see the beast, because it once was, now is not, and yet will come.

⁹'This calls for a mind with wisdom. The seven heads are seven hills on which the woman sits. ¹⁰They are also seven kings. Five have fallen, one is, the other has not yet come; but when he does come, he must remain for a little while. ¹¹The beast who once was, and now is not, is an eighth king. He belongs to the seven and is going to his destruction.

¹²'The ten horns you saw are ten kings who have not yet received a kingdom, but who for one hour will receive authority as kings along with the beast. ¹³They have one purpose and will give their power and authority to the beast. ¹⁴They will make war against the Lamb, but the Lamb will triumph over them because he is Lord of lords and King of kings—and with him will be his called, chosen and faithful followers.'

¹⁵Then the angel said to me, 'The waters you saw, where the prostitute sits, are peoples, multitudes, nations and languages. ¹⁶The beast and the ten horns you saw will hate the prostitute. They will bring her to ruin and leave her naked; they will eat her flesh and burn her with fire. ¹⁷For God has put it into their hearts to accomplish his purpose by agreeing to give the beast their power to rule, until God's words are fulfilled. ¹⁸The woman you saw is the great city that rules over the kings of the earth.'

Lament over fallen Babylon

18 After this I saw another angel coming down from heaven. He had great authority, and the earth was illuminated by his splendour. ²With a mighty voice he shouted:

'"Fallen! Fallen is Babylon the Great!"[a]
  She has become a dwelling for demons
    and a haunt for every evil[b] spirit,
  a haunt for every unclean bird,
  a haunt for every unclean and
    detestable animal.
³For all the nations have drunk
  the maddening wine of her adulteries.
The kings of the earth committed
    adultery with her,
  and the merchants of the earth grew
    rich from her excessive luxuries.'

Warning to escape Babylon's judgment

⁴Then I heard another voice from heaven say:

'"Come out of her, my people,"[c]
  so that you will not share in her sins,
  so that you will not receive any of her
    plagues;
⁵for her sins are piled up to heaven,
  and God has remembered her crimes.
⁶Give back to her as she has given;
  pay her back double for what she has
    done.

---

a 2 Isaiah 21:9 *b* 2 Greek *unclean* *c* 4 Jer. 51:45

Pour her a double portion from her
  own cup.
⁷Give her as much torment and grief
  as the glory and luxury she gave herself.
In her heart she boasts,
  "I sit enthroned as queen.
I am not a widow;[a]
I will never mourn."
⁸Therefore in one day her plagues will
  overtake her:
  death, mourning and famine.
She will be consumed by fire,
  for mighty is the Lord God who judges
  her.

Threefold woe over Babylon's fall

⁹'When the kings of the earth who committed adultery with her and shared her luxury see the smoke of her burning, they will weep and mourn over her. ¹⁰Terrified at her torment, they will stand far off and cry:

'"Woe! Woe to you, great city,
  you mighty city of Babylon!
In one hour your doom has come!"

¹¹'The merchants of the earth will weep and mourn over her because no-one buys their cargoes any more— ¹²cargoes of gold, silver, precious stones and pearls; fine linen, purple, silk and scarlet cloth; every sort of citron wood, and articles of every kind made of ivory, costly wood, bronze, iron and marble; ¹³cargoes of cinnamon and spice, of incense, myrrh and frankincense, of wine and olive oil, of fine flour and wheat; cattle and sheep; horses and carriages; and human beings sold as slaves.

¹⁴'They will say, "The fruit you longed for is gone from you. All your luxury and splendour have vanished, never to be recovered." ¹⁵The merchants who sold these things and gained their wealth from her will stand far off, terrified at her torment. They will weep and mourn ¹⁶and cry out:

'"Woe! Woe to you, great city,
  dressed in fine linen, purple and
    scarlet,
  and glittering with gold, precious
    stones and pearls!

¹⁷In one hour such great wealth has been
  brought to ruin!"

'Every sea captain, and all who travel by ship, the sailors, and all who earn their living from the sea, will stand far off. ¹⁸When they see the smoke of her burning, they will exclaim, "Was there ever a city like this great city?" ¹⁹They will throw dust on their heads, and with weeping and mourning cry out:

'"Woe! Woe to you, great city,
  where all who had ships on the sea
    became rich through her wealth!
In one hour she has been brought to
  ruin!"

²⁰'Rejoice over her, you heavens!
  Rejoice, you people of God!
  Rejoice, apostles and prophets!
For God has judged her
  with the judgment she imposed on
    you.'

The finality of Babylon's doom

²¹Then a mighty angel picked up a boulder the size of a large millstone and threw it into the sea, and said:

'With such violence
  the great city of Babylon will be thrown
    down,
  never to be found again.
²²The music of harpists and musicians,
  pipers and trumpeters,
  will never be heard in you again.
No worker of any trade
  will ever be found in you again.
The sound of a millstone
  will never be heard in you again.
²³The light of a lamp
  will never shine in you again.
The voice of bridegroom and bride
  will never be heard in you again.
Your merchants were the world's
  important people.
By your magic spell all the nations were
  led astray.
²⁴In her was found the blood of prophets
  and of God's people,
  of all who have been slaughtered on the
    earth.'

---

[a] 7 See Isaiah 47:7,8.

IN OTHER WORDS

Hallelujah
Revelation 19:1
Hallelujah is Hebrew for 'praise the Lord'. It often appears at the beginning or end of a psalm, and it might have been a standard call to worship in the temple.

Threefold hallelujah over Babylon's fall

19 After this I heard what sounded like the roar of a great multitude in heaven shouting:

'Hallelujah!
Salvation and glory and power belong to our God,
2 for true and just are his judgments.
He has condemned the great prostitute
    who corrupted the earth by her adulteries.
He has avenged on her the blood of his servants.'

3And again they shouted:

'Hallelujah!
The smoke from her goes up for ever and ever.'

4The twenty-four elders and the four living creatures fell down and worshipped God, who was seated on the throne. And they cried:

'Amen, Hallelujah!'

5Then a voice came from the throne, saying:

'Praise our God,
    all you his servants,
you who fear him,
    both great and small!'

6Then I heard what sounded like a great multitude, like the roar of rushing waters and like loud peals of thunder, shouting:

'Hallelujah!
For our Lord God Almighty reigns.
7Let us rejoice and be glad
    and give him glory!
For the wedding of the Lamb has come,
    and his bride has made herself ready.
8Fine linen, bright and clean,
    was given her to wear.'

(Fine linen stands for the righteous acts of God's people.)

9Then the angel said to me, 'Write: "Blessed are those who are invited to the wedding supper of the Lamb!"' And he added, 'These are the true words of God.'

10At this I fell at his feet to worship him. But he said to me, 'Don't do that! I am a fellow-servant with you and with your brothers and sisters who hold to Jesus' testimony. Worship God! For the testimony of Jesus is the Spirit of prophecy.'

The heavenly warrior defeats the beast

11I saw heaven standing open and there before me was a white horse, whose rider is called Faithful and True. With justice he judges and makes war. 12His eyes are like blazing fire, and on his head are many crowns. He has a name written on him that no-one knows but he himself. 13He is dressed in a robe dipped in blood, and his name is the Word of God. 14The armies of heaven were following him, riding on white horses and dressed in fine linen, white and clean. 15Coming out of his mouth is a sharp sword with which to strike down the nations. 'He will rule them with an iron sceptre.'[a] He treads the winepress of the fury of the wrath of God Almighty. 16On his robe and on his thigh he has this name written:

KING OF KINGS AND LORD OF LORDS.

17And I saw an angel standing in the sun, who cried in a loud voice to all the birds flying in mid-air, 'Come, gather together for the great supper of God, 18so that you may eat the flesh of kings, generals, and the mighty, of horses and their riders, and the flesh of all people, free and slave, great and small.'

19Then I saw the beast and the kings of the earth and their armies gathered together to make war against the rider on the horse and his army. 20But the beast was captured, and

---

[a] 15 Psalm 2:9

with him the false prophet who had performed the signs on his behalf. With these signs he had deluded those who had received the mark of the beast and worshipped his image. The two of them were thrown alive into the fiery lake of burning sulphur. 21The rest were killed with the sword coming out of the mouth of the rider on the horse, and all the birds gorged themselves on their flesh.

The thousand years

20 And I saw an angel coming down out of heaven, having the key to the Abyss and holding in his hand a great chain. 2He seized the dragon, that ancient snake, who is the devil, or Satan, and bound him for a thousand years. 3He threw him into the Abyss, and locked and sealed it over him, to keep him from deceiving the nations any more until the thousand years were ended. After that, he must be set free for a short time.

4I saw thrones on which were seated those who had been given authority to judge. And I saw the souls of those who had been beheaded because of their testimony about Jesus and because of the word of God. They had not worshipped the beast or his image and had not received his mark on their foreheads or their hands. They came to life and reigned with Christ for a thousand years. 5(The rest of the dead did not come to life until the thousand years were ended.) This is the first resurrection. 6Blessed and holy are those who have part in the first resurrection. The second death has no power over them, but they will be priests of God and of Christ and will reign with him for a thousand years.

The judgment of Satan

7When the thousand years are over, Satan will be released from his prison 8and will go out to deceive the nations in the four corners of the earth—Gog and Magog—and to gather them for battle. In number they are like the sand on the seashore. 9They marched across the breadth of the earth and surrounded the camp of God's people, the city he loves. But fire came down from heaven and devoured them. 10And the devil, who deceived them, was thrown into the lake of burning sulphur, where the beast and the false prophet had been thrown. They will be tormented day and night for ever and ever.

The judgment of the dead

11Then I saw a great white throne and him who was seated on it. The earth and the heavens fled from his presence, and there was no place for them. 12And I saw the dead, great and small, standing before the throne, and books were opened. Another book was opened, which is the book of life. The dead were judged according to what they had done as recorded in the books. 13The sea gave up the dead that were in it, and death and Hades gave up the dead that were in them, and everyone was judged according to what they had done. 14Then death and Hades were thrown into the lake of fire. The lake of fire is the second death. 15All whose names were not found written in the book of life were thrown into the lake of fire.

A new heaven and a new earth

21 Then I saw 'a new heaven and a new earth,'[a] for the first heaven and the first earth had passed away, and there was no longer any sea. 2I saw the Holy City, the new Jerusalem, coming down out of heaven from God, prepared as a bride beautifully dressed for her husband. 3And I heard a loud voice from the throne saying, 'Look! God's dwelling-place is now among the people, and he will dwell with them. They will be his people, and God himself will be with them and be their God. 4"He will wipe every tear from their eyes. There will be no more death"[b] or mourning or crying or pain, for the old order of things has passed away.'

5He who was seated on the throne said, 'I am making everything new!' Then he said, 'Write this down, for these words are trustworthy and true.'

6He said to me: 'It is done. I am the Alpha and the Omega, the Beginning and the End. To the thirsty I will give water without cost from the spring of the water of

---

[a] 1 Isaiah 65:17 [b] 4 Isaiah 25:8

making Connections

New heavens and new earth
Revelation 21:1

John looks forward to a future time when the heavens and earth will be renewed to the state that God originally intended. All evil, sickness and conflict will be destroyed and there will be peace and prosperity for all. The prophet Isaiah also looked forward to this time in Isaiah 65:17.

life. 7Those who are victorious will inherit all this, and I will be their God and they will be my children. 8But the cowardly, the unbelieving, the vile, the murderers, the sexually immoral, those who practise magic arts, the idolaters and all liars—they will be consigned to the fiery lake of burning sulphur. This is the second death.'

The new Jerusalem, the bride of the Lamb

9One of the seven angels who had the seven bowls full of the seven last plagues came and said to me, 'Come, I will show you the bride, the wife of the Lamb.' 10And he carried me away in the Spirit to a mountain great and high, and showed me the Holy City, Jerusalem, coming down out of heaven from God. 11It shone with the glory of God, and its brilliance was like that of a very precious jewel, like a jasper, clear as crystal. 12It had a great, high wall with twelve gates, and with twelve angels at the gates. On the gates were written the names of the twelve tribes of Israel. 13There were three gates on the east, three on the north, three on the south and three on the west. 14The wall of the city had twelve foundations, and on them were the names of the twelve apostles of the Lamb.

15The angel who talked with me had a measuring rod of gold to measure the city, its gates and its walls. 16The city was laid out like a square, as long as it was wide. He measured the city with the rod and found it to be 12,000 stadia^a in length, and as wide and high as it is long. 17He measured its wall and it was 144 cubits^b thick,^{c} by human measurement, which the angel was using. 18The wall was made of jasper, and the city of pure gold, as pure as glass. 19The foundations of the city walls were decorated with every kind of precious stone. The first foundation was jasper, the second sapphire, the third agate, the fourth emerald, 20the fifth onyx, the sixth ruby, the seventh chrysolite, the eighth beryl, the ninth topaz, the tenth turquoise, the eleventh jacinth, and the twelfth amethyst.^{d} 21The twelve gates were twelve pearls, each gate made of a single pearl. The great street of the city was of gold, as pure as transparent glass.

22I did not see a temple in the city, because the Lord God Almighty and the Lamb are its temple. 23The city does not need the sun or the moon to shine on it, for the glory of God gives it light, and the Lamb is its lamp. 24The nations will walk by its light, and the kings of the earth will bring their splendour into it. 25On no day will its gates ever be shut, for there will be no night there. 26The glory and honour of the nations will be brought into it. 27Nothing impure will ever enter it, nor will anyone who does what is shameful or deceitful, but only those whose names are written in the Lamb's book of life.

Eden restored

22 Then the angel showed me the river of the water of life, as clear as crystal, flowing from the throne of God and of the Lamb 2down the middle of the great street of the city. On each side of the river stood the tree of life, bearing twelve crops of fruit, yielding its fruit every month. And the leaves of the tree are for the healing of the nations. 3No longer will there be any curse. The throne of God and of the Lamb will be in the city, and his servants will serve him.

---

^{a}16 That is, about 1,400 miles or about 2,200 kilometres ^{b}17 That is, about 65 metres) ^{c}17 Or *high* ^{d}20 The precise identification of some of these precious stones is uncertain.

4They will see his face, and his name will be on their foreheads. 5There will be no more night. They will not need the light of a lamp or the light of the sun, for the Lord God will give them light. And they will reign for ever and ever.

John and the angel

6The angel said to me, 'These words are trustworthy and true. The Lord, the God who inspires the prophets, sent his angel to show his servants the things that must soon take place.'

7'Look, I am coming soon! Blessed are those who keep the words of the prophecy in this scroll.'

8I, John, am the one who heard and saw these things. And when I had heard and seen them, I fell down to worship at the feet of the angel who had been showing them to me. 9But he said to me, 'Don't do that! I am a fellow-servant with you and with your fellow-prophets and with all who keep the words of this scroll. Worship God!'

10Then he told me, 'Do not seal up the words of the prophecy of this scroll, because the time is near. 11Let those who do wrong continue to do wrong; let those who are vile continue to be vile; let those who do right continue to do right; and let those who are holy continue to be holy.'

Epilogue: invitation and warning

12'Look, I am coming soon! My reward is with me, and I will give to everyone according to what they have done. 13I am the Alpha and the Omega, the First and the Last, the Beginning and the End.

14'Blessed are those who wash their robes, that they may have the right to the tree of life and may go through the gates into the city. 15Outside are the dogs, those who practise magic arts, the sexually immoral, the murderers, the idolaters and everyone who loves and practises falsehood.

16'I, Jesus, have sent my angel to give you[a] this testimony for the churches. I am the Root and the Offspring of David, and the bright Morning Star.'

17The Spirit and the bride say, 'Come!' And let those who hear say, 'Come!' Let those who are thirsty come; and let all who wish take the free gift of the water of life.

18I warn everyone who hears the words of the prophecy of this scroll: if any one of you adds anything to them, God will add to you the plagues described in this scroll. 19And if any one of you takes words away from this scroll of prophecy, God will take away from you your share in the tree of life and in the Holy City, which are described in this scroll.

20He who testifies to these things says, 'Yes, I am coming soon.'

Amen. Come, Lord Jesus.

21The grace of the Lord Jesus be with God's people. Amen.

---

[a] 16 The Greek is plural.

HOW TO READ THE BIBLE

Each time you set out to explore a bit more of the Bible, you need to make some simple preparations. Otherwise, it's far too easy to get lost!

Thank God

Thank God for being there, even if you can't feel him or are not sure about him. Pray that the Holy Spirit will breathe his truth into your mind and heart. Pray that you will learn something useful you can apply in your life over the next 24 hours. Open yourself to be rebuked and corrected (you know you are not quite perfect!) so that you can become more of the person God wants you to be. And expect to learn something to bring you closer to God or to equip you to know and serve him better. If you find praying difficult, just turn this paragraph into a simple prayer. Instead of 'you/your' say 'I/my'.

Take it steady

Now you are almost ready to set off. But there is one rule of the road to observe at all times: 'Take it steady'. Sometimes it can be helpful to jog round a part of the Bible quite fast just to get the feel of it. But most of the time you need to stroll slowly, pausing to think about the things you come across.

Ask questions

Ask questions of what you are reading. What does this tell me about God? About the world? About myself? What challenge is there here for me? What is there to put right? What does this tell me about Jesus, and what does it mean for me to trust him? What positive thing can I learn to bring me closer to God and make me more useful to him? Of course, not every passage will answer all these questions; but every passage deals with some of them.

Plan your journey

Finally, choose a starting point and a specific path to follow. The **What's in the Bible?** section near the front of this book can help you to get an overview of the Bible.

Once you have a basic overview of the Bible, you could work through whole books, beginning perhaps with a Gospel (say Luke), then one of Paul's letters (Ephesians or Philippians) and an Old Testament book. Your local church or Christian bookshop will be able to advise you on other Bible reading schemes and notes to help you continue – and vary – your explorations.

Many people find it helpful to set aside the same period of time each day for their Bible journey. Often, they will follow it by praying about what they have read and bringing to God the needs of the world and other people who they know. It helps to keep daily life in God's perspective. Try it!

ONE-YEAR BIBLE READING PLAN

There are many different paths for reading through the entire Bible. This plan is a suggestion only, but offers a balanced approach to trying to read the whole book in one year. Each daily reading contains a passage from the Old Testament, the New Testament, and from Psalms or Proverbs. The Old Testament is in broadly chronological order; otherwise, traditional Bible order is maintained.

The names of the books of the Bible are abbreviated as follows:

THE OLD TESTAMENT		THE NEW TESTAMENT	
Genesis	Ge	Matthew	Mt
Exodus	Ex	Mark	Mk
Leviticus	Lev	Luke	Lk
Numbers	Nu	John	Jn
Deuteronomy	Dt	Acts	Ac
Joshua	Jos	Romans	Ro
Judges	Jdg	1 Corinthians	1 Cor
Ruth	Ru	2 Corinthians	2 Cor
1 Samuel	1Sa	Galatians	Gal
2 Samuel	2Sa	Ephesians	Eph
1 Kings	1Ki	Philippians	Php
2 Kings	2Ki	Colossians	Col
1 Chronicles	1Ch	1 Thessalonians	1 Th
2 Chronicles	2Ch	2 Thessalonians	2Th
Ezra	Ezr	1 Timothy	1Ti
Nehemiah	Ne	2 Timothy	2Ti
Esther	Est	Titus	Tit
Job	Job	Philemon	Phm
Psalms	Ps	Hebrews	Heb
Proverbs	Pr	James	Jas
Ecclesiastes	Ecc	1 Peter	1Pe
Song of Songs	SS	2 Peter	2Pe
Isaiah	Isa	1 John	1Jn
Jeremiah	Jer	2 John	2Jn
Lamentations	Lam	3 John	3Jn
Ezekiel	Eze	Jude	Jude
Daniel	Dan	Revelation	Rev
Hosea	Hos		
Joel	Joel		
Amos	Am		
Obadiah	Ob		
Jonah	Jnh		
Micah	Mic		
Nahum	Na		
Habakkuk	Hab		
Zephaniah	Zep		
Haggai	Hag		
Zechariah	Zec		
Malachi	Mal		

JANUARY

1	Ge 1:1–2:17	Mt 1:1–17	Ps 1:1–6
2	Ge 2:18–4:16	Mt 1:18–2:18	Ps 2:1–12
3	Ge 4:17–6:22	Mt 2:19–3:17	Ps 3:1–8
4	Ge 7:1–9:17	Mt 4:1–22	Pr 1:1–7
5	Ge 9:18–11:9	Mt 4:23–5:20	Ps 4:1–8
6	Ge 11:10–13:18	Mt 5:21–42	Ps 5:1–12
7	Ge 14:1–16:16	Mt 5:43–6:24	Ps 6:1–10
8	Ge 17:1–18:33	Mt 6:25–7:23	Ps 1:8–19
9	Ge 19:1–20:18	Mt 7:24–8:22	Ps 7:1–9
10	Ge 21:1–23:20	Mt 8:23–9:13	Ps 7:10–17
11	Ge 24:1–67	Mt 9:14–38	Ps 8:1–9
12	Ge 25:1–26:35	Mt 10:1–31	Ps 1:20–33
13	Ge 27:1–28:22	Mt 10:32–11:10	Ps 9:1–6
14	Ge 29:1–30:43	Mt 11:11–30	Ps 9:7–12
15	Ge 31:1–55	Mt 12:1–21	Ps 9:13–20
16	Ge 32:1–33:20	Mt 12:22–45	Pr 2:1–11
17	Ge 34:1–35:29	Mt 12:46–13:17	Ps 10:1–11
18	Ge 36:1–37:36	Mt 13:18–35	Ps 10:12–18
19	Ge 38:1–39:23	Mt 13:36–58	Ps 11:1–7
20	Ge 40:1–41:40	Mt 14:1–21	Pr 2:12–22
21	Ge 41:41–42:38	Mt 14:22–15:9	Pr 12:1–8
22	Ge 43:1–44:34	Mt 15:10–39	Ps 13:1–6
23	Ge 45:1–46:34	Mt 16:1–20	Ps 14:1–7
24	Ge 47:1–48:22	Mt 16:21–17:13	Pr 3:1–10
25	Ge 49:1–50:26	Mt 17:14–18:9	Ps 15:1–5
26	Job 1:1–4:11	Mt 18:10–35	Ps 16:1–11
27	Job 4:12–7:21	Mt 19:1–15	Ps 17:1–5
28	Job 8:1–10:22	Mt 19:16–30	Pr 3:11–20
29	Job 11:1–14:22	Mt 20:1–19	Ps 17:6–12
30	Job 15:1–18:21	Mt 20:20–34	Ps 17:13–15
31	Job 19:1–21:34	Mt 21:1–17	Ps 18:1–6

FEBRUARY

1	Job 22:1–24:25	Mt 21:18–32	Pr 3:21–35
2	Job 25:1–29:25	Mt 21:33–22:14	Ps 18:7–15
3	Job 30:1–32:22	Mt 22:15–45	Ps 18:16–24
4	Job 33:1–35:16	Mt 23:1–39	Ps 18:25–36
5	Job 36:1–38:41	Mt 24:1–31	Pr 4:1–9
6	Job 39:1–42:17	Mt 24:32–25:13	Ps 18:37–42
7	Ex 1:1–2:25	Mt 25:14–46	Ps 18:43–50
8	Ex 3:1–4:31	Mt 26:1–30	Ps 19:1–6
9	Ex 5:1–6:27	Mt 26:31–46	Pr 4:10–19
10	Ex 6:28–8:32	Mt 26:47–68	Ps 19:7–14
11	Ex 9:1–10:29	Mt 26:69–27:10	Ps 20:1–9
12	Ex 11:1–12:51	Mt 27:11–44	Ps 21:1–7
13	Ex 13:1–14:31	Mt 27:45–66	Pr 4:20–27
14	Ex 15:1–16:36	Mt 28:1–20	Ps 21:8–13
15	Ex 17:1–18:27	Mk 1:1–28	Ps 22:1–11
16	Ex 19:1–20:26	Mk 1:29–2:17	Ps 22:12–21
17	Ex 21:1–22:31	Mk 2:18–3:30	Pr 5:1–14
18	Ex 23:1–24:18	Mk 3:31–4:29	Ps 22:22–31
19	Ex 25:1–26:37	Mk 4:30–5:20	Ps 23:1–6
20	Ex 27:1–28:43	Mk 5:21–6:6a	Ps 24:1–10
21	Ex 29:1–30:38	Mk 6:6b–29	Pr 5:15–23
22	Ex 31:1–33:6	Mk 6:30–56	Ps 25:1–7
23	Ex 33:7–34:35	Mk 7:1–30	Ps 25:8–15
24	Ex 35:1–36:38	Mk 7:31–8:13	Ps 25:16–22
25	Ex 37:1–38:31	Mk 8:14–9:1	Pr 6:1–11
26	Ex 39:1–40:38	Mk 9:2–32	Ps 26:1–12
27	Lev 1:1–2:16	Mk 9:33–10:12	Ps 27:1–6
28	Lev 3:1–4:35	Mk 10:13–31	Ps 27:7–14

MARCH

1	Lev 5:1–7:10	Mk 10:32–52	Pr 6:12–19
2	Lev 7:11–8:36	Mk 11:1–26	Ps 28:1–9

3	Lev 9:1–10:20	Mk 11:27–12:12	Ps 29:1–11
4	Lev 11:1–12:9	Mk 12:13–27	Ps 30:1–7
5	Lev 13:1–59	Mk 12:28–44	Pr 6:20–29
6	Lev 14:1–57	Nk 13:1–31	Ps 30:8–12
7	Lev 15:1–16:34	Mk 13:32–14:16	Ps 31:1–8
8	Lev 17:1–18:30	Mk 14:17–42	Ps 31:9–18
9	Lev 19:1–20:27	Mk 14:43–72	Pr 6:30–35
10	Lev 21:1–22:33	Mk 15:1–32	Ps 31:19–24
11	Lev 23:1–24:23	Mk 15:33–47	Ps 32:1–11
12	Lev 25:1–26:13	Mk 16:1–20	Ps 33:1–11
13	Lev 26:14–27:34	Lk 1:1–25	Pr 7:1–9
14	Nu 1:1–29	Lk 1:26–38	Ps 33:12–22
15	Nu 2:10–3:51	Lk 1:39–56	Ps 34:1–10
16	Nu 4:1–5:10	Lk 1:57–80	Ps 34:11–22
17	Nu 5:11–6:27	Lk 2:1–20	Pr 7:10–20
18	Nu 7:1–65	Lk 2:21–40	Ps 35:1–10
19	Nu 7:66–9:14	Lk 2:41–52	Ps 35:11–18
20	Nu 9:15–11:23	Lk 3:1–22	Ps 35:19–28
21	Nu 11:24–13:33	Lk 3:23–4:13	Pr 7:21–27
22	Nu 14:1–15:21	Lk 4:14–37	Ps 36:1–12
23	Nu 15:22–16:35	Lk 4:38–5:16	Ps 37:1–9
24	Nu 16:36–18:32	Lk 5:17–32	Ps 37:10–20
25	Nu 19:1–21:3	Lk 5:33–6:11	Pr 8:1–11
26	Nu 21:4–22:20	Lk 6:12–36	Ps 37:21–31
27	Nu 22:21–23:30	Lk 6:37–7:10	Ps 37:32–40
28	Nu 24:1–26:11	Lk 7:11–35	Ps 38:1–12
29	Nu 26:12–27:11	Lk 7:36–50	Pr 8:12–21
30	Nu 27:12–29:11	Lk 8:1–18	Ps 38:13–22
31	Nu 29:12–31:24	Lk 8:19–39	Ps 39:1–13

APRIL

1	Nu 31:25–32:42	Lk 8:40–9:9	Ps 40:1–8
2	Nu 33:1–34:29	Lk 9:10–27	Pr 8:22–31
3	Nu 35:1–36:13	Lk 9:28–56	Ps 40:9–17
4	Dt 1:1–2:37	Lk 9:57–10:24	Ps 41:1–6
5	Dt 3:1–4:49	Lk 10:25–11:4	Ps 41:7–13
6	Dt 5:1–6:25	Lk 11:5–32	Pr 8:32–36
7	Dt 7:1–8:20	Lk 11:33–54	Ps 42:1–6a
8	Dt 9:1–10:22	Lk 12:1–34	Ps 42:6b–11
9	Dt 11:1–12:32	Lk 12:35–39	Ps 43:1–5
10	Dt 13:1–14:29	Lk 13:1–30	Pr 9:1–12
11	Dt 15:1–16:20	Lk 13:31–14:14	Ps 44:1–12
12	Dt 16:21–18:22	Lk 14:15–35	Ps 44:13–26
13	Dt 19:1–20:20	Lk 15:1–32	Ps 45:1–9
14	Dt 21:1–22:30	Lk 16:1–18	Pr 9:13–18
15	Dt 23:1–25:19	Lk 16:19–17:10	Ps 45:10–17
16	Dt 26:1–28:14	Lk 17:11–37	Ps 46:1–11
17	Dt 28:15–68	Lk 18:1–30	Ps 47:1–9
18	Dt 29:1–30:10	Lk 18:31–19:10	Ps 48:1–8
19	Dt 30:11–31:30	Lk 19:11–44	Ps 48:9–14
20	Dt 32:1–52	Lk 19:45–20:26	Ps 49:1–20
21	Dt 33:1–34:12	Lk 20:27–21:4	Pr 10:1–10
22	Jos 1:1–2:24	Lk 21:5–38	Pr 10:11–20
23	Jos 3:1–5:12	Lk 22:1–38	Ps 50:1–15
24	Jos 5:13–7:26	Lk 22:39–62	Ps 50:16–23
25	Jos 8:1–9:15	Lk 22:63–23:25	Ps 51:1–9
26	Jos 9:16–10:43	Lk 23:26–56	Pr 10:21–30
27	Jos 11:1–12:24	Lk 24:1–35	Ps 51:10–19
28	Jos 13:1–14:15	Lk 24:36–53	Ps 52:1–9
29	Jos 15:1–63	John 1:1–28	Ps 53:1–6
30	Jos 16:1–18:28	Jn 1:29–51	Pr 10:31–11:8

MAY

1	Jos 19:1–20:9	Jn 2:1–25	Ps 54:1–7
2	Jos 21:1–22:34	Jn 3:1–21	Ps 55:1–11
3	Jos 23:1–24:33	Jn 3:22–36	Ps 55:12–23

4	Jdg 1:1–2:5	Jn 4:1–26	Pr 11:9–18
5	Jdg 2:6–3:31	Jn 4:27–42	Ps 56:1–13
6	Jdg 4:1–5:31	Jn 4:43–5:15	Ps 57:1–6
7	Jdg 6:1–7:8a	Jn 5:16–30	Ps 57:7–11
8	Jdg 7:8b–8:35	Jn 5:31–47	Pr 11:19–28
9	Jdg 9:1–57	Jn 6:1–24	Ps 58:1–11
10	Jdg 10:1–11:28	Jn 6:25–59	Ps 59:1–8
11	Jdg 11:29–13:25	Jn 6:60–7:13	Ps 59:9–17
12	Jdg 14:1–15:20	Jn 7:14–44	Pr 11:29–12:7
13	Jdg 16:1–17:13	Jn 7:45–8:11	Ps 60:1–4
14	Jdg 18:1–19:30	Jn 8:12–30	Ps 60:5–12
15	Jdg 20:1–21:25	Jn 8:31–59	Ps 61:1–8
16	Ru 1:1–2:23	Jn 9:1–34	Pr 12:8–17
17	Ru 3:1–4:22	Jn 9:35–10:21	Ps 62:1–12
18	1Sa 1:1–2:26	Jn 10:22–42	Ps 63:1–11
19	1Sa 2:27–4:22	Jn 11:1–44	Ps 64:1–10
20	1Sa 5:1–7:17	Jn 11:45–12:11	Pr 12:18–27
21	1Sa 8:1–10:8	Jn 12:12–36	Ps 65:1–13
22	1Sa 10:9–12:25	Jn 12:37–13:17	Ps 66:1–12
23	1Sa 13:1–14:23	Jn 13:18–38	Ps 66:13–20
24	1Sa 14:24–15:35	Jn 14:1–31	Pr 12:28–13:9
25	1Sa 16:1–17:37	Jn 15:1–16:4	Ps 67:1–7
26	1Sa 17:38–18:30	Jn 16:5–17:5	Ps 68:1–6
27	1Sa 19:1–20:42	Jn 17:6–26	Ps 68:7–14
28	1Sa 21:1–23:29	Jn 18:1–24	Pr 13:10–19
29	1Sa 24:1–25:44	Jn 18:25–40	Ps 68:15–20
30	1Sa 26:1–28:25	Jn 19:1–27	Ps 68:21–27
31	1Sa 29:1–31:13	Jn 19:28–20:9	Ps 68:28–35

JUNE

1	2Sa 1:1–2:7	Jn 20:10–31	Pr 13:20–14:4
2	2Sa 2:8–3:21	Jn 21:1–25	Ps 69:1–12
3	2Sa 3:22–5:16	Ac 1:1–22	Ps 69:13–28
4	2Sa 5:17–6:23	Ac 1:23–2:21	Ps 69:29–36
5	2Sa 7:1–8:18	Ac 2:22–47	Pr 14:5–14
6	2Sa 9:1–10:19	Ac 3:1–26	Ps 70:1–5
7	2Sa 11:1–12:31	Ac 4:1–22	Ps 71:1–8
8	2Sa 13:1–39	Ac 4:23–5:11	Ps 71:9–18
9	2Sa 14:1–15:12	Ac 5:12–42	Pr 14:15–24
10	2Sa 15:13–16:23	Ac 6:1–7:19	Ps 71:19–24
11	2Sa 17:1–18:18	Ac 7:20–43	Ps 72:1–20
12	2Sa 18:19–19:43	Ac 7:44–8:3	Ps 73:1–14
13	2Sa 20:1–21:22	Ac 8:4–40	Pr 14:25–35
14	2Sa 22:1–23:7	Ac 9:1–31	Ps 73:15–28
15	2Sa 23:8–24:25	Ac 9:32–10:23a	Ps 74:1–9
16	1Ki 1:1–2:12	Ac 10:23b–11:18	Ps 74:10–17
17	1Ki 2:13–3:15	Ac 11:19–12:19a	Ps 15:1–10
18	1Ki 3:16–5:18	Ac 12:19b–13:15	Ps 74:18–23
19	1Ki 6:1–7:22	Ac 13:16–41	Ps 75:1–10
20	1Ki 7:23–8:21	Ac 13:42–14:7	Ps 76:1–12
21	1Ki 8:22–9:9	Ac 14:8–28	Pr 15:11–20
22	1Ki 9:10–11:13	Ac 15:1–21	Ps 77:1–9
23	1Ki 11:14–12:24	Ac 15:22–41	Ps 77:10–20
24	1Ki 12:25–14:20	Ac 16:1–15	Ps 78:1–8
25	1Ki 14:21–16:7	Ac 16:16–40	Pr 15:21–30
26	1Ki 16:8–18:15	Ac 17:1–21	Ps 78:9–16
27	1Ki 18:16–19:21	Ac 17:22–18:8	Ps 78:17–31
28	1Ki 20:1–21:29	Ac 18:9–28	Ps 78:32–39
29	1Ki 22:1–53	Ac 19:1–41	Pr 15:31–16:7
30	2 Kings 1:1–2:25	Ac 20:1–38	Ps 78:40–55

JULY

1	2Ki 3:1–4:37	Ac 21:1–26	Ps 78:56–72
2	2Ki 4:38–6:23	Ac 21:27–22:16	Ps 79:1–13
3	2Ki 6:24–8:15	Ac 22:17–23:11	Pr 16:8–17
4	2Ki 8:16–9:37	Ac 23:12–35	Ps 80:1–7

5	2Ki 10:1–11:21	Ac 24:1–27	Ps 80:8–19
6	2Ki 12:1–14:22	Ac 25:1–22	Ps 81:1–7
7	2Ki 14:23–15:38	Ac 25:23–26:23	Pr 16:18–27
8	2Ki 16:1–17:41	Ac 26:24–27:12	Ps 81:8–16
9	2Ki 18:1–19:13	Ac 27:13–32	Ps 82:1–8
10	2Ki 19:14–20:21	Ac 27:33–28:16	Ps 83:1–18
11	2Ki 21:1–23:7	Ac 28:17–31	Pr 16:28–17:4
12	2Ki 23:8–24:17	Ro 1:1–17	Ps 84:1–7
13	2Ki 24:18–25:30	Ro 1:18–32	Ps 84:8–12
14	Jnh 1:1–4:11	Ro 2:1–24	Ps 85:1–7
15	Am 1:1–2:16	Ro 2:25–3:8	Pr 17:5–14
16	Am 3:1–4:13	Ro 3:9–31	Ps 85:8–13
17	Am 5:1–27	Ro 4:1–15	Ps 86:1–10
18	Am 6:1–7:17	Ro 4:16–5:11	Ps 86:11–17
19	Am 8:1–9:15	Ro 5:12–6:10	Pr 17:15–24
20	Hos 1:1–2:23	Ro 6:11–23	Ps 87:1–7
21	Hos 3:1–5:15	Ro 7:1–13	Ps 88:1–9a
22	Hos 6:1–7:16	Ro 7:14–8:8	Ps 88:9b–18
23	Hos 8:1–9:17	Ro 8:9–27	Pr 17:25–18:6
24	Hos 10:1–11:11	Ro 8:28–39	Ps 89:1–8
25	Hos 11:12–14:9	Ro 9:1–21	Ps 89:9–13
26	1Ch 1:1–2:17	Ro 9:22–10:4	Ps 89:14–18
27	1Ch 2:18–4:8	Ro 10:5–11:10	Pr 18:7–16
28	1Ch 4:9–5:26	Ro 11:11–32	Ps 89:19–29
29	1Ch 6:1–81	Ro 11:33–12:21	Ps 89:30–37
30	1Ch 7:1–8:28	Ro 13:1–14	Ps 89:38–45
31	1Ch 8:29–10:14	Ro 14:1–18	Pr 18:17–19:2

AUGUST

1	1Ch 11:1–12:18	Ro 14:19–15:13	Ps 89:46–52
2	1Ch 12:19–14:17	Ro 15:14–33	Ps 90:1–10
3	1Ch 15:1–16:36	Ro 16:1–27	Ps 90:11–17
4	1Ch 16:37–18:17	1Co 1:1–17	Pr 19:3–12
5	1Ch 19:1–22:1	1Co 1:18–2:5	Ps 91:1–8
6	1Ch 22:2–23:32	1Co 2:6–16	Ps 91:9–16
7	1Ch 24:1–26:13	1Co 3:1–23	Ps 92:1–15
8	1Ch 26:14–27:34	1Co 4:1–21	Pr 19:13–22
9	1Ch 28:1–29:30	1Co 5:1–13	Ps 93:1–5
10	2Ch 1:1–17	1Co 6:1–20	Ps 94:1–11
11	Ecc 1:1–3:22	1Co 7:1–16	Ps 94:12–23
12	Ecc 4:1–6:12	1Co 7:17–31	Pr 19:23–20:4
13	Ecc 7:1–9:12	1Co 7:32–8:13	Ps 95:1–11
14	Ecc 9:13–12:14	1Co 9:1–18	Ps 96:1–13
15	2Ch 2:1–5:1	1Co 9:19–10:13	Ps 97:1–12
16	2Ch 5:2–7:10	1Co 10:14–11:1	Pr 20:5–14
17	2Ch 7:11–9:31	1Co 11:2–34	Ps 98:1–9
18	SS 1:1–4:16	1Co 12:1–26	Ps 99:1–9
19	SS 5:1–8:14	1Co 12:27–13:13	Ps 100:1–5
20	2Ch 10:1–12:16	1Co 14:1–17	Pr 20:15–24
21	2Ch 13:1–15:19	1Co 14:18–40	Ps 101:1–8
22	2Ch 16:1–18:27	1Co 15:1–34	Ps 102:1–11
23	2Ch 18:28–21:3	1Co 15:35–49	Ps 102:12–17
24	2Ch 21:4–23:21	1Co 15:50–16:4	Pr 20:25–21:4
25	2Ch 24:1–25:28	1Co 16:5–24	Ps 102:18–28
26	2Ch 26:1–28:27	2Co 1:1–11	Ps 103:1–12
27	2Ch 29:1–31:1	2Co 1:12–22	Ps 103:13–22
28	2Ch 31:2–33:20	2Co 1:23–2:11	Pr 21:5–16
29	2Ch 33:21–35:19	2Co 2:12–3:6	Ps 104:1–18
30	2Ch 35:20–36:23	2Co 3:7–18	Ps 104:19–30
31	Mic 1:1–4:13	2Co 4:1–18	Ps 104:31–35

SEPTEMBER

1	Mic 5:1–7:20	2Co 5:1–10	Pr 21:17–26
2	Isa 1:1–2:22	2Co 5:11–6:2	Ps 105:1–11
3	Isa 3:1–5:7	2Co 6:3–7:1	Ps 105:12–22
4	Isa 5:8–8:10	2Co 7:2–16	Ps 105:23–36

5	Isa 8:11–10:19	2Co 8:1–15	Pr 21:27–22:6
6	Isa 10:20–13:22	2Co 8:16–9:5	Ps 105:37–45
7	Isa 14:1–16:14	2Co 9:6–15	Ps 106:1–15
8	Isa 17:1–19:25	2Co 10:1–18	Ps 106:16–31
9	Isa 20:1–23:18	2Co 11:1–15	Pr 22:7–16
10	Isa 24:1–26:21	2Co 11:16–33	Ps 106:32–39
11	Isa 27:1–28:29	2Co 12:1–10	Ps 106:40–48
12	Isa 29:1–30:18	2Co 12:11–21	Ps 107:1–9
13	Isa 30:19–32:20	2Co 13:1–14	Pr 22:17–27
14	Isa 33:1–35:10	Gal 1:1–24	Ps 107:10–22
15	Isa 36:1–37:38	Gal 2:1–10	Ps 107:23–32
16	Isa 38:1–40:31	Gal 2:11–3:9	Ps 107:33–43
17	Isa 41:1–42:25	Gal 3:10–25	Pr 22:28–23:9
18	Isa 43:1–44:23	Gal 3:26–4:20	Ps 108:1–5
19	Isa 44:24–46:13	Gal 4:21–5:6	Ps 108:6–13
20	Isa 47:1–49:7	Gal 5:7–26	Ps 109:1–20
21	Isa 49:8–51:16	Gal 6:1–18	Pr 23:10–18
22	Isa 51:17–54:17	Eph 1:1–23	Ps 109:21–31
23	Isa 55:1–57:13	Eph 2:1–22	Ps 110:1–7
24	Isa 57:14–59:21	Eph 3:1–21	Ps 111:1–10
25	Isa 60:1–62:12	Eph 4:1–16	Pr 23:19–28
26	Isa 63:1–65:16	Eph 4:17–5:7	Ps 112:1–10
27	Isa 65:17–66:24	Eph 5:8–33	Ps 113:1–9
28	Na 1:1–3:19	Eph 6:1–24	Ps 114:1–8
29	Zep 1:1–3:20	Php 1:1–26	Pr 23:29–24:4
30	Jer 1:1–2:30	Php 1:27–2:11	Ps 115:1–11

OCTOBER

1	Jer 2:31–4:9	Php 2:12–30	Ps 115:12–18
2	Jer 4:10–5:31	Php 3:1–4:1	Ps 116:1–11
3	Jer 6:1–7:29	Php 4:2–23	Pr 24:5–14
4	Jer 7:30–9:16	Col 1:1–23	Ps 116:12–19
5	Jer 9:17–11:13	Col 1:24–2:5	Ps 117:1–2
6	Jer 11:14–13:27	Col 2:6–23	Ps 118:1–16
7	Jer 14:1–15:21	Col 3:1–4:1	Pr 24:15–22
8	Jer 16:1–17:27	Col 4:2–18	Ps 118:17–29
9	Jer 18:1–20:18	1Th 1:1–2:16	Ps 119:1–8
10	Jer 21:1–23:8	1Th 2:17–3:13	Ps 119:9–16
11	Jer 23:9–25:14	1Th 4:1–18	Pr 24:23–34
12	Jer 25:15–26:24	1Th 5:1–28	Ps 119:17–24
13	Jer 27:1–29:23	2Th 1:1–12	Ps 119:25–32
14	Jer 29:24–31:14	2Th 2:1–17	Ps 119:33–40
15	Jer 31:15–32:25	2Th 3:1–18	Pr 25:1–10
16	Jer 32:26–34:22	1Ti 1:1–20	Ps 119:41–48
17	Jer 35:1–37:21	1Ti 2:1–15	Ps 119:49–56
18	Jer 38:1–40:6	1Ti 3:1–16	Ps 119:57–64
19	Jer 40:7–42:22	1Ti 4:1–16	Pr 25:11–20
20	Jer 43:1–45:5	1Ti 5:1–6:2	Ps 119:65–72
21	Jer 46:1–47:7	1Ti 6:3–21	Ps 119:73–80
22	Jer 48:1–49:6	2Ti 1:1–18	Ps 119:81–88
23	Jer 49:7–50:10	2Ti 2:1–26	Pr 25:21–26:2
24	Jer 50:11–51:14	2Ti 3:1–17	Ps 119:89–96
25	Jer 51:15–64	2Ti 4:1–22	Ps 119:97–104
26	Jer 52:1–34	Tit 1:1–16	Ps 119:105–112
27	Hab 1:1–3:19	Tit 2:1–15	Pr 26:3–12
28	Lam 1:1–2:6	Tit 3:1–15	Ps 119:113–120
29	La 2:7–3:39	Phm 1–25	Ps 119:121–128
30	La 3:40–5:22	Heb 1:1–14	Ps 119:129–136
31	Ob 1–21	Heb 2:1–18	Pr 26:13–22

NOVEMBER

1	Joel 1:1–2:17	Heb 3:1–19	Ps 119:137–144
2	Joel 2:18–3:21	Heb 4:1–13	Ps 119:145–152
3	Eze 1:1–3:27	Heb 4:14–5:10	Ps 119:153–160
4	Eze 4:1–6:14	Heb 5:11–6:12	Pr 26:23–27:4
5	Eze 7:1–9:11	Heb 6:13–7:10	Ps 119:161–168

6	Eze 10:1–12:28	Heb 7:11–28	Ps 119 169–176
7	Eze 13:1–15:18	Heb 8:1–13	Ps 120:1–7
8	Eze 16:1–63	Heb 9:1–15	Pr 27:5–14
9	Eze 17:1–18:32	Heb 9:16–28	Ps 121:1–8
10	Eze 19:1–20:44	Heb 10:1–18	Ps 122:1–9
11	Eze 20:45–22:22	Heb 10:19–39	Ps 123:1–4
12	Eze 22:23–23:49	Heb 11:1–16	Pr 27:15–22
13	Eze 24:1–25:17	Heb 11:17–40	Ps 124:1–8
14	Eze 26:1–27:36	Heb 12:1–13	Ps 125:1–5
15	Eze 28:1–29:21	Heb 12:14–29	Ps 126:1–6
16	Eze 30:1–31:18	Heb 13:1–25	Pr 27:23–28:6
17	Eze 32:1–33:20	Jas 1:1–27	Ps 127:1–5
18	Eze 33:21–34:31	Jas 2:1–26	Ps 128:1–6
19	Eze 35:1–37:14	Jas 3:1–18	Ps 129:1–8
20	Eze 37:15–39:20	Jas 4:1–17	Pr 28:7–17
21	Eze 39:21–40:49	Jas 5:1–20	Ps 130:1–8
22	Eze 41:1–42:20	1Pe 1:1–2:3	Ps 131:1–3
23	Eze 43:1–44:31	1Pe 2:4–25	Ps 132:1–18
24	Eze 45:1–46:24	1Pe 3:1–22	Pr 28:18–28
25	Eze 47:1–48:35	1Pe 4:1–19	Ps 133:1–3
26	Da 1:1–2:23	1Pe 5:1–14	Ps 134:1–3
27	Da 2:24–3:12	2Pe 1:1–21	Ps 135:1–12
28	Da 3:13–4:18	2Pe 2:1–22	Pr 29:1–9
29	Da 4:19–5:16	2Pe 3:1–18	Ps 135:13–21
30	Da 5:17–6:28	1Jn 1:1–2:1	Ps 136:1–12

DECEMBER

1	Da 7:1–8:14	1Jn 2:12–27	Ps 136:13–26
2	Da 8:15–9:19	1Jn 2:28–3:10	Pr 29:10–18
3	Da 9:20–11:1	1Jn 3:11–4:6	Ps 137:1–9
4	Da 11:2–35	1Jn 4:7–21	Ps 138:1–8
5	Da 11:36–12:13	1Jn 5:1–21	Ps 139:1–10
6	Hag 1:1–2:23	2Jn 1–13	Pr 29:19–27
7	Zec 1:1–4:14	3Jn 1–14	Ps 139:11–16
8	Zec 5:1–8:23	Jude 1–25	Ps 139:17–24
9	Zec 9:1–11:17	Rev 1:1–20	Ps 140:1–5
10	Zec 12:1–14:21	Rev 2:1–17	Pr 30:1–10
11	Est 1:1–2:18	Rev 2:18–3:6	Ps 140:6–13
12	Est 2:19–5:14	Rev 3:7–22	Ps 141:1–10
13	Est 6:1–8:17	Rev 4:1–5:5	Ps 142:1–7
14	Est 9:1–10:3	Rev 5:6–14	Pr 30:11–23
15	Mal 1:1–2:16	Rev 6:1–17	Ps 143:1–12
16	Mal 2:17–4:6	Rev 7:1–17	Ps 144:1–8
17	Ezr 1:1–2:67	Rev 8:1–9:12	Ps 144:9–15
18	Ezr 2:68–4:5	Rev 9:13–10:11	Pr 30:24–33
19	Ezr 4:6–5:17	Rev 11:1–19	Ps 145:1–7
20	Ezr 6:1–7:10	Rev 12:1–13:1a	Ps 145:8–13a
21	Ezr 7:11–8:14	Rev 13:1b–18	Ps 145:13b–21
22	Ezr 8:15–9:15	Rev 14:1–13	Pr 31:1–9
23	Ezr 10:1–44	Rev 14:14–15:8	Ps 146:1–10
24	Neh 1:1–2:20	Rev 16:1–21	Ps 147:1–11
25	Ne 3:1–4:23	Rev 17:1–18	Ps 147:12–20
26	Ne 5:1–7:3	Rev 18:1–17a	Pr 31:10–20
27	Ne 7:4–8:18	Rev 18:17b–19:10	Ps 148:1–6
28	Ne 9:1–37	Rev 19:11–20:6	Ps 148:7–14
29	Ne 9:38–11:21	Rev 20:7–21:4	Ps 149:1–9
30	Ne 11:22–12:47	Rev 21:5–27	Pr 31:21–31
31	Ne 13:1–31	Rev 22:1–21	Ps 150:1–6

A Word to the Reader

Today's New International Version (TNIV) is a revision of the New International Version (NIV). Among the many English versions of the Bible that appeared in the twentieth century, the NIV (1973, 1978, 1984) has gained the widest readership in all parts of the English-speaking world. It was a completely new translation made by over a hundred scholars working directly from the best available Hebrew, Aramaic and Greek texts. The fact that participants from the United States, Great Britain, Canada, Australia and New Zealand worked together gave the project its international scope. That they were from many denominations—including Anglican, Assemblies of God, Baptist, Brethren, Christian Reformed, Church of Christ, Evangelical Covenant, Evangelical Free, Lutheran, Mennonite, Methodist, Nazarene, Presbyterian, Wesleyan and other churches—helped to safeguard the translation from sectarian bias. Responsibility for the NIV text, and now also for the text of the TNIV, is held by a self-governing body, the Committee on Bible Translation (CBT), composed of biblical scholars from colleges, universities and seminaries. During the revision process, many of the original members of CBT have been replaced by other scholars owing to retirement and other causes, but a similar geographical and denominational mix has been maintained.

From the beginning the translators have been united in their commitment to the authority and infallibility of the Bible as God's Word in written form. For them, the Bible contains the divine answer to the deepest needs of humanity, sheds unique light on our path in a dark world and sets forth the way to our eternal well-being. Out of this deep conviction, the Committee has held to certain goals for the NIV and for the present revision: that it would be an accurate translation and one that would have clarity and literary quality and so prove suitable for public and private reading, teaching, preaching, memorising and liturgical use. The Committee has also sought to preserve a measure of continuity with the long tradition of translating the Scriptures into English.

There is a sense in which the work of translating the Bible is never finished. This very fact has prompted the Committee to engage in an ongoing review of the text of the NIV with the assistance of many other scholars. The chief goal of this review has always been to bring the text of the NIV abreast of contemporary biblical scholarship and of shifts in English idiom and usage. Already in 1978 and again in 1984 various corrections and revisions to the NIV text were made. In the TNIV the Committee offers to the reading public the latest fruits of its review.

The first concern of the translators has continued to be the accuracy of the translation and its faithfulness to the intended meaning of the biblical writers. This has moved the translators to go beyond a formal word-for-word rendering of the original texts. Because thought patterns and syntax differ from language to language, accurate communication of the meaning of the biblical authors demands constant regard for varied contextual uses of words and idioms and for frequent modifications in sentence structures.

To achieve clarity the translators have sometimes supplied words not in the original texts but required by the context. In a few instances, where some uncertainty about such material remained, it is enclosed in corner brackets. As an aid to the reader, italicised sectional headings have been inserted. They are not to be regarded as part of the biblical text and are not intended for oral reading. It is the Committee's hope that these headings may prove more helpful to the reader than the traditional chapter divisions (which were introduced in the thirteenth century).

For the Old Testament the standard Hebrew text, the Masoretic Text as published in the latest editions of Biblia Hebraica, has been used throughout. The Masoretic Text tradition contains marginal notations that offer variant readings. These have sometimes been followed instead of the text itself. Because such instances involve variants within the Masoretic tradition, they have not been indicated in the textual notes. In a few cases, words in the basic consonantal text have been divided differently than in the Masoretic Text. Such cases are usually indicated in the textual footnotes. The Dead Sea Scrolls contain biblical texts that represent an earlier stage of the transmission of the Hebrew text. They have been consulted, as have been the Samaritan Pentateuch and the ancient scribal traditions concerning deliberate textual changes. The translators also consulted the more important early versions-the Greek Septuagint, Aquila, Symmachus and Theodotion, the Latin Vulgate, the Syriac Peshitta, the Aramaic Targums, and for the Psalms the Juxta Hebraica of Jerome. Readings from the Dead Sea Scrolls, the scribal traditions and these versions were occasionally followed where the Masoretic Text seemed doubtful and where accepted principles of textual criticism showed that one or more of these textual witnesses appeared to provide the correct reading. In rare cases, the translators have emended the Hebrew text where it appears to have become corrupted at an even earlier stage of its transmission. These departures from the Masoretic Text are also indicated in the textual footnotes. Sometimes the vowel indicators (which are later additions to the basic consonantal text) found in the Masoretic Text did not, in the judgment of the translators, represent the correct vowels for the original text. Accordingly, some words have been read with a different set of vowels. These instances are usually not indicated in the footnotes.

The Greek text used in translating the New Testament has been an eclectic one, based on the latest editions of the Nestle-Aland/United Bible Societies' Greek New Testament. The translators have made their choices among the variant readings in accordance with widely accepted principles of New Testament textual criticism. Footnotes call attention to places where uncertainty remains.

The New Testament authors, writing in Greek, often quote the Old Testament from its ancient Greek version, the Septuagint. This is one reason why some of the Old Testament quotations in the TNIV New Testament are not identical to the corresponding passages in the TNIV Old Testament. Such quotations in the New Testament are indicated with the footnote '(see Septuagint)'.

Other footnotes in this version are of several kinds, most of which need no explanation. Those giving alternative translations begin with 'Or' and generally introduce the alternative with the last word preceding it in the text, except when it is a single-word alternative. In poetry quoted in a footnote a slash mark indicates a line division.

It should be noted that references to diseases, minerals, flora and fauna, architectural details, clothing, jewellery, musical instruments and other articles cannot always be identified with precision. Also, linear measurements and measures of capacity can only be approximated (see Appendix I). The manner in which Hebrew proper names are to be represented in English has not become fully standardised. In the TNIV the spelling of many names has been revised to conform more closely to current scholarly practice and to the phonetics of the Hebrew originals. A list of such changes can be found in Appendix II, following the biblical text. A parallel list provides the spelling of these names in the NIV. Although Selah, used mainly in the Psalms, is probably a musical term, its meaning is uncertain. Since it may interrupt reading and distract the reader, this word has not been kept in the English text, but every occurrence has been signalled by a footnote.

Three changes of special note in the TNIV are the frequent substitution of 'Messiah' for the more traditional 'Christ,' the replacement of 'saints' in most cases with alternative renderings, and a greater sensitivity to shifts in English idiom.. A word about each is in order.

While 'Messiah' (from the Hebrew) and 'Christ' (from the Greek) both mean 'Anointed One,' what began as a title full of meaning to the early Jewish hearers of the gospel tended in the later Greek-speaking churches to become just another name for Jesus. So where the term is clearly used to designate the God-sent deliverer of Jewish expectations (primarily in the Gospels and Acts), it was judged more appropriate to use 'Messiah.' However, where this sense seems less prominent (primarily in the Epistles), the transliteration of the Greek word ('Christ') has been retained.

Concerning 'saints,' current usage (as reflected in major dictionaries of the English language) burdens it with meanings that lie outside the sense of the original-language words. The main Old Testament term that has traditionally been rendered 'saints' refers to those who are faithful to God. The New Testament term primarily designates those who have become followers of the Christian Way as people consecrated to God and thus belonging to the Lord in a special sense.

Although a basic core of the English language remains relatively stable, many diverse and complex cultural forces continue to bring about subtle shifts in the meanings and/or connotations of even old, well-established words and phrases. Among the more programmatic changes in the TNIV are the removal of nearly all vocative 'O's and the elimination of most instances of the generic use of masculine nouns and pronouns. Relative to the second of these, the so-called singular 'they/their/them,' which has been gaining acceptance among careful writers and which actually has a venerable place in English idiom, has been employed to fill in the vocabulary gap in generic nouns and pronouns referring to human beings. Where an individual emphasis is deemed to be present, 'anyone' or everyone' or some other equivalent is generally used as the antecedent of such pronouns.

Sometimes the chapter and/or verse numbering in English translations of the Old Testament differs from that found in published Hebrew texts. This is particularly the case in the Psalms, where the traditional titles are included in the Hebrew verse numbering. Such differences are marked by asterisks (*) in the text and informative footnotes set off in a separate line (or lines) at the bottom of the page. In the New Testament, verse numbers that marked off portions of the traditional English text not supported by the best Greek manuscripts are now set alongside the immediately preceding verse numbers and placed in brackets (see, for example, Matthew 17:20[21]).

Mark 16:9–20 and John 7:53–8: 11, although long accorded virtually equal status with the rest of the Gospels in which they stand, have a very questionable—and confused—standing in the textual history of the New Testament, as noted in the bracketed annotations with which they are set off. A different typeface has now been chosen for these passages to indicate even more clearly their uncertain status.

Basic formatting of the text, such as lining the poetry, paragraphing (both prose and poetry), setting up of (administrative-like) lists, indenting letters and lengthy prayers within narratives and the insertion of sectional headings, has been the work of the Committee. However, the choice between single-column and double-column formats has been left to the publishers. Also the issuing of 'red-letter' editions is a publisher's choice—one that the Committee does not endorse.

The Committee has again been reminded that every human effort is flawed—including this revision of the NIV. We trust, however, that many will find in it an improved representation of the Word of God, through which they hear his call to faith in our Lord Jesus Christ and to service in his kingdom. We offer this version of the Bible to him in whose name and for whose glory it has been made.

The Committee on Bible Translation
August 2003